**Collins** COBUILD

# SCHOOL
# DICTIONARY
## of American English

HEINLE
CENGAGE Learning

Australia • Brazil • Japan • Korea • Mexico • Singapore • Spain • United Kingdom • United States

**HEINLE** CENGAGE Learning™

**Collins** | COBUILD

**Collins COBUILD School Dictionary of American English**

**Heinle Cengage Learning**

President: Dennis Hogan
Editorial Director: Joe Dougherty
Publisher: Sherrise Roehr
Development Editor: Katherine Carroll
Director of Global Marketing: Ian Martin
Director of U.S. Marketing: Jim McDonough
Product Marketing Manager: Katie Kelley
Content Project Manager: Dawn Marie Elwell
Asset Development Coordinator: Noah Vincelette
Sr. Frontlist Buyer: Mary Beth Hennebury
Editors: Carol Braham, Amy Lawler, Tessa Stevens, Christina Terranova, Catherine Weller, Lynne Wilkins
History of English written by Daniel M. Short
Front and End Matter Typeset: Parkwood Composition Service, Inc.
Illustrators: See pgs. 1131–1134 for illustration and photo credits.
Cover Layout: Linda Beaupre

©2009 Heinle Cengage Learning

In-text features including: Picture Dictionary, Thesaurus, Usage Notes, Word Links, Word Partnerships, Word Webs, and supplements including: Guide to Key Features, History of English, Activity Guide, Brief Grammar Reference, Brief Writer's Handbook, Brief Speaker's Handbook, Text Messaging and Emoticons, Academic Word List, Presidents of the United States of America, USA States and Capitals, Geographical Place and Nationalities

**Heinle Cengage Learning**
25 Thomson Place
Boston, MA 02210
USA

Cengage Learning products are represented in Canada by Nelson Education, Ltd.

Visit Heinle online at **elt.heinle.com**

Visit our corporate website at **www.cengage.com**

**4WELL0003255**

Printed in China by China Translation & Printing Services Limited
2 3 4 5 6 7 8 9 10  11  10  09

**Collins**

Founding Editor-in-Chief: John Sinclair
Publishing Management: Morven Dooner, Elaine Higgleton
Project Management: Helen Forrest, Lisa Sutherland
Assistant Project Manager: Anne Robertson
Editors: Sandra Anderson, Carol Braham, Katharine Coates, Rosalind Combley, Robert Grossmith, Penny Hands, Lucy Hollingworth, Alison Macaulay, Enid Pearsons, Elizabeth Potter, Laura Wedgeworth
Computing support by Thomas Callan
Typeset by Wordcraft

First Edition 2008

Dictionary Text, Introduction and Defining Vocabulary copyright © HarperCollins Publishers 2008

**Harper Collins Publishers**
Westerhill Road
Bishopbriggs
Glasgow
G64 2QT
Great Britain

**www.collins.co.uk**

Library of Congress Control Number: 2007932910

Softcover: 978-1-4240-0082-1
Softcover + CD-ROM: 978-1-4240-0787-5
Hardcover: 978-1-4240-1894-9
Hardcover + CD-ROM: 978-1-4240-1895-6
CD-ROM: 978-1-4240-0793-6

Photo and illustration credits can be found on pages 1131–1134, which constitutes a continuation of this copyright page.

# CONTENTS

# Acknowledgements

The publishers would like to acknowledge the following for their invaluable contribution to the original COBUILD concept:

John Sinclair
Patrick Hanks
Gwyneth Fox
Richard Thomas

Stephen Bullion, Jeremy Clear, Rosalind Combley, Susan Hunston, Ramesh Krishnamurthy, Rosamund Moon, Elizabeth Potter

Jane Bradbury, Joanna Channell, Alice Deignan, Andrew Delahunty, Sheila Dignen, Gill Francis, Helen Liebeck, Elizabeth Manning, Carole Murphy, Michael Murphy, Jonathan Payne, Elaine Pollard, Christina Rammell, Penny Stock, John Todd, Jenny Watson, Laura Wedgeworth, John Williams

We would like to acknowledge the assistance of the many hundreds of individuals and companies who have kindly given permission for copyright material to be used in the Bank of English™. The written sources include many national and regional newspapers in Britain and overseas; magazines and periodical publishers; and book publishers in Britain, the United States and Australia. Extensive spoken data has been provided by radio and television broadcasting companies; research workers at many universities and other institutions; and numerous individual contributors. We are grateful to them all.

Consultant
Paul Nation

# John Sinclair

Founding Editor-in-Chief, Collins COBUILD Dictionaries
1933-2007

John Sinclair was Professor of Modern English Language at the University of Birmingham for most of his career; he was an outstanding scholar, one of the very first modern corpus linguists, and one of the most open-minded and original thinkers in the field. The COBUILD project in lexical computing, funded by Collins, revolutionized lexicography in the 1980s, and resulted in the creation of the largest corpus of English language texts in the world.

Professor Sinclair personally oversaw the creation of this very first electronic corpus, and was instrumental in developing the tools needed to analyze the data. Having corpus data allowed Professor Sinclair and his team to find out how people really use the English language, and to develop new ways of structuring dictionary entries. Frequency information, for example, allowed him to rank senses by importance and usefulness to the learner (thus the most common meaning should be put first); and the corpus highlights collocates (the words which go together), information which had only been sketchily covered in previous dictionaries. Under his guidance, his team also developed a full-sentence defining style, which not only gave the user the sense of a word, but showed that word in grammatical context.

When the first *Collins COBUILD Dictionary of English* was published in 1987, it revolutionized dictionaries for learners, completely changed approaches to dictionary-writing, and led to a new generation of corpus-driven dictionaries and reference materials for English language learners.

Professor Sinclair worked on the Collins COBUILD range of titles until his retirement, when he moved to Florence, Italy and became president of the Tuscan Word Centre, an association devoted to promoting the scientific study of language. He remained interested in dictionaries until his death, and the Collins COBUILD range of dictionaries remains a testament to his revolutionary approach to lexicography and English language learning. Professor Sinclair will be sorely missed by everyone who had the great pleasure of working with him.

# Guide to Key Features

Through a collaborative initiative, Collins COBUILD and Heinle is co-publishing a dynamic new line of learners dictionaries offering unparalleled pedagogy and learner resources.

With innovations such as Definitions*PLUS* and vocabulary builders, the *Collins COBUILD School Dictionary of American English* transforms the learner's dictionary from an occasional reference into the ultimate resource and must-have dictionary for language learners. The definitions have been created using a controlled vocabulary, and each definition has been reviewed by a team of classroom teachers to ensure that they are appropriate for learners at the intermediate level.

Definitions *PLUS*
- **Collocations:** Each definition is written using the high-frequency words native speakers naturally use with the target word.
- **Grammar:** Each definition includes naturally occurring grammatical patterns to improve accurate language use.
- **Natural English:** Each definition is a model of how to use the language appropriately.
- **Word Origin:** Each definition includes the word origin information.

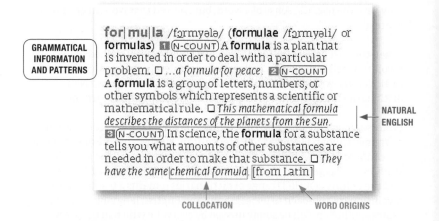

GRAMMATICAL INFORMATION AND PATTERNS

NATURAL ENGLISH

COLLOCATION

WORD ORIGINS

## Academic Vocabulary

*The Collins COBUILD School Dictionary of American English* includes more than 1,000 curriculum terms that students need to know for state examinations and to succeed in all of their classes.

**BANK of ENGLISH**

The Bank of English™ is the original and the most current computerized corpus of authentic American English. This robust research tool was used to create each definition with language appropriate for intermediate level learners. All sample sentences are drawn from the rich selection that the corpus offers which also allows for level appropriate sentences.

## Vocabulary Builders

Over 2,400 pedagogical features encourage curiosity and exploration, which in turn builds the learner's bank of active and passive vocabulary knowledge. The "Vocabulary Builders" outlined here enhance vocabulary acquisition, increase language fluency, and improve accurate communication. They provide the learner with a greater depth and breadth of knowledge of the English language. The *Collins COBUILD School Dictionary of American English* offers a level of content and an overall learning experience unmatched in other dictionaries.

"Picture Dictionary" boxes illustrate vocabulary and concepts. The words are chosen for their usefulness in an academic setting, frequently showing a concept or process that benefits from a visual presentation.

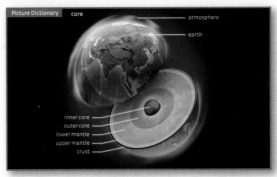

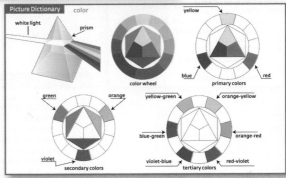

"Word Webs" present topic-related vocabulary through encyclopedia-like readings combined with stunning art, creating opportunities for deeper understanding of the language and concepts. All key words in bold are defined in the dictionary. Upon looking up one word, learners discover other related words that draw them further into the dictionary and the language. The more sustained time learners spend exploring words, the greater and richer their language acquisition is. The "Word Webs" encourage language exploration.

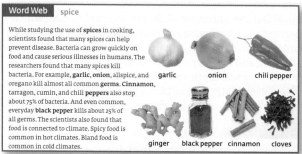

**Word Web**   spice

While studying the use of **spices** in cooking, scientists found that many spices can help prevent disease. Bacteria can grow quickly on food and cause serious illnesses in humans. The researchers found that many spices kill bacteria. For example, **garlic, onion,** allspice, and oregano kill almost all common **germs. Cinnamon,** tarragon, cumin, and chili **peppers** also stop about 75% of bacteria. And even common, everyday **black pepper** kills about 25% of all germs. The scientists also found that food is connected to climate. Spicy food is common in hot climates. Bland food is common in cold climates.

garlic   onion   chili pepper

ginger   black pepper   cinnamon   cloves

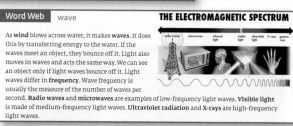

**Word Web**   wave

**THE ELECTROMAGNETIC SPECTRUM**

As **wind** blows across water, it makes **waves.** It does this by transferring energy to the water. If the waves meet an object, they bounce off it. Light also moves in waves and acts the same way. We can see an object only if light waves bounce off it. Light waves differ in **frequency.** Wave frequency is usually the measure of the number of waves per second. **Radio waves** and **microwaves** are examples of low-frequency light waves. **Visible light** is made of medium-frequency light waves. **Ultraviolet radiation** and **X-rays** are high-frequency light waves.

Chosen based on frequency in the Bank of English™, "Word Partnerships" show high-frequency word patterns, giving the complete collocation with the headword in place to clearly demonstrate use. The numbers refer the student to the correct meaning within the definition of the word that collocates with the headword.

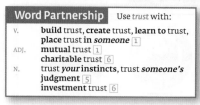

**Word Partnership**   Use *trust* with:

| | |
|---|---|
| V. | **build** trust, **create** trust, **learn to** trust, **place** trust **in *someone*** [1] |
| ADJ. | **mutual** trust [1] **charitable** trust [6] |
| N. | trust ***your* instincts,** trust ***someone's* judgment** [5] **investment** trust [6] |

**Word Partnership**   Use *moment* with:

| | |
|---|---|
| ADV. | **a moment ago, just a** moment [1] |
| N. | moment **of silence,** moment **of thought** [1] |
| V. | **stop for a** moment, **take a** moment, **think for a** moment, **wait a** moment [1] |
| ADJ. | **an awkward** moment, **a critical** moment, **the right** moment [2] |

"Word Links" exponentially increase language awareness by showing how words are built in English, something that will be useful for learners in all areas of academic work as well as in daily communication. Focusing on prefixes, suffixes, and word roots, each "Word Link" provides a simple definition of the building block and then gives three examples of it used in a word. Providing three examples encourages learners to look up these words to further solidify understanding.

"Thesaurus" entries offer both synonyms and antonyms for high frequency words. An extra focus on synonyms offers learners an excellent way to expand vocabulary knowledge and usage by directing them to other words they can research in the dictionary. The numbers refer the student to the correct meaning within the definition of the headword.

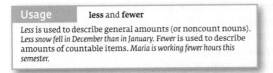

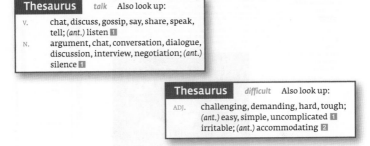

"Usage" notes highlight explain shades of meaning, clarify cultural references, and highlight important grammatical information.

**Usage**     **less** and **fewer**

*Less* is used to describe general amounts (or noncount nouns). *Less snow fell in December than in January.* *Fewer* is used to describe amounts of countable items. *Maria is working fewer hours this semester.*

**Usage**     **one** and **you**

Sometimes *one* is used to refer to any person or to people in general, but it sounds formal: *One has to be smart about buying a computer.* In everyday English, use *you* instead of *one*: *You should only call 911 in an emergency.*

## CD-ROM

A valuable enhancement to the learning experience, the *Collins COBUILD Intermediate Dictionary of American English* CD-ROM offers learners a fast and simple way to explore words and their meanings while working on a computer.

- **Search** definitions, sample sentences, Word Webs, and Picture Dictionary boxes.

- **"PopUp" Dictionary:** Find the definition of a word while working in any computer application.

- **Audio pronunciation with record and playback** provides pronunciation practice.

- **"My Dictionary"** allows learners to create a personalized tool by adding their own words, definitions, and sample sentences.

- **Bookmarks** allow learners to save and organize vocabulary.

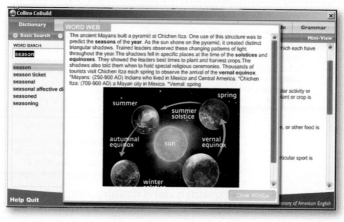

By using the resources found in this volume, learners will discover that the *Collins COBUILD School Dictionary of American English* is something that they want to delve into and spend time exploring, not just something to flip through for a quick answer. As they investigate options for words that will best serve their individual communicative needs at any given point, learners will find more opportunities for learning than they have ever seen in a traditional reference tool. This will become their ultimate resource and partner in their language learning journey.

# Introduction

A dictionary is probably the single most important reference book that a student of English can buy. The *Collins COBUILD School Dictionary of American English* is especially important, because it may be the first dictionary entirely in English that you use.

Like all COBUILD dictionaries, the *Collins COBUILD School Dictionary of American English* is based on a huge database of text, both written and spoken, called The Bank of English™. At this printing, The Bank of English™ contains over 650 million words, and it is the basis of all the statements that COBUILD makes about the language. It allows the dictionary editors to study the way the language works, and shows the patterns and systems of the English language.

The Bank of English™ gives fast and accurate access to all sorts of information about the language. One major area is word frequency. This information is very important in helping to prepare dictionary entries, both because it helps in the choice of words that are suitable for dictionary definitions, and because it provides a sensible list of words that need to be included.

The words explained in this dictionary account for over 90% of the language that is written and spoken. That is because there is a relatively small number of words which are used over and over again, while there is a large number of words which are not used very often. For example, in this introduction, there are 694 words in total. Of these, the word "the" occurs 67 times, while 132 words occur only once. In fact, there are only 223 different words in this introduction. In a much larger amount of text, the words that do not occur very often are much less important. That is why this dictionary concentrates on the words that occur over and over again, and why the entries represent the language that you really do need to know and to use.

One of the main aims of a learner's dictionary is to provide information about those words that the user already "knows", as well as to provide information that the user does not know. Many words have several uses and meanings, and we do not really "know" a word until we are familiar with its full range of meaning and grammatical behavior.

The entries contain a detailed account of the main uses and meanings of each word. Each of the forms is listed at the start of each entry, along with information about alternative spellings, if any exist. Explanations are written in full sentences, and show typical grammatical behavior. The explanations also give a clear description of meaning. And, of course, the thousands of examples are taken directly from The Bank of English™, showing typical patterns of use and grammatical structure. The information in this dictionary has been carefully chosen in order to allow the dictionary user to be a confident language user. It will enable you to write better English as well as understand English better.

The *Collins COBUILD School Dictionary of American English* is printed in full color, which helps the entries to stand out on the page. Over 3,000 of the most frequent English words in the dictionary are clearly shown by having the headword highlighted in pink. These have been identified by using the frequency information in the Bank of English™.

Entries which are very long or complex are treated differently to make it easier to find exactly what you are looking for. A menu shows the sections the entry is divided into, and how they are ordered, so that you can immediately go to the correct section to find the meaning you want. For example, **hand** is divided into two sections, showing its noun and verb uses. The entry for **fire** has three sections showing different groups of meaning.

There are a number of language and usage notes which supplement the information already provided in the dictionary entries. In many cases, these language notes draw together information that helps to clarify the differences that exist between some items.

# Guide to the Dictionary Entries

### Entries and letter index
The main text of the dictionary is made up of entries from A to Z. An **entry** is a complete explanation of a word and all its meanings. For example, the first entries on page 61 are *babble, babe,* and *baby.* Entries are shown under the letter that they begin with. On left-hand pages, the letter is shown as a capital letter, and on right-hand pages, it is shown as a small letter.

### Guide words
At the top of every page you will see a word. This is called a **running head**. On left-hand pages, the running head is the same as the first complete entry on that page. For example, on page 2 the first complete entry is *abide* and this is the running head at the top of the page. On right-hand pages, the running head is the same as the last entry that begins on that page. On page 3, for example, the running head is *absolute zero* because that is the last entry which begins on the page.

### Entry order
Entries are ordered alphabetically and spaces, hyphens, apostrophes, and accents do not make any difference to this. For example, *up-to-date* comes after *uptight* and before *uptown*, and *director general* comes after *director* and before *directory.* In the same way, abbreviations and entries beginning with capital letters are treated like ordinary words, so *B & B* comes after *bandage* and before *bandit*, and *April* comes between *apricot* and *apron.*

### Headwords and superheadwords

Every entry begins with a **headword,** starting at the left-hand edge of the column. Most of the headwords are printed in blue. Words which are closely related in meaning to the headword are also printed in blue, with a black circle before them. For example, on page 1 of the main text, *abdominal* appears as part of the entry for *abdomen*.

Some entries are very long or have very different meanings. These entries are called **superheadwords.** They are divided into numbered sections, with a menu at the beginning of the entry to guide you to the correct section for the meaning you are looking for. For example, *ahead* on page 20 is divided into two sections; section 1 is adverb uses and section 2 is preposition uses.

### Inflected forms and alternative spellings

**Inflected forms** are the different grammatical forms that a word can have. Different forms are shown after the pronunciation. Verbs are shown with the 3rd person singular, the *–ing* form, the past tense, and, where it is different from the past tense, the past participle. Adjectives and adverbs are shown with their comparative forms and nouns are shown with their plural forms. Where a noun does not change its form in the plural, this information is also given. Where there are **alternative spellings** for the headword, these are given in blue before the pronunciation.

### Definitions, meanings, and set structures

**Definitions** are written in full sentences using simple words and show the common ways in which the headword is used. When there is more than one **meaning,** the different meanings are numbered. If a word or expression is used to show approval or disapproval, this information is also given in the definition.

Many words are used in particular grammatical patterns. The definitions show you these important patterns by highlighting these **set structures** in **bold** (black) print.

For example, if you look at the entry for the verb *agree* on page 20, you can see that the preposition *with* is also bold to show that it is used with this verb.

### Examples

The **examples** follow the definitions and are written in *italics*. They are all examples of real language taken from the Bank of English™. They show how the word or phrase is generally used, and give more information about the grammatical patterns in which it is most often used.

### Grammatical labels

Before a definition, there is a **grammatical label.** These labels are explained on pages xvii–xxiii. Where a word has more than one meaning, there is a grammatical label at the beginning of each numbered meaning.

## Style

Some words are used in particular contexts. This is shown in the dictionary by a label in square brackets and in small capitals after the definition.

Style labels:

[BUSINESS]: used mainly when talking about the field of business, e.g. *asset*

[COMPUTING]: used mainly when talking about the field of computing, e.g. *chat room*

[DIALECT]: used in some dialects of English, e.g. *howdy*

[FORMAL]: used mainly in official situations such as politics and business, e.g. *allege*

[INFORMAL]: used mainly in informal situations, conversations, and personal letters, e.g. *pal*

[LEGAL]: used mainly in legal documents, in law courts, and by the police in official situations, e.g. *accused*

[LITERARY]: used mainly in novels, poetry, and other forms of literature, e.g. *aloft*

[MEDICAL]: used mainly in medical texts, and by doctors in official situations, e.g. *psychosis*

[SPOKEN]: used mainly in speech rather than in writing, e.g. *pardon*

[TECHNICAL]: used mainly when talking or writing about specialist subjects, such as science or music, e.g. *biotechnology*

[WRITTEN]: used mainly in writing rather than in speech, e.g. *avail*

# Pronunciation

The suggested pronunciations in this dictionary use the principle that "If you pronounce it like this, most people will understand you." They are based on the most widely taught accent of American English, General American.

The system of showing pronunciations developed from original work by Dr. David Brazil for the *Collins COBUILD English Language Dictionary*. The symbols used in the dictionary are adapted from those of the International Phonetic Alphabet (IPA).

## IPA Symbols

| Vowel | Sounds | Consonant | Sounds |
|---|---|---|---|
| ɑ | calm, ah | b | bed, rub |
| æ | act, mass | d | done, red |
| ɑɪ | dive, cry | f | fit, if |
| ɑɪə | fire, tire | g | good, dog |
| ɑʊ | out, down | h | hat, horse |
| ɑʊə | flour, sour | j | yellow, you |
| ɛ | met, lend, pen | k | king, pick |
| eɪ | say, weight | l | lip, bill |
| ɛə | fair, care | ᵊl | handle, panel |
| ɪ | fit, win | m | mat, ram |
| i | seem, me | n | not, tin |
| ɪə | near, beard | ᵊn | hidden, written |
| ɒ | lot, spot | p | pay, lip |
| oʊ | note, coat | r | run, read |
| ɔ | claw, more | s | soon, bus |
| ɔɪ | boy, joint | t | talk, bet |
| ʊ | could, stood | v | van, love |
| u | you, use | w | win, wool |
| ʊə | lure, pure | x | loch |
| ɛr | turn, third | z | zoo, buzz |
| ʌ | fund, must | ʃ | ship, wish |
| ə | *the first vowel in* **a**bout | ʒ | measure, leisure |
| i | *the second vowel in* ve**ry** | ŋ | sing, working |
| u | the *second vowel in* act**u**al | tʃ | cheap, witch |
| | | θ | thin, myth |
| | | ð | then, bathe |
| | | dʒ | joy, bridge |

## Stress

Stress is shown by underlining the vowel in the stressed syllable:

**two** /tu̲/

**result** /rɪzʌ̲lt/

**disappointing** /dɪsəpɔɪ̲ntɪŋ/

When a word is spoken in isolation, stress falls on the syllables which have vowels which are underlined. If there is one syllable underlined, it will have primary stress.

"TWO"

"reSULT"

If two syllables are underlined, the first will have secondary stress, and the second will have primary stress:

"DISapPOINTing"

A few words are shown with three underlined syllables, for example "disqualification" /dɪskwɒlɪfɪkeɪ̲ʃ°n/. In this case, the third underlined syllable will have primary stress, while the secondary stress may be on the first or second syllable:

"DISqualifiCAtion" or "disQUALifiCAtion"

In the case of compound words, where the pronunciation of each part is given separately, the stress pattern is shown by underlining the headword: "o̲ff-pe̲ak", "fi̲rst-cla̲ss", but "ca̲ke pan".

## Stressed syllables

When words are used in context, the way in which they are pronounced depends upon the information units that are constructed by the speaker. For example, a speaker could say:

1 "the reSULT was disapPOINTing"

2 "it was a DISappointing reSULT"

3 "it was VERy disappointing inDEED"

In (3), neither of the two underlined syllables in disappointing /dɪsəpɔɪntɪŋ/ receives either primary or secondary stress. This shows that it is not possible for a dictionary to predict whether a particular syllable will be stressed in context.

It should be noted, however, that in the case of adjectives with two stressed syllables, the second syllable often loses its stress when it is used before a noun:

"an OFF-peak FARE"

"a FIRST-class SEAT"

Two things should be noted about the marked syllables:

1 They can take primary or secondary stress in a way that is not shared by the other syllables.

2 Whether they are stressed or not, the vowel must be pronounced distinctly; it cannot be weakened to /ə/, /ɪ/, or /ʊ/.

These features are shared by most of the one-syllable words in English, which are therefore transcribed in this dictionary as stressed syllables:

**two** /tu/

**inn** /ɪn/

**tree** /tri/

### Unstressed syllables

It is an important characteristic of English that vowels in unstressed syllables tend not to be pronounced clearly. Many unstressed syllables contain the vowel /ə/, a neutral vowel which is not found in stressed syllables. The vowels /ɪ/, or /ʊ/. which are relatively neutral in quality, are also common in unstressed syllables.

Single-syllable grammatical words such as "shall" and "at" are often pronounced with a weak vowel such as /ə/. However, some of them are pronounced with a more distinct vowel under certain circumstances, for example when they occur at the end of a sentence. This distinct pronunciation is generally referred to as the strong form, and is given in this dictionary after the word rsqnmf .

**shall** /ʃəl, STRONG ʃæl/

**at** /ət, STRONG æt/

# GRAMMATICAL LABELS USED IN THE DICTIONARY

Nearly all the words that are explained in this dictionary have grammar information given about them. For each word or meaning, its word class is shown in capital letters, just before the definition. Examples of word classes are N-COUNT, VERB, PRON and ADV.

The sections below contain further information about each word class.

### Verbs

A verb is a word which is used to say what someone or something does or what happens to them, or to give information about them.

### V-I

An **intransitive verb** is one which takes an indirect object or no object, e.g.:

    bake: I love to <u>bake</u>.

## V-T

A **transitive verb** is one which takes a direct object, e.g.:

mail: *He mailed me the contract.*

## V-T/V-I

Some verbs may be **transitive** or **intransitive** depending on how they are used, e.g.:

open: *He opened the window.* (transitive) *The doors opened.* (intransitive)

## V-T PASSIVE

**V-T PASSIVE** means **passive verb.** A passive verb is a verb that is formed using a form of *be* followed by the past participle of the main verb. Passive verbs focus on the person or thing that is affected by the action, e.g.:

born: *She was born in Milan on April 29, 1923.*

## PHR-VERB

**PHR-VERB** means **phrasal verb.** A phrasal verb is a combination of a verb and an adverb (e.g., *catch up*) or a verb and a preposition (e.g., *call for*), which together have a particular meaning. Some phrasal verbs have both an adverb and a preposition (for example *add up to*).

catch up: *I stopped and waited for her to catch up.*

call for: *I will call for you at seven o'clock.*

add up to: *Profits can add up to millions of dollars.*

## V-LINK

**V-LINK** means **link verb.** A **link verb** is a verb such as *be*, *feel*, or *seem*. These verbs connect the subject of a sentence to a complement. Most link verbs do not occur in the passive, e.g.:

be: *She is my mother.*

feel: *It feels good to finish a piece of work.*

seem: *Everyone seems busy.*

## V-RECIP

**V-RECIP** means **reciprocal verb.** A reciprocal verb describes a process in which two or more people, groups, or things do the same thing to each other, or take part in the same action or event. Reciprocal verbs are used where the subject is both people, e.g. *Fred and Sally met.* The people can also be referred to separately, e.g. *Fred met Sally. Fred argued with Sally.* These patterns are reciprocal because they also mean that *Sally met Fred* and *Sally argued with Fred.* Many reciprocal verbs can also be used in a way that is not reciprocal. For example, *Fred and Sally spoke* is reciprocal, but *Fred spoke to Sally* is not reciprocal (because it does not mean that Sally also spoke to Fred).

### V-RECIP-PASSIVE
**V-RECIP-PASSIVE** means **passive reciprocal verb**. A passive reciprocal verb behaves like both a passive verb and a reciprocal verb, e.g., *I don't think Susan and I will be reconciled*.

### MODAL
A **modal** is a **modal verb** such as *may*, *must*, or *would*. A **modal** is used before the infinitive form of a verb, e.g., *I must go home now*. In questions, it comes before the subject, e.g., *May we come in?* In negatives, it comes before the negative word, e.g., *She wouldn't say where she bought her shoes*. It does not inflect, for example, it does not take an *-s* in the third person singular, e.g., *I can take care of myself*.

### Nouns

### N-COUNT
**N-COUNT** means a **count noun**. Count nouns refer to things which can be counted, and they have both the singular and plural forms. When a count noun is used in the singular, it must normally have a word such as *a*, *an*, *the*, or *her* in front of it, e.g.:

> head: *She turned her head away from him*.

> room: *A minute later he left the room*.

### N-UNCOUNT
**N-UNCOUNT** means an **uncount noun**. Uncount nouns refer to things that are not normally counted or which we do not think of as individual items. Uncount nouns do not have a plural form, and are used with a singular verb, e.g.:

> help: *He shouted for help*.

> rain: *We got very wet in the rain*.

> bread: *She bought a loaf of bread*.

### N-VAR
**N-VAR** means a **variable noun**. Variable nouns are uncount when they refer to something in general, and count nouns when they refer to a particular instance of something, e.g.:

> night: *The rain continued all night*.

> > *Night finally fell*.

Other variable nouns refer to substances. They are uncount when they refer to a mass of the substance, and count nouns when they refer to types or brands, e.g.:

> coffee: *Would you like some coffee?*

> > *We had a coffee*.

### N-SING

**N-SING** means a **singular noun**. A singular noun is always singular and must have a word such as *a*, *an*, *the*, or *my* in front of it, e.g.:

sun: *The sun was high in the sky.*

fault: *The accident was all my fault.*

### N-PLURAL

**N-PLURAL** means a **plural noun**. A plural noun is always plural and is used with plural verbs, e.g.:

clothes: *Moira went upstairs to change her clothes.*

feelings: *I'm sorry if I hurt your feelings.*

### N-TITLE

**N-TITLE** means a noun that is used to refer to someone who has a particular role or position. Titles come before the name of the person and begin with a capital letter, e.g., *President Obama, Queen Elizabeth.*

### N-VOC

**N-VOC** means a **vocative noun**. A vocative noun is a noun that is used when speaking directly to someone or writing to them, e.g.:

darling: *Thank you, darling.*

dear: *Are you feeling better, dear?*

### N-PROPER

**N-PROPER** means a **proper noun**. A proper noun refers to one person, place, thing, or institution, and begins with a capital letter, e.g.:

Earth: *We don't know everything about the Earth.*

Pentagon: *There was a news conference at the Pentagon.*

## Other Word Classes

### ADJ

**ADJ** means an **adjective**. An adjective is a word which is used to tell you more about a person or thing, such as its appearance, color, size, or other qualities, e.g.:

angry: *An angry crowd gathered.*

brown: *She has brown eyes.*

wet: *My gloves were wet.*

### ADV

**ADV** means an **adverb**. An adverb is a word that gives more information about when, how, or where something happens, e.g.:

tomorrow: *Bye, see you tomorrow.*

slowly: *He spoke slowly and clearly.*

home: *She wanted to go home.*

## AUX
**AUX** means an **auxiliary verb**. An auxiliary verb is used with another verb to add particular meanings to that verb, for example, to form the continuous or the passive, or to form negatives and questions. The verbs *be, do, get* and *have* are used as auxiliary verbs in some meanings, e.g.:

be: *She didn't always think carefully about what she was doing.*

do: *They don't want to work.*

have: *Alex has already gone.*

get: *A pane of glass got broken.*

## COLOR
A **color** word refers to a color. It is like an adjective, e.g., *the blue sky . . . The sky was blue,* and also like a noun, e.g., *She was dressed in red. . . . several shades of yellow.*

## CONJ
**CONJ** means a **conjunction**. Conjunctions are words such as *and, but, although,* or *since,* which are used to link two words or two clauses in a sentence, e.g.:

although: *Although I was only six, I remember it.*

but: *I'm sorry, but it's true.*

since: *So much has changed since I was a teenager.*

## CONVENTION
A **convention** is a word or fixed phrase which is used in conversation, for example when greeting someone, apologizing, or replying. Examples of conventions are *hello, sorry,* and *I'm afraid,* e.g.:

hello: *Hello, this is Susan. Could I speak to Nancy please?*

sorry: *Sorry I took so long.*

I'm afraid: *I'm afraid I don't agree.*

## DET
**DET** means a **determiner**. A determiner is a word such as *a, the, my,* or *every* which is used at the beginning of a noun group, e.g.:

an: *One way of making friends is to go to an evening class.*

the: *Daily walks are the best exercise.*

every: *Every room has a window facing the ocean.*

## EXCLAM

**EXCLAM** means an **exclamation**. An exclamation is a word or phrase which is spoken suddenly or loudly in order to express a strong emotion, e.g.:

oh: "_Oh!_" _Kenny said._ "_Has everyone gone?_"

wow: _Wow, this is so exciting!_

## FRACTION

A **fraction** is used in numbers, e.g., _five and a half, two and two thirds;_ before _of_ and a noun group, e.g., _half of the money, a third of the children, an eighth of a gallon;_ after _in_ or _into_, e.g., _in half, into thirds._ A fraction is also used like a count noun, e.g., _two halves, the first quarter of the year._

## QUANT

**QUANT** means a **quantifier**. A quantifier is a word or phrase like _plenty_ or _a lot_ which allows you to say in a general way how many there are of something, or how much there is of something. Quantifiers are often followed by _of_, e.g.:

all: _He was talking to all of us._

enough: _They had enough money for a one-way ticket._

whole: _We spent the whole summer in Italy._

## NEG

**NEG** means **negative**. This is used to describe _not_, which is used to make negative statements and questions. Please see the entry for _not_.

## NUM

**NUM** means **number,** e.g.:

ten: _It took almost ten years._

billion: _. . . 3 billion dollars._

## ORD

**ORD** means **ordinal**. An ordinal is a number that is used like an adjective or an adverb, e.g.:

hundredth: _The bank's hundredth anniversary is in December._

first: _January is the first month of the year._

## PHRASE

A **phrase** is a group of words which have a particular meaning when they are used together. This meaning is not always understandable from the separate parts, e.g.:

change hands: _The company has changed hands many times._

sit tight: _Sit tight, I'll be right back._

### PREDET

**PREDET** means a **predeterminer**. A predeterminer is a word such as *all* or *half* which can come before a determiner, e.g.:

all: *She's worked all her life.*

half: *She's half his age*

### PREP

**PREP** means a **preposition**. A preposition is a word such as *by*, *with*, or *from* which is always followed by a noun group or the *-ing* form of a verb, e.g.:

near: *He stood near the door.*

of: *She is a young woman of twenty-six.*

### PRON

**PRON** means a **pronoun**. A pronoun is used to refer to someone or something that has already been mentioned or whose identity is already known, e.g.:

she: *When Ann arrived home she found Brian watching TV.*

they: *She said goodbye to the children as they left for school.*

this: *I have seen many movies, but never one like this.*

### PRON-NEG

**PRON-NEG** means a negative pronoun such as *neither*, e.g.:

neither: *Neither one noticed him leave the room.*

Some meanings in entries have more than one word class. For example:

officer 2: N-COUNT; N-VOC

This means that *officer* is both a count noun and a vocative noun for meaning 2.

*The officer saw no sign of a break-in.*

*Officer Montoya was the first on the scene.*

# Irregular Verbs

| Infinitive | Past Tense | Past Participle |
|---|---|---|
| arise | arose | arisen |
| be | was, were | been |
| beat | beat | beaten |
| become | became | become |
| begin | began | begun |
| bend | bent | bent |
| bet | bet | bet |
| bind | bound | bound |
| bite | bit | bitten |
| bleed | bled | bled |
| blow | blew | blown |
| break | broke | broken |
| bring | brought | brought |
| build | built | built |
| burn | burned or burnt | burned or burnt |
| burst | burst | burst |
| buy | bought | bought |
| can | could | – |
| cast | cast | cast |
| catch | caught | caught |
| choose | chose | chosen |
| cling | clung | clung |
| come | came | come |
| cost | cost or costed | cost or costed |
| creep | crept | crept |
| cut | cut | cut |
| deal | dealt | dealt |
| dig | dug | dug |
| dive | dived or dove | dived |
| do | did | done |
| draw | drew | drawn |
| dream | dreamed or dreamt | dreamed or dreamt |
| drink | drank | drunk |
| drive | drove | driven |
| eat | ate | eaten |
| fall | fell | fallen |
| feed | fed | fed |
| feel | felt | felt |
| fight | fought | fought |
| find | found | found |
| fly | flew | flown |
| forbid | forbade | forbidden |
| forget | forgot | forgotten |
| freeze | froze | frozen |
| get | got | gotten, got |

| give | gave | given |
|------|------|-------|
| go | went | gone |
| grind | ground | ground |
| grow | grew | grown |
| hang | hung *or* hanged | hung *or* hanged |
| have | had | had |
| hear | heard | heard |
| hide | hid | hidden |
| hit | hit | hit |
| hold | held | held |
| hurt | hurt | hurt |
| keep | kept | kept |
| kneel | kneeled *or* knelt | kneeled *or* knelt |
| know | knew | known |
| lay | laid | laid |
| lead | led | led |
| lean | leaned *or* leant | leaned *or* leant |
| leap | leaped *or* leapt | leaped *or* leapt |
| leave | left | left |
| lend | lent | lent |
| let | let | let |
| lie | lay | lain |
| light | lit *or* lighted | lit *or* lighted |
| lose | lost | lost |
| make | made | made |
| may | might | – |
| mean | meant | meant |
| meet | met | met |
| pay | paid | paid |
| put | put | put |
| quit | quit | quit |
| read | read | read |
| rid | rid | rid |
| ride | rode | ridden |
| ring | rang | rung |
| rise | rose | risen |
| run | ran | run |
| say | said | said |
| see | saw | seen |
| seek | sought | sought |
| sell | sold | sold |
| send | sent | sent |
| set | set | set |
| shake | shook | shaken |
| shed | shed | shed |
| shine | shined *or* shone | shined *or* shone |

| | | |
|---|---|---|
| shoe | shod | shod |
| shoot | shot | shot |
| show | showed | shown |
| shrink | shrank | shrunk |
| shut | shut | shut |
| sing | sang | sung |
| sink | sank | sunk |
| sit | sat | sat |
| sleep | slept | slept |
| slide | slid | slid |
| speak | spoke | spoken |
| speed | sped *or* speeded | sped *or* speeded |
| spend | spent | spent |
| spill | spilled *or* spilt | spilled *or* spilt |
| spit | spit *or* spat | spit *or* spat |
| spoil | spoiled *or* spoilt | spoiled *or* spoilt |
| spread | spread | spread |
| spring | sprang | sprung |
| stand | stood | stood |
| steal | stole | stolen |
| stick | stuck | stuck |
| sting | stung | stung |
| stink | stank | stunk |
| strike | struck | struck *or* stricken |
| swear | swore | sworn |
| sweep | swept | swept |
| swell | swelled | swollen |
| swim | swam | swum |
| swing | swung | swung |
| take | took | taken |
| teach | taught | taught |
| tear | tore | torn |
| tell | told | told |
| think | thought | thought |
| throw | threw | thrown |
| wake | woke *or* waked | woken *or* waked |
| wear | wore | worn |
| weep | wept | wept |
| win | won | won |
| wind | wound | wound |
| write | wrote | written |

# Suffixes and prefixes

Suffixes are word endings which can be added to words, usually to make a new word with a similar meaning but different part of speech. In this dictionary some words have a black circle in front of them and have an example but no definition. These words are formed by adding a suffix.

The list of suffixes is followed by a list of the most frequent prefixes. Prefixes are beginnings of words, which have a regular meaning.

## Suffixes

**-ability** and **-ibility** replace *-able* and *-ible* at the end of adjectives to form nouns which refer to a particular state or quality. For example, *reliability* is the state or quality of being reliable.

**-able** forms adjectives which indicate what someone or something can have done to them. For example, if something is *readable*, it is possible to read it.

**-al** forms adjectives which indicate what something is connected with. For example, *environmental* problems are problems connected with the environment.

**-ally** is added to adjectives ending in *-ic* to form adverbs which indicate how something is done or what something relates to. For example, if something is done *enthusiastically*, it is done in an enthusiastic way.

**-ance** and **-ence** form nouns which refer to a particular action, state, or quality. For example, *brilliance* is the state or quality of being brilliant, and *reappearance* is the action of reappearing.

**-ation, -ication, -sion** and **-tion** form nouns which refer to a state or process, or to an instance of that process. For example, the *protection* of something is the process of protecting it.

**-cy** forms nouns which refer to a particular state or quality. For example, *accuracy* is the state or quality of being accurate.

**-ed** is added to verbs to make the past tense and past participle. Past participles formed are often used as adjectives which indicate that something has been affected in some way. For example, *cooked* food is food that has been cooked.

**-ence** see **-ance**

**-er** and **-or** form nouns which refer to a person who performs a particular action, often because it is their job. For example, a *teacher* is someone who teaches. **-er** and **-or** also form nouns which refer to tools and machines that perform a particular action. For example, a *boiler* is a machine that boils things.

**-ful** forms nouns which refer to the amount of a substance that something contains or can contain. For example, a *handful* of sand is the amount of sand that you can hold in your hand.

**-ibility** see **-ability**

**-ic** forms adjectives which indicate that something or someone is connected with a particular thing. For example, *photographic* equipment is equipment connected with photography.

**-ication,** see **-ation**

**-ing** is added to verbs to make the *-ing* form, or present participle. Present participle forms are often used as adjectives describing a person or thing who is doing something. For example, a *sleeping* baby is a baby that is sleeping and an *amusing* joke is a joke that amuses people. Present participle forms are also used as nouns which refer to activities. For example, if you say you like *dancing*, you mean that you like to dance.

**-ish** forms adjectives which indicate that someone or something has a quality to a small extent. For example, if you say that something is *largish*, you mean it is fairly large, and something that is *yellowish* is slightly yellow in color.

**-ish** also forms words that indicate that a particular time or age mentioned is approximate. For example, if someone is *fortyish*, they are about forty years old.

**-ism** forms nouns which refer to particular beliefs, or to behaviour based on these beliefs. For example, *professionalism* is behaviour that is professional and *racism* is the beliefs and behavior of a racist.

**-ist** forms nouns which refer to people who do a particular kind of work. For example, a *scientist* is someone whose work is connected with science.

**-ist** also forms nouns which refer to people who play a particular musical instrument, often as their job. For example, a *violinist* is someone who plays the violin.

**-ity** forms nouns which refer to a particular state or quality. For example, *solidity* is the state or quality of being solid.

**-less** forms adjectives which indicate that someone or something does not have a particular thing. For example, someone who is *childless* does not have any children.

**-ly** forms adverbs which indicate how something is done. For example, if someone speaks *cheerfully*, they speak in a cheerful way.

**-ment** forms nouns which refer to the process of making or doing something, or to the result of this process. For example, *replacement* is the process of replacing something or the thing which replaces it.

**-ness** forms nouns which refer to a particular state or quality. For example, *gentleness* is the state or quality of being gentle.

**-or** see **-er**

**-ous** forms adjectives which indicate that someone or something has a particular quality. For example, a person who is *humorous* has a lot of humor.

**-sion, -tion,** see **-ation**

**-y** forms adjectives which indicate that something is full of something else or covered in it. For example, if something is *dirty*, it is covered with dirt.

**-y** also forms adjectives which mean that something is like something else. For example, if something tastes *chocolatey*, it tastes like chocolate, although it is not actually chocolate.

### Prefixes

**a-** forms adjectives which have *not*, *without*, or *opposite* in their meaning. For example, *atypical* behavior is not typical of someone.

**anti-** forms nouns and adjectives which refer to some sort of opposition. For example, if something is an *anti-virus*, it protects against a virus.

**auto-** forms words which refer to someone doing something to, for, or about themselves. For example, your *autobiography* is an account of your life, which you write yourself.

**bi-** forms nouns and adjectives which have *two* as part of their meaning. For example, if someone is *bilingual*, they speak two languages.

**bi-** also forms adjectives and adverbs which refer to something happening twice in a period of time, or once in two consecutive periods of time. A **bimonthly** event happens twice a month, or once every two months.

**co-** forms verbs and nouns which refer to people sharing things or doing things together. For example, if two people *co-write* a book, they write it together. The *co-author* of a book is one of the people who have written it.

**counter-** forms words which refer to actions or activities that oppose another action or activity. For example, a *counter-measure* is an action you take to weaken the effect of another action or situation.

**de-** is added to some verbs to make verbs which mean the opposite. For example, to *deactivate* a mechanism means to switch it off so that it cannot work.

**dis-** can be added to some words to form words which have the opposite meaning. For example, if someone is *dishonest*, they are not honest.

**eco-** forms nouns and adjectives which refer to something related to the environment. For example, *eco-friendly* products do not harm the environment.

**ex-** forms words which refer to people who are no longer a particular thing. For example, an *ex-police officer* is someone who is no longer a police officer.

**extra-** forms adjectives which refer to something being outside or beyond something else. For example, something which is *extraordinary* is more than ordinary, that is, very special.

**extra-** also forms adjectives which refer to something having a large amount of a particular quality. For example, if something is *extra-strong*, it is very strong.

**hyper-** forms adjectives which refer to people or things which have a large amount of, or too much, of a particular quality. For example, *hyperinflation* is very extreme inflation.

**il-, im-, in-,** and **ir-** can be added to some words to form words which have the opposite meaning. For example, if an activity is *illegal*, it is not legal. If someone is *impatient*, they are not patient.

**inter-** forms adjectives which refer to things that move, exist, or happen between two or more people or things. For example, *inter-city* trains travel between cities.

**ir-** see **il-**

**kilo-** forms words which refer to things which have a thousand parts. For example, a *kilometer* is a thousand meters.

**mal-** forms words which refer to things that are bad or unpleasant, or that are unsuccessful or imperfect. For example, if a machine *malfunctions*, it does not work properly.

**mega-** forms words which refer to units which are a million times bigger. For example, a *megawatt* is a million watts.

**micro-** forms nouns which have *small* as part of their meaning. For example, a *micro-organism* is a very small living thing that you cannot see with your eyes alone.

**mid-** forms nouns and adjectives which refer to the middle part of a particular period of time, or the middle part of a particular place. For example, *mid-June* is the middle of June.

**milli-** forms nouns which refer to units which are a thousand times smaller. For example, a *millimeter is a thousandth of a meter.*

**mini-** forms nouns which refer to things which are a smaller version of something else. For example, a *minibus* is a small bus.

**mis-** forms verbs and nouns which refer to something being done badly or wrongly. For example, if you *misbehave*, you behave badly.

**mono-** forms nouns and adjectives which have *one* or *single* as part of their meaning. For example, *monogamy* is the custom of being married to one person.

**multi-** forms adjectives which refer to something that consists of many things of a particular kind. For example, a *multi-colored* object has many different colors.

**neo-** forms nouns and adjectives which refer to modern versions of styles and particular groups of the past. For example, *neo-classical* architecture is based on ancient Greek or Roman architecture.

**non-** forms nouns and adjectives which refer to people or things that do not have a particular quality or characteristic. For example, a *non-fatal* accident is not fatal.

**non-** also forms nouns which refer to situations where a particular action has not taken place. For example, someone's *non-attendance* at a meeting is the fact that they did not go to the meeting.

**out-** forms verbs which refer to an action as being done better by one person than by another. For example, if you can *outswim* someone, you can swim further or faster than they can.

**over-** forms words which refer to a quality of action that exists or is done to too great an extent. For example, if someone is being *over-cautious*, they are being too cautious.

**part-** forms words which refer to something that is partly but not completely a particular thing. For example, *partly-baked bread* is only partly baked.

**poly-** forms nouns and adjectives which have *many* as part of their meaning. For example, a *polysyllabic* word contains many syllables.

**post-** forms words that refer to something that takes place after a particular date, period, or event. For example, a *postscript* (PS) to a letter is extra information that you write at the end, after you have signed it.

**pre-** forms words that refer to something that takes place before a particular date, period, or event. For example, *pregame* activities take place before a game or sporting event.

**pro-** forms adjectives which refer to people who strongly support a particular person or thing. For example, if you are *pro-democracy*, you support democracy.

**pseudo-** forms nouns and adjectives which refer to something which is not really what it seems or claims to be. For example, a *pseudo-science* is something that claims to be a science, but is not.

**re-** forms verbs and nouns which refer to an action or process being repeated. For example, if you *re-read* something, you read it again.

**semi-** forms nouns and adjectives which refer to people and things that are partly, but not completely, in a particular state. For example, if you are *semi-conscious*, you are partly, but not wholly, conscious.

**sub-** forms nouns which refer to things that are part of a larger thing. For example, a *subcommittee* is a small committee made up of members of a larger committee.

**sub-** also forms adjectives which refer to people or things that are inferior. For example, *substandard* living conditions are inferior to normal living conditions.

**super-** forms nouns and adjectives which refer to people and things that are larger, better, or more advanced than others. For example, a *super-fit* athlete is extremely fit, and a *supertanker* is a very large tanker.

**tri-** forms nouns and adjectives which have 'three' as part of their meaning. For example, a *tricycle* is a cycle with three wheels.

**ultra-** forms adjectives which refer to people and things that possess a quality to a very large degree. For example, an *ultra-light* fabric is extremely light.

**un-** can be added to some words to form words which have the opposite meaning. For example, if something is *unacceptable*, it is not acceptable.

**under-** forms words which refer to an amount or value being too low or not enough. For example, if someone is *underweight*, their weight is lower than it should be.

# History of English

The English language has been spoken for about 1,500 years. Its family roots reach back further, even beyond England, to the tribes and kingdoms of northern Europe, and yet further, to an ancient people living in central Asia more than 5,000 years ago. We can reconstruct the history of our language through careful study of the few written records that we have, through related historical records, and even through the similarities of English to other related languages.

Languages, like humans, exist in families, and have brothers and sisters, parents, grandparents, close cousins, and distant cousins. Some researchers believe that *all* human languages have a common ancestor. The study of the origins and development of languages is called historical linguistics, and a person who studies historical linguistics is called a *philologist*. The word *philology* comes to English from French, and to French from the ancient Greek words *philos*, meaning *love*, and *logos*, meaning *word, reason, learning*.

Perhaps 5,000 to 7,000 years ago or more—no one knows for certain—an ancient people dwelt on the steppes of central Asia. We know little about these people, and in fact we have no actual proof that they existed, nor that they lived there on the steppes. Everything we suppose about these people is called a *hypothesis*—a theory that makes sense based on the known facts. These people lived in the lands between the Black Sea and the Caspian Sea, around an area named the Caucasus. Today this area is largely located in southwestern Russia, and also includes areas in the present-day nations of Armenia, Azerbaijan, and Georgia. We do not know the name of this people, so we refer to them as the Indo-Europeans, for reasons which will become clear.

Perhaps 5,000 to 6,000 years ago, about the time that the Egyptian pharaohs were building the great pyramids at Giza, the Indo-European people began spreading out, moving north, east, west, and south. It is unclear why they began migrating: They may have wanted to conquer their neighboring peoples, or they may have been simply looking for more farmland to till. We know that they had carts with wheels, and horses to ride and pull the carts. They probably had tools and weapons made of copper or bronze. They had their own gods, which they would have taken with them when they migrated. In any event, over the centuries they spread farther and farther from their ancestral homelands, traveling over the steppes, forests, and mountains of Asia and Europe. Eventually, many generations later, their descendants reached as far east as India and as far west as Europe. Thus, because they had spread far and wide, we call these original people the Indo-Europeans.

When the original Indo-Europeans dwelt in the Caucasus, they most likely all spoke a common language, or different dialects of their common language. But languages evolve and change over time. When groups of people, who speak a common language, are separated from one another and no longer speak with one another, the languages of the separated groups may evolve differently. Even today, although England and America have been separated for only a little more than 200 years, there are differences between British English and American English. After many generations, the Indo-European travelers had been separated from their ancestral homeland for hundreds or thousands of years. Their once-common language evolved along separate paths. Eventually the languages spoken by the different groups had changed so much that they were completely different languages. If one of the European travelers had met one of the Indian travelers, they would not have been able to understand each other.

Some of these early wandering tribes reached present-day Europe about 4,000 to 5,000 years ago. Their migrations took them all the way to the shores of the Atlantic Ocean in present-day France, Spain, and Portugal. Today we call these people the Celts, or Celtic people, although we do not know if they had a name for themselves. Their original Indo-European language had evolved into a group of Celtic languages. Eventually they built boats, crossed the English Channel, and populated the British Isles. These were the first Britons, speaking Celtic languages. Their language is the ancestor of modern-day Gaelic, Welsh, and Manx.

Other Indo-European tribes migrated toward northern Europe, possibly a thousand years later than the Celts. They settled in the forests and fields of northern Germany and along the cold shores of the Baltic Sea. The Indo-European language of these people had evolved into what we today call

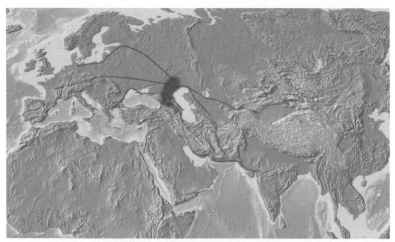

Migration of Indo-European people.

Proto-Germanic (*proto-* means *first* or *earliest*). This language is the ancestor of the German, Dutch, and the Scandinavian languages.

Some of the migrating Indo-European tribes moved into southern Europe along the rocky steep shores of the Mediterranean Sea and the Aegean Sea. The language of these people became the Greek language, for which we have written records dating back at least 3,500 years.

Several hundred years after the Greeks had established their civilization, some of the Celtic and Greek peoples moved into the Italian peninsula. They brought their languages with them and eventually their languages evolved to become the Italic languages. As their civilization grew, their languages began to dominate the peninsula. The non-Indo-European languages that had existed there in ancient times withered away. Eventually the region in the center of present-day Italy, known as Latium, would dominate the other areas. This area is around the ancient city of Rome, and the language spoken there was Latin. When Rome became the dominant power in the Mediterranean area and spread its civilization, the Latin language was carried far and wide. In the centuries following the fall of Roman civilization, other languages began to evolve, which were based on Latin. These languages are known as the *Romance languages*, and include Italian, French, Spanish, Portuguese, and others.

Around the year 55 BC, the mighty army of the Roman empire had reached the British Isles and began the process of subduing the original Celtic inhabitants of the isles. Within eight years, the Roman conquest was complete, and by 43 BC Rome had control of most of the area that is now England. The colony was named Britannia (which is where we get the name Britain). The language of the ruling class was, of course, Latin, which the army had brought with them from Rome. Some of the original Celts became Romanized and spoke Latin, but most likely they would have spoken their Celtic languages among themselves.

While Rome was occupied with its Mediterranean and western European empire, the proto-Germanic tribes of Scandinavia and northern Germany were pushing south and conquering the earlier Celtic tribes of western Europe. Eventually the tribes pushed clear down into the Italian peninsula and sacked Rome itself in 410 AD and again in 455 AD. The destruction of 410 was accomplished by a Germanic tribe named the Visigoths (*Visi-* means western—The *Ostrogoths* were the eastern Goths). The Goths even set themselves up as Roman emperors.

Even before the ruin of Rome, the once-vast Roman empire had been steadily collapsing in the 4th century AD. Rome no longer had the strength, the will, or the resources to continue their constant battles against the Celts. So in the year 410, the year in which the Visigoths laid waste to Rome, Roman armies sailed away from the isles and left the original inhabitants to fend for themselves. After this time the Latin language was not spoken much in England, but was still used in the monasteries as the language of the Christian church, as the British Isles had been Christianized during the Roman reign.

Unfortunately for the Britons, they did not get much respite from conquering armies after Rome departed. Within a short period of time, fierce northern Germanic tribes began arriving in the British Isles. These tribes were notably the Jutes, Frisians, Angles, and Saxons. The Jutes came from an area of Germany that is still today called Jutland, which is the northern peninsula of Germany that stretches up toward Denmark and Scandinavia, and encloses the Baltic Sea. The Frisians were close neighbors of the Jutes, inhabiting the low-lying islands on the northern coast of Germany and what is today the Netherlands. The Angles were also close neighbors of the Jutes and Frisians in an area of modern Germany named Schleswig-Holstein. Likewise, the Saxons lived in the same area between the Angles and the Frisians. The modern English word *Anglo-Saxon* comes from the names of these latter two peoples.

By the time of the Germanic invasions of Britain, each of the invading tribes already had its own language, descended from the ancient Indo-European travelers of thousands of years ago. However, their languages were closely related, and it is likely that they could have talked with one another with only a moderate level of difficulty. In those days there were no nations such as Germany and Netherlands, only tribes and clans.

After many fierce battles with the Germanic invaders, over the next two hundred years or so the original Celts were pushed aside. Many fled west to Wales and Cornwall, and across the Irish Sea to Ireland. Others fled north to Scotland and some went south to northwestern France, to an area that is today named Brittany. Today the people of those countries still speak the Celtic-based languages: Welsh, Cornish, Irish Gaelic, Scots Gaelic, and Breton.

The conquering Germanic tribes set up seven kingdoms in the southwest of England called the Anglo-Saxon Heptarchy (*hept-* means seven, and *-arch* means *ruling*, as in *monarch*), which were Mercia, Northumbria, Kent, Wessex, Sussex, Essex, and East Anglia. They spoke a number of different Germanic dialects, but probably could talk with one another. By about the year 600 AD, their languages had more-or-less merged into a new language, and this language was distinct from their original Germanic languages. This was the beginning of the English language, and began what we now call the Old English period.

This early language was eventually called *Englisc* (English), but was probably first called *Anglisc*, named for the Angles who had invaded and ruled. The name *England*, was of course derived from Angle-land, also named for the Angles.

Around the year 731 lived a remarkable man named Bede, known as Venerable Bede. He was a Benedictine monk who lived at the Northumbrian monastery of Saint Peter at Monkwearmouth in the northeast of England. He is well known as an author and scholar, and his most famous work was *Historia ecclesiastica gentis Anglorum* (Latin: The Ecclesiastical History of the English People). This work gained him the title The Father of English History. This is the first recorded use of the term English for a people or a language, and it is one of the earliest records we have that is written in Old English.

Around this time, another group of Germanic peoples had their eye on England as a potential for loot and new lands to conquer, and they saw England as ripe for the plucking. These were the fierce Viking warriors, who hailed from the fjords of the Norwegian coast, and the Danes from Denmark, just a few hundred miles to the east across the cold North Sea. In the year 793 came the first serious and damaging raid by the Vikings: They sailed across the sea in their great longboats and sacked the monastery at Lindisfarne, in Northumberland in far northeast England.

Over the next 200 years, the Vikings and Danes continually attacked the kingdoms in the east of England. Many pitched battles were fought but the English were unable to completely drive the Viking warriors from the isles. In the year 878 King Alfred called for a truce with the Vikings and signed the Treaty of Wedmore, which gave the northeast half of England to the Danes for settlement. This was called the "Danelaw." The Danes of course had their own Germanic language but because the languages were so similar to Old English, the Danes quickly assimilated (a Latin word that means *becoming alike*) and intermarried into the English society. As a result of this settlement, many old words of Danish were brought into the English language.

In the year 1014, the Aethelred, the king of England, fled to France in the face of unrelenting attacks by the Danes and Vikings. The Danish ruler Canute (or *Cnut* or *Knut*), son of the Danish king, became the king of England. Despite his Danish origins, Canute considered himself English, and encouraged English literature and culture. Canute died in 1035, leaving no heir, so the throne reverted back to the Englishman Edward. Edward (known as "Edward the Confessor") died in January 1066, again leaving no heir, but he had recommended Harold Godwinson, the son of a powerful Wessex duke, to be the next king. Harold was duly crowned king.

However, William, the Duke of Normandy from across the English Channel, and descendent of English nobility, had claimed the rights to the throne, and expected to be named king upon the death of Edward. When he was not so named, in September 1066 he sailed across the English Channel with his army of Normans to take the throne by force. In a decisive battle at Hastings

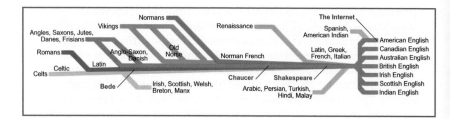

in Sussex, England, William defeated the army of Harold, thus gaining the throne of England. This was a defining moment in the history of England and forever changed the English language as well as English history.

This event marks the close of the age of Old English and the beginning of Middle English. When William became king, he brought with him all of his courtiers and advisers from France. Thus the royal court of England became a French-speaking court, and anyone of power and influence, or anyone who simply wanted to do business with the court, had to learn to speak French. However, the lower classes, the Anglo-Saxons, were mostly farmers and continued to speak English.

A word or two about the French language: In the fifth century after the breakup of the Roman Empire, in which Latin was spoken, the peoples who were formerly subjects of Rome were left to their own devices. They were widely dispersed throughout Europe and their languages began to evolve by separate paths from the original Latin. Thus the Italian, Spanish, Portuguese, and French languages—and others—began to diverge from their Latin source. By 1066 when William conquered England, more than 600 years after the fall of Rome, these had become separate languages, but all with recognizable Latin roots. Today we call these languages the *Romance languages*—not because they are romantic, but because the are descended from the Roman language: Latin. Even today, a thousand year later, speakers of these languages often are able to recognize words in one another's languages.

Over the next 200 years or so, French began to lose its prestige as the royal language. The English language began to become more prominent at court as the nobility began to consider themselves English. In 1272, Edward I assumed the throne, and he used only English at court. Nevertheless, over the previous 200 years, many French words and phrases had become firmly fixed in the English language. Today at least half of the English vocabulary consists of words which are derived from French, while the original English vocabulary has not been lost. One interesting aspect of this fact is that the English language has different words for animals and the meat that comes from them. The Anglo-Saxon farmers tended the animals in the fields: the sheep, cows, chickens, and pigs. The wealthier Normans, who purchased and ate the meat from these animals, used the French words. They bought *mouton* (mutton), *bouef* (beef), *poulet* (poultry), and *porc* (pork).

During this period the English language continued to evolve, as all languages do. We have little literature preserved from these early years, and much of what is preserved is religious works written by monks of the church, who most often used Latin in their writings. Around the year 1380, Geoffrey Chaucer wrote in English a series of stories named *The Canterbury Tales*. Some scholars credit this work as the first one that demonstrated the artistic worth of English works written in the *vernacular* (native, or common language). You would not find it easy to read *The Canterbury Tales* in the original Middle English, as Modern English has evolved greatly in the 600 years since Chaucer wrote them.

In the year 1474 William Caxton brought the first movable-type printing press to England from Germany, where it had been invented by Johannes Gutenberg. The printing press is one of the most significant inventions in the history of mankind. It made large-scale printing of books possible, which enabled many more people to have access to literature, Bibles, and other printed works. Until the invention of the printing press, most writing was done laboriously by hand, which severely limited the amount of written materials available to the common people. The printing press was likely a major contributor to the European Renaissance, which was beginning about that time.

Around this time there occurred fairly rapid change in Middle English known as The Great Vowel Shift. This did not happen all at once, but over a period of one or two hundred years. The pronunciation of many words was changed, and many words changed form. For example, the *-eth* ending on many verbs changed to *-s*: *hath* became *has*, *loveth* became *loves*.

At the end of the 16th century, William Shakespeare lived and wrote plays and poetry. His works have had more influence on the English language than any other. It is said that Shakespeare coined some 1,600 new words in English, many of which are still used today. To call someone "a piece of work," to say "to be or not to be," or to say "O, woe is me" is to quote Shakespeare.

Shakespeare's work was produced during a long period in European history that is commonly called the Renaissance—a French word that means rebirth (*re-* meaning *again*, and *-naissance*, which means *birth*, and is related to the words *native* and *natal*). The name refers to the rebirth of learning and culture, which is thought to have been lost during medieval times after the fall of Rome. During the Renaissance there was a great flowering of arts, music, culture, and literature. This period also marked the end of the age of Middle English and the beginning of early Modern English. While you would find it difficult to read Chaucer's works, written in Middle English, you will have little difficulty reading Shakespeare. Some of the words used in Shakespeare's works may seem a little odd to the modern reader, and the meanings of some words have altered since his time 400 years ago, but in large part the modern reader can understand and enjoy Shakespeare's works.

During the Renaissance period, English gained many new words from Latin, Greek, French, and Italian. Writers of the period learned from, and borrowed from writings in ancient and modern foreign languages. It became quite stylish for writers to use foreign words and phrases in their writings.

The 16th to 18th centuries were also an age of worldwide exploration. British sailors such as Captain James Cook, Sir Walter Raleigh, and George Vancouver sailed the oceans of the world and brought back new ideas and new words for things they had seen in the far corners of the earth. New words such as *cashmere* from India, *typhoon* from China, and *bamboo* from Malaya were introduced into the language.

The American settlers in the early 17th century encountered many new thing in the New World. In the Americas they discovered delightful things like the *tomato* and the *raccoon*, and terrible things like a *hurricane*. They learned how to cook food on a *barbecue*. Because these things were all new to them, they had to learn the names of these things from the natives of the land, who were the American Indians.

When the American settlers pushed the frontier far west to the Pacific Ocean in the 19th century, they encountered the lands that then belonged to Mexico, where Spanish was spoken. The cowboys and settlers again had to learn new words for new things: words like *adobe*, *pueblo*, and *tortilla*. Some Spanish words were changed into western slang, such as *hoosegow* (jail) from Spanish *juzgado*.

During the age of exploration in the 16th to 18th centuries the British had established colonies all around the world, in places as near as North America and as far away as Australia, Hong Kong, and Singapore. Naturally the first inhabitants of these colonies spoke proper English, but as time passed, the variety of English spoken in the colonies began to change, as languages will, and diverged somewhat from the mother tongue. Today India, Australia, Hong Kong, North America, and other former British colonies all speak somewhat different versions of the English language, though we have little difficulty understanding one another.

The scientific, industrial, and technical revolutions of the 18th to 20th centuries created many new ideas and things, with the corresponding need for new words to describe those things. The language created new words, mostly from ancient Latin and Greek roots, for new things like *electricity*, *bacteria*, *automobile*, and *computer*.

Finally, in the late 20th century, the internet was created. The internet not only enabled nearly instant communication among the peoples of the world, but also required the invention of new terms and words for new things. Before the internet there was no such thing as a *blog* or *e-mail*.

In the 21st century, English is spoken as a first language by about 400 million people around the world, and about twice that many people as a second or foreign language. English has proved to be quite adept at adopting new words from foreign languages when new words are needed, and creating new words. English has become a lingua franca—a language spoken between two or more people who have different native languages around the world. Over the coming centuries the language will continue to evolve.

# ACTIVITY GUIDE CONTENTS

# Activity Guide

## 1. USING YOUR BRAIN

| Word Web Activities<br>Choosing the Right Definition | Word Link Activities<br>Practice with Pragmatics |
| --- | --- |

1. **Word Web Activities**
   Use the Word Web feature entitled *brain* to answer the following
   questions about the brain.
   a. Which part tells you it's time to eat?                    _____
   b. Which part helps you learn to speak?                  _____
   c. Which part makes sure you stand up
      straight?                                                              _____
   d. Which part controls your heartbeat?               _____
   e. Which part is wrapped around the
      outside of the brain?                                        _____

2. **Choosing the Right Definition**
   Study the numbered definitions for *brain*. Then write the number of the
   definition that relates to each sentence below.
   a. _____    Angela mastered the new computer program in one day.
               She has some <u>brain</u>!
   b. _____    Some studies show that people with larger <u>brains</u> are more
               intelligent than people with smaller <u>brains</u>.
   c. _____    They say that Martin is the <u>brains</u> behind the success of
               the company.
   d. _____    If you'll just use your <u>brain</u>, you'll make the right decision.
   e. _____    In proportion to the size of its body, the elephant's <u>brain</u> is
               very small.

3. Word Link Activities
   a. The definition of *brain* says that it "enables you to think."
      The prefix in the word *enable* is _____.

   b. Find the Word Link for this prefix.
      What does the prefix mean? _____

   c. What two other words with this prefix do you find?

      _____          _____

      Guess what each word means. Then check your answers by looking
      up the words.

4. Practice with Pragmatics
   Study the information about the fourth meaning of the definition of
   *brain*. Read the four sentences below. Write *Yes* if the sentence uses the
   term appropriately, and *No* if the usage is inappropriate.
   a. _____   I think Anna was the brains behind the kids' plan to skip
                school on Friday.
   b. _____   History states that Einstein was the brains behind the
                discovery of the theory of relativity.
   c. _____   The president said that the governor was the brains
                behind the economic recovery in her state.
   d. _____   I supplied the money, but Mike was the brains behind the
                surprise party.

**ANSWER KEY:**
1. **a.** medulla oblongata; **b.** cerebrum; **c.** cerebellum; **d.** medulla
   oblongata; **e.** cerebrum
2. **a.** 2, **b.** 1, **c.** 4; **d.** 2; **e.** 1
3. **a.** en; **b.** making or putting; **c.** enact, encode
4. **a.** Yes; **b.** No; **c.** No; **d.** Yes

## 2. GOING IN CIRCLES

| Grammar Activities<br>Picture Dictionary Activities | Word Link Activities |
| --- | --- |

1. **Grammar Activities**

   Many different words are based on the word *circle*. Write the part of speech of each underlined word—noun, verb, or adjective. Use your dictionary to check your answers.

   **a.** The moon was perfectly <u>circular</u> last night. _____

   **b.** The students arranged the chairs in a <u>circle</u>. _____

   **c.** Vitamin E improves the <u>circulation</u> of the blood. _____

   **d.** Airplanes sometimes <u>circle</u> several times before landing. _____

   **e.** Please open the window so the air can <u>circulate</u>. _____

   **f.** What is the <u>circulation</u> of *The Times*? _____

   **g.** Did the teacher <u>circle</u> your mistakes? _____

   **h.** I like <u>circular</u> eyeglasses, not square ones. _____

2. **Picture Dictionary Activities—A**

   **a.** How many other shapes can you think of besides the circle? Write your list below.

   _____

   Look at the Picture Dictionary feature *shapes* and check your answers.

   **b.** Which two shapes most closely resemble the circle?

   _____        _____

3. **Picture Dictionary Activities—B**

   Look at the Picture Dictionary feature entitled *area*. Pay special attention to how to find the area of a circle.

   **a.** What do you call the distance from the center of the circle to the outside edge? _____

   **b.** What do you call the line that runs around the outside of the circle? _____

   **c.** What do you call the line that runs across the circle from one side to the other? _____

   **d.** What is the formula for finding the area of a circle? _____

   **e.** If a circle has a radius of 3 inches, what is its area? Use $\pi = 3.14$. _____

4. Word Link Activities
   a. The first four letters of the word *circle* form a Word Link. What is that link? _____

   b. Look up the words *circle, circuit* and, *circulate*. Notice the Word Link *circ-* in those words. Write each word below.
   Then look it up in the dictionary and identify it as *verb, noun,* or *both*.

   _____, _____
   (word)                    (part of speech)

   _____, _____
   (word)                    (part of speech)

   _____, _____
   (word)                    (part of speech)

   c. Complete each sentence below with the correct word from item **b**.
      1. Blood _____ around the body.
      2. A _____ is a shape with all points the same distance from the center.
      3. A tree fell on the power lines and broke the electrical _____.

**ANSWER KEY:**
1. **a.** adjective; **b.** noun; **c.** noun; **d.** verb; **e.** verb; **f.** noun; **g.** verb; **h.** adjective
2. **a.** Answers will vary; **b.** ellipse, oval
3. **a.** radius; **b.** circumference; **c.** diameter; **d.** $\pi r^2$; **e.** 28.26 inches
4. **a.** circ; **b.** circle, both; circuit, noun; circulate, verb; **c1.** circulates; **c2.** circle; **c3.** circuit

# 3. TRANSPORTATION

| Choosing the Right Definition<br>Word Web Activities | Dictionary Research<br>Word Link Activities |
|---|---|

1. **Choosing the Right Definition**
   Study the numbered definitions for *transportation*. Then write the
   number of the definition that relates to each sentence below.
   a. _____ The <u>transportation</u> of nuclear waste through large cities
            can be dangerous.
   b. _____ Using mass <u>transportation</u> helps the environment.
   c. _____ Many schools provide <u>transportation</u> for children in the
            form of school buses.
   d. _____ Subways provide rapid <u>transportation</u>.
   e. _____ Bad weather slows down most forms of <u>transportation</u>.

2. **Word Web Activities—A**
   Use the Word Web feature entitled *transportation* to answer the following
   questions.

   What are the three names for underground transportation systems?
   s_____  m_____  t_____

3. **Word Web Activities—B**
   Use the Word Web feature entitled *ship* to answer the following
   questions.
   Look up these words in the dictionary to check your answers.
   a. What do you call things other than people
      that are carried on ships?                    _____
   b. What do you call the place where a ship stops?  _____
   c. What do you call the person who steers a
      large ship?                                   _____
   d. What do you call the place where a plane can
      land on a large ship?                         _____

4. Dictionary Research
   a. Reread the definition of *transportation*. Write your own definition of the word *goods* as it is used in the definition.

   _____

   b. Look up the word *goods* in the dictionary and complete these sentences.

   *Goods* are things that people make and then later _____.

   *Goods* are things that people _____ and can move from one place to another.

5. Word Link Activities
   The first five letters of the word *transportation* form a Word Link.
   a. What is the Word Link? _____
   b. What does the Word Link *trans* mean? _____
   c. Look up the words *transfer*, *transition* and *translate*. Notice the Word Link *trans* in those words. Read the definitions.
   d. Complete each sentence below with the correct word from item **c**. Check your answers by looking up each word in the dictionary.
      1. I don't know how to read Chinese. Can you _____ this letter for me?
      2. After the president of the college left, there was a period of _____ before a new one was appointed.
      3. You'll have to take two buses to get there. You can _____ from the 101 to the 145 at Main Street.

**ANSWER KEY:**

1. **a.** 3, **b.** 2, **c.** 1; **d.** 2; **e.** 3
2. subway, metro, tube
3. **a.** cargo; **b.** port; **c.** captain; **d.** flight deck
4. **a.** Answers will vary; **b.** sell; own, or make
5. **a.** trans; **b.** across; **d1.** translate; **d2.** transition; **d3.** transfer

# 4. TRIAL BY JURY

| Dictionary Research<br>Word Web Activities<br>Word Partnership Activities | Word Link Activities<br>Choosing the Right<br>Definition |
|---|---|

1. **Dictionary Research**

   Study the first numbered definition for *trial*. Think about the meaning of the four words listed below. Then match each word with the correct definition below. Look up these words in the dictionary if you are not sure.

   _____ **a.** judge

   _____ **b.** guilty

   _____ **c.** jury

   _____ **d.** evidence

   1. something you see that causes you to believe something is true
   2. a person who decides how a law is applied
   3. responsible for a crime
   4. group of people who decide if a person is guilty or not

2. **Word Web Activities**

   Study the Word Web feature entitled *trial*. Then use bold words from this Word Web feature to complete the following sentences. Look up any words you aren't sure of.

   **a.** The defendant will get a trial by _____.

   **b.** The defendant may or may not _____ guilty.

   **c.** The person who accused the defendant is the _____.

   **d.** The _____ will tell what they know about the crime.

   **e.** The words the witnesses say is called their _____.

   **f.** In the end, the jury will deliver a _____.

3. Word Partnership Activities
   Study the Word Partnership feature for *jury*. Pay special attention to the phrases below. Then match each phrase with the correct definition. Look up the words in the dictionary if you are not sure.
   
   _____ **a.** jury convicts
   _____ **b.** hung jury
   _____ **c.** jury duty
   
   **1.** a jury that can't agree on a verdict
   **2.** a jury finds someone guilty
   **3.** a citizen's obligation to serve on a jury

4. Word Link Activities
   Study the Word Link feature for the words *illegal, illiterate,* and *illogical.* Read the definitions.
   **a.** What is the meaning of the Word Link *il*? _____
   
   Which of these words (*illegal, illiterate, illogical*) names or describes the following? Read the definitions again if you are not sure.
   **b.** a person who is unable to read _____
   **c.** something that does not make sense _____
   **d.** something that is against the law _____

5. Choosing the Right Definition
   Study the definition of *trial.* Then write the number of the definition that relates to each sentence below.
   **a.** _____ Elena learned to bake bread by <u>trial and error</u>.
   **b.** _____ You should give aspirin a <u>trial</u> before you ask for anything stronger.
   **c.** _____ The murderer's <u>trial</u> lasted for six weeks.
   **d.** _____ The boss gave me a three-week <u>trial</u> to see if I could handle the responsibilities.

**ANSWER KEY:**

1. **a.** 2; **b.** 3; **c.** 4; **d.** 1
2. **a.** jury; **b.** plead; **c.** plaintiff; **d.** witnesses; **e.** testimony; **f.** verdict
3. **a.** 2; **b.** 1; **c.** 3
4. **a.** not; **b.** illiterate; **c.** illogical; **d.** illegal
5. **a.** 3; **b.** 2; **c.** 1; **d.** 2

# 5. ORCHESTRA

| Word Web Activities<br>Word Partnership Activities | Word Link Activities<br>Choosing the Right Definition |
| --- | --- |

1. **Word Web Activities**
   Study the information in the Word Web feature entitled *orchestra*. Then answer the questions below. Write T for *true* or F for *false*.
   _____ **a.** A symphony orchestra usually has more than 100 players.
   _____ **b.** The largest section of the orchestra is the string section.
   _____ **c.** The double bass plays in the string section.
   _____ **d.** The brass section needs to play very loud.
   _____ **e.** The timpani is part of the brass section.

2. **Word Partnership Activities**
   The job of a symphony orchestra is to *perform* for the public. Look up the word *perform* in the dictionary.
   **a.** Write the number of the definition that applies to music.                                              _____

   Study the Word Partnership feature for *perform*. Then complete the four sentences below using the word *perform* before or after one of these words or phrases: *tasks*, *able to*, *miracles*, *well*. Use each of these words or phrases one time.
   **b.** Some people believe holy people can _____ _____.
   **c.** The violinist felt ill and was not _____ _____.
   **d.** The new tires _____ _____ on icy roads.
   **e.** Doctors believe the brains of adults and children _____ _____ in different ways.

3. **Word Link Activities**
   Symphony. Look up *symphony* and read the Word Links *sym* and *phon*.
   **d.** What does *sym* mean? _____
   **e.** What does *phon* mean? _____
   **f.** So *symphony* means to make _____ _____.

4. **Choosing the Right Definition**
   Reread the Word Web feature for *orchestra*. Several of the bold words in this feature have multiple meanings.

   Study the numbered definitions for *composition*. Then write the number of the definition that relates to each sentence below.
   _____ **a.** The <u>composition</u> of furniture in the store window was very attractive.
   _____ **b.** Have you written any new <u>compositions</u> lately?

   Study the numbered definitions for *instrument*. Then write the number of the definition that relates to each sentence below.
   _____ **c.** The piano is my favorite <u>instrument.</u>
   _____ **d.** The dentist placed the <u>instruments</u> on the shelf.

**ANSWER KEY:**
1. **a.** F; **b.** T; **c.** T; **d.** F; **e.** F
2. **a.** 2; **b.** perform miracles; **c.** able to perform; **d.** performed well;
   **e.** perform tasks
3. **a.** together; **b.** sound; **c.** sound together
4. **a.** 1; **b.** 2 or 3; **c.** 2; **d.** 1

# 6. COOKING

| Word Web Activities | Thesaurus Activities |
|---|---|
| Picture Dictionary Activities | Grammar Activities |
| | Dictionary Research |

1. **Word Web Activities**

   As you complete this activity, look up any words you aren't sure of.

   Read the definitions for *cook* and *cooking*. Then use the Word Web feature entitled *cooking* to answer the following questions.
   a. Which bold word means the opposite of *tough*? _____
   b. Which bold word means *absorb food into your body*? _____

   Now use the Word Web feature entitled *spice* to answer the following questions.
   c. Which spice is the least effective in killing germs? _____
   d. What kind of food do people in cold climates usually like? _____

   Now use the Word Web feature entitled *pan* to answer the following questions.
   e. Cooking pans are very heavy when made of what material? _____
   f. Copper pans are usually covered with a thin layer of what metal? _____

2. **Picture Dictionary Activities—A**

   Look at the Picture Dictionary feature for *cook*. Then complete the sentences correctly.
   a. If you want to make tea, you have to _____ the water.
   b. You need an oven if you want to _____, _____, or _____ food.
   c. When you put food in a wire container with boiling water under it, you _____ the food.
   d. When you make a slice of bread brown by cooking it you _____ it.
   e. When you cook food in an oven very close to the flame, you _____ it.

3. **Picture Dictionary Activities—B**

   Look at the Picture Dictionary feature for *egg*. Then answer the questions below. Look up any words you aren't sure of. Write T for *true* or F for *false*.
   _____ a. The scrambled eggs have peppers in them.
   _____ b. The hard-boiled egg has a round yolk.
   _____ c. The fried egg is in a frying pan.

4. Thesaurus Activities
   Find the Thesaurus feature with the word *cook*. Then complete the sentences using words from the feature. Look up any words you aren't sure of.
   a. A _____ works in a restaurant.
   b. Yeast is the ingredient that _____ bread rise.
   c. If the meal was cooked but it has gotten cold, you might _____ _____ the food.
   d. Busy people tend to eat meals that are simple to _____.

5. Grammar Activities
   Write the part of speech of each underlined word—noun or verb.
   a. I don't like <u>cooking</u> vegetables.              _____
   b. My sister's <u>cooking</u> is fantastic.             _____
   c. Which do you prefer <u>cooking</u> or baking?        _____
   d. On Sunday I <u>cooked</u> dinner for my family.      _____
   e. My husband is a very good <u>cook</u>.               _____

6. Dictionary Research
   Look at other words and phrases that follow the word *cook* in the dictionary.
   a. Which one describes a collection of recipes?        _____
   b. Which one describes something you eat?              _____
   c. Which one describes how someone plans to do something?                                  _____
   d. Which one describes cooking outside?                _____

**ANSWER KEY:**
1. **a.** tender; **b.** digest; **c.** black pepper; **d.** bland; **e.** cast iron; **f.** tin
2. **a.** boil; **b.** roast, bake, broil; **c.** steam; **d.** toast; **e.** broil
3. **a.** F; **b.** T; **c.** T
4. **a.** chef; **b.** makes; **c.** heat up; **d.** prepare
5. **a.** verb; **b.** noun; **c.** verb; **d.** verb; **e.** noun
6. **a.** cookbook; **b.** cookie; **c.** cook up; **d.** cookout

# 7. ENERGY

| Choosing the Right Definition Word Web Activities | Word Link Activities Grammar Activities |
|---|---|

1.  **Choosing the Right Definition**
    Study the numbered definitions for *energy*. Then write the number of the definition that relates to each sentence below.
    a.  _____ She's putting all her <u>energies</u> into her school work.
    b.  _____ My children have more <u>energy</u> than I do.
    c.  _____ One problem with nuclear <u>energy</u> is that it produces radioactive waste.
    d.  _____ You should put more <u>energy</u> into your homework.
    e.  _____ Which <u>energy</u> source do you think is the cleanest?
    f.  _____ Conserve your <u>energy</u>. Go to bed early.

2.  **Word Web Activities**
    Use the Word Web feature entitled *energy* to answer the following questions. Answer each question with one of the bold words in the Word Web feature.
    a.  What kind of power plants were built in the 1970s?   _____
    b.  What kind of gas is still used for home heating?   _____
    c.  What was the primary energy source for American settlers?   _____
    d.  What was the source of electrical power in the early 1900s?   _____

3.  **Word Link Activities**
    Look up the words below to find the Word Link in the word. Write the Word Link.
    a.  hydraulic  _____      d.  complicate  _____
    b.  carefree  _____       e.  seller  _____
    c.  electricity  _____

    Match the Word Link with the correct definition.

| Word Link | Definition |
|---|---|
| _____ f. hydr | 1. without |
| _____ g. free | 2. causing to be |
| _____ h. electr | 3. one who acts as |
| _____ i. ate | 4. water |
| _____ j. er | 5. electric |

Now look back at the Word Web feature for *energy*. Write the three words from this feature that are formed from these Word Links.

**k.** g_____       **l.** h_____       **m.** e_____

4. **Grammar Activities**

   Review the dictionary entry for *energy* and *energetic*. Then complete each sentence with the correct form of a word starting with the letters *energ-*. Identify the part of speech of each word you use—noun, verb, adjective, or adverb.

|  | Part of Speech |
|---|---|
| **a.** Celia is very _____ today. | _____ |
| **b.** I don't know what happened to all my _____. I'm really tired. | _____ |
| **c.** David washed the car _____. | _____ |

**ANSWER KEY:**

1. **a.** 2; **b.** 1; **c.** 3; **d.** 2 **e.** 3; **f.** 1
2. **a.** nuclear; **b.** natural; **c.** wood; **d.** coal
3. **a.** hydr; **b.** free; **c.** electr; **d.** ate; **e.** er; **f.** 4; **g.** 1; **h.** 5; **i.** 2; **j.** 3; **k.** generate; **l.** hydroelectric ; **m.** electrical
4. **a.** energetic, adjective; **b.** energy, noun; **c.** energetically, adverb

# 8. SEEDS AND PLANTS

| Choosing the Right Definition<br>Picture Dictionary Activities | Dictionary Research<br>Word Link Activities |
| --- | --- |

1. **Choosing the Right Definition**

   Study the numbered definitions for *plant*. Then write the number of the definition that relates to each sentence below.

   _____ **a.** The child shouted "No" and <u>planted</u> her feet firmly on the ground.

   _____ **b.** I brought a <u>plant</u> as a housewarming present.

   _____ **c.** My brother works in a power <u>plant</u> in Milwaukee.

   Study the definition of *seed*. Then write the number of the definition that relates to each sentence below.

   _____ **d.** I bought a package of flower <u>seeds</u> to plant in the garden.

   _____ **e.** I didn't have all the details worked out, but I did have the <u>seed</u> of an idea.

2. **Picture Dictionary Activities**

   Use the Picture Dictionary feature entitled *plants* to answer the following questions. Look up the meaning of any words you don't know.

   **a.** What tree loses its leaves?   _____

   **b.** What tree is always green?   _____

3. **Dictionary Research**

   Study the first four numbered definitions for *plant*. Think about the meaning of the four words listed below. Then match each word with the correct definition. Look up these words in the dictionary if you are not sure.

   _____ **a.** root

   _____ **b.** exotic

   _____ **c.** produce

   _____ **d.** stem

   **1.** very unusual

   **2.** the long thin part of a plant that is above ground

   **3.** the part of a plant that is underground

   **4.** to make something

4. Word Link Activities
   a. Some plants are *annual* plants. These plants bloom for only one year or season. Notice the root word *ann* in the word *annual*. Look up *annual* and find the Word Link. What does *ann* mean? _____
   b. What other words with the root *ann* do you find?
      _____      _____
   c. Which word in item b means a particular amount each year? _____
   d. Which word in item b means something you celebrate every year? _____

**ANSWER KEY:**
1. **a.** 6; **b.** 1; **c.** 4; **d.** 1; **e.** 2
2. **a.** deciduous; **b.** evergreen
3. **a.** 3; **b.** 1; **c.** 4; **d.** 2
4. **a.** year; **b.** anniversary, annum; **c.** annum; **d.** anniversary

# 9. STARS AND ASTRONOMERS

| Word Web Activities<br>Choosing the Right Definition | Word Partnership Activities<br>Thesaurus Activities<br>Word Link Activities |
|---|---|

1. **Word Web Activities**
   Use the Word Web feature entitled *star* to answer the following
   questions. Look up each word in the dictionary to check your answers.
   a. What is a group of stars called?                               a _____
   b. What do people call the idea that the stars control
      our lives?                                                     _____
   c. What is the scientific study of the stars called?             _____
   d. Which star is used to guide ships on the sea?       the _____

   Use the Word Web feature entitled *astronomer* to answer this question:
   e. Copernicus was an astronomer who thought that the center of the
      universe was the _____.

2. **Choosing the Right Definition**
   Study the six numbered definitions for *star*. Then write the number of
   the definition that relates to each sentence below.
   a. _____ Eric is starring in a new TV comedy called *Just for You*.
   b. _____ It was cloudy last night, and we couldn't see any stars.
   c. _____ Madonna is my favorite singing star.
   d. _____ The flag of the United States has 50 stars on it.

3. **Word Partnership Activities**
   Reread the Word Web feature for *star*. Find the word *object* in the
   second sentence. Look up the word *object* in the dictionary and read the
   definitions.
   a. The first meaning of *object* is *something that has a fixed _____ or*
      _____.
   b. The second meaning of *object* is _____ or _____.

   Study the Word Partnership feature for the noun form of *object*. Then
   complete the four sentences below using the word *object* and one of
   these words: *foreign, inanimate, moving, solid*. Use each of these words one
   time. Look up any words you aren't sure of.
   c. Dogs are not usually interested in an _____ _____.
   d. We watched as the magician passed a _____ _____ through
      a mirror.
   e. A fast-_____ _____ has a high speed.
   f. If a child swallows a _____ _____ call a doctor for advice.

4. **Thesaurus Activities**

Reread the Word Web feature entitled *astronomer*. Notice the word *study* in the second sentence of the feature. A synonym for *study* is *observe*. Look up *observe* in the dictionary and study the Thesaurus entry that accompanies it. Which of the words in the box goes with each sentence below?

| notice    watch    study |
|---|

   **a.** I'll show you how to do it. _____ me. _____

   **b.** I checked the level of the water every hour, but
   I didn't <u>observe</u> any change. _____

   **c.** Jane Goodall would <u>observe</u> the chimps carefully
   for hours without moving. _____

5. **Word Link Activities**

The first five letters of the word *astronomer* form a Word Link. Look at the information in the Word Link for *astro*.

   **a.** What does the Word Link *astro* mean? _____

   **b.** What are the three Word Links for *astro*?

   _____  _____  _____

   **c.** Complete each sentence below with the correct word from item b. Check your answers by looking up each word in the dictionary.

   **1.** This symbol (*) is called the _____.

   **2.** You need a telescope to study _____.

   **3.** You have to know how to fly a plane before you can study to become an _____.

   **d.** Reread the Word Web feature for *star*. Find the word *astrology*. It contains two Word Links. You have studied the Word Link *astro*. Now look up *geology* find the Word Link *logy*.

   **1.** What does *logy* mean? _____

   **2.** So the literal meaning of *astrology* is the _____ of _____.

**ANSWER KEY:**

1. **a.** constellation; **b.** astrology; **c.** astronomy; **d.** North Star; **e.** Sun
2. **a.** 4; **b.** 1; **c.** 3; **d.** 2
3. **a.** shape, form; **b.** aim, purpose; **c.** inanimate object; **d.** solid object;
   **e.** moving object; **f.** foreign object
4. **a.** watch; **b.** notice; **c.** study
5. **a.** star; **b.** asterisk, astronaut, astronomy; **c.** **1.** asterisk, **2.** astronomy,
   **3.** astronaut; **d.** **1.** study of, **2.** study, stars

# 10. FOOD

| Word Web Activities<br>Thesaurus Activities<br>Picture Dictionary Activities | Choosing the Right Definition<br>Dictionary Research |
|---|---|

1. **Word Web Activities**
   Study the information in the Word Web feature entitled *food*. Then answer the questions below. Write T for *true* or F for *false*.
   
   _____ **a.** Snakes are herbivores.
   
   _____ **b.** Mice are predators.
   
   _____ **c.** Green plants store energy from the sun.

2. **Thesaurus Activities**
   The Word Web feature for *food* says that a hawk is a *top predator*. Look at the Thesaurus feature for the word *top*. Then complete the sentences using words from the feature. Look up any words you aren't sure of.
   **a.** The adjective meaning for *top* is _____.
   **b.** Which adjective best describes the hawk's position as a top predator? _____
   **c.** Which two noun meanings describe the <u>top</u> of a mountain? _____ and _____.

3. **Picture Dictionary Activities**
   Look at the Picture Dictionary feature for *dessert*. Then answer the questions below. Look up any words you aren't familiar with.
   **a.** Which two desserts don't have to be cooked? _____, and _____
   **b.** Which dessert is usually very cold? _____
   **c.** Which desserts are always brown? _____ _____
   **d.** Which dessert is made mostly of eggs? _____
   **e.** Which dessert is made mostly of a white grain? _____

4. Choosing the Right Definition

The word *feed* is related to the word *food*. Look up the word *feed* and study the numbered definitions. Then write the number of the definition that relates to each sentence below.

a. _____ My mother always <u>feeds</u> the children dinner early on Friday nights.

b. _____ The squirrels in our yard like to <u>feed</u> on the seed we leave for the birds.

c. _____ Newborn babies usually <u>feed</u> every three hours.

d. _____ We collected money to <u>feed</u> the hurricane victims in Louisiana.

5. Dictionary Research

a. Look up the word *nutrient*. Write a sentence with the word *nutrient*.

_____

b. Use the definition of *nutrients* to complete this sentence.

Nutrients are things that plants and animals _____ .

c. Study the words following *nutrient* in the dictionary. Which words also contain the prefix *nutri* ?

_____  _____  _____

**ANSWER KEY:**

1. **a.** F; **b.** F; **c.** T
2. **a.** best; **b.** best; **c.** peak, summit
3. **a.** ice cream, fruit salad; **b.** ice cream; **c.** brownie, chocolate mousse; **d.** custard; **e.** rice pudding
4. **a.** 1; **b.** 3; **c.** 4; **d.** 2
5. **a.** Answers will vary; **b.** need; **c.** nutrition, nutritional, nutritious

# 11. ART

| Word Web Activities<br>Thesaurus Activities | Word Link Activities<br>Choosing the Right Definition |
|---|---|

1. **Word Web Activities**
   Use the Word Web feature entitled *art* to answer the following questions.
   a. What inspired the term "impressionist"?    a painting by _____
   b. In what part of the world did impressionism start?    in _____
   c. What did the impressionists usually paint?    _____
   d. What elements did they emphasize in their paintings?
   _____ and color
   e. The art of what country influenced the impressionists?    _____

2. **Thesaurus Activities**
   The Word Web feature for *art* says that the impressionists were interested in light and color. Find the Thesaurus feature with the word *light*. Then complete the sentences using words from the feature. Look up any words you aren't sure of.
   a. The noun meanings for *light* are _____, _____, _____, and _____.
   b. Which noun meaning best describes the soft light of a fire when there are no flames?    _____
   c. Which noun meaning describes the happiness on a person's face?    _____
   d. Which adjective describes a room with a lot of windows facing south?    _____

3. **Word Link Activities**
   Review the Word Web feature for *art* noting the words *realistic* and *depiction*. Look up the words below and study the Word Links. Then answer the questions. Look up *reality, realize, really*
   a. What does the Word Link *real* mean?    _____
   b. Which word in this link means "to make something happen"?    _____
   c. Which word in this link means "actually"?    _____

Look up *biologist, chemist, journalist*. Look at the Word Link for *-ist*.

    **d.** What does *ist* mean?     _____

    **e.** Which word in this link means someone who
       studies objects from the past?     _____

    **f.** Which word describes someone who works in a
       drug store?     _____

Look up *depict, picture, picturesque*. Look at the Word Link for *pict*.

    **g.** What does the Word Link *pict* mean?     _____

    **h.** Which word in this link means "attractive
       and interesting"?     _____

    **i.** Which word in this link means "show or
       represent"?     _____

4. **Choosing the Right Definition**

   The Word Web feature for *art* says that the impressionists stopped
   painting in their *studios*. Study the numbered definitions for *studio*. Then
   write the number of the definition that relates to each sentence below.

   **a.** \_\_\_\_\_ The TV show originated in a <u>studio</u> in New York City.

   **b.** \_\_\_\_\_ The photographer has a large <u>studio</u> with large windows.

**ANSWER KEY:**

1. **a.** Monet; **b.** Europe; **c.** landscapes; **d.** light; **e.** Japan
2. **a.** brightness, glow, radiance, shine; **b.** glow; **c.** radiance/glow;
   **d.** sunny
3. **a.** actual; **b.** realize; **c.** really; **d.** one who practices; **e.** archaeologist;
   **f.** pharmacist; **g.** painting; **h.** picturesque; **i.** depict
4. **a.** 2; **b.** 1

# 12. TELEVISION

| Word Web Activities<br>Thesaurus Activities<br>Word Link Activities | Choosing the Right Definition<br>Grammar Activities |
| --- | --- |

1. **Word Web Activities**

   Use the Word Web feature entitled *television* to answer the following questions. Look up any words you don't know in the dictionary.

   **a.** What kind of tube was used in old-fashioned televisions?

   _____

   **b.** What are the tiny dots of light on a TV screen called? _____

   **c.** What are the three sources of TV signals?

   _____, _____ and _____

2. **Thesaurus Activities**

   The Word Web feature for *television* says that high-definition televisions have a very *clear image*.

   **a.** Read the dictionary definition for *clear*. *Clear* is used to describe a TV picture that is easy to _____.

   Find the Thesaurus feature for *clear*. Then complete the sentences using words from the feature. Look up any words you aren't sure of.

   **b.** These words describe something that is easy to understand.

   _____ _____ _____

   Read the dictionary definition for *picture*. Then study the Thesaurus feature for this word and answer the questions below.

   **c.** Which meaning of the word *picture* applies to a television picture?

   _____

   **d.** Look at the verb meanings of *picture* in the Thesaurus entry. They describe a picture that exists only in a person's _____.

3. **Word Link Activities**

   Television

   **a.** Look up the Word Link for *tele*. What does *tele* mean? _____

   **b.** Look up the word *visible*. Read the the Word Link above *visible*. What does the prefix *vis* mean? _____

   **c.** So television is something that lets you _____ things at a _____.

4. Choosing the Right Definition

   Reread the Word Web feature for *television*. Pay special attention to the words *screen* and *station*. Then look up these words in the dictionary. Study the numbered definitions for *screen*. Then write the number of the definition that relates to each sentence below.

   _____ **a.** At the movies a tall person sat in front of me and it was hard to see the screen.

   _____ **b.** Blood samples are screened in a laboratory

   Study the numbered definitions for *station*. Then write the number of the definition that relates to each sentence below.

   _____ **c.** We live only three blocks from the subway station.

   _____ **d.** Which station is showing the soccer game tonight?

5. Grammar Activities

   The Word Web feature says that cathode ray tubes are used to *produce* a television picture. Many different words are based on the word *produce*. Write the part of speech of each underlined word—noun, verb, adjective, or adverb. Use your dictionary to check your answers.

   **a.** I always buy my produce from the fruit market on the corner. _____

   **b.** There are so many new products on the market, I don't know which to buy. _____

   **c.** A lot of movie production takes place on the streets of New York. _____

   **d.** I am the most productive early in the morning. _____

   **e.** The thief produced a gun from his pocket. _____

**ANSWER KEY:**

1. **a.** cathode ray; **b.** pixels; **c.** ground stations, satellites, cables
2. **a.** see; **b.** obvious, plain, straightforward; **c.** 3; **d.** mind
3. **a.** distance; **b.** seeing; **c.** see, distance
4. **a.** 1; **b.** 6; **c.** 1; **d.** 3
5. **a.** noun; **b.** noun; **c.** noun; **d.** adjective; **e.** verb

## 13. MONEY

| Word Web Activities<br>Word Partnership Activities<br>Thesaurus Activities | Choosing the Right Definition<br>Dictionary Research |
| --- | --- |

1. **Word Web Activities**
   Use the Word Web feature entitled *money* to answer the following questions.
   **a.** Which word in the feature means the same as *trade*? _____
   **b.** What form of ocean life was used as money at one time? _____
   **c.** Were the first coins round? _____
   **d.** What country had the first circular coins? _____
   **e.** Which two metals were used by the Lydians to make coins? _____ and _____

2. **Word Partnership Activities**
   Look up the word *buy* in the dictionary.
   **a.** What is the past tense of the verb *buy*? _____
   **b.** Which meaning of *buy* is found in this sentence?
   *I bought myself a few minutes to think of the answer to the question.*
   sense number _____

   Study the Word Partnership feature for *buy*. Then complete the four sentences below using the word *buy* before or after one of these words or phrases: *online, and sell, tickets, afford to*. Use each of these items once.

   **c.** I can't _____ _____ a flat screen TV. I don't have enough money.
   **d.** If you _____ _____ stocks at the right time, you can get rich.
   **e.** Is it safe to _____ _____ ?
   **f.** Let's _____ _____ to the concert.

3. **Thesaurus Activities**
   Find the Thesaurus feature with the word *money*. Then complete the sentences using words from the feature. Look up any words you aren't sure of.
   **a.** A single _____ is now in use in all European Union countries.
   **b.** I never use _____. I prefer to pay by credit card or check.
   **c.** I don't have the amount of _____ I need to start my own business.
   **d.** The group decided to raise _____ to help people with AIDS.
   **e.** The discovery of oil brought great _____ to the Middle East.

4. **Choosing the Right Definition**
   Study the numbered definitions for *bill*. Then write the number of the definition that relates to each sentence below.
   _____ a. Please ask the waiter to bring the <u>bill</u>.
   _____ b. My electric <u>bill</u> this month was over $100.
   _____ c. He handed me three crisp dollar <u>bills</u>.
   _____ d. The mechanic <u>billed</u> us for some work he didn't do.
   _____ e. Congress passed a <u>bill</u> that prohibited smoking in hospitals.

5. **Dictionary Research**
   The Word Web feature for *money* says that the Lydians *minted* three types of coins. Look up the word *mint* in the dictionary.

   **Meaning number**

   a. Which numbered meaning of *mint* is used in the
      Word Web feature?                                        _____
   b. Which meaning names an herb people cook with?           _____
   c. Which meaning names a type of candy?                    _____
   d. Which meaning tells where money is manufactured?        _____

**ANSWER KEY:**
1. **a.** barter; **b.** cowrie shells; **c.** no; **d.** China; **e.** gold, silver
2. **a.** bought; **b.** 2; **c.** afford to, buy; **d.** buy, and sell; **e.** buy, online;
   **f.** buy, tickets
3. **a.** currency; **b.** cash; **c.** capital; **d.** funds; **e.** wealth
4. **a.** 1; **b.** 1; **c.** 3; **d.** 2; **e.** 4
5. **a.** 4; **b.** 1; **c.** 2; **d.** 3

# 14. POLLUTION AND THE GREENHOUSE EFFECT

| Word Web Activities<br>Word Partnership Activities<br>Word Link Activities | Choosing the Right Definition |
|---|---|

1. **Word Web Activities**
   Use the Word Web feature entitled *pollution* to answer the following questions. Look up any words you aren't sure of.
   **a.** *Smog* is a combination of smoke and _____.
   **b.** Factories in the Midwest cause _____ that falls in the East.
   **c.** A substance used to kill insects is called a _____.

   Use the Word Web feature entitled *the greenhouse effect* to answer these questions.
   **d.** Energy that comes from the sun is called _____ radiation.
   **e.** Gasoline is an example of a _____ fuel.

2. **Word Partnership Activities**
   Notice how the word *cause* is used in the Word Web features for *pollution* and *the greenhouse effect*. Next study the Word Partnership feature for *cause*. Use the correct Word Partnership phrase to complete each sentence below. If necessary, look up new words in the dictionary.
   **a.** Scientists are looking for answers. They want to _____ of global warming.
   **b.** My cold isn't serious at all. There's no _____ .
   **c.** They want to know why their dog died. The vet is looking for the _____ .

3. **Word Link Activities**
   **a.** The prefix in the word *explode* is _____.
   **b.** Find the Word Link at the entry for *explode*. What does the prefix mean? _____ _____ _____

   Which of the words in the *ex* Word Link means the same as the following? Look up the words in the dictionary if you are not sure.
   **c.** to leave _____
   **d.** to break into many pieces _____
   **e.** to go beyond _____

4. **Choosing the Right Definition**

The Word Web feature for *the greenhouse effect* mentions carbon dioxide and other *gases*. Study the numbered definitions for *gas*. Then write the number of the definition that relates to each sentence below.

_____ **a.** I need to put some gas in the car before we leave this afternoon.

_____ **b.** The soldiers were gassed by a small group of enemy troops.

_____ **c.** Our new stove uses gas instead of electricity.

_____ **d.** Cigarette smoke contains poisonous gases.

_____ **e.** Oxygen is a gas that plants give off.

5. **Dictionary Research**

The Word Web feature for *greenhouse effect* says that global average *temperature* has risen over the past 100 years. Search the Word Webs to find the answers to the following questions about temperature.

|    | Word Web | Fill in the Blank |
|----|----------|-------------------|
| **a.** | thermometer | On the Fahrenheit scale water boils at _____. |
| **b.** | climate | In the last 100 years, the earth's temperature has increased by _____. |
| **c.** | wind | Air flows from one place to another because of the _____ in temperature from one area to another. |
| **d.** | cooking | Heating food to a high temperature kills _____. |

**ANSWER KEY:**

1. **a.** fog; **b.** acid rain; **c.** pesticide; **d.** solar; **e.** fossil
2. **a.** determine the cause; **b.** cause for concern; **c.** cause of death
3. **a.** ex; **b.** away, from, out; **c.** exit; **d.** explode; **e.** exceed
4. **a.** 3; **b.** 4; **c.** 1; **d.** 2; **e.** 1
5. **a.** 212 degrees; **b.** about 1° Fahrenheit; **c.** difference; **d.** bacteria

# 15. BRIDGES AND DAMS

| Word Web Activities | Grammar Activities |
|---|---|
| Thesaurus Activities | Word Partnership Activities |

1. **Word Web Activities**
   Study the Word Web feature for *bridge*. Then match each number below with the correct description.

   1. The height in feet of the Akashi Kaikyo Bridge
   2. When the Brooklyn Bridge was built
   3. The length of the Evergreen Point Floating Bridge
   4. How many vehicles cross the Brooklyn Bridge every day
   5. The strength of an earthquake that the Akashi Kaikyo Bridge can withstand
   6. The length of the Akashi Kaikyo Bridge

   _____ **a.** over 1 mile
   _____ **b.** 1883
   _____ **c.** 120,000
   _____ **d.** 1,000
   _____ **e.** 8.5
   _____ **f.** 12,828 feet

   Study the Word Web feature for *dam*. Then answer the questions below. Write T for *true* or F for *false*.
   _____ **g.** The world's first dam was built near Memphis, Egypt.
   _____ **h.** The world's first dam prevented flooding.
   _____ **i.** Hydroelectric dams provide 20% of the world's electricity.
   _____ **j.** The Itapu Dam took 10 years to build.

2. **Thesaurus Activities**
   The Word Web feature for *dam* states that dams sometimes damage valuable forest *lands*. Find the Thesaurus feature with the word *land*. Then complete the sentences below using words from the feature. Look up any words you aren't sure of.
   **a.** Someday I will return to the _____ of my birth.
   **b.** Harry doesn't own a house, but he does own some _____ _____ outside of town.
   **c.** We weren't sure when the plane would _____.
   **d.** Do you live in a safe _____ ?

3. Grammar Activities

   The Word Web feature for *dam* describes the world's longest *suspension* bridge. Study the list of words that are formed from the root word *suspend*. Write the part of speech of each underlined word—noun, verb, or adjective. Use your dictionary to check your answers.

   a. I drove over a large rock and damaged the car's <u>suspension</u>.      _____

   b. The airline <u>suspends</u> flights during storms.      _____

   c. I use <u>suspenders</u> instead of a belt.      _____

   d. I couldn't stand the <u>suspense</u>, so I asked the teacher what my grade was.      _____

4. Word Partnership Activities

   Study the Word Partnership feature for *build*. Use one of the phrases in this feature to complete each sentence below. If necessary, look up new words in these phrases in the dictionary.

   a. Leo works out at the gym and has a very _____.

   b. Many female ballet dancers have a _____.

   c. The government will _____ to connect all the major cities in the country.

   d. Tax revenue often helps to _____ and _____.

**ANSWER KEY:**

1. **a.** 3; **b.** 2; **c.** 4; **d.** 1; **e.** 5; **f.** 6; **g.** T; **h.** F; **i.** T; **j.** F
2. **a.** country; **b.** real estate; **c.** arrive *or* touch down; **d.** area
3. **a.** noun; **b.** verb; **c.** noun; **d.** noun
4. **a.** athletic/strong build; **b.** slender build; **c.** build roads; **d.** build bridges, build schools

## 16. CLONE

| Word Web Activities<br>Thesaurus Activities | Word Link Activities<br>Choosing the Right Definition |
|---|---|

1. **Word Web Activities**
   Use the Word Web feature entitled *clone* to answer the following questions. Answer each question with one of the bold words in the Word Web feature. Look up any words you aren't sure of.
   **a.** Maria and her sister are _____.
   **b.** I need to give them a _____ of my driver's license.
   **c.** The girls look like _____ , but they were born a year apart.
   **d.** Each _____ in your body contains DNA.
   **e.** Scientists use _____ to create new types of plants.

2. **Thesaurus Activities**
   Find the Thesaurus feature for the word *natural*. Then complete the sentences using words from the feature. Look up any words you aren't sure of.
   **a.** It is _____ for new students to be a little nervous at first.
   **b.** This doesn't look like _____ leather to me. I think it's plastic.
   **c.** Please accept my _____ apology for what I said.
   **d.** Farm-grown strawberries are good, but _____ strawberries are better.

3. **Word Link Activities**

Find the word *identical* in the Word Web feature for *clone*. Look up *identical*. Study the Word Link feature for the root *ident*.

**a.** What does the Word Link *ident* mean? _____

Write the word in this Word Link that matches each definition below. Look up the words in the dictionary if you are not sure.

**b.** your passport or driver's license _____

**c.** exactly the same _____

**d.** unknown or nameless _____

Find the word *donor* in the Word Web feature for *clone*. Look up *donor*. Study the Word Link feature for the root *don*.

**e.** What does the Word Link *don* mean? _____

Write the word in this Word Link that matches each definition below. Look up the words in the dictionary if you are not sure.

**f.** to forgive someone _____

**g.** someone who gives something away _____

**h.** to give money or goods to an organization _____

4. **Choosing the Right Definition**

Scientists produce clones by *genetic engineering*. Study the numbered definitions for *engineer*. Then write the number of the definition that relates to each sentence below.

_____ **a.** The building <u>engineer</u> repaired the water heater.

_____ **b.** My "accidental" meeting with Rosa was actually <u>engineered</u> by her sister.

_____ **c.** A famous civil <u>engineer</u> designed that bridge.

_____ **d.** They <u>engineered</u> the car in such a way that it would get good gas mileage.

**ANSWER KEY:**

1. **a.** identical; **b.** copy; **c.** twins; **d.** cell; **e.** genetic engineering
2. **a.** normal; **b.** genuine; **c.** sincere; **d.** wild
3. **a.** same; **b.** identification; **c.** identical; **d.** unidentified; **e.** giving; **f.** pardon; **g.** donor; **h.** donate
4. **a.** 2; **b.** 4; **c.** 1; **d.** 3

# Aa

**a** /ə, STRONG eɪ/ also **an** /ən, STRONG æn/

**A** or **an** is the indefinite article. It is used at the beginning of noun groups that refer to only one person or thing. The form **an** is used in front of words that begin with vowel sounds.

**1** DET You use **a** or **an** when you are referring to someone or something for the first time or when people may not know which particular person or thing you are talking about. ❑ *A waiter entered with a glass and a bottle of water.* ❑ *He started eating an apple.* **2** DET You use **a** or **an** when you are referring to any person or thing of a particular type and do not want to be specific. ❑ *You should leave it to an expert.* ❑ *Bring a sleeping bag.* **3** DET You use **a** or **an** in front of a noun when that noun is followed by words that describe it more fully. ❑ *They shared a love of music.* **4** DET You use **a** or **an** instead of the number "one" in front of some numbers or measurements. ❑ *...a hundred miles.* **5** DET You use **a** or **an** in expressions such as **eight hours a day** to express a rate or ratio. ❑ *Prices start at $13.95 a yard for cotton.*

**AB** /eɪ bi/ N-UNCOUNT A piece of music or a poem that has an **AB** form or structure consists of two separate parts.

**ABA** /eɪ bi eɪ/ N-UNCOUNT A piece of music or a poem that has an **ABA** form or structure consists of three separate parts. The second part contrasts with the first part, and the third part repeats the first part in a different form.

**aback** /əbæk/ PHRASE If you are **taken aback by** something, you are surprised or shocked by it. ❑ *Frank was taken aback by the question.* [from Old English]

**aban|don** /əbændən/ (**abandons, abandoning, abandoned**) **1** V-T If you **abandon** a place, thing, or person, you leave the place, thing, or person permanently or for a long time, especially when you should not do so. ❑ *He claimed that his parents had abandoned him.* ● **aban|doned** ADJ ❑ *...a network of abandoned tunnels.* ● **aban|don|ment** N-UNCOUNT ❑ *...her father's abandonment of her.* **2** V-T If you **abandon** an activity or piece of work, you stop doing it before it is finished. ❑ *The authorities have abandoned any attempt to distribute food.* ● **aban|don|ment** N-UNCOUNT ❑ *Rain forced the abandonment of the game.* **3** V-T If you **abandon** an idea or way of thinking, you stop having that idea or thinking in that way. ❑ *She abandoned the idea of going to nursing school.* **4** N-UNCOUNT If you do something **with abandon**, you behave in a wild, uncontrolled way. ❑ *He lived life with reckless abandon.* [from Old French]

| **Thesaurus** | *abandon* | Also look up : |
|---|---|---|

v.   desert, leave, quit; (ant.) stay **1**
break off, give up, quit, stop; (ant.) continue **2**

**abate** /əbeɪt/ (**abates, abating, abated**) V-I If something bad **abates**, it becomes much less strong or severe. [FORMAL] ❑ *The rain showed no sign of abating.* [from Old French]

**ab|bey** /æbi/ (**abbeys**) N-COUNT An **abbey** is a church with buildings attached to it in which monks or nuns live or used to live. [from Old French]

**ab|bre|vi|ate** /əbrivi]eɪt/ (**abbreviates, abbreviating, abbreviated**) V-T If you **abbreviate** something, especially a word or a piece of writing, you make it shorter. ❑ *"Compact disc" is often abbreviated to "CD."* [from Late Latin]

**ab|bre|via|tion** /əbrivieɪʃᵊn/ (**abbreviations**) N-COUNT An **abbreviation** is a short form of a word or phrase, made by leaving out some of the letters or by using only the first letter of each word. ❑ *The abbreviation for Kansas is KS.* [from Late Latin]

**ABC's** also **ABCs** /eɪ bi siz/ **1** N-PLURAL The **ABC's of** a subject or activity are the parts of it that you have to learn first because they are the most important and basic. ❑ *...the ABC's of cooking.* **2** N-PLURAL Children who have learned their **ABC's** have learned to recognize, write, or say the alphabet. [INFORMAL]

**ab|di|cate** /æbdɪkeɪt/ (**abdicates, abdicating, abdicated**) **1** V-I If a king or queen **abdicates**, he or she gives up being king or queen. ❑ *The last French king was called Louis Philippe, and he abdicated in 1848.* ● **ab|di|ca|tion** /æbdɪkeɪʃᵊn/ N-UNCOUNT ❑ *...the abdication of Edward VIII.* **2** V-T If you **abdicate** responsibility for something, you refuse to accept responsibility for it any longer. [FORMAL] ❑ *Many parents simply abdicate all responsibility for their children.* ● **ab|di|ca|tion** N-UNCOUNT ❑ *There had been a complete abdication of responsibility.* [from Latin]

**ab|do|men** /æbdəmən/ (**abdomens**) N-COUNT Your **abdomen** is the part of your body below your chest where your stomach is. [FORMAL] ❑ *The pain in my abdomen grew worse.* ● **ab|domi|nal** /æbdɒmɪnᵊl/ ADJ [FORMAL] ❑ *...the abdominal muscles.* [from Latin]
→ see **insect**

**ab|duct** /æbdʌkt/ (**abducts, abducting, abducted**) V-T If someone **is abducted** by another person, he or she is taken away illegally, usually using force. ❑ *He was going to the airport when he was abducted by four gunmen.* ● **ab|duc|tion** (**abductions**) N-VAR ❑ *The company confirmed the abduction of eight of its workers.* [from Latin]

**ab|er|ra|tion** /æbəreɪʃᵊn/ (**aberrations**) N-VAR An **aberration** is an incident or way of behaving that is not typical. [FORMAL] ❑ *I think this attack was an aberration, something that does not occur regularly.* [from Latin]

A

**abide** /əbaɪd/ (**abides, abiding, abided**)
**1** PHRASE If you **can't abide** someone or
something, you dislike them very much. □ *Sally
can't abide cats.* [from Old English] **2** → see also
**abiding, law-abiding**
▶ **abide by** PHR-VERB If you **abide by** a law,
agreement, or decision, you do what it says you
should do. □ *They have to abide by the rules.*
**abid|ing** /əbaɪdɪŋ/ ADJ An **abiding** feeling,
memory, or interest is one that you have for a very
long time. □ *He has a deep and abiding love of jazz.*
[from Old English]
**abil|ity** /əbɪlɪti/ (**abilities**) N-VAR Your **ability**
is the quality or skill that you have which makes
it possible for you to do something. □ *Her drama
teacher spotted her acting ability.* □ *His mother had
strong musical abilities.* [from Old French]

| Thesaurus | *ability* | Also look up : |
|---|---|---|

N. capability, competence, craft, knack, skill,
technique

| Word Partnership | Use *ability* with : |
|---|---|

V. ability **to handle, have the** ability, **lack
the** ability
N. **lack of** ability
ADJ. **natural** ability

**abiot|ic** /eɪbaɪɒtɪk/ ADJ **Abiotic** factors in the
environment are things such as the climate and
the quality of the soil, which affect the ability of
organisms to survive. [TECHNICAL] [from Greek]
**ab|ject** /æbdʒɛkt/ ADJ You use **abject** to
emphasize that a situation or quality is extremely
bad. □ *Both of them died in abject poverty.* [from
Latin]
**ablaze** /əbleɪz/ ADJ Something that is **ablaze**
is burning very strongly. □ *Stores and houses were
set ablaze.*
**able** /eɪbəl/ (**abler** /eɪblər/, **ablest**) **1** PHRASE If
you **are able to** do something, you have skills or
qualities which make it possible for you to do it.
□ *The 10-year-old child should be able to prepare a simple
meal.* □ *The company says they're able to keep prices
low.* **2** PHRASE If you **are able to** do something,
you have enough freedom, power, time, or money
to do it. □ *You'll be able to read in peace.* □ *Are you able
to help me or not?* **3** ADJ Someone who is **able** is
very intelligent or very good at doing something.
□ *Mr. Nicholas was one of the most able men in the
industry.* ● **ably** /eɪbli/ ADV □ *He was ably assisted by
Robert James.* [from Latin]

| Usage | **be able to** and **could** |
|---|---|

*Could* is used to refer to ability in the past:
*When I was younger I could swim very fast.* When
referring to single events in the past, use *be able
to* instead: *I was able to finish my essay last night.* In
negative sentences or when referring to things
that happened frequently or over a period
of time, you can use either *be able to* or *could*:
*I wasn't able to/couldn't finish my essay last night.*
*When you were in college could you usually/were you
usually able to get your work done on time?*

**ab|nor|mal** /æbnɔrməl/ ADJ Someone or
something that is **abnormal** is unusual, especially
in a way that is troublesome. □ *...an abnormal*

heartbeat. ● **ab|nor|mal|ly** ADV □ *...abnormally high
ocean temperatures.* [from Medieval Latin]
**ab|nor|mal|ity** /æbnɔrmælɪti/ (**abnormalities**)
N-VAR An **abnormality** in something is an
unusual part or feature of it that may be a concern
or dangerous. □ *...a genetic abnormality.* [from
Medieval Latin]
**aboard** /əbɔrd/ PREP If you are **aboard** a ship or
plane, you are on it or in it. □ *He's invited us aboard
his boat.* ● **Aboard** is also an adverb. □ *It took two
hours to get all the people aboard.*
**abol|ish** /əbɒlɪʃ/ (**abolishes, abolishing,
abolished**) V-T If someone in authority **abolishes**
a system or practice, they put an end to it. □ *The
committee voted Thursday to abolish the death penalty.*
● **abo|li|tion** /æbəlɪʃən/ N-UNCOUNT □ *I support the
total abolition of slavery.* [from Old French]

| Thesaurus | *abolish* | Also look up : |
|---|---|---|

V. eliminate, end; (*ant.*) continue

**abomi|nable** /əbɒmɪnəbəl/ ADJ Something
that is **abominable** is very unpleasant or bad.
□ *The president said the killings were an abominable
crime.* [from Latin]
**Abo|rigi|nal** /æbərɪdʒɪnəl/ (**Aboriginals**)
also **aboriginal** **1** N-COUNT An **Aboriginal**
is an Australian Aborigine. □ *He was fascinated
by the Aboriginals' tales.* **2** ADJ **Aboriginal**
means belonging or relating to the Australian
Aborigines. □ *...aboriginal art.* [from Latin]
**Abo|rigi|ne** /æbərɪdʒɪni/ (**Aborigines**) N-COUNT
**Aborigines** are members of the tribes that were
living in Australia when Europeans arrived there.
□ *...an area sacred to Aborigines.* [from Latin]
**abort** /əbɔrt/ (**aborts, aborting, aborted**) **1** V-T
If you **abort** a process, plan, or activity, you stop
it before it has been completed. □ *The decision was
made to abort the mission.* **2** V-T If an unborn baby
**is aborted**, the pregnancy is ended deliberately
and the baby is not born alive. □ *He was the last of
10 children and his mother was advised to abort him for
health reasons.* [from Latin]
**abor|tion** /əbɔrʃən/ (**abortions**) N-VAR If a
woman has an **abortion**, she ends her pregnancy
deliberately so that the baby is not born alive.
□ *This drug is not used as a method of abortion in the
U.S.* [from Latin]
**abor|tive** /əbɔrtɪv/ ADJ An **abortive** attempt
or action is unsuccessful. [FORMAL] □ *I was there
during the abortive raid last August.* [from Latin]
**abound** /əbaʊnd/ (**abounds, abounding,
abounded**) V-I If things **abound**, or if a place
**abounds** with things, there are very large
numbers of them. [FORMAL] □ *Stories abound that he
traveled to India.* [from Old French]
**about** /əbaʊt/ **1** PREP You use **about** to
introduce who or what something relates to or
concerns. □ *She knew a lot about food.* □ *He never
complains about his wife.* **2** PREP When you say that
there is a particular quality **about** someone or
something, you mean that they have this quality.
□ *There was something special about her.* □ *There was a
warmth and passion about him you never knew.* **3** ADV
**About** is used in front of a number to show that
the number is not exact. □ *The child is about eight
years old.* □ *The rate of inflation is about 2.7 percent.*
**4** ADJ If you are **about to** do something, you are

going to do it very soon. ❑ *I think he's about to leave.* ❑ *Visas are about to be abolished.* [from Old English] **5 how about →** see **how 6 what about →** see **what 7 just about →** see **just**

---

**Usage** | **about to**

*About to* is used to say that something is going to happen very soon without specifying exactly when. A time expression is not necessary and should be avoided: *The concert is about to start.* means that it is imminent; *The concert starts in five minutes.* tells us exactly when.

---

**above** /əbˈʌv/ **1** PREP If one thing is **above** another one, it is directly over it or higher than it. ❑ *He lifted his hands above his head.* ❑ *Apartment 46 was a quiet apartment, unlike the one above it.* ● **Above** is also an adverb. ❑ *A long scream sounded from somewhere above.* ❑ *...a picture of the new house as seen from above.* **2** PREP If an amount or measurement is **above** a particular level, it is greater than that level. ❑ *The temperature rose to just above 40 degrees.* ❑ *Victoria Falls has had above average levels of rainfall this year.* ● **Above** is also an adverb. ❑ *Banks have been charging 25 percent and above for loans.* **3** PREP If someone is **above** you, they are in a higher social position than you or in a position of authority over you. ❑ *You have people above you making decisions.* ● **Above** is also an adverb. ❑ *The policemen were acting on orders from above.* **4** PREP If someone thinks they are **above** something, they act as if they are too good or important for it. ❑ *He thought he was above failure.* **5** PREP If someone is **above** criticism or suspicion, they cannot be criticized or suspected because of their good qualities or their position. ❑ *He was a respected academic and above suspicion.* **6** ADV In writing, you use **above** to refer to something that has already been mentioned or discussed. ❑ *Several conclusions could be drawn from the results described above.* ● **Above** is also a noun. ❑ *For additional information, contact any of the above.* ● **Above** is also an adjective. ❑ *For a copy of their brochure, write to the above address.* [from Old English] **7 over and above →** see **over** → see **location**

**abra|sion** N-UNCOUNT **Abrasion** is the gradual wearing away of the surface of rock as a result of other rock or sand particles rubbing against it. [from Medieval Latin]

**abra|sive** /əbreɪsɪv/ **1** ADJ Someone who has an **abrasive** manner is unkind and rude. ❑ *His voice was abrasive.* **2** ADJ An **abrasive** substance is rough and can be used to clean hard surfaces. ❑ *...a new, non-abrasive cleaner.* [from Medieval Latin]

**abreast** /əbrɛst/ **1** ADV If people or things walk or move **abreast**, they are side by side. ❑ *The sidewalk was too narrow for them to walk abreast.* **2** PHRASE If you **keep abreast** of a subject, you know all the most recent facts about it. ❑ *He will be keeping abreast of the news.*

**abroad** /əbrɔd/ ADV If you go **abroad**, you go to a foreign country. ❑ *I would love to go abroad this year.* ❑ *The owner of the house is abroad.*

**ab|rupt** /əbrʌpt/ **1** ADJ An **abrupt** change or action is very sudden, often in a way that is unpleasant. ❑ *His career came to an abrupt end in 1998.* ● **ab|rupt|ly** ADV ❑ *He stopped abruptly and looked my way.* **2** ADJ Someone who is **abrupt**

speaks or acts in a rude, unfriendly way. ❑ *His voice was abrupt.* ● **ab|rupt|ly** ADV ❑ *"Good night, then," she said abruptly.* [from Latin]

**ab|sence** /æbsˈns/ (**absences**) **1** N-VAR Someone's **absence** from a place is the fact that they are not there. ❑ *A letter from my mother arrived for me in my absence.* **2** N-SING The **absence** of something from a place is the fact that it is not there or does not exist. ❑ *She told the child that in the absence of his father, he was the head of the family.* [from Old French]

**ab|sent** /æbsˈnt/ **1** ADJ If someone or something is **absent** from a place or situation, they are not there. ❑ *He has been absent from his desk for two weeks.* ❑ *The pictures, too, were absent from the walls.* **2** ADJ If someone appears **absent**, they are not paying attention. ❑ *"Nothing," Rosie said in an absent way.* ● **ab|sent|ly** ADV ❑ *He nodded absently.* [from Latin]

**ab|sen|tee** /æbsˈnti/ (**absentees**) **1** N-COUNT An **absentee** is a person who should be in a particular place but who is not there. ❑ *Two of the absentees had good reasons for being away.* **2** ADJ In elections in the United States, if you vote by **absentee** ballot or if you are an **absentee** voter, you vote in advance because you will be unable to go to the polling place. ❑ *He voted by absentee ballot.* [from Latin] → see **election**

**absent-minded** ADJ Someone who is **absent-minded** forgets things or does not pay attention to what they are doing. ❑ *In his later life he became even more absent-minded.* ● **absent-mindedly** ADV ❑ *Elliot absent-mindedly scratched his head.*

**ab|so|lute** /æbsəlut/ (**absolutes**) **1** ADJ **Absolute** means total and complete. ❑ *It's not really suitable for absolute beginners.* ❑ *...absolute proof.* **2** ADJ **Absolute** rules and principles are believed to be true or right in all situations. ❑ *There are no absolute rules.* **3** N-COUNT An **absolute** is a rule or principle that is believed to be true or right in all situations. ❑ *This is one of the few absolutes in U.S. law.* [from Latin]

**ab|so|lute dat|ing** N-UNCOUNT In archeology, **absolute dating** is a method of estimating the age of something such as a building or tool by examining its physical or chemical properties.

**ab|so|lute|ly** /æbsəlutli/ **1** ADV **Absolutely** means totally and completely. ❑ *Joan is absolutely right.* ❑ *I absolutely refuse to get married.* **2** ADV **Absolutely** is an emphatic way of saying yes or of agreeing with someone. **Absolutely not** is an emphatic way of saying no or of disagreeing with someone. ❑ *"It's worrying though, isn't it?" — "Absolutely."* [from Latin]

**ab|so|lute mag|ni|tude** (**absolute magnitudes**) N-COUNT The **absolute magnitude** of a star or galaxy is a measure of its actual brightness, after its distance from the Earth has been taken into account. [TECHNICAL]

**ab|so|lute value** (**absolute values**) N-COUNT In mathematics, the **absolute value** of a number is the difference between that number and zero. The absolute value of -4 is 4, and the absolute value of +4 is 4.

**ab|so|lute zero** N-UNCOUNT **Absolute zero** is a theoretical temperature that is thought to be the lowest possible temperature.

**ab|sorb** /əbsɔrb, -zɔrb/ (**absorbs, absorbing, absorbed**) ◼ V-T To **absorb** a substance means to soak it up or take it in. ❑ *Cook the rice until it absorbs the water.* ● **ab|sorp|tion** /əbsɔrpʃən, -zɔrp!-/ N-UNCOUNT ❑ *The heat of the water helps the absorption of the oil through the skin.* ◼ V-T If a group **is absorbed into** a larger group, it becomes part of the larger group. ❑ *In 1662, the New Haven colony was absorbed into Connecticut.* ● **ab|sorp|tion** N-UNCOUNT ❑ *…the absorption of the old East Germany into the new republic.* ◼ V-T If something **absorbs** a force or shock, it reduces its effect. ❑ *…shoes that absorb the impact of running.* ◼ V-T If you **absorb** information, you learn and understand it. ❑ *Often he only absorbs half the information in the instruction manual.* ◼ V-T If something **absorbs** you, it interests you a lot and takes up all your attention and energy. ❑ *Her new career absorbed her completely.*

**ab|sorbed** /əbsɔrbd, -zɔrbd/ ADJ If you are **absorbed in** something or someone, they take up all your attention and energy. ❑ *They were completely absorbed in each other.* [from Old French]

**ab|sorb|ing** /əbsɔrbɪŋ, -zɔrbɪŋ/ ADJ An **absorbing** task or activity interests you a great deal and takes up all your attention and energy. ❑ *This is a very absorbing game.* [from Old French]

**ab|stain** /æbsteɪn/ (**abstains, abstaining, abstained**) ◼ V-I If you **abstain from** something you like doing, you deliberately do not do it. [FORMAL] ❑ *Many Catholics abstain from meat on Friday.* ◼ V-I If you **abstain** during a vote, you do not use your vote. ❑ *Three countries abstained in the vote.* [from Old French]

**ab|sti|nence** /æbstɪnəns/ N-UNCOUNT **Abstinence** is the practice of abstaining from something such as alcoholic drink or sex, often for health or religious reasons. ❑ *…six months of abstinence.* [from Old French]

**ab|stract** /æbstrækt/ (**abstracts**) ◼ ADJ An **abstract** idea or way of thinking is based on general ideas rather than on real things and events. ❑ *…starting with a few abstract ideas.* ◼ ADJ **Abstract** art makes use of shapes and patterns rather than showing people or things. ❑ *…a modern abstract painting.* ◼ N-COUNT An **abstract** is an abstract work of art. ❑ *His abstracts are held in many collections.* ◼ PHRASE When you talk or think about something **in the abstract**, you talk or think about it in a general way, rather than considering particular things or events. ❑ *Money was something she only thought about in the abstract.* [from Latin]

**ab|strac|tion** /æbstrækʃⁿn/ (**abstractions**) N-VAR An **abstraction** is a general idea rather than one relating to a particular object, person, or situation. [FORMAL] ❑ *It is better to start with a firm opinion than with an abstraction.* [from Latin]

**ab|surd** /æbsɜrd, -zɜrd/ ADJ If you say that something is **absurd**, you are criticizing it because you think that it is ridiculous or that it does not make sense. ❑ *That's absurd.* ❑ *It's absurd to suggest that they knew what was going on but did nothing.* ● **The absurd** is something that is absurd. ❑ *She has a strong sense of the absurd.* ● **ab|surd|ly** ADV ❑ *Prices were still absurdly low.* ● **ab|surd|ity** /æbsɜrdɪti, -zɜrd-/ (**absurdities**) N-VAR ❑ *…the absurdity of the situation.* [from French]

**abun|dance** /əbʌndəns/ N-SING An **abundance of** something is a large quantity of it. ❑ *This area of Mexico has an abundance of safe beaches.* [from Old French]

**abun|dant** /əbʌndənt/ ADJ Something that is **abundant** is present in large quantities. ❑ *…an abundant supply of food.* [from Latin]

**abuse** (**abuses, abusing, abused**)

The noun is pronounced /əbyus/. The verb is pronounced /əbyuz/.

◼ N-VAR **Abuse** of someone or something is cruel and violent treatment of it. ❑ *…child abuse.* ❑ *…victims of physical abuse.* ◼ N-UNCOUNT **Abuse** is extremely rude and insulting things that people say when they are angry. ❑ *I shouted abuse as the car drove off.* ◼ N-VAR **Abuse** of something is the use of it in a wrong way or for a bad purpose. ❑ *…the abuse of power.* ◼ V-T If someone **is abused**, they are treated cruelly and violently. ❑ *The film is about her daughter, who was abused as a child.* ❑ *A person who abuses animals is likely to be violent with people.* ◼ V-T You can say that someone **is abused** if extremely rude and insulting things are said to them. ❑ *He said that he was verbally abused by other soldiers.* ◼ V-T If you **abuse** something, you use it in a wrong way or for a bad purpose. ❑ *The rich and powerful sometimes abuse their position.* [from Old French]

**abu|sive** /əbyusɪv/ ◼ ADJ Someone who is **abusive** behaves in a cruel and violent way toward other people. ❑ *He was violent and abusive toward Ben's mother.* ◼ ADJ **Abusive** language is extremely rude and insulting. ❑ *I did not use any bad or abusive language.* [from Old French]

**abys|mal** /əbɪzm²l/ ADJ Something that is **abysmal** is very bad or poor in quality. ❑ *The sound was so abysmal that you couldn't hear it properly.* ● **abys|mal|ly** ADV ❑ *The standard of education was abysmally low.* [from Old French]

**abyss** /əbɪs/ (**abysses**) ◼ N-COUNT An **abyss** is a very deep hole in the ground. [LITERARY] ❑ *They could see the river disappearing into a black abyss.* ◼ N-COUNT If someone is on the edge or brink of an **abyss**, they are about to enter into a very frightening or threatening situation. [LITERARY] ❑ *…a warning that the Middle East was on the brink of an abyss.* [from Late Latin]

**abys|sal plain** /əbɪsəl pleɪn/ (**abyssal plains**) N-COUNT An **abyssal plain** is a wide, flat area at the bottom of an ocean.

**a/c** also **A/C** /eɪ si/ N-UNCOUNT **a/c** is an abbreviation for **air-conditioning**. ❑ *Keep your windows closed and the a/c on high.* ❑ *60 Motel Units. All Units A/C, Heat, Cable TV.*

**aca|dem|ic** /ækədɛmɪk/ (**academics**) ◼ ADJ **Academic** means relating to the work done in schools, colleges, and universities, especially work that involves studying and reasoning rather than practical or technical skills. ❑ *Their academic standards are high.* ❑ *...the start of the academic year.* • **aca|dem|ical|ly** ADV ❑ *He is academically gifted.* **2** N-COUNT An **academic** is a member of a university or college who teaches or does research. ❑ *...a group of academics.* [from Latin]

**acad|emy** /əkǽdəmi/ (**academies**) **1** N-COUNT **Academy** is sometimes used in the names of schools and colleges, especially those specializing in particular subjects or skills, or private high schools in the United States. ❑ *He is an English teacher at the Seattle Academy for Arts and Sciences.* **2** N-COUNT **Academy** appears in the names of some societies formed to improve or maintain standards in a particular field. ❑ *...the National Academy of Sciences.* [from Latin]

**ac|cel|er|ate** /æksɛ́ləreɪt/ (**accelerates, accelerating, accelerated**) **1** V-T/V-I If the process or rate of something **accelerates** or if something **accelerates** it, it gets faster and faster. ❑ *Growth will accelerate to 2.9 percent next year.* • **ac|cel|era|tion** /æksɛ́ləreɪʃ°n/ N-UNCOUNT ❑ *...the acceleration of knowledge this century.* **2** V-I When a moving vehicle **accelerates**, it goes faster and faster. ❑ *Suddenly the car accelerated.* • **ac|cel|era|tion** N-UNCOUNT ❑ *Acceleration to 60 mph takes just 5.7 seconds.* [from Latin]
→ see **motion**

**ac|cel|era|tion** /æksɛ́ləreɪʃ°n/ **1** N-UNCOUNT **Acceleration** is the rate at which the speed of an object increases. [TECHNICAL] [from Latin] **2** → see also **accelerate**

**ac|cel|era|tor** /æksɛ́ləreɪtər/ (**accelerators**) N-COUNT The **accelerator** in a car or other vehicle is the pedal that you press with your foot in order to make the vehicle go faster. ❑ *He took his foot off the accelerator.* [from Latin]

**ac|cent** /æksɛnt/ (**accents**) **1** N-COUNT Someone who speaks with a particular **accent** pronounces the words of a language in a distinctive way that shows which country, region, or background they come from. ❑ *He had a slight southern accent.* **2** N-COUNT An **accent** is a short line or other mark which is written above certain letters in some languages and which indicates the way those letters are pronounced. ❑ *Some languages use accents to change the sound of a letter.* [from Old French]

**Word Partnership** Use *accent* with :

| | |
|---|---|
| ADJ. | **American/French** accent, **regional** accent, **thick** accent **1** |
| ADV. | **heavily** accented **1** |
| V. | **do an** accent, **have an** accent **1** **put the** accent **on 2** |

**ac|cen|tu|ate** /æksɛ́ntʃueɪt/ (**accentuates, accentuating, accentuated**) V-T To **accentuate** something means to emphasize it or make it more noticeable. ❑ *His bald head accentuates his large round face.* [from Old French]

**ac|cept** /æksɛ́pt/ (**accepts, accepting, accepted**) **1** V-T/V-I If you **accept** something that you have been offered, you say yes to it or agree to take it. ❑ *She accepted his offer of marriage.* ❑ *All those invited to next week's peace conference have accepted.* • **ac|cept|ance** N-UNCOUNT ❑ *...his*

*acceptance speech for the Nobel Peace Prize.* **2** V-T If you **accept** an idea, statement, or fact, you believe that it is true or valid. ❑ *I accept that I cannot be perfect.* ❑ *I don't think they will accept that view.* • **ac|cept|ance** N-UNCOUNT ❑ *The theory is gaining acceptance.* **3** V-T If you **accept** an unpleasant fact or situation, you get used to it or recognize that it is necessary or cannot be changed. ❑ *People often accept noise as part of city life.* • **ac|cept|ance** N-UNCOUNT ❑ *...his acceptance of pain.* **4** V-T If an organization or group **accepts** you, you are allowed to join the organization or become part of the group. ❑ *We do not accept all-male groups.* ❑ *Some men find it difficult to accept a woman as a business partner.* • **ac|cept|ance** N-UNCOUNT ❑ *...his acceptance into American society.* **5** V-T If you **accept** the responsibility or blame for something, you recognize that you are responsible for it. ❑ *The company cannot accept responsibility for loss or damage.* [from Latin] **6** → see also **accepted**

**Usage** **accept** and **except**
*Accept* and *except* sound similar but have different meanings. *Accept* means "to receive." *Monique accepted her diploma.* *Except* means "other than." *Everyone in the class knew the answer except John.*

**Thesaurus** *accept* Also look up :

| | |
|---|---|
| V. | receive, take; (*ant.*) refuse, reject **1** acknowledge, agree to, recognize; (*ant.*) object, oppose, refuse **2** endure, live with, tolerate; (*ant.*) disallow, reject **3** |

**Word Link** *able* ≈ able to be : accept*able*, incur*able*, port*able*

**ac|cept|able** /æksɛ́ptəb°l/ **1** ADJ **Acceptable** activities and situations are those that most people approve of or consider to be normal. ❑ *This is not acceptable behavior.* • **ac|cept|abil|ity** /æksɛptəbílɪti/ N-UNCOUNT ❑ *...public acceptability of the plan.* • **ac|cept|ably** ADV ❑ *The aim of discipline is to teach children to behave acceptably.* **2** ADJ If something is **acceptable**, it is good enough or fairly good. ❑ *On the far side of the street was a restaurant that looked acceptable.* [from Latin]

**ac|cept|ed** /æksɛ́ptɪd/ **1** ADJ **Accepted** ideas are agreed by most people to be correct or reasonable. ❑ *It was not a widely accepted idea.* [from Latin] **2** → see also **accept**

**ac|cess** /ǽksɛs/ (**accesses, accessing, accessed**) **1** N-UNCOUNT If you have **access to** a building or other place, you are able or allowed to go into it. ❑ *The general public does not have access to the White House.* **2** N-UNCOUNT If you have **access to** something such as information or equipment, you have the opportunity or right to see it or use it. ❑ *Patients have access to their medical records.* **3** N-UNCOUNT If you have **access to** a person, you have the opportunity or right to see them or meet them. ❑ *He was not allowed access to a lawyer.* **4** V-T If you **access** something, especially information held on a computer, you succeed in finding or obtaining it. ❑ *The software lets parents see which sites their children have accessed.* [from Old French]

**ac|ces|sible** /æksɛ́sɪb°l/ **1** ADJ If a place or building is **accessible to** people, it is easy for

**A**

them to reach it or get into it. ❑ *The center is easily accessible to the general public.* • **ac|ces|sibil|ity** /æksɛsɪbɪlɪti/ N-UNCOUNT ❑ *...the easy accessibility of the area.* ◼ ADJ If something is **accessible to** people, they can easily use it or obtain it. ❑ *The computer system is accessible to all our workers.* • **ac|ces|sibil|ity** N-UNCOUNT ❑ *...growing public concern about the cost, quality and accessibility of health care.* [from Old French]
→ see **disability**

**ac|ces|so|ry** /æksɛsəri/ (**accessories**)
◼ N-COUNT **Accessories** are items of equipment that are not usually essential, but can be used with or added to something else in order to make it more efficient, useful, or decorative. ❑ *...bathroom accessories.* ◼ N-COUNT **Accessories** are articles such as belts and scarves which you wear or carry but which are not part of your main clothing. ❑ *...handbags, scarves and other accessories.* ◼ N-COUNT An **accessory to** a crime is someone who helps the person who commits it, or knew it was being committed but did not tell the police. [LEGAL] ❑ *The fact that you have that key could make you an accessory to murder.* [from Late Latin]

**ac|ci|dent** /æksɪdənt/ (**accidents**) ◼ N-COUNT An **accident** happens when a vehicle hits a person, an object, or another vehicle, causing injury or damage. ❑ *She had a serious car accident last week.* ◼ N-COUNT If someone has an **accident**, something unpleasant happens to them that was not intended, sometimes causing injury or death. ❑ *5,000 people die every year because of accidents in the home.* ◼ PHRASE If something happens **by accident**, it happens completely by chance. ❑ *She discovered the problem by accident during a visit to a nearby school.* [from Old French]

| **Word Partnership** | Use *accident* with : |
|---|---|
| N. | **car** accident ◼ |
| | **the cause of an** accident ◼ ◼ |
| ADJ. | **bad** accident, **a tragic** accident ◼ ◼ |
| V. | **cause an** accident, **insure against** accident, **report an** accident ◼ ◼ |
| PREP. | **without** accident ◼ |
| | **by** accident ◼ |

**ac|ci|den|tal** /æksɪdɛntᵊl/ ADJ An **accidental** event happens by chance or as the result of an accident, and is not intended. ❑ *...the accidental death of his younger brother.* • **ac|ci|den|tal|ly** /æksɪdɛntli/ ADV ❑ *Names were accidentally removed from computer disks.* [from Old French]

| **Word Link** | *claim ≈ shouting : ac*claim, clam*or,* ex*claim* |
|---|---|

**ac|claim** /əkleɪm/ (**acclaims, acclaiming, acclaimed**) ◼ V-T If someone or something is **acclaimed**, they are praised enthusiastically. [FORMAL] ❑ *The restaurant has been widely acclaimed for its excellent French food.* ❑ *He was acclaimed as America's greatest filmmaker.* • **ac|claimed** ADJ ❑ *She has published six highly acclaimed novels.* ◼ N-UNCOUNT **Acclaim** is public praise for someone or something. [FORMAL] ❑ *Angela Bassett has won acclaim for her excellent performance.* [from Latin]

**ac|cli|mate** /æklɪmeɪt, əklaɪmɪt/ (**acclimates, acclimating, acclimated**) V-T/V-I also **ac|cli|ma|tize** /əklaɪmətaɪz/ When you **acclimate** or **are acclimated to** a new situation,

place, or climate, you become used to it. ❑ *I help them acclimate to living in the U.S.* ❑ *I hadn't had any time to acclimate myself.* • **ac|cli|ma|tion** /æklɪmeɪʃən/ N-UNCOUNT ❑ *...acclimation to physical exercise.* [from Late Latin]

**ac|co|lade** /ækəleɪd/ (**accolades**) N-COUNT An **accolade** is something that is done or said about someone which shows how much people admire them. [FORMAL] ❑ *The Nobel Prize is the ultimate accolade in the sciences.* ❑ *When you win games everyone receives accolades.* [from French]

**ac|com|mo|date** /əkɒmədeɪt/ (**accommodates, accommodating, accommodated**) ◼ V-T If a building or space can **accommodate** someone or something, it has enough room for them. ❑ *The school was not big enough to accommodate all the children.* ◼ V-T To **accommodate** someone means to provide them with a place to live or stay. ❑ *The hotel can accommodate up to seventy-five people.* [from Latin]

**ac|com|mo|dat|ing** /əkɒmədeɪtɪŋ/ ADJ If you describe someone as **accommodating**, you like the fact that they are willing to do things in order to please you or help you. ❑ *Eddie was always very accommodating to me.* [from Latin]

**ac|com|mo|da|tion** /əkɒmədeɪʃᵊn/ (**accommodations**) N-VAR **Accommodations** are buildings or rooms where people live or stay. ❑ *The government will provide accommodations for up to three thousand homeless people.* [from Latin]

**ac|com|pa|ni|ment** /əkʌmpənɪmənt/ (**accompaniments**) ◼ N-VAR The **accompaniment** to a song or tune is the music that is played at the same time as it and forms a background to it. ❑ *He sang "Happy Birthday" to piano accompaniment.* ◼ N-COUNT An **accompaniment** is something that goes with another thing. ❑ *Strawberries make a good accompaniment to ice cream.* ◼ PHRASE If one thing happens **to the accompaniment of** another, they happen at the same time. [from Old French]

**ac|com|pa|ny** /əkʌmpəni/ (**accompanies, accompanying, accompanied**) ◼ V-T If you **accompany** someone, you go somewhere with them. [FORMAL] ❑ *Ken agreed to accompany me on a trip to Africa.* ❑ *She was accompanied by her younger brother.* ◼ V-T If one thing **accompanies** another, the two things happen or exist at the same time. [FORMAL] ❑ *Stress accompanies change of any sort.* ◼ V-T If you **accompany** a singer or a musician, you play one part of a piece of music while they sing or play the main tune. ❑ *Eddie Higgins accompanies her on all the songs on her new CD.* [from Old French]

**ac|com|plice** /əkɒmplɪs/ (**accomplices**) N-COUNT An **accomplice** is a person who helps someone to commit a crime. ❑ *Police believe that he had an accomplice.*

**ac|com|plish** /əkɒmplɪʃ/ (**accomplishes, accomplishing, accomplished**) V-T If you **accomplish** something, you succeed in doing it. ❑ *If we all work together, I think we can accomplish our goal.* • **ac|com|plish|ment** /əkɒmplɪʃmənt/ N-UNCOUNT ❑ *...the accomplishment of his highly important mission.* [from Old French]

| **Thesaurus** | *accomplish* | Also look up : |
|---|---|---|
| V. | achieve, complete, gain, realize, succeed | |

**ac|com|plished** /əkɒmplɪʃt/ ADJ If someone is **accomplished** at something, they are very good at it. [FORMAL] ❑ *He is an accomplished painter.* [from Old French]

**ac|com|plish|ment** /əkɒmplɪʃmənt/ (**accomplishments**) **1** N-COUNT An **accomplishment** is something unusual or special that has been done or achieved. ❑ *This is the proudest accomplishment of my life.* [from Old French] **2** → see also **accomplish**

**ac|cord** /əkɔrd/ (**accords, according, accorded**) **1** N-COUNT An **accord** between countries or groups of people is a formal agreement; for example, to end a war. ❑ *...the 1991 peace accords.* **2** V-T If you **are accorded** a particular kind of treatment, people act toward you or treat you in that way. [FORMAL] ❑ *He was accorded the very highest status.* ❑ *The government accorded him the rank of Colonel.* **3** → see also **according to** **4** PHRASE If something happens **of its own accord**, it seems to happen by itself, without anyone making it happen. ❑ *In many cases the disease will clear up of its own accord.* **5** PHRASE If you do something **of your own accord**, you do it because you want to, without being asked or forced. ❑ *He left his job of his own accord.* [from Old French]

**ac|cord|ance** /əkɔrdᵊns/ PHRASE If something is done **in accordance with** a particular rule or system, it is done in the way that the rule or system says that it should be done. ❑ *This decision is in accordance with the law.* [from Old French]

**ac|cord|ing|ly** /əkɔrdɪŋli/ ADV You use **accordingly** to say that one thing happens as a result of another. ❑ *It is a difficult job and we should pay them accordingly.* [from Old French]

**ac|cord|ing to** **1** PHRASE If something is true **according to** a particular person, book, or other source of information, that is where the information comes from. ❑ *The van raced away, according to police reports.* **2** PHRASE If something is done **according to** a particular set of principles, these principles are used as a basis for the way it is done. ❑ *They played the game according to the rules.* **3** PHRASE If something happens **according to plan**, it happens in exactly the way that it was intended to happen. ❑ *Everything is going according to plan.*

**ac|count** /əkaʊnt/ (**accounts, accounting, accounted**) **1** N-COUNT If you have an **account** with a bank, you leave your money there and take some out when you need it. ❑ *Some banks make it difficult to open an account.* **2** N-COUNT In business, a regular customer of a company can be referred to as an **account**. [BUSINESS] ❑ *Already Transamerica has two major accounts.* **3** N-COUNT **Accounts** are detailed records of all the money that a person or business receives and spends. [BUSINESS] ❑ *He kept detailed accounts.* **4** N-COUNT An **account** is a written or spoken report of something that has happened. ❑ *He gave a detailed account of what happened.* **5** → see also **accounting, checking account** **6** PHRASE If you tell someone not to do something **on your account**, you mean that they should do it only if they want to, and not because they think it will please you. [SPOKEN] ❑ *Don't leave on my account.* **7** PHRASE If you say that something should **on no account** be done, you are emphasizing that it should not be done under any circumstances. ❑ *On no account should the liquid boil.*

**8** PHRASE If you **take** something **into account**, or **take account of** something, you consider it when you are thinking about a situation or deciding what to do. ❑ *You have to take everyone into account before making a decision as it will affect us all.* [from Old French] → see **history**

▶ **account for** **1** PHR-VERB If a particular thing **accounts for** a part of something, that part consists of that thing, or is used or produced by it. ❑ *Computers account for 5% of the country's electricity use.* **2** PHR-VERB If you can **account for** something, you can explain it or give the necessary information about it. ❑ *How do you account for these differences?*

**ac|count|able** /əkaʊntəbᵊl/ ADJ If you are **accountable for** something that you do, you are responsible for it. ❑ *We are accountable to taxpayers.* ● **ac|count|abil|ity** /əkaʊntəbɪlɪti/ N-UNCOUNT ❑ *There's too much waste and too little accountability.* [from Old French]

**ac|count|ant** /əkaʊntənt/ (**accountants**) N-COUNT An **accountant** is a person whose job is to keep financial accounts. [from Old French]

**ac|count|ing** /əkaʊntɪŋ/ N-UNCOUNT **Accounting** is the theory or practice of keeping financial accounts. [from Old French]

**ac|cu|mu|late** /əkyumyəleɪt/ (**accumulates, accumulating, accumulated**) V-T/V-I When you **accumulate** things or when they **accumulate**, they collect or are gathered over a period of time. ❑ *He accumulated $42,000 in 6 years.* ● **ac|cu|mu|la|tion** /əkyumyəleɪʃᵊn/ (**accumulations**) N-VAR ❑ *...the accumulation of wealth.* [from Latin]

**ac|cu|rate** /ækyərɪt/ **1** ADJ **Accurate** information, measurements, and statistics are correct to a very detailed level. ❑ *This is the most accurate description of the killer we have.* ● **ac|cu|ra|cy** N-UNCOUNT ❑ *...the accuracy of weather reports.* ● **ac|cu|rate|ly** ADV ❑ *He described it quite accurately.* **2** ADJ A person, device or machine that is **accurate** is able to perform a task without making a mistake. ❑ *We require grammar and spelling to be accurate.* ● **ac|cu|ra|cy** N-UNCOUNT ❑ *We edit letters for length and accuracy.* ● **ac|cu|rate|ly** ADV ❑ *He hit the golf ball powerfully and accurately.* [from Latin]

| Thesaurus | accurate | Also look up : |
|---|---|---|

ADJ. right, true; (*ant.*) inaccurate **1** correct, precise, rigorous **2**

**ac|cu|sa|tion** /ækyuzeɪʃᵊn/ (**accusations**) N-VAR If you make an **accusation** against someone, you criticize them or express the belief that they have done something wrong. ❑ *...an accusation of murder.* [from Old French]

**ac|cuse** /əkyuz/ (**accuses, accusing, accused**) **1** V-T If you **accuse** someone **of** something, you say that you believe they did something wrong or dishonest. ❑ *They accused her of lying.* ❑ *Her assistant was accused of theft by the police.* [from Old French] **2** → see also **accused**

| Thesaurus | accuse | Also look up : |
|---|---|---|

V. blame, charge, implicate

**ac|cused** /əkyuzd/ (**accused**) N-COUNT The **accused** refers to a person or a group of people

**A**

charged with a crime or on trial for it. [LEGAL] ❑ *The accused is a high school senior.* [from Old French]

**ac|cus|tom** /əkʌstəm/ (**accustoms, accustoming, accustomed**) V-T If you **accustom yourself** to something, you make yourself become used to it. [FORMAL] ❑ *She tried to accustom herself to the darkness.* ● **ac|cus|tomed** ADJ ❑ *I was accustomed to being the only child among adults.* [from Old French]

**ace** /eɪs/ (**aces**) **1** N-COUNT An **ace** is a playing card with a single symbol on it. ❑ *...the ace of hearts.* **2** N-COUNT If you describe someone such as a sports player as an **ace**, you mean that they are very good at what they do. ❑ *...former tennis ace John McEnroe.* ● **Ace** is also an adjective. ❑ *...ace film producer Lawrence Woolsey.* **3** N-COUNT In tennis, an **ace** is a serve which is so fast that the other player cannot return the ball. ❑ *Agassi served three aces in the final set of the tennis match.* [from Old French]

ace

**ache** /eɪk/ (**aches, aching, ached**) **1** V-I If you **ache** or a part of your body **aches**, you feel a steady, fairly strong pain. ❑ *Her head was hurting and she ached all over.* ❑ *My leg still aches when I sit down.* **2** N-COUNT An **ache** is a steady, fairly strong pain in a part of your body. ❑ *She had an ache in the knee she hurt last year.* [from Old English] **3** → see also **headache, heartache**

| Thesaurus | *ache* | Also look up : |
|---|---|---|
| N. | hurt, pain, pang **2** | |
| V. | throb **2** | |

**achieve** /ətʃiv/ (**achieves, achieving, achieved**) V-T If you **achieve** a particular aim or effect, you succeed in doing or causing it to happen, usually after a lot of effort. ❑ *He worked hard to achieve his goals.* [from Old French]

| Thesaurus | *achieve* | Also look up : |
|---|---|---|
| V. | accomplish, bring about; (*ant.*) fail, lose, miss | | |

**achieve|ment** /ətʃivmənt/ (**achievements**) **1** N-COUNT An **achievement** is something that someone has succeeded in doing, especially after a lot of effort. ❑ *It was a great achievement to reach this agreement so quickly.* **2** N-UNCOUNT **Achievement** is the process of achieving something. ❑ *Only the achievement of these goals will bring peace.* [from Old French]

**achiev|er** /ətʃivər/ (**achievers**) N-COUNT A high **achiever** is someone who is successful in their studies or their work, usually as a result of their efforts. A low **achiever** is someone who achieves less than those around them. ❑ *He's been a high achiever from the moment he got here.* [from Old French]

**achoo** /ɑtʃu/ **Achoo** is used, especially in writing, to represent the sound that you make when you sneeze. ❑ *"Achoo!", she sneezed. And then, "Achoo!", she sneezed again.*

**acid** /æsɪd/ (**acids**) **1** N-VAR An **acid** is a chemical substance, usually a liquid, which contains hydrogen and can react with other substances to form salts. Some acids burn or dissolve other substances that they come into contact with. ❑ *...citric acid.* **2** ADJ An **acid** substance contains acid. ❑ *These plants must have an acid soil.* ● **acid|ity** /əsɪdɪti/ N-UNCOUNT ❑ *...the acidity of rainwater.* [from French]

**acid|ic** /əsɪdɪk/ ADJ **Acidic** substances contain acid. ❑ *Blueberries need acidic soil.* [from French]

**acid rain** also **acid precipitation** N-UNCOUNT **Acid rain** is rain polluted by acid that has been released into the atmosphere from factories and other industrial processes. Acid rain is harmful to the environment.
→ see **pollution**

**ac|knowl|edge** /æknɒlɪdʒ/ (**acknowledges, acknowledging, acknowledged**) **1** V-T If you **acknowledge** a fact or a situation, you accept or admit that it is true or that it exists. [FORMAL] ❑ *He acknowledged that he was wrong.* ❑ *At last, the government has acknowledged the problem.* **2** V-T If you **acknowledge** a message or letter, you write to the person who sent it in order to say that you have received it. ❑ *The army sent me a postcard acknowledging my request.* **3** V-T If you **acknowledge** someone, for example, by moving your head or smiling, you show that you have seen and recognized them. ❑ *He saw her but refused to acknowledge her.* [from Old English]

**ac|knowl|edg|ment** /æknɒlɪdʒmənt/ (**acknowledgments**) also **acknowledgement** **1** N-SING An **acknowledgment** is a statement or action which recognizes that something exists or is true. ❑ *It's an acknowledgment that there is a problem.* **2** N-PLURAL The **acknowledgments** in a book are the section in which the author thanks all the people who have helped him or her. ❑ *...two whole pages of acknowledgments.* [from Old English]

**acne** /ækni/ N-UNCOUNT If someone has **acne**, they have a skin condition which causes a lot of pimples on their face and neck. ❑ *...a new treatment for mild to severe acne.* [from New Latin]

**acorn** /eɪkɔrn/ (**acorns**) N-COUNT An **acorn** is a pale oval nut that is the fruit of an oak tree. [from Old English]

acorn

**acous|tic** /əkustɪk/ (**acoustics**) **1** ADJ An **acoustic** guitar or other instrument is one whose sound is produced without any electrical equipment. **2** N-PLURAL The **acoustics** of a space are the structural features which determine how well you can hear music or speech in it. ❑ *The theater's acoustics are very clear.* **3** N-UNCOUNT **Acoustics** is the scientific study of sound. ❑ *...his work in acoustics.* [from Greek]
→ see **string**

**ac|quaint** /əkweɪnt/ (**acquaints, acquainting, acquainted**) **1** V-T If you **acquaint** someone **with** something, you tell them about it so that they know it. [FORMAL] ❑ *This chapter will acquaint you with some standard business writing styles.* [from Old French] **2** → see also **acquainted**

**ac|quaint|ance** /əkweɪntəns/ (**acquaintances**) **1** N-COUNT An **acquaintance** is someone who you have met, but don't know well. ❑ *He spoke to the owner, an old acquaintance of his.* **2** N-VAR If you have an **acquaintance with** someone, you have met them and you know them. ❑ *The author talks about his personal acquaintance with Picasso.* [from Old French]

**ac|quaint|ed** /əkweɪntɪd/ **1** ADJ If you are **acquainted with** something, you know about it because you have learned it or experienced it. [FORMAL] ❑ *I became acquainted with the way they liked to work.* **2** ADJ If you get or become **acquainted with** someone, you talk to each other or do something together so that you get to know each other. You can also say that two people get or become **acquainted**. ❑ *At first the meetings were a way to get acquainted with each other.* [from Old French] **3** → see also **acquaint**

**ac|quire** /əkwaɪər/ (**acquires, acquiring, acquired**) **1** V-T If you **acquire** something, you obtain it. [FORMAL] ❑ *Recently, I acquired two new printers.* **2** V-T If you **acquire** a skill or a habit, you learn it or develop it. ❑ *I've never acquired a taste for coffee.* [from Old French]

**ac|qui|si|tion** /ækwɪzɪʃən/ (**acquisitions**) **1** N-VAR If a company or business person makes an **acquisition**, they buy another company or part of a company. [BUSINESS] ❑ *...the acquisition of a profitable recycling company.* **2** N-COUNT If you make an **acquisition**, you buy or obtain something, often to add to things that you already have. ❑ *Her acquisition of a computer music program helped her to start writing music.* **3** N-UNCOUNT The **acquisition** of a skill or a particular type of knowledge is the process of learning it or developing it. ❑ *...language acquisition.* [from Latin]

**ac|quit** /əkwɪt/ (**acquits, acquitting, acquitted**) V-T If someone **is acquitted of** a crime in a court of law, they are formally declared not to have committed the crime. ❑ *Mr. Castorina was acquitted of attempted murder.* [from Old French]

**ac|quit|tal** /əkwɪtəl/ (**acquittals**) N-VAR **Acquittal** is a formal declaration in a court of law that someone who has been accused of a crime is innocent. ❑ *Irene's chances for aquittal were good.* [from Old French]

**acre** /eɪkər/ (**acres**) N-COUNT An **acre** is an area of land measuring 4,840 square yards or 4,047 square meters. ❑ *The property has two acres of land.* [from Old English]

**ac|ri|mo|ni|ous** /ækrɪmoʊniəs/ ADJ **Acrimonious** words or quarrels are bitter and angry. [FORMAL] ❑ *Talks were acrimonious and lasted for ten years.* [from Latin]

| Word Link | onym ≈ name : acronym, anonymous, synonym |
| --- | --- |

**ac|ro|nym** /ækrənɪm/ (**acronyms**) N-COUNT An **acronym** is a word composed of the first letters of the words in a phrase, especially when this is used as a name. An example of an acronym is NATO which is made up of the first letters of the "North Atlantic Treaty Organization."

**across** /əkrɔs/

In addition to the uses shown below, **across** is used in phrasal verbs such as "come across," "get across," and "put across."

**1** PREP If someone or something goes **across** a place or a boundary, they go from one side of it to the other. ❑ *She walked across the floor and sat down.* ❑ *Karl ran across the street.* ● **Across** is also an adverb. ❑ *Richard stood up and walked across to the window.* **2** PREP If something is situated or stretched **across** something else, it is situated or stretched from one side of it to the other. ❑ *...the bridge across the lake.* ❑ *He wrote his name across the bill.* ● **Across** is also an adverb. ❑ *Cut across using scissors.* **3** PREP When something happens **across** a place or organization, it happens equally everywhere within it. ❑ *The movie opens across the country on May 11.* **4** ADV If you look **across** at a place, person, or thing, you look toward them. ❑ *He looked across at his sleeping wife.* **5** ADV **Across** is used in measurements to show the width of something. ❑ *This plate is 14 inches across.* [from Old French]

**acryl|ic** /əkrɪlɪk/ N-UNCOUNT **Acrylic** material is artificial and is manufactured by a chemical process. ❑ *...her pink acrylic sweater.*

**act** /ækt/ (**acts, acting, acted**) **1** V-I When you **act**, you do something for a particular purpose. ❑ *The police acted to stop the riot.* **2** V-I If someone **acts** in a particular way, they behave in that way. ❑ *...youths who were acting suspiciously.* ❑ *He acted as if he hadn't heard any of it.* **3** V-I If someone or something **acts as** a particular thing, they have that role or function. ❑ *He acted as the ship's doctor.* **4** V-I If someone **acts** in a particular way, they pretend to be something that they are not. ❑ *He acted surprised when I talked about Japan.* **5** V-I If you **act** in a play or film, you have a part in it. ❑ *He acted in many films, including "Reds."* **6** N-COUNT An **act** is a single thing that someone does. [FORMAL] ❑ *As a child I loved the act of writing.* **7** N-COUNT An **Act** is a law passed by the government. ❑ *...an Act of Congress.* **8** N-COUNT An **act** in a play, opera, or ballet is one of the main parts into which it is divided. ❑ *Act II contained a really funny scene.* **9** N-COUNT An **act** in a show is a short performance which is one of several in the show. ❑ *This year many bands are playing, as well as comedy acts.* **10** N-SING If you say that someone's behavior is an **act**, you mean that it does not express their real feelings. ❑ *His anger was real. It wasn't an act.* [from Latin] **11** to **act the fool** → see **fool**

**act|ing** /æktɪŋ/ **1** N-UNCOUNT **Acting** is the activity or profession of performing in plays or films. ❑ *I'd like to do a little acting some day.* **2** ADJ You use **acting** before the title of a job to indicate that someone is doing that job temporarily. ❑ *...the new acting president.* [from Latin]

**act|ing area** (**acting areas**) N-COUNT In a theater, the **acting areas** are the different parts of the stage such as the front or back of the stage.

**ac|tion** /ækʃən/ (**actions**) **1** N-UNCOUNT **Action** is doing something for a particular purpose. ❑ *The government is taking emergency action.* **2** N-UNCOUNT The fighting which takes place in a war can be referred to as **action**. ❑ *Our leaders have generally supported military action if it proves necessary.* **3** N-COUNT An **action** is something that you do on a particular occasion. ❑ *Peter had a reason for*

A

*his action.* **4** N-SING In physics, **action** is the force that is applied to an object. **5** N-UNCOUNT The **action** of a chemical is the way that it works, or the effect that it has. **6** PHRASE If someone or something is **out of action**, they are injured or damaged and cannot work or be used. *He's been out of action for 16 months with a knee injury.* **7** PHRASE If you **put** an idea or policy **into action**, you begin to use it or cause it to operate. *Agnes decided to put her plan into action.* [from Latin]
→ see **genre, motion**

| **Word Partnership** | Use *action* with : |
| --- | --- |

| N. | **course of** action, **plan of** action **1** |
| V. | **take** action **1** |
| ADJ. | **disciplinary** action **1** |
| | **military** action **2** |

**ac|ti|vate** /ǽktɪveɪt/ (**activates, activating, activated**) V-T If a device or process **is activated**, something causes it to start working. *Video cameras can be activated by movement.* [from Latin]

**ac|ti|va|tion en|er|gy** N-SING In chemistry and biology, the **activation energy** is the minimum amount of energy that is needed in order for a chemical reaction to occur.

**ac|tive** /ǽktɪv/ **1** ADJ Someone who is **active** moves around a lot or does a lot of things. *With three active kids, I was very busy.* **2** ADJ If someone is **active** in an organization or cause, they do things for it rather than just giving it their support. *We should play an active role in politics.* ● **ac|tive|ly** ADV *They are actively involved in job training.* **3** ADJ **Active** is used to emphasize that someone is taking action in order to achieve something, rather than just waiting for it to happen. *Companies need to take active steps to increase exports.* ● **ac|tive|ly** ADV *Many adults are actively looking for work.* **4** ADJ An **active** volcano has erupted recently and is expected to erupt soon. *...lava from an active volcano.* [from Latin]

| **Word Partnership** | Use *active* with : |
| --- | --- |

| ADV. | **politically** active **2** |
| N. | active **role 2** |

**ac|tive duty** N-UNCOUNT Someone who is on **active duty** is taking part in a war as a member of the armed forces.

**ac|tive so|lar heat|ing** N-UNCOUNT **Active solar heating** is a method of heating a building by using solar collectors and pipes to distribute energy from the sun throughout the building.

**ac|tive trans|port** N-UNCOUNT In biology, **active transport** is the movement of chemicals and other substances through the membranes of cells, which requires the cells to use energy.

**ac|tive voice** N-SING In grammar, *the* **active voice** means the forms of a verb which are used when the subject of the sentence refers to a person or thing that does something. For example, in "I saw her yesterday," the verb is in the active voice.

**ac|tiv|ist** /ǽktɪvɪst/ (**activists**) N-COUNT An **activist** is a person who works to bring about political or social changes. *...animal rights activists.* [from Latin]

**ac|tiv|ity** /æktɪvɪti/ (**activities**) **1** N-UNCOUNT **Activity** is a situation in which a lot of things

are happening. *Children are supposed to get 60 minutes of physical activity every day.* **2** N-COUNT An **activity** is something that you spend time doing. *Activities for small children and adults.* **3** N-PLURAL The **activities** of a group are the things that they do in order to achieve their aims. *...criminal activities.* [from Latin]

**ac|tor** /ǽktər/ (**actors**) N-COUNT An **actor** is someone whose job is acting in plays or movies. "Actor" in the singular usually refers to a man, but some women who act prefer to be called "actors" rather than "actresses." *His father was an actor.* [from Latin]
→ see **drama, theater**

**ac|tor's po|si|tion** (**actor's positions** or **actors' positions**) N-COUNT In the theater, an **actor's position** is the position that an actor occupies in relation to the audience, for example facing toward the audience or facing away from the audience.

**ac|tress** /ǽktrɪs/ (**actresses**) N-COUNT An **actress** is a woman whose job is acting in plays or movies. *She's a really good actress.* [from Latin]

**ac|tual** /ǽktʃuəl/ **1** ADJ You use **actual** to emphasize that you are referring to something real or genuine. *The stories in this book are based on actual people.* **2** ADJ You use **actual** to contrast the important aspect of something with a less important aspect. *The movie lasts 100 minutes, but the actual story is 90 minutes.* [from Late Latin]

**ac|tu|al|ly** /ǽktʃuəli/ **1** ADV You use **actually** to indicate that a situation exists or that it is true. *One afternoon I actually fell asleep for a few minutes.* **2** ADV You use **actually** when you are correcting or contradicting someone, or to introduce a new topic into a conversation. *No, I'm not a student. I'm a doctor, actually.* *Actually, that's not quite right.* [from Late Latin]

**acu|men** /əkyúmən, ǽkyʊmən/ N-UNCOUNT **Acumen** is the ability to make good judgments and quick decisions. *...business acumen.* [from Latin]

**acu|punc|ture** /ǽkyʊpʌŋktʃər/ N-UNCOUNT **Acupuncture** is the treatment of a person's illness or pain by sticking small needles into their body at certain places. *I had acupuncture in my lower back.* [from Latin]

**acute** /əkyút/ **1** ADJ An **acute** situation or feeling is very severe or intense. *He was in acute pain.* ● **acute|ly** ADV *People were acutely interested in what we did.* **2** ADJ If a person's or animal's senses are **acute**, they are sensitive and powerful. *When she lost her sight, her other senses grew more acute.* ● **acute|ly** ADV *He was acutely aware of the smell.* **3** ADJ An **acute** angle is less than 90°. Compare **obtuse** angle. [from Latin]

**ad** /ǽd/ (**ads**) N-COUNT An **ad** is an advertisement. [INFORMAL] *...a "help wanted" ad.*

**AD** /eɪ díː/ You use **AD** in dates to indicate the number of years or centuries that have passed since the year in which Jesus Christ is believed to have been born. Compare **BC**. *The building dates from 600 AD.* [from Latin]

**ad agen|cy** (**ad agencies**) N-COUNT An **ad agency** is a company whose business is to create advertisements for other companies or organizations.

**ada|mant** /ǽdəmənt/ ADJ If someone is **adamant about** something, they are determined not to change their mind about it. □ *The president is adamant that he will not resign.* ● **ada|mant|ly** ADV □ *She was adamantly opposed to her husband taking this trip.* [from Old English]

**a|dapt** /ədæpt/ (**adapts, adapting, adapted**) **1** V-I If you **adapt to** a new situation, you change your ideas or behavior in order to deal with it. □ *The world will be different in the future, and we will have to adapt to the change.* **2** V-T If you **adapt** something, you change it to make it suitable for a new purpose or situation. □ *They adapted the library for use as an office.* □ *She'll adapt the rooms to her needs.* [from Latin] **3** → see also **adapted**

**Usage**    **adapt** and **adopt**

*Adapt* and *adopt* sound similar and have similar meanings, but be careful not to confuse them. When you *adapt* something, you change it to make it fit your purpose: *Gilberto tried to adapt the recipe to cook a fish instead of a chicken – what a mistake!* When you *adopt* something, you use it unchanged: *Lucas adopted his boss's technique for dealing with rude customers – he ignored them!*

**Thesaurus**    *adapt*    Also look up :

v.    acclimate, adjust, conform **1** modify, revise **2**

**adapt|able** /ədæptəbəl/ ADJ Someone or something that is **adaptable** is able to change in order to deal with new situations. □ *Dogs and cats are easily adaptable to new homes.* ● **adapt|abil|ity** /ədæptəbɪlɪti/ N-UNCOUNT □ *The adaptability of wool is one of its great attractions.* [from Latin]

**ad|ap|ta|tion** /ædæpteɪʃ°n/ (**adaptations**) **1** N-COUNT An **adaptation** of a book or play is a film or a television program that is based on it. □ *...his screen adaptation of Shakespeare's "Henry the Fifth."* **2** N-UNCOUNT **Adaptation** is the act of changing something to make it suitable for a new purpose or situation. □ *Most living creatures are capable of adaptation.* [from Latin]

**a|dapt|ed** /ədæptɪd/ ADJ If something is **adapted to** a particular situation or purpose, it is especially suitable for it. □ *The house is well adapted to extreme heat.* [from Latin]

**ad cam|paign** (**ad campaigns**) N-COUNT An **ad campaign** is a planned series of advertisements. □ *...a $50 million government ad campaign.*

**add** /æd/ (**adds, adding, added**) **1** V-T If you **add** one thing **to** another, you put it with the other thing, to complete or improve it. □ *Add the grated cheese to the sauce.* □ *Vinegar is added to improve the flavor.* **2** V-T If you **add** numbers or amounts **together**, you calculate their total. □ *If there is more than one number, add these together.* **3** V-I If one thing **adds to** another, it makes the other thing greater in degree or amount. □ *The cosy look of the fireplace adds to the room.* ● **add|ed** ADJ □ *For added protection choose lipsticks with a sunscreen.* **4** V-T To **add** a particular quality **to** something means to cause it to have that quality. □ *The generous amount of garlic adds flavor.* **5** V-T If you **add** something when you are speaking, you say something more. □ *"He's very angry," Mr. Smith added.* **6** V-I If you can **add**, you are able to calculate the total of numbers or amounts. □ *Many seven-year-olds cannot add properly.* [from Latin]

▶ **add in** PHR-VERB If you **add in** something, you include it as a part of something else. □ *Once the vegetables start to cook add in a couple of tablespoons of water.*

▶ **add on** **1** PHR-VERB If you **add on** an extra amount or item to a list or total, you include it. □ *Many tour operators add on extra charges.* **2** PHR-VERB If you **add on**, you increase the size of a house or other building by constructing one or more extra rooms. □ *We've added on two bedrooms and a bathroom.*

▶ **add up** **1** PHR-VERB If you **add up** numbers or amounts, or if you **add** them **up**, you calculate their total. □ *Add up the total of those six games.* □ *We just added all the numbers up.* **2** PHR-VERB If facts or events do not **add up**, they make you confused about a situation because they do not seem to be consistent. If something that someone has said or done **adds up**, it is reasonable and sensible. □ *His story did not add up.* **3** PHR-VERB If small amounts of something **add up**, they gradually increase. □ *Even small savings, 5 cents here or there, can add up.*

▶ **add up to** PHR-VERB If amounts **add up to** a particular total, they result in that total when they are put together. □ *Profits can add up to millions of dollars.*

→ see **fraction**

**Thesaurus**    *add*    Also look up :

v.    put on, throw in **1** calculate, tally, total; (ant.) reduce, subtract **2** augment, increase; (ant.) lessen, reduce **3**

**ad|dict** /ædɪkt/ (**addicts**) **1** N-COUNT An **addict** is someone who cannot stop doing something harmful or dangerous, such as taking harmful drugs. □ *...a drug addict.* **2** N-COUNT You can say that someone is an **addict** when they like a particular activity very much. □ *She is a TV addict.* [from Latin]

**ad|dict|ed** /ədɪktɪd/ **1** ADJ Someone who is **addicted to** a harmful drug cannot stop taking it. □ *Many of the women are addicted to heroin and cocaine.* **2** ADJ If someone is **addicted to** something, they like it very much. □ *She had become addicted to golf.* [from Latin]

**ad|dic|tion** /ədɪkʃ°n/ (**addictions**) **1** N-VAR **Addiction** is the condition of being addicted to drugs. □ *She helped him fight his drug addiction.* **2** N-VAR An **addiction to** something is a very strong desire or need for it. □ *...his addiction to winning.* [from Latin]

**ad|dic|tive** /ədɪktɪv/ **1** ADJ If a drug is **addictive**, people who take it cannot stop taking it. □ *Cigarettes are highly addictive.* **2** ADJ Something that is **addictive** is so enjoyable that it makes you want to do it or have it a lot. □ *...an addictive cream cheese icing.* [from Latin]

**ad|di|tion** /ədɪʃ°n/ (**additions**) **1** PHRASE You use **in addition** when you want to mention another item connected with the subject you are discussing. □ *He had nine children in addition to his son Steve.* **2** N-COUNT An **addition to** something is a thing which is added to it. □ *This is a fine book; a fine addition to the series.* ● **ad|di|tion|al** /ədɪʃən°l/ ADJ □ *Add the garlic and cook for an additional three minutes.* **3** N-COUNT An **addition** is a new room or building which is added to an existing building or

group of buildings. ❑ *They spent $20,000 on building an addition to their kitchen.* ◳ N-UNCOUNT **Addition** is the process of calculating the total of two or more numbers. ❑ *...simple addition and subtraction problems.* [from Latin]
→ see **mathematics**

**ad|di|tion|al|ly** /ədɪʃənᵊli/ ADV You use **additionally** to introduce an extra fact or reason. ❑ *Nurses spend two hours each day washing their hands. Additionally, washing very often can make the skin dry out.* [from Latin]

**ad|di|tive** /ædɪtɪv/ (**additives**) ◳ N-COUNT An **additive** is a substance which is added to foods in order to improve them or to make them last longer. ❑ *...food additives.* ◳ ADJ **Additive** sculpture is sculpture that is created by adding material such as clay or wax until the sculpture is complete. [from Late Latin]

**ad|dress** (**addresses, addressing, addressed**)

The noun is pronounced /ədrɛs/ or /ædrɛs/. The verb is pronounced /ədrɛs/.

◳ N-COUNT Your **address** is the number of the house or apartment and the name of the street and the town where you live or work. ❑ *The address is 2025 M Street, NW, Washington, DC, 20036.* ◳ N-COUNT The **address** of a website is its location on the Internet, for example, http://www.thomson.com. [COMPUTING] ❑ *Full details, including the website address, are at the bottom of this page.* ◳ V-T If a letter, envelope, or parcel **is addressed to** you, your name and address have been written on it. ❑ *One of the letters was addressed to her.* ◳ V-T If you **address** a group of people, you give a speech to them. ❑ *He addressed the crowd of 17,000 people.* ● **Address** is also a noun. ❑ *...an address to the American people.* [from Old French]

**Thesaurus**    address    Also look up :
N.    lecture, speech, talk ◳

**Word Partnership**    Use *address* with :
N.    **name and** address, **street** address ◳
      address **remarks to** ◳
ADJ.  **permanent** address ◳
      **inaugural** address, **public** address ◳

**ad|enine** /ædᵊnin, -nɪn/ (**adenines**) N-VAR **Adenine** is an organic molecule that forms an important part of the structure of DNA. [TECHNICAL] [from German]

**adept** /ædɛpt/ ADJ Someone who is **adept at** something can do it skillfully. ❑ *He is adept at avoiding difficult questions.* [from Medieval Latin]

**ad|equate** /ædɪkwɪt/ ADJ If something is **adequate**, there is enough of it or it is good enough to be used or accepted. ❑ *One in four people worldwide do not have adequate homes.* ● **ad|equa|cy** /ædɪkwəsi/ N-UNCOUNT ❑ *...the adequacy of their work.* ● **ad|equate|ly** ADV ❑ *Many students are not adequately prepared for higher education.* [from Latin]

**ad|here** /ædhɪər/ (**adheres, adhering, adhered**) ◳ V-I If you **adhere to** a rule or agreement, you act in the way that it says you should. ❑ *Different churches adhere to different teachings.* ● **ad|her|ence** /ædhɪərəns/ N-UNCOUNT ❑ *...strict adherence to the constitution.* ◳ V-I If something **adheres to** something else, it sticks firmly to it. ❑ *The self-stick*

backing adheres to metal and plastic.* [from Medieval Latin]

**ad|he|sive** /ædhisɪv/ (**adhesives**) ◳ N-VAR An **adhesive** is a substance such as glue, which is used to make things stick firmly together. ❑ *Glue the mirror in with a strong adhesive.* ◳ ADJ An **adhesive** substance is able to stick firmly to something else. ❑ *...adhesive tape.* [from Medieval Latin]

**ad hoc** /æd hɒk/ ADJ An **ad hoc** activity or organization is not planned in advance, but is done or formed only because a particular situation has made it necessary. ❑ *A lot of the work is done in ad hoc teams.* [from Latin]

**ad ho|mi|nem** /æd hɒmɪnɛm, -nəm/ ADJ; ADV In logic, an ad hominem argument is an argument which attacks the motives or character of the person presenting a claim rather than the claim itself.

**ad|ja|cent** /ædʒeɪsᵊnt/ ADJ If two things are **adjacent**, they are next to each other. ❑ *He sat in an adjacent room and waited.* ❑ *The schools were adjacent but there were separate doors.* [from Latin]

**ad|jec|tive** /ædʒɪktɪv/ (**adjectives**) N-COUNT An **adjective** is a word such as "big," "dead," or "financial" that describes a person or thing, or gives extra information about them. Adjectives usually come before nouns or after linking verbs. [from Late Latin]

**ad|jec|tive phrase** (**adjective phrases**) N-COUNT An **adjective phrase** or **adjectival phrase** is a group of words based on an adjective, such as "very nice" or "interested in football." An adjective phrase can also consist simply of an adjective.

**ad|join** /ædʒɔɪn/ (**adjoins, adjoining, adjoined**) V-T If one room, place, or object **adjoins** another, they are next to each other. [FORMAL] ❑ *The school adjoined the teacher's house.* [from Old French]

**ad|journ** /ædʒɜrn/ (**adjourns, adjourning, adjourned**) V-T/V-I If a meeting or trial **is adjourned** or if it **adjourns**, it is stopped for a short time. ❑ *The trial has been adjourned until next week.* ● **ad|journ|ment** /ædʒɜrnmənt/ (**adjournments**) N-COUNT ❑ *The court ordered a four-month adjournment.* [from Old French]

**ad|just** /ædʒʌst/ (**adjusts, adjusting, adjusted**) ◳ V-T/V-I When you **adjust to** a new situation, you get used to it by changing your behavior or your ideas. ❑ *We have been preparing our fighters to adjust themselves to civil society.* ❑ *She has adjusted to the idea of being a mother very well.* ● **ad|just|ment** /ædʒʌstmənt/ (**adjustments**) N-COUNT ❑ *He will have to make adjustments to his thinking.* ◳ V-T If you **adjust** something, you change it so that it is more effective or appropriate. ❑ *The company adjusted gas prices once a year.* ● **ad|just|ment** N-COUNT ❑ *...a new monthly cost adjustment.* ◳ V-T If you **adjust** something such as your clothing or a machine, you correct or alter its position or setting. ❑ *Liz adjusted her mirror and then moved the car out of its parking space.* ● **ad|just|ment** N-COUNT ❑ *...a large workshop for repairs and adjustments.* [from Old French]

**ad|just|able** /ædʒʌstəbᵊl/ ADJ If something is **adjustable**, it can be changed to different positions or sizes. ❑ *The bags have adjustable shoulder straps.* [from Old French]

**a**

## Thesaurus

*adjustable* Also look up :

ADJ. adaptable; (*ant.*) fixed

**ad|min|is|ter** /ædmɪnɪstər/ (**administers, administering, administered**) **1** V-T If someone **administers** something such as a country, the law, or a test, they take responsibility for organizing and supervising it. ❑ *Who will administer these accounts and what will it cost?* **2** V-T If a doctor or a nurse **administers** a drug, they give it to a patient. [FORMAL] ❑ *The tests will focus on how to administer the drug safely.* [from Old French]

**ad|min|is|tra|tion** /ædmɪnɪstreɪʃ³n/ (**administrations**) **1** N-UNCOUNT **Administration** is the range of activities connected with organizing and supervising the way that an organization or institution functions. ❑ *We spend too much time on administration.* **2** N-SING **The administration** of a company or institution is the group of people who organize and supervise it. ❑ *The administration wants to increase spending.* **3** N-COUNT You can refer to a country's government as **the administration**; used especially in the United States. ❑ *…the Bush administration.* [from Old French]

**ad|min|is|tra|tive** /ædmɪnɪstreɪtɪv/ ADJ **Administrative** work involves organizing and supervising an organization or institution. ❑ *…administrative costs.* [from Old French]

**ad|min|is|tra|tor** /ædmɪnɪstreɪtər/ (**administrators**) N-COUNT An **administrator** is a person whose job involves helping to organize and supervise the way that an organization or institution functions. ❑ *Students and parents met with school administrators.* [from Old French]

**ad|mi|rable** /ædmɪrəb³l/ ADJ An **admirable** quality or action is one that deserves to be praised and admired. ❑ *She did an admirable job of holding their attention.* ● **ad|mi|rably** /ædmɪrəbli/ ADV ❑ *Peter dealt admirably with the questions.* [from Latin]

**ad|mi|ral** /ædmərəl/ (**admirals**) N-COUNT; N-TITLE An **admiral** is a very senior officer who commands a navy. ❑ *…Admiral Hodges.* [from Old French]

**ad|mi|ra|tion** /ædmɪreɪʃ³n/ N-UNCOUNT **Admiration** is a feeling of great liking and respect. ❑ *I have the greatest admiration for him.* [from Latin]

**ad|mire** /ædmaɪər/ (**admires, admiring, admired**) **1** V-T If you **admire** someone or something, you like and respect them. ❑ *I admired her when I first met her and I still think she's marvelous.* ● **ad|mir|er** (**admirers**) N-COUNT ❑ *He was an admirer of her grandfather's paintings.* **2** V-T If you **admire** someone or something, you look at them with pleasure. ❑ *We took time to stop and admire the view.* [from Latin]

## Thesaurus

*admire* Also look up :

V. adore, esteem, honor, look up to, respect **1**

**ad|mis|sion** /ædmɪʃ³n/ (**admissions**) **1** N-VAR **Admission** is permission given to a person to enter a place, or permission given to a country to enter an organization. **Admission** is also the act of entering a place. ❑ *Yesterday was the anniversary of Bosnia's admission to the United Nations.* **2** N-VAR An **admission** is a statement that something bad, unpleasant, or embarrassing is true. ❑ *By his*

own admission, he is not playing well. **3** N-UNCOUNT **Admission** at a park, museum, or other place is the amount of money that you pay to enter it. ❑ *Gates open at 10:30 a.m. and admission is free.* ● **Admission** is also used before a noun. ❑ *The admission price is $8 for adults.* [from Latin]
→ see **hospital**

**ad|mit** /ædmɪt/ (**admits, admitting, admitted**) **1** V-T/V-I If you **admit** that something bad, unpleasant, or embarrassing is true, you agree, often unwillingly, that it is true. ❑ *I am willing to admit that I make mistakes.* ❑ *They didn't admit to doing anything wrong.* ❑ *None of these people will admit responsibility.* **2** V-T If someone **is admitted to** a hospital, they are taken into the hospital for treatment. ❑ *She was admitted to the hospital with a very high temperature.* **3** V-T If someone **is admitted to** a place or organization, they are allowed to enter it or join it. ❑ *She was admitted to law school.* ❑ *Security officers refused to admit him or his wife.* [from Latin]

## Word Partnership

Use *admit* with :

V. **ashamed to** admit, **be the first to** admit, **must** admit, **willing to** admit **1**
N. admit **defeat 1**
CONJ. admit **that 1**

**ad|mit|ted|ly** /ædmɪtɪdli/ ADV You use **admittedly** when you are saying something that weakens the importance or force of your statement. ❑ *Some of it admittedly is my fault.* [from Latin]

**ado|les|cent** /æd³lɛs³nt/ (**adolescents**) ADJ **Adolescent** is used to describe young people who are no longer children but who have not yet become adults. ❑ *…an adolescent boy.* ● An **adolescent** is an adolescent boy or girl. ❑ *Adolescents are happiest with small groups of close friends.* ● **ado|les|cence** /æd³lɛs³ns/ N-UNCOUNT ❑ *…the early part of my life from childhood through adolescence.* [from Old French]
→ see **age, child**

## Word Link

*opt ≈ choosing : adopt, option, optional*

**adopt** /ædɒpt/ (**adopts, adopting, adopted**) **1** V-T If you **adopt** a new attitude, plan, or way of behaving, you begin to have it. ❑ *Students should adopt a more positive attitude to the environment.* ● **adop|tion** /ædɒpʃ³n/ N-UNCOUNT ❑ *The meeting ended with the adoption of a plan of action.* **2** V-T/V-I If you **adopt** someone else's child, you take it into your own family and make it legally your son or daughter. ❑ *There are hundreds of people who want to adopt a child.* ❑ *They really want to adopt.* ● **adop|tion** (**adoptions**) N-VAR ❑ *They gave their babies up for adoption.* [from Latin] **3** → see also **adapt**

## Thesaurus

*adopt* Also look up :

V. approve, endorse, support; (*ant.*) refuse, reject **1**
care for, raise, take in **2**

**adop|tive** /ædɒptɪv/ ADJ Someone's **adoptive** family is the family that adopted them. ❑ *He grew up with adoptive parents in Kentucky.* [from Latin]

**ador|able** /ædɔrəb³l/ ADJ If you say that someone or something is **adorable**, you are

**A**

emphasizing that they are very attractive and you feel great affection for them. ❑ *We had three adorable children.* [from French]

**adore** /əd‌ɔ‌r/ (**adores, adoring, adored**) **1** V-T If you **adore** someone, you feel great love and admiration for them. ❑ *She adored her parents and would do anything to please them.* ● **ado‌ra‌tion** /æ‌d‌ɔreɪ‌ʃ‌ə‌n/ N-UNCOUNT ❑ *The adoration of his fans has helped him.* **2** V-T If you **adore** something, you like it very much. [INFORMAL] ❑ *Robyn adores university life.* [from French]
→ see **emotion**

**ador‌ing** /əd‌ɔrɪŋ/ ADJ An **adoring** person loves and admires another person very much. ❑ *Jackson waved to the adoring crowd.* ● **ador‌ing‌ly** ADV ❑ *She looked adoringly at him.* [from French]

**adorn** /əd‌ɔrn/ (**adorns, adorning, adorned**) V-T If something **adorns** a place or an object, it makes it look more beautiful. ❑ *Large photographs of waterfalls and mountains adorn the walls.*
● **adorn‌ment** /əd‌ɔrnmənt/ (**adornments**) N-VAR ❑ *The building had no adornment or decoration.* [from Old French]

**adrena‌lin** /ədrɛnə‌lɪn/ also **adrenaline** N-UNCOUNT **Adrenalin** is a substance which your body produces when you are angry, scared, or excited. It makes your heart beat faster and gives you more energy. ❑ *That was my first big game in months and the adrenalin was going through me.*

**adrift** /ədrɪft/ **1** ADJ If a boat is **adrift**, it is floating on the water and is not tied to anything or controlled by anyone. ❑ *They spent three hours adrift in a small boat.* **2** ADJ If someone is **adrift**, they feel alone with no clear idea of what they should do. ❑ *Amy felt adrift and isolated.*

**adult** /əd‌ʌlt/ (**adults**) **1** N-COUNT An **adult** is a mature, fully developed person or animal. ❑ *Becoming a father meant that he was now an adult.* ❑ *...a pair of adult birds.* **2** ADJ **Adult** means relating to the time when you are an adult, or typical of adult people. ❑ *I've lived most of my adult life in Arizona.* [from Latin]
→ see **age**

| **Thesaurus** | *adult* | Also look up : |

| ADJ. | full-grown **1** |
| N. | grown-up, man, woman **1** |

**adul‌tery** /əd‌ʌltəri/ N-UNCOUNT If a married person commits **adultery**, they have sex with someone that they are not married to. ❑ *She is going to divorce him on the grounds of adultery.* [from Latin]

| **Word Link** | *hood ≈ state, condition : adulthood, childhood, manhood* |

**adult‌hood** /əd‌ʌlthʊd/ N-UNCOUNT **Adulthood** is the state of being an adult. ❑ *During the past twelve years they've grown to adulthood.* [from Latin]

**ad‌vance** /æd‌væns/ (**advances, advancing, advanced**) **1** V-I To **advance** means to move forward, in order to attack someone. ❑ *Soldiers are advancing on the capital.* ❑ *The water is advancing at a rate of between 8 and 10 inches a day.* **2** V-I To **advance** means to make progress, especially in your knowledge of something. ❑ *Science advanced greatly in the last 100 years.* **3** → see also **advanced** **4** V-T If you **advance**

someone a sum of money, you lend it to them, or pay it to them earlier than arranged. ❑ *I advanced him some money, which he repaid on our way home.* **5** V-T To **advance** an event, or the time or date of an event, means to bring it forward to an earlier time or date. ❑ *A poor diet may advance the aging process.* **6** N-COUNT An **advance** is money lent or paid to someone before they would normally receive it. ❑ *She was paid a $100,000 advance for her next two novels.* **7** N-VAR An **advance** is a forward movement of people or vehicles, usually as part of a military operation. ❑ *Hitler's army began its advance on Moscow in June 1941.* **8** N-VAR An **advance** in a particular subject or activity is progress in understanding it or in doing it well. ❑ *...advances in medicine and public health.* **9** ADJ **Advance** booking, notice, or warning is done or given before an event happens. ❑ *You must give 30 days' advance notice.* **10** PHRASE If you do something **in advance**, you do it before a particular date or event. ❑ *The theater sells tickets in advance.* [from Latin]

**ad‌vanced** /æd‌vænst/ **1** ADJ An **advanced** system, method, or design is modern and has been developed from an earlier version of the same thing. ❑ *...one of the most advanced phones available.* **2** ADJ A country that is **advanced** has reached a high level of industrial or technological development. ❑ *...advanced countries like the United States.* **3** ADJ An **advanced** student has already learned the basic facts of a subject and is doing more difficult work. ❑ *This course is for advanced students only.* [from Latin]

| **Thesaurus** | *advanced* | Also look up : |

| ADJ. | cutting-edge, foremost, latest, sophisticated **1** |

**ad‌vance‌ment** /æd‌vænsmənt/ (**advancements**) **1** N-UNCOUNT **Advancement** is progress in your job or in your social position. ❑ *He didn't care about social advancement.* **2** N-VAR The **advancement** of something is the process of helping it to progress. ❑ *...the advancement of learning.* [from Latin]

**ad‌van‌tage** /æd‌væntɪdʒ/ (**advantages**) **1** N-COUNT An **advantage** is something that puts you in a better position than other people. ❑ *They think that going to a private school will give them an advantage in getting into college.* **2** N-COUNT An **advantage** is a way in which one thing is better than another. ❑ *The advantage of home-grown oranges is their great flavor.* **3** N-UNCOUNT **Advantage** is the state of being in a better position than others who are competing against you. ❑ *We were in a position of advantage before this game.* **4** PHRASE If you **take advantage of** something, you make good use of it while you can. ❑ *I'm going to take advantage of this trip to go shopping.* **5** PHRASE If someone **takes advantage of** you, they treat you unfairly for their own benefit, especially when you are trying to be kind or to help them. ❑ *She took advantage of him even after they were divorced.* **6** PHRASE If you use or turn something **to** your **advantage**, you use it in order to benefit from it. ❑ *He could turn any situation to his advantage.* [from Latin]

### Word Partnership    Use *advantage* with :

ADJ.    **competitive** advantage, **unfair**
       advantage **1**
V.     **have an** advantage **1**
       **take** advantage **of** *something* **4**
       **use to** *someone's* advantage **5**

**ad|van|ta|geous** /ˌædvənˈteɪdʒəs/ ADJ If
something is **advantageous** to you, it is likely to
benefit you. ❑ *It's advantageous to have an unusual
name.* [from Latin]

**ad|vent** /ˈædvɛnt/ N-UNCOUNT The **advent of**
something is the fact of it starting or coming into
existence. [FORMAL] ❑ *...the advent of the computer.*
[from Latin]

**ad|ven|ture** /ædˈvɛntʃər/ (**adventures**)
N-VAR An **adventure** is a series of events that is
unusual, exciting, and perhaps dangerous. ❑ *I
set off for a new adventure in Alaska.* ❑ *...a spirit of
adventure.* ● **ad|ven|tur|er** (**adventurers**) N-COUNT
❑ *...American adventurer Steve Fossett.* [from Latin]

**ad|ven|tur|ous** /ædˈvɛntʃərəs/ also
**adventuresome** /ædˈvɛntʃərsəm/ ADJ Someone
who is **adventurous** is willing to take risks
and have new experiences. Something that is
**adventurous** involves new things or ideas. ❑ *...an
adventurous life in the tropics.* [from Latin]

### Word Link    *verb ≈ word : adverb, proverb, verbal*

**ad|verb** /ˈædvɜrb/ (**adverbs**) N-COUNT An
**adverb** is a word such as "slowly," "now," "very,"
"politically," or "happily" which adds information
about an action, event, or situation. [from Latin]

**ad|verb phrase** (**adverb phrases**) N-COUNT An
**adverb phrase** or **adverbial phrase** is a group of
words based on an adverb, such as "very slowly"
or "fortunately for us." An adverb phrase can also
consist simply of an adverb.

**ad|ver|sary** /ˈædvərsɛri/ (**adversaries**) N-COUNT
Your **adversary** is someone you are competing
with, or arguing or fighting against. ❑ *...political
adversaries.* [from Latin]

**ad|verse** /ædˈvɜrs/ ADJ **Adverse** decisions,
conditions, or effects are unfavorable to you.
❑ *There may be adverse effects as a result of this
treatment.* ● **ad|verse|ly** ADV ❑ *The change didn't
adversely affect him.* [from Latin]

**ad|ver|sity** /ædˈvɜrsɪti/ (**adversities**) N-VAR
**Adversity** is a very difficult or unfavorable
situation. ❑ *He showed courage in adversity.* [from
Latin]

**ad|ver|tise** /ˈædvərtaɪz/ (**advertises,
advertising, advertised**) **1** V-T/V-I If you
**advertise** something such as a product, an event,
or a job, you tell people about it in newspapers,
on television, or on posters. ❑ *They are advertising
houses for sale.* ❑ *We advertise on radio stations* **2** V-I
If you **advertise for** someone to do something
for you, for example, to work for you or share
your accommodation, you announce it in a
newspaper, on television, or on a bulletin board.
❑ *We advertised in a local newspaper.* ● **ad|ver|tis|er**
(**advertisers**) N-COUNT ❑ *...television advertisers.*
[from Old French] **3** → see also **advertising**

**ad|ver|tise|ment** /ˈædvərtaɪzmənt/
(**advertisements**) N-COUNT An **advertisement** is
an announcement in a newspaper, on television,
or on a poster about something such as a product,
event, or job. [WRITTEN] ❑ *Miss Parrish placed an
advertisement in the local newspaper.* [from Old
French]

**ad|ver|tis|ing** /ˈædvərtaɪzɪŋ/ N-UNCOUNT
**Advertising** is the activity of creating
advertisements and making sure people see them.
❑ *I work in advertising.* [from Old French]

**ad|vice** /ædˈvaɪs/ N-UNCOUNT If you give
someone **advice**, you tell them what you think
they should do in a particular situation. ❑ *I'll give
you some advice that will change your life.* ❑ *Take my
advice and stay away from him!* [from Old French]

### Usage    *advice* and *advise*

Be careful not to confuse *advice* and *advise*. *Advice*
is a noun, and the *c* is pronounced like the *ss*
in *less*; *advise* is a verb, and the *s* is pronounced
like the *z* in *size*: *Quang advised Tuyet not to give
people advice!*

### Thesaurus    *advice*    Also look up :

N.    counsel, encouragement, guidance,
      help, information, input, opinion,
      recommendation, suggestion

### Word Partnership    Use *advice* with :

PREP.    **against** advice
V.      **ask for** advice, **give** advice, **need some**
        advice, **take** advice
ADJ.    **bad/good** advice, **expert** advice

**ad|vice col|umn** (**advice columns**) N-COUNT
In a newspaper or magazine, the **advice column**
contains letters from readers about their personal
problems, and advice on what to do about them.

**ad|vice col|umn|ist** (**advice columnists**)
N-COUNT An **advice columnist** is a person who
writes a column in a newspaper or magazine in
which they reply to readers who have written to
them for advice on their personal problems.

**ad|vis|able** /ædˈvaɪzəbᵊl/ ADJ If you tell
someone that it is **advisable to** do something, you
are suggesting that they should do it, because it
is sensible or is likely to achieve the result they
want. [FORMAL] ❑ *It is advisable to book hotels in
advance.* [from Old French]

**ad|vise** /ædˈvaɪz/ (**advises, advising, advised**)
**1** V-T If you **advise** someone **to** do something, you
tell them what you think they should do. ❑ *The
minister advised him to leave as soon as possible.* ❑ *I
would strongly advise against it.* **2** V-T If an expert
**advises** people **on** a particular subject, he or she
gives them help and information on that subject.
❑ *...an officer who advises students on money matters.*
[from Old French] **3** → see also **advice**

**ad|vis|er** /ædˈvaɪzər/ (**advisers**) also **advisor**
N-COUNT An **adviser** is an expert whose job is
to give advice to another person or to a group of
people. ❑ *The president and his advisers spent the day
in meetings.* [from Old French]

### Word Link    *ory ≈ relating to : advisory,
contradictory, sensory*

**ad|vi|so|ry** /ædˈvaɪzəri/ (**advisories**) **1** N-COUNT
An **advisory** is an official announcement or report
that warns people about bad weather, diseases,

or other dangers or problems. ❑ ...*public health advisories.* **2** ADJ An **advisory** group regularly gives suggestions and help to people or organizations, especially about a particular subject or area of activity. [FORMAL] ❑ ...*an advisory group on oil and gas.* [from Old French]

**ad|vo|ca|cy** /ǽdvəkəsi/ **1** N-SING **Advocacy of** a particular action or plan is the act of recommending it publicly. [FORMAL] ❑ *She was loved by many people here for her advocacy of peace.* **2** N-UNCOUNT An **advocacy** group or organization is one that tries to influence the decisions of a government or other authority. ❑ ...*a workers' advocacy group.* [from Old French]

Word Link **voc ≈ speaking : a*voc*ate, *voc*abulary, *voc*al**

**ad|vo|cate** (**advocates, advocating, advocated**)

The verb is pronounced /ǽdvəkeɪt/. The noun is pronounced /ǽdvəkɪt/.

**1** V-T If you **advocate** a particular action or plan, you recommend it publicly. [FORMAL] ❑ *He advocates improvements to the bus service.* **2** N-COUNT An **advocate of** a particular action or plan is someone who recommends it publicly. [FORMAL] ❑ *He was a great advocate of checking other people's work.* **3** N-COUNT An **advocate for** a particular group is a person who works for the interests of that group. ❑ ...*advocates for the homeless.* **4** N-COUNT An **advocate** is a lawyer who speaks in favor of someone or defends them in a court of law. [LEGAL] [from Old French]

Word Link **aer ≈ air : *aer*ial, *aer*obics, *aer*osol**

**aer|ial** /ɛ́əriəl/ (**aerials**) ADJ **Aerial** means from an airplane. ❑ *The aerial attacks may continue for weeks more.* ❑ ...*an aerial photograph.* [from Latin]

**aer|ial per|spec|tive** (**aerial perspectives**) N-VAR In a painting or drawing, **aerial perspective** is a method of representing more distant objects by using lighter or duller colors.

**aero|bics** /ɛəroʊbɪks/ N-UNCOUNT **Aerobics** is a form of exercise which increases the amount of oxygen in your blood, and strengthens your heart and lungs. The verb that follows **aerobics** may be either singular or plural. ❑ ...*an aerobics class.* [from Greek]

**aero|phone** /ɛ́ərəfoʊn/ (**aerophones**) N-COUNT An **aerophone** is a musical instrument such as a trumpet or flute which produces sound by causing the air to vibrate.

**aero|sol** /ɛ́ərəsɔl/ (**aerosols**) N-COUNT An **aerosol** is a small container in which a liquid such as paint or deodorant is kept under pressure. When you press a button, the liquid is forced out as a fine spray or foam. ❑ ...*an aerosol can of insecticide.*

**aes|thet|ic** /ɛsθɛ́tɪk/ also **esthetic** ADJ **Aesthetic** is used to talk about beauty or art, and people's appreciation of beautiful things. ❑ *We chose the products for their aesthetic appeal.* ● **aes|thet|ic|al|ly** /ɛsθɛ́tɪkli/ ADV ❑ ...*an aesthetically pleasing product.* [from Greek]

**aes|thet|ic cri|te|ria** N-PLURAL **Aesthetic criteria** are standards that are used in making judgments about the artistic value of a work of art.

**aes|thet|ics** /ɛsθɛ́tɪks/ also **esthetics** N-UNCOUNT **Aesthetics** is a branch of philosophy concerned with the study of the idea of beauty. [from Greek]

**af|fable** /ǽfəbᵊl/ ADJ Someone who is **affable** is pleasant and friendly. ❑ *Mr. Brooke is an affable and friendly man.* [from Latin]

**af|fair** /əfɛ́ər/ (**affairs**) **1** N-SING You can refer to an event as **an affair** when you are talking about it in a general way. ❑ *He has handled the whole affair badly.* **2** N-COUNT If two people who are not married to each other have an **affair**, they have a sexual relationship. ❑ *He was having an affair with the woman next door.* **3** → see also **love affair** **4** N-PLURAL You can use **affairs** to refer to all the important facts or activities that are connected with a particular subject. ❑ *He does not want to interfere in the affairs of another country.* **5** → see also **current affairs, state of affairs** **6** N-PLURAL Your **affairs** are all the matters connected with your life that you consider to be private. ❑ *He was unable to make important decisions or handle his affairs.* [from Old French]

**af|fect** /əfɛ́kt/ (**affects, affecting, affected**) **1** V-T If something **affects** a person or thing, it influences or causes them to change in some way. ❑ *This problem affects all of us.* ❑ *We were close to the area affected by the earthquake.* **2** V-T If a disease **affects** you it makes you ill. ❑ *Arthritis is a disease which affects people all over the world.* [from Latin] **3** → see also **effect**

**af|fec|tion** /əfɛ́kʃᵊn/ **1** N-UNCOUNT If you regard someone or something with **affection**, you are fond of them. ❑ *She thought of him with affection.* **2** N-PLURAL Your **affections** are your feelings of love or fondness for someone. ❑ *Caroline is the object of his affections.* [from Latin] → see **love**

**af|fec|tion|ate** /əfɛ́kʃənɪt/ ADJ If you are **affectionate**, you show your fondness for another person in your behavior. ❑ *They were openly affectionate.* ● **af|fec|tion|ate|ly** ADV ❑ *He looked affectionately at his niece.* [from Latin]

**af|fi|da|vit** /ǽfɪdeɪvɪt/ (**affidavits**) N-COUNT An **affidavit** is a written statement that you swear is true and that may be used as evidence in a court of law. [LEGAL] ❑ *She signed the affidavit.* [from Medieval Latin]

**af|fili|ate** (**affiliates, affiliating, affiliated**)

The noun is pronounced /əfɪliɪt/. The verb is pronounced /əfɪlieɪt/.

**1** N-COUNT An **affiliate** is an organization which is officially connected with another, larger organization or is a member of it. [FORMAL] ❑ *The World Chess Federation has affiliates in around 120 countries.* **2** V-I If an organization **affiliates with** another larger organization, it forms a close connection with the larger organization or becomes a member of it. [FORMAL] ❑ *Local parent groups are welcome to affiliate with us.* ● **af|filia|tion** /əfɪlieɪʃᵊn/ (**affiliations**) N-VAR [FORMAL] ❑ *They had no affiliation with any other group.* **3** V-I If a professional person such as a lawyer or doctor **affiliates with** an organization, they become officially connected with that organization. [FORMAL] ❑ *He wanted to affiliate with a U.S. firm because he needed "expert advice."* [from Medieval Latin]

**af|fin|ity** /əfɪ́nɪti/ (**affinities**) N-SING If you have an **affinity** with someone or something, you feel that you are similar to them or that you know and understand them very well. □ *He has a close affinity with the landscape.* [from Old French]

| **Word Link** | firm ≈ making strong : af**firm**, con**firm**, reaf**firm** |

af|**firm** /əfɜ́rm/ (**affirms, affirming, affirmed**)
■ V-T If you **affirm** that something is true, you state firmly and publicly that it is true. [FORMAL] □ *The newspaper report affirmed that the story was true.* ● af|**fir**|**ma**|**tion** /ǽfərmeɪʃ°n/ (**affirmations**) N-VAR □ *...an affirmation of support.* ■ V-T If an event **affirms** something, it shows that it is true or exists. [FORMAL] □ *Everything I did seemed to affirm that opinion.* ● af|**fir**|**ma**|**tion** N-UNCOUNT; N-SING □ *Maguire's performance is an affirmation of his talent.* [from Old French]

af|**firma**|**tive** /əfɜ́rmətɪv/ ADJ An **affirmative** word or gesture indicates that you agree with what someone has said or that the answer to a question is "yes." [FORMAL] □ *Haig was eager for an affirmative answer.* [from Old French]

af|**firma**|**tive ac**|**tion** N-UNCOUNT **Affirmative action** is the policy of giving jobs and other opportunities to members of groups such as racial minorities or women who might not otherwise have them.

af|**fix** /ǽfɪks/ (**affixes**) N-COUNT An **affix** is a letter or group of letters, for example, "un-" or "-y," which is added to either the beginning or the end of a word to form a different word with a different meaning. For example, "un-" is added to "kind" to form "unkind." Compare **prefix** and **suffix**. [from Medieval Latin]

af|**flict** /əflɪ́kt/ (**afflicts, afflicting, afflicted**)
V-T If you **are afflicted by** something, it affects you badly. [FORMAL] □ *We live on a street afflicted by traffic.* □ *There are two main problems which afflict people with hearing difficulties.* [from Latin]

| **Word Link** | flict ≈ striking : af**flic**tion, con**flict**, in**flict** |

af|**flic**|**tion** /əflɪ́kʃ°n/ (**afflictions**) N-VAR An **affliction** is something that causes physical or mental suffering. [FORMAL] □ *Not one of them was willing to talk about their affliction.* [from Latin]

af|**flu**|**ent** /ǽfluənt/ ADJ If you are **affluent**, you have a lot of money. □ *It is one of the most affluent areas in the country.* ● **The affluent** are people who are affluent. □ *These tax changes let the affluent keep more of their money.* ● af|**flu**|**ence** N-UNCOUNT □ *They enjoyed a lifetime of affluence.* [from Latin]

af|**ford** /əfɔ́rd/ (**affords, affording, afforded**)
■ V-T If you **can afford** something, you have enough money to pay for it. □ *Some people can't even afford a new refrigerator.* ■ V-T If you cannot **afford to** do something or allow it to happen, you must not do it or must prevent it from happening because it would be harmful or embarrassing to you. □ *We can't afford to wait.* [from Old English]

| **Word Partnership** | Use *afford* with : |
| v. | afford **to buy/pay** ■ |
| | can/could afford, **can't/** |
| | **couldn't** afford ■ ■ |
| | afford **to lose** ■ |
| ADJ. | **able/unable to** afford ■ ■ |

af|**ford**|**able** /əfɔ́rdəb°l/ ADJ If something is **affordable**, most people have enough money to buy it. □ *...affordable housing.* ● af|**ford**|**abil**|**ity** /əfɔ́rdəbɪ́lɪti/ N-UNCOUNT *Affordability* is a problem for students going to college. [from Old English]

af|**front** /əfrʌ́nt/ (**affronts, affronting, affronted**) ■ V-T If something **affronts** you, you feel insulted and hurt because of it. [FORMAL] □ *I am affronted by some of their habits.* ■ N-COUNT If something is an **affront to** you, it is an obvious insult to you. □ *The killings were an affront to humanity.* [from Old French]

afloat /əflóʊt/ ■ ADV If someone or something is **afloat**, they remain partly above the surface of water and do not sink. □ *They tried to keep the ship afloat.* ■ ADV If a person, business, or country stays **afloat** or is kept **afloat**, they have just enough money to pay their debts and continue operating. [BUSINESS] □ *Many businesses are finding it hard to stay afloat.*

afoot /əfʊ́t/ ADJ If a plan or scheme is **afoot**, it is already happening or being planned, but you do not know much about it. □ *Everybody knew that something awful was afoot.*

afore|men|tioned /əfɔ́rmɛnʃ°nd/ ADJ If you refer to **the aforementioned** person or subject, you mean the person or subject that has already been mentioned. [FORMAL] □ *Joseph and Miller are two of the aforementioned newcomers.*

afraid /əfréɪd/ ■ ADJ If you are **afraid of** someone or **afraid to** do something, you are frightened because you think that something very unpleasant is going to happen to you. □ *She was not at all afraid.* □ *I was afraid of the other boys.* ■ ADJ If you are **afraid for** someone else, you are worried that something horrible is going to happen to them. □ *She's afraid for her family in Somalia.* ■ ADJ If you are **afraid** that something unpleasant will happen, you are worried that it may happen. □ *I was afraid that nobody would believe me.* ■ PHRASE If you want to apologize to someone or to disagree with them in a polite way, you can say **I'm afraid**. [SPOKEN] □ *We don't have anything like that, I'm afraid.*

| **Thesaurus** | afraid | Also look up : |
| ADJ. | alarmed, fearful, frightened, petrified, scared; (ant.) terrified, worried ■ | | |

afresh /əfrɛ́ʃ/ ADV If you do something **afresh**, you do it again in a different way. □ *The only hope is to start afresh.*

Af|ri|can /ǽfrɪkən/ (**Africans**) ■ ADJ **African** means belonging or relating to the continent of Africa, or to its countries or people. □ *...the African continent.* □ *...traditional African culture.* ■ ADJ **African** is used to describe someone who comes from Africa. □ *...African women.* ● An **African** is someone who is African. □ *Fish is an important part of the diet of many Africans.* [from Latin]

**African-American** (**African-Americans**) N-COUNT **African-Americans** are people living in the United States who are descended from families that originally came from Africa. □ *Today African-Americans are 12 percent of the population.*
● **African-American** is also an adjective. □ *She is the daughter of an African-American father and an East Indian mother.*

**African-Caribbean** (**African-Caribbeans**)
ADJ **African-Caribbean** refers to people from the Caribbean whose ancestors came from Africa. ❏ *...modern African-Caribbean culture.* ● An **African-Caribbean** is someone who is African-Caribbean.

**af|ter** /ǽftər/

> In addition to the uses shown below, **after** is used in phrasal verbs such as "look after," and "take after."

**1** PREP If something happens or is done **after** a particular date or event, it happens or is done during the period of time that follows that date or event. ❏ *He died after a long illness.* ❏ *After breakfast Amy took a taxi to the station.* ● **After** is also a conjunction. ❏ *After Don told me this, he spoke of his mother.* **2** PREP If you go **after** someone, you follow or chase them. ❏ *Alice said to Gina, "Why don't you go after him, he's your son."* **3** PREP If you are **after** something, you are trying to get it. ❏ *They were after the money.* **4** PREP If you call or shout **after** someone, you call or shout at them as they move away from you. ❏ *"Come back!" he called after me.* **5** PREP You use **after** in order to give the most important aspect of something when comparing it with another aspect. ❏ *After Germany, America is Britain's second-biggest customer.* **6** PREP To be named **after** someone means to be given the same name as them. ❏ *He wanted Virginia to name the baby after him.* **7** PREP **After** is used when telling the time. If it is, for example, **ten after six**, the time is ten minutes past six. **8** CONVENTION If you say "**after you**" to someone, you are being polite and allowing them to go in front of you or through a doorway before you do. [from Old English] **9** **after all** → see **all**

**after|math** /ǽftərmæθ/ N-SING The **aftermath of** an important event, especially a harmful one, is the situation that results from it. ❏ *The team worked closely together in the aftermath of the fire.* [from Old English]

**after|noon** /ǽftərnuːn/ (**afternoons**) N-VAR The **afternoon** is the part of each day that begins at lunchtime and ends at about six o'clock. ❏ *He arrived in the afternoon.* ❏ *He stayed at home all afternoon.* → see **time**

**after|ward** /ǽftərwərd/ also **afterwards** ADV If you do something or if something happens **afterward**, you do it or it happens after a particular event or time that has already been mentioned. ❏ *Shortly afterward, the police arrived.* [from Old English]

**again** /əgɛ́n, əgéɪn/ **1** ADV You use **again** to indicate that something happens a second time, or after it has already happened before. ❏ *He kissed her again.* ❏ *Again there was a short silence.* **2** ADV You use **again** to indicate that something is now in a particular state or place that it used to be in. ❏ *He opened his case, took out a folder, then closed it again.* **3** PHRASE You can use **again and again** or **time and again** to emphasize that something happens many times. ❏ *He would go over his work again and again until he thought it was right.* [from Old English] **4** **now and again** → see **now**

**against** /əgɛ́nst, əgéɪnst/

> In addition to the uses shown below, **against** is used in phrasal verbs such as "come up against," "guard against," and "hold against."

**1** PREP If one thing is leaning or pressing **against** another, it is touching it. ❏ *She leaned against him.* **2** PREP If you are **against** something such as a plan, policy, or system, you think it is wrong, bad, or stupid. ❏ *He was against the war.* ● **Against** is also an adverb. ❏ *66 percent were in favor of the decision and 34 against.* **3** PREP If you compete **against** someone in a game, you try to beat them. ❏ *This is the first of two games against Denver.* **4** PREP If you take action **against** someone or something, you try to harm them. ❏ *Security forces are still using violence against opponents of the government.* **5** PREP If you do something **against** someone's wishes, advice, or orders, you do not do what they want you to do or tell you to do. ❏ *Against medical advice, she left the hospital.* **6** PREP If you do something in order to protect yourself **against** something unpleasant or harmful, you do something that will make its effects on you less serious if it happens. ❏ *Any business needs insurance against fire, flood, and breakage.* **7** PREP If something is **against** the law or **against** the rules, there is a law or a rule which says that you must not do it. ❏ *It is against the law to help others kill themselves.* **8** PREP The odds **against** something happening are the chances or odds that it will not happen. ❏ *The odds against him surviving are very great.* ● **Against** is also an adverb. ❏ *What were the odds against?*

**age** /éɪdʒ/ (**ages, aging** or **ageing, aged**) **1** N-VAR Your **age** is the number of years that you have lived. ❏ *She has a nephew who is ten years of age.* ❏ *Demi left school at the age of 16.* **2** N-UNCOUNT **Age** is the state of being old or the process of becoming older. ❏ *He has grown wiser with age.* **3** V-T/V-I When someone **ages**, or when something **ages** them, they seem much older and less strong or less alert. ❏ *Both parents said they have aged in the past six months.* ❏ *Worry had aged him.* ● **aging** N-UNCOUNT ❏ *He isn't showing any signs of aging.* **4** N-COUNT An **age** is a period in history. ❏ *...the age of silent films.* [from Old French] **5** → see also **aged, middle age**
→ see Picture Dictionary: **age**

**aged**

> Pronounced /éɪdʒd/ for meaning **1**, and /éɪdʒɪd/ for meanings **2** and **3**.

**1** ADJ You use **aged** followed by a number to say how old someone is. ❏ *Alan has two children, aged eleven and nine.* **2** ADJ **Aged** means very old. ❏ *She has an aged parent who can be very difficult.* **3** N-PLURAL You can refer to all people who are very old as **the aged**. ❏ *...daycare centers and homes for the aged.* [from Old French] **4** → see also **middle-aged**

**agen|cy** /éɪdʒənsi/ (**agencies**) **1** N-COUNT An **agency** is a business that provides a service on behalf of other businesses. [BUSINESS] ❏ *...an advertising agency.* **2** → see also **ad agency** **3** N-COUNT An **agency** is a government organization responsible for a certain area of administration. ❏ *...local, state and federal agencies.* [from Medieval Latin]

**agen|da** /ədʒɛ́ndə/ (**agendas**) **1** N-COUNT You can refer to the political issues that are important at a particular time as an **agenda**. ❏ *...the president's education agenda.* **2** N-COUNT An **agenda** is a list of the items that have to be discussed at a meeting. ❏ *...an item on Monday's meeting agenda.* [from Latin]

a

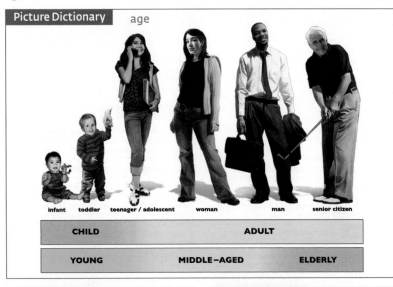

**Picture Dictionary**   age

infant    toddler    teenager / adolescent    woman      man      senior citizen

| CHILD | ADULT |
| --- | --- |

| YOUNG | MIDDLE-AGED | ELDERLY |
| --- | --- | --- |

---

**Word Partnership**   Use *agenda* with :

| | |
| --- | --- |
| ADJ. | **domestic/legislative/political** agenda, **hidden** agenda ■ |
| PREP. | **on the** agenda ■ |
| V. | **set the** agenda ■ |

**agent** /ˈeɪdʒənt/ (**agents**) ■ N-COUNT An **agent** is a person who arranges work or business for someone else or does business on their behalf. [BUSINESS] ❑ *You are buying direct, not through an agent.* ■ → see also **travel agent** ■ N-COUNT An **agent** is a person who works for a country's secret service. ❑ *...world-famous secret agent James Bond.* ■ N-COUNT A chemical that has a particular effect or is used for a particular purpose can be referred to as a particular kind of **agent**. ❑ *...the bleaching agent in flour.* [from Latin]
→ see **concert**

**age-old** ADJ An **age-old** story, tradition, or problem has existed for many generations or centuries. [WRITTEN] ❑ *...the age-old problem of what to wear.*

**ag|gra|vate** /ˈæɡrəveɪt/ (**aggravates, aggravating, aggravated**) ■ V-T If someone or something **aggravates** a situation, they make it worse. ❑ *Stress and lack of sleep can aggravate the situation.* ■ V-T If someone or something **aggravates** you, they make you annoyed. [INFORMAL] ❑ *What aggravates you most about this country?* ● **ag|gra|vat|ing** ADJ ❑ *You don't realize how aggravating you can be.* ● **ag|gra|va|tion** /ˌæɡrəˈveɪʃ³n/ (**aggravations**) N-VAR ❑ *I just couldn't take the aggravation.* [from Latin]

**ag|gres|sion** /əˈɡrɛʃ³n/ N-UNCOUNT **Aggression** is violent and attacking behavior. ❑ *They are using aggression and violence against their neighbours.* [from Latin]
→ see **anger**

---

**Word Partnership**   Use *aggression* with :

| | |
| --- | --- |
| N. | **act of** aggression |
| PREP. | aggression **against** |
| ADJ. | **military** aggression, **physical** aggression |

**ag|gres|sive** /əˈɡrɛsɪv/ ■ ADJ An **aggressive** person or animal behaves angrily or violently toward other people. ❑ *Some children are much more aggressive than others.* ● **ag|gres|sive|ly** ADV ❑ *They'll react aggressively.* ■ ADJ People who are **aggressive** in their work or other activities behave in a forceful way because they are very eager to succeed. ❑ *He was an aggressive manager.* ● **ag|gres|sive|ly** ADV ❑ *They want to play aggressively and do what is necessary to be successful.* [from Latin]

**ag|gres|sor** /əˈɡrɛsər/ (**aggressors**) N-COUNT The **aggressor** in a fight or battle is the person, group, or country that starts it. ❑ *They have been the aggressors in this conflict.* [from Latin]

---

**Word Link**   *griev* ≈ heavy, serious : ag*griev*ed, *griev*ance, *griev*e

**ag|grieved** /əˈɡriːvd/ ADJ If you feel **aggrieved**, you feel upset and angry because of the way in which you have been treated. ❑ *I really feel aggrieved at this sort of thing.* [from Old French]

**aghast** /əˈɡæst/ ADJ If you are **aghast**, you are filled with horror and surprise. [FORMAL] ❑ *We all stared, aghast at what had happened.* [from Old English]

**ag|ile** /ˈædʒəl/ ■ ADJ Someone who is **agile** can move quickly and easily. ❑ *At 20 years old he was not as agile as he is now.* ● **agil|ity** /əˈdʒɪlɪti/ N-UNCOUNT ❑ *She was surprised at his agility.* ■ ADJ If you have an **agile** mind, you think quickly and intelligently. ● **agil|ity** N-UNCOUNT ❑ *His mental agility has never been in doubt.* [from Latin]

**A**

**agi|tate** /ˈædʒɪteɪt/ (**agitates, agitating, agitated**) v-ɪ If people **agitate for** something, they protest or take part in political activity in order to get it. ❑ *The workers were agitating for better conditions.* ● **agi|ta|tion** /ˌædʒɪteɪʃən/ N-UNCOUNT ❑ *...continuing agitation against the decision.* [from Latin]

**agi|tat|ed** /ˈædʒɪteɪtɪd/ ADJ If someone is **agitated**, they are very worried or upset, and show this in their behavior, movements, or voice. ❑ *Susan seemed agitated about something.* [from Latin]

**agi|ta|tion** /ˌædʒɪteɪʃən/ N-UNCOUNT If someone is in a state of **agitation**, they are very worried or upset, and show this in their behavior, movements, or voice. ❑ *In his state of agitation he couldn't think clearly.* [from Latin]

**ago** /əˈɡoʊ/ ADV You use **ago** when you are referring to past time. For example, if something happened one year **ago**, it is one year since it happened. If it happened a long time **ago**, it is a long time since it happened. ❑ *I got your letter a few days ago.* [from Old English]

**Word Link** agon ≈ struggling : **agon**ize, **agon**y, prot**agon**ist

**ago|nize** /ˈæɡənaɪz/ (**agonizes, agonizing, agonized**) v-ɪ If you **agonize over** something, you feel very anxious about it and spend a long time thinking about it. ❑ *He was agonizing over a difficult decision.* [from Medieval Latin]

**ago|niz|ing** /ˈæɡənaɪzɪŋ/ **1** ADJ Something that is **agonizing** causes you to feel great physical or mental pain. ❑ *He did not wish to die the agonizing death of his mother and brother.* **2** ADJ **Agonizing** decisions and choices are very difficult to make. ❑ *He now faced an agonizing decision about his future.* [from Medieval Latin]

**ago|ny** /ˈæɡəni/ (**agonies**) N-VAR **Agony** is great physical or mental pain. ❑ *He tried to move but screamed in agony.* [from Late Latin]

**agree** /əˈɡri/ (**agrees, agreeing, agreed**) **1** v-RECIP If people **agree with** each other about something, they have the same opinion about it or say that they have the same opinion. ❑ *Both have agreed on the need for money.* ❑ *Do we agree there's a problem?* ❑ *I agree with you.* ❑ *"It's a shame." — "It is. I agree."* ❑ *I agree with every word you've just said.* **2** v-RECIP If people **agree on** something, they all decide to accept or do something. ❑ *They agreed on a price of $85,000.* **3** v-T/v-ɪ If you **agree to** do something, you say that you will do it. If you **agree to** a proposal, you accept it. ❑ *He agreed to pay me for the drawings.* **4** v-ɪ If you **agree with** an action or suggestion, you approve of it. ❑ *Most people agreed with what we did.* **5** v-RECIP If one account of an event or one set of figures **agrees with** another, the two accounts or sets of figures are the same or are consistent with each other. ❑ *His second statement agrees with mine.* [from Old French]

**agree|able** /əˈɡriəbəl/ **1** ADJ If something is **agreeable**, it is pleasant and you enjoy it. ❑ *...workers in more agreeable and better paid jobs.* **2** ADJ If someone is **agreeable**, they are pleasant and try to please people. ❑ *...an agreeable companion.* [from Old French]

**Word Link** ment ≈ state, condition : agree**ment**, manage**ment**, move**ment**

**agree|ment** /əˈɡrimənt/ (**agreements**) **1** N-COUNT An **agreement** is a formal decision about future action that is made by two or more countries, groups, or people. ❑ *Government officials reached agreement late Sunday.* **2** N-UNCOUNT **Agreement** with someone means having the same opinion as they have. ❑ *The doctors were in agreement.* **3** PHRASE If you are **in agreement with** someone, you have the same opinion as they have. ❑ *We are all in agreement with her.* [from Old French]

**Word Partnership** Use agreement with :

| | |
|---|---|
| N. | peace agreement, **terms of an** agreement, **trade** agreement **1** |
| V. | **enter into an** agreement, **sign an** agreement **1** |
| | **reach an** agreement **1 2** |

**ag|ri|cul|ture** /ˈæɡrɪkʌltʃər/ N-UNCOUNT **Agriculture** is farming and the methods that are used to raise and take care of crops and animals. ❑ *Governments must invest more in agriculture and farmers.* ● **ag|ri|cul|tur|al** /ˌæɡrɪkʌltʃərəl/ ADJ ❑ *...agricultural land.* [from Latin]
→ see **farm, grassland, industry**

**ahead**

**❶** ADVERB USES
**❷** PREPOSITION USES

**❶ ahead** /əˈhɛd/

In addition to the uses shown below, **ahead** is used in phrasal verbs such as "get ahead," "go ahead," and "press ahead."

**1** ADV Something that is **ahead** is in front of you. If you look **ahead**, you look directly in front of you. ❑ *Brett looked straight ahead.* ❑ *The road ahead was now blocked solid.* **2** ADV If you are **ahead** in your work or achievements, you have made more progress than you expected to and are performing well. ❑ *He wanted a good job, a home, and a chance to get ahead.* **3** ADV If a person or a team is **ahead** in a competition, they are winning. ❑ *Australia was ahead throughout the game.* **4** ADV **Ahead** means in the future. ❑ *A much bigger battle is ahead for the president.* **5** ADV If you go **ahead**, or if you go on **ahead**, you go in front of someone who is going to the same place so that you arrive there some time before they do. ❑ *I went ahead and waited with Sean.*

**Word Partnership** Use ahead with :

| | |
|---|---|
| ADV. | **straight** ahead **❶ 1** |
| V. | lie ahead, **look** ahead **❶ 1 4** |
| | **get** ahead **❶ 2** |
| | **go** ahead **❶ 5** |
| PREP. | ahead **of schedule/time ❶ 2** |
| | **in the days/months/years** ahead **❶ 4** |

**❷ ahead of 1** PHRASE If someone is **ahead of** you, they are in front of you. ❑ *I saw a man thirty yards ahead of me.* **2** PHRASE If an event or period of time lies **ahead of** you, it is going to happen or take place soon or in the future. ❑ *Heather was thinking about the future that lay ahead of her.* **3** PHRASE If something happens **ahead of** schedule or **ahead of** time, it happens earlier than was planned. ❑ *We were a week ahead of schedule.* **4** PHRASE If someone is **ahead of** someone else, they have made more progress and are more advanced in what they are doing. ❑ *Henry was ahead of the others in most subjects.* ❑ **one step ahead of** someone or something → see **step** ❑ **ahead of** your **time** → see **time**

**ahold** /əhoʊld/ ❶ PHRASE If you **get ahold of** someone or something, you manage to contact, find, or get them. [INFORMAL] ❑ *I tried to get ahold of my cousin Joan.* ❷ PHRASE If you **get ahold of yourself**, you force yourself to become calm and sensible after a shock or in a difficult situation. [INFORMAL] ❑ *I'm going to have to get ahold of myself.*

**aid** /eɪd/ (**aids, aiding, aided**) ❶ N-UNCOUNT **Aid** is money, equipment, or services that are provided for people, countries, or organizations who need them but cannot provide them for themselves. ❑ *They have promised billions of dollars in aid.* ❷ V-T To **aid** a country, organization, or person means to provide them with money, equipment, or services that they need. ❑ *...a $1 billion fund to aid storm victims.* ❸ V-T To **aid** someone means to help or assist them. [WRITTEN] ❑ *He is doing what he can to aid his friend.* ● **Aid** is also a noun. ❑ *He fell into the water and shouted for aid.* ❹ V-T/V-I If something **aids** a process, it makes it easier or more likely to happen. ❑ *The design of the pages might aid the reader's understanding.* ❑ *...a medicine that will aid in the treatment of cancer.* ❺ N-COUNT An **aid** is an object, device, or technique that makes something easier to do. ❑ *The book is a valuable aid to teachers of literature.* ❻ → see also **first aid** ❼ PHRASE If you **come** or **go to** someone's **aid**, you try to help them when they are in danger or difficulty. ❑ *Dr. Fox went to the aid of the dying man.* [from Old French]

**aide** /eɪd/ (**aides**) ❶ N-COUNT An **aide** is an assistant to someone who has an important job, especially in government or in the armed forces. ❑ *An aide to the president described the meeting as very useful.* [from Old French] ❷ → see also **teacher's aide**

**AIDS** /eɪdz/ N-UNCOUNT **AIDS** is a disease that destroys the natural system of protection that the body has against other diseases. **AIDS** is an abbreviation for **acquired immune deficiency syndrome**. ❑ *...people suffering from AIDS.*

| Word Partnership | Use *AIDS* with : |
| --- | --- |
| N. | AIDS **activists**, AIDS **epidemic**, AIDS **patient**, AIDS **research**, **spread of** AIDS, AIDS **victims** |
| V. | **infected with** AIDS |

**ail|ing** /eɪlɪŋ/ ADJ An **ailing** organization or society is in difficulty and is becoming weaker. ❑ *...the ailing airline industry.* [from Old English]

**ail|ment** /eɪlmənt/ (**ailments**) N-COUNT An **ailment** is an illness, especially one that is not very serious. ❑ *Her father had an eye ailment.* [from Old English]

**aim** /eɪm/ (**aims, aiming, aimed**) ❶ V-T/V-I If you **aim for** something or **aim to** do something, you plan or hope to achieve it. ❑ *He is aiming for the 100 meter world record.* ❑ *The appeal aims to raise money for children with special needs.* ❷ V-T If you **aim to** do something, you decide or want to do it. [INFORMAL] ❑ *I aim to please.* ❸ V-T If your actions or remarks **are aimed at** a particular person or group, you intend that the person or group should notice them and be influenced by them. ❑ *Most of their advertisements are aimed at women.* ❹ V-T If you **aim** a weapon or object **at** something or someone, you point it toward them before firing or throwing it. ❑ *He was aiming the rifle at Wright.* ❺ N-COUNT The **aim** of something that you do is the purpose for which you do it or the result that it is intended to achieve. ❑ *The aim of the event is to bring parents and children together.* ❻ V-T If an action or plan **is aimed at** achieving something, it is intended or planned to achieve it. ❑ *The plan is aimed at reaching an agreement.* ❼ N-SING Your **aim** is your skill or action in pointing a weapon or other object at its target. ❑ *His aim was good.* ❽ PHRASE When you **take aim**, you point a weapon or object at someone or something. ❑ *She saw a man with a shotgun taking aim.* [from Old French]

**aim|less** /eɪmləs/ ADJ A person or activity that is **aimless** has no clear purpose or plan. ❑ *They all led aimless lives.* ● **aim|less|ly** ADV ❑ *I wandered around aimlessly.* [from Old French]

**air** /ɛər/ (**airs, airing, aired**) ❶ N-UNCOUNT **Air** is the mixture of gases that forms the earth's atmosphere and that we breathe. ❑ *Keith opened the window and leaned out into the cold air.* ❷ N-UNCOUNT **Air** is used to refer to travel in aircraft. ❑ *Air travel will continue to grow at about 6% per year.* ❸ N-SING The **air** is the space around things or above the ground. ❑ *He was waving his arms in the air.* ❹ V-T If a broadcasting company **airs** a television or radio program, they show it on television or broadcast it on the radio. ❑ *Tonight PBS will air a documentary called "Democracy In Action."* ● **air|ing** N-SING ❑ *...the airing of a new television commercial.* ❺ V-T If you **air** a room or building, you let fresh air into it. ❑ *One day a week her mother cleaned and aired each room.* ❻ PHRASE If you do something to **clear the air**, you do it in order to resolve any problems or disagreements that there might be. ❑ *...an meeting to clear the air and agree on the facts.* ❼ PHRASE If someone is **on the air**, they are broadcasting on radio or television. If a program is **on the air**, it is being broadcast on radio or television. If it is **off the air**, it is not being broadcast. ❑ *We go on the air at 11:30 a.m.* [from Old French]
→ see Word Web: **air**
→ see **erosion, respiration, wind**

**air base** (**air bases**) also **airbase** N-COUNT An **air base** is a center where military aircraft take off or land and are serviced, and where many of the center's staff live. ❑ *...the largest U.S. air base in Saudi Arabia.*

**air|borne** /ɛərbɔrn/ ADJ **Airborne** means flying in the air or coming from the air. ❑ *The pilot did manage to get airborne.*
→ see **pollution**

**air-conditioned** ADJ If a room or vehicle is **air-conditioned**, the air in it is kept cool and dry by means of a special machine. ❑ *...air-conditioned trains.*

**air-condition|ing** N-UNCOUNT **Air-conditioning** is a method of providing buildings and vehicles with cool dry air.

**air|craft** /ɛərkræft/ (**aircraft**) N-COUNT An **aircraft** is a vehicle that can fly, for example, an airplane or a helicopter. ❑ *The aircraft landed safely.*
→ see **fly, ship**

**air|field** /ɛərfild/ (**airfields**) N-COUNT An **airfield** is an area of ground where aircraft take off and

**A**

## Word Web　air

The **air** we breathe has seventeen different **gases**. It is made up mostly of **nitrogen**, not **oxygen**. Recently, human activities have changed the balance in the earth's **atmosphere**. The widespread burning of coal and oil increases the levels of **carbon dioxide** gas. Scientists believe this air **pollution** may cause **global warming**. Certain chemicals used in air conditioners, farming, and manufacturing are the problem. With less protection from the sun, the air temperature rises and makes the earth warmer. This leads to harmful effects on people, farming, animals, and the natural environment.

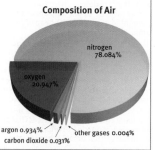

**Composition of Air**

nitrogen 78.084%
oxygen 20.947%
argon 0.934%　other gases 0.004%
carbon dioxide 0.031%

land. It is smaller than an airport.

**air force** (**air forces**) N-COUNT An **air force** is the part of a country's armed forces that is concerned with fighting in the air. ❑ ...the United States Air Force.

**air|lift** /ɛ́ərlɪft/ (**airlifts, airlifting, airlifted**) **1** N-COUNT An **airlift** is an operation to move people, troops, or goods by air, especially in a war or when land routes are closed. ❑ ...an airlift of food, medicines and blankets. **2** V-T If people, troops, or goods **are airlifted** somewhere, they are carried by air, especially in a war or when land routes are closed. ❑ The injured were airlifted to a hospital in Dayton.

**air|line** /ɛ́ərlaɪn/ (**airlines**) N-COUNT An **airline** is a company that provides regular services carrying people or goods in airplanes. ❑ ...the world's largest airline.

**air|lin|er** /ɛ́ərlaɪnər/ (**airliners**) N-COUNT An **airliner** is a large airplane that is used for carrying passengers.

**air mass** (**air masses**) N-COUNT An **air mass** is a large area of air that has the same temperature and amount of moisture throughout.

**air|plane** /ɛ́ərpleɪn/ (**airplanes**) N-COUNT An **airplane** is a vehicle with wings and one or more engines that enable it to fly through the air. [from French]
→ see **fly**

**air|port** /ɛ́ərpɔrt/ (**airports**) N-COUNT An **airport** is a place where planes take off and land, and that has buildings and facilities for passengers. ❑ Heathrow Airport is the busiest international airport in the world.

**air pres|sure** N-UNCOUNT **Air pressure** is a measure of the force with which air presses against a surface.

**air raid** (**air raids**) N-COUNT An **air raid** is an attack by military aircraft in which bombs are dropped. ❑ The war began with overnight air raids on Baghdad and Kuwait.

**air sac** (**air sacs**) N-UNCOUNT An **air sac** is a very small, round structure in the lungs of some animals that helps them to breathe.

**air|space** /ɛ́ərspeɪs/ also **air space** N-UNCOUNT A country's **airspace** is the part of the sky that is over that country and is considered to belong to it. ❑ Forty minutes later, they left Colombian airspace.

**air|tight** /ɛ́ərtaɪt/ also **air-tight 1** ADJ If a container is **airtight**, its lid fits so tightly that no

air can get in or out. ❑ Store the cookies in an airtight container. **2** ADJ An **airtight** alibi, case, argument, or agreement is one that has been so carefully put together that nobody will be able to find a fault in it. ❑ He has an airtight alibi for the time of the murder.

**air|waves** /ɛ́ərweɪvz/ also **air waves** N-PLURAL **The airwaves** is used to refer to the activity of broadcasting on radio and television. For example, if someone says something over **the airwaves**, they say it on the radio or television. ❑ The announcement came over the airwaves.

**airy** /ɛ́əri/ (**airier, airiest**) ADJ If a building or room is **airy**, it is large and has a lot of fresh air inside. ❑ The bathroom has a light and airy feel. [from Old French]

**aisle** /aɪl/ (**aisles**) N-COUNT An **aisle** is a long narrow gap that people can walk along between rows of seats in a public building such as a church or between rows of shelves in a store. ❑ ...the frozen food aisle. [from Old French]

**akin** /əkɪ́n/ ADJ If one thing is **akin to** another, it is similar to it in some way. [FORMAL] ❑ His life story is akin to a good adventure story.

**à la mode** /ɑ lə moʊd/ also **a la mode** ADJ A dessert **à la mode** is served with ice cream. ❑ ...apple pie à la mode. ● **A'la mode** is also used as an adverb. ❑ ...served à la mode with vanilla ice cream.

**alarm** /əlɑ́rm/ (**alarms, alarming, alarmed**) **1** N-UNCOUNT **Alarm** is a feeling of fear or anxiety that something unpleasant or dangerous might happen. ❑ She greeted the news with alarm. **2** V-T If something **alarms** you, it makes you afraid or anxious that something unpleasant or dangerous might happen. ❑ I don't know what alarmed him. ● **alarmed** ADJ ❑ They should not be alarmed by the press reports. ● **alarm|ing** ADJ ❑ The disease has spread at an alarming rate. ● **alarm|ing|ly** ADV ❑ ...the alarmingly high rate of heart disease. **3** N-COUNT An **alarm** is an automatic device that warns you of danger, for example, by ringing a bell. ❑ He heard the alarm go off and went to investigate. **4** N-COUNT An **alarm** is the same as an **alarm clock**. ❑ Dad set the alarm for eight the next day. [from Old French] **5** → see also **false alarm**, **fire alarm**

## Word Partnership　Use *alarm* with :

| | |
|---|---|
| V. | **cause** alarm **1** |
| | **set** the alarm **3 4** |
| N. | **alarm** system **3** |

**alarm clock** (**alarm clocks**) N-COUNT An **alarm clock** is a clock that you can set to make a noise so that it wakes you up at a particular time. ❑ *I set my alarm clock for 4:30.*

**alas** /əlǽs/ ADV You use **alas** to say that you think that the facts you are talking about are sad or unfortunate. [FORMAL] ❑ *I thought he was getting better but, alas, I was wrong.* [from Old French]

**al|be|it** /ɔːlbíːɪt/ ADV You use **albeit** to introduce a fact or comment that reduces the force or significance of what you have just said. [FORMAL] ❑ *It was just another work day, albeit a quieter one.*

**al|bum** /ǽlbəm/ (**albums**) **1** N-COUNT An **album** is a collection of songs that is available on a CD, record, or cassette. ❑ *Chris has a large collection of albums.* ❑ *Oasis released their new album on July 1.* **2** N-COUNT An **album** is a book in which you keep things such as photographs or stamps that you have collected. ❑ *Theresa showed me her photo album.* [from Latin]

**al|co|hol** /ǽlkəhɔl/ **1** N-UNCOUNT Drinks that can make people drunk, such as beer, wine, and whiskey, can be referred to as **alcohol**. ❑ *Do either of you drink alcohol?* **2** N-UNCOUNT **Alcohol** is a colorless liquid that is found in drinks such as beer, wine, and whiskey. It is also used in products such as perfumes and cleaning fluids. ❑ *...low-alcohol beer.* [from New Latin]

**al|co|hol|ic** /ǽlkəhɔlɪk/ (**alcoholics**) **1** N-COUNT An **alcoholic** is someone who cannot stop drinking alcohol, even when this is making them ill. ❑ *He admitted that he is an alcoholic.* ● **al|co|hol|ism** /ǽlkəhɒlɪzəm/ N-UNCOUNT ❑ *She was treated for alcoholism.* **2** ADJ **Alcoholic** drinks are drinks that contain alcohol. ❑ *Wine and beer are alcoholic drinks.* [from New Latin]

**ale** /eɪl/ (**ales**) N-VAR **Ale** is a kind of strong beer. ❑ *We sell ales and spirits.* [from Old English]

**alert** /əlɜːrt/ (**alerts, alerting, alerted**) **1** ADJ If you are **alert**, you are paying full attention to things around you and are able to deal with anything that might happen. ❑ *We all have to stay alert.* ● **alert|ness** N-UNCOUNT ❑ *Coffee may increase alertness.* **2** ADJ If you are **alert to** something, you are fully aware of it. ❑ *He is alert to the danger.* **3** N-COUNT An **alert** is a situation in which people prepare themselves for something dangerous that might happen soon. ❑ *...last week's storm alert.* **4** V-T If you **alert** someone **to** a situation, especially a dangerous or unpleasant situation, you tell them about it. ❑ *He wanted to alert people to the danger.* **5** PHRASE When soldiers, police or other authorities are **on alert** they are ready to deal with anything that may happen. ❑ *Health officials have put hospitals on alert.* [from Italian]

**al|gae** /ǽldʒi/ N-PLURAL **Algae** are plants with no stems or leaves that grow in water or on damp surfaces. [from Latin]

**al|ge|bra** /ǽldʒɪbrə/ N-UNCOUNT **Algebra** is a type of mathematics in which letters are used to represent possible quantities. [from Medieval Latin]
→ see **mathematics**

**al|go|rithm** /ǽlgərɪðəm/ (**algorithms**) N-COUNT An **algorithm** is a series of mathematical steps, especially in a computer program, which will give you the answer to a particular kind of problem or question. [from Greek]

**ali|as** /eɪliəs/ (**aliases**) **1** N-COUNT An **alias** is a false name, especially one used by a criminal. ❑ *Using an alias, he rented a house in Des Moines.* **2** PREP You use **alias** when you are mentioning another name that someone, especially a criminal or an actor, is known by. ❑ *...Richard Thorp, alias Alan Turner.* [from Latin]

**ali|bi** /ǽlɪbaɪ/ (**alibis**) N-COUNT If you have an **alibi**, you can prove that you were somewhere else when a crime was committed. ❑ *His wife gave him an alibi.* [from Latin]

**al|ien** /eɪliən/ (**aliens**) **1** ADJ **Alien** means belonging to a different country, race, or group, usually one you do not like or are frightened of. [FORMAL] ❑ *The group sings about growing up in an alien culture.* **2** ADJ If something is **alien to** you or **to** your normal feelings or behavior, it is not the way you would normally feel or behave. [FORMAL] ❑ *Such behavior is alien to most people.* **3** N-COUNT An **alien** is someone who is not a legal citizen of the country in which they live. [LEGAL] ❑ *He's an illegal alien.* **4** N-COUNT In science fiction, an **alien** is a creature from outer space. ❑ *...aliens from another planet.* **5** N-COUNT An **alien** is a plant or an animal that lives in a different geographical area from the place where it originally lived. [TECHNICAL] [from Latin]

**al|ien|ate** /eɪliəneɪt/ (**alienates, alienating, alienated**) **1** V-T If you **alienate** someone, you make them become unfriendly or unsympathetic toward you. ❑ *We do not want to alienate anybody.* **2** V-T To **alienate** a person **from** someone or something that they are normally linked with means to cause them to be emotionally or intellectually separated from them. ❑ *His second wife, Alice, wanted to alienate him from his two boys.* ● **alienated** ADJ ❑ *Most of these students feel alienated from their parents.* ● **alienation** N-UNCOUNT ❑ *...her sense of alienation from the world.* [from Latin]

**alight** /əlaɪt/ (**alights, alighting, alighted**) **1** ADJ If something is **alight**, it is burning. ❑ *Several buildings were set alight.* **2** ADJ If your eyes are **alight** or if your face is **alight**, your expression shows that you are feeling a strong emotion such as excitement or happiness. [LITERARY] ❑ *She turned toward him, her face alight with happiness.* **3** V-I When you **alight** from a train, bus, or other vehicle, you get out of it after a trip. [FORMAL] [from Old English]

**align** /əlaɪn/ (**aligns, aligning, aligned**) **1** V-T If you **align yourself with** a particular group, you support their political aims. ❑ *He aligned himself with the Republican Party.* ● **align|ment** /əlaɪnmənt/ (**alignments**) N-VAR ❑ *The church should have no political alignment.* **2** V-T If you **align** something, you place it in a certain position in relation to something else, usually parallel to it. ❑ *Wilson managed to align the plane with the runway.* ● **align|ment** N-UNCOUNT ❑ *...the alignment of the planets.* [from Old French]

**align|ment** /əlaɪnmənt/ **1** N-UNCOUNT The **alignment** of a person's body is the relationship between the position of their spine and their feet when they are standing or sitting. [from Old French] **2** → see also **align**

A

**alike** /əlaɪk/ ■ ADJ If two or more things are **alike**, they are similar in some way. ❑ We looked very alike. ■ ADV **Alike** means in a similar way. ❑ They even dressed alike. [from Old English]

**A-list** ADJ An **A-list** celebrity is a celebrity who is very famous. ❑ …an A-list Hollywood actress.

**alive** /əlaɪv/ ■ ADJ If people or animals are **alive**, they are not dead. ❑ She does not know if he is alive or dead. ■ ADJ If you say that someone seems **alive**, you mean that they seem to be very lively and to enjoy everything that they do. ❑ She seemed more alive and looked forward to getting up in the morning. ■ ADJ If an activity, organization, or situation is **alive**, it continues to exist or function. ❑ The big factories are trying to stay alive by cutting costs. ■ ADJ If a place is **alive with** something, there are a lot of people or things there and it seems busy or exciting. ❑ The river was alive with birds. ■ PHRASE If people, places, or events **come alive**, they start to be lively again after a quiet period. ❑ John's voice came alive and his eyes shone. [from Old English]

**al|ka|li met|al** (**alkali metals**) N-COUNT **Alkali metals** are a group of metallic elements that includes sodium and potassium. [TECHNICAL]

**alkaline-earth met|al** also **alkaline earth** (**alkaline-earth metals**) N-COUNT **Alkaline-earth metals** are a group of metallic elements that includes calcium and strontium. [TECHNICAL]

**all**

❶ EVERYTHING, THE WHOLE OF SOMETHING
❷ EMPHASIS
❸ OTHER PHRASES

❶ **all** /ɔl/ ■ PREDET You use **all** to indicate that you are referring to the whole of a particular group or thing or to everyone or everything of a particular kind. ❑ …the restaurant that Hugh and all his friends go to. ● **All** is also a determiner. ❑ There is storage space in all bedrooms. ❑ He loved all literature. ● **All** is also a quantifier. ❑ He threw away all of his letters. ■ DET You use **all** to refer to the whole of a particular period of time. ❑ He watched TV all day. ● **All** is also a predeterminer. ❑ She's worked all her life. ■ PRON You use **all** to refer to the whole of a situation or to life in general. ❑ All is silent on the island now. ■ PHRASE **In all** means in total. ❑ There was a $5,000 first prize and 30 prizes in all. ■ PHRASE You use **all in all** to introduce a summary or general statement. ❑ We both thought that all in all it wasn't a bad idea. [from Old English]

❷ **all** /ɔl/ ■ ADV You use **all** to emphasize the extent to which something happens or is true. ❑ I ran away and left her all alone. ❑ …universities all around the world. ■ ADV **All** is used in structures such as **all the more** or **all the better** to mean even more or even better than before. ❑ The fact that it's hard to get there makes it all the more exciting. ■ PHRASE You say **above all** to indicate that the thing you are mentioning is the most important point. ❑ Above all, chairs should be comfortable. ■ PHRASE You use **at all** at the end of a clause to give emphasis in negative statements, conditional clauses, and questions. ❑ Richard never really liked him at all. ■ PHRASE You use **of all** to emphasize the words "first" or "last," or a superlative adjective or adverb. ❑ First of all, answer these questions. [from Old English]

❸ **all** /ɔl/ ■ ADV You use **all** when you are talking about an equal score in a game. For example, if the score is three **all**, both players or teams have three points. ■ PHRASE You use **after all** when introducing a statement that supports or helps explain something you have just said. ❑ I thought you might know somebody. After all, you live here. ■ PHRASE You use **after all** when you are saying that something that you thought might not be true is in fact true. ❑ There may be a way out after all. ■ PHRASE You use **for all** to indicate that the thing mentioned does not affect or contradict the truth of what you are saying. ❑ For all its faults, the movie instantly became a classic. [from Old English]

**Allah** /ɑlə, ælə, ɑlɑ/ N-PROPER **Allah** is the name of God in Islam. ❑ Allah be praised! [from Arabic]

**all-American** ADJ If you describe someone as an **all-American** boy or girl, you mean that they seem to have all the typical qualities that are valued by ordinary Americans, such as good looks and love of their country. ❑ Billy was an all-American kid from Long Island.

**all-around** ■ ADJ An **all-around** person is good at a lot of different skills, academic subjects, or sports. ❑ He is a great all-around player. ■ ADJ **All-around** means doing or relating to all aspects of a job or activity. ❑ She has a great all-around game.

**al|lay** /əleɪ/ (**allays, allaying, allayed**) V-T If you **allay** someone's fears or doubts, you stop them feeling afraid or doubtful. [FORMAL] ❑ He did what he could to allay his wife's fears. [from Old English]

**al|le|ga|tion** /æligeɪʃⁿn/ (**allegations**) N-COUNT An **allegation** is a statement saying that someone has done something wrong. ❑ The company denied the allegations. [from Latin]

**al|lege** /əlɛdʒ/ (**alleges, alleging, alleged**) V-T If you **allege that** something bad is true, you say it but do not prove it. [FORMAL] ❑ They alleged that the murder resulted from a quarrel between the two men. ❑ The accused is alleged to have killed a man. ● **al|leg|ed|ly** /əlɛdʒɪdli/ ADV ❑ His van allegedly hit them as they were crossing the street. [from Latin]

**al|le|giance** /əlíːdʒⁿns/ (**allegiances**) N-VAR Your **allegiance** is your support for and loyalty to a particular group, person, or belief. ☐ *My allegiance to Kendall was very strong.* [from Old French]

**al|lele** /əlíl/ (**alleles**) N-COUNT **Alleles** are different forms of a particular gene within an organism. [TECHNICAL] [from German]

**al|ler|gic** /əlɜ́rdʒɪk/ **1** ADJ If you are **allergic to** something, you become ill or get a rash when you eat it, smell it, or touch it. ☐ *I'm allergic to cats.* **2** ADJ If you have an **allergic** reaction to something, you become ill or get a rash when you eat it, smell it, or touch it. ☐ *He had an allergic reaction to oranges.* [from German]
→ see **peanut**

**al|ler|gy** /ǽlərdʒi/ (**allergies**) N-VAR If you have a particular **allergy**, you become ill or get a rash when you eat, smell, or touch something that does not normally make people ill. ☐ *He has an allergy to nuts.* [from German]

**al|le|vi|ate** /əlíːvieɪt/ (**alleviates, alleviating, alleviated**) V-T If you **alleviate** pain, suffering, or an unpleasant condition, you make it less intense or severe. [FORMAL] ☐ *Nowadays, a lot can be done to alleviate back pain.* ● **al|le|via|tion** /əlíːvieɪʃⁿn/ N-UNCOUNT ☐ *Yoga can help in the alleviation of illness.* [from Late Latin]

**al|ley** /ǽli/ (**alleys**) N-COUNT An **alley** is a narrow passage or street with buildings or walls on both sides. [from Old French]

**al|li|ance** /əlaɪəns/ (**alliances**) **1** N-COUNT An **alliance** is a group of countries or political parties that are formally united and working together because they have similar aims. ☐ *The two parties formed an alliance.* **2** N-COUNT An **alliance** is a relationship in which two countries, political parties, or organizations work together for some purpose. ☐ *...Britain's alliance with the United States.* [from Old French]

**al|lied** /əlaɪd/ **1** ADJ **Allied** countries, troops, or political parties are united by a political or military agreement. ☐ *...forces from three allied nations.* **2** ADJ If one thing or group is **allied to** another, it is related to it because the two things have particular qualities or characteristics in common. ☐ *...books on subjects allied to health, beauty and fitness.* [from Old French]

**al|li|ga|tor** /ǽlɪgeɪtər/ (**alligators**) N-COUNT An **alligator** is a large reptile with short legs, a long tail, and very powerful jaws. ☐ *Do not feed the alligators.* [from Spanish]

alligator

**all-in-one** **1** ADJ **All-in-one** means having several different parts or several different functions. ☐ *...an all-in-one printer that's also a scanner, fax and copier.* **2** → see also **one**

**al|lit|era|tion** /əlɪtərеɪʃən/ (**alliterations**) N-VAR **Alliteration** is the use in speech or writing of several words close together that all begin with the same letter or sound. [TECHNICAL] [from Medieval Latin]

**al|lo|cate** /ǽləkeɪt/ (**allocates, allocating, allocated**) V-T If one item or share of something is **allocated to** a particular person or **for** a particular purpose, it is given to that person or used for that purpose. ☐ *Tickets will be allocated to those who apply first.* ☐ *Our plan is to allocate one member of staff to handle appointments.* ● **al|lo|ca|tion** /ǽləkeɪʃⁿn/ N-UNCOUNT ☐ *...the allocation of land for new homes.* [from Medieval Latin]

**al|lot** /əlɒt/ (**allots, allotting, allotted**) V-T If something **is allotted to** someone, it is given to them as their share. ☐ *We were allotted half an hour to discuss the subject.* ● **al|lot|ment** (**allotments**) N-VAR ☐ *Their usual allotment of water has been cut by two thirds.* [from Old French]

**all-out** also **all out** ADJ You use **all-out** to describe actions that are carried out in a very energetic and determined way, using all the resources available. ☐ *It was an all-out group effort.*

**all-over** ADJ You can use **all-over** to describe something that covers an entire surface. ☐ *They got great all-over suntans.*

**al|low** /əlaʊ/ (**allows, allowing, allowed**) **1** V-T If someone **is allowed to** do something, it is all right for them to do it. ☐ *The children are allowed to watch TV after school.* **2** V-T If you **are allowed** something, you are given permission to have it or are given it. ☐ *Gifts like chocolates or flowers are allowed.* **3** V-T If you **allow** something **to** happen, you do not prevent it. ☐ *He won't allow himself to fail.* **4** V-T If one thing **allows** another thing **to** happen, the first thing creates the opportunity for the second thing to happen. ☐ *A period of rest will allow me to become stronger.* **5** V-T If you **allow** a particular length of time or a particular amount of something **for** a particular purpose, you include it in your planning. ☐ *Please allow 28 days for delivery.* [from Old French]
▸ **allow for** PHR-VERB If you **allow for** certain problems or expenses, you include some extra time or money in your planning so that you can deal with them if they occur. ☐ *They allowed for a public meeting.*

| Thesaurus | allow | Also look up : |
|---|---|---|
| v. | approve, consent, let, tolerate; (ant.) disallow, forbid, prohibit, prevent **4** | |

**al|low|ance** /əlaʊəns/ (**allowances**) **1** N-COUNT An **allowance** is money that is given regularly to someone. ☐ *She gets an allowance for taking care of Amy.* **2** N-COUNT A child's **allowance** is money that is given to him or her every week or every month by his or her parents. ☐ *When you give kids an allowance make sure they save some of it.* **3** PHRASE If you **make allowances for** something, you take it into account in your decisions, plans, or actions. ☐ *She tried to make allowances for his age.* **4** PHRASE If you **make allowances for** someone, you accept behavior from them that you would not normally accept, because of a problem that they have. ☐ *He's tired so I'll make allowances for him.* [from Old French]

**al|loy** /ǽlɔɪ/ (**alloys**) N-VAR An **alloy** is a metal that is made by mixing two or more types of metal together. [from Old French]

**all-points bul|letin** (**all-points bulletins**) N-COUNT An **all-points bulletin** is a message sent by a police force to all its officers. The abbreviation **APB** is also used. ☐ *An all-points bulletin gave out their names and addresses.*

**A**

**all right** ■ ADJ If you say that someone or something is **all right**, you mean that they are satisfactory or acceptable. ❑ *I'll do that if it's all right with you.* ● **All right** is also used before a noun. [INFORMAL] ❑ *He's an all right kind of guy really.* ■ ADJ If someone or something is **all right**, they are well or safe. ❑ *Are you all right?* ■ CONVENTION You say "**all right**" when you are agreeing to something. ❑ *"I think you should go now." —"All right."*

**all-time** ADJ You use **all-time** when you are comparing all the things of a particular type that there have ever been. For example, if you say that something is the **all-time** best, you mean that it is the best thing of its type that there has ever been. ❑ *It's one of my all-time favorite movies.*

**al|lude** /əlu̱d/ (**alludes, alluding, alluded**) V-I If you **allude to** something, you mention it in an indirect way. [FORMAL] ❑ *He alluded to the problem.* [from Latin]

**al|lure** /əlʊ̱ər/ N-UNCOUNT The **allure** of something or someone is the pleasing or exciting quality that they have. ❑ *…the allure of shopping.* [from Old French]

**al|lu|sion** /əlu̱ʒᵊn/ (**allusions**) N-VAR An **allusion** is an indirect reference to someone or something. ❑ *She made an allusion to the events in Los Angeles.* [from Late Latin]

**al|lu|vial cone** also **alluvial cone** /əlu̱viəl fæn/ (**alluvial fans**) N-COUNT An **alluvial fan** is material such as sand and gravel, shaped like a fan, that is deposited on the land by a fast-flowing river. [TECHNICAL]

**al|lu|vium** /əlu̱viəm/ N-UNCOUNT **Alluvium** is soil or rock that has been deposited by a river. [TECHNICAL] [from Latin]

**ally** (**allies, allying, allied**)

> The noun is pronounced /æ̱laɪ/. The verb is pronounced /əla̱ɪ/.

■ N-COUNT A country's **ally** is another country that has an agreement to support it, especially in war. ❑ *…the Western allies.* ■ N-COUNT If you describe someone as your **ally**, you mean that they help and support you, especially when other people are opposing you. ❑ *He is a close ally of the president.* ■ V-T If you **ally yourself with** someone or something, you give your support to them. ❑ *He allied himself with his father-in-law.* [from Old French] ■ → see also **allied**

**al|mighty** /ɔlma̱ɪti/ N-PROPER The **Almighty** is another name for God. You can also refer to **Almighty God**. ❑ *He put his faith in the Almighty.* [from Old English]

**al|mond** /ɑ̱mənd, æ̱m-, æ̱lm-/ (**almonds**) N-VAR **Almonds** are pale oval nuts. ❑ *…sponge cake flavored with almonds.* [from Old French]

**Word Link**    **most ≈ superlative degree : al**most, **fore**most, **ut**most

**al|most** /ɔ̱lmoʊst/ ADV **Almost** means very nearly but not completely. ❑ *We have been married for almost three years.* ❑ *He caught Spanish flu, which almost killed him.*

**Usage**    **almost** and **most**
Be sure to use **almost**, not **most**, before such words as *all, any, anyone, every,* and *everyone*: *Almost all people like chocolate. Almost anyone can learn to ride a bike. Strangely, almost every student in the class is left-handed.*

**Thesaurus**    almost    Also look up :

ADV. about, most, practically, virtually

**Word Link**    **loft ≈ air : a**loft, **loft, loft**y

**aloft** /əlɔ̱ft/ ADV Something that is **aloft** is in the air or off the ground. [LITERARY] ❑ *He held aloft a sign reading "We will not forget."* [from Old Norse]

**alone** /əloʊ̱n/ ■ ADJ When you are **alone**, you are not with any other people. ❑ *She wanted to be alone.* ● **Alone** is also an adverb. ❑ *He lived alone in this house for almost five years.* ■ ADJ If one person is **alone with** another person, or if two or more people are **alone**, they are together, without anyone else present. ❑ *He wanted to be alone with her.* ❑ *We were alone together.* ■ ADJ If you say that you are **alone** or feel **alone**, you mean that nobody who is with you, or nobody at all, cares about you. ❑ *She had never felt so alone.* ■ ADV You say that one person or thing **alone** does something when you are emphasizing that only one person or thing is involved. ❑ *You alone should decide what is right for you.* ■ ADV When someone does something **alone**, they do it without help from other people. ❑ *Bringing up a child alone is very difficult.* [from Old English] ■ to **leave** someone or something **alone** → see **leave** ■ **let alone** → see **let**

**Thesaurus**    alone    Also look up :

ADJ. solitary; (*ant.*) crowded, together ■

**along** /əlɔ̱ŋ/

> In addition to the uses shown below, **along** is used in phrasal verbs such as "go along with," "play along," and "string along."

■ PREP If you move or look **along** something such as a road, you move or look toward one end of it. ❑ *Pedro walked along the street.* ■ PREP If something is situated **along** a road, river, aisle or hallway, it is situated in it or beside it. ❑ *There were traffic jams all along the roads.* ■ ADV When someone or something moves **along**, they keep moving in a particular direction. ❑ *He was talking as they walked along.* ■ ADV If you say that something is going **along** in a particular way, you mean that it is progressing in that way. ❑ *The discussions are moving along very slowly.* ■ ADV If you take someone or something **along** when you go somewhere, you take them with you. ❑ *Bring along your friends and family.* ■ ADV If someone or something is coming **along** or is sent **along**, they are coming or being sent to a particular place. ❑ *He's coming along to help me.* ■ PHRASE You use **along with** to mention someone or something else that is also involved in an action or situation. ❑ *She escaped from the fire along with her two children.* ■ PHRASE If something has been true or been present **all along**, it has been true or been present throughout a period of time. ❑ *I was right all along.* [from Old English]

**along|side** /əlɔ̱ŋsaɪd/ ■ PREP If one thing

is **alongside** another thing, the first thing is next to the second. ❑ *He crossed the street and walked alongside Central Park.* ● **Alongside** is also an adverb. ❑ *He waited several minutes for a car to pull up alongside.* **2** PREP If you work **alongside** other people, you all work together in the same place. ❑ *He worked alongside Frank and Mark and they became friends.*

**aloof** /əlúf/ ADJ If you say that someone is **aloof**, you think they are not very friendly and do not like to spend time with other people. ❑ *He seemed aloof and detached.*

**aloud** /əláʊd/ ADV When you speak, read, or laugh **aloud**, you speak or laugh so that other people can hear you. ❑ *When we were children, our father read aloud to us.*

**al|pha|bet** /ǽlfəbɛt, -bɪt/ (**alphabets**) N-COUNT An **alphabet** is a set of letters usually presented in a fixed order which is used for writing the words of a language. ❑ *The modern Russian alphabet has 31 letters.* [from Late Latin]

**al|pha|beti|cal** /ǽlfəbɛtɪkᵊl/ ADJ **Alphabetical** means arranged according to the normal order of the letters in the alphabet. ❑ *The books are arranged in alphabetical order.* [from Late Latin]

**al|pha|bet|ic prin|ci|ple** N-SING The **alphabetic principle** is the idea that each of the letters of an alphabet represents a particular sound in the language.

**al|pha par|ti|cle** /ǽlfəpɑrtɪkᵊl/ (**alpha particles**) N-COUNT **Alpha particles** are subatomic particles that are emitted by radioactive substances such as uranium and radium.

**al|pine** /ǽlpaɪn/ ADJ **Alpine** means existing in or relating to mountains. ❑ *...grassy, alpine meadows.* [from French]

**al|ready** /ɔlrɛdi/ **1** ADV You use **already** to show that something has happened, or that something had happened before the moment you are referring to. Some speakers use **already** with the simple past tense of the verb instead of a perfect tense. ❑ *They've spent nearly a billion dollars on it already.* ❑ *She says she already told the neighbors not to come over for a couple of days.* **2** ADV You use **already** to show that a situation exists at this present moment or that it exists at an earlier time than expected. You use **already** after the verb "be" or an auxiliary verb, or before a verb if there is no auxiliary. When you want to add emphasis, you can put **already** at the beginning of a sentence. ❑ *He was already rich.* ❑ *Already, she is thinking ahead.* [from Middle English]

<table>
<tr><td>**Usage**</td><td>**already** and **all ready**</td></tr>
</table>

It's easy to confuse *already* and *all ready*. *Already* means "before now" : *Have you finished eating already? Akiko had already heard the good news.* *All ready* means "completely prepared" : *Jacob is all ready to leave, but Michelle still has to get dressed.*

**also** /ɔlsoʊ/ **1** ADV You can use **also** to give more information about a person or thing. ❑ *The book also includes an index of all U.S. presidents.* ❑ *We've got a big table and also some stools and benches.* **2** ADV You can use **also** to indicate that something you have just said about one person or thing is true of another person or thing. ❑ *I was surprised but also thankful that people remembered us.* [from Old English]

<table>
<tr><td>**Thesaurus**</td><td>also</td><td>Also look up :</td></tr>
<tr><td>ADV.</td><td colspan="2">additionally, furthermore, plus, still **1**</td></tr>
<tr><td>CONJ.</td><td colspan="2">and, likewise, too **2**</td></tr>
</table>

<table>
<tr><td>**Word Link**</td><td>alt ≈ high : altar, altitude, alto</td></tr>
</table>

**al|tar** /ɔltər/ (**altars**) N-COUNT An **altar** is a holy table in a church or temple. ❑ *...the high altar of the cathedral.* [from Old English]

**al|ter** /ɔltər/ (**alters, altering, altered**) V-T/V-I If something **alters** or if you **alter** it, it changes. ❑ *World War II altered American life in many ways.* ● **al|tera|tion** /ɔltəreɪʃᵊn/ (**alterations**) N-VAR ❑ *...clothing alterations.* [from Old French]

**al|ter|nate** (**alternates, alternating, alternated**)

The verb is pronounced /ɔltərneɪt/. The adjective and noun are pronounced /ɔltɜrnɪt/.

**1** V-RECIP When you **alternate** two things, you keep using one then the other. When one thing **alternates with** another, the first regularly occurs after the other. ❑ *Rain alternated with wet snow.* ❑ *Starting with the onions, alternate meat and onions until they are all used.* **2** ADJ **Alternate** actions, events, or processes regularly occur after each other. ❑ *...alternate bands of color.* ● **al|ter|nate|ly** ADV ❑ *He lived alternately in New York and Seattle.* **3** ADJ If something happens on **alternate** days, it happens on one day, then happens on every second day after that. In the same way, something can happen in **alternate** weeks, years, or other periods of time. ❑ *Jim went skiing in alternate years.* **4** ADJ You use **alternate** to describe a plan, idea, or system which is different from the one already in operation and can be used instead of it. ❑ *His group was forced to turn back and take an alternate route.* **5** N-COUNT An **alternate** is a person or thing that replaces another, and can act or be used instead of them. ❑ *...a jury of twelve jurors and two alternates.* [from Latin] **6** → see also **alternative**

**al|ter|na|tive** /ɔltɜrnətɪv/ (**alternatives**) **1** N-COUNT If one thing is an **alternative** to another, the first can be found, used, or done instead of the second. ❑ *The new treatment may provide an alternative to painkillers.* **2** ADJ An **alternative** plan or offer is different from the one that you already have, and can be done or used instead. ❑ *Alternative methods of travel were available.* **3** ADJ **Alternative** is used to describe something that is different from the usual things of its kind, or the usual ways of doing something. ❑ *...alternative health care.* [from Latin]

**al|ter|na|tive|ly** /ɔltɜrnətɪvli/ ADV You use **alternatively** to introduce a suggestion or to mention something different from what has just been stated. ❑ *Hotels are not too expensive. Alternatively you could stay in an apartment.* [from Latin]

<table>
<tr><td>**Usage**</td><td>**alternatively** and **alternately**</td></tr>
</table>

*Alternatively* and *alternately* are often confused. *Alternatively* is used to talk about a choice between different things: *Sheila might go to the beach tomorrow; alternatively, she could go to the museum.* *Alternately* is used to talk about things that regularly occur after each other: *The traffic light was alternately green, yellow, and red. The days have been alternately sunny and rainy.*

A

**al|though** /ɔlðoʊ/ ■ CONJ You use **although** to introduce a statement that contrasts with something else that you are saying. ❑ *Their system worked, although no one knew how.* ❑ *Although I was only six, I can remember seeing it on TV.* ■ CONJ You use **although** to introduce clauses that modify what is being said or give further information. ❑ *They all play basketball, although on different teams.* [from Middle English]

| **Thesaurus** | *although* | Also look up : |
|---|---|---|
| CONJ. | despite, though, while ■ ■ | |

| **Word Link** | *alt* ≈ *high : altar, altitude, alto* |
|---|---|

**al|ti|tude** /æltɪtud/ (**altitudes**) N-VAR If something is at a particular **altitude**, it is at that height above sea level. ❑ *The aircraft reached an altitude of about 39,000 feet.* [from Latin]

**alto** /æltoʊ/ (**altos**) ■ N-COUNT An **alto** is a woman who has a low singing voice. ■ N-COUNT An **alto** or a **male alto** is a man who has the highest male singing voice. [from Italian]

**al|to|geth|er** /ɔltəgɛðər/ ■ ADV You use **altogether** to emphasize that something has stopped, been done, or finished completely. ❑ *Babies should stay out of the sun altogether.* ■ ADV You use **altogether** in front of an adjective or adverb to emphasize a quality that someone or something has. ❑ *That's an altogether different story.* ■ ADV If several amounts add up to a particular amount **altogether**, that amount is their total. ❑ *There were eleven of us altogether.*

| **Usage** | **altogether** and **all together** |
|---|---|

*Altogether* and *all together* are easily confused. *Altogether* means "in all" : *Altogether, I saw four movies at the film festival last week. All together* means "together in a group" : *It was the first time we were all together in four years and it meant a lot to me.*

**al|to|stra|tus** /æltoʊstreɪtəs, -stræt-/ (**altostrati**) N-VAR **Altostratus** is a type of thick gray cloud that forms at intermediate altitudes. [TECHNICAL]

**altricial** /æltrɪʃəl/ ADJ An **altricial** chick is a young bird that is weak and blind when it is born and is dependent on its parents for food and care. [TECHNICAL] [from New Latin]

**al|tru|ism** /æltruɪzəm/ N-UNCOUNT **Altruism** is unselfish concern for other people's happiness and welfare. ❑ *Volunteers act out of altruism.* ● **al|tru|is|tic** /æltruɪstɪk/ ADJ ❑ *The company was not being entirely altruistic.* [from French]

**alum** /əlʌm/ (**alums**) N-COUNT An **alum** is the same as an **alumnus**. [INFORMAL] ❑ *...a University of Chicago alum.* [from Old French]

**alu|mi|num** /əluminəm/ N-UNCOUNT **Aluminum** is a lightweight metal used, for example, for making cooking equipment and aircraft parts. ❑ *...aluminum cans.* [from Latin]

**alum|nus** /əlʌmnəs/ (**alumni** /əlʌmnaɪ/) N-COUNT The **alumni** of a school, college, or university are the people who used to be students there. [from Latin]

**al|veo|lus** /ælvɪələs/ (**alveoli**) N-COUNT **Alveoli** are hollow structures in the lungs of mammals, which carry oxygen to the bloodstream. [TECHNICAL] [from Latin]

**al|ways** /ɔlweɪz/ ■ ADV If you **always** do something, you do it whenever a particular situation occurs. If you **always** did something, you did it whenever a particular situation occurred. ❑ *She's always late for everything.* ❑ *Always lock your door.* ■ ADV If you **always** do particular thing, you do it all the time, continuously. ❑ *They always talked sports together.* ■ ADV You use **always** in expressions such as **can always** or **could always** when you are making suggestions or suggesting an alternative approach or method. ❑ *If you don't know, you can always ask me.* [from Old English]

| **Thesaurus** | *always* | Also look up : |
|---|---|---|
| ADV. | consistently, constantly ■ ■ continuously, endlessly, repeatedly; (ant.) never, rarely ■ ■ | |

**am** /əm, STRONG æm/ **Am** is the first person singular of the present tense of **be**. **Am** is often shortened to **'m** in spoken English. The negative forms are "I am not" and "I'm not." In questions and tags in spoken English, these are usually changed to "aren't I." [from Old English]

**a.m.** /eɪ ɛm/ **a.m.** after a number indicates that the number refers to a particular time between midnight and noon. ❑ *The program starts at 9 a.m.* [from Latin]

**amal|gam|ate** /əmælgəmeɪt/ (**amalgamates, amalgamating, amalgamated**) V-RECIP When two or more organizations **amalgamate** or **are amalgamated**, they become one large organization. ❑ *The two firms have amalgamated.* ● **amal|gama|tion** /əmælgəmeɪʃᵊn/ (**amalgamations**) N-VAR ❑ *Athletics South Africa was formed by an amalgamation of two organizations.* [from Medieval Latin]

**amass** /əmæs/ (**amasses, amassing, amassed**) V-T If you **amass** something such as money or information, you gradually get a lot of it. ❑ *How had he amassed his fortune?* [from Old French]

| **Word Link** | *eur* ≈ *one who does : amateur, chauffeur, entrepreneur* |
|---|---|

**ama|teur** /æmətʃər, -tʃʊər/ (**amateurs**) N-COUNT An **amateur** is someone who does something as a hobby and not as a job. ❑ *Jerry is an amateur who dances because he likes it.* ❑ *...amateur runners.* [from French]

**amaze** /əmeɪz/ (**amazes, amazing, amazed**) V-T/V-I If something **amazes** you, it surprises you very much. ❑ *Colorado history.* ❑ *14-year-old Michelle Wie continued to amaze.* ● **amazed** ADJ ❑ *I was amazed at how difficult it was.* [from Old English]

| **Word Partnership** | Use *amaze* with : |
|---|---|
| V. | **continue to** amaze, **never cease to** amaze |
| N. | amaze **your friends** |

**amaze|ment** /əmeɪzmənt/ N-UNCOUNT **Amazement** is the feeling you have when something surprises you very much. ❑ *I looked at her in amazement.* [from Old English]

**amaz|ing** /əmeɪzɪŋ/ ADJ You say that something is **amazing** when it is very surprising and makes you feel pleasure, approval, or wonder. ❑ *It's amazing what we can remember if we try.* ● **amaz|ing|ly** ADV ❑ *She was an amazingly good cook.* [from Old English]

| **Thesaurus** | *amazing* Also look up : |
| --- | --- |
| ADJ. | astonishing, astounding, extraordinary, incredible, stunning, wonderful |

**am|bas|sa|dor** /æmbæsədər/ (**ambassadors**) N-COUNT An **ambassador** is an important official who lives in a foreign country and represents his or her own country's interests there. ❑ *...the ambassador to Poland.* [from Old French]

**am|ber** /æmbər/ **1** N-UNCOUNT **Amber** is a hard yellowish-brown substance used for making jewelry. ❑ *...an amber necklace.* **2** COLOR **Amber** is used to describe things that are yellowish-brown in color. ❑ *...a row of amber lights.* [from Medieval Latin]

**am|bi|ence** /æmbiəns/ also **ambiance** N-SING The **ambience** of a place is the character and atmosphere that it seems to have. [LITERARY] ❑ *The hotel has a relaxed ambience.* [from French]

**am|bi|gu|ity** /æmbɪgyuɪti/ (**ambiguities**) N-VAR If you say that there is **ambiguity** in something, you mean that it is unclear or confusing, or it can be understood in more than one way. ❑ *There is ambiguity about what this actually means.* [from Latin]

**am|bigu|ous** /æmbɪgyuəs/ ADJ If you describe something as **ambiguous**, you mean that it is unclear or confusing because it can be understood in more than one way. ❑ *This agreement is very ambiguous.* ● **am|bigu|ous|ly** ADV ❑ *...an ambiguously worded statement.* [from Latin]

**am|bi|tion** /æmbɪʃ°n/ (**ambitions**) **1** N-COUNT If you have an **ambition** to do or achieve something, you want very much to do it or achieve it. ❑ *His ambition is to sail around the world.* **2** N-UNCOUNT **Ambition** is the desire to be successful, rich, or powerful. ❑ *Even when I was young I never had any ambition.* [from Old French]

**am|bi|tious** /æmbɪʃəs/ **1** ADJ Someone who is **ambitious** has a strong desire to be successful, rich, or powerful. ❑ *Chris is very ambitious.* **2** ADJ An **ambitious** idea or plan is on a large scale and needs a lot of work to be carried out successfully. ❑ *He has ambitious plans for the firm.* [from Old French]

**am|biva|lent** /æmbɪvələnt/ ADJ If you are **ambivalent about** something, you are not sure exactly what you think about it. ❑ *Some women are ambivalent about having children.* [from German]

**am|ble** /æmb°l/ (**ambles, ambling, ambled**) V-I When you **amble**, you walk slowly and in a relaxed manner. ❑ *They ambled slowly back to the car.* [from Old French]

**am|bu|lance** /æmbyələns/ (**ambulances**) N-COUNT An **ambulance** is a vehicle for taking people to and from a hospital. [from French]

**am|bush** /æmbʊʃ/ (**ambushes, ambushing, ambushed**) **1** V-T If a group of people **ambush** their enemies, they attack them after hiding and waiting for them. ❑ *Gunmen ambushed and killed 10 soldiers.* **2** N-VAR An **ambush** is an attack on someone by people who have been hiding and waiting for them. ❑ *Three civilians were killed in an ambush.* [from Old French]

**amen** /ɑmɛn, eɪ-/ CONVENTION **Amen** is said by Christians at the end of a prayer. ❑ *In the name of the Father and of the Son and of the Holy Spirit, amen.* [from Late Latin]

**amend** /əmɛnd/ (**amends, amending, amended**) **1** V-T If you **amend** something that has been written such as a law, or something that is said, you change it in order to improve it or make it more accurate. ❑ *The governor tried to amend the law.* **2** PHRASE If you **make amends** when you have harmed someone, you show that you are sorry by doing something to please them. ❑ *He wanted to make amends for his mistakes.* [from Old French]

**amend|ment** /əmɛndmənt/ (**amendments**) N-VAR An **amendment** is a section that is added to a law or rule in order to change it. ❑ *...an amendment to the defense bill.* [from Old French]

**amen|ity** /əmɛnɪti/ (**amenities**) N-COUNT **Amenities** are things such as shopping centers or sports facilities that are provided for people's convenience, enjoyment, or comfort. ❑ *Amenities include a heated swimming pool.* [from Latin] → see **hotel**

**Ameri|can** /əmɛrɪkən/ (**Americans**) **1** ADJ **American** means belonging to or coming from the United States of America. ❑ *...the American ambassador at the United Nations.* ❑ *...American television and movies.* **2** → see also **Latin American** ● An **American** is someone who is American. ❑ *He's an American living in Canada.* [from Latin]

**Ameri|cas** /əmɛrɪkəz/ N-PLURAL People sometimes refer to North America, Central America, and South America collectively as **the Americas**. ❑ *...music of the Americas.* [from Latin]

**ami|able** /eɪmiəb°l/ ADJ Someone who is **amiable** is friendly and pleasant to be with. [WRITTEN] ❑ *She was surprised at how amiable and polite he was.* ● **ami|ab|ly** ADV ❑ *We chatted amiably about old friends.* [from Old French]

**ami|cable** /æmɪkəb°l/ ADJ When people have an **amicable** relationship, they are pleasant to each other and solve their problems without quarreling. ❑ *The meeting ended on amicable terms.* ● **ami|cably** /æmɪkəbli/ ADV ❑ *He and his partner separated amicably earlier this year.* [from Late Latin]

**Amish** /ɑmɪʃ/ **1** N-PLURAL **The Amish** are members of a Protestant group who have a strict and simple way of life. ❑ *Many Amish are moving to other regions.* **2** ADJ **Amish** means relating to the Amish people or their religion. ❑ *...an Amish community.* [from German]

**amiss** /əmɪs/ ADJ If you say that something is **amiss**, you mean there is something wrong. ❑ *I had a feeling that something was amiss.*

**am|mo|nia** /əmoʊniə/ N-UNCOUNT **Ammonia** is a colorless liquid or gas with a strong, sharp smell. [from New Latin]

**am|mu|ni|tion** /æmyʊnɪʃ°n/ **1** N-UNCOUNT **Ammunition** is bullets and rockets that are made to be fired from weapons. ❑ *He had only seven rounds of ammunition.* **2** N-UNCOUNT You can describe information that you can use against someone in an argument or discussion as **ammunition**. ❑ *The data in the study might be used as ammunition.* [from French]

**am|nes|ty** /ˈæmnɪsti/ (**amnesties**) ◼ N-VAR An **amnesty** is an official pardon granted to a group of prisoners by the state. □ *...an amnesty for political prisoners.* ◼ N-COUNT An **amnesty** is a period of time during which people can admit to a crime or give up weapons without being punished. □ *The government announced an immediate amnesty.* [from Latin]

**am|ni|on** /ˈæmniɒn, -ən/ (**amnions**) N-COUNT The **amnion** is a thin covering that surrounds and protects an embryo in reptiles, birds, and mammals. [TECHNICAL] [from New Latin]

**amoe|ba** /əˈmiːbə/ (**amoebae** /əˈmiːbiː/ or **amoebas**) N-COUNT An **amoeba** is the smallest kind of living creature. Amoebae consist of only one cell, and are found in water or soil. [from New Latin]

**among** /əˈmʌŋ/ ◼ PREP Someone or something that is **among** a group of things or people is surrounded by them. □ *...teenagers sitting among adults.* □ *They walked among the crowds.* ◼ PREP If someone or something is **among** a group, they are a member of that group and share its characteristics. □ *A young girl was among the injured.* ◼ PREP If something happens **among** a group of people, it happens within the whole of that group or between the members of that group. □ *We discussed it among ourselves.* ◼ PREP If something such as a feeling, opinion, or situation exists **among** a group of people, most of them have it or experience it. □ *There is concern among parents about teaching standards.* ◼ PREP If something is shared **among** a number of people, some of it is given to all of them. □ *The money will be shared among family members.* [from Old English] ◼ → see also **between**

**amount** /əˈmaʊnt/ (**amounts, amounting, amounted**) ◼ N-VAR The **amount of** something is how much there is, or how much you have, need, or get. □ *He needs that amount of money to live.* □ *I still do a certain amount of work for them.* ◼ V-I If something **amounts to** a particular total, all the parts of it add up to that total. □ *The payment amounted to $42 billion.* [from Old French]
▸ **amount to** PHR-VERB If you say that one thing **amounts to** something else, you consider the first thing to be the same as the second thing. □ *The proposal amounts to less money for us.*

**Usage** **amount** and **number**
*Number* is used to talk about how many there are of something: *Madhu was surprised at the large number of students in the class. Amount* is used to talk about how much there is of something: *There is only a small amount of water in the glass.*

**amp** /æmp/ (**amps**) N-COUNT An **amp** is a unit which is used for measuring electric current □ *...a 3 amp fuse.*

**am|per|sand** /ˈæmpərsænd/ (**ampersands**) N-COUNT An **ampersand** is the sign &, used to represent the word "and."

**am|phib|ian** /æmˈfɪbiən/ (**amphibians**) N-COUNT **Amphibians** are animals such as frogs and toads that can live both on land and in water. [from Latin]
→ see Word Web: **amphibian**

**am|phi|thea|ter** /ˈæmfɪθiətər/ (**amphitheaters**) N-COUNT An **amphitheater** is a large open area surrounded by rows of seats sloping upward. Amphitheaters were built mainly in Greek and Roman times for the performance of plays.

**Word Link** *ampl ≈ large : ample, amplifier, amplify*

**am|ple** /ˈæmpəl/ (**ampler, amplest**) ADJ If there is an **ample** amount of something, there is enough of it and usually some extra. □ *There'll be ample opportunity to relax.* ● **am|ply** ADV □ *He has amply shown his ability.* [from Old French]

**am|pli|fi|er** /ˈæmplɪfaɪər/ (**amplifiers**) N-COUNT An **amplifier** is an electronic device in a radio or stereo system that causes sounds or signals to get louder. [from Old French]

**am|pli|fy** /ˈæmplɪfaɪ/ (**amplifies, amplifying, amplified**) V-T If you **amplify** a sound, you make it louder, usually by using electronic equipment. □ *The band amplified the music with microphones.* ● **am|pli|fi|ca|tion** /ˌæmplɪfɪˈkeɪʃən/ N-UNCOUNT □ *Her voice did not need any amplification.* [from Old French]

**am|pli|tude** /ˈæmplɪtud/ (**amplitudes**) N-VAR In physics, the **amplitude** of a sound wave or electrical signal is its strength. [TECHNICAL] [from Latin]
→ see **sound**

**am|pu|tate** /ˈæmpyuteɪt/ (**amputates, amputating, amputated**) V-T To **amputate** someone's arm or leg means to cut all or part of it off in an operation because it is diseased or badly damaged. □ *To save his life, doctors amputated his legs.* ● **am|pu|ta|tion** /ˌæmpyuˈteɪʃən/ (**amputations**) N-VAR □ *He lived only hours after the amputation.* [from Latin]

**amu** /ˈeɪ ɛm ˈyu/ (**amu**) **amu** is an abbreviation for **atomic mass unit.**

**amuse** /əˈmyuz/ (**amuses, amusing, amused**) ◼ V-T If something **amuses** you, it makes you want to laugh or smile. □ *The thought amused him.* ◼ V-T If you **amuse yourself**, you do something in order to pass the time and not become bored. □ *I wrote the story for children and to amuse myself.* [from Old French] ◼ → see also **amusing**

**amused** /əˈmyuzd/ ADJ If you are **amused by** something, it makes you want to laugh or smile. □ *Sara was amused by his jokes.* [from Old French]

**amuse|ment** /əˈmyuzmənt/ (**amusements**) ◼ N-UNCOUNT **Amusement** is the feeling that you have when you think that something is funny or amusing. □ *Tom watched them with amusement.* ◼ N-UNCOUNT **Amusement** is the pleasure that you get from being entertained or from doing something interesting. □ *I fell, much to everyone's amusement.* ◼ N-COUNT **Amusements** are ways of passing the time pleasantly. □ *People did not have many amusements to choose from.* ◼ N-PLURAL **Amusements** are games, rides, and other things that you can enjoy, for example, at an amusement park or resort. □ *...a place full of swings and amusements.* [from Old French]

**amuse|ment park** (**amusement parks**) N-COUNT An **amusement park** is a place where people pay to ride on various machines for pleasure or try to win prizes in games.

**amus|ing** /əˈmyuzɪŋ/ ADJ Someone or something that is **amusing** makes you laugh or

## Word Web — amphibian

**Amphibians** were the first four-legged animals to develop **lungs**. They were the dominant animal on Earth for nearly 75 million years. Amphibians lay eggs in water. The **larvae** use **gills** to breathe. During **metamorphosis**, the larvae begin to breathe with lungs and move on to land. **Frogs** follow this cycle, going from egg to **tadpole** to adult. Amphibians have **permeable** skin. They are extremely sensitive to changes in their **environment**. This makes them a bellwether **species**. Scientists use the disappearance of amphibians as an early warning sign of damage to the local **ecology**.

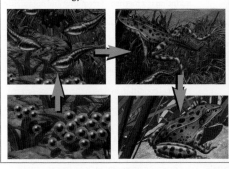

smile. ❑ *He had a great sense of humor and could be very amusing.* • **amus|ing|ly** ADV ❑ *The article was very amusingly written.* [from Old French]

**an** /ən, STRONG æn/ DET **An** is used instead of "a" in front of words that begin with vowel sounds. [from Old English]

**an|aero|bic** /ænər<u>ou</u>bɪk/ ADJ **Anaerobic** creatures or processes do not need oxygen in order to function or survive.

**anal** /<u>eɪ</u>nᵊl/ ADJ **Anal** means relating to the anus. ❑ ...*anal injuries.* [from New Latin]

**ana|log** /ænəlɔg/ also **analogue** ■ ADJ **Analog** technology involves measuring, storing, or recording information by using physical quantities such as voltage. ❑ ...*the change from analog to digital television.* ■ ADJ An **analog** watch or clock shows what it is measuring with a pointer on a dial rather than with a number display. Compare **digital**. [from Latin]

**analo|gous** /ənæləgəs/ ADJ **Analogous** colors are colors that are similar or related to one another such as yellow and green. [from Latin]

**anal|ogy** /ənælədʒi/ (**analogies**) N-COUNT If you make or draw an **analogy between** two things, you show that they are similar in some way. ❑ *The analogy between light and sound is clear.* • **analo|gous** /ənæləgəs/ ADJ [FORMAL] ❑ *Swimming has no event that is analogous to the 100 meters in track and field.* [from Greek]

## Word Partnership — Use *analogy* with :

| | |
|---|---|
| PREP. | analogy **between** |
| V. | **draw an** analogy, **make an** analogy |
| ADJ. | **false** analogy |

**analy|sis** /ənæləsɪs/ (**analyses** /ənæləsiz/) ■ N-VAR **Analysis** is the process of considering something carefully or using statistical methods in order to understand it or explain it. ❑ ...*a careful analysis of the situation.* ■ N-VAR **Analysis** is the scientific process of examining something in order to find out what it consists of. ❑ *They collect blood samples for analysis.* [from New Latin]

**ana|lyst** /ænəlɪst/ (**analysts**) ■ N-COUNT An **analyst** is a person whose job is to analyze a subject and give opinions about it. ❑ ...*a political analyst.* ■ N-COUNT An **analyst** is someone who examines and treats people who have emotional problems. ❑ *My analyst helped me to feel better about myself.*

**ana|lyti|cal** /ænəlɪtɪkᵊl/ also **analytic** ADJ An **analytical** way of doing something involves the use of logical reasoning. ❑ *You need analytical skills.* [from Late Latin]

**ana|lyze** /ænəlaɪz/ (**analyzes, analyzing, analyzed**) V-T If you **analyze** something, you consider it carefully in order to fully understand it or to find out what it consists of. ❑ *We need more time to analyze the decision.* ❑ *They haven't analyzed those samples yet.*

A

**ana|phase** /ˈænəfeɪz/ N-UNCOUNT **Anaphase** is a stage in the process of cell division that takes place within animals and plants. [TECHNICAL]

**an|ar|chist** /ˈænərkɪst/ (**anarchists**) N-COUNT An **anarchist** is a person who believes that the laws and power of governments should be replaced by people working together freely.. ❑ ...*an anarchist group.* ● **an|ar|chism** N-UNCOUNT ❑ *He saw anarchism as the answer to social problems.* [from Medieval Latin]

**an|ar|chy** /ˈænərki/ N-UNCOUNT If you describe a situation as **anarchy**, you disapprove of it because nobody seems to be paying any attention to rules or laws. ❑ *If we follow our own rules, it could lead to anarchy.* ● **an|ar|chic** /ænˈɑrkɪk/ ADJ ❑ ...*anarchic attitudes.* [from Medieval Latin]

**anato|my** /əˈnætəmi/ N-UNCOUNT **Anatomy** is the study of the structure of the bodies of people or animals. ❑ ...*a course in anatomy.* ● **ana|tomi|cal** /ˌænəˈtɒmɪkªl/ ADJ ❑ ...*anatomical differences between insects.* [from Latin]
→ see **medicine**

**an|ces|tor** /ˈænsɛstər/ (**ancestors**) N-COUNT Your **ancestors** are the people from whom you are descended. ❑ *Our daily lives are so different from those of our ancestors.* ● **an|ces|tral** /ænˈsɛstrəl/ ADJ ❑ ...*the family's ancestral home.* [from Old French]

**an|ces|try** /ˈænsɛstri/ (**ancestries**) N-COUNT Your **ancestry** is the fact that you are descended from certain people. ❑ *They've traced their ancestry back to the sixteenth century.* [from Old French]

**an|chor** /ˈæŋkər/ (**anchors, anchoring, anchored**) ■ N-COUNT An **anchor** is a heavy hooked object that is dropped from a boat into the water at the end of a chain in order to make the boat stay in one place. ■ V-T/V-I When a boat **anchors** or when you **anchor** it, its anchor is dropped into the water in order to make it stay in one place. ❑ *The boat anchored off the island.* ■ V-T If an object **is anchored** somewhere, it is fixed to something to prevent it moving from that place. ❑ *The roots anchor the plant in the earth.* ■ V-T The person who **anchors** a television or radio program, especially a news program. [from Old English]

anchor

**an|cient** /ˈeɪnʃənt/ ADJ **Ancient** means very old, or having existed for a long time. ❑ ...*ancient Jewish traditions.* [from Old French]
→ see **history**

**and** /ənd, STRONG ænd/ ■ CONJ You use **and** to link two or more words, groups, or clauses. ❑ *She and Simon have already gone.* ❑ *I'm 53 and I'm very happy.* ■ CONJ You use **and** to link two words or phrases that are the same in order to emphasize the degree of something, or to suggest that something continues or increases over a period of time. ❑ *Learning becomes more and more difficult as we get older.* ❑ *We talked for hours and hours.* ■ CONJ You use **and** to link two statements about events when one of the events follows the other. ❑ *I waved goodbye and went down the steps.* ■ CONJ You use **and** to link two statements when the second statement continues the point that has been made in the first statement. ❑ *You can only really tell the effects of the disease over a long time, and five years isn't long enough.* ❑ *"He used to be so handsome." —"And now?"* ■ CONJ You use **and** to indicate that two numbers are to be added together. ❑ *What does two and two make?* [from Old English]

**an|ec|do|tal** /ˌænɪkˈdoʊtªl/ ADJ **Anecdotal** evidence is based on individual accounts, rather than on reliable research or statistics, and so may not be valid. ❑ *Anecdotal evidence suggests that sales have fallen.* [from Medieval Latin]

**an|ec|do|tal script|ing** N-UNCOUNT **Anecdotal scripting** is a method of recording and organizing information about a text such as a play or novel by writing notes in the margins of the text. [TECHNICAL]

**an|ec|dote** /ˈænɪkdoʊt/ (**anecdotes**) N-VAR An **anecdote** is a short, amusing account of something that has happened. ❑ *Pete told them an anecdote about their mother.* [from Medieval Latin]

**anemia** /əˈnimiə/ N-UNCOUNT **Anemia** is a medical condition in which there are too few red cells in your blood, causing you to feel tired and look pale. ❑ *She suffered from anemia.* [from New Latin]

**anemic** /əˈnimɪk/ ADJ Someone who is **anemic** suffers from anemia. ❑ *Tests showed that she was anemic.* [from New Latin]

**an|emom|eter** /ˌænɪˈmɒmɪtər/ (**anemometers**) N-COUNT An **anemometer** is an instrument that is used to measure wind speeds.

**an|es|the|si|olo|gist** /ˌænɪsˌθiziˈɒlədʒɪst/ (**anesthesiologists**) N-COUNT An **anesthesiologist** is a doctor who specializes in giving anaesthetics to patients. [from New Latin]

**an|es|thet|ic** /ˌænɪsˈθɛtɪk/ (**anesthetics**) N-VAR **Anesthetic** is a substance that doctors use to stop you feeling pain during an operation, either in the whole of your body when you are unconscious, or in a part of your body when you are awake. ❑ *The operation was carried out under a general anesthetic.* [from New Latin]

**anes|the|tist** /əˈnɛsθətɪst/ (**anesthetists**) N-COUNT An **anesthetist** is a nurse or other person who gives an anesthetic to a patient. [from New Latin]

**anew** /əˈnu/ ADV If you do something **anew**, you do it again, often in a different way from before. [WRITTEN] ❑ *She's ready to start anew.* [from Old English]

**an|gel** /ˈeɪndʒªl/ (**angels**) ■ N-COUNT **Angels** are spiritual beings that some people believe are God's servants in heaven. ❑ *My daughter believes in angels.* ■ N-COUNT If you describe someone as an **angel**, you mean that they seem to be very kind and good. ❑ *Thank you so much, you're an angel.* [from Old English]

**an|gel|ic** /ænˈdʒɛlɪk/ ADJ You can describe

## Word Web anger

**Anger** can be a positive thing. Until we feel anger, we may not know how **upset** we are about a situation. Anger can give us a sense of our own power. Showing someone how **annoyed** we are with them may lead them to change. Anger also helps us to let go of **tension** in **frustrating** situations. This allows us to move on with our lives. But anger has its downside. It's hard to think clearly when we're **furious**. We may use bad judgment. **Rage** can also keep us from seeing the truth about ourselves. And when anger turns into **aggression**, people get hurt.

someone as **angelic** if they are, or seem to be, very good, kind, and gentle. ❑ *...an angelic face.* [from Old English]

**an|ger** /ˈæŋgər/ (**angers, angering, angered**) **1** N-UNCOUNT **Anger** is the strong emotion that you feel when you think that someone has behaved in an unfair, cruel, or unacceptable way. ❑ *He cried with anger.* **2** V-T If something **angers** you, it makes you feel angry. ❑ *The decision angered some Californians.* [from Old Norse]
→ see Word Web: **anger**
→ see **emotion**

**anger man|age|ment** N-UNCOUNT **Anger management** is a set of guidelines that are designed to help people control their anger. ❑ *...anger management courses.*

**an|gio|sperm** /ˈændʒiəspɜrm/ (**angiosperms**) N-COUNT An **angiosperm** is a plant that produces seeds within its flowers. [TECHNICAL]

**an|gle** /ˈæŋgᵊl/ (**angles**) **1** N-COUNT An **angle** is the difference in direction between two lines or surfaces. Angles are measured in degrees. ❑ *...a 30 degree angle.* **2** → see also **right angle** **3** N-COUNT An **angle** is the direction from which you look at something. ❑ *From this angle, he looks young.* **4** N-COUNT You can refer to a way of presenting something or thinking about it as a particular **angle**. ❑ *He was considering the idea from all angles.* **5** PHRASE If something is **at an angle**, it is leaning in a particular direction so that it is not straight, horizontal, or vertical. ❑ *An iron bar stuck out at an angle.* [from Old English]
→ see **mathematics**

90°

angle

**an|gling** /ˈæŋglɪŋ/ N-UNCOUNT **Angling** is the activity or sport of fishing with a fishing rod. [from French]

**an|glo|phone** /ˈæŋgləfoʊn/ (**anglophones**) **1** ADJ **Anglophone** communities are English-speaking communities in areas where more than one language is commonly spoken. ❑ *...anglophone Canadians.* **2** N-COUNT **Anglophones** are people whose native language is English or who speak English because they live in a country where English is one of the official languages.

**an|gry** /ˈæŋgri/ (**angrier, angriest**) ADJ When you are **angry**, you feel strong dislike or impatience about something. ❑ *Are you angry with me for some reason?* ❑ *I was angry about the rumors.* ❑ *An angry crowd gathered.* ● **an|gri|ly** /ˈæŋgrɪli/ ADV ❑ *"Do you know what this means?" she said angrily.* [from Middle English]

## Thesaurus angry Also look up :

| | |
|---|---|
| ADJ. | bitter, enraged, mad; (ant.) content, happy, pleased |

**angst** /ˈæŋst/ N-UNCOUNT **Angst** is a feeling of anxiety and worry. ❑ *Many kids suffer from angst.* [from German]

**an|guish** /ˈæŋgwɪʃ/ N-UNCOUNT **Anguish** is great mental suffering or physical pain. ❑ *Mark looked at him in anguish.* [from Old French]

**an|guished** /ˈæŋgwɪʃt/ ADJ **Anguished** means showing or feeling great mental suffering or physical pain. [WRITTEN] ❑ *She let out an anguished cry.* [from Old French]

**an|gu|lar** /ˈæŋgyʊlər/ ADJ **Angular** things have shapes that seem to contain a lot of straight lines and sharp points. ❑ *He had an angular face.* [from Latin]

## Word Link anim ≈ alive, mind : animal, animated, unanimous

**ani|mal** /ˈænɪmᵊl/ (**animals**) **1** N-COUNT An **animal** is a living creature such as a dog, lion, or rabbit, rather than a bird, fish, insect, or human being. ❑ *He was attacked by wild animals.* **2** N-COUNT Any living creature, including a human being, can be referred to as an **animal**. [from Latin]
→ see **earth, pet**

## Word Partnership Use *animal* with :

| | |
|---|---|
| N. | **cruelty to** animals, animal **hide**, animal **kingdom**, animal **noises, plant and** animal, animal **shelter** **1** |
| ADJ. | **domestic** animal, **stuffed** animal, **wild** animal **1** |

**Ani|ma|lia** /ˌænɪˈmeɪlyə, -liə/ N-PLURAL All the animals, birds, and insects in the world can be referred to together as **Animalia**. [TECHNICAL]

**ani|mate** /ˈænɪmət/ ADJ Something that is **animate** has life, in contrast to things like stones and machines which do not. ❑ *...animate beings.* [from Latin]

**ani|mat|ed** /ˈænɪmeɪtɪd/ **1** ADJ Someone who is **animated** or who is having an **animated**

## Word Web animation

TV **cartoons** are one of the most popular forms of **animation**. Each **episode,** or show, begins with a storyline. Once the **script** is final, cartoonists make up storyboards. The director uses them to plan how the **artists** will **illustrate** the episode. First the illustrators **draw** some **sketches**. Next they draw a few important **frames** for each **scene**. **Animators** turn these into moving storyboards. This form of the cartoon looks unfinished. The producers then look at the storyboard and suggest changes. After they make these changes, the artists fill in the missing frames. This makes the movements of the characters look smooth and natural.

conversation is lively and is showing their feelings. ❑ *Jessica was making animated conversation with Andrew.* ❷ ADJ An **animated** film is one in which puppets or drawings appear to move. ❑ *Disney's animated film "The Lion King."* [from Latin]

**ani|ma|tion** /ænɪmeɪʃⁿn/ N-UNCOUNT **Animation** is the process of making films in which drawings or puppets appear to move. ❑ *…computer animation.* [from Latin] → see Word Web: **animation**

**ani|mos|ity** /ænɪmɒsɪti/ (**animosities**) N-VAR **Animosity** is a strong feeling of dislike and anger. ❑ *The animosity between the two men grew.* [from Late Latin]

**an|kle** /æŋkⁿl/ (**ankles**) N-COUNT Your **ankle** is the joint where your foot joins your leg. ❑ *John twisted his ankle badly.* [from Old Norse] → see **body, foot**

**an|nex** (**annexes, annexing, annexed**)

The verb is pronounced /æneks/. The noun is pronounced /æneks/.

❶ V-T If a country **annexes** another country or an area of land, it seizes it and takes control of it. ❑ *Chicago annexed Pullman in 1889.* ● **an|nexa|tion** /ænekseɪʃⁿn/ (**annexations**) N-COUNT ❑ *…the annexation of Texas in 1845.* ❷ N-COUNT An **annex** is a building joined to or next to a larger main building. ❑ *There is a museum in an annex to the theater.* [from Medieval Latin]

**an|ni|hi|late** /ənaɪleɪt/ (**annihilates, annihilating, annihilated**) V-T To **annihilate** something means to destroy it completely. ❑ *The fire annihilated everything.* ● **an|ni|hi|la|tion** /ənaɪleɪʃⁿn/ N-UNCOUNT ❑ *They fought to save themselves from annihilation.* [from Late Latin]

### Word Link ann ≈ year : anniversary, annual, annum

**an|ni|ver|sa|ry** /ænɪvɜrsəri/ (**anniversaries**) N-COUNT An **anniversary** is a date that is remembered or celebrated because a special event happened on that date in a previous year. ❑ *…their fiftieth wedding anniversary.* [from Latin]

**an|no|ta|ted bib|li|og|ra|phy** (**annotated bibliographies**) N-COUNT An **annotated bibliography** is a list of books or articles on a particular subject that contains additional comments such as a summary of each book or article.

### Word Link nounce ≈ repoting : announce, denounce, pronounce

**an|nounce** /ənaʊns/ (**announces, announcing, announced**) ❶ V-T If you **announce** something, you tell people about it publicly or officially. ❑ *He will announce tonight that he is resigning from office.* ❑ *She was planning to announce her engagement.* ❷ V-T If you **announce** a piece of news or an intention, you say it loudly and clearly, so that everyone you are with can hear it. ❑ *Peter announced that he was not going to university.* [from Old French]

### Thesaurus announce Also look up :

V. advertise, declare, make public, reveal; (*ant.*) withhold ❶

**an|nounce|ment** /ənaʊnsmənt/ (**announcements**) ❶ N-COUNT An **announcement** is a public statement that gives information about something that has happened or that will happen. ❑ *She made her announcement after talks with the president.* ❷ N-SING The **announcement of** something that has happened is the act of telling people about it. ❑ *…the announcement of their engagement.* [from Old French]

### Word Partnership Use announcement with:

V. **make an** announcement ❶
ADJ. **formal** announcement, **official** announcement, **public** announcement, **surprise** announcement ❶

**an|nounc|er** /ənaʊnsər/ (**announcers**) N-COUNT An **announcer** is someone who introduces programs on radio or television. ❑ *The radio announcer said it was nine o'clock.* [from Old French]

**an|noy** /ənɔɪ/ (**annoys, annoying, annoyed**) ❶ V-T If someone or something **annoys** you, it makes you feel angry and impatient. ❑ *Rosie said she didn't mean to annoy anyone.* ❑ *It annoyed me that she believed him.* [from Old French] ❷ → see also **annoyed, annoying** → see **anger**

**an|noy|ance** /ənɔɪəns/ N-UNCOUNT **Annoyance** is the feeling that you get when someone makes you feel fairly angry or impatient. ❑ *To her annoyance he did not go away.* [from Old French]

**an|noyed** /ənɔɪd/ ❶ ADJ If you are **annoyed**, you are fairly angry about something. ❑ *She was*

*annoyed that Sasha was there.* [from Old French]
**2** → see also **annoy**

**an|noy|ing** /ənɔɪɪŋ/ **1** ADJ Someone or something that is **annoying** makes you feel fairly angry and impatient. □ *It's very annoying when this happens.* **2** → see also **annoy** [from Old French]

**an|nual** /ænyuəl/ **1** ADJ **Annual** events happen once every year. □ *They held their annual meeting May 20.* ● **an|nual|ly** ADV □ *The prize is awarded annually.* **2** ADJ **Annual** quantities or rates relate to a period of one year. □ *The company has annual sales of about $80 million.* ● **an|nual|ly** ADV □ *El Salvador produces 100,000 tons of copper annually.* [from Late Latin]

**an|nual ring** (**annual rings**) N-COUNT An **annual ring** is the layer of wood that forms during a single year in a plant such as a tree. Annual rings can be used to measure the age of plants.

**an|nu|lar eclipse** /ænyələr ɪklɪps/ (**annular eclipses**) N-COUNT An **annular eclipse** is a solar eclipse in which the edge of the sun can be seen around the moon. [TECHNICAL]

**an|num** /ænəm/ → see **per annum**

**anoma|ly** /ənɒməli/ (**anomalies**) N-COUNT If something is an **anomaly**, it is different from what is usual or expected. [FORMAL] □ *This song is an anomaly for the group.* [from Late Latin]

**anony|mous** /ənɒnɪməs/ ADJ If you remain **anonymous** when you do something, you do not let people know that you were the person who did it. □ *You can remain anonymous if you wish.* ● **ano|nym|ity** /ænɒnɪmɪti/ N-UNCOUNT □ *Both mother and daughter have requested anonymity.* ● **anony|mous|ly** ADV □ *The photographs were sent anonymously to the magazine's offices.* [from Late Latin]

**ano|rexia** /ænərɛksiə/ N-UNCOUNT **Anorexia** or **anorexia nervosa** is an illness in which a person has an overwhelming fear of becoming fat, and so refuses to eat enough and becomes thinner and thinner. [from New Latin]

**an|oth|er** /ənʌðər/ **1** DET **Another** thing or person means an additional thing or person of the same type as one that already exists. □ *We're going to have another baby.* ● **Another** is also a pronoun. □ *He said one thing and did another.* **2** DET You use **another** when you want to emphasize that an additional thing or person is different from one that already exists. □ *I think he's going to deal with this problem another day.* ● **Another** is also a pronoun. □ *I don't believe that one person can read another's mind.* **3** PRON You use **one another** to indicate that each member of a group does something to or for the other members. □ *...women learning to help themselves and one another.* **4** PHRASE If you talk about **one** thing **after another**, you are referring to a series of repeated or continuous events. □ *They faced one difficulty after another.*

**an|swer** /ænsər/ (**answers, answering, answered**) **1** V-T/V-I When you **answer** someone who has asked you something, you say something back to them. □ *Just answer the question.* □ *I asked him but he didn't answer.* □ *Williams answered that he didn't know.* **2** V-T/V-I If you **answer** a letter or advertisement, you write to the person who wrote it. □ *I wrote to him but he didn't answer.* **3** V-T/V-I When you **answer** the telephone, you pick it up when it rings. When you **answer** the door, you open it when you hear a knock or the bell. □ *Why didn't you answer when I called?* ● **Answer** is also a noun. □ *I knocked at the front door and there was no answer.* **4** V-T When you **answer** a question in a test or quiz, you write or say something in an attempt to give the facts that are asked for. □ *Always read an exam through at least once before you start to answer any questions.* **5** N-COUNT An **answer** is something that you say or write when you answer someone. □ *Without waiting for an answer, he turned and went in through the door.* □ *I wrote to him but I never had an answer back.* **6** N-COUNT An **answer to** a problem is a solution to it. □ *There are no easy answers to this problem.* **7** N-COUNT An **answer to** a question in a test or quiz is what someone writes or says in an attempt to give the facts that are asked for. □ *Simply marking an answer wrong will not help the student to get future questions correct.* [from Old English]
▸ **answer for** PHR-VERB If you have to **answer for** something bad or wrong you have done, you are punished for it. □ *He must be made to answer for his crime.*
→ see Picture Dictionary: **answer**

**an|swer|ing ma|chine** (**answering machines**) N-COUNT An **answering machine** is a device which records telephone messages.

**ant** /ænt/ (**ants**) **1** N-COUNT **Ants** are small crawling insects that live in large groups. [from Old English] **2** see also **aunt**
→ see **insect**

**an|tago|nism** /æntægənɪzəm/ (**antagonisms**) N-VAR **Antagonism** between people is hatred or dislike between them. □ *There is a lot of antagonism*

## Picture Dictionary     answer

**Check**

Check the correct answer.

"Small" is a/an ___.
- ✓ noun
- ___ adjective
- ___ verb

**Choose**

Choose the correct answer.

_b_ Q: Is he a waiter?
A: Yes, he ___.
- a. am
- b. is
- c. are

**Circle**

Circle the best answer.

She isn't tall. She's
( thin /(short)/ little ).

**Cross out**

Cross out the word
that doesn't belong.

chicken
dog
t~~able~~
cow

**Match**

Match the words
that go together.

savings    dispenser
cash    guard
security    account

**Fill in the circle**

Fill in the oval.

Ann ___ with her family.
- ○ live
- ○ living
- ● lives

**Fill in the blank**

Fill in the blank.

Q: Have you met Bill?
A: Yes, I _have_ .

**Underline**

Underline the adjectives.

The <u>young</u> woman was talking
with a <u>tall</u> man.

**Unscramble**

Unscramble the words.

(been / you / where / have)
_Where have you been?_

---

between the two groups. [from Greek]

**an|tago|nist** /æntǽgənɪst/ (**antagonists**)
■ N-COUNT Your **antagonist** is your opponent
or enemy. ❑ _He expected his antagonist to lose._
■ N-COUNT In literature, a character's **antagonist**
is another person or a situation that makes it
harder for the character to achieve what they
want. [from Greek]

**an|tago|nize** /æntǽgənaɪz/ (**antagonizes,
antagonizing, antagonized**) V-T If you **antagonize**
someone, you make them feel angry or hostile
toward you. ❑ _He didn't want to antagonize her._ [from
Greek]

**ante|ced|ent** /æntɪsiːdᵊnt/ (**antecedents**)
N-COUNT In grammar, an **antecedent** is a word,
phrase, or clause to which a pronoun that occurs
later in the sentence refers. For example, in the
sentence "Mary tried but she failed," "Mary" is the
antecedent of "she." [from Latin]

**an|ten|na** /æntɛnə/ (**antennae**
/æntɛni/ or **antennas**)

**Antennas** is the usual plural form for meaning
■.

■ N-COUNT The **antennae** of something such as
an insect are the two long, thin parts attached
to its head that it uses to feel things with.
■ N-COUNT An **antenna** is a device that sends and
receives television or radio signals. [from Latin]
→ see **insect**

**an|them** /ǽnθəm/ (**anthems**) N-COUNT An
**anthem** is a song that is used to represent a
particular nation, society, or group and that is
sung on special occasions. ❑ _The band played the
national anthem._ [from Old English]

**an|ther** /ǽnθər/ (**anthers**) N-COUNT The **anther**

is the male part of a flower, which produces
pollen. [TECHNICAL] [from New Latin]

**an|thol|ogy** /ænθɒlədʒi/ (**anthologies**)
N-COUNT An **anthology** is a collection of writings
by different writers published together in one
book. ❑ _...an anthology of poetry._ [from Medieval
Latin]

**Word Link**    _logy, ology ≈ study of : anthropology,
biology, geology_

**an|thro|pol|ogy** /ænθrəpɒlədʒi/ N-UNCOUNT
**Anthropology** is the scientific study of people,
society, and culture. ● **an|thro|polo|gist**
(**anthropologists**) N-COUNT ❑ _...an anthropologist
who worked in the South Pacific._ [from Greek]
→ see **evolution**

**Word Link**    _anti ≈ against : antibiotic, antibody,
antidote_

**anti|bi|ot|ic** /æntibaɪɒtɪk, æntaɪ-/ (**antibiotics**)
N-COUNT **Antibiotics** are medical drugs used to
kill bacteria and treat infections. ❑ _Your doctor may
prescribe antibiotics._ [from Greek]
→ see **medicine**

**anti|body** /ǽntɪbɒdi, æntaɪ-/ (**antibodies**)
N-COUNT **Antibodies** are substances that your
body produces in order to fight diseases. ❑ _Your
body produces antibodies to fight disease._ [from Old
English]

**an|tici|pate** /æntɪsɪpeɪt/ (**anticipates,
anticipating, anticipated**) ■ V-T If you **anticipate**
an event, you realize in advance that it may
happen and you are prepared for it. ❑ _We couldn't
have anticipated the result of our campaign._ ❑ _It is
anticipated that 192 jobs will be lost._ ■ V-T If you
**anticipate** a question, request, or need, you do

a

what is necessary or required before the question, request, or need occurs. ❏ *Jeff anticipated my next question.* [from Latin]

**an|tici|pa|tion** /æntɪsɪpeɪʃ°n/ **1** N-UNCOUNT **Anticipation** is a feeling of excitement about something pleasant or exciting that you know is going to happen. ❏ *There's been an atmosphere of anticipation around here for a few days now.* **2** PHRASE If something is done **in anticipation of** an event, it is done because people believe that event is going to happen. ❏ *Some schools were closed in anticipation of the weather getting worse.* [from Latin]

**anti|cline** /æntɪklaɪn/ (**anticlines**) N-COUNT An **anticline** is a rock formation in which layers of rock are folded so that they resemble an arch. [TECHNICAL]

**an|tics** /æntɪks/ N-PLURAL **Antics** are funny, silly, or unusual ways of behaving. ❏ *She laughed at their antics.* [from Italian]

**anti|dote** /æntɪdoʊt/ (**antidotes**) N-COUNT An **antidote** is a chemical substance that stops or controls the effect of a poison. ❏ *He noticed their sickness and prepared an antidote.* [from Latin]

**an|ti|per|spi|rant** /æntipɜrspɪrənt, æntaɪ-/ (**antiperspirants**) N-VAR **Antiperspirant** is a substance that you can use on your body, especially under your arms, to prevent or reduce sweating. ADJ ❏ *...an antiperspirant for sensitive skins.*

| Word Link | *antiq ≈ old* : *antiquated, antique, antiquity* |

**anti|quat|ed** /æntɪkweɪtɪd/ ADJ If you describe something as **antiquated**, you are criticizing it because it is very old or old-fashioned. ❏ *Many factories are so antiquated they are not worth saving.* [from Latin]

**an|tique** /æntik/ (**antiques**) N-COUNT An **antique** is an old object such as a piece of china or furniture that is valuable because of its beauty or rarity. ❏ *...a genuine antique.* [from Latin]

**an|tiq|uity** /æntɪkwɪti/ (**antiquities**) **1** N-UNCOUNT **Antiquity** is the distant past, especially the time of the ancient Egyptians, Greeks, and Romans. ❏ *He is a historian of classical antiquity.* **2** N-COUNT **Antiquities** are things such as buildings, statues, or coins that were made in ancient times and have survived to the present day. ❏ *...collectors of Roman antiquities.* [from Latin]

**anti|sep|tic** /æntəsɛptɪk/ (**antiseptics**) N-VAR **Antiseptic** is a substance that kills germs and harmful bacteria. ❏ *She washed the cut with antiseptic.*
→ see **medicine**

**anti|so|cial** /æntisoʊʃ°l, æntaɪ-/ ADJ Someone who is **antisocial** is unwilling to meet and be friendly with other people. ❏ *...antisocial behavior.* [from Latin]

**anti-virus** also **antivirus** ADJ **Anti-virus** software is software that protects a computer against viruses.

**anus** /eɪnəs/ (**anuses**) N-COUNT A person's **anus** is the hole from which feces leaves their body. [MEDICAL] [from Latin]

**anxi|ety** /æŋzaɪɪti/ (**anxieties**) N-VAR **Anxiety** is a feeling of nervousness or worry. ❏ *Her voice was full of anxiety.* [from Latin]

**anx|ious** /æŋkʃəs/ **1** ADJ If you are **anxious to** do something or **anxious that** something should happen, you very much want to do it or very much want it to happen. ❏ *He is anxious to go back to work.* ❏ *I'm anxious that we succeed.* **2** ADJ If you are **anxious**, you are nervous or worried about something. ❏ *She became very anxious.* ● **anx|ious|ly** ADV ❏ *They are waiting anxiously for news.* [from Latin]

**any** /ɛni/ **1** DET You use **any** in statements with negative meaning to indicate that no thing or person of a particular type exists, is present, or is involved in a situation. ❏ *I'm not making any promises.* ❏ *We are doing this all without any support.* ❏ *It is too early to say what effect, if any, there will be.* ● **Any** is also a quantifier. ❏ *You don't know any of my friends.* ● **Any** is also a pronoun. ❏ *The children needed new clothes and Kim couldn't afford any.* **2** DET You use **any** in questions and conditional clauses to ask whether there is some of a particular thing or some of a particular group of people, or to suggest that there might be. ❏ *Do you speak any foreign languages?* ● **Any** is also a quantifier. ❏ *Do you use any of the following?* ● **Any** is also a pronoun. ❏ *I'll be happy to answer questions if there are any.* **3** DET You use **any** in positive statements when you are referring to someone or something of a particular kind that might exist, occur, or be involved in a situation, when their exact identity or nature is not important. ❏ *He admired any person who did their job well.* ● **Any** is also a quantifier. ❏ *I'm prepared to take any advice.* ● **Any** is also a pronoun. ❏ *We looked at several programs but didn't find any that were good enough.* **4** ADV You can also use **any** to emphasize a comparative adjective or adverb in a negative statement. ❏ *I can't see things getting any easier.* **5** PHRASE If something does not happen or is not true **any longer**, it has stopped happening or is no longer true. ❏ *I couldn't keep the tears hidden any longer.* [from Old English] **6 any old** → see **old** **7 at any rate** → see **rate**

**any|body** /ɛnibɒdi, -bʌdi/ PRON **Anybody** means the same as **anyone**.

**any|how** /ɛnihaʊ/ ADV **Anyhow** means the same as **anyway**.

**any|more** /ɛnimɔr/ also **any more** ADV If something does not happen or is not true **anymore**, it has stopped happening or is no longer true. ❏ *I don't ride my motorbike much anymore.* ❏ *I couldn't trust him anymore.*

| Usage | **anymore** and **any more** |

**Anymore** and **any more** are different. *Anymore* means "from now on" : *Jacqueline doesn't wear glasses anymore, so she won't have to worry anymore about losing them. Any more* means "an additional quantity of something": *Please don't give me any more cookies – I don't have any more room in my stomach!*

**any|one** /ɛniwʌn/

| The form **anybody** is also used. |

**1** PRON You use **anyone** or **anybody** in negative statements to indicate in a general way that nobody is present or involved in an action. ❏ *I won't tell anyone I saw you here.* ❏ *You needn't talk to anyone if you don't want to.* **2** PRON You use **anyone** or **anybody** in questions and conditional clauses to ask or talk about whether someone is present or doing something. ❑ *Why would anyone want that job?* ❑ *If anybody wants me, I'll be in my office.* **3** PRON You use **anyone** or **anybody** before words that indicate the kind of person you are talking about. ❑ *It's not a job for anyone who is slow with numbers.* **4** PRON You use **anyone** or **anybody** to refer to a person when you are emphasizing that it could be any person out of a very large number of people. ❑ *Anyone could do what I'm doing.*

> ### Usage  **anyone** and **any one**
> *Anyone* and *any one* are different. *Anyone* can refer to an unspecified person: *Does anyone know the answer? Any one* refers to an unspecified individual person or thing in a group: *Any one of the players is capable of winning. All those desserts look good-please give me any one with strawberries on it.*

**any|place** /ɛnipleɪs/ ADV **Anyplace** means the same as **anywhere**. [INFORMAL] ❑ *She didn't have anyplace to go.*

**any|thing** /ɛniθɪŋ/ **1** PRON You use **anything** in negative statements to indicate in a general way that nothing is present or that an action or event does not or cannot happen. ❑ *We can't do anything.* ❑ *She couldn't see or hear anything at all.* **2** PRON You use **anything** in questions and conditional clauses to ask or talk about whether something is present or happening. ❑ *What happened, is anything wrong?* ❑ *Did you find anything?* **3** PRON You can use **anything** before words that indicate the kind of thing you are talking about. ❑ *More than anything else, he wanted to become a teacher.* ❑ *Anything that's cheap this year will be even cheaper next year.* **4** PRON You use **anything** to emphasize a possible thing, event, or situation, when you are saying that it could be any one of a very large number of things. ❑ *He is young and ready for anything.* **5** PRON You use **anything** in expressions such as **anything near**, **anything close to** and **anything like** to emphasize a statement that you are making. ❑ *This is the only way he can live anything near a normal life.*

**any|time** /ɛnitaɪm/ ADV You use **anytime** to mean a point in time that is not fixed or set. ❑ *The college admits students anytime during the year.* ❑ *He can leave anytime he wants.*

**any|way** /ɛniweɪ/

> The form **anyhow** is also used.

**1** ADV You use **anyway** or **anyhow** to indicate that a statement explains or supports a previous point. ❑ *I'm sure David told you. Anyway, everyone knows that he owes money.* **2** ADV You use **anyway** or **anyhow** to suggest that a statement is true or relevant in spite of other things that have been said. ❑ *I don't know why I went there, but anyway I did.* **3** ADV You use **anyway** or **anyhow** to correct or modify a statement. ❑ *Mary Ann doesn't want to have children. Not right now, anyway.* **4** ADV You use **anyway** or **anyhow** to change the topic or return to a previous topic. ❑ *I found Z in the last book with W, X, and Y. Which is understandable. Anyway, I took it back to my room.* [from Old English]

> ### Usage  **anyway** and **any way**
> Be sure to use *anyway* and *any way* correctly. *Anyway* can mean "in any situation, no matter what": *Its raining, but lets go for a walk anyway. Any way* means "by any method": *Its not far to Tom's house, so we can walk, drive, or ride our bikes – any way you want.*

**any|where** /ɛniwɛər/ **1** ADV You use **anywhere** in negative statements, questions and conditional clauses to refer to a place without saying exactly where you mean. ❑ *Did you try to get help from anywhere?* ❑ *I haven't got anywhere to live.* **2** ADV You use **anywhere** in positive statements to emphasize an expression that refers to a place or area. ❑ *He'll meet you anywhere you want.* **3** ADV When you do not want to be exact, you use **anywhere** to refer to a particular range of things. ❑ *His shoes cost anywhere from $200 up.*

> **apart**
> ❶ POSITIONS AND STATES
> ❷ INDICATING EXCEPTIONS AND FOCUSING

**❶ apart** /əpɑrt/

> In addition to the uses shown below, **apart** is used in phrasal verbs such as "grow apart" and "take apart."

**1** ADV When people or things are **apart**, they are some distance from each other. ❑ *He was standing a bit apart from the rest of us.* ❑ *Ray and his sister lived just 25 miles apart.* **2** ADV If two people are **apart**, they are no longer living together or spending time together. ❑ *It was the first time Jane and I had been apart for more than a few days.* **3** ADV If you take something **apart**, you separate it into the pieces that it is made of. If it comes or falls **apart**, its parts separate from each other. ❑ *When the clock stopped he took it apart, found what was wrong, and put it together again.* [from Old French]

> ### Word Partnership  Use *apart* with:
> ADV. **far** apart ❶ **1**
> N. **miles** apart ❶ **1**
> V. **take** apart ❶ **3**

**❷ apart** /əpɑrt/ **1** PHRASE **Apart from** means the same as **aside from**. **2** ADV You use **apart** when you are making an exception to a general statement. ❑ *The room was empty apart from one man sitting beside the fire.* [from Old French]

**apart|heid** /əpɑrthaɪt/ N-UNCOUNT **Apartheid** was a political system in South Africa in which people were divided into racial groups and kept apart by law. ❑ *...the struggle against apartheid.* [from Afrikaans]

**apart|ment** /əpɑrtmənt/ (**apartments**) N-COUNT An **apartment** is a separate set of rooms for living in, in a house or a building with other apartments. ❑ *Christina has her own apartment.* [from French]
→ see **city**

**apart|ment build|ing** (**apartment buildings**) also **apartment house** N-COUNT An **apartment building** or **apartment house** is a tall building which contains different apartments on different floors. ❑ *They live in a Manhattan apartment house.*

**apart|ment com|plex** (**apartment complexes**) N-COUNT An **apartment complex** is a group of buildings that contain apartments and are managed by the same company. ❑ *...a 10-story apartment complex.*

> **Word Link**    *path ≈ feeling : a*path*y, em*path*y,* sym*pathy*

**apa|thy** /ˈæpəθi/ N-UNCOUNT You can use **apathy** to talk about someone's state of mind if you are criticizing them because they do not seem to be interested in or enthusiastic about anything. ❑ *...political apathy.* ● **apa|thet|ic** /ˌæpəˈθɛtɪk/ ADJ ❑ *Even the most apathetic students are beginning to listen.* [from Latin]

**ape** /eɪp/ (**apes, aping, aped**) **1** N-COUNT **Apes** are chimpanzees, gorillas, and other animals in the same family. ❑ *...chimpanzees and other apes.* **2** V-T If you **ape** someone's speech or behavior, you imitate it. ❑ *People began to ape European customs.* [from Old English]
→ see **primate**

*ape*

**ap|er|ture** /ˈæpərtʃər/ (**apertures**) **1** N-COUNT An **aperture** is a narrow hole or gap. [FORMAL] ❑ *Through the aperture he could see daylight.* **2** N-COUNT In photography, the **aperture** of a camera is the size of the hole through which light passes to reach the image sensor. ❑ *Use a small aperture and position the camera carefully.* [from Late Latin]

**apex** /ˈeɪpɛks/ (**apexes**) **1** N-SING The apex of an organization or system is the highest and most important position in it. ❑ *At the apex of the party was its central committee.* **2** N-COUNT The apex of something is its pointed top or end. ❑ *...the apex of a pyramid.* [from Latin]

**aphe|li|on** /əˈfiliən, -liən, æfˈhil-/ (**aphelia**) N-SING The **aphelion** of a planet is the point in its orbit at which it is furthest from the sun. [TECHNICAL] [from New Latin]

**apiece** /əˈpis/ ADV If people have a particular number of things **apiece**, they have that number each. ❑ *Barrett and Allen had 16 points apiece.*

**apolo|get|ic** /əˌpɒləˈdʒɛtɪk/ ADJ If you are **apologetic**, you show or say that you are sorry for causing trouble for someone, for hurting them, or for disappointing them. ❑ *The man was apologetic for his actions.* ● **apolo|geti|cal|ly** /əˌpɒləˈdʒɛtɪkli/ ADV ❑ *"It's not very good," he said, almost apologetically.* [from Old French]

**apolo|gize** /əˈpɒlədʒaɪz/ (**apologizes, apologizing, apologized**) V-I When you **apologize to** someone, you say that you are sorry that you have hurt them or caused trouble for them. You can say "**I apologize**" as a formal or polite way of saying sorry. ❑ *I apologize for being late.* ❑ *He apologized to everyone.* [from Old French]

> **Word Link**    *log ≈ reason, speech : a*pology*,* dia*logue,* logic

**apol|ogy** /əˈpɒlədʒi/ (**apologies**) N-VAR An

**apology** is something that you say or write in order to tell someone that you are sorry that you have hurt them or caused trouble for them. ❑ *I didn't get an apology.* ❑ *We received a letter of apology.* [from Old French]

> **Word Partnership**    Use *apology* with :
>
> | | |
> |---|---|
> | V. | **demand an** apology, **make an** apology, **owe** *someone* **an** apology |
> | ADJ. | **formal/public** apology |
> | N. | **letter of** apology |

**apos|tro|phe** /əˈpɒstrəfi/ (**apostrophes**) N-COUNT An **apostrophe** is the mark ' when it is written to indicate that one or more letters have been left out of a word, as in "isn't" and "we'll." It is also added to nouns to form possessives, as in "Mike's car." [from Latin]
→ see **punctuation**

**ap|pall** also **ap|pal** /əˈpɔl/ (**appalls, appalling, appalled**) V-T If something **appalls** you, it shocks you because it seems so bad or unpleasant. ❑ *His rudeness appalled me.* ❑ *We are appalled by the news.* [from Old French]

**ap|pall|ing** /əˈpɔlɪŋ/ **1** ADJ Something that is **appalling** is so bad that it shocks you. ❑ *They have been living under the most appalling conditions.* ● **ap|pal|ling|ly** ADV ❑ *...an appallingly bad speech.* [from Old French] **2** → see also **appall**

**ap|pa|rat|us** /ˌæpəˈrætəs, -ˈreɪ-/ (**apparatuses**) N-VAR **Apparatus** is the equipment, such as tools and machines, which is used to do a particular job or activity. ❑ *The firemen wore breathing apparatus.* [from Latin]

**ap|par|ent** /əˈpærənt/ **1** ADJ An **apparent** situation, quality, or feeling seems to exist, although you cannot be certain that it does exist. ❑ *I was worried by our apparent lack of progress.* **2** ADJ If something is **apparent**, it is clear and obvious. ❑ *It's apparent that standards have improved.* [from Latin]

**ap|par|ent|ly** /əˈpærəntli/ ADV You use **apparently** to refer to something that seems to be true, although you are not sure whether it is or not. ❑ *Apparently the girls are not at all amused.* [from Latin]

**ap|par|ent mag|ni|tude** (**apparent magnitudes**) N-COUNT The **apparent magnitude** of a star or galaxy is a measure of how bright it appears to an observer on Earth.

**ap|peal** /əˈpil/ (**appeals, appealing, appealed**) **1** V-I If you **appeal to** someone **to** do something, you make a serious and urgent request to them. ❑ *Police appealed to the public for help.* ❑ *The country's prime minister appealed for calm.* **2** V-T If you **appeal** a decision **to** someone in authority, you formally ask them to change it. ❑ *We intend to appeal the verdict.* **3** V-I If something **appeals to** you, you find it attractive or interesting. ❑ *The idea appealed to him.* **4** N-COUNT An **appeal** is a serious and urgent request. ❑ *...an appeal for help.* **5** N-VAR An **appeal** is a formal request for a decision to be changed. ❑ *They took their appeal to the Supreme Court.* **6** N-UNCOUNT The **appeal** of something is a quality that people find attractive or interesting. ❑ *...tiny dolls with great appeal to young girls.* [from Old French]
→ see **trial**

## Word Partnership    Use *appeal* with :

| | |
|---|---|
| PREP. | appeal **to someone** 🔢 🔢 🔢 |
| | appeal **to a court**, appeal **for** |
| | **something** 🔢 |
| V. | **make an** appeal 🔢 🔢 |

**ap|peal|ing** /əpiːlɪŋ/ ADJ Someone or something that is **appealing** is pleasing and attractive. ❑ *I found his sense of humor very appealing.* [from Old French]

**ap|peals court** (**appeals courts**) N-COUNT An **appeals court** is the same as an **appellate court.**

**ap|peal to author|ity** (**appeals to authority**) N-VAR In logic, an **appeal to authority** is a type of argument in which someone tries to support their view by referring to an expert on the subject who shares their view.

**ap|peal to emo|tion** (**appeals to emotion**) N-VAR In logic, an **appeal to emotion** is a type of argument in which someone tries to support their view by using emotional language that is intended to arouse feelings such as excitement, anger or hatred.

**ap|peal to pa|thos** also **appeal to pity** (**appeals to pathos**) N-VAR In logic, an **appeal to pathos** is a type of argument in which someone tries to support their view by using language that is intended to arouse feelings of pity or mercy.

**ap|peal to rea|son** (**appeals to reason**) N-VAR In logic, an **appeal to reason** is a type of argument in which someone tries to support their view by showing that it is based on good reasoning.

**ap|pear** /əpɪər/ (**appears, appearing, appeared**) 🔢 V-LINK If you say that something **appears** to be the way you describe it, you are reporting what you believe or what you have been told, though you cannot be sure it is true. ❑ *The aircraft appears to have crashed.* 🔢 V-LINK If someone or something **appears to** have a particular quality or characteristic, they give the impression of having that quality or characteristic. ❑ *She appeared more confident than she felt.* ❑ *There appeared to be a problem with the baby's breathing..* 🔢 V-I When someone or something **appears**, it becomes possible to see them or obtain them. ❑ *A woman appeared at the far end of the street.* ❑ *...small white flowers which appear in early summer.* 🔢 V-I When someone **appears in** something such as a play, a show, or a television program, they take part in it. ❑ *Jill Bennett appeared in several of Osborne's plays.* 🔢 V-I When someone **appears before** a court of law or **before** an official committee, they go there in order to answer questions or to give information as a witness. ❑ *They will appear in federal court today.* [from Old French]

## Thesaurus    *appear*    Also look up :

| | |
|---|---|
| V. | seem 🔢 |
| | look like, resemble, seem 🔢 |
| | arrive, show up, turn up; *(ant.)* |
| | disappear, vanish 🔢 |

**ap|pear|ance** /əpɪərəns/ (**appearances**) 🔢 N-COUNT When someone makes an **appearance** at a public event or in a broadcast, they take part in it. ❑ *It was the president's second public appearance.* 🔢 N-SING Someone's or something's **appearance** is the way that they look. ❑ *She used to care a lot about her appearance.* 🔢 N-SING The **appearance of** someone or something in a place is the fact of their arriving or becoming visible there. ❑ *...the welcome appearance of Uncle John.* ❑ *Flowering plants were making their first appearance.* [from Old French]

## Word Partnership    Use *appearance* with :

| | |
|---|---|
| N. | **court** appearance 🔢 |
| ADJ. | **public** appearance, **sudden** |
| | appearance 🔢 |
| | **physical** appearance 🔢 |
| V. | **make an** appearance 🔢 |
| | **change your** appearance 🔢 |

**ap|pease** /əpiːz/ (**appeases, appeasing, appeased**) V-T If you try to **appease** someone, you try to stop them from being angry by giving them what they want, even though this is not the right thing to do. ❑ *The government tried to appease angry workers.* ● **ap|pease|ment** N-UNCOUNT ❑ *...an act of appeasement.* [from Old French]

**ap|pel|late court** /əpelɪt kɔrt/ (**appellate courts**) N-COUNT In the United States, an **appellate court** is a special court where people who have been convicted of a crime can appeal against their conviction. ❑ *An appellate court overturned his conviction.*

**ap|pen|dix** /əpendɪks/ (**appendixes**)

The plural form **appendices** /əpendɪsiːz/ is usually used for meaning 🔢.

🔢 N-COUNT Your **appendix** is a small closed tube inside your body that is attached to your digestive system. ❑ *...a burst appendix.* 🔢 N-COUNT An **appendix to** a book is extra information that is placed after the end of the main text. ❑ *...an appendix to the main document.* [from Latin]

**ap|pe|tite** /æpɪtaɪt/ (**appetites**) 🔢 N-VAR Your **appetite** is your desire to eat. ❑ *He has a healthy appetite.* 🔢 N-COUNT Someone's **appetite for** something is their strong desire for it. ❑ *...his appetite for success.* [from Old French]

**ap|pe|tiz|ing** /æpɪtaɪzɪŋ/ ADJ **Appetizing** food looks and smells good, so that you want to eat it. ❑ *...the appetizing smell of freshly baked bread.* [from Old French]

**ap|plaud** /əplɔd/ (**applauds, applauding, applauded**) 🔢 V-T/V-I When a group of people **applaud**, they clap their hands in order to show approval, for example, when they have enjoyed a play or concert. ❑ *The audience laughed and applauded.* ❑ *We applauded him for his bravery.* 🔢 V-T When an attitude or action **is applauded**, people praise it. ❑ *He should be applauded for his courage.* ❑ *We applaud her determination.* [from Latin]

**ap|plause** /əplɔz/ N-UNCOUNT **Applause** is the noise made by a group of people clapping their hands to show approval. ❑ *...a round of applause.* [from Latin]

**ap|ple** /æpᵊl/ (**apples**) N-VAR An **apple** is a round fruit with smooth skin and firm white flesh. ❑ *I want an apple.* ❑ *...the finest apples in the world.* [from Old English]
→ see **fruit**

**ap|pli|ance** /əplaɪəns/ (**appliances**) N-COUNT An **appliance** is a device or machine in your home that you use to do a job such as cleaning or cooking. [FORMAL] ❑ *This shop sells all sorts of appliances — refrigerators, heaters, stoves and washing machines.* [from Old French]

**ap|pli|ca|ble** /ˈæplɪkəbəl, əˈplɪkə-/ ADJ Something that is **applicable to** a particular situation is relevant to it or can be applied to it. ❑ *Write down your name and, where applicable, your present occupation.* [from Old French]

**ap|pli|cant** /ˈæplɪkənt/ (**applicants**) N-COUNT An **applicant for** something such as a job or a college is someone who makes a formal written request to be considered for it. ❑ *We've had many applicants for these positions.* [from Latin]

**ap|pli|ca|tion** /ˌæplɪˈkeɪʃən/ (**applications**) ◼ N-COUNT An **application for** something such as a job or membership of an organization is a formal written request for it. ❑ *We are unable to accept your application.* ◼ N-COUNT In computing, an **application** is a piece of software designed to carry out a particular task. ❑ *...a software application that is accessed via the Internet.* ◼ N-VAR The **application of** a rule or piece of knowledge is the use of it in a particular situation. ❑ *...the practical application of the theory.* [from Old French]

**Word Partnership** Use *application* with :

| | |
|---|---|
| v. | **accept/reject an** application, **file/submit an** application, **fill out an** application ◼ |
| N. | **college** application, application **form**, **grant/loan** application, **job** application, **membership** application ◼ application **software** ◼ |

**ap|plied** /əˈplaɪd/ ADJ An **applied** subject of study has a practical use, rather than being concerned only with theory. ❑ *...Applied Physics.* [from Old French] → see **science**

**ap|ply** /əˈplaɪ/ (**applies, applying, applied**) ◼ V-T/V-I If you **apply for** something such as a job or membership of an organization, you write a letter or fill out a form in order to ask formally for it. ❑ *I am applying for jobs.* ❑ *They applied to join the organization.* ◼ V-T If you **apply yourself to** something or **apply** your mind **to** something, you concentrate hard on it. ❑ *He has applied himself to this task with great energy.* ◼ V-I If something such as a rule or a remark **applies to** a person or a situation, it is relevant to them. ❑ *The rule does not apply to them.* ◼ V-T If you **apply** something such as a rule, system, or skill, you use it in a situation or activity. ❑ *We are applying technology to reduce costs.* ◼ V-T If you **apply** something **to** a surface, you put it on or rub it into the surface. ❑ *Apply direct pressure to the wound.* [from Old French] ◼ → see also **applied** → see **makeup**

**Word Partnership** Use *apply* with :

| | |
|---|---|
| PREP. | apply **for admission**, apply **for a job** ◼ |
| N. | **laws/restrictions/rules** apply ◼ apply **makeup**, apply **pressure** ◼ |

**ap|point** /əˈpɔɪnt/ (**appoints, appointing, appointed**) ◼ V-T If you **appoint** someone **to** a job or official position, you formally choose them for it. ❑ *Mr. Putin appointed him to the job in 2000.* ❑ *The bank appointed Kenneth Conley as manager of its office*

in Aurora. ● **ap|point|ment** N-UNCOUNT ❑ *...his appointment to the position of manager.* [from Old French] ◼ → see also **appointed**

**ap|point|ed** /əˈpɔɪntɪd/ ADJ If something happens at the **appointed** time, it happens at the time that was decided in advance. [FORMAL] ❑ *He arrived at the appointed hour.* [from Old French]

**ap|point|ment** /əˈpɔɪntmənt/ (**appointments**) ◼ N-COUNT An **appointment** is a job or position of responsibility. ❑ *I decided to accept the appointment as music director.* ◼ N-COUNT If you have an **appointment with** someone, you have arranged to see them at a particular time, usually in connection with their work or for a serious purpose. ❑ *She has an appointment with her doctor.* ◼ PHRASE If something can be done **by appointment**, people can arrange in advance to do it at a particular time. ❑ *Groups are welcome by appointment only.* ◼ → see also **appoint** [from Old French]

**Thesaurus** *appointment* Also look up :
| | |
|---|---|
| N. | date, engagement, meeting ◼ |

**ap|posi|tive** /əˈpɒzɪtɪv/ (**appositives**) ADJ In grammar, an **appositive** word or phrase is a word or phrase that modifies the meaning of the noun that comes before it. For example, in the sentence "My son David got married," "David" is appositive. ● **Appositive** is also a noun. [from Latin]

**ap|prais|al** /əˈpreɪzəl/ (**appraisals**) ◼ N-VAR If you make an **appraisal** of something, you consider it carefully and form an opinion about it. ❑ *We need a calm appraisal of the situation.* ◼ N-COUNT An **appraisal** is a judgment that someone makes about how much money something such as a house or a company is worth. ❑ *We may need to get a new appraisal of the property.* [from Old French]

**ap|praise** /əˈpreɪz/ (**appraises, appraising, appraised**) ◼ V-T If you **appraise** something or someone, you consider them carefully and form an opinion about them. [FORMAL] ❑ *I carefully appraised the situation.* ◼ V-T When experts **appraise** something, they decide how much money it is worth. ❑ *The house was recently appraised at $405,000.* [from Old French]

**ap|pre|ci|ate** /əˈpriːʃieɪt/ (**appreciates, appreciating, appreciated**) ◼ V-T If you **appreciate** something, you like it because you recognize its good qualities. ❑ *Anyone can appreciate our music.* ● **ap|pre|cia|tion** /əˌpriːʃiˈeɪʃən/ N-SING ❑ *...children's appreciation of art.* ◼ V-T If you **appreciate** a situation or problem, you understand it and know what it involves. ❑ *I don't think we appreciated how much time it would take.* ● **ap|pre|cia|tion** N-SING ❑ *...an appreciation of each patient's needs.* ◼ V-T If you **appreciate** something that someone has done for you or is going to do for you, you are grateful for it. ❑ *Peter helped me when I most needed it. I'll always appreciate that.* ● **ap|pre|cia|tion** N-SING ❑ *He expressed his appreciation for their help.* ◼ V-I If something that you own **appreciates** over a period of time, its value increases. ❑ *People feel their houses will appreciate in value.* ● **ap|pre|cia|tion** N-UNCOUNT ❑ *You have to take appreciation of the property into account.* [from Medieval Latin]

**ap|pre|cia|tive** /əˈpriːʃiətɪv, -ʃətɪv/ ADJ If you are **appreciative of** something, you are grateful

**A**

for it. ❑ *We have been very appreciative of their support.* ● **ap|pre|cia|tive|ly** ADV ❑ *Michael smiled appreciatively.* [from Medieval Latin]

**ap|pre|hen|sion** /ˌæprɪˈhɛnʃən/ (**apprehensions**) N-VAR **Apprehension** is a feeling of fear that something bad may happen. [FORMAL] ❑ *…apprehension about the future.* [from Latin]

**ap|pre|hen|sive** /ˌæprɪˈhɛnsɪv/ ADJ Someone who is **apprehensive** is afraid that something bad may happen. ❑ *People are still terribly apprehensive about the future.* [from Latin]

**ap|pren|tice** /əˈprɛntɪs/ (**apprentices**) N-COUNT An **apprentice** is a young person who works for someone in order to learn their skill. ❑ *Their son Dominic is an apprentice woodworker.* [from Old French]

**ap|pren|tice|ship** /əˈprɛntɪsʃɪp/ (**apprenticeships**) N-VAR Someone who has an **apprenticeship** works for a fixed period of time for a person who has a particular skill in order to learn the skill. **Apprenticeship** is the system of learning a skill like this. ❑ *After serving his apprenticeship, he became a manager.* [from Old French]

**ap|proach** /əˈproʊtʃ/ (**approaches, approaching, approached**) ■ V-T/V-I When you **approach** something, you get closer to it. ❑ *He approached the front door.* ❑ *When I approached, they grew silent.* ● **Approach** is also a noun. ❑ *At their approach the little boy ran away and hid.* ■ V-T If you **approach** someone **about** something, you speak to them about it for the first time, often making an offer or request. ❑ *Robinson first approached him about the job in late September.* ❑ *He approached me about the job.* ● **Approach** is also a noun. ❑ *There have already been approaches from buyers.* ■ V-T When you **approach** a task, problem, or situation in a particular way, you deal with it or think about it in that way. ❑ *The bank has approached the situation in a practical way.* ■ V-I As a future time or event **approaches**, it gradually gets nearer as time passes. ❑ *As autumn approached, the plants and colors in the garden changed.* ● **Approach** is also a noun. ❑ *…the approach of Christmas.* ■ V-T As you **approach** a future time or event, time passes so that you get gradually nearer to it. ❑ *We are approaching the end of the year.* ■ V-T If something **approaches** a particular level or state, it almost reaches that level or state. ❑ *…speeds approaching 200mph.* ■ N-COUNT An **approach to** a place is a road, path, or other route that leads to it. ❑ *Two men stood on the approach to the bridge.* ■ N-COUNT Your **approach** to a task, problem, or situation is the way you deal with it or think about it. ❑ *There are two approaches: spend less money or find a new job.* [from Old French]

| Thesaurus | *approach* Also look up : |
| --- | --- |
| V. | close in, near; (ant.) go away, leave ■ |
| N. | attitude, method, technique ■ |

**ap|pro|pri|ate** /əˈproʊpriɪt/ ADJ Something that is **appropriate** is suitable or acceptable for a particular situation. ❑ *Is it appropriate that they pay for it?* ❑ *Wear clothes appropriate to the job.* ● **ap|pro|pri|ate|ly** ADV ❑ *Behave appropriately and ask intelligent questions.* [from Late Latin]

| Thesaurus | *appropriate* Also look up : |
| --- | --- |
| ADJ. | correct, fitting, relevant, right; (ant.) improper, inappropriate, incorrect |

**ap|prov|al** /əˈpruvəl/ ■ N-UNCOUNT If you get someone's **approval for** something that you ask for or suggest, they agree to it. ❑ *The chairman gave his approval for an investigation.* ■ N-UNCOUNT If someone or something has your **approval**, you like and admire them. ❑ *She wanted her father's approval.* [from Old French]

**ap|prove** /əˈpruv/ (**approves, approving, approved**) ■ V-I If you **approve of** someone or something, you like them or think they are good. ❑ *My father approves of you.* ■ V-T If someone in a position of authority **approves** a plan or idea, they formally agree to it and say that it can happen. ❑ *The directors have approved the change.* [from Old French]

**ap|proved** /əˈpruvd/ ADJ An **approved** method or course of action is officially accepted as appropriate in a particular situation. ❑ *There is an approved method of dealing with these things.* [from Old French]

**ap|prov|ing** /əˈpruvɪŋ/ ADJ An **approving** reaction or remark shows support for something, or satisfaction with it. ❑ *His mother leaned forward and gave him an approving look.* ● **ap|prov|ing|ly** ADV ❑ *He nodded approvingly.* [from Old French]

| Word Link | *proxim ≈ near : approximate, approximation, proximity* |
| --- | --- |

**ap|proxi|mate** (**approximates, approximating, approximated**)

The adjective is pronounced /əˈprɒksɪmət/. The verb is pronounced /əˈprɒksɪmeɪt/.

■ ADJ An **approximate** number, time, or position is close to the correct number, time, or position, but is not exact. ❑ *What is its approximate age?* ● **ap|proxi|mate|ly** ADV ❑ *They've spent approximately $150 million.* ■ V-T If something **approximates** something else, it is similar to it but is not exactly the same. ❑ *The test approximates the students' daily math program.* [from Late Latin]

**ap|proxi|ma|tion** /əˌprɒksɪˈmeɪʃən/ (**approximations**) N-COUNT An **approximation** is a fact, calculation, or description that is not exact. ❑ *As we know, this is only an approximation.* [from Late Latin]

**apri|cot** /ˈæprɪkɒt, ˈeɪp-/ (**apricots**) N-VAR An **apricot** is a small, soft, round fruit with yellowish-orange flesh and a large seed inside. ❑ *…12 oz. fresh apricots.* [from Portuguese]

**April** /ˈeɪprɪl/ (**Aprils**) N-VAR **April** is the fourth month of the year in the Western calendar. ❑ *I'm getting married in April.* [from Latin]

**apron** /ˈeɪprən/ (**aprons**) N-COUNT An **apron** is a piece of clothing that you put on over the front of your normal clothes and tie around your waist, especially when you are cooking, in order to prevent your clothes from getting dirty. [from Old French]

**apt** /æpt/ ■ ADJ An **apt** remark, description, or choice is especially suitable. ❑ *"Happy" is an apt description of Maggie.* ● **apt|ly** ADV ❑ *…the aptly named town of Oceanside.* ■ ADJ If someone is **apt**

to do something, they often do it and so it is likely that they will do it again. ❑ *She was apt to raise her voice.* [from Latin]

**ap|ti|tude** /ˈæptɪtud/ (**aptitudes**) N-VAR If you have an **aptitude for** something, you are able to learn it quickly and to do it well. ❑ *He had an aptitude for working with numbers.* [from Latin]

**aquat|ic** /əˈkwætɪk/ **1** ADJ An **aquatic** animal or plant lives or grows on or in water. ❑ *...aquatic plants.* **2** ADJ **Aquatic** means relating to water. ❑ *...our aquatic resources.* [from Latin]

**aqui|fer** /ˈækwɪfər/ (**aquifers**) N-COUNT In geology, an **aquifer** is an area of rock underneath the surface of the earth which absorbs and holds water. [TECHNICAL] [from New Latin]

**ar|able** /ˈærəbᵊl/ ADJ **Arable** farming involves growing crops rather than keeping animals. **Arable** land is land that is used for arable farming. ❑ *...arable farmers.* [from Latin]

**arach|nid** /əˈræknɪd/ (**arachnids**) N-COUNT **Arachnids** are a group of small insects such as spiders and scorpions that have eight legs and no antennae. [TECHNICAL] [from New Latin]

**ar|bi|trary** /ˈɑrbɪtreri/ ADJ An **arbitrary** action, rule, or decision is not based on any principle, plan, or system. It often seems unfair because of this. ❑ *This arbitrary arrangement often fails to work.* ● **ar|bi|trari|ly** /ˈɑrbɪtreərɪli/ ADV ❑ *The victims were not chosen arbitrarily.* [from Latin]

**ar|bi|trary col|or** (**arbitrary colors**) N-VAR An artist who uses **arbitrary colors** paints things in colors that do not naturally belong to the object being painted, for example a blue horse, in order to express their feelings about the object.

**ar|bi|trate** /ˈɑrbɪtreɪt/ (**arbitrates, arbitrating, arbitrated**) V-T When someone in authority **arbitrates** a dispute, they consider all the facts and make an official decision about who is right. ❑ *The organization arbitrates trade rows.* ● **ar|bi|tra|tion** /ˈɑrbɪtreɪʃᵊn/ N-UNCOUNT ❑ *The matter is likely to go to arbitration.* [from Latin]

**arc** /ˈɑrk/ (**arcs**) N-COUNT An **arc** is a smoothly curving line or movement. ❑ *...the rainbow's arc.* [from Old French]

**ar|cade** /ɑrˈkeɪd/ (**arcades**) **1** N-COUNT An **arcade** is a place where you can play games on machines which work when you put money in them. **2** → see also **video arcade** [from French]

**arch** /ˈɑrtʃ/ (**arches, arching, arched**) **1** N-COUNT An **arch** is a structure that is curved at the top and is supported on either side by a pillar, post, or wall. ❑ *The bridge is 65 feet at the top of the main arch.* **2** → see also **arched** **3** V-T/V-I If you **arch** a part of your body such as your back or if it **arches**, you bend it so that it forms a curve. ❑ *Don't arch your back.* [from Old French]
→ see **architecture, foot**

**Ar|chae|bac|te|ria** /ˈɑrkibæktɪəriə/ N-PLURAL **Archaebacteria** are a type of bacteria that can live in extreme environments such as volcanoes. [TECHNICAL]

**ar|chae|ol|ogy** /ˈɑrkiɒlədʒi/ also **archeology** N-UNCOUNT **Archaeology** is the study of the past by examining the remains of things

such as buildings, tools, and other objects. ● **ar|chaeo|logi|cal** /ˈɑrkiəlɒdʒɪkᵊl/ ADJ ❑ *...one of the region's most important archaeological sites.* ● **ar|chae|olo|gist** /ˈɑrkiɒlədʒɪst/ (**archaeologists**) N-COUNT ❑ *The archaeologists found a house built around 300 BC.* [from Late Latin]
→ see **history**

**ar|cha|ic** /ɑrˈkeɪɪk/ ADJ **Archaic** means extremely old or extremely old-fashioned. ❑ *...archaic laws.* [from French]

**arch|bishop** /ˈɑrtʃbɪʃəp/ (**archbishops**) N-COUNT; N-TITLE In the Roman Catholic, Orthodox, and Anglican Churches, an **archbishop** is a bishop of the highest rank. ❑ *...the Roman Catholic archbishop of Colorado Springs.*

**arched** /ˈɑrtʃt/ **1** ADJ An **arched** roof, window, or doorway is curved at the top. ❑ *An arched doorway leads in to the hall.* **2** ADJ An **arched** bridge has arches as part of its structure. ❑ *She led them across a little arched stone bridge.* [from Old French]

**ar|che|ol|ogy** /ˈɑrkiɒlədʒi/ → see **archaeology**

**ar|che|typ|al criti|cism** N-UNCOUNT **Archetypal criticism** is a type of literary criticism that interprets a literary work by emphasizing its use of archetypes such as ancient myths and symbols. [TECHNICAL]

**ar|che|type** /ˈɑrkɪtaɪp/ (**archetypes**) N-COUNT An **archetype** is something that is considered to be a perfect or typical example of a particular kind of person or thing, because it has all their most important characteristics. [FORMAL] ❑ *He is the archetype of the successful businessman.* ● **ar|che|typ|al** /ˈɑrkɪtaɪpᵊl/ ADJ [FORMAL] ❑ *...the archetypal American middle-class family.* [from Latin]
→ see **myth**

**Archimedes' prin|ci|ple** /ˈɑrkɪmidɪz prɪnsɪpᵊl/ N-UNCOUNT **Archimedes' principle** is a law of physics which states that, when an object is in a fluid such as water, its apparent loss of weight is equal to the weight of the fluid that the object has displaced.

**archi|tect** /ˈɑrkɪtɛkt/ (**architects**) **1** N-COUNT An **architect** is a person who designs buildings. **2** N-COUNT The **architect of** an idea, event, or institution is the person who invented it or made it happen. ❑ *Robert Moses was the architect of New York State's highway system.* [from French]

**archi|tec|ture** /ˈɑrkɪtɛktʃər/ **1** N-UNCOUNT **Architecture** is the art of planning, designing, and constructing buildings. ❑ *He studied architecture in Rome.* ● **archi|tec|tur|al** /ˈɑrkɪtɛktʃərəl/ ADJ ❑ *...architectural drawings.* ● **archi|tec|tur|al|ly** ADV ❑ *The old city center is architecturally rich.* **2** N-UNCOUNT The **architecture** of a building is the style in which it is designed and constructed. ❑ *...modern architecture.* [from French]
→ see Word Web: **architecture**

**ar|chive** /ˈɑrkaɪv/ (**archives**) N-COUNT **Archives** are a collection of documents and records that contain historical information. ❑ *...the State Library's archives.* [from Late Latin]

**ar|dent** /ˈɑrdᵊnt/ ADJ **Ardent** is used to describe someone who has extremely strong feelings about something or someone. ❑ *...ardent fans* [from Latin]

**ar|du|ous** /ˈɑrdʒuəs/ ADJ Something that is **arduous** is difficult and tiring, and involves a lot of effort. ❑ *...a long, hot and arduous trip.* [from Latin]

## Word Web  architecture

The Colosseum (sometimes spelled Coliseum) in Rome is a great **architectural** success of the ancient world. This amphitheater, built in the first century BC, could hold 50,000 people. It was used for animal fights, human executions, and staged battles. The oval shape allowed people to be closer to the action. It also prevented participants from hiding in the corners. The **arches** are an important part of the **building**. They are an example of a Roman improvement to the simple arch. Each arch is supported by a **keystone** in the top center. The **design** of the Colosseum has influenced the design of thousands of other public places. Many modern day sports stadiums are the same shape.

**are** /ər, STRONG ɑr/ **Are** is the plural and the second person singular of the present tense of the verb **be**. **Are** is often shortened to **-'re** after pronouns in spoken English. [from Old English]

**area** /ˈɛəriə/ (**areas**) **1** N-COUNT An **area** is a particular part of a town, a country, a region, or the world. ❑ *There are 11,000 people living in the area.* **2** N-COUNT A particular **area** is a piece of land or part of a building that is used for a particular activity. ❑ *...a picnic area.* **3** N-COUNT You can use **area** to refer to a particular subject or topic, or to a particular part of a larger, more general situation or activity. ❑ *...the area of child care.* **4** N-VAR The **area** of a surface such as a piece of land is the amount of flat space or ground that it covers, measured in square units. ❑ *The islands cover a total area of 400 square miles.* [from Latin] **5** → see also **gray area**
→ see Picture Dictionary: **area**

### Word Partnership  Use *area* with :

| | |
|---|---|
| N. | **downtown** area, **tourist** area **1** |
| ADJ. | **local** area, **metropolitan** area, **remote** area, **surrounding** area **1** **residential** area, **restricted** area **2** |
| PREP. | **throughout** the area **1** **2** area **of expertise** **3** |

**area code** (**area codes**) N-COUNT The **area code** for a particular city or region is the series of numbers that you have to dial before someone's personal number if you are making a telephone call to that place from a different area. ❑ *The area code for western Pennsylvania is 412.*

**arena** /əˈriːnə/ (**arenas**) **1** N-COUNT An **arena** is a place where sports, entertainments, and other public events take place. ❑ *We went to watch them at the largest indoor sports arena in the world.* **2** N-COUNT You can refer to a field of activity, especially one where there is a lot of conflict or action, as an **arena** of a particular kind. ❑ *He entered the political arena in 1987.* [from Latin]

**aren't** /ɑrnt, ˈɑrənt/ **1** **Aren't** is the usual spoken form of "are not." **2** **Aren't** is the form of "am not" that is used in questions or tags in spoken English.

**arête** /əˈreɪt/ (**arêtes**) N-COUNT An **arête** is a thin ridge of rock separating two valleys in mountainous regions. [from French]

**arguably** /ˈɑrgyuəbli/ ADV You can use **arguably** when you are stating your opinion or belief, as a way of giving more authority to it. ❑ *It was arguably the most important day of his life.* [from Old French]

**ar|gue** /ˈɑrgyu/ (**argues, arguing, argued**) **1** V-RECIP If you **argue with** someone, you disagree with them about something, often angrily. ❑ *He was arguing with his wife about their daughter.* ❑ *They are arguing over details.* **2** V-T If you **argue that** something is true, you state it and give the reasons why you think it is true. ❑ *They are arguing that the money belongs to them.* **3** V-I If you **argue for** something, you say why you agree with it, in order to persuade people that it is right. If you **argue against** something, you say why you disagree with it, in order to persuade people that it is wrong. ❑ *He argued against having the meeting.* [from Old French]

### Thesaurus  argue  Also look up :

| | |
|---|---|
| V. | bicker, debate, disagree, dispute, fight, quarrel; (*ant.*) agree **1** claim **2** discuss, dispute |

**ar|gu|ment** /ˈɑrgyəmənt/ (**arguments**) **1** N-VAR An **argument** is a statement or set of statements that you use in order to try to convince people that your opinion about something is correct. ❑ *There's a strong argument for lowering the price.* **2** N-COUNT An **argument** is a conversation in which people disagree with each other angrily or noisily. ❑ *Annie had an argument with one of the other girls.* [from Old French]

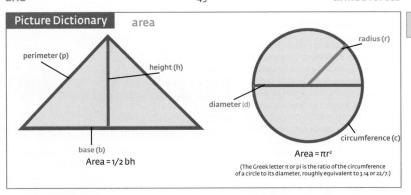

## Picture Dictionary — area

perimeter (p)

height (h)

base (b)

Area = 1/2 bh

radius (r)

diameter (d)

circumference (c)

Area = πr²

(The Greek letter π or pi is the ratio of the circumference of a circle to its diameter, roughly equivalent to 3.14 or 22/7.)

**arid** /ǽrɪd/ ADJ **Arid** land is so dry that very few plants can grow on it. ❑ *...crops that can grow in arid conditions.* [from Latin]

**arise** /əráɪz/ (**arises, arising, arose, arisen** /ərɪ́zən/) ◼ V-I If a situation or problem **arises**, it begins to exist or people start to become aware of it. ❑ *When the opportunity finally arose, thousands of workers left.* ◻ V-I If something **arises from** a particular situation, or **arises out of** it, it is created or caused by the situation. ❑ *The idea arose from discussions held last year.* [from Old English]

**a·ris·toc·ra·cy** /ǽrɪstɒkrəsi/ (**aristocracies**) N-COUNT The **aristocracy** is a class of people in some countries who have a high social rank and special titles. ❑ *...a member of the aristocracy.* [from Late Latin]

**aris·to·crat** /ərɪ́stəkræt, ǽrɪst-/ (**aristocrats**) N-COUNT An **aristocrat** is someone whose family has a high social rank, especially someone who has a title. ❑ *...a wealthy southern aristocrat.* ● **aris·to·crat·ic** /ərɪ́stəkrǽtɪk/ ADJ ❑ *...an aristocratic family.* [from Late Latin]

**arith·me·tic** /ərɪ́θmɪtɪk/ N-UNCOUNT **Arithmetic** is the part of mathematics that is concerned with the addition, subtraction, multiplication, and division of numbers. ❑ *...teaching the basics of reading, writing and arithmetic.* [from Latin]
→ see **mathematics**

**ar·ith·met·ic se·quence** /ǽrɪθmɛtɪk síkwəns/ also **arithmetic progression** (**arithmetic sequences**) N-COUNT An **arithmetic sequence** is a series of numbers in which each number differs from the one before it by the same amount, for example the sequence 3, 6, 9, 12.

**arm** /ɑrm/ (**arms, arming, armed**) ◼ N-COUNT Your **arms** are the two parts of your body between your shoulders and your hands. ❑ *She stretched her arms out.* ◻ N-COUNT The **arm** of a chair is the part on which you rest your arm when you are sitting down. ❑ *Mack held the arms of the chair.* ◼ N-COUNT The **arm** of a piece of clothing is the part of it that covers your arm. ❑ *The coat was short in the arms.* ◼ N-PLURAL **Arms** are weapons, especially bombs and guns. ❑ *Soldiers searched their house for illegal arms.* ◼ V-T If you **arm** someone **with** a weapon, you provide them with a weapon. ❑ *She was so frightened that she armed herself with a rifle.* [Senses 1, 2 and 3 from Old English. Senses 4 and 5 from Old French] ◼ → see also **armed**
→ see **body, war**

**ar·ma·ments** /ɑ́rməmənts/ N-PLURAL **Armaments** are weapons and military equipment belonging to an army or country. ❑ *They had a limited number of ships, planes and armaments.* [from Latin]

**arm·chair** /ɑ́rmtʃeər/ (**armchairs**) N-COUNT An **armchair** is a big comfortable chair that has a support on each side for your arms. ❑ *She was sitting in an armchair.*

**armed** /ɑrmd/ ◼ ADJ Someone who is **armed** is carrying a weapon, usually a gun. ❑ *City police said the man was armed with a gun.* ❑ *...armed guards.* ◻ ADJ An **armed** attack or conflict involves people fighting with guns or carrying weapons. ❑ *They were found guilty of armed robbery.* [from Old French] ◼ → see also **arm**

**armed forces** N-PLURAL The **armed forces** or the **armed services** of a country are its military forces, usually the army, navy, marines, and air force. ❑ *...members of the armed forces.*

## Word Web army

The first Roman **army** was a poorly
organized **militia band**. Its members had
no **weapons** such as **swords** or **spears**.
Things changed after the Etruscans, an
advanced society from west-central Italy,
**conquered** Rome. Then the Roman army
became more powerful. They learned how
to **deploy** their **troops** to **fight** better in
**battles**. By the first century BC, the

Roman army learned the importance of protective equipment. They started using bronze **helmets**,
**armor**, and wooden **shields**. They fought many **military campaigns** and won many **wars**.

**ar|mor** /ɑrmər/ ■ N-UNCOUNT In former times,
**armor** was special metal clothing that soldiers
wore for protection in battle. ❑ ...*knights in armor.*
■ N-UNCOUNT **Armor** is a hard, usually metal,
covering that protects a vehicle against attack.
❑ ...*armor-piercing bullets.* [from Old French]
→ see **army**

**ar|mored** /ɑrmərd/ ADJ **Armored** vehicles are
equipped with a hard metal covering in order to
protect them from gunfire and other missiles.
❑ *More than forty armored vehicles have gone into the
area.* [from Old French]

**arm|pit** /ɑrmpɪt/ (**armpits**) N-COUNT Your
**armpits** are the areas of your body under your
arms where your arms join your shoulders. ❑ *I
shave my armpits every couple of days.*

**army** /ɑrmi/ (**armies**) ■ N-COUNT An **army** is
a large organized group of people who are armed
and trained to fight on land in a war. Most armies
are organized and controlled by governments.
❑ *Perkins joined the Army in 1990.* ■ N-COUNT An
**army of** people, animals, or things is a large
number of them, especially when they are
regarded as a force of some kind. ❑ ...*an army of
volunteers.* [from Old French]
→ see Word Web: **army**

**aro|ma** /əroʊmə/ (**aromas**) N-COUNT An **aroma**
is a strong, pleasant smell. ❑ ...*the wonderful aroma
of fresh bread.* [from Latin]

**aro|mat|ic** /ærəmætɪk/ ADJ An **aromatic** plant
or food has a strong, pleasant smell of herbs
or spices. ❑ ...*an evergreen shrub with dark green,
aromatic leaves.* [from Latin]

**arose** /əroʊz/ **Arose** is the past tense of **arise**.

**around** /əraʊnd/

Around is an adverb and a preposition. **Around**
is often used with verbs of movement, such as
"walk" and "drive," and also in phrasal verbs
such as "get around" and "turn around."

■ PREP To be positioned **around** a place or object
means to surround it or be on all sides of it. To
move **around** a place means to go around its edge,
back to your starting point. ❑ *She looked at the
papers around her.* ❑ *She wore her hair down around
her shoulders.* ● **Around** is also an adverb. ❑ ...*a
village with hills all around.* ❑ *They celebrated their
win by running around on the football field.* ■ PREP If
you move **around** a corner or obstacle, you move
to the other side of it. If you look **around** a corner

or obstacle, you look to see what is on the other
side. ❑ *The photographer stopped taking pictures and
hurried around the corner.* ■ PREP You use **around**
to say that something happens in different parts
of a place or area. ❑ *Police say ten people have died
in violence around the country.* ● **Around** is also an
adverb. ❑ *Why are you following me around?* ■ ADV If
you move things **around**, you move them so that
they are in different places. ❑ *She moved things
around so the table was underneath the window.* ■ ADV
If someone or something is **around**, they exist or
are present in a place. ❑ *You haven't seen my wife
anywhere around, have you?* ■ ADV **Around** means
approximately. ❑ *My salary was around $45,000.*
● **Around** is also a preposition. ❑ *We're leaving
around May 15.* ■ **the other way around** → see **way**

**arous|al** /əraʊzəl/ N-UNCOUNT **Arousal** is a state
in which you feel excited or very alert.

**arouse** /əraʊz/ (**arouses, arousing, aroused**)
V-T If something **arouses** a particular reaction or
feeling in you, it causes you to have that reaction
or feeling. ❑ *The smell of frying bacon aroused his
hunger.*

**ar|range** /əreɪndʒ/ (**arranges, arranging,
arranged**) ■ V-T If you **arrange** an event or
meeting, you make plans for it to happen. ❑ *She
arranged an appointment for Friday afternoon.* ❑ *I've
arranged to see him Thursday.* ❑ *I will arrange for
someone to take you around.* ■ V-T If you **arrange**
things somewhere, you place them in a particular
position, usually in order to make them look
attractive or neat. ❑ *She enjoys arranging dried
flowers.* [from Old French]

**ar|range|ment** /əreɪndʒmənt/
(**arrangements**) ■ N-COUNT **Arrangements** are
plans and preparations that you make so that
something can happen. ❑ *They're working on
final arrangements for the meeting.* ■ N-COUNT An
**arrangement** of things, for example, flowers
or furniture, is a group of them displayed in a
particular way. ❑ ...*flower arrangements.* [from Old
French]

**ar|ray** /əreɪ/ (**arrays**) N-COUNT An **array of**
different things or people is a large number or
wide range of them. ❑ ...*a wide array of products.*
[from Old French]

**ar|rears** /ərɪərz/ ■ N-PLURAL **Arrears** are
amounts of money that you owe, especially
regular payments that you should have made
earlier. ❑ *They promised to pay the arrears over the next*

**a**

## Word Web    art

The Impressionist movement in **painting** began in Europe during the second half of the 19th century. The Impressionists no longer used traditional **realistic depictions** of people and objects painted in **studios**. They often painted **landscapes**, with more light and color in

their **interpretations** of everyday life.

Among these painters were French artists Paul Cézanne, Pierre Renoir, and Claude Monet. The word "Impressionist" comes from the name of a Monet painting, "Impression, Sunrise." Japanese prints also had an effect on the Impressionist movement. The Impressionists liked the use of contrasting dark and bright colors found in these prints.

five years. **2** PHRASE If someone is **in arrears with** their payments, or falls **into arrears,** they have not paid the regular amounts of money that they should have paid. ☐ *They are more than six months in arrears with their payments.* [from Old French]

**ar|rest** /ərɛst/ (**arrests, arresting, arrested**) **1** V-T If the police **arrest** you, they take charge of you and take you to a police station, because they believe you may have committed a crime. ☐ *Police arrested five young men in connection with the attacks.* ● **Arrest** is also a noun. ☐ *Police later made two arrests.* [from Old French] **2** → see also **house arrest**

**ar|ri|val** /əraɪvᵊl/ (**arrivals**) **1** N-VAR When a person or vehicle arrives at a place, you can refer to their **arrival.** ☐ *...the day after his arrival in Wichita.* **2** N-SING When something is brought to you or becomes available, you can refer to its **arrival.** ☐ *I read the newspaper while I was waiting for the arrival of orange juice and coffee.* **3** N-COUNT You can refer to someone who has just arrived at a place as a new **arrival.** ☐ *Many of the new arrivals are skilled professionals.* [from Old French]

**ar|rive** /əraɪv/ (**arrives, arriving, arrived**) **1** V-I When a person or vehicle **arrives** at a place, they come to it from somewhere else. ☐ *Their train arrived on time.* **2** V-I When something **arrives,** it is brought to you or becomes available. ☐ *The movie will finally arrive in the stores this month.* **3** V-I When you **arrive at** something such as a decision, you decide something after thinking about it or discussing it. ☐ *John was unable to arrive at a decision.* [from Old French]

| Thesaurus | *arrive* | Also look up : |
|---|---|---|
| v. | enter, land, pull in, reach; (*ant.*) depart **1** | |

**ar|ro|gant** /ærəgənt/ ADJ Someone who is **arrogant** behaves in a proud, unpleasant way toward other people because they believe that they are more important than others. ☐ *He was so arrogant.* ☐ *That sounds arrogant, doesn't it?* ● **ar|ro|gance** N-UNCOUNT ☐ *...the arrogance of powerful people.* ● **ar|ro|gant|ly** ADV ☐ *The doctor arrogantly dismissed their cry for help.* [from Latin]

**ar|row** /æroʊ/ (**arrows**) **1** N-COUNT An **arrow** is a long thin weapon that is sharp and pointed at one end. An arrow is shot from a bow. ☐ *They were armed with bows and arrows.* **2** N-COUNT An

**arrow** is a written or printed sign that points in a particular direction to indicate where something is. ☐ *The arrow pointed down.* [from Old English]

**ar|se|nal** /ɑrsənᵊl/ (**arsenals**) N-COUNT An **arsenal** is a large collection of weapons and military equipment. ☐ *...a secret arsenal of weapons.* [from Italian]

**ar|son** /ɑrsᵊn/ N-UNCOUNT **Arson** is the crime of deliberately setting fire to a building or vehicle. ☐ *The wooden building burned to the ground in an arson attack on January 4.* [from Old French]

**art** /ɑrt/ (**arts**) **1** N-UNCOUNT **Art** consists of paintings, sculpture, and other pictures or objects that are created for people to look at. ☐ *...modern American art.* **2** N-UNCOUNT **Art** is the activity or educational subject that consists of creating paintings, sculptures, and other pictures or objects for people to look at. ☐ *...art classes.* ☐ *...Savannah College of Art and Design.* **3** N-PLURAL **The arts** are activities such as music, painting, literature, film, and dance. ☐ *...people working in the arts.* **4** N-PLURAL At a university or college, **arts** are subjects such as history, literature, or languages in contrast to scientific subjects. ☐ *...arts and social science graduates.* **5** N-COUNT If you describe an activity as an **art,** you mean that it requires skill and that people learn to do it by instinct or experience, rather than by learning facts or rules. ☐ *...the art of acting.* [from Old French] **6** → see also **fine art, martial art, state-of-the-art, work of art**

→ see Word Web: **art**
→ see **culture**

**art criti|cism** N-UNCOUNT **Art criticism** is the study and evaluation of the visual arts, especially painting.

**art el|ement** (**art elements**) N-COUNT **Art elements** are the basic parts that a painting or drawing consists of, such as lines, colors and shapes.

**ar|tery** /ɑrtəri/ (**arteries**) N-COUNT **Arteries** are the tubes in your body that carry blood from your heart to the rest of your body. Compare **vein.** ☐ *...patients suffering from blocked arteries.* [from Latin]
→ see **cardiovascular system**

**ar|te|sian spring** /ɑrtiʒən sprɪŋ/ (**artesian springs**) N-COUNT An **artesian spring** is a place where water rises naturally through holes or cracks in the ground.

**A**

| Word Link | itis ≈ inflammation : arthritis, hepatitis, meningitis |

**ar|thri|tis** /ɑrθraɪtɪs/ N-UNCOUNT **Arthritis** is a medical condition in which the joints in your body are swollen and painful. □ *I have a touch of arthritis in the wrist.* ● **ar|thrit|ic** /ɑrθrɪtɪk/ ADJ □ *...arthritic hands.* [from Latin]

**ar|ti|choke** /ɑrtɪtʃoʊk/ (**artichokes**) N-VAR **Artichokes** or **globe artichokes** are round green vegetables that have fleshy leaves arranged like the petals of a flower. [from Italian]

| Word Link | cle ≈ small : article, cubicle, particle |

**ar|ti|cle** /ɑrtɪkªl/ (**articles**) **1** N-COUNT An **article** is a piece of writing that is published in a newspaper or magazine. □ *...a newspaper article.* **2** N-COUNT You can refer to objects as **articles** of some kind. □ *...articles of clothing.* ● *He removed all articles of value.* **3** N-COUNT An **article of** a formal agreement or document is a section of it that deals with a particular point. □ *...Article 50 of the UN charter.* [from Old French]

**ar|ticu|late** (**articulates, articulating, articulated**)

The adjective is pronounced /ɑrtɪkyəlɪt/. The verb is pronounced /ɑrtɪkyəleɪt/.

**1** ADJ If you describe someone as **articulate,** you mean that they are able to express their thoughts and ideas easily and well. □ *She is an articulate young woman.* **2** V-T When you **articulate** your ideas or feelings, you express them clearly in words. [FORMAL] □ *She articulated her views.* [from Latin]

**ar|ticu|lat|ed** /ɑrtɪkyəleɪtɪd/ ADJ An **articulated** vehicle is made in two or more sections that are joined together by metal bars, so that the vehicle can turn more easily. [from Latin]

**ar|ticu|la|tion** /ɑrtɪkyəleɪʃªn/ N-UNCOUNT **Articulation** is the action of producing a sound or word clearly, in speech or music. [FORMAL] [from Latin]

| Word Link | fact, fic ≈ making : artifact, artificial, factor |

**ar|ti|fact** /ɑrtɪfækt/ (**artifacts**) N-COUNT An **artifact** is an ornament, tool, or other object that is made by a human being, especially one that is historically or culturally interesting. □ *They repair broken religious artifacts.* [from Latin]
→ see **history**

**ar|ti|fi|cial** /ɑrtɪfɪʃªl/ **1** ADJ **Artificial** objects, materials, or processes do not occur naturally and are created by human beings. □ *The city has many small lakes, natural and artificial.* □ *...a diet free from artificial additives.* ● **ar|ti|fi|cial|ly** ADV □ *...artificially sweetened lemonade.* **2** ADJ An **artificial** state or situation exists only because someone has created it, and therefore often seems unnatural or unnecessary. □ *...a fixed, artificial smile.* ● **ar|ti|fi|cial|ly** ADV □ *...artificially low prices.* [from Latin]

| **Thesaurus** | artificial | Also look up : |

| ADJ. | manmade, manufactured, synthetic, unnatural; (ant.) natural **1** **2** |

**ar|ti|fi|cial in|tel|li|gence** N-UNCOUNT **Artificial intelligence** is a type of computer technology concerned with making machines work in a similar way to the human mind.

**ar|ti|fi|cial light** (**artificial lights**) N-VAR **Artificial light** is light from a source such as an electric light or a gas lamp rather than from the sun.

**ar|til|lery** /ɑrtɪləri/ **1** N-UNCOUNT **Artillery** consists of large, powerful guns that are transported on wheels. □ *...tanks and heavy artillery.* **2** N-SING **The artillery** is the section of an army that is trained to use large, powerful guns. □ *From 1935 to 1937 he was in the artillery.* [from Old French]

**art|ist** /ɑrtɪst/ (**artists**) **1** N-COUNT An **artist** is someone who draws, paints or produces other works of art. □ *Each poster is signed by the artist.* □ *She considers herself a serious artist.* **2** N-COUNT An **artist** is a performer such as a musician, actor, or dancer. □ *...a popular artist who has sold millions of records.* [from Old French]
→ see **animation**

**ar|tis|tic** /ɑrtɪstɪk/ **1** ADJ Someone who is **artistic** is good at drawing or painting, or arranging things in a beautiful way. □ *The boys are sensitive and artistic.* **2** ADJ **Artistic** means relating to art or artists. □ *He's the artistic director of the Montreal Opera.* ● **ar|tis|ti|cal|ly** /ɑrtɪstɪkli/ ADV □ *...artistically gifted children.* [from Old French]

**art|ist|ry** /ɑrtɪstri/ N-UNCOUNT **Artistry** is the creative skill of an artist, writer, actor, or musician. □ *...musical artistry.* [from Old French]

---

**as**

**❶** CONJUNCTION AND PREPOSITION USES
**❷** USED WITH OTHER PREPOSITIONS AND CONJUNCTIONS

---

**❶ as** /əz, STRONG æz/ **1** CONJ If one thing happens **as** something else happens, it happens at the same time. □ *We shut the door behind us as we entered.* **2** CONJ You use **as** to say how something happens or is done. □ *Today, as usual, he was wearing a suit.* **3** CONJ You can use **as** to mean "because." □ *This is important as it sets the mood for the rest of the day.* **4** PHRASE You use **as...as** when you are comparing things, or emphasizing how large or small something is. □ *This was not as easy as we imagined.* □ *She gets as many as eight thousand letters a month.* ● **As** is also a conjunction. □ *Being a mother isn't as bad as I thought at first!* **5** PREP You use **as** when you are indicating what someone or something is or is thought to be. □ *The news came as a complete surprise.* **6** PREP You use **as** in expressions like **as a result** and **as a consequence** to indicate how two situations or events are linked to each other. □ *She was unable to walk as a result of her injuries.* [from Old English] **7 as ever** → see **ever 8 as a matter of fact** → see **fact 9 as follows** → see **follow 10 as long as** → see **long 11 as opposed to** → see **opposed 12 as regards** → see **regard 13 as soon as** → see **soon 14 as such** → see **such 15 as well** → see **well 16 as well as** → see **well**

**❷ as** /əz, STRONG æz/ **1** PHRASE You use **as for** and **as to** in order to introduce a slightly different subject. □ *I don't know why he shouted at me. And as for going back there, certainly I would never go back.* **2** PHRASE You use **as to** to indicate what something refers to. □ *They should make*

a

decisions as to whether the student needs more help with tuition. **3** PHRASE If you say that something will happen **as of** a particular date or time, you mean that it will happen from that time on. □ *The store will be open as of January the 1st.* **4** PHRASE You use **as if** and **as though** when you are giving a possible explanation for something or saying that something appears to be the case when it is not. □ *Anne stopped, as if she didn't know what to do or say next.*

**as|bes|tos** /æsbɛstəs, æz-/ N-UNCOUNT **Asbestos** is a gray material that does not burn. □ *...those old brick houses with green asbestos roofs.* [from Latin]

| Word Link | scend ≈ climbing : ascend, condescend, descend |
|---|---|

**as|cend** /əsɛnd/ (**ascends, ascending, ascended**) **1** V-T If you **ascend** a hill or staircase, you go up it. [WRITTEN] □ *Mrs. Clayton held Lizzie's hand as they ascended the steps.* **2** V-I If a staircase or path **ascends**, it leads up to a higher position. [WRITTEN] □ *A number of staircases ascend from the streets.* [from Latin]

**as|cend|ing** /əsɛndɪŋ/ ADJ If a group of things is arranged in **ascending** order, each thing is bigger, greater, or more important than the thing before it. □ *List the numbers in ascending order.* [from Latin]

**as|cent** /əsɛnt/ (**ascents**) **1** N-COUNT An **ascent** is an upward journey or movement. □ *...the first ascent of the world's highest mountain.* **2** N-COUNT An **ascent** is an upward slope or path, especially when you are walking or climbing. □ *It was a difficult course over a gradual ascent.* □ *The elevator began its slow ascent.* [from Latin]

| Word Link | cert ≈ determined, true : ascertain, certificate, certify |
|---|---|

**as|cer|tain** /æsərteɪn/ (**ascertains, ascertaining, ascertained**) V-T If you **ascertain** the truth about something, you find out what it is. [FORMAL] □ *We'll call him and ascertain the facts.* □ *They ascertained that he was telling the truth.* [from Old French]

**as|cribe** /əskraɪb/ (**ascribes, ascribing, ascribed**) V-T If you **ascribe** something **to** a person, event or thing, you believe that they cause it or have it. [FORMAL] □ *I don't ascribe much importance to what he says.* [from Latin]

**asexu|al re|pro|duc|tion** N-UNCOUNT **Asexual reproduction** is a form of reproduction that involves no sexual activity.

**ash** /æʃ/ (**ashes**) **1** N-VAR **Ash** is the gray or black powdery substance that is left after something is burned. You can also refer to this substance as **ashes**. □ *...a cloud of ash.* **2** N-VAR An **ash** is a tree that has smooth gray bark and loses its leaves in winter. ● **Ash** is the wood from this tree. □ *The chairs are made from ash.* [from Old English]
→ see **fire, glass, volcano**

**ashamed** /əʃeɪmd/ **1** ADJ If someone is **ashamed**, they feel embarrassed or guilty because of something they do or they have done, or because of their appearance. □ *I felt ashamed of myself for getting so angry.* **2** ADJ If you are **ashamed** of someone or something, you feel embarrassed or

guilty because of them. □ *I was ashamed of myself.* □ *She was ashamed that she looked so messy.* [from Old English]

**ashore** /əʃɔr/ ADV Someone or something that comes **ashore** comes from the sea onto the shore. □ *Oil has come ashore east of Anchorage.* □ *He came ashore to buy supplies for his sailing trip.*

**ash|tray** /æʃtreɪ/ (**ashtrays**) N-COUNT An **ashtray** is a small dish in which smokers can put the ash from their cigarettes and cigars.

**Asian** /eɪʒⁿn/ (**Asians**) ADJ Someone or something that is **Asian** comes from or is associated with Asia, for example China, Korea, Thailand, Japan, or Vietnam. □ *I'm listening to a lot of Asian music right now.* ● An **Asian** is a person who comes from or is associated with a country or region in Asia.

**aside** /əsaɪd/

In addition to the uses shown below, **aside** is used in phrasal verbs such as "cast aside," "stand aside," and "step aside."

**1** ADV If you move something **aside**, you move it to one side of you. □ *Sarah closed the book and laid it aside.* **2** ADV If you take or draw someone **aside**, you take them a little way away from a group of people in order to talk to them in private. □ *I took him aside and discussed it with him.* **3** ADV If you move **aside**, you get out of someone's way. □ *She stepped aside to let them pass as they appeared to be in a hurry.* **4** PHRASE You use **aside from** when you are making an exception to a general statement. □ *The room was empty aside from one man seated beside the fire.* **5** PHRASE You use **aside from** to indicate that you are aware of one aspect of a situation, but that you are going to focus on another aspect. □ *Aside from the bruises, there were no other injuries.*

**ask** /æsk/ (**asks, asking, asked**) **1** V-T/V-I If you **ask** someone something, you say something to them in the form of a question because you want to know the answer. □ *"How is Frank?" he asked.* □ *I asked him his name.* □ *She asked me if I'd enjoyed my dinner.* □ *All you have to do is ask.* **2** V-T If you **ask** someone **to** do something, you tell them that you want them to do it. □ *We had to ask him to leave.* **3** V-T If you **ask to** do something, you tell someone that you want to do it. □ *I asked to see the director.* **4** V-I If you **ask for** something, you say that you would like it. □ *She asked for my address, which I didn't want to give her.* **5** V-I If you **ask for** someone, you say that you would like to speak to them. □ *There's a man at the gate asking for you.* **6** V-T If you **ask** someone's permission, opinion, or forgiveness, you try to obtain it. □ *He asked permission to leave.* **7** V-T If you **ask** someone **to** an event or place, you invite them to go there. □ *I asked Juan to the party.* **8** PHRASE You can say "**if you ask me**" to emphasize that you are stating your personal opinion. □ *He was nuts, if you ask me.* [from Old English]

| Thesaurus | | ask | | Also look up : |
|---|---|---|---|---|
| v. | | demand, interrogate, question, quiz; (ant.) answer, reply, respond **1** | | |
| | | beg, plead, request; (ant.) command, insist **6** | | |

A

| ADJ. | **afraid to** ask ■ |
| V. | **come to** ask, **have to** ask ■ |
| DET. | ask **how/what/when/where/who/ why** ■ |
| CONJ. | ask **if/whether** ■ |
| PREP. | ask **about** ■ |
| | ask **to** ■ ■ ■ |
| | ask **for** ■ ■ |
| N. | ask **a question** ■ |
| | ask **for help** ■ |
| | ask **forgiveness**, ask *someone's* **opinion**, |
| | ask **permission** ■ |

**asleep** /əsl**i**p/ ■ ADJ Someone who is **asleep** is sleeping. ❑ *My daughter was asleep on the sofa.* ■ PHRASE When you **fall asleep**, you start sleeping. ❑ *Sam soon fell asleep.* ■ PHRASE Someone who is **fast asleep** or **sound asleep** is sleeping deeply. ❑ *They were both fast asleep in their beds.*
→ see **sleep**

**as|para|gus** /əsp**æ**rəgəs/ N-UNCOUNT **Asparagus** is a vegetable that is long and green and has small shoots at one end. [from Latin]
→ see **vegetable**

**as|pect** /**æ**spɛkt/ (aspects) ■ N-COUNT An **aspect** of something is one of the parts of its character or nature. ❑ *Climate and weather affect every aspect of our lives.* ❑ *He was interested in all aspects of the work here.* ■ N-COUNT The **aspect** of a building or window is the direction in which it faces. [FORMAL] ❑ *The house had a southwest aspect.* [from Latin]

**as|pi|ra|tion** /æspɪr**eɪ**ʃ°n/ (aspirations) N-VAR Someone's **aspirations** are their desire to achieve things. ❑ *The girl had aspirations to a movie career.* [from Latin]

**as|pire** /əsp**aɪ**ər/ (aspires, aspiring, aspired) ■ V-I If you **aspire to** something such as an important job, you have a strong desire to achieve it. ❑ *...people who aspire to public office.* ❑ *James aspired to go to college.* [from Latin] ■ → see also **aspiring**

**as|pi|rin** /**æ**spərɪn, -prɪn/ (aspirins)

The form **aspirin** can also be used for the plural.

N-VAR **Aspirin** is a mild drug that reduces pain and fever. [from German]

**as|pir|ing** /əsp**aɪ**ərɪŋ/ ■ ADJ If you use **aspiring** to describe someone who is starting a particular career, you mean that they are trying to become successful in it. ❑ *...aspiring young artists.* [from Latin] ■ → see also **aspire**

**as|sail|ant** /əs**eɪ**lənt/ (assailants) N-COUNT Someone's **assailant** is a person who has physically attacked them. [FORMAL] ❑ *Friends rescued the injured man from his assailant.* [from Old French]

**as|sas|sin** /əs**æ**sɪn/ (assassins) N-COUNT An **assassin** is a person who assassinates someone. ❑ *The assassin shot the wrong man.* [from Medieval Latin]

**as|sas|si|nate** /əs**æ**sɪneɪt/ (assassinates, assassinating, assassinated) V-T When someone important **is assassinated**, they are murdered as a political act. ❑ *Robert Kennedy was assassinated in 1968.* ● **as|sas|si|na|tion** /əsæsɪn**eɪ**ʃ°n/ (assassinations) N-VAR ❑ *She wants an investigation into the assassination of her husband.* ❑ *He lives in fear of assassination.* [from Medieval Latin]

**as|sault** /əs**ɔ**lt/ (assaults, assaulting, assaulted) ■ N-COUNT An **assault** by an army is a strong attack made against an enemy. ❑ *They are making a new assault.* ■ N-VAR An **assault on** a person is a physical attack on them. ❑ *...a series of assaults in the university area.* ■ V-T To **assault** someone means to physically attack them. ❑ *The gang assaulted him with iron bars.* [from Old French]

**as|sem|blage** /əs**ɛ**mblɪdʒ/ (assemblages) N-COUNT An **assemblage** is a piece of sculpture that combines a number of different objects. [from Old French]

**as|sem|ble** /əs**ɛ**mb°l/ (assembles, assembling, assembled) ■ V-T/V-I When people **assemble** or when someone **assembles** them, they come together in a group. ❑ *There was nowhere for students to assemble between classes.* ■ V-T To **assemble** something means to collect it together or to fit the different parts of it together. ❑ *Workers were assembling airplanes.* [from Old French]
→ see **industry**

**as|sem|bly** /əs**ɛ**mbli/ (assemblies) ■ N-COUNT An **assembly** is a group of people gathered together for a particular purpose. ❑ *He waited until complete quiet settled on the assembly.* ■ N-UNCOUNT The **assembly** of a machine, device, or object is the process of fitting its different parts together. ❑ *...final assembly of the cars.* [from Old French]

**as|sem|bly line** (assembly lines) N-COUNT An **assembly line** is an arrangement of workers and machines in a factory, where each worker deals with only one part of a product. The product passes from one worker to another until it is finished.

**as|sent** /əs**ɛ**nt/ (assents, assenting, assented) ■ N-UNCOUNT If someone gives their **assent to** something, they formally agree to it. ❑ *He gave his assent to the plan.* ■ V-I If you **assent to** something, you agree to it or agree with it. ❑ *I assented to their request.* [from Old French]

**as|sert** /əs**ɜ**rt/ (asserts, asserting, asserted) ■ V-T If you **assert** a fact or belief, you state it firmly. [FORMAL] ❑ *He asserted that he had a right to go anywhere.* ❑ *He asserted his innocence.* ● **as|ser|tion** /əs**ɜ**rʃ°n/ (assertions) N-VAR ❑ *There is nothing to support these assertions.* ■ V-T If you **assert yourself** or **assert** your authority, you speak and act in a forceful way. ❑ *He's speaking up and asserting himself.* ● **as|ser|tion** N-UNCOUNT ❑ *The decision is an assertion of his authority.* [from Latin]

**as|ser|tive** /əs**ɜ**rtɪv/ ADJ Someone who is **assertive** states their needs and opinions clearly, so that people take notice. ❑ *I learned to be more assertive.* ● **as|ser|tive|ness** N-UNCOUNT ❑ *...assertiveness training.* [from Latin]

**as|sess** /əs**ɛ**s/ (assesses, assessing, assessed) V-T When you **assess** a person, thing, or situation, you consider them in order to make a judgment about them. ❑ *I looked around and assessed the situation.* ❑ *The doctor is assessing whether she is well* enough to travel. ● as|sess|ment (**assessments**) N-VAR ❑ ...the assessment of senior managers. [from Old French]

as|set /ǽsɛt/ (**assets**) **1** N-COUNT An **asset** is something or someone that is considered useful or helps a person or organization to be successful. ❑ He is a great asset to the company. **2** N-PLURAL The **assets** of a company or a person are all the things that they own. [BUSINESS] ❑ In 1989 the group had assets of $3.5 billion.

as|sign /əsáɪn/ (**assigns, assigning, assigned**) **1** V-T If you **assign** a piece of work to someone, you give them the work to do. ❑ I assign a topic to the children for them to write about. ❑ The teacher will assign them homework. **2** V-T If someone **is assigned** to a particular place, group, or person, they are sent to work there. ❑ He was assigned to head office. ❑ Did you choose Russia or were you assigned there? [from Old French]

as|sign|ment /əsáɪnmənt/ (**assignments**) N-COUNT An **assignment** is a task or piece of work that you are given to do, especially as part of your job or studies. ❑ ...written assignments and practical tests. [from Old French]

| **Thesaurus** | assignment | Also look up : |
|---|---|---|
| N. | chore, duty, job, task | |

as|simi|late /əsíməleɪt/ (**assimilates, assimilating, assimilated**) **1** V-T/V-I When people such as immigrants **assimilate into** a community or when that community **assimilates** them, they become an accepted part of it. ❑ School should help assimilate immigrants. ● as|simi|la|tion /əsíməléɪʃᵊn/ N-UNCOUNT ❑ ...the assimilation of minority groups. **2** V-T If you **assimilate** new ideas, customs, or techniques, you learn them or adopt them. ❑ You need to relax and assimilate the changes in your life. ● as|simi|la|tion N-UNCOUNT ❑ ...assimilation of knowledge. [from Latin]
→ see **culture**

as|sist /əsíst/ (**assists, assisting, assisted**) V-T/ V-I If someone or something **assists** you, they help you. ❑ The family decided to assist me with my work. ❑ Please do all you can to assist us in this work. ❑ They assisted with serving meals. [from French]

as|sis|tance /əsístəns/ N-UNCOUNT If you give someone **assistance**, you help them. ❑ We greatly welcome any assistance. **2** PHRASE Someone or something that **is of assistance** to you is helpful or useful to you. ❑ Can I be of any assistance? [from French]

| **Word Partnership** | Use assistance with : |
|---|---|
| ADJ. | emergency assistance, financial assistance, assistance, technical assistance **1** |
| V. | need/require assistance, provide assistance **1** |

as|sis|tant /əsístənt/ (**assistants**) **1** ADJ **Assistant** is used in front of titles or jobs to indicate a slightly lower rank. For example, an assistant director is one rank lower than a director in an organization. ❑ ...the assistant secretary of defense. **2** N-COUNT Someone's **assistant** is a person who helps them in their work. ❑ Kalan called his assistant, Hashim, to take over while he went out. **3** N-COUNT An **assistant** is a person who works in a store selling things to customers. ❑ The assistant took the book and checked the price. [from French]

as|sis|tant pro|fes|sor (**assistant professors**) N-COUNT; N-TITLE An **assistant professor** is a college teacher who ranks above an instructor but below an associate professor. ❑ ...an assistant professor of mathematics. ❑ ...Assistant Professor Rob Nideffer.

as|sis|ted liv|ing N-UNCOUNT **Assisted living** is a type of housing specially designed for people who need help in their everyday lives, but who do not need specialist nursing care. In **assisted living facilities**, residents live in independent rooms or apartments, but receive help with day-to-day activities, for example bathing, dressing, preparing meals, and taking their medicines. ❑ One million elderly Americans live in assisted living facilities. ❑ Now she's in assisted living, and her niece and nephew are helping with her affairs.

| **Word Link** | soci ≈ companion : associate, social, sociology |
|---|---|

as|so|ci|ate (**associates, associating, associated**)

The verb is pronounced /əsóʊʃieɪt, -sieɪt/. The noun and adjective are pronounced /əsóʊʃiɪt, -siɪt/.

**1** V-T If you **associate** someone or something **with** another thing, the two are connected in your mind. ❑ Some people associate thinness with happiness. **2** V-T If you **are associated with** a particular organization, cause, or point of view, or if you **associate yourself with** it, you support it publicly. ❑ We're associated with the U.S. Airways group. **3** V-I If you say that someone **is associating with** another person or group of people, you mean they are spending a lot of time in the company of people you do not approve of. ❑ I think she's associating with a bad crowd. **4** N-COUNT Your **associates** are the people you are closely connected with, especially at work. ❑ ...business associates. [from Latin]

as|so|ci|ate de|gree (**associate degrees**) N-COUNT An **associate degree** is a college degree that is awarded to a student who has completed a two-year course of study. ❑ She has an associate degree in food management.

as|so|ci|ate pro|fes|sor (**associate professors**) N-COUNT; N-TITLE An **associate professor** is a college teacher who ranks above an assistant professor but below a professor. ❑ ...an associate professor of psychiatry. ❑ ...Associate Professor Saifi Karibash.

as|so|cia|tion /əsóʊʃiéɪʃᵊn, -sié-/ (**associations**) **1** N-COUNT An **association** is an official group of people who have the same job, aim, or interest. ❑ ...the National Basketball Association. **2** N-COUNT Your **association with** a person or a thing such as an organization is the connection that you have with them. ❑ ...the company's association with retailer J.C. Penney. **3** N-COUNT If something has particular **associations** for you, it is connected in your mind with a particular memory, idea, or feeling. ❑ He has lots of things which have happy associations for him. **4** PHRASE If you do something **in association with** someone else, you do it together. ❑ The book was

**A**

*published in association with the Walden Woods Project.* [from Latin]

**as|sort|ed** /əsɔrtɪd/ ADJ A group of **assorted** things is a group of similar things that are of different sizes or colors or have different qualities. ❑ *...cotton-knit sweaters in assorted colors.* [from Old French]

**as|sort|ment** /əsɔrtmənt/ (**assortments**) N-COUNT An **assortment** is a group of similar things that are of different sizes or colors or have different qualities. ❑ *...an assortment of books.* [from Old French]

**Word Link** | *sume ≈ taking : assume, consume, presume*
---|---

**as|sume** /əsum/ (**assumes, assuming, assumed**) ◼ V-T If you **assume that** something is true, you suppose that it is true, sometimes wrongly. ❑ *I assume the eggs will be fresh.* ◻ V-T If someone **assumes** power or responsibility, they take power or responsibility. ❑ *Mr. Cross will assume the role of CEO.* ◼ V-T If you **assume** a particular expression or way of behaving, you start to look or behave in this way. ❑ *He assumed an air of calm.* [from Latin]

**Word Partnership** Use *assume* with :

| V. | tend to assume, lets assume *that* ◼ |
|---|---|
| ADV. | assume so ◼ |
| | automatically assume ◼ ◻ |
| N. | assume the worst ◼ |
| | assume power/control, assume responsibility, assume a role ◻ |

**as|sum|ing** /əsumɪn/ CONJ You use **assuming** or **assuming that** when you are considering a possible situation or event, so that you can think about the consequences. ❑ *"Assuming you're right," he said, "there's not much I can do about it, is there?"* [from Latin]

**Word Link** | *sumpt ≈ taking : assumption, consumption, presumption*
---|---

**as|sump|tion** /əsʌmpʃ⁰n/ (**assumptions**) N-COUNT If you make an **assumption** that something is true or will happen, you suppose that it is true or will happen, often wrongly. ❑ *You are making an assumption that I agree with you.* [from Latin]

**as|sur|ance** /əʃʊərəns/ (**assurances**) ◼ N-VAR If you give someone an **assurance that** something is true or will happen, you say that it is definitely true or will definitely happen, in order to make them feel less worried. ❑ *I gave him an assurance that it wouldn't happen again.* ◻ N-UNCOUNT If you do something **with assurance**, you do it with a feeling of confidence and certainty. ❑ *Masur led the orchestra with assurance.* [from Old French]

**as|sure** /əʃʊər/ (**assures, assuring, assured**) ◼ V-T If you **assure** someone **that** something is true or will happen, you tell them that it is definitely true or will definitely happen, often in order to make them less worried. ❑ *He assured me that there was nothing wrong.* ❑ *"Are you sure it's safe?" she asked anxiously. "It couldn't be safer," Max assured her.* ◻ → see also **assured** ◼ V-T To **assure** someone **of** something means to make certain that they will get it. ❑ *His performance yesterday*

*assured him of a medal.* [from Old French]

**as|sured** /əʃʊərd/ ADJ Someone who is **assured** is very confident and relaxed. ❑ *He gave an assured performance.* [from Old French]

**Word Link** | *aster, astro ≈ star : asterisk, astronaut, astronomy*
---|---

**as|ter|isk** /æstərɪsk/ (**asterisks**) N-COUNT An **asterisk** is the sign . [from Late Latin]

**as|ter|oid** /æstərɔɪd/ (**asteroids**) N-COUNT An **asteroid** is one of the very small planets that move around the sun between Mars and Jupiter. [from Greek]

**as|ter|oid belt** (**asteroid belts**) N-COUNT The **asteroid belt** is the region of the solar system between Mars and Jupiter where most asteroids occur.

**as|theno|sphere** /æsθɛnəsfɪər/ N-SING The **asthenosphere** is the region of the Earth which lies between approximately 70 and 120 miles below the surface. [TECHNICAL] [from Greek]

**asth|ma** /æzmə/ N-UNCOUNT **Asthma** is a lung condition that causes difficulty in breathing. [from Greek]

**asth|mat|ic** /æzmætɪk/ (**asthmatics**) N-COUNT People who suffer from asthma are sometimes referred to as **asthmatics**. ❑ *I have been an asthmatic from childhood.* ● **Asthmatic** is also an adjective. ❑ *Ten percent of children are asthmatic.* [from Greek]

**as|ton|ish** /əstɒnɪʃ/ (**astonishes, astonishing, astonished**) V-T If something or someone **astonishes** you, they surprise you very much. ❑ *My news will astonish you.* ● **aston|ished** ADJ ❑ *They were astonished to find the driver was a six-year-old boy.* [from Old French]

**as|ton|ish|ing** /əstɒnɪʃɪŋ/ ADJ Something that is **astonishing** is very surprising. ❑ *...an astonishing display of strength.* ● **aston|ish|ing|ly** ADV ❑ *Andrea was an astonishingly beautiful young woman.* [from Old French]

**aston|ish|ment** /əstɒnɪʃmənt/ N-UNCOUNT **Astonishment** is a feeling of great surprise. ❑ *He looked at her in astonishment.* [from Old French]

**as|tound** /əstaʊnd/ (**astounds, astounding, astounded**) V-T If something **astounds** you, you are very surprised by it. ❑ *These low prices will astound you.* ● **astound|ing** /əstaʊndɪŋ/ ADJ ❑ *The results are astounding.* [from Old French]

**as|tray** /əstreɪ/ ◼ PHRASE If you **are led astray** by someone or something, you behave badly or foolishly because of them. ❑ *He was led astray by older children.* ◻ PHRASE If something **goes astray**, it gets lost. ❑ *Many items of mail go astray every day.* [from Old French]

**as|tride** /əstraɪd/ ADV If you sit or stand **astride** something, you sit or stand with one leg on each side of it. ❑ *...three boys who stood astride their bicycles.*

**as|trol|ogy** /əstrɒlədʒi/ N-UNCOUNT **Astrology** is the study of the movements of the planets, sun, moon, and stars in the belief that these movements can have an influence on people's lives. ● **as|trolo|ger** (**astrologers**) N-COUNT ❑ *He went to see an astrologer.* [from Old French] → see **star**

## Word Web    astronomer

The Italian **astronomer** Galileo Galilei did not invent the telescope. However, he was the first person to use it to study **celestial** bodies. He recorded his findings. What Galileo saw through the telescope supported the theory that the **planet** Earth is not the center of the universe. This theory was written by the Polish astronomer Nicolaus Copernicus in 1530. Copernicus said that all of the planets in the universe revolve around the **sun**. In 1609, Galileo used a telescope to see the **craters** on Earth's **moon**. He also discovered the four largest **satellites** of the planet Jupiter. These four bodies are called the Galilean moons.

## Word Link    aster, astro ≈ star : aster**isk**, astro**naut**, astro**nomy**

astronaut

**as|tro|naut** /ǽstrənɔt/ (**astronauts**) N-COUNT An **astronaut** is a person who is trained for traveling in a spacecraft. [from Greek]

**as|tro|nomi|cal** /ǽstrənɒmɪkəl/ **1** ADJ If you describe an amount as **astronomical**, you are emphasizing that it is very large. ❏ *Houses are selling for astronomical prices.* **2** ADJ **Astronomical** means relating to astronomy. ❏ *...the American Astronomical Society.* [from Old French]

**as|tro|nomi|cal unit** (**astronomical units**) N-COUNT An **astronomical unit** is a unit of distance used in astronomy that is equal to the average distance between the Earth and the sun. The abbreviation *AU* is also used.

## Word Link    er, or ≈ one who does, that which does : astronom**er**, auth**or**, writ**er**

**as|trono|my** /əstrɒnəmi/ N-UNCOUNT **Astronomy** is the scientific study of the stars, planets, and other natural objects in space. ● **as|trono|mer** (**astronomers**) N-COUNT ❏ *...an amateur astronomer.* [from Old French]
→ see Word Web: **astronomer**
→ see **galaxy, telescope, star**

**A-student** (**A-students**) also A student N-COUNT An **A-student** is a student who regularly receives the highest grades for his or her work. ❏ *...good, hard-working A students.*

**as|tute** /əstut/ ADJ Someone who is **astute** shows understanding of behavior and situations, and is skillful at using this knowledge to their own advantage. ❏ *He's an astute businessman.* [from Latin]

**asy|lum** /əsaɪləm/ (**asylums**) N-UNCOUNT If a government gives a person from another country **asylum**, they allow them to stay, usually because they are unable to return home safely for political reasons. ❏ *He applied for asylum in 1987.* [from Latin]

**asym|met|ri|cal** /eɪsɪmétrɪkəl/ ADJ Something that is **asymmetrical** has two sides or halves that are different in shape, size, or style.

**asym|me|try** /eɪsɪmətri/ (**asymmetries**) N-VAR **Asymmetry** is the appearance that something has when its two sides or halves are different in shape, size, or style.

**asymp|tote** /ǽsɪmtoʊt, -ɪmp-/ (**asymptotes**) N-COUNT An **asymptote** is a straight line to which a curved line approaches closer and closer as one moves along it. [TECHNICAL] [from Greek]

**at** /ət, STRONG æt/

> In addition to the uses shown below, **at** is used after some verbs, nouns, and adjectives to introduce extra information. **At** is also used in phrasal verbs such as "get at" and "play at."

**1** PREP You use **at** to say where something happens or is situated. ❏ *He will be at the airport to meet her.* ❏ *I didn't like being alone at home.* ❏ *They agreed to meet at a restaurant.* **2** PREP You use **at** to say when something happens. ❏ *The funeral will be this afternoon at 3:00.* ❏ *Zachary started playing violin at age 4.* **3** PREP You use **at** to express a rate, frequency, level, or price. ❏ *I drove back down the highway at normal speed.* ❏ *...at a rate of about 1 centimeter a month.* **4** PREP If you look **at** someone or something, you look toward them. If you direct an object or a comment **at** someone, you direct it toward them. ❏ *He looked at Michael and laughed.* **5** PREP If you are working **at** something, you are dealing with it. If you are aiming **at** something, you are trying to achieve it. ❏ *She has worked hard at her marriage.* **6** PREP If something is done **at** your invitation or request, it is done as a result of it. ❏ *She closed the window at his request.* **7** PREP You use **at** to say that someone or something is in a particular state or condition. ❏ *The two nations are living at peace with each other.* **8** PREP You use **at** to say how something is being done. ❏ *We'll pick three winners at random from correct entries.* **9** PREP You use **at** to indicate an activity or task when saying how well someone does it. ❏ *I'm good at my work.* **10** PREP You use **at** to indicate what someone is reacting to. ❏ *Elena was annoyed at having to wait so long.* [from Old English] **11** **at all** → see **all**

**ate** /eɪt/ **Ate** is the past tense of **eat**.

A

**athe|ism** /eɪθiɪzəm/ N-UNCOUNT **Atheism** is the belief that there is no God. ● **athe|ist** /eɪθiɪst/ (**atheists**) N-COUNT ❑ *Lambert said he had been an atheist since ninth grade.* [from French]

**ath|lete** /æθlit/ (**athletes**) N-COUNT An **athlete** is a person who does any kind of physical sports, exercise, or games, especially in competitions. ❑ *Jesse Owens was one of the greatest athletes of the twentieth century.* [from Latin]

**ath|let|ic** /æθlɛtɪk/ ■ ADJ **Athletic** means relating to athletes and athletics. ❑ *He comes from an athletic family.* ◨ ADJ An **athletic** person is fit, and able to perform energetic movements easily. ❑ *Sandra is an athletic 36-year-old.* [from Latin]

**ath|let|ics** /æθlɛtɪks/ N-UNCOUNT **Athletics** refers to any kind of physical sports, exercise, or games. ❑ *...college athletics.* [from Latin]

**at|las** /ætləs/ (**atlases**) N-COUNT An **atlas** is a book of maps. [from Latin]

**ATM** /eɪ ti: ɛm/ (**ATMs**) N-COUNT An **ATM** is a machine built into the wall of a bank or other building, which allows people to take out money from their bank account by using a special card. **ATM** is an abbreviation for "automated teller machine."

**at|mos|phere** /ætməsfɪər/ (**atmospheres**) ■ N-COUNT A planet's **atmosphere** is the layer of air or other gases around it. ❑ *The shuttle Columbia will re-enter Earth's atmosphere tomorrow morning.* ● **at|mos|pher|ic** /ætməsfɛrɪk/ ADJ ❑ *...atmospheric gases.* ◨ N-COUNT The **atmosphere** of a place is the air that you breathe there. ❑ *Gases from the power plant rise into the atmosphere.* ◳ N-SING The **atmosphere** of a place is the general impression that you get of it. ❑ *The rooms are warm and the atmosphere is welcoming.* [from New Latin] → see **air, biosphere, core, earth, greenhouse effect, meteor, moon, ozone, water**

**at|mos|pher|ic per|spec|tive** (**atmospheric perspectives**) N-VAR **Atmospheric perspective** means the same as **aerial perspective**.

**atmos|pher|ic pres|sure** (**atmospheric pressures**) N-VAR **Atmospheric pressure** is the amount of pressure that is produced by the weight of the Earth's atmosphere.

**atom** /ætəm/ (**atoms**) N-COUNT An **atom** is the smallest amount of a substance that can take part in a chemical reaction. [from Old French] → see **element**

**atom|ic** /ətɒmɪk/ ADJ **Atomic** means relating atoms or to power that is produced by splitting atoms. ❑ *...atomic energy.* ❑ *...the atomic number of an element.* [from Old French]

**atom|ic mass** (**atomic masses**) N-VAR The **atomic mass** of a chemical element is the weight of one atom of that element, usually expressed in atomic mass units. [TECHNICAL] → see **periodic table**

**atom|ic mass unit** (**atomic mass units**) N-COUNT An **atomic mass unit** is a unit that is used to measure the atomic mass of chemical

elements. The abbreviation *amu* is also used. [TECHNICAL]

**atom|ic num|ber** (**atomic numbers**) N-COUNT The **atomic number** of a chemical element is the number of protons in the nucleus of one atom of the element. [TECHNICAL]

**aton|al** /eɪtoʊnᵊl/ ADJ **Atonal** music is music that is not written or played in any key or system of scales.

**ATP** /eɪ ti pi/ N-UNCOUNT **ATP** is a molecule that is found in all plant and animals cells and provides the cells with their main source of energy. **ATP** is an abbreviation for "adenosine triphosphate."

**atrium** /eɪtriəm/ (**atria**) N-COUNT The *left* **atrium** and the *right* **atrium** are the two upper chambers of the heart. [from Latin]

**atro|cious** /ətroʊʃəs/ ADJ If you describe something as **atrocious**, you are emphasizing that it is very bad. ❑ *The food is atrocious.* ❑ *...atrocious crimes.* [from Latin]

**atroc|ity** /ətrɒsɪti/ (**atrocities**) N-VAR An **atrocity** is a very cruel, shocking action. ❑ *The people who committed this atrocity should be punished.* [from Latin]

**at|tach** /ətætʃ/ (**attaches, attaching, attached**) ■ V-T If you **attach** something **to** an object, you join it or fasten it to the object. ❑ *We attach labels to things before we store them.* ❑ *Please use the attached form.* ◨ V-T In computing, if you **attach** a file **to** a message that you send to someone, you send it with the message but separate from it. ❑ *It is possible to attach program files to e-mail.* [from Old French] ◳ → see also **attached** ◳ **no strings attached** → see **string**

**at|tached** /ətætʃt/ ADJ If you are **attached to** someone or something, you like them very much. ❑ *She is very attached to her family and friends.* [from Old French]

**at|tach|ment** /ətætʃmənt/ (**attachments**) ■ N-VAR If you have an **attachment to** someone or something, you are fond of them. ❑ *Mother and child form a close attachment.* ◨ N-COUNT An **attachment** is a device that can be fixed onto a machine in order to enable it to do different jobs. ❑ *Some cleaners come with an attachment for brushing.* ◳ N-COUNT In computing, an **attachment** is a file which is attached separately to a message that you send to someone. ❑ *When you send an e-mail you can also send a file as an attachment.* [from Old French]

**at|tack** /ətæk/ (**attacks, attacking, attacked**) ■ V-T/V-I To **attack** a person or place means to try to hurt or damage them using physical violence. ❑ *I thought he was going to attack me.* ❑ *He was in the yard when the dog attacked.* ● **Attack** is also a noun. ❑ *...an attack on a police officer.* ● **at|tack|er** (**attackers**) N-COUNT ❑ *She struggled with her attacker.* ◨ V-T If you **attack** a person, belief, idea, or act, you criticize them strongly. ❑ *He attacked bosses for giving themselves big pay raises.* ● **Attack** is also a noun. ❑ *...his response to attacks on his work.* ◳ V-T If you **attack** a job or a problem, you start to deal with it in an energetic way. ❑ *Parents shouldn't attack the problem on their own.* ◳ V-T/V-I In games such as soccer, when one team **attacks** the opponent's goal, they try to score a goal. ❑ *Now the U.S. is attacking the other side's goal.* ❑ *They attacked constantly in the second half.* ◵ N-COUNT An

**attack of** an illness is a short period in which you suffer badly from it. ❏ ...*an attack of asthma.* [from French] **6** → see also **counterattack, heart attack** → see **war**

at|tain /əteɪn/ (**attains, attaining, attained**) v-T If you **attain** something, you gain it or achieve it, often after a lot of effort. [FORMAL] ❏ *Jim is about to attain his pilot's license.* ● at|tain|ment N-UNCOUNT ❏ ...*the attainment of independence.* [from Old French]

at|tempt /ətempt/ (**attempts, attempting, attempted**) **1** v-T If you **attempt to** do something, you try to do it. ❏ *He attempted to enter law school.* ● at|tempt|ed ADJ ❏ ...*a case of attempted murder.* **2** N-COUNT If you make an **attempt to** do something, you try to do it, often without success. ❏ *He was standing in the middle of the street in an attempt to stop the traffic.* **3** N-COUNT An **attempt on** someone's life is an attempt to kill them. ❏ ...*an attempt on the life of the president.* [from Old French]

| Thesaurus | attempt | Also look up : |
|---|---|---|
| V. | strive, tackle, take on, try **1** | |
| N. | effort, try, venture **2** | |

**Word Partnership** Use *attempt* with :

| | | |
|---|---|---|
| N. | attempt **suicide 1** | |
| | **assassination** attempt **3** | |
| ADJ. | **any** attempt, **desperate** attempt, **failed/ successful** attempt **2** | |
| V. | attempt **to control/find/prevent/solve,** make an attempt **2** | |

at|tend /ətend/ (**attends, attending, attended**) **1** v-T/v-I If you **attend** a meeting or other event, you are present at it. ❏ *Thousands of people attended the wedding.* ❏ *I was invited but was unable to attend.* ● at|tend|ance N-UNCOUNT ❏ ...*his poor attendance at classes.* **2** v-T If you **attend** an institution such as a school, college, or church, you go there regularly. ❏ *They attended college together.* ● at|tend|ance N-UNCOUNT ❏ *Attendance at the school is above average.* **3** v-I If you **attend to** something, you deal with it. If you **attend to** someone who is hurt or injured, you care for them. ❏ *The staff will attend to your needs.* [from Old French]

at|tend|ance /ətendəns/ (**attendances**) N-VAR The **attendance** at an event is the number of people who are present at it. ❏ *People had a good time, and attendance was high.* [from Old French]

at|tend|ant /ətendənt/ (**attendants**) **1** N-COUNT An **attendant** is someone whose job is to serve or help people in a place such as a gas station or a parking lot. ❏ *Tony Williams was working as a parking lot attendant in Los Angeles.* **2** N-COUNT The **attendants** at a wedding are people such as the bridesmaids and the ushers, who accompany or help the bride and groom. ❏ *The bride will choose the dresses her attendants will wear to the wedding.* [from Old French]

at|tend|ee /ətendi/ (**attendees**) N-COUNT The **attendees** at something such as a meeting or a conference are the people who are attending it.

❏ *Only half the attendees could fit into the large hall at any one time.* [from Old French]

at|ten|tion /ətenʃⁿn/ **1** N-UNCOUNT If you give someone or something your **attention**, you look at them, listen to them, or think about them carefully. ❏ *Can I have your attention?* **2** N-UNCOUNT If someone or something is getting **attention**, they are being dealt with or cared for. ❏ *Each year more than two million people need medical attention.* **3** PHRASE If you **pay attention to** someone, you watch them, listen to them, or take notice of them. If you **pay no attention to** someone, you behave as if you are not aware of them or as if they are not important. ❏ *Everyone is paying attention.* [from Latin]

**Word Partnership** Use *attention* with :

| | | |
|---|---|---|
| PREP. | attention **to detail 1** | |
| ADJ. | **careful/close/undivided** attention **1** **special** attention **1 2** **unwanted** attention **2** | |
| V. | **attract** attention, **call/direct** someone's attention, **catch someone's** attention, **draw** attention, **focus** attention, attention **to** *someone/something* **1** **pay** attention **3** | |
| N. | **center of** attention **2** | |

at|ten|tive /ətentɪv/ **1** ADJ If you are **attentive**, you are paying close attention to what is being said or done. ❏ ...*an attentive audience.* ● at|ten|tive|ly ADV ❏ *He listened attentively to what Chris told him.* **2** ADJ Someone who is **attentive** is helpful and polite. ❏ *He is attentive to his wife.* [from Latin]

at|test /ətest/ (**attests, attesting, attested**) v-T/v-I To **attest** something or **attest to** something means to say, show, or prove that it is true. [FORMAL] ❏ *Police records attest to his history of violence.* [from Latin]

at|tic /ætɪk/ (**attics**) N-COUNT An **attic** is a room at the top of a house just below the roof. → see **house**

at|ti|tude /ætɪtud/ (**attitudes**) N-VAR Your **attitude** to something is the way that you think and feel about it. ❏ *We needed to change our attitude.* ❏ ...*negative attitudes to work.* [from French]

**Word Partnership** Use *attitude* with :

| | | |
|---|---|---|
| PREP. | attitude **toward/about** | |
| ADJ. | **bad** attitude, **new** attitude, **positive/ negative** attitude, **progressive** attitude | |
| V. | **change your** attitude | |

at|tor|ney /ətɜrni/ (**attorneys**) N-COUNT In the United States, an **attorney** or **attorney-at-law** is a lawyer. ❏ ...*a prosecuting attorney.* ❏ *At the hearing, her attorney did not enter a plea.* [from Old French] → see **trial**

at|tract /ətrækt/ (**attracts, attracting, attracted**) **1** v-T If something **attracts** people or animals, it has features that cause them to come to it. ❏ *The museum is attracting many visitors.* **2** v-T If someone or something **attracts** you, they have particular qualities which cause you to like or admire them. ❏ *May's boldness surprised and attracted him.* ● at|tract|ed ADJ ❏ *I wasn't very*

A

*attracted to him.* **3** V-T If something **attracts** support, publicity, or money, it receives it. □ *We're hoping to attract money into women's golf.* [from Latin] → see **magnet**

**at|trac|tion** /ətrækʃ°n/ (**attractions**)
**1** N-UNCOUNT **Attraction** is a feeling of liking someone. □ *His attraction to her was growing.* **2** N-COUNT An **attraction** is a feature that makes something interesting or desirable. □ *...the attractions of living on the waterfront.* **3** N-COUNT An **attraction** is something that people can go to for interest or enjoyment, for example, a famous building. □ *Disney World is an important tourist attraction.* **4** N-UNCOUNT **Attraction** is the force that exists between two objects when they are pulled toward one another, for example by magnetism or gravity. [from Latin]

**at|trac|tive** /ətræktɪv/ **1** ADJ An **attractive** person or thing is pleasant to look at. □ *She's a very attractive woman.* □ *The apartment was small but attractive.* ● **at|trac|tive|ness** N-UNCOUNT □ *...the attractiveness of the country.* **2** ADJ You can describe something as **attractive** when it seems worth having or doing. □ *Younger players are more attractive to major-league teams.* [from Latin]

**Thesaurus** *attractive* Also look up :

ADJ. appealing, charming, good-looking, pleasant; (*ant.*) repulsive, ugly, unattractive **1**

**Word Link** *tribute ≈ giving : at*tribute, *con*tribute, *dis*tribute

**at|trib|ute** (**attributes, attributing, attributed**)

The verb is pronounced /ətrɪbyut/. The noun is pronounced /ætrɪbyut/.

**1** V-T If you **attribute** something **to** a person, thing, or event, you think that it was caused by that event or situation. □ *I attributed my success to luck.* **2** V-T If a piece of writing, a work of art, or a remark **is attributed** to someone, people say that they wrote it, created it, or said it. □ *For a long time the painting was attributed to Rembrandt.* **3** N-COUNT An **attribute** is a quality or feature that someone or something has. □ *He had most of the attributes of a really great reporter.* [from Latin]

**AU** /eɪ yu/ (**AU**) **AU** is an abbreviation for **astronomical unit.**

**auburn** /ɔbərn/ COLOR **Auburn** hair is reddish brown. □ *...a tall woman with long auburn hair.* [from Old French]

**auc|tion** /ɔkʃ°n/ (**auctions, auctioning, auctioned**) **1** N-VAR An **auction** is a public sale where items are sold to the person who offers the highest price. □ *The painting sold for $400,000 at auction.* **2** V-T If something **is auctioned**, it is sold in an auction. □ *Eight drawings by French artist Jean Cocteau will be auctioned next week.* [from Latin]
▶ **auction off** PHR-VERB If you **auction off** something, you sell it to the person who offers most for it, often at an auction. □ *They're coming to auction off my farm.*

**Word Link** *eer ≈ one who does : auction*eer, *mountain*eer, *volunt*eer

**auc|tion|eer** /ɔkʃənɪər/ (**auctioneers**) N-COUNT An **auctioneer** is a person in charge of an auction.

[from Latin]

**auda|cious** /ɔdeɪʃəs/ ADJ Someone who is **audacious** takes risks in order to achieve something. □ *...an audacious plan to win the presidency.* ● **audac|ity** /ɔdæsɪti/ N-UNCOUNT □ *I was shocked at his audacity.* [from Latin]

**Word Link** *ible ≈ able to be : au*dible, *flex*ible, *poss*ible

**audible** /ɔdɪb°l/ ADJ A sound that is **audible** is loud enough to be heard. □ *Her voice was barely audible.* ● **audibly** /ɔdɪbli/ ADV □ *Frank sighed audibly.* [from Late Latin]

**Word Link** *audi ≈ hearing : audi*ence, *audi*tion, *audi*torium

**audi|ence** /ɔdiəns/ (**audiences**) **1** N-COUNT The **audience** of a play, concert, movie, or television program is all the people who are watching or listening to it. □ *...a TV audience of 35 million.* **2** N-COUNT The **audience** of a writer or artist is the people who read their books or look at their work. □ *His books reached a wide audience during his lifetime.* [from Old French]
→ see **concert**

**Word Partnership** Use *audience* with :

PREP. **before/in front of an** audience **1**
N. audience **participation, studio** audience, **audience 1**
ADJ. **captive** audience, **general** audience, **live** audience, audience, **wide** audience **1** **large** audience **1** **2**
V. **reach an** audience **2**

**audio** /ɔdioʊ/ ADJ **Audio** equipment is used for recording and reproducing sound. □ *...audio and video files.*

**audit** /ɔdɪt/ (**audits, auditing, audited**) V-T When an accountant **audits** an organization's accounts, he or she examines the financial records officially in order to make sure that they are correct. □ *Each year they audit our financial records.* ● **Audit** is also a noun. □ *The bank learned of the problem when it carried out an internal audit.* ● **audi|tor** (**auditors**) N-COUNT □ *...the group's internal auditors.* [from Latin]

**audi|tion** /ɔdɪʃ°n/ (**auditions, auditioning, auditioned**) **1** N-COUNT An **audition** is a short performance given by an actor, dancer, or musician so that a director or conductor can decide if they are good enough to be in a play, film, or orchestra. □ *...an audition for a Broadway musical.* **2** V-T/V-I If you **audition** or if someone **auditions** you, you do an audition. □ *They're auditioning new members for the cast of "Miss Saigon" today.* [from Latin]
→ see **theater**

**audi|to|rium** /ɔdɪtɔriəm/ (**auditoriums** or **auditoria** /ɔdɪtɔriə/) **1** N-COUNT An **auditorium** is the part of a theater or concert hall where the audience sits. □ *...a 250-seat auditorium.* **2** N-COUNT An **auditorium** is a large room, hall, or building that is used for events such as meetings and concerts. □ *...a high school auditorium.* [from Latin]

**aug|ment** /ɔgmɛnt/ (**augments, augmenting,**

augmented) v-t To **augment** something means to make it larger, stronger, or more effective by adding something to it. [FORMAL] ❑ *She was looking for a way to augment the family income.* [from Late Latin]

**aug|ment|ed in|ter|val** (**augmented intervals**) N-COUNT In music, an **augmented interval** is an interval that is increased by half a step or half a tone.

**August** /ˈɔgəst/ (**Augusts**) N-VAR **August** is the eighth month of the year in the Western calendar. ❑ *The movie opened in August.* ❑ *The trial will start on August twenty-second.* [from Old English]

**aunt** /ænt, ɑnt/ (**aunts**) N-COUNT; N-TITLE Your **aunt** is the sister of your mother or father, or the wife of your uncle. ❑ *She wrote to her aunt in Alabama.* [from Old French]
→ see **family**

> ### Usage     **aunt** and **ant**
>
> Be sure not to confuse *aunt* and *ant*, which many English speakers pronounce the same way. Your *aunt* is a sister of your parent; an *ant* is an insect: *Linh's aunt has an unusual fear – she's terrified of stepping on ants.*

**au pair** /ˌoʊ ˈpɛər/ (**au pairs**) N-COUNT An **au pair** is a young person usually from a foreign country who lives with a family to help take care of the children and often to learn the language. [from French]

**aura** /ˈɔrə/ (**auras**) N-COUNT An **aura** is a quality or feeling that seems to surround a person or place. ❑ *She had an aura of authority.* [from Latin]

**aural** /ˈɔrəl/ ADJ **Aural** means related to the sense of hearing. Compare **oral**. ❑ *…astonishing visual and aural effects.* [from Latin]

**aus|pices** /ˈɔspɪsɪz/ PHRASE If something is done **under the auspices of** a particular person or organization, or **under** their **auspices**, it is done with their support and approval. [FORMAL] ❑ *They met under the auspices of the United Nations.* [from Latin]

**aus|tere** /ɔˈstɪər/ ■ ADJ Something that is **austere** has a plain and simple appearance. ❑ *…an austere black blouse.* ■ ADJ If you describe someone as **austere**, you disapprove of them because they are strict and serious. ❑ *I found her an austere, distant person.* ■ ADJ An **austere** way of life is one that is simple and without luxuries. ❑ *Their life was somewhat austere.* ● **aus|ter|ity** /ɔˈstɛrɪti/ N-UNCOUNT ❑ *Years of austerity followed the war.* [from Old French]

**Aus|tra|lo|pithe|cine** also **australopithecine** /ˌɔstreɪloʊpɪˈθəsɪn, -saɪn, ɔstrə-/ (**Australopithecines**) N-COUNT **Australopithecines** were a species of primates, resembling early human beings, that lived over 3 million years ago. [from New Latin]

**authen|tic** /ɔˈθɛntɪk/ ADJ An **authentic** person, object, or emotion is genuine. ❑ *…authentic Italian food.* ❑ *She has authentic charm.* ● **au|then|tic|ity** /ˌɔθɛnˈtɪsɪti/ N-UNCOUNT ❑ *Some people doubt the statue's authenticity.* [from Late Latin]

> ### Word Link     *er, or ≈ one who does, that which does : astronomer, author, writer*

**author** /ˈɔθər/ (**authors**) ■ N-COUNT The **author**

of a piece of writing is the person who wrote it. ❑ *…Jill Phillips, author of the book "Give Your Child Music."* ■ N-COUNT An **author** is a person whose job is writing books. ❑ *Haruki Murakami is Japan's best-selling author.* [from Old French]

**authori|tar|ian** /əθɔrɪˈtɛəriən/ ADJ If you describe a person or an organization as **authoritarian**, you are critical of them controlling everything rather than letting people decide things for themselves. ❑ *…authoritarian governments.* ● An **authoritarian** is someone who is authoritarian. [from French]

**authori|ta|tive** /əˈθɔrɪteɪtɪv/ ■ ADJ Someone or something that is **authoritative** gives an impression of power and importance and is likely to be obeyed. ❑ *He has a deep, authoritative voice.* ■ ADJ Someone or something that is **authoritative** has a lot of knowledge of a particular subject. ❑ *The first authoritative study of the disease.* [from French]

**author|ity** /əˈθɔrɪti/ (**authorities**) ■ N-PLURAL The **authorities** are the people who have the power to make decisions and to make sure that laws are obeyed. ❑ *The authorities stopped more than 100 cars Friday.* ■ N-COUNT An **authority** is an official organization or government department that has the power to make decisions. ❑ *…the Philadelphia Parking Authority.* ■ N-COUNT Someone who is an **authority on** a particular subject knows a lot about it. ❑ *He's an authority on Russian music.* ■ N-UNCOUNT **Authority** is the right to command and control other people. ❑ *…a position of authority.* ■ N-UNCOUNT **Authority** is official permission to do something. ❑ *They acted without authority.* [from French]

**author|ize** /ˈɔθəraɪz/ (**authorizes, authorizing, authorized**) v-t If someone **authorizes** something, they give their official permission for it to happen. ❑ *Only the president could authorize its use.* ● **authori|za|tion** /ˌɔθərɪˈzeɪʃᵊn/ (**authorizations**) N-VAR ❑ *We didn't have authorization to go.* [from Old French]

**auto|bi|og|ra|phy** /ˌɔtəbaɪˈɒgrəfi/ (**autobiographies**) N-COUNT Your **autobiography** is an account of your life, which you write yourself. ❑ *He published his autobiography last fall.* ● **auto|bio|graphi|cal** /ˌɔtoʊbaɪəˈgræfɪkᵊl/ ADJ ❑ *…an autobiographical novel.*

> ### Word Link     *graph ≈ riting : auto*graph, bio*graphy, graph*

**auto|graph** /ˈɔtəgræf/ (**autographs, autographing, autographed**) ■ N-COUNT An **autograph** is the signature of someone famous that is specially written for a fan to keep. ❑ *He asked for her autograph.* ■ v-t If someone famous **autographs** something, they put their signature on it. ❑ *I autographed a copy of one of my books.* [from Late Latin]

**auto|maker** /ˈɔtoʊmeɪkər/ (**automakers**) N-COUNT An **automaker** is a company that manufactures cars. ❑ *…General Motors Corp., the world's largest automaker.*

**auto|mat|ed** /ˈɔtəmeɪtɪd/ ADJ An **automated** factory, office, or industrial process uses machines to do the work instead of people. ❑ *The equipment was made on automated production lines.* [from Greek]

**Word Link** auto ≈ self : *auto*matic, *auto*mobile, *auto*nomy

**auto|mat|ic** /ɔtəmætɪk/ (**automatics**) **1** ADJ An **automatic** machine or device can keep running without someone operating its controls. ❑ *Modern trains have automatic doors.* **2** ADJ An **automatic** weapon is one that keeps firing shots until you stop pulling the trigger. ❑ *Three gunmen with automatic rifles opened fire.* ● **Automatic** is also a noun. ❑ *He drew his automatic and began running in the direction of the sounds.* **3** ADJ An **automatic** action is one that you do without thinking about it. ❑ *All of the automatic body functions, even breathing, are affected.* ● **auto|mati|cal|ly** /ɔtəmætɪkli/ ADV ❑ *You will automatically wake up after 30 minutes.* [from Greek]

**Word Link** mobil ≈ moving : *auto*mobile, *mobile*, *mobilize*

**auto|mo|bile** /ɔtəməbil/ (**automobiles**) N-COUNT An **automobile** is a car. ❑ *...the automobile industry.*
→ see **car**

**autono|my** /ɔtɒnəmi/ **1** N-UNCOUNT **Autonomy** is the control or government of a country, organization, or group by itself rather than by others. ❑ *Reagan spoke about his idea of greater autonomy for individual states.* ● **autono|mous** ADJ ❑ *...the autonomous region of Andalucia.* **2** N-UNCOUNT **Autonomy** is the ability to make your own decisions about what to do rather than being influenced by someone else or told what to do. [FORMAL] ❑ *Each of the area managers has a great deal of autonomy in the running of his own area.* ● **autono|mous** ADJ ❑ *...autonomous business managers.* [from Greek]

**autop|sy** /ɔtɒpsi/ (**autopsies**) N-COUNT An **autopsy** is an examination of a dead body by a doctor who cuts it open in order to try to discover the cause of death. [from New Latin]

**auto|worker** /ɔtoʊwɜrkər/ (**autoworkers**) N-COUNT An **autoworker** is a person who works in the automobile manufacturing industry. ❑ *...an autoworker from Cleveland.*

**autumn** /ɔtəm/ (**autumns**) N-VAR **Autumn** is the season between summer and winter when the weather becomes cooler and the leaves fall off the trees. [AM usually **fall**] [from Latin]

**aux|ilia|ry** /ɔgzɪlyəri, -zɪləri/ (**auxiliaries**) **1** ADJ **Auxiliary** equipment is extra equipment that is available for use when necessary. ❑ *...an auxiliary motor.* **2** ADJ **Auxiliary** staff assist other staff. ❑ *...auxiliary nurses.* **3** N-COUNT An **auxiliary** is an organization that is connected with, but less important than, another organization. ❑ *...the Stanford Hospital Auxiliary.* **4** N-COUNT An **auxiliary** is a person who is employed to assist other people in their work. Auxiliaries are often medical workers or members of the armed forces. ❑ *Nursing auxiliaries provide basic care.* **5** N-COUNT In grammar, an **auxiliary** or **auxiliary verb** is a verb that is used with a main verb, for example, to form different tenses or to make the verb passive. In English, the basic auxiliary verbs are "be," "have," and "do." [from Latin]

**avail** /əveɪl/ PHRASE If you do something **to no avail** or **to little avail**, what you do fails to achieve what you want. [WRITTEN] ❑ *His efforts were to no avail.* [from Old French]

**avail|able** /əveɪləbəl/ **1** ADJ If something you want or need is **available**, you can find it or obtain it. ❑ *Breakfast is available from 6 a.m.* ● **avail|abil|ity** /əveɪləbɪliti/ N-UNCOUNT ❑ *...the availability of health care.* **2** ADJ Someone who is **available** is not busy and is therefore free to talk to you or to do a particular task. ❑ *Mr. Leach is not available for comment.* [from Old French]

**Thesaurus** available Also look up :

ADJ. accessible, handy, obtainable, usable **1** free **2**

**ava|lanche** /ævəlæntʃ/ (**avalanches**) N-COUNT An **avalanche** is a large mass of snow that falls down the side of a mountain. [from French]
→ see **snow**

**avant-garde** /ævɒŋgɑrd/ ADJ **Avant-garde** art, music, theater, and literature is very modern and experimental. ❑ *...avant-garde concert music.* [from French]

**avenge** /əvɛndʒ/ (**avenges, avenging, avenged**) V-T If you **avenge** a wrong or harmful act, you hurt or punish the person who is responsible for it. ❑ *He is determined to avenge his daughter's death.* [from Old French]

**av|enue** /ævɪnyu, -nu/ (**avenues**) **1** N-COUNT **Avenue** is sometimes used in the names of streets. The written abbreviation **Ave.** is also used. ❑ *...the most expensive apartments on Park Avenue.* **2** N-COUNT An **avenue** is a wide, straight road, especially one with trees on either side. [from French]

**av|er|age** /ævərɪdʒ, ævrɪdʒ/ (**averages, averaging, averaged**) **1** N-COUNT An **average** is the result that you get when you add two or more numbers together and divide the total by the number of numbers you added together. ❑ *The average age was 63.* ● **Average** is also an adjective. ❑ *The average price of goods rose by just 2.2%.* **2** N-SING An amount or quality that is **the average** is the normal amount or quality for a particular group of things or people. ❑ *Rainfall was nearly twice the average for this time of year.* ● **Average** is also an adjective. ❑ *The average adult man burns 1,500 to 2,000 calories per day.* **3** V-T To **average** a particular amount means to do, get, or produce that amount as an average over a period of time. ❑ *We averaged 42 miles per hour.* **4** PHRASE You say **on average** or **on the average** to indicate that a number is the average of several numbers. ❑ *Women are, on average, paid 25 per cent less than men.* [from Old Italian]

**av|er|age speed** (**average speeds**) N-COUNT The **average speed** of a moving object is the overall rate at which it moves, which you calculate by dividing the distance that the object travels by the time it takes to travel that distance.

**averse** /əvɜrs/ ADJ If you say that you are **averse** to something, you mean that you like it or want to do it. [FORMAL] ❑ *He's not averse to publicity.* [from Latin]

**aver|sion** /əvɜrʒən/ (**aversions**) N-VAR If you have an **aversion** to someone or something, you dislike them very much. ❑ *Many people have a natural aversion to insects.* [from Latin]

**avert** /əvɜrt/ (**averts, averting, averted**) **1** v-t
If you **avert** something unpleasant, you prevent
it from happening. ❑ *They managed to avert war.*
**2** v-t If you **avert** your eyes or gaze **from** someone
or something, you look away from them. ❑ *I saw
her but I averted my eyes.* [from Old French]

**aviary** /eɪvieri/ (**aviaries**) N-COUNT An **aviary**
is a large cage or covered area in which birds are
kept. [from Latin]

**avia|tion** /eɪvieɪʃⁿn/ N-UNCOUNT **Aviation** is
the operation and production of aircraft. ❑ *...the
aviation industry.* [from French]
→ see **oil**

**avid** /ævɪd/ ADJ You use **avid** to describe
someone who is very enthusiastic about
something that they do. ❑ *He's an avid reader.*
● **av|id|ly** ADV ❑ *I read the magazine avidly each
month.* [from Latin]

**avo|ca|do** /ævəkɑdoʊ/ (**avocados**) N-VAR
**Avocados** are pear-shaped vegetables, with hard
skins and large seeds, which are usually eaten
raw. [from Spanish]

**avoid** /əvɔɪd/ (**avoids, avoiding, avoided**) **1** v-t
If you **avoid** something unpleasant that might
happen, you take action in order to prevent it
from happening. ❑ *...a last-minute attempt to avoid
a disaster.* **2** v-t If you **avoid** doing something,
you choose not to do it, or you put yourself in a
situation where you do not have to do it. ❑ *I avoid
working in places which are too public.* **3** v-t If you
**avoid** a person or thing, you keep away from them.
❑ *She locked herself in the women's restroom to avoid
him.* **4** v-t If a person or vehicle **avoids** someone
or something, they change the direction they
are moving in, so that they do not hit them.
❑ *The driver only just avoided the woman.* [from Old
French]

**avoid|ance** /əvɔɪdⁿns/ N-UNCOUNT **Avoidance
of** someone or something is the act of avoiding
them. ❑ *...the avoidance of stress.* [from Old French]

**aw** /ɔ/ **1** EXCLAM People sometimes use **aw**
to express disapproval, disappointment, or
sympathy. [INFORMAL] ❑ *"Aw, leave her alone," Paul
said.* **2** EXCLAM People sometimes use **aw** to
express encouragement or approval. [INFORMAL]
❑ *Aw, she's got her mother's nose!*

**await** /əweɪt/ (**awaits, awaiting, awaited**)
**1** v-t If you **await** someone or something, you
wait for them. [FORMAL] ❑ *We awaited the arrival of
the chairman.* **2** v-t Something that **awaits** you
is going to happen or come to you in the future.
[FORMAL] ❑ *A surprise awaited them inside the store.*

| Word Link | wak ≈ *being awake : awake,
awakening, wake* |

**awake** /əweɪk/ **1** ADJ Someone who is **awake** is
not sleeping. ❑ *I stayed awake worrying.* **2** PHRASE
Someone who is **wide awake** is fully awake and
unable to sleep. ❑ *I could not relax and still felt wide
awake.* [from Old English]
→ see **sleep**

| Word Partnership | Use *awake* with : |
| --- | --- |
| v. | **keep** *someone* **awake, lie** awake, **stay**
awake **1** |
| ADV. | **fully** awake, **half** awake **1**
**wide** awake **2** |

**awak|en** /əweɪkən/ (**awakens, awakening,
awakened**) **1** v-t To **awaken** a feeling in a
person means to cause them to start having this
feeling. [LITERARY] ❑ *The aim of the cruise was to
awaken an interest in foreign cultures.* ● **awak|en|ing**
(**awakenings**) N-COUNT ❑ *...the awakening of
nationalism.* **2** v-t/v-i When you **awaken**, or when
something or someone **awakens** you, you wake
up. [LITERARY] ❑ *Grandma always awakens very early.*
❑ *He was snoring when José awakened him.* [from
English]

**award** /əwɔrd/ (**awards, awarding, awarded**)
**1** N-COUNT An **award** is a prize or certificate that a
person is given for doing something well. ❑ *...the
National Book Award for fiction.* **2** N-COUNT In law,
an **award** is a sum of money that a court decides
should be given to someone. ❑ *He received an award
of nearly $400,000.* **3** v-t If someone **is awarded**
something such as a prize or an examination
mark, it is given to them. ❑ *She was awarded the
prize for both films.* **4** v-t To **award** something **to**
someone means to decide that it will be given
to that person. ❑ *We have awarded the contract to a
company in New York.* [from Old Northern French]

| Usage | **award** and **reward** |

Be careful not to confuse *award* and *reward*. You
get an *award* for doing something well, and you
get a *reward* for doing a good deed or service:
*Tuka got an award for writing the best short story, and
Gina got a $50 reward for giving a lost wallet back to
the owner–so they went out and had a fancy dinner at
a fine restaurant.*

| Word Link | ness ≈ *state, condition : awareness,
consciousness, kindness* |

| Word Link | war ≈ *watchful : aware, beware,
warning* |

**aware** /əweɛr/ **1** ADJ If you are **aware of**
something, you know about it. ❑ *They are well
aware of the danger.* ● **aware|ness** N-UNCOUNT
❑ *...public awareness of the problem.* **2** ADJ If you are
**aware of** something, you realize that it is present
or is happening because you hear it, see it, smell
it, or feel it. ❑ *She was very aware of the noise of the
city.* [from Old English]

| Word Partnership | Use *aware* with : |
| --- | --- |
| ADV. | **painfully** aware, **well** aware **1 2**
**acutely/vaguely** aware,
**fully** aware **1 2** |
| PREP. | aware **of** *something/someone*,
aware **that 1 2** |
| v. | **become** aware **1 2** |

**awash** /əwɒʃ/ ADJ If the ground or a floor is
**awash**, it is covered in water, often because of
heavy rain or as the result of an accident. ❑ *The
bathroom floor was awash.*

**away** /əweɪ/

**Away** is often used with verbs of movement,
such as "go" and "drive," and also in phrasal
verbs such as "do away with" and "fade away."

**1** ADV If someone or something moves or is
moved **away from** a place, they move or are moved
so that they are no longer there. If you are **away
from** a place, you are not in the place where

people expect you to be. ❑ *He walked away from his car.* ❑ *Jason was away from home.* **2** ADV If you put something **away**, you put it where it should be. If you hide someone or something **away**, you put them in a place where nobody can see them or find them. ❑ *I put my book away and went to bed.* ❑ *All her letters were carefully filed away.* **3** ADV You use **away** to talk about future events. For example, if an event is a week **away**, it will happen after a week. ❑ *Christmas is now only two weeks away.* **4** ADV When a sports team plays **away**, it plays on its opponents' playing court or field. ❑ *...a 4-3 victory for the team playing away.* ● **Away** is also an adjective. ❑ *Pittsburgh is about to play an important away game.* **5** ADV You can use **away** to say that something slowly disappears, becomes less significant, or changes so that it is no longer the same. ❑ *The snow has already melted away.* **6** ADV You can use **away** to emphasize a continuous or repeated action. ❑ *He often worked away late into the night.* **7** PHRASE If something is **away from** a person or place, it is at a distance from that person or place. ❑ *The two women were sitting as far away from each other as possible.* [from Old English] **8** **right away** → see **right**

**awe** /ɔ/ (**awes, awed**) **1** N-UNCOUNT **Awe** is the feeling of respect and amazement that you have when you are faced with something wonderful and often rather frightening. ❑ *She looked in awe at the great stones.* **2** V-T If you **are awed by** someone or something, they make you feel respectful and amazed, though often rather frightened. ❑ *I am still awed by David's courage.* [from Old Norse]

**awe|some** /ɔsəm/ **1** ADJ An **awesome** person or thing is very impressive and often frightening. ❑ *...the awesome power of the ocean waves.* **2** ADJ If you describe someone or something as **awesome**, you are emphasizing that they are very impressive or extraordinary. [INFORMAL] ❑ *I thought he was awesome in the game.* [from Old Norse]

**aw|ful** /ɔfəl/ **1** ADJ If you say that someone or something is **awful**, you think they are very bad. ❑ *I thought he was awful.* ❑ *...an awful smell of paint.* **2** ADJ You can use **awful** with noun groups that refer to an amount in order to emphasize how large that amount is. ❑ *I've got an awful lot of work to do.* ● **aw|ful|ly** ADV ❑ *The cake looks awfully good.* **3** ADV You can use **awful** with adjectives that describe a quality in order to emphasize that particular quality. [INFORMAL] ❑ *Gosh, you're awful pretty.*

**awhile** /əwaɪl/ ADV **Awhile** means for a short time. ❑ *I waited awhile.*

**awk|ward** /ɔkwərd/ **1** ADJ An **awkward** situation is embarrassing and difficult to deal with. ❑ *...awkward questions.* ● **awk|ward|ly** ADV ❑ *There was an awkwardly long silence.* **2** ADJ Something that is **awkward** to use or carry is difficult to use or carry because of its design. A job that is **awkward** is difficult to do. ❑ *It was small but awkward to carry.* ● **awk|ward|ly** ADV ❑ *...an awkwardly shaped room.* **3** ADJ An **awkward** movement or position is uncomfortable or clumsy. ❑ *Amy made an awkward movement with her hands.* ● **awk|ward|ly** ADV ❑ *He fell awkwardly.* **4** ADJ Someone who is **awkward** deliberately creates problems for other people. ❑ *Please try not to be so awkward!* [from Old English]

**awoke** /əwoʊk/ **Awoke** is the past tense of **awake**.

**awok|en** /əwoʊkən/ **Awoken** is the past participle of **awake**.

**ax** /æks/ (**axes, axing, axed**) **1** N-COUNT An **ax** is a tool used for cutting wood. It consists of a heavy metal blade that is sharp at one edge and attached by its other edge to the end of a long handle. **2** V-T If someone's job or something such as a public service or a television program **is axed**, it is ended suddenly and without discussion. ❑ *Thousands of jobs were axed.* [from Old English]

**ax|ial move|ment** /æksiəl muvmənt/ (**axial movements**) N-VAR **Axial movement** is movement such as bending or stretching, which does not involve moving from one place to another.

**axi|om** /æksiəm/ (**axioms**) N-COUNT An **axiom** is a statement or idea that people accept as being true. [FORMAL] [from Latin]

**axis** /æksɪs/ (**axes**) **1** N-COUNT An **axis** is an imaginary line through the middle of something. ❑ *...the Earth's axis.* **2** N-COUNT An **axis** of a graph is one of the two lines on which the scales of measurement are marked. [from Latin] → see **graph, moon**

**axle** /æksəl/ (**axles**) N-COUNT An **axle** is a rod connecting a pair of wheels on a car or other vehicle. [from Old Norse] → see **wheel**

**axon** /æksɒn/ (**axons**) N-COUNT **Axons** are the long, thin parts of a nerve cell that carry electrical impulses to other parts of the nervous system. [TECHNICAL] [from New Latin]

**azi|muth|al pro|jec|tion** /æzɪmʌθəl prədʒɛkʃən/ (**azimuthal projections**) N-VAR An **azimuthal projection** is an image of a map that is made by projecting the map on a globe onto a flat surface. [TECHNICAL]

# Bb

**bab|ble** /ˈbæbᵊl/ (babbles, babbling, babbled)
■ V-I If someone **babbles**, they talk in a confused
or excited way. ❑ Mom babbled on about how messy I
was. ❑ They all babbled together. ■ N-SING You can
refer to people's voices as a **babble of** sound when
they are excited and confused, preventing you
from understanding what they are saying. ❑ Kemp
knocked loudly so that they could hear him above the
babble of voices. [from Dutch]

**babe** /beɪb/ (babes) N-VOC Some people
use **babe** as an affectionate way of addressing
someone they love. [INFORMAL] ❑ I'm sorry, babe. I
didn't mean it.

**baby** /ˈbeɪbi/ (babies) ■ N-COUNT A **baby**
is a very young child that cannot yet walk or
talk. ❑ She used to take care of me when I was a
baby. ❑ My wife just had a baby. ■ N-VOC; N-COUNT
Some people use **baby** as an affectionate way of
addressing someone. [INFORMAL] ❑ "Be careful,
baby," he said.
→ see child

### Word Partnership    Use baby with:

| | |
|---|---|
| N. | baby **boy/girl/sister**, baby **clothes**, baby **food**, baby **names**, baby **talk** ■ |
| V. | **deliver** a baby, **have** a baby ■ |
| ADJ. | **new/newborn** baby, **unborn** baby ■ |

**baby car|riage** (baby carriages) N-COUNT A
**baby carriage** is a small vehicle in which a baby
can lie as it is pushed along.

**baby|sit** /ˈbeɪbisɪt/ (babysits, babysitting,
babysat) V-T/V-I If you **babysit for** someone
or **babysit** their children, you look after their
children while they are out. ❑ I promised to babysit
for Mrs. Plunkett. ❑ She was babysitting him and
his little sister. ● **baby|sitter** N-COUNT ❑ It can be
difficult to find a good babysitter.

**baby tooth** (baby teeth) N-COUNT Your **baby
teeth** are the first teeth that grow in your mouth,
which later fall out and are replaced by a second
set.

**bach|elor** /ˈbætʃələr/ (bachelors) N-COUNT A
**bachelor** is a man who has never married. [from
Old French]

**bach|elor|ette** /ˌbætʃələˈrɛt/ (bachelorettes)
N-COUNT A **bachelorette** is a woman who has
never married.

**bach|elor|ette par|ty** (bachelorette parties)
N-COUNT A **bachelorette party** is a party for a
woman who is getting married very soon, to
which only women are invited.

**bach|elor par|ty** (bachelor parties) N-COUNT A
**bachelor party** is a party for a man who is getting
married very soon, to which only men are invited.

### back

❶ ADVERB USES
❷ OPPOSITE OF FRONT; NOUN AND ADJECTIVE USES
❸ VERB USES

❶ **back** /bæk/

In addition to the uses shown below, **back** is also
used in phrasal verbs such as "date back" and
"fall back on."

■ ADV If you move **back**, you move in the opposite
direction to the one in which you are facing or in
which you were moving before. ❑ She stepped back
from the door. ■ ADV If you go **back** somewhere,
you return to where you were before. ❑ I went
back to bed. ❑ I'll be back as soon as I can. ■ ADV If
someone or something is **back** in a particular
state, they were in that state before and are now
in it again. ❑ The bus company expects service to
get slowly back to normal. ■ ADV If you give or put
something **back**, you return it to the person who
had it or to the place where it was before you
took it. If you get or take something **back**, you
then have it again after not having it for a while.
❑ You'll get your money back. ❑ Put the meat back in
the freezer. ■ ADV If you write or call **back**, you
write to or telephone someone after they have
written to or telephoned you. If you look **back** at
someone, you look at them after they have started
looking at you. ❑ They wrote back to me and told me
I didn't have to do it. ❑ If the phone rings, you should
say you'll call back after dinner. ■ ADV If someone or
something is kept or situated **back from** a place,
they are at a distance away from it. ❑ Keep back
from the edge of the train platform. ■ ADV If you talk
about something that happened **back** in the past
or several years **back**, you are emphasizing that it
happened quite a long time ago. ❑ The story starts
back in 1950. ■ PHRASE If someone moves **back and
forth**, they repeatedly move in one direction and
then in the opposite direction. ❑ He paced back and
forth. [from Old English]

❷ **back** /bæk/ (backs) ■ N-COUNT Your **back** is
the part of your body from your neck to your waist
that is on the opposite side to your chest. ❑ Her
son was lying on his back. ❑ She turned her back to him.
■ N-COUNT The **back of** something is the side or
part of it that is toward the rear or farthest from
the front. ❑ ...a room at the back of the store. ❑ ...the
back of her neck. ■ ADJ **Back** is used to refer to the
side or part of something that is toward the rear or
farthest from the front. ❑ She opened the back door.
❑ Ann sat in the back seat of their car. ■ N-COUNT The
**back** of a chair is the part that you lean against.
❑ There was a pink sweater on the back of the chair.
■ N-UNCOUNT You use **out back** to refer to the

area behind a house or other building. You also use **in back** to refer to the rear part of something, especially a car or building. ❑ *Dan was out back in the yard cleaning his shoes.* ❑ *…the trees in back of the building.* **6** PHRASE If you say or do something **behind** someone's **back**, you do it without them knowing about it. ❑ *You eat at her house, and then criticize her behind her back.* [from Old English] **7** to **take a back seat** → see **seat**
→ see **body, horse**

**❸ back** /bæk/ (**backs, backing, backed**)
**1** V-I If a building **backs onto** something, the back of it faces in the direction of that thing or touches the edge of that thing. ❑ *He lives in an apartment that backs onto Friedman's Restaurant.* **2** V-T/V-I When you **back** a vehicle somewhere or when it **backs** somewhere, it moves backward. ❑ *He backed his car out of the driveway.* **3** V-T If you **back** a person or a course of action, you support them. ❑ *We told them what we wanted to do, and they agreed to back us.* [from Dutch]
▸ **back away** PHR-VERB If you **back away**, you move away, often because you are frightened of them. ❑ *James stood up, but the girl backed away.*
▸ **back down** PHR-VERB If you **back down**, you withdraw a claim or demand that you made earlier. ❑ *It's too late to back down now.*
▸ **back off** PHR-VERB If you **back off**, you move away in order to avoid problems or a fight. ❑ *They backed off in fright.*
▸ **back out** PHR-VERB If you **back out**, you decide not to do something that you previously agreed to do. ❑ *The Hungarians backed out of the project.*
▸ **back up** **1** PHR-VERB If someone or something **backs up** a statement, they supply evidence to suggest that it is true. ❑ *He didn't have any proof to back up his story.* **2** PHR-VERB If you **back up** a computer file, you make a copy of it that you can use if the original file is damaged or lost. [COMPUTING] ❑ *Make sure you back up your files every day.* **3** PHR-VERB If you **back** someone **up**, you show your support for them. ❑ *His employers backed him up.* **4** PHR-VERB If you **back** someone **up**, you help them by confirming that what they are saying is true. ❑ *The girl denied being there, and the man backed her up.* **5** PHR-VERB When a car **backs up** or when you **back** it **up**, the car is driven backward. **6** → see also **backup**

**back|board** /bǽkbɔrd/ (**backboards**) N-COUNT In basketball, the **backboard** is the flat board above each of the baskets. [from Old English]
→ see **basketball**

**back|bone** /bǽkboʊn/ (**backbones**)
**1** N-COUNT Your **backbone** is the column of small linked bones down the middle of your back. **2** N-UNCOUNT If you say that someone has no **backbone**, you think that they do not have the courage to do things which need to be done. ❑ *He doesn't have the backbone to admit to his mistakes.*

**back|court** /bǽkkɔrt/ (**backcourts**) N-COUNT In sports such tennis and badminton, the **backcourt** is the section of each side of the court that is furthest from the net. In basketball, the **backcourt** is the rear part of the court, where the defense plays. You can also use **backcourt** to refer to the members of a team who play mainly in this part of the court.
→ see **tennis**

**back|er** /bǽkər/ (**backers**) N-COUNT A **backer** is

someone who gives support or financial help to a person or project. ❑ *I was looking for a backer to help me with my business.* [from Old English]

**back|fire** /bǽkfaɪər/ (**backfires, backfiring, backfired**) **1** V-I If a plan or project **backfires**, it has the opposite result to the one that was intended. **2** V-I When a motor vehicle or its engine **backfires**, it produces an explosion in the exhaust pipe. ❑ *A car backfired in the outside.*

---

**Word Link** ground ≈ bottom : back**ground**, **ground**work, under**ground**

---

**back|ground** /bǽkgraʊnd/ (**backgrounds**)
**1** N-COUNT Your **background** is the kind of family you come from and the kind of education you have had. ❑ *The Warners were from a Jewish working-class background.* **2** N-COUNT The **background** to an event or situation consists of the facts that explain what caused it. ❑ *…the background to the current problems.* **3** N-SING The **background** is sounds, such as music, that you can hear but that you are not listening to with your full attention. ❑ *I heard the sound of music in the background.* **4** N-COUNT You can use **background** to refer to the things in a picture or scene that are less noticeable or important than the main things or people in it. ❑ *…roses on a blue background.*

---

**Word Partnership** Use *background* with :

| | |
|---|---|
| N. | background **check** **1** |
| | background **information/** **knowledge** **1** **2** |
| | background **story** **2** |
| | background **music/noise** **3** |
| ADJ. | **cultural/ethnic/family** background, **educational** background **1** |
| PREP. | **in the** background **3** **4** |
| | **against a** background **4** |
| V. | **blend into the** background **4** |

---

**back|hoe** /bǽkhoʊ/ (**backhoes**) N-COUNT A **backhoe** is a large vehicle which is used for moving large amounts of earth.

**back|ing** /bǽkɪŋ/ (**backings**) **1** N-UNCOUNT **Backing** is money, resources, or support given to a person or organization. ❑ *The president had the full backing of his government.* **2** N-VAR A **backing** is a layer of something such as cloth that is put onto the back of something to strengthen or protect it. ❑ *The mats have a non-slip backing.* [from Old English]

**back|lash** /bǽklæʃ/ N-SING A **backlash against** a tendency or recent development in society or politics is a sudden, strong reaction against it. ❑ *…a backlash against healthy-eating messages.*

**back|log** /bǽklɔg/ (**backlogs**) N-COUNT A **backlog** is a number of things which have not yet been done but which need to be done. ❑ *…a backlog of repairs in schools.*

**back|pack** /bǽkpæk/ (**backpacks**) N-COUNT A **backpack** is a bag with straps that go over your shoulders, so that you can carry things on your back when you are walking.

**back|side** /bǽksaɪd/ (**backsides**) N-COUNT Your **backside** is the part of your body

backpack

that you sit on. [INFORMAL] ❑ *He fell backwards and landed on his backside.*

**back|stage** /bæksteɪdʒ/ ADV In a theater, **backstage** refers to the areas behind the stage. ❑ *He went backstage and asked for her autograph.*

**back|stroke** /bækstroʊk/ N-UNCOUNT **Backstroke** is a swimming stroke that you do lying on your back. ❑ *"You swim very well," she said, watching him do the backstroke.*

**back talk** also **backtalk** N-UNCOUNT If you refer to something that someone says as **back talk**, you mean that it is rude or shows a lack of respect.

**back|up** /bækʌp/ (backups) also **back-up** **1** N-VAR **Backup** consists of extra equipment, resources, or people that you can get help or support from if necessary. ❑ *He drove to answer another officer's call for backup.* **2** N-VAR If you have something such as a second set of plans as **backup**, you have arranged for them to be available for use if the first one does not work. ❑ *Every part of the system has a backup.* **3** N-COUNT A **backup** is a long line of traffic stretching back along a road, which moves very slowly or not at all, for example, because of roadwork or an accident. ❑ *There was a seven-mile backup on the highway.*

> **Word Link**    *ward ≈ in the direction of : back*ward, for*ward, in*ward

**back|ward** /bækwərd/ **1** ADJ A **backward** movement or look is in the direction that your back is facing. ❑ *...a backward glance.* **2** ADV If you move or look **backward**, you move or look in the direction that your back is facing. ❑ *He took two steps backward.* **3** ADV If you do something **backward**, you do it in the opposite way to the usual way. ❑ *Start at the end of the alphabet and work backward.* **4** PHRASE If someone or something moves **backward and forward**, they move repeatedly first in one direction and then in the opposite direction. ❑ *I started moving backward and forward in time with the music.* **5** ADJ A **backward** country or society does not have modern industries and machines. [from Old English]

**back|water** /bækwɔːtər/ (backwaters) N-COUNT A **backwater** is a place or an institution that is isolated from modern ideas and influences. ❑ *...a quiet rural backwater.* ❑ *He turned Seattle from a backwater into a modern city.*

**back|yard** /bækyɑːrd/ (backyards) also **back yard** N-COUNT A **backyard** is an area of land at the back of a house. [from Old English]

**ba|con** /beɪkən/ N-UNCOUNT **Bacon** is salted or smoked meat which comes from the back or sides of a pig. ❑ *...bacon and eggs.* [from Old French]

**bac|te|ria** /bæktɪəriə/ N-PLURAL **Bacteria** are very small organisms which can cause disease. ❑ *Chlorine is added to the water to kill bacteria.* ● **bac|te|rial** ADJ ❑ *...a bacterial infection.* [from New Latin]

**bad** /bæd/ (worse, worst) **1** ADJ Something that is **bad** is unpleasant, harmful, or undesirable. ❑ *...bad weather.* ❑ *...a bad idea.* ❑ *...bad news.* ❑ *Too much coffee is bad for you.* ❑ *The floods are the worst in nearly fifty years.* **2** ADJ Something that is **bad** is of an unacceptably low standard, quality, or amount. ❑ *...bad housing.* ❑ *The school's main problem is that teachers' pay is so bad.* **3** ADJ Someone who is **bad at** doing something is not skillful or successful at it.

❑ *Howard was bad at basketball.* ❑ *He was a bad driver.* **4** ADJ You can say that something is **not bad** to mean that it is quite good or acceptable, especially when you are rather surprised about this. ❑ *"How much is he paying you?" — "Oh, five thousand." — "Not bad."* ❑ *That's not a bad idea.* **5** ADJ If you are in a **bad** mood, you are angry and behave unpleasantly to people. ❑ *She is in a bad mood because she had to get up early.* **6** ADJ If you **feel bad about** something, you feel sorry or guilty about it. ❑ *You don't have to feel bad about relaxing.* ❑ *I feel bad that he's doing most of the work.* **7** ADJ If you have a **bad** back, heart, leg, or eye, there is something wrong with it. ❑ *Joe has to be careful because of his bad back.* **8** ADJ **Bad** language is language that contains vulgar or offensive words. ❑ *I don't like to hear bad language in the street.* [from Old English] **9** → see also **worse**, **worst** **10** **bad luck** → see **luck**

> **Thesaurus**    *bad*    Also look up :
>
> ADJ.   damaging, dangerous, harmful; *(ant.)* good **1**
>      inferior, poor, unsatisfactory; *(ant.)* acceptable, good, satisfactory **2**

**bad check** (bad checks) N-COUNT A **bad check** is a check that will not be paid because there is a mistake on it, or because there is not enough money in the account of the person who wrote it.

**badge** /bædʒ/ (badges) N-COUNT A **badge** is a piece of metal, cloth or plastic which you wear or carry to show that you work for a particular organization, or that you have achieved something. ❑ *...a police officer's badge.* [from Norman French]

**badg|er** /bædʒər/ (badgers, badgering, badgered) **1** N-COUNT A **badger** is a wild animal which has a white head with two wide black stripes on it. Badgers live underground and usually come up to feed at night. **2** V-T If you **badger** someone, you repeatedly tell them to do something or repeatedly ask them questions. ❑ *She badgered him to let her play the role of Juliet.* ❑ *They kept phoning — badgering me to go back.*

**bad|ly** /bædli/ (worse, worst) **1** ADV If something is done **badly** or goes **badly**, it is not very successful or effective. ❑ *I was angry because I played so badly.* ❑ *The whole project was badly managed.* **2** ADV If someone or something is **badly** hurt or **badly** affected, they are severely hurt or affected. ❑ *The fire badly damaged a church.* ❑ *One man was killed and another badly injured.* **3** ADV If you want or need something **badly**, you want or need it very much. ❑ *Why do you want to go so badly?* [from Old English] **4** → see also **worse**, **worst**

**bad|min|ton** /bædmɪntən/ N-UNCOUNT **Badminton** is a game played by two or four players on a rectangular court with a high net across the middle. The players try to score points by hitting a small object called a shuttlecock across the net using a racket.

**bad off** (worse off, worst off) **1** ADJ If you are **bad off**, you are in a bad situation. ❑ *The people I write about are usually pretty bad off.* **2** ADJ If you are **bad off**, you do not have much money. ❑ *The owners are not so bad off; most are making money.*

**bad-tempered** ADJ Someone who is **bad-tempered** is not very cheerful and gets angry easily. ❑ *I was tired and bad-tempered on Friday evening.*

**baf|fle** /bǽfˀl/ (**baffles, baffling, baffled**) v-t If something **baffles** you, you cannot understand it or explain it. ❑ *These ancient markings in the desert have baffled experts for many years.* ● **baf|fling** ADJ ❑ *I was ill, with a baffling set of symptoms.* [from Scottish]

**bag** /bæg/ (**bags**) ◼ N-COUNT A **bag** is a container made of paper, plastic, or leather which is to carry things. ❑ *...a bag of candy.* ❑ *...a shopping bag.* ◻ N-PLURAL If you have **bags** under your eyes, you have folds of skin there, usually because you have not had enough sleep. ❑ *The bags under his eyes have grown darker.* ◼ PHRASE [INFORMAL] If you say that something is **in the bag**, you mean that you are certain to get it or achieve it. ❑ *"I'll win this time," he assured me. "It's in the bag."* ◼ PHRASE If you **are left holding the bag**, you are put in a situation where you are responsible for something, often in an unfair way because other people fail or refuse to take responsibility for it. [INFORMAL] ❑ *I don't want to be left holding the bag if something goes wrong.* [from Old Norse] ◼ → see also **sleeping bag** → see **container**

**bag|gage** /bǽgɪdʒ/ ◼ N-UNCOUNT Your **baggage** consists of the bags that you take with you when you travel. ❑ *He collected his baggage and left the airport.* ◻ N-UNCOUNT You can use **baggage** to refer to someone's problems or prejudices. ❑ *How much emotional baggage is he bringing with him into the relationship?* [from Old French]

**bag|gage car** (**baggage cars**) N-COUNT A **baggage car** is a railroad car, often without windows, which is used to carry luggage, goods, or mail.

**bag|gage claim** N-SING At an airport, the **baggage claim** is the area where you collect your baggage at the end of your trip. ❑ *Luke followed the signs to the baggage claim.*

**bag|ger** /bǽgər/ (**baggers**) N-COUNT A **bagger** is a person whose job is to put customers' purchases into bags at a supermarket or other store. ❑ *As well as being a bagger, he's worked at a fast-food restaurant.*

**bag|gy** /bǽgi/ (**baggier, baggiest**) ADJ If a piece of clothing is **baggy**, it hangs loosely on your body. ❑ *...a baggy sweater.*

**bail** /beɪl/ (**bails, bailing, bailed**)

> The spelling **bale** is also used for meaning ◼, and for meaning ◼ of the phrasal verb.

◼ N-UNCOUNT **Bail** is permission for an arrested person to be released after a sum of money has been paid as a guarantee that they will attend their trial. ❑ *He was held without bail after a court appearance in Detroit.* ◻ V-T/V-I If you **bail**, or **bail** water from a boat or from a place which is flooded, you use a container to remove water from it. ❑ *We kept the boat afloat for a couple of hours by bailing frantically.* ◼ PHRASE If someone who has been arrested **is freed on bail**, or **released on bail**, or **makes bail**, or if another person **makes bail** for them, the arrested person is released because a sum of money has been paid as a guarantee that they will attend their trial. ❑ *Guerrero was finally arrested, but he made bail and fled to Colombia.* ❑ *He was freed on bail pending an appeal.* [from Old French] ▶ **bail out** ◼ PHR-VERB If you **bail** someone **out**, you help them out of a difficult situation, often by giving them money. ❑ *They will discuss how to bail out the country's banking system.* ◻ → see also **bailout** ◼ PHR-VERB If you **bail** an arrested person **out**, you pay a sum of money as a guarantee that they will attend their trial. ❑ *He has been arrested eight times. Each time, friends bailed him out.*

**bail|iff** /beɪlɪf/ (**bailiffs**) N-COUNT A **bailiff** is an official in a court of law who deals with tasks such as keeping control in court. ❑ *The court bailiff said jurors did not wish to speak to newspaper reporters.* [from Old French]

**bail|out** /beɪlaʊt/ (**bailouts**) N-COUNT A **bailout** of an organization or individual that has financial problems is the act of helping them by giving them money. ❑ *...one of the biggest government bailouts of a private company in years.*

**bait** /beɪt/ (**baits, baiting, baited**) ◼ N-VAR **Bait** is food which you put on a hook or in a trap in order to catch fish or animals. ❑ *...a shop selling fishing bait.* ◻ V-T If you **bait** a hook or trap, you put bait on it or in it. ❑ *He baited his hook with worms.* ◼ N-UNCOUNT; N-SING To use something as **bait** means to use it to trick or persuade someone to do something. ❑ *Television programs are just bait to attract an audience for commercials.* ◼ V-T If you **bait** someone, you deliberately try to make them angry by teasing them. ❑ *He delighted in baiting his mother.* ◼ **Bait and switch** is used to refer to a sales technique in which goods are advertised at low prices in order to attract customers, although only a small number of the low-priced goods are available. ❑ *The restaurant really sells 11 dishes for the advertised price. There's no bait or switch here.* [from Old Norse]

**bake** /beɪk/ (**bakes, baking, baked**) ◼ V-T/V-I If you **bake**, you spend some time preparing and mixing together ingredients to make bread, cakes, pies, or other food which is cooked in the oven. ❑ *How did you learn to bake cakes?* ❑ *I love to bake.* ● **bak|ing** N-UNCOUNT ❑ *On a Thursday she used to do all the baking.* ◻ V-T/V-I When a cake or bread **bakes** or when you **bake** it, it cooks in the oven without any extra liquid or fat. ❑ *Bake the cake for 35 to 50 minutes.* ❑ *The batter rises as it bakes.* [from Old English] ◼ → see also **baking** → see **cook**

**bake-off** (**bake-offs**) N-COUNT A **bake-off** is a cooking competition. ❑ *If you win the bake-off, you'll get a prize.*

**bak|er** /beɪkər/ (**bakers**) N-COUNT A **baker** is a person whose job is to bake and sell bread, pastries, and cakes. [from Old English]

| Word Link | *ery ≈ place where something happens: bakery, cemetery, refinery* |
|---|---|

**bak|ery** /beɪkəri, beɪkri/ (**bakeries**) N-COUNT A **bakery** is a building where bread, pastries, and cakes are baked, or the store where they are sold. ❑ *...the smell of bread from a bakery.* [from Old English]

**bak|ing** /beɪkɪŋ/ ◼ ADJ You can use **baking** to describe weather or a place that is very hot indeed. ❑ *...a baking July day.* ❑ *...in the baking heat of the desert.* [from Old English] ◻ → see also **bake**

**bal|ance** /bǽləns/ (**balances, balancing, balanced**) ◼ V-T/V-I If you **balance** something somewhere, or if it **balances** there, it remains steady and does not fall. ❑ *I balanced on the window ledge.* ◻ N-UNCOUNT **Balance** is the ability to

remain steady when you are standing up. ❑ *The medicines you are taking could be affecting your balance.* ◻ V-RECIP If you **balance** one thing **with** something different, each of the things has the same strength or importance. ❑ *Balance spicy dishes with mild ones.* ❑ *The government has to find some way to balance these two needs.* ◻ N-SING A **balance** is a situation in which all the different parts are equal in strength or importance. ❑ *...the ecological balance of the forest.* ◻ V-T If you **balance** one thing **against** another, you consider its importance in relation to the other one. ❑ *...trying to balance professional success against motherhood.* ◻ V-T If someone **balances** their budget or if a government **balances** the economy of a country, they make sure that the amount of money that is spent is not greater than the amount that is received. ❑ *He balanced his budgets by tightly controlling spending.* ◻ V-T/V-I If you **balance** your books or make them **balance**, you prove by calculation that the amount of money you have received is equal to the amount that you have spent. ❑ *...teaching them to balance the books.* ◻ N-COUNT The **balance** in your bank account is the amount of money you have in it. ❑ *I'd like to check the balance in my account please.* ◻ N-SING The **balance** of an amount of money is what remains to be paid for something or what remains when part of the amount has been spent. ❑ *You sign the final agreement and pay the balance.* ◻ N-UNCOUNT In a painting or drawing, **balance** is a sense of harmony in the arrangement of the different parts of the painting or drawing. ◻ N-UNCOUNT If two or more physical objects are in a state of **balance**, their weight is evenly distributed around a central point. ◻ N-COUNT A **balance** is a scientific instrument that is used for weighing things. ◻ PHRASE You can say **on balance** to indicate that you are stating an opinion after considering all the relevant facts or arguments. ❑ *On balance he agreed with Christine.* [from Old French]
→ see **brain**

| **Word Partnership** | Use *balance* with : |
|---|---|
| V. | keep/lose *your* balance, restore balance ◻ |
| | check a balance, maintain a balance ◻ |
| | pay a balance ◻ |
| ADJ. | delicate balance ◻ |
| | balance due, outstanding balance ◻ |
| N. | balance a budget ◻ |
| | account balance, balance transfer ◻ ◻ |

**bal|anced** /bǽlənst/ ◻ ADJ A **balanced** account or report is fair and reasonable; used to show approval. ❑ *...a fair, balanced, comprehensive report.* ◻ ADJ Something that is **balanced** is pleasing or useful because its different parts are in the correct proportions. ❑ *...a balanced diet of nutritious food.* [from Old French] ◻ → see also **balance**

**bal|anced forces** N-PLURAL In physics, **balanced forces** are forces that are equal and opposite to each other, so that an object to which the forces are applied does not move.

**bal|co|ny** /bǽlkəni/ (**balconies**) ◻ N-COUNT A **balcony** is a platform on the outside of a building, above ground level, with a wall or railing around it. ◻ N-SING The **balcony** in a theater is an area of seats above the main seating area. [from Italian]

**bald** /bɔːld/ (**balder, baldest**) ◻ ADJ Someone who is **bald** has little or no hair on the top of their head. ● **bald|ness** N-UNCOUNT ❑ *He wears a cap to cover a spot of baldness.* ◻ ADJ If a tire is **bald**, its surface has worn down and it is no longer safe to use. ◻ ADJ A **bald** statement has no unnecessary words in it. ❑ *The bald truth is that he's just not happy.* ● **bald|ly** ADV ❑ *"I don't think these stories are true," said Phillips, baldly.* [from Danish]

**bald|ing** /bɔːldɪŋ/ ADJ Someone who is **balding** is beginning to lose the hair on the top of their head. ❑ *...a balding man in his late forties.* [from Danish]

**bale** /beɪl/ (**bales, baling, baled**) ◻ N-COUNT A **bale** is a large quantity of something such as hay, cloth, or paper, tied together tightly. ❑ *...bales of hay.* ◻ V-T If something such as hay, cloth, or paper **is baled**, it is tied together tightly. ❑ *...a quantity of hay, some baled, some loose.* [from Old French] ◻ → see also **bail**

**balk** /bɔːk/ (**balks, balking, balked**) also **baulk** V-I If you **balk at** something, you are very reluctant to do it. ❑ *Even biology students may balk at animal experiments.* ❑ *When the company stopped offering online ordering, customers balked.* [from Old English]

**ball** /bɔːl/ (**balls, balling, balled**) ◻ N-COUNT A **ball** is a round or oval object that is used in games such as tennis, baseball, football, basketball, and soccer. ❑ *...a golf ball.* ◻ N-COUNT A **ball** is something that has a round shape. ❑ *Thomas squeezed the letter up into a ball.* ◻ N-COUNT The **ball of** your foot or **the ball of** your thumb is the rounded part where your toes join your foot or where your thumb joins your hand. ◻ N-COUNT A **ball** is a large formal dance. ❑ *My Mama and Daddy used to have a grand Christmas ball every year.* ◻ PHRASE If you **are having a ball**, you are having a very enjoyable time. [INFORMAL] ❑ *The boys were sitting outside having a ball.* [Senses 1 to 3 from Old Norse. Sense 4 from French]
→ see **foot, golf, soccer**

| **Word Partnership** | Use *ball* with : |
|---|---|
| V. | bounce/catch/hit/kick/throw a ball ◻ |
| | roll into a ball ◻ |
| N. | bowling/golf/soccer/tennis ball, ball field, ball game ◻ |
| | snow ball ◻ |
| PREP. | ball of *something* ◻ |

**bal|lad** /bǽləd/ (**ballads**) ◻ N-COUNT A **ballad** is a long song or poem which tells a story in simple language. ❑ *...an eighteenth century ballad.* ◻ N-COUNT A **ballad** is a slow, romantic, popular song. ❑ *"You Don't Know Paris" is one of the most beautiful ballads that he ever wrote.* [from Old French]

**bal|let** /bǽleɪ/ (**ballets**) ◻ N-UNCOUNT **Ballet** is a type of artistic dancing with carefully planned movements. ❑ *I trained as a ballet dancer.* ◻ N-COUNT A **ballet** is an artistic work that is performed by ballet dancers. ❑ *The performance will include three new ballets.* [from French]
→ see **dance**

**ball game** (**ball games**) ◻ N-COUNT **Ball games** are games that are played with a ball such as tennis, baseball, and football. ◻ N-COUNT A **ball game** is a baseball match. ❑ *I'd like to go to a ball game.* ◻ N-SING You can use **ball game** to describe any situation or activity, especially one that involves competition. ❑ *Two of his biggest competitors are out of the ball game.*

**bal|loon** /bəlun/ (**balloons, ballooning, ballooned**) **1** N-COUNT A **balloon** is a small, thin, rubber bag that you blow air into so that it becomes larger. ❑ *She popped a balloon with her fork.* **2** N-COUNT A **balloon** is a large, strong bag filled with gas or hot air, which can carry passengers in a container that hangs underneath it. ❑ *They will attempt to circle the Earth by balloon.* **3** V-I When something **balloons**, it increases rapidly in size or amount. ❑ *The jail's female population has ballooned in recent years.* [from Italian]
→ see **fly**

**bal|lot** /bælət/ (**ballots**) N-COUNT A **ballot** is a secret vote in which people select a candidate in an election, or express their opinion about something. ❑ *The result of the ballot will not be known for two weeks.* [from Italian]
→ see **election, vote**

**ball|player** /bɔlpleɪər/ (**ballplayers**) also **ball player** N-COUNT A **ballplayer** is a baseball player.

**balm** /bɑm/ (**balms**) N-VAR **Balm** is a sweet-smelling oil that is obtained from some tropical trees and used to make creams that heal wounds or reduce pain. ❑ *She applied some lip balm.* [from Old French]

**ba|lo|ney** /bəlouni/ N-UNCOUNT If you say that an idea or statement is **baloney**, you disapprove of it and think it is foolish or wrong. [INFORMAL]

**bam|boo** /bæmbu/ (**bamboos**) N-VAR **Bamboo** is a tall tropical plant with hard, hollow stems. ❑ *...huts with walls made of bamboo.* [from Malay]

**ban** /bæn/ (**bans, banning, banned**) **1** V-T To **ban** something means to state officially that it must not be done, shown, or used. ❑ *Scotland will ban hunting with dogs today.* **2** N-COUNT A **ban** is an official ruling that something must not be done, shown, or used. ❑ *The general lifted the ban on political parties.* **3** V-T If you **are banned from** doing something, you are officially prevented from doing it. ❑ *He was banned from driving for three years.* [from Old English]

**ba|nal** /bənɑl, -næl, beɪnɑl/ ADJ If you describe something as **banal**, you do not like it because you think it is so ordinary that it is not at all effective or interesting. ❑ *The text is banal.* ● **banality** /bənɑliti/ N-VAR (**banalities**) ❑ *...the banality of life.* [from Old French]

**ba|na|na** /bənænə/ (**bananas**) N-VAR **Bananas** are long curved fruit with yellow skins. ❑ *...a bunch of bananas.* [from Spanish]
→ see **fruit**

**band** /bænd/ (**bands, banding, banded**) **1** N-COUNT A **band** is a group of musicians who play popular music such as jazz, rock, or pop. ❑ *He was a drummer in a rock band.* **2** N-COUNT A **band** is a group of musicians who play brass and percussion instruments. ❑ *Bands played German marches.* **3** N-COUNT A **band of** people is a group of people who have joined together because they share an interest or belief. ❑ *...bands of rebels.* **4** N-COUNT A **band** is a flat, narrow strip of cloth which you wear around your head or wrists, or which forms part of a piece of clothing. ❑ *Almost all hospitals use a wrist-band of some kind.* **5** N-COUNT A **band** is a strip or loop of metal or other strong material which strengthens something, or which

holds several things together. ❑ *His hand was like an iron band around her arm.* **6** N-COUNT A **band** is a range of numbers or values within a system of measurement. ❑ *A 10 megahertz-wide band of frequencies will be needed.* [Senses 1 to 3 from French. Senses 4 and 5 from Old French.]
→ see **concert, theater**

▸ **band together** PHR-VERB If people **band together**, they meet and act as a group in order to try and achieve something. ❑ *Women banded together to protect each other.*

**band|age** /bændɪdʒ/ (**bandages, bandaging, bandaged**) **1** N-COUNT A **bandage** is a long strip of cloth that is wrapped around a wounded part of your body to support it. ❑ *We put a bandage on his knee.* **2** V-T If you **bandage** a wound or part of someone's body, you tie a bandage around it. ❑ *Apply a dressing to the wound and bandage it.* [from French]

**B&B** /bi ən bi/ (**B&Bs**) → see **bed and breakfast**

**ban|dit** /bændɪt/ (**bandits**) N-COUNT Robbers are sometimes called **bandits**, especially if they are found in areas where the law has broken down. [from Italian]

**band|wagon** /bændwægən/ (**bandwagons**) N-COUNT If you say that someone jumps or climbs **on the bandwagon**, they become involved in an activity only because it is fashionable; used to show disapproval. ❑ *Many companies tried to jump on the dot-com bandwagon in the late 1990s.*

**band|width** /bændwɪdθ, -wɪtθ/ (**bandwidths**) N-VAR A **bandwidth** is the range of frequencies used for a particular telecommunications signal, radio transmission, or computer network. ❑ *To cope with this amount of data, the system will need a bandwidth of around 100 megahertz.*

**bang** /bæŋ/ (**bangs, banging, banged**) **1** N-COUNT A **bang** is a sudden loud noise such as the noise of an explosion. ❑ *I heard four or five loud bangs.* ❑ *She slammed the door with a bang.* **2** V-T/V-I If you **bang** a door, or if it **bangs**, it closes suddenly with a loud noise. ❑ *...the sound of doors banging.* ❑ *All up and down the street the windows bang shut.* **3** V-T/V-I If you **bang on** something or if you **bang** it, you hit it hard, making a loud noise. ❑ *We decided to bang on the desks and shout till they let us out.* **4** V-T If you **bang** a part of your body, you accidentally knock it against something and hurt yourself. ❑ *She fainted and banged her head.* **5** N-PLURAL **Bangs** are hair which is cut so that it hangs over your forehead. ❑ *My bangs were cut short, but the rest of my hair was long.* [from Old Norse]
→ see **hair**

**bang-up** also **bang up** ADJ Some people use **bang-up** to describe something they think is very good or enjoyable. [INFORMAL] ❑ *NET has done a bang-up job of designing its products for young people.*

**ban|ish** /bænɪʃ/ (**banishes, banishing, banished**) **1** V-T If someone or something **is banished from** a place or area of activity, they are sent away from it and prevented from entering it. ❑ *John was banished from England.* ❑ *I was banished to the small bedroom upstairs.* **2** V-T If you **banish** something unpleasant, you get rid of it. ❑ *I'm trying to banish that idea from my head.* [from Old French]

## bank

❶ FINANCE AND STORAGE
❷ AREAS AND MASSES
❸ VERB USES

❶ **bank** /bæŋk/ (**banks**) **1** N-COUNT A **bank** is a place where people can keep their money. □ *Students should see which bank offers them the service that best suits their financial needs.* **2** N-COUNT You use **bank** to refer to a store of something. For example, a blood **bank** is a store of blood. □ *…a national data bank of information on hospital employees.* [from Italian]

❷ **bank** /bæŋk/ (**banks**) **1** N-COUNT The **banks of** a river, canal, or lake are the raised areas of ground along its edge. □ *We walked along the east bank of the river.* **2** N-COUNT A **bank** of ground is a raised area of it with a flat top and one or two sloping sides. □ *…resting on the grassy bank.* **3** N-COUNT A **bank of** something is a long high mass of it. □ *…a bank of clouds.* [of Scandinavian origin]

❸ **bank** /bæŋk/ (**banks, banking, banked**)
▸ **bank on** PHR-VERB If you **bank on** something happening, you rely on it happening. □ *Everyone is banking on his recovery.*

**bank card** (**bank cards**) also **ATM card** N-COUNT A **bank card** is a plastic card which your bank gives you so you can get money from your bank account using a cash machine.

**bank check** (**bank checks**) N-COUNT A **bank check** is a check that you can buy from a bank in order to pay someone who is not willing to accept a personal check. □ *Payments should be made by bank check in U.S. dollars.*

**bank|er** /bæŋkər/ (**bankers**) N-COUNT A **banker** is someone who works in banking at a senior level. □ *…an investment banker.* [from Italian]

**bank|ing** /bæŋkɪŋ/ N-UNCOUNT **Banking** is the business activity of banks and similar institutions. □ *…online banking.* [from Italian]
→ see **industry**

**bank|note** /bæŋknoʊt/ (**banknotes**) also **bank note** N-COUNT **Banknotes** are pieces of paper money. □ *…a shopping bag full of banknotes.*

**bank|rupt** /bæŋkrʌpt/ (**bankrupts, bankrupting, bankrupted**) **1** ADJ People or organizations that go **bankrupt** do not have enough money to pay their debts. [BUSINESS] □ *If the firm cannot sell its products, it will go bankrupt.* **2** V-T To **bankrupt** a person or organization means to make them go bankrupt. [BUSINESS] □ *It became known as the most expensive film ever made and almost bankrupted the studio.* **3** ADJ If you say that something is **bankrupt**, you are emphasizing that it lacks any value or worth. □ *He thinks that European civilization is morally bankrupt.* [from Old French]

**bank|rupt|cy** /bæŋkrʌptsi/ (**bankruptcies**) **1** N-UNCOUNT **Bankruptcy** is the state of being bankrupt. [BUSINESS] □ *He was brought in to rescue the company from bankruptcy.* **2** N-COUNT A **bankruptcy** is an instance of an organization or person going bankrupt. [BUSINESS] □ *The number of corporate bankruptcies climbed in August.* [from Old French]

**Word Partnership** Use *bankruptcy* with :

V. **force into** bankruptcy **1**
**avoid** bankruptcy **1 2**
**declare** bankruptcy, **file for** bankruptcy **2**

N. bankruptcy **law**,
bankruptcy **protection 1 2**

**b**

**ban|ner** /bænər/ (**banners**) N-COUNT A **banner** is a long strip of cloth with something written on it. □ *The crowd danced and sang, and waved banners, flags, and caps.* [from Old French]

**ban|ner ad** (**banner ads**) N-COUNT A **banner ad** is a rectangular advertisement on a web page that contains a link to the advertiser's website. □ *See our banner ad at this site!*

**ban|quet** /bæŋkwɪt/ (**banquets**) N-COUNT A **banquet** is a grand formal dinner. □ *The traditional New Year's Eve banquet was canceled.* □ *…a wedding banquet.* [from Old French]

**ban|ter** /bæntər/ N-UNCOUNT **Banter** is friendly teasing or joking talk. □ *She heard Tom exchanging friendly banter with Jane.*

**bap|tism** /bæptɪzəm/ (**baptisms**) N-VAR A **baptism** is a Christian ceremony in which a person is baptized. □ *Infants prepared for baptism should be dressed in pure white.* [from Late Latin]

**bap|tize** /bæptaɪz/ (**baptizes, baptizing, baptized**) V-T When someone **is baptized,** water is put on their heads or they are covered with water as a sign that they have become a member of the Christian church. □ *At this time she decided to become a Christian and was baptized.* [from Late Latin]

**bar** /bɑr/ (**bars, barring, barred**) **1** N-COUNT A **bar** is a place where you can buy and drink alcoholic drinks. □ *…the city's most popular bar.* **2** → see also **wine bar 3** N-COUNT A **bar** is a counter on which alcoholic drinks are served. □ *Michael was standing alone by the bar when Brian joined him.* **4** N-COUNT A **bar** is a long, straight, stiff piece of metal. □ *…a building with bars across the ground floor windows.* **5** N-COUNT A **bar of** something is a piece of it which is roughly rectangular. □ *What is your favorite chocolate bar?* **6** V-T If you **bar** someone's way, you prevent them from going somewhere or entering a place, by blocking their path. □ *Harry moved to bar his way.* **7** V-T If someone **is barred from** a place or from doing something, they are officially forbidden to go there or to do it. □ *He has been barred from working in this country.* **8** N-COUNT If something is a **bar to** doing a particular thing, it prevents someone from doing it. □ *One of the bars to communication is the lack of a common language.* **9** N-SING **The bar** is used to refer to the profession of any kind of lawyer in the United States, or of a barrister in England. □ *Very few graduates from the law school pass the bar exam on the first try.* **10** N-COUNT In music, a **bar** is one of the several short parts of the same length into which a piece of music is divided. □ *The opening bars of a waltz filled the room.* **11** PHRASE If you say that someone is **behind bars**, you mean that they are in prison. □ *Fisher was behind bars last night, charged with attempted murder.* [from Old French]
→ see **chart, soap**

**bar|bar|ic** /bɑrbærɪk/ ADJ If you describe someone's behavior as **barbaric**, you strongly disapprove of it because it is extremely cruel. ❑ *This barbaric treatment of animals has no place in any decent society.* ● **barbarism** /bɑrbərɪzəm/ N-UNCOUNT ❑ *...the wicked barbarism of the attacks.* ● **bar|bar|ity** /bɑrbærɪti/ (**barbarities**) N-VAR ❑ *...the barbarity of war.* [from Latin]

**bar|becue** /bɑrbɪkyu/ (**barbecues, barbecuing, barbecued**) also **barbeque** or **Bar-B-Q**
**1** N-COUNT A **barbecue** is a piece of equipment which you use for cooking on outdoors.
**2** N-COUNT If someone has a **barbecue**, they cook food on a barbecue in the open air. ❑ *On New Year's Eve we had a barbecue on the beach.* **3** V-T If you **barbecue** food, you cook it on a barbecue. ❑ *Tuna can be grilled, fried or barbecued.* ❑ *Here's a way of barbecuing fish that I learned from my uncle.* [from American Spanish]
→ see **cook**

**barbed wire** /bɑrbd waɪər/ N-UNCOUNT **Barbed wire** is strong wire with sharp points sticking out of it, and is used to make fences. ❑ *The factory was surrounded by barbed wire.*

**bar|bell** /bɑrbɛl/ (**barbells**) N-COUNT A **barbell** is a long bar with adjustable weights on either side that people lift to strengthen their arm and shoulder muscles. ❑ *She lifted the barbell in her left hand.*

**bar|ber** /bɑrbər/ (**barbers**) N-COUNT A **barber** is a man whose job is cutting men's hair. [from Old French]

**bare** /bɛər/ (**barer, barest, bares, baring, bared**)
**1** ADJ If a part of your body is **bare**, it is not covered by any clothing. ❑ *Her feet were bare.* **2** ADJ A **bare** surface is not covered or decorated with anything. ❑ *...bare wooden floors.* **3** ADJ If a room, cupboard, or shelf is **bare**, it is empty. ❑ *His refrigerator was bare.* **4** ADJ If someone gives you the **bare** facts or the **barest** details of something, they tell you only the most basic and important things. ❑ *Newspaper reporters were given only the bare facts by the officer in charge of the investigation.* **5** ADJ If you talk about the **bare** minimum or the **bare** essentials, you mean the very least that is necessary. ❑ *We learned that it was all right to do the bare minimum at school.* **6** V-T If you **bare** something, you uncover it and show it. [WRITTEN] ❑ *Walsh bared his teeth in a grin.* **7** PHRASE If you do something **with** your **bare hands**, you do it without using any weapons or tools. ❑ *Rescuers used their bare hands to reach the trapped miners.* [from Old English]

**bare-bones** ADJ If you describe something as **bare-bones**, you mean that it is reduced to the smallest size, amount, or number that you need. ❑ *...the city's bare-bones budget.*

**bare|foot** /bɛərfʊt/ ADJ Someone who is **barefoot** is not wearing anything on their feet. ❑ *I wore a white dress and was barefoot.*

**bare|ly** /bɛərli/ **1** ADV You use **barely** to say that something is only just true or possible ❑ *Anastasia could barely remember the ride to the hospital.* ❑ *It was 90 degrees and the air conditioning barely cooled the room.* **2** ADV If you say that one thing had **barely** happened when something else happened, you mean that the first event was followed immediately by the second. ❑ *She had barely sat down at the awards ceremony when she was called on*

stage. [from Old English]

**barf** (**barfs, barfing, barfed**) V-I If someone **barfs**, they vomit. [INFORMAL] ❑ *When I first tasted it I almost barfed.*

**bar|gain** /bɑrgɪn/ (**bargains, bargaining, bargained**) **1** N-COUNT Something that is a **bargain** is good value, usually because it has been sold at a lower price than normal. ❑ *At this price the dress is a bargain.* **2** N-COUNT A **bargain** is an agreement in which two people or groups agree what each of them will do, pay, or receive. ❑ *I'll make a bargain with you. I'll be the hostess if you'll include Matthew in your guest list.* **3** V-I When people **bargain** with each other, they discuss what each of them will do, pay, or receive. ❑ *They prefer to bargain with individual clients, for cash.* ● **bar|gain|ing** N-UNCOUNT ❑ *The pay rise was the subject of intense bargaining last night.* **4** PHRASE You use **into the bargain** or **in the bargain** when mentioning an additional quantity, feature, fact, or action, to emphasize the fact that it is also involved. ❑ *The taxis here are cheap, and you can have a great conversation with the driver thrown into the bargain.* [from Old French]
▶ **bargain for** or **bargain on** PHR-VERB If you have not **bargained for** or **bargained on** something that happens, you did not expect it to happen and so feel surprised or worried by it. ❑ *The effects of this policy are more than the government bargained for.*

| **Thesaurus** | *bargain* | Also look up : |
|---|---|---|
| N. | deal, discount, markdown **1** | |
| | agreement, deal, understanding **2** | |
| V. | barter, haggle, negotiate **3** | |

| **Word Partnership** | Use *bargain* with : |
|---|---|
| V. | **find/get a** bargain **1** |
| | **make/strike a** bargain **2** |
| N. | bargain **hunter**, bargain **price**, bargain **rates 1** |
| | **part of the** bargain **2** |
| PREP. | bargain **with** *someone* **3** |

**barge** /bɑrdʒ/ (**barges, barging, barged**)
**1** N-COUNT A **barge** is a long, narrow boat with a flat bottom, used for carrying heavy loads. **2** V-I If you **barge into** a place or **barge through** it, you rush or push into it in a rough and rude way. [INFORMAL] ❑ *Please knock before you barge into my room.* **3** V-I If you **barge into** someone or **barge past** them, you bump against them roughly and rudely. [INFORMAL] ❑ *He barged into them and kicked them.* [from Old French]
→ see **ship**

**bar graph** (**bar graphs**) N-COUNT A **bar graph** is a graph which uses parallel rectangular shapes to represent changes in the size, value or rate of something.

**bari|tone** /bærɪtoʊn/ (**baritones**) N-COUNT A **baritone** is a man with a fairly deep singing voice that is lower than that of a tenor but higher than that of a bass. ❑ *...the American baritone Monte Pederson.* [from Italian]

**bark** /bɑrk/ (**barks, barking, barked**) **1** V-I When a dog **barks**, it makes a short, loud noise. ❑ *Don't let the dogs bark.* ● **Bark** is also a noun. ❑ *Your child may be afraid of a dog's bark, its smell or its size.* **2** N-UNCOUNT **Bark** is the tough material that

## Picture Dictionary    barn

barn

hay

pasture

orchard

greenhouse

livestock

tractor    plow    barnyard

**b**

covers the outside of a tree. [Sense 1 from Old English. Sense 2 from Old Norse]

**bar|ley** /bɑrli/ N-UNCOUNT **Barley** is a grain that is used to make food, beer, and whiskey. □ ...*fields of ripening wheat and barley.* [from Old English]

**barn** /bɑrn/ (**barns**) N-COUNT A **barn** is a building on a farm in which animals, animal food, or crops can be kept. [from Old English] → see Picture Dictionary: **barn**

**ba|rom|eter** /bərɒmɪtər/ (**barometers**) N-COUNT A **barometer** is an instrument that measures air pressure and shows when the weather is changing.

**baro|met|ric** /bærəmɛtrɪk/ ADJ **Barometric** pressure is the atmospheric pressure that is shown by a barometer.

**bar|on** /bærən/ (**barons**) N-COUNT You can use **baron** to refer to someone who controls a large part of a particular industry or activity and who is therefore extremely powerful. □ ...*the oil barons of Texas.* [from Old French]

**bar|racks** /bærəks/ (**barracks**) N-COUNT A **barracks** is a building or group of buildings where soldiers or other members of the armed forces live and work. □ ...*an army barracks in the north of the city.* [from French]

**bar|rage** /bərɑʒ/ (**barrages**) ◼ N-COUNT A **barrage** is continuous firing on an area with large guns and tanks. □ ...*a barrage of gunfire.* ◻ N-COUNT A **barrage of** something such as criticism or complaints is a large number of them directed at someone, often in an aggressive way. □ *He was faced with a barrage of angry questions.* [from French]

**bar|rel** /bærəl/ (**barrels**) ◼ N-COUNT A **barrel** is a large, round container for liquids or food. □ ...*oak barrels.* ◻ N-COUNT The **barrel** of a gun is the tube through which the bullet moves when the gun is fired. [from Old French]

**barrel-chested** ADJ A **barrel-chested** man has

a large, rounded chest. □ *A barrel-chested young man entered the room.*

**bar|ren** /bærən/ ADJ **Barren** land consists of soil that is so poor that plants cannot grow in it. □ ...*barren desert land.* [from Old French]

**bar|rette** /bərɛt/ (**barrettes**) N-COUNT A **barrette** is a small metal or plastic device that a woman uses to hold her hair in position. □ *Sarah's hair was held back by a barrette.* [from French]

**bar|ri|cade** /bærɪkeɪd/ (**barricades, barricading, barricaded**) ◼ N-COUNT A **barricade** is a line of vehicles or other objects placed across a road or open space to stop people from getting past, for example, during street fighting or as a protest. □ *Large areas of the city were blocked by barricades.* ◻ V-T If you **barricade** something such as a road or an entrance, you place a barricade or barrier across it, usually to stop someone from getting in. □ *Youths barricaded streets with burning tires.* ◼ V-T If you **barricade** yourself inside a room or building, you place barriers across the door or entrance so that other people cannot get in. □ *The students have barricaded themselves into their dormitory building.* [from Old French]

barrier

**bar|ri|er** /bæriər/ (**barriers**) ◼ N-COUNT A **barrier** is something such as a rule, law, or policy that makes it difficult or impossible for something to happen or be achieved. □ *Taxes are the most obvious barrier to free trade.* ◻ N-COUNT A **barrier** is something such as a fence or wall that prevents people or things from moving from one area to another. □ *A police barrier still blocked the road.* [from Old French]

B

**bar|ring** /bɑrɪŋ/ PREP You use **barring** to indicate that the person, thing, or event that you are mentioning is an exception to your statement. ❑ *Barring accidents, I believe they will succeed.* [from Old French]

**bar|rio** /bɑrioʊ/ (**barrios**) **1** N-COUNT A **barrio** is a mainly Spanish-speaking area in an American city. ❑ *...the barrios of Santa Cruz.* **2** N-COUNT A **barrio** is an urban district in a Spanish-speaking country. ❑ *...the barrios of Mexico City.* [from Spanish]

**bar|ris|ter** /bærɪstər/ (**barristers**) N-COUNT In England and Wales, a **barrister** is a lawyer who represents clients in the higher courts of law.

**bar|tender** /bɑrtɛndər/ (**bartenders**) N-COUNT A **bartender** is a person who serves drinks behind a bar.

**bar|ter** /bɑrtər/ (**barters, bartering, bartered**) V-T/V-I If you **barter** goods, you exchange them for other goods, rather than selling them for money. ❑ *They have been bartering wheat for cotton and timber.* ❑ *The men were trading animal skins, bartering for jewellery.* ● **Barter** is also a noun. [from Old French]
→ see **money**

**bas|alt** /bəsɔlt, beɪsɔlt/ N-UNCOUNT **Basalt** is a type of black rock that is produced by volcanoes. [from Late Latin]

**base** /beɪs/ (**bases, basing, based**) **1** N-COUNT The **base** of something is its lowest edge or part. ❑ *...a bright red candle with artificial roses around its base.* ❑ *...the base of the skull.* **2** N-COUNT The **base** of an object is the lower surface or section of it. ❑ *Put the base of the pan into a bowl of very cold water.* ❑ *The mattress is best on a solid bed base.* **3** N-COUNT A position or thing that is a **base** for something is one from which that thing can be developed or achieved. ❑ *The company has developed a plan to establish a base for future growth.* **4** V-T If you **base** one thing **on** another thing, the first thing develops from the second thing. ❑ *He based his conclusions on the evidence.* ❑ *...products based on traditional herbal medicines.* ❑ *The film is based on a novel by Alexander Trocchi.* **5** N-COUNT A military **base** is a place that part of the armed forces works from. ❑ *...an army base close to the airport.* **6** N-COUNT Your **base** is the main place where you work, stay, or live. ❑ *For most of the summer her base was her home in Connecticut.* **7** N-COUNT A **base** in baseball or softball is one of the places at each corner of the diamond on the field. A player who is at **first base, second base,** or **third base,** is standing at the first, second, or third base in a counterclockwise direction from home plate. ❑ *The first runner to reach second base was John Flaherty.* **8** N-COUNT In chemistry, a **base** is a substance which has the opposite effect to an acid. Bases react with acids to form salts and turn red litmus paper blue. **9** PHRASE If you say that someone is **off base,** you mean that they are wrong. [INFORMAL] [from Old French]
→ see **area, baseball**

**base|ball** /beɪsbɔl/ N-UNCOUNT **Baseball** is a game played by two teams of nine players. Each player from one team hits a ball with a bat and then tries to run around three bases and get to home plate before the other team can get the ball back.
→ see Picture Dictionary: **baseball**
→ see **park**

**base|ball cap** (**baseball caps**) N-COUNT A **baseball cap** is a close-fitting cap with a curved part at the front that sticks out above your eyes.

**base|ment** /beɪsmənt/ (**basements**) N-COUNT The **basement** of a building is a floor built partly or completely below ground level. ❑ *They built a workshop in the basement.* [from Old French]
→ see **house**

**bases**

Pronounced /beɪsɪz/ for meaning **1**. Pronounced /beɪsiz/ and hyphenated ba|ses for meaning **2**.

**1 Bases** is the plural of **base**. **2 Bases** is the plural of **basis**. [from Old French]

**base word** (**base words**) N-COUNT A **base word** is a word that you can add a prefix or suffix to in order to create other related words. [TECHNICAL]

**bash** /bæʃ/ (**bashes, bashing, bashed**) **1** N-COUNT A **bash** is a party or celebration. [INFORMAL] ❑ *...birthday bashes.* **2** V-T If you **bash** someone or something, you hit them hard in a rough way. [INFORMAL] ❑ *I bashed him on the head.*

**ba|sic** /beɪsɪk/ **1** ADJ You use **basic** to describe the most important or simplest aspects of something. ❑ *...the basic skills of reading and writing.* ❑ *Access to justice is a basic right.* **2** ADJ **Basic** goods and services are very simple ones which every human being needs. ❑ *...shortages of even the most basic foods.* ❑ *Hospitals lack even basic drugs for surgical operations.* **3** ADJ If one thing is **basic to** another, it is absolutely necessary to it. ❑ *...an oily liquid, basic to the manufacture of many other chemical substances.* **4** ADJ You can use **basic** to describe something that has only the most necessary features, without any luxuries. ❑ *We provide basic cooking and camping equipment.* [from Old French]

## Picture Dictionary  baseball

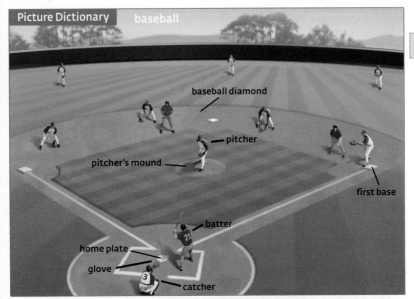

baseball diamond

pitcher

pitcher's mound

first base

batter

home plate

glove

catcher

**ba|si|cal|ly** /beɪsɪkli/ ■ ADV You use **basically** for emphasis when you are stating an opinion, or when you are making an important statement about something. ▢ *Basically, the whole thing was extremely dull.* ❷ ADV You use **basically** to show that you are describing a situation in a simple, general way. ▢ *Basically you have two choices.* [from Old French]

**ba|sics** /beɪsɪks/ N-PLURAL The **basics** of something are its most important or simplest aspects. ▢ *...the basics of arithmetic.* [from Old French]

**ba|sin** /beɪs³n/ (**basins**) ■ N-COUNT A **basin** is a large or deep bowl that you use for holding liquids. ▢ *Water dripped into a basin at the back of the room.* ❷ N-COUNT A **basin** is a sink. ▢ *...a white bathtub with a matching basin.* ❸ N-COUNT The **basin** of a large river is the area of land around it from which streams run down into it. ▢ *The river flows into the Amazon basin.* [from Old French]
→ see **lake**

**ba|sis** /beɪsɪs/ (**bases** /beɪsiz/) ■ N-SING If something is done on a particular **basis**, it is done according to that method, system, or principle. ▢ *We're going to be meeting there on a regular basis.* ▢ *They want all groups to be treated on an equal basis.* ❷ N-SING If you say that you are acting on the **basis** of something, you are giving that as the reason for your action. ▢ *McGregor must remain in bed, on the basis of the medical reports.* ❸ N-COUNT The **basis** of something is the central or most important part of it from which it can be further developed. ▢ *The UN plan is a possible basis for peace talks.* [from Latin]

### Word Partnership   Use *basis* with :

| | |
|---|---|
| ADJ. | **equal** basis, **on a daily/regular/weekly** basis, **on a voluntary** basis ■ |
| PREP. | **on the** basis **of** ❷ basis **for** *something* ❸ |
| V. | **provide a** basis, **serve as a** basis ❸ |

**bask** /bæsk/ (**basks, basking, basked**) ■ V-I If you **bask in** the sunshine, you lie somewhere sunny and enjoy the heat. ▢ *We basked in the sun on the hotel terrace.* ❷ V-I If you **bask in** someone's approval, favor, or admiration, you greatly enjoy it. ▢ *He spent a month basking in the admiration of the fans back in Jamaica.* [from Old Norse]

**bas|ket** /bæskɪt/ (**baskets**) N-COUNT A **basket** is a stiff container that is used for carrying or storing objects. Baskets are made from thin strips of materials such as straw, plastic, or wire woven together. ▢ *...picnic baskets filled with sandwiches.* [from Old Northern French]
→ see **basketball**

**basket|ball** /bæskɪtbɔl/ N-UNCOUNT **Basketball** is a game in which two teams of five players each try to score points by throwing a large ball through a circular net attached to a metal ring at each end of the court.
→ see Picture Dictionary: **basketball**

**bas|ket sponge** (**basket sponges**) N-COUNT A **basket sponge** is a type of primitive sea creature with a hollow body that is open at the top.

**bass** /beɪs/ (**basses**) ■ N-COUNT A **bass** is a man with a very deep singing voice. ▢ *...the great Russian bass Chaliapin.* ❷ ADJ A **bass** drum, guitar, or other musical instrument is one that produces a very deep sound. ▢ *...bass guitarist Dee Murray.* [from Italian]

B

**Picture Dictionary** **basketball**

- basketball
- backboard
- basket
- sideline
- referee
- free throw line
- uniform
- player

**bass clef** (**bass clefs**) N-COUNT A **bass clef** is a symbol that you use when writing music in order to show that the notes on the staff are below middle C.

**bas|ti|on** /bǽstʃən/ (**bastions**) N-COUNT If a system or organization is described as a **bastion of** a particular way of life, it is seen as being important and effective in defending that way of life. [FORMAL] ❑ The university is a bastion of free speech. ❑ He sees the Church as a bastion of spiritual freedom. [from French]

**bat** /bǽt/ (**bats, batting, batted**) ■ N-COUNT A **bat** is a specially shaped piece of wood that is used for hitting the ball in baseball, softball, or cricket. ❑ ...a baseball bat. ■ V-I When you **bat**, you have a turn at hitting the ball with a bat in baseball, softball, or cricket. ❑ Paxton hurt his elbow while he was batting. ■ N-COUNT A **bat** is a small flying animal that looks like a mouse with wings made of skin. Bats are active at night. [Senses 1 and 2 from Old English. Sense 3 of Scandinavian origin] → see Word Web: **bat**

**batch** /bǽtʃ/ (**batches**) N-COUNT A **batch of** things or people is a group of things or people of the same kind, especially a group that is dealt with at the same time. ❑ They announced the first batch of players for the team. ❑ She brought a large batch of newspaper clippings. ❑ I baked a batch of cookies. [from Old English]

**bath** /bǽθ/ (**baths, bathing, bathed**)

> When the form **baths** is the plural of the noun it is pronounced /bǽðz/. When it is used in the present tense of the verb, it is pronounced /bɑ̱θs/ or /bǽθs/.

■ N-COUNT A **bath** is the process of washing your body in a bathtub. ❑ The nurse gave him a warm bath. ■ N-COUNT When you take a **bath**, you sit or lie in a bathtub filled with water in order to wash your body. ❑ Take a shower instead of a bath. [from Old English]

**bathe** /bḛɪð/ (**bathes, bathing, bathed**) ■ V-I When you **bathe**, you take a bath. ❑ Most of us now bathe or shower once a day. ■ V-T If you **bathe** someone, especially a child, you wash them in a bathtub. ❑ Back home, Shirley feeds and bathes the baby. ■ V-T If you **bathe** a part of your body or a wound, you wash it gently or soak it in a liquid. ❑ Bathe the infected area in a salt solution. ■ V-T If a place **is bathed in** light, it is covered with light, especially a gentle, pleasant light. ❑ The garden was bathed in warm sunshine. ❑ ...a room bathed in soft red light. [from Old English] ■ → see also **sunbathe**

**bath|room** /bǽθrum/ (**bathrooms**) ■ N-COUNT A **bathroom** is a room in a house that contains

b

## Word Web    bat

**Bats** fly like birds, but they are **mammals**. Female bats give birth to their young and produce milk to feed them. Bats are **nocturnal**. They search for food at night and sleep during the day. They **roost** upside down in dark, quiet places such as caves and attics. People think that bats drink blood, but only **vampire bats** do this. Most bats eat fruit or insects. As bats fly they make high-pitched sounds that bounce off objects. This echolocation is a kind of **radar** that guides them as they fly.

a bathtub or shower, a sink, and sometimes a toilet. ◼ N-SING A **bathroom** is a room in a house or public building that contains a sink and toilet. ❑ She asked if she could use the bathroom.
→ see Picture Dictionary: **bathroom**
→ see **house**

## Thesaurus    bathroom   Also look up :

N.   lavatory, boy's/girl's/ladies'/men's/ womens room, powder room, restroom, toilet, washroom ◼

**bath salts** N-PLURAL You dissolve **bath salts** in bath water to make the water smell pleasant and as a water softener. ❑ She poured all of the bath salts into the swirling water of the tub.

**bath|tub** /bæθtʌb/ (**bathtubs**) N-COUNT A **bathtub** is a long, usually rectangular container that you fill with water and sit in to wash your body. ❑ ...a huge pink marble bathtub.
→ see **bathroom**

**ba|ton** /bətɒn/ (**batons**) ◼ N-COUNT A **baton** is a light, thin stick used by a conductor to conduct an orchestra or a choir. ❑ The conductor raises his baton. ◼ N-COUNT In track and field or track events, a **baton** is a short stick that is passed from one runner to another in a relay race. ❑ He passed

the baton to the runner in front of him. [from French]

**bats|man** /bætsmən/ (**batsmen**) N-COUNT The **batsman** in a game of cricket is the player who is batting. ❑ He was the greatest batsman of his generation.

**bat|tal|ion** /bətælyən/ (**battalions**) N-COUNT A **battalion** is a large group of soldiers that consists of three or more companies. ❑ Anthony was ordered to return to his battalion. [from French]

**bat|ter** /bætər/ (**batters, battering, battered**)
◼ V-T To **batter** someone or something means to hit them many times. ❑ The East Coast was battered by an unusually severe storm. ❑ They were battering the door, trying to get in. ◼ N-VAR **Batter** is a mixture of flour, eggs, and milk that is used in cooking. ❑ ...pancake batter. ◼ N-COUNT In sports such as baseball and softball, a **batter** is a person who hits the ball. ❑ ...batters and pitchers. ◼ → see also **battered, battering**
→ see **baseball**

**bat|tered** /bætərd/ ADJ Something that is **battered** is old and in poor condition. ❑ ...a battered old car.

**bat|ter|ing** /bætərɪŋ/ (**batterings**) N-COUNT If something takes a **battering**, it suffers very badly as a result of a particular event or action. ❑ The

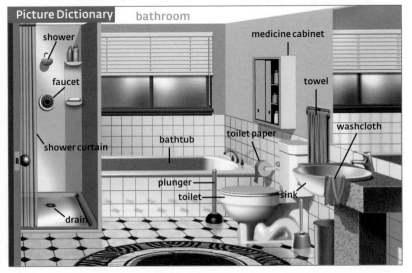

## Picture Dictionary    bathroom

shower

faucet

shower curtain

drain

medicine cabinet

towel

bathtub

toilet paper

washcloth

plunger

toilet

sink

*industry's reputation has taken a battering.*

**bat|tery** /bǽtəri/ (**batteries**) **1** N-COUNT **Batteries** are small devices that provide the power for electrical items such as radios and children's toys. ❑ *The shavers come complete with batteries.* ❑ *...a battery-operated watch.* **2** N-COUNT A car **battery** is a rectangular box containing acid that is found in a car engine. It provides the electricity needed to start the car. ❑ *...a car with a dead battery.* **3** N-UNCOUNT **Battery** is the crime of hitting or beating someone. [LEGAL] ❑ *Lawrence was charged with battery.* **4** N-COUNT A **battery of** people or things is a very large number of them. ❑ *...a battery of journalists and television cameras.* [from Old French]
→ see **cellphone**

**bat|tle** /bǽtəl/ (**battles, battling, battled**) **1** N-VAR A **battle** is a violent fight between groups of people, especially one between military forces during a war. ❑ *...the Battle of the Boyne.* ❑ *...a gun battle.* **2** N-COUNT A **battle** is a conflict in which different people or groups compete in order to achieve success or control. ❑ *...a political battle over jobs and the economy.* ❑ *...the eternal battle between good and evil in the world.* **3** V-RECIP To **battle with** an opposing group means to take part in a fight or contest against them. You can also say that one group or person **is battling** another. ❑ *Thousands of people battled with police.* ❑ *The two players battled for a place in the final.* **4** V-T/V-I To **battle** means to try hard to do something in spite of very difficult circumstances. You can also **battle** something, or **battle against** something or **with** something. ❑ *Doctors battled throughout the night to save her life.* ❑ *Firefighters are still battling the two blazes.* [from Old French]
→ see **army**

| Word Partnership | Use *battle* with : |
| --- | --- |
| ADJ. | **bloody** battle, **major** battle **1** **constant** battle, **legal** battle, **losing** battle, **uphill** battle **2** |
| V. | **prepare for** battle **1** **fight** a battle, **lose/win** a battle **1** **2** |
| N. | battle **of wills 2** |

**battle|field** /bǽtəlfild/ (**battlefields**) **1** N-COUNT A **battlefield** is a place where a battle is fought. ❑ *...the struggle to save America's Civil War battlefields.* **2** N-COUNT You can refer to an issue or field of activity over which people disagree or compete as a **battlefield.** ❑ *...the battlefield of family life.*

**battle|ship** /bǽtəlʃɪp/ (**battleships**) N-COUNT A **battleship** is a very large, heavily armed warship. [from Old French]

**baulk** /bɔk/ → see **balk**

**bawl** /bɔl/ (**bawls, bawling, bawled**) **1** V-I If a child **is bawling,** it is crying loudly. ❑ *One of the boys was bawling loudly.* **2** V-T/V-I If you **bawl,** you shout in a very loud voice. ❑ *When I came back to the hotel Laura and Peter were bawling at each other.* ❑ *Then a voice bawled: "Get out!"* [from Icelandic]

**bay** /beɪ/ (**bays, baying, bayed**) **1** N-COUNT A **bay** is a part of a coast where the land curves inward. ❑ *...a short ferry ride across the bay.* ❑ *...the Bay of Bengal.* **2** N-COUNT A **bay** is a partly enclosed area, inside or outside a building, that is used for

a particular purpose. ❑ *The animals are herded into a bay.* ❑ *...a cargo loading bay.* **3** V-I If a number of people **are baying for** something, they are demanding something angrily, usually that someone should be punished. ❑ *...voices from the crowd baying for a penalty.* ❑ *Opposition politicians have been baying for his blood.* **4** PHRASE If you **keep** something or someone **at bay,** or **hold** them **at bay,** you prevent them from reaching, attacking, or affecting you. ❑ *Eating oranges keeps colds at bay.* [from Old French]

**bayo|net** /beɪənɪt, beɪənɛt/ (**bayonets**) N-COUNT A **bayonet** is a long, sharp blade that can be attached to the end of a rifle and used as a weapon. [from French]

**ba|zaar** /bəzɑr/ (**bazaars**) **1** N-COUNT In areas such as the Middle East and India, a **bazaar** is a place where there are many small stores and stalls. ❑ *...Cairo's open-air bazaar.* **2** N-COUNT A **bazaar** is a sale to raise money for charity. ❑ *...a church bazaar.* [from Persian]

**BB gun** /bi gʌn/ (**BB guns**) N-COUNT A **BB gun** is a type of airgun that fires small round bullets that are called **BBs.** ❑ *Sims was carrying a BB gun when he was shot.*

**BC** /bi si/ also **B.C.** You use **BC** in dates to indicate a number of years or centuries before the year in which Jesus Christ is believed to have been born. ❑ *The necklace dates back to the fourth century BC.*

**BCE** /bi si i/ also **B.C.E.** Non-Christians often use **BCE** instead of **BC** in dates to indicate a number of years or centuries before the year in which Jesus Christ is believed to have been born. **BCE** is an abbreviation for "Before the Common Era." ❑ *...Lao-tzu, a sixth-century BCE Chinese teacher.* ❑ *The Babylonian Empire was conquered by the Persian Empire in 539 BCE.*

| **be** |
| --- |
| ❶ AUXILIARY VERB USES |
| ❷ OTHER VERB USES |

**❶ be** /bi, STRONG bi/ (**am, are, is, being, was, were, been**)

In spoken English, forms of **be** are often shortened, for example "I am" can be shortened to "I'm" and "was not" can be shortened to "wasn't."

**1** AUX You use **be** with a present participle to form the continuous tenses of verbs. ❑ *This is happening in every school throughout the country.* ❑ *She didn't always think carefully about what she was doing.* **2** **be going to** → see **going** **3** AUX You use **be** with a past participle to form the passive voice. ❑ *Her husband was killed in a car crash.* ❑ *Similar action is being taken by the U.S. government.* **4** AUX You use **be** with an infinitive to indicate that something is planned to happen, that it will definitely happen, or that it must happen. ❑ *The talks are to begin tomorrow.* ❑ *It was to be Johnson's first meeting with the board.* [from Old English] **5** **be about to** → see **about**

**❷ be** /bi, STRONG bi/ (**am, are, is, being, was, were, been**)

In spoken English, forms of **be** are often shortened, for example "I am" can be shortened to "I'm" and "was not" can be shortened to "wasn't."

**1** V-LINK You use **be** to introduce more information about the subject, such as its identity, nature, qualities, or position. ❑ *She's my mother.* ❑ *He is a very attractive man.* ❑ *He is fifty and has been married twice.* ❑ *The sky was black.* ❑ *His house is next door.* ❑ *He's still alive, isn't he?* **2** V-LINK You use **be**, with "it" as the subject, in clauses where you are describing something or giving your judgment of a situation. ❑ *It was too chilly for swimming.* ❑ *Sometimes it is necessary to say no.* ❑ *It is likely that investors will face losses.* ❑ *It's nice having friends to chat with.* **3** V-LINK You use **be** with "there" in expressions like **there is** and **there are** to say that something exists or happens. ❑ *Clearly there is a problem here.* ❑ *There are very few cars on this street.* **4** V-LINK You use **be** as a link between a subject and a clause and in certain other clause structures, as shown below. ❑ *Our greatest problem is convincing them.* ❑ *All she knew was that she was feeling very lonely.* ❑ *Local residents say it was as if there were two explosions.* [from Old English]

**beach** /biːtʃ/ (beaches) N-COUNT A **beach** is an area of sand or stones beside the ocean. ❑ *...a beautiful sandy beach.* [from Old English]
→ see Word Web: **beach**

**beach chair** (beach chairs) N-COUNT A **beach chair** is a simple chair with a folding frame, and a piece of canvas as the seat and back.

**beacon** /biːkən/ (beacons) N-COUNT A **beacon** is a light or a fire, usually on a hill or tower, that acts as a signal or a warning. ❑ *...a huge office tower with aircraft warning beacons on the roof.* [from Old English]

**bead** /biːd/ (beads) **1** N-COUNT **Beads** are small pieces of colored glass, wood, or plastic with a hole through the middle which are used for jewelry or

beak

decoration. ❑ *...a string of beads.* **2** N-COUNT A **bead of** liquid or moisture is a small drop of it. ❑ *...beads of blood.* [from Old English]
→ see **glass**

**beak** /biːk/ (beaks) N-COUNT A bird's **beak** is the hard curved or pointed part of its mouth. ❑ *...a*

black bird with a yellow beak. [from Old French]
→ see **bird**

**beaker** /biːkər/ (beakers) N-COUNT A **beaker** is a glass cup with straight sides used in a laboratory. [from Old Norse]
→ see **laboratory**

**beam** /biːm/ (beams, beaming, beamed) **1** V-T/V-I If someone or something **is beaming**, they are smiling because they are happy. [WRITTEN] ❑ *Frances beamed at her friend.* ❑ *"Welcome back," she beamed.* **2** V-T/V-I If radio signals or television pictures **are beamed** somewhere, they are sent there by means of electronic equipment. ❑ *The interview was beamed live across America.* ❑ *The Sci-Fi Channel began beaming into 10 million American homes this week.* **3** N-COUNT A **beam of** light is a line of light that shines from an object such as a lamp. **4** N-COUNT A **beam** is a long thick bar of wood, metal, or concrete, especially one used to support the roof of a building. ❑ *The ceilings are supported by oak beams.* [from Old English]
→ see **laser**

**bean** /biːn/ (beans) **1** N-COUNT **Beans** are the pods of a climbing plant, or the seeds that the pods contain, eaten as a vegetable. **2** N-COUNT **Beans** such as coffee **beans** or cocoa **beans** are the seeds of plants that are used to produce coffee, cocoa, and chocolate. [from Old English]

---

### bear

❶ VERB USES
❷ NOUN USE

---

❶ **bear** /bɛər/ (bears, bearing, bore, borne) **1** V-T If someone or something **bears** something somewhere, they carry it there. [LITERARY] ❑ *The wind bore coldness with it.* **2** V-T If one thing **bears** the weight of something else, it supports the weight of that thing. ❑ *The ice was not thick enough to bear their weight.* **3** V-T If you **bear** an unpleasant experience, you accept it because you are unable to do anything about it. ❑ *They will have to bear the misery of living in constant fear.* **4** V-T If you can't **bear** someone or something, you dislike them very much. ❑ *I can't bear people who talk during movies.* **5** → see also **bore, borne** [from Old English] **6** to **bear the brunt of** → see **brunt 7** to **bear fruit** → see **fruit 8** to **bear in mind** → see **mind**
▶ **bear out** PHR-VERB If someone or something **bears** a person **out** or **bears out** what that person is saying, they support what that person is saying. ❑ *Studies have borne out claims that perfume can change the way you feel.*
▶ **bear with** PHR-VERB If you ask someone to **bear with** you, you are asking them to be patient. ❑ *If*

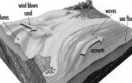

*you'll bear with me, Frank, just let me explain.*

| **Thesaurus** | *bear* | Also look up : |
| --- | --- | --- |

v.    carry, lug, move, transport ❶ ▪

      endure, put up with, stand, tolerate ❶ ▪

bear

❷ **bear** /bɛər/
(**bears**) N-COUNT A
**bear** is a large, strong
wild animal with
thick fur and sharp
claws. [from Old
English]
→ see **carnivore**

**bear|able**
/bɛərəbᵊl/ ADJ If
something is
**bearable**, you feel that you can accept it or deal
with it. ❏ *A cool breeze made the heat bearable.* [from
Old English]

**beard** /bɪərd/ (**beards**) N-COUNT A man's **beard**
is the hair that grows on his chin and cheeks.
❏ *He's decided to grow a beard.* [from Old English]
→ see **hair**

**beard|ed** /bɪərdɪd/ ADJ A **bearded** man has a
beard. ❏ *...a bearded 40-year-old professor.* [from Old
English]

**bear|er** /bɛərər/ (**bearers**) ■ N-COUNT The
**bearer of** something such as a document or a
message is the person who has it or brings it to
you. ❏ *I hate to be the bearer of bad news.* ■ N-COUNT
A **bearer** of a particular thing is a person who
carries it, especially in a ceremony. [FORMAL] ❏ *He
was the U.S. flag bearer at the 1976 Montreal Games.*
[from Old English]

**bear|ing** /bɛərɪŋ/ (**bearings**) ■ PHRASE If
something **has a bearing on** a situation or event, it
is relevant to it. ❏ *The food you eat has an important
bearing on your general health.* ■ PHRASE If you **get**
your **bearings** or **find** your **bearings**, you find out
where you are or what you should do next. If you
**lose** your **bearings**, you do not know where you are
or what you should do next. ❏ *A bus tour of the city
will help you get your bearings.* [from Old English]

**beast** /bist/ (**beasts**) N-COUNT A **beast** is an
animal, especially a large and dangerous one.
[LITERARY] ❏ *...wild beasts.* [from Old French]

**beat** /bit/ (**beats, beating, beaten**)

> The form **beat** is used in the present tense and is
> the past tense.

■ V-T To **beat** someone or something means to
hit them very hard. ❏ *My wife tried to stop them and
they beat her.* ❏ *There was silence except for a fly beating
against the glass.* • **beat|ing** (**beatings**) N-COUNT
❏ *...the investigation into the beating of a car thief.* ❏ *All
we heard was the beating of the rain.* ■ V-I When your
heart or pulse **beats**, it continually makes regular
rhythmic movements. ❏ *I felt my heart beating
faster.* • **Beat** is also a noun. ❏ *He could hear the beat
of his heart.* • **beat|ing** N-SING ❏ *I could hear the
beating of my heart.* ■ N-COUNT The **beat** of a piece
of music is the main rhythm that it has. ❏ *...the
pounding beat of rock music.* ■ V-T If you **beat** eggs,
cream, or butter, you mix them thoroughly using
a fork or beater. ❏ *Beat the eggs and sugar until they
start to thicken.* ■ V-T If you **beat** someone in a
competition or election, you defeat them. ❏ *In
yesterday's game, Switzerland beat the United States*

two to one. • **beat|ing** N-SING ❏ *Our firm has taken
a terrible beating in recent years.* [from Old English]
■ → see also **beating** ■ to **beat** someone **at their
own game** → see **game**
▸ **beat up** PHR-VERB If someone **beats** a person
**up**, they hit or kick the person many times. ❏ *Then
they beat her up as well.*

| **Usage** | **beat** |
| --- | --- |

As a verb, **beat** is commonly used to talk about
fighting an illness or addiction: *Lance Armstrong
beat cancer. She just can't beat her addiction to
cocaine.*

| **Thesaurus** | *beat* | Also look up : |
| --- | --- | --- |

v.    hit, pound, punch; (*ant.*) caress, pat,
      pet ■
      mix, stir, whip ■

| **Word Partnership** | Use *beat* with : |
| --- | --- |

N.    beat a **rug** ■
      **heart** beat ■
      beat **eggs** ■
PREP.   beat **against**, beat **on** ■
      **on/to** a beat ■

| **Word Link** | ful ≈ filled with : beautiful, careful, dreadful |
| --- | --- |

**beau|ti|ful** /byutɪfəl/ ■ ADJ A **beautiful** person
is very attractive to look at. ❏ *She was a very beautiful
woman.* ■ ADJ Something that is **beautiful** is
very attractive or pleasing. ❏ *New England is
beautiful.* ❏ *It was a beautiful morning.* • **beau|ti|ful|ly**
/byutɪfli/ ADV ❏ *The children behaved beautifully.*
■ ADJ You can describe something that someone
does as **beautiful** when they do it very skillfully.
❏ *...a beautiful throw to first base.* • **beau|ti|ful|ly**
ADV ❏ *The Sixers played beautifully.* [from Old French]

| **Thesaurus** | *beautiful* | Also look up : |
| --- | --- | --- |

ADJ.   gorgeous, lovely, pretty, ravishing,
      stunning; (*ant.*) grotesque, hideous,
      homely, ugly ■

**beau|ty** /byuti/ (**beauties**) ■ N-UNCOUNT
**Beauty** is the state or quality of being beautiful.
❏ *...an area of outstanding natural beauty.* ■ N-COUNT
A **beauty** is a beautiful woman. ❏ *She is known
as a great beauty.* ■ N-COUNT The **beauties** of
something are its attractive qualities or features.
[LITERARY] ❏ *He was beginning to enjoy the beauties
of nature.* ■ PHRASE If you say that a particular
feature is **the beauty of** something, you mean
that this feature is what makes the thing so good.
❏ *The beauty of this type of paint is that it washes off
easily.* [from Old French]

**beau|ty mark** (**beauty marks**) N-COUNT A
**beauty mark** is a small, dark spot on the skin that
is supposed to add to a woman's beauty.

**beau|ty pag|eant** (**beauty pageants**) N-COUNT
A **beauty pageant** is a competition in which
young women are judged to decide which one is
the most beautiful.

**beau|ty shop** (**beauty shops**) also **beauty
parlor** N-COUNT A **beauty shop** is a place where
women can go to have beauty treatments, for

example, to have their hair, nails, or makeup done.

**bea|ver** /bívər/ (**beavers**) N-COUNT A **beaver** is a furry animal with a big flat tail and large teeth. [from Old English]

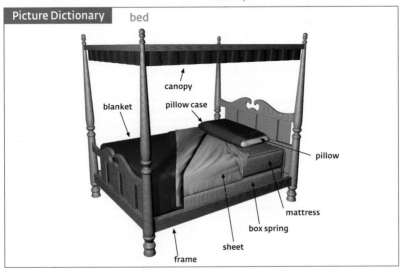

beaver

**be|came** /bɪkeɪm/ **Became** is the past tense of **become**.

**be|cause** /bɪkɒz, -kɒz/ ■ CONJ You use **because** when stating the reason or explanation for something. □ He is called Mitch, because his name is Mitchell. □ Because it is an area of natural beauty, the number of boats on the river is limited. □ I'm miserable because he didn't even ask me. ■ PHRASE If an event or situation occurs **because of** something, that thing is the reason or cause. □ He's retiring because of ill health.

**beck|on** /bɛkən/ (**beckons, beckoning, beckoned**) ■ V-T/V-I If you **beckon to** someone, you signal to them to come to you. □ He beckoned to the waiter. □ I beckoned her over. ■ V-I If something **beckons**, it is so attractive to someone that they feel they must become involved in it. □ All the attractions of the island beckon. [from Old English]

**be|come** /bɪkʌm/ (**becomes, becoming, became**)

The form **become** is used in the present tense and is the past participle.

■ V-LINK If someone or something **becomes** a particular thing, they start to change into that thing, or start to develop the characteristics mentioned. □ I became interested in Islam while I was doing my nursing training. ■ V-LINK If you wonder what has **become of** someone or something you wonder what will **become of** them, you wonder what has happened to them or what will happen to them. □ ...the need for families to discover what has become of their relatives. [from Old English]

**Usage**    **become**

Become is a linking verb and may be followed by a noun: I'd like to become a teacher. or by an adjective: In the summer the weather becomes hot.

**bed** /bɛd/ (**beds**) ■ N-COUNT A **bed** is a piece of furniture that you lie on when you sleep. □ We finally went to bed at about 4 a.m. □ Nona was already in bed. ■ N-COUNT A **bed** in a garden or park is an area of ground that has been specially prepared so that plants can be grown in it. □ ...beds of strawberries. ■ N-COUNT The sea **bed** or a river **bed** is the ground at the bottom of the sea or of a river. □ ...an operation to recover the wreckage from the sea bed. ■ → see also **bedding** [from Old English]
→ see Picture Dictionary: **bed**
→ see **lake, sleep**

**Word Partnership**    Use *bed* with :

| | |
|---|---|
| ADJ. | **asleep in** bed, **double/single/twin** bed, **ready for** bed ■ |
| V. | **be sick in** bed, **get into** bed, **go to** bed, **lie (down)** bed, **put** *someone* **to** bed ■ |
| PREP. | **in/out of** bed, **under the** bed ■ bed **of** *something* ■ |

**bed and break|fast** also **bed-and-breakfast** N-UNCOUNT **Bed and breakfast** is accommodation in a hotel or guest house, in which you pay for a room for the night and for breakfast the following morning. The abbreviation **B&B** is also used. □ Bed and breakfast costs from $50 per person per night.

**bed|ding** /bɛdɪŋ/ N-UNCOUNT **Bedding** is sheets, blankets, and covers that are used on beds. □ ...a crib with two full sets of bedding. [from Old English]

**bed|rock** /bɛdrɒk/ N-SING The **bedrock** of something is the principles, ideas, or facts on which it is based. □ Trust is the bedrock of a relationship.

---

**Picture Dictionary**    bed

canopy

blanket    pillow case

pillow

mattress

box spring

sheet

frame

**bed|room** /bɛdrum/ (**bedrooms**) 🔳 N-COUNT
A **bedroom** is a room used for sleeping in. ❑ …*an extra bedroom.* 🔳 ADJ If you refer to a place as a **bedroom community** or **suburb**, you mean that most of the people who live there travel to work in a city or another, larger town a short distance away. ❑ *This town is becoming a bedroom community of Columbus, 20 miles to the north.*
→ see **house**

**bed|side** /bɛdsaɪd/ 🔳 N-SING Your **bedside** is the area beside your bed. ❑ *She put a cup of tea down on the bedside table.* 🔳 N-SING If you are at someone's **bedside**, you are near them when they are ill in bed. ❑ *She remained at the bedside of her critically ill son.*

**bed|sore** /bɛdsɔr/ (**bedsores**) N-COUNT
**Bedsores** are sore places on a person's skin, caused by having to lie in bed for a long time without changing position.

**bee** /biː/ (**bees**) N-COUNT A **bee** is an insect with a yellow-and-black striped body that makes a buzzing noise as it flies. Bees make honey, and can sting. ❑ *A bee buzzed in the flowers.* [from Old English]

**beef** /biːf/ (**beefs, beefing, beefed**) N-UNCOUNT
**Beef** is the meat of a cow, bull, or ox. ❑ …*roast beef.* ❑ …*beef stew.* [from Old French]
→ see **meat**
▶ **beef up** PHR-VERB If you **beef up** something, you increase, strengthen, or improve it. ❑ …*to beef up security.* ❑ *Both sides are still beefing up their military strength.*

**been** /bɪn/ 🔳 **Been** is the past participle of **be**. 🔳 V-I If you have **been** to a place, you have gone to it or visited it. ❑ *He's already been to Tunisia, and has now moved on to Morocco.* [from Old English]

**beer** /bɪər/ (**beers**) N-VAR **Beer** is an alcoholic drink made from grain. A **beer** is a glass, can, or bottle of beer. ❑ *He sat in the kitchen drinking beer.* ❑ *Would you like a beer?* [from Old English]

**beet** /biːt/ (**beets**) 🔳 N-UNCOUNT **Beet** is a crop with a thick round root. ❑ …*fields of sweet corn and beet.* 🔳 N-VAR **Beets** are dark red roots that are eaten as a vegetable. They are often preserved in vinegar. ❑ *The roll comes with red beets, cottage cheese and blueberries.* [from Old English]
→ see **sugar**

**bee|tle** /biːtᵊl/ (**beetles**) N-COUNT A **beetle** is an insect with a hard covering on its body. [from Old English]

**be|fall** /bɪfɔl/ (**befalls, befalling, befell, befallen**) V-T If something bad or unlucky **befalls** you, it happens to you. [LITERARY] ❑ …*the disaster that befell the island of Flores.* [from Old English]

**be|fit** /bɪfɪt/ (**befits, befitting, befitted**) V-T If something **befits** a person or thing, it is suitable or appropriate for them. [FORMAL] ❑ *They offered him a job befitting his experience.*

**be|fore** /bɪfɔr/ 🔳 PREP If something happens **before** a particular date, time, or event, it happens earlier than that date, time, or event. ❑ *Annie was born a few weeks before Christmas.* ● **Before** is also a conjunction. ❑ *They decided to get married just before he got on the plane.* 🔳 ADV You use **before** when you are talking about time. For example, if something happened the day **before**, it happened during the previous day. ❑ *Carlton's girlfriend had moved to Denver a month before.* 🔳 ADV If someone has done

something **before**, they have done it on a previous occasion. If someone has never done something **before**, they have never done it. ❑ *I've been here before.* ❑ *I have met Professor Lown before.* 🔳 PREP If someone is **before** something, they are in front of it. [FORMAL] ❑ *They drove through the tall gates, and stopped before a large white house.* 🔳 PREP If you have something such as a trip, a task, or a stage of your life **before** you, you must do it or live through it in the future. ❑ *Everyone in the room knew it was the hardest task before them.* [from Old English]
🔳 **before long** → see **long**

| Thesaurus | before | Also look up : |
|---|---|---|
| ADV. | already, earlier, previously; (ant.) after 🔳 | |

**before|hand** /bɪfɔrhænd/ ADV If you do something **beforehand**, you do it earlier than a particular event. ❑ *How did she know beforehand that I was going to go out?*

**be|friend** /bɪfrɛnd/ (**befriends, befriending, befriended**) V-T If you **befriend** someone, you make friends with them. ❑ *The movie is about an elderly woman and a young nurse who befriends her.*

**beg** /bɛg/ (**begs, begging, begged**) 🔳 V-T/V-I If you **beg** someone **to** do something, you ask them very anxiously or eagerly to do it. ❑ *I begged him to come back to New York with me.* ❑ *We are not going to beg for help anymore.* 🔳 V-T/V-I If someone who is poor **is begging**, they are asking people to give them food or money. ❑ *I was surrounded by people begging for food.* ❑ …*homeless people begging on the streets.* ❑ *She was living alone, begging food from neighbors.* [from Old English] 🔳 **I beg your pardon** → see **pardon**

**be|gan** /bɪgæn/ **Began** is the past tense of **begin**. [from Old English]

**beg|gar** /bɛgər/ (**beggars**) N-COUNT A **beggar** is someone who lives by asking people for money or food. ❑ *There are no beggars on the streets in Vienna.* [from Old English]

**be|gin** /bɪgɪn/ (**begins, beginning, began, begun**) 🔳 V-T To **begin to** do something means to start doing it. ❑ *He stood up and began to move around the room.* ❑ *The damage began to look more serious.* ❑ *"Professor Theron," he began, "I'm very pleased to see you."* 🔳 V-T/V-I When something **begins** or when you **begin** it, it takes place from a particular time onward. ❑ *The problems began last November.* ❑ *He has just begun his fourth year in hiding.* 🔳 PHRASE You use **to begin with** when you are talking about the first stage of a situation, event, or process, to introduce the first of several things that you want to say. ❑ *It was great to begin with but now it's difficult.* ❑ *"What do scientists think about that?" — "Well, to begin with, they doubt it's going to work."* [from Old English]

| Thesaurus | begin | Also look up : |
|---|---|---|
| V. | commence, kick off, start; (ant.) end, stop 🔳 🔳 | |

**be|gin|ner** /bɪgɪnər/ (**beginners**) N-COUNT A **beginner** is someone who has just started learning to do something and cannot do it very well yet. ❑ *The course is suitable for both beginners and advanced students.* [from Old English]

**be|gin|ning** /bɪgɪnɪŋ/ (**beginnings**) N-COUNT
The **beginning of** something is the first part of it.

❑ *This was the beginning of her career.* ❑ *The wedding will be at the beginning of March.* ❑ *I had the beginnings of a headache.* [from Old English]

**be|gun** /bɪgʌn/ **Begun** is the past participle of **begin**. [from Old English]

**be|half** /bɪhæf/ PHRASE If you do something on someone's **behalf**, you do it for that person as their representative. ❑ *She thanked us all on her son's behalf.* [from Old English]

**be|have** /bɪheɪv/ (behaves, behaving, behaved) ■ V-I The way that you **behave** is the way that you do and say things, and the things that you do and say. ❑ *I couldn't believe these people were behaving in this way.* ■ V-T/V-I If you **behave** or **behave yourself**, you act in the way that people think is correct and proper. ❑ *You have to behave.*

**be|hav|ior** /bɪheɪvyər/ (behaviors) ■ N-VAR A person's **behavior** is the way that they behave. ❑ *Make sure that good behavior is rewarded.* ❑ *...human social behavior.* ■ N-UNCOUNT In science, the **behavior** of something is the way that it behaves. [from Middle English]

| Word Partnership | Use *behavior* with : |
| --- | --- |
| ADJ. | **aggressive/criminal** behavior, **bad/ good** behavior, **learned** behavior ■ |
| V. | **change** *someone's* behavior ■ |
| N. | **human** behavior, behavior **pattern**, behavior **problems** ■ ■ |

**be|hav|ior|al** /bɪheɪvyərəl/ ADJ **Behavioral** means relating to the behavior of a person or animal, or to the study of their behavior. ❑ *...emotional and behavioral problems.* [from Middle English]

**be|hav|ior|ism** /bɪheɪvyərɪzəm/ N-UNCOUNT **Behaviorism** is the belief held by some psychologists that the only valid method of studying the psychology of people or animals is to observe how they behave. ● **be|hav|ior|ist** (behaviorists) N-COUNT ❑ *Animal behaviorists have been studying these monkeys for years.* [from Middle English]

**be|hind** /bɪhaɪnd/ (behinds)

> In addition to the uses shown below, **behind** is also used in a few phrasal verbs, such as "fall behind" and "lie behind."

■ PREP If something is **behind** a thing or person, it is on the other side of them from you, or nearer their back rather than their front. ❑ *I put one of the cushions behind his head.* ❑ *They were parked behind the truck.* ● **Behind** is also an adverb. ❑ *...wonderful views of the canal and the hills behind.* ■ PREP If you are walking or traveling **behind** someone or something, you are following them. ❑ *Keith wandered along behind him.* ● **Behind** is also an adverb. ❑ *The other guards followed behind in a second vehicle.* ■ N-COUNT Your **behind** is the part of your body that you sit on. ■ PREP If something or someone is **behind** you, they support you and help you. ❑ *The new government must get the country behind them.* ■ PREP If something is **behind** schedule, it is not as far advanced as people had planned. If someone is **behind** schedule, they are not progressing as quickly at something as they had planned. ❑ *The work is 22 weeks behind schedule.* ■ ADV If you stay **behind**, you remain in a place

after other people have gone. ❑ *Some of us stayed behind to tidy up.* ■ ADV If you leave something or someone **behind**, you do not take them with you when you go. ❑ *The soldiers escaped into the mountains, leaving behind their weapons and supplies.* [from Old English] ■ to do something **behind** someone's **back** → see **back** ■ **behind bars** → see **bar** ■ **behind the scenes** → see **scene** → see **location**

| Usage | **behind** |
| --- | --- |

*Behind* and *in back of* have similar meanings, but *behind* is not generally used with *of*. *A police officer pulled up behind/in back of us and signaled us to stop.*

**beige** /beɪʒ/ COLOR Something that is **beige** is pale brown in color. ❑ *The walls are beige.* [from Old French]

**be|ing** /biɪŋ/ (beings) ■ **Being** is the present participle of **be**. ■ N-COUNT You can refer to any real or imaginary creature as a **being**. ❑ *Remember you are dealing with a living being — consider the horse's feelings too.* ■ → see also **human being** ■ N-UNCOUNT **Being** is existence. Something that is in **being** or comes **into being** exists. ❑ *Abraham Maslow described psychology as "the science of being."* [from Old English] ■ → see also **well-being** ■ **other things being equal** → see **equal** ■ **for the time being** → see **time**

**be|jew|eled** /bɪdʒuºld/ also **bejewelled** ADJ A **bejeweled** person or object is wearing a lot of jewelry or is decorated with jewels. ❑ *...bejeweled women.* ❑ *...a bejeweled golden crown.*

**be|la|bor** /bɪleɪbər/ (belabors, belaboring, belabored) V-T If someone **belabors** a point, they keep on talking about it. ❑ *I won't belabor the point, for this is a familiar story.*

**be|lat|ed** /bɪleɪtɪd/ ADJ A **belated** action happens later than it should have. [FORMAL] ❑ *...a belated attempt to improve conditions.* [from Old English]

**belch** /bɛltʃ/ (belches, belching, belched) ■ V-I If someone **belches**, they make a sudden noise in their throat because air has risen up from their stomach. ❑ *Bardo belched again and coughed in embarrassment.* ● **Belch** is also a noun. ❑ *He laughed and let out a belch.* ■ V-T/V-I If a machine or chimney **belches** smoke or fire, or if smoke or fire **belches** from it, large amounts of smoke or fire come from it. ❑ *Trucks were struggling up the road, belching black smoke.* [from Old English]

**be|lea|guered** /bɪligərd/ ADJ A **beleaguered** person, organization, or project is being attacked or criticized. [FORMAL] ❑ *...a final attack on the beleaguered city.*

**be|lie** /bɪlaɪ/ (belies, belying, belied) V-T If one thing **belies** another, it creates a false idea or image of someone or something. ❑ *Her looks belie her 50 years.* [from Old English]

**be|lief** /bɪlif/ (beliefs) N-VAR **Belief** is a feeling of certainty that something exists, is true, or is good. ❑ *One billion people throughout the world are Muslims, united by belief in one god.* [from Old English]

**be|liev|able** /bɪlivəbºl/ ADJ Something that is **believable** makes you think that it could be true or real. ❑ *This book is full of believable characters.* [from Old English]

**be|lieve** /bɪliːv/ (**believes, believing, believed**)
■ V-T If you **believe** that something is true, you
think it is true. [FORMAL] ❑ *Many experts believe
that prices will continue to rise.* ❑ *We believe them to be
hidden here in this apartment.* ■ V-T If you **believe**
someone, you accept that they are telling the
truth. ❑ *Of course I believe you!* ❑ *Never believe what
you read in the newspapers.* ■ V-I If you **believe in**
fairies, ghosts, or miracles, you are sure that they
exist or happen. If you **believe in** a god, you are
sure of the existence of that god. ❑ *I don't believe
in ghosts.* ■ V-I If you **believe in** a way of life or an
idea, you think it is good or right. ❑ *He believed in
honesty and trust.* [from Old English]

| **Thesaurus** | *believe* | Also look up : |
|---|---|---|
| v. | consider, guess, speculate, think ■ | |
| | accept, buy, trust ■ | |

**be|liev|er** /bɪliːvər/ (**believers**) ■ N-COUNT If
you are a **believer in** something, you think that it
is good or right. ❑ *Mom was a great believer in herbal
medicines.* ■ N-COUNT A **believer** is someone who
is sure that God exists or that their religion is true.
❑ *It was no secret that I was not a believer.* [from Old
English]

**bell** /bɛl/ (**bells**) ■ N-COUNT A **bell** is a device
that makes a ringing sound and is used to attract
people's attention. ❑ *I had just enough time to finish
eating before the bell rang.* ■ N-COUNT A **bell** is a
hollow metal object with a loose piece hanging
inside it that hits the sides and makes a sound.
❑ *My brother was born on a Sunday, when all the church
bells were ringing.* [from Old English]

**bell|hop** /bɛlhɒp/ (**bellhops**) N-COUNT A **bellhop**
is a man or boy who works in a hotel, carrying
bags or bringing things to the guests' rooms.

**bel|lig|er|ent** /bɪlɪdʒərənt/ ADJ A **belligerent**
person or action is hostile and aggressive.
❑ *…belligerent statements from both sides.*
● **bel|lig|er|ence** N-UNCOUNT ❑ *He could be accused
of passion, but never belligerence.* [from Latin]

**bel|low** /bɛloʊ/ (**bellows, bellowing, bellowed**)
■ V-T/V-I If someone **bellows**, they shout angrily
in a loud, deep voice. ❑ *"You're not leaving yet!" she
bellowed.* ❑ *She came in and found them there, bellowing
at each other.* ● **Bellow** is also a noun. ❑ *I let out a
bellow of tearful rage.* ■ N-COUNT A **bellows** is or
**bellows** are a device used for blowing air into a fire
in order to make it burn more fiercely. [from Old
English]

**bell pep|per** (**bell peppers**) N-COUNT A **bell
pepper** is a hollow green, red, or yellow vegetable
with seeds.

**bell|weth|er** /bɛlwɛðər/ (**bellwethers**) N-COUNT
If you describe something as a **bellwether**, you
mean that it is an indication of the way a situation
is changing. [JOURNALISM] ❑ *IBM is considered the
bellwether of the stock market.*

**bel|ly** /bɛli/ (**bellies**) N-COUNT The **belly** of a
person or animal is their stomach or abdomen.
❑ *She laid her hands on her swollen belly.* [from Old
English]
→ see **horse**

**be|long** /bɪlɔŋ/ (**belongs, belonging, belonged**)
■ V-I If something **belongs to** you, you own
it. ❑ *The house had belonged to her family for three
generations.* ■ V-I If someone or something

**belongs to** a particular group, they are a member
of that group. ❑ *I used to belong to a youth club.*
■ V-I If something or someone **belongs in** or **to**
a particular category, type, or group, they are of
that category, type, or group. ❑ *The judges could not
decide which category it belonged in.* [from Old High
German]

**be|long|ings** /bɪlɔŋɪŋz/ N-PLURAL Your
**belongings** are the things that you own. ❑ *I
collected my belongings and left.* [from Old High
German]

**be|lov|ed** /bɪlʌvɪd, -lʌvd/ ADJ A **beloved** person,
thing, or place is one that you feel great affection
for. ❑ *He lost his beloved wife last year.* [from Old
English]

**be|low** /bɪloʊ/ ■ PREP If something is **below**
something else, it is in a lower position. ❑ *He
appeared from the apartment directly below Leonard's.*
❑ *The sun has already sunk below the horizon.* ● **Below**
is also an adverb. ❑ *We climbed down a rope-ladder to
the boat below.* ❑ *…a view to the street below.* ■ PREP
If something is **below** a particular amount,
rate, or level, it is less than that amount, rate, or
level. ❑ *Night temperatures can drop below 15 degrees.*
● **Below** is also an adverb. ❑ *…temperatures at zero or
below.* ■ below par → see **par**

| **Word Partnership** | Use *below* with : |
|---|---|
| ADV. | **directly** below, **far/significantly/
substantially/well** below, **just/slightly**
below ■ |
| N. | below **the surface** ■
below **cost**, below **freezing**, below
**ground** below **the poverty level/line**,
below **zero** ■ |
| V. | **dip/drop/fall** below ■ ■ |
| ADJ. | below **average**, below **normal** ■ |

**belt** /bɛlt/ (**belts, belting, belted**) ■ N-COUNT A
**belt** is a strip of leather or cloth that you fasten
around your waist. ❑ *He wore a belt with a large
brass buckle.* ■ → see also **seat belt** ■ N-COUNT A
**belt** in a machine is a circular strip of rubber that
is used to drive moving parts or to move objects
along. ❑ *I started the car: the fan belt made a strange
noise.* ■ → see also **conveyor belt** ■ N-COUNT A
**belt** of land or sea is a long, narrow area of it that
has some special feature. ❑ *…the country's cocoa
belt.* ■ V-T If someone **belts** you, they hit you very
hard. If someone **belts** something, they hit it very
hard. [INFORMAL] ❑ *She belted poor old George in the
stomach.* ● **Belt** is also a noun. ❑ *She gave him a belt
with her umbrella as he tried to run away.* ■ PHRASE If
you have to **tighten** your **belt**, you have to manage
without things because you have less money than
you used to have. ❑ *If you are spending more than your
income, you'll need to tighten your belt.* ■ PHRASE If
you have something **under** your **belt**, you have
already achieved it or done it. ❑ *Clare is now a full-
time author with six books under her belt.* [from Old
English]
→ see **button**

**be|mused** /bɪmyuːzd/ ADJ If you are **bemused**,
you are puzzled or confused. ❑ *He was rather
bemused by children.* [rom old French]

**bench** /bɛntʃ/ (**benches**) ■ N-COUNT A **bench**
is a long seat of wood or metal. ❑ *He sat down on a
park bench.* ■ N-COUNT A **bench** is a long, narrow
table in a factory or laboratory. ❑ *…the laboratory*

bench. **3** N-SING In a court of law, **the bench** is the judge or magistrates. ❑ *The Pollards and their lawyers approached the bench.* [from Old English]

**bend** /bɛnd/ (**bends, bending, bent**) **1** V-I When you **bend**, you move the top part of your body downward and forward. ❑ *I bent over and kissed her cheek.* ❑ *She bent and picked up a plastic bucket.* **2** V-T/V-I When you **bend** a part of your body such as your arm or leg, or when it **bends**, you change its position so that it is no longer straight. ❑ *Bend your legs and leap as far as you can.* ● **bent** ADJ ❑ *Keep your knees slightly bent.* **3** V-T If you **bend** something that is flat or straight, you use force to make it curved or to put an angle in it. ❑ *Bend the bar into a horseshoe.* ● **bent** ADJ ❑ *...a length of bent wire.* **4** V-T/V-I When a road, beam of light, or other long thin thing **bends**, or when something **bends** it, it changes direction to form a curve or angle. ❑ *The road bent slightly to the right.* **5** N-COUNT A **bend** in a road, pipe, or other long thin object is a curve or angle in it. ❑ *The crash occurred on a sharp bend.* **6** V-T If you **bend** rules or laws, you interpret them in a way that allows you to do something they would not normally allow you to do. ❑ *A few officers were prepared to bend the rules.* [from Old English] **7** → see also **bent**

**be|neath** /bɪniθ/ PREP Something that is **beneath** another thing is under the other thing. ❑ *She could see the muscles of his shoulders beneath his T-shirt.* ❑ *Four levels of parking beneath the theater was not enough.* ADV ● **Beneath** is also an adverb. ❑ *On a shelf beneath he spotted a photo album.* [from Old English]

**ben|efac|tor** /bɛnɪfæktər/ (**benefactors**) N-COUNT A **benefactor** is someone who helps a person or organization by giving them money. ❑ *In his old age he became a benefactor of the arts.* [from Late Latin]

**ben|efi|cial** /bɛnɪfɪʃ°l/ ADJ Something that is **beneficial** helps people or improves their lives. ❑ *...vitamins that are beneficial to our health.* [from Late Latin]

**bene|fi|ciary** /bɛnɪfɪʃieri/ (**beneficiaries**) N-COUNT Someone who is a **beneficiary of** something is helped by it. ❑ *One of the main beneficiaries of the early election is the former president.* [from Late Latin]

**ben|efit** /bɛnɪfɪt/ (**benefits, benefiting** or **benefitting, benefited** or **benefitted**) **1** N-VAR The **benefit of** something is the help that you get from it or the advantage that results from it. ❑ *It was his task to give them the benefit of his experience in academic matters.* ❑ *I'm a great believer in the benefits of this form of therapy.* **2** N-UNCOUNT If something is **to** your **benefit** or is **of benefit to** you, it helps you or improves your life. ❑ *This could now work to Albania's benefit.* **3** V-T/V-I If you **benefit from** something or if it **benefits** you, it helps you or improves your life. ❑ *Both sides have benefited from the talks.* **4** N-UNCOUNT If you have the **benefit of** some information, knowledge, or equipment, you are able to use it so that you can achieve something. ❑ *Steve didn't have the benefit of a formal*

college education. **5** N-VAR **Benefits** are money or other advantages which come from your job, the government, or an insurance company. ❑ *McCary will receive about $921,000 in retirement benefits.* ❑ *...the rising cost of health care and medical benefits.* **6** PHRASE If you give someone **the benefit of the doubt**, you treat them as if they are telling the truth or as if they have behaved properly, even though you are not sure that this is the case. ❑ *At first I gave him the benefit of the doubt.* [from Latin]

**be|nevo|lent** /bɪnɛvələnt/ ADJ A **benevolent** person is kind and fair. ❑ *The company has proved to be a most benevolent employer.* ● **be|nevo|lence** N-UNCOUNT ❑ *He tried to help with his small acts of benevolence.* [from Latin]

**be|nign** /bɪnaɪn/ **1** ADJ You use **benign** to describe someone who is kind, gentle, and harmless. ❑ *They are normally a more benign audience.* ● **be|nign|ly** ADV ❑ *I just smiled benignly.* **2** ADJ A **benign** substance or process does not have any harmful effects. ❑ *This is a relatively benign medicine.* **3** ADJ A **benign** tumor will not cause death or serious harm. [MEDICAL] ❑ *It wasn't cancer, only a benign tumor.* [from Old French]

**bent** /bɛnt/ **1** **Bent** is the past tense and past participle of **bend**. **2** ADJ If someone is **bent on** doing something, especially something harmful, they are determined to do it. ❑ *...the leader of a group bent on world domination.* **3** N-SING If you have a **bent for** something, you have a natural ability to do it or a natural interest in it. ❑ *His bent for natural history directed him toward his first job.* [from Old English]

**ben|thic en|vir|on|ment** /bɛnθɪk ɪnvaɪrənmənt, -vaɪərn-/ also **benthic zone** N-SING The **benthic environment** or **benthic zone** is the area on or near the bottom of seas, rivers, and lakes, and all the organisms that live there. Compare **pelagic**. [TECHNICAL]

**ben|thos** /bɛnθɒs/ N-PLURAL **Benthos** are plants and animals that live in or near the bottoms of seas, rivers, and lakes. You can also use **benthos** to mean the areas at the bottoms of seas, rivers, and lakes. [TECHNICAL] [from Greek]

**be|queath** /bɪkwið/ (**bequeaths, bequeathing, bequeathed**) V-T If you **bequeath** your money or property **to** someone, you legally state that they should have it when you die. [FORMAL] ❑ *He bequeathed all his silver to his children.* [from Old English]

**be|reaved** /bɪrivd/ ADJ A **bereaved** person is one who has a relative or close friend who has recently died. ❑ *Mr. Dinkins visited the bereaved family to offer comfort.* ● **be|reave|ment** /bɪrivmənt/ (**bereavements**) N-VAR ❑ *When Mary died, Anne did not share her brother's sense of bereavement.* [from Old English]

**be|reft** /bɪrɛft/ ADJ If a person or thing is **bereft of** something, they no longer have it. [FORMAL] ❑ *The place seemed to be utterly bereft of human life.* [from Old English]

**Bernoulli's prin|ci|ple** /bərnuliz prɪnsɪp°l/ N-UNCOUNT **Bernoulli's principle** is a law in physics which states that the pressure of a moving fluid decreases as its speed increases. [TECHNICAL] [after Daniel Bernoulli (1700–82), a Swiss mathematician and physicist]

**ber|ry** /bɛri/ (berries) N-COUNT **Berries** are small, round fruit that grow on a bush or a tree. [from Old English]

**berth** /bɜrθ/ (berths, berthing, berthed)
■ N-COUNT A **berth** is a bed on a ship or train. ■ N-COUNT A **berth** is a space in a harbor where a ship stays for a period of time. □ ...the slow passage through the docks to the ship's berth. ■ V-I When a ship **berths**, it sails into harbor and stops at the quay. □ The ship berthed in New York.

**be|set** /bɪsɛt/ (besets, besetting, beset) V-T If someone or something **is beset by** problems or fears, they have many problems or fears which affect them severely. □ The country is beset by severe economic problems. □ The discussions were beset with difficulties. [from Old English]

**be|side** /bɪsaɪd/ ■ PREP Something that is **beside** something else is at the side of it or next to it. □ On the table beside an empty plate was a pile of books. ■ → see also **besides** ■ PHRASE If you are **beside yourself** with anger or excitement, you are extremely angry or excited. □ He shouted at her, beside himself with anxiety. [from Old English] ■ **beside the point** → see **point**

**be|sides** /bɪsaɪdz/ ■ PREP **Besides** something or **beside** something means in addition to it. □ She has many good qualities besides being very beautiful. ● **Besides** is also an adverb. □ You get to sample some baking, and take home some cookies besides. ■ ADV **Besides** is used to emphasize an additional point that you are making. □ The house is out of our price range. Besides, I am fond of our little apartment. [from Old English] ■ → see also **except**

**Usage** besides

*Besides* and *beside* are often confused. *Besides* means "in addition (to)" : *What are you doing today besides working? Beside* means "next to" : *Come sit beside me.*

**be|siege** /bɪsidʒ/ (besieges, besieging, besieged) ■ V-T If you **are besieged by** people, many people want something from you and continually bother you. □ She was besieged by journalists and the public. ■ V-T If soldiers **besiege** a place, they surround it and wait for the people in it to stop fighting or resisting. □ The main part of the army moved to Sevastopol to besiege the town. [from Middle English]

**best** /bɛst/ ■ **Best** is the superlative of **good**. □ The best thing to do is ask the driver as you get on the bus. ■ **Best** is the superlative of **well**. □ James Fox is best known as the author of "White Mischief." ■ N-SING **The best** is used to refer to things of the highest quality or standard. □ We offer only the best to our clients. ■ N-SING Someone's **best** is the greatest effort or highest achievement or standard that they are capable of. □ Miss Blockey was at her best when she played the piano. ■ ADV If you like something **best** or like it **the best**, you prefer it. □ The thing I liked best about the show was the music. □ Mother liked it best when Daniel did the cooking. ■ **Best** is used to form the superlative of compound adjectives beginning with "good" and "well." For example, the superlative of "well-known" is "best-known." ■ → see also **second best** ■ PHRASE You use **at best** to indicate that

even if you describe something as favorably as possible or if it performs as well as it possibly can, it is still not very good. □ At best his grade will be a B or B-minus. [from Old English] ■ to **hope for the best** → see **hope** ■ to **the best of** your **knowledge** → see **knowledge** ■ **best of luck** → see **luck** ■ **the best of both worlds** → see **world**

**be|stow** /bɪstoʊ/ (bestows, bestowing, bestowed) V-T To **bestow** something on someone means to give or present it to them. [FORMAL] □ The United States bestowed honorary citizenship upon Sir Winston Churchill. [from Middle English]

**best|sell|er** /bɛstsɛlər/ (bestsellers) N-COUNT A **bestseller** is a book of which a great number of copies has been sold. □ By mid-August the book was a bestseller.

**best-selling** also bestselling ■ ADJ A **best-selling** product such as a book is very popular and a large quantity of it has been sold. ■ ADJ A **best-selling** author is an author who has sold a very large number of copies of his or her book.

**bet** /bɛt/ (bets, betting)

The form **bet** is used in the present tense and is the past tense and past participle.

■ V-T/V-I If you **bet on** the result of a horse race, football game, or other event, you give someone a sum of money which they give you back with extra money if the result is what you predicted, or which they keep if it is not. □ Jockeys are forbidden to bet on the outcome of races. □ I bet $20 on a horse called Bright Boy. ● **Bet** is also a noun. □ Do you always have a bet on the Kentucky Derby? ● **bet|ting** N-UNCOUNT □ ...his thousand-dollar fine for illegal betting. ■ PHRASE You use expressions such as "I bet," "I'll bet," and "**you can bet**" to indicate that you are sure something is true. [INFORMAL] □ I bet you were good at games when you were at school. □ I'll bet they'll taste wonderful.

**beta par|ti|cle** /beɪtəpɑrtɪkəl/ (beta particles) N-COUNT **Beta particles** are atomic particles that are released by the nuclei of certain radioactive substances. Compare alpha particle and gamma ray. [TECHNICAL]

**be|tray** /bɪtreɪ/ (betrays, betraying, betrayed) ■ V-T If you **betray** someone who loves or trusts you, your actions hurt and disappoint them. □ She betrayed him by starting a relationship with another writer. ■ V-T If someone **betrays** their country or their friends, they give information to an enemy, putting their country's security or their friends' safety at risk. □ They offered me money if I would betray my friends. ■ V-T If you **betray** a feeling or quality, you show it without intending to. □ She studied his face, but it betrayed nothing. [from Old French]

**be|tray|al** /bɪtreɪəl/ (betrayals) N-VAR A **betrayal** is an action which betrays someone or something. □ She felt that what she had done was a betrayal of Patrick. [from Old French]

---

**better**

❶ COMPARING STATES AND QUALITIES

❷ GIVING ADVICE

---

❶ **bet|ter** /bɛtər/ ■ **Better** is the comparative of **good**. ■ **Better** is the comparative of **well**. ■ ADV

If you like one thing **better than** another, you like it more. ❑ *I like your poem better than mine.* ❑ *They liked it better when it rained.* ◳ ADJ If you are **better** after an illness or injury, you have recovered from it. If you feel **better**, you no longer feel so ill. ❑ *He is much better now; he's fine.* ◳ **Better** is used to form the comparative of compound adjectives beginning with "good" and "well." For example, the comparative of "well-off" is "better-off." ◳ PHRASE If something changes **for the better**, it improves. ❑ *He dreams of changing the world for the better.* ◪ PHRASE If a feeling such as jealousy, curiosity, or anger **gets the better of** you, it becomes too strong for you to hide or control. ❑ *She didn't allow her emotions to get the better of her.* [from Old English]

❷ **bet|ter** /bɛtər/ PHRASE You use **had better** or **'d better** when you are advising, warning, or threatening someone, or expressing an opinion about what should happen. ❑ *It's half past two. I think we had better go home.* ❑ *You'd better run if you're going to get your ticket.* ● In spoken English, people sometimes use **better** without "had" or "be" before it. It has the same meaning. ❑ *Better not say too much aloud.* [from Old English]

**be|tween** /bɪtwin/

In addition to the uses shown below, **between** is used in a few phrasal verbs, such as "come between."

❶ PREP If something is **between** two things or is **in between** them, it has one of the things on one side of it and the other thing on the other side. ❑ *She left the table to stand between the two men.* ❷ PREP If people or things travel **between** two places, they travel regularly from one place to the other and back again. ❑ *I spent a lot of time traveling between Waco and El Paso.* ❸ PREP A relationship, discussion, or difference **between** two people, groups, or things is one that involves them both or relates to them both. ❑ *...the relationship between patients and doctors.* ❑ *...long discussions between the two governments.* ◳ PREP If something stands **between** you and what you want, it prevents you from having it. ❑ *His sense of duty often stood between him and his enjoyment of life.* ◳ PREP If something is **between** two amounts or ages, it is greater or older than the first one and smaller or younger than the second one. ❑ *Increase the time you spend exercising by walking between 15 and 20 minutes every day.* ◳ PREP If something happens **between** or **in between** two times or events, it happens after the first time or event and before the second one. ❑ *The canal was built between 1793 and 1797.* ● **Between** or **in between** is also an adverb. ❑ *My life had been a journey from one crisis to another with only a brief time in between.* ◪ PREP If you must choose **between** two or more things, you must choose just one of them. ❑ *Students will be able to choose between English, French and Russian as their first* foreign language. ◳ PREP If people or places have a particular amount of something **between** them, this is the total amount that they have. ❑ *The three companies employ 12,500 people between them.* ◳ PREP When something is divided or shared **between** people, they each have a share of it. ❑ *There is only one bathroom shared between eight bedrooms.* [from Old English]
→ see **location**

**bev|er|age** /bɛvərɪdʒ, bɛvrɪdʒ/ (**beverages**) N-COUNT **Beverages** are drinks. [WRITTEN] [from Old French]
→ see **sugar**

**be|ware** /bɪwɛər/

Beware is only used as an imperative or infinitive. It does not have any other forms.

V-I If you tell someone to **beware of** a person or thing, you are warning them that the person or thing may harm them or be dangerous. ❑ *Beware of being too impatient with others.* ❑ *Drivers were warned to beware of icy conditions.*

**be|wil|dered** /bɪwɪldərd/ ADJ If you are **bewildered**, you are very confused and cannot understand something or decide what you should do. ❑ *Some shoppers looked bewildered by the huge variety of goods for sale.* ● **be|wil|der|ing** ADJ ❑ *His bookshelves revealed a bewildering range of interests.*

**be|wil|der|ment** /bɪwɪldərmənt/ N-UNCOUNT **Bewilderment** is the feeling of being bewildered. ❑ *He shook his head in bewilderment.*

**be|witch** /bɪwɪtʃ/ (**bewitches, bewitching, bewitched**) V-T If someone or something **bewitches** you, you are so attracted to them that you cannot think about anything else. ❑ *She was not moving, as if someone bewitched her.* ● **be|witch|ing** ADJ ❑ *...bewitching brown eyes.*

**be|yond** /bɪyɒnd/ ❶ PREP If something is **beyond** a place or barrier, it is on the other side of it. ❑ *On his right was a vegetable garden and beyond it a few apple trees.* ● **Beyond** is also an adverb. ❑ *The house had a fabulous view out to the Strait of Georgia and the Rockies beyond.* ❷ PREP If something happens **beyond** a particular time or date, it continues after that time or date has passed. ❑ *Few jockeys continue riding beyond the age of 40.* ● **Beyond** is also an adverb. ❑ *...through the 1990s and beyond.*

**B**

**3** PREP If something extends **beyond** a particular thing, it affects or includes other things. ❏ *His interests extended beyond the fine arts to politics and philosophy.* **4** PREP If something is, for example, **beyond** understanding or **beyond** belief, it is so extreme in some way that it cannot be understood or believed. ❏ *What Jock had done was beyond my comprehension.* **5** PREP If you say that something is **beyond** someone, you mean that they cannot deal with it. ❏ *The situation was beyond her control.* [from Old English]

**B-grade** /biː greɪd/ ADJ A **B-grade** person or thing is one that you consider to be inferior or of poor quality. ❏ *...a B-grade action movie star.*

**bias** /baɪəs/ (**biases**) N-VAR **Bias** is a tendency to prefer one person or thing to another, and to favor that person or thing. ❏ *...his desire to avoid the appearance of bias in favor of one candidate or another.* [from Old French]

**bi|ased** /baɪəst/ **1** ADJ If someone is **biased**, they prefer one group of people to another, and behave unfairly as a result. ❏ *He seemed a bit biased against women in my opinion.* **2** ADJ If something is **biased toward** one thing, it is more concerned with it than with other things. ❏ *University funding was biased toward scientists.* [from Old French]

**Bible** /baɪbəl/ (**Bibles**) N-PROPER **The Bible** is the sacred book of the Christian and Jewish religion. ● **biblical** /bɪblɪkəl/ ADJ ❏ *...the biblical story of creation.*

**bib|li|og|ra|phy** /bɪbliɒgrəfi/ (**bibliographies**) **1** N-COUNT A **bibliography** is a list of books on a particular subject. ❏ *At the end of this chapter there is a bibliography of useful books.* **2** N-COUNT A **bibliography** is a list of the books and articles that are referred to in a particular book. ❏ *The full bibliography is printed at the end of the second volume.* [from French]

**Word Link** **bi ≈ two** : *bi*centennial, *bi*cycle, *bi*lingual

**bi|cen|ten|nial** /baɪsɛntɛniəl/ (**bicentennials**) **1** N-COUNT A **bicentennial** is a year in which you celebrate something important that happened exactly two hundred years ago. ❏ *...the Bicentennial of the U.S. Constitution.* **2** ADJ **Bicentennial** celebrations are held to celebrate a bicentennial. ❏ *...the bicentennial celebration of the American Revolution.*

**bick|er** /bɪkər/ (**bickers, bickering, bickered**) V-RECIP When people **bicker**, they argue or quarrel

about unimportant things. ❏ *My partner and I spend too much time bickering.* ❏ *...as states bicker over territory.* ● **bick|er|ing** N-UNCOUNT ❏ *...political bickering.*

**bi|coas|tal** /baɪkoʊstəl/ ADJ Someone or something that is **bicoastal** lives or occurs on both the east coast and the west coast of the U.S.

**Word Link** **cycl ≈ circle** : *bi*cycle, cycle, cyclical

**bi|cy|cle** /baɪsɪkəl/ (**bicycles**) N-COUNT A **bicycle** is a vehicle with two wheels which you ride by sitting on it and pushing two pedals with your feet. [from Late Latin] → see Word Web: **bicycle**

**bid** /bɪd/ (**bids, bidding**)

The form **bid** is used in the present tense and is the past tense and past participle.

**1** N-COUNT A **bid for** something or a **bid to** do something is an attempt to obtain it or do it. ❏ *...Sydney's successful bid for the 2000 Olympic Games.* **2** N-COUNT A **bid** is an offer to pay a particular amount of money for something that is being sold. ❏ *They are hoping to make a bid for the company before Christmas.* **3** V-I If you **bid for** something or **bid to** do something, you try to obtain it or do it. ❏ *Several well-known firms are bidding for the work.* **4** V-T/V-I If you **bid for** something that is being sold, you offer to pay a particular amount of money for it. ❏ *She wanted to bid for the painting.* ❏ *The bank announced its intention to bid.* ❏ *The manager is prepared to bid $2 million for the soccer player.* ● **bid|der** (**bidders**) N-COUNT ❏ *The sale will be made to the highest bidder.* [from Old English]

**Word Link** **er ≈ more** : big*ger*, loud*er*, tall*er*

**big** /bɪg/ (**bigger, biggest**) **1** ADJ A **big** person or thing is large in degree or great in importance, or importance.. ❏ *Australia's a big country.* ❏ *Her husband was a big man.* ❏ *The crowd included a big group from Cleveland.* ❏ *Her problem was just too big for her to solve on her own.* ❏ *...one of the biggest companies in Italy.* **2** ADJ Children often refer to their older brother or sister as their **big** brother or sister. ❏ *She always introduces me as her big sister.* [of Scandinavian origin]

**Thesaurus** big Also look up :

ADJ. enormous, huge, large, massive; (ant.) little, small, tiny **1**

**Word Web** bicycle

A Scotsman named Kirkpatrick MacMillan invented the first **bicycle** with **pedals** around 1840. Early bicycles had wooden or metal **wheels**. However, by the mid-1800s **tires** with tubes appeared. Modern **racing bikes** are very lightweight and aerodynamic. The wheels have fewer **spokes** and the tires are very thin and smooth. **Mountain bikes** allow riders to ride up and down steep hills on dirt trails. These bikes have fat, knobby tires for extra traction. The **tandem** is a bicycle for two people. It has about the same **wind resistance** as a one-person bike. But with twice the power, it goes faster.

handle bars · seat · front brakes · rear brake · tire · spoke · wheel · pedal · chain

**big bang theo|ry** N-SING In astronomy **the big bang theory** is a theory that suggests that the universe was created as a result of an extremely large explosion.

**big-box** ADJ A **big-box** store or retailer is a very large store where a great variety of goods is sold. □ ...big-box stores spreading an hour west of Manhattan.

**big bucks** N-PLURAL If someone earns or spends **big bucks**, they earn or spend a lot of money. [INFORMAL] □ Plastic pipe is easy to install, and doing it yourself saves big bucks.

**big busi|ness** N-UNCOUNT Something that is **big business** is something which people spend a lot of money on, and which has become an important commercial activity. □ Online dating is big business in the United States.

**big deal** ■ N-SING If you say that something is a **big deal**, you mean that it is important or significant. [INFORMAL] □ Winning was such a big deal for the whole family. ■ CONVENTION You can say "**big deal**" to someone to show that you are not impressed by something that they consider important or impressive. [INFORMAL] □ "You'll miss dinner." — "Big deal."

**big|ot** /bɪɡət/ (**bigots**) N-COUNT If you describe someone as a **bigot**, you disapprove of them because they have strong, unreasonable prejudices and opinions. □ Anyone who opposes them is labeled a racist or a bigot. [from Old French]

**big|ot|ry** /bɪɡətri/ N-UNCOUNT **Bigotry** is the possession or expression of strong, unreasonable prejudices or opinions. □ ...religious bigotry. [from Old French]

**big-ticket** ADJ If you describe something as a **big-ticket** item, you mean that it costs a lot of money. □ Supercomputers are big-ticket items.

**big time** ADV You can use **big time** if you want to emphasize the importance or extent of something that has happened. [INFORMAL] □ You've upset her big-time.

**bike** /baɪk/ (**bikes**) N-COUNT A **bike** is a bicycle or a motorcycle. [INFORMAL] □ When you ride a bike, you exercise all of the leg muscles.

**bike path** (**bike paths**) N-COUNT A **bike path** is a special path on which people can travel by bicycle separately from motor vehicles.

**bik|er** /baɪkər/ (**bikers**) ■ N-COUNT **Bikers** are people who ride around on motorcycles, usually in groups. ■ N-COUNT People who ride bicycles are called **bikers**.

**bi|ki|ni** /bɪkini/ (**bikinis**) N-COUNT A **bikini** is a two-piece swimsuit worn by women.

**bi|lat|er|al sym|me|try** N-UNCOUNT An organism that has **bilateral symmetry** has a body that consists of two halves which are exactly the same, except that one half is the mirror image of the other. Compare **radial symmetry**. [TECHNICAL]

| **Word Link** | bi ≈ two : bicentennial, bicycle, bilingual |
|---|---|

| **Word Link** | lingu ≈ language : bilingual, linguist, linguistics |
|---|---|

**bi|lin|gual** /baɪlɪŋɡwəl/ ADJ **Bilingual** means involving or using two languages. □ ...bilingual education. □ He is bilingual in Mandarin and English.

**bill** /bɪl/ (**bills, billing, billed**) ■ N-COUNT A **bill** is a written statement of money that you owe for goods or services. □ They couldn't afford to pay the bills. □ He paid his bill for the newspapers promptly. ■ V-T If you **bill** someone **for** goods or services you have provided them with, you give or send them a bill stating how much money they owe you for these goods or services. □ Are you going to bill me for this? ■ N-COUNT A **bill** is a piece of paper money. □ The case contained a large quantity of U.S. dollar bills. ■ N-COUNT In government, a **bill** is a formal statement of a proposed new law that is discussed and then voted on. □ This is the toughest crime bill that Congress has passed in years. [from Old English]

| **Word Partnership** | Use bill with : |
|---|---|
| N. | **electricity/gas/phone** bill, **hospital/ hotel** bill ■ **dollar** bill ■ |
| V. | **pay a** bill ■ **pass a** bill, **sign a** bill, **vote on a** bill ■ |

**bill|board** /bɪlbɔrd/ (**billboards**) N-COUNT A **billboard** is a very large board on which advertising is displayed.

**bill|fold** /bɪlfoʊld/ (**billfolds**) N-COUNT A **billfold** is a small flat folded case, usually made of leather or plastic, where you can keep banknotes and credit cards. [from Late Latin]

**bil|liards** /bɪliərdz/

The form **billiard** is used as a modifier.

N-UNCOUNT **Billiards** is a game played on a large table, in which you use a long stick called a cue to hit balls against each other or against the walls around the sides of the table. [from Old French]

**bil|lion** /bɪlyən/ (**billions**)

The plural form is **billion** after a number, or after a word or expression referring to a number, such as "several" or "a few."

■ NUM A **billion** is a thousand million. □ The Ethiopian foreign debt has risen to 3 billion dollars. ■ QUANT You can use **billions** to mean an extremely large amount. □ The Universe is billions of years old. ● You can also use **billions** as a pronoun. □ It must be worth billions.

**bil|lion|aire** /bɪlyənɛər/ (**billionaires**) N-COUNT A **billionaire** is an extremely rich person who has money or property worth at least a thousand million dollars. [from French]

**bil|low** /bɪloʊ/ (**billows, billowing, billowed**) V-I When something **billows**, it swells out and moves slowly in the wind. □ The curtains billowed in the breeze. □ Her pink dress billowed out around her. □ ...thick smoke billowing from factory chimneys. □ Steam billowed out from under the hood of the car. [from Old Norse]

**bi|me|tal|lic strip** /baɪmətælɪk strɪp/ (**bimetallic strips**) N-COUNT A **bimetallic strip** is a long thin piece of material containing two different metals which expand at different rates when heated. Bimetallic strips are used in devices such as thermostats. [TECHNICAL]

**bin** /bɪn/ (**bins**) N-COUNT A **bin** is a container that you keep or store things in. □ There is a storage bin under the passenger seat. [from Old English]

**bi|na|ry fis|sion** N-UNCOUNT **Binary fission**

b

is the biological process by which a single cell divides to form two new cells. [TECHNICAL]

**bind** /baɪnd/ (**binds, binding, bound**) **1** V-T If something **binds** people **together**, it makes them feel as if they are all part of the same group. □ *It is the threat of attack that binds them together.* □ *The contract will bind the coach to the football team for two more seasons.* **2** V-T If you **are bound** by something such as a rule, agreement, or restriction, you are forced or required to act in a certain way. □ *You are bound by law to make sure that the information you receive remains secret.* □ *The authorities are legally bound to arrest any troublemakers.* **3** V-T If you **bind** something or someone, you tie rope, string, tape, or other material around them so that they are held firmly. □ *Bind the ends of the cord together with thread.* □ *…the red tape which was used to bind the files.* **4** V-T When a book **is bound**, the pages are joined together and the cover is put on. □ *Each volume is bound in bright-colored cloth.* □ *Their business is from a few big publishers, all of whose books they bind.* [from Old English] **5** → see also **bound**

**bind|ing** /baɪndɪŋ/ (**bindings**) **1** ADJ A **binding** promise, agreement, or decision must be obeyed or carried out. □ *It can take months to enter into a legally binding contract to buy a house.* **2** N-VAR The **binding** of a book is its cover. □ *Its books are noted for the quality of their paper and bindings.* [from Old English] **3** → see also **bind**

**binge** /bɪndʒ/ (**binges, bingeing, binged**) **1** N-COUNT If you go on a **binge**, you do too much of something, such as eating or spending money. [INFORMAL] □ *She went on occasional junk food binges.* **2** V-I If you **binge**, you do too much of something, such as drinking alcohol, eating, or spending money. [INFORMAL] □ *I haven't binged since 1986.* [from French]

**bin|go** /bɪŋgoʊ/ N-UNCOUNT **Bingo** is a game in which each player has a card with numbers on it. Someone calls out numbers and if you are the first person to have all your numbers called out, you win the game. □ *…a bingo hall.*

**bin|ocu|lars** /bɪnɒkyələrz/ N-PLURAL **Binoculars** consist of two small telescopes joined together side by side, which you look through in order to look at things that are a long distance away. [from Latin]

binoculars

**bi|no|mial** /baɪnoʊmiəl/ (**binomials**) **1** N-COUNT A **binomial** is an expression in algebra that consists of two terms, for example "3x + 2y." Compare **monomial, polynomial.** [TECHNICAL] **2** ADJ **Binomial** means relating to binomials. [from Medieval Latin]

**bi|no|mial dis|tri|bu|tion** (**binomial distributions**) N-COUNT A **binomial distribution** is a calculation that measures the probability of a particular outcome resulting from an event that has two possible outcomes. [TECHNICAL]

**bi|no|mial no|men|cla|ture** /baɪnoʊmiəl noʊmənkleɪtʃər/ N-UNCOUNT **Binomial nomenclature** is a system of scientifically classifying plants and animals by giving them a name consisting of two parts, first the genus and then the species. [TECHNICAL]

**bi|no|mial theo|rem** (**binomial theorems**) N-COUNT The **binomial theorem** is a mathematical formula that is used to calculate the value of a binomial that has been multiplied by itself a particular number of times. [TECHNICAL]

**bio|chemi|cal** /baɪoʊkɛmɪkʰl/ (**biochemicals**) **1** ADJ **Biochemical** changes, reactions, and mechanisms relate to the chemical processes that happen in living things. □ *Starvation causes biochemical changes in the body.* **2** N-COUNT **Biochemicals** are chemicals that are made by living things, for example hormones and enzymes.

Word Link    chem ≈ chemical : biochemist, chemical, chemistry

**bio|chem|is|try** /baɪoʊkɛmɪstri/ N-UNCOUNT **Biochemistry** is the study of the chemical processes that occur in living things. ● **bio|chem|ist** (**biochemists**) N-COUNT

**bio|degrad|able** /baɪoʊdɪgreɪdəbʰl/ ADJ Something that is **biodegradable** breaks down or decays naturally without any special scientific treatment, and can therefore be thrown away without causing pollution.

**bio|di|ver|sity** /baɪoʊdaɪvɜrsɪti/ N-UNCOUNT **Biodiversity** is the existence of a wide variety of plant and animal species living in their natural environment.

**bi|og|raph|er** /baɪɒgrəfər/ (**biographers**) N-COUNT Someone's **biographer** is a person who writes an account of their life. □ *…Picasso's biographer.* [from Late Greek]

Word Link    bio ≈ life : biography, biology, biotechnology

Word Link    graph ≈ writing : autograph, biography, graph

**bi|og|ra|phy** /baɪɒgrəfi/ (**biographies**) N-COUNT A **biography** of someone is an account of their life, written by someone else. □ *…recent biographies of Stalin.* ● **bio|graphi|cal** /baɪəgræfɪkʰl/ ADJ □ *The book contains few biographical details.* [from Late Greek]
→ see **library**

**bio|logi|cal** /baɪəlɒdʒɪkʰl/ **1** ADJ **Biological** is used to describe processes and states that occur in the bodies and cells of living things. □ *…biological processes.* ● **bio|logi|cal|ly** /baɪəlɒdʒɪkli/ ADV □ *Much of our behavior is biologically determined.* **2** ADJ **Biological** is used to describe activities concerned with the study of living things. □ *…all aspects of biological research.* **3** ADJ **Biological** weapons and **biological** warfare involve the use of bacteria or other living organisms in order to attack human beings, animals, or plants. □ *…chemical and biological weapons.* [from French]
→ see **war, zoo**

**bio|logi|cal clock** (**biological clocks**) N-COUNT Your **biological clock** is your body's way of registering time. It does not rely on events such as day or night, but on factors such as your habits, your age, and chemical changes taking place in your body.

### Word Web    biosphere

Earth is the only place in the **universe** where we are sure that **life** exists. A **geologist**, Eduard Suess*, invented the term **biosphere** in 1875. For him it included the **land**, **water**, and **atmosphere** in which all life occurs. Later scientists studied the relationships among living things and the biosphere. They created the term **ecosystem** to describe these interactions. In the 1980s, scientists built a research center called Biosphere 2 in Arizona. They hoped to create an artificial biosphere for people to use on the moon. Today, the center performs research into the effects of **greenhouse gases** on the environment.

*Eduard Suess (1831-1914): an Austrian geologist.*

### Word Link    ist ≈ one who practices : archaeolog**ist**, biolog**ist**, pharmac**ist**

### Word Link    logy, ology ≈ study of : anthropo**logy**, bio**logy**, geo**logy**

**bi|ol|ogy** /baɪɒlədʒi/ N-UNCOUNT **Biology** is the science which is concerned with the study of living things. ● **bi|olo|gist** /baɪɒlədʒɪst/ (**biologists**) N-COUNT ❏ ...biologists studying the fruit fly. [from French]

**bio|mass** /baɪoʊmæs/ **1** N-UNCOUNT The **biomass** of a particular area is the total number of organisms that live there. [TECHNICAL] **2** N-UNCOUNT **Biomass** is biological material such as dead plants that is used to provide fuel or energy. [TECHNICAL]

**bi|ome** /baɪoʊm/ (**biomes**) N-COUNT A **biome** is a group of plants and animals that live in a particular region because they are suited to its physical environment.
→ see **habitat**

**bio|sphere** /baɪəsfɪər/ N-SING The **biosphere** is the part of the Earth's surface and atmosphere where there are living things. [TECHNICAL]
→ see Word Web: **biosphere**

**bio|tech|nol|ogy** /baɪoʊtɛknɒlədʒi/ N-UNCOUNT **Biotechnology** is the use of living parts such as cells or bacteria in industry and technology. [TECHNICAL] ❏ ...the Scottish biotechnology company that developed Dolly the cloned sheep.
→ see **technology**

**bi|ot|ic** /baɪɒtɪk/ ADJ **Biotic** means relating to plants, animals, and other living organisms. [TECHNICAL] [from Greek]

**bio|weap|on** /baɪoʊwɛpən/ (**bioweapons**) N-COUNT **Bioweapons** are biological weapons.

**bi|po|lar dis|or|der** (**bipolar disorders**) N-VAR **Bipolar disorder** is a mental illness in which a person's state of mind changes between extreme happiness and extreme depression.

**birch** /bɜrtʃ/ (**birches**) N-VAR A **birch** is a type of tall tree with thin branches. [from Old English]

**bird** /bɜrd/ (**birds**) N-COUNT A **bird** is a creature with feathers and wings. [from Old English]
→ see Word Web: **bird**
→ see **pet**

**bird feed|er** (**bird feeders**) also **birdfeeder** N-COUNT A **bird feeder** is an object that you fill with seeds or nuts and hang up outside in order attract birds.

**bird flu** N-UNCOUNT **Bird flu** is a virus that can be transmitted from chickens, ducks, and other birds to people.

**bird|seed** /bɜrdsid/ N-UNCOUNT **Birdseed** is seeds that you give to birds as food. ❏ She bought a supply of birdseed for the winter.

**birth** /bɜrθ/ (**births**) **1** N-VAR When a baby is born, you refer to this event as his or her **birth**. ❏ His bad behavior started after the birth of his brother. ❏ She weighed 5 lbs 7 oz at birth. **2** N-UNCOUNT You can refer to the beginning or origin of something as its **birth**. ❏ ...the birth of democracy. **3** PHRASE When a woman **gives birth**, she produces a baby from her body. ❏ She's just given birth to a baby girl. ❏ I'd like to be with my wife when she give's birth. [from Old Norse]
→ see **reproduction**

### Word Web    bird

Many scientists today believe that birds evolved from avian dinosaurs. Recently many links have been found. Like birds, these dinosaurs laid their **eggs** in **nests**. Some had **wings**, **beaks**, and **claws** similar to modern birds. But perhaps the most dramatic link was found in 2001. Scientists in China discovered a well-preserved *Sinornithosaurus*, a bird-like dinosaur with **feathers**. This dinosaur is believed to be related to a prehistoric bird, the *Archaeopteryx*.

Sinornithosaurus

| Word Partnership | Use *birth* with : |
| --- | --- |
| PREP. | **at** birth, **before** birth ◼ |
| ADJ. | **premature** birth ◼ |
| N. | birth **of a baby/child**, birth **certificate**, birth **control**, birth **and death**, birth **defect**, birth **rate** ◼ |
| | **date of** birth ◼ ◼ |
| | **birth of a** nation ◼ |
| V. | **give** birth ◼ |

**birth con|trol** N-UNCOUNT **Birth control** means planning whether to have children, and using contraception to prevent unwanted pregnancy. ❑ ...*today's methods of birth control.*

**birth|day** /bɜrθdeɪ, -di/ (**birthdays**) N-COUNT Your **birthday** is the anniversary of the date on which you were born. ❑ *On his birthday she sent him presents.*

**birth|place** /bɜrθpleɪs/ (**birthplaces**) ◼ N-COUNT Your **birthplace** is the place where you were born. [WRITTEN] ❑ ...*Bob Marley's birthplace in the village of Nine Mile.* ◼ N-COUNT The **birthplace of** something is the place where it began. ❑ ...*Athens, the birthplace of the ancient Olympics.*

**birth rate** (**birth rates**) also **birth-rate** N-COUNT The **birth rate** is the number of babies born for every 1000 people during a particular period. ❑ *America's birth rate fell last year.*

**bi|sex|ual** /baɪsɛkʃuəl/ (**bisexuals**) ADJ Someone who is **bisexual** is sexually attracted to both men and women. ● **Bisexual** is also a noun. ❑ *He was an active bisexual.*

**bish|op** /bɪʃəp/ (**bishops**) ◼ N-COUNT; N-TITLE; N-VOC A **bishop** is a high-ranking member of the clergy. ◼ N-COUNT In chess a **bishop** is a piece that can be moved diagonally across the board on squares that are the same color. [from Old English] → see **chess**

**bis|tro** /bistroʊ, bɪs-/ (**bistros**) N-COUNT A **bistro** is a small, informal restaurant or a bar where food is served. [from French]

**bit** /bɪt/ (**bits**) ◼ QUANT A **bit of** something is a small amount of it, or a small part or section of it. ❑ *All it required was a bit of work.* ❑ *Only a bit of the barley remained.* ❑ *Now comes the really important bit.* ◼ PHRASE A **bit** means to a small extent or degree. It is sometimes used to make a statement less extreme. ❑ *This girl was a bit strange.* ❑ *I think people feel a bit more confident.* ◼ PHRASE You can use **a bit of** to make a statement less forceful. ❑ *It's all a bit of a mess.* ❑ *Students have always been portrayed as a bit of a joke.* ◼ PHRASE **Quite a bit** means quite a lot. ❑ *They're worth quite a bit of money.* ❑ *Things have changed quite a bit.* ◼ PHRASE If you do something **a bit** or do something **for a bit**, you do it for a short time. ❑ *Let's wait a bit.* ❑ *I hope there will be time to talk a bit this evening.* ◼ N-COUNT In computing, a **bit** is the smallest unit of information that is held in a computer's memory. It is either 1 or 0. Several bits form a byte. ◼ N-COUNT A **bit** is a piece of metal that is held in a horse's mouth and is used to control the horse when you are riding. ◼ **Bit** is the past tense of **bite**. ◼ PHRASE If you say that something is **a bit much**, you are annoyed because you think someone has behaved in an unreasonable way. [INFORMAL] ❑ *Her bright red outfit was a bit much.* ◼ PHRASE You say that

one thing is **every bit as** good, interesting, or important **as** another to emphasize that the first thing is just as good, interesting, or important as the second. ❑ *My jacket is every bit as good as his.* [from Old English]

**bitch** /bɪtʃ/ (**bitches**) N-COUNT A **bitch** is a female dog. [from Old English]

**bite** /baɪt/ (**bites, biting, bit, bitten**) ◼ V-T/V-I If you **bite** something, you use your teeth to cut into it or through it. ❑ *Both sisters bit their nails as children.* ❑ *He bit into his sandwich.* ❑ *She bit the end off the chocolate bar.* ◼ N-COUNT A **bite** of something, especially food, is the action of biting it. ❑ *He took another bite of apple.* ◼ V-T/V-I If a snake or insect **bites** you, it makes a mark or hole in your skin. ❑ *Mosquitoes spread the virus when they bite humans.* ❑ *Do these flies bite?* ◼ N-COUNT A **bite** is an injury or a mark on your body where an animal, snake, or insect has bitten you. ❑ *Any dog bite needs immediate medical*

bite

*attention.* ◼ V-I When an action or policy begins to **bite**, it begins to have a serious or harmful effect. ❑ *The spending cuts will begin to bite from November onward.* ◼ PHRASE If you **bite** your **lip** or your **tongue**, you stop yourself from saying something that you want to say, because it would be the wrong thing to say in the circumstances. ❑ *I must learn to bite my lip.* [from Old English]

**bit|ing** /baɪtɪŋ/ ◼ ADJ **Biting** wind or cold is extremely cold. ❑ ...*a raw, biting northerly wind.* ◼ ADJ **Biting** criticism or wit is very harsh or unkind, and is often caused by such feelings as anger or dislike. ❑ ...*the author's biting criticism of the church.* [from Old English]

**bit|ten** /bɪtⁿn/ **Bitten** is the past participle of **bite**. [from Old English]

**bit|ter** /bɪtər/ (**bitterest**) ◼ ADJ In a **bitter** argument or conflict, people argue very angrily or fight very fiercely. ❑ ...*the scene of bitter fighting.* ❑ ...*a bitter attack on the government.* ◼ ADJ If someone is **bitter**, they feel angry and resentful. ❑ *She is very bitter about the way she was fired from her job.* ● **bit|ter|ly** ADV ❑ *"And he sure didn't help us," Grant said bitterly.* ● **bit|ter|ness** N-UNCOUNT ❑ *I still feel bitterness and anger toward the person who knocked me down.* ◼ ADJ A **bitter** taste is sharp, not sweet, and often slightly unpleasant. ❑ *The leaves taste bitter.* ◼ ADJ A **bitter** experience makes you feel very disappointed. You can also use **bitter** to emphasize feelings of disappointment. ❑ *The decision was a bitter blow from which he never recovered.* ❑ *Bitter experience has taught him how to lose gracefully.* ● **bit|ter|ly** ADV ❑ *I was bitterly disappointed to have lost yet another race.* ◼ ADJ **Bitter** weather, or a **bitter** wind, is extremely cold. ❑ ...*a bitter east wind.* ● **bit|ter|ly** ADV ❑ *It's been bitterly cold here in Moscow.* [from Old English] → see **taste**

**bi|week|ly** /baɪwikli/ ADJ A **biweekly** event or publication happens or appears once every two weeks. ❑ *He used to see them at the biweekly meetings.*

**bi|zarre** /bɪzɑr/ ADJ Something that is **bizarre** is very odd and strange. ❑ ...*the bizarre behavior of the team's manager.* ● **bi|zarre|ly** ADV ❑ *She dressed*

bizarrely. [from French]

**black** /blæk/ (**blacker, blackest, blacks, blacking, blacked**) **1** COLOR Something that is **black** is of the darkest color that there is, the color of the sky at night when there is no light at all. ❏ *She was wearing a black coat with a white collar.* ❏ *He had thick black hair.* ● **black|ness** N-UNCOUNT [LITERARY] ❏ *…the blackness of the night.* **2** ADJ A **black** person belongs to a race of people with dark skins, especially a race originally from Africa. ❏ *He worked for the rights of black people.* ❏ *Sharon is black, tall, and slender.* **3** N-COUNT Black people are sometimes referred to as **blacks**, especially when comparing different groups of people. Other uses of the word could cause offense. ❏ *There are about thirty-one million blacks in the U.S.* **4** ADJ **Black** coffee or tea has no milk or cream added to it. ❏ *A cup of black tea or black coffee contains no calories.* **5** ADJ If you describe a situation as **black**, you are emphasizing that it is very bad indeed. ❏ *It was one of the blackest days of his political career.* [from Old English]
→ see **hair, spice**
▸ **black out** **1** PHR-VERB If you **black out**, you lose consciousness for a short time. ❏ *I felt as if I was going to black out.* **2** → see also **blackout**

**black and white** also **black-and-white** **1** COLOR In a **black and white** photograph or film, everything is shown in black, white, and gray. ❏ *…old black and white films.* ❏ *…a black-and-white photo of the two of us.* **2** PHRASE You say that something is **in black and white** when it has been written or printed, and not just said. ❏ *He has seen the proof in black and white.*

**black|berry** /blækbɛri/ (**blackberries**) N-COUNT A **blackberry** is a small, soft black or dark purple fruit.

**black|board** /blækbɔrd/ (**blackboards**) N-COUNT A **blackboard** is a dark-colored board that you can write on with chalk. [AM also **chalkboard**] [from Old English]

**black|en** /blækən/ (**blackens, blackening, blackened**) V-T To **blacken** something means to make it black or very dark in color. ❏ *Smoke from the fire blackened the kitchen walls.* [from Old English]

**black eye** (**black eyes**) N-COUNT If someone has a **black eye**, they have a dark-colored bruise around their eye. ❏ *He arrived at the hospital with a broken nose and a black eye.*

**black-eyed pea** (**black-eyed peas**) N-COUNT **Black-eyed peas** are beige seeds with black marks that are eaten as a vegetable. They are from a plant called the cowpea.

**black hole** (**black holes**) N-COUNT **Black holes** are areas in space where gravity is so strong that nothing, not even light, can escape from them. Black holes are thought to be formed by collapsed stars.

**black|jack** /blækdʒæk/ (**blackjacks**) **1** N-UNCOUNT **Blackjack** is a card game in which players try to obtain a combination of cards worth 21 points. ❏ *Vicky lost five hundred dollars playing blackjack.* **2** N-COUNT A **blackjack** is a short, thick stick that is used as a weapon. [INFORMAL] ❏ *Police searched the house for knives and blackjacks.*

**black|mail** /blækmeɪl/ (**blackmails, blackmailing, blackmailed**) **1** N-UNCOUNT **Blackmail** is the action of threatening to do something unpleasant to someone unless they do something you tell them to do, such as giving you money. ❏ *It looks like the pictures were being used for blackmail.* **2** V-T If one person **blackmails** another person, they use blackmail against them. ❏ *He suddenly realized that she was blackmailing him.* ❏ *The president insisted that he would not be blackmailed by violence.* ● **black|mail|er** (**blackmailers**) N-COUNT ❏ *The nasty thing about a blackmailer is that his starting point is usually the truth.*

**black mar|ket** (**black markets**) N-COUNT If something is bought or sold **on the black market**, it is bought or sold illegally. ❏ *They bought their gasoline on the black market.*

**black|out** /blækaʊt/ (**blackouts**) also **black-out** **1** N-COUNT A **blackout** is a period of time during a war in which towns and buildings are made dark so that they cannot be seen by enemy planes. ❏ *…blackout curtains.* **2** N-COUNT If a **blackout** is imposed on a particular piece of news, journalists are prevented from broadcasting or publishing it. ❏ *The government has ordered a media blackout.* **3** N-COUNT If you have a **blackout**, you temporarily lose consciousness. ❏ *I suffered a blackout which lasted for several minutes.*

**black rhi|no** also **black rhinoceros** (**black rhinos**) N-COUNT A **black rhino** is a type of rhinoceros with gray skin and two horns on its nose, that lives in Africa.

**black|smith** /blæksmɪθ/ (**blacksmiths**) N-COUNT A **blacksmith** is a person whose job is making things by hand out of metal.

**black|top** /blæktɒp/ N-UNCOUNT **Blacktop** is a hard black substance which is used as a surface for roads. ❏ *…waves of heat rising from the blacktop.*

**blad|der** /blædər/ (**bladders**) N-COUNT Your **bladder** is the part of your body where urine is stored until it leaves your body. ❏ *…a full bladder.* [from Old English]

**blade** /bleɪd/ (**blades**) **1** N-COUNT The **blade** of a knife, ax, or saw is the edge, which is used for cutting. ❏ *Many of them will have sharp blades.* **2** N-COUNT The **blades** of a propeller are the long, flat parts that turn around. [from Old English]

blade

**blame** /bleɪm/ (**blames, blaming, blamed**) **1** V-T If you **blame** a person or thing **for** something bad, or if you **blame** something bad **on** somebody, you believe or say that they are responsible for it or that they caused it. ❏ *He can blame Greg for his failure.* ❏ *The company blames its problems on the new computer system.* ● **Blame** is also a noun. ❏ *Nothing could relieve my terrible sense of blame.* **2** N-UNCOUNT The **blame for** something bad that has happened is the responsibility for causing it or letting it happen. ❏ *I'm not going to take the blame for a mistake he made.* **3** V-T If you say that you do not **blame** someone **for** doing something, you mean that you consider it was a reasonable thing to do in the circumstances. ❏ *I don't blame them for trying to make some money.* **4** PHRASE If someone is **to blame for** something bad that has happened, they are responsible for causing it. ❏ *You are not to blame for your illness.* [from Old French]

**Word Partnership** Use *blame* with :

N. blame **the victim** ■
V. **tend to** blame ■
lay blame, **share the** blame ■
**can hardly** blame someone ■

**blanch** /blæntʃ/ (**blanches, blanching, blanched**) v-i If you **blanch**, you suddenly become very pale. □ *Simon's face blanched as he looked at Sharpe's torn uniform.* [from Old French]

**bland** /blænd/ (**blander, blandest**) ■ ADJ If you describe someone or something as **bland**, you mean that they are rather dull and unexciting. □ *Serle has a blander personality than Howard.* □ *It sounds like a commercial: bland and forgettable.* ■ ADJ Food that is **bland** has very little flavor. □ *It tasted bland, like warmed cardboard.* [from Latin] → see **spice**

**blank** /blæŋk/ ■ ADJ Something that is **blank** has nothing on it. □ *We could put the pictures on that blank wall.* □ *He tore a blank page from his notebook.* ■ ADJ If you look **blank**, your face shows no feeling, understanding, or interest. □ *Abbot looked blank. "I don't know him, sir."* ● **blank|ly** ADV □ *She stared at him blankly.* ■ N-SING If your mind or memory is **a blank**, you cannot think of anything or remember anything. □ *I'm sorry, but my mind is a blank.* ■ → see **point-blank** ■ PHRASE If your mind **goes blank**, you are suddenly unable to say anything appropriate to say, for example in reply to a question. [from Old French]

**blank check** (**blank checks**) N-COUNT If someone is given a **blank check**, they are given the authority to spend as much money as they need or want. □ *We will not write a blank check for companies that are in trouble.*

**blan|ket** /blæŋkɪt/ (**blankets, blanketing, blanketed**) ■ N-COUNT A **blanket** is a large square or rectangular piece of thick cloth, especially one that you put on a bed to keep you warm. ■ N-COUNT A **blanket of** something such as snow is a continuous layer of it which hides what is below or beyond it. □ *The mud disappeared under a blanket of snow.* ■ V-T If something such as snow **blankets** an area, it covers it. □ *More than a foot of snow blanketed parts of Michigan.* ■ ADJ You use **blanket** to describe something when you want to emphasize that it affects or refers to every person or thing in a group. □ *...a blanket ban on courtroom cameras.* [from Old French] → see **bed**

**blare** /blɛər/ (**blares, blaring, blared**) v-i If something such as a siren or radio **blares**, it makes a loud, unpleasant noise. □ *The fire engines were just arriving, sirens blaring.* □ *Music blared from the apartment behind me.* ● **Blare** is also a noun. □ *...the blare of a radio through a thin wall.* ● **Blare out** means the same as **blare**. □ *Music blares out from every cafe.* [from Middle Dutch]

**blas|phe|my** /blæsfəmi/ (**blasphemies**) N-VAR You can describe something that shows disrespect for God or a religion as **blasphemy**. □ *He has acted out every kind of blasphemy, including dressing up as the pope.* ● **blas|phe|mous** /blæsfəməs/ ADJ □ *She was accused of being blasphemous.* □ *Critics attacked the film as blasphemous.* [from Late Latin]

**blast** /blæst/ (**blasts, blasting, blasted**)

■ N-COUNT A **blast** is a big explosion, especially one caused by a bomb. □ *250 people were killed in the blast.* ■ V-T If something **is blasted** into a particular place or state, an explosion causes it to be in that place or state. If a hole **is blasted** in something, it is created by an explosion. □ *...There is a risk that harmful chemicals might be blasted into the atmosphere.* □ *The explosion blasted out the wall of her apartment.* ■ V-T If workers **are blasting** rock, they are using explosives to make holes in it or destroy it, for example, so that a road or tunnel can be built. □ *Workers were blasting the rock beside the train track.* ■ V-T To **blast** someone means to shoot them with a gun. □ *He blasted his rival to death.* ■ N-SING If you say that something was a **blast**, you mean that you enjoyed it very much. [INFORMAL] □ *He went skiing with his daughter. "It was a blast," he said later.* [from Old English] ▶ **blast off** PHR-VERB When a space rocket **blasts off**, it leaves the ground at the start of its journey. □ *Columbia is expected to blast off at 1:20 am Eastern Time tomorrow.*

**bla|tant** /bleɪtᵊnt/ ADJ You use **blatant** to describe something bad that is done in an open or very obvious way. □ *They tell blatant lies.* □ *...a blatant attempt to win the support of the people.* ● **bla|tant|ly** ADV □ *...a blatantly hostile question.* □ *...blatantly false statements.* [from Old English]

**blaze** /bleɪz/ (**blazes, blazing, blazed**) ■ V-I When a building or a fire **blazes**, it burns strongly and brightly. □ *Three people died as the building blazed.* □ *The log fire was blazing merrily.* ■ N-COUNT A **blaze** is a large fire which is difficult to control and which destroys a lot of things. □ *More than 4,000 firefighters are battling the blaze.* ■ V-I If something **blazes with** light or color, it is extremely bright. [LITERARY] □ *The gardens blazed with color.* ● **Blaze** is also a noun. □ *I wanted the front garden to be a blaze of color.* ■ N-SING A **blaze of** publicity or attention is a great amount of it. □ *He was arrested in a blaze of publicity.* [from Old English]

**blaz|er** /bleɪzər/ (**blazers**) N-COUNT A **blazer** is a kind of light jacket for men or women. [from Old English]

blazer

**blaz|ing** /bleɪzɪŋ/ ADJ The **blazing** sun or **blazing hot** weather is very hot. □ *A few people were eating outside in the blazing sun.* [from Old English]

**bleach** /blitʃ/ (**bleaches, bleaching, bleached**) ■ V-T If you **bleach** something, you use a chemical to make it white or pale in color. □ *These products don't bleach the hair.* □ *...bleached pine tables.* ■ V-T/V-I If the sun **bleaches** something, or if something bleaches, its color gets paler until it is almost white. □ *The cloth was laid out on the grass to bleach in the sun..* □ *His hair has been bleached by the sun.* ■ N-UNCOUNT **Bleach** is a chemical that is used to make cloth white, or to clean things thoroughly and kill germs. [from Old English]

**bleach|ers** /blitʃərz/ N-PLURAL The **bleachers** are a part of an outdoor sports stadium, or the seats in that area, which are usually uncovered and are the least expensive place where people can sit. [from Old English]

**bleak** /blik/ (**bleaker, bleakest**) ■ ADJ If a situation is **bleak**, it is bad, and seems unlikely to improve. □ *The outlook remains bleak.* ● **bleak|ness**

N-UNCOUNT ❏*We tried to get used to the bleakness of life after the war.* **2** ADJ If you describe a place as **bleak**, you mean that it looks cold, empty, and unattractive. ❏*The island's pretty bleak.* **3** ADJ When the weather is **bleak**, it is cold, dull, and unpleasant. ❏*The weather can be quite bleak on the coast.* **4** ADJ If someone looks or sounds **bleak**, they look or sound depressed. ❏*His face was bleak.* ● **bleak|ly** ADV ❏*"There is nothing left," she says bleakly.* [from Old English]

**bleed** /blid/ (**bleeds, bleeding, bled**) V-I When you **bleed**, you lose blood from your body as a result of injury or illness. ❏*His lip was bleeding.* ❏*He was bleeding heavily from the cut on his arm.* ● **bleed|ing** N-UNCOUNT ❏*We tried to stop the bleeding.* [from Old English]

**blem|ish** /blɛmɪʃ/ (**blemishes, blemishing, blemished**) **1** N-COUNT A **blemish** is a small mark on something that spoils its appearance. ❏*...a slight blemish on his skin.* **2** N-COUNT A **blemish** on something is a small fault in it. ❏*This is the one blemish on an otherwise outstanding success.* **3** V-T If something **blemishes** your character or reputation, it spoils it or makes it seem less good than it was in the past. ❏*He wasn't about to blemish that perfect record.* [from Old French]

**blend** /blɛnd/ (**blends, blending, blended**) **1** V-RECIP If you **blend** substances together or if they **blend**, you mix them together so that they become one substance. ❏*Blend the butter with the sugar and beat until light and creamy.* ❏*Blend the ingredients until you have a smooth cream.* **2** N-COUNT A **blend of** things is a mixture or combination of them that is useful or pleasant. ❏*My album is a blend of jazz and rock'n'roll.* ❏*...a blend of natural cheeses and other fine ingredients.* **3** V-RECIP When colors, sounds, or styles **blend**, they come together or are combined in a pleasing way. ❏*You could paint the walls and ceilings the same color so they blend together.* **4** N-COUNT In linguistics, a **blend** is a combination of sounds that are represented by letters, for example the sound "spl" in "splash". [TECHNICAL] [from Old English]

**bless** /blɛs/ (**blesses, blessing, blessed**) **1** V-T When someone such as a priest **blesses** people or things, he or she asks for God's favor and protection for them. ❏*We have come together to bless this couple and their love for each other.* **2** CONVENTION **Bless** is used in expressions such as "God bless" or "bless you" to express affection, thanks, or good wishes. [INFORMAL, SPOKEN] ❏*"Bless you, Eva," he whispered.* **3** CONVENTION You can say "**bless you**" to someone who has just sneezed. [SPOKEN] [from Old English] **4** → see also **blessed, blessing**

**bless|ed** /blɛsɪd/ **1** ADJ You use **blessed** to describe something that you are grateful for or relieved about. ❏*The birth of a healthy baby is a truly blessed event.* ● **bless|ed|ly** ADV ❏*...a wall still blessedly warm from the day's sun.* [from Old English] **2** → see also **bless**

**bless|ing** /blɛsɪŋ/ (**blessings**) **1** N-COUNT A **blessing** is something good that you are grateful for. ❏*Rivers are a blessing for an agricultural country.* **2** N-COUNT If something is done with your **blessing**, it is done with your approval and support. ❏*Hailey quit school with the blessing of her parents.* [from Old English] **3** → see also **bless**

**blew** /blu/ **Blew** is the past tense of **blow**. [from Old English]

**blight** /blaɪt/ (**blights, blighting, blighted**) **1** N-VAR You can refer to something as a **blight** when it causes great difficulties, and damages or spoils other things. ❏*This unfair policy has really been a blight on America.* **2** V-T If something **blights** your life or your hopes, it damages and spoils them. If something **blights** an area, it spoils it and makes it unattractive. ❏*An embarrassing mistake nearly blighted his career.* ❏*...families whose lives were blighted by unemployment.* [from Old English]

**blind** /blaɪnd/ (**blinds, blinding, blinded**) **1** ADJ Someone who is **blind** is unable to see because their eyes are damaged. ❏*I started helping him with the business when he went blind.* ● **The blind** are people who are blind. ❏*He was a teacher of the blind.* ● **blind|ness** N-UNCOUNT ❏*Early treatment can usually prevent blindness.* **2** V-T If something **blinds** you, it makes you unable to see, either for a short time or permanently. ❏*The sun hit the windshield, momentarily blinding him.* **3** ADJ If you are **blind to** a fact or a situation, you ignore it or are unaware of it; used to show disapproval. ❏*David's good looks and manners made her blind to his faults.* ● **blind|ness** N-UNCOUNT ❏*...his blindness in the face of his son's guilt.* **4** V-T If something **blinds** you **to** the real situation, it prevents you from realizing that it exists or from understanding it properly. ❏*He never allowed his love of Australia to blind him to its faults.* **5** ADJ You can describe someone's beliefs or actions as **blind** when you disapprove of them because they do not question or think about what they are doing. ❏*...her blind faith in the wisdom of the church.* **6** N-COUNT A **blind** is a roll of cloth or paper which you can pull down over a window as a covering. ❏*Pulling the blinds up, she let some of the bright sunlight in.* **7** → see also **blinding, blindly** **8** PHRASE If someone **is turning a blind eye to** something bad or illegal that is happening, they are pretending not to notice that it is happening so that they will not have to do anything about it. ❏*Officers say they are turning a blind eye to minor crimes.* [from Old English]

→ see **disability**

| Word Partnership | Use *blind* with : |
| --- | --- |
| ADJ. | blind **and deaf 1** |
| ADV. | **legally** blind, **partially** blind **1** |
| N. | blind **person 1** |
| | blind **faith 5** |

**blind|ers** /blaɪndərz/ N-PLURAL **Blinders** are two pieces of leather that are placed at the side of a horse's eyes so that it can only see straight ahead. [from Old English]

**blind|fold** /blaɪndfoʊld/ (**blindfolds, blindfolding, blindfolded**) **1** N-COUNT A **blindfold** is a strip of cloth that is tied over your eyes so that you cannot see. **2** V-T If you **blindfold** someone, you tie a blindfold over their eyes. ❏*Two men blindfolded him and drove him to an apartment in southern Beirut.* [from Old English]

**blind|ing** /blaɪndɪŋ/ ADJ A **blinding** light is extremely bright. ❏*The doctor worked beneath the blinding lights of the operating room.* [from Old English]

**blind|ly** /blaɪndli/ **1** ADV If someone does something **blindly**, they do it without having enough information, or without thinking about it. ❑ *Don't just blindly follow what he says.* ❑ *Without enough information, many students choose a college almost blindly.* [from Old English] **2** → see also **blind**

**blind|side** /ˈblaɪndsaɪd/ (**blindsides, blindsiding, blindsided**) V-T If you say that you **were blindsided** by something, you mean that it surprised you in a negative way; used to show disapproval. ❑ *He complained about being blindsided by the decision.*

**bling** /blɪŋ/ also **bling-bling** N-UNCOUNT Some people refer to expensive or fancy jewelry or clothes as **bling** or **bling-bling.** [INFORMAL] ❑ *Famous jewelers want to see celebrities to wear their bling.* ❑ *...the rap star's love of bling-bling.*

**blink** /blɪŋk/ (**blinks, blinking, blinked**) **1** V-T/V-I When you **blink** or when you **blink** your eyes, you shut your eyes and very quickly open them again. ❑ *Kathryn blinked and forced a smile.* ❑ *She was blinking her eyes rapidly.* ● **Blink** is also a noun. ❑ *She gave a couple of blinks and her eyes cleared.* **2** V-I When a light **blinks**, it flashes on and off. ❑ *Green and yellow lights blinked on the surface of the water.* ❑ *The plane was flying for about 15 minutes before a warning light blinked on.* [from Middle Dutch]

**bliss** /blɪs/ N-UNCOUNT **Bliss** is a state of complete happiness. ❑ *It took them a long time to find romantic bliss.* [from Old English]

**bliss|ful** /ˈblɪsfəl/ ADJ A **blissful** situation or period of time is one in which you are extremely happy. ❑ *We spent a blissful week together.* ● **bliss|ful|ly** ADV ❑ *We're blissfully happy.* [from Old English]

**blis|ter** /ˈblɪstər/ (**blisters, blistering, blistered**) **1** N-COUNT A **blister** is a painful swelling containing a clear liquid on the surface of your skin. **2** V-T/V-I When your skin **blisters** or when something **blisters** it, blisters appear on it. ❑ *The skin turns red and may blister.* ❑ *Be careful: this plant blisters the skin.* [from Old French]

**blis|ter|ing** /ˈblɪstərɪŋ/ ADJ **Blistering** heat is very great heat. ❑ *...a blistering summer day.* ADJ A **blistering** remark expresses great anger or dislike. ❑ *The president responded with a blistering attack on his critics.* [from Old French]

**blithe** /blaɪð/ ADJ You use **blithe** to indicate that something is done casually, without serious or careful thought; used to show disapproval. ❑ *...the blithe disregard that boys had for private property.* ● **blithe|ly** ADV ❑ *Your report blithely ignores the main facts.* [from Old English]

**blitz** /blɪts/ (**blitzes, blitzing, blitzed**) **1** N-COUNT If you have a **blitz** on something, you make a big effort to deal with it or to improve it. [INFORMAL] ❑ *We're having a blitz on incorrect grammar.* **2** N-PROPER The heavy bombing of British cities by German aircraft in 1940 and 1941 is referred to as **the Blitz.** **3** V-T If a city or building is **blitzed** during a war, it is attacked by bombs dropped by enemy aircraft. ❑ *In the autumn of 1940 London was blitzed by an average of two hundred aircraft a night.* [from German]

**bliz|zard** /ˈblɪzərd/ (**blizzards**) N-COUNT A **blizzard** is a very bad snowstorm with strong winds.
→ see **snow, storm, weather**

**bloat|ed** /ˈbloʊtɪd/ ADJ If your body or a part of your body is **bloated**, it is much larger than normal, usually because it has a lot of liquid or gas

inside it. ❑ *...the bloated body of a dead cow.* [from Old Norse]

**blob** /blɒb/ (**blobs**) N-COUNT A **blob of** thick or sticky liquid is a small, often round, amount of it. [INFORMAL] ❑ *...a blob of chocolate pudding.*

**bloc** /blɒk/ (**blocs**) N-COUNT A **bloc** is a group of countries that have similar political aims and interests and that act together over some issues. ❑ *...the former Soviet bloc.* [from French]

**block** /blɒk/ (**blocks, blocking, blocked**) **1** N-COUNT A **block** of a substance is a large rectangular piece of it. ❑ *...a block of ice.* **2** N-COUNT A **block** in a town or city is an area

**block**

of land with streets on all its sides, or the area or distance between such streets. ❑ *He walked around the block three times.* ❑ *She walked four blocks down High Street.* **3** V-T To block a road, channel, or pipe means to put an object across it or in it so that nothing can pass through it or along it. ❑ *Students blocked a highway through the center of the city.* **4** V-T If something **blocks** your view, it prevents you from seeing something because it is between you and that thing. ❑ *A row of trees blocked his view of the north slope of the mountain.* **5** V-T If you **block** something that is being arranged, you prevent it from being done. ❑ *The country has tried to block imports of cheap foreign products.* [from Old French] **6** → see also **stumbling block**

▶ **block out** PHR-VERB If you **block out** a thought, you try not to think about it. ❑ *She accused me of blocking out the past.*

**block|ade** /blɒˈkeɪd/ (**blockades, blockading, blockaded**) **1** N-COUNT A **blockade** of a place is an action that is taken to prevent goods or people from entering or leaving it. ❑ *It's not yet clear who will enforce the blockade.* **2** V-T If a group of people **blockade** a place, they stop goods or people from reaching that place. If they **blockade** a road or a port, they stop people from using that road or port. ❑ *The town has been blockaded for 40 days.*

**block|age** /ˈblɒkɪdʒ/ (**blockages**) N-COUNT A **blockage** in a pipe, tube, or tunnel is an object which blocks it, or the state of being blocked. ❑ *The logical treatment is to remove this blockage.* [from Old French]

**block and tack|le** (**block and tackles** or **blocks and tackles**) N-COUNT A **block and tackle** is a device consisting of two or more pulleys connected by a rope or cable, which is used for lifting heavy objects.

**block|bust|er** /ˈblɒkbʌstər/ (**blockbusters**) N-COUNT A **blockbuster** is a movie or book that is very popular and successful, usually because it is very exciting. [INFORMAL] ❑ *...the latest Hollywood blockbuster.*

**blocked** /blɒkt/ also **blocked up** ADJ If something is **blocked** or **blocked up**, it is completely closed so that nothing can get through it. ❑ *The main drain was blocked.* ❑ *His arteries were blocked up and he needed surgery.* [from Old French]

**block|ing** **1** N-UNCOUNT In the theater, **blocking** is the process of planning the movements that

## Word Web blog

The word **blog** is a combination of the words **web** and **log**. It is a **website** that has many dated **entries**. A blog can focus on one subject of interest. Most blogs are written by one person. But sometimes a political committee, corporation, or other group keeps a blog. Many blogs ask readers to leave comments on the site. This often results in a group of readers who write back and forth to each other. The total group of web logs is the blogosphere. A blogstorm occurs when there are many people using blogs about the same topic.

the actors will make on the stage during the performance of a play. [TECHNICAL] [from Old French] **2** → see also **block**

**block par|ty** (**block parties**) N-COUNT A **block party** is an outdoor party for all the residents of a block or neighborhood. □ ...the Fourth of July parade and block party.

**blog** /blɒg/ (**blogs**) N-COUNT A **blog** is a website containing a diary or journal on a particular subject. [COMPUTING] □ There are many ways to add entries and edit your blog. ● **blog|ger** (**bloggers**) N-COUNT □ Most bloggers comment on news reported elsewhere, while others do their own reporting.
● **blog|ging** N-UNCOUNT □ ...the enormous popularity of blogging.
→ see Word Web: **blog**

## Word Link sphere ≈ ball : atmosphere, blogosphere, hemisphere

**blogo|sphere** /blɒgəsfɪər/ also **blogsphere** /blɒgsfɪər/ N-SING In computer technology, **the blogosphere** or **the blogsphere** is all the blogs on the Internet, considered collectively. □ The blogosphere continues to expand.

**blonde** /blɒnd/ (**blondes, blonder, blondest**)
**1** COLOR Someone who has **blonde** hair has pale-colored hair. □ ...a little girl with blonde hair. **2** ADJ Someone who is **blonde** has blonde hair. □ He was blonder than his brother. **3** N-COUNT A **blonde** is a woman who has blonde hair. □ ...a stunning blonde in her early thirties. [from Old French]
→ see **hair**

**blood** /blʌd/ **1** N-UNCOUNT **Blood** is the red liquid that flows inside your body, which you can see if you cut yourself. □ His shirt was covered in blood. **2** N-UNCOUNT You can use **blood** to refer to the race or social class of someone's parents or ancestors. □ There was Greek blood in his veins. **3** PHRASE If something violent and cruel is done **in cold blood**, it is done deliberately and in an unemotional way. □ The crime was committed in cold blood. **4** → see also **cold-blooded 5** PHRASE You can use the expressions **new blood, fresh blood,** or **young blood** to refer to people who are brought into an organization to improve it by thinking of new ideas or new ways of doing things. □ There's been a major effort to bring in new blood. [from Old English] **6** **own flesh and blood** → see **flesh**
→ see **cardiovascular system, donor**

## Word Partnership Use blood with :

| | |
|---|---|
| N. | (red/white) blood **cells**, blood **clot**, blood **disease**, blood **loss**, **pool of** blood, blood **sample**, blood **stream**, blood **supply**, blood **test**, blood **transfusion 1** |
| ADJ. | **covered in** blood, blood **stained 1** |
| V. | **donate/give** blood **1** |

**blood pres|sure** N-UNCOUNT Your **blood pressure** is the amount of force with which your blood flows around your body. □ Your doctor will take your blood pressure. □ What are the causes of high blood pressure?
→ see **diagnosis**

**blood|shed** /blʌdʃɛd/ N-UNCOUNT **Bloodshed** is violence in which people are killed or wounded. □ The government must avoid further bloodshed.

**blood|stream** /blʌdstrim/ (**bloodstreams**) N-COUNT Your **bloodstream** is the blood that flows around your body. □ The virus stays in the bloodstream for only a short time.

**blood test** (**blood tests**) N-COUNT A **blood test** is a medical examination of a small amount of your blood.

**blood ves|sel** (**blood vessels**) N-COUNT **Blood vessels** are the narrow tubes through which your blood flows.

**bloody** /blʌdi/ (**bloodier, bloodiest**) ADJ
**1** Something that is **bloody** is covered in blood. □ ...a bloody nose. **2** A situation or event that is **bloody** is one in which there is a lot of violence and people are killed. □ ...a long and bloody battle. [from Old English]

**bloom** /blum/ (**blooms, blooming, bloomed**)
**1** N-COUNT A **bloom** is the flower on a plant. [LITERARY] □ ...the sweet smell of the white blooms. **2** PHRASE A plant or tree that is **in bloom** has flowers on it. □ ...a pink rose in full bloom. **3** V-I When a plant or tree **blooms**, it produces flowers. When a flower **blooms**, it opens. □ This plant blooms between May and June. [from Old English]

**bloop|er** /blupər/ (**bloopers**) N-COUNT A **blooper** is a silly mistake. [INFORMAL] □ ...the funniest television bloopers.

**blos|som** /blɒsəm/ (**blossoms, blossoming, blossomed**) **1** N-VAR **Blossom** is the flowers that appear on a tree before the fruit. □ ...cherry blossoms. **2** V-I If someone or something **blossoms**, they develop good, attractive, or successful qualities. □ Some people take longer than others to blossom. □ Our local festival has blossomed

B

*into an international event.* ◾ V-I When a tree **blossoms**, it produces blossom. ❑ *Rain begins to fall and peach trees blossom.* [from Old English]

**blot** /blɒt/ (**blots, blotting, blotted**) N-COUNT A **blot** is a drop of liquid that has fallen onto a surface and dried. ❑ *...an ink blot.* [of Germanic origin]

▶ **blot out** ◾ PHR-VERB If one thing **blots out** another thing, it is in front of the other thing and prevents it from being seen. ❑ *Clouds blotted out the sun.* ◾ PHR-VERB If you try to **blot out** a memory, you try to forget it. If one thought or memory **blots out** other thoughts or memories, it becomes the only one that you can think about. ❑ *She's trying to blot out all memory of the incident.* ❑ *I wanted to sleep all the time to blot things out.*

**blotch** /blɒtʃ/ (**blotches**) N-COUNT A **blotch** is a small unpleasant-looking area of color, for example, on your skin. ❑ *His face was covered in red blotches.*

**blouse** /blaʊs/ (**blouses**) N-COUNT A **blouse** is a kind of shirt worn by a girl or woman. [from French]
→ see **clothing**

---
**blow**

❶ VERB USES
❷ NOUN USES
---

❶ **blow** /bloʊ/ (**blows, blowing, blew, blown**) ◾ V-I When a wind or breeze **blows**, the air moves. ❑ *A cold wind blew at the top of the hill.* ◾ V-T/V-I If the wind **blows** something somewhere or if it **blows** there, the wind moves it there. ❑ *The wind blew her hair back from her forehead.* ❑ *Sand blew in our eyes.* ◾ V-I If you **blow**, you send out a stream of air from your mouth. ❑ *Danny blew on his fingers to warm them.* ◾ V-T/V-I When a whistle or horn **blows** or someone **blows** it, they make a sound by blowing into it. ❑ *The whistle blew and the train moved forward.* ◾ V-T When you **blow** your nose, you force air out of it through your nostrils in order to clear it. ❑ *He took out a handkerchief and blew his nose.* ◾ V-T To **blow** something **out, off**, or **away** means to remove or destroy it violently with an explosion. ❑ *The can exploded, blowing out the kitchen windows.* ◾ V-T If you **blow** a chance or attempt to do something, you make a mistake which wastes the chance or causes the attempt to fail. [INFORMAL] ❑ *One careless word could blow the whole deal.* ❑ *Oh you fool! You've blown it!* ◾ V-T If you **blow** a large amount of money, you spend it quickly on luxuries. [INFORMAL] ❑ *My brother lent me some money and I went out and blew it all.* [from Old English] ◾ → see also **full-blown**
→ see **glass, wind**

▶ **blow off** PHR-VERB If you **blow** something **off**, you ignore it or choose not to deal with it. [INFORMAL] ❑ *I don't think we can just blow this off.*
▶ **blow out** PHR-VERB If you **blow out** a flame or a candle, you blow at it so that it stops burning. ❑ *I blew out the candle.*
▶ **blow over** PHR-VERB If something such as trouble or an argument **blows over**, it ends without any serious consequences. ❑ *Wait, and it'll all blow over.*
▶ **blow up** ◾ PHR-VERB If someone **blows** something **up** or if it **blows up**, it is destroyed by

an explosion. ❑ *He was jailed for 45 years for trying to blow up a plane.* ◾ PHR-VERB If you **blow up** something such as a balloon or a tire, you fill it with air. ❑ *Take some slow, deep breaths, as if you are blowing up a balloon.*

❷ **blow** /bloʊ/ (**blows**) ◾ N-COUNT If someone receives a **blow**, they are hit with a fist or weapon. ❑ *He went to the hospital after a blow to the face.* ◾ N-COUNT If something that happens is a **blow** to someone or something, it is very upsetting, disappointing, or damaging to them. ❑ *The increase in tax was a blow to the industry.* [from Old English]

| **Word Partnership** | Use *blow* with : |
| --- | --- |
| ADV. | blow **away** ❶ ◾ ◾ |
| N. | blow **away**, blow **smoke** ❶ ◾ <br> blow **a whistle** ❶ ◾ <br> blow **your nose** ❶ ◾ |
| V. | **deliver/strike** a blow ❷ ◾ <br> **cushion/soften** a blow, **suffer** a blow ❷ ◾ ◾ |
| ADJ. | **crushing/devastating/heavy** blow ❷ ◾ ◾ |
| PREP. | blow **to the head** ❷ ◾ <br> blow **to someone** ❷ ◾ |

**blown** /bloʊn/ **Blown** is the past participle of **blow**. [from Old English]

**bludg|eon** /blʌdʒˀn/ (**bludgeons, bludgeoning, bludgeoned**) V-T To **bludgeon** someone means to hit them several times with a heavy object. ❑ *He bludgeoned the man with a hammer.*

**blue** /blu/ (**bluer, bluest, blues**) ◾ COLOR Something that is **blue** is the color of the sky on a sunny day. ❑ *...the cloudless blue sky.* ❑ *...pale blue eyes.* ◾ N-PLURAL The **blues** is a type of music which was developed by African American musicians in the southern United States. It is characterized by a slow tempo and a strong rhythm. ❑ *...to sing the blues.* ◾ ADJ If a U.S. state is described as **blue**, it means that the majority of its residents vote for the Democrats in elections, especially in the presidential elections. ❑ *...the red and blue states.* [from Old French]
→ see **color, rainbow**

**blue-collar** ADJ **Blue-collar** workers work in industry, doing physical work, rather than in offices. ❑ *It wasn't just the blue-collar workers who lost their jobs, it was everyone.*

**blue|print** /bluprɪnt/ (**blueprints**) N-COUNT A **blueprint for** something is a plan or set of proposals that shows how it is expected to work. ❑ *The president will announce his blueprint for the country's future.*

**bluff** /blʌf/ (**bluffs, bluffing, bluffed**) ◾ N-VAR A **bluff** is an attempt to make someone believe that you will do something when you do not really intend to do it. ❑ *The letter was a bluff.* ❑ *"We must act now," he said, hoping that it was all just a bluff or a terrible mistake.* ◾ PHRASE If you **call** someone's **bluff**, you tell them to do what they have been threatening to do, because you are sure that they will not really do it. ❑ *If you think I'm lying, you're welcome to call my bluff.* ◾ V-T/V-I If you **bluff**, you make someone believe that you will do something when you do not really intend to do it, or that you know something when you do not really know it.

❑ *Either side, or both, could be bluffing.* ❑ *The hijackers bluffed the airline crew using fake weapons.* [from Dutch]

**blun|der** /blʌndər/ (**blunders, blundering, blundered**) **1** N-COUNT A **blunder** is a stupid or careless mistake. ❑ *...a medical blunder.* **2** V-I If you **blunder**, you make a stupid or careless mistake. ❑ *No doubt I have blundered again.* **3** V-I If you **blunder** somewhere, you move there in a clumsy and careless way. ❑ *He blundered into the table, knocking down the flowers.* [of Scandinavian origin]

**blunt** /blʌnt/ (**blunter, bluntest, blunts, blunting, blunted**) **1** ADJ If you are **blunt**, you say exactly what you think without trying to be polite. ❑ *She is blunt about her personal life.* ● **blunt|ly** ADV ❑ *"I don't believe you!" Jeanne said bluntly.* ● **blunt|ness** N-UNCOUNT ❑ *His bluntness got him into trouble.* **2** ADJ A **blunt** object has a rounded or flat end rather than a sharp one. ❑ *Carefully draw round the shapes with a blunt pencil..* **3** ADJ A **blunt** knife or blade is no longer sharp and does not cut well. ❑ *The edge is as blunt as a butter knife.* **4** V-T If something **blunts** an emotion, a feeling, or a need, it weakens it ❑ *Norway blunted England's hopes of qualifying for the Soccer World Cup by beating them 2–1.* [of Scandinavian origin]

**blur** /blɜr/ (**blurs, blurring, blurred**) **1** N-COUNT A **blur** is a shape or area which you cannot see clearly because it has no distinct outline or because it is moving very fast. ❑ *I saw a blur of movement on the other side of the glass door.* **2** V-T/V-I When a thing **blurs** or when something **blurs** it, you cannot see it clearly because its edges are no longer distinct. ❑ *Removing your eyeglasses blurs the image.* ● **blurred** ADJ ❑ *...blurred black and white photographs.* **3** V-T If something **blurs** an idea or a distinction between things, that idea or distinction no longer seems clear. ❑ *She constantly blurs the line between work, personal life and love.* ● **blurred** ADJ ❑ *The line between fact and fiction is becoming blurred.*

**blurt** /blɜrt/ (**blurts, blurting, blurted**) ▸ **blurt out** PHR-VERB If someone **blurts** something **out**, they say it suddenly, after trying hard to keep quiet or to keep it secret. [INFORMAL] ❑ *"You're mad," the driver blurted out.*

**blush** /blʌʃ/ (**blushes, blushing, blushed**) V-I When you **blush**, your face becomes redder than usual because you are ashamed or embarrassed. ❑ *"Hello, Maria," he said, and she blushed again.* ● **Blush** is also a noun. ❑ *"The most important thing is to be honest," she says, without the trace of a blush.* [from Old English]

**blus|ter** /blʌstər/ (**blusters, blustering, blustered**) V-T/V-I If you say that someone **is blustering**, you mean that they are speaking aggressively but without authority, often because they are angry or offended. ❑ *"That's crazy," he blustered.* ❑ *He was still blustering, and there was panic in his eyes.* ● **Bluster** is also a noun. ❑ *...the bluster of the presidential campaign.* [from Middle Low German]

**BMI** /biː ɛm aɪ/ **BMI** is an abbreviation for **body mass index**. [MEDICAL] ❑ *A BMI greater than 30 is considered obese.*

**boar** /bɔr/ (**boars**)

The plural **boar** can also be used for meaning **1**.

**1** N-COUNT A **boar** or a **wild boar** is a wild pig. ❑ *Wild boar are numerous in the valleys.* **2** N-COUNT A **boar** is a male pig. [from Old English]

**board** /bɔrd/ (**boards, boarding, boarded**) **1** N-COUNT A **board** is a flat, thin, rectangular piece of wood or plastic which is used for a particular purpose. ❑ *After using cutting boards and knives, immediately wash them with hot soapy water.* **2** N-COUNT A **board** is a square piece of wood or stiff cardboard that you use for playing games such as chess. ❑ *...a checkers board.* **3** N-COUNT You can refer to a blackboard or a bulletin board as a **board**. ❑ *He wrote a few more notes on the board.* **4** N-COUNT The **board** of a company or organization is the group of people who control it and direct it. [BUSINESS] ❑ *The board has asked me to continue as chief executive.* **5** V-T When you **board** a train, ship, or aircraft, you get on it in order to travel somewhere. [FORMAL] ❑ *I boarded the plane to Boston.* **6** N-UNCOUNT **Board** is the food which is provided when you stay somewhere, for example in a hotel. ❑ *Free room and board are provided for all hotel staff.* **7** PHRASE If a policy or a situation applies **across the board**, it affects everything or everyone in a particular group. ❑ *The job cuts will take place across the board, from senior managers to mailmen.* **8** PHRASE When you are **on board** a train, ship, or aircraft, you are on it or in it. ❑ *All 269 people on board the plane were killed.* **9** PHRASE If you **take on board** an idea or a problem, you begin to accept it or understand it. ❑ *We hope that they will take on board some of what you have said.* ❑ *I'm glad you can take that on board.* [from Old English] ▸ **board up** PHR-VERB If you **board up** a door or window, you fix pieces of wood over it so that it is covered up. ❑ *Shopkeepers have boarded up their windows.*

| Word Partnership | Use *board* with : |
| --- | --- |
| N. | **cutting** board, **diving** board **1** |
| | board **game 2** |
| | **bulletin** board, **message** board **3** |
| | **chair/member of the** board, |
| | board **of directors**, board |
| | **meeting 4** |
| | board **a flight/plane/ship 5** |
| | **room and** board **6** |

**board|ing pass** (**boarding passes**) N-COUNT A **boarding pass** is a card that a passenger must have when boarding a plane or a boat.

**board|ing school** (**boarding schools**) also **boarding-school** N-VAR A **boarding school** is a school that some or all of the students live in during the school term.

**board|room** /bɔrdrum/ (**boardrooms**) also **board room** N-COUNT The **boardroom** is a room where the board of a company meets. [BUSINESS] ❑ *Everyone assembled in the boardroom for the 9:00 a.m. session.*

**board|walk** /bɔrdwɔk/ (**boardwalks**) N-COUNT A **boardwalk** is a path made of wooden boards, especially one along a beach.

**boast** /boʊst/ (**boasts, boasting, boasted**) V-T/V-I If someone **boasts** about something that they have done or that they own, they talk about it very proudly, in a way that other people may find irritating or offensive. ❑ *He boasted that the police would never catch him.* ❑ *Carol boasted about her*

**Word Web**   boat

People once used **boats** only for transportation. But today millions of people enjoy boating as a form of recreation. Weekend **captains** enjoy quietly **sailing** their **small boats** along the shore. However, other boaters like to ride around in motorboats. Any **rowboat** can become a motorboat just by attaching an outboard **motor** to the back. Inboard motors are quieter, but they're more expensive. Fishermen usually like to use a rowboat with **oars**. That way they won't scare the fish away. For an even more peaceful ride, some people **paddle** around in **canoes**. But really adventurous folks like the thrill of white-water **rafting**.

costume. ● **Boast** is also a noun. ❑ *It is the charity's proud boast that it has never turned anyone away.* [from French]

**boat** /boʊt/ (**boats**) ◼ N-COUNT A **boat** is something in which people can travel across water. ❑ *One of the best ways to see the area is in a small boat.* ◼ N-COUNT You can refer to a passenger ship as a **boat**. ❑ *When the boat reached Cape Town, we said goodbye.* [from Old English]
→ see Word Web: **boat**
→ see **ship**

**boat|ing** /boʊtɪŋ/ N-UNCOUNT **Boating** is traveling on a lake or river in a small boat for pleasure. ❑ *You can go boating or play tennis.* [from Old English]

**bob** /bɒb/ (**bobs, bobbing, bobbed**) V-I If something **bobs**, it moves up and down, like something does when it is floating on water. ❑ *Huge balloons bobbed about in the sky above.*

**bob|ble** /bɒbəl/ (**bobbles, bobbling, bobbled**) V-T If a player **bobbles** a ball, they drop it or fail to control it. ❑ *The ball was bobbled momentarily, allowing Holloway to race home.*

**bob|by pin** /bɒbi pɪn/ (**bobby pins**) N-COUNT A **bobby pin** is a small piece of metal or plastic bent back on itself, which a woman uses to hold her hair in position.

**bob|sled** /bɒbslɛd/ (**bobsleds**) N-COUNT A **bobsled** is a vehicle with long thin strips of metal fixed to the bottom, which is used for racing downhill on ice.

**bo|da|cious** /boʊdeɪʃəs/ ◼ ADJ If you say that someone or something is **bodacious**, you mean that they are very good or impressive. [INFORMAL] ❑ *This is a bodacious opportunity for him.* ◼ ADJ If you say that someone is **bodacious**, you mean that they are appealing or sexually attractive. [INFORMAL] ❑ *...such bodacious models as Elle Macpherson and Rachel Williams.* ❑ *...a bodacious physique.* [from English dialect]

**bode** /boʊd/ (**bodes, boding, boded**) V-I If something **bodes** ill, it makes you think that something bad will happen in the future. If something **bodes** well, it makes you think that something good will happen. [FORMAL] ❑ *All this bodes ill for a peaceful resolution to the problem.* [from Old English]

**bodi|ly** /bɒdɪli/ ◼ ADJ Your **bodily** needs and functions are the needs and functions of your body. ❑ *...circulation, respiration, and other bodily functions.* ◼ ADV You use **bodily** to indicate that an action involves the whole of someone's body. ❑ *I was hurled bodily to the floor.* [from Old English]

**body** /bɒdi/ (**bodies**) ◼ N-COUNT Your **body** is all your physical parts, including your head, arms, and legs. ❑ *The largest organ in the body is the liver.* ◼ N-COUNT You can refer to the main part of your body, except for your arms, head, and legs, as your **body**. ❑ *Lying flat on your back, twist your body onto one side.* ◼ N-COUNT You can refer to a person's dead body as a **body**. ❑ *Two days later, her body was found in a wood.* ◼ N-COUNT A **body** is an organized group of people who deal with something officially. ❑ *She was elected student body president at the University of North Carolina.* ◼ N-COUNT The **body** of a car or airplane is the main part of it, not including its engine, wheels, or wings. ❑ *The only shade was under the body of the plane.* [from Old English]
→ see Picture Dictionary: **body**

**body|guard** /bɒdigɑrd/ (**bodyguards**) N-COUNT A **bodyguard** is a person or a group of people employed to protect someone. ❑ *Three of his bodyguards were injured in the attack.*

**body image** (**body images**) N-VAR A person's **body image** is their perception of their physical appearance. Someone with a good body image thinks they are attractive, while someone with a poor body image thinks they are unattractive.

**body lan|guage** N-UNCOUNT Your **body language** is the way in which you show your feelings or thoughts to other people by means of the movements of your body ❑ *I could tell by his body language that he was happy with the decision.*

**body mass in|dex** N-SING A person's **body mass index** is a measurement that represents the relationship between their weight and their height. [MEDICAL] ❑ *...those with a body mass index of 30 and over.*

**body odor** N-UNCOUNT **Body odor** is an unpleasant smell caused by sweat on a person's body.

**body position** (**body positions**) N-VAR An actor's **body position** is their posture at a particular point in a play or other theatrical production, for example whether they are sitting or standing. [TECHNICAL]

**bog** /bɒg/ (**bogs**) N-COUNT A **bog** is an area of land that is very wet and muddy. [from Gaelic]

**bogged down** ADJ If you get **bogged down in** something, it prevents you from making progress or getting something done. ❑ *Why get bogged down in legal details?*

**bog|gle** /bɒgəl/ (**boggles, boggling, boggled**) V-T/V-I If you say that something **boggles** at something, or that it **boggles your mind**, you mean that it is so strange or amazing that it is difficult to imagine or understand. ❑ *The mind*

b

body

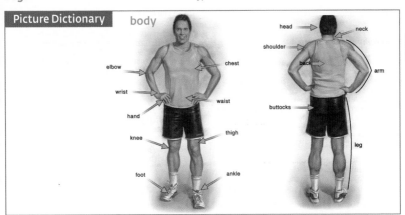

boggles at what he was able to achieve with so little.

**bo|gus** /boʊɡəs/ ADJ If you describe something as **bogus**, you mean that it is not genuine. ❑ ...bogus insurance claims.

**bo|he|mian** /boʊhimiən/ (**bohemians**) ADJ You can use **bohemian** to describe artistic people who live in an unconventional way. ❑ ...a bohemian writer. ❑ ...the bohemian lifestyle of the French capital. ● A **bohemian** is someone who lives in a bohemian way. ❑ ...this community of writers, artists, and other bohemians.

**boil** /bɔɪl/ (**boils, boiling, boiled**) ■ V-T/V-I When a hot liquid **boils** or when you **boil** it, bubbles appear in it and it starts to change into steam or vapor. ❑ I stood in the kitchen, waiting for the water to boil. ❑ Boil the water in the saucepan and add the salt. ■ V-T/V-I When you **boil** a pot or a kettle, or put it on to **boil**, you heat the water inside it until it boils. ❑ He had nothing to do but boil the kettle and make the tea. ■ V-T/V-I When you **boil** food, or when it **boils**, it is cooked in boiling water. ❑ Boil the chickpeas, then add garlic and lemon juice. ❑ I peeled potatoes and put them in a pot to boil. ■ N-COUNT A **boil** is a red, painful swelling on your skin. ■ → see also **boiling** ■ PHRASE When you **bring** a liquid **to a boil**, you heat it until it boils. When it **comes to a boil**, it begins to boil. ❑ Put the milk into a saucepan and bring it slowly to a boil. [Senses 1–3 from Old French. Sense 4 from Old English.] → see **cook, egg, thermometer**

▸ **boil down to** PHR-VERB If you say that a situation or problem **boils down to** a particular thing or can **be boiled down to** a particular thing, you mean that this is the most important or the most basic aspect of it. ❑ What they want boils down to just one thing: land.

▸ **boil over** PHR-VERB When a liquid that is being heated **boils over**, it rises and flows over the edge of the container. ❑ Heat the liquid in a large, wide container so it doesn't boil over.

**boil|er** /bɔɪlər/ (**boilers**) N-COUNT A **boiler** is a device that uses gas, oil, electricity, or coal in order to provide hot water. [from Old French]

**boil|ing** /bɔɪlɪŋ/ ADJ Something that is **boiling** or **boiling hot** is very hot. ❑ "It's boiling in here," complained Miriam. [from Old French]

**boil|ing point** N-UNCOUNT The **boiling point** of a liquid is the temperature at which it starts to change into steam or vapor. For example, the boiling point of water is 212°Fahrenheit.

**bois|ter|ous** /bɔɪstərəs, -strəs/ ADJ Someone who is **boisterous** is noisy, lively, and full of energy. ❑ ...a boisterous but good-natured crowd.

**bold** /boʊld/ (**bolder, boldest**) ■ ADJ Someone who is **bold** is not afraid to do things that involve risk or danger. ❑ Amrita becomes a bold, daring rebel. ❑ In 1960 this was a bold move. ● **bold|ly** ADV ❑ You must act boldly and confidently. ● **bold|ness** N-UNCOUNT ❑ ...the boldness of his economic program. ■ ADJ A **bold** color or pattern is very bright and noticeable. ❑ ...bold flowers in shades of red, blue or white. ■ ADJ **Bold** lines or designs are drawn in a clear, strong way. ❑ Each picture is shown in color on one page and as a bold outline on the opposite page. [from Old English]

**bo|lo|gna** /bəloʊni/ (**bolognas**) N-VAR **Bologna** is a type of large smoked sausage, usually made of beef, veal, or pork. ❑ ...a bologna sandwich. [from Italian]

**bol|ster** /boʊlstər/ (**bolsters, bolstering, bolstered**) V-T If you **bolster** someone's confidence or courage, you increase it. ❑ The president is attempting to bolster confidence in the economy. [from Old English]

**bolt** /boʊlt/ (**bolts, bolting, bolted**) ■ N-COUNT A **bolt** is a long metal object that screws into a nut and is used to fasten things together. ■ V-T When you **bolt** one thing to another, you fasten them firmly together, using a bolt. ❑ Perkins bolted the new parts to the old engine. ❑ Bolt the parts together. ■ N-COUNT A **bolt** on a door or window is a metal bar that you can slide across in order to fasten the door or window. ❑ I heard the sound of a bolt being slowly slid open. ■ V-T When you **bolt** a door or window, you slide the bolt across to fasten it. ❑ He locked and bolted the kitchen door after her. ■ V-I If a person or animal

bolt

B

bolts, they suddenly start to run very fast, often because something has frightened them. ❑ *The pig rose squealing, and bolted.* [from Old English]
→ see **lightning**

**bomb** /bɒm/ (**bombs, bombing, bombed**)
■ N-COUNT A **bomb** is a device that explodes and damages or destroys a large area. ❑ *Bombs went off at two London train stations.* ❑ *It's not known who planted the bomb.* ② V-T When people **bomb** a place, they attack it with bombs. ❑ *Air force jets bombed the airport.* ● **bomb|ing** (**bombings**) N-VAR ❑ *...the bombing of Pearl Harbor.* ❑ *The city was destroyed by the bombing.* [from French]

| **Word Partnership** | Use *bomb* with : |
| --- | --- |
| ADJ. | **atomic/nuclear** bomb, **live** bomb ■ |
| N. | bomb **blast, car** bomb, **pipe** bomb, bomb **shelter,** bomb **squad,** bomb **threat** ■ |
| V. | **drop/plant** a bomb, **set off** a bomb ② |

**bom|bard** /bɒmbɑrd/ (**bombards, bombarding, bombarded**) ■ V-T If you **bombard** someone **with** something, you make them face a great deal of it. ❑ *He bombarded Catherine with questions.* ② V-T When soldiers **bombard** a place, they attack it with continuous heavy gunfire or bombs. ❑ *From where he stood, he could see the Army bombarding local villages.* ● **bom|bard|ment** (**bombardments**) N-VAR A **bombardment** is a strong and continuous attack of gunfire or bombing. ❑ *...a fierce all-night bombardment of Fort McHenry.* [from Old French]

**bomb|er** /bɒmər/ (**bombers**) ■ N-COUNT **Bombers** are people who cause bombs to explode in public places. ❑ *Detectives hunting the bombers will be eager to interview him.* ② N-COUNT A **bomber** is a military aircraft which drops bombs. ❑ *...a high-speed bomber with twin engines.* [from French]

**bomb|shell** /bɒmʃɛl/ (**bombshells**) N-COUNT A **bombshell** is a sudden piece of bad or unexpected news. ❑ *His resignation is a political bombshell.*

**bo|nan|za** /bənænzə/ (**bonanzas**) N-COUNT You can refer to a sudden great increase in wealth, success, or luck as a **bonanza**. ❑ *The wedding season is a bonanza for florists.* [from Spanish]

**bond** /bɒnd/ (**bonds, bonding, bonded**)
■ N-COUNT A **bond between** people is a strong feeling of friendship, love, or shared beliefs and experiences that unites them. ❑ *The experience created a very special bond between us.* ② V-RECIP When people **bond** with each other, they form a relationship based on love or shared beliefs and experiences. ❑ *Belinda was having difficulty bonding with the baby.* ❑ *They all bonded while writing the book together.* ⓷ N-COUNT A **bond between** people or groups is a close connection that they have with each other. ❑ *...the strong bond between church and nation.* ④ V-RECIP When one thing **bonds with** another, it sticks to it or becomes joined to it in some way. ❑ *Strips of wood are bonded together and shaped by machine.* ⑤ N-COUNT When a government or company issues a **bond**, it borrows money from investors. The certificate that is issued to investors who lend money is also called a **bond**. [BUSINESS] ❑ *Most of it will be financed by government bonds.* [from Old Norse]
→ see **love**

**bond|age** /bɒndɪdʒ/ N-UNCOUNT **Bondage** is the condition of being someone's property and having to work for them. ❑ *...a life of bondage.*

[from Old Norse]

**bone** /boʊn/ (**bones, boning, boned**) ■ N-VAR Your **bones** are the hard parts inside your body that together form your skeleton. ❑ *Many passengers suffered broken bones.* ❑ *The body is made up primarily of bone, muscle, and fat.* ② V-T If you **bone** a piece of meat or fish, you remove the bones from it before cooking it. ❑ *Make sure that you do not pierce the skin when boning the chicken thighs.* [from Old English]

**bon|fire** /bɒnfaɪər/ (**bonfires**) N-COUNT A **bonfire** is a fire that is made outdoors, usually to burn waste. ❑ *Bonfires are not allowed in urban areas.* [from French]

**bon|net** /bɒnɪt/ (**bonnets**) N-COUNT A **bonnet** is a hat with ribbons that are tied under the chin. [from Old French]
→ see **hat**

**bo|nus** /boʊnəs/ (**bonuses**) ■ N-COUNT A **bonus** is an extra amount of money that is added to your pay, usually because you have worked very hard. ❑ *Workers in big firms receive a part of their pay in the form of bonuses.* ❑ *...a $60 bonus.* ② N-COUNT A **bonus** is something good that you get in addition to something else, and which you would not usually expect. ❑ *We might finish third. Any better would be a bonus.* [from Latin]

**bony** /boʊni/ ADJ Someone who has a **bony** face or **bony** hands, for example, has a very thin face or very thin hands, with very little flesh covering their bones. ❑ *...an old man with a bony face and white hair.* [from Old English]

**boo** /buː/ (**boos, booing, booed**) V-T/V-I If you **boo** a speaker or performer, you shout "boo" or make other loud sounds to indicate that you do not like them. ❑ *People were booing and throwing things at them.* ❑ *When he entered the game, the crowd booed him loudly.* ● **Boo** is also a noun. ❑ *She was greeted with boos and hisses.* ● **boo|ing** N-UNCOUNT ❑ *The fans are entitled to their opinion but booing doesn't help anyone.*

**boo-boo** (**boo-boos**) ■ N-COUNT A **boo-boo** is a silly mistake or blunder. [INFORMAL] ❑ *O.K. I made a boo-boo. I apologize.* ② N-COUNT **Boo-boo** is a child's word for a cut or other minor injury. [INFORMAL]

**book** /bʊk/ (**books, booking, booked**)
■ N-COUNT A **book** is a number of pieces of paper, usually with words printed on them, which are fastened together and fixed inside a cover of strong paper or cardboard. ❑ *His eighth book was an instant best-seller.* ❑ *...the author of a book on politics.* ❑ *I can't wait to read the new book by Rosella Brown.* ② N-COUNT A **book of** something such as stamps, matches, or tickets is a small number of them fastened together between thin cardboard covers. ❑ *Can I have a book of stamps please?* ⓷ V-T When you **book** something such as a hotel room or a ticket, you arrange to have it or use it at a particular time. ❑ *The club has booked hotel rooms for the women and children.* ❑ *Laurie booked herself a flight home.* ④ N-PLURAL A company's or organization's **books** are its records of money that has been spent and earned or of the names of people who belong to it. [BUSINESS] ❑ *He left the books to his managers and accountants.* ⑤ PHRASE If transportation or a hotel, restaurant, or theater is **booked up, fully booked**, or **booked solid**, it has no tickets, rooms, or tables left for a particular time or date. ❑ *The*

*ferries are often fully booked by February.* [from Old English]

→ see **concert, library**

**Word Partnership** Use *book* with :

| | |
|---|---|
| N. | **address** book, book **award, children's** book, book **club, comic** book, **copy of a** book, book **cover, library** book, **phone** book, book **review, subject of a** book, **title of a** book ◼ |
| ADJ. | **latest/new/recent** book ◼ |
| V. | **read a** book, **publish a** book, **write a** book ◼ |

**book|case** /bʊkkeɪs/ (**bookcases**) N-COUNT A **bookcase** is a piece of furniture with shelves that you keep books on.

**book group** (**book groups**) N-COUNT A **book group** is a group of people who meet regularly to discuss books that they have read.

**Word Link** *let ≈ little : booklet, droplet, inlet*

**book|let** /bʊklɪt/ (**booklets**) N-COUNT A **booklet** is a very thin book that has a paper cover and that gives you information about something. ❑ *...a 48-page booklet of notes.*

**Word Link** *mark ≈ boundary, sign : bookmark, earmark, landmark*

**book|mark** /bʊkmɑrk/ (**bookmarks, bookmarking, bookmarked**) ◼ N-COUNT A **bookmark** is a narrow piece of card or leather that you put between the pages of a book so that you can find a particular page easily. ◼ N-COUNT In computing, a **bookmark** is the address of an Internet site that you put into a list on your computer so that you can return to it easily. [COMPUTING] ❑ *It is simple to save what you find with an electronic bookmark; that way you can return to it later.* ● **Bookmark** is also a verb. [COMPUTING] ❑ *You should bookmark this website and use it in the future.*

**book|store** /bʊkstɔr/ (**bookstores**) N-COUNT A **bookstore** is a store where books are sold.

**boom** /bum/ (**booms, booming, boomed**) ◼ N-COUNT If there is a **boom** in the economy, there is an increase in economic activity, for example, in the number of things that are being bought and sold. ❑ *An economic boom followed, especially in housing and construction.* ❑ *The 1980s were indeed boom years.* ◼ V-T/V-I When something such as your voice, a cannon, or a big drum **booms**, it makes a loud, deep sound that lasts for several seconds. ❑ *"Ladies," boomed Helena, without a microphone, "We all know why we're here tonight."* ❑ *Thunder boomed over Crooked Mountain.* ● **Boom out** means the same as **boom.** ❑ *Music boomed out from loudspeakers.* ❑ *A megaphone boomed out, "This is the police."* ● **Boom** is also a noun. ❑ *...the boom of a cannon.* [from Dutch]

→ see **sound**

**Thesaurus** *boom* Also look up :

| | |
|---|---|
| V. | flourish, prosper, succeed, thrive; (*ant.*) fail ◼ |
| N. | explosion, roar ◼ |

**boom box** (**boom boxes**) N-COUNT A **boom box** is a large portable machine for playing music,

especially one that is played loudly in public by young people. [INFORMAL]

**boon** /bun/ (**boons**) N-COUNT You can describe something as a **boon** when it makes life better or easier for someone. ❑ *Internet shopping has proved to be a real boon for working parents.* [from Old Norse]

**boost** /bust/ (**boosts, boosting, boosted**) ◼ V-T If one thing **boosts** another, it causes it to increase, improve, or be more successful. ❑ *Lower interest rates can boost the economy by reducing borrowing costs for consumers and businesses.* ● **Boost** is also a noun. ❑ *It would get the economy going and give us the boost that we need.* ◼ V-T If something **boosts** your confidence or morale, it improves it. ❑ *We need a big win to boost our confidence.* ● **Boost** is also a noun. ❑ *Scoring that goal gave me a real boost.*

**boot** /but/ (**boots, booting, booted**) ◼ N-COUNT **Boots** are shoes that cover your whole foot and the lower part of your leg. ❑ *He reached down and pulled off his boots.* ◼ N-COUNT **Boots** are strong, heavy shoes that cover your ankle and that have thick soles. ❑ *...the regular beat of the soldiers' boots.* ◼ V-T To **boot** an illegally parked car means to fit a device to one of its wheels so that it cannot be driven away. ❑ *The city will no longer boot cars.* ◼ V-T/V-I If a computer **boots** or you **boot** it, it is made ready to use by putting in the instructions it needs in order to start working. [COMPUTING] ❑ *The computer won't boot.* ❑ *Put the CD into the drive and boot the machine.* ● **Boot up** means the same as **boot.** ❑ *Go over to your PC and boot it up.* ◼ PHRASE If you **get the boot** or **are given the boot**, you are told that you are not wanted anymore, either in your job or by someone you are having a relationship with. [INFORMAL] ❑ *She didn't enjoy her job, and after a year she got the boot.* [from Old French]

→ see **clothing, shoe**

**boot camp** (**boot camps**) N-VAR In the United States, a **boot camp** is a camp where people who have just joined the army, navy, or marines are trained.

**booth** /buθ/ (**booths**) ◼ N-COUNT A **booth** is a small area separated from a larger public area by screens or thin walls where, for example, people can make a telephone call or vote in private. ❑ *...a public phone booth.* ◼ N-COUNT A **booth** in a restaurant or café consists of a table with long fixed seats on two or sometimes three sides of it. ❑ *They sat in a corner booth, away from other diners.* ◼ N-COUNT A **booth** is a stall at an exhibition, for example with a display of goods for sale or with information leaflets. [of Scandinavian origin]

**booze** /buz/ (**boozes, boozing, boozed**) ◼ N-UNCOUNT **Booze** is alcoholic drink. [INFORMAL] ◼ V-I If people **booze**, they drink alcohol. [INFORMAL] [from Middle Dutch]

**bor|der** /bɔrdər/ (**borders, bordering, bordered**)

border

◼ N-COUNT The **border** between two countries or regions is the dividing line between them. Sometimes **the border** also refers to the land close to this line. ❑ *They fled across the border.* ❑ *Soldiers closed the border between the two countries.* ◼ V-T A country that **borders** another country, a sea, or a river is next to it. ❑ ...the countries bordering the Mediterranean Sea. ⊠ N-COUNT A **border** is a strip or band around the edge of something. ❑ ...pillowcases trimmed with a lace border. [from Old French]

| **Thesaurus** | border | Also look up : |
|---|---|---|
| N. | boundary, end, extremity, perimeter; (ant.) center, inside, middle ⊡ | |

**bore** /bɔr/ (**bores, boring, bored**) ⊡ V-T If someone or something **bores** you, you find them dull and uninteresting. ❑ Dickie bored him with stories of the navy. ⊠ N-COUNT You describe someone as a **bore** when you think that they talk in a very uninteresting way. ❑ He's a bore and a fool. ⊠ N-SING You can describe a situation as **a bore** when you find it annoying. ❑ It's a bore to be sick. ⊠ V-T If you **bore** a hole in something, you make a deep round hole in it using a special tool. ❑ Bore a hole through the window frame and pass the cable through it. ⊠ **Bore** is the past tense of **bear.** [from Old Norse] ⊠ → see also **bored, boring**

**bored** /bɔrd/ ADJ If you are **bored**, you feel tired and impatient because you have lost interest in something or because you have nothing to do. ❑ I am getting very bored with this.

| **Word Link** | dom ≈ state of being : bore*dom,* free*dom,* wis*dom* |
|---|---|

**bore|dom** /bɔrdəm/ N-UNCOUNT **Boredom** is the state of being bored. ❑ Students never complain of boredom when great teachers are teaching. [from Old English]

**bor|ing** /bɔrɪŋ/ ADJ Someone or something **boring** is so dull and uninteresting that they make people tired and impatient. ❑ ...boring work. [from Old English]

| **Thesaurus** | boring | Also look up : |
|---|---|---|
| ADJ. | dull, tedious; (ant.) exciting, fun, interesting, lively | |

**born** /bɔrn/ ⊡ V-T PASSIVE When a baby **is born**, it comes out of its mother's body. In formal English, if you say that someone **is born of** someone or **to** someone, you mean that person is their parent. ❑ She was born in Milan on April 29, 1923. ❑ He was born of German parents and lived most of his life abroad. ⊠ ADJ You use **born** to describe someone who has a natural ability to do a particular activity or job. ❑ Jack was a born teacher. [from Old English] ⊠ → see also **newborn**

**borne** /bɔrn/ **Borne** is the past participle of **bear.** [from Old English]

**bor|ough** /bɜroʊ/ (**boroughs**) N-COUNT A **borough** is a town, or a district within a large city, which has its own council, government, or local services. ❑ ...the New York City borough of Brooklyn. [from Old English]

**bor|row** /bɒroʊ/ (**borrows, borrowing, borrowed**) V-T If you **borrow** something that belongs to someone else, you take it or use it for a period of time, usually with their permission. ❑ Can I borrow a pen please? ● **bor|row|ing** N-UNCOUNT ❑ We have allowed spending and borrowing to rise. [from Old English] → see **library**

**bor|row|er** /bɒroʊər/ (**borrowers**) N-COUNT A **borrower** is a person or organization that borrows money. ❑ Borrowers of more than $100,000 pay less interest. [from Old English]

**bos|om** /buzəm/ ⊡ N-SING A woman's **bosom** is her chest. ❑ She was a smallish woman with a large bosom. ⊠ ADJ A **bosom** buddy is a friend who you know very well and like very much. ❑ They were bosom buddies. [from Old English]

**boss** /bɒs/ (**bosses, bossing, bossed**) ⊡ N-COUNT Your **boss** is the person in charge of the organization or department where you work. ❑ He hates his boss. ⊠ V-T If someone **bosses** you, they keep telling you what to do in a way that is irritating. ❑ We cannot boss them into doing more. ● **Boss around** means the same as **boss.** ❑ He started bossing people around. [from Dutch]

| **Thesaurus** | boss | Also look up : |
|---|---|---|
| N. | chief, director, employer, foreman, manager, owner, superintendent, supervisor ⊡ | |

**bossy** /bɒsi/ ADJ If you describe someone as **bossy**, you disapprove of the fact that they enjoy telling people what to do. ❑ ...a bossy little girl. [from Dutch]

| **Word Link** | botan ≈ plant : botan*ical,* botan*ist,* botan*y* |
|---|---|

**bota|ny** /bɒtəni/ N-UNCOUNT **Botany** is the scientific study of plants. ● **bo|tani|cal** /bətænɪkªl/ ADJ ❑ The area is of great botanical interest. ● **bota|nist** (**botanists**) N-COUNT

**botch** /bɒtʃ/ (**botches, botching, botched**) V-T If you **botch** something that you are doing, you do it badly or clumsily. [INFORMAL] ❑ ...a botched job. ● **Botch up** means the same as **botch.** ❑ I hate it when workers botch up repairs on my house.

**both** /boʊθ/ ⊡ DET You use **both** when you are referring to two people or things and saying that something is true about each of them. ❑ She threw both arms up to protect her face. ● **Both** is also a quantifier. ❑ Both of these women have strong memories of the Vietnam War. ● **Both** is also a pronoun. ❑ Miss Brown and her friend are both from Brooklyn. ❑ They both worked at the University of Havana. ● **Both** is also a predeterminer. ❑ Both the horses were out, ready for the ride. ⊠ CONJ You use the structure **both...and** when you are giving two facts or alternatives and emphasizing that each of them is true or possible. ❑ Now women work both before and after having their children. [from Old Norse]

**both|er** /bɒðər/ (**bothers, bothering, bothered**) ⊡ V-T/V-I If you do not **bother to** do something or if you do not **bother with** it, you do not do it, consider it, or use it because you think it is unnecessary or because you are too lazy. ❑ *Lots of people don't bother to get married these days.* ❑ *Nothing I do makes any difference anyway, so why bother?* ◾ N-UNCOUNT; N-SING **Bother** means trouble or difficulty. ❑ *I usually buy sliced bread — it's less bother.* ◾ V-T If something **bothers** you, it worries, annoys, or upsets you. ❑ *Is something bothering you?* ❑ *It bothered me that boys weren't interested in me.* ● **both|ered** ADJ ❑ *I was bothered about the blister on my hand.* ◾ V-T If someone **bothers** you, they talk to you when you want to be left alone or they interrupt you when you are busy. ❑ *...a man who keeps bothering me.* ◾ PHRASE If you say that you **can't be bothered to** do something, you mean that you are not going to do it because you think it is unnecessary or because you are too lazy. ❑ *I can't be bothered to clean the house.* ◾ **hot and bothered** → see **hot**

**bot|tle** /bɒtᵊl/ (**bottles, bottling, bottled**) ◾ N-COUNT A **bottle** is a glass or plastic container in which drinks and other liquids are kept. ❑ *There were two empty water bottles on the table.* ❑ *She drank half a bottle of lemonade.* ◾ V-T To **bottle** a drink or other liquid means to put it into bottles after it has been made. ❑ *...equipment to automatically bottle the soda.* [from Old French] → see **container, glass**

**bot|tom** /bɒtəm/ (**bottoms**) ◾ N-COUNT The **bottom** of something is the lowest or deepest part of it. ❑ *He sat at the bottom of the stairs.* ❑ *Answers can be found at the bottom of page 8.* ❑ *...the bottom of their shoes.* ◾ ADJ The **bottom** thing or layer in a series of things or layers is the lowest one. ❑ *...the bottom drawer of the desk.* ◾ N-SING If someone is at **the bottom** in a survey, test, or league, their performance is worse than that of all the other people involved. ❑ *He was always at the bottom of the class in school.* ◾ PHRASE If you want to **get to the bottom of** a problem, you want to solve it by finding out its real cause. ❑ *I have to get to the bottom of this.* [from Old English]

| **Thesaurus** | *bottom* | Also look up : |
|---|---|---|
| N. | base, floor, foundation, ground; (*ant.*) peak, top ◾ | |

| **Word Partnership** | Use *bottom* with : |
|---|---|
| N. | bottom **of a hill**, bottom **of the page/ screen** ◾ bottom **drawer**, bottom **of the pool**, bottom **of the sea, river** bottom ◾ ◾ bottom **lip**, bottom **rung** ◾ |
| PREP. | **along the** bottom, **on the** bottom ◾ ◾ **at/near the** bottom ◾ – ◾ |
| V. | **reach the** bottom, **sink to the** bottom ◾ ◾ |

**bot|tom line** (**bottom lines**) N-COUNT The **bottom line** in a decision or situation is the most important factor that you have to consider. ❑ *The bottom line is that we can't afford it.*

**bought** /bɔt/ **Bought** is the past tense and past participle of **buy**. [from Old English]

**bouil|lon cube** (**bouillon cubes**) N-COUNT A **bouillon cube** is a solid cube made from dried meat or vegetable juices and other flavorings.

**boul|der** /boʊldər/ (**boulders**) N-COUNT A **boulder** is a large rounded rock. ❑ *It is thought that the train hit a boulder.* [of Scandinavian origin]

**boule|vard** /bʊləvɑrd/ (**boulevards**) N-COUNT A **boulevard** is a wide street in a city, usually with trees along each side. ❑ *...Lenton Boulevard.* [from French]

**bounce** /baʊns/ (**bounces, bouncing, bounced**) ◾ V-T/V-I When an object such as a ball **bounces** or when you **bounce** it, it moves upward from a surface or away from it immediately after hitting it. ❑ *My father came into the kitchen bouncing a tennis ball.* ❑ *...a falling pebble, bouncing down the cliff.* ● **Bounce** is also a noun. ❑ *...two bounces of the ball.* ◾ V-T/V-I If something **bounces** or if something **bounces** it, it swings or moves up and down. ❑ *Her long black hair bounced as she walked.* ❑ *The car was bouncing up and down as if someone were jumping on it.* ◾ V-I If you **bounce** on a soft surface, you jump up and down on it repeatedly. ❑ *She lets us do anything, even bounce on our beds.* ◾ V-T/V-I If a check **bounces** or if someone **bounces** it, the bank refuses to accept it and pay out the money, because the person who wrote it does not have enough money in their account. ❑ *Our only complaint would be if the check bounced.* ◾ V-I If an e-mail or other electronic message **bounces**, it is returned to the person who sent it because the address was wrong or because of a problem with one of the computers involved in sending it. [COMPUTING] ❑ *...a message saying that your mail has bounced or was unable to be delivered.* [from Low German]

**bounc|er** /baʊnsər/ (**bouncers**) N-COUNT A **bouncer** is someone who stands at the door of a club, prevents unwanted people from coming in, and makes people leave if they cause trouble. [from Low German]

**bouncy** /baʊnsi/ ADJ Someone or something that is **bouncy** is very lively. ❑ *She was bouncy and full of energy.* [from Low German]

| **bound** |
|---|
| ❶ BE BOUND |
| ❷ OTHER USES |

❶ **bound** /baʊnd/ ◾ **Bound** is the past tense and past participle of **bind**. ◾ PHRASE If something **is bound to** happen or be true, it is certain to happen or be true. ❑ *There are bound to be price increases next year.* ❑ *I'll show it to Benjamin. He's bound to know.* ◾ ADJ If a vehicle or person is **bound for** a particular place, they are traveling toward it. ❑ *The ship was bound for Italy.* [from Old Norse]

| **Word Partnership** | Use *bound* with : |
|---|---|
| N. | bound **by duty** ❶ ◾ |
| ADV. | **legally** bound, **tightly** bound ❶ ◾ |
| V. | bound **and gagged** ❶ ◾ bound **to fail** ❶ ◾ |
| N. | **feet/hands/wrists** bound, **leather** bound, **spiral** bound, bound **with tape** ❶ ◾ **a flight/plane/ship/train** bound **for** ❶ ◾ |

❷ **bound** /baʊnd/ (**bounds, bounding, bounded**) ◾ N-PLURAL **Bounds** are limits which normally restrict what can happen or what people can do. ❑ *You can use the time, within certain bounds, as you wish.* ❑ *...beyond the bounds of polite conversation.*

**B**

② v-i If a person or animal **bounds** in a particular direction, they move quickly with large steps or jumps. ❑ *He bounded up the steps.* ③ PHRASE If a place is **out of bounds**, people are not allowed to go there. ❑ *For the last few days the area has been out of bounds to foreign journalists.* [from Old French]

**boun|da|ry** /ˈbaʊndəri, -dri/ (**boundaries**) ❶ N-COUNT The **boundary of** an area of land is an imaginary line that separates it from other areas. ❑ *The river forms the western boundary of the wood.* ❷ N-COUNT In linguistics, a **boundary** is a division between one word and another or between the different parts of a word. [TECHNICAL] [from Old French]

| **Word Partnership** | Use *boundary* with : |
| --- | --- |
| PREP. | boundary **around places/things**, boundary **between places/things**, **beyond** a boundary, boundary **of someplace/something** ❶ |
| V. | **cross** a boundary, **mark/set** a boundary ❶ |
| N. | boundary **dispute**, boundary **line** ❶ |

**boun|ty** /ˈbaʊnti/ (**bounties**) ❶ N-VAR You can refer to something that is provided in large amounts as **bounty**. [LITERARY] ❑ *...autumn's bounty of fruits, seeds and berries.* ❷ N-COUNT A **bounty** is money that is offered as a reward for doing something, especially for finding or killing a particular person. ❑ *There was a bounty of more than $3m for his capture.* [from Old French]

**bou|quet** /boʊˈkeɪ, bu-/ (**bouquets**) N-COUNT A **bouquet** is a bunch of flowers which is attractively arranged. ❑ *The woman carried a bouquet of dried roses.* [from French]

**bour|geois** /bʊərˈʒwɑ/ ADJ If you describe people, their way of life, or their attitudes as **bourgeois**, you disapprove of them because you consider them typical of conventional middle-class people. ❑ *He accused them of having a bourgeois and limited view of life.* [from French]

**bout** /baʊt/ (**bouts**) ❶ N-COUNT If you have a **bout of** an illness, you have it for a short period. ❑ *He was recovering from a severe bout of flu.* ❷ N-COUNT A **bout of** something that is unpleasant is a short time during which it occurs a great deal. ❑ *...the latest bout of violence.* [from German]

**bou|tique** /buˈtik/ (**boutiques**) N-COUNT A **boutique** is a small store that sells fashionable clothes, shoes, or jewelry. [from French]

---
**bow**
---
❶ BENDING OR SUBMITTING
❷ OBJECTS
---

❶ **bow** /baʊ/ (**bows, bowing, bowed**) ❶ v-i When you **bow** to someone, you briefly bend your body toward them as a formal way of greeting them or showing respect. ❑ *They bowed low to the king and moved quickly out of his way.* ● **Bow** is also a noun. ❑ *I gave a theatrical bow and waved.* ❷ v-t If you **bow** your head, you bend it downward so that you are looking toward the ground. ❑ *The colonel bowed his head and whispered a prayer.* ❸ v-i If you **bow to** pressure or to someone's wishes, you agree to what they want you to do. ❑ *Some stores are*

bowing to consumer pressure and offering organically grown vegetables. [from Old English]
▸ **bow out** PHR-VERB If you **bow out** of something, you stop taking part in it. [WRITTEN] ❑ *The executives were happy to let him bow out after 26 years in the job.*

❷ **bow** /boʊ/ (**bows**) ❶ N-COUNT A **bow** is a knot with two loops and two loose ends that is used

in tying shoelaces and ribbons. ❑ *Add some ribbon tied in a bow.* ❷ N-COUNT A **bow** is a weapon for shooting arrows that consists of a long piece of curved wood with a string attached to both its ends. ❑ *Some of them were armed with bows and arrows.* ❸ N-COUNT The **bow** of a violin or other stringed instrument is a long thin piece of wood with fibers stretched along it that you move across the strings of the instrument in order to play it. [from Old English]

**bowed**

Pronounced /boʊd/ for meaning ❶, and /baʊd/ for meaning ❷.

❶ ADJ Something that is **bowed** is curved. ❑ *...an old lady with bowed legs.* ❷ ADJ If a person's body is **bowed**, it is bent forward. ❑ *He walked along the street, head down and shoulders bowed.* [from Old English]

**bow|el** /ˈbaʊəl/ (**bowels**) N-COUNT Your **bowels** are the tubes in your body through which digested food passes from your stomach to your anus. ❑ *Eating fruit and vegetables can help to keep your bowels healthy.* [from Old French]

**bowl** /boʊl/ (**bowls, bowling, bowled**) ❶ N-COUNT A **bowl** is a round container with a wide uncovered top that is used for mixing and serving food. ❑ *Put all the ingredients into a large bowl.* ❑ *...a bowl of soup.* ❷ N-COUNT You can refer to the hollow rounded part of an object as its **bowl**. ❑ *...toilet bowl cleaners.* ❸ A **bowl** or **bowl game** is a competition in which the best college teams play, after the main season has ended. N-COUNT ❑ *...the Fiesta college football bowl.* ❹ v-t/v-i In a sport such as bowling or lawn bowling, when a bowler **bowls**, or **bowls** a ball, he or she rolls it down a narrow track or field of grass. ❑ *Neither finalist bowled a very strong game.* ❺ v-t/v-i In a sport such as cricket, when a bowler **bowls**, or **bowls** a ball, he or she throws it down the field toward a batsman. ❑ *Lee bowled a ball to Walsh at 161.8 kph.* [Senses 1–3 from Old English. Senses 4–55 from French.] ❻ → see also **bowling**
→ see **dish, utensil**

**bowl|er** /ˈboʊlər/ (**bowlers**) N-COUNT A **bowler** is someone who goes **bowling** or plays **lawn bowling**. [from French]

**bowl|ing** /ˈboʊlɪŋ/ N-UNCOUNT **Bowling** is a game in which you roll a heavy ball down a narrow track toward a group of wooden objects and try to knock down as many of them as possible. ❑ *I go bowling for relaxation.* [from French]

**box** /bɒks/ (**boxes, boxing, boxed**) ❶ N-COUNT A **box** is a square or rectangular container with hard or stiff sides. Boxes often have lids. ❑ *He reached into the cardboard box beside him.* ❑ *They sat on wooden* boxes. ❑ …boxes of chocolates. **2** N-COUNT A **box** is a square or rectangle that is printed or drawn on a piece of paper, a road, or on some other surface. ❑ For more information, just check the box and send us the form. **3** N-COUNT A **box** is a small separate area in a theater or at a sports arena or stadium, where a small number of people can sit to watch the performance or game. ❑ Jim watched the game from a private box. **4** V-I To **box** means to fight someone according to the rules of boxing. ❑ At school I boxed and played rugby. ● **boxer** (**boxers**) N-COUNT ❑ …a professional boxer. [from Old English] **5** → see also boxing

→ see **container**

▶ **box in** PHR-VERB If you **are boxed in**, you are unable to move from a particular place because you are surrounded by other people or cars. ❑ The police boxed in his white van outside his apartment.

**box|ing** /bɒksɪŋ/ N-UNCOUNT **Boxing** is a sport in which two people wearing large padded gloves fight according to special rules. [from Old English]

**box lunch** (**box lunches**) N-COUNT A **box lunch** is food, for example sandwiches, which you take to work, to school, or on a trip and eat as your lunch.

**box of|fice** (**box offices**) also **box-office** **1** N-COUNT The **box office** in a theater or concert hall is the place where the tickets are sold. ❑ …the long line of people outside the box office. **2** N-SING When people talk about **the box office**, they are referring to the degree of success of a film or play in terms of the number of people who go to watch it or the amount of money it makes. ❑ The film has earned $180 million at the box office.

**box plot** (**box plots**) also **box-and-whisker plot, box-and-whisker chart** N-COUNT A **box plot** is a graph that shows the distribution of a set of data by using the middle fifty percent of the data. [TECHNICAL]

**box spring** (**box springs**) N-COUNT A **box spring** is a frame containing rows of coiled springs that is used to provide support for a mattress. You can also use **box springs** to refer to the springs themselves.

**boy** /bɔɪ/ (**boys**) **1** N-COUNT A **boy** is a male child. ❑ He was still just a boy. **2** N-COUNT You can refer to a young man as a **boy**, especially when talking about relationships between boys and girls. ❑ …the age when girls get interested in boys. [from Latin]

**boy band** (**boy bands**) N-COUNT A **boy band** is a band consisting of young men who sing pop music and dance.

**boy|cott** /bɔɪkɒt/ (**boycotts, boycotting, boycotted**) V-T If a country, group, or person **boycotts** a country, organization, or activity, they refuse to be involved with it in any way because they disapprove of it. ❑ The main opposition parties are boycotting the elections. ● **Boycott** is also a noun. ❑ The boycott of British beef was finally lifted in June. [from Irish]

**boy|friend** /bɔɪfrɛnd/ (**boyfriends**) N-COUNT Someone's **boyfriend** is a man or boy with whom they are having a romantic or sexual relationship. ❑ …Brenda and her boyfriend Anthony.

**boy|hood** /bɔɪhʊd/ N-UNCOUNT **Boyhood** is the period of a male person's life during which he is a boy. ❑ They have known each other since boyhood. [from Latin]

**boy|ish** /bɔɪɪʃ/ ADJ If you describe a man as **boyish**, you mean that he is like a boy in his appearance or behavior, and you find this attractive. ❑ …a rich man with a boyish liking for spaceships. ● **boy|ish|ly** ADV ❑ John grinned boyishly. [from Latin]

**Boyle's law** /bɔɪlz lɔ/ N-UNCOUNT **Boyle's law** is a law in physics which describes the relationship between the pressure of a gas and its volume. [TECHNICAL] [from Irish]

**bra** /brɑ/ (**bras**) N-COUNT A **bra** is a piece of underwear that women wear to support their breasts. [from French]

**brace** /breɪs/ (**braces, bracing, braced**) **1** V-T If you **brace yourself for** something unpleasant or difficult, you prepare yourself for it. ❑ He braced himself for the icy dive into the black water. **2** V-T If you **brace yourself against** something or **brace** part of your body **against** it, you press against something in order to steady your body or to avoid falling. ❑ Elaine braced herself against the table. **3** N-COUNT A **brace** is a device attached to a part of a person's body to strengthen or support it. ❑ They make wheelchairs and leg braces for children. **4** N-PLURAL **Braces** are a metal device that can be fastened to a person's teeth in order to help them grow straight. ❑ I used to have to wear braces. [from Old French]

→ see **teeth**

**brace|let** /breɪslɪt/ (**bracelets**) N-COUNT A **bracelet** is a piece of jewelry that you wear around your wrist. [from Old French]

→ see **jewelry**

**brac|ing** /breɪsɪŋ/ ADJ If you describe a place, climate, or activity as **bracing**, you mean that it makes you feel fresh and full of energy. ❑ …a bracing walk. [from Old French]

**brack|et** /brækɪt/ (**brackets, bracketing, bracketed**) **1** N-COUNT If you say that someone or something is in a particular **bracket**, you mean that they come within a particular range. ❑ People in higher income brackets are less likely to need health care. **2** N-COUNT **Brackets** are pieces of metal, wood, or plastic that are fastened to a wall in order to support something such as a shelf. ❑ There was a TV on a wall bracket in one corner. **3** N-COUNT **Brackets** are a pair of written marks [ ] that you place around a word, expression, or sentence in order to indicate that you are giving extra information. [from Old French]

**brag** /bræg/ (**brags, bragging, bragged**) V-T/V-I If you **brag**, you say in a very proud way that you have something or have done something; used to show disapproval. ❑ He's always bragging that he's a great artist. ❑ He'll probably go around bragging to his friends. ❑ He never brags about his charity work.

**braid** /breɪd/ (**braids, braiding, braided**) **1** N-UNCOUNT **Braid** is a narrow piece of decorated cloth or twisted threads, which is used to decorate clothes or curtains. ❑ …a plum-colored uniform with lots of gold braid. **2** V-T If you **braid** hair or a group of threads, you twist three or more lengths of the hair or threads over and under each other to make one thick length. ❑ She has almost finished braiding Louisa's hair. **3** N-COUNT A **braid** is a length of hair that has been divided into three or more lengths and then braided. ❑ …a woman with her hair in braids. [from Old English]

B

## Word Web brain

The human **brain** weighs about three pounds. It contains seven distinct sections. The largest are the cerebrum, the cerebellum, and the medulla oblongata. The cerebrum wraps around the outside of the brain. It handles **learning**, **communication**, and voluntary **movement**. The cerebellum controls **balance**, **posture**, and movement. The medulla oblongata joins the **spinal cord** with other parts of the brain. This part of the brain controls automatic actions such as breathing, heartbeat, and swallowing. It also tells us when we are hungry and when we need to sleep.

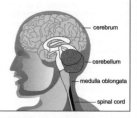

cerebrum

cerebellum

medulla oblongata

spinal cord

**brain** /breɪn/ (**brains**) **1** N-COUNT Your **brain** is the organ inside your head that controls your body's activities and enables you to think and to feel things such as heat and pain. **2** N-COUNT Your **brain** is your mind and the way that you think. ❑ *Sports are good for your brain as well as your body.* **3** N-COUNT If someone has **brains** or a good **brain**, they have the ability to learn and understand things quickly, to solve problems, and to make good decisions. ❑ *The final competitors all had brains and imagination.* **4** PHRASE If someone is **the brains** behind an idea or an organization, he or she had that idea or makes the important decisions about how that organization is managed. [INFORMAL] ❑ *Mr. White was the brains behind the plan.* [from Old English] **5** to **rack** your **brains** → see **rack**
→ see Word Web: **brain**
→ see **nervous system**

**brain|child** /breɪntʃaɪld/ N-SING Someone's **brainchild** is an idea or invention that they have thought up or created. ❑ *The record was the brainchild of rock star Bob Geldof.*

**brain|storm** /breɪnstɔrm/ N-COUNT If you have a **brainstorm**, you suddenly have a clever idea. ❑ *"Look," she said, getting a brainstorm, "Why don't you invite them here?"*

**brake** /breɪk/ (**brakes, braking, braked**) **1** N-COUNT **Brakes** are devices in a vehicle that make it go slower or stop. **2** V-T/V-I When a vehicle or its driver **brakes**, the driver makes it slow down or stop by using the brakes. ❑ *The car braked to avoid a collision.* ❑ *He braked the car slightly.* [from Middle Dutch]

### Usage brake and break

*Brake* and *break* sound the same, but they have very different meanings. You step on the *brake* to make your car slow down or stop: *Sometimes, Nayana steps on the accelerator when she means to step on the brake.* If you *break* something, you damage it: *I learned something today — if your laptop falls off your desk, it will probably break!*

**bran** /bræn/ N-UNCOUNT **Bran** is the outer skin of grain that is left when the grain has been used to make flour. ❑ *...oat bran.* [from Old French]

**branch** /bræntʃ/ (**branches, branching, branched**) **1** N-COUNT The **branches** of a tree are the parts that grow out from its trunk. ❑ *...the upper branches of a row of pines.* **2** N-COUNT A **branch** of a business or other organization is one of the offices, stores, or groups which belong to it and which are located in different places. ❑ *The local branch of Bank of America is handling the accounts.*

**3** N-COUNT A **branch of** a subject is a part or type of it. ❑ *Astronomy is a branch of science.* [from Old French]
▶ **branch off** PHR-VERB A road or path that **branches off** from another one starts from it and goes in a slightly different direction. If you **branch off** somewhere, you change the direction in which you are going. ❑ *After a few miles, a small road branched off to the right.*
▶ **branch out** PHR-VERB If a person or an organization **branches out**, they do something that is different from their normal activities or work. ❑ *I continued studying moths, and branched out to other insects.*

**brand** /brænd/ (**brands, branding, branded**) **1** N-COUNT A **brand** of a product is the version of it that is made by one particular manufacturer. ❑ *...a brand of cereal.* ❑ *I bought one of the leading brands.* **2** V-T If someone **is branded** as something bad, people think they are that thing. ❑ *I was instantly branded as a rebel.* ❑ *Journalists who disagree have been branded unpatriotic.* **3** V-T If you **brand** an animal, you put a permanent mark on its skin in order to show who it belongs to, usually by burning a mark onto its skin. ❑ *The owner didn't bother to brand the cattle.* [from Old English]

**bran|dish** /brændɪʃ/ (**brandishes, brandishing, brandished**) V-T If you **brandish** something, especially a weapon, you hold it in a threatening way. ❑ *He appeared in the kitchen brandishing a knife.* [from Old French]

**brand name** (**brand names**) N-COUNT The **brand name** of a product is the name the manufacturer gives it and under which it is sold. [BUSINESS] ❑ *The drug is marketed under the brand name Viramune.*

**brand-name prod|uct** (**brand-name products**) N-COUNT A **brand-name product** is one which is made by a well-known manufacturer and has the manufacturer's label on it. [BUSINESS] ❑ *In buying footwear, 66% prefer brand-name products.*

**brand-new** ADJ A **brand-new** object is completely new. ❑ *Yesterday he went off to buy himself a brand-new car.*

**bran|dy** /brændi/ (**brandies**) N-VAR **Brandy** is a strong alcoholic drink that is made from wine. [from Dutch]

**brash** /bræʃ/ (**brasher, brashest**) ADJ If you describe someone as **brash**, you disapprove of them because you think that they are too confident and aggressive. ❑ *He is now a brash, successful businessman.* ● **brash|ly** ADV ❑ *Hampton brashly accepted the challenge.*

**brass** /bræs/ **1** N-UNCOUNT **Brass** is a yellow-

## Picture Dictionary    brass

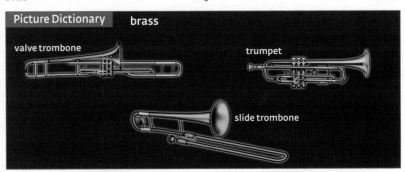

valve trombone

trumpet

slide trombone

colored metal made from copper and zinc. ❑ *The instrument is beautifully made in brass.* **2** N-SING **The brass** is the section of an orchestra which consists of brass wind instruments such as trumpets and horns. ❑ *The drum solo gives the brass section a chance to recover.* **3** N-SING In the army or in other organizations, **the brass** are the people in the highest positions. [INFORMAL] ❑ *Simmons admitted to being satisfied with most of the brass's answers.* [from Old English]
→ see Picture Dictionary: **brass**
→ see **orchestra**

**brat** /bræt/ (**brats**) N-COUNT If you call a child a **brat**, you disapprove of their bad or annoying behavior. [INFORMAL] ❑ *He's a spoiled brat.* [from Old English]

**bra|va|do** /brəvɑdoʊ/ N-UNCOUNT **Bravado** is an appearance of courage or confidence that someone shows in order to impress other people. ❑ *"Ridiculous," she said, with more bravado than she felt.* [from Spanish]

**brave** /breɪv/ (**braver, bravest, braves, braving, braved**) **1** ADJ Someone who is **brave** is willing to do things that are dangerous, and does not show fear in difficult or dangerous situations. ❑ *He was not brave enough to report the loss of the documents.* ● **brave|ly** ADV ❑ *The enemy fought bravely and well.* **2** V-T If you **brave** unpleasant or dangerous conditions, you deliberately expose yourself to them, usually in order to achieve something. [WRITTEN] ❑ *Thousands have braved icy rain to show their support.* [from French]
→ see **hero**

**brav|ery** /breɪvəri, breɪvri/ N-UNCOUNT **Bravery** is brave behavior or the quality of being brave. ❑ *He deserves the highest praise for his bravery.* [from French]

**brawl** /brɔl/ (**brawls, brawling, brawled**) **1** N-COUNT A **brawl** is a rough disorganized fight. ❑ *He was arrested in a street brawl.* **2** V-RECIP If people **brawl** with each other, they fight in a rough disorganized way. ❑ *He was arrested for brawling outside a nightclub.* [from Dutch]

**bra|zen** /breɪzᵊn/ ADJ If you describe a person or their behavior as **brazen**, you mean that they are very bold and do not care what other people think about them. ❑ *I am completely brazen about asking for things.* ● **bra|zen|ly** ADV ❑ *He consistently and brazenly laughed off the rules.* [from Old English]

**breach** /britʃ/ (**breaches, breaching, breached**) **1** V-T If you **breach** an agreement, a law,

or a promise, you break it. ❑ *The newspaper breached the rules on privacy.* **2** N-VAR A **breach of** an agreement, a law, or a promise is an act of breaking it. ❑ *Their actions are a breach of contract.* **3** N-COUNT A **breach in** a relationship is a serious disagreement which often results in the relationship ending. [FORMAL] ❑ *…a serious breach in relations between the two countries.* **4** V-T If someone or something **breaches** a barrier, they make an opening in it, usually leaving it weakened or destroyed. [FORMAL] ❑ *Tree roots have breached the roof of the cave.* **5** V-T If you **breach** security or someone's defenses, you manage to get through and attack an area that is heavily guarded and protected. ❑ *The bomber breached security by hurling his dynamite from a roof.* ● **Breach** is also a noun. ❑ *…serious breaches of security.* [from Old English]

**bread** /brɛd/ (**breads**) N-VAR **Bread** is a food made from flour, water, and usually yeast. ❑ *…a loaf of bread.* ❑ *…bread and butter.* [from Old English]
→ see Picture Dictionary: **bread**

**breadth** /brɛdθ, brɛtθ/ **1** N-UNCOUNT The **breadth** of something is the distance between its two sides. ❑ *…a river seven times the breadth of the Mississippi.* **2** N-UNCOUNT The **breadth of** something is its quality of consisting of or involving many different things. ❑ *Older people have a tremendous breadth of experience.* [from Old English]

**bread|winner** /brɛdwɪnər/ (**breadwinners**) also **bread-winner** N-COUNT The **breadwinner** in a family is the person in it who earns the money that the family needs. ❑ *I've always paid the bills and been the breadwinner.*

---

| **break** |
| --- |
| **❶** DAMAGE OR DESTROY |
| **❷** STOP OR CHANGE SOMETHING |
| **❸** OTHER USES |
| **❹** PHRASAL VERBS |

**❶ break** /breɪk/ (**breaks, breaking, broke, broken**)
**1** V-T/V-I When an object **breaks** or when you **break** it, it suddenly separates into two or more pieces, often because it has been hit or dropped. ❑ *He fell through the window, breaking the glass.* ❑ *The plate broke.* ❑ *The plane broke into three pieces.* **2** V-T/V-I If you **break** a part of your body such

## Picture Dictionary

bread

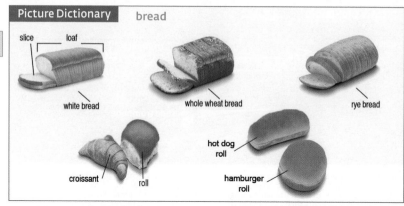

slice · loaf

white bread · whole wheat bread · rye bread

hot dog roll

croissant · roll · hamburger roll

as your leg, your arm, or your nose, or if a bone **breaks**, you are injured because a bone cracks or splits. ❑ *She broke a leg in a skiing accident.* ❑ *Old bones break easily.* ● **Break** is also a noun. ❑ *Gabriella had a bad break in her leg.* ❸ V-T/V-I When a tool or piece of machinery **breaks** or when you **break** it, it is damaged and no longer works. ❑ *The cable on the elevator broke, and it crashed to the ground.* [from Old English] ❹ → see also **brake., tear**

❷ **break** /breɪk/ (**breaks, breaking, broke, broken**)
❶ V-T If someone **breaks** a habit, or a difficult or unpleasant situation that has existed for some time, they end it or change it. ❑ *Here's a good way to break the habit of eating too quickly.* ❑ *There have been suggestions of breaking the military's hold on power.* ❷ V-I If someone **breaks for** a short period of time, they rest or change from what they are doing for a short period. ❑ *They broke for lunch.* ❸ N-COUNT A **break** is a short period of time when you have a rest or a change from what you are doing, especially if you are working or if you are in a boring or unpleasant situation. ❑ *They may be able to help with childcare so that you can have a break.* ❑ *...a 15 minute break from work.* [from Old English]

❸ **break** /breɪk/ (**breaks, breaking, broke, broken**)
❶ V-T If you **break** a rule, promise, or agreement, you do something that you should not do according to that rule, promise, or agreement. ❑ *We didn't know we were breaking the law.* ❑ *...no more lies, no more broken promises.* ❷ V-I If you **break** free or loose, you free yourself from something or escape from it. ❑ *She broke free by thrusting her elbow into his chest.* ❸ V-T To **break** the force of something such as a blow or fall means to weaken its effect, for example, by getting in the way of it. ❑ *He suffered serious neck injuries after he broke someone's fall.* ❹ V-T When you **break** a piece of bad news to someone, you tell it to them, usually in a kind way. ❑ *Then Louise broke the news that she was leaving me.* ❺ N-COUNT A **break** is a lucky opportunity that someone gets to achieve something. [INFORMAL] ❑ *My first break came when I was 16.* ❻ V-T If you **break** a record, you beat the previous record for a particular achievement. ❑ *Carl Lewis has broken the world record in the 100 meters.* ❼ V-I When day or dawn **breaks**, it starts to grow light after the night has ended. ❑ *They continued the search as dawn broke.* ❽ V-I When a

wave **breaks**, it passes its highest point and turns downward, for example, when it reaches the shore. ❑ *Danny listened to the waves breaking against the shore.* ❾ V-T If you **break** a secret code, you work out how to understand it. ❑ *The machines worked on finding the numbers that would break the code.* ❿ V-I When a boy's voice **breaks**, it becomes deeper and sounds more like a man's voice. ❑ *He sings with the strained discomfort of someone whose voice hasn't quite broken.* [from Old English] ⓫ → see also **broke, broken, heartbreak, heartbreaking, heartbroken, outbreak** ⓬ to **break even** → see **even**
→ see **crash, factory**

### Word Partnership    Use *break* with :

| | |
|---|---|
| N. | break **a bone**, break **your arm/leg/ neck** ❶ ❷ |
| | break **a habit**, break **the silence** ❷ ❶ **coffee/lunch** break ❷ ❸ |
| | break **the law**, break **a promise**, break **a rule** ❸ ❶ |
| | break **a record** ❸ ❻ |
| V. | **need a** break, **take a** break ❷ ❸ |

❹ **break** /breɪk/ (**breaks, breaking, broke, broken**)
▶ **break down** ❶ PHR-VERB If a machine or a vehicle **breaks down**, it stops working. ❑ *Their car broke down.* ❷ PHR-VERB If a discussion, relationship, or system **breaks down**, it fails because of a problem or disagreement. ❑ *Talks with business leaders broke down last night.* ❸ PHR-VERB When a substance **breaks down** or when something **breaks** it **down**, a biological or chemical process causes it to separate into the substances which make it up. ❑ *White pasta breaks down into sugars almost as fast as table sugar does.* ❹ PHR-VERB If someone **breaks down**, they lose control of themselves and start crying. ❑ *Because he was being so kind and concerned, I broke down and cried.* ❺ PHR-VERB If you **break down** a door or barrier, you hit it so hard that it falls to the ground. ❑ *An angry mob broke down police barricades and rushed into the courtroom.* ❻ → see also **breakdown**
▶ **break in** ❶ PHR-VERB If someone **breaks in**, they get into a building by force. ❑ *Masked robbers broke in and stole $8,000.* ❷ → see also **break-**

**in** ③ PHR-VERB If you **break in** on someone's conversation or activity, you interrupt them. ❑ *O'Leary broke in on his thoughts.* ❑ *"Oh yes, immediately!" Mollie broke in.*

▶ **break into** ■ PHR-VERB If someone **breaks into** a building, they get into it by force. ❑ *There was no one nearby who might see him trying to break into the house.* ② PHR-VERB If someone **breaks into** something they suddenly start doing it. ❑ *The moment she was out of sight she broke into a run.* ③ PHR-VERB If you **break into** a profession or area of business, especially one that is difficult to succeed in, you manage to have some success in it. ❑ *She finally broke into films after a successful stage career.*

▶ **break off** ■ PHR-VERB If part of something **breaks off** or if you **break** it **off**, it comes off or is removed by force. ❑ *The two wings of the aircraft broke off in the crash.* ❑ *Grace broke off a large piece of the clay.* ② PHR-VERB If you **break off** when you are doing or saying something, you suddenly stop doing it or saying it. ❑ *Barry broke off in the middle of a sentence.* ③ PHR-VERB If someone **breaks off** a relationship, they end it. ❑ *The two West African states broke off relations two years ago.*

▶ **break out** ■ PHR-VERB If something such as war, fighting, or disease **breaks out**, it begins suddenly. ❑ *He was 29 when war broke out.* ② PHR-VERB If you **break out in** a rash or a sweat, a rash or sweat appears on your skin. ❑ *My skin tends to break out in a rash when I get nervous.*

▶ **break through** ■ PHR-VERB If you **break through** a barrier, you succeed in forcing your way through it. ❑ *Protesters tried to break through a police barricade.* ② → see also **breakthrough**

▶ **break up** ■ PHR-VERB When something **breaks up** or when you **break** it **up**, it separates or is divided into several smaller parts. ❑ *There could be a civil war if the country breaks up.* ❑ *Break up the chocolate and melt it.* ② PHR-VERB If you **break up with** someone, your relationship with that person ends. ❑ *My girlfriend has broken up with me.* ❑ *He hated the idea of marriage so we broke up.* ③ PHR-VERB When a meeting or gathering **breaks up** or when someone **breaks** it **up**, it is brought to an end and the people involved in it leave. ❑ *A neighbor asked for the music to be turned down and the party broke up.* ❑ *Police used clubs to break up a demonstration.*

**break|away** /bre͟ɪkəweɪ/ ADJ A **breakaway** group is a group of people who have separated from a larger group, for example, because of a disagreement. ❑ *...a breakaway party that split form the Conservatives.* [from Old English]

**break|down** /bre͟ɪkdaʊn/ (**breakdowns**) ■ N-COUNT The **breakdown** of something such as a relationship, plan, or discussion is its failure or ending. ❑ *...the breakdown of talks between the U.S. and European Union officials.* ❑ *...the breakdown of a marriage.* ② N-COUNT If you have a **breakdown**, you become very depressed, so that you are unable to cope with your life. ❑ *My mother died, and a couple of years later I had a breakdown.* ③ N-COUNT If a car or a piece of machinery has a **breakdown**, it stops working. ❑ *Her old car was unreliable, so the trip was ruined by breakdowns.*

**breakdown** ④ N-COUNT A **breakdown**

of something is a list of its separate parts. ❑ *The organizers were given a breakdown of the costs.*
→ see **traffic**

**breaker zone** (**breaker zones**) N-COUNT The **breaker zone** is the area of water near a shoreline where waves begin to fall downward and hit the shore. [TECHNICAL]

**break|fast** /bre͟kfəst/ (**breakfasts**) ■ N-VAR **Breakfast** is the first meal of the day. It is usually eaten in the early part of the morning. ❑ *What's for breakfast?* ② → see also **bed and breakfast**
→ see **meal**

**break-in** (**break-ins**) N-COUNT If there is a **break-in**, someone gets into a building by force. ❑ *The break-in occurred just before midnight.*

**break|ing point** N-UNCOUNT If something or someone has reached the **breaking point**, they have so many problems or difficulties that they can no longer cope with them, and may soon collapse or be unable to continue. ❑ *This race tests horse and rider to the breaking point.*

**break|neck** /bre͟ɪknɛk/ ADJ Something happens or travels at **breakneck** speed happens or travels very fast. ❑ *Jack drove to the hospital at breakneck speed.*

**break|out** /bre͟ɪkaʊt/ (**breakouts**) N-COUNT If there has been a **breakout**, someone has escaped from prison. ❑ *The police are looking for two men after a prison breakout last night.*

**break|through** /bre͟ɪkθruː/ (**breakthroughs**) N-COUNT A **breakthrough** is an important development or achievement. ❑ *The company is about to make a significant breakthrough in Europe.*

**break|up** /bre͟ɪkʌp/ (**breakups**) N-COUNT The **breakup of** a marriage, relationship, or association is its end. ❑ *...the sudden breakup of the meeting.*

**breast** /brɛ͟st/ (**breasts**) ■ N-COUNT A woman's **breasts** are the two soft, round parts on her chest that can produce milk to feed a baby. ② N-COUNT A person's **breast** is the upper part of his or her chest. [LITERARY] ❑ *He struck his breast in a dramatic gesture.* ③ N-COUNT A bird's **breast** is the front part of its body. ❑ *...the robin's red breast.* ④ N-VAR You can refer to piece of meat that is cut from the front of a bird as **breast**. ❑ *...a chicken breast with vegetables.* [from Old English]

**breast|stroke** /brɛ͟ststroʊk, brɛ͟sstroʊk/ N-UNCOUNT **Breaststroke** is a swimming stroke that you do lying on your front, moving your arms and legs horizontally in a circular motion. ❑ *I do not know how to swim breaststroke.*

**breath** /brɛ͟θ/ (**breaths**) ■ N-VAR Your **breath** is the air that you let out through your mouth when you breathe. If someone has **bad breath**, their breath smells unpleasant. ❑ *I could smell peppermint on his breath.* ② N-VAR When you take a **breath**, you breathe in once. ❑ *He took a deep breath, and began to climb the stairs.* ❑ *Gasping for breath, she leaned against the door.* ③ PHRASE If you describe something new or different as a **breath of fresh air**, you mean that it makes a situation or subject more interesting or exciting. ❑ *I thought it was my job to bring a breath of fresh air to the company.* ④ PHRASE If you are **out of breath**, you are breathing very quickly and with difficulty because you have been doing something energetic. ❑ *She was slightly out of breath from running.* ⑤ PHRASE If you say something **under**

your **breath**, you say it in a very quiet voice, often because you do not want other people to hear what you are saying. ❑ *Walsh muttered something under his breath.* [from Old English]

| Word Partnership | Use *breath* with : |
|---|---|

| ADJ. | **bad** breath, **fresh** breath **1** |
| | **deep** breath **2** |
| V. | **hold** *your* breath **1** |
| | **gasp for** breath, **take a** breath **2** |

**breatha|lyze** /brɛθəlaɪz/ (**breathalyzes, breathalyzing, breathalyzed**) V-T If the driver of a car **is breathalyzed** by the police, they ask him or her to breathe into a special bag or device in order to test whether he or she has drunk too much alcohol. ❑ *She was breathalyzed and found to be over the legal limit.*

**breathe** /briːð/ (**breathes, breathing, breathed**) V-T/V-I When people or animals **breathe**, they take air into their lungs and let it out again. When they **breathe** smoke or a particular kind of air, they take it into their lungs and let it out again as they breathe. ❑ *He stood there breathing deeply and evenly.* ❑ *No American should have to drive out of town to breathe clean air.* ● **breath|ing** N-UNCOUNT ❑ *Her breathing became slow and heavy.* → see **sigh**
→ see **respiration**

▶ **breathe in** PHR-VERB When you **breathe in**, you take some air into your lungs. ❑ *She breathed in deeply.*

▶ **breathe out** PHR-VERB When you **breathe out**, you send air out of your lungs through your nose or mouth. ❑ *Breathe out and bring your knees in toward your chest.*

**breath|er** /briːðər/ (**breathers**) N-COUNT If you take a **breather**, you stop what you are doing for a short time in order to rest. [INFORMAL] ❑ *Relax and take a breather whenever you feel that you need one.*

**breath|ing space** (**breathing spaces**) N-VAR A **breathing space** is a short period of time between two activities in which you can recover from the first activity and prepare for the second one. ❑ *Firms need a breathing space if they are to recover.* ❑ *We hope that it will give us some breathing space.*

**breath|less** /brɛθlɪs/ ADJ If you are **breathless**, you have difficulty in breathing properly, for example, because you have been running or because you are afraid or excited. ❑ *I was a little breathless.* ● **breath|less|ly** ADV ❑ *"I'll go in," he said breathlessly.* ● **breath|less|ness** N-UNCOUNT ❑ *A slow heart rate causes breathlessness.* [from Old English]

**breath|taking** /brɛθteɪkɪŋ/ also **breath-taking** ADJ If you say that something is **breathtaking**, you are emphasizing that it is extremely beautiful or amazing. ❑ *The house has breathtaking views from every room.* ❑ *The scale of the damage was breathtaking.*

**breed** /briːd/ (**breeds, breeding, bred**) **1** N-COUNT A **breed** of animal is a particular type of it. For example, terriers are a breed of dog. ❑ *...rare breeds of cattle.* **2** V-T If you **breed** animals or plants, you keep them for the purpose of producing more animals or plants with particular qualities, in a controlled way. ❑ *He lived alone, breeding horses and dogs.* ❑ *He used to breed dogs for the police.* ● **breed|er** (**breeders**) N-COUNT ❑ *Her father was a well-known racehorse breeder.* ● **breed|ing**

N-UNCOUNT ❑ *They are involved in the breeding of guide dogs for blind people.* **3** V-I When animals **breed**, they have babies. ❑ *Frogs will usually breed in any convenient pond.* ● **breed|ing** N-UNCOUNT ❑ *During the breeding season the birds come ashore.* **4** V-T If you say that something **breeds** bad feeling or bad behavior, you mean that it causes bad feeling or bad behavior to develop. ❑ *If they are unemployed it may breed resentment.* [from Old English] **5** → see also **breeding**
→ see **zoo**

**breeze** /briːz/ (**breezes, breezing, breezed**) **1** N-COUNT A **breeze** is a gentle wind. ❑ *...a cool summer breeze.* **2** V-I If you **breeze into** a place or a position, you enter it in a very casual or relaxed manner. ❑ *Lopez breezed into the finals of the tournament.* [from Old Spanish]
→ see **wind**

**breezy** /briːzi/ ADJ If you describe someone as **breezy**, you mean that they behave in a casual, cheerful, and confident manner. ❑ *...his bright and breezy personality.* [from French]

**brew** /bruː/ (**brews, brewing, brewed**) **1** V-T If you **brew** tea or coffee, you make it by pouring hot water over tea leaves or ground coffee. ❑ *He brewed a pot of coffee.* **2** N-COUNT A **brew** is a particular kind of tea or coffee. It can also be a pot of tea or coffee. ❑ *She swallowed a mouthful of the hot strong brew.* **3** V-T If someone **brews** beer, they make it. ❑ *I brew my own beer.* **4** V-I If an unpleasant or difficult situation **is brewing**, it is starting to develop. ❑ *At home a crisis was brewing.* [from Old English]
→ see **tea**

**brew|er** /bruːər/ (**brewers**) N-COUNT **Brewers** are people or companies who make beer. [from Old English]

**brew|ery** /bruːəri/ (**breweries**) N-COUNT A **brewery** is a place where beer is made. [from Old English]

**bribe** /braɪb/ (**bribes, bribing, bribed**) **1** N-COUNT A **bribe** is a sum of money or something valuable that one person offers or gives to another in order to persuade him or her to do something. ❑ *He was accused of receiving bribes.* **2** V-T If one person **bribes** another, they give them a bribe. ❑ *He was accused of bribing a bank official.* [from Old French]

**brib|ery** /braɪbəri/ N-UNCOUNT **Bribery** is the act of offering someone money or something valuable in order to persuade them to do something for you. ❑ *He was jailed on charges of bribery.* [from Old French]

**brick** /brɪk/ (**bricks**) N-VAR **Bricks** are rectangular blocks of baked clay used for building walls, which are usually red or brown. **Brick** is the material made up of these blocks. ❑ *She built bookshelves out of bricks and boards.* [from Old French]

**bride** /braɪd/ (**brides**) N-COUNT A **bride** is a woman who is getting married or who has just gotten married. ❑ *...the bride and groom.* ● **brid|al** ADJ ❑ *She wore a floor length bridal gown.* [from Old English]
→ see **wedding**

**bride|groom** /braɪdgrum/ (**bridegrooms**) N-COUNT A **bridegroom** is a man who is getting married. [from Old English]

## Word Web    bridge

The world's longest and tallest **suspension bridge** is the Akashi Kaikyo Bridge. It is 12,828 feet long and almost 1,000 feet tall. It can withstand an 8.5 magnitude earthquake. Another famous **span**, the Brooklyn Bridge in New York City, dates from 1883. It was the first suspension bridge to use **steel** for its **cable** wire. More than 120,000 vehicles still use the bridge every day. The Evergreen Point Floating Bridge near Seattle, Washington, floats on pontoons. It's over a mile long. During windy weather the drawbridge in the middle must stay open to protect the bridge from damage.

**brides|maid** /ˈbraɪdzmeɪd/ (**bridesmaids**) N-COUNT A **bridesmaid** is a woman or a girl who accompanies a bride on her wedding day.
→ see **wedding**

**bridge** /brɪdʒ/ (**bridges, bridging, bridged**) **1** N-COUNT A **bridge** is a structure that is built over a railroad, river, or road so that people or vehicles can cross from one side to the other. □ *He walked back across the railroad bridge.* **2** V-T To **bridge** the gap between two people or things means to reduce it or get rid of it. □ *It is unlikely that the two sides will be able to bridge their differences.* **3** V-T Something that **bridges** the gap between two very different things has some of the qualities of each of these things. □ *…a singer who bridged the gap between pop music and opera.* **4** N-COUNT If something or someone acts as a **bridge** between two people, groups, or things, they connect them. □ *We hope this book will act as a bridge between doctor and patient.* **5** N-UNCOUNT **Bridge** is a card game for four players in which the players begin by declaring how many tricks they expect to win. [from Old English]
→ see Word Web: **bridge**

**bridge loan** (**bridge loans**) N-COUNT A **bridge loan** is money that a bank lends you for a short time, for example, so that you can buy a new house before you have sold the one you already own.

**bri|dle** /ˈbraɪdᵊl/ (**bridles**) N-COUNT A **bridle** is a set of straps that is put around a horse's head and mouth so that the person riding or driving the horse can control it. [from Old English]

**brief** /briːf/ (**briefer, briefest, briefs, briefing, briefed**) **1** ADJ Something that is **brief** lasts for only a short time. □ *She once made a brief appearance on television.* **2** ADJ A **brief** speech or piece of writing does not contain too many words or details. □ *In a brief statement, he concentrated on international affairs.* **3** ADJ If you are **brief**, you say what you want to say in as few words as possible. □ *Now please be brief — my time is valuable.* **4** ADJ You can describe a period of time as **brief** if you want to emphasize that it is very short. □ *For a few brief minutes we forgot our worries.* **5** N-PLURAL Men's or women's underpants can be referred to as **briefs**. □ *…a pair of briefs.* **6** V-T If someone **briefs** you, especially about a piece of work or a serious matter, they give you information that you need before you do it or consider it. □ *A Defense Department spokesman briefed reporters.* [from Old French] **7** → see also **briefing**

### Word Partnership    Use *brief* with :

| | |
|---|---|
| N. | brief **appearance**, brief **conversation**, brief **pause** **1** |
| | brief **description**, brief **explanation**, brief **history**, brief **speech**, brief **statement** **2** |

**brief|case** /ˈbriːfkeɪs/ (**briefcases**) N-COUNT A **briefcase** is a case used for carrying documents in.

**brief|ing** /ˈbriːfɪŋ/ (**briefings**) **1** N-VAR A **briefing** is a meeting at which information or instructions are given to people. □ *They're holding a press briefing tomorrow.* [from Old French] **2** → see also **brief**

**brief|ly** /ˈbriːfli/ **1** ADV Something that happens **briefly** happens for a very short period of time. □ *He smiled briefly.* **2** ADV If you say or write something **briefly**, you use very few words or give very few details. □ *There are lots of basic choices; they are described briefly below.* □ *Briefly, he believes that Europe should unite politically.* [from Old French]

**bri|gade** /brɪˈɡeɪd/ (**brigades**) N-COUNT A **brigade** is one of the groups which an army is divided into. □ *…the soldiers of the 173rd Airborne Brigade.* [from Old French]

**bright** /braɪt/ (**brights, brighter, brightest**) **1** ADJ A **bright** color is strong and noticeable, and not dark. □ *…a bright red dress.* ● **bright|ly** ADV □ *…a display of brightly colored flowers.* **2** ADJ A **bright** light, object, or place is shining strongly or is full of light. □ *…a bright October day.* ● **bright|ly** ADV □ *…a warm, brightly lit room.* ● **bright|ness** N-UNCOUNT □ *An astronomer can determine the brightness of each star.* **3** ADJ If you describe someone as **bright**, you mean that they are quick at learning things. □ *I was convinced that he was brighter than average.* **4** ADJ A **bright** idea is clever and original. □ *There are lots of books filled with bright ideas.* **5** ADJ If someone looks or sounds **bright**, they look or sound cheerful and lively. □ *Bamber spoke twice, sounding bright and eager.* ● **bright|ly** ADV □ *He smiled brightly as Ben approached.* **6** ADJ If the future is **bright**, it is likely to be pleasant or successful. □ *Both had successful careers and the future looked bright.* **7** N-PLURAL The **brights** on a vehicle are its headlights when they are set to shine their brightest. □ *…a Bronco with its brights on, parked in the middle of the street.* [from Old English]

**bright|en** /ˈbraɪtᵊn/ (**brightens, brightening, brightened**) **1** V-I If someone **brightens** or their face **brightens**, they suddenly look happier. □ *Seeing him, she seemed to brighten a little.* ● **Brighten**

**up** means the same as **brighten**. ❑ *He brightened up a bit when he saw the food.* **2** V-T If someone or something **brightens** a place, they make it more colorful and attractive. ❑ *Pots planted with flowers brightened the area outside the door.* ● **Brighten up** means the same as **brighten**. ❑ *She thought the pink lampshade would brighten up the room.* **3** V-T/V-I If someone or something **brightens** a situation or the situation **brightens**, it becomes more pleasant, enjoyable, or favorable. ❑ *This piece of news should brighten your day.* [from Old English]

**bril|liant** /brɪlyənt/ **1** ADJ A **brilliant** person, idea, or performance is extremely clever or skillful. ❑ *She had a brilliant mind.* ● **bril|liant|ly** ADV ❑ *It is a very high quality show, brilliantly written and acted.* ● **bril|liance** N-UNCOUNT ❑ *He is a serious musician who showed his brilliance very early.* **2** ADJ A **brilliant** career or success is very successful. ● **bril|liant|ly** ADV ❑ *The strategy worked brilliantly.* **3** ADJ A **brilliant** light or color is extremely bright. ❑ *The woman had brilliant green eyes.* ● **bril|liant|ly** ADV ❑ *Many of the patterns show brilliantly colored flowers.* ● **bril|liance** N-UNCOUNT ❑ *…a blue butterfly in all its brilliance.* [from French]

**brim** /brɪm/ (**brims**, **brimming**, **brimmed**) **1** N-COUNT The **brim** of a hat is the wide part that sticks outward at the bottom. ❑ *Rain dripped from the brim of his baseball cap.* **2** V-I If someone or something **is brimming with** something, they are full of it. ❑ *The team is brimming with confidence after two straight wins.* ❑ *Michael looked at her, his eyes brimming with tears.* [from Middle High German]

**bring** /brɪŋ/ (**brings**, **bringing**, **brought**) **1** V-T If you **bring** someone or something **with** you when you come to a place, they come with you or you have them with you. ❑ *Remember to bring an old shirt to protect your clothes.* ❑ *Someone went upstairs and brought down a huge box.* **2** V-T If you **bring** something somewhere, you move it there. ❑ *Reaching into her pocket, she brought out a dollar bill.* **3** V-T If you **bring** something that someone wants or needs, you get it for them or carry it to them. ❑ *He poured a glass of milk for Dena and brought it to her.* **4** V-T To **bring** something or someone to a place or position means to cause them to come to the place or move into that position. ❑ *I told you what brought me here.* ❑ *The shock of her husband's arrival brought her to her feet.* **5** V-T To **bring** someone or something into a particular state or condition means to cause them to be in that state or condition. ❑ *He brought the car to a stop in front of the store.* ❑ *They have brought down income taxes.* **6** V-T If something **brings** a particular feeling, situation, or quality, it makes people experience it or have it. ❑ *He called on the United States to play a role in bringing peace to the region.* ❑ *Her three children brought her much joy.* **7** V-T If you cannot **bring yourself to** do something, you cannot do it because you find it too upsetting, embarrassing, or disgusting. ❑ *It is all very sad and I just cannot bring myself to talk about it.* [from Old English]

▸ **bring about** PHR-VERB To **bring** something **about** means to cause it to happen. ❑ *They can bring about political change.*

▸ **bring along** PHR-VERB If you **bring** someone or something **along**, you bring them with you when you come to a place. ❑ *They brought baby Michael along in a carrier.*

▸ **bring back** **1** PHR-VERB Something that **brings**

**back** a memory makes you think about it. ❑ *Your article brought back sad memories for me.* **2** PHR-VERB When people **bring back** a practice or fashion that existed at an earlier time, they introduce it again. ❑ *We've brought back long skirts so it's easier to walk.*

▸ **bring down** PHR-VERB When people or events **bring down** a government or ruler, they cause the government or ruler to lose power. ❑ *They were threatening to bring down the government.*

▸ **bring forward** PHR-VERB If you **bring forward** a meeting or event, you arrange for it to take place at an earlier date or time than had been planned. ❑ *He had to bring forward an 11 o'clock meeting.*

▸ **bring in** **1** PHR-VERB When a government or organization **brings in** a new law or system, they introduce it. ❑ *The government brought in a law under which it could take any land it wanted.* **2** PHR-VERB Someone or something that **brings in** money makes it or earns it. ❑ *I have three part-time jobs, which bring in about $24,000 a year.*

▸ **bring out** **1** PHR-VERB When a person or company **brings out** a new product, especially a new book or CD, they produce it and put it on sale. ❑ *A journalist all his life, he's now brought out a book.* **2** PHR-VERB Something that **brings out** a particular kind of behavior or feeling in you causes you to show it, especially when it is something you do not normally show. ❑ *He brings out the best in his pupils.*

▸ **bring up** **1** PHR-VERB When someone **brings up** a child, they look after it until it is an adult. ❑ *She brought up four children on her own.* ❑ *He was brought up in Nebraska.* **2** PHR-VERB If you **bring up** a particular subject, you introduce it into a discussion or conversation. ❑ *Her mother brought up the subject of going back to work.*

| **Thesaurus** | bring | Also look up : |
|---|---|---|
| V. | accompany, bear, carry, take; (*ant.*) drop, leave **1** | |
| | move, take, transfer **2** | |

| **Word Partnership** | Use *bring* with : |
|---|---|
| N. | bring **bad/good luck**, bring *someone/ something* **home** **1** |
| | bring to *someone's* **attention**, bring **to a boil**, bring **to justice**, bring **to life**, bring **to mind**, bring **together** **5** |

**brink** /brɪŋk/ N-SING If you are **on the brink of** something important, terrible, or exciting, you are just about to do it or experience it. ❑ *Their economy is on the brink of collapse.* [from Middle Dutch]

**brisk** /brɪsk/ (**brisker**, **briskest**) **1** ADJ A **brisk** activity or action is done quickly and in an energetic way. ❑ *He put out his hand for a brisk, firm handshake.* ● **brisk|ly** ADV ❑ *Eve walked briskly down the hall to her son's room.* **2** ADJ If the weather is **brisk**, it is cold and fresh. ❑ *…a brisk winter's day on the south coast.* **3** ADJ Someone who is **brisk** behaves in a busy, confident way which shows that they want to get things done quickly. ❑ *The chief was brisk and businesslike.* ● **brisk|ly** ADV ❑ *"Anyhow," she added briskly, "it's none of my business."*

**bris|tle** /brɪsᵊl/ (**bristles**) **1** N-COUNT **Bristles** are the short hairs that grow on a man's face after he has shaved. The hairs on the top of a man's head can also be called **bristles** when they are cut very short. ❑ *...two days' growth of bristles.* **2** N-COUNT The **bristles** of a brush are the thick hairs attached to it. ❑ *As soon as the bristles on your toothbrush begin to wear, throw it out.* **3** N-COUNT **Bristles** are thick, strong animal or plant hairs that feel hard and rough. ❑ *The plant is covered with bristles that are uncomfortable to touch.* [from Old English]

**Brit|ish** /brɪtɪʃ/ **1** ADJ **British** means belonging or relating to the United Kingdom, or to its people or culture. **2** N-PLURAL **The British** are the people of Great Britain. [from Old English]

**Brit|on** /brɪtᵊn/ (**Britons**) N-COUNT A **Briton** is a British citizen, or a person of British origin. [FORMAL] ❑ *The role of the daughter is played by seventeen-year-old Briton Jane March.* [from Old French]

**brit|tle** /brɪtᵊl/ ADJ An object or substance that is **brittle** is hard but easily broken. ❑ *...a treatment for brittle nails.* [from Old English]

**bro** /broʊ/ (**bros**) **1** N-VOC Some men use **bro** as a friendly way of addressing other men when they are talking to them. [INFORMAL] ❑ *What do you mean, bro?* **2** N-COUNT **Bro** is the same as **brother**. [INFORMAL] ❑ *Bryant said his bro did a great job.* [from Afrikaans]

**broach** /broʊtʃ/ (**broaches, broaching, broached**) V-T When you **broach** a subject, you mention it in order to start a discussion on it. ❑ *Eventually I broached the subject of her early life.* [from Old French]

**broad** /brɔd/ (**broader, broadest**) **1** ADJ Something that is **broad** is wide. ❑ *His shoulders were broad and his waist narrow.* ❑ *...the broad river.* **2** ADJ A **broad** smile is one in which your mouth is stretched very wide. ❑ *He greeted them with a wave and a broad smile.* ● **broad|ly** ADV ❑ *Charles grinned broadly.* **3** ADJ You use **broad** to describe something that includes a large number of different things or people. ❑ *A broad range of issues was discussed.* ● **broad|ly** ADV ❑ *It's a broadly-based group of people.* **4** ADJ You use **broad** to describe a word or meaning which covers or refers to a wide range of different things. ❑ *A theater director is, in the broad sense of the word, an artist.* ● **broad|ly** ADV ❑ *The authors define leadership broadly to include political figures and even parents.* **5** ADJ You use **broad** to describe a feeling or opinion that is shared by many people, or by people of many different kinds. ❑ *The agreement won broad support in the U.S. Congress.* ● **broad|ly** ADV ❑ *The law has been broadly welcomed.* [from Old English] **6** → see also **broadly**

---

**Word Partnership** Use *broad* with :

N.  broad **expanse**, broad **shoulders** **1**
    broad **smile** **2**
    broad **range**, broad **spectrum** **3**
    broad **definition**, broad **strokes**, broad
    **view** **4**

---

**broad|band** /brɔdbænd/ N-UNCOUNT **Broadband** is a method of sending many electronic messages at the same time by using a wide range of frequencies. [COMPUTING] ❑ *The telecommunications company announced big price cuts for broadband customers.*

**broad|cast** /brɔdkæst/ (**broadcasts, broadcasting**)

> The form **broadcast** is used in the present tense and is the past tense and past participle of the verb.

**1** N-COUNT A **broadcast** is a program, performance, or speech on the radio or on television. ❑ *...a live television broadcast of Saturday's game.* **2** V-T/V-I To **broadcast** a program means to send it out by radio waves, wires, or satellites so that it can be heard on the radio or seen on television. ❑ *The concert will be broadcast live on television and radio.* ❑ *CNN also broadcasts in Europe.* ● **broad|cast|ing** N-UNCOUNT ❑ *...religious broadcasting.*

**broad|cast|er** /brɔdkæstər/ (**broadcasters**) N-COUNT A **broadcaster** is someone who gives talks or takes part in interviews and discussions on radio or television programs. ❑ *...the naturalist and broadcaster, Sir David Attenborough.*

**broad|en** /brɔdᵊn/ (**broadens, broadening, broadened**) **1** V-I When something **broadens**, it becomes wider. ❑ *The trails broadened into roads.* **2** V-T/V-I When you **broaden** something or when it **broadens**, the number of things or people that it includes becomes greater. ❑ *We must broaden our appeal.* ❑ *Gradually the fair has broadened to include big London dealers.* [from Old English]

**broad|ly** /brɔdli/ **1** ADV You can use **broadly** to indicate that something is generally true. ❑ *The president broadly got what he wanted out of his meeting.* [from Old English] **2** → see also **broad**

**broad-minded** also **broadminded** ADJ If you describe someone as **broad-minded**, you approve of them because they are willing to accept types of behavior that other people consider immoral. ❑ *...a fair and broad-minded man.*

**broc|co|li** /brɒkəli, brɒkli/ N-UNCOUNT **Broccoli** is a vegetable with green stalks and green or purple tops. [from Italian]
→ see **vegetable**

**bro|chure** /broʊʃʊər/ (**brochures**) N-COUNT A **brochure** is a thin magazine with pictures that gives you information about a product or service. ❑ *...travel brochures.* [from French]

**broil** /brɔɪl/ (**broils, broiling, broiled**) V-T When you **broil** food, you cook it using very strong heat directly above it. ❑ *I'll broil the lobster.* [from Old French]

**broil|er** /brɔɪlər/ (**broilers**) N-COUNT A **broiler** is a part of a stove which produces strong heat and cooks food placed underneath it. [from Old French]

**broke** /broʊk/ **1** **Broke** is the past tense of **break**. **2** ADJ If you are **broke**, you have no money. [INFORMAL] ❑ *I'm as broke as you are.* **3** PHRASE If a company or person **goes broke**, they lose money and are unable to continue in business or to pay their debts. [INFORMAL] ❑ *Balton went broke twice in his career.* [from Old English]

---

**Thesaurus**    *broke*    Also look up :

ADJ.  bankrupt, destitute, impoverished, penniless, poor; (ant.) rich, wealthy, well-to-do **2**

---

**bro|ken** /broʊkən/ **1** **Broken** is the past

participle of **break**. ◳ ADJ A **broken** line is not continuous but has gaps or spaces in it. ❑ *...a broken blue line.* ◳ ADJ You can use **broken** to describe a marriage that has ended in divorce, or a home in which the parents of the family are divorced, when you think this is a sad thing. ❑ *...the pain of a broken marriage.* ◳ ADJ If someone talks in **broken** English, for example, or in **broken** French, they speak slowly and make a lot of mistakes because they do not know the language very well. ❑ *Eric could only respond in broken English.* [from Old English]

**bro|ker** /br<u>oʊ</u>kər/ (**brokers, brokering, brokered**) ◳ N-COUNT A **broker** is a person whose job is to buy and sell securities, foreign money, real estate, or goods for other people. [BUSINESS] ◳ V-T If a country or government **brokers** an agreement, a ceasefire, or a round of talks, they try to negotiate or arrange it. ❑ *The United Nations brokered a peace agreement at the end of March.* [from Old Northern French]

**bron|chi** /br<u>ɒ</u>ŋki, -kaɪ/ N-PLURAL The **bronchi** are the two large tubes in your body that connect your windpipe to your lungs. [TECHNICAL] [from New Latin]

**Bronx cheer** /br<u>ɒ</u>ŋks tʃ<u>ɪə</u>r/ (**Bronx cheers**) N-COUNT A **Bronx cheer** is a sound that people make by vibrating their lips in order to express disapproval or contempt. [INFORMAL]

**bronze** /br<u>ɒ</u>nz/ ◳ N-UNCOUNT **Bronze** is a yellowish-brown metal which is a mixture of copper and tin. ❑ *...a bronze statue of Giorgi Dimitrov.* ◳ COLOR Something that is **bronze** is yellowish-brown in color. ❑ *Her hair shone bronze and gold.* [from French]

**bronze med|al** (**bronze medals**) N-COUNT A **bronze medal** is a medal made of bronze or bronze-colored metal that is given as a prize to the person who comes third in a competition, especially a sports contest.

**brooch** /br<u>oʊ</u>tʃ/ (**brooches**) N-COUNT A **brooch** is a piece of jewelry that has a pin at the back so it can be fastened on a dress, blouse, or coat. [from Old French]
→ see **jewelry**

**brood** /br<u>u</u>d/ (**broods, brooding, brooded**) ◳ N-COUNT A **brood** is a group of baby birds that were born at the same time to the same mother. ❑ *...a brood of 14 ducklings.* ◳ N-COUNT You can refer to someone's young children as their **brood** when you want to emphasize that there are a lot of them. ❑ *...a large brood of children.* ◳ V-I If someone **broods** over something, they think about it a lot, seriously and often unhappily. ❑ *She constantly broods about her family.* [from Old English]

**brood|ing** /br<u>u</u>dɪŋ/ (**broodings**) ◳ ADJ **Brooding** is used to describe an atmosphere or feeling that makes you feel anxious or slightly afraid. [LITERARY] ❑ *...a heavy, brooding silence.* ◳ N-COUNT **Brooding** is the process by which birds help their eggs to hatch by sitting on them. [TECHNICAL] [from Old English]

**brook** /br<u>ʊ</u>k/ (**brooks**) N-COUNT A **brook** is a small stream. [from Old English]

**broom** /br<u>u</u>m/ (**brooms**) N-COUNT A **broom** is a kind of brush with a long handle. You use a broom for sweeping the floor. [from Old English]

**broth** /br<u>ɒ</u>θ/ (**broths**) N-VAR **Broth** is a kind of soup made by boiling meat or vegetables. [from Old English]

**broth|el** /br<u>ɒ</u>θ<sup>ə</sup>l/ (**brothels**) N-COUNT A **brothel** is a building where men pay to have sex with prostitutes. [from Old English]

**broth|er** /br<u>ʌ</u>ðər/ (**brothers**) ◳ N-COUNT Your **brother** is a boy or a man who has the same parents as you. ❑ *Oh, so you're Peter's younger brother.* ❑ *My brother is living in Europe.* ◳ N-COUNT You can describe a man as your **brother** if he belongs to the same race, religion, country, or profession as you, or if he has similar ideas to you. ❑ *He told reporters he'd come to be with his Latvian brothers.* ◳ N-TITLE; N-COUNT; N-VOC **Brother** is a title given to a man who belongs to a religious community such as a monastery. ❑ *...Brother Otto.* [from Old English]
→ see **family**

**broth|er|hood** /br<u>ʌ</u>ðərhʊd/ (**brotherhoods**) ◳ N-UNCOUNT **Brotherhood** is the affection and loyalty that you feel for people who you have something in common with. ❑ *...spreading the message of peace, love and brotherhood among all people.* ◳ N-COUNT A **brotherhood** is an organization whose members all have the same political aims and beliefs or the same job or profession. ❑ *...the International Brotherhood of Electrical Workers.* [from Old English]

**brother-in-law** (**brothers-in-law**) N-COUNT Someone's **brother-in-law** is the brother of their husband or wife, or the man who is married to their sister.
→ see **family**

**brought** /br<u>ɔ</u>t/ **Brought** is the past tense and past participle of **bring**. [from Old English]

**brow** /br<u>aʊ</u>/ (**brows**) ◳ N-COUNT Your **brow** is your forehead. ❑ *He wiped his brow with the back of his hand.* ◳ N-COUNT Your **brows** are your eyebrows. ❑ *...his thick dark brows.* ◳ N-COUNT The **brow of** a hill is the top part of it. ❑ *A helicopter came over the brow of the hill.* [from Old English]

**brown** /br<u>aʊ</u>n/ (**browner, brownest, browns, browning, browned**) ◳ COLOR Something that is **brown** is the color of earth or of wood. ❑ *...her brown eyes.* ◳ ADJ **Brown** is used to describe grains that have not had their outer layers removed, and foods made from these grains. ❑ *...brown bread.* ❑ *...brown rice.* ◳ V-T/V-I When food **browns** or when you **brown** it, you cook it, usually for a short time on a high flame. ❑ *Cook for ten minutes until the sugar browns.* [from Old English]
→ see **hair**

**brown-bag** (**brown-bags, brown-bagging, brown-bagged**) ◳ V-T If you **brown-bag** your lunch or you **brown-bag it**, you bring your lunch in a bag to work or school. ❑ *Most of the time I brown-bagged my lunch.* ◳ ADJ A **brown-bag** lunch is a meal that you bring in a bag to work or school. ❑ *Members should bring a brown-bag lunch.*

**brown sugar** N-UNCOUNT **Brown sugar** is sugar that has not been refined, or is only partly refined. It is golden brown in color.

**browse** /br<u>aʊ</u>z/ (**browses, browsing, browsed**) ◳ V-I If you **browse** in a store, you look at things in a casual way, in the hope that you might find something you like. ❑ *I stopped in several bookstores to browse.* ❑ *She browsed in an antiques shop.* ● **Browse** is also a noun. ❑ *...a browse around the gift shop.*

**browse** V-I If you **browse through** a book or magazine, you look through it in a casual way. ❑ *...sitting on the sofa browsing through the TV magazine.* ◪ V-T/ V-I If you **browse** the Internet or **browse** on a computer, you search for information in computer files or on the Internet, especially on the World Wide Web. [COMPUTING] ❑ *...an Internet café where they can browse during their free time.* [from French]

**brows|er** /braʊzər/ (**browsers**) N-COUNT A **browser** is a piece of computer software that you use to search for information on the Internet, especially on the World Wide Web. [COMPUTING] ❑ *You need an up-to-date Web browser.* [from French]

**bruise** /bruːz/ (**bruises, bruising, bruised**)
◪ N-COUNT A **bruise** is an injury that appears as a purple mark on your body. ❑ *How did you get that bruise on your cheek?* ◪ V-T/V-I If you **bruise** a part of your body, a bruise appears on it, for example, because something hits you. If you **bruise** easily, bruises appear when something hits you only slightly. ❑ *I bruised my knee.* ● **bruised** ADJ ❑ *I escaped with severely bruised legs.* [from Old English]

**brunt** /brʌnt/ PHRASE To **bear the brunt** or **take the brunt** of something unpleasant means to suffer the main part or force of it. ❑ *Areas south of Miami bore the brunt of the storm.*

**brush** /brʌʃ/ (**brushes, brushing, brushed**)
◪ N-COUNT A **brush** is an object that has a large number of bristles or hairs fixed to it. You use brushes for painting, for cleaning things, and for making your hair neat. ❑ *We gave him paint and brushes.* ❑ *...buckets of soapy water and scrubbing brushes.* ◪ V-T If you **brush** something or **brush** something such as dirt off it, you clean it or make it neat using a brush. ❑ *Have you brushed your teeth?* ❑ *She brushed the powder out of her hair.* ● **Brush** is also a noun. ❑ *I gave my hair a quick brush.* ◪ V-T If you **brush** something somewhere, you remove it with quick light movements of your hands. ❑ *He brushed his hair back with both hands.* ❑ *He brushed the snow off his suit.* ◪ V-T/V-I If one thing **brushes against** another or if you **brush** one thing **against** another, the first thing touches the second thing lightly while passing it. ❑ *Something brushed against her leg.* ❑ *I felt her dark hair brushing the back of my shoulder.* [from Old French]
→ see **teeth**
▸ **brush aside** or **brush away** PHR-VERB If you **brush aside** or **brush away** an idea, remark, or feeling, you refuse to consider it because you think it is not important or useful, even though it may be. ❑ *Perhaps you shouldn't brush the idea aside.*
▸ **brush up** or **brush up on** PHR-VERB If you **brush up** something, you practice it or improve your knowledge of it. ❑ *I had hoped to brush up on my Spanish.*

**brusque** /brʌsk/ ADJ If you describe a person or their behavior as **brusque**, you mean that they deal with people quickly and shortly, so that they seem to be rude. ❑ *The doctors are brusque and busy.* [from French]

**brus|sels sprout** /brʌsəlz spraʊt/ (**brussels sprouts**) also **Brussels sprout** N-COUNT **Brussels sprouts** are vegetables that look like tiny cabbages.

**bru|tal** /bruːtᵊl/ ◪ ADJ A **brutal** act or person is cruel and violent. ❑ *...brutal punishment.* ● **bru|tal|ly** ADV ❑ *Her parents were brutally murdered.* ◪ ADJ If someone expresses something unpleasant with **brutal** honesty or frankness, they express it in a clear and accurate way, without attempting to disguise its unpleasantness. ❑ *It was good to talk about our feelings with brutal honesty.* ● **bru|tal|ly** ADV ❑ *The talks have been brutally frank.* [from Latin]

**bru|tal|ity** /bruːtæləti/ (**brutalities**) N-VAR **Brutality** is cruel and violent treatment or behavior. A **brutality** is an instance of cruel and violent treatment or behavior. ❑ *...police brutality.* ❑ *Memories of wartime brutalities remain vivid in their minds.* [from Latin]

**brute** /bruːt/ (**brutes**) N-COUNT If you call someone, usually a man, a **brute**, you mean that they are rough, violent, and insensitive. ❑ *He was an idiot and a brute and he deserved his fate.* [from Latin]

**BSE** /bi ɛs i/ N-UNCOUNT **BSE** is a disease that affects the nervous system of cattle and kills them. **BSE** is an abbreviation for "bovine spongiform encephalopathy." ❑ *...meat from cattle infected with BSE, or mad cow disease.*

**BTW** **BTW** is the written abbreviation for "by the way," often used in e-mail. ❑ *BTW, the machine is simply amazing.*

**bub|ble** /bʌbᵊl/ (**bubbles, bubbling, bubbled**)
◪ N-COUNT **Bubbles** are small balls of air or gas in a liquid. ❑ *Air bubbles rise to the surface.* ◪ N-COUNT A **bubble** is a hollow ball of soapy liquid that is floating in the air or standing on a surface. ❑ *With soap and water, bubbles and boats, children love bathtime.* ◪ V-I When a liquid **bubbles**, bubbles move in it, for example, because it is boiling or moving quickly. ❑ *Heat the soup until it is bubbling.* ❑ *...the well where oil first bubbled up in Nigeria 43 years ago.* [of Scandinavian origin]
→ see **soap**

**bub|bly** /bʌbli/ ◪ ADJ Someone who is **bubbly** is very lively and cheerful and talks a lot; used to show approval. ❑ *...a bubbly girl who loves to laugh.* ◪ ADJ If something is **bubbly**, it has a lot of bubbles in it. ❑ *When the butter is melted and bubbly, put in the flour.* [of Scandinavian origin]

**buck** /bʌk/ (**bucks, bucking, bucked**)
◪ N-COUNT A **buck** is a U.S. or Australian dollar. [INFORMAL] ❑ *That would probably cost you about fifty bucks.* ❑ *Why can't you spend a few bucks on a coat?* ◪ N-COUNT A **buck** is the male of various animals, including the deer, antelope, rabbit, and kangaroo. ◪ V-I If a horse **bucks**, it kicks both of its back legs wildly into the air, or jumps into the air wildly with all four feet off the ground. ❑ *The stallion bucked and kicked.* ◪ PHRASE If you **pass the buck**, you refuse to accept responsibility for something, and say that someone else is responsible. [INFORMAL] ❑ *They are trying to pass the buck and blame teachers.* [from Old English]

**buck|et** /bʌkɪt/ (**buckets**) N-COUNT A **bucket** is a round metal or plastic container with a handle attached to its sides. Buckets are often used for holding and carrying water. ❑ *...a blue bucket.* ❑ *...a bucket of water.* [from Old English]

**buck|le** /bʌkᵊl/ (**buckles, buckling, buckled**)
◪ N-COUNT A **buckle** is a piece of metal or plastic attached to one end of a belt or strap, which is used to fasten it. ❑ *He wore a belt with a large silver buckle.* ◪ V-T When you **buckle** a belt or strap, you fasten it. ❑ *A door slammed and a man came out buckling his belt.* ◪ V-T/V-I If an object **buckles** or if something

B

buckles it, it becomes bent as a result of very great heat or force. ◻ *The door was beginning to buckle from the extreme heat.* ◢◢ V-I If your legs or knees **buckle**, they bend because they have become very weak or tired. ◻ *His knees buckled and he fell to the floor.* [from Old French]

→ see **button, crash**

▶ **buckle up** PHR-VERB When you **buckle up** in a car or airplane, you fasten your seat belt. [INFORMAL] ◻ *A sign ahead of me said, "Buckle Up. It's the Law in Illinois."*

**bud** /bʌd/ (buds) ◼ N-COUNT A **bud** is a small pointed lump that appears on a tree or plant and develops into a leaf or flower. ◻ *Rosanna's favorite time is early summer, just before the buds open.* ◢ N-VOC Some men use **bud** as a way of addressing other men. [INFORMAL] ◻ *You heard what the boss said, bud.* ◢ → see also **budding** ◢ PHRASE If you **nip** something such as bad behavior **in the bud**, you stop it before it can develop very far. [INFORMAL] ◻ *It is important to recognize jealousy and to nip it in the bud.* [from Middle English]

→ see **flower, taste**

**Bud|dhism** N-UNCOUNT Buddhism is a religion which teaches that the way to end suffering is by overcoming your desires. [from Sanskrit]

**Bud|dhist** /bʊdɪst, bʊd-/ (Buddhists) ◼ N-COUNT A **Buddhist** is a person whose religion is Buddhism. ◢ ADJ **Buddhist** means relating or referring to Buddhism. ◻ *...Buddhist monks.* [from Sanskrit]

**bud|ding** /bʌdɪŋ/ ◼ ADJ If you describe someone as, for example, a **budding** businessman or a **budding** artist, you mean that they are starting to succeed or become interested in business or art. ◻ *...budding writers.* ◢ ADJ You use **budding** to describe a situation that is just beginning. ◻ *Our budding romance was over.* ◢ N-UNCOUNT **Budding** is a type of reproductive process in which a new cell or organism grows on the surface of its parent's body and then separates from it. [TECHNICAL] [from Germanic]

**bud|dy** /bʌdi/ (buddies) ◼ N-COUNT A **buddy** is a close friend, usually a male friend of a man. ◻ *We became great buddies.* ◢ N-VOC Men sometimes address other men as **buddy**. [INFORMAL] ◻ *Hey, buddy, do me a favor.* ◢ PHRASE If one person is **buddy buddy with** another, they are very close friends. [INFORMAL]

**budge** /bʌdʒ/ (budges, budging, budged) ◼ V-T/V-I If someone will not **budge** on a matter, or if nothing **budges** them, they refuse to change their mind or to come to an agreement. ◻ *The Americans will not budge on this point.* ◢ V-T/V-I If someone or something will not **budge**, they will not move. If you cannot **budge** them, you cannot make them move. ◻ *Her mother refused to budge from Omaha.* ◻ *The window wouldn't budge.* [from Old French]

**budg|et** /bʌdʒɪt/ (budgets, budgeting, budgeted) ◼ N-COUNT Your **budget** is the amount of money that you have available to spend. The **budget** for something is the amount of money that a person, organization, or country has available to spend on it. [BUSINESS] ◻ *She will design a fantastic new kitchen for you — and all within your budget.* ◻ *Our low budget means we have to be careful with our money.* ◢ V-T/V-I If you **budget**

certain amounts of money for particular things, you decide that you can afford to spend those amounts on those things. ◻ *The company has budgeted $10 million for advertising.* ◻ *The movie is only budgeted at $10 million.* ◻ *I'm learning how to budget.* ● **budg|et|ing** N-UNCOUNT ◻ *...our budgeting for the current year.* ◢ ADJ **Budget** is used in advertising to suggest that something is being sold cheaply. ◻ *Cheap flights are available from budget travel agents.* [from Old French]

**buff** /bʌf/ (buffs) ◼ COLOR Something that is **buff** is pale brown in color. ◻ *He took a buff envelope from his pocket.* ◢ N-COUNT You use **buff** to describe someone who knows a lot about a particular subject. For example, if you describe someone as a movie **buff**, you mean that they know a lot about movies. [INFORMAL] ◻ *Henry is a real movie buff.* [from Old French]

**buf|fa|lo** /bʌfəloʊ/ (buffalo)

The plural can be either **buffaloes** or **buffalo**.

N-COUNT A **buffalo** is a wild animal like a large cow with horns that curve upward. [from Italian]

→ see **grassland**

buffalo

**buff|er** /bʌfər/ (buffers) ◼ N-COUNT A **buffer** is something that prevents something else from being harmed or that prevents two things from harming each other. ◻ *Keep savings as a buffer against unexpected cash needs.* ◢ N-COUNT A **buffer** is an area in a computer's memory where information can be stored for a short time. [COMPUTING] [from Old French]

**buf|fet** (buffets, buffeting, buffeted)

Pronounced /bʊfeɪ/ for meaning ◼ and /bʌfɪt/ for meaning ◢.

◼ N-COUNT A **buffet** is a meal of food that is displayed on a long table at a party or public occasion. Guests usually serve themselves. ◻ *...a buffet lunch.* ◢ V-T If something **is buffeted** by strong winds or by stormy seas, it is repeatedly struck or blown around by them. ◻ *Their plane was severely buffeted by storms.* [from Old French]

**bug** /bʌg/ (bugs, bugging, bugged) ◼ N-COUNT A **bug** is an insect or similar small creature. [INFORMAL] ◻ *We noticed tiny bugs that were all over the walls.* ◢ N-COUNT A **bug** is an illness which is caused by small organisms such as bacteria. [INFORMAL] ◻ *I think I've got a stomach bug.* ◢ N-COUNT If there is a **bug** in a computer program, there is a mistake in it. [COMPUTING] ◻ *There is a bug in the software.* ◢ V-T If someone **bugs** a place, they hide tiny microphones in it that transmit what people are saying. ◻ *He heard that they were planning to bug his office.* ◢ V-T If someone or something **bugs** you, they worry or annoy you.

[INFORMAL] ❏ *I only did it to bug my parents.*

| **Thesaurus** | *bug* | Also look up : |
| --- | --- | --- |

N.   disease, germ, infection, microorganism, virus **2**
     breakdown, defect, error, glitch, hitch, malfunction **3**

**build** /bɪld/ (**builds, building, built**) **1** V-T If you **build** something, you make it by joining things together. ❏ *They are going to build a hotel on the site.* ❏ *The house was built in the early 19th century.* ● **build|ing** N-UNCOUNT ❏ *In Japan, the building of Kansai airport continues.* ● **built** ADJ ❏ *Even newly built houses can need repairs.* ❏ *It's a product that has been built for safety.* **2** V-T If you **build** something **into** a wall or object, you make it in such a way that it is in the wall or object, or is part of it. ❏ *The TV was built into the wall.* **3** V-T If people **build** an organization, a society, or a relationship, they gradually form it. ❏ *He and a partner built a successful fashion company.* ❏ *Their purpose is to build a fair society and a strong economy.* ● **build|ing** N-UNCOUNT ❏ *...the building of the great civilizations of the ancient world.* **4** V-T If you **build** an organization, system, or product **on** something, you base it on it. ❏ *Science involves building theories from logical processes.* **5** V-T If you **build** something **into** a policy, system, or product, you make it part of it. ❏ *We have to build computers into the school curriculum.* **6** N-VAR Someone's **build** is the shape that their bones and muscles give to their body. ❏ *He's described as six feet tall and of medium build.* [from Old English] **7** → see also **building, built**
→ see **muscle**

▶ **build up** **1** PHR-VERB If you **build up** something or if it **builds up**, it gradually becomes bigger, for example, because more is added to it. ❏ *I worked really hard building up the business.* ❏ *The collection has been built up over the last seventeen years.* **2** PHR-VERB If you **build** someone **up**, you help them to feel stronger or more confident, especially when they have had a bad experience or have been ill. ❏ *Build her up with kindness.* **3** → see also **build-up, built-up**

| **Thesaurus** | *build* | Also look up : |
| --- | --- | --- |

V.   assemble, make, manufacture, produce, put together, set up; (*ant.*) demolish, destroy, knock down **1**

| **Word Partnership** | Use *build* with : |
| --- | --- |

N.   build **bridges**, build **roads**, build **schools** **1**
V.   **plan to** build **1**
ADJ.   **athletic** build, **slender** build, **strong** build **6**

**build|er** /bɪldər/ (**builders**) N-COUNT A **builder** is a person whose job is to build or repair houses and other buildings. ❏ *The builders have finished the roof.* [from Old English]

**build|ing** /bɪldɪŋ/ (**buildings**) N-COUNT A **building** is a structure that has a roof and walls. ❏ *They were on the upper floor of the building.* [from Old English]
→ see **architecture**

**build-up** (**build-ups**) also buildup, build up **1** N-COUNT A **build-up** is a gradual increase in

something. ❏ *There will be a slight build-up of cloud later on this afternoon.* **2** N-COUNT The **build-up** to an event is the way that journalists, advertisers, or other people talk about it a lot in the period of time immediately before it, and try to make it seem important and exciting. ❏ *...the excitement of the build-up to Christmas.*

**built** /bɪlt/ **1** **Built** is the past tense and past participle of **build**. **2** ADJ If you say that someone is **built** in a particular way, you are describing the kind of body they have. ❏ *...a strong, powerfully-built man of 60.* ❏ *He wasn't very well built.* [from Old English]

**built-in** ADJ **Built-in** devices or features are included in something as a part of it, rather than being separate. ❏ *...a computer with a built-in camera.*

**built-up** ADJ A **built-up** area is an area such as a town or city which has a lot of buildings in it. ❏ *A speed limit of 30 mph was introduced in built-up areas.*

**bulb** /bʌlb/ (**bulbs**) **1** N-COUNT A **bulb** is the glass part of an electric light or lamp, which gives out light when electricity passes through it. ❏ *The room was lit by a single bulb.* **2** N-COUNT A **bulb** is a root shaped like an onion that grows into a flower or plant. ❏ *...tulip bulbs.* [from Latin]
→ see **flower**

**bulge** /bʌldʒ/ (**bulges, bulging, bulged**) **1** V-I If something **bulges**, it sticks out. ❏ *His eyes were bulging with terror.* ❏ *He bulges out of his black T-shirt.* **2** V-I If something **is bulging** with things, it is full of them. ❏ *They returned home, the car bulging with boxes.* **3** N-COUNT **Bulges** are lumps that stick out from a surface which is otherwise flat or smooth. ❏ *Why won't those bulges on your hips and thighs go?* [from Old French]

**bu|limia** /bulɪmiə, -lɪm-/ N-UNCOUNT **Bulimia** or **bulimia nervosa** is an illness in which a person has a very great fear of becoming fat, and so they make themselves vomit after eating. ● **bu|limic** /bulɪmɪk, -lɪm-/ ADJ ❏ *...bulimic patients.* [from New Latin]

**bulk** /bʌlk/ (**bulks, bulking, bulked**) **1** N-SING You can refer to the **bulk** of a person or thing when you want to emphasize that they are very large and heavy. [WRITTEN] ❏ *Despite its bulk, it's a beautiful bike.* ❏ *Bannol lowered his bulk carefully into the chair.* **2** QUANT The **bulk of** something is most of it. ❏ *The bulk of the money will go to the children's hospital in Dublin.* ● **Bulk** is also a pronoun. ❏ *They come from all over the world, but the bulk is from India.* **3** PHRASE If you buy or sell something **in bulk**, you buy or sell it in large quantities. ❏ *It is cheaper to buy supplies in bulk.* [from Old Norse]

**bulky** /bʌlki/ (**bulkier, bulkiest**) ADJ Something that is **bulky** is large and heavy. ❏ *...bulky items like lawn mowers.* [from Old Norse]

**bull** /bʊl/ (**bulls**) **1** N-COUNT A **bull** is a male animal of the cow family. **2** N-COUNT Some other male animals, including elephants and whales, are called **bulls**. ❏ *...a bull elephant with huge tusks.* [from Old English]

**bull|dog** /bʊldɔg/ (**bulldogs**) N-COUNT A **bulldog** is a small dog with a large square head and short hair.

**bull|doze** /bʊldoʊz/ (**bulldozes, bulldozing, bulldozed**) V-T If people **bulldoze** something such as a building, they knock it down using a bulldozer. ❑ *They wanted to bulldoze her home to build a supermarket.*

**bull|doz|er** /bʊ̱ldoʊzər/ (**bulldozers**) N-COUNT A **bulldozer** is a large vehicle with a broad metal blade at the front, which is used for knocking down buildings or moving large amounts of earth.

**bul|let** /bʊ̱lɪt/ (**bullets**) N-COUNT A **bullet** is a small piece of metal which is fired out of a gun. ❑ *Two of the police fired 16 bullets each.* [from French]

**bul|letin** /bʊ̱lɪtɪn/ (**bulletins**) ■ N-COUNT A **bulletin** is a short news report on the radio or television. ❑ *...the early morning news bulletin.* ◪ N-COUNT A **bulletin** is a regular newspaper or leaflet that is produced by an organization or group such as a school or church. [from French]

**bul|letin board** (**bulletin boards**) ■ N-COUNT A **bulletin board** is a board which is usually attached to a wall in order to display notices giving information about something. ◪ N-COUNT In computing, a **bulletin board** is a system that allows users to send and receive messages of general interest. ❑ *The Internet is the largest computer bulletin board in the world, and it's growing.*

**bul|let point** (**bullet points**) N-COUNT A **bullet point** is one of a series of important items for discussion or action in a document, usually marked by a square or round symbol. ❑ *Use bold type for headings and bullet points for lists.*

**bullet|proof** /bʊ̱lɪtpruf/ also **bullet-proof** ADJ Something that is **bulletproof** is made of a strong material that bullets cannot pass through. ❑ *...bulletproof glass.*
→ see **glass**

**bull|horn** /bʊ̱lhɔrn/ (**bullhorns**) N-COUNT A **bullhorn** is a device for making your voice sound louder in the open air.

**bul|lion** /bʊ̱lyən/ N-UNCOUNT **Bullion** is gold or silver, usually in the form of bars. ❑ *Traders expect the gold bullion price to rise over the next few days.* [from Old French]

**bull|ock** /bʊ̱lək/ (**bullocks**) N-COUNT A **bullock** is a young bull that has been castrated. [from Old English]

**bull|pen** /bʊ̱lpɛn/ (**bullpens**) N-COUNT In baseball, a **bullpen** is an area alongside the playing field, where pitchers can practice or warm up. ❑ *Players from both bullpens ran onto the field.*

**bull ses|sion** (**bull sessions**) N-COUNT A **bull session** is an informal conversation among a small group of people. [INFORMAL] ❑ *The production actually started as an after-work bull session at a restaurant.*

**bul|ly** /bʊ̱li/ (**bullies, bullying, bullied**) ■ N-COUNT A **bully** is someone who uses their strength or power to hurt or frighten other people. ❑ *He was the office bully.* ◪ V-T If someone **bullies** you, they use their strength or power to hurt or frighten you. ❑ *I wasn't going to let him bully me.* ● **bul|ly|ing** N-UNCOUNT ❑ *...schoolchildren who were victims of bullying.* ◪ V-T If someone **bullies** you **into** something, they make you do it by using force or threats. ❑ *Mary bullies me into a stroll every day.* ❑ *She used to bully me into doing my schoolwork.* [from Middle Dutch]

**bump** /bʌ̱mp/ (**bumps, bumping, bumped**) ■ V-T/V-I If you **bump into** something or someone, you accidentally hit them while you

are moving. ❑ *They stopped walking and he almost bumped into them.* ❑ *She bumped her head against a low branch.* ● **Bump** is also a noun. ❑ *Small children often cry after a minor bump.* ◪ N-COUNT A **bump** is a minor injury or swelling that you get if you bump into something or if something hits you. ❑ *She fell against our coffee table and got a large bump on her forehead.* ◖ V-I If a vehicle **bumps over** a surface, it travels in a rough, bouncing way because the surface is very uneven. ❑ *We left the road, and again bumped over the mountainside.*
▸ **bump into** PHR-VERB If you **bump into** someone you know, you meet them unexpectedly. [INFORMAL] ❑ *I happened to bump into Mervyn Johns in the hallway.*

**bump|er** /bʌ̱mpər/ (**bumpers**) ■ N-COUNT **Bumpers** are bars at the front and back of a vehicle that protect it if it bumps into something. ❑ *What stickers do you have on the bumper?* ◪ ADJ A **bumper** crop or harvest is one that is larger than usual. ❑ *...a bumper crop of rice.*

**bumpy** /bʌ̱mpi/ (**bumpier, bumpiest**) ■ ADJ A **bumpy** road or path has a lot of bumps on it. ❑ *...bumpy streets.* ◪ ADJ A **bumpy** ride is uncomfortable and rough, usually because you are traveling over an uneven surface. ❑ *...a hot and bumpy ride across the desert.*

**bun** /bʌ̱n/ (**buns**) ■ N-COUNT **Buns** are small bread rolls. ❑ *...a cinnamon bun.* ◪ N-COUNT If a woman has her hair in a **bun**, she has fastened it tightly on top of her head or at the back of her head in the shape of a ball.
→ see **bread**

**bunch** /bʌ̱ntʃ/ (**bunches, bunching, bunched**) ■ N-COUNT A **bunch of** people is a group of people who share one or more characteristics or who are doing something together. [INFORMAL] ❑ *We were a pretty inexperienced bunch of people really.* ❑ *Before she graduated, she and a bunch of friends started the Actors Company.* ◪ N-COUNT A **bunch of** flowers is a number of flowers with their stalks held or tied together. ❑ *He left a huge bunch of flowers in her hotel room.* ◖ N-COUNT A **bunch of** bananas or grapes is a group of them growing on the same stem. ◗ QUANT A **bunch of** things is a number of things, especially a large number. [INFORMAL] ❑ *We recorded a bunch of songs together.* ● **Bunch** is also a pronoun.
▸ **bunch up** or **bunch together** PHR-VERB If people or things **bunch up** or if you **bunch** them **up**, they move close to each other so that they form a small tight group. **Bunch together** means the same as **bunch up**. ❑ *They were bunching up, almost stepping on each other's heels.* ❑ *People were bunched up at all the exits.*

**bun|dle** /bʌ̱ndəl/ (**bundles, bundling, bundled**) ■ N-COUNT A **bundle of** things is a number of them that are tied together or wrapped in a cloth or bag so that they can be carried or stored. ❑ *...a bundle of papers.* ❑ *...bundles of clothing.* ◪ N-SING If you describe someone as, for example, a **bundle of** fun, you are emphasizing that they are full of fun. If you describe someone as a **bundle of** nerves, you are emphasizing that they are very nervous. ❑ *I remember Mickey as a bundle of fun, great to be with.* ❑ *Life at high school wasn't a bundle of laughs.* ◖ V-T If someone **is bundled** somewhere, someone pushes them there in a rough and hurried way. ❑ *He was bundled into a car.* [from Middle Dutch]

**bun|ga|low** /bʌŋgəloʊ/ (**bungalows**) N-COUNT A **bungalow** is a very small house that usually has only one level and no stairs. [from Hindi]

**bun|gle** /bʌŋgᵊl/ (**bungles, bungling, bungled**) V-T If you **bungle** something, you fail to do it properly, because you make mistakes or are clumsy. □ *Two prisoners bungled an escape attempt.* ● **Bungle** is also a noun. □ *...a legal bungle.* [of Scandinavian origin]

**bunk** /bʌŋk/ (**bunks**) N-COUNT A **bunk** is a narrow bed that is usually attached to a wall, especially in a ship. □ *He left his bunk and went up on deck again.*

**bun|ker** /bʌŋkər/ (**bunkers**) ■ N-COUNT A **bunker** is a place, usually underground, that has been built with strong walls to protect it against heavy gunfire and bombing. □ *...an extensive network of underground bunkers.* ■ N-COUNT A **bunker** is a container for coal or other fuel. ■ N-COUNT On a golf course, a **bunker** is a large area filled with sand that is deliberately put there as an obstacle that golfers must try to avoid. [from Scottish]

**bun|ny** /bʌni/ (**bunnies**) N-COUNT A **bunny** or a **bunny rabbit** is a child's word for a rabbit. [INFORMAL] [from Scottish Gaelic]

**bunt** /bʌnt/ (**bunts, bunting, bunted**) ■ V-T/V-I In baseball, if you **bunt** or if you **bunt** the ball, you deliberately hit the ball softly, in order to gain an advantage. □ *With runners on first and second, he tried to bunt.* □ *Richard Becker bunted a ball on the third-base side.* ■ N-COUNT In baseball, a **bunt** is the act of bunting a ball or a hit made by bunting the ball. □ *Then came a bunt from Russ Davis.* [from Old French]

**buoy** /bui/ (**buoys, buoying, buoyed**) ■ N-COUNT A **buoy** is a floating object that is used to show ships and boats where they can go and to warn them of danger. ■ PHR-VERB If someone is in a difficult situation **is buoyed up** by something, it makes them feel more cheerful and optimistic. □ *They are buoyed up by a sense of hope.* [from Middle Dutch]
→ see **tsunami**

**buoy|ant** /bɔɪənt/ ■ ADJ If you are in a **buoyant** mood, you feel cheerful and behave in a lively way. □ *You will feel more buoyant than you have for a long time.* ● **buoy|an|cy** /bɔɪənsi/ N-UNCOUNT □ *...a mood of buoyancy.* ■ ADJ A **buoyant** object floats on a liquid. □ *These boats are surprisingly buoyant.* ● **buoy|an|cy** N-UNCOUNT □ *Air can be pumped into the diving suit to increase buoyancy.* [from Spanish]

**buoy|ant force** (**buoyant forces**) N-COUNT The **buoyant force** of an object immersed in a fluid is the physical force that causes the object to float or to rise upward. [TECHNICAL]

**'burbs** /bɜrbz/ also **burbs** N-PLURAL The **'burbs** are the same as the **suburbs**. [INFORMAL] □ *...a quiet kid from the 'burbs.*

**bur|den** /bɜrdᵊn/ (**burdens, burdening, burdened**) ■ N-COUNT If you describe a problem or a responsibility as a **burden**, you mean that it causes someone a lot of difficulty, worry, or hard work. □ *...the families who bear the burden of looking after aging relatives.* □ *Her death will be an impossible burden on Paul.* ■ N-COUNT A **burden** is a heavy load that is difficult to carry. [FORMAL] □ *...African women carrying burdens on their heads.* ■ V-T If

someone **burdens** you **with** something that is likely to worry you, for example, a problem or a difficult decision, they tell you about it. □ *We decided not to burden him with the news.* [from Old English]

**bur|dened** /bɜrdᵊnd/ ADJ If you are **burdened** with something, it causes you a lot of worry or hard work. □ *Nicaragua was burdened with a foreign debt of $11 billion.* [from Old English]

**bu|reau** /byʊəroʊ/ (**bureaus**) ■ N-COUNT A **bureau** is an office, organization, or government department that collects and distributes information. □ *...the Federal Bureau of Investigation.* ■ N-COUNT A **bureau** is an office of a company or organization that has its main office in another city or country. [BUSINESS] □ *...the Wall Street Journal's Washington bureau.* ■ N-COUNT A **bureau** is a low piece of furniture with drawers in which you keep clothes or other things. [from French]

**Word Link**    cracy ≈ rule by : aristo**cracy**, bureau**cracy**, demo**cracy**

**bu|reau|cra|cy** /byʊrɒkrəsi/ (**bureaucracies**) ■ N-COUNT A **bureaucracy** is an administrative system operated by a large number of officials. □ *He blames the big bureaucracies for his troubles.* ■ N-UNCOUNT **Bureaucracy** refers to all the rules and procedures followed by government departments and similar organizations, especially when you think that these are complicated and cause long delays. □ *People usually complain about too much bureaucracy.* [from French]

**Word Link**    crat ≈ power : aristo**crat**, bureau**crat**, demo**crat**

**bu|reau|crat** /byʊərəkræt/ (**bureaucrats**) N-COUNT **Bureaucrats** are officials who work in a large administrative system, especially ones who seem to follow rules and procedures too strictly. □ *The economy is still controlled by bureaucrats.* [from French]

**bu|reau|crat|ic** /byʊərəkrætɪk/ ADJ **Bureaucratic** means involving complicated rules and procedures which can cause long delays; used to show disapproval. □ *...bureaucratic delays.* [from French]

**bur|geon** /bɜrdʒᵊn/ (**burgeons, burgeoning, burgeoned**) V-I If something **burgeons**, it grows or develops rapidly. [LITERARY] □ *Plants burgeon from every available space.* □ *My confidence began to burgeon later in life.* [from Old French]

**burg|er** /bɜrgər/ (**burgers**) N-COUNT A **burger** is a flat round mass of ground meat or minced vegetables that is fried and often eaten in a bread roll. □ *...a burger and fries.* [after Hamburg, a city in Germany]

**bur|glar** /bɜrglər/ (**burglars**) N-COUNT A **burglar** is a thief who enters a house or other building by force. □ *...the ability of the police to catch burglars.* [from Medieval Latin]

**bur|glar|ize** /bɜrgləraɪz/ (**burglarizes, burglarizing, burglarized**) V-T If a building **is burglarized**, a thief enters it by force and steals things. □ *Her home was burglarized.* [from Medieval Latin]

**bur|gla|ry** /bɜrgləri/ (**burglaries**) N-VAR If someone commits a **burglary**, they enter a building by force and steal things. **Burglary** is the

**B**

act of doing this. ❑ *An 11-year-old boy committed a burglary.* [from Medieval Latin]
→ see **crime**

**bur|ial** /bɛriəl/ (**burials**) N-VAR A **burial** is the act or ceremony of putting a dead body into a grave in the ground. ❑ *The priest prepared the body for burial.* [from Old English]

**burka** /bɜrkə/ (**burkas**) → see **burqa**

**bur|ly** /bɜrli/ (**burlier, burliest**) ADJ A **burly** man has a broad body and strong muscles. ❑ *He was a big, burly man.* [from Old High German]

**burn** /bɜrn/ (**burns, burning, burned** or **burnt**)
■ V-I If there is a fire or a flame somewhere, you say that there is a fire or flame **burning** there. ❑ *Fires were burning out of control in the center of the city.* ❑ *There was a fire burning in the fireplace.* ■ V-I If something **is burning**, it is on fire. ❑ *When I arrived, one of the vehicles was still burning.* ❑ *The building burned for hours.* ● **burn|ing** N-UNCOUNT ❑ *When we arrived in our village, there was a terrible smell of burning.* ■ V-T If you **burn** something, you destroy or damage it with fire. ❑ *Protesters burned a building.* ❑ *They use the equipment to burn household waste.* ● **burn|ing** N-UNCOUNT ❑ *...the burning of a U.S. flag outside the American embassy.* ■ V-T If you **burn** part of your body, **burn yourself,** or **are burned** or **burnt,** you are injured by fire or by something very hot. ❑ *Take care not to burn your fingers.* ● **Burn** is also a noun. ❑ *She suffered burns to her back.* ■ V-T If a substance **burns,** it produces flames or smoke when heated [TECHNICAL] ■ V-T To **burn** a CD means to write or copy data onto it. [COMPUTING] ❑ *I have the equipment to burn audio CDs.* [from Old English] ■ → see also **burning**
→ see **calorie, fire**
▶ **burn down** PHR-VERB If a building **burns down** or if someone **burns** it **down,** it is completely destroyed by fire. ❑ *Six months after Bud died, the house burned down.*

| Thesaurus | *burn* | Also look up : |
| --- | --- | --- |
| v. | ignite, incinerate, kindle, scorch, singe; (*ant.*) extinguish, put out ■ – ■ | |

| Word Partnership | Use *burn* with : |
| --- | --- |
| N. | **fires** burn ■<br>burn **victim** ■<br>burn **a CD** ■ |
| V. | **watch** *something* burn ■ ■ |
| ADJ. | **first/second/third degree** burn ■ |

**burn|er** /bɜrnər/ (**burners**) N-COUNT A **burner** is a device which produces heat or a flame, especially as part of a stove or heater. ❑ *He put the frying pan on the gas burner.* [from Old English]
→ see **laboratory**

**burn|ing** /bɜrnɪŋ/ ADJ You use **burning** to describe something that is extremely hot. ❑ *...the burning desert of central Asia.* ● **Burning** is also an adverb. ❑ *He touched the boy's forehead. It was burning hot.* [from Old English]

**burnt** /bɜrnt/ **Burnt** is a past tense and past participle of **burn.** [from Old English]

**burqa** /bɜrkə/ (**burqas**) also **burka** N-COUNT A **burqa** is a long garment that covers the head and body and is traditionally worn by some women in Islamic countries. [from Arabic]

**bur|ri|to** /bəritoʊ/ (**burritos**) N-COUNT A **burrito** is a tortilla containing a filling of ground beef, chicken, cheese, or beans. [from Mexican Spanish]

**bur|row** /bɜroʊ/ (**burrows, burrowing, burrowed**) ■ N-COUNT A **burrow** is a tunnel or hole in the ground that is dug by an animal such as a rabbit. ❑ *The squirrels were sleeping safely in their burrows.* ■ V-I If an animal **burrows** into the ground or into a surface, it moves through it by making a tunnel or hole. ❑ *The ants burrow into cracks in the floor.*

**burst** /bɜrst/ (**bursts, bursting**)

> The form **burst** is used in the present tense and is the past tense and past participle.

■ V-T/V-I If something **bursts** or if you **burst** it, it suddenly breaks open or splits open and the air or other substance inside it comes out. ❑ *The driver lost control when a tire burst.* ❑ *It is not a good idea to burst a blister.* ■ V-I To **burst into** or **out** of a place means to enter or leave it suddenly with a lot of energy or force. ❑ *Gunmen burst into his home.* ■ N-COUNT A **burst of** something is a sudden short period of it. ❑ *...a burst of energy.* [from Old English]
→ see **crash, cry, laugh**

burst

▶ **burst into** ■ PHR-VERB If you **burst into** tears, laughter, or song, you suddenly begin to cry, laugh, or sing. ❑ *She burst into tears and ran from the kitchen.* ❑ *I was so happy I burst into song.* ■ to **burst into flames** → see **flame**
▶ **burst out** PHR-VERB If someone **bursts out** laughing, crying, or making another noise, they suddenly start to make that noise. ❑ *The class burst out laughing.*

| Thesaurus | *burst* | Also look up : |
| --- | --- | --- |
| v. | blow, explode, pop, rupture ■ | |

| Word Partnership | Use *burst* with : |
| --- | --- |
| N. | burst **appendix, bubble** burst, **pipe** burst ■<br>burst **of air,** burst **of energy,** burst **of laughter** ■ |
| ADJ. | **ready to** burst ■<br>**sudden** burst ■ |

**burst|ing** /bɜrstɪŋ/ ■ ADJ If a place is **bursting with** people or things, it is full of them. ❑ *The place appears to be bursting with women directors.* ■ ADJ If you are **bursting with** a feeling or quality, you are full of it. ❑ *I was bursting with curiosity.* [from Old English] ■ → see also **burst**

**bury** /bɛri/ (**buries, burying, buried**) ■ V-T To **bury** something means to put it into a hole in the ground and cover it up. ❑ *They make the charcoal by burying wood in the ground and then slowly burning it.* ❑ *Squirrels bury nuts and seeds.* ■ V-T To **bury** a dead person means to put their body into a grave and cover it with earth. ❑ *Soldiers helped to bury the dead.* ❑ *People might think I was dead, and bury me*

**b**

alive. ■ V-T If something **buries** a place or person, it falls on top of them so that it completely covers them and often harms them in some way. □ *Latest reports say that mud slides buried entire villages.* □ *The village was buried under seven feet of snow.* [from Old English]

**bus** /bʌs/ (**buses, busing, bused**)

The spellings **busses, bussing, bussed** are also used for the verb.

■ N-COUNT A **bus** is a large motor vehicle that carries passengers. □ *He missed his last bus home.* ■ V-T To **bus** tables means to clear away dirty dishes and reset the tables in a restaurant. □ *I used to bus tables, and then I became a waitress.*
→ see **transportation**

**bus boy** (**bus boys**) N-COUNT A **bus boy** is someone whose job is to set or clear tables in a restaurant.

**bush** /bʊʃ/ (**bushes**) ■ N-COUNT A **bush** is a large plant which is smaller than a tree and has a lot of branches. □ *Trees and bushes grew down to the water's edge.* ■ N-SING The wild, uncultivated parts of some hot countries are referred to as **the bush.** □ *They walked through the thick Mozambican bush for thirty-six hours.* [of Germanic origin]
→ see **plant**

**bushy** /bʊʃi/ (**bushier, bushiest**) ■ ADJ **Bushy** hair or fur is very thick. □ *...bushy eyebrows.* ■ ADJ A **bushy** plant has a lot of leaves very close together. □ *...strong, sturdy, bushy plants.* [of Germanic origin]

**busi|ly** /bɪzɪli/ ADV If you do something **busily**, you do it in a very active way. □ *Members of his staff were busily trying to repair the damage.* [from Old English]

**busi|ness** /bɪznɪs/ (**businesses**) ■ N-UNCOUNT **Business** is work relating to the production, buying, and selling of goods or services. □ *...a career in business.* □ *Jennifer has an impressive academic and business background.* □ *...Harvard Business School.* ■ N-UNCOUNT **Business** is used when talking about how many products or services a company is able to sell. If **business** is good, a lot of products or services are being sold and if **business** is bad, few of them are being sold. □ *They worried that German companies would lose business.* ■ N-COUNT A **business** is an organization that produces and sells goods or that provides a service. □ *...a family business.* □ *...small businesses.* ■ N-UNCOUNT If you say that something is your **business**, you mean that it concerns you personally and that other people have no right to ask questions about it or disagree with it. □ *If she doesn't want the police involved, that's her business.* ■ N-SING You can use **business** to refer in a general way to an event, situation, or activity. □ *I hope this unpleasant business will soon be over.* ■ → see also **big business, show business** ■ PHRASE If you say that someone **has no business to** be in a place or **to** do something, you mean that they have no right to be there or to do it. □ *Really I had no business to be there at all.* [from Old English]
→ see **city**

N.   company, corporation, firm,
     organization ■ – ■

N.   **close of** business, business
     **opportunity,** business **school** ■
     business **administration,** business
     **decision,** business **expense,** business
     **hours,** business **owner,** business
     **partner,** business **practices** ■ – ■
ADJ. **family** business, **online** business, **small**
     business ■
     **your own** business ■ ■
V.   **go out of** business, **run a** business ■

**business|like** /bɪznɪslaɪk/ ADJ Someone who is **businesslike** deals with things in an efficient way without wasting time. □ *Mr. Penn sounds quite businesslike.* [from Old English]

**business|man** /bɪznɪsmæn/ (**businessmen**) N-COUNT A **businessman** is a man who works in business. □ *...a wealthy businessman who owns a printing business in Orlando.*

**business|woman** /bɪznɪswʊmən/ (**businesswomen**) N-COUNT A **businesswoman** is a woman who works in business. □ *...a successful businesswoman who runs her own cosmetics company.*

**bust** /bʌst/ (**busts, busting, busted**)

The form **bust** is used as the present tense of the verb, and can also be used as the past tense and past participle.

■ V-T If you **bust** something, you break it or damage it so badly that it cannot be used.

[INFORMAL] □ *They will have to bust the door to get him out.* ■ PHRASE If a company **goes bust,** it loses so much money that it is forced to close down. [INFORMAL] □ *...a Swiss company which went bust last May.* ■ N-COUNT A **bust** is a statue of the head and shoulders of a person. □ *...a bronze bust of Thomas Jefferson.* [from French]

**bust**

**bus|tle** /bʌsəl/ (**bustles, bustling, bustled**) ■ V-I If someone **bustles** somewhere, they move there in a hurried way. □ *My mother bustled around the kitchen.* ■ V-I A place that **is bustling** or **bustling with** people or activity is full of people who are very busy or lively. □ *The sidewalks are bustling with people.* ■ N-UNCOUNT **Bustle** is busy, noisy activity. □ *...the bustle of modern life.* [from Old Norse]

**busy** /bɪzi/ (**busier, busiest, busies, busying, busied**) ■ ADJ When you are **busy,** you are working hard or concentrating on a task, so that you are not free to do anything else. □ *What is it? I'm busy.* □ *They are busy preparing for a day's activity on Saturday.* ■ V-T If you **busy yourself** with something, you occupy yourself by dealing with it. □ *He busied himself with the camera.* □ *She busied herself getting towels ready.* ■ ADJ A **busy** place is full of people who are doing things or moving around. □ *...a busy city street.* ■ ADJ When a telephone line is **busy,** you cannot make your call because the line is already being used by someone else. □ *I tried to reach him, but the line was busy.* [from Old English] ■ → see also **busily**

**busy sig|nal** (**busy signals**) N-COUNT If you try

to make a telephone call and get a **busy signal**, it means that you cannot make the call because the line is already being used by someone else. ❑ *I tried the number again, but got a busy signal.*

**busy|work** /bɪziwɜrk/ N-UNCOUNT **Busywork** is work that is intended to keep someone occupied and is not completely necessary. ❑ *...meaningless busywork.*

**but** /bət, STRONG bʌt/ ■ CONJ You use **but** to introduce something that contrasts with what you have just said, or to introduce something that adds to what you have just said. ❑ *"You said you'd stay till tomorrow." — "I know, but I think I would rather go back."* ❑ *Heat the cider until it is very hot but not boiling.* ◢ CONJ You use **but** when you are about to add something further in a discussion or to change the subject. ❑ *After three weeks, they reduced their sleep to eight hours. But another interesting thing happened.* ◣ CONJ You use **but** after you have made an excuse or apologized for what you are just about to say. ❑ *Please excuse me, but there is something I must say.* ❑ *I'm sorry, but it's true.* ◪ CONJ You use **but** to introduce a reply to someone when you want to indicate surprise, disbelief, refusal, or protest. ❑ *"I don't think I should stay in this house." — "But why?"* ◧ PREP **But** is used to mean "except." ❑ *Europe will be represented in all but two of the seven races.* ❑ *He didn't speak anything but Greek.* ◨ ADV **But** is used to mean "only." [FORMAL] ❑ *He is but one among many who are fighting for equality.* ◩ PHRASE You use **but for** to introduce the only factor that causes a particular thing not to happen or not to be completely true. ❑ *The street below was empty but for a white van.* [from Old English] ◪ **all but** → see **all** ◫ **anything but** → see **anything**

> ### Usage    **but** and **yet**
>
> *But* is used to add something to what has been said: *Lisa tried to bake cookies, but she didn't have enough sugar. Yet* is used to indicate an element of surprise: *He doesn't eat much, yet he is gaining weight.*

**butch|er** /bʊtʃər/ (**butchers, butchering, butchered**) ■ N-COUNT A **butcher** is a storekeeper who cuts up and sells meat. ◢ V-T You can say that someone **has butchered** people when they have killed a lot of people in a very cruel way, and you want to express your horror and disgust. ❑ *Eight tourists were butchered in Bwindi national park.* [from Old French]

**but|ler** /bʌtlər/ (**butlers**) N-COUNT A **butler** is the most important male servant in a wealthy house. ❑ *I called for the butler to clear up the broken glass.* [from Old French]

**butt** /bʌt/ (**butts, butting, butted**) ■ N-COUNT Someone's **butt** is the part of their body that they sit on. [INFORMAL] ◢ N-COUNT The **butt** or the **butt end of** a weapon or tool is the thick end of its handle. ❑ *They beat him with their rifle butts.* ◣ N-COUNT The **butt of** a cigarette or cigar is the small part of it that is left when someone has finished smoking it. ◪ N-SING If someone or something is **the butt of** jokes or criticism, people often make fun of them or criticize them. ❑ *He is still often the butt of cruel jokes.* [from Old English]

▶ **butt in** PHR-VERB If you say that someone is **butting in**, you are criticizing the fact that they are joining in a conversation or activity without being asked to. ❑ *Sorry, I don't mean to butt in.*

▶ **butt out** PHR-VERB If someone tells you to **butt out**, they are telling you rudely to go away or not to interfere with what they are doing. [INFORMAL] ❑ *She wanted to tell him to butt out.*

**but|ter** /bʌtər/ (**butters, buttering, buttered**) ■ N-UNCOUNT **Butter** is a soft yellow substance made from cream. You spread it on bread or use it in cooking. ❑ *...bread and butter.* ◢ V-T If you **butter** something such as bread or toast, you spread butter on it. ❑ *She put two pieces of bread on the counter and buttered them.* [from Old English]

**butter|fly** /bʌtərflaɪ/ (**butterflies**) N-COUNT A **butterfly** is an insect with large colorful wings and a thin body. ❑ *Butterflies are attracted to the wild flowers.* [from Old English]
→ see **insect**

**but|tock** /bʌtək/ (**buttocks**) N-COUNT Your **buttocks** are the two rounded fleshy parts of your body that you sit on. ❑ *He had scars on his back and his buttocks.* [from Old English]
→ see **body**

**but|ton** /bʌtᵊn/ (**buttons, buttoning, buttoned**) ■ N-COUNT **Buttons** are small hard objects sewn onto shirts, coats, or other pieces of clothing. You fasten the clothing by pushing the buttons through holes called buttonholes. ❑ *...a coat with blue buttons.* ◢ V-T If you **button** a shirt, coat, or other piece of clothing, you fasten it by pushing its buttons through the buttonholes. ❑ *Ferguson stood up and buttoned his coat.* ● **Button up** means the same as **button**. ❑ *I buttoned up my coat; it was chilly.* ❑ *The young man put on the shirt and buttoned it up.* ◣ N-COUNT A **button** is a small object on a machine or electrical device that you press in order to operate it. ❑ *He pressed the "play" button.* ◪ N-COUNT A **button** is a small piece of metal or plastic that you wear in order to show that you support a particular movement, organization, or person. You fasten a button to your clothes with a pin. ❑ *People wore campaign buttons saying "Vote Clinton."* [from Old French]

▶ **button up** → see **button 2**
→ see Picture Dictionary: **buttons and fasteners**
→ see **photography**

> ### Word Partnership   Use *button* with :
>
> | N. | **shirt** button ■ |
> | --- | --- |
> | V. | **sew on a** button ■ |
> | | **press a** button, **push a** button ◣ |
> | PREP. | button **up** *something* ◢ |

**button|hole** /bʌtᵊnhoʊl/ (**buttonholes**) N-COUNT A **buttonhole** is a hole that you push a button through in order to fasten a shirt, coat, or other piece of clothing. [from Old French]
→ see **button**

**but|tress** /bʌtrɪs/ (**buttresses**) N-COUNT **Buttresses** are supports, usually made of stone or brick, that support a wall. ❑ *...the cathedral's massive buttresses.* [from Old French]

> ### Word Link   *ar, er ≈ one who acts as* : **buy**er, **li**ar, **sell**er

**buy** /baɪ/ (**buys, buying, bought**) ■ V-T If you **buy** something, you obtain it by paying money for it. ❑ *He could not afford to buy a house.* ❑ *Lizzie bought herself a bike.* ● **buy|er** (**buyers**) N-COUNT ❑ *Car buyers are more interested in safety than speed.* ◢ V-T If you **buy** something like time, freedom, or

b

## Picture Dictionary   buttons and fasteners

**button, buttonhole**   **zipper**   **hook and loop tape**

**snap**   **belt, buckle**   **shoelace**

victory, you obtain it but only by offering or giving up something in return. ▢ *It was a risky operation, but might buy more time.* ▪ N-COUNT If something is a good **buy**, it is of good quality and not very expensive. ▢ *This was still a good buy even at the higher price.* [from Old English]

▶ **buy into** PHR-VERB If you **buy into** a company or an organization, you buy part of it, often in order to gain some control of it. [BUSINESS] ▢ *Other companies could buy into the firm.*

▶ **buy out** PHR-VERB If you **buy** someone **out**, you buy their share of something such as a company or piece of property that you previously owned together. [BUSINESS] ▢ *The bank bought out most of the 200 former partners.* → see also **buyout**

▶ **buy up** PHR-VERB If you **buy up** land, property, or a commodity, you buy large amounts of it, or all that is available. ▢ *The mention of price increases sent people out to buy up as much as they could.*

### Thesaurus   *buy*   Also look up :

| | |
|---|---|
| V. | acquire, bargain, barter, get, obtain, pay, purchase ▪ |

### Word Partnership   Use *buy* with :

| | |
|---|---|
| V. | **afford to** buy, buy **and/or sell** ▪ |
| N. | buy **in bulk**, buy **clothes**, buy a **condo/ house**, buy **food**, buy **shares/stocks**, buy **tickets** ▪ |
| ADV. | buy **direct**, buy **online**, buy **retail**, buy **secondhand**, buy **wholesale** ▪ |

**buy|out** /ˈbaɪaʊt/ (**buyouts**) ▪ N-COUNT A **buyout** is the buying of a company, especially by its managers or employees. [BUSINESS] ▢ *A management buyout is one option.*

**buzz** /bʌz/ (**buzzes, buzzing, buzzed**) ▪ V-I If something **buzzes** or **buzzes** somewhere, it makes a long continuous sound, like the noise a bee makes when it is flying. ▢ *Her doorbell buzzed.* ● **Buzz** is also a noun. ▢ *...the annoying buzz of an insect.* ▪ V-I If a place **is buzzing with** activity or conversation, there is a lot of activity or conversation there, especially because something important or exciting is about to happen. ▢ *The*

rehearsal studio is buzzing with lunchtime activity.
▪ N-SING If a place or event has a **buzz** around it, it has a lively, interesting, and modern atmosphere. ▢ *There is a real buzz around the place. Everyone is really excited.*

**buzz cut** (**buzz cuts**) N-COUNT A **buzz cut** is hairstyle in which the hair is cut very close to the head. ▢ *He seemed even bigger than before, and he has a buzz cut now.*

**buzz|er** /ˈbʌzər/ (**buzzers**) N-COUNT A **buzzer** is an electrical device that is used to make a buzzing sound, for example, to attract someone's attention. ▢ *She rang a buzzer at the information desk.*

**buzz saw** /ˈbʌzsɔ/ (**buzzsaws**) N-COUNT A **buzzsaw** is an electric saw consisting of a round metal disk with a row of V-shaped points along the edge. It is powered by an electric motor and is used for cutting wood and other materials.

**buzz|word** /ˈbʌzwɜrd/ (**buzzwords**) also **buzz word** N-COUNT A **buzzword** is a word or expression that has become fashionable in a particular field and is being used a lot by the media. ▢ *Globalization is the buzzword for big businesses.*

### by

❶ WHO DOES SOMETHING OR HOW IT IS DONE
❷ POSITION OR PLACE
❸ TIMES AND AMOUNTS

In addition to the uses shown below, **by** is used in phrasal verbs such as "abide by," "put by," and "stand by."

The preposition is pronounced /baɪ/. The adverb is pronounced /baɪ/.

❶ **by** ▪ PREP If something is done **by** a person or thing, that person or thing does it. ▢ *The feast was served by his mother and sisters.* ▢ *She was woken by a loud noise in the street.* ▪ PREP If you say that something such as a book, a piece of music, or a painting is **by** a particular person, you mean that this person wrote it or created it. ▢ *...a painting by*

*Van Gogh.* ◼ PREP **By** is used to say how something is done. ❑ *…traveling by car.* ❑ *Make the sauce by boiling the cream and stock together.* ❑ *The all-female yacht crew made history by becoming the first to sail around the world.* ◼ PREP If you hold someone or something by a particular part of them, you hold that part. ❑ *He caught her by the shoulder and turned her around.* ❑ *She was led by the arm to a small room.* ◼ PHRASE If you are **by yourself**, you are alone. ❑ *…a dark-haired man sitting by himself in a corner.* ◼ PHRASE If you do something **by yourself**, you succeed in doing it without anyone helping you. ❑ *I didn't know if I could raise a child by myself.* [from Old English]

❷ **by** ◼ PREP Someone or something that is **by** something else is beside it and close to it. ❑ *Judith was sitting in a chair by the window.* ❑ *Jack stood by the door, ready to leave.* ● **By** is also an adverb. ❑ *Large numbers of police stood by.* ◼ PREP If a person or vehicle goes **by** you, they move past you without stopping. ❑ *A few cars passed close by me.* ● **By** is also an adverb. ❑ *Those who knew her waved or smiled as she went by.* [from Old English]

❸ **by** /baɪ/ ◼ PREP If something happens **by** a particular time, it happens at or before that time. ❑ *He arrived at my hotel by eight o'clock.* ◼ PREP If something increases or decreases **by** a particular amount, that amount is gained or lost. ❑ *Violent crime has increased by 10 percent since last year.* ◼ PREP Things that are made or sold **by** the million or **by** the dozen are made or sold in those quantities. ❑ *Packages arrived by the dozen from America.* ◼ PREP You use **by** in expressions such as "minute by minute" and "drop by drop" to talk about things that happen gradually, not all at once. ❑ *His father began to lose his memory bit by bit.* [from Old English]

**bye** /baɪ/ also **bye-bye** CONVENTION **Bye** and **bye-bye** are informal ways of saying goodbye. ❑ *Bye, Daddy.*

**by|gone** /baɪɡɔn/ ADJ **Bygone** means happening or existing a very long time ago. ❑ *The book recalls memories of a bygone age.*

**by|law** /baɪlɔ/ (**bylaws**) N-COUNT A **bylaw** is a rule which controls the way an organization is run. ❑ *Under the company's bylaws, he can continue as chairman until the age of 70.* [of Scandinavian origin]

**by|pass** /baɪpæs/ (**bypasses, bypassing, bypassed**) ◼ V-T If you **bypass** someone or something that you would normally have to get involved with, you ignore them, often because you want to achieve something more quickly. ❑ *The president gives radio interviews to bypass the newspapers.* ◼ N-COUNT A **bypass** is a surgical operation performed on or near the heart, in which the flow of blood is redirected so that it does not flow through a part of the heart that is diseased or blocked. ❑ *…heart bypass surgery.* ◼ N-COUNT A **bypass** is a main road that takes traffic around the edge of a town or city rather than through its center. ❑ *A new bypass around the city is being built.* ◼ V-T If you **bypass** a place when you are traveling, you avoid going through it. ❑ *His bus trip to the Midwest bypassed all the big cities.*

**by|product** /baɪprɒdʌkt/ (**byproducts**) also **by-product** N-COUNT A **byproduct** is something that is produced during the manufacture or processing of another product. ❑ *For decades gas was regarded as a useless byproduct of oil production.*

**by|stander** /baɪstændər/ (**bystanders**) N-COUNT A **bystander** is a person who is present when something happens and who sees it but does not take part in it. ❑ *An innocent bystander was killed in the attack.*

**byte** /baɪt/ (**bytes**) N-COUNT In computing, a **byte** is a unit of storage approximately equivalent to one printed character. ❑ *…two million bytes of data.*

# Cc

**cab** /kæb/ (**cabs**) **1** N-COUNT A **cab** is a taxi.
❑ *Can I call a cab?* **2** N-COUNT The **cab** of a truck or train is the front part in which the driver sits.
❑ *...the driver's cab.*

**caba|ret** /kæbəreɪ/ N-UNCOUNT **Cabaret** is live entertainment consisting of dancing, singing, or comedy acts that are performed in the evening in restaurants or nightclubs. ❑ *Helen made a successful career in cabaret.* [from Norman French]

**cab|bage** /kæbɪdʒ/ (**cabbages**) N-VAR A **cabbage** is a round vegetable with white, green, or purple leaves that is usually eaten cooked. [from Norman French]

**cab|in** /kæbɪn/ (**cabins**) **1** N-COUNT A **cabin** is a small wooden house, especially one in an area of forests or mountains. ❑ *...a log cabin.* **2** N-COUNT A **cabin** is a small room in a ship or boat. ❑ *He showed her to a small cabin.* **3** N-COUNT A **cabin** is one of the areas inside a plane. ❑ *He sat in the first class cabin.* [from Old French]

**cabi|net** /kæbɪnɪt/ (**cabinets**) **1** N-COUNT A **cabinet** is a cupboard used for storing things such as medicine or for displaying decorative things in. ❑ *...the medicine cabinet.* **2** N-COUNT The **cabinet** is a group of the most senior advisers or ministers in a government. ❑ *...a cabinet meeting.* [from Old French]
→ see **bathroom**

**ca|ble** /keɪbᵊl/ (**cables**) **1** N-VAR A **cable** is a kind of very strong, thick rope, made of wires twisted together. ❑ *...a cable made of steel wire.* **2** N-VAR A **cable** is a thick wire, or a group of wires inside a rubber or plastic covering, which is used to carry electricity or electronic signals. ❑ *...underground power cables.* **3** N-UNCOUNT **Cable** is used to refer to television systems in which the signals are sent along underground wires rather than by radio waves. ❑ *We don't have cable TV.* [from Old Norman French]
→ see **bridge, computer, laser, television**

**ca|boose** /kəbus/ (**cabooses**) N-COUNT On a freight train, a **caboose** is a small car, usually at the rear, in which the crew travels. [from Dutch]

**cab stand** also **cabstand** (**cab stands**) N-COUNT A **cab stand** is a place where taxis wait for passengers, for example, at an airport or outside a station.

**cache** /kæʃ/ (**caches**) **1** N-COUNT A **cache** is a quantity of things such as weapons that have been hidden. ❑ *We found a cache of documents that may give us more information.* **2** N-COUNT A **cache** or **cache memory** is an area of computer memory that is used for temporary storage of data and can be accessed more quickly than the main memory. [COMPUTING] ❑ *In your Web browser's cache are the most recent Web files that you have downloaded.* [from French]

cactus

**cac|tus** /kæktəs/ (**cactuses** or **cacti** /kæktaɪ/) N-COUNT A **cactus** is a desert plant with a thick stem, often with spikes. [from Latin]
→ see **desert**

**ca|det** /kədɛt/ (**cadets**) N-COUNT A **cadet** is a young person who is being trained in the armed services or the police force. ❑ *...army cadets.* [from French]

**café** /kæfeɪ/ (**cafés**) also **cafe** N-COUNT A **café** is a place where you can buy drinks, simple meals, and snacks. ❑ *...an Italian café.* ❑ *...sidewalk cafés and boutiques.* [from French]

**caf|eteria** /kæfɪtɪəriə/ (**cafeterias**) N-COUNT A **cafeteria** is a self-service restaurant, usually in a public building such as a hospital, college, or office. [from American Spanish]

**caf|feine** /kæfin/ N-UNCOUNT **Caffeine** is a chemical substance found in coffee, tea, and cocoa, which affects your brain and body and makes you more active. [from German]

**cage** /keɪdʒ/ (**cages**) N-COUNT A **cage** is a structure of wire or metal bars in which birds or animals are kept. ❑ *I hate to see birds in cages.* [from Old French]

**caged** /keɪdʒd/ ADJ A **caged** bird or animal is inside a cage. ❑ *...a caged lion.* [from Old French]

**ca|jole** /kədʒoʊl/ (**cajoles, cajoling, cajoled**) V-T If you **cajole** someone, you get them to do something after persuading them for some time. ❑ *He cajoled her into going to the movies with him.* [from French]

**cake** /keɪk/ (**cakes**) **1** N-VAR A **cake** is a sweet food made by baking a mixture of flour, eggs, sugar, and fat. ❑ *...a piece of chocolate cake.* ❑ *...a birthday cake.* **2** N-COUNT Food that is formed into flat round shapes before it is cooked can be referred to as **cakes**. ❑ *...fish cakes.* **3** PHRASE If someone has done something very stupid, rude, or selfish, you can say that they **take the cake** or that what they have done **takes the cake**, to emphasize your surprise at their behavior. [from Old Norse]
→ see **dessert**

**cake pan** (**cake pans**) N-COUNT A **cake pan** is a metal container that you bake a cake in.

**cake|walk** /keɪkwɔk/ N-SING If you describe something as a **cakewalk**, you mean that it is very easy to do or achieve. [INFORMAL] ❑ *Tomorrow's game against Italy should be a cakewalk.*

**ca|lam|ity** /kəlæmɪti/ (**calamities**) N-VAR A **calamity** is an event that causes a great deal of damage or distress. [FORMAL] ❑ *...the calamity of war.* [from French]

**cal|cium** /kǽlsiəm/ N-UNCOUNT **Calcium** is a soft white chemical element which is found in bones and teeth, and also in limestone, chalk, and marble. [from New Latin]

**cal|cu|late** /kǽlkyəleɪt/ (**calculates, calculating, calculated**) **1** V-T If you **calculate** a number or amount, you work it out using arithmetic. ❑ ...a course in how to calculate business costs. ❑ We calculate that the average farm in Lancaster County is 65 acres. • **cal|cu|la|tion** /kǽlkyəleɪʃ°n/ (**calculations**) N-VAR ❑ Leonard made a quick calculation: he'd never get there in time. **2** → see also **mathematics 3** V-T If you **calculate** the effects of something, you consider what they will be. ❑ We are calculating the consequences of his actions. [from Late Latin]
→ see **mathematics**

**cal|cu|lat|ed** /kǽlkyəleɪtɪd/ ADJ If something is **calculated**, it is deliberately planned to have a particular effect. ❑ Everything she said seemed calculated to make him feel guilty. [from Late Latin]

**cal|cu|lat|ing** /kǽlkyəleɪtɪŋ/ ADJ If you describe someone as **calculating**, you disapprove of the fact that they deliberately plan to get what they want, often by hurting or harming other people. ❑ Watson is a calculating and clever criminal. [from Late Latin]

**cal|cu|la|tor** /kǽlkyəleɪtər/ (**calculators**) N-COUNT A **calculator** is a small electronic device that you use for making mathematical calculations. ❑ ...a pocket calculator. [from Late Latin]
→ see **office**

**cal|de|ra** /kældɛ́ərə/ (**calderas**) N-COUNT A **caldera** is a large crater at the top of a volcano that is formed when a volcano collapses. [TECHNICAL] [from Spanish]

**cal|en|dar** /kǽlɪndər/ (**calendars**) **1** N-COUNT A **calendar** is a chart or device which displays the date and the day of the week, and often the whole of a particular year. ❑ There was a calendar on the wall with large squares around the dates. **2** N-COUNT A **calendar** is a list of dates within a year that are important for a particular organization or activity. ❑ The meeting wasn't on the secretary's calendar. [from Norman French]
→ see **year**

**calf** /kǽf/ (**calves** /kǽvz/) **1** N-COUNT A **calf** is a young cow. **2** N-COUNT Some other young animals, including elephants and whales, are called **calves**. **3** N-COUNT Your **calf** is the thick part at the back of your leg, between your ankle and your knee. ❑ He injured his calf during the game. [Senses 1 and 2 from Old English. Sense 3 from Old Norse.]

**cali|ber** /kǽlɪbər/ (**calibers**) **1** N-UNCOUNT The **caliber of** someone or something is their qualities, abilities, or high standards. ❑ The caliber of the teaching was very high. ❑ I was impressed by the high caliber of the researchers. **2** N-COUNT The **caliber** of a gun is the width of the inside of its barrel. [TECHNICAL] ❑ ...a small-caliber rifle. **3** N-COUNT The **caliber** of a bullet is its diameter. [TECHNICAL] ❑ ...a .22-caliber bullet. [from Old French]

---

┌─────────────────────────────────┐
│ **call** │
│ **❶** NAMING │
│ **❷** DECLARING, ANNOUNCING, AND │
│ DEMANDING │
│ **❸** TELEPHONING AND VISITING │
│ **❹** PHRASAL VERBS │
└─────────────────────────────────┘

**❶ call** /kɔ́l/ (**calls, calling, called**) **1** V-T If you **call** someone or something **by** a particular name or title, you give them that name or title. ❑ Everybody called each other by their first names. ❑ I wanted to call the dog Mufty. ❑ There are two men called Buckley in the office. **2** V-T If you **call** a person or situation something, that is how you describe them. ❑ They called him a traitor. ❑ She calls me lazy. [from Old English] **3** → see also **so-called 4** to **call** something your **own** → see **own 5** to **call it quits** → see **quit**

**❷ call** /kɔ́l/ (**calls, calling, called**) **1** V-T If you **call** something, or if you **call** it **out**, you say it in a loud voice. ❑ He could hear the others calling his name. • **Call out** means the same as **call**. ❑ The butcher called out a greeting. **2** V-T If you **call** a meeting, you arrange for it to take place. ❑ We're going to call a meeting for next week. **3** V-T To **call** a game or sporting event means to cancel it, for example because of rain or bad light. ❑ We called the next game. **4** N-COUNT If there is a **call for** something, someone demands that it should happen. ❑ There have been calls for new security arrangements. **5** PHRASE If someone is **on call**, they are ready to go to work at any time if they are needed. ❑ ...a doctor on call. [from Old English] **6** to **call** someone's **bluff** → see **bluff 7** to **call a halt** → see **halt 8** to **call** something **into question** → see **question 9** to **call the tune** → see **tune**

┌─────────────────────────────────────────┐
│ **Thesaurus** call Also look up : │
│ V. cry, holler, scream, shout **❷ 1** │
└─────────────────────────────────────────┘

**❸ call** /kɔ́l/ (**calls, calling, called**) **1** V-T If you **call** someone, you telephone them. ❑ Would you call me as soon as you find out? ❑ I think we should call the doctor. ❑ She told me to call this number. **2** V-I If you **call** somewhere, you make a short visit there. ❑ A salesman called at the house. • **Call** is also a noun. ❑ The police van was out on a call. **3** N-COUNT When you make a telephone **call**, you telephone someone. ❑ I made a phone call to the United States. ❑ I've had hundreds of calls from victims. • PHRASE If you **call collect** when you make a telephone call, the person who you are phoning pays the cost of the call and not you. [AM] [from Old English] **4** → see also **collect call**

**❹ call** /kɔ́l/ (**calls, calling, called**)
▸ **call back** PHR-VERB If you **call** someone **back**, you telephone them again or in return for a telephone call that they have made to you. ❑ We'll call you back.
▸ **call for 1** PHR-VERB If something **calls for** a particular action or quality, it needs it. ❑ The situation calls for quick action. **2** PHR-VERB If you **call for** someone, you go to the building where they are, so that you can both go somewhere. ❑ I'll call for you at seven o'clock. **3** PHR-VERB If you **call for** something, you demand that it should happen. ❑ He called for further discussions on the issue.
▸ **call in 1** PHR-VERB If you **call** someone **in**, you

ask them to come and help you or do something for you. ❏ *Call in a builder to do the work.* ◷ PHR-VERB If you **call in** somewhere, you make a short visit there. ❏ *He calls in occasionally.*

▶ **call off** PHR-VERB If you **call off** an event that has been planned, you cancel it. ❏ *He called off the trip.*

▶ **call on** or **call upon** ◷ PHR-VERB If you **call on** someone to do something, you say publicly that you want them to do it. ❏ *He called on the government to resign.* ◷ PHR-VERB If you **call on** someone, you visit them for a short time. ❏ *Sofia was intending to call on Miss Kitts.*

▶ **call out** ◷ PHR-VERB If you **call** someone **out**, you order them to come to help, especially in an emergency. ❏ *Colombia has called out the army.* [from Old English] ◷ → see also **call ◷** 1

▶ **call up** ◷ PHR-VERB If you **call** someone **up**, you telephone them. ❏ *When I'm in Pittsburgh, I call him up.* ❏ *He called up the museum.* ◷ PHR-VERB If someone **is called up**, they are ordered to join the army, navy, or air force. ❏ *The United States Army has called up about 150,000 men and women.*

▶ **call upon** → see **call on**

**call cen|ter** (**call centers**) N-COUNT A **call center** is an office where people work answering or making telephone calls for a company.

**call|er** /kɔlər/ (**callers**) ◷ N-COUNT A **caller** is a person who is making a telephone call. ❏ *A caller told police what happened.* ◷ N-COUNT A **caller** is a person who comes to see you for a short visit. ❏ *She took her callers into the living room.*

**call|er ID** N-UNCOUNT A telephone that has **caller ID** displays the telephone number and name of the person who is calling you. ❏ *The cell phone's caller ID display told her Frank Montoya was calling.*

**cal|lous** /kæləs/ ADJ A **callous** person or action is cruel and shows no concern for other people. ❏ *...the callous treatment he received.* ● **cal|lous|ness** N-UNCOUNT ❏ *...the callousness of the sick woman's family.* ● **cal|lous|ly** ADV ❏ *I did not want to abandon my parents callously.* [from Latin]

**calm** /kɑm/ (**calmer, calmest, calms, calming, calmed**) ◷ ADJ A **calm** person does not show or feel any worry, anger, or excitement. ❏ *...a calm, patient woman.* ❏ *Try to keep calm.* ● **Calm** is also a noun. ❏ *He felt a sudden sense of calm.* ● **calm|ly** ADV ❏ *Alan said calmly, "I don't believe you."* ◷ ADJ If water is **calm**, it is not moving very much. ❏ *...the calm waters of the canals.* ◷ ADJ If the weather is **calm**, there is little or no wind. ❏ *It was a fine, calm day.* ◷ N-UNCOUNT **Calm** is a state of being quiet and

peaceful. ❏ *...the calm of Grand Rapids, Michigan.* ◷ V-T If you **calm** someone, you do something to make them less upset or excited. ❏ *She tried to calm herself.* ● **calm|ing** ADJ ❏ *Yoga can have a very calming effect on the mind.* [from French]

▶ **calm down** PHR-VERB If you **calm down**, or if someone **calms** you **down**, you become less upset or excited. ❏ *Calm down for a minute and listen to me.* ❏ *I'll try to calm him down.*

| **Thesaurus** | *calm* | Also look up : |
| --- | --- | --- |

ADJ. laid-back, relaxed; (ant.) excited, upset ◷ mild, peaceful, placid, serene, tranquil; (ant.) rough ◷ – ◷

**calo|rie** /kæləri/ (**calories**) ◷ N-COUNT **Calories** are units used to measure the energy value of food. ❏ *Sweet drinks contain a lot of calories.* ◷ N-COUNT In physics, a **calorie** is the amount of heat that is needed to increase the temperature of one gram of water by one degree centigrade. **Calorie** is also sometimes used to mean a **kilocalorie**. [TECHNICAL] [from French]

→ see Word Web: **calories**
→ see **diet**

**calo|rim|eter** /kælərɪmɪtər/ (**calorimeters**) N-COUNT A **calorimeter** is a scientific instrument that measures the amount of heat given off or absorbed in a chemical reaction.

**cam|cord|er** /kæmkɔrdər/ (**camcorders**) N-COUNT A **camcorder** is a small video camera that records both pictures and sound.

**came** /keɪm/ **Came** is the past tense of **come**.

**cam|el** /kæməl/ (**camels**) ◷ N-COUNT A **camel** is a desert animal with one or two humps on its back. [from Old English] ◷ **the straw that broke the camel's back** → see **straw**

camel

**cameo** /kæmioʊ/ (**cameos**) ◷ N-COUNT A **cameo** is a short descriptive piece of acting or writing. ❏ *...cameos of American history.* ◷ N-COUNT A **cameo** is a piece of jewelry with a raised stone design on a flat stone of another color. [from Italian]

**cam|era** /kæmrə/ (**cameras**) ◷ N-COUNT A **camera** is a piece of equipment for taking photographs or making movies. ❏ *...a video*

---

## Word Web    calories

**Calories** are a measure of **energy**. One calorie of heat raises the **temperature** of 1 gram of water by 1°C*. However, we usually think of calories in relation to food and exercise. A person eating a cup of vanilla ice cream **takes in** 270 calories. Walking a mile **burns** 66 calories. Different types of foods store different amounts of energy. **Proteins** and **carbohydrates** contain 4 calories per gram. However **fat** contains 9 calories per gram. Our bodies store extra calories in the form of fat. For every 3,500 extra calories we take in, we gain a pound of fat.

*0°Celsius = 32° Fahrenheit*

*camera.* **2** PHRASE If someone or something is **on camera**, they are being filmed. ❑ *I won't be on camera, will I?* [from Latin]
→ see **photography**

**camera|man** /kǽmrəmæn/ (**cameramen**) N-COUNT A **cameraman** is a person who operates a camera for television or movies.

**camera phone** (**camera phones**) N-COUNT A **camera phone** is a cellphone that can also take photographs.

**camera|wom|an** /kǽmrəwʊmən/ (**camerawomen**) N-COUNT A **camerawoman** is a person who operates a camera for television or movies.

**camou|flage** /kǽməflɑʒ/ (**camouflages, camouflaging, camouflaged**) **1** N-UNCOUNT; N-SING **Camouflage** consists of things such as leaves, branches, or paint, used to make someone or something difficult to see. ❑ *They were dressed in camouflage.* ❑ *...a camouflage jacket.* **2** N-UNCOUNT; N-SING **Camouflage** is the way in which some animals are colored and shaped so that they cannot easily be seen in their natural surroundings. ❑ *...the natural camouflage patterns of insects.* **3** V-T If military buildings or vehicles **are camouflaged**, things such as leaves, branches, or paint are used to make it difficult to see them. ❑ *The entrance was camouflaged with bricks and dirt.* [from French]

**camp** /kǽmp/ (**camps, camping, camped**) **1** N-COUNT A **camp** is a place where people live or stay in tents or trailers. ❑ *...a refugee camp.* **2** V-I If you **camp** somewhere, you stay there in a tent or trailer. ❑ *We camped near the beach.* ❑ *They camped out in a meadow.* • **camp|ing** N-UNCOUNT ❑ *They went camping in the wild.* [from Old French] **3** → see also **concentration camp**

**cam|paign** /kǽmpeɪn/ (**campaigns, campaigning, campaigned**) **1** N-COUNT A **campaign** is a planned set of activities aimed at achieving a particular result. ❑ *...a campaign to improve the training of staff.* ❑ *...a bombing campaign.* **2** V-I To **campaign** means to carry out a planned set of activities aimed at achieving a particular result. ❑ *We are campaigning for law reform.* • **cam|paign|er** (**campaigners**) N-COUNT ❑ *Anti-war campaigners marched through the city.* [from French]
→ see **army, election**

**camp|er** /kǽmpər/ (**campers**) **1** N-COUNT A **camper** is a person who goes camping. ❑ *Campers were already packing up their tents.* **2** N-COUNT A **camper** is a motor vehicle equipped with beds and cooking equipment so that you can live, sleep, and cook in it. [from Old French]

**camp|ground** /kǽmpgraʊnd/ (**campgrounds**) N-COUNT A **campground** is the same as a **campsite.**

**Word Link** | site, situ ≈ position, location : campsite, situation, website

**camp|site** /kǽmpsaɪt/ (**campsites**) N-COUNT A **campsite** is a place where people who are on vacation can stay in tents.

**cam|pus** /kǽmpəs/ (**campuses**) N-COUNT A **campus** is an area of land that contains the main buildings of a university or college. [from Latin]

**can**

**❶** MODAL USES
**❷** CONTAINER

**❶ can** /kən, STRONG kæn/

**Can** is a modal verb. It is used with the base form of a verb. The form **cannot** is used in negative statements. The usual spoken form of **cannot** is **can't**, pronounced /kǽnt/.

**1** MODAL If you **can** do something, you have the ability or opportunity to do it. ❑ *I can take care of myself.* ❑ *The United States will do whatever it can to help Greece.* **2** MODAL You use **can** to indicate that something is true sometimes or is true in some circumstances. ❑ *...long-term therapy that can last five years or more.* ❑ *Exercising alone can be boring.* **3** MODAL You use **cannot** and **can't** to state that you are certain that something is not the case or will not happen. ❑ *Things can't be that bad.* ❑ *That person can't be Douglas!* **4** MODAL If you **can** do something, you are allowed to do it. ❑ *Can I have your jeans when you go?* ❑ *We can't answer any questions, I'm afraid.* **5** MODAL You use **can** in order to make suggestions or requests, or to offer to do something. ❑ *You can always try the pasta.* ❑ *Can I have a look at that?* ❑ *Can I help you?* [from Old English]

**Usage** | **can and may**

Both *can* and *may* are used to talk about possibility and permission: *Highway traffic can/may be heavier in the summer than in the winter. Can/May I interrupt you for a moment?* To talk about ability, use *can* but not *may*: *Kazuo can run a mile in five minutes.*

**❷ can** /kǽn/ (**cans, canning, canned**) **1** N-COUNT A **can** is a sealed metal container for food, drink, or paint. ❑ *Several young men were kicking a tin can along the middle of the road.* **2** V-T When food or drink **is canned**, it is put into a metal container and sealed. ❑ *Fruit and vegetables were canned in large quantities.* [from Old English]
→ see **container**

**ca|nal** /kənǽl/ (**canals**) N-COUNT A **canal** is a long, narrow, man-made stretch of water. ❑ *...the Grand Union Canal.* [from Latin]

**can|cel** /kǽnsºl/ (**cancels, canceling** or **cancelling, canceled** or **cancelled**) **1** V-T/V-I If you **cancel** something that has been arranged, you stop it from happening. If you **cancel** an order for goods or services, you tell the person or organization supplying them that you no longer wish to receive them. ❑ *The governor yesterday canceled his visit to Washington.* ❑ *The customer called to cancel.* • **can|cel|la|tion** /kǽnsəleɪʃºn/ (**cancellations**) N-VAR ❑ *The cancellation of his visit has disappointed many people.* **2** V-T If someone in authority **cancels** a document or a debt, they officially declare that it is no longer valid or no longer legally exists. ❑ *...a government order canceling his passport.* • **can|cel|la|tion** N-UNCOUNT ❑ *...cancellation of Third World debt.* [from Old French]

▸ **cancel out** PHR-VERB If one thing **cancels out** another thing, the two things have opposite effects which combine to produce no real effect. ❑ *The different influences might cancel each other out.*

## Word Web    cancer

The traditional **treatments** for **cancer** are **surgery**, **radiation therapy**, and chemotherapy. However, there is a new type of treatment called targeted therapy. This treatment uses new drugs that target specific types of cancer cells. Targeted therapy does not have many of the **toxic** effects on healthy **tissue** that traditional chemotherapy can have. One of these drugs helps stop blood vessels that feed a **tumor** from growing. Another drug kills cancer cells.

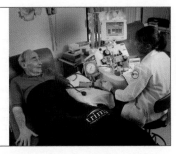

**C**

---

### Thesaurus    *cancel*    Also look up :

v.    break, call off, scrap, undo ■

**can|cer** /kænsər/ (**cancers**) N-VAR **Cancer** is a serious disease in which abnormal body cells increase, producing growths. ❑ *Her mother died of breast cancer.* ❑ *Jane was 25 when she learned she had cancer.* ● **can|cer|ous** ADJ ❑ *...the production of cancerous cells.* [from Latin]
→ see Word Web: **cancer**

**can|did** /kændɪd/ ADJ If you are **candid** about something or with someone, you speak honestly. ❑ *Natalie is candid about the problems she is having with Steve.* ❑ *I haven't been completely candid with him.* [from Latin]

**can|di|da|cy** /kændɪdəsi/ (**candidacies**) N-VAR Someone's **candidacy** is their position of being a candidate in an election. ❑ *Today he is formally announcing his candidacy for president.* [from Latin]

**can|di|date** /kændɪdeɪt/ (**candidates**)
■ N-COUNT A **candidate** is someone who is being considered for a position, for example in an election or for a job. ❑ *...the Democratic candidate.* ❑ *He is a candidate for the office of governor.* ② N-COUNT A **candidate** is someone who is studying for a degree at a college. ❑ *He is now a candidate for a master's degree in social work.* [from Latin]
→ see **election, vote**

**can|dle** /kænd°l/ (**candles**) N-COUNT A **candle** is a stick of hard wax with a piece of string called a wick through the middle, that you set fire to in order to provide light. ❑ *The bedroom was lit by a single candle.* [from Old English]

**can|dor** /kændər/ N-UNCOUNT **Candor** is the quality of speaking honestly and openly. ❑ *He was noted for his candor.* [from Latin]

**can|dy** /kændi/ (**candies**) N-VAR **Candy** is sweet foods such as chocolate or taffy. ❑ *...a piece of candy.* [from Old French]

**can|dy apple** (**candy apples**) N-COUNT A **candy apple** is an apple coated with hard red sugar syrup and fixed on a stick.

**can|dy bar** (**candy bars**) N-COUNT A **candy bar** is a long, thin, sweet food, usually covered in chocolate.

**candy cane** (**candy canes**) N-COUNT A **candy cane** is a stick of red and white candy with a curve at one end.

**cane** /keɪn/ (**canes**) ■ N-VAR **Cane** is the long, hollow, hard stems of plants such as bamboo.

❑ *...cane furniture.* ❑ *...cane sugar.* ② N-COUNT A **cane** is a long narrow stick. ❑ *He leaned heavily on his cane.* [from Old French]
→ see **disability, sugar**

**ca|nine** /keɪnaɪn/ ADJ **Canine** means relating to dogs. ❑ *...research into canine diseases.* [from Latin]

**can|is|ter** /kænɪstər/ (**canisters**) N-COUNT A **canister** is a metal container. ❑ *They stole big canisters of gasoline from the air base.* [from Latin]

**can|na|bis** /kænəbɪs/ N-UNCOUNT **Cannabis** is a drug made from the hemp plant. [from Latin]

**can|ni|bal** /kænɪb°l/ (**cannibals**) N-COUNT A **cannibal** is a person who eats human flesh. ● **can|ni|bal|ism** /kænɪbəlɪzəm/ N-UNCOUNT ❑ *They were forced to practice cannibalism in order to survive.* [from Spanish]

**can|non** /kænən/ (**cannons**) ■ N-COUNT A **cannon** is a large gun on wheels, which was used in battles in the past. ❑ *The soldiers marched beside the gigantic cannons.* ② N-COUNT A **cannon** is a heavy automatic gun, especially one fired from an aircraft. [from Old French]

**can|not** /kænɒt, kənɒt/ **Cannot** is the negative form of **can**.

canoe

**ca|noe** /kənu/ (**canoes**) N-COUNT A **canoe** is a small, narrow boat that you move through the water using a paddle. [from Spanish]
→ see **boat**

**ca|no|la** /kənoʊlə/ N-UNCOUNT **Canola** or **canola oil** is a type of vegetable oil used in cooking.

**can|on** /kænən/ (**canons**) ■ N-COUNT A **canon** is a member of the clergy on the staff of a cathedral. ② N-COUNT A **canon** is a piece of music in which several voices or instruments perform the same melody but start at different times. A **canon** is also a dance form in which the dancers perform the same movements but start at different times. [TECHNICAL] [Sense 1 from Anglo-French. Sense 2 from Old English.]

**cano|py** /kænəpi/ (**canopies**) N-COUNT A **canopy** is a decorated cover which hangs above something such as a bed or a seat. [from Medieval Latin]
→ see **bed**

**can't** /kænt/ **Can't** is the usual spoken form of "cannot."

**can|teen** /kæntin/ (**canteens**) N-COUNT A

**canteen** is a place in a factory or military base where workers can have meals or snacks. ❑ *Rennie ate his supper in the canteen.* [from French]

**can|ter** /kǽntər/ (**canters, cantering, cantered**) v-i When a horse **canters**, it moves at a speed between a gallop and a trot. ❑ *The horses cantered into the arena.* • **Canter** is also a noun. ❑ *Carnac set off at a canter.*

**can|vas** /kǽnvəs/ (**canvases**) **1** N-UNCOUNT **Canvas** is a strong, heavy cloth that is used for making tents, sails, and bags. ❑ *...a canvas bag.* **2** N-VAR A **canvas** is a piece of canvas on which an oil painting is done, or the painting itself. ❑ *...canvases by Italian painters.* [from Norman French]
→ see **painting**

**can|vass** /kǽnvəs/ (**canvasses, canvassing, canvassed**) **1** v-i If you **canvass for** a particular person or political party, you try to persuade people to vote for them. ❑ *I'm canvassing for the Republican Party.* **2** v-t If you **canvass** public opinion, you find out how people feel about something. ❑ *Members of Congress are canvassing opinion.*

**can|yon** /kǽnyən/ (**canyons**) N-COUNT A **canyon** is a long, narrow valley with very steep sides. ❑ *...the Grand Canyon.* [from Spanish]

**cap** /kǽp/ (**caps, capping, capped**) **1** N-COUNT A **cap** is a soft, flat hat with a curved part at the front which is called a visor. ❑ *...a dark blue baseball cap.* **2** N-COUNT The **cap** of a bottle is its lid. ❑ *She unscrewed the cap of her water bottle and gave him a drink.* **3** v-t You can say that the last event in a series **caps** the others. ❑ *The arrests capped a four-month investigation by the Internal Revenue Service.* [from Old English]
→ see **clothing, hat**

**ca|pable** /kéɪpəb³l/ **1** ADJ If you are **capable of** doing something, you are able to do it. ❑ *He was hardly capable of standing up.* • **ca|pa|bil|ity** /kéɪpəbɪlɪti/ (**capabilities**) N-VAR ❑ *She has lost all her physical capabilities.* **2** ADJ Someone who is **capable** has the ability to do something well. ❑ *She's a very capable speaker.* • **ca|pably** /kéɪpəbli/ ADV ❑ *It was all dealt with very capably.* [from French]

**ca|pac|ity** /kəpǽsɪti/ (**capacities**) **1** N-VAR Your **capacity for** something is your ability to do it. ❑ *...our capacity for giving care, love, and attention.* ❑ *Her mental capacity is remarkable.* **2** N-VAR The **capacity** of something is the maximum amount that it can hold or produce. ❑ *...containers with a maximum capacity of 200 gallons of water.* ❑ *Each stadium had a seating capacity of about 50,000.* ❑ *Bread factories are working at full capacity.* **3** N-COUNT If you do something **in** a particular **capacity**, you do it as part of your job. [WRITTEN] ❑ *She was there in her capacity as U.S. ambassador.* **4** ADJ A **capacity** crowd or audience completely fills a theater, sports stadium, or other place. ❑ *A capacity crowd of 76,000 people was at the stadium for the event.* [from Old French]

**cape** /kéɪp/ (**capes**) **1** N-COUNT A **cape** is a large piece of land that sticks out into the sea from the coast. ❑ *...the storms of the cape.* **2** N-COUNT A **cape** is a type of long coat with no sleeves that hangs from your shoulders. ❑ *...a woolen cape.* [Sense 1 from Old French. Sense 2 from French.]

**ca|pil|lary** /kǽpəleri/ (**capillaries**) N-COUNT **Capillaries** are tiny blood vessels in your body. [from Latin]

**capi|tal** /kǽpɪt³l/ (**capitals**) **1** N-UNCOUNT **Capital** is a sum of money used to start a business or invested to make more money. [BUSINESS] ❑ *Companies are having difficulty in raising capital.* **2** N-COUNT The **capital** of a country is the city where its government meets. ❑ *...Kathmandu, the capital of Nepal.* **3** N-COUNT A **capital** or a **capital letter** is the large form of a letter used at the beginning of sentences and names. ❑ *The name and address are written in capitals.* **4** ADJ A **capital** offense is one that is punished by death. [from Latin]
→ see **city, country**

**capi|tal|ism** /kǽpɪt³lɪzəm/ N-UNCOUNT **Capitalism** is an economic and political system in which property, business, and industry are owned by private individuals and not by the state. ❑ *Nobody ever said capitalism was fair.* • **capi|tal|ist** (**capitalists**) N-COUNT ❑ *They argue that only private capitalists can remake Poland's economy.* ❑ *...Western capitalists.* [from Latin]

**capi|tal|ize** /kǽpɪt³laɪz/ (**capitalizes, capitalizing, capitalized**) v-i If you **capitalize on** a situation, you use it to gain some advantage for yourself. ❑ *The other parties will try to capitalize on the government's mistake.* [from Latin]

**capi|tal pun|ish|ment** N-UNCOUNT **Capital punishment** is the legal killing of a person who has committed a serious crime. ❑ *Most democracies have outlawed capital punishment.*

**capi|tol** /kǽpɪt³l/ also **Capitol** (**capitols**) **1** N-COUNT A **capitol** is a government building in which a state legislature meets. [AM] ❑ *...the construction of the state capitol in 1908.* **2** N-PROPER The **Capitol** is the government building in Washington, D.C., in which the U.S. Congress meets. [AM] ❑ *Thousands of demonstrators gathered in front of the Capitol.* [from Latin]

capitol

**ca|pitu|late** /kəpɪtʃəleɪt/ (**capitulates, capitulating, capitulated**) v-i If you **capitulate**, you stop resisting and do what someone else wants you to do. ❑ *The club finally capitulated and now grants equal rights to women.* [from Medieval Latin]

**cap|let** /kǽplɪt/ (**caplets**) N-COUNT A **caplet** is an oval tablet of medicine.

**cap|size** /kǽpsaɪz/ (**capsizes, capsizing, capsized**) v-t/v-i If you **capsize** a boat or if it **capsizes**, it turns upside down in the water. ❑ *The sea got very rough and the boat capsized.*

**cap|sule** /kǽps³l/ (**capsules**) **1** N-COUNT A **capsule** is a very small tube containing

C

### Word Web — car

The first mass-produced **automobile** in the U.S. was the Model T. In 1909, Ford sold over 10,000 of these **vehicles**. They all had the same basic **engine** and chassis. For years the only color choice was black. Three different bodies were available—roadster, **sedan,** and coupe. Today car makers offer many more choices. These include **convertibles, sports cars, station wagons, vans, pick-up trucks** and SUVs. Laws now require **seat belts** and airbags to make **driving** safer.

Some car makers now offer **hybrid** vehicles. They combine an electrical engine with an **internal combustion engine** to improve **fuel** economy.

powdered or liquid medicine, which you swallow. **2** N-COUNT The **capsule** of a spacecraft is the part in which the astronauts travel. ❑ ...*a Russian space capsule.* [from French]

**cap|tain** /kæptɪn/ (**captains, captaining, captained**) **1** N-COUNT; N-TITLE; N-VOC In the army, navy, and some other armed forces, a **captain** is an officer of middle rank. ❑ ...*Captain Mark Phillips.* ❑ ...*a captain in the army.* **2** N-COUNT The **captain of** a sports team is the player in charge of it. ❑ ...*Mickey Thomas, the captain of the tennis team.* **3** N-COUNT The **captain** of an airplane or ship is the person in charge of it. ❑ ...*the captain of the boat.* **4** N-COUNT; N-TITLE In the United States and some other countries, a **captain** is a high-ranking police officer or firefighter. ❑ ...*a former police captain.* **5** V-T If you **captain** a team or a ship, you are the captain of it. ❑ *He captained the winning team in 1991.* [from Old French]
→ see **boat, ship**

**cap|tain|cy** /kæptɪnsi/ N-UNCOUNT The **captaincy** of a team is the position of being captain. ❑ *His captaincy of the team was ended by eye trouble.* [from Old French]

**cap|tion** /kæpʃⁿn/ (**captions**) N-COUNT A **caption** of a picture consists of the words which are printed underneath. ❑ *The photo had the caption, "Home for the holidays."* [from Latin]

### Word Link — cap ≈ seize : captivate, captive, capture

**cap|ti|vate** /kæptɪveɪt/ (**captivates, captivating, captivated**) V-T If you **are captivated** by someone or something, you find them fascinating and attractive. ❑ *I was captivated by her brilliant mind.* ● **cap|ti|vat|ing** ADJ ❑ ...*her captivating smile.*

**cap|tive** /kæptɪv/ (**captives**) **1** ADJ A **captive** animal or person is being kept in a place and is not allowed to escape. [LITERARY] ❑ ...*captive rats, mice, and monkeys.* ● A **captive** is a prisoner. ❑ *He survived for four months as a captive.* **2** PHRASE If you **take** someone **captive** or **hold** someone **captive**, you take or keep them as a prisoner. ❑ *The kidnappers held Richard captive for a year.* [from Latin]

**cap|tiv|ity** /kæptɪvɪti/ N-UNCOUNT **Captivity** is the state of being kept imprisoned or enclosed. ❑ *The birds were bred in captivity.* [from Latin]

**cap|ture** /kæptʃər/ (**captures, capturing, captured**) **1** V-T If you **capture** someone or something, you catch them or take possession of them, especially in a war. ❑ *The enemy shot down one airplane and captured the pilot.* ● **Capture** is also a noun. ❑ ...*the final battles which led to the army's capture of the town.* **2** V-T If someone or something **captures** a quality, feeling, or atmosphere, they represent or express it successfully. ❑ ...*food that captures the spirit of the Mediterranean.* [from Latin]

### Word Partnership — Use capture with :

| | |
|---|---|
| V. | **avoid** capture, **escape** capture, **fail to** capture **1** |
| N. | capture **territory 1** capture *your* **attention**, capture *your* **imagination 2** |

**car** /kɑr/ (**cars**) **1** N-COUNT A **car** is a motor vehicle with room for a small number of passengers. ❑ *He had left his tickets in his car.* ❑ *They arrived by car.* **2** N-COUNT A **car** is one of the separate, long sections of a train. ❑ *The company manufactured railroad cars.* ❑ *He made his way into the dining car.* [from Latin]
→ see Word Web: **car**
→ see **train**

**cara|mel** /kærəmɛl, -məl, kɑrməl/ (**caramels**) **1** N-VAR A **caramel** is a chewy sweet food made from sugar, butter, and milk. **2** N-UNCOUNT **Caramel** is burnt sugar used for coloring and flavoring food. [from French]

**car|at** /kærət/ (**carats**) N-COUNT A **carat** is a unit equal to 0.2 grams used for measuring the weight of diamonds and other precious stones. ❑ ...*a huge eight-carat diamond.* [from Old French]

**cara|van** /kærəvæn/ (**caravans**) N-COUNT A **caravan** is a group of people and animals or vehicles who travel together. ❑ ...*the old caravan routes from Central Asia to China.* [from Italian]

### Word Link — hydr ≈ water : carbohydrate, dehydrate, hydraulic

**car|bo|hy|drate** /kɑrboʊhaɪdreɪt/ (**carbohydrates**) N-VAR **Carbohydrates** are energy-giving substances found in foods such as sugar and bread. ❑ ...*carbohydrates such as bread, pasta, or potatoes.*
→ see **calorie, diet**

C

## Word Web　cardiovascular system

The **cardiovascular** or **circulatory system** carries **oxygen** and **nutrients** to **cells** in all parts of the body. It also removes waste from these cells. The **heart** pumps the **blood** through the **veins** and **arteries**. A human body contains more than 100,000 kilometers of veins and arteries. The blood follows two main routes. **Pulmonary circulation** carries blood through the **lungs** where it absorbs oxygen. The **systemic route** carries the oxygen-rich blood from the lungs to the rest of the body. Blood contains three types of cells. **Red blood cells** carry oxygen. **White blood cells** help fight disease. **Platelets** help the blood clot when there is an injury.

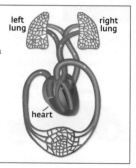

left lung　　right lung

heart

**car|bon** /kɑrbən/ N-UNCOUNT **Carbon** is a chemical element that diamonds and coal are made of. [from French]
→ see **fossil**

**car|bon|at|ed** /kɑrbəneɪtɪd/ ADJ **Carbonated** drinks are drinks that contain small bubbles of carbon dioxide. ❏ …*colas and other carbonated soft drinks.* [from French]

**car|bon di|ox|ide** /kɑrbən daɪɒksaɪd/ N-UNCOUNT **Carbon dioxide** is a gas that animals and people breathe out.
→ see **air, greenhouse effect, ozone, photosynthesis, respiration**

**car|bon mon|ox|ide** /kɑrbən mənɒksaɪd/ N-UNCOUNT **Carbon monoxide** is a poisonous gas produced especially by the engines of vehicles.
→ see **ozone**

**car|bu|re|tor** /kɑrbəreɪtər/ (**carburetors**) N-COUNT A **carburetor** is the part of an engine, usually in a car, in which air and gasoline are mixed together to form a vapor which can be burned.

**car|cass** /kɑrkəs/ (**carcasses**) N-COUNT A **carcass** is the body of a dead animal. ❏ *We drove past the carcass of a dead buffalo.* [from Old French]

**card** /kɑrd/ (**cards, carding, carded**) ◼ N-COUNT A **card** is a piece of stiff paper or thin cardboard on which something is written or printed. ❏ *He carries a card with details of his illness on it.* ◻ N-COUNT A **card** is a small piece of cardboard or plastic that you use, for example, to prove your identity, to pay for things, or to give information about yourself. ❏ *Members must show their membership card.* ❏ *He paid the bill with a credit card.* ◼ N-COUNT A **card** is a piece of stiff paper with a picture and a message which you send to someone on a special occasion. ❏ *She sends me a card on my birthday.* ◼ N-COUNT **Cards** are thin pieces of cardboard with numbers or pictures on them which are used to play various games. ❏ …*a deck of cards.* ❏ *They enjoy themselves playing cards.* ◼ N-UNCOUNT **Card** is strong, stiff paper or thin cardboard. ❏ *She put the pieces of card in her pocket.* ◼ V-T If you **are carded**, someone asks you to show a document to prove that you are old enough to do something, for example, to buy alcohol. ❏ *For the first time in many years, I got carded.* [from Old French] ◼ → see also **bank card, credit card, debit card, greeting card, identity card, playing card**

**card|board** /kɑrdbɔrd/ N-UNCOUNT **Cardboard** is thick, stiff paper that is used to make boxes and other containers. ❏ …*a cardboard box.* [from Old French]

**car|di|ac** /kɑrdiæk/ ADJ **Cardiac** means relating to the heart. [MEDICAL] ❏ *The man was suffering from cardiac weakness.* [from Latin]
→ see **muscle**

**car|di|ac mus|cle** (**cardiac muscles**) N-VAR **Cardiac muscle** is the muscle in the heart that pumps blood around the body by contracting.

**car|di|gan** /kɑrdɪgən/ (**cardigans**) N-COUNT A **cardigan** is a sweater that fastens at the front. [after James Thomas Brudenell, 7th Earl of Cardigan (1797–1868), a British cavalry officer]

**car|di|nal** /kɑrdⁿnⁿl/ (**cardinals**) ◼ N-COUNT; N-TITLE A **cardinal** is a high-ranking priest in the Catholic church. ❏ *In 1448, Nicholas became a cardinal.* ◻ ADJ A **cardinal** rule or quality is extremely important. [FORMAL] ❏ *As a salesman, your cardinal rule is to do everything you can to satisfy a customer.* ◼ N-COUNT A **cardinal** is a common North American bird. The male has bright red feathers. [from Latin]

**car|di|nal di|rec|tion** (**cardinal directions**) N-COUNT The **cardinal directions** are the same as the **cardinal points**.

**car|dio|vas|cu|lar sys|tem** (**cardiovascular systems**) N-COUNT The **cardiovascular system** carries blood to and from the body's cells. The organs in this system include the heart, the arteries, and the veins.
→ see Word Web: **cardiovascular system**

**care** /kɛər/ (**cares, caring, cared**) ◼ V-T/V-I If you **care** about something, you are concerned about it or interested in it. ❏ …*a company that cares about the environment.* ❏ …*young men who did not care whether they lived or died.* ◻ V-I If you **care for** someone, you feel a lot of affection for them. ❏ *He still cared for me.* ◼ V-I If you **care for** someone or something, you look after them and keep them in a good state or condition. ❏ *They hired a nurse to care for her.* ● **Care** is also a noun. ❏ *Sensitive teeth need special care.* ◼ V-T/V-I You can ask someone if they would **care for** something or if they would **care to** do something as a polite way of asking if they would like to have or do something. ❏ *Would you care for some orange juice?* ◼ N-UNCOUNT If you do something **with care**, you do it with careful attention to avoid mistakes or damage. ❏ *He took care to close the door.* ◼ N-COUNT Your **cares** are your worries, anxieties, or fears. ❏ *Lean back in a hot bath and forget all the cares of the day.* ◼ → see also **caring, day care, intensive care** ◻ PHRASE If you **take care of** someone or something, you look after them and prevent them from being harmed or damaged. ◻ *There was no one else to take care of their children.* [from Old English]

---

**Word Partnership** Use *care* with :

ADJ. **good** care, **loving** care ◻
v. **provide** care, **receive** care ◻

---

ca|reen /kərin/ (**careens, careening, careened**)
v-i If a person or vehicle **careens** somewhere, they move fast and in an uncontrolled way. ◻ *He stood to one side as they careened past him.* [from French]

ca|reer /kəriər/ (**careers, careering, careered**)
■ N-COUNT A **career** is a job or profession. ◻ *...a career as a fashion designer.* ◻ *...a political career.*
■ N-COUNT Your **career** is the part of your life that you spend working. ◻ *During his career, he wrote more than fifty plays.* ■ v-i If a person or vehicle **careers** somewhere, they move fast and in an uncontrolled way. ◻ *His car careered into a river.* [from French]

---

**Thesaurus** *career* Also look up :

N. field, job, profession, specialty, vocation, work ■

---

**Word Partnership** Use *career* with :

N. career **advancement**, career **goals**, career **opportunities**, career **path** ■ ■
ADJ. **political** career, **professional** career ■ ■
V. **pursue a** career ■ ■

---

**Word Link** free ≈ without : *carefree, duty-free, toll-free*

---

care|free /kɛərfri/ ADJ A **carefree** person or period of time is without problems or responsibilities. ◻ *Chantal remembered carefree summers at the beach.*

---

**Word Link** ful ≈ filled with : *beautiful, careful, dreadful*

---

care|ful /kɛərfəl/ ■ ADJ If you are **careful**, you give serious attention to what you are doing, in order to avoid damage or mistakes. ◻ *Be very careful with this stuff, it can be dangerous.* ◻ *Careful on those stairs!* ● care|ful|ly ADV ◻ *Have a nice time, and drive carefully.* ■ ADJ **Careful** work, thought, or examination is thorough and shows a concern for details. ◻ *The trip needs careful planning.* ● care|ful|ly ADV ◻ *All her letters were carefully filed away.* [from Old English]

---

**Word Partnership** Use *careful* with :

ADV. **better be** careful ■
**extremely** careful, **very** careful ■ ■
N. careful **attention**, careful **consideration**, careful **planning** ■

---

care|giv|er /kɛərgɪvər/ (**caregivers**) also care giver N-COUNT A **caregiver** is someone who looks after another person, for example, a person who is disabled, ill, or very young. ◻ *It is nearly always women who are the main caregivers.*

care|less /kɛərlɪs/ ADJ If you are **careless**, you do not pay enough attention to what you are doing, and so you make mistakes. ◻ *I'm sorry. How careless of me.* ◻ *Some parents are careless with their children's health.* ● care|less|ly ADV ◻ *She was fined $200 for driving carelessly.* ● care|less|ness N-UNCOUNT ◻ *Errors are sometimes made from simple carelessness.* [from Old English]

---

**Thesaurus** *careless* Also look up :

ADJ. absent-minded, forgetful, irresponsible, reckless, sloppy; (ant.) attentive, careful, cautious

---

ca|ress /kərɛs/ (**caresses, caressing, caressed**)
v-t If you **caress** someone or something, you stroke them gently and affectionately. [WRITTEN] ◻ *He was gently caressing her golden hair.* ● **Caress** is also a noun. ◻ *...a gentle caress.* [from French]

care|tak|er /kɛərteɪkər/ (**caretakers**)
■ N-COUNT A **caretaker** is a person who takes care of a house or property when the owner is not there. ◻ *Slater acted as caretaker when the family was away.* ■ N-COUNT A **caretaker** is someone who looks after another person, for example, a person who is disabled, ill, or very young. ◻ *His caretakers called him severely disabled.*

car|go /kɑrgoʊ/ (**cargoes**) N-VAR The **cargo** of a ship or plane is the goods that it is carrying. ◻ *...a cargo of bananas.* [from Spanish]
→ see **ship, train**

car|go pants N-PLURAL **Cargo pants** are large, loose pants with lots of pockets. ◻ *...a pair of brown cargo pants.*

cari|ca|ture /kærɪkətʃər, -tʃʊər/ (**caricatures, caricaturing, caricatured**) ■ N-COUNT A **caricature** is a drawing or description of someone that exaggerates their appearance or behavior. ◻ *...a caricature of Hitler.* ■ v-t If you **caricature** someone, you draw or describe them in an exaggerated way in order to be humorous or critical. ◻ *He was caricatured as a fool.* [from Italian]

car|ing /kɛərɪŋ/ ADJ A **caring** person is affectionate, helpful, and sympathetic. ◻ *He is a lovely boy, very gentle and caring.* [from Old English]

---

**Word Link** carn ≈ flesh : *carnage, carnation, incarnation*

---

car|nage /kɑrnɪdʒ/ N-UNCOUNT **Carnage** is the violent killing of large numbers of people, especially in a war. [LITERARY] ◻ *...his strategy for stopping the carnage.* [from French]

car|na|tion /kɑrneɪʃᵊn/ (**carnations**) N-COUNT A **carnation** is a plant with white, pink, or red flowers. [from French]

car|ni|val /kɑrnɪvᵊl/ (**carnivals**) ■ N-COUNT A **carnival** is a public festival with music, processions, and dancing. ■ N-COUNT A **carnival** is a traveling show held in a park or field, with machines to ride on, entertainments, and games. [from Italian]

car|ni|vore /kɑrnɪvɔr/ (**carnivores**) ■ N-COUNT A **carnivore** is an animal that eats meat. [TECHNICAL] ■ N-COUNT If you describe someone as a **carnivore**, you are saying, especially in a humorous way, that they eat meat.
→ see Word Web: **carnivore**

C

**Carnivores** are at the top of the **food chain**. These **predators** have to catch and kill their **prey**, so they must be fast and agile. They also have specialized teeth in the front of their mouths. Large, strong canine teeth allow them to **stab** their prey. Sharp **incisors** work almost like scissors as they tear into animal **flesh**. Carnivores include large **wild** animals such as **lions** and **wolves**. Many people think of **bears** as carnivores, but they are **omnivorous**. They eat plants and berries as well as **meat**. There are many more **herbivores** than carnivores in the world.

**car|ol** /kǽrəl/ (**carols**) N-COUNT **Carols** are Christian religious songs that are sung at Christmas. ◻ *The children all sang carols as loudly as they could.* [from Old French]

**car|pen|ter** /kɑ́rpɪntər/ (**carpenters**) N-COUNT A **carpenter** is a person whose job is making and repairing wooden things. [from Latin]

**car|pet** /kɑ́rpɪt/ (**carpets**) N-VAR A **carpet** is a thick covering of soft material which is laid over a floor or a staircase. ◻ *They laid new carpets.* [from Old French]

**carpet|bag|ger** /kɑ́rpɪtbægər/ (**carpetbaggers**) N-COUNT If you call someone a **carpetbagger**, you disapprove of them because they are trying to become a politician in an area which is not their home, because they think they are more likely to succeed there. ◻ *He was called a carpetbagger because he lived outside the district.*

**car|pool** /kɑ́rpul/ (**carpools, carpooling, carpooled**) also **car pool** or **car-pool** V-I If a group of people **carpool**, they take turns driving each other to work, or driving each other's children to school. ◻ *The government says fewer Americans are carpooling to work.*

**car|rel** /kǽrəl/ (**carrels**) N-COUNT A **carrel** is a desk with low walls on three sides, at which a student can work in private, especially in a library.

**car|riage** /kǽrɪdʒ/ (**carriages**) N-COUNT A **carriage** is an old-fashioned vehicle pulled by horses. ◻ *…an open carriage pulled by six beautiful gray horses.* [from Old Northern French]

**car|ri|er** /kǽriər/ (**carriers**) **1** N-COUNT A **carrier** is a vehicle that is used for carrying people, especially soldiers, or things. ◻ *…a helicopter carrier.* **2** N-COUNT A **carrier** is a company that provides telecommunications services, such as telephone and Internet services. ◻ *The company is Japan's top wireless carrier.* **3** N-COUNT A **carrier** is a passenger airline. ◻ *The airline is the third-largest carrier at Denver International Airport.* [from Old Northern French]
→ see **ship**

**car|rot** /kǽrət/ (**carrots**) **1** N-VAR **Carrots** are long, thin, orange-colored vegetables that grow under the ground. **2** N-COUNT Something that is offered to people in order to persuade them to do something can be referred to as a **carrot**. ◻ *They are given targets, with a carrot of extra pay if they achieve them.* [from Old French]
→ see **vegetable**

**car|ry** /kǽri/ (**carries, carrying, carried**) **1** V-T If you **carry** something, you take it with you, holding it so that it does not touch the ground. ◻ *He was carrying a briefcase.* ◻ *She carried her son to the car.* **2** V-T If you **carry** something, you have it with you wherever you go. ◻ *You have to carry a passport.* **3** V-T To **carry** someone or something means to take them somewhere. ◻ *Insects carry the pollen from plant to plant.* ◻ *They were carrying a message of thanks to President Mubarak.* **4** V-T If someone **is carrying** a disease, they are infected with it and can pass it on to others. ◻ *…people carrying the virus.* **5** V-T If an action or situation **carries** a particular quality or consequence, it has it. ◻ *The medication carries no risk for your baby.* ◻ *It was a crime that carried the death penalty.* **6** V-T If you **carry** an idea or a method to a particular extent, you use or develop it to that extent. ◻ *It's not a new idea, but I carried it to extremes.* **7** V-T If a newspaper or poster **carries** a picture or an article, it contains it. ◻ *Several papers carry the photograph of Mr. Anderson.* **8** V-T In a debate, if a proposal or motion **is carried**, a majority of people vote in favor of it. ◻ *The motion was carried by 322 votes to 296.* **9** V-I If a sound **carries**, it can be heard a long way away. ◻ *He doubted if the sound would carry far.* **10** PHRASE If you **get carried away**, you are so eager or excited about something that you do something hasty or foolish. ◻ *I got completely carried away and almost cried.* [from Old Northern French] **11** to **carry weight** → see **weight**

▸ **carry on** **1** PHR-VERB If you **carry on** doing something, you continue to do it. ◻ *The assistant carried on talking.* ◻ *Her bravery has given him the will to carry on with his life.* ◻ *His eldest son Joseph carried on his father's traditions.* **2** PHR-VERB If you **carry on** an activity, you do it or take part in it for a period of time. ◻ *They carried on a conversation all morning.*

▸ **carry out** PHR-VERB If you **carry out** a threat, task, or instruction, you do it or act according to it. ◻ *The Social Democrats could still carry out their threat to leave the government.* ◻ *Police believe the attacks were carried out by nationalists.*

▸ **carry through** PHR-VERB If you **carry** something **through**, you do it, often in spite of difficulties. ◻ *We don't have the confidence that the UN will carry through this program.*

| **Thesaurus** | carry | Also look up : |
|---|---|---|
| v. | bear, bring, cart, haul, lug, move, truck **1** | |

**car|ry|ing ca|pac|ity** (**carrying capacities**) N-COUNT The **carrying capacity** of a particular area is the maximum number of people or animals that can live there on a long-term basis. [TECHNICAL]

**car|ry-on** ADJ Your **carry-on** bags are bags you have with you in an airplane, rather than ones that are carried in the hold. ❑ *Passengers' carry-on bags are put through X-ray machines.*

**car|ry|over** /kǽriouvər/ (**carryovers**) N-COUNT If something is a **carryover from** an earlier time, it began during an earlier time but still exists or happens now. ❑ *His team's success is a carryover from the high school season.*

**car|sick** /kɑ́rsɪk/ ADJ If someone feels **carsick**, they feel sick as a result of traveling in a car. ❑ *My son always gets carsick if we have to travel far.*

**cart** /kɑ́rt/ (**carts, carting, carted**) **1** N-COUNT A **cart** is an old-fashioned wooden vehicle, usually pulled by an animal. ❑ *...a country where there are more horse-drawn carts than cars.* **2** N-COUNT A **cart** is a small vehicle with a motor. ❑ *Transportation is by electric cart.* **3** N-COUNT A **cart** or a **shopping cart** is a large metal basket on wheels which is provided by stores such as supermarkets for customers to use while they are in the store. **4** V-T If you **cart** things or people somewhere, you carry them or transport them there, often with difficulty. [INFORMAL] ❑ *He carted off the entire contents of the house.* ❑ *...a bag for carting around your child's books or toys.* [from Old Norse]
→ see **golf**

**car|tel** /kɑrtɛ́l/ (**cartels**) N-COUNT A **cartel** is an association of similar companies or businesses that have grouped together in order to prevent competition and to control prices. [BUSINESS] ❑ *...the OPEC oil cartel.* [from German]

**car|ti|lage** /kɑ́rtɪlɪdʒ/ (**cartilages**) N-VAR **Cartilage** is a strong, flexible substance which surrounds joints in your body. ❑ *The player tore cartilage in his chest.* [from Latin]
→ see **shark**

**car|ton** /kɑ́rtªn/ (**cartons**) **1** N-COUNT A **carton** is a plastic or cardboard container in which food or drink is sold. ❑ *...a quart carton of milk.* **2** N-COUNT A **carton** is a large, strong cardboard box. ❑ *There were 10,000 letters, 12 cartons full.* [from French]
→ see **container**

**car|toon** /kɑrtún/ (**cartoons**) **1** N-COUNT A **cartoon** is a humorous drawing in a newspaper or magazine. ❑ *...cartoon characters.* **2** N-COUNT A **cartoon** is a film in which all the characters and scenes are drawn rather than being real people or objects. [from Italian]
→ see **animation**

**car|toon|ist** /kɑrtúnɪst/ (**cartoonists**) N-COUNT A **cartoonist** is a person whose job is to draw cartoons for newspapers and magazines. [from Italian]

**car|tridge** /kɑ́rtrɪdʒ/ (**cartridges**) **1** N-COUNT In a gun, a **cartridge** is a tube containing a bullet and an explosive substance. **2** N-COUNT A **cartridge** is part of a machine that can be easily removed and replaced when it is worn out or empty. ❑ *Change the filter cartridge.*

**carve** /kɑ́rv/ (**carves, carving, carved**) **1** V-T/V-I If you **carve** an object, you cut it out of wood or stone. If you **carve** wood or stone, you make an object by cutting it out. ❑ *One of the prisoners has carved a beautiful wooden chess set.* ❑ *I picked up a piece of wood and started carving.* **2** → see also **carving** **3** V-T If you **carve** writing or a design **on** an object, you cut it into the surface. ❑ *He carved his*

name on his desk. **4** V-T If you **carve** meat, you cut slices from it. ❑ *Andrew began to carve the chicken.* [from Old English]
▸ **carve out** PHR-VERB If you **carve** or **carve out** a niche or a career, you succeed in getting the position or the career that you want by your own efforts. ❑ *Vick carved out his niche as the fastest quarterback in football.*
▸ **carve up** PHR-VERB If you say that someone **carves** something **up**, you disapprove of the way they have divided it into small parts. ❑ *He has carved up the company that Smith created.*

**carv|ing** /kɑ́rvɪŋ/ (**carvings**) **1** N-COUNT A **carving** is an object or a design that has been cut out of stone or wood. ❑ *...a wood carving of a human hand.* **2** N-UNCOUNT **Carving** is the act of carving objects or designs. ❑ *I found wood carving satisfying.* [from Old English]

**cas|cade** /kæskéɪd/ (**cascades, cascading, cascaded**) **1** N-COUNT A **cascade of** something is a large amount of it. [LITERARY] ❑ *...cascades of black hair.* **2** V-I If water **cascades**, it pours downward very fast and in large quantities. ❑ *The freezing, rushing water cascaded past her.* [from French]

---

**case**

❶ INSTANCES AND OTHER ABSTRACT MEANINGS
❷ CONTAINERS
❸ GRAMMAR TERM

---

| **Word Link** | cas ≈ box, hold : case, encase, suitcase |

❶ **case** /kéɪs/ (**cases**) **1** N-COUNT A **case** is a particular situation or instance, especially one that you are using as an example of something more general. ❑ *Prices of these goods have fallen, especially in the case of computers.* ❑ *In some cases, it can be very difficult.* **2** N-COUNT A **case** is a person that a professional such as a doctor is dealing with. ❑ *Doctors were meeting to discuss her case.* **3** N-COUNT A crime, or the trial that takes place after a crime, can be called a **case**. ❑ *...a murder case.* **4** → see also **test case 5** N-COUNT The **case for** or **against** a plan or idea consists of the facts and reasons used to support it or oppose it. ❑ *He sat there while I made the case for his dismissal.* **6** PHRASE You say **in any case** when you are adding another reason for something you have just said or done. ❑ *The concert was sold out, and in any case, most people could not afford the price of a ticket.* **7** PHRASE If you do something **in case** or **just in case** a particular thing happens, you do it because that thing might happen. ❑ *In case anyone was following me, I jumped on a bus.* ❑ *We've already talked about this but I'll ask you again just in case.* **8** PHRASE You say **in that case** or **in which case** to indicate that what you are going to say is true if the possible situation that has just been mentioned actually exists. ❑ *Perhaps you've some doubts about the attack. In that case it may interest you to know that Miss Woods witnessed it.* **9** PHRASE If you say that a task or situation is a **case of** a particular thing, you mean that it consists of that thing or can be described as that thing. ❑ *Every team has a weakness; it's just a case of finding it.* [from Old English]
→ see **hospital**

**❷ case** /keɪs/ (**cases**) ■ N-COUNT A **case** is a container that is designed to hold or protect something. □ ...*a black case for his glasses.* [from Old English] ❷ → see also **bookcase, briefcase**

**❸ case** /keɪs/ (**cases**) N-COUNT In the grammar of many languages, the **case** of a group such as a noun group or adjective group is the form it has which shows its relationship to other groups in the sentence. [from Old English]

**case-sensitive** ADJ If a word is **case-sensitive**, it must be written in a particular form, for example using all capital letters or all small letters, in order for a computer to recognize it. [COMPUTING]

**case study** (**case studies**) N-COUNT A **case study** is a written account that gives detailed information about a person, group, or thing and their development over a period of time. □ *He did a large case study of malaria in West African children as part of his course.*

**cash** /kæʃ/ (**cashes, cashing, cashed**)
■ N-UNCOUNT **Cash** is money, especially money in the form of bills and coins rather than checks. □ ...*two thousand dollars in cash.* □ ...*a financial-services group with plenty of cash.* ❷ V-T If you **cash** a check, you exchange it at a bank for the amount of money that it is worth. □ *If you cash a check, they ask for an ID.* [from Old Italian]
▶ **cash in** PHR-VERB If someone **cashes in on** a situation, they use it to gain an advantage, often in an unfair or dishonest way. □ *Private hospitals were trying to cash in on the growing number of elderly patients.*

**cash bar** (**cash bars**) N-COUNT A **cash bar** is a bar at a party or similar event where guests can buy drinks. □ *At 6 p.m. there will be a reception and cash bar.*

**cash|ier** /kæʃɪər/ (**cashiers**) N-COUNT A **cashier** is a person to whom customers pay money to or get money from in places such as stores or banks. [from Dutch or French]

**cash|ier's check** (**cashier's checks**) N-COUNT A **cashier's check** is one which a cashier signs and which is drawn on a bank's own funds. [AM]

**cash|mere** /kæʒmɪər/ N-UNCOUNT **Cashmere** is a kind of very fine, soft wool. □ ...*a big, soft cashmere sweater.* [after Kashmir, a region in central Asia]

**cash on de|liv|ery** PHRASE If you pay for goods **cash on delivery**, you pay for them in cash when they are delivered. The abbreviation **C.O.D.** is also used. □ ...*an option of paying cash on delivery or by credit card.*

**ca|si|no** /kəsiːnoʊ/ (**casinos**) N-COUNT A **casino** is a building where people play gambling games. [from Italian]

**cas|ket** /kæskɪt/ (**caskets**) N-COUNT A **casket** is a **coffin**. [from Old French]

**cas|se|role** /kæsəroʊl/ (**casseroles**) ■ N-VAR A **casserole** is a meal made by cooking food slowly in a liquid. □ *She made a huge beef casserole, full of herbs and vegetables.* ❷ N-COUNT A **casserole** or a **casserole dish** is a large heavy container with a lid used for cooking casseroles. □ *Place all the chopped vegetables into a casserole dish.* [from French]

| Word Link | ette ≈ small : cas*ette*, gaz*ette*, pal*ette* |

**cas|sette** /kəsɛt/ (**cassettes**) N-COUNT A **cassette** is a small, flat, rectangular plastic case containing magnetic tape which is used for recording and playing back sound. [from French]

**cast** /kæst/ (**casts, casting**)

The form **cast** is used in the present tense and is the past tense and past participle.

■ N-COUNT The **cast** of a play or movie is all the people who act in it. □ *The show is very amusing and the cast is very good.* ❷ V-T To **cast** an actor means to choose them to act a particular role. □ *He was cast as a college professor.* ❸ V-T If you **cast** your eyes or **cast** a look somewhere, you look there. [WRITTEN] □ *He cast a glance at the two men.* □ *I cast my eyes down briefly.* ❹ V-T If something **casts** a light or shadow somewhere, it causes it to appear there. [WRITTEN] □ *The moon cast a bright light over the yard.* ❺ V-T To **cast** doubt **on** something means to cause people to be unsure about it. □ *Last night a top psychologist cast doubt on the theory.* ❻ V-T When you **cast** your vote in an election, you vote. □ *The people will cast their votes in the country's first elections.* ❼ V-T To **cast** an object means to make it by pouring a liquid such as hot metal into a specially shaped container and leaving it there until it becomes hard. □ *Our door knocker is cast in solid brass.* [from Old Norse] ❽ to **cast** your **mind back** → see **mind**
→ see **election, theater, vote**
▶ **cast aside** PHR-VERB If you **cast aside** someone or something, you get rid of them. □ *We need to cast aside outdated policies.*

**caste** /kæst/ (**castes**) N-VAR A **caste** is one of the social classes into which people are divided in a Hindu society. □ *Most of the upper castes worship the goddess Kali.* [from Portuguese]

**cas|ti|gate** /kæstɪgeɪt/ (**castigates, castigating, castigated**) V-T If you **castigate** someone or something, you speak to them angrily or criticize them severely. [FORMAL] □ *Opponents were quick to castigate yesterday's agreement.* [from Latin]

**cas|tle** /kæsəl/ (**castles**) N-COUNT A **castle** is a large building with thick, high walls that was built in the past to protect people during wars and battles. [from Latin]

**cas|trate** /kæstreɪt/ (**castrates, castrating, castrated**) V-T To **castrate** a male animal means to remove its testicles. □ ...*castrated roosters.*
● **cas|tra|tion** /kæstreɪʃən/ (**castrations**) N-VAR □ ...*the castration of male farm animals.* [from Latin]

**cas|ual** /kæʒuəl/ ■ ADJ If you are **casual**, you are relaxed and not very concerned about what is happening. □ *It's difficult for me to be casual about anything.* ● **casu|al|ly** ADV □ "*No need to hurry,*" Ben said casually. ❷ ADJ A **casual** event or situation happens by chance or without planning. □ ...*a casual remark.* ❸ ADJ **Casual** clothes are ones that you normally wear at home or on vacation, and not on formal occasions. □ *I also bought some casual clothes for the weekend.* ● **casu|al|ly** ADV □ *They were casually dressed.* [from Late Latin]

**cas|ual Fri|day** (**casual Fridays**) also **Casual Friday** N-COUNT In some companies, a **casual Friday** is a Friday when employees are allowed to wear clothes that are more informal than usual.

❏ *This denim shirt is as great with jeans as it is for work on casual Fridays.*

**casu|al|ty** /kǽʒuəlti/ (**casualties**) **1** N-COUNT A **casualty** is a person who is injured or killed in a war or in an accident. ❏ *Police fired on the demonstrators causing many casualties.* **2** N-COUNT A **casualty of** an event or situation is a person or a thing that has suffered badly as a result of it. ❏ *One casualty of the battle for power may be the prime minister.* [from Late Middle English]

**cat** /kǽt/ (**cats**) **1** N-COUNT A **cat** is a small furry animal that has a long tail and sharp claws. Cats are often kept as pets. **2** N-COUNT **Cats** are lions, tigers, and other animals in the same family. ❏ *The lion is perhaps the most famous member of the cat family.* [from Old English]
→ see **pet**

**cata|log** /kǽtᵊlɒg/ (**catalogs**) also **catalogue** **1** N-COUNT A **catalog** is a list of things such as the goods you can buy from a particular company, the objects in a museum, or the books in a library. ❏ *...the world's biggest seed catalog.* **2** N-COUNT A **catalog of** similar things, especially bad things, is a number of them considered or discussed one after another. ❏ *His story is a catalog of bad luck.* [from Late Latin]
→ see **library**

**cata|lyst** /kǽtᵊlɪst/ (**catalysts**) **1** N-COUNT You can describe a person or thing that causes a change or event to happen as a **catalyst**. ❏ *I hope that this event will be a catalyst for change.* **2** N-COUNT In chemistry, a **catalyst** is a substance that causes a chemical reaction to take place more quickly. [from New Latin]

**cata|lyze** /kǽtᵊlaɪz/ (**catalyzes, catalyzing, catalyzed**) **1** V-T If something **catalyzes** a change or event, it makes it happen. [FORMAL] ❏ *This new report should catalyze further public debate.* **2** V-T In chemistry, if something **catalyzes** a reaction, it causes it to happen. [TECHNICAL] ❏ *The wires do not have a large enough surface to catalyze a big explosion.* [from New Latin]

**cata|pult** /kǽtəpʌlt/ (**catapults, catapulting, catapulted**) V-T/V-I If someone or something **catapults** through the air, they move or are thrown very suddenly and violently through it. ❏ *His car catapulted off the curb and into a tree.* [from Latin]

**cata|ract** /kǽtərækt/ (**cataracts**) N-COUNT **Cataracts** are layers over a person's eyes that prevent them from seeing properly. ❏ *The majority of people get cataracts when they are older.* [from Latin]

**ca|tas|tro|phe** /kətǽstrəfi/ (**catastrophes**) N-COUNT A **catastrophe** is an unexpected event that causes great suffering or damage. ❏ *From all points of view, war would be a catastrophe.* [from Greek]

**cata|stroph|ic** /kǽtəstrɒfɪk/ ADJ **Catastrophic** means extremely bad or serious, often causing great suffering or damage. ❏ *A storm caused catastrophic damage to the coast.* ❏ *...a catastrophic mistake.* [from Greek]

---

**catch**

❶ HOLD OR TOUCH
❷ MANAGE TO SEE, HEAR, OR TALK TO
❸ OTHER USES
❹ PHRASAL VERBS

❶ **catch** /kǽtʃ/ (**catches, catching, caught**) **1** V-T If you **catch** a person or animal, you capture them. ❏ *Police say they are confident of catching the gunman.* ❏ *Where did you catch the fish?* **2** V-T If you **catch** an object that is moving through the air, you grab it with your hands. ❏ *I jumped up to catch a ball and fell over.* ● **Catch** is also a noun. ❏ *He missed the catch and the game was lost.* **3** V-T If one thing **catches** another, it hits it. ❏ *I caught him with my elbow but it was an accident.* **4** V-I If something **catches on** or **in** an object, it accidentally becomes attached to the object or stuck in it. ❏ *Her ankle caught on a root, and she fell over.* [from Old Northern French] **5** to **catch hold of** something → see **hold**

| **Thesaurus** | catch | Also look up : |
|---|---|---|

v. arrest, capture, grab, seize, snatch, trap; (ant.) free, let go, let off, release ❶ **1**

❷ **catch** /kǽtʃ/ (**catches, catching, caught**) **1** V-T When you **catch** a bus, train, or plane, you get on it in order to travel somewhere. ❏ *We were in plenty of time for Anthony to catch the ferry.* **2** V-T If you **catch** someone doing something wrong, you see or find them doing it. ❏ *He caught a man breaking into a car.* ❏ *They caught him with $30,000 cash in a briefcase.* **3** V-T If you **catch** something that someone has said, you manage to hear it. ❏ *I didn't catch your name.* [from Old Northern French] **4** to **catch sight of** something → see **sight**

❸ **catch** /kǽtʃ/ (**catches, catching, caught**) **1** V-T If something **catches** your attention or your eye, you notice it or become interested in it. ❏ *My shoes caught his attention.* **2** V-T If you **catch** a cold or a disease, you become ill with it. ❏ *The more stress you are under, the more likely you are to catch a cold.* **3** V-T If something **catches** the light or if the light **catches** it, it reflects the light and looks bright or shiny. ❏ *They saw the ship's guns, catching the light of the moon.* **4** V-T PASSIVE If you **are caught** in a storm or other unpleasant situation, it happens when you cannot avoid its effects. ❏ *He was caught in a storm and almost drowned.* **5** N-COUNT A **catch** on a window, door, or container is a device that fastens it. ❏ *She opened the catch of her bag.* **6** N-COUNT A **catch** is a hidden problem or difficulty in a plan or an offer. ❏ *The catch is that some of the students in need of help do not ask for it.* [from Old Northern French] **7** to **catch fire** → see **fire**

❹ **catch** /kǽtʃ/ (**catches, catching, caught**) [from Old Northern French]
▶ **catch on** **1** PHR-VERB If you **catch on to** something, you understand it, or realize that it is happening. ❏ *I was slow to catch on to what she was trying to tell me.* **2** PHR-VERB If something **catches on**, it becomes popular. ❏ *The idea has been around for years without catching on.*
▶ **catch up** **1** PHR-VERB If you **catch up with** someone, you reach them by walking faster than they are walking. ❏ *I stopped and waited for her to*

C

*catch up.* **2** PHR-VERB To **catch up with** someone means to reach the same standard or level that they have reached. ❑ *Most late developers will catch up with their friends.* ❑ *John began the season better than me but I fought to catch up.* **3** PHR-VERB If you **catch up on** an activity that you have not had much time to do, you spend time doing it. ❑ *I was catching up on a bit of reading.* **4** PHR-VERB If you **are caught up in** something, you are involved in it, usually unwillingly. ❑ *The people weren't part of the conflict; they were just caught up in it.*
▶ **catch up with** **1** PHR-VERB When people **catch up with** someone who has done something wrong, they succeed in finding them. ❑ *The police caught up with him yesterday.* **2** PHR-VERB If something **catches up with** you, you are forced to deal with an unpleasant situation that you have been able to avoid until now. ❑ *His criminal past caught up with him.*

**catch|ment area** (**catchment areas**) N-COUNT In geography, the **catchment area** of a river is the area of land from which water flows into the river. [TECHNICAL]

**catch-up** PHRASE If someone **is playing catch-up,** they are trying to equal or better someone else's performance. ❑ *We were playing catch-up for most of the game.*

**catch|word** also **catch phrase** /kætʃwɜrd/ (**catchwords**) N-COUNT A **catchword** is a word or phrase that becomes popular or well-known. ❑ *The catchword he and his supporters have been using is "consolidation."*

**catchy** /kætʃi/ (**catchier, catchiest**) ADJ A **catchy** tune, name, or phrase is attractive and easy to remember. ❑ *The songs were catchy.* [from Old Northern French]

**cat|egori|cal** /kætɪgɔrɪk⁰l/ ADJ If you are **categorical** about something, you state your views very definitely and firmly. ❑ *...his categorical denial of the charges.* ● **cat|egori|cal|ly** /kætɪgɔrɪkli/ ADV ❑ *I categorically refused to leave.* [from Late Latin]

**cat|ego|rize** /kætɪgəraɪz/ (**categorizes, categorizing, categorized**) V-T If you **categorize** people or things, you say which set they belong to. ❑ *His movies are hard to categorize.* ❑ *The novel was wrongly categorized as a children's story.* ● **cat|ego|ri|za|tion** /kætɪgərɪzeɪʃⁿn/ (**categorizations**) N-VAR ❑ *...attempts at categorization.* [from Late Latin]

**cat|ego|ry** /kætɪgɔri/ (**categories**) N-COUNT If people or things are divided into **categories**, they are divided into groups according to their qualities and characteristics. ❑ *This book clearly falls into the category of autobiography.* [from Late Latin]

| **Thesaurus** | *category* | Also look up : |
|---|---|---|
| N. | class, grouping, kind, rank, sort, type | |

**ca|ter** /keɪtər/ (**caters, catering, catered**) V-I To **cater to** a group of people means to provide all the things that they need or want. ❑ *...businesses that cater to local trade.* [from Latin]

**ca|ter|er** /keɪtərər/ (**caterers**) N-COUNT A **caterer** is a person or a company that provides food in a particular place or on a special occasion. ❑ *The caterers were already laying out the tables for lunch.* [from Latin]

**ca|ter|ing** /keɪtərɪŋ/ N-UNCOUNT **Catering** is the activity or business of providing food for large numbers of people. ❑ *His catering business made him a millionaire at 41.* [from Latin]

**cat|er|pil|lar** /kætərpɪlər/ (**caterpillars**) N-COUNT A **caterpillar** is a small, worm-like animal that eventually develops into a butterfly or moth. [from Old Northern French]

**ca|thar|sis** /kəθɑrsɪs/ N-UNCOUNT **Catharsis** is getting rid of unhappy memories or strong emotions such as anger or sadness by expressing them in some way. [from New Latin]

**ca|thedral** /kəθidrəl/ (**cathedrals**) N-COUNT A **cathedral** is a large and important church which has a bishop in charge of it. ❑ *...St. Paul's Cathedral.* [from Late Latin]

**Catho|lic** /kæθlɪk/ (**Catholics**) **1** ADJ The **Catholic** Church is the branch of the Christian Church that accepts the Pope as its leader and is based in the Vatican in Rome. ❑ *...Catholic priests.* ● **Ca|tholi|cism** /kəθɒlɪsɪzəm/ N-UNCOUNT ❑ *...her interest in Catholicism.* **2** N-COUNT A **Catholic** is a member of the Catholic Church. ❑ *At least nine out of ten Mexicans are Catholics.* [from Latin]

**cat|nip** /kætnɪp/ N-UNCOUNT **Catnip** is an herb with scented leaves, which cats are fond of.

**cat|tle** /kæt⁰l/ N-PLURAL **Cattle** are cows and bulls. ❑ *...the finest herd of beef cattle for two hundred miles.* [from Old Northern French]
→ see **dairy, herbivore**

**catty-corner** also **kitty-corner** ADV Something that is **catty-corner** or **kitty-corner** from another thing is placed or arranged diagonally from it. ❑ *There was a police car catty-corner across the street.* ❑ *Two tall, steel and aluminum towers stood kitty-corner from each other.*

**cat|walk** /kætwɔk/ (**catwalks**) **1** N-COUNT At a fashion show, the **catwalk** is a narrow platform that models walk along to display clothes. **2** N-COUNT A **catwalk** is a narrow bridge high in the air, for example between two parts of a tall building, on the outside of a large structure, or over a stage.

**cau|cus** /kɔkəs/ (**caucuses**) N-COUNT A **caucus** is an influential group of people within an organization who share similar aims and interests. [FORMAL] ❑ *The new members agreed to form their own caucus.* [from Algonquian]

**caught** /kɔt/ **Caught** is the past tense and past participle of **catch.**

**cau|li|flow|er** /kɔliflaʊər/ (**cauliflowers**) N-VAR A **cauliflower** is a large, round, white vegetable surrounded by green leaves. [from Italian]
→ see **vegetable**

**caulk** /kɔk/ (**caulks, caulking, caulked**) **1** V-T If you **caulk** something, you fill small cracks in its surface in order to prevent it from leaking. ❑ *He offered to caulk the windows.* ● **caulk|ing** /kɔkɪŋ/ N-UNCOUNT ❑ *...easy jobs like caulking.* **2** N-UNCOUNT **Caulk** is a soft substance that is used to caulk something. [from Old Northern French]

**cause** /kɔz/ (**causes, causing, caused**) **1** N-COUNT The **cause of** an event, usually a bad event, is the thing that makes it happen. ❑ *Pollution is the commonest cause of death for birds.*

**2** N-COUNT A **cause** is an aim or principle which a group of people supports or is fighting for. ❑ *Refusing to have one leader has not helped the cause.* **3** V-T To **cause** something, usually something bad, means to make it happen. ❑ *Stress can cause health problems.* ❑ *This was a genuine mistake, but it did cause me some worry.* **4** N-UNCOUNT If you have **cause for** a particular feeling or action, you have good reasons for feeling it or doing it. ❑ *Only a few people can find any cause for celebration.* [from Latin]

**cau|tion** /kɔʃ°n/ (cautions, cautioning, cautioned) **1** N-UNCOUNT **Caution** is great care which you take in order to avoid possible danger. ❑ *You should use caution when buying used tires.* **2** V-T/V-I If someone **cautions** you, they warn you about problems or danger. ❑ *Tony cautioned against believing everything in the newspapers.* ❑ *His lawyers have cautioned him against saying anything.* ● **Caution** is also a noun. ❑ *There was a note of caution in her voice.* [from Old French] **3** to **err on the side of** caution → see **err**

**cau|tion|ary** /kɔʃəneri/ ADJ A **cautionary** story is intended to give a warning to people. ❑ *...a cautionary tale about the dangers of the Internet.* [from Old French]

**cau|tious** /kɔʃəs/ ADJ Someone who is **cautious** acts very carefully in order to avoid danger. ❑ *Scientists are cautious about using the therapy on humans.* ● **cau|tious|ly** ADV ❑ *David moved cautiously forward and looked over the edge.* [from Old French]

**cava|lier** /kævəlɪər/ ADJ If you describe a person as **cavalier**, you disapprove of them because you think that they do not consider other people's feelings or take account of the seriousness of a situation. ❑ *...a cavalier attitude toward the law.* [from Italian]

**cav|al|ry** /kæv°lri/ **1** N-SING The **cavalry** is the part of an army that uses armored vehicles for fighting. ❑ *...the 3rd Cavalry.* **2** N-SING In the past, **the cavalry** was the group of soldiers in an army who rode horses. ❑ *...a young cavalry officer.* [from French]

**cave** /keɪv/ (caves, caving, caved) N-COUNT A **cave** is a large hole in the side of a cliff or hill or under the ground. [from Old French]
▶ **cave in 1** PHR-VERB If a roof or a wall **caves in**, it collapses inward. ❑ *Part of the roof caved in.* **2** PHR-VERB If you **cave in**, you suddenly stop arguing or resisting. ❑ *The judge caved in to political pressure.*
→ see Picture Dictionary: **cave**

**cav|ern** /kævərn/ (caverns) N-COUNT A **cavern** is a large, deep cave. [from Old French]

**cavi|ar** /kæviɑr/ also **caviare** N-UNCOUNT **Caviar** is the salted eggs of a fish called a sturgeon. [from Old Italian]

**cav|ity** /kæviti/ (cavities) **1** N-COUNT A **cavity** is a small space or hole in something solid. [FORMAL] ❑ *...a cavity in the roof.* **2** N-COUNT In dentistry, a **cavity** is a hole in a tooth, caused by

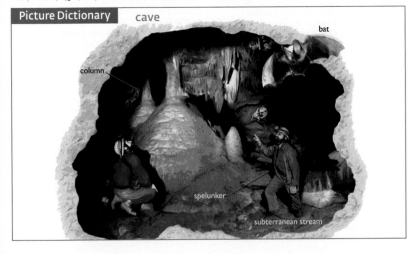

**Picture Dictionary** cave

bat

column

spelunker

subterranean stream

decay. [TECHNICAL] [from French]
→ see **smell**, **teeth**

**cc** /ˌsiː ˈsiː/ **1** **cc** is an abbreviation for "cubic centimeters," used when referring to the volume or capacity of something such as the size of a car engine. ❑ …1,500 cc sports cars. **2** **cc** is used in e-mail headers or at the end of a business letter to indicate that a copy is being sent to another person. [BUSINESS] ❑ …cc j.jones@harpercollins.co.uk.

**CCTV** /ˌsiː siː tiː ˈviː/ N-UNCOUNT **CCTV** is an abbreviation for "closed-circuit television." ❑ …a CCTV camera.

**CD** /ˌsiː ˈdiː/ (CDs) N-COUNT A **CD** is a small shiny disc on which music or computer data is stored.
→ see **laser**

**CD burn|er** (CD burners) N-COUNT A **CD burner** is a piece of computer equipment that you use for copying data from a computer onto a CD. [COMPUTING]

**CD play|er** (CD players) N-COUNT A **CD player** is a machine on which you can play CDs.

**CD-ROM** /ˌsiː diː ˈrɒm/ (CD-ROMs) N-COUNT A **CD-ROM** is a CD on which a very large amount of information can be stored and then read using a computer. [COMPUTING]
→ see **computer**

**CD writ|er** (CD writers) N-COUNT A **CD writer** is the same as a **CD burner**. [COMPUTING]

**cease** /siːs/ (ceases, ceasing, ceased) **1** V-I If something **ceases**, it stops happening or existing. [FORMAL] ❑ At one o'clock the rain ceased. **2** V-T If you **cease to** do something, you stop doing it. [FORMAL] ❑ He never ceases to amaze me. ❑ The newspaper ceased publication this week. [from Old French]

| **Thesaurus** | cease | Also look up : |
|---|---|---|
| v. | end, finish, halt, quit, shut down, stop; (ant.) begin, continue, start **1** | |

**cease|fire** /ˈsiːsfaɪər/ (ceasefires) N-COUNT A **ceasefire** is an arrangement in which countries at war agree to stop fighting for a time. ❑ They have agreed to a ceasefire after three years of conflict.

**ce|dar** /ˈsiːdər/ (cedars) N-VAR A **cedar** is a kind of evergreen tree. ● **Cedar** is the wood of this tree. ❑ The boat is built of cedar. [from Old French]

**cede** /siːd/ (cedes, ceding, ceded) V-T If someone in a position of authority **cedes** land or power to someone else, they let them have it. [FORMAL] ❑ After the war Spain ceded the island to America. [from Latin]

**ceil|ing** /ˈsiːlɪŋ/ (ceilings) **1** N-COUNT A **ceiling** is the top inside surface of a room. ❑ The rooms were large, with high ceilings. **2** N-COUNT A **ceiling** is an official upper limit on prices or wages. ❑ …an informal agreement to put a ceiling on salaries.

**cel|ebrate** /ˈsɛlɪbreɪt/ (celebrates, celebrating, celebrated) **1** V-T/V-I If you **celebrate** something, you do something enjoyable because of a special occasion. ❑ I was in a mood to celebrate. ❑ Dick celebrated his 60th birthday Monday. ● **cel|ebra|tion** /ˌsɛlɪbreɪʃ°n/ (celebrations) N-VAR ❑ There was a celebration in our house that night. ❑ Few people can find any cause for celebration. **2** V-T When priests **celebrate** Holy Communion or Mass, they officially perform the actions and ceremonies that are involved. ❑ The Pope celebrated Mass today in Saint Peter's Square. [from Latin]

**cel|ebrat|ed** /ˈsɛlɪbreɪtɪd/ ADJ A **celebrated** person or thing is famous and much admired. ❑ …one of the most celebrated young painters in England. [from Latin]

**ce|leb|rity** /sɪlɛbrɪti/ (celebrities) N-COUNT A **celebrity** is someone who is famous. ❑ At the age of 30, Hersey suddenly became a celebrity. [from Latin]

**cel|ery** /ˈsɛləri/ N-UNCOUNT **Celery** is a vegetable with long, pale green stalks. ❑ …a stick of celery. [from French]

**ce|les|tial** /sɪlɛstʃəl/ ADJ **Celestial** is used to describe things relating to heaven or to the sky. [LITERARY] ❑ …the Sun, Moon, and other celestial bodies. [from Medieval Latin]
→ see **astronomer**

**celi|bate** /ˈsɛlɪbɪt/ ADJ Someone who is **celibate** does not marry or have sex. ❑ The Pope has told priests to stay celibate. ● **celi|ba|cy** /ˈsɛlɪbəsi/ N-UNCOUNT ❑ …vows of celibacy. [from Latin]

**cell** /sɛl/ (cells) **1** N-COUNT A **cell** is the smallest part of an animal or plant. Every animal or plant is made up of millions of cells. ❑ …blood cells. **2** N-COUNT A **cell** is a small room in which a prisoner is locked. ❑ How many prisoners were in each cell? **3** N-COUNT A **cell** is a device that produces electricity as the result of a chemical reaction. [from Medieval Latin]
→ see **cardiovascular system**, **cellphone**, **clone**, **skin**

**cel|lar** /ˈsɛlər/ (cellars) N-COUNT A **cellar** is a room underneath a building. ❑ He kept the box of papers in the cellar. [from Latin]

**cell cy|cle** (cell cycles) N-COUNT A **cell cycle** is the series of changes that a biological cell goes through from the beginning of its life until its death.

**cell di|vi|sion** N-UNCOUNT **Cell division** is the biological process by which a cell inside an animal or a plant divides into two new cells during growth or reproduction.

**cell mem|brane** (cell membranes) N-COUNT **Cell membranes** are the thin outer layers of the cells inside an animal.

**cel|lo** /ˈtʃɛloʊ/ (cellos) N-VAR A **cello** is a musical instrument that looks like a large violin. You hold it upright and play it sitting down. ● **cel|list** /ˈtʃɛlɪst/ (cellists) N-COUNT ❑ …the world's greatest cellist.
→ see **orchestra**, **string**

**cell|phone** /ˈsɛlfoʊn/ (cellphones) N-COUNT A **cellphone** is a type of telephone which does not need wires to connect it to a telephone system.
→ see Word Web: **cellphone**

**cell theo|ry** N-SING The **cell theory** is a set of basic principles relating to biological cells, such as the principle that all living creatures are composed of cells and that all cells come from other cells.

**cel|lu|lar** /ˈsɛlyələr/ ADJ **Cellular** means relating to the cells of animals or plants. ❑ …cellular growth. [from Medieval Latin]
→ see **cell**

**cel|lu|lar phone** (cellular phones) N-COUNT A **cellular phone** is the same as a **cellphone**.
→ see **cellphone**

## Word Web    cellphone

The word **"cell"** is not something inside the **cellular phone** itself. It describes the area around the **wireless transmitter** that your phone uses to make a call. The electrical system and **battery** in today's **mobile** phones are tiny. This makes their electronic **signals** weak. They can't travel very far. Therefore today's **cellular** phone systems need a lot of cells close together. When you make a call, your phone connects to the wireless transmitter with the strongest signal. Then it chooses a radio **channel** and connects you to the number you dialed. If you are riding in a car, **stations** in several different cells may handle your call.

**cel|lu|lar res|pi|ra|tion** N-UNCOUNT **Cellular respiration** is the biological process by which cells convert substances such as sugar into energy. [TECHNICAL]

**cel|lu|lite** /sɛlyəlaɪt/ N-UNCOUNT **Cellulite** is lumpy fat which people may get under their skin, especially on their thighs. [from French]

**cell wall** (**cell walls**) N-COUNT **Cell walls** are the thin outer layers of the cells inside plants and bacteria.

**Celsius** /sɛlsiəs/ ADJ **Celsius** is a scale for measuring temperature, in which water freezes at 0° and boils at 100°. [TECHNICAL] ❑ *It's 11° Celsius today, that's 52° Fahrenheit.* [from Swedish]
→ see **thermometer**

### Usage    Celsius and Fahrenheit

The Celsius or centigrade scale is rarely used to express temperature in the U.S. The Fahrenheit scale is used instead.

**ce|ment** /sɪmɛnt/ (**cements, cementing, cemented**) ■ N-UNCOUNT **Cement** is a gray powder which is mixed with sand and water in order to make concrete. ② V-T Something that **cements** a relationship or agreement makes it stronger. ❑ *Nothing cements a friendship between countries so much as trade.* ③ V-T If things **are cemented** together, they are stuck or fastened together. ❑ *...a street sign cemented into the wall.* [from Old French]

### Word Link    ery ≈ place where something happens : bakery, cemetery, refinery

**cem|etery** /sɛmətɛri/ (**cemeteries**) N-COUNT A **cemetery** is a place where dead people's bodies or their ashes are buried. [from Late Latin]

**Ce|no|zo|ic era** /siːnəzoʊɪk, sɛn-/ N-SING The **Cenozoic era** is the most recent period in the history of the Earth, from 65 million years ago to the present day. [TECHNICAL]

**cen|sor** /sɛnsər/ (**censors, censoring, censored**) ■ V-T If someone **censors** a letter or the media, they officially examine it and cut out any parts that they consider unacceptable. ❑ *The government has heavily censored the news.* ② N-COUNT A **censor** is a person who has been officially appointed to censor things. ❑ *The censors wouldn't accept the movie until cuts were made.* [from Latin]

### Word Link    ship ≈ condition or state : censorship, citizenship, friendship

**cen|sor|ship** /sɛnsərʃɪp/ N-UNCOUNT **Censorship** is the censoring of the media or of letters. ❑ *Censorship is stricter than ever.* [from Latin]

**cen|sure** /sɛnʃər/ (**censures, censuring, censured**) V-T If you **censure** someone **for** something that they have done, you criticize them strongly. [FORMAL] ❑ *The committee may decide to censure him.* ● **Censure** is also a noun. ❑ *...a policy which has attracted international censure.* [from Latin]

**cen|sus** /sɛnsəs/ (**censuses**) N-COUNT A **census** is an official survey of the population of a country. ❑ *...a detailed assessment of the latest census.* [from Latin]

### Word Link    cent ≈ hundred : cents, century, percentage

**cent** /sɛnt/ (**cents**) N-COUNT A **cent** is a small unit of money worth one hundredth of some currencies, for example the dollar and the euro. ❑ *...a cup of rice which cost thirty cents.* [from Latin]

### Word Link    enn ≈ year : centennial, millennium, perennial

**cen|ten|nial** /sɛntɛniəl/ N-SING A **centennial** is the one hundredth anniversary of an event. [FORMAL] ❑ *The centennial Olympics will be in Atlanta, Georgia.* [from Latin]

**cen|ter** /sɛntər/ (**centers, centering, centered**) ■ N-COUNT The **center** of something is the middle of it. ❑ *...the center of the room.* ② N-COUNT A **center** is a place where people have meetings, take part in a particular activity, or get help of some kind. ❑ *After school, Room 250 is a tutoring center.* ③ N-COUNT If an area or town is a **center** for an industry or activity, that industry or activity is very important there. ❑ *New York is a major international financial center.* ④ N-COUNT If someone or something is the **center of** attention or interest, people are giving them a lot of attention. ❑ *She was used to being the center of attention.* ⑤ V-T/V-I If something **centers on** or **is centered on** a particular thing or person, that thing or person is the main subject of attention. ❑ *...a plan which centered on academic achievement.* ❑ *All his concerns were centered around himself rather than Rachel.* ● **-centered** ADJ ❑ *...child-centered teaching methods.* ⑥ V-T If something **is centered** in a place, it happens or is based there. ❑ *The fighting centered around the town of Vucovar.* ⑦ → see also **community center, shopping center** [from Latin]
→ see **soccer**

**Word Partnership**    Use *center* with :

N.     center **of a circle** 1
      **convention** center, **research** center 2
      center **of attention** 4

**cen|ter stage** N-UNCOUNT In a theater, **center stage** is the middle part of the stage.

**cen|ti|li|ter** /sɛntɪlitər/ (**centiliters**) N-COUNT A **centiliter** is a unit of volume in the metric system equal to ten milliliters or one-hundredth of a liter.

**cen|ti|me|ter** /sɛntɪmitər/ (**centimeters**) N-COUNT A **centimeter** is a unit of length in the metric system equal to ten millimeters or one-hundredth of a meter. ❑ *...a tiny plant, only a few centimeters high.*
→ see **measurement**

**cen|ti|pede** /sɛntɪpid/ (**centipedes**) N-COUNT A **centipede** is a long, thin creature with a lot of legs.

**cen|tral** /sɛntrəl/ 1 ADJ Something that is **central** is in the middle of a place or area. ❑ *...Central America.* ● **cen|tral|ly** ADJ ❑ *...a centrally located office.* 2 ADJ A **central** group or organization makes all the important decisions for a larger organization or a country. ❑ *...the central government in Rome.* ● **cen|tral|ly** ADV ❑ *...an international organization, centrally controlled by one country.* 3 ADJ The **central** person or thing in a situation is the most important one. ❑ *Black dance music has been central to pop since the early '60s.* [from Latin]

**Word Partnership**    Use *central* with :

N.     central **location** 1
      central **government** 2

**cen|tral heat|ing** N-UNCOUNT **Central heating** is a heating system in which air or water is heated and passed around a building through pipes and radiators.

**cen|tral|ize** /sɛntrəlaɪz/ (**centralizes, centralizing, centralized**) V-T To **centralize** a country or organization means to create a system in which one central group of people gives instructions to regional groups. ❑ *Very large firms usually centralize their operations.* ● **cen|tral|i|za|tion** /sɛntrəlɪzeɪ˺ən/ N-UNCOUNT ❑ *...the centralization of power.* [from Latin]

**cen|tral nerv|ous sys|tem** (**central nervous systems**) N-COUNT Your **central nervous system** is the part of your nervous system that consists of the brain and spinal cord.

**cen|trip|etal ac|cel|era|tion** /sɛntrɪpɪt˺l ækseləreɪ˺ən/ N-UNCOUNT **Centripetal acceleration** is the acceleration that is required to keep an object traveling at a constant speed when it is moving in a circle. [TECHNICAL]

**cen|tro|mere** /sɛntrəmɪər/ (**centromeres**) N-COUNT The **centromere** is the central part of a chromosome where the two ends of the chromosome are connected. [TECHNICAL] [from Latin]

**cen|tu|ry** /sɛntʃəri/ (**centuries**) 1 N-COUNT A **century** is a period of a hundred years that is used when stating a date. For example, the 19th century was the period from 1801 to 1900. ❑ *...the late eighteenth century.* 2 N-COUNT A **century** is any period of a hundred years. ❑ *The winter was the worst in a century.* [from Latin]

**cephalo|tho|rax** /sɛfələθɔ˺ræks/ (**cephalothoraces** or **cephalothoraxes**) N-COUNT In animals such as spiders and crabs, the **cephalothorax** is the front part of the body consisting of the head and thorax. [TECHNICAL]

**ce|ram|ic** /sɪræmɪk/ (**ceramics**) 1 N-UNCOUNT **Ceramic** is clay that has been heated to a very high temperature so that it becomes hard. ❑ *...ceramic tiles.* 2 N-COUNT **Ceramics** are ceramic ornaments or objects. ❑ *...a collection of Chinese ceramics.* 3 N-UNCOUNT **Ceramics** is the art of making artistic objects out of clay. ❑ *...courses in ceramics and art.* [from Greek]
→ see **pottery**

**ce|real** /sɪəriəl/ (**cereals**) 1 N-VAR **Cereal** is a food made from grain, usually mixed with milk and eaten for breakfast. ❑ *I have a bowl of cereal every morning.* 2 N-COUNT **Cereals** are plants such as wheat, corn, or rice that produce grain. ❑ *...the cereal-growing districts of the Midwest.* [from Latin]

**cer|ebel|lum** /sɛrəbɛləm/ (**cerebellums** or **cerebella**) N-COUNT The **cerebellum** is a part of the brain in humans and other mammals that controls the body's movements and balance. [MEDICAL] [from Latin]

**cere|bral** /sərɪbrəl/ 1 ADJ **Cerebral** means relating to thought and reasoning rather than to emotions. [FORMAL] ❑ *Some think he is too cerebral to win the support of voters.* 2 ADJ **Cerebral** means relating to the brain. [MEDICAL] ❑ *...a cerebral hemorrhage.* [from Latin]

**cer|ebrum** /sərɪbrəm, sɛrə-/ (**cerebrums** or **cerebra**) N-COUNT The **cerebrum** is the large, front part of the brain, which is divided into two halves and controls activities such as thinking and memory. [MEDICAL] [from Latin]

**cer|emo|nial** /sɛrɪmoʊniəl/ ADJ Something that is **ceremonial** relates to a ceremony or is used in a ceremony. ❑ *He represented the nation on ceremonial occasions.* [from Medieval Latin]

**cer|emo|ny** /sɛrɪmoʊni/ (**ceremonies**) 1 N-COUNT A **ceremony** is a formal event such as a wedding. ❑ *His grandmother's funeral was a private ceremony attended only by the family.* 2 N-UNCOUNT **Ceremony** consists of the special things that are said and done on very formal occasions. ❑ *The historic meeting took place with great ceremony.* [from Medieval Latin]
→ see **graduation, wedding**

**cer|tain** /sɜrt˺n/ 1 ADJ If you are **certain** about something or if it is **certain**, you firmly believe it is true and have no doubt about it. ❑ *She's absolutely certain she's going to make it.* ❑ *We are not certain whether the airline will be able to stay profitable.* ❑ *One thing is certain, both have the greatest respect for each other.* 2 ADJ You use **certain** to indicate that you are referring to one particular thing or person, although you are not saying exactly which it is. ❑ *There will be certain people who'll say "I told you so!"* ❑ *You owe a certain person a sum of money.* 3 PHRASE If you know something **for certain**, you have no doubt at all about it. ❑ *She didn't know for certain if he'd go or not.* 4 PHRASE If you **make certain that** something is the way you want or expect it to be, you take action to ensure that it is. ❑ *Parents should make certain that children spend enough time doing homework.* [from Old French]

**Thesaurus**　　*certain*　　Also look up :

ADJ. definite, known, positive, sure, true, unmistakable ∎

cer|tain|ly /ˈsɜrtᵊnli/ ∎ ADV You use **certainly** to emphasize what you are saying. ❑ *The public is certainly getting tired of hearing about it.* ❑ *The meeting will almost certainly start late.* ∎ ADV You use **certainly** when you are agreeing or disagreeing strongly with what someone has said. ❑ *"In any case you remained friends." — "Certainly."* ❑ *"Perhaps it would be better if I left." — "Certainly not!"* [from Old French]

cer|tain|ty /ˈsɜrtᵊnti/ (**certainties**) ∎ N-UNCOUNT **Certainty** is the state of having no doubts at all. ❑ *I can tell you this with absolute certainty.* ∎ N-COUNT **Certainties** are things that nobody has any doubts about. ❑ *There are no certainties in modern life.* [from Old French]

**Word Link**　*cert ≈ determined, true : ascertain, certificate, certify*

cer|tifi|cate /sərˈtɪfɪkɪt/ (**certificates**) N-COUNT A **certificate** is an official document stating that particular facts are true, or that you have successfully completed a course of study or training. ❑ *Please bring your birth certificate with you when you come to the bank to open an account.* [from Old French]
→ see **wedding**

cer|ti|fied check (**certified checks**) N-COUNT A **certified check** is a check that is guaranteed by a bank, because the bank has set aside sufficient money in the account.

cer|ti|fied mail N-UNCOUNT If you send a letter or package by **certified mail**, you send it using a mail service which gives you an official record of the fact that it has been mailed and delivered. ❑ *We recommend that you send your certificates by certified mail.*

cer|ti|fied pub|lic ac|count|ant (**certified public accountants**) N-COUNT A **certified public accountant** is someone who has received a certificate stating that he or she is qualified to work as an accountant within a particular state. The abbreviation **CPA** is also used. [AM]

cer|ti|fy /ˈsɜrtɪfaɪ/ (**certifies, certifying, certified**) ∎ V-T If someone in an official position **certifies** something, they officially state that it is true. ❑ *The president certified that the project would receive at least $650 million.* ❑ *The National Election Council is supposed to certify the results.* ● cer|tifi|ca|tion /ˌsɜrtɪfɪˈkeɪʃᵊn/ (**certifications**) N-VAR ❑ *An employer can demand written certification that the relative is really ill.* ∎ V-T If someone is **certified as** a particular kind of worker, they are given a certificate stating that they have successfully completed a course of training in their profession. ❑ *They wanted to get certified as divers.* ● cer|ti|fi|ca|tion N-UNCOUNT ❑ *...training leading to the certification of their skill in a particular field.* [from Old French]

cer|vix /ˈsɜrvɪks/ (**cervixes** or **cervices** /sərˈvaɪsiz, ˈsɜrvɪsiz/) N-COUNT The **cervix** is the entrance to the womb. [MEDICAL] ● cer|vi|cal /ˈsɜrvɪkᵊl/ ADJ ❑ *...cervical cancer.* [from Latin]

CFC /ˌsi ɛf ˈsi/ (**CFCs**) N-COUNT **CFCs** are chemicals that are used in aerosols, refrigerators, and cooling systems that can cause damage to the ozone layer. **CFC** is an abbreviation for "chlorofluorocarbon." ❑ *...the drop in CFC emissions.*

CGI /ˌsi dʒi ˈaɪ/ N-UNCOUNT **CGI** is a type of computer technology that is used to make special effects in movies and on television. **CGI** is an abbreviation for "computer-generated imagery."

chain /tʃeɪn/ (**chains, chaining, chained**) ∎ N-COUNT A **chain** consists of metal rings connected together in a line. ❑ *Around his neck he wore a gold chain.* ∎ N-COUNT A **chain of** things is a group of them existing or arranged in a line. ❑ *...a chain of islands known as the Windward Islands.* ∎ N-COUNT A **chain of** stores, hotels, or other businesses is a number of them owned by the same company. ❑ *...a large supermarket chain.* ∎ V-T If a person or thing **is chained to** something, they are fastened to it with a chain. ❑ *The dogs were chained to a fence.* ❑ *We were sitting together in our cell, chained to the wall.* ∎ N-SING A **chain of** events is a series of them happening one after another. ❑ *...the chain of events that led to his departure.* [from Old French]
→ see **food**

chair /tʃɛər/ (**chairs, chairing, chaired**) ∎ N-COUNT A **chair** is a piece of furniture for one person to sit on, with a back and four legs. ❑ *He rose from his chair and walked to the window.* ∎ N-COUNT At a university, a **chair** is the position or job of professor. ❑ *He has been named chair of the sociology department.* ∎ N-COUNT The **chair of** a committee or meeting is the person in charge of it. ❑ *She is the chair of the Defense Advisory Committee on Women in the Military.* ∎ V-T If you **chair** a meeting or a committee, you are the person in charge of it. ❑ *He was about to chair a meeting.* [from Old French]

chair|man /ˈtʃɛərmən/ (**chairmen**) N-COUNT The **chairman** of a meeting or organization is the person in charge of it. ❑ *He is chairman of the committee which produced the report.*

chair|person /ˈtʃɛərpɜrsᵊn/ (**chairpersons**) N-COUNT The **chairperson** of a meeting or organization is the person in charge of it. ❑ *She's the chairperson of the safety committee.*

chair|woman /ˈtʃɛərwʊmən/ (**chairwomen**) N-COUNT The **chairwoman** of a meeting or organization is the woman in charge of it. ❑ *Primakov was meeting with the chairwoman of the Party.*

cha|let /ʃæˈleɪ/ (**chalets**) N-COUNT A **chalet** is a small wooden house, especially in a mountain area. ❑ *...Swiss ski chalets.* [from Swiss French]

chalk /tʃɔk/ (**chalks, chalking, chalked**) ∎ N-UNCOUNT **Chalk** is a type of soft, white rock. ❑ *...white cliffs made of chalk.* ∎ N-VAR **Chalk** is small sticks of chalk used for writing or drawing. ❑ *...colored chalk.* [from Old English]
▶ chalk up PHR-VERB If you **chalk up** a success, you achieve it. ❑ *The team chalked up another victory.*

chalk|board /ˈtʃɔkbɔrd/ (**chalkboards**) N-COUNT A **chalkboard** is a dark-colored board that you can write on with chalk. [from Old English]

chal|lenge /ˈtʃælɪndʒ/ (**challenges, challenging, challenged**) ∎ N-VAR A **challenge** is something new and difficult which requires great effort and determination. ❑ *His first challenge was winning* the respect of his players. **2** PHRASE If someone **rises to the challenge**, they act in response to a difficult situation which is new to them and are successful. ❑ *Germany must rise to the challenge of its responsibilities.* **3** V-T If you **challenge** ideas or people, you question their truth, value, or authority. ❑ *They challenged the laws and tried to change them.* ❑ *The move was challenged by two of the republics.* ● **Challenge** is also a noun. ❑ *...a challenge to his authority.* **4** V-T If you **challenge** someone, you invite them to fight or compete with you in some way. ❑ *Woods challenged O'Meara to a friendly game.* ❑ *He left a note at the crime scene, challenging detectives to catch him.* ● **Challenge** is also a noun. ❑ *Both the Swiss and the German team will provide a serious challenge for the gold medals.* [from Old French] **5** → see also **challenging**

---

**Word Partnership** Use *challenge* with :

| | | |
|---|---|---|
| ADJ. | **biggest** challenge, **new** challenge **1** **3** **4** | |
| | **legal** challenge **3** | |
| V. | **accept a** challenge, **present a** challenge **1** **3** **4** | |
| | **dare to** challenge **3** **4** | |

---

**chal|leng|er** /tʃælɪndʒər/ (**challengers**) N-COUNT A **challenger** is someone who competes for a position or title. ❑ *...a challenger for the Americas Cup.* [from Old French]

**chal|leng|ing** /tʃælɪndʒɪŋ/ **1** ADJ A **challenging** task or job requires great effort and determination. ❑ *Mike found a challenging job as a computer programmer.* **2** ADJ **Challenging** behavior seems to be inviting people to argue or compete. ❑ *Mona gave him a challenging look.* [from Old French]

**cham|ber** /tʃeɪmbər/ (**chambers**) **1** N-COUNT A **chamber** is a large room that is designed and equipped for a particular purpose, for example for formal meetings. ❑ *...the council chamber.* ❑ *...a burial chamber.* **2** N-COUNT You can refer to a country's legislature or to one section of it as a **chamber**. ❑ *...a two-chamber parliament.* [from Old French]

**cham|ber of com|merce** (**chambers of commerce**) N-COUNT A **chamber of commerce** is an organization of businesspeople that promotes local commercial interests. [BUSINESS]

**champ** /tʃæmp/ (**champs**) N-COUNT A **champ** is the same as a **champion**. [INFORMAL] ❑ *...boxing champ Mike Tyson.*

**cham|pagne** /ʃæmpeɪn/ (**champagnes**) N-VAR **Champagne** is an expensive French white wine with bubbles in it.

**cham|pi|on** /tʃæmpiən/ (**champions, championing, championed**) **1** N-COUNT A **champion** is someone who has won the first prize in a competition. ❑ *...a former Olympic champion.* ❑ *Kasparov became world champion.* **2** N-COUNT If you are a **champion of** a person, a cause, or a principle, you support or defend them. ❑ *...a champion of freedom.* **3** V-T If you **champion** a person, a cause, or a principle, you support or defend them. ❑ *He passionately championed the poor.* [from Old French]

**cham|pi|on|ship** /tʃæmpiənʃɪp/ (**championships**) **1** N-COUNT A **championship** is a competition to find the best player or team in a

particular sport. ❑ *...the world chess championship.* **2** N-SING **The championship** refers to the title or status of being a sports champion. ❑ *He went on to win the championship.* [from Old French]

**chance** /tʃæns/ (**chances, chancing, chanced**) **1** N-VAR If there is a **chance of** something happening, it is possible that it will happen. ❑ *Do you think they have a chance of beating Australia?* ❑ *There was very little chance that Ben would ever lead a normal life.* **2** N-SING If you have a **chance to** do something, you have the opportunity to do it. ❑ *Everyone will get a chance to vote.* ❑ *One hundred and fifty million never get the chance to go to school.* **3** PHRASE Something that happens **by chance** was not planned by anyone. ❑ *He met Mr. Maude by chance.* **4** PHRASE If you say that someone **stands a chance of** achieving something, you mean that they are likely to achieve it. If you say that someone **doesn't stand a chance of** achieving something, you mean that they cannot possibly achieve it. ❑ *I stood a good chance of gaining high grades.* **5** PHRASE When you **take a chance**, you try to do something although there is a large risk of danger or failure. ❑ *You take a chance on the weather if you vacation in Maine.* ❑ *Retailers are not taking any chances on unknown brands.* [from Old French]

---

**Word Partnership** Use *chance* with :

| | | |
|---|---|---|
| N. | chance **of success**, chance **of survival**, chance **of winning** **1** | |
| ADJ. | **fair** chance, **good** chance, **slight** chance **1** **2** | |
| V. | **give** *someone/something* a chance, **have a** chance, **miss a** chance **1** **2** | |
| | **get a** chance **2** | |

---

**chan|cel|lor** /tʃænsələr, -slər/ (**chancellors**) **1** N-TITLE; N-COUNT **Chancellor** is the title of the head of government in Germany and Austria. ❑ *...Chancellor Angela Merkel of Germany.* **2** N-COUNT The head of some American universities is called the **chancellor**. **3** N-COUNT In Britain, the **Chancellor** or **Chancellor of the Exchequer** is the minister in charge of finance and taxes. [from Late Latin]

**chan|de|lier** /ʃændəˈlɪər/ (**chandeliers**) N-COUNT A **chandelier** is an ornamental frame hanging from a ceiling, which holds light bulbs or candles. [from French]

**change** /tʃeɪndʒ/ (**changes, changing, changed**) **1** N-VAR If there is a **change** in something, it becomes different. ❑ *...a change in U.S. policy.* ❑ *There are going to be some big changes.* **2** N-SING If you say that something is a **change** or **makes** a **change**, you mean that it is enjoyable because it is different from what you are used to. ❑ *It is a complicated system, but it certainly makes a change.* **3** V-T/V-I When something **changes** or when you **change** it, it becomes different. ❑ *We are trying to understand how the climate changes.* ❑ *The color of the sky changed from pink to blue.* ❑ *She has now changed into a happy, self-confident woman.* ❑ *They should change the law.* **4** V-T/V-I To **change** something means to replace it with something new or different. ❑ *All they did was change a light bulb.* ❑ *He changed to a different medication.* ● **Change** is also a noun. ❑ *A change of leadership alone will not be enough.* **5** V-T/V-I When you **change** your clothes, you take them off and put on different ones. ❑ *Ben changed his shirt.* ❑ *They allowed her to shower and change.* ◾ V-T When you **change** a bed or **change** the sheets, you take off the dirty sheets and put on clean ones. ❑ *After changing the bed, I would usually fall asleep quickly.* ◾ V-T When you **change** a baby or **change** its diaper, you take off the dirty one and put on a clean one. ❑ *She criticizes me for the way I change him.* ◾ V-T/V-I When you **change** buses, trains, or planes, you get off one and get on to another in order to continue your journey. ❑ *I changed planes in Chicago.* ◾ N-UNCOUNT Your **change** is the money that you receive when you pay for something with more money than it costs. ❑ *"There's your change."* — *"Thanks very much."* ◾ N-UNCOUNT **Change** is coins, rather than paper money. ❑ *...a bag of loose change.* ◾ PHRASE If you say that you are doing something or something is happening **for a change**, you mean that you do not usually do it or it does not usually happen, and you are happy to be doing it or that it is happening. ❑ *Now let me ask you a question, for a change.* ◾ PHRASE When a substance undergoes a **change of state**, it changes from one form to another, for example from a solid to a liquid. [from Old French] ◾ to change **for the better** → see **better** ◾ to change **hands** → see **hand** ◾ a change **of heart** → see **heart** ◾ to change your **mind** → see **mind** ◾ to change **places** → see **place** ◾ to change the **subject** → see **subject** ◾ to change **tack** → see **tack** ◾ to change **your tune** → see **tune** ◾ to change **for the worse** → see **worse**

▶ **change over** PHR-VERB If you **change over from** one thing **to** another, you stop doing one thing and start doing the other. ❑ *We are gradually changing over to a completely metric system.*

| **Thesaurus** | *change* | Also look up : |
|---|---|---|
| N. | adjustment, alteration ◾ | |
| V. | adapt, modify, transform, vary ◾ | |

| **Word Partnership** | Use *change* with : |
|---|---|
| V. | adapt to change, resist change ◾ make a change ◾◾ |
| ADJ. | gradual change, social change, sudden change ◾ loose change, spare change ◾ |
| N. | change of pace, policy change ◾ change of address, change clothes, change color, change direction, change the subject ◾◾ |

**chan|nel** /tʃænᵊl/ (**channels, channeling** or **channelling, channeled** or **channelled**) ◾ N-COUNT A **channel** is a television station. ❑ *...the huge number of television channels in America.* ◾ N-COUNT If you do something through a particular **channel**, that is the system or organization that you use in order to do it. ❑ *Very few details of the talks are available through official channels.* ◾ N-COUNT A **channel** is a narrow passage along which water flows. ❑ *...a drainage channel.* ◾ V-T If you **channel** money into something, you arrange for it to be used for that purpose. ❑ *...a system to channel funds to poor countries.* [from Old French]
→ see **cellphone**

**channel-surfing** N-UNCOUNT **Channel-surfing** means switching quickly between different

television channels looking for something interesting to watch.

**chant** /tʃænt/ (**chants, chanting, chanted**) ◾ N-COUNT A **chant** is a word or group of words that is repeated over and over again. ❑ *Then the crowd started the chant of "U-S-A!"* ◾ N-COUNT A **chant** is a religious song or prayer that is sung on only a few notes. ❑ *...a Gregorian chant.* ◾ V-T/V-I If you **chant** something, you repeat the same words over and over again. ❑ *The crowd chanted his name.* ❑ *The crowd chanted "We are with you."* ● **chant|ing** N-UNCOUNT ❑ *A lot of the chanting was in support of the prime minister.* [from Old French]

**cha|os** /keɪɒs/ N-UNCOUNT **Chaos** is a state of complete disorder and confusion. ❑ *The race ended in chaos.* [from Latin]

| **Word Partnership** | Use *chaos* with : |
|---|---|
| V. | bring chaos, cause chaos |
| ADJ. | complete chaos, total chaos |
| N. | chaos and confusion |

| **Word Link** | *otic ≈ affecting, causing* : *chaotic, neurotic, patriotic* |
|---|---|

**cha|ot|ic** /keɪɒtɪk/ ADJ Something that is **chaotic** is in a state of complete disorder and confusion. ❑ *My house feels as chaotic as a bus terminal.* [from Latin]

**chap|el** /tʃæpᵊl/ (**chapels**) ◾ N-COUNT A **chapel** is a part of a church which has its own altar and which is used for private prayer. ◾ N-COUNT A **chapel** is a small church in or attached to a hospital, school, or prison. ❑ *We married in the college chapel.* [from Old French]

**chap|lain** /tʃæplɪn/ (**chaplains**) N-COUNT A **chaplain** is a member of the Christian clergy who does religious work in a place such as a hospital, school, prison, or in the armed forces. ❑ *...an army chaplain.* [from Old French]

**chapped** /tʃæpt/ ADJ If your skin is **chapped**, it is dry, cracked, and sore. ❑ *...chapped lips.* [from Germanic]

**chap|ter** /tʃæptər/ (**chapters**) ◾ N-COUNT A **chapter** is one of the parts that a book is divided into. ❑ *See Chapter 4.* ◾ N-COUNT You can refer to part of your life or a period in history as a **chapter**. [WRITTEN] ❑ *This is a difficult chapter in Lebanon's history.* [from Old French]

**char|ac|ter** /kærɪktər/ (**characters**) ◾ N-COUNT The **character** of a person or place consists of all the qualities they have that make them distinct. ❑ *There is a negative side to his character that you haven't seen yet.* ◾ N-COUNT You can refer to a person as a **character**, especially when describing their qualities. ❑ *It's his courage that makes him such a remarkable character.* ◾ N-COUNT The **characters** in a movie, book, or play are the people in it. ❑ *The central character is played by Collard himself.* ◾ N-COUNT A **character** is a letter, number, or other symbol that is written or printed. ❑ *...a shopping list written in Chinese characters.* ◾ N-VAR Your **character** is your reputation. ❑ *...a series of personal attacks on my character.* [from Latin]
→ see **printing**

## Word Partnership   Use *character* with :

| | |
|---|---|
| N. | character **flaw**, character **trait** ■ |
| | character **development** ■ ■ |
| | character **in a book/movie**, **cartoon** |
| | character ■ |
| ADJ. | **moral** character ■ |
| | **fictional** character, **main** character, |
| | **minor** character ■ |

char|ac|ter|is|tic /kærɪktərɪstɪk/
(**characteristics**) ■ N-COUNT A **characteristic** is
a quality or feature that is typical of someone or
something. ❑ *Genes determine the characteristics
of every living thing.* ■ ADJ If something is
**characteristic** of a person, thing, or place, it
is typical of them. ❑ *Refusal to admit defeat was
characteristic of Davis.* ❑ *Churches are a characteristic
feature of the English countryside.*
• char|ac|ter|is|ti|cal|ly /kærɪktərɪstɪkli/ ADV
❑ *He was characteristically impatient.* [from Latin]

char|ac|ter|is|tic prop|er|ty (**characteristic
properties**) N-COUNT A **characteristic property**
of a substance is a quality of the substance that
distinguishes it from other substances, for
example the fact that it melts at a particular
temperature.

char|ac|teri|za|tion /kærɪktərɪzeɪʃ°n/
(**characterizations**) N-VAR **Characterization** is the
way an author or an actor describes or shows what
a character is like. [from Latin]

char|ac|ter|ize /kærɪktəraɪz/ (**characterizes,
characterizing, characterized**) ■ V-T If
something **is characterized by** a particular feature
or quality, that feature or quality is an obvious
part of it. [FORMAL] ❑ *This election campaign has been
characterized by violence.* ■ V-T If you **characterize**
someone or something **as** a particular thing,
you describe them in that way. [FORMAL] ❑ *Both
companies characterized the relationship as "friendly."*
• char|ac|teri|za|tion /kærɪktərɪzeɪʃ°n/
(**characterizations**) N-VAR ❑ *...his characterization of
other designers as "thieves."* [from Latin]

cha|rade /ʃəreɪd/ (**charades**) N-COUNT A
**charade** is a situation in which people pretend
to think or feel a certain way, even though it is
obvious that they do not. [from French]

char|broiled /tʃɑrbrɔɪld/ also **char-grilled** ADJ
**Charbroiled** meat or fish has been cooked so that it
burns slightly and turns black.

char|coal /tʃɑrkoʊl/ N-UNCOUNT **Charcoal** is
a black substance used as a fuel and for drawing,
obtained by burning wood without much air.
→ see **firework**

charge /tʃɑrdʒ/ (**charges, charging, charged**)
■ V-T/V-I If you **charge** someone an amount
of money, you ask them to pay that amount for
something. ❑ *The newspaper charges $5 a week for car
ads.* ❑ *Some banks charge if you access your account to
determine your balance.* ❑ *The architect charged us a fee
of seven hundred and fifty dollars.* ■ V-T If you **charge**
something **to** an organization or your account,
it will be paid for later by the organization or
added to your account and paid for later. ❑ *Go out
and buy a pair of glasses, and charge it to us.* ■ V-T
When the police **charge** someone, they formally
accuse them of having done something illegal.
❑ *They have the evidence to charge him.* ■ V-I If you

**charge** toward someone or something, you move
quickly and aggressively toward them. ❑ *He
charged through the door to my mother's office.* ❑ *He
ordered us to charge.* ■ V-T To **charge** a battery
means to pass an electrical current through it
in order to make it more powerful or to make
it last longer. ❑ *Alex forgot to charge the battery.*
■ N-COUNT An electrical **charge** is an amount
of electricity that is held in or carried by something.
[TECHNICAL] ■ N-COUNT A **charge** is an amount
of money that you have to pay for a service. ❑ *We
can arrange this for a small charge.* ■ N-COUNT A
**charge** is a formal accusation that someone has
committed a crime. ❑ *He may still face criminal
charges.* ■ N-UNCOUNT If you have **charge of** or
are **in charge of** someone or something, you are
responsible for them. ❑ *A few years ago Bacryl
took charge of the company.* ❑ *Who's in charge here?*
■ PHRASE If something is **free of charge**, it does
not cost anything. ❑ *The leaflet is available free of
charge from post offices.* [from Old French]
→ see **lightning, magnet, trial**

## Word Partnership   Use *charge* with :

| | |
|---|---|
| N. | charge **a fee** ■ |
| | charge **a battery** ■ |
| ADJ. | **criminal** charge, **guilty of a** charge ■ |
| V. | **deny a** charge ■ |
| | **lead a** charge ■ |

charge card N-COUNT A **charge card** is the same
as a **credit card**.

cha|ris|ma /kərɪzmə/ N-UNCOUNT You say that
someone has **charisma** when they can attract,
influence, and inspire people by their personal
qualities. ❑ *He doesn't have the personal charisma
to inspire people.* • char|is|mat|ic /kærɪzmætɪk/
ADJ ❑ *With her charismatic personality, she is noticed
wherever she goes.* [from Church Latin]

chari|table /tʃærɪtəb°l/ ■ ADJ A **charitable**
organization or activity helps and supports people
who are ill, disabled, or very poor. ❑ *...charitable
work.* ■ ADJ Someone who is **charitable** is kind
and tolerant. ❑ *They were not very charitable toward
the referee.* [from Old French]

char|ity /tʃærɪti/ (**charities**) ■ N-VAR A **charity**
is an organization which raises money in order to
help people who are ill, disabled, or very poor. If
you give money **to charity**, you give it to a charity.
❑ *...an AIDS charity.* ❑ *Gooch is raising money for
charity.* ■ N-UNCOUNT People who live on **charity**
live on money or goods which other people give
them because they are poor. ❑ *Her husband is
unemployed and the family depends on charity.* [from
Old French]

## Word Partnership   Use *charity* with :

| | |
|---|---|
| V. | **collect for** charity, **donate to** charity, |
| | **give to** charity ■ |
| N. | **donation to** charity, charity |
| | **event**, **money for** charity, charity |
| | **organization**, charity **work** ■ |
| ADJ. | **local** charity, **private** charity ■ |

Charles's law /tʃɑrlzɪz lɔ/ also **Charles' law**
N-UNCOUNT **Charles's law** is a principle in physics
which states that the volume of a gas increases
when the gas gets hotter. [TECHNICAL]

charm /tʃɑrm/ (**charms, charming, charmed**)

## Picture Dictionary    chart

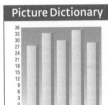

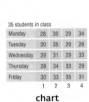

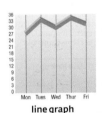

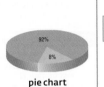

| bar graph | chart | line graph | pie chart |

**C**

■ N-VAR **Charm** is the quality of being pleasant and attractive. □ *The original movie has lost none of its charm.* ■ V-T If you **charm** someone, you please them by using your charm. □ *He charmed all of us.* ■ N-COUNT A **charm** is an act, saying, or object that is believed to have magic powers. □ *...a good luck charm.* [from Old French]
→ see **jewelry**

**charm|ing** /tʃɑrmɪŋ/ ADJ If someone or something is **charming**, they are very pleasant and attractive. □ *...a charming little fishing village.* □ *...a charming young man.* ● **charm|ing|ly** ADV □ *Calder smiled charmingly.* □ *There's something charmingly old-fashioned about him.* [from Old French]

**charred** /tʃɑrd/ ADJ Something that is **charred** is black as a result of being badly burned. □ *...the charred remains of the building.*

**chart** /tʃɑrt/ (**charts, charting, charted**)
■ N-COUNT A **chart** is a diagram or graph which displays information. □ *Male unemployment was 14.2%, compared with 5.8% for women.* ■ → see also **flow chart, pie chart** ■ N-COUNT A **chart** is a map of the ocean or stars. □ *...charts of the Pacific Ocean.* ■ V-T If you **chart** the development or progress of something, you observe and record it carefully. □ *The book charts the history of four generations of the family.* [from Latin]
→ see Picture Dictionary: **chart**

**char|ter** /tʃɑrtər/ (**charters, chartering, chartered**) ■ N-COUNT A **charter** is a formal document describing the rights, aims, or principles of an organization. □ *...the United Nations Charter.* ■ ADJ A **charter** plane or boat is one which is rented for use by a particular person or group. □ *The plane was a charter flight.* ■ V-T If someone **charters** a plane or boat, they rent it for their own use. □ *He chartered a jet to fly her home.* [from Old French]

**char|ter mem|ber** (**charter members**) N-COUNT A **charter member** of a club or organization is one of the people who first joined or started it.

**chase** /tʃeɪs/ (**chases, chasing, chased**) ■ V-T If you **chase** someone, you run after them or follow them in order to catch them or force them to leave a place. □ *She chased the thief for 100 yards.* □ *Many farmers will chase you off their land.* ● **Chase** is also a noun. □ *The chase ended at about 10:30 p.m. on Highway 522.* ■ V-T/V-I If you **are chasing** something you want, such as work or money, you are trying hard to get it. □ *In some areas, 14 people are chasing every job.* □ *There are too many schools chasing after too few students.* [from Old French]
▸ **chase down** PHR-VERB If you **chase** someone **down**, you run after them or follow them quickly

and catch them. □ *Ness chased the thief down and held him until police arrived.*

**chasm** /kæzəm/ (**chasms**) ■ N-COUNT A **chasm** is a very deep crack in rock, earth, or ice. □ *...a fourteen-foot-deep chasm in the riverbed.* ■ N-COUNT If you say that there is a **chasm** between two things or between two groups, you mean that there is a very large difference between them. □ *...the chasm that divides the worlds of university and industry.* [from Latin]

**chat** /tʃæt/ (**chats, chatting, chatted**) V-RECIP When people **chat**, they talk in an informal and friendly way. □ *The women were chatting.* □ *I was chatting to him the other day.* ● **Chat** is also a noun. □ *I had a chat with John.*

**châ|teau** /ʃætoʊ/ (**châteaux** /ʃætoʊz/) also **chateau** N-COUNT A **château** is a large country house or castle in France. [from French]

**chat room** (**chat rooms**) also **chatroom** N-COUNT A **chat room** is a site on the Internet where people can exchange messages about a particular subject. [COMPUTING]

**chat|ter** /tʃætər/ (**chatters, chattering, chattered**) ■ V-I If you **chatter**, you talk quickly and continuously about unimportant things. □ *Everyone's chattering away in different languages.* □ *Erica chattered about Andrew's children.* ● **Chatter** is also a noun. □ *...their noisy chatter.* ■ V-I If your teeth **chatter**, they keep knocking together because you are cold. □ *She was so cold her teeth chattered.*

**Word Link**    *eur ≈ one who does : amateur, chauffeur, entrepreneur*

**chauf|feur** /ʃoʊfər, ʃoʊfɜr/ (**chauffeurs, chauffeuring, chauffeured**) ■ N-COUNT A **chauffeur** is a person whose job is to drive and look after another person's car. ■ V-T If you **chauffeur** someone somewhere, you drive them there in a car, usually as part of your job. □ *It was useful to have her there to chauffeur him around.* [from French]

**chau|vin|ism** /ʃoʊvɪnɪzəm/ N-UNCOUNT **Chauvinism** is a strong, unreasonable belief that your own country, sex, race, or religion, is better and more important than any other. ● **chau|vin|ist** (**chauvinists**) N-COUNT □ *He is a bit of a chauvinist.* [from French]

**cheap** /tʃip/ (**cheaper, cheapest**) ■ ADJ Goods or services that are **cheap** cost less money than usual or than you expected. □ *I'm going to live off campus if I can find somewhere cheap enough.* □ *Costs are coming down because of cheaper fuel.* ● **cheap|ly** ADV □ *It will produce electricity more cheaply than a nuclear plant.* ■ ADJ **Cheap** goods cost less money than similar products but their quality is poor. □ *Don't buy cheap imitations.* ❸ ADJ **Cheap** remarks are unkind and unnecessary. □ *...a series of cheap insults.* ❹ ADJ If you describe someone as **cheap**, you are criticizing them for being unwilling to spend money. □ *Oh, please, Dad, just this once don't be cheap.* [from Old English]

**Thesaurus** *cheap* Also look up :

ADJ. budget, economical, low-cost, reasonable; (ant.) costly, expensive ❶ second-rate ❷

**cheat** /tʃit/ (**cheats, cheating, cheated**) ❶ V-I If someone **cheats**, they do not obey a set of rules which they should be obeying, for example in a game or exam. □ *Students may be tempted to cheat in order to get into top schools.* ● **Cheat** is also a noun. □ *Cheats will be disqualified.* ● **cheat|ing** N-UNCOUNT □ *He was accused of cheating by his opponent.* ❷ V-T If someone **cheats** you **out of** something, they get it from you by behaving dishonestly. □ *It was a deliberate effort to cheat them out of their money.*
▸ **cheat on** ❶ PHR-VERB If someone **cheats on** their husband, wife, or partner, they have a sexual relationship with another person. [INFORMAL] ❷ PHR-VERB If someone **cheats on** something such as an agreement or their taxes, they do not do what they should do under a set of rules. □ *Their job is to check that none of the countries is cheating on the agreement.*

**cheat|er** /tʃitər/ (**cheaters**) N-COUNT A **cheater** is someone who cheats.

**check** /tʃɛk/ (**checks, checking, checked**)
❶ V-T/V-I If you **check** something, you make sure that it is correct, satisfactory, or safe. □ *Check the meanings of the words in a dictionary.* □ *I think there is an age limit, but I'd have to check.* □ *She checked whether she had a clean, ironed shirt.* □ *Stephen checked on her several times during the night.* ● **Check** is also a noun. □ *...regular checks on his blood pressure.* ❷ V-T If you **check** something that is written on a piece of paper, you put a mark, like a V with the right side extended, next to it. □ *Please check the box below.* ❸ V-T To **check** something, usually something bad, means to stop it from spreading or continuing. □ *How can we check the spread of this disease?* ❹ V-T When you **check** your luggage at an airport, you give it to an official so that it can be taken onto your plane. □ *We checked our baggage and walked around the gift shops.* ❺ N-COUNT The **check** in a restaurant is a piece of paper on which the price of your meal is written and which you are given before you pay. ❻ N-COUNT A pattern of squares, usually of two colors, can be referred to as **checks** or a **check**. □ *Styles include stripes and checks.* ❼ N-COUNT A **check** is a printed form on which you write an amount of money and who it is to be paid to. Your bank then passes the money to that person from your account. □ *He handed me a check for $1,500.* ❽ → see also **blank check, traveler's check** ❾ PHRASE If something or someone **is held in check** or **is kept in check**, they are controlled and prevented from becoming too great or powerful. □ *Life on Earth will become impossible unless population growth is held in check.* [from Old French] ❿ → see also **rain check**
→ see **answer, hotel**
▸ **check in** ❶ PHR-VERB When you **check in** or

**check into** a hotel or clinic, you arrive and go through the necessary procedures before you stay there. □ *I'll tell the hotel we'll check in tomorrow.* □ *He has checked into a clinic.* ❷ PHR-VERB When you **check in** at an airport, you arrive and show your ticket before going on a flight. □ *He checked in at Amsterdam's Schiphol airport for a flight to Atlanta.* ❸ → see also **check-in**
▸ **check out** ❶ PHR-VERB When you **check out of** a hotel, you pay the bill and leave. □ *They packed and checked out of the hotel.* □ *They checked out yesterday morning.* ❷ PHR-VERB If you **check out** something or someone, you find out information about them. □ *Maybe we ought to go down to the library and check it out.* □ *We ought to check him out on the computer.* ❸ → see also **checkout**
▸ **check up** ❶ PHR-VERB If you **check up on** something or someone, you find out information about them. □ *Are you asking me to check up on my colleagues?* ❷ → see also **checkup**

**Thesaurus** *check* Also look up :

V. confirm, find out, make sure, verify; (ant.) ignore, overlook ❶

**Word Partnership** Use *check* with :

PREP. check **for/that** *something*, check **with** *someone* ❶
N. **background** check, **credit** check, **security** check ❶
check your **baggage/luggage** ❹
V. **cash** a check, **deposit** a check, **pay with** a check ❼

**checked** /tʃɛkt/ ADJ Something that is **checked** has a pattern of small squares, usually of two colors. □ *...a checked shirt.* [from Old French]
→ see **pattern**

**checker|board** ❶ N-COUNT A **checkerboard** is a square board with 64 black and white squares that is used for playing checkers or chess. ❷ ADJ A **checkerboard** pattern is made up of equal-sized squares of two different colors, usually black and white.

**check|ers** N-UNCOUNT **Checkers** is a game for two people, played with 24 round pieces on a board.

**check-in** (**check-ins**) N-COUNT At an airport, a **check-in** is the counter or desk where you check in.

**check|ing ac|count** (**checking accounts**) N-COUNT A **checking account** is a personal bank account that you can take money out of at any time.

**check mark** (**check marks**) N-COUNT A **check mark** is a written mark like a V with the right side extended. It is used to show that something is correct or has been selected or dealt with.

**check|out** /tʃɛkaʊt/ (**checkouts**) N-COUNT In a supermarket, a **checkout** is a counter where you pay for things you are buying.

**check|point** /tʃɛkpɔɪnt/ (**checkpoints**) N-COUNT A **checkpoint** is a place where traffic is stopped so that it can be checked.

**check|up** /tʃɛkʌp/ (**checkups**) N-COUNT A **checkup** is an examination by your doctor or dentist.

**cheek** /tʃik/ (**cheeks**) N-COUNT Your **cheeks** are

the sides of your face below your eyes. [from Old English]

→ see face, kiss

**cheek|bone** /tʃikboʊn/ (**cheekbones**) N-COUNT Your **cheekbones** are the two bones in your face just below your eyes.

**cheer** /tʃɪər/ (**cheers, cheering, cheered**) ◼ V-T/ V-I When people **cheer**, they shout loudly to show approval or encouragement. ❑ *The crowd cheered as she went up the steps to the stage.* ❑ *Thousands of Americans cheered him on his return.* ● **Cheer** is also a noun. ❑ *...a loud cheer.* ◼ V-T If you **are cheered by** something, it makes you happier. ❑ *The people around him looked cheered by his presence.* ● **cheer|ing** ADJ ❑ *...very cheering news.* [from Old French]

▶ **cheer on** PHR-VERB When you **cheer** someone **on**, you shout loudly in order to encourage them, for example when they are taking part in a game. ❑ *A thousand supporters packed into the stadium to cheer them on.*

▶ **cheer up** PHR-VERB When you **cheer up** or when someone or something **cheers** you **up**, you stop feeling sad and become more cheerful. ❑ *I think he misses her terribly. You might cheer him up.* ❑ *I wrote that song just to cheer myself up.*

**cheer|ful** /tʃɪərfəl/ ◼ ADJ Someone who is **cheerful** is happy and shows this in their behavior. ❑ *Paddy was always cheerful and jolly.* ● **cheer|ful|ly** ADV ❑ *"We've come with good news," Pat said cheerfully.* ● **cheer|ful|ness** N-UNCOUNT ❑ *...a youthful cheerfulness.* ◼ ADJ Something that is **cheerful** is pleasant and makes you feel happy. ❑ *The nursery is bright and cheerful.* [from Old French]

**cheery** /tʃɪəri/ (**cheerier, cheeriest**) ADJ **Cheery** means cheerful and happy. ❑ *She was cheery and talked to them about their problems.* ● **cheer|i|ly** ADV ❑ *"Come on in," she said cheerily.* [from Old French]

**cheese** /tʃiz/ (**cheeses**) N-VAR **Cheese** is a solid food made from milk. It is usually white or yellow. ❑ *...bread and cheese.* ❑ *...delicious French cheeses.* [from Old English]

**chef** /ʃɛf/ (**chefs**) N-COUNT A **chef** is a cook in a restaurant or hotel. [from French]

**chef's sal|ad** (**chef's salads**) N-VAR A **chef's salad** is a green salad with hard-boiled egg and strips of meat and cheese on top.

| Word Link | chem ≈ chemical : biochemist, chemical, chemistry |
| --- | --- |

**chemi|cal** /kɛmɪkˀl/ (**chemicals**) ◼ ADJ **Chemical** means involving or resulting from a reaction between two or more substances, or relating to the substances that something consists of. ❑ *...chemical reactions.* ❑ *Almost all of the natural chemical elements are found in the ocean.* ● **chemi|cal|ly** /kɛmɪkli/ ADV ❑ *...chemically related drugs.* ◼ N-COUNT **Chemicals** are substances that are used in a chemical process or made by a chemical process. ❑ *...the overuse of chemicals in agriculture.* [from French]

→ see farm, firework, periodic table, war

**chemi|cal bond** (**chemical bonds**) N-COUNT A **chemical bond** is the force that holds atoms together to make molecules.

**chemi|cal bond|ing** N-UNCOUNT **Chemical bonding** is the joining together of atoms to make molecules.

**chemi|cal change** (**chemical changes**)

N-COUNT A **chemical change** is a change in a substance that results in a new or different substance, such as the conversion of wood to smoke and ash when it is burned.

**chemi|cal en|er|gy** N-UNCOUNT **Chemical energy** is the energy that is released during a chemical reaction or a chemical change.

**chemi|cal equa|tion** (**chemical equations**) N-COUNT A **chemical equation** is an equation that describes a chemical reaction.

**chemi|cal for|mu|la** (**chemical formulas** or **chemical formulae**) N-COUNT A **chemical formula** is the scientific name for a substance, based on the number and type of atoms in one molecule of the substance. For example, $H_2O$ is the chemical formula for water.

**chemi|cal prop|er|ty** (**chemical properties**) N-COUNT The **chemical properties** of a substance are the physical qualities that determine how it will react with other substances.

**chemi|cal re|ac|tion** (**chemical reactions**) N-COUNT A **chemical reaction** is the change that happens when two or more substances are mixed and a new substance is formed.

**chemi|cal weath|er|ing** N-UNCOUNT **Chemical weathering** is the change that takes place in the structure of rocks and minerals as a result of their exposure to water and the atmosphere.

**chem|ist** /kɛmɪst/ (**chemists**) N-COUNT A **chemist** is a person who does research connected with chemistry or who studies chemistry. [from New Latin]

**chem|is|try** /kɛmɪstri/ N-UNCOUNT **Chemistry** is the scientific study of the structure of substances and of the way that they react with other substances.

**chemo|thera|py** /kimoʊθɛrəpi/ N-UNCOUNT **Chemotherapy** is the treatment of disease using chemicals. It is often used in treating cancer. ❑ *He is having chemotherapy for lung cancer.*

**cher|ish** /tʃɛrɪʃ/ (**cherishes, cherishing, cherished**) ◼ V-T If you **cherish** something such as a hope or a pleasant memory, you keep it in your mind for a long period of time. ❑ *The president will cherish the memory of this visit to Ohio.* ● **cher|ished** ADJ ❑ *...the cherished dream of a world without wars.* ◼ V-T If you **cherish** someone or something, you take good care of them because you love them. ❑ *He genuinely loved and cherished her.* ● **cher|ished** ADJ ❑ *...his most cherished possession.* ◼ V-T If you **cherish** a right or a privilege, you regard it as important and try hard to keep it. ❑ *They cherish their independence.* ● **cher|ished** ADJ ❑ *...deeply cherished beliefs.* [from Old French]

**cher|ry** /tʃɛri/ (**cherries**) ◼ N-COUNT **Cherries** are small, round fruit with red skins. ◼ N-COUNT A **cherry** or a **cherry tree** is a tree that cherries grow on. [from Old English]

**chess** /tʃɛs/ N-UNCOUNT **Chess** is a game for two people, played on a chessboard. Each player has 16 pieces, including a king. The aim is to trap your opponent's king. ❑ *He was playing chess with his uncle.* [from Old French]

→ see Word Web: chess

**chest** /tʃɛst/ (**chests**) ◼ N-COUNT Your **chest** is the top part of the front of your body. ❑ *He crossed his arms over his chest.* ❑ *He was shot in the chest.*

### Word Web    chess

Scholars disagree on the origin of the game of **chess**. Some say it started in China around 570 AD. Others say it was invented later in India. In early versions of the **game**, the **king** was the most powerful **chess piece**. But when the game was brought to Europe in the Middle Ages, a new form appeared. It was called Queen's Chess. Modern chess is based on this game. The king is the most important piece, but the **queen** is the most powerful. Chess **players** use rooks, **bishops**, **knights**, and **pawns** to protect their king and to put their **opponent** in checkmate.

**2** N-COUNT A **chest** is a large, heavy box used for storing things. ❑ *...a treasure chest.* [from Old English]
→ see **body**

**chest|nut** /tʃɛsnʌt, -nət/ (**chestnuts**) **1** N-VAR A **chestnut** or **chestnut tree** is a tall tree with broad leaves. **2** N-COUNT **Chestnuts** are the reddish brown nuts that grow on chestnut trees. **3** COLOR Something that is **chestnut** is dark reddish brown in color. ❑ *...chestnut hair.* [from Old French]

**chew** /tʃu/ (**chews, chewing, chewed**) V-T/V-I When you **chew** food, you break it up with your teeth so that it becomes easier to swallow. ❑ *Eat slowly and chew your food well.* ❑ *He chewed on his toast.* [from Old English]

**chic** /ʃik/ ADJ Something or someone that is **chic** is fashionable and sophisticated. ❑ *Her dress was French and very chic.* [from French]

**Chi|ca|na** /tʃɪkɑnə/ (**Chicanas**) N-COUNT A **Chicana** is an American girl or woman whose family originally came from Mexico. ❑ *...a Chicana from Michigan.* [from Spanish]

**Chi|ca|no** /tʃɪkɑnoʊ/ (**Chicanos**) N-COUNT A **Chicano** is an American boy or man whose family originally came from Mexico. [from Spanish]

chick

**chick** /tʃɪk/ (**chicks**) N-COUNT **1** A **chick** is a baby bird. ❑ *...newly-hatched chicks.* **2** N-COUNT Some men refer to women as **chicks**. This use could cause offense.

**chicka|dee** /tʃɪkədi/ (**chickadees**) N-COUNT A **chickadee** is a small North American bird with gray and black feathers.

**chick|en** /tʃɪkɪn/ (**chickens, chickening, chickened**) **1** N-COUNT **Chickens** are birds which are kept on a farm for their eggs and for their meat. ● **Chicken** is the flesh of this bird eaten as food. ❑ *...roast chicken.* [from Old English] **2** **chickens come home to roost** → see **roost**
→ see **meat**

▸ **chicken out** PHR-VERB If someone **chickens out** of something, they do not to do it because they are afraid. [INFORMAL] ❑ *He makes excuses to chicken out of family occasions such as weddings.*

**chick flick** (**chick flicks**) N-COUNT A **chick flick** is a romantic film that is not very serious and is intended to appeal to women. [INFORMAL]

**chief** /tʃif/ (**chiefs**) **1** N-COUNT The **chief** of an organization or group is its leader or the person who is in charge of it. ❑ *The police chief has said very little about it.* **2** ADJ **Chief** is used in the job titles of the most senior worker or workers of a particular kind in an organization. ❑ *...the chief test pilot.* **3** ADJ The **chief** cause, part, or member of something is the most important one. ❑ *Lack of water is the chief problem in Ethiopia.* [from Old French]

### Thesaurus    chief    Also look up :

N.    boss, director, head, leader **1**
ADJ.  key, main, major; (ant.) minor, unimportant **3**

**chief jus|tice** (**chief justices**) N-COUNT; N-TITLE A **chief justice** is the most important judge in a court of law, especially a supreme court.

**chief|ly** /tʃifli/ ADV You use **chiefly** to indicate that a particular reason, emotion, method, or feature is the main or most important one. ❑ *He painted chiefly portraits.* [from Old French]

**chief of staff** (**chiefs of staff**) N-COUNT The **chiefs of staff** are the highest-ranking officers of each service of the armed forces.

**chif|fon** /ʃɪfɒn/ N-UNCOUNT **Chiffon** is a kind of very thin silk or nylon cloth. [from French]

**child** /tʃaɪld/ (**children**) **1** N-COUNT A **child** is a human being who is not yet an adult. ❑ *When I was a child I lived in a village.* ❑ *...a child of six.* **2** N-COUNT Someone's **children** are their sons and daughters of any age. ❑ *How are the children?* ❑ *His children have left home.* [from Old English]
→ see Word Web: **child**
→ see **age**

### Word Partnership    Use *child* with :

N.    child **abuse**, child **care 1**
V.    **adopt** a child, **have** a child, **raise** a child **1**
ADJ.  **difficult** child, **happy** child, **small/young** child, **unborn** child **1**

**child|birth** /tʃaɪldbɜrθ/ N-UNCOUNT **Childbirth** is the act of giving birth to a child. ❑ *She died in childbirth.*

### Word Link    hood ≈ state, condition : adulthood, childhood, manhood

**child|hood** /tʃaɪldhʊd/ (**childhoods**) N-VAR A person's **childhood** is the period of their life when

### Word Web  child

In the Middle Ages, only **infants** and **toddlers** enjoyed the freedoms of **childhood**. A **child** of seven or eight helped the family by working. In the countryside, **sons** started working on the family's farm. **Daughters** did important housework. In cities, children became laborers and worked along with adults. Today **parents** treat children with special care. **Babies** play with toys to help them learn. There are educational programs for **preschoolers**. The idea of **adolescence** as a separate stage of life appeared about 100 years ago. Today **teenagers** often have part-time jobs while they go to school.

they are a child. ❑ *She had a happy childhood.* ❑ *...a story heard in childhood.* [from Old English]
→ see **child**

**child|ish** /tʃaɪldɪʃ/ **1** ADJ **Childish** means relating to or typical of a child. ❑ *...childish enthusiasm.* **2** ADJ If you describe someone, especially an adult, as **childish**, you disapprove of them because they behave in an immature way. ❑ *...Penny's selfish and childish behavior.* [from Old English]

**child|less** /tʃaɪldlɪs/ ADJ Someone who is **childless** has no children. ❑ *...childless couples.* [from Old English]

### Word Link   like ≈ similar : alike, childlike, unlike

**child|like** /tʃaɪldlaɪk/ ADJ You describe someone as **childlike** when they seem like a child in their character, appearance, or behavior. ❑ *...childlike innocence.* [from Old English]

**chil|dren** /tʃɪldrən/ **Children** is the plural of **child**. [from Old English]

**child sup|port** N-UNCOUNT If a parent pays **child support**, they legally have to pay money to help provide things such as food and clothing for a child with whom they no longer live. ❑ *He went to prison for failing to pay child support.*

**chili** /tʃɪli/ (**chilies** or **chilis**) **1** N-VAR **Chilies** are small red or green peppers with a hot, spicy taste. **2** N-UNCOUNT **Chili** is a dish made from meat or beans, or sometimes both, with chilies and a thick sauce of tomatoes. [from Spanish]
→ see **spice**

**chil|i con car|ne** /tʃɪli kɒn kɑrni/ N-UNCOUNT **Chili con carne** is a dish made from meat, with chilies and a thick sauce of tomatoes.

**chill** /tʃɪl/ (**chills, chilling, chilled**) **1** V-T/V-I To **chill** something means to make it cold. ❑ *Chill the fruit salad until serving time.* ❑ *Put the pastry in the fridge to chill.* ❑ *Smith placed his chilled hands on the radiator.* **2** N-COUNT If something sends a **chill** through you, it gives you a sudden feeling of fear or anxiety. ❑ *He felt a chill of fear.* **3** N-COUNT A **chill** is a mild illness which can give you a slight fever and headache. ❑ *He caught a chill.* [from Old English]
→ see **illness**

▶ **chill out** PHR-VERB To **chill out** means to relax after you have done something tiring or stressful. [INFORMAL] ❑ *After school, we used to chill out and watch TV.*

**chill|ing** /tʃɪlɪŋ/ ADJ If you describe something as **chilling**, you mean it is frightening. ❑ *...a chilling warning.* ● **chill|ing|ly** ADV ❑ *The threat of war became chillingly real.* [from Old English]

**chil|ly** /tʃɪli/ (**chillier, chilliest**) ADJ **Chilly** means uncomfortably cold. ❑ *It was a chilly afternoon.* ❑ *I'm a bit chilly.* [from Old English]

**chime** /tʃaɪm/ (**chimes, chiming, chimed**) **1** V-T/V-I When a bell or a clock **chimes**, it makes ringing sounds. ❑ *He heard the front doorbell chime.* ❑ *The clock chimed three o'clock.* **2** N-COUNT A **chime** is a ringing sound made by a bell, especially when it is part of a clock. ❑ *Did you hear a chime?* [from Latin]
→ see **percussion**

▶ **chime in** PHR-VERB If you **chime in**, you say something just after someone else has spoken. ❑ *"Why?" Pete asked impatiently. — "Yes, why?" Bob chimed in.*

**chim|ney** /tʃɪmni/ (**chimneys**) N-COUNT A **chimney** is a pipe above a fireplace or furnace through which smoke can go up into the air. ❑ *Smoke poured out of the chimneys.* [from Old French]

*chimney*

**chim|pan|zee** /tʃɪmpænzi/ (**chimpanzees**) N-COUNT A **chimpanzee** is a kind of small African ape. [from Kongo]
→ see **primate, zoo**

**chin** /tʃɪn/ (**chins**) N-COUNT Your **chin** is the part of your face that is below your mouth and above your neck. [from Old English]

**chi|na** /tʃaɪnə/ **1** N-UNCOUNT **China** is a hard white substance made from clay, used to make cups, plates, and ornaments. ❑ *...a small bowl made of china.* **2** N-UNCOUNT Cups, plates, and ornaments made of china are referred to as **china**. ❑ *Judy collects blue and white china.* [from Persian]
→ see **pottery**

**chink** /tʃɪŋk/ (**chinks**) N-COUNT A **chink** is a very narrow crack or opening. ❑ *...a chink in the wall.* [from Old English]

**chip** /tʃɪp/ (**chips, chipping, chipped**) **1** N-COUNT **Chips** or **potato chips** are very thin slices of fried potato that are eaten as a snack. ❑ *...a packet of potato chips.* **2** N-COUNT A silicon **chip** is a very small piece of silicon with electronic circuits on it.

❏ ...*an electronic card containing a chip.* ❸ N-COUNT
A **chip** is a small piece of something or a small
piece which has been broken off something. ❏ *It
contains real chocolate chips.* ❹ V-T/V-I If you **chip**
something, a small piece is broken off it. ❏ *The
apple chipped the woman's tooth.* ● **chipped** ADJ ❏ *The
paint was badly chipped.* [from Old English]
▶ **chip in** PHR-VERB When a number of people
**chip in**, each person gives some money so that
they can pay for something together. [INFORMAL]
❏ *They all chipped in for the gas.*

**chis|el** /tʃɪzᵊl/ (**chisels, chiseling** or **chiselling,
chiseled** or **chiselled**) ❶ N-COUNT A **chisel** is a tool
that has a long metal blade with a sharp edge at
the end. It is used for cutting and shaping wood
and stone. ❏ ...*a hammer and chisel.* ❷ V-T If you
**chisel** wood or stone, you cut and shape it using
a chisel. ❏ *He chiseled a dog out of stone.* [from Old
French]

**chlo|rine** /klɔrin/ N-UNCOUNT **Chlorine** is a
gas that is used to disinfect water and to make
cleaning products.

**chlo|ro|phyll** /klɔrəfɪl/ N-UNCOUNT **Chlorophyll**
is a green substance in plants which enables them
to use the energy from sunlight in order to grow.
→ see **photosynthesis**

**chlo|ro|plast** /klɔrəplæst/ (**chloroplasts**)
N-COUNT **Chloroplasts** are the parts of cells in
plants and algae where photosynthesis takes
place. [TECHNICAL]

**choco|late** /tʃɔkəlɪt, tʃɔklɪt/ (**chocolates**)
❶ N-UNCOUNT **Chocolate** is a sweet food made
from cocoa and eaten as a candy. ❏ ...*a bar of
chocolate.* ❷ N-VAR **Chocolate** or **hot chocolate**
is a hot drink made from a powder containing
chocolate. ❏ ...*a small cafeteria where the visitors can
buy tea, coffee and chocolate.* ❸ N-COUNT **Chocolates**
are small candies or nuts covered with a layer of
chocolate. ❏ *He gave me a box of chocolates to say
"thankyou".* [from Spanish]

**choice** /tʃɔɪs/ (**choices, choicer, choicest**)
❶ N-COUNT If there is a **choice of** things, there are
several of them and you can choose the one you
want. ❏ *It's available in a choice of colors.* ❏ *There's a
choice between meat or a vegetarian dish.* ❷ N-COUNT
Your **choice** is the thing or things that you choose.
❏ *His choice of words made Rodney angry.* ❏ ...*tickets
to see the football team of your choice.* ❸ ADJ **Choice**
means of very high quality. [FORMAL] ❏ ...*choice
cuts of beef.* ❹ PHRASE If you **have no choice but** to
do something or **have little choice but** to do it, you
cannot avoid doing it. ❏ *They had little choice but to
agree.* ❺ PHRASE The item **of choice** is the one that
someone likes best, or that most people prefer.
❏ *Coffee is their drink of choice.* [from Old French]

**choir** /kwaɪər/ (**choirs**) N-COUNT A **choir** is a
group of people who sing together. ❏ *He has been
singing in his church choir since he was six.* [from Old
French]

**choke** /tʃoʊk/ (**chokes, choking, choked**)
❶ V-T/V-I If you **choke** on something, it prevents

you from breathing properly. ❏ *A small child could
choke on the toy.* ❏ *The smoke was choking her.* ❏ *The
girl choked to death after breathing in smoke.* ❷ V-T To
**choke** someone means to squeeze their neck until
they are dead. ❏ *They choked him with his tie.* ❸ V-T
If a place **is choked with** things or people, it is full
of them and they prevent movement in it. ❏ *The
village's roads are choked with traffic.* ❹ N-COUNT
A vehicle's **choke** is a device that reduces the
amount of air going into the engine and makes it
easier to start. ❏ *He pulled out the choke and turned
the key.* [from Old English]

**chol|era** /kɒlərə/ N-UNCOUNT **Cholera** is a
serious disease that affects your digestive system.
❏ ...*a cholera epidemic.* [from Latin]

**cho|les|ter|ol** /kəlɛstərɔl/ N-UNCOUNT
**Cholesterol** is a substance that exists in the
fat, tissues, and blood of all animals. Too much
cholesterol in the blood can cause heart disease.
❏ ...*a dangerously high cholesterol level.* [from Greek]

**choose** /tʃuz/ (**chooses, choosing, chose,
chosen**) ❶ V-T/V-I If you **choose** someone or
something, you decide to have that person
or thing. ❏ *They will choose their own leaders in
democratic elections.* ❏ *There are several patterns
to choose from.* ❷ V-T/V-I If you **choose to** do
something, you do it because you want to or
because you feel that it is right. ❏ *They chose to
ignore what was going on.* ❏ *You have the right to remain
silent if you choose.* [from Old English]
→ see **answer**

**chop** /tʃɒp/ (**chops, chopping, chopped**) ❶ V-T
If you **chop** something, you cut it into pieces with
a knife and an ax. ❏ *Chop the butter into small pieces.*
❏ *We set to work chopping wood.* ❷ N-COUNT A **chop**
is a small piece of meat cut from the ribs of a sheep
or pig. ❏ ...*lamb chops.* [of Germanic origin]
→ see **cut**
▶ **chop down** PHR-VERB If you **chop down** a tree,
you cut through its trunk with an ax so that it falls
to the ground. ❏ *Sometimes they chop down a tree for
firewood.*
▶ **chop off** PHR-VERB To **chop off** something such
as a part of your body means to cut it off. ❏ *She
chopped off her hair.*
▶ **chop up** PHR-VERB If you **chop** something **up**,
you chop it into small pieces. ❏ *Chop up three firm
tomatoes.*

**chop|per** /tʃɒpər/ (**choppers**) N-COUNT A
**chopper** is a helicopter. [INFORMAL]

**cho|ral** /kɔrəl/ ADJ **Choral** music is sung by a
choir. ❏ ...*choral music from around the world.* [from
German]

**cho|rale** /kəræl, -rɑl/ (**chorales**) N-COUNT A
**chorale** is a group of people who sing together.
❏ ...*the Seattle Symphony Chorale.* [from German]

**chord** /kɔrd/ (**chords**) N-COUNT A **chord** is a
number of musical notes played or sung at the
same time with a pleasing effect. ❏ *I could play a
few chords on the guitar.* [from Latin]

**chor|do|phone** /kɔrdəfoʊn/ (**chordophones**)
N-COUNT A **chordophone** is any musical
instrument which produces its sound by means of

vibrating strings, for example a harp or a guitar. [TECHNICAL]

**chore** /tʃɔr/ (**chores**) N-COUNT A **chore** is an unpleasant task. ❑ *She sees exercise as a chore.* [from Middle English]

**cho|reo|graph** /kɔriəgræf/ (**choreographs, choreographing, choreographed**) V-T When someone **choreographs** a ballet or other dance, they invent the steps and movements and tell the dancers how to perform them. ❑ *Achim had choreographed the dance himself.* ● **cho|reog|ra|pher** /kɔriŋgrəfər/ (**choreographers**) N-COUNT ❑ *...dancer and choreographer Rudolph Nureyev.* [from Greek]

**cho|reog|ra|phy** /kɔriŋgrəfi/ N-UNCOUNT **Choreography** is the inventing of steps and movements for ballets and other dances. ❑ *...the choreography of Eric Hawkins.* ● **cho|reo|graph|ic** /kɔriəgræfɪk/ ADJ ❑ *...his choreographic work for The Royal Ballet.* [from Greek]

**cho|rus** /kɔrəs/ (**choruses, chorusing, chorused**) ◼ N-COUNT A **chorus** is a part of a song which is repeated after each verse. ❑ *Caroline sang two verses and the chorus of her song.* ◼ N-COUNT A **chorus** is a large group of people who sing together. ❑ *The chorus was singing "The Ode to Joy."* ◼ N-COUNT When there is a **chorus of** criticism, disapproval, or praise, that attitude is expressed by a lot of people at the same time. ❑ *There is a growing chorus of criticism against the government.* ◼ V-T When people **chorus** something, they say it or sing it together. [WRITTEN] ❑ *"Hi," they chorused.* [from Latin]

**chose** /tʃoʊz/ **Chose** is the past tense of **choose**.

**cho|sen** /tʃoʊzᵊn/ **Chosen** is the past participle of **choose**.

**chris|ten** /krɪsᵊn/ (**christens, christening, christened**) V-T When a baby **is christened**, he or she is given a name during a Christian ceremony. ❑ *She was born in March and christened in June.* [from Old English]

**chris|ten|ing** /krɪsᵊnɪŋ/ (**christenings**) N-COUNT A **christening** is a ceremony in which a baby is made a member of the Christian church and is officially given his or her name. ❑ *...my granddaughter's christening.* [from Old English]

**Christian** /krɪstʃən/ (**Christians**) ◼ N-COUNT A **Christian** is someone who follows the teachings of Jesus Christ. ◼ ADJ **Christian** means relating to Christianity or Christians. ❑ *...the Christian Church.* ❑ *Most of my friends are Christian.* [from Old English]

**Chris|ti|an|ity** /krɪstʃiænɪti/ N-UNCOUNT **Christianity** is a religion based on the teachings of Jesus Christ. ❑ *He converted to Christianity.* [from Old English]

**Christ|mas** /krɪsməs/ (**Christmases**) N-VAR **Christmas** is the day or period around the day of the 25th of December, when Christians celebrate the birth of Jesus Christ. ❑ *...the day after Christmas.* ❑ *...the Christmas holidays.* [from Old English]

**Christ|mas Day** N-UNCOUNT **Christmas Day** is the 25th of December.

**Christ|mas Eve** N-UNCOUNT **Christmas Eve** is the 24th of December, the day before Christmas Day.

**Christ|mas tree** (**Christmas trees**) N-COUNT A **Christmas tree** is a real or artificial fir tree, which people put in their houses at Christmas and decorate with lights and ornaments.

**chro|ma|tid** /kroʊmətɪd/ (**chromatids**) N-COUNT A **chromatid** is one of the two identical halves of a chromosome. [TECHNICAL] [from Greek]

**chrome** /kroʊm/ N-UNCOUNT **Chrome** is metal plated with chromium. ❑ *...old-fashioned chrome faucets.* [from French]

**chro|mium** /kroʊmiəm/ N-UNCOUNT **Chromium** is a hard, shiny, metallic element, used to make steel alloys and to coat other metals. ❑ *...a bathroom mirror with a chromium frame.* [from New Latin]

**chro|mo|some** /kroʊməsoʊm/ (**chromosomes**) N-COUNT A **chromosome** is a part of a cell in an animal or plant. It contains genes which determine what characteristics the animal or plant will have. ❑ *Each cell of our bodies contains 46 chromosomes.*

**chro|mo|sphere** /kroʊməsfɪər/ N-SING The **chromosphere** is the thin, middle layer of the sun's atmosphere. [TECHNICAL]

**chron|ic** /krɒnɪk/ ◼ ADJ A **chronic** illness lasts for a very long time. ❑ *...chronic back pain.* ● **chroni|cal|ly** /krɒnɪkli/ ADV ❑ *Most of them were chronically ill.* ◼ ADJ A **chronic** situation is very severe and unpleasant. ❑ *...chronic poverty.* ● **chroni|cal|ly** ADV ❑ *His wife is chronically ill.* [from Latin]

**chroni|cle** /krɒnɪkᵊl/ (**chronicles, chronicling, chronicled**) ◼ V-T To **chronicle** a series of events means to describe them in the order in which they happened. ❑ *The series chronicles the adventures of two friends.* ◼ N-COUNT A **chronicle** is an account or record of a series of events. ❑ *...a chronicle of the civil rights movement.* [from Latin]
→ see **diary**

**chrono|logi|cal** /krɒnᵊlɒdʒɪkᵊl/ ADJ If things are described or shown in **chronological** order, they are described or shown in the order in which they happened. ❑ *I have arranged these stories in chronological order.* ● **chrono|logi|cal|ly** ADV ❑ *The exhibition is organized chronologically.*

**chrysa|lis** /krɪsəlɪs/ (**chrysalises**) ◼ N-COUNT A **chrysalis** is a butterfly or moth in the stage between being a larva and an adult. ◼ N-COUNT A **chrysalis** is the hard, protective covering that a chrysalis has. [from Latin]

**chry|san|themum** /krɪsænθəməm/ (**chrysanthemums**) N-COUNT A **chrysanthemum** is a large garden flower with many long, thin petals. [from Latin]

**chub|by** /tʃʌbi/ (**chubbier, chubbiest**) ADJ A **chubby** person is somewhat fat. ❑ *Do you think I'm too chubby?*

**chuck** /tʃʌk/ (**chucks, chucking, chucked**) V-T When you **chuck** something somewhere, you throw it there in a casual or careless way. [INFORMAL] ❑ *I chucked the clock in the trash.*

**chuck|le** /tʃʌkᵊl/ (**chuckles, chuckling, chuckled**) V-I When you **chuckle**, you laugh quietly. ❑ *He chuckled and said, "Of course not."* ● **Chuckle** is also a noun. ❑ *He gave a little chuckle.*

**chug** /tʃʌg/ (**chugs, chugging, chugged**) **1** V-I When a vehicle **chugs** somewhere, it goes there slowly, with its engine making short thudding sounds. ❑ *The train chugs down the track.* **2** V-T If you **chug** something, you drink it very quickly without stopping. [INFORMAL] ❑ *Nadine chugged her lemonade and ordered another.*

**chunk** /tʃʌŋk/ (**chunks**) **1** N-COUNT **Chunks of** something are thick, solid pieces of it. ❑ *...floating chunks of ice.* ❑ *a chunk of meat.* **2** N-COUNT A **chunk of** something is a large amount or large part of it. [INFORMAL] ❑ *...a chunk of farmland near the airport.*

**chunky** /tʃʌŋki/ (**chunkier, chunkiest**) ADJ A **chunky** person or thing is large and heavy. ❑ *...a chunky girl from California.* ❑ *...a chunky sweater.*

**church** /tʃɜrtʃ/ (**churches**) **1** N-VAR A **church** is a building in which Christians worship. ❑ *...one of the country's most historic churches.* ❑ *...St Helen's Church.* ❑ *The family has gone to church.* **2** N-COUNT A **Church** is one of the groups of people within the Christian religion that have their own beliefs, clergy, and forms of worship. ❑ *...the Catholic Church.* [from Old English]

**churn** /tʃɜrn/ (**churns, churning, churned**) **1** N-COUNT A **churn** is a container which is used for making butter. **2** V-T If something **churns** water, mud, or dust, it moves it about violently. ❑ *The dirt roads were churned into mud by the rain.* ● **Churn up** means the same as **churn**. ❑ *Passing trucks churned up the dust.* **3** V-I If you say that your stomach **is churning**, you mean that you feel sick. ❑ *My stomach churned as I stood up.* [from Old English]
▶ **churn out** PHR-VERB To **churn out** something means to produce large quantities of it very quickly. [INFORMAL] ❑ *He began to churn out novels.*
▶ **churn up** → see **churn 2**

**chute** /ʃut/ (**chutes**) **1** N-COUNT A **chute** is a steep, narrow slope down which people or things can slide. ❑ *...the plane's emergency chutes.* **2** N-COUNT A **chute** is a parachute. ❑ *You can release the chute with either hand.* [Sense 1 from Old French]

**chut|ney** /tʃʌtni/ (**chutneys**) N-VAR **Chutney** is a cold sauce made from fruit, vinegar, sugar, and spices. ❑ *...mango chutney.* [from Hindi]

**ci|der** /saɪdər/ (**ciders**) N-VAR **Cider** is a drink made from apples. In Britain, **cider** is an alcoholic drink made from apples. ❑ *He ordered a cider.* [from Old French]

**ci|gar** /sɪgɑr/ (**cigars**) N-COUNT **Cigars** are rolls of dried tobacco leaves which people smoke. [from Spanish]

**ciga|rette** /sɪgərɛt/ (**cigarettes**) N-COUNT **Cigarettes** are small tubes of paper containing tobacco which people smoke. [from French]

**ci|lan|tro** /sɪlæntroʊ/ N-UNCOUNT **Cilantro** is the leaves of the coriander plant that are used as an herb. ❑ *Put a little cilantro on the side of each plate.* [from Spanish]

**cilia** /sɪliə/ N-PLURAL **Cilia** are short thin structures, resembling hairs, on the surfaces of some types of cells and organisms. [TECHNICAL]

**cin|der** /sɪndər/ (**cinders**) N-COUNT **Cinders** are the pieces of blackened material that are left after

wood or coal has burned. [from Old English]

**cin|der block** (**cinder blocks**) also **cinderblock** N-COUNT A **cinder block** is a large gray brick made from coal cinders and cement which is used for building.

**cin|der cone** (**cinder cones**) also **cinder cone volcano** N-COUNT A **cinder cone** or a **cinder cone volcano** is a small volcano with steep sides, made from pieces of rock and ash.

**cin|ema** /sɪnɪmə/ N-UNCOUNT **Cinema** is the business and art of making movies. ❑ *...the history of cinema.* ● **cin|emat|ic** /sɪnɪmætɪk/ ADJ ❑ *...the director's cinematic style.*

**cin|na|mon** /sɪnəmən/ N-UNCOUNT **Cinnamon** is a sweet spice used for flavoring food. [from French]
→ see **spice**

**cir|ca** /sɜrkə/ PREP If you write **circa** in front of a date, you mean that the date is approximate. [FORMAL] ❑ *...circa 1850.* [from Latin]

**cir|ca|dian rhythm** /sɜrkeɪdiən rɪðəm/ (**circadian rhythms**) N-COUNT **Circadian rhythms** are patterns in the function or behavior of living organisms that are repeated every 24 hours.

**cir|cle** /sɜrkəl/ (**circles, circling, circled**) **1** N-COUNT A **circle** is a round shape. Every part of its edge is the same distance from the center. ❑ *The flag was red, with a large white circle in the center.* ❑ *Cut out 4 circles of pastry.* **2** N-COUNT You can refer to a group of people as a **circle**. ❑ *He has a small circle of friends.* **3** V-T/V-I To **circle** someone or something means to move around them in a circle. ❑ *The plane circled above the airport, waiting to land.* ❑ *There were two helicopters circling around.* [from Latin] **4** → see also **inner circle, vicious circle**
→ see Word Web: **circle**
→ see **shape**

**cir|cuit** /sɜrkɪt/ (**circuits**) **1** N-COUNT An electrical **circuit** is a complete route which an electric current can flow around. ❑ *The electrical circuit was broken.* **2** → see also **closed-circuit** **3** N-COUNT A **circuit** is a series of places that are visited regularly by a person or group. ❑ *...the lecture circuit.* [from Latin]

**cir|cu|lar** /sɜrkyələr/ (**circulars**) **1** ADJ Something that is **circular** is shaped like a circle. ❑ *...a circular hole twelve feet wide.* **2** N-COUNT A **circular** is a letter or advertisement that is sent to a large number of people at the same time. ❑ *Information circulars were sent to 1,800 newspapers.* [from Latin]
→ see **circle**

**cir|cu|late** /sɜrkyəleɪt/ (**circulates, circulating, circulated**) **1** V-T/V-I When something **circulates** or **is circulated**, it is passed around or spread among a group of people. ❑ *Rumors were beginning to circulate that the project might have to be abandoned.* ❑ *She circulated a letter explaining why she was leaving.*

**Word Web** circle

During the 1970s crop **circles** began to appear in England and the U.S. Something creates these mysterious **rings** in fields of crops such as wheat or corn. Are they messages left by visitors from other worlds? Most people think they are made by humans. The **diameter** of each crop circle ranges from a few inches to a few hundred feet. Sometimes the patterns have **shapes** that are not **circular**, such as **ovals**, **triangles**, and **spirals**. Occasionally the shapes seem to represent something, such as a face or a flower. One pattern even had a written message: *We are not alone.*

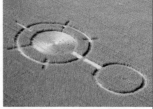

● **cir|cu|la|tion** /sɜrkyəleɪʃ°n/ N-UNCOUNT
❏ ...*the circulation of leaflets attacking him*. **2** V-I
When something **circulates**, it moves easily and freely within a closed place or system. ❏ *The virus circulates throughout the body.* ● **cir|cu|la|tion** N-UNCOUNT ❏ ...*the circulation of air.* [from Latin]

**cir|cu|la|tion** /sɜrkyəleɪʃ°n/ (**circulations**)
**1** N-COUNT The **circulation** of a newspaper or magazine is the number of copies that are sold each time it is produced. ❏ *The Daily News once had the highest circulation in the country.* **2** N-UNCOUNT
Your **circulation** is the movement of blood through your body. ❏ ...*cold spots in the fingers caused by poor circulation.* **3** → see also **circulate**
**4** PHRASE If something such as money is **in circulation**, it is being used by the public. ❏ *In Spain, seven million credit cards are in circulation.* [from Latin]
→ see **cardiovascular system**

**Word Link** circum ≈ around : circumcise, circumference, circumstance

**cir|cum|cise** /sɜrkəmsaɪz/ (**circumcises, circumcising, circumcised**) V-T If a boy or man **is circumcised**, the loose skin at the end of his penis is cut off. ❏ *He was circumcised within eight days of birth.* ● **cir|cum|ci|sion** /sɜrkəmsɪʒ°n/ (**circumcisions**) N-VAR ❏ *Jews and Moslems practice circumcision for religious reasons.* [from Latin]

**cir|cum|fer|ence** /sərkʌmfrəns/ N-UNCOUNT
The **circumference** of a circle, place, or round object is the distance around its edge. ❏ ...*the Earth's circumference.* [from Old French]
→ see **area**

**cir|cum|stance** /sɜrkəmstæns/
(**circumstances**) **1** N-COUNT **Circumstances** are the conditions which affect what happens in a particular situation. ❏ *Under certain circumstances, it may be necessary to fight a war.* ❏ *You're doing a wonderful job in the circumstances.* ❏ *I'm making inquiries about the circumstances of Mary Dean's murder.* **2** N-PLURAL Your **circumstances** are the conditions of your life, especially the amount of money that you have. ❏ ...*help and support for the single mother, whatever her circumstances.* [from Old French]

**Word Partnership** Use *circumstances* with :

ADJ. **certain** circumstances, **different/ similar** circumstances, **difficult** circumstances, **exceptional** circumstances **1** **2**
PREP. **under the** circumstances **1** **2**

**cir|cus** /sɜrkəs/ (**circuses**) N-COUNT A **circus** is a group that consists of clowns, acrobats, and animals that travels around to different places and performs shows. ❏ *My real ambition was to work in a circus.* [from Latin]

**cir|rus** /sɪrəs/ (**cirri** /sɪraɪ/) N-VAR **Cirrus** is a type of thin white cloud that forms at high altitudes. [TECHNICAL] [from Latin]

**ci|ta|tion** /saɪteɪʃ°n/ (**citations**) **1** N-COUNT A **citation** is an official document or speech which praises a person for something brave or special that they have done. ❏ *His citation says he showed extraordinary courage.* **2** N-COUNT A **citation** from a book or other piece of writing is a passage or phrase from it. [FORMAL] ❏ ...*citations from the Koran.* **3** N-COUNT A **citation** is the same as a **summons**. ❏ *The court issued a citation to Ms. Robbins.* **4** N-COUNT A **citation** is an official piece of paper which orders you to pay a fine or to appear in court because you have committed a traffic offense. ❏ *The Highway Patrol this year issued 1,018 speeding citations.* [from Old French]

**cite** /saɪt/ (**cites, citing, cited**) **1** V-T If you **cite** something, you quote it or mention it, especially as an example or proof of what you are saying. [FORMAL] ❏ *She cited a favorite poem by George Herbert.* ❏ *Pilot error was cited as the main cause of the accident.* **2** V-T If someone **is cited**, they are officially ordered to appear before a court or criticized in court. [LEGAL] ❏ *He was cited for driving without a license.* [from Old French]

**citi|zen** /sɪtɪz°n/ (**citizens**) **1** N-COUNT Someone who is a **citizen** of a particular country is legally accepted as belonging to that country. ❏ ...*American citizens.* **2** N-COUNT The **citizens** of a town or city are the people who live there. ❏ ...*the citizens of Buenos Aires.* **3** → see also **senior citizen** [from Old French]
→ see **citizenship, election**

**citi|zen's ar|rest** (**citizen's arrests**) N-COUNT
If someone **makes a citizen's arrest**, they catch someone who they believe has committed a crime and inform the police. ❏ *Police do not advise the average person to make a citizen's arrest.*

**citi|zens band** N-PROPER **Citizens band** is a range of radio frequencies which the general public is allowed to use to send messages to each other. The abbreviation **CB** is often used. ❏ ...*citizens band radios.*

**Word Link** ship ≈ condition or state : censorship, citizenship, friendship

**citi|zen|ship** /sɪtɪz°nʃɪp/ N-UNCOUNT If you have **citizenship** of a country, you are legally

---

**Word Web**    citizenship

**Citizenship** gives people important **rights**. In most countries **citizens** have the right to **vote** in **elections**. Citizens can hold government jobs and travel with a **passport**. They are also free to **demonstrate** to show disagreement with the government. In addition, citizens have **duties** and **responsibilities**. Two main duties of citizens are obeying the law and paying **taxes**. They may also be asked to be a **juror** in a court case. In some countries citizens have to do **military service**.

accepted as belonging to it. ❏ *He decided to apply for American citizenship.* [from Old French]
→ see Word Web: **citizenship**

**cit|rus** /sɪtrəs/ ADJ A **citrus** fruit is a juicy fruit with a sharp taste such as an orange, lemon, or grapefruit. ❏ *...citrus fruit.* [from Latin]

**city** /sɪti/ (**cities**) N-COUNT A **city** is a large town. ❏ *...the city of Bologna.* [from Old French]
→ see Word Web: **city**

**city cen|ter** (**city centers**) N-COUNT The **city center** is the busiest part of a city, where most of the stores and businesses are. ❏ *Our offices are in the city center.*

**city plan|ning** N-UNCOUNT **City planning** is the planning and design of all the new buildings, roads, and parks in a place in order to make them attractive and convenient for the people who live there. ❏ *...city planning officials.*

**city|wide** /sɪtiwaɪd/ ADJ **Citywide** activities or situations happen or exist in all parts of a city. ❏ *This is a citywide problem.*

**Word Link**    *civ ≈ citizen : civic, civil, civilian*

**civ|ic** /sɪvɪk/ **1** ADJ You use **civic** to describe people or things that have an official status in a city or town. ❏ *Civic leaders say they want the city to look its best.* **2** ADJ You use **civic** to describe the duties or feelings that people have because they belong to a particular community. ❏ *...a sense of civic pride.* [from Latin]

**civic cen|ter** (**civic centers**) N-COUNT In a city or town, a **civic center** is a building or buildings that contain local government offices. Sporting events

and concerts are also often held at **civic centers**. ❏ *The city council wants more parks and a civic center.*

**civ|ics** /sɪvɪks/ N-UNCOUNT **Civics** is the study of the rights and duties of the citizens of a society. ❏ *...my high-school civics class.* [from Latin]

**civ|il** /sɪvəl/ **1** ADJ You use **civil** to describe things that relate to the people of a country, and their rights and activities, often in contrast with the armed forces. ❏ *He is a trained civil engineer.* ❏ *...civil disturbances in the city.* ❏ *...civil and political rights.* **2** ADJ Someone who is **civil** is polite in a formal way, but not particularly friendly. [FORMAL] ❏ *The least we can do is be civil to people.* ● **civ|il|ity** /sɪvɪlɪti/ N-UNCOUNT ❏ *...an atmosphere of civility.* [from Old French]

**Word Partnership**    Use *civil* with :

| N. | civil **disobedience**, civil **liberties/ rights**, civil **unrest** **1** |
|---|---|

**civ|il de|fense** N-UNCOUNT **Civil defense** is the organization and training of ordinary people in a country so that they can help the armed forces in an emergency. ❏ *...a civil defense exercise.*

**ci|vil|ian** /sɪvɪlyən/ (**civilians**) **1** N-COUNT In a military situation, a **civilian** is anyone who is not a member of the armed forces. ❏ *He assured me the soldiers were not shooting at civilians.* **2** ADJ In a military situation, **civilian** is used to describe people or things that are not military. ❏ *...the country's civilian population.* [from Latin]
→ see **war**

**civi|li|za|tion** /sɪvɪlɪzeɪʃən/ (**civilizations**) **1** N-VAR A **civilization** is a human society with

**Word Web**    city

For the past 6,000 years people have been moving from the **countryside** to **urban** centers. The world's oldest **capital** is Damascus, Syria. People have lived there for over 2,500 years. Cities are usually economic, commercial, cultural, political, social, and transportation centers. **Tourists** travel to cities for shopping and **sightseeing**. In some big cities, **skyscrapers** have **apartments**, **businesses**, **restaurants**, **theaters**, and **retail stores**. People never have to leave their building. Sometimes cities become overpopulated and **crime rates** soar. Then people move to the **suburbs**. In recent decades this trend has been reversed in some places and **inner cities** are being rebuilt.

its own social organization and culture. ❑ *...the ancient civilizations of Central and Latin America.* **2** N-UNCOUNT **Civilization** is the state of having an advanced level of social organization and a comfortable way of life. ❑ *...our advanced state of civilization.* [from Old French]
→ see **history**

**civi|lized** /sɪvɪlaɪzd/ **1** ADJ A **civilized** society has an advanced level of social organization. ❑ *This is not what we expect of a civilized society.* **2** ADJ If you describe a person or their behavior as **civilized**, you mean that they are polite and reasonable. ❑ *She was very civilized about it.* [from Old French]

**civ|il rights** N-PLURAL **Civil rights** are the rights that people have in a society to equal treatment and equal opportunities, whatever their race, sex, or religion. ❑ *...the civil rights movement.*

**civ|il serv|ant** (**civil servants**) N-COUNT A **civil servant** is a person who works for the **civil service**. ❑ *...two senior civil servants.*

**civ|il ser|vice** N-SING The **civil service** of a country consists of its government departments and all the people who work in them. ❑ *...a job in the civil service.*

**civ|il war** (**civil wars**) N-COUNT A **civil war** is a war which is fought between different groups of people who live in the same country. ❑ *...the American Civil War.*

**CJD** /si dʒeɪ di/ N-UNCOUNT **CJD** is an incurable brain disease that affects human beings and is believed to be caused by eating beef from cows infected with BSE. **CJD** is an abbreviation for "Creutzfeldt-Jakob disease."

**clad** /klæd/ ADJ If you are **clad** in particular clothes, you are wearing them. [LITERARY] ❑ *...the figure of a woman, clad in black.* [from Old French]

**claim** /kleɪm/ (**claims, claiming, claimed**) **1** V-T If someone **claims that** something is true, they say that it is true but they have not proved it and it may be false. ❑ *He claimed that the people supported his action.* ❑ *..a man claiming to be a journalist.* **2** V-T If someone **claims** responsibility or credit for something, they say that they are responsible for it. ❑ *A little-known group has claimed responsibility for the attack.* **3** V-T If you **claim** something, you try to get it because you think you have a right to it. ❑ *Now they are returning to claim their land.* ● **Claim** is also a noun. ❑ *...claims for improved working conditions.* ❑ *...rival claims to the territory.* **4** V-T If something **claims** someone's life, they are killed by it or because of it. [FORMAL] ❑ *The civil war claimed the life of a U.N. official yesterday.* **5** N-COUNT A **claim** is something which someone says which they have not proved and which may be false. ❑ *He repeated his claim that the people supported his actions.* **6** N-COUNT If you have a **claim on** someone or their attention, you have the right to demand things from them or to demand their attention. ❑ *She had no claims on him now.* [from Old French] **7** to **stake a claim** → see **stake**

**claim|ant** /kleɪmənt/ (**claimants**) N-COUNT A **claimant** is someone who asks to be given something which they think they are entitled to. [from Old French]

**clam** /klæm/ (**clams**) N-COUNT **Clams** are a kind of shellfish. [from Old English]
→ see **shellfish**

**clam|bake** /klæmbeɪk/ (**clambakes**) N-COUNT A **clambake** is a picnic at which clams and other food are served.

**clam|ber** /klæmbər/ (**clambers, clambering, clambered**) V-I If you **clamber** somewhere, you climb there with difficulty. ❑ *They clambered up the stone walls.*

**clam|or** /klæmər/ (**clamors, clamoring, clamored**) V-I If people **are clamoring for** something, they are demanding it in a noisy or angry way. ❑ *Both parties are clamoring for the attention of the voter.* [from Old French]

**clamp** /klæmp/ (**clamps, clamping, clamped**) **1** N-COUNT A **clamp** is a device that holds two things firmly together. ❑ *Many can openers have a set of clamps to grip the lid.* **2** V-T When you **clamp** one thing to another, you fasten the two things together with a clamp. ❑ *Clamp the microphone to the stand.* **3** V-T To **clamp** something in a particular place means to put it or hold it there firmly and tightly. ❑ *Simon clamped the phone to his ear.* ❑ *He clamped his lips together.* [from Dutch or Low German]
→ see **laboratory**
▶ **clamp down** PHR-VERB To **clamp down on** people or activities means to take strong official action to stop or control them. ❑ *The authorities are determined to clamp down on the media.*

**clan** /klæn/ (**clans**) N-COUNT A **clan** is a group which consists of families that are related to each other. ❑ *...enemy clans.* [from Scottish Gaelic]

**clan|des|tine** /klændestɪn/ ADJ Something that is **clandestine** is hidden or secret. [FORMAL] ❑ *...clandestine meetings.* [from Latin]

**clang|or** /klæŋər, klæŋgər/ N-SING A **clangor** is a loud or harsh noise. ❑ *Suddenly, the clangor and shouting ceased.* [from Latin]

**clap** /klæp/ (**claps, clapping, clapped**) **1** V-T/V-I When you **clap**, you hit your hands together to express appreciation or attract attention. ❑ *The men danced and the women clapped.* ❑ *Midge clapped her hands.* **2** V-T If you **clap** your hand or an object onto something, you put it there quickly and firmly. ❑ *I clapped a hand over her mouth.* **3** N-COUNT A **clap of thunder** is a sudden and loud noise of thunder. [from Old English]

**clari|fy** /klærɪfaɪ/ (**clarifies, clarifying, clarified**) V-T To **clarify** something means to make it easier to understand, usually by explaining it in more detail. [FORMAL] ❑ *Thank you for clarifying the position.* ● **clari|fi|ca|tion** /klærɪfɪkeɪʃ°n/ (**clarifications**) N-VAR ❑ *The union has asked for clarification of the situation.* [from Latin]

**clari|net** /klærɪnɛt/ (**clarinets**) N-VAR A **clarinet** is a wind instrument with a single reed in its mouthpiece. [from French]
→ see **orchestra**

**clar|ity** /klærɪti/ N-UNCOUNT **Clarity** is the quality of being clear and easy to understand. ❑ *...the clarity of his writing.* [from Latin]

**clash** /klæʃ/ (**clashes, clashing, clashed**)
**1** V-RECIP When people **clash**, they fight, argue, or disagree with each other. ❏ He often clashed with his staff when human projects. ❏ The two countries clashed over human rights. ● **Clash** is also a noun. ❏ There have been a number of clashes between police and demonstrators. **2** V-RECIP Beliefs, ideas, or qualities that **clash with** each other are very different from each other and therefore are opposed. ❏ We hope that the Internet will not clash with local customs and culture. ● **Clash** is also a noun. ❏ ...a clash of views. **3** V-RECIP If one color **clashes with** another, they look ugly together. ❏ The red door clashed with the soft, natural color of the stone walls.

**clasp** /klæsp/ (**clasps, clasping, clasped**) **1** V-T If you **clasp** someone or something, you hold them tightly. ❏ She clasped the children to her. **2** N-COUNT A **clasp** is a small device that fastens something. ❏ ...the clasp of her handbag. [from Old English]

**class** /klæs/ (**classes, classing, classed**)
**1** N-COUNT A **class** is a group of students who are taught together. ❏ He spent six months in a class with younger students. **2** N-COUNT A **class** is a course of teaching in a particular subject. ❏ She got her law degree by taking classes at night. **3** N-COUNT A **class of** things is a group of them with similar characteristics. ❏ Measurements for the same class of boats often varied. **4** N-UNCOUNT If you do something **in class**, you do it during a lesson in school. ❏ We do lots of reading in class. **5** N-UNCOUNT If you say that someone or something has **class**, you mean that they are elegant and sophisticated. [INFORMAL] **6** N-SING The students in a school or college who finish their course in a particular year are often referred to as the **class of** that year. ❏ ...Evergreen High School's Class of 2002. **7** N-VAR **Class** refers to the division of people in a society into groups according to their social status. ❏ ...the relationship between social classes. **8** → see also **middle class, upper class, working class** **9** V-T If someone or something **is classed as** a particular thing, they are regarded as belonging to that group of things. ❏ They cannot be classed as different species. ❏ I class myself as an ordinary working person. [from Latin] **10** → see also **second-class, world-class**

| **Word Partnership** | Use *class* with : |
| --- | --- |
| N. | **class for beginners**, class **size**, **students in a** class **1 2** |
| | **freshman/senior** class, |
| | **graduating** class **6** |
| | **leisure** class, class **struggle**, |
| | **working** class **7** |
| V. | **take a** class, **teach a** class **1 2** |
| ADJ. | **social** class **7** |

**class act** (**class acts**) N-COUNT If you describe someone or something as a **class act**, you mean that they are impressive and of high quality. ❏ This Broadway show will run a long time because it's a class act.

**clas|sic** /klæsɪk/ (**classics**) **1** ADJ A **classic** example of something has all the features which you expect such a thing to have. ❏ It's a classic example of racism in our country. **2** ADJ A **classic** movie or piece of writing is of very high quality and has become a standard against which

similar things are judged. ❏ ...the classic movie "Huckleberry Finn." ● **Classic** is also a noun. ❏ ...one of the classics of modern popular music. **3** N-UNCOUNT **Classics** is the study of the ancient Greek and Roman civilizations, especially their languages, literature, and philosophy. ❏ ...a classics degree. [from Latin]

**clas|si|cal** /klæsɪkᵊl/ **1** ADJ You use **classical** to describe something that is traditional in form, style, or content. ❏ ...classical ballet. ❏ ...a classical composer like Beethoven. ● **clas|si|cal|ly** /klæsɪkli/ ADV ❏ ...a classically trained pianist. **2** ADJ **Classical** is used to describe things which relate to the ancient Greek or Roman civilizations. ❏ ...ancient Egypt and classical Greece. [from Latin]
→ see **genre**

**clas|si|fied** /klæsɪfaɪd/ ADJ **Classified** information is officially secret. ❏ He had access to classified information.

**clas|si|fy** /klæsɪfaɪ/ (**classifies, classifying, classified**) V-T To **classify** things means to divide them into groups or types so that things with similar characteristics are in the same group. ❏ It is necessary to classify the headaches into certain types. ● **clas|si|fi|ca|tion** /klæsɪfɪkeɪʃᵊn/ (**classifications**) N-VAR ❏ ...the classification of knowledge into fields of study.

**class|less** /klæslɪs/ ADJ A **classless** society is one in which people are not affected by social status. ❏ ...the Western concept of a classless society. [from Latin]

**class|mate** /klæsmeɪt/ (**classmates**) N-COUNT Your **classmates** are students who are in the same class as you at school or college.

**class|room** /klæsrum/ (**classrooms**) N-COUNT A **classroom** is a room in a school where lessons take place.

**class sched|ule** (**class schedules**) N-COUNT In a school or college, a **class schedule** is a list that shows the times when particular subjects are taught.

**classy** /klæsi/ (**classier, classiest**) ADJ If you describe someone or something as **classy**, you mean that they are stylish and sophisticated. [INFORMAL] ❏ The German star gave a classy performance. [from Latin]

**clat|ter** /klætər/ (**clatters, clattering, clattered**) V-I If you say that people or things **clatter** somewhere, you mean that they move there noisily. ❏ He turned and clattered down the stairs. [from Old English]

**clause** /klɔz/ (**clauses**) **1** N-COUNT A **clause** is a section of a legal document. ❏ There is a clause in his contract about company cars. **2** N-COUNT In grammar, a **clause** is a group of words containing a verb. [from Old French]

**claw** /klɔ/ (**claws, clawing, clawed**)
**1** N-COUNT The **claws** of a bird or animal are the thin, hard, curved nails at the end of its feet. ❏ The cat tried to cling to the edge by its claws. **2** V-I If an animal **claws at** something, it scratches or damages it with its claws. ❏ The wolf clawed at the tree and howled.

claw

C

**3** V-I To **claw at** something mean to try very hard to get hold of it. ❑ *His fingers clawed at Blake's wrist.* [from Old English]
→ see **bird, shellfish**

**clay** /kleɪ/ N-UNCOUNT **Clay** is a kind of earth that is soft when it is wet and hard when it is dry. Clay is shaped and baked to make things such as pots and bricks. ❑ *He shaped and squeezed the lump of clay.* [from Old English]
→ see **pottery**

**clean** /klin/ (**cleaner, cleanest, cleans, cleaning, cleaned**) **1** ADJ Something that is **clean** is free from dirt or unwanted marks. ❑ *The subway is efficient and clean.* ❑ *Tiled kitchen floors are easy to keep clean.* **2** ADJ If something such as a book, joke, or lifestyle is **clean**, it is good because it is not immoral or offensive. ❑ *...clean, decent movies.* **3** ADJ If someone has a **clean** reputation or record, they have never done anything illegal or wrong. ❑ *I've been driving for 40 years with a clean license.* **4** V-T/V-I If you **clean**, or **clean** something, you make it free from dirt and unwanted marks. ❑ *Her father cleaned his glasses with a paper napkin.* ❑ *It took half an hour to clean the orange powder off the bathtub.* ● **cleaning** N-UNCOUNT ❑ *The windows were given a thorough cleaning.* [from Old English] **5** to **clean up** your **act** → see **act 6** to **keep** your **nose clean** → see **nose 7** a **clean slate** → see **slate 8** a **clean sweep** → see **sweep 9 clean as a whistle** → see **whistle**
→ see **soap**

▶ **clean out** PHR-VERB If you **clean out** something such as a closet or room, you take everything out of it and clean it thoroughly. ❑ *Mr. Peters asked if I would help him clean out the basement.*

▶ **clean up** PHR-VERB If you **clean up** something, you clean it thoroughly. ❑ *Hundreds of workers are cleaning up the beaches.*

| Thesaurus | *clean* | Also look up : |
|---|---|---|
| ADJ. | neat, pure; (*ant.*) dirty, filthy **1** | |
| V. | rinse, wash; (*ant.*) dirty, soil, stain **4** | |

**cleaner** /klinər/ (**cleaners**) **1** N-COUNT A **cleaner** is someone who is employed to clean the rooms and furniture inside a building. ❑ *...the hospital where Sid worked as a cleaner.* **2** N-COUNT A **cleaner** is a substance or device used for cleaning things. ❑ *...oven cleaner.* ❑ *...an air cleaner.* **3** → see also **vacuum cleaner 4** N-COUNT A **cleaner** or a **cleaner's** is a store where things such as clothes are dry-cleaned. ❑ *Did you pick up my suit from the cleaner's?* [from Old English]

**cleanliness** /klɛnlɪnɪs/ N-UNCOUNT **Cleanliness** is the degree to which people keep themselves and their surroundings clean. ❑ *Many of the state's beaches fail to meet minimum standards of cleanliness.* [from Old English]

**cleanse** /klɛnz/ (**cleanses, cleansing, cleansed**) **1** V-T To **cleanse** a place, person, or organization of something dirty, unpleasant, or evil means to make them free from it. ❑ *He tried to cleanse the house of bad memories.* **2** V-T If you **cleanse** your skin or a wound, you clean it. ❑ *Catherine demonstrated the proper way to cleanse the face.* [from Old English]

**cleanser** /klɛnzər/ (**cleansers**) N-VAR A **cleanser** is a liquid or cream that you use for cleaning something, especially your skin. ❑ *...an*

effective cleanser for dry and sensitive skin.* [from Old English]

---

**clear**

**1** FREE FROM CONFUSION
**2** FREE FROM PHYSICAL OBSTACLES
**3** MORALLY OR LEGALLY RIGHT, POSSIBLE, OR PERMITTED
**4** PHRASAL VERBS

**1 clear** /klɪər/ (**clearer, clearest, clears, clearing, cleared**) **1** ADJ Something that is **clear** is easy to understand, see, or hear. ❑ *The book is clear and readable.* ❑ *The space telescope has taken the clearest pictures ever of Pluto.* ● **clearly** ADV ❑ *Whales journey up the coast, clearly visible from the beach.* **2** ADJ Something that is **clear** is obvious. ❑ *It was a clear case of homicide.* ❑ *It became clear that I wouldn't be able to convince Mike.* ● **clearly** ADV ❑ *Clearly, the police cannot break the law in order to enforce it.* **3** ADJ If you are **clear about** something, you understand it completely. ❑ *It is important to be clear about what Chomsky is doing here.* **4** V-T/V-I If you **clear**, you are able to think sensibly and logically. ❑ *She needed a clear head to carry out her instructions.* ● **clearly** ADV ❑ *The only time I can think clearly is when I'm alone.* [from Old French]

**2 clear** /klɪər/ (**clearer, clearest, clears, clearing, cleared**) **1** ADJ If a substance is **clear**, it has no color and you can see through it. ❑ *...a clear glass panel.* ❑ *...a clear gel.* **2** ADJ If a surface, place, or view is **clear**, it is free of unwanted objects or obstacles. ❑ *The runway is clear — go ahead and land.* **3** ADJ If it is a **clear** day or if the sky is **clear**, there is no mist, rain, or cloud. ❑ *On a clear day you can see the coast.* **4** ADJ **Clear** eyes or skin look healthy and attractive. ❑ *...clear blue eyes.* **5** ADJ If one thing is **clear of** another, it is not touching it or is a safe distance away from it. ❑ *As soon as he was clear of the building he looked around.* **6** ADV If you drive **clear** to a place, especially a place that is far away, you go all the way there without delays. ❑ *They drove clear over to St Paul.* **7** V-T When you **clear** an area or place, you remove unwanted things from it. ❑ *They needed to clear the land.* ❑ *Workers could not clear the tunnels of smoke.* **8** V-I When fog or mist **clears**, it gradually disappears. ❑ *The early morning mist has cleared.* [from Old French] **9** to **clear the air** → see **air 10** → see also **clearing, crystal clear 11** to **clear** your **throat** → see **throat**

| Thesaurus | *clear* | Also look up : |
|---|---|---|
| ADJ. | obvious, plain, straightforward **1 1** | |
| | bright, cloudless, sunny **2 3** | |

| Word Partnership | | Use *clear* with : |
|---|---|---|
| N. | clear **goals/purpose**, clear **picture** **1 1** | |
| | clear **idea**, clear **understanding** **1 1 2** | |
| | clear **the way** **2 7** | |
| V. | **be** clear, **seem** clear **1 1 2** | |
| | **make it** clear **1 1 2** | |
| ADJ. | **crystal** clear **1 1 – 3 2 1 2** | |

**3 clear** /klɪər/ (**clearer, clearest, clears, clearing, cleared**) **1** ADJ If you say that your conscience is

**clear**, you mean you do not think you have done anything wrong. ▢ *Mr. Garcia said his conscience was clear.* **2** V-T If a course of action **is cleared**, people in authority give permission for it to happen. ▢ *The helicopter was cleared for take-off.* **3** V-T If someone **is cleared**, they are proved to be not guilty of a crime or mistake. ▢ *She was cleared of the murder.* [from Old French]

**❹ clear** /klɪər/ (**clears, clearing, cleared**)
▸ **clear away** PHR-VERB When you **clear** things **away** or **clear away**, you put away the things that you have been using. ▢ *The waitress cleared away the plates.*
▸ **clear out** **1** PHR-VERB If you tell someone to **clear out of** a place or to **clear out**, you are telling them rather rudely to leave. [INFORMAL] ▢ *She turned to the others in the room. "The rest of you clear out of here."* **2** PHR-VERB If you **clear out** a closet or place, you make it neat and throw away the things in it that you no longer want. ▢ *I cleared out my desk before I left.*
▸ **clear up** **1** PHR-VERB When you **clear up** or **clear** a place **up**, you make things neat and put them away. ▢ *After breakfast they played while I cleared up.* **2** PHR-VERB To **clear up** a problem, misunderstanding, or mystery means to settle it or find a satisfactory explanation for it. ▢ *The purpose of the meeting is to clear up these disagreements.* **3** PHR-VERB When the weather **clears up**, it stops raining or being cloudy. ▢ *It all depends on the weather clearing up.*

**clear|ance** /klɪərəns/ (**clearances**) **1** N-VAR **Clearance** is the removal of old buildings, trees, or other things that are not wanted from an area. ▢ *...the clearance of new lands for farming.* **2** N-VAR If you need **clearance to** do or have something, you get official approval or permission to do or have it. ▢ *The plane was given clearance to land.* [from Old French]

**clear-cut** also **clear cut** ADJ Something that is **clear-cut** is easy to understand and is definite or distinct. ▢ *There are no clear-cut answers.*

**clear|ing** /klɪərɪŋ/ (**clearings**) N-COUNT A **clearing** is a small area in a forest where there are no trees or bushes. ▢ *The helicopter landed in a clearing in the dense jungle.* [from Old French]

**cleats** /klit/ N-PLURAL **Cleats** are shoes with metal pieces attached to the soles that stop you slipping when you are playing football or other sports. ▢ *...my brother's football cleats.* [from Germanic]

**cleav|age** /klivɪdʒ/ (**cleavages**) N-COUNT **Cleavage** is the tendency of a mineral such as a gemstone to split along smooth, regular surfaces. [TECHNICAL] [from Old English]

**clef** /klɛf/ (**clefs**) **1** N-COUNT A **clef** is a symbol at the beginning of a line of music that indicates the pitch of the written notes. [from French] **2** → see also **bass clef, treble clef**

**clench** /klɛntʃ/ (**clenches, clenching, clenched**) **1** V-T/V-I When you **clench** your fist or your fist **clenches**, you curl your fingers up tightly, usually because you are very angry. ▢ *Alex clenched her fists.* **2** V-T/V-I When you **clench** your teeth or your teeth **clench**, you squeeze them together firmly, usually because you are angry or upset. ▢ *She clenched her teeth in frustration.* [from Old English]

**cler|gy** /klɜrdʒi/ N-PLURAL The **clergy** are the official religious leaders of a particular group of believers. ▢ *...Catholic clergy.* [from Old French]

**clergy|man** /klɜrdʒimən/ (**clergymen**) N-COUNT A **clergyman** is a male member of the clergy.

**cler|ic** /klɛrɪk/ (**clerics**) N-COUNT A **cleric** is a member of the clergy. ▢ *...a Muslim cleric.* [from Church Latin]

**cleri|cal** /klɛrɪkʰl/ **1** ADJ **Clerical** jobs, skills, and workers are concerned with work that is done in an office. ▢ *...a strike by clerical staff.* **2** ADJ **Clerical** means relating to the clergy. ▢ *...Iran's clerical leadership.* [from Church Latin]

**clerk** /klɜrk/ (**clerks, clerking, clerked**) **1** N-COUNT A **clerk** is a person who works in an office, bank, or law court and whose job is to keep the records or accounts, and sometimes to answer the telephone and deal with customers. ▢ *She works as a clerk with a travel agency.* **2** N-COUNT A **clerk** is someone who sells things to customers in a store. ▢ *Thomas was working as a clerk in a store that sold leather goods.* **3** V-I To **clerk** means to work as a clerk. ▢ *He clerked for a New York judge.* [from Old English]
→ see **hotel**

**clev|er** /klɛvər/ (**cleverer, cleverest**) **1** ADJ A **clever** idea, book, or invention is extremely effective and shows the skill of the people involved. ▢ *It is a clever novel.* ● **clev|er|ly** ADV ▢ *...a cleverly designed swimsuit.* **2** ADJ Someone who is **clever** is intelligent and able to understand things easily or plan things well. ▢ *He's a very clever man.* ● **clev|er|ly** ADV ▢ *...asks cleverly thought-out questions.* ● **clev|er|ness** N-UNCOUNT ▢ *Her cleverness seems to get in the way of her emotions.*

| **Thesaurus** | clever | Also look up : |
|---|---|---|
| ADJ. | bright, ingenious, smart; (*ant.*) dumb, stupid **1** **2** | |

**cli|ché** /kliʃeɪ/ (**clichés**) N-COUNT A **cliché** is an idea or phrase which has been used so much that it is no longer interesting or effective or no longer has much meaning. ▢ *I've learned that the cliché about life not being fair is true.* [from French]

**click** /klɪk/ (**clicks, clicking, clicked**) **1** V-T/V-I If something **clicks** or if you **click** it, it makes a short, sharp sound. ▢ *Hundreds of cameras clicked as she stepped out of the car.* ▢ *He clicked off the radio.* ● **Click** is also a noun. ▢ *I heard a click and then her recorded voice.* **2** V-T/V-I If you **click** on an area of a computer screen, you point the cursor at that area and press one of the buttons on the mouse in order to make something happen. [COMPUTING] ▢ *I clicked on a link.* ● **Click** is also a noun. ▢ *You can check your email with a click of your mouse.* **3** V-I When you suddenly understand something, you can say that it **clicks**. [INFORMAL] ▢ *When I saw the television report it all clicked.* **4** to **click into place** → see **place**

**cli|ent** /klaɪənt/ (**clients**) N-COUNT A **client** is someone for whom a professional person or organization provides a service or does some work. [BUSINESS] ▢ *...a lawyer and his client.* [from Latin]
→ see also **customer**
→ see **trial**

**cli|en|tele** /klaɪəntɛl, kliɒn-/ N-SING The **clientele** of a place or organization are its

## Word Web climate

During the past 100 years, the air **temperature** of the earth has increased by about 1° **Fahrenheit** (F). Alaska has warmed by about 4° F. At the same time, precipitation over the northern hemisphere increased by 10%. This suggests that the increase in rain and snow has caused the sea level to rise 4-8 inches around the world. The years 1998, 2001, and 2002 were the three hottest ever recorded. This warm period followed what some

scientists call the "Little Ice Age." Researchers found that from the 1400s to the 1800s the Earth cooled by about 6° F. Air and water temperatures were lower, **glaciers** grew quickly, and **ice** floes came further south than usual.

*St. Mark's Square in Venice flooded 111 times in 2002.*

customers or clients. ❑ *The restaurant's clientele includes all age groups.* [from Latin]

**cliff** /klɪf/ (**cliffs**) N-COUNT A **cliff** is a high area of land with a very steep side, especially one next to the sea. ❑ *The car rolled over the edge of a cliff.* [from Old English]
→ see **mountain**

**cli|mate** /klaɪmɪt/ (**climates**) **1** N-VAR The **climate** of a place is the general weather conditions that are typical of it. ❑ *...the hot and humid climate of Florida.* **2** N-COUNT You can use **climate** to refer to the general atmosphere or situation somewhere. ❑ *When the political climate changes, they will return to their home in Cuba.* [from Late Latin]
→ see Word Web: **climate**

**cli|max** /klaɪmæks/ (**climaxes, climaxing, climaxed**) **1** N-COUNT The **climax of** something is the most exciting or important moment in it, usually near the end. ❑ *Reaching the Olympics was the climax of her career.* **2** V-T/V-I The event that **climaxes** a sequence of events is an exciting or important event that comes at the end. You can also say that a sequence of events **climaxes with** a particular event. ❑ *The evening climaxed with an amazing firework display.* [from Late Latin]

**climb** /klaɪm/ (**climbs, climbing, climbed**) **1** V-T/V-I If you **climb** something such as a tree, mountain, or ladder, or **climb up** it, you move toward the top of it. ❑ *Climbing the hill took half an hour.* ❑ *Climb up the steps onto the bridge.* ● **Climb** is also a noun. ❑ *...an hour's climb through the woods.* **2** V-I If you **climb** somewhere, you move there carefully, for example because you are moving into a small space or trying to avoid falling. ❑ *The girls climbed into the car and drove off.* ❑ *He must have climbed out of his bed.* **3** V-I When something such as an airplane **climbs**, it moves upward. ❑ *The plane lost an engine as it climbed.* **4** V-I When something **climbs**, it increases in value or amount. ❑ *The nation's unemployment rate has been climbing steadily since last June.* ❑ *Prices have climbed by 21% since the beginning of the year.* [from Old English] **5** → see also **climbing**

### Word Partnership Use *climb* with :

| N. | climb **the stairs** **1** |
| | **prices** climb **4** |
| PREP. | climb **in/on,** climb **down/up** **1** |
| V. | **begin/continue to** climb **3** **4** |

**climb|er** /klaɪmər/ (**climbers**) N-COUNT A **climber** is someone who climbs rocks or mountains as a sport or a hobby. ❑ *She was an experienced climber.* [from Old English]

**climb|ing** /klaɪmɪŋ/ N-UNCOUNT **Climbing** is the activity of climbing rocks or mountains. ❑ *I have done no skiing, no climbing, and no hiking.* [from Old English]

**clinch** /klɪntʃ/ (**clinches, clinching, clinched**) V-T If you **clinch** something you are trying to achieve, you succeed in getting it. ❑ *The Lakers scored the next ten points to clinch the victory.*

**cling** /klɪŋ/ (**clings, clinging, clung**) **1** V-I If you **cling to** someone or something, you hold onto them tightly. ❑ *The man was rescued as he clung to the riverbank.* ❑ *She had to cling onto the door handle.* **2** V-I If you **cling to** a position or way of behaving, you try very hard to keep it or continue it. ❑ *He appears determined to cling to power.* [from Old English]

**clin|ic** /klɪnɪk/ (**clinics**) N-COUNT A **clinic** is a building where people receive medical advice or treatment. [from Latin]

**clini|cal** /klɪnɪkªl/ **1** ADJ **Clinical** means involving or relating to the direct medical treatment or testing of patients. [MEDICAL] ❑ *...her clinical training.* ● **clini|cal|ly** /klɪnɪkli/ ADV ❑ *She was clinically depressed.* **2** ADJ **Clinical** thought or behavior is very logical and does not involve any emotion, often when it would be more appropriate to show emotion. ❑ *He didn't like the clinical way she talked about their love.* [from Latin]

**clink** /klɪŋk/ (**clinks, clinking, clinked**) V-RECIP If glass or metal objects **clink** or if you **clink** them, they touch each other and make a short, light sound. ❑ *She clinked her glass against his.* ❑ *They clinked glasses.* ❑ *The empty bottle clinked against the seat.* ● **Clink** is also a noun. ❑ *...the clink of a spoon in a cup.* [from Middle Dutch]

**clip** /klɪp/ (**clips, clipping, clipped**) **1** N-COUNT
A **clip** is a small metal or plastic device that is
used for holding things together. ❑ *She took the
clip out of her hair.* **2** N-COUNT A **clip** from a movie
or a radio or television program is a short piece
of it that is broadcast separately. ❑ *...a film clip of
the Apollo moon landing.* **3** V-T/V-I When you **clip**
things together or when things **clip** together, you
fasten them together using a clip. ❑ *Clip the rope
onto the ring.* **4** V-T If you **clip** something, you cut
small pieces from it. ❑ *I saw an old man clipping his
hedge.* [Senses 1 and 3 from Old English. Senses
2 and 4 from Old Norse.] **5** → see also **clipped,
clipping**

**clipped** /klɪpt/ **1** ADJ **Clipped** means neatly cut.
❑ *...a quiet street of clipped hedges.* **2** ADJ If you have
a **clipped** way of speaking, you speak with quick,
short sounds. ❑ *A woman's clipped voice answered the
phone.* [from Old Norse]

**clip|ping** /klɪpɪŋ/ (**clippings**) N-COUNT A
**clipping** is an article, picture, or advertisement
that has been cut from a newspaper or magazine.
❑ *...newspaper clippings.* [from Old Norse]

**clique** /klik, klɪk/ (**cliques**) N-COUNT If you
describe a group of people as a **clique**, you mean
that they spend a lot of time together and seem
unfriendly towards people who are not in the
group. ❑ *He was accepted into the most popular
clique on campus.* ● **cli|quish** /klikɪʃ, klɪk-/ ADJ
❑ *...cliquish gossip.* [from French]

**cloak** /kloʊk/ (**cloaks**) **1** N-COUNT A **cloak** is
a long, loose, sleeveless piece of clothing which
people used to wear over their clothes when
they went out. **2** N-SING If you refer to something
as a **cloak**, you mean that it is intended to hide
the truth about something. ❑ *Preparations for the
wedding were made under a cloak of secrecy.* [from Old
French]

**clob|ber** /klɒbər/ (**clobbers, clobbering,
clobbered**) V-T If you **clobber** someone, you hit
them. [INFORMAL] ❑ *Hillary clobbered him with a vase.*

**clock** /klɒk/ (**clocks**) **1** N-COUNT A **clock** is
an instrument, for example in a room or on the
outside of a building, that shows what time of day
it is. ❑ *He could hear a clock ticking.* **2** → see also
**alarm clock, o'clock 3** PHRASE If something is
done **around the clock** or **round the clock**, it is done
all day and all night without stopping. ❑ *Rescue
services have been working round the clock.* [from
Middle Dutch]
→ see **time**

N.     **hands of a** clock, clock **radio 1**
V.     **look at a** clock, **put/turn the** clock
       **forward/back, set a** clock, clock
       **strikes,** clock **ticks 1**

**Word Link**   *wise ≈ in the direction or manner of :*
*clockwise, likewise, otherwise*

clockwise

**clock|wise** /klɒkwaɪz/
ADV When something is
moving **clockwise**, it is
moving in a circle in the
same direction as the hands
on a clock. ❑ *The children
started moving clockwise
around the room.* ● **Clockwise**
is also an adjective. ❑ *Gently
swing your right arm in a
clockwise direction.* [from
Middle Dutch]

**clock|work** /klɒkwɜrk/ **1** ADJ A **clockwork** toy
or device has machinery inside it which makes it
move or operate when it is wound up with a key.
❑ *...a clockwork train set.* **2** PHRASE If you say that
something happens **like clockwork**, you mean
that it happens without any problems or delays.
❑ *The president's trip went like clockwork.*

**clog** /klɒg/ (**clogs, clogging, clogged**) **1** V-T
When something **clogs** a hole or place, it blocks it
so that nothing can pass through. ❑ *Traffic clogged
the bridges.* **2** N-COUNT **Clogs** are heavy leather or
wooden shoes with thick, wooden soles.
→ see **shoe**

**cloister** /klɔɪstər/ (**cloisters**) N-COUNT A
**cloister** is a covered area around a square in a
monastery or a cathedral.

**clone** /kloʊn/ (**clones, cloning, cloned**)
**1** N-COUNT A **clone** is an animal or plant that
has been produced artificially from a cell of
another animal or plant, and is exactly the same
as it. ❑ *...the world's first human clone.* **2** N-COUNT
If someone or something is a **clone** of another
person or thing, they are so similar to this person
or thing that they seem to be exactly the same as
them. ❑ *Tom was in some ways a younger clone of his
father.* **3** V-T To **clone** an animal or plant means
to produce it as a clone. ❑ *The lecture was given by
the scientist who helped to clone Dolly the sheep.* [from
Greek]
→ see Word Web: **clone**

**Word Web**   clone

Clones have always existed. For example, a plant can be
duplicated by using a leaf cutting to produce an **identical** new
plant. Identical **twins** are also natural clones of each other.
Recently however, scientists have started using **genetic
engineering** to produce artificial clones of animals. The first step
involves removing the genetic information called **DNA** from a
**cell**. Next, the genetic information is placed into an egg cell. The
egg then grows into a **copy** of the donor animal. The first animal experiments in the 1970s involved
tadpoles. In 1997 a sheep named Dolly became the first successfully cloned mammal.

---

**close**

❶ SHUTTING OR COMPLETING
❷ NEARNESS; ADJECTIVE USES
❸ NEARNESS; VERB USES

---

❶ **close** /kloʊz/ (**closes, closing, closed**) ■ V-T/
V-I When you **close** a door, window, or lid, or when
it **closes**, it moves so that a hole, gap, or opening
is covered. ❏ *If you are cold, close the window.* ❏ *Zac
heard the door close.* ❏ The man
moved closer. ● **close**|**ly** ADV ❏ *They crowded more
closely around the fire.* ❷ ADJ People who are **close**
**to** each other like each other very much and know
each other very well. ❏ *She was closest to her sister
Gail.* ❏ *...a close friend from school.* ● **close**|**ness**
N-UNCOUNT ❏ *...her closeness to her mother.* ❸ ADJ
Your **close** relatives are the members of your
family who are most directly related to you, for
example your parents and your brothers or sisters.
❏ *...the death of a close relative.* ❹ ADJ **Close** contact
or cooperation involves seeing or communicating
with someone often. ❏ *Both nations are seeking
closer links with the West.* ● **close**|**ly** ADV ❏ *We
work closely with local groups.* ❺ ADJ If there is a
**close** connection or resemblance between two
things, they are strongly connected or are very
similar. ❏ *There is a close connection between income
and education.* ● **close**|**ly** ADV ❏ *The two problems
are closely linked.* ❻ ADJ **Close** inspection or
observation of something is careful and thorough.
❏ *Let's have a closer look.* ● **close**|**ly** ADV ❏ *You
have to look closely to find the café.* ❼ ADJ A **close**
competition or election is won or seems likely to
be won by only a small amount. ❏ *...a close contest
for a Senate seat.* ● **close**|**ly** ADV ❏ *This will be a closely
fought race.* ❽ ADJ If you are **close to** something,
or if it is **close**, it is likely to happen or come soon.
❏ *She sounded close to tears.* ❏ *At the end of January,
agreement seemed close.* ❾ ADJ If the atmosphere
somewhere is **close**, it is unpleasantly warm
with not enough air. ❿ PHRASE Something that
is **close by** or **close at hand** is near to you. ❏ *Did a
new hair salon open close by?* ⓫ PHRASE **Close to** a
particular amount or distance means slightly less
than that amount or distance. ❏ *He spent close to 30
years in prison.* ⓬ PHRASE If you look at something
**close up**, you look at it when you are very near

to it. ❏ *The airplane looked smaller close up.* [from
Old French] ⓭ → see also **close-up** ⓮ **at close
quarters** → see **quarter** ⓯ **at close range** → see
**range**

---

**Word Partnership**   Use *close* with :

| | |
|---|---|
| N. | close **a door**, close *your eyes* ❶ ■ |
| | close **friend**, close **to** *someone* ❷ ❷ |
| | close **family/relative** ❷ ❷ ❸ |
| | close **attention/scrutiny** ❷ ❻ |
| | close **election**, close **race** ❷ ❼ |
| ADV. | close **enough, so/too/very** |
| | close ❷ ❺ – ❽ |

---

❸ **close** /kloʊz/ (**closes, closing, closed**) V-I If
you **are closing on** someone or something that you
are following, you are getting nearer and nearer to
them. ❏ *I was closing on the guy in second place.* [from
Old French]
▶ **close in** PHR-VERB If a group of people **close in
on** a person or place, they come nearer and nearer
to them and gradually surround them. ❏ *Soviet
forces were closing in on Berlin.*

**closed** /kloʊzd/ ■ ADJ A **closed** group of people
does not welcome new people or ideas from
outside. ❏ *It is a closed society.* [from Old French]
❷ → see also **close** ❶

**closed-circuit** ADJ **Closed-circuit** television is
a television system used to film people within a
limited area such as a building. ❏ *There's a closed-
circuit television camera in the reception area.*

**closed cir|cu|la|tory sys|tem** (**closed
circulatory systems**) N-COUNT In animals that
have a **closed circulatory system**, their blood
flows through vessels such as veins and arteries
and never flows through other parts of their
body.

**closed sys|tem** (**closed systems**) N-COUNT In
a **closed system**, matter cannot enter or leave
the system and the system cannot be affected by
anything outside it.

**close-mouthed** ADJ Someone who is **close-
mouthed** about something does not say much
about it. ❏ *Lionel was close-mouthed about his private
life.*

**close|out** /kloʊzaʊt/ (**closeouts**) N-COUNT A
**closeout** at a store is a sale at which goods are
sold at reduced prices. ❏ *...a closeout sale at the
department store.*

**clos|et** /klɒzɪt/ (**closets**) ■ N-COUNT A **closet**
is a very small room for storing things, especially
clothing and linens. ❷ ADJ **Closet** is used to
describe a person who has beliefs, habits, or
feelings which they keep secret. ❏ *He is a closet
Fascist.* [from Old French]
→ see **house**

**close-up** /kloʊs ʌp/ (**close-ups**) N-COUNT A
**close-up** is a photograph or a picture in a film that
shows a lot of detail because it is taken very near
to the subject. ❏ *...a close-up of Harvey's face.*

**clos|ing** /kloʊzɪŋ/ (**closings**) ■ ADJ The **closing**
part of an activity or period of time is its final part.
❏ *...the closing minutes of the game.* ❷ N-COUNT A
**closing** is the final meeting between the buyer
and seller of a property. [from Old French]

**clos|ing ar|gu|ment** (**closing arguments**)
N-COUNT In a court case, a lawyer's **closing
argument** is their final speech, in which they give

---

**Thesaurus**   *close*   Also look up :

| | |
|---|---|
| V. | fasten, seal, shut, slam; (*ant.*) open ❶ ■ |

❷ **close** /kloʊs/ (**closer, closest**) ■ ADJ
Something that is **close to** something else is near
to it. ❏ *Her lips were close to his head.*

C

**Picture Dictionary** clothing

jacket
shawl
sweatshirt
blouse
T-shirt
skirt
jeans
sock
sweatpants
shoes
sneakers
high heels
baseball cap
shirt
tie
sweater
coat
suit
pants
boots

a summary of their case. ❑ *Both sides presented closing arguments.*

**clos|ing date** (**closing dates**) N-COUNT The **closing date** for a competition or offer is the final date by which entries or applications must be received. ❑ *The closing date for entries is Friday, January 11.*

**clo|sure** /klo͟ʊʒər/ (**closures**) **1** N-VAR The **closure** of a place such as a business or factory is the permanent ending of work or activity there. ❑ *...the closure of the steel mill.* **2** N-COUNT The **closure** of a road or border is the blocking of it in order to prevent people from using it. ❑ *Storms forced the closure of many roads.* [from Old French]

**clot** /klɒ͟t/ (**clots, clotting, clotted**) **1** N-COUNT A **clot** is a sticky lump that forms when blood dries up or becomes thick. ❑ *Surgeons removed a blood clot from his brain.* **2** V-I When blood **clots**, it becomes thick and forms a lump. ❑ *The patient's blood refused to clot.* [from Old English]

**cloth** /klɔ͟θ/ (**cloths**) **1** N-UNCOUNT **Cloth** is fabric which is made by weaving or knitting a substance such as cotton or wool. ❑ *...a piece of cloth.* **2** N-COUNT A **cloth** is a piece of cloth which you use for a particular purpose, such as cleaning. ❑ *Clean the surface with a damp cloth.* [from Old English]

**clothed** /klo͟ʊðd/ ADJ If you are **clothed in** a certain way, you are dressed in that way. ❑ *He lay down on the bed fully clothed.* ❑ *She was clothed in a flowered dress.* [from Old English]

**clothes** /klo͟ʊz, klo͟ʊðz/ N-PLURAL **Clothes** are the things that people wear, such as shirts, coats, pants, and dresses. ❑ *Moira went upstairs to change her clothes.* [from Old English]

**cloth|ing** /klo͟ʊðɪŋ/ N-UNCOUNT **Clothing** is the things that people wear. ❑ *...a women's clothing store.* [from Old English]
→ see Picture Dictionary: **clothing**

**cloud** /kla͟ʊd/ (**clouds, clouding, clouded**)
**1** N-VAR A **cloud** is a mass of water vapor that can be seen as a white or gray mass in the sky. ❑ *...the varied shapes of the clouds.* ❑ *...a black mass of cloud.* **2** N-COUNT A **cloud of** smoke or dust is a mass of it floating in the air. ❑ *We saw a huge cloud of dust.* **3** V-T If you say that something **clouds** your view of a situation, you mean that it makes you unable to understand the situation or judge it properly. ❑ *Perhaps anger clouded his vision.* **4** V-T If something **clouds** an event or situation, it makes it less pleasant. ❑ *Anger clouded his thinking.* [from Old English]
→ see Picture Dictionary: **clouds**
→ see **precipitation, water**

**cloudy** /kla͟ʊdi/ (**cloudier, cloudiest**) **1** ADJ If it is **cloudy**, there are a lot of clouds in the sky. ❑ *...a windy, cloudy day.* **2** ADJ A **cloudy** liquid is less clear than it should be. ❑ *The water was cloudy.* [from Old English]

**clout** /kla͟ʊt/ (**clouts, clouting, clouted**) **1** V-T If you **clout** someone, you hit them. [INFORMAL] ❑ *Rachel clouted him.* ● **Clout** is also a noun. ❑ *I gave him a clout across the shoulders.* **2** N-UNCOUNT A person or institution that has **clout** has influence and power. [INFORMAL] ❑ *The insurance companies have a lot of clout.* [from Old English]

**clove** /klo͟ʊv/ (**cloves**) **1** N-VAR **Cloves** are small dried flower buds which are used as a spice. ❑ *...chicken soup with cloves.* **2** N-COUNT A **clove of** garlic is one of the sections of a garlic bulb. [Sense 1 from Old French. Sense 2 from Old English.]

**clo|ver** /klo͟ʊvər/ (**clovers**) N-VAR **Clover** is a small plant with pink or white ball-shaped flowers and usually three round leaves. [from Old English]

**clover|leaf** /klo͟ʊvərlif/ (**cloverleafs, cloverleaves**) N-COUNT A **cloverleaf** is an arrangement of curved roads, resembling a four-

**Picture Dictionary**    clouds

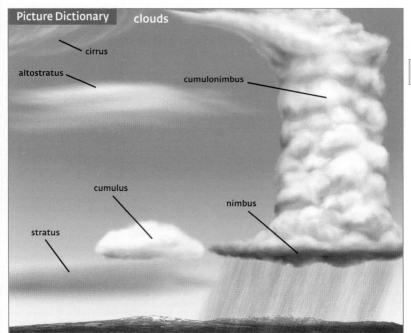

- cirrus
- altostratus
- cumulonimbus
- cumulus
- nimbus
- stratus

C

leaf clover, that joins two main roads. ❑ ...*the new route 29 cloverleaf.*

**clown** /kla͟ʊn/ (**clowns, clowning, clowned**)
■ N-COUNT A **clown** is a performer who wears funny clothes and bright makeup, and does silly things to make people laugh. ■ V-I If you **clown around**, you do silly things in order to make people laugh. ❑ *He was clowning around with his umbrella.* [from Low German]

**club** /klʌ̱b/ (**clubs, clubbing, clubbed**)
■ N-COUNT A **club** is an organization of people who are all interested in a particular activity. ❑ *...the Young Republicans Club.* ❑ *...a chess club.*
■ N-COUNT A **club** is a place where the members of a club meet. ❑ *I stopped in at the club.* ■ N-COUNT A **club** is a team which competes in sports competitions. ❑ *...the New York Yankees baseball club.* ■ N-COUNT A **club** is the same as a **nightclub.** ❑ *It's a big dance hit in the clubs.* ■ N-COUNT A **club** is a long, thin, metal stick with a piece of wood or metal at one end that you use to hit the ball in golf. ❑ *...a six-iron club.* ■ N-COUNT A **club** is a thick, heavy stick that can be used as a weapon. ❑ *...men armed with knives and clubs.* ■ V-T To **club** a person or animal means to hit them hard with a thick heavy stick or a similar weapon. ❑ *Someone clubbed him over the head.* ■ N-UNCOUNT **Clubs** is one of the four suits in a pack of playing cards. Each card in the suit is marked with one or more black symbols: ♣. ❑ *...the ace of clubs.* ● A **club** is a playing card of this suit. ❑ *The next player put down a club.* [from Old Norse]
→ see **golf**

**club|house** /klʌ̱bhaʊs/ (**clubhouses**) N-COUNT A **clubhouse** is a place where the members of a sports club meet.
→ see **golf**

**club soda** N-UNCOUNT **Club soda** is carbonated water used for mixing with alcoholic drinks and fruit juice.

**clue** /klu̱/ (**clues**) ■ N-COUNT A **clue to** a problem, mystery, or puzzle is something that helps you to find the answer. ❑ *The police are looking for clues to his disappearance.* ❑ *I'll give you a clue and then you have to think of the next word.* ■ PHRASE If you **don't have a clue** about something, you do not know anything about it or you have no idea what to do about it. [INFORMAL] ❑ *I don't have a clue what I'll give Carl for his birthday.*

**clump** /klʌ̱mp/ (**clumps**) N-COUNT A **clump of** things is a small group of them growing together or collected together in one place. ❑ *...a clump of trees.* ❑ *Her hair fell out in clumps.* [from Old English]

**clum|sy** /klʌ̱mzi/ (**clumsier, clumsiest**) ■ ADJ A **clumsy** person moves or handles things in an awkward way. ❑ *As a child she was very clumsy.*
● **clum|si|ly** /klʌ̱mzɪli/ ADV ❑ *He fell clumsily onto the bed.* ● **clum|si|ness** N-UNCOUNT ❑ *His clumsiness embarrassed him.* ■ ADJ A **clumsy** action or statement is not skillful and is likely to fail or to upset people. ❑ *...a clumsy attempt to bring down the government.* ● **clum|si|ly** ADV ❑ *The matter was handled clumsily.* ● **clum|si|ness** N-UNCOUNT ❑ *My clumsiness upset him.* [of Scandinavian origin]

**clung** /klʌ̱ŋ/ **Clung** is the past tense and past participle of **cling.**

**clunk|er** /klʌŋkər/ (clunkers) N-COUNT If you describe a machine, especially a car, as a **clunker**, you mean that it is very old and almost falling apart. [INFORMAL]

**clus|ter** /klʌstər/ (clusters, clustering, clustered) **1** N-COUNT A **cluster of** people or things is a small group of them close together. □ ...clusters of men in formal clothes. **2** V-I If people **cluster together**, they gather together in a small group. □ The passengers clustered together in small groups. [from Old English]

**clus|ter|ing** /klʌstərɪŋ/ N-UNCOUNT **Clustering** is a teaching method in which information is presented as a group of ideas in order to help students to remember it better. [from Old English]

**clutch** /klʌtʃ/ (clutches, clutching, clutched) **1** V-T/V-I If you **clutch** something, you hold it very tightly. □ Michelle clutched my arm. □ I clutched at a chair for support. **2** N-PLURAL If you are in someone's **clutches**, they have power over you. □ Tony fell into the clutches of an evil gang. **3** N-COUNT In a vehicle, the **clutch** is the pedal that you press before you change gear. □ Laura let out the clutch and pulled slowly away. [from Old English] **4** to **clutch at straws** → see **straw**

**clut|ter** /klʌtər/ (clutters, cluttering, cluttered) **1** N-UNCOUNT **Clutter** is a lot of unnecessary or useless things in a messy state. □ We started by getting rid of all the clutter. **2** V-T If things or people **clutter** a place, they fill it in a messy way. □ Empty soft-drink cans clutter the desks.

**cm** cm is the written abbreviation for **centimeter** or **centimeters**.

**coach** /koʊtʃ/ (coaches, coaching, coached) **1** N-COUNT A **coach** is someone who is in charge of training a person or sports team. □ ...the women's soccer coach at Rowan University. **2** N-COUNT A **coach** is an enclosed vehicle with four wheels which is pulled by horses, and in which people used to travel. □ ...a coach pulled by six black horses. **3** N-COUNT A **coach** is a large, comfortable bus that carries passengers on long trips. **4** V-T If you **coach** someone, you help them to become better at a particular sport or subject. □ She coached a golf team in San José. [from French]

**coal** /koʊl/ (coals) **1** N-UNCOUNT **Coal** is a hard, black substance that is extracted from the ground and burned as fuel. □ Gas is cheaper than coal. **2** N-PLURAL **Coals** are burning pieces of coal. [from Old English]
→ see **energy**

<table><tr><td>**Word Link**</td><td>co ≈ together : coalition, collaborate, collect</td></tr></table>

**coa|li|tion** /koʊəlɪʃ°n/ (coalitions) **1** N-COUNT A **coalition** is a government consisting of people from two or more political parties. □ The country has a coalition government. **2** N-COUNT A **coalition** is a group consisting of people from different political or social groups. □ ...a coalition of women's organizations. [from Medieval Latin]

**coarse** /kɔrs/ (coarser, coarsest) **1** ADJ **Coarse** things have a rough texture. □ ...a jacket made of very coarse cloth. ● **coarse|ly** ADV □ ...coarsely ground black pepper. **2** ADJ A **coarse** person talks and behaves in a rude and offensive way. □ ...coarse humor. ● **coarse|ly** ADV □ The women laughed coarsely at the joke.

**coarse ad|just|ment** N-UNCOUNT The part of a microscope that controls the **coarse adjustment** is the part that allows you to obtain the correct general focus for the object you are looking at. [TECHNICAL]

**coast** /koʊst/ (coasts) N-COUNT The **coast** is an area of land that is next to the sea. □ We stayed at a camp site on the coast. ● **coast|al** /koʊst°l/ ADJ □ ...coastal areas. [from Old French]
→ see **beach**

**Coast Guard** N-PROPER The **Coast Guard** is a part of a country's military forces and is responsible for protecting the coast, carrying out rescues, and doing police work along the coast. [AM] □ The U.S. Coast Guard is searching for a missing airplane.

**coast|line** /koʊstlaɪn/ (coastlines) N-VAR A country's **coastline** is the edge of its coast. □ ...the Pacific coastline.

**coast-to-coast** ADJ A **coast-to-coast** journey or route is one that goes from one coast of a country or region to the opposite coast. □ ...a coast-to-coast tour across the United States. ● **Coast-to-coast** is also an adverb. □ I drove coast-to-coast in two hours.

**coat** /koʊt/ (coats, coating, coated) **1** N-COUNT A **coat** is a piece of clothing with long sleeves which you wear over your other clothes when you go outside. □ He put on his coat and walked out. **2** N-COUNT An animal's **coat** is its fur or hair. **3** N-COUNT A **coat of** paint or varnish is a thin layer of it. □ The front door needs a new coat of paint. **4** V-T If you **coat** something **with** a substance, you cover it with a thin layer of the substance. □ Coat the fish with flour. [from Old French]
→ see **clothing, painting**

**coat check** (coat checks) also **coat-check** N-COUNT The **coat check** at a public building such as a theater or club is the place where customers can leave their coats. □ Let's get our coats at the coat check.

**coat|ing** /koʊtɪŋ/ (coatings) N-COUNT A **coating of** a substance is a thin layer of it. □ ...a coating of dust. [from Old French]

**coat|room** /koʊtrum/ (coatrooms) also **coat room** N-COUNT A **coatroom** is the same as a **coat check**.

**coax** /koʊks/ (coaxes, coaxing, coaxed) V-T If you **coax** someone **into** doing something, you gently try to persuade them to do it. □ They kept trying to coax me into talking.

**cob|ble** /kɒb°l/ (cobbles, cobbling, cobbled) ▸ **cobble together** PHR-VERB If you say that someone has **cobbled** something **together**, you mean that they have made or produced it roughly or quickly. □ The group cobbled together a few songs.

**co|bra** /koʊbrə/ (cobras) N-COUNT A **cobra** is a kind of poisonous snake. [from Portuguese]

**cob|web** /kɒbwɛb/ (cobwebs) N-COUNT A **cobweb** is the fine net that a spider makes for catching insects. □ The windows are cracked and covered in cobwebs. [from Old English]

**co|caine** /koʊkeɪn/ N-UNCOUNT **Cocaine** is an addictive drug which some people take for pleasure.

**coch|lea** /kɒkliə, koʊ-/ (cochleae) N-COUNT The **cochlea** is the spiral-shaped part of the inner ear. [from Latin]

**cock|pit** /ˈkɒkpɪt/ (cockpits) N-COUNT In an airplane or racing car, the **cockpit** is the part where the pilot or driver sits.

**cock|roach** /ˈkɒkroʊtʃ/ (cockroaches) N-COUNT A **cockroach** is a large brown insect that is sometimes found in warm places or where food is kept. [from Spanish]
→ see **insect**

**cock|tail** /ˈkɒkteɪl/ (cocktails) **1** N-COUNT A **cocktail** is an alcoholic drink that contains several ingredients. ❑ Guests are offered a champagne cocktail. **2** N-COUNT A **cocktail** is a mixture of a number of different things. ❑ ...a cocktail of chemicals.

**cocky** /ˈkɒki/ (cockier, cockiest) ADJ Someone who is **cocky** is so confident and sure of their abilities that they annoy other people. [INFORMAL] ❑ He was a little bit cocky because he was winning.

**co|coa** /ˈkoʊkoʊ/ **1** N-UNCOUNT **Cocoa** is a brown powder used in making chocolate. ❑ The Ivory Coast became the world's leading cocoa producer. **2** N-UNCOUNT **Cocoa** is a hot drink made from cocoa powder and milk or water. ❑ He made himself a cup of cocoa.

**coco|nut** /ˈkoʊkənʌt/ (coconuts) **1** N-COUNT A **coconut** is a very large nut with a hairy shell, white flesh, and milky juice inside it. **2** N-UNCOUNT **Coconut** is the white flesh of a coconut. ❑ ...two cups of grated coconut.

**co|coon** /kəˈkun/ (cocoons) **1** N-COUNT A **cocoon** is a covering of silky threads made by the larvae of moths and other insects before they grow into adults. ❑ ...like a butterfly emerging from a cocoon. **2** N-COUNT You can use **cocoon** to refer to an environment in which you feel protected and safe. ❑ ...a cocoon of love. [from French]

**cod** /ˈkɒd/ (cod) N-VAR A **cod** is a large sea fish with white flesh. ● **Cod** is this fish eaten as food. ❑ ...fried cod. [of Germanic origin]

**C.O.D.** /ˈsi oʊ ˈdi/ PHRASE **C.O.D.** is an abbreviation for **cash on delivery.** ❑ Phone orders are accepted for C.O.D. payment.

---

**Word Link** cod ≈ writing : code, decode, encode

---

**code** /ˈkoʊd/ (codes) **1** N-COUNT A **code** is a set of rules about how people should behave or about how something must be done. ❑ ...a strict moral code. **2** N-COUNT A **code** is a system of replacing the words in a message with other words or symbols, so that nobody can understand it unless they know the system. ❑ They used secret codes. **3** N-COUNT A **code** is a group of numbers or letters which is used to identify something such as a mailing address. ❑ The area code for western Pennsylvania is 412. **4** N-VAR A **code** is any system of signs or symbols that has a meaning. ❑ ...digital code. ❑ She began writing software code at the age of nine. [from French] **5** → see also **zip code**

**cod|ed** /ˈkoʊdɪd/ ADJ **Coded** messages have words or symbols which represent other words, so that the message is secret unless you know the system behind the code. ❑ There was a coded warning shortly before the blast. [from French]

**cod|ing** /ˈkoʊdɪŋ/ N-UNCOUNT **Coding** is a method of making something easy to recognize or distinct, for example by coloring it. ❑ ...a color coding system. [from French]

**co|ed** /ˈkoʊɛd, -ˌɛd/ **1** ADJ A **coed** school or facility is one that includes or involves both males and females. ❑ He was educated at a coed school. ❑ You have a choice of coed or single-sex exercise classes. **2** ADJ A **coed** sports facility or sport is one that both males and females use or take part in at the same time. ❑ We have coed and single-sex swimming pools.

**co|ef|fi|cient** /ˌkoʊɪˈfɪʃənt/ (coefficients) N-COUNT A **coefficient** is a number that expresses a measurement of a particular quality of a substance or object under specified conditions. [TECHNICAL] [from New Latin]

**coe|lom** /ˈsiləm/ (coeloms) N-COUNT The **coelom** is a hollow space in the body of an animal which contains organs such as the heart and kidneys. [TECHNICAL] [from Greek]

**co|erce** /koʊˈɜrs/ (coerces, coercing, coerced) V-T If you **coerce** someone **into** doing something, you make them do it, although they do not want to. [FORMAL] ❑ Poole argued that the government coerced him into pleading guilty. ● **co|er|cion** /koʊˈɜrʃən/ N-UNCOUNT ❑ Elections should be free of coercion. [from Latin]

**co|evo|lu|tion** /ˌkoʊɛvəˈluʃən/ N-UNCOUNT **Coevolution** is a process in which different species of animals or plants evolve in a particular way because of their close interaction with each other. [TECHNICAL]

**cof|fee** /ˈkɒfi/ (coffees) **1** N-VAR **Coffee** is the roasted beans of the coffee plant. ❑ Brazil is the world's largest coffee producer. **2** N-VAR **Coffee** is a drink made from boiling water and ground or powdered coffee beans. ❑ Would you like some coffee? ● A **coffee** is a cup of coffee. ❑ We had a coffee. [from Italian]

**cof|fee shop** (coffee shops) N-COUNT A **coffee shop** is an informal restaurant that sells food and drink, but not normally alcoholic drinks.

**cof|fin** /ˈkɒfɪn/ (coffins) N-COUNT A **coffin** is a box in which a dead body is buried or cremated. [from Old French]

**cog|nac** /ˈkoʊnyæk/ (cognacs) also Cognac N-VAR **Cognac** is a type of brandy. [after Cognac, a town in France]

**cog|ni|tive** /ˈkɒgnɪtɪv/ ADJ **Cognitive** means relating to the mental process involved in knowing, learning, and understanding things. [FORMAL] ❑ ...cognitive development. [from Latin]

**co|her|ent** /koʊˈhɪərənt, -ˈhɛrənt/ **1** ADJ If something is **coherent**, it is well planned, so that it is clear and sensible. ❑ We need a coherent policy. ● **co|her|ence** /koʊˈhɪərəns, -ˈhɛrəns/ N-UNCOUNT ❑ I thought the speech lacked coherence. **2** ADJ If someone is **coherent**, they express their thoughts in a clear and calm way. ❑ He wasn't capable of holding a coherent conversation. ● **co|her|ent|ly** ADV ❑ Many young people are unable to express themselves coherently. [from Latin]

**co|he|sion** /koʊˈhiʒən/ N-UNCOUNT If there is **cohesion** within a society, organization, or group, the different members fit together well and form a united whole. ❑ ...the cohesion of the armed forces. [from Latin]

**co|he|sive** /koʊˈhisɪv/ ADJ Something that is **cohesive** consists of parts that fit together well and form a united whole. ❑ ...a cohesive family unit. [from Latin]

**coil** /kɔɪl/ (**coils**) N-COUNT A **coil** of rope or wire is a length of it that has been wound into a series of loops. ❑ *He was carrying a coil of rope.* [from Old French]

**coin** /kɔɪn/ (**coins, coining, coined**) ■ N-COUNT A **coin** is a small piece of metal which is used as money. ❑ *…a few loose coins.* ■ V-T If you **coin** a word or a phrase, you are the first person to use it. ❑ *Jaron Lanier coined the term "virtual reality."* [from Old French]
→ see **English, money**

**coin|age** /kɔɪnɪdʒ/ N-UNCOUNT **Coinage** is the coins which are used in a country. ❑ *The city produced its own coinage from 1325 to 1864.* ■ N-UNCOUNT **Coinage** is the system of money used in a country. ❑ *…changes to U.S. coinage.* [from Old French]

**co|in|cide** /koʊɪnsaɪd/ (**coincides, coinciding, coincided**) ■ V-RECIP If one event **coincides with** another, they happen at the same time. ❑ *The exhibition coincides with the 50th anniversary of his death.* ■ V-RECIP If the ideas or interests of two or more people **coincide**, they are the same. ❑ *The kids' views on life don't always coincide.* [from Medieval Latin]

**co|in|ci|dence** /koʊɪnsɪdəns/ (**coincidences**) N-VAR A **coincidence** is when two or more similar or related events occur at the same time by chance. ❑ *Mr. Barry said the timing was a coincidence.* [from Medieval Latin]

**co|in|ci|dent|al|ly** /koʊɪnsɪdɛntli/ ADV You use **coincidentally** when you want to draw attention to a coincidence. ❑ *Coincidentally, I had once found myself in a similar situation.* [from Medieval Latin]

**coke** /koʊk/ ■ N-UNCOUNT **Coke** is a solid, black substance that is produced from coal and is burned as a fuel. ❑ *…a coke-burning stove.* ■ N-UNCOUNT **Coke** is the same as **cocaine**. [INFORMAL] [Sense 1 from northern English dialect]

**cola** /koʊlə/ (**colas**) N-VAR **Cola** is a sweet, brown, nonalcoholic carbonated drink. ❑ *…a can of cola.*

**cold** /koʊld/ (**colder, coldest, colds**) ■ ADJ If something or someone is **cold**, they have a very low temperature. ❑ *…cold running water.* ❑ *The house is cold because I can't afford to turn the heat on.* ❑ *I was freezing cold.* ● **cold|ness** N-UNCOUNT ❑ *She complained about the coldness of his hands.* ■ ADJ A **cold** person does not show much emotion or affection, and therefore seems unfriendly. ❑ *She was a cold, unfeeling woman.* ● **cold|ly** ADV ❑ *"I'll see you in the morning," Hugh said coldly.* ● **cold|ness** N-UNCOUNT ❑ *His coldness angered her.* ■ N-UNCOUNT Cold weather or low temperatures can be referred to as **the cold**. ❑ *He must have come inside to get out of the cold.* ■ **in cold blood** → see **blood** ■ to get **cold feet** → see **foot** ■ to **blow hot and cold** → see **hot** ■ to **pour cold water on** something → see **water** ■ N-COUNT If you have a **cold**, you have a mild, very common illness which makes you sneeze a lot and gives you a sore throat or a cough. ❑ *I had a pretty bad cold.* ■ PHRASE If you **catch cold**, or **catch a cold**, you become ill with a cold. ❑ *Let's dry our hair so we don't catch cold.* [from Old English]

**Thesaurus**    *cold*    Also look up :

| | |
|---|---|
| ADJ. | bitter, chilly, cool, freezing, frozen, raw; (ant.) hot, warm ■ |
| | cool, distant; (ant.) friendly, warm ■ |

**Word Partnership**    Use *cold* with :

| | |
|---|---|
| ADV. | **bitterly** cold ■ **freezing** cold ■ ■ |
| V. | **feel** cold, **get** cold ■ **catch/get** a cold ■ |
| N. | cold **air**, **dark** and cold, cold **night**, cold **rain**, cold **water**, cold **weather**, cold **wind** ■ ■ |

**cold-blooded** ADJ **Cold-blooded** animals have a body temperature that changes according to the surrounding temperature. Reptiles, for example, are cold-blooded.

**cold cuts** N-PLURAL **Cold cuts** are thin slices of cooked meat which are served cold.

**cold read|ing** (**cold readings**) N-COUNT A **cold reading** is a reading of the script of a play, read aloud for the first time by actors who are going to perform the play.

**Word Link**    *co = together : coalition, collaborate, collect*

**Word Link**    *labor ≈ working : collaborate, elaborate, laboratory*

**col|labo|rate** /kəlæbəreɪt/ (**collaborates, collaborating, collaborated**) ■ V-RECIP When people **collaborate**, they work together on a particular project. ❑ *He collaborated with his son Michael on the English translation.* ❑ *Students collaborate in group exercises.* ● **col|labo|ra|tion** /kəlæbəreɪʃⁿn/ (**collaborations**) N-VAR ❑ *…collaboration between parents and schools.* ❑ *…scientific collaborations.* ● **col|labo|ra|tor** /kəlæbəreɪtər/ (**collaborators**) N-COUNT ❑ *He and his collaborator completed the book in two years.* ■ V-I If someone **collaborates with** an enemy that is occupying their country during a war, they help them. ❑ *He was accused of collaborating with the secret police.* ● **col|labo|ra|tion** N-UNCOUNT ❑ *…collaboration with the enemy.* ● **col|labo|ra|tor** N-COUNT ❑ *He was suspected of being a collaborator.* [from Late Latin]

**col|labo|ra|tive** /kəlæbəreɪtɪv, -ərətɪv/ ADJ A **collaborative** piece of work is done by two or more people or groups working together. [FORMAL] ❑ *…a collaborative research project.* [from Late Latin]

**col|lage** /kəlɑʒ/ (**collages**) ■ N-COUNT A **collage** is a picture that has been made by sticking pieces of colored paper and cloth onto paper. ❑ *…a collage of words and pictures from magazines.* ■ N-UNCOUNT **Collage** is the method of making pictures by sticking pieces of colored paper and cloth onto paper. ❑ *The illustrations make use of collage and watercolor.* [from French]

**Word Link**    *lapse ≈ falling : collapse, elapse, lapse*

**col|lapse** /kəlæps/ (**collapses, collapsing, collapsed**) ■ V-I If a building or other structure **collapses**, it falls down very suddenly. ❑ *A section of the Bay Bridge collapsed.* ● **Collapse** is also a noun.

❑ ...*an inquiry into the freeway's collapse.* **2** v-i If a system or institution **collapses**, it fails completely and suddenly. ❑ *His business empire collapsed overnight.* ● **Collapse** is also a noun. ❑ *The medical system is facing collapse.* **3** v-i If you **collapse**, you suddenly fall down because you are very ill or tired. ❑ *He collapsed at his home.* ● **Collapse** is also a noun. ❑ *A few days after his collapse he was sitting up in bed.* [from Latin]

**col|lar** /kɒlər/ (**collars**) **1** N-COUNT The **collar** of a shirt or coat is the part which fits around the

neck and is usually folded over. ❑ *His tie was loose and his collar was open.* **2** → see also **blue-collar, white-collar**

collar

**3** N-COUNT A **collar** is a band of leather or plastic which is put around the neck of a dog or cat. [from Latin]

**col|late** /kəleɪt/ (**collates, collating, collated**) v-t When you **collate** pieces of information, you gather them all together and examine them. ❑ *Roberts spent years collating the data on which the study was based.* [from Latin]

**col|lat|er|al** /kəlætərəl/ N-UNCOUNT **Collateral** is money or property which is used as a guarantee that someone will repay a loan. [FORMAL] ❑ *They used their house as collateral for the loan.* [from Medieval Latin]

**col|league** /kɒliɡ/ (**colleagues**) N-COUNT Your **colleagues** are the people you work with, especially in a professional job. ❑ *...a business colleague.* [from French]

> **Word Link** *co ≈ together : coalition, collaborate, collect*

**col|lect** /kəlɛkt/ (**collects, collecting, collected**) **1** v-t If you **collect** a number of things, you bring them together from several places or from several people. ❑ *Two young girls were collecting firewood.* ● **col|lec|tion** N-UNCOUNT ❑ *Computer systems can speed up collection of information.* **2** v-t If you **collect** things, such as stamps or books, as a hobby, you get a large number of them over a period of time because they interest you. ❑ *I used to collect key rings.* ● **col|lect|ing** N-UNCOUNT ❑ *...hobbies like stamp collecting.* ● **col|lec|tor** (**collectors**) N-COUNT ❑ *...a respected collector of Indian art.* **3** v-t/v-i If a substance **collects** somewhere, or if something **collects** it, it comes arriving over a period of time and is held in that place or thing. ❑ *Gas does collect in the mines around here.* ❑ *...tanks which collect rainwater.* **4** v-t/v-i If you **collect for** a charity or for a present for someone, you ask people to give you money for it. ❑ *Are you collecting for charity?* ❑ *The organization has collected $2.5 million for the relief effort.* ● **col|lec|tion** N-COUNT ❑ *We held a collection for a children's charity.* [from Latin]

> **Thesaurus** collect Also look up :
>
> v. accumulate, compile, gather; (ant.) scatter **1**

**col|lect call** (**collect calls**) **1** N-COUNT A **collect call** is a telephone call which is paid for by the person who receives the call, rather than the person who makes the call. ❑ *I want to make a collect call.* **2** → see also **call**

**col|lec|tion** /kəlɛkʃən/ (**collections**) **1** N-COUNT A **collection** of things is a group of similar or related things. ❑ *...the world's largest collection of sculptures by Henry Moore.* ❑ *...a collection of short stories called "Facing The Music."* ❑ *...a collection of modern glass office buildings.* [from Latin] **2** → see also **collect**

**col|lec|tion agen|cy** (**collection agencies**) N-COUNT A **collection agency** is an organization that obtains payments from people who owe money to others. ❑ *...a debt collection agency.*

**col|lec|tive** /kəlɛktɪv/ (**collectives**) **1** ADJ **Collective** means shared by every member of a group. ❑ *It was a collective decision.* ● **col|lec|tive|ly** ADV ❑ *They collectively decided to move on.* **2** N-COUNT A **collective** is a business or farm which is run, and often owned, by a group of people. [BUSINESS] ❑ *He participates in all the decisions of the collective.* [from Latin] → see **union**

**col|lec|tor** /kəlɛktər/ (**collectors**) **1** N-COUNT A **collector** is someone whose job is to take something such as money, tickets, or garbage from people. ❑ *He earned his living as a tax collector.* [from Latin] **2** → see also **collect** → see **solar**

**col|lege** /kɒlɪdʒ/ (**colleges**) **1** N-VAR A **college** is an institution where students study after they have left secondary school. ❑ *Joanna is taking business courses at a local college.* ❑ *Stephanie left art college this summer.* **2** N-COUNT At some universities in the United States, **colleges** are divisions which offer degrees in particular subjects. ❑ *...a professor at the University of Florida College of Law.* **3** N-COUNT A **college** is one of the institutions which some British universities are divided into. ❑ *He was educated at Balliol College, Oxford.* [from Latin] → see **graduation**

**col|le|gi|ate** /kəlidʒɪt, -dʒiɪt/ ADJ **Collegiate** means belonging or relating to a college or to college students. ❑ *...the national collegiate football championship.* ❑ *...collegiate life.* [from Latin]

**col|lide** /kəlaɪd/ (**collides, colliding, collided**) v-RECIP If people or vehicles **collide**, they crash into one another. ❑ *Two trains collided head-on.* ❑ *Racing up the stairs, he almost collided with Daisy.* [from Latin]

> **Thesaurus** collide Also look up :
>
> v. bump, clash, crash, hit, smash; (ant.) avoid

**col|li|sion** /kəliʒən/ (**collisions**) N-VAR A **collision** occurs when a moving object crashes into something. ❑ *Their van was involved in a collision with a car.* [from Late Latin]

**col|loid** /kɒlɔɪd/ (**colloids**) N-COUNT A **colloid** is a mixture containing tiny particles of a substance that do not dissolve or settle at the bottom of the mixture. [TECHNICAL] [from Greek]

**col|lude** /kəlud/ (**colludes, colluding, colluded**) v-RECIP If one person **colludes with** another, they cooperate with them secretly or illegally. ❑ *Several local officials are in jail on charges of colluding with the Mafia.* ❑ *The police and army colluded in the attacks.* ● **col|lu|sion** /kəluʒən/ N-UNCOUNT [FORMAL] ❑ *He* *found no evidence of collusion between record companies and retailers.* [from Latin]

**co|lon** /kóʊlən/ (**colons**) ■ N-COUNT A **colon** is the punctuation mark (:). ■ N-COUNT Your **colon** is the part of your intestine above your rectum. □ *...deaths from colon cancer.* [from Latin]
→ see **punctuation**

**colo|nel** /kɜrnᵊl/ (**colonels**) N-COUNT; N-TITLE; N-VOC A **colonel** is a senior officer in an army, air force, or the marines. □ *...an ex-army colonel.* [from Old French]

**co|lo|nial** /kəlóʊniəl/ ■ ADJ **Colonial** means relating to countries that are colonies, or to colonialism. □ *...Jamaica's independence from British colonial rule.* ■ ADJ A **colonial** building or piece of furniture was built or made in a style that was popular in America in the 17th and 18th centuries. □ *...big white colonial houses.* [from Latin]

**co|lo|ni|al|ism** /kəlóʊniəlɪzəm/ N-UNCOUNT **Colonialism** is the practice by which a powerful country directly controls less powerful countries. □ *...the fight against colonialism.* [from Latin]

**colo|nist** /kɒlənɪst/ (**colonists**) N-COUNT **Colonists** are the people who start a colony or the people who are among the first to live in a particular colony. □ *...the early American colonists.* [from Latin]

**colo|nize** /kɒlənaɪz/ (**colonizes, colonizing, colonized**) V-T If people **colonize** a foreign country, they go to live there and take control of it. □ *...the first British attempt to colonize Ireland.* [from Latin]

**colo|ny** /kɒləni/ (**colonies**) ■ N-COUNT A **colony** is a country which is controlled by a more powerful country. □ *...France's former North African colonies.* ■ N-COUNT A **colony** is a group of people or animals of a particular sort living together. □ *...an artists' colony.* □ *...colonies of sea birds.* ■ N-PLURAL **The colonies** means the 13 British

colonies in North America which formed the original United States. [AM] □ *Philadelphia was the most important city in the colonies.* [from Latin]

**col|or** /kʌlər/ (**colors, coloring, colored**) ■ N-COUNT The **color** of something is the appearance that it has as a result of the way in which it reflects light. Red, blue, and green are colors. □ *"What color is the car?" — "Red."* □ *Judi's favorite color is pink.* ■ N-COUNT Someone's **color** is the color of their skin. People often use **color** in this way to refer to a person's race. □ *I don't care what color she is.* ■ V-T If you **color** something, you use something such as dyes or paint to change its color. □ *Many women begin coloring their hair in their mid-30s.* ■ V-T If something **colors** your opinion or judgment, it affects the way that you think about something. □ *He sometimes let emotion color his judgment.* ■ ADJ A **color** television, photograph, or picture is one that shows things in all their colors, and not just in black, white, and gray. □ *...a color television set.* ■ N-UNCOUNT **Color** is a quality that makes something especially interesting or exciting. □ *Travel adds color to our lives.* [from Old French] ■ → see also **colored, coloring**
→ see Picture Dictionary: **color**
→ see **painting**

▶ **color in** PHR-VERB If you **color in** a drawing, you give it different colors using crayons or paints. □ *They colored in all the black and white pictures.*

| Word Partnership | Use *color* with : |
| --- | --- |
| ADJ. | **bright** color, **favorite** color ■ |
| N. | color **blind**, **eye/hair** color ■ |
| | **skin** color ■ |
| | color **film/photograph**, |
| | color **television** ■ |

**color-blind** ■ ADJ Someone who is **color-blind** cannot see the difference between colors, especially between red and green. □ *Far more*

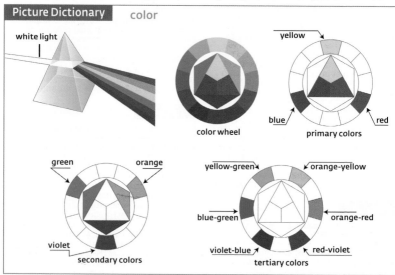

**Picture Dictionary**    color

white light

color wheel

yellow
blue    red
primary colors

green     orange
violet
secondary colors

yellow-green    orange-yellow
blue-green    orange-red
violet-blue    red-violet
tertiary colors

men are color-blind than women. ● **color-blindness**
N-UNCOUNT ❑ *What exactly is color-blindness?* **2** ADJ
A **color-blind** system or organization does not treat
people differently according to their race or color.
❑ *Their goal is a color-blind society.*

**color-coded** ADJ Things that are **color-coded**
use colors to represent different features or
functions. ❑ *...color-coded buckets.*

**col|ored** /kʌlərd/ ADJ **Colored** means having
a particular color. ❑ *...colored scarves.* [from Old
French]

**col|or|ful** /kʌlərfəl/ **1** ADJ Something that
is **colorful** has bright colors or a lot of different
colors. ❑ *The flowers were colorful.* **2** ADJ **Colorful**
means interesting and exciting. ❑ *The story she told
was certainly colorful.* ❑ *...probably the most colorful
character in baseball.* [from Old French]

| **Thesaurus** | *colorful* | Also look up : |
|---|---|---|
| ADJ. | bright, lively, vibrant, vivid; (*ant.*) bland, colorless, dull **1** animated, dramatic, interesting **2** | |

**col|or|ing** /kʌlərɪŋ/ **1** N-UNCOUNT Someone's
**coloring** is the color of their hair, skin, and
eyes. ❑ *None of them had their father's dark coloring.*
**2** N-UNCOUNT **Coloring** is a substance that is used
to give color to food. ❑ *...green food coloring.* [from
Old French] **3** → see also **color**

**col|or|ing book** (**coloring books**) N-COUNT A
**coloring book** is a book of simple drawings which
children can color in.

**col|or|less** /kʌlərlɪs/ **1** ADJ Something that is
**colorless** has no color at all. ❑ *...a colorless liquid.*
**2** ADJ **Colorless** people or places are dull and
uninteresting. ❑ *...a colorless little town.* [from Old
French]

**col|or re|la|tion|ship** (**color relationships**) also
color harmony also **color scheme** **1** N-COUNT
**Color relationships** are pleasing combinations of
colors that are based on the position of colors on
the color wheel. **2** → see also **color**

**col|or scheme** (**color schemes**) N-COUNT In
a room or house, the **color scheme** is the way in
which colors have been used to decorate it. ❑ *...a
color scheme of green and pink.*

**col|or the|ory** (**color theories**) N-VAR **Color
theory** is a set of rules for mixing colors in order to
achieve a particular result in a painting.

**co|los|sal** /kəlɒsᵊl/ ADJ Something that is
**colossal** is very large. ❑ *...a colossal waste of public
money.* [from Latin]

**colt** /koʊlt/ (**colts**) N-COUNT A **colt** is a young
male horse. [from Old English]

**col|umn** /kɒləm/ (**columns**) **1** N-COUNT A
**column** is a tall, solid cylinder, especially one
supporting part of a building. ❑ *The house had six
white columns across the front.* **2** N-COUNT A **column**
is something that has a tall, narrow shape. ❑ *...a
column of smoke.* **3** N-COUNT A **column** is a group
of people or animals which moves in a long line.
❑ *...columns of military vehicles.* **4** N-COUNT In a
newspaper or magazine, or a printed chart, a
**column** is a vertical section of writing, or a section
that is always written by the same person. ❑ *He
writes a column for the Wall Street Journal.* [from Latin]

**col|um|nist** /kɒləmnɪst, -əmɪst/ (**columnists**)
N-COUNT A **columnist** is a journalist who writes a

regular article in a newspaper or magazine. ❑ *...a
columnist for the Chicago Tribune.* [from Latin]

**coma** /koʊmə/ (**comas**) N-COUNT If someone is
in a **coma**, they are deeply unconscious. ❑ *She was
in a coma for seven weeks.* [from Medieval Latin]

**comb** /koʊm/ (**combs, combing, combed**)
**1** N-COUNT A **comb** is a flat piece of plastic or
metal with narrow, pointed teeth along one side,
which you use to make your hair neat. **2** V-T
When you **comb** your hair, you make it neat using
a comb. ❑ *Salvatore combed his hair carefully.* **3** V-T
If you **comb** a place for something, you search
thoroughly for it. ❑ *Police combed the area for the boy.*
[from Old English]

**com|bat** (**combats, combating** or
**combatting, combated** or **combatted**)

> The noun is pronounced /kɒmbæt/. The verb is
> pronounced /kəmbæt/.

**1** N-UNCOUNT **Combat** is fighting that takes place
in a war. ❑ *Over 16 million men had died in combat.*
**2** V-T If people in authority **combat** something,
they try to stop it from happening. ❑ *...new laws to
combat crime.* [from French]
→ see **war**

| **Word Partnership** | Use *combat* with : |
|---|---|
| ADJ. | **hand-to-hand** combat, **heavy** combat **1** |
| N. | combat **forces/troops/units**, combat **gear** **1** combat **crime**, combat **disease**, combat **terrorism** **2** |

**com|bat|ive** /kəmbætɪv/ ADJ A person who
is **combative** is aggressive and eager to fight
or argue. ❑ *He conducted the meeting in his usual
combative style.* [from French]

**com|bi|na|tion** /kɒmbɪneɪʃᵊn/ (**combinations**)
N-COUNT A **combination** of things is a mixture of
them. ❑ *...a fantastic combination of colors.* [from
Late Latin]

| **Word Link** | com ≈ with, together : *combine, compact, companion* |
|---|---|

**com|bine** /kəmbaɪn/ (**combines, combining,
combined**) **1** V-RECIP If you **combine** two or
more things or if they **combine**, they exist or join
together. ❑ *Combine the flour with 3 tablespoons of
water.* ❑ *Disease and hunger combine to kill thousands.*
● **com|bined** /kəmbaɪnd/ ADJ ❑ *The companies had
combined sales of $90 million.* **2** V-T If someone or
something **combines** two qualities or features,
they have both of them. ❑ *Their system seems to
combine the two ideals.* ❑ *His latest movie combines
comedy with mystery.* **3** V-T If someone **combines**
two activities, they do them both at the same
time. ❑ *It is possible to combine a career with being a
mother.* [from Late Latin]

| **Thesaurus** | *combine* | Also look up : |
|---|---|---|
| V. | blend, fuse, incorporate, join, mix, unite; (*ant.*) detach, disconnect, divide, separate **1** – **3** | |

**com|bus|tion** /kəmbʌstʃən/ N-UNCOUNT
**Combustion** is the act of burning something or
the process of burning. [TECHNICAL] ❑ *The energy is
released by combustion.* [from Old French]
→ see **engine**

C

---

## come

**❶ ARRIVE AT A PLACE**
**❷ OTHER USES**
**❸ PHRASAL VERBS**

---

**Come** is used in a large number of expressions which are explained under other words in this dictionary. For example, the expression "to come to terms with something" is explained at "term."

**❶ come** /kʌm/ (comes, coming, came)

The form **come** is used in the present tense and is the past participle.

**1** V-I You use **come** to say that someone or something arrives somewhere, or moves toward you. ❑ *Two police officers came into the hall.* ❑ *He came to a door.* ❑ *Eleanor came to see her.* ❑ *Come here, Tom.* ❑ *We heard the train coming.* ❑ *The windows broke and the sea came rushing in.* **2** V-I If something **comes to** a particular point, it reaches it. ❑ *The water came up to my chest.* [from Old English]

**❷ come** /kʌm/ (comes, coming, came)

The form **come** is used in the present tense and is the past participle.

**1** V-I You can use **come** in expressions which state what happens to someone or something. ❑ *The lid won't come off.* ❑ *Their worst fears may be coming true.* **2** V-T If someone **comes to** do something, they gradually start to do it. ❑ *She said it so many times that she came to believe it.* **3** V-T/V-I When a particular event or time **comes**, it arrives or happens. ❑ *The announcement came after a meeting at the White House.* ❑ *There will come a time when they will have to negotiate.* ● **coming** N-SING ❑ *Most people welcome the coming of summer.* **4** V-I If a thought, idea, or memory **comes to** you, you suddenly think of it or remember it. ❑ *He was about to shut the door when an idea came to him.* **5** V-I If something **comes to** a particular amount, it adds up to it. ❑ *Lunch came to $80.* **6** V-I If someone or something **comes from** a particular place or thing, that place or thing is their origin, source, or starting point. ❑ *Nearly half the students come from overseas.* ❑ *Most of Germany's oil comes from the North Sea.* **7** V-I Something that **comes from** something else or **comes of** it is the result of it. ❑ *...a feeling of power that comes from driving fast.* ❑ *Some good might come of this.* **8** V-T If someone or something **comes** first, next, or last, they are first, next, or last in a series, list, or competition. ❑ *The two countries cannot agree what should come next.* **9** V-I If a type of thing **comes in** a particular range of colors, forms, styles, or sizes, it can have any of those colors, forms, styles, or sizes. ❑ *Bikes come in all shapes and sizes.* [from Old English]

**❸ come** /kʌm/ (comes, coming, came)

The form **come** is used in the present tense and is the past participle.

▸ **come about** PHR-VERB When you say how or when something **came about**, you say how or when it happened. ❑ *How did this situation come about?*

▸ **come across** **1** PHR-VERB If you **come across** something or someone, you find them or meet them by chance. ❑ *I came across a photo of my grandparents.* **2** PHR-VERB The way that someone **comes across** is the impression that they make on other people. ❑ *He comes across as an extremely pleasant young man.*

▸ **come along** **1** PHR-VERB You ask someone to **come along** to invite them in a friendly way to do something with you or go somewhere. ❑ *There's a party tonight and you're very welcome to come along.* **2** PHR-VERB When something or someone **comes along**, they occur or arrive by chance. ❑ *It was lucky you came along.* **3** PHR-VERB If something **is coming along**, it is developing or making progress. ❑ *The talks are coming along quite well.*

▸ **come around** **1** PHR-VERB If someone **comes around**, they come to your house to see you. ❑ *Beth came around this morning to apologize.* **2** PHR-VERB If you **come around to** an idea, you eventually change your mind and accept it. ❑ *It looks like they're coming around to our way of thinking.* **3** PHR-VERB When something **comes around**, it happens as a regular or predictable event. ❑ *I hope to be fit when the World Championship comes around.* **4** PHR-VERB When someone who is unconscious **comes around**, they become conscious again. ❑ *When I came around I was on the kitchen floor.*

▸ **come at** PHR-VERB If a person or animal **comes at** you, they move toward you in a threatening way and try to attack you. ❑ *Mr. Cox came at him with a wild expression.*

▸ **come back** **1** PHR-VERB If someone comes back to a place, they return to it. ❑ *He wanted to come back to Washington.* ❑ *She just wanted to go home and not come back.* **2** PHR-VERB If something that you had forgotten **comes back to** you, you remember it. ❑ *I'll tell you his name when it comes back to me.* **3** PHR-VERB When something **comes back**, it becomes fashionable again. ❑ *I'm glad hats are coming back.* **4** → see also **comeback**

▸ **come by** PHR-VERB To **come by** something means to obtain it or find it. ❑ *How did you come by that check?*

▸ **come down** **1** PHR-VERB If the cost, level, or amount of something **comes down**, it becomes less than it was before. ❑ *Interest rates should come down.* ❑ *If you buy three, the price comes down to $10.* **2** PHR-VERB If something **comes down**, it falls to the ground. ❑ *The cold rain came down for hours.*

▸ **come down on** **1** PHR-VERB If you **come down on** one side of an argument, you declare that you support that side. ❑ *He clearly came down on the side of the president.* **2** PHR-VERB If you **come down on** someone, you criticize them severely or treat them strictly. ❑ *If Douglas comes down hard on him, Dale will rebel.*

▸ **come down to** PHR-VERB If a problem, decision, or question **comes down to** a particular thing, that thing is the most important factor involved. ❑ *The problem comes down to money.*

▸ **come down with** PHR-VERB If you **come down with** an illness, you get it. ❑ *Thomas came down with a cold.*

▸ **come for** PHR-VERB If people such as soldiers or police **come for** you, they come to find you. ❑ *Tanya was ready to fight if they came for her.*

▸ **come forward** PHR-VERB If someone **comes forward**, they make themselves known and offer to help. ❑ *Police asked witnesses to come forward.*

▸ **come in** **1** PHR-VERB If information, a report, or a telephone call **comes in**, it is received. ❑ *Reports are coming in of trouble at another jail.* **2** PHR-VERB If you have some money **coming in**, you receive it regularly as your income. ❑ *She had no money* *coming in and no savings.* **3** PHR-VERB If someone or something **comes in**, they are involved in a situation or discussion. ❑ *Rose asked again, "But where do we come in, Henry?"* **4** PHR-VERB When a new idea, fashion, or product **comes in**, it becomes popular or available. ❑ *Lots of new ideas were coming in.*

▶ **come in for** PHR-VERB If someone or something **comes in for** criticism or blame, they receive it. ❑ *The plans have already come in for criticism.*

▶ **come into** **1** PHR-VERB If someone **comes into** some money, some property, or a title, they inherit it. ❑ *My father has just come into a fortune.* **2** PHR-VERB If someone or something **comes into** a situation, they have a role in it. ❑ *We don't really know where Harry comes into all this.*

▶ **come off** PHR-VERB If something **comes off**, it is successful or effective. ❑ *It was a good try but it didn't really come off.*

▶ **come on** **1** CONVENTION You say **"Come on"** to someone to encourage them to do something or be quicker. [SPOKEN] ❑ *Come on Doreen, let's dance.* ❑ *Come on, or we'll be late.* **2** PHR-VERB If you have an illness or a headache **coming on**, you can feel it starting. ❑ *Tiredness and fever are likely to be a sign of the flu coming on.* **3** PHR-VERB If something or someone **is coming on**, they are developing well or making good progress. ❑ *Leah is coming on very well now.* **4** PHR-VERB When a machine **comes on**, it starts working. ❑ *The central heating came on.*

▶ **come out** **1** PHR-VERB When a new product **comes out**, it becomes available to the public. ❑ *The book comes out this week.* **2** PHR-VERB If a fact **comes out**, it becomes known to people. ❑ *The truth is beginning to come out about what happened.* **3** PHR-VERB If you **come out for** or **against** something, you declare that you do or do not support it. ❑ *France came out against the plan on Friday.* **4** PHR-VERB When the sun, moon, or stars **come out**, they appear in the sky. ❑ *Oh, look! The sun's coming out!*

▶ **come over** **1** PHR-VERB If a feeling **comes over** you, it affects you. ❑ *A strange feeling came over me.* **2** PHR-VERB The way that someone or something **comes over** is the impression they make on people. ❑ *You come over as capable and amusing.*

▶ **come round** → see **come around**

▶ **come through** **1** PHR-VERB To **come through** a dangerous or difficult situation means to survive it and recover from it. ❑ *The city had faced the crisis and come through it.* **2** PHR-VERB If something **comes through**, you receive it. ❑ *The message that comes through is that taxes will have to be raised.*

▶ **come to** PHR-VERB When someone who is unconscious **comes to**, they become conscious. ❑ *He came to and raised his head.*

▶ **come under** **1** PHR-VERB If you **come under** attack or pressure, for example, people attack you or put pressure on you. ❑ *The police came under attack from angry crowds.* **2** PHR-VERB If something **comes under** a particular authority, it is managed or controlled by that authority. ❑ *Their troops will come under U.S. command.*

▶ **come up** **1** PHR-VERB If a person or animal **comes up** to you, they approach you. ❑ *Her cat came up and rubbed itself against their legs.* **2** PHR-VERB If something **comes up** in a conversation, it is mentioned. ❑ *The subject came up at work.* **3** PHR-VERB If something **is coming up**, it is about to happen or take place. ❑ *We do have elections*

*coming up.* **4** PHR-VERB If something **comes up**, it happens unexpectedly. ❑ *I was delayed — something came up at home.* **5** PHR-VERB If a job **comes up** or if something **comes up for** sale, it becomes available. ❑ *A job came up and I applied for it.* **6** PHR-VERB When the sun or moon **comes up**, it rises. ❑ *It will be so great watching the sun come up.*

▶ **come up against** PHR-VERB If you **come up against** a problem or difficulty, you are faced with it and have to deal with it. ❑ *We came up against a few problems in dealing with the case.*

**come|back** (**comebacks**) **1** N-COUNT If a well-known person makes a **comeback**, they return to their profession or sport after a period away. ❑ *At the age of 65 he's trying to make a comeback.* **2** N-COUNT If something makes a **comeback**, it becomes fashionable again. ❑ *Tight fitting T-shirts are making a comeback.*

**co|median** /kəmiːdiən/ (**comedians**) N-COUNT A **comedian** is an entertainer whose job is to make people laugh, by telling jokes or funny stories. ❑ *...comedian Jay Leno.* [from Old French]

**com|edy** /kɒmədi/ (**comedies**) **1** N-UNCOUNT **Comedy** consists of types of entertainment that are intended to make people laugh. ❑ *...his career in comedy.* **2** N-COUNT A **comedy** is a play, movie, or television program that is intended to make people laugh. ❑ *The movie is a romantic comedy.* [from Old French]
→ see **genre**

**com|et** /kɒmɪt/ (**comets**) N-COUNT A **comet** is a bright object with a long tail that travels around the sun. ❑ *Halley's Comet is going to come back in 2061.* [from Old French]
→ see **solar system**

**com|fort** /kʌmfərt/ (**comforts, comforting, comforted**) **1** N-UNCOUNT **Comfort** is the state of being physically or mentally relaxed. ❑ *The audience can sit in comfort while watching the show.* **2** N-UNCOUNT **Comfort** is a style of life in which you have enough money to have everything you need. ❑ *We don't earn enough to live in comfort.* **3** N-UNCOUNT If something offers **comfort**, it makes you feel less worried or unhappy. ❑ *They will be able to take some comfort from the news.* **4** N-COUNT **Comforts** are things which make your life easier and more pleasant. ❑ *She enjoys the comforts married life has brought her.* **5** V-T If you **comfort** someone, you make them feel less worried or unhappy. ❑ *Ned put his arm around her, trying to comfort her.* [from Old French]

**com|fort|able** /kʌmftəbəl, -fərtəbəl/ **1** ADJ If something such as furniture is **comfortable**, it makes you feel physically relaxed. ❑ *...a comfortable chair.* ❑ *A home should be comfortable and friendly.* ❑ *Lie down on your bed and make yourself comfortable.* ● **com|fort|ably** ADV ❑ *...the comfortably furnished living room.* ❑ *Are you sitting comfortably?* **2** ADJ If someone is **comfortable**, they have enough money to be able to live without financial problems. ❑ *"Is he rich?" — "He's comfortable."* ● **com|fort|ably** ADV ❑ *Cayton lives very comfortably.* **3** ADJ If you feel **comfortable with** a particular situation or person, you feel confident and relaxed with them. ❑ *He liked me and I felt comfortable with him.* [from Old French]

## Thesaurus    *comfortable*    Also look up :

ADJ. comfy, cozy, soft; (*ant.*) uncomfortable 1
well-off 2

**com|fort|er** /kʌmfərtər/ (**comforters**) N-COUNT
A **comforter** is a large cover filled with feathers or
soft material which you put over yourself in bed.
[from French]

**com|fort|ing** /kʌmfərtɪŋ/ ADJ If something
is **comforting**, it makes you feel less worried or
unhappy. □ *I found the book very comforting.* [from
Old French]

**com|ic** /kɒmɪk/ (**comics**) 1 ADJ Something
that is **comic** makes you want to laugh. □ *The
novel is comic and tragic.* □ *Grodin is a fine comic
actor.* 2 N-COUNT A **comic** is an entertainer who
tells jokes in order to make people laugh. □ *...the
funniest comic in America.* [from Latin]

**comi|cal** /kɒmɪkⁿl/ ADJ If something is **comical**,
it makes you want to laugh because it is funny or
silly. □ *Her expression was comical.* [from Latin]

**com|ic book** (**comic books**) N-COUNT A **comic
book** is a magazine that contains stories told in
pictures. □ *...comic book heroes such as Spider Man.*

**com|ing** /kʌmɪŋ/ 1 ADJ A **coming** event or time
is an event or time that will happen soon. □ *...the
weather in the coming months.* [from Old English]
2 → see also **come**

**com|ma** /kɒmə/ (**commas**) N-COUNT A **comma**
is the punctuation mark (,). [from Latin]
→ see **punctuation**

**com|mand** /kəmænd/ (**commands,
commanding, commanded**) 1 V-T If someone in
authority **commands** you to do something, they
tell you that you must do it. [mainly WRITTEN]
□ *He commanded his troops to attack.* □ *"Get in your car
and follow me," she commanded.* ● **Command** is also
a noun. □ *The driver failed to respond to a command
to stop.* □ *I closed my eyes at his command.* 2 V-T
If you **command** something such as respect or
obedience, you obtain it because you are popular
or important. □ *She commanded the respect of all
her colleagues.* 3 V-T An officer who **commands**
part of an army, navy, or air force is responsible
for controlling and organizing it. □ *...the French
general who commands the UN troops in the region.*
● **Command** is also a noun. □ *The force will be under
the command of an American general.* 4 N-UNCOUNT
Your **command of** something is your knowledge
of it and your ability to use it. □ *His command of
English was excellent.* [from Old French]

**com|mand|er** /kəmændər/ (**commanders**)
1 N-COUNT; N-TITLE; N-VOC A **commander** is
an officer in charge of a military operation or
organization. □ *The commander and some of the
men were released.* 2 N-COUNT; N-TITLE; N-VOC A
**commander** is an officer in the U.S. Navy or the
Royal Navy. [from Old French]

**com|mand|ing** /kəmændɪŋ/ 1 ADJ If you are
in a **commanding** position, you are in a strong or
powerful position. □ *They remain in a commanding
position to win their second game..* 2 ADJ If you
describe someone as **commanding**, you mean
that they seem powerful and confident. □ *...a tall,
commanding man.* [from Old French] 3 → see also
**command**

**com|mand mod|ule** (**command modules**)
N-COUNT The **command module** is the part of
a spacecraft in which the astronauts live and
operate the controls.

**com|man|do** /kəmændoʊ/ (**commandos** or
**commandoes**) N-COUNT A **commando** is a soldier
who been specially trained to carry out surprise
attacks. □ *...small groups of American commandos.*
[from Afrikaans]

**com|media dell'ar|te** /kəmeɪdiədɛlɑrti, -teɪ/
N-UNCOUNT **Commedia dell'arte** was a form
of improvised theater that began in Italy in
the sixteenth century and used well-known
characters and stories. [from Italian]

### Word Link    *memor ≈ memory : com*memorate, *
*memorial, memory*

**com|memo|rate** /kəmɛməreɪt/
(**commemorates, commemorating,
commemorated**) V-T To **commemorate** an
important event or person means to remember
them by means of a special action, ceremony,
or specially created object. □ *...paintings
commemorating great moments in baseball history.*
● **com|memo|ra|tion** /kəmɛməreɪʃⁿn/
(**commemorations**) N-VAR □ *...a commemoration of
victory.* [from Latin]

**com|memo|ra|tive** /kəmɛmərətɪv, -əreɪtɪv/
ADJ A **commemorative** object or event is intended
to make people remember a particular event or
person. □ *...a commemorative stamp.* [from Latin]

**com|mence** /kəmɛns/ (**commences,
commencing, commenced**) V-T/V-I When
something **commences** or you **commence** it, it
begins. [FORMAL] □ *The school year commences in the
fall.* □ *They commenced a thorough search.* [from Old
French]

**com|mence|ment** /kəmɛnsmənt/
(**commencements**) 1 N-UNCOUNT The
**commencement** of something is its beginning.
[FORMAL] □ *Students must register before the
commencement of classes.* 2 N-VAR **Commencement**
is a ceremony at a university, college, or high
school at which students formally receive their
degrees or diplomas. □ *President Bush gave the
commencement address today at the University of Notre
Dame.* [from Old French]

**com|mend** /kəmɛnd/ (**commends,
commending, commended**) V-T If you **commend**
someone or something, you praise them for it.
[FORMAL] □ *I commended her for that action.* □ *The
reports commend her bravery.* ● **com|men|da|tion**
/kɒmɛndeɪʃⁿn/ (**commendations**) N-COUNT
□ *Clare won a commendation for bravery.* [from Latin]

**com|mend|able** /kəmɛndəbⁿl/ ADJ If you
describe someone's behavior as **commendable**,
you approve of it. [FORMAL] □ *He has acted with
commendable speed.* [from Latin]

**com|men|sal|ism** /kəmɛnsəlɪzəm/
(**commensalisms**) N-VAR A **commensalism**
between two species of plants or animals is a
relationship which benefits one of the species
and does not harm the other species. [TECHNICAL]
[from Middle English]

**com|ment** /kɒmɛnt/ (**comments,
commenting, commented**) 1 V-T/V-I If you
**comment on** something, you give your opinion
about it or make a statement about it. □ *Mr. Cooke
has not commented on these reports.* □ *You really can't*

comment until you know the facts. ▢ One student commented that she preferred literature to social science. **2** N-VAR A **comment** is a statement that you make or opinion that you give about something. ▢ He made his comments at a news conference. ▢ There's been no comment so far from police. [from Latin]

com|men|tary /kɒmənteri/ (commentaries) **1** N-VAR A **commentary** is a description of an event that is broadcast on radio or television while the event is taking place. ▢ He turned on his car radio to listen to the commentary. **2** N-COUNT A **commentary** is an article or book which explains or discusses something. ▢ ...a commentary on American society and culture. [from Latin]

com|men|tate /kɒmənteɪt/ (commentates, commentating, commentated) V-I To **commentate** means to give a radio or television commentary on an event. ▢ They are in New Hampshire to commentate on the ice hockey. [from Latin]

com|men|ta|tor /kɒmənteɪtər/ (commentators) **1** N-COUNT A **commentator** is a broadcaster who gives a commentary on an event. ▢ ...a sports commentator. **2** N-COUNT A **commentator** is someone who often writes or broadcasts about a particular subject. ▢ ...a political commentator. [from Latin]

| Word Link | merc ≈ trading : com**merce**, **merc**handise, **merc**hant |
|---|---|

com|merce /kɒmɜrs/ **1** N-UNCOUNT **Commerce** is the activities and procedures involved in buying and selling things. ▢ They made their fortunes from industry and commerce. [from Latin] **2** → see also **chamber of commerce**

com|mer|cial /kəmɜrʃəl/ (commercials) **1** ADJ **Commercial** means relating to the buying and selling of goods. ▢ ...a major center of commercial activity. **2** ADJ **Commercial** organizations and activities are concerned with making profits. ▢ The company has become more commercial over the past few years. ● com|mer|cial|ly ADV ▢ ...a commercially successful movie. **3** ADJ **Commercial** television and radio are paid for by advertising. ▢ ...commercial radio stations. **4** N-COUNT A **commercial** is an advertisement that is broadcast on television or radio. ▢ There are too many commercials. [from Latin]

com|mis|sion /kəmɪʃⁿn/ (commissions, commissioning, commissioned) **1** V-T If you **commission** something or **commission** someone to do something, you formally arrange for someone to do a piece of work for you. ▢ They have commissioned a study of the town's nightclubs. ▢ You can commission them to paint something especially for you. ● **Commission** is also a noun. ▢ He began making practical furniture by commission. **2** N-COUNT A **commission** is a piece of work that someone is asked to do and is paid for. ▢ Just a few days ago, I finished a commission. **3** N-VAR **Commission** is a sum of money paid to a salesperson for every sale that he or she makes. If a salesperson is paid **on commission**, the amount they receive depends on the amount they sell. ▢ The salespeople work on commission. **4** N-COUNT A **commission** is a group of people who have been appointed to find out about something or to control something. ▢ The government has set up a commission to look into those crimes. **5** N-COUNT If a member of the armed

forces receives a **commission**, he or she becomes an officer. ▢ He accepted a commission as a naval officer. [from Old French]

com|mis|sion|er /kəmɪʃənər/ (commissioners) also Commissioner N-COUNT A **commissioner** is an important official in a government department or other organization. ▢ ...Alaska's commissioner of education. [from Old French]

com|mit /kəmɪt/ (commits, committing, committed) **1** V-T If someone **commits** a crime or a sin, they do something illegal or bad. ▢ I have never committed any crime. **2** V-T If you **commit** money or resources **to** something, you decide to use them for a particular purpose. ▢ They called on Western nations to commit more money to the poorest nations. **3** V-T If you **commit yourself to** something, you accept it fully or say that you will definitely do it. ▢ People should think carefully about committing themselves to working Sundays. **4** V-T If someone **is committed to** a mental hospital or prison, they are officially sent there. ▢ Arthur was committed to the hospital. [from Latin]

com|mit|ment /kəmɪtmənt/ (commitments) **1** N-UNCOUNT **Commitment** is a strong belief in an idea or system. ▢ ...his commitment to democracy. **2** N-COUNT A **commitment** is a regular task that takes up some of your time. ▢ I've got a lot of commitments. **3** N-COUNT If you make a **commitment to** do something, you promise that you will do it. ▢ We made a commitment to keep working together. [from Latin]

| Word Partnership | Use commitment with : |
|---|---|
| ADJ. | deep/firm/strong commitment **1** |
| | long-term commitment, prior commitment **2** **3** |
| N. | someone's commitment **1** – **3** |
| PREP. | commitment to someone/something **1** **3** |
| V. | make a commitment **3** |

com|mit|tee /kəmɪti/ (committees) N-COUNT A **committee** is a group of people who meet to make decisions or plans for a larger group or organization that they represent. ▢ ...the school yearbook committee.

com|mod|ity /kəmɒdɪti/ (commodities) N-COUNT A **commodity** is something that is sold for money. [BUSINESS] ▢ ...basic commodities like bread and meat. [from Old French]

com|mon /kɒmən/ (commons) **1** ADJ If something is **common**, it is found in large numbers or it happens often. ▢ His name was Hansen, a common name in Norway. ▢ Oil pollution is the most common cause of death for seabirds. ● com|mon|ly ADV ▢ Parsley is one of the most commonly used herbs. **2** ADJ If something is **common** to two or more people or groups, it is done, possessed, or used by them all. ▢ The two groups share a common language. **3** ADJ You can use **common** to describe knowledge, an opinion, or a feeling that is shared by people in general. ▢ It is common knowledge that swimming is one of the best forms of exercise. ● com|mon|ly ADV ▢ It was commonly believed that the earth was just 6000 years old. **4** N-COUNT A **common** is an area of grassy land, usually in or near a village or small town, where the public is allowed to go. ▢ We are warning women not to go out onto the common alone. **5** PHRASE

If people or things have something **in common**, they have the same characteristics, features, or interests. ❑ *He had very little in common with his sister.* [from Old French] ◳ **common ground** → see **ground**

**Thesaurus** *common* Also look up :

ADJ. frequent, typical, usual ◳
accepted, standard, universal ◳

**Word Partnership** Use *common* with :

N. common **belief**, common **language**, common **practice**, common **problem** ◳
ADV. **fairly/increasingly/more/most** common ◳
V. **have** *something* in common ◳

**com|mon an|ces|tor** (**common ancestors**) N-COUNT The **common ancestor** of a group of human beings or animals is the individual who is an ancestor of all of them.

**com|mon law** ◳ N-UNCOUNT **Common law** is the system of law which is based on judges' decisions and on custom rather than on written laws. ❑ *Most American law is based on English common law.* ◳ ADJ A **common law** relationship is regarded as a marriage because it has lasted a long time, although no official marriage contract has been signed. ❑ *...his common law wife.*

**common|place** /kɒmənpleɪs/ ADJ If something is **commonplace**, it happens often or is often found. ❑ *Home computers have become commonplace.* [from Latin]

**com|mon sense** also **commonsense** N-UNCOUNT Your **common sense** is your natural ability to make good judgments and to behave sensibly. ❑ *Use your common sense.* ❑ *She always had a lot of common sense.*

**com|mon stock** N-UNCOUNT **Common stock** refers to the shares in a company that are owned by people who have a right to vote at the company's meetings and to receive part of the company's profits after the holders of preferred stock have been paid. [AM, BUSINESS] ❑ *...2.7 million shares of common stock at 20 cents a share.*

**com|mo|tion** /kəmoʊʃ⁰n/ (**commotions**) N-VAR A **commotion** is a lot of noise and confusion. ❑ *He heard a commotion outside.* [from Latin]

**com|mu|nal** /kəmyʊn⁰l/ ◳ ADJ **Communal** means relating to particular groups in a country or society. ❑ *These groups developed strong communal ties.* ◳ ADJ You use **communal** to describe something that is shared by a group of people. ❑ *They ate in a communal dining room.*

**com|mune** /kɒmyun/ (**communes**) N-COUNT A **commune** is a group of people who live together and share everything. ❑ *Mack lived in a commune.* [from French]

**Word Link** *commun ≈ sharing :* communicate, communism, community

**com|mu|ni|cate** /kəmyunɪkeɪt/ (**communicates, communicating, communicated**) ◳ V-RECIP If you **communicate with** someone, you share information, for example by speaking, writing, or sending radio signals. ❑ *They communicate with their friends by cell*

phone. ❑ *They use e-mail to communicate with each other.* ● **com|mu|ni|ca|tion** /kəmyunɪkeɪʃ⁰n/ N-UNCOUNT ❑ *There has been no direct communication with Moscow.* ❑ *...communication between parents and teachers.* ◳ V-RECIP If people are able to **communicate**, they are able to talk to each other openly, so that they understand each other's feelings. ❑ *We had to learn how to communicate with each other.* ● **com|mu|ni|ca|tion** N-UNCOUNT ❑ *There was a lack of communication between us.* ◳ V-T If you **communicate** an idea or a feeling to someone, you let them know about it. ❑ *They successfully communicate their knowledge to others.* [from Latin]

**com|mu|ni|ca|tion** /kəmyunɪkeɪʃ⁰n/ (**communications**) ◳ N-PLURAL **Communications** are the systems and processes that are used to communicate or broadcast information. ❑ *...a communications satellite.* ◳ N-COUNT A **communication** is a message. [FORMAL] ❑ *The ambassador has brought with him a communication from the president.* [from Latin] ◳ → see also **communicate**
→ see **brain**, **radio**

**com|mun|ion** /kəmyunyən/ (**communions**) ◳ N-UNCOUNT; N-SING **Communion** with nature or with a person is the feeling that you are sharing thoughts or feelings with them. ❑ *...communion with nature.* ◳ also **Communion** N-VAR **Communion** is the Christian ceremony in which people eat bread and drink wine in memory of Christ's death. [from Latin]

**com|mu|ni|qué** /kəmyunɪkeɪ/ (**communiqués**) N-COUNT A **communiqué** is an official statement. [FORMAL] ❑ *The communiqué said military targets were hit.* [from French]

**Word Link** *ism ≈ action or state :* communism, optimism, patriotism

**com|mun|ism** /kɒmyənɪzəm/ also **Communism** N-UNCOUNT **Communism** is the political belief that all people are equal, that there should be no private ownership and that workers should control the means of producing things. ❑ *...the fight against communism.* ● **com|mun|ist** /kɒmyənɪst/ (**communists**) also **Communist** N-COUNT ❑ *The communists seized power in 1947.* ADJ ❑ *...the Communist Party.* [from French]

**com|mu|ni|ty** /kəmyunɪti/ (**communities**) ◳ N-SING A **community** is a group of people who live in a particular area or are alike in some way. ❑ *He's well liked by people in the community.* ❑ *...the black community.* ◳ N-UNCOUNT **Community** is friendship between different people or groups, and a sense of having something in common. ❑ *...a neighborhood with no sense of community.* ◳ N-COUNT A **community** is a group of plants and animals that live in the same region and interact with one another. [from Latin]

**Thesaurus** *community* Also look up :

N. neighborhood, public, society ◳

**com|mu|ni|ty cen|ter** (**community centers**) N-COUNT A **community center** is a place that is specially provided for the people, groups, and organizations in a particular area, where they can go in order to meet one another and do things.

**com|mu|ni|ty col|lege** (**community colleges**)

N-COUNT A **community college** is a local college where students from the surrounding area can take courses in practical or academic subjects. [AM]

**com|mu|ni|ty ser|vice** ■ N-UNCOUNT **Community service** is unpaid work that criminals sometimes do as a punishment instead of being sent to prison. □ *He was sentenced to 140 hours community service.* ■ N-UNCOUNT **Community service** is unpaid voluntary work that a person performs for the benefit of his or her local community. □ *I have been doing community service in Oakland for several years.*

**com|mute** /kəmyut/ (**commutes, commuting, commuted**) V-I If you **commute**, you travel a long distance to work every day. □ *Mike commutes to Miami.* □ *McLaren began commuting between Philadelphia and New York.* ● **com|mut|er** (**commuters**) N-COUNT □ *There are large numbers of commuters using our streets.* [from Latin]
→ see **traffic, transportation**

**comp** /kɒmp/ (**comps, comping, comped**) ■ N-UNCOUNT **Comp** is short for **compensation**. [INFORMAL] □ *Workers' comp pays for work-related medical problems.* ■ V-T If someone, or if a place such as a hotel or a restaurant **comps** you, they give you a room or a meal without charging you for it. [INFORMAL] □ *I comped him his lunch.*

---

**Word Link** com ≈ with, together : combine, compact, companion

**com|pact** /kəmpækt/ ADJ **Compact** things are small or take up very little space. □ *...my compact office in Washington.* [from Latin]

**com|pact bone** N-UNCOUNT **Compact bone** is very hard, dense bone that exists in the arms and legs and forms the outer layer of other bones. [MEDICAL]

**com|pact disc** (**compact discs**) also **compact disk** N-COUNT **Compact discs** are small shiny discs that contain music or computer information. The abbreviation **CD** is also used.

**com|pact|ed** /kəmpæktɪd/ ADJ **Compacted** rock is rock that is formed when layers of material such as clay or sand press against each other over a long period of time. [from Latin]

**com|pan|ion** /kəmpænyən/ (**companions**) N-COUNT A **companion** is someone who you spend time with or who you are traveling with. □ *Her traveling companion was a middle-aged man.* [from Late Latin]
→ see **pet**

**com|pan|ion|ship** /kəmpænyənʃɪp/ N-UNCOUNT **Companionship** is having someone you know and like with you, instead of being on your own. □ *I depended on his companionship.* [from Late Latin]

**com|pa|ny** /kʌmpəni/ (**companies**) ■ N-COUNT A **company** is a business organization that makes money by selling goods or services. □ *...an insurance company.* ■ N-COUNT A **company** is a group of opera singers, dancers, or actors who work together. □ *...the Phoenix Dance Company.* ■ N-UNCOUNT **Company** is having another person or other people with you. □ *"I won't stay long."* — *"No, please do stay. I need the company."* ■ PHRASE If you **keep** someone **company**, you spend time with them and stop them from feeling lonely

or bored. □ *Why don't you stay here and keep Emma company?* [from Old French]
→ see **electricity**

---

**Word Partnership** Use company with:

| | |
|---|---|
| ADJ. | **foreign** company, **parent** company ■ |
| V. | **buy/own/sell/start** a company, company **employs**, company **makes** ■ **have** company, **keep** company, **part** company ■ |

---

**com|pa|rable** /kɒmpərəbᵊl/ ■ ADJ Something that is **comparable** to something else is roughly similar, for example in amount or importance. □ *Farmers' incomes should be comparable to those of townspeople.* ■ ADJ If two or more things are **comparable**, they are similar and so they can reasonably be compared. □ *In comparable countries wages increased much more rapidly.* [from Old French]

**com|para|tive** /kəmpærətɪv/ (**comparatives**) ■ ADJ You use **comparative** to show that you are judging something against a previous or different situation. □ *...a life of comparative ease.* ● **com|para|tive|ly** ADV □ *...a comparatively small nation.* ■ ADJ A **comparative** study is a study that involves the comparison of two or more things of the same kind. □ *...a comparative study of the two writers.* ■ ADJ In grammar, the **comparative** form of an adjective or adverb shows that something has more of a quality than something else has. For example, "bigger" is the comparative form of "big." ● **Comparative** is also a noun. □ *The comparative of "pretty" is "prettier."* [from Old French]

---

**Word Link** par ≈ equal : compare, disparate, part

**com|pare** /kəmpɛər/ (**compares, comparing, compared**) ■ V-T When you **compare** things, you consider them and discover the differences or similarities between them. □ *Compare the two illustrations in Figure 60.* □ *You can't compare my situation with hers.* ■ V-T If you **compare** one person or thing **to** another, you say that they are like the other person or thing. □ *Some critics compared his work to that of James Joyce.* [from Old French] ■ → see also **compared**

---

**Thesaurus** compare Also look up :

| | |
|---|---|
| V. | analyze, consider, contrast, examine ■ equate, match ■ |

---

**com|pared** /kəmpɛərd/ PHRASE If you say, for example, that one thing is large or small **compared with** another or **compared to** another, you mean that it is larger or smaller than the other thing. □ *Your bag is light compared to mine.* [from Old French]

**com|pari|son** /kəmpærɪsən/ (**comparisons**) ■ N-VAR When you make a **comparison**, you consider two or more things and discover the differences between them. □ *...a comparison of the two teams' performances this year.* ■ N-COUNT When you make a **comparison**, you say that one thing is like another in some way. □ *...the comparison of her life to a journey.* [from Old French]

**com|part|ment** /kəmpɑrtmənt/ (**compartments**) ■ N-COUNT A **compartment** is one of the separate parts of an object that is used for keeping things in. □ *The fire started in the baggage compartment.* ■ N-COUNT A **compartment**

**C**

is one of the separate spaces into which a railroad car is divided. ❑ *...a first class compartment.* [from French]

**com|pass** /kʌmpəs/ (**compasses**) N-COUNT A **compass** is an instrument that you use for finding directions. It has a dial and a magnetic needle that always points to the north. ❑ *We had to use a compass to get here.* [from Old French] → see **magnet, navigation**

compass

**com|pas|sion** /kəmpæʃ⁰n/ N-UNCOUNT **Compassion** is a feeling of pity, sympathy, and understanding for someone who is suffering. ❑ *Elderly people need compassion from their doctors.* [from Old French]

**com|pas|sion|ate** /kəmpæʃⁱnɪt/ ADJ A **compassionate** person feels pity, sympathy, and understanding for people who are suffering. ❑ *My father was a deeply compassionate man.* [from Old French]

**com|pat|ible** /kəmpætɪb⁰l/ ■ ADJ If things, systems, or ideas are **compatible**, they work well together or can exist together successfully. ❑ *He argues that religious beliefs are compatible with modern society.* ● **com|pat|ibil|ity** /kəmpætɪbɪliti/ N-UNCOUNT ❑ *...Islam and its compatibility with democracy.* ■ ADJ If you are **compatible** with someone, you have a good relationship with them because you have similar opinions and interests. ❑ *Millie and I are very compatible.* ● **com|pat|ibil|ity** N-UNCOUNT ❑ *The basis of friendship is compatibility.* [from Medieval Latin]

> **Word Link** pel ≈ driving, forcing : com**pel**, ex**pel**, pro**pel**

**com|pel** /kəmpɛl/ (**compels, compelling, compelled**) V-T If a situation, a rule, or a person **compels** you to do something, they force you to do it. ❑ *...a law to compel cyclists to wear a helmet.* [from Latin]

**com|pel|ling** /kəmpɛlɪŋ/ ADJ A **compelling** argument or reason is one that convinces you that something is true or that something should be done. ❑ *...a compelling reason to spend money.* [from Latin]

**com|pen|sate** /kɒmpənseɪt/ (**compensates, compensating, compensated**) ■ V-T To **compensate** someone **for** money or things that they have lost means to pay them money or give them something to replace those things. ❑ *Some say that the government should compensate farmers for their losses.* ■ V-I To **compensate for** something, especially something harmful or unwanted, means to do something which balances it or reduces its effects. ❑ *Her sense of humor and friendliness compensate for her lack of experience.* [from Latin]

**com|pen|sa|tion** /kɒmpənseɪʃ⁰n/ (**compensations**) ■ N-UNCOUNT **Compensation** is money that someone who has experienced loss or suffering claims from the person or organization responsible. ❑ *They want $20,000 in compensation.* ■ N-VAR If something is a **compensation**, it reduces the effects of something bad that has happened. ❑ *Age does have some compensations.* [from Latin]

**com|pete** /kəmpit/ (**competes, competing, competed**) ■ V-RECIP When one firm or country **competes with** another for something, it tries to get that thing for themselves and stop the other from getting it. ❑ *Hardware stores are competing for business.* ❑ *Books compete with TV and movies for teenagers' attention.* ■ V-I If you **compete** in a contest or a game, you take part in it. ❑ *He will be competing in the 100 meter race.* [from Late Latin]

**com|pe|tence** /kɒmpɪtəns/ N-UNCOUNT **Competence** is the ability to do something well or effectively. ❑ *No one doubts his competence.* [from Latin]

**com|pe|tent** /kɒmpɪtənt/ ADJ Someone who is **competent** is efficient and effective. ❑ *He was a very competent salesman.* ● **com|pe|tent|ly** ADV ❑ *The government performed competently.* [from Latin]

**com|pe|ti|tion** /kɒmpɪtɪʃ⁰n/ (**competitions**) ■ N-UNCOUNT **Competition** is a situation in which two or more people or groups are trying to get something which not everyone can have. ❑ *There's been a lot of competition for the prize.* ■ N-VAR A **competition** is an event in which many people take part in order to find out who is best at a particular activity. ❑ *...a surfing competition.* [from Late Latin]

**com|peti|tive** /kəmpɛtɪtɪv/ ■ ADJ **Competitive** situations or activities are ones in which people or companies compete with each other. ❑ *Japan is a highly competitive market system.* ● **com|peti|tive|ly** ADV ❑ *He's now skiing competitively again.* ■ ADJ A **competitive** person is eager to be more successful than other people. ❑ *He has always been very competitive.* ● **com|peti|tive|ly** ADV ❑ *People do better when they work in teams than when they work competitively.* ● **com|peti|tive|ness** N-UNCOUNT ❑ *I can't stand the competitiveness.* ■ ADJ Goods or services that are **competitive** are likely to be bought because they are less expensive than other goods of the same quality. ❑ *...homes for sale at competitive prices.* ● **com|peti|tive|ly** ADV ❑ *...a competitively priced product.* ● **com|peti|tive|ness** N-UNCOUNT ❑ *...the competitiveness of the U.S. economy.* [from Late Latin]

> **Word Partnership** Use *competitive* with :
>
> | N. | competitive **sport** ■ |
> |---|---|
> | | competitive **person** ■ |
> | ADV. | **fiercely** competitive, **highly** competitive, **more** competitive ■ ■ |

**com|peti|tor** /kəmpɛtɪtər/ (**competitors**) ■ N-COUNT A company's **competitors** are companies that are trying to sell similar goods or services to the same people. ❑ *The bank isn't performing as well as some of its competitors.* ■ N-COUNT A **competitor** is a person who takes part in a competition or contest. ❑ *One of the oldest competitors won the silver medal.* [from Late Latin]

**com|pi|la|tion** /kɒmpɪleɪʃ⁰n/ (**compilations**) N-COUNT A **compilation** is a book, CD, or program that contains many different items that have been gathered together, usually ones which have already appeared in other places. ❑ *His latest CD is a compilation of his jazz works.* [from Latin]

**com|pile** /kəmpaɪl/ (**compiles, compiling, compiled**) V-T When you **compile** something such as a report, book, or program, you produce it by collecting and putting together many pieces of information. ❑ *The book took 10 years to compile.* [from Latin]

**com|pla|cent** /kəmpleɪsᵊnt/ ADJ If someone is **complacent** about a threat or danger, they wrongly behave as if there is nothing to worry about. ❑ *We cannot afford to be complacent about our health.* ● **com|pla|cen|cy** /kəmpleɪsᵊnsi/ N-UNCOUNT ❑ *...complacency about the risks of infection.* [from Latin]

**com|plain** /kəmpleɪn/ (**complains, complaining, complained**) ◼ V-T/V-I If you **complain about** something, you say that you are not satisfied with it. ❑ *Voters complained that the government did not fulfill its promises.* ❑ *The couple complained about the high cost of visiting Europe.* ❑ *I shouldn't complain, I've got a good job.* ❑ *"I wish someone would do something about it," he complained.* ◼ V-I If you **complain of** pain or illness, you say that you are feeling pain or feeling ill. ❑ *He complained of a headache.* [from Old French]

**com|plaint** /kəmpleɪnt/ (**complaints**) ◼ N-VAR A **complaint** is a statement of dissatisfaction or a reason for it. ❑ *...complaints about the standard of service.* ◼ N-COUNT A **complaint** is an illness. ❑ *Eczema is a common skin complaint.* [from Old French]

**com|ple|ment** (**complements, complementing, complemented**)

The verb is pronounced /kɒmplɪmɛnt/. The noun is pronounced /kɒmplɪmənt/.

◼ V-T If people or things **complement** each other, they have different qualities that go together well. ❑ *There will be a written examination to complement the listening test.* ◼ N-COUNT Something that is a **complement to** something else complements it. ❑ *Our sauces are the perfect complement to your favorite dishes.* ◼ N-COUNT In grammar, the **complement** of a link verb is an adjective group or noun group which comes after the verb and describes or identifies the subject. For example, in the sentence "They felt very tired," "very tired" is the complement. In "They were students," "students" is the complement. [TECHNICAL] [from Latin]

**com|ple|men|tary** /kɒmplɪmɛntəri, -mɛntri/ ◼ ADJ **Complementary** things are different from each other but make a good combination. [FORMAL] ❑ *Their complementary talents make them a good team.* ◼ ADJ **Complementary** medicine refers to ways of treating patients which are different from the ones used by most Western doctors, for example acupuncture and homeopathy. ❑ *...a wide range of complementary therapies.* ◼ ADJ **Complementary colors** are colors that are directly opposite each other on the color wheel, such as red and green. [from Latin]

**com|plete** /kəmplit/ (**completes, completing, completed**) ◼ ADJ You use **complete** to emphasize that something is as great in extent, degree, or amount as it possibly can be. ❑ *The house is a complete mess.* ❑ *His resignation came as a complete surprise.* ● **com|plete|ly** ADV ❑ *Dozens of homes*

have been completely destroyed. ◼ ADJ If something is **complete**, it contains all the parts that it should contain. ❑ *The list may not be complete.* ❑ *...a complete set of novels by Henry James.* ◼ ADJ If something is **complete**, it has been finished. ❑ *The repairs to the house are complete.* ◼ V-T To **complete** a set or group means to provide the last item that is needed to make it a full set or group. ❑ *Children don't complete their set of 20 baby teeth until they are two to three years old.* ◼ V-T If you **complete** something, you finish doing, making, or producing it. ❑ *Peter Mayle has just completed his first novel.* ● **com|ple|tion** /kəmpliʃᵊn/ (**completions**) N-VAR ❑ *The project is nearing completion.* ◼ V-T To **complete** a form means to write the necessary information on it. ❑ *Complete part 1 of the application.* ◼ PHRASE If one thing comes **complete with** another, it has that thing as an additional part. ❑ *The diary comes complete with a gold pen.* [from Latin]

**com|plex** (**complexes**)

The adjective is pronounced /kəmplɛks/ or sometimes /kɒmplɛks/. The noun is pronounced /kɒmplɛks/.

◼ ADJ Something that is **complex** has many different parts, and is difficult to understand. ❑ *...a complex system of voting.* ◼ N-COUNT A **complex** is a group of buildings used for a particular purpose. ❑ *...a low-cost apartment complex.* [from Latin]

**com|plex|ion** /kəmplɛkʃᵊn/ (**complexions**) N-COUNT Your **complexion** is the natural color or condition of the skin on your face. ❑ *She had a pale complexion.* [from Latin]
→ see **makeup**

**com|plex|ity** /kəmplɛksiti/ N-VAR **Complexity** is the state of having many different parts connected or related to each other in a complicated way. ❑ *...the complexity of the problem.* ❑ *...the legal complexities of the issue.* [from Latin]

**com|plex num|ber** (**complex numbers**) N-COUNT **Complex numbers** are numbers of the form a+bi, where a and b are real numbers and i is the square root of -1. [TECHNICAL]

**com|pli|ance** /kəmplaɪəns/ N-UNCOUNT **Compliance** with something, for example a law or agreement, means doing what you are required or expected to do. [FORMAL] ❑ *The company says it is in full compliance with labor laws.* [from Italian]

**com|pli|cate** /kɒmplɪkeɪt/ (**complicates, complicating, complicated**) V-T To **complicate** something means to make it more difficult to understand or deal with. ❑ *This would only complicate the task.* [from Latin]

**com|pli|cat|ed** /kɒmplɪkeɪtɪd/ ADJ Something that is **complicated** has many parts and is therefore difficult to understand. ❑ *The situation is very complicated.* [from Latin]

**com|pli|ca|tion** /kɒmplɪkeɪʃᵊn/ (**complications**) N-COUNT A **complication** is a problem or difficulty. ❑ *There were a number of complications.* [from Latin]

**com|plic|ity** /kəmplɪsɪti/ N-UNCOUNT
**Complicity** is involvement with other people in an illegal activity. [FORMAL] ❑ *He was charged with complicity in the attack.* [from Old French]

**com|pli|ment** (**compliments, complimenting, complimented**)

The verb is pronounced /kɒmplɪment/. The noun is pronounced /kɒmplɪmənt/.

**1** N-COUNT A **compliment** is something nice that you say to someone about them. ❑ *You can do no harm by giving a compliment.* **2** V-T If you **compliment** someone, you give them a compliment. ❑ *They complimented me on the way I looked.* [from French]

### Usage  compliment

**Compliment** and **complement** are easily confused. **Compliment** means to say something nice to or about someone. *Jack complimented Rita on her pronunciation.* **Complement** means to go well together or to make something good seem even better. *The wine complemented the meal.*

**com|pli|men|tary** /kɒmplɪmɛntəri, -mɛntri/
**1** ADJ If you are **complimentary** about something, you express admiration for it. ❑ *They have been very complimentary.* **2** ADJ A **complimentary** seat, ticket, or book is given to you free. ❑ *He had complimentary tickets to take his wife to see the movie.* [from French]

**com|ply** /kəmplaɪ/ (**complies, complying, complied**) V-I If you **comply with** a demand or rule, you do what is required. ❑ *Our changes comply with the new law.* [from Italian]

**com|po|nent** /kəmpoʊnənt/ (**components**)
N-COUNT The **components** of something are its parts. ❑ *The plan has four main components.* [from Latin]

### Word Partnership  Use *component* with :

| ADJ. | **key** component, **main** components, **separate** components |
| N. | component **parts** |

**com|pose** /kəmpoʊz/ (**composes, composing, composed**) **1** V-T The things that something **is composed of** are its parts or members. The separate things that **compose** something are the parts or members that form it. ❑ *The band is composed of police officers from all over the county.* ❑ *...the cells that compose muscles.* **2** V-T/V-I When someone **composes** a piece of music, a speech, or a letter, they write it. ❑ *Vivaldi composed a large number of concertos.* ❑ *I'd like more time to play the piano and compose.* [from Old French]
→ see **music**

**com|posed** /kəmpoʊzd/ ADJ If someone is **composed**, they are calm and able to control their feelings. ❑ *Laura was very calm and composed.* [from Old French]

**com|pos|er** /kəmpoʊzər/ (**composers**) N-COUNT A **composer** is a person who writes music, especially classical music. ❑ *...Mozart, Beethoven, and other great composers.* [from Old French]
→ see **music**

**com|po|site** /kəmpɒzɪt/ (**composites**) ADJ A

composite object or item is made up of several different things, parts, or substances. ❑ *...skis made from layers of different composite materials.*
● **Composite** is also a noun. ❑ *The book is a composite of two real-life stories.* [from Latin]

**com|pos|ite vol|ca|no** (**composite volcanoes**)
N-COUNT A **composite volcano** is a volcano with steep sides composed of layers of lava and rock. [TECHNICAL]

**com|po|si|tion** /kɒmpəzɪʃ°n/ (**compositions**)
**1** N-UNCOUNT The **composition** of something is the things that it consists of and the way that they are arranged. ❑ *...the composition of the audience.* **2** N-COUNT A composer's **compositions** are the pieces of music that he or she has written. ❑ *Mozart's compositions are among the world's greatest.* **3** N-COUNT A **composition** is a piece of written work that children do at school. ❑ *We had to write a composition on the subject "My Pet."* **4** N-UNCOUNT **Composition** is the technique or skill involved in composing something such as a piece of music or a poem. [from Old French]
→ see **orchestra**

**com|post** /kɒmpoʊst/ N-UNCOUNT **Compost** is a mixture of decayed plants that is used to improve soil. ❑ *...a small compost pile.* [from Old French]
→ see **dump**

**com|po|sure** /kəmpoʊʒər/ N-UNCOUNT **Composure** is the appearance or feeling of calm and the ability to control your feelings. [FORMAL] ❑ *She was a little nervous at first but soon found her composure.* [from Old French]

**com|pound** /kɒmpaʊnd/ (**compounds, compounding, compounded**)

The noun is pronounced /kɒmpaʊnd/. The verb is pronounced /kəmpaʊnd/.

**1** N-COUNT A **compound** is an enclosed area of land that is used for a particular purpose. ❑ *...a military compound.* **2** N-COUNT In chemistry, a **compound** is a substance that consists of two or more elements. ❑ *...a chemical compound consisting of two different elements.* **3** V-T To **compound** a problem means to make it worse by adding to it. ❑ *Additional loss of life will only compound the tragedy.* ❑ *The problem is compounded by the medical system here.* **4** ADJ In grammar, a **compound** noun, adjective, or verb is one that is made up of two or more words, for example "fire truck." **5** ADJ In grammar, a **compound** sentence is one that is made up of two or more main clauses. [TECHNICAL] [Sense 1 from Malay. Senses 2–5 from Old French.]
→ see **element, rock**

**com|pound eye** (**compound eyes**) N-COUNT A **compound eye** is a type of eye found in some creatures that is made up of many identical elements that work together.

**com|pound light micro|scope** (**compound light microscopes**) N-COUNT A **compound light microscope** is a microscope that uses glass lenses and light to produce an image.

**com|pound ma|chine** (**compound machines**)
N-COUNT A **compound machine** is a machine that consists of two or more smaller machines working together. Compare **simple machine**.

**com|pound me|ter** (**compound meters**) N-VAR
In a piece of music written in **compound meter**, the beat is divided into three parts. [TECHNICAL]

**com|pre|hend** /kɒmprɪhɛnd/ (**comprehends, comprehending, comprehended**) V-T If you cannot **comprehend** something, you cannot understand it. [FORMAL] ❑ *I just cannot comprehend your attitude.* [from Latin]

**com|pre|hen|sion** /kɒmprɪhɛnʃⁿn/ N-UNCOUNT **Comprehension** is the ability to understand something or the process of understanding something. [FORMAL] ❑ *This was completely beyond her comprehension.* [from Latin]

**com|pre|hen|sive** /kɒmprɪhɛnsɪv/ ADJ Something that is **comprehensive** includes everything that is needed or relevant. ❑ *...a comprehensive guide to the region.* ● **com|pre|hen|sive|ly** /kɒmprɪhɛnsɪvli/ ADV ❑ *The book is comprehensively illustrated.* [from Latin]

**com|press** /kəmprɛs/ (**compresses, compressing, compressed**) V-T/V-I When you **compress** something or when it **compresses**, it is pressed or squeezed so that it takes up less space. ❑ *Compressing a gas heats it up.* ● **com|pres|sion** /kəmprɛʃⁿn/ N-UNCOUNT ❑ *The compression of the wood is an easy process.* [from Late Latin]

**com|prise** /kəmpraɪz/ (**comprises, comprising, comprised**) V-T If something **comprises** or **is comprised of** a number of things or people, it has them as its parts or members. [FORMAL] ❑ *The exhibit comprises 50 paintings.* ❑ *American society is comprised of people from many different backgrounds.* [from French]

**com|pro|mise** /kɒmprəmaɪz/ (**compromises, compromising, compromised**) ■ N-VAR A **compromise** is a situation in which people accept something slightly different from what they really want. ❑ *Try to reach a compromise between what he wants and what you want.* ■ V-RECIP If you **compromise with** someone, you reach an agreement with them in which you both give up something that you originally wanted. ❑ *The government has compromised with its critics.* ❑ *"Nine," I said. "Nine thirty," he replied. We compromised on 9:15.* ■ V-T If someone **compromises** themselves or their beliefs, they do something which damages their reputation for honesty, loyalty, or high moral principles. ❑ *He would never compromise his*

principles. [from Old French]

**com|pro|mis|ing** /kɒmprəmaɪzɪŋ/ ADJ If you describe information or a situation as **compromising**, you mean that it reveals an embarrassing or guilty secret about someone. ❑ *...compromising photographs.* [from Old French]

**comp time** N-UNCOUNT **Comp time** is time off that an employer gives to an employee because the employee has worked overtime. **Comp time** is short for "compensation time." [AM] ❑ *Comp time is often promised to firefighters and police officers.*

**Word Link**  puls ≈ driving, pushing : compulsion, expulsion, impulse

**com|pul|sion** /kəmpʌlʃⁿn/ (**compulsions**) ■ N-COUNT A **compulsion** is a strong desire to do something. ❑ *He felt a sudden compulsion to run away.* ■ N-UNCOUNT If someone uses **compulsion** to make you do something, they force you to do it. ❑ *They were in classes out of choice rather than compulsion.* [from Old French]

**com|pul|sive** /kəmpʌlsɪv/ ADJ You use **compulsive** to describe people who cannot stop doing something. ❑ *...a compulsive liar.* [from Old French]

**com|pul|so|ry** /kəmpʌlsəri/ ADJ If something is **compulsory**, you must do it because a law or someone in authority says you must. ❑ *In East Germany learning Russian was compulsory.* [from Old French]

**Word Link**  put ≈ thinking : computer, dispute, undisputed

**com|put|er** /kəmpyutər/ (**computers**) ■ N-COUNT A **computer** is an electronic machine that can store and deal with large amounts of information. ❑ *The data are then fed into a computer.* ❑ *The company installed a $650,000 computer system.* [from Latin] ■ → see also **personal computer** → see Picture Dictionary: **computer** → see **office**

**com|put|er|ize** /kəmpyutəraɪz/ (**computerizes, computerizing, computerized**) V-T To **computerize** a system or type of work means to arrange for a lot of the work to be done

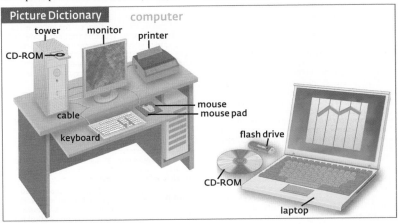

**Picture Dictionary**  computer

tower
monitor
printer
CD-ROM
cable
keyboard
mouse
mouse pad
flash drive
CD-ROM
laptop

by computer. ❏ *I'm trying to computerize everything.*
● **com|put|er|ized** /kəmpyu̱təraɪzd/ ❏ *...a computerized system.* [from Latin]

**com|pu|ting** /kəmpyu̱tɪŋ/ N-UNCOUNT
**Computing** is the activity of using a computer and writing programs for it. ❏ *Courses range from cooking to computing.* [from Latin]

**com|rade** /kɒmræd/ (**comrades**) N-COUNT
Your **comrades** are your friends or companions. [LITERARY] ❏ *Unlike so many of his comrades, he survived the war.* [from French]

**con** /kɒn/ (**cons, conning, conned**) ■ V-T If someone **cons** you, they persuade you to do something or believe something by telling you things that are not true. [INFORMAL] ❏ *He claimed that the businessman conned him of $10,000.* ❏ *White conned his way into a job.* ■ N-COUNT A **con** is a trick in which someone deceives you by telling you something that is not true. [INFORMAL] ❏ *It was all a con.* ■ **pros and cons** → see **pro**

**con|cave lens** (**concave lenses**) N-COUNT A **concave lens** is a lens that is thinner in the middle than at the edges. Compare **convex lens.**

**con|ceal** /kənsi̱l/ (**conceals, concealing, concealed**) V-T To **conceal** something means to hide it or keep it secret. ❏ *The hat concealed her hair.* ❏ *Robert could not conceal his happiness.*
● **con|ceal|ment** /kənsi̱lmənt/ N-UNCOUNT
❏ *...the concealment of his true identity.* [from Old French]

**con|cede** /kənsi̱d/ (**concedes, conceding, conceded**) V-T If you **concede** something, you admit, often unwillingly, that it is true or correct. ❏ *Bess finally conceded that Nancy was right.* ❏ *"Well," he conceded, "there have been a few problems."* [from Latin]

**con|ceiv|able** /kənsi̱vəb³l/ ADJ If something is **conceivable**, you can imagine it or believe it. ❏ *Without their support the project would not have been conceivable.* [from Old French]

**con|ceive** /kənsi̱v/ (**conceives, conceiving, conceived**) ■ V-T/V-I If you cannot **conceive of** something, you cannot imagine it or believe it. ❏ *I can't even conceive of that quantity of money.* ❏ *We could not conceive that he might soon be dead.* ■ V-T If you **conceive** a plan or idea, you think of it and work out how it can be done. ❏ *She conceived the idea of a series of novels.* ■ V-T/V-I When a woman **conceives**, she becomes pregnant. ❏ *...women who want to conceive.* ❏ *...peoople trying to conceive a child.*
● **con|cep|tion** /kənsɛp³n/ (**conceptions**) N-VAR
❏ *Six weeks after conception your baby is the size of your little fingernail.* [from Old French]

**con|cen|trate** /kɒns³ntreɪt/ (**concentrates, concentrating, concentrated**) ■ V-I If you **concentrate on** something, you give it all your attention. ❏ *He should concentrate on his studies.* ❏ *At work you need to be able to concentrate.* ■ V-T If something **is concentrated in** one place, it is all there rather than being spread around. ❏ *Italy's industrial cities are concentrated in the north.* [from Latin]

**con|cen|trat|ed** /kɒns³ntreɪtɪd/ ■ ADJ A **concentrated** liquid has been increased in strength by having water removed from it. ❏ *...concentrated apple juice.* ■ ADJ A **concentrated** activity is done with great intensity. ❏ *...a concentrated effort to control his temper.* [from Latin]

**con|cen|tra|tion** /kɒns³ntreɪʃ³n/ (**concentrations**) ■ N-UNCOUNT **Concentration** on something involves giving all your attention to it. ❏ *Neal kept talking, breaking my concentration.* ■ N-VAR A **concentration of** something is a large amount of it or large numbers of it in a small area. ❏ *The area has one of the world's greatest concentrations of wildlife.* ■ N-VAR The **concentration of** a substance is the proportion of essential ingredients or substances in it. [from Latin]

**con|cen|tra|tion camp** (**concentration camps**) N-COUNT A **concentration camp** is a prison in which large numbers of ordinary people are kept in very bad conditions, usually during a war. ❏ *...the ruins of the Nazi concentration camp at Buchenwald.*

**con|cept** /kɒnsɛpt/ (**concepts**) N-COUNT A **concept** is an idea or abstract principle. ❏ *...the concept of human rights.* ● **con|cep|tual** /kənsɛptʃuəl/ ADJ ❏ *...difficult conceptual problems.* [from Latin]

**con|cep|tion** /kənsɛpʃ³n/ (**conceptions**) ■ N-VAR A **conception** of something is an idea that you have of it in your mind. ❏ *...my conception of a garden.* [from Latin] ■ → see also **conceive**

**con|cern** /kənsɜ̱rn/ (**concerns, concerning, concerned**) ■ N-UNCOUNT **Concern** is worry about a situation. ❏ *There is no cause for concern.* ■ V-T If something **concerns** you, it worries you. ❏ *It concerns me that we were not told about this.* ● **con|cerned** ADJ ❏ *I've been concerned about you lately.* ■ V-T If you **concern yourself with** something, you give it attention because you think that it is important. ❏ *I didn't concern myself with politics.* ■ V-T If a book or a piece of information **concerns** a particular subject, it is about that subject. ❏ *The book concerns Sandy's two children.* ● **con|cerned** ADJ ❏ *Randolph's work is concerned with the effects of pollution.* ■ V-T If a situation, event, or activity **concerns** you, it affects or involves you. ❏ *It doesn't concern you at all.* ● **con|cerned** ADJ ❏ *It's a very stressful situation for everyone concerned.* ■ N-COUNT A **concern** is a fact or situation that worries you. ❏ *His concern was that people would know that he was responsible.* ■ N-COUNT A **concern** is a company or business. [FORMAL, BUSINESS] ❏ *The Minos Beach Hotel is a family concern.* ■ N-VAR **Concern for** someone is a feeling that you want them to be happy, safe, and well. ❏ *Without her care and concern, he had no chance at all.* ■ N-SING If a situation or problem is your **concern**, it is your duty or responsibility. ❏ *The technical details were the concern of the army.* [from Late Latin]

**con|cern|ing** /kənsɜ̱rnɪŋ/ PREP You use **concerning** to indicate what question or piece of information is about. [FORMAL] ❏ *For more information concerning the club, contact Mr. Coldwell.* [from Late Latin]

**con|cert** /kɒnsərt/ (**concerts**) N-COUNT A **concert** is a performance of music. ❏ *...a short concert of piano music.* ❏ *...live rock concerts.* [from French]
→ see Word Web: **concert**

**con|cert|ed** /kənsɜ̱rtɪd/ ■ ADJ A **concerted** action is done by several people or groups working together. ❏ *It's time for concerted action by world leaders.* ■ ADJ If you make a **concerted** effort to do

## Word Web    concert

A **rock concert** is much more than a group of **musicians**
playing **music** on a **stage**. It is a full-scale **performance**.
Each **band** must have a **manager** and an **agent** who **books**
the **venue** and **promotes** the **show** in each new location.
The band's assistants, called roadies, set up the stage, test
the **microphones**, and tune the **instruments**. **Sound
engineers** make sure the band sounds as good as possible.
There's always **lighting** to **spotlight** the **lead singer** and
**backup** singers. The bright, moving lights help to build

excitement. The **fans** scream and yell when they hear their favorite **songs**. The **audience** never wants
the show to end.

something, you try very hard to do it. ❑ *I'm going
to make a concerted effort to write more letters.* [from
French]

**con|cer|to** /kənt**ʃɛər**toʊ/ (**concertos**) N-COUNT
A **concerto** is a piece of music for one or more solo
instruments and an orchestra. ❑ *...Tchaikovsky's
First Piano Concerto.* [from Italian]
→ see **music**

**con|ces|sion** /kən**sɛ**ʃ°n/ (**concessions**)
■ N-COUNT If you make a **concession to** someone,
you agree to let them do or have something,
especially in order to end an argument or conflict.
❑ *We made too many concessions to the workers and we
got too little in return.* ■ N-COUNT A **concession** is
an arrangement where someone is given the right
to sell a product or to run a business, especially
in a building belonging to another business.
[BUSINESS] ❑ *Concession sales at the airport are up 15%.*
[from Latin]

**con|cili|ation** /kənsɪli**eɪ**ʃ°n/ N-UNCOUNT
**Conciliation** is trying to end a disagreement. ❑ *...a
mood of conciliation on both sides.* [from Latin]

**con|cilia|tory** /kən**sɪ**liətɔri/ ADJ When you are
**conciliatory** in your actions or behavior, you show
that you are willing to end a disagreement with
someone. ❑ *He used a more conciliatory tone.* [from
Latin]

**con|cise** /kən**saɪs**/ ADJ Something that is
**concise** gives all the necessary information in
a very brief form. ❑ *Burton's text is concise and
informative.* ● **con|cise|ly** ADV ❑ *He delivered his
report clearly and concisely.* [from Latin]

**con|clude** /kən**klud**/ (**concludes, concluding,
concluded**) ■ V-T If you **conclude** that something
is true, you decide that it is true using the facts
you know. ❑ *Larry concluded that he had no choice
but to accept.* ❑ *So what can we conclude from this
debate?* ■ V-T/V-I When something **concludes**, or
when you **conclude** it, you end it. [FORMAL] ❑ *The
evening concluded with dinner and speeches.* ■ V-RECIP
If people or groups **conclude** a treaty or business
deal, they arrange it or agree to it. [FORMAL] ❑ *We
have concluded 81 trade agreements in the last two years.*
[from Latin]

**con|clu|sion** /kən**kluʒ**°n/ (**conclusions**)
■ N-COUNT When you come to a **conclusion**,
you decide that something is true after you
have thought about it carefully. ❑ *I've come to the
conclusion that she's a great musician.* ■ N-SING The
**conclusion** of something is its ending. ❑ *...the*

*conclusion of the program.* ■ PHRASE You say "**in
conclusion**" to indicate that what you are about
to say is the last thing that you want to say. ❑ *In
conclusion, walking is cheap, safe, and enjoyable.* [from
Old French]

### Word Partnership    Use *conclusion* with :

| | |
|---|---|
| V. | come to a conclusion, draw a conclusion, reach a conclusion ■ |
| N. | conclusion of *something* ■ ■ |
| PREP. | in conclusion ■ |

**con|clu|sive** /kən**klu**sɪv/ ADJ **Conclusive**
evidence shows that something is certainly true.
❑ *There is no conclusive evidence that any crime took
place.* [from Old French]

**con|coct** /kən**kɒkt**/ (**concocts, concocting,
concocted**) ■ V-T If you **concoct** an excuse, you
invent one. ❑ *The prisoner concocted the story.* ■ V-T
If you **concoct** something, especially something
unusual, you make it by mixing several things
together. ❑ *Eugene was concocting a new pudding.*
[from Latin]

**con|coc|tion** /kən**kɒk**ʃ°n/ (**concoctions**)
N-COUNT A **concoction** is something that has been
made out of several things mixed together. ❑ *...a
concoction of honey, yogurt, oats, and apples.* [from
Latin]

**con|crete** /**kɒn**krit/ ■ N-UNCOUNT **Concrete** is
a substance used for building which is made from
cement, sand, small stones, and water. ❑ *The fence
posts have to be set in concrete.* ❑ *We sat on the concrete
floor.* ■ ADJ Something that is **concrete** is definite
and specific. ❑ *I had no concrete evidence.* ❑ *There
were no concrete proposals.* ■ ADJ A **concrete** object
is a real, physical object. A **concrete** image is an
image of a real, physical object. [from Latin]

**con|cur** /kən**kɜr**/ (**concurs, concurring,
concurred**) V-RECIP If two or more people **concur**,
they agree. [FORMAL] ❑ *Local people do not necessarily
concur with this view.* [from Latin]

### Word Link    *curr, curs ≈ running, flowing :
con**cur**rent, **curr**ent, ex**curs**ion*

**con|cur|rent** /kən**kɜr**ənt/ ADJ **Concurrent**
events or situations happen at the same time.
❑ *The gallery is holding three concurrent exhibitions.*
❑ *He will serve three concurrent five-year sentences.*
● **con|cur|rent|ly** ADV ❑ *There were three races
running concurrently.* [from Latin]

**con|cus|sion** /kənkʌʃⁿn/ (concussions)
N-VAR If you suffer a **concussion** after a blow to your head, you lose consciousness or feel sick or confused. ❑ *Nicky was rushed to the hospital with a concussion.* [from Latin]

**con|demn** /kəndɛm/ (condemns, condemning, condemned) **1** V-T If you **condemn** something, you say that it is very bad and unacceptable. ❑ *Political leaders yesterday condemned the violence.* ● **con|dem|na|tion** /kɒndɛmneɪʃⁿn/ (condemnations) N-VAR ❑ *There was widespread condemnation of the decision.* **2** V-T If someone **is condemned to** a punishment, they are given this punishment. ❑ *He was condemned to life imprisonment.* **3** V-T If authorities **condemn** a building, they officially decide that it is not safe and must be pulled down or repaired. ❑ *The town council has condemned all these houses.* [from Old French] **4** → see **condemned**

**con|demned** /kəndɛmd/ ADJ A **condemned** prisoner is going to be executed. ❑ *Prison officers sat with the condemned man.* [from Old French]

**con|den|sa|tion** /kɒndɛnseɪʃⁿn/ N-UNCOUNT **Condensation** consists of small drops of water which form when warm water vapor or steam touches a cold surface such as a window. [from Latin]

**con|den|sa|tion point** (condensation points) N-VAR The **condensation point** of a gas or vapor is the temperature at which it becomes a liquid.

**con|dense** /kəndɛns/ (condenses, condensing, condensed) **1** V-T If you **condense** something, especially a piece of writing or a speech, you make it shorter. ❑ *To save time, teachers condense lesson plans.* **2** V-T/V-I When a gas or vapor **condenses**, or **is condensed**, it changes into a liquid. ❑ *Water vapor condenses to form clouds.* [from Latin]
→ see **matter, water**

---
**Word Link**    scend ≈ climbing : ascend, condescend, descend
---

**con|de|scend** /kɒndɪsɛnd/ (condescends, condescending, condescended) **1** V-T If someone **condescends to** do something, they agree to do it, but in a way which shows that they think they are better than other people and should not have to do it. ❑ *He wouldn't condescend to talk to the nurse.* **2** V-I If you say that someone **condescends to** other people, you are showing your disapproval of the fact that they behave in a way which shows that they think they are superior. ❑ *Don't condescend to me.* ● **con|de|scend|ing** /kɒndɪsɛndɪŋ/ ADJ ❑ *...a condescending attitude.* ● **con|de|scen|sion** /kɒndɪsɛnʃⁿn/ N-UNCOUNT ❑ *There was a note of condescension in her greeting.* [from Church Latin]

**con|di|tion** /kəndɪʃⁿn/ (conditions, conditioning, conditioned) **1** N-SING The **condition** of someone or something is the state they are in. ❑ *He remains in a critical condition in a California hospital.* ❑ *The two-bedroom house is in good condition.* **2** N-PLURAL The **conditions** in which people live or do things are the factors which affect their comfort, safety, or success. ❑ *People are living in terrible conditions.* ❑ *...ideal weather conditions.* **3** N-COUNT A **condition** is something which must happen or be done in order for something else to be possible, especially when this is written into a contract or law. ❑ *A*

condition of our release was that we left the country immediately. ❑ *...terms and conditions of employment.* . **4** N-COUNT If someone has a particular **condition**, they have an illness or other medical problem. ❑ *Doctors suspect he may have a heart condition.* **5** V-T If someone **is conditioned** by their experiences or environment, they are influenced by them over a period of time so that they do certain things or think in a particular way. ❑ *We are all conditioned by early experiences.* ❑ *Some people are conditioned to eating particular foods, especially junk food.* ● **con|di|tion|ing** N-UNCOUNT ❑ *...social conditioning.* **6** PHRASE When you agree to do something **on condition that** something else happens, you mean that you will only do it if this other thing also happens. ❑ *He agreed to speak to reporters on condition that he was not identified.* [from Latin]
→ see **factory**

**con|di|tion|al** /kəndɪʃənⁿl/ ADJ If a situation or agreement is **conditional on** something, it will only take place if this thing happens. ❑ *Our second offer will be conditional on the success of the first.* ❑ *...a conditional offer.* [from Latin]

**con|do|lence** /kəndoʊləns/ (condolences) N-PLURAL; N-UNCOUNT When you offer your **condolences**, or when you send a message of **condolence**, you express your sympathy for someone whose friend or relative has died recently. ❑ *He expressed his condolences to the families of the victims.* [from Church Latin]

**con|dom** /kɒndəm/ (condoms) N-COUNT A **condom** is a rubber covering which a man wears on his penis as a contraceptive or as protection against disease during sex.

**con|do|min|ium** /kɒndəmɪniəm/ (condominiums) **1** N-COUNT A **condominium** is an apartment building in which each apartment is owned by the person who lives there. **2** N-COUNT A **condominium** is one of the privately owned apartments in a condominium. [from New Latin]

**con|done** /kəndoʊn/ (condones, condoning, condoned) V-T If someone **condones** behavior that is morally wrong, they accept it and allow it to happen. ❑ *I have never condoned violence.* [from Latin]

**con|du|cive** /kənduːsɪv/ ADJ If one thing is **conducive to** another thing, it makes the other thing likely to happen. ❑ *Make your bedroom as conducive to sleep as possible.* [from Latin]

**con|duct** (conducts, conducting, conducted)

---
The verb is pronounced /kəndʌkt/. The noun is pronounced /kɒndʌkt/.
---

**1** V-T When you **conduct** an activity or task, you organize it and do it. ❑ *I decided to conduct an experiment.* **2** V-T If you **conduct** yourself in a particular way, you behave in that way. ❑ *The way he conducts himself reflects on the family.* **3** V-T/V-I When someone **conducts** an orchestra or choir, they stand in front of it and direct its performance. ❑ *He will be conducting the orchestra and chorus.* ❑ *Solti continued to conduct here and abroad.* **4** V-T If something **conducts** heat or electricity, it allows heat or electricity to pass through it or along it. ❑ *Water conducts heat faster than air.* **5** N-SING The **conduct of** a task or activity is the way in which it is organized and carried out. ❑ ...the conduct of free and fair elections. **5** N-UNCOUNT Someone's **conduct** is the way they behave in particular situations. ❑ ...a prize for good conduct. [from Medieval Latin]

| **Thesaurus** | conduct | Also look up : |
| --- | --- | --- |

v. control, direct, manage **1**
N. attitude, behavior, manner **5**

| **Word Partnership** | Use conduct with : |
| --- | --- |

N. conduct **business**, conduct **an experiment 1**
**code** of conduct **5**

con|duc|tion /kəndʌkʃ°n/ N-UNCOUNT **Conduction** is the process by which heat or electricity passes through or along something. [TECHNICAL] [from Medieval Latin]

con|duc|tor /kəndʌktər/ (**conductors**) **1** N-COUNT A **conductor** is a person who stands in front of an orchestra or choir and directs its performance. **2** N-COUNT On a train, a **conductor** is a person whose job is to travel on the train in order to help passengers and check tickets. **3** N-COUNT On a streetcar or a bus, the **conductor** is the person whose job is to sell tickets to the passengers. **4** N-COUNT A **conductor** is a substance that heat or electricity can pass through or along. ❑ ...a highly efficient conductor of electricity. [from Medieval Latin] **5** → see also **semiconductor**
→ see **metal**

cone /koʊn/ (**cones**) **1** N-COUNT A **cone** is a shape with a circular base ending in a point at the top. ❑ ...bright-orange traffic cones to stop people parking on the bridge. **2** N-COUNT A **cone** is the fruit of a tree such as a pine or fir. ❑ ...a bowl of fir cones. **3** N-COUNT **Cones** are cells in the eye that detect bright light and help you to see colors. [MEDICAL] [from Latin]
→ see **solid, volcano, volume**

cone

con|fec|tion|ers' sug|ar N-UNCOUNT **Confectioners' sugar** is very fine white sugar that is used for making frosting and candy.

con|fed|era|tion /kənfɛdəreɪʃ°n/ (**confederations**) N-COUNT A **confederation** is an organization or group consisting of smaller groups or states, especially one that exists for business or political purposes. ❑ ...the Confederation of Indian Industry. [from Late Latin]

con|fer /kənfɜr/ (**confers, conferring, conferred**) **1** V-RECIP When you **confer with** someone, you discuss something with them in order to make a decision. ❑ He conferred with Hill and the others in his office. ❑ His doctors conferred by telephone. **2** V-T To **confer** something such as power or an honor **on** someone means to give it to them. [FORMAL] ❑ The constitution confers large powers on Brazil's 25 states. [from Latin]

con|fer|ence /kɒnfərəns, -frəns/ (**conferences**) **1** N-COUNT A **conference** is a meeting, often lasting a few days, which is organized on a particular subject. ❑ ...a conference on education. ❑ ...the Alternative Energy conference. [from Medieval Latin] **2** → see also **press conference**

con|fess /kənfɛs/ (**confesses, confessing, confessed**) V-T/V-I If you **confess** to doing something wrong or something you are ashamed of, you admit that you did it. ❑ He confessed to seventeen murders. ❑ Ed confessed that he was worried. ❑ He claimed that he was forced to confess. [from Old French]

con|fes|sion /kənfɛʃ°n/ (**confessions**) **1** N-COUNT A **confession** is a signed statement by someone in which they admit that they have committed a particular crime. ❑ They forced him to sign a confession. **2** N-VAR **Confession** is the act of admitting that you have done something that you are ashamed of or embarrassed about. ❑ I have a confession to make. [from Old French]

con|fide /kənfaɪd/ (**confides, confiding, confided**) V-T/V-I If you **confide in** someone, you tell them a secret. ❑ She confided in me earlier. ❑ He confided to me that he felt lonely. [from Latin]

con|fi|dence /kɒnfɪdəns/ **1** N-UNCOUNT If you have **confidence in** someone, you feel that you can trust them. ❑ I have great confidence in you. **2** N-UNCOUNT If you have **confidence**, you feel sure about your abilities, qualities, or ideas. ❑ The band is full of confidence. **3** N-UNCOUNT If you tell someone something **in confidence**, you tell them a secret. ❑ We told you all these things in confidence. [from Latin]

con|fi|dent /kɒnfɪdənt/ **1** ADJ If you are **confident** about something, you are certain that it will happen in the way you want it to. ❑ I am confident that everything will come out right. ❑ Mr. Ryan is confident of success. ● con|fi|dent|ly ADV ❑ I can confidently promise that this year is going to be very different. **2** ADJ People who are **confident** feel sure about their own abilities, qualities, or ideas. ❑ In time he became more confident and relaxed. ● con|fi|dent|ly ADV ❑ She walked confidently across the hall. [from Latin]

con|fi|den|tial /kɒnfɪdɛnʃ°l/ ADJ Information that is **confidential** is meant to be kept secret. ❑ ...confidential information about her private life. ● con|fi|den|tial|ly ADV ❑ Any information they give will be treated confidentially. ● con|fi|den|ti|al|ity /kɒnfɪdɛnʃiælɪti/ N-UNCOUNT ❑ ...the confidentiality of the doctor-patient relationship. [from Latin]

| **Thesaurus** | confidential | Also look up : |
| --- | --- | --- |

ADJ. private, restricted; (ant.) public

con|figu|ra|tion /kənfɪgyəreɪʃ°n/ (**configurations**) N-COUNT A **configuration** is an arrangement of a group of things. [FORMAL] ❑ ...an ancient configuration of giant stones. [from Late Latin]

| **Word Link** | fig ≈ form, shape : configure, disfigure, figure |
| --- | --- |

con|fig|ure /kənfɪgyər/ (**configures, configuring, configured**) V-T If you **configure** a piece of computer equipment, you set it up so that it is ready for use. [COMPUTING] ❑ How easy was it to configure the software? [from Late Latin]

**con|fine** /kənfaɪn/ (**confines, confining, confined**) ◼ V-T To **confine** something **to** a particular place or group means to prevent it from spreading beyond it or from leaving it. ◻ *Health officials have confined the disease to the Tabatinga area.* ◻ *He was confined in a cell measuring 8 feet by 8 feet.* ● **con|fine|ment** /kənfaɪnmənt/ N-UNCOUNT ◻ *…my two-year confinement in a hospital.* ◼ V-T If you **confine yourself** or your activities to something, you do only that thing. ◻ *He did not confine himself to one language.* [from Medieval Latin]

**con|fined** /kənfaɪnd/ ◼ ADJ If something is **confined to** a particular place, it exists only in that place. If it is **confined to** a particular group, only members of that group have it. ◻ *The problem is not confined to Georgia.* ◼ ADJ A **confined** space or area is small and enclosed by walls. ◻ *I don't like confined spaces.* [from Medieval Latin]

---

**Word Link**   *firm ≈ making strong : af*firm*, con*firm*, reaf*firm*

---

**con|firm** /kənfɜrm/ (**confirms, confirming, confirmed**) ◼ V-T If something **confirms** what you believe, it shows that it is definitely true. ◻ *Doctors have confirmed that he has not broken any bones.* ◻ *This news confirms our worst fears.* ● **con|fir|ma|tion** /kɒnfərmeɪʃⁿn/ N-UNCOUNT ◻ *They took her words as confirmation of their suspicions.* ◼ V-T If you **confirm** something that has been stated or suggested, you say that it is true because you know about it. ◻ *Edith confirmed that every detail Peter gave was correct.* ● **con|fir|ma|tion** N-UNCOUNT ◻ *She glanced over at James for confirmation.* ◼ V-T If you **confirm** an arrangement or appointment, you make it definite. ◻ *You make the reservation, and I'll confirm it in writing.* ● **con|fir|ma|tion** N-UNCOUNT ◻ *Travel arrangements are subject to confirmation.* [from Old French]

**con|fis|cate** /kɒnfɪskeɪt/ (**confiscates, confiscating, confiscated**) V-T If you **confiscate** something **from** someone, you take it away from them, usually as a punishment. ◻ *The court confiscated his passport.* [from Latin]

---

**Word Link**   *flict ≈ striking : af*fliction*, con*flict*, in*flict

---

**con|flict** (**conflicts, conflicting, conflicted**)

The noun is pronounced /kɒnflɪkt/. The verb is pronounced /kənflɪkt/.

◼ N-UNCOUNT **Conflict** is serious disagreement and argument. If two people or groups are **in conflict**, they have had a serious disagreement or argument and have not yet reached agreement. ◻ *I don't like being in conflict with people.* ◼ N-VAR **Conflict** is fighting between countries or groups of people. [WRITTEN] ◻ *…a military conflict.* ◼ V-RECIP If ideas, beliefs, or accounts **conflict**, they are very different from each other and it seems impossible for them to exist together. ◻ *He held firm opinions which usually conflicted with mine.* [from Latin] → see **war**

**con|form** /kənfɔrm/ (**conforms, conforming, conformed**) ◼ V-I If something **conforms to** something such as a law or standard, it is of the required type or quality. ◻ *The lamp conforms to new safety standards.* ◼ V-I If you **conform**, you behave in the way that you are expected or supposed to behave. ◻ *Many children who don't conform are bullied.* [from Old French]

**con|form|ity** /kənfɔrmɪti/ N-UNCOUNT **Conformity** means behaving in the same way as most other people. ◻ *…social conformity.* [from Old French]

**con|found** /kənfaʊnd/ (**confounds, confounding, confounded**) V-T If someone or something **confounds** you, they make you feel surprised or confused. ◻ *His performance confounded all his critics.* [from Old French]

**con|front** /kənfrʌnt/ (**confronts, confronting, confronted**) ◼ V-T If you **are confronted with** a problem or task, you have to deal with it. ◻ *She was confronted with serious money problems.* ◻ *We are learning how to confront death.* ◼ V-T If you **confront** someone, you stand or sit in front of them, especially when you are going to fight or argue with them. ◻ *She confronted him face to face.* ◼ V-T If you **confront** someone **with** evidence, you present it to them in order to accuse them of something. ◻ *She decided to confront Kathryn with the truth.* ◻ *I could not bring myself to confront him about it.* [from Medieval Latin]

**con|fron|ta|tion** /kɒnfrʌnteɪʃⁿn/ (**confrontations**) N-VAR A **confrontation** is a dispute, fight, or battle. ◻ *…confrontation with the enemy.* ● **con|fron|ta|tion|al** /kɒnfrʌnteɪʃənⁿl/ ADJ ◻ *…his confrontational style.* [from Medieval Latin]

**con|fuse** /kənfyuz/ (**confuses, confusing, confused**) ◼ V-T If you **confuse** two things, you get them mixed up, so that you think one of them is the other one. ◻ *I always confuse my left with my right.* ● **con|fu|sion** /kənfyuʒⁿn/ N-UNCOUNT ◻ *Use different colors to avoid confusion.* ◼ V-T To **confuse** someone means to make it difficult for them to know exactly what is happening or what to do. ◻ *My words surprised and confused him.* ◼ V-T To **confuse** a situation means to make it complicated or difficult to understand. ◻ *In attempting to present two sides, you only confused the issue.* [from Latin]

**con|fused** /kənfyuzd/ ◼ ADJ If you are **confused**, you do not know exactly what is happening or what to do. ◻ *People are confused about what they should eat to stay healthy.* ◼ ADJ Something that is **confused** does not have any order or pattern and is difficult to understand. ◻ *The situation remains confused.* [from Latin]

**con|fus|ing** /kənfyuzɪŋ/ ADJ Something that is **confusing** makes it difficult for people to know exactly what is happening or what to do. ◻ *The statement is really confusing.* [from Latin]

**con|fu|sion** /kənfyuʒⁿn/ (**confusions**) ◼ N-VAR If there is **confusion** about something, it is not clear what the true situation is. ◻ *There's still confusion about the number of students.* ◼ N-UNCOUNT **Confusion** is a situation in which everything is in disorder, especially because there are lots of things happening at the same time. ◻ *There was confusion when a man fired shots.* [from Latin] ◼ → see also **confuse**

**con|gen|ial** /kəndʒinyəl/ ADJ A **congenial** person, place, or environment is pleasant. [FORMAL] ◻ *…the congenial company of friends.*

**con|gest|ed** /kəndʒɛstɪd/ ADJ A **congested** road or area is extremely crowded and blocked with traffic or people. ◻ *He promised to clear the city's* *congested roads.* [from Latin]

**con|ges|tion** /kəndʒɛstʃ°n/ N-UNCOUNT If there is **congestion** in a place, the place is extremely congested. ❑ *...the problems of traffic congestion.* [from Latin]

→ see **traffic**

**con|glom|er|ate** /kənglɒmərɪt/ (**conglomerates**) N-COUNT A **conglomerate** is a large business firm consisting of several different companies. [BUSINESS] ❑ *the world's second-largest media conglomerate.* [from Latin]

---

**Word Link**    *grat ≈ pleasing : congratulate, gratify, gratitude*

---

**con|gratu|late** /kəngrætʃəleɪt/ (**congratulates, congratulating, congratulated**) V-T If you **congratulate** someone, you express pleasure about something nice that has happened to them, or something good that they have done. ❑ *She congratulated him on the birth of his son.*
● **con|gratu|la|tion** /kəngrætʃəleɪ°n/ N-UNCOUNT ❑ *...letters of congratulation.* [from Latin]

**con|gratu|la|tions** /kəngrætʃəleɪ°nz/ CONVENTION You say "**Congratulations**" to someone in order to congratulate them. ❑ *Congratulations, you have a healthy baby girl.* ❑ *Congratulations on your interesting article.* [from Latin]

**con|gre|gate** /kɒŋgrɪgeɪt/ (**congregates, congregating, congregated**) V-I When people **congregate**, they gather together and form a group. ❑ *Young people love to congregate here in the evenings.* [from Latin]

**con|gre|ga|tion** /kɒŋgrɪgeɪ°n/ (**congregations**) N-COUNT The people who attend a religious service are the **congregation**. ❑ *Members of the congregation began arriving.* [from Latin]

**con|gress** /kɒŋgrɪs/ (**congresses**) N-COUNT A **congress** is a large meeting that is held to discuss ideas and policies. ❑ *A lot has changed after the party congress.* [from Latin]

**Con|gress** N-PROPER **Congress** is the elected group of politicians that is responsible for making laws in the United States. ❑ *We want to cooperate with both the administration and Congress.* ● **con|gres|sion|al** /kəngrɛʃən°l/ also **Congressional** ADJ ❑ *The president explained his plans to congressional leaders.* [from Latin]

**congress|man** /kɒŋgrɪsmən/ (**congressmen**) N-COUNT; N-TITLE A **congressman** is a male member of the U.S. Congress, especially of the House of Representatives.

**congress|person** /kɒŋgrɪspɜrs°n/ (**congresspeople**) N-COUNT A **congressperson** is a member of the U.S. Congress, especially of the House of Representatives.

**congress|woman** /kɒŋgrɪswʊmən/ (**congresswomen**) N-COUNT; N-TITLE A **congresswoman** is a female member of the U.S. Congress, especially of the House of Representatives.

**con|gru|ent** /kɒŋgruənt, kəngru-/ ADJ In geometry, two shapes are **congruent** if they are the same size and shape but in different positions. [TECHNICAL] [from Latin]

**con|ic pro|jec|tion** /kɒnɪk prədʒɛkʃən/ (**conic**

projections**) N-VAR A **conic projection** is an image of a map that is made by projecting the map on a globe onto a cone. Compare **azimuthal projection**, **Mercator projection**. [TECHNICAL]

**co|ni|fer** /kɒnɪfər/ (**conifers**) N-COUNT **Conifers** are a type of tree and shrub such as pine trees and fir trees. They have fruit called cones, and very thin leaves called needles which they do not normally lose in winter. [from Latin]

**con|jec|ture** /kəndʒɛktʃər/ (**conjectures**) N-VAR A **conjecture** is a guess based on information that is not certain or complete. [FORMAL] ❑ *That was a conjecture, not a fact.* [from Latin]

**con|joined twin** /kəndʒɔɪnd twɪn/ (**conjoined twins**) N-COUNT **Conjoined twins** are twins who are born with their bodies joined.

**con|junc|tion** /kəndʒʌŋkʃ°n/ (**conjunctions**)
■ N-COUNT In grammar, a **conjunction** is a word or group of words that joins together words, groups, or clauses. For example, "and" and "or" are conjunctions. ■ PHRASE If one thing is done **in conjunction with** another, the two things are done or used together. ❑ *Textbooks are designed to be used in conjunction with classroom teaching.* [from Latin]

**con|jure** /kɒndʒər/ (**conjures, conjuring, conjured**) V-T If you **conjure** something out of nothing, you make it appear as if by magic. ❑ *She found herself having to conjure a career from thin air.*
● **Conjure up** means the same as **conjure**. ❑ *Phyllis conjured up a delicious dinner.* [from Old French]
▶ **conjure up** ■ PHR-VERB If you **conjure up** a memory, picture, or idea, you create it in your mind. ❑ *Try to conjure up that pleasant thought again.* ■ → see **conjure**

**con|nect** /kənɛkt/ (**connects, connecting, connected**) ■ V-RECIP If something or someone **connects** one thing to another, or if one thing **connects to** another, or if two things **connect**, the two things are joined together. ❑ *You can connect the speakers to your CD player.* ❑ *I connected the wires.* ■ V-I If one train, plane, or boat **connects with** another, it arrives at a time which allows passengers to change to the other one in order to continue their trip. ❑ *The train connects with a ferry to Ireland.* ■ V-T If a piece of equipment or a place **is connected to** a source of power or water, it is joined to that source. ❑ *The house is not yet connected to the water supply.* ● **Connect up** means the same as **connect**. ❑ *The shower needs to be connected up to the hot and cold water supply.* ■ V-T If you **connect** a person or thing **with** something, you realize that there is a link or relationship between them. ❑ *I hoped he would not connect me with the article.* [from Latin]

**con|nect|ed** /kənɛktɪd/ ■ ADJ If one thing is **connected with** another, there is a link or relationship between them. ❑ *...problems connected with a high-fat diet.* ❑ *Your breathing is directly connected to your heart rate.* [from Latin] ■ → see also **connect**

**con|nec|tion** /kənɛkʃ°n/ (**connections**)
■ N-VAR A **connection** is a relationship between two things, people, or groups. ❑ *I felt a strong connection between us.* ■ N-COUNT A **connection** is a joint where two wires or pipes are joined together. ❑ *...pipework connections.* ■ N-COUNT If a place has good road, rail, or air **connections**, many places can be directly reached from there by car,

C

train, or plane. ❑ *Mexico City has excellent air and rail connections.* ◳ N-COUNT If you get a **connection** at a station or airport, you continue your trip by catching another train, bus, or plane. ❑ *My flight was late and I missed the connection.* [from Latin]

**con|nec|tive tis|sue** N-UNCOUNT **Connective tissue** is the substance in the bodies of animals and people which fills in the spaces between organs and connects muscles and bones. [TECHNICAL]

**con|nois|seur** /kɒnəsɜr, -suər/ (**connoisseurs**) N-COUNT A **connoisseur** is someone who knows a lot about the arts, food, or drink. ❑ *...connoisseurs of good food.* [from French]

**con|no|ta|tion** /kɒnəteɪʃ°n/ (**connotations**) N-COUNT The **connotations** of a particular word or name are the ideas or qualities which it makes you think of. ❑ *...words that have negative connotations.* [from Medieval Latin]

**con|quer** /kɒŋkər/ (**conquers, conquering, conquered**) ◱ V-T If one country or group of people **conquers** another, they take complete control of their land. ❑ *Germany conquered France in 1940.* ● **con|quer|or** /kɒŋkərər/ (**conquerors**) N-COUNT ❑ *They obeyed their conquerors because they wanted to go on living.* ◲ V-T If you **conquer** something such as a problem, you succeed in ending it or dealing with it. ❑ *Love was enough to conquer our differences.* [from Old French]
→ see **army, empire**

**con|quest** /kɒŋkwɛst/ N-UNCOUNT **Conquest** is the act of conquering a country or group of people. ❑ *...the Spanish conquest of Mexico.* [from Old French]

**Word Link**   sci ≈ knowing : conscience, conscious, science

**con|science** /kɒnʃ°ns/ (**consciences**) ◱ N-COUNT Your **conscience** is the part of your mind that tells you if what you are doing is wrong. If you have a **guilty conscience**, or if you have something **on** your **conscience**, you feel guilty about something because you know it was wrong. ❑ *My conscience is completely clear on this point.* ❑ *He got a guilty conscience and brought it back.* ◲ N-UNCOUNT **Conscience** is doing what you believe is right even though it might be unpopular or difficult. ❑ *He refused for reasons of conscience to eat meat.* [from Old French]

**con|sci|en|tious** /kɒnʃiɛnʃəs/ ADJ Someone who is **conscientious** is very careful to do their work properly. ❑ *We are generally very conscientious about our work.* ● **con|sci|en|tious|ly** ADV ❑ *He studied conscientiously.* [from Old French]

**con|scious** /kɒnʃəs/ ◱ ADJ If you are **conscious of** something, you notice it or realize that it is happening. ❑ *She was very conscious of Max studying her.* ◲ ADJ If you are **conscious of** something, you think about it a lot, especially because you think it is important. ❑ *I'm very conscious of my weight.* ◳ ADJ A **conscious** decision or effort is one that you are aware of making. ❑ *I don't think we ever made a conscious decision to have a big family.* ● **con|scious|ly** ADV ❑ *Sophie was not consciously seeking a replacement after her father died.* ◴ ADJ Someone who is **conscious** is awake rather than asleep or unconscious. ❑ *She was fully conscious throughout the operation.* [from Latin]

**Thesaurus**   conscious Also look up :

ADJ. calculated, deliberate, intentional, rational ◳
     awake, aware, responsive; (ant.) unaware, unconscious ◴

**Word Link**   ness ≈ state, condition : awareness, consciousness, kindness

**con|scious|ness** /kɒnʃəsnɪs/ (**consciousnesses**) ◱ N-COUNT Your **consciousness** is your mind, thoughts, beliefs, and attitudes. ❑ *...ideas about the nature of consciousness.* ◲ N-UNCOUNT If you **lose consciousness**, you become unconscious, and if you **regain consciousness**, you become conscious again. ❑ *She banged her head and lost consciousness.* [from Latin]

**con|script** (**conscripts, conscripting, conscripted**)

The noun is pronounced /kɒnskrɪpt/. The verb is pronounced /kənskrɪpt/.

◱ N-COUNT A **conscript** is a person who has been made to join the armed forces of a country. ❑ *Most of the soldiers are conscripts.* ◲ V-T If someone **is conscripted**, they are officially made to join the armed forces of a country. ❑ *He was conscripted into the U.S. army.* ● **con|scrip|tion** /kənskrɪpʃ°n/ N-UNCOUNT [FORMAL] ❑ *...the necessity for conscription.* [from Latin]

**con|se|crate** /kɒnsɪkreɪt/ (**consecrates, consecrating, consecrated**) V-T When a building, place, or object **is consecrated**, it is officially declared to be holy. ❑ *The church was consecrated in 1234.* [from Latin]

**con|secu|tive** /kənsɛkyətɪv/ ADJ **Consecutive** periods of time or events happen one after the other without interruption. ❑ *The Cup was won for the third consecutive year by the Toronto Maple Leafs.* [from French]

**Word Link**   con ≈ together, with : consensus, construct, convene

**con|sen|sus** /kənsɛnsəs/ N-SING A **consensus** is general agreement among a group of people. ❑ *The consensus among scientists is that the world is likely to warm up.* [from Latin]

**con|sent** /kənsɛnt/ (**consents, consenting, consented**) ◱ N-UNCOUNT If you give your **consent to** something, you give someone permission to do it. [FORMAL] ❑ *Pollard finally gave his consent to the search.* ◲ V-T/V-I If you **consent to** something, you agree to do it or to allow it to be done. [FORMAL] ❑ *He finally consented to go.* [from Old French]

**Word Link**   sequ ≈ following : consequence, sequel, sequence

**con|se|quence** /kɒnsɪkwɛns, -kwəns/ (**consequences**) ◱ N-COUNT The **consequences** of something are the results or effects of it. ❑ *She understood the consequences of her actions.* ◲ PHRASE If one thing happens and then another thing happens **in consequence** or **as a consequence**, the second thing happens as a result of the first. ❑ *His death was unexpected and, in consequence, no plans have been made for his replacement.* [from Latin]

**con|se|quent** /kɒnsɪkwɛnt, -kwənt/ ADJ
**Consequent** means happening as a direct result of
something. [FORMAL] □ ...the warming of the Earth
and the consequent climatic changes. [from Latin]

**con|se|quent|ly** /kɒnsɪkwɛntli, -kwəntli/
ADV **Consequently** means as a result. [FORMAL]
□ Grandfather broke his back while working in the mines.
Consequently, he spent the rest of his life in a wheelchair.
[from Latin]

**con|ser|va|tion** /kɒnsərveɪʃⁿn/ ■ N-UNCOUNT
**Conservation** is saving and protecting the
environment. □ ...elephant conservation.
■ N-UNCOUNT The **conservation** of a supply of
something is the careful use of it so that it lasts for
a long time. [from Latin]

**con|ser|va|tion|ist** /kɒnsərveɪʃənɪst/
(**conservationists**) N-COUNT A **conservationist**
is someone who works and campaigns
for the conservation of the environment.
□ Conservationists say the law must be strengthened.
[from Latin]

**con|ser|va|tion of en|er|gy** N-UNCOUNT
The law of **conservation of energy** is a principle
in physics which states that energy cannot be
created or destroyed.

**con|ser|va|tion of mass** also conservation
of matter N-UNCOUNT The law of **conservation
of mass** is a principle in physics which states that
matter cannot be created or destroyed.

**con|serva|tive** /kənsɜrvətɪv/ (**conservatives**)

The spelling **Conservative** is also used for
meaning ■.

■ ADJ Someone who is **conservative** has views
that are toward the political right. □ ...the
most conservative candidate. ● **Conservative** is
also a noun. □ The new judge is a conservative.
● **con|serva|tism** /kənsɜrvətɪzəm/ N-UNCOUNT
□ ...the philosophy of modern conservatism. ■ ADJ
Someone who is **conservative** is unwilling to
accept changes and new ideas. □ People tend to be
more conservative as they get older. ● **con|serva|tism**
N-UNCOUNT □ ...the traditional conservatism of the
countryside. ■ ADJ A **conservative** estimate is very
cautious and probably less than the real amount.
□ Conservative estimates put her wealth at $15 million.
● **con|serva|tive|ly** ADV □ The cost is conservatively
estimated at $30 million. ■ ADJ A **Conservative**
politician or voter is a member of or votes for the
Conservative Party in Britain and in various other
countries. □ ...Conservative MPs. ● **Conservative**
is also a noun. □ The Conservatives won the election.
[from Latin]

| **Thesaurus** | conservative | Also look up : |

| ADJ. conventional, right-wing, traditional; (ant.)
left-wing, liberal, radical ■ |

| **Word Link** | ory ≈ place where something
happens : conservatory, factory,
territory |

**con|serva|tory** /kənsɜrvətɔri/
(**conservatories**) N-COUNT A **conservatory** is a
glass room built onto a house. [from Latin]

| **Word Link** | serv ≈ keeping : conserve, observe,
preserve |

**con|serve** /kənsɜrv/ (**conserves, conserving,**

**conserved**) ■ V-T If you **conserve** a supply of
something, you use it carefully so that it lasts for a
long time. □ The factories have closed for the weekend
to conserve energy. ■ V-T To **conserve** something
means to protect it from harm, loss, or change.
□ We want to conserve this natural beauty for ever.
[from Latin]

**con|sid|er** /kənsɪdər/ (**considers, considering,
considered**) ■ V-T If you **consider** a person or
thing to be something, you think it is your opinion
of them. □ We don't consider our customers to be
just consumers. □ I had always considered myself a
strong, competent woman. ■ V-T If you **consider**
something, you think about it carefully. □ The
administration continues to consider ways to resolve the
situation. □ You do have to consider the feelings of those
around you. ● **con|sid|era|tion** N-UNCOUNT □ There
should be careful consideration about the use of these
chemicals. [from Latin] ■ → see also **considering**

| **Thesaurus** | consider | Also look up : |

| V. contemplate, examine, study, think about,
think over; (ant.) dismiss, forget, ignore ■ |

**con|sid|er|able** /kənsɪdərəbⁿl/ ADJ
**Considerable** means great in amount or degree.
[FORMAL] □ ...his considerable wealth. □ Their fees
can be considerable. ● **con|sid|er|ably** ADV □ The
process is considerably faster now that we have our new
computer system. [from Latin]

**con|sid|er|ate** /kənsɪdərɪt/ ADJ Someone
who is **considerate** pays attention to the needs,
wishes, or feelings of other people. □ He's the most
charming, most considerate man I've ever known. [from
Latin]

**con|sid|era|tion** /kənsɪdəreɪʃⁿn/
(**considerations**) ■ N-UNCOUNT If you show
**consideration**, you pay attention to the needs,
wishes, or feelings of other people. □ Show
consideration for your neighbors. ■ N-COUNT A
**consideration** is something that should be
thought about when you are planning or
deciding something. □ Price has become a more
important consideration for shoppers. ■ → see also
**consider** ■ PHRASE If you take something **into
consideration**, you think about it because it is
relevant to what you are doing. □ Safe driving takes
into consideration the lives of other people. ■ PHRASE
If something is **under consideration**, it is being
discussed. □ Several ideas are under consideration.
[from Latin]

**con|sid|er|ing** /kənsɪdərɪŋ/ PREP You use
**considering** to indicate that you are thinking
about a particular fact when making a judgment
or giving an opinion. □ Considering the current
situation, he may be hoping for too much. □ Graham
did very well considering that he hasn't been playing
regularly. [from Latin]

**con|sign** /kənsaɪn/ (**consigns, consigning,
consigned**) V-T To **consign** something or someone
to a particular place means to put them there.
[FORMAL] □ She consigned all the junk to the garage.
[from Old French]

**con|sign|ment** /kənsaɪnmənt/
(**consignments**) N-COUNT A **consignment of**
goods is a load that is being delivered to a place
or person. □ The first consignment of food arrived
yesterday. [from Old French]

**con|sist** /kənsɪst/ (consists, consisting, consisted) V-I Something that **consists of** particular things or people is formed from them. ❏ *My diet consisted of cookies and milk.* [from Latin]

**con|sist|en|cy** /kənsɪstənsi/ N-UNCOUNT The **consistency** of a substance is how thick or smooth it is. ❏ *Add water to the paint until it is the consistency of milk.* [from Latin]

**con|sist|ent** /kənsɪstənt/ **1** ADJ Someone who is **consistent** always behaves or responds in the same way. ❏ *He was a very consistent player.* ● **con|sist|en|cy** N-UNCOUNT ❏ *She scores goals with great consistency.* ● **con|sist|ent|ly** ADV ❏ *He has consistently denied it.* **2** ADJ If one fact or idea is **consistent with** another, they do not contradict each other. ❏ *This result is consistent with the theory.* [from Latin]

**con|sole** (consoles, consoling, consoled)

> The verb is pronounced /kənsoʊl/. The noun is pronounced /kɒnsoʊl/.

**1** V-T If you **console** someone who is unhappy, you try to make them feel more cheerful. ❏ *"Never mind, Ned," he consoled me.* ❏ *I can console myself with the fact that I'm not alone.* ● **con|so|la|tion** /kɒnsəleɪʃⁿn/ (consolations) N-VAR ❏ *The only consolation for the team is that they will get another chance.* **2** N-COUNT A **console** is a panel with a number of switches or knobs that is used to operate a machine. ❏ *...a console of flashing lights.* [Sense 1 from Latin. Sense 2 from French.]

**con|soli|date** /kənsɒlɪdeɪt/ (consolidates, consolidating, consolidated) V-T If you **consolidate** something such as your power or success, you strengthen it so that it becomes more effective or secure. ❏ *The government consolidated its power by force.* [from Latin]

**con|so|nant** /kɒnsənənt/ (consonants) N-COUNT A **consonant** is a sound such as "p" or "f" which you pronounce by stopping the air from flowing freely through your mouth. [from Latin]

**con|so|nant dou|bling** N-UNCOUNT In grammar, **consonant doubling** is the repetition of the final consonant in certain words when a suffix is added, for example the repetition of the "r" in "occur" to make "occurred." [TECHNICAL]

**con|sor|tium** /kənsɔrʃiəm, -tɪ-/ (consortia /kənsɔrʃiə, -tɪ-/ or consortiums) N-COUNT A **consortium** is a group of people or companies who have agreed to work together. [FORMAL] ❏ *The consortium includes some of the biggest firms in North America.* [from Latin]

**con|spicu|ous** /kənspɪkyuəs/ ADJ If someone or something is **conspicuous**, people can see or notice them very easily. ❏ *Most people don't want to be too conspicuous.* ● **con|spicu|ous|ly** ADV ❏ *Johnston's name was conspicuously absent from the list.* [from Latin]

**con|spira|cy** /kənspɪrəsi/ (conspiracies) N-VAR **Conspiracy** is secret planning by a group of people to do something wrong or illegal. ❏ *Seven men admitted conspiracy to commit murder.* [from Old French]

**con|spira|tor** /kənspɪrətər/ (conspirators) N-COUNT A **conspirator** is a person who joins a conspiracy. ❏ *He was killed by a group of conspirators.* [from Old French]

**con|spire** /kənspaɪər/ (conspires, conspiring, conspired) **1** V-RECIP If two or more people or groups **conspire to** do something illegal or harmful, they make a secret agreement to do it. ❏ *They conspired to overthrow the government.* ❏ *He was accused of conspiring with his brother to commit robberies.* **2** V-T If events **conspire to** produce a particular result, they seem to work together to cause this result. ❏ *High prices and bad weather conspired to keep the crowds away.* [from Old French]

**con|sta|ble** /kʌnstəbᵊl, kɒn-/ (constables) **1** N-COUNT; N-TITLE In the United States, a **constable** is an official who helps keep the peace in a town. They are lower in rank than a sheriff. ❏ *Courts cannot work without sheriffs and constables.* **2** N-COUNT; N-TITLE; N-VOC In Britain and some other countries, a **constable** is a police officer of the lowest rank. [from Old French]

**con|stant** /kɒnstənt/ **1** ADJ You use **constant** to describe something that happens all the time or is always there. ❏ *Women are under constant pressure to be thin.* ● **con|stant|ly** ADV ❏ *The direction of the wind is constantly changing.* **2** ADJ If an amount or level is **constant**, it stays the same over a particular period of time. ❏ *The temperature remains more or less constant.* [from Old French]

**con|stel|la|tion** /kɒnstəleɪʃⁿn/ (constellations) N-COUNT A **constellation** is a group of stars which form a pattern. [from Late Latin]
→ see **star**

**con|ster|na|tion** /kɒnstərneɪʃⁿn/ N-UNCOUNT **Consternation** is a feeling of anxiety or fear. [FORMAL] ❏ *His decision caused consternation.* [from Old French]

**con|sti|pa|tion** /kɒnstɪpeɪʃⁿn/ N-UNCOUNT **Constipation** is a medical condition which causes people to have difficulty getting rid of solid waste from their body. ❏ *Do you suffer from constipation?* [from Old French]

**con|stitu|en|cy** /kənstɪtʃuənsi/ (constituencies) **1** N-COUNT A **constituency** is a section of society that may give political support to a particular party or politician. ❏ *In Iowa, farmers are a powerful political constituency.* **2** N-COUNT A **constituency** is an area for which someone is elected as the representative in a legislature or government. ❏ *Voters in 17 constituencies are voting today.* [from Latin]

**con|stitu|ent** /kənstɪtʃuənt/ (constituents) **1** N-COUNT A **constituent** is someone who lives in a particular constituency. ❏ *He told his constituents that he would continue to represent them.* **2** N-COUNT A **constituent of** something is one of the things from which it is formed. [FORMAL] ❏ *Caffeine is one of the main constituents of coffee.* ● **Constituent** is also an adjective. ❏ *...a plan to split the company into its constituent parts.* [from Latin]

**con|sti|tute** /kɒnstɪtut/ (constitutes, constituting, constituted) **1** V-LINK If something **constitutes** a particular thing, it can be regarded as being that thing. ❏ *Testing patients without their consent would constitute a legal offense.* **2** V-LINK If a number of things or people **constitute** something, they are the parts or members that form it. ❏ *Hindus constitute 83% of India's population.* [from Latin]

**con|sti|tu|tion** /kɒnstɪtuʃⁿn/ (constitutions) **1** N-COUNT The **constitution** of a country or organization is the system of laws which formally states people's rights and duties. ❑ *The king was forced to adopt a new constitution.* ● **con|sti|tu|tion|al** /kɒnstɪtuʃənᵊl/ ADJ ❑ *The issue is one of constitutional and civil rights.* **2** N-COUNT Your **constitution** is the state of your health. ❑ *He must have an extremely strong constitution.* [from Latin]

**con|strain** /kənstreɪn/ (**constrains, constraining, constrained**) V-T To **constrain** someone or something means to limit their development or activities. [FORMAL] ❑ *Women are often constrained by family commitments.* [from Old French]

**con|straint** /kənstreɪnt/ (**constraints**) **1** N-COUNT A **constraint** is something that limits or controls what you can do. ❑ *...financial constraints.* **2** N-UNCOUNT **Constraint** is control over the way you behave which prevents you from doing what you want to do. ❑ *Journalists must be free to report without constraint.* [from Old French]

**con|strict** /kənstrɪkt/ (**constricts, constricting, constricted**) **1** V-T/V-I If a part of your body, especially your throat, **constricts** or **is constricted**, something causes it to become narrower. ❑ *Don't scream as this constricts the throat.* ● **con|stric|tion** /kənstrɪkʃᵊn/ N-UNCOUNT ❑ *...constriction of air passages in the lungs.* **2** V-T If something **constricts** you, it limits your actions so that you cannot do what you want to do. ❑ *The constant testing constricts her teaching style.* ● **con|stric|tion** (**constrictions**) N-COUNT [FORMAL] ❑ *I hated the constrictions of school.* [from Latin]

| Word Link | *con ≈ together, with : consensus, construct, convene* |
|---|---|

| Word Link | *struct ≈ building : construct, destructive, instruct* |
|---|---|

**con|struct** /kənstrʌkt/ (**constructs, constructing, constructed**) V-T If you **construct** something, you build, make, or create it. ❑ *His company recently constructed an office building in downtown Denver.* ❑ *He eventually constructed a huge business empire.* [from Latin]

**con|struc|tion** /kənstrʌkʃᵊn/ (**constructions**) **1** N-UNCOUNT **Construction** is the building or creating of something. ❑ *He has started construction on a swimming pool.* ❑ *...the construction of an equal society.* **2** N-COUNT A **construction** is an object that has been made or built. ❑ *...an impressive steel and glass construction.* [from Latin]

**con|struc|tion pa|per** N-UNCOUNT **Construction paper** is a type of stiff, colored paper that children use for drawing and for making things. ❑ *...animals cut out of brown construction paper.*

**con|struc|tive** /kənstrʌktɪv/ ADJ A **constructive** discussion, comment, or approach is useful and helpful. ❑ *She welcomes constructive criticism.* [from Latin]

**con|strue** /kənstru/ (**construes, construing, construed**) V-T If something **is construed** in a particular way, its nature or meaning is interpreted in that way. [FORMAL] ❑ *Her attempts to be helpful were construed as interference.* [from Latin]

**con|sul** /kɒnsᵊl/ (**consuls**) N-COUNT; N-TITLE A **consul** is an official who lives in a foreign city and helps other citizens from his or her country who are there. ❑ *...the American Consul in London.*

● **con|su|lar** /kɒnsələr/ ADJ ❑ *...U.S. Consular officials.* [from Latin]

**con|su|late** /kɒnsəlɪt/ (**consulates**) N-COUNT A **consulate** is the place where a consul works. ❑ *He has an appointment at the Canadian consulate in Seattle.* [from Latin]

**con|sult** /kənsʌlt/ (**consults, consulting, consulted**) V-T/V-I If you **consult** someone or something, you refer to them for advice or permission. ❑ *Consult your doctor about how much exercise you should get.* ❑ *He needed to consult with an attorney.* ● **con|sul|ta|tion** (**consultations**) N-VAR ❑ *...a consultation with a lawyer.* [from French]

**con|sul|tan|cy** /kənsʌltənsi/ (**consultancies**) N-COUNT A **consultancy** is a company that gives expert advice on a particular subject. ❑ *A management consultancy carried out a survey on the local hospital.* [from French]

**con|sult|ant** /kənsʌltənt/ (**consultants**) N-COUNT A **consultant** is a person who gives expert advice on a particular subject. ❑ *She is a consultant to the government.* [from French]

**con|sul|ta|tion** /kɒnsəlteɪʃᵊn/ (**consultations**) **1** N-VAR A **consultation** is a meeting to discuss something. ❑ *The unions want consultations with the employers.* [from French] **2** → see also **consult**

**con|sul|ta|tive** /kənsʌltətɪv/ ADJ A **consultative** committee or document gives advice or makes proposals about a particular problem or subject. ❑ *...the consultative committee on local government finance.* [from French]

| Word Link | *sume ≈ taking : assume, consume, presume* |
|---|---|

**con|sume** /kənsum/ (**consumes, consuming, consumed**) **1** V-T If you **consume** something, you eat or drink it. [FORMAL] ❑ *Martha consumed nearly a pound of cheese per day.* **2** V-T To **consume** an amount of fuel, energy, or time means to use it up. ❑ *The most efficient refrigerators consume 70 percent less electricity.* [from Latin] **3** → see also **consuming**

**con|sumed** /kənsumd/ ADJ If you are **consumed with** a feeling or idea, it affects you very strongly. [LITERARY] ❑ *They are consumed with jealousy at her success.* [from French]

**con|sum|er** /kənsumər/ (**consumers**) **1** N-COUNT A **consumer** is a person who buys things or uses services. ❑ *...consumer rights.* **2** N-COUNT A **consumer** is a plant or animal that obtains energy by eating other plants or animals. [TECHNICAL] [from Latin]

**con|sum|er con|fi|dence** N-UNCOUNT If there is **consumer confidence**, people generally are willing to spend money and buy things. ❑ *Consumer confidence rose in July.*

**Con|sum|er Price In|dex** N-PROPER The **consumer price index** is an official measure of the rate of inflation within a country's economy. The abbreviation **CPI** is also used. ❑ *The Consumer Price Index fell by 1.1 per cent.*

**con|sum|ing** /kənsumɪŋ/ **1** ADJ A **consuming** passion or interest is more important to you than anything else. ❑ *He has developed a consuming passion for chess.* [from Latin] **2** → see also **consume**

**con|sum|mate** (**consummates, consummating, consummated**)

> The adjective is pronounced /kɒnsəmɪt, kənsʌmɪt/. The verb is pronounced /kɒnsəmeɪt/.

**1** ADJ You use **consummate** to describe someone who is extremely skillful. [FORMAL] □ *He acted the part with consummate skill.* **2** V-T If two people **consummate** a marriage or relationship, they make it complete by having sex. [FORMAL] [from Latin]

| **Word Link** | sumpt ≈ taking : assumption, consumption, presumption |
|---|---|

**con|sump|tion** /kənsʌmpʃⁿn/ **1** N-UNCOUNT The **consumption** of fuel or energy is the act of using it or the amount that is used. □ *...a reduction in fuel consumption.* **2** N-UNCOUNT The **consumption** of food or drink is the act of eating or drinking something. [FORMAL] □ *Most of the meat was unfit for human consumption.* **3** N-UNCOUNT **Consumption** is the act of buying and using things. □ *...the production and consumption of goods and services.* [from Latin]

**con|tact** /kɒntækt/ (**contacts, contacting, contacted**) **1** N-UNCOUNT **Contact** involves meeting or communicating with someone. □ *I had very little contact with teenagers.* □ *He was in direct contact with the kidnappers.* □ *How did you make contact with the author?* **2** N-UNCOUNT If you come **into contact with** something, you have some experience of it in the course of your work or other activities. □ *The college has brought me into contact with western ideas.* **3** N-UNCOUNT If people or things are in **contact**, they are touching each other. □ *There was no physical contact.* **4** V-T If you **contact** someone, you telephone them or send them a message or letter. □ *Contact our head office for further details.* **5** N-COUNT A **contact** is someone you know in an organization or profession who helps you or gives you information. □ *Their contact at the United States embassy was Phil.* [from Latin]

**con|tact lens** (**contact lenses**) N-COUNT **Contact lenses** are small plastic lenses that you put on the surface of

contact lens

your eyes to help you see better.
→ see **eye**

**con|ta|gious** /kənteɪdʒəs/ **1** ADJ A **contagious** disease can be caught by touching people or things that are infected with it. □ *...a highly contagious disease.* **2** ADJ A feeling or attitude that is **contagious** spreads quickly among a group of people. □ *Laughing is contagious.* [from Latin]

**con|tain** /kənteɪn/ (**contains, containing, contained**) **1** V-T If something such as a box or room **contains** things, those things are in it. □ *The envelope contained a Christmas card.* □ *The first two floors of the building contain stores and a restaurant.* **2** V-T If something **contains** a substance, that substance is a part of it. □ *Apples contain vitamins.* **3** V-T To **contain** something means to control it and prevent it from spreading or increasing. □ *Firefighters are still trying to contain the fire.* [from Old French] **4** → see also **self-contained**

**con|tain|er** /kənteɪnər/ (**containers**) **1** N-COUNT A **container** is something such as a box or bottle that is used to hold or store things. □ *The fish are stored in plastic containers.* **2** N-COUNT A **container** is a very large metal or wooden box used for transporting goods so that they can be loaded easily onto ships and trucks. □ *The train carried loaded containers.* [from Old French]
→ see Picture Dictionary: **container**
→ see **ship**

**con|tami|nate** /kəntæmɪneɪt/ (**contaminates, contaminating, contaminated**) V-T If something **is contaminated** by dirt, chemicals, or radiation, they make it dirty or harmful. □ *Have any fish been contaminated?* ● **con|tami|na|tion** /kəntæmɪneɪʃⁿn/ N-UNCOUNT □ *...the contamination of the ocean.* [from Latin]

**con|tem|plate** /kɒntəmpleɪt/ (**contemplates, contemplating, contemplated**) **1** V-T If you **contemplate** an action, you consider it as a possibility. □ *For a time he contemplated a career as a doctor.* **2** V-T If you **contemplate** an idea or subject, you think about it carefully for a long time. □ *He cried as he contemplated his future.* ● **con|tem|pla|tion** /kɒntəmpleɪʃⁿn/ N-UNCOUNT □ *It is a place of quiet contemplation.* **3** V-T If you **contemplate** something or someone, you look at them for a long time. □ *He contemplated his hands.* [from Latin]

**Picture Dictionary**    container

bag

packet

carton

container

tube

package

bottle

jar

can

carton

**Word Link**    *tempo ≈ time : con*tempo*rary,* *tempo*ral*, temporary*

con|tem|po|ra|ry /kəntɛmpəreri/
(**contemporaries**) **1** ADJ **Contemporary** means existing now or at the time you are talking about. ❏ *...contemporary music.* **2** N-COUNT Someone's **contemporary** is a person who is or was alive at the same time as them. ❏ *...Shakespeare and his contemporaries.* [from Medieval Latin]

con|tempt /kəntɛmpt/ N-UNCOUNT If you have **contempt for** someone or something, you have no respect for them. ❏ *He has contempt for politicians of all parties.* [from Latin]

con|temp|tu|ous /kəntɛmptʃuəs/ ADJ If you are **contemptuous** of someone or something, you have no respect for them. ❏ *He was contemptuous of the poor.* ❏ *He's openly contemptuous of all the major political parties.* [from Latin]

con|tend /kəntɛnd/ (**contends, contending, contended**) **1** V-I If you have to **contend with** a problem or difficulty, you have to deal with it or overcome it. ❏ *It is time, once again, to contend with racism.* **2** V-T If you **contend that** something is true, you state or argue that it is true. [FORMAL] ❏ *Evans contends that he has been falsely accused.* **3** V-RECIP If you **contend with** someone **for** something, you compete with them to try to get it. ❏ *...the two main groups contending for power.* ❏ *Clubs such as the Kansas City Royals have had trouble contending with richer teams.* ● con|tend|er /kəntɛndər/ (**contenders**) N-COUNT ❏ *...a strong contender for a place on the Olympic team.* [from Latin]

---

**content**

❶ NOUN USES
❷ ADJECTIVE USES

❶ con|tent /kɒntɛnt/ (**contents**) **1** N-PLURAL The **contents** of a container such as a bottle, box, or room are the things inside it. ❏ *Empty the contents of the pan into a bowl.* **2** N-PLURAL The **contents** of a book are its different chapters and sections. ❏ *There is no table of contents.* **3** N-VAR The **content** of a book, television program, or website is its subject and the ideas expressed in it. ❏ *She refused to discuss the content of the letter.* **4** N-SING You can use **content** to refer to the amount or proportion of something that a substance contains. ❏ *Margarine has the same fat content as butter.* [from Latin]

❷ con|tent /kəntɛnt/ **1** ADJ If you are **content with** something, you are willing to accept it, rather than wanting something more or something better. ❏ *I am content to admire the mountains from below.* ❏ *I'm perfectly content with the way the campaign has gone.* **2** ADJ If you are **content**, you are happy or satisfied. ❏ *He says his daughter is quite content.* [from Old French] **3 to** your **heart's content** → see **heart**

con|tent|ed /kəntɛntɪd/ ADJ If you are **contented**, you are satisfied with your life or the situation you are in. ❏ *Whenever he returns to this place he is happy and contented.* [from Latin]

con|ten|tion /kəntɛnʃ°n/ (**contentions**) **1** N-COUNT Someone's **contention** is the opinion that they are expressing. ❏ *It is my contention that everyone wants to be loved.* **2** N-UNCOUNT If something is a cause **of contention**, it is a cause of

disagreement or argument. ❏ *What happened next is a matter of contention.* [from Latin]

con|ten|tious /kəntɛnʃəs/ ADJ A **contentious** issue causes a lot of disagreement or arguments. [FORMAL] ❏ *...contentious issues such as workers' rights.* [from Latin]

con|tent|ment /kəntɛntmənt/ N-UNCOUNT **Contentment** is a feeling of happiness and satisfaction. ❏ *...a feeling of contentment.* [from Latin]

con|test (**contests, contesting, contested**)

The noun is pronounced /kɒntɛst/. The verb is pronounced /kəntɛst/.

**1** N-COUNT A **contest** is a competition or game. ❏ *It was a thrilling contest.* **2** N-COUNT A **contest** is a struggle to win power or control. ❏ *...next year's presidential contest.* **3** V-T If you **contest** a statement or decision, you object to it formally. ❏ *He has to reply within 14 days in order to contest the case.* [from Latin]

**Thesaurus**    *contest*    Also look up :

N.    competition, game, match **1** fight, struggle **2**

con|test|ant /kəntɛstənt/ (**contestants**) N-COUNT A **contestant** in a competition or game show is a person who takes part in it. ❏ *He applied to be a contestant on the television show.* [from Latin]

con|text /kɒntɛkst/ (**contexts**) **1** N-VAR The **context** of an idea or event is the general situation in which it occurs. ❏ *It helps to understand the historical context in which Chaucer wrote.* **2** N-VAR The **context** of a word, sentence, or text consists of the words, sentences, or text before and after it which help to make its meaning clear. ❏ *Thomas says that he has been quoted out of context.* [from Latin]

con|text clue (**context clues**) N-COUNT **Context clues** are words or phrases that surround a particular word and help the reader to understand the word's meaning or pronunciation.

con|ti|nent /kɒntɪnənt/ (**continents**) N-COUNT A **continent** is a very large area of land, such as Africa or Asia, that consists of several countries. ❏ *She loved the African continent.* ● con|ti|nen|tal ADJ ❏ *...continental Europe.* ❏ *...the UK and continental economy.* [from Latin]
→ see Word Web: **continents**
→ see **earth**

con|ti|nen|tal /kɒntɪnɛnt°l/ **1** ADJ The **continental** United States consists of all the states which are situated on the continent of North America, as opposed to Hawaii and territories such as the Virgin Islands. ❏ *Shipping is included on orders sent within the continental U.S.* **2** → see also **continent**
→ see **meal**

con|ti|nen|tal drift N-UNCOUNT **Continental drift** is the slow movement of the Earth's continents toward and away from each other.

con|ti|nen|tal mar|gin (**continental margins**) N-COUNT The **continental margin** is the part of the ocean floor between the edge of a continent and the deepest part of the ocean.

con|ti|nen|tal rise (**continental rises**) N-COUNT The **continental rise** is the part of the ocean floor

C

## Word Web  continents

In 1912, Alfred Wegener* made an important discovery. The shapes of the various **continents** seemed to fit together like the pieces of a puzzle. He decided they had once been a single **land mass**, which he called Pangaea. He thought the continents had slowly moved apart. Wegener called this theory **continental drift**. He said the earth's **crust** is not a single, solid piece. It's full of cracks which allow huge pieces to move around on the earth's mantle. The movement of these tectonic **plates** increases the distance between Europe and North America by about 20 millimeters every year.

**Major Plates of the Earth's Crust**

*Alfred Wegener (1880-1930): a German scientist.*

that lies at the base of a continental slope.

**con|ti|nen|tal shelf** N-UNCOUNT **The continental shelf** is the area which forms the edge of a continent, ending in a steep slope to the depths of the ocean.

**con|ti|nen|tal slope** (**continental slopes**) N-COUNT The **continental slope** is the steepest part of the continental margin.

**con|tin|gen|cy** /kəntɪndʒ³nsi/ (**contingencies**) N-VAR A **contingency** is something that might happen in the future. [FORMAL] □ *I need to examine all possible contingencies.* ● **Contingency** is also an adjective. [FORMAL] □ *We have contingency plans.* [from Latin]

**con|tin|gent** /kəntɪndʒ³nt/ (**contingents**) N-COUNT A **contingent** is a group of people representing a country or organization at a meeting or other event. [FORMAL] □ *The American contingent will stay overnight in London.* [from Latin]

**con|tin|ual** /kəntɪnyuəl/ ADJ **Continual** means happening without stopping or happening again and again. □ *The school has been in continual use since 1883.* □ *...the government's continual demands for cash.* ● **con|tinu|al|ly** ADV □ *She cried almost continually.* □ *Malcolm was continually changing his mind.* [from Old French]

### Thesaurus    continual    Also look up :

ADJ. ongoing, constant, repeated, unending

**con|tinu|ation** /kəntɪnyueɪʃ³n/ (**continuations**) ◼ N-VAR The **continuation of** something is the fact that it continues to happen or exist. □ *...the continuation of the war.* ◼ N-COUNT Something that is a **continuation of** something else is closely connected with it or forms part of it. □ *This chapter is a continuation of Chapter 8.* [from Old French]

**con|tinue** /kəntɪnyu/ (**continues, continuing, continued**) ◼ V-T/V-I If something **continues**, it does not stop. If you **continue** to do something, you do not stop doing it. □ *The conflict continued for another four years.* □ *Outside the building people continue their protest.* □ *I hope they continue to fight for equal justice.* □ *Diana and Roy are determined to continue working.* ◼ V-T/V-I If something **continues** or if you **continue** it, it starts again after a break or

interruption. □ *The trial continues today.* □ *I went up to my room to continue with my packing.* □ *She looked up for a minute and then continued drawing.* ◼ V-T/V-I If you **continue**, you begin speaking again after a pause or interruption. □ *"You have no right to threaten this man," Alison continued.* □ *Tony drank some coffee before he continued.* ◼ V-I If you **continue** in a particular direction, you keep going in that direction. □ *He continued rapidly up the path.* [from Old French]

### Thesaurus    continue    Also look up :

v.    go on, persist; (ant.) stop ◼
      carry on, resume ◼

**con|ti|nu|ity** /kɒntɪnuiti/ (**continuities**) N-VAR **Continuity** is the fact that something continues to happen or exist, without stopping or changing suddenly. □ *...continuity of fuel supply.* [from Old French]

**con|tinu|ous** /kəntɪnyuəs/ ◼ ADJ A **continuous** process or event continues for a period of time without stopping. □ *They heard continuous gunfire.* ● **con|tinu|ous|ly** ADV □ *Detectives are working continuously on the case.* ◼ ADJ A **continuous** line or surface has no gaps or holes in it. □ *...a continuous line of cars.* ◼ ADJ In English grammar, **continuous** verb groups are formed using the auxiliary "be" and the present participle of a verb, as in "I'm feeling a bit tired." Compare **simple**. [from Latin]

**con|tort** /kəntɔrt/ (**contorts, contorting, contorted**) V-T/V-I If something **contorts**, or is **contorted**, it moves into an unnatural or unusual shape. □ *His face contorted with pain.* ● **con|tor|tion** /kəntɔrʃ³n/ (**contortions**) N-COUNT □ *...the contortions of the gymnasts.* [from Latin]

**con|tour** /kɒntʊər/ (**contours**) ◼ N-COUNT You can refer to the general shape or outline of an object as its **contours**. [LITERARY] □ *...the contours of the body.* ◼ N-COUNT A **contour** on a map is a line joining points of equal height. □ *...a contour map showing two hills.* [from French]

**con|tour draw|ing** (**contour drawings**) N-VAR **Contour drawing** is a method of drawing in which you draw the outline of an object in a single, continuous line without looking at the drawing as a whole. A **contour drawing** is a drawing that is made using this method.

**con|tour feath|er** (**contour feathers**) N-COUNT **Contour feathers** are the outermost feathers on the body of an adult bird.

**con|tour in|ter|val** (**contour intervals**) N-COUNT A **contour interval** on a map is the difference in height between one contour line and the contour line next to it.

**con|tour line** (**contour lines**) N-COUNT **Contour lines** on a map are the same as **contours**.

**contra|cep|tion** /kɒntrəsɛpʃ°n/ N-UNCOUNT **Contraception** refers to methods of preventing pregnancy. □ *Use a reliable method of contraception.*

**contra|cep|tive** /kɒntrəsɛptɪv/ (**contraceptives**) N-COUNT A **contraceptive** is a device or drug that prevents a woman from becoming pregnant. □ *...oral contraceptives.*

> **Word Link** tract ≈ dragging, drawing : contract, subtract, tractor

**con|tract** (**contracts, contracting, contracted**)

> The noun is pronounced /kɒntrækt/. The verb is pronounced /kəntrækt/.

■ N-COUNT A **contract** is a legal agreement, usually between two companies or between an employer and employee, which involves doing work for a stated sum of money. □ *The company won a contract for work on Chicago's tallest building.* ■ V-T If you **contract with** someone **to** do something, you legally agree to do it for them or for them to do it for you. [FORMAL] □ *You can contract with us to deliver your goods.* ■ V-T/V-I When something **contracts**, or something **contracts** it, it becomes smaller or shorter. □ *When you are anxious, your muscles contract.* ● **con|trac|tion** /kəntrækʃ°n/ (**contractions**) N-VAR □ *...the contraction and expansion of blood vessels.* ■ V-T If you **contract** a serious illness, you become ill with it. □ *He contracted malaria in Africa.* [FORMAL] [from Latin] → see **illness, muscle**

> **Word Partnership** Use contract with :
>
> V. **sign a** contract ■
> N. **terms of a** contract ■
> contract **with someone** ■
> contract **a disease** ■

**con|trac|tor** /kɒntræktər, kəntræk-/ (**contractors**) N-COUNT A **contractor** is a person or company that does work for other people or organizations. [BUSINESS] □ *...a building contractor.* [from Latin]

**con|trac|tual** /kəntræktʃuəl/ ADJ A **contractual** arrangement or relationship involves a legal agreement between people. [FORMAL] □ *The company has not fulfilled its contractual obligations.* ● **con|trac|tu|al|ly** ADV □ *You are contractually entitled to six months' salary.* [from Latin]

> **Word Link** contra ≈ against : contradict, contrary, contrast

> **Word Link** dict ≈ speaking : contradict, dictate, predict

**contra|dict** /kɒntrədɪkt/ (**contradicts, contradicting, contradicted**) ■ V-T If you

contradict someone, you say or suggest that what they have just said is wrong. □ *She did not contradict him.* ■ V-T If one statement or piece of evidence **contradicts** another, the first one makes the second one appear to be wrong. □ *Her version of the story contradicted her daughter's.* [from Latin]

**contra|dic|tion** /kɒntrədɪkʃ°n/ (**contradictions**) N-COUNT A **contradiction** is an aspect of a situation that appears to conflict with other aspects, so that they cannot all exist or be true. □ *...the contradiction between his private life and her public image.* [from Latin]

> **Word Link** ory ≈ relating to : advisory, contradictory, sensory

**contra|dic|tory** /kɒntrədɪktəri/ ADJ If two or more facts, ideas, or statements are **contradictory**, they state or imply that opposite things are true. □ *...a series of contradictory statements.* [from Latin]

**con|tra|ry** /kɒntreri/ ■ ADJ **Contrary** ideas or opinions are completely different from each other. □ *Contrary to popular belief, moderate exercise actually decreases your appetite.* ■ PHRASE You use **on the contrary** when you disagree with something and are going to say that the opposite is true. □ *"People just don't do things like that."—"On the contrary, they do them all the time."* ■ PHRASE When a particular idea is being considered, evidence or statements **to the contrary** suggest that it is not true or that the opposite is true. □ *He continued to claim that he did nothing wrong, despite clear evidence to the contrary.* [from Latin]

**con|trast** (**contrasts, contrasting, contrasted**)

> The noun is pronounced /kɒntræst/. The verb is pronounced /kəntræst/.

■ N-VAR A **contrast** is a great difference between two or more things. □ *...the contrast between town and country.* ■ PHRASE You say **by contrast** or **in contrast**, or **in contrast to** something, to show that you are mentioning a very different situation from the one you have just mentioned. □ *His brother, by contrast, has plenty of money to spend.* □ *In contrast, the lives of girls were often very restricted.* ■ V-T If you **contrast** one thing **with** another, you show or consider the differences between them. □ *She contrasted the situation then with the present crisis.* □ *In this section we contrast four different ideas.* ■ V-RECIP If one thing **contrasts with** another, it is very different from it. □ *The latest news contrasts with earlier reports.* □ *Paint the wall in a contrasting color.* ■ N-UNCOUNT **Contrast** is the degree of difference between the darker and lighter parts of a photograph, television picture, or painting. [from French]

**contra|vene** /kɒntrəvin/ (**contravenes, contravening, contravened**) V-T To **contravene** a law or rule means to do something that is forbidden by it. [FORMAL] □ *The film contravenes the law.* ● **contra|ven|tion** /kɒntrəvɛnʃ°n/ (**contraventions**) N-VAR □ *Child labor is in contravention of labor laws.* [from Late Latin]

> **Word Link** tribute ≈ giving : attribute, contribute, distribute

**con|trib|ute** /kəntrɪbyut/ (**contributes, contributing, contributed**) ■ V-I If you **contribute** to something, you say or do something to help make it successful. □ *The three sons also contribute to*

C

*the family business.* **2** V-T/V-I To **contribute** money or resources **to** something means to help pay for it or achieve it. □ *The U.S. is contributing $4 billion in loans.* □ *Local businesses have agreed to contribute.* ● **con|tribu|tor** /kəntrɪbyətər/ (**contributors**) N-COUNT □ *Candidates for Congress received 53 percent of their funds from individual contributors.* **3** V-I If something **contributes to** an event or situation, it is one of the causes of it. □ *The wet road contributed to the accident.* [from Latin]

### Thesaurus
*contribute* Also look up :

V.    aid, assist, chip in, commit, donate, give, grant, help, support; (*ant.*) neglect, take away **2**

**con|tribu|tor** (**contributors**) N-COUNT □ *Old buses are major contributors to pollution in cities.*

**con|tri|bu|tion** /kɒntrɪbyuʃ°n/ (**contributions**) **1** N-COUNT If you make a **contribution to** something, you do something to help make it successful or to produce it. □ *He received an award for his contribution to world peace.* **2** N-COUNT A **contribution** is a sum of money that you give in order to help pay for something. □ *...contributions to charity.* [from Latin]

### Word Partnership
Use *contribution* with :

ADJ.  **important** contribution, **significant** contribution **1 2**
V.    **make a** contribution, **send a** contribution **1 2**

**con|trive** /kəntraɪv/ (**contrives, contriving, contrived**) **1** V-T If you **contrive** to do something difficult, you manage to do it. [FORMAL] □ *He contrived to see her most days.* **2** V-T If you **contrive** an event or situation, you succeed in making it happen, often by tricking someone. [FORMAL] □ *The oil companies were accused of contriving a shortage of gasoline.* [from Old French]

**con|trived** /kəntraɪvd/ ADJ If you say that something someone says or does is **contrived**, you think it is false and unconvincing, rather than natural or sincere. □ *There was nothing contrived about what he said.* [from Old French]

**con|trol** /kəntroʊl/ (**controls, controlling, controlled**) **1** N-UNCOUNT **Control of** an organization, place, or system is the power to make all the important decisions about the way that it is run. □ *Mr. Ronson is giving up control of the company.* **2** PHRASE If you are **in control of** something, you have the power to make all the important decisions about the way it is run. □ *Nobody knows who is in control of the club.* **3** PHRASE If something is **under** your **control**, you have the power to make all the important decisions about the way that it is run. □ *All the newspapers are under government control.* **4** V-T If someone **controls** an organization, place, or system, they have the power to make all the important decisions about the way that it is run. □ *He controls the largest software company in California.* ● **con|trol|ler** (**controllers**) N-COUNT □ *He became controller of Continental Airlines.* **5** V-T If you **control** a person or machine, you are able to make them do what you want them to do. □ *...a computerized system to control the gates.* □ *I can't control what the judge says.* ● **Control** is also a noun. □ *He lost control of his car.*

**6** V-T To **control** prices, wages, or undesirable activities means to deal with them or restrict them to an acceptable level. □ *The government tried to control rising health-care costs.* ● **Control** is also a noun. □ *...control of inflation.* **7** PHRASE If something is **out of control**, it cannot be dealt with or restricted to an acceptable level. □ *The fire is burning out of control.* **8** PHRASE If something is **under control**, it is being dealt with or kept at an acceptable level. □ *The situation is under control.* **9** V-T If you **control yourself** or your feelings, you make yourself behave calmly even though you are feeling angry, excited, or upset. □ *Jo should learn to control herself.* ● **Control** is also a noun. □ *Sometimes he would completely lose control.* ● **con|trolled** ADJ □ *Her manner was quiet and very controlled.* **10** N-COUNT A **control** is a device such as a switch or lever which you use in order to operate a machine or piece of equipment. □ *I practiced operating the controls.* **11** N-VAR **Controls** are the methods an organization uses to restrict something. □ *...price controls.* **12** N-COUNT In a scientific experiment such as a test of a new drug or treatment, a **control** is the use of a group of people or animals that do not receive the drug or treatment, so that the two groups can be compared to see if the drug or treatment works. **13** V-I In a scientific experiment, to **control for** a particular variable means to carry out a second experiment in which the variable does not occur, so that the results of the two experiments can be compared and the effect of the variable seen. [from Old French] **14** → see also **birth control, remote control**
→ see **experiment**

**con|trolled ex|peri|ment** (**controlled experiments**) N-COUNT A **controlled experiment** is a scientific experiment which examines the effect of a single variable by keeping all the other variables fixed.

**con|tro|ver|sial** /kɒntrəvɜrʃ°l/ ADJ Something or someone that is **controversial** is the subject of intense public argument, disagreement, or disapproval. □ *...a controversial new book.* [from Latin]

**con|tro|ver|sy** /kɒntrəvɜrsi/ (**controversies**) N-VAR **Controversy** is a lot of discussion and argument about something, often involving strong anger or disapproval. □ *The proposals have caused controversy.* [from Latin]

**con|va|lesce** /kɒnvəlɛs/ (**convalesces, convalescing, convalesced**) V-I If you are **convalescing**, you are resting and getting your health back after an illness or operation. [FORMAL] □ *I convalesced at home for three months.* ● **con|va|les|cence** /kɒnvəlɛs°ns/ N-UNCOUNT [FORMAL] □ *They invited me to stay with them during my convalescence.* ● **con|va|les|cent** /kɒnvəlɛs°nt/ ADJ [FORMAL] □ *...convalescent hospitals.* [from Latin]

**con|vec|tion** /kənvɛkʃ°n/ N-UNCOUNT **Convection** is the process by which heat travels through air, water, and other gases and liquids. [TECHNICAL] [from Late Latin]

**con|vec|tion cur|rent** (**convection currents**) N-COUNT A **convection current** is a circular current within a substance such as air or water resulting from a difference in density between warm and cool parts of the substance. [TECHNICAL]

con|vec|tive zone /kənvɛktɪv zoʊn/
(**convective zones**) N-COUNT The **convective zone**
is the area of the sun where energy is carried
toward the surface by convection currents.
[TECHNICAL]

**Word Link**    con ≈ together, with : consensus,
construct, convene

con|vene /kənvin/ (**convenes, convening,
convened**) V-T/V-I If you **convene** a meeting,
you arrange for it to take place. You can also say
that people **convene** at a meeting. [FORMAL] ❑ He
convened a meeting of his closest advisers. [from
Latin]

con|veni|ence /kənvinyəns/ (**conveniences**)
**1** N-UNCOUNT If something is done for your
**convenience**, it is done in a way that is useful
or suitable for you. ❑ We have enclosed a pre-
paid envelope for your convenience. **2** N-COUNT A
**convenience** is something that is very useful.
❑ Mail order is a convenience for buyers who are too
busy to shop. **3** N-COUNT **Conveniences** are pieces
of equipment designed to make your life easier.
❑ She moved into an apartment with all the modern
conveniences. [from Latin] **4** → see also
**convenient**

con|veni|ent /kənvinyənt/ **1** ADJ Something
that is **convenient** is easy, useful, or suitable for a
particular purpose. ❑ ...a convenient way of paying.
● con|veni|ence N-UNCOUNT ❑ They may use a
credit card for convenience. ● con|veni|ent|ly ADV
❑ ...conveniently placed cupholders. **2** ADJ A place
that is **convenient** is near to where you are, or
near to another place where you want to go. ❑ The
town is convenient to Dulles Airport. ● con|veni|ent|ly
ADV ❑ It was very conveniently situated just across the
road. **3** ADJ A **convenient** time to do something
is a time when you are free to do it or would like
to do it. ❑ She will try to arrange a convenient time.
[from Latin]

con|vent /kɒnvɛnt, -vᵊnt/ (**convents**) N-COUNT
A **convent** is a building in which a community of
nuns live. [from Old French]

con|ven|tion /kənvɛnʃn/ (**conventions**)
**1** N-VAR A **convention** is an accepted way of
behaving or of doing something. ❑ It's a social
convention that men don't wear skirts. **2** N-COUNT
A **convention** is an official agreement between
countries or organizations. ❑ ...the UN convention
on climate change. **3** N-COUNT A **convention** is
a large meeting of an organization or group.
❑ ...the annual convention of the Society of Professional
Journalists. **4** N-COUNT In art, literature, or the
theater, a **convention** is a traditional method or
style. [from Latin]

con|ven|tion|al /kənvɛnʃᵊnᵊl/ **1** ADJ
**Conventional** people behave in a way that
is accepted as normal in their society. ❑ ...a
respectable married woman with conventional
opinions. ● con|ven|tion|al|ly ADV ❑ Men still
wore their hair short and dressed conventionally.
**2** ADJ A **conventional** method or product is
one that is usually used. ❑ ...a conventional oven.
● con|ven|tion|al|ly ADV ❑ ...conventionally grown
crops. **3** ADJ **Conventional** weapons and wars
do not include nuclear, chemical, or biological
weapons. [from Latin]

**Word Link**    verg, vert ≈ turning : converge,
diverge, subvert

con|verge /kənvɜrdʒ/ (**converges, converging,
converged**) **1** V-I If people or vehicles **converge**
on a place, they move toward it from different
directions. ❑ Thousands of protesters will converge on
the capital. **2** V-I If roads or lines **converge**, they
meet or join. [FORMAL] ❑ As they flow south, the five
rivers converge. [from Late Latin]

con|ver|gent bounda|ry (**convergent
boundaries**) N-COUNT A **convergent boundary** is
an area in the Earth's crust where two tectonic
plates are moving toward each other. [TECHNICAL]

con|ver|sa|tion /kɒnvərseɪʃᵊn/
(**conversations**) N-COUNT If you have a
**conversation with** someone, you talk with
them, usually in an informal situation.
❑ I had an interesting conversation with him.
● con|ver|sa|tion|al ADJ ❑ ...the author's easy,
conversational style. [from Old French]

con|verse (**converses, conversing, conversed**)

> The verb is pronounced /kənvɜrs/. The noun is
> pronounced /kɒnvɜrs/.

**1** V-RECIP If you **converse with** someone, you
talk to them. You can also say that two people
**converse**. [FORMAL] ❑ Luke conversed with the
pilot. **2** N-SING The **converse** of a statement
is its opposite or reverse. [FORMAL] ❑ If great
events produce great men, the converse is also true.
● con|verse|ly /kɒnvɜrsli, kənvɜrs-/ ADV
[FORMAL] ❑ Some people mistake politeness for
weakness, and conversely, they think that rudeness is a
sign of strength. [Sense 1 from Old French. Sense 2
from Latin.]

con|vert (**converts, converting, converted**)

> The verb is pronounced /kənvɜrt/. The noun is
> pronounced /kɒnvɜrt/.

**1** V-T To **convert** one thing **into** another means
to change it into a different shape or form. ❑ The
signal will be converted into digital code. ❑ He wants
to convert County Hall into a hotel. ● con|ver|sion
/kənvɜrʒᵊn/ (**conversions**) N-VAR ❑ ...the
conversion of unused rail lines into bike paths. **2** V-T/V-I
If someone **converts** you, they persuade you to
change your religious or political beliefs. ❑ If you
try to convert him, you could find he just walks away.
❑ He converted her to Catholicism. ● con|ver|sion
N-VAR ❑ ...his conversion to Christianity. **3** N-COUNT
A **convert** is someone who has changed their
religious or political beliefs. ❑ She was a convert to
Roman Catholicism. [from Old French]

**Thesaurus**    convert    Also look up :

V.    adapt, alter, change, modify, transform **1**

con|vert|ible /kənvɜrtɪbᵊl/ (**convertibles**)
**1** N-COUNT A **convertible** is a car with a soft roof
that can be folded down or removed. ❑ Her car is
a yellow convertible. **2** ADJ In finance, **convertible**
investments or money can be easily exchanged for
other forms of investments or money. [BUSINESS]
❑ ...the introduction of a convertible currency. [from
Old French]
→ see car

con|vex lens (**convex lenses**) N-COUNT A
**convex lens** is a lens that is thicker in the middle
than at the edges. Compare **concave**.

**con|vey** /kənveɪ/ (**conveys, conveying, conveyed**) v-t To **convey** information or feelings means to cause them to be known or understood. ❑ *I tried to convey the wonder of this machine to my husband.* [from Old French]

**con|vey|or belt** /kənveɪər bɛlt/ (**conveyor belts**) N-COUNT A **conveyor belt** or a **conveyor** is a continuously moving strip which is used in factories for moving objects along. ❑ *The damp bricks went along a conveyor belt into another room to dry.*

**Word Link** vict, vinc ≈ conquering : convict, convince, invincible

**con|vict** (**convicts, convicting, convicted**)

The verb is pronounced /kənvɪkt/. The noun is pronounced /kɒnvɪkt/.

■ v-t If someone **is convicted of** a crime, they are found guilty of it in a court of law. ❑ *He was convicted of murder.* ❑ *There was insufficient evidence to convict him.* ■ N-COUNT A **convict** is someone who is in prison. ❑ *...escaped convicts.* [from Latin]

**con|vic|tion** /kənvɪkʃ³n/ (**convictions**) ■ N-COUNT A **conviction** is a strong belief or opinion. ❑ *It is our firm conviction that a step forward has been taken.* ■ N-COUNT If someone has a **conviction**, they have been found guilty of a crime in a court of law. ❑ *He will appeal against his conviction.* [from Latin]

**con|vince** /kənvɪns/ (**convinces, convincing, convinced**) ■ v-t If someone or something **convinces** you **to** do something, they persuade you to do it. ❑ *He convinced her to go ahead and marry Bud.* ■ v-t If someone or something **convinces** you **of** something, they make you believe that it is true or that it exists. ❑ *I soon convinced him of my innocence.* ● **con|vinced** /kənvɪnst/ ADJ ❑ *He was convinced that I was part of the problem.* [from Latin]

**Thesaurus** convince Also look up :

v. argue, brainwash, persuade, sell, talk into, win over; (ant.) discourage ■ ■

**con|vinc|ing** /kənvɪnsɪŋ/ ADJ If someone or something is **convincing**, you believe them. ❑ *There is no convincing evidence that power lines cause cancer.* ● **con|vinc|ing|ly** ADV ❑ *He argued convincingly.* [from Latin]

**con|voy** /kɒnvɔɪ/ (**convoys**) N-COUNT A **convoy** is a group of vehicles or ships traveling together. ❑ *...a U.N. convoy carrying food and medical supplies.* [from Old French]

**con|vul|sion** /kənvʌlʃ³n/ (**convulsions**) N-COUNT If someone has **convulsions**, they suffer uncontrollable movements of their muscles. ❑ *5 percent suffered convulsions.* [from French]

**cook** /kʊk/ (**cooks, cooking, cooked**) ■ v-t/v-i When you **cook** a meal, you prepare and heat food so it can be eaten. ❑ *I have to go and cook dinner.* ❑ *...some basic instructions on how to cook a turkey.* ❑ *Let the vegetables cook gently for about 10 minutes.* ❑ *Chefs at the restaurant once cooked for President Kennedy.* ● **cook|ing** N-UNCOUNT ❑ *Her hobbies include dancing and cooking.* ■ N-COUNT A **cook** is a person who prepares and cooks food. ❑ *They had a butler, a cook, and a maid.* ❑ *I'm a terrible cook.* [from Old English]

▶ **cook up** PHR-VERB If someone **cooks up** a dishonest scheme, they plan it. [INFORMAL] ❑ *They cooked up the plan between them.*

→ see Picture Dictionary: **cook**

**Usage** cook and make

*Cook* is used when referring to the preparation of food using a process involving heat. If preparation only involves assembling ingredients which may have previously been cooked, then *make* is used. "Who made this salad? It's delicious!" "Oh, I just threw it together while I was cooking/making the rest of the dinner."

**Thesaurus** cook Also look up :

v. heat up, make, prepare ■
n. chef ■

**cook|book** /kʊkbʊk/ (**cookbooks**) N-COUNT A **cookbook** is a book that contains recipes for preparing food.

**cookie** /kʊki/ (**cookies**) ■ N-COUNT A **cookie** is a small sweet cake. ■ N-COUNT A **cookie** is a piece of computer software which enables a website you have visited to recognize you if you visit it again. [COMPUTING] [from Dutch]

→ see **dessert**

**cookie cut|ter** (**cookie cutters**) also **cookie-cutter** ■ N-COUNT A **cookie cutter** is a tool that

---

**Picture Dictionary** cook

boil

steam

roast

fry

stir fry

bake

microwave

toast

barbecue

broil

## Word Web cooking

Scientists that study humans believe ancestors began to experiment with **cooking** about 1.5 million years ago. Cooking made some poisonous or **inedible** plants safe to **eat**. It made tough meat **tender** and easier for our bodies to **digest**. It also improved the flavor of the food they ate. **Heating up food** to a high **temperature** killed dangerous bacteria. **Cooked** food could be stored longer. This all helped increase the amount of food available to our ancestors.

**c**

is used for cutting cookies into a particular shape. ❑ *…heart-shaped cookie cutters.* **2** ADJ A **cookie-cutter** style is one in which the same approach is always used and there are not enough individual differences. ❑ *Too many cookie-cutter houses were built.*

**cookie sheet** (cookie sheets) N-COUNT A **cookie sheet** is a flat piece of metal on which you bake foods such as cookies in an oven.

**cook|ing** /kʊkɪŋ/ **1** N-UNCOUNT **Cooking** is food which has been cooked. ❑ *The menu is based on classic French cooking.* **2** N-UNCOUNT **Cooking** is the activity of preparing food. ❑ *He did the cooking, cleaning, and home repairs.* [from Old English] **3** → see also **cook**
→ see Word Web: **cooking**

**cook|out** /kʊkaʊt/ (cookouts) N-COUNT A **cookout** is the same as a **barbecue**.

**cool** /kul/ (cooler, coolest, cools, cooling, cooled) **1** ADJ Something that is **cool** has a low temperature but is not cold. ❑ *I felt a current of cool air.* ❑ *The water was cool.* **2** ADJ If you stay **cool** in a difficult situation, you remain calm. ❑ *He was marvelously cool, smiling as if nothing had happened.* ● **cool|ly** ADV ❑ *Everyone must think this situation through calmly and coolly.* **3** ADJ If you say that a person or their behavior is **cool**, you mean that they are unfriendly or not enthusiastic. ❑ *The idea has received a cool response.* ● **cool|ly** ADV ❑ *"It's your choice, Nina," David said coolly.* **4** ADJ If you say that a person or thing is **cool**, you mean that they are fashionable and attractive. [INFORMAL] ❑ *He was trying to be really cool and trendy.* ❑ *That's a cool hat.* **5** V-T/V-I When something **cools** or when you **cool** it, it becomes lower in temperature. ❑ *Drain the meat and allow it to cool.* ❑ *Huge fans cool the room.* ● To **cool down** means the same as to **cool**. ❑ *Avoid putting your car away until the engine has cooled down.* **6** ADJ **Cool** colors are colors that suggest coolness, especially the colors blue, green, and violet. [from Old English]
▸ **cool down 1** PHR-VERB → see **cool 5**
**2** PHR-VERB If someone **cools down** or if you **cool** them **down**, they become less angry. ❑ *He has had time to cool down.*
▸ **cool off** PHR-VERB If someone or something **cools off**, or if you **cool** them **off**, they become cooler after being hot. ❑ *He's trying to cool off out there in the rain.* ❑ *She jumped in the pool to cool herself off.*

### Thesaurus    cool    Also look up :
ADJ. chilly, cold, nippy; (ant.) warm **1**
distant, unfriendly **3**

### Word Partnership    Use *cool* with :
N.    cool **air**, cool **breeze** **1**

### Word Link    oper ≈ work : cooperate, opera, operation

**co|oper|ate** /koʊɒpəreɪt/ (cooperates, cooperating, cooperated) **1** V-RECIP If you **cooperate with** someone, you work with them or help them. ❑ *The UN has been cooperating with the State Department.* ● **co|opera|tion** /koʊɒpəreɪʃⁿn/ N-UNCOUNT ❑ *…economic cooperation with East Asia.* **2** V-I If you **cooperate**, you do what someone has asked or told you to do. ❑ *He agreed to cooperate with the police investigation.* ● **co|opera|tion** N-UNCOUNT ❑ *…the importance of the public's cooperation in the hunt for the bombers.* [from Late Latin]

### Word Partnership    Use *cooperate* with :
V.    **agree to** cooperate, **continue to** cooperate, **fail to** cooperate, **refuse to** cooperate **1** **2**
ADV.    cooperate **fully** **1** **2**
N.    **willingness to** cooperate **1** **2**

**co|opera|tive** /koʊɒpərətɪv/ (cooperatives) **1** N-COUNT A **cooperative** is a business or organization run by the people who work for it, who share its benefits and profits. [BUSINESS] ❑ *…a housing cooperative.* **2** ADJ A **cooperative** activity is done by people working together. ❑ *…a smooth cooperative effort between Egyptian and U.S. authorities.* ● **co|opera|tive|ly** ADV ❑ *They agreed to work cooperatively.* **3** ADJ Someone who is **cooperative** does what you ask them to without complaining or arguing. ❑ *I made every effort to be cooperative.* [from Late Latin]

### Thesaurus    cooperative    Also look up :
ADJ. combined, shared, united; (ant.) independent, private, separate **2** accommodating **3**

**co|or|di|nate** (coordinates, coordinating, coordinated)
The verb is pronounced /koʊɔrdⁿneɪt/. The noun is pronounced /koʊɔrdənət/.
**1** V-T If you **coordinate** an activity, you organize it. ❑ *…a committee to coordinate police work.* ● **co|or|di|nat|ed** ADJ ❑ *…a well-coordinated surprise attack.* ● **co|or|di|na|tion** /koʊɔrdⁿneɪʃⁿn/ N-UNCOUNT ❑ *…the coordination of educational policy.* ● **co|or|di|na|tor** (coordinators) N-COUNT ❑ *…the party's campaign coordinator.* **2** V-T If you **coordinate** the parts of your body, you make them

work together efficiently. ❏ *You need to coordinate legs, arms, and breathing.* ● **co|or|di|na|tion** N-UNCOUNT ❏ *Symptoms of the disease are clumsiness and lack of coordination.* **3** N-COUNT The **coordinates** of a point on a map or graph are the two sets of numbers or letters that you need in order to find that point. [TECHNICAL] ❏ *Can you give me your coordinates?*

---

**Thesaurus** *coordinate* Also look up :

V. direct, manage, organize **1**

---

**co|or|di|nate sys|tem** (**coordinate systems**) N-COUNT A **coordinate system** is a system that uses coordinates to describe the position of objects on a map or graph.

**cootie** /kúti/ (**cooties**) N-COUNT **Cooties** are the same as **lice**. [INFORMAL] [from Malay]

**cop** /kɒp/ (**cops, copping, copped**) N-COUNT A **cop** is a policeman or policewoman. [INFORMAL] ❏ *The cops know where to find him.* [from Old French]
▸ **cop to** PHR-VERB If you **cop to** something bad or wrong that you have done, you admit that you have done it. [INFORMAL] ❏ *...a chance to cop to all the mistakes we made.*

**cope** /koʊp/ (**copes, coping, coped**) V-I If you **cope with** a problem or task, you deal with it successfully. ❏ *My mother coped with bringing up three children on thirty dollars a week when my father was away.* [from Old French]

---

**Word Partnership** Use *cope* with :

| | |
|---|---|
| N. | **ability to** cope, cope **with loss** |
| ADV. | **how to** cope |
| V. | **learn to** cope, **manage to** cope |
| ADJ. | **unable to** cope |

---

**cop|ier** /kɒpiər/ (**copiers**) N-COUNT A **copier** is a machine which makes exact copies of writing or pictures on paper, usually by a photographic process. [from Medieval Latin]

**co|pi|ous** /koʊpiəs/ ADJ A **copious** amount of something is a large amount of it. ❏ *...copious amounts of food.* ● **co|pi|ous|ly** ADV ❏ *She wept copiously.* [from Latin]

**cop|per** /kɒpər/ N-UNCOUNT **Copper** is a soft reddish brown metal. ❏ *Chile is the world's largest producer of copper.* [from Old English]
→ see **metal, mineral, pan**

**cop|per wire** (**copper wires**) N-VAR **Copper wire** is a type of cable made of copper that is good at conducting heat and electricity.

**copy** /kɒpi/ (**copies, copying, copied**)
**1** N-COUNT If you make a **copy of** something, you produce something that looks like the original thing. ❏ *...a copy of Steve's letter.* **2** N-COUNT A **copy** of a book, newspaper, or CD is one of many that are exactly the same. ❏ *...a copy of "USA Today."* **3** V-T If you **copy** something, you produce or write something that is exactly like the original thing. ❏ *...companies who unlawfully copy computer programs.* ❏ *We're copying from textbooks.* **4** V-T If you **copy** a person or their ideas, you try to do what they do or try to be like them. ❏ *Children copy the behavior of people they admire.* [from Medieval Latin]
→ see **clone, draw**

---

**Thesaurus** *copy* Also look up :

| | |
|---|---|
| N. | likeness, photocopy, replica, reprint; (ant.) master, original **1** |
| V. | reproduce; (ant.) originate **3** imitate, mimic **4** |

---

**copy ma|chine** (**copy machines**) N-COUNT A **copy machine** is the same as a **copier**.

**copy|right** /kɒpiraɪt/ (**copyrights**) N-VAR If someone has the **copyright** on a piece of writing or music, it is illegal to reproduce or perform it without their permission. ❏ *Who owns the copyright on this movie?*

**cor|al** /kɔrəl/ (**corals**) **1** N-VAR **Coral** is a hard substance formed from the bones of very small sea animals. **2** N-COUNT **Corals** are very small sea animals formed from coral. [from Old French]

**cord** /kɔrd/ (**cords**) **1** N-VAR **Cord** is strong, thick string. ❏ *...a length of nylon cord.* **2** N-VAR **Cord** is electrical wire covered in rubber or plastic. ❏ *...the iron's electrical cord.* [from Old French]

**cor|dial** /kɔrdʒəl/ ADJ **Cordial** means friendly. [FORMAL] ❏ *He was chatty and cordial.* ● **cor|di|al|ly** ADV ❏ *They all greeted me very cordially.* [from Medieval Latin]

**cor|don** /kɔrdən/ (**cordons, cordoning, cordoned**) N-COUNT A **cordon** is a line or ring of police, soldiers, or vehicles preventing people from entering or leaving an area. ❏ *Police formed a cordon between the two crowds.* [from Old French]
▸ **cordon off** PHR-VERB If police or soldiers **cordon off** an area, they prevent people from entering or leaving it. ❏ *Police cordoned off part of the city center.*

**core** /kɔr/ (**cores**) **1** N-COUNT The **core** of a fruit is the central part of it that contains seeds. ❏ *...an apple core.* **2** N-COUNT The **core** of something is the central or most important part of it. ❏ *...the earth's core.* ❏ *...the ability to get straight to the core of a problem.*
→ see Picture Dictionary: **core**

---

**Word Partnership** Use *core* with :

| | |
|---|---|
| N. | **apple** core **1** core **curriculum, Earth's** core, core **group 2** |

---

**Coriolis ef|fect** /kɔrioʊlɪs ɪfɛkt/ (**Coriolis effects**) N-COUNT The **Coriolis effect** is the tendency of moving objects to turn to the right in the northern hemisphere and to the left in the southern hemisphere, because of the Earth's rotation. [TECHNICAL]

**cork** /kɔrk/ (**corks**) **1** N-UNCOUNT **Cork** is a soft, light substance which forms the bark of a type of Mediterranean tree. ❏ *...cork floors.* **2** N-COUNT A **cork** is a piece of cork or plastic that is pushed into the opening of a bottle to close it. [from Arabic]

**cork|screw** /kɔrkskru/ (**corkscrews**) N-COUNT A **corkscrew** is a device for pulling corks out of bottles.

**corn** /kɔrn/ **1** N-UNCOUNT **Corn** is a tall plant which produces long vegetables covered with yellow seeds, or the seeds of this plant. ❏ *...rows of corn in an Iowa field.* [from Old English] **2** → see also **popcorn, sweetcorn**
→ see **grain, vegetable**

**cor|ner** /kɔrnər/ (**corners, cornering, cornered**)

C

## Picture Dictionary    core

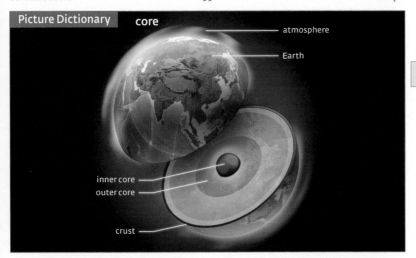

atmosphere

Earth

inner core
outer core

crust

1 N-COUNT A **corner** is a point or an area where two sides or edges of something meet, or where a road meets another road. ❑ *There was a table in the corner of the living room.* ❑ *...street corners.* 2 V-T If you **corner** a person or animal, you force them into a place they cannot escape from. ❑ *The gang was cornered by armed police.* 3 V-T If a company or organization **corners** an area of trade, they gain control over it so that no one else can have any success in that area. [BUSINESS] ❑ *They have cornered the market in MP3 players.* 4 PHRASE If you say that something is **around the corner**, you mean that it will happen very soon. ❑ *Economic recovery is just around the corner.* [from Old French]

### Word Partnership   Use *corner* with :

| | |
|---|---|
| ADJ. | **far** corner, **sharp** corner 1 |
| V. | **round/turn** a corner, **sit in** a corner 1 |
| N. | **street** corner 1 |
| PREP. | **in** a corner 1 |
| | **around the** corner 4 |

**corner|stone** /kɔrnərstoʊn/ (**cornerstones**) N-COUNT The **cornerstone of** something is the basis of its existence or success. [FORMAL] ❑ *Free speech is the cornerstone of journalism.* [from Old French]

**corn|row** /kɔrnroʊ/ (**cornrows**) also corn row N-COUNT If someone wears their hair in **cornrows**, they braid their hair in parallel rows that lie flat upon their head. ❑ *...a tall woman in cornrows.*
→ see **hair**

**corn|starch** /kɔrnstɑrtʃ/ also corn starch N-UNCOUNT **Cornstarch** is a fine white powder made from corn that is used to make sauces thicker.

**corny** /kɔrni/ (**cornier, corniest**) ADJ If you describe something as **corny**, you mean that it is obvious or sentimental and not at all original. ❑ *I know it sounds corny, but I'm really not interested in money.* ❑ *...a corny old war movie.*

**co|ro|na** /kəroʊnə/ N-SING The sun's **corona** is

its outer atmosphere. [TECHNICAL] [from Latin]

**coro|nary** /kɔrənɛri/ (**coronaries**) 1 ADJ **Coronary** means relating to the heart. [MEDICAL] ❑ *...the coronary arteries.* 2 N-COUNT If someone has a **coronary**, they collapse because the flow of blood to their heart is blocked by a blood clot. [from Latin]

**coro|na|tion** /kɔrəneɪʃ°n/ (**coronations**) N-COUNT A **coronation** is the ceremony at which a king or queen is crowned. [from Old French]

**coro|ner** /kɔrənər/ (**coroners**) N-COUNT A **coroner** is an official who is responsible for investigating sudden or unusual deaths. ❑ *The coroner said Kerkowski was dead by December if not earlier.* [from Old French]

**cor|po|ral** /kɔrpərəl, -prəl/ (**corporals**) N-COUNT; N-TITLE; N-VOC A **corporal** is a noncommissioned officer in the army or United States Marines. ❑ *The corporal shouted an order at the men.* ❑ *Corporal Jones.* [from Old French]

**cor|po|ral pun|ish|ment** N-UNCOUNT **Corporal punishment** is the punishment of people by hitting them. ❑ *Corporal punishment in public schools is forbidden.*

**cor|po|rate** /kɔrpərit, -prit/ ADJ **Corporate** means relating to business corporations. [BUSINESS] ❑ *...top U.S. corporate executives.* [from Latin]

### Word Partnership   Use *corporate* with :

| | |
|---|---|
| N. | corporate **clients**, corporate **culture**, corporate **hospitality**, corporate **image**, corporate **lawyer**, corporate **sector**, corporate **structure** |

**cor|po|ra|tion** /kɔrpəreɪʃ°n/ (**corporations**) N-COUNT A **corporation** is a large business or company. [BUSINESS] ❑ *...multinational corporations.* [from Latin]

**corps** /kɔr/ (**corps**) 1 N-COUNT A **corps** is a part of the army which has special duties. ❑ *...the Army Medical Corps.* 2 N-COUNT A **corps** is a small group of people who do a special job. ❑ *He traveled to Uganda with the U.S. diplomatic corps.* [from French]

**corpse** /kɔrps/ (**corpses**) N-COUNT A **corpse** is a dead body. [from Old French]

**cor|ral** /kəræl/ (**corrals, corralling, corralled**)
■ N-COUNT A **corral** is a space surrounded by a fence where cattle or horses are kept. ■ V-T To **corral** a person or animal means to capture or trap them. ❑ *Within hours, police corralled the three men.* [from Spanish]

**Word Link**    rect ≈ right, straight : cor**rect**, rect**angle**, rect**ify**

**cor|rect** /kərɛkt/ (**corrects, correcting, corrected**) ■ ADJ If something is **correct**, it is right and true. ❑ *The correct answers can be found on page 8.* ● **cor|rect|ly** ADV ❑ *Did I pronounce your name correctly?* ● **cor|rect|ness** N-UNCOUNT ❑ *Ask him to check the correctness of what he has written.* ■ ADJ If you are **correct**, what you have said or thought is true. [FORMAL] ❑ *You are absolutely correct.* ■ ADJ The **correct** thing or method is the one that is most suitable in a particular situation. ❑ *The use of the correct materials was essential.* ● **cor|rect|ly** ADV ❑ *The exercises, correctly performed, will stretch and tone muscles.* ■ ADJ **Correct** behavior is in accordance with social rules. ❑ *He was very polite and very correct.* ● **cor|rect|ly** ADV ❑ *She began speaking politely, even correctly.* ● **cor|rect|ness** N-UNCOUNT ❑ *...his old-fashioned correctness.* ■ V-T If you **correct** a problem, mistake, or fault, you put it right. ❑ *He may need surgery to correct the problem.* ● **cor|rec|tion** /kərɛkʃən/ (**corrections**) N-VAR ❑ *...the correction of factual errors.* ■ V-T If you **correct** someone, you say something which is more accurate or appropriate than what they have just said. ❑ *"Actually, that isn't what happened," George corrects me.* ■ V-T When someone **corrects** a piece of writing, they look at it and mark the mistakes in it. ❑ *He was correcting his students' work.* [from Latin]
→ see **answer**

**Thesaurus**    correct    Also look up :

| | |
|---|---|
| ADJ. | accurate, legitimate, precise, right, true; (ant.) false, inaccurate, incorrect, wrong ■ |
| V. | fix, rectify, repair; (ant.) damage, hurt ■ |

**Word Partnership**    Use correct with :

| | |
|---|---|
| N. | correct **answer**, correct **response** ■ ■ correct **a mistake**, correct **a situation** ■ correct *someone* ■ |

**cor|rec|tion** /kərɛkʃən/ (**corrections**)
■ N-COUNT **Corrections** are marks or comments made on a piece of written work which indicate where there are mistakes and what are the right answers. ❑ *...corrections to the text.* ■ N-UNCOUNT **Correction** is the punishment of criminals. ❑ *...jails and other parts of the correction system.* ● **cor|rec|tion|al** /kərɛkʃənəl/ ADJ ❑ *He is currently in a city correctional center.* [from Latin] ■ → see also **correct**

**cor|rec|tion|al fa|cil|ity** (**correctional facilities**) N-COUNT A **correctional facility** is a prison or similar institution. ❑ *...the Utah state correctional facility.*

**cor|rec|tions of|fi|cer** (**corrections officers**) N-COUNT A **corrections officer** is someone who works as a guard at a prison.

**cor|rec|tive** /kərɛktɪv/ ADJ **Corrective** measures or techniques are intended to put right something that is wrong. ❑ *...corrective surgery.* [from Latin]

**Word Link**    cor ≈ with : cor**relate**, cor**respond**, cor**roborate**

**cor|re|late** /kɔrəleɪt/ (**correlates, correlating, correlated**) V-RECIP If one thing **correlates with** another, there is a close similarity or connection between them. [FORMAL] ❑ *Cellphone use correlates with age.* [from Medieval Latin]

**cor|re|la|tion** /kɔrəleɪʃən/ (**correlations**) N-COUNT A **correlation between** things is a link between them. [FORMAL] ❑ *...the correlation between exercise and mental health.* [from Medieval Latin]

**cor|re|la|tion|al de|sign** /kɔrəleɪʃənəl dɪzaɪn/ (**correlational designs**) N-VAR Research that has a **correlational design** involves studying the relationship between two or more things.

**cor|re|spond** /kɔrəspɒnd/ (**corresponds, corresponding, corresponded**) ■ V-RECIP If one thing **corresponds to** another, there is a close similarity or connection between them. ❑ *All buttons were clearly numbered to correspond to the chart on the wall* ❑ *The two maps of the Rockies correspond closely.* ● **cor|re|spond|ing** ADJ ❑ *...anger and its corresponding rise in blood pressure.* ● **cor|re|spond|ing|ly** /kɔrɪspɒndɪŋli/ ADV ❑ *As he gets older, he is growing correspondingly more dependent on his daughters.* ■ V-RECIP If you **correspond with** someone, you write letters to them. ❑ *She still corresponds with her American friends.* ❑ *We corresponded regularly.* [from Medieval Latin]

**cor|re|spond|ence** /kɔrɪspɒndəns/ (**correspondences**) ■ N-UNCOUNT; N-SING **Correspondence** is the act of writing letters to someone. ❑ *...a long correspondence with a college friend.* ■ N-UNCOUNT Someone's **correspondence** is the letters that they receive or send. ❑ *He always replied to his correspondence.* ■ N-COUNT If there is a **correspondence between** two things, there is a similarity or connection between them. ❑ *In African languages there is a close correspondence between sounds and letters.* [from Medieval Latin]

**cor|re|spond|ent** /kɔrɪspɒndənt/ (**correspondents**) N-COUNT A **correspondent** is a newspaper or television journalist. ❑ *...White House correspondent for The New Republic magazine.* [from Medieval Latin]

**cor|robo|rate** /kərɒbəreɪt/ (**corroborates, corroborating, corroborated**) V-T To **corroborate** something that has been said means to provide evidence that supports it. [FORMAL] ❑ *...documents which corroborated the story.* ● **cor|robo|ra|tion** /kərɒbəreɪʃən/ N-UNCOUNT ❑ *...independent corroboration.* [from Latin]

**cor|rode** /kəroʊd/ (**corrodes, corroding, corroded**) V-T/V-I If metal or stone **corrodes** or is **corroded**, it is gradually destroyed by a chemical or by rust. ❑ *...gold wires which do not corrode.* ❑ *The structure is being corroded by moisture.* ● **cor|rod|ed** ADJ ❑ *The underground pipes were badly corroded.* ● **cor|ro|sion** /kəroʊʒən/ N-UNCOUNT ❑ *Watch for signs of corrosion.* [from Latin]

C

**cor|ru|gat|ed** /kɔrəgeɪtɪd/ ADJ **Corrugated** metal or cardboard has been folded into a series of small parallel folds to make it stronger. ❑ ...*a hut with a corrugated iron roof.* [from Latin]

**cor|rupt** /kərʌpt/ (**corrupts, corrupting, corrupted**) ◼ ADJ A **corrupt** person behaves in a way that is morally wrong, especially by doing illegal things for money. ❑ ...*corrupt politicians.* ◼ V-T/V-I If someone **is corrupted by** something, it causes them to become dishonest and unable to be trusted. ❑ *He was corrupted by the desire for money.* ❑ *Power corrupts.* [from Latin]

**cor|rup|tion** /kərʌpʃ°n/ N-UNCOUNT **Corruption** is dishonesty and illegal behavior by people in positions of power. ❑ *The president faces charges of corruption.* [from Latin]

**co|sine** /koʊsaɪn/ (**cosines**) N-COUNT A **cosine** is a mathematical calculation that is used especially in the study of triangles. The abbreviation **cos** is also used. [TECHNICAL] [from New Latin]

**cos|met|ic** /kɒzmɛtɪk/ (**cosmetics**) ◼ N-COUNT **Cosmetics** are substances such as lipstick or face powder. ❑ ...*the cosmetics counter of a department store.* ◼ ADJ **Cosmetic** changes are not very effective because they improve the appearance of something without changing its basic character or solving a basic problem. ❑ ...*parts of the building where cosmetic improvements have been made.* [from Greek]
→ see **makeup**

**cos|mic** /kɒzmɪk/ ADJ **Cosmic** means occurring in, or coming from, the part of space that lies outside Earth and its atmosphere. ❑ ...*cosmic radiation.* [from Greek]

**cos|mic back|ground ra|dia|tion** N-UNCOUNT **Cosmic background radiation** is the heat that is present throughout the universe as a result of the original explosion which started the universe.

**cos|mol|ogy** /kɒzmɒlədʒi/ N-UNCOUNT **Cosmology** is the study of the origin and nature of the universe. [from Greek]

> **Word Link** *poli ≈ city : cosmopolitan, metropolis, politics*

**cos|mo|poli|tan** /kɒzməpɒlɪtən/ ADJ **Cosmopolitan** means influenced by many different countries and cultures. ❑ ...*a cosmopolitan city.* [from French]

**cos|mos** /kɒzməs, -moʊs/ N-SING The **cosmos** is the universe. [LITERARY] ❑ ...*the natural laws of the cosmos.* [from Greek]

**cost** /kɔst/ (**costs, costing, cost**) ◼ N-COUNT The **cost of** something is the amount of money that is needed in order to buy, do, or make it. ❑ *The cost of a loaf of bread has increased.* ❑ *The price did not even cover the cost of production.* ◼ V-T If something **costs** a particular amount of money, you can buy, do, or make it for that amount. ❑ *This course is limited to 12 people and costs $150.* ❑ *It's going to cost me over $100,000 to buy new trucks.* ◼ V-T If an event or mistake **costs** you something, you lose that thing as the result of it. ❑ ...*an operation that cost him his sight.* ◼ N-SING The **cost of** something is the loss, damage, or injury that is involved in trying to achieve it. ❑ *He shut down the city's oil refinery at a cost of 5,000 jobs.* ◼ PHRASE If you say that something must be avoided **at all costs**, you

are emphasizing that it must not be allowed to happen under any circumstances. ❑ *A world trade war must be avoided at all costs.* [from Old French]

> **Thesaurus** *cost* Also look up :
>
> | N. | fee, price ◼ |
> | | harm, loss, sacrifice ◼ |

> **Word Partnership** Use *cost* with :
>
> | ADJ. | **additional** costs ◼ |
> | N. | cost **of living** ◼ |
> | V. | **cover the** cost, **cut** costs, **keep** costs **down** ◼ ◼ |

**co|star** /koʊstɑr/ (**costars, costarring, costarred**) ◼ N-COUNT An actor who is a **costar** in a movie has one of the main parts in it. ❑ *Curtis fell in love with his costar.* ◼ V-RECIP If actors **costar** in a particular movie, they have the main parts in it. ❑ *They costarred in the movie "State of Grace."* ❑ ...*a movie in which she costarred with her father.*

**cost-effective** ADJ Something that is **cost-effective** saves or makes more money than it costs to make or run. ❑ *The bank must be run in a cost-effective way.*

**cost|ly** /kɔstli/ (**costlier, costliest**) ADJ Something that is **costly** is very expensive. ❑ *The project could be very costly.* [from Old French]

**cost of liv|ing** N-SING The **cost of living** is the average amount of money that people need to spend on food, housing, and clothing. ❑ *The cost of living has increased dramatically.*

**cos|tume** /kɒstum/ (**costumes**) ◼ N-VAR A **costume** is a set of clothes worn as part of a performance. ❑ *His costume was stunning.* ◼ N-UNCOUNT The clothes worn by people at a particular time in history, or in a particular country, are referred to as a particular type of **costume**. ❑ ...*men and women in eighteenth-century costume.* [from French]
→ see **drama, theater**

**cos|tume par|ty** (**costume parties**) also **costume ball** N-COUNT A **costume party** or **costume ball** is a party at which the guests dress to look like famous people or people from history. ❑ *I went to a costume party a few weeks ago dressed as an angel.*

**cot** /kɒt/ (**cots**) N-COUNT A **cot** is a narrow bed, usually made of canvas fitted over a frame which can be folded up. [from Hindi]

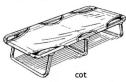
cot

**cot|tage** /kɒtɪdʒ/ (**cottages**) N-COUNT A **cottage** is a small house, usually in the country. ❑ *They have a cottage in Scotland.*

**cot|ton** /kɒt°n/ (**cottons**) ◼ N-VAR **Cotton** is cloth made from the soft fibers of the cotton plant. ❑ ...*a cotton shirt.* ◼ N-UNCOUNT **Cotton** is a plant which produces soft fibers used in making cloth. ❑ ...*a large cotton plantation in Tennessee.* ◼ N-UNCOUNT **Cotton** is a soft mass of cotton, used especially for putting liquids or creams onto your skin. ❑ ...*cotton balls.* [from Old French]

**cot|ton can|dy** N-UNCOUNT **Cotton candy** is a pink or white mass of sugar threads that is eaten from a paper cone.

**cot|ton swab** (**cotton swabs**) N-COUNT A **cotton swab** is the same as a **swab**.

**cotton|tail** /kɒtənteɪl/ (**cottontails**) N-COUNT A **cottontail** is a type of rabbit commonly found in North America.

**coty|ledon** /kɒtəlidən/ (**cotyledons**) N-COUNT A **cotyledon** is the first leaf to grow after a seed germinates, before the proper leaves grow. [TECHNICAL] [from Latin]

**couch** /kaʊtʃ/ (**couches**) N-COUNT A **couch** is a long, comfortable seat for two or three people. [from Old French]

couch

**cou|gar** /kugər/ (**cougars**) N-COUNT A **cougar** is a wild member of the cat family that has brownish-gray fur and lives in mountain regions of North and South America. [from French]

**cough** /kɔf/ (**coughs, coughing, coughed**)
**1** V-I When you **cough**, you force air out of your throat with a sudden, harsh noise. □ *Graham began to cough violently.* ● **Cough** is also a noun. □ *Coughs and sneezes spread infections.* ● **cough|ing** N-UNCOUNT □ *...a terrible fit of coughing.* **2** V-T If you **cough** blood, it comes up out of your throat or mouth when you cough. □ *I started coughing blood.* **3** N-COUNT A **cough** is an illness in which you cough. □ *I had a cough for over a month.* [from Old English]
→ see **illness**
▸ **cough up** **1** PHR-VERB If you **cough up** money, you pay or spend it, usually when you would prefer not to. [INFORMAL] □ *I'll have to cough up $30,000 a year for tuition.* **2** → see also **cough**

**could** /kəd, STRONG kʊd/

Could is a modal verb. It is used with the base form of a verb. **Could** is sometimes considered to be the past form of **can**, but in this dictionary the two words are dealt with separately.

**1** MODAL If you **could** do something, you were able to do it. □ *I could see that something was terribly wrong.* □ *When I left school at 16, I couldn't read or write.* **2** MODAL You use **could** to indicate that something sometimes happened. □ *He could be very pleasant when he wanted to.* **3** MODAL You use **could have** to indicate that something was a possibility in the past, although it did not actually happen. □ *He could have made a lot of money as a lawyer.* **4** MODAL You use **could** to indicate that something is possibly true, or that it may possibly happen. □ *Food which is high in fat could cause health problems.* **5** MODAL You use **could** after "if" when you are imagining what would happen if something was true. □ *If I could afford it I'd have four television sets.* **6** MODAL You use **could** when you are making offers and suggestions. □ *I could call the doctor.* □ *Couldn't we call a special meeting?* **7** MODAL You use **could** in questions to make polite requests. □ *Could I stay tonight?* □ *He asked if he could have a cup of coffee.* [from Old English] **8** **could do with** → see **do** **9** → see also **able**

**couldn't** /kʊdənt/ **Couldn't** is the usual spoken form of "could not."

**could've** /kʊdəv/ **Could've** is the usual spoken form of "could have" when "have" is an auxiliary verb.

**coun|cil** /kaʊnsəl/ (**councils**) N-COUNT A **council** is a group of people who are elected to govern a local area such as a city. □ *The city council has decided to build a new school.* [from Old French]

**coun|ci|lor** /kaʊnsələr/ (**councilors**) N-COUNT; N-TITLE A **councilor** is a member of a local council. □ *...Councilor Michael Poulter.* [from Old French]

**coun|sel** /kaʊnsəl/ (**counsels, counseling** or **counselling, counseled** or **counselled**)
**1** N-UNCOUNT **Counsel** is advice. [FORMAL] □ *If you have a problem, it is a good idea to ask for help and counsel.* **2** V-T If you **counsel** someone to do something, you advise them to do it. [FORMAL] □ *My advisers counseled me to do nothing.* **3** V-T If you **counsel** people, you listen to them talk about their problems and help them to resolve them. □ *She counsels people with eating disorders.* ● **coun|sel|ing** also **counselling** N-UNCOUNT □ *She will need counseling to overcome the tragedy.* ● **coun|se|lor** (**counselors**) also **counsellor** N-COUNT □ *Children who have suffered like this should see a counselor.* **4** N-COUNT Someone's **counsel** is the lawyer who gives advice on a legal case and speaks for them in court. □ *Singleton's counsel said that he would appeal.* [from Old French]

**coun|se|lor** /kaʊnsələr/ (**counselors**) also **counsellor** **1** N-COUNT A **counselor** is a young person who supervises children at a summer camp. □ *Hicks worked with children as a camp counselor.* [from Old French] **2** → see also **counsel**

**count** /kaʊnt/ (**counts, counting, counted**)
**1** V-I When you **count**, you say all the numbers in order up to a particular number. □ *Nancy forced herself to count slowly to five.* **2** V-T If you **count** all the things in a group, you add them up in order to find how many there are. □ *I counted the money.* □ *I counted 34 wild goats grazing.* ● **Count up** means the same as **count**. □ *They counted up all the hours the villagers work.* **3** V-I If something or someone **counts for** something or **counts**, they are important or valuable. □ *It doesn't matter where charities get their money: what counts is what they do with it.* **4** V-I If something **counts as** a particular thing, it is regarded as being that thing. □ *No one agrees on what counts as a desert.* **5** N-COUNT A **count** is the action of counting, or the number that you get after counting. □ *The final count showed 56.7 percent in favor.* **6** N-COUNT; N-TITLE; N-VOC A **count** is a European nobleman. □ *Her father was a Polish count.* **7** PHRASE If you **keep count of** a number of things, you keep a record of how many have occurred. If you **lose count of** a number of things, you cannot remember how many have occurred. □ *Keep count of the number of hours you work.* [Senses 1–5 and 7 from Anglo-French. Sense 6 from Old French.]
→ see **mathematics, zero**
▸ **count against** PHR-VERB If something **counts against** you, it may cause you to be rejected or punished. □ *His youth might count against him.*
▸ **count on** or **count upon** PHR-VERB If you **count on** someone or something, you rely on them to support you. □ *They did not know how much support they could count on.*

▶ **count out** PHR-VERB If you **count out** a sum of money, you count the bills or coins as you put them in a pile one by one. ❑ *Mr. Rohmbauer counted out the money.*

▶ **count up** → see **count 2**

▶ **count upon** → see **count on**

**count|able noun** /ka͟ʊntəbᵊl na͟ʊn/ (**countable nouns**) N-COUNT A **countable noun** is the same as a **count noun**.

**count|down** /ka͟ʊntda͟ʊn/ N-SING A **countdown** is the counting aloud of numbers in reverse order before something happens. ❑ *The countdown has begun for the launch of the space shuttle.*

**coun|te|nance** /ka͟ʊntɪnəns/ (**countenances, countenancing, countenanced**) **1** V-T If someone will not **countenance** something, they do not agree with it and will not allow it to happen. [FORMAL] ❑ *Jake would not countenance Janis's marrying Frank.* **2** N-COUNT Someone's **countenance** is their face. [FORMAL] [from Old French]

**coun|ter** /ka͟ʊntər/ (**counters, countering, countered**) **1** N-COUNT In a store or café, a **counter** is a long flat surface at which customers are served. ❑ *...guys working behind the counter at our local DVD rental store.* **2** N-COUNT A **counter** is a device which keeps a count of something. ❑ *The new answering machine has a call counter.* **3** N-COUNT A **counter** is a very small object used in board games. ❑ *...boards and counters for fifteen different games.* **4** V-T/V-I If you **counter** something that is being done, you take action to make it less effective. ❑ *...more police officers to counter the increase in crime.* ❑ *He countered by filing a lawsuit.* **5** N-SING If something is **counter to** something else, it is the opposite. ❑ *It was counter to what I believed in.* [from Old French]

**counter|act** /ka͟ʊntəræ̱kt/ (**counteracts, counteracting, counteracted**) V-T To **counteract** something means to reduce its effect by doing something that produces an opposite effect. ❑ *...pills to counteract high blood pressure.*

**counter|at|tack** /ka͟ʊntərətæ̱k/ (**counterattacks, counterattacking, counterattacked**) V-I If you **counterattack**, you attack someone who has attacked you. ❑ *The security forces counterattacked the following day.* ● **Counterattack** is also a noun. ❑ *The army began its counterattack this morning.*

**counter|bal|ance** /ka͟ʊntərbæ̱ləns/ (**counterbalances**) N-COUNT A **counterbalance** is a weight that balances another weight.

**counter|clockwise** /ka͟ʊntərklɒ̱kwaɪz/ ADV If something is moving **counterclockwise**, it is moving in a circle in the opposite direction to the hands of a clock. ❑ *Winds blow counterclockwise around storm centers.*

**counter clockwise**

● **Counterclockwise** is also an adjective. ❑ *The dance moves in a counterclockwise direction.*

**counter|feit** /ka͟ʊntərfɪt/ (**counterfeits, counterfeiting, counterfeited**) **1** ADJ **Counterfeit** money, goods, or documents are not genuine, but have been made to look exactly like genuine ones in order to deceive people. ❑ *He admitted using*

counterfeit currency. ● **Counterfeit** is also a noun. ❑ *Counterfeits of the company's jeans are flooding Europe.* **2** V-T To **counterfeit** something means to make a counterfeit version of it. ❑ *Davies was accused of counterfeiting the coins.* [from Old French]

**counter|of|fer** /ka͟ʊntərɔfər/ (**counteroffers**) N-COUNT A **counteroffer** is an offer that someone makes in response to an offer by another person or group. ❑ *Many would welcome a counteroffer from a foreign bidder.*

**counter|part** /ka͟ʊntərpɑrt/ (**counterparts**) N-COUNT Someone's or something's **counterpart** is another person or thing that has a similar function in a different place. ❑ *The Foreign Secretary telephoned his German and Italian counterparts.*

**counter|pro|duc|tive** /ka͟ʊntərprədʌ̱ktɪv/ ADJ Something that is **counterproductive** achieves the opposite result from what you intended. ❑ *In practice, such an attitude is counterproductive.*

**counter|top** /ka͟ʊntərtɒp/ (**countertops**) N-COUNT A **countertop** is a flat surface in a kitchen on which you can prepare food.

**coun|tess** /ka͟ʊntɪs/ (**countesses**) N-COUNT; N-TITLE; N-VOC A **countess** is a female member of the European nobility. ❑ *...the Countess of Lichfield.* [from Old French]

**count|less** /ka͟ʊntlɪs/ ADJ **Countless** means very many. ❑ *She made countless people happy through her music.* [from Old French]

**count noun** (**count nouns**) N-COUNT A **count noun** is a noun such as "bird," "chair," or "year" which has a singular and a plural form and is always used after a determiner in the singular.

**coun|try** /kʌ̱ntri/ (**countries**) **1** N-COUNT A **country** is one of the political units which the world is divided into, covering a particular area of land. ❑ *This is the greatest country in the world.* ❑ *...the border between the two countries.* **2** N-SING **The country** is land that is away from cities and towns. ❑ *...a healthy life in the country.* ❑ *She was cycling along a country road.* **3** N-UNCOUNT A particular kind of **country** is an area of land which has particular characteristics. ❑ *...mountainous country.* **4** N-UNCOUNT **Country** music is a style of popular music from the southern United States. ❑ *I just wanted to play country music.* [from Old French]

→ see Word Web: **country**

**country|man** /kʌ̱ntrimən/ (**countrymen**) N-COUNT Your **countrymen** are people from your own country. ❑ *He beat his fellow countryman, Agassi.*

**country|side** /kʌ̱ntrisaɪd/ N-UNCOUNT The **countryside** is land that is away from cities and towns. ❑ *I've always loved the English countryside.* → see **city**

**coun|ty** /ka͟ʊnti/ (**counties**) N-COUNT A **county** is a region of the U.S., Britain, or Ireland, which has its own local government. ❑ *...Palm Beach County.* [from Old French]

**coup** /ku̱/ (**coups**) **1** N-COUNT When there is a **coup**, a group of people seize power in a country. ❑ *...a military coup.* **2** N-COUNT A **coup** is an achievement which is thought to be especially good because it was very difficult. ❑ *The sale is a big coup for them.* [from French]

**coup d'état** /ku̱ deɪtɑ̱/ (**coups d'état**) N-COUNT → see **coup**

C

C

### Word Web country

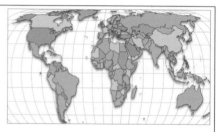

The largest **country** in the world geographically is Russia. It has an area of six million square miles and a **population** of more than 142 million people. Russia is a federal state with a republican form of **government**. The government is based in Russia's **capital** city, Moscow.

One of the smallest countries in the world is Nauru. This tiny island **nation** in the South Pacific Ocean is 8.1 square miles in size. Many of Nauru's more than 13,000 **residents** live in Yaren, which is the largest city, but not the capital. The Republic of Nauru is the only nation in the world without an official capital.

**cou|ple** /kʌpᵊl/ (couples, coupling, coupled) ■ QUANT If you refer to **a couple of** people or things, you mean two or approximately two of them. ❑ *There are a couple of police officers outside.* ❑ *I think the trouble will clear up in a couple of days.* ● **Couple** is also a determiner in spoken American English. ❑ *...a couple weeks before the election.* ● **Couple** is also a pronoun. ❑ *I've got a couple that don't look too bad.* ② N-COUNT A **couple** is two people who are married or having a sexual or romantic relationship. ❑ *The couple have no children.* ❑ *Burglars broke into an elderly couple's home.* ③ N-COUNT A **couple** is two people that you see together on a particular occasion or that have some association. ❑ *The four couples began the opening dance.* ④ V-T If one thing produces a particular effect when it **is coupled with** another, the two things combine to produce that effect. ❑ *High temperatures coupled with strong winds can mean fire danger.* [from Old French]

**cou|pon** /kupɒn, kyu-/ (coupons) ■ N-COUNT A **coupon** is a piece of printed paper which allows you to pay less money than usual for a product, or to get it free. ❑ *...a money-saving coupon.* ② N-COUNT A **coupon** is a small form which you send off to ask for information, to order something, or to enter a competition. ❑ *Mail this coupon with your check.* [from French]

### Word Link age ≈ state of, related to : courage, marriage, percentage

**cour|age** /kɜrɪdʒ/ ■ N-UNCOUNT **Courage** is the quality shown by someone who does something difficult or dangerous, even though they may be afraid. ❑ *The girl had the courage to tell the police.* [from Old French] ② to **pluck up the courage** → see **pluck**

**cou|ra|geous** /kəreɪdʒəs/ ADJ Someone who is **courageous** shows courage. ❑ *The children were very courageous.* [from Old French]

**cou|ri|er** /kuəriər, kɜr-/ (couriers, couriering, couriered) ■ N-COUNT A **courier** is a person who is paid to take letters and packages direct from one place to another. ❑ *...a motorcycle courier.* ② V-T If you **courier** something somewhere, you send it there by courier. ❑ *I couriered it to Darren in New York.* [from Old French]

**course** /kɔrs/ (courses) ■ **Course** is often used in the expression "of course," or instead of "of course" in informal spoken English. See **of**

**course.** ② N-UNCOUNT; N-SING The **course** of a vehicle is the route along which it is traveling. ❑ *Aircraft can avoid each other by altering course.* ③ N-COUNT A **course of** action is an action or a series of actions that you can take in a particular situation. ❑ *My best course of action was to help Gill.* ④ N-COUNT A **course** is a series of lessons or lectures on a particular subject. ❑ *...a course in business administration.* ⑤ N-COUNT A **course of** medical treatment is a series of treatments that a doctor gives someone. ❑ *...a course of antibiotics.* ⑥ N-COUNT A **course** is one part of a meal. ❑ *Lunch was excellent, especially the first course.* ⑦ N-COUNT In sports, a **course** is an area of land where races are held or golf is played. ❑ *Only 12 seconds separated the first three riders on the course.* ⑧ **in due course** → see **due** ⑨ PHRASE If you are **on course for** something, you are likely to achieve it. ❑ *The company is on course for profits of $20 million.* [from Old French]

### court

❶ NOUN USES
❷ VERB USES

**❶ court** /kɔrt/ (courts) ■ N-COUNT A **court** is a place where legal matters are decided by a judge and jury or by a magistrate. You can also refer to a judge, jury, or magistrates as a **court**. ❑ *Would she be willing to testify in court?* ❑ *The court awarded the man one and a half million dollars.* ② N-COUNT A **court** is an area for playing a game such as tennis or squash. ❑ *The hotel has several tennis courts.* ③ N-COUNT The **court** of a king or queen is the place where he or she lives and carries out duties. ❑ *...the court of James I.* ④ PHRASE Your **day in court** is your chance to give your side of an argument. ❑ *All we wanted was our day in court.* [from Old French] → see **park**

**❷ court** /kɔrt/ (courts, courting, courted) ■ V-T If you **court** something such as publicity or popularity, you try to attract it. ❑ *He spent a lifetime courting publicity.* ② V-T If you **court** disaster, you act in a way that makes it likely to happen. ❑ *I knew I was courting disaster in asking her to stay.* [from Old French]

**cour|teous** /kɜrtiəs/ ADJ Someone who is **courteous** is polite and respectful. ❑ *He was a kind and courteous man.* ● **cour|teous|ly** ADV ❑ *He nodded courteously to me.* [from Old French]

**cour|tesy** /kɜrtɪsi/ (**courtesies**) **1** N-UNCOUNT **Courtesy** is politeness, respect, and consideration for others. [FORMAL] ❑ ...*a gentleman who always behaves with courtesy.* **2** N-COUNT A **courtesy** is something polite and respectful that you say or do. [FORMAL] ❑ *I wanted to give you the courtesy of returning your call.* **3** ADJ **Courtesy** is used to describe services that are provided free of charge by an organization to its customers, or to the general public. ❑ *A courtesy shuttle bus operates between the hotel and the town.* [from Old French]

**court|house** /kɔrthaʊs/ (**courthouses**) **1** N-COUNT A **courthouse** is a building in which a court of law meets. **2** N-COUNT A **courthouse** is a building used by the government of a county. ❑ *They were married at the Los Angeles County Courthouse.*

**court|ier** /kɔrtiər/ (**courtiers**) N-COUNT **Courtiers** were members of the nobility who spent a lot of time at the court of a king or queen. [from Old French]

**Court of Ap|peals** (**Courts of Appeals**) N-COUNT A **Court of Appeals** is a court which deals with appeals against legal judgments. ❑ ...*the Oregon Court of Appeals.*

**court|room** /kɔrtrum/ (**courtrooms**) N-COUNT A **courtroom** is a room in which a law court meets.

**court|yard** /kɔrtyɑrd/ (**courtyards**) N-COUNT A **courtyard** is an open area of ground which is surrounded by buildings or walls. ❑ *They walked into the courtyard.* [from Old French]

**cous|in** /kʌzªn/ (**cousins**) N-COUNT Your **cousin** is the child of your uncle or aunt. ❑ *My cousin Mark helped me to bring in the bags.* [from Old French]

**co|va|lent bond** /koʊveɪlənt bɒnd/ (**covalent bonds**) N-COUNT A **covalent bond** is the force that holds together two atoms that share a pair of electrons. [TECHNICAL]

**co|va|lent com|pound** /koʊveɪlənt kɒmpaʊnd/ (**covalent compounds**) N-COUNT A **covalent compound** is a chemical compound made of molecules in which the atoms are held together by covalent bonds. [TECHNICAL]

**cove** /koʊv/ (**coves**) N-COUNT A **cove** is a small bay on the coast. [from Old English]

**cov|enant** /kʌvənənt/ (**covenants**) N-COUNT A **covenant** is a formal written agreement between two or more people or groups of people which is recognized in law. ❑ ...*the International Covenant on Civil and Political Rights.* [from Old French]

---

**cover**

❶ VERB USES
❷ NOUN USES

---

❶ **cov|er** /kʌvər/ (**covers, covering, covered**) **1** V-T If you **cover** something, you place something else over it in order to protect it, hide it, or close it. ❑ *Cover the dish with a tight-fitting lid.* ❑ *A black patch covered his left eye.* **2** V-T If one thing **covers** another, it forms a layer over its surface. ❑ *The clouds had spread and covered the entire sky.* ❑ *The desk was covered with papers.* **3** V-T If you **cover** a particular distance, you travel that distance. ❑ *It would not be easy to cover ten miles on that amount of gas.* **4** V-T An insurance policy that **covers** a person or thing guarantees that money

will be paid by the insurance company in relation to that person or thing. ❑ *Our insurance does not cover damage caused by floods.* **5** V-T If you **cover** a particular topic, you discuss it in a lecture, course, or book. ❑ *Introduction to Chemistry aims to cover the main topics in chemistry.* **6** V-T If a sum of money **covers** something, it is enough to pay for it. ❑ *Send $2.50 to cover postage.* [from Old French]
▶ **cover up 1** PHR-VERB If you **cover** something or someone **up**, you put something over them in order to protect or hide them. ❑ *I covered him up with a blanket.* **2** PHR-VERB If you **cover up** something that you do not want people to know about, you hide the truth about it. ❑ *They tried to cover up the crime.* ❑ *They knew they did something terribly wrong and lied to cover it up.* **3** → see also **cover-up**

❷ **cov|er** /kʌvər/ (**covers**) **1** N-COUNT A **cover** is something which is put over an object, usually in order to protect it. ❑ ...*a sofa with washable covers.* **2** N-COUNT The **cover** of a book or a magazine is the outside part of it. ❑ ...*a small book with a green cover.* **3** N-UNCOUNT **Cover** is trees, rocks, or other things that give protection from the weather or from an attack. ❑ *The rain started and they ran for cover.* **4** N-PLURAL Bed **covers** are sheets, blankets, and comforters. ❑ *She slid under the covers.* [from Old French] **5** → see also **covering**

**cov|er|age** /kʌvərɪdʒ/ **1** N-UNCOUNT The **coverage** of something in the news is the reporting of it. ❑ *A special TV network gives live coverage of most races.* **2** N-UNCOUNT **Coverage** is a guarantee from an insurance company that money will be paid by them in particular situations. ❑ *Make sure that your insurance coverage is adequate.* [from Old French]

**cover|alls** /kʌvərɔlz/ N-PLURAL **Coveralls** are a single piece of clothing that combines pants and a jacket, worn over your clothes to protect them. ❑ ...*a man in white coveralls.*

**cov|er|ing** /kʌvərɪŋ/ (**coverings**) N-COUNT A **covering** is a layer of something that protects or hides something else. ❑ ...*a light covering of snow.* [from Old French]

**cov|er let|ter** (**cover letters**) N-COUNT A **cover letter** is a letter that you send with something else in order to provide information about it.

**cov|ert** /koʊvɜrt, kʌvərt/ ADJ **Covert** activities or situations are secret or hidden. [FORMAL] ❑ *A covert radio station broadcast news across the border.* • **cov|ert|ly** ADV ❑ *They covertly observed Lauren.* [from Old French]

**cover-up** (**cover-ups**) also **coverup** N-COUNT A **cover-up** is an attempt to hide a crime or mistake. ❑ *The general denied there was a cover-up.*

**cov|et** /kʌvɪt/ (**covets, coveting, coveted**) V-T If you **covet** something, you strongly want to have it for yourself. [FORMAL] ❑ *She openly coveted his job.* [from Old French]

**cov|et|ed** /k**ʌ**vɪtɪd/ ADJ You use **coveted** to describe something that very many people would like to have. ❑ *...the coveted title of reporter of the year.* ❑ *...one of sport's most coveted prizes.* [from Old French]

**cow** /ka**ʊ**/ (**cows, cowing, cowed**) ◼ N-COUNT A **cow** is a large female animal that is kept on farms for its milk. ❑ *He kept a few dairy cows.* ❑ *Dad went out to milk the cows.* ◢ N-COUNT Some female animals, including elephants and whales, are called **cows**. ❑ *...a cow elephant.* ◣ V-T If someone **is cowed**, they are made to behave in a particular way because they have been frightened. [FORMAL] ❑ *The government was not cowed by these threats.* ● **cowed** ADJ ❑ *She was so cowed that she obeyed at once.* [Senses 1 and 2 from Old English. Sense 3 from Old Norse.]
→ see **dairy, meat**

**cow|ard** /ka**ʊ**ərd/ (**cowards**) N-COUNT A **coward** is someone who is easily frightened and avoids dangerous or difficult situations. ❑ *She accused her husband of being a coward.* [from Old French]

**cow|ard|ice** /ka**ʊ**ərdɪs/ N-UNCOUNT **Cowardice** is cowardly behavior. ❑ *He accused his opponents of cowardice.* [from Old French]

**cow|ard|ly** /ka**ʊ**ərdli/ ADJ Someone who is **cowardly** is easily frightened and avoids doing dangerous and difficult things; used showing disapproval. ❑ *I was too cowardly to complain.* [from Old French]

**cow|boy** /ka**ʊ**bɔɪ/ (**cowboys**) ◼ N-COUNT A **cowboy** is a male character in a western. ❑ *...cowboy movies.* ◢ N-COUNT A **cowboy** is a man employed to look after cattle in North America, especially in former times.
→ see **hat**

**cow|boy boots** N-PLURAL **Cowboy boots** are high leather boots, similar to those worn by cowboys. ❑ *He showed up in jeans and cowboy boots.*

**coy** /kɔɪ/ ◼ ADJ If you describe someone as **coy**, you disapprove of them for pretending to be shy and modest in order to attract attention. ❑ *Carol charmed all the men by turning coy.* ● **coy|ly** ADV ❑ *She smiled coyly at Algie.* ◢ ADJ If someone is being **coy**, they are unwilling to talk about something that they feel guilty or embarrassed about. ❑ *Mr. Alexander is not the slightest bit coy about his ambitions.* ● **coy|ly** ADV ❑ *The administration coyly refused to put a price tag on the war's costs.* [from Old French]

**cozy** /ko**ʊ**zi/ (**cozier, coziest**) ◼ ADJ A **cozy** house or room is comfortable and warm. ❑ *Guests can relax in the cozy lounge.* ◢ ADJ You use **cozy** to describe activities that are pleasant and friendly. ❑ *...a cozy chat between friends.* [from Scots]

**CPA** /si pi e**ɪ**/ (**CPAs**) N-COUNT **CPA** is an abbreviation for **certified public accountant.** [AM] ❑ *He is a CPA in both New York and New Jersey.*

**CPI** /si pi a**ɪ**/ N-SING **CPI** is an abbreviation for **consumer price index.** ❑ *The CPI was up 6/10 of a percent in October.*

**CPR** /si pi ɑr/ N-UNCOUNT **CPR** is a medical technique for reviving someone whose heart has stopped beating by pressing on their chest and breathing into their mouth. **CPR** is an abbreviation for "cardiopulmonary resuscitation."

[MEDICAL] ❑ *Robert McMullen performed CPR while someone called 911 on their cellphone.*

**crab** /kræb/ (**crabs**) ◼ N-COUNT A **crab** is a sea creature with a flat round body covered by a shell, and five pairs of legs with large claws on the front pair. Crabs usually move sideways. ● **Crab** is the flesh of this creature eaten as food. ❑ *I can't remember when I last had crab.* [from Old English]
→ see **shellfish**

---

### crack
❶ VERB USES
❷ NOUN AND ADJECTIVE USES

---

❶ **crack** /kræk/ (**cracks, cracking, cracked**) ◼ V-T/V-I If something hard **cracks**, or if you **crack** it, it becomes slightly damaged, with lines appearing on its surface. ❑ *A gas pipe cracked and gas leaked into our homes.* ❑ *...a cracked mirror.* ◢ V-T When you **crack** something hard, you hit it and it breaks or is damaged. ❑ *Crack the eggs into a bowl.* ❑ *He cracked his head on the pavement.* ◣ V-T If you **crack** a problem or a code, you solve it, especially after a lot of thought. ❑ *He has finally cracked the system after years of research.* ◤ V-I If someone **cracks**, they lose control of their emotions or actions because they are under a lot of pressure. [INFORMAL] ❑ *She's calm and strong, and she is just not going to crack.* ◥ V-I If your voice **cracks** when you are speaking or singing, it changes in pitch because you are feeling a strong emotion. ❑ *Her voice cracked and she began to cry.* ◙ V-T If you **crack** a joke, you tell it. ❑ *He cracked jokes, and talked about girls.* [from Old English]
→ see **crack**

▶ **crack down** ◼ PHR-VERB If people in authority **crack down** on a group of people, they become stricter in making them obey rules or laws. ❑ *Police are cracking down on people who ride their bikes on the sidewalk.* ◢ → see also **crackdown**

▶ **crack up** PHR-VERB If someone **cracks up**, they are under such emotional strain that they become mentally ill. [INFORMAL] ❑ *She'll crack up if she doesn't have some fun.*

❷ **crack** /kræk/ (**cracks**) ◼ N-COUNT A **crack** is a very narrow gap between two things. ❑ *Kathryn saw him through a crack in the curtains.* ◢ N-COUNT A **crack** is a line that appears on the surface of something when it is slightly damaged. ❑ *The plate had a crack in it.* ◣ N-COUNT A **crack** is a sharp sound, like the sound of a piece of wood breaking. ❑ *Suddenly there was a loud crack and glass flew into the car.* ◤ ADJ A **crack** soldier or sportsman is highly trained and very skillful. ❑ *...a crack police officer.* ◥ N-COUNT A **crack** is a slightly rude or cruel joke. ❑ *Tell Tracy you're sorry for that crack about her weight.* ◙ N-UNCOUNT **Crack** is a very pure form of the drug **cocaine.** [from Old English]

---

### Word Partnership  Use *crack* with :

| | |
|---|---|
| ADJ. | crack **open** ❶ ◼ |
| N. | crack **a code**, crack **the system** ❶ ◣ |
| | crack **jokes** ❶ ◙ |
| ADJ. | **deep** crack ❷ ◼ ◢ |
| V. | **have a** crack ❷ ◼ ◢ |

---

**crack|down** /krækda**ʊ**n/ (**crackdowns**) N-COUNT A **crackdown** is strong official action that is taken to punish people who break laws.

❏ *The unrest ended with a violent crackdown.*

**crack|er** /krǽkər/ (**crackers**) N-COUNT A **cracker** is a thin, crisp piece of baked bread which is often eaten with cheese. [from Old English]

**crack|le** /krǽkᵊl/ (**crackles, crackling, crackled**) V-I If something **crackles**, it makes a series of short, harsh noises. ❏ *The radio crackled again.* ● **Crackle** is also a noun. ❏ *…the crackle of flames.* [from Old English]

**crack-up** (**crack-ups**) ◼ N-COUNT A **crack-up** is a mental breakdown. [INFORMAL] ❏ *You're clearly having some kind of a crack-up.* ◼ N-COUNT A **crack-up** is a motor vehicle accident. [INFORMAL] ❏ *In one recent crack-up, two drivers survived with only minor injury.*

cradle

**cra|dle** /kréɪdᵊl/ (**cradles, cradling, cradled**) ◼ N-COUNT A **cradle** is a baby's small bed with high sides, which can be rocked from side to side. ◼ V-T If you **cradle** someone or something in your arms, you hold them carefully and gently. ❏ *I cradled her in my arms.* [from Old English]

**craft** /kræft/ (**crafts, crafting, crafted**)

> **Craft** is both the singular and the plural form for meaning ◼.

◼ N-COUNT You can refer to a boat, a spacecraft, or an aircraft as a **craft**. ❏ *The fisherman guided his small craft close to the shore.* ◼ N-COUNT A **craft** is an activity such as weaving, carving, or pottery that involves making things skillfully with your hands. ❏ *…the crafts of the people of Oceania.* ◼ V-T If something **is crafted**, it is made skillfully. ❏ *The windows were probably crafted in the late Middle Ages.* [from Old English]
→ see **fly, ship**

**crafts|man** /kræftsmən/ (**craftsmen**) N-COUNT A **craftsman** is a man who makes things skillfully with his hands. ❏ *The table in the kitchen was made by a local craftsman.*

**crafts|man|ship** /kræftsmənʃɪp/ N-UNCOUNT **Craftsmanship** is the skill that someone uses when they make beautiful things with their hands. ❏ *…good materials and fine craftsmanship.*

**crafty** /kræfti/ (**craftier, craftiest**) ADJ If you describe someone as **crafty**, you mean that they achieve what they want in a clever way, often by deceiving people. ❏ *…a crafty, lying character.* [from Old English]

**cram** /kræm/ (**crams, cramming, crammed**) V-T/V-I If you **cram** things or people **into** a container or place, or if they **cram into** it, there are so many of them in it at one time that it is completely full. ❏ *Terry crammed the dirty clothes into his bag.* ❏ *She crammed her mouth with cake.* ❏ *We crammed into my car and set off.* [from Old English]

**crammed** /kræmd/ ADJ If a place is **crammed with** things or people, it is full of them, so that there is hardly room for anything or anyone else. ❏ *The house is crammed with antiques.* [from Old English]

**cramp** /kræmp/ (**cramps**) N-VAR A **cramp** is a sudden strong pain caused by a muscle suddenly contracting. ❏ *He had a cramp in his leg.* [from Old French]

**cramped** /kræmpt/ ADJ A **cramped** room or building is not big enough for the people or things in it. ❏ *…families living in cramped conditions.* [from Old French]

crane

**crane** /kreɪn/ (**cranes, craning, craned**) ◼ N-COUNT A **crane** is a large machine that moves heavy things by lifting them in the air. ❏ *…a huge crane.* ◼ N-COUNT A **crane** is a kind of large bird with a long neck and long legs. ◼ V-T If you **crane** your neck or head, you stretch your neck in a particular direction in order to see or hear something better. ❏ *She craned her neck to get a better view.* [from Old English]

**crank** /kræŋk/ (**cranks, cranking, cranked**) ◼ N-COUNT If you call someone a **crank**, you think their ideas or behavior are strange. [INFORMAL] ❏ *Everyone thought he was a crank.* ◼ V-T If you **crank** an engine or machine, you make it move by turning a handle. ❏ *The driver got out to crank the motor.* [from Old English]

**cranky** /krǽŋki/ ADJ **Cranky** means bad-tempered. [INFORMAL] ❏ *Jack and I both started to get cranky.*

**crap|shoot** /krǽpʃut/ N-SING If you describe something as a **crapshoot**, you mean that what happens depends entirely on luck or chance. ❏ *Is buying a computer always a crapshoot?*

**crash** /kræʃ/ (**crashes, crashing, crashed**) ◼ N-COUNT A **crash** is an accident in which a moving vehicle hits something and is damaged or destroyed. ❏ *His elder son was killed in a car crash.* ◼ N-COUNT A **crash** is a sudden, loud noise. ❏ *Two people recalled hearing a loud crash about 1:30 a.m.* ◼ V-T/V-I If a moving vehicle **crashes** or if the driver **crashes** it, it hits something and is damaged or destroyed. ❏ *The plane crashed mysteriously.* ❏ *Her car crashed into the rear of a van.* ◼ V-I To **crash** means to move or fall violently, making a loud noise. ❏ *The walls above us crashed down.* ◼ V-I If a business or financial system **crashes**, it fails suddenly, often with serious effects. [BUSINESS] ❏ *When the market crashed, the deal was canceled.* ● **Crash** is also a noun. ❏ *…a stock market crash.* ◼ V-I If a computer or a computer program **crashes**, it fails suddenly. ❏ *My computer crashed for the second time in 10 days.*
→ see Word Web: **crash**

| Thesaurus | crash | Also look up : |
|---|---|---|
| N. | collision, wreck ◼ | |
| | bang ◼ | |
| | collide, hit, smash ◼ | |
| V. | fail ◼ ◼ | |

**crass** /kræs/ (**crasser, crassest**) ADJ **Crass** behavior is stupid and does not show consideration for other people. ❏ *The government has behaved with crass insensitivity.* [from Latin]

**crate** /kreɪt/ (**crates**) N-COUNT A **crate** is a large box used for transporting or storing things. ❏ *…a pile of wooden crates.* [from Latin]

---

**Word Web**   crash

Every year the National Highway Traffic Safety Administration* conducts crash tests on new cars. They evaluate exactly what happens during an accident. How fast do you have to be going to **buckle** a bumper during a collision? Does the gas tank **rupture**? Do the tires **burst**? What happens when the windshield **breaks**? Does it **crack**, or does it **shatter** into a thousand pieces? Does the force of the **impact crush** the front of the car completely? This is actually a good thing. It means that the engine and hood would protect the passengers during the crash.

*National Highway Traffic Safety Administration: a U.S. government agency that sets safety standards.*

---

**cra|ter** /kreɪtər/ (**craters**) N-COUNT A **crater** is a very large hole in the ground, which has been caused by something hitting it or by an explosion. ❑ *The bomb left a ten foot crater in the street.* [from Latin]
→ see **astronomer, lake, meteor, moon, solar system**

crater

**crave** /kreɪv/ (**craves, craving, craved**) V-T If you **crave** something, you want to have it very much. ❑ *...an unhappy girl who craves affection.* ● **crav|ing** (**cravings**) N-COUNT ❑ *...a craving for sugar.* [from Old English]

**craw|fish** /krɔfɪʃ/ (**crawfish**) N-COUNT A **crawfish** is a small shellfish with five pairs of legs which lives in rivers and streams. [from Old French]
→ see **shellfish**

**crawl** /krɔl/ (**crawls, crawling, crawled**) **1** V-I When you **crawl**, you move forward on your hands and knees. ❑ *Don't worry if your baby seems a little slow to crawl.* ❑ *I began to crawl on my hands and knees toward the door.* **2** V-I If something or someone **crawls** somewhere, they move there slowly. ❑ *He crawled from the car after the accident.* ● **Crawl** is also a noun. ❑ *The traffic slowed to a crawl.* **3** V-I If you say that a place **is crawling** with people or things, you are emphasizing that it is full of them. [INFORMAL] ❑ *This place is crawling with police.* **4** N-SING The **crawl** is a kind of swimming stroke which you do lying on your front, swinging one arm over your head, and then the other arm. ❑ *I did 50 lengths of the crawl.* [from Old Norse]

crawl

**crawl space** (**crawl spaces**) N-COUNT A **crawl space** is a narrow space under the roof or floor of a building that provides access to the wiring or plumbing. ❑ *...a crawl space between the basement and the kitchen.*

**cray|on** /kreɪɒn/ (**crayons**) N-COUNT A **crayon** is a stick of colored wax used for drawing. [from French]

**craze** /kreɪz/ (**crazes**) N-COUNT If there is a **craze** for something, it is very popular for a short time. ❑ *...the latest fitness craze.* [of Scandinavian origin]

**crazed** /kreɪzd/ ADJ **Crazed** people are wild and uncontrolled, and perhaps insane. [WRITTEN] ❑ *He was crazed with shock.* [of Scandinavian origin]

**cra|zy** /kreɪzi/ (**crazier, craziest, crazies**) **1** ADJ If you describe someone or something as **crazy**, you think they are very foolish or strange. [INFORMAL] ❑ *People thought they were crazy.* ● **cra|zi|ly** ADV ❑ *...a flock of sheep running crazily in every direction.* **2** ADJ Someone who is **crazy** is insane. [INFORMAL] ❑ *If I sat home and worried about all this stuff, I'd go crazy.* ● **Crazy** is also a noun. ❑ *...one of New York's crazies.* **3** ADJ If you are **crazy about** something, you are very enthusiastic about it. If you are **crazy about** someone, you are deeply in love with them. [INFORMAL] ❑ *He's still crazy about his work.* ❑ *We're crazy about each other.* [of Scandinavian origin]

**creak** /krik/ (**creaks, creaking, creaked**) V-I If something **creaks**, it makes a short, high-pitched sound when it moves. ❑ *The steps creaked beneath his feet.* ❑ *The bed creaked when she turned over.* ● **Creak** is also a noun. ❑ *The door was pulled open with a creak.*

**cream** /krim/ (**creams**) **1** N-UNCOUNT **Cream** is a thick liquid that is produced from milk. You can use it in cooking or put it on fruit or desserts. ❑ *...strawberries and cream.* **2** N-VAR A **cream** is a substance that you rub onto your skin, for example, to keep it soft or to heal or protect it. ❑ *Gently apply the cream to the skin.* **3** COLOR Something that is **cream** is yellowish-white in color. ❑ *...a cream silk shirt.* [from Old French] **4** → see also **ice cream**

**cream|er** /krimər/ (**creamers**) N-COUNT A **creamer** is a small pitcher used for pouring cream or milk. [from Old French]
→ see **dish**

**creamy** /krimi/ (**creamier, creamiest**) **1** ADJ Food or drink that is **creamy** contains a lot of cream or milk. ❑ *...rich, creamy coffee.* **2** ADJ Food that is **creamy** has a soft smooth texture and appearance. ❑ *...creamy mashed potato.* [from Old French]

**crease** /kris/ (**creases, creasing, creased**) **1** N-COUNT **Creases** are lines that are made in cloth or paper when it is crushed or folded. ❑ *...pants with sharp creases.* **2** N-COUNT **Creases**

in your skin are lines which form where your skin folds when you move. ❏ ...*the tiny creases at the corners of his eyes.* ● **creased** ADJ ❏ *Sweat poured down her deeply creased face.* ❸ V-T/V-I If cloth or paper **creases** or if you **crease** it, lines form in it when it is crushed or folded. ❏ *Most clothes crease a bit when you are traveling.* ● **creased** ADJ ❏ *His clothes were creased.* [from Old French]

| Word Link | ator ≈ one who does : creator, narrator, translator |
| --- | --- |

**cre|ate** /kri**eɪ**t/ (**creates, creating, created**) V-T To **create** something means to cause it to happen or exist. ❏ *It is really great for a radio producer to create a show like this.* ❏ *She could create a fight out of anything.* ● **crea|tion** /kri**eɪ**ʃᵊn/ N-UNCOUNT ❏ ...*the creation of local jobs.* ● **crea|tor** /kri**eɪ**tər/ (**creators**) N-COUNT ❏ ...*Ian Fleming, the creator of James Bond.* [from Latin]

| Thesaurus | create | Also look up : |
| --- | --- | --- |
| v. | produce, make; (*ant.*) destroy | |

| Word Link | creat ≈ making : creation, creature, recreate |
| --- | --- |

**crea|tion** /kri**eɪ**ʃᵊn/ (**creations**) ❶ N-UNCOUNT In many religions, **creation** is the making of the universe, earth, and creatures by God. ❏ ...*the Creation of the universe as told in Genesis Chapter One.* ❷ N-COUNT You can refer to something that someone has made as a **creation**. ❏ *The bathroom is entirely my own creation.* [from Latin] ❸ → see also **create**

**crea|tive** /kri**eɪ**tɪv/ ❶ ADJ A **creative** person has the ability to invent and develop original ideas, especially in the arts. ❏ *Like many creative people, he was never satisfied.* ● **crea|tiv|ity** /kri**eɪ**tɪvɪti/ N-UNCOUNT ❏ *American art reached a peak of creativity in the '50s and '60s.* ❷ ADJ If you use something in a **creative** way, you use it in a new way that produces interesting and unusual results. ❏ ...*his creative use of words.* [from Latin]

**crea|tive dra|ma** (**creative dramas**) N-VAR **Creative drama** is a form of improvised drama that is often used in teaching.

**crea|tive writ|ing** N-UNCOUNT **Creative writing** is writing such as novels, stories, poems, and plays. ❏ ...*a creative writing class.*

**crea|ture** /kri**tʃ**ər/ (**creatures**) N-COUNT You can refer to any living thing that is not a plant as a **creature**. ❏ *Like all living creatures, birds need a good supply of water.* [from Church Latin]

**cre|dence** /kri**d**ᵊns/ N-UNCOUNT If something lends or gives **credence to** a theory or story, it makes it easier to believe. [FORMAL] ❏ *Studies are needed to lend credence to the idea.* [from Medieval Latin]

| Word Link | cred ≈ to believe : credentials, credibility, incredible |
| --- | --- |

**cre|den|tials** /krɪd**ɛ**nʃ**ᵊ**lz/ ❶ N-PLURAL Your **credentials** are your previous achievements, training, and general background, which indicate that you are qualified to do something. ❏ ...*her credentials as a teacher.* ❷ N-PLURAL Someone's **credentials** are a letter or certificate that proves their identity or qualifications. ❏ *The new*

*ambassador presented his credentials to the president.* [from Medieval Latin]

**cred|ible** /kr**ɛ**dɪbᵊl/ ❶ ADJ **Credible** means able to be trusted or believed. ❏ *Her claims seem credible to many.* ● **cred|ibil|ity** /kr**ɛ**dɪbɪlɪti/ N-UNCOUNT ❏ *The police have lost their credibility.* ❷ ADJ A **credible** candidate, policy, or system is one that appears to have a chance of being successful. ❏ *Mr. Robertson is a credible candidate.* [from Latin]

**cred|it** /kr**ɛ**dɪt/ (**credits, crediting, credited**) ❶ N-UNCOUNT If you are given **credit** for goods or services, or buy them **on credit** you are allowed to pay for them several weeks or months after you have received them. ❏ *The group can't get credit to buy farming machinery.* ❷ N-UNCOUNT If you get **the credit for** something good, people praise you because you are thought to be responsible for it. ❏ *We don't mind who gets the credit so long as we don't get the blame.* ❏ *It would be wrong for us to take all the credit.* ❸ V-T If people **credit** someone **with** an achievement, people say or believe that they were responsible for it. ❏ *The staff are crediting him with having saved Hythe's life.* ❹ N-COUNT A **credit** is one part of a course of study at a school or college that has been successfully completed. ❏ *He doesn't have enough credits to graduate.* ❺ N-PLURAL The list of people who helped to make a movie, a CD, or a television program is called **the credits.** ❏ *It was fantastic seeing my name in the credits.* ❻ PHRASE If something is **to** your **credit**, you deserve praise for it. ❏ *To her credit, she continued to look upon life as a positive experience.* [from Old French]

| Word Partnership | Use credit with : |
| --- | --- |
| N. | credit **history, letter of** credit ❶ |
| V. | **provide** credit ❶ |
| | **deserve** credit, **take** credit ❷ |
| ADJ. | **personal** credit ❶ ❷ |

**cred|it|able** /kr**ɛ**dɪtəbᵊl/ ADJ A **creditable** performance or achievement is of a reasonably high standard. [from Old French]

**cred|it card** (**credit cards**) N-COUNT A **credit card** is a plastic card that you use to buy goods on credit. Compare **charge card.**

**cred|it hour** (**credit hours**) N-COUNT A **credit hour** is a credit that a school or college awards to students who have completed a course of study. [AM] ❏ *Now he needs only two credit hours to graduate.*

**cred|it lim|it** (**credit limits**) N-COUNT Your **credit limit** is the amount of debt that you are allowed, for example, by a credit card company. ❏ *If you exceed your credit limit, we have the right to close your account.*

**cred|it line** (**credit lines**) N-COUNT Your **credit line** is the same as your **credit limit.**

**credi|tor** /kr**ɛ**dɪtər/ (**creditors**) N-COUNT Your **creditors** are the people who you owe money to. ❏ *The company said it would pay all its creditors.* [from Old French]

**cred|it trans|fer** (**credit transfers**) N-COUNT If a student has a **credit transfer** when they change to a new school or college, their credits are transferred from their old school or college to their new one. [AM]

**cred|it un|ion** (**credit unions**) N-COUNT A **credit union** is a financial institution that offers its members low-interest loans.

**creed** /kriːd/ (**creeds**) **1** N-COUNT A **creed** is a set of beliefs or principles that influence the way people live or work. [FORMAL] ❑ ...*their creed of self-help.* **2** N-COUNT A **creed** is a religion. [FORMAL] ❑ *The center is open to all, of every race or creed.* [from Old English]

**creek** /kriːk/ (**creeks**) N-COUNT A **creek** is a small stream or river. ❑ *Follow Austin Creek for a few miles.* [from Old Norse]

**creep** /kriːp/ (**creeps, creeping, crept**) **1** V-I To **creep** somewhere means to move there quietly and slowly. ❑ *He crept up the stairs.* ❑ *Mist crept in from the sea.* **2** V-I If something **creeps** in or **creeps** back, it gradually starts happening or returning without people realizing or without them wanting it. ❑ *Problems can creep in.* ❑ *The inflation rate has been creeping up.* ❑ *Mistakes started to creep into her game.* **3** N-UNCOUNT In geology, **creep** is the very slow downhill movement of rocks and soil as a result of gravity. [TECHNICAL] [from Old English] **4** to **make** someone's **flesh creep** → see **flesh**

---

**Word Partnership**    Use *creep* with :

PREP.    creep **into**, creep **toward**, creep **up** **1**
            creep **in** **2**

---

**creepy** /kriːpi/ (**creepier, creepiest**) ADJ If you say that something or someone is **creepy**, you mean they make you feel nervous or frightened. [INFORMAL] ❑ ...*places that were really creepy at night.* [from Old English]

**cre|mate** /krɪmeɪt/ (**cremates, cremating, cremated**) V-T When someone **is cremated**, their dead body is burned, usually as part of a funeral service. ❑ *She wants Chris to be cremated.* ● **cre|ma|tion** /krɪmeɪ˞ʃ⁰n/ (**cremations**) N-VAR ❑ *There was a cremation after a private ceremony.* [from Latin]

**crept** /krɛpt/ **Crept** is the past tense and past participle of **creep**. [from old English]

**cre|scen|do** /krɪʃɛndoʊ/ (**crescendos**) N-COUNT A **crescendo** is a noise that gets louder and louder. Some people also use **crescendo** to refer to the point when a noise is at its loudest. ❑ *She spoke in a crescendo.* [from Italian]

---

**Word Link**    cresc, creas ≈ growing : *cresc*ent,
                 de*creas*e, in*creas*e

---

**cres|cent** /krɛs⁰nt/ (**crescents**) N-COUNT A **crescent** is a curved shape like the shape of the moon during its first and last quarters. It is the most important symbol of the Islamic faith. [from Latin]

**crest** /krɛst/ (**crests**) **1** N-COUNT The **crest of** a hill or a wave is the top of it. **2** N-COUNT A **crest** is a design that is the symbol of a noble family, a town, or an organization. ❑ *On the wall is the family crest.* [from Old French]
→ see **sound**

**cre|vasse** /krɪvæs/ (**crevasses**) N-COUNT A **crevasse** is a large, deep crack in thick ice or rock. [from French]

**crev|ice** /krɛvɪs/ (**crevices**) N-COUNT A **crevice** is a narrow crack in a rock. ❑ ...*a huge rock with plants growing in every crevice.* [from Old French]

**crew** /kruː/ (**crews**) **1** N-COUNT The **crew** of a ship, an aircraft, or a spacecraft is the people who work on and operate it. ❑ ...*the crew of the space shuttle.* ❑ *These ships carry small crews, usually of around twenty men.* **2** N-COUNT A **crew** is a group of people with special technical skills who work together on a task or project. ❑ ...*a two-man film crew.* [from Old French]
→ see **theater**

crib

**crib** /krɪb/ (**cribs**) N-COUNT A **crib** is a bed for a baby. [from Old English]

**crick|et** /krɪkɪt/ (**crickets**) **1** N-UNCOUNT **Cricket** is an outdoor game played between two teams who try to score points, called runs, by hitting a ball with a wooden bat. ❑ *During the summer term we played cricket.* **2** N-COUNT A **cricket** is a small jumping insect that produces short, loud sounds by rubbing its wings together. [from Old French]
→ see **insect**

**crick|et|er** /krɪkɪtər/ (**cricketers**) N-COUNT A **cricketer** is a person who plays cricket. [from Old French]

**crime** /kraɪm/ (**crimes**) N-VAR A **crime** is an illegal action or activity for which a person can be punished by law. ❑ ...*the scene of the crime.* ❑ *This is a good example of the growing problem of organized crime.* [from Old French]
→ see Picture Dictionary: **crime**
→ see **city**

---

**Word Partnership**    Use *crime* with :

V.      **commit** a crime, **fight against** crime
ADJ.    **organized** crime, **terrible** crime,
        **violent** crime
N.      **partner in** crime, crime **prevention**,
        crime **scene**, crime **wave**

---

**Picture Dictionary**    crime

graffiti

mugging

theft

burglary

shoplifting

**crimi|nal** /krɪmɪnᵊl/ (**criminals**) **1** N-COUNT A **criminal** is a person who has committed a crime. ❑ *They attacked the prison and set free nine criminals.* **2** ADJ **Criminal** means connected with crime. ❑ *Her husband faces various criminal charges.* [from Late Latin]

**crim|son** /krɪmzᵊn/ (**crimsons**) COLOR Something that is **crimson** is deep red in color. ❑ *He walked through a field of crimson flowers.* [from Old Spanish]

**cringe** /krɪndʒ/ (**cringes, cringing, cringed**) V-I If you **cringe at** something, you feel embarrassed or disgusted, and perhaps show this in your expression or by making a slight movement. ❑ *Molly cringed when Ann picked up the guitar.* ❑ *Chris cringed at the thought of using her own family for publicity.* [from Old English]

**crinkle** /krɪŋkᵊl/ (**crinkles, crinkling, crinkled**) **1** V-T/V-I If something **crinkles** or you **crinkle** it, becomes slightly creased or folded. ❑ *When she laughs she crinkles her nose.* **2** N-COUNT **Crinkles** are small creases or folds. [from Old English]

**crip|ple** /krɪpᵊl/ (**cripples, crippling, crippled**) V-T If someone **is crippled** by an injury, it is so serious that they can never move their body properly again. ❑ *Mr. Easton was crippled in an accident.* ❑ *Another bad fall could cripple him for life.* [from Old English]

**crip|pling** /krɪplɪŋ/ **1** ADJ A **crippling** illness or disability is one that severely damages your health or your body. ❑ *Arthritis is a crippling disease.* **2** ADJ If you say that an action, policy, or situation has a **crippling** effect on something, you mean it has a very serious, harmful effect. ❑ *High costs can have a crippling effect on small firms.* [from Old English]

**cri|sis** /kraɪsɪs/ (**crises** /kraɪsiz/) **1** N-VAR A **crisis** is a situation in which something or someone is affected by one or more very serious problems. ❑ *Natural disasters are the cause of the continent's economic crisis.* ❑ *Everyone needs someone special to turn to in moments of crisis.* **2** N-COUNT The **crisis** is the most dramatic part of a play or movie, or the most important part of its plot. [from Latin]

**crisp** /krɪsp/ (**crisper, crispest**) **1** ADJ Food that is **crisp** is pleasantly hard and crunchy. ❑ *Bake the potatoes for 15 minutes, till they're nice and crisp.* ❑ *...crisp bacon.* **2** ADJ Weather that is pleasantly fresh, cold, and dry can be described as **crisp**. ❑ *...a crisp autumn day.* [from Old English]

**crispy** /krɪspi/ (**crispier, crispiest**) ADJ Food that is **crispy** is pleasantly hard, or has a pleasantly hard surface. ❑ *...crispy fried onions.* ❑ *...crispy bread rolls.*

**criss-cross** /krɪs krɔs/ (**criss-crosses, criss-crossing, criss-crossed**) also **crisscross** **1** V-T If a person or thing **criss-crosses** an area, they travel from one side to the other and back again many times. If a number of things **criss-cross** an area, they cross it, and cross over each other. ❑ *They criss-crossed the country by bus.* **2** ADJ A **criss-cross** pattern or design consists of lines crossing each other. ❑ *Make a criss-cross pattern in the tops of the loaves.*

**cri|teri|on** /kraɪtɪəriən/ (**criteria** /kraɪtɪəriə/) N-COUNT A **criterion** is a factor on which you judge or decide something. ❑ *The bank is reviewing its criteria for lending money.* ❑ *There's one more criterion:*

*Internet access must be free.* [from Greek]

**Word Link**   *crit ≈ to judge : critic, critical, criticize*

**crit|ic** /krɪtɪk/ (**critics**) **1** N-COUNT A **critic** is a person who writes about and expresses opinions about books, movies, music, or art. ❑ *Mather was a film critic for many years.* **2** N-COUNT Someone who is a **critic** of a person or system disapproves of them and criticizes them publicly. ❑ *He has been one of the most consistent critics of the government.* [from Latin]

**criti|cal** /krɪtɪkᵊl/ **1** ADJ A **critical** time or situation is extremely important. ❑ *The incident happened at a critical point in the campaign.* ❑ *He says setting deadlines is of critical importance.* ● **criti|cal|ly** /krɪtɪkli/ ADV ❑ *It is critically important for people to be prepared.* **2** ADJ A **critical** situation is very serious and dangerous. ❑ *The situation may become critical.* ● **criti|cal|ly** ADV ❑ *Food supplies are running critically low.* **3** ADJ To be **critical of** someone or something means to criticize them. ❑ *His report is highly critical of the trial judge.* ● **criti|cal|ly** ADV ❑ *She spoke critically of Lara.* **4** ADJ A **critical** approach to something involves examining and judging it carefully. ❑ *...a critical examination of political ideas.* ● **criti|cal|ly** ADV ❑ *Wyman watched them critically.* [from Latin]

**Word Partnership**   Use *critical* with :

| | |
|---|---|
| N. | critical **issue**, critical **role** **1** |
| | critical **state** **1** **2** |
| | critical **condition** **2** |
| V. | **become** critical **1** **2** |
| PREP. | critical **of** *someone*, critical **of** *something* **3** |

**criti|cism** /krɪtɪsɪzəm/ (**criticisms**) **1** N-VAR **Criticism** is the action of expressing disapproval of something or someone. A **criticism** is a statement that expresses disapproval. ❑ *This policy has come under strong criticism.* **2** N-UNCOUNT **Criticism** is a serious examination and judgment of something such as a book or play. ❑ *She has published more than 20 books including novels, poetry, and literary criticism.* [from Latin]

**Thesaurus**   *criticism*   Also look up :

| | |
|---|---|
| N. | disapproval, judgment; (ant.) approval, flattery, praise **1** |
| | commentary, critique, evaluation, review **2** |

**Word Partnership**   Use *criticism* with :

| | |
|---|---|
| PREP. | criticism **against** *something*, criticism **from** *something*, criticism **of** *something* **1** |
| | **public** criticism **1** **2** |
| ADJ. | **constructive** criticism, **open to** criticism **1** **2** |
| N. | **literary** criticism **2** |

**criti|cize** /krɪtɪsaɪz/ (**criticizes, criticizing, criticized**) V-T If you **criticize** someone or something, you express your disapproval of them by saying what you think is wrong with them. ❑ *His mother rarely criticized him or any of her other children.* [from Latin]

**cri|tique** /krɪtik/ (**critiques**) N-COUNT A **critique** is a written examination and judgment of a situation or of a person's work or ideas. [FORMAL] ❑ …*a critique of the power of newspapers.* [from French]

**crit|ter** /krɪtər/ (**critters**) N-COUNT A **critter** is a living creature. [INFORMAL] ❑ …*little furry critters.* [from U.S. and Canadian dialect]

**croak** /kroʊk/ (**croaks, croaking, croaked**) ◼ V-I When a frog or bird **croaks**, it makes a harsh, low sound. ❑ *Frogs croaked in the river.* ◼ V-T If someone **croaks** something, they say it in a low, rough voice. ❑ *Tiller moaned and managed to croak, "Help me."* [from Old English]

**croco|dile** /krɒkədaɪl/ (**crocodiles**) N-COUNT A **crocodile** is a large reptile with a long body and strong jaws. Crocodiles live in rivers. [from Old French]

**cro|cus** /kroʊkəs/ (**crocuses**) N-COUNT **Crocuses** are small white, yellow, or purple flowers that are grown in parks and gardens in the early spring. [from New Latin]

**crois|sant** /krwɑsɒn, krəsɑnt/ (**croissants**) N-VAR **Croissants** are bread rolls in the shape of a crescent that are eaten for breakfast. [from French]
→ see **bread**

**Cro-Magnon** /kroʊ mægnən, mænyən/ (**Cro-Magnons**) N-COUNT **Cro-Magnons** were a species of early human being who lived between 50,000 and 100,000 years ago. ● **Cro-Magnon** is also an adjective. ❑ *Cro-Magnon man used relatively advanced tools made from wood and stone.*

**cro|ny** /kroʊni/ (**cronies**) N-COUNT You can refer to friends that someone spends a lot of time with as their **cronies**, especially when you disapprove of them. [INFORMAL] ❑ …*lunches with his business cronies.* [from Greek]

**crook** /krʊk/ (**crooks**) ◼ N-COUNT A **crook** is a dishonest person or a criminal. [INFORMAL] ❑ *The man is a crook and a liar.* ◼ N-COUNT The **crook** of your arm or leg is the soft inside part where you bend your elbow or knee. ❑ *She hid her face in the crook of her arm.* [from Old Norse]

**crook|ed** /krʊkɪd/ ◼ ADJ If you describe something as **crooked**, especially something that is usually straight, you mean that it is bent or twisted. ❑ …*the crooked line of his broken nose.* ◼ ADJ A **crooked** smile is uneven and bigger on one side than the other. ❑ *Polly gave her a crooked smile.* ◼ ADJ If you describe a person or an activity as **crooked**, you mean that they are dishonest or criminal. [INFORMAL] ❑ …*a crooked cop.* [from Old Norse]

**croon** /krun/ (**croons, crooning, crooned**) V-T/ V-I If you **croon**, you sing or say something quietly and gently. ❑ *Lewis began to croon another song.* [from Middle Dutch]

**crop** /krɒp/ (**crops, cropping, cropped**) ◼ N-COUNT **Crops** are plants such as wheat and potatoes that are grown in large quantities for food. ❑ *Rice farmers here still plant and harvest their crops by hand.* ◼ N-COUNT The plants or fruits that are collected at harvest time are referred to as a **crop**. ❑ *Each year it produces a fine crop of fruit.* ❑ *The U.S. government says this year's corn crop should be about 8 percent more than last year.* ◼ N-SING You can refer to a group of people or things that have appeared together as a **crop of** people or things. [INFORMAL] ❑ …*a crop of books about Marilyn Monroe.*

◼ V-T To **crop** your hair means to cut it short. ❑ *She cropped her hair and dyed it blonde.* [from Old English]
→ see **farm, grain, photography, plant**
▶ **crop up** PHR-VERB If something **crops up**, it appears or happens unexpectedly. ❑ *His name has cropped up at every meeting.*

**crop dust|ing** also **crop-dusting** N-UNCOUNT **Crop dusting** is the spreading of pesticides on crops, usually from an aircraft. ❑ …*a crop-dusting plane.*

**cro|quet** /kroʊkeɪ/ N-UNCOUNT **Croquet** is a game played on grass in which the players use long wooden sticks called mallets to hit balls through metal arches. ❑ *Every summer the family plays croquet on the front lawn.* [from French]

| cross |
|---|
| ❶ MOVING ACROSS |
| ❷ ANGRY |

❶ **cross** /krɔs/ (**crosses, crossing, crossed**) ◼ V-T/V-I If you **cross** a room, a road, or an area of land, you move to the other side of it. If you **cross** to a place, you move or travel over a room, road, or area in order to reach that place. ❑ *She failed to look as she crossed the road.* ❑ *Egan crossed to the window and looked out.* ◼ V-T A road, railroad, or bridge that **crosses** an area of land or water passes over it. ❑ *The road crosses the river half a mile outside the town.* ◼ V-T If an expression **crosses** your face, it appears briefly on your face. [WRITTEN] ❑ *A sad look crossed his face.* ◼ V-T If you **cross** your arms, legs, or fingers, you put one of them on top of the other. ❑ *Jill crossed her legs.* ◼ V-RECIP Lines or roads that **cross** meet and go across each other. ❑ …*the place where Main and Center Streets cross.* ◼ N-COUNT A **cross** is a shape that consists of a vertical line or piece with a shorter horizontal line or piece across it. It is the most important Christian symbol. ❑ *Around her neck was a cross on a silver chain.* ◼ N-COUNT A **cross** is a written mark in the shape of an X. ❑ *Put a cross next to those activities you like.* ◼ N-SING Something that is **a cross between** two things is neither one thing nor the other, but a mixture of both. ❑ *"Ha!" It was a cross between a laugh and a bark.* [from Old English] ◼ → see also **crossing** ◼ to **cross** your **fingers** → see **finger** ◼ I **cross** my **heart** → see **heart** ◼ to **cross** your **mind** → see **mind** ◼ to **cross swords** → see **sword**
▶ **cross out** PHR-VERB If you **cross out** words, you draw a line through them. ❑ *He crossed out her name and added his own.*

❷ **cross** /krɔs/ (**crosser, crossest**) ADJ Someone who is **cross** is angry or irritated. ❑ *I'm terribly cross with him.* ● **cross|ly** ADV ❑ *"No, no, no," Morris said crossly.* [from Old English]

**cross-country** ◼ N-UNCOUNT **Cross-country** is the sport of running, riding, or skiing across open countryside. ❑ *She finished third in the world cross-country championships.* ◼ ADJ A **cross-country** trip takes you from one side of a country to the other. ❑ …*cross-country rail services.* ● **Cross-country** is also an adverb. ❑ *I drove cross-country in his van.*

**cross-examine** (**cross-examines, cross-examining, cross-examined**) V-T When a lawyer **cross-examines** someone during a trial or hearing, he or she questions them about the evidence that they have given. ❑ *His lawyers will get a chance to*

cross-examine him. ● **cross-examination** (**cross-examinations**) N-VAR ❑ ...the cross-examination of a witness.
→ see **trial**

**cross|ing** /krɒsɪŋ/ (**crossings**) **1** N-COUNT A **crossing** is a boat journey to a place on the other side of an ocean, river, or lake. ❑ He made the crossing from Cape Town to Sydney. **2** N-COUNT A **crossing** is a place where you can cross something such as a road or a border. [from Old English]

**cross|ing over** N-UNCOUNT In biology, **crossing over** is a process in which genetic material is exchanged between one type of activity to another. ❑ ...the crossover from actress to singer.

**cross|over** /krɒsoʊvər/ (**crossovers**) **1** N-VAR A **crossover** of one style and another is a combination of the two different styles. ❑ ...the crossover hit song "I Need To Know." **2** N-SING A **crossover** is a change from one type of activity to another. ❑ ...the crossover from actress to singer.

**cross|roads** /krɒsroʊdz/ (**crossroads**) **1** N-COUNT A **crossroads** is a place where two roads meet and cross each other. ❑ Turn right at the first crossroads. **2** N-SING A **crossroads** is an important or central place. ❑ ...a small town at the crossroads of agriculture in central Florida.

**cross-section** (**cross-sections**) also **cross section** **1** N-COUNT A **cross-section of** something such as a group of people is a typical or representative sample. ❑ The jury should represent a cross-section of the community. **2** N-COUNT A **cross-section** of an object is what you would see if you could cut straight through the middle of it. ❑ ...a cross-section of an airplane.

**cross|town** /krɒstaʊn/ also **cross-town** ADJ A **crosstown** bus or route is one that crosses the main roads or transportation lines of a city or town. ❑ ...the crosstown bus that takes me to work. ❑ ...a crosstown subway. ● **Crosstown** is also an adverb. ❑ I have trouble these days getting crosstown in Manhattan.

**cross|walk** /krɒswɔk/ (**crosswalks**) N-COUNT A **crosswalk** is a place where drivers must stop to let pedestrians cross a street. ❑ I stood on the curb and watched people come and go in the crosswalk.

**cross|word** /krɒswɜrd/ (**crosswords**) N-COUNT A **crossword** or **crossword puzzle** is a word game in which you work out the answers and write them in the white squares of a pattern of black and white squares. ❑ He could do the Times crossword in 15 minutes.

**crossword puzzle**

**crotch** /krɒtʃ/ (**crotches**) **1** N-COUNT Your **crotch** is the part of your body between the tops of your legs. **2** N-COUNT The **crotch** of something such as a pair of pants is the part that covers the area between the tops of your legs. ❑ The pants were too long in the crotch.

**crouch** /kraʊtʃ/ (**crouches, crouching, crouched**) V-I If you **are crouching**, your legs are bent under you so that you are close to the ground and leaning forward slightly. ❑ We were crouching in the bushes. ❑ I crouched on the ground. ● **Crouch** is also a noun. ❑ They walked along in a crouch each bent over close to the ground. ● **Crouch down** means the same as

**crouch**. ❑ He crouched down and reached under the bed. [from Old French]

**crow** /kroʊ/ (**crows, crowing, crowed**) **1** N-COUNT A **crow** is a large black bird which makes a loud, harsh noise. **2** V-I When a rooster **crows**, it makes a loud sound, often early in the morning. ❑ The rooster crowed for many hours past dawn. [from Old English]

**crowd** /kraʊd/ (**crowds, crowding, crowded**) **1** N-COUNT A **crowd** is a large group of people who have gathered together. ❑ A huge crowd gathered in the square. **2** N-COUNT A particular **crowd** is a group of friends, or a set of people who share the same interests or job. [INFORMAL] ❑ All the old crowd were there. **3** V-I When people **crowd around** someone or something, they gather closely together around them. ❑ The children crowded around him. **4** V-T/V-I If people **crowd into** a place or **are crowded into** a place, large numbers of them enter it so that it becomes very full. ❑ Hundreds of thousands of people have crowded into the center. ❑ One group of journalists were crowded into a bus. [from Old English]

**crowd|ed** /kraʊdɪd/ ADJ If a place is **crowded**, it is full of people. ❑ He looked slowly around the small crowded room. ❑ ...a crowded city of 2 million. [from Old English]

**crown** /kraʊn/ (**crowns, crowning, crowned**) **1** N-COUNT A **crown** is a circular ornament, usually made of gold and jewels, which a king or queen wears on their head at official ceremonies. **2** N-COUNT Your **crown** is the top part of your head, at the back. ❑ He laid his hand gently on the crown of her head. **3** N-COUNT

**crown**

A **crown** is an artificial top piece fixed over a broken or decayed tooth. ❑ How long does it take to have crowns fitted? **4** V-T When a king or queen **is crowned**, a crown is placed on their head as part of a ceremony in which they are officially made king or queen. ❑ Two days later, Juan Carlos was crowned king. [from Old French]
→ see **teeth**

| Word Link | cruc ≈ cross : crucial, crucifixion, crucify |
| --- | --- |

**cru|cial** /kruʃⁱl/ ADJ Something that is **crucial** is extremely important. ❑ He made all the crucial decisions himself. ● **cru|cial|ly** ADV ❑ Chewing properly is crucially important. [from French]

**cru|ci|fy** /krusɪfaɪ/ (**crucifies, crucifying, crucified**) V-T In former times, if someone **was crucified**, they were killed by being tied or nailed to a cross and left to die. ❑ ...the day that Christ was crucified. ● **cru|ci|fix|ion** /krusɪfɪkʃⁿn/ (**crucifixions**) N-VAR ❑ ...the crucifixion of Christians in Rome. [from Old French]

**crud** /krʌd/ N-UNCOUNT You use **crud** to refer to any disgusting dirty or sticky substance. [INFORMAL] ❑ Remember the motel with all the crud in the pool?

**crude** /krud/ (**cruder, crudest**) **1** ADJ Something that is **crude** is simple and rough rather than precise or sophisticated. ❑ ...a crude way of assessing the risk of heart disease. ❑ ...*crude wooden boxes*. ● **crude|ly** ADV ❑ ...*a crudely carved wooden form*. ❷ ADJ If you describe someone as **crude**, you disapprove of them because they speak or behave in a rude or offensive way. ❑ *Must you be quite so crude?* ● **crude|ly** ADV ❑ *He hated it when she spoke so crudely*. ❸ N-UNCOUNT **Crude** is the same as **crude oil**. [from Latin]

→ see **petroleum**

**crude oil** N-UNCOUNT **Crude oil** is oil in its natural state before it has been processed or refined. ❑ *A thousand tons of crude oil has spilled into the sea from an oil tanker*.

→ see **oil**

**cru|el** /krˈuəl/ (**crueler** or **crueller, cruelest** or **cruellest**) ADJ Someone who is **cruel** deliberately causes pain or distress to people or animals. ❑ *Children can be so cruel*. ● **cru|el|ly** ADV ❑ *Douglas was often treated cruelly by his jealous sisters*. ● **cru|el|ty** /krˈuəlti/ (**cruelties**) N-VAR ❑ *The U.S. has several laws against cruelty to animals*. [from Old French]

| **Thesaurus** | *cruel* | Also look up : |
| --- | --- | --- |
| ADJ. | harsh, mean, nasty, unkind; (*ant.*) gentle, kind | |

**cruise** /krˈuz/ (**cruises, cruising, cruised**) ❶ N-COUNT A **cruise** is a vacation during which you travel on a ship or boat and visit a number of places. ❑ *He and his wife went on a world cruise*. ❷ V-T/V-I If you **cruise** an ocean, river, or canal, you travel around it or along it on a cruise. ❑ *She wants to cruise the canals of France*. ❑ ...*a vacation cruising around the Caribbean*. ❸ V-I If a car, ship, or aircraft **cruises** somewhere, it moves there at a steady comfortable speed. ❑ *A black and white police car cruised past*. [from Dutch]

→ see **ship**

**cruise con|trol** N-UNCOUNT In a car or other vehicle, **cruise control** is a system that automatically keeps the vehicle's speed at the same level. ❑ *My new car has air-conditioning and cruise control*.

**cruis|er** /krˈuzər/ (**cruisers**) ❶ N-COUNT A **cruiser** is a motorboat which has an area for people to live or sleep. ❑ ...*a small cruiser with indoor and outdoor seating*. ❷ N-COUNT A **cruiser** is a large fast warship. ❑ *Italy lost three cruisers and two destroyers*. ❸ N-COUNT A **cruiser** is a police car. ❑ *Police cruisers surrounded the bank throughout the day*. [from Dutch]

**crumb** /krˈʌm/ (**crumbs**) N-COUNT **Crumbs** are tiny pieces that fall from bread, cookies, or cake when you cut it or eat it. ❑ *I stood up, brushed crumbs from my pants, and went out of the room*. [from Old English]

**crum|ble** /krˈʌmbəl/ (**crumbles, crumbling, crumbled**) ❶ V-T/V-I If something **crumbles**, or if you **crumble** it, it breaks into a lot of small pieces. ❑ *The rock crumbled into pieces*. ❷ V-I If an old building or piece of land **is crumbling**, parts of it keep breaking off. ❑ *Apartment buildings built in the 1960s are crumbling*. ● **Crumble away** means the same as **crumble**. ❑ *Much of the coastline is crumbling away*. ❸ V-I If something such as a system, relationship, or hope **crumbles**, it comes to an end. ❑ *Their economy crumbled as a result of the war*. [from Old English]

**crum|bly** /krˈʌmbli/ (**crumblier, crumbliest**) ADJ Something that is **crumbly** is easily broken into a lot of little pieces. ❑ ...*crumbly cheese*. [from Old English]

**crum|ple** /krˈʌmpəl/ (**crumples, crumpling, crumpled**) V-T/V-I If you **crumple** something such as paper or cloth, or if it **crumples**, it is squashed and becomes full of untidy creases and folds. ❑ *She crumpled the paper in her hand*. ● **Crumple up** means the same as **crumple**. ❑ *She crumpled up the note*. ● **crum|pled** ADJ ❑ *His uniform was crumpled and untidy*. [from Old High German]

**crunch** /krˈʌntʃ/ (**crunches, crunching, crunched**) ❶ V-T/V-I If you **crunch** something hard, you crush it noisily between your teeth. ❑ *She sucked an ice cube into her mouth and crunched it loudly*. ❷ V-I If something **crunches**, it makes a breaking or crushing noise, for example, when you step on it. ❑ *A piece of china crunched under my foot*. ● **Crunch** is also a noun. ❑ *She heard the crunch of tires on the driveway, and ran outside*.

**crunchy** /krˈʌntʃi/ (**crunchier, crunchiest**) ADJ Food that is **crunchy** is pleasantly hard or crisp so that it makes a noise when you eat it. ❑ ...*fresh, crunchy vegetables*.

**cru|sade** /kruseˈɪd/ (**crusades**) N-COUNT A **crusade** is a long and determined attempt to achieve something for a cause that you feel strongly about. ❑ *He made it his crusade to teach children to love books*. ● **cru|sad|er** (**crusaders**) N-COUNT ❑ ...*a crusader for higher standards in journalism*. [from Old French]

**crush** /krˈʌʃ/ (**crushes, crushing, crushed**) ❶ V-T To **crush** something means to press it very hard so that its shape is destroyed or so that it breaks into pieces. ❑ *Andrew crushed his empty can*. ❑ ...*crushed ice*. ❷ V-T To **crush** a protest or movement, or a group of opponents, means to defeat it completely. ❑ ...*a plan to crush the protests*. ● **crush|ing** N-UNCOUNT ❑ ...*the violent crushing of anti-government demonstrations*. ❸ V-T If you **are crushed** against someone or something, you are pushed or pressed against them. ❑ *We were at the front, crushed against the stage*. ❹ N-COUNT A **crush** is a crowd of people pressed close together. ❑ *His thirteen-year-old son somehow got separated in the crush*. ❺ N-COUNT If you have a **crush on** someone, you are in love with them but do not have a relationship with them. [INFORMAL] ❑ *She had a crush on you all through high school, you know*. [from Old French]

→ see **crash**

**crust** /krˈʌst/ (**crusts**) ❶ N-COUNT The **crust** on a loaf of bread or pie is the hard, crisp outside part. ❑ *Cut the crusts off and soak the bread in the milk*. ❷ N-COUNT The Earth's **crust** is its outer layer. ❑ *Earthquakes leave scars in the Earth's crust*. [from Latin]

→ see **continent, core, earthquake**

**crusty** /krˈʌsti/ (**crustier, crustiest**) ADJ **Crusty** bread has a hard, crisp outside. ❑ ...*crusty French loaves*. [from Latin]

**crutch** /krˈʌtʃ/ (**crutches**) N-COUNT A **crutch** is a stick which someone with an injured foot or leg uses to support them when walking. ❑ *I can walk without crutches*. [from Old English]

**crux** /krˈʌks/ N-SING The **crux of** a problem or argument is the most important or difficult part

## Word Web    cry

Have you ever seen someone **burst into tears** when something wonderful happened to them? We expect people to **cry** when they are **sad** or upset. But why do people sometimes **weep** when they are happy? Scientists have found there are three different types of **tears**. Basal tears keep the **eyes** moist. Reflex tears clear the eyes of dirt or smoke. The third type, emotional tears, occur when people experience strong feelings, either good or bad. These tears have high levels of chemicals called manganese and prolactin. Decreasing the amount of these chemicals in the body helps us feel better. When people experience strong feelings, **shedding tears** may help restore emotional balance.

of it, which affects everything else. ❑ *The said that the crux of the matter was economic policy.* [from Latin]

**cry** /kraɪ/ (**cries, crying, cried**) **1** V-I When you **cry**, tears come from your eyes, usually because you are unhappy or hurt. ❑ *I hung up the phone and started to cry.* ❑ *He cried with anger and frustration.* ● **Cry** is also a noun. ❑ *You have a good cry, dear.* ● **cry|ing** N-UNCOUNT ❑ *She was unable to sleep because of her baby son's crying.* **2** V-T If you **cry** something, you shout it or say it loudly. ❑ *"Nancy Drew," she cried, "you're under arrest!"* ● **Cry out** means the same as **cry**. ❑ *"You're wrong, quite wrong!" Henry cried out.* **3** N-COUNT A **cry** is a loud, high sound that you make when you feel a strong emotion such as fear, pain, or pleasure. ❑ *...a cry of horror.* **4** N-COUNT A bird's or an animal's **cry** is the loud, high sound that it makes. ❑ *...the cry of a seagull.* [from Old French] **5** → see also **crying** **6** to **cry** your **eyes out** → see **eye** **7** a **shoulder to cry on** → see **shoulder**

▶ **cry out** **1** PHR-VERB If you **cry out**, you call out loudly because you are frightened, unhappy, or in pain. ❑ *He was crying out in pain when the ambulance arrived.* **2** → see also **cry 2**

▶ **cry out for** PHR-VERB If you say that something **cries out for** a particular thing, you mean that it needs that thing very much. ❑ *His body was crying out for some exercise.*

→ see Word Web: **cry**

## Thesaurus    cry    Also look up :

| | |
|---|---|
| V. | sob, weep **1** |
| | call, shout, yell **2** |
| N. | howl, moan, shriek **3** |

## Word Partnership    Use *cry* with :

| | |
|---|---|
| V. | **begin to** cry, **start to** cry **1** |
| N. | cry **with anger 1 2** |
| | cry **for help**, cry **with joy**, cry **with horror**, cry **of pain 2** |

**cryp|tic** /krɪptɪk/ ADJ A **cryptic** remark or message contains a hidden meaning or is difficult to understand. ❑ *...a short, cryptic statement.* ● **cryp|ti|cal|ly** ADV ❑ *"Not necessarily," she says cryptically.* [from Late Latin]

**crys|tal** /krɪstəl/ (**crystals**) **1** N-COUNT A **crystal** is a small piece of a substance that has formed naturally into a regular symmetrical shape. ❑ *...salt crystals.* ❑ *...ice crystals.* **2** N-VAR **Crystal** is a transparent rock used in jewelry and ornaments. ❑ *She wore a string of crystal beads around her neck.* **3** N-UNCOUNT **Crystal** is high quality glass, usually with patterns cut into its surface. ❑ *Some of the finest drinking glasses are made from crystal.* [from Old English] → see Word Web: **crystal** → see **precipitation**, **rock**, **sugar**

**crys|tal clear** ADJ Something that is **crystal clear** is very easy to understand. ❑ *The message is crystal clear — if you lose weight, you will have a better life.*

**crys|tal lat|tice** (**crystal lattices**) N-COUNT A **crystal lattice** is a symmetrical arrangement of atoms in a crystal. [TECHNICAL]

**crys|tal|lize** /krɪstəlaɪz/ (**crystallizes, crystallizing, crystallized**) **1** V-T/V-I If you **crystallize** an opinion or idea, or if it **crystallizes**, it becomes fixed and definite in your mind. ❑ *I hope our discussion has helped to crystallize your thoughts.* **2** V-I If a substance **crystallizes**, it turns into crystals. ❑ *Don't stir the jam or the sugar will*

## Word Web    crystal

The outsides of **crystals** have smooth flat planes. These surfaces form because of the repeating patterns of atoms, molecules, or ions inside the crystal. Evaporation, temperature changes, and pressure can all help to form crystals. Crystals grow when sea water evaporates and leaves behind **salt**. When water freezes, **ice** crystals form. When melted rock cools, it becomes **rock** with a crystalline structure. Pressure can create one of the hardest, most beautiful crystals—the **diamond**.

crystallize. [from Old English]

**CST** /ˌsi ɛs ˈti/ (**CST**) CST is an abbreviation for "Central Standard Time." [AM] ❑ *Calls are taken between 7 a.m. and 8 p.m., CST.*

**cub** /kʌb/ (**cubs**) N-COUNT A cub is a young wild animal such as a lion, wolf, or bear. ❑ *...young lion cubs.* [from Old Norse]

**cube** /kyub/ (**cubes**) N-COUNT A cube is a solid object with six square surfaces which are all the same size. ❑ *...cold water with ice cubes in it.* ❑ *...a box of sugar cubes.* [from Latin]
→ see **solid, volume**

**cu|bic** /ˈkyubɪk/ ADJ Cubic is used to express units of volume. ❑ *...3 billion cubic meters of earth.* [from Latin]

> **Word Link** cle ≈ small : article, cubicle, particle

**cu|bi|cle** /ˈkyubɪkəl/ (**cubicles**) N-COUNT A cubicle is a very small enclosed area, for example, one where you can take a shower or change your clothes. ❑ *The bathroom contains a small shower cubicle.* [from Latin]
→ see **office**

**cuckoo** /ˈkuku, ˈkuku/ (**cuckoos**) N-COUNT A cuckoo is a bird that has a call of two quick notes, and lays its eggs in other birds' nests. [from Old French]

**cu|cum|ber** /ˈkyukʌmbər/ (**cucumbers**) N-VAR A cucumber is a long dark green vegetable that is eaten raw in salads. ❑ *...a cheese and cucumber sandwich.* [from Latin]
→ see **vegetable**

**cud|dle** /ˈkʌdəl/ (**cuddles, cuddling, cuddled**) V-RECIP If you cuddle someone, you put your arms around them and hold them close as a way of showing your affection. ❑ *He cuddled the baby girl.* ● Cuddle is also a noun. ❑ *It would have been nice to give him a cuddle.*

**cud|dly** /ˈkʌdli/ (**cuddlier, cuddliest**) ADJ A cuddly person or animal is plump or soft and looks nice to cuddle. ❑ *He is a small, cuddly man with spectacles and a beard.*

**cue** /kyu/ (**cues**) ◼ N-COUNT A cue is something said or done by a performer that is a signal for another performer to begin speaking, playing, or doing something. ❑ *The actors sit at the side of the stage, waiting for their cues.* ◼ N-COUNT If you say that something that happens is a cue for an action, you mean that people start doing that action when it happens. ❑ *That was the cue for several months of fighting.* ◼ N-COUNT A cue is a long, thin wooden stick that is used to hit the ball in games such as billiards, pool, and snooker. [from Latin]

**cuff** /kʌf/ (**cuffs**) ◼ N-COUNT The cuffs of a shirt or dress are the end parts of the sleeves. ❑ *...a pale blue shirt with white collar and cuffs.* ◼ N-COUNT The cuffs on a pair of pants are the end parts of the legs which are folded up. ◼ PHRASE An off-the-cuff remark is made without being prepared or thought about in advance. ❑ *It was an off-the-cuff remark.*

**cui|sine** /kwɪˈzin/ (**cuisines**) N-VAR The cuisine of a region or district is its characteristic style of cooking. ❑ *The cuisine of Japan is low in fat.* [from French]

**culi|nary** /ˈkyulənɛri, ˈkʌlə-/ ADJ Culinary means concerned with cooking. [FORMAL] ❑ *...advanced culinary skills.* [from Latin]

**cull** /kʌl/ (**culls, culling, culled**) ◼ V-T If items or ideas are culled from a particular source or number of sources, they are taken and gathered together. ❑ *All this information was culled from radio reports.* ◼ V-T To cull animals means to kill some of them in order to reduce their numbers. ❑ *The national parks department is planning to cull 2000 elephants.* ❑ Cull is also a noun. ❑ *...the annual seal cull.* ● cull|ing N-UNCOUNT ❑ *...the culling of seal cubs.* [from Old French]

**cul|mi|nate** /ˈkʌlmɪneɪt/ (**culminates, culminating, culminated**) V-I If you say that an activity, process, or series of events culminates in or with a particular event, you mean that event happens at the end of it. ❑ *They had an argument, which culminated in Tom leaving the house.* ● cul|mi|na|tion /ˌkʌlmɪˈneɪʃən/ N-SING ❑ *The event was the culmination of a week of celebrations.* [from Late Latin]

**cul|prit** /ˈkʌlprɪt/ (**culprits**) ◼ N-COUNT The person who committed a crime or did something wrong can be referred to as the culprit. ❑ *We do not know who the culprits are.* ◼ N-COUNT The cause of a problem or bad situation can be referred to as the culprit. ❑ *About 10% of Japanese teenagers are overweight. Experts say the main culprit is eating Western fast food.*

**cult** /kʌlt/ (**cults**) ◼ N-COUNT A cult is a fairly small religious group, especially one which is considered strange. ◼ ADJ Cult is used to describe things that are very popular or fashionable among a particular group. ❑ *The movie became a cult classic.* [from Latin]

**cul|ti|vate** /ˈkʌltɪveɪt/ (**cultivates, cultivating, cultivated**) ◼ V-T If you cultivate land, you prepare it and grow crops on it. ❑ *She cultivated a small garden of her own.* ● cul|ti|va|tion /ˌkʌltɪˈveɪʃən/ N-UNCOUNT ❑ *...the cultivation of fruits and vegetables.* ◼ V-T If you cultivate an attitude, image, or skill, you develop it and make it stronger. ❑ *He has written eight books and has cultivated the image of an artist.* ● cul|ti|va|tion N-UNCOUNT ❑ *...the cultivation of a positive approach to life.* [from Medieval Latin]
→ see **farm, grain**

**cul|ti|vat|ed** /ˈkʌltɪveɪtɪd/ ◼ ADJ If you describe someone as cultivated, you mean they are well educated and have good manners. [FORMAL] ❑ *His mother was an elegant, cultivated woman.* ◼ ADJ Cultivated plants have been developed for growing on farms or in gardens. ❑ *The park boaasts a mixture of wild and cultivated flowers.* [from Medieval Latin]

**cul|tur|al** /ˈkʌltʃərəl/ ADJ Cultural means relating to the arts, or to the arts, ideas, and customs of a particular society. ❑ *...sports and cultural events.* ❑ *...cultural and educational exchanges.* ● cul|tur|al|ly ADV ❑ *Culturally, the two countries have much in common.* ❑ *...a guide to culturally and historically significant sites.* [from Old French]

**cul|ture** /ˈkʌltʃər/ (**cultures**) ◼ N-UNCOUNT Culture consists of activities such as the arts and philosophy, which are considered to be important for the development of civilization and of people's minds. ❑ *There is just not enough fun in culture today.* ❑ *Movies are part of our popular culture.* ◼ N-COUNT

## Word Web culture

Each **society** has its own **culture** which influences how people live their lives. Culture includes **customs, language, art**, and other shared **traits**. When people move from one culture to another, there is often cultural **diffusion**. For example, European artists first saw Japanese art about 150 years ago. This caused a change in their painting style. The new style was called Impressionism. **Assimilation** happens when people enter a new culture. For instance, **immigrants** may start to follow American customs when they move to the U.S. People whose ideas differ from **mainstream** society may also form **subcultures** within the society.

A **culture** is a particular society or civilization, especially considered in relation to its beliefs, way of life, or art. ❑ ...*people from different cultures.*
**3** N-COUNT In science, a **culture** is a group of bacteria or cells grown in a laboratory as part of an experiment. [TECHNICAL] ❑ ...*a culture of human cells.* [from Old French]
→ see Word Web: **culture**
→ see **myth**

## Word Partnership Use *culture* with :

| ADJ. | **ancient** culture, **popular** culture **1** |
|---|---|
| N. | culture **and religion, richness of** culture, culture **shock, society and** culture **1 2** |

**cul|tured** /kʌltʃərd/ ADJ If you describe someone as **cultured**, you mean that they are well educated and know a lot about the arts. ❑ *He is a cultured man with a wide circle of friends.* [from Old French]

**cul|ture shock** N-UNCOUNT **Culture shock** is a feeling of anxiety, loneliness, and confusion that people sometimes experience when they first arrive in another country. ❑ *John is homeless, friendless, and suffering from culture shock.*

**cum|ber|some** /kʌmbərsəm/ **1** ADJ Something that is **cumbersome** is large and heavy and difficult to carry, wear, or handle. ❑ *Although the machine looks cumbersome, it is actually easy to use.* **2** ADJ A **cumbersome** system or process is very complicated and inefficient. ❑ ...*an old and cumbersome computer system.*

**cum laude** /cʊm laʊdeɪ/ ADV If a college student graduates **cum laude**, they receive the third highest honor that is possible. [AM] ❑ *She graduated cum laude from Harvard.* [from Latin]

**cu|mu|la|tive** /kyuːmyələtɪv/ ADJ If something has a **cumulative** effect, it makes the effect greater by adding to it gradually. ❑ *The benefits from eating fish are cumulative.* [from Latin]

**cu|mu|lo|nim|bus** /kyuːmyəloʊnɪmbəs/ (**cumulonimbi** /kyuːmyəloʊnɪmbaɪ/) also **cumulo-nimbus** N-VAR **Cumulonimbus** is a type of cloud, similar to cumulus, that extends to a great height and is associated with thunderstorms. [TECHNICAL]
→ see **cloud**

**cu|mu|lus** /kyuːmyələs/ (**cumuli** /kyuːmyəlaɪ/) N-VAR **Cumulus** is a type of thick white cloud formed when hot air rises very quickly. [from Latin]
→ see **cloud**

**cun|ning** /kʌnɪŋ/ **1** ADJ A **cunning** person is clever and deceitful. ❑ *These kids can be cunning.*
● **cun|ning|ly** ADV ❑ *They were cunningly disguised in golf clothes.* **2** N-UNCOUNT **Cunning** is the ability to achieve things in a clever way, often by deceiving people. ❑ *This most recent theft is an example of the cunning of today's art thieves.* [from Old English]

**cup** /kʌp/ (**cups, cupping, cupped**) **1** N-COUNT A **cup** is a small round container with a handle, that you drink from. ❑ ...*cups and saucers.* ❑ ...*a cup of coffee.* **2** N-COUNT A **cup** is a unit of measurement used in cooking, equal to 16 tablespoons or 8 fluid ounces. ❑ *Gradually add 1 cup of milk.* ❑ ...*half a cup of sugar.* **3** N-COUNT Something that is small, round, and hollow can be referred to as a **cup**. ❑ ...*flower cups.* **4** N-COUNT A **cup** is a large metal cup with two handles that is given to the winner of a game or competition. ❑ *The Stars won the Stanley Cup in 1999.* **5** V-T If you **cup** your **hands**, you make them into a curved shape like a cup. ❑ *He cupped his hands around his mouth and called out for Diane.* **6** V-T If you **cup** something in your hands, you make your hands into a curved dish-like shape and support it or hold it gently. ❑ *He cupped her chin in his hand.* [from Old English]
→ see **dish, tea, utensil**

**cup|board** /kʌbərd/ (**cupboards**) N-COUNT A **cupboard** is a piece of furniture that has one or two doors, usually contains shelves, and is used to store things. ❑ *The kitchen cupboard was full of cans of soup.* [from Old English]

**cur|able** /kyʊərəbəl/ ADJ A **curable** disease or illness can be cured. ❑ *The disease is 95 percent curable.* [from Old French]

**cu|rate** /kyʊərət/ (**curates**) N-COUNT A **curate** is a clergyman who helps a vicar or priest. [from Medieval Latin]

**cu|ra|tor** /kyʊəreɪtər, kyʊər[ei]tər/ (**curators**) N-COUNT A **curator** is someone who is in charge of the objects or works of art in a museum or art gallery. ❑ *Peter Forey is a curator at the Natural History Museum.* [from Latin]

**curb** /kɜrb/ (**curbs, curbing, curbed**) **1** V-T If you **curb** something, you control it and keep it within limits. ❑ ...*advertisements aimed at curbing the spread of AIDS.* ● **Curb** is also a noun. ❑ *He called for much*

curb

*stricter curbs on immigration.* 🔳 N-COUNT **The curb** is the raised edge of a sidewalk which separates it from the road. ❏ *I pulled over to the curb and waved at him.* [from Old French]

**curb|stone** /kɜrbstoʊn/ (**curbstones**) N-COUNT A **curbstone** is one of the stones that form a curb. ❏ *There are people sitting on the curbstones.* [from Old French]

**cure** /kyʊər/ (**cures, curing, cured**) 🔳 V-T If doctors or medical treatments **cure** someone or **cure** an illness or injury, they make the person well again. ❏ *An operation finally cured his leg injury.* ❏ *Almost overnight I was cured.* 🔳 V-T If someone or something **cures** a problem, they bring it to an end. ❏ *We need to cure our economic problems.* 🔳 V-T When food, tobacco, or animal skin **is cured**, it is dried, smoked, or salted so that it will last for a long time. ❏ *Legs of pork were cured and smoked over the fire.* 🔳 N-COUNT A **cure for** an illness or a medicine or other treatment that cures the illness. ❏ *There is still no cure for the common cold.* [from Old French]

**cur|few** /kɜrfyu/ (**curfews**) N-VAR A **curfew** is a law stating that people must stay inside their houses after a particular time at night, for example during a war. ❏ *The village was placed under curfew.* [from Old French]

**cu|ri|os|ity** /kyʊərɪɒsɪti/ (**curiosities**) 🔳 N-UNCOUNT **Curiosity** is a desire to know about something. ❏ *Ryle accepted more out of curiosity than anything else.* ❏ *...curiosity about the past.* 🔳 N-COUNT A **curiosity** is something that is interesting and fairly rare. ❏ *There is much to see in the way of castles, curiosities, and museums.* ❏ *The house is full of curiosities, collected during their travels.* [from Latin]

**cu|ri|ous** /kyʊəriəs/ 🔳 ADJ If you are **curious about** something, you are interested in it and want to know more about it. ❏ *Steve was curious about the place I came from.* ● **cu|ri|ous|ly** ADV ❏ *The woman in the shop looked at them curiously.* 🔳 ADJ If you describe something as **curious**, you mean that it is unusual or difficult to understand. ❏ *The play is a curious mixture of old and new.* ● **cu|ri|ous|ly** ADV ❏ *Harry was curiously silent through all this.* [from Latin]

**curl** /kɜrl/ (**curls, curling, curled**) 🔳 N-COUNT If you have **curls**, your hair is in the form of curves and spirals. ❏ *She was a pretty little girl with blonde curls.* 🔳 N-COUNT A **curl of** something is a piece or quantity of it that is curved or spiral in shape. ❏ *A thin curl of smoke rose from the fire.* 🔳 V-T/V-I If your hair **curls** or if you **curl** it, it is full of curls. ❏ *She has hair that refuses to curl.* ❏ *Maria curled her hair for the party.* 🔳 V-I If something **curls** somewhere, it moves there in a circles or spirals. ❏ *Smoke was curling up the chimney.* ❏ *He curled the ball into the net.* 🔳 V-I If a person or animal **curls into** a ball, they move their arms and legs toward their stomach so that their body makes a rounded shape. ❏ *He wanted to curl into a tiny ball.* ● **Curl up** means the same as **curl**. ❏ *She curled up next to him.* 🔳 V-I When a leaf, a piece of paper, or another flat object

**curls**, its edges bend toward the center. ❏ *The rose leaves have curled because of a disease.* ● **Curl up** means the same as **curl**. ❏ *The corners of the rug were curling up.* [from Middle Dutch]
▸ **curl up** → see **curl 5, 6**

**curly** /kɜrli/ (**curlier, curliest**) 🔳 ADJ **Curly** hair is full of curls. ❏ *I've got naturally curly hair.* 🔳 ADJ **Curly** objects are curved or spiral in shape. ❏ *...cauliflowers with extra long curly leaves.* [from Middle Dutch]
→ see **hair**

**cur|ren|cy** /kɜrənsi/ (**currencies**) N-VAR The money used in a particular country is referred to as its **currency**. ❏ *Tourism is the country's top earner of foreign currency.* ❏ *...a single European currency.* [from Medieval Latin]
→ see **money**

**Word Link**    *curr, curs ≈ running, flowing :*
*concurrent, current, excursion*

**cur|rent** /kɜrənt/ (**currents**) 🔳 N-COUNT A **current** is a steady, continuous flowing movement of water or air. ❏ *Under normal conditions, the ocean currents of the Pacific travel from east to west.* ❏ *I felt a current of cool air.* 🔳 N-COUNT An electric **current** is a flow of electricity through a wire or circuit. ❏ *...a powerful electric current.* 🔳 ADJ **Current** means happening, being used, or being done at the present time. ❏ *The current situation is very different to that in 1990.* ● **cur|rent|ly** ADV ❏ *He is currently unmarried.* [from Old French]
→ see **beach, erosion, ocean, tide**

**cur|rent af|fairs** also current events N-PLURAL → see **current events**

**cur|rent elec|tric|ity** N-UNCOUNT **Current electricity** is electricity that is flowing through a circuit. Compare **static electricity**.

**cur|rent ev|ents** also current affairs N-PLURAL **Current events** are political events and problems which are discussed in the media. ❏ *I know nothing about current affairs.*

**cur|ricu|lum** /kərɪkyələm/ (**curriculums** or **curricula** /kərɪkyələ/) 🔳 N-COUNT A **curriculum** is all the different courses of study that are taught in a school, college, or university. ❏ *Business skills should be part of the regular school curriculum.* 🔳 N-COUNT A particular **curriculum** is one particular course of study that is taught in a school, college, or university. ❏ *...the history curriculum.* [from Latin]

**cur|ry** /kɜri/ (**curries**) N-VAR **Curry** is a dish, originally from Asia, consisting of vegetables and sometimes meat cooked with hot spices. ❏ *I would like to make a vegetable curry, but I cannot find a recipe that is easy to follow.* [from Tamil]

**curse** /kɜrs/ (**curses, cursing, cursed**) 🔳 V-I If you **curse**, you use very impolite or offensive language, usually because you are angry about something. [WRITTEN] ❏ *I cursed and got to my feet.* ● **Curse** is also a noun. 🔳 V-T If you **curse** someone or something, you say impolite or insulting things about them because you are angry. ❏ *He cursed her and rudely pushed her aside.* ❏ *We set off again, cursing the delay.* 🔳 N-COUNT If you say that there is a **curse on** someone, you mean that there seems to be a supernatural power causing unpleasant things to happen to them. ❏ *Maybe there is a curse on my family.* 🔳 N-COUNT You can refer to something that causes a lot of trouble as a **curse**. ❏ *...the curse of high unemployment.* [from Old English]

**cur|sor** /kɜrsər/ (**cursors**) N-COUNT On a computer screen, the **cursor** is a small shape that indicates where anything that is typed by the user will appear. [COMPUTING] ❏ *He moved the cursor and clicked the mouse.* [from Old English]

**curt** /kɜrt/ ADJ If someone is **curt**, they speak in a brief and rather rude way. ❏ *"The matter is closed," was the curt reply.* • **curt|ly** ADV ❏ *"I'm leaving," she said curtly.* [from Latin]

**cur|tail** /kɜrteɪl/ (**curtails, curtailing, curtailed**) V-T If you **curtail** something, you reduce or limit it. [FORMAL] ❏ *There are plans to curtail the number of troops being sent to the region.* • **cur|tail|ment** /kɜrteɪlmənt/ N-SING [FORMAL] ❏ *...the curtailment of presidential power.*

**cur|tain** /kɜrtⁿn/ (**curtains**) ■ N-COUNT **Curtains** are pieces of material which hang from the top of a window. ❏ *...her bedroom curtains.* ■ N-SING In a theater, **the curtain** is the large piece of material that hangs in front of the stage until a performance begins. ❏ *The curtain rose.* [from Old French]

**cur|tain rod** (**curtain rods**) N-COUNT A **curtain rod** is a long, narrow pole on which you hang curtains.

**cur|va|ture** /kɜrvətʃər, -tʃuər/ N-UNCOUNT The **curvature of** something is its curved shape, especially when this shape is part of the circumference of a circle. [TECHNICAL] [from Latin]

**curve** /kɜrv/ (**curves, curving, curved**) ■ N-COUNT A **curve** is a smooth, gradually bending line, for example, part of the edge of a circle. ❏ *...the curve of his lips.* ■ N-COUNT You can refer to a change in something as a particular **curve**, especially when it is represented on a graph. ❏ *Youth crime is on a slow downward curve.* ■ V-I If something **curves**, it has the shape of a curve or moves in a curve. ❏ *Her spine curved.* ❏ *The ball curved strangely in the air.* • **curved** ADJ ❏ *...curved lines of the chairs.* [from Latin]

**cur|vi|lin|ear** /kɜrvɪlɪliər/ ADJ A **curvilinear** shape has curving lines. Compare **rectilinear**.

**cush|ion** /kʊʃⁿn/ (**cushions, cushioning, cushioned**) ■ N-COUNT A **cushion** is a fabric case filled with soft material, which you put on a seat to make it more comfortable. ❏ *...a beautiful, purple velvet cushion.* ■ V-T To **cushion** an impact means to reduce its effect. ❏ *We tried to cushion the blow.* [from Latin]

**cus|tard** /kʌstərd/ (**custards**) N-VAR **Custard** is a baked dessert made of milk, eggs, and sugar. ❏ *...a custard with a caramel sauce.* [from Middle English]
→ see **dessert**

**Word Link** custod ≈ guarding : custodial, custodian, custody

**cus|to|dial** /kʌstoudiəl/ ADJ If a child's parents are divorced or separated, the **custodial** parent is the parent who has custody of the child. [LEGAL] ❏ *...expenses that come with being the custodial parent.* [from Latin]

**cus|to|dian** /kʌstoudiən/ (**custodians**) ■ N-COUNT The **custodian** of an official building,

a company's assets, or something else valuable is the person who is officially in charge of it. ❏ *...the custodian of the holy shrines in Mecca and Medina.* ■ N-COUNT The **custodian** of a large building such as an office or a school is responsible for cleaning and maintaining it. ❏ *He served as an elementary-school custodian for 20 years.* [from Latin]

**cus|to|dy** /kʌstədi/ ■ N-UNCOUNT **Custody** is the legal right to keep and take care of a child, especially the right given to a child's mother or father when they get divorced. ❏ *I'm going to court to get custody of the children.* ❏ *Child custody is normally given to the mother.* ■ PHRASE Someone who is **in custody** has been arrested and is being kept in prison. [from Latin]

**cus|tom** /kʌstəm/ (**customs**) ■ N-VAR A **custom** is an activity, a way of behaving, or an event which is usual or traditional in a particular society or in particular circumstances. ❏ *...an ancient Japanese custom.* ❏ *It was the custom to give presents to visitors.* [from Old French] ■ → see also **customs**
→ see **culture**

**cus|tom|ary** /kʌstəmeri/ ADJ **Customary** means usual. [FORMAL] ❏ *It is customary to offer a drink or a snack to guests.* ❏ *Yvonne took her customary seat.* [from Old French]

**cus|tom|er** /kʌstəmər/ (**customers**) N-COUNT A **customer** is someone who buys goods or services, especially from a store. ❏ *...a satisfied customer.* [from Old French]

**Usage** customers, patients, and clients

Stores have *customers*: *Many small bookstores don't have enough customers to stay in business.* Professionals have *clients*: *The husband is a lawyer and the wife is an accountant, and they have many clients in common.* Doctors, dentists, nurses, and other medical practitioners have *patients*: *There were so many patients in my doctor's waiting room, I couldn't find a place to sit.*

**Word Partnership** Use customer with :

| | |
|---|---|
| N. | customer **account**, customer **loyalty**, customer **satisfaction** |
| V. | **greet** customers, **satisfy** a customer |

**cus|tom|er ser|vice** N-UNCOUNT **Customer service** refers to the way that companies behave toward their customers, for example, how well they treat them. [BUSINESS] ❏ *...a business with a strong reputation for customer service.* ❏ *The firm has an excellent customer service department.*

**cus|tom|ize** /kʌstəmaɪz/ (**customizes, customizing, customized**) V-T If you **customize** something, you change its appearance or features to suit your tastes or needs. ❏ *You can customize the camera's basic settings.* ❏ *Every year, people spend thousands of dollars customizing their cars.* [from Old French]

**cus|toms** /kʌstəmz/ ■ N-PROPER **Customs** is the official organization responsible for collecting taxes on goods coming into a country and preventing illegal goods from being brought in. ❏ *What right does Customs have to search my car?* ■ N-UNCOUNT **Customs** is the place where people arriving from a foreign country have to declare goods that they bring with them. ❏ *He walked*

C

through customs. [from Old French] 🔞 → see also
**custom**
→ see **culture**

---

## cut

❶ PHYSICAL ACTION
❷ SHORTEN OR REDUCE AMOUNT
❸ PHRASAL VERBS

---

❶ **cut** /kʌt/ (**cuts, cutting**)

The form **cut** is used in the present tense and is the past tense and past participle.

🔟 V-T/V-I If you **cut** something, you use a knife or a similar tool to remove part of it, or to mark it or damage it. ❑ *Mrs. Haines cut the ribbon.* ❑ *Cut the tomatoes in half.* ❑ *The thieves cut a hole in the fence.* ❑ *You had your hair cut, it looks great.* ❑ *This little knife cuts really well.* • **Cut** is also a noun. ❑ *Carefully make a cut in the shell with a small knife.* 🔁 V-T If you **cut yourself**, you accidentally injure yourself on a sharp object so that you bleed. ❑ *Johnson cut himself shaving.* ❑ *I started to cry because I cut my finger.* • **Cut** is also a noun. ❑ *He had a cut on his left eyebrow.* [of Scandinavian origin]
→ see Picture Dictionary: **cut**

❷ **cut** /kʌt/ (**cuts, cutting**)

The form **cut** is used in the present tense and is the past tense and past participle.

🔟 V-T If you **cut** something, you reduce it. ❑ *The aim is to cut costs.* ❑ *The UN force is to be cut by 90%.* • **Cut** is also a noun. ❑ *The economy needs an immediate 2 percent cut in interest rates.* 🔁 V-T If you **cut** part of a piece of writing or a performance, you do not publish, broadcast, or perform that part of it. ❑ *Branagh has cut the play a little.* • **Cut** is also a noun. ❑ *It was necessary to make some cuts in the text.* 🔢 V-I If you **cut across** or **through** a place, you go through it because it is the shortest route to another place. ❑ *Jesse cut across the parking lot.* 🔢 V-T To **cut** a supply of something means to stop providing it or stop it from being provided. ❑ *Winds have knocked down power lines, cutting electricity to thousands of people.* • **Cut** is also a noun. ❑ *...cuts in electricity and water supplies.* [of Scandinavian origin] 🔢 to cut something **to the bone** → see **bone** 🔢 to **cut corners** → see **corner**

❸ **cut** /kʌt/ (**cuts, cutting**)

The form **cut** is used in the present tense and is the past tense and past participle.

▶ **cut across** PHR-VERB If an issue or problem **cuts across** the division between two or more groups of people, it affects or matters to people in all the groups. ❑ *The issue of health care cuts across all age groups.*
▶ **cut back** 🔟 PHR-VERB If you **cut back** something such as expenditure or **cut back on** it, you reduce it. ❑ *Customers cut back spending in January and February.* ❑ *The government has cut back on defense spending.* 🔁 → see also **cutback**
▶ **cut down** 🔟 PHR-VERB If you **cut down on** something or **cut down** something, you use or do less of it. ❑ *He cut down on coffee and ate a balanced diet.* ❑ *Car owners were asked to cut down travel.* 🔁 PHR-VERB If you **cut down** a tree, you cut through its trunk so that it falls to the ground. ❑ *They cut down several trees.*
▶ **cut off** 🔟 PHR-VERB If you **cut** something **off**, you remove it with a knife or a similar tool. ❑ *Mrs. Johnson cut off a large piece of the meat.* ❑ *He threatened to cut my hair off.* 🔁 PHR-VERB To **cut** someone or something **off** means to separate them from things that they are normally connected with. ❑ *They cut off the army from its supplies.* • **cut off** ADJ ❑ *Without a car we still felt very cut off.* 🔢 PHR-VERB To **cut off** a supply of something means to stop providing it or stop it from being provided. ❑ *They have cut off electricity from the nation's capital.* 🔢 PHR-VERB If you get **cut off** when you are on the telephone, the line is suddenly disconnected. ❑ *When you get through, you've got to speak quickly before you get cut off.* 🔢 → see also **cutoff** 🔢 to **cut off** your **nose to spite** your **face** → see **spite**
▶ **cut out** 🔟 PHR-VERB If you **cut** something **out**, you remove or separate it from what surrounds it using scissors or a knife. ❑ *I cut the picture out and pinned it to my wall.* 🔁 PHR-VERB If you **cut**

---

## Picture Dictionary — cut

chop up     peel     slice     dice     mince

grate     saw     chop down     tear off     rip up

out a part of a text, you do not print, publish, or broadcast that part, because to include it would make the text too long or unacceptable. ❑ *They cut out all the best bits.* ■ PHR-VERB To **cut** something **out** of something means to completely remove it or stop doing or having it. ❑ *It is wise to cut out coffee during pregnancy.* ❑ *I've cut out eating eggs entirely.* ■ PHR-VERB If an object **cuts out** the light, it prevents light from reaching a place. ❑ *The curtains cut out the sunlight.* ■ PHR-VERB If an engine **cuts out**, it suddenly stops working. ❑ *The plane crashed when one of its engines cut out.*
▶ **cut up** ■ PHR-VERB If you **cut** something **up**, you cut it into several pieces. ❑ *Halve the tomatoes, then cut them up.* ■ → see also **cut up**

**cut|back** /kʌtbæk/ (**cutbacks**) N-COUNT A **cutback** is a reduction that is made in something. ❑ *...cutbacks in spending on education.*

**cute** /kyut/ (**cuter, cutest**) ■ ADJ **Cute** means pretty or attractive. [INFORMAL] ❑ *Oh, look at that dog! He's so cute.* ■ ADJ If you describe someone as **cute**, you think they are pretty or attractive. [INFORMAL] ❑ *There was this girl, and I thought she was really cute.*

| **Thesaurus** | cute | Also look up : |
|---|---|---|

ADJ. adorable, charming, pretty; (ant.) homely, ugly

**cu|ti|cle** /kyutɪkᵊl/ (**cuticles**) N-VAR **Cuticle** is a protective covering on the surface of leaves and other parts of a plant. [TECHNICAL] [from Latin]

**cut|lery** /kʌtləri/ N-UNCOUNT You can refer to knives and tools used for cutting as **cutlery**. ❑ *The catalog featured shavers, accessories, and cutlery.* [from French]

**cut|let** /kʌtlɪt/ (**cutlets**) N-COUNT A **cutlet** is a small piece of meat which is usually fried or grilled. ❑ *...grilled lamb cutlets.* [from Old French]

**cut|off** /kʌtɔf/ (**cutoffs**) ■ N-COUNT A **cutoff** or a **cutoff** point is the level or limit at which you decide that something should stop happening. ❑ *The cutoff has not yet been announced.* ■ N-PLURAL **Cut-offs** are short pants made by cutting part of the legs off old pants.

**cut|ter** /kʌtər/ (**cutters**) N-COUNT A **cutter** is a tool that you use for cutting something. ❑ *...wire cutters.* [of Scandinavian origin]

**cut|ting** /kʌtɪŋ/ (**cuttings**) ■ N-COUNT A **cutting** is a part of a plant that you have cut off so that you can grow a new plant from it. ❑ *Take cuttings from garden tomatoes in late summer.* ■ ADJ A **cutting** remark is unkind and hurts your feelings. ❑ *People make cutting remarks to help themselves feel superior.* [of Scandinavian origin]

**cut|ting board** (**cutting boards**) N-COUNT A **cutting board** is a wooden or plastic board that you chop meat or vegetables on. ❑ *She took out a cutting board and started chopping the lemons.*

**cut|ting edge** N-SING If you are **at the cutting edge** of a field of activity, you are involved in its most important or most exciting developments. ❑ *The firm of architects is at the cutting edge of modern design.*
→ see **technology**

**cuz** /kʌz/ also '**cuz** CONJ **Cuz** is an informal way of saying **because**. [SPOKEN] ❑ *I can't go 'cuz I'm a boy.*

**cya|nide** /saɪənaɪd/ N-UNCOUNT **Cyanide** is a highly poisonous substance. ❑ *His death has all the signs of cyanide poisoning.*

**cyano|bac|te|ria** /saɪənoʊbæktɪəriə/ N-PLURAL **Cyanobacteria** are bacteria that obtain their energy through photosynthesis. [TECHNICAL]

**cy|ber|café** /saɪbərkæfeɪ/ (**cybercafés**) N-COUNT A **cybercafé** is a café where people can pay to use the Internet. ❑ *The cybercafé charged $5 an hour for Internet use.*

**cy|ber|space** /saɪbərspeɪs/ N-UNCOUNT In computer technology, **cyberspace** refers to data banks and networks, considered as a space. [COMPUTING] ❑ *...a report on global warming circulating in cyberspace.*

| **Word Link** | cycl ≈ circle : bicycle, cycle, cyclical |
|---|---|

**cy|cle** /saɪkᵊl/ (**cycles, cycling, cycled**) ■ N-COUNT A **cycle** is a series of events or processes that is repeated again and again, always in the same order. ❑ *...the life cycle of the plant.* ■ N-COUNT A **cycle** is a single complete series of movements in an electrical, electronic, or mechanical process. ❑ *...10 cycles per second.* ■ N-COUNT A **cycle** is the same as a **motorcycle**. ■ V-I If you **cycle**, you ride a bicycle. ❑ *He cycled to Ingwold and back in less than two hours.* ● **cy|cling** N-UNCOUNT ❑ *The quiet country roads are ideal for cycling.* [from Late Latin]
→ see **hat, water**

**cy|clic** /saɪklɪk, saɪk-/ ADJ **Cyclic** means the same as **cyclical**. [from Late Latin]

**cy|cli|cal** /sɪklɪkᵊl, saɪk-/ ADJ A **cyclical** process is one in which a series of events happens again and again in the same order. ❑ *Human beings can do nothing to stop the cyclical progress of the changing seasons.* [from Late Latin]

**cy|clist** /saɪklɪst/ (**cyclists**) N-COUNT A **cyclist** is someone who rides a bicycle. ❑ *...better protection for cyclists.* [from Late Latin]
→ see **park**

**cy|clone** /saɪkloʊn/ (**cyclones**) N-COUNT A **cyclone** is a violent tropical storm in which the air goes around and around. ❑ *The race was called off as a cyclone struck.* [from Greek]
→ see **hurricane**

**cyl|in|der** /sɪlɪndər/ (**cylinders**) N-COUNT A **cylinder** is a shape or container with flat circular ends and long straight sides. ❑ *It was recorded on a wax cylinder.* ❑ *...oxygen cylinders.* [from Latin]
→ see **engine, solid, volume**

**cym|bal** /sɪmbᵊl/ (**cymbals**) N-COUNT A **cymbal** is a flat circular brass object that is used as a musical instrument. You hit it with a stick or clash two cymbals together, making a loud noise. [from Old English]

**cyn|ic** /sɪnɪk/ (**cynics**) N-COUNT A **cynic** is someone who believes that people usually act selfishly or dishonestly. ❑ *I have come to be very much of a cynic in matters relating to international trade agreements.* [from Latin]

**cyni|cal** /sɪnɪkᵊl/ ADJ If someone is **cynical**, they believe that people are usually selfish or dishonest. ❑ *...his cynical view of the world.* ❑ *It has made me more cynical about relationships.* ● **cyni|cal|ly** ADV ❑ *He laughed cynically.* ● **cyni|cism** /sɪnɪsɪzəm/ N-UNCOUNT ❑ *...a time of growing cynicism about* *politicians.* [from Latin]

**cy|press** /sаɪprɪs/ (**cypresses**) N-COUNT A **cypress** is a type of tree. [from Old English]

**cyst** /sɪst/ (**cysts**) N-COUNT A **cyst** is a growth containing liquid that appears inside your body or under your skin. □ ...*a minor operation to remove a cyst*. [from New Latin]

**cy|to|ki|nesis** /saɪtoʊkɪnisɪs/ N-UNCOUNT **Cytokinesis** is the stage in cell division at which the cytoplasm of the cell divides in two. [TECHNICAL]

**cyto|plasm** /saɪtəplæzəm/ N-UNCOUNT **Cytoplasm** is the material that surrounds the nucleus of a plant or animal cell. [TECHNICAL]

**cyto|sine** /saɪtəsin, -sɪn/ (**cytosines**) N-VAR **Cytosine** is one of the four basic components of the DNA molecule. It bonds with guanine. [TECHNICAL]

**czar** /zɑr/ (**czars**) N-COUNT; N-TITLE In former times, the **czar** was the ruler of Russia. [from Russian]

# Dd

**D.A.** /di eı/ (**D.A.s**) N-COUNT A **D.A.** is a **District Attorney.** [AM]

**dab** /dæb/ (**dabs, dabbing, dabbed**) ■ V-T If you **dab** something, you touch it several times using quick, light movements. □ *She was crying and dabbing her eyes with a tissue.* □ *She dabbed some perfume on her wrists.* ■ N-COUNT A **dab of** something is a small amount of it that is put onto a surface. [INFORMAL] □ *...a dab of glue.*

**dab|ble** /dæbᵊl/ (**dabbles, dabbling, dabbled**) V-I If you **dabble in** something, you are involved with it, but not very seriously. □ *He dabbled in business.* [from Dutch]

**dad** /dæd/ (**dads**) N-COUNT Your **dad** is your father. [INFORMAL] □ *How are you, Dad?* [from Greek]

**dad|dy** /dædi/ (**daddies**) N-COUNT Children often call their father **daddy**. [INFORMAL] □ *Look at me, Daddy!* [from Greek]

daffodil

**daf|fo|dil** /dæfədıl/ (**daffodils**) N-COUNT A **daffodil** is a yellow spring flower with a central part shaped like a tube and a long stem. [from Dutch]

**dag|ger** /dægər/ (**daggers**) N-COUNT A **dagger** is a weapon like a knife with two sharp edges.

**dai|ly** /deıli/ ■ ADV If something happens **daily**, it happens every day. □ *The airline flies daily to Hong Kong.* ● **Daily** is also an adjective. □ *They had daily meetings.* ■ ADJ **Daily** quantities or rates relate to a period of one day. □ *...their daily dose of vitamins.* ■ PHRASE Your **daily life** is the things that you do every day as part of your normal life. □ *Laughter was part of their daily life then.* [from Old English]

**dain|ty** /deınti/ (**daintier, daintiest**) ADJ If you describe a movement, person, or object as **dainty**, you mean that they are small, delicate, and pretty. □ *The girls were dainty.* ● **dain|ti|ly** ADV □ *She walked daintily down the steps.* [from Old French]

**dairy** /dɛəri/ (**dairies**) ■ N-COUNT A **dairy** is a company that sells milk and food made from milk, such as butter, cream, and cheese. □ *Local dairies bought milk from local farmers.* ■ ADJ **Dairy** is used to refer to foods such as butter and cheese that are made from milk. □ *He can't eat dairy products.* ■ ADJ **Dairy** is used to refer to cattle that produce milk rather than meat. □ *...a dairy farm.* [from Old English]
→ see Word Web: **dairy**

**dai|sy** /deızi/ (**daisies**) N-COUNT A **daisy** is a small wildflower with a yellow center and white petals. [from Old English]

dam

**dam** /dæm/ (**dams**) N-COUNT A **dam** is a wall that is built across a river in order to stop the water from flowing and to make a lake. **Dams** are often used to produce electricity. □ *Before the dam was built, the Campbell River used to flood.* [from Middle Low German]
→ see Word Web: **dam**

**dam|age** /dæmıdʒ/ (**damages, damaging, damaged**) ■ V-T To **damage** something means to break it, harm it, or stop it from working properly. □ *He damaged a car with a baseball bat.* □ *Failure to pay will damage the company's reputation.* ● **dam|ag|ing** ADJ □ *...the damaging effects of pollution on the environment.* ■ N-UNCOUNT **Damage** is physical harm that is caused to an object. □ *The explosion caused a lot of damage to the house.* ■ N-PLURAL If a court of law awards **damages** to someone, it orders money to be paid to them by a person who has damaged their reputation or property, or who has injured them. □ *She won more than $75,000 in damages.* [from Old French]
→ see **disaster**

## Word Web    dairy

Farmers no longer **milk** one **cow** at a time. Today most dairy **farms** use machines instead. The **milk** is taken from the cow by a vacuum-powered **milking machine**. Then it travels through a pipeline to be stored in a **refrigerated** storage tank. From there it goes to the factory for pasteurization and packaging. The largest such dairy farm in the world is the Al Safi Dairy Farm in Saudi Arabia. It has 24,000 head of **cattle** and produces about 33 million gallons of milk each year.

D

## Word Web — dam

The Egyptians built the world's first **dam** in about 2900 BC. The dam sent water into a **reservoir** near the capital city of Memphis*. Later they built another dam to prevent **flooding** south of Cairo*. Today, dams are used with **irrigation** systems to prevent **droughts**. Modern hydroelectric dams also provide more than 20% of the world's electricity. Brazil and Paraguay built the largest hydroelectric power station in the world—the Itaipu Dam. It took 18 years to build and cost 18 billion dollars! Hydroelectric power is non-polluting. However, the dams endanger some species of fish and sometimes destroy valuable forest lands.

*Memphis: an ancient city in Egypt.*
*Cairo: the capital of Egypt.*

## Thesaurus — damage — Also look up :

| | |
|---|---|
| V. | break, harm, hurt, ruin, wreck **1** |
| N. | harm, loss **2** |

**dame** /deɪm/ (**dames**) N-COUNT A **dame** is a woman. This use is old-fashioned and could cause offense. [INFORMAL] ❑ *Who does that dame think she is?* [from Old French]

**damn** /dæm/ (**damns, damning, damned**) V-T To **damn** someone or something means to criticize them severely. ❑ *His report damns the proposed law.* [from Old French]

**damn|ing** /dæmɪŋ/ ADJ If you describe evidence or a report as **damning**, you mean that it suggests very strongly that someone is guilty of a crime or has made a serious mistake. ❑ *...a damning report on the state of schools.* [from Old French]

**damp** /dæmp/ (**damper, dampest**) ADJ Something that is **damp** is slightly wet. ❑ *Her hair was still damp.* ❑ *...the damp, cold air.* ● **damp|ness** N-UNCOUNT ❑ *It was cooler, and there was dampness in the air.* [from Middle Low German]
→ see **weather**

**damp|en** /dæmpən/ (**dampens, dampening, dampened**) V-T To **dampen** something such as your enthusiasm or excitement means to make it less lively or intense. ❑ *Nothing seems to dampen his enthusiasm.* [from Middle Low German]

**dance** /dæns/ (**dances, dancing, danced**) **1** V-I When you **dance**, you move your body and feet in a way that follows a rhythm, usually to music. ❑ *He doesn't like to dance.* ● **danc|ing** N-UNCOUNT ❑ *Let's go dancing tonight.* **2** N-COUNT A **dance** is a particular series of graceful movements of your body and feet, which you usually do in time to music. ❑ *...a traditional Scottish dance.* **3** N-COUNT A **dance** is a social event where people dance with each other. ❑ *At the school dance he talked to her all evening.* **4** V-RECIP When you **dance with** someone, the two of you take part in a dance together, as partners. You can also say that two people **dance**. ❑ *Nobody wanted to dance with him.* ❑ *Shall we dance?* ● **Dance** is also a noun. ❑ *Come and have a dance with me.* **5** N-UNCOUNT **Dance** is the activity of performing dances, as a public entertainment or an art form. ❑ *...international*

dance and music. [from Old French]
→ see Picture Dictionary: **dance**

## Word Partnership — Use *dance* with :

| | |
|---|---|
| V. | let's dance **1** **4** |
| | choreograph a dance, learn to dance **2** **5** |
| N. | dance **class**, dance **moves**, dance **music**, dance **partner** **2** **5** |

**dance floor** (**dance floors**) N-COUNT In a restaurant or night club, the **dance floor** is the area where people can dance. ❑ *Everybody was on the dance floor.*

**dance form** (**dance forms**) N-COUNT A **dance form** is a type of dancing, such as ballet or tap dancing.

**dance phrase** (**dance phrases**) N-COUNT A **dance phrase** is a short section of a dance consisting of a series of interconnected movements.

**danc|er** /dænsər/ (**dancers**) N-COUNT A **dancer** is a person who earns money by dancing, or a person who is dancing. ❑ *She was a dancer with the New York City Ballet.* [from Old French]

**dance se|quence** (**dance sequences**) N-COUNT A **dance sequence** is a section of a dance that develops a particular theme or idea.

**dance struc|ture** (**dance structures**) N-VAR **Dance structure** is the general way in which a dance is organized and the way that the parts of the dance relate to one another.

**dance study** (**dance studies**) N-VAR A **dance study** is a series of movements that a dance teacher or student performs in order to develop an idea for a dance.

**dan|de|lion** /dændɪlaɪən/ (**dandelions**) N-COUNT A **dandelion** is a wild plant which has yellow flowers with lots of thin petals. When the petals of each flower drop off, a fluffy white ball of seeds grows. [from Old French]

**dan|ger** /deɪndʒər/ (**dangers**) **1** N-UNCOUNT **Danger** is the possibility that someone may be harmed or killed. ❑ *He faced great danger with wonderful bravery.* **2** N-COUNT A **danger** is something or someone that can hurt or harm you. ❑ *...the dangers of speeding.* **3** N-SING If there is a

**danger that** something unpleasant will happen, it is possible that it will happen. ❑ *There is a real danger that this crisis will spread across the country.* ❑ *There was no danger that the prisoner would escape.* [from Old French]
→ see **hero**

| Word Link | *ous* ≈ *having the qualities of :* *danger*ous*, fabul*ous*, nutriti*ous* |

**dan|ger|ous** /de̱ɪndʒərəs, de̱ɪndʒrəs/ ADJ If something is **dangerous**, it is able or likely to hurt or harm you. ❑ *It's a dangerous road.* ❑ *...dangerous dogs.* ● **dan|ger|ous|ly** ADV ❑ *He is dangerously ill.* [from Old French]

| Thesaurus | *dangerous* Also look up : |
| ADJ. | risky, threatening, unsafe |

| Word Partnership | Use *dangerous* with : |
| N. | dangerous **area**, dangerous **criminal**, dangerous **driving**, dangerous **man**, dangerous **situation** |
| ADJ. | **potentially** dangerous |

**dan|gle** /dæ̱ŋgəl/ (**dangles, dangling, dangled**) V-T/V-I If something **dangles from** somewhere or if you **dangle** it somewhere, it hangs or swings loosely. ❑ *A gold bracelet dangled from his left wrist.* [from Danish]

**dare** /de̱ər/ (**dares, daring, dared**) ■ V-T If you do not **dare to** do something, you do not have enough courage to do something, or you do not want to do it because you fear what might happen as a result. If you **dare to** do something, you do something which requires a lot of courage. ❑ *Most people hate Harry but they don't dare to say so.* ● **Dare** is also a modal. ❑ *Dare she risk staying where she was?* ❑ *She dare not leave the house.* ■ V-T If you **dare** someone **to** do something, you challenge them to prove that they are not frightened of doing it. ❑ *His friends dared him to ask Randle for a job.* ■ N-COUNT A **dare** is a challenge which one person gives to another to do something dangerous or frightening. ❑ *Jones stole the car on a dare.* ■ PHRASE You say "**how dare you**" when you are very shocked and angry about something that someone has done. [SPOKEN] ❑ *How dare you pick up the phone and listen in on my conversations!* [from Old English]

**dar|ing** /de̱ərɪŋ/ ■ ADJ A **daring** person is willing to do things that might be dangerous or shocking. ❑ *His daring rescue saved the lives of the boys.* ❑ *Bergit was more daring than I was.* ■ N-UNCOUNT **Daring** is the courage to do things which might be dangerous or which might shock or anger other people. ❑ *We all admired his daring when we were boys.* [from Old English]

**dark** /dɑ̱rk/ (**darker, darkest**) ■ ADJ When it is **dark**, there is not enough light to see properly. ❑ *It was too dark to see much.* ❑ *People usually shut the curtains when it gets dark.* ● **dark|ness** N-UNCOUNT ❑ *The light went out, and we were in total darkness.* ● **dark|ly** ADV ❑ *...a darkly lit hall.* ■ ADJ If you describe something as **dark**, you mean that it is black in color, or a shade that is close to black. ❑ *He wore a dark suit.* ❑ *...a dark blue dress.* ● **dark|ly** ADV ❑ *His skin was darkly tanned.* ■ ADJ If someone has **dark** hair, eyes, or skin, they have brown or black hair, eyes, or skin. ❑ *He had dark, curly hair.* ■ ADJ **Dark** thoughts are sad, and show that you are expecting something unpleasant to happen. [LITERARY] ❑ *Troy's chatter stopped me from thinking dark thoughts.* ● **dark|ly** ADV ❑ *"I might need to talk to you," he said darkly.* ■ N-SING **The dark** is the lack of light in a place. ❑ *Children are often afraid of the dark.* ■ PHRASE If you are **in the dark about** something, you do not know anything about it. ❑ *He was still in the dark about what was happening.* [from Old English]

| Word Partnership | Use *dark* with : |
| V. | **get** dark ■ |
| | **afraid of the** dark, **scared of the** dark ■ |
| N. | dark **clouds**, dark **suit** ■ |

**dark choco|late** N-UNCOUNT **Dark chocolate** is dark brown chocolate that has a stronger and less sweet taste than milk chocolate. ❑ *I don't like dark chocolate.*

---

## Picture Dictionary    dance

dancing

folk dancing

tap dancing

ballroom dancing

modern dance

ballet

**dark|en** /dɑrkən/ (**darkens, darkening, darkened**) **1** V-T/V-I If something **darkens** or if a person or thing **darkens** it, it becomes darker. □ *The sky darkened suddenly.* **2** V-T/V-I If your mood **darkens** or if something **darkens** your mood, you suddenly become unhappy. [LITERARY] □ *My happy mood suddenly darkened.* [from Old English]

**dark|room** /dɑrkrum/ (**darkrooms**) N-COUNT A **darkroom** is a room which can be completely closed off from natural light and is lit only by red light. It is used for developing photographs.

**dar|ling** /dɑrlɪŋ/ (**darlings**) **1** N-VOC You call someone **darling** if you love them or like them very much. □ *Thank you, darling.* **2** ADJ Some people use **darling** to describe someone or something that they love or like very much. [INFORMAL] □ *They have a darling baby boy.* **3** N-COUNT If you describe someone as a **darling**, you are fond of them and think that they are nice. [INFORMAL] □ *He's such a darling.* [from Old English]

**darn** /dɑrn/ (**darns, darning, darned**) **1** V-T If you **darn** something knitted or made of cloth, you repair a hole in it by sewing stitches across the hole and then weaving stitches in and out of them. □ *Aunt Emilie darned old socks.* **2** ADJ People sometimes use **darn** or **darned** to emphasize what they are saying, often when they are annoyed. [INFORMAL] □ *There's not a darn thing he can do.* ● **Darn** is also an adverb. □ *We'll do what we darn well want.* **3** EXCLAM You can say **darn it** to show that you are very annoyed about something. [INFORMAL] □ *Darn it! Why didn't I think of that idea?* **4** PHRASE You can say **I'll be darned** to show that you are very surprised about something. [INFORMAL] □ *"A talking pig!" he exclaimed. "Well, I'll be darned."* [Sense 1 from French]

**dart** /dɑrt/ (**darts, darting, darted**) **1** V-I If a person or animal **darts** somewhere, they move there suddenly and quickly. [WRITTEN] □ *Ingrid darted across the street.* **2** V-T/V-I If you **dart** a look at someone or something, or if your eyes **dart to** them, you look at them very quickly. [LITERARY] □ *She darted a sly glance at Bramwell.* **3** N-COUNT A **dart** is a small, narrow object with a sharp point which can be thrown or shot. □ *The idea was to burst a balloon by throwing a dart.* **4** N-UNCOUNT **Darts** is a game in which you throw darts at a round board which has numbers on it. □ *I enjoy playing darts.* [from Old French]

**dash** /dæʃ/ (**dashes, dashing, dashed**) **1** V-I If you **dash** somewhere, you run or go there quickly and suddenly. □ *Suddenly she dashed downstairs.* ● **Dash** is also a noun. □ *...a quick dash to the store.* **2** V-T If an event or person **dashes** your hopes, it destroys them by making it impossible that the thing that is hoped for will ever happen. [LITERARY] □ *The fighting dashed hopes for a return to peace.* **3** N-COUNT A **dash of** something is a small quantity or amount of it. □ *Pour over olive oil and a dash of vinegar.* **4** N-COUNT A **dash** is a straight, horizontal line used in writing, for example, to separate two main clauses whose meanings are closely connected. □ *Sometimes the dash ( — ) is used in places where a colon could also be used.* **5** N-COUNT A **dash** is a short fast race. [from Middle English]
▶ **dash off 1** PHR-VERB If you **dash off to** a place, you go there very quickly. □ *He dashed off to the restaurant.* **2** PHR-VERB If you **dash off** a piece of writing, you write or compose it very quickly,

without thinking about it very much. □ *In the waiting room, he dashed off a short poem.*

**dash|board** /dæʃbɔrd/ (**dashboards**) N-COUNT The **dashboard** in a car is the panel facing the driver's seat where most of the instruments and switches are. □ *The clock on the dashboard said it was two o'clock.* [from Middle English]

dashboard

**da|ta** /deɪtə, dætə/ **1** N-PLURAL You can refer to information as **data**, especially when it is in the form of facts or statistics that you can analyze. □ *The study was based on data from 2,100 women.* **2** N-UNCOUNT **Data** is information that can be stored and used by a computer program. [COMPUTING] □ *A CD-ROM can hold huge amounts of data.* [from Latin]
→ see **forecast**

| **Thesaurus** | data | Also look up : |
| --- | --- | --- |
| N. | facts, figures, information, results, statistics **1** | |

**data|base** /deɪtəbeɪs, dætə-/ (**databases**) also **data base** N-COUNT A **database** is a collection of data that is stored in a computer and that can easily be used and added to. □ *There is a database of names of people who are allowed to vote.*

**da|ta en|try** N-UNCOUNT **Data entry** is the activity of putting data into a computer, for example, by using a keyboard. □ *A simple data entry mistake was the cause of the computer error.*

**da|ta ta|ble** (**data tables**) N-COUNT A **data table** is a chart containing a set of data.

**date** /deɪt/ (**dates, dating, dated**) **1** N-COUNT A **date** is a specific time that can be named, for example, a particular day or a particular year. □ *What's the date today?* **2** N-COUNT A **date** is an appointment to meet someone or go out with them, especially someone with whom you are having, or would like to have, a romantic relationship. □ *I have a date with Bob.* **3** V-RECIP If you **are dating** someone, you go out with them regularly because you are having a romantic relationship with them. You can also say that two people **are dating**. □ *I dated a woman who was a teacher.* **4** N-COUNT If you have a date with someone with whom you are having, or may soon have, a romantic relationship, you can refer to that person as your **date**. □ *His date was one of the girls in the show.* **5** N-COUNT A **date** is a small, dark-brown, sticky fruit with a stone inside. Dates grow on palm trees in hot countries. **6** V-T If you **date** something, you give or discover the date when it was made or when it began. □ *Experts have dated the jug to the fifteenth century.* **7** V-T When you **date** something such as a letter or a check, you write that day's date on it. □ *He dated and signed the letter.* **8** V-I If something **dates**, it goes out of fashion and becomes unacceptable to modern tastes. □ *...a classic style which never dates.* ● **dat|ed** ADJ □ *Some of his ideas are dated.* **9** → see also **out of date 10** PHRASE **To date** means up until the present time. □ *"Dottie" is his best novel to date.* [from Old French]
→ see **fossil**

▶ **date back** PHR-VERB If something **dates back to** a particular time, it started or was made at that time. ❑ *The issue dates back to the 1930s.*

N.  **birth** date, **cut-off** date, **due** date, **expiration** date ❶
V.  **set a** date ❶ ❷
    date **and sign** ❼

**date rape** N-UNCOUNT **Date rape** is when a man rapes a woman after having spent the evening socially with her.

**daub** /dɔb/ (**daubs, daubing, daubed**) V-T When you **daub** a substance such as mud or paint on something, you spread it on that thing in a rough or careless way. ❑ *The children daubed wet mud all over the place.* [from Old French]

**daugh|ter** /dɔtər/ (**daughters**) N-COUNT Someone's **daughter** is their female child. ❑ *...Flora and her daughter Catherine.* ❑ *...the daughter of a university professor.* [from Old English]
→ see **child**

**daugh|ter cell** (**daughter cells**) N-COUNT A **daughter cell** is one of the two cells that are formed when a single cell divides. [TECHNICAL]

**daughter-in-law** (**daughters-in-law**) N-COUNT Someone's **daughter-in-law** is the wife of their son.

**daunt** /dɔnt/ (**daunts, daunting, daunted**) V-T If something **daunts** you, it makes you feel slightly afraid or worried about dealing with it. ❑ *Nothing daunted her.* ● **daunt|ed** ADJ ❑ *It is hard not to feel a little daunted.* ● **daunt|ing** ADJ ❑ *...the daunting task of cooking a meal for 100 people.* [from Old French]

**dawn** /dɔn/ (**dawns, dawning, dawned**)
❶ N-VAR **Dawn** is the time of day when light first appears in the sky, just before the sun rises. ❑ *Nancy woke at dawn.* ❷ N-SING **The dawn of a** period of time or a situation is the beginning of it. [LITERARY] ❑ *...the dawn of a new age in computing.* ❸ V-I If something **is dawning**, it is beginning to develop or come into existence. [WRITTEN] ❑ *A new century was dawning.* ● **dawn|ing** N-SING ❑ *...the dawning of the space age.* [from Old English]
▶ **dawn on** or **dawn upon** PHR-VERB If a fact or idea **dawns on** you, you realize it. ❑ *It took a while to dawn on me that I was trapped.*

**day** /deɪ/ (**days**) ❶ N-COUNT A **day** is one of the seven twenty-four hour periods of time in a week. ❑ *It snowed every day last week.* ❷ N-COUNT You can refer to a particular period in history as a particular **day** or as particular **days**. ❑ *...the most famous artist of his day.* ❑ *...the early days of the war.* ❸ N-VAR **Day** is the time when it is light, or the time when you are up and doing things. ❑ *Twenty-seven million working days are lost each year due to work accidents and sickness.* ❑ *The streets are busy during the day.* ❹ PHRASE If you **call it a day**, you decide to stop what you are doing because you are tired of it or because it is not successful. ❑ *They had no money left so decided to call it a day.* ❺ PHRASE **One day** or **some day** or **one of these days** means at some time in the future. ❑ *I dreamed of living in Dallas one day.* ❑ *I hope some day you will find the woman who will make you happy.* [from Old English]
→ see **year**

**day care** also **daycare** N-UNCOUNT **Day care** is care that is provided during the day for people who cannot take care of themselves, such as small children, old people, or people who are ill. Day care is provided by paid workers. ❑ *The day care for her 2-year-old son was canceled.* ❑ *...a daycare center for elderly people.*

**day|dream** /deɪdrim/ (**daydreams, daydreaming, daydreamed**) ❶ V-I If you **daydream**, you think about pleasant things for a period of time, usually about things you would like to happen. ❑ *I've been daydreaming about a job in France.* ❑ *He daydreams of being a famous journalist.* ❷ N-COUNT A **daydream** is a series of pleasant thoughts, usually about things that you would like to happen. ❑ *He escaped into daydreams of handsome men and beautiful women.*

**day|light** /deɪlaɪt/ ❶ N-UNCOUNT **Daylight** is the natural light that there is during the day, before it gets dark. ❑ *Lack of daylight often makes people feel depressed.* ❷ PHRASE If you say that a crime is committed **in broad daylight**, you are expressing your surprise that it is done during the day when people can see it, rather than at night. ❑ *He was attacked in broad daylight.*

**day|light sav|ing time** also **daylight savings time**, **daylight savings** N-UNCOUNT **Daylight saving time** is a period of time in the spring when the clocks are set one hour forward, so that people can have extra light in the evening. [AM]

**day|time** /deɪtaɪm/ N-SING **The daytime** is the part of a day between the time when it gets light and the time when it gets dark. ❑ *In the daytime he stayed in his room, sleeping, or listening to music.*

**day-to-day** ADJ **Day-to-day** things or activities exist or happen every day as part of ordinary life. ❑ *I pay our day-to-day expenses in cash.*

**dazed** /deɪzd/ ADJ If someone is **dazed**, they are confused and unable to think clearly, often because of shock or a blow to the head. ❑ *The former hostages were exhausted, hungry and dazed.* [from Old Norse]

**daz|zle** /dæzªl/ (**dazzles, dazzling, dazzled**) ❶ V-T If someone or something **dazzles** you, you are extremely impressed by their skill, qualities, or beauty. ❑ *George dazzled her with his knowledge of the world.* ❷ V-T If a bright light **dazzles** you, it makes you unable to see properly for a short time. ❑ *The sun, reflected on the water, dazzled me.*

**dazz|ling** /dæzlɪŋ/ ❶ ADJ Something that is **dazzling** is very impressive or beautiful. ❑ *Lydia gave Paige a dazzling smile.* ● **dazz|ling|ly** ADV ❑ *The view was dazzlingly beautiful.* ❷ ADJ A **dazzling** light is very bright and makes you unable to see properly for a short time. ❑ *He shielded his eyes against the dazzling sun.* ● **dazz|ling|ly** ADV ❑ *The sun was dazzlingly bright.*

**dead** /dɛd/ ❶ ADJ A person, animal, or plant that is **dead** is no longer living. ❑ *"Do you live on your own?" — "Yes. My husband's dead."* ❑ *The group had shot dead another hostage.* ● **The dead** are people who are dead. ❑ *Two soldiers were among the dead.* ❷ ADJ A telephone or piece of electrical equipment that is **dead** is no longer functioning, for example, because it no longer has any electrical power. ❑ *I answered the phone and the line went dead.* **3** ADJ **Dead** is used to mean "complete" or "absolute," especially before the words "center," "silence," and "stop." ❑ *They hurried about in dead silence.* **4** ADV **Dead** means "precisely" or "exactly." ❑ *Mars was visible, dead in the center of the telescope.* **5** PHRASE To **stop dead** means to suddenly stop happening or moving. To **stop** someone or something **dead** means to cause them to suddenly stop happening or moving. ❑ *We all stopped dead and looked at it.* [from Old English] **6** to **stop dead in** your **tracks** → see **track**

| Thesaurus | dead | Also look up : |
|---|---|---|
| ADJ. | deceased, lifeless; (ant.) alive, living **1** | |

**dead end (dead ends) 1** N-COUNT If a street is a **dead end**, there is no way out at one end of it. ❑ *There was another alleyway which came to a dead end.* **2** ADJ A **dead-end** job or course of action is one that you think is bad because it does not lead to further developments or progress. ❑ *Waitressing was a dead-end job.*

**dead|line** /dɛdlaɪn/ **(deadlines)** N-COUNT A **deadline** is a time or date before which a particular task must be finished or a particular thing must be done. ❑ *We were not able to meet the deadline because of several delays.*

**dead|lock** /dɛdlɒk/ **(deadlocks)** N-VAR If a dispute or series of negotiations reaches **deadlock**, neither side is willing to give in at all and no agreement can be made. ❑ *It looks as if the peace talks could end in deadlock.*

**dead|ly** /dɛdli/ **(deadlier, deadliest) 1** ADJ If something is **deadly**, it is likely or able to cause death, or has already caused death. ❑ *...assault with a deadly weapon.* ❑ *...a deadly disease currently affecting dolphins.* **2** ADJ If you describe a person or their behavior as **deadly**, you mean that they will do or say anything to get what they want, without caring about other people. ❑ *She gave me a deadly look.* **3** ADJ A **deadly** situation has unpleasant or dangerous consequences. ❑ *...a deadly combination of hunger and war.* [from Old English]

**deaf** /dɛf/ **(deafer, deafest) 1** ADJ Someone who is **deaf** is unable to hear anything or is unable to hear very well. ❑ *She is now totally deaf.* ● **The deaf** are people who are deaf. ❑ *Many regular TV programs are captioned for the deaf.* ● **deaf|ness** N-UNCOUNT ❑ *Because of her deafness she found conversations difficult.* [from Old English] **2** to **fall on deaf ears** → see **ear 3** to **turn a deaf ear** → see **ear** → see **disability**

**deaf|en** /dɛfən/ **(deafens, deafening, deafened)** V-T If a noise **deafens** you, it is so loud that you cannot hear anything else at the same time. ❑ *The noise of the engine deafened her.* [from Old English]

**deaf|en|ing** /dɛfənɪŋ/ ADJ A **deafening** noise is a very loud noise. ❑ *...the deafening sound of gunfire.* [from Old English]

| deal |
|---|
| ❶ QUANTIFIER USES |
| ❷ VERB AND NOUN USES |

**❶ deal** /dil/ QUANT If you say that you need or have **a great deal of** or **a good deal of** a particular thing, you are emphasizing that you need or have

a lot of it. ❑ *...a great deal of money.* ❑ *She knew a good deal more than she admitted.* [from Old English]

**❷ deal** /dil/ **(deals, dealing, dealt) 1** N-COUNT If you **make a deal, do a deal,** or **cut a deal,** you complete an agreement or an arrangement with someone, especially in business. [BUSINESS] ❑ *They made a deal to split the money between them.* ❑ *Japan did a deal with the U.S. on rice imports.* **2** V-I If a person, company, or store **deals in** a particular type of goods, their business involves buying or selling those goods. [BUSINESS] ❑ *They deal in antiques.* ● **deal|er (dealers)** N-COUNT ❑ *...an antique dealer.* **3** V-T If you **deal** playing cards, you give them out to the players in a game of cards. ❑ *She dealt each player a card.* ● **Deal out** means the same as **deal**. ❑ *Dalton dealt out five cards to each player.* [from Old English] **4** → see also **dealings**
▸ **deal out 1** PHR-VERB If someone **deals out** a punishment or harmful action, they punish or harm someone. [WRITTEN] ❑ *I'll leave you to deal out whatever punishment you feel is appropriate.* **2** → see also **deal ❷ 3**
▸ **deal with 1** PHR-VERB When you **deal with** something or someone that needs attention, you give your attention to them, and often solve a problem or make a decision concerning them. ❑ *...the way that banks deal with complaints.* **2** PHR-VERB If a book, speech, or movie **deals with** a particular thing, it has that thing as its subject or is concerned with it. ❑ *This is a sad story dealing with love and grief.* **3** PHR-VERB If you **deal with** a particular person or organization, you have business relations with them. ❑ *When I worked in Florida I dealt with tourists all the time.*

**deal|ings** /dilɪŋz/ N-PLURAL Someone's **dealings with** a person or organization are the relations that they have with them or the business that they do with them. ❑ *He has learned little in his dealings with the community.* [from Middle Low German]

**dean** /din/ **(deans) 1** N-COUNT A **dean** is an important official at a university or college. ❑ *She was dean of the University of Washington's Graduate School.* **2** N-COUNT A **dean** is a priest who is the main administrator of a large church. ❑ *...Bob Gregg, dean of the Chapel, Stanford Memorial Church.* **3** N-COUNT The **dean** of a group is the most important member of that group. ❑ *Aaron Copland was known as the dean of American composers.* [from Old English]

**dear** /dɪər/ **(dearer, dearest, dears) 1** ADJ You use **dear** to describe someone or something that you feel affection for. ❑ *Mrs. Cavendish is a dear friend of mine.* **2** ADJ If something is **dear to** you or **dear to** your **heart**, you care deeply about it. ❑ *This is a subject very dear to the hearts of teachers.* **3** ADJ **Dear** is written at the beginning of a letter, followed by the name or title of the person you are writing to. ❑ *Dear Peter, How are you?* ❑ *...Dear Sir or Madam.* **4** N-VOC You can call someone **dear** as a sign of affection. ❑ *Are you feeling better, dear?* [from Old English]

**dear|est** /dɪərɪst/ ADJ When you are writing to someone you are very fond of, you can use **dearest** at the beginning of a letter before the person's name or the word you are using to address them. ❑ *Dearest Maria, I hope you are well.* [from Old English]

**dear|ly** /dɪ̯ərli/ ■ ADV If you love someone **dearly**, you love them very much. [FORMAL] ❑ *She loved her father dearly.* ② ADV If you would **dearly** like to do or have something, you would very much like to do it or have it. [FORMAL] ❑ *I would dearly love to marry.* ③ PHRASE If you **pay dearly for** doing something or if it **costs** you **dearly**, you suffer a lot as a result. [FORMAL] ❑ *He paid dearly for his mistakes.* [from Old English]

**death** /dɛθ/ (**deaths**) ■ N-VAR **Death** is the permanent end of the life of a person or animal. ❑ *1.5 million people are in danger of death from hunger.* ❑ *…the thirtieth anniversary of her death.* ② PHRASE If you say that something is a matter **of life and death**, you are emphasizing that it is extremely important, often because someone may die or suffer great harm if people do not act immediately. ❑ *Never mind, John, it's not a matter of life and death.* ③ PHRASE If someone **is put to death**, they are executed. [FORMAL] ❑ *He was put to death for his crimes.* ④ PHRASE You use **to death** after an adjective or a verb to emphasize the action, state, or feeling mentioned. For example, if you are **frightened to death** or **bored to death**, you are extremely frightened or bored. ❑ *I was scared to death just watching him climbing the cliff.* [from Old English]

**Word Partnership** Use *death* with :

| ADJ. | **accidental** death, **sudden** death, **violent** death ■ |
| N. | **brush with** death, **cause of** death, death **threat**, *someone's* death ■ |

**death pen|al|ty** N-SING The **death penalty** is the punishment of death used in some countries for people who have committed very serious crimes. ❑ *Both men could face the death penalty.*

**death row** /dɛθroʊ/ N-UNCOUNT If someone is **on death row**, they are in the part of a prison which contains the cells for criminals who have been sentenced to death. ❑ *He was on death row for 11 years.*

**death toll** (**death tolls**) also **death-toll** N-COUNT The **death toll** of an accident, disaster, or war is the number of people who die in it. ❑ *The death toll from the crash rose to 83.*

**de|ba|cle** /dɪbɑk³l, -bæk³l/ (**debacles**) N-COUNT A **debacle** is an event or attempt that is a complete failure. ❑ *The government wants to avoid another election debacle.* [from French]

**de|bat|able** /dɪbe̯ɪtəb³l/ ADJ If you say that something is **debatable**, you mean that it is not certain. ❑ *It is debatable whether or not he was right to stay.* [from Old French]

**de|bate** /dɪbe̯ɪt/ (**debates, debating, debated**) ■ N-VAR A **debate** is a discussion about a subject on which people have different views. ❑ *An intense debate is going on within the government.* ❑ *There has been a lot of debate among teachers about this subject.* ② N-COUNT A **debate** is a formal discussion, for example, in a parliament or institution, in which people express different opinions about a particular subject and then vote on it. ❑ *There was a debate in Congress on immigration reform.* ③ V-RECIP If people **debate** a topic, they discuss it fairly formally, putting forward different views. You can also say that one person **debates** a topic **with**

another person. ❑ *The committee will debate the issue today.* ❑ *NASA officials are debating whether the space flight should end early.* ④ V-T If you **debate** whether to do something or what to do, you think or talk about possible courses of action before deciding exactly what you are going to do. ❑ *Emma was debating whether to go or not.* [from Old French] → see **election**

**Word Partnership** Use *debate* with :

| V. | **open to** debate ■ ② |
| ADJ. | **major** debate, **ongoing** debate, **televised** debate ■ ② **political** debate, **presidential** debate ② |
| N. | debate **over** *something*, debate **the issue** ③ ④ |

**deb|it** /dɛbɪt/ (**debits, debiting, debited**) ■ V-T When your bank **debits** your account, money is taken from it and paid to someone else. ❑ *We will confirm the amount before debiting your account.* ② N-COUNT A **debit** is a record of the money taken from your bank account, for example, when you write a check. ❑ *The total of debits must balance the total of credits.* [from Latin]

**deb|it card** (**debit cards**) N-COUNT A **debit card** is a bank card that you can use to pay for things. When you use it the money is taken out of your bank account immediately.

**de|bris** /dəbri, deɪ-/ N-UNCOUNT **Debris** is pieces from something that has been destroyed or pieces of trash or unwanted material that are spread around. ❑ *Several people were killed by flying debris.* [from French]

**debt** /dɛt/ (**debts**) ■ N-VAR A **debt** is a sum of money that you owe someone. ❑ *He is still paying off his debts.* ② N-UNCOUNT **Debt** is the state of owing money. ❑ *…a report on the amount of debt people owe.* ③ PHRASE If you are **in debt** or **get into debt**, you owe money. If you are **out of debt** or **get out of debt**, you succeed in paying all the money that you owe. ❑ *Many students get into debt.* [from Old French]

**Word Partnership** Use *debt* with :

| V. | **incur** debt, **pay off a** debt, **reduce** debt, **repay a** debt ■ |
| ADV. | **deeply in** debt ③ |

**debt|or** /dɛtər/ (**debtors**) N-COUNT A **debtor** is a country, organization, or person who owes money. ❑ *…the question of how best to help the world's poorest debtor nations.* [from Old French]

**de|but** /deɪbyu/ (**debuts**) N-COUNT The **debut** of a performer or sports player is their first public performance, appearance, or recording. ❑ *She made her debut in a 1937 production of "Hamlet."* [from French]

**dec|ade** /dɛkeɪd/ (**decades**) N-COUNT A **decade** is a period of ten years, especially one that begins with a year ending in 0, for example, 1980 to 1989. ❑ *…the last decade of the nineteenth century.* [from Old French]

**deca|dent** /dɛkədənt/ ADJ If you say that a person or society is **decadent**, you disapprove of them because you think that they have low moral standards and are interested mainly in pleasure. ❑ *…the decadent lifestyles of some famous people.*

**d**

● **deca|dence** N-UNCOUNT ❑ *The empire was falling into decadence.* [from French]

**de|cal** /dikæl/ (**decals**) N-COUNT **Decals** are pieces of paper with a design on one side. The design can be transferred onto a surface by heating it, soaking it in water, or pressing it hard. [from French]

**de|cay** /dikeɪ/ (**decays, decaying, decayed**)
◼ V-I When something such as a dead body, a dead plant, or a tooth **decays**, it is gradually destroyed by a natural process. ❑ *The bodies slowly decayed.* ● **Decay** is also a noun. ❑ *Eating too much candy causes tooth decay.* ● **de|cayed** ADJ ❑ *Even young children can have teeth so decayed they need to be pulled.* ◼ V-I If something such as a society, system, or institution **decays**, it gradually becomes weaker or its condition gets worse. ❑ *The old standards have decayed.* ● **Decay** is also a noun. ❑ *There are problems of urban decay.* [from Old Northern French]
→ see **teeth**

**de|ceased** /dɪsist/ (**deceased**) ◼ N-SING OR N-PLURAL **The deceased** is used to refer to a particular person or to particular people who have recently died. [LEGAL] ❑ *Police will inform the families of the deceased.* ◼ ADJ A **deceased** person is one who has recently died. [FORMAL] ❑ *...his recently deceased mother.* [from Old French]

**de|ceit** /dɪsit/ (**deceits**) N-VAR **Deceit** is behavior that is deliberately intended to make people believe something which is not true. ❑ *Losing with honor is better than winning by lies and deceit.* [from Old French]

**de|ceit|ful** /dɪsitfəl/ ADJ If you say that someone is **deceitful**, you mean that they behave in a dishonest way by making other people believe something that is not true. ❑ *The report was deceitful and misleading.* [from Old French]

**de|ceive** /dɪsiv/ (**deceives, deceiving, deceived**)
V-T If you **deceive** someone, you make them believe something that is not true, usually in order to get some advantage for yourself. ❑ *He has deceived us all.* [from Old French]

**De|cem|ber** /dɪsɛmbər/ (**Decembers**) N-VAR **December** is the twelfth and last month of the year in the Western calendar. ❑ *...a bright morning in December.* [from Old French]

**de|cen|cy** /disənsi/ N-UNCOUNT **Decency** is the quality of following accepted moral standards. ❑ *His sense of decency forced him to resign.* [from Latin]

**de|cent** /disənt/ ◼ ADJ **Decent** is used to describe something which is considered to be of an acceptable standard or quality. ❑ *He didn't get a decent explanation.* ● **de|cent|ly** ADV ❑ *They treated their prisoners decently.* ◼ ADJ **Decent** is used to describe something which is morally correct or acceptable. ❑ *After a decent interval, she married again.* ● **de|cent|ly** ADV ❑ *Can't you dress more decently?* [from Latin]

**de|cen|tral|ize** /disɛntrəlaɪz/ (**decentralizes, decentralizing, decentralized**) V-T/V-I To **decentralize** government or a large organization means to move some departments away from the main administrative area, or to give more power to local departments. ❑ *The company began to decentralize thirty years ago.* ● **de|cen|trali|za|tion** /disɛntrəlizeɪʃᵊn/ N-UNCOUNT ❑ *He is against the*

*idea of increased decentralization.*

**de|cep|tion** /dɪsɛpʃᵊn/ (**deceptions**) N-VAR **Deception** is the act of deceiving someone or the state of being deceived by someone. ❑ *He admitted obtaining property by deception.* [from Old French]

**de|cep|tive** /dɪsɛptɪv/ ADJ If something is **deceptive**, it encourages you to believe something which is not true. ❑ *He looked quite happy, but appearances can be deceptive.* ● **de|cep|tive|ly** ADV ❑ *The atmosphere was deceptively peaceful.* [from Old French]

**deci|bel** /dɛsɪbɛl/ (**decibels**) N-COUNT A **decibel** is a unit of measurement which is used to indicate how loud a sound is. ❑ *80 decibels is about the level of a ringing alarm clock.*

**de|cide** /dɪsaɪd/ (**decides, deciding, decided**)
◼ V-T/V-I If you **decide** to do something, you choose to do it, usually after you have thought carefully about the other possibilities. ❑ *She decided to take a course in philosophy.* ❑ *Think about it very carefully before you decide.* ◼ V-T If a person or group of people **decides** something, they choose what something should be like or how a particular problem should be solved. ❑ *Schools need to decide the best way of testing students.* ◼ V-T If an event or fact **decides** something, it makes it certain that a particular choice will be made or that there will be a particular result. ❑ *This goal decided the game.* ❑ *The election will decide if either party controls both houses of Congress.* ◼ V-T If you **decide** that something is true, you form that opinion about it after considering the facts. ❑ *He decided Franklin was suffering from a bad cold.* [from Old French]
▶ **decide on** PHR-VERB If you **decide on** something or **decide upon** something, you choose it from two or more possibilities. ❑ *Have you decided on a name for the baby?*

| **Thesaurus** | *decide* | Also look up : |
|---|---|---|
| v. | choose, elect, pick, select ◼ ◼ | |

| **Word Partnership** | Use *decide* with : |
|---|---|
| v. | **help (to)** decide, **let** *someone* decide **try to** decide ◼ ◼ |
| ADJ. | **unable to** decide ◼ ◼ ◼ |

**de|cid|ed** /dɪsaɪdɪd/ ADJ **Decided** means clear and definite. ❑ *She is a decided improvement on my last boss.* [from Old French]

**de|cid|ed|ly** /dɪsaɪdɪdli/ ADV **Decidedly** means to a great extent and in a way that is very obvious. ❑ *She was looking decidedly unwell.* [from Old French]

**de|cidu|ous** /dɪsɪdʒuəs/ ADJ A **deciduous** tree or bush is one that loses its leaves in the fall every year. [from Latin]
→ see **plant, tree**

**deci|mal** /dɛsɪmᵊl/ ◼ ADJ A **decimal** system involves counting in units of ten. ❑ *The mathematics of ancient Egypt used a decimal system.* ◼ N-COUNT A **decimal** is a fraction that is written in the form of a dot followed by one or more numbers which represent tenths, hundredths, and so on: for example, .5, .51, .517. ❑ *...simple math concepts, such as decimals and fractions.* [from Medieval Latin]
→ see **fraction**

**deci|mal point** (**decimal points**) N-COUNT A **decimal point** is the dot in front of a decimal fraction. □ *A waiter omitted the decimal point in the $13.09 bill.*

**deci|mate** /dɛsɪmeɪt/ (**decimates, decimating, decimated**) V-T To **decimate** something such as a group of people or animals means to destroy a very large number of them. □ *The pollution could decimate the river's birds.* [from Latin]

**de|ci|pher** /dɪsaɪfər/ (**deciphers, deciphering, deciphered**) V-T If you **decipher** a piece of writing or a message, you work out what it says, even though it is very difficult to read or understand. □ *I still can't decipher the code.*

**de|ci|sion** /dɪsɪʒən/ (**decisions**) **1** N-COUNT When you make a **decision**, you choose what should be done or which is the best of various possible actions. □ *I don't want to make the wrong decision and regret it later.* **2** N-UNCOUNT **Decision** is the act of deciding something or the need to decide something. □ *First plan carefully, then act with decision.* [from Old French]

**de|ci|sive** /dɪsaɪsɪv/ **1** ADJ If a fact, action, or event is **decisive**, it makes certain a particular result. □ *...his decisive victory in the presidential elections.* • **de|ci|sive|ly** ADV □ *The plan was decisively rejected by Congress.* **2** ADJ If someone is **decisive**, they have or show an ability to make quick decisions in a difficult or complicated situation. □ *He was a decisive leader.* • **de|ci|sive|ly** ADV □ *"I'll call you at ten," she said decisively.* • **de|ci|sive|ness** N-UNCOUNT □ *His supporters admire his decisiveness.* [from Old French]

**deck** /dɛk/ (**decks**) **1** N-COUNT A **deck** on a vehicle such as a bus or ship is a lower or upper area of it. □ *...a luxury ship with five passenger decks.* **2** N-COUNT The **deck** of a ship is the top part of it that forms a floor in the open air which you can

walk on. □ *She stood on the deck and waved as the boat moved off.* **3** N-COUNT A **deck** is a flat wooden area next to a house, where people can sit and relax or eat. □ *A deck leads into the main room of the home.* **4** N-COUNT A **deck** of cards is a complete set of playing cards. □ *Matt picked up the cards and shuffled the deck.* [from Middle Dutch]
→ see **ship**

deck

**dec|la|ra|tion** /dɛkləreɪʃən/ (**declarations**) **1** N-COUNT A **declaration** is an official announcement or statement. □ *...a declaration of war.* **2** N-COUNT A **declaration** is a firm, emphatic statement which shows that you have no doubts about what you are saying. □ *...declarations of love.* [from Latin]

**de|clara|tive** /dɪklɛərətɪv/ ADJ A **declarative** sentence is a sentence that expresses a statement, for example "My car is blue." [from Latin]

**de|clare** /dɪklɛər/ (**declares, declaring, declared**) **1** V-T If you **declare** that something is true, you say that it is true in a firm, deliberate way. You can also **declare** an attitude or intention. [WRITTEN] □ *He declared he would not seek re-election as president.* □ *He declared his intention to become the best golfer in the world.* **2** V-T If you **declare** something, you state officially and formally that it exists or is the case. □ *Neither leader was willing to declare an end to the war.* □ *The judges declared Mr. Stevens innocent.* **3** V-T If you **declare** goods that you have bought in another country or money that you have earned, you say how much you have bought or earned so that you can pay tax on it. □ *Declaring the wrong income will lead to a fine.* [from Latin]
→ see **war**

**de|cline** /dɪklaɪn/ (**declines, declining, declined**) **1** V-I If something **declines**, it becomes less in quantity, importance, or strength. □ *The number of staff has declined from 217,000 to 114,000.* □ *Exports rose 1.5% while imports declined 3.6%.* **2** V-T/V-I If you **decline** something or **decline to** do something, you politely refuse to accept it or do it. [FORMAL] □ *He declined their invitation.* □ *He offered the boys some coffee. They declined politely.* **3** N-VAR If there is a **decline in** something, it becomes less in quantity, importance, or quality. □ *Official records show a sharp decline in the number of foreign tourists.* **4** PHRASE If something is **in decline** or **on the decline**, it is gradually decreasing in importance, quality, or power. □ *Thankfully the disease is on the decline.* **5** PHRASE If something **goes** or **falls into decline**, it begins to gradually decrease in importance, quality, or power. □ *Libraries should not be allowed to fall into decline.* [from Old French]

**de|code** /dikoʊd/ (**decodes, decoding, decoded**) V-T If you **decode** a message that has been written or spoken in a code, you change it into ordinary language. □ *If you know both these numbers, you can decode the message.*

**de|cod|ing** /dikoʊdɪŋ/ N-UNCOUNT **Decoding** is the process that is involved in understanding the meaning of a written word. [TECHNICAL]

**de|com|pose** /dikəmpoʊz/ (**decomposes, decomposing, decomposed**) V-T/V-I When things such as dead plants or animals **decompose**, or when something **decomposes** them, they change chemically and begin to decay. □ *The waste slowly decomposes into compost.* • **de|com|po|si|tion** /dikɒmpəzɪʃən/ N-UNCOUNT □ *The body was in an advanced stage of decomposition.* [from French]

**de|com|pos|er** /dikəmpoʊzər/ (**decomposers**) N-COUNT **Decomposers** are organisms such as bacteria, fungi, and earthworms that feed on dead plants and animals and convert them into soil. [TECHNICAL] [from French]

**de|com|po|si|tion re|ac|tion** (**decomposition reactions**) N-COUNT A **decomposition reaction** is a chemical reaction in which a compound is broken down into two or more simpler substances. [TECHNICAL]

**de|cor** /deɪkɔr/ N-UNCOUNT The **decor** of a house or room is its style of furnishing and decoration. ❑ *The decor is simple — white walls.* [from French]

**deco|rate** /dɛkəreɪt/ (**decorates, decorating, decorated**) ◼ V-T If you **decorate** something, you make it more attractive by adding things to it. ❑ *He decorated his room with pictures of sports figures.* ❑ *I would like to decorate this room to reflect my taste.* ◼ V-T/V-I If you **decorate** a room or the inside of a building, you put new paint or wallpaper on the walls and ceiling, and paint the woodwork. ❑ *They were decorating Jemma's bedroom.* ❑ *They are planning to decorate when they get the time.* ● **deco|rat|ing** N-UNCOUNT ❑ *I did a lot of the decorating myself.* ● **deco|ra|tor** (**decorators**) N-COUNT ❑ *…Bloomberg's private palace, with its interior design by decorator Jamie Drake.* [from Latin]

**deco|ra|tion** /dɛkəreɪʃⁿn/ (**decorations**) ◼ N-UNCOUNT The **decoration** of a room is its furniture, wallpaper, and ornaments. ❑ *The decoration and furnishings were practical for a family home.* ◼ N-VAR **Decorations** are things that are added to something in order to make it look more attractive. ❑ *The only wall decorations are candles and a single mirror.* ❑ *Colorful paper decorations were hanging from the ceiling.* [from Latin] ◼ → see also **decorate**

**deco|ra|tive** /dɛkərətɪv, -əreɪtɪv/ ADJ Something that is **decorative** is intended to look pretty or attractive. ❑ *The drapes are for decorative purposes and do not open or close.* [from Latin]

**de|coy** /dikɔɪ/ (**decoys**) N-COUNT If you refer to something or someone as a **decoy**, you mean that they are intended to attract people's attention and deceive them, for example, by leading them into a trap or away from a particular place. ❑ *A plane was waiting at the airport but this was just one of the decoys.* [from Dutch]

| Word Link | *cresc, creas ≈ growing* : cresc**ent**, de**crease**, in**crease** |

**de|crease** (**decreases, decreasing, decreased**)

The verb is pronounced /dɪkris/. The noun is pronounced /dikris/ or /dɪkris/.

◼ V-T/V-I When something **decreases** or when you **decrease** it, it becomes less in quantity, size, or intensity. ❑ *Population growth is decreasing by 1.4% each year.* ❑ *The average price decreased from $134,000 to $126,000.* ❑ *Since 1945 air forces have decreased in size.* ◼ N-COUNT A **decrease in** the quantity, size, or intensity of something is a reduction in it. ❑ *There has been a decrease in the number of people without a job.* [from Old French]

| Thesaurus | *decrease* Also look up : |
| v. | decline, diminish, go down; (*ant.*) increase ◼ |

**de|cree** /dɪkri/ (**decrees, decreeing, decreed**) ◼ N-COUNT A **decree** is an official order or decision, especially one made by the ruler of a country. ❑ *The decree banned all meetings, strikes, parades and protests.* ◼ N-COUNT A **decree** is a judgment made by a law court. ❑ *…court decrees.* ◼ V-T If someone in authority **decrees** that

something must happen, they decide or state this officially. ❑ *The government decreed that all children should have an education.* [from Old French]

**dedi|cate** /dɛdɪkeɪt/ (**dedicates, dedicating, dedicated**) ◼ V-T If you say that someone **has dedicated** themselves **to** something, they have decided to give a lot of time and effort to it because they think that it is important. ❑ *For the next few years, she dedicated herself to her work.* ● **dedi|cat|ed** ADJ ❑ *He's dedicated to his students.* ● **dedi|ca|tion** /dɛdɪkeɪʃⁿn/ N-UNCOUNT ❑ *We admire her dedication to achieving peace.* ◼ V-T If someone **dedicates** something such as a book, play, or piece of music **to** you, they mention your name, for example, in the front of a book or when a piece of music is performed, as a way of showing affection or respect for you. ❑ *She dedicated her first book to her sons.* ● **dedi|ca|tion** (**dedications**) N-COUNT ❑ *…the dedication at the beginning of the book.* [from Latin]

**de|duce** /dɪdus/ (**deduces, deducing, deduced**) V-T If you **deduce** something or **deduce** that something is true, you reach that conclusion because of other things that you know to be true. ❑ *Alison cleverly deduced that I was the author of the letter.* ❑ *The date of the document can be deduced from references to the Civil War.* [from Latin]

**de|duct** /dɪdʌkt/ (**deducts, deducting, deducted**) V-T When you **deduct** an amount from a total, you subtract it from the total. ❑ *The company deducted the money from his wages.* [from Latin]

**de|duct|ible** /dɪdʌktɪbəl/ (**deductibles**) ◼ ADJ If a payment or expense is **deductible**, it can be deducted from another sum such as your income, for example, when calculating how much income tax you have to pay. ❑ *Travel is deductible as a business expense.* ❑ *…deductible expenses.* ◼ N-COUNT A **deductible** is a sum of money which an insured person has to pay toward the cost of an insurance claim. The insurance company pays the rest. ❑ *Each time they go to a hospital, they have to pay a deductible of $628.* [from Latin]

**de|duc|tion** /dɪdʌkʃⁿn/ (**deductions**) ◼ N-COUNT A **deduction** is an amount that has been subtracted from a total. ❑ *…an income tax deduction.* ◼ N-COUNT A **deduction** is a conclusion that you have reached about something because of other things that you know to be true. ❑ *It was a pretty clever deduction.* [from Latin] → see **science**

**deed** /did/ (**deeds**) ◼ N-COUNT A **deed** is something that is done, especially something that is very good or very bad. [LITERARY] ❑ *The people who did this evil deed must be punished.* ◼ N-COUNT A **deed** is a document containing the terms of an agreement, especially an agreement about the ownership of land or a building. [LEGAL] ❑ *Do you have the deeds to the property?* [from Old English]

**dee|jay** /didʒeɪ/ (**deejays, deejaying, deejayed**) ◼ N-COUNT A **deejay** is the same as a **disc jockey**. [INFORMAL] ◼ V-I If someone **deejays**, they introduce and play music on the radio or at a nightclub. ❑ *Ronson deejays every weekend.*

**deem** /dim/ (**deems, deeming, deemed**) V-T If something **is deemed to** have a particular quality or **to** do a particular thing, it is considered to have that quality or do that thing. [FORMAL] ❑ *A car was deemed essential to get around the many places to* see and visit. ❑ *He will support the use of force if the government deems it necessary.* [from Old English]

**deep** /diːp/ (**deeper, deepest**) **1** ADJ If something is **deep**, it extends a long way down from the ground or from the top surface of something. ❑ *The water is very deep.* ❑ *Den dug a deep hole in the center of the garden.* ● **Deep** is also an adverb. ❑ *She put her hand in deeper, to the bottom.* ● **deep|ly** ADV ❑ *When planting a tree, the soil should be dug deeply.* **2** ADJ A **deep** container, such as a closet, extends or measures a long distance from front to back. ❑ *...a deep cupboard.* **3** ADJ You use **deep** to emphasize the seriousness, strength, importance, or degree of something. ❑ *I had a deep admiration for Sartre.* ❑ *He expressed his deep sympathy to the family.* ● **deep|ly** ADV ❑ *He loved his brother deeply.* **4** ADJ If you are in a **deep** sleep, you are sleeping peacefully and it is difficult to wake you. ❑ *Una fell into a deep sleep.* ❑ *She slept deeply but woke early.* **5** ADJ A **deep** breath or sigh uses or fills the whole of your lungs. ❑ *Cal took a long, deep breath, struggling to control his emotions.* ● **deep|ly** ADV ❑ *She sighed deeply.* **6** ADJ A **deep** sound is low in pitch. ❑ *His voice was deep.* **7** ADJ If you describe something such as a problem or a piece of writing as **deep**, you mean that it is important, serious, or complicated. ❑ *They're adventure stories. They're not intended to be deep.* **8** ADV If you experience or feel something **deep inside** you or **deep down**, you feel it very strongly even though you do not necessarily show it. ❑ *I have fear deep down, but I can't show it.* **9** ADJ You use **deep** to describe colors that are strong and fairly dark. ❑ *...cushions in deep colors.* ❑ *The sky was deep blue and starry.* **10** PHRASE If you say that something **goes deep** or **runs deep**, you mean that it is very serious or strong and is hard to change. ❑ *His anger clearly went deep.* [from Old English]

**deep cur|rent** (**deep currents**) N-COUNT A **deep current** is a current of water that flows far below the surface of an ocean.

**deep|en** /diːpən/ (**deepens, deepening, deepened**) **1** V-T/V-I If a situation or emotion **deepens** or if something **deepens** it, it becomes stronger and more intense. ❑ *These friendships will probably deepen in your teenage years.* **2** V-T/V-I When a sound **deepens** or **is deepened**, it becomes lower in tone. ❑ *"Go and speak to her," he said deepening his voice.* **3** V-T If people **deepen** something, they increase its depth by digging out its lower surface. ❑ *There are plans to deepen the river from 40 to 45 feet, to allow for larger ships.* [from Old English]

**deep ocean ba|sin** (**deep ocean basins**) N-COUNT The **deep ocean basin** is the part of the Earth's surface that lies beneath the ocean.

**deep-seated** ADJ A **deep-seated** problem, feeling, or belief is difficult to change because its causes have been there for a long time. ❑ *The country still has deep-seated economic problems.*

**deep-water zone** (**deep-water zones**) N-COUNT The **deep-water zone** of a lake or pond is the area furthest from the surface, where no sunlight reaches.

**deer** /dɪər/ (**deer**) N-COUNT A **deer** is a large wild animal that eats grass and leaves. A male deer usually has large, branching horns. [from Old English]

**de|face** /dɪfeɪs/ (**defaces, defacing, defaced**) V-T If someone **defaces** something such as a wall or a notice, they spoil it by writing or drawing things on it. ❑ *It's illegal to deface buildings.* [from Middle English]

**de|fault** /dɪfɔlt/ (**defaults, defaulting, defaulted**) **1** V-I If a person, company, or country **defaults on** something that they have legally agreed to do, such as paying some money or doing a piece of work before a particular time, they fail to do it. [LEGAL] ❑ *More borrowers are defaulting on loan repayments.* ● **Default** is also a noun. ❑ *...a default on $1.3 billion in loans.* **2** N-UNCOUNT In computing, the **default** is a particular set of instructions which the computer always uses unless the person using the computer gives other instructions. [COMPUTING] ❑ *The default setting on the printer is for color.* **3** PHRASE If something happens **by default**, it happens only because something else which might have prevented it or changed it has not happened. [FORMAL] ❑ *He kept his title by default because no one else wanted to compete for it.* [from Old French]

**de|feat** /dɪfiːt/ (**defeats, defeating, defeated**) **1** V-T If you **defeat** someone, you win a victory over them in a battle, game, or contest. ❑ *They defeated the army in 1954.* **2** V-T If a task or a problem **defeats** you, it is so difficult that you cannot do it or solve it. ❑ *The task of writing the book nearly defeated him.* **3** V-T To **defeat** an action or plan means to cause it to fail. ❑ *The navy had an important role in defeating the rebellion.* **4** N-VAR **Defeat** is the experience of being beaten in a battle, game, or contest, or of failing to achieve what you wanted to. ❑ *He didn't want to admit defeat.* ❑ *...the team's 31-point defeat at Sacramento.* [from Old French]

**de|fect** (**defects, defecting, defected**)

> The noun is pronounced /diːfɛkt/. The verb is pronounced /dɪfɛkt/.

**1** N-COUNT A **defect** is a fault or imperfection in a person or thing. ❑ *He was born with a hearing defect.* ❑ *The report shows the defects of the present system.* **2** V-I If you **defect**, you leave your country, political party, or other group, and join an opposing country, party, or group. ❑ *...a Democrat who defected in 2004.* ● **de|fec|tion** /dɪfɛkʃⁿn/ (**defections**) N-VAR ❑ *...the defection of ten Republicans.* ● **de|fec|tor** /dɪfɛktər/ (**defectors**) N-COUNT ❑ *The government has attracted defectors from other parties.* [from Latin]

**de|fec|tive** /dɪfɛktɪv/ ADJ If something is **defective**, there is something wrong with it and it does not work properly. ❑ *...defective equipment.* [from Latin]

| **Word Link** | *fend ≈ striking : de***fend**, ***fend***er, of***fend*** |
| --- | --- |

**de|fend** /dɪfɛnd/ (**defends, defending, defended**) **1** V-T If you **defend** someone or something, you take action in order to protect them. ❑ *He has always defended religious rights.* **2** V-T If you **defend** someone or something when they have been criticized, you argue in support of them. ❑ *The president defended his decision to go to war.* **3** V-T When a lawyer **defends** a person who has been accused of something, the lawyer argues on their behalf in a court of law that the

charges are not true. ❑ ...*a lawyer who defended political prisoners.* ❑ *He has hired a lawyer to defend him in court.* **4** V-T When a sports player plays in the tournament which they won the previous time it was held, you can say that they **are defending** their title. ❑ *Torrence hopes to defend her title successfully in the next Olympics.* [from Old French]
→ see **hero**

**Word Link** ant ≈ one who does, has : defend*ant*, depend*ant*, occup*ant*

**de|fend|ant** /dɪfɛndənt/ (**defendants**) N-COUNT A **defendant** is a person who has been accused of breaking the law and is being tried in court. ❑ *The defendant pleaded guilty and was fined $500.* [from Old French]
→ see **trial**

**de|fend|er** /dɪfɛndər/ (**defenders**) **1** N-COUNT If you are a **defender of** a particular thing or person that has been criticized, you argue or act in support of that thing or person. ❑ *He was known as a defender of human rights.* **2** N-COUNT A **defender** in a game such as soccer or hockey is a player whose main task is to try and stop the other side from scoring. ❑ *Lewis was the team's top defender.* [from Old French]

**de|fense** /dɪfɛns/ (**defenses**)

Defense in meaning **7** is pronounced /diːfɛns/.

**1** N-UNCOUNT **Defense** is action that is taken to protect someone or something against attack. ❑ *The land was flat which made defense difficult.* **2** N-UNCOUNT **Defense** is the organization of a country's armies and weapons, and their use to protect the country or its interests. ❑ *Twenty-eight percent of the country's money is spent on defense.* **3** N-PLURAL The **defenses** of a country or region are all its armed forces and weapons. ❑ *...his promise to rebuild the country's defenses.* **4** N-COUNT A **defense** is something that people or animals can use or do to protect themselves. ❑ *The immune system is the human body's main defense against disease.* **5** N-COUNT A **defense** is something that you say or write which supports ideas or actions that have been criticized or questioned. ❑ *...his defense of the government's performance.* **6** N-SING The **defense** is the case that is presented by a lawyer in a trial for the person who has been accused of a crime. You can also refer to this person's lawyers as **the defense.** ❑ *The defense was that the police had not kept full records of the interviews.* **7** N-SING In games such as soccer or hockey, the **defense** is the group of players in a team who try to stop the opposing players from scoring a goal or a point. ❑ *Their defense was weak and allowed in 12 goals in six games.* [from Old French]

**de|fense|less** /dɪfɛnslɪs/ ADJ If someone or something is **defenseless,** they are weak and unable to defend themselves properly. ❑ *He was a defenseless old man.* [from Old French]

**de|fense mecha|nism** (**defense mechanisms**) N-COUNT A **defense mechanism** is a way of behaving or thinking which is not conscious or deliberate and is an automatic reaction to unpleasant experiences or feelings such as anxiety and fear.

**de|fen|sive** /dɪfɛnsɪv/ **1** ADJ You use **defensive** to describe things that are intended to protect someone or something. ❑ *The Government*

*organized defensive measures to protect the city.* **2** ADJ Someone who is **defensive** is behaving in a way that shows they feel unsure or threatened. ❑ *She heard the defensive note in his voice and knew that he was ashamed.* ● **de|fen|sive|ly** ADV ❑ *"I know," said Kate, defensively.* **3** PHRASE If someone is **on the defensive,** they are trying to protect themselves or their interests because they feel unsure or threatened. ❑ *Do not let one difficult student put you on the defensive.* [from Old French]

**de|fer** /dɪfɜr/ (**defers, deferring, deferred**) **1** V-T If you **defer** an event or action, you arrange for it to happen at a later date, rather than immediately or at the previously planned time. ❑ *Customers often defer payment for as long as possible.* **2** V-I If you **defer to** someone, you accept their opinion or do what they want you to do, even when you do not agree with it yourself, because you respect them or their authority. ❑ *They deferred to their doctors.* [Sense 1 from Old French. Sense 2 from Latin.]

**def|er|ence** /dɛfərəns/ N-UNCOUNT **Deference** is a polite and respectful attitude toward someone, especially because they have an important position. ❑ *It was a gesture of deference to the new king.* [from French]

**de|fi|ance** /dɪfaɪəns/ N-UNCOUNT **Defiance** is behavior or an attitude which shows that you are not willing to obey someone. ❑ *...his brave defiance of the government.* [from Middle English]

**de|fi|ant** /dɪfaɪənt/ ADJ If you say that someone is **defiant,** you mean they show aggression or independence by refusing to obey someone. ❑ *The players are in a defiant mood as they prepare for tomorrow's game.* ● **de|fi|ant|ly** ADV ❑ *They defiantly rejected the plan.* [from French]

**de|fi|cien|cy** /dɪfɪʃənsi/ (**deficiencies**) **1** N-VAR **Deficiency in** something, especially something that your body needs, is not having enough of it. ❑ *He had blood tests for signs of vitamin deficiency.* **2** N-VAR A **deficiency** that someone or something has is a weakness or imperfection in them. [FORMAL] ❑ *The company failed to correct deficiencies in the system.* [from Latin]

**de|fi|cient** /dɪfɪʃənt/ ADJ If someone or something is **deficient in** a particular thing, they do not have the full amount of it that they need in order to function normally or work properly. [FORMAL] ❑ *...a diet deficient in vitamin B.* [from Latin]

**defi|cit** /dɛfəsɪt/ (**deficits**) **1** N-COUNT A **deficit** is the amount by which something is less than is needed, especially the amount by which the total money received is less than the total money spent. ❑ *...a deficit of five billion dollars.* **2** PHRASE If an account or organization is **in deficit,** more money has been spent than has been received. [from Latin]

**defi|cit spend|ing** N-UNCOUNT **Deficit spending** is an economic policy in which a government spends more money raised by borrowing than it receives in revenue. ❑ *...plans to end deficit spending.*

**de|fine** /dɪfaɪn/ (**defines, defining, defined**) V-T If you **define** something, you show, describe, or state clearly what it is and what its limits are, or what it is like. ❑ *The government defines a household as a group of people who live in the same house.* [from Old French]

**defi|nite** /dɛfɪnɪt/ **1** ADJ If something such as a decision or an arrangement is **definite**, it is firm and clear, and unlikely to be changed. □ *It's too soon to give a definite answer.* □ *She made no definite plans for her future.* **2** ADJ **Definite** evidence or information is true, rather than being an opinion or guess. □ *We didn't have any definite proof.* [from Latin]

| Thesaurus | *definite* | Also look up : |
| --- | --- | --- |
| ADJ. | clear-cut, distinct, precise, specific; (*ant.*) ambiguous, vague **1** | |

**defi|nite ar|ti|cle** (**definite articles**) N-COUNT The word "the" is sometimes called **the definite article.**

**defi|nite|ly** /dɛfɪnɪtli/ ADV You use **definitely** to emphasize that something is true, and will not change. □ *This game is definitely more fun.* □ *The extra money will definitely help.* [from Latin]

**defi|ni|tion** /dɛfɪnɪʃ°n/ (**definitions**) **1** N-COUNT A **definition** is a statement giving the meaning of a word or expression, especially in a dictionary. □ *There is no agreement on a standard definition of intelligence.* **2** PHRASE If you say that something has a particular quality **by definition**, you mean that it has this quality simply because of what it is. **3** N-UNCOUNT **Definition** is the quality of being clear and distinct. □ *They criticized Prof. Johnson's program for its lack of definition.* [from Latin]

**defini|tive** /dɪfɪnɪtɪv/ **1** ADJ Something that is **definitive** provides a firm conclusion that cannot be questioned. □ *The study provides definitive proof that the drug is safe.* ● **de|fini|tive|ly** ADV □ *He wasn't able to answer the question definitively.* **2** ADJ A **definitive** book or performance is thought to be the best of its kind that has ever been done or that will ever be done. □ *...a definitive book on Spanish history.* [from Latin]

| Word Link | *de ≈ from, down, away : deflate, descend, detach* |
| --- | --- |

**de|flate** /dɪfleɪt/ (**deflates, deflating, deflated**) **1** V-T If you **deflate** someone or something, you take away their confidence or make them seem less important. □ *The mention of her name seemed to deflate him.* ● **de|flat|ed** ADJ □ *When she refused I felt deflated.* **2** V-T/V-I When something such as a tire or balloon **deflates**, or when you **deflate** it, all the air comes out of it. □ *We drove a few miles until the tire deflated.*

**de|fla|tion** /dɪfleɪʃ°n/ N-UNCOUNT In geology, **deflation** is the removal of soil and other material from the surface of the Earth by wind. [TECHNICAL]

**de|flect** /dɪflɛkt/ (**deflects, deflecting, deflected**) **1** V-T If you **deflect** something such as criticism or attention, you act in a way that prevents it from being directed toward you or affecting you. □ *The president talks about family values to deflect attention from his political failure.* **2** V-T If you **deflect** something that is moving, you make it go in a slightly different direction, for example, by hitting or blocking it. □ *My forearm deflected the first punch.* ● **de|flec|tion** (**deflections**) N-VAR □ *Look at the deflection of light as it passes through the gap in the curtains.* [from Latin]

**de|fog|ger** /difɒgər/ (**defoggers**) N-COUNT A **defogger** is a device that removes condensation from the window of a vehicle by blowing warm air onto it. □ *...rear window defoggers.*

**de|for|esta|tion** /difɔrɪsteɪʃ°n/ N-UNCOUNT **Deforestation** is the cutting down of trees over a large area. □ *...the deforestation of the Amazon.* → see **greenhouse effect**

**de|form** /dɪfɔrm/ (**deforms, deforming, deformed**) V-T/V-I If something **deforms** a person's body or something else, it causes it to have an unnatural shape. In technical English, you can also say that the second thing **deforms** when it changes to an unnatural shape. □ *The disease deforms arms and legs.* ● **de|formed** ADJ □ *He had a deformed right leg.* [from Latin]

**de|for|ma|tion** /difɔrmeɪʃ°n/ (**deformations**) N-VAR **Deformation** is a change in the shape of a rock as a result of pressure, for example in an earthquake. [TECHNICAL] [from Latin]

**de|form|ity** /dɪfɔrmɪti/ (**deformities**) **1** N-COUNT A **deformity** is a part of someone's body which is not the normal shape because of injury or illness, or because they were born this way. □ *...facial deformities.* **2** N-UNCOUNT **Deformity** is the condition of having a deformity. □ *The aim of these exercises is to prevent deformity of joints.* [from Latin]

**de|fraud** /dɪfrɔd/ (**defrauds, defrauding, defrauded**) V-T If someone **defrauds** you, they take something away from you or stop you from getting what belongs to you by means of tricks and lies. □ *He intended to defraud his clients.* [from Late Middle English]

**deft** /dɛft/ (**defter, deftest**) ADJ A **deft** action is skillful and often quick. [WRITTEN] □ *With a deft kick, he put the ball in the back of the net.* ● **deft|ly** ADV □ *She deftly caught him as he fell.*

**de|funct** /dɪfʌŋkt/ ADJ If something is **defunct**, it no longer exists or has stopped functioning or operating. □ *...the leader of the now defunct Social Democratic Party.* [from Latin]

**de|fuse** /difyuz/ (**defuses, defusing, defused**) **1** V-T If you **defuse** a dangerous or tense situation, you calm it. □ *He defused a violent situation.* **2** V-T If someone **defuses** a bomb, they remove the fuse so that it cannot explode. □ *Police have defused a bomb found in a building.*

**de|fy** /dɪfaɪ/ (**defies, defying, defied**) **1** V-T If you **defy** someone or something that is trying to make you behave in a particular way, you refuse to obey them and behave in that way. □ *This was the first time I defied my mother.* **2** V-T If you **defy** someone **to** do something, you challenge them to do it when you think that they will be unable to do it or too frightened to do it. □ *I defy you to think of a better answer.* **3** V-T If something **defies** description or understanding, it is so strange, extreme, or surprising that it is almost impossible to understand or explain. □ *This decision defies logic.* [from Old French]

**de|gen|er|ate** (**degenerates, degenerating, degenerated**)

The verb is pronounced /dɪdʒɛnəreɪt/. The adjective is pronounced /dɪdʒɛnərɪt/.

**1** V-I If you say that someone or something **degenerates**, you mean that they become worse in

**D**

some way, for example, weaker, lower in quality, or more dangerous. ❏ *Your bones may begin to degenerate if you are too inactive.* ● **de|gen|era|tion** /dɪdʒɛnəreɪʃᵊn/ N-UNCOUNT ❏ *...various forms of physical and mental degeneration.* **2** ADJ If you describe a person or their behavior as **degenerate**, you disapprove of them because you think they have low standards of behavior or morality. ❏ *...the effects of a degenerate lifestyle.* [from Latin]

**de|grade** /dɪgreɪd/ (**degrades, degrading, degraded**) **1** V-T Something that **degrades** someone causes people to have less respect for them. ❏ *...a poster which degrades women.* ● **deg|ra|da|tion** /dɛgrədeɪʃᵊn/ (**degradations**) N-VAR ❏ *The scenes of misery and degradation sickened them.* ● **de|grad|ing** ADJ ❏ *...the degrading treatment of the prisoners.* **2** V-T To **degrade** something means to cause it to get worse. [FORMAL] ❏ *...the ability to satisfy human needs without degrading the environment.* ● **deg|ra|da|tion** N-UNCOUNT ❏ *...air pollution and the steady degradation of our quality of life.* [from Late Latin]

**de|gree** /dɪgri/ (**degrees**) **1** N-COUNT You use **degree** to indicate the extent to which something happens or is the case, or the amount which something is felt. ❏ *He treated her with a high degree of respect.* ❏ *They tried it, with varying degrees of success.* **2** N-COUNT A **degree** is a unit of measurement that is used to measure temperatures. It is often written as °, for example, 23°. ❏ *It's over 80 degrees outside.* **3** N-COUNT A **degree** is a unit of measurement that is used to measure angles, and also longitude and latitude. It is often written as °, for example, 23°. ❏ *It was pointing outward at an angle of 45 degrees.* **4** N-COUNT A **degree** is a title or rank given by a university or college when you have completed a course of study there. It can also be given as an honorary title. ❏ *...an engineering degree.* [from Old French] → see **graduation, thermometer**

| Word Partnership | Use *degree* with : |
| --- | --- |
| N. | degree **of certainty**, degree **of difficulty 1** 45/90 degree **angle 2** bachelor's/master's degree, college degree, degree **program 4** |
| ADJ. | high degree **1** honorary degree **4** |

| Word Link | hydr ≈ water : carbo**hydr**ate, de**hydr**ate, **hydr**aulic |
| --- | --- |

| Word Link | ation ≈ state of : de**hydr**ation, elev**ation**, preserv**ation** |
| --- | --- |

**de|hy|drate** /dihaɪdreɪt/ (**dehydrates, dehydrating, dehydrated**) **1** V-T When something such as food **is dehydrated**, all the water is removed from it, often in order to preserve it. ❏ *The food was dehydrated.* **2** V-T/V-I If you **dehydrate** or if something **dehydrates** you, you lose too much water from your body so that you feel weak or ill. ❏ *People can dehydrate in hot weather like this.* ● **de|hy|dra|tion** /dihaɪdreɪʃᵊn/ N-UNCOUNT ❏ *The child is suffering from dehydration.*

**de|ity** /diɪti/ (**deities**) N-COUNT A **deity** is a god or goddess. [FORMAL] ❏ *...a deity worshipped by thousands of Hindus.* [from Old French]

**de|lay** /dɪleɪ/ (**delays, delaying, delayed**) **1** V-T/V-I If you **delay** doing something, you do not do it immediately or at the planned or expected time, but you leave it until later. ❏ *I delayed the decision until I had spoken to my mother.* ❏ *They delayed having children until they had more money.* ❏ *There was no time to delay.* **2** V-T To **delay** someone or something means to make them late or to slow them down. ❏ *Can you delay him in some way?* ❏ *Several problems delayed production.* **3** N-VAR If there is a **delay**, something does not happen until later than planned or expected. ❏ *He apologized for the delay.* [from Old French]

| Thesaurus | delay | Also look up : |
| --- | --- | --- |
| V. | hold up, postpone, stall; *(ant.)* hurry, rush **1** | |
| N. | interruption, lag; *(ant.)* rush **3** | |

**del|egate** (**delegates, delegating, delegated**)

The noun is pronounced /dɛlɪgɪt/. The verb is pronounced /dɛlɪgeɪt/.

**1** N-COUNT A **delegate** is a person who is chosen to vote or make decisions on behalf of a group of other people, especially at a conference or a meeting. ❏ *The Canadian delegate didn't reply.* **2** V-T/V-I If you **delegate** duties, responsibilities, or power **to** someone, you give them those duties, those responsibilities, or that power so that they can act on your behalf. ❏ *He wants to delegate more tasks to his employees.* ❏ *As a team leader, you must delegate effectively.* ● **del|ega|tion** N-UNCOUNT ❏ *The delegation of responsibility is very important in a business.* [from Latin]

**del|ega|tion** /dɛlɪgeɪʃᵊn/ (**delegations**) **1** N-COUNT A **delegation** is a group of people who have been sent somewhere to have talks with other people on behalf of a larger group of people. ❏ *...the Chinese delegation to the UN talks in New York.* [from Latin] **2** → see also **delegate**

**de|lete** /dɪlit/ (**deletes, deleting, deleted**) V-T If you **delete** something that has been written down or stored in a computer, you cross it out or remove it. ❏ *He deleted old files from the computer.* [from Latin]

| Thesaurus | delete | Also look up : |
| --- | --- | --- |
| V. | cut out, erase, remove | |

**deli** /dɛli/ (**delis**) N-COUNT A **deli** is a **delicatessen**. [INFORMAL]

**de|lib|er|ate** (**deliberates, deliberating, deliberated**)

The adjective is pronounced /dɪlɪbərɪt/. The verb is pronounced /dɪlɪbəreɪt/.

**1** ADJ If you do something that is **deliberate**, you planned or decided to do it beforehand, and so it happens on purpose rather than by chance. ❏ *It was a deliberate attempt to upset him.* ● **de|lib|er|ate|ly** ADV ❏ *He started the fire deliberately.* **2** ADJ If a movement or action is **deliberate**, it is done slowly and carefully. ❏ *She folded her scarf with slow, deliberate movements.* ● **de|lib|er|ate|ly** ADV ❏ *He spoke slowly and deliberately, as if Rae were a very young child.* **3** V-I If you **deliberate**, you think about something carefully, especially before making a very important decision. ❏ *She deliberated over the*

*decision before she made up her mind.* [from Latin]
→ see **trial**

**de|lib|era|tion** /dɪlɪbəreɪʃ°n/ (**deliberations**)
**1** N-UNCOUNT **Deliberation** is the long and careful consideration of a subject. ❑ *After much deliberation, he decided to go.* **2** N-PLURAL **Deliberations** are formal discussions where an issue is considered carefully. ❑ *The judge sent the jury to begin its deliberations.* [from Latin]

**deli|ca|cy** /dɛlɪkəsi/ (**delicacies**) N-COUNT
A **delicacy** is a rare or expensive food that is considered especially nice to eat. ❑ *Smoked salmon was an expensive delicacy.* [from Latin]

**deli|cate** /dɛlɪkɪt/ **1** ADJ Something that is **delicate** is small and beautifully shaped. ❑ *He had delicate hands.* ● **deli|ca|cy** N-UNCOUNT ❑ *...the delicacy of a flower.* ● **deli|cate|ly** ADV ❑ *She was a delicately pretty girl.* **2** ADJ Something that is **delicate** has a color, taste, or smell which is pleasant and not strong or intense. ❑ *The beans have a delicate flavor.* ● **deli|cate|ly** ADV ❑ *...a soup delicately flavored with nutmeg.* **3** ADJ If something is **delicate**, it is easy to harm, damage, or break, and needs to be handled or treated carefully. ❑ *The china is very delicate.* **4** ADJ Someone who is **delicate** is not healthy and strong, and becomes ill easily. ❑ *She was physically delicate.* **5** ADJ You use **delicate** to describe a situation, problem, matter, or discussion that needs to be dealt with carefully and sensitively in order to avoid upsetting things or offending people. ❑ *There's a delicate balance between the need for people to travel freely and the need for security.* ● **deli|ca|cy** N-UNCOUNT ❑ *This was a subject of delicacy on which he wanted her advice.* ● **deli|cate|ly** ADV ❑ *Shawn sent a delicately worded memo.* [from Latin]

**deli|ca|tes|sen** /dɛlɪkətɛs°n/ (**delicatessens**) N-COUNT A **delicatessen** is a store that sells cold cuts, cheeses, salads, and often a selection of imported foods. [from German]

**de|li|cious** /dɪlɪʃəs/ ADJ Food that is **delicious** has a very pleasant taste. ❑ *There was a wide choice of delicious meals.* ● **de|li|cious|ly** ADV ❑ *This yogurt has a deliciously creamy flavor.* [from Old French]

**de|light** /dɪlaɪt/ (**delights, delighting, delighted**) **1** N-UNCOUNT **Delight** is a feeling of very great pleasure. ❑ *He expressed delight at the news.* ❑ *Andrew laughed with delight.* **2** PHRASE If someone **takes delight** or **takes a delight in** something, they get a lot of pleasure from it. ❑ *Haig took obvious delight in his children.* **3** N-COUNT You can refer to someone or something that gives you great pleasure or enjoyment as a **delight**. ❑ *The aircraft was a delight to fly.* **4** V-T If something **delights** you, it gives you a lot of pleasure. ❑ *She created a style of music which delighted audiences everywhere.* [from Old French]

**de|light|ed** /dɪlaɪtɪd/ ADJ If you are **delighted**, you are extremely pleased and excited about something. ❑ *Frank was delighted to see her.* ● **de|light|ed|ly** ADV ❑ *"Look at that!" Jackson exclaimed delightedly.* [from Old French]

**de|light|ful** /dɪlaɪtfəl/ ADJ If you describe something or someone as **delightful**, you mean they are very pleasant. ❑ *...a delightful garden.* ● **de|light|ful|ly** ADV ❑ *...a delightfully refreshing perfume.* [from Old French]

**de|lin|quent** /dɪlɪŋkwənt/ (**delinquents**)
ADJ Someone, usually a young person, who is **delinquent** repeatedly commits minor crimes. ❑ *...homes for delinquent children.* ● **Delinquent** is also a noun. ❑ *...a nine-year-old delinquent.* ● **de|lin|quen|cy** N-UNCOUNT ❑ *...a study of delinquency.* [from Latin]

**de|liri|ous** /dɪlɪəriəs/ **1** ADJ Someone who is **delirious** is unable to think or speak in a sensible and reasonable way, usually because they are very ill and have a fever. ❑ *I was delirious and fainted several times.* **2** ADJ Someone who is **delirious** is extremely excited and happy. ❑ *A crowd of 25,000 delirious fans waited outside the singer's hotel.* ● **de|liri|ous|ly** ADV ❑ *Dora returned from her vacation deliriously happy.* [from Latin]

**de|liv|er** /dɪlɪvər/ (**delivers, delivering, delivered**) **1** V-T If you **deliver** something somewhere, you take it there. ❑ *The Canadians plan to deliver more food to Somalia.* **2** V-T If you **deliver** a lecture or speech, you give it in public. [FORMAL] ❑ *The president will deliver a speech about schools.* **3** V-T When someone **delivers** a baby, they help the woman who is giving birth to the baby. ❑ *He didn't expect to deliver his own baby!* **4** V-T If someone **delivers** a blow to someone else, they hit them. [WRITTEN] ❑ *He delivered the blow with a hammer.* [from Old French]

| Word Partnership | Use *deliver* with : |
| --- | --- |
| N. | deliver **a letter**, deliver **mail**, deliver **a message**, deliver **news**, deliver **a package** **1** |
| | deliver **a lecture**, deliver **a speech** **2** |
| | deliver **a baby** **3** |
| | deliver **a blow** **4** |

**de|liv|ery** /dɪlɪvəri/ (**deliveries**) **1** N-VAR
**Delivery** or a **delivery** is the bringing of letters, packages, or other goods to your house or to another place where you want them. ❑ *Please allow 28 days for delivery.* ❑ *The fighting is threatening the delivery of food and medicine.* **2** N-COUNT A **delivery** of something is the goods that are delivered. ❑ *I got a delivery of fresh eggs this morning.* **3** N-VAR **Delivery** is the process of giving birth to a baby. ❑ *It was an easy delivery.* **4** N-UNCOUNT You talk about someone's **delivery** when you are referring to the way in which they give a speech or lecture. ❑ *His speeches were well written but his delivery was hopeless.* [from Old French]

**de|liv|ery charge** (**delivery charges**) N-COUNT
A **delivery charge** is the cost of transporting or delivering goods. ❑ *Delivery charges are included in the price.* [FORMAL]

**del|ta** /dɛltə/ (**deltas**) N-COUNT A **delta** is an area of low, flat land shaped like a triangle, where a river splits and spreads out into several branches before entering the sea. ❑ *...the Mississippi delta.* [from Latin] → see **river**

**de|lude** /dɪlud/ (**deludes, deluding, deluded**)
V-T If you **delude** someone, you make them believe something that is not true. ❑ *He was deluding himself about the state of their relationship.* ❑ *Anna deluded him into thinking that she loved him.* [from Latin]

**de|luge** /dɛlyudʒ/ (**deluges, deluging, deluged**)
**1** N-COUNT A **deluge of** things is a large number of them which arrive or happen at the same

time. ❑ *There was a deluge of requests for interviews.*
**2** V-T If a place or person **is deluged with** things,
a large number of them arrive or happen at the
same time. ❑ *The office was deluged with complaints.*
**3** N-COUNT A **deluge** of rain is a very heavy fall of
rain. ❑ *The deluge was too much for the drains.* [from
Old French]

de|lu|sion /dɪluʒ³n/ (**delusions**) N-VAR A
**delusion** is a false idea. ❑ *I was under the delusion
that he intended to marry me.* ❑ *...a form of mental
delusion.* [from Latin]

deluxe /dɪlʌks/ ADJ **Deluxe** goods or services
are better in quality and more expensive than
ordinary ones. ❑ *...deluxe hotel suites.* [from French]

delve /dɛlv/ (**delves, delving, delved**) V-I If you
**delve into** something, you try to discover new
information about it. ❑ *Jenny delved into her mother's
past.* [from Old English]

de|mand /dɪmænd/ (**demands, demanding,
demanded**) **1** V-T If you **demand** something such
as information or action, you ask for it in a very
forceful way. ❑ *The victim's family is demanding an
investigation into the shooting.* ❑ *He demanded that
I give him an answer.* **2** V-T If one thing **demands**
another, the first needs the second in order to
happen or be dealt with successfully. ❑ *The job
demands much patience and hard work.* **3** N-COUNT A
**demand** is a firm request for something. ❑ *There
were demands for better services.* **4** N-UNCOUNT
If you refer to **demand**, or to the **demand for**
something, you are referring to how many people
want to have it, do it, or buy it. ❑ *Demand for the
product has increased.* **5** N-PLURAL The **demands of**
something or its **demands on** you are the things
which it needs or the things which you have to
do for it. ❑ *...the demands and challenges of a new job.*
**6** PHRASE If someone or something is **in demand**
or **in great demand**, they are very popular and a
lot of people want them. ❑ *He was much in demand
as a lecturer in the U.S.* **7** PHRASE If something is
available or happens **on demand**, you can have it
or it happens whenever you want it or ask for it.
❑ *...an entertainment system that offers 25 movies on
demand.* [from Medieval Latin]

| Thesaurus | *demand* | Also look up : |
| --- | --- | --- |
| V. | command, insist on, order; (*ant.*) give, grant, offer **1** | |
| | necessitate, need, require; (*ant.*) give, supply **2** | |

de|mand|ing /dɪmændɪŋ/ **1** ADJ A **demanding**
job or task requires a lot of your time, energy,
or attention. ❑ *He could no longer cope with his
demanding job.* **2** ADJ People who are **demanding**
are not easily satisfied or pleased. ❑ *Ricky was a
very demanding child.* [from Medieval Latin]

de|mean /dɪmin/ (**demeans, demeaning,
demeaned**) V-T To **demean** someone or something
means to make people have less respect for
them. ❑ *Books like these demean religious believers.*
● **de|mean|ing** ADJ ❑ *In the past, it was demeaning for
a man to help with housework.*

de|mean|or /dɪminər/ N-UNCOUNT Your
**demeanor** is the way you behave, which gives
people an impression of your character and
feelings. [FORMAL] ❑ *...her calm and cheerful
demeanor.*

**Word Link** *ment ≈ mind : demented, mental, mentality*

de|ment|ed /dɪmɛntɪd/ ADJ If you describe
someone as **demented**, you disapprove of them
because you think that their actions are strange,
foolish, or uncontrolled. [INFORMAL] ❑ *...demented
laughter.* [from Latin]

de|men|tia /dɪmɛnʃə/ (**dementias**) N-VAR
**Dementia** is a serious illness of the mind.
[MEDICAL] ❑ *...a treatment for conditions such as
dementia and Alzheimer's disease.* [from Latin]

**Word Link** *milit ≈ soldier : demilitarize, military, militia*

de|mili|ta|rize /dɪmɪlɪtəraɪz/ (**demilitarizes,
demilitarizing, demilitarized**) V-T To **demilitarize**
an area means to ensure that all military forces
are removed from it. ❑ *...a demilitarized zone.*

de|mise /dɪmaɪz/ N-SING The **demise** of
something or someone is their end or death.
[FORMAL] ❑ *...the demise of his father.* [from Old
French]

demo /dɛmoʊ/ (**demos**) **1** N-COUNT A **demo** is
a sample recording of music to allow a recording
company to listen to it in order to hear how good
it is. [INFORMAL] ❑ *They recorded a demo of the
songs.* **2** N-COUNT A **demo** is a demonstration of
something. [INFORMAL] ❑ *Download free demos of
our newest software.*

de|mo|bi|lize /dimoʊbɪlaɪz/ (**demobilizes,
demobilizing, demobilized**) V-T/V-I If a country or
armed force **demobilizes** its troops, or if its troops
**demobilize**, its troops are released from service
and allowed to go home. ❑ *He demanded that the
army demobilize its troops.* ● **de|mo|bi|li|za|tion**
/dimoʊbɪlɪzeɪʃ³n/ N-UNCOUNT ❑ *The government
was opposed to the demobilization of its army.*

**Word Link** *cracy ≈ rule by : aristocracy, bureaucracy, democracy*

de|moc|ra|cy /dɪmɒkrəsi/ (**democracies**)
**1** N-UNCOUNT **Democracy** is a system of
government in which people choose their rulers
by voting for them in elections. ❑ *...the spread
of democracy in Eastern Europe.* **2** N-COUNT A
**democracy** is a country in which the people
choose their government by voting for it. ❑ *The
new democracies face tough challenges.* [from French]
→ see **vote**

**Word Link** *crat ≈ power : aristocrat, bureaucrat, democrat*

demo|crat /dɛməkræt/ (**democrats**)
**1** N-COUNT A **Democrat** is a member or
supporter of a particular political party which
has the word "democrat" or "democratic" in its
title, for example, the Democratic Party in the
United States. ❑ *Democrats voted against the plan.*
**2** N-COUNT A **democrat** is a person who believes
in the ideals of democracy, personal freedom,
and equality. ❑ *This is the time for democrats and not
dictators.* [from French]

demo|crat|ic /dɛməkrætɪk/ **1** ADJ A
**democratic** country, government, or political
system is governed by representatives who
are elected by the people. ❑ *Bolivia returned
to democratic rule in 1982.* ● **demo|crati|cal|ly**

/dɛməkrætɪkli/ ADV ❏ *Yeltsin became Russia's first democratically elected president.* **2** ADJ Something that is **democratic** is based on the idea that everyone should have equal rights and should be involved in making important decisions. ❏ *Education is the basis of a democratic society.* ● **demo|crati|cal|ly** ADV ❏ *This committee tries to make decisions democratically.* [from French]

**de|mol|ish** /dɪmɒlɪʃ/ (**demolishes, demolishing, demolished**) **1** V-T To **demolish** something such as a building means to destroy it completely. ❏ *The storm demolished buildings and flooded streets.* ● **demo|li|tion** /dɛməlɪʃ°n/ (**demolitions**) N-VAR ❏ *...the total demolition of the old bridge.* **2** V-T If you **demolish** someone's ideas or arguments, you prove that they are completely wrong or unreasonable. ❏ *Our intention was to demolish the rumors about him.* [from French]

**de|mon** /dimən/ (**demons**) N-COUNT A **demon** is an evil spirit. ❏ *She ran out of the room as if she was being chased by demons.* ● **de|mon|ic** /dɪmɒnɪk/ ADJ ❏ *...a demonic grin.* [from Latin]

**dem|on|strate** /dɛmənstreɪt/ (**demonstrates, demonstrating, demonstrated**) **1** V-T To **demonstrate** a fact means to make it clear to people. ❏ *Studies have demonstrated the link between what we eat and the diseases we may suffer from.* ❏ *The party wants to demonstrate to the voters that they have practical policies.* ● **dem|on|stra|tion** /dɛmənstreɪʃ°n/ (**demonstrations**) N-COUNT ❏ *It was a demonstration of power by the people of Moscow.* **2** V-T If you **demonstrate** a particular skill, quality, or feeling, you show by your actions that you have it. ❏ *They have demonstrated their ability to work together.* ● **dem|on|stra|tion** N-COUNT ❏ *There's been no public demonstration of opposition to the president.* **3** V-I When people **demonstrate**, they march or gather somewhere to show their opposition to something or their support for something. ❏ *200,000 people demonstrated against the war.* ❏ *In the cities, crowds demonstrated for change.* ● **dem|on|stra|tion** N-COUNT ❏ *...an anti-government demonstration.* ● **de|mon|stra|tor** (**demonstrators**) N-COUNT ❏ *Police were dealing with a crowd of demonstrators.* **4** V-T If you **demonstrate** something, you show people how it works or how to do it. ❏ *Several companies will be demonstrating their new products.* ● **dem|on|stra|tion** N-COUNT ❏ *...a cooking demonstration.* [from Latin]
→ see **citizenship**

**de|mor|al|ize** /dɪmɔrəlaɪz/ (**demoralizes, demoralizing, demoralized**) V-T If something **demoralizes** someone, it makes them lose so much confidence in what they are doing that they want to give up. ❏ *Bad conditions in schools demoralize teachers and students.* ● **de|mor|al|ized** ADJ ❏ *...demoralized young people who have done badly in tests.* ● **de|mor|al|iz|ing** ADJ ❏ *Losing their star player was demoralizing for the team.* [from French]

**de|mote** /dɪmoʊt/ (**demotes, demoting, demoted**) V-T If someone **demotes** you, they give you a lower rank or a less important position than you already have, often as a punishment. ❏ *He was demoted from train driver to ticket inspector.*

● **de|mo|tion** /dɪmoʊʃ°n/ (**demotions**) N-VAR ❏ *He believes it was an unfair demotion.*

**den** /dɛn/ (**dens**) **1** N-COUNT A **den** is the home of certain types of wild animals such as lions or foxes. **2** N-COUNT Your **den** is a quiet room in your house where you can go to study, work, or relax without being disturbed. ❏ *He sits in his den surrounded by photos of boats.* **3** N-COUNT A **den** is a secret place where people meet, usually for a dishonest purpose. ❏ *The building was a den of thieves.* [from Old English]

**den|drite** /dɛndraɪt/ (**dendrites**) N-COUNT **Dendrites** are thin fibers with which nerve cells receive messages from other nerve cells. [TECHNICAL] [from Greek]

**de|ni|al** /dɪnaɪəl/ (**denials**) **1** N-VAR A **denial** of something is a statement that it is not true, does not exist, or did not happen. ❏ *...official denials of the government's involvement.* **2** N-UNCOUNT The **denial of** something to someone is the act of refusing to let them have it. [FORMAL] ❏ *...the denial of visas to international workers.* [from Old French]

**den|i|grate** /dɛnɪgreɪt/ (**denigrates, denigrating, denigrated**) V-T If you **denigrate** someone or something, you criticize them unfairly or insult them. ❏ *...a campaign to denigrate the role of the police.* ● **deni|gra|tion** /dɛnɪgreɪʃ°n/ N-UNCOUNT ❏ *...the denigration of minorities in this country.* [from Latin]

**den|im** /dɛnɪm/ N-UNCOUNT **Denim** is a thick cotton cloth, usually blue, which is used to make clothes. Jeans are made from denim. ❏ *...a denim jacket.* [from French]

**de|nomi|na|tion** /dɪnɒmɪneɪʃ°n/ (**denominations**) **1** N-COUNT A particular **denomination** is a particular religious group which has slightly different beliefs from other groups within the same faith. ❏ *Acceptance of women priests varies greatly from denomination to denomination.* **2** N-COUNT The **denomination** of a banknote or coin is its official value. ❏ *She paid in cash, in bills of large denominations.* [from Latin]

**de|note** /dɪnoʊt/ (**denotes, denoting, denoted**) V-T If one thing **denotes** another, it is a sign or indication of it. [FORMAL] ❏ *Red eyes often denote tiredness.* [from Latin]

**de|noue|ment** /deɪnuːmɒn/ (**denouements**) also **dénouement** N-COUNT In a book, play, or series of events, the **denouement** is the sequence of events at the end, when things come to a conclusion. [from French]

**de|noue|ment de|sign** (**denouement designs**) N-COUNT In a book or play, the **denouement design** is the way that the main theme of the book or play is resolved. [TECHNICAL]

**de|nounce** /dɪnaʊns/ (**denounces, denouncing, denounced**) V-T If you **denounce** a person or an action, you criticize them severely and publicly because you feel strongly that they are wrong or evil. ❏ *German leaders denounced the attacks.* [from Old French]

**dense** /dɛns/ (**denser, densest**) **1** ADJ Something that is **dense** contains a lot of things or people in a small area. ❏ *...a large, dense forest.*

● **dense|ly** ADV ❏ *Java is a densely populated island.*
**2** ADJ **Dense** fog or smoke is difficult to see
through because it is very heavy and dark. ❏ *Dense
smoke rose several miles into the air.* **3** ADJ In science,
a **dense** substance is very heavy in relation to its
volume. [TECHNICAL] ❏ *…a small dense star.* [from
Latin]

**den|sity** /dɛnsɪti/ (**densities**) **1** N-VAR **Density**
is the extent to which something is filled or
covered with people or things. ❏ *The area has a
very high population density.* **2** N-VAR In science,
the **density** of a substance or object is the relation
of its mass or weight to its volume. [TECHNICAL]
❏ *Jupiter's moon Io has a density of 3.5 grams per cubic
centimeter.* [from Latin]

**dent** /dɛnt/ (**dents, denting, dented**) **1** V-T If
you **dent** the surface of
something, you make
a hollow area in it by
hitting or pressing it.
❏ *The stone dented the
car's fender.* **2** V-T If
something **dents** your
confidence or your pride,
it makes you realize
that you are not as good
or successful as you
thought. ❏ *Her comments
dented Sebastian's pride.* **3** N-COUNT A **dent** is a
hollow in the surface of something which has
been caused by hitting or pressing it. ❏ *There was a
dent in the car door.* [from Old English]

dent

**Word Link**     dent, dont ≈ tooth : **dent**al, **dent**ist,
                  **dent**ures

**den|tal** /dɛnt³l/ ADJ **Dental** is used to describe
things that relate to teeth or to the care and
treatment of teeth. ❏ *Regular dental care is
important.* [from Medieval Latin]

**den|tist** /dɛntɪst/ (**dentists**) N-COUNT A
**dentist** is a medical practitioner who is qualified
to examine and treat people's teeth. ❏ *Visit your
dentist twice a year for a checkup.* ● **The dentist** or
**the dentist's** is used to refer to the office or clinic
where a dentist works. ❏ *I'm going to the dentist's.*
[from French]
→ see **teeth**

**den|tist's of|fice** (**dentist's offices**) N-COUNT
A **dentist's office** is the room or house where a
dentist works.

**den|tures** /dɛntʃərz/

The form **denture** is used as a modifier.

N-PLURAL **Dentures** are artificial teeth worn by
people who no longer have all their own teeth.
❏ *He had a new set of dentures.* [from French]
→ see **teeth**

**de|nun|cia|tion** /dɪnʌnsieɪʃ³n/ (**denunciations**)
N-VAR **Denunciation of** someone or something is
severe public criticism of them. ❏ *He wrote an angry
denunciation of his critics.* [from Old French]

**deny** /dɪnaɪ/ (**denies, denying, denied**) **1** V-T
When you **deny** something, you state that it is
not true. ❏ *She denied both accusations.* ❏ *He denied
that he was involved in the crime.* **2** V-T If you **deny**
someone something that they need or want, you
refuse to let them have it. ❏ *The military cannot deny
prisoners access to lawyers.* [from Old French]

**Word Partnership**     Use *deny* with :

N.      deny **a charge**, officials deny **1**
        deny **access**, deny **entry**,
        deny **a request** **2**
V.      **confirm or** deny **1**

**de|odor|ant** /dioʊdərənt/ (**deodorants**) N-VAR
**Deodorant** is a substance that you can use on your
body to hide or prevent the smell of sweat.

**de|part** /dɪpɑrt/ (**departs, departing, departed**)
V-T/V-I When something or someone **departs**
**from** a place, they leave it and start a trip to
another place. You can also say that something
**departs** a place ❏ *Flight 43 will depart from Denver at
11:45 a.m.* ❏ *In the morning Mr. McDonald departed for
Sydney.* [from Old French]

**de|part|ment** /dɪpɑrtmənt/ (**departments**)
N-COUNT A **department** is one of the sections in
an organization such as a government, business,
or university. A department is also one of the
sections in a large store. ❏ *…the U.S. Department
of Health and Human Services.* ❏ *He moved to the sales
department.* ● **de|part|men|tal** /dɪpɑrtmɛnt³l/
ADJ ❏ *The Secretary of Education wants a bigger
departmental budget.* [from French]

**de|part|ment store** (**department stores**)
N-COUNT A **department store** is a large store
which sells many different kinds of goods.
❏ *…famous department stores such as Macy's and
Bloomingdales.*

**de|par|ture** /dɪpɑrtʃər/ (**departures**) **1** N-VAR
**Departure** or a **departure** is the act of going away
from somewhere. ❏ *…the president's departure for
Helsinki.* ❏ *They wanted the departure of all foreign
soldiers from the country.* **2** N-COUNT If someone
does something different or unusual, you can
refer to their action as a **departure**. ❏ *This was an
unusual departure from tradition.* [from Old French]

**de|par|tures** /dɪpɑrtərz/ N-SING In an airport,
**departures** is the place where passengers wait
before they get onto their plane. [from Old French]

**de|pend** /dɪpɛnd/ (**depends, depending,
depended**) **1** V-I If you say that one thing
**depends on** another, you mean that the first
thing will be affected or determined by the
second. ❏ *The cooking time needed depends on the size
of the potato.* **2** V-I If you **depend on** someone or
something, you need them in order to be able to
survive physically, financially, or emotionally.
❏ *He depended on his writing for his income.* **3** V-I If
you can **depend on** a person, organization, or law,
you know that they will support you or help you
when you need them. ❏ *"You can depend on me," I
assured him.* **4** V-I You use **depend** in expressions
such as **it depends** to indicate that you cannot give
a clear answer to a question because the answer
will be affected or determined by other factors.
❏ *"How long can you stay?" —"I don't know. It depends."*
**5** PHRASE You use **depending on** when you are
saying that something varies according to the
circumstances mentioned. ❏ *The trip takes between
two and three hours, depending on the traffic.* [from
Old French]

**de|pend|able** /dɪpɛndəb³l/ ADJ If you say that
someone or something is **dependable**, you approve
of them because you feel that you can be sure that
they will always act consistently or sensibly, or do

what you need them to do. ❑ *He was a dependable friend.* [from Old French]

| **Word Link** | ant ≈ one who does, has : defend**ant**, depend**ant**, occup**ant** |
|---|---|

| **Word Link** | ence ≈ state, condition : depend**ence**, excell**ence**, independ**ence** |
|---|---|

| **Word Link** | ent ≈ one who does, has : depend**ent**, resid**ent**, superintend**ent** |
|---|---|

**de|pend|ent** /dɪpɛndənt/ (**dependents**) also **dependant** ◼ ADJ To be **dependent on** something or someone means to need them in order to succeed or be able to survive. ❑ *The local economy is dependent on oil.* ● **de|pend|ence** N-UNCOUNT ❑ *...the city's dependence on tourism.* ● **de|pend|en|cy** N-UNCOUNT ❑ *...the dependency on chemicals for growing crops.* ◼ N-COUNT Your **dependents** are the people you support financially, such as your children. ❑ *...a single man with no dependents.* [from Old French]

| **Word Link** | pict ≈ painting : de**pict**, **pict**ure, **pict**uresque |
|---|---|

**de|pict** /dɪpɪkt/ (**depicts, depicting, depicted**) V-T To **depict** someone or something means to show or represent them in a work of art such as a drawing or painting. ❑ *...pictures depicting Lee's most famous battles.* ● **de|pic|tion** (**depictions**) N-VAR ❑ *...their depiction in the book as thieves.* [from Latin]
→ see **art**

| **Word Link** | ple ≈ filling : com**ple**ment, com**ple**te, de**ple**te |
|---|---|

**de|plete** /dɪplit/ (**depletes, depleting, depleted**) V-T To **deplete** a stock or amount of something means to reduce it. [FORMAL] ❑ *...substances that deplete the ozone layer.* ● **de|plet|ed** ADJ ❑ *...Lee's tired and depleted army.* ● **de|ple|tion** /dɪplijⁿn/ N-UNCOUNT ❑ *...the depletion of water supplies.* [from Latin]

**de|plor|able** /dɪplɔrəb³l/ ADJ If you say that something is **deplorable**, you think that it is very bad and unacceptable. [FORMAL] ❑ *Many people live in the country in deplorable conditions.* [from Old French]

**de|plore** /dɪplɔr/ (**deplores, deploring, deplored**) V-T If you say that you **deplore** something, you think it is very wrong or immoral. [FORMAL] ❑ *Both leaders issued statements deploring the violence.* [from Old French]

**de|ploy** /dɪplɔɪ/ (**deploys, deploying, deployed**) V-T To **deploy** troops or military resources means to organize or position them so that they are ready to be used. ❑ *The president has no intention of deploying troops.* ● **de|ploy|ment** (**deployments**) N-VAR ❑ *...the deployment of soldiers.* [from French]
→ see **army**

**de|port** /dɪpɔrt/ (**deports, deporting, deported**) V-T If a government **deports** someone, usually someone who is not a citizen of that country, it sends them out of the country because they have committed a crime or because it believes they do not have the right to be there. ❑ *...a government decision to deport all illegal immigrants.* ● **de|por|ta|tion** /dipɔrteɪʃⁿn/ (**deportations**)

N-VAR ❑ *Thousands of people face deportation.* [from French]

**de|pose** /dɪpoʊz/ (**deposes, deposing, deposed**) V-T If a ruler or political leader **is deposed**, they are forced to give up their position. ❑ *Mr. Ben Bella was deposed in a coup in 1965.* [from Old French]

| **Word Link** | pos ≈ placing : depo**si**t, pre**pos**ition, re**pos**itory |
|---|---|

**de|pos|it** /dɪpɒzɪt/ (**deposits, depositing, deposited**) ◼ N-COUNT A **deposit** is a sum of money which is part of the full price of something, and which you pay when you agree to buy it or rent it. ❑ *He put down a deposit of $500 for the car.* ◼ N-COUNT A **deposit** is an amount of a substance that has been left somewhere as a result of a chemical or geological process. ❑ *...underground deposits of gold.* ◼ N-COUNT A **deposit** is a sum of money which you put into a bank account. ❑ *I made a deposit every week.* ◼ V-T If you **deposit** a sum of money, you put it into a bank account or savings account. ❑ *The customer has to deposit a minimum of $100 monthly.* [from Medieval Latin]

**depo|si|tion** /dɛpəzɪʃⁿn/ N-UNCOUNT **Deposition** is a geological process in which material that has been carried by the wind or water from one area is left on the surface of another area. [TECHNICAL] [from Late Latin]

**de|pot** /dipoʊ/ (**depots**) ◼ N-COUNT A **depot** is a bus station or train station. ❑ *She met him in the bus depot of Ozark, Alabama.* ◼ N-COUNT A **depot** is a place where large amounts of raw materials, equipment, arms, or other supplies are kept until they are needed. ❑ *...food depots.* [from French]

**de|pre|ci|ate** /dɪpriʃieɪt/ (**depreciates, depreciating, depreciated**) V-T/V-I If something such as a currency **depreciates** or if something **depreciates** it, it loses some of its original value. ❑ *Inflation is rising rapidly; the yuan is depreciating.* ❑ *The demand for foreign currency depreciates the real value of local currencies.* ● **de|pre|cia|tion** /dɪpriʃieɪʃⁿn/ (**depreciations**) N-VAR ❑ *...cost, including machinery depreciation.* [from Late Latin]

**de|press** /dɪprɛs/ (**depresses, depressing, depressed**) ◼ V-T If someone or something **depresses** you, they make you feel sad and disappointed. ❑ *The state of the country depresses me.* ◼ V-T If something **depresses** prices, wages, or figures, it causes them to become less. ❑ *The stronger U.S. dollar depressed sales.* [from Old French]

**de|pressed** /dɪprɛst/ ◼ ADJ If you are **depressed**, you are sad and feel that you cannot enjoy anything. ❑ *She was very depressed after her husband died.* ◼ ADJ A **depressed** place or industry does not have enough business or employment to be successful. ❑ *...plans to encourage more business in depressed areas.* [from Old French]

**de|press|ing** /dɪprɛsɪŋ/ ADJ Something that is **depressing** makes you feel sad and disappointed. ❑ *The view from the window was gray and depressing.* ● **de|press|ing|ly** ADV ❑ *The story sounded depressingly familiar to Janet.* [from Old French]

**de|pres|sion** /dɪprɛʃⁿn/ (**depressions**) ◼ N-VAR **Depression** is a mental state in which you are sad and feel that you cannot enjoy anything. ❑ *Mr. Thomas was suffering from depression.* ◼ N-COUNT A **depression** is a time when there is very little economic activity, which causes a lot of unemployment and poverty. □ …*the Great Depression of the 1930s*. **3** N-COUNT A **depression** in a surface is an area which is lower than the parts surrounding it. □ …*rain-filled depressions*. [from Old French]

**de|prive** /dɪpraɪv/ (**deprives, depriving, deprived**) V-T If you **deprive** someone **of** something that they want or need, you take it away from them, or you prevent them from having it. □ *They were deprived of fuel to heat their homes.* ● **dep|ri|va|tion** /dɛprɪveɪʃ⁰n/ (**deprivations**) N-VAR □ *Many people suffer from sleep deprivation caused by long work hours.* ● **de|prived** ADJ □ …*the most severely deprived children in the country.* [from Old French]

**depth** /dɛpθ/ (**depths**) **1** N-VAR The **depth** of something such as a river or hole is the distance downward from its top surface, or between its upper and lower surfaces. □ *The depth of the hole is 520 yards.* □ *The lake is fourteen feet in depth.* **2** N-VAR The **depth** of something such as a closet or drawer is the distance between its front surface and its back. **3** N-VAR If an emotion is very strongly or intensely felt, you can talk about its **depth**. □ …*the depth of feeling on the subject.* **4** N-UNCOUNT The **depth** of a situation is its extent and seriousness. □ *The president underestimated the depth of the crisis.* **5** N-UNCOUNT The **depth** of someone's knowledge is the great amount that they know. □ *We were impressed with the depth of her knowledge.* **6** N-PLURAL If you talk about **the depths of** an area, you mean the parts of it which are very far from the edge. □ …*the depths of the countryside.* **7** N-PLURAL If you are **in the depths of** an unpleasant emotion, you feel that emotion very strongly. □ *I was in the depths of despair before I met you.* **8** PHRASE If you deal with a subject **in depth**, you deal with it very thoroughly and consider all the aspects of it. □ *We will discuss these three areas in depth.* **9** → see also **in-depth** **10** PHRASE If you say that someone is **out of** their **depth**, you mean that they are in a situation that is much too difficult for them to be able to cope with it. □ *Mr. Gibson is intellectually out of his depth.*

**depu|ty** /dɛpjəti/ (**deputies**) **1** N-COUNT A **deputy** is the second most important person in an organization such as a business or government department. Someone's deputy acts on their behalf when they are not there. □ …*Jack Lang, France's minister for culture, and his deputy, Catherine Tasca.* **2** N-COUNT A **deputy** is a police officer. □ *Robyn asked the deputy if she could speak with Sheriff Adkins.* [from Old French]

**de|rail** /dɪreɪl/ (**derails, derailing, derailed**) **1** V-T If you **derail** something such as a plan or a series of negotiations, you prevent it from continuing as planned. □ *The killing is the work of people who are trying to derail peace talks.* **2** V-T/V-I If a train **is derailed** or if it **derails**, it comes off the track on which it was running. □ *Twenty people were injured when a train was derailed.* ● **de|rail|ment** (**derailments**) N-VAR □ *Several people suffered injuries in a train derailment.*

**de|ranged** /dɪreɪndʒd/ ADJ Someone who is **deranged** behaves in a wild and uncontrolled way, often as a result of mental illness. □ *A deranged man shot and killed 14 people in the main square.* [from Old French]

**der|by** /dɑrbi/ (**derbies**) **1** N-COUNT A **derby** is a sports competition or race where there are no restrictions or limits on who can enter. □ …*the annual fishing derby at Lake Winnipesaukee.* **2** N-COUNT A **derby** is a round, hard hat with a narrow brim which is worn by men. Derbies are no longer very common.

**der|elict** /dɛrɪlɪkt/ ADJ A place or building that is **derelict** is empty and in a bad state of repair because it has not been used or lived in for a long time. □ …*a derelict house.* [from Latin]

<table>
<tr><td>Word Link</td><td>rid, ris ≈ laughing : deride, derision, ridicule</td></tr>
</table>

**de|ride** /dɪraɪd/ (**derides, deriding, derided**) V-T If you **deride** someone or something, you say that they are stupid or have no value. [FORMAL] □ *Critics derided the decision.* ● **de|ri|sion** /dɪrɪʒ⁰n/ N-UNCOUNT □ *There was general derision over the idea.* [from Latin]

**de|riva|tive** /dɪrɪvətɪv/ (**derivatives**) N-COUNT A **derivative** is something which has been developed or obtained from something else. □ *Turkmeni is a derivative of Turkish spoken in Turkmenistan.* [from Old French]

**de|rive** /dɪraɪv/ (**derives, deriving, derived**) **1** V-T If you **derive** something such as pleasure or benefit **from** a person or from something, you get it from them. [FORMAL] □ *Many people derive pleasure from helping others.* **2** V-T/V-I If you say that something such as a word or feeling **derives** or **is derived from** something else, you mean that it comes from that thing. □ *The name Anastasia is derived from a Greek word.* [from Old French]

**der|ma|tolo|gist** /dɜrmətɒlədʒɪst/ (**dermatologists**) N-COUNT A **dermatologist** is a doctor who specializes in the study of skin and the treatment of skin diseases. ● **der|ma|tol|ogy** N-UNCOUNT □ …*drugs used in dermatology.* → see **skin**

**der|mis** /dɜrmɪs/ N-SING The **dermis** is the layer of skin beneath the epidermis. [TECHNICAL] [from New Latin]

**de|sali|na|tion** /disælɪneɪʃ⁰n/ N-UNCOUNT **Desalination** is the process of removing salt from sea water so that it can be used for drinking, or for watering crops.

**des|cant** /dɛskænt/ (**descants**) N-COUNT A **descant** is a tune which is played or sung above the main tune in a piece of music. [from Old Northern French]

<table>
<tr><td>Word Link</td><td>de ≈ from, down, away : deflate, descend, detach</td></tr>
</table>

<table>
<tr><td>Word Link</td><td>scend ≈ climbing : ascend, condescend, descend</td></tr>
</table>

**de|scend** /dɪsɛnd/ (**descends, descending, descended**) **1** V-T/V-I If you **descend** or if you **descend** a staircase, you move downward from a higher to a lower level. [FORMAL] □ *We descended to the basement.* **2** V-I If a large group of people arrive to see you, especially if their visit is unexpected or causes you a lot of work, you can say that they **have descended on** you. □ *Thousands of tourists descend on the area each year.* **3** V-I When you want to emphasize that the situation that someone is entering is very bad, you can say that they **are**

descending into that situation. ❑ *The country descended into chaos.* ◳ v-i If you say that someone **descends to** behavior which you consider unacceptable, you are expressing your disapproval of the fact that they do it. ❑ *We're not going to descend to such methods.* [from Old French]

**de|scend|ant** /dɪsɛndənt/ (**descendants**) N-COUNT Someone's **descendants** are the people in later generations who are related to them. ❑ *…a descendant of King David.* [from Old French]

**de|scend|ed** /dɪsɛndɪd/ ADJ A person who is **descended from** someone who lived a long time ago is directly related to them. ❑ *Anna is descended from people who settled in Colorado in 1898.* [from Old French]

**de|scent** /dɪsɛnt/ (**descents**) ◳ N-VAR A **descent** is a movement from a higher to a lower level or position. ❑ *Fasten your seatbelts for the descent into San Francisco International Airport.* ◳ N-COUNT A **descent** is a surface that slopes downward, for example, the side of a steep hill. ❑ *On the descents cyclists pass cars at tremendous speed.* ◳ N-UNCOUNT You use **descent** to talk about a person's family background, for example, their nationality or social status. [FORMAL] ❑ *All the writers were of African descent.* [from Old French]

**de|scribe** /dɪskraɪb/ (**describes, describing, described**) ◳ v-t If you **describe** a person, object, event, or situation, you say what they are like or what happened. ❑ *She described what she did in her spare time.* ❑ *The poem describes their life together.* ◳ v-t If you **describe** someone or something **as** a particular thing, you say that they are like that thing. ❑ *He described it as the worst job in the world.* ❑ *Even his closest friends describe him as forceful and determined.* [from Latin]

**de|scrip|tion** /dɪskrɪpʃ°n/ (**descriptions**) N-VAR A **description** of someone or something is an account which explains what they are or what they look like. ❑ *Police have issued a description of the man.* ❑ *He gave a detailed description of how the new system will work.* [from Latin]

| **Thesaurus** | *description* | Also look up : |
|---|---|---|
| N. | account, characterization, summary | |

| **Word Partnership** | Use *description* with : |
|---|---|
| ADJ. | **accurate** description, **brief** description, **detailed** description, **physical** description, **vague** description |
| V. | **fit a** description, **give a** description, **match a** description |

**de|scrip|tive** /dɪskrɪptɪv/ ADJ **Descriptive** language or writing indicates what someone or something is like. ❑ *Being descriptive doesn't require a string of adjectives and adverbs. Often a strong verb gives a more precise picture in fewer words.* [from Latin]

**de|scrip|tive de|sign** (**descriptive designs**) N-VAR Research that has a **descriptive design** involves studying the similarities and differences between two or more things.

**des|ecrate** /dɛsɪkreɪt/ (**desecrates, desecrating, desecrated**) v-t If someone **desecrates** something which is considered to be holy or very special, they deliberately damage

or insult it. ❑ *She shouldn't desecrate the picture of a religious leader.* ● **des|ecra|tion** /dɛsɪkreɪʃ°n/ N-UNCOUNT ❑ *Everyone was shocked by the desecration of the church.*

**des|ert** (**deserts, deserting, deserted**)

The noun is pronounced /dɛzərt/. The verb is pronounced /dɪzɜrt/ and is hyphenated de|sert.

◳ N-VAR A **desert** is a large area of land, usually in a hot region, where there is almost no water, rain, trees, or plants. ❑ *…the Sahara Desert.* ◳ v-t If people or animals **desert** a place, they leave it and it becomes empty. ❑ *Poor farmers are deserting their fields and coming to the cities to find jobs.* ● **de|sert|ed** ADJ ❑ *She led them into a deserted street.* ◳ v-t If someone **deserts** you, they go away and leave you, and no longer help or support you. ❑ *Mrs. Roding's husband deserted her years ago.* ● **de|ser|tion** /dɪzɜrʃ°n/ (**desertions**) N-VAR ❑ *…her father's desertion.* ◳ v-t/v-i If someone **deserts**, or **deserts** a job, especially a job in the armed forces, they leave that job without permission. ❑ *He was an officer in the army until he deserted.* ❑ *He deserted from the army last month.* ● **de|sert|er** /dɪzɜrtər/ (**deserters**) N-COUNT ❑ *Two deserters were shot.* ● **de|ser|tion** N-VAR ❑ *Two soldiers face charges of desertion.* [Sense 1 from Old French. Senses 2, 3 and 4 from French.]
→ see Picture Dictionary: **desert**
→ see **habitat**

**de|serve** /dɪzɜrv/ (**deserves, deserving, deserved**) v-t If you say that a person or thing **deserves** something, you mean that they should have it or receive it because of their actions or qualities. ❑ *Government officials clearly deserve some of the blame.* ❑ *These people deserve to get more money.* [from Old French]

| **Word Partnership** | Use *deserve* with : |
|---|---|
| N. | deserve **a chance**, deserve **credit**, deserve **recognition**, deserve **respect** |
| V. | **don't** deserve, deserve **to know** |
| PRON. | deserve **nothing** |

**de|serv|ing** /dɪzɜrvɪŋ/ ADJ If you describe a person, organization, or cause as **deserving**, you mean that you think they should be helped. ❑ *The money should be used for more deserving causes.* [from Old French]

**de|sign** /dɪzaɪn/ (**designs, designing, designed**) ◳ v-t When you **design** something new, you plan what it should be like. ❑ *They wanted to design a machine that was both attractive and practical.* ◳ N-UNCOUNT **Design** is the process and art of planning and making detailed drawings of something. ❑ *He had a talent for design.* ◳ N-UNCOUNT The **design** of something is the way in which it has been planned and made. ❑ *…a new design of clock.* ◳ N-COUNT A **design** is a drawing which someone produces to show how they would like something to be built or made. ❑ *They drew up the design for the house.* ◳ N-COUNT A **design** is a pattern of lines, flowers, or shapes which is used to decorate something. ❑ *Many pictures are based on simple designs.* ◳ N-UNCOUNT In the theater, **design** is the planning and making of things such as the costumes, sets, and lighting for a play or other production. [from Latin]
→ see **architecture, quilt**

**d**

D

**Picture Dictionary**

desert

cactus

palm tree

oasis

sand dune

lizard

sand

snake

---

**des|ig|nate** (**designates, designating, designated**)

> The verb is pronounced /dɛzɪgneɪt/. The adjective is pronounced /dɛzɪgnɪt/.

**1** V-T When you **designate** someone or something **as** a particular thing, you formally give them that description or name. ❑ *The president designated Sunday, February 3rd, as a national day of prayer for peace.* ❑ *...plans to designate the hotel a historic building.* ● **des|ig|na|tion** /dɛzɪgneɪʃᵊn/ (**designations**) N-VAR ❑ *The NC-17 designation for motion pictures stands for no children under 17 admitted.* **2** V-T If something **is designated for** a particular purpose, it is set aside for that purpose. ❑ *Some of the rooms were designated as offices.* **3** ADJ **Designate** is used to describe someone who has been formally chosen to do a particular job, but has not yet started doing it. ❑ *...Japan's prime minister-designate.* [from Latin]

**de|sign|er** /dɪzaɪnər/ (**designers**) **1** N-COUNT A **designer** is a person whose job is to design things by making drawings of them. ❑ *Carolyne is a fashion designer.* **2** ADJ **Designer** clothes or **designer** labels are expensive, fashionable clothes made by a famous designer, rather than being made in large quantities in a factory. ❑ *He wears designer clothes.* [from Latin]

**de|sir|able** /dɪzaɪərəbᵊl/ ADJ Something that is **desirable** is worth having or doing because it is useful, necessary, or popular. ❑ *The house is in a desirable neighborhood, close to schools.* ● **de|sir|abil|ity** /dɪzaɪərəbɪlɪti/ N-UNCOUNT ❑ *...the desirability of political change.* ● **de|sir|abil|ity** N-UNCOUNT ❑ *...our attractiveness and desirability as a partner.* [from Old French]

**de|sire** /dɪzaɪər/ (**desires, desiring, desired**) **1** N-COUNT A **desire** is a strong wish to do or have something. ❑ *I had a strong desire to help people.*

**2** V-T If you **desire** something, you want it. [FORMAL] ❑ *She desired a child with her new husband.* ● **de|sired** ADJ ❑ *This will produce the desired effect.* [from Old French]

---

**Word Partnership**   Use *desire* with :

| | |
|---|---|
| N. | **heart's** desire **1** |
| ADJ. | **strong** desire **1** |
| V. | **express** desire, **have no** desire, **satisfy a** desire **1** |
| | desire **to change** **1** **2** |

---

**desk** /dɛsk/ (**desks**) **1** N-COUNT A **desk** is a table, often with drawers, which you sit at to write or work. **2** N-SING The place in a hotel, hospital, airport, or other building where you check in or obtain information is referred to as a particular **desk**. ❑ *They asked at the desk for Miss Minton.* [from Medieval Latin]
→ see **office**

**desk|top** /dɛsktɒp/ (**desktops**) also **desk-top** **1** ADJ **Desktop** computers are a convenient size for using on a desk or table, but are not designed to be portable. ❑ *It was the smallest desktop computer ever produced.* ● **Desktop** is also a noun. ❑ *We have stopped making desktops.* **2** N-COUNT The **desktop** of a computer is the display of icons that you see on the screen when the computer is ready to use. ❑ *You can rearrange the icons on the desktop.*

**deso|late** /dɛsəlɪt/ **1** ADJ A **desolate** place is empty of people and lacking in comfort. ❑ *...a desolate landscape of flat green fields.* **2** ADJ If someone is **desolate**, they feel very sad, alone, and without hope. [LITERARY] ❑ *He was desolate without her.* [from Latin]

**deso|la|tion** /dɛsəleɪʃᵊn/ **1** N-UNCOUNT **Desolation** is a feeling of great unhappiness and hopelessness. ❑ *Kozelek expresses his sense* of desolation. **2** N-UNCOUNT If you refer to **desolation** in a place, you mean that it is empty and frightening, for example, because it has been destroyed by a violent force or army. ❑ *We looked out at a scene of desolation and ruin.* [from Latin]

**des|pair** /dɪspɛ̱ər/ (**despairs, despairing, despaired**) **1** N-UNCOUNT **Despair** is the feeling that everything is wrong and that nothing will improve. ❑ *I looked at my wife in despair.* **2** V-I If you **despair,** you feel that everything is wrong and that nothing will improve. ❑ *"Oh, I despair sometimes," he said.* **3** V-I If you **despair of** something, you feel that there is no hope that it will happen or improve. If you **despair of** someone, you feel that there is no hope that they will improve. ❑ *She despaired of making him understand her.* [from Old French]

**Word Link**     sper ≈ hope : de*sper*ate, exa*sper*ate, pro*sper*ity

**des|per|ate** /dɛ̱spərɪt/ **1** ADJ If you are **desperate,** you are in such a bad situation that you are willing to try anything to change it. ❑ *Troops helped to get food to places where people are in desperate need.* ● **des|per|ate|ly** ADV ❑ *Thousands of people are desperately trying to leave the country.* **2** ADJ If you are **desperate for** something or **desperate to** do something, you want or need it very much indeed. ❑ *June was desperate to have a baby.* ● **des|per|ate|ly** ADV ❑ *He was a boy who desperately needed affection.* **3** ADJ A **desperate** situation is very difficult, serious, or dangerous. ❑ *...his desperate financial position.* [from Latin]

**Word Partnership**     Use *desperate* with :

| | |
|---|---|
| N. | desperate **act,** desperate **attempt,** desperate **measures,** desperate **need,** desperate **struggle** **1** desperate **situation** **3** |
| V. | **sound** desperate **1** **grow** desperate **1** – **3** |

**des|pera|tion** /dɛ̱spəreɪ̱ʃ⁰n/ N-UNCOUNT **Desperation** is the feeling that you have when you are in such a bad situation that you will try anything to change it. ❑ *..this feeling of desperation and helplessness that most of the refugees had.* [from Latin]

**des|pic|able** /dɛ̱spɪkəb⁰l/ ADJ If you say that a person or action is **despicable,** you are

emphasizing that they are extremely nasty, cruel, or evil. ❑ *...a despicable crime.* [from Late Latin]

**des|pise** /dɪspaɪ̱z/ (**despises, despising, despised**) V-T If you **despise** something or someone, you dislike them and have a very low opinion of them. ❑ *I can never forgive him. I despise him.* [from Old French]

**de|spite** /dɪspaɪ̱t/ PREP You use **despite** to introduce a fact which makes something surprising. ❑ *The event was a success, despite the rain.* [from Old French]

**des|sert** /dɪzɜ̱rt/ (**desserts**) N-VAR **Dessert** is something sweet, such as fruit, pastry, or ice cream, that you eat at the end of a meal. ❑ *She had ice cream for dessert.* [from French]
→ see Picture Dictionary: **dessert**

**Word Link**     stab ≈ steady : de*stab*ilize, e*stab*lish, in*stab*ility

**de|sta|bi|lize** /disteɪ̱bəlaɪz/ (**destabilizes, destabilizing, destabilized**) V-T To **destabilize** something such as a country or government means to create a situation which reduces its power or influence. ❑ *Their aim is to destabilize the Indian government.*

**des|ti|na|tion** /dɛ̱stɪneɪ̱ʃⁿn/ (**destinations**) N-COUNT Your **destination** is the place you are going to. ❑ *Ellis Island is one of America's most popular tourist destinations.* [from Old French]

**des|tined** /dɛ̱stɪnd/ ADJ If something is **destined to** happen or if someone is **destined to** behave in a particular way, that thing seems certain to happen or be done. ❑ *The plan is destined to fail.* [from Old French]

**des|ti|ny** /dɛ̱stɪni/ (**destinies**) **1** N-COUNT A person's **destiny** is everything that happens to them during their life, including what will happen in the future, especially when it is considered to be controlled by someone or something else. ❑ *Do we control our own destiny?* **2** N-UNCOUNT **Destiny** is the force which some people believe controls the things that happen to you in your life. ❑ *Is it destiny that brings people together, or is it accident?* [from Old French]

**des|ti|tute** /dɛ̱stɪtut/ ADJ Someone who is **destitute** has no money or possessions. [FORMAL] ❑ *...destitute children who live on the streets.* [from Latin]

**de|stroy** /dɪstrɔ̱ɪ/ (**destroys, destroying, destroyed**) V-T To **destroy** something means to

**Picture Dictionary**     dessert

ice cream | cake | pie | cookies | cheesecake
custard | brownie | chocolate mousse | rice pudding | fruit salad

cause so much damage to it that it is completely ruined or does not exist any more. ❑ *The plan will destroy the economy.* ● de|**struc**|**tion** /dɪstrʌkʃ°n/ N-UNCOUNT ❑ *...an international agreement aimed at stopping the destruction of the ozone layer.* [from Old French]

| **Thesaurus** | *destroy* | Also look up : |
| --- | --- | --- |
| v. | annihilate, crush, demolish, eradicate, ruin, wipe out; *(ant.)* build, construct, create, repair | |

| **Word Link** | *struct ≈ building : con***struct**, de***struct***ive |
| --- | --- |

de|**struc**|**tive** /dɪstrʌktɪv/ ADJ Something that is **destructive** causes or is capable of causing great damage, harm, or injury. ❑ *...the destructive power of nuclear weapons.* [from Old French]

| **Word Link** | *de ≈ from, down, away : de*flate, *de*scend, *de*tach |
| --- | --- |

de|**tach** /dɪtætʃ/ (**detaches, detaching, detached**) V-T/V-I If you **detach** one thing **from** another that it is attached to, you remove it. If one thing **detaches from** another, it becomes separated from it. [FORMAL] ❑ *Detach the card and mail it to this address.* ❑ *They tried to detach the kite from the tree.* [from Old French]

de|**tached** /dɪtætʃt/ **1** ADJ Someone who is **detached** is not personally involved in something or has no emotional interest in it. ❑ *They tried to remain emotionally detached from the prisoners.* **2** ADJ A **detached** building is one that is not joined to any other building. ❑ *...a house with a detached garage.* [from Old French]

de|**tach**|**ment** /dɪtætʃmənt/ N-UNCOUNT **Detachment** is the feeling of not being personally involved in something or of having no emotional interest in it. ❑ *The work requires detachment.* [from Old French]

de|**tail** /dɪteɪl/ (**details, detailing, detailed**)

The pronunciation /dɪteɪl/ is also used for the noun.

**1** N-COUNT The **details of** something are its small, individual features or elements. ❑ *The details of the plan are still being worked out.* ❑ *They gave no details of the discussions.* **2** N-PLURAL **Details** about someone or something are facts or pieces of information about them. ❑ *See the bottom of this page for details of how to apply for this offer.* **3** V-T If you **detail** things, you list them or give information about them. ❑ *The report detailed the mistakes which were made.* **4** PHRASE If you examine or discuss something **in detail**, you do it thoroughly and carefully. ❑ *Examine the contract in detail before signing it.* [from French]

| **Thesaurus** | *detail* | Also look up : |
| --- | --- | --- |
| N. | component, element, feature, point **1** **2** fact, information **2** | |
| V. | depict, describe, specify; *(ant.)* approximate, generalize **3** | |

de|**tailed** /dɪteɪld/ ADJ A **detailed** report or plan contains a lot of details. ❑ *The letter contains a detailed account of the decisions.* [from French]

| **Word Partnership** | Use *detailed* with : |
| --- | --- |
| N. | detailed **account**, detailed **analysis**, detailed **description**, detailed **instructions**, detailed **plan**, detailed **record** |

de|**tain** /dɪteɪn/ (**detains, detaining, detained**) **1** V-T When people such as the police **detain** someone, they keep them in a place under their control. [FORMAL] ❑ *Police have detained two people in connection with the attack.* **2** V-T To **detain** someone means to delay them, for example, by talking to them. [FORMAL] ❑ *Could I ask just one more question — if I'm not detaining you?* [from Old French]

de|**tainee** /dɪteɪni/ (**detainees**) N-COUNT A **detainee** is someone who is held prisoner by a government because of his or her political views or activities. ❑ *...the release of political detainees.* [from Old French]

| **Word Link** | *tect ≈ covering : de***tect**, *pro***tect**, *pro***tect***ive* |
| --- | --- |

de|**tect** /dɪtɛkt/ (**detects, detecting, detected**) V-T If you **detect** something, you find it or notice it. ❑ *...a piece of equipment used to detect heat.* ❑ *Arnold could detect a sadness in the old man's face.* ● de|**tec**|**tion** N-UNCOUNT ❑ *...the early detection of cancer.* [from Latin]

de|**tec**|**tive** /dɪtɛktɪv/ (**detectives**) N-COUNT A **detective** is someone whose job is to discover what has happened in a crime or other situation and to find the people involved. Some detectives work in the police force and others work privately. ❑ *Detectives are appealing for witnesses to the attack.* [from Latin]

de|**tec**|**tor** /dɪtɛktər/ (**detectors**) N-COUNT A **detector** is an instrument which is used to discover that something is present somewhere, or to measure how much of something there is. ❑ *...a metal detector.* [from Latin]

de|**tente** /deɪtɒnt/ also **détente** N-UNCOUNT; N-SING **Detente** is a state of friendly relations between two countries when previously there had been problems between them. [FORMAL] ❑ *...a policy of detente.* [from French]

de|**ten**|**tion** /dɪtɛnʃ°n/ (**detentions**) **1** N-UNCOUNT **Detention** is when someone is arrested or put into prison. ❑ *...the detention of people involved in crime.* **2** N-VAR **Detention** is a punishment for students who misbehave, who are made to stay at school after the other students have gone home. ❑ *He kept most of the class after school for detention.* [from Latin]

de|**ten**|**tion** cen|**ter** (**detention centers**) N-COUNT A **detention center** is a sort of prison, for example, a place where people who have entered a country illegally are kept while a decision is made about what to do with them.

de|**ter** /dɪtɜr/ (**deters, deterring, deterred**) V-T To **deter** someone **from** doing something means to make them not want to do it or continue doing it. ❑ *High prices deter people from buying.* [from Latin]

de|**ter**|**gent** /dɪtɜrdʒ°nt/ (**detergents**) N-VAR **Detergent** is a chemical substance, usually in the form of a powder or liquid, which is used for washing things such as clothes or dishes. ❑ *...a*

*type of detergent.* [from Latin]
→ see **soap**

**de|te|rio|rate** /dɪtɪəriəreɪt/ (**deteriorates, deteriorating, deteriorated**) V-I If something **deteriorates**, it becomes worse in some way. ❑ *The situation might deteriorate into war.* ● **de|terio|ra|tion** /dɪtɪəriəreɪ⁰n/ N-UNCOUNT ❑ *...concern about the deterioration in relations between the two countries.* [from Late Latin]

**de|ter|mi|na|tion** /dɪtɜrmɪneɪ⁰n/
■ N-UNCOUNT **Determination** is the quality that you show when you have decided to do something and you will not let anything stop you. ❑ *Everyone behaved with courage and determination.* [from Old French] ■ → see also **determine**

**de|ter|mine** /dɪtɜrmɪn/ (**determines, determining, determined**) ■ V-T If something **determines** what will happen, it controls it. [FORMAL] ❑ *The size of the chicken pieces will determine the cooking time.* ● **de|ter|mi|na|tion** N-UNCOUNT ❑ *This gene is responsible for eye color determination.* ■ V-T To **determine** a fact means to discover it as a result of investigation. [FORMAL] ❑ *The investigation will determine what really happened.* ❑ *Testing must be done to determine the long-term effects on humans.* ● **de|ter|mi|na|tion** N-UNCOUNT ❑ *...a determination of guilt or innocence.* [from Old French]

**de|ter|mined** /dɪtɜrmɪnd/ ADJ If you are **determined to** do something, you have made a firm decision to do it and will not let anything stop you. ❑ *His enemies are determined to ruin him.* [from Old French]

**de|ter|min|er** /dɪtɜrmɪnər/ (**determiners**) N-COUNT In grammar, a **determiner** is a word which is used at the beginning of a noun group to indicate, for example, which thing you are referring to or whether you are referring to one thing or several. Common English determiners are "a," "the," "some," "this," and "each." [from Old French]

**de|ter|rent** /dɪtɜrənt/ (**deterrents**) N-COUNT A **deterrent** is something that prevents people from doing something by making them afraid of what will happen to them if they do it. ❑ *...months of debate over whether arming pilots would be a deterrent to hijackers.* ● **de|ter|rence** N-UNCOUNT ❑ *...policies of nuclear deterrence.* [from Latin]

**de|test** /dɪtɛst/ (**detests, detesting, detested**) V-T If you **detest** someone or something, you dislike them very much. ❑ *My mother detested him.* [from Latin]

**deto|nate** /dɛt⁰neɪt/ (**detonates, detonating, detonated**) V-T/V-I If someone **detonates** a device such as a bomb, or if it **detonates**, it explodes. ❑ *The country detonated its first nuclear device.* ● **deto|na|tion** /dɛt⁰neɪ⁰n/ (**detonations**) ❑ *...detonation of nuclear weapons.* [from Latin]

**de|tour** /ditʊər/ (**detours**) ■ N-COUNT If you make a **detour** on a trip, you go by a route which is not the shortest way, because you want to avoid something such as a traffic jam, or because there is something you want to do on the way. ❑ *He did not take the direct route to his home, but made a detour.* ■ N-COUNT A **detour** is a special route for traffic to follow when the normal route is blocked, for

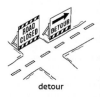

detour

example, because it is being repaired. ❑ *A detour in the road is causing major problems for businesses.* [from French]

**de|tract** /dɪtrækt/ (**detracts, detracting, detracted**) ■ V-I If one thing **detracts from** another, it makes it seem less good or impressive. ❑ *The injury did not detract from her beauty.* [from Latin] ■ → see also **distract**

**det|ri|ment** /dɛtrɪmənt/ PHRASE If something happens **to the detriment of** something or **to** a person's **detriment**, it causes harm or damage to them. [FORMAL] ❑ *These tests give too much importance to written exams to the detriment of other skills.* [from Latin]

**det|ri|men|tal** /dɛtrɪmɛnt⁰l/ ADJ Something that is **detrimental to** something else has a harmful or damaging effect on it. ❑ *Many foods are detrimental to health because of the chemicals they contain.* [from Latin]

**de|value** /divælyu/ (**devalues, devaluing, devalued**) ■ V-T To **devalue** something means to cause it to be thought less impressive or less deserving of respect. ❑ *They tried to devalue her work.* ■ V-T To **devalue** the currency of a country means to reduce its value in relation to other currencies. ❑ *India has devalued the rupee by about eleven percent.* ● **de|valua|tion** /divælyueɪ⁰n/ (**devaluations**) N-VAR ❑ *It resulted in the devaluation of several currencies.*

**dev|as|tate** /dɛvəsteɪt/ (**devastates, devastating, devastated**) V-T If something **devastates** an area or a place, it damages it very badly or destroys it totally. ❑ *The earthquake devastated parts of Indonesia.* ● **dev|as|ta|tion** /dɛvəsteɪ⁰n/ N-UNCOUNT ❑ *The war brought massive devastation to the area.* [from Latin]

**dev|as|tat|ed** /dɛvəsteɪtɪd/ ADJ If you are **devastated** by something, you are very shocked and upset by it. ❑ *Teresa was devastated when Scott ended their marriage.* [from Latin]

**dev|as|tat|ing** /dɛvəsteɪtɪŋ/ ADJ If you describe something as **devastating**, you are emphasizing that it is very harmful or upsetting. ❑ *We must find a cure for this devastating disease.* ❑ *When I heard about my dad's illness, it was devastating.* [from Latin]

**de|vel|op** /dɪvɛləp/ (**develops, developing, developed**) ■ V-I When something **develops**, it grows or changes over a period of time and usually becomes more advanced, complete, or severe. ❑ *It's difficult to know how the market will develop.* ❑ *This violence could develop into war.* ● **de|vel|oped** ADJ ❑ *Their bodies were well developed and super fit.* ● **de|vel|op|ment** N-UNCOUNT ❑ *...the development of language.* ■ V-I If a problem or difficulty **develops**, it begins to occur. ❑ *A problem developed with an experiment aboard the space shuttle.* ■ V-I If you say that a country **develops**, you mean that it changes from being a poor agricultural country to being a rich industrial country. ❑ *All of these countries developed fast.* ● **de|vel|oped** ADJ ❑ *Family size is smaller in more developed countries.* ■ → see also **developing** ■ V-T To **develop** land or property means to make it more profitable,

d

by building houses or factories or by improving the existing buildings. ❑ *Local business people developed fashionable restaurants in the area.*
● de|vel|oped ADJ ❑ *Developed land grew from 5.3% to 6.9%.* ● de|vel|op|er (**developers**) N-COUNT ❑ *The land has a high value if it is sold to developers.*
● de|vel|op|ment (**developments**) N-COUNT ❑ *...a 16-house development.* ◳ V-T If someone **develops** a new product, they design it and produce it. ❑ *Several countries developed nuclear weapons secretly.*
● de|vel|op|er N-COUNT ❑ *...a developer of computer software.* ● de|vel|op|ment N-VAR ❑ *The company is spending $850M on research and development.* ◷ V-T To **develop** photographs means to make negatives or prints from a photographic film. ❑ *She developed one roll of film.* [from Old French]
→ see **photography**

de|vel|op|ing /dɪvɛləpɪŋ/ ADJ If you talk about **developing** countries or the **developing** world, you mean the countries or the parts of the world that are poor and have few industries. ❑ *Pollution is increasing in the developing world.* [from Old French]

de|vel|op|ment /dɪvɛləpmənt/ (**developments**) ◰ N-UNCOUNT **Development** is the growth of something such as a business or an industry. [BUSINESS] ❑ *A country's economic development is a key factor to progress.* ◳ N-COUNT A **development** is an event or incident which has recently happened and is likely to have an effect on the present situation. ❑ *Police say this is an important development in the investigation.* [from Old French]

de|vi|ant /dɪviənt/ ADJ **Deviant** behavior or thinking is different from what people normally consider to be acceptable. ❑ *...deviant and criminal behavior.* ● de|vi|ance N-UNCOUNT ❑ *...social deviance.* [from Late Latin]

de|vi|ate /dɪvieɪt/ (**deviates, deviating, deviated**) V-I To **deviate from** something means to start doing something different or not planned, especially in a way that causes problems for others. ❑ *The message deviated from the government's policy.* ● de|via|tion /dɪvieɪʃⁿn/ (**deviations**) N-VAR ❑ *...a deviation from your daily routine.* [from Late Latin]

de|vice /dɪvaɪs/ (**devices**) N-COUNT A **device** is an object that has been invented for a particular purpose, for example, for recording or measuring something. ❑ *He used an electronic device to measure the rooms.* [from Old French]

dev|il /dɛvⁿl/ (**devils**) ◰ N-PROPER In Judaism, Christianity, and Islam, the **Devil** is the most powerful evil spirit. ◳ N-COUNT A **devil** is an evil spirit. ❑ *...the idea of angels with wings and devils with horns.* [from Old English]

de|vi|ous /dɪviəs/ ADJ If you describe someone as **devious** you think they are dishonest and like to keep things secret, often in a complicated way. ❑ *He used every devious trick to get his friend out of prison.* [from Latin]

de|vise /dɪvaɪz/ (**devises, devising, devised**) V-T If you **devise** a plan, system, or machine, you have the idea for it and design it. ❑ *We devised a plan to help him.* [from Old French]

de|void /dɪvɔɪd/ ADJ If you say that someone or something is **devoid of** a quality or thing, you are emphasizing that they have none of it. [FORMAL] ❑ *His face was devoid of emotion.* [from Old French]

de|volve /dɪvɒlv/ (**devolves, devolving, devolved**) V-T/V-I If you **devolve** power, authority, or responsibility or if it **devolves upon** them, it is transferred to them. ❑ *...the need to devolve power to local governments.* ● de|vo|lu|tion /dɪvəluʃⁿn, dɛv-/ N-UNCOUNT ❑ *...the devolution of power to the regions.* [from Latin]

de|vote /dɪvoʊt/ (**devotes, devoting, devoted**) V-T If you **devote** yourself, your time, or your energy **to** something, you spend all or most of your time or energy on it. ❑ *He devoted the rest of his life to science.* ❑ *A lot of money was devoted to the project.* [from Latin]

de|vot|ed /dɪvoʊtɪd/ ADJ Someone who is **devoted to** a person loves that person very much. ❑ *...a devoted husband.* [from Latin]

devo|tee /dɛvəti/ (**devotees**) N-COUNT Someone who is a **devotee of** a subject or activity is very enthusiastic about it. ❑ *Mr. Carpenter is a devotee of Britten's music.* [from Latin]

de|vo|tion /dɪvoʊʃⁿn/ N-UNCOUNT **Devotion to** someone or something is great love of them and commitment to them. ❑ *I've never seen such devotion between a brother and sister before.* ❑ *...their devotion to religion.* [from Latin]

de|vour /dɪvaʊər/ (**devours, devouring, devoured**) V-T If a person or animal **devours** something, they eat it quickly and eagerly. ❑ *The dog devoured a whole can of food.* [from Old French]

de|vout /dɪvaʊt/ ◰ ADJ A **devout** person has deep religious beliefs. ❑ *She was a devout Christian.* ● **The devout** are people who are devout. ❑ *...priests instructing the devout.* ◳ ADJ If you describe someone as a **devout** supporter or a **devout** opponent of something, you mean that they support it enthusiastically or oppose it strongly. ❑ *He was a devout fan of the TV show.* [from Old French]

dew /du/ N-UNCOUNT **Dew** is small drops of water that form on the ground and other surfaces outdoors during the night. ❑ *The dew gathered on the leaves.* [from Old English]

dew point (**dew points**) N-COUNT The **dew point** is the temperature at which water vapor in the air becomes liquid and dew begins to form. [TECHNICAL]

dia|be|tes /daɪəbitɪs, -tiz/ N-UNCOUNT **Diabetes** is a medical condition in which someone has too much sugar in their blood. [from Latin]
→ see **sugar**

dia|bet|ic /daɪəbɛtɪk/ (**diabetics**) ◰ N-COUNT A **diabetic** is a person who suffers from diabetes. ❑ *...food that is suitable for diabetics.* ● **Diabetic** is also an adjective. ❑ *...diabetic patients.* ◳ ADJ **Diabetic** means relating to diabetes. ❑ *He found her in a diabetic coma.* [from Latin]

| Word Link | *dia* ≈ *across, through* : *dia*gnose, *dia*gonal, *dia*logue |
| --- | --- |

di|ag|nose /daɪəgnoʊs/ (**diagnoses, diagnosing, diagnosed**) V-T If someone or something **is diagnosed as** having a particular illness or problem, their illness or problem is identified. If an illness or problem **is diagnosed**, it is identified. ❑ *The soldiers were diagnosed as having the flu.* [from New Latin]
→ see **diagnosis, illness**

| Word Web | diagnosis |

Many doctors suggest that their **patients** get a routine **physical examination** once a year—even if they're feeling healthy. This enables the **physician** to see any **symptoms** early and **diagnose** possible **diseases** at an early stage. The doctor may begin by using a **tongue** depressor to look down the patient's throat for possible **infections**. Then he or she may use a stethoscope to listen to subtle sounds in the heart, lungs, and stomach. A **blood pressure** reading is always part of the physical exam.

**di|ag|no|sis** /daɪəgnoʊsɪs/ (**diagnoses**) N-VAR **Diagnosis** is the discovery and naming of what is wrong with someone who is ill or with something that is not working properly. ❑ *I had a second test to confirm the diagnosis.* [from New Latin]
→ see Word Web: **diagnosis**

**di|ag|nos|tic** /daɪəgnɒstɪk/ ADJ **Diagnostic** equipment, methods, or systems are used for discovering what is wrong with people who are ill or with things that do not work properly. ❑ *...X-rays and other diagnostic tools.* [from New Latin]

| Word Link | dia ≈ across, through : *diagnose, diagonal, dialogue* |

**di|ago|nal** /daɪæɡənᵊl, -æɡnᵊl/ ADJ A **diagonal** line or movement goes in a sloping direction, for example, from one corner of a square across to the opposite corner. ❑ *...a pattern of diagonal lines.*
● **di|ago|nal|ly** ADV ❑ *He ran diagonally across the field.* [from Latin]

square
diagonal line
diagonal

| Word Link | gram ≈ writing : *diagram, program, telegram* |

**dia|gram** /daɪəgræm/ (**diagrams, diagramming** or **diagraming, diagrammed** or **diagramed**) ◼ N-COUNT A **diagram** is a simple drawing which consists mainly of lines and is used, for example, to explain how a machine works. ❑ *...a diagram of a computer.* ◼ V-T To **diagram** something means to draw a diagram of it or to explain it using a diagram. [FORMAL] ❑ *The process can be diagramed.* [from Latin]

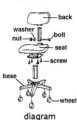
back
washer
nut
bolt
seat
screw
base
wheel
diagram

| Thesaurus | diagram | Also look up : |

N. blueprint, chart, design, illustration, plan ◼

**dial** /daɪəl/ (**dials, dialing, dialed**) ◼ N-COUNT A **dial** is the part of a machine or instrument such as a clock or watch which shows you the time or a measurement that has been recorded. ❑ *The dial on the clock showed five minutes to seven.* ◼ N-COUNT A **dial** is a control on a device or piece of equipment which you can move in order to adjust the setting, for example, to select or change the frequency

on a radio or the temperature of a heater. ❑ *He turned the dial on the radio.* ◼ V-T/V-I If you **dial** or if you **dial** a number, you press the buttons on a telephone, or turn the dial on an old-fashioned telephone, in order to phone someone. ❑ *He lifted the phone and dialed her number.* [from Medieval Latin]

dial

**dia|lect** /daɪəlɛkt/ (**dialects**) N-COUNT A **dialect** is a form of a language that is spoken in a particular area. ❑ *...speaking in the local dialect.* [from Latin]
→ see **English**

**dia|log box** (**dialog boxes**) N-COUNT A **dialog box** is a small area containing information or questions that appears on a computer screen when you are performing particular operations. [COMPUTING] ❑ *Clicking this brings up another dialog box.*

| Word Link | log ≈ reason, speech : *apology, dialogue, logic* |

**dia|logue** /daɪəlɔg/ (**dialogues**) also **dialog** ◼ N-VAR **Dialogue** is communication or discussion between people or groups of people such as governments or political parties. ❑ *The dialogue continued for months.* ◼ N-VAR A **dialogue** is a conversation between two people in a book, film, or play. ❑ *He writes very funny dialogue.* [from Old French]

**dial tone** (**dial tones**) N-COUNT The **dial tone** is the noise you hear when you pick up a telephone receiver, and which means that you can dial the number that you want.

**dial-up** ADJ A **dial-up** connection to the Internet is a connection that uses a modem and a conventional telephone line. ❑ *...more than 200 times the speed of a regular dial-up connection.*

**di|am|eter** /daɪæmɪtər/ (**diameters**) N-COUNT The **diameter** of a round object is the length of a straight line that can be drawn across it, passing through the middle of it. ❑ *The tube is much smaller than the diameter of a human hair.* [from Medieval Latin]
→ see **area, circle**

**dia|mond** /daɪmənd, daɪə-/ (**diamonds**) ◼ N-VAR A **diamond** is a hard, bright, precious stone which is clear and colorless. Diamonds are used in jewelry and for cutting very hard substances. ❑ *...a pair of diamond earrings.*

**2** N-COUNT A **diamond** is a shape with four straight sides of equal length where the opposite angles are the same, but none of the angles is equal to 90°: ◇. □ *He formed his hands into the shape of a diamond.* **3** N-UNCOUNT **Diamonds** is one of the four suits of cards in a pack of playing cards. Each card in the suit is marked with one or more red symbols in the shape of a diamond. □ *He picked the seven of diamonds.* ● A **diamond** is a playing card of this suit. □ *Win the ace of clubs and play a diamond.* **4** N-COUNT In baseball, the **diamond** is the square formed by the four bases, or the whole of the playing area. □ *He was the best player to walk out onto the diamond.* [from Old French]
→ see **baseball, crystal, park**

**dia|per** /dáɪpər, dáɪə-/ (**diapers**) N-COUNT A **diaper** is a piece of soft towel or paper, which you fasten around a baby's bottom in order to contain its urine and feces. □ *He never changed her diapers.* [from Old French]

**dia|phragm** /dáɪəfræm/ (**diaphragms**) N-COUNT Your **diaphragm** is a muscle between your lungs and your stomach. It is used when you breathe. □ *...the skill of breathing from the diaphragm.* [from Late Latin]
→ see **respiration**

**di|ar|rhea** /dáɪəríə/ N-UNCOUNT If someone has **diarrhea**, a lot of liquid feces comes out of their body because they are ill. □ *Many team members suffered from diarrhea.* [from Late Latin]

**dia|ry** /dáɪəri/ (**diaries**) N-COUNT A **diary** is a book which has a separate space for each day of the year. You use a diary to write down things you plan to do, or to record what happens in your life day by day. □ *I read the entry from his diary for July 10, 1940.* [from Latin]
→ see Word Web: **diary**
→ see **history**

**dia|ton|ic scale** /dáɪətɒnɪk skéɪl/ (**diatonic scales**) N-COUNT A **diatonic scale** is the sequence of musical notes that make up a major or minor scale. [TECHNICAL]

**dice** /dáɪs/ (**dices, dicing, diced**) **1** N-COUNT A **dice** is a small cube which has between one and six spots or numbers on its sides, and which is used in games to provide random numbers. In old-fashioned English, "dice" was used only as a plural form, and the singular was **die**, but now "dice" is used as both the singular and the plural form. □ *I throw both dice and get double 6.* **2** V-T If you **dice** food, you cut it into small cubes. □ *Dice the onion and boil in the water.*

→ see **cut**

**di|choto|mous key** /daɪkɒtəməs kí/ (**dichotomous keys**) N-COUNT A **dichotomous key** is a system for identifying species of plants or animals based on pairs of questions. [TECHNICAL]

> **Word Link**    dict ≈ speaking : contra**dict**, **dict**ate, pre**dict**

**dic|tate** (**dictates, dictating, dictated**)

The verb is pronounced /díkteɪt, dɪktéɪt/. The noun is pronounced /díkteɪt/.

**1** V-T If you **dictate** something, you say or read it aloud for someone else to write down. □ *She dictated a letter to her secretary.* **2** V-T If you **dictate to** someone, you tell them what they must do. □ *Why should one country dictate the policy of another country?* □ *What gives them the right to dictate to us what we should eat?* **3** V-T If one thing **dictates** another, the first thing causes or influences the second thing. □ *The movie's budget dictated a tough schedule.* □ *Several factors dictate how long an apple tree can live.* [from Latin]

**dic|ta|tion** /dɪktéɪʃⁿn/ N-UNCOUNT **Dictation** is the speaking or reading aloud of words for someone else to write down. □ *...taking dictation from the dean of the graduate school.* [from Latin]

**dic|ta|tor** /díkteɪtər/ (**dictators**) N-COUNT A **dictator** is a ruler who has complete power in a country, especially power which was obtained by force and is used unfairly or cruelly. □ *...foreign dictators.* [from Latin]

**dic|ta|tor|ial** /dɪktətɔ́riəl/ ADJ If you describe someone's behavior as **dictatorial**, you do not like the fact that they tell people what to do in a forceful and unfair way. □ *...his dictatorial management style.* [from Latin]

**dic|ta|tor|ship** /dɪktéɪtərʃɪp/ (**dictatorships**) **1** N-VAR **Dictatorship** is government by a dictator. □ *...a long period of military dictatorship in the country.* **2** N-COUNT A **dictatorship** is a country which is ruled by a dictator or by a very strict and harsh government. □ *Every country in the region was a military dictatorship.* [from Latin]

**dic|tion** /díkʃⁿn/ N-UNCOUNT Someone's **diction** is how clearly they speak or sing. □ *She has very good diction.* [from Latin]

**dic|tion|ary** /díkʃəneri/ (**dictionaries**) N-COUNT A **dictionary** is a book in which the words and phrases of a language are listed alphabetically,

---

> ### Word Web    diary
>
> Someone writes in a **diary** to tell about the things that happen in their daily life. Most diaries are private **documents** and are not shared with others. But sometimes an important diary is published as a book. One such example is *The Diary of a Young Girl*. This is Anne Frank's World War II **chronicle** of her family's experience as they hid from the Nazis. They were found and arrested, and later Anne died in a concentration camp. This **primary source** document tells Anne's story in her own words. It is full of rich details that are often missing from other historical **texts**. The book is now available in 60 different languages.
>
>

# did · 251 · difference

**d**

together with their meanings or their translations in another language. ❑ ...*a Spanish-English dictionary.* [from Medieval Latin]

**did** /dɪd/ **Did** is the past tense of **do.** [from Old English]

**didn't** /dɪdᵊnt/ **Didn't** is the usual spoken form of "did not."

**die** /daɪ/ (**dies, dying, died**) **1** V-I When people, animals, and plants **die,** they stop living. ❑ *My dog died.* ❑ *Sadly, my mother died of cancer.* **2** V-I You can say that you **are dying** of thirst, hunger, boredom, or curiosity to emphasize that you are very thirsty, hungry, bored, or curious. [INFORMAL] ❑ *Order me a drink, I'm dying of thirst.* **3** V-T/V-I You can say that you **are dying for** something or **are dying to** do something to emphasize that you very much want to have it or do it. [INFORMAL] ❑ *I'm dying for some fresh air.* **4** → see also **dying** **5** V-I When something **dies,** or when it **dies away** or **dies down,** it gradually becomes weaker, until it no longer exists. ❑ *My love for you will never die.* ❑ *The thunder was dying away across the mountains.* ❑ *The wind died down.* [from Old English]
▸ **die out** PHR-VERB If something **dies out,** it becomes less and less common and eventually disappears completely. ❑ *Use of the Internet won't die out.*

**die|sel** /diːzᵊl/ (**diesels**) **1** N-UNCOUNT **Diesel** or **diesel oil** is the heavy fuel used in a diesel engine. **2** N-COUNT A **diesel** is a vehicle which has a diesel engine. ❑ *Diesels are better now than they used to be.* [after Rudolf Diesel (1858–1913), a German engineer]

**diet** /daɪɪt/ (**diets, dieting, dieted**) **1** N-VAR Your **diet** is the type and variety of food that you regularly eat. ❑ *It's never too late to improve your diet.* **2** N-COUNT If you are on a **diet,** you eat special kinds of food or you eat less food than usual because you are trying to lose weight. ❑ *Have you been on a diet? You've lost a lot of weight.* ● **di|et|er** /daɪətər/ (**dieters**) N-COUNT ❑ *More than 90 percent of dieters gain back every pound they lose.* **3** V-I If you **are dieting,** you eat special kinds of food or you eat

less food than usual because you are trying to lose weight. ❑ *I've been dieting since the birth of my child.* [from Old French]
→ see Word Web: **diet**
→ see **vegetarian**

**di|etary** /daɪətɛri/ ADJ You can use **dietary** to describe anything that concerns a person's diet. ❑ *Dr. Susan Hankinson studied the dietary habits of 50,000 women.* [from Old French]

**dif|fer** /dɪfər/ (**differs, differing, differed**) **1** V-RECIP If two or more things **differ,** they are unlike each other in some way. ❑ *The story he told police differed from the one he told his mother.* **2** V-RECIP If people **differ** about something, they do not agree with each other about it. ❑ *The two leaders differed on the issue.* ❑ *That is where we differ.* [from Latin] **3** to **agree to differ** → see **agree**

**dif|fer|ence** /dɪfərəns, dɪfrəns/ (**differences**) **1** N-COUNT The **difference** between two things is the way in which they are unlike each other. ❑ *That is the main difference between the two societies.* ❑ *...the great difference in size.* **2** N-COUNT If people have their **differences** about something, they disagree about it. ❑ *The two groups are learning how to resolve their differences.* **3** N-SING A **difference** between two quantities is the amount by which one quantity is less than the other. ❑ *The difference is 8532.* **4** PHRASE If something **makes a difference** or **makes** a lot of **difference,** it affects you and helps you in what you are doing. If something **makes** no **difference,** it does not have any effect on what you are doing. ❑ *Where you live makes such a difference to the way you feel.* [from Latin]

**Word Web** diet

Recent U.S. government reports show that about 64% of American adults are **overweight** or **obese.** The number of people on **weight loss diets** is the highest ever. Many people are trying **fad** diets to lose weight. One diet tells people to eat mostly **protein**—meat, fish, and cheese—and very few **carbohydrates.** However, another diet tells people to eat at least 40% carbohydrates. A weight-loss diet works when you burn more **calories** than you eat. Most doctors agree that a balanced diet with plenty of exercise is the best way to lose weight.

**D**

**dif|fer|ent** /dɪfərənt, dɪfrənt/ 🔟 ADJ If two people or things are **different**, they are not like each other. ❑ *London was different from most European capital cities.* ❑ *Things would be different if he went to music school.* ● **dif|fer|ent|ly** ADV ❑ *Every person learns differently.* 🔟 ADJ You use **different** to indicate that you are talking about two or more separate and distinct things of the same kind. ❑ *Different countries export different products.* 🔟 ADJ You can describe something as **different** when it is unusual and not like others of the same kind. ❑ *The result is interesting and different.* [from Latin]

**dif|fer|en|tial** /dɪfərɛnʃ°l/ (**differentials**) N-COUNT In mathematics and economics, a **differential** is a difference between two values in a scale. ❑ *...the wage differential between factory workers and office workers.* [from Latin]

**dif|fer|en|ti|ate** /dɪfərɛnʃieɪt/ (**differentiates, differentiating, differentiated**) 🔟 V-T/V-I If you **differentiate between** things or if you **differentiate** one thing **from** another, you recognize or show the difference between them. ❑ *A child may not differentiate between his imagination and the real world.* 🔟 V-T A quality or feature that **differentiates** one thing **from** another makes the two things different. ❑ *...unusual policies that differentiate them from the other parties.* ● **dif|fer|en|tia|tion** /dɪfərɛnʃieɪʃ°n/ N-UNCOUNT ❑ *...a strict differentiation between men and women.* [from Latin]

**dif|fi|cult** /dɪfɪkʌlt, -kəlt/ 🔟 ADJ Something that is **difficult** is not easy to do, understand, or deal with. ❑ *The lack of childcare made it difficult for mothers to get jobs.* ❑ *It was a very difficult decision to make.* 🔟 ADJ Someone who is **difficult** behaves in an unreasonable and unhelpful way. ❑ *I knew you were going to be difficult about this.*

**dif|fi|cul|ty** /dɪfɪkʌlti, -kəlti/ (**difficulties**) 🔟 N-COUNT A **difficulty** is a problem. ❑ *...the difficulty of getting information.* 🔟 N-UNCOUNT If you have **difficulty** doing something, you are not able to do it easily. ❑ *Do you have difficulty walking?* 🔟 PHRASE If someone or something is **in difficulty**, they are having a lot of problems. ❑ *The city's movie industry is in difficulty.* [from Latin]

**dif|fi|dent** /dɪfɪdənt/ ADJ Someone who is **diffident** is rather shy and lacks confidence. ❑ *Helen was diffident.* ● **dif|fi|dence** /dɪfɪdəns/ N-UNCOUNT ❑ *My initial diffidence has given way to confidence over the years.* [from Latin]

**dif|frac|tion** /dɪfrækʃən/ N-UNCOUNT In physics, **diffraction** is a change in the direction of a sound wave or a light wave caused by the presence of an obstacle in its path. ❑ *...the diffraction of light that occurs in rainbows.* [from New Latin]

**dif|fuse** /dɪfyuz/ (**diffuses, diffusing, diffused**) V-T/V-I If something such as knowledge or information **is diffused**, or if it **diffuses** somewhere, it is made known over a wide area or to a lot of people. [WRITTEN] ❑ *The technology is diffused and used by other countries.* ❑ *...to diffuse new ideas obtained from elsewhere.* ● **dif|fu|sion** /dɪfyuʒ°n/ N-UNCOUNT ❑ *...the development and diffusion of ideas.* [from Latin]

→ see **culture**

**dig** /dɪg/ (**digs, digging, dug**) 🔟 V-T/V-I If people or animals **dig**, they make a hole in the ground or in a pile of something such as earth or stones. ❑ *I grabbed the shovel and started digging.* ❑ *Dig a large hole.* 🔟 V-T/V-I If you **dig** one thing **into** another or if one thing **digs into** another, the first thing is pushed hard into the second, or presses hard into it. ❑ *She dug her spoon into the chocolate pudding.* 🔟 N-COUNT If you have a **dig at** someone, you say something which is intended to make fun of them or upset them. ❑ *She couldn't resist a dig at Dave after he lost the game.*

dig

→ see **tunnel**

▸ **dig out** PHR-VERB If you **dig** something **out**, you find it after it has been stored, hidden, or forgotten for a long time. [INFORMAL] ❑ *Recently, I dug out the book and read it again.*

**di|gest** (**digests, digesting, digested**)

The verb is pronounced /dɪdʒɛst/. The noun is pronounced /daɪdʒɛst/.

🔟 V-T/V-I When food **digests** or when you **digest** it, it passes through your body to your stomach. Your stomach removes the substances that your body needs and gets rid of the rest. ❑ *Do not swim for an hour after a meal to allow food to digest.* ❑ *She couldn't digest food properly.* ● **di|ges|tion** /daɪdʒɛstʃən/ N-UNCOUNT ❑ *Peppermint aids digestion.* 🔟 V-T If you **digest** information, you think about it carefully so that you understand it. ❑ *You need time to digest the information.* [from Late Latin]

→ see **cooking**

**di|ges|tive** /daɪdʒɛstɪv/ ADJ You can describe things that are related to the digestion of food as **digestive**. ❑ *Digestive juices break down our food.* [from Late Latin]

**dig|it** /dɪdʒɪt/ (**digits**) N-COUNT A **digit** is a written symbol for any of the ten numbers from 0 to 9. ❑ *Her telephone number differs from mine by one digit.* [from Latin]

**digi|tal** /dɪdʒɪt°l/ 🔟 ADJ **Digital** systems record or transmit information in the form of thousands of very small signals. ❑ *...the new digital technology.* 🔟 ADJ **Digital** devices such as watches or clocks give information by displaying numbers rather than by having a pointer which moves around a dial. Compare **analog**. ❑ *...a digital watch.* [from Latin]

→ see **technology, time, television**

**dig|i|tal cam|er|a** (**digital cameras**) N-COUNT A **digital camera** is a camera that produces digital images that can be stored on a computer. ❑ *"Star Wars Attack of the Clones" was made using digital cameras.*

**dig|i|tal ra|dio** (**digital radios**) ■ N-UNCOUNT **Digital radio** is radio in which the signals are transmitted in digital form and decoded by the radio receiver. ❑ *...people with access to digital radio.* ■ N-COUNT A **digital radio** is a radio that can receive digital signals. ❑ *...more than 100 digital radio channels.*

**dig|i|tal tele|vi|sion** (**digital televisions**) ■ N-UNCOUNT **Digital television** is television in which the signals are transmitted in digital form and decoded by the television receiver. ❑ *At present only 31 percent of the population has access to digital television.* ■ N-COUNT A **digital television** is a television that can receive digital signals. ❑ *...wide screen digital televisions.*

**Word Link** *dign ≈ proper, worthy : dignified, dignitary, indignant*

**dig|ni|fied** /ˈdɪgnɪfaɪd/ ADJ Someone or something that is **dignified** is calm, impressive, and deserves respect. ❑ *He was a very dignified and charming man.* [from Old French]

**dig|ni|tary** /ˈdɪgnɪtɛri/ (**dignitaries**) N-COUNT **Dignitaries** are people who have a high rank in government or in a church. ❑ *...money used for entertaining visiting dignitaries.* [from Old French]

**dig|nity** /ˈdɪgnɪti/ ■ N-UNCOUNT If someone behaves or moves with **dignity**, they are serious, calm, and controlled. ❑ *...her extraordinary dignity.* ■ N-UNCOUNT **Dignity** is the quality of being worthy of respect. ❑ *...the sense of human dignity.* [from Old French]

**di|graph** /ˈdaɪgræf/ (**digraphs**) N-COUNT A **digraph** is a combination of two letters that represents a single speech sound, such as "ea" in "bread." [TECHNICAL]

**dike** /daɪk/ (**dikes**) N-COUNT A **dike** is a thick wall that is built to stop water flooding onto very low-lying land from a river or from the ocean. [from Old English]

dike

**di|lapi|da|ted** /dɪˈlæpɪdeɪtɪd/ ADJ A **dilapidated** building is old and in a generally bad condition. ❑ *...an old dilapidated farmhouse.* [from Latin]

**di|late** /daɪˈleɪt/ (**dilates, dilating, dilated**) V-T/V-I When things such as blood vessels or the pupils of your eyes **dilate** or when something **dilates** them, they become wider or bigger. ❑ *At night, the pupils dilate to allow in more light.* ● **di|lat|ed** ADJ ❑ *His eyes seemed slightly dilated.* [from Latin]

**di|la|tion** /daɪˈleɪʃⁿn/ (**dilations**) N-VAR In mathematics, a **dilation** is a procedure in which a figure such as a triangle is made bigger or smaller but its shape stays the same. [TECHNICAL] [from Latin]

**Word Link** *di ≈ two : dilemma, diverge, diverse*

**di|lem|ma** /dɪˈlɛmə/ (**dilemmas**) N-COUNT A **dilemma** is a difficult situation in which you have to choose between two or more alternatives. ❑ *He was facing the dilemma of whether or not to return to his country.* [from Latin]

**dili|gent** /ˈdɪlɪdʒⁿnt/ ADJ Someone who is **diligent** works hard in a careful and thorough way. ❑ *...a diligent student.* ● **dili|gence** /ˈdɪlɪdʒⁿns/ N-UNCOUNT ❑ *He performed his duties with diligence.* ● **dili|gent|ly** ADV ❑ *He was diligently searching the house.* [from Old French]

**di|lute** /daɪˈlut/ (**dilutes, diluting, diluted**) V-T If a liquid **is diluted**, it is added to water or another liquid, and becomes weaker. ❑ *If you give your baby juice, dilute it with water.* ❑ *The liquid is then diluted.* [from Latin]

**dim** /dɪm/ (**dimmer, dimmest, dims, dimming, dimmed**) ■ ADJ **Dim** light is not bright. ❑ *She waited in the dim light.* ● **dim|ly** ADV ❑ *Two lamps burned dimly.* ■ ADJ A **dim** figure, place or object is not very easy to see, because the light is not bright enough. ❑ *Pete's flashlight showed the dim figures of Bob and Chang.* ● **dim|ly** ADV ❑ *The shoreline could be dimly seen.* ■ V-T/V-I If you **dim** a light or if it **dims**, it becomes less bright. ❑ *Dim the lighting.* ❑ *Dim your lights behind that car.* [from Old English]

**dime** /daɪm/ (**dimes**) N-COUNT A **dime** is a U.S. coin worth ten cents. [from Old French]

**di|men|sion** /dɪˈmɛnʃⁿn, daɪ-/ (**dimensions**) ■ N-COUNT A particular **dimension** of something is a particular aspect of it. ❑ *There is a political dimension to the accusations.* ■ N-PLURAL The **dimensions** of something are its measurements. ❑ *We do not yet know the exact dimensions of the new oilfield.* [from Old French]

**di|men|sion|al analy|sis** /dɪˈmɛnʃⁿl ənæləsɪs, daɪ-/ (**dimensional analyses**) N-VAR **Dimensional analysis** is a method used by scientists to understand the relationships between things that are measured in different sorts of units. [TECHNICAL]

**Word Link** *min ≈ small, lessen : diminish, minus, minute*

**di|min|ish** /dɪˈmɪnɪʃ/ (**diminishes, diminishing, diminished**) V-T/V-I When something **diminishes**, or when something **diminishes** it, it becomes reduced in size, importance, or intensity. ❑ *The threat of war has diminished.* ❑ *This doesn't diminish what he has achieved.* [from Latin]

**di|min|ished in|ter|val** (**diminished intervals**) N-COUNT In music, a **diminished interval** is an interval that is reduced by half a step or half a tone. [TECHNICAL]

**di|minu|tive** /dɪˈmɪnyətɪv/ ADJ A **diminutive** person or object is very small. ❑ *A diminutive figure stood at the entrance.* [from Latin]

**dim sum** /dɪm sʊm, sʌm/ N-UNCOUNT **Dim sum** is a Chinese dish of dumplings filled with meat or other ingredients. ❑ *...dim sum restaurants.* [from Cantonese]

**din** /dɪn/ N-SING A **din** is a very loud and unpleasant noise that lasts for some time. ❑ *They tried to talk over the din of the crowd.* [from Old English]

**dine** /daɪn/ (**dines, dining, dined**) V-I When you

**dine**, you have dinner. [FORMAL] ❑ *He dines alone most nights.* [from Old French]

**din|er** /daɪnər/ (**diners**) **1** N-COUNT A **diner** is a small cheap restaurant that is often open all day. **2** N-COUNT The people who are having dinner in a restaurant can be referred to as **diners**. ❑ *They sat in a corner, away from other diners.* [from Old French]

**ding|bat** /dɪŋbæt/ (**dingbats**) N-COUNT People sometimes refer to a person who they think is crazy or stupid as a **dingbat**. [INFORMAL] ❑ *I hope people realize I'm not a dingbat.*

**din|ghy** /dɪŋgi/ (**dinghies**) N-COUNT A **dinghy** is a small open boat that you sail or row. ❑ *...a rubber dinghy.* [from Hindi]

**din|gy** /dɪndʒi/ (**dingier, dingiest**) ADJ A **dingy** building or place is dark and depressing. ❑ *Shaw took me to his dingy office.* [from Old English]

**din|ing room** (**dining rooms**) N-COUNT The **dining room** is the room in a house where people have their meals, or a room in a hotel where meals are served.
→ see **house**

**din|ner** /dɪnər/ (**dinners**) **1** N-VAR **Dinner** is the main meal of the day, usually served in the early part of the evening. ❑ *She invited us for dinner.* ❑ *Would you like to stay and have dinner?* **2** N-VAR Some people refer to the meal you eat in the middle of the day as **dinner**. **3** N-COUNT A **dinner** is a formal social event in the evening at which a meal is served. ❑ *...a series of official dinners.* [from Old French]
→ see **meal**

**dino|flag|el|late** /daɪnoʊflædʒəlɪt, -leɪt/ (**dinoflagellates**) N-COUNT; ADJ **Dinoflagellates** are tiny organisms that live in sea water and fresh water and are found in plankton. [TECHNICAL] [from New Latin]

**di|no|saur** /daɪnəsɔr/ (**dinosaurs**) N-COUNT **Dinosaurs** were large reptiles which lived millions of years ago. [from New Latin]

**dio|ra|ma** /daɪəræmə, -rɑmə/ (**dioramas**) N-COUNT A **diorama** is a miniature three-dimensional scene in which models of figures are arranged against a background. ❑ *...a superb diorama of Quebec City.* [from French]

dinosaur

**dip** /dɪp/ (**dips, dipping, dipped**) **1** V-T If you **dip** something in a liquid, you put it in and then quickly take it out again. ❑ *Dip each apple in the syrup.* **2** N-COUNT A **dip** is a thick sauce that you dip pieces of food into before eating them. ❑ *...avocado dip.* **3** V-I If something **dips**, it makes a downward movement. ❑ *The boat dipped slightly as he got in.* **4** V-I If an area of land, a road, or a path **dips**, it goes down quite suddenly to a lower level. ❑ *The road dipped and rose again.* ● **Dip** is also a noun. ❑ *Where the road makes a dip, turn right.* [from Old English]

**di|plo|ma** /dɪploʊmə/ (**diplomas**) N-COUNT A **diploma** is a document which may be awarded to a student who has completed a course of study by a university or college, or by a high school in the United States. ❑ *...a diploma in social work.* [from Latin]
→ see **graduation**

**di|plo|ma|cy** /dɪploʊməsi/ **1** N-UNCOUNT **Diplomacy** is the activity or profession of managing relations between the governments of different countries. ❑ *...a success for American diplomacy.* **2** N-UNCOUNT **Diplomacy** is the skill of saying or doing things which will not offend people. ❑ *...Jane's powers of persuasion and diplomacy.* [from French]

**dip|lo|mat** /dɪpləmæt/ (**diplomats**) N-COUNT A **diplomat** is a senior official who discusses affairs with another country on behalf of his or her own country, usually working as a member of an embassy. ❑ *...a Western diplomat with long experience in Asia.* [from French]

**dip|lo|mat|ic** /dɪpləmætɪk/ **1** ADJ **Diplomatic** means relating to diplomacy and diplomats. ❑ *...diplomatic relations.* ● **dip|lo|mati|cal|ly** /dɪpləmætɪkli/ ADV ❑ *The conflict was resolved diplomatically.* **2** ADJ Someone who is **diplomatic** is careful to say or do things without offending people. ❑ *She is very direct, but I'm more diplomatic.* ● **dip|lo|mati|cal|ly** ADV ❑ *"Of course," agreed Sloan diplomatically.* [from French]

**dire** /daɪər/ ADJ **Dire** is used to emphasize how serious or terrible a situation or event is. ❑ *He was in dire need of help.* [from Latin]

**di|rect** /dɪrɛkt, daɪ-/ (**directs, directing, directed**) **1** ADJ **Direct** means moving toward a place or object, without changing direction and without stopping, for example, in a trip. ❑ *They took a direct flight to Athens.* ● **Direct** is also an adverb. ❑ *You can fly direct from Seattle to London.* ● **di|rect|ly** ADV ❑ *On arriving in New York, Dylan went directly to Greenwich Village.* **2** ADJ You use **direct** to describe an experience, activity, or system which only involves the people, actions, or things that are necessary to make it happen. ❑ *He has direct experience of the process.* ● **Direct** is also an adverb. ❑ *More farms are selling direct to consumers.* ● **di|rect|ly** ADV ❑ *We cannot measure pain directly.* **3** ADJ If you describe a person or their behavior as **direct**, you mean that they are honest and open, and say exactly what they mean. ❑ *He avoided giving a direct answer.* ● **di|rect|ly** ADV ❑ *Explain simply and directly what you hope to achieve.* ● **di|rect|ness** N-UNCOUNT ❑ *He spoke with rare directness.* **4** V-T If something **is directed at** a particular person or thing, it is aimed at them or intended to affect them. ❑ *The question was directed toward her.* ❑ *The abuse was directed at the manager.* **5** V-T If you **direct** someone somewhere, you tell them how to get there. ❑ *Could you direct them to Dr. Lamont's office, please?* **6** V-T When someone **directs** a project or a group of people, they are responsible for organizing the people and activities that are involved. ❑ *Christopher will direct day-to-day operations.* ● **di|rec|tion** /dɪrɛkʃⁿn, daɪ-/ N-UNCOUNT ❑ *Organizations need clear direction.* ● **di|rec|tor** (**directors**) N-COUNT ❑ *...the director of the project.* **7** V-T/V-I When someone **directs** a movie, play, or television program, they are responsible for the way in which it is performed and for telling the actors and assistants what to do. ❑ *He directed several TV shows.* ❑ *Branagh himself will star and direct.* ● **di|rec|tor** /dɪrɛktər, daɪ-/ (**directors**) N-COUNT ❑ *"Cut!" the director yelled. "That was perfect."* [from Latin] **8** → see also **direction, directly**

**Thesaurus**   *direct*   Also look up :

| | |
|---|---|
| ADJ. | nonstop, straight **1** |
| | firsthand, personal **2** |
| | candid, frank, plain **3** |

**di|rect dis|course** N-UNCOUNT In grammar, **direct discourse** is speech which is reported by using the exact words that the speaker used.

**di|rect|ing** /dɪrɛkt, daɪ-/ N-UNCOUNT **Directing** is the work that the director of a movie, play, or television program does. [from Latin]

**di|rec|tion** /dɪrɛkʃ°n, daɪ-/ (**directions**) **1** N-VAR A **direction** is the general line that someone or something is moving or pointing in. ❑ *The nearest town was ten miles in the opposite direction.* ❑ *He set off in the direction of Larry's shop.* **2** N-PLURAL **Directions** are instructions that tell you what to do, how to do something, or how to get somewhere. ❑ *She stopped the car to ask for directions.* [from Latin] **3** → see also **direct**

**Word Partnership**   Use *direction* with :

| | |
|---|---|
| ADJ. | **general** direction, **opposite** direction, **right** direction, **wrong** direction **1** |
| N. | **sense of** direction **1** |
| V. | **change** direction, **move in a** direction **1** **lack** direction, **take** direction **2** |

**di|rec|tive** /dɪrɛktɪv, daɪ-/ (**directives**) N-COUNT A **directive** is an official instruction that is given by someone in authority. ❑ *The new directive means that food labeling will be more specific.* [from Latin]

**di|rect|ly** /dɪrɛktli, daɪ-/ **1** ADV If something is **directly** above, below, or in front of something, it is in exactly that position. ❑ *...the apartment directly above us.* **2** ADV If you do one action **directly after** another, you do the second action as soon as the first one is finished. ❑ *Most guests left directly after the meal.* [from Latin] **3** → see also **direct**

**di|rect ob|ject** (**direct objects**) N-COUNT In grammar, the **direct object** of a transitive verb is the noun group which refers to someone or something directly affected by or involved in the action performed by the subject. For example, in "I saw him yesterday," "him" is the direct object. Compare **indirect object**.

**di|rec|tor** /dɪrɛktər, daɪ-/ (**directors**) **1** N-COUNT The **directors** of a company are its most senior managers, who meet regularly to make important decisions about how it will be run. [BUSINESS] ❑ *...the directors of the bank.* **2** N-COUNT The **director** of a choir is the person

who is conducting it. **3** N-COUNT The **director** of a play, movie, or television program is the person who decides how it will appear on stage or screen, and who tells the actors and technical staff what to do. [from Latin]
→ see **theater**

**di|rec|tor gen|er|al** (**directors general**) N-COUNT The **director general** of a large organization is the person who is in charge of it. [BUSINESS]

**di|rec|tor's cut** (**director's cuts**) N-COUNT A **director's cut** is a version of a movie chosen by the movie's director, which expresses the director's artistic aims more fully than the original version. ❑ *I saw the director's cut of "Amadeus."*

**di|rec|tory** /dɪrɛktəri, daɪ-/ (**directories**) **1** N-COUNT A **directory** is a book which gives lists of facts, for example, people's names, addresses, and telephone numbers, or the names and addresses of business companies, usually arranged in alphabetical order. ❑ *...a telephone directory.* **2** N-COUNT A **directory** is an area of a computer disk which contains one or more files or other directories. [COMPUTING] ❑ *You can search the directory for files by date or name.* [from Latin]

**di|rec|tory as|sis|tance** N-UNCOUNT **Directory assistance** is a service which you can telephone to find out someone's telephone number. ❑ *He dialed directory assistance.*

**dirt** /dɜrt/ **1** N-UNCOUNT If there is **dirt** on something, there is dust, mud, or a stain on it. ❑ *I started to scrub off the dirt.* **2** N-UNCOUNT You can refer to the earth on the ground as **dirt**. ❑ *They all sat on the dirt under a tree.* [from Old Norse]
→ see **erosion**

**dirty** /dɜrti/ (**dirtier, dirtiest, dirties, dirtying, dirtied**) **1** ADJ If something is **dirty**, it is marked or covered with stains, spots, or mud, and needs to be cleaned. ❑ *She collected the dirty plates from the table.* **2** ADJ If you describe something such as a joke, a book, or someone's language as **dirty**, you mean that it refers to sex in a way that some people find offensive. ❑ *He laughed at their dirty jokes.* ● **Dirty** is also an adverb. ❑ *"Don't talk dirty, Roger."* **3** V-T To **dirty** something means to cause it to become dirty. ❑ *The dog's hairs will dirty the seats.* [from Old Norse]

**dis|abil|ity** /dɪsəbɪlɪti/ (**disabilities**) N-COUNT A **disability** is a permanent injury, illness, or physical or mental condition that restricts the way that someone can live their life. ❑ *We're building a new changing room for people with disabilities.* [from Old French]
→ see Word Web: **disability**

**Word Web**   disability

Careful planning is making public places more **accessible** for people with **disabilities**. For hundreds of years **wheelchairs** have helped **paralyzed** people move around their homes. Today, **ramps** help these people cross the street, enter buildings, and get to work. Extra-wide doorways allow them to use public restrooms. **Blind** people are also more active and independent. **Seeing Eye dogs**, **canes**, and beeping crosswalks all help them get around town safely. Some movie theaters rent headsets for the **hearing-impaired**. **Hearing dogs** help **deaf** people stay connected. And sign language allows people who are deaf or **dumb** to communicate.

**dis|able** /dɪseɪbᵊl/ (**disables, disabling, disabled**)
**1** V-T If an injury or illness **disables** someone, it affects them so badly that it restricts the way that they can live their life. ❑ *The damage to her leg disabled her.* **2** V-T To **disable** a system or mechanism means to stop it from working. ❑ *He disabled the car alarm.* [from Latin]

**dis|abled** /dɪseɪbᵊld/ ADJ Someone who is **disabled** has an illness, injury, or condition that tends to restrict the way that they can live their life, especially by making it difficult for them to move about. ❑ *...the practical problems that disabled people face in the workplace.* ● People who are disabled are sometimes referred to as **the disabled**. ❑ *There are toilet facilities for the disabled.* [from Latin]

**dis|ad|vant|age** /dɪsədvæntɪdʒ/ (**disadvantages**) **1** N-COUNT A **disadvantage** is a factor which makes someone or something less useful, acceptable, or successful than other people or things. ❑ *The big disadvantage of this computer is its size.* **2** PHRASE If you are **at a disadvantage**, you have a problem or difficulty that many other people do not have, which makes it harder for you to be successful. ❑ *The children from poor families were at a distinct disadvantage.* [from Latin]

**dis|ad|van|taged** /dɪsədvæntɪdʒd/ ADJ People who are **disadvantaged** live in bad economic or social conditions. ❑ *...the educational problems of disadvantaged children.* [from Latin]

**dis|af|fect|ed** /dɪsəfɛktɪd/ ADJ **Disaffected** people no longer fully support something such as an organization or political ideal which they previously supported. ❑ *He attracts disaffected voters.*

---

**Word Link** dis ≈ negative, not : *disagree, discomfort, disconnect*

---

**dis|agree** /dɪsəgri/ (**disagrees, disagreeing, disagreed**) **1** V-RECIP If you **disagree** with someone, you do not accept that what they say is true or correct. ❑ *You must continue to see them even if you disagree with them.* ❑ *They can communicate even when they strongly disagree.* **2** V-I If you **disagree with** a particular action or proposal, you disapprove of it. ❑ *I respect the president but I disagree with his decision.* [from Old French]

**dis|agree|ment** /dɪsəgrimənt/ (**disagreements**) **1** N-UNCOUNT **Disagreement** means objecting to something. ❑ *Britain and France have expressed some disagreement with the plan.* **2** N-VAR When there is **disagreement** about something, people disagree or argue about what should be done. ❑ *The United States Congress and the president are still in disagreement over the plans.* [from Old French]

**dis|al|low** /dɪsəlaʊ/ (**disallows, disallowing, disallowed**) V-T If something is **disallowed**, it is not allowed or accepted officially, because it has not been done correctly. ❑ *The goal was disallowed.* [from Old French]

**dis|ap|pear** /dɪsəpɪər/ (**disappears, disappearing, disappeared**) **1** V-I If someone or something **disappears**, they go away or are taken away somewhere where nobody can find them. ❑ *She disappeared thirteen years ago.* ● **dis|ap|pear|ance** (**disappearances**) N-VAR ❑ *Her disappearance is a mystery.* **2** V-I If something **disappears**, it stops existing or happening. ❑ *The*

*immediate threat has disappeared.* ● **dis|ap|pear|ance** N-UNCOUNT ❑ *...the disappearance of the dinosaurs.* [from Old French]

**dis|ap|point** /dɪsəpɔɪnt/ (**disappoints, disappointing, disappointed**) V-T If things or people **disappoint** you, they are not as good as you had hoped, or do not do what you hoped they would do. ❑ *I don't want to disappoint him.* ● **dis|ap|point|ing** ADJ ❑ *The restaurant looked lovely, but the food was disappointing.* ● **dis|ap|point|ing|ly** ADV ❑ *Progress is disappointingly slow.* [from Old French]

**dis|ap|point|ed** /dɪsəpɔɪntɪd/ ADJ If you are **disappointed**, you are sad because something has not happened or because something is not as good as you had hoped. ❑ *Adamski was very disappointed with the mayor's decision.* ❑ *I was disappointed that John was not there.* [from Old French]

**dis|ap|point|ment** /dɪsəpɔɪntmənt/ (**disappointments**) **1** N-UNCOUNT **Disappointment** is the state of feeling disappointed. ❑ *She couldn't hide the disappointment in her voice.* **2** N-COUNT Something or someone that is a **disappointment** is not as good as you had hoped. ❑ *The result was a terrible disappointment.* [from Old French]

**dis|ap|prov|al** /dɪsəpruvᵊl/ N-UNCOUNT If you feel or show **disapproval** of something or someone, you feel or show that you do not approve of them. ❑ *He stared at Marina with disapproval.* [from Old French]

**dis|ap|prove** /dɪsəpruv/ (**disapproves, disapproving, disapproved**) V-I If you **disapprove of** something or someone, you feel or show that you do not like them or do not approve of them. ❑ *Most people disapprove of such violent methods.* ● **dis|ap|prov|ing** ADJ ❑ *Janet gave him a disapproving look.* ● **dis|ap|prov|ing|ly** ADV ❑ *Antonio looked at him disapprovingly.* [from Old French]

**dis|arm** /dɪsɑrm/ (**disarms, disarming, disarmed**) **1** V-T To **disarm** a person or group means to take away all their weapons. ❑ *We will agree to disarming troops.* **2** V-I If a country or group **disarms**, it gives up the use of weapons, especially nuclear weapons. ❑ *The guerrillas refused to disarm.* **3** V-T If a person or their behavior **disarms** you, they cause you to feel less angry, hostile, or critical toward them. ❑ *He started crying, which disarmed Judy.* ● **dis|arm|ing** ADJ ❑ *Leonard approached with a disarming smile.* ● **dis|arm|ing|ly** ADV ❑ *He is disarmingly honest.* [from Old English]

**dis|arma|ment** /dɪsɑrməmənt/ N-UNCOUNT **Disarmament** is the act of reducing the number of weapons, especially nuclear weapons, that a country has. ❑ *...nuclear disarmament.*

**dis|ar|ray** /dɪsəreɪ/ N-UNCOUNT If people or things are in **disarray**, they are disorganized and confused. ❑ *The country is in disarray following the fighting.* [from Old French]

**dis|as|ter** /dɪzæstər/ (**disasters**) **1** N-COUNT A **disaster** is a very bad accident such as an earthquake or a plane crash. ❑ *It was the second air disaster that month.* **2** N-COUNT If you refer to something as a **disaster**, you are emphasizing that you think it is extremely bad. ❑ *The whole event was just a disaster!* **3** N-UNCOUNT **Disaster** is something which has very bad consequences

d

## Word Web    disaster

We are learning more about nature's cycles. But natural **disasters** remain a big challenge. We can predict some disasters, such as **hurricanes** and **floods**. However, we still can't avoid the **damage** they do. Each year **monsoons** strike southern Asia. Monsoons are a combination of **typhoons**, **tropical storms**, and heavy **rains**. In addition to the damage caused by floods, **landslides** and mudslides add to the problem. In 2005 more than 90 million people suffered from disaster in China alone. Over 700 people died in that country and millions of acres of crops were destroyed. The **economic loss** totaled nearly 6 billion dollars.

for you. ❑ *The government is facing financial disaster.* [from Italian]
→ see Word Web: **disaster**

**dis|as|trous** /dɪzæstrəs/ ADJ A **disastrous** event has extremely bad consequences and effects or is very unsuccessful. ❑ *...the recent, disastrous earthquake.* ❑ *...their disastrous performance in the election.* ● **dis|as|trous|ly** ADV ❑ *...the company's disastrously low profits.* [from Italian]

**dis|band** /dɪsbænd/ (**disbands, disbanding, disbanded**) V-T/V-I If someone **disbands** a group of people, or if the group **disbands**, it stops operating as a single unit. ❑ *All the armed groups were disbanded.* [from French]

**dis|be|lief** /dɪsbɪlif/ N-UNCOUNT **Disbelief** is not believing that something is true or real. ❑ *She looked at him in disbelief.*

**disc** /dɪsk/ → see **disk**

**dis|card** /dɪskɑrd/ (**discards, discarding, discarded**) V-T If you **discard** something, you get rid of it because you no longer want it or need it. ❑ *Read the instructions before discarding the box.* [from Old French]

**dis|cern** /dɪsɜrn/ (**discerns, discerning, discerned**) ■ V-T If you can **discern** something, you are aware of it and know what it is. ❑ *...an effort to discern the truth.* ② V-T If you can **discern** something, you can just see it, but not clearly. [FORMAL] ❑ *Below the bridge we could just discern a car.* [from Old French]

**dis|cern|ible** /dɪsɜrnəbᵊl/ ADJ If something is **discernible**, you can see it or recognize that it exists. [FORMAL] ❑ *The outline of the island is just discernible.* [from Old French]

**dis|cern|ing** /dɪsɜrnɪŋ/ ADJ If you describe someone as **discerning**, you approve of the fact that they are able to judge which things of a particular kind are good and which are bad. ❑ *...educated and discerning readers.* [from Old French]

**dis|charge** (**discharges, discharging, discharged**)

The verb is pronounced /dɪstʃɑrdʒ/. The noun is pronounced /dɪstʃɑrdʒ/.

■ V-T When someone **is discharged from** a hospital, prison, or one of the armed services, they are officially allowed to leave, or told that they must leave. ❑ *He was discharged from hospital today.* ● **Discharge** is also a noun. ❑ *...his discharge from the army.* ② V-T If someone **discharges** their duties or responsibilities, they do everything that needs to be done in order to complete them. [FORMAL]

❑ *...the quiet skill with which he discharged his duties.* ③ V-T If something **is discharged** from inside a place, it comes out. [FORMAL] ❑ *The salty water was discharged at sea.* ④ N-VAR When there is a **discharge** of a substance, the substance comes out from inside somewhere. [FORMAL] ❑ *The disease causes a discharge from the eyes.* ⑤ N-COUNT The **discharge** of a river is the amount of water that it carries from one place to another in a particular period of time. [TECHNICAL] [from Old French]
→ see **lightning**

**dis|ci|ple** /dɪsaɪpᵊl/ (**disciples**) N-COUNT If you are someone's **disciple**, you are influenced by their teachings and try to follow their example. ❑ *...a leader with disciples throughout Europe.* [from Old English]

**dis|ci|pli|nary** /dɪsɪplɪnɛri/ ADJ **Disciplinary** bodies or actions are concerned with making sure that people obey rules or regulations and that they are punished if they do not. ❑ *He is facing disciplinary action.* [from Latin]

**dis|ci|pline** /dɪsɪplɪn/ (**disciplines, disciplining, disciplined**) ■ N-UNCOUNT **Discipline** is the practice of making people obey rules or standards of behavior, and punishing them when they do not. ❑ *...poor discipline in schools.* ② N-UNCOUNT **Discipline** is the quality of being able to behave and work in a controlled way which involves obeying particular rules or standards. ❑ *He was impressed by their speed and discipline.* ③ V-T If someone **is disciplined** for something that they have done wrong, they are punished for it. ❑ *The workman was disciplined by his company but not dismissed.* ④ N-COUNT A **discipline** is a particular area of study, especially a subject of study in a college or university. [FORMAL] ❑ *We're looking for people from a wide range of disciplines.* [from Latin]

**disc jock|ey** (**disc jockeys**) also **disk jockey** N-COUNT A **disc jockey** is someone who plays and introduces music on the radio or at a disco.

**dis|close** /dɪsklouz/ (**discloses, disclosing, disclosed**) V-T If you **disclose** new or secret information, you tell people about it. ❑ *They refused to disclose details of the deal.* [from Old French]

**dis|clo|sure** /dɪsklouʒər/ (**disclosures**) N-VAR **Disclosure** is the act of giving people new or secret information. ❑ *...disclosure of negative information about the company.* [from Old French]

**dis|co** /dɪskou/ (**discos**) N-COUNT A **disco** is a place or event at which people dance to pop music. ❑ *Fridays and Saturdays are regular disco nights.*

**Word Link** dis ≈ negative, not : disagree, discomfort, disconnect

**dis|com|fort** /dɪskʌmfərt/ (**discomforts**)
**1** N-UNCOUNT **Discomfort** is a painful feeling in part of your body when you have been hurt slightly or when you have been uncomfortable for a long time. ❑ Steve had some discomfort, but no real pain. **2** N-UNCOUNT **Discomfort** is a feeling of worry caused by shame or embarrassment. ❑ She hears the discomfort in his voice. **3** N-COUNT **Discomforts** are conditions which cause you to feel physically uncomfortable. ❑ ...the discomforts of camping. [from Old French]

**dis|con|cert|ing** /dɪskənsɜrtɪŋ/ ADJ If something is **disconcerting**, it makes you feel anxious, confused, or embarrassed. ❑ He had a disconcerting habit of staring into your eyes when talking to you. ● **dis|con|cert|ing|ly** ADV ❑ Her reaction was disconcertingly calm. [from Old French]

**dis|con|nect** /dɪskənɛkt/ (**disconnects, disconnecting, disconnected**) V-T If you **disconnect** a piece of equipment, you separate it from its source of power or break a connection that it needs in order to work. ❑ Complete peace and quiet may mean disconnecting the telephone for a while. [from Latin]

**dis|con|nect|ed** /dɪskənɛktɪd/ ADJ **Disconnected** things are not linked in any way. ❑ ...sequences of disconnected events. [from Latin]

**dis|con|tent** /dɪskəntɛnt/ N-UNCOUNT **Discontent** is the feeling that you have when you are not satisfied with your situation. ❑ There are reports of widespread discontent in the city. [from Latin]

**dis|con|tinue** /dɪskəntɪnyu/ (**discontinues, discontinuing, discontinued**) **1** V-T If you **discontinue** something that you have been doing regularly, you stop doing it. [FORMAL] ❑ Do not discontinue the treatment without consulting your doctor. **2** V-T If a product **is discontinued**, the manufacturer stops making it. ❑ This camera model was discontinued in 1967. [from Old French]

**dis|cord** /dɪskɔrd/ N-UNCOUNT **Discord** is disagreement and argument between people. [LITERARY] [from Old French]

**dis|count** (**discounts, discounting, discounted**)

Pronounced /dɪskaʊnt/ for meaning **1**, and /dɪskaʊnt/ for meaning **2**.

**1** N-COUNT A **discount** is a reduction in the usual price of something. ❑ You can buy them at a discount. ❑ All staff get a 20 percent discount. **2** V-T If you **discount** an idea, fact, or theory, you consider that it is not true, not important, or not relevant. ❑ He quickly discounted the idea. [from Old French]

**dis|count store** (**discount stores**) N-COUNT A **discount store** is a store that sells goods at lower prices than usual. ❑ A growing number of shoppers buy food at discount stores.

**dis|cour|age** /dɪskɜrɪdʒ/ (**discourages, discouraging, discouraged**) **1** V-T If someone or something **discourages** you, they cause you to lose your enthusiasm about your actions. ❑ It may be difficult to do at first. Don't let this discourage you. ● **dis|cour|aged** ADJ ❑ He felt discouraged by his lack of progress. ● **dis|cour|ag|ing** ADJ ❑ Today's report is extremely discouraging for the economy. **2** V-T To **discourage** an action or to **discourage** someone

from doing it means to make them not want to do it. ❑ High prices discourage many people from traveling by train. ● **dis|cour|age|ment** N-UNCOUNT ❑ Her family supported her when she experienced discouragement. [from Old French]

**dis|course** /dɪskɔrs/ N-UNCOUNT **Discourse** is spoken or written communication between people. ❑ ...political discourse. [from Medieval Latin]

**dis|cov|er** /dɪskʌvər/ (**discovers, discovering, discovered**) **1** V-T If you **discover** something that you did not know about before, you become aware of it or learn of it. ❑ She discovered that they'd escaped. ❑ They needed to discover who the thief was. **2** V-T If a person or thing **is discovered**, someone finds them, either by accident or because they have been looking for them. ❑ The car was discovered on a roadside outside the city. **3** V-T When someone **discovers** a new place, substance, scientific fact, or scientific technique, they are the first person to find it or become aware of it. ❑ ...the first European to discover America. [from Old French]

**Thesaurus** discover Also look up :

V. detect, find out, learn, uncover; (ant.) ignore, miss, overlook **1**

**dis|cov|ery** /dɪskʌvəri/ (**discoveries**) **1** N-VAR If someone makes a **discovery**, they become aware of something that they did not know about before. ❑ I made an incredible discovery. **2** N-VAR If someone makes a **discovery**, they are the first person to find or become aware of a place, substance, or scientific fact that no one knew about before. ❑ In that year, two important discoveries were made. **3** N-VAR When the **discovery** of people or objects happens, someone finds them. ❑ ...the discovery of a box of cellphones. [from Old French]

**dis|cred|it** /dɪskrɛdɪt/ (**discredits, discrediting, discredited**) V-T To **discredit** someone or something means to cause them to lose people's respect or trust. ❑ ...research which discredits the theory. ● **dis|cred|it|ed** ADJ ❑ The government is thoroughly discredited. [from Old French]

**dis|creet** /dɪskrit/ ADJ If you are **discreet**, you are polite and careful in what you do or say, because you want to avoid embarrassing or offending someone. ❑ They were gossipy and not always discreet. ● **dis|creet|ly** ADV ❑ I took the phone, and she went discreetly into the living room. [from Old French]

**dis|crep|an|cy** /dɪskrɛpənsi/ (**discrepancies**) N-VAR If there is a **discrepancy between** two things that ought to be the same, there is a noticeable difference between them. ❑ ...the discrepancy between newspaper reports. [from Latin]

**dis|cre|tion** /dɪskrɛʃən/ **1** N-UNCOUNT **Discretion** is the quality of behaving in a quiet and controlled way without drawing attention to yourself or giving away personal or private information. [FORMAL] ❑ Angela was a model of discretion and didn't ask what had been in the letter. **2** N-UNCOUNT If someone in a position of authority uses their **discretion** or has the **discretion** to do something in a particular situation, they have the freedom and authority to decide what to do. [FORMAL] ❑ City departments have wide discretion on the contracts. ❑ We may change the

*rate at our discretion and will notify you of any change.*
[from Old French]

**dis|cre|tion|ary** /dɪskrɛʃənɛri/ ADJ
**Discretionary** things are not fixed by rules but are decided on by people in authority, who consider each individual case. ❑ *They were given wider discretionary powers.* [from Old French]

**dis|crimi|nate** /dɪskrɪmɪneɪt/ (**discriminates, discriminating, discriminated**) **1** V-I If you can **discriminate between** two things, you can recognize that they are different. ❑ *He is unable to discriminate between a good idea and a terrible one.* **2** V-I To **discriminate against** a group of people or **in favor of** a group of people means to unfairly treat them worse or better than other groups. ❑ *They believe the law discriminates against women.* ❑ *The company plan discriminated in favor of top executives.* [from Latin]

**dis|crimi|na|tion** /dɪskrɪmɪneɪʃən/
**1** N-UNCOUNT **Discrimination** is the practice of treating one person or group of people less fairly or less well than other people or groups. ❑ *...sex discrimination laws.* **2** N-UNCOUNT **Discrimination** is knowing what is good or of high quality. ❑ *They cooked without skill and ate without discrimination.* [from Latin]

**dis|crimi|na|tory** /dɪskrɪmɪnətɔri/ ADJ
**Discriminatory** laws or practices are unfair because they treat one group of people worse than other groups. ❑ *...racially discriminatory laws.* [from Latin]

**dis|cuss** /dɪskʌs/ (**discusses, discussing, discussed**) V-T If people **discuss** something, they talk about it, often in order to reach a decision. ❑ *I will discuss the situation with colleagues tomorrow.* [from Late Latin]

| Word Partnership | Use *discuss* with : |
|---|---|
| v. | **meet to** discuss, **refuse to** discuss |
| N. | discuss **options**, discuss **problems**, discuss **an issue**, discuss **a matter**, discuss **plans** |

**dis|cus|sion** /dɪskʌʃən/ (**discussions**) **1** N-VAR If there is **discussion** about something, people talk about it, often in order to reach a decision. ❑ *There was a lot of discussion about the report.* ❑ *Managers are having informal discussions later today.* **2** PHRASE If something is **under discussion**, it is still being talked about and a final decision has not yet been reached. [from Late Latin]

| Thesaurus | *discussion* Also look up : |
|---|---|
| N. | conference, conversation, debate, talk |

**dis|dain** /dɪsdeɪn/ N-UNCOUNT If you feel **disdain for** someone or something, you dislike them because you think that they are inferior or unimportant. ❑ *Janet looked at him with disdain.* [from Old French]

**dis|ease** /dɪziz/ (**diseases**) N-VAR A **disease** is an illness which affects people, animals, or plants. ❑ *...the rapid spread of disease.* [from Old French]
→ see **diagnosis, illness, medicine**

**dis|eased** /dɪzizd/ ADJ Something that is **diseased** is affected by a disease. ❑ *...diseased animals.* [from Old French]

**dis|en|chant|ed** /dɪsɪntʃæntɪd/ ADJ If you are **disenchanted with** something, you are disappointed with it and no longer believe that it is good or worthwhile. ❑ *Voters are disenchanted with politics.* ● **dis|en|chant|ment** N-UNCOUNT ❑ *There is growing public disenchantment with the educational system.*

**dis|en|gage** /dɪsɪngeɪdʒ/ (**disengages, disengaging, disengaged**) V-T/V-I If you **disengage** something, or if it **disengages**, it becomes separate from something which it has been attached to. ❑ *The fisherman ran to disengage the anchor as the water level rose in the harbor.* ❑ *Dennis was definitely disengaged from reality.* [from Old French]

**dis|en|gage|ment** /dɪsɪngeɪdʒmənt/
N-UNCOUNT **Disengagement** is a process by which people gradually stop being involved in a conflict, activity, or organization. ❑ *...a policy of disengagement from the war.* [from Old French]

| Word Link | *fig* ≈ *form, shape* : *configure, disfigure, figure* |
|---|---|

**dis|fig|ure** /dɪsfɪgyər/ (**disfigures, disfiguring, disfigured**) V-T If someone **is disfigured**, their appearance is harmed or damaged. ❑ *Many of the injured people had been badly disfigured.* ● **dis|fig|ured** ADJ ❑ *She tried not to look at the disfigured face.* [from Latin]

| Word Link | *grac* ≈ *pleasing* : *disgrace, grace, graceful* |
|---|---|

**dis|grace** /dɪsgreɪs/ (**disgraces, disgracing, disgraced**) **1** N-UNCOUNT If you say that someone is **in disgrace**, you are emphasizing that other people disapprove of them and do not respect them because of something that they have done. ❑ *The vice president resigned in disgrace.* **2** N-SING If you say that something is **a disgrace**, you are emphasizing that it is very bad or wrong, and that you find it completely unacceptable. ❑ *His behavior was a complete disgrace.* **3** V-T If you say that someone **disgraces** someone else, you are emphasizing that their behavior causes the other person to feel ashamed. ❑ *I have disgraced my family.* [from Old French]

**dis|graced** /dɪsgreɪst/ ADJ You use **disgraced** to describe someone whose bad behavior has caused them to lose the approval and respect of the public or of people in authority. ❑ *...the disgraced leader of the party.* [from Old French]

**dis|grace|ful** /dɪsgreɪsfəl/ ADJ If you say that something such as behavior or a situation is **disgraceful**, you disapprove of it strongly, and feel that the person or people responsible should be ashamed of it. ❑ *The way they treated him was disgraceful.* ● **dis|grace|ful|ly** ADV ❑ *His brother behaved disgracefully.* [from Old French]

**dis|grun|tled** /dɪsgrʌntəld/ ADJ If you are **disgruntled**, you are angry and dissatisfied because things have not happened the way that you wanted them to happen. ❑ *Disgruntled employees complained about the situation.*

**dis|guise** /dɪsgaɪz/ (**disguises, disguising, disguised**) **1** N-VAR If you are **in disguise**, you are not wearing your usual clothes or you have altered your appearance in other ways, so that people will not recognize you. ❑ *He traveled in disguise.* **2** V-T

If you **disguise yourself**, you put on clothes which make you look like someone else or alter your appearance in other ways, so that people will not recognize you. ❑ *She disguised herself as a man so she could fight on the battlefield.* ● **dis|guised** ADJ ❑ *The robber entered the hospital disguised as a medical worker.* **3** V-T To **disguise** something means to hide it or make it appear different so that people will not know about it or will not recognize it. ❑ *He made no attempt to disguise his anger.* ● **dis|guised** ADJ ❑ *The book was actually a thinly disguised autobiography.* [from Old French]

**dis|gust** /dɪsgʌst/ (**disguists, disgusting, disgusted**) **1** N-UNCOUNT **Disgust** is a feeling of very strong dislike or disapproval. ❑ *George watched in disgust.* **2** V-T To **disgust** someone means to make them feel a strong sense of dislike and disapproval. ❑ *He disgusted many people with his behavior.* [from Old French]

**dis|gust|ed** /dɪsgʌstɪd/ ADJ If you are **disgusted**, you feel a strong sense of dislike and disapproval. ❑ *I'm disgusted with the way that he was treated.* ● **dis|gust|ed|ly** ADV ❑ *"It's a little late for that," Ritter said disgustedly.* [from Old French]

**dis|gust|ing** /dɪsgʌstɪŋ/ ADJ If you say that something is **disgusting**, you think it is extremely unpleasant or unacceptable. ❑ *It tasted disgusting.* ❑ *It's disgusting the way we were treated.* [from Old French]

**dish** /dɪʃ/ (**dishes, dishing, dished**) **1** N-COUNT A **dish** is a shallow container used for cooking or serving food. ❑ *…plastic bowls and dishes.* **2** N-COUNT Food that is prepared in a particular style or combination can be referred to as a **dish**. ❑ *There are plenty of vegetarian dishes to choose from.* **3** N-COUNT You can use **dish** to refer to anything that is round and hollow in shape with a wide uncovered top. ❑ *…a dish used to receive satellite broadcasts.* [from Old English] **4** → see also **satellite dish**

→ see Picture Dictionary: **dish**

→ see **pottery**

▶ **dish out 1** PHR-VERB If you **dish out** something, you distribute it among a number of people. [INFORMAL] ❑ *…dishing out money.* **2** PHR-VERB If someone **dishes out** criticism or punishment, they give it to someone. [INFORMAL] ❑ *It was his job to dish out the punishment.*

**3** PHR-VERB If you **dish out** food, you serve it to people at the beginning of each course of a meal. [INFORMAL] ❑ *Annie dished out the curry.*

▶ **dish up** PHR-VERB If you **dish up** food, you serve it. [INFORMAL] ❑ *They dished up a lovely meal.*

**di|shev|eled** /dɪʃɛvᵊld/ also **dishevelled** ADJ If you describe someone's hair, clothes, or appearance as **disheveled**, you mean that it is very untidy. ❑ *She arrived tired and disheveled.* [from Old French]

**dis|hon|est** /dɪsɒnɪst/ ADJ If you say that a person or their behavior is **dishonest**, you mean that they are not truthful or honest and that you cannot trust them. ❑ *I was dishonest with him.* ● **dis|hon|est|ly** ADV ❑ *He dishonestly received $500,000.* [from Old French]

**dis|hon|es|ty** /dɪsɒnɪsti/ N-UNCOUNT **Dishonesty** is dishonest behavior. ❑ *She accused the government of dishonesty.*

**dis|hon|or** /dɪsɒnər/ (**dishonors, dishonoring, dishonored**) **1** V-T If you **dishonor** someone, you behave in a way that damages their good reputation. [FORMAL] ❑ *He had insulted and dishonored these people.* **2** V-T If someone **dishonors** an agreement, they refuse to act according to its conditions. ❑ *I do not think I dishonored my oath.* **3** N-UNCOUNT **Dishonor** is a state in which people disapprove of you and lose their respect for you. [FORMAL] ❑ *I have brought shame and dishonor on my family.* [from Old French]

**dis|hon|or|able** /dɪsɒnərəbᵊl/ ADJ Someone who is **dishonorable** is not honest and does things which you consider to be morally unacceptable. ❑ *Actresses were considered slightly dishonorable in those days.* ● **dis|hon|or|ably** ADV ❑ *He didn't want to behave dishonorably.* [from Old French]

**dish|rag** /dɪʃræg/ (**dishrags**) N-COUNT A **dishrag** is a cloth used for washing dishes, pans, and flatware.

**dish|wash|er** /dɪʃwɒʃər/ (**dishwashers**) **1** N-COUNT A **dishwasher** is an electrically operated machine that washes and dries dishes, pans and flatware. **2** N-COUNT A **dishwasher** is a person who is employed to wash dishes, for example at a restaurant, or who usually washes the dishes at home. ❑ *I was a short-order cook and a dishwasher.*

**Picture Dictionary**    dish

salt & pepper shakers

butter dish

gravy boat

cup & saucer

creamer

sugar bowl

mug

dinner plate

salad plate

bread plate

bowl

platter

**dish|washing liq|uid** /dɪʃwɒʃɪŋlɪkwɪd/ (**dishwashing liquids**) N-VAR **Dishwashing liquid** is a thick soapy liquid which you add to hot water to clean dirty dishes.

**dis|il|lu|sion** /dɪsɪluːʒ³n/ (**disillusions, disillusioning, disillusioned**) ■ V-T If a person or thing **disillusions** you, they make you realize that something is not as good as you thought. ❑ Well you certainly have disillusioned me about Miami. ● **dis|il|lu|sioned** ADJ ❑ I'm very disillusioned with politics. ■ N-UNCOUNT **Disillusion** is the same as **disillusionment**. ❑ There is disillusion with political parties. [from Latin]

**dis|il|lu|sion|ment** /dɪsɪluːʒ³nmənt/ N-UNCOUNT **Disillusionment** is the disappointment that you feel when you discover that something is not as good as you had expected or thought. ❑ ...his disillusionment with his job. [from Latin]

**dis|in|fect** /dɪsɪnfɛkt/ (**disinfects, disinfecting, disinfected**) V-T If you **disinfect** something, you clean it using a substance that kills germs. ❑ Chlorine is used for disinfecting water. [from Latin]

**dis|in|fect|ant** /dɪsɪnfɛktənt/ (**disinfectants**) N-VAR **Disinfectant** is a substance that kills germs. It is used, for example, for cleaning kitchens and bathrooms. ❑ They washed their hands with disinfectant. [from Latin]

**dis|in|te|grate** /dɪsɪntɪgreɪt/ (**disintegrates, disintegrating, disintegrated**) ■ V-I If something **disintegrates**, it becomes seriously weakened, and is divided or destroyed. ❑ The empire began to disintegrate. ● **dis|in|te|gra|tion** /dɪsɪntɪgreɪʃ³n/ N-UNCOUNT ❑ ...the violent disintegration of Yugoslavia. ■ V-I If an object or substance **disintegrates**, it breaks into many small pieces or parts and is destroyed. ❑ At 420 mph the windshield disintegrated. [from Latin]

**dis|in|ter|est|ed** /dɪsɪntərɛstɪd, -ɪntrɪstɪd/ ■ ADJ Someone who is **disinterested** is not involved in a particular situation or not likely to benefit from it and is therefore able to act in a fair and unselfish way. ❑ ...an independent and disinterested committee. ■ ADJ If you are **disinterested in** something, you are not interested in it. Some users of English believe that it is not correct to use **disinterested** with this meaning. ❑ Doran was disinterested in food.

**disk** /dɪsk/ (**disks**) also **disc** ■ N-COUNT A **disk** is a flat, circular shape or object. ❑ The food processor has thin, medium, and thick slicing disks. ■ N-COUNT A **disk** is one of the thin, circular pieces of cartilage which separate the bones in your back. ❑ I had slipped a disk and was in pain. ■ N-COUNT In a computer, the **disk** is the part where information is stored. ❑ The program takes up 2.5 megabytes of disk space. ■ N-COUNT A disk is the same as a **compact disk**. [from Latin] ■ → see also **floppy disk, hard disk**

**disk drive** (**disk drives**) N-COUNT The **disk drive** on a computer is the part that contains the disk or into which a disk can be inserted. The disk drive allows you to read information from the disk and store information on the disk.

**dis|like** /dɪslaɪk/ (**dislikes, disliking, disliked**) ■ V-T If you **dislike** someone or something, you think they are unpleasant and do not like them. ❑ Many people dislike the taste. ■ N-UNCOUNT **Dislike** is the feeling that you do not like

someone or something. ❑ ...his dislike of publicity. ■ N-COUNT Your **dislikes** are the things that you do not like. ❑ Consider what your likes and dislikes are about your job. [from Old English]

**dis|lo|cate** /dɪsloʊkeɪt, dɪsloʊkeɪt/ (**dislocates, dislocating, dislocated**) V-T If you **dislocate** a bone or joint in your body, or in someone else's body, it moves out of its proper position in relation to other bones, usually in an accident. ❑ Harrison dislocated a finger. [from Late Middle English]

**dis|lodge** /dɪslɒdʒ/ (**dislodges, dislodging, dislodged**) V-T To **dislodge** something means to remove it from where it was fixed or held. ❑ Rainfall dislodged the rocks from the hillside. [from Old French]

**dis|mal** /dɪzm³l/ ■ ADJ Something that is **dismal** is bad in a sad or depressing way. ❑ ...the team's dismal performance. ■ ADJ Something that is **dismal** is sad and depressing, especially in appearance. ❑ The hospital is pretty dismal. [from Medieval Latin]

**dis|man|tle** /dɪsmænt³l/ (**dismantles, dismantling, dismantled**) V-T If you **dismantle** a machine or structure, you carefully separate it into its different parts. ❑ Expertly he dismantled the gun. [from Old French]

**dis|may** /dɪsmeɪ/ (**dismays, dismaying, dismayed**) ■ N-UNCOUNT **Dismay** is a strong feeling of fear, worry, or sadness that is caused by something unpleasant and unexpected. [FORMAL] ❑ Local people reacted with dismay. ■ V-T If you **are dismayed** by something, it makes you feel afraid, worried, or sad. [FORMAL] ❑ The committee was dismayed by the news. ● **dis|mayed** ADJ ❑ Glen was shocked and dismayed at her reaction. [from Old French]

**dis|mem|ber** /dɪsmɛmbər/ (**dismembers, dismembering, dismembered**) V-T To **dismember** the body of a dead person or animal means to cut or pull it into pieces. ❑ He killed, skinned, and dismembered a rabbit. ● **dis|mem|ber|ment** /dɪsmɛmbərmənt/ N-UNCOUNT ❑ ...dismemberment of the body. [from Latin]

**Word Link**    miss ≈ sending : dismiss, missile, missionary

**dis|miss** /dɪsmɪs/ (**dismisses, dismissing, dismissed**) ■ V-T If you **dismiss** something, you decide or say that it is not important enough for you to think about or consider. ❑ He dismissed the plan as nonsense. ■ V-T When an employer **dismisses** an employee, the employer tells the employee that they are no longer needed to do the job that they have been doing. ❑ Locke was dismissed from the team after admitting to stealing an ATM card. ■ V-T If you **are dismissed** by someone in authority, they tell you that you can go away from them. ❑ Two more witnesses were called, heard, and dismissed. [from Medieval Latin]

**Word Partnership**    Use dismiss with :

| | |
|---|---|
| ADJ. | easy to dismiss ■ |
| N. | dismiss **an idea**, dismiss **a possibility** ■ |
| | dismiss **an employee** ■ |
| | dismiss **a case** ■ |

**dis|mis|sal** /dɪsmɪs³l/ (**dismissals**) ■ N-VAR When an employee is dismissed from their job, you call this their **dismissal**. ❑ …*Mr. Low's dismissal from his job.* 🔢 N-UNCOUNT **Dismissal of** something means deciding or saying that it is not important. ❑ …*dismissal of public opinion.* [from Medieval Latin]

**dis|miss|ive** /dɪsmɪsɪv/ ADJ If you are **dismissive** of someone or something, you say or show that you think they are not important or have no value. ❑ *Mr. Jones was dismissive of the report.* ● **dis|miss|ive|ly** ADV ❑ *"Forget it," he replied dismissively.* [from Medieval Latin]

**dis|obedi|ence** /dɪsəbidiəns/ N-UNCOUNT **Disobedience** is deliberately not doing what someone tells you to do, or what a rule or law says that you should do. ❑ …*an act of disobedience.*

**dis|obey** /dɪsəbeɪ/ (**disobeys, disobeying, disobeyed**) V-T/V-I When someone **disobeys** a person or an order, they deliberately do not do what they have been told to do. ❑ *He often disobeyed his mother and father.* ❑ *He will not dare disobey.* [from Old French]

**dis|or|der** /dɪsɔrdər/ (**disorders**) 🔢 N-VAR A **disorder** is a problem or illness which affects your mind or body. ❑ …*a rare blood disorder.* 🔢 N-UNCOUNT **Disorder** is violence or rioting in public. ❑ *America's worst civil disorder erupted in the city of Los Angeles.* 🔢 N-UNCOUNT **Disorder** is a state of being untidy, badly prepared, or badly organized. ❑ *The emergency room was in disorder.* [from Old French]

**dis|or|der|ly** /dɪsɔrdərli/ ADJ If you describe something as **disorderly**, you mean that it is messy, irregular, or disorganized. [FORMAL] ❑ …*the large and disorderly room.* [from Old French]

**dis|or|der|ly con|duct** N-UNCOUNT In law, **disorderly conduct** is the offense of behaving in a dangerous or disruptive way in public. ❑ *The group was charged with disorderly conduct.*

**dis|or|gan|ized** /dɪsɔrgənaɪzd/ 🔢 ADJ Something that is **disorganized** is in a confused state or is badly planned or managed. ❑ *He stepped into the large, disorganized office.* 🔢 ADJ Someone who is **disorganized** is very bad at organizing things in their life. ❑ *My boss is completely disorganized.*

**dis|own** /dɪsoʊn/ (**disowns, disowning, disowned**) V-T If you **disown** someone or something, you say or show that you no longer want to have any connection with them or any responsibility for them. ❑ *Her family have disowned her because of the scandal.* [from Old English]

**dis|par|age** /dɪspærɪdʒ/ (**disparages, disparaging, disparaged**) V-T If you **disparage** someone or something, you speak about them in a way which shows that you do not have a good opinion of them. [FORMAL] ❑ *Helena is keen to disparage such an idea.* ● **dis|par|age|ment** N-UNCOUNT ❑ …*the reviewers' disparagement of this book.* ● **dis|par|ag|ing** ADJ ❑ *He was disparaging of their rude manners.* [from Old French]

| **Word Link** | *par* ≈ *equal : compare, disparate, part* |

**dis|par|ate** /dɪspərɪt/ ADJ **Disparate** things are completely different from each other in quality or type. [FORMAL] ❑ …*disparate ideas.* [from Latin]

**dis|par|ity** /dɪspærɪti/ (**disparities**) N-VAR A **disparity between** two or more things is a noticeable difference between them. [FORMAL]

❑ …*the health disparities between different ethnic groups in the U.S.* [from Late Latin]

**dis|patch** /dɪspætʃ/ (**dispatches, dispatching, dispatched**) V-T If you **dispatch** someone or something to a place, you send them there. [FORMAL] ❑ *He dispatched another letter to his cousin.* ● **Dispatch** is also a noun. ❑ *We have 125 cases ready for dispatch.* [from Italian]

**dis|patch|er** /dɪspætʃər/ (**dispatchers**) N-COUNT A **dispatcher** is someone who works for an organization such as the police or the fire department and whose job is to send members of the organization to the places where they are needed. ❑ *The police dispatcher received the call at around 10:30 a.m.* [from Italian]

**dis|pel** /dɪspɛl/ (**dispels, dispelling, dispelled**) V-T To **dispel** an idea or feeling that people have means to stop them having it. ❑ *Leonard could not dispel his doubts.* [from Latin]

**dis|pense** /dɪspɛns/ (**dispenses, dispensing, dispensed**) 🔢 V-T If someone **dispenses** something that they own or control, they give or provide it to a number of people. [FORMAL] ❑ *The union dispensed $60,000 in grants.* 🔢 V-T When a pharmacist **dispenses** medicine, he or she prepares it, and gives or sells it to the patient or customer. ❑ *Information was given to the people who dispense the drug.* [from Medieval Latin] ▸ **dispense with** PHR-VERB If you **dispense with** something, you stop using it or get rid of it completely, especially because you no longer need it. ❑ *It was warm enough to dispense with gloves.*

**dis|pens|er** /dɪspɛnsər/ (**dispensers**) N-COUNT A **dispenser** is a machine or container from which you can get things. ❑ …*cash dispensers.* [from Medieval Latin]

**dis|perse** /dɪspɜrs/ (**disperses, dispersing, dispersed**) 🔢 V-T/V-I When something **disperses** or when you **disperse** it, it spreads over a wide area. ❑ *When the sandbags open, the sand is dispersed on the ocean floor.* 🔢 V-T/V-I When a group of people **disperses** or when someone **disperses** them, the group splits up and the people leave in different directions. ❑ *Police used tear gas to disperse the demonstrators.* [from Latin]

**dis|place** /dɪspleɪs/ (**displaces, displacing, displaced**) 🔢 V-T If one thing **displaces** another, it forces the other thing out and then occupies its position. ❑ *These factories have displaced tourism as the country's main source of income.* 🔢 V-T If a person or group of people **is displaced**, they are forced to move away from the area where they live. ❑ *More than 600,000 people were displaced by the earthquake.* ● **dis|place|ment** N-UNCOUNT ❑ …*the gradual displacement of Native Americans.* [from Old French]

**dis|play** /dɪspleɪ/ (**displays, displaying, displayed**) 🔢 V-T If you **display** something, you put it in a place where people can see it. ❑ *Old soldiers proudly displayed their medals.* ● **Display** is also a noun. ❑ …*the artists whose work is on display.* 🔢 V-T If you **display** a characteristic, quality, or emotion, you behave in a way which shows that you have it. ❑ *Gordon didn't often display his feelings.* ● **Display** is also a noun. ❑ *He reserved displays of affection for his mother.* 🔢 N-COUNT A **display** is an arrangement of things that have been put in a particular place, so that people can see them easily. ❑ …*a display of your work.* 🔢 N-COUNT A

**display** is a public performance or other event which is intended to entertain people. ❑ …*a fireworks display.* [from Late Latin]

**dis|pleas|ure** /dɪsplɛʒər/ N-UNCOUNT **Displeasure** is a feeling of annoyance toward someone or something. ❑ *Alexander tried not to show his displeasure.* [from Old French]

**dis|pos|able** /dɪspoʊzəbªl/ ADJ A **disposable** product is designed to be thrown away after it has been used. ❑ …*disposable diapers.* [from Old French]

**dis|pos|al** /dɪspoʊzªl/ ◼ PHRASE If you have something **at** your **disposal**, you are able to use it whenever you want, and for whatever purpose you want. If you are **at** someone's **disposal**, you are willing to help them in any way you can. ❑ *Do you have this information at your disposal?* ◻ N-UNCOUNT **Disposal** is the act of getting rid of something that is no longer wanted or needed. ❑ …*the disposal of waste.* [from Old French]

**dis|pose** /dɪspoʊz/ (**disposes, disposing, disposed**) [from Old French]
▸ **dispose of** PHR-VERB If you **dispose of** something that you no longer want or need, you get rid of it. ❑ …*ways of disposing of nuclear waste.*

**dis|posed** /dɪspoʊzd/ ◼ ADJ If you are **disposed to** do something, you are willing or eager to do it. [FORMAL] ❑ *We were not disposed to stop.* ◻ ADJ You can use **disposed** when you are talking about your general attitude or opinion. For example, if you are well or favorably **disposed to** or **toward** someone or something, you like them or approve of them. [FORMAL] ❑ *The publishers were well disposed toward my book.* [from Old French]

**dis|po|si|tion** /dɪspəzɪʃªn/ (**dispositions**) N-COUNT Someone's **disposition** is the way that they tend to behave or feel. ❑ *Her happy disposition always brought a smile to my face.* [from Late Latin]

**dis|prove** /dɪspruv/ (**disproves, disproving, disproved, disproven**) V-T To **disprove** an idea, belief, or theory means to show that it is not true. ❑ *The research disproved his theory.* [from Old French]
→ see **science**

**dis|pute** /dɪspyut/ (**disputes, disputing, disputed**) ◼ N-VAR A **dispute** is an argument or disagreement between people or groups. ❑ *They won a pay dispute with the government.* ◻ V-T If you **dispute** a fact, statement, or theory, you say that it is incorrect or untrue. ❑ *He disputed the idea that he had made a mistake.* ❑ *Nobody disputed that Davey was clever.* ◼ V-RECIP When people **dispute** something, they fight for control or ownership of it. ❑ *Russia and Ukraine were disputing the ownership of the ships.* ◼ PHRASE If something is **in dispute**, people are questioning it or arguing about it. ❑ *The contract is in dispute.* [from Late Latin]

**dis|quali|fy** /dɪskwɒlɪfaɪ/ (**disqualifies, disqualifying, disqualified**) V-T When someone is **disqualified**, they are officially stopped from taking part in a particular event, activity, or competition. ❑ *Thomson was disqualified from the race.* ● **dis|quali|fi|ca|tion** /dɪskwɒlɪfɪkeɪʃªn/ (**disqualifications**) N-VAR ❑ …*her disqualification from next year's Olympic Games.* [from Old French]

**dis|qui|et** /dɪskwaɪɪt/ N-UNCOUNT **Disquiet** is a feeling of worry or anxiety. [FORMAL] ❑ *There is growing public disquiet about the cost.* [from Latin]

**dis|re|gard** /dɪsrɪgɑrd/ (**disregards, disregarding, disregarded**) V-T If you **disregard** something, you ignore it or do not take account of it. ❑ *He disregarded the advice of his parents.* ● **Disregard** is also a noun. ❑ *These terrorists had a total disregard for human life.* [from Old French]

**dis|re|pute** /dɪsrɪpyut/ PHRASE If something **is brought into disrepute** or **falls into disrepute**, it loses its good reputation, because it is connected with activities that people do not approve of. ❑ *She brought the profession into disrepute.*

**dis|rupt** /dɪsrʌpt/ (**disrupts, disrupting, disrupted**) V-T If someone or something **disrupts** an event, system, or process, they cause difficulties that prevent it from continuing or operating in a normal way. ❑ *Anti-war protesters disrupted the debate.* ● **dis|rup|tion** (**disruptions**) N-VAR ❑ *The bad weather caused disruption at many airports.* [from Latin]

**dis|rup|tive** /dɪsrʌptɪv/ ADJ If someone is **disruptive**, they prevent something from continuing or operating in a normal way. ❑ *He was a disruptive influence.* [from Latin]

**dis|sat|is|fac|tion** /dɪssætɪsfækʃªn, dɪssæt-/ (**dissatisfactions**) N-VAR If you feel **dissatisfaction with** something, you are not content or pleased with it. ❑ *She expressed her dissatisfaction.* [from French]

**dis|sat|is|fied** /dɪssætɪsfaɪd/ ADJ If you are **dissatisfied with** something, you are not content or pleased with it. ❑ *Eighty-two percent of voters are dissatisfied with the way their country is being governed.*

**dis|sect** /dɪsɛkt, daɪ-/ (**dissects, dissecting, dissected**) V-T If someone **dissects** the body of a dead person or animal, they cut it up in order to examine it scientifically. ❑ *We dissected a frog in biology class.* ● **dis|sec|tion** /dɪsɛkʃªn, daɪ-/ (**dissections**) N-VAR ❑ *Researchers need a supply of bodies for dissection.* [from Latin]

**dis|semi|nate** /dɪsɛmɪneɪt/ (**disseminates, disseminating, disseminated**) V-T To **disseminate** information or knowledge means to distribute it so that it reaches many people or organizations. [FORMAL] ❑ …*programs to disseminate information.* ● **dis|semi|na|tion** /dɪsɛmɪneɪʃªn/ N-UNCOUNT ❑ …*the dissemination of scientific ideas.* [from Latin]

**dis|sent** /dɪsɛnt/ (**dissents, dissenting, dissented**) ◼ N-UNCOUNT **Dissent** is strong disagreement with a decision or opinion, especially one that is supported by most people or by people in authority. ❑ …*political dissent.* ◻ V-I If you **dissent**, you express disagreement with a decision or opinion, especially one that is supported by most people or by people in authority. [FORMAL] ❑ *Just one of the 10 members dissented.* ❑ *No one dissents from the decision.* ● **dis|sent|er** (**dissenters**) N-COUNT ❑ *The party* *does not tolerate dissenters.* ● **dis|sent|ing** ADJ ❑ *He ignored dissenting views.* [from Latin]

**dis|ser|ta|tion** /dɪsərteɪʃ³n/ (**dissertations**) N-COUNT A **dissertation** is a long formal piece of writing on a particular subject, especially for an advanced university degree. ❑ *He is writing a dissertation on the civil war.* [from Latin]

**dis|si|dent** /dɪsɪdənt/ (**dissidents**) N-COUNT **Dissidents** are people who disagree with and criticize their government, especially because it is undemocratic. ❑ *...political dissidents.* [from Latin]

**dis|si|pate** /dɪsɪpeɪt/ (**dissipates, dissipating, dissipated**) ■ V-T/V-I When something **dissipates** or when you **dissipate** it, it becomes less or becomes less strong until it disappears or goes away completely. [FORMAL] ❑ *The gas clouds dissipated by late morning.* ■ V-T When someone **dissipates** money, time, or effort, they waste it in a foolish way. [FORMAL] ❑ *He dissipates his time and energy on too many different things.* ● **dis|si|pa|tion** /dɪsɪpeɪʃ³n/ N-UNCOUNT [LITERARY] ❑ *...the dissipation of wealth.* [from Latin]

**dis|so|ci|ate** /dɪsoʊʃieɪt, -sieɪt/ (**dissociates, dissociating, dissociated**) V-T If you **dissociate yourself from** something or someone, you say or show that you are not connected with them. ❑ *The president is unable to dissociate himself from the scandals.*

**dis|solve** /dɪzɒlv/ (**dissolves, dissolving, dissolved**) ■ V-T/V-I If a substance **dissolves** in liquid or if you **dissolve** it, it becomes mixed with the liquid and disappears. ❑ *Heat the mixture gently until the sugar dissolves.* ■ V-T When something **is dissolved**, it is officially ended or broken up. ❑ *The committee was dissolved.* ● **dis|so|lu|tion** /dɪsəluʃ³n/ N-UNCOUNT; N-SING ❑ *He stayed until the dissolution of the company.* [from Latin]

**Word Link** suad, suas ≈ urging : dissuade, persuade, persuasive

**dis|suade** /dɪsweɪd/ (**dissuades, dissuading, dissuaded**) V-T If you **dissuade** someone **from** doing or believing something, you persuade them not to do or believe it. [FORMAL] ❑ *Nothing can dissuade him from that decision.* [from Latin]

**dis|tance** /dɪstəns/ (**distances, distancing, distanced**) ■ N-VAR The **distance between** two places is the amount of space between them. ❑ *...the distance between the island and the shore.* ■ N-UNCOUNT **Distance** is coolness or unfriendliness in the way that someone behaves toward you. [FORMAL] ❑ *There were periods of distance, of coldness.* ■ V-T If you **distance yourself from** a person or thing, or if something **distances** you **from** them, you feel less friendly or positive toward them, or become less involved with them. ❑ *The author distanced himself from some of the comments in his book.* ● **dis|tanced** ADJ ❑ *She had become distanced from Derek.* ■ PHRASE If you are **at a distance** from something, or if you see it or remember it **from a distance**, you are a long way away from it in space or time. ❑ *At a distance, the lake looked beautiful.* ❑ *Now I can think about what happened from a distance of almost forty years.* [from Latin]

**Word Partnership** Use *distance* with :

| ADJ. | **safe** distance, **short** distance ■ |
|---|---|
| PREP. | distance **between**, **within walking** distance ■ |
| | **at a** distance, **from a** distance ■ |

**dis|tant** /dɪstənt/ ■ ADJ **Distant** means very far away. ❑ *The mountains were on the distant horizon.* ● **dis|tant|ly** ADV [LITERARY] ❑ *Distantly, she could just see the town of Chiffa.* ■ ADJ You use **distant** to describe a time or event that is very far away in the future or in the past. ❑ *Things will improve in the not too distant future.* ■ ADJ A **distant** relative is one who you are not closely related to. ❑ *He's a distant relative of the mayor.* ● **dis|tant|ly** ADV ❑ *The O'Shea girls are distantly related to our family.* ■ ADJ If you describe someone as **distant**, you mean that you find them cold and unfriendly. ❑ *She seemed cold and distant.* ■ ADJ If you describe someone as **distant**, you mean that they are not concentrating on what they are doing because they are thinking about other things. ❑ *There was a distant look in her eyes.* ● **dis|tant|ly** ADV ❑ *"He's in the kitchen," she said distantly.* [from Latin]

**Thesaurus** *distant* Also look up :

| ADJ. | faraway, remote; (*ant.*) close, near ■ |
|---|---|
| | aloof, cool, unfriendly ■ |

**dis|taste** /dɪsteɪst/ N-UNCOUNT If you feel **distaste for** someone or something, you dislike them or disapprove of them. ❑ *He showed his distaste for everything related to money.* [from Old French]

**dis|taste|ful** /dɪsteɪstfʊl/ ADJ If something is **distasteful** to you, you think it is unpleasant, disgusting, or immoral. ❑ *He found the whole subject distasteful.* [from Old French]

**dis|till** /dɪstɪl/ (**distills, distilling, distilled**) V-T If a liquid such as whiskey or water **is distilled**, it is heated until it changes into steam or vapor and then cooled until it becomes liquid again. ❑ *...a gallon of distilled water.* ● **dis|til|la|tion** /dɪstɪleɪʃ³n/ N-UNCOUNT ❑ *The water is warm because of the distillation process.* [from Latin]

**dis|tinct** /dɪstɪŋkt/ ■ ADJ If something is **distinct from** something else of the same type, it is different or separate from it. ❑ *Engineering and technology are distinct from one another.* ● **dis|tinct|ly** ADV ❑ *...a banking industry with two distinctly different sectors.* ■ ADJ If something is **distinct**, you can hear, see, or taste it clearly. ❑ *Each vegetable has its own distinct flavor.* ● **dis|tinct|ly** ADV ❑ *I distinctly heard the loudspeaker calling passengers for the Washington-Miami flight.* ■ ADJ If an idea, thought, or intention is **distinct**, it is clear and definite. ❑ *There was a distinct change in her attitude.* ● **dis|tinct|ly** ADV ❑ *I distinctly remember wishing I wasn't there.* [from Latin]

**Usage** **distinct and distinctive**

*Distinct* and *distinctive* are easy to confuse. You use *distinct* to say that something is separate, different, clear, or noticeable; you use *distinctive* to say that something is special and easily recognized: *The distinct taste of lemon gave Elena's cake a distinctive and delicious flavor.*

**dis|tinc|tion** /dɪstɪŋkʃən/ (**distinctions**)
**1** N-COUNT A **distinction** is a difference between similar things. ❑ *There are obvious distinctions between the two areas.* ❑ *...the distinction between craft and fine art.* **2** PHRASE If you **draw a distinction** or **make a distinction**, you say that two things are different. ❑ *He draws a distinction between art and culture.* **3** N-UNCOUNT **Distinction** is the quality of being excellent. [FORMAL] ❑ *Lewis is a writer of distinction.* [from Latin]

**dis|tinc|tive** /dɪstɪŋktɪv/ **1** ADJ Something that is **distinctive** has a special quality or feature which makes it easily recognizable. ❑ *...the distinctive smell of gas.* ● **dis|tinc|tive|ly** ADV ❑ *...distinctively American music.* [from Latin] **2** → see also **distinct**

**dis|tin|guish** /dɪstɪŋgwɪʃ/ (**distinguishes, distinguishing, distinguished**) **1** V-T/V-I If you can **distinguish** one thing **from** another or **distinguish between** two things, you can see or understand how they are different. ❑ *Could he distinguish right from wrong?* ❑ *Research suggests that babies learn to see by distinguishing between areas of light and dark.* **2** V-T A feature or quality that **distinguishes** one thing **from** another causes the two things to be regarded as different. ❑ *There is something about music that distinguishes it from other art forms.* **3** V-T If you can **distinguish** something, you can see, hear, or taste it although it is very difficult to detect. [FORMAL] ❑ *He could distinguish voices.* **4** V-T If you **distinguish yourself**, you do something that makes you famous or important. ❑ *He distinguished himself as a scientist.* [from Latin]

**dis|tin|guished** /dɪstɪŋgwɪʃt/ ADJ If you describe a person or their work as **distinguished**, you mean that they have been very successful in their career and have a good reputation. ❑ *...a distinguished academic family.* [from Latin]

**dis|tort** /dɪstɔrt/ (**distorts, distorting, distorted**) **1** V-T If you **distort** a statement, fact, or idea, you report or represent it in an untrue way. ❑ *The media distorts reality.* ● **dis|tort|ed** ADJ ❑ *These figures give a distorted view of the situation.* ● **dis|tor|tion** (**distortions**) N-VAR ❑ *...a gross distortion of reality.* **2** V-T/V-I If something you can see or hear **is distorted** or **distorts**, its appearance or sound is changed so that it seems unclear. ❑ *An artist may distort shapes in a painting.* ● **dis|tort|ed** ADJ ❑ *The sound was becoming distorted.* ● **dis|tor|tion** N-VAR ❑ *Audio signals can travel along cables without distortion.* [from Latin]

**dis|tract** /dɪstrækt/ (**distracts, distracting, distracted**) V-T If something **distracts** you or your attention **from** something, it takes your attention away from it. ❑ *Tom admits that playing video games sometimes distracts him from his homework.* ❑ *Don't let yourself be distracted by fears about the future.* ● **dis|tract|ing** ADJ ❑ *I find it distracting if someone watches me while I work.* [from Latin]

**Usage** **distract** and **detract**
Be careful not to confuse *distract* and *detract*, which have some similarity in meaning. *Distract* means taking away attention, whereas *detract* means taking away importance or value: *Jose's torn pants really detracted from his appearance; he'd been distracted by Rosa and had fallen down.*

**dis|tract|ed** /dɪstræktɪd/ ADJ If you are **distracted**, you are not concentrating on something because you are worried or are thinking about something else. ❑ *She seemed distracted.* ● **dis|tract|ed|ly** ADV ❑ *He looked up distractedly. "Be with you in a second."* [from Latin]

**dis|trac|tion** /dɪstrækʃən/ (**distractions**) N-VAR A **distraction** is something that turns your attention away from something you want to concentrate on. ❑ *This is a distraction from what I really want to do.* [from Latin]

**dis|traught** /dɪstrɔt/ ADJ If someone is **distraught**, they are so upset and worried that they cannot think clearly. ❑ *...distraught relatives of people killed in the plane crash.*

**dis|tress** /dɪstrɛs/ (**distresses, distressing, distressed**) **1** N-UNCOUNT **Distress** is a state of extreme sorrow, suffering, or pain. ❑ *Jealousy causes distress and painful emotions.* **2** N-UNCOUNT **Distress** is the state of being in extreme danger and needing urgent help. ❑ *The ship was in distress.* **3** V-T If someone or something **distresses** you, they cause you to be upset or worried. ❑ *The idea distressed him greatly.* ● **dis|tressed** ADJ ❑ *I feel very distressed about my problem.* ● **dis|tress|ing** ADJ ❑ *It is very distressing when your baby is sick.* ● **dis|tress|ing|ly** ADV ❑ *A distressingly large number of firms are ignoring the rules.* [from Old French]

**Word Link** tribute ≈ giving : at**tribute**, con**tribute**, dis**tribute**

**dis|trib|ute** /dɪstrɪbyut/ (**distributes, distributing, distributed**) **1** V-T If you **distribute** things, you hand them or deliver them to a number of people. ❑ *They distributed free tickets to young people.* ● **dis|tri|bu|tion** /dɪstrɪbyuʃən/ N-UNCOUNT ❑ *...the distribution of information.* **2** V-T When a company **distributes** goods, it supplies them to the stores or businesses that sell them. [BUSINESS] ❑ *We didn't understand how difficult it was to distribute a national paper.* ● **dis|tri|bu|tion** /dɪstrɪbyuʃən/ N-UNCOUNT ❑ *...the distribution of goods and services.* ● **dis|tribu|tor** (**distributors**) N-COUNT ❑ *...Spain's largest distributor of oranges.* **3** V-T To **distribute** a substance **over** something means to scatter it over it. [FORMAL] ❑ *Distribute the cheese evenly over the vegetables.* [from Latin]

**dis|tri|bu|tion** /dɪstrɪbyuʃən/ (**distributions**) N-VAR The **distribution** of something is how much of it there is in each place or at each time, or how much of it each person has. ❑ *...a fairer distribution of wealth.* [from Latin]

**dis|trict** /dɪstrɪkt/ (**districts**) N-COUNT A **district** is a particular area of a town or country. ❑ *I drove around the business district.* [from Medieval Latin]

**dis|trict at|tor|ney** (**district attorneys**) N-COUNT A **district attorney** is a lawyer who works for a city, state, or federal government and puts on trial people who are accused of crimes. The abbreviation **D.A.** is also used. [AM]

**dis|trict court** (**district courts**) N-COUNT In the United States, a **district court** is a state or federal court that has jurisdiction in a particular district. [AM] ❑ *A Miami district court has scheduled a hearing for Friday.*

**dis|trust** /dɪstrʌst/ (**distrusts, distrusting, distrusted**) **1** V-T If you **distrust** someone or something, you think they are not honest, reliable, or safe. ❑ *I don't have any reason to distrust them.* ❷ N-UNCOUNT; N-SING **Distrust** is the feeling of doubt that you have toward someone or something you distrust. ❑ *...a distrust of all politicians.* [from Old Norse]

**dis|turb** /dɪstɜrb/ (**disturbs, disturbing, disturbed**) ❶ V-T If you **disturb** someone, you interrupt what they are doing and upset them. ❑ *I didn't want to disturb you. You looked so peaceful.* ❷ V-T If something **disturbs** you, it makes you feel upset or worried. ❑ *My dreams are so vivid that they disturb me for days.* ❸ V-T If something **is disturbed**, its position or shape is changed. ❑ *The books had not been disturbed for a long time and were covered in dust.* [from Latin]

| | Word Partnership | Use *disturb* with : |
|---|---|---|
| V. | be careful not to disturb, do not disturb ❶ be sorry to disturb ❶ ❷ | |
| N. | disturb the neighbors ❷ | |

**dis|turb|ance** /dɪstɜrbəns/ (**disturbances**) ❶ N-COUNT A **disturbance** is an incident in which people behave violently in public. ❑ *During the disturbance, three men were hurt.* ❷ N-UNCOUNT **Disturbance** means upsetting or disorganizing something which was previously in a calm and well-ordered state. ❑ *There must be no disturbance in the treatment room.* [from Latin]

**dis|turbed** /dɪstɜrbd/ ADJ A **disturbed** person is very upset emotionally, and often needs special care or treatment. ❑ *...emotionally disturbed children.* [from Latin]

**dis|turb|ing** /dɪstɜrbɪŋ/ ADJ Something that is **disturbing** makes you feel worried or upset. ❑ *...disturbing news.* ● **dis|turb|ing|ly** ADV ❑ *...the disturbingly high frequency of racial attacks.* [from Latin]

**dis|used** /dɪsyuzd/ ADJ A **disused** place or building is empty and is no longer used. ❑ *...a disused gas station.*

**ditch** /dɪtʃ/ (**ditches, ditching, ditched**) ❶ N-COUNT A **ditch** is a long narrow channel cut into the ground at the side of a road or field. ❑ *Both vehicles landed in a ditch.* ❷ V-T If you **ditch** something, you get rid of it. [INFORMAL] ❑ *I decided to ditch the bed.* [from Old English] ❸ → see also **last-ditch**

**dive** /daɪv/ (**dives, diving, dived, dove, dived**) ❶ V-I If you **dive** into some water, you jump in head first with your arms held straight above your head. ❑ *He tried to escape by diving into a river.* ❑ *She was standing by a pool, about to dive in.* ● **Dive** is also a noun. ❑ *Pam made a dive of 80 feet from the Chasm Bridge.* ● **div|ing** N-UNCOUNT ❑ *Weight is important in diving.* ❷ V-I If you **dive**, you go under the surface of the sea or a lake, using special breathing equipment. ❑ *Bezanik is diving to look at fish.* ● **Dive** is also a noun. ❑ *He is already planning the next dive.* ● **div|er** (**divers**) N-COUNT ❑ *Divers have discovered the wreck of a ship.* ● **div|ing** N-UNCOUNT ❑ *...equipment for diving.* ❸ V-I When birds and animals **dive**, they go quickly downward, head first, through the air or through water. ❑ *The pelican was diving for a fish.* ❹ V-I If you **dive** in a particular direction or into a particular place, you

jump or move there quickly. ❑ *They dived into a taxi.* ● **Dive** is also a noun. ❑ *David made a dive for the door.* [from Old English]

| | Word Link | di ≈ two : di*lemma*, di*verge*, di*verse* |
|---|---|---|

| | Word Link | verg, vert ≈ turning : con*verge*, di*verge*, sub*vert* |
|---|---|---|

**di|verge** /dɪvɜrdʒ, daɪ-/ (**diverges, diverging, diverged**) ❶ V-RECIP When two things **diverge**, they are different or become different. ❑ *His interests diverged from those of his colleagues.* ❷ V-RECIP If roads or lines **diverge**, they separate and go in different directions. [from Medieval Latin]

**di|ver|gent** /dɪvɜrdʒənt, daɪ-/ ADJ **Divergent** things are different from each other. [FORMAL] ❑ *They have divergent views on this question.* ● **di|ver|gence** (**divergences**) N-VAR [FORMAL] ❑ *There's a great divergence of opinion within the party.* [from Medieval Latin]

**di|ver|gent bounda|ry** (**divergent boundaries**) N-COUNT A **divergent boundary** is an area in the Earth's crust where two tectonic plates are moving away from each other. [TECHNICAL]

**di|verse** /dɪvɜrs, daɪ-/ ADJ If a group of things is **diverse**, it is made up of a wide variety of things. ❑ *...a diverse group of students.* [from Latin]

| | Word Link | ify ≈ making : cla*ify*, divers*ify*, intens*ify* |
|---|---|---|

**di|ver|si|fy** /dɪvɜrsɪfaɪ, daɪ-/ (**diversifies, diversifying, diversified**) V-T/V-I When an organization or person **diversifies** into other things, or **diversifies** their product line, they increase the variety of things that they do or make. ❑ *The company's troubles started when it diversified into new products.* ❑ *Manufacturers need to diversify and improve quality.* ● **di|ver|si|fi|ca|tion** /dɪvɜrsɪfɪkeɪʃən, daɪ-/ (**diversifications**) N-VAR ❑ *...diversification of teaching methods.* [from Old French]

**di|ver|sion** /dɪvɜrʒən, daɪ-/ (**diversions**) N-COUNT A **diversion** is an action or event that attracts your attention away from what you are doing. ❑ *The robbers escaped after throwing smoke bombs to create a diversion.* ● **di|ver|sion|ary** ADJ ❑ *The fires were started by the prisoners as a diversionary tactic.* [from Latin]

**di|ver|sity** /dɪvɜrsɪti, daɪ-/ (**diversities**) ❶ N-VAR The **diversity** of something is the fact that it contains many very different elements. ❑ *...the cultural diversity of Latin America.* ❷ N-SING A **diversity of** things is a range of things which are very different from each other. ❑ *There was a diversity of attitudes about race.* [from Latin] → see **zoo**

**di|vert** /dɪvɜrt, daɪ-/ (**diverts, diverting, diverted**) ❶ V-T/V-I To **divert** vehicles or travelers means to make them follow a different route or go to a different destination than they originally intended. You can also say that someone or something **diverts from** a particular route or **to** a particular place. ❑ *We diverted a plane to rescue 100 passengers.* ❑ *The hospital diverted patients to other hospitals because it did not have enough beds.* ❷ V-T To **divert** money or resources means to cause them to be used for a different purpose. ❑ *This will divert*

D

*money from patient care.* ● **di**|**ver**|**sion** N-UNCOUNT
❑ *...the diversion of funds from other parts of the economy.* **3** V-T If someone **diverts** your attention from something important or serious, they behave or talk in a way that stops you thinking about it. ❑ *I don't want to divert attention from the project.* [from French]

**di**|**vide** /dɪvaɪd/ (**divides, dividing, divided**)
**1** V-T/V-I When people or things **are divided** or **divide into** smaller groups or parts, they become separated into smaller parts. ❑ *Divide the pastry in half and roll out each piece.* ❑ *The class was divided into two groups of six.* **2** V-T If you **divide** a larger number **by** a smaller number or **divide** a smaller number **into** a larger number, you calculate how many times the smaller number can fit exactly into the larger number. ❑ *Measure the floor area and divide it by six.* **3** V-T If a border or line **divides** two areas or **divides** an area into two, it keeps the two areas separate from each other. ❑ *A long frontier divides Mexico from the United States.* **4** V-T/V-I If people **divide** over something or if something **divides** them, it causes strong disagreement between them. ❑ *Major issues divided the country.* ● **di**|**vid**|**ed** ADJ ❑ *The democrats are divided over whether to agree to the plan.* **5** N-COUNT A **divide** is a significant distinction between two groups. ❑ *...a deliberate attempt to create a Hindu-Muslim divide in India.* **6** N-COUNT A **divide** is a line of high ground between areas that are drained by different rivers. [from Latin]
▶ **divide up** PHR-VERB If you **divide** something **up**, you separate it into smaller or more useful groups. ❑ *The idea is to divide up the country into four areas.*

| **Thesaurus** | *divide* | Also look up : |
|---|---|---|
| v. | categorize, group, segregate, separate, split **1** | |
| | part, separate, split; (ant.) unite **4** | |

**di**|**vid**|**ed high**|**way** (**divided highways**)
N-COUNT A **divided highway** is a road which has two lanes of traffic traveling in each direction with a strip of grass or concrete down the middle to separate the two lots of traffic.

**divi**|**dend** /dɪvɪdɛnd/ (**dividends**) **1** N-COUNT A **dividend** is the part of a company's profits which is paid to people who own shares in the company. [BUSINESS] ❑ *The dividend has increased by 4 percent.* **2** PHRASE If something **pays dividends**, it brings advantages at a later date. ❑ *Things you do now to improve your health will pay dividends later on.* [from Latin]

**di**|**vine** /dɪvaɪn/ ADJ You use **divine** to describe something that is provided by or relates to a god or goddess. ❑ *...a divine punishment.* ● **di**|**vine**|**ly** ADV ❑ *The work was divinely inspired.* ● **di**|**vin**|**ity** /dɪvɪnɪti/ N-UNCOUNT ❑ *...the divinity of Christ's word.* [from Latin]

**div**|**ing** /daɪvɪŋ/ → see **dive**

**di**|**vi**|**sion** /dɪvɪʒⁿn/ (**divisions**) **1** N-UNCOUNT The **division of** something is the act of separating it **into** two or more distinct parts. ❑ *...the unification of Germany, after its division into two states.* ❑ *The division of labor between workers and management will change.* **2** N-UNCOUNT **Division** is the arithmetical process of dividing one number into another number. ❑ *I taught my daughter how to do division.* **3** N-VAR A **division** is a significant

distinction or argument between two groups. ❑ *The division between the rich West and the poor East remains.* **4** N-COUNT In a large organization, a **division** is a group of departments whose work is done in the same place or is connected with similar tasks. ❑ *...the bank's Latin American division.* ● **di**|**vi**|**sion**|**al** ADJ ❑ *She is divisional sales manager for the Philadelphia region.* [from Latin]
→ see **mathematics**

**di**|**vi**|**sive** /dɪvaɪsɪv/ ADJ Something that is **divisive** causes unfriendliness and argument between people. ❑ *The subject of women priests is a divisive issue among Christians.* [from Latin]

**di**|**vorce** /dɪvɔrs/ (**divorces, divorcing, divorced**)
**1** N-VAR A **divorce** is the formal ending of a marriage by law. ❑ *Many marriages end in divorce.* **2** V-RECIP If a man and woman **divorce** or if one of them **divorces** the other, their marriage is legally ended. ❑ *He and Lillian got divorced.* ❑ *He divorced me and married my friend.* **3** V-T If one thing cannot **be divorced from** another, the two things cannot be considered as different and separate things. ❑ *Democracy cannot be divorced from social and economic progress.* [from Old French]

**di**|**vor**|**cé** /dɪvɔrseɪ, -vɔrseɪ/ (**divorcés**) N-COUNT A **divorcé** is a man who is divorced. [from Old French]

**di**|**vorced** /dɪvɔrst/ **1** ADJ Someone who **is divorced** from their former husband or wife has separated from them and is no longer legally married to them. ❑ *He is divorced, with a young son.* **2** ADJ If you say that one thing **is divorced from** another, you mean that the two things are very different and separate from each other. ❑ *...theories divorced from reality.* [from Old French]

**di**|**vor**|**cée** /dɪvɔrseɪ, -si/ (**divorcées**) N-COUNT A **divorcée** is a woman who is divorced. ❑ *He married Clare Hollway, a divorcée.* [from Old French]

**di**|**vulge** /dɪvʌldʒ, daɪ-/ (**divulges, divulging, divulged**) V-T If you **divulge** a piece of secret or private information, you tell it to someone. [FORMAL] ❑ *Officials refuse to divulge details of the talks.* [from Latin]

**DIY** /di aɪ waɪ/ N-UNCOUNT **DIY** is the activity of making or repairing things yourself, especially in your home. **DIY** is an abbreviation for **do-it-yourself.** ❑ *He's useless at DIY. He won't even put up a shelf.*

**diz**|**zy** /dɪzi/ (**dizzier, dizziest**) ADJ If you feel **dizzy**, you feel that you are losing your balance and are about to fall. ❑ *Her head hurt, and she felt slightly dizzy.* ● **diz**|**zi**|**ness** N-UNCOUNT ❑ *His head injury caused dizziness.* [from Old English]

**diz**|**zy**|**ing** /dɪziɪŋ/ ADJ You can use **dizzying** to emphasize that something impresses you, though it makes you a bit confused or unsteady. ❑ *...one of the dizzying changes that have taken place.* ❑ *We're descending now at dizzying speed.* [from Old English]

**DJ** /di dʒeɪ/ (**DJs**) also **D.J.** or **dj** N-COUNT A **DJ** is the same as a **disc jockey.**

**DNA** /di ɛn eɪ/ N-UNCOUNT **DNA** is an acid in the chromosomes in the center of the cells of living things. DNA determines the particular structure and functions of every cell and is responsible for characteristics being passed on from parents to their children. **DNA** is an abbreviation for "deoxyribonucleic acid." ❑ *A DNA sample was taken.*
→ see **clone**

d

**DNA finger|print|ing** N-UNCOUNT
**DNA fingerprinting** is the same as **genetic fingerprinting**.

---

**do**

❶ AUXILIARY VERB USES
❷ OTHER VERB USES

---

❶ **do** /də, STRONG duː/ (**does, doing, did, done**)

> **Do** is used as an auxiliary with the simple present tense. **Did** is used as an auxiliary with the simple past tense. In spoken English, negative forms of **do** are often shortened, for example, **do not** is shortened to **don't** and **did not** is shortened to **didn't**.

**1** AUX **Do** is used to form the negative of main verbs, by putting "not" after "do" and before the main verb without "to." ❑ *They don't work very hard.* ❑ *I did not know Jamie had a knife.* **2** AUX **Do** is used to form questions, by putting the subject after "do" and before the main verb without "to." ❑ *Do you like music?* ❑ *What did he say?* **3** AUX **Do** is used in question tags. ❑ *You know about Andy, don't you?* **4** AUX You use **do** when you are confirming or contradicting a statement containing "do," or giving a negative or positive answer to a question. ❑ *"Do you think he is telling the truth?"* — *"Yes, I do."* **5** V-T/V-I **Do** can be used to refer back to another verb group when you are comparing or contrasting two things, or saying that they are the same. ❑ *I earn more money than he does.* ❑ *I have dreams, as do all mothers, about what life will be like when my girls are grown.* **6** V-T You use **do** after "so" and "nor" to say that the same statement is true for two people or groups. ❑ *You know that's true, and so do I.* [from Old English]

❷ **do** /duː/ (**does, doing, did, done**) **1** V-T When you **do** something, you take some action or perform an activity or task. **Do** is often used instead of a more specific verb, to talk about a common action involving a particular thing. ❑ *I was trying to do some work.* ❑ *After lunch Elizabeth and I did the dishes.* **2** V-T If you **do** something **about** a problem, you take action to try to solve it. ❑ *They refuse to do anything about the real cause of crime: poverty.* **3** V-T If an action or event **does** a particular thing, such as harm or good, it has that result or effect. ❑ *A few bombs can do a lot of damage.* **4** V-T If you ask someone what they **do**, you want to know what their job or profession is. ❑ *"What does your father do?"* — *"He's a doctor."* **5** V-T If you **are doing** something, you are busy or active in some way, or have planned an activity for some time in the future. ❑ *Are you doing anything tomorrow night?* **6** V-I If someone or something **does** well or badly, they are successful or unsuccessful. ❑ *Connie did well at school and graduated with honors.* **7** V-T You can use **do** when referring to the speed or rate that something or someone achieves or is able to achieve. ❑ *They were doing 70 miles an hour.* **8** V-T/V-I If you say that something **will do** or **will do** you, you mean that it is satisfactory. ❑ *Wear suitable clothes — anything warm will do.* ❑ *Twenty dollars will do me fine thanks.* **9** PHRASE If you say that you **could do with** something, you mean that you need it or would benefit from it. ❑ *I could do with a cup of tea.* **10** PHRASE If you ask **what** someone or something **is doing** in a particular place, you are asking why they are there. ❑ *"What are you*

doing here?" he said, clearly surprised.* **11** PHRASE If you say that one thing **has** something **to do with** or is something **to do with** another thing, you mean that the two things are connected or that the first thing is about the second thing. ❑ *Mr. Butterfield denies having anything to do with it.* [from Old English]

▶ **do away with** PHR-VERB If you **do away with** something, you remove it completely or put an end to it. ❑ *This device does away with the need for batteries.*

▶ **do over** PHR-VERB If you **do** a task **over**, you perform it again from the beginning. ❑ *He made me do it over twice.*

▶ **do up** PHR-VERB If you **do** something **up**, you fasten it. ❑ *Mari did up the buttons.*

▶ **do without** PHR-VERB If you **do without** something you need, want, or usually have, you are able to survive, continue, or succeed although you do not have it. ❑ *We can't do without the help of your organization.*

**DOB** also **d.o.b.** **DOB** is a written abbreviation for **date of birth**, used especially on official forms.

**dock** /dɒk/ (**docks, docking, docked**) **1** N-COUNT A **dock** is an enclosed area in a harbor where

dock

ships go to be loaded, unloaded, and repaired. ❑ *She headed for the docks.* **2** N-COUNT A **dock** is a platform for loading vehicles or trains. ❑ *The truck left the loading dock.* **3** N-COUNT A **dock** is a small structure at the

edge of water where boats can tie up, especially one that is privately owned. ❑ *He had a house and a dock and a little boat.* **4** V-T/V-I When a ship **docks** or **is docked**, it is brought into a dock. ❑ *The crash happened as the ferry tried to dock on Staten Island.* **5** V-T If you **dock** someone's pay or money, you take some of the money away. ❑ *He threatens to dock her fee.* **6** V-RECIP When one spacecraft **docks** or **is docked with** another, the two craft join together in space. ❑ *The space shuttle Atlantis is scheduled to dock with Russia's Mir space station.* **7** N-SING In a law court, **the dock** is where the person accused of a crime stands or sits. ❑ *…the prisoner in the dock.* [Senses 1–4 and 6 from Middle Dutch. Sense 7 from Flemish.]

**dock|et** /dɒkɪt/ (**dockets**) N-COUNT A **docket** is a list of cases waiting for trial in a law court. [mainly AM] ❑ *The Court has 1,400 appeals on its docket.*

**doc|tor** /dɒktər/ (**doctors, doctoring, doctored**) **1** N-COUNT; N-TITLE; N-VOC A **doctor** is someone who has a degree in medicine and treats people who are sick or injured. ❑ *Do not discontinue the treatment without consulting your doctor.* **2** N-COUNT; N-TITLE; N-VOC A **dentist** or **veterinarian** can also be called **doctor**. **3** N-COUNT; N-TITLE A **doctor** is someone who has been awarded the highest academic degree by a university. ❑ *He is a doctor of philosophy.* **4** V-T If someone **doctors** something, they change it in order to deceive people. ❑ *…a doctored photo.* [from Latin]

**doc|tor|ate** /dɒktərɪt/ (**doctorates**) N-COUNT A **doctorate** is the highest degree awarded by a university. ❑ *She has a doctorate in psychology from the University of Michigan.* [from Latin]

**doc|tor of phi|loso|phy** (**doctors of philosophy**) N-COUNT A **doctor of philosophy** is someone who has a **PhD**.

**doc|tor's of|fice** (**doctor's offices**) N-COUNT A **doctor's office** is the room or clinic where a doctor works. ❑ *...a visit to the doctor's office.*

**doc|trine** /dɒktrɪn/ (**doctrines**) **1** N-VAR A **doctrine** is a set of principles or beliefs. ❑ *...Christian doctrine.* ● **doc|tri|nal** /dɑktrɪnᵊl/ ADJ [FORMAL] ❑ *...doctrinal differences.* **2** N-COUNT A **doctrine** is a statement of official government policy, especially foreign policy. ❑ *...Bush's doctrine on terrorism.* [from Old French]

**docu|ment** (**documents, documenting, documented**)

> The noun is pronounced /dɒkyəmənt/. The verb is pronounced /dɒkyəmɛnt/.

**1** N-COUNT A **document** is one or more official pieces of paper with writing on them. ❑ *...legal documents.* **2** N-COUNT A **document** is a piece of text or graphics that is stored as a file on a computer. [COMPUTING] ❑ *Remember to save your document.* **3** V-T If you **document** something, you make a detailed record of it in writing or on film or tape. ❑ *He wrote a book documenting his prison experiences.* [from Latin]
→ see **diary, history, printing**

**docu|men|tary** /dɒkyəmɛntəri, -tri/ (**documentaries**) **1** N-COUNT A **documentary** is a television or radio program, or a movie, which shows real events or provides information about a particular subject. ❑ *...a TV documentary on crime.* **2** ADJ **Documentary** evidence consists of things that are written down. ❑ *The government has documentary evidence that the two countries are planning military action.* [from Latin]

**docu|men|ta|tion** /dɒkyəmɛnteɪʃᵊn/ N-UNCOUNT **Documentation** consists of documents which provide proof or evidence of something, or are a record of something. ❑ *Passengers must carry proper documentation.* [from Latin]

**dodge** /dɒdʒ/ (**dodges, dodging, dodged**) **1** V-I If you **dodge**, you move suddenly, often to avoid being hit, caught, or seen. ❑ *I dodged back into the alley and waited a minute.* **2** V-T If you **dodge** something, you avoid it by quickly moving aside or out of reach so that it cannot hit or reach you. ❑ *He desperately dodged a speeding car.* **3** V-T If you **dodge** something, you deliberately avoid doing it, thinking about it or dealing with it, often by being deceitful. ❑ *He dodged military service by pretending to be sick.*

**dodo** /doʊdoʊ/ (**dodos** or **dodoes**) N-COUNT A **dodo** was a very large bird that was unable to fly. Dodos are now extinct. [from Portuguese]

**does** /dəz, STRONG dʌz/ **Does** is the third person singular in the present tense of **do**. [from Old English]

**doesn't** /dʌzᵊnt/ **Doesn't** is the usual spoken form of "does not."

**dog** /dɒg/ (**dogs, dogging, dogged**) **1** N-COUNT A **dog** is an animal that is often kept by people as a pet. ❑ *He was walking his dog.* **2** V-T If problems or injuries **dog** you, they are with you all the time.

❑ *His career has been dogged by bad luck.* [from Old English]
→ see **disability, pet**

**dog days** N-PLURAL The hottest part of the summer is sometimes referred to as the **dog days**. ❑ *We're into the dog days of summer.* [from Late Latin]

**dog|ged** /dɒgɪd/ ADJ If you describe someone's actions as **dogged**, you mean that they are determined to continue with something even if it becomes difficult or dangerous. ❑ *By dogged determination, he improved.* ● **dog|ged|ly** ADV ❑ *She fought doggedly for her rights.* ● **dog|ged|ness** N-UNCOUNT ❑ *His doggedness was his great strength.* [from Old English]

**dog|gone** /dɒgɔn/ ADJ People sometimes use **doggone** to emphasize what they are saying, especially when they are annoyed. [INFORMAL] ❑ *The doggone business just keeps getting worse.* ● **Doggone** is also an adverb. ❑ *It was so doggone hot yesterday.*

**dog|house** /dɒghaʊs/ (**doghouses**) N-COUNT A **doghouse** is a small building made especially for a dog to sleep in.

**dog|ma** /dɒgmə/ (**dogmas**) N-VAR If you refer to a belief or a system of beliefs as a **dogma**, you disapprove of it because people are expected to accept that it is true, without questioning it. ❑ *Practical action is more important than political dogma.* [from Latin]

**dog|mat|ic** /dɒgmætɪk/ ADJ If you say that someone is **dogmatic**, you are critical of them because they are convinced that they are right, and refuse to consider that other opinions might also be justified. ❑ *Many writers had very dogmatic views.* ● **dog|mati|cal|ly** /dɒgmætɪkli/ ADV ❑ *He dogmatically opposed the plan.* ● **dog|ma|tism** /dɒgmətɪzəm/ N-UNCOUNT ❑ *We cannot allow dogmatism to stop progress.* [from Latin]

**doh** /doʊ/ also **d'oh** EXCLAM People sometimes say **doh** to show that they have made a silly mistake. [INFORMAL] ❑ *Doh! What are you doing?*

**do-it-yourself** N-UNCOUNT **Do-it-yourself** is the same as **DIY**.

**dol|drums** /doʊldrəmz/ PHRASE If an activity or situation is **in the doldrums**, it is very quiet and nothing new or exciting is happening. ❑ *The economy is in the doldrums.* [from Old English]

**doll** /dɒl/ (**dolls**) N-COUNT A **doll** is a child's toy which looks like a small person or baby.

**dol|lar** /dɒlər/ (**dollars**) N-COUNT The **dollar** is the unit of money used in the U.S., Canada, Australia, and some other countries. It is represented by the symbol $. ❑ *She earns seven dollars an hour.* [from Low German]

**doll|house** /dɒlhaʊs/ (**dollhouses**) N-COUNT A **dollhouse** is a toy in the form of a small house, which contains tiny dolls and furniture for children to play with.

**dol|phin** /dɒlfɪn/ (**dolphins**) N-COUNT A **dolphin** is a mammal with fins and a pointed mouth which lives in the sea. [from Old French]
→ see **whale**

dolphin

Word Link **dom ≈ home :** domain, dome, dome**stic**

Word Link **dom, domin ≈ rule, master :** dominate, domain, pre**dominant**

**do|main** /doʊmeɪn/ (**domains**) **1** N-COUNT A **domain** is a particular field of thought, activity, or interest. [FORMAL] ❑ ...a theory which is accepted in the domain of science. **2** N-COUNT On the Internet, a **domain** is a set of addresses that shows, for example, the category or geographical area that an Internet address belongs to. [COMPUTING] ❑ ...a domain name. [from French]

dome

**dome** /doʊm/ (**domes**) N-COUNT A **dome** is a round roof. ❑ ...the dome of the building. [from French]

**do|mes|tic** /dəmɛstɪk/ **1** ADJ **Domestic** political activities, events, and situations happen or exist within one particular country. ❑ ...over 100 domestic flights a day. **2** ADJ **Domestic** means relating to or concerned with the home and family. ❑ ...a plan for sharing domestic chores. ❑ ...domestic appliances such as washing machines. **3** ADJ A **domestic** animal is one that is not wild and is kept either on a farm or as a pet. ❑ A domestic cat is a great companion. [from Old French]

**domi|nant** /dɒmɪnənt/ **1** ADJ Someone or something that is **dominant** is more powerful, successful, influential, or noticeable than other people or things. ❑ ...his party's dominant position in politics. ● **domi|nance** N-UNCOUNT ❑ By 1942 Hitler had achieved dominance in all of Europe except Britain. **2** ADJ A **dominant** gene is one that produces a particular characteristic, whether a person has only one of these genes from one parent, or two genes, one from each parent. Compare **recessive**. [from Latin]

**domi|nate** /dɒmɪneɪt/ (**dominates, dominating, dominated**) **1** V-T/V-I To **dominate** a situation means to be the most powerful or important person or thing in it. ❑ The book dominated the bestseller lists. ❑ ...countries where life is dominated by war. ❑ At the conference, issues about the environment will dominate. ● **domi|na|tion** /dɒmɪneɪʃⁿn/ N-UNCOUNT ❑ ...the domination of the market by a small number of organizations. **2** V-T If one country or person **dominates** another, they have power over them. ❑ He denied that his country wants to dominate Europe. ❑ Women are no longer dominated by men. ● **domi|nat|ing** ADJ ❑ She was a dominating woman. ● **domi|na|tion** N-UNCOUNT ❑ ...domination by a foreign country. [from Latin]

**do|min|ion** /dəmɪnyən/ (**dominions**) N-COUNT A **dominion** is an area of land that is controlled by a ruler. ❑ The area is a dominion of the Brazilian people. [from Latin]

**domi|no** /dɒmɪnoʊ/ (**dominoes**) N-VAR **Dominoes** is a game played with small rectangular blocks, called

dominoes

dominoes, that are marked with two groups of spots on one side. [from French]

Word Link **don ≈ giving :** donate, donor, par**don**

**do|nate** /doʊneɪt, doʊneɪt/ (**donates, donating, donated**) **1** V-T If you **donate** something to a charity or other organization, you give it to them. ❑ He often donates large amounts of money to charity. ● **do|na|tion** /doʊneɪʃⁿn/ (**donations**) N-VAR ❑ ...the donation of his collection to the art gallery. ❑ Employees make regular donations to charity. **2** V-T If you **donate** your blood or a part of your body, you allow doctors to use it to help someone who is ill. ❑ ...people who donate their organs for use after death. ● **do|na|tion** N-UNCOUNT ❑ ...ways of encouraging organ donation. [from Latin]
→ see **donor**

**done** /dʌn/ **1 Done** is the past participle of **do**. **2** ADJ A task or activity that is **done** has been completed successfully. ❑ We thought the deal was done. **3** ADJ When something that you are cooking is **done**, it has been cooked long enough and is ready. ❑ As soon as the cake is done, remove it from the oven. [from Old English]

**don|key** /dɒŋki/ (**donkeys**) N-COUNT A **donkey** is an animal which is like a small horse with long ears.

**do|nor** /doʊnər/ (**donors**) **1** N-COUNT A **donor** is someone who gives a part of their body or some of their blood to be used by doctors to help a person who is ill. ❑ ...a blood donor. **2** N-COUNT A **donor** is a person or organization who gives something, especially money, to a charity, organization, or country that needs it. ❑ The money was provided by a wealthy donor. [from Old French]
→ see Word Web: **donor**

**don't** /doʊnt/ **Don't** is the usual spoken form of "do not."

**do|nut** /doʊnʌt, -nət/ (**donuts**) → see **doughnut**

**doom** /dum/ N-UNCOUNT **Doom** is a terrible future state or event which you cannot prevent. ❑ ...his warnings of doom. [from Old English]

**doomed** /dumd/ **1** ADJ If something **is doomed** to happen, or if you **are doomed to** a particular state, something unpleasant is certain to happen, and you can do nothing to prevent it. ❑ Their plans seemed doomed to failure. **2** ADJ Someone or something that is **doomed** is certain to fail or be destroyed. ❑ The project was doomed from the start. [from Old English]

**door** /dɔr/ (**doors**) **1** N-COUNT A **door** is a piece of wood, glass, or metal, which is moved to open and close the entrance to a building, room, closet, or vehicle. ❑ I knocked at the front door but there was no answer. **2** N-COUNT A **door** is the space in a wall when a door is open. ❑ She looked through the door of the kitchen. **3** PHRASE When you **answer the door**, you go and open the door because a visitor has knocked on it or rung the bell. ❑ Carol answered the door as soon as I knocked. **4** PHRASE If someone goes **from door to door** or goes **door to door**, they go along a street stopping at each house in turn, for example, selling something. ❑ They are going from door to door collecting money. **5** PHRASE When you are **out of doors**, you are not inside a building, but in the open air. ❑ The weather was fine enough for working out of doors. [from Old English]

**Word Web** donor

Many people **give donations**. They like to **help** others. They **donate money**, clothes, food, or volunteer their time. Some people even give parts of their bodies. Doctors performed the first successful human **organ transplants** in the 1950s. Today this type of operation is very common. The problem now is finding enough **donors** to meet the needs of potential **recipients**. Organs such as the **kidney** often come from a living donor. **Hearts, lungs**, and other vital organs come from donors who have died. Of course our health care system relies on **blood** donors. They help save lives every day.

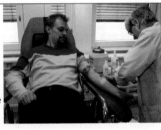

d

**do-or-die** ◼ ADJ A **do-or-die** battle or struggle is one that involves a determined or desperate effort to succeed. ❑ *The management team are making a do-or-die effort to turn the company into a successful business.* ◼ PHRASE If something is **do-or-die for** someone or something, it will determine whether they succeed or fail. ❑ *Nobody will know until Monday, when it is do-or-die for the deal.*

**door|step** /dɔrstɛp/ (**doorsteps**) ◼ N-COUNT A **doorstep** is a step in front of a door on the outside of a building. ❑ *I went and sat on the doorstep.* ◼ PHRASE If a place is **on** your **doorstep**, it is very near to where you live. ❑ *It is easy to forget what is happening on our own doorstep.*

**door|way** /dɔrweɪ/ (**doorways**) N-COUNT A **doorway** is a space in a wall where a door opens and closes. ❑ *David was standing in the doorway.* [from Old English]

**dope** /doʊp/ (**dopes, doping, doped**) ◼ N-UNCOUNT **Dope** is an illegal drug, especially marijuana. [INFORMAL] ◼ V-T If someone **dopes** a person or animal or **dopes** their food, they force them to take drugs or put drugs into their food. ❑ *He doped the drink.* ❑ *She was doped with painkilling drugs.* [from Dutch]

**dor|mant** /dɔrmənt/ ADJ Something that is **dormant** has not been active or used for a long time. ❑ *The dormant volcano of Mount St. Helens erupted in 1980.* [from Old French]

**dor|mi|tory** /dɔrmɪtɔri/ (**dormitories**) ◼ N-COUNT A **dormitory** is a building at a college or university where students live. ❑ *She lived in a college dormitory.* ◼ N-COUNT A **dormitory** is a large bedroom where several people sleep, for example, in a boarding school. ❑ *...the boys' dormitory.* [from Latin]

**dos|age** /doʊsɪdʒ/ (**dosages**) N-COUNT A **dosage** is the amount of a medicine or drug that someone takes or should take. ❑ *He was put on a high dosage of the drug.* [from French]

**dose** /doʊs/ (**doses**) N-COUNT A **dose of** medicine or a drug is a measured amount of it which is intended to be taken at one time. ❑ *One dose of penicillin can get rid of the infection.* [from French]

**dos|si|er** /dɒsieɪ/ (**dossiers**) N-COUNT A **dossier** is a collection of papers containing information on a particular subject. ❑ *They published a dossier of evidence on the subject.* [from French]

**dot** /dɒt/ (**dots**) N-COUNT A **dot** is a very small round mark, for example, one that is used as the top part of the letter "i," as a period, or in the names of websites. ❑ *...a system of painting using small dots of color.* [from Old English]

**dot-com** (**dot-coms**) also **dotcom** N-COUNT A **dot-com** is a company that does all or most of its business on the Internet. ❑ *In 1999, dot-coms spent more than $1 billion on TV advertising.*

**dote** /doʊt/ (**dotes, doting, doted**) V-I If you **dote on** someone, you love them very much and ignore their faults. ❑ *He dotes on his son.* ● **dot|ing** ADJ ❑ *His doting parents bought him his first racing bike.* [from Middle Dutch]

**dot|ted** /dɒtɪd/ ◼ ADJ A **dotted** line is a line which is made of a row of dots. ❑ *Cut along the dotted line.* ◼ PHRASE If you **sign on the dotted line**, you formally agree to something by signing an official document. ◼ ADJ If a place or object is **dotted with** things, it has many of those things scattered over its surface. ❑ *The maps were dotted with the names of towns.* ❑ *Many plants are dotted around the house.* [from Old English]

**dou|ble** /dʌbᵊl/ (**doubles, doubling, doubled**) ◼ ADJ You use **double** to indicate that something includes or is made of two things of the same kind. ❑ *...a pair of double doors.* ❑ *...a double murder.* ◼ ADJ You use **double** to describe something which is twice the normal size or can hold twice the normal quantity of something. ❑ *...a double helping of ice cream.* ◼ ADJ A **double** room is a room intended for two people, usually a couple, to stay or live in. ❑ *The hotel charges $180 for a double room.* ● **Double** is also a noun. ❑ *The Grand Hotel costs around $300 a night for a double.* ◼ ADJ A **double** bed is a bed that is wide enough for two people to sleep in. ❑ *One bedroom had a double bed.* ◼ V-T/V-I When something **doubles** or when you **double** it, it becomes twice as great in number, amount, or size. ❑ *The number of students has doubled from 50 to 100.* ◼ V-I If a person or thing **doubles as** someone or something else, they have a second job or purpose as well as their main one. ❑ *Lots of homes double as businesses.* ◼ N-UNCOUNT In tennis or badminton, when people play **doubles**, two teams consisting of two players on each team play against each other on the same court. ❑ *In the doubles, they beat the Williams sisters.* [from Old French] ◼ in **double figures** → see **figure** → see **hotel, tennis**

▸ **double over** PHR-VERB If you **double over**, you bend your body quickly or violently, for example, because you are laughing a lot or because you are feeling a lot of pain. ❑ *Everyone doubled over in laughter.*

**double-barreled** ◼ ADJ A **double-barreled** gun has two barrels. ❑ *…a double-barreled shotgun.* ◼ ADJ **Double-barreled** is used to describe something such as a plan which has two main parts.

**dou|ble bass** /dʌbᵊl beɪs/ (**double basses**) also **double-bass** N-VAR A **double bass** is the largest instrument in the violin family.
→ see **orchestra, string**

**double-click** (**double-clicks, double-clicking, double-clicked**) V-T If you **double-click on** an area of a computer screen, you point the cursor at that area and press one of the buttons on the mouse twice quickly in order to make something happen. [COMPUTING] ❑ *Go to Control Panel and double-click on Sounds for a list of sounds.*

**double-header** (**double-headers**) N-COUNT A **double-header** is a sporting contest between two teams that involves two separate games being played, often on the same day.

**dou|ble he|lix** /dʌbᵊl hiːlɪks/ N-SING The **double helix** is a term used to describe the shape of the DNA molecule, which resembles a long ladder twisted into a coil.

**dou|ble-re|place|ment re|ac|tion** (**double-replacement reactions**) N-COUNT A **double-replacement reaction** is a chemical reaction between two compounds in which some of the atoms in each compound switch places and form two new compounds. [TECHNICAL]

**double-space** (**double-spaces, double-spacing, double-spaced**) also **double space** ◼ V-T If you **double-space** something you are writing or typing, you include a full line of space between each line of writing. ❑ *Double-space the list.*
● **double-spaced** ADJ ❑ *…forty pages of double-spaced text.* ● **dou|ble spac|ing** N-UNCOUNT ❑ *Single spacing is used within paragraphs, double spacing between paragraphs.* ◼ N-COUNT A **double space** is a full line of space between each line of a piece of writing. ❑ *Leave a double space between entries.*

**dou|bly** /dʌbli/ ◼ ADV You use **doubly** to indicate that a situation has two aspects or features. ❑ *The funeral was a doubly sad occasion — burying my father and realizing that I could never say sorry to him.* ◼ ADV You use **doubly** to emphasize that something exists or happens to a greater degree than usual. ❑ *In pregnancy, eating well is doubly important.* [from Old French]

**doubt** /daʊt/ (**doubts, doubting, doubted**) ◼ N-VAR If you have **doubt** or **doubts** about something, you feel uncertain about it. ❑ *Rendell raised doubts about the plan.* ❑ *There is little doubt that the Earth's climate is changing.* ◼ V-T If you **doubt** something, or if you **doubt** whether something is true, genuine or possible, you believe that it is probably not true, genuine or possible. ❑ *Many people doubted whether it would happen.* ❑ *No one doubted his ability.* ◼ V-T If you **doubt** someone or **doubt** their word, you think that they may not be telling the truth. ❑ *No one doubted him.* ◼ PHRASE You say that something is **beyond doubt** or **beyond reasonable doubt** when you are certain that it is true and it cannot be contradicted or disproved. ❑ *The vote showed beyond doubt that people wanted independence.* ◼ PHRASE If you are **in doubt** about something, you feel unsure or uncertain about it. ❑ *He is in no doubt about what to do.* ◼ PHRASE If you

say that something is **in doubt** or **open to doubt**, you consider it to be uncertain or unreliable. ❑ *The future of the business was still in doubt.* ◼ PHRASE You use **no doubt** to emphasize that something seems certain or very likely to you. ❑ *She will no doubt be here soon.* ◼ PHRASE If you say that something is true **without doubt** or **without a doubt**, you are emphasizing that it is definitely true. ❑ *This was without doubt the best day of Amanda's life.* [from Old French] ◼ **the benefit of the doubt** → see **benefit** ◼ **a shadow of a doubt** → see **shadow**

**doubt|ful** /daʊtfᵊl/ ◼ ADJ If it is **doubtful that** something will happen, it seems unlikely to happen or you are uncertain whether it will happen. ❑ *After the accident, it seemed doubtful that he would be able to walk again.* ◼ ADJ If you are **doubtful about** something, you feel unsure or uncertain about it. ❑ *I was still very doubtful about the chances for success.* ● **doubt|ful|ly** ADV ❑ *Keeton shook his head doubtfully.* [from Old French]

**doubt|less** /daʊtlɪs/ ADV If you say that something is **doubtless** true, you mean that you think it is probably or almost certainly true. ❑ *He will doubtless try and persuade his colleagues to change their minds.* [from Old French]

**dough** /doʊ/ N-UNCOUNT **Dough** is a mixture of flour, water, and sometimes also fat and sugar. It can be cooked to make bread or pastry. ❑ *Roll out the dough into one large circle.* [from Old English]

**dough|nut** /doʊnʌt, -nət/ (**doughnuts**) also **donut** N-COUNT A **doughnut** is a piece of sweet dough that has been cooked in hot oil.

**dour** /dʊər, daʊər/ ADJ If you describe someone as **dour**, you mean that they are very serious and unfriendly. ❑ *He was often dour.* [from Latin]

**douse** /daʊs/ (**douses, dousing, doused**) also **dowse** ◼ V-T If you **douse** a fire, you stop it from burning by pouring a lot of water over it. ❑ *The firefighters began to douse the fire with water.* ◼ V-T If you **douse** someone or something **with** a liquid, you throw a lot of that liquid over them. ❑ *He doused his french fries with ketchup.*

**dove** (**doves**)

Pronounced /dʌv/ for meaning ◼, and /doʊv/ for meaning ◼.

◼ N-COUNT A **dove** is a bird that looks like a pigeon but is smaller and lighter in color. Doves are often used as a symbol of peace. ◼ **Dove** is sometimes used as the past tense of **dive**. [from Old English]

dove

# down

**❶ PREPOSITION AND ADVERB USES**
**❷ ADJECTIVE USES**
**❸ NOUN USES**

**❶ down** /daʊn/

**Down** is often used with verbs of movement, such as "fall" and "pull," and also in phrasal verbs such as "bring down" and "calm down."

◼ PREP **Down** means toward the ground or a lower level, or in a lower place. ❑ *I marched down the hill.* ❑ *A man came down the stairs to meet them.* ❑ *He*

was already halfway down the hill. ❑ She was looking
down at her papers. ● **Down** is also an adverb. ❑ She
went down to the kitchen. ② PREP If you go or look
**down** something such as a road or river, you go or
look along it. If you are **down** a road or river, you
are somewhere along it. ❑ They set off up one street
and down another. ③ ADV If you put something
**down**, you put it onto a surface. ❑ Danny put
down his glass. ④ ADV If an amount or level of
something goes **down**, it decreases. ❑ Prices
came down today. ❑ Inflation is down to three percent.
⑤ PHRASE If someone or something is **down for** a
particular thing, it has been arranged that they
will do that thing, or that thing will happen.
❑ Mark was down for an interview. [from Old English]
⑥ **up and down** → see **up**

❷ **down** /daʊn/ ① ADJ If you are feeling **down**,
you are feeling unhappy or depressed. [INFORMAL]
❑ The man sounded really down. ② ADJ If something
is **down on** paper, it has been written on the paper.
❑ That meeting wasn't down on the calendar. ③ ADJ If a
piece of equipment, especially a computer system,
is **down**, it is temporarily not working. Compare
**up**. ❑ The computer's down again. [from Old
English]

❸ **down** /daʊn/ N-UNCOUNT **Down** consists of
the small, soft feathers on young birds. **Down** is
used to make bed-covers and pillows. ❑ ...goose
down. [of Scandinavian origin]

**down|draft** /daʊndræft/ (**downdrafts**)
N-COUNT A **downdraft** is a downward current of
air, usually accompanied by rain.

> **Word Link** down ≈ below, lower : down**fall**,
> down**hill**, down**stairs**

**down|fall** /daʊnfɔl/ (**downfalls**) ① N-COUNT
The **downfall** of a successful or powerful person or
institution is their loss of success or power. ❑ His
lack of experience led to his downfall. ② N-COUNT The
thing that was a person's **downfall** caused them
to fail or lose power. ❑ Jeremy's honesty was his
downfall.

**down feath|er** (**down feathers**) N-COUNT
**Down feathers** are the soft feathers on the bodies
of young birds. [TECHNICAL]

**down|grade** /daʊngreɪd/ (**downgrades,
downgrading, downgraded**) V-T If someone or
something **is downgraded**, their situation is
changed to a lower level of importance or value.
❑ The boy's condition was downgraded from critical to
serious. ❑ There was no criticism of her work until after
she was downgraded.

**down|hill** /daʊnhɪl/ ① ADV If something or
someone is moving **downhill** or is **downhill**, they
are moving down a slope or are located toward
the bottom of a hill. ❑ He walked downhill toward the
river. ● **Downhill** is also an adjective. ❑ ...downhill
ski runs. ② ADV If you say that something **is going
downhill**, you mean that it is becoming worse or
less successful. ❑ Since I started to work longer hours
things have gone steadily downhill.

**down|load** /daʊnloʊd/ (**downloads,
downloading, downloaded**) V-T To **download** data
means to transfer it to or from a computer along
a line such as a telephone line, a radio link, or a
computer network. ❑ You can download the software
from the Internet.

**down|load|able** /daʊnloʊdəbᵊl/ ADJ If a

computer file or program is **downloadable**, it can
be downloaded to another computer. [COMPUTING]
❑ ...downloadable computer games.

**down pay|ment** (**down payments**) also
**downpayment** N-COUNT If you make a **down
payment on** something, you pay only a percentage
of the total cost when you buy it. You then finish
paying for it later, usually by paying a certain
amount every month. ❑ The money was used as a
down payment on a house.

**down|pour** /daʊnpɔr/ (**downpours**) N-COUNT
A **downpour** is a sudden and unexpected heavy fall
of rain. ❑ ...a sudden downpour of rain.

**down|right** /daʊnraɪt/ ADV You use **downright**
to emphasize unpleasant or bad qualities or
behavior. ❑ It is downright dangerous to drive with
a broken leg. ● **Downright** is also an adjective.
❑ ...downright bad manners.

**down|scale** /daʊnskeɪl/ ADJ If you describe
a product or service as **downscale**, you think
that it is cheap and not very good in quality.
❑ ...downscale stores.

**down|side** /daʊnsaɪd/ N-SING The **downside of**
a situation is the aspect of it which is less positive,
pleasant, or useful than its other aspects. ❑ The
downside of buying cars on the Internet is that you can't
really see what they're like.

**down|stage** /daʊnsteɪdʒ/ ADV When an actor
is **downstage** or moves **downstage**, he or she
is or moves toward the front part of the stage.
[TECHNICAL] ● **Downstage** is also an adjective.
❑ ...downstage members of the cast.

**down|stairs** /daʊnstɛərz/ ① ADV If you go
**downstairs** in a building, you go down a staircase
toward the ground floor. ❑ Denise went downstairs
and made some tea. ② ADV If something or someone
is **downstairs** in a building, they are on the ground
floor or on a lower floor than you. ❑ The telephone
was downstairs in the kitchen. ③ ADJ **Downstairs**
means situated on the ground floor of a building
or on a lower floor than you are. ❑ She painted the
downstairs rooms.

**Down's syn|drome** N-UNCOUNT **Down's
syndrome** is a disorder that some people are born
with. People who have Down's syndrome have
a flat forehead and sloping eyes and lower than
average intelligence.

**down|stream** /daʊnstrim/ ADV **Downstream**
means toward the mouth of a river. ❑ We sailed
downstream. ● **Downstream** is also an adjective.
❑ The dam broke and flooded downstream cities such as
Wuhan.

**down|time** /daʊntaɪm/ ① N-UNCOUNT In
computing, **downtime** is time when a computer
is not working. ② N-UNCOUNT **Downtime** is time
when people are not working. ❑ Downtime can cost
businesses a lot of money.

**down-to-earth** ADJ If you say that someone
is **down-to-earth**, you approve of the fact that
they concern themselves with practical things
and actions, rather than with abstract theories.
❑ Gloria is the most down-to-earth person I've ever
met.

**down|town** /daʊntaʊn/ ADJ **Downtown**
places are in or toward the center of a large town
or city, where the stores and places of business
are. ❑ ...We have an office in downtown Chicago.
● **Downtown** is also an adverb. ❑ He worked

*downtown for an insurance firm.*

**down|turn** /daʊntɜrn/ (**downturns**) N-COUNT
If there is a **downturn** in the economy or in a
company or industry, it becomes worse or less
successful than it had been. ❑ *They predicted a
severe economic downturn.*

**down|ward** /daʊnwərd/

> The form **downwards** is also used for the adverb.

**1** ADJ A **downward** movement or look is directed
toward a lower place or a lower level. ❑ *...a
downward movement of the hands.* **2** ADJ If you refer
to a **downward** trend, you mean that something
is decreasing or that a situation is getting
worse. ❑ *There has actually been a downward trend in
summer temperatures.* **3** ADV If you move or look
**downward**, you move or look toward the ground
or a lower level. ❑ *Benedict pointed downward
with his stick.* **4** ADV If an amount or rate moves
**downward**, it decreases. ❑ *Inflation is moving firmly
downward.* [from Old English]

**dowse** /daʊs/ (**dowses, dowsing, dowsed**) → see
**douse**

**doze** /doʊz/ (**dozes, dozing, dozed**) V-I When
you **doze**, you sleep lightly or for a short period.
❑ *She dozed for a while in the cabin.* [from Old Norse]
→ see **sleep**

▶ **doze off** PHR-VERB If you **doze off**, you fall into a
light sleep. ❑ *I closed my eyes and dozed off.*

**doz|en** /dʌzᵊn/ (**dozens**)

> The plural form is **dozen** after a number, or after
> a word or expression referring to a number, such
> as "several" or "a few."

**1** NUM A **dozen** means twelve. ❑ *The bus had
room for two dozen people.* ❑ *In half a dozen words, he
explained what was wrong.* **2** QUANT If you refer to
**dozens of** things or people, you are emphasizing
that there are very many of them. ❑ *Last week's
storm destroyed dozens of buildings.* [from Old
French]

**Dr.** (**Drs.**) **Dr.** is a written abbreviation for **Doctor**.
❑ *...Dr. John Hardy of St. Mary's Hospital.*

**drab** /dræb/ (**drabber, drabbest**) ADJ Something
that is **drab** is dull and boring. ❑ *...his drab little
office.* ● **drab|ness** N-UNCOUNT ❑ *...the drabness of
the small room.* [from Old French]

**dra|co|nian** /dreɪkoʊniən, drə-/ ADJ **Draconian**
laws or measures are extremely harsh and severe.
[FORMAL] ❑ *There will be no draconian measures to
lower health care costs.* [after Draco, a 7th century
Athenian statesman]

**draft** /dræft/ (**drafts, drafting, drafted**)
**1** N-COUNT A **draft** is an early version of a letter,
book, or speech. ❑ *I rewrote the rough draft.* ❑ *I
e-mailed a first draft of the article to him.* **2** N-COUNT
A **draft** is a current of air that comes into a place
in an undesirable way. ❑ *Block drafts around doors
and windows.* **3** V-T When you **draft** a letter, book,
or speech, you write the first version of it. ❑ *He
drafted a letter to the manager.* **4** V-T If you **are
drafted**, you are ordered to serve in the armed
forces, usually for a limited period of time. ❑ *He
was drafted into the U.S. Army.* **5** V-T If people **are
drafted** to do something, they are asked to do
a particular job. ❑ *Foxton was drafted to run the
organization.* **6** N-SING **The draft** is the practice
of ordering people to serve in the armed forces,
usually for a limited period of time. ❑ *...his effort*

*to avoid the draft.* [from Old Norse]

| **Word Partnership** | Use *draft* with : |
|---|---|
| ADJ. | **final** draft, **rough** draft **1** |
| V. | **revise** a draft, **write** a draft **1**<br>**feel** a draft **2**<br>**dodge** the draft **6** |
| N. | draft **a letter**, draft **a speech** **3** |

**draft dodg|er** (**draft dodgers**) N-COUNT A **draft
dodger** is someone who avoids joining the armed
forces when normally they would have to join.

**drag** /dræg/ (**drags, dragging, dragged**) **1** V-T If
you **drag** something, you pull it along the ground,
often with difficulty. ❑ *He dragged his chair toward*

**drag**

*the table.* **2** V-T If
you **drag** a computer
image, you use the
mouse to move
the position of
the image on the
screen, or to change
its size or shape.
[COMPUTING] ❑ *Use
your mouse to drag
the pictures.* **3** V-T

If someone **drags** you somewhere, they pull
you there, or force you to go there by physically
threatening you. ❑ *They dragged the men out of the
car.* **4** V-T If you **drag** someone somewhere they
do not want to go, you make them go there. ❑ *He's
very friendly, when you can drag him away from his work!*
❑ *I find it really hard to drag myself out and exercise
regularly.* **5** V-T If the police **drag** a river or lake,
they pull nets or hooks across the bottom of it in
order to look for something. ❑ *Police are planning to
drag the pond.* **6** V-I If a period of time or an event
**drags**, it is very boring and seems to last a long
time. ❑ *The minutes dragged past.* **7** N-UNCOUNT
**Drag** is the resistance to movement that is
experienced by something that is moving through
air or through a fluid. [TECHNICAL] **8** PHRASE If
you **drag** your **feet** or **drag** your **heels**, you delay
doing something or do it very slowly because you
do not want to do it. ❑ *The government was dragging
its feet on the issue.* **9** PHRASE If a man is **in drag**,
he is wearing women's clothes; if a woman is **in
drag**, she is wearing men's clothes. [from Old
English]

▶ **drag out** **1** PHR-VERB If you **drag** something
**out**, you make it last for longer than is necessary.
❑ *They did everything they could to drag out the process.*
**2** PHR-VERB If you **drag** something **out of** a
person, you persuade them to tell you something
that they do not want to tell you. ❑ *She didn't want
to tell me what happened, but I dragged it out of her.*

**drag and drop** (**drags and drops, dragging and
dropping, dragged and dropped**) also **drag-and-
drop** **1** V-T If you **drag and drop** computer files or
images, you move them from one place to another
by clicking on them with the mouse and moving
them across the screen. ❑ *Drag and drop the folder
to the hard drive.* **2** N-UNCOUNT **Drag and drop** is a
method of moving computer files or images from
one place to another by clicking on them with
the mouse and moving them across the screen.
❑ *Copying software onto an iPod is as easy as drag and
drop.* ● **Drag and drop** is also an adjective. ❑ *...a
drag-and-drop text.*

**drag|on** /drǽgən/ (**dragons**) N-COUNT In stories and legends, a **dragon** is an animal like a big lizard. It has wings and claws, and breathes out fire. [from Old French]
→ see **fantasy**

**dragon|fly** /drǽgənflaɪ/ (**dragonflies**) N-COUNT **Dragonflies** are brightly colored insects with long, thin bodies and two sets of wings.
→ see **insect**

**drain** /dreɪn/ (**drains, draining, drained**) **1** V-T/ V-I If you **drain** a liquid from a place or object, you remove the liquid by causing it to flow somewhere else. If a liquid **drains** somewhere, it flows there. ❑ They built the tunnel to drain water out of the mines. ❑ ...springs and rivers that drain into lakes. **2** V-T/V-I If you **drain** a place or object, you dry it by causing water to flow out of it. If a place or object **drains**, water flows out of it until it is dry. ❑ ...attempts to drain flooded land. **3** V-T/V-I If you **drain** food or if food **drains**, you remove the liquid that it has been in, especially after it has been cooked or soaked in water. ❑ Drain the pasta well. **4** V-T If something **drains** you, it makes you feel physically and emotionally exhausted. ❑ All the worry drained me. ● **drained** ADJ ❑ I suffer from headaches, which make me feel completely drained. ● **drain|ing** ADJ ❑ This work is physically tiring and emotionally draining. **5** N-COUNT A **drain** is a pipe that carries water or sewage away from a place, or an opening in a surface that leads to the pipe. ❑ Tony built his own house and laid his own drains. **6** N-SING If you say that something is a **drain on** an organization's finances or resources, you mean that it costs the organization a large amount of money, and you do not think that it is worth it. ❑ Her fuel bills were a constant drain on her cash. **7** PHRASE If you say that something **is going down the drain**, you mean that it is being destroyed or wasted. [INFORMAL] ❑ These dreams were soon down the drain. [from Old English]
→ see **bathroom**

**drain|age** /dreɪnɪdʒ/ N-UNCOUNT **Drainage** is the system or process by which water or other liquids are drained from a place. ❑ Plant pots need good drainage. [from Old English]
→ see **farm**

**drain|age ba|sin** (**drainage basins**) N-COUNT A **drainage basin** is the same as a **catchment area**. [TECHNICAL]

**dra|ma** /drɑmə, drǽmə/ (**dramas**) **1** N-COUNT A **drama** is a serious play for the theater, television, or radio, or a serious movie. ❑ He acted in radio dramas. ❑ The movie is a drama about a woman searching for her children. **2** N-UNCOUNT You use **drama** to refer to plays and the theater in general. ❑ He knew nothing of Greek drama. **3** N-VAR You can refer to a real situation which is exciting or distressing as **drama**. ❑ He slept through all the drama. [from Late Latin]
→ see Picture Dictionary: **drama**
→ see **genre**

**dra|mat|ic** /drəmǽtɪk/ **1** ADJ A **dramatic** change or event happens suddenly and is very noticeable and surprising. ❑ The reduction in sales had a dramatic effect on profits. ● **dra|mati|cal|ly** /drəmǽtɪkli/ ADV ❑ The climate has changed dramatically. **2** ADJ A **dramatic** action, event, or situation is exciting and impressive. ❑ His dramatic escape involved a helicopter and a submarine. [from Late Latin]

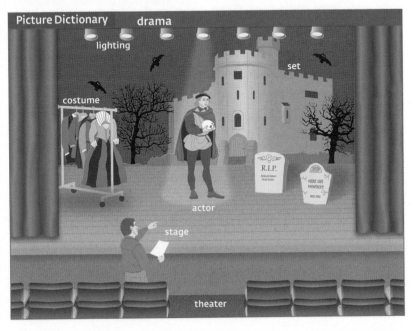

Picture Dictionary    drama

lighting

set

costume

R.I.P.

HERE LIES
MONTECO

actor

stage

theater

**dra|mat|ic play** N-UNCOUNT **Dramatic play** is children's play that involves imagined characters and situations.

**dra|mat|ics** /drəmætɪks/ N-UNCOUNT You use **dramatics** to refer to activities connected with the theater and drama. ❑ *...an amateur dramatics class.* ❑ *...the university dramatics society.* [from Late Latin]

**dra|mat|ic struc|ture** (**dramatic structures**) N-VAR The **dramatic structure** of a play or other story is the different parts into which it can be divided, such as the climax and the denouement.

**drama|tist** /dræmətɪst/ (**dramatists**) N-COUNT A **dramatist** is someone who writes plays. [from Late Latin]

**drama|tize** /dræmətaɪz/ (**dramatizes, dramatizing, dramatized**) ■ V-T If a book or story **is dramatized**, it is written or presented as a play, movie, or television drama. ❑ *The event was dramatized in the movie "The Right Stuff."* ● **drama|ti|za|tion** /dræmətɪzeɪʃ°n/ (**dramatizations**) N-COUNT ❑ *...a dramatization of Hemingway's "Capital of the World."* ■ V-T If you say that someone **dramatizes** a situation or event, you disapprove of the fact that they try to make it seem more serious, more important, or more exciting than it really is. ❑ *He dramatizes almost every situation.* [from Late Latin]

**drama|turg** /dræmətɜrdʒ/ also **dramaturge** (**dramaturgs** or **dramaturges**) N-COUNT A **dramaturg** is a person who works with writers and theaters to help them to develop and produce plays. [TECHNICAL] [from French]

**drank** /dræŋk/ **Drank** is the past tense of **drink**. [from Old English]

**drape** /dreɪp/ (**drapes, draping, draped**) ■ V-T If you **drape** a piece of cloth somewhere, you place it there so that it hangs down. ❑ *Natasha draped the coat over her shoulders.* ❑ *A U.S. flag was draped across the window.* ■ N-COUNT **Drapes** are pieces of heavy fabric that you hang from the top of a window and can close to keep the light out or stop people looking in. ❑ *He pulled the drapes shut.* [from Old French]

**dras|tic** /dræstɪk/ ■ ADJ If you have to take **drastic** action in order to solve a problem, you have to do something extreme to solve it. ❑ *Drastic measures are needed to improve the situation.* ■ ADJ A **drastic** change is a very great change. ❑ *...drastic alterations to Microsoft's products.* ● **dras|ti|cal|ly** ADV ❑ *Services have been drastically reduced.* [from Greek]

---

**draw**

❶ MAKE A PICTURE
❷ MOVE, PULL, OR TAKE
❸ OTHER USES AND PHRASAL VERBS

---

❶ **draw** /drɔ/ (**draws, drawing, drew, drawn**) ■ V-T/V-I When you **draw**, or when you **draw** something, you use a pencil or pen to produce a picture, pattern, or diagram. ❑ *She was drawing with a pencil.* ● **draw|ing** N-UNCOUNT ❑ *I like dancing, singing, and drawing.* [from Old English] ■ to **draw the line** → see **line**
→ see Picture Dictionary: **draw**
→ see **animation**

❷ **draw** /drɔ/ (**draws, drawing, drew, drawn**) ■ V-I If a person or vehicle **draws** somewhere, they move there. [WRITTEN] ❑ *She drew away and did not smile.* ❑ *Claire saw the taxi drawing away.* ■ V-T If you **draw** something or someone in a particular direction, you move them in that direction. [WRITTEN] ❑ *He drew his chair nearer the fire.* ❑ *He put his arm around Caroline's shoulders and drew her close to him.* ■ V-T When you **draw** a drape or blind, you pull it across a window, either to cover or to uncover it. ❑ *He went to the window and drew the drapes.* ■ V-T If someone **draws** a gun, knife, or other weapon, they pull it out of its container so that it is ready to use. ❑ *He drew his knife and turned to face them.* ■ V-T If you **draw** a deep breath, you breathe in deeply once. ❑ *He paused, and drew a deep breath.* ■ V-T To **draw** something such as water or energy **from** a particular source means to take it from that source. ❑ *Villagers still have to draw their water from wells.* ■ V-T If you **draw** money out of a bank account, you get it from the account so that you can use it. ❑ *A few months ago he drew out nearly all his savings.* [from Old English] ■ to **draw lots** → see **lot**

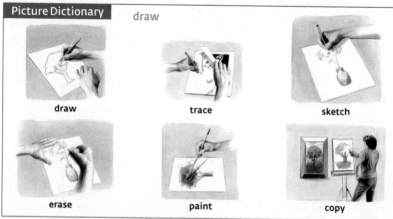

**Picture Dictionary** draw

draw

trace

sketch

erase

paint

copy

**❸ draw** /drɔ/ (**draws, drawing, drew, drawn**)

**1** V-T If you **draw** a comparison, conclusion, or distinction, you decide that it exists or is true. ❑ *Fonda's performance drew comparisons with his famous father, Henry.* ❑ *He draws two conclusions from this.* **2** V-T If you **draw** someone's attention to something, you make them aware of it or make them think about it. ❑ *He was waving his arms to draw their attention.* **3** V-T If someone or something **draws** a particular reaction, people react to it in that way. ❑ *The suggestion drew laughter from everyone there.* **4** → see also **drawing** **5** PHRASE When an event or period of time **draws to a close** or **draws to an end**, it finishes. ❑ *Another celebration drew to its close.* [from Old English]

▸ **draw in** PHR-VERB If you **draw** someone **in** or **draw** them **into** something you are involved with, you cause them to become involved with it. ❑ *It won't be easy for you to draw him in.*

▸ **draw on** PHR-VERB If you **draw on** or **draw upon** something such as your skill or experience, you make use of it in order to do something. ❑ *He drew on his experience to write a book.*

▸ **draw up** PHR-VERB If you **draw up** a document, list, or plan, you prepare it and write it out. ❑ *They drew up a formal agreement.*

▸ **draw upon** → see **draw on**

| Thesaurus | *draw* | Also look up : |
|---|---|---|
| v. | illustrate, sketch, trace ❶ **1** | |
| | bring out, pull out, take out ❷ **4** | |
| | inhale ❷ **5** | |
| | extract, take ❷ **5** | |
| | conclude, decide, make a decision, settle on ❸ **1** | |

**draw|back** /drɔbæk/ (**drawbacks**) N-COUNT A **drawback** is an aspect of something or someone that you do not like. ❑ *The apartment's only drawback was that it was too small.*

drawer

**drawer** /drɔr/ (**drawers**) N-COUNT A **drawer** is part of a desk, chest, or other piece of furniture that is shaped like a box. You pull it toward you to open it. ❑ *She opened her desk drawer and took out the book.* [from Old English]

**draw|ing** /drɔɪŋ/ (**drawings**) **1** N-COUNT A **drawing** is a picture made with a pencil or pen. ❑ *She did a drawing of me.* [from Old English] **2** → see also **draw ❶**

**drawl** /drɔl/ (**drawls, drawling, drawled**) V-T/V-I If someone **drawls**, they speak slowly and not very clearly, with long vowel sounds. ❑ *"Very funny," the president drawled.* ❑ *He has a deep voice, and he drawls slightly.* ● **Drawl** is also a noun. ❑ *Jack's southern drawl became more obvious as they traveled southward.*

**drawn** /drɔn/ **1** **Drawn** is the past participle of **draw**. **2** ADJ If someone or their face looks **drawn**, their face is thin and they look tired or ill. ❑ *She looked drawn and tired.* [from Old English]

**drawn-out** ADJ You can describe something as **drawn-out** when it lasts or takes longer than you would like it to. ❑ *...a long, drawn-out conversation.*

**dread** /drɛd/ (**dreads, dreading, dreaded**) **1** V-T If you **dread** something which may happen, you feel very anxious and unhappy about it because you think it will be unpleasant or upsetting. ❑ *I'm dreading Christmas this year.* ❑ *I dreaded coming back.* **2** N-UNCOUNT **Dread** is a feeling of great anxiety and fear about something that may happen. ❑ *She thought with dread of the cold winters.* [from Old English]

**dread|ed** /drɛdɪd/ ADJ **Dreaded** means terrible and greatly feared. ❑ *No one knew how to treat this dreaded disease.* [from Old English]

| Word Link | ful ≈ filled with : beautiful, careful, dreadful |
|---|---|

**dread|ful** /drɛdfəl/ ADJ If you say that something is **dreadful**, you mean that it is very bad or unpleasant, or very poor in quality. ❑ *They told us the dreadful news.* ● **dread|fully** ADV ❑ *You behaved dreadfully.* [from Old English]

**dream** /drim/ (**dreams, dreaming, dreamed** or **dreamt**) **1** N-COUNT A **dream** is a series of events that you experience only in your mind while you are asleep. ❑ *He had a dream about Claire.* **2** N-COUNT You can refer to a situation or event as a **dream** if you often think about it because you would like it to happen. ❑ *He finally achieved his dream of becoming a pilot.* **3** V-T/V-I When you **dream**, you experience events in your mind while you are asleep. ❑ *Ivor dreamed that he was on a bus.* ❑ *She dreamed about her baby.* **4** V-T/V-I If you often think about something that you would very much like to happen or have, you can say that you **dream of** it. ❑ *She dreamed of becoming an actress.* ❑ *For most people, a life without work is something we can only dream about.* ❑ *I dream that my son will attend college.* **5** V-I If you say that you **would not dream of** doing something, you are emphasizing that you would never do it because you think it is wrong or is not possible or suitable for you. ❑ *I wouldn't dream of laughing at you.* [from Old English]

▸ **dream up** PHR-VERB If you **dream up** a plan or idea, you work it out or create it in your mind. ❑ *I dreamed up a plan to solve the problem.*

| Thesaurus | *dream* | Also look up : |
|---|---|---|
| N. | nightmare, reverie, vision **1** | |
| | ambition, aspiration, design, hope, wish **2** | |
| V. | hope, long for, wish **4** | |

| Word Partnership | Use *dream* with : |
|---|---|
| v. | **have a** dream **1** |
| | **fulfill a** dream, **pursue a** dream, **realize a** dream **2** |
| N. | dream **interpretation 1** |
| | dream **home**, dream **vacation 2** |

**dream|er** /drimər/ (**dreamers**) N-COUNT Someone who is a **dreamer** spends a lot of time thinking about and planning for things that may never happen. ❑ *Harry was a dreamer.* [from Old English]

**dreamy** /drimi/ (**dreamier, dreamiest**) ADJ If someone has a **dreamy** expression, they are not paying attention to things around them and look as if they are thinking about something pleasant. ❑ *His face had a dreamy expression.* [from Old English]

**dreary** /drɪɑri/ (**drearier, dreariest**) ADJ If you describe something as **dreary**, you mean that it is dull and depressing. ❑ ...*a dreary little town.* [from Old English]

**dredge** /drɛdʒ/ (**dredges, dredging, dredged**)
v-т When people **dredge** a harbor, river, or other area of water, they remove mud and unwanted material from the bottom with a special machine in order to make it deeper or to look for something. ❑ *Police dredged the lake but didn't find his body.* [from Old English]

▸ **dredge up** PHR-VERB If someone **dredges up** a piece of information they learned a long time ago, or if they **dredge up** a distant memory, they manage to remember it. ❑ *He dredged up some of the French he had learned in high school.*

**drench** /drɛntʃ/ (**drenches, drenching, drenched**) v-т To **drench** something or someone means to make them completely wet. ❑ *They turned fire hoses on the people and drenched them.* ❑ *He got drenched by the icy water.* • **drenched** ADJ ❑ *We were completely drenched and cold.* [from Old English]

**dress** /drɛs/ (**dresses, dressing, dressed**)
■ N-COUNT A **dress** is a piece of clothing worn by a woman or girl. It covers her body and part of her legs. ❑ *She was wearing a black dress.* ■ N-UNCOUNT You can refer to clothes worn by men or women as **dress**. ❑ *He wore formal evening dress.* ■ V-T/V-I When you **dress** or **dress yourself**, you put on clothes. ❑ *Sarah waited while he dressed.* [from Old French] ■ → see also **dressing, dressed**

▸ **dress down** PHR-VERB If you **dress down**, you wear clothes that are less formal than usual. ❑ *She dressed down in dark glasses and baggy clothes.*

▸ **dress up** PHR-VERB If you **dress up** or **dress yourself up**, you put on different clothes, in order to make yourself look more formal than usual or to disguise yourself. ❑ *You do not need to dress up for dinner.* ❑ *I love the fun of dressing up in nice clothing.*

| Word Partnership | Use *dress* with : |
| --- | --- |
| V. | **put on** a dress, **wear** a dress ■ |
| ADJ. | **casual** dress, **formal** dress, **traditional** dress ■ |
| ADV. | dress **appropriately**, dress **casually**, dress **well** ■ |

**dressed** /drɛst/ ■ ADJ If you are **dressed**, you are wearing clothes rather than being naked or wearing your nightclothes. ❑ *He was fully dressed, including shoes.* ■ ADJ If you are **dressed** in a particular way, you are wearing clothes of a particular color or kind. ❑ ...*a tall woman dressed in black.* [from Old French] ■ → see also **well-dressed**

**dress|er** /drɛsər/ (**dressers**) N-COUNT A **dresser** is a chest of drawers, sometimes with a mirror on the top. [from Old French]

**dress|ing** /drɛsɪŋ/ (**dressings**) ■ N-VAR A salad **dressing** is a mixture of oil, vinegar, and herbs or flavorings, which you pour over salad. ❑ *Mix the ingredients for the dressing.*

**dresser**

■ N-COUNT A **dressing** is a covering that is put on a wound to protect it while it heals. ❑ *He applied a fresh dressing to her hand.* ■ N-UNCOUNT **Dressing** is a mixture of food that is cooked and then put inside a bird such as a turkey before it is cooked and eaten. ❑ ...*cornbread dressing.* [from Old French]

**dress|ing room** (**dressing rooms**) also **dressing-room** N-COUNT A **dressing room** is a room in a theater where performers can dress and get ready for their performance.

**dress re|hears|al** (**dress rehearsals**) N-COUNT The **dress rehearsal** of a play, opera, or show is the final rehearsal before it is performed, in which the performers wear their costumes and the lights and scenery are all used as they will be in the performance.

**dress-up** ■ N-UNCOUNT When children play **dress-up**, they put on special or different clothes and pretend to be different people. ■ ADJ **Dress-up** clothes are stylish clothes which you wear when you want to look elegant or formal. ❑ *The hotel is very informal and you do not need dress-up clothes.*

**drew** /dru/ **Drew** is the past tense of **draw.** [from Old English]

**drib|ble** /drɪbᵊl/ (**dribbles, dribbling, dribbled**)
■ V-T/V-I If a liquid **dribbles** somewhere, or if you **dribble** it, it drops down slowly or flows in a thin stream. ❑ *Sweat dribbled down Hart's face.* ■ V-T/V-I When players **dribble** the ball in a game such as basketball or soccer, they keep kicking or tapping it quickly in order to keep it moving. ❑ *He dribbled the ball toward Ferris.* ❑ *He dribbled past four players.* ■ V-I If a person **dribbles**, saliva drops slowly from their mouth. ❑ ...*to protect sheets when the baby dribbles.*

**dried** /draɪd/ ■ ADJ **Dried** food or milk has had all the water removed from it so that it will last for a long time. ❑ ...*dried herbs.* [from Old English] ■ → see also **dry**

**dri|er** /draɪər/ → see **dry, dryer**

**drift** /drɪft/ (**drifts, drifting, drifted**) ■ V-I When something **drifts** somewhere, it is carried there by the movement of wind or water. ❑ *We drifted up the river.* ■ V-I To **drift** somewhere means to move there slowly or gradually. ❑ *People drifted toward the cities as there were fewer jobs on farms.* ■ N-COUNT A **drift** is a movement away from somewhere or something, or a movement toward somewhere or something different. ❑ ...*the drift toward the cities.* ■ N-COUNT A **drift** is a mass of snow that has built up into a pile as a result of the movement of wind. ❑ *A boy was trapped in a snow drift.* [from Old Norse] → see **continent, snow**

▸ **drift off** PHR-VERB If you **drift off** to sleep, you gradually fall asleep. ❑ *He finally drifted off to sleep.*

**drill** /drɪl/ (**drills, drilling, drilled**) ■ N-COUNT A **drill** is a tool or machine that you use for making holes. ❑ ...*a dentist's drill.* ■ V-T/V-I When you **drill into** something or **drill** a hole in something, you make a hole in it using a drill. ❑ *He drilled the wall.* ■ N-VAR A **drill** is repeated training for a group of people, especially soldiers, so that they can do something quickly and efficiently. ❑ ...*a drill that included 18 ships and 90 planes.* [from Middle Dutch]

→ see **oil, tools**

**drink** /drɪŋk/ (**drinks, drinking, drank, drunk**)
■ V-T/V-I When you **drink** a liquid, you take it into your mouth and swallow it. ❑ *He drank his cup of tea.* ❑ *He drank thirstily.* • **drink|er** (**drinkers**) N-COUNT ❑ ...*coffee drinkers.* ■ V-I To **drink** means to drink alcohol. ❑ *He drank too much.* • **drink|er** N-COUNT ❑ *I'm not a heavy drinker.* • **drink|ing**

N-UNCOUNT ❑ *She left him because of his drinking.*
**❸** N-COUNT A **drink** is an amount of a liquid which
you drink. ❑ *I'll get you a drink of water.* **❹** N-COUNT
A **drink** is an alcoholic drink. ❑ *They only had one
drink each.* [from Old English]
▸ **drink to** PHR-VERB When people **drink to**
someone or something, they wish them success,
good luck, or good health before having an
alcoholic drink. ❑ *We drank to our success.*

**drip** /drɪp/ (**drips, dripping, dripped**) **❶** V-T/
V-I When liquid **drips** somewhere, or you **drip**

it somewhere, it falls in
individual small drops. ❑ *The
rain dripped down my face.* **❷** V-I
When something **drips**, drops of
liquid fall from it. ❑ *A faucet in
the kitchen was dripping.* ❑ *Lou was
dripping with sweat.* **❸** N-COUNT
A **drip** is a small individual drop

drip

of a liquid. ❑ *...little drips of
candle-wax.* **❹** N-COUNT A **drip**
is a piece of medical equipment by which a liquid
is slowly passed through a tube into a patient's
blood. ❑ *He was put on a drip to treat his dehydration.*
[from Old English]

**drive** /draɪv/ (**drives, driving, drove, driven**)
**❶** V-T/V-I When you **drive** somewhere, you
operate a car or other vehicle and control its
movement and direction. ❑ *I drove into town.*
❑ *She never learned to drive.* ❑ *We drove the car down
to Richmond.* ● **driving** N-UNCOUNT ❑ *...a driving
instructor.* ● **driver** (**drivers**) N-COUNT ❑ *The driver
got out of his truck.* **❷** V-T If you **drive** someone
somewhere, you take them there in a car or other
vehicle. ❑ *She drove him to the train station.* **❸** V-T
If something **drives** a machine, it supplies the
power that makes it work. ❑ *Electric motors drive
the wheels.* **❹** V-T If you **drive** something such
as a nail **into** something else, you push it in or
hammer it in using a lot of effort. ❑ *Drive the
pegs into the ground.* **❺** V-T If you **drive** people or
animals somewhere, you make them go to or from
that place. ❑ *The war drove thousands of people into
Thailand.* **❻** V-T The desire or feeling that **drives**
a person **to** do something, especially something
extreme, is the desire or feeling that causes them
to do it. ❑ *His unhappiness drove him to ask for help.*
❑ *Jealousy can drive people to murder.* **❼** N-COUNT A
**drive** is a trip in a car or other vehicle. ❑ *Let's go for
a drive on Sunday.* **❽** N-COUNT A **drive** is a wide piece
of hard ground, or sometimes a private road, that
leads from the road to a person's house. ❑ *The boys
followed Eleanor up the drive to the house.* **❾** N-COUNT
You use **drive** to refer to the mechanical part of
a computer which reads the data on disks and
tapes, or writes data onto them. ❑ *The firm supplies
tape drives and printers.* **❿** → see also **disk drive**
**⓫** N-UNCOUNT **Drive** is energy and determination.
❑ *John has a lot of drive and enthusiasm.* **⓬** N-SING A
**drive** is a special effort made by a group of people
for a particular purpose. ❑ *...a drive toward personal
happiness.* [from Old English] **⓭** → see also **driving**
→ see **car**
▸ **drive away** PHR-VERB To **drive** people **away**
means to make them want to go away or stay
away. ❑ *Patrick's rudeness drove Monica's friends away.*

**drive-by** ADJ A **drive-by** shooting or a **drive-by**
murder involves shooting someone from a moving
car. ❑ *He was killed in a drive-by shooting.*

**driv|er** /draɪvər/ (**drivers**) **❶** → see also **drive** 1
**❷** N-COUNT A **driver** is a computer program that
controls a device such as a printer. [COMPUTING]
❑ *...printer driver software.* [from Old English]

**driv|er's li|cense** (**driver's licenses**) N-COUNT
A **driver's license** is a card showing that you are
qualified to drive because you have passed a
driving test.

**drive-through** also **drive-thru** ADJ A **drive-
through** store, bank, or restaurant is one where
you can be served without leaving your car. ❑ *...a
drive-through restaurant.*

**drive|way** /draɪvweɪ/
(**driveways**) N-COUNT A
**driveway** is a piece of hard
ground that leads from
the road to the front of a
house, garage, or other
building. ❑ *I ran down the
driveway to the car.* [from
Old English]

driveway

**driv|ing** /draɪvɪŋ/
**❶** ADJ The **driving** force
or idea behind something that happens or is done
is the main thing that has a strong effect on it
and makes it happen or be done in a particular
way. ❑ *Increased sales were the driving force behind
the economic growth.* [from Old English] **❷** → see
also **drive**

**driz|zle** /drɪzᵊl/ (**drizzles, drizzling, drizzled**)
**❶** N-UNCOUNT; N-SING **Drizzle** is light rain falling
in fine drops. ❑ *The drizzle stopped and the sun came
out.* **❷** V-I If it **is drizzling**, it is raining very lightly.
❑ *It was starting to drizzle.* [from Old English]
→ see **precipitation**

**drone** /droʊn/ (**drones, droning, droned**) **❶** V-I
If something **drones**, it makes a low, continuous,
dull noise. ❑ *Above him a plane droned through the
sky.* ● **Drone** is also a noun. ❑ *I hear the drone of an
airplane.* **❷** V-I If you say that someone **drones**, you
mean that they keep talking about something in
a boring way. ❑ *Chambers' voice droned.* ● **Drone** is
also a noun. ❑ *The minister's voice was a relentless
drone.* ● **Drone on** means the same as **drone**. ❑ *Aunt
Maimie's voice droned on.* [from Middle Dutch]

**drool** /druːl/ (**drools, drooling, drooled**) **❶** V-I To
**drool over** someone or something means to look
at them with great pleasure, in an exaggerated or
ridiculous way. ❑ *They were drooling over the pictures
of food.* **❷** V-I If a person or animal **drools**, saliva
drops slowly from their mouth. ❑ *My dog is drooling
on my shoulder.*

**droop** /druːp/ (**droops, drooping, drooped**) V-I If
something **droops**, it hangs or leans downward
with no strength or firmness. ❑ *Crook's eyelids
drooped and he yawned.* [from Old Norse]

**drop** /drɒp/ (**drops, dropping, dropped**)
**❶** V-T/V-I If a level or amount **drops** or if someone
or something **drops** it, it quickly becomes less.
❑ *Temperatures can drop to freezing at night.* ❑ *His
blood pressure had dropped severely.* ● **Drop** is also a
noun. ❑ *He took a drop in wages.* **❷** V-T/V-I If you
**drop** something or it drops, it falls straight down.
❑ *I dropped my glasses and broke them.* ❑ *He felt tears
dropping onto his fingers.* **❸** V-T/V-I If you **drop**
something somewhere or if it **drops** there, you
deliberately let it fall there. ❑ *Drop the pasta into
the water.* ❑ *Bombs dropped on the city.* ● **drop|ping**

d

N-UNCOUNT ❑ …*the dropping of the first atomic bomb.* ◼ V-T/V-I If a person or a part of their body **drops** to a lower position, or if they **drop** a part of their body to a lower position, they move to that position, often in a tired and lifeless way. ❑ *Nancy dropped into a chair.* ❑ *She let her head drop.* ◼ V-T/V-I If your voice **drops** or if you **drop** your voice, you speak more quietly. ❑ *Her voice dropped to a whisper.* ◼ V-T If you **drop** someone or something somewhere, you take them somewhere and leave them there, usually in a car or other vehicle. ❑ *He dropped me outside the hotel.* ● **Drop off** means the same as **drop**. ❑ *Just drop me at the airport.* ◼ V-T If you **drop** an idea, course of action, or habit, you do not continue with it. ❑ *He decided to drop the idea.* ◼ N-COUNT A **drop of** a liquid is a very small amount of it shaped like a little ball. ❑ …*a drop of ink.* ◼ N-COUNT You use **drop** to talk about vertical distances. ❑ *The most impressive of the waterfalls had a drop of 741 feet.* [from Old English]

▸ **drop by** PHR-VERB If you **drop by**, you visit someone informally. ❑ *She will drop by later.*
▸ **drop in** PHR-VERB If you **drop in on** someone, you visit them informally, usually without having arranged it. ❑ *Why not drop in for a chat?*
▸ **drop off** ◼ → see **drop 6** ◼ PHR-VERB If you **drop off** to sleep, you go to sleep. [INFORMAL] ❑ *I lay down on the bed and dropped off to sleep.*
▸ **drop out** PHR-VERB If someone **drops out of** college or a race, for example, they leave it without finishing what they started. ❑ *He dropped out of high school at the age of 16.*

| **Word Partnership** | Use *drop* with : |
|---|---|
| N. | drop **in sales** ◼ |
| | drop **a ball** ◼ |
| | drop **a bomb** ◼ |
| | drop **of blood**, **tear** drop, drop **of water** ◼ |
| ADJ. | **sudden** drop ◼ |
| | **steep** drop ◼ |

**drop-down menu** (drop-down menus) N-COUNT On a computer screen, a **drop-down menu** is a list of choices that appears when you give the computer a command. ❑ *In the drop-down menu right-click on any item.*

**drop kick** (drop kicks) N-COUNT In sports such as football and rugby, a **drop kick** is a kick in which the ball is dropped to the ground and kicked at the moment that it bounces.

| **Word Link** | *let ≈ little : book**let**, drop**let**, in**let*** |
|---|---|

**drop|let** /drɒplɪt/ (droplets) N-COUNT A **droplet** is a very small drop of liquid. ❑ …*droplets of sweat.*
→ see **precipitation**

**drop-off** (drop-offs) N-COUNT A **drop-off in** something such as sales or orders is a decrease in them. ❑ …*a sharp drop-off in orders.*

**drought** /draʊt/ (droughts) N-VAR A **drought** is a long period of time during which no rain falls. ❑ *Drought and famines have killed more than two million people.* [from Old English]
→ see **dam**

**drove** /droʊv/ **Drove** is the past tense of **drive**. [from Old English]

**drown** /draʊn/ (drowns, drowning, drowned) ◼ V-T/V-I When someone **drowns** or **is drowned**, they die because they have gone under water and

cannot breathe. ❑ *A child can drown in only a few inches of water.* ❑ *Last night a boy was drowned in the river.* ◼ V-T If something **drowns** a sound, it is so loud that you cannot hear that sound properly. ❑ *Clapping drowned the speaker's words.* ● **Drown out** means the same as **drown**. ❑ *Their cheers drowned out the protests of demonstrators.* [from Old English]

**drowsy** /draʊzi/ (drowsier, drowsiest) ADJ If you feel **drowsy**, you feel sleepy and cannot think clearly. ❑ *He felt pleasantly drowsy.* ● **drowsi|ness** N-UNCOUNT ❑ *Big meals during the day cause drowsiness.* [from Old English]

**drug** /drʌg/ (drugs, drugging, drugged) ◼ N-COUNT A **drug** is a chemical which is given to people in order to treat or prevent an illness or disease. ❑ *The drug is useful to hundreds of thousands of people.* ◼ N-COUNT **Drugs** are illegal substances that some people take because they enjoy their effects. ❑ *She hoped he wouldn't spend the money on drugs.* ❑ *She was sure Leo was taking drugs.* ◼ V-T If you **drug** a person or animal, you give them a chemical substance in order to make them sleepy or unconscious. ❑ *She was drugged and robbed.* [from Old French]

**drug ad|dict** (drug addicts) N-COUNT A **drug addict** is someone who is addicted to illegal drugs.

**drug|store** /drʌgstɔr/ (drugstores) N-COUNT A **drugstore** is a store where medicines, cosmetics, and some other goods are sold.

**drum** /drʌm/ (drums, drumming, drummed) ◼ N-COUNT A **drum** is a musical instrument consisting of a skin stretched tightly over a round frame. ● **drum|mer** (drummers) N-COUNT ❑ *He was a drummer in a band.* ◼ N-COUNT A **drum** is a large cylindrical container which is used to store fuel or other substances. ❑ …*an oil drum.* ◼ V-T/V-I If something **drums on** a surface, or if you **drum** something **on** a surface, it hits it regularly, making a continuous beating sound. ❑ *He drummed his fingers on the top of his desk.* [from Middle Dutch]
→ see **percussion**

▸ **drum into** PHR-VERB If you **drum** something **into** someone, you keep saying it to them until they understand it or remember it. ❑ *The information was drummed into students' heads.*
▸ **drum up** PHR-VERB If you **drum up** support or business, you try to get it. ❑ …*drumming up new clients.*

**drum|beat** /drʌmbit/ (drumbeats) N-COUNT People sometimes describe a series of warnings or continuous pressure on someone to do something as a **drumbeat**. [JOURNALISM] ❑ …*a continuous drumbeat of protest.*

**drum ma|jor** (drum majors) N-COUNT A **drum major** is a man who leads a marching band by walking in front of them.

**drum ma|jor|ette** /drʌm meɪʒərɛt/ (drum majorettes) N-COUNT A **drum majorette** is a girl or young woman who leads a marching band by walking in front of them.

**drunk** /drʌŋk/ (drunks) ◼ ADJ Someone who is **drunk** has drunk so much alcohol that they cannot speak clearly or behave sensibly. ❑ *He got drunk and was carried home.* ◼ N-COUNT A **drunk** is someone who is drunk or frequently gets drunk. ❑ *A drunk lay in the alley.* ◼ **Drunk** is the past participle of **drink**. [from Old English]

**drunk driv|er** (**drunk drivers**) N-COUNT A **drunk driver** is someone who drives after drinking more than the amount of alcohol that is legally allowed. ❑ *The car accident was caused by a drunk driver.* ● **drunk driv|ing** N-UNCOUNT ❑ *He was arrested for drunk driving.*

**drunk|en** /drʌŋkən/ ADJ A **drunken** person is drunk or is frequently drunk. ❑ *Groups of drunken people smashed windows.* ● **drunk|en|ly** ADV ❑ *Bob stormed drunkenly into the house and smashed some chairs.* ● **drunk|en|ness** N-UNCOUNT ❑ *He was arrested for drunkenness.* [from Old English]

**dry** /draɪ/ (**drier** or **dryer, driest, dries, drying, dried**) **1** ADJ If something is **dry**, there is no water or moisture on it or in it. ❑ *Clean the metal with a soft dry cloth.* ❑ *Pat it dry with a soft towel.* ● **dry|ness** N-UNCOUNT ❑ *...the dryness of the air.* **2** ADJ If your skin or hair is **dry**, it is less oily than, or not as soft as, normal. ❑ *She had dry, cracked lips.* ● **dry|ness** N-UNCOUNT ❑ *...dryness of the skin.* **3** ADJ If the weather, a place or a period of time is **dry**, there is no rain or there is much less rain than average. ❑ *Exceptionally dry weather ruined crops.* ❑ *It was one of the driest places in Africa.* **4** ADJ **Dry** humor is subtle and clever. ❑ *He kept his dry humor in spite of all the stress.* ● **dry|ly** ADV ❑ *"I have been just a little busy," he said dryly.* **5** ADJ If you describe something such as a book, play, or activity as **dry**, you mean that it is dull and uninteresting. ❑ *...dry, academic phrases.* **6** V-T/V-I When something **dries** or when you **dry** it, it becomes dry. ❑ *Let your hair dry naturally whenever possible.* ❑ *Mrs. Madrigal picked up a towel and began drying dishes.* [from Old English]
→ see **weather**

▶ **dry out** PHR-VERB If something **dries out** or **is dried out**, it loses all the moisture that was in it and becomes hard. ❑ *If the soil dries out, the tree could die.*

▶ **dry up 1** PHR-VERB If something **dries up** or if something **dries** it **up**, it loses all its moisture and becomes completely dry and shriveled or hard. ❑ *The river dried up.* **2** PHR-VERB If a supply of something **dries up**, it stops. ❑ *With the economic crisis there, work has dried up.*

**dry-clean** (**dry-cleans, dry-cleaning, dry-cleaned**) V-T When things such as clothes **are dry-cleaned**, they are cleaned with a liquid chemical rather than with water. ❑ *The suit must be dry-cleaned.*

**dry|er** /draɪər/ (**dryers**) also **drier 1** N-COUNT A **dryer** is a machine for drying things, for example, clothes or people's hair. ❑ *...the hot air hand dryers in the restroom.* **2** → see also **dry**

**dry goods** N-PLURAL **Dry goods** are cloth, thread, flour, tea, and coffee, that contain no liquid.

**dry ice** N-UNCOUNT **Dry ice** is a form of solid carbon dioxide that is used to keep things cold and to create smoke in stage shows.

**dry run** (**dry runs**) N-COUNT If you have a **dry run**, you practice something to make sure that you are ready to do it properly. ❑ *The competition is a dry run for the World Cup finals.*

**DSL** /di es el/ **DSL** is a method of transmitting digital information at high speed over telephone lines. **DSL** is an abbreviation for "digital subscriber line." [COMPUTING]

**dual** /duəl/ ADJ **Dual** means having two parts, functions, or aspects. ❑ *...his dual role as head of the party and head of state.* [from Latin]

**dub** /dʌb/ (**dubs, dubbing, dubbed**) **1** V-T If someone or something **is dubbed** a particular thing, they are given that description or name. ❑ *...a man dubbed as the "biggest nuisance in the U.S."* **2** V-T If a movie or soundtrack in a foreign language **is dubbed**, a new soundtrack is added with actors giving a translation. ❑ *It was dubbed into Spanish for Mexican audiences.* [from Old English]

**du|bi|ous** /dubiəs/ **1** ADJ If you describe something as **dubious**, you think it is not completely honest, safe, or reliable. ❑ *This claim seems to be rather dubious.* ● **du|bi|ous|ly** ADV ❑ *The government was dubiously re-elected.* **2** ADJ If you are **dubious about** something, you are not completely sure about it and have not yet made up your mind about it. ❑ *Hayes was originally dubious about becoming involved with the project.* ● **du|bi|ous|ly** ADV ❑ *He looked at Coyne dubiously.* [from Latin]

**duch|ess** /dʌtʃɪs/ (**duchesses**) N-COUNT A **duchess** is a woman who has the same rank as a duke, or who is a duke's wife or widow. ❑ *...the Duchess of Kent.* [from Old French]

**duck** /dʌk/ (**ducks, ducking, ducked**) **1** N-VAR A **duck** is a water bird with short legs, a short neck, and a large flat beak. ❑ *Chickens and ducks walk around outside.* ● **Duck** is the flesh of this bird when it is eaten as food. ❑ *...roasted duck.* **2** V-T/V-I If you **duck**, you move your head or the top half of your body quickly downward to avoid something that might hit you or to avoid being seen. ❑ *There was a loud noise and I ducked.* ❑ *Hans deftly ducked their blows.* **3** V-T If you **duck** your head, you move it quickly downward to hide the expression on your face. ❑ *Davy ducked his head to hide his tears.* **4** V-T You say that someone **ducks** a duty or responsibility when you disapprove of the fact that they avoid it. [INFORMAL] ❑ *The defense secretary ducked the question of whether the United States was winning the war.* [Sense 1 from Old English. Senses 2–4 from Old High German.]

▶ **duck out** PHR-VERB If you **duck out of** something that you are supposed to do, you avoid doing it. [INFORMAL] ❑ *George ducked out of the meeting early.*

**duct** /dʌkt/ (**ducts**) N-COUNT A **duct** is a pipe, tube, or channel which carries a liquid or gas. ❑ *...a big air duct in the ceiling.* [from Latin]

**duc|til|ity** /dʌktɪlɪti/ N-UNCOUNT The **ductility** of a metal is its ability to be stretched without breaking. [TECHNICAL] [from Old French]

**duct tape** N-UNCOUNT **Duct tape** is a strong, sticky tape that you use to bind things together or to seal cracks in something. ❑ *...a broken lid held on with duct tape.*

**dud** /dʌd/ (**duds**) ADJ **Dud** means not working properly or not successful. [INFORMAL] ❑ *He replaced a dud battery.* ● **Dud** is also a noun. ❑ *The celebration was a dud.*

**dude** /dud/ (**dudes**) N-COUNT A **dude** is a man. In very informal situations, **dude** is sometimes used as a greeting or form of address to a man. [INFORMAL] ❑ *He's a real cool dude.*

**due** /du/ **1** PHRASE If an event or situation is **due to** something, it happens or exists as a direct result of that thing. ❑ *She couldn't do the job, due to pain in her hands.* ❑ *Due to the large number of letters* he receives, he cannot answer them all. **2** PHRASE If you say that something will happen or take place **in due course**, you mean that you cannot make it happen any quicker and it will happen when the time is right for it. ❑ *In due course the baby was born.* **3** PHRASE You can say **"with due respect"** when you are about to disagree politely with someone. ❑ *With all due respect, I think you're asking the wrong question.* **4** ADJ If something is **due** at a particular time, it is expected to happen, be done, or arrive at that time. ❑ *The results are due at the end of the month.* ❑ *Mr. Carter is due in Washington on Monday.* **5** ADJ **Due** attention or consideration is the proper, reasonable, or deserved amount of it under the circumstances. ❑ *We'll give due consideration to any serious offer.* **6** ADJ Something that is **due**, or that is **due to** someone, is owed to them, either as a debt or because they have a right to it. ❑ *I was told that no more payments were due.* **7** ADJ If someone is **due for** something, that thing is planned to happen or be given to them now, or very soon, often after they have been waiting for it for a long time. ❑ *The prisoner is due for release next year.* [from Old French]

**duel** /dˈuəl/ (**duels**) N-COUNT A **duel** is a formal fight between two people in which they use guns or swords in order to settle a quarrel. ❑ *He killed a man in one duel.* [from Medieval Latin]

**due pro|cess** N-UNCOUNT In law, **due process** refers to the carrying out of the law according to established rules and principles. ❑ *The principles of fairness and due process were not followed.*

**duet** /dˈuɛt/ (**duets**) N-COUNT A **duet** is a piece of music sung or played by two people. ❑ *She sang a duet with Maurice Gibb.* [from Italian]

**dug** /dˈʌg/ **Dug** is the past tense and past participle of **dig**. [from Scandinavian]

**DUI** /dˈiː yuː aɪ/ N-UNCOUNT **DUI** is the offense of driving after drinking more than the amount of alcohol that is legally allowed. **DUI** is an abbreviation for "driving under the influence." [AM] ❑ *He was arrested for DUI.* ❑ *...DUI offenders.*

**duke** /dˈuːk/ (**dukes**) N-COUNT A **duke** is a man with a very high social rank in the nobility of some countries. ❑ *...the Duke of Edinburgh.* [from Old French]

**dull** /dˈʌl/ (**duller, dullest, dulls, dulling, dulled**) **1** ADJ If you describe someone or something as **dull**, you mean they are not interesting or exciting. ❑ *I thought he was boring and dull.* ● **dull|ness** N-UNCOUNT ❑ *...the dullness of their routine life.* **2** ADJ A **dull** color or light is not bright. ❑ *The stamp was a dark, dull blue color.* ● **dul|ly** ADV ❑ *The street lamps gleamed dully.* **3** ADJ **Dull** sounds are not very clear or loud. ❑ *The lid closed with a dull thud.* ● **dul|ly** ADV ❑ *He heard his heart thump dully but more quickly.* **4** ADJ **Dull** feelings are weak and not intense. ❑ *The pain was a dull ache.* ● **dul|ly** ADV ❑ *His arm throbbed dully.* **5** V-T/V-I If something **dulls** or if it **is dulled**, it becomes less intense, bright, or lively. ❑ *Her eyes dulled.* [from Old English]

| Thesaurus | *dull* | Also look up : |
|---|---|---|
| ADJ. | dingy, drab, faded, plain **2** | |

**duly** /dˈuːli/ ADV If something **duly** happened or was done, it happened or was done at the correct

time or in the correct way. ❑ *Westcott asked for an apology, which he duly received.* ❑ *He is the duly elected president of the country.*

**dumb** /dˈʌm/ (**dumber, dumbest, dumbs, dumbing, dumbed**) **1** ADJ Someone who is **dumb** is completely unable to speak. ❑ *...a young deaf and dumb man.* **2** ADJ If someone is **dumb** on a particular occasion, they cannot speak because they are angry, shocked, or surprised. [LITERARY] ❑ *The guards were struck dumb, in fear.* **3** ADJ If you call a person **dumb**, you mean that they are stupid or foolish. [INFORMAL] ❑ *He was a brilliant guy. He made me feel dumb.* **4** ADJ If you say that something is **dumb**, you think that it is silly and annoying. [INFORMAL] ❑ *He had this dumb idea.* [from Old English]

→ see **disability**

▶ **dumb down** PHR-VERB If you **dumb down** something, you make it easier for people to understand, especially when this oversimplifies it. ❑ *The channel has dumbed down its news programs.* ● **dumb|ing down** N-UNCOUNT ❑ *...the dumbing down of modern culture.*

**dum|my** /dˈʌmi/ (**dummies**) **1** N-COUNT A **dummy** is a model of a person, often used to display clothes. **2** ADJ You can use **dummy** to refer to things that are not real, but have been made to look or behave as if they are real. ❑ *There are dummy police cars beside highways to frighten speeding motorists.* **3** N-COUNT If you call a person a **dummy**, you mean that they are stupid or foolish. [INFORMAL]

**dump** /dˈʌmp/ (**dumps, dumping, dumped**) **1** V-T If you **dump** something somewhere, you put it or unload it there quickly and carelessly. [INFORMAL] ❑ *We dumped our bags at the hotel and went to the market.* **2** V-T If something **is dumped** somewhere, it is put or left there because it is no longer wanted or needed. [INFORMAL] ❑ *The getaway car was dumped near the freeway.* ● **dump|ing** N-UNCOUNT ❑ *German law forbids the dumping of hazardous waste.* **3** N-COUNT A **dump** is a place where garbage and waste material are left. ❑ *He took his father's trash to the dump.* **4** N-COUNT If you say that a place is a **dump**, you think it is ugly and unpleasant to live in or visit. [INFORMAL] ❑ *"What a dump!" Christabel said, standing in the doorway of the house.* [of Scandinavian origin]

→ see Word Web: **dump**

**dune** /dˈuːn/ (**dunes**) N-COUNT A **dune** is a hill of sand near the ocean or in a desert. ❑ *Large dunes make access to the beach difficult.* [from Old French]

→ see **beach, desert**

**dung** /dˈʌŋ/ N-UNCOUNT **Dung** is feces from large animals. ❑ *...cow dung.* [from Old English]

**dun|geon** /dˈʌndʒən/ (**dungeons**) N-COUNT A **dungeon** is a dark underground prison in a castle. [from Old French]

**dun|no** /dənˈoʊ/ **Dunno** is sometimes used in written English to represent an informal way of saying "don't know." ❑ *"How did she get it?" — "I dunno."*

| Word Link | *du ≈ two : **du**o, **du**plex, **du**plicate* |
|---|---|

**duo** /dˈuːoʊ/ (**duos**) N-COUNT A **duo** is two musicians, singers, or other performers who perform together as a pair. ❑ *...a famous singing duo.* [from Italian]

## Word Web dump

Most communities used to dispose of **solid waste** in **dumps**. However, more **environmentally friendly** methods are common today. There are alternatives to dumping **refuse** in a **landfill**. **Reduction** means creating less waste. For example, using washable napkins instead of paper napkins. **Reuse** involves finding a second use for something without processing it. For instance, giving old clothing to a charity. **Recycling** and **composting** involve finding a new use for something by processing it—using food scraps to fertilize a garden. **Incineration** involves burning solid waste and using the heat for another useful purpose.

**dupe** /dup/ (**dupes, duping, duped**) V-T If a person **dupes** you, they trick you into doing something or into believing something which is not true. ❑ *A boy of 16 duped people into believing he was running a huge computer company.* [from French]

**du|ple me|ter** /dup³l mitər/ (**duple meters**) N-VAR Music that is written in **duple meter** has a beat that is repeated in groups of two. [TECHNICAL]

### Word Link du ≈ two : duo, duplex, duplicate

**du|plex** /dupleks/ (**duplexes**) N-COUNT A **duplex** is a house which has been divided into two separate units for two different families or groups of people. [from Latin]

**du|pli|cate** (**duplicates, duplicating, duplicated**)

> The verb is pronounced /duplıkeıt/. The noun and adjective are pronounced /duplıkıt/.

■ V-T If you **duplicate** something that has already been done, you repeat or copy it. ❑ *His task will be to duplicate his overseas success here at home.* ● **Duplicate** is also a noun. ❑ *…a duplicate of the elections in Georgia and South Dakota last month.* ● **du|pli|ca|tion** /duplıkeıʃᵊn/ N-UNCOUNT ❑ *…unnecessary duplication of resources.* ■ V-T To **duplicate** something which has been written, drawn, or recorded onto tape means to make exact copies of it. ❑ *The business duplicates video tapes for movie makers.* ● **Duplicate** is also a noun. ❑ *I've lost my card. I've got to get a duplicate.* ■ ADJ **Duplicate** is used to describe things that have been made as an exact copy of other things, usually in order to serve the same purpose. ❑ *He unlocked the door with a duplicate key.* [from Latin]

**du|rable** /duərəb³l/ ADJ Something that is **durable** is strong and lasts a long time without breaking or becoming weaker. ❑ *…a sofa covered with soft, durable leather.* ● **du|rabil|ity** /duərəbılıti/ N-UNCOUNT ❑ *Airlines recommend hard-sided cases for durability.* [from Old French]

**du|ra|tion** /duəreıʃᵊn/ N-UNCOUNT The **duration of** an event or state is the time during which it happens or exists. ❑ *The hotel was my home for the duration of my stay.* [from Medieval Latin]

**dur|ing** /duərıŋ/ ■ PREP If something happens **during** a period of time or an event, it happens continuously, or happens several times between the beginning and end of that period or event. ❑ *Storms are common during the winter.* ■ PREP An event that happens **during** a period of time

happens at some point or moment in that period. ❑ *During his visit, the president will visit the new hospital.* [from Latin]

### Usage during

**During** and **for** are often confused. *During* answers the question "When?" : *Bats hibernate during the winter. For* answers the question "How long?" : *Carla talks on the phone to her boyfriend for an hour every night.*

**dusk** /dʌsk/ N-UNCOUNT **Dusk** is the time just before night when the daylight has almost gone but when it is not completely dark. ❑ *We arrived home at dusk.* [from Old English]

**dust** /dʌst/ (**dusts, dusting, dusted**) ■ N-UNCOUNT **Dust** is very small dry particles of earth, sand or dirt. ❑ *Tanks raise huge trails of dust when they move.* ❑ *I could see a thick layer of dust on the stairs.* ■ V-T/V-I When you **dust** something such as furniture, you remove dust from it, usually using a cloth. ❑ *I vacuumed and dusted the living room.* ■ PHRASE If you say that something will happen when **the dust settles**, you mean that a situation will be clearer after it has calmed down. If you let **the dust settle** before doing something, you let a situation calm down before you try to do anything else. [INFORMAL] ❑ *Once the dust had settled Beck defended his decision.* [from Old English]

**dust bowl** (**dust bowls**) also **dustbowl** N-COUNT A **dust bowl** is an area of land, especially in the southern or central United States, that is dry and arid because the soil has been eroded by the wind. ❑ *…the midwestern dust bowl.*

**dust|pan** /dʌstpæn/ (**dustpans**) N-COUNT A **dustpan** is a small flat container made of metal or plastic. You hold it flat on the floor and put dirt and dust into it using a brush.

**dusty** /dʌsti/ (**dustier, dustiest**) ADJ If something is **dusty**, it is covered with dust. ❑ *…a dusty room.* [from Old English]

**du|ti|ful** /dutıfəl/ ADJ If you are **dutiful**, you do everything that you are expected to do. ❑ *She was a dutiful daughter.* ● **du|ti|ful|ly** ADV ❑ *The inspector dutifully recorded the date.* [from Old French]

**duty** /duti/ (**duties**) ■ N-VAR **Duty** is work that you have to do for your job. ❑ *Staff must report for duty at 8 a.m.* ■ N-SING If you say that something is your **duty**, you believe that you ought to do it because it is your responsibility. ❑ *I consider it my* duty to write to you and thank you. ❸ N-VAR **Duties** are taxes which you pay to the government on goods that you buy. ❏ *Import duties are around 30%.* ❹ PHRASE If someone such as a police officer or a nurse is **off duty**, they are not working. If someone is **on duty**, they are working. ❏ *I'm off duty.* [from Old French] → see **citizenship**

| **Thesaurus** | *duty* | Also look up : |
| --- | --- | --- |

| N. | assignment, responsibility, task ❶ ❷ |
| --- | --- |
| | obligation ❷ |

| **Word Partnership** | Use *duty* with : |
| --- | --- |

| N. | **guard** duty ❶ |
| --- | --- |
| ADJ. | **civic** duty, **military** duty, **patriotic** duty, |
| | **sense of** duty ❷ |
| PREP. | **off** duty, **on** duty ❹ |

| **Word Link** | *free ≈ without : care*free*, duty-*free*,* |
| --- | --- |
| | *toll-*free |

**duty-free** ADJ **Duty-free** goods are sold at airports or on planes or ships at a cheaper price than usual because you do not have to pay import tax on them. ❏ *...duty-free perfume.*

**DVD** /di vi di/ (**DVDs**) N-COUNT A **DVD** is a disk on which a movie or music is recorded. DVD disks are similar to compact disks but hold more information. **DVD** is an abbreviation for "digital video disk" or "digital versatile disk." ❏ *...a DVD player.* → see **laser**

**DVD burn|er** (**DVD burners**) also **DVD writer** N-COUNT A **DVD burner** is a piece of computer equipment that you use for copying data from a computer onto a DVD. [COMPUTING]

**DVT** /di vi ti/ (**DVTs**) N-VAR **DVT** is a serious medical condition caused by blood clots in the legs moving up to the lungs. **DVT** is an abbreviation for "deep vein thrombosis." [MEDICAL]

**dwarf** /dwɔrf/ (**dwarves, dwarfs, dwarfing, dwarfed**)

The spellings **dwarves** or **dwarfs** are used for the plural form of the noun.

❶ V-T If one person or thing **is dwarfed** by another, the second is so much bigger than the first that it makes them look very small. ❏ *The money he makes is dwarfed by his wife's salary.* ❷ N-COUNT In children's stories, a **dwarf** is an imaginary creature that is like a small man. [from Old English]

**dwarf planet** (**dwarf planets**) N-COUNT A **dwarf planet** is a round object that orbits the sun and is larger than an asteroid but smaller than a planet.

**dwell** /dwɛl/ (**dwells, dwelling, dwelt** or **dwelled**) ❶ V-I If you **dwell on** something, especially something unpleasant, you think, speak, or write about it a lot or for a long time. ❏ *"I don't want to dwell on the past," he told me.* [from Old English] ❷ → see also **dwelling**

**dwell|er** /dwɛlər/ (**dwellers**) N-COUNT A city **dweller** or slum **dweller**, for example, is a person who lives in the kind of place or house indicated. ❏ *The number of city dwellers is growing.* [from Old English]

**dwell|ing** /dwɛlɪŋ/ (**dwellings**) N-COUNT A **dwelling** or a **dwelling place** is a place where someone lives. [FORMAL] ❏ *3,500 new dwellings are*

planned for the area. [from Old English]

**dwelt** /dwɛlt/ **Dwelt** is the past tense and past participle of **dwell**. [from Old English]

**DWI** /di dʌbəlyu aɪ/ N-UNCOUNT **DWI** is the offense of driving after drinking more than the amount of alcohol that is legally allowed. **DWI** is an abbreviation for "driving while intoxicated." [AM] ❏ *He paid a fine for charges of DWI.*

**dwin|dle** /dwɪnd²l/ (**dwindles, dwindling, dwindled**) V-I If something **dwindles**, it becomes smaller, weaker, or less in number. ❏ *The factory's workforce dwindled from over 4,000 to a few hundred.* [from Old English]

**dye** /daɪ/ (**dyes, dyeing, dyed**) ❶ V-T If you **dye** something such as hair or cloth, you change its color by soaking it in a special liquid. ❏ *The women spun and dyed the wool.* ❷ N-VAR **Dye** is a substance made from plants or chemicals which is mixed into a liquid and used to change the color of something such as cloth or hair. ❏ *...bottles of hair dye.* [from Old English]

**dy|ing** /daɪɪŋ/ ❶ **Dying** is the present participle of **die**. ❷ ADJ A **dying** person or animal is very ill and likely to die soon. ❏ *...a dying man.* ● **The dying** are people who are dying. ❏ *By the time our officers arrived, the dead and the dying were everywhere.* ❸ ADJ A **dying** tradition or industry is becoming less important and is likely to disappear completely. ❏ *Shipbuilding is a dying business.* [from Old English]

| **Word Link** | *dyn ≈ power : *dyn*amic, *dyn*amite,* |
| --- | --- |
| | *dyn*amo |

**dy|nam|ic** /daɪnæmɪk/ (**dynamics**) ❶ ADJ If you describe someone as **dynamic**, you approve of them because they are full of energy or full of new and exciting ideas. ❏ *He was a dynamic and energetic leader.* ● **dy|nami|cal|ly** /daɪnæmɪkli/ ADV ❏ *He's the most dynamically imaginative jazz musician of our time.* ● **dy|na|mism** /daɪnəmɪzəm/ N-UNCOUNT ❏ *The situation needs dynamism and new thinking.* ❷ N-PLURAL The **dynamics** of a situation or group of people are the opposing forces within it that cause it to change. ❏ *...an understanding of family dynamics.* ❸ N-PLURAL **Dynamics** are forces which produce power or movement. [TECHNICAL] ❹ N-UNCOUNT **Dynamics** is the scientific study of motion, energy, and forces. [TECHNICAL] ❺ N-PLURAL The **dynamics** of a piece of music is how softly or loudly it is being played. [TECHNICAL] [from French]

**dy|nam|ic mark|ing** (**dynamic markings**) N-COUNT **Dynamic markings** are words and symbols in a musical score which show how softly or loudly the music should be played. [TECHNICAL]

**dy|na|mite** /daɪnəmaɪt/ N-UNCOUNT **Dynamite** is a type of explosive. ❏ *Fifty yards of track was blown up with dynamite.*

**dy|na|mo** /daɪnəmoʊ/ (**dynamos**) N-COUNT A **dynamo** is a device that uses the movement of a machine or vehicle to produce electricity.

**dyn|as|ty** /daɪnəsti/ (**dynasties**) N-COUNT A **dynasty** is a series of rulers of a country who all belong to the same family. ❏ *The Seljuk dynasty of Syria was founded in 1094.* [from Late Latin]

**dys|lexia** /dɪslɛksiə/ N-UNCOUNT If someone has **dyslexia**, they have difficulty with reading because of a slight disorder of their brain. [from Greek]

# Ee

**each** /iᴛʃ/ **1** DET If you refer to **each** thing or **each** person in a group, you are referring to every member of the group and considering them as individuals. ❑ *Each book is beautifully illustrated.* ❑ *The library buys $12,000 worth of books each year.* ● **Each** is also a pronoun. ❑ *…two bedrooms, each with three beds.* ❑ *We each have different needs and interests.* ● **Each** is also an adverb. ❑ *Tickets are six dollars each.* ● **Each** is also a quantifier. ❑ *He handed each of them a page of photos.* ❑ *Each of these exercises takes one or two minutes to do.* **2** QUANT If you refer to **each one of** the members of a group, you are emphasizing that something applies to every one of them. ❑ *He bought all her books and read each one of them.* **3** PRON You use **each other** when you are saying that each member of a group does something to the others or has a particular connection with the others. ❑ *We looked at each other in silence.* [from Old English]

> **Usage** each
>
> Sentences that begin with *each* take a singular verb. *Each of the drivers has a license.*

**eager** /igər/ ADJ If you are **eager to** do or have something, you want to do or have it very much. ❑ *Robert was eager to talk.* ❑ *I became eager for another baby.* ● **eager|ly** ADV *"So what do you think will happen?" he asked eagerly.* ● **eager|ness** N-UNCOUNT ❑ *…an eagerness to learn.* [from Old French]

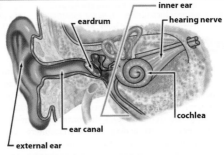

**eagle** /igᵊl/ (**eagles**) N-COUNT An **eagle** is a large bird that lives by eating small animals. [from Old French]

eagle

**ear** /ɪər/ (**ears**) **1** N-COUNT Your **ears** are the two parts of your body with which you hear sounds. ❑ *He whispered something in her ear.* **2** N-SING If you have **an ear for** music or language, you are able to hear its sounds accurately and to interpret them or reproduce them well. ❑ *Moby certainly has a fine ear for a tune.* **3** N-COUNT The **ears** of a cereal plant such as corn or barley are the top parts that contain the seeds. ❑ *…ears of corn.* [from Old English] **4** **music to** your **ears** → see **music** → see Word Web: **ear** → see **face**

**ear|li|er** /ɜrliər/ **1** **Earlier** is the comparative of **early**. **2** ADV **Earlier** is used to refer to a point or period in time before the present or before the one you are talking about. ❑ *They finished making the movie earlier this year.* ● **Earlier** is also an adjective. ❑ *Earlier reports suggested that the fire started accidentally.* [from Old English]

**ear|li|est** /ɜrliɪst/ **1** **Earliest** is the superlative of **early**. **2** PHRASE **At the earliest** means not before the date or time mentioned. ❑ *The official results are not expected until Tuesday at the earliest.* [from Old English]

**ear|lobe** /ɪərloʊb/ (**earlobes**) also **ear lobe** N-COUNT Your **earlobes** are the soft parts at the bottom of your ears. ❑ *…the holes in her earlobes.* → see **face**

**ear|ly** /ɜrli/ (**earlier, earliest**) **1** ADV **Early** means before the usual time that something happens or before the time that was arranged or expected. ❑ *I knew I had to get up early.* ❑ *She arrived early to get a place at the front.* ● **Early** is also an adjective. ❑ *I want to get an early start in the morning.* **2** ADJ **Early** means near the beginning of an activity, process, or period of time. ❑ *…the early stages of pregnancy.* ❑ *…the early 1980s.* ❑ *She was in her early teens.* ● **Early** is also an adverb. ❑ *We'll see you some time early next week.* ❑ *…an accident that happened earlier in the week.* [from Old English]

## Word Web ear

The **ear** collects **sound waves** and sends them to the brain. First the **external ear** picks up sound waves. Then these sound **vibrations** travel along the **ear canal** and strike the **eardrum**. The eardrum pushes against a series of tiny bones. These bones carry the vibrations into the **inner ear**. There they are picked up by the hair cells in the cochlea. At that point, the vibrations turn into electronic impulses. The cochlea is connected to the hearing **nerve**. It sends the electronic impulses to the brain.

inner ear
eardrum
hearing nerve
cochlea
ear canal
external ear

**Word Link**     *mark ≈ boundary, sign : book*mark, ear*mark*, land*mark*

**ear|mark** /ˈɪərmɑrk/ (**earmarks, earmarking, earmarked**) V-T If something is **earmarked for** a particular purpose, it is reserved for that purpose. ❑ *Extra money is being earmarked for the new projects.* ❑ *China has earmarked more than $20 billion for oil exploration.*

**earn** /ɜrn/ (**earns, earning, earned**) **1** V-T If you **earn** money, you receive money in return for work that you do. ❑ *She earns $37,000 a year.* **2** V-T If something **earns** money, it produces money as profit or interest. ❑ *...a bank account that earns interest.* **3** V-T If you **earn** something such as praise, you get it because you deserve it. ❑ *Companies must earn a reputation for honesty.* [from Old English]

**Thesaurus**    *earn*    Also look up :

| | |
|---|---|
| v. | bring in, make, take in **1** |

**earn|er** /ˈɜrnər/ (**earners**) N-COUNT An **earner** is someone or something that earns money or produces profit. ❑ *...a typical wage earner.* [from Old English]

**ear|nest** /ˈɜrnɪst/ **1** PHRASE If something is done or happens **in earnest**, it happens to a much greater extent and more seriously than before. ❑ *He'll start work in earnest next week.* **2** ADJ **Earnest** people are very serious and sincere. ❑ *Catherine was an earnest woman.* • **ear|nest|ly** ADV ❑ *She always listened earnestly.* [from Old English]

**earn|ings** /ˈɜrnɪŋz/ N-PLURAL Your **earnings** are the sums of money that you earn by working. ❑ *Average weekly earnings rose by 1.5% in July.* [from Old English]

**ear|phone** /ˈɪərfoʊn/ (**earphones**) **1** N-COUNT **Earphones** are a small piece of equipment which you wear over or inside your ears so that you can listen to a radio or mp3 player without anyone else hearing. **2** N-COUNT An **earphone** is the part of a telephone receiver or other device that you hold up to your ear or put into your ear.

**ear|ring** /ˈɪərɪŋ/ (**earrings**) N-COUNT **Earrings** are pieces of jewelry that you attach to your ears. ❑ *...an expensive pair of diamond earrings.* [from Old English]
→ see **jewelry**

**earth** /ɜrθ/ **1** N-PROPER **Earth** or **the Earth** is the planet on which we live. ❑ *The space shuttle Atlantis returned safely to Earth today.* **2** N-SING **The**

**earth** is the land surface on which we live and move around. ❑ *The earth shook and the walls fell around them.* **3** N-UNCOUNT **Earth** is the substance on the land surface of the earth in which plants grow. ❑ *...a huge pile of earth.* **4** → see also **down-to-earth** **5** PHRASE **On earth** is used for emphasis in questions that begin with words such as "how," "why," "what," or "where." ❑ *How on earth did that happen?* **6** PHRASE If you come **down to earth** or **back to earth**, you have to face the reality of everyday life after a period of great excitement. ❑ *When he came down to earth after his win he admitted: "It was an amazing feeling."* [from Old English]
→ see Word Web: **earth**
→ see **core, eclipse, erosion**

**earth|ly** /ˈɜrθli/ **1** ADJ **Earthly** means happening in the material world of our life on earth and not in any spiritual life or life after death. ❑ *...earthly pleasures.* **2** ADJ If you say that there is **no earthly reason** for something, you are emphasizing that there is no possible reason for it. ❑ *There is no earthly reason why they should ever change.* [from Old English]

**earth|quake** /ˈɜrθkweɪk/ (**earthquakes**) N-COUNT An **earthquake** is a shaking of the ground caused by movement of the Earth's crust. ❑ *...the San Francisco earthquake of 1906.*
→ see Word Web: **earthquake**
→ see **tsunami**

**earth sci|ence** (**earth sciences**) also **Earth science** N-VAR **Earth sciences** are sciences such as geology and geography that are concerned with the study of the earth.

**earthy** /ˈɜrθi/ (**earthier, earthiest**) **1** ADJ If you describe someone as **earthy**, you mean that they are open and direct about subjects that other people avoid or feel ashamed about. ❑ *...earthy humor.* **2** ADJ If you describe something as **earthy**, you mean it looks, smells, or feels like earth. ❑ *...warm, earthy colors.* [from Old English]

**earth|worm** /ˈɜrθwɜrm/ (**earthworms**) N-COUNT An **earthworm** is a kind of worm that lives in the ground.

**ear|wig** /ˈɪərwɪg/ (**earwigs**) N-COUNT An **earwig** is a small, thin, brown insect that has a pair of claws at the back end of its body. [from Old English]

**ease** /iz/ (**eases, easing, eased**) **1** PHRASE If you do something **with ease**, you do it without difficulty or effort. ❑ *Anne passed her exams with ease.* **2** N-UNCOUNT If you talk about the **ease of** a particular activity, you are referring to the way that it has been made easier to do, or to

**Word Web**    earth

The **earth** is made of material left over after the **sun** formed. In the beginning, about 4 billion years ago, the earth was made of liquid **rock**. During its first million years, it cooled into solid rock. **Life**, in the form of bacteria, began in the **oceans** about 3.5 billion years ago. During the next billion years, the **continents** formed. At the same time, the level of **oxygen** in the **atmosphere** increased. **Life forms evolved**, and some of them began to use oxygen. **Evolution** allowed **plants** and **animals** to move from the oceans onto the **land**.

## Word Web · earthquake

**Earthquakes** occur when two **tectonic plates** meet and start to move past each other. This meeting point is called the focus. It may be located anywhere from a few hundred meters to a few hundred kilometers below the surface of the earth. The resulting pressure causes a split in the earth's **crust** called a **fault**. Vibrations move out from the focus in all directions. These **seismic waves** cause little damage until they reach the surface. The **epicenter**, directly above the focus, receives the greatest damage. **Seismologists** use **seismographs** to measure the amount of ground movement during an earthquake.

*A seismograph recording a major earthquake.*

the fact that it is already easy to do. ❏ *For ease of reference, use the index to find the page.* **3** V-T/V-I If something unpleasant **eases** or if you **ease** it, it is reduced in degree, speed, or intensity. ❏ *Tensions had eased.* ❏ *I gave him some aspirin to ease the pain.* **4** V-T/V-I If you **ease your way** somewhere or **ease** somewhere, you move there slowly, carefully, and gently. If you **ease** something somewhere, you move it there slowly, carefully, and gently. ❏ *I eased my way toward the door.* ❏ *He eased his foot off the gas pedal.* **5** PHRASE If you are **at ease**, you are feeling confident and relaxed, and are able to talk to people without feeling nervous or anxious. ❏ *It is important that you feel at ease with your doctor.* **6** PHRASE If you are **ill at ease**, you feel somewhat uncomfortable, anxious, or worried. ❏ *He seemed embarrassed and ill at ease when everyone applauded.* [from Old French]
▶ **ease up** **1** PHR-VERB If something **eases up**, it is reduced in degree, speed, or intensity. ❏ *The rain started to ease up.* **2** PHR-VERB If you **ease up**, you start to make less effort. ❏ *He told supporters not to ease up even though he's in the lead.*

**easel** /iz³l/ (easels) N-COUNT An **easel** is a frame that supports a picture which an artist is painting or drawing. ❏ *I set up my easel in the garden.* [from Dutch]
→ see **painting**

**easi|ly** /izɪli/ **1** ADV You use **easily** to emphasize that something is very likely to happen, or is very likely to be true. ❏ *It could easily be another year before things improve.* **2** ADV You use **easily** to say that something happens more quickly or more often than is usual or normal. ❏ *He has always cried very easily.* [from Old French] **3** → see also **easy**

### Thesaurus · easily · Also look up :

| | |
|---|---|
| ADV. | quickly, readily **2** |

**east** /ist/ also East **1** N-UNCOUNT The **east** is the direction where the sun rises. ❏ *The city lies to the east of the river.* **2** N-SING The **east of** a place, country, or region is the part which is in the east. ❏ *They live in a village in the east of the country.* ● **East** is also an adjective. ❏ *...a line of hills along the east coast.* **3** ADV **East** means toward the east, or positioned to the east of a place or thing. ❏ *Go east on Route 9.* ❏ *...just east of the center of town.* **4** ADJ

An **east** wind is a wind that blows from the east. ❏ *...a cold east wind.* **5** N-SING **The East** is used to refer to the southern and eastern part of Asia, including India, China, and Japan. ❏ *Every so often, a new fashion arrives from the East.* [from Old English] **6** → see also **Middle East, Far East**

**East|er** /istər/ (Easters) N-VAR **Easter** is a Christian festival in March or April when Jesus Christ's return to life is celebrated. [from Old English]

**east|er|ly** /istərli/ (easterlies) **1** ADJ An **easterly** point, area, or direction is to the east or toward the east. ❏ *He progressed slowly along the coast in an easterly direction.* **2** ADJ An **easterly** wind is a wind that blows from the east. ❏ *It was a beautiful September day, with cool easterly winds.* **3** N-COUNT An **easterly** is a wind that blows from the east. [from Old English]

**east|ern** /istərn/ **1** ADJ **Eastern** means in or from the east of a region, state, or country. ❏ *...Eastern Europe.* **2** ADJ **Eastern** means coming from or associated with the people or countries of the East, such as India, China, or Japan. ❏ *Exports to Eastern countries have gone down.* [from Old English]

**east|ern|er** /istərnər/ (easterners) N-COUNT An **easterner** is a person who was born in or who lives in the eastern part of a place or country, especially an American from the East Coast of the U.S. [from Old English]

**east|ward** /istwərd/

The form **eastwards** is also used.

ADV **Eastward** or **eastwards** means toward the east. ❏ *A powerful snow storm is moving eastward.* ● **Eastward** is also an adjective. ❏ *...the eastward expansion of the city.* [from Old English]

**easy** /izi/ (easier, easiest) **1** ADJ If a job or action is **easy**, you can do it without difficulty. ❏ *The shower is easy to install.* ❏ *This is not an easy task.* ● **easi|ly** ADV ❏ *Dress your baby in clothes you can remove easily.* **2** ADJ If you say that someone has an **easy** life, you mean that they live comfortably without any problems or worries. ❏ *She has not had an easy life.* **3** PHRASE If someone tells you to **take it easy** or **take things easy**, they mean that you should relax and not do very much at all. [INFORMAL] ❏ *It is best to take things easy for a week or two.* [from Old French] **4** → see also **easily**

| **Thesaurus** | *easy* | Also look up : |

ADJ. basic, elementary, simple, uncomplicated; (*ant.*) complicated, difficult, hard ◼

**easy|going** /ízigoʊɪŋ/ ADJ If you describe someone as **easygoing**, you mean that they are not easily annoyed, worried, or upset, and you think this is a good quality. ❑ *He was easygoing and good-natured.*

**eat** /ít/ (**eats, eating, ate, eaten**) ◼ V-T/V-I When you **eat** something, you put it into your mouth, chew it, and swallow it. ❑ *She was eating a sandwich.* ❑ *I ate slowly and without speaking.* [from Old English] ◻ **dog eat dog** → see **dog** ◼ to **eat crow** → see **crow**
→ see **cooking, food**
▸ **eat away** PHR-VERB If one thing **eats away** another or **eats away at** another, it gradually destroys or uses it up. ❑ *The sea eats away at rocks.*
▸ **eat into** PHR-VERB If something **eats into** your time or your resources, it uses them, when they should be used for other things. ❑ *Responsibilities at home and work eat into his time.*

| **Thesaurus** | *eat* | Also look up : |

V. chew, consume, munch, nibble, taste ◼

| **Word Partnership** | Use *eat* with : |

ADV. eat **alone**, eat **properly**, eat **together**, eat **too much**, eat **well** ◼
V. eat **and drink**, eat **and sleep**, **want** *something* to eat ◼

**eat|er** /ítər/ (**eaters**) N-COUNT You use **eater** to refer to someone who eats in a particular way or who eats particular kinds of food. ❑ *a meat eater.* [from Old English]

**eat|ing dis|or|der** (**eating disorders**) N-COUNT An **eating disorder** is a medical condition such as bulimia or anorexia in which a person does not eat in a normal or healthy way. ❑ *Anyone can develop an eating disorder.*

**eaves|drop** /ívzdrɒp/ (**eavesdrops, eavesdropping, eavesdropped**) V-I If you **eavesdrop on** someone, you listen secretly to what they are saying. ❑ *They illegally eavesdropped on his telephone conversations.* [from Old English]

**ebb** /ɛb/ (**ebbs, ebbing, ebbed**) ◼ V-I When the tide or the sea **ebbs**, its level gradually falls. ❑ *When the tide ebbs, you can walk out for a mile.* ◼ N-COUNT The **ebb** or the **ebb** tide is one of the regular periods, usually two per day, when the sea gradually falls to a lower level as the tide moves away from the land. ◼ V-I If a feeling or the strength of something **ebbs**, it becomes weaker and gradually disappears. [FORMAL] ❑ *Were there times when enthusiasm ebbed?* ● **Ebb away** means the same as **ebb**. ❑ *The government's popular support is ebbing away.* ◼ PHRASE If someone or something is **at a low ebb** or **at their lowest ebb**, they are not very successful or profitable. ❑ *a time when everyone is tired and at a low ebb.* [from Old English]
→ see **ocean, tide**

**Ebola** /iboulə/ also **Ebola virus** N-UNCOUNT **Ebola** or the **Ebola virus** is a virus that causes a fever and internal bleeding, usually resulting in death. [after the Ebola River, the Democratic Republic of Congo]

**ebul|lient** /ɪbʌliənt, -bʊl-/ ADJ If you describe someone as **ebullient**, you mean that they are lively and full of enthusiasm or excitement about something. [FORMAL] ❑ *She has an ebullient sense of humor.* ● **ebul|lience** /ɪbʌliəns, -bʊl-/ N-UNCOUNT ❑ *His natural ebullience began to return.* [from Latin]

| **Word Link** | *ec ≈ away, from, out : eccentric, eclectic, ecstatic* |

**ec|cen|tric** /ɪksɛntrɪk/ (**eccentrics**) ADJ If you say that someone is **eccentric**, you mean that they behave in a strange way, and have habits or opinions that are different from those of most people. ❑ *He is an eccentric character who likes wearing unusual clothes.* ● An **eccentric** is an eccentric person. ❑ *Askew had a reputation as an eccentric.* ● **ec|cen|tric|ity** /ɛksɛntrɪsɪti/ (**eccentricities**) N-VAR ❑ *She is unusual to the point of eccentricity.* ❑ *We all have our eccentricities.* [from Medieval Latin]

**ec|cle|si|as|ti|cal** /ɪklíziǽstɪkᵊl/ ADJ **Ecclesiastical** means belonging to or connected with the Christian Church. ❑ *ecclesiastical law.* [from Late Middle English]

**eche|lon** /ɛʃəlɒn/ (**echelons**) N-COUNT An **echelon** in an organization or society is a level or rank in it. [FORMAL] ❑ *the lower echelons of society.* [from French]

**echo** /ɛkoʊ/ (**echoes, echoing, echoed**) ◼ N-COUNT An **echo** is a sound caused by a noise being reflected off a surface such as a wall. ❑ *He heard nothing but the echoes of his own voice.* ◼ V-I If a sound **echoes**, or a place **echoes with** sounds, sounds are reflected off a surface and there can be heard again. ❑ *His feet echoed on the floor.* ❑ *The hall echoed with the barking of a dozen dogs.* ◼ V-T If you **echo** someone's words, you repeat what they have said or express the same opinion. ❑ *Their views often echo each other.* ◼ N-COUNT A detail or feature that reminds you of something else can be referred to as an **echo**. ❑ *The accident has echoes of past disasters.* [from Latin]
→ see Word Web: **echo**
→ see **sound**

**ec|lec|tic** /ɪklɛktɪk/ ADJ An **eclectic** collection of objects, ideas, or beliefs is wide-ranging and comes from many different sources. [FORMAL] ❑ *an eclectic collection of paintings, drawings, and prints.* [from Greek]

**eclipse** /ɪklɪps/ (**eclipses, eclipsing, eclipsed**) ◼ N-COUNT An **eclipse of** the sun is an occasion when the moon is between the Earth and the sun, so that for a short time you cannot see part or all of the sun. An **eclipse of** the moon is an occasion when the Earth is between the sun and the moon, so that for a short time you cannot see part or all of the moon. ❑ *the solar eclipse on May 21.* ◼ V-T If one thing **is eclipsed by** a second thing that is bigger, newer, or more important than it, the first thing is no longer noticed because the second thing gets all the attention. ❑ *The space program has been eclipsed by other needs.* [from Old English]
→ see Word Web: **eclipse**

**eco-friendly** ADJ **Eco-friendly** products or services are less harmful to the environment than other similar products or services. ❑ *eco-friendly laundry detergent.*

## Word Web echo

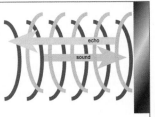

We can learn a lot from studying **echoes**. Geologists use **sound reflection** to predict how earthquake waves will travel through the earth. They also use echolocation to find underground oil reservoirs. Oceanographers use sonar to explore the ocean. Marine mammals, bats, and humans also use sonar for navigation. Architects study building materials and surfaces to understand how they absorb or **reflect** sound **waves**. They may use hard reflective surfaces to help create a noisy, exciting atmosphere in a restaurant. They may suggest soft drapes and carpeting to create a quiet, calm library.

**eco|logi|cal suc|ces|sion** N-UNCOUNT
**Ecological succession** is the process in which one population of plants and animals gradually replaces another population in a particular area as a result of changing environmental conditions. [TECHNICAL]

**ecol|ogy** /ɪkɒlədʒi/ (**ecologies**) ■ N-UNCOUNT **Ecology** is the study of the relationships between animals, plants, people, and their environment, and the balances between these relationships. □ ...a professor of ecology. ● **ecolo|gist** (**ecologists**) N-COUNT □ Ecologists are concerned that these chemicals might be polluting lakes. ■ N-VAR When you talk about the **ecology** of a place, you are referring to the pattern and balance of relationships between plants, animals, people, and the environment in that place. □ ...the ecology of the desert. ● **eco|logi|cal** /ɛkəlɒdʒɪkˀl, ik-/ ADJ □ ...Siberia's delicate ecological balance. ● **eco|logi|cal|ly** /ɛkəlɒdʒɪkli, ik-/ ADV □ This product can be recycled and is ecologically harmless. [from German]
→ see **amphibian**

**eco|nom|ic** /ɛkənɒmɪk, ik-/ ■ ADJ **Economic** means concerned with the organization of the money, industry, and trade of a country, region, or society. □ ...economic reforms. □ ...economic growth. ● **eco|nomi|cal|ly** /ɛkənɒmɪkli, ik-/ ADV □ ...an economically depressed area. ■ ADJ If something is **economic**, it produces a profit. □ The main purpose of most companies is economic and not charitable. [from Latin]
→ see **disaster**

**eco|nomi|cal** /ɛkənɒmɪkˀl, ik-/ ■ ADJ Something that is **economical** does not require a lot of money to operate. □ ...smaller and more economical cars. ● **eco|nomi|cal|ly** ADV □ Services could be operated more efficiently and economically.

■ ADJ Someone who is **economical** spends money sensibly and does not want to waste it on things that are unnecessary. A way of life that is **economical** does not require a lot of money. □ ...ideas for economical housekeeping. [from Latin]

### Thesaurus economical Also look up :

ADJ.  cost-effective, inexpensive ■
careful, frugal, practical, thrifty ■

### Word Link ics ≈ system, knowledge : economics, electronics, ethics

**eco|nom|ics** /ɛkɒnɒmɪks, ik-/ N-UNCOUNT **Economics** is the study of the way in which money, industry, and commerce are organized in a society. □ His sister is studying economics. [from Latin]

**econo|mist** /ɪkɒnəmɪst/ (**economists**) N-COUNT An **economist** is a person who studies, teaches, or writes about economics. [from Latin]

**econo|my** /ɪkɒnəmi/ (**economies**) ■ N-COUNT An **economy** is the system according to which the money, industry, and commerce of a country or region are organized. □ The Indian economy is changing fast. ■ N-UNCOUNT **Economy** is the use of the minimum amount of money, time, or other resources needed to achieve something, so that nothing is wasted. □ The biggest single step we can take to stop global warming is to raise the fuel economy of our vehicles. [from Latin]

**eco|sys|tem** /ɛkoʊsɪstəm, ik-/ (**ecosystems**) N-COUNT An **ecosystem** is all the plants and animals that live in a particular area together with the complex relationship that exists between them and their environment. [TECHNICAL] □ ...the forest ecosystem.
→ see **biosphere**

## Word Web eclipse

There is more than one kind of eclipse. When the **earth** passes between the **sun** and the **moon**, we see a **lunar eclipse**. When the moon passes between the sun and the earth, we see a **solar eclipse**. A total eclipse of the sun happens when the moon covers the sun completely. In the past, people were frightened of eclipses. Some civilizations understood eclipses. Their leaders pretended to control the sun in order to gain the respect of their people. On July 22, 2009, a total eclipse of the sun will be visible in North America.

Sun
Moon
Earth
orbit of the moon

**ec|sta|sy** /ɛkstəsi/ (**ecstasies**) N-VAR **Ecstasy** is a feeling of very great happiness. □ *...a state of religious ecstasy.* [from Old French]

**ec|stat|ic** /ɛkstætɪk/ ADJ If you are **ecstatic**, you feel very happy and full of excitement. □ *He was ecstatic about the birth of their first child.* □ *They gave an ecstatic reception to the speech.* ● **ec|stati|cal|ly** /ɛkstætɪkli/ ADV □ *We are both ecstatically happy.* [from Old French]

**ec|to|therm** /ɛktəθɜrm/ (**ectotherms**) N-COUNT An **ectotherm** is a cold-blooded animal, such as a reptile, whose body temperature depends on the temperature of the environment around it. Compare **endotherm**. [TECHNICAL]

**ec|ze|ma** /ɛksəmə, ɛgzə-, ɪgzi-/ N-UNCOUNT **Eczema** is a skin condition that makes your skin itch and become sore, rough, and broken. [from New Latin]

**edge** /ɛdʒ/ (**edges, edging, edged**) **1** N-COUNT The **edge** of something is the place or line where it stops, or the part of it that is farthest from the

edge

middle. □ *We were on a hill, right on the edge of town.* □ *She was standing at the water's edge.* **2** N-COUNT The **edge** of something sharp such as a knife or an ax is its sharp or narrow side. □ *...the sharp edge of the sword.* **3** V-I If someone or something **edges** somewhere, they move very slowly in that direction. □ *He edged closer to the telephone.* **4** N-SING If someone or

something has an **edge**, they have an advantage. □ *Mature students have skills and experience that can give them the edge over younger graduates.* **5** → see also **cutting edge, leading edge** **6** PHRASE If you or your nerves are **on edge**, you are tense, nervous, and unable to relax. □ *My nerves were constantly on edge.* [from Old English]

▶ **edge out** PHR-VERB If someone **edges out** someone else, they just manage to beat them or get in front of them in a game, race, or contest. □ *France edged out the American team by less than a second.*

**edge|wise** /ɛdʒwaɪz/ PHRASE If you say that you **cannot get a word in edgewise**, you are complaining that you do not have the opportunity to speak because someone else is talking so much. [INFORMAL] [from Old English]

**edgy** /ɛdʒi/ (**edgier, edgiest**) ADJ If someone is **edgy**, they are nervous and anxious, and seem likely to lose control of themselves. [INFORMAL] □ *Interviews make him edgy, he says.* [from Old English]

**ed|ible** /ɛdɪbəl/ ADJ If something is **edible**, it is safe to eat and not poisonous. □ *...edible mushrooms.* [from Late Latin]

**edict** /idɪkt/ (**edicts**) N-COUNT An **edict** is a command or instruction given by someone in authority. [FORMAL] □ *Officials issued an edict that*

*no cars could be left within 75 feet of an airport terminal.* [from Latin]

**edi|fice** /ɛdɪfɪs/ (**edifices**) N-COUNT An **edifice** is a large and impressive building. [FORMAL] □ *...a list of historic edifices.* [from Old French]

**edit** /ɛdɪt/ (**edits, editing, edited**) **1** V-T If you **edit** a text such as an article or a book, you correct and adapt it so that it is suitable for publishing. □ *She helped him edit his book.* **2** V-T If you **edit** a book, you collect several pieces of writing by different authors and prepare them for publishing. □ *This collection of essays is edited by Ellen Knight.* **3** V-T If you **edit** a movie or a television or radio program, you choose some of what has been filmed or recorded and arrange it in a particular order. □ *He taught me to edit film.* **4** V-T Someone who **edits** a newspaper, magazine, or journal is in charge of it. □ *I used to edit the college paper.*

**edi|tion** /ɪdɪʃən/ (**editions**) **1** N-COUNT An **edition** is a particular version of a book, magazine, or newspaper that is printed at one time. □ *The second edition was published only in Canada.* □ *...a paperback edition.* **2** N-COUNT An **edition** is a single television or radio program that is one of a series about a particular subject. □ *...last week's edition of "60 Minutes."* [from Latin]

**edi|tor** /ɛdɪtər/ (**editors**) **1** N-COUNT An **editor** is the person who is in charge of a newspaper or magazine, or a section of a newspaper or magazine, and who decides what will be published in each edition of it. □ *Her father was the editor of the Saturday Review.* **2** N-COUNT An **editor** is a person who checks and corrects texts before they are published. □ *He works as an editor of children's books.* **3** N-COUNT An **editor** is a person who prepares a movie, or a radio or television program, by selecting some of what has been filmed or recorded and putting it in a particular order. □ *She worked at 20th Century Fox as a film editor.* **4** N-COUNT An **editor** is a person who collects pieces of writing by different authors and prepares them for publication in a book or a series of books. □ *Michael Rosen is the editor of the book.* **5** N-COUNT An **editor** is a computer program that enables you to change and correct stored data. [COMPUTING] [from Late Latin]

**edi|to|rial** /ɛdɪtɔriəl/ (**editorials**) **1** ADJ **Editorial** means involved in preparing a newspaper, magazine, or book for publication. □ *I went to the editorial meetings when I had time.* **2** ADJ **Editorial** means involving the attitudes, opinions, and contents of something such as a newspaper, magazine, or television program. □ *The editorial standpoint of the magazine is right-wing.* **3** N-COUNT An **editorial** is an article in a newspaper, or an item on television or radio, that gives the opinion of the newspaper, network, or radio station. □ *...an editorial in The New York Times.* [from Late Latin]

**edu|cate** /ɛdʒukeɪt/ (**educates, educating, educated**) **1** V-T When someone **is educated**, he or she is taught at a school or college. ❑ *He was educated at Yale and Stanford.* **2** V-T To **educate** people means to teach them better ways of doing something or a better way of living. ❑ *...a program to help educate people about disabilities.* [from Latin]

**Thesaurus** educate Also look up :

v. coach, instruct, teach, train **2**

**edu|cat|ed** /ɛdʒʊkeɪtɪd/ ADJ Someone who is **educated** has a high standard of learning. ❑ *...an educated and decent man.* [from Latin]

**edu|ca|tion** /ɛdʒʊkeɪʃⁿn/ (**educations**) **1** N-VAR **Education** involves teaching and learning. ❑ *They're cutting funds for education.* ❑ *...better health education.* ● **edu|ca|tion|al** /ɛdʒʊkeɪʃənⁿl/ ADJ ❑ *...the Japanese educational system.* [from Latin] **2** → see also **further education, higher education**

**edu|ca|tive** /ɛdʒʊkeɪtɪv/ ADJ Something that has an **educative** role teaches you something. [FORMAL] ❑ *...an educative experience.*

**edu|ca|tor** /ɛdʒʊkeɪtər/ (**educators**) N-COUNT An **educator** is someone who is specialized in the theories and methods of education. [from Latin]

**eel** /il/ (**eels**) N-VAR An **eel** is a long, thin fish that looks like a snake. ● **Eel** is the flesh of this fish eaten as food. ❑ *...smoked eel.* [from Old English]

**eerie** /ɪəri/ (**eerier, eeriest**) ADJ Something that is **eerie** is strange and frightening. ❑ *I walked down the eerie dark path.* ● **eeri|ly** /ɪərɪli/ ADV ❑ *After the snowfall the city was eerily quiet.* [from Scottish]

**ef|fect** /ɪfɛkt/ (**effects, effecting, effected**) **1** N-VAR An **effect** is a change, reaction, or impression that is caused by something or is the result of something. ❑ *Parents worry about the effect of junk food on their child's behavior.* ❑ *The overall effect is cool, light, and airy.* **2** V-T If you **effect** something that you are trying to achieve, you succeed in causing it to happen. [FORMAL] ❑ *Effecting real change does not come quickly.* **3** → see also **greenhouse effect, side effect, special effect** **4** PHRASE You add **in effect** to a statement or opinion that you feel is a reasonable description or summary of a particular situation. ❑ *The deal would create, in effect, the world's biggest airline.* **5** PHRASE When something **takes effect, comes into effect**, or is **put into effect**, it begins to apply or starts to have results. ❑ *The second injection should be given once the first drug takes effect.* ❑ *These measures were put into effect in 2005.* **6** PHRASE You use **effect** in expressions such as **to good effect** and **to no effect** in order to indicate how successful or impressive an action is. ❑ *The museum is using advertising to good effect.* **7** PHRASE You use **to this effect, to that effect**, or **to the effect that** to indicate that you have given or are giving a summary of something that was said or written, and not the actual words used. ❑ *A public warning was issued to this effect.* [from Latin]

**Usage** effect and affect

*Effect* and *affect* are often confused. *Effect* means "to bring about": *Voters hope the election will effect change. Affect* means "to change": *The cloudy weather affected his mood.*

**Word Partnership** Use *effect* with :

| | |
|---|---|
| ADJ. | **adverse** effect, **desired** effect, **immediate** effect, **lasting** effect, **negative/positive** effect **1** |
| V. | **have an** effect **1** **produce an** effect, **take** effect **5** |
| N. | effect **a change 2** |

**ef|fec|tive** /ɪfɛktɪv/ **1** ADJ Something that is **effective** works well and produces the results that were intended. ❑ *We could be more effective in encouraging students to enter teacher training.* ❑ *No drugs are effective against this disease.* ● **ef|fec|tive|ly** ADV ❑ *Services need to be organized more effectively.* ● **ef|fec|tive|ness** N-UNCOUNT ❑ *...the effectiveness of computers as an educational tool.* **2** ADJ **Effective** means having a particular role or result in practice, though not officially or in theory. ❑ *...an agreement giving Rubin effective control of the company.* **3** ADJ When something such as a law or an agreement becomes **effective**, it begins officially to apply or be valid. ❑ *The new rules will become effective in the next few days.* [from Latin]

**Word Partnership** Use *effective* with :

| | |
|---|---|
| N. | effective **means**, effective **method**, effective **treatment**, effective **use 1** |
| ADV. | **highly** effective **1** effective **immediately 3** |

**ef|fec|tive|ly** /ɪfɛktɪvli/ ADV You use **effectively** with a statement to show that it is not accurate in every detail, but that you feel it is a reasonable description of a particular situation. ❑ *The region was effectively independent.* [from Latin]

**ef|fi|cient** /ɪfɪʃⁿnt/ ADJ If something or someone is **efficient**, they are able to do tasks successfully, without wasting time or energy. ❑ *Cycling is the most efficient form of transport.* ● **ef|fi|cien|cy** /ɪfɪʃⁿnsi/ N-UNCOUNT ❑ *...ways to increase efficiency.* ● **ef|fi|cient|ly** ADV ❑ *...a campaign to encourage people to use energy more efficiently.* [from Latin] → see also **effective**

**Usage** effective and efficient

*Effective* and *efficient* are often confused. If you are *effective*, you get the job done properly; if you are *efficient*, you get the job done quickly and easily: *Doing research at the library can be effective, but using the Internet is often more efficient.*

**Word Partnership** Use *efficient* with :

| | |
|---|---|
| N. | **energy** efficient, **fuel** efficient, efficient **method**, efficient **system**, efficient **use** of *something* |
| ADV. | **highly** efficient |

**ef|fort** /ɛfərt/ (**efforts**) **1** N-VAR If you make an **effort** to do something, you try very hard to do it. ❑ *He made no effort to hide his disappointment.* ❑ *Finding a cure takes a lot of time and effort.* **2** N-UNCOUNT; N-SING If you do something **with effort**, or if it is **an effort**, you mean it is difficult to do. [WRITTEN] ❑ *She sat up slowly and with great effort.* ❑ *Carrying the equipment while hiking in the forest was*

*an effort*. [from Old French]

| **Thesaurus** | *effort* | Also look up : |

| | |
|---|---|
| N. | attempt **1** |
| | exertion, labor, work **2** |

**ef|fort force** N-UNCOUNT In physics, **effort force** is force that is used to move an object. [TECHNICAL]

**ef|fort|less** /ɛfərtlɪs/ ADJ Something that is **effortless** is done easily and well. ❑ …*effortless Italian cooking*. ● **ef|fort|less|ly** ADV ❑ *Peter adapted effortlessly to his new surroundings*. [from Old French]

**EFL** /i ɛf ɛl/ N-UNCOUNT **EFL** is the teaching of English to people whose first language is not English. **EFL** is an abbreviation for "English as a Foreign Language." ❑ …*an EFL teacher*.

**e.g.** /i dʒi/ **e.g.** is an abbreviation that means "for example." It is used before a noun, or to introduce another sentence. ❑ *We need professionals of all types, e.g., teachers*. [from Latin]

**egg** /ɛg/ (**eggs, egging, egged**) **1** N-COUNT An **egg** is an oval object that is produced by a female bird and contains a baby bird. Other animals such as reptiles and fish also lay eggs. ❑ …*a baby bird hatching from its egg*. **2** N-VAR In many countries, an **egg** means a hen's egg, eaten as food. ❑ *Break the eggs into a shallow bowl*. **3** N-COUNT An **egg** is a cell that is produced in the bodies of female animals and humans. If it is fertilized by a sperm, a baby develops from it. ❑ *It only takes one sperm to fertilize an egg*. [Senses 1, 2 and 3 from Old Norse.]
→ see **bird, reproduction**
▶ **egg on** PHR-VERB If you **egg** a person **on**, you encourage them to do something, especially something dangerous or foolish. ❑ *She was laughing and egging him on*.
→ see Picture Dictionary: **egg**

**egg|plant** /ɛgplænt/ (**eggplants**) N-VAR An **eggplant** is a vegetable with a smooth, dark purple skin.
→ see **vegetable**

**ego** /igoʊ, ɛgoʊ/ (**egos**) N-VAR Someone's **ego** is their sense of their own worth. ❑ *He had a big ego and never admitted that he was wrong*. [from Latin]

**eight** /eɪt/ (**eights**) NUM **Eight** is the number 8. ❑ *The McEwans have eight children*. [from Old English]

| **Word Link** | *teen ≈ plus ten, from 13-19 :* **eight***teen,* **seven***teen,* **teen***ager* |

**eight|een** /eɪtin/ NUM **Eighteen** is the number 18. ❑ *He worked for them for eighteen years*. [from Old English]

**eight|eenth** /eɪtinθ/ ORD The **eighteenth** item in a series is the one that you count as number eighteen. ❑ *The talks are now in their eighteenth day*. [from Old English]

**eighth** /eɪtθ/ (**eighths**) **1** ORD The **eighth** item in a series is the one that you count as number eight. ❑ …*the eighth prime minister of India*. **2** ORD An **eighth** is one of eight equal parts of something. ❑ *The area produces an eighth of Russia's grain, meat, and milk*. [from Old English]

**eighth note** (**eighth notes**) N-COUNT An **eighth note** is a musical note that has a time value equal to half a quarter note.

**eighti|eth** /eɪtiəθ/ ORD The **eightieth** item in a series is the one that you count as number eighty. ❑ *Mr. Stevens recently celebrated his eightieth birthday*. [from Old English]

**eighty** /eɪti/ (**eighties**) **1** NUM **Eighty** is the number 80. ❑ *Eighty horses trotted up*. **2** N-PLURAL When you talk about the **eighties**, you are referring to numbers between 80 and 89. For example, if you are **in** your **eighties**, you are aged between 80 and 89. If the temperature is **in the eighties**, the temperature is between 80 and 89 degrees. ❑ *He was in his late eighties*. **3** N-PLURAL The **eighties** is the decade between 1980 and 1989. ❑ *He died in the eighties*. [from Old English]

**either** /iðər, aɪðər/ **1** CONJ You use **either** in front of the first of two or more alternatives, when you are stating the only possibilities or choices that there are. The other alternatives are introduced by "or." ❑ *Either she goes or I go*. ❑ *He should be either put on trial or set free*. **2** CONJ You use **either** in a negative statement in front of the first of two alternatives to indicate that the negative statement refers to both the alternatives. ❑ *There is no sign of either brain damage or memory loss*. ● **Either** is also a pronoun. ❑ *She said I'd never marry or have children. I don't want either*. ● **Either** is also a quantifier. ❑ *There are no simple answers to either of those questions*. ● **Either** is also a determiner. ❑ *He couldn't remember either man's name*. **3** PRON You can use **either** to refer to one of two things, people, or situations, when you want to say that they are both possible and it does not matter which one is chosen or considered. ❑ *You can contact him either by phone or by email*. ● **Either** is also a quantifier. ❑ *It's quick and convenient and requires little effort from either of you*. ● **Either** is also a determiner. ❑ *You can choose either date to send in your completed application form*. **4** ADV You use **either** by itself in negative statements to indicate that there is a similarity or connection with a person or thing that you have just mentioned. ❑ *He did not say anything to her, and she did not speak to him either*. **5** DET You can use **either** to introduce a noun that refers to each of two things when you are talking about both of them. ❑ *The basketball nets hung down from the ceiling at either end of the gym*. [from Old English]

| **Word Link** | *e ≈ away, out :* **e***ject,* **e***migrate,* **e***mit* |

**eject** /ɪdʒɛkt/ (**ejects, ejecting, ejected**) **1** V-T If you **eject** someone **from** a place, you force them

**Picture Dictionary**    **egg**

fried egg      scrambled eggs      hard-boiled egg

soft-boiled egg

omelet

to leave. ❏ *Officials used guard dogs to eject the protesters.* ● **ejec|tion** /ɪdʒɛkʃ°n/ (**ejections**) N-VAR ❏ *...the ejection of the New York Mets' manager from Saturday night's game.* **2** V-T To **eject** something means to remove it or push it out forcefully. ❏ *Sometimes the disc can't be ejected from the computer.* [from Latin]

> **Word Link** labor ≈ working : col**labor**ate, e**labor**ate, **labor**atory

**elabo|rate** (**elaborates, elaborating, elaborated**)

The adjective is pronounced /ɪlæbərɪt/. The verb is pronounced /ɪlæbəreɪt/.

**1** ADJ You use **elaborate** to describe something that is very complex because it has a lot of different parts. ❏ *...an elaborate research project.* ● **elabo|rate|ly** ADV ❏ *It was an elaborately planned operation.* **2** V-I If you **elaborate on** something that has been said, you say more about it, or give more details. ❏ *A spokesman declined to elaborate on yesterday's statement.* [from Latin]

> **Word Link** lapse ≈ falling : col**lapse**, e**lapse**, **lapse**

**elapse** /ɪlæps/ (**elapses, elapsing, elapsed**) V-I When time **elapses**, it passes. [FORMAL] ❏ *Forty-eight hours have elapsed since his arrest.* [from Latin]

**elas|tic** /ɪlæstɪk/ **1** N-UNCOUNT **Elastic** is a rubber material that stretches when you pull it and returns to its original size and shape when you let it go. ❏ *It has a piece of elastic that goes around the back of the head.* **2** ADJ Something that is **elastic** is able to stretch easily. ❏ *Beat the dough until it is slightly elastic.* [from New Latin]

**elas|tic|ity** /ɪlæstɪsɪti, ɪlæst-/ N-UNCOUNT The **elasticity** of a material or substance is its ability to return to its original shape, size, and condition after it has been stretched. ❏ *Daily facial exercises help to retain the skin's elasticity.* [from New Latin]

**elas|tic re|bound** (**elastic rebounds**) N-VAR **Elastic rebound** is a geological process associated with earthquakes, in which rock is stretched and then contracts as a result of energy stored within it. [TECHNICAL]

**elat|ed** /ɪleɪtɪd/ ADJ If you are **elated**, you are extremely happy and excited because of something that has happened. ❏ *I was elated by the news.* ● **ela|tion** /ɪleɪʃ°n/ N-UNCOUNT ❏ *His supporters reacted to the news with elation.* [from Latin]
→ see **emotion**

**el|bow** /ɛlboʊ/ (**elbows, elbowing, elbowed**) **1** N-COUNT Your **elbow** is the joint where your arm bends in the middle. ❏ *He slipped and fell, badly bruising an elbow.* **2** V-T If you **elbow** people **aside** or **elbow** your **way** somewhere, you push people with your elbows in order to move somewhere. ❏ *Jake came up to her, elbowing Susan aside.* [from Old English] **3** to **rub elbows with** → see **rub**
→ see **body**

**el|der** /ɛldər/ (**elders**) **1** ADJ The **elder of** two people is the one who was born first. ❏ *...his elder brother.* **2** N-COUNT A person's **elder** is someone who is older than them, especially someone quite a lot older. [FORMAL] ❏ *They have no respect for their elders.* **3** N-COUNT In some societies, an **elder** is one of the respected older people who have influence and authority. ❏ *...a meeting of tribal elders.* [from Old English]

**el|der|ly** /ɛldərli/ ADJ You use **elderly** as a polite way of saying that someone is old. ❏ *There was an elderly couple on the porch.* ● **The elderly** are people who are old. ❏ *...health care for the elderly.* [from Old English]
→ see **age**

**eld|est** /ɛldɪst/ ADJ The **eldest** person in a group is the one who was born before all the others. ❏ *The eldest child was a daughter called Elizabeth.* ❏ *David was the eldest of three boys.* [from Old English]

**elect** /ɪlɛkt/ (**elects, electing, elected**) **1** V-T When people **elect** someone, they choose that person to represent them, by voting for them. ❏ *The people have voted to elect a new president.* ❏ *The University of Washington elected him dean in 1976.* **2** V-T If you **elect to** do something, you choose to do it. [FORMAL] ❏ *He elected to stay in India.* [from Latin]
→ see **election**

**elec|tion** /ɪlɛkʃ°n/ (**elections**) **1** N-VAR An **election** is a process in which people vote to choose a person or group of people to hold an official position. ❏ *...the country's first free elections for more than fifty years.* ❏ *...his election campaign.* **2** N-UNCOUNT The **election** of a particular person or group of people is their success in winning an election. ❏ *...the election of the Democrat candidate last year.* ❏ *...his election as president of the United States.* [from Latin]
→ see Word Web: **election**
→ see **citizenship**

> **Word Web** election
>
> **Presidential candidates** spend millions of dollars on their **campaigns**. They give **speeches**. They appear on TV and **debate**. On election day, **voters cast** their **votes** at local **polling places**. **Citizens** living outside of the US mail in **absentee ballots**. But voters don't **elect** the **president** directly. States send representatives to the **electoral college**. There, representatives from all but two states must cast all their votes for one candidate—even if 49% of the people wanted the other candidate. Four times a candidate has **won** the popular vote and lost the election. This happened when George W. Bush won in 2000.

E

---

**Word Partnership** Use *election* with :

N. election **campaign**, election **day**,
election **official**, election **results** ◼

V. **hold an** election, **lose an** election,
election, **win an** election ◼

---

**elec|tive** /ɪlɛktɪv/ (**electives**) N-COUNT An
**elective** is a subject which a student can choose to
study as part of his or her course. ◻ *I took most of my
electives in English.* [from Latin]

**elec|tor** /ɪˈlɛktə/ (**electors**) N-COUNT An **elector**
is a person who has the right to vote in an election.
[from Latin]

**elec|tor|al** /ɪlɛktərəl/ ADJ **Electoral** is used to
describe things that are connected with elections.
◻ *...electoral reform.* ● **elec|tor|al|ly** ADV ◻ *The
government's tax increases were electorally unpopular.*
[from Latin]

**elec|tor|al col|lege** N-SING The **electoral
college** is the system that is used in the United
States in presidential elections. The electors in
the electoral college act as representatives for
each state, and they elect the president and vice
president.

**elec|tor|ate** /ɪlɛktərɪt/ (**electorates**) N-COUNT
The **electorate** of a country or area is all the people
in it who have the right to vote in an election. ◻ *He
has the support of almost a quarter of the electorate.*
[from Latin]

**elec|tric** /ɪlɛktrɪk/ ◼ ADJ An **electric** device or
machine works by means of electricity, rather
than using some other source of power. ◻ *...her
electric guitar.* ◻ ADJ An **electric** current, voltage,
or charge is one that is produced by electricity.
◼ ADJ **Electric** plugs, sockets, or power lines are
designed to carry electricity. ◼ ADJ If you describe
the atmosphere of a place or event as **electric**,
you mean that people are in a state of great
excitement. ◻ *The mood in the hall was electric.* [from
New Latin]
→ see **keyboard**

**elec|tri|cal** /ɪlɛktrɪkəl/ ◼ ADJ **Electrical** goods,
equipment, or appliances work by means of
electricity. ◻ *...electrical equipment.* ● **elec|tri|cal|ly**
/ɪlɛktrɪkli/ ADV ◻ *...electrically powered vehicles.*
◻ ADJ **Electrical** industries, engineers, or workers
are involved in the production and supply of
electricity or electrical products. ◻ *...company
representatives from the electrical industry.* [from New
Latin]
→ see **electricity, energy**

**elec|tri|cal charge** N-SING The **law of electrical
charges** is a principle in physics which states that
two electrical charges will attract one another if
they are opposite and repel one another if they are
the same. [TECHNICAL]

**elec|tri|cal en|er|gy** N-UNCOUNT **Electrical
energy** is the form of energy that is produced by
electricity.

**elec|tric force** (**electric forces**) N-VAR An
**electric force** is the force that exists between two
objects with an electric charge.

**elec|tric gen|era|tor** (**electric generators**)
N-COUNT An electric generator is a machine which
produces electricity.

---

**Word Link** *electr ≈ electric : electrician,
electricity, electron*

---

**Word Link** *ician ≈ person who works at :
electrician, musician, physician*

---

**elec|tri|cian** /ɪlɛktrɪʃⁿn, ilɛk-/ (**electricians**)
N-COUNT An **electrician** is a person whose job is
to install and repair electrical equipment. [from
New Latin]

**elec|tric|ity** /ɪlɛktrɪsiti, ilɛk-/ N-UNCOUNT
**Electricity** is a form of energy that can be carried
by wires and is used for heating and lighting, and
to provide power for machines. ◻ *We moved into a
house with electricity but no running water.* [from New
Latin]
→ see Word Web: **electricity**
→ see **energy, light bulb**

**elec|tric pow|er** N-UNCOUNT **Electric power** is
the same as **electricity**.

**elec|tric shock** (**electric shocks**) N-COUNT If
you get an **electric shock**, you get a sudden painful
feeling when you touch something connected to a
supply of electricity.

**elec|tri|fy** /ɪlɛktrɪfaɪ/ (**electrifies, electrifying,
electrified**) ◼ V-T If people **are electrified by**
an event or experience, it makes them feel very
excited and surprised. ◻ *The world was electrified
by his courage.* ● **elec|tri|fy|ing** ADJ ◻ *He gave an
electrifying performance.* ◻ V-T When a rail system
or rail line **is electrified**, electric cables are put over
the tracks, or electric rails are put beside them, so
that the trains can be powered by electricity. ◻ *The
railroad line was electrified in 1974.* ● **elec|tri|fi|ca|tion**
/ɪlɛktrɪfɪkeɪʃⁿn/ N-UNCOUNT ◻ *...the electrification
of the Toronto tramway system.* [from New Latin]

**elec|tro|cute** /ɪlɛktrəkyut/ (**electrocutes,
electrocuting, electrocuted**) V-T If someone **is**

---

**Word Web** electricity

The need for **electrical** power in the U.S. may rise by 35 percent
over the next 20 years. **Power companies** are working hard
to meet this need. At the center of every **power station** are
electrical **generators**. Traditionally, they ran on hydroelectric
power or **fossil fuel**. However, today new sources of **energy**
are available. On **wind farms**, wind **turbines** use the power
of moving air to run generators. Seaside tidal power stations
make use the forces of rising and falling tides to turn
turbines. And in sunny climates, **photovoltaic cells** produce electrical power from the sun's rays.

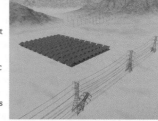

**electrocuted**, they are killed or badly injured when they touch something connected to a source of electricity. ❑ *Three people were electrocuted by falling power lines.* ● **elec|tro|cu|tion** /ɪlɛktrəkyuˈʃ°n/ (**electrocutions**) N-VAR ❑ *The court sentenced him to death by electrocution.*

**elec|tro|mag|net** /ɪlɛktroʊmægnɪt/ (**electromagnets**) N-COUNT An **electromagnet** is a magnet that consists of a piece of iron or steel surrounded by a coil. The metal becomes magnetic when an electric current is passed through the coil.

**elec|tro|mag|net|ic spec|trum** N-SING The **electromagnetic spectrum** is the complete range of electromagnetic radiation, from the longest radio waves to the shortest gamma rays.

**elec|tro|mag|net|ic wave** (**electromagnetic waves**) N-COUNT **Electromagnetic** waves are waves of energy inside an electromagnetic field.

| Word Link | electr ≈ electric : electrician, electricity, electron |
|---|---|

**elec|tron** /ɪlɛktrɒn/ (**electrons**) N-COUNT An **electron** is a tiny particle of matter that is smaller than an atom and has a negative electrical charge. [TECHNICAL]
→ see **television**

**elec|tron cloud** (**electron clouds**) N-COUNT An **electron cloud** is an area inside an atom where electrons are likely to exist. [TECHNICAL]

**elec|tron|ic** /ɪlɛktrɒnɪk, i-/ ◼ ADJ An **electronic** device has transistors or silicon chips that control and change the electric current passing through the device. ❑ *...expensive electronic equipment.* ◼ ADJ An **electronic** process or activity involves the use of electronic devices. ❑ *...electronic music.* ● **elec|troni|cal|ly** ADV ❑ *The gates are operated electronically.*

**elec|tron|ic me|dia** N-PLURAL **Electronic media** are means of communication such as radio, television, and the Internet, which use technology to produce information. Compare **print media**.

| Word Link | ics ≈ system, knowledge : economics, electronics, ethics |
|---|---|

**elec|tron|ics** /ɪlɛktrɒnɪks, i-/ N-UNCOUNT **Electronics** is the technology of using transistors and silicon chips, especially in devices such as radios, televisions, and computers. ❑ *...Ohio's three main electronics companies.*

**elec|tron micro|scope** (**electron microscopes**) N-COUNT An **electron microscope** is a type of very powerful microscope that uses electrons instead of light to produce a magnified image of something.

**elec|tro|stat|ic dis|charge** /ɪlɛktrəstætɪk dɪstʃɑrdʒ/ (**electrocstatic discharges**) N-VAR An **electrostatic discharge** is the sudden release of static electricity that can occur when two objects with different electrical charges are brought close together.

**el|egant** /ɛlɪgənt/ ◼ ADJ If you describe a person or thing as **elegant**, you mean that they are pleasing and graceful in appearance or style. ❑ *Patricia looked beautiful and elegant as always.* ● **el|egance** N-UNCOUNT ❑ *...the elegance of the hotel.* ● **el|egant|ly** ADV ❑ *...a tall, elegantly dressed man.* ◼ ADJ If you describe a piece of writing, an idea, or a plan as **elegant**, you mean that it is simple, clear, and clever. ❑ *The document impressed me with its elegant simplicity.* ● **el|egant|ly** ADV ❑ *...an elegantly simple idea.* [from Latin]

| Thesaurus | elegant | Also look up : |
|---|---|---|
| ADJ. | chic, exquisite, luxurious, stylish ◼ | |

**el|ement** /ɛlɪmənt/ (**elements**) ◼ N-COUNT The different **elements** of something are the different parts it contains. ❑ *The exchange of prisoners was a key element of the UN's peace plan.* ❑ *Physical fitness has now become an important element in our lives.* ◼ N-COUNT When you talk about **elements** within a society or organization, you are referring to groups of people who have similar aims, beliefs, or habits. ❑ *...criminal elements, such as thieves, murderers and hooligans.* ◼ N-COUNT If something has an **element** of a particular quality or emotion, it has a certain amount of this quality or emotion. ❑ *Many of the complaints contain an element of truth.* ◼ N-COUNT An **element** is a substance such as gold, oxygen, or carbon that consists of only one type of atom. ◼ N-COUNT The **element** in an electric or water heater is the metal part that changes the electric current into heat. ◼ N-PLURAL You can refer to the weather, especially wind and rain, as **the elements**. ❑ *Their open boat was exposed to the elements.* ◼ PHRASE If

| Word Web | element |
|---|---|

**Elements**—like copper, sodium, and oxygen—are made from only one type of **atom**. Each element has its own unique **properties**. For example, oxygen is a gas at room temperature and copper is a solid. Often elements come together with other types of elements to make **compounds**. When the atoms in a compound bind together, they form a **molecule**. One of the best known molecules is $H_2O$. It is made up of two hydrogen atoms and one oxygen atom. This molecule is also known as water. The **periodic table** is a complete listing of all the elements.

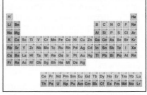

The Periodic Table of Elements

you say that someone is **in** their **element**, you mean that they are in a situation they enjoy. ❑ *My mother was in her element, organizing everything.* [from Latin]

→ see Word Web: **element**

→ see **periodic table, rock**

**el|ement|al** /ˌɛlɪˈmɛntᵊl/ ADJ **Elemental** feelings and types of behavior are simple, basic, and forceful. [LITERARY] ❑ *...the elemental life they would be living in this new colony.* [from Latin]

**el|emen|ta|ry** /ˌɛlɪˈmɛntəri, -tri/ ADJ Something that is **elementary** is very simple and basic. ❑ *...elementary computer skills.* [from Latin]

**el|emen|ta|ry school** (**elementary schools**) N-VAR An **elementary school** is a school where children are taught for the first six or sometimes eight years of their education.

**el|ements of art** N-PLURAL The **elements of art** are the basic components of a painting or drawing, such as line, color, and shape. [TECHNICAL]

**el|ements of mu|sic** N-PLURAL The **elements of music** are the basic components of a piece of music, such as melody, harmony, and rhythm. [TECHNICAL]

elephant

**el|ephant** /ˈɛlɪfənt/ (**elephants**) N-COUNT An **elephant** is a very large animal with a long, flexible nose called a trunk. [from Latin]

→ see **herbivore**

**el|evate** /ˈɛlɪveɪt/ (**elevates, elevating, elevated**) **1** V-T When someone or something **is elevated to** a more important rank or status, they achieve it. [FORMAL] ❑ *He was elevated to the post of president.* ● **el|eva|tion** /ˌɛlɪˈveɪʃᵊn/ N-UNCOUNT ❑ *...the elevation of the assistant coach to the head coaching position.* **2** V-T To **elevate** something means to increase it in amount or intensity. [FORMAL] ❑ *Emotional stress can elevate blood pressure.* **3** V-T If you **elevate** something, you raise it higher. ❑ *I built a platform to elevate the bed.* [from Latin]

**Word Link** ation ≈ state of: dehydr**ation**, elev**ation**, preserv**ation**

**el|eva|tion** /ˌɛlɪˈveɪʃᵊn/ (**elevations**) N-COUNT The **elevation** of a place is its height above sea level. ❑ *We're at an elevation of 13,000 feet above sea level.* [from Latin]

**el|eva|tor** /ˈɛlɪveɪtər/ (**elevators**) N-COUNT An **elevator** is a device that carries people or goods up and down inside tall buildings. ❑ *We took the elevator to the fourteenth floor.* [from Latin]

**elev|en** /ɪˈlɛvᵊn/ (**elevens**) NUM **Eleven** is the number 11. ❑ *Josh invited eleven friends to his party.* [from Old English]

**elev|enth** /ɪˈlɛvᵊnθ/ ORD The **eleventh** item in a series is the one that you count as number eleven. ❑ *We were working on the eleventh floor.* [from Old English]

**elic|it** /ɪˈlɪsɪt/ (**elicits, eliciting, elicited**) **1** V-T If you **elicit** a response or a reaction, you do or say something that makes other people respond or react. ❑ *He was hopeful that his request would elicit a positive response.* **2** V-T If you **elicit** a piece

of information, you get it by asking the right questions. [FORMAL] ❑ *Several phone calls elicited no further information.* [from Latin]

**eli|gible** /ˈɛlɪdʒɪbᵊl/ ADJ Someone who is **eligible to** do something is qualified or able to do it, for example, because they are old enough. ❑ *Almost half the population are eligible to vote.* ● **eli|gibil|ity** /ˌɛlɪdʒɪˈbɪlɪti/ N-UNCOUNT ❑ *...the rules covering eligibility for benefits.* [from Late Latin]

**elimi|nate** /ɪˈlɪmɪneɪt/ (**eliminates, eliminating, eliminated**) **1** V-T To **eliminate** something means to remove it completely. [FORMAL] ❑ *Recent measures have not eliminated discrimination in employment.* ● **elimi|na|tion** N-UNCOUNT ❑ *...the elimination of chemical weapons.* **2** V-T PASSIVE When a person or team **is eliminated from** a competition, they are defeated and so stop participating in the competition. ❑ *I was eliminated from the 400 meters in the semi-finals.* [from Latin]

**elite** /ɪˈlit, eɪ-/ (**elites**) N-COUNT You can refer to the most powerful, rich, or talented people within a particular group, place, or society as the **elite**. ❑ *...the political elite.* ● **Elite** is also an adjective. ❑ *...the elite troops of the president's bodyguard.* [from French]

**elit|ist** /ɪˈlitɪst, eɪ-/ (**elitists**) **1** ADJ **Elitist** systems, practices, or ideas favor the most powerful, rich, or talented people within a group, place, or society. ❑ *College athletics could become even more elitist than they are now.* ● **elit|ism** /ɪˈlitɪzəm, eɪ-/ N-UNCOUNT ❑ *...the elitism of certain universities.* **2** N-COUNT If you say someone is an **elitist**, you disapprove of them because they believe that they are part of an elite. ❑ *They're elitists who think they're smarter than the rest of us.* [from French]

**Eliza|bethan thea|ter** /ɪˌlɪzəbiθᵊn θiətər/ N-UNCOUNT **Elizabethan theater** is the plays that were written or performed in England during the reign of Queen Elizabeth I.

**el|lipse** /ɪˈlɪps/ (**ellipses**) N-COUNT An **ellipse** is an oval shape similar to a circle but longer and flatter.

**el|lip|ti|cal gal|axy** (**elliptical galaxies**) N-COUNT An **elliptical galaxy** is a galaxy containing mainly older stars, which are distributed in an elliptical pattern. [TECHNICAL]

**elm** /ɛlm/ (**elms**) N-VAR An **elm** is a tree that has broad leaves which it loses in winter. ● **Elm** is the wood of this tree. ❑ *...a good table, constructed of elm.* [from Old English]

**El Niño** /ɛl ˈninyou/ N-PROPER **El Niño** is a current of warm water that occurs every few years in the Pacific Ocean and can affect the weather throughout the world. [from Spanish]

**elo|quent** /ˈɛləkwənt/ ADJ A person who is **eloquent** is good at speaking and able to persuade people. ❑ *He was eloquent about his love of books.* ❑ *I heard him make a very eloquent speech.* ● **elo|quence** N-UNCOUNT ❑ *...the eloquence of his writing.* ● **elo|quent|ly** ADV ❑ *Juanita speaks eloquently about her art.* [from Latin]

**else** /ɛls/ **1** ADJ You use **else** after words such as "anywhere," "someone," "what," "everyone," and "everything" to refer in a vague way to another person, place, or thing, or to all other people, places, or things. ❑ *If I can't do it myself I'll ask someone else.* ❑ *She is much taller than everyone* *else.* ❑ *I try to be truthful, and I expect everyone else to be truthful.* ● **Else** is also an adverb. ❑ *I never wanted to live anywhere else.* **2** PHRASE You use **or else** after stating a logical conclusion, to indicate that what you are about to say is evidence for that conclusion. ❑ *No lessons were learned or else they would not have handled the problem so badly.* **3** PHRASE You use **or else** to introduce a possibility or alternative. ❑ *Hold on tight or else you will fall out.* ❑ *He is either a total genius or else totally crazy.* **4** PHRASE You can say **"if nothing else"** to indicate that what you are mentioning is, in your opinion, the only good thing in a particular situation. ❑ *If nothing else, you'll really enjoy meeting them.* [from Old English]

**else|where** /ɛlsweər/ ADV **Elsewhere** means in other places or to another place. ❑ *Almost 80 percent of the state's residents were born elsewhere.* ❑ *They were living well, in comparison with people elsewhere in the world.* [from Old English]

**elude** /ɪlud/ (**eludes, eluding, eluded**) **1** V-T If something that you want **eludes** you, you fail to obtain it. ❑ *Sleep eluded her.* ❑ *The appropriate word eluded him.* **2** V-T If you **elude** someone or something, you avoid them or escape from them. ❑ *He eluded the police for 13 years.* [from Latin]

**elu|sive** /ɪlusɪv/ ADJ Something or someone that is **elusive** is difficult to find, describe, remember, or achieve. ❑ *In Denver late-night taxis are elusive.* [from Latin]

**e-mail** (**e-mails, e-mailing, e-mailed**) also E-Mail, email **1** N-VAR **E-mail** is a system of sending written messages electronically from one computer to another. **E-mail** is an abbreviation of **electronic mail.** ❑ *You can contact us by e-mail.* ❑ *Do you want to send an E-mail?* **2** V-T If you **e-mail** someone, you send them an e-mail. ❑ *Jamie e-mailed me to say he couldn't come.*
→ see **Internet**

**ema|nate** /ɛmaneɪt/ (**emanates, emanating, emanated**) **1** V-T/V-I If a quality **emanates from** you, or if you **emanate** a quality, you give people a strong sense that you have that quality. [FORMAL] ❑ *Intelligence emanated from him.* **2** V-I If something **emanates from** somewhere, it comes from there. [FORMAL] ❑ *The smell of fresh bread emanated from the oven.* [from Latin]

> **Word Link**    *man ≈ hand : e*man*cipate, *man*acle,* man*icure*

**eman|ci|pate** /ɪmænsɪpeɪt/ (**emancipates, emancipating, emancipated**) V-T If people **are emancipated,** they are freed from unpleasant or unfair social, political, or legal restrictions. [FORMAL] ❑ *Catholics were emancipated in 1792.* ❑ *The war preserved the Union and emancipated the slaves.* ● **eman|ci|pa|tion** /ɪmænsɪpeɪʃ³n/ N-UNCOUNT ❑ *...the emancipation of women.* [from Latin]

**em|bank|ment** /ɪmbæŋkmənt/ (**embankments**) N-COUNT An **embankment** is a thick wall of earth that is built to carry a road or railroad track over an area of low ground, or to prevent water from a river or the sea from flooding the area. ❑ *They climbed a steep embankment.*

**em|bar|go** /ɪmbɑrgoʊ/ (**embargoes**) N-COUNT If one country or group of countries imposes an **embargo** against another, it forbids trade with that country. ❑ *The United Nations imposed an*

*embargo.* [from Spanish]

**em|bark** /ɪmbɑrk/ (**embarks, embarking, embarked**) **1** V-I If you **embark on** something new, difficult, or exciting, you start doing it. ❑ *He's embarking on a new career as a writer.* **2** V-I When you **embark on** a ship, you go on board before the start of a journey. ❑ *They embarked on a ship bound for Europe.* [from French]

**em|bar|rass** /ɪmbærəs/ (**embarrasses, embarrassing, embarrassed**) **1** V-T If something or someone **embarrasses** you, they make you feel shy or ashamed. ❑ *His clumsiness embarrassed him.* ● **em|bar|rass|ing** ADJ ❑ *That was an embarrassing situation for me.* ● **em|bar|rass|ing|ly** ADV ❑ *It became embarrassingly clear that Lionel wasn't coming home for Christmas.* **2** V-T If something **embarrasses** a public figure such as a politician or an organization such as a political party, it causes problems for them. ❑ *They destroyed documents that would embarrass the governor.* ● **em|bar|rass|ing** ADJ ❑ *He has put the administration in an embarrassing position.* [from French]

**em|bar|rassed** /ɪmbærəst/ ADJ A person who is **embarrassed** feels shy, ashamed, or guilty about something. ❑ *He looked a bit embarrassed.* [from French]

**em|bar|rass|ment** /ɪmbærəsmənt/ (**embarrassments**) **1** N-VAR **Embarrassment** is the feeling you have when you are embarrassed. ❑ *We apologize for any embarrassment this may have caused.* **2** N-SING If you refer to a person as **an embarrassment,** you mean that you disapprove of them but cannot avoid your connection with them. ❑ *You have been an embarrassment to us from the day Doug married you.* [from French]

**em|bas|sy** /ɛmbəsi/ (**embassies**) N-COUNT An **embassy** is a group of government officials, headed by an ambassador, who represent their government in a foreign country. The building in which they work is also called an **embassy.** ❑ *The American embassy has already complained.* [from Old French]

> **Word Link**    *em ≈ making, putting : e*mbellish, e*mbody, e*mpower*

**em|bel|lish** /ɪmbɛlɪʃ/ (**embellishes, embellishing, embellished**) **1** V-T If something **is embellished with** decorative features, they have been added to make it more attractive. ❑ *The boat was embellished with carvings.* ❑ *He embellished the garden with statues.* ● **em|bel|lish|ment** /ɪmbɛlɪʃmənt/ N-VAR ❑ *...buildings with little bits of embellishment.* **2** V-T If you **embellish** a story, you make it more interesting by adding details that may be untrue. ❑ *Every time she told the story, she embellished it further.* [from Old French]

**em|bel|lish|ment** /ɪmbɛlɪʃmənt/ (**embellishments**) N-COUNT In music, **embellishments** are extra notes that area added to a melody or rhythm to make it more pleasing. [TECHNICAL] [from Old French]

**em|bez|zle** /ɪmbɛz³l/ (**embezzles, embezzling, embezzled**) V-T If someone **embezzles** money that their organization or company has placed in their care, they take it and use it illegally for their own purposes. ❑ *One former director embezzled $34 million in company funds.* ● **em|bez|zle|ment** N-UNCOUNT

❏ *He was later charged with embezzlement.* [from Old French]

**em|blem** /ɛmbləm/ (**emblems**) **1** N-COUNT An **emblem** is a design representing a country or organization. ❏ *...the emblem of the Red Cross.* **2** N-COUNT An **emblem** is something that represents a quality or idea. ❏ *The eagle was an emblem of strength and courage.* [from Latin]

**em|bodi|ment** /ɪmbɒdimənt/ N-SING If you say that someone or something is the **embodiment** of a quality or idea, you mean that that is their most noticeable characteristic or the basis of all they do. [FORMAL] ❏ *She is the embodiment of normality.*

> **Word Link** em ≈ making, putting : embellish, embody, empower

**em|body** /ɪmbɒdi/ (**embodies, embodying, embodied**) **1** V-T To **embody** an idea or quality means to be a symbol or expression of that idea or quality. ❏ *Jack Kennedy embodied all the hopes of the 1960s.* **2** V-T If something **is embodied in** a particular thing, the second thing contains or consists of the first. ❏ *Their belief in the importance of good design is embodied in everything they do, from architecture to interior design.*

**em|brace** /ɪmbreɪs/ (**embraces, embracing, embraced**) **1** V-RECIP If you **embrace** someone, you put your arms around them in order to show affection for them. You can also say that two people **embrace**. ❏ *Penelope came forward and embraced her sister.* ❏ *People were crying for joy and embracing.* ● **Embrace** is also a noun. ❏ *...a young couple locked in an embrace.* **2** V-T If you **embrace** a change, political system, or idea, you accept it and start supporting it or believing in it. [FORMAL] ❏ *He embraces the new information age.* ● **Embrace** is also a noun. ❏ *...James's embrace of the Catholic faith.* **3** V-T If something **embraces** a group of people, things, or ideas, it includes them in a larger group or category. [FORMAL] ❏ *Paulin's poetry embraces a wide range of subjects.* [from Old French]

**em|broi|der** /ɪmbrɔɪdər/ (**embroiders, embroidering, embroidered**) V-T If something such as clothing or cloth **is embroidered with** a design, the design is stitched into it. ❏ *The collar was embroidered with small red flowers.* ❏ *I have a pillow with my name embroidered on it.* [from Old French]

**em|broi|dery** /ɪmbrɔɪdəri/ (**embroideries**) **1** N-VAR **Embroidery** consists of designs stitched into cloth. ❏ *The shorts had blue embroidery over the pockets.* **2** N-UNCOUNT **Embroidery** is the activity of stitching designs onto cloth. ❏ *She learned sewing, knitting, and embroidery.* [from Old French]
→ see **quilt**

**em|broiled** /ɪmbrɔɪld/ ADJ If you become **embroiled** in a fight or argument, you become deeply involved in it. ❏ *The two sides became embroiled in a long conflict.* [from French]

**em|bryo** /ɛmbrioʊ/ (**embryos**) N-COUNT An **embryo** is an unborn animal or human being in the very early stages of development. [from Late Latin]
→ see **reproduction**

**em|bry|on|ic** /ɛmbriɒnɪk/ ADJ **Embryonic** means in the very early stages of development. [FORMAL] ❏ *...an embryonic airline.* [from Late Latin]

**em|cee** /ɛmsi/ (**emcees, emceeing, emceed**) **1** N-COUNT An **emcee** is the same as a **master of ceremonies**. **2** V-T To **emcee** an event means to act as master of ceremonies for it. ❏ *I'm going to be emceeing a costume contest.*

**em|er|ald** /ɛmərəld, ɛmrəld/ (**emeralds**) N-COUNT An **emerald** is a bright green precious stone. [from Old French]

> **Word Link** merg ≈ sinking : emerge, merge, submerge

**emerge** /ɪmɜrdʒ/ (**emerges, emerging, emerged**) **1** V-I To **emerge** means to come out from a place where you could not be seen. ❏ *Richard was waiting outside the door as she emerged.* ❏ *She then emerged from the courthouse to thank her supporters.* **2** V-I If you **emerge from** a difficult or bad experience, you come to the end of it. ❏ *Emerging from the illness was like coming out of a fog.* **3** V-I When something such as an organization or an industry **emerges**, it comes into existence. ❏ *...the new republic that emerged in October 1917.* ● **emer|gence** N-UNCOUNT ❏ *...the emergence of new democracies in Latin America.* [from Latin]

**emer|gen|cy** /ɪmɜrdʒ³nsi/ (**emergencies**) **1** N-COUNT An **emergency** is an unexpected and serious situation, such as an accident, that must be dealt with quickly. ❏ *He deals with emergencies promptly.* **2** ADJ An **emergency** action is one that is done or arranged quickly and not in the normal way, because an emergency has occurred. ❏ *The board held an emergency meeting.* **3** ADJ **Emergency** equipment or supplies are those intended for use in an emergency. ❏ *The plane is carrying emergency supplies for refugees.* [from Latin]
→ see **hospital**

> **Word Partnership** Use *emergency* with :
>
> | | |
> |---|---|
> | ADJ. | **major** emergency, **medical** emergency, **minor** emergency **1** |
> | N. | **state of** emergency **1** emergency **care**, emergency **surgery** **2** emergency **supplies**, emergency **vehicle** **3** |

**emer|gen|cy brake** (**emergency brakes**) N-COUNT In a vehicle, the **emergency brake** is a brake which the driver operates with his or her hand.

**emer|gen|cy room** (**emergency rooms**) N-COUNT The **emergency room** is the room or department in a hospital where people who have severe injuries or sudden illnesses are taken for emergency treatment. The abbreviation **ER** is often used.

> **Word Link** e ≈ away, out : eject, emigrate, emit

**emi|grate** /ɛmɪgreɪt/ (**emigrates, emigrating, emigrated**) V-I If you **emigrate**, you leave your own country to live in another country. ❏ *He emigrated to Belgium.* ● **emi|gra|tion** /ɛmɪgreɪʃ³n/ N-UNCOUNT ❏ *...the huge emigration of workers to the West.* [from Latin]

**emi|nent** /ɛmɪnənt/ ADJ An **eminent** person is well-known and highly respected. ❏ *...an eminent scientist.* ● **emi|nence** /ɛmɪnəns/ N-UNCOUNT ❏ *He was a man of great eminence.* [from Latin]

**emi|nent|ly** /ɛmɪnəntli/ ADV You use

## Word Web    emotion

Scientists believe that animals experience **emotions** such as **happiness** and **sadness** just like humans do. Research shows animals also feel **anger, fear, love,** and **hate.** Biochemical changes in mammals' brains cause these emotions. When an elephant gives birth, a **hormone** goes through her bloodstream. This causes feelings of **adoration** for her baby. The same thing happens to human mothers. When a dog chews on a bone, a chemical increases in its brain to produce feelings of **joy.** The same chemical produces **elation** in humans. Scientists aren't sure whether animals experience **shame.** However, they do know that animals experience **stress.**

**eminently** in front of an adjective describing a positive quality in order to emphasize the quality expressed by that adjective. ❑ *His books were eminently readable.* [from Latin]

**emis|sion** /ɪmɪʃ°n/ (**emissions**) N-VAR An **emission** of something such as gas or radiation is the release of it into the atmosphere. [FORMAL] ❑ *...the emission of gases such as carbon dioxide.* [from Latin]
→ see **pollution**

**Word Link**    *e ≈ away, out : eject, emigrate, emit*

**emit** /ɪmɪt/ (**emits, emitting, emitted**) V-T To **emit** a sound, smell, or substance means to produce it or send it out. [FORMAL] ❑ *Whitney blinked and emitted a long, low whistle.* [from Latin]

**emo|tion** /ɪmoʊʃ°n/ (**emotions**) N-VAR **Emotion** is feeling such as joy or love. An **emotion** is one of these feelings. ❑ *Mr. Anderson was a professional man who never showed his emotions at work.* ❑ *Wanda's voice was full of emotion and there were tears in her eyes.* [from French]
→ see Word Web: **emotion**

**emo|tion|al** /ɪmoʊʃən°l/ **1** ADJ **Emotional** means concerned with emotions and feelings. ❑ *I needed emotional support.* ● **emo|tion|al|ly** ADV ❑ *Are you becoming emotionally involved with her?* **2** ADJ If someone is **emotional**, they show their feelings very openly, especially because they are upset. ❑ *He is a very emotional man.* [from French]

**emo|tive** /ɪmoʊtɪv/ ADJ An **emotive** situation or issue is likely to make people feel strong emotions. ❑ *Hunting is an emotive issue.* [from French]

**Word Link**    *path ≈ feeling : apathy, empathy, sympathy*

**em|pa|thy** /ɛmpəθi/ N-UNCOUNT **Empathy** is the ability to share another person's feelings and emotions as if they were your own. ❑ *Very young children are capable of empathy.* [from Greek]

**em|per|or** /ɛmpərər/ (**emperors**) N-COUNT; N-TITLE An **emperor** is a man who rules an empire or is the head of state in an empire. ❑ *...the emperor of Japan.* [from Old French]
→ see **empire**

**em|pha|sis** /ɛmfəsɪs/ (**emphases** /ɛmfəsiz/) **1** N-VAR **Emphasis** is special or extra importance that is given to an activity or to a part or aspect of something. ❑ *Too much emphasis is placed on research.* **2** N-VAR **Emphasis** is extra force that

you put on a syllable, word, or phrase when you are speaking in order to make it seem more important. ❑ *The emphasis is on the first syllable of the word.* [from Latin]

**em|pha|size** /ɛmfəsaɪz/ (**emphasizes, emphasizing, emphasized**) V-T To **emphasize** something means to indicate that it is particularly important or true, or to draw special attention to it. ❑ *She emphasized that no major changes can be expected.* [from Latin]

**em|phat|ic** /ɪmfætɪk/ **1** ADJ An **emphatic** response or statement is one made in a forceful way. ❑ *His response was immediate and emphatic.* ● **em|phati|cal|ly** /ɪmfætɪkli/ ADV ❑ *"No fast food,"* she said emphatically. **2** ADJ An **emphatic** victory is one in which the winner has won by a large amount or distance. ❑ *Yesterday's emphatic victory was their fifth this season.* [from Greek]

**em|pire** /ɛmpaɪər/ (**empires**) **1** N-COUNT An **empire** is a number of individual nations that are all controlled by the government or ruler of one particular country. ❑ *...the Roman Empire.* **2** N-COUNT You can refer to a group of companies controlled by one person as an **empire**. ❑ *...a global media empire.* [from Old French]
→ see Word Web: **empire**
→ see **history**

**em|piri|cal** /ɪmpɪrɪk°l/ ADJ **Empirical** evidence or knowledge is based on observation, experiment, and experience rather than theories. ❑ *There is no empirical evidence to support his thesis.* ● **em|piri|cal|ly** ADV ❑ *They approached this part of their task empirically.* [from Latin]
→ see **science**

**em|ploy** /ɪmplɔɪ/ (**employs, employing, employed**) **1** V-T If a person or company **employs** you, they pay you to work for them. ❑ *The company employs 18 workers.* ❑ *More than 3,000 local workers are employed in the tourism industry.* **2** V-T If you **employ** methods, materials, or expressions, you use them. ❑ *All good teachers employ a variety of methods to teach reading.* [from Old French]

**em|ploy|ee** /ɪmplɔɪi/ (**employees**) N-COUNT An **employee** is a person who is paid to work for an organization or for another person. ❑ *He is an employee of Fuji Bank.* [from Old French]
→ see **factory, union**

**em|ploy|er** /ɪmplɔɪər/ (**employers**) N-COUNT Your **employer** is the person or organization that you work for. ❑ *He was sent to Rome by his employer.* [from Old French]

e

## Word Web    empire

An **empire** is formed when a strong nation-state **conquers** other states and creates a larger **political union**. An early example is the Roman Empire which began in 31 BC. The Roman **emperor** Augustus Caesar* ruled a large area from the Mediterranean Sea* to Western Europe. Later, the British Empire ruled from about 1600 to 1900 AD. Queen Victoria's* empire spread across oceans and continents. One of her many titles was **Empress** of India. Both of these empires spread their political influence as well as their language and culture over large areas.

■ British Empire (1900 AD)
■ Roman Empire (117 AD)
■ British and Roman Empires

*Augustus Caesar: the first emperor of Rome.*
*Mediterranean Sea: between Europe and Africa.*
*Queen Victoria (1819-1901): queen of the United Kingdom.*

**em|ploy|ment** /ɪmplɔɪmənt/ N-UNCOUNT
**Employment** is the fact of having a paid job. ◻ *She was unable to find employment.* [from Old French]

### Word Link    em ≈ making, putting : embellish, embody, empower

**em|power** /ɪmpaʊər/ (**empowers, empowering, empowered**) V-T To **empower** someone means to give them the means or the power to achieve something for themselves. ◻ *We must continue to empower young people.* ● **em|pow|er|ment** N-UNCOUNT ◻ *...the empowerment of women.*

**em|press** /ɛmprɪs/ (**empresses**) N-COUNT; N-TITLE An **empress** is a woman who rules an empire or who is the wife of an emperor. ◻ *...Catherine II, Empress of Russia.* [from Old French] → see **empire**

**emp|ty** /ɛmpti/ (**emptier, emptiest, empties, emptying, emptied**) **1** ADJ An **empty** place, vehicle, or container is one that has no people or things in it. ◻ *The room was bare and empty.* ◻ *...empty cans of soda.* ● **emp|ti|ness** N-UNCOUNT ◻ *...the emptiness of the desert.* **2** ADJ If you describe something as **empty**, you mean that it has no real value or meaning. ◻ *She made empty threats to leave.* ● **emp|ti|ness** N-UNCOUNT ◻ *...feelings of emptiness and depression.* **3** V-T If you **empty** a container, or **empty** something out of it, you remove its contents, especially by tipping it up. ◻ *I emptied the bottle.* ◻ *Empty the rice into a serving bowl.* **4** V-T/V-I If someone **empties** a room or place, or if it **empties**, everyone in it goes away. ◻ *The stadium emptied after the game.* [from Old English]

### Thesaurus    empty    Also look up :

| | |
|---|---|
| ADJ. | vacant; (ant.) full, occupied **1** |
| | meaningless **2** |
| V. | drain out, pour out **3** |
| | evacuate, go out, leave **4** |

### Word Partnership    Use empty with :

| | |
|---|---|
| N. | empty **bottle**, empty **box**, empty **building**, empty **seat**, empty **space**, empty **stomach** **1** |
| | empty **promise**, empty **threat** **2** |
| | empty **the trash** **3** |

**empty-handed** ADJ If you come away from somewhere **empty-handed**, you have failed to get what you wanted. ◻ *I have no intention of going home empty-handed.*

**emu|late** /ɛmyʊleɪt/ (**emulates, emulating, emulated**) V-T If you **emulate** something or someone, you imitate them because you admire them a great deal. ◻ *Sons are traditionally expected to emulate their fathers.* [from Latin]

### Word Link    en ≈ making, putting : enable, enact, encode

**en|able** /ɪneɪbəl/ (**enables, enabling, enabled**) V-T If someone or something **enables** you to do a particular thing, they make it possible for you to do it. ◻ *The new test should enable doctors to detect the disease early.*

**en|act** /ɪnækt/ (**enacts, enacting, enacted**) **1** V-T When a government or authority **enacts** a proposal, they make it into a law. [TECHNICAL] ◻ *President Johnson led the battle to enact civil-rights laws.* ● **en|act|ment** (**enactments**) N-VAR ◻ *...the enactment of a Bill of Rights.* **2** V-T If people **enact** a story or play, they perform it by acting. ◻ *She often enacted the stories told to her by her father.*

**enam|el** /ɪnæməl/ (**enamels**) N-UNCOUNT **Enamel** is a substance like glass that can be heated and put onto metal, glass, or pottery in order to decorate or protect it. ◻ *...a white enamel saucepan.* [from Old French]

**en|cap|su|late** /ɪnkæpsəleɪt, -syʊ-/ (**encapsulates, encapsulating, encapsulated**) V-T To **encapsulate** particular facts or ideas means to represent them in a very small space or in a single object or event. ◻ *The article encapsulated the views of many conservatives.*

### Word Link    cas ≈ box, hold : case, encase, suitcase

**en|case** /ɪnkeɪs/ (**encases, encasing, encased**) V-T If a person or an object is **encased** in something, they are completely covered or surrounded by it. ◻ *Nuclear fuel is encased in metal cans.*

**en|chant** /ɪntʃænt/ (**enchants, enchanting, enchanted**) **1** V-T If you **are enchanted by** someone or something, they cause you to have feelings of great delight or pleasure. ❑ *Dena was enchanted by the house.* ● **en|chant|ing** ADJ ❑ *She's an absolutely enchanting child.* **2** v-T In fairy tales and legends, to **enchant** someone or something means to put a magic spell on them. ❑ *...stories of enchanted princesses.* [from Old French]

**en|cir|cle** /ɪnsɜrkᵊl/ (**encircles, encircling, encircled**) v-T To **encircle** something or someone means to surround or enclose them, or to go around them. ❑ *A forty-foot-high concrete wall encircles the jail.*

**en|clave** /ɛnkleɪv, ɒn-/ (**enclaves**) N-COUNT An **enclave** is an area within a country or a city where people live who have a different nationality or culture from the people living in the surrounding country or city. ❑ *...an English-speaking enclave in the Montreal region.* [from French]

**en|close** /ɪnkloʊz/ (**encloses, enclosing, enclosed**) **1** v-T If a place or object **is enclosed** by something, the place or object is inside that thing or completely surrounded by it. ❑ *Samples must be enclosed in two watertight containers.* ❑ *Enclose the meat in a plastic bag.* **2** v-T If you **enclose** something with a letter, you put it in the same envelope as the letter. ❑ *I have enclosed a check for $100.*

**en|clo|sure** /ɪnkloʊʒər/ (**enclosures**) N-COUNT An **enclosure** is an area of land that is surrounded by a wall or fence and that is used for a particular purpose. ❑ *Visitors watch the bears at play in an outdoor enclosure.*

| Word Link | cod ≈ writing : code, decode, encode |
|---|---|

| Word Link | en ≈ making, putting : enable, enact, encode |
|---|---|

**en|code** /ɪnkoʊd/ (**encodes, encoding, encoded**) v-T If you **encode** a message or some information, you put it into a code. ❑ *Both sender and receiver can encode and decode messages.*

**en|com|pass** /ɪnkʌmpəs/ (**encompasses, encompassing, encompassed**) v-T If something **encompasses** particular things, it includes them. ❑ *The western region encompasses nine states.*

**en|core** /ɒŋkɔr, -kɔr/ (**encores**) N-COUNT An **encore** is a short extra performance at the end of a longer one, that an entertainer gives because the audience asks for it. ❑ *Lang's final encore last night was "Barefoot."* [from French]

**en|coun|ter** /ɪnkaʊntər/ (**encounters, encountering, encountered**) **1** v-T If you **encounter** problems or difficulties, you experience them. ❑ *Every day of our lives we encounter stress.* **2** v-T If you **encounter** someone, you meet them, usually unexpectedly. [FORMAL] ❑ *Did you encounter anyone in the building?* ● **Encounter** is also a noun. ❑ *...a remarkable encounter with a group of soldiers.* [from Old French]

| Thesaurus | *encounter* Also look up : |
|---|---|
| v. | bump into, come across, run into; (*ant.*) avoid, miss **1** **2** |

**en|cour|age** /ɪnkɜrɪdʒ/ (**encourages, encouraging, encouraged**) **1** v-T If you **encourage** someone, you give them confidence, for example by letting them know that what they are doing is good. ❑ *When things aren't going well,*

*he encourages me.* **2** v-T If someone **is encouraged by** something that happens, it gives them hope or confidence. ❑ *She has been encouraged by the support of her family.* ● **en|cour|aged** ADJ ❑ *He was encouraged that there seemed to be some progress.* **3** v-T If you **encourage** someone to do something, you try to persuade them to do it, for example, by trying to make it easier for them to do it. ❑ *We want to encourage people to go fishing.* ❑ *Their task is to encourage private investment.* **4** v-T If something **encourages** a particular activity or state, it causes it to happen or increase. ❑ *...a drug that encourages cell growth.*

**en|cour|age|ment** /ɪnkɜrɪdʒmənt/ (**encouragements**) N-VAR **Encouragement** is the activity of encouraging someone, or something that is said or done in order to encourage them. ❑ *Friends gave me a great deal of encouragement.*

**en|cour|ag|ing** /ɪnkɜrɪdʒɪŋ/ ADJ Something that is **encouraging** gives people hope or confidence. ❑ *The results have been encouraging.* ● **en|cour|ag|ing|ly** ADV ❑ *...encouragingly large audiences.*

**en|croach** /ɪnkroʊtʃ/ (**encroaches, encroaching, encroached**) **1** v-I If one thing **encroaches on** another, it spreads or becomes stronger, and slowly begins to restrict the power, range, or effectiveness of the second thing. [FORMAL] ❑ *The church is resisting attempts to encroach on its authority.* ● **en|croach|ment** (**encroachments**) N-VAR ❑ *...preserving wildlife against the encroachment of hotels and homes.* **2** v-I If something **encroaches on** a place, it spreads and takes over more and more of that place. [FORMAL] ❑ *The bushes kept encroaching on the path.* [from Old French]

**en|cy|clo|pedia** /ɪnsaɪkləpidiə/ (**encyclopedias**) also **encyclopaedia** N-COUNT An **encyclopedia** is a book, set of books, or CD-ROM in which facts about many different subjects or about one particular subject are arranged for reference, usually in alphabetical order. [from New Latin]

---

**end**

❶ NOUN USES
❷ VERB USES
❸ PHRASAL VERBS

---

❶ **end** /ɛnd/ (**ends**) **1** N-SING **The end of** something such as a period of time, an event, a book, or a movie is the last part of it or the final point in it. ❑ *The report is expected by the end of the year.* ❑ *...families who settled in the region at the end of the 17th century.* **2** N-COUNT An **end to** something or the **end of** it is the fact that it finishes and does not continue any longer. You can also say that something **comes to an end** or **is at an end**. ❑ *The government today called for an end to the violence.* ❑ *The hot weather came to an end at the beginning of October.* **3** N-COUNT The **end of** a long, narrow object is the tip or farthest part of it. ❑ *He tapped the ends of his fingers together.* ❑ *...both ends of the tunnel.* **4** N-COUNT An **end** is the purpose for which something is done or toward which you are working. ❑ *The church should not be used for political ends.* **5** PHRASE If you find it difficult to **make ends meet**, you do not have enough money for the things you need. ❑ *With Betty's salary they* barely made ends meet. **6** PHRASE When something happens for hours, days, weeks, or years **on end**, it happens continuously and without stopping for the amount of time that is mentioned. ❑ *We can talk for hours on end.* [from Old English] **7 the end of** your **tether** → see **tether 8** to **make** your **hair stand on end** → see **hair 9** to **be on the receiving end** → see **receive**

**❷ end** /ɛnd/ (**ends, ending, ended**) **1** V-T/V-I When a situation, process, or activity **ends**, or when something or someone **ends** it, it reaches its final point and stops. ❑ *The meeting quickly ended.* ❑ *She began to weep. That ended our discussion.* ● **end|ing** N-SING ❑ *...the ending of a marriage.* **2** V-I A journey, road, or river that **ends** at a particular place stops there and goes no further. ❑ *The highway ended at an intersection.* [from Old English]

| **Thesaurus** | *end* | Also look up : |
| --- | --- | --- |
| N. | close, conclusion, finale, finish, stop; (*ant.*) beginning **❶ 1 2** | |
| V. | conclude, finish, wrap up **❷ 1** | |

**❸ end** /ɛnd/ (**ends, ending, ended**)
▶ **end up** PHR-VERB If you **end up** in a particular place or situation, you are in that place or situation after a series of events. ❑ *The painting ended up at the Museum of Modern Art.* ❑ *You might end up getting something you don't want.*

**en|dan|ger** /ɪndeɪndʒər/ (**endangers, endangering, endangered**) V-T To **endanger** something or someone means to put them in a situation where they might be harmed or destroyed completely. ❑ *The debate could endanger the peace talks.* ❑ *The beetles are on the list of endangered species.*

**en|dan|gered spe|cies** (**endangered species**) N-COUNT An **endangered species** is an animal species that is in danger of becoming extinct. ❑ *These African beetles are on the list of endangered species.*

**en|dear** /ɪndɪər/ (**endears, endearing, endeared**) V-T If something **endears** you to someone or if you **endear yourself to** them, you become popular with them and well liked by them. ❑ *Jason's arrogance did not endear him to Rachel.* ● **en|dear|ing** ADJ ❑ *...an endearing personality.*

**en|deav|or** /ɪndɛvər/ (**endeavors, endeavoring, endeavored**) **1** V-I If you **endeavor to** do something, you try very hard to do it. [FORMAL] ❑ *They are endeavoring to protect labor union rights.* **2** N-VAR An **endeavor** is an attempt to do something, especially something new or original. [FORMAL] ❑ *...the company's creative endeavors.* [from Old French]

**en|dem|ic** /ɛndɛmɪk/ ADJ If a disease or illness is **endemic** in a place, it is frequently found among the people who live there. [TECHNICAL] ❑ *The disease was then endemic among children my age.* [from New Latin]

**end|ing** /ɛndɪŋ/ (**endings**) **1** N-COUNT You can refer to the last part of a book, story, play, or movie as the **ending**, especially when you are considering the way that the story ends. ❑ *The film has a Hollywood happy ending.* [from Old English] **2** → see also **end**

**en|dive** /ɛndaɪv/ (**endives**) N-VAR **Endive** is a type of plant with crisp bitter leaves that can be cooked or eaten raw in salads. [from Old French]

**end|less** /ɛndlɪs/ ADJ If you say that something is **endless**, you mean that it is very large or lasts for a very long time, and it seems as if it will never stop. ❑ *...the endless hours I spent on homework.* ● **end|less|ly** ADV ❑ *They talk about it endlessly.* [from Old English]

**endo|crine** /ɛndəkrɪn, -kraɪn/ ADJ The **endocrine** system is the system of glands that produce hormones for the bloodstream, such as the pituitary or thyroid glands. [MEDICAL] [from Greek]

**endo|cy|to|sis** /ɛndoʊsaɪtoʊsɪs/ N-UNCOUNT **Endocytosis** is a process in which a cell absorbs material from outside the cell by enclosing the material within a part of the cell membrane. Compare **exocytosis**. [TECHNICAL]

**endo|plas|mic re|ticu|lum** /ɛndoʊplæzmɪk rɪtɪkyələm/ (**endoplasmic reticulums** or **endoplasmic reticula**) N-COUNT The **endoplasmic reticulum** is a network of tubes and membranes within cells that is involved in the making and movement of proteins. [TECHNICAL]

**en|dorse** /ɪndɔrs/ (**endorses, endorsing, endorsed**) **1** V-T If you **endorse** someone or something, you say publicly that you support or approve of them. ❑ *I can endorse his opinion wholeheartedly.* ● **en|dorse|ment** (**endorsements**) N-COUNT ❑ *This is a powerful endorsement for his softer style of government.* **2** V-T If you **endorse** a product or company, you appear in advertisements for it. ❑ *The twins endorsed a line of household cleaning products.* ● **en|dorse|ment** N-COUNT ❑ *...his commercial endorsements for breakfast cereals.* [from Old French]

**endo|skel|eton** /ɛndoʊskɛlɪtᵊn/ (**endoskeletons**) N-COUNT Animals with an **endoskeleton** have their skeleton inside their body, like humans. [TECHNICAL]

**endo|therm** /ɛndəθɜrm/ (**endotherms**) N-COUNT An **endotherm** is a warm-blooded animal, such as a bird or mammal, that can keep its body temperature above or below that of the surrounding environment. Compare **ectotherm**. [TECHNICAL]

**endo|ther|mic** /ɛndoʊθɜrmɪk/ ADJ An **endothermic** chemical reaction or process is one that takes in heat from its surroundings, such as when ice melts. [TECHNICAL]

**en|dow** /ɪndaʊ/ (**endows, endowing, endowed**) **1** V-T If someone **is endowed with** a quality, they have it or are given it. ❑ *You are endowed with good health.* ❑ *Herbs endow food with subtle flavors.* **2** V-T If someone **endows** an institution, they provide it with a large amount of money that will produce an income. ❑ *The ambassador has endowed a $1 million public-service program.* [from Old French]

**en|dow|ment** /ɪndaʊmənt/ (**endowments**) N-COUNT An **endowment** is a gift of money that is made to an institution or community in order to provide it with an annual income. ❑ *...the National Endowment for the Arts.* [from Old French]

**end re|sult** (**end results**) N-COUNT The **end result** of an activity or a process is the final result that it produces. ❑ *The end result is very good and very successful.*

**en|dur|ance** /ɪndʊ̯ərəns/ N-UNCOUNT
**Endurance** is the ability to continue with an
unpleasant or difficult situation, experience, or
activity over a long period of time. ❑ *The exercise
will improve strength and endurance.* [from Old
French]

**en|dure** /ɪndʊ̯ər/ (**endures, enduring, endured**)
■ V-T If you **endure** a painful or difficult
situation, you experience it, usually because you
have no other choice. ❑ *The company endured heavy
financial losses.* ■ V-I If something **endures**, it
continues to exist without any loss in quality or
importance. ❑ *Somehow the language endures and
continues to survive.* ● **en|dur|ing** ADJ ❑ *...the start of
an enduring friendship.* [from Old French]

**end user** (**end users**) N-COUNT The **end user** of
a piece of equipment is the user that it has been
designed for, rather than the person who installs
or maintains it. [COMPUTING] ❑ *You have to describe
things in a form that the end user can understand.*

**en|emy** /ɛnəmi/ (**enemies**) ■ N-COUNT If
someone is your **enemy**, they hate you or want to
harm you. ❑ *...her many enemies.* ■ N-SING The
**enemy** is an army or other force that is opposed to
you in a war, or a country with which your country
is at war. ❑ *They pursued the enemy for two miles.*
[from Old French]

**en|er|get|ic** /ɛnərdʒɛtɪk/ ADJ An **energetic**
person has a lot of energy. **Energetic** activities
require a lot of energy. ❑ *Young children are incredibly
energetic.* ● **en|er|geti|cal|ly** ADV ❑ *David chewed
energetically on the steak.* [from Late Latin]

**en|er|gy** /ɛnərdʒi/ (**energies**) ■ N-UNCOUNT
**Energy** is the ability and strength to do active
physical things. ❑ *He was saving his energy for next
week's race.* ■ N-COUNT Your **energies** are the
efforts and attention that you can direct toward
a particular aim. ❑ *She started to devote her energies
to teaching rather than performing.* ■ N-UNCOUNT
**Energy** is the power from sources such as
electricity and coal that makes machines work or
provides heat. ❑ *...Many people favor nuclear energy.*
[from Late Latin]
→ see Word Web: **energy**
→ see **calorie, electricity, food, petroleum,
photosynthesis, solar**

---

| **Word Partnership** | Use *energy* with : |
| --- | --- |
| ADJ. | **full of** energy, **physical** energy ■ <br> **atomic** energy, **nuclear** energy, **solar** energy ■ |
| V. | **focus** energy ■ ■ <br> **conserve/save** energy ■ |

---

**en|er|gy con|ver|sion** N-UNCOUNT **Energy
conversion** is the changing of energy from one
form to another, for example from mechanical
energy to electrical energy.

**en|er|gy ef|fi|cien|cy** N-UNCOUNT **Energy
efficiency** is the careful use of resources such as
electricity or fuel in order to reduce the amount of
energy that is wasted.

**energy-efficient** also **energy efficient** ADJ
A device or building that is **energy-efficient** uses
relatively little energy to provide the power it
needs. ❑ *...energy-efficient light bulbs.*

**en|er|gy pyra|mid** (**energy pyramids**) N-COUNT
An **energy pyramid** is a diagram that shows the
amount of energy that is available at each level of
a food chain. [TECHNICAL]

**en|er|gy re|source** (**energy resources**)
N-COUNT An **energy resource** is a source of energy
such as oil, coal, and wind.

**en|er|gy source** (**energy sources**) N-COUNT An
**energy source** is any substance or system from
which energy can be obtained, such as coal, gas,
water, or sunlight.

**en|force** /ɪnfɔ̯rs/ (**enforces, enforcing, enforced**)
V-T If people in authority **enforce** a law or a
rule, they make sure that it is obeyed, usually by
punishing people who do not obey it. ❑ *Many states
enforce drug laws.* ● **en|force|ment** /ɪnfɔ̯rsmənt/
N-UNCOUNT ❑ *The doctors want stricter enforcement
of existing laws.*

**en|gage** /ɪngeɪdʒ/ (**engages, engaging,
engaged**) ■ V-I If you **engage in** an activity, you
do it or are actively involved with it. [FORMAL]
❑ *They've never engaged in typical father-son activities
like sports.* ■ V-T If something **engages** you, it
keeps you interested in it and thinking about
it. ❑ *They never learned skills to engage the attention
of the others.* ■ V-T If you **engage** someone **in**
conversation, you have a conversation with them.
❑ *They tried to engage him in conversation.* ■ V-T If
you **engage** someone to do a particular job, you
appoint them to do it. [FORMAL] ❑ *We engaged
the services of a famous engineer.* [from Old French]
■ → see also **engaged, engaging**

**en|gaged** /ɪngeɪdʒd/ ■ ADJ Someone who
is **engaged in** a particular activity is doing that
thing. [FORMAL] ❑ *...the various projects he was
engaged in.* ■ ADJ When two people are **engaged**,
they have agreed to marry each other. ❑ *We got
engaged on my eighteenth birthday.* [from Old French]

**en|gage|ment** /ɪngeɪdʒmənt/ (**engagements**)
■ N-COUNT An **engagement** is an arrangement
that you have made to do something at a

---

---

**Word Web**    energy

Wood was the most important **energy** source for American settlers.
Then, as industry developed, factories began to use **coal**. Coal was also
used to **generate** most of the **electrical power** in the early 1900s.
However, the popularity of automobile use soon made **petroleum** the
most important **fuel**. **Natural gas** remains popular for home heating and
industrial use. Hydroelectric power isn't a major source of energy in the
U.S. It requires too much land and water to produce. Some companies
built **nuclear** power plants to make **electricity** in the 1970s. Today **solar**
panels convert sunlight and giant wind farms convert wind into electricity.

E

## Word Web engine

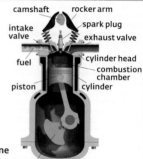

In the **internal combustion engine** found in most cars, there are four, six, or eight **cylinders**. To start an engine, the **intake valve** opens and a small amount of **fuel** enters the **combustion** chamber of the cylinder. A **spark plug** ignites the fuel and air mixture, causing it to explode. This **combustion** moves the **cylinder head**, which causes the crankshaft to turn and the car to move. Next, the **exhaust valve** opens and the burned gases are drawn out. As the cylinder head returns to its original position, it compresses the new gas and air mixture and the process repeats itself.

**internal combustion engine**

particular time. [FORMAL] ❑ *He had an engagement at a restaurant at eight.* **2** N-COUNT An **engagement** is an agreement that two people have made with each other to get married. ❑ *I've broken off my engagement to Arthur.* **3** N-VAR A military **engagement** is a battle. [from Old French]

**en|gag|ing** /ɪngeɪdʒɪŋ/ ADJ An **engaging** person or thing is pleasant, interesting, and entertaining. ❑ *...one of her most engaging and least known novels.* [from Old French]

**en|gen|der** /ɪndʒɛndər/ (**engenders, engendering, engendered**) V-T If someone or something **engenders** a particular feeling or situation, they cause it. [FORMAL] ❑ *Companies give away free gifts to engender good will and repeat sales.* [from Old French]

**en|gine** /ɛndʒɪn/ (**engines**) **1** N-COUNT The **engine** of a car or other vehicle is the part that produces the power which makes the vehicle move. ❑ *He got into the driving seat and started the engine.* **2** N-COUNT An **engine** is also the large vehicle that pulls a train. ❑ *In 1941, trains were pulled by steam engines.* [from Old French]
→ see Word Web: **engine**
→ see **car**

**en|gi|neer** /ɛndʒɪnɪər/ (**engineers, engineering, engineered**) **1** N-COUNT An **engineer** is a skilled person who uses scientific knowledge to design, construct, and maintain engines and machines or structures such as roads, railroads, and bridges. **2** N-COUNT An **engineer** is a person who repairs mechanical or electrical devices. ❑ *They sent a service engineer to fix the disk drive.* **3** V-T When a vehicle, bridge, or building **is**

**engineered**, it is planned and constructed using scientific methods. ❑ *The spaceship was engineered by Bert Rutan.* **4** V-T If you **engineer** an event or situation, you arrange for it to happen, in a clever or indirect way. ❑ *Did she engineer the murder of her boss?* [from Old French]

**en|gi|neer|ing** /ɛndʒɪnɪərɪŋ/ **1** N-UNCOUNT **Engineering** is the work involved in designing and constructing engines and machinery or structures such as roads and bridges. **Engineering** is also the subject studied by people who want to do this work. ❑ *...graduates with degrees in engineering.* [from Old French] **2** → see also **genetic engineering**
→ see **clone**

**Eng|lish** /ɪŋglɪʃ/ **1** N-UNCOUNT **English** is the language spoken by people who live in Great Britain and Ireland, the United States, Canada, Australia, and many other countries. **2** ADJ **English** means belonging or relating to England. ❑ *...the English way of life.* ● The **English** are English people. ❑ *It is often said that the English are reserved.* [from Old English]
→ see Word Web: **English**

**Eng|lish muf|fin** (**English muffins**) N-COUNT **English muffins** are flat, round bread rolls that you split in half and usually eat hot with butter.

**en|graved** /ɪngreɪvd/ ADJ If an object is **engraved**, a design or some writing has been cut into its surface. ❑ *...beautiful engraved glass.*

**en|grossed** /ɪngroʊst/ ADJ If you are **engrossed** in something, it holds your attention completely. ❑ *Tony didn't notice because he was too engrossed in his*

## Word Web English

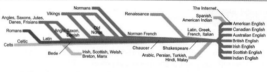

The **English language** has more **words** than any other language. Early English grew out of a Germanic language.
Much of its **grammar** and basic **vocabulary** came from that language. But in 1066, England was conquered by the Normans. Norman French became the language of the rulers. Therefore many French and Latin words came into the English language. The playwright Shakespeare* **coined** over 1,600 new words in his plays. English has become an international language with many regional **dialects**.

*William Shakespeare (1564-1616): an English playwright and poet.*

*work.* [from Old French]

**en|gulf** /ɪnɡʌlf/ (**engulfs, engulfing, engulfed**)
**1** V-T If one thing **engulfs** another, it completely covers or hides it, often in a sudden and unexpected way. ❑ *The apartment building was engulfed in flames.* **2** V-T If a feeling or emotion **engulfs** you, you are strongly affected by it. ❑ *...the pain that engulfed him.*

**en|hance** /ɪnhæns/ (**enhances, enhancing, enhanced**) V-T To **enhance** something means to improve its value, quality, or attractiveness. ❑ *They are eager to protect and enhance their reputation.* ● **en|hance|ment** (**enhancements**) N-VAR ❑ *Music is merely an enhancement to the power of her words.* [from Old French]

**enig|ma** /ɪnɪɡmə/ (**enigmas**) N-COUNT If you describe something or someone as an **enigma**, you mean they are mysterious or difficult to understand. ❑ *The country remains an enigma for the outside world.* [from Latin]

**en|ig|mat|ic** /ɛnɪɡmætɪk/ ADJ **Enigmatic** means mysterious and difficult to understand. ❑ *...one of the most enigmatic movies ever made.* ● **en|ig|mati|cal|ly** ADV ❑ *"He didn't deserve this," she said enigmatically.* [from Latin]

---

**Word Link**     joy ≈ being glad : en**joy**, **joy**ful, **joy**ous

**en|joy** /ɪndʒɔɪ/ (**enjoys, enjoying, enjoyed**)
**1** V-T If you **enjoy** something, you find pleasure and satisfaction in doing it or experiencing it. ❑ *Ross has always enjoyed the company of women.* ❑ *I enjoyed playing basketball.* **2** V-T If you **enjoy yourself**, you do something that you like doing or you take pleasure in the situation that you are in. ❑ *I am really enjoying myself at the moment.* **3** V-T If you **enjoy** something such as a privilege, you have it. [FORMAL] ❑ *The average German will enjoy 40 days' paid vacation this year.* [from Old French]

**en|joy|able** /ɪndʒɔɪəbᵊl/ ADJ Something that is **enjoyable** gives you pleasure. ❑ *It was much more enjoyable than I expected.* [from Old French]

**en|joy|ment** /ɪndʒɔɪmənt/ N-UNCOUNT **Enjoyment** is the feeling of pleasure and satisfaction that you have when you do or experience something that you like. ❑ *He took great enjoyment from traveling.* [from Old French]

**en|large** /ɪnlɑrdʒ/ (**enlarges, enlarging, enlarged**) **1** V-T/V-I When you **enlarge** something or when it **enlarges**, it becomes bigger. ❑ *The college plans to enlarge its stadium.* ● **en|large|ment** N-UNCOUNT ❑ *There is not enough space for enlargement of the buildings.* **2** V-I If you **enlarge on** something that has been mentioned, you give more details about it. [FORMAL] ❑ *He didn't enlarge on the form that the government would take.*
→ see **photography**

---

**Word Link**     light ≈ shining : day**light**, en**light**en, head**light**

**en|light|en** /ɪnlaɪtᵊn/ (**enlightens, enlightening, enlightened**) V-T To **enlighten** someone means to give them more knowledge and greater understanding about something. [FORMAL] ❑ *This book will entertain and enlighten the reader.* ● **en|light|en|ing** ADJ ❑ *...an enlightening talk on the work done at the zoo.*

**en|light|ened** /ɪnlaɪtᵊnd/ ADJ If you describe someone or their attitudes as **enlightened**,

you admire them for having sensible, modern attitudes and ways of dealing with things. ❑ *...an enlightened policy.*

**en|list** /ɪnlɪst/ (**enlists, enlisting, enlisted**)
**1** V-T/V-I If someone **enlists** or **is enlisted**, they join the army, navy, marines, or air force. ❑ *He enlisted in the 82nd Airborne.* ❑ *He enlisted as a private in the Mexican War.* **2** V-T If you **enlist** the help of someone, you persuade them to help or support you in doing something. ❑ *I enlisted the help of several neighbors.*

**en|liv|en** /ɪnlaɪvᵊn/ (**enlivens, enlivening, enlivened**) V-T To **enliven** events, situations, or people means to make them more lively or cheerful. ❑ *Even the most boring meeting was enlivened by Dan's presence.*

**en masse** /ɒn mæs/ ADV If a group of people do something **en masse**, they do it all together and at the same time. ❑ *The people marched en masse.* [from French]

**enor|mous** /ɪnɔrməs/ ADJ Something that is **enormous** is extremely large in size, amount, or degree. ❑ *The main bedroom is enormous.* ❑ *It was an enormous disappointment.* ● **enor|mous|ly** ADV ❑ *I admired him enormously.* [from Latin]

**enough** /ɪnʌf/ **1** DET **Enough** means as much as you need or as much as is necessary. ❑ *They had enough cash for a one-way ticket.* ● **Enough** is also an adverb. ❑ *I was old enough to work and earn money.* ❑ *Do you believe that sentences for criminals are tough enough?* ● **Enough** is also a pronoun. ❑ *Although efforts are being made, they are not doing enough.* ● **Enough** is also a quantifier. ❑ *Is your child getting enough of the right foods?* **2** ADV You can use **enough** to say that something is the case to a moderate or fairly large degree. ❑ *Winters is a common enough surname.* **3** ADV You use **enough** in expressions such as **strangely enough** and **interestingly enough** to indicate that you think a fact is strange or interesting. ❑ *Strangely enough, the last thing he thought of was Tanya.* [from Old English] **4** fair enough → see **fair 5** sure enough → see **sure**

---

**Thesaurus**     enough     Also look up :

| | |
|---|---|
| ADJ. | adequate, complete, satisfactory, sufficient; (ant.) deficient, inadequate, insufficient **1** |

---

**en|quire** /ɪnkwaɪər/ → see **inquire**

**en|quiry** /ɪnkwaɪəri/ → see **inquiry**

**en|rage** /ɪnreɪdʒ/ (**enrages, enraging, enraged**) V-T If you **are enraged** by something, it makes you extremely angry. ❑ *Many were enraged by the news.*

**en|rich** /ɪnrɪtʃ/ (**enriches, enriching, enriched**) V-T To **enrich** something means to improve its quality, usually by adding something to it. ❑ *It is important to enrich the soil before planting.* ● **en|rich|ment** N-UNCOUNT ❑ *...spiritual enrichment.*

**en|roll** /ɪnroʊl/ (**enrolls, enrolling, enrolled**) V-T/V-I If you **enroll** or **are enrolled** at an institution or in a class, you officially join it. ❑ *Cherny was enrolled at the University in 1945.* ❑ *Her mother enrolled her in acting classes.* ● **en|roll|ment** N-UNCOUNT ❑ *A fee is payable at enrollment.*

**en route** /ɒn rut/ → see **route**

**en|sem|ble** /ɑnsɑmbᵊl/ (**ensembles**) N-COUNT An **ensemble** is a group of musicians, actors, or dancers who regularly perform together. [from French]

**en|sue** /ɪnsu/ (**ensues, ensuing, ensued**) v-ɪ If something **ensues**, it happens immediately after another event, usually as a result of it. □ *A brief but embarrassing silence ensued.* [from Old French]

**en|su|ing** /ɪnsuɪŋ/ ADJ **Ensuing** events happen immediately after other events. □ *The ensuing argument was bitter.* [from Old French]

**en|sure** /ɪnʃʊər/ (**ensures, ensuring, ensured**) v-ɪ To **ensure** something, or to **ensure that** something happens, means to make certain that it happens. [FORMAL] □ *We must ensure that all patients have access to high quality care.*

---

> ### Usage    ensure and insure
>
> *Ensure* and *insure* both mean "to make certain." *Automobile inspections ensure that a car is safe to drive. Insure* can also mean "to protect against loss." *Drivers should also insure their cars against theft.*

---

**en|tail** /ɪnteɪl/ (**entails, entailing, entailed**) v-ɪ If one thing **entails** another, it involves it or causes it. [FORMAL] □ *Such a decision would entail a huge risk.*

**en|tan|gle** /ɪntæŋgəl/ (**entangles, entangling, entangled**) **1** v-ɪ If something **is entangled in** something such as a rope or a net, it is caught in it very tightly. □ *A whale was entangled in their nets.* **2** v-ɪ If something **entangles** you **in** problems or difficulties, it causes you to become involved in problems or difficulties from which it is hard to escape. □ *These events could entangle us in a war.* ● **en|tan|gled** ADJ □ *The case got entangled in international politics.* ● **en|tan|gle|ment** (**entanglements**) N-COUNT □ *...a military entanglement.*

**en|ter** /ɛntər/ (**enters, entering, entered**) **1** v-ɪ/v-ɪ When you **enter** a place such as a room or building, you go into it or come into it. [FORMAL] □ *He entered the room and stood near the door.* □ *When Spinks entered they all turned to look at him.* **2** v-ɪ If you **enter** an organization or institution, you start to work there or become a member of it. □ *He entered the firm as a junior assistant.* **3** v-ɪ If someone or something **enters** a particular situation or period of time, they start to be in it or part of it. □ *The war has entered its second month.* **4** v-ɪ If you **enter** a competition, race, or examination, you officially state that you will compete or take part in it. □ *I'm planning to enter some races.* □ *His wife entered him for the championship.* **5** v-ɪ If you **enter** something in a book or computer, you write or type it in. □ *When a baby is born, they enter that baby's name into the computer.* [from Old French]

▸ **enter into** PHR-VERB If you **enter into** something such as an agreement, discussion, or relationship, you become involved in it. [FORMAL] □ *I have not entered into any agreements with them.* □ *The strike was cancelled when the nurses entered into talks with the government.*

**en|ter|prise** /ɛntərpraɪz/ (**enterprises**) **1** N-COUNT An **enterprise** is a company or business. [BUSINESS] □ *There are plenty of small industrial enterprises.* **2** N-COUNT An **enterprise** is something new, difficult, or important that you do or try to do. □ *Horse breeding is indeed a risky enterprise.* **3** N-UNCOUNT **Enterprise** is the ability and willingness to try out new ways of doing

things, especially in order to make money. □ *...the spirit of enterprise.* ● **en|ter|pris|ing** ADJ □ *...an enterprising young man.* [from Old French]

**en|ter|tain** /ɛntərteɪn/ (**entertains, entertaining, entertained**) **1** v-ɪ If you **entertain** people, you do something that amuses or interests them. □ *They were entertained by singers and dancers.* ● **en|ter|tain|ing** ADJ □ *The sport needs to become more entertaining.* **2** v-ɪ/v-ɪ If you **entertain** guests, you give them food and hospitality. □ *I don't like to entertain guests anymore.* □ *He loves to entertain.* ● **en|ter|tain|ing** N-UNCOUNT □ *...a cozy area for entertaining and relaxing.* **3** v-ɪ If you **entertain** an idea or suggestion, you consider it. [FORMAL] □ *They refused to entertain the idea.* [from Old French]

**en|ter|tain|er** /ɛntərteɪnər/ (**entertainers**) N-COUNT An **entertainer** is a person whose job is to entertain audiences, for example, by telling jokes, singing, or dancing. □ *Some people called him the greatest entertainer of the twentieth century.* [from Old French]

**en|ter|tain|ment** /ɛntərteɪnmənt/ (**entertainments**) N-VAR **Entertainment** consists of performances of plays and movies, and activities such as reading and watching television, that give people pleasure. □ *...celebrities from the world of entertainment.* [from Old French] → see **radio**

**en|thrall** /ɪnθrɔl/ (**enthralls, enthralling, enthralled**) v-ɪ If you **are enthralled by** something, you enjoy it and give it your complete attention and interest. □ *The passengers were enthralled by the scenery.*

**en|thuse** /ɪnθuz/ (**enthuses, enthusing, enthused**) **1** v-ɪ If you **enthuse about** something, you talk about it in a way that shows how excited you are about it. □ *"We had a fantastic time!" she enthused.* **2** v-ɪ If you **are enthused** by something, it makes you feel excited and enthusiastic. □ *I was immediately enthused.* [from Late Latin]

**en|thu|si|asm** /ɪnθuziæzəm/ (**enthusiasms**) **1** N-VAR **Enthusiasm** is great eagerness to be involved in a particular activity that you like and enjoy or that you think is important. □ *Their skill and enthusiasm has gotten them on the team.* **2** N-COUNT An **enthusiasm** is an activity or subject that interests you very much and that you spend a lot of time on. □ *Find out about his enthusiasms and future plans.* [from Late Latin]

---

> ### Thesaurus    enthusiasm    Also look up :
>
> N.    eagerness, energy, excitement, passion, zest; (ant.) apathy, indifference **1**

---

**en|thu|si|ast** /ɪnθuziæst/ (**enthusiasts**) N-COUNT An **enthusiast** is a person who is very interested in a particular activity or subject and who spends a lot of time on it. □ *He is a great sports enthusiast.* [from Late Latin]

**en|thu|si|as|tic** /ɪnθuziæstɪk/ ADJ If you are **enthusiastic about** something, you show how much you like or enjoy it by the way that you behave and talk. □ *Tom was very enthusiastic about the place.* ● **en|thu|si|as|ti|cal|ly** /ɪnθuziæstɪkli/ ADV □ *The announcement was greeted enthusiastically.* [from Late Latin]

**en|tice** /ɪntaɪs/ (**entices, enticing, enticed**) v-ɪ To **entice** someone means to try to persuade them to go somewhere or to do something. ❑ *They enticed doctors to move to rural areas by paying them more.* ● **en|tice|ment** /ɪntaɪsmənt/ (**enticements**) N-VAR ❑ *Banks offer a range of enticements to open an account.* [from Old French]

**en|tic|ing** /ɪntaɪsɪŋ/ ADJ Something that is **enticing** is extremely attractive and makes you want to get it or to become involved with it. ❑ *The whole menu is enticing.* [from Old French]

**en|tire** /ɪntaɪər/ ADJ You use **entire** when you want to emphasize that you are referring to the whole of something, for example, the whole of a place, time, or population. ❑ *He spent his entire life in China.* ❑ *There are only 60 swimming pools in the entire country.* [from Old French]

| Thesaurus | *entire* | Also look up : |
|---|---|---|
| ADJ. | absolute, complete, total, whole; (*ant.*) incomplete, limited, partial | |

**en|tire|ly** /ɪntaɪərli/ ADV **Entirely** means completely and not just partly. ❑ *...an entirely new approach.* ❑ *I agree entirely.* [from Old French]

**en|tirety** /ɪntaɪərti, -taɪrɪti/ PHRASE If something is used or affected in its **entirety**, the whole of it is used or affected. ❑ *The plan has not been accepted in its entirety.* [from Old French]

**en|ti|tle** /ɪntaɪtᵊl/ (**entitles, entitling, entitled**) ■ V-T If you **are entitled** to something, you have the right to have it or do it. ❑ *A student card will entitle you to discounts at a variety of local clubs.* ❑ *They are entitled to first class travel.* ● **en|ti|tle|ment** (**entitlements**) N-VAR [FORMAL] ❑ *They lose their entitlement to welfare when they start work.* ■ V-T You say that a book, movie, or painting is **entitled** a particular thing when you are mentioning its title. ❑ *...a performance entitled "United States."* [from Old French]

**en|tity** /ɛntɪti/ (**entities**) N-COUNT An **entity** is something that exists separately from other things and has a clear identity of its own. [FORMAL] ❑ *The earth is a living entity.* [from Medieval Latin]

**en|tou|rage** /ɒntʊrɑːʒ/ (**entourages**) N-COUNT A famous or important person's **entourage** is the group of assistants, servants, or other people who travel with them. ❑ *Rachel was surrounded by her entourage.* [from French]

---
**entrance**

❶ NOUN USES
❷ VERB USE
---

❶ **en|trance** /ɛntrəns/ (**entrances**) ■ N-COUNT The **entrance to** a place is the way into it, for example, a door or gate. ❑ *Beside the entrance to the church, turn right.* ❑ *He came out of a side entrance.* ■ N-COUNT Someone's **entrance** is their arrival in a room. ❑ *She noticed her father's entrance.* ■ N-UNCOUNT If you gain **entrance to** a particular place, profession, or institution, you are allowed to go into it or accepted as a member of it. ❑ *Many students fail to gain entrance to the university of their choice.* [from French]

| Thesaurus | *entrance* | Also look up : |
|---|---|---|
| N. | doorway, entry; (*ant.*) exit ❶ ■ | |
| | appearance, approach, debut ❶ ■ | |

❷ **en|trance** /ɪntræns/ (**entrances, entrancing, entranced**) V-T If something or someone **entrances** you, they cause you to feel delight and wonder. ❑ *He entranced me because he has a lovely voice.* ● **en|tranced** ADJ ❑ *For the next three hours we sat entranced.* [from French]

**en|trant** /ɛntrənt/ (**entrants**) N-COUNT An **entrant** is a person who officially enters a competition or institution. ❑ *All items entered for the competition must be the entrant's own work.* [from French]

**en|trench** /ɪntrɛntʃ/ (**entrenches, entrenching, entrenched**) V-T If something such as power, a custom, or an idea is **entrenched**, it is firmly established, so that it would be difficult to change it. ❑ *...laws designed to entrench democracy.* ● **en|trenched** ADJ ❑ *Religious differences remain deeply entrenched.*

| Word Link | *eur ≈ one who does : amateur, chauffeur, entrepreneur* |
|---|---|

**en|tre|pre|neur** /ɒntrəprənɜːr, -nʊər/ (**entrepreneurs**) N-COUNT An **entrepreneur** is a person who sets up businesses and business deals. [BUSINESS] ● **en|tre|pre|neur|ial** /ɒntrəprənɜːrial, -nʊər-/ ADJ ❑ *...her entrepreneurial husband.* [from French]

**en|trust** /ɪntrʌst/ (**entrusts, entrusting, entrusted**) V-T If you **entrust** something important to someone or **entrust** them **with** it, you make them responsible for looking after it or dealing with it. ❑ *He entrusted his cash to a business partner.* ❑ *She was entrusted with the children's education.*

**en|try** /ɛntri/ (**entries**) ■ N-UNCOUNT If you gain **entry to** a particular place, you are able to go in. ❑ *No entry after 11 pm.* ❑ *Entry to the museum is free.* ■ PHRASE **No Entry** is used on signs to indicate that you are not allowed to go into a particular area or go through a particular door or gate. ■ N-UNCOUNT Someone's **entry into** a particular society or group is their joining of it. ❑ *...China's entry into the World Trade Organization.* ■ N-COUNT An **entry** in a diary or other book or in a computer file is a short piece of writing in it. ❑ *...Violet's diary entry for April 20, 1917.* ■ N-COUNT An **entry for** a competition is something that you complete in order to take part, for example the answers to a set of questions. ❑ *The closing date for entries is December 31.* ■ N-COUNT The **entry to** a place is the way into it, for example a door or gate. ❑ *The entry was blocked.* [from Old French] → see **blog**

**en|vel|op** /ɪnvɛləp/ (**envelops, enveloping, enveloped**) V-T If one thing **envelops** another, it covers or surrounds it completely. ❑ *The smell of the forest enveloped us.* [from Old French]

**en|velope** /ɛnvəloʊp, ɒn-/ (**envelopes**) N-COUNT An **envelope** is the rectangular paper cover in which you send a letter to someone through the mail. [from French] → see **office**

**en|vi|able** /ɛnviəbᵊl/ ADJ You describe something such as a quality as **enviable** when someone else has it and you wish that you had it too. ❑ *Their athletes have an enviable reputation.* [from Old French]

**en|vi|ous** /ɛnviəs/ ADJ If you are **envious of**

someone, you want something that they have. ❑ *I'm not envious of your success.* ● **en|vi|ous|ly** ADV ❑ *People talked enviously about his good luck.* [from Latin]

**en|vi|ron|ment** /ɪnvaɪrənmənt, -vaɪərn-/ (**environments**) **1** N-VAR Someone's **environment** is their surroundings, especially the conditions in which they grow up, live, or work. ❑ *Students in our schools are taught in a safe, secure environment.* **2** N-SING **The environment** is the natural world of land, sea, air, plants, and animals. ❑ *...persuading people to respect the environment.* ● **en|vi|ron|men|tal** /ɪnvaɪrənmɛntəl, -vaɪərn-/ ADJ ❑ *Environmental groups plan to hold public protests during the conference.* ● **en|vi|ron|men|tal|ly** ADV ❑ *...the high price of environmentally friendly goods.* [from Old French]
→ see **amphibian, dump, habitat, pollution**

| Word Partnership | Use *environment* with : |
| --- | --- |
| ADJ. | **hostile** environment, **safe** environment, **supportive** environment, **unhealthy** environment **1** **natural** environment **2** |
| V. | **damage the** environment, **protect the** environment **2** |

**en|vi|ron|men|tal|ist** /ɪnvaɪrənmɛntəlɪst, -vaɪərn-/ (**environmentalists**) N-COUNT An **environmentalist** is a person who is concerned with protecting and preserving the natural environment. [from Old French]

**en|vis|age** /ɪnvɪzɪdʒ/ (**envisages, envisaging, envisaged**) V-T If you **envisage** something, you imagine that it is true, real, or likely to happen. ❑ *I don't envisage spending my whole life in this job.* [from French]

**en|vi|sion** /ɪnvɪʒⁿn/ (**envisions, envisioning, envisioned**) V-T If you **envision** something, you envisage it. ❑ *We can envision a better future.*

**en|voy** /ɛnvɔɪ, ɒn-/ (**envoys**) **1** N-COUNT An **envoy** is someone who is sent as a representative from one government or political group to another. ❑ *A U.S. envoy is expected in the region this month.* **2** N-COUNT An **envoy** is a diplomat in an embassy who is immediately below the ambassador in rank. [from French]

**envy** /ɛnvi/ (**envies, envying, envied**) V-T If you **envy** someone, you wish that you had the same things or qualities that they have. ❑ *I don't envy young people.* ● **Envy** is also a noun. ❑ *...his feelings of envy towards his mother.* [from Old French]

**en|zyme** /ɛnzaɪm/ (**enzymes**) N-COUNT An **enzyme** is a chemical substance found in living creatures that produces changes in other substances without being changed itself. [TECHNICAL] [from Medieval Greek]

**epic** /ɛpɪk/ (**epics**) **1** N-COUNT An **epic** is a long book, poem, or movie whose story extends over a long period of time or tells of great events. ❑ *...Mel Gibson's historical epic "Braveheart."* ● **Epic** is also an adjective. ❑ *...epic narrative poems.* **2** ADJ Something that is **epic** is very impressive or ambitious. ❑ *...Columbus's epic voyage of discovery.* [from Latin]
→ see **hero**

**epi|cen|ter** /ɛpɪsɛntər/ (**epicenters**) N-COUNT The **epicenter** of an earthquake is the place on the earth's surface directly above the point where it starts, and is the place where it is felt most strongly. [from New Latin]

**epic thea|ter** N-UNCOUNT **Epic theater** is a style of theater that uses non-realistic devices such as songs and captions to illustrate social or political ideas.

**epi|dem|ic** /ɛpɪdɛmɪk/ (**epidemics**) N-COUNT If there is an **epidemic of** a particular disease somewhere, it affects a very large number of people there and spreads quickly to other areas. ❑ *...a flu epidemic.* [from French]
→ see **illness**

**epi|der|mis** /ɛpɪdɜrmɪs/ N-SING Your **epidermis** is the thin, protective, outer layer of your skin. [TECHNICAL] [from Late Latin]

**epi|di|dy|mis** /ɛpɪdɪdəmɪs/ (**epididymes**) N-COUNT The **epididymis** is a long, narrow tube behind the testicles of male animals, where sperm is stored. [TECHNICAL] [from Greek]

**epi|lep|sy** /ɛpɪlɛpsi/ N-UNCOUNT **Epilepsy** is a brain condition that causes a person to suddenly lose consciousness and sometimes to have seizures. ❑ *Shawna suffers from epilepsy.* [from Late Latin]

**epi|lep|tic** /ɛpɪlɛptɪk/ (**epileptics**) ADJ Someone who is **epileptic** suffers from epilepsy. ❑ *He was epileptic and refused to take medication for his condition.* ● An **epileptic** is someone who is epileptic. ❑ *His wife is an epileptic.* [from Late Latin]

**epi|sode** /ɛpɪsoʊd/ (**episodes**) **1** N-COUNT You can refer to an event or a short period of time as an **episode** if you want to suggest that it is important or unusual, or has some particular quality. ❑ *This episode is deeply embarrassing for Washington.* **2** N-COUNT An **episode** is one of the separate parts of a story broadcast on television or radio, or published in a magazine. ❑ *The final episode will be shown next Sunday.* [from Greek]
→ see **animation**

**epi|the|lial tis|sue** /ɛpɪθiliəl tɪʃu/ (**epithelial tissues**) N-VAR **Epithelial tissue** is a layer of cells in animals that covers the skin and other surfaces of the body. [TECHNICAL]

**epito|me** /ɪpɪtəmi/ N-SING If you say that a person or thing is **the epitome of** something, you are emphasizing that they are the best possible example of it. [FORMAL] ❑ *George was the epitome of good sense.* [from Latin]

**epito|mize** /ɪpɪtəmaɪz/ (**epitomizes, epitomizing, epitomized**) V-T If you say that something or someone **epitomizes** a particular thing, you mean that they are a perfect example of it. ❑ *Her clothes epitomized French style.* [from Latin]

**epoch** /ɛpək/ (**epochs**) N-COUNT If you refer to a long period of time as an **epoch**, you mean that important events or great changes took place during it. ❑ *The birth of Christ was the beginning of a major epoch of world history.* [from New Latin]

**equal** /ikwəl/ (**equals, equaling, equaled**) **1** ADJ If two things are **equal** or if one thing is **equal** to another, they are the same in size, number, or value. ❑ *Research and teaching are of equal importance.* ❑ *...equal numbers of men and women.* ● **equal|ly** ADV ❑ *All these techniques are equally effective.* ❑ *Eat three small meals a day, at equally spaced intervals.* **2** ADJ If different groups of people are **equal** or are given **equal** treatment, they have the same rights or are treated in the same way. ❏ *We demand equal rights at work.* ❏ *They have agreed to meet on equal terms.* ● **equal|ly** ADV ❏ *The court system is supposed to treat everyone equally.* **3** N-COUNT Someone who is your **equal** has the same ability, status, or rights as you have. ❏ *It was a marriage of equals.* **4** ADJ If someone is **equal to** a particular job or situation, they have the necessary ability, strength, or courage to deal successfully with it. ❏ *She is equal to any situation in which she finds herself.* **5** V-LINK If something **equals** a particular number or amount, it is the same as that amount or the equivalent of that amount. ❏ *9 minus 7 equals 2.* **6** V-T To **equal** something or someone means to be as good or as great as them. ❏ *The victory equaled the team's best in history.* [from Latin]

**Word Partnership** Use *equal* with :

N. equal **importance**, equal **number**, equal **parts**, equal **pay**, equal **share** **1**
equal **rights**, equal **treatment** **2**

**equal|i|ty** /ɪkwɒlɪti/ N-UNCOUNT **Equality** is the same status, rights, and responsibilities for all the members of a society, group, or family. ❏ *…equality of the sexes.* [from Latin]

**equal|ize** /ikwəlaɪz/ (**equalizes, equalizing, equalized**) V-T To **equalize** a situation means to give everyone the same rights or opportunities, for example, in education, wealth, or social status. ❏ *Modern divorce laws equalize the rights of husbands and wives.* ● **equali|za|tion** /ikwəlɪzeɪʃⁿn/ N-UNCOUNT ❏ *…the equalization of opportunities for men and women.* [from Latin]

**equal|ly** /ikwəli/ **1** ADV **Equally** is used to introduce another comment on the same topic, that balances or contrasts with the previous comment. ❏ *I think it is a serious issue, but equally I don't think it is a matter of life and death.* [from Latin] **2** → see also **equal**

**equal op|por|tu|nity** N-UNCOUNT **Equal opportunity** refers to the policy of giving everyone the same opportunities for employment, pay, and promotion, without discriminating against particular groups. [BUSINESS] ❏ *…equal opportunity for women.*

**equal op|por|tu|nity em|ploy|er** (**equal opportunity employers**) N-COUNT An **equal opportunity employer** is an employer who gives people the same opportunities for employment, pay, and promotion, without discrimination against anyone. [BUSINESS]

**equate** /ɪkweɪt/ (**equates, equating, equated**) V-T/V-I If you **equate** one thing **with** another, or if you say that one thing **equates** with another, you believe that they are strongly connected. ❏ *I equate being thin with ill health.* ❏ *The authors equate mind and brain.* [from Latin]

**equa|tion** /ɪkweɪʒⁿn/ (**equations**) N-COUNT An **equation** is a mathematical statement saying that two amounts or values are the same, for example 6x4=24. [from Latin]

**equa|tor** /ɪkweɪtər/ N-SING The **equator** is an imaginary line around the middle of the earth at an equal distance from the North Pole and the South Pole. [from Medieval Latin]
→ see **globe**

**eques|trian** /ɪkwɛstriən/ ADJ **Equestrian**

means connected with the activity of riding horses. ❏ *…his equestrian skills.* [from Latin]

**Word Link** equi ≈ equal : equilibrium, equitable, equivalent

**equi|lib|rium** /ikwɪlɪbriəm/ (**equilibria**) N-VAR **Equilibrium** is a state of balance and stability in a situation or in someone's emotions. [FORMAL] ❏ *Prices found a new level of equilibrium.* ❏ *I took three deep breaths to restore my equilibrium.* [from Latin]

**equip** /ɪkwɪp/ (**equips, equipping, equipped**) **1** V-T If you **equip** a person or thing **with** something, you give them the tools or equipment that are needed. ❏ *Seattle police have equipped their cars with cameras.* **2** V-T If something **equips** you **for** a particular task or experience, it gives you the skills and attitudes you need for it, especially by educating you in a particular way. ❏ *These skills will equip you for the future.* [from Old French]

**equip|ment** /ɪkwɪpmənt/ N-UNCOUNT **Equipment** consists of the things that are used for a particular purpose, such as a hobby or job. ❏ *…computers and electronic equipment.* [from Old French]

**Thesaurus** equipment Also look up :

N. accessories, facilities, gear, machinery, supplies; (ant.) tools, utensils

**equi|table** /ɛkwɪtəbⁿl/ ADJ Something that is **equitable** is fair and reasonable in a way that gives equal treatment to everyone. ❏ *He urged them to come to an equitable compromise.* [from French]

**equiva|lent** /ɪkwɪvələnt/ (**equivalents**) **1** N-SING If one amount or value is **the equivalent of** another, they are the same. ❏ *Mr. Li's pay is the equivalent of about $80 a month.* ● **Equivalent** is also an adjective. ❏ *If you don't have apples, you can use an equivalent amount of pears.* **2** N-COUNT The **equivalent** of someone or something is a person or thing that has the same function in a different place, time, or system. ❏ *…the Red Cross, and its equivalent in Muslim countries, the Red Crescent.* ● **Equivalent** is also an adjective. ❏ *…a decrease of 10% compared with the equivalent period in 1991.* [from Late Latin]

**Thesaurus** equivalent Also look up :

N. counterpart, match, parallel, peer, substitute **2**
ADJ. equal, similar; (ant.) different **2**

**er** /ɜr/ **Er** is used in writing to represent the sound that people make when they hesitate, especially while they decide what to say next. ❏ *I'm just, er, mentioning the opportunity as I see it.*

**ER** /i ɑr/ (**ERs**) N-COUNT The **ER** is the part of a hospital where people who have severe injuries or sudden illnesses are taken for emergency treatment. **ER** is an abbreviation for **emergency room.** ❏ *People come to the ER with heart attacks.*

**era** /ɪərə/ (**eras**) N-COUNT An **era** is a period of time that is considered as a single unit because it has a particular feature. ❏ *…the nuclear era.* ❏ *…the Reagan-Bush era.* [from Latin]

**eradi|cate** /ɪrædɪkeɪt/ (**eradicates, eradicating, eradicated**) V-T To **eradicate** something means to get rid of it completely. [FORMAL] ❏ *We are trying*

e

*to eradicate illnesses such as malaria.* ● **eradi|ca|tion** /ɪrædɪkeɪʃ°n/ N-UNCOUNT ❑ *...the eradication of corruption.* [from Latin]

**erase** /ɪreɪs/ (**erases, erasing, erased**) **1** V-T If you **erase** a thought or feeling, you destroy it completely so that you can no longer remember something or no longer feel a particular emotion. ❑ *They are desperate to erase the memory of that last defeat.* **2** V-T If you **erase** sound that has been recorded on a tape or information which has been stored in a computer, you completely remove or destroy it. ❑ *The names were accidentally erased from computer files.* **3** V-T If you **erase** something such as writing or a mark, you remove it, usually by rubbing it. ❑ *She erased his name from her address book.* [from Latin]
→ see **draw**

**eras|er** /ɪreɪsər/ (**erasers**) N-COUNT An **eraser** is an object, usually a piece of rubber or plastic, which is used to remove writing in pencil or a pen. ❑ *...a large, pink eraser.* [from Latin]

**erect** /ɪrɛkt/ (**erects, erecting, erected**) **1** V-T If people **erect** something such as a building, bridge, or barrier, they build it or create it. [FORMAL] ❑ *The building was erected in 1900.* ● **erec|tion** N-UNCOUNT ❑ *...the erection of temporary fences.* **2** ADJ People or things that are **erect** are straight and upright. ❑ *Stand erect, with your arms straight.* [from Latin]

**erec|tion** /ɪrɛkʃ°n/ (**erections**) N-COUNT If a man has an **erection**, his penis is stiff and sticking up because he is sexually aroused. [from Latin]

**erode** /ɪroʊd/ (**erodes, eroding, eroded**) **1** V-T/V-I If rock or soil **erodes** or **is eroded** by the weather, sea, or wind, it cracks and breaks so that it is gradually destroyed. ❑ *The storm washed away buildings and eroded beaches.* ● **ero|sion** /ɪroʊʒ°n/ N-UNCOUNT ❑ *...erosion of the river valleys.* **2** V-T/V-I If something **erodes** or **is eroded**, it gradually weakens or loses value. ❑ *Competition has eroded profits.* ● **ero|sion** N-UNCOUNT ❑ *...the erosion of moral standards.* [from Latin]
→ see Word Web: **erosion**
→ see **beach, rock**

**erot|ic** /ɪrɒtɪk/ ADJ If you describe something as **erotic**, you mean that it involves sexual feelings or arouses desire. ❑ *...an erotic experience.* [from Greek]

**err** /ɜr, ɛr/ (**errs, erring, erred**) **1** V-I If you **err**, you make a mistake. [FORMAL] ❑ *The firm erred in its estimates.* **2** PHRASE If you **err on the side of** caution, for example, you decide to act in a cautious way, rather than take risks. ❑ *They may be wise to err on the side of caution.* [from Old French]

**er|rand** /ɛrənd/ (**errands**) N-COUNT An **errand** is a short trip that you make in order to do a job, for example, when you go to a store to buy something.

❑ *She went off on some errand.* [from Old English]

**er|rat|ic** /ɪrætɪk/ ADJ Something that is **erratic** happens at unexpected times or moves in an irregular way. ❑ *...Argentina's erratic inflation rate.* ● **er|rati|cal|ly** /ɪrætɪkli/ ADV ❑ *Police stopped him for driving erratically.* [from Latin]

**er|ro|neous** /ɪroʊniəs/ ADJ Beliefs, opinions, or methods that are **erroneous** are incorrect. ❑ *They reached some erroneous conclusions.* ● **er|ro|neous|ly** ADV ❑ *It was erroneously reported that Armstrong refused to give evidence.* [from Latin]

**er|ror** /ɛrər/ (**errors**) N-VAR An **error** is a mistake. ❑ *There was a mathematical error in the calculations.* ❑ *The man was shot in error.* [from Latin]

| Word Partnership | Use *error* with : |
| --- | --- |
| ADJ. | **clerical** error, **common** error, **fatal** error, **human** error |
| V. | **commit an** error, **correct an** error, **make an** error |

| Word Link | *rupt ≈ breaking : dis*rupt, *e*rupt, *inter*rupt |
| --- | --- |

**erupt** /ɪrʌpt/ (**erupts, erupting, erupted**) **1** V-I When a volcano **erupts**, it throws out a lot of hot, melted rock called lava, as well as ash and steam. ❑ *The volcano erupted in 1980.* ● **erup|tion** /ɪrʌpʃ°n/ (**eruptions**) N-VAR ❑ *...the volcanic eruption of Tambora.* **2** V-I If something such as violence **erupts**, it suddenly begins or gets more intense. ❑ *Heavy fighting erupted there today.* ● **erup|tion** N-COUNT ❑ *...this sudden eruption of violence.* [from Latin]
→ see **rock, volcano**

| Word Link | *scal, scala ≈ ladder, stairs : e*scalate, *e*scalator, *scale* |
| --- | --- |

**es|ca|late** /ɛskəleɪt/ (**escalates, escalating, escalated**) V-T/V-I If a bad situation **escalates** or if someone or something **escalates** it, it becomes worse. ❑ *Nobody wants the situation to escalate; everybody wants the nation to return to peace and order.* ❑ *The protests escalated into five days of rioting.* ● **es|ca|la|tion** /ɛskəleɪʃ°n/ (**escalations**) N-VAR ❑ *...the threat of nuclear escalation.*

**es|ca|la|tor** /ɛskəleɪtər/ (**escalators**) N-COUNT An **escalator** is a moving staircase. ❑ *Take the escalator.*

**es|cape** /ɪskeɪp/ (**escapes, escaping, escaped**) **1** V-I If you **escape from** a place, you succeed in getting away from it. ❑ *A prisoner has escaped from a*

escalator

## Word Web   erosion

There are two main causes of **soil erosion—water** and **wind. Rainfall**, especially heavy **thunderstorms**, breaks down **dirt**. Small particles of **earth, sand,** and **silt** are then carried away by the water. The runoff may form **gullies** on hillsides. Heavy rain sometimes even causes a large, flat soil surface to wash away all at once. This is called sheet erosion. When the soil contains too much water, **mudslides** occur. Strong **currents** of **air** cause wind erosion. There are two major ways to prevent this damage. Permanent **vegetation** anchors the soil and **windbreaks** reduce the force of the wind.

jail in northern Texas. ❑ *They escaped to the other side of the border.* ● **Escape** is also a noun. ❑ *The man made his escape.* **2** V-T/V-I You can say that you **escape** when you survive something such as an accident. ❑ *The two officers were extremely lucky to escape serious injury.* ❑ *The man's girlfriend managed to escape unhurt.* ● **Escape** is also a noun. ❑ *I had a very narrow escape on the bridge.* **3** N-COUNT If something is an **escape**, it is a way of avoiding difficulties or responsibilities. ❑ *For me television is an escape.* **4** V-T If something **escapes** you or **escapes** your attention, you do not know about it, do not remember it, or do not notice it. ❑ *His name escapes me for the moment.* [from Old Northern French]

**es|cap|ism** /ɪskeɪpɪzəm/ N-UNCOUNT If you describe an activity or type of entertainment as **escapism**, you mean that it makes people think about pleasant things instead of the uninteresting or unpleasant aspects of their life. ❑ *The movie is pure escapism.* ● **es|cap|ist** ADJ ❑ *...a little escapist fantasy.* [from Old Northern French]

**es|cort** (**escorts, escorting, escorted**)

The noun is pronounced /ɛskɔrt/. The verb is pronounced /ɪskɔrt/.

**1** V-T If you **escort** someone somewhere, you accompany them there, usually in order to make sure that they go. ❑ *I escorted him to the door.* **2** N-COUNT An **escort** is a person who travels with someone in order to protect or guard them. ❑ *He arrived with a police escort.* **3** PHRASE If someone is taken somewhere **under escort**, they are accompanied by guards. **4** N-COUNT An **escort** is a person who accompanies another person of the opposite sex to a social event. Sometimes people are paid to be escorts. ❑ *I needed an escort for a company dinner.* [from French]

**eso|ter|ic** /ɛsətɛrɪk/ ADJ Something that is **esoteric** is known or understood by only a small number of people. [FORMAL] ❑ *...esoteric knowledge.* [from Greek]

**es|pe|cial|ly** /ɪspɛʃ°li/ **1** ADV You use **especially** to emphasize that what you are saying applies to one person, thing, time, or area than to any others. ❑ *Wild flowers grow in the valleys, especially in April.* **2** ADV You use **especially** to emphasize a characteristic or quality. ❑ *The brain is especially sensitive to lack of oxygen.* [from Old French]

**es|pio|nage** /ɛspiənɑʒ/ N-UNCOUNT **Espionage** is the activity of finding out the political, military, or industrial secrets of your enemies or rivals by using spies. [FORMAL] ❑ *The authorities have arrested several people suspected of espionage.* [from French]

**es|pouse** /ɪspaʊz/ (**espouses, espousing, espoused**) V-T If you **espouse** a policy or cause, you support it. [FORMAL] ❑ *She ran away to Mexico and espoused the revolutionary cause.* [from Old French]

**es|say** /ɛseɪ/ (**essays**) N-COUNT An **essay** is a short piece of writing on a particular subject. ❑ *...an essay about politics.* [from Old French]

**es|sence** /ɛs°ns/ (**essences**) **1** N-UNCOUNT The **essence of** something is its basic and most important characteristic that gives it its individual identity. ❑ *The essence of being a customer is choice.* **2** PHRASE You use **in essence** to emphasize that you are talking about the most important aspect of an idea, situation, or event. [FORMAL] ❑ *Local taxes are in essence simple.* **3** PHRASE If you say that something **is of the essence**, you mean that it is absolutely necessary in order for a particular action to be successful. [FORMAL] ❑ *Speed was of the essence in this project.* [from Medieval Latin]

**es|sen|tial** /ɪsɛnʃ°l/ (**essentials**) **1** ADJ Something that is **essential** is absolutely necessary. ❑ *It was essential to separate crops from the areas used by animals.* ❑ *Play is an essential part of a child's development.* **2** N-COUNT The **essentials** are the things that are absolutely necessary in a situation. ❑ *The apartment contained the basic essentials.* [from Medieval Latin]

**es|sen|tial|ly** /ɪsɛnʃəli/ **1** ADV You use **essentially** to emphasize a quality that someone or something has, and to say that it is their most important or basic quality. [FORMAL] ❑ *He was essentially a simple man.* **2** ADV You use **essentially** to indicate that what you are saying is mainly true, although some parts of it are wrong or more complicated than has been stated. ❑ *His guess proved essentially correct.* [from Medieval Latin]

**es|tab|lish** /ɪstæblɪʃ/ (**establishes, establishing, established**) **1** V-T If someone **establishes** an organization or system, they create it. ❑ *...the right to establish trade unions.* ● **es|tab|lish|ment** N-SING ❑ *...the establishment of the regional government in 1980.* **2** V-RECIP If you **establish** contact with someone, you start to have contact with them. You can also say that two people, groups, or countries **establish** contact. [FORMAL] ❑ *We have already established contact with the museum.* **3** V-T If you **establish that** something is true, you discover facts that show that it is definitely true. [FORMAL] ❑ *Medical tests established that she had a heart defect.* ● **es|tab|lished** ADJ ❑ *This is an established medical fact.* [from Old French]

e

**es|tab|lished** /ɪstæblɪʃt/ ADJ If you use **established** to describe something such as an organization, you mean that it is well known because it has existed for a long time. ❑ ...old established companies. [from Old French]

**es|tab|lish|ment** /ɪstæblɪʃmənt/ (**establishments**) **1** N-COUNT An **establishment** is a store, business, or organization occupying a particular building or place. [FORMAL] ❑ ...food establishments such as cafeterias and restaurants. **2** N-SING You refer to the people who have power and influence in the running of a country, society, or organization as **the establishment**. ❑ Scientists are now part of the establishment. [from Old French] **3** → see also **establish**

**es|tate** /ɪsteɪt/ (**estates**) **1** N-COUNT An **estate** is a large area of land in the country which is owned by a person, family, or organization. ❑ He spent the holidays at the 300-acre estate of his aunt and uncle. **2** N-COUNT Someone's **estate** is all the money and property that they leave behind when they die. [LEGAL] ❑ His estate was valued at $150,000. [from Old French] **3** → see also **real estate**

**es|teem** /ɪstim/ **1** N-UNCOUNT **Esteem** is admiration and respect. [FORMAL] ❑ He is held in high esteem by colleagues. [from Old French] **2** → see also **self-esteem**

**es|thet|ic** /ɛsθɛtɪk/ ADJ **Esthetic** is used to talk about beauty or art, and people's appreciation of beautiful things. ❑ ...products chosen for their esthetic appeal. [from Greek]

**es|ti|mate** (**estimates, estimating, estimated**)

The verb is pronounced /ɛstɪmeɪt/. The noun is pronounced /ɛstɪmɪt/.

**1** V-T If you **estimate** a quantity or value, you make an approximate judgment or calculation of it. ❑ It's difficult to estimate how much money is involved. ❑ I estimate that the total cost for treatment will go from $9,000 to $12,500. ● **Estimate** is also a noun. ❑ ...the official estimate of the election result. ● **es|ti|mat|ed** ADJ ❑ There are an estimated 90,000 foreigners in the country. **2** N-COUNT An **estimate** is a judgment about a person or situation that you make based on the available evidence. ❑ I was right in my estimate of his capabilities. [from Latin]

**es|ti|va|tion** also **aestivation** /ɛstɪveɪʃⁿn/ N-UNCOUNT **Estivation** is a period during which some animals are inactive because the weather is very hot or dry. [TECHNICAL] [from Latin]

**es|tranged** /ɪstreɪndʒd/ ADJ If you are **estranged from** your family or friends, you have quarreled with them and are not communicating with them. [FORMAL] ❑ ...his estranged wife. ❑ Joanna was estranged from her father. ● **es|trange|ment** N-UNCOUNT ❑ ...years of estrangement between them. [from Old French]

**es|tu|ary** /ɛstʃuɛri/ (**estuaries**) N-COUNT An **estuary** is the wide part of a river where it joins the sea. [from Latin]

**etc.** /ɛt sɛtərə, -sɛtrə/ **etc.** is used at the end of a list to indicate that you have mentioned only some of the items involved and have not given a full list. **etc.** is a written abbreviation for "etcetera." ❑ She knew all about my schoolwork, my hospital work, etc.

**et|cet|era** /ɛtsɛtərə, -sɛtrə/ also **et cetera** → see **etc.**

**etch** /ɛtʃ/ (**etches, etching, etched**) **1** V-T If a line or pattern **is etched into** a surface, it is cut into the surface by means of acid or a sharp tool. ❑ Crosses were etched into the walls. **2** V-T PASSIVE If something **is etched on** your memory, you remember it very clearly because it made a strong impression on you. [LITERARY] ❑ The ugly scene in the study was still etched on her mind. [from Dutch]

**etch|ing** /ɛtʃɪŋ/ (**etchings**) N-COUNT An **etching** is a picture printed from a metal plate that has had a design cut into it. [from Dutch]

**eter|nal** /ɪtɜrnⁿl/ ADJ Something that is **eternal** lasts forever. ❑ ...the desire for eternal youth. ● **eter|nal|ly** ADV ❑ She is eternally grateful to her family for their support. [from Late Latin]

**eter|nity** /ɪtɜrnɪti/ **1** N-UNCOUNT **Eternity** is time without an end or a state of existence outside time, especially the state that some people believe they will pass into after they have died. ❑ I find the thought of eternity terrifying. **2** N-SING If you say that a situation lasted for **an eternity**, you mean that it seemed to last an extremely long time, usually because it was boring or unpleasant. ❑ The war continued for an eternity. [from Late Latin]

**ethe|real** /ɪθɪəriəl/ ADJ Someone or something that is **ethereal** has a delicate beauty that seems almost supernatural. [FORMAL] [from Latin]

**eth|ic** /ɛθɪk/ (**ethics**) **1** N-PLURAL **Ethics** are moral beliefs and rules about right and wrong. ❑ Its members are bound by a strict code of ethics. **2** N-SING An **ethic** of a particular kind is an idea or moral belief that influences the behavior, attitudes, and philosophy of a group of people. ❑ ...the ethic of public service. [from Latin]

**ethi|cal** /ɛθɪkⁿl/ **1** ADJ **Ethical** means relating to beliefs about right and wrong. ❑ ...ethical issues surrounding terminally-ill people. ● **ethi|cal|ly** /ɛθɪkli/ ADV ❑ We can defend ethically everything we do. **2** ADJ If you describe something as **ethical**, you mean that it is morally right or morally acceptable. ❑ ...ethical business practices. ● **ethi|cal|ly** ADV ❑ Companies should behave ethically. [from Latin]

**eth|nic** /ɛθnɪk/ ADJ **Ethnic** means connected with or relating to different racial or cultural groups of people. ❑ ...a survey of ethnic minorities. ● **eth|ni|cal|ly** /ɛθnɪkli/ ADV ❑ ...a young, ethnically mixed audience. [from Late Latin]

**ethos** /iθɒs/ N-SING The **ethos** of a group of people is the set of ideas and attitudes associated with it. [FORMAL] ❑ The whole ethos of the hotel is one of service. [from Late Latin]

**eti|quette** /ɛtɪkɪt, -kɛt/ N-UNCOUNT **Etiquette** is a set of customs and rules for polite behavior.

❏ ...*the rules of etiquette.* [from French]

**ety|mol|ogy** /ɛtɪmɒlədʒi/ (**etymologies**)
■ N-UNCOUNT **Etymology** is the study of the origins and historical development of words.
② N-COUNT The **etymology** of a particular word is its history. [from Latin]

**EU** /i yu/ N-PROPER The **EU** is an organization of European countries that have the same policies on matters such as trade, agriculture, and finance. **EU** is an abbreviation for **European Union**.

**eu|bac|te|ria** /yubæktɪəriə/ N-PLURAL **Eubacteria** are bacteria that have a rigid cell wall. Compare **archaebacteria**. [TECHNICAL] [from New Latin]

**eu|glena** /yuglinə/ (**euglena**) N-COUNT **Euglena** is a type of single-celled organism that lives mainly in fresh water. [TECHNICAL] [from New Latin]

**eu|karyot|ic cell** /yukæriɒtɪk sɛl/ (**eukaryotic cells**) N-COUNT **Eukaryotic cells** are cells that have a nucleus, such as the cells in animals and plants. Compare **prokaryotic cell**. [TECHNICAL]

**eulo|gize** /yulədʒaɪz/ (**eulogizes, eulogizing, eulogized**) V-T If you **eulogize** someone who has died, you make a speech praising them. ❏ *Leaders from around the world eulogized the president.* [from Late Latin]

**eulogy** /yulədʒi/ (**eulogies**) N-COUNT A **eulogy** is a speech, usually at a funeral, in which a person who has just died is praised. [from Late Latin]

**euphemism** /yufəmɪzəm/ (**euphemisms**) N-COUNT A **euphemism** is a polite word or expression that is used to talk about something unpleasant or embarrassing, for example death or sex. ❏ *He prefers the word "chubby" as a euphemism for fat.* [from Greek]

**euphemis|tic** /yufəmɪstɪk/ ADJ **Euphemistic** language uses polite words and expressions to refer to unpleasant or embarrassing things.
❏ ...*a euphemistic way of saying that someone is lying.* ● **euphemis|ti|cal|ly** /yufəmɪstɪkli/ ADV ❏ ...*political prisons, called euphemistically "reeducation camps."* [from Greek]

**eupho|ria** /yufɔriə/ N-UNCOUNT **Euphoria** is a feeling of intense happiness. ❏ *There was euphoria after the election.* ● **euphor|ic** /yufɒrɪk/ ADJ ❏ *The war received euphoric support from the public.* [from Greek]

**euro** /yʊəroʊ/ (**euros**) N-COUNT The **euro** is a unit of currency that is used by most member countries of the European Union.

**Word Link** an, ian ≈ one of, relating to : Christian, European, pedestrian

**Euro|pean** /yʊərəpiən/ (**Europeans**) ■ ADJ **European** means belonging or relating to, or coming from Europe. ❏ *She plans to visit several European countries.* ② N-COUNT A **European** is a person who comes from Europe. [from French]

**Euro|pean Un|ion** N-PROPER The **European Union** is an organization of European countries that have the same policies on matters such as trade, agriculture, and finance.

**eutha|na|sia** /yuθəneɪʒə/ N-UNCOUNT **Euthanasia** is the practice of painlessly killing a dying person in order to end their suffering, usually done with their consent. ❏ ...*those in favor of voluntary euthanasia.* [from New Latin]

**Word Link** vac ≈ empty : evacuate, vacant, vacate

**evacu|ate** /ɪvækyueɪt/ (**evacuates, evacuating, evacuated**) V-T If people are **evacuated from** a place, or if they **evacuate** a place, they move out of it because it has become dangerous. ❏ *The fire is threatening about sixty homes, and residents have evacuated the area.* ❏ *Officials ordered the residents to evacuate.* ● **evacu|ation** /ɪvækyueɪʃən/ (**evacuations**) N-VAR ❏ *An evacuation of the city's four million inhabitants is planned.* [from Latin]

**evac|uee** /ɪvækyui/ (**evacuees**) N-COUNT An **evacuee** is someone who has been sent away from a dangerous place to somewhere safe, especially during a war. [from Latin]

**evade** /ɪveɪd/ (**evades, evading, evaded**) V-T If you **evade** something unpleasant or difficult, you avoid it. ❏ *He admits he evaded taxes.* [from French]

**evalu|ate** /ɪvælyueɪt/ (**evaluates, evaluating, evaluated**) V-T If you **evaluate** something or someone, you consider them in order to make a judgment about them, for example about how good or bad they are. ❏ *The situation is difficult to evaluate.* ● **evalu|ation** /ɪvælyueɪʃən/ (**evaluations**) N-VAR ❏ ...*the opinions and evaluations of college supervisors.* [from French]

**evapo|rate** /ɪvæpəreɪt/ (**evaporates, evaporating, evaporated**) V-I When a liquid **evaporates**, it changes into a gas, because its temperature has increased. ❏ *Moisture is drawn to the surface of the fabric so that it evaporates.* ● **evapo|ra|tion** /ɪvæpəreɪʃən/ N-UNCOUNT ❏ ...*the evaporation of sweat on the skin.* [from Late Latin]
→ see **matter, water**

**eva|sion** /ɪveɪʒən/ (**evasions**) N-VAR **Evasion** means deliberately avoiding something that you are supposed to do or deal with. ❏ *He was arrested for tax evasion.* [from Late Latin]

**eva|sive** /ɪveɪsɪv/ ADJ If you describe someone as **evasive**, you mean that they deliberately avoid giving clear answers to questions. ❏ *He was evasive about the circumstances of their meeting.* ● **eva|sive|ly** ADV ❏ *"I can't come to any conclusion about that," Manuel said evasively.* [from Late Latin]

**eve** /iv/ (**eves**) ■ N-COUNT The **eve of** a particular event or occasion is the day before it, or the period of time just before it. ❏ ...*on the eve of his 27th birthday.* ② → see also **Christmas Eve**

---
**even**

❶ DISCOURSE USES
❷ ADJECTIVE USES
❸ PHRASAL VERB USES
---

❶ **even** /ivən/ ■ ADV You use **even** to suggest that what comes just after or just before it in the sentence is rather surprising. ❏ *He would call me and text me about 10 times a day, even when I asked him to stop.* ❏ *Rob remains good-natured, even after the death of his wife.* ② ADV You use **even** with comparative adjectives and adverbs to emphasize a quality that someone or something has. ❏ *On television he made an even stronger impact.* ③ PHRASE You use **even if** or **even though** to indicate that a particular fact does not make the rest of your statement untrue. ❏ *Cynthia is not ashamed of* *what she does, even if she ends up doing something wrong.* **4** PHRASE You use **even so** to introduce a surprising fact that relates to what you have just said. ❏ *The bus was only half full. Even so, a man asked Nina if the seat next to her was taken.* [from Old English]

❷ **even** /iˈvᵊn/ **1** ADJ An **even** measurement or rate stays at about the same level. ❏ *How important is it to have an even temperature?* • **even|ly** ADV ❏ *He looked at Ellen, breathing evenly in her sleep.* **2** ADJ An **even** surface is smooth and flat. ❏ *The table has a glass top which provides an even surface.* **3** ADJ If there is an **even** distribution or division of something, each person, group, or area involved has an equal amount. ❏ *Divide the dough into 12 even pieces.* • **even|ly** ADV ❏ *The money was divided evenly.* **4** ADJ An **even** contest or competition is equally balanced between the two sides who are taking part. ❏ *It was an even game.* • **even|ly** ADV ❏ *...two evenly matched candidates.* **5** ADJ An **even** number can be divided exactly by the number two. **6** PHRASE When a company or a person running a business **breaks even**, they make neither a profit nor a loss. [BUSINESS] ❏ *The airline hopes to break even next year.* [from Old English] **7** to **be on an even keel** → see **keel**

❸ **even** /iˈvᵊn/ (**evens, evening, evened**)
▸ **even out** PHR-VERB If something **evens out**, or if you **even** it **out**, the differences between the different parts of it are reduced. ❏ *The power balance has evened out in the government.*

**eve|ning** /ivnɪŋ/ (**evenings**) N-VAR The **evening** is the part of each day between the end of the afternoon and the time when you go to bed. ❏ *All he did that evening was sit around the house.* ❏ *Supper is from 5:00 to 6:00 in the evening.* [from Old English]
→ see **time**

**event** /ɪvɛnt/ (**events**) **1** N-COUNT An **event** is something that happens. ❏ *Yesterday's events took everyone by surprise.* **2** N-COUNT An **event** is a planned and organized occasion. ❏ *...major sports events.* **3** PHRASE You use **in the event of, in the event that**, and **in that event** when you are talking about a possible future situation, especially when you are planning what to do if it occurs. ❏ *The bank has agreed to give an immediate refund in the unlikely event of an error.* [from Latin]
→ see **graduation, history**

**even|tual** /ɪvɛntʃuəl/ ADJ The **eventual** result of something is what happens at the end of it. ❏ *There are many who believe that civil war will be the eventual outcome.* [from Latin]

**even|tu|al|ity** /ɪvɛntʃuælɪti/ (**eventualities**) N-COUNT An **eventuality** is a possible future event or result. [FORMAL] ❏ *Every eventuality is covered, from running out of gas to needing water.* [from Latin]

**even|tu|al|ly** /ɪvɛntʃuəli/ **1** ADV **Eventually** means in the end, especially after a lot of delays, problems, or arguments. ❏ *The flight eventually got*

*away six hours late.* **2** ADV **Eventually** means at the end of a situation or process or as the final result of it. ❏ *Eventually your child will leave home.* [from Latin]

**ever** /ɛvər/

**1** ADV **Ever** means at any time. It is used in questions and negative statements. ❏ *I'm not sure I'll ever trust people again.* ❏ *Neither of us has ever skied.* ❏ *Have you ever seen anything like it?* **2** ADV You use **ever** after comparatives and superlatives to emphasize the degree to which something is true. ❏ *She is singing better than ever.* ❏ *Japan is wealthier and more powerful than ever before.* **3** PHRASE You say **as ever** in order to indicate that something is not unusual. ❏ *As ever, the meals are mainly fish-based.* **4** PHRASE If something has been the case **ever since** a particular time, it has been the case all the time from then until now. ❏ *He's been there ever since you left!* [from Old English] **5** → see also **forever 6 hardly ever** → see **hardly**

**ever|green** /ɛvərgrin/ (**evergreens**) N-COUNT An **evergreen** is a tree or bush that has green leaves all year long. • **Evergreen** is also an adjective. ❏ *Plant evergreen shrubs around the end of the month.*
→ see **plant**

**every** /ɛvri/ **1** DET You use **every** to indicate that you are referring to all the members of a group or all the parts of something. ❏ *Every room has a window facing the ocean.* ❏ *Record every purchase you make.* • **Every** is also an adjective. ❏ *...parents who fulfill his every need.* **2** DET You use **every** in order to say how often something happens or to indicate that something happens at regular intervals. ❏ *We had to attend meetings every day.* ❏ *A burglary occurs every three minutes in the city.* **3** DET You can use **every** before some nouns in order to emphasize what you are saying. ❏ *He has every intention of staying.* ❏ *There is every chance that you will succeed.* **4** PHRASE You use **every** in the expressions **every now and then, every now and again, every once in a while,** and **every so often** in order to indicate that something happens occasionally. ❏ *Stir the mixture every now and then to keep it from separating.* **5** PHRASE If something happens **every other day** or **every second day,** for example, it happens one day, then does not happen the next day, then happens the day after that, and so on. You can also say that something happens **every third week, every fourth year,** and so on. ❏ *I went home every other week.* [from Old English] **6 every bit as** good **as** → see **bit**

**every|body** /ɛvribɒdi, -bʌdi/ **Everybody** means the same as **everyone.**

**every|day** /ɛvrideɪ/ ADJ You use **everyday** to describe something that happens or is used every day, or forms a regular and basic part of your life. ❏ *In the course of my everyday life, I had very little contact with teenagers.*

**Usage**    **everyday** and **every day**

*Everyday* and *every day* are often confused. *Everyday* means "ordinary, unsurprising"; *every day* means "something happens daily": *The everyday things are the things that happen every day.*

**every|one** /ɛvriwʌn/

The form **everybody** is also used.

PRON **Everyone** or **everybody** means all the people in a particular group or all people in general. □ *Everyone on the street was shocked when they heard the news.* □ *Not everyone thinks that the government is being fair.* □ *Everyone feels like a failure at times.*

**Usage**    **everyone** and **every one**

*Everyone* and *every one* are different. *Everyone* refers to all people or to all the people in some group being discussed, while *every one* refers to every single person or thing in some group being discussed: *Luisa offered everyone a copy of her new book; unfortunately, she had only twelve copies, and every one was gone before I could get one.*

**every|place** /ɛvripleɪs/ → see **everywhere**

**every|thing** /ɛvriθɪŋ/ **1** PRON You use **everything** to refer to all the objects, actions, activities, or facts in a situation. □ *Everything else in his life has changed.* □ *Najib and I do everything together.* **2** PRON You use **everything** to refer to a whole situation or to life in general. □ *She says everything is going smoothly.* □ *Is everything all right?*

**every|where** /ɛvriwɛər/ also **everyplace** **1** ADV You use **everywhere** to refer to a whole area or to all the places in a particular area. □ *Working people everywhere object to paying taxes.* □ *We went everywhere together.* **2** ADV You use **everywhere** to refer to all the places that someone goes to. □ *Mary Jo is accustomed to traveling everywhere in style.* **3** ADV If you say that someone or something is **everywhere**, you mean that they are present in a place in very large numbers. □ *There were ambulances and police cars everywhere.*

**evict** /ɪvɪkt/ (**evicts, evicting, evicted**) V-T If someone **is evicted**, they are officially forced to leave the place where they live. □ *They were evicted from their apartment.* □ *The city police evicted ten families.* ● **evic|tion** (**evictions**) N-VAR □ *He was facing eviction, along with his wife and family.* [from Late Latin]

**evi|dence** /ɛvɪdəns/ **1** N-UNCOUNT **Evidence** is anything that makes you believe that something is true or has really happened. □ *There is no evidence that he committed the offenses.* □ *The evidence against him is very strong.* **2** PHRASE If you **give evidence** in a court of law, you give a statement saying what you know about something. □ *Scientists will be called to give evidence.* **3** PHRASE If someone or something **is in evidence**, they are present and can be clearly seen. □ *Few soldiers were in evidence.* [from Latin]
→ see **experiment, trial**

**Word Partnership**    Use *evidence* with :

| ADJ. | **circumstantial** evidence, **new** evidence, **physical** evidence **1** |
| V. | **find** evidence, **gather** evidence, **present** evidence, evidence **to support something 1** |

**evi|dent** /ɛvɪdənt/ ADJ If something is **evident**, you notice it easily and clearly. □ *His footprints were clearly evident in the heavy dust.* □ *It was evident that she had once been a beauty.* [from Latin]

**evi|dent|ly** /ɛvɪdəntli, -dɛnt-/ ADV You use **evidently** to say that something is true, for example, because you have seen evidence of it yourself or because someone has told you it is true. □ *The two Russians evidently knew each other.* [from Latin]

**evil** /iv<sup>ə</sup>l/ (**evils**) **1** N-UNCOUNT **Evil** is used to refer to all the wicked and bad things that happen in the world. □ *...a conflict between good and evil.* **2** N-COUNT An **evil** is a very unpleasant or harmful situation or activity. □ *...the evils of prejudice.* **3** ADJ If you describe something or someone as **evil**, you mean that you think they are morally very bad and cause harm to people. □ *...the country's most evil terrorists.* □ *He condemned slavery as evil.* [from Old English]

**evoca|tive** /ɪvɒkətɪv/ ADJ If something is **evocative**, it strongly reminds you of something or gives you a powerful impression of something. [FORMAL] □ *Her story is strongly evocative of Italian life.* [from Latin]

**evoke** /ɪvoʊk/ (**evokes, evoking, evoked**) V-T To **evoke** a particular memory, idea, emotion, or response means to cause it to occur. [FORMAL] □ *The scene evoked memories of those old movies.* [from Latin]

**evo|lu|tion** /ɛvəluʃⁿn, iv-/ (**evolutions**) **1** N-UNCOUNT **Evolution** is a process of gradual change that takes place over many generations, during which species of animals, plants, or insects slowly change some of their physical characteristics. □ *...the evolution of plants and animals.* **2** N-VAR **Evolution** is a process of gradual development in a particular situation or thing over a period of time. [FORMAL] □ *...a crucial period in the evolution of modern physics.* [from Latin]
→ see Word Web: **evolution**
→ see **earth**

**evo|lu|tion|ary** /ɛvəluʃənɛri, iv-/ ADJ **Evolutionary** means relating to a process of gradual change and development. □ *...an evolutionary process.* [from Latin]

**evolve** /ɪvɒlv/ (**evolves, evolving, evolved**) **1** V-I When animals or plants **evolve**, they gradually change and develop into different forms. □ *Corn evolved from a wild grass.* **2** V-T/V-I If something **evolves** or you **evolve** it, it gradually develops over a period of time into something different and usually more advanced. □ *...a tiny airline which eventually evolved into Pakistan International Airlines.* □ *Popular music evolved from folk songs.* [from Latin]
→ see **earth**

**ewe** /yu/ (**ewes**) N-COUNT A **ewe** is an adult female sheep. [from Old English]

## Word Web    evolution

The **theory** of **human evolution** states that humans **evolved** from an ape-like ancestor. In 1856 the **fossils** of a **Neanderthal** were found. This was the first time that **scientists** realized time that there were earlier forms of humans. **Anthropologists** have found other fossils that show how **hominids** changed over time. One of the earliest ancestors that has been found is called **Australopithecus**. This **species** lived about 4 million years ago in Africa. The most famous specimen of this species is named 'Lucy'. Scientists believe that she was among the first hominids to walk upright. The oldest fossils of **Homo sapiens** date back to approximately 130,000 years ago.

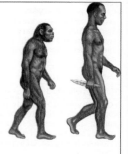

**ex|ac|er|bate** /ɪgzǽsərbeɪt/ (**exacerbates, exacerbating, exacerbated**) V-T If something **exacerbates** a bad situation, it makes it worse. [FORMAL] ❑ *Heavy rains exacerbated flooding problems in the area.* ● **ex|ac|er|ba|tion** /ɪgzæsərbeɪʃⁿn/ N-UNCOUNT ❑ *…the exacerbation of global problems.* [from Latin]

**ex|act** /ɪgzǽkt/ (**exacts, exacting, exacted**) ■ ADJ **Exact** means correct, accurate, and complete in every way. ❑ *I don't remember the exact words.* ❑ *The exact number of protest calls has not been revealed.* ● **ex|act|ly** ADV ❑ *Both drugs will be exactly the same.* ■ ADJ You use **exact** before a noun to emphasize that you are referring to that particular thing and no other. ❑ *…the exact moment when he realized the truth.* ● **ex|act|ly** ADV ❑ *These are exactly the people who do not vote.* ■ V-T When someone **exacts** something, they demand and obtain it from another person. [FORMAL] ❑ *Already he has exacted a written apology from the chairman.* [from Latin] ■ → see also **exactly**

### Thesaurus    exact    Also look up :

ADJ.    accurate, clear, precise, true; (*ant.*) wrong ■

### Word Partnership    Use *exact* with :

N.    exact **change**, exact **duplicate**, exact **number**, exact, exact **replica**, exact **science**, exact **words** ■
exact **cause**, exact **location**, exact **moment** ■
exact **revenge** ■

**ex|act|ing** /ɪgzǽktɪŋ/ ADJ An **exacting** person or task requires you to work very hard. ❑ *He was not well enough to carry out such an exacting task.* [from Latin]

**ex|act|ly** /ɪgzǽktli/ ■ ADV **Exactly** means precisely, and not just approximately. ❑ *The tower was exactly ten meters in height.* ■ ADV If you say "**Exactly**," you are agreeing with someone or emphasizing the truth of what they say. If you say "**Not exactly**," you are telling them politely that they are wrong in part of what they are saying. ❑ *Eve nodded. "Exactly."* ■ ADV You use **not exactly** to indicate that a meaning or situation is slightly different from what people think or expect. ❑ *He's not exactly homeless, he just hangs out in this park.* [from Latin] ■ → see **exact**

**ex|ag|ger|ate** /ɪgzǽdʒəreɪt/ (**exaggerates, exaggerating, exaggerated**) ■ V-T/V-I If you **exaggerate**, you indicate that something is bigger, worse, or more important than it really is. ❑ *He thinks I'm exaggerating.* ❑ *She sometimes exaggerates the demands of her job.* ● **ex|ag|gera|tion** /ɪgzǽdʒəreɪʃⁿn/ N-VAR ❑ *He was accused of exaggeration.* ■ V-T If something **exaggerates** a situation, quality, or feature, it makes it appear greater, more obvious, or more important than it really is. ❑ *These figures exaggerate the size of the loss.* [from Latin]

**ex|ag|ger|at|ed** /ɪgzǽdʒəreɪtɪd/ ADJ Something that is **exaggerated** is or seems larger, better, worse, or more important than it actually needs to be. ❑ *Western fears, he insists, are greatly exaggerated.* [from Latin]

**ex|alt|ed** /ɪgzɔ́ltɪd/ ADJ Someone who is **exalted** is at a very high rank or level. [FORMAL] ❑ *You must decide how to make the best use of your exalted position.* [from Latin]

**exam** /ɪgzǽm/ (**exams**) ■ N-COUNT An **exam** is a formal test that you take to show your knowledge of a subject. ❑ *I don't want to take any more exams.* ■ N-COUNT If you have a medical **exam**, a doctor looks at your body or does simple tests in order to check how healthy you are. ❑ *These medical exams have shown I am in perfect physical condition.*

**ex|ami|na|tion** /ɪgzæmɪneɪʃⁿn/ (**examinations**) N-COUNT An **examination** is the same as an **exam**. [FORMAL] [from Old French] → see **diagnosis**

**ex|am|ine** /ɪgzǽmɪn/ (**examines, examining, examined**) ■ V-T If you **examine** something or someone, you look at them carefully. ❑ *He examined her passport.* ❑ *A doctor examined her and could find nothing wrong.* ● **ex|ami|na|tion** /ɪgzæmɪneɪʃⁿn/ (**examinations**) N-VAR ❑ *The navy is to carry out an examination of the ship.* ❑ *The government said the proposals required careful examination.* ■ V-T If you **are examined**, you are given a formal test in order to show your knowledge of a subject. ❑ *…the pressures of being judged and examined by our teachers.* [from Old French]

### Thesaurus    examine    Also look up :

V.    analyze, go over, inspect, investigate, research; (*ant.*) scrutinize ■

**ex|am|in|er** /ɪgzǽmɪnər/ (**examiners**)

example 317 excess

■ N-COUNT An **examiner** is a person who conducts an examination. ❑ *They have asked a judge to appoint an independent examiner.* [from Old French] ② → see also **medical examiner**

**ex|am|ple** /ɪgzæmpᵊl/ (**examples**) ■ N-COUNT An **example** is something that represents or is typical of a particular group of things. ❑ *There are examples of this type of architecture among many different cultures around the world.* ❑ *This story was a perfect example of how men and women communicate differently.* ② N-COUNT If you refer to a person or their behavior as an **example to** other people, you mean that he or she behaves in a good way that other people should copy. ❑ *He is an example to the younger boys.* ③ PHRASE You use **for example** to introduce and emphasize something that shows that something is true. ❑ *Take, for example, the simple sentence: "The man climbed up the hill."* ④ PHRASE If you **follow** someone's **example**, you copy their behavior, especially because you admire them. ❑ *Following the example set by her father, she has done her duty.* ⑤ PHRASE If you **set an example**, you encourage or inspire people by your behavior to behave or act in a similar way. ❑ *An officer's job is to set an example.* [from Old French]

| Thesaurus | *example* | Also look up : |
|---|---|---|
| N. | model, representation, sample ■ |
| | ideal, role model, standard ② |

| Word Partnership | Use *example* with : |
|---|---|
| ADJ. | **classic** example, **good** example, **obvious** example, **typical** example ■ |
| V. | **give an** example ■ |
| | **follow an** example ④ |

**Word Link** *sper ≈ hope : de*sper*ate, exa*sper*ate, pro*sper*ity*

**ex|as|per|ate** /ɪgzæspəreɪt/ (**exasperates, exasperating, exasperated**) V-T If someone or something **exasperates** you, they annoy you and make you feel frustrated or upset. ❑ *His children exasperated him with their bad behavior.* ● **ex|as|per|at|ed** ADJ ❑ *The president was clearly exasperated by the story.* ● **ex|as|pera|tion** /ɪgzæspəreɪʃᵊn/ N-UNCOUNT ❑ *Mahoney clenched his fist in exasperation.* [from Latin]

**Word Link** *cav ≈ hollow : *cav*e, *cav*ity, ex*cav*ate*

**ex|ca|vate** /ɛkskəveɪt/ (**excavates, excavating, excavated**) V-T When archaeologists or other people **excavate** a piece of land, they remove earth carefully from it and look for the remains of objects or buildings, in order to discover information about the past. ❑ *A new Danish expedition is excavating the site.* ● **ex|ca|va|tion** /ɛkskəveɪʃᵊn/ (**excavations**) N-VAR ❑ *An excavation of the site is essential.* [from Latin]

**Word Link** *ex ≈ away, from, out : *ex*ceed, *ex*it, *ex*plode*

**ex|ceed** /ɪksid/ (**exceeds, exceeding, exceeded**) ■ V-T If something **exceeds** a particular amount, it is greater than that amount. [FORMAL] ❑ *Its research budget exceeds $700 million a year.* ② V-T If you **exceed** a limit, you go beyond it. [FORMAL] ❑ *He accepts that he was exceeding the speed limit.*

[from Latin]

**ex|cel** /ɪksɛl/ (**excels, excelling, excelled**) V-I If someone **excels in** something or **excels at** it, they are very good at doing it. ❑ *Mary excelled at outdoor sports.* ❑ *Academically he began to excel.* [from Latin]

**Word Link** *ence ≈ state, condition : depend*ence*, excell*ence*, independ*ence*

**ex|cel|lence** /ɛksələns/ N-UNCOUNT **Excellence** is the quality of being extremely good in some way. ❑ *...the top award for excellence in journalism.* [from Latin]

**Ex|cel|len|cy** /ɛksələnsi/ (**Excellencies**) N-VOC You use expressions such as **Your Excellency** or **His Excellency** when you are addressing or referring to officials of very high rank, such as ambassadors or governors. ❑ *I am reluctant to trust anyone totally, Your Excellency.* [from Latin]

**ex|cel|lent** /ɛksələnt/ ADJ Something that is **excellent** is extremely good. ❑ *The recording quality is excellent.* ● **ex|cel|lent|ly** ADV ❑ *They're both playing excellently.* [from Latin]

**ex|cept** /ɪksɛpt/ PREP You use **except** or **except for** to introduce the only thing or person that a statement does not apply to, or a fact that prevents a statement from being completely true. ❑ *I wouldn't have accepted anything except a job in New York.* ❑ *He hasn't eaten a thing except for a bit of salad.* ● **Except** is also a conjunction. ❑ *Freddie would tell me nothing about what he was writing, except that it was a play.* [from Old French]

| Usage | **except** and **besides** |
|---|---|

*Except* and *besides* are often confused. *Except* refers to someone or something that is not included: *I've taken all my required courses except psychology. I'm going to take it next term. Besides* means "in addition to." *What courses should I take next term besides psychology?*

**ex|cep|tion** /ɪksɛpʃᵊn/ (**exceptions**) ■ N-COUNT An **exception** is a particular thing, person, or situation that is not included in a general statement. ❑ *Few guitarists can sing as well as they can play; Eddie, however, is an exception.* ❑ *The law makes no exceptions.* ② PHRASE If you **take exception to** something, you feel offended or annoyed by it, usually with the result that you complain about it. ❑ *He took exception to being spied on.* [from Old French]

**ex|cep|tion|al** /ɪksɛpʃənᵊl/ ■ ADJ You use **exceptional** to describe someone or something that has a particular quality, usually a good quality, to an unusually high degree. ❑ *...children with exceptional ability.* ● **ex|cep|tion|al|ly** ADV ❑ *He's an exceptionally talented dancer.* ② ADJ **Exceptional** situations are very unusual or rare. [FORMAL] ❑ *The time limit can be extended in exceptional circumstances.* ● **ex|cep|tion|al|ly** ADV ❑ *Exceptionally, in times of emergency, we may send a team of experts.* [from Old French]

**ex|cerpt** /ɛksɜrpt/ (**excerpts**) N-COUNT An **excerpt** is a short piece of writing or music taken from a larger piece. ❑ *...an excerpt from Tchaikovsky's "Nutcracker."* [from Latin]

**ex|cess** (**excesses**)

The noun is pronounced /ɪksɛs/ or /ɛksɛs/. The adjective is pronounced /ɛksɛs/.

**1** N-VAR An **excess of** something is a larger amount than is needed, allowed, or usual. □ ...*the problems created by an excess of wealth.* ● **Excess** is also an adjective. □ *After cooking the fish, pour off any excess fat.* **2** PHRASE **In excess of** means more than a particular amount. [FORMAL] □ *The value of the company is in excess of $2 billion.* **3** PHRASE If you do something **to excess**, you do it too much; used showing disapproval. □ *At Christmas, people sometimes eat to excess.* [from Latin]

**ex|ces|sive** /ɪksɛsɪv/ ADJ If you describe the amount or level of something as **excessive**, you disapprove of it because it is more or higher than is necessary or reasonable. □ *Their spending on research is excessive.* ● **ex|ces|sive|ly** ADV □ *Managers are paying themselves excessively high salaries.* [from Latin]

**ex|change** /ɪkstʃeɪndʒ/ (**exchanges, exchanging, exchanged**) **1** V-RECIP If two or more people **exchange** things of a particular kind, they give them to each other at the same time. □ *We exchanged addresses.* □ *The two men exchanged glances.* ● **Exchange** is also a noun. □ *He ruled out any exchange of prisoners.* **2** V-T If you **exchange** something, you replace it with a different thing, especially something that is better or more satisfactory. □ ...*the chance to exchange goods.* **3** N-COUNT An **exchange** is a brief conversation. [FORMAL] □ *There have been some bitter exchanges between the two groups.* **4** → see also **foreign exchange, stock exchange** **5** PHRASE If you do or give something **in exchange for** something else, you do it or give it in order to get that thing. □ *It is illegal for public officials to receive gifts or money in exchange for favors.* [from Vulgar Latin]

<table>
<tr><td colspan="2">**Word Partnership**    Use *exchange* with:</td></tr>
<tr><td>N.</td><td>**currency** exchange, exchange **gifts,** exchange **greetings 1**</td></tr>
<tr><td>ADJ.</td><td>**cultural** exchange **1** <br> **brief** exchange **3**</td></tr>
</table>

**ex|change rate** (**exchange rates**) N-COUNT The **exchange rate** of a country's unit of currency is the amount of another country's currency that you get in exchange for it. □ ...*a high exchange rate for the Canadian dollar.*

**ex|cise** /ɛksaɪz/ (**excises**) N-VAR **Excise** is a tax that the government of a country puts on certain goods produced for sale in that country. □ ...*an excise tax on gasoline.* [from Middle Dutch]

**ex|cit|able** /ɪksaɪtəbªl/ ADJ An **excitable** person becomes excited very easily. □ *Mary sat beside Elaine, who seemed excitable.* [from Latin]

**ex|cite** /ɪksaɪt/ (**excites, exciting, excited**) **1** V-T If something **excites** you, it makes you feel very happy or enthusiastic. □ *This is what excites me about the trip.* **2** V-T If something **excites** a particular feeling or reaction, it causes it. □ *Auto racing did not excite his interest.* [from Latin]

**ex|cit|ed** /ɪksaɪtɪd/ ADJ If you are **excited**, you are looking forward to something eagerly. □ *I was excited about the possibility of playing football again.* ● **ex|cit|ed|ly** ADV □ *"You're coming?" he said excitedly. "That's fantastic!"* [from Latin]

**ex|cite|ment** /ɪksaɪtmənt/ (**excitements**) N-VAR You use **excitement** to refer to the state of being excited, or to something that excites you.

□ *Everyone is in a state of great excitement.* [from Latin]

**ex|cit|ing** /ɪksaɪtɪŋ/ ADJ If something is **exciting**, it makes you feel very happy or enthusiastic. □ *The race itself is very exciting.* [from Latin]

<table>
<tr><td colspan="2">**Word Link**    *claim, clam = shouting : ac*claim, *clam*or, *ex*claim</td></tr>
</table>

**ex|claim** /ɪkskleɪm/ (**exclaims, exclaiming, exclaimed**) V-T Writers sometimes use **exclaim** to show that someone is speaking suddenly, loudly, or emphatically, often because they are excited, shocked, or angry. □ *"There!" Jackson exclaimed delightedly.* [from Latin]

**ex|cla|ma|tion point** (**exclamation points**) also **exclamation mark** N-COUNT An **exclamation point** is the sign ! which is used in writing to show that a word, phrase, or sentence is an exclamation.
→ see **punctuation**

**ex|cla|ma|tory** /ɪksklæmətɔri/ ADJ An **exclamatory** sentence is a sentence that is spoken suddenly, loudly, or emphatically, for example "We won!" [from Latin]

**ex|clude** /ɪksklud/ (**excludes, excluding, excluded**) **1** V-T If you **exclude** someone **from** a place or activity, you prevent them from entering it or taking part in it. □ *The academy excluded women from its classes.* □ *Many of the youngsters feel excluded.* ● **ex|clu|sion** /ɪkskluʒªn/ (**exclusions**) N-VAR □ ...*women's exclusion from political power.* **2** V-T If you **exclude** something that has some connection with what you are doing, you deliberately do not use it or consider it. □ *The university excluded women from its classes until 1968.* ● **ex|clu|sion** N-VAR □ *Their kids play video games to the exclusion of everything else.* **3** V-T To **exclude** a possibility means to decide or prove that it is wrong and not worth considering. □ *They do not exclude the possibility of hiring a foreigner.* [from Latin]

**ex|clud|ing** /ɪkskludɪŋ/ PREP You use **excluding** before mentioning a person or thing to show that you are not including them in your statement. □ *Excluding water, half of the body's weight is protein.* [from Latin]

**ex|clu|sive** /ɪksklusɪv/ (**exclusives**) **1** ADJ Something that is **exclusive** is available only to people who are rich or privileged. □ *It used to be a private, exclusive club.* **2** ADJ **Exclusive** means used or owned by only one person or group. □ *Our group will have exclusive use of a 60-foot boat.* **3** PHRASE If two things are **mutually exclusive**, they cannot exist together. □ *Career ambition and successful fatherhood can be mutually exclusive.* [from Latin]

**ex|clu|sive|ly** /ɪksklusɪvli/ ADV **Exclusively** is used to refer to situations or activities that involve only the thing or things mentioned, and nothing else. □ ...*an exclusively male group.* [from Latin]

**ex|crete** /ɪkskrit/ (**excretes, excreting, excreted**) V-T When you **excrete** waste matter from your body, you get rid of it. [FORMAL] □ *The kidneys excrete the extra fluid.* [from Latin]

**ex|cru|ci|at|ing** /ɪkskruʃieɪtɪŋ/ ADJ **Excruciating** means extremely painful. □ *I was in excruciating pain.* [from Latin]

| **Word Link** | curr, curs ≈ running, flowing : concurrent, current, excursion |
|---|---|

**ex|cur|sion** /ɪkskɜrʒ°n/ (**excursions**) N-COUNT An **excursion** is a short trip, especially one taken for pleasure. ❏ Sam's father took him on an excursion. [from Latin]

**ex|cuse** (**excuses, excusing, excused**)

The noun is pronounced /ɪkskyus/. The verb is pronounced /ɪkskyuz/.

**1** N-COUNT An **excuse** is a reason that you give in order to explain why something has been done or has not been done, or in order to avoid doing something. ❏ ...trying to find excuses for their failure. ❏ Just stop making excuses and do it. **2** PHRASE If you say that there is **no excuse for** something, you are emphasizing that it should not happen, or expressing disapproval that it has happened. ❏ There's no excuse for behavior like that. **3** V-T To **excuse** someone or **excuse** their behavior means to provide reasons for their actions, especially when other people disapprove of these actions. ❏ He excused himself by saying that his English was not good enough. **4** V-T If you **excuse** someone **for** something wrong that they have done, you forgive them for it. ❏ I'm not excusing him for what he did. **5** V-T If someone **is excused from** a duty or responsibility, they are told that they do not have to carry it out. ❏ She is usually excused from her duties during summer vacation. **6** V-T If you **excuse yourself**, you use a phrase such as "Excuse me" as a polite way of saying that you are about to leave. ❏ He excused himself and went up to his room. **7** CONVENTION You say "**Excuse me**" when you want to politely get someone's attention. ❏ Excuse me, but are you Mr. Honig? **8** CONVENTION You use **excuse me** to apologize to someone, for example when you interrupt them, bump into them, or do something slightly impolite such as burping or sneezing. ❏ Excuse me, but there's something I need to say. [from Latin]

| **Thesaurus** | excuse | Also look up : |
|---|---|---|
| N. | apology, explanation, reason **1** | |
| V. | forgive, pardon, spare; (ant.) accuse, blame, punish **3** | |

**ex|ecute** /ɛksɪkyut/ (**executes, executing, executed**) **1** V-T To **execute** someone means to kill them as a punishment. ❏ Harris was executed this morning. ❏ One group claimed to have executed the hostage. ● **ex|ecu|tion** /ɛksɪkyuʃ°n/ (**executions**) N-VAR ❏ ...execution by lethal injection. ● **ex|ecu|tion|er** (**executioners**) N-COUNT ❏ ...the executioner's ax. **2** V-T If you **execute** a plan, you carry it out. [FORMAL] ❏ He decided to execute his plan to kill the king. ● **ex|ecu|tion** N-UNCOUNT ❏ U.S. forces are fully prepared for the execution of any action. **3** V-T If you **execute** a difficult action or movement, you successfully perform it. ❏ The landing was skillfully executed. [from Old French]

**ex|ecu|tive** /ɪgzɛkyətɪv/ (**executives**) **1** N-COUNT An **executive** is someone who is employed by a business at a senior level. ❏ ...an advertising executive. **2** N-SING The **executive** of an organization is a committee that has the authority to make important decisions. ❏ Some members of the executive have called for his resignation. **3** N-SING The **executive** is the part of the government of a country that is concerned with carrying out decisions or orders, as opposed to the part that makes laws or the part that deals with criminals. ❏ Her brother, David, works for the Scottish Executive in Edinburgh. [from Old French]

**ex|ecu|tive or|der** (**executive orders**) N-COUNT An **executive order** is a regulation issued by a member of the executive branch of government. It has the same authority as a law. ❏ The president issued an executive order.

**ex|em|pla|ry** /ɪgzɛmpləri/ ADJ If you describe someone or something as **exemplary**, you think they are extremely good. ❏ ...an exemplary record. [from Latin]

**ex|em|pli|fy** /ɪgzɛmplɪfaɪ/ (**exemplifies, exemplifying, exemplified**) V-T If a person or thing **exemplifies** something, they are a typical example of it. [FORMAL] ❏ The room's style exemplifies their ideal of "beauty and practicality." [from Old French]

**ex|empt** /ɪgzɛmpt/ (**exempts, exempting, exempted**) **1** ADJ If someone is **exempt from** a rule or duty, they do not have to obey it or perform it. ❏ Men in college were exempt from military service. **2** V-T To **exempt** a person **from** a rule or duty means to state officially that they are not bound or affected by it. ❏ He was exempted from the full course because of his experience. ● **ex|emp|tion** /ɪgzɛmpʃ°n/ (**exemptions**) N-VAR ❏ ...the exemption of health insurance from taxation. [from Latin]

**ex|er|cise** /ɛksərsaɪz/ (**exercises, exercising, exercised**) **1** V-T If you **exercise** something such as your authority, your rights, or a good quality, you use it or put it into effect. [FORMAL] ❏ They are merely exercising their right to free speech. ● **Exercise** is also a noun. ❏ ...the exercise of political and economic power. **2** V-I When you **exercise**, you move your body energetically in order to get in shape and to remain healthy. ❏ She exercises two or three times a week. ● **Exercise** is also a noun. ❏ Lack of exercise can lead to feelings of depression. **3** N-COUNT **Exercises** are a series of movements or actions that you do in order to get in shape, remain healthy, or practice for a particular physical activity. ❏ I do special neck and shoulder exercises. **4** N-COUNT **Exercises** are activities that you do in order to maintain or practice a skill. ❏ ...military exercises. ❏ ...creative writing exercises. [from Old French]
→ see **muscle**

**ex|ert** /ɪgzɜrt/ (**exerts, exerting, exerted**) **1** V-T If someone or something **exerts** influence or pressure, they use their influence or put pressure on someone else in order to produce a particular effect. [FORMAL] ❏ Parents exert a huge influence over their children when it comes to diet and exercise. **2** V-T If you **exert yourself**, you make a physical or mental effort to do something. ❏ Do not exert yourself unnecessarily. ● **ex|er|tion** (**exertions**) N-UNCOUNT ❏ ...the stress of physical exertion. [from Latin]
→ see **motion**

**ex|hale** /ɛkshe͟ɪl/ (**exhales, exhaling, exhaled**) V-I When you **exhale**, you breathe out the air that is in your lungs. [FORMAL] ❏ Hold your breath for a moment and exhale. [from Latin]
→ see **respiration**

exhale

**ex|haust** /ɪgzɔst/ (**exhausts, exhausting, exhausted**) **1** V-T If something **exhausts** you,

it makes you very tired. ❑ *Don't exhaust him.*
● **ex|haust|ed** ADJ ❑ *She was too exhausted to talk.*
● **ex|haust|ing** ADJ ❑ *It was an exhausting schedule.*
● **ex|haus|tion** /ɪgzɔstʃ ᵊn/ N-UNCOUNT ❑ *He is suffering from exhaustion.* **2** V-T If you **exhaust** something such as money or food, you use or finish it all. ❑ *We have exhausted all our material resources.* **3** V-T If you **have exhausted** a subject or topic, you have talked about it so much that there is nothing more to say about it. ❑ *She and Chantal must have exhausted the subject of clothes.* **4** N-UNCOUNT **Exhaust** is the gas or steam that is produced when the engine of a vehicle is running. ❑ *...the exhaust from a car engine.* [from Latin]
→ see **engine, pollution**

**ex|haus|tive** /ɪgzɔstɪv/ ADJ An **exhaustive** study or search is very thorough and complete. ❑ *This is not an exhaustive list.* ● **ex|haust|ive|ly** ADV ❑ *The book is exhaustively researched.* [from Latin]

**ex|haust pipe** (**exhaust pipes**) N-COUNT The **exhaust pipe** is the pipe that carries the gas out of the engine of a vehicle.

**ex|hib|it** /ɪgzɪbɪt/ (**exhibits, exhibiting, exhibited**) **1** V-T To **exhibit** a particular quality, feeling, or type of behavior means to show it. [FORMAL] ❑ *He exhibited symptoms of anxiety.* **2** V-T When an object of interest **is exhibited**, it is put in a public place such as a museum or art gallery so that people can come to look at it. ❑ *His work was exhibited in the best galleries.* ● **ex|hi|bi|tion** N-UNCOUNT ❑ *Five of her paintings are currently on exhibition.* **3** V-I When artists **exhibit**, they show their work in public. ❑ *He has exhibited at galleries and museums in New York.* **4** N-COUNT An **exhibit** is an object of interest that is displayed to the public in a museum or art gallery. ❑ *Shona showed me around the exhibits.* **5** N-COUNT An **exhibit** is a public display of art or objects of interest in a museum or art gallery. ❑ *...an exhibit at the Metropolitan Museum of Art.* **6** N-COUNT An **exhibit** is an object that a lawyer shows in court as evidence in a legal case. ❑ *The jury has already asked to see more than 40 exhibits.* [from Latin]

**ex|hi|bi|tion** /ɛksɪbɪʃ ᵊn/ (**exhibitions**) **1** N-COUNT An **exhibition** is a public event at which art or objects of interest are displayed, for example at a museum or art gallery. ❑ *...an exhibition of modern art.* **2** N-SING An **exhibition** of a particular skillful activity is a display or example of it. ❑ *He treated the fans to an exhibition of power and speed.* [from Latin] **3** → see also **exhibit 2**

**ex|hi|bi|tion game** (**exhibition games**) N-COUNT In sports, an **exhibition game** is a game that is not part of a competition, and is played for entertainment or practice.

**ex|hibi|tor** /ɪgzɪbɪtər/ (**exhibitors**) N-COUNT An **exhibitor** is a person or company whose work or products are being shown in an exhibition. ❑ *Schedules will be sent out to all exhibitors.* [from Latin]

**ex|hil|arat|ing** /ɪgzɪləreɪtɪŋ/ ADJ If you describe an experience or feeling as **exhilarating**, you mean that it makes you feel very happy and excited. ❑ *It was exhilarating to be at the top of the mountain.* [from Latin]

**ex|hort** /ɪgzɔrt/ (**exhorts, exhorting, exhorted**) V-T If you **exhort** someone to do something, you try hard to persuade them to do

it. [FORMAL] ❑ *Kennedy exhorted his listeners to turn away from violence.* ● **ex|hor|ta|tion** /ɛgzɔrteɪʃ ᵊn/ (**exhortations**) N-VAR ❑ *...exhortations to reform.* [from Latin]

**ex|ile** /ɛksaɪl, ɛgz-/ (**exiles, exiling, exiled**) **1** V-T If someone **is exiled**, they are living in a foreign country because they cannot live in their own country, usually for political reasons. ❑ *His wife, Hilary, was exiled from South Africa.* ❑ *They threatened to exile her in southern Spain.* ● **Exile** is also a noun. ❑ *He is now living in exile in Egypt.* ❑ *He returned from exile earlier this year.* **2** N-COUNT An **exile** is someone who has been exiled. ❑ *He is an exile who has given up the idea of going home.* [from Latin]

---

**Word Partnership** Use *exile* with :

| | |
|---|---|
| V. | **force into** exile, **go into** exile, **live in** exile, **return from** exile, **send into** exile **1** |
| ADJ. | **self-imposed** exile **1** **political** exile **1 2** |

---

**ex|ist** /ɪgzɪst/ (**exists, existing, existed**) V-I If something **exists**, it is present in the world as a real thing. ❑ *He thought that if he couldn't see something, it didn't exist.* ❑ *Research opportunities exist in a wide range of areas.* [from Latin]

**ex|ist|ence** /ɪgzɪstəns/ (**existences**) **1** N-UNCOUNT The **existence** of something is the fact that it is present in the world as a real thing. ❑ *...the existence of other worlds.* **2** N-COUNT You can refer to someone's way of life as a particular **existence**. ❑ *...a miserable existence.* [from Latin]

---

**Word Partnership** Use *existence* with :

| | |
|---|---|
| V. | **come into** existence, **deny the** existence **1** |
| ADJ. | **continued** existence, **daily** existence, **everyday** existence **1 2** |

---

**ex|ist|ing** /ɪgzɪstɪŋ/ ADJ **Existing** is used to describe something that is now present, available, or in operation, especially when you are contrasting it with something that is planned for the future. ❑ *...the need to improve existing products.* [from Latin]

---

**Word Link** *ex ≈ away, from, out* : ex**ceed**, **exit**, **ex**plode

---

**exit** /ɛgzɪt, ɛksɪt/ (**exits, exiting, exited**) **1** N-COUNT The **exit** is the door through which you can leave a public building. ❑ *He picked up the box and walked toward the exit.* **2** N-COUNT An **exit** on a highway is a place where traffic can leave it. ❑ *She continued to the next exit.* **3** N-COUNT If you refer to someone's **exit**, you are referring to the way that they left a room or building. [FORMAL] ❑ *I made a quick exit.* **4** V-T/V-I If you **exit** a room or building or **exit from** it, you leave it. [FORMAL] ❑ *She exited into the night.* ❑ *I exited the elevator and stepped into the lobby of the hotel.* **5** V-T If you **exit** a computer program or system, you stop running it. [COMPUTING] ❑ *Do you want to exit this program?* ● **Exit** is also a noun. ❑ *Press "exit" to return to your document.* [from Latin]

**exit poll** (**exit polls**) N-COUNT An **exit poll** is a survey in which people who have just voted in an election are asked which candidate they voted for.

**exit strat|egy** (**exit strategies**) N-COUNT In politics and business, an **exit strategy** is a way of ending your involvement in a situation. ❑ *We have no exit strategy from this conflict.*

**exo|cy|to|sis** /ɛksoʊsaɪtoʊsɪs/ N-UNCOUNT **Exocytosis** is a process in which a cell releases material from inside itself by sending the material to the surface of the cell. Compare **endocytosis**. [TECHNICAL]

**exo|dus** /ɛksədəs/ N-SING If there is an **exodus** of people **from** a place, a lot of people leave at the same time. ❑ *The hospital is in trouble because of an exodus of doctors.* [from Latin]

**exo|skel|eton** /ɛksoʊskɛlɪtᵊn/ (**exoskeletons**) N-COUNT Animals with an **exoskeleton** have their skeleton on the outside of their body, like insects. [TECHNICAL]

**exo|sphere** /ɛksəsfɪər/ N-SING The **exosphere** is the highest layer of the Earth's atmosphere. [TECHNICAL]

**exo|ther|mic** /ɛksoʊθɜrmɪk/ ADJ An **exothermic** chemical reaction or process is one that releases heat. [TECHNICAL]

**ex|ot|ic** /ɪgzɒtɪk/ ADJ Something that is **exotic** is unusual and interesting, usually because it comes from or is related to a distant country. ❑ *...brilliantly colored, exotic flowers.* ● **ex|oti|cal|ly** ADV ❑ *...exotically beautiful scenery.* [from Latin]

**ex|pand** /ɪkspænd/ (**expands, expanding, expanded**) V-T/V-I If something **expands** or **is expanded**, it becomes larger. ❑ *The industry expanded toward the middle of the 19th century.* ❑ *We have to expand the size of the image.* ● **ex|pan|sion** /ɪkspænʃᵊn/ (**expansions**) N-VAR ❑ *...the rapid expansion of private health insurance.* [from Latin]
▶ **expand on** or **expand upon** PHR-VERB If you **expand on** or **expand upon** something, you give more information about it. ❑ *The president used today's speech to expand on remarks he made last month.*

**ex|pand|ed form** (**expanded forms**) N-COUNT In mathematics, the **expanded form** of an expression is a version of the expression that is written in full, for example without any brackets. [TECHNICAL]

**ex|panse** /ɪkspæns/ (**expanses**) N-COUNT An **expanse of** something, usually sea, sky, or land, is a very large amount of it. ❑ *...a vast expanse of grassland.* [from New Latin]

**ex|pan|sive** /ɪkspænsɪv/ ADJ If you are **expansive**, you talk a lot, or are friendly or generous, because you are feeling happy and relaxed. ❑ *He was becoming more expansive as he relaxed.* [from New Latin]

**ex|pat|ri|ate** /ɛkspeɪtriət, -pæt-/ (**expatriates**) N-COUNT An **expatriate** is someone who is living in a country that is not their own. ❑ *...British expatriates in Spain.* [from Medieval Latin]

**ex|pect** /ɪkspɛkt/ (**expects, expecting, expected**) ◼ V-T If you **expect** something **to** happen, you believe that it will happen. ❑ *He expects to lose his job in the next few weeks.* ❑ *The talks are expected to continue until tomorrow.* ◻ V-T If you **are expecting** something or someone, you believe that they will be delivered or arrive soon. ❑ *I wasn't expecting a visitor.* ◾ V-T If you **expect** something, or **expect** a person **to** do something, you believe that it is your right to have that thing, or the person's duty to do it for you. ❑ *I don't expect*

*your help.* ❑ *I do expect to have some time to myself.* ◢ V-T/V-I If a woman **is expecting** a baby, she is pregnant. ❑ *She was expecting another baby.* ❑ *I hear Dawn's expecting.* [from Latin]

**ex|pec|tant** /ɪkspɛktənt/ ◼ ADJ If someone is **expectant**, they are excited because they think something interesting is about to happen. ❑ *An expectant crowd gathered.* ● **ex|pec|tan|cy** N-UNCOUNT ❑ *...a tremendous air of expectancy.* ● **ex|pect|ant|ly** ADV ❑ *The others waited, looking at him expectantly.* ◻ ADJ An **expectant** mother or father is someone whose baby is going to be born soon. ❑ *...a magazine for expectant mothers.* [from Latin]

**ex|pec|ta|tion** /ɛkspɛkteɪʃᵊn/ (**expectations**) ◼ N-VAR Your **expectations** are your beliefs that something will happen or that you will get something that you want. ❑ *Their expectation was that she was going to be found safe.* ◻ N-COUNT A person's **expectations** are strong beliefs they have about the proper way someone should behave or something should happen. ❑ *He was determined to live up to the expectations of his parents.* [from Latin]

**ex|pedi|ent** /ɪkspidiənt/ (**expedients**) ◼ N-COUNT An **expedient** is an action that achieves a particular purpose, but may not be morally right. ❑ *The restrictions are a temporary expedient.* ◻ ADJ If it is **expedient to** do something, it is useful or convenient to do it, even though it may not be morally right. ❑ *It was expedient to be nice to him if you wanted to do well.* ● **ex|pedi|en|cy** N-UNCOUNT ❑ *This was a matter less of morals than of expediency.* [from Latin]

**ex|pedi|tion** /ɛkspɪdɪʃᵊn/ (**expeditions**) N-COUNT An **expedition** is an organized trip made for a particular purpose such as exploration. ❑ *...an expedition to Antarctica.* [from Latin]

| **Word Link** | *pel* ≈ *driving, forcing* : *com*pel, *ex*pel, *pro*pel |
|---|---|

**ex|pel** /ɪkspɛl/ (**expels, expelling, expelled**) ◼ V-T If someone **is expelled from** a school or organization, they are officially told to leave because they have behaved badly. ❑ *High school students have been expelled for cheating.* ◻ V-T If people **are expelled from** a place, they are made to leave it, often by force. ❑ *An American was expelled from the country yesterday.* ◾ V-T To **expel** something means to force it out from a container or from your body. ❑ *He groaned, expelling the air from his lungs.* [from Latin]

**ex|pend** /ɪkspɛnd/ (**expends, expending, expended**) V-T To **expend** energy, time, or money means to use it or spend it. [FORMAL] ❑ *Young children expend a lot of energy.* [from Latin]

**ex|pendi|ture** /ɪkspɛndɪtʃər/ (**expenditures**) N-VAR **Expenditure** is the spending of money on something, or the money that is spent on something. [FORMAL] ❑ *The total expenditure of the administration was $11.4 billion.* [from Latin]

**ex|pense** /ɪkspɛns/ (**expenses**) ◼ N-VAR **Expense** is the money that something costs you or that you need to spend in order to do something. ❑ *He's bought a big TV at great expense.* ◻ N-PLURAL **Expenses** are amounts of money that you spend while doing something in the course of your work, which will be paid back to you afterwards. [BUSINESS] ❑ *Her hotel expenses were paid by the* *committee.* ③ PHRASE If you do something **at** someone's **expense**, they provide the money for it. ❑ *Architects are trained for five years at public expense.* ④ PHRASE If someone laughs or makes a joke **at** your **expense**, they do it to make you seem foolish. ❑ *I think he's having fun at our expense.* [from Late Latin]

**ex|pen|sive** /ɪkspɛnsɪv/ ADJ If something is **expensive**, it costs a lot of money. ❑ *Broadband is still more expensive than dial-up services.*
● **ex|pen|sive|ly** ADV ❑ *She was expensively dressed.* [from Late Latin]

### Thesaurus    *expensive*   Also look up :

ADJ.   costly, pricey, upscale; (*ant.*) cheap, economical, inexpensive

**ex|peri|ence** /ɪkspɪəriəns/ (**experiences, experiencing, experienced**) ① N-UNCOUNT **Experience** is knowledge or skill in a particular job or activity that you have gained because you have done that job or activity for a long time. ❑ *He has managerial experience.* ● **ex|peri|enced** ADJ ❑ *...a team packed with experienced professionals.* ② N-UNCOUNT **Experience** is used to refer to the past events, knowledge, and feelings that make up your life or character. ❑ *Experience has taught me caution.* ③ N-COUNT An **experience** is something that you do or that happens to you, especially something important that affects you. ❑ *His only experience of gardening so far proved very satisfying.* ④ V-T If you **experience** a particular situation or feeling, it happens to you or you are affected by it. ❑ *I have never experienced true love.* [from Latin]

### Thesaurus    *experience*   Also look up :

N.   know-how, knowledge, wisdom; (*ant.*) inexperience ①

### Word Partnership    Use *experience* with :

| | |
|---|---|
| ADJ. | **professional** experience ① |
| | **valuable** experience ① – ③ |
| | **past** experience, **shared** experience ② ③ |
| | **learning** experience, **religious** experience, **traumatic** experience ③ |
| N. | **work** experience ① |
| | **life** experience ② |
| | experience **a loss**, experience **symptoms** ④ |

**ex|peri|ment** (**experiments, experimenting, experimented**)

The noun is pronounced /ɪkspɛrɪmənt/. The verb is pronounced /ɪkspɛrɪment/.

① N-VAR An **experiment** is a scientific test done in order to discover what happens to something in particular conditions. ❑ *...experiments to learn how the body reacts in space.* ② V-I If you **experiment with** something or **experiment on** it, you do a scientific test on it in order to discover what happens to it in particular conditions. ❑ *The scientists have experimented on rats.* ● **ex|peri|men|ta|tion** /ɪkspɛrɪmɛnteɪʃən/ N-UNCOUNT ❑ *...animal experimentation.* ③ N-VAR An **experiment** is the trying out of a new idea or method in order to see what it is like and what effects it has. ❑ *They started the magazine as an experiment.* ④ V-I To **experiment** means to try out a new idea or method to see what it is like and what effects it has. ❑ *I like cooking and have the time to experiment.* ● **ex|peri|men|ta|tion** N-UNCOUNT ❑ *Experimentation must be encouraged.* [from Latin]
→ see Word Web: **experiment**
→ see **laboratory, science**

### Word Partnership    Use *experiment* with :

| | |
|---|---|
| V. | **conduct an** experiment ① |
| | **perform an** experiment, **try an** experiment ① ③ |
| ADJ. | **scientific** experiment ① |
| | **simple** experiment ① ③ |

**ex|peri|men|tal** /ɪkspɛrɪmɛntəl/ ① ADJ Something that is **experimental** is new or uses new ideas or methods. ❑ *...an experimental air-conditioning system.* ② ADJ **Experimental** means relating to scientific experiments. ❑ *...experimental science.* ● **ex|peri|men|tal|ly** ADV ❑ *...a laboratory where animals can be studied experimentally.* [from Latin]

**ex|peri|men|tal de|sign** (**experimental designs**) N-VAR Research that has an **experimental design** involves carrying out scientific experiments.

**ex|pert** /ɛkspɜrt/ (**experts**) ① N-COUNT An **expert** is a person who is very skilled at doing something or who knows a lot about a particular subject. ❑ *...a computer expert.* ● **Expert** is also an adjective. ❑ *...an expert gardener.* ● **ex|pert|ly** ADV ❑ *He drove expertly down the twisting mountain road.* ② ADJ **Expert** advice or help is given by someone who has studied a subject thoroughly or who is very skilled at a particular job. ❑ *We'll need an expert opinion.* [from Latin]

### Word Web    experiment

**Scientists** learn much of what they know through **controlled experiments.** The **scientific method** provides a dependable way to understand natural **phenomena.** The first step in any experiment is **observation.** During this stage researchers examine the situation and ask a question about it. They may also read what others have discovered about it. Next, they state a **hypothesis.** Then they use the hypothesis to design an experiment and **predict** what will happen. Next comes the **testing** phase. Often researchers do several experiments using different **variables.** If all of the **evidence** supports the hypothesis, it becomes a new **theory.**

E

**Word Partnership** Use *expert* with:

ADJ. **leading** expert 1
N. expert **advice**, expert **opinion**, expert **witness** 2

**ex|per|tise** /ɛkspɜrtiz/ N-UNCOUNT **Expertise** is special skill or knowledge. ❑ *She didn't have the expertise to deal with all the financial details.* [from French]

**ex|pert wit|ness** (**expert witnesses**) N-COUNT In a court case, an **expert witness** is a professional person, such as a doctor, who testifies about issues that have been raised in the case.

**ex|pi|ra|tion date** /ɛkspɪreɪʃᵊn deɪt/ (**expiration dates**) N-COUNT The **expiration date** on a food container is the date by which the food should be sold or eaten. ❑ *We checked the expiration date on the carton and it was fine.*

**ex|pire** /ɪkspaɪər/ (**expires, expiring, expired**) V-I When something such as a contract, deadline, or visa **expires**, it comes to an end or is no longer valid. ❑ *My passport has expired.* [from Old French]

**ex|plain** /ɪkspleɪn/ (**explains, explaining, explained**) 1 V-T/V-I If you **explain** something, you give details about it or describe it so that it can be understood. ❑ *...the ability to explain the law in simple terms.* ❑ *Don't sign anything until your lawyer has explained the contract to you.* ❑ *Professor Griffiths explained how the drug works.* 2 V-T/V-I If you **explain**, or **explain** something that has happened, you give reasons for it. ❑ *Let me explain, sir.* ❑ *Before she ran away, she left a note explaining her actions.* ❑ *Explain why you didn't telephone.* [from Latin]
▸ **explain away** PHR-VERB If someone **explains away** a mistake or a bad situation they are responsible for, they try to indicate that it is unimportant or that it is not really their fault. ❑ *They tried to explain away any problems as temporary.*

**Thesaurus** *explain* Also look up:

V. describe, tell 1
account for, justify 2

**ex|pla|na|tion** /ɛkspləneɪʃᵊn/ (**explanations**) N-COUNT If you give an **explanation**, you give reasons why something happened, or describe something in detail. ❑ *There was no apparent explanation for the crash.* ❑ *She gave a full explanation of the decision.* [from Latin]

**Word Partnership** Use *explanation* with:

ADJ. **brief** explanation, **detailed** explanation, **logical** explanation, **only** explanation, **possible** explanation
V. **give an** explanation, **offer an** explanation, **provide** explanation

**ex|plana|tory** /ɪksplænətɔri/ ADJ Something that is **explanatory** explains something by giving details about it. [FORMAL] ❑ *...a series of explanatory notes.* [from Latin]

**ex|plic|it** /ɪksplɪsɪt/ 1 ADJ Something that is **explicit** is expressed or shown clearly and openly, without hiding anything. ❑ *...the increase in explicit violence on television.* ● **ex|plic|it|ly** ADV ❑ *...programs that deal explicitly with death.* 2 ADJ If you are **explicit about** something, you speak about it very openly and clearly. ❑ *He was explicit about his intention to reform the party.* ● **ex|plic|it|ly** ADV ❑ *She has been talking very explicitly about AIDS.* [from Latin]

**Word Link** *ex ≈ away, from, out : exceed, exit, explode*

**ex|plode** /ɪksploʊd/ (**explodes, exploding, exploded**) 1 V-T/V-I If an object such as a bomb **explodes**, it bursts with great force. ❑ *They were clearing up when the second bomb exploded.* ❑ *...gunfire which exploded the fuel tank.* 2 V-I If someone **explodes**, they express strong feelings suddenly and violently. ❑ *Do you fear that you'll explode with anger?* [from Latin]
→ see **firework**

**Thesaurus** *explode* Also look up:

V. blow up, erupt, go off 1

**Word Partnership** Use *explode* with:

N. **bombs** explode, **missiles** explode 1
ADJ. **about to** explode, **ready to** explode 1 2

**ex|ploit** (**exploits, exploiting, exploited**)

The verb is pronounced /ɪksplɔɪt/. The noun is pronounced /ɛksplɔɪt/.

1 V-T If someone **exploits** you, they treat you unfairly by using your work or ideas and giving you very little in return. ❑ *They claim he exploited other musicians.* ● **ex|ploi|ta|tion** /ɛksplɔɪteɪʃᵊn/ N-UNCOUNT ❑ *We should prevent exploitation.* 2 V-T To **exploit** a situation means to use it to gain an advantage for yourself. ❑ *They exploit the troubles to their advantage.* ● **ex|ploi|ta|tion** N-SING ❑ *...the exploitation of the situation by local politicians.* 3 V-T To **exploit** resources or raw materials means to develop them and use them for industry or commercial activities. ❑ *We're being very short-sighted in not exploiting our own coal.* ● **ex|ploi|ta|tion** N-UNCOUNT ❑ *...the planned exploitation of oil and natural gas reserves.* 4 N-COUNT Someone's **exploits** are the brave or interesting things that they have done. ❑ *...his wartime exploits.* [from Old French]

**ex|plora|tory** /ɪksplɔrətɔri/ ADJ **Exploratory** actions are done in order to discover or learn something. ❑ *...exploratory surgery.* [from Latin]

**ex|plore** /ɪksplɔr/ (**explores, exploring, explored**) 1 V-T/V-I If you **explore**, or **explore** a place, you travel around it to find out what it is like. ❑ *I just wanted to explore on my own.* ❑ *The best way to explore the area is in a boat.* ● **ex|plo|ra|tion** /ɛkspləreɪʃᵊn/ (**explorations**) N-VAR ❑ *...space exploration.* ● **ex|plor|er** (**explorers**) N-COUNT ❑ *...the travels of Columbus, Magellan, and many other explorers.* 2 V-T If you **explore** an idea, you carefully think about or discuss its different aspects. ❑ *The movie explores the relationship between artist and model.* ● **ex|plo|ra|tion** N-VAR ❑ *...the exploration of their theories.* 3 V-I If people **explore for** a substance such as oil or minerals, they study an area and do tests on the land to see whether they can find it. ❑ *They dug a mile-deep well to explore for oil.* ● **ex|plo|ra|tion** N-UNCOUNT ❑ *...gas exploration.* [from Latin]

**ex|plo|sion** /ɪksploʊʒᵊn/ (**explosions**) 1 N-COUNT An **explosion** is a sudden, violent

e

burst of energy, such as one caused by a bomb. □ *Six soldiers were injured in the explosion.* **2** N-COUNT An **explosion** is a large rapid increase in the number or amount of something. □ *...an explosion in the diet soft-drink market.* [from Latin]

**ex|plo|sive** /ɪksplousɪv/ (**explosives**) **1** N-VAR An **explosive** is a substance or device that can cause an explosion. □ *...150 pounds of explosive.* ● **Explosive** is also an adjective. □ *The explosive device was timed to go off at the rush hour.* **2** ADJ An **explosive** situation is likely to have serious or dangerous effects. □ *...a potentially explosive situation.* [from Latin]
→ see **tunnel**

**ex|po|nent** /ɪkspounənt/ (**exponents**) **1** N-COUNT An **exponent** of an idea, theory, or plan is a person who supports and explains it. [FORMAL] □ *...an exponent of free speech.* **2** N-COUNT An **exponent** of a particular skill or activity is a person who is good at it. □ *...a leading exponent of modern dance.* **3** N-COUNT In mathematics, an **exponent** is a number that indicates how many times a particular quantity should be multiplied by itself. For example, the exponent of $2^3$ is 3. [TECHNICAL] [from Latin]

**ex|po|nen|tial func|tion** /ɛkspənɛnʃəl fʌŋkʃⁿ/ (**exponential functions**) N-COUNT An **exponential function** is a mathematical calculation that is used to study processes which increase at a constant rate, such as population growth or compound interest. [TECHNICAL]

**Word Link** port ≈ carrying : ex**port**, im**port**, **port**able

**ex|port** (**exports, exporting, exported**)

The verb is pronounced /ɪkspɔrt/. The noun is pronounced /ɛkspɔrt/.

**1** V-T/V-I To **export** products or raw materials means to sell them to another country. □ *They also export beef.* □ *The company now exports to Japan.* ● **Export** is also a noun. □ *A lot of our land is used to grow crops for export.* ● **ex|port|er** /ɛkspɔrtər, ɪkspɔrtər/ (**exporters**) N-COUNT □ *France is the world's second-biggest exporter of agricultural products.* **2** N-COUNT **Exports** are goods sold to another country and sent there. □ *Ghana's main export is cocoa.* [from Latin]

**ex|pose** /ɪkspouz/ (**exposes, exposing, exposed**) **1** V-T To **expose** something means to uncover it so that it can be seen. □ *Water levels fell and exposed the wrecked boat.* **2** V-T To **expose** a person or situation means to reveal the truth about them. □ *Officials exposed him as a fake.* **3** V-T If someone **is exposed to** something dangerous or unpleasant, they are put in a situation in which it might affect them. □ *They have not been exposed to these diseases.* [from Old French]

**ex|po|si|tion** /ɛkspəzɪʃⁿn/ (**expositions**) **1** N-COUNT An **exposition of** an idea or theory is a detailed explanation or account of it. [FORMAL] □ *...a clear exposition of the problem.* **2** N-VAR In a story or play, the **exposition** is the part, usually near the beginning, where important information about the characters and the situation is given. [TECHNICAL] [from Latin]

**ex|po|sure** /ɪkspouʒər/ (**exposures**) **1** N-UNCOUNT **Exposure to** something dangerous means being in a situation where it might affect

you. □ *Exposure to the sun can damage your skin.* **2** N-UNCOUNT **Exposure** is the harmful effect on your body caused by very cold weather. □ *He was suffering from exposure and shock.* **3** N-UNCOUNT The **exposure** of a well-known person is the revealing of the fact that they are bad or immoral in some way. □ *...his exposure as a spy.* **4** N-UNCOUNT **Exposure** is publicity that a person, company, or product receives. □ *All the candidates have been getting an enormous amount of exposure on television.* **5** N-COUNT In photography, an **exposure** is a single photograph. [TECHNICAL] [from Old French]

**ex|pound** /ɪkspaund/ (**expounds, expounding, expounded**) V-T If you **expound** an idea or opinion, you give a clear and detailed explanation of it. [FORMAL] □ *Schmidt continued to expound his views.* [from Old French]

**ex|press** /ɪksprɛs/ (**expresses, expressing, expressed**) **1** V-T When you **express** an idea or feeling, or **express yourself**, you show what you think or feel. □ *He expressed concern at American attitudes.* **2** V-T If an idea or feeling **expresses itself** in some way, it can be clearly seen in your actions or in its effects on a situation. □ *Anxiety often expresses itself as anger.* **3** ADJ An **express** command or order is one that is clearly and deliberately stated. [FORMAL] □ *This power station was built on the express orders of the president.* ● **ex|press|ly** ADV □ *He has expressly forbidden her to go out on her own.* **4** ADJ An **express** intention or purpose is deliberate and specific. □ *The express purpose of the flights was to get Americans out of the danger zone.* ● **ex|press|ly** ADV □ *...projects expressly designed to support cattle farmers.* **5** ADJ An **express** service is one in which things are sent or done faster than usual. □ *A special express service is available.* ● **Express** is also an adverb. □ *Send it express.* **6** N-COUNT An **express** or an **express** train is a fast train that stops at very few stations. □ *The express to Kuala Lumpur left Singapore station.* [from Latin]

**Word Partnership** Use *express* with :

| N. | express **appreciation**, express **your emotions**, express **gratitude**, express **sympathy**, **words** to express *something* **1** express **purpose** **4** express **mail**, express **service** **5** |
|---|---|

**ex|pres|sion** /ɪksprɛʃⁿn/ (**expressions**) **1** N-VAR The **expression of** ideas or feelings is the showing of them through words, actions, or artistic activities. □ *Your baby's smiles are expressions of happiness.* □ *...the rights of the individual to freedom of expression.* **2** N-VAR Your **expression** is the way that your face looks at a particular moment. It shows what you are thinking or feeling. □ *Levin sat there, an expression of sadness on his face.* **3** N-COUNT An **expression** is a word or phrase. □ *When writing an essay it is important to avoid using slang expressions.* [from Latin]

**ex|pres|sive** /ɪksprɛsɪv/ ADJ Something that is **expressive** clearly indicates a person's feelings or intentions. □ *You can train people to be more expressive.* □ *...expressive poetry.* ● **ex|pres|sive|ly** ADV □ *He moved his hands expressively.* [from Latin]

**ex|pres|sive con|tent** N-UNCOUNT **Expressive content** is writing, speech, or another form of communication which expresses someone's feelings about a particular subject.

**ex|pres|sive writ|ing** N-UNCOUNT **Expressive writing** is writing such as diaries and letters that describes the writer's feelings, ideas, or beliefs.

---

**Word Link**    puls ≈ driving, pushing : compulsion, expulsion, impulse

---

**ex|pul|sion** /ɪkspʌlʃ°n/ (**expulsions**) **1** N-VAR **Expulsion** is when someone is forced to leave a school, university, or organization. □ ...her expulsion from high school. **2** N-VAR **Expulsion** is when someone is forced to leave a place. [FORMAL] □ ...the expulsion of foreign workers. [from Latin]

**ex|quis|ite** /ɪkskwɪzɪt, ɛkskwɪzɪt/ ADJ **Exquisite** means extremely beautiful. □ The Indians brought in exquisite things to sell. ● **ex|quis|ite|ly** ADV □ ...exquisitely made dollhouses. [from Latin]

**ex|tend** /ɪkstɛnd/ (**extends, extending, extended**) **1** V-I If you say that something, usually something large, **extends for** a particular distance or **extends from** one place to another, you are indicating its size or position. □ The caves extend for 12 miles. □ The main stem will extend to around 12 feet. **2** V-I If an object **extends from** a surface or place, it sticks out from it. □ A table extended from the front of her desk. **3** V-I If something **extends to** a group of people, things, or activities, it includes or affects them. □ The service extends to delivering gifts. **4** V-T If you **extend** something, you make it bigger, make it last longer, or make it include more. □ This year they have introduced three new products to extend their range. □ They have extended the deadline by twenty-four hours. **5** V-T If someone **extends** their hand, they stretch out their arm and hand to shake hands with someone. □ The man extended his hand: "I'm Chuck." [from Latin]

**ex|ten|sion** /ɪkstɛnʃ°n/ (**extensions**) **1** N-COUNT An **extension** is a new room or building that is added to an existing building. □ We are thinking of having an extension built. **2** N-COUNT An **extension** is an extra period of time for which something lasts or is valid, usually as a result of official permission. □ He was given a six-month extension to his visa. **3** N-COUNT Something that is an **extension of** something else is a development of it that includes or affects more people, things, or activities. □ They did not agree with the extension of police powers. **4** N-COUNT An **extension** is a telephone line that is connected to the switchboard of a company or institution, and that has its own number. The written abbreviation **ext.** is also used. □ She can get me on extension 308. [from Late Latin]

**ex|ten|sive** /ɪkstɛnsɪv/ **1** ADJ Something that is **extensive** covers or includes a large physical area. □ ...an extensive tour of Latin America. ● **ex|ten|sive|ly** ADV □ Mark travels extensively. **2** ADJ Something that is **extensive** covers a wide range of details, ideas, or items. □ She recently completed an extensive study of elected officials. ● **ex|ten|sive|ly** ADV □ All these issues have been extensively researched. **3** ADJ If something is **extensive**, it is very great. □ The security forces have extensive powers. ● **ex|ten|sive|ly** ADV □ Hydrogen is used extensively in industry. [from Late Latin]

**ex|ten|sor** /ɪkstɛnsər/ (**extensors**) N-COUNT **Extensors** are muscles that extend or straighten a part of your body. [TECHNICAL] [from New Latin]

**ex|tent** /ɪkstɛnt/ **1** N-SING If you are talking about how great, important, or serious a difficulty or situation is, you can refer to **the extent of** it. □ The government has little information on the extent of industrial pollution. **2** N-SING **The extent of** something is its length, area, or size. □ Their commitment was to maintain the extent of forests. **3** PHRASE You use expressions such as **to a large extent**, **to what extent**, or **to the extent that** in order to say how far something is true. □ To some extent this was the truth. □ I was getting more nervous to the extent that I was almost physically sick. [from Old French]

---

**Word Partnership**    Use extent with :

| | |
|---|---|
| N. | extent **of the damage** **1** |
| V. | **determine the** extent, **know the** extent **1** |
| ADJ. | **lesser** extent **1** **full** extent **1** **2** **a certain** extent **3** |

---

**ex|te|ri|or** /ɪkstɪəriər/ (**exteriors**) **1** N-COUNT The **exterior** of something is its outside surface. □ ...the exterior of the building. **2** N-COUNT You can refer to someone's usual appearance or behavior as their **exterior**. □ Pat's tough exterior hides a shy and sensitive soul. **3** ADJ You use **exterior** to refer to the outside parts of something or things that are outside something. □ ...exterior walls. [from Latin]

---

**Thesaurus**    exterior    Also look up :

| | |
|---|---|
| N. | coating, cover, shell, skin **1** |
| ADJ. | external, outer, surface **3** |

---

**ex|ter|mi|nate** /ɪkstɜrmɪneɪt/ (**exterminates, exterminating, exterminated**) V-T To **exterminate** a group of people or animals means to kill all of them. □ A huge effort was made to exterminate the rats. ● **ex|ter|mi|na|tion** /ɪkstɜrmɪneɪʃ°n/ N-UNCOUNT □ ...the extermination of wild dogs. [from Latin]

**ex|ter|nal** /ɪkstɜrn°l/ ADJ **External** means happening, coming from, or existing outside a place, person, or area. □ ...heat loss through external walls. ● **ex|ter|nal|ly** ADV □ Vitamins can be applied externally to the skin. [from Latin]
→ see **ear**

**ex|ter|nal com|bus|tion en|gine** (**external combustion engines**) N-COUNT An **external combustion engine** is an engine that burns fuel outside the engine. [TECHNICAL]

**ex|ter|nal fer|ti|li|za|tion** N-UNCOUNT **External fertilization** is a method of reproduction in some animals in which the egg and sperm join together outside the female's body, for example in water. Compare **internal fertilization**. [TECHNICAL]

**ex|ter|nal fuel tank** (**external fuel tanks**) N-COUNT An **external fuel tank** is a container for fuel that is fitted to the outside of a spacecraft.

**ex|tinct** /ɪkstɪŋkt/ **1** ADJ A species of animal or plant is **extinct** no longer has any living members. □ Many animals could become extinct in less than 10 years. **2** ADJ An **extinct** volcano does not erupt or is not expected to erupt anymore. □ Its tallest volcano is long extinct. [from Latin]

**ex|tinc|tion** /ɪkstɪŋkʃ°n/ N-UNCOUNT The **extinction** of a species of animal or plant is the

e

death of all its remaining living members. □ *We want to save the species from extinction.* [from Latin]

**ex|tin|guish** /ɪkstɪ́ŋgwɪʃ/ (**extinguishes, extinguishing, extinguished**) V-T If you **extinguish** a fire or a light, you stop it from burning or shining. [FORMAL] □ *It took about 50 minutes to extinguish the fire.* [from Latin]

**ex|tol** /ɪkstóʊl/ (**extols, extolling, extolled**) also **extoll** V-T If you **extol** something, you praise it enthusiastically. □ *The book extols the joys of living in the country.* [from Latin]

**ex|tra** /ɛ́kstrə/ (**extras**) ◼ ADJ An **extra** amount, person, or thing is another one that is added to others of the same kind. □ *Police warned drivers to allow extra time to get to work.* □ *There's an extra blanket in the bottom drawer.* ● **Extra** is also an adverb. □ *You may be charged 10% extra for this service.* ● **Extra** is also a pronoun. □ *She won't pay any extra.* ◼ N-COUNT **Extras** are additional amounts of money that are added to the price that you have to pay for something. □ *There are no hidden extras.* ◼ N-COUNT **Extras** are things that are not necessary in a situation, activity, or object, but that make it more comfortable, useful, or enjoyable. □ *Optional extras include cooking classes.* ◼ N-COUNT The **extras** in a movie are the people who play unimportant parts, for example, as members of a crowd. □ *In 1944, Kendall entered films as an extra.* ◼ ADV You can use **extra** in front of adjectives and adverbs to emphasize the quality that they are describing. [INFORMAL] □ *You have to be extra careful.*

---

**Word Link** | extra ≈ outside of : extract, extradite, extraordinary

**ex|tract** (**extracts, extracting, extracted**)

The verb is pronounced /ɪkstrǽkt/. The noun is pronounced /ɛ́kstrækt/.

◼ V-T To **extract** a substance means to obtain it from something else, for example, by using industrial or chemical processes. □ *...the traditional method of extracting coal.* ● An **extract** is a substance that has been obtained in this way. □ *...plant extracts.* ● **ex|trac|tion** N-UNCOUNT □ *...the extraction of oil.* ◼ V-T If you **extract** something **from** a place, you take it out or pull it out. □ *He extracted a small notebook from his pocket.* ◼ V-T When a dentist **extracts** a tooth, he or she removes it from a patient's mouth. □ *A dentist may decide to extract the tooth.* ● **ex|trac|tion** (**extractions**) N-VAR □ *The extraction was painless.* ◼ N-COUNT An **extract from** a book or piece of writing is a small part of it that is printed or published separately. □ *Read this extract from an information booklet.* [from Latin] → see **industry, mineral**

**ex|tra|dite** /ɛ́kstrədaɪt/ (**extradites, extraditing, extradited**) V-T If someone **is extradited,** they are officially sent back to their own or another country or state to be tried for a crime. [FORMAL] □ *A judge agreed to extradite him to Texas.* ● **extra|di|tion** /ɛ̀kstrədɪ́ʃ³n/ (**extraditions**) N-VAR □ *A New York court turned down the British government's request for his extradition.*

**extraor|di|nary** /ɪkstrɔ́rd³nɛri/ ◼ ADJ If you describe something or someone as **extraordinary,** you mean that they have some extremely good or special quality. □ *We've made extraordinary progress.* □ *The task requires extraordinary patience.*

● **extraor|di|nari|ly** /ɪkstrɔ́rd³nɛ́rɪli/ ADV □ *She's extraordinarily kind.* ◼ ADJ If you describe something as **extraordinary,** you mean that it is very unusual or surprising. □ *What an extraordinary thing to happen!* ● **extraor|di|nari|ly** ADV □ *Apart from the hair, he looked extraordinarily unchanged.* [from Latin]

**ex|trava|gance** /ɪkstrǽvəgəns/ (**extravagances**) ◼ N-COUNT An **extravagance** is something that you spend money on but cannot really afford. □ *Why waste money on such extravagances?* [from Medieval Latin] ◼ → see also **extravagant**

**ex|trava|gant** /ɪkstrǽvəgənt/ ◼ ADJ Someone who is **extravagant** spends more money than they can afford or uses more of something than is reasonable. □ *We are not extravagant; restaurant meals are a luxury.* ● **ex|trava|gance** N-UNCOUNT □ *Tales of his extravagance were common.* ● **ex|trava|gant|ly** ADV □ *Jeff shopped extravagantly for presents.* ◼ ADJ Something that is **extravagant** costs more money than you can afford or uses more of something than is reasonable. □ *Her aunt gave her an extravagant gift.* ● **ex|trava|gant|ly** ADV □ *...an extravagantly expensive machine.* ◼ ADJ **Extravagant** behavior is extreme behavior that is often done for a particular effect. □ *He was extravagant in his admiration of her.* ● **ex|trava|gant|ly** ADV □ *She praised him extravagantly.* [from Medieval Latin]

**ex|trava|gan|za** /ɪkstræ̀vəgǽnzə/ (**extravaganzas**) N-COUNT An **extravaganza** is a very elaborate and expensive show or performance. □ *...a magnificent fireworks extravaganza.* [from Italian]

**ex|treme** /ɪkstrím/ (**extremes**) ◼ ADJ **Extreme** means very great in degree or intensity. □ *...people living in extreme poverty.* ● **ex|treme|ly** ADV □ *My cellphone is extremely useful.* ◼ ADJ You use **extreme** to describe situations and behavior that are much more severe or unusual than you would expect, especially when you disapprove of them because of this. □ *It is hard to imagine Jesse capable of anything so extreme.* ◼ N-COUNT You can use **extremes** to refer to situations or types of behavior that have opposite qualities to each other, especially when each situation or type of behavior has such a quality to the greatest degree possible. □ *...a middle way between the extremes of success and failure.* ◼ ADJ The **extreme** end or edge of something is its farthest end or edge. □ *...the room at the extreme end of the corridor.* [from Latin]

---

**Word Partnership** | Use *extreme* with :

| | |
|---|---|
| N. | extreme **caution**, extreme **difficulty** ◼ extreme **case**, extreme **left**, extreme **right**, extreme **sports**, extreme **views** ◼ |
| ADJ. | **the opposite** extreme ◼ |

**ex|trem|ist** /ɪkstrímɪst/ (**extremists**) N-COUNT If you describe someone as an **extremist,** you disapprove of them because they try to bring about political change by using violent or extreme methods. □ *...foreign extremists.* ● **ex|trem|ism** N-UNCOUNT □ *...left and right-wing extremism.* [from Latin]

**extro|vert** /ɛ́kstrəvɜrt/ (**extroverts**) N-COUNT An **extrovert** is someone who is extroverted. [from Latin]

**extro|vert|ed** /ˈɛkstrəvɜrtɪd/ ADJ Someone who is **extroverted** is very active, lively, and friendly. ❑ ...*young people who were easy-going and extroverted as children.* [from Latin]

**ex|tru|sive** /ɪkstruˈsɪv/ ADJ **Extrusive** rock is rock that forms on the surface of the Earth after lava has been released and has cooled. Compare **intrusive**. [TECHNICAL] [from Latin]

**exu|ber|ant** /ɪgˈzubərənt/ ADJ If you are **exuberant**, you are full of energy, excitement, and cheerfulness. ❑ ...*the exuberant young girl with dark hair and blue eyes.* ● **exu|ber|ance** N-UNCOUNT ❑ ...*a burst of exuberance.* ● **exu|ber|ant|ly** ADV ❑ *They both laughed exuberantly.* [from Latin]

**ex|ude** /ɪgˈzud, ɪkˈsud/ (**exudes, exuding, exuded**) **1** V-T If someone **exudes** a quality or feeling, or if it **exudes**, they show that they have a lot of it. [FORMAL] ❑ *She exudes an air of relaxed calm.* **2** V-T/V-I If something **exudes** a liquid or smell or if a liquid or smell **exudes from** it, the liquid or smell comes out of it slowly and steadily. [FORMAL] ❑ ...*a factory which exuded a strong smell.* [from Latin]

---

**eye**

❶ PART OF THE BODY, ABILITY TO SEE
❷ PART OF AN OBJECT

---

❶ **eye** /aɪ/ (**eyes, eyeing** or **eying, eyed**) **1** N-COUNT Your **eyes** are the parts of your body with which you see. ❑ *I opened my eyes and looked.* ❑ ...*a tall lady with dark brown eyes.* **2** V-T If you **eye** someone or something in a particular way, you look at them carefully in that way. ❑ *Sally eyed Claire with interest.* ❑ *Martin eyed the money.* **3** N-COUNT You use **eye** when you are talking about a person's ability to judge things or about the way in which they are considering or dealing with things. ❑ ...*a man with an eye for quality.* ❑ *He learned to fish under the watchful eye of his grandmother.* **4** → see also **black eye** **5** PHRASE If you say that something happens **before** your **eyes, in front of** your **eyes,** or **under** your **eyes,** you are emphasizing that it happens where you can see it clearly or while you are watching it. ❑ *A lot of them died in front of our eyes.* **6** PHRASE If something **catches** your **eye,** you suddenly notice it. ❑ *A movement across the garden caught her eye.* **7** → see also **eye-catching** **8** PHRASE If you **catch** someone's **eye,** you do something to attract their attention, so that you can speak to them. ❑ *He tried to catch Annie's eye.* **9** PHRASE If you **keep** your **eyes open** or **keep an eye out for** someone or something, you watch for them carefully. [INFORMAL] ❑ *I asked the patrol to keep their eyes open.* **10** PHRASE If you **have** your **eye on** something,

you want to have it. [INFORMAL] ❑ ...*a new outfit you've had your eye on.* [from Old English] **11** to **turn a blind eye** → see **blind** **12** to **feast** your **eyes** → see **feast** **13** in your **mind's eye** → see **mind**
→ see Word Web: **eye**
→ see **cry, face, hurricane**

❷ **eye** /aɪ/ (**eyes**) **1** N-COUNT An **eye** is a small metal loop that a hook fits into, as a fastening on a piece of clothing. ❑ ...*hooks and eyes.* **2** N-COUNT The **eye** of a needle is the small hole at one end that the thread passes through. ❑ *The difficult part was threading the cotton thread through the eye of the needle.* [from Old English]

**eye|ball** /ˈaɪbɔl/ (**eyeballs**) N-COUNT Your **eyeballs** are the parts of your eyes that are like white balls.

**eye|brow** /ˈaɪbraʊ/ (**eyebrows**) **1** N-COUNT Your **eyebrows** are the lines of hair that grow above your eyes. **2** PHRASE If something causes you to **raise an eyebrow** or to **raise** your **eyebrows,** it causes you to feel surprised or disapproving. ❑ *He raised his eyebrows over some of the suggestions.*
→ see **face**

**eye can|dy** also **eye-candy** N-UNCOUNT **Eye candy** is used to refer to people or things that are attractive to look at but are not interesting in other ways. [INFORMAL] ❑ *Back then, women on TV were mostly seen as eye candy.*

**eye-catching** ADJ Something that is **eye-catching** is very noticeable. ❑ ...*a series of eye-catching ads.*

**eye|glasses** /ˈaɪglæsɪz/ N-PLURAL **Eyeglasses** are the same as **glasses** or **spectacles**.

**eye|lash** /ˈaɪlæʃ/ (**eyelashes**) N-COUNT Your **eyelashes** are the hairs that grow on the edges of your eyelids.
→ see **face**

**eye|lid** /ˈaɪlɪd/ (**eyelids**) N-COUNT Your **eyelids** are the two pieces of skin that cover your eyes when they are closed.
→ see **face**

**eye|piece** /ˈaɪpis/ (**eyepieces**) N-COUNT The **eyepiece** of a microscope or telescope is the piece of glass at one end, where you put your eye in order to look through the instrument.

**eye-popping** ADJ Something that is **eye-popping** is very impressive or striking. ❑ ...*a plan to raise property taxes by an eye-popping $2 billion.*

**eye|sight** /ˈaɪsaɪt/ N-UNCOUNT Your **eyesight** is your ability to see. ❑ *He suffered from poor eyesight.*

**eye|witness** /ˈaɪwɪtnɪs/ (**eyewitnesses**) N-COUNT An **eyewitness** is a person who was present at an event and can therefore describe it, for example in a law court. ❑ *She was an eyewitness to the assassination of President Kennedy.*

---

**Word Web** eye

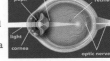

**Light** enters the **eye** through the **cornea**. The cornea bends the light and directs it through the **pupil**. The colored **iris** opens and closes the **lens**. This helps focus the **image** clearly on the **retina**. Nerve cells in the retina change the light into electrical signals. The **optic nerve** then carries these signals to the brain. In a **nearsighted** person the light rays focus in front of the lens. The image comes onto focus in back of the lens in a **farsighted** person. An irregularity in the cornea can cause **astigmatism**. Glasses or **contact lenses** can correct all three problems.

# Ff

**fa|ble** /ˈfeɪbᵊl/ (**fables**) N-VAR A **fable** is a traditional story which teaches a moral lesson. [from Latin]

**fab|ric** /ˈfæbrɪk/ (**fabrics**) **1** N-VAR **Fabric** is cloth produced by weaving together cotton, silk, or other threads. ❑ ...red cotton fabric. **2** N-SING The **fabric** of a society or system is its basic structure, with all the customs and beliefs that make it work successfully. ❑ The fabric of society was damaged by the previous government. [from Latin]
→ see **quilt**

**fab|ri|cate** /ˈfæbrɪkeɪt/ (**fabricates, fabricating, fabricated**) V-T If someone **fabricates** information, they invent it in order to deceive people. ❑ Jones fabricated details about his education to get the job. ● **fab|ri|ca|tion** /ˌfæbrɪˈkeɪʃᵊn/ (**fabrications**) N-VAR ❑ She described the interview as a "complete fabrication." [from Latin]

---

> **Word Link**    *ous ≈ having the qualities of :*    *danger*ous, *fabul*ous, *nutriti*ous

---

**fabu|lous** /ˈfæbyələs/ ADJ If you describe something as **fabulous**, you like it a lot or think that it is very good. [INFORMAL] [from Latin]

**fa|cade** /fəˈsɑd/ (**facades**) also **façade**
**1** N-COUNT The **facade** of a large building is its front wall. ❑ ...repairs to the building's facade.
**2** N-SING A **facade** is an outward appearance which deliberately gives you a wrong impression about someone or something. ❑ A facade of happiness hides the anger between them. [from French]

---

### face

① NOUN USES
② VERB USES

---

**① face** /feɪs/ (**faces**) **1** N-COUNT Your **face** is the front part of your head from your chin to the top of your forehead. ❑ She had a beautiful face. ❑ He was hit in the face. **2** N-COUNT The **face** of a cliff, mountain, or building is a vertical surface or side of it. ❑ ...the north face of the Eiger. **3** N-COUNT The **face** of a clock or watch is the surface with the numbers or hands on it, which shows the time. **4** N-SING If you refer to one particular **face of** something, you mean one particular aspect of it. ❑ ...the unacceptable face of politics. **5** N-UNCOUNT If you lose **face**, you do something which makes people respect or admire you less. If you do something in order to save **face**, you do it in order to avoid losing people's respect or admiration. ❑ They don't want a war, but they don't want to lose face. **6** → see also **face value** **7** PHRASE If you come **face to face** with someone, you meet them and can talk to them or look at them directly. ❑ We were walking into the town when we came face to face

with Jacques Dubois. **8** PHRASE If an action or belief **flies in the face of** accepted ideas or rules, it seems to completely oppose or contradict them. ❑ These ideas fly in the face of common sense. **9** PHRASE If you take a particular action or attitude **in the face of** a problem or difficulty, you respond to that problem or difficulty in that way. ❑ ...Harrison's courage in the face of cancer. **10** PHRASE If you **make a face**, you show a feeling such as dislike for something by twisting your face into an ugly expression. ❑ Opening the door, she made a face at the horrible smell. **11** PHRASE If you manage to keep a **straight face**, you manage to look serious, although you want to laugh. [from Old French]
→ see Picture Dictionary: **face**
→ see **makeup**

**② face** /feɪs/ (**faces, facing, faced**) **1** V-T/V-I To **face** a particular direction means to look in that direction from a position directly opposite it. ❑ They stood facing each other. ❑ Our house faces south. **2** V-T If you **face** or **are faced** with something difficult or unpleasant, or if it **faces** you, you have to deal with it. ❑ Williams faces life in prison. **3** V-T If you **cannot face** something, you do not feel able to do it because it seems so difficult or unpleasant. ❑ I can't face telling my girlfriend. [from Old French]

**face card** (**face cards**) N-COUNT A **face card** is any of the twelve cards in a deck of cards which has a picture of a face. The face cards are kings, queens, and jacks.

**face|less** /ˈfeɪslɪs/ ADJ If you describe someone or something as **faceless**, you dislike them because they are uninteresting and have no character. ❑ ...faceless managers. [from Old French]

**face mask** (**face masks**) **1** N-COUNT A **face mask** is something that you wear over your face to prevent yourself from breathing bad air or from spreading germs, or to protect your face.
**2** N-COUNT A **face mask** is a substance that you spread on your face, allow to dry and then remove, in order to clean your skin.

**face-off** (**face-offs**) N-COUNT A **face-off** is an argument or conflict that is intended to settle a dispute. ❑ ...a face-off between Congress and the White House.

**fac|et** /ˈfæsɪt/ (**facets**) N-COUNT A **facet** of something is a single part or aspect of it. ❑ ...every facet of American life. [from French]

**face value** **1** N-SING The **face value** of things such as coins, paper money, or tickets is the amount of money that they are worth, and that is written on them. ❑ Tickets were selling at twice their face value. **2** PHRASE If you take something **at face value**, you accept it and believe it without thinking about it very much, even though it might be untrue. ❑ Public statements should not necessarily be taken at face value.

## Picture Dictionary: face

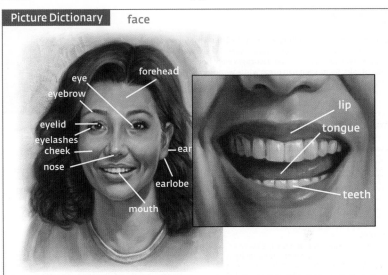

eye
forehead
eyebrow
eyelid
eyelashes
cheek
nose
ear
earlobe
mouth
lip
tongue
teeth

f

**fa|cial** /ˈfeɪʃᵊl/ ADJ **Facial** means appearing on or being part of your face. ❑ *His facial expression didn't change.* [from Old French]

**fa|cili|tate** /fəˈsɪlɪteɪt/ (**facilitates, facilitating, facilitated**) V-T To **facilitate** an action or process means to make it easier or more likely to happen. ❑ *The new airport will facilitate the development of tourism.* [from Latin]

**fa|cil|ity** /fəˈsɪlɪti/ (**facilities**) **1** N-COUNT **Facilities** are buildings, pieces of equipment, or services that are provided for a particular purpose. ❑ *...excellent kitchen and bathroom facilities.* **2** N-COUNT A **facility** is a useful service or feature provided by an organization or machine. ❑ *...a website's search facility.* [from Latin]

**fact** /fækt/ (**facts**) **1** N-COUNT **Facts** are pieces of information that are true. ❑ *...the facts about the murder.* **2** PHRASE You use **the fact that** after some verbs or prepositions, especially in expressions such as **in view of the fact that**, **apart from the fact that**, and **despite the fact that**, to link the verb or preposition with a clause. ❑ *My family now accepts the fact that I don't eat sugar or bread.* **3** PHRASE You use **in fact**, **in actual fact**, or **in point of fact** to indicate that you are giving more detailed information about what you have just said. ❑ *I don't watch television. In fact, I no longer even own a TV.* **4** N-VAR When you refer to something as a **fact** or as **fact**, you mean that you think it is true or correct. ❑ *...a statement of historical fact.* [from Latin]
→ see **history**

### Word Partnership    Use *fact* with :

| | |
|---|---|
| V. | **accept a** fact, **check the** facts, **face a** fact **1** |
| N. | fact **and fiction 1** |
| ADJ. | **hard** fact, **historical** fact, **important** fact, **obvious** fact, **random** fact, **simple** fact **1** |

**fac|tion** /ˈfækʃᵊn/ (**factions**) N-COUNT A **faction** is an organized group of people within a larger group, which opposes some of the ideas of the larger group and fights for its own ideas. ❑ *...the leaders of the country's warring factions.* ● **fac|tion|al** ADJ ❑ *...factional disputes between the various groups in the party.* [from Latin]

### Word Link    fact, fic ≈ making : artifact, artificial, factor

**fac|tor** /ˈfæktər/ (**factors, factoring, factored**) **1** N-COUNT A **factor** is one of the things that affects an event, decision, or situation. ❑ *Exercise is an important factor in maintaining physical and mental health.* **2** N-COUNT In mathematics, a **factor** is one of the numbers that you multiply when you multiply two or more numbers together. [TECHNICAL] [from Latin]
▶ **factor in** or **factor into** PHR-VERB If you **factor** a particular cost or element **into** a calculation you are making, or if you **factor** it **in**, you include it. ❑ *You'd better consider this and factor it into your decision making.*

### Word Link    ory ≈ place where something happens : conservatory, factory, territory

**fac|to|ry** /ˈfæktəri, -tri/ (**factories**) N-COUNT A **factory** is a large building where machines are used to make large quantities of goods. [from Late Latin]
→ see Word Web: **factory**

**fac|tual** /ˈfæktʃuəl/ ADJ Something that is **factual** is concerned with facts, rather than theories or personal interpretations. ❑ *The article contained several factual errors.* [from Latin]

**fac|ul|ty** /ˈfækᵊlti/ (**faculties**) **1** N-COUNT Your **faculties** are your physical and mental abilities. ❑ *X-rays showed fractures in my left arm, legs and skull*

## Word Web   factory

Life in a 19th-century **factory** was very difficult. **Employees** often **worked** twelve hours a day, six days a week. **Wages** were low and **child labor** was common. Many **workers** were not allowed to take **breaks**. Some even had to eat while working. As early as 1832, doctors started warning about the dangers of **air pollution**. The 20th century brought some big changes. Workers began to join **unions**. During World War I, **government regulations** set standards for **minimum wages** and better **working conditions**. In addition, automation took over some of the most difficult and dangerous jobs.

*but I was in full control of my faculties.* **2** N-VAR A **faculty** is all the teaching staff of a university or college, or of one department. □ *Good faculties are essential to a good college.* [from Latin]

**fad** /fæd/ (**fads**) N-COUNT A **fad** is an activity or topic of interest that is very popular for a short time, but which people become bored with very quickly. □ *In 1981, some people thought the new mountain bikes were a fad.*
→ see **diet**

**fade** /feɪd/ (**fades, fading, faded**) **1** V-T/V-I When a colored object **fades** or when the light **fades** it, it gradually becomes paler. □ *Color fades under direct sunlight.* □ *No matter how soft the light is, it still fades carpets.* ● **fad|ed** ADJ □ *...a girl in a faded dress.* **2** V-I If memories, feelings, or possibilities **fade**, they slowly become less intense or less strong. □ *My wish to live here has started to fade.* [from Old French]

### Word Partnership   Use *fade* with :

| | |
|---|---|
| N. | **colors** fade, **images** fade **1** |
| | **memories** fade **2** |
| V. | **begin to** fade **1** **2** |
| ADV. | fade **quickly** **1** **2** |

**Fahr|en|heit** /fæɹənhaɪt/ ADJ **Fahrenheit** is a scale for measuring temperature, in which water freezes at 32 degrees and boils at 212 degrees. It is represented by the symbol °F. □ *The temperature was above 100 degrees Fahrenheit.* [from German]
→ see **climate, thermometer**

### Usage   Fahrenheit and Celsius

The Fahrenheit scale is commonly used to express temperature in the U.S. rather than the Celsius (or centigrade) scale.

**fail** /feɪl/ (**fails, failing, failed**) **1** V-T/V-I If you **fail** to do something that you were trying to do, you do not succeed in doing it. □ *The party failed to win the election.* □ *He failed in his attempt to take control of the company.* **2** V-T If someone or something **fails** to do a particular thing that they should have done, they do not do it. [FORMAL] □ *He failed to file his tax return.* **3** V-T If someone **fails** you, they do not do what you had expected or trusted them to do. □ *All the doctors have failed me — they don't know what's wrong.* **4** V-T If someone **fails** a test or examination, they do not reach the standard that is required. □ *I lived in fear of failing my final exams.* **5** PHRASE You use **without fail** to emphasize that something always happens or must definitely happen. □ *He attended every meeting without fail.* □ *You must without fail give the*

*money to Alex.* [from Old French]

**fail|ing** /feɪlɪŋ/ (**failings**) **1** N-COUNT The **failings** of someone or something are their faults or unsatisfactory features. □ *It's easy to blame your failings on your parents.* **2** PHRASE You say **failing that** to introduce an alternative, in case what you have just said is not possible. □ *More than anything else, I wanted to sleep, or, failing that, to read.* [from Old French]

**fail|ure** /feɪlyər/ (**failures**) **1** N-UNCOUNT **Failure** is a lack of success in doing or achieving something. □ *This policy is doomed to failure.* □ *Three attempts on the 200-meter record ended in failure.* **2** N-UNCOUNT Your **failure to** do a particular thing is the fact that you do not do it. □ *They were upset by his failure to tell the truth.* **3** N-COUNT If something is a **failure**, it is not a success. □ *The marriage was a failure.* **4** N-VAR If there is a **failure** of something, it goes wrong and stops working or developing properly. □ *Several accidents were caused by engine failures.* [from Old French]

### Word Partnership   Use *failure* with :

| | |
|---|---|
| ADJ. | **afraid of** failure, **doomed to** failure **1** |
| | **complete** failure **1** – **3** |
| | **dismal** failure **3** |
| N. | **feelings of** failure, **risk of** failure, **success or** failure **1** |
| | **engine** failure, **heart** failure, **kidney** failure **4** |
| V. | failure **to communicate** **1** **2** |

**faint** /feɪnt/ (**fainter, faintest, faints, fainting, fainted**) **1** ADJ A **faint** sound, color, mark, or quality is not strong or intense. □ *...the soft, faint sounds of water dripping.* □ *There was still the faint hope that she might return.* ● **faint|ly** ADV □ *The room smelled faintly of paint.* **2** ADJ Someone who is **faint** feels weak and unsteady as if they are about to lose consciousness. □ *He was unsteady on his feet and felt faint.* **3** V-I If you **faint**, you lose consciousness for a short time. □ *She suddenly fell forward and fainted.* [from Old French]

**fair** /fɛər/ (**fairer, fairest, fairs**) **1** ADJ Something or someone that is **fair** is reasonable and right. □ *It didn't seem fair to leave out her father.* □ *Do you feel they're paying their fair share?* □ *I wanted to get them a fair deal.* ● **fair|ly** ADV □ *We solved the problem quickly and fairly.* ● **fair|ness** N-UNCOUNT □ *...concerns about the fairness of the election campaign.* **2** ADJ A **fair** amount, degree, size, or distance is quite a large amount, degree, size, or distance. □ *My neighbors travel a fair amount.* **3** ADJ Someone who is **fair**, or who has **fair** hair, has light-colored hair.

**4** ADJ **Fair** skin is very pale and usually burns easily under strong sunlight. **5** ADJ When the weather is **fair**, it is quite sunny and not raining. [FORMAL] **6** N-COUNT A county, state, or country **fair** is an event where there are, for example, displays of goods and animals, and amusements, games, and competitions. **7** N-COUNT A **fair** is an event at which people display and sell goods. ❑ *I got a great bargain at an antiques fair.* **8** PHRASE You use **fair enough** when you want to say that a statement, decision, or action seems reasonable to a certain extent, but that perhaps there is more to be said or done. [mainly SPOKEN] ❑ *"I need a holiday."* — *"That's fair enough. Can I come too?"* [Senses 1–5 from Old English. Senses 6 and 7 from Old French.]

**Usage** **fair** and **fare**

Avoid confusing *fair* and *fare*, which sound exactly the same. The adjective *fair* means reasonable, or attractive, or light in color; the noun *fare* refers to the price of a bus, train, ferry, or airplane ticket, while the verb *fare* refers to how well someone is doing in a particular situation: *Was it fair that all the fair-haired people on the boat fared well, while all the dark-haired people got seasick? After all, everyone had paid the same fare.*

**Word Partnership** Use *fair* with:

ADJ. fair **and balanced** **1**
N. fair **chance**, fair **deal**, fair **fight**, fair **game**, fair **play**, fair **price**, fair **share**, fair **trade**, fair **treatment**, fair **trial** **1**
  fair **amount** **2**
  fair **hair** **3**
  fair **skin** **4**
  **science** fair **6**
  **craft** fair **6** **7**

**fair|ground** /fɛərɡraʊnd/ (**fairgrounds**) N-COUNT A **fairground** is an area of land where a fair is held.

**fair|ly** /fɛərli/ **1** ADV **Fairly** means to quite a large degree. ❑ *We did fairly well.* ❑ *Were you always fairly bright at school?* [from Old English] **2** → see also **fair**

**fairy** /fɛəri/ (**fairies**) N-COUNT A **fairy** is an imaginary creature with magical powers. Fairies are often represented as small people with wings. [from Old French]
→ see **fantasy**

**fairy tale** (**fairy tales**) also **fairytale** N-COUNT A **fairy tale** is a story for children involving magical events and imaginary creatures.

**faith** /feɪθ/ (**faiths**) **1** N-UNCOUNT If you have **faith in** someone or something, you feel confident about their ability or goodness. ❑ *People have lost faith in the government.* **2** N-UNCOUNT **Faith** is strong religious belief in a particular God. ❑ *They respect his faith.* **3** N-COUNT A **faith** is a particular religion, for example, Christianity, Buddhism, or Islam. ❑ *The college welcomes students of all faiths.* **4** PHRASE If you do something **in good faith**, you seriously believe that what you are doing is right, even though it may not be. [from Latin]

**faith|ful** /feɪθfəl/ **1** ADJ Someone who is **faithful to** a person, organization or idea, remains firm in their support for them. ❑ *Help your brothers and sisters and be faithful to your friends.* ● The **faithful** are people who are faithful to someone or something. ❑ *...the Democratic Party faithful.* ● **faith|ful|ly** ADV ❑ *He has faithfully supported every government policy.* **2** ADJ Someone who is **faithful to** their husband, wife, or lover does not have a sexual relationship with anyone else. **3** ADJ A **faithful** account, translation, or copy of something represents or reproduces the original accurately. ❑ *His movie is not faithful to the book.* ● **faith|ful|ly** ADV ❑ *The story is told faithfully.* [from Latin]

**faith|ful|ly** /feɪθfəli/ **1** CONVENTION When you start a formal or business letter with "Dear Sir" or "Dear Madam," you can write **Yours faithfully** before your signature at the end. [from Latin] **2** → see also **faithful**

**fa|ji|ta** /fəhitə/ (**fajitas**) N-COUNT A **fajita** is a Mexican dish consisting of a tortilla wrapped around strips of meat and vegetables. ❑ *...chicken fajitas.* [from Mexican Spanish]

**fake** /feɪk/ (**fakes, faking, faked**) **1** ADJ **Fake** things have been made to look valuable or genuine, although they are not. ❑ *The bank manager issued fake certificates.* ● A **fake** is something that is fake. ❑ *Every one of the works of art is a fake.* **2** V-T If someone **fakes** something, they try to make it look genuine although it is not. ❑ *It's easy to fake a suntan with make-up.* ❑ *...faked evidence.* [from Italian]

**Thesaurus** *fake* Also look up :

ADJ. artificial, counterfeit, imitation **1**
V. falsify, pretend **2**

**fall** /fɔl/ (**falls, falling, fell, fallen**) **1** V-I If someone or something **falls**, they move quickly downward, by accident or because of a natural force. ❑ *He has fallen from his horse.* ❑ *Bombs fell on the town.* **2** V-I If a person or structure that is standing somewhere **falls**, they move from their upright position, so that they are then lying on the ground. ❑ *The woman tried to stop herself from falling.* ❑ *He lost his balance and fell backwards.* ❑ *He broke her right leg in a bad fall.* ● **Fall down** means the same as **fall**. ❑ *I hit him so hard he fell down.* **3** V-I When rain or snow **falls**, it comes down from the sky. **4** V-I When something **falls**, it decreases in amount, value, or strength. ❑ *His income will fall by almost 70 percent.* ❑ *The number of Americans without jobs has fallen to 9.8 million.* ● **Fall** is also a noun. ❑ *...a sharp fall in the value of the dollar.* **5** V-I If a powerful or successful person **falls**, they suddenly lose their power or position. ❑ *Leaders fall, revolutions come and go, but places never really change.* ● **Fall** is also a noun. ❑ *...the fall of the military dictator.* **6** V-I If you say that something or someone **falls into** a particular group or category, you mean that they belong in that group or category. ❑ *The problems fall into two categories.* **7** V-I When light or shadow **falls** on something, it covers it. ❑ *A shadow suddenly fell across the doorway.* **8** V-I When night or darkness **falls**, night begins and it becomes dark. ❑ *As darkness fell outside, they sat down to eat.* **9** V-LINK You can use **fall** to show that someone or something passes into another state. For example, if someone **falls ill**, they become ill. ❑ *It is almost impossible to visit Florida without falling in love with it.*

*Shakespeare's tragic heroine, Desdemona, fell victim to the jealousy of her husband.* **10** N-PLURAL You can refer to a **waterfall** as the **falls**. **11** N-VAR **Fall** is the season between summer and winter when the weather becomes cooler. □ *...the fall of 1991.* [from Old English] **12** → see also **fallen** **13** to **fall foul of** → see **foul** **14** to **fall flat** → see **flat** **15** to **fall into place** → see **place**

▶ **fall apart** **1** PHR-VERB If something **falls apart**, it breaks into pieces because it is old or badly made. □ *Bit by bit the building fell apart.* **2** PHR-VERB If an organization or system **falls apart**, it becomes disorganized and inefficient. □ *Europe's monetary system is falling apart.*

▶ **fall back on** PHR-VERB If you **fall back on** something, you do it or use it after other things have failed. □ *When things get tricky, you fall back on your experience.*

▶ **fall behind** PHR-VERB If you **fall behind**, you do not make progress or move forward as fast as other people. □ *He is falling behind all the top players.*

▶ **fall for** **1** PHR-VERB If you **fall for** someone, you are strongly attracted to them and start loving them. □ *I just fell for him right away.* **2** PHR-VERB If you **fall for** a lie or trick, you believe it or are deceived by it. □ *He pretended he was famous, but none of us fell for it.*

▶ **fall off** PHR-VERB If something **falls off**, it separates from the thing to which it was attached. □ *When the exhaust pipe falls off your car, you have to replace it.*

▶ **fall out** **1** PHR-VERB If a person's hair or a tooth **falls out**, it comes out. **2** PHR-VERB If you **fall out** with someone, you have an argument and stop being friendly with them. You can also say that two people **fall out**. □ *She fell out with her husband.* **3** → see also **fallout**

▶ **fall through** PHR-VERB If an arrangement, plan, or deal **falls through**, it fails to happen. □ *They wanted to turn the estate into a private golf course, but the deal fell through.*

▶ **fall to** PHR-VERB If a responsibility, duty, or opportunity **falls to** someone, it becomes their responsibility, duty, or opportunity. □ *It fell to me to make a speech.*

| Thesaurus | *fall* | Also look up : |
| --- | --- | --- |
| v. | fall down, plunge, topple **1** **2** | |
| | come down **3** | |
| | drop, plunge; (*ant.*) increase, rise **4** | |

**fal|la|cy** /fǽləsi/ (**fallacies**) N-VAR A **fallacy** is an idea which many people believe to be true, but which is in fact false. □ *It's a fallacy that you can't earn money by doing what you really like.* [from Latin]

**fall|en** /fɔ́lən/ **Fallen** is the past participle of **fall**. [from Old English]

**fal|lo|pian tube** /fəlóupiən tub/ (**fallopian tubes**) N-COUNT A woman's **fallopian tubes** are the two tubes in her body along which eggs pass from her ovaries to her womb.

**fall|out** /fɔ́laʊt/ N-UNCOUNT **Fallout** is the radiation that affects a place after a nuclear explosion. □ *...radioactive fallout.*

**false** /fɔls/ **1** ADJ If something is **false**, it is incorrect, untrue, or mistaken. □ *The president received false information from those around him.* □ *You do not know whether what you're told is true or false.* ● **false|ly** ADV □ *She falsely accused him of the crime.* **2** ADJ You use **false** to describe objects which are artificial but which are intended to look like the real thing or to be used instead of the real thing. □ *...a set of false teeth.* **3** ADJ If you describe a person or their behavior as **false**, you are criticizing them for being insincere or for hiding their real feelings. □ *"Thank you," she said with false enthusiasm.* ● **false|ly** ADV □ *They smiled at one another, somewhat falsely.* [from Old English]

**false alarm** (**false alarms**) N-COUNT When you think something dangerous is about to happen, but then discover that you were mistaken, you can say that it was a **false alarm**. □ *The bomb threat turned out to be a false alarm.*

**false cau|sal|ity** N-UNCOUNT In logic, **false causality** is an error that occurs when one event is wrongly considered to be the cause of another event. [TECHNICAL]

**false start** (**false starts**) N-COUNT A **false start** is an attempt to start something, such as a speech, project, or plan, which fails because you were not properly prepared or ready to begin. □ *There was a false start because the singer's microphone was turned off.*

**fal|si|fy** /fɔ́lsɪfaɪ/ (**falsifies, falsifying, falsified**) V-T If someone **falsifies** something, they change it or add untrue details to it in order to deceive people. □ *The charges against him include falsifying business records.* [from Old French]

**fal|ter** /fɔ́ltər/ (**falters, faltering, faltered**) **1** V-I If something **falters**, it weakens and seems likely to collapse or to stop. □ *The economy is faltering.* **2** V-I If you **falter**, you hesitate and become unsure or unsteady. □ *So far loyal Mary has not faltered in her support.* [of Scandinavian origin]

**fame** /feɪm/ N-UNCOUNT If you achieve **fame**, you become very well-known. □ *The film earned him international fame.* [from Latin]

### Word Partnership Use *fame* with :

| | |
| --- | --- |
| v. | **bring** fame, **gain** fame, **rise to** fame |
| N. | **claim to** fame, fame **and fortune, hall of** fame |
| ADJ. | **international** fame |

**famed** /feɪmd/ ADJ If people, places, or things are **famed for** a particular thing, they are very well known for it. □ *The city is famed for its outdoor restaurants.* [from Latin]

**fa|mili|ar** /fəmɪ́lyər/ **1** ADJ If someone or something is **familiar** to you, you recognize them or know them well. □ *...a culture that was quite familiar to him.* □ *They are already familiar faces on our TV screens.* ● **fa|mili|ar|ity** /fəmɪliǽrɪti/ N-UNCOUNT □ *...the comforting familiarity of her face.* **2** ADJ If you are **familiar with** something, you know or understand it well. □ *Are you familiar with the region?* ● **fa|mili|ar|ity** N-UNCOUNT □ *...familiarity with advanced technology.* **3** ADJ If someone you do not know well behaves in a **familiar** way toward you, they treat you very informally in a way that you might find offensive. □ *The women suggested that his behavior was "too familiar."* ● **fa|mili|ar|ity** N-UNCOUNT □ *She spoke to the waiter with easy familiarity.* ● **fa|mili|ar|ly** ADV □ *"Gerald, isn't it?" I began familiarly.* [from Latin]

**fa|mili|ar|ly** /fəmɪ́lyərli/ PHRASE If you say that something or someone is **familiarly known as** a

## Picture Dictionary   family

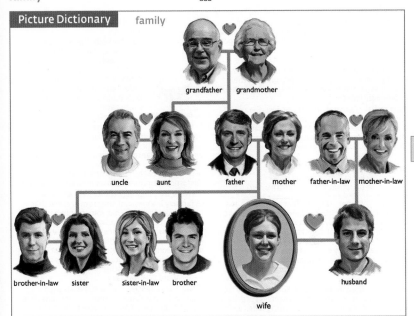

grandfather    grandmother

uncle    aunt    father    mother    father-in-law    mother-in-law

brother-in-law    sister    sister-in-law    brother       husband

wife

f

particular thing or **familiarly called** a particular thing, you are giving the name that people use informally to refer to it or them. ❑ ...*Ann Hamilton's father, familiarly known as "Hank."* [from Latin]

**fam|i|ly** /fǽmɪli, fǽmli/ (**families**) **1** N-COUNT A **family** is a group of people who are related to each other, especially parents and their children. ❑ ...*a family of five.* ❑ *Does he have any family?* **2** N-COUNT When people talk about their **family,** they sometimes mean their ancestors. ❑ *My father's family came from Ireland.* **3** N-COUNT A **family** of animals or plants is a group of related species. [from Latin]
→ see Picture Dictionary: **family**

**fam|i|ly plan|ning** N-UNCOUNT **Family planning** is the practice of using contraception to control the number of children you have. ❑ ...*a family planning clinic.*

**fam|i|ly room** (**family rooms**) N-COUNT A **family room** in a house is a room where a family watches television or plays games. ❑ *The present owners added a new kitchen, a front porch and a family room.*

**fam|i|ly val|ues** N-PLURAL People sometimes refer to traditional moral values and standards as **family values.** ❑ *Reverend Jackson called for a return to family values.*

**fam|ine** /fǽmɪn/ (**famines**) N-VAR **Famine** is a situation in which large numbers of people have little or no food, and many of them die. ❑ ...*refugees trapped by war and famine.* [from Old French]

**fa|mous** /féɪməs/ ADJ Someone or something that is **famous** is very well known. ❑ ...*one of Kentucky's most famous landmarks.* [from Latin]

**Thesaurus**    *famous*    Also look up :

ADJ.   acclaimed, celebrated, prominent, renowned; (*ant.*) anonymous, obscure, unknown

**fa|mous|ly** /féɪməsli/ ADV You use **famously** to refer to a fact that is well known, usually because it is remarkable. ❑ ...*a famously modest, reluctant hero.* [from Latin]

**fan** /fǽn/ (**fans, fanning, fanned**) **1** N-COUNT If you are a **fan** of someone or something, you like them very much and are very interested in them. ❑ *If you're a Billy Crystal fan, you'll love this movie.* ❑ *I am a great fan of rave music.* **2** N-COUNT A **fan** is a piece of electrical equipment that keeps a room or machine cool. **3** N-COUNT A **fan** is a flat object that you wave to keep yourself cool. **4** V-T If you **fan** yourself when you are hot, you wave a fan or other flat object in order to make yourself feel cooler. ❑ *She waited in the truck, fanning herself with a piece of cardboard.* [Senses 2–4 from Old English.]

fan

→ see **concert**

▶ **fan out** PHR-VERB If a group of people or things **fan out,** they move forward away from a particular point in different directions. ❑ *The troops have fanned out to the west.*

**fa|nat|ic** /fənǽtɪk/ (**fanatics**) **1** N-COUNT If you describe someone as a **fanatic,** you disapprove of them because you think their behavior or opinions are very extreme. ❑ *I am not a religious* *fanatic but I am a Christian.* ● **fa|nati|cal** ADJ ❑ *They're fanatical about what they eat.* **2** N-COUNT If you say that someone is a **fanatic**, you mean that they are very enthusiastic about a particular activity, sport, or way of life. ❑ *…football fanatics.* **3** ADJ **Fanatic** means the same as **fanatical**. [from Latin]

**fan base** (**fan bases**) also **fanbase** N-COUNT The **fan base** of a pop star or a pop group is their fans, considered as a whole. ❑ *His fan base is mostly middle-aged ladies.*

**fan|ci|ful** /fǽnsɪfəl/ ADJ If you describe an idea as **fanciful**, you disapprove of it because you think it comes from someone's imagination, and is therefore unrealistic or unlikely to be true. ❑ *…fanciful ideas about life on Mars.*

---

### fancy

❶ ELABORATE OR EXPENSIVE
❷ WANTING, LIKING, OR THINKING

---

❶ **fan|cy** /fǽnsi/ (**fancier, fanciest**) **1** ADJ If you describe something as **fancy**, you mean that it is special, unusual, or elaborate, for example because it has a lot of decoration. ❑ *…fancy jewelry.* **2** ADJ If you describe something as **fancy**, you mean that it is very expensive or of very high quality, and you often dislike it because of this. [INFORMAL] ❑ *My parents sent me to a fancy private school.*

❷ **fan|cy** /fǽnsi/ **1** EXCLAM You say "**fancy**" or "**fancy that**" when you want to express surprise or disapproval. **2** PHRASE If something **takes** your **fancy**, you like it a lot when you see it or think of it. ❑ *She makes her own clothes, copying any fashion which takes her fancy.*

**fan|fare** /fǽnfɛər/ (**fanfares**) N-COUNT A **fanfare** is a short, loud tune played on trumpets to announce a special event. [from French]

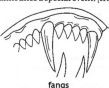

fangs

**fang** /fǽŋ/ (**fangs**) N-COUNT **Fangs** are the two long, sharp, upper teeth that some animals have. ❑ *…the snake's venomous fangs.* [from Old English]

**fan mail** N-UNCOUNT **Fan mail** is mail that is sent to a famous person by their fans.

**fan|ny pack** (**fanny packs**) N-COUNT A **fanny pack** is a small bag attached to a belt which you

fanny pack

wear around your waist. You use it to carry things such as money and keys.

**fan|ta|size** /fǽntəsaɪz/ (**fantasizes, fantasizing, fantasized**) V-I If you **fantasize** about something, you give yourself pleasure by imagining it, although it is unlikely to happen. ❑ *I fantasized about writing music.* [from Latin]

**fan|tas|tic** /fæntǽstɪk/ **1** ADJ If you say that something is **fantastic**, you are emphasizing that you think it is very good. [INFORMAL] ❑ *I have a fantastic social life.* **2** ADJ A **fantastic** amount or quantity is an extremely large one. ❑ *…fantastic sums of money.* ● **fan|tas|ti|cal|ly** /fæntǽstɪkli/ ADV ❑ *…a fantastically expensive restaurant.* [from Late Latin]

**fan|ta|sy** /fǽntəsi/ (**fantasies**) **1** N-COUNT A **fantasy** is a pleasant situation or event that you think about and that you want to happen, especially one that is unlikely to happen. ❑ *…fantasies of romance and true love.* **2** N-VAR You can refer to a story or situation that someone creates from their imagination and that is not based on reality as **fantasy**. ❑ *The film is a science-fiction fantasy.* [from Latin]
→ see Word Web: fantasy

**FAQ** /fæk/ (**FAQs**) N-PLURAL **FAQ** is used especially on websites to refer to questions about a particular topic. **FAQ** is an abbreviation for "frequently asked questions."

---

### far

❶ DISTANT IN SPACE OR TIME
❷ THE EXTENT TO WHICH SOMETHING HAPPENS
❸ EMPHATIC USES

---

**Far** has two comparatives, **farther** and **further**, and two superlatives, **farthest** and **furthest**. **Farther** and **farthest** are used mainly in sense **1**, and are dealt with here. **Further** and **furthest** are dealt with in separate entries.

❶ **far** /fɑr/ **1** ADV If one place, thing, or person is **far** away from another, there is a great distance between them. ❑ *He was too far from the car to go back now.* ❑ *My sisters moved even farther away from home.* **2** ADV You use **far** in questions and statements about distances. ❑ *How far is it to San*

---

## Word Web    fantasy

All **fictional** writing involves the use of **imaginary** situations and characters. However, **fantasy** goes even further. This **genre** uses more **imagination** than **reality**. Authors create new creatures, **myths**, and **legends**. A **novelist** may use **realistic** people and settings. But a fantasy writer is free to create a whole different world where earthly laws no longer apply. Contemporary movies have found a rich source

of stories in the genre. Today you can see many different films about **fairies**, **wizards**, and **dragons**.

## Word Web    farm

Farmers no longer simply plant a **crop** and **harvest** it. Today's **farmer** uses engineering and technology to make a living. Careful **irrigation** and **drainage** control the amount of water **plants** receive. **Insecticides** and fungicides protect plants from insects. **Fertilizers** make things grow. High-tech **agricultural** methods may increase the world's **food** supply. Using **hydroponic** methods, farmers use **chemical** solutions to **cultivate** plants. This has several advantages. **Soil** can contain **pests** and diseases not present in water alone. Growing plants hydroponically also requires less water and less labor than conventional growing methods.

*Francisco?* ❑ *She followed the tracks as far as the road.* **3** ADV A time or event that is **far** away in the future or the past is a long time from the present or from a particular point in time. ❑ *...conflicts whose roots lie far back in time.* ❑ *I can't plan any farther than the next six months.* **4** ADJ You can use **far** to refer to the part of an area or object that is the greatest distance from the center in a particular direction. ❑ *Port Angeles is in the far north of Washington State.* [from Old English] **5 near and far → see near**

**❷ far** /fɑr/ **1** ADV You can use **far** to talk about the extent to which something happens. ❑ *How far did the film tell the truth about his life?* **2** ADV You can talk about how **far** someone or something gets to describe the progress that they make. ❑ *Discussions never progressed very far.* ❑ *Think of how far we have come in a short time.* **3** ADV You can talk about how **far** a person or action goes to describe the degree to which someone's behavior or actions are extreme. ❑ *This time he's gone too far.* **4** PHRASE If you talk about what has happened **so far**, you talk about what has happened up until the present point in a situation or story. ❑ *So far, they have failed.* [from Old English]

**❸ far** /fɑr/ **1** ADV You can use **far** to mean "very much" when you are comparing two things and emphasizing the difference between them. ❑ *Women who eat a healthy diet are far less likely to suffer anxiety.* ❑ *The police say the response has been far better than expected.* **2** PHRASE You use the expression **by far** when you are comparing something or someone with others of the same kind, in order to emphasize how great the difference is between them. ❑ *By far the most important issue for them is unemployment.* **3** PHRASE If you say that something is **far from** a particular thing or **far from** being true, you are emphasizing that it is not that particular thing or not true at all. ❑ *Much of what they said was far from the truth.* ❑ *Far from being relaxed, we both felt very uncomfortable.* [from Old English]

**far|away** /fɑrəweɪ/ ADJ A **faraway** place is a long distance from you or from a particular place. ❑ *...photographs of a faraway country.* [from Old English]

**farce** /fɑrs/ (**farces**) **1** N-COUNT A **farce** is a humorous play in which the characters become involved in complicated and unlikely situations. **2** N-SING If you describe a situation or event as a **farce**, you disapprove of it and think it is so disorganized or ridiculous that you cannot take it seriously. ❑ *The elections have been reduced to a farce.* ● **far|ci|cal** ADJ ❑ *...a farcical nine months' jail sentence for a killer.* [from Old French]

**fare** /fɛər/ (**fares, faring, fared**) **1** N-COUNT A **fare** is the money that you pay for a trip that you make, for example, in a bus, train, or taxi. ❑ *He could not afford the fare.* **2** V-I If you say that someone or something **fares** well or badly, you are referring to the degree of success they have in a particular situation or activity. ❑ *Of course, some vice presidents fare better than others.* [from Old English]
→ see also **fair**

**Far East** N-PROPER The **Far East** consists of all the countries of Eastern Asia, including China, Japan, North and South Korea, and Indonesia.

**far-fetched** ADJ If you describe a story or idea as **far-fetched**, you are criticizing it because you think it is unlikely to be true or practical.

**farm** /fɑrm/ (**farms, farming, farmed**) **1** N-COUNT A **farm** is an area of land, together with the buildings on it, that is used for growing crops or raising animals. ❑ *Both boys like to work on the farm.* **2** V-T/V-I If you **farm** an area of land, you grow crops or keep animals on it. ❑ *They farmed some of the best land in the country.* ❑ *Bease has been farming for 30 years.* [from Old French]
→ see Word Web: **farm**
→ see **dairy**

**farm|er** /fɑrmər/ (**farmers**) N-COUNT A **farmer** is a person who owns or manages a farm. [from Old French]
→ see **farm**

**farm|house** /fɑrmhaʊs/ (**farmhouses**) N-COUNT A **farmhouse** is the main house on a farm, and is usually where the farmer lives.

**farm|ing** /fɑrmɪŋ/ N-UNCOUNT **Farming** is the activity of growing crops or keeping animals on a farm. [from Old French]

**farm|land** /fɑrmlænd/ N-UNCOUNT **Farmland** is land which is farmed, or which is suitable for farming.

**farm|yard** /fɑrmyɑrd/ (**farmyards**) N-COUNT On a farm, the **farmyard** is an area of land near the farmhouse which is enclosed by walls or buildings. [from Old French]

**far off** (**further off, furthest off**) **1** ADJ **Far-off** time is a long way in the future or past. ❑ *In those far-off days no one imagined that a woman could be prime minister.* **2** ADJ A **far-off** place is a long distance away. ❑ *...far-off galaxies.* ❑ *The woman was too far off to hear.* ● **Far off** is also an adverb. ❑ *The band was playing far off.*

**far-reaching** ADJ **Far-reaching** actions, events, or changes have a very great influence and affect a great number of things. ❑ *New technology can have* *far-reaching effects on society.*

**Farsi** /fɑrsi/ N-UNCOUNT **Farsi** is a language that is spoken in Iran. [from Arabic]

**far-sighted** ADJ **Far-sighted** people cannot see things clearly that are close to them, and therefore need to wear glasses.

**far|ther** /fɑrðər/ **Farther** is a comparative of **far**.

**far|thest** /fɑrðɪst/ **Farthest** is a superlative of **far**.

**fas|ci|nate** /fæsɪneɪt/ (**fascinates, fascinating, fascinated**) V-T If something **fascinates** you, you find it extremely interesting. □ *Politics fascinated Franklin's father.* [from Latin]

**fas|ci|nat|ed** /fæsɪneɪtɪd/ ADJ If you are **fascinated by** something, you find it extremely interesting. □ *I am fascinated by cities.* [from Latin]

**fas|ci|nat|ing** /fæsɪneɪtɪŋ/ ADJ If you describe something as **fascinating**, you find it extremely interesting. □ *Madagascar is a fascinating place.* [from Latin]

**fas|ci|na|tion** /fæsɪneɪʃ°n/ N-UNCOUNT **Fascination** is the state of being extremely interested in something. □ *I've had a lifelong fascination with the sea.* [from Latin]

**fas|cist** /fæʃɪst/ (**fascists**) ADJ Someone with **fascist** views has right-wing political beliefs that include strong control by the state and a powerful role for the armed forces. □ *...extreme fascist organizations.* ● A **fascist** is someone who has fascist views. ● **fas|cism** N-UNCOUNT □ *...the rise of fascism in the 1930s.* [from Italian]

**fash|ion** /fæʃ°n/ (**fashions**) **1** N-UNCOUNT **Fashion** is the area of activity that involves styles of clothing and appearance. □ *...20 full-color pages of fashion for men.* **2** N-COUNT A **fashion** is a style of clothing or a way of behaving that is popular at a particular time. □ *Long dresses were in fashion back then.* **3** N-SING If you do something **in** a particular **fashion** or **after** a particular **fashion**, you do it in that way. □ *According to investigators, all of the fires were set in a similar fashion.* **4** → see also **old-fashioned 5** PHRASE If something is **in fashion**, it is popular and approved of at a particular time. If it is **out of fashion**, it is not popular or approved of. □ *That sort of house is back in fashion.* [from Old French]

**fash|ion|able** /fæʃənəb°l/ ADJ Something or someone that is **fashionable** is popular or approved of at a particular time. □ *It became fashionable to eat certain kinds of fish.* ● **fash|ion|ably** ADV □ *She is fashionably dressed.* [from Old French]

**fast** /fæst/ (**faster, fastest, fasts, fasting, fasted**) **1** ADJ **Fast** means happening, moving, or doing something at great speed. You also use **fast** in questions or statements about speed. □ *fast cars.* □ *How fast will the process will be?* ADV ● **Fast** is also an adverb. □ *They work terrifically fast.* □ *It would be nice to go faster and break the world record.* **2** ADJ If a watch or clock is **fast**, it is showing a time that is later than the real time. □ *That clock's an hour fast.* **3** ADV You use **fast** to say that something happens without any delay. □ *You need professional help — fast!* ● **Fast** is also an adjective. □ *...surprisingly fast action by Congress.* **4** ADV If you hold something **fast**, you hold it tightly and firmly. If something is stuck **fast**, it is stuck very firmly and cannot move. □ *She climbed the staircase cautiously, holding fast to the rail.* **5** ADV If you hold **fast** to a principle or idea, or if you stand **fast**, you do not change your mind about it, even though people are trying to persuade you to. □ *We try to hold fast to the values of honesty and concern for others.* **6** V-I If you **fast**, you eat no food for a period of time, usually for either religious or medical reasons, or as a protest. ● **Fast** is also a noun. □ *The fast is over at sunset.* **7** PHRASE Someone who is **fast asleep** is completely asleep. □ *When he went upstairs five minutes later, she was fast asleep.* [from Old English] **8** to **make a fast buck** → see **buck**

| Thesaurus | | *fast* | Also look up : |
| --- | --- | --- | --- |
| ADJ. | hasty, quick, rapid, speedy, swift; (ant.) leisurely, slow **1** | | |
| ADV. | quickly, rapidly, soon, swiftly; (ant.) leisurely, slowly **1** | | |
| | firmly, tightly; (ant.) loosely, unsteadily **4** | | |

**fas|ten** /fæs°n/ (**fastens, fastening, fastened**) **1** V-T/V-I When you **fasten** something, you close it by means of buttons or a strap, or some other device. If something **fastens** with buttons or straps, you can close it in this way. □ *She got quickly into her car and fastened the seat-belt.* □ *Her long hair was fastened at her neck by an elastic band.* **2** V-T If you **fasten** one thing **to** another, you attach the first thing to the second. □ *...instructions on how to fasten the strap to the box.* [from Old English] **3** → see also **fastening**

**fas|ten|ing** /fæsənɪŋ/ (**fastenings**) N-COUNT A **fastening** is something such as a clasp or zipper that you use to fasten something. □ *The dress has a back zipper fastening.* [from Old English]

**fast food** N-UNCOUNT **Fast food** is hot food, such as hamburgers and French fries, which is served quickly after you order it.
→ see **meal**

**fas|tidi|ous** /fæstɪdiəs, fə-/ ADJ If you say that someone is **fastidious**, you mean that they pay great attention to detail because they like everything to be very neat and in good order. □ *He was fastidious about his appearance.* [from Latin]

**fast lane** (**fast lanes**) **1** N-COUNT On a highway, the **fast lane** is the part of the road where the vehicles that are traveling fastest go. **2** N-SING If someone is living **in the fast lane**, they have a very busy, exciting life, although they sometimes seem to take a lot of risks. □ *...a tale of life in the fast lane.*

**fat** /fæt/ (**fats, fatter, fattest**) **1** ADJ A **fat** person has a lot of flesh on his or her body and weighs too much. □ *I ate what I liked and began to get fat.* ● **fat|ness** N-UNCOUNT □ *...an increase in fatness in adults.* **2** N-VAR **Fat** is a substance contained in foods such as meat, cheese, and butter which stores energy in your body. □ *Cut the amount of fat in your diet by avoiding red meats.* **3** N-VAR **Fat** is a solid or liquid substance obtained from animals or vegetables, which is used in cooking. □ *Use as little oil or fat as possible.* **4** ADJ A **fat** object, especially a book, is very thick or wide. **5** N-UNCOUNT **Fat** is the extra flesh that animals and humans have under their skin, which is used to store energy and to help keep them warm. □ *If you don't exercise, everything you eat turns to fat.* [from Old English]
→ see **calorie**

| Thesaurus | *fat* | Also look up : |
|---|---|---|
| ADJ. | big, chunky, heavy, obese, overweight, stout, thick; (*ant.*) lean, skinny, slim, thin 1 | |

**fa|tal** /feɪtᵊl/ 1 ADJ A **fatal** action has very undesirable effects. ❑ *He made the fatal mistake of lending her some money.* • **fa|tal|ly** ADV ❑ *This could fatally damage his chances of becoming president.* 2 ADJ A **fatal** accident or illness causes someone's death. ❑ *...the fatal stabbing of a police officer.* • **fa|tal|ly** ADV ❑ *The soldier was fatally wounded in the chest.* [from Old French]

**fa|tal|ity** /fətælɪti/ (**fatalities**) N-COUNT A **fatality** is a death caused by an accident or by violence. [FORMAL] ❑ *...rising highway fatalities.* [from Old French]

**fate** /feɪt/ (**fates**) 1 N-UNCOUNT **Fate** is a power that some people believe controls and decides everything that happens. ❑ *I believe in fate and that things happen for a reason.* 2 N-COUNT A person's or thing's **fate** is what happens to them. ❑ *His fate is now in the hands of the governor.* [from Latin]

**fate|ful** /feɪtfəl/ ADJ If you describe an action or a time when something happened as **fateful**, you mean that it had an important, and often very bad, effect on future events. ❑ *...the fateful decision to drop the bombs.* [from Latin]

**fa|ther** /fɑðər/ (**fathers, fathering, fathered**) 1 N-COUNT Your **father** is your male parent. ❑ *His father was a painter.* 2 V-T When a man **fathers** a child, he makes a woman pregnant and their child is born. ❑ *She claims Mark fathered her child.* 3 N-COUNT The man who invented or started something is sometimes referred to as the **father of** that thing. ❑ *...Max Dupain, the father of modern photography.* [from Old English]
→ see **family**

**father|hood** /fɑðərhʊd/ N-UNCOUNT **Fatherhood** is the state of being a father. ❑ *...the joys of fatherhood.* [from Old English]

**father-in-law** (**fathers-in-law**) N-COUNT Your **father-in-law** is the father of your husband or wife.
→ see **family**

**fath|om** /fæðəm/ (**fathoms, fathoming, fathomed**) 1 N-COUNT A **fathom** is a measurement of 6 feet or 1.8 meters, used when referring to the depth of water. ❑ *They found the wrecked boat in only fifteen fathoms of water.* 2 V-T If you cannot **fathom** something, you are unable to understand it, although you think carefully about it. ❑ *I really couldn't fathom what Steiner was talking about.* • **Fathom out** means the same as **fathom.** ❑ *We're trying to fathom out what's going on.* [from Old English]

**fa|tigue** /fətiɡ/ (**fatigues**) 1 N-UNCOUNT **Fatigue** is a feeling of extreme physical or mental tiredness. ❑ *She continued to have severe stomach cramps and fatigue.* 2 N-PLURAL **Fatigues** are clothes that soldiers wear when they are fighting or when they are doing routine jobs. [from French]

**fat|so** /fætsoʊ/ (**fatsos** or **fatsoes**) N-COUNT; N-VOC If someone calls another person a **fatso**, they are saying in an unkind way that the person is fat. [INFORMAL]

**fat|ten|ing** /fætᵊnɪŋ/ ADJ Food that is **fattening** is considered to make people fat easily. ❑ *Hamburgers and French fries are fattening.* [from Old English]

**fat|ty** /fæti/ (**fattier, fattiest**) 1 ADJ **Fatty** food contains a lot of fat. ❑ *Don't eat fatty food or chocolates.* 2 ADJ **Fatty** acids or **fatty** tissues contain a lot of fat. [from Old English]

**fau|cet** /fɔsɪt/ (**faucets**) N-COUNT A **faucet** is a device that controls the flow of a liquid or gas from a pipe or container. Sinks and baths have faucets attached to them. ❑ *She turned off the faucet and dried her hands.* [from Old French]
→ see **bathroom**

**fault** /fɔlt/ (**faults, faulting, faulted**) 1 N-SING If a bad or undesirable situation is your **fault**, you caused it or are responsible for it. ❑ *The accident was my fault.* 2 N-COUNT A **fault** in someone or something is a weakness in them or something that is not perfect. ❑ *His manners made her forget his faults.* 3 N-COUNT A **fault** is a large crack in the surface of the Earth. ❑ *...the San Andreas Fault.* 4 V-T If you **cannot fault** someone, you cannot find any reason for criticizing them or the things that they are doing. ❑ *You can't fault their determination.* 5 PHRASE If someone or something is **at fault**, they are responsible for something that has gone wrong. ❑ *He could not accept that he was at fault.* 6 PHRASE If you **find fault with** something or someone, you complain about them. ❑ *He says you're always finding fault with him.* [from Old French]
→ see **earthquake**

| Thesaurus | *fault* | Also look up : |
|---|---|---|
| N. | blunder, error, mistake, wrongdoing 1<br>defect, flaw, imperfection, weakness 2 | |

**fault block** (**fault blocks**) N-COUNT A **fault block** is a large area of rock that is separated from other rock by faults in the Earth's surface. [TECHNICAL]

**fault-block moun|tain** (**fault-block mountains**) N-COUNT A **fault-block mountain** is a mountain that is formed when the land between two fault lines rises up or the land outside the fault lines drops down. [TECHNICAL]

**fault|less** /fɔltlɪs/ ADJ Something that is **faultless** is perfect and has no mistakes at all. ❑ *...Mary Thomson's faultless performance.* [from Old French]

**faulty** /fɔlti/ ADJ A **faulty** piece of equipment has something wrong with it and is not working properly. ❑ *The money will be used to repair faulty equipment.* [from Old French]

**fau|na** /fɔnə/ N-UNCOUNT Animals, especially the animals in a particular area, can be referred to as **fauna.** [TECHNICAL] ❑ *...the flora and fauna of the African jungle.* [from New Latin]

**fava bean** /fɑvəbin/ (**fava beans**) N-COUNT **Fava beans** are flat round beans that are light green in color and are eaten as a vegetable. [from Italian]

**fa|vor** /feɪvər/ (**favors, favoring, favored**) 1 N-UNCOUNT If you regard something or someone with **favor**, you like or support them. ❑ *She wished that she could look with favor on her new boss.* 2 N-COUNT If you **do** someone **a favor**, you do something to help them even though you do not have to. ❑ *I've come to ask you to do me a favor.* 3 V-T If you **favor** something, you prefer it to the other

f

choices available. ❑ *The majority of Americans favor raising taxes on the rich.* **4** V-T If you **favor** someone, you treat them better or in a kinder way than you treat other people. ❑ *The company favors U.S. citizens.* **5** PHRASE If you are **in favor of** something, you support it and think that it is a good thing. ❑ *I wouldn't be in favor of income tax cuts.* **6** PHRASE If someone makes a judgment **in** your **favor**, they say that you are right about something. ❑ *The Supreme Court ruled in Fitzgerald's favor.* **7** PHRASE If something is **in** your **favor**, it helps you or gives you an advantage. ❑ *This is a career where age works in your favor.* **8** PHRASE If one thing is rejected **in favor of** another, the second thing is done or chosen instead of the first. ❑ *The writing program is being rejected in favor of computer classes.* **9** PHRASE If someone or something is **in favor**, people like or support them. If they are **out of favor**, people no longer like or support them. ❑ *Governments only remain in favor with the public for so long.* [from Latin]

F

**fa|vor|able** /feɪvərəbᵊl/ **1** ADJ If your opinion or your reaction is **favorable** to something, you agree with it and approve of it. ❑ *The president's speech received favorable reviews.* **2** ADJ **Favorable** conditions make something more likely to succeed or seem more attractive. ❑ *Under favorable conditions, these tiny cells divide every 22 minutes.* **3** ADJ If you make a **favorable** comparison between two things, you say that the first is better than or as good as the second. [from Latin]

**fa|vor|ite** /feɪvərɪt, feɪvrɪt/ (**favorites**) **1** ADJ Your **favorite** thing or person is the one you like most. ❑ *...his favorite music.* • **Favorite** is also a noun. ❑ *That hotel is my favorite.* **2** N-COUNT The **favorite** in a race or contest is the competitor that is expected to win. ❑ *The U.S. team is one of the favorites in next month's games.* [from Italian]

**fa|vor|it|ism** /feɪvərɪtɪzəm, feɪvrɪt-/ N-UNCOUNT If you accuse someone of **favoritism**, you disapprove of them because they unfairly help or favor one person or group much more than another. ❑ *Maria loved both the children. There was never a hint of favoritism.* [from Italian]

**fawn** /fɔn/ (**fawns**) **1** N-COUNT A **fawn** is a very young deer. **2** COLOR **Fawn** is a pale yellowish-brown color. [from Old French]

**fax** /fæks/ (**faxes, faxing, faxed**) **1** N-COUNT A **fax** or a **fax machine** is a piece of equipment used to send and receive documents electronically using a telephone line. **2** N-COUNT You can refer to a copy of a document that is sent or received by a fax machine as a **fax**. ❑ *I sent him a long fax.* **3** V-T If you **fax** a document to someone, you send it from one fax machine to another. ❑ *I faxed a copy of the agreement to each of the investors.* ❑ *Did you fax him a reply?*

**FDA** /ɛf di eɪ/ N-PROPER **FDA** is an abbreviation for **Food and Drug Administration.** ❑ *The FDA has approved a new treatment for a rare blood disorder.*

**fear** /fɪər/ (**fears, fearing, feared**) **1** N-VAR **Fear** is the unpleasant feeling you have when you think that you are in danger. ❑ *I sat shivering with fear because a bullet was fired through a window.* **2** N-VAR A **fear** is a thought that something unpleasant might happen or might have happened. ❑ *These youngsters have a fear of failure.* ❑ *His worst fears were confirmed.* **3** N-VAR If you have **fears for** someone or something, you are very worried because you think that they might be in danger. ❑ *He also spoke of his fears for the future of his country.* **4** V-T If you **fear** something unpleasant or undesirable, you are worried that it might happen or might have happened. ❑ *She feared she was losing her memory.* **5** V-I If you **fear for** someone or something, you are very worried because you think that they might be in danger. ❑ *Carla fears for her son.* **6** PHRASE If you do not do something **for fear of** another thing happening, you do not do it because you do not wish that other thing to happen. ❑ *He did not move his feet for fear of making a noise.* [from Old English]

→ see **emotion**

**Thesaurus** *fear* Also look up:

N. alarm, dread, panic, terror **1**
concern, worry **2**

**Word Partnership** Use *fear* with:

ADJ. **constant** fear **1**
**irrational** fear **1 2**
**worst** fear **2**
V. **face** ***your*** fear, **hide** ***your*** fear, **live in** fear, ***your*** fear **1 2**
N. fear **of failure**, fear **of rejection**, fear **of the unknown 2**
fear **change, nothing to** fear, fear **the worst 4**

**fear|ful** /fɪərfəl/ **1** ADJ If you are **fearful of** something, you are afraid of it. [FORMAL] ❑ *Bankers were fearful of a world banking crisis.* **2** ADJ You use **fearful** to emphasize how serious or bad a situation is. [FORMAL] ❑ *The world's in such a fearful mess.* [from Old English]

**fear|less** /fɪərlɪs/ ADJ If you say that someone is **fearless**, you mean that they are not afraid at all, and you admire them for this. ❑ *...his fearless campaigning for racial justice.* [from Old English]

**Word Link** ***some ≈ causing : awesome, fearsome, troublesome***

**fear|some** /fɪərsəm/ ADJ **Fearsome** is used to describe things that are frightening. ❑ *He had a fearsome reputation for threatening people.* [from Old English]

**fea|sible** /fizəbᵊl/ ADJ If something is **feasible**, it can be done. ❑ *She questioned whether it was feasible to travel to these regions.* • **fea|sibil|ity** /fizəbɪlɪti/ N-UNCOUNT ❑ *They discussed the feasibility of building a stadium in downtown Los Angeles.* [from Latin]

**feast** /fist/ (**feasts, feasting, feasted**) **1** N-COUNT A **feast** is a large and special meal. ❑ *...wedding feasts.* **2** V-I If you **feast on** a particular food, you eat a large amount of it with great enjoyment. ❑ *They feasted on Indian food.* **3** V-I If you **feast**, you take part in a feast. ❑ *They feasted in the castle's main hall.* [from Old French]

**feat** /fit/ (**feats**) N-COUNT If you refer to something as a **feat**, you admire it because it is an impressive and difficult achievement. ❑ *A racing car is an extraordinary feat of engineering.* [from Anglo-French]

**feath|er** /fɛðər/ (**feathers**) **1** N-COUNT A bird's **feathers** are the light soft things covering its body. ❑ *...black ostrich feathers.* [from Old English] **2** → see also **feathered**

→ see **bird**

feather

**feath|ered** /fɛðərd/ ADJ
**Feathered** things have feathers on them. ❑ ...*the lady in the feathered hat.* [from Old English]

**fea|ture** /fitʃər/ (**features, featuring, featured**) **1** N-COUNT
A **feature of** something is an interesting or important part or characteristic of it. ❑ *The flower gardens are a special feature of this property.* **2** N-COUNT A **feature** is a special article in a newspaper or magazine, or a special program on radio or television. ❑ *There was a feature on Marvin Gaye in the New York Times.* **3** N-COUNT A **feature** or a **feature** film or movie is a full-length film about a fictional situation. **4** N-PLURAL Your **features** are your eyes, nose, mouth, and other parts of your face. ❑ ...*his mother's fine, delicate features.* **5** V-T When something such as a movie or exhibition **features** a particular person or thing, they are an important part of it. ❑ *The program will feature highlights from recent games.* **6** V-I If someone or something **features in** something such as a show, exhibition, or magazine, they are an important part of it. ❑ *Jon featured in one of the show's most thrilling episodes.* [from Latin]

### Word Partnership
Use *feature* with :

| ADJ. | **key** feature **1** |
| | **special** feature **1 2** |
| | **best** feature, **striking** feature **1 4** |
| | **animated** feature, **double** feature, |
| | **full-length** feature **3** |
| | **facial** feature **4** |

**Feb|ru|ary** /fɛbyuɛri, fɛbru-/ (**Februaries**)
N-VAR **February** is the second month of the year in the Western calendar. ❑ *His exhibition opens on February 5.* [from Latin]

**fe|ces** /fisiz/ N-UNCOUNT **Feces** is the solid waste substance that leaves the body through the anus. [FORMAL] [from Latin]

**fed** /fɛd/ (**feds**) **1** **Fed** is the past tense and past participle of **feed. 2** → see also **fed up 3** N-SING The **Fed** is the **Federal Reserve.** [INFORMAL] ❑ *The Fed has lowered interest rates three times since late October.* **4** N-COUNT The **feds** are federal agents, for example of the American security agency, the FBI. [INFORMAL] [Sense 1 from old English.]

**fed|er|al** /fɛdərəl/ **1** ADJ In a **federal** country or system, a group of states is controlled by a central government. **2** ADJ **Federal** means belonging or relating to the national government of a federal country rather than to one of the states within it. ❑ ...*federal judges.* ● **fed|er|al|ly** ADV ❑ ...*federally-regulated companies.* [from Latin]

**Fed|er|al Re|serve** N-SING In the United States, the **Federal Reserve** is the central banking system, responsible for national financial matters such as interest rates.

**fed|era|tion** /fɛdəreɪʃ°n/ (**federations**)
**1** N-COUNT A **federation** is a federal country. ❑ ...*He is moving to the Russian Federation.* **2** N-COUNT A **federation** is a group of organizations which have joined together for a common purpose. ❑ ...*the American Federation of Government Employees.* [from Latin]

**fed up** ADJ If you are **fed up**, you are unhappy, bored, or tired of something. [INFORMAL] ❑ *He became fed up with city life.*

**fee** /fi/ (**fees**) **1** N-COUNT A **fee** is a sum of money that you pay to be allowed to do something. ❑ *He paid his license fee, and walked out with a new driver's license.* **2** N-COUNT A **fee** is the amount of money that a person or organization is paid for a particular job or service that they provide. ❑ ...*lawyer's fees.* [from Old French]

**fee|ble** /fib°l/ (**feebler, feeblest**) **1** ADJ If you describe someone or something as **feeble**, you mean that they are weak. ❑ *He was old and feeble and was not able to walk far.* ● **fee|bly** ADV ❑ *His left hand moved feebly at his side.* **2** ADJ If you describe something that someone says as **feeble**, you mean that it is not very good or convincing. ❑ ...*a feeble argument.* ● **fee|bly** ADV ❑ *I said "Sorry," very feebly, feeling rather embarrassed.* [from Old French]

**feed** /fid/ (**feeds, feeding, fed**) **1** V-T If you **feed** a person or animal, you give them food. ❑ *We brought along pieces of old bread and fed the birds.* ● **feed|ing** N-UNCOUNT ❑ ...*the feeding of dairy cows.* **2** V-T To **feed** a family or a community means to supply food for them. ❑ *Feeding a hungry family can be expensive.* **3** V-I When an animal **feeds**, it eats or drinks something. ❑ *Some insects feed on wood.* **4** V-T/V-I When a baby **feeds**, or when you **feed** it, it drinks breast milk or milk from a bottle. ❑ *When a baby is thirsty, it feeds more often.* **5** V-T To **feed** something to a place, means to supply it to that place in a steady flow. ❑ *The blood vessels feed blood to the brain.* [from Old English] **6** to **bite the hand that feeds** you → see **bite 7** **mouths to feed** → see **mouth**

### Word Partnership
Use *feed* with :

| N. | **feed the baby**, **feed the cat**, **feed the children**, **feed your family**, **feed the hungry 1** |
| V. | **feed and clothe 2** |

**feed|back** /fidbæk/ N-UNCOUNT If you get **feedback on** your work or progress, someone tells you how well or badly you are doing. ❑ *Continue to ask for feedback on your work.*

**feed|back con|trol** N-UNCOUNT **Feedback control** is a system that regulates a process by using the output of the system in order to make changes to the input of the system. [TECHNICAL]

**feel** /fil/ (**feels, feeling, felt**) **1** V-LINK If you **feel** a particular emotion or physical sensation, you experience it. ❑ *I am feeling very depressed.* ❑ *I felt a sharp pain in my shoulder.* **2** V-LINK If you talk about how an experience or event **feels**, you talk about the emotions and sensations connected with it. ❑ *It feels good to finish a piece of work.* ❑ *The speed at which everything moved felt strange.* **3** V-LINK If you talk about how an object **feels**, you talk about the physical quality that you notice when you touch or hold it. ❑ *The metal felt smooth and cold.* ● **Feel** is also a noun. ❑ ...*the feel of her skin.* **4** V-T/V-I If you **feel** an object, you touch it deliberately with your hand, so that you learn what it is like. ❑ *The doctor felt his head.* ❑ *Feel how soft the skin is.* **5** V-T If you can **feel** something, you are aware of it because you touch it or it touches you. ❑ *Joe felt a bump on the back of his brother's head.* ❑ *She felt something being pressed into her hands.* **6** V-T If you **feel yourself**

doing something or being in a particular state, you are aware that something is happening to you which you are unable to control. □ *I felt myself blush.* ☷ V-T If you **feel** the presence of someone or something, you become aware of them, even though you cannot see or hear them. □ *He felt her eyes on him.* □ *I could feel that a man was watching me.* ☷ V-T If you **feel** that something is true, you have a strong idea in your mind that it is true. □ *I feel that not enough is being done.* □ *She felt certain that it wasn't the same guy.* ☷ V-T If you **feel** that you should do something, you think that you should do it. □ *I feel that I should resign.* ☷ V-I If you talk about how you **feel about** something, you talk about your opinion, attitude, or reaction to it. □ *We'd like to know what you feel about the new rules.* □ *She feels guilty about spending less time lately with her two kids.* ☷ V-I If you **feel like** doing something or having something, you want to do it or have it because you are in the right mood for it and think you would enjoy it. □ *Neither of them felt like going back to sleep.* [from Old English] ☷ → see also **feeling, felt** ☷ **feel free** → see **free**

▶ **feel for** ☷ PHR-VERB If you **feel for** something, you try to find it by moving your hand around until you touch it. □ *I felt for my wallet in my pocket.* ☷ PHR-VERB If you **feel for** someone, you have sympathy for them. □ *She cried on the phone and I really felt for her.*

**feel|good** /fílgʊd/ also **feel-good** ADJ A **feelgood** movie is a movie which presents people and life in a way which makes the people who watch it feel happy and optimistic.

**feel|ing** /fílɪŋ/ (**feelings**) ☷ N-COUNT A **feeling** is an emotion. □ *It gave me a feeling of satisfaction.* ☷ N-COUNT If you have **a feeling that** something is the case or **that** something is going to happen, you think that it is probably the case or that it is probably going to happen. □ *I have a feeling that everything will be all right.* ☷ N-PLURAL Your **feelings** about something are the things that you think and feel about it, or your attitude toward it. □ *They have strong feelings about politics.* ☷ N-PLURAL When you refer to your **feelings**, you are talking about the things that might embarrass, offend, or upset you. For example, if someone hurts your **feelings**, he or she upsets you by something that he or she says or does. □ *I'm sorry if I hurt your feelings.* ☷ N-UNCOUNT **Feeling** for someone is love, affection, sympathy, or concern for them. □ *Thomas never lost his feeling for Harriet.* ☷ N-UNCOUNT **Feeling** in part of your body is the ability to experience the sense of touch in this part of the body. □ *After the accident he had no feeling in his legs.* ☷ N-SING If you have a **feeling of** being in a particular situation, you feel that you are in that situation. □ *I had the terrible feeling of being left behind to bring up the baby on my own.* ☷ → see also **feel** ☷ PHRASE **Bad feeling** or **ill feeling** is bitterness or anger which exists between people. □ *There's been some bad feeling between the two families.* [from Old English]

**feet** /fít/ **Feet** is the plural of **foot**. [from Old English]

**feign** /feɪn/ (**feigns, feigning, feigned**) V-T If someone **feigns** a particular feeling or attitude, they try to make other people think that they have it or are experiencing it, although this is not true. [FORMAL] □ *I didn't want to go to school, and decided to*

feign illness. [from Old French]

**feld|spar** /fɛldspɑr, fɛl-/ (**feldspars**) N-VAR **Feldspar** is a mineral that forms rocks and makes up most of the Earth's crust. [from German]

**fell** /fɛl/ (**fells, felling, felled**) ☷ **Fell** is the past tense of **fall**. ☷ V-T If trees **are felled**, they are cut down. [Senses 1 and 2 from Old English.] ☷ **in one fell swoop** → see **swoop**

**fel|low** /fɛloʊ/ (**fellows**) ☷ ADJ You use **fellow** to describe people who are in the same situation as you, or people you feel you have something in common with. □ *...a talent for making her fellow guests laugh.* ☷ N-COUNT A **fellow of** an academic or professional association is someone who is a specially elected member of it. □ *...a fellow of the New York Academy of Medicine.* [from Old English]

**fel|low|ship** /fɛloʊʃɪp/ (**fellowships**) ☷ N-COUNT A **fellowship** is a group of people that join together for a common purpose. □ *...the Fellowship of World Christians.* ☷ N-UNCOUNT **Fellowship** is a feeling of friendship that people have when they are talking or doing something together and sharing their experiences. □ *...a sense of community and fellowship.* [from Old English]

**felo|ny** /fɛləni/ (**felonies**) N-COUNT A **felony** is a very serious crime such as armed robbery. [LEGAL] □ *He was guilty of six felonies.* [from Medieval Latin]

**fel|sic** /fɛlsɪk/ ADJ **Felsic** rocks are igneous rocks that contain a lot of lighter elements such as silicon, aluminum, sodium, and potassium. Compare **mafic**. [TECHNICAL]

**felt** /fɛlt/ ☷ **Felt** is the past tense and past participle of **feel**. ☷ N-UNCOUNT **Felt** is a thick cloth made from wool or other fibers packed tightly together. □ *...an old felt hat.* [from Old English]

| Word Link | *fem, femin* ≈ *woman* : *female, feminine, feminist* |
|---|---|

**fe|male** /fímeɪl/ (**females**) ☷ ADJ Someone who is **female** is a woman or a girl. □ *...a female singer.* ☷ ADJ **Female** matters and things relate to or affect women rather than men. □ *...female diseases.* ☷ N-COUNT Women and girls are sometimes referred to as **females** when they are being considered as a type. □ *Hay fever affects males more than females.* ☷ N-COUNT You can refer to any creature that can lay eggs or produce babies from its body as a **female**. □ *Each female will lay just one egg.* ● **Female** is also an adjective. □ *...the female gorillas.* [from Latin] → see **reproduction**

| Usage | **female** and **woman** |
|---|---|

In everyday situations, you should avoid using *female* to refer to women, because that can sound offensive. When used as a noun, *female* is mainly used in scientific or medical contexts. *The leader of the herd of elephants is usually the oldest female.*

**femi|nine** /fɛmɪnɪn/ ADJ **Feminine** qualities and things relate to or are considered typical of women, in contrast to men. □ *...traditional feminine roles.* ● **femi|nin|ity** /fɛmɪnɪnɪti/ N-UNCOUNT □ *...ideals of femininity.* [from Latin]

**femi|nism** /fɛmɪnɪzəm/ N-UNCOUNT **Feminism** is the belief and aim that women should have the same rights, power, and opportunities as men. [from Latin]

> **Word Link**    *fem, femin ≈ woman : female, feminine, feminist*

**femi|nist** /fɛmɪnɪst/ (**feminists**) **1** N-COUNT A **feminist** is a person who believes in and supports feminism. □ *...one of the earliest feminists to speak up in this country.* **2** ADJ **Feminist** groups, ideas, and activities are involved in feminism. □ *...the feminist movement.* [from Latin]

**fence** /fɛns/ (**fences, fencing, fenced**) **1** N-COUNT A **fence** is a barrier made of wood or wire supported by posts. **2** V-T If you **fence** an area of land, you surround it with a fence. □ *The owner has fenced the property.* **3** PHRASE If you **sit on the fence**, you avoid supporting a particular side in a discussion or argument. □ *I'm sitting on the fence until I know what happened.*

**fenc|ing** /fɛnsɪŋ/ **1** N-UNCOUNT **Fencing** is a sport in which two competitors fight each other using very thin swords. **2** N-UNCOUNT Materials such as wood or wire that are used to make fences are called **fencing**.

**fend** /fɛnd/ (**fends, fending, fended**) V-I If you have to **fend** for yourself, you have to look after yourself without relying on anyone else. □ *The woman and her young baby were left to fend for themselves.*
▸ **fend off** **1** PHR-VERB If you **fend off** someone or something, you defend yourself against them using words. □ *Henry fended off questions about his future.* **2** PHR-VERB If you **fend off** someone who is attacking you, you use your arms or something such as a stick to defend yourself from their blows. □ *He raised his hand to fend off the blow.*

> **Word Link**    *fend ≈ striking : defend, fender, offend*

**fend|er** /fɛndər/ (**fenders**) N-COUNT The **fender** of a car is a bar at the front or back that protects the car if it bumps into something.

**fer|ment** (**ferments, fermenting, fermented**)

> The noun is pronounced /fɜrment/. The verb is pronounced /fərmɛnt/.

**1** N-UNCOUNT **Ferment** is excitement and trouble caused by change or uncertainty. □ *The whole country was in a state of political ferment.* **2** V-T/V-I If a food, drink, or other natural substance **ferments**, or if it **is fermented**, a chemical change takes place in it so that alcohol is produced. □ *The dried grapes are allowed to ferment until there is no sugar left.* ● **fer|men|ta|tion** /fɜrmɛnteɪʃᵊn/ N-UNCOUNT □ *Fermentation produces alcohol.* [from Latin]
→ see **fungus**

**fern** /fɜrn/ (**ferns**) N-VAR A **fern** is a plant that has long stems with feathery leaves and no flowers. [from Old English]

**fe|ro|cious** /fəroʊʃəs/ **1** ADJ A **ferocious** animal, person, or action is very fierce and violent. □ *...a pack of ferocious dogs.* **2** ADJ A **ferocious** war, argument, or other form of conflict involves a great deal of anger, bitterness, and determination. □ *Fighting has been ferocious.* [from Latin]

**fe|roc|ity** /fərɒsɪti/ N-UNCOUNT The **ferocity** of something is its fierce or violent nature. □ *The armed forces were surprised by the ferocity of the attack.* [from Latin]

**Fer|ris wheel** (**Ferris wheels**) also **ferris wheel** N-COUNT A **Ferris wheel** is a very large wheel with carriages for people to ride in, especially at a theme park or fair. [from American English]

**fer|ry** /fɛri/ (**ferries, ferrying, ferried**) **1** N-COUNT A **ferry** is a boat that transports passengers and sometimes also vehicles, usually across rivers or short stretches of sea. □ *They crossed the River Gambia by ferry.* **2** V-T If a vehicle **ferries** people or goods, it transports them, usually by means of regular trips between the same two places. □ *A plane arrived to ferry guests to and from Bird Island Lodge.* [from Old English]
→ see **ship**

**fer|tile** /fɜrtᵊl/ **1** ADJ Land or soil that is **fertile** is able to support the growth of a large number of strong healthy plants. ● **fer|til|ity** /fɜrtɪlɪti/ N-UNCOUNT □ *...the fertility of the soil.* **2** ADJ A situation or environment that is **fertile** in relation to a particular activity or feeling encourages the activity or feeling. □ *She says Seattle is fertile ground for small businesses.* **3** ADJ A person or animal that is **fertile** is able to reproduce and have babies or young. ● **fer|til|ity** N-UNCOUNT □ *In the cities, fertility levels are lower.* [from Latin]
→ see **grassland**

**fer|ti|lize** /fɜrtᵊlaɪz/ (**fertilizes, fertilizing, fertilized**) **1** V-T When an egg from the ovary of a woman or female animal **is fertilized**, a sperm from the male joins with the egg, causing a baby or young animal to begin forming. A female plant **is fertilized** when its reproductive parts come into contact with pollen from the male plant. □ *...the normal sperm levels needed to fertilize the egg.* ● **fer|ti|li|za|tion** /fɜrtᵊlɪzeɪʃᵊn/ N-UNCOUNT □ *From fertilization until birth is about 266 days.* **2** V-T To **fertilize** land means to improve its quality in order to make plants grow well on it, by spreading solid animal waste or a chemical mixture on it. □ *The fields are fertilized, usually with animal manure.* [from Latin]
→ see **reproduction**

**fer|ti|liz|er** /fɜrtᵊlaɪzər/ (**fertilizers**) N-UNCOUNT **Fertilizer** is a substance such as solid animal waste or a chemical mixture that you spread on the ground in order to make plants grow more successfully. [from Latin]
→ see **farm, pollution**

**fer|vent** /fɜrvᵊnt/ ADJ A **fervent** person has strong feelings about something, and is very enthusiastic about it. □ *...a fervent admirer of Morisot's work.* ● **fer|vent|ly** ADV □ *Their claims will be fervently denied.* [from Latin]

**fer|vor** /fɜrvər/ N-UNCOUNT **Fervor** for something is a very strong feeling for or belief in it. [FORMAL] □ *...their religious fervor.* [from Latin]

**fes|ter** /fɛstər/ (**festers, festering, festered**) **1** V-I If a situation or problem **is festering**, it is getting worse because it is not being properly recognized or dealt with. □ *These misunderstandings could start to fester.* **2** V-I If a wound **festers**, it becomes infected. [from Old French]

**fes|ti|val** /fɛstɪvᵊl/ (**festivals**) **1** N-COUNT A **festival** is an organized series of events such as musical concerts or drama productions. □ *...festivals of music, theater, and dance.* **2** N-COUNT A **festival** is a day or time of the year when people do not go to work or school and celebrate some special event, often a religious event. ❑ *Shavuot is a two-day festival for Jews.* [from Church Latin]

**fes|tive** /fɛstɪv/ **1** ADJ Something that is **festive** is special, colorful, or exciting, especially because of a holiday or celebration. ❑ *Parades and street parties add to the festive atmosphere.* **2** ADJ **Festive** means relating to a holiday or celebration, especially Christmas. ❑ *With Christmas almost here, you should start your festive cooking now.* [from Latin]

| **Thesaurus** | *festive* | Also look up : |
| --- | --- | --- |
| ADJ. | happy, joyous, merry; (*ant.*) gloomy, somber **1** | |

**fes|tiv|ity** /fɛstɪvɪti/ (**festivities**) **1** N-UNCOUNT **Festivity** is the celebration of something in a happy way. ❑ *There was a general air of festivity.* **2** N-COUNT **Festivities** are events that are organized in order to celebrate something. ❑ *The festivities included a huge display of fireworks.* [from Latin]

**fe|tal po|si|tion** (**fetal positions**) N-COUNT If someone is in the **fetal position**, their body is curled up like a fetus in the womb. ❑ *She lay in a fetal position, turned away from him.*

**fetch** /fɛtʃ/ (**fetches, fetching, fetched**) **1** V-T If you **fetch** something or someone, you go and get them from the place where they are. ❑ *Sylvia fetched a towel from the bathroom.* ❑ *Fetch me a glass of water.* **2** V-T If something **fetches** a particular sum of money, it is sold for that amount. ❑ *The painting fetched three million dollars.* [from Old English] **3** → see also **far-fetched**

**fete** /feɪt, fɛt/ (**fetes, feting, feted**) also **fête** **1** N-COUNT A **fete** is a fancy party or celebration. ❑ *The pop star flew 100 friends in from London and Paris for a two-day fete.* **2** V-T If someone **is feted**, they are celebrated, welcomed, or admired by the public. ❑ *Vera Wang was feted in New York at a spectacular dinner.* [from French]

**fe|tus** /fitəs/ (**fetuses**) N-COUNT A **fetus** is an animal or human being in its later stages of development before it is born. [from Latin]
→ see **reproduction**

**feud** /fyud/ (**feuds, feuding, feuded**) **1** N-COUNT A **feud** is a quarrel in which two people or groups remain angry with each other for a long time. ❑ *...a long and bitter feud between the government and the villagers.* **2** V-RECIP If two people or groups **feud**, they have a quarrel and remain angry with each other for a long time. ❑ *He feuded with all his neighbors.* [from Old French]

**feu|dal** /fyudᵊl/ ADJ **Feudal** means relating to the system or the time of feudalism. [from Medieval Latin]

**fe|ver** /fivər/ (**fevers**) **1** N-VAR If you have a **fever** when you are ill, your body temperature is higher than usual. ❑ *Jim had a high fever.* [from Old English] **2** → see also **hay fever**
→ see **illness**

**fe|ver blis|ter** (**fever blisters**) N-COUNT **Fever blisters** are small sore spots that sometimes appear on someone's lips and nose when they have a cold.

**fe|ver|ish** /fivərɪʃ/ **1** ADJ **Feverish** activity is done extremely quickly, often in a state of nervousness or excitement because you want to finish it as soon as possible. ❑ *Hours of feverish*

activity lay ahead as we prepared the show. **2** ADJ If you are **feverish**, you are suffering from a fever. ❑ *A feverish child refuses to eat and asks only for cold drinks.* [from Old English]

**few** /fyu/ (**fewer, fewest**) **1** DET You use **a few** to indicate that you are talking about a small number of people or things. ❑ *...a dinner party for a few close friends.* ❑ *Here are a few more ideas to consider.* ● **Few** is also a pronoun. ❑ *Most were Americans but a few were British.* ● **Few** is also a quantifier. ❑ *There are many ways eggs can be prepared; here are a few of them.* **2** DET You use **few** to indicate that you are talking about a small number of people or things. ❑ *She had few friends.* ● **Few** is also a pronoun. ❑ *Few can survive more than a week without water.* ● **Few** is also a quantifier. ❑ *Few of the houses still had lights on.* ● **Few** is also an adjective. ❑ *She spent her few waking hours in front of the TV.* **3** PHRASE You use **as few as** before a number to suggest that it is surprisingly small. ❑ *Some people put on weight eating as few as 800 calories a day.* **4** PHRASE Things that are **few and far between** are very rare or do not happen very often. ❑ *Kelly's trips to the hairdresser were few and far between.* **5** PHRASE You use **no fewer than** to emphasize that a number is surprisingly large. ❑ *No fewer than thirteen foreign ministers attended the session.* [from Old English]
→ see also **less**

| **Usage** | **few** and **a few** |
| --- | --- |

Be careful to use *few* and a *few* correctly. *Few* means "not many," and is used to emphasize that the number is very small: *He had few complaints about his workload.* A *few* means "more than one or two," and is used when we wish to imply a small but significant number: *He had a few complaints about his workload.*

**fi|an|cé** /fiɑnseɪ, fiɑnseɪ/ (**fiancés**) N-COUNT A woman's **fiancé** is the man to whom she is engaged to be married. [from French]

**fi|an|cée** /fiɑnseɪ, fiɑnseɪ/ (**fiancées**) N-COUNT A man's **fiancée** is the woman to whom he is engaged to be married. [from French]

**fi|as|co** /fiæskoʊ/ (**fiascos**) N-COUNT If you describe an event or attempt to do something as a **fiasco**, you are emphasizing that it fails completely. ❑ *The race was a complete fiasco.* [from Italian]

**fi|ber** /faɪbər/ (**fibers**) **1** N-COUNT A **fiber** is a thin thread of a natural or artificial substance, especially one that is used to make cloth or rope. ❑ *If you look at the paper under a microscope you will see the fibers.* **2** N-COUNT A **fiber** is a thin piece of flesh like a thread which connects nerve cells in your body or which muscles are made of. **3** N-UNCOUNT **Fiber** consists of the parts of plants or seeds that your body cannot digest. ❑ *Most vegetables contain fiber.* [from Latin]
→ see **paper**

**fiber|glass** /faɪbərglæs/ N-UNCOUNT **Fiberglass** is a material made from short, thin threads of glass which can be used to stop heat from escaping.

**fi|ber op|tics**

| The form **fiber optic** is used as a modifier. |
| --- |

**1** N-UNCOUNT **Fiber optics** is the use of long thin threads of glass to carry information in the form

of light. **2** ADJ **Fiber optic** means relating to or involved in fiber optics. ❑ ...*fiber optic cables.*
→ see **laser**

**fi|brous root** (**fibrous roots**) N-COUNT Plants with **fibrous roots** have a series of thin roots which branch out from the stem of the plant. [TECHNICAL]

**fick|le** /ˈfɪkᵊl/ **1** ADJ If you describe someone as **fickle**, you disapprove of them because they keep changing their mind about what they like or want. ❑ *A recent poll puts the president's approval rating at 80%. But the public can be fickle.* **2** ADJ If you say that something is **fickle**, you mean that it often changes and is unreliable. ❑ *New England's weather can be fickle.* [from Old English]

**fic|tion** /ˈfɪkʃᵊn/ **1** N-UNCOUNT **Fiction** refers to books and stories about imaginary people and events. ● **fictional** ADJ ❑ ...*fictional characters.* **2** N-UNCOUNT A statement or account that is **fiction** is not true. ❑ *The truth or fiction of this story has never really been determined.* [from Latin]
→ see **fantasy, genre, library**

**fic|ti|tious** /fɪkˈtɪʃəs/ ADJ **Fictitious** is used to describe something that is false or does not exist, although some people claim that it is true or exists. ❑ *We're interested in the source of these fictitious rumors.* [from Latin]

**fid|dle** /ˈfɪdᵊl/ (**fiddles, fiddling, fiddled**) **1** V-I If you **fiddle with** an object, you keep moving it or touching it with your fingers. ❑ *Harriet fiddled with a pen.* **2** N-VAR Some people call violins **fiddles.** [from Old English]

**fi|del|ity** /fɪˈdɛlɪti/ N-UNCOUNT **Fidelity** is loyalty to a person, organization, or set of beliefs. [FORMAL] ❑ *Your lawyer will serve you with total fidelity.* [from Latin]

**fidg|et** /ˈfɪdʒɪt/ (**fidgets, fidgeting, fidgeted**) V-I If you **fidget**, you keep moving your hands or feet slightly or changing your position slightly, because you are nervous or bored. ❑ *Brenda fidgeted in her seat.* [from Old Norse]

**field** /fild/ (**fields, fielding, fielded**) **1** N-COUNT A **field** is an enclosed area of land where crops are grown, or where animals are kept. ❑ ...*a field of wheat.* **2** N-COUNT A sports **field** is an area of grass where sports are played. ❑ ...*a baseball field.* **3** N-COUNT A **field** is an area of land or seabed under which large amounts of a particular mineral have been found. ❑ ...*a natural gas field in Alaska.* **4** N-COUNT A particular **field** is a particular subject of study or type of activity. ❑ *Each of the authors is an expert in his field.* **5** N-COUNT Your **field** of vision is the area that you can see without turning your head. **6** ADJ **Field** work involves research that is done in a real, natural environment rather than in a theoretical way or in controlled conditions. ❑ *She did her field work in Somalia in the late 1980s.* **7** V-I In a game of baseball or cricket, the team that is **fielding** is trying to catch the ball, while the other team is trying to hit it. ● **field|er** (**fielders**) N-COUNT ❑ *He hit 10 home runs and he's also a good fielder.* [from Norwegian] **8** → see also **minefield, playing field**

**Word Partnership** Use *field* with :

| | |
|---|---|
| ADJ. | **open** field **1** |
| N. | **ball** field, field **hockey, track and** field **2** |
| | **oil** field **3** |
| | **expert in a** field, field **trip 4** |
| | field **of vision 5** |
| V. | **work in a** field **4** |

**field goal** (**field goals**) N-COUNT In football, a **field goal** is a score of three points that is gained by kicking the ball through the opponent's goalposts above the crossbar.

**field hand** (**field hands**) N-COUNT A **field hand** is someone who is employed to work on a farm.

**field hock|ey** N-UNCOUNT **Field hockey** is an outdoor game played between two teams of 11 players who use long curved sticks to hit a small ball and try to score goals.

**field trip** (**field trips**) N-COUNT A **field trip** is a trip made by students and a teacher to see something, for example a museum, or a historical site.

**fierce** /fɪərs/ (**fiercer, fiercest**) **1** ADJ A **fierce** animal or person is very aggressive or angry. ● **fierce|ly** ADV ❑ *"Go away!" she said fiercely.* **2** ADJ **Fierce** feelings or actions are very intense or enthusiastic, or involve great activity. ❑ *Consumers have a wide range of choices and price competition is fierce.* ● **fierce|ly** ADV ❑ *He is ambitious and fiercely competitive.* [from Old French]

**fiery** /ˈfaɪəri/ (**fierier, fieriest**) **1** ADJ Something that is **fiery**, is burning strongly or contains fire. [LITERARY] ❑ *A helicopter crashed in a fiery explosion.* **2** ADJ You can use **fiery** for emphasis when you are referring to bright colors such as red or orange. [LITERARY] ❑ *The sky turned from fiery orange to lemon yellow.* [from Old English]

**fif|teen** /ˈfɪfˈtin/ (**fifteens**) NUM **Fifteen** is the number 15. [from Old English]

**fif|teenth** /ˈfɪfˈtinθ/ ORD The **fifteenth** item in a series is the one that you count as number fifteen. ❑ ...*the fifteenth century.* [from Old English]

**fifth** /fɪfθ/ (**fifths**) **1** ORD The **fifth** item in a series is the one that you count as number five. ❑ ...*his fifth trip to Australia.* **2** N-COUNT A **fifth** is one of five equal parts of something. ❑ *India spends over a fifth of its budget on defense.* [from Old English]

**Fifth Amend|ment** N-SING In American law, if someone **takes the Fifth Amendment**, they refuse to answer a question because they think it might show that they are guilty of a crime.

**fif|ti|eth** /ˈfɪftiəθ/ ORD The **fiftieth** item in a series is the one that you count as number fifty. ❑ ...*his fiftieth birthday.* [from Old English]

**fif|ty** /ˈfɪfti/ (**fifties**) **1** NUM **Fifty** is the number 50. **2** N-PLURAL When you talk about the **fifties**, you are referring to numbers between 50 and 59. For example, if you are in your **fifties**, you are aged between 50 and 59. If the temperature is in the **fifties**, the temperature is between 50 and 59 degrees. **3** N-PLURAL The **fifties** is the decade between 1950 and 1959. ❑ *They first met in the early Fifties.* [from Old English]

**fig** /fɪg/ (**figs**) N-COUNT A **fig** is a soft sweet fruit full of tiny seeds. Figs grow on trees in hot countries. [from Old French]
→ see **fruit**

**fight** /faɪt/ (fights, fighting, fought) ■ V-T/V-I
If you **fight** something unpleasant, you try in
a determined way to prevent it or stop it from
happening. ❑ *Prison inmates are being trained to
fight forest fires.* ❑ *I've spent a lifetime fighting against
racism and prejudice.* ● **Fight** is also a noun. ❑ *...the
fight against crime.* ■ V-I If you **fight** for something,
you try in a determined way to get it or achieve
it. ❑ *Lee had to fight hard for his place on the team.* ❑ *I
told him how we had fought to hold on to the company.*
● **Fight** is also a noun. ❑ *...the fight for justice.*
■ V-T/V-I If a person or army **fights** or **fights in** a
battle or a war, they take part in it. ❑ *He fought in
the war and was taken prisoner.* ❑ *I would sooner go to
prison than fight for this country.* ❑ *The United States
is fighting a new war against terrorism.* ● **fighting**
N-UNCOUNT ❑ *More than nine hundred people have
died in the fighting.* ■ V-T If you **fight** your way to
a place, you move toward it with great difficulty,
because there are a lot of people or things in your
way. ❑ *The firefighters fought their way through the
flames into the house.* ■ V-T If you **fight** an election,
you are a candidate in the election and try to win
it. ■ V-T If you **fight** an emotion or desire, you
try very hard not to feel it, show it, or act on it. ❑ *I
desperately fought the urge to giggle.* ■ V-RECIP If one
person **fights** with another, the two people hit or
kick each other because they want to hurt each
other. ❑ *As a child she fought with her younger sister.*
❑ *He looked like he wanted to fight with me.* ● **Fight** is
also a noun. ❑ *Had had a fight with Smith.* ● V-RECIP
If one person **fights** with another, they have an
angry disagreement or quarrel. [INFORMAL] ❑ *She
was always fighting with him.* ● **Fight** is also a noun.
❑ *He had a big fight with his dad when he came home
late.* [from Old English]
→ see **army**

▶ **fight back** ■ PHR-VERB If you **fight back**
against someone or something that is attacking or
harming you, you defend yourself by taking action
against them. ❑ *The passengers and crew chose to
fight back against the hijackers.* ■ PHR-VERB If you
**fight back** an emotion, you try very hard not to feel
it, show it, or act on it. ❑ *She fought back the tears.*
▶ **fight off** ■ PHR-VERB If you **fight off** something
such as an illness or an unpleasant feeling, you
succeed in getting rid of it and in not letting it
overcome you. ❑ *...the body's ability to fight off
infection.* ■ PHR-VERB If you **fight off** someone
who has attacked you, you fight with them, and
succeed in making them go away or stop attacking
you. ❑ *She fought off three armed robbers.*

| Thesaurus | *fight* | Also look up : |
|---|---|---|
| v. | scuffle, squabble ■ | |
| | argue, bicker, quarrel ■ | |
| N. | fist fight ■ | |
| | argument, disagreement, squabble, tiff ■ | |

| Word Partnership | Use *fight* with : |
|---|---|
| N. | fight **crime**, fight **fire** ■ |
| | fight **a battle/war**, fight **an enemy** ■ |
| v. | **join a** fight ■ ■ ■ |
| | **lose a** fight, **win a** fight ■ ■ ■ ■ |
| | **stay and** fight ■ ■ ■ |
| | **break up a** fight, **have a** fight, **pick a**
fight, **start a** fight ■ ■ |

**fight|er** /faɪtər/ (fighters) ■ N-COUNT A **fighter**
or a **fighter plane** is a fast military aircraft that is
used for destroying other aircraft. ■ N-COUNT A
**fighter** is a person who physically fights another
person, especially a professional boxer. ❑ *...a real
street fighter.* [from Old English] ■ → see also
**firefighter**

**fight|ing chance** N-SING If you say that
someone has a **fighting chance** of success, you
are emphasizing that they have some chance of
success after a hard struggle. ❑ *The airline has a
fighting chance of surviving.*

**fig|ura|tive** /fɪgyərətɪv/ ■ ADJ If you use a
word or expression in a **figurative** sense, you use
it with a more abstract or imaginative meaning
than its ordinary literal one. ❑ *"Like I said before, I'm
in a different place." His statement was both literal and
figurative.* ● **fig|ura|tive|ly** ADV ❑ *Figuratively, the
world is standing still, waiting to see what will happen.*
■ ADJ **Figurative** art is a style of art in which
people and things are shown in a realistic way.
[from Latin]

| Word Link | fig ≈ form, shape : configure,
disfigure, figure |
|---|---|

**fig|ure** /fɪgyər/ (figures, figuring, figured)
■ N-COUNT A **figure** is a particular amount
expressed as a number, especially a statistic. ❑ *We
need a true figure of how many people in this country
do not have a job.* ■ N-COUNT A **figure** is any of the
ten written symbols from 0 to 9 that are used to
represent a number. ❑ *...the glowing red figures on
the radio alarm clock.* ■ N-COUNT A **figure** is the
shape of a person you cannot see clearly. ❑ *Ernie
saw the dim figure of Rose in the chair.* ■ N-COUNT In
art, a **figure** is a person in a drawing or a painting,
or a statue of a person. ❑ *...a life-size bronze figure
of a woman.* ■ N-COUNT Your **figure** is the shape
of your body. ❑ *Take pride in your health and your
figure.* ■ N-COUNT Someone who is referred to
as a **figure** of a particular kind is a person who is
well-known and important in some way. ❑ *...key
figures in the three main political parties.* ■ N-COUNT
If you say that someone is, for example, a mother
**figure** or a hero **figure**, you mean that other
people regard them as the type of person stated
or suggested. ■ N-PLURAL An amount or number
that is in single **figures** is between zero and nine.
An amount or number that is in double **figures**
is between ten and ninety-nine. ■ V-T If you
**figure** that something is true, you think or guess
that it is true. [INFORMAL] ❑ *She figured that she had
learned a lot from the experience.* ■ V-I If a person
or thing **figures in** something, they appear in or
are included in it. ❑ *Human rights violations figured
heavily in the report.* [from Latin]
▶ **figure out** PHR-VERB If you **figure out** a
solution to a problem or the reason for something,
you succeed in solving it or understanding it.
[INFORMAL] ❑ *It took them about one month to figure
out how to use the equipment.*
▶ **figure up** PHR-VERB If you **figure up** a cost or
amount, you add numbers together to get the
total. ❑ *He figured up the balance in their checking
account.*

**fig|ure eight** (figure eights) N-COUNT A **figure
eight** is something that has the same shape as
a number 8, for example a movement done by a
skater.

**figure|head** /fɪɡyərhɛd/ (figureheads)
N-COUNT If someone is the **figurehead** of an
organization or movement, they are recognized
as being its leader, although they have little real
power. ❑ *He is little more than a figurehead.*

**file** /faɪl/ (files, filing, filed) **1** N-COUNT A **file** is
a box or folder in which letters or documents are
kept. ❑ *...a file of insurance papers.* **2** N-COUNT A **file**
is a collection of information about a particular
person or thing. ❑ *We have files on people's tax
details.* **3** N-COUNT In computing, a **file** is a set
of related data that has its own name. ❑ *Save
the revised version of the file under a new filename.*
**4** N-COUNT A **file** is a tool which is used for
rubbing hard objects to make them smooth or to
shape them. **5** V-T If you **file** a document, you put
it in the correct file. ❑ *They are all filed alphabetically
under author.* **6** V-T/V-I If you **file** a formal or legal
accusation, complaint, or request, you make it
officially. ❑ *I filed for divorce.* **7** V-T If you **file** an
object, you smooth it, shape it, or cut it with a file.
❑ *She was shaping and filing her nails.* **8** → see also
**rank and file** **9** PHRASE A group of people who
are walking or standing **in single file** are in a line,
one behind the other. [Senses 1–3, 5 and 6 from Old
French. Senses 4 and 7 from Old English.]
→ see **tools**

**file|name** /faɪlneɪm/ (filenames) N-COUNT In
computing, a **filename** is a name that you give to a
particular document.

**file-sharing** also **file sharing** N-UNCOUNT
**File-sharing** is a method of distributing computer
files, for example, files containing music, among
a large number of users. [COMPUTING]

**fi|let** /fɪleɪ, fɪleɪ/ (filets) N-COUNT A **filet** of meat
or fish is the same as a **fillet**. [from French]

**fili|bus|ter** /fɪlɪbʌstər/ (filibusters) N-COUNT
A **filibuster** is a long slow speech made to use up
time so that a vote cannot be taken and a law
cannot be passed. [from Spanish]

**fil|ings** N-PLURAL Court **filings** are cases filed in
a court of law. ❑ *In court filings, they argued that the
payment was inadequate.* [from Old English]

**fill** /fɪl/ (fills, filling, filled) **1** V-T/V-I If you **fill**
a container or area, or if it **fills**, an amount of
something enters it that is enough to make it full.
❑ *She went to the bathroom and filled a glass with water.*
❑ *The boy's eyes filled with tears.* ● **Fill up** means the
same as **fill**. ❑ *Warehouses fill up with sacks of rice
and flour.* **2** V-T If something **fills** a space, it is so
big, or there are such large quantities of it, that
there is very little room left. ❑ *Rows of cabinets
filled the enormous work area.* ● **Fill up** means the
same as **fill**. ❑ *Complicated machines fill up today's
laboratories.* ● **filled** ADJ ❑ *...museum buildings filled
with historical objects.* **3** V-T If you **fill** a crack or
hole, you put a substance into it in order to make
the surface smooth again. ❑ *You should fill cracks
between plaster walls and window frames.* ● **Fill in**
means the same as **fill**. ❑ *Start by filling in any cracks.*
**4** V-T If something **fills** you **with** an emotion, you
experience this emotion strongly. ❑ *My father's
work filled me with awe.* **5** V-T If you **fill** a period of
time with a particular activity, you spend the time
in this way. ❑ *We fill our days with swimming and
sailing.* ● **Fill up** means the same as **fill**. ❑ *She went
to her yoga class, glad to have something to fill up the
evening.* **6** V-T If something **fills** a need or a gap, it
makes this need or gap no longer exist. ❑ *Her sense*

*of fun filled a gap in his life.* **7** V-T If something **fills**
a role or position, that is their role or function.
❑ *Dena filled the role of diplomat's wife with skill.* [from
Old English] **8** to **fill the bill** → see **bill**
▶ **fill in** **1** PHR-VERB If you **fill in** a form, you write
information in the spaces on it. ❑ *Fill in the coupon
and send it to the address shown.* **2** PHR-VERB If you
**fill** someone **in**, you give them more details about
something that you know about. [INFORMAL] ❑ *He
filled her in on Wilbur Kantor's visit.* **3** PHR-VERB If
you **fill in** for someone, you do the work that they
normally do because they are unable to do it.
**4** → see also **fill 3**
▶ **fill out** PHR-VERB If you **fill out** a form, you
write information in the spaces on it. ❑ *Fill out the
application carefully.*
▶ **fill up** **1** PHR-VERB A type of food that **fills** you
**up** makes you feel that you have eaten a lot, even
though you have only eaten a small amount.
**2** → see also **fill 1, 2, 5**

| **Thesaurus** | *fill* | Also look up : |
|---|---|---|
| v. | inflate, load, pour into, put into; (*ant.*) empty, pour out **1** | |
| | crowd, take up **2** | |
| | block, close, plug, seal **3** | |

**fil|let** /fɪleɪ/ (fillets, filleting, filleted) **1** N-VAR
A **fillet** is a strip of meat that has no bones in it.
❑ *...chicken breast fillets.* **2** N-COUNT A **fillet** of
fish is the side of a fish with the bones removed.
❑ *...anchovy fillets.* **3** V-T When you **fillet** fish or
meat, you prepare it by taking the bones out. [from
Old French]

**fill|ing** /fɪlɪŋ/ (fillings) **1** N-COUNT A **filling** is
a small amount of metal or plastic that a dentist
puts in a hole in a tooth. **2** N-VAR The **filling** in a
cake, pie, or sandwich is what is inside it. **3** ADJ
Food that is **filling** makes you feel full when you
have eaten it. [from Old English]
→ see **teeth**

**film** /fɪlm/ (films, filming, filmed) **1** N-COUNT
A **film** consists of moving pictures that have been
recorded so that they can be shown in a theater or
on television. ❑ *Everything about the film was good.*
**2** N-COUNT A **film of** powder, liquid, or oil is a very
thin layer of it. ❑ *The sea is coated with a film of oil.*
**3** V-T If you **film** something, you use a camera to
take moving pictures of it. ❑ *He filmed her life story.*
● **filming** N-UNCOUNT ❑ *Filming is due to start next
month.* **4** N-VAR A **film** is the narrow roll of plastic
that is used in a camera to take photographs.
❑ *...rolls of film.* [from Old English]
→ see **genre, photography**

| **Word Partnership** | Use *film* with : |
|---|---|
| N. | film **clip**, film **critic**, film **director**, film **festival**, film **producer**, film **studio** **1** roll of film **4** |
| v. | **direct** a film, **edit** film, **watch a** film **1** **develop** film **4** |

**fil|ter** /fɪltər/ (filters, filtering, filtered) **1** V-T
To **filter** a substance means to pass it through
a device which is designed to remove certain
particles contained in it. ❑ *The best prevention for
cholera is to boil or filter water.* **2** V-I If light or sound
**filters into** a place, it comes in faintly. ❑ *Light
filtered into my kitchen through the tree.* **3** V-I When

**f**

news or information **filters** through to people, it gradually reaches them. ❑ *It took months before the findings began to filter through to the politicians.* ❑ *News of the attack filtered through the college.* ❹ N-COUNT A **filter** is a device through which a substance is passed when it is being filtered. ❑ *...a coffee filter.* ❺ N-COUNT A **filter** is a device through which sound or light is passed and which blocks or reduces particular sound or light frequencies. ❑ *A blue filter gives the correct color balance.* [from Medieval Latin]

**filth** /fɪlθ/ N-UNCOUNT **Filth** is a disgusting amount of dirt. ❑ *Tons of filth and sewage pour into the Ganges every day.* [from Old English]

**filthy** /fɪlθi/ (**filthier, filthiest**) ADJ Something that is **filthy** is very dirty. ❑ *He always wore a filthy old jacket.* [from Old English]

**fin** /fɪn/ (**fins**) ❶ N-COUNT A fish's **fins** are the flat parts which stick out of its body and help it to swim. ❷ N-COUNT A **fin** on something such as an airplane, rocket, or bomb is a flat part which sticks out and helps control its movement. [from Old English]
→ see **fish**

| Word Link | fin ≈ end : final, finale, finish |

**fi|nal** /faɪnᵊl/ (**finals**) ❶ ADJ In a series of events, things, or people, the **final** one is the last one. ❑ *Astronauts will make a final attempt today to rescue a communications satellite.* ❷ ADJ If a decision is **final**, it cannot be changed or questioned. ❑ *The judges' decision is final.* ❸ N-COUNT The **final** is the last game or contest in a series and decides who is the winner. ❑ *...the Gold Cup final.* [from Latin] ❹ → see also **quarterfinal, semifinal**

| Thesaurus | final | Also look up : |

ADJ.  last, ultimate ❶
      absolute, decisive, definite, settled ❷

**fi|na|le** /fɪnɑli, -næli/ (**finales**) N-COUNT The **finale** of a show, piece of music, or series of shows is the last part of it or the last one of them, especially when this is exciting or impressive. ❑ *...the finale of Shostakovich's Fifth Symphony.* [from Italian]

**fi|nal|ist** /faɪnᵊlɪst/ (**finalists**) N-COUNT A **finalist** is someone who reaches the last stages of a competition or tournament. ❑ *The twelve finalists were listed in the school newspaper.* [from Italian]

| Word Link | ize ≈ making : finalize, modernize, normalize |

**fi|nal|ize** /faɪnᵊlaɪz/ (**finalizes, finalizing, finalized**) V-T If you **finalize** something such as a plan or an agreement, you complete the arrangements for it. ❑ *James Baker arrived in Israel to finalize the details of the conference.* [from Italian]

**fi|nal|ly** /faɪnᵊli/ ❶ ADV You use **finally** to suggest that something happens after a long period of time, usually later than you wanted or expected it to happen. ❑ *The food finally arrived at the end of last week.* ❷ ADV You use **finally** to indicate that something is last in a series of actions or events. ❑ *The action slips from comedy to melodrama and finally to tragedy.* [from Latin]

**fi|nance** /faɪnæns, fɪnæns/ (**finances, financing, financed**) ❶ V-T When someone **finances** a project or a purchase, they provide the money to pay for it. ❑ *The fund has been used to finance the building of prisons.* ● **Finance** is also a noun. ❑ *They are looking for finance for a major new project.* ❷ **Finance** is the commercial or government activity of managing money. ❑ *It is their job to inform consumers about the world of finance.* ❸ N-PLURAL You can refer to the amount of money that you have and how well it is organized as your **finances**. ❑ *Take control of your finances now and save thousands.* [from Old French]

**fi|nance charge** (**finance charges**) N-COUNT **Finance charges** are fees or interest that you pay when you borrow money or buy something on credit. ❑ *...credit cards with reduced finance charges.*

**fi|nan|cial** /faɪnænʃᵊl, fɪn-/ ADJ **Financial** means relating to or involving money. ❑ *The company is in financial difficulties.* ● **fi|nan|cial|ly** ADV ❑ *She would like to be more financially independent.* [from Old French]

**fi|nan|cial ad|vis|er** (**financial advisers**) N-COUNT A **financial adviser** is someone whose job it is to advise people about financial products and services. [BUSINESS]

**fi|nan|cial ser|vices**

The form **financial service** is used as a modifier.

N-PLURAL A company or organization that provides **financial services** is able to help you do things such as make investments or get a mortgage. [BUSINESS]

**fi|nan|ci|er** /fɪnənsɪər, faɪn-/ (**financiers**) N-COUNT A **financier** is a person who provides money for projects or businesses. [BUSINESS] [from Old French]

**finch** /fɪntʃ/ (**finches**) N-COUNT A **finch** is a small bird with a short strong beak. [from Old English]

**find** /faɪnd/ (**finds, finding, found**) ❶ V-T If you **find** someone or something, you see them or learn where they are. ❑ *The police found a pistol.* ❷ V-T If you **find** something that you need or want, you succeed in getting it. ❑ *Many people here cannot find work.* ❑ *We have to find him a job.* ❸ V-T If you **find yourself** doing something, you are doing it without deciding or intending to do it. ❑ *It's not the first time that you've found yourself in this situation.* ❑ *I found myself having a good time.* ❹ V-T If you **find** that something is true, you become aware of it or realize that it is true. ❑ *They awoke to find that he was no longer there.* ❑ *I find that I am very happy in my life at the moment.* ❺ V-T When a court or jury decides that a person on trial is guilty or innocent, you say that the person **has been found** guilty or not guilty. ❻ V-T You can use **find** to express your reaction to someone or something. ❑ *I find his behavior extremely rude.* ❑ *I find it shocking that nothing has been done to protect passengers from fire.* ❼ V-T PASSIVE If something **is found** in a particular place or thing, it exists in that place. ❑ *Many species of flowering plants are found in the park.* ❽ N-COUNT If you describe someone or something that has been discovered as a **find**, you mean that they are valuable, interesting, good, or useful. ❑ *...a lucky find at a local yard sale.* ❾ → see also **finding, found** ❿ PHRASE If you **find your way** somewhere, you successfully get there by choosing the right way to go. ❑ *He was an expert at finding his way, even in strange surroundings.* [from Old English] ⓫ to **find fault with** → see **fault** ⓬ to **find**

one's **feet** → see **foot**

▸ **find out** ◼ PHR-VERB If you **find** something **out**, you learn something that you did not already know, especially by making a deliberate effort to do so. ❑ *I'll watch the next episode to find out what happens.* ❑ *I was relieved to find out that my illness was not serious.* ◼ PHR-VERB If you **find** someone **out**, you discover that they have been doing something dishonest. ❑ *I've spent months filled with shame that they might find me out.*

**find|ing** /ˈfaɪndɪŋ/ (**findings**) N-COUNT Someone's **findings** are the information they get as the result of an investigation or some research. ❑ *...one of the main findings of the survey.* [from Old English]

→ see **laboratory, science**

---
**fine**
❶ ADJECTIVE USES
❷ PUNISHMENT
---

❶ **fine** /ˈfaɪn/ (**finer, finest**) ◼ ADJ You use **fine** to describe something that you think is very good. ❑ *There is a fine view of the countryside.* ● **fine|ly** ADV ❑ *They are finely engineered boats.* ◼ ADJ If you say that you are **fine**, you mean that you are in good health or reasonably happy. ❑ *Lina is fine and sends you her love.* ◼ ADJ If you say that something is **fine**, you mean that it is satisfactory or acceptable. ❑ *Everything was going to be just fine.* ● **Fine** is also an adverb. ❑ *All the instruments are working fine.* ◼ ADJ Something that is **fine** is very delicate, narrow, or small. ❑ *...the fine hairs on her arms.* ● **fine|ly** ADV ❑ *Chop the onions finely.* ◼ ADJ A **fine** detail or distinction is very small or exact. ❑ *Johnson likes the broad outline but is critical of the fine detail.* ● **fine|ly** ADV ❑ *The smallest mistake could ruin the whole finely-balanced process.* ◼ ADJ When the weather is **fine**, the sun is shining and it is not raining. [from Italian]

❷ **fine** /ˈfaɪn/ (**fines, fining, fined**) ◼ N-COUNT A **fine** is a punishment in which a person is ordered to pay a sum of money because they have done something illegal or broken a rule. ◼ V-T If someone **is fined**, they are punished by being ordered to pay a sum of money because they have done something illegal or broken a rule. ❑ *She was fined $300 and banned from driving for one month.* [from Old French]

**fine ad|just|ment** N-UNCOUNT The part of a microscope that controls the **fine adjustment** is the part that allows you to obtain the best possible focus for the object you are looking at. [TECHNICAL]

**fine art** (**fine arts**) N-VAR Painting and sculpture, in which objects are produced that are beautiful rather than useful, can be referred to as **fine art** or as the **fine arts**.

**fi|nesse** /fɪˈnɛs/ N-UNCOUNT If you do something with **finesse**, you do it with great skill and style. ❑ *He handles diplomatic challenges with finesse.* [from French]

**fine-tune** (**fine-tunes, fine-tuning, fine-tuned**) V-T If you **fine-tune** something, you make very small and precise changes to it in order to make it work better. ❑ *The staff help to fine-tune business plans.*

**fin|ger** /ˈfɪŋɡər/ (**fingers, fingering, fingered**) ◼ N-COUNT Your **fingers** are the long thin parts at the end of each hand. ❑ *She ran her fingers through her hair.* ◼ V-T If you **finger** something, you touch or feel it with your fingers. ❑ *He fingered the coins in his pocket.* ◼ PHRASE If you **cross** your **fingers**, you put one finger on top of another and hope for good luck. If you say that someone **is keeping their fingers crossed**, you mean they are hoping for good luck. ◼ PHRASE If you **point the finger at** someone, you blame them or accuse them of doing something wrong. ❑ *He said he wasn't pointing an accusing finger at anyone in the government.* ◼ PHRASE If you **put** your **finger on** something, for example, a reason or problem, you see and identify exactly what it is. ❑ *We couldn't put our finger on what went wrong.* [from Old English]

→ see **hand**

**finger|nail** /ˈfɪŋɡərneɪl/ (**fingernails**) N-COUNT Your **fingernails** are the thin hard areas at the end of each of your fingers.

→ see **hand**

**finger|print** /ˈfɪŋɡərprɪnt/ (**fingerprints**) N-COUNT ◼ **Fingerprints** are marks made by a person's fingers which show the lines on the skin. ❑ *His fingerprints were found on the murder weapon.* ◼ PHRASE If the police **take** someone's **fingerprints**, they make that person press their fingers onto a pad covered with ink, and then onto paper, so that they know what that person's fingerprints look like.

**finger|tip** /ˈfɪŋɡərtɪp/ (**fingertips**) also **finger-tip** ◼ N-COUNT Your **fingertips** are the ends of your fingers. ❑ *He plays the drum very lightly with his fingertips.* ◼ PHRASE If you say that something is **at** your **fingertips**, you can get it or reach it easily. ❑ *I had the information at my fingertips.*

| **Word Link** | fin ≈ end : final, finale, finish |

**fin|ish** /ˈfɪnɪʃ/ (**finishes, finishing, finished**) ◼ V-T When you **finish** doing something, you do the last part of it, so that there is no more for you to do. ❑ *As soon as he finished eating, he excused himself.* ❑ *Mr. Gould was given loud cheers when he finished his speech.* ● **Finish up** means the same as **finish**. ❑ *We waited a few minutes outside his office while he finished up his meeting.* ◼ V-I When something such as a course, show, or sale **finishes**, especially at a planned time, it ends. ❑ *The teaching day finishes at around 4 p.m.* ◼ N-SING **The finish** of something is the end of it or the last part of it. ❑ *I'll see the job through to the finish.* ◼ N-COUNT If the surface of something that has been made has a particular kind of **finish**, it has the appearance or texture mentioned. ❑ *The anchors are made from stainless steel and are polished to a shiny finish.* ◼ → see also **finished** ◼ PHRASE If you add the **finishing touches** to something, you add or do the last things that are necessary to complete it. ❑ *She was adding the finishing touches to her novel.* [from Old French]

▸ **finish off** ◼ PHR-VERB If you **finish off** something that you have been eating or drinking, you eat or drink the last part of it with the result that there is none left. ❑ *Kelly finished off his coffee.* ◼ → see also **finish 2** ◼ PHR-VERB If you **finish up** something that you have been eating or drinking, you eat or drink the last part of it. ❑ *Finish up your soup now, please.* ◼ → see also **finish 1, 2**

### Thesaurus    *finish*    Also look up :

v.    conclude, end, wrap up; *(ant.)* begin, start **1** **2**

### Word Partnership    Use *finish* with :

N.    finish **a conversation**, finish **school**, finish **work 1**
finish **a job, time to** finish **1 2**

**fin|ished** /fɪnɪʃt/ **1** ADJ Someone who is **finished with** something is no longer doing it or dealing with it or is no longer interested in it. ❏ *He says he is finished with police work.* **2** ADJ Someone or something that is **finished** is no longer important, powerful, or effective. ❏ *Her power over me is finished.* [from Old French]

**fin|ish line** (**finish lines**) N-COUNT In a race, the **finish line** is the place on the track or course where the race officially ends.

**fi|nite** /faɪnaɪt/ ADJ Something that is **finite** has a definite fixed size or extent. [FORMAL] ❏ *...the realization that life is finite.* [from Latin]

**fir** /fɜr/ (**firs**) N-VAR A **fir** or a **fir tree** is a tall evergreen tree that has thin needle-like leaves. [from Old English]

---

#### fire

❶ BURNING, HEAT
❷ SHOOTING OR ATTACKING
❸ DISMISSAL

---

**❶ fire** /faɪər/ (**fires**) **1** N-UNCOUNT **Fire** is the hot, bright flames produced by things that are burning. ❏ *They saw a huge ball of fire reaching hundreds of feet into the sky.* **2** N-VAR **Fire** or a **fire** is an occurrence of uncontrolled burning which destroys buildings, forests, or other things. ❏ *87 people died in a fire at the Social Club.* ❏ *...a forest fire.* **3** N-COUNT A **fire** is a burning pile of wood, coal, or other fuel that you make. ❏ *There was a fire in the fireplace.* **4** PHRASE If an object or substance **catches fire**, it starts burning. ❏ *The blast caused several buildings to catch fire.* **5** PHRASE If something is **on fire**, it is burning and being damaged by a fire. **6** PHRASE If you **set fire to** something or you **set** it **on fire**, you start it burning in order to damage or destroy it. [from Old English] **7** to **have irons on the fire** → see **iron** **8** **like a house on fire** → see **house** **9** **there's no smoke without fire** → see **smoke**
→ see Word Web: **fire**
→ see **pottery**

**❷ fire** /faɪər/ (**fires, firing, fired**) **1** V-T/V-I If someone **fires** a gun or a bullet, or if they **fire**, a bullet is sent from a gun that they are using. ❏ *Soldiers fired rubber bullets into the crowd.* ● **fir|ing** N-UNCOUNT ❏ *The firing got heavier and we moved inside the building.* **2** V-T If you **fire** questions at someone, you ask them a lot of questions very quickly, one after another. **3** N-UNCOUNT You can use **fire** to refer to the shots fired from a gun or guns. ❏ *...fire from automatic weapons.* [from Old English]

**❸ fire** /faɪər/ (**fires, firing, fired**) V-T If an employer **fires** you, they dismiss you from your job. ❏ *This guy's lying. Do we fire him?* [from Old English]

**fire alarm** (**fire alarms**) N-COUNT A **fire alarm** is a device that makes a noise, for example, with a bell, to warn people when there is a fire.

**fire|arm** /faɪərɑrm/ (**firearms**) N-COUNT **Firearms** are guns. [FORMAL] ❏ *Security guards were carrying firearms.*
→ see **war**

**fire blan|ket** (**fire blankets**) N-COUNT A **fire blanket** is a thick cloth made from fire-resistant material that is designed to put out small fires.

**fire de|part|ment** (**fire departments**) N-COUNT The **fire department** is an organization which has the job of putting out fires.

**fire en|gine** (**fire engines**) N-COUNT A **fire engine** is a large vehicle which carries firefighters and equipment for putting out fires.

**fire ex|tin|guish|er** (**fire extinguishers**) also **fire-extinguisher** N-COUNT A **fire extinguisher** is a metal cylinder which contains water or chemicals at high pressure which can put out fires.

**fire|fight|er** /faɪərfaɪtər/ (**firefighters**) N-COUNT A **firefighter** is a person whose job is to put out fires.

extinguisher

**fire|place** /faɪərpleɪs/ (**fireplaces**) N-COUNT In a room, the **fireplace** is the place where a fire can be lit and the area on the wall and floor surrounding this place.
→ see **fire**

**fire|power** /faɪərpaʊər/ N-UNCOUNT The **firepower** of an army, ship, tank, or aircraft is the amount of ammunition it can fire. ❏ *The U.S. had superior firepower.*

**fire|storm** /faɪərstɔrm/ (**firestorms**) N-COUNT If you say that there is a **firestorm of** protest or

---

### Word Web    fire

A single **match**, a **campfire**, or even a bolt of lightning can **spark** a **wild fire**. Wild fires can spread across grasslands and **burn down** forests. Huge **firestorms** can **burn** out of control for days. They cause death and destruction. However, some ecosystems depend on fire. Once the fire passes, the **smoke** clears, the **smoldering** embers cool, and the **ash** settles, then the cycle of life begins again. Humans have learned to use fire. The **heat** cooks our food. People build fires in **fireplaces** and **wood** stoves. The **flames** warm our hands. And before electricity, the **glow** of candlelight lit our homes.

## Word Web fireworks

**Fireworks** were created in China more than a thousand years ago. Historians believe that the discovery was made by alchemists. They heated **sulfur**, potassium **nitrate**, **charcoal**, and arsenic together and the mixture **exploded**. It made a very hot, bright fire. Later they mixed these **chemicals** in a hollow bamboo tube and threw it in the fire. Thus the firecracker was born. Marco Polo brought firecrackers to Europe from the Orient in 1292. Soon the Italians began experimenting with ways of producing elaborate, colorful fireworks displays. This launched the era of modern pyrotechnics.

criticism, you are emphasizing that there is a great deal of fierce protest or criticism.

**fire truck** (fire trucks) N-COUNT A **fire truck** is a large vehicle which carries firefighters and equipment for putting out fires.

**fire|wood** /faɪərwʊd/ N-UNCOUNT **Firewood** is wood that has been cut into pieces so that it can be burned on a fire.

**fire|work** /faɪərwɜrk/ (fireworks) N-COUNT **Fireworks** are small objects that are lit to entertain people on special occasions. They burn brightly in an attractive way, and often make a loud noise.
→ see Word Web: **fireworks**

**firm** /fɜrm/ (firms, firmer, firmest) **1** N-COUNT A **firm** is an organization which sells or produces something or which provides a service which people pay for. ❑ …a Chicago law firm. **2** ADJ If something is **firm**, it does not change much in shape when it is pressed but is not completely hard. ❑ Fruit should be firm and in excellent condition. **3** ADJ A **firm** physical action is strong and controlled. ❑ The quick handshake was firm and cool. ● **firm|ly** ADV ❑ She held me firmly by the elbow. **4** ADJ A **firm** person behaves in a way that shows that they are not going to change their mind. ❑ She had to be firm with him. "I don't want to see you again." ● **firm|ly** ADV ❑ "A good night's sleep is what you want," he said firmly. **5** ADJ A **firm** decision or opinion is definite and unlikely to change. ❑ He made a firm decision to leave. ● **firm|ly** ADV ❑ Political values and opinions are firmly held. **6** ADJ **Firm** evidence or information is based on facts and so is likely to be true. **7** PHRASE If someone **stands firm**, they refuse to change their mind about something. ❑ The council is standing firm against the protest. [sense **1** from Spanish, senses **2**–**6** from Latin]

### Thesaurus firm Also look up :

| | |
|---|---|
| N. | business, company, enterprise, organization **1** |
| ADJ. | dense, hard, sturdy **2** |

**first** /fɜrst/ **1** ORD The **first** thing, person, event, or period of time is the one that happens or comes before all the others of the same kind. ❑ …the first month of the year. ❑ …the first few flakes of snow. ● **First** is also a pronoun. ❑ I've seen the movie twice and the second time I liked it even better than the first. **2** ORD You use **first** to refer to the best or most important thing or person of a particular kind. ❑ The first duty of any government must be to protect the interests of the taxpayers. **3** ADV If you do something **first**, you do it before anyone else does, or before you do anything else. ❑ I do

not remember who spoke first. ❑ First, tell me what you think of my products. **4** ADV You use **first** when you are talking about what happens in the early part of an event or experience, in contrast to what happens later. ❑ When we first came here there were a lot of kids. ● **First** is also an ordinal. ❑ She told him that her first reaction was disgust. **5** N-SING An event that is described as **a first** has never happened before and is important or exciting. ❑ It is a first for New York: an outdoor exhibition of Botero's sculpture on Park Avenue. **6** PRON The **first** you hear of something or **the first** you know about it is the time when you first become aware of it. ❑ We heard it on TV last night — that was the first we heard of it. **7** PHRASE You use **first of all** to introduce the first of a number of things that you want to say. ❑ First of all, he's far too old to work as a spy, and secondly, he's completely honest. **8** PHRASE You use **at first** when you are talking about what happens in the early stages of an event or experience, or just after something else has happened, in contrast to what happens later. ❑ At first, he seemed surprised by my questions. [from Old English] **9 first and foremost** → see **foremost**

**first aid** N-UNCOUNT **First aid** is simple medical treatment given as soon as possible to a sick or injured person. ❑ …emergencies which need prompt first aid treatment.

**first aid kit** (first aid kits) N-COUNT A **first aid kit** is a bag or case containing basic medical supplies that are designed to be used on someone who is injured or who suddenly becomes ill.

**First Amend|ment** N-SING The **First Amendment** is the part of the U.S. Constitution that guarantees people the right of free speech, and freedom of religion, assembly, and petition.

**First Fami|ly** N-SING The **First Family** is the U.S. president and their spouse and children.

**first floor** (first floors) N-COUNT The **first floor** of a building is the one at ground level.

**First Lady** (First Ladies) N-COUNT The **First Lady** in a country or state is the wife of the president or state governor, or a woman who performs the official duties normally performed by the wife.

**first|ly** /fɜrstli/ ADV You use **firstly** in speech or writing when you want to mention an item that will be followed by others connected with it. ❑ The program is behind schedule as a result firstly of increased costs, then of technical problems. [from Old English]

**first name** (first names) N-COUNT Your **first name** is the first of the names that were given to you when you were born. ❑ Her first name was Mary.

**fis|cal** /fɪskəl/ ADJ **Fiscal** is used to describe

f

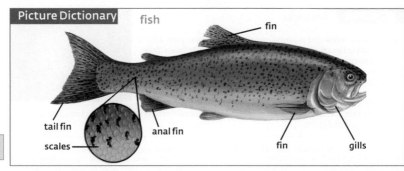

**Picture Dictionary**

fish

fin

tail fin

anal fin

scales

fin

gills

something that relates to government money or public money, especially taxes. ❑ ...*fiscal policy*. [from Latin]

**fish** /fɪʃ/ (**fish** or **fishes, fishes, fishing, fished**) **1** N-COUNT A **fish** is a creature that lives in water and has a tail and fins. **2** N-UNCOUNT **Fish** is the flesh of a fish eaten as food. **3** V-I If you **fish**, you try to catch fish, either for food or as a form of sport or recreation. ❑ *Brian learned to fish in the Colorado River*. [from Old English] **4** → see also **fishing**
→ see Picture Dictionary: **fish**
→ see **aquarium, pet, shark**

**fish and chips** N-PLURAL **Fish and chips** are fish fillets coated with batter and deep-fried, eaten with French fries. ❑ *We were too tired to cook, so instead bought some fish and chips to eat.*

**fish|bowl** /fɪʃboʊl/ (**fishbowls**) also **fish bowl** **1** N-COUNT A **fishbowl** is a glass bowl in which you can keep fish as pets. **2** N-COUNT You can use **fishbowl** to describe a place or situation that is open to observation. ❑ *The yacht's crew must get used to working in a fishbowl.*

**fisher|man** /fɪʃərmən/ (**fishermen**) N-COUNT A **fisherman** is a person who catches fish as a job or for sport.

**fish|ing** /fɪʃɪŋ/ N-UNCOUNT **Fishing** is the sport, hobby, or business of catching fish. [from Old English]

**fish stick** (**fish sticks**) N-COUNT **Fish sticks** are small long pieces of fish covered in breadcrumbs, usually sold in frozen form.

**fish|tail** /fɪʃteɪl/ (**fishtails, fishtailing, fishtailed**) V-I If a vehicle **fishtails**, the rear of the vehicle swings around in an uncontrolled way while the vehicle is moving.

**fist** /fɪst/ (**fists**) N-COUNT Your hand is referred to as your **fist** when you have bent your fingers in toward the palm in order to hit someone, to make an angry gesture, or to hold something. ❑ *He shouted and shook his fist at me*. [from Old English]

**fist|fight** /fɪstfaɪt/ (**fistfights**) also **fist fight** N-COUNT A **fistfight** is a fight in which people punch each other. ❑ *Their argument almost ended in a fistfight.*

**fit**

**1** BEING RIGHT OR GOING IN THE RIGHT PLACE
**2** HEALTHY
**3** UNCONTROLLABLE MOVEMENTS OR EMOTIONS

**1 fit** /fɪt/ (**fits, fitting, fitted** or **fit**) **1** V-T/V-I If something **fits**, it is the right size and shape to go onto a person's body or onto a particular object. ❑ *The kimono fit the child perfectly*. ❑ *She has to go to the men's department to find trousers that fit at the waist*. **2** V-I If something **fits** somewhere, it can be put there or is designed to be put there. ❑ *The pocket computer is small enough to fit into your pocket*. **3** V-T If you **fit** something into a particular space or place, you put it there. ❑ *She fitted the book back on the shelf*. **4** V-T If you **fit** something somewhere, you attach it there, or put it there carefully and securely. ❑ *Fit locks on outside doors and install a visible burglar alarm*. ❑ *Peter built the overhead ladders and fitted them to the wall*. **5** N-SING If something is a good **fit**, it fits well. ❑ *He was happy that the doors were a reasonably good fit*. **6** ADJ If something is **fit** for a particular purpose, it is suitable for that purpose. ❑ *Only two of the bicycles were fit for the road*. **7** ADJ If someone is **fit** to do something, they have the appropriate qualities or skills that will allow them to do it. ❑ *You're not fit to be a mother!* ● **fit|ness** N-UNCOUNT ❑ *There is a debate about his fitness for the job*. **8** PHRASE If you say that someone **sees fit to** do something, you mean that they are entitled to do it, but that you disapprove of their decision to do it. [FORMAL] ❑ *He's not a friend, you say, yet you saw fit to lend him money*. [from Middle Dutch] **9** → see also **fitted, fitting** **10** fit the bill → see bill **11** to fit like a glove → see glove **12** not in a fit state → see state
▸ **fit in** **1** PHR-VERB If you manage to **fit** a person or task **in**, you manage to find time to deal with them. ❑ *We work long hours and we rush around trying to fit everything in*. **2** PHR-VERB If you **fit in** as part of a group, you seem to belong there because you are similar to the other people in it. ❑ *She was great with the children and fitted in beautifully.*
▸ **fit out** PHR-VERB If you **fit** someone or something **out**, or you **fit** them **up**, you provide them with equipment and other things that they need. ❑ *We helped to fit him out for a trip to the Baltic*. ❑ *Within an hour, Saab had fitted me up with another car.*

**❷ fit** /fɪt/ (**fitter, fittest**) ADJ Someone who is **fit** is healthy and physically strong. ❏ *An averagely fit person can master easy ski runs within a few days.* ● **fit|ness** N-UNCOUNT ❏ *Squash was once thought to offer all-round fitness.* [from Middle Dutch]

**❸ fit** /fɪt/ (**fits**) **1** N-COUNT If you have a **fit of** coughing or laughter, you suddenly start coughing or laughing in an uncontrollable way. ❏ *Part of the way through my speech I had a fit of coughing.* **2** N-COUNT If someone has a **fit** they suddenly lose consciousness and their body makes uncontrollable movements. ❏ *Place a pillow under the head of the person suffering a fit.* [from Old English]

**fit|ted** /fɪtɪd/ ADJ A **fitted** piece of clothing is designed so that it is the same size and shape as your body rather than being loose. ❏ *…fitted jackets.* [from Middle Dutch]

**fit|ting** /fɪtɪŋ/ (**fittings**) **1** ADJ Something that is **fitting** is right or suitable. ❏ *A solitary man, it was perhaps fitting that he died alone.* ● **fit|ting|ly** ADV ❏ *He ended his baseball career, fittingly, by hitting a home run.* **2** N-COUNT A **fitting** is one of the smaller parts on the outside of a piece of equipment or furniture, for example, a handle or a faucet. ❏ *…brass light fittings.* **3** N-PLURAL **Fittings** are things such as ovens or heaters, that are fitted inside a building, but can be removed if necessary. [from Middle Dutch]

**five** /faɪv/ (**fives**) NUM **Five** is the number 5. ❏ *I spent five years there.* [from Old English]

**fix** /fɪks/ (**fixes, fixing, fixed**) **1** V-T If you **fix** something which is damaged or which does not work properly, you repair it. ❏ *This morning, a man came to fix my washing machine.* **2** V-T If you **fix** something, for example, a date, price, or policy, you decide and say exactly what it will be. ❏ *He's going to fix a time when I can see him.* **3** V-T If something **is fixed** somewhere, it is attached there firmly or securely. ❏ *It is fixed on the wall.* **4** V-T/V-I If you **fix** your eyes **on** someone or something or if your eyes **fix on** them, you look at them with complete attention. ❏ *Gregory fixed his eyes on the floor.* **5** V-T If someone **fixes** a race, election, contest, or other event, they make unfair or illegal arrangements to affect the result. ❏ *They offered players bribes to fix the game.* ● **Fix** is also a noun. ❏ *It's all a fix, a deal they've made.* [from Medieval Latin] **6** → see also **fixed**

▸ **fix up** PHR-VERB If you **fix** someone **up with** something they need, you provide it for them. ❏ *We'll fix him up with a tie.*

| **Thesaurus** | *fix* | Also look up : |
|---|---|---|
| v. | adjust, correct, repair, restore **1** | |
| | agree on, decide, establish, work out **2** | |

**fixed** /fɪkst/ **1** ADJ You use **fixed** to describe something which stays the same and does not or cannot vary. ❏ *The company issues a fixed number of shares.* ❏ *…fixed-price menus.* [from Medieval Latin] **2** → see also **fix**

**fixed pul|ley** (**fixed pulleys**) N-COUNT A **fixed pulley** is a pulley that is attached to something that does not move.

| **Word Link** | *fix ≈ fastening : fixture, prefix, suffix* |

**fix|ture** /fɪkstʃər/ (**fixtures**) N-COUNT **Fixtures** are fittings or furniture which belong to a building and are legally part of it, for example, a bathtub or a toilet. ❏ *…fixtures and fittings are included in the purchase price.* [from Late Latin]

**fizz** /fɪz/ (**fizzes, fizzing, fizzed**) V-I If a drink **fizzes**, it produces a lot of little bubbles of gas and makes a sound like a long "s." ● **Fizz** is also a noun. ❏ *I wonder if there's any fizz left in the soda.*

**fizzy** /fɪzi/ (**fizzier, fizziest**) ADJ **Fizzy** liquids contain small bubbles of carbon dioxide. ❏ *…fizzy water.*

**flag** /flæg/ (**flags, flagging, flagged**) **1** N-COUNT A **flag** is a piece of colored cloth which can be attached to a pole and is used as a sign for something or as a signal. ❏ *…the American flag.* **2** V-I If you **flag** or if your spirits **flag**, you begin to lose enthusiasm or energy.

**fla|gella** /flədʒɛlə/ N-PLURAL **Flagella** are the long, thin extensions of cells in some microorganisms that help them move. [TECHNICAL]

**fla|grant** /fleɪgrənt/ ADJ You can use **flagrant** to describe an action, situation, or behavior that you find extremely bad or shocking in a very obvious way. ❏ *…a flagrant act of aggression.* [from Latin]

**flag|ship** /flægʃɪp/ (**flagships**) N-COUNT The **flagship** of a group of things that are owned or produced by a particular organization is the most important one. ❏ *The company plans to open a flagship store in New York.*

**flail** /fleɪl/ (**flails, flailing, flailed**) V-T/V-I If your arms or legs **flail** or if you **flail** them about, they wave about in an energetic but uncontrolled way. ❏ *His arms were flailing in all directions.* ● **Flail around** means the same as **flail**. ❏ *He started flailing around and hitting Vincent in the chest.* [from Late Latin]

**flair** /flɛər/ **1** N-SING If you have a **flair for** a particular thing, you have a natural ability to do it well. ❏ *My friend has a flair for languages.* **2** N-UNCOUNT If you have **flair**, you do things in an original, interesting, and stylish way. ❏ *Each of these groups is producing jazz with flair.* [from French]

**flak** /flæk/ also **flack** N-UNCOUNT If you get a lot of **flak** from someone, they criticize you severely. If you take **flak**, you get the blame for something. [INFORMAL] ❏ *the company took flak for high prices and slow delivery of services.* [from German]

**flake** /fleɪk/ (**flakes, flaking, flaked**) **1** N-COUNT A **flake** is a small thin piece of something, especially one that has broken off a larger piece. ❏ *…flakes of paint.* ❏ *Large flakes of snow began to fall.* **2** V-I If something such as paint **flakes**, small thin pieces of it come off. ● **Flake off** means the same as **flake**. ❏ *The paint is flaking off.* [of Scandinavian origin]

| **Word Link** | *flam ≈ burning : flame, flamboyant, inflame* |

**flam|boy|ant** /flæmbɔɪənt/ ADJ If you say that someone or something is **flamboyant**, you mean that they are very noticeable, stylish, and exciting. ❏ *Freddie Mercury was a flamboyant star.* ● **flam|boy|ance** N-UNCOUNT ❏ *Campese was his usual mixture of flamboyance and flair.* [from French]

**flame** /fleɪm/ (**flames**) **1** N-VAR A **flame** is a hot bright stream of burning gas that comes from something that is burning. ❏ *The heat from the flames was so intense that roads melted.* **2** → see

also **flaming** ⬛ PHRASE If something **bursts into flames** or **bursts into flame**, it suddenly starts burning strongly. ⬛ PHRASE Something that is **in flames** is on fire. [from Old French]
→ see **fire, laboratory**

**flam|ing** /ˈfleɪmɪŋ/ ADJ **Flaming** is used to describe something that is burning and producing a lot of flames. ❑ *The plane scattered flaming fragments over a large area.* [from Old French]

**fla|min|go** (**flamingos** or **flamingoes**) N-COUNT A **flamingo** is a bird with pink feathers, long thin legs, a long neck, and a curved beak. Flamingos live near water in warm areas. [from Portuguese]

**flank** /flæŋk/ (**flanks, flanking, flanked**) ⬛ N-COUNT An animal's **flank** is its side, between the ribs and the hip. ⬛ N-COUNT A **flank** of an army or navy force is one side of it when it is organized for battle. ⬛ V-T If something **is flanked by** things, it has them on both sides of it, or sometimes on one side of it. ❑ *The altar was flanked by two Christmas trees.* [from Old French]
→ see **horse**

**flan|nel** /ˈflænᵊl/ N-UNCOUNT **Flannel** is a soft cloth, usually made of cotton or wool, that is used for making clothes. ❑ *...a red flannel shirt.* [from Welsh]

**flap** /flæp/ (**flaps, flapping, flapped**) ⬛ V-T/V-I If something such as a piece of cloth or paper **flaps** or if you **flap** it, it moves quickly up and down or from side to side. ❑ *Gray sheets flapped on the clothes line.* ⬛ V-T/V-I If a bird or insect **flaps** its wings or if its wings **flap**, the wings move quickly up and down. ⬛ N-COUNT A **flap** of cloth or skin is a flat piece of it that can move freely up and down or from side to side because it is attached by only one edge. ❑ *He drew back the tent flap.*

**flare** /flɛər/ (**flares, flaring, flared**) ⬛ N-COUNT A **flare** is a small device that produces a bright flame. Flares are used as distress signals, for example, on ships. ⬛ V-I If a fire **flares**, the flames suddenly become larger. • **Flare up** means the same as **flare**. ❑ *Don't spill too much fat on the barbecue as it could flare up.* ⬛ V-I If something such as trouble, violence, or conflict **flares**, it starts or becomes more violent. ❑ *Trouble flared in several American cities.* • **Flare up** means the same as **flare**. ❑ *Dozens of people were injured as fighting flared up.*

**flare-up** (**flare-ups**) N-COUNT If there is a **flare-up** of violence or of an illness, it suddenly starts or gets worse.

**flash** /flæʃ/ (**flashes, flashing, flashed**) ⬛ N-COUNT A **flash** is a sudden burst of light or of something shiny or bright. ❑ *...a sudden flash of lightning.* ⬛ V-T/V-I If a light **flashes** or if you **flash** a light, it shines with a sudden bright light, especially as quick, regular flashes of light. ❑ *Lightning flashed among the dark clouds.* ❑ *Frightened drivers flashed their headlights at him as he drove down the wrong side of the road.* ⬛ V-I If something **flashes** past or by, it moves past you so fast that you cannot see it properly. ❑ *It was a busy road, and cars flashed by every few minutes.* ⬛ N-COUNT A **flash** is the same as a **flashlight**. [INFORMAL] ❑ *Stopping to rest, Pete shut off the flash.* ⬛ PHRASE If you say that something happens **in a flash**, you mean that it happens suddenly and lasts only a very short time. ❑ *The answer came to him in a flash.*

**flash|back** /ˈflæʃbæk/ (**flashbacks**) ⬛ N-COUNT In a movie, novel, or play, a **flashback** is a scene that returns to events in the past. ❑ *There is even a flashback to the murder itself.* ⬛ N-COUNT If you have a **flashback** to a past experience, you have a sudden and very clear memory of it. ❑ *I had a flashback to a birthday party when I was eight.*

**flash drive** (**flash drives**) N-COUNT A **flash drive** is a small, lightweight smart card that can be plugged into a computer where it functions as a portable hard drive.
→ see **computer**

**flash flood** (**flash floods**) N-COUNT A **flash flood** is a sudden rush of water over dry land, usually caused by a great deal of rain.

**flash|light** /ˈflæʃlaɪt/ (**flashlights**) N-COUNT A **flashlight** is a small electric light which gets

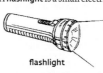

its power from batteries and which you can carry in your hand.

**flashy** /ˈflæʃi/ (**flashier, flashiest**) ADJ If you describe a person or thing

flashlight

as **flashy**, you mean they are fashionable and noticeable, but in a somewhat vulgar way. [INFORMAL] ❑ *...a flashy sports car.*

**flask** /flæsk/ (**flasks**) N-COUNT A **flask** is a bottle which you use for carrying alcoholic or hot drinks around with you. ❑ *...a flask of coffee.* [from Old French]
→ see **laboratory**

---

### flat

**❶** SURFACES, SHAPES, AND POSITIONS
**❷** OTHER USES

---

**❶ flat** /flæt/ (**flatter, flattest**) ⬛ ADJ Something that is **flat** is level, smooth, or even, rather than sloping, curved, or uneven. ❑ *Tiles can be fixed to any surface as long as it's flat.* ❑ *...a flat roof.* ⬛ ADJ A **flat** object is not very tall or deep in relation to its length and width. ❑ *...a square flat box.* ⬛ ADJ A **flat** tire or ball does not have enough air in it. [from Old Norse]

| **Thesaurus** | *flat* | Also look up : |
|---|---|---|
| ADJ. | even, horizontal, level, smooth **❶** ⬛ | |

**❷ flat** /flæt/ (**flatter, flattest**) ⬛ ADJ If you say that something happens, for example, in ten seconds **flat** or ten minutes **flat**, you are emphasizing that it happened surprisingly quickly and only took ten seconds or ten minutes. ❑ *The engine will take you from 0 to 60 mph in six seconds flat.* ⬛ ADJ A **flat** rate, price, or percentage is one that is fixed and which applies in every situation. ❑ *Fees are charged at a flat rate.* ⬛ ADJ **Flat** is used after a letter representing a musical note, to show that the note should be played or sung half a tone lower than the note which otherwise matches that letter. **Flat** is often represented by the symbol ♭ after the letter. ❑ *...Schubert's B flat Piano Trio.* ⬛ ADV If someone sings **flat** or if a musical instrument is **flat**, their singing or the instrument is slightly lower in pitch than it should be. ● **Flat** is also an adjective. ❑ *He was fired from the choir because his singing was flat.* **5** ADJ A **flat** denial or refusal is definite and firm. ❑ *The Foreign Ministry has issued a flat denial of any involvement.* ● **flat|ly** ADV ❑ *He flatly refused to discuss it.* **6** PHRASE If an event or attempt **falls flat** or **falls flat on its face**, it is unsuccessful. ❑ *Liz meant it as a joke but it fell flat.* **7** PHRASE If you do something **flat out**, you do it as fast or as hard as you can. ❑ *Everyone is working flat out to try to find those responsible.* ❑ *...almost 20 minutes of flat-out rowing.* [from Old Norse]

**flat|lands** /flǽtlændz/ N-PLURAL **Flatlands** are areas where the land is very flat. ❑ *...the featureless flatlands of the Midwest.*

**flat|ten** /flǽtᵊn/ (**flattens, flattening, flattened**) **1** V-T/V-I If you **flatten** something or if it **flattens**, it becomes flat or flatter. ❑ *Flatten the dough with your hands to a thickness of about 1 inch.* ❑ *The dog's ears flattened slightly as Chris spoke his name.* ● **Flatten out** means the same as **flatten**. ❑ *The hills flattened out just south of the mountain.* **2** V-T If you **flatten yourself against** something, you press yourself flat against it, for example, to avoid getting in the way or being seen. ❑ *He flattened himself against a brick wall as I passed.* [from Old Norse]

**flat|ter** /flǽtər/ (**flatters, flattering, flattered**) **1** V-T If someone **flatters** you, they praise you in an exaggerated way that is not sincere. ❑ *I knew she was just flattering me.* **2** V-T If you **flatter yourself that** something good is true, you believe that it is true, although others may disagree. ❑ *I flatter myself that I've done it all very well.* [from Old French] **3** → see also **flat, flattered, flattering**

**flat|tered** /flǽtərd/ ADJ If you are **flattered** by something that has happened, you are pleased about it because it makes you feel important or special. ❑ *She was flattered by Roberto's long letter.* [from Old French]

**flat|ter|ing** /flǽtərɪŋ/ **1** ADJ If something is **flattering**, it makes you appear more attractive. ❑ *It wasn't a very flattering photograph.* **2** ADJ If someone's remarks are **flattering**, they praise you and say nice things about you. ❑ *Most of his colleagues had positive, even flattering things to say.* [from Old French]

**flat|ware** /flǽtweər/ N-UNCOUNT You can refer to knives, forks, and spoons that you eat food with as **flatware**.

**flaunt** /flɔnt/ (**flaunts, flaunting, flaunted**) V-T If you say that someone **flaunts** their possessions, abilities, or qualities, you disapprove of them because they display them in a very obvious way. ❑ *They drove around in Rolls-Royces, openly flaunting their wealth.* [of Scandinavian origin]

**fla|vor** /fléɪvər/ (**flavors, flavoring, flavored**) **1** N-VAR The **flavor** of a food or drink is its taste. ❑ *I always add some paprika for extra flavor.* **2** V-T If you **flavor** food or drink, you add something to it to give it a particular taste. ❑ *Flavor your favourite dishes with herbs and spices.* [from Old French]

**fla|vored** /fléɪvərd/ ADJ If a food is **flavored**, various ingredients have been added to it so that it has a distinctive flavor. ❑ *Many of these recipes are highly flavored.* [from Old French]

**fla|vor|ful** /fléɪvərfəl/ ADJ **Flavorful** food has a strong, pleasant taste and is good to eat. ❑ *...flavorful recipes for everyday cooking.* [from Old

French]

**fla|vor|ing** /fléɪvərɪŋ/ (**flavorings**) N-VAR **Flavorings** are substances that are added to food or drink to give it a particular taste. [from Old French]

**fla|vor|less** /fléɪvərlɪs/ ADJ **Flavorless** food is uninteresting because it does not taste strongly of anything. [from Old French]

**flaw** /flɔ/ (**flaws**) **1** N-COUNT A **flaw in** something such as a theory or argument is a mistake in it, which causes it to be less effective or valid. ❑ *There were a number of flaws in his theory.* **2** N-COUNT A **flaw in** your character is an undesirable quality that you have. ❑ *The only flaw in his character seems to be a bad temper.* [from Old Norse]

**flawed** /flɔd/ ADJ Something that is **flawed** has a mark, fault, or mistake in it. ❑ *These tests were seriously flawed.* [from Old Norse]

**flaw|less** /flɔlɪs/ ADJ If you say that something or someone is **flawless**, you mean that they are extremely good and that there are no faults or problems with them. ❑ *Discovery's takeoff from Cape Canaveral was flawless.* ● **flaw|less|ly** ADV ❑ *Each stage of the battle was carried out flawlessly.* [from Old Norse]

**flea** /fli/ (**fleas**) N-COUNT A **flea** is a very small jumping insect that has no wings and feeds on the blood of humans or animals. [from Old English]

**fleck** /flɛk/ (**flecks**) N-COUNT **Flecks** are small marks on a surface, or objects that look like small marks. ❑ *He washed the flecks of blood from his shirt.* [from Old Norse]

**fled** /flɛd/ **Fled** is the past tense and past participle of **flee**. [from Old English]

**fledg|ling** /flɛdʒlɪŋ/ (**fledglings**) **1** N-COUNT A **fledgling** is a young bird that is learning to fly. **2** ADJ You use **fledgling** to describe a person, organization, or system that is new or without experience. ❑ *...Russia's fledgling democracy.* [from Old English]

**flee** /fli/ (**flees, fleeing, fled**) V-T/V-I If you **flee from** something or someone, or **flee** a person or thing, you escape from them. [WRITTEN] ❑ *He slammed the door behind him and fled.* ❑ *...refugees fleeing torture.* [from Old English]

**fleece** /flis/ (**fleeces, fleecing, fleeced**) **1** N-COUNT A sheep's **fleece** is the coat of wool that covers it. **2** N-COUNT A **fleece** is the wool that is cut off one sheep in a single piece. **3** V-T If you **fleece** someone, you get a lot of money from them by tricking them or charging them too much. [INFORMAL] ❑ *She claims she fleeced her out of thousands of dollars.* [from Old English]

**fleet** /flit/ (**fleets**) **1** N-COUNT A **fleet** is a group of ships organized to do something together. ❑ *...local fishing fleets.* **2** N-COUNT A **fleet** of vehicles is a group of them, especially when they all belong to a particular organization or business. ❑ *With its own fleet of trucks, the company delivers most orders overnight.* [from Old English]

**fleet|ing** /flitɪŋ/ ADJ **Fleeting** is used to describe something which lasts only for a very short time. ❑ *The girls caught only a fleeting glimpse of the driver.* ● **fleet|ing|ly** ADV ❑ *A smile passed fleetingly across his face.* [from Old English]

**f**

**flesh** /flɛʃ/ (fleshes, fleshing, fleshed)
**1** N-UNCOUNT **Flesh** is the soft part of a person's or animal's body between the bones and the skin. □ ...*the pale pink flesh of trout.* **2** N-UNCOUNT You can use **flesh** to refer to human skin and the human body. □ ...*the warmth of her flesh.* **3** N-UNCOUNT The **flesh** of a fruit or vegetable is the soft inside part. **4** PHRASE If you say that someone is your **own flesh and blood**, you are emphasizing that they are a member of your family. **5** PHRASE If you meet or see someone **in the flesh**, you actually meet or see them in person. □ *The first thing people usually say when they see me in the flesh is "You're smaller than you look on TV."* [from Old English]
→ see **carnivore**
▶ **flesh out** PHR-VERB If you **flesh out** something such as a story or plan, you add details and more information to it. □ *We need to flesh out the details of the agreement.*

**flesh-colored** ADJ Something that is **flesh-colored** is yellowish pink in color.

**flew** /flu/ **Flew** is the past tense of **fly**. [from Old English]

> **Word Link** flex ≈ bending : flex, flexible, reflex

**flex** /flɛks/ (flexes, flexing, flexed) **1** V-T If you **flex** your muscles or parts of your body, you bend, move, or stretch them for a short time in order to exercise them. [from Latin] **2** to **flex** your **muscles** → see **muscle**

> **Word Link** ible ≈ able to be : audible, flexible, possible

**flex|ible** /flɛksəbəl/ **1** ADJ A **flexible** object or material can be bent easily without breaking. □ ...*brushes with long, flexible bristles.* ● **flexi|bil|ity** /flɛksɪbɪlɪti/ N-UNCOUNT □ ...*exercises to enhance the body's flexibility and strength.* **2** ADJ If you say that something or someone is **flexible**, you approve of them because they are able to change easily and adapt to different conditions and circumstances. □ ...*flexible working hours.* ● **flexi|bil|ity** N-UNCOUNT □ ...*the flexibility of the seating arrangements.* [from Latin]

**flex|or** /flɛksər/ (flexors) N-COUNT A **flexor** is a muscle that bends a part of your body. [TECHNICAL] [from New Latin]

**flex|time** /flɛkstaɪm/ also flexitime N-UNCOUNT **Flextime** is a system that allows employees to vary the time that they start or finish work, provided that an agreed total number of hours are spent at work. [BUSINESS]

**flick** /flɪk/ (flicks, flicking, flicked) **1** V-T/V-I If something **flicks** in a particular direction, or if someone **flicks** it, it moves with a short, sudden movement. □ *His tongue flicked across his lips.* □ *He shook his head to flick hair out of his eyes.* ● **Flick** is also a noun. □ ...*a flick of a paintbrush.* **2** V-T If you **flick** a switch, or **flick** an electrical appliance on or off, you press the switch quickly. □ *Sam was flicking a flashlight on and off.* **3** V-I If you **flick through** a book or magazine, you turn its pages quickly.

**flick|er** /flɪkər/ (flickers, flickering, flickered) V-I If a light or flame **flickers**, it shines unsteadily. □ *Lights flickered, and then the room was very bright.* ● **Flicker** is also a noun. □ ...*the flicker of flames.* [from Old English]

**flight** /flaɪt/ (flights) **1** N-COUNT A **flight** is a trip made by flying, usually in an airplane. □ *The flight will take four hours.* **2** N-COUNT You can refer to an airplane carrying passengers on a particular trip as a particular **flight**. □ *BA flight 286 was two hours late.* **3** N-COUNT A **flight** of steps or stairs is a set of steps or stairs that lead from one level to another. **4** N-UNCOUNT **Flight** is the action of flying, or the ability to fly. □ ...*the first commercial space flight.* **5** N-UNCOUNT **Flight** is the act of running away from a dangerous or unpleasant situation or place. □ *The family was often in flight, hiding out in friends' houses.* [from Old English]
→ see **fly**

**flim|sy** /flɪmzi/ (flimsier, flimsiest) **1** ADJ A **flimsy** object is easily damaged because it is made of a weak material, or is badly made. □ ...*a flimsy wooden door.* **2** ADJ **Flimsy** cloth or clothing is thin and does not give much protection. □ ...*a flimsy pink nightgown.* **3** ADJ If you describe something such as evidence or an excuse as **flimsy**, you mean that it is not very good or convincing.

**flinch** /flɪntʃ/ (flinches, flinching, flinched) **1** V-I If you **flinch**, you make a small sudden movement, especially when something surprises you or hurts you. □ *Leo stared back at him without flinching.* **2** V-I If you do not **flinch from** something unpleasant, you do not attempt to avoid it. □ *We should not flinch in the face of this challenge.* [from Old French]

**fling** /flɪŋ/ (flings, flinging, flung) **1** V-T If you **fling** something somewhere, you throw it there using a lot of force. □ *The woman flung the cup at him.* **2** N-COUNT If two people have **a fling**, they have a brief romantic relationship. [INFORMAL] □ *She had a brief fling with him 30 years ago.* [of Scandinavian origin]

**flip** /flɪp/ (flips, flipping, flipped) **1** V-I If you **flip** through the pages of a book, you turn the pages quickly. □ *He was flipping through a magazine in the living room.* **2** V-T/V-I If something **flips** over, or if you **flip** it over or into a different position, it moves or is moved into a different position. □ *The car flipped over and burst into flames.*

**flip-flop** (flip-flops, flip-flopping, flip-flopped) V-I If you say that someone, especially a politician, **flip-flops** on a decision, you are critical of them because they change their decision, so that they do or think the opposite. [INFORMAL] □ *He was criticized for flip-flopping on several key issues.*

**flirt** /flɜrt/ (flirts, flirting, flirted) **1** V-RECIP If you **flirt with** someone, you behave as if you are attracted to them, in a playful or not very serious way. □ *He's flirting with all the ladies.* ● **flir|ta|tion** /flɜrteɪʃən/ (flirtations) N-VAR □ *She was aware of his attempts at flirtation.* **2** N-COUNT Someone who is a **flirt** likes to flirt a lot. □ *I'm not a flirt. I like being with one person.* **3** V-I If you **flirt with** the idea of something, you consider it but do not do anything about it. □ *Sadat also flirted with socialism.* ● **flir|ta|tion** N-VAR □ ...*a flirtation with danger that excited me.*

**flit** /flɪt/ (flits, flitting, flitted) **1** V-I If you **flit** around or **flit** between one place and another, you go to lots of places without staying for very long in any of them. □ *Sylvia knew a lot of people at the party and was flitting around chatting.* **2** V-I If someone **flits from** one thing or situation **to** another, they move or turn their attention from one to the other very quickly. ❑ *He flits easily between subjects.* **3** V-I If something such as a bird or a bat **flits** about, it flies quickly from one place to another. ❑ *The bird flitted from tree to tree.* [from Old Norse]

**float** /floʊt/ (**floats, floating, floated**) **1** V-T/V-I If something or someone **is floating** in a liquid, they are in the liquid, on or just below the surface, and are being supported by it. You can also **float** something on a liquid. ❑ *They noticed fifty-dollar bills floating in the water.* ❑ *It's below freezing and small icebergs are floating by.* **2** V-I Something that **floats** in or through the air hangs in it or moves slowly and gently through it. ❑ *The white cloud of smoke floated away.* **3** V-T If a company director **floats** their company, they start to sell shares in it to the public. [BUSINESS] ❑ *He floated his firm on the stock market.* **4** N-COUNT A **float** is a light object that is used to help someone or something float. ❑ *First, the children learn to swim using floats.* [from Old English]

**flock** /flɒk/ (**flocks, flocking, flocked**) **1** N-COUNT A **flock of** birds, sheep, or goats is a group of them. **2** N-COUNT You can refer to a group of people or things as a **flock of** them to emphasize that there are a lot of them. ❑ *A flock of small children came running.* **3** V-I If people **flock to** a particular place or event, a lot of them go there. ❑ *The public has flocked to the show.* ❑ *The criticisms will not stop people from flocking to see the film.* [from Old English]

**flog** /flɒg/ (**flogs, flogging, flogged**) V-T If someone **is flogged**, they are hit very hard with a whip or stick as a punishment. ● **flog|ging** (**floggings**) N-VAR ❑ *He was sentenced to a flogging and life imprisonment.* [from Latin]

**flood** /flʌd/ (**floods, flooding, flooded**) **1** N-VAR If there is a **flood**, a large amount of water covers an area which is usually dry, for example, when a river flows over its banks or a pipe bursts. ❑ *More than 70 people died in the floods.* **2** V-T/V-I If something such as a river or a burst pipe **floods** an area that is usually dry or if the area **floods**, it becomes covered with water. ❑ *The kitchen flooded.* ● **flood|ing** N-UNCOUNT ❑ *The flooding is the worst in sixty-five years.* **3** V-I If you say that people or things **flood** into a place, you are emphasizing that they arrive there in large numbers. ❑ *Thousands of immigrants flooded into the area.* **4** N-COUNT If you say that a **flood of** people or things arrive somewhere, you are emphasizing that a very large number of them arrive there. ❑ *...the flood of refugees out of Haiti and into Florida.* [from Old English]
→ see **dam, disaster, storm**

**flood|light** /flʌdlaɪt/ (**floodlights, floodlighting, floodlit**) **1** N-COUNT **Floodlights** are very powerful lamps that are used outside to light public buildings, sports grounds, and other places at night. **2** V-T If a building or place **is floodlit**, it is lit by floodlights. ❑ *In the evening the theater is floodlit.*

**flood plain** (**flood plains**) also **floodplain** N-COUNT A **flood plain** is a flat area on the edge of a river, where the ground consists of soil, sand, and rock left by the river when it floods.

**floor** /flɔr/ (**floors, flooring, floored**) **1** N-COUNT The **floor** of a room is the part of it that you walk on. ❑ *Jack's sitting on the floor watching TV.* **2** N-COUNT A **floor** of a building is all the rooms

that are on a particular level. ❑ *The café was on the top floor.* ❑ *I live on the second floor of the apartment block.* **3** N-COUNT The ocean **floor** is the ground at the bottom of an ocean. The valley **floor** is the ground at the bottom of a valley. **4** V-T If you **are floored by** something, you are unable to respond to it because you are so surprised by it. ❑ *He was floored by the announcement.* [from Old English] **5** → see also **dance floor, first floor, shop floor**

**floor|board** /flɔrbɔrd/ (**floorboards**) N-COUNT **Floorboards** are the long pieces of wood that a wooden floor is made up of. [from Old English]

**floor lamp** (**floor lamps**) N-COUNT A **floor lamp** is a tall electric light which stands on the floor in a living room.

**flop** /flɒp/ (**flops, flopping, flopped**) **1** V-I If you **flop** into a chair, for example, you sit down suddenly and heavily because you are so tired. ❑ *Ben flopped down upon the bed and rested his tired feet.* **2** V-I If something **flops** onto something else, it falls there heavily or untidily. ❑ *The briefcase flopped onto the desk.* **3** V-I If something **flops**, it is completely unsuccessful. [INFORMAL] ❑ *The movie flopped badly at the box office.* **4** N-COUNT If something is a **flop**, it is completely unsuccessful. [INFORMAL] ❑ *It is the public who decides whether a film is a hit or a flop.*

**flop|py** /flɒpi/ (**floppier, floppiest**) ADJ **Floppy** things are loose rather than stiff, and hang downward. ❑ *...the girl with the floppy hat.*

**flop|py disk** (**floppy disks**) N-COUNT A **floppy disk** is a small magnetic disk that is used for storing computer data and programs.

**flo|ra** /flɔrə/ N-UNCOUNT You can refer to plants, especially the plants growing in a particular area. [FORMAL] ❑ *...the variety of flora which now exists in Dominica.* [from New Latin]

**flo|ral** /flɔrəl/ **1** ADJ A **floral** fabric or design has flowers on it. **2** ADJ You can use **floral** to describe something that contains flowers or is made of flowers. ❑ *...floral arrangements.* [from New Latin]

**flo|rist** /flɔrɪst/ (**florists**) **1** N-COUNT A **florist** is a storekeeper who arranges and sells flowers and sells houseplants. **2** N-COUNT A **florist** or a **florist's** is a store where flowers and houseplants are sold. [from New Latin]

**floun|der** /flaʊndər/ (**flounders, floundering, floundered**) **1** V-I If something **is floundering**, it has many problems and may soon fail completely. ❑ *What a pity that his career was left to flounder.* **2** V-I If you say that someone **is floundering**, you are criticizing them for not making decisions or for not knowing what to say or do. ❑ *Right now, you've got a president who's floundering.*

**flour** /flaʊər/ N-UNCOUNT **Flour** is a white or brown powder that is made by grinding grain. It is used to make bread, cakes, and pastry.
→ see **grain**

f

**flour|ish** /flɜrɪʃ/ (flourishes, flourishing, flourished) **1** V-I If something **flourishes**, it is successful, active, or common, and is developing quickly and strongly. ❑ *Translations of Western literature have flourished in China since the 19th century.* ● **flour|ish|ing** ADJ ❑ *Boston quickly became a flourishing port.* **2** V-I If a plant or animal **flourishes**, it grows well or is healthy. ❑ *The plant flourishes well in warm climates.* ● **flour|ish|ing** ADJ ❑ *...a flourishing fox population.* **3** N-COUNT If you do something with a **flourish**, you do it with a bold sweeping movement, intended to make people notice it. ❑ *He took his cap from under his arm with a flourish.* [from Old French]

**flout** /flaʊt/ (flouts, flouting, flouted) V-T If you **flout** a law, an order, or an accepted way of behaving, you deliberately do not obey it or follow it. ❑ *Illegal campers are flouting the law.* [from Middle English]

**flow** /floʊ/ (flows, flowing, flowed) **1** V-I If a liquid, gas, or electrical current **flows** somewhere, it moves there steadily and continuously. ❑ *A stream flowed gently down into the valley.* ● **Flow** is also a noun. ❑ *In the veins, the blood flow is slower.* **2** V-I If a number of people or things **flow** from one place to another, they move there steadily in large groups. ❑ *Large numbers of refugees continue to flow from the troubled region.* ● **Flow** is also a noun. ❑ *...the flow of cars and buses along the street.* **3** V-I If information or money **flows** somewhere, it moves freely between people or organizations. ❑ *A lot of this information flowed through other police departments.* ● **Flow** is also a noun. ❑ *...the opportunity to control the flow of information.* [from Old English]

→ see **ocean, traffic**

**flow chart** (flow charts) N-COUNT A **flow chart** or a **flow diagram** is a diagram which represents the sequence of actions in a particular process or activity.

**flow|er** /flaʊər/ (flowers, flowering, flowered) **1** N-COUNT A **flower** is the part of a plant which is often brightly colored and grows at the end of a stem. ❑ *...a bunch of flowers.* **2** V-I When a plant or tree **flowers**, its flowers appear and open. ❑ *These plants will flower this year for the first time.* **3** V-I When something **flowers**, for example, a political movement or a relationship, it gets stronger and more successful. ● **flow|er|ing** N-UNCOUNT ❑ *...the flowering of new thinking.* [from Old French]

→ see Picture Dictionary: **flower**
→ see **plant**

**flow|er|ing** /flaʊərɪŋ/ ADJ **Flowering** shrubs, trees, or plants are those which produce noticeable flowers. [from Old French]

**flown** /floʊn/ **Flown** is the past participle of **fly**.

**flu** /flu/ N-UNCOUNT **Flu** is an illness which is similar to a bad cold but more serious. It is an abbreviation for "influenza." ❑ *I got the flu and felt dreadful.*

**flub** /flʌb/ (flubs, flubbing, flubbed) **1** V-T If you **flub** something that you are trying to do, you are unsuccessful or you do it badly. [INFORMAL] ❑ *If you try a sales technique and flub it, will you try it again?* **2** N-COUNT A **flub** is a mistake or an unsuccessful attempt to do something. [INFORMAL] ❑ *...her biggest flub of the day.*

**fluc|tu|ate** /flʌktʃueɪt/ (fluctuates, fluctuating, fluctuated) V-I If something **fluctuates**, it changes a lot in an irregular way. ❑ *Body temperature can fluctuate if you are ill.* ● **fluc|tua|tion** /flʌktʃueɪʃⁿ/ (fluctuations) N-VAR ❑ *Don't worry about tiny fluctuations in your weight.* [from Latin]

**flu|ent** /fluənt/ **1** ADJ Someone who is **fluent** in a particular language can speak the language easily and correctly. You can also say that someone speaks **fluent** French, Chinese, or some other language. ● **flu|en|cy** /fluənsi/ N-UNCOUNT ❑ *To work as a translator, you need fluency in at least one foreign language.* ● **flu|ent|ly** ADV ❑ *He spoke three languages fluently.* **2** ADJ If your speech, reading, or writing is **fluent**, you speak, read, or write easily, smoothly, and clearly with no mistakes. ❑ *...a fluent debater.* ● **flu|ent|ly** ADV ❑ *Alex didn't read fluently till he was nearly seven.* [from Latin]

**fluff** /flʌf/ N-UNCOUNT **Fluff** consists of soft threads or fibers in the form of small, light balls or lumps. ❑ *The chicks were just small gray balls of fluff.*

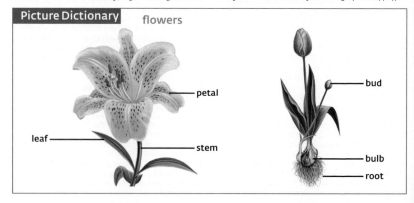

**Picture Dictionary** flowers

petal

leaf

stem

bud

bulb

root

**fluffy** /flˈʌfi/ (**fluffier, fluffiest**) ADJ If you describe something such as a towel or a toy animal as **fluffy**, you mean that it is very soft.

**fluid** /flˈuɪd/ (**fluids**) **1** N-VAR A **fluid** is a liquid. [FORMAL] ❑ *Make sure that you drink plenty of fluids.* **2** ADJ **Fluid** movements, lines, or designs are smooth and graceful. ❑ *His painting became more fluid.* [from Latin]

**fluke** /flˈuk/ (**flukes**) N-COUNT If you say that something good is a **fluke**, you mean that it happened accidentally rather than by being planned or arranged. [INFORMAL] ❑ *The discovery was actually a fluke.*

**flung** /flˈʌŋ/ **Flung** is the past tense and past participle of **fling**. [of Scandinavian origin]

**flunk** /flˈʌŋk/ (**flunks, flunking, flunked**) V-T If you **flunk** an exam or a course, you fail to reach the required standard. [INFORMAL]

**fluo|res|cent** /flʊrˈɛsᵊnt/ **1** ADJ A **fluorescent** surface, substance, or color has a very bright appearance when light is directed onto it. ❑ *...a piece of fluorescent tape.* **2** ADJ A **fluorescent** light shines with a very hard, bright light and is usually in the form of a long strip.
→ see **light bulb**

**flur|ry** /flˈɜri/ (**flurries**) **1** N-COUNT A **flurry** of something such as activity or excitement is a short intense period of it. ❑ *...a flurry of diplomatic activity aimed at ending the war.* **2** N-COUNT A **flurry** of something such as snow is a small amount of it that suddenly appears for a short time and moves in a quick, swirling way. ❑ *...We should expect light snow flurries.*

**flush** /flˈʌʃ/ (**flushes, flushing, flushed**) **1** V-I If you **flush**, your face gets red because you are hot or ill, or because you are feeling a strong emotion such as embarrassment or anger. ● **Flush** is also a noun. ❑ *There was a slight flush on his cheeks.* ● **flushed** ADJ ❑ *Her face was flushed with anger.* **2** V-T/V-I When someone **flushes** a toilet after using it, they press a handle and water flows into the toilet bowl, cleaning it. ❑ *I heard the toilet flush.* ● **Flush** is also a noun. ❑ *He heard the flush of a toilet.* **3** V-T If you **flush** people or animals **out** of a place where they are hiding, you find or capture them by forcing them to come out of that place. ❑ *They flushed them out of their hiding places.*

**flushed** /flˈʌʃt/ ADJ If you say that someone is **flushed with** success or pride you mean that they are very excited by their success or pride. ❑ *Grace was flushed with the success of the venture.*

**flus|ter** /flˈʌstər/ (**flusters, flustering, flustered**) V-T If you **fluster** someone, you make them feel nervous and confused by rushing them and preventing them from concentrating on what they are doing. ❑ *The General refused to be flustered.* ● **flus|tered** ADJ ❑ *She was so flustered that she forgot her reply.* [of Scandinavian origin]

**flute** /flˈut/ (**flutes**) N-VAR A **flute** is a musical instrument of the woodwind family. You play it by blowing over a hole near one end while holding it sideways to your mouth. [from Old French]
→ see **orchestra**

**flut|ist** /flˈutɪst/ (**flutists**) N-COUNT A **flutist** is someone who plays the flute. [from Italian]

**flut|ter** /flˈʌtər/ (**flutters, fluttering, fluttered**) V-T/V-I If something thin or light **flutters**, or if you **flutter** it, it moves up and down or from side to side with a lot of quick, light movements. ❑ *Her silk skirt was fluttering in the breeze.* ❑ *The butterfly fluttered its wings.* ● **Flutter** is also a noun. ❑ *...a flutter of white cloth.* [from Old English]

**flux** /flˈʌks/ N-UNCOUNT If something is in a state of **flux**, it is constantly changing. ❑ *...a period of economic flux.* [from Latin]

**fly** /flˈaɪ/ (**flies, flying, flew, flown**) **1** N-COUNT A **fly** is a small insect with two wings. **2** N-COUNT The front opening on a pair of pants is referred to as the **fly**. **3** V-I When something such as a bird, insect, or aircraft **flies**, it moves through the air. ❑ *The planes flew through the clouds.* ● **fly|ing** ADJ ❑ *...flying insects.* **4** V-I If you **fly** somewhere, you travel there in an aircraft. ❑ *He flew to Los Angeles.* **5** V-T/V-I When someone **flies** an aircraft, they control its movement in the air. ❑ *He flew a small plane to Cuba.* ❑ *I learned to fly in Vietnam.* ● **fly|er** (**flyers**) N-COUNT ❑ *The American flyers ran for their planes and got in.* **6** V-T To **fly** someone or something somewhere means to take or send them there in an aircraft. ❑ *It may be possible to fly the women out on Thursday.* **7** V-I If something such as your hair **is flying** about, it is moving about freely and loosely in the air. ❑ *His long, uncovered hair flew back in the wind.* **8** V-T/V-I If you **fly** a flag or if it **is flying**, you display it at the top of a pole. ❑ *He flies the American flag on his front lawn.* **9** V-I If you say that someone or something **flies** in a particular direction, you are emphasizing that they move there with a lot of speed or force. ❑ *She flew to their bedsides when they were ill.* [from Old English] **10** → see also **flying** **11** to **fly in the face of** → see **face** **12** to **fly off the handle** → see **handle** **13** a **fly in the ointment** → see **ointment** **14** when **pigs fly** → see **pig** **15** **sparks fly** → see **spark** **16** time **flies** → see **time**
→ see **insect**

▸ **fly into** PHR-VERB If you **fly into** a bad temper or a panic, you suddenly become very angry or anxious and show this in your behavior. ❑ *Losing a game would cause him to fly into a rage.*
→ see Word Web: **fly**

**fly ball** (**fly balls**) also **flyball** N-COUNT In baseball, a **fly ball** is a ball that is hit very high.

**fly|er** /flˈaɪər/ (**flyers**) also **flier** N-COUNT A **flyer** is a small printed notice which is used to advertise a particular company, service, or event. ❑ *Flyers advertising the tour were handed out.* [from Old English]

**fly|ing** /flˈaɪɪŋ/ PHRASE If someone or something **gets off to a flying start**, or **makes a flying start**, they start very well. ❑ *The bank has gotten off to a flying start and profits are well ahead of last year.* [from Old English]

**foal** /fˈoʊl/ (**foals**) N-COUNT A **foal** is a very young horse. [from Old English]

**foam** /fˈoʊm/ **1** N-UNCOUNT **Foam** consists of a mass of small bubbles that are formed when air and a liquid are mixed together. ❑ *The water curved round the rocks in great bursts of foam.* **2** N-UNCOUNT **Foam** or **foam rubber** is soft rubber full of small holes which is used, for example, to make mattresses and cushions. [from Old English]

**fo|cal point** /fˈoʊkᵊl pɔɪnt/ (**focal points**) **1** N-COUNT The **focal point** of something is the thing that people concentrate on or pay most attention to. ❑ *The focal point for the town's many visitors is the museum.* **2** N-COUNT The **focal point**

F

---

### Word Web    fly

About 500 years ago, Leonardo da Vinci* designed some simple flying machines. His sketches look a lot like modern **parachutes** and **helicopters**. About 300 years later, the Montgolfier Brothers amazed the king of France with hot-air **balloon** flights. Soon inventors in many countries began experimenting with blimps, **hang gliders**, and human-powered **aircraft**. Most inventors tried to imitate the **flight** of birds. Then in 1903, the Wright brothers invented the first true **airplane**. Their gasoline-powered **craft** carried one **passenger**. The trip lasted 59 seconds. And amazingly, 70 years later **jumbo jets** carrying 400 passengers became an everyday occurrence.

*Leonardo da Vinci (1452-1519): an Italian artist.*

---

of a painting or drawing is the part of the picture that the viewer spends most time looking at.

**fo|cus** /foʊkəs/ (**focuses, focusing** or **focussing, focused** or **focussed**)

> The plural of the noun can be either **focuses** or **foci** /foʊsaɪ/.

**1** V-T/V-I If you **focus on** a particular topic or if your attention **is focused on** it, you concentrate on it and deal with it, rather than dealing with other topics. ❑ *The research focused on these effects.* **2** V-T/V-I If you **focus** your eyes or if your eyes **focus**, your eyes adjust so that you can clearly see the thing that you want to look at. If you **focus** a camera, telescope, or other instrument, you adjust it so that you can see clearly through it. ❑ *Kelly couldn't focus his eyes well enough to tell if the figure was male or female.* ❑ *His eyes began to focus on what looked like a small ball.* **3** V-T If you **focus** rays of light on a particular point, you pass them through a lens or reflect them from a mirror so that they meet at that point. ❑ *They move the mirrors to focus the sun's rays onto a piece of glass.* **4** N-COUNT The **focus** of something is the main topic or main thing that it is concerned with. ❑ *The new system is the focus of controversy.* **5** N-COUNT Your **focus on** something is the special attention that you pay it. ❑ *...his sudden focus on foreign policy.* **6** N-COUNT The **focus** of an earthquake is the point within the Earth where the earthquake starts. **7** PHRASE If an image or a camera, telescope, or other instrument is **in focus**, the edges of what you see are clear and sharp. **8** PHRASE If an image or a camera, telescope, or other instrument is **out of focus**, the edges of what you see are unclear. [from New Latin]
→ see **photography, telescope**

**fo|cus group** (**focus groups**) N-COUNT A **focus group** is a specially selected group of people who are intended to represent the general public. Focus groups have discussions in which their opinions are recorded as a form of market research.

**fod|der** /fɒdər/ N-UNCOUNT **Fodder** is food that is given to cows, horses, and other animals. [from Old English]

**foe** /foʊ/ (**foes**) N-COUNT Someone's **foe** is their enemy. [WRITTEN] [from Old English]

**fog** /fɒg/ (**fogs**) N-VAR When there is **fog**, there are tiny drops of water in the air which form a thick cloud and make it difficult to see things. ❑ *The crash happened in thick fog.* [from Scandinavian]

fog

**fog|gy** /fɒgi/ (**foggier, foggiest**) ADJ When it is foggy, there is fog.

**foil** /fɔɪl/ (**foils, foiling, foiled**) **1** N-UNCOUNT **Foil** consists of sheets of metal as thin as paper. It is used to wrap food in. **2** V-T If someone **foils** your plan or attempt to do something, he or she succeeds in stopping you from doing what you want. ❑ *A brave police chief foiled an armed robbery.* [from Old French]

**fold** /foʊld/ (**folds, folding, folded**) **1** V-T If you **fold** a piece of paper or cloth, you bend it so that one part covers another part. ❑ *He folded the paper carefully.* ❑ *Fold the towel in half.* **2** V-T/V-I If a piece of furniture or equipment **folds** or if you can **fold** it, you can make it smaller by bending or closing parts of it. ❑ *The back of the bench folds forward to make a table.* ❑ *This portable seat folds flat for easy storage.*

fold

● **Fold up** means the same as **fold**. ❑ *When not in use, the table folds up out of the way.* **3** V-T If you **fold** your arms or hands, you bring them together and cross or link them, for example, over your chest. **4** N-COUNT A **fold** in a piece of paper or cloth is a bend that you make in it when you put one part of it over another part and press the edge. ❑ *Make another fold and turn the ends together.* **5** N-COUNT The **folds** in a piece of cloth are the curved shapes which are formed when it is not hanging or lying flat. **6** N-COUNT A **fold** is a bend in a layer of rock that occurs when the rock is compressed. ● **fold|ing** N-UNCOUNT ❑ *...where the fracturing has resulted from folding of the rock.* [from Old English]
▶ **fold up 1** PHR-VERB If you **fold** something **up**, you make it into a smaller, neater shape by folding it, usually several times. ❑ *I folded up the map and put it away.* **2** → see also **fold 2**

---

### Word Partnership    Use **fold** with :

| | |
|---|---|
| ADV. | fold **carefully**, fold **gently**, fold **neatly** **1** |
| N. | fold **clothes**, fold **paper** **1** |
| | fold *your* **arms/hands** **3** |

---

**fold|ed moun|tain** (**folded mountains**) N-COUNT A **folded mountain** is a mountain that forms when rock is bent or folded because of stresses in the Earth's crust. [TECHNICAL]

**fold|er** /foʊldər/ (**folders**) **1** N-COUNT A **folder** is a thin piece of cardboard in which you can keep loose papers. **2** N-COUNT A **folder** is a group of files that are stored together on a computer. [from Old English]
→ see **office**

**fo|li|age** /foʊliɪdʒ/ N-UNCOUNT The leaves of a plant are referred to as its **foliage**. □ ...plants with gray or silver foliage. [from Old French]

**fo|li|at|ed** /foʊlieɪtɪd/ ADJ **Foliated** rock is rock that consists of lots of thin layers. [TECHNICAL] [from Old French]

**folk** /foʊk/ (**folks**)

> **Folk** can also be used as the plural form for meaning **1**.

**1** N-PLURAL You can refer to people as **folk** or **folks**. □ ...country folk. □ These are the folks from the local TV station. **2** N-PLURAL You can refer to your close family, especially your mother and father, as your **folks**. [INFORMAL] □ I'll introduce you to my folks. **3** ADJ **Folk** art and customs are traditional or typical of a particular community or nation. □ ...South American folk art. **4** ADJ **Folk** music is music which is traditional or typical of a particular community or nation. [from Old English]
→ see **dance**

**folk|lore** /foʊklɔr/ N-UNCOUNT **Folklore** consists of the traditional stories, customs, and habits of a particular community or nation. □ In Chinese folklore the bat is a symbol of good fortune.

**fol|li|cle** /fɒlɪkəl/ (**follicles**) N-COUNT A **follicle** is one of the small hollows in the skin which hairs grow from. [from Latin]

┌─────────────────────────┐
│ **follow** │
│ **1** GO OR COME AFTER │
│ **2** ACT ACCORDING TO │
│    SOMETHING, OBSERVE │
│    SOMETHING │
│ **3** UNDERSTAND │
│ **4** PHRASAL VERBS │
└─────────────────────────┘

**1 fol|low** /fɒloʊ/ (**follows, following, followed**) **1** V-T/V-I If you **follow** someone who is going somewhere, you move along behind them. □ We followed him up the steps. □ Please follow me, madam. □ They took him into a small room and I followed. **2** V-T If you **follow** someone who is going somewhere, you move along behind them without their knowledge, in order to catch them or find out where they are going. □ She realized that the car was following her. **3** V-T If you **follow** someone to a place, you join them there at a later time. □ He followed Janice to New York. **4** V-T/V-I An event, activity, or period of time that **follows** a particular thing happens or comes after that thing, at a later time. □ Great celebrations followed the announcement. □ Other problems may follow. **5** V-T If you **follow** one thing **with** another, you do or say the second thing after you have done or said the first thing. □ Warm up first then follow this with a series of simple stretching exercises. ● **Follow up** means the same as **follow**. □ The Phillies followed up a five-game winning streak with three straight losses. **6** V-T/V-I If it **follows** that

a particular thing is true, that thing is a logical result of something else being true. □ With ten new families moving to the neighborhood, it follows that there will be more children in school. □ If the explanation is right, two things follow. **7** V-T If you **follow** a path, route, or set of signs, you go somewhere using the path, route, or signs to direct you. □ All we had to do was follow the map. **8** PHRASE You use **as follows** in writing or speech to introduce something such as a list, description, or an explanation. □ The winners are as follows: E. Walker; R. Foster; R. Gates. **9** PHRASE You use **followed by** to say what comes after something else in a list or ordered set of things. □ Potatoes are still the most popular food, followed by white bread. [from Old English] **10** → see also **following 11** to **follow in** someone's **footsteps** → see **footstep 12** to **follow** your **nose** → see **nose 13** to **follow suit** → see **suit**

**2 fol|low** /fɒloʊ/ (**follows, following, followed**) **1** V-T If you **follow** advice, an instruction, or a recipe, you act or do something in the way that it indicates. □ Follow the instructions carefully. **2** V-T If you **follow** something, you take an interest in it and keep informed about what happens. □ Millions of people follow football. [from Old English]

**3 fol|low** /fɒloʊ/ (**follows, following, followed**) **1** V-T/V-I If you are able to **follow** something such as an explanation or the story of a movie, you understand it. □ Can you follow the plot so far? □ I'm sorry, I don't follow. [from Old English] **2** → see also **following**

┌────────────────────────────────────────────┐
│ **Word Partnership** Use *follow* with : │
├────────────────────────────────────────────┤
│ ADV. **closely** follow **1 1 2** │
│    **blindly** follow **2 1 2** │
│ N. follow **a road**, follow **signs**, │
│    follow **a trail 1 7** │
│    follow **orders**, follow **rules 2 1** │
│    follow **advice**, follow **directions**, follow │
│    **instructions**, follow **a story 3 1** │
└────────────────────────────────────────────┘

**4 fol|low** /fɒloʊ/ (**follows, following, followed**) ▶ **follow through** PHR-VERB If you **follow through** an action, plan, or idea or **follow through** with it, you continue doing or thinking about it until you have done everything possible. □ The leadership has been unwilling to follow through with these ideas. □ I was trained to be an actress but I didn't follow it through.

**fol|low|er** /fɒloʊər/ (**followers**) N-COUNT A **follower** of a particular person, group, or belief is someone who supports or admires this person, group, or belief. □ ...followers of Judaism. [from Old English]

**fol|low|ing** /fɒloʊɪŋ/ (**followings**) **1** PREP **Following** a particular event means after that event. □ He took four months off work following the birth of his first child. **2** ADJ The **following** day, week, or year is the day, week, or year after the one you have just mentioned. □ We went to dinner the following Monday evening. **3** ADJ You use **following** to refer to something that you are about to mention. □ Write down the following information: name of product, date purchased and price. ● **The following** refers to the thing or things that you are about to mention. □ The following is a summary of what was said. **4** N-COUNT A person or organization that has a **following** has a group of people who support or admire their beliefs or actions. ❑ *Australian rugby league enjoys a huge following in New Zealand.* [from Old English]

**follow-up** (**follow-ups**) N-VAR A **follow-up** is something that is done to continue or add to something done previously. ❑ *They are recording a follow-up to their 2005 album.*

**fol|ly** /fɒli/ (**follies**) N-VAR If you say that a particular action or way of behaving is **folly** or a **folly**, you mean that it is foolish. ❑ *It's folly to build nuclear power stations in a country that has earthquakes every year.* [from Old French]

**fond** /fɒnd/ (**fonder, fondest**) **1** ADJ If you are **fond of** someone, you feel affection for them. ❑ *I am very fond of Michael.* ● **fond|ness** N-UNCOUNT ❑ *...a great fondness for children.* **2** ADJ You use **fond** to describe people or their behavior when they show affection. ❑ *...a fond father.* ● **fond|ly** ADV ❑ *Their eyes met fondly across the table.* **3** ADJ If you are **fond of** something, you like it or you like doing it very much. ❑ *He was fond of singing.* ● **fond|ness** N-UNCOUNT ❑ *...a fondness for chocolate cake.* **4** ADJ If you have **fond** memories of someone or something, you remember them with pleasure. ● **fond|ly** ADV ❑ *My dad took us there and I remembered it fondly.*

**food** /fud/ (**foods**) **1** N-VAR **Food** is what people and animals eat. ❑ *Enjoy your food.* ❑ *...frozen foods.* **2** → see also **fast food 3** PHRASE If you give someone **food for thought**, you make them think carefully about something. ❑ *Her speech offers much food for thought.* [from Old English]
→ see Word Web: **food**
→ see **cooking, farm, habitat, rice, sugar, vegetarian**

**Food and Drug Ad|min|is|tra|tion** N-PROPER In the United States, the **Food and Drug Administration** is a government department that is responsible for making sure that foods and drugs are safe.

**food bank** (**food banks**) N-COUNT A **food bank** is a place that collects food that has been donated and gives it to people who are poor or homeless.

**food chain** (**food chains**) N-COUNT The **food chain** is a series of living things which are linked to each other because each thing feeds on the one next to it in the series.
→ see **carnivore**

**food court** (**food courts**) N-COUNT A **food court** is a place, for example, in a shopping mall, that has several small restaurants and a common eating area.

**food|stuff** /fudstʌf/ (**foodstuffs**) N-VAR **Foodstuffs** are substances which people eat.

❑ *...basic foodstuffs such as sugar, cooking oil and cheese.*

**food web** (**food webs**) N-COUNT A **food web** is a network of interconnected food chains.

**fool** /ful/ (**fools, fooling, fooled**) **1** N-COUNT If you call someone a **fool**, you are indicating that you think they are not at all sensible and show a lack of good judgment. ❑ *"You fool!" she shouted.* **2** V-T If someone **fools** you, they deceive or trick you. ❑ *Art dealers fool a lot of people.* ❑ *Don't be fooled by his appearance.* **3** PHRASE If you **make a fool of** someone, you make them seem silly by telling people about something stupid that they have done, or by tricking them. ❑ *Your brother is making a fool of you.* [from Old French]
▶ **fool around** PHR-VERB If you **fool around**, you behave in a silly or dangerous way. ❑ *They fool around and get into trouble at school.*

**fool|ish** /fulɪʃ/ ADJ If your behavior or action is **foolish**, it is not sensible and shows a lack of good judgment. ❑ *It would be foolish to raise their hopes.* ● **fool|ish|ly** ADV ❑ *He admitted that he had acted foolishly.* ● **fool|ish|ness** N-UNCOUNT ❑ *They don't accept any foolishness.* [from Old French]

---

**foot**

❶ PART OF BODY
❷ UNIT OF MEASUREMENT
❸ LOWER END OF SOMETHING

---

❶ **foot** /fut/ (**feet**) **1** N-COUNT Your **feet** are the parts of your body that are at the ends of your legs, and that you stand on. ❑ *She stamped her foot again.* ❑ *...a foot injury.* **2** → see also **footing 3** PHRASE If you go somewhere **on foot**, you walk, rather than using any form of transport. ❑ *We rowed ashore, then explored the island on foot.* **4** PHRASE If you are **on your feet**, you are standing up. ❑ *Everyone was on their feet applauding.* **5** PHRASE If you say that someone or something is **on its feet** again after an illness or difficult period, you mean that they have recovered and are back to normal. ❑ *You need someone to help you get back on your feet.* **6** PHRASE If someone **puts their foot down**, they use their authority in order to stop something from happening. ❑ *He wanted to go skiing in March but his wife put her foot down.* **7** PHRASE If you **put your feet up**, you relax or have a rest, especially by sitting or lying with your feet supported off the ground. ❑ *After supper he put his feet up and read.* **8** PHRASE If you get or rise **to your feet**, you stand up. ❑ *Malone got to his feet and followed us out.* [from Old English] **9** **foot in the door** → see **door 10** to **drag** your **feet** → see **drag 11** to **vote with** your

---

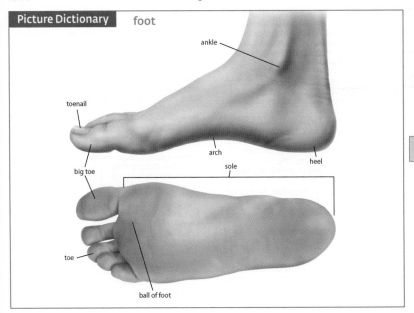

**Picture Dictionary**    foot

- ankle
- toenail
- big toe
- toe
- arch
- sole
- heel
- ball of foot

**feet** → see **vote**
→ see Picture Dictionary: **foot**
→ see **body**

**❷ foot** /fʊt/ (**feet**) N-COUNT A **foot** is a unit of length equal to 12 inches or 30.48 centimeters. The plural form **foot** is also sometimes used. □ ...*six thousand feet above sea level.* □ ...*a cell 10 foot long, 6 foot wide and 10 foot high.* [from Old English]
→ see **measurement**

**❸ foot** /fʊt/ N-SING The **foot of** something is the part that is farthest from its top. □ ...*the foot of the stairs.* [from Old English]

**foot|age** /fʊtɪdʒ/ N-UNCOUNT **Footage** of a particular event is a film of it or the part of a film which shows this event. □ ...*footage from this summer's festivals.* [from Old English]

**foot|ball** /fʊtbɔl/ (**footballs**) **1** N-UNCOUNT **Football** is a game played by two teams of eleven players using an oval ball. Players carry the ball in their hands or throw it to each other as they try to score goals that are called touchdowns. □ ...*a field where boys played football.* **2** N-COUNT A **football** is

a ball that is used for playing football. □ ...*a heavy leather football.*
→ see Picture Dictionary: **football**

**foot|ball field** (**football fields**) N-COUNT A **football field** is an area of grass where football is played.

**foot|er** /fʊtər/ (**footers**) N-COUNT A **footer** is text such as a name or page number that can be automatically displayed at the bottom of each page of a printed document. Compare **header**. [COMPUTING]

**foot|hills** /fʊthɪlz/ N-PLURAL The **foothills** of a mountain or a range of mountains are the lower hills or mountains around its base. □ *Pasadena lies in the foothills of the San Gabriel mountains.*

**foot|hold** /fʊthoʊld/ (**footholds**) **1** N-COUNT A **foothold** is a strong position from which further advances or progress may be made. □ *Businesses are investing millions of dollars to gain a foothold in this new market.* **2** N-COUNT A **foothold** is a place such as a small hole or area of rock where you can safely put your foot when climbing.

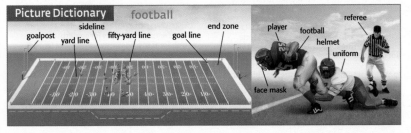

**Picture Dictionary**    football

- goalpost
- sideline
- yard line
- fifty-yard line
- goal line
- end zone
- player
- football
- referee
- helmet
- uniform
- face mask

**foot|ing** /fʊtɪŋ/ ■ N-UNCOUNT You use **footing** to describe the basis on which something is done or exists. ❑ *The research is aimed at placing training on a more scientific footing.* ■ N-UNCOUNT You use **footing** to refer to your position and how securely your feet are placed on the ground. ❑ *He lost his footing and slid into the water.* [from Old English]

**foot|lock|er** /fʊtlɒkər/ (**footlockers**) also **foot locker** N-COUNT A **footlocker** is a large box for keeping personal possessions in, especially one that is placed at the end of a bed.

**foot|note** /fʊtnoʊt/ (**footnotes**) N-COUNT A **footnote** is a note at the bottom of a page in a book which provides more detailed information about something that is mentioned on that page.

**foot|path** /fʊtpæθ/ (**footpaths**) N-COUNT A **footpath** is a path for people to walk on, especially in the countryside.

**foot|print** /fʊtprɪnt/ (**footprints**) N-COUNT A **footprint** is the mark of a person's or animal's foot left on a surface.
→ see **fossil**

**foot|step** /fʊtstɛp/ (**footsteps**) ■ N-COUNT A **footstep** is the sound that is made by someone walking each time their foot touches the ground. ❑ *I heard footsteps outside.* ■ PHRASE If you **follow in** someone's **footsteps**, you do the same things as he or she did earlier. ❑ *My father is proud that I followed in his footsteps and became a doctor.*

**foot|wall** /fʊtwɔl/ (**footwalls**) N-COUNT A **footwall** is the rock beneath a geological fault. Compare **hanging wall**. [TECHNICAL]

**foot|wear** /fʊtwɛər/ N-UNCOUNT **Footwear** refers to things that people wear on their feet, for example, shoes and boots.

### for

① SAYING WHO OR WHAT SOMETHING RELATES TO, OR WHO BENEFITS
② MENTIONING A PURPOSE, REASON, OR DESTINATION
③ BEFORE NUMBERS, AMOUNTS, AND TIMES
④ WANTING OR SUPPORTING

In addition to the uses shown below, **for** is used after some verbs, nouns, and adjectives in order to introduce extra information, and in phrasal verbs such as "account for" and "make up for." It is also used with some verbs that have two objects in order to introduce the second object.

① **for** /fər, STRONG fɔr/ ■ PREP If something is **for** someone, they are intended to have it or benefit from it. ❑ *Isn't that enough for you?* ❑ *...a table for two.* ■ PREP If you work or do a job **for** someone, you are employed by them. ❑ *He worked for a security firm.* ■ PREP If someone does something **for** you, they do it so that you do not have to do it. ❑ *I held the door open for the next person.* ■ PREP If you feel a particular emotion **for** someone or something, they are the object of that emotion. ❑ *I'm sorry for Steve, but I think you've made the right decision.* ■ PREP You use **for** after words such as "time," "space," "money," or "energy" when you say how much there is or whether there is enough of it in order to be able to do or use a particular thing. ❑ *...a huge house with plenty of room for books.* ■ PREP After some adjective, noun, and verb phrases, you use **for** when you are saying how something affects someone. ❑ *I have made arrangements for my affairs to be dealt with by my children.* ■ PREP A word or term **for** something, is another way of referring to it. ❑ *The technical term for sunburn is erythema.* ■ PREP To be named **for** someone means to be given the same name as them. ❑ *The Brady Bill is named for former White House Press Secretary James Brady.* [from Old English] ■ **as for** → see **as** ■ **but for** → see **but** ■ **for all** → see **all**

② **for** /fər, STRONG fɔr/ ■ PREP You use **for** when you are describing the purpose of something. ❑ *...laboratory equipment for genetic research.* ❑ *...a knife for cutting sausage.* ■ PREP You use **for** when you are describing the reason for something or the cause of something. ❑ *...his reasons for going.* ❑ *The hospital could find no physical cause for Sumner's problems.* ■ PREP If you leave **for** a place or if you take a bus, train, plane, or boat **for** a place, you are going there. ❑ *They left for Rio early the next morning.* [from Old English]

③ **for** /fər, STRONG fɔr/ ■ PREP You use **for** to say how long something lasts or continues. ❑ *The toaster was on for more than an hour.* ❑ *They talked for a bit.* ■ PREP You use **for** to say how far something extends. ❑ *We drove on for a few miles.* ■ PREP If something is bought, sold, or done **for** a particular amount of money, that amount of money is its price. ❑ *The Martins sold their house for about 1.4 million dollars.* ■ PREP If something is planned **for** a particular time, it is planned to happen then. ❑ *The Baltimore Boat Show is planned for January 21 – 29.* ■ PHRASE You use expressions such as **for the first time** and **for the last time** when you are talking about how often something has happened before. ❑ *He was married for the second time.* ■ PREP You use **for** when you say that an aspect of something or someone is surprising in relation to other aspects of them. ❑ *He was tall for an eight-year-old.* ■ PREP You use **for** with "every" when you state the second part of a ratio. ❑ *There is one manager for every six employees.* [from Old English]

④ **for** /fər, STRONG fɔr/ ■ PREP If you say that you are **for** a particular activity, you mean that this is what you want or intend to do. ❑ *Who's for a toasted sandwich?* ■ PREP If you are **for** something, you agree with it or support it. ❑ *He wasn't sure whether he was for or against what Quayle had said.* [from Old English]

**for|age** /fɔrɪdʒ/ (**forages, foraging, foraged**) ■ V-I If someone **forages for** something, they search for it in a busy way. ❑ *They were forced to forage for clothing and fuel.* ■ V-I When animals **forage**, they search for food. ❑ *A wild rabbit was foraging by the roadside.* [from Old French]

**for|ay** /fɔreɪ/ (**forays**) ■ N-COUNT If you make a **foray into** a new or unfamiliar type of activity, you start to become involved in it. ❑ *The Italian fashion house made a foray into furnishings.* ■ N-COUNT If a group of soldiers make a **foray into** enemy territory, they make a quick attack there, and then return to their own territory. [from Old French]

**for|bid** /fərbɪd, fɔr-/ (**forbids, forbidding, forbade, forbidden**) **1** v-T If you **forbid** someone **to** do something, or if you **forbid** an activity, you order that it must not be done. ❑ *They'll forbid you to marry.* ❑ *...regulations that forbid the use of torture.* **2** v-T If something **forbids** a particular course of action or state of affairs, it makes it impossible. ❑ *His own pride forbids him to ask for Arthur's help.* [from Old English]

**for|bid|den** /fərbɪdªn, fɔr-/ ADJ If something is **forbidden**, you are not allowed to do it or have it. ❑ *Loud noise was forbidden everywhere.* [from Old English]

---
**force**

❶ VERB USES
❷ NOUN USES: POWER OR STRENGTH
❸ THE ARMY, POLICE, ETC.
---

❶ **force** /fɔrs/ (**forces, forcing, forced**) **1** v-T If someone **forces** you **to** do something, they make you do it even though you do not want to. ❑ *He forced them to drive away from the area.* ❑ *They were grabbed by three men who forced them into a car.* **2** v-T If you **force** something into a particular position, you use a lot of strength to make it move there. ❑ *She forced her key into the lock.* **3** v-T If someone **forces** a lock, a door, or a window, they break the lock or fastening in order to get into a building without using a key. ❑ *Police forced the door of the apartment and arrested Mr. Roberts.* [from Old French]

❷ **force** /fɔrs/ (**forces**) **1** N-UNCOUNT If someone uses **force** to do something, strong and violent physical action is taken in order to achieve it. ❑ *The government decided against using force to break up the demonstrations.* **2** N-UNCOUNT **Force** is the power or strength which something has. ❑ *...the force of the explosion.* **3** N-COUNT If you refer to someone or something as a **force** in a particular type of activity, you mean that they have a strong influence on it. ❑ *The army was the most powerful political force in the country.* **4** N-VAR In physics, a **force** is the pulling or pushing effect that something has on something else. ❑ *...the Earth's gravitational force.* **5** PHRASE A law, rule, or system that is **in force** exists or is being used. ❑ *The new tax is already in force.* **6** PHRASE If you **join forces with** someone, you work together in order to achieve a common aim or purpose. ❑ *He joined forces with his brother to start the company.* [from Old French]
→ see **motion**

❸ **force** /fɔrs/ (**forces**) **1** N-COUNT **Forces** are groups of soldiers or military vehicles that are organized for a particular region. ❑ *...the presence of American forces in the region.* [from Old French] **2** → see also **air force, armed forces, labor force, workforce**

| **Thesaurus** | *force* | Also look up : |
|---|---|---|
| v. | coerce, make ❶ **1** | |
| | push, thrust ❶ **2** | |
| | break in, break open ❶ **3** | |
| N. | energy, pressure, strength ❷ **2** | |

| **Word Partnership** | Use *force* with : |
|---|---|
| V. | force **to resign** ❶ **1** |
| N. | force a **smile** ❶ **2** |
| | **use of** force ❷ **1** |
| | force **of gravity** ❷ **4** |
| ADJ. | **excessive** force, **necessary** force ❷ **1** |
| | **driving** force, **powerful** force ❷ **3** |
| | **enemy** forces, **military** forces ❸ **1** **2** |

**forced** /fɔrst/ ADJ If you describe something as **forced**, you mean it does not happen naturally and easily. ❑ *...a forced smile.* [from Old French]

**force field** (**force fields**) N-COUNT A **force field** is an area of energy, such as magnetic energy, that surrounds an object or place. ❑ *A giant force field protects the planet from solar winds.*

**force|ful** /fɔrsfəl/ **1** ADJ Someone who is **forceful** expresses their opinions and wishes in a strong and confident way. ❑ *He was a man of forceful character.* ● **force|ful|ly** ADV ❑ *He argued forcefully against this course of action.* **2** ADJ Something that is **forceful** causes you to think or feel something very strongly. ❑ *It made a very forceful impression on me.* [from Old French]

**for|cible** /fɔrsɪbªl/ ADJ **Forcible** action involves physical force or violence. ❑ *...the forcible resettlement of villagers.* [from Old French]

**ford** /fɔrd/ (**fords**) N-COUNT A **ford** is a shallow place in a river or stream where it is possible to cross safely without using a boat. [from Old English]

**fore** /fɔr/ **1** PHRASE If someone or something comes **to the fore**, they become important or popular. ❑ *A number of independent films brought new directors to the fore.* **2** ADJ **Fore** is used to refer to parts at the front of an animal, ship, or aircraft. ❑ *...the fore part of the ship.* [from Old English]

**fore|arm** /fɔrɑrm/ (**forearms**) N-COUNT Your **forearm** is the part of your arm between your elbow and your wrist.

| **Word Link** | *fore* ≈ *before* : *forecast, foreman, foresight* |
|---|---|

**fore|cast** /fɔrkæst/ (**forecasts, forecasting, forecasted**)

> The forms **forecast** and **forecasted** can both be used for the past tense and past participle.

**1** N-COUNT A **forecast** is a statement of what is expected to happen in the future, especially in relation to a particular event or situation. ❑ *...a forecast of a 2.25 percent growth in the economy.* **2** v-T If you **forecast** future events, you say what you think is going to happen in the future. ❑ *They forecast a defeat for the president.* ● **fore|cast|er** (**forecasters**) N-COUNT ❑ *...the nation's top economic forecasters.* **3** → see also **weather forecast**
→ see Word Web: **forecast**
→ see **tsunami**

**fore|finger** /fɔrfɪŋgər/ (**forefingers**) N-COUNT Your **forefinger** is the finger that is next to your thumb.

**fore|front** /fɔrfrʌnt/ N-SING If you are at **the forefront** of a campaign or other activity, you have a leading and influential position in it. ❑ *They have been at the forefront of the movement for political change.*

F

## Word Web — forecast

Meteorologists depend on good information. They make **observations**. They gather **data** about barometric **pressure**, **temperature**, and **humidity**. They track **storms** with **radar** and **satellites**. They track cold **fronts** and warm fronts. They put all of this information into their computers and **model** possible weather patterns. Today scientists are trying to make better **weather forecasts**. They are installing thousands of small, inexpensive **radar** units on rooftops and cell phone towers. They will gather information near the Earth's surface and high in the sky. This will give meteorologists more information to help them **predict** tomorrow's weather.

**fore|go** /fɔrgoʊ/ (**foregoes, foregoing, forewent, foregone**) also **forgo** v-т If you **forego** something, you decide not to have it or do it, although you would like to have it or do it. [FORMAL] □ *Many skiers are happy to forego a summer vacation to go skiing.* [from Old English]

**fore|ground** /fɔrgraʊnd/ (**foregrounds**)
**1** N-VAR The **foreground** of a picture or scene is the part that is nearest to you. □ *There are five figures and a dog in the foreground of the painting.*
**2** N-SING If something or someone is **in the foreground**, they receive a lot of attention. □ *This worry has come to the foreground in recent years.*

**fore|head** /fɔrhɛd, fɔrɪd/ (**foreheads**) N-COUNT Your **forehead** is the area at the front of your head between your eyebrows and your hair. [from Old English]
→ see **face**

**for|eign** /fɔrɪn/ **1** ADJ Something or someone that is **foreign** comes from or relates to a country that is not your own. □ *...her first foreign vacation without her parents.* □ *...a foreign language.* **2** ADJ In politics and journalism, **foreign** is used to describe people, jobs, and activities relating to countries that are not the country of the person or government concerned. □ *...the German foreign minister.* □ *...American foreign policy.* **3** ADJ A **foreign** object is something that has got into something else, usually by accident, and should not be there. [FORMAL] □ *...a foreign body in the eye.* [from Old French]

### Thesaurus — foreign Also look up:

ADJ. alien, exotic, strange; (*ant.*) domestic, native **1**

**for|eign|er** /fɔrɪnər/ (**foreigners**) N-COUNT A **foreigner** is someone who belongs to a country that is not your own. [from Old French]

**for|eign ex|change** (**foreign exchanges**)
**1** N-PLURAL **Foreign exchanges** are the institutions or systems involved with changing one currency into another. □ *On the foreign exchanges, the U.S. dollar is up point forty-five.*
**2** N-UNCOUNT **Foreign exchange** is used to refer to foreign currency that is obtained through the foreign exchange system. □ *...an important source of foreign exchange.*

**for|eign ser|vice** N-SING The **foreign service** is the government department that employs diplomats to work in foreign countries.

### Word Link
fore ≈ before : fore**cast**, fore**man**, fore**sight**

### Word Link
man ≈ human being : fore**man**, hu**man**e, wo**man**

**fore|man** /fɔrmən/ (**foremen**) N-COUNT A **foreman** is a person who is in charge of a group of workers.

### Word Link
most ≈ superlative degree : al**most**, fore**most**, ut**most**

**fore|most** /fɔrmoʊst/ **1** ADJ The **foremost** thing or person in a group is the most important or best. □ *...one of the world's foremost scholars of ancient Indian culture.* **2** PHRASE You use **first and foremost** to emphasize the most important quality of something or someone. □ *It is first and foremost a trade agreement.* [from Old English]

**fo|ren|sic** /fərɛnsɪk/ ADJ **Forensic** is used to describe the work of scientists who examine evidence in order to help the police solve crimes. □ *They were convicted on forensic evidence alone.* □ *Forensic experts searched the area.* [from Latin]

**fore|run|ner** /fɔrrʌnər/ (**forerunners**) N-COUNT The **forerunner of** something is a similar thing that existed before it and influenced its development. □ *This machine was the forerunner of the modern helicopter.*

**fore|see** /fɔrsi/ (**foresees, foreseeing, foresaw, foreseen**) v-т If you **foresee** something, you expect and believe that it will happen. □ *He did not foresee any problems.*

**fore|see|able** /fɔrsiəbᵊl/ **1** ADJ If a future event is **foreseeable**, you know that it will happen or that it can happen, because it is a natural or obvious consequence of something else that you know. □ *It seems to me that this crime was foreseeable.* **2** PHRASE If you say that something will happen **for the foreseeable future**, you think that it will continue to happen for a long time. □ *She doesn't want to leave for the foreseeable future.*

**fore|sight** /fɔrsaɪt/ N-UNCOUNT If someone says that you have **foresight**, he or she approves of you because you have the ability to see what is likely to happen in the future and to take appropriate action. □ *They had the foresight to invest in new technology.*

**for|est** /fɔrɪst/ (**forests**) N-VAR A **forest** is a large area where trees grow close together. [from Old French]
→ see Word Web: **forest**
→ see **habitat**

---

### Word Web    forest

Four hundred years ago, settlers in North America found endless **forests**. This large supply of **wood** helped them. They used **timber** to build homes and make furniture. They burned wood for cooking and heat. They cut down the **woods** to create farmland. By the late 1800s, most of the old growth forests on the East Coast had disappeared. The **lumber** industry has also destroyed millions of trees. Reforestation has replaced some of them. However, **logging** companies usually plant single species forests. Some people say these are not really forests at all—just **tree** farms.

---

**fore|stall** /fɔrstɔl/ (**forestalls, forestalling, forestalled**) v-T If you **forestall** someone, you realize what they are likely to do and prevent them from doing it. ❑ *Police were there to forestall any demonstrations.* [from Old English]

**for|est land** (**forest lands**) also **forestland** N-VAR **Forest land** is land that is mainly covered by forest.

**for|est|ry** /fɔrɪstri/ N-UNCOUNT **Forestry** is the science or skill of growing and taking care of trees in forests. [from Old French]
→ see **industry**

**for|ever** /fɔrɛvər, fər-/ **1** ADV If you say that something will happen or continue **forever**, you mean that it will always live together forever. **2** ADV If something has gone or changed **forever**, it has gone or changed **forever**, it has gone or changed and will never come back or return to the way it was. ❑ *After his operation, his pain was gone forever.*

#### Thesaurus    forever    Also look up :

| ADV. | always, endlessly, eternally **1** |
| --- | --- |
| | permanently **2** |

**fore|went** /fɔrwɛnt/ **Forewent** is the past tense of **forego**. [from Old English]

**for|feit** /fɔrfɪt/ (**forfeits, forfeiting, forfeited**) **1** v-T If you **forfeit** a right, privilege, or possession, you have to give it up because you have done something wrong. ❑ *He was ordered to forfeit more than 1.5 million dollars.* **2** N-COUNT A **forfeit** is something that you have to give up because you have done something wrong. ❑ *That is the forfeit he must pay.* [from Old French]

**for|gave** /fərɡeɪv/ **Forgave** is the past tense of **forgive**. [from Old English]

**forge** /fɔrdʒ/ (**forges, forging, forged**) **1** v-RECIP If one person or institution **forges** an agreement or relationship with another, they succeed in creating it. ❑ *The prime minister is determined to forge a good relationship with the country's new leader.* ❑ *They agreed to forge closer economic ties.* **2** v-T If someone **forges** paper money, a document, or a painting, they make false copies of it in order to deceive people. ❑ *He admitted forging passports.* ❑ *They used forged documents to leave the country.*
●**forg|er** (**forgers**) N-COUNT ❑ *...an art forger.* [from Old French]
▶ **forge ahead** PHR-VERB If you **forge ahead** with something, you continue with it and make a lot of progress with it. ❑ *He forged ahead with his plans for reform.*

#### Word Partnership    Use *forge* with :

| N. | forge **a bond**, forge **a friendship**, forge **links**, forge **ties** **1** |
| --- | --- |
| | forge **documents**, forge **an identity**, forge **a signature** **2** |

**for|gery** /fɔrdʒəri/ (**forgeries**) **1** N-UNCOUNT **Forgery** is the crime of forging money, documents, or paintings. **2** N-COUNT You can refer to a forged document, bill, or painting as a **forgery**. ❑ *The letter was a forgery.* [from Old French]

**for|get** /fərɡɛt/ (**forgets, forgetting, forgot, forgotten**) **1** v-T If you **forget** something or **forget** how to do something, you cannot think of it or think how to do it, although you knew in the past. ❑ *She forgot where she left the car.* **2** v-T/v-I If you **forget** something or **forget** to do it, you do not remember it or remember to do it. ❑ *She never forgets her dad's birthday.* ❑ *She forgot to lock her door.* ❑ *When I close my eyes, I forget about everything.* ❑ *I meant to ask you about it but I forgot.* **3** v-T If you **forget** something that you had intended to bring with you, you do not remember to bring it. ❑ *Once when we were going to Paris, I forgot my passport.* **4** v-T/v-I If you **forget** something or someone, you deliberately put them out of your mind and do not think about them any more. ❑ *I hope you will forget the bad experience you had today.* ❑ *I found it very easy to forget about Sumner.* [from Old English]

#### Thesaurus    forget    Also look up :

| V. | neglect, overlook **2** |
| --- | --- |
| | disregard, ignore **4** |

#### Word Partnership    Use *forget* with :

| ADV. | **never** forget, **quickly** forget, **soon** forget **1** |
| --- | --- |
| | **almost** forget **1** – **3** |
| ADJ. | **easy/hard to** forget **1** – **4** |

**for|get|ful** /fərɡɛtfəl/ ADJ Someone who is **forgetful** often forgets things. ❑ *My mother has become very forgetful and confused.* [from Old English]

**for|give** /fərɡɪv/ (**forgives, forgiving, forgave, forgiven**) v-T If you **forgive** someone who has done something bad or wrong, you stop being angry with them and no longer want to punish them. ❑ *Hopefully Jane will understand and forgive you.* ❑ *Irene forgave Terry for stealing her money.*
●**for|giv|ing** ADJ ❑ *I don't think people are in a very*

**forgiving** mood. ● **for|give|ness** N-UNCOUNT ❑ ...*a spirit of forgiveness.* [from Old English]

**for|go** /fɔrgoʊ/ → see **forego**

**for|got** /fərgɒt/ **Forgot** is the past tense of **forget**. [from Old English]

**for|got|ten** /fərgɒtⁿn/ **Forgotten** is the past participle of **forget**. [from Old English]

**fork** /fɔrk/ (**forks, forking, forked**) **1** N-COUNT A **fork** is a tool used for eating food which has a row of three or four long metal points at the end. ❑ ...*knives and forks.* **2** N-COUNT A **fork** in a road, path, or river is a point at which it divides into two parts and forms a "Y" shape. ❑ *We arrived at a fork in the road.* **3** V-I If a road, path, or river **forks**, it forms a fork. [from Old English]

▶ **fork out** PHR-VERB If you **fork out for** something, you spend a lot of money on it. [INFORMAL] ❑ *Visitors to the castle had to fork out for a guidebook.* ❑ *I forked out $530 on a ticket for a month's train travel in Europe.*

**for|lorn** /fɔrlɔrn/ **1** ADJ If someone is **forlorn**, they feel alone and unhappy. [LITERARY] ❑ *One of the demonstrators sat forlorn on the sidewalk.* **2** ADJ A **forlorn** hope or attempt is one that you think has no chance of success. ❑ *Peasants have left the land in the forlorn hope of finding a better life in cities.* [from Old English]

**form** /fɔrm/ (**forms, forming, formed**) **1** N-COUNT A **form of** something is a type or kind of it. ❑ ...*a rare form of the disease.* ❑ *I am against violence in any form.* **2** N-COUNT The **form** of something is its shape. ❑ ...*the form of the body.* **3** N-COUNT You can refer to something that you can see as a **form** if you cannot see it clearly, or if its outline is the clearest aspect of it. ❑ *His form lay still under the blankets.* **4** N-COUNT A **form** is a paper with questions on it and spaces marked where you should write the answers. ❑ *You will be asked to fill in a form with details of your birth and occupation.* **5** V-T/V-I When a particular shape **forms** or is **formed**, people or things move or are arranged so that this shape is made. ❑ *A line formed to use the bathroom.* ❑ *The 12 students formed a circle with their arms around each other.* **6** V-T If something is arranged or changed so that it becomes similar to a thing with a particular structure or function, you can say that it **forms** that thing. ❑ *These panels fold up to form a screen.* **7** V-T If something consists of particular things, people, or features, you can say that they **form** that thing. ❑ *These articles formed the basis of Randolph's book.* **8** V-T If you **form** an organization, group, or company, you start it. ❑ *They tried to form a study group on human rights.* **9** V-T/V-I When something natural **forms** or is **formed**, it begins to exist and develop. ❑ *The stars formed 10 to 15 billion years ago.* **10** N-UNCOUNT In sports, **form** refers to the ability or success of a person or animal over a period of time. ❑ *His form this season has been brilliant.* [from French]

| Thesaurus | *form* | Also look up : |
|---|---|---|
| N. | class, description, kind **1** | |
| | body, figure, frame, shape **2** | |
| | application, document, sheet **4** | |
| V. | construct, create, develop, | |
| | establish **5** – **9** | |

**for|mal** /fɔrmⁿl/ **1** ADJ **Formal** speech or behavior is very correct and serious rather than

relaxed and friendly, and is used especially in official situations. ❑ *I received a very formal letter of apology from my father.* ● **for|mal|ly** ADV ❑ *He took her home, saying goodnight formally on the doorstep.* ● **for|mal|ity** N-UNCOUNT ❑ *Lillith's formality and seriousness amused him.* **2** ADJ A **formal** action, statement, or request is an official one. ❑ *No formal announcement has been made.* ● **for|mal|ly** ADV ❑ *Officials haven't formally agreed to Anderson's plan.* **3** ADJ **Formal** education or training is given officially, usually in a school, college, or university. ❑ *Wendy didn't have any formal dance training.* ● **for|mal|ly** ADV ❑ ...*formally-trained artists from established schools.* [from Latin] **4** → see also **formality**
→ see also **formerly**

**for|mal|ity** /fɔrmælɪti/ (**formalities**) **1** N-COUNT **Formalities** are formal actions or procedures that are carried out as part of a particular activity or event. ❑ ...*immigration and customs formalities.* [from Latin] **2** → see also **formal**

**for|mal|ize** /fɔrməlaɪz/ (**formalizes, formalizing, formalized**) V-T If you **formalize** a plan, idea, arrangement, or system, you make it formal and official. ❑ *Russia, Canada and Japan formalized an agreement to work together on climate change.* [from Latin]

**for|mal thea|ter** N-UNCOUNT **Formal theater** is entertainment consisting of plays performed before an audience in a theater.

**for|mat** /fɔrmæt/ (**formats, formatting, formatted**) **1** N-COUNT The **format** of something is the way or order in which it is arranged and presented. ❑ *I met with him to explain the format of the program.* **2** V-T To **format** a computer disk means to run a program so that the disk can be written on. [COMPUTING] [from French]

**for|ma|tion** /fɔrmeɪʃⁿn/ (**formations**) **1** N-UNCOUNT The **formation of** something is the starting or creation of it. ❑ ...*the formation of a new government.* **2** N-COUNT If people or things are **in formation**, they are arranged in a particular pattern as they move. ❑ *He was flying in formation with seven other jets.* **3** N-COUNT A rock or cloud **formation** is rock or cloud of a particular shape or structure. [from French]

**forma|tive** /fɔrmətɪv/ ADJ A **formative** period of time or experience is one that has an important and lasting influence on a person's character and attitudes. ❑ *She spent her formative years growing up in Miami.* [from French]

**for|mer** /fɔrmər/ **1** ADJ **Former** is used to describe someone who used to have a particular job, position, or role, but no longer has it. ❑ *The unemployed executives include former sales managers, directors and accountants.* ❑ ...*former president Richard Nixon.* **2** PRON When two people, things, or groups have just been mentioned, you can refer to the first of them as **the former**. The second of them is called **the latter**. ❑ *If you want a career and children, then plan the latter as carefully as the former.*

| Thesaurus | *former* | Also look up : |
|---|---|---|
| ADJ. | prior **1** | |
| | past, previous **1** **2** | |

**for|mer|ly** /fɔrmərli/ ADV If something happened or was true **formerly**, it happened or was true in the past. ❑ *He was formerly in the navy.* [from Old French]

**form-fitting** ADJ **Form-fitting** clothes fit very closely to the body of the person who is wearing them. ❑ *...a black, form-fitting designer dress.*

**for|mi|da|ble** /fɔrmɪdəbᵊl, fərmɪd-/ ADJ If you describe something or someone as **formidable**, you mean that you feel slightly frightened by them because they are very great or impressive. ❑ *We have a formidable task ahead of us.* [from Latin]

**form let|ter** (**form letters**) N-COUNT A **form letter** is a single copy of a letter that has been reproduced in large numbers and sent to many people.

**for|mu|la** /fɔrmyələ/ (**formulae** /fɔrmyəli/ or **formulas**) ◼ N-COUNT A **formula** is a plan that is invented in order to deal with a particular problem. ❑ *...a formula for peace.* ◼ N-COUNT A **formula** is a group of letters, numbers, or other symbols which represents a scientific or mathematical rule. ❑ *This mathematical formula describes the distances of the planets from the Sun.* ◼ N-COUNT In science, the **formula** for a substance tells you what amounts of other substances are needed in order to make that substance. ❑ *They have the same chemical formula.* [from Latin]

**for|mu|late** /fɔrmyəleɪt/ (**formulates, formulating, formulated**) ◼ V-T If you **formulate** something such as a plan or proposal, you invent it, thinking about the details carefully. ❑ *Little by little, he formulated his plan for escape.* ● **for|mu|la|tion** N-UNCOUNT ❑ *...the formulation of U.S. environmental policies.* ◼ V-T If you **formulate** a thought, opinion, or idea, you express it or describe it in words. ❑ *I was impressed by the way he formulated his ideas.* ● **for|mu|la|tion** N-UNCOUNT ❑ *The formulation of the question is important.* [from Latin]

**for-profit** ADJ A **for-profit** organization is one that is run with the aim of making a profit. [BUSINESS] ❑ *Gerber has been running her own for-profit school in southern Florida for 17 years.*

**for|sake** /fərseɪk/ (**forsakes, forsaking, forsook** /fɔrsʊk/, **forsaken**) ◼ V-T If you **forsake** someone, you leave them when you should have stayed, or you stop helping them or looking after them. [LITERARY] ❑ *I still love him and I would never forsake him.* ◼ V-T If you **forsake** something, you stop doing it, using it, or having it. [LITERARY] ❑ *He has forsaken gambling.* [from Old English]

**fort** /fɔrt/ (**forts**) N-COUNT A **fort** is a strong building that is used as a military base. [from Old French]

**forth** /fɔrθ/

In addition to the uses shown below, **forth** is also used in the phrasal verbs "put forth" and "set forth."

◼ ADV When someone goes **forth** from a place,

they leave it. [LITERARY] ❑ *Go forth into the desert.* ◼ ADV If one thing brings **forth** another, the first thing produces the second. [LITERARY] ❑ *My reflections brought forth no conclusion.* [from Old English] ◼ **back and forth** → see **back** ◼ to **hold forth** → see **hold**

**forth|com|ing** /fɔrθkʌmɪŋ/ ◼ ADJ A **forthcoming** event is planned to happen soon. ❑ *...the forthcoming elections.* ◼ ADJ If something that you want, need, or expect is **forthcoming**, it is given to you or it happens. [FORMAL] ❑ *They promised that the money would be forthcoming.* ❑ *No major shift in policy will be forthcoming.* ◼ ADJ If you say that someone is **forthcoming**, you mean that they willingly give information when you ask them. ❑ *William was not very forthcoming about where he lived.*

**forth|right** /fɔrθraɪt/ ADJ If you describe someone as **forthright**, you admire them because they show clearly and strongly what they think and feel. ❑ *...a man with forthright opinions.*

**for|ti|eth** /fɔrtiəθ/ ORD The **fortieth** item in a series is the one that you count as number forty. ❑ *It was the fortieth anniversary of the death of the composer.* [from Old English]

**for|ti|fy** /fɔrtɪfaɪ/ (**fortifies, fortifying, fortified**) ◼ V-T To **fortify** a place means to make it stronger and more difficult to attack, often by building a wall or ditch around it. ❑ *Soldiers worked to fortify the airbase.* ◼ V-T If food or drink **is fortified**, another substance is added to it to make it healthier or stronger. ❑ *...margarine fortified with vitamin D.* [from Old French]

**for|tress** /fɔrtrɪs/ (**fortresses**) N-COUNT A **fortress** is a castle or other large strong building, or a well-protected place, which is intended to be difficult for enemies to enter. [from Old French]

**for|tu|nate** /fɔrtʃənɪt/ ADJ If someone or something is **fortunate**, they are lucky. ❑ *He was extremely fortunate to survive.* ❑ *She is in the fortunate position of having plenty of choice.* [from Old French]

**for|tu|nate|ly** /fɔrtʃənɪtli/ ADV **Fortunately** is used to introduce or indicate a statement about an event or situation that is good. ❑ *Fortunately, the weather last winter was reasonably mild.* [from Old French]

**for|tune** /fɔrtʃən/ (**fortunes**) ◼ N-COUNT You can refer to a large sum of money as **a fortune** or **a small** fortune to emphasize how large it is. ❑ *He made a small fortune in the property boom.* ◼ N-COUNT Someone who has a **fortune** has a very large amount of money. ❑ *He made his fortune in car sales.* ◼ N-UNCOUNT **Fortune** or good **fortune** is good luck. Ill **fortune** is bad luck. ❑ *Investors are starting to wonder how long their good fortune can last.* ◼ N-PLURAL If you talk about someone's **fortunes** or the **fortunes** of something, you are talking about the extent to which they are doing well or being successful. ❑ *The company had to do something to reverse its sliding fortunes.* [from Old French]

**for|ty** /fɔrti/ (**forties**) ◼ NUM **Forty** is the number 40. ◼ N-PLURAL The **forties** is the decade between 1940 and 1949. ❑ *They met in London in the Forties.* [from Old English]

**fo|rum** /fɔrəm/ (**forums**) N-COUNT A **forum** is a place, situation, or group in which people exchange ideas and discuss issues. ❑ *The discussion groups are an open forum for listening.* [from Latin]

**F**

> **Word Link**   *ward ≈ in the direction of : back*ward, *for*ward, *in*ward

**for|ward** /fˈɔrwərd/ (**forwards, forwarding, forwarded**) **1** ADV If you move or look **forward**, you move or look in a direction that is in front of you. ❑ *He came forward with his hand out. "Mr. and Mrs. Selby?" he said.* ❑ *She fell forward on to her face.* **2** ADV **Forward** means in a position near the front of something such as a building or a vehicle. ❑ *The best seats in the theater are as far forward as possible.* ● **Forward** is also an adjective. ❑ *The troops moved to forward positions.* **3** ADV You use **forward** to indicate that something progresses or improves. ❑ *By boosting economic prosperity in Mexico, Canada and the United States, it will help us move forward on issues that concern all of us.* ❑ *They just couldn't see any way forward.* **4** ADV If something or someone is put **forward**, or comes **forward**, they are suggested or offered as suitable for a particular purpose. ❑ *Several similar theories have been put forward.* ❑ *No witnesses came forward.* **5** V-T If a letter or message **is forwarded to** someone, it is sent to the place where they are, after having been sent to a different place earlier. ❑ *When he's out on the road, office calls are forwarded to his cellphone.* [from Old English] **6 backward and forward** → see **backward**

**for|ward slash** (**forward slashes**) N-COUNT A **forward slash** is the sloping line / that separates letters, words, or numbers.

**fos|sil** /fˈɒsˀl/ (**fossils**) N-COUNT A **fossil** is the hard remains of a prehistoric animal or plant that are found inside a rock. [from Latin]
→ see Word Web: **fossil**
→ see **evolution**

**fos|sil fuel** also **fossil-fuel** N-VAR **Fossil fuel** is fuel such as coal or oil that is formed from the decayed remains of plants or animals. ❑ *Burning fossil fuels uses oxygen and produces carbon dioxide.*
→ see **electricity, greenhouse effect, solar**

**fos|sil rec|ord** (**fossil records**) N-COUNT The **fossil record** is the history of life on Earth that is recorded in fossils found in rocks.

**fos|ter** /fˈɔstər/ (**fosters, fostering, fostered**) **1** ADJ **Foster** parents are people who officially take a child into their family for a period of time, without becoming the child's legal parents. The child is referred to as their **foster** child. **2** V-T If you **foster** a child, you take it into your family for a period of time, without becoming its legal parent. **3** V-T If you **foster** a feeling, activity, or idea, you help it to develop. ❑ *These organizations fostered a strong sense of pride within the black*

community. [from Old English]

**fought** /fˈɔt/ **Fought** is the past tense and past participle of **fight**. [from Old English]

**foul** /fˈaʊl/ (**fouler, foulest, fouls**) **1** ADJ If you describe something as **foul**, you mean it is dirty and smells or tastes unpleasant. ❑ *...foul, polluted water.* **2** ADJ **Foul** language is offensive and contains swear words or rude words. **3** ADJ If someone has a **foul** temper or is in a **foul** mood, they become angry or violent very suddenly and easily. **4** N-COUNT A **foul** is an act in a game or sport that is not allowed according to the rules. **5** PHRASE If you **run foul of** someone or **fall foul of** them, you do something which gets you into trouble with them. ❑ *He had fallen foul of the FBI.* [from Old English]

**foul line** (**foul lines**) N-COUNT In basketball, **the foul line** is the line from which a player tries to throw the ball through the basket after they have been fouled.

**found** /fˈaʊnd/ (**founds, founding, founded**) **1 Found** is the past tense and past participle of **find**. **2** V-T When an institution, company, or organization **is founded** by someone, he or she gets it started, often by providing the necessary money. ❑ *The New York Free-Loan Society was founded in 1892.* ❑ *His father founded the American Socialist Party.* ● **foun|da|tion** /faʊndˈeɪʃˀn/ N-SING ❑ *...the foundation of the National Association of Evangelicals in 1942.* ● **found|er** (**founders**) N-COUNT ❑ *...one of the founders of the United Nations.* ● **found|ing** N-SING ❑ *The firm has had great success since its founding 65 years ago.* [Sense 1 from Old English. Sense 2 from Old French.] **3** → see also **founded, founding**

> **Word Link**   *found ≈ base : found*ation, *found*ed, *found*er

**foun|da|tion** /faʊndˈeɪʃˀn/ (**foundations**) **1** N-COUNT The **foundation of** something such as a belief or way of life is the things on which it is based. ❑ *Best friends are the foundation of my life.* ❑ *The issue strikes at the very foundation of our community.* **2** N-COUNT A **foundation** is an organization which provides money for a special purpose. ❑ *...the National Foundation for Educational Research.* **3** N-PLURAL The **foundations** of a building or other structure are the layer of bricks or concrete below the ground that it is built on. **4** N-UNCOUNT If a story, idea, or argument has **no foundation**, there are no facts to prove that it is true. ❑ *The rumors were without foundation.* [from Old French] **5** → see also **found**
→ see **makeup**

**found|ed** /fˈaʊndɪd/ **1** ADJ If something is **founded on** a particular thing, it is based on

---

> **Word Web**   fossil

There are two types of animal **fossils**—body fossils and **trace** fossils. Body fossils help us understand how the animal looked when it was alive. Trace fossils, such as **tracks** and **footprints**, show us how the animal moved. Since we don't find tracks of dinosaurs' tails, we know they lifted them up as they walked. Footprints tell us about the weight of the dinosaur and how fast it moved. Scientists use two methods to calculate the date of a fossil. They sometimes count the number of **rock** layers covering it. They also use **carbon** dating.

## Picture Dictionary: fractions

| fraction | decimal | percentage |
|---|---|---|
| 1/4 | 0.25 | 25% |

| fraction | decimal | percentage |
|---|---|---|
| 1/3 | 0.33 | 33% |

| fraction | decimal | percentage |
|---|---|---|
| 1/2 | 0.50 | 50% |

**adding fractions**

| problem: | solution: |
|---|---|
| 1 1/4 | 1 1/4 |
| +2 1/2 | +2 2/4 |
| ? | 3 3/4 |

**subtracting fractions**

| problem: | solution: |
|---|---|
| 5 2/3 | 5 4/6 |
| - 1 1/6 | - 1 1/6 |
| ? | 4 3/6 = 4 1/2 |

f

it. ❑ *The criticisms are founded on facts.* [from Old French] ② → see also **found**

**Word Link** found ≈ base : found**ation**, found**ed**, found**er**

**found|er** /fa͟ʊndər/ (**founders, foundering, foundered**) V-I If something such as a plan or project **founders**, it fails. ❑ *The talks foundered, without agreement.* [from Old French]

**found|ing mem|ber** (**founding members**) N-COUNT A **founding member** of a club, group, or organization is one of the first members, often one who was involved in setting it up.

**foun|dry** /fa͟ʊndri/ (**foundries**) N-COUNT A **foundry** is a place where metal or glass is melted and formed into particular shapes. [from Old French]

**foun|tain** /fa͟ʊntɪn/ (**fountains**) ① N-COUNT A **fountain** is an ornamental feature in a pool or lake which consists of a jet of water that is forced up into the air by a pump. ② N-COUNT A **fountain of** a liquid is an amount of it which is sent up into the air and falls back. [LITERARY] ❑ *A fountain of liquid rock rose from the volcano.* [from Old French]

**four** /fɔ͟r/ (**fours**) ① NUM **Four** is the number 4. ② PHRASE If you are **on all fours**, your knees, feet, and hands are on the ground. ❑ *She crawled on all fours over to the window.* [from Old English]

**four|some** /fɔ͟rsəm/ (**foursomes**) N-COUNT A **foursome** is a group of four people or things. ❑ *The foursome released their second CD this month.* [from Old English]

**four|teen** /fɔ͟rti͟n/ (**fourteens**) NUM **Fourteen** is the number 14. [from Old English]

**four|teenth** /fɔ͟rti͟nθ/ ORD The **fourteenth** item in a series is the one that you count as number fourteen. ❑ *The festival is now in its fourteenth year.* [from Old English]

**fourth** /fɔ͟rθ/ (**fourths**) ① ORD The **fourth** item in a series is the one that you count as number four. ❑ *Last year's winner finished in fourth place.* ② N-COUNT A **fourth** is one of four equal parts of something. ❑ *Three-fourths of the public say they favor a national vote on the issue.* [from Old English]

**four-wheel drive** (**four-wheel drives**) N-COUNT A **four-wheel drive** is a vehicle in which all four wheels receive power from the engine to help with steering.

**fowl** /fa͟ʊl/ (**fowls**)

The form **fowl** is usually used for the plural, but **fowls** can also be used.

N-COUNT A **fowl** is a bird, especially one that can be eaten as food, such as a duck or a chicken. [from Old English]

**fox** /fɒ͟ks/ (**foxes**) N-COUNT A **fox** is a wild animal which looks like a dog and has reddish-brown fur, a pointed face and ears, and a thick

fox

tail. [from Old English]

**foxy** /fɒ͟ksi/ (**foxier, foxiest**) ADJ If a man calls a woman **foxy**, he means that she is physically attractive. [INFORMAL] ❑ *...a foxy blonde.* [from Old English]

**foy|er** /fɔ͟ɪər, fɔ͟ɪeɪ, fwɑ͟yeɪ/ (**foyers**) N-COUNT The **foyer** is the large area where people meet or wait just inside the main doors of a building such as a theater or hotel. [from French]

**Word Link** fract, frag ≈ breaking : **fract**ion, **fract**ure, **frag**ile

**frac|tion** /fræ͟kʃⁿn/ (**fractions**) ① N-COUNT A **fraction** of something is a tiny amount or proportion of it. ❑ *She hesitated for a fraction of a second before answering.* ② N-COUNT A **fraction** is a number that can be expressed as a proportion of two whole numbers. For example, ½ and ⅓ are both fractions. [from Late Latin] → see Picture Dictionary: **fractions**

**frac|ture** /fræ͟ktʃər/ (**fractures, fracturing, fractured**) ① N-COUNT A **fracture** is a crack or break in something, especially a bone. ❑ *...a hip fracture.* ② V-T/V-I If something such as a bone **is fractured** or **fractures**, it gets a crack or break in it. ❑ *You've fractured a rib, maybe more than one.* ❑ *The mast of his boat fractured in two places and fell into the sea.* [from Old French]

**frag|ile** /fræ͟dʒⁿl/ ① ADJ If you describe a situation as **fragile**, you mean that it is weak or uncertain, and is unlikely to be able to resist strong pressure or attack. ❑ *The fragile economies of several southern African nations could be damaged.* ● **fra|gil|ity** /frədʒɪlɪti/ N-UNCOUNT ❑ *...the fragility of the peace process.* **2** ADJ Something that is **fragile** is easily broken or damaged. ❑ *...fine, fragile crystal.* ● **fra|gil|ity** N-UNCOUNT ❑ *...the fragility of their bones.* [from Latin]

| **Thesaurus** | *fragile* | Also look up : |
| --- | --- | --- |

ADJ. unstable, weak **1**
breakable, delicate; (*ant.*) sturdy **2**

**frag|ment** (**fragments, fragmenting, fragmented**)

The noun is pronounced /frǽgmənt/. The verb is pronounced /frægmɛ́nt/.

**1** N-COUNT A **fragment of** something is a small piece or part of it. ❑ *...tiny fragments of glass.* ❑ *She read every fragment of news.* **2** V-T/V-I If something **fragments** or **is fragmented**, it breaks or separates into small pieces or parts. ❑ *The clouds fragmented and out came the sun.* ● **frag|men|ta|tion** /frǽgmənteɪ⁰n/ N-UNCOUNT ❑ *...the fragmentation of the Soviet Union.* [from Latin]

**frag|men|ta|tion** /frǽgmənteɪ⁰n/
**1** N-UNCOUNT **Fragmentation** is a type of reproduction in some worms and other organisms, in which the organism breaks into several parts and each part grows into a new individual. [TECHNICAL] [from Latin] **2** → see also **fragment**

**fra|grance** /freɪgrəns/ (**fragrances**) N-VAR A **fragrance** is a pleasant or sweet smell. ❑ *...a plant with a strong fragrance.* [from Latin]

**fra|grant** /freɪgrənt/ ADJ Something that is **fragrant** has a pleasant, sweet smell. ❑ *...fragrant oils and perfumes.* [from Latin]

**frail** /freɪl/ (**frailer, frailest**) **1** ADJ Someone who is **frail** is not very strong or healthy. ❑ *She lay in bed looking frail.* **2** ADJ Something that is **frail** is easily broken or damaged. ❑ *The frail boat rocked as he climbed in.* [from Old French]

**frame** /freɪm/ (**frames, framing, framed**)
**1** N-COUNT The **frame** of a picture or mirror is the wood, metal, or plastic that is fitted around it. ❑ *...a photograph of her mother in a silver frame.* **2** N-COUNT The **frame** of an object such as a building, chair, or window is the arrangement of wooden, metal, or plastic bars between which other material is fitted, and which gives the object its strength and shape. ❑ *He supplied builders with door and window frames.* ❑ *With difficulty he released the mattress from the metal frame.* **3** N-COUNT A **frame** of movie film is one of the many separate photographs that it consists of. ❑ *...films shot at 4000 frames per second.* **4** V-T When a picture or photograph **is framed**, it is put in a frame. ❑ *The picture is now ready to be mounted and framed.* **5** V-T If someone **frames** an innocent person, they make other people think that that person is guilty of a crime, by lying or inventing evidence. [INFORMAL] ❑ *I'm trying to find out who tried to frame me.* **6** N-COUNT You can refer to someone's body as their **frame**, especially when you are describing the general shape of it. ❑ *Their belts are pulled tight against their bony frames.* [from Old English] → see **animation, bed, painting**

**frame of mind** (**frames of mind**) N-COUNT Your **frame of mind** is the mood that you are in,

which causes you to have a particular attitude to something. ❑ *I was not in the right frame of mind to play golf.*

**frame|work** /freɪmwɜrk/ (**frameworks**)
**1** N-COUNT A **framework** is a particular set of rules, ideas, or beliefs which you use in order to decide what to do. ❑ *...the framework of federal regulations.* **2** N-COUNT A **framework** is a structure that forms a support or frame for something. ❑ *...wooden shelves on a steel framework.*

**fran|chise** /frǽntʃaɪz/ (**franchises**) **1** N-COUNT A **franchise** is an authority that is given by an organization to someone, allowing them to sell its goods or services or to take part in an activity which the organization controls. [BUSINESS] ❑ *...a franchise to develop Hong Kong's first cable TV system.* **2** N-UNCOUNT **Franchise** is the right to vote in an election. ❑ *...the introduction of universal franchise.* [from Old French]

**frank** /frǽŋk/ (**franker, frankest**) ADJ If someone is **frank**, they state or express things in an open and honest way. ❑ *My husband has not been frank with me.* ● **frank|ly** ADV ❑ *You can talk frankly to me.* ● **frank|ness** N-UNCOUNT ❑ *The reaction to his frankness was hostile.* [from Old French]

**frank|ly** /frǽŋkli/ **1** ADV You use **frankly** when you are expressing an opinion or feeling to emphasize that you mean what you are saying, especially when the person you are speaking to may not like it. ❑ *Frankly, this whole thing is getting boring.* [from Old French] **2** → see also **frank**

**fran|tic** /frǽntɪk/ ADJ If you are **frantic**, you are behaving in a wild and uncontrolled way because you are frightened or worried. ❑ *A bird was trapped in the room and was by now quite frantic.* ● **fran|ti|cal|ly** /frǽntɪkli/ ADV ❑ *She clutched frantically at Emily's arm.* [from Old French]

**fra|ter|nity** /frətɜrnɪti/ (**fraternities**)
**1** N-COUNT You can refer to people who have the same profession or the same interests as a particular **fraternity**. ❑ *...the spread of stolen guns among the criminal fraternity.* **2** N-UNCOUNT **Fraternity** refers to friendship and support between people who feel they are closely linked to each other. [FORMAL] ❑ *Bob needs the fraternity of others who share his ideas.* **3** N-COUNT In the United States, a **fraternity** is a society of male university or college students. [from Latin]

**fraud** /frɔd/ (**frauds**) **1** N-VAR **Fraud** is the crime of gaining money or financial benefits by a trick or by lying. ❑ *He was jailed for two years for fraud and deception.* **2** N-COUNT A **fraud** is something or someone that deceives people in a way that is illegal or dishonest. ❑ *He's a fraud and a cheat.* [from Old French]

**fraudu|lent** /frɔdʒələnt/ ADJ A **fraudulent** activity is deceitful or dishonest. ❑ *...fraudulent claims about being a nurse.* ● **fraudu|lent|ly** ADV ❑ *She was fraudulently using a credit card.* [from Latin]

**fraught** /frɔt/ **1** ADJ If a situation or action is **fraught with** problems or risks, it is filled with them. ❑ *The earliest operations using this technique were fraught with dangers.* **2** ADJ If you say that a situation or action is **fraught**, you mean that it is worrisome or difficult. ❑ *It has been a somewhat fraught day.* [from Middle Dutch]

**fray** /freɪ/ (**frays, fraying, frayed**) V-T/V-I If something such as cloth or rope **frays**, or if something **frays** it, its threads or fibers start to come apart from each other and spoil its appearance. □ *The fabric is very fine and frays easily.* [from French]

**fraz|zle** /fræzəl/ PHRASE If you **wear** yourself **to a frazzle**, or if you **are worn to a frazzle**, you feel mentally and physically exhausted because you have been working too hard or because you have been constantly worrying about something. □ *She's worn to a frazzle preparing for the competition.* [from Middle English]

**fraz|zled** /fræzəld/ ADJ If you are **frazzled**, or if your nerves are **frazzled**, you feel mentally and physically exhausted. □ *…a place to calm the most frazzled tourist.* [from Middle English]

**freak** /friːk/ (**freaks**) ◼ ADJ A **freak** event or action is one that is a very unusual or extreme example of its type. □ *Weir broke his leg in a freak accident playing golf.* ◼ N-COUNT People are sometimes referred to as **freaks** when their behavior or attitude is very different from that of the majority of people and other people do not like them because of this. □ *It's the story of a troupe of circus freaks.*

**freck|le** /frɛkᵊl/ (**freckles**) N-COUNT **Freckles** are small light brown spots on your skin, especially on your face. □ *He had short ginger-colored hair and freckles.* [from Old Norse]

**free** /friː/ (**freer, freest, frees, freeing, freed**) ◼ ADJ If something is **free**, you can have it or use it without paying for it. □ *The classes are free, with lunch provided.* ◼ **free of charge** → see **charge** ◼ ADJ Someone or something that is **free** is not restricted, controlled, or limited, for example, by rules, customs, or other people. □ *The government will be free to pursue its economic policies.* □ *The elections were free and fair.* ● **free|ly** ADV □ *They cast their votes freely on election day.* ◼ ADJ Someone who is **free** is no longer a prisoner or a slave. □ *He walked from the court house a free man.* ◼ ADJ If someone or something is **free of** or **free from** an unpleasant thing, they do not have it or they are not affected by it. □ *…a future free of fear.* □ *She still has her slim figure and is free of wrinkles.* ◼ ADJ If you have a **free** period of time or are **free** at a particular time, you are not working or occupied then. □ *She spent her free time shopping.* □ *I used to write during my free periods at school.* ◼ ADJ If something such as a table or seat is **free**, it is not being used or occupied by anyone, or is not reserved for anyone to use. ◼ ADJ If you get something **free** or if it gets **free**, it is no longer trapped by anything or attached to anything. □ *He pulled his arm free.* ◼ V-T If you **free** someone of something that is unpleasant or restricting, you remove it from them. □ *It will free us of debt.* ◼ V-T To **free** a prisoner or a slave means to release them. ◼ V-T To **free** someone or something means to make them available for a task or function that they were previously not available for. □ *Choosing the play early frees the director to make other decisions.* □ *His contract will run out soon, freeing him to pursue his own projects.* ◼ V-T If you **free** someone or something, you remove them from the place in which they have been trapped or become fixed. □ *Rescue workers freed him by cutting away part of the car.* ◼ PHRASE You say **"feel free"** when you want to give someone permission to do something, in a very willing way. [INFORMAL] □ *If you have any questions at all,*

*please feel free to ask me.* [from Old English] ◼ to **give** someone **a free hand** → see **hand** ◼ to **give** someone **free rein** → see **rein**

**free agent** (**free agents**) N-COUNT If a sports player is a **free agent**, he or she is free to sign a contract with any team.

**free as|so|cia|tion** N-UNCOUNT **Free association** is a psychological technique in which words or images are used to suggest other words or images in a non-logical way.

**free|dom** /friːdəm/ (**freedoms**) ◼ N-VAR **Freedom** is the state of being allowed to do what you want to do. □ *…individual freedoms and human rights.* ◼ N-UNCOUNT When prisoners or slaves are set free or escape, they gain their **freedom**. □ *…the agreement under which all hostages would gain their freedom.* ◼ N-UNCOUNT **Freedom from** something you do not want means not being affected by it. □ *…the freedom from pain that medicine could provide.* [from Old English]

**free|dom of speech** N-UNCOUNT **Freedom of speech** is the same as **free speech**. □ *…a country where freedom of speech may not be allowed.*

**free en|ter|prise** N-UNCOUNT **Free enterprise** is an economic system in which businesses compete for profit without much government control. [BUSINESS]

**free fall** (**free falls**) also **free-fall** N-UNCOUNT An object that is **in free fall** is falling through the air because of gravity, and no other forces are affecting it.

**free|lance** /friːlæns/ ADJ Someone who does **freelance** work or who is, for example, a **freelance** journalist or photographer is not employed by one organization, but is paid for each piece of work they do by the organization they do it for. [BUSINESS] ● **Freelance** is also an adverb. □ *He is now working freelance from his home.*

**free|ly** /friːli/ ◼ ADV **Freely** means many times or in large quantities. □ *We have referred freely to his ideas.* □ *George was spending very freely.* ◼ ADV If you can talk **freely**, you can talk without needing to be careful about what you say. ◼ ADV If someone gives or does something **freely**, they give or do it willingly, without being ordered or forced to do it. □ *Danny shared his knowledge freely with anyone interested.* ◼ ADV If something or someone moves **freely**, they move easily and smoothly, without any obstacles or resistance. □ *Traffic is flowing freely.*

f

[from Old English] **5** → see also **free**

**free ride** (**free rides**) N-COUNT If you say that someone is getting **a free ride** in a particular situation, you mean that they are getting some benefit from it without putting any effort into achieving it themselves, and you disapprove of this. ❑ *I didn't want anyone to think I was getting a free ride from the boss.*

**free speech** N-UNCOUNT **Free speech** is the right to express your opinions in public.

**free trade** N-UNCOUNT **Free trade** is trade between different countries that is carried on without particular government regulations such as subsidies or taxes. ❑ *...the idea of a free trade pact between the U.S. and Mexico.*

**free|way** /frɪweɪ/ (**freeways**) N-COUNT A **freeway** is a major road that has been specially built for fast travel over long distances. [from Old English]

**free will** PHRASE If you do something **of** your **own free will**, you do it by choice and not because you are forced to do it. ❑ *She stayed of her own free will.*

**freeze** /friz/ (**freezes, freezing, froze, frozen**) **1** V-T/V-I If a liquid or a substance containing a liquid **freezes**, or if something **freezes** it, it becomes solid because of low temperatures. ❑ *If the temperature drops below 32°F, water freezes.* ❑ *The ground froze solid.* ● **freez|ing** N-UNCOUNT ❑ *...damage due to freezing and thawing.* **2** V-T If you **freeze** something such as food, you preserve it by storing it at a temperature below freezing point. **3** V-I If you **freeze**, you feel extremely cold. ❑ *The windows didn't fit properly so in winter we froze.* **4** V-I If someone who is moving **freezes**, they suddenly stop and become completely still and quiet. [WRITTEN] ❑ *She froze when the beam of the flashlight struck her.* **5** V-T If the government or a company **freeze** things such as prices or wages, they state officially that they will not allow them to increase for a fixed period of time. [BUSINESS] ❑ *They want the government to freeze prices.* ● **Freeze** is also a noun. ❑ *A wage freeze was imposed on all staff.* **6** V-T If someone in authority **freezes** something such as a bank account, fund, or property, they obtain a legal order which states that it cannot be used or sold for a particular period of time. [BUSINESS] [from Old English] **7** → see also **freezing, frozen** → see **thermometer, water**

**freez|er** /frizər/ (**freezers**) N-COUNT A **freezer** is a large container like a refrigerator in which the temperature is kept below freezing point so that you can store food inside it for long periods. [from Old English]

**freez|ing** /frizɪŋ/ **1** ADJ If you say that something is **freezing** or **freezing cold**, you are emphasizing that it is very cold. ❑ *The movie theater was freezing.* **2** ADJ If you say that you are **freezing** or **freezing cold**, you are emphasizing that you feel very cold. ❑ *"You must be freezing," she said.* [from Old English] **3** → see also **freeze** → see **precipitation**

**freez|ing point** (**freezing points**) also **freezing-point 1** N-UNCOUNT **Freezing point** is 32°Fahrenheit or 0°Celsius, the temperature at which water freezes. Freezing point is often used when talking about the weather. **2** N-COUNT The **freezing point** of a particular substance is the temperature at which it freezes.

**freight** /freɪt/ **1** N-UNCOUNT **Freight** is the movement of goods by trucks, trains, ships, or airplanes. ❑ *Most shipments went by air freight.* **2** N-UNCOUNT **Freight** is goods that are transported by trucks, trains, ships, or airplanes. ❑ *...26 tons of freight.* [from Middle Dutch] → see **train**

**freight car** (**freight cars**) N-COUNT On a train, a **freight car** is a large container in which goods are transported.

**freight|er** /freɪtər/ (**freighters**) N-COUNT A **freighter** is a large ship or airplane that is designed for carrying freight. [from Middle Dutch]

**French fries** N-PLURAL **French fries** are long, thin pieces of potato fried in oil or fat.

**French toast** N-UNCOUNT **French toast** is toast made by dipping a slice of bread into beaten egg and milk and then frying it.

**fre|net|ic** /frɪnɛtɪk/ ADJ **Frenetic** activity is fast and energetic, but rather uncontrolled. ❑ *...the frenetic pace of life in New York.* [from Old French]

**fren|zied** /frɛnzid/ ADJ **Frenzied** activities or actions are wild, excited, and uncontrolled. ❑ *...the frenzied activity of the election.* [from Old French]

**fren|zy** /frɛnzi/ (**frenzies**) N-VAR **Frenzy** or a **frenzy** is great excitement or wild behavior that often results from losing control of your feelings. ❑ *"Get out!" she ordered in a frenzy.* [from Old French]

**fre|quen|cy** /frikwənsi/ (**frequencies**) **1** N-UNCOUNT The **frequency** of an event is the number of times it happens. ❑ *The frequency of Kara's phone calls increased.* **2** N-VAR The **frequency** of a sound wave or a radio wave is the number of times it vibrates within a period of time. ❑ *You can't hear waves of such a high frequency.* [from Latin] → see **sound, wave**

**fre|quent** /frikwənt/ ADJ If something is **frequent**, it happens often. ❑ *Bordeaux is on the main Paris-Madrid line so there are frequent trains.* ● **fre|quent|ly** ADV ❑ *He was frequently unhappy.* [from Latin]

| **Thesaurus** | *frequent* | Also look up : |
|---|---|---|
| ADJ. | common, everyday, habitual; (*ant.*) occasional, rare | |

**fres|co** /frɛskoʊ/ (**frescoes** or **frescos**) N-COUNT A **fresco** is a picture that is painted on a plastered wall when the plaster is still wet. [from Italian]

**fresh** /frɛʃ/ (**fresher, freshest**) **1** ADJ A **fresh** thing or amount replaces or is added to a previous thing or amount. ❑ *He asked the police to make fresh inquiries.* **2** ADJ Something that is **fresh** has been done, made, or experienced recently. ❑ *There were fresh car tracks in the snow.* ● **fresh|ly** ADV ❑ *...freshly-baked bread.* **3** ADJ **Fresh** food has been picked or produced recently, and has not been preserved. ❑ *...locally-caught fresh fish.* **4** ADJ If you describe something as **fresh**, you like it because it is new and exciting. ❑ *These designers are full of fresh ideas.* **5** ADJ If something smells, tastes, or feels **fresh**, it is clean or cool. ❑ *The air was fresh and for a moment she felt revived.* **6** ADJ **Fresh** paint is not yet dry. [from Old English] → see **glacier**

**fresh air** N-UNCOUNT You can describe the air outside as **fresh air**, especially when you mean that it is good for you. ❑ *Let's take the baby outside — we all need some fresh air.*

**fresh|man** /frɛʃmən/ (**freshmen**) N-COUNT In the United States, a **freshman** is a student who is in their first year at a high school or college.

**fresh|water** /frɛʃwɔtər/ ADJ A **freshwater** lake contains water that is not salty, usually in contrast to the sea. ❑ *...Lake Balaton, the largest freshwater lake in Europe.*

**fret** /frɛt/ (**frets, fretting, fretted**) V-T/V-I If you **fret** about something, you worry about it. ❑ *I was constantly fretting about everyone else's problems.* ❑ *Members of Congress fret that the project will eventually cost billions.* [from Old English]

**fric|tion** /frɪkʃ°n/ (**frictions**) **1** N-UNCOUNT **Friction** between people is disagreement and argument between them. ❑ *Sara sensed that there had been friction between her children.* **2** N-UNCOUNT **Friction** is the force that makes it difficult for things to move freely when they are touching each other. [from French]

**Fri|day** /fraɪdeɪ, -di/ (**Fridays**) N-VAR **Friday** is the day after Thursday and before Saturday. ❑ *He is intending to go home on Friday.* ❑ *...Friday November 6.* [from Old English]

**fridge** /frɪdʒ/ (**fridges**) N-COUNT A **fridge** is the same as a **refrigerator**. [INFORMAL]

**friend** /frɛnd/ (**friends**) **1** N-COUNT A **friend** is someone who you know well and like, but who is not related to you. ❑ *...my best friend.* ❑ *She never was a close friend of mine.* **2** N-PLURAL If you are **friends** with someone, you are their friend and they are yours. ❑ *I still wanted to be friends with Alison.* ❑ *We remained good friends.* **3** N-PLURAL The **friends of** a country, cause, or organization are the people and organizations who help and support them. ❑ *...the friends of Israel.* **4** PHRASE If you **make friends with** someone, you begin a friendship with them. ❑ *He has made friends with the kids on the street.* ❑ *Dennis made friends easily.* [from Old English]

| Word Partnership | Use *friend* with : |
| --- | --- |
| ADJ. | **best** friend, **close** friend, **dear** friend, **faithful** friend, **good** friend, **loyal** friend, **mutual** friend, **old** friend, **personal** friend, **trusted** friend ■ |
| N. | **childhood** friend, friend **of the family**, friend **or foe** ■ |
| V. | **tell** a friend ■<br>**make** a friend ■ ■ |

**friend|ly** /frɛndli/ (**friendlier, friendliest, friendlies**) **1** ADJ If someone is **friendly**, they behave in a pleasant, kind way, and like to be with other people. ❑ *Godfrey was friendly to me.* ❑ *The man had a pleasant, friendly face.* ● **friend|li|ness** N-UNCOUNT ❑ *She loves the friendliness of the people in Russia.* **2** ADJ If you are **friendly with** someone, you like each other and enjoy spending time together. ❑ *I'm friendly with his mother.* **3** [from Old English]

| Word Partnership | Use *friendly* with : |
| --- | --- |
| N. | friendly **atmosphere**, friendly **face**, friendly **neighbors**, friendly **relationship**, friendly **service**, friendly **voice** ■ |
| V. | **become** friendly ■ |

**friend|ly fire** N-UNCOUNT If you come under **friendly fire** during a battle, you are accidentally shot at by people on your own side, rather than by your enemy. ❑ *A high percentage of casualties were caused by friendly fire.*

| Word Link | *ship ≈ condition or state :* censor**ship**, citizen**ship**, friend**ship** |
| --- | --- |

**friend|ship** /frɛndʃɪp/ (**friendships**) N-VAR A **friendship** is a relationship between two or more friends. ❑ *She ended our friendship by sending me a hurtful letter.* [from Old English]

**fries** /fraɪz/ N-PLURAL **Fries** are the same as **French fries.** [from Old French]

**frig|ate** /frɪgət/ (**frigates**) N-COUNT A **frigate** is a fairly small ship owned by the navy that can move at fast speeds. [from French]

**fright** /fraɪt/ (**frights**) **1** N-UNCOUNT **Fright** is a sudden feeling of fear. ❑ *The steam pipes rattled suddenly, and Franklin jumped with fright.* **2** N-COUNT A **fright** is an experience which makes you suddenly afraid. ❑ *The snake raised its head, which gave everyone a fright.* [from Old English]

**fright|en** /fraɪt°n/ (**frightens, frightening, frightened**) V-T If something or someone **frightens** you, they cause you to suddenly feel afraid, anxious, or nervous. ❑ *He knew that Soli was trying to frighten him.* [from Old English]
▶ **frighten away** or **frighten off** **1** PHR-VERB If you **frighten away** a person or animal or **frighten** them **off**, you make them afraid so that they run away or stay some distance away from you. ❑ *The boats were frightening away the fish.* **2** PHR-VERB To **frighten** someone **away** or **frighten** them **off** means to make them nervous so that they decide not to become involved with a particular person or activity. ❑ *High prices have frightened buyers off.*
▶ **frighten off** → see **frighten away**

**fright|ened** /fraɪt°nd/ ADJ If you are **frightened**, you are anxious or afraid. ❑ *She was frightened of making a mistake.* [from Old English]

**fright|en|ing** /fraɪt°nɪŋ/ ADJ If something is **frightening**, it makes you feel afraid, anxious, or nervous. ❑ *It was a very frightening experience.* ● **fright|en|ing|ly** ADV ❑ *The country is frighteningly close to war.* [from Old English]

**frill** /frɪl/ (**frills**) **1** N-COUNT A **frill** is a long narrow strip of cloth or paper with many folds in it, which is attached to something as a decoration. ❑ *...curtains with frills.* **2** PHRASE If you describe something as having **no frills**, you mean that it has no extra features, but is acceptable or good if you want something simple. [from Flemish]

**fringe** /frɪndʒ/ (**fringes**) **1** N-COUNT A **fringe** is a decoration attached to clothes, or other objects such as curtains, consisting of a row of hanging threads. ❑ *The jacket had leather fringes.* **2** N-COUNT To be **on the fringe** or **the fringes of** a place means to be on the outside edge of it. ❑ *...a small town on the fringes of the city.* **3** N-COUNT The **fringe** or **the**

**fringes of** an activity or organization are its less important, least typical, or most extreme parts. ❑ *This political party is the fringe of the political scene.* [from Old French]

**fringed** /frɪndʒd/ **1** ADJ **Fringed** clothes, curtains, or lampshades are decorated with fringes. ❑ *…a fringed scarf.* **2** ADJ If a place or object **is fringed with** something, that thing forms a border around it. ❑ *Her eyes were fringed with long lashes.* [from Old French]

**frivo|lous** /frɪvələs/ **1** ADJ If you describe someone as **frivolous,** you mean they behave in a silly or light-hearted way, rather than being serious and sensible. ❑ *I was a bit too frivolous to be a doctor.* **2** ADJ If you describe an activity as **frivolous,** you disapprove of it because it is not useful and wastes time or money. ❑ *The group wants politicians to stop wasting money on what it believes are frivolous projects.* [from Latin]

**fro** /froʊ/ **to and fro** → see **to**

**frog** /frɒg/ (**frogs**) N-COUNT A **frog** is a small creature with smooth skin, big eyes, and long back legs which it uses for jumping. [from Old English] → see **amphibian**

**frol|ic** /frɒlɪk/ (**frolics, frolicking, frolicked**) V-I When people or animals **frolic,** they play or move in a lively, happy way. ❑ *Tourists sunbathe and frolic in the ocean.* [from Dutch]

---

**from**

❶ MENTIONING THE SOURCE, ORIGIN, OR STARTING POINT
❷ MENTIONING A RANGE OF TIMES, AMOUNTS, OR THINGS
❸ MENTIONING SOMETHING YOU WANT TO PREVENT OR AVOID

---

In addition to the uses shown below, **from** is used in phrasal verbs such as "date from" and "grow away from."

❶ **from** /frəm, STRONG frʌm/ **1** PREP If something comes **from** a particular person or thing, or if you get something **from** them, they give it to you or they are the source of it. ❑ *He appealed for information from anyone who saw the attackers.* ❑ *…an anniversary present from his wife.* **2** PREP Someone who comes **from** a particular place lives in that place or originally lived there. Something that comes **from** a particular place was made in that place. ❑ *…an art dealer from Zurich.* **3** PREP If someone or something moves or is moved **from** a place, they leave it or are removed, so that they are no longer there. ❑ *The guests watched as she fled from the room.* **4** PREP If you take one thing or person **from** another, you move that thing or person so that they are no longer with the other or attached to the other. ❑ *In many bone transplants, bone can be taken from other parts of the patient's body.* **5** PREP If you take something **from** an amount, you reduce the amount by that much. ❑ *The $103 was deducted from Mrs. Adams' salary.* **6** PREP If you return **from** a place or an activity, you return after being in that place or doing that activity. ❑ *My son has just returned from Amsterdam.* **7** PREP If you see or hear something **from** a particular place, you are in that place when you see it or hear it. ❑ *Visitors see the painting from behind*

*a plate glass window.* **8** PREP If something hangs or sticks out **from** an object, it is attached to it or held by it. ❑ *Hanging from her right wrist is a gold bracelet.* ❑ *Large fans hang from the ceilings.* **9** PREP You can use **from** when giving distances. For example, if a place is fifty miles **from** another place, the distance between the two places is fifty miles. ❑ *The park is only a few hundred yards from Zurich's main shopping center.* ❑ *How far is it from here?* **10** PREP If a road or railroad line goes **from** one place to another, you can travel along it between the two places. ❑ *…the road from St. Petersburg to Tallinn.* **11** PREP **From** is used, especially in the expression **made from,** to say what substance has been used to make something. ❑ *…bread made from white flour.* **12** PREP If something changes **from** one thing to another, it stops being the first thing and becomes the second thing. ❑ *The expression on his face changed from sympathy to surprise.* ❑ *Unemployment has fallen from 7.5 to 7.2%.* **13** PREP You use **from** after some verbs and nouns when mentioning the cause of something. ❑ *The problem simply resulted from a difference of opinion.* **14** PREP You use **from** when you are giving the reason for an opinion. ❑ *She knew from experience that Dave was telling her the truth.* [from Old English]

❷ **from** /frəm, STRONG frʌm/ **1** PREP You can use **from** when you are talking about the beginning of a period of time. ❑ *She studied painting from 1926.* ❑ *Breakfast is available from 6 a.m.* **2** PREP You say **from** one thing **to** another when you are stating the range of things that are possible. ❑ *There are 94 countries represented, from Algeria to Zimbabwe.* [from Old English]

❸ **from** /frəm, STRONG frʌm/ PREP **From** is used after verbs with meanings such as "protect," "free," "keep," and "prevent" to introduce the action that does not happen, or that someone does not want to happen. ❑ *Such laws could protect the consumer from harm.* [from Old English]

**front** /frʌnt/ (**fronts**) **1** N-COUNT The **front** of something is the part of it that faces you, or that faces forward. ❑ *Stand at the front of the line.* **2** N-COUNT In a war, the **front** is a line where two opposing armies are fighting each other. ❑ *Sonja's husband is fighting at the front.* **3** → see also **front line 4** N-COUNT If you say that something is happening on a particular **front,** you mean that it is happening with regard to a particular situation or field of activity. ❑ *…research across a wide academic front.* **5** N-COUNT If someone puts on a particular kind of **front,** they pretend to have a particular quality. ❑ *Michael kept up a brave front to the world.* **6** N-COUNT An organization or activity that is a **front for** one that is illegal or secret is used to hide it. ❑ *…The charity was set up as a front for their criminal activities.* **7** N-COUNT In relation to the weather, a **front** is a line where a mass of cold air meets a mass of warm air. **8** PHRASE If a person or thing is **in front,** they are ahead of others in a moving group. ❑ *Don't drive too close to the car in front.* **9** PHRASE Someone who is **in front** in a competition or contest at a particular point is winning at that point. ❑ *Richard Dunwoody is in front in the race.* **10** PHRASE If someone or something is **in front of** a particular thing, they are facing it, ahead of it, or close to the front part of it. ❑ *She sat down in front of her mirror.* ❑ *Something ran out in front of my car.* **11** PHRASE If you do or say

something **in front of** someone else, you do or say it when they are present. ☐ *They never argued in front of their children.* [from Latin]
→ see **forecast**

**front|al** /frʌntªl/ ADJ **Frontal** means relating to or involving the front of something. [FORMAL] ☐ *The plan is to avoid the enemy's frontal attack.* [from Old French]

**front and cen|ter** ADJ If a topic or question is **front and center**, a lot of attention is being paid to it or a lot of people are talking about it. ☐ *The media has kept the story front and center.*

**front desk** N-SING The **front desk** in a hotel is the desk or office that books rooms for people and answers their questions. ☐ *Call the hotel's front desk and cancel your morning wake-up call.*
→ see **hotel**

**fron|tier** /frʌntɪ̯ər, frɒn-/ (**frontiers**)
**1** N-COUNT The **frontiers** of something are the limits to which it extends. ☐ *...expanding the frontiers of science.* **2** N-COUNT A **frontier** is a border between two countries. ☐ *They showed their passports at the Russian frontier.* [from Old French]

**front line** (**front lines**) also **front-line** N-COUNT The **front line** is the place where two opposing armies are fighting each other. ☐ *...taking supplies to soldiers on the front line.*

**front of|fice** (**front offices**) N-COUNT The **front office** of a company or other organization is the room or rooms where staff deal with the public. The executives of a company or other organization are sometimes referred to collectively as the **front office**. ☐ *Information is available at the front office of the Cultural Center.*

**front-page** ADJ A **front-page** article or picture appears on the front page of a newspaper because it is very important or interesting.

**front-runner** (**front-runners**) N-COUNT In a competition or contest, the **front-runner** is the person who seems most likely to win it. ☐ *Neither of the front-runners in the presidential election is a mainstream politician.*

**frost** /frɔst/ (**frosts, frosting, frosted**) **1** N-VAR When there is **frost** or a **frost**, the temperature outside falls below freezing point and the ground becomes covered in ice crystals. ☐ *There is frost on the ground and snow is forecast.* **2** V-T If you **frost** a cake, you cover and decorate it with frosting. [from Old English]
→ see **snow**

**frost|ing** /frɔstɪŋ/ N-UNCOUNT **Frosting** is a sweet substance made from powdered sugar that is used to decorate cakes. [from Old English]

**frosty** /frɔsti/ (**frostier, frostiest**) **1** ADJ If the weather is **frosty**, the temperature is below freezing. ☐ *...winter's cold and frosty nights.* **2** ADJ You describe the ground or an object as **frosty** when it is covered with frost. ☐ *...the frosty road.* [from Old English]

**froth** /frɔθ/ (**froths, frothing, frothed**) **1** N-UNCOUNT **Froth** is a mass of small bubbles on the surface of a liquid. ☐ *Use a straw to blow a froth of bubbles.* **2** V-I If a liquid **froths**, small bubbles appear on its surface. ☐ *The sea frothed over my feet.* [from Old Norse]

**frown** /fraʊn/ (**frowns, frowning, frowned**) V-I When someone **frowns**, their eyebrows become drawn together, because they are annoyed, worried, or puzzled, or because they are concentrating. ☐ *Nancy shook her head, frowning.* ☐ *He frowned at her anxiously.* ● **Frown** is also a noun. ☐ *There was a deep frown on the boy's face.* [from Old French]
▸ **frown upon** or **frown on** PHR-VERB If something is **frowned upon** or is **frowned on**, people disapprove of it. ☐ *This practice is frowned upon as being wasteful.*

**froze** /froʊz/ **Froze** is the past tense of **freeze**. [from Old English]

**fro|zen** /froʊzªn/ **1** **Frozen** is the past participle of **freeze**. **2** ADJ If the ground is **frozen** it has become very hard because the weather is very cold. ☐ *It was bitterly cold and the ground was frozen hard.* **3** ADJ **Frozen** food has been preserved by being kept at a very low temperature. ☐ *Frozen fish is a healthy convenience food.* **4** ADJ If you say that you are **frozen**, or a part of your body is **frozen**, you are emphasizing that you feel very cold. ☐ *He put one hand up to his frozen face.* ☐ *I'm frozen out here.* [from Old English]
→ see **glacier**

**fru|gal** /fruːgªl/ **1** ADJ People who are **frugal** or who live **frugal** lives do not spend much money on themselves. ● **fru|gal|ity** /frugælɪti/ N-UNCOUNT ☐ *His frugality allowed him to save $3,000.* **2** ADJ A **frugal** meal is small and not expensive. ☐ *The diet was frugal: cheese and water, rice and beans.* [from Latin]

**fruit** /fruːt/ (**fruit, fruits**)

> The plural form is usually **fruit**, but can also be **fruits**.

**1** N-VAR **Fruit** is something which grows on a tree or bush and which contains seeds or a pit covered by a substance that you can eat. ☐ *Fresh fruit and vegetables provide fiber and vitamins.* ☐ *...bananas and other tropical fruits.* **2** N-COUNT The **fruits** or the **fruit** of your work or activity are the good things that result from it. ☐ *We will have a meeting to share the fruits of your investigations.* **3** → see also **kiwi fruit** **4** PHRASE If an action **bears fruit**, it produces good results. ☐ *Eleanor's work will, I hope, bear fruit.* [from Old French]
→ see Picture Dictionary: **fruit**
→ see **dessert, grain**

**fruit|ful** /fruːtfəl/ ADJ Something that is **fruitful** produces good and useful results. ☐ *We had a long, happy, fruitful relationship.* [from Old French]

**frui|tion** /fruːɪ̯ªn/ N-UNCOUNT If something comes **to fruition**, it starts to produce the intended results. [FORMAL] ☐ *These plans will take time to come to fruition.* [from Late Latin]

**fruit|less** /fruːtlɪs/ ADJ **Fruitless** actions, events, or efforts do not achieve anything at all. ☐ *It was a fruitless search.* [from Old French]

**fruity** /fruːti/ (**fruitier, fruitiest**) **1** ADJ Something that is **fruity** smells or tastes of fruit. ☐ *This shampoo smells fruity.* **2** ADJ A **fruity** voice or laugh is pleasantly rich and deep. [from Old French]

**frus|trate** /frʌstreɪt/ (**frustrates, frustrating, frustrated**) **1** V-T If something **frustrates** you, it upsets or angers you because you are unable to do anything about the problems it creates. ☐ *These questions frustrated me.* ● **frus|trat|ed** ADJ ☐ *Roberta felt frustrated and angry.* ● **frus|trat|ing** ADJ ☐ *This*

f

**Picture Dictionary**   fruit

peel — apple, banana, lemon

figs

skin — kiwi

grapes

seeds

segment — orange

pear

pineapple

watermelon

situation is very frustrating for us. ● **frus|tra|tion** /frʌstreɪ<sup>ə</sup>n/ (**frustrations**) N-VAR ❑ ...frustration among hospital doctors. **2** V-T If someone or something **frustrates** a plan or attempt to do something, they prevent it from succeeding. ❑ The government has frustrated his efforts to employ foreign workers. [from Latin]
→ see **anger**

**fry** /fraɪ/ (**fries, frying, fried**) **1** V-T When you **fry** food, you cook it in a pan that contains hot fat or oil. ❑ Fry the breadcrumbs until golden brown. **2** N-PLURAL **Fries** are the same as **French fries.** [from Old French]
→ see **egg**

**fry|ing pan** (**frying pans**) N-COUNT A **frying pan** is a flat metal pan with a long handle, in which you fry food.
→ see **pan**

**fudge** /fʌdʒ/ (**fudges, fudging, fudged**) **1** N-UNCOUNT **Fudge** is a soft brown candy that is made from butter, cream, and sugar. **2** V-T If you **fudge** something, you avoid making a clear and definite decision, distinction, or statement about it. ❑ They have fudged their calculations.

**fuel** /fyuəl/ (**fuels**) N-VAR **Fuel** is a substance such as coal, oil, or gasoline that is burned to provide heat or power. ❑ They ran out of fuel. [from Old French]
→ see **car, energy, engine, oil, petroleum**

**fuel cell** (**fuel cells**) N-COUNT A **fuel cell** is a device, similar to a battery, that converts chemicals into electricity.

**fueled** /fyuəld/ also **fuelled** ADJ A machine or vehicle that **is fueled by** a particular substance works by burning that substance. ❑ She's cooking on a stove fueled by natural gas. [from Old French]

**fu|gi|tive** /fyudʒɪtɪv/ (**fugitives**) N-COUNT A **fugitive** is someone who is running away or hiding, usually in order to avoid being caught by the police. ❑ The rebel leader was a fugitive from justice. [from Latin]

**fugue** /fyug/ (**fugues**) N-COUNT A **fugue** is a piece of music that begins with a simple tune which is then repeated by other voices or instrumental parts with small variations. [TECHNICAL] [from French]

**ful|crum** /fʊlkrəm/ N-SING In physics, the **fulcrum** is the central point on which a lever balances when it is lifting or moving something. [from Latin]

**ful|fill** /fʊlfɪl/ (**fulfills, fulfilling, fulfilled**) **1** V-T If you **fulfill** a promise, dream, or hope, you do what you said or hoped you would do. ❑ She fulfilled her dream of starting law school. **2** V-T To **fulfill** a task, role, or requirement means to do or be what is required, necessary, or expected. ❑ Without their help you will not be able to fulfill the tasks you have before you. **3** V-T If something **fulfills** you, you feel happy and satisfied with what you are doing or with what you have achieved. ❑ Rachel knew that a life of luxury could not fulfill her. ● **ful|filled** ADJ ❑ ...a fulfilled life. ● **ful|fill|ing** ADJ ❑ ...a fulfilling career. ● **ful|fill|ment** N-UNCOUNT ❑ ...professional fulfillment. [from Old English]

---

**full**

❶ CONTAINING AS MANY PEOPLE/ THINGS AS POSSIBLE
❷ COMPLETE, INCLUDING THE MAXIMUM POSSIBLE
❸ OTHER USES

---

❶ **full** /fʊl/ (**fuller, fullest**) **1** ADJ If something is **full**, it contains as much of a substance or as many objects as it can. ❑ Once the container is full, close it. **2** ADJ If a place or thing **is full of** things or people, it contains a large number of them. ❑ The case was full of clothes. ❑ The streets are still full of garbage from two nights of rioting. **3** ADJ If you feel **full**, you have eaten or drunk so much that you do not want anything else. ❑ It's healthy to eat when you're hungry and to stop when you're full. ● **full|ness** N-UNCOUNT ❑ High-fiber diets give the feeling of fullness. [from Old English]

## Thesaurus    *full*    Also look up :

ADJ.    brimming; (ant.) empty ❶ 🔢
        loaded ❶ 🔢 🔢
        bursting ❶ 🔢

❷ **full** /fʊl/ (**fuller, fullest**) 🔢 ADJ If someone or something **is full of** a particular feeling or quality, they have a lot of it. ❑ *I feel full of confidence.* ❑ *Mom's face was full of pain.* 🔢 ADJ You use **full** before a noun to indicate that you are referring to all the details, things, or people that it can possibly include. ❑ *Full details will be sent to you once your application has been accepted.* ❑ *May I have your full name?* 🔢 ADJ **Full** is used to describe a sound, light, or physical force which is being produced with the greatest possible power or intensity. ❑ *...the sound of Mahler, playing at full volume.* ❑ *The operation will be carried out in full daylight.* 🔢 ADJ If you say that someone has or leads a **full** life, you approve of the fact that they are always busy and do a lot of different things. 🔢 PHRASE You say that something has been done or described **in full** when everything that was necessary has been done or described. ❑ *The medical experts have yet to report in full.* 🔢 PHRASE Something that is done or experienced **to the full** is done to as great an extent as is possible. ❑ *A good mind should be used to the full.* [from Old English] 🔢 **full blast** → see **blast** 🔢 to **have** your **hands full** → see **hand** 🔢 **in full swing** → see **swing**

❸ **full** /fʊl/ (**fuller, fullest**) 🔢 ADJ A **full** flavor is strong and rich. ❑ *Italian plum tomatoes have a full flavor.* 🔢 ADJ When there is a **full** moon, the moon appears as a bright, complete circle. [from Old English]

**full-blown** ADJ **Full-blown** means having all the characteristics of a particular type of thing or person. ❑ *Before becoming a full-blown director, he worked as a film editor.*

**full-flavored** ADJ **Full-flavored** food or drink has a pleasant fairly strong taste.

**full-length** 🔢 ADJ A **full-length** book, record, or movie is the normal length, rather than being shorter than normal. 🔢 ADJ A **full-length** coat or skirt is long enough to reach the lower part of a person's leg. 🔢 ADJ A **full-length** mirror or painting shows the whole of a person. 🔢 ADV Someone who is lying **full-length**, is lying down flat and stretched out. ❑ *She stretched herself out full-length.*

**full-scale** 🔢 ADJ **Full-scale** means as complete, intense, or great in extent as possible. ❑ *...a full-scale nuclear war.* 🔢 ADJ A **full-scale** drawing or model is the same size as the thing that it represents. ❑ *The artist drew a full-scale sketch.*

**full-size** also **full-sized** ADJ A **full-size** or **full-sized** model or picture is the same size as the thing or person that it represents.

**full-time** also **full time** ADJ **Full-time** work or study involves working or studying for the whole of each normal working week. ❑ *...a full-time job.* ● **Full-time** is also an adverb. ❑ *Deirdre works full-time.*

**ful|ly** /fʊli/ 🔢 ADV **Fully** means to the greatest degree or extent possible. ❑ *She was fully aware of my thoughts.* 🔢 ADV If you describe, answer, or deal with something **fully**, you leave out nothing that

should be mentioned or dealt with. ❑ *He promised to answer fully and truthfully.* [from Old English]

## Word Partnership    Use *fully* with :

ADJ.    fully **adjustable**, fully **aware**, fully **clothed**, fully **functional**, fully **operational**, fully **prepared** 🔢
V.      fully **agree**, fully **expect**, fully **extend**, fully **understand** 🔢
        fully **explain** 🔢

**fum|ble** /fʌmbᵊl/ (**fumbles, fumbling, fumbled**) V-I If you **fumble for** something or **fumble with** something, you try to reach for it or hold it in a clumsy way. ❑ *She got out of bed and fumbled for her bathrobe.* [of Scandinavian origin]

**fume** /fyum/ (**fumes, fuming, fumed**) 🔢 N-PLURAL **Fumes** are the unpleasant and often unhealthy smoke and gases that are produced by fires or by things such as chemicals, fuel, or cooking. ❑ *...car exhaust fumes.* 🔢 V-T If you **fume** over something, you express annoyance and anger about it. ❑ *"It's appalling!" Jackie fumed.* [from Old French]

**fun** /fʌn/ 🔢 N-UNCOUNT You refer to an activity or situation as **fun** if you think it is pleasant and enjoyable. ❑ *It's been a learning adventure and it's also been great fun.* ❑ *It could be fun to watch them.* 🔢 N-UNCOUNT If you say that someone is **fun**, you mean that you enjoy being with them because they say and do interesting or amusing things. ❑ *Liz was fun to be with.* 🔢 PHRASE If you do something **in fun**, you do it as a joke or for amusement, without intending to cause any harm. ❑ *Don't say such things, even in fun.* 🔢 PHRASE If you **make fun of** someone or something or **poke fun at** them, you laugh at them, tease them, or make jokes about them in a way that causes them to seem ridiculous. ❑ *Don't make fun of me.*

## Thesaurus    *fun*    Also look up :

N.      amusement, enjoyment, play; (ant.) misery 🔢
ADJ.    amusing, enjoyable, entertaining, happy, pleasant; (ant.) boring 🔢

**func|tion** /fʌŋkʃᵊn/ (**functions, functioning, functioned**) 🔢 N-COUNT The **function** of something or someone is the useful thing that they do or are intended to do. ❑ *The main function of fat is as a store of energy.* 🔢 N-COUNT A **function** is a large formal dinner or party. ❑ *...a private function hosted by one of his students.* 🔢 V-I If a machine or system **is functioning**, it is working or operating. ❑ *The prison is now functioning normally.* 🔢 V-I If someone or something **functions as** a particular thing, they do the work or fulfill the purpose of that thing. ❑ *On weekdays, one third of the living room functions as workspace.* 🔢 N-COUNT If you say that one thing is a **function** of another, you mean that its amount or nature depends on the other thing. [FORMAL] [from Latin]

**func|tion|al** /fʌŋkʃənᵊl/ 🔢 ADJ **Functional** things are useful rather than decorative. ❑ *...modern, functional furniture.* 🔢 ADJ **Functional** equipment works or operates in the way that it is supposed to. ❑ *We have fully functional smoke alarms on all staircases.* [from Latin]

f

**fund** /fʌnd/ (funds, funding, funded)
**1** N-PLURAL **Funds** are amounts of money that are available to be spent, especially money that is given to an organization or person for a particular purpose. ❑ *The concert will raise funds for research into cancer.* **2** → see also **fund-raising** **3** N-COUNT A **fund** is an amount of money that is collected or saved for a particular purpose. ❑ *...a scholarship fund for undergraduate engineering students.* **4** V-T When a person or organization **funds** something, they provide money for it. ❑ *The Foundation has funded a variety of programs.* [from Latin]

**fun|da|men|tal** /fʌndəmɛntᵊl/ ADJ You use **fundamental** to describe things, activities, and principles that are very important or essential. ❑ *...the fundamental principles of democracy.* ❑ *...a fundamental human right.* ● **fun|da|men|tal|ly** ADV ❑ *He is fundamentally a good man.* [from Latin]

**fun|da|men|tal|ism** /fʌndəmɛntᵊlɪzəm/ N-UNCOUNT **Fundamentalism** is the belief in the original form of a religion or theory, without accepting any later ideas. ❑ *...religious fundamentalism.* ● **fun|da|men|tal|ist** (fundamentalists) N-COUNT ❑ *...Christian fundamentalists.* [from Latin]

**fun|da|men|tals** /fʌndəmɛntᵊlz/ N-PLURAL The **fundamentals** of something are its simplest, most important elements, ideas, or principles. ❑ *Come and learn the fundamentals of effective speaking.* [from Latin]

**fund|ing** /fʌndɪŋ/ N-UNCOUNT **Funding** is money which a government or organization provides for a particular purpose. ❑ *They hope for government funding for the program.* [from Latin]

**fund man|ag|er** (fund managers) N-COUNT A **fund manager** is someone whose job involves investing the money contained in a fund, for example, a mutual fund, on behalf of another person or organization.

**fund|rais|er** /fʌndreɪzər/ (fundraisers) also **fund-raiser** **1** N-COUNT A **fundraiser** is an event which is intended to raise money for a particular purpose. ❑ *Organize a fundraiser for your church.* **2** N-COUNT A **fundraiser** is someone who works to raise money for a particular purpose, for example, for a charity. ❑ *...a fundraiser for the Democrats.*

**fund-raising** also **fundraising** N-UNCOUNT **Fund-raising** is the activity of collecting money to support a charity or political campaign or organization.

**fu|ner|al** /fyunərəl/ (funerals) N-COUNT A **funeral** is the ceremony that is held when the body of someone who has died is buried or cremated. ❑ *The funeral will be held in Joplin, Missouri.* [from Medieval Latin]

**fu|ner|al home** (funeral homes) N-COUNT A **funeral home** is a place where the body of a dead person is taken to be prepared for burial or cremation.

**fu|ner|al par|lor** (funeral parlors) N-COUNT A **funeral parlor** is the same as a **funeral home**.

**fun|gus** /fʌŋgəs/ (fungi /fʌndʒaɪ, -ŋgaɪ/ or **funguses**) N-VAR A **fungus** is a plant that has no flowers, leaves, or green coloring, such as a mushroom or a toadstool. ● **fun|gal** ADJ ❑ *...fungal growth.* [from Latin]
→ see Word Web: **fungus**

**funky** /fʌŋki/ (funkier, funkiest) ADJ If you describe something or someone as **funky**, you like them because they are unconventional or unusual. [INFORMAL] ❑ *It had a certain funky charm, but it wasn't a place to raise a kid.*

**fun|nel** /fʌnᵊl/ (funnels, funneling or funnelling, funneled or funnelled) **1** N-COUNT A **funnel** is an object with a wide, circular top and a narrow short tube at the bottom. ❑ *Rain falls through the funnel into the jar below.* **2** N-COUNT A **funnel** is a chimney on a ship or railroad engine. **3** V-T/V-I If something **funnels** somewhere or is **funneled** there, it is directed through a narrow space. ❑ *The winds came across the plains, funneling down the valley.* **4** V-T If you **funnel** money, goods, or information from one place or group to another, you cause it to be sent there as it becomes available. ❑ *He secretly funneled credit card information to criminals.* **5** N-COUNT A **funnel** is an organ on the bodies of some animals such as octopuses, which is used for breathing, laying eggs, and getting rid of waste. **6** N-COUNT A **funnel** or **funnel cloud** is a rotating column of air below a cumulonimbus cloud, which can become part of a tornado. [from Old Provençal]

funnel

**fun|ny** /fʌni/ (funnier, funniest) **1** ADJ Someone or something that is **funny** is amusing and likely to make you smile or laugh. ❑ *I'll tell you a funny story.* **2** ADJ If you describe something as **funny**, you think it is strange, surprising, or puzzling. ❑ *Children get some very funny ideas sometimes!* ❑ *There's something funny about him.*

---

**Word Web** fungus

**Fungi** can be both harmful and helpful. For example, **mold** and mildew destroy crops, ruin clothing, cause diseases, and can even lead to death. But many fungi are useful. For instance, a single-cell fungus called **yeast** makes bread rise. Another form of yeast makes wine **ferment**. It turns the sugar in grape juice into alcohol. And **mushrooms** are a part of the diet of people all over the world. Cheese makers use a specific fungus to produce the creamy white skin on brie. A different **microorganism** gives blue cheese its characteristic color. Truffles, the most expensive fungi, cost more than $100 an ounce.

**3** ADJ If you feel **funny**, you feel slightly ill. [INFORMAL] ❑ *My head began to ache and my stomach felt funny.*

| **Thesaurus** | *funny* | Also look up : |
|---|---|---|
| ADJ. | amusing, comical, entertaining; (ant.) serious **1** bizarre, odd, peculiar **2** | |

**fur** /f<u>3</u>r/ (**furs**) **1** N-UNCOUNT **Fur** is the thick and usually soft hair that grows on the bodies of many mammals. ❑ *This creature's fur is short, dense and silky.* **2** N-COUNT A **fur** is a coat made from fur. ❑ *...women in furs.* [from Old French]

**fu|ri|ous** /fy<u>ua</u>riəs/ **1** ADJ Someone who is **furious** is extremely angry. ❑ *He is furious at the way his wife has been treated.* ● **fu|ri|ous|ly** ADV ❑ *He stormed out of the apartment, slamming the door furiously behind him.* **2** ADJ **Furious** is used to describe something that is done with great energy, effort, speed, or violence. ❑ *...a furious gunbattle.* ● **fu|ri|ous|ly** ADV ❑ *Doctors worked furiously to save their friend's life.* [from Latin]
→ see **anger**

**fur|long** /f<u>3</u>rlɔŋ/ (**furlongs**) N-COUNT A **furlong** is a unit of length that is equal to 220 yards or 201.2 meters. [from Old English]

**fur|nace** /f<u>3</u>rnɪs/ (**furnaces**) N-COUNT A **furnace** is a container or enclosed space in which a very hot fire is made, for example, to melt metal, burn trash, or produce heat for a building or house. [from Old French]

**fur|nish** /f<u>3</u>rnɪʃ/ (**furnishes, furnishing, furnished**) **1** V-T If you **furnish** a room or building, you put furniture and furnishings into it. ❑ *Many owners try to furnish their hotels with antiques.* ● **fur|nished** ADJ ❑ *...his sparsely furnished house.* **2** V-T If you **furnish** someone **with** something, you provide or supply it. [FORMAL] ❑ *They'll be able to furnish you with the rest of the details.* [from Old French]

**fur|nish|ings** /f<u>3</u>rnɪʃɪŋz/ N-PLURAL The **furnishings** of a room or house are the furniture, curtains, carpets, and decorations such as pictures. ❑ *...luxurious furnishings.* [from Old French]

**fur|ni|ture** /f<u>3</u>rnɪtʃər/ N-UNCOUNT **Furniture** consists of large objects such as tables, chairs, or beds that are used in a room for sitting or lying on or for putting things on. ❑ *Each piece of furniture suited the style of the house.* [from French]

**fu|ror** /fy<u>ua</u>rɔr, -ər/ N-SING A **furor** is a very angry or excited reaction by people to something. ❑ *...an international furor over the plan.* [from Latin]

**fur|row** /f<u>3</u>roʊ/ (**furrows**) **1** N-COUNT A **furrow** is a long line in the earth which a farmer makes in order to plant seeds. **2** N-COUNT A **furrow** is a deep fold or line in the skin of your face. ❑ *Deep furrows marked the corners of his mouth.* [from Old English]

**fur|ry** /f<u>3</u>ri/ (**furrier, furriest**) **1** ADJ A **furry** animal is covered with thick, soft hair. **2** ADJ If you describe something as **furry**, you mean that it has a soft rough texture like fur. ❑ *The leaves are soft and furry.* [from Old French]

**fur|ther** /f<u>3</u>rðər/ (**furthers, furthering, furthered**)

> **Further** is a comparative form of **far**. It is also a verb.

**1** ADV **Further** means to a greater extent or degree. ❑ *Inflation is below 5% and set to fall further.* ❑ *The rebellion further damaged the country's image.* **2** ADV If you go or get **further with** something, or take something **further**, you make some progress. ❑ *We've got a great chance of going further in this competition.* **3** ADV **Further** means a greater distance than before or than something else. ❑ *People are living further away from their jobs.* ❑ *...a main road fifty yards further on.* **4** ADV **Further** is used in expressions such as "**further back**" and "**further ahead**" to refer to a point in time that is earlier or later than the time you are talking about. ❑ *Looking still further ahead, by the end of the next century world population is expected to be about ten billion.* **5** ADJ A **further** thing, number of things, or amount of something is an additional thing, number of things, or amount. ❑ *...further evidence of slowing economic growth.* **6** V-T If you **further** something, you help it to progress, to be successful, or to be achieved. ❑ *Education isn't only about furthering your career, it's about improving your mind.* [from Old English]

**fur|ther edu|ca|tion** N-UNCOUNT **Further education** is the education of people who have left school but who are not at a university or a college of education.

**further|more** /f<u>3</u>rðərmɔr/ ADV **Furthermore** is used to introduce a piece of information or opinion that adds to or supports the previous one. [FORMAL] ❑ *It's nearly dark, and furthermore it's going to rain.*

**fur|thest** /f<u>3</u>rðɪst/

> **Furthest** is a superlative form of **far**.

**1** ADV **Furthest** means to a greater extent or degree than ever before or than anything or anyone else. ❑ *Prices have fallen furthest in the south.* **2** ADV **Furthest** means at a greater distance from a particular point than anyone or anything else, or for a greater distance than anyone or anything else. ❑ *...those areas furthest from the coast.* ● **Furthest** is also an adjective. ❑ *...the furthest point from earth that any spacecraft has ever been.* [from Old English]

**fur|tive** /f<u>3</u>rtɪv/ ADJ If you describe someone's behavior as **furtive**, you disapprove of them behaving as if they want to keep something secret or hidden. ❑ *With a furtive glance over her shoulder, she entered the house.* [from Latin]

**fury** /fy<u>ua</u>ri/ N-UNCOUNT **Fury** is violent or very strong anger. ❑ *She screamed, her face distorted with fury.* [from Latin]

**fuse** /fy<u>u</u>z/ (**fuses, fusing, fused**)

> The spelling **fuze** is also used for meaning **2**.

**1** N-COUNT A **fuse** is a safety device in an electric plug or circuit. It contains a piece of wire which melts when there is a fault so that the flow of electricity stops. ❑ *The fuse blew as he pressed the button to start the motor.* **2** N-COUNT A **fuse** is a device on a bomb or firework which delays the explosion so that people can move a safe distance away. ❑ *Some witnesses said he lit the fuse, others that he made the bomb.* **3** V-RECIP When things **fuse** or **are fused**, they join together physically or chemically, usually to become one thing. ❑ *The* *skull bones fuse between the ages of fifteen and twenty-five.* ❑ *Manufactured glass is made by fusing various types of sand.* [Senses 1 and 3 from Latin. Sense 2 from Italian.]

**fu|selage** /fyu̱sɪlɑʒ, -lɪdʒ, -zɪ-/ (**fuselages**) N-COUNT The **fuselage** is the main body of an airplane, missile, or rocket. ❑ *The force of the impact ripped apart the plane's fuselage.* [from French]

**fu|sion** /fyu̱ʒ³n/ (**fusions**) ◼ N-VAR The **fusion** of two or more things involves joining them together to form one thing. ❑ *...a delicate fusion of Eastern and Western art.* ◼ N-UNCOUNT In physics, **fusion** is the process in which atomic particles combine and produce a large amount of nuclear energy. ❑ *...research into nuclear fusion.* [from Latin] → see **sun**

**fuss** /fʌ̱s/ (**fusses, fussing, fussed**) ◼ N-SING **Fuss** is anxious or excited behavior which serves no useful purpose. ❑ *I don't know what all the fuss is about.* ◼ V-I If you **fuss**, you worry or behave in a nervous, anxious way about unimportant matters or rush around doing unnecessary things. ❑ *Carol fussed about getting me a drink.* ❑ *My wife was fussing over the clothing we were going to take.* ◼ V-I If you **fuss over** someone, you pay them a lot of attention and do things to make them happy or comfortable. ❑ *Aunt Laura fussed over him all afternoon.*

**fussy** /fʌ̱si/ (**fussier, fussiest**) ADJ Someone who is **fussy** is very concerned with unimportant details and is difficult to please. ❑ *She is very fussy about her food.*

**fu|tile** /fyu̱t³l/ ADJ If you say that something is **futile**, you mean there is no point in doing it, usually because it has no chance of succeeding. ❑ *He lifted his arm in a futile attempt to avoid the blow.* ● **fu|til|ity** /fyuti̱lɪti/ N-UNCOUNT ❑ *...the futility of war.* [from Latin]

**fu|ture** /fyu̱tʃər/ (**futures**) ◼ N-SING The **future** is the period of time that will come after the present. ❑ *No decision on the proposal is likely in the immediate future.* ❑ *He was making plans for the future.* ◼ ADJ **Future** things will happen or exist after the present time. ❑ *...the future king and queen.* ◼ N-COUNT Someone's **future**, or the **future of** something, is what will happen to them or what they will do after the present time. ❑ *His future depends on the outcome of the elections.* ◼ PHRASE You use **in the future** when you are saying what will happen from now on, and you are emphasizing that this will be different from what has previously happened. ❑ *I asked her to be more careful in the future.* [from Latin]

| Word Partnership | Use *future* with : |
| --- | --- |
| ADJ. | **bright** future, **distant** future, **immediate** future, **near** future, **uncertain** future ◼ |
| V. | **discuss the** future, **have a** future, **plan for the** future, **predict/see the** future ◼ |
| N. | future **date**, future **events**, future **generations**, future **plans**, for future **reference** ◼ |

**fu|tur|is|tic** /fyu̱tʃərɪstɪk/ ADJ Something that is **futuristic** looks or seems very modern and unusual, like something from the future. ❑ *The theater is a futuristic steel and glass structure.* [from Latin]

**fuzzy** /fʌ̱zi/ (**fuzzier, fuzziest**) ◼ ADJ **Fuzzy** hair sticks up in a soft, curly mass. ◼ ADJ A **fuzzy** picture, image, or sound is unclear and hard to see or hear. ❑ *A couple of fuzzy pictures have been published.*

**FYI** **FYI** is a written abbreviation for "for your information," often used in notes and documents when giving someone additional information about something. ❑ *The town's postmaster is called Jamie Ablerd [FYI she's a female].*

# Gg

**gadg|et** /ɡædʒɪt/ (**gadgets**) N-COUNT A **gadget** is a small machine or device which does something useful. ❑ *...kitchen gadgets such as can openers and bottle openers.* [from French]
→ see **technology**

**gag** /ɡæɡ/ (**gags, gagging, gagged**) **1** N-COUNT A **gag** is something such as a piece of cloth that is tied around or put inside someone's mouth in order to stop them from speaking. ❑ *The prisoner had a gag over his mouth.* **2** V-T If someone **gags** you, they tie a piece of cloth around your mouth to stop you from speaking or shouting. ❑ *They gagged him with a towel.* **3** V-T If a person **is gagged** by someone in authority, they are prevented from expressing their opinion or from publishing certain information. ❑ *Judges must not be gagged.* **4** N-COUNT A **gag** is a joke. [INFORMAL] ❑ *He told some funny gags.* **5** N-COUNT A **gag** is a humorous trick that you play on someone. [INFORMAL] ❑ *Richard thought they were playing a gag on him.*

**gag or|der** (**gag orders**) N-COUNT If a judge puts a **gag order** on information relating to a legal case, people involved in the case are banned from discussing it in public or writing about it.

**gag rule** (**gag rules**) N-COUNT A **gag rule** is an official restriction that forbids people from discussing something in a particular place.

**gain** /ɡeɪn/ (**gains, gaining, gained**) **1** V-T If you **gain** something, you acquire it gradually. ❑ *Students can gain valuable experience by working during their vacations.* **2** V-T/V-I If you **gain from** something such as an event or situation, you get some advantage from it. ❑ *The company expects to gain billions from the deal.* ❑ *Everybody is going to gain from working together.* **3** V-T To **gain** something such as weight or speed means to have an increase in that particular thing. ❑ *Some women gain weight after they have a baby.* ❑ *The car was gaining speed as it approached.* ● **Gain** is also a noun. ❑ *Sales showed a gain of nearly 8% last month.* **4** V-T If you **gain** something, you obtain it, usually after a lot of effort. ❑ *To gain a promotion, you might have to work overtime.* **5** PHRASE If something such as an idea or an ideal **gains ground**, it gradually becomes more widely known or more popular. ❑ *His views are gaining ground.* [from Old French]

**gait** /ɡeɪt/ (**gaits**) N-COUNT A particular kind of **gait** is a particular way of walking. [WRITTEN] ❑ *He had a strange, uneven gait.*

**gala** /ɡeɪlə, ɡæl-/ (**galas**) N-COUNT A **gala** is a special public celebration, entertainment, performance, or festival. ❑ *...a gala evening at the Metropolitan Opera House.* [from French]

**gal|axy** /ɡæləksi/ (**galaxies**) also **Galaxy** N-COUNT A **galaxy** is an extremely large group of stars and planets that extends over many billions of light years. ❑ *Astronomers have discovered a distant galaxy.* [from Medieval Latin]
→ see Word Web: **galaxy**
→ see **star**

**gale** /ɡeɪl/ (**gales**) N-COUNT A **gale** is a very strong wind. ❑ *There could be gales over the next few days.*
→ see **wind**

**gall** /ɡɔl/ (**galls, galling, galled**) **1** N-UNCOUNT If you say that someone has **the gall to** do something, you are criticizing them for behaving in a rude or disrespectful way. ❑ *He had the gall to accuse me of cheating.* **2** V-T If someone's action **galls** you, it makes you angry or annoyed because it is unfair and you cannot do anything about it. ❑ *It galled him that Nick won every game.* [Sense 1 from Old Norse. Sense 2 of Germanic origin.]

**gal|lery** /ɡæləri/ (**galleries**) **1** N-COUNT A **gallery** is a place where people go to look at works of art. ❑ *...an art gallery.* **2** N-COUNT The **gallery** in a theater or concert hall is an area high above the ground that usually contains the cheapest seats. ❑ *They got cheap tickets in the gallery.* [from Old French]

## Word Web  galaxy

The word **galaxy** with a small g refers to an extremely large group of **stars** and **planets**. It measures billions of **light years** wide. There are about 100 billion galaxies in the **universe**. **Astronomers** classify galaxies into four different types. Irregular galaxies have no particular shape. Elliptical galaxies look like flattened spheres. Spiral galaxies have long curving arms. A barred spiral galaxy has straight lines of stars extending from its nucleus. Galaxy with a capital G refers to our own **solar system**. The name of this galaxy is the **Milky Way**. It is about 100,000 light years wide.

**gal|ley** /gǽli/ (**galleys**) N-COUNT On a ship or aircraft, the **galley** is the kitchen. [from Old French]

**gal|lon** /gǽlən/ (**gallons**) N-COUNT A **gallon** is a unit of measurement for liquids that is equal to eight pints or 3.785 liters. ❑ ...80 million gallons of water. [from Old Northern French]
→ see **measurement**

**gal|lop** /gǽləp/ (**gallops, galloping, galloped**) ◼ V-T/V-I When a horse **gallops**, it runs very fast so that all four legs are off the ground at the same time. If you **gallop** a horse, you make it gallop. ❑ The horses galloped away. ◼ V-I If you **gallop**, you ride a horse that is galloping. ❑ The captain galloped into the distance. ◼ N-SING A **gallop** is a ride on a horse that is galloping. ❑ He rode off at a gallop. [from Old French]

**ga|lore** /gəlɔ́r/ ADJ You use **galore** to emphasize that something you like exists in very large quantities. [INFORMAL, WRITTEN] ❑ You'll be able to win prizes galore. [from Irish Gaelic]

**gal|va|nize** /gǽlvənaɪz/ (**galvanizes, galvanizing, galvanized**) V-T To **galvanize** someone means to cause them to take action, for example by making them feel very excited, afraid, or angry. ❑ The disaster galvanized local people to work together. [from French]

**gam|ble** /gǽmbəl/ (**gambles, gambling, gambled**) ◼ N-COUNT A **gamble** is a risky action or decision that you take in the hope of gaining money, success, or an advantage over other people. ❑ She took a gamble and started up her own business. ◼ V-T/V-I If you **gamble on** something, you take a risky action or decision in the hope of gaining money, success, or an advantage over other people. ❑ Companies sometimes have to gamble on new products. ❑ He gambled his career on this movie. ◼ V-T/V-I If you **gamble**, you bet money in a game or on the result of a race or competition. ❑ Most people visit Las Vegas to gamble their money. ❑ John gambled heavily on horse racing.

**gam|bler** /gǽmblər/ (**gamblers**) ◼ N-COUNT A **gambler** is someone who gambles regularly, for example in card games or horse racing. ❑ Her husband was a heavy gambler. ◼ N-COUNT If you describe someone as a **gambler**, you mean that they are ready to take risks in order to gain advantages or success. ❑ He had never been afraid of failure: he was a gambler.

**gam|bling** /gǽmblɪŋ/ N-UNCOUNT **Gambling** is the act or activity of betting money, for example in card games or on horse racing. ❑ The gambling laws are quite tough.

**game** /geɪm/ (**games**) ◼ N-COUNT A **game** is an activity or sport usually involving skill, knowledge, or chance, in which you follow fixed rules and try to win against an opponent or to solve a puzzle. ❑ Football is a popular game. ❑ ...a game of cards. ◼ N-COUNT A **game** is one particular occasion on which a game is played. ❑ It was the first game of the season. ◼ N-COUNT In sports such as tennis, a **game** is a part of a match. ❑ She won the first game of the tennis match. ◼ N-PLURAL **Games** are an organized event in which competitions in several sports take place. ❑ ...the 1996 Olympic Games in Atlanta. ◼ N-COUNT You can describe a way of behaving as a **game** when a person uses it to gain an advantage. ❑ The Americans are playing a very delicate political game. ◼ N-UNCOUNT **Game**

is wild animals or birds that are hunted for sport or food. ❑ The men shot game for food. ◼ ADJ If you are **game for** something, you are willing to do something new, unusual, or risky. ❑ He's always game for a challenge. ◼ PHRASE If you beat someone at their **own game**, you use the same methods that they have used, but more successfully, so that you gain an advantage over them. ❑ He must beat the other lawyers at their own game. ◼ PHRASE If someone or something **gives the game away**, they reveal a secret or reveal their feelings, and this puts them at a disadvantage. ❑ Their faces gave the game away. [from Old English]
→ see **chess, mammal**

**ga|meto|phyte** /gəmíːtəfaɪt/ (**gametophytes**) N-COUNT A **gametophyte** is a stage in the life of a plant when it produces eggs and sperm, or a plant during this stage of its life. [TECHNICAL]

**gam|ing** /geɪmɪŋ/ N-UNCOUNT **Gaming** means the same as **gambling**. ❑ Gaming is illegal in some places. [from Old English]

**gam|ma rays** N-PLURAL **Gamma rays** are a type of electromagnetic radiation that has a shorter wavelength and higher energy than X-rays.

**gang** /gǽŋ/ (**gangs, ganging, ganged**) ◼ N-COUNT A **gang** is a group of people, especially young people, who go around together and often deliberately cause trouble. ❑ ...a fight with a rival gang. ◼ N-COUNT A **gang** is a group of criminals who work together to commit crimes. ❑ Police are hunting for a gang that have stolen several cars. ◼ N-COUNT A **gang** is a group of workers who do physical work together. ❑ ...a gang of laborers. [from Old English]
▶ **gang up** PHR-VERB If people **gang up on** someone, they unite against them. [INFORMAL] ❑ Harrison complained that his colleagues ganged up on him. ❑ All the other parties ganged up to keep them out of power.

| **Thesaurus** | gang | Also look up : |
|---|---|---|
| N. | crowd, group, pack ◼ mob, ring ◼ | |

**gan|gli|on** /gǽŋgliən/ (**ganglia**) N-COUNT **Ganglia** are groups of nerve cells, usually outside the central nervous system. [TECHNICAL] [from Late Latin]

**gang|ster** /gǽŋstər/ (**gangsters**) N-COUNT A **gangster** is a member of an organized group of violent criminals. ❑ ...a gangster movie. [from Old English]

**gap** /gǽp/ (**gaps**) ◼ N-COUNT A **gap** is a space between two things or a hole in the middle of something solid. ❑ There was a narrow gap between the curtains. ◼ N-COUNT A **gap** is a period of time when you are not busy or when you stop doing something that you normally do. ❑ There was a gap of five years between the birth of her two children. ◼ N-COUNT If there is something missing from a situation that prevents it from being complete or satisfactory, you can say that there is a **gap**. ❑ We need more young teachers to fill the gap left by retirements. ◼ N-COUNT A **gap between** two groups of people, things, or sets of ideas is a big difference between them. ❑ ...the gap between rich and poor. [from Old Norse]

**gape** /geɪp/ (**gapes, gaping, gaped**) ◼ V-I If you **gape**, you look at someone or something in surprise, usually with an open mouth. ❑ *She gaped at me in shock.* **2** V-I If you say that something such as a hole or a wound **gapes**, you are emphasizing that it is big or wide. ❑ *A hole gaped in the roof.* ● **gap|ing** ADJ ❑ *The aircraft took off with a gaping hole in it.* [from Old Norse]

**gap hy|poth|esis** N-SING The **gap hypothesis** is a theory in geology which states that strong earthquakes are more likely to occur close to fault lines that have had few earthquakes in the past. [TECHNICAL]

**gar|age** /gəɾɑʒ/ (**garages**) **1** N-COUNT A **garage** is a building in which you keep a car. ❑ *They have turned the garage into a study.* **2** N-COUNT A **garage** is a place where you can get your car repaired. ❑ *Nancy took her car to a local garage.* [from French]

**gar|age sale** (**garage sales**) N-COUNT If you have a **garage sale**, you sell things such as clothes, toys and household items that you do not want, usually in your garage.

**gar|bage** /gɑrbɪdʒ/ **1** N-UNCOUNT **Garbage** is waste material, especially waste from a kitchen. ❑ *...a garbage bag.* **2** N-UNCOUNT If someone says that an idea or opinion is **garbage**, they are emphasizing that they believe it is untrue or unimportant. [INFORMAL] ❑ *I think this theory is garbage.* [from Old Italian]
→ see **pollution**

| Thesaurus | garbage | Also look up : |
| --- | --- | --- |

N.    junk, litter, rubbish, trash **1**
      foolishness, nonsense **2**

**gar|bage can** (**garbage cans**) N-COUNT A **garbage can** is a container that you put rubbish into.

**gar|bage col|lec|tor** (**garbage collectors**) N-COUNT A **garbage collector** is a person whose job is to take people's garbage away.

garbage can

**gar|bage dis|pos|al** (**garbage disposals**) N-COUNT

A **garbage disposal** or a **garbage disposal unit** is a small machine in the kitchen sink that breaks down waste matter so that it does not block the sink.

**gar|bage dump** (**garbage dumps**) N-COUNT A **garbage dump** is a place where garbage is left.

**gar|bage man** (**garbage men**) N-COUNT A **garbage man** is the same as a **garbage collector**.

**gar|bage truck** (**garbage trucks**) N-COUNT A **garbage truck** is a large truck which collects the garbage from outside people's houses.

**gar|den** /gɑrdᵊn/ (**gardens, gardening, gardened**) **1** N-COUNT A **garden** is the part of a yard which is used for growing flowers and vegetables. ❑ *She had a beautiful garden.* **2** V-I If you **garden**, you do work in your garden such as weeding or planting. ❑ *Jim gardened on weekends.* ● **gar|den|er** N-COUNT (**gardeners**) ❑ *She employed a gardener.* ● **gar|den|ing** N-UNCOUNT ❑ *My favorite hobby is gardening.* **3** N-PLURAL **Gardens** are a places with plants, trees, and grass, that people can visit. ❑ *The gardens are open from 10:30 a.m. until 5:00 p.m.* [from Old French]
→ see Picture Dictionary: **garden**
→ see **park**

**garden-variety** ADJ You can use **garden-variety** to describe something you think is ordinary and not special in any way. ❑ *The experiment is garden-variety science.*

**gar|ish** /gɛərɪʃ/ ADJ You describe something as **garish** when you dislike it because it is very bright in an unattractive way. ❑ *The stairs had a garish purple carpet.*

**gar|land** /gɑrlənd/ (**garlands**) N-COUNT A **garland** is a circular decoration made from flowers and leaves. People sometimes wear garlands on their heads or around their necks. ❑ *They wore garlands of summer flowers in their hair.* [from Old French]

**gar|lic** /gɑrlɪk/ N-UNCOUNT **Garlic** is the small, white, round bulb of a plant. It has a strong flavor and is used in cooking. ❑ *...a clove of garlic.* [from Old English]
→ see **spice**

**Picture Dictionary**   garden

hose

sprinkler

trowel   wheelbarrow

hoe

lawnmower    rake    spade    shovel

**g**

**gar|ment** /gɑrmənt/ (**garments**) N-COUNT
A **garment** is a piece of clothing. ❑ *Exports of garments to the U.S. fell 3%.* [from Old French]

**gar|ner** /gɑrnər/ (**garners, garnering, garnered**)
V-T If someone **has garnered** something useful or valuable, they have gained it or collected it. [FORMAL] ❑ *He has garnered a lot of support for his proposals.* [from Old French]

**gar|nish** /gɑrnɪʃ/ (**garnishes, garnishing, garnished**) **1** N-VAR A **garnish** is a small amount of salad, herbs, or other food that is used to decorate cooked or prepared food. ❑ *…a garnish of chopped tomato.* **2** V-T If you **garnish** cooked or prepared food, you decorate it with a garnish. ❑ *She was garnishing the chicken.* [from Old French]

**gar|ri|son** /gærɪsⁿn/ (**garrisons**) N-COUNT A **garrison** is a group of soldiers whose task is to guard the town or building where they live. You can also refer to the buildings which the soldiers live in as a **garrison**. ❑ *…a five-hundred-soldier garrison.* [from Old French]

**gas** /gæs/ (**gases, gasses, gassing, gassed**)

The form **gases** is the plural of the noun. The form **gasses** is the third person singular of the verb.

**1** N-VAR A **gas** is any substance that is neither liquid nor solid, for example oxygen or hydrogen. ❑ *Hydrogen is a gas, not a metal.* **2** N-VAR **Gas** is a poisonous gas that can be used as a weapon. ❑ *…a gas attack.* **3** N-UNCOUNT **Gas** is the fuel which is used to drive motor vehicles. ❑ *…a tank of gas.* **4** V-T To **gas** a person or animal means to kill them by making them breathe poisonous gas. ❑ *They attempted to gas the rats.* **5** PHRASE If you **step on the gas** when you are driving a vehicle, you go faster. [INFORMAL] [from Flemish] **6** → see also **gas mask, greenhouse gas, tear gas**
→ see **air, energy, greenhouse effect, matter, petroleum, solar system**

**gas ex|change** N-UNCOUNT **Gas exchange** is the same as **respiration**. [TECHNICAL]

**gas gi|ant** (**gas giants**) N-COUNT A **gas giant** is a large planet that is composed mainly of gas, such as Neptune or Jupiter. [TECHNICAL]

**gas guz|zler** (**gas guzzlers**) also **gas-guzzler** N-COUNT If you say that a car is a **gas guzzler** you mean that it uses a lot of fuel and is not cheap to run. [INFORMAL] ❑ *He drives one of those big gas guzzlers.*

**gash** /gæʃ/ (**gashes, gashing, gashed**)
**1** N-COUNT A **gash** is a long, deep cut in your skin or in the surface of something. ❑ *There was a gash above his right eye.* **2** V-T If you **gash** something, you accidentally make a long and deep cut in it. ❑ *He gashed his leg while cutting down trees.* [from Old French]

**gas mask** (**gas masks**) N-COUNT A **gas mask** is a device that you wear over your face in order to protect yourself from poisonous gases.

**gaso|hol** /gæsəhɔl/ N-UNCOUNT **Gasohol** is a mixture of gasoline and alcohol that can be used instead of gasoline in cars.

**gaso|line** /gæsəlin/ N-UNCOUNT **Gasoline** is the fuel which is used to drive motor vehicles.
→ see **oil, petroleum**

**gasp** /gæsp/ (**gasps, gasping, gasped**)
**1** N-COUNT A **gasp** is a short, quick breath of air that you take in through your mouth, especially when you are surprised, shocked, or in pain. ❑ *A gasp went around the court as the jury announced the verdict.* **2** V-I When you **gasp**, you take a short, quick breath through your mouth, especially when you are surprised, shocked, or in pain. ❑ *She gasped for air.* **3** PHRASE You describe something as **the last gasp** to emphasize that it is the final part of something or happens at the last possible moment. ❑ *…the last gasp of the Roman Empire.* [from Old Norse]

**gas pe|dal** (**gas pedals**) N-COUNT The **gas pedal** is another name for the **accelerator**.

**gas sta|tion** (**gas stations**) N-COUNT A **gas station** is a place where you can buy fuel for your car.

**gas tank** (**gas tanks**) N-COUNT The **gas tank** in a motor vehicle is the container for gas. ❑ *The gas tank holds 15 gallons.*

**gas|tric** /gæstrɪk/ ADJ You use **gastric** to describe processes, pain, or illnesses that occur in someone's stomach. [MEDICAL] ❑ *…gastric flu.* [from Greek]

**gate** /geɪt/ (**gates**) **1** N-COUNT A **gate** is a structure like a door which is used at the entrance to a field, a garden, or the grounds of a building. ❑ *He opened the gate and walked up to the house.* **2** N-COUNT In an airport, a **gate** is a place where passengers leave the airport and get on their airplane. ❑ *Please go to gate 15.* [from Old English]

**gat|ed com|mu|nity** (**gated communities**) N-COUNT A **gated community** is an area of houses and sometimes stores that is surrounded by a wall or fence and has an entrance that is guarded.

**gate|way** /geɪtweɪ/ (**gateways**) **1** N-COUNT A **gateway** is an entrance where there is a gate. ❑ *He walked across the park and through a gateway.* **2** N-COUNT A **gateway to** somewhere is a way of reaching, achieving, or discovering it. ❑ *Denver is the gateway to some great skiing.* [from Old English]
→ see **Internet**

**gath|er** /gæðər/ (**gathers, gathering, gathered**)
**1** V-T/V-I If people **gather** somewhere, or if someone **gathers** them, they come together in a group. ❑ *We gathered around the fireplace and talked.* **2** V-T If you **gather** things, you collect them together so that you can use them. ❑ *They gathered enough firewood to last the night.* ❑ *He used a hidden tape recorder to gather information.* ● **Gather up** means the same as **gather**. ❑ *Steve gathered up his papers and went out.* **3** V-T If something **gathers** speed, momentum, or force, it gradually becomes faster or more powerful. ❑ *Demands for reform gathered momentum.* **4** V-T You use **gather** in expressions such as "I gather" and "as far as I can gather" to introduce information that you have found out, especially when you have found it out in an indirect way. ❑ *I gather he didn't enjoy the show.* ❑ *"He speaks English," she said to Graham. "I gathered that."* [from Old English] **5** to **gather dust** → see **dust**
▶ **gather up** → see **gather 2**

**gath|er|ing** /gæðərɪŋ/ (**gatherings**) N-COUNT A **gathering** is a group of people meeting together for a particular purpose. ❑ *…a large family gathering.* [from Old English]

**gator** /geɪtər/ (**gators**) also **'gator** N-COUNT A **gator** is the same as an **alligator**. [INFORMAL]

**gaudy** /ˈgɔdi/ (**gaudier, gaudiest**) ADJ If something is **gaudy**, it is very brightly colored in a way you find unattractive. □ …*a gaudy orange and purple hat.* [from Old French]

**gauge** /geɪdʒ/ (**gauges, gauging, gauged**) ■ V-T If you **gauge** something, you measure it or judge it. □ *She found it hard to gauge his mood.* ■ N-COUNT A **gauge** is a device that measures the amount or quantity of something and shows the amount measured. □ …*temperature gauges.* ■ N-SING A **gauge of** a situation is a fact or event that can be used to judge it. □ *Letters to the newspapers are a gauge of how people feel.* [from Old Northern French]

**gaunt** /gɔnt/ ADJ If someone looks **gaunt**, they look very thin, usually because they have been very ill or worried. □ *He looked gaunt and tired after a sleepless night.* [of Scandinavian origin]

**gaunt|let** /ˈgɔntlɪt/ (**gauntlets**) ■ N-COUNT **Gauntlets** are long, thick, protective gloves. □ *Bikers should wear boots, gauntlets, and protective clothing.* ■ PHRASE If you **pick up the gauntlet** or **take up the gauntlet**, you accept the challenge that someone has made. □ *She picked up the gauntlet thrown down by her rival.* ■ PHRASE If you **run the gauntlet**, you go through an unpleasant experience in which a lot of people criticize or attack you. □ *He ran the gauntlet of press photographers on his way into the building.* ■ PHRASE If you **throw down the gauntlet to** someone, you say or do something that challenges them to argue or compete with you. □ *The firm has thrown down the gauntlet to competitors by cutting its prices.* [from Old French]

**gave** /geɪv/ **Gave** is the past tense of **give**. [from Old English]

**gay** /geɪ/ ADJ A **gay** person is homosexual. □ *The quality of life for gay men has improved.* ● **Gay** people are sometimes referred to as **gays**, especially when comparing different groups of people. Other uses of the word could cause offense. □ *It's a friendly city for gays to move to.* [from Old French]

**gaze** /geɪz/ (**gazes, gazing, gazed**) ■ V-I If you **gaze at** someone or something, you look steadily at them for a long time, for example because you find them attractive or interesting, or because you are thinking about something else. □ *She was gazing at herself in the mirror.* □ *He gazed into the fire.* ■ N-COUNT You can talk about someone's **gaze** as a way of describing how they are looking at something, especially when they are looking steadily at it. [WRITTEN] □ *She felt uncomfortable under the woman's steady gaze.* [from Swedish]

**Word Link**    ette ≈ small : cas*ette*, gaz*ette*, pal*ette*

**ga|zette** /gəˈzɛt/ (**gazettes**) N-COUNT **Gazette** is often used in the names of newspapers. □ …*the Arkansas Gazette.* [from French]

**gear** /gɪər/ (**gears, gearing, geared**) ■ N-COUNT The **gears** on a machine or vehicle are a device for changing the rate at which energy is changed into motion. □ *On a hill, use low gears.* □ *The car was in fourth gear.* ■ N-UNCOUNT The **gear** involved in a particular activity is the equipment or special clothing that you use. □ …*100 police officers in riot gear.* □ …*fishing gear.* ■ V-T PASSIVE If someone or something **is geared to** or **toward** a particular

purpose, they are organized or designed in order to achieve that purpose. □ *Colleges are not always geared to the needs of part time students.* □ *My training was geared toward winning the gold medal.* [from Old Norse]

▶ **gear up** PHR-VERB If someone **is gearing up for** a particular activity, they are preparing to do it. If they **are geared up to** do a particular activity, they are prepared to do it. □ *The country is gearing up for an election.*

**gear|box** /ˈgɪərbɒks/ (**gearboxes**) N-COUNT A **gearbox** is the system of gears in an engine or vehicle.

**gear|shift** /ˈgɪərʃɪft/ (**gearshifts**) N-COUNT The **gearshift** is the lever that you use to change gear in a car or other vehicle.

**GED** /dʒi i di/ (**GEDs**) N-COUNT A **GED** is an American educational qualification which is equivalent to a high school diploma. **GED** is an abbreviation for "General Equivalency Diploma."

**geese** /gis/ **Geese** is the plural of **goose**. [from Old English]

**gel** /dʒɛl/ (**gels, gelling, gelled**)

The spelling **jell** is sometimes used for meanings ■ and ■.

■ V-RECIP If people **gel with** each other, or if two groups of people **gel**, they work well together because their skills and personalities fit together well. □ *He has gelled very well with the rest of the team.* □ *The two writers gelled, and scriptwriting for television followed.* ■ V-I If a vague shape, thought, or creation **gels**, it becomes clearer or more definite. □ *Her idea has not yet gelled into a satisfying whole.* ■ N-VAR **Gel** is a thick, jelly-like substance, especially one used to keep your hair in a particular style.

**gela|tin** /ˈdʒɛlətən/ (**gelatins**) also **gelatine** N-VAR **Gelatin** is a clear tasteless powder that is used to make liquids become firm, for example when you are making desserts. [from French]

**gem** /dʒɛm/ (**gems**) ■ N-COUNT A **gem** is a jewel or stone that is used in jewelry. □ …*precious gems.* ■ N-COUNT If you describe something or someone as a **gem**, you mean that they are especially good or helpful. [INFORMAL] □ …*a gem of a hotel.* [from Old French]

**gen|der** /ˈdʒɛndər/ (**genders**) ■ N-VAR A person's **gender** is the fact that they are male or female. □ *Women are sometimes denied opportunities because of their gender.* ■ N-COUNT You can refer to all male people or all female people as a particular **gender**. □ *She made some general comments about the male gender.* ■ N-VAR In grammar, the **gender** of a noun, pronoun, or adjective is whether it is masculine, feminine, or neuter. A word's gender can affect its form and behavior. In English, only personal pronouns such as "she," reflexive pronouns such as "itself," and possessive determiners such as "his" have gender. □ *In French the word for "moon" is of feminine gender.* [from Old French]

**gene** /dʒin/ (**genes**) N-COUNT A **gene** is the part of a cell in a living thing which controls its physical characteristics, growth, and development. □ …*the gene for left-handedness.* [from German]

**ge|neal|ogy** /dʒinɪˈɒlədʒi, -æl-/ N-UNCOUNT **Genealogy** is the study of the history of families. ● gen|ea|logi|cal /dʒiːniəlɒdʒɪkᵊl/ ADJ ❑ ...genealogical research. [from Old French]

gen|er|al /dʒɛnərəl/ (generals) ■ N-COUNT; N-TITLE; N-VOC A general is a high-ranking officer in the armed forces, usually in the army. ❑ The troops received a visit from the general. ◨ ADJ If you talk about the general situation somewhere or talk about something in general terms, you are describing the situation as a whole rather than considering its details or exceptions. ❑ There has been a general fall in unemployment. ❑ In general terms life has gotten better. ◨ ADJ You use general to describe something that involves or affects most people, or most people in a particular group. ❑ There is not enough general awareness of this problem. ◨ ADJ If you describe something as general, you mean that it is not limited to any one thing or area. ❑ ...a general ache across her upper body. ◨ ADJ General is used to describe a person's job, usually as part of their title, to indicate that they have complete responsibility for the administration of an organization or business. [BUSINESS] ❑ He became general manager of the company. ◨ → see also generally ◨ PHRASE You use in general to indicate that you are talking about something as a whole, rather than about part of it. ❑ We need to improve our educational system in general. ◨ PHRASE You say in general to indicate that you are referring to most people or things in a particular group. ❑ People in general will support us. [from Latin]

gen|er|al elec|tion (general elections) N-COUNT In the United States, a general election is a local, state, or national election where the candidates have been selected by a primary election. Compare primary.

gen|er|al hos|pi|tal (general hospitals) N-COUNT A general hospital is a hospital that does not specialize in the treatment of particular illnesses or patients.

gen|er|al|ize /dʒɛnrəlaɪz/ (generalizes, generalizing, generalized) V-I If you generalize, you say something that seems to be true in most situations or for most people, but that may not be completely true in all cases. ❑ You shouldn't generalize and say that all men are the same. ● gen|er|ali|za|tion (generalizations /dʒɛnrəlaɪzeɪʃᵊn/) N-VAR ❑ He made sweeping generalizations about politicians. [from Latin]

gen|er|al|ized /dʒɛnrəlaɪzd/ ■ ADJ Generalized means involving many different things, rather than one or two specific things. ❑ ...a generalized discussion about music. ◨ ADJ You use generalized to describe medical conditions or problems which affect the whole of your body, or the whole of a part of your body. [MEDICAL] ❑ The patient experienced generalized aches and pains. [from Latin]

gen|er|al|ly /dʒɛnrəli/ ■ ADV You use generally to give a summary of a situation, activity, or idea without referring to the particular details of it. ❑ Teachers generally are enthusiastic about their subjects. ◨ ADV You use generally to say that something happens or is used on most occasions but not on every occasion. ❑ It is generally true that darker fruits contain more iron than paler ones. [from Latin]

| Thesaurus | generally | Also look up : |
| --- | --- | --- |
| ADV. | commonly, mainly, usually ■ ◨ | |

gen|er|al pub|lic N-SING You can refer to the people in a society as the general public, especially when you are contrasting people in general with a small group. ❑ Charities depend on the generosity of the general public.

gen|er|al store (general stores) N-COUNT A general store is a store, especially in a small town, where many different sorts of goods are sold.

gen|er|ate /dʒɛnəreɪt/ (generates, generating, generated) ■ V-T To generate something means to cause it to begin and develop. ❑ The reforms will generate new jobs. ◨ V-T To generate a form of energy or power means to produce it. ❑ We burn coal to generate power. [from Latin]
→ see energy

gen|era|tion /dʒɛnəreɪʃᵊn/ (generations) ■ N-COUNT A generation is all the people in a group or country who are of a similar age, especially when they are considered as having the same experiences or attitudes. ❑ ...the current generation of teens. ◨ N-COUNT A generation is the period of time, usually considered to be about thirty years, that it takes for children to grow up and become adults and have children of their own. ❑ Within a generation, flying has become a very common method of travel. ◨ N-COUNT You can use generation to refer to a stage of development in the design and manufacture of machines or equipment. ❑ ...a new generation of computers. [from Latin]

gen|era|tion time (generation times) N-VAR The generation time of an organism is the average time between the birth of one generation of the organism and the birth of the next generation. [TECHNICAL]

gen|era|tor /dʒɛnəreɪtər/ (generators) N-COUNT A generator is a machine which produces electricity. ❑ The house has its own power generators. [from Latin]
→ see electricity

ge|ner|ic /dʒɪnɛrɪk/ (generics) ■ ADJ You use generic to describe something that refers or relates to a whole class of similar things. ❑ As a boy, I said "pop" as a generic term for all soft drinks. ◨ ADJ A generic drug or other product is one that does not have a trademark and that is known by a general name, rather than the manufacturer's name. ❑ Doctors sometimes prescribe cheaper generic drugs instead of more expensive brand names. ● Generic is also a noun. ❑ The program saved $11 million by substituting generics for brand-name drugs. [from French]

gen|er|ous /dʒɛnərəs/ ■ ADJ A generous person gives more of something, especially money, than is usual or expected. ❑ He is generous with his money. ● gen|er|os|ity /dʒɛnərɒsɪti/ N-UNCOUNT ❑ There are many stories about his generosity. ● gen|er|ous|ly ADV ❑ We would like to thank everyone who generously gave their time. ◨ ADJ A generous person is friendly, helpful, and willing to see the good qualities in someone or something. ❑ He was always generous in sharing his knowledge. ● gen|er|ous|ly ADV ❑ He generously offered some advice. ◨ ADJ A generous amount of something is much larger than is usual or necessary. ❑ The house has a generous amount of storage space. ● gen|er|ous|ly ADV ❑ Season the steaks generously with salt and pepper. [from Old French]

**ge|net|ic** /dʒɪnɛtɪk/ ADJ You use **genetic** to describe something that is concerned with genetics or with genes. ❑ ...a rare genetic disease. ● **ge|neti|cal|ly** /dʒɪnɛtɪkli/ ADV ❑ Some people are genetically more likely to suffer from diabetes.

**ge|neti|cal|ly modi|fied** ADJ Genetically **modified** plants and animals have had one or more genes changed. The abbreviation **GM** is often used. ❑ ...genetically modified foods.

**ge|net|ic en|gi|neer|ing** N-UNCOUNT Genetic **engineering** is the science or activity of changing the genetic structure of an animal, plant, or other organism in order to make it stronger or more suitable for a particular purpose.

**ge|net|ics** /dʒɪnɛtɪks/ N-UNCOUNT Genetics is the study of how characteristics are passed on from one generation to another by means of genes. ❑ Genetics is changing our understanding of cancer.
→ see **clone**

**gen|ial** /dʒinyəl/ ADJ Someone who is **genial** is kind and friendly. ❑ Bob was always genial and welcoming. ● **gen|ial|ly** ADV ❑ "Come in!" she said genially. ● **ge|ni|al|ity** /dʒiniæliti/ N-UNCOUNT ❑ He greeted them with his usual geniality. [from Latin]

**ge|ni|us** /dʒinyəs/ (**geniuses**) **1** N-UNCOUNT Genius is very great ability or skill in a particular subject or activity. ❑ ...her genius as a designer. **2** N-COUNT A **genius** is a highly talented, creative, or intelligent person. ❑ Chaplin was a genius. [from Latin]

**geno|cide** /dʒɛnəsaɪd/ N-UNCOUNT Genocide is the deliberate murder of a whole community or race. [from Greek]

**geno|type** /dʒinətaɪp, dʒɛn-/ (**genotypes**) N-VAR A **genotype** is the particular set of genes possessed by an individual organism. Compare **phenotype**. [TECHNICAL]

**gen|re** /ʒɒnrə/ (**genres**) N-COUNT A **genre** is a particular type of literature, painting, music, film, or other art form which people consider as a class

because it has special characteristics. [FORMAL] ❑ ...novels in the romance genre. [from French]
→ see Word Web: **genre**
→ see **fantasy**

**gen|teel** /dʒɛntil/ ADJ A **genteel** person is respectable and well-mannered, and comes or seems to come from a high social class. ❑ It was a place where genteel families came in search of peace and quiet. [from French]

**gen|tle** /dʒɛntᵊl/ (**gentler, gentlest**) **1** ADJ Someone who is **gentle** is kind, mild, and calm. ❑ My husband was a quiet and gentle man. ● **gen|tly** ADV ❑ She smiled gently at him. ● **gen|tle|ness** N-UNCOUNT ❑ She treated her mother with great gentleness. **2** ADJ **Gentle** actions or movements are performed in a calm and controlled manner, with little force. ❑ ...a gentle game of tennis. ● **gen|tly** ADV ❑ Patrick took her gently by the arm. **3** ADJ A **gentle** slope or curve is not steep or severe. ❑ ...an easy walk up a gentle slope. ● **gen|tly** ADV ❑ Tuscany is known for its gently rolling hills. **4** ADJ A **gentle** heat is a fairly low heat. ❑ Cook the sauce over a gentle heat. ● **gen|tly** ADV ❑ Cook the onion gently for about 15 minutes. [from Old French]

**gentle|man** /dʒɛntᵊlmən/ (**gentlemen**) **1** N-COUNT A **gentleman** is a man who is polite and educated, and can be trusted. ❑ He was always such a gentleman. **2** N-COUNT A **gentleman** is a man who comes from a family of high social standing. ❑ Her parents wanted her to marry a gentleman. **3** N-COUNT; N-VOC You can address men as **gentlemen**, or refer politely to them as **gentlemen**. ❑ This way, please, ladies and gentlemen.

**genu|ine** /dʒɛnyuɪn/ **1** ADJ **Genuine** is used to describe people and things that are exactly what they appear to be, and are not false or an imitation. ❑ He's a genuine American hero. ❑ ...genuine leather. **2** ADJ **Genuine** refers to things such as emotions that are real and not pretended. ❑ This is a genuine offer to help. ● **genu|ine|ly** ADV ❑ He was genuinely surprised. **3** ADJ Someone who is **genuine** is honest, truthful, and sincere. ❑ She is very caring and very genuine. [from Latin]

**ge|nus** /dʒinəs/ (**genera** /dʒɛnərə/) N-COUNT A **genus** is a class of similar animals or plants.

[TECHNICAL] ❑ …*a genus of plants called Sinningia.*
[from Latin]

**geo|graphi|cal** /dʒiəgræfɪkᵊl/ also
**geographic** /dʒiəgræfɪk/ ADJ **Geographical** or
**geographic** means concerned with or relating
to geography. ❑ …*a vast geographical area.*
● **geo|graphi|cal|ly** /dʒiəgræfɪkli/ ADV ❑ *It is
geographically a very diverse continent.* [from French]

> **Word Link** geo ≈ earth : geography, geology,
> geothermal

**ge|og|ra|phy** /dʒiɒgrəfi/ **1** N-UNCOUNT
**Geography** is the study of the countries of the
world and of such things as the land, seas,
climate, towns, and population. **2** N-UNCOUNT
The **geography** of a place is the way that features
such as rivers, mountains, towns, or streets are
arranged within it. ❑ …*policemen who knew the local
geography.* [from French]

**geo|logi|cal time scale** also **geological
timescale** (**geological time scales**) N-COUNT
The **geological time scale** is an arrangement of
the main geological and biological events in the
history of the Earth.

> **Word Link** logy, ology ≈ study of : anthropology,
> biology, geology

**ge|ol|ogy** /dʒiɒlədʒi/ **1** N-UNCOUNT **Geology**
is the study of the Earth's structure, surface, and
origins. ❑ *He was professor of geology at the University
of Georgia.* ● **geo|logi|cal** /dʒiɒlɒdʒɪkᵊl/ ADJ
❑ …*a geological survey.* ● **ge|olo|gist** (**geologists**)
N-COUNT ❑ *Geologists have studied the way that heat
flows from the earth.* **2** N-UNCOUNT The **geology** of
an area is the structure of its land, together with
the types of rocks and minerals that exist within
it. ❑ …*the geology of Asia.* [from Latin]
→ see **biosphere**

**geo|met|ric** /dʒiəmɛtrɪk/ also **geometrical**
/dʒiəmɛtrɪkᵊl/ **1** ADJ **Geometric** or **geometrical**
patterns or shapes consist of regular shapes or
lines. ❑ …*geometric designs.* **2** ADJ **Geometric** or
**geometrical** means relating to or involving the
principles of geometry. ❑ …*geometric laws.* [from
Latin]

**geo|met|ric se|quence** (**geometric sequences**)
also **geometric progression** N-COUNT A
**geometric sequence** is a series of numbers in
which there is the same ratio between each
number and the next one, for example the series 1,
2, 4, 8, 16. [TECHNICAL]

**ge|om|etry** /dʒiɒmɪtri/ **1** N-UNCOUNT
**Geometry** is the branch of mathematics
concerned with the properties and relationships
of lines, angles, curves, and shapes. ❑ …*the way
in which mathematics and geometry describe nature.*
**2** N-UNCOUNT The **geometry** of an object is its
shape or the relationship of its parts to each other.
❑ …*the geometry of the curved roof.* [from Latin]
→ see **mathematics**

**geo|sta|tion|ary** /dʒioʊsteɪʃənɛri/ also
**geosynchronous** /dʒioʊsɪŋkrənəs/ ADJ
A satellite that is in **geostationary** orbit is
positioned directly above the equator and moves
at the same speed as the Earth's rotation, so that it
appears to be stationary.

**geo|ther|mal en|er|gy** /dʒioʊθɜrmᵊl ɛnərdʒi/
ADJ **Geothermal** energy is heat that comes from

hot water and steam beneath the Earth's surface.
[TECHNICAL] ❑ *The house is heated and cooled with
geothermal energy.*

> **Word Link** iatr ≈ healing : geriatric, pediatrics,
> psychiatry

**geri|at|ric** /dʒɛriætrɪk/ ADJ **Geriatric** is used
to describe things relating to the illnesses and
medical care of elderly people. [MEDICAL] ❑ …*the
cost of geriatric care.* [from Greek]

**germ** /dʒɜrm/ (**germs**) **1** N-COUNT A **germ** is a
very small organism that causes disease. ❑ *This
chemical is used to kill germs.* **2** N-SING The **germ**
**of** something such as an idea is the beginning of
it. ❑ *The incident gave him the germ of a book.* [from
French]
→ see **medicine, spice**

**Ger|man shep|herd** /dʒɜrmən ʃɛpərd/
(**German shepherds**) N-COUNT A **German shepherd**
is a large, usually fierce dog that is used to guard
buildings or by the police to help them find
criminals.

**ger|mi|nate** /dʒɜrmɪneɪt/ (**germinates,
germinating, germinated**) **1** V-T/V-I If a seed
**germinates** or if it is **germinated**, it starts to
grow. ❑ *Some seeds germinate in just a few days.*
● **ger|mi|na|tion** /dʒɜrmɪneɪ͡ʃᵊn/ N-UNCOUNT ❑ *If
the soil is too cold it can stop germination.* **2** V-I If an
idea, plan, or feeling **germinates**, it comes into
existence and begins to develop. ❑ *A book was
germinating in his mind.* [from Latin]
→ see **tree**

**ges|ta|tion pe|ri|od** (**gestation periods**)
N-COUNT The **gestation period** of a particular
species of animal is the length of time that
animals belonging to it are pregnant
for. [TECHNICAL]

**ges|ture** /dʒɛstʃər/ (**gestures, gesturing,
gestured**) **1** N-COUNT A **gesture** is a movement
that you make with a part of your body, especially
your hands, to express emotion or information.
❑ *Sarah made a gesture with her fist.* **2** N-COUNT A
**gesture** is something that you say or do in order
to express your attitude or intentions, often
something that you know will not have much
effect. ❑ *He asked the government to make a gesture of
good will.* **3** V-I If you **gesture**, you use movements
of your hands or head in order to tell someone
something or draw their attention to something.
❑ *I gestured toward the house.* [from Medieval Latin]

**ges|ture draw|ing** (**gesture drawings**)
N-COUNT A **gesture drawing** is a quick, simple
drawing that aims to represent the movements or
gestures of a body. [TECHNICAL]

---

**get**

❶ CHANGING, CAUSING, MOVING,
OR REACHING
❷ OBTAINING, RECEIVING, OR
CATCHING
❸ PHRASAL VERBS

---

❶ **get** /gɛt/ (**gets, getting, got, gotten** or **got**)

In most of its uses **get** is a fairly informal word.

**1** V-LINK You use **get** with adjectives to mean
"become." For example, if someone **gets cold**, they
become cold, and if they **get angry**, they become

angry. ❑ *The boys were getting bored.* ❑ *Things will get better.* **2** V-LINK **Get** is used with expressions referring to states or situations. For example, to **get into trouble** means to start being in trouble. ❑ *She was getting ready to go out for the evening.* ❑ *If you do that you might get into trouble.* **3** V-T To **get** someone or something into a particular state or situation means to cause them to be in it. ❑ *I can't get the windows clean.* ❑ *Brian will get them out of trouble.* **4** V-T If you **get** someone **to** do something, you cause them to do it by asking, persuading, or telling them to do it. ❑ *...a campaign to get politicians to take AIDS more seriously.* **5** V-T If you **get** something done, you cause it to be done. ❑ *Why don't you get your car fixed?* **6** V-I To **get** somewhere means to move there. ❑ *I got off the bed and opened the door.* ❑ *How can I get past her without her seeing me?* **7** V-T To **get** something or someone into a place or position means to cause them to move there. ❑ *Mack got his wallet out.* ❑ *Go and get your coat on.* **8** AUX **Get** is often used in place of "be" as an auxiliary verb to form passives. ❑ *A window got broken.* **9** V-T If you **get to** do something, you manage to do it or have the opportunity to do it. ❑ *How did he get to be the boss of a major company?* ❑ *Do you get to see him often?* **10** V-T You can use **get** in expressions like **get moving, get going,** and **get working** when you want to tell people to begin moving, going, or working quickly. ❑ *The train leaves in 30 minutes, so let's get moving.* **11** V-I If something that has continued for some time **gets to** you, it starts causing you to suffer. ❑ *The pressure was getting to him and he lost his temper.* [from Old English]

> **Usage** **get**
>
> In conversation *get* is often used instead of *become.* We're getting worried about her.

**❷ get** /gɛt/ (**gets, getting, got, gotten** or **got**) **1** V-T If you **get** something that you want or need, you obtain it. ❑ *I got a job at the store.* **2** V-T If you **get** something, you receive it or are given it. ❑ *I'm getting a bike for my birthday.* ❑ *He gets a lot of letters from fans.* **3** V-T If you **get** someone or something, you go and bring them to a particular place. ❑ *I went downstairs to get the newspaper.* ❑ *Go and get me a drink of water.* **4** V-T If you **get** a particular price **for** something that you sell, you obtain that amount of money by selling it. ❑ *He can't get a good price for his crops.* **5** V-T If you **get** an idea, impression, or feeling, you begin to have that idea, impression, or feeling as you learn or understand more about something. ❑ *I get the feeling that you're an honest man.* **6** V-T If you **get** a joke or **get** the point of something that is said, you understand it. ❑ *Did you get that joke?* **7** V-T If you **get** an illness or disease, you become ill with it. ❑ *When I was five I got the measles.* **8** V-T When you **get** a train, bus, plane, or boat, you leave a place on a particular train, bus, plane, or boat. ❑ *It's quicker to get the bus.* [from Old English] **9** → see also **got**

| **Thesaurus** | *get* | Also look up : |
|---|---|---|
| V-LINK. | become **❶ 1** | |
| V. | bring, collect, pick up **❷ 3** | |
| | know, sense **❷ 5** | |

**❸ get** /gɛt/ (**gets, getting, got, gotten** or **got**) ▸ **get across** PHR-VERB When an idea **gets across** or when you **get** it **across**, you succeed in making other people understand it. ❑ *People felt their opinions were not getting across to the government.*
▸ **get along** PHR-VERB If you **get along with** someone, you have a friendly relationship with them. You can also say that two people **get along.** ❑ *It's impossible to get along with him.*
▸ **get around** **1** PHR-VERB To **get around** a problem or difficulty means to overcome it. ❑ *We need to find a way to get around the problem of kids missing school.* **2** PHR-VERB If you **get around** a rule or law, you find a way of doing something that the rule or law is intended to prevent, without actually breaking it. ❑ *Companies find ways to get around the ban.* **3** PHR-VERB If news **gets around,** it becomes well known as a result of being told to lots of people. ❑ *Word got around that he was going to leave.* **4** PHR-VERB If you **get around,** you visit a lot of different places as part of your way of life. ❑ *He was a journalist, and he got around.* **5** PHR-VERB The way that someone **gets around** is the way that they walk or go from one place to another. ❑ *It is difficult for Gail to get around since she broke her leg.*
▸ **get around to** PHR-VERB When you **get around to** doing something that you have delayed doing or have been too busy to do, you finally do it. ❑ *I said I would write you, but I never got around to it.*
▸ **get at** **1** PHR-VERB To **get at** something means to succeed in reaching it. ❑ *She walked on the grass to get at the flowers in front of the house.* **2** PHR-VERB If you **get at** the truth about something, you succeed in discovering it. ❑ *We want to get at the truth. Who killed him? And why?* **3** PHR-VERB If you ask someone what they **are getting at,** you are asking them to explain what they mean, usually because you think that they are being unpleasant or are suggesting something that is untrue. ❑ *I don't understand what you're getting at.*
▸ **get away** **1** PHR-VERB If you **get away,** you succeed in leaving a place or a person's company. ❑ *She wanted to get away from the city for a while.* **2** PHR-VERB If you **get away,** you go away for a period of time in order to have a vacation. ❑ *He is too busy to get away.* **3** PHR-VERB When someone or something **gets away,** or when you **get** them **away,** they escape. ❑ *The thieves got away through an upstairs window.*
▸ **get away with** PHR-VERB If you **get away with** doing something wrong or risky, you do not suffer any punishment or other bad consequences because of it. ❑ *Criminals know how to steal and get away with it.*
▸ **get back** PHR-VERB If you **get** something **back** after you have lost it or after it has been taken from you, you then have it again. ❑ *You have the right to cancel the contract and get your money back.*
▸ **get back to** **1** PHR-VERB If you **get back to** an activity, you start doing it again after you have stopped doing it. ❑ *Let's get back to work.* **2** PHR-VERB If you **get back to** someone, you contact them again after a short period of time, often by telephone. ❑ *We'll get back to you as soon as possible.*
▸ **get by** PHR-VERB If you can **get by** with what you have, you can manage to live or do things in a satisfactory way. ❑ *I'm a survivor. I'll get by.*
▸ **get down** **1** PHR-VERB If something **gets you down,** it makes you unhappy. ❑ *Sometimes my work gets me down.* **2** PHR-VERB If you **get down,** you lower your body until you are sitting, kneeling,

or lying on the ground. ❏ *Everybody got down and started looking for the earring.*

▶ **get down to** PHR-VERB If you **get down to** something, you begin doing it. ❏ *It's time for us to stop talking and get down to business.*

▶ **get in** ■ PHR-VERB If a political party or a politician **gets in**, they are elected. ❏ *If the Democrats get in everything will change.* ■ PHR-VERB If you **get** something **in**, you manage to do it at a time when you are very busy doing other things. ❏ *I managed to get a trip to the gym in.* ■ PHR-VERB When a train, bus, or plane **gets in**, it arrives. ❏ *Our flight got in late.*

▶ **get into** ■ PHR-VERB If you **get into** a particular kind of work or activity, you manage to become involved in it. ❏ *He wanted to get into politics.* ■ PHR-VERB If you **get into** a school, college, or university, you are accepted there as a student. ❏ *I was working hard to get into Yale.*

▶ **get off** ■ PHR-VERB If someone who has broken a law or rule **gets off**, they are not punished, or are given only a very small punishment. ❏ *He got off with a small fine.* ■ PHR-VERB If you tell someone to **get off** a piece of land or a property, you are telling them to leave, because they have no right to be there and you do not want them there. ❏ *I told the dog to get off the grass.*

▶ **get on** ■ PHR-VERB If you **get on with** something, you continue doing it or start doing it. ❏ *Jane got on with her work.*

▶ **get on to** PHR-VERB If you **get on to** a topic when you are speaking, you start talking about it. ❏ *We got on to the subject of relationships.*

▶ **get out** ■ PHR-VERB If you **get out**, you leave a place because you want to escape from it, or because you are made to leave it. ❏ *They wanted to get out of the country.* ■ PHR-VERB If you **get out**, you go to places and meet people, usually in order to have a more enjoyable life. ❏ *Get out and enjoy yourself, make new friends.* ■ PHR-VERB If news or information **gets out**, it becomes known. ❏ *News got out about their relationship.*

▶ **get out of** PHR-VERB If you **get out of** doing something that you do not want to do, you succeed in avoiding doing it. ❏ *Some people will do anything to get out of paying taxes.*

▶ **get over** ■ PHR-VERB If you **get over** an unpleasant or unhappy experience or an illness, you recover from it. ❏ *It took me a long time to get over her death.* ■ PHR-VERB If you **get over** a problem or difficulty, you overcome it. ❏ *I don't know how they'll get over that problem.*

▶ **get through** ■ PHR-VERB If you **get through** a task or an amount of work, you complete it. ❏ *I managed to get through the first two chapters.* ■ PHR-VERB If you **get through** a difficult or unpleasant period of time, you manage to live through it. ❏ *It is hard to see how people will get through the winter.* ■ PHR-VERB If you **get through** to someone, you succeed in making them understand something that you are trying to tell them. ❏ *An old friend might be able to get through to her and help her.* ■ PHR-VERB If you **get through to** someone, you succeed in contacting them on the telephone. ❏ *I can't get through to this number.*

▶ **get together** ■ PHR-VERB When people **get together**, they meet in order to discuss something or to spend time together. ❏ *This is a time for families to get together and enjoy themselves.* ■ PHR-VERB If you **get** something **together**, you organize it.

❏ *Paul and I got a band together.* ■ PHR-VERB If you **get** an amount of money **together**, you succeed in getting all the money that you need in order to pay for something. ❏ *We've finally got enough money together to buy a home.*

▶ **get up** ■ PHR-VERB When someone who is sitting or lying down **gets up**, they rise to a standing position. ❏ *I got up and walked over to where he was.* ■ PHR-VERB When you **get up**, you get out of bed. ❏ *They have to get up early in the morning.*

**get|away** /gɛtəweɪ/ (**getaways**) N-COUNT If someone makes a **getaway**, they leave a place quickly, especially after committing a crime or when trying to avoid someone. ❏ *They made their getaway on a stolen motorcycle.* [from Old English]

**get-go** PHRASE If something happens or is true **from the get-go**, it happens or is true from the beginning of a process or activity. [INFORMAL] ❏ *From the get-go, we knew he could do the job.*

**ghast|ly** /gæstli/ ADJ If you describe someone or something as **ghastly**, you mean that you find them very unpleasant or shocking. [INFORMAL] ❏ *It was the worst week of my life. It was ghastly.* [from Old English]

**ghet|to** /gɛtoʊ/ (**ghettos** or **ghettoes**) N-COUNT A **ghetto** is a part of a city in which many poor people or many people of a particular race, religion, or nationality live separately from everyone else. ❏ *...the ghettos of New York.* [from Italian]

**ghost** /goʊst/ (**ghosts**) N-COUNT A **ghost** is the spirit of a dead person that someone believes they can see or feel. ❏ *...the ghost of Marie Antoinette.* [from Old English]

**ghost|ly** /goʊstli/ ADJ Something that is **ghostly** seems unreal or unnatural and may be frightening because of this. ❏ *...ghostly laughter.* [from Old English]

**GI** /dʒi aɪ/ (**GIs**) N-COUNT A **GI** is a soldier in the United States armed forces, especially the army. ❏ *...the GIs who came to Europe to fight the Nazis.*

**gi|ant** /dʒaɪənt/ (**giants**) ■ ADJ Something that is described as **giant** is much larger or more important than most others of its kind. ❏ *America's giant car makers are located in Detroit.* ❏ *...a giant oak table.* ■ N-COUNT **Giant** is often used to refer to any large, successful business organization or country. ❏ *Japan is an electronics giant.* ■ N-COUNT A **giant** is an imaginary person who is very big and strong, especially one mentioned in old stories. [from Old French]

| **Thesaurus** | *giant* | Also look up : |
|---|---|---|
| ADJ. | colossal, enormous, gigantic, huge, immense, mammoth; (*ant.*) miniature ■ | |

**gi|ant pan|da** (**giant pandas**) N-COUNT A **giant panda** is the same as a **panda**.

**gid|dy** /gɪdi/ (**giddier, giddiest**) ADJ ■ If you feel **giddy**, you feel unsteady and think that you are about to fall over, usually because you are not well. ❏ *He felt giddy and light-headed.* ■ ADJ If you feel **giddy with** delight or excitement, you feel so happy or excited that you find it hard to think or act normally. ❏ *Anthony was giddy with excitement before the prom.* [from Old English]

**gift** /gɪft/ (**gifts**) ■ N-COUNT A **gift** is something that you give someone as a present. ❏ *...a birthday* *gift.* **2** N-COUNT If someone has a **gift for** doing something, they have a natural ability for doing it. ☐ *He found he had a gift for teaching.* [from Old English]

**gift cer|tifi|cate** (**gift certificates**) N-COUNT A **gift certificate** is a card or piece of paper that you buy at a store and give to someone, which entitles the person to exchange it for goods worth the same amount. ☐ *...a $25 gift certificate.*

**gift|ed** /ɡɪftɪd/ **1** ADJ Someone who is **gifted** has a natural ability to do something well. ☐ *...one of the most gifted players in the world.* **2** ADJ A **gifted** child is much more intelligent or talented than average. [from Old English]

**gig** /ɡɪɡ/ (**gigs**) N-COUNT A **gig** is a live performance by someone such as a musician or a comedian. [INFORMAL] ☐ *We went to a gig at Madison Square Garden.* [of Scandinavian origin]

**gi|ga|byte** /ɡɪɡəbaɪt/ (**gigabytes**) N-COUNT In computing, a **gigabyte** is one thousand and twenty-four megabytes.

**gi|gan|tic** /dʒaɪɡæntɪk/ ADJ If you describe something as **gigantic**, you are emphasizing that it is extremely large in size, amount, or degree. ☐ *There are gigantic rocks along the roadside.* [from Greek]

**gig|gle** /ɡɪɡ°l/ (**giggles, giggling, giggled**) V-T/ V-I If someone **giggles**, they laugh in a childlike way, because they are amused, nervous, or embarrassed. ☐ *The girls began to giggle.* ☐ *"I beg your pardon?" she giggled.* ● **Giggle** is also a noun. ☐ *He gave a little giggle.*
→ see **laugh**

**gill** /ɡɪl/ (**gills**) N-COUNT **Gills** are the organs on the sides of fish and other water creatures through which they breathe. [from Old Norse]
→ see **amphibian, fish**

**gilt** /ɡɪlt/ ADJ A **gilt** object is covered with a thin layer of gold or gold paint. ☐ *...thick paper with gilt edges.* [from Old English]

**gim|mick** /ɡɪmɪk/ (**gimmicks**) N-COUNT A **gimmick** is an unusual and unnecessary feature or action whose purpose is to attract attention or publicity; used to show disapproval. ☐ *It is just a gimmick to attract the public's attention.*

**gin** /dʒɪn/ (**gins**) N-VAR **Gin** is a strong, colorless, alcoholic drink. [from Dutch]

**gin|ger** /dʒɪndʒər/ **1** N-UNCOUNT **Ginger** is the root of a plant that is used to flavor food. It has a sweet, spicy flavor and is often sold in powdered form. **2** COLOR **Ginger** is used to describe things that are orangey brown in color. ☐ *She had ginger hair and pale skin.* [from Old French]

**gin|ger|ly** /dʒɪndʒərli/ ADV If you do something **gingerly**, you do it in a careful manner, usually because you expect it to be dangerous, unpleasant, or painful. [WRITTEN] ☐ *He stepped gingerly into the elevator.* [from Old French]

**gi|raffe** /dʒɪræf/ (**giraffes**) N-COUNT A **giraffe** is a large African animal with a very long neck, long legs, and dark patches on its body. [from Italian]

giraffe

**girl** /ɡɜrl/ (**girls**) **1** N-COUNT A **girl** is a female child. ☐ *...an eleven-year-old girl.* ☐ *They have two girls and a boy.* **2** N-COUNT Young women are often referred to as **girls**. This use could cause offense. ☐ *He married a girl ten years younger.* [from Low German]

<table>
<tr><td>Usage</td><td>girl</td></tr>
</table>

Don't refer to an adult female as a *girl*. This may cause offense. Use *woman*. *I'm studying with Diana. She's a woman from my English class.*

**girl|friend** /ɡɜrlfrɛnd/ (**girlfriends**) **1** N-COUNT Someone's **girlfriend** is a girl or woman with whom they are having a romantic or sexual relationship. ☐ *Does he have a girlfriend?* **2** N-COUNT A **girlfriend** is a female friend. ☐ *I had lunch with my girlfriends.*

**girth** /ɡɜrθ/ (**girths**) N-VAR The **girth** of an object, for example a person's or an animal's body, is its width or thickness, considered as the measurement around its circumference. [FORMAL] ☐ *She noticed his increasing girth.* [from Old Norse]

**gist** /dʒɪst/ N-SING The **gist of** a speech, conversation, or piece of writing is its general meaning. ☐ *He told me the gist of their conversation.* [from Old French]

> **give**
> **❶** USED WITH NOUNS DESCRIBING ACTIONS
> **❷** TRANSFERRING
> **❸** OTHER USES, PHRASES, AND PHRASAL VERBS

**❶ give** /ɡɪv/ (**gives, giving, gave, given**) **1** V-T You can use **give** with nouns that refer to physical actions. The whole expression refers to the performing of the action. For example, **She gave a smile** means almost the same as "She smiled." ☐ *She gave a big yawn.* ☐ *He gave her a friendly smile.* **2** V-T You use **give** to say that a person does something for another person. For example, if you **give** someone a lift, you take them somewhere in your car. ☐ *I gave her a lift back to her house.* ☐ *She began to give piano lessons to children.* **3** V-T You use **give** with nouns that refer to information, opinions, or greetings to indicate that something is communicated. For example, if you **give** someone some news, you tell it to them. ☐ *He gave no details.* ☐ *Would you please give me your name?* **4** V-T You use **give** to say how long you think something will last or how much you think something will be. ☐ *The doctors gave her a year to live.* **5** V-T If someone or something **gives** you a particular idea, impression, or feeling, they cause you to have it. ☐ *They gave me the impression that they were very happy.* ☐ *He gave me a shock.* **6** V-T If you **give** a performance or speech, you perform or speak in public. ☐ *She gives a wonderful performance in the movie.* **7** V-T If you **give** something thought or attention, you think about it, concentrate on it, or deal with it. ☐ *I've given the matter some thought.* **8** V-T If you **give** a party or other social event, you organize it. ☐ *I gave a dinner party for a few friends.* [from Old English]
→ see **donor**

**❷ give** /ɡɪv/ (**gives, giving, gave, given**) **1** V-T/V-I If you **give** someone something that you own or have bought, you provide them with

## Word Web  glacier

Two-thirds of all **fresh water** is **frozen**. The largest **glaciers** in the world are the **polar ice caps** of Antarctica and Greenland. They cover more than six million square miles. Their average depth is almost one mile. If all the glaciers **melted**, the average **sea level** would rise by more than 250 feet. Glaciologists have noted that the Antarctic is about 1°C* warmer than it was 50 years ago. Some of them are worried. Continued warming might cause floating **ice** shelves there to begin to fall apart. This, in turn, could cause disastrous coastal flooding around the world.

*1° Celsius = 33.8° Fahrenheit*

it, so that they have it or can use it. ❑ *They gave us T-shirts and stickers.* ❑ *He gave money to the World Health Organization.* ❑ *Most Americans give to charity.* **2** V-T If you **give** someone something that you are holding or that is near you, you pass it to them, so that they are then holding it. ❑ *Give me that pencil.* **3** V-T To **give** someone or something a particular power or right means to allow them to have it. ❑ *The new law would give the president more power.* [from Old English]

**❸ give** /gɪv/ (**gives, giving, gave, given**) **1** V-I If something **gives**, it collapses or breaks under pressure. ❑ *My knees gave under me.* **2** V-T PASSIVE You say that you **are given to** understand or believe that something is the case when you do not want to say how you found out about it, or who told you. [FORMAL] ❑ *We were given to understand that he was sick.* **3** → see also **given** **4** PHRASE You use **give me** to say that you would rather have one thing than another, especially when you have just mentioned the thing that you do not want. ❑ *I hate rain. Give me cold, dry weather any day.* **5** PHRASE If you say that something requires **give-and-take**, you mean that people must compromise or cooperate for it to be successful. ❑ *In a happy relationship there has to be give-and-take.* **6** PHRASE **Give or take** is used to indicate that an amount is approximate. For example, if you say that something is fifty years old, **give or take** a few years, you mean that it is approximately fifty years old. ❑ *They grow to a height of 12 inches — give or take a couple of inches.* [from Old English] **7** to **give the game away** → see **game** **8** to **give notice** → see **notice** **9** to **give rise to** → see **rise** **10** to **give way** → see **way**

▸ **give away** **1** PHR-VERB If you **give away** something that you own, you give it to someone, rather than selling it, often because you no longer want it. ❑ *She likes to give away plants from her garden.* **2** PHR-VERB If you **give away** information that should be kept secret, you reveal it to other people. ❑ *Her face gave nothing away.*

▸ **give back** PHR-VERB If you **give** something **back**, you return it to the person who gave it to you. ❑ *I gave the book back to him.* ❑ *Give me back my camera.*

▸ **give in** **1** PHR-VERB If you **give in**, you admit that you are defeated or that you cannot do something. ❑ *It was tough, but we were determined not to give in.* **2** PHR-VERB If you **give in**, you agree to do something that you do not want to do. ❑ *My parents finally gave in and let me have driving lessons.*

▸ **give off** or **give out** PHR-VERB If something **gives off** or **gives out** a gas, heat, or a smell, it produces it and sends it out into the air. ❑ *Natural gas gives off less carbon dioxide than coal.*

▸ **give out** **1** PHR-VERB If you **give out** a number of things, you distribute them among a group of people. ❑ *There were people at the entrance giving out tickets.* **2** → see **give off**

▸ **give over to** or **give up to** PHR-VERB If something **is given over** or **given up to** a particular use, it is used entirely for that purpose. ❑ *Much of the garden was given over to vegetables.*

▸ **give up** **1** PHR-VERB If you **give up** something, you stop doing it or having it. ❑ *The Coast Guard have given up all hope of finding the divers alive.* **2** PHR-VERB If you **give up**, you decide that you cannot do something and stop trying to do it. ❑ *I give up. I'll never understand this.* **3** PHR-VERB If you **give up** your job, you resign from it. ❑ *She gave up her job to join her husband's campaign.*

▸ **give up to** → see **give over to**

**giv|en** /gɪvˀn/ **1** **Given** is the past participle of **give**. **2** ADJ If you talk about, for example, any **given** position or a **given** time, you mean any particular position or any particular time. ❑ *There are usually about 250 students in the building at any given time.* **3** PREP **Given** is used when indicating a possible situation in which someone has the opportunity or ability to do something. For example, **given the chance** means "if I had the chance." ❑ *Given the opportunity, I'd like to travel more.* **4** PHRASE If you say **given** something, or **given that** something is true, you mean taking that thing into account. ❑ *Given the difficulties, I think we did very well.* ❑ *I have to be careful with money, given that I don't earn very much.* [from Old English]

**gla|cial** /ɡleɪʃˀl/ ADJ **Glacial** means relating to or produced by glaciers or ice. [TECHNICAL] ❑ *...a glacial landscape.* [from French]
→ see **lake**

**gla|cial drift** N-UNCOUNT **Glacial drift** is rocks that have been carried and left by a glacier. [TECHNICAL]

**gla|ci|er** /ɡleɪʃər/ (**glaciers**) N-COUNT A **glacier** is an extremely large mass of ice which moves very slowly, often down a mountain valley. [from French Savoy]
→ see Word Web: **glacier**
→ see **climate, mountain**

**glad** /ɡlæd/ **1** ADJ If you are **glad** about something, you are happy and pleased about it.

❑ They seemed glad to see me. ❑ I'd be glad if the boys slept a little longer. ● **glad|ly** ADV ❑ Malcolm gladly accepted the invitation. ② ADJ If you say that you will be **glad to** do something, usually for someone else, you mean that you are willing and eager to do it. ❑ I'll be glad to show you everything. ● **glad|ly** ADV ❑ She'll gladly baby-sit for you if she's free. [from Old English]

**glam|or** /ɡlǽmər/ N-UNCOUNT → see **glamour**

**glam|or|ous** /ɡlǽmərəs/ ADJ If you describe someone or something as **glamorous**, you mean that they are more attractive, exciting, or interesting than ordinary people or things. ❑ ...beautiful and glamorous women. [from Scottish]

**glam|our** /ɡlǽmər/ also **glamor** N-UNCOUNT **Glamour** is the quality of being more attractive, exciting, or interesting than ordinary people or things. ❑ ...the glamour of show biz. [from Scottish]

**glance** /ɡlæns/ (**glances, glancing, glanced**) ① V-I If you **glance at** something or someone, you look at them very quickly and then look away again immediately. ❑ He glanced at his watch. ② V-I If you **glance through** or **at** a newspaper, report, or book, you spend a short time looking at it without reading it very carefully. ❑ I picked up the book and glanced through it. ③ N-COUNT A **glance** is a quick look at someone or something. ❑ Trevor and I exchanged a glance. ④ PHRASE If you say that something is true or seems to be true **at first glance**, you mean that it seems to be true when you first see it or think about it, but that your first impression may be wrong. ❑ At first glance, the new car looks like the old one. [from Old French]

**gland** /ɡlænd/ (**glands**) N-COUNT A **gland** is an organ in the body which produces chemical substances for the body to use or get rid of. ❑ ...sweat glands. [from Latin]

**glare** /ɡlɛər/ (**glares, glaring, glared**) ① V-I If you **glare at** someone, you look at them with an angry expression on your face. ❑ The old woman glared at him. ❑ Jacob glared angrily. ② N-COUNT A **glare** is an angry, hard, and unfriendly look. ❑ She gave him a furious glare. ③ V-I If the sun or a light **glares**, it shines with a very bright light which is difficult to look at. ❑ Blinding white light glared in his eyes. ④ N-UNCOUNT **Glare** is very bright light that is difficult to look at. ❑ ...the glare of a car's headlights. ⑤ N-SING If someone is in **the glare of** publicity or public attention, they are constantly being watched and talked about by a lot of people. ❑ The president's wife disliked the glare of publicity. [from Middle Low German]

**glar|ing** /ɡlɛərɪŋ/ ① ADJ If you describe something bad as **glaring**, you are emphasizing that it is very obvious and easily seen or noticed. ❑ This was a glaring mistake. ❑ It was glaringly obvious. [from Middle Low German] ② → see also **glare**

**glass** /ɡlæs, ɡlæs/ (**glasses**) ① N-UNCOUNT **Glass** is a hard, transparent substance that is used to make things such as windows and bottles. ❑ ...a bowl made of glass. ② N-COUNT A **glass** is a container made from glass, which you can drink from and which does not have a handle. ❑ He picked up his glass and drank. ❑ ...a glass of milk. ③ N-UNCOUNT **Glass** is used to mean objects made of glass. ❑ They sell beautiful silver and glass. ④ N-PLURAL **Glasses** are two lenses in a frame that some people wear in front of their eyes in order to help them see better. ❑ He took off his glasses. [from Old English]
→ see Word Web: **glass**
→ see **aquarium, light bulb**

**glass slide** (**glass slides**) → see **slide**

**glaze** /ɡleɪz/ (**glazes**) N-COUNT A **glaze** is a thin layer of a hard shiny substance which is put on a piece of pottery. ❑ ...tiles with decorative glazes.
→ see **pottery**

**glazed** /ɡleɪzd/ ① ADJ If someone's eyes are **glazed**, their expression is dull or dreamy, because they are tired or having difficulty concentrating. ❑ He sat with glazed eyes in front of the TV. ② ADJ **Glazed** pottery is covered with a thin layer of a hard, shiny substance. ❑ ...a large glazed pot. ③ ADJ A **glazed** window or door has glass in it. ❑ Her new office had a glazed door with her name on it.

**gleam** /ɡliːm/ (**gleams, gleaming, gleamed**) ① V-I If an object or a surface **gleams**, it reflects light because it is shiny and clean. ❑ His black hair gleamed in the sun. ② N-COUNT A **gleam of** something is a faint sign of it. ❑ There was a gleam of hope for peace. [from Old English]

**glean** /ɡliːn/ (**gleans, gleaning, gleaned**) V-T If you **glean** information or knowledge, you learn or collect it slowly and patiently. ❑ We're trying to glean information from all sources. [from Old French]

**glee** /ɡliː/ N-UNCOUNT **Glee** is a feeling of happiness and excitement, often caused by your own good luck or someone else's bad luck. ❑ His victory was greeted with glee. [from Old English]

**glee|ful** /ɡliːfəl/ ADJ Someone who is **gleeful** is happy and excited, often because of someone else's bad luck. [WRITTEN] ❑ He took a gleeful delight

---

## Word Web    glass

The basic ingredients for **glass** are silica (found in **sand**) and **ash** (left over from burning wood). The earliest glass objects are glass **beads** made in Egypt around 3500 BC. By 14 AD, the Syrians had learned how to **blow** glass to form hollow containers. These included primitive **bottles** and **vases**. By 100 AD, the Romans were making clear glass windowpanes. Modern factories now produce **safety glass** which doesn't **shatter** when it breaks. It includes a layer of cellulose between two **sheets** of glass. **Bulletproof** glass consists of several layers of glass with a tough, **transparent** plastic between the layers.

in proving her wrong. ● **glee|ful|ly** ADV ❑ *She gleefully told us every detail of the story.* [from Old English]

**glib** /glɪb/ ADJ If you describe what someone says as **glib**, you disapprove of it because it implies that something is simple or easy, or that there are no problems involved, when this is not the case. ❑ *This glib talk shows no real understanding of their misery.* ● **glib|ly** ADV ❑ *We talk glibly of equality of opportunity.* [from Middle Low German]

**glide** /glaɪd/ (**glides, gliding, glided**) **1** V-I If you **glide** somewhere, you move silently and smoothly. ❑ *Waiters glide around carrying trays.* **2** V-I When birds or airplanes **glide**, they float on air currents. ❑ *Geese glide over the lake.* [from Old English]

**glid|er** /glaɪdər/ (**gliders**) N-COUNT A **glider** is an aircraft without an engine, which flies by floating on air currents. [from Old English]

**glim|mer** /glɪmər/ (**glimmers, glimmering, glimmered**) **1** V-I If something **glimmers**, it produces a faint, unsteady light. ❑ *The moon glimmered through the mist.* **2** N-COUNT A **glimmer** is a faint, unsteady light. ❑ *In the east there was a glimmer of light.* **3** N-COUNT A **glimmer of** something is a faint sign of it. ❑ *...a glimmer of hope.* [from Middle High German]

**glimpse** /glɪmps/ (**glimpses, glimpsing, glimpsed**) **1** N-COUNT If you get a **glimpse of** someone or something, you see them very briefly and not very well. ❑ *Fans waited outside the hotel to catch a glimpse of the star.* **2** V-T If you **glimpse** someone or something, you see them very briefly and not very well. ❑ *She glimpsed a boat out on the ocean.* **3** N-COUNT A **glimpse of** something is a brief experience of it or an idea about it that helps you understand or appreciate it better. ❑ *The movie offers a glimpse into the lives of these women.* [from Old English]

**glint** /glɪnt/ (**glints, glinting, glinted**) **1** V-I If something **glints**, it produces or reflects a quick flash of light. [WRITTEN] ❑ *The sea glinted in the sun.* ❑ *Sunlight glinted on his glasses.* **2** N-COUNT A **glint** is a quick flash of light. [WRITTEN] ❑ *...glints of sunlight.* [of Scandinavian origin]

**glis|ten** /glɪsªn/ (**glistens, glistening, glistened**) V-I If something **glistens**, it shines, usually because it is wet or oily. ❑ *The sea glistened in the sunlight.* ❑ *David's face was glistening with sweat.* [from Old English]

**glit|ter** /glɪtər/ (**glitters, glittering, glittered**) **1** V-I If something **glitters**, light comes from or is reflected off different parts of it. ❑ *The bay glittered in the sunshine.* **2** N-UNCOUNT You can use **glitter** to refer to superficial attractiveness or the excitement connected with something. ❑ *She loved the glitter of show business.* [from Old Norse]

**gloat** /gloʊt/ (**gloats, gloating, gloated**) V-I If someone **is gloating**, they are showing pleasure at their own success or at other people's failure. ❑ *They're all gloating over the result.* [of Scandinavian origin]

**glob|al** /gloʊbªl/ **1** ADJ **Global** means concerning or including the whole world. ❑ *...a global ban on nuclear testing.* ● **glob|al|ly** ADV ❑ *The company employs 5,800 people globally, including 2,000 in Colorado.* **2** ADJ A **global** view or vision of a situation is one in which all the different aspects of it are considered. ❑ *We need to take a global view of economic and social problems.* [from Old French]

**glob|al vil|lage** N-SING People sometimes refer to the world as a **global village** when they want to emphasize that all the different parts of the world form one community linked together by electronic communications, especially the Internet. ❑ *We are all part of the global village.* [coined by Marshall McLuhan (1911–80), a Canadian author]

**glob|al warm|ing** N-UNCOUNT **Global warming** is the gradual rise in the earth's temperature caused by high levels of carbon dioxide and other gases in the atmosphere. ❑ *...the threat of global warming.*
→ see **air, greenhouse effect, ozone**

**globe** /gloʊb/ (**globes**) **1** N-SING You can refer to the world as **the globe** when you are emphasizing how big it is or that something happens in many different parts of it. ❑ *...people from every part of the globe.* ❑ *70% of our globe's surface is water.* **2** N-COUNT A **globe** is a ball-shaped object with a map of the world on it. It is usually fixed on a stand. ❑ *A large globe stood on his desk.* [from Old French]

**globu|lar clus|ter** (**globular clusters**) N-COUNT A **globular cluster** is a dense group of older stars that is roughly the shape of a sphere. [TECHNICAL]

**gloom** /glum/ **1** N-SING **The gloom** is a state of near darkness. ❑ *...the gloom of a foggy November morning.* **2** N-UNCOUNT **Gloom** is a feeling of sadness and lack of hope. ❑ *There is increasing gloom over the economy.* [from Norwegian]

**gloomy** /glumi/ (**gloomier, gloomiest**) **1** ADJ If a place is **gloomy**, it is almost dark so that you cannot see very well. ❑ *Inside it's gloomy after all that sunshine.* **2** ADJ If people are **gloomy**, they are unhappy and have no hope. ❑ *He is gloomy about the future of television.* ● **gloom|i|ly** ADV ❑ *He told me gloomily that he had to leave.* **3** ADJ If a situation is **gloomy**, it does not give you much hope of success or happiness. ❑ *The economic prospects for next year are gloomy.* [from Norwegian]
→ see **weather**

**glo|ri|fy** /glɔrɪfaɪ/ (**glorifies, glorifying, glorified**) V-T To **glorify** something means to praise it or make it seem good or special, usually when it is not. ❑ *He denies that the film glorifies war.* ● **glo|ri|fi|ca|tion** /glɔrɪfɪkeɪʃªn/ N-UNCOUNT ❑ *...the glorification of violence.* [from Old French]

**glo|ri|ous** /glɔriəs/ **1** ADJ Something that is **glorious** is very beautiful and impressive. ❑ *...a glorious rainbow.* ● **glo|ri|ous|ly** ADV ❑ *The trees are gloriously colored in the fall.* **2** ADJ If you describe something as **glorious**, you are emphasizing that it is wonderful and it makes you feel very happy. ❑ *...glorious memories of his days as a champion.* ● **glo|ri|ous|ly** ADV ❑ *...a gloriously sunny morning.* **3** ADJ A **glorious** career, victory, or occasion involves great fame or success. ❑ *He had a glorious career as a writer.* ● **glo|ri|ous|ly** ADV ❑ *The mission was gloriously successful.* [from Old French]

**glo|ry** /glɔri/ (**glories**) **1** N-UNCOUNT **Glory** is the fame and admiration that you gain by doing something impressive. ❑ *He had his moment of glory when he won a 20 km race.* **2** N-PLURAL A person's **glories** are the occasions when they have done something people greatly admire which makes them famous. ❑ *Instead of remembering past glories we need to create something new.* [from Old French]

| Word Partnership | Use *glory* with : |
| --- | --- |
| V. | **bask in the** glory ◼ |
| N. | **blaze of** glory, glory **days**, **hope and** glory ◼ |

**gloss** /glɒs/ (**glosses, glossing, glossed**)
◼ N-SING A **gloss** is a bright shine on the surface of something. ❑ *The rain produced a black gloss on the sidewalks.* ◻ N-UNCOUNT **Gloss** or **gloss paint** is paint that forms a shiny surface when it dries. [of Scandinavian origin]
▸ **gloss over** PHR-VERB If you **gloss over** a problem, a mistake, or an embarrassing moment, you try to make it seem unimportant by ignoring it or by dealing with it very quickly. ❑ *Some governments gloss over human rights abuses.*

**glossy** /glɒsi/ (**glossier, glossiest**) ◼ ADJ **Glossy** means smooth and shiny. ❑ *...glossy black hair.* ◻ ADJ **Glossy** magazines, books, and photographs are produced on expensive, shiny paper. ❑ *...a glossy magazine aimed at teenage girls.* [of Scandinavian origin]

**glove** /glʌv/ (**gloves**) N-COUNT **Gloves** are pieces of clothing which cover your hands and wrists and have individual sections for each finger. You wear gloves to keep your hands warm or dry or to protect them. ❑ *He put his gloves in his pocket.* [from Old English]
→ see **baseball**

**glow** /gloʊ/ (**glows, glowing, glowed**)
◼ N-COUNT A **glow** is a dull, steady light, for example the light produced by a fire when there are no flames. ❑ *She saw the red glow of a fire.*
◻ N-SING A **glow** is a pink color on a person's face, usually because they are healthy or have been exercising. ❑ *The moisturizer gave my face a healthy glow.* ◼ N-SING If you feel a **glow of** satisfaction or achievement, you have a strong feeling of pleasure because of something that you have done or that has happened. ❑ *Exercise will give you a glow of satisfaction.* ◼ V-I If something **glows,** it produces a dull, steady light. ❑ *The lantern glowed softly in the darkness.* ◼ V-I If someone's skin **glows,** it looks pink because they are healthy or excited, or have been doing physical exercise. ❑ *Her skin glowed with health.* ◼ V-I If someone **glows with** an emotion such as pride or pleasure, the expression on their face shows how they feel. ❑ *Her mother glowed with pride.* [from Old English]
→ see **fire, light bulb**

| Thesaurus | *glow* | Also look up : |
| --- | --- | --- |
| N. | beam, glimmer, light ◼ | |
| | blush, flush, radiance ◻ | |
| V. | gleam, radiate, shine ◼ ◼ | |

**glowing** /gloʊɪŋ/ ◼ ADJ A **glowing** description or opinion about someone or something praises them highly or supports them strongly. ❑ *The media spoke in glowing terms of his latest movie.* [from Old English] ◻ → see also **glow**

**glucose** /gluːkoʊs/ N-UNCOUNT **Glucose** is a type of sugar. [from French]
→ see **photosynthesis**

**glue** /gluː/ (**glues, glueing** or **gluing, glued**)
◼ N-VAR **Glue** is a sticky substance used for joining things together. ❑ *...a tube of glue.* ◻ V-T If you **glue** one object to another, you stick them together using glue. ❑ *Glue the fabric around the picture.* ❑ *The material is cut and glued in place.* ◼ V-T PASSIVE If you say that someone **is glued to** something, you mean that they are giving it all their attention. ❑ *They were all glued to the game on TV.* [from Old French]

**glum** /glʌm/ (**glummer, glummest**) ADJ Someone who is **glum** is sad and quiet because they are disappointed or unhappy about something. ❑ *She was very glum and was obviously missing her children.* ● **glumly** ADV ❑ *He was sitting glumly on the couch.*

**glut** /glʌt/ (**gluts, glutting, glutted**) ◼ N-COUNT If there is a **glut of** something, there is so much of it that it cannot all be sold or used. ❑ *...a glut of apples.* ◻ V-T If a market **is glutted with** something, there is a glut of that thing. [BUSINESS] ❑ *The region is glutted with hospitals.* [from Old French]

**GM** /dʒiː ɛm/ ADJ **GM** crops have had one or more genes changed, for example in order to make them resist pests better. **GM** is an abbreviation for **genetically modified.** ❑ *We may be eating food containing GM ingredients without realizing it.*

**GM-free** ADJ **GM-free** products or crops are products or crops that do not contain any genetically modified material. ❑ *...GM-free soy.*

**GMO** /dʒiː ɛm oʊ/ (**GMOs**) N-COUNT A **GMO** is an animal, plant, or other organism whose genetic structure has been changed by genetic engineering. **GMO** is an abbreviation for "genetically modified organism." ❑ *...the presence of GMOs in many processed foods.*

**GMT** /dʒiː ɛm tiː/ **GMT** is the standard time in Great Britain which is used to calculate the time in the rest of the world. **GMT** is an abbreviation for **Greenwich Mean Time.** ❑ *New Mexico is seven hours behind GMT.*

**gnaw** /nɔː/ (**gnaws, gnawing, gnawed**) ◼ V-T/V-I If people or animals **gnaw** something or **gnaw on** it, they bite it repeatedly. ❑ *...a hungry dog gnawing on a bone.* ◻ V-I If a feeling or thought **gnaws at** you, it causes you to keep worrying. [WRITTEN] ❑ *Worry gnawed at him for days.* [from Old English]

**gnome** /noʊm/ (**gnomes**) N-COUNT In children's stories, a **gnome** is an imaginary creature that is like a tiny old man with a beard and pointed hat. [from French]

| | go |
| --- | --- |
| ◉ | MOVING OR LEAVING |
| ◉ | LINK VERB USES |
| ◉ | OTHER VERB USES, NOUN USES, AND PHRASES |
| ◉ | PHRASAL VERBS |

◉ **go** /goʊ/ (**goes, going, went, gone**)

In most cases the past participle of **go** is **gone,** but occasionally you use "been": see **been.**

◼ V-T/V-I When you **go** somewhere, you move or travel there. ❑ *We went to Rome.* ❑ *I went home for the weekend.* ❑ *It took an hour to go three miles.* ◻ V-I When you **go,** you leave the place where you are. ❑ *It's time for me to go.* ◼ V-T/V-I You use **go** to say that someone leaves the place where they are and does an activity, often a leisure activity. ❑ *We*

*g*

went swimming early this morning. ❑ They've gone shopping. ❑ He went for a walk. **4** V-I When you **go** do something, you move to a place in order to do it and you do it. You can also **go and** do something, but you always say that someone **went and** did something. ❑ I have to go see the doctor. ❑ I finished my drink, then went and got another. **5** V-I If you **go** **to** school, work, or church, you attend it regularly as part of your normal life. ❑ Does your daughter go to school yet? **6** V-I When you say where a road or path **goes**, you are saying where it begins or ends, or what places it is in. ❑ There's a road that goes from Blairstown to Millbrook Village. **7** V-I If you say where money **goes**, you are saying what it is spent on. ❑ Most of my money goes toward bills. **8** V-I If you say that something **goes to** someone, you mean that it is given to them. ❑ A lot of credit should go to his father. **9** V-I If something **goes**, someone gets rid of it. ❑ Hundreds of jobs could go. **10** V-I If something **goes into** something else, it is put in it as one of the parts or elements that form it. ❑ …the ingredients that go into the dish. **11** V-I If something **goes** in a particular place, it belongs there or should be put there, because that is where you normally keep it. ❑ The shoes go on the shoe shelf. **12** V-I If one of a person's senses, such as their sight or hearing, **is going**, it is getting weak and they may soon lose it completely. [INFORMAL] ❑ His eyes are going. **13** V-I If something such as a light bulb or a part of an engine **goes**, it is no longer working and needs to be replaced. ❑ A light bulb has gone in the bathroom. [from Old English]

**❷ go** /goʊ/ (**goes, going, went, gone**) V-LINK You can use **go** to say that a person or thing changes to another state or condition. For example, if someone **goes crazy**, they become crazy, and if something **goes bad**, it deteriorates. ❑ I'm going bald. ❑ The meat has gone bad. [from Old English]

**❸ go** /goʊ/ (**goes, going, went, gone**) **1** V-I You use **go** to talk about the way something happens. For example, if an event or situation **goes well**, it is successful. ❑ Everything is going wrong. **2** V-I If a machine or device **is going**, it is working. ❑ Can you get my car going again? **3** V-RECIP If something **goes** **with** something else, or if two things **go together**, they look or taste good together. ❑ Those pants would go with my new shirt. ❑ Some colors go together and some don't. **4** N-COUNT A **go** is an attempt at doing something. ❑ I wanted to have a go at football. ❑ She won on her first go. **5** N-COUNT If it is your **go** in a game, it is your turn to do something, for example to play a card or move a piece. ❑ Now whose go is it? **6** → see also **going**, **gone** **7** PHRASE If you say that someone **is making a go of** something such as a business or relationship, you mean that they are having some success with it. ❑ I knew we could make a go of it and be happy. **8** PHRASE If you say that someone is always **on the go**, you mean that they are always busy and active. [INFORMAL] ❑ In my job I am on the go all the time. **9** PHRASE If you say that there is a certain amount of time **to go**, you mean that there is that amount of time left before something happens or ends. ❑ There is a week to go until the party. **10** PHRASE If

you are in a café or restaurant and ask for an item of food **to go**, you mean that you want to take it with you and not eat it there. ❑ …large fries to go. [from Old English]

**❹ go** /goʊ/ (**goes, going, went, gone**)
▸ **go about** **1** PHR-VERB The way you **go about** a task or problem is the way you approach it and deal with it. ❑ I want to work in journalism, but I don't know how to go about it. **2** PHR-VERB When you **are going about** your normal activities, you are doing them. ❑ People were going about their business when they heard an explosion.
▸ **go after** PHR-VERB If you **go after** something, you try to get it, catch it, or hit it. ❑ This year he's going after the championship.
▸ **go against** **1** PHR-VERB If a person or their behavior **goes against** your wishes, beliefs, or expectations, their behavior is the opposite of what you want, believe in, or expect. ❑ These changes go against my principles.
▸ **go ahead** **1** PHR-VERB If someone **goes ahead with** something, they begin to do it or make it, especially after planning, promising, or asking permission to do it. ❑ The board will vote on whether to go ahead with the plan. **2** PHR-VERB If a process or an organized event **goes ahead**, it takes place or is carried out. ❑ The event will go ahead as planned next summer.
▸ **go along with** **1** PHR-VERB If you **go along with** a rule, decision, or policy, you accept it and obey it. ❑ I'll go along with whatever the others decide.
▸ **go around** **1** PHR-VERB If you **go around to** someone's house, you go to visit them at their house. ❑ He went around to her house to see if she was there. **2** PHR-VERB If there is enough of something **to go around**, there is enough of it to be shared among a group of people, or to do all the things for which it is needed. ❑ In the future we may not have enough water to go around.
▸ **go away** **1** PHR-VERB If you **go away**, you leave a place or a person's company. ❑ I need to go away and think about this. **2** PHR-VERB If you **go away**, you leave a place and spend a period of time somewhere else, especially as a vacation. ❑ Why don't you and I go away this weekend?
▸ **go back on** PHR-VERB If you **go back on** a promise or agreement, you do not do what you promised or agreed to do. ❑ The president has gone back on his promise.
▸ **go back to** PHR-VERB If you **go back to** a task or activity, you start doing it again after you have stopped doing it for a period of time. ❑ I want to go back to work as soon as possible.
▸ **go before** PHR-VERB To **go before** a judge, tribunal, or court of law means to be present there as part of an official or legal process. ❑ The case went before the judge on December 23.
▸ **go by** PHR-VERB If you say that time **goes by**, you mean that it passes. ❑ I gradually forgot about him as the years went by.
▸ **go down** **1** PHR-VERB If a price, level, or amount **goes down**, it becomes lower or less than it was. ❑ Inflation went down last month. ❑ Crime has gone down 70 percent. **2** PHR-VERB If you **go down on** your knees or **on** all fours, you lower your body until it is supported by your knees, or by your hands and knees. ❑ I went down on my knees and prayed. **3** PHR-VERB When the sun **goes down**, it goes below the horizon. ❑ It gets cold after the sun goes down. **4** PHR-VERB If a ship **goes down**, it

sinks. If a plane **goes down**, it crashes out of the sky. ❏ *Their aircraft went down.*

▶ **go for** 1 PHR-VERB If you **go for** a particular thing or way of doing something, you choose it. ❏ *He decided to go for a smaller computer.* 2 PHR-VERB If you **go for** someone, you attack them. ❏ *The dog suddenly went for him.*

▶ **go in** PHR-VERB If the sun **goes in**, a cloud comes in front of it and it can no longer be seen. ❏ *The sun went in, and it felt cold.*

▶ **go in for** PHR-VERB If you **go in for** a particular activity, you do it as a hobby. ❏ *They go in for tennis.*

▶ **go into** 1 PHR-VERB If you **go into** something, you describe or examine it fully or in detail. ❏ *I don't want to go into details about what was said.* 2 PHR-VERB If you **go into** something, you decide to do it as your job or career. ❏ *Sam has gone into the tourism business.*

▶ **go off** 1 PHR-VERB If an explosive device or a gun **goes off**, it explodes or fires. ❏ *A bomb went off, destroying the vehicle.* 2 PHR-VERB If an alarm bell **goes off**, it makes a sudden loud noise. ❏ *The fire alarm went off and everybody ran out.* 3 PHR-VERB If an electrical device **goes off**, it stops operating. ❏ *All the lights went off.*

▶ **go on** 1 PHR-VERB If you **go on** doing something, or **go on with** an activity, you continue to do it. ❏ *Go on with your work.* 2 PHR-VERB If something **is going on**, it is happening. ❏ *While this conversation was going on, I was listening.* 3 PHR-VERB If a process or institution **goes on**, it continues to happen or exist. ❏ *Why is it necessary for the war to go on?* 4 PHR-VERB If an electrical device **goes on**, it begins operating. ❏ *A light went on at seven every evening.*

▶ **go out** 1 PHR-VERB If you **go out**, you leave your home in order to do something enjoyable, for example to go to a party, a bar, or the movies. ❏ *I'm going out tonight.* 2 PHR-VERB If you **go out with** someone, the two of you have a romantic or sexual relationship. ❏ *I once went out with a French man.* 3 PHR-VERB If a light **goes out**, it stops shining. ❏ *The bedroom light went out after a moment.* 4 PHR-VERB If something that is burning **goes out**, it stops burning. ❏ *The fire seemed to be going out.* 5 PHR-VERB When the tide **goes out**, the water in the sea gradually moves back to a lower level. ❏ *The tide was going out.*

▶ **go over** PHR-VERB If you **go over** a document, incident, or problem, you examine, discuss, or think about it very carefully. ❏ *We went over everything, searching for errors.*

▶ **go round** → see **go around** 1 PHR-VERB If you **go through** a difficult experience or a period of time, you experience it. ❏ *He was going through a very difficult time.* 2 PHR-VERB If you **go through** a lot of things such as papers or clothes, you look at them, usually in order to sort them into groups or to search for a particular item. ❏ *Someone has gone through my possessions.* 3 PHR-VERB If a law, agreement, or official decision **goes through**, it is approved by a legislature or committee. ❏ *The bill probably won't go through.*

▶ **go through with** PHR-VERB If you **go through with** an action you have decided on, you do it, even though it may be very unpleasant or difficult for you. ❏ *Richard pleaded with Bella not to go through with the divorce.*

▶ **go under** PHR-VERB If a business or project **goes under**, it becomes unable to continue in operation or in existence. [BUSINESS] ❏ *Many small businesses have gone under.*

▶ **go up** 1 PHR-VERB If a price, amount, or level **goes up**, it becomes higher or greater than it was. ❏ *Interest rates went up.* ❏ *The cost has gone up to $1.95 a minute.* 2 PHR-VERB If something **goes up**, it explodes or starts to burn, usually suddenly and with great intensity. ❏ *The hotel went up in flames.*

▶ **go with** 1 PHR-VERB If one thing **goes with** another thing, the two things officially belong together, so that if you get one, you also get the other. ❏ *A $250,000 salary goes with the job.* 2 PHR-VERB If one thing **goes with** another thing, it is usually found or experienced together with the other thing. ❏ *...the pain that goes with defeat.*

▶ **go without** PHR-VERB If you **go without** something that you need or usually have or do, you do not get it or do it. ❏ *They had to go without food for days.*

**goad** /goʊd/ (**goads, goading, goaded**) V-T If you **goad** someone, you deliberately make them angry, often causing them to react by doing something. ❏ *Charles was always goading me.* ● **Goad** is also a noun. ❏ *Her presence was just one more goad to Joanna.* [from Old English]

**go-ahead** 1 N-SING If you give someone or something **the go-ahead**, you give them permission to start doing something. ❏ *He got the go-ahead to start the project.* 2 ADJ A **go-ahead** person or organization tries hard to succeed, often by using new methods.

**goal** /goʊl/ (**goals**) 1 N-COUNT In games such as soccer or hockey, the **goal** is the space into which the players try to get the ball in order to score a point for their team. ❏ *The ball went straight into the goal.* 2 N-COUNT In games such as soccer or hockey, a **goal** is when a player gets the ball into the goal, or the point that is scored by doing this. ❏ *They scored five goals in the first half of the match.* 3 N-COUNT Your **goal** is something that you hope to achieve, especially when much time and effort will be needed. ❏ *You need to decide your own goals.* [from Middle English]
→ see **football, soccer**

| **Word Partnership** | Use *goal* with : |
|---|---|
| V. | **shoot at a goal** 1 |
| | **score a goal** 2 |
| | **accomplish a** goal, **share a** goal 3 |
| ADJ. | **winning** goal 2 |
| | **attainable** goal, **main** goal 3 |

**goalie** /goʊli/ (**goalies**) N-COUNT A **goalie** is the same as a **goalkeeper**. [INFORMAL] [from Middle English]

**goalkeeper** /goʊlkipər/ (**goalkeepers**) N-COUNT A **goalkeeper** is the player on a sports team whose job is to guard the goal.

**goalpost** /goʊlpoʊst/ (**goalposts**) also **goal post** N-COUNT A **goalpost** is one of the two upright wooden posts that are connected by a crossbar and form the goal in games such as soccer and hockey.
→ see **football**

**goat** /goʊt/ (**goats**) N-COUNT A **goat** is an animal that is about the size of a sheep. Goats have horns, and hairs on their chin which resemble a beard. [from Old English]

**gob** /gɒb/ (**gobs**) **1** N-COUNT A **gob of** something is a lump of it. □ *...a gob of ice.* **2** N-PLURAL **Gobs of** something means a lot of it. [INFORMAL] □ *We're getting input from gobs of sources.* [from Old French]

**gob|ble** /gɒbᵊl/ (**gobbles, gobbling, gobbled**) V-T If you **gobble** food, you eat it quickly and greedily. □ *Pete gobbled all the cake.*

**go-between** (**go-betweens**) N-COUNT A **go-between** is a person who takes messages between people who are unable or unwilling to meet each other. □ *He will act as a go-between to try and reach an agreement.*

**go-cart** (**go-carts**) also **go-kart** N-COUNT A **go-cart** is a very small motor vehicle with four wheels, used for racing.

**god** /gɒd/ (**gods**) **1** N-PROPER The name **God** is given to the spirit or being who is worshipped as the creator and ruler of the world, especially by Jews, Christians, and Muslims. □ *He believes in God.* **2** CONVENTION People sometimes use **God** in exclamations to emphasize something that they are saying, or to express surprise, fear, or excitement. This use could cause offense. □ *Oh my God, it's snowing.* □ *Good God, it's Mr. Harper!* **3** N-COUNT In many religions, a **god** is one of the spirits or beings that are believed to have power over a particular part of the world or nature. □ *...Zeus, king of the gods.* [from Old English] **4 thank God** → see **thank**

**god|dess** /gɒdɪs/ (**goddesses**) N-COUNT In many religions, a **goddess** is a female spirit or being that is believed to have power over a particular part of the world or nature. □ *...Diana, the goddess of hunting.* [from Old English]

**GOES** /dʒi oʊ e ɛs/ The **GOES** program is a series of satellites that send back information to Earth about environmental and weather conditions. **GOES** is an abbreviation for "Geostationary Operational Environmental Satellite."

goggles

**gog|gles** /gɒgᵊlz/ N-PLURAL **Goggles** are large glasses that fit closely to your face around your eyes to protect them from such things as water or wind.

**going** /goʊɪŋ/ **1** PHRASE If you say that something **is going to** happen, you mean that it will happen in the future, usually quite soon. □ *I think it's going to be successful.* □ *You're going to enjoy this.* **2** PHRASE You say that you **are going to** do something to express your intention or determination to do it. □ *I'm going to go to bed.* □ *He announced that he's going to resign.* **3** N-UNCOUNT You use **the going** to talk about how easy or difficult it is to do something. You can also say that something is, for example, **hard going** or **tough going**. □ *She will support him when the going gets tough.* **4** ADJ The **going** rate for something is the usual amount of money that you expect to pay or receive for it. □ *...the going price for oil.* **5** → see also **go** **6** PHRASE If someone or something **has a** lot **going for** them, they have a lot of advantages. □ *This school has a lot going for it.* **7** PHRASE When you **get going**, you start doing something or start

a journey, especially after a delay. □ *The plane leaves in two hours so I've got to get going.* **8** PHRASE If you **keep going**, you continue doing things or doing a particular thing. □ *She kept going even when she was sick.* [from Old English]
→ see also **will**

### Usage   going to

*Going to* and the present continuous are both used to talk about the future. *Going to* is used to describe things that you intend to do: *I'm going to call my sister tonight.* The present continuous is used to talk about things that are already planned or decided: *We are meeting for lunch on Saturday at noon.*

**goings-on** N-PLURAL If you describe events or activities as **goings-on**, you mean that they are strange, interesting, amusing, or dishonest. □ *A reporter found out about all the goings-on in the company.*

**gold** /goʊld/ (**golds**) **1** N-UNCOUNT **Gold** is a valuable, yellow-colored metal that is used for making jewelry and ornaments, and as an international currency. □ *...a ring made of gold.* □ *The price of gold was going up.* **2** N-UNCOUNT **Gold** is jewelry and other things that are made of gold. □ *We handed over all our gold and money.* **3** COLOR Something that is **gold** is a bright yellow color, and is often shiny. □ *He wore a black and gold shirt.* [from Old English]
→ see **metal, mineral, money**

**gold|en** /goʊldᵊn/ **1** ADJ Something that is **golden** is bright yellow in color. □ *She combed her golden hair.* **2** ADJ **Golden** things are made of gold. □ *...a golden chain.* **3** ADJ If you describe something as **golden**, you mean it is wonderful because it is likely to be successful and rewarding, or because it is the best of its kind. □ *This is a golden opportunity for peace.* [from Old English]

**gold|fish** /goʊldfɪʃ/ (**goldfish**) N-COUNT **Goldfish** are small gold or orange fish which are often kept as pets.
→ see **aquarium**

**gold med|al** (**gold medals**) N-COUNT A **gold medal** is a medal made of gold which is awarded as first prize in a contest or competition. □ *Her dream is to win a gold medal at the Winter Olympics.*

**golf** /gɒlf/ N-UNCOUNT **Golf** is a game in which you use long sticks called clubs to hit a small, hard ball into holes that are spread out over a large area of grassy land. □ *Do you play golf?* ● **golf|er** (**golfers**) N-COUNT □ *...one of the world's best golfers.* ● **golf|ing** N-UNCOUNT □ *You can play tennis or go golfing.* □ *...golfing buddies.* [from Middle Dutch]
→ see Picture Dictionary: **golf**
→ see **golf**

**golf club** (**golf clubs**) **1** N-COUNT A **golf club** is a long, thin, metal stick with a piece of wood or metal at one end that you use to hit the ball in golf. **2** N-COUNT A **golf club** is a social organization which provides a golf course and a building to meet in for its members.

**golf course** (**golf courses**) N-COUNT A **golf course** is a large area of grass which is specially designed for people to play golf on.

**Golgi com|plex** /gɔldʒi kɒmplɛks, goʊl-/ also **Golgi body, Golgi apparatus** (**Golgi complexes**) N-COUNT The **Golgi complex** is a

**Picture Dictionary** golf

clubhouse

cart path

sand trap

green

golfer

sand trap

golf cart

golf club

golf ball

hole

green

g

structure inside the cells of animals and plants, which controls the production and secretion of substances such as proteins. [TECHNICAL] [from Italian]

**gone** /gɔn/ **1** Gone is the past participle of **go**. **2** ADJ When someone is **gone**, they have left the place where you are and are no longer there. When something is **gone**, it is no longer present or no longer exists. ❏ Things were hard for her while he was gone. ❏ He's already been gone four hours! [from Old English]

**gong** /gɔŋ/ (**gongs**) N-COUNT A gong is a large, flat, circular piece of metal that you hit with a hammer to make a sound like a loud bell. Gongs are sometimes used as musical instruments, or to give a signal that it is time to do something. [from Malay]
→ see **percussion**

**gon|na** /gɔnə/ Gonna is used in written English to represent the words "going to" when they are pronounced informally. ❏ What am I gonna do?

---

**good**

**❶** DESCRIBING QUALITY, EXPRESSING APPROVAL
**❷** BENEFIT
**❸** MORALLY RIGHT
**❹** OTHER USES

---

**❶ good** /gʊd/ (**better, best**) **1** ADJ **Good** means pleasant or enjoyable. ❏ We had a really good time. ❏ They wanted a better life. **2** ADJ **Good** means of a high quality, standard, or level. ❏ Good food is important to health. ❏ His parents wanted him to have the best possible education. **3** ADJ If you are **good at** something, you are skillful and successful at doing it. ❏ He was very good at his work. ❏ I'm not very good at singing. **4** ADJ A **good** idea, reason, method, or decision is a sensible or valid one. ❏ It's a good idea to keep your desk tidy. ❏ There is good reason to suspect that he's guilty. **5** ADJ Someone who is in a **good** mood is cheerful and pleasant to be with. ❏ She woke up in a good mood. ❏ He is full of charm and good humor. **6** ADJ You use **good** to emphasize the great extent or degree of something. ❏ We waited a good fifteen minutes. [from Old English] **7** → see also **best, better**

**Thesaurus** good Also look up :

ADJ. agreeable, enjoyable, nice, pleasant; (ant.) unpleasant **❶ 1**
able, capable, skilled; (ant.) unqualified, unskilled **❶ 3**

**❷ good** /gʊd/ **1** N-SING If something is done for **the good** of a person or organization, it is done in order to benefit them. ❏ He should resign for the good of the country. **2** N-UNCOUNT If you say that doing something is **no good** or does **not** do **any good**, you mean that doing it is not of any use or will not bring any success. ❏ It's no good worrying about it now. ❏ We gave them water, but it didn't do any good. [from Old English] **3** → see also **goods**

**❸ good** /gʊd/ (**better, best**) **1** N-UNCOUNT **Good** is what is considered to be right according to moral standards or religious beliefs. ❏ ...the battle between good and evil. **2** ADJ Someone, especially a child, who is **good** is well-behaved. ❏ The children were very good. ❏ I'm going to be a good boy now. **3** ADJ Someone who is **good** is kind and thoughtful. ❏ You are good to me. ❏ Her good intentions did not work out the way she wanted. [from Old English] **4** → see also **best, better**

**❹ good** /gʊd/ **1** PHRASE **"As good as"** can be used to mean "almost." ❏ His career is as good as finished. **2** PHRASE If something changes or disappears **for good**, it never changes back or comes back as it was before. ❏ These forests may be gone for good. **3** PHRASE If someone **makes good** a threat or promise or **makes good on** it, they do what they have threatened or promised to do. ❏ I am sure they will make good on their promises. [from Old English]

**good after|noon** CONVENTION You say "**Good afternoon**" when you are greeting someone in the afternoon. [FORMAL]

**good|bye** /gʊdbaɪ/ (**goodbyes**) also **good-bye**
**1** CONVENTION You say "**Goodbye**" to someone when you or they are leaving, or at the end of a telephone conversation. **2** N-COUNT When you say your **goodbyes**, you say something such as "Goodbye" when you leave. ❏ They said their goodbyes at the airport. ❏ Perry and I exchanged goodbyes.

**good eve|ning** CONVENTION You say "**Good evening**" when you are greeting someone in the evening. [FORMAL]

**good guy** (**good guys**) N-COUNT You can refer to the good characters in a movie or story as the **good guys**. You can also refer to the **good guys** in a situation in real life. [INFORMAL] ❑ *We're the good guys in this situation.*

**good-humored** ADJ A **good-humored** person or atmosphere is pleasant and cheerful. ❑ *Charles remained very good-humored.* ❑ *It was a good-humored meeting.*

**goodie** /gʊdi/ (**goodies**) → see **goody**

**good-looking** (**better-looking**, **best-looking**) ADJ Someone who is **good-looking** has an attractive face. ❑ *Katy noticed him because he was good-looking.*

**good morn|ing** CONVENTION You say "Good morning" when you are greeting someone in the morning. [FORMAL]

**good-natured** ADJ A **good-natured** person or animal is naturally friendly and does not get angry easily. ❑ *He seems like a good-natured person.*

**good|ness** /gʊdnɪs/ ■ EXCLAM People sometimes say "**goodness**" or "**my goodness**" to express surprise. ❑ *Goodness, I wonder how that happened?* ■ **thank goodness** → see **thank** ■ N-UNCOUNT **Goodness** is the quality of being kind, helpful, and honest. ❑ *He has faith in human goodness.* [from Old English]

**goods** /gʊdz/ N-PLURAL **Goods** are things that are made to be sold. ❑ *Companies sell goods or services.* [from Old English]

| **Word Partnership** | Use *goods* with : |
| --- | --- |
| V. | **buy** goods, **sell** goods, **transport** goods |
| N. | **consumer** goods, **delivery of** goods, **exchange of** goods, **variety of** goods |
| ADJ. | **sporting** goods, **stolen** goods |

**good|will** /gʊdwɪl/ N-UNCOUNT **Goodwill** is a friendly or helpful attitude toward other people, countries, or organizations. ❑ *I invited them to dinner to show my goodwill.*

**goody** /gʊdi/ (**goodies**) also **goodie** N-COUNT You can refer to pleasant, exciting, or attractive things as **goodies**. [INFORMAL] ❑ *...a little bag of goodies.*

**goody bag** (**goody bags**) ■ N-COUNT A **goody bag** is a bag of little gifts, often given away by manufacturers in order to encourage people to try their products. [INFORMAL] ■ N-COUNT A **goody bag** is a bag of little gifts or candy that children are sometimes given at a children's party.

**goof** /guf/ (**goofs**, **goofing**, **goofed**) [from Old French]
▸ **goof off** PHR-VERB If someone **goofs off**, they spend their time doing nothing, often when they should be working. [INFORMAL] ❑ *I goofed off all day.*

**goose** /gus/ (**geese**) ■ N-COUNT A **goose** is a large bird that has a long neck and webbed feet. ❑ *Geese are often raised for their meat.* ■ N-UNCOUNT **Goose** is the meat from a goose that has been cooked. ❑ *...roast goose.* [from Old English]

**gore** /gɔr/ (**gores**, **goring**, **gored**) ■ V-T If someone **is gored** by an animal, they are badly wounded by its horns or tusks. ❑ *The farmer was gored by a bull.* ■ N-UNCOUNT **Gore** is blood from a wound that has become thick. ❑ *There was blood and gore on the sidewalk.* [from Old English]

**gorge** /gɔrdʒ/ (**gorges**, **gorging**, **gorged**) ■ N-COUNT A **gorge** is a deep, narrow valley with very steep sides, usually where a river passes through mountains or an area of hard rock. ❑ *...the deep gorge between the hills.* ■ V-T/V-I If you **gorge on** something or **gorge yourself on** it, you eat lots of it in a very greedy way. ❑ *We gorged on chocolate.* [from Old French]
→ see **river**

**gor|geous** /gɔrdʒəs/ ADJ Someone or something that is **gorgeous** is very pleasant or attractive. [INFORMAL] ❑ *It's a gorgeous day.* ❑ *You look gorgeous.* [from Old French]

**go|ril|la** /gərɪlə/ (**gorillas**) N-COUNT A **gorilla** is a very large ape. [from New Latin]
→ see **primate**

**gos|pel** /gɒspəl/ (**gospels**) ■ N-COUNT In the New Testament of the Bible, the **Gospels** are the four books which describe the life and teachings of Jesus Christ. ❑ *...St. Matthew's Gospel.* ■ N-UNCOUNT **Gospel** or **gospel music** is a style of religious music that uses strong rhythms and vocal harmony. ❑ *I used to sing gospel.* ■ N-UNCOUNT If you take something **as gospel**, or as **the gospel truth**, you believe that it is completely true. ❑ *This is the gospel truth, I promise.* [from Old English]

**gos|sip** /gɒsɪp/ (**gossips**, **gossiping**, **gossiped**) ■ N-UNCOUNT; N-SING **Gossip** is informal conversation, often about other people's private business. ❑ *There has been gossip about the reasons for his absence.* ■ V-RECIP If you **gossip with** someone, you talk informally, especially about other people or local events. You can also say that people **gossip**. ❑ *They sat at the kitchen table gossiping.* ❑ *Eva gossiped with Sarah.* ■ N-COUNT If you describe someone as a **gossip**, you disapprove of them because they enjoy talking about the private business of other people. ❑ *He was a terrible gossip.* [from Old English]

**got** /gɒt/ ■ **Got** is the past tense and sometimes the past participle of **get**. ■ PHRASE You use **have got** to say that someone has a particular thing, or to mention a quality or characteristic that someone or something has. In informal American English, people sometimes just use "got." [SPOKEN] ❑ *I've got a coat just like this.* ❑ *He asked, "You got any identification?"* ■ PHRASE You use **have got to** when you are saying that something is necessary or must happen in the way stated. In informal American English, the "have" is sometimes omitted. [SPOKEN] ❑ *I'm not happy with the situation, but I've got to accept it.* ❑ *Sometimes you got to admit you're wrong.* ■ PHRASE People sometimes use **have got to** in order to emphasize that they are certain that something is true, because of the facts or circumstances involved. In informal American English, the "have" is sometimes omitted. [SPOKEN] ❑ *"You've got to be joking!" he replied.* [from Old English]

**Goth|ic** /gɒθɪk/ ■ ADJ **Gothic** architecture and religious art was produced in the Middle Ages. Its features include tall pillars, high curved ceilings, and pointed arches. ❑ *...a huge Gothic cathedral.* ❑ *...Gothic stained glass windows.* ■ ADJ In **Gothic** stories, strange, mysterious adventures happen in dark and lonely places such as graveyards and old castles. ❑ *This novel is typical Gothic horror.* [from French]

**got|ta** /gɒtə/ **Gotta** is used in written English to represent the words "got to" when they are pronounced informally, with the meaning "have to" or "must." ❑ *We gotta eat.*

**got|ten** /gɒtᵊn/ **Gotten** is the past participle of **get** in American English. ❑ *Since then, the company has gotten much bigger.*

**gouge** /ɡaʊdʒ/ (**gouges, gouging, gouged**) **1** V-T If you **gouge** something, you make a hole or a long cut in it, usually with a pointed object. ❑ *He gouged the desk with a screwdriver.* **2** V-T If you say that a business **gouges** its customers, you mean that it forces them to pay an unfairly high price for its goods or services. [INFORMAL] ❑ *Banks have been accused of gouging their customers.* [from French] ▸ **gouge out** PHR-VERB To **gouge out** a piece or part of something means to cut, dig, or force it from the surrounding surface. You can also **gouge out** a hole in the ground. ❑ *He gouged a rock out of the dirt.*

**gour|met** /ɡʊərmeɪ, ɡʊərmeɪ / (**gourmets**) **1** ADJ **Gourmet** food is nicer or more unusual or sophisticated than ordinary food. ❑ *…gourmet food stores.* ❑ *Both of us love gourmet cooking and fine wine.* **2** N-COUNT A **gourmet** is someone who enjoys good food and drink, and knows a lot about them. ❑ *…a restaurant popular with gourmets.* [from French]

**gov|ern** /ɡʌvərn/ (**governs, governing, governed**) **1** V-T To **govern** a place such as a country, or its people, means to officially control and organize its economic, social, and legal systems. ❑ *The people choose who they want to govern their country.* **2** V-T If a situation or activity **is governed by** a particular factor, rule, or force, it is controlled by that factor, rule, or force. ❑ *The insurance industry is governed by strict rules.* [from Old French]

| **Thesaurus** | *govern* | Also look up : |

V. administer, command, control, direct, guide, head up; (ant.) lead, manage, reign **1**

**gov|ern|ment** /ɡʌvərnmənt/ (**governments**) **1** N-COUNT The **government** of a country is the group of people who are responsible for governing it. ❑ *The government has decided to make changes.* ❑ *…democratic governments in countries like Britain and the U.S.* **2** N-UNCOUNT **Government** consists of the activities, methods, and principles involved in governing a country or other political unit. ❑ *…our system of government.* ● **gov|ern|men|tal** /ɡʌvərnmentᵊl/ ADJ **Governmental** means relating to a particular government, or to the practice of governing a country. ❑ *…a governmental agency.* [from Old French]
→ see **country**

**gov|er|nor** /ɡʌvərnər/ (**governors**) **1** N-COUNT; N-TITLE In some systems of government, a **governor** is a person who is in charge of the political administration of a state, colony, or region. ❑ *He was governor of Iowa.* **2** N-COUNT A **governor** is a member of a committee which controls an organization such as a university or a hospital. ❑ *…the board of governors at City University, Bellevue.* [from Old French]

**gown** /ɡaʊn/ (**gowns**)

**1** N-COUNT A **gown** is a long dress which women wear on formal occasions. ❑ *She was wearing a ball gown.* **2** N-COUNT A **gown** is a loose black garment worn on formal occasions by people such as lawyers and academics. ❑ *…a headmaster in a long black gown.* [from Old French]

gown

**GP** /dʒi pi/ (**GPs**) also **G.P.** N-COUNT A **GP** is a doctor who does not specialize in any particular area of medicine, but who has a medical practice in which he or she treats all types of illness. **GP** is an abbreviation for "general practitioner." ❑ *Her husband called their local GP.*

**GPA** /dʒi pi eɪ/ (**GPAs**) N-COUNT **GPA** is an abbreviation for **grade point average**. ❑ *You need a good GPA to get into graduate school.*

**grab** /ɡræb/ (**grabs, grabbing, grabbed**) **1** V-T If you **grab** something, you take it or pick it up suddenly and roughly. ❑ *I grabbed her hand.* **2** V-I If you **grab at** something, you try to grab it. ❑ *He was grabbing at the handle.* ● **Grab** is also a noun. ❑ *I made a grab for the letter.* **3** to **grab hold of** → see **hold** **4** PHRASE If something is **up for grabs**, it is available to anyone who is interested. [INFORMAL] ❑ *His job is up for grabs.* [from Middle Low German]

| **Thesaurus** | *grab* | Also look up : |

V. capture, catch, seize, snap up; (ant.) release **1**

**grab bag** (**grab bags**) **1** N-COUNT A **grab bag** is a game in which you take a prize out of a container full of hidden prizes. **2** N-COUNT A **grab bag of** things, ideas, or people is a varied group of them. ❑ *The movie is just a grab bag of jokes.*

| **Word Link** | *grac ≈ pleasing : dis*grace, grace, graceful |

**grace** /ɡreɪs/ (**graces, gracing, graced**) **1** N-UNCOUNT If someone moves with **grace**, they move in a smooth, controlled, and attractive way. ❑ *He moved with the grace of a dancer.* **2** V-T If you say that something **graces** a place or a person, you mean that it makes them more attractive. [FORMAL] ❑ *Beautiful antique furniture graces their home.* **3** N-VAR When someone says **grace** before or after a meal, they say a prayer in which they thank God for the food and ask Him to bless it. ❑ *Will you say grace?* [from Old French]

**grace|ful** /ɡreɪsfᵊl/ **1** ADJ Someone or something that is **graceful** moves in a smooth and controlled way that is attractive to watch. ❑ *His movements were smooth and graceful.* ● **grace|ful|ly** ADV ❑ *She stepped gracefully onto the stage.* **2** ADJ Something that is **graceful** is attractive because it has a pleasing shape or style. ❑ *His handwriting was flowing and graceful.* [from Old French]

**gra|cious** /ɡreɪʃəs/ **1** ADJ If someone is **gracious**, they are polite and considerate. [FORMAL] ❑ *She gave a gracious speech of thanks.* ● **gra|cious|ly** ADV ❑ *They graciously declined our invitation.* **2** ADJ You use **gracious** to describe the comfortable way of life of wealthy people. ❑ *…gracious suburbs with swimming pools and tennis courts.* [from Old French]

**grad** /ɡræd/ (**grads**) N-COUNT A **grad** is a **graduate**. [INFORMAL]

**grade** /ɡreɪd/ (**grades, grading, graded**) ◼ V-T If something **is graded**, its quality is judged, and it is often given a number or a name that indicates how good or bad it is. ❑ *Restaurants are graded according to the quality of the food and service.* ❑ *Teachers grade the students' work from A to E.* ◼ N-COUNT The **grade** of a product is its quality. ❑ *...a good grade of wood.* ◼ N-COUNT Your **grade** in an examination or piece of written work is the mark you get, usually in the form of a letter or number, that indicates your level of achievement. ❑ *The best grade you can get is an A.* ◼ N-COUNT Your **grade** in a company or organization is your level of importance or your rank. ❑ *She thinks she should move to a higher grade.* ◼ N-COUNT In the United States, a **grade** is a group of classes in which all the children are of a similar age. When you are six years old you go into the first grade and you leave school after the twelfth grade. ❑ *Mr. White teaches first grade.* ◼ N-COUNT A **grade** is a slope. ❑ *She drove up a steep grade.* ◼ N-COUNT Someone's **grade** is their military rank. ❑ *I was a naval officer, lieutenant junior grade.* ◼ PHRASE If someone **makes the grade**, they succeed, especially by reaching a particular standard. ❑ *She wanted to be a dancer but failed to make the grade.* [from French]

**grade point av|er|age** (**grade point averages**) also **grade-point average** N-COUNT A student's **grade point average** is a measure of their academic achievement, based on an average of all the grades they receive. ❑ *She had the highest grade point average in the class.*

**gradu|al** /ɡrædʒuəl/ ADJ A **gradual** change or process occurs in small stages over a long period of time, rather than suddenly. ❑ *Losing weight is a gradual process.* ● **gradu|al|ly** /ɡrædʒuəli/ ADV ❑ *We are gradually learning to use the new computer system.* [from Medieval Latin]

**gradu|ate** (**graduates, graduating, graduated**)

> The noun is pronounced /ɡrædʒuɪt/. The verb is pronounced /ɡrædʒueɪt/.

◼ N-COUNT A **graduate** is a student who has successfully completed a course at a high school, college, or university. ❑ *His parents are both college graduates.* ◼ V-I When a student **graduates**, they complete their studies successfully and leave their school or university. ❑ *Her son just graduated from high school.* ◼ V-I If you **graduate from** one thing **to** another, you go from a less important job or position to a more important one. ❑ *He graduated to a job as assistant manager.* [from Medieval Latin] → see **graduation**

**gradu|at|ed** /ɡrædʒueɪtɪd/ ADJ **Graduated** jars are marked with lines and numbers which show particular measurements. [from Medieval Latin]

**gradu|ate stu|dent** (**graduate students**) N-COUNT In the United States, a **graduate student** is a student with a first degree from a university who is studying or doing research at a more advanced level.

**gradua|tion** /ɡrædʒueɪʃⁿn/ (**graduations**) ◼ N-UNCOUNT **Graduation** is the successful completion of a course of study at a university, college, or school, for which you receive a degree or diploma. ❑ *What are your plans after graduation?* ◼ N-COUNT A **graduation** is a special ceremony at a university, college, or school, at which certificates are given to students who have completed their studies. ❑ *Her parents came to her graduation.* [from Medieval Latin] → see Word Web: **graduation**

**graf|fi|ti** /ɡrəfiti/ N-UNCOUNT **Graffiti** is words or pictures that are written or drawn in public places, for example on walls or posters. ❑ *There was graffiti all over the walls.* [from Italian] → see **crime**

**graft** /ɡræft/ (**grafts, grafting, grafted**) ◼ N-COUNT A **graft** is a piece of healthy skin or bone, or a healthy organ, which is attached to a damaged part of your body by a medical operation in order to replace it. ❑ *She had a skin graft on her arm.* ◼ V-T If a piece of healthy skin or bone or a healthy organ **is grafted onto** a damaged part of your body, it is attached to that part of your body by a medical operation. ❑ *A layer of skin is grafted onto the burns.* ◼ V-T If a part of one plant or tree **is grafted** onto another plant or tree, they are joined together so that they will become one plant or tree, often in order to produce a new variety. [from Old French]

**gra|ham crack|er** /ɡreɪəm krækər/ (**graham crackers**) N-COUNT A **graham cracker** is a thin, crisp cookie made from wholewheat flour.

**grain** /ɡreɪn/ (**grains**) ◼ N-COUNT A **grain of** wheat, rice, or other cereal crop is a seed from it. ❑ *...a grain of wheat.* ◼ N-VAR **Grain** is a cereal crop, especially wheat or corn, that has been harvested and is used for food or in trade. ❑ *...a bag of grain.* ◼ N-COUNT A **grain of** something such as sand or salt is a tiny, hard piece of it. ❑ *...a grain of sand.* ◼ N-SING A **grain of** a quality is a very small amount of it. ❑ *There's a grain of truth in what he says.* ◼ N-SING The **grain** of a piece of wood is the direction of its fibers. You can also refer to the pattern of lines on the surface of the wood as the **grain**. ❑ *Paint the wood in the direction of the grain.* ◼ PHRASE If an idea or action **goes against the**

---

**Word Web**        graduation

**High school** and **college graduations** are important **events** for students. This **ceremony** tells the world that the **student** is educated. In college, **graduates** receive different types of **diplomas** depending on their subject and level of study. After four years of study, students earn a Bachelor of Arts or Bachelor of Science **degree**. A Master of Arts or Master of Science usually takes one or two more years. The PhD, or doctor of philosophy degree, may require several more years. In addition, a PhD student must write a **thesis** and defend it in front of a group of **professors**.

**g**

| Word Web | grain |
|---|---|

People first began **cultivating grain** about 10,000 years ago in Asia. Working in groups made growing and **harvesting** the **crop** easier. This probably led Stone Age people to live in communities. Today grain is still the principal food source for humans and domestic animals. Half of all the farmland in the world is used to produce grain. The most popular are **wheat, rice, corn,** and **oats.** An individual kernel of grain is actually a dry, one-seeded **fruit.** It combines the walls of the seed and the flesh of the fruit. Grain is often **ground** into **flour** or meal.

**grain,** it is very difficult for you to accept it or do it, because it conflicts with your ideas, beliefs, or principles. ❏ *Paying more taxes goes against the grain for him.* [from Old French]
→ see Word Web: **grain**
→ see **rice**

**gram** /græm/ (**grams**) N-COUNT A **gram** is a unit of weight. One thousand grams are equal to one kilogram. ❏ *A soccer ball weighs about 400 grams.* [from French]

**gram|mar** /græmər/ **1** N-UNCOUNT **Grammar** is the ways that words can be put together in order to make sentences. ❏ *You need to know the basic rules of grammar.* **2** N-UNCOUNT Someone's **grammar** is the way in which they obey or do not obey the rules of grammar when they write or speak. ❏ *His vocabulary was large and his grammar was excellent.* [from Old French]
→ see **English**

**gram|mar school** (**grammar schools**) N-VAR A **grammar school** is the same as an **elementary school.** ❏ *Jenny came home from grammar school.*

**gram|mati|cal** /grəmætɪkªl/ **1** ADJ **Grammatical** is used to indicate that something relates to grammar. ❏ *...a book of grammatical rules.* **2** ADJ If language is **grammatical,** it is considered correct because it obeys the rules of grammar. ❏ *The test will show whether students can write grammatical English.* [from Old French]

**gramme** /græm/ (**grammes**) → see **gram**

**grand** /grænd/ (**grander, grandest, grand**)

The form **grand** is used as the plural for meaning **5**.

**1** ADJ If you describe a building or a piece of scenery as **grand,** you mean that its size or appearance is very impressive. ❏ *The courthouse is a grand building in the center of town.* **2** ADJ **Grand** plans or actions are intended to achieve important results. ❏ *He had a grand design to change the entire future of the United States.* **3** ADJ People who are **grand** think they are important or socially superior. ❏ *He is grander than the Prince of Wales.* **4** ADJ A **grand** total is one that is the final amount or the final result of a calculation. ❏ *We collected a grand total of $220,329.* **5** N-COUNT A **grand** is a thousand dollars or a thousand pounds. [INFORMAL] ❏ *She makes at least 80 grand a year.* [from Old French]

**gran|dad** /grændæd/ (**grandads**) → see **granddad**

**grand|child** /græntʃaɪld/ (**grandchildren**) N-COUNT Someone's **grandchild** is the child of their son or daughter. ❏ *Mary loves her grandchildren.*

**grand|dad** /grændæd/ (**granddads**) N-COUNT,

N-VOC Your **granddad** is your grandfather. [INFORMAL] ❏ *My granddad is 85.*

**grand|daugh|ter** /grændɔtər/ (**granddaughters**) N-COUNT Someone's **granddaughter** is the daughter of their son or daughter. ❏ *This is my granddaughter Amelia.*

**gran|deur** /grændʒər/ **1** N-UNCOUNT If something such as a building or a piece of scenery has **grandeur,** it is impressive because of its size, its beauty, or its power. ❏ *...the grandeur and beauty of the landscape of South America.* **2** N-UNCOUNT Someone's **grandeur** is the great importance and social status that they have, or think they have. ❏ *He is too concerned with his own grandeur.* [from Old French]

**grand|fa|ther** /grænfɑðər/ (**grandfathers**) N-COUNT Your **grandfather** is the father of your father or mother. ❏ *His grandfather was a professor.*
→ see **family**

**gran|di|ose** /grændiouss/ ADJ If you describe something as **grandiose,** you mean it is bigger or more elaborate than necessary; used to show disapproval. ❏ *None of his grandiose plans worked.* [from French]

**grand jury** (**grand juries**) N-COUNT A **grand jury** is a jury, usually in the United States, which considers a criminal case in order to decide if someone should be tried in a court of law. ❏ *They gave evidence before a grand jury in Washington.*

**grand|ma** /grænmɑ/ (**grandmas**) N-COUNT Your **grandma** is your grandmother. [INFORMAL] ❏ *Grandma was from Scotland.*

**grand|moth|er** /grænmʌðər/ (**grandmothers**) N-COUNT Your **grandmother** is the mother of your father or mother. ❏ *My grandmothers were both teachers.*
→ see **family**

**grand|pa** /grænpɑ/ (**grandpas**) N-COUNT Your **grandpa** is your grandfather. [INFORMAL] ❏ *Grandpa was sitting in the yard.*

**grand|par|ent** /grænpeərənt, -pær-/ (**grandparents**) N-COUNT Your **grandparents** are the parents of your father or mother. ❏ *Tammy was raised by her grandparents.*

**grand slam** (**grand slams**) **1** ADJ In sports, a **grand slam** tournament is a major one. ❏ *She won 39 grand slam titles.* ● **Grand slam** is also a noun. ❏ *It's my first grand slam.* **2** N-COUNT If someone wins a **grand slam,** they win all the major tournaments in a season in a particular sport, for example in golf or tennis. ❏ *They won the grand slam in 1990.* **3** N-COUNT In baseball, a **grand slam** is a home run that is hit when there are players standing at all of the bases.

G

## Word Web   graph

There are three main elements in a **line** or **bar graph**:
- a **vertical axis** (the y-axis)
- a **horizontal axis** (the x-axis)
- at least one line or set of bars.

To understand a **graph**, do the following:
1. Read the **title** of the graph.
2. Read the **labels** and the **range** of numbers along the side (the **scale** or vertical axis).
3. Read the information along the bottom (horizontal axis) of the graph.
4. Determine what **units** the graph uses. This information can be found on the axis or in the **key**.
5. Look for patterns, groups, and differences.

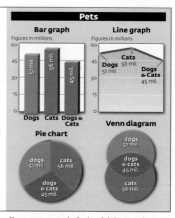

**grand|son** /ɡrænsʌn/ (**grandsons**) N-COUNT Someone's **grandson** is the son of their son or daughter. ❑ *My grandson's birthday was on Tuesday.*

**grand|stand** /ɡrændstænd/ (**grandstands**) N-COUNT A **grandstand** is a covered stand with rows of seats for people to sit on at sporting events.

| Word Link | ite ≈ mineral, rock : granite, graphite, meteorite |
|---|---|

**gran|ite** /ɡrænɪt/ (**granites**) N-UNCOUNT **Granite** is a very hard rock used in building. [from Italian]

**gran|ny** /ɡræni/ (**grannies**) also **grannie** N-COUNT Some people refer to their grandmother as **granny**. [INFORMAL] ❑ *I hugged my granny.*

**gra|no|la** /ɡrənoʊlə/ N-UNCOUNT **Granola** is a breakfast cereal that contains cereals, dried fruit and nuts. ❑ *I usually have granola for breakfast.*

**grant** /ɡrænt/ (**grants, granting, granted**) **1** N-COUNT A **grant** is an amount of money that a government or other institution gives to an individual or to an organization for a particular purpose such as education or home improvements. ❑ *They got a grant to research the disease.* **2** V-T If someone in authority **grants** you something, you are allowed to have it. [FORMAL] ❑ *France granted him political asylum.* ❑ *We should grant more independence to our children.* **3** V-T If you **grant that** something is true, you accept that it is true, even though your opinion about it does not change. ❑ *We grant that we made a mistake, but it was not intentional.* **4** PHRASE If you say that someone **takes** you **for granted**, you are complaining that they benefit from your help, efforts, or presence without showing that they are grateful. ❑ *She feels that her family take her for granted.* **5** PHRASE If you **take** something **for granted**, you believe that it is true or accept it as normal without thinking about it. ❑ *We take things like electricity and running water for granted.* **6** PHRASE If you **take it for granted that** something is true, you believe that it is true or you accept it as normal without thinking about it. ❑ *He seemed to take it for granted that everyone agreed with him.* [from Old French]

**grape** /ɡreɪp/ (**grapes**) **1** N-COUNT **Grapes** are small green or purple fruit which grow in bunches. ❑ *...a bunch of grapes.* **2** PHRASE If you describe someone's attitude as **sour grapes**, you mean that they say something is worthless or undesirable because they want it themselves but cannot have it. ❑ *These accusations are just sour grapes.* [from Old French]
→ see **fruit**

**grape|fruit** /ɡreɪpfrut/ (**grapefruit**)

The plural can also be **grapefruits**.

N-VAR A **grapefruit** is a large, round, yellow fruit that has a sharp, slightly bitter taste.

grapevines

**grape|vine** /ɡreɪpvaɪn/ N-SING If you hear or learn something **on** or **through the grapevine**, you hear it or learn it in casual conversation with other people. ❑ *I heard through the grapevine that he was planning to visit.*

| Word Link | graph ≈ writing : autograph, biography, graph |
|---|---|

**graph** /ɡræf/ (**graphs**) N-COUNT A **graph** is a mathematical diagram which shows the relationship between two or more sets of numbers or measurements. ❑ *The graph shows that prices have risen about 20 percent over the past five years.*
→ see Word Web: **graph**
→ see **chart**

**graph|ic** /ɡræfɪk/ (**graphics**) **1** ADJ If you say that a description or account of something unpleasant is **graphic**, you are emphasizing that it is clear and detailed. ❑ *...graphic descriptions of violence.* ● **graph|ical|ly** /ɡræfɪkli/ ADV ❑ *War was very graphically depicted in the movie.* **2** N-UNCOUNT **Graphics** is the activity of drawing or making pictures, especially in publishing, industry, or computing. ❑ *...a computer manufacturer that specializes in graphics.* **3** N-COUNT **Graphics** are drawings and pictures that are composed using simple lines. ❑ *The organization chose a new graphic to replace the old logo.* [from Latin]

| Word Link | ite ≈ mineral, rock : granite, graphite, meteorite |

**graph|ite** /grǽfaɪt/ N-UNCOUNT **Graphite** is a soft black substance that is a form of carbon. It is used in pencils and electrical equipment. [from German]

**grap|ple** /grǽpəl/ (**grapples, grappling, grappled**) **1** V-I If you **grapple with** a problem or difficulty, you try hard to solve it. ❑ *The new boss has to grapple with many tough problems.* **2** V-RECIP If you **grapple with** someone, you take hold of them and struggle with them, as part of a fight. You can also say that two people **grapple**. ❑ *He was grappling with another man.* [from Old French]

**grasp** /grǽsp/ (**grasps, grasping, grasped**) **1** V-T If you **grasp** something, you take it in your hand and hold it very firmly. ❑ *He grasped both my hands.* **2** N-SING A **grasp** is a very firm hold or grip. ❑ *He took her hand in a firm grasp.* **3** N-SING If something is **in** your **grasp**, you possess or control it. If something slips **from** your **grasp**, you lose it or lose control of it. ❑ *Victory slipped from her grasp.* **4** V-T If you **grasp** something that is complicated or difficult to understand, you understand it. ❑ *I don't think you have grasped how serious this problem is.* **5** N-SING A **grasp of** something is an understanding of it. ❑ *They have a good grasp of foreign languages.* **6** PHRASE If something is **within** someone's **grasp**, it is very likely that they will achieve it. ❑ *Peace is now within our grasp.* [from Low German]

**grass** /grǽs/ (**grasses**) N-VAR **Grass** is a very common plant consisting of large numbers of thin, spiky, green leaves that cover the surface of the ground. ❑ *We sat on the grass and ate our picnic.* [from Old English]
→ see **grassland, habitat, herbivore, plant**

**grass|hop|per** /grǽshɒpər/ (**grasshoppers**) N-COUNT A **grasshopper** is an insect that jumps high into the air and makes a high, vibrating sound with its long back legs .

**grass|land** /grǽslænd/ (**grasslands**) N-VAR **Grassland** is land covered with wild grass. ❑ *...areas of open grassland.*
→ see Word Web: **grassland**
→ see **habitat**

**grass|roots** /grǽsruːts/ N-PLURAL The **grassroots** of an organization or movement are the ordinary people who form the main part of it, rather than its leaders. ❑ *The grassroots of the party should help to choose its leader.*

**grassy** /grǽsi/ (**grassier, grassiest**) ADJ A **grassy** area of land is covered in grass. ❑ *Next to the river was a grassy bank.* [from Old English]

**grate** /greɪt/ (**grates, grating, grated**) **1** N-COUNT A **grate** is a framework of metal bars in a fireplace, which holds the wood or coal. ❑ *A fire burned in the grate.* **2** V-T If you **grate** food such as cheese or carrots, you rub it over a metal tool called a grater so that the food is cut into very small pieces. ❑ *Grate the cheese into a bowl.* **3** V-I When something **grates**, it rubs against something else, making a harsh, unpleasant sound. ❑ *His chair grated as he stood up.* **4** V-I If something such as someone's behavior **grates on** you or **grates**, it makes you feel annoyed. ❑ *His voice grates on me.* [from Old French]
→ see **cut**

**grate|ful** /greɪtfəl/ ADJ If you are **grateful for** something that someone has given you or done for you, you have warm, friendly feelings towards them and wish to thank them. ❑ *She was grateful to him for being so helpful.* ● **grate|ful|ly** ADV ❑ *"That's kind of you," Claire said gratefully.* [from Latin]

| Word Link | grat ≈ pleasing : congratulate, gratify, gratitude |

**grati|fy** /grǽtɪfaɪ/ (**gratifies, gratifying, gratified**) **1** V-T If you **are gratified** by something, it gives you pleasure or satisfaction. [FORMAL] ❑ *The teacher was gratified by her students' success.* ● **grati|fy|ing** ADJ ❑ *It's very gratifying when people appreciate what you do.* ● **grati|fi|ca|tion** /grǽtɪfɪkeɪʃən/ N-UNCOUNT ❑ *To his gratification, they all knew who he was.* **2** V-T If you **gratify** your own or another person's desire, you do what is necessary to please yourself or them. [FORMAL] ❑ *Gratify my curiosity and tell me why you're here.* ● **grati|fi|ca|tion** N-UNCOUNT ❑ *Children want instant gratification.* [from Latin]

**grati|tude** /grǽtɪtud/ N-UNCOUNT **Gratitude** is the state of feeling grateful. ❑ *I want to express my gratitude to everyone who has helped.* [from Medieval Latin]

**gra|tui|tous** /grətuːɪtəs/ ADJ If you describe something as **gratuitous**, you mean that it is unnecessary, and often harmful or upsetting. ❑ *There's too much gratuitous violence on TV.* ● **gra|tui|tous|ly** ADV ❑ *His comments were gratuitously offensive.* [from Latin]

**grave** /greɪv/ (**graves, graver, gravest**) **1** N-COUNT A **grave** is a place where a dead person is buried. ❑ *They visit her grave twice a year.* **2** ADJ A

---

| Word Web | grassland |

**Grasslands** are flat, open areas of land covered with **grass**. They get from 10 to 30 inches of rain per year. The **soil** there is deep and **fertile**. The **prairies** in the American Midwest used to be mostly grasslands. At that time, herds of bison, or **buffalo**, lived there along with antelopes. Because of the rich soil, almost all this prairie land has been converted to **agricultural** use. Very few buffalo or antelopes are still there. There are grasslands on every continent except Antarctica. In South America they are called pampas. In Europe they call them steppes and in Africa, savannas.

**grave** event or situation is very serious, important, and worrying. ❑ *The situation in his country is very grave.* • **grave|ly** ADV ❑ *They have gravely damaged the government's reputation.* **3** ADJ A **grave** person is quiet and serious in their appearance or behavior. ❑ *He looked grave and worried.* • **grave|ly** ADV ❑ *She said gravely that they were in danger.* [Sense 1 from Old English. Senses 2 and 3 from Old French.]

**grav|el** /ɡrǽvªl/ N-UNCOUNT **Gravel** consists of very small stones. It is often used to make paths. ❑ *...a gravel path.* [from Old French]

**grav|eled** /ɡrǽvªld/ ADJ A **graveled** path, road, or area has a surface made of gravel. [from Old French]

**grave|yard** /ɡréɪvɑrd/ (**graveyards**) N-COUNT A **graveyard** is an area of land where dead people are buried. ❑ *They went to the graveyard to put flowers on her grave.* [from Old English]

**grave|yard shift** (**graveyard shifts**) N-COUNT If someone works **the graveyard shift**, they work during the night.

**gravi|ta|tion|al** /ɡrævɪtéɪʃənªl/ ADJ **Gravitational** means relating to or resulting from the force of gravity. [TECHNICAL] ❑ *...the earth's gravitational pull.* [from Latin]
→ see **tide**

**gravi|ta|tion|al po|ten|tial en|er|gy** N-UNCOUNT **Gravitational potential energy** is the stored energy that an object has because of its height above the Earth. [TECHNICAL]

**gra|vit|ro|pism** /ɡrǽvɪtrəpɪzəm/ N-UNCOUNT **Gravitropism** is the tendency of a plant to grow either downward or upward in response to the force of gravity. [TECHNICAL]

**grav|ity** /ɡrǽvɪti/ **1** N-UNCOUNT **Gravity** is the force that causes things to drop to the ground. ❑ *...the force of gravity.* **2** N-UNCOUNT The **gravity of** a situation or event is its extreme importance or seriousness. ❑ *We didn't understand the gravity of the situation.* [from Latin]
→ see **moon**

**gra|vy** /ɡréɪvi/ (**gravies**) N-UNCOUNT **Gravy** is a sauce made from the juices that come from meat when it cooks. [from Old French]

**gray** /ɡréɪ/ (**grayer, grayest**) COLOR **Gray** is the color of ashes or of clouds on a rainy day. ❑ *...a gray suit.* [from Old English]
→ see **hair**

N. gray **eyes**, gray **hair**, **shades of** gray, gray **sky**, gray **suit**

**gray area** (**gray areas**) N-COUNT If you refer to something as a **gray area**, you mean that it is unclear. ❑ *At the moment, the law on discrimination is a gray area.*

**gray mat|ter** N-UNCOUNT You can refer to your intelligence or your brains as **gray matter**. [INFORMAL] ❑ *These puzzles will exercise your gray matter.*

**graze** /ɡréɪz/ (**grazes, grazing, grazed**) **1** V-T/V-I When animals **graze** or **are grazed**, they eat the grass or other plants that are growing in a particular place. You can also say that a field **is grazed** by animals. ❑ *Cows were grazing peacefully in the field.* ❑ *Horses grazed the meadow.* **2** V-T If

you **graze** a part of your body, you injure your skin by scraping against something. ❑ *I fell and grazed my knees.* **3** N-COUNT A **graze** is a small wound caused by scraping against something. ❑ *Cuts and grazes can be quite painful.* **4** V-T If something **grazes** another thing, it touches that thing lightly as it passes by. ❑ *The ball grazed the hitter's face.* [from Old English]
→ see **herbivore**

**grease** /ɡrís/ (**greases, greasing, greased**) **1** N-UNCOUNT **Grease** is a thick, oily substance which is put on the moving parts of cars and other machines in order to make them work smoothly. ❑ *His hands were covered in grease.* **2** V-T If you **grease** a part of a car, machine, or device, you put grease on it in order to make it work smoothly. ❑ *I greased the wheels.* **3** N-UNCOUNT **Grease** is an oily substance that is produced by your skin. ❑ *He needs to wash the grease out of his hair.* **4** N-UNCOUNT **Grease** is animal fat that is produced by cooking meat. ❑ *I could smell bacon grease.* **5** V-T If you **grease** a dish, you put a small amount of fat or oil around the inside of it in order to prevent food from sticking to it during cooking. ❑ *Grease two baking sheets.* [from Old French]

**greasy** /ɡrísi, -zi/ (**greasier, greasiest**) ADJ Something that is **greasy** has grease on it or in it. ❑ *He wiped the greasy counter.* [from Old French]

**great** /ɡréɪt/ (**greater, greatest, greats**) **1** ADJ You use **great** to describe something that is very large. ❑ *Inside the castle was a great hall.* **2** ADJ **Great** means large in amount or degree. ❑ *She lived to a great age.* • **great|ly** ADV [FORMAL] ❑ *He will be greatly missed.* **3** ADJ You use **great** to describe someone or something that is important, famous, or exciting. ❑ *...great scientific discoveries.* ❑ *He has the ability to be a great player.* • **great|ness** N-UNCOUNT ❑ *She dreamed of achieving greatness.* **4** EXCLAM If something is **great**, it is very good. ❑ *I thought it was a great idea.* ❑ *Oh great! You made a cake.* [from Old English]

**Great Red Spot** N-SING The **Great Red Spot** is a large area in the atmosphere of the planet Jupiter where a powerful storm has been taking place for hundreds of years.

**greed** /ɡríd/ N-UNCOUNT **Greed** is the desire to have more of something, such as food or money, than is necessary or fair. ❑ *People say that the world economy is based on greed.*

**greedy** /ɡrídi/ (**greedier, greediest**) ADJ If you describe someone as **greedy**, you mean that they want to have more of something such as food or money than is necessary or fair. ❑ *He criticized greedy bosses for giving themselves big raises.* • **greed|ily** ADV ❑ *Laurie ate the pastries greedily.* [from Old English]

**Greek thea|ter** N-UNCOUNT **Greek theater** is the style of theater associated with ancient Greece.

## Word Web  greenhouse effect

Over the past 100 years, the global average **temperature** has risen dramatically. Researchers believe that this **global warming** comes from added **carbon dioxide** and other **gases** in the **atmosphere**. With **water vapor**, they form a layer that holds in heat. It acts like the glass in a greenhouse. Scientists call this the **greenhouse effect**. Some natural causes of this warming may include increased **solar radiation** and tiny changes in the earth's orbit. However, human activities, such as **deforestation** and the use of **fossil fuels**, seem to be important causes.

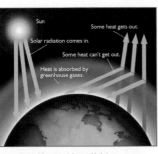

Sun
Solar radiation comes in.
Some heat gets out.
Some heat can't get out.
Heat is absorbed by greenhouse gases.

**green** /ɡriːn/ (**greener, greenest, greens**)
■ COLOR **Green** is the color of grass or leaves. ❑ *She wore a green dress.* ■ ADJ A place that is **green** is covered with grass, plants, and trees. ❑ *The city has lots of parks and green spaces.* ● **green|ness** N-UNCOUNT ❑ *...the greenness of the river valley.* ■ ADJ **Green** issues and political movements relate to or are concerned with the protection of the environment. ❑ *...the Green movement.* ■ N-COUNT A **green** is a smooth, flat area of grass around a hole on a golf course. ❑ *...the 18th green.* [from Old English]
→ see color, golf, rainbow

**green|ery** /ɡriːnəri/ N-UNCOUNT Plants that make a place look attractive are referred to as **greenery**. ❑ *Adriana misses the greenery of the mountains where she grew up.* [from Old English]

**green|house** /ɡriːnhaʊs/ (**greenhouses**) N-COUNT A **greenhouse** is a glass building in which you grow plants that need to be protected from bad weather.
→ see barn

**green|house ef|fect** N-SING The greenhouse **effect** is the problem caused by increased quantities of gases such as carbon dioxide in the air. ❑ *...gases that contribute to the greenhouse effect.*
→ see Word Web: greenhouse effect
→ see ozone

**green|house gas** (**greenhouse gases**) N-VAR **Greenhouse gases** are the gases responsible for causing the greenhouse effect. The main greenhouse gas is carbon dioxide. ❑ *...an international treaty to limit greenhouse gases.*
→ see biosphere

**green on|ion** (**green onions**) N-COUNT **Green onions** are small onions with long green leaves.

**green plant** (**green plants**) N-COUNT **Green plants** are plants that get their energy by means of photosynthesis.

**green tea** (**green teas**) N-VAR **Green tea** is tea made from tea leaves that have been steamed and dried quickly. ❑ *...a cup of green tea.*

**greet** /ɡriːt/ (**greets, greeting, greeted**) ■ V-T When you **greet** someone, you say "Hello" or shake hands with them. ❑ *She greeted him when he came in from school.* ■ V-T If something **is greeted** in a particular way, people react to it in that way. ❑ *His comments were greeted with anger.* [from Old English]

**greet|ing** /ɡriːtɪŋ/ (**greetings**) N-VAR A **greeting** is something friendly that you say or do when you meet someone. ❑ *...a friendly greeting.* ❑ *They*

exchanged greetings. [from Old English]

**greet|ing card** (**greeting cards**) N-COUNT A **greeting card** is a folded card with a picture on the front and greetings inside that you give or send to someone, for example on their birthday.

**gre|nade** /ɡrɪneɪd/ (**grenades**) N-COUNT A **grenade** or a **hand grenade** is a small bomb that can be thrown by hand. ❑ *He threw a hand grenade.* [from French]

**grew** /ɡruː/ **Grew** is the past tense of **grow**. [from Old English]

**grey|hound** /ɡreɪhaʊnd/ (**greyhounds**) N-COUNT A **greyhound** is a dog with a thin body and long thin legs, which can run very fast. Greyhounds sometimes run in races and people bet on them. ❑ *...greyhound racing.*

**grid** /ɡrɪd/ (**grids**) ■ N-COUNT A **grid** is something which is in a pattern of straight lines that cross over each other, forming squares. On maps, the grid is used to help you find a particular thing or place. ❑ *...a metal grid.* ❑ *...a grid of narrow streets.* ■ N-COUNT A **grid** is a network of wires and cables by which sources of power, such as electricity, are distributed throughout a country or area. ❑ *...a breakdown in the power grids.*

**grid|lock** /ɡrɪdlɒk/ ■ N-UNCOUNT **Gridlock** is the situation that exists when all the roads in a particular place are so full of vehicles that none of them can move. ❑ *There was an accident on the freeway, creating gridlock.* ■ N-UNCOUNT You can use **gridlock** to refer to a situation in an argument or dispute when neither side is prepared to give in, so no agreement can be reached. ❑ *...political gridlock.*
→ see traffic

**grief** /ɡriːf/ (**griefs**) ■ N-VAR **Grief** is a feeling of extreme sadness. ❑ *She experienced terrible grief after he died.* ■ PHRASE If something **comes to grief**, it fails. If someone **comes to grief**, they fail in something they are doing, and may be hurt. ❑ *Their friendship came to grief over lack of money.*

### Word Link  griev ≈ heavy, serious : ag**griev**ed, **griev**ance, grie**v**e

**griev|ance** /ɡriːvəns/ (**grievances**) N-VAR If you have a **grievance** about something that has happened or been done, you believe that it was unfair. ❑ *She had a grievance against her employer.* [from Old French]

**grieve** /ɡriːv/ (**grieves, grieving, grieved**) V-I If you **grieve over** something, especially someone's death, you feel very sad about it. ❑ *He's grieving over* his dead wife. ❑ *I didn't have any time to grieve.* [from Old French]

**griev|ous** /grĩvəs/ ADJ If you describe something such as a loss as **grievous**, you mean that it is extremely serious or worrying in its effects. ❑ *There has been a very grievous mistake.* ● **griev|ous|ly** ADV ❑ *All these people have suffered grievously.* [from Old French]

**grill** /grɪl/ (**grills, grilling, grilled**) ◼ N-COUNT A **grill** is a flat frame of metal bars on which food

**grill**

can be cooked over a fire. ❑ *We cooked the fish on a grill over the fire.* ◻ V-T When you **grill** food, you cook it on metal bars above a fire or barbecue. ❑ *Grill the steaks for about 5 minutes each side.* ◼ V-T If you **grill** someone **about** something, you ask them a lot of questions for a long period of time. [INFORMAL] ❑ *The*

*teacher grilled us about what had happened.* ● **grill|ing** (**grillings**) N-COUNT ❑ *He got a grilling from the committee.* [from French]
→ see **cook**

**grille** /grɪl/ (**grilles**) also **grill** N-COUNT A **grille** is a framework of metal bars or wire which is placed in front of a window or a piece of machinery, in order to protect it or to protect people. ❑ *The window was protected by an iron grille.* [from Old French]

**grim** /grɪm/ (**grimmer, grimmest**) ◼ ADJ A situation or piece of information that is **grim** is unpleasant, depressing, and difficult to accept. ❑ *There was grim news about the economy yesterday.* ❑ *With rising crime and violence, the situation is grim.* ◻ ADJ A place that is **grim** is unattractive and depressing. ❑ *…a grim, industrial city.* [from Old English]

**gri|mace** /grɪməs, grɪmeɪs/ (**grimaces, grimacing, grimaced**) V-I If you **grimace**, you twist your face in an ugly way because you are annoyed, disgusted, or in pain. [WRITTEN] ❑ *When she tried to get up she grimaced.* ● **Grimace** is also a noun. ❑ *"This coffee is awful," he said with a grimace.* [from French]

**grin** /grɪn/ (**grins, grinning, grinned**) ◼ V-I When you **grin**, you smile broadly. ❑ *He grinned, delighted at the memory.* ❑ *Phillip grinned at her.* ◻ N-COUNT A **grin** is a broad smile. ❑ *She had a big grin on her face.* [from Old English]

**grind** /graɪnd/ (**grinds, grinding, ground**) ◼ V-T If you **grind** a substance such as corn, you crush it until it becomes a fine powder. ❑ *Grind some pepper into the sauce.* ◻ V-T If you **grind** something **into** a surface, you press and rub it hard into the surface using small circular or sideways movements. ❑ *He ground the toe of his boot into the gravel path.* ◼ N-SING If you refer to routine tasks or activities as a **grind**, you mean they are boring and take up a lot of time and effort. [INFORMAL] ❑ *Life is a terrible grind for most people.* ◼ PHRASE If a country's economy or something such as a process **grinds to a halt**, it gradually becomes slower or less active until it stops. ❑ *The peace process has ground to a halt.* ◼ PHRASE If a vehicle **grinds to a halt**, it stops slowly and noisily. ❑ *The truck ground to a halt after a*

hundred yards. [from Old English]
▶ **grind down** PHR-VERB If you say that someone **grinds** you **down**, you mean that they treat you very harshly and cruelly, reducing your confidence or your will to resist them. ❑ *Don't let people grind you down.*

**grind|er** /graɪndər/ (**grinders**) N-COUNT In a kitchen, a **grinder** is a device for crushing food such as coffee or meat into small pieces or into a powder. ❑ *…an electric coffee grinder.* [from Old English]

**grip** /grɪp/ (**grips, gripping, gripped**) ◼ V-T If you **grip** something, you take hold of it with your hand and continue to hold it firmly. ❑ *She gripped the rope.* ◻ N-COUNT A **grip** is a firm, strong hold on something. ❑ *He pulled the bag from her grip.* ◼ N-SING Someone's **grip on** something is the power and control they have over it. ❑ *The president maintains a strong grip on his country.* ◼ V-T If you **are gripped by** something, it affects you strongly and your attention is concentrated on it. ❑ *The audience was gripped by the dramatic story.* ● **grip|ping** ADJ ❑ *The film was a gripping thriller.* ◼ PHRASE If you **come to grips with** a problem, you consider it seriously, and start taking action to deal with it. ❑ *Our first job is to come to grips with the economy.* ◼ PHRASE If you **get a grip** on yourself, you make an effort to control or improve your behavior or work. ❑ *I was very frightened and I had to get a grip on myself.* [from Old English]

**gripe** /graɪp/ (**gripes, griping, griped**) ◼ V-I If you say that someone **is griping**, you mean they are annoying you because they keep on complaining about something. [INFORMAL] ❑ *Why is he griping when he has so much money?* ● **grip|ing** N-UNCOUNT ❑ *I don't like this constant griping.* ◻ N-COUNT A **gripe** is a complaint about something. [INFORMAL] ❑ *My only gripe is that the soup was a little cold.* [from Old English]

**gris|ly** /grɪzli/ (**grislier, grisliest**) ADJ Something that is **grisly** is extremely unpleasant, and usually involves death and violence. ❑ *…a story about a grisly murder.* [from Old English]

**grit** /grɪt/ (**grits, gritting, gritted**) ◼ N-UNCOUNT **Grit** is very small pieces of stone. ❑ *Tiny pieces of grit were stuck in his knee.* ◻ N-UNCOUNT If someone has **grit**, they have the determination and courage to continue doing something even though it is very difficult. ❑ *She showed a lot of grit.* ◼ N-PLURAL **Grits** are coarsely ground grains of corn which are cooked and eaten for breakfast or as part of a meal in the southern United States. ❑ *I want grits with my eggs.* ◼ PHRASE If you **grit** your **teeth**, you make up your mind to carry on even if the situation is very difficult. ❑ *We have to grit our teeth and finish the job.* [from Old English]

**grit|ty** /grɪti/ (**grittier, grittiest**) ◼ ADJ Something that is **gritty** contains grit, is covered with grit, or has a texture like that of grit. ❑ *The sheets fell on the gritty floor.* ◻ ADJ Someone who is **gritty** is brave and determined. ❑ *She proved how gritty she is.* [from Old English]

**groan** /groʊn/ (**groans, groaning, groaned**) ◼ V-I If you **groan**, you make a long, low sound because you are in pain, or because you are upset or unhappy about something. ❑ *He began to groan with pain.* ❑ *The man on the floor was groaning.* ● **Groan** is also a noun. ❑ *She let out a groan.* ◻ V-T If you **groan** something, you say it in a low, unhappy voice. ❏ *"My head hurts," Eric groaned.* [from Old English]

**gro|cer** /gr**ou**sər/ (**grocers**) N-COUNT A **grocer** is a storekeeper who sells foods such as flour, sugar, and canned foods. [from Old French]

**gro|cery** /gr**ou**səri, gr**ou**sri/ (**groceries**) **1** N-COUNT A **grocery** or a **grocery store** is a small store that sells foods such as flour, sugar, and canned goods. ❏ *They run a small grocery store.* **2** → see also **supermarket 3** N-PLURAL **Groceries** are foods you buy at a grocery or at a supermarket. ❏ *...a small bag of groceries.* [from Old French]

**groin** /gr**oi**n/ (**groins**) N-COUNT Your **groin** is the front part of your body between your legs. ❏ *He felt a pain in his groin.* [from English]

**groom** /gr**u**m/ (**grooms, grooming, groomed**) **1** N-COUNT A **groom** is the same as a **bridegroom**. ❏ *...the bride and groom.* **2** N-COUNT A **groom** is someone whose job is to look after the horses in a stable and to keep them clean. **3** V-T If you **groom** an animal, you clean its fur, usually by brushing it. ❏ *She groomed the horses regularly.* **4** V-T If you **are groomed for** a special job, someone prepares you for it by teaching you the skills you will need. ❏ *George was being groomed for the manager's job.* [from Old English]

**groomed** /gr**u**md/ ADJ You use **groomed** in expressions such as **well groomed** and **badly groomed** to say how neat and clean a person is. ❏ *...a very well groomed man.* [from Old English]

**groom|ing** /gr**u**mɪŋ/ N-UNCOUNT **Grooming** refers to the things that people do to keep themselves clean and make their face, hair, and skin look nice. ❏ *Men today take more care with personal grooming.* [from Old English]

**groove** /gr**u**v/ (**grooves**) N-COUNT A **groove** is a deep line cut into a surface. ❏ *Grooves had been worn in the table.* [from Dutch]

**grope** /gr**ou**p/ (**gropes, groping, groped**) **1** V-I If you **grope for** something that you cannot see, you try to find it by moving your hands around in order to feel it. ❏ *He groped for the door handle in the dark.* **2** V-T If you **grope** your **way** to a place, you move there, holding your hands in front of you and feeling the way because you cannot see anything. ❏ *I didn't turn on the light, but groped my way across the room.* **3** V-I If you **grope for** something, for example the solution to a problem, you try to think of it, when you have no real idea what it could be. ❏ *He groped for solutions to his problems.* [from English]

**gross** /gr**ou**s/ (**grosser, grossest, grosses, grossing, grossed**) **1** ADJ You use **gross** to describe something unacceptable or unpleasant to a very great amount, degree, or intensity. ❏ *...gross abuse of human rights.* ● **gross|ly** ADV ❏ *He was sentenced to nine years in prison after a grossly unfair trial.* **2** ADJ If you describe someone or something as **gross**, you think they are very unpleasant. [INFORMAL] ❏ *Some scenes in the movie were really gross.* **3** ADJ **Gross** means the total amount of something, especially money, before any has been taken away, for example in tax. ❏ *The account gives 10.4% gross interest or 7.8% net interest.* ● **Gross** is also an adverb. ❏ *Interest is paid gross.* [from Old French]

**Word Partnership** Use *gross* with :

| | |
|---|---|
| N. | act of gross **injustice**, gross **mismanagement**, gross **negligence 1** gross **income**, gross **margin 3** |
| V. | feel gross **2** |

**gro|tesque** /grout**ɛ**sk/ (**grotesques**) **1** ADJ You say that something is **grotesque** when it is so unnatural, unpleasant, and exaggerated that it upsets or shocks you. ❏ *The difference between the wealthy and the poor is grotesque.* ● **gro|tesque|ly** ADV ❏ *It was a grotesquely awful experience.* **2** ADJ If someone or something is **grotesque**, they are very ugly. ❏ *...a nightmare about grotesque monsters.* ● **gro|tesque|ly** ADV ❏ *...grotesquely ugly creatures.* [from French]

ground

**1** NOUN USES
**2** VERB AND ADJECTIVE USES
**3** PHRASES

**❶ ground** /gr**au**nd/ (**grounds**) **1** N-SING The **ground** is the surface of the earth or the floor of a room. ❏ *They were sitting on the ground.* ❏ *He fainted and fell to the ground.* **2** N-SING If you say that something takes place **on the ground**, you mean it takes place on the surface of the earth and not in the air. ❏ *Repairs are done while the plane is on the ground.* **3** N-COUNT You can use **ground** to refer to an area of land, sea, or air which is used for a particular activity. ❏ *There are great fishing grounds around the islands.* **4** N-PLURAL The **grounds** of a large or important building are the garden or area of land which surrounds it. ❏ *...the palace grounds.* **5** N-VAR You can use **ground** to refer to a place or situation in which particular methods or ideas can develop and be successful. ❏ *This company is a developing ground for new ideas.* **6** N-UNCOUNT **Ground** is used in expressions such as **gain ground**, **lose ground**, and **give ground** in order to indicate that someone gets or loses an advantage. ❏ *The team has won its last three games and is gaining ground.* **7** N-VAR If something is **grounds for** a feeling or action, it is a reason for it. If you do something **on the grounds of** a particular thing, that thing is the reason for your action. ❏ *There are some grounds for optimism.* ❏ *They denied his request on the grounds that it would cost too much money.* **8** N-COUNT The **ground** in an electric plug or piece of electrical equipment is the wire through which electricity passes into the ground and which makes the equipment safe. [from Old English]

**❷ ground** /gr**au**nd/ (**grounds, grounding, grounded**) **1** V-T If an argument, belief, or opinion **is grounded** in something, that thing is used to justify it. ❏ *Her argument was grounded in fact.* **2** V-T If an aircraft or its passengers **are grounded**, they are made to stay on the ground and are not allowed to take off. ❏ *Planes were grounded because of the bad weather.* **3** ADJ **Ground** meat has been cut into very small pieces in a machine. ❏ *The sausages are made of ground pork.* **4** **Ground** is the past tense and past participle of **grind.** [from Old English] **5** → see also **grounding** → see **grain**

**❸ ground** /gr**au**nd/ **1** PHRASE If something such as a project gets **off the ground**, it begins or

g

starts functioning. ❑ *We help small companies to get off the ground.* **2** PHRASE If you **stand** your **ground** or **hold** your **ground**, you do not run away from a situation, but face it bravely. ❑ *He was angry, but she stood her ground.* **3** PHRASE In a painting, the **middle ground** is the area between the foreground and the background. [from Old English]

**ground|ing** /ˈgraʊndɪŋ/ N-SING If you have a **grounding in** a subject, you know the basic facts or principles of that subject, especially as a result of a particular course of training or instruction. ❑ *The course provides a good grounding in mathematics.* [from Old English]

**ground rule** (**ground rules**) N-COUNT The **ground rules for** something are the basic principles on which future action will be based. ❑ *Parents and teenagers need to agree some ground rules.*

**grounds|keeper** /ˈgraʊndzkiːpər/ (**groundskeepers**) N-COUNT A **groundskeeper** is a person whose job is to look after a park or sports ground.

**ground|water** /ˈgraʊndwɔːtər/ N-UNCOUNT **Groundwater** is water that is found under the ground. Groundwater has usually passed down through the soil and become trapped by rocks.

**Word Link** ground ≈ bottom : back*ground*, *ground*work, under*ground*

**ground|work** /ˈgraʊndwɜːrk/ N-SING The **groundwork for** something is the early work on it which forms the basis for further work. ❑ *This meeting will prepare the groundwork for the task ahead.*

**ground zero** also **Ground Zero** N-UNCOUNT People sometimes use **ground zero** to refer to the site of a disaster such as a nuclear explosion. It is used especially to refer to the site of the destruction of the World Trade Center in New York City on September 11, 2001.

**group** /ˈgruːp/ (**groups, grouping, grouped**) **1** N-COUNT A **group of** people or things is a number of people or things that are together in one place at one time. ❑ *A small group of people stood on the street corner.* **2** N-COUNT A **group** is a set of people who have the same interests or aims, and who organize themselves to work or act together. ❑ *...members of an environmental group.* **3** N-COUNT A **group** is a set of people, organizations, or things which are considered together because they have something in common. ❑ *She is among the best players in her age group.* **4** N-COUNT A **group** is a number of musicians who perform together, especially ones who play popular music. ❑ *He played guitar in a rock group.* **5** V-T/V-I If a number of things or people **are grouped together** or **group together**, they are together in one place or within one organization or system. ❑ *Plants are grouped into botanical "families."* ❑ *We group the students together according to ability.* **6** N-COUNT In chemistry, a **group** of elements is a number of them that are in the same column in the periodic table of elements. [from French] **7** → see also **grouping, pressure group** → see **periodic table**

**Thesaurus** group Also look up :

| N. | collection, crowd, gang **1** organization, society **2** |
|----|---|
| V. | arrange, categorize, class, order, rank, sort **5** |

**group|ing** /ˈgruːpɪŋ/ (**groupings**) N-COUNT A **grouping** is a set of people or things that have something in common. ❑ *They were part of a political grouping that campaigned for independence.* [from French]

**grouse** /ˈgraʊs/ (**grouses, grousing, groused**)

The form **grouse** is used as the plural for meaning **1**.

**1** N-COUNT A **grouse** is a wild bird with a round body. Grouse are often shot for sport and can be eaten. ❑ *We saw several grouse in the field.* ● **Grouse** is the flesh of this bird eaten as food. ❑ *The menu included roast grouse.* **2** V-T/V-I If you **grouse**, you complain. ❑ *"How come we never know what's going on?" he groused.* ❑ *They groused about the parking rules.* **3** N-COUNT A **grouse** is a complaint. ❑ *There have been grouses about housing prices.*

**grove** /ˈɡroʊv/ (**groves**) N-COUNT A **grove** is a group of trees that are close together. ❑ *...an olive grove.* [from Old English] → see **tree**

**grov|el** /ˈgrɑːvəl, ˈgrʌv-/ (**grovels, groveling, groveled**) **1** V-I If you say that someone **grovels**, you think they are showing too much respect towards another person, for example because they are frightened or because they want something. ❑ *I won't grovel to anybody.* ❑ *She wants respect, but she doesn't expect her staff to grovel.* **2** V-I If you **grovel**, you crawl on the ground, for example in order to find something. ❑ *We groveled on the floor searching for his contact lens.* [from Middle English]

**grow** /ˈgroʊ/ (**grows, growing, grew, grown**) **1** V-I When people, animals, and plants **grow**, they increase in size and change physically over a period of time. ❑ *All children grow at different rates.* **2** V-I If a plant or tree **grows** in a particular place, it is alive there. ❑ *There were roses growing by the side of the door.* **3** V-T If you **grow** a particular type of plant, you put seeds or young plants in the ground and take care of them as they develop. ❑ *I always grow a few red onions.* ● **grow|er** (**growers**) N-COUNT ❑ *...apple growers.* **4** V-T/V-I When your hair or nails **grow**, they gradually become longer. If you **grow** your hair or nails, you stop cutting them so that they become longer. ❑ *My hair grows really fast.* ❑ *He's growing a beard.* **5** V-LINK You use **grow** to say that someone or something gradually changes until they have a new quality, feeling, or attitude. ❑ *I grew a little afraid of him.* ❑ *He's growing old.* **6** V-I If something **grows**, it becomes bigger, greater or more intense. ❑ *The number of unemployed people grew to 4 million.* ❑ *The public's anger is growing.* ❑ *The economy continues to grow.* [from Old English] **7** → see also **grown**

▶ **grow apart** PHR-VERB If people who have a close relationship **grow apart**, they gradually start to have different interests and opinions from each other, and their relationship starts to fail. ❑ *He and his wife grew apart.*

▶ **grow into** PHR-VERB When a child **grows into** an item of clothing, they become taller or bigger so that it fits them properly. ❑ *The coat is too big, but she'll soon grow into it.*

▸ **grow on** PHR-VERB If someone or something **grows on** you, you start to like them more and more. ❑ *Slowly the place began to grow on me.*

▸ **grow out of** 1 PHR-VERB If you **grow out of** a type of behavior or an interest, you stop behaving in that way or having that interest, as you develop or change. ❑ *Most children who bite their nails grow out of it.* 2 PHR-VERB When a child **grows out of** an item of clothing, they become so tall or big that it no longer fits them properly. ❑ *You've grown out of your shoes again.*

▸ **grow up** 1 PHR-VERB When someone **grows up**, they gradually change from being a child into being an adult. ❑ *She grew up in Tokyo.* 2 → see also **grown-up** 3 PHR-VERB If something **grows up**, it starts to exist and then becomes larger or more important. ❑ *New housing grew up alongside the port.*

<table>
<tr><td colspan="2">**Word Partnership** Use *grow* with :</td></tr>
<tr><td>v.</td><td>**continue to** grow 1 – 3<br>**try to** grow 3</td></tr>
<tr><td>N.</td><td>grow **food** 3</td></tr>
<tr><td>ADJ.</td><td>grow **older** 5</td></tr>
</table>

**growl** /gra͟ʊl/ (**growls, growling, growled**) 1 V-I When a dog or other animal **growls**, it makes a low noise in its throat, usually because it is angry. ❑ *The dog was growling and showing its teeth.* ● **Growl** is also a noun. ❑ *The animal gave a growl.* 2 V-T If someone **growls** something, they say something in a low, rough, and angry voice. [WRITTEN] ❑ *He growled some instructions at Pete.* [from Old French]

**grown** /gro͟ʊn/ ADJ A **grown** man or woman is one who is fully grown and mature, both physically and mentally. ❑ *Why do grown men love games so much?* [from Old English]

**grown-up** (**grown-ups**)

The spelling **grownup** is also used. The syllable **up** is not stressed when it is a noun.

1 N-COUNT A **grown-up** is an adult; used by or to children. ❑ *Jan was almost a grown-up.* 2 ADJ Someone who is **grown-up** is physically and mentally mature and no longer depends on their parents or another adult. ❑ *She has two grown-up children who both live nearby.*

**growth** /gro͟ʊθ/ (**growths**) 1 N-UNCOUNT The **growth** of something such as an industry, organization, or idea is its development in size, wealth, or importance. ❑ *...Japan's enormous economic growth.* 2 N-UNCOUNT **Growth** in a person, animal, or plant is the process of increasing in physical size and development. ❑ *...hormones which control growth.* 3 N-COUNT A **growth** is a lump caused by a disease that grows inside or on a person, animal, or plant. ❑ *He had a growth on his back.* [from Old English]

**grub** /gra͟ʌb/ (**grubs**) 1 N-COUNT A **grub** is a young insect which has just come out of an egg and looks like a short, fat worm. 2 N-UNCOUNT **Grub** is food. [INFORMAL] ❑ *Let's have some grub.* [from Old English]

**grub|by** /gra͟ʌbi/ (**grubbier, grubbiest**) 1 ADJ A **grubby** person or object is rather dirty. ❑ *His face was grubby.* 2 ADJ If you call an activity or someone's behavior **grubby**, you disapprove of it because it is not completely honest or respectable.

❑ *...the grubby business of politics.* [from Germanic]

**grudge** /gra͟ʌdʒ/ (**grudges**) N-COUNT If you have or bear a **grudge against** someone, you have unfriendly feelings toward them because of something they did in the past. ❑ *He seems to have a grudge against me.* [from Old French]

**grudg|ing** /gra͟ʌdʒɪŋ/ ADJ A **grudging** feeling or action is felt or done very unwillingly. ❑ *He earned his opponents' grudging respect.* ● **grudg|ing|ly** ADV ❑ *The company grudgingly agreed to allow him to continue working.* [from Old French]

**gru|el|ing** /gru͟əlɪŋ/ ADJ A **grueling** activity is extremely difficult and tiring to do. ❑ *The president has a grueling schedule.*

**grue|some** /gru͟səm/ ADJ Something that is **gruesome** is extremely unpleasant and shocking. ❑ *There has been a series of gruesome murders.* [from Northern English]

**grum|ble** /gra͟ʌmbəl/ (**grumbles, grumbling, grumbled**) V-T/V-I If someone **grumbles**, they complain about something in a bad-tempered way. ❑ *They grumble about how hard they have to work.* ● **Grumble** is also a noun. ❑ *Its high price has brought grumbles from some customers.* [from Middle Low German]

**grumpy** /gra͟ʌmpi/ (**grumpier, grumpiest**) ADJ If you say that someone is **grumpy**, you mean that they are bad tempered and miserable. ❑ *...a grumpy old man.* ● **grump|i|ly** ADV ❑ *"I'm busy," said Ken grumpily.*

**grunge** /gra͟ʌndʒ/ 1 N-UNCOUNT **Grunge** is the name of a fashion and of a type of music. **Grunge** fashion involves wearing clothes which look old and untidy. **Grunge** music is played on guitars and is very loud. 2 N-UNCOUNT **Grunge** is dirt. [INFORMAL] ● **grungy** ADJ ❑ *...grungy motel rooms.*

**grunt** /gra͟ʌnt/ (**grunts, grunting, grunted**) 1 V-T/V-I If you **grunt**, you make a low sound, especially because you are annoyed or not interested in something. ❑ *When I said hello he just grunted.* ❑ *"Huh," he grunted.* ● **Grunt** is also a noun. ❑ *Her reply was no more than a grunt.* 2 V-I When an animal **grunts**, it makes a low, rough noise. ❑ *...the sound of a pig grunting.* 3 N-COUNT A **grunt** is a soldier of low rank in the infantry or the marines. [INFORMAL] ❑ *I'm just a grunt. I have to follow orders.* [from Old English]

**grunt work** N-UNCOUNT The **grunt work** is the hard work or the less interesting part of the work that needs to be done. [INFORMAL] ❑ *She didn't have enough patience for the grunt work.*

**gua|nine** /gwɑ͟nin, -nɪn/ (**guanines**) N-VAR **Guanine** is one of the four basic components of the DNA molecule. It bonds with cytosine. [TECHNICAL]

**guar|an|tee** /gæ͟rənti͟/ (**guarantees, guaranteeing, guaranteed**) 1 V-T If one thing **guarantees** another, the first is certain to cause the second thing to happen. ❑ *Hard work does not guarantee success.* 2 N-COUNT Something that is a **guarantee of** something else makes it certain that it will happen or that it is true. ❑ *A famous company name is not a guarantee of quality.* 3 V-T If you **guarantee** something, you promise that it will definitely happen, or that you will do or provide it for someone. ❑ *We guarantee the safety of our products.* ❑ *I guarantee that you will enjoy this movie.* ● **Guarantee** is also a noun. ❑ *He gave me a guarantee*

**g**

*he would finish the job.* **4** N-COUNT A **guarantee** is a written promise by a company to replace or repair a product free of charge if it has any faults within a particular time. ▢ *Keep the guarantee in case something goes wrong.* **5** V-T If a company **guarantees** its product or work, they provide a guarantee for it. ▢ *All our computers are guaranteed for 12 months.* [from Spanish]

**guard** /gɑrd/ (**guards, guarding, guarded**)
**1** V-T If you **guard** a place, person, or object, you stand near them in order to watch and protect them. ▢ *Armed police guarded the court.* **2** V-T If you **guard** someone, you watch them and keep them in a particular place to stop them from escaping. ▢ *Marines with rifles guarded them.* **3** N-COUNT A

**guard**

**guard** is someone such as a soldier, police officer, or prison officer who is guarding a particular place or person. ▢ *The prisoners attacked their guards.* **4** N-SING A **guard** is a specially organized group of people, such as soldiers or police officers, who protect or watch someone or something. ▢ *We hired a security guard.*
**5** V-T If you **guard** some information or advantage that you have, you try to protect it or keep it for yourself. ▢ *He closely guarded his information.*
**6** N-COUNT A **guard** is a protective device which covers a part of your body or a dangerous part of a piece of equipment. ▢ *...the chin guard of my helmet.*
**7** → see also **bodyguard, lifeguard** **8** PHRASE If someone **catches** you **off guard**, they surprise you by doing something you do not expect. If something **catches** you **off guard**, it surprises you by happening when you are not expecting it. ▢ *He likes to catch the audience off guard.* **9** PHRASE If you are **on** your **guard** or **on guard**, you are being very careful because you think a situation might become difficult or dangerous. ▢ *He was on his guard when the police arrived.* [from Old French]
▶ **guard against** PHR-VERB If you **guard against** something, you are careful to prevent it from happening, or to avoid being affected by it. ▢ *Wear gloves to guard against infection.*

**Word Partnership** Use *guard* with :

| | |
|---|---|
| N. | guard **a door/house/prisoner** **1** **2** **prison** guard, **security** guard **3** **4** |
| V. | **catch** *someone* **off** guard **8** **be on** guard **9** |

**guard cell** (**guard cells**) N-COUNT **Guard cells** are pairs of cells on the leaves of plants, which control things such as how much air a plant takes in and how much water it releases.

**guard|ian** /gɑrdiən/ (**guardians**) **1** N-COUNT A **guardian** is someone who has been legally appointed to take charge of the affairs of another person, for example a child or someone who is mentally ill. ▢ *Diana's grandmother was her legal guardian.* **2** N-COUNT The **guardian** of something is someone who defends and protects it. ▢ *He sees himself as the guardian of democracy.* [from Old French]

**guer|ril|la** /gərɪlə/ (**guerrillas**) also **guerilla** N-COUNT A **guerrilla** is someone who fights as part

of an unofficial army. ▢ *...a guerrilla war.* [from Spanish]

**guess** /gɛs/ (**guesses, guessing, guessed**)
**1** V-T/V-I If you **guess** something, you give an answer or provide an opinion which may not be true because you do not have definite knowledge about the matter concerned. ▢ *Yvonne guessed that he was around 40 years old.* **2** V-T If you **guess that** something is the case, you correctly form the opinion that it is the case, although you do not have definite knowledge about it. ▢ *I guessed that he was American.* ▢ *He should have guessed what would happen.* **3** N-COUNT A **guess** is an attempt to give an answer or provide an opinion which may not be true because you do not have definite knowledge about the matter concerned. ▢ *My guess is that this solution will not work.* ▢ *He made a guess at her age.* **4** PHRASE You say "**I guess**" to show that you are slightly uncertain or reluctant about what you are saying. [INFORMAL] ▢ *I guess he's right.* [of Scandinavian origin]

**Thesaurus** *guess* Also look up :

| | |
|---|---|
| V. | estimate, predict, suspect **1** |
| N. | assumption, prediction, theory **3** |

**Word Partnership** Use *guess* with :

| | |
|---|---|
| N. | guess **a secret** **2** |
| V. | **make** a guess **3** |
| ADJ. | **educated** guess, **good** guess, **wild** guess **3** |

**guest** /gɛst/ (**guests**) **1** N-COUNT A **guest** is someone who is visiting you or is at an event because you have invited them. ▢ *She was a guest at the wedding.* **2** N-COUNT A **guest** is someone who visits a place or organization or appears on a radio or television show because they have been invited to do so. ▢ *...a frequent talk show guest.* ▢ *Dr. Gerald Jeffers is the guest speaker.* **3** N-COUNT A **guest** is someone who is staying in a hotel. [from Old English]
→ see **hotel**

**Word Partnership** Use *guest* with :

| | |
|---|---|
| ADJ. | **unwelcome** guest **1** **2** |
| V. | **be** *someone's* guest, **entertain** a guest **1** **2** **accommodate** a guest **1** – **3** |
| N. | guest **appearance**, guest **list**, guest **speaker** **1** **2** **hotel** guest **3** |

**guest house** N-COUNT A **guest house** is a small house on the grounds of a large house, where visitors can stay.

**guest of hon|or** (**guests of honor**) N-COUNT The **guest of honor** at a dinner or other social occasion is the most important guest.

**GUI** /gui/ (**GUIs**) N-COUNT In computing, a **GUI** is a type of screen interface that is found on most computers, consisting of menus and icons that can be controlled by a mouse. **GUI** is an abbreviation for "graphical user interface."

**guid|ance** /gaɪdᵊns/ N-UNCOUNT **Guidance** is help and advice. ▢ *My tennis game improved under his guidance.* [from Old French]

**guid|ance coun|se|lor** (**guidance counselors**) N-COUNT A **guidance counselor** is a person who works in a school giving students advice about careers and personal problems.

**guide** /gaɪd/ (**guides, guiding, guided**) **1** N-COUNT A **guide** is a book that gives you information or instructions to help you do or understand something. □ ...*a step-by-step guide to building your own home.* **2** N-COUNT A **guide** is a book that gives tourists information about a town, area, or country. □ *The guide to Paris lists hotel rooms for as little as $35 a night.* **3** N-COUNT A **guide** is someone who shows tourists around places such as museums or cities. □ *A guide will take you on a tour of the city.* **4** V-T If you **guide** someone around a city, museum, or building, you show it to them and explain points of interest. □ *She guided him around Berlin.* **5** N-COUNT A **guide** is someone who shows people the way to a place in a difficult or dangerous region. □ *With guides, the journey can be done in fourteen days.* **6** N-COUNT A **guide** is something that can be used to help you plan your actions or to form an opinion about something. □ *As a rough guide, you need about half a loaf of bread per person.* **7** V-T If you **guide** someone somewhere, you go there with them in order to show them the way. □ *He took her by the arm and guided her out.* **8** V-T If you **guide** a vehicle somewhere, you control it carefully to make sure that it goes in the right direction. □ *Captain Shelton guided his plane along the runway.* **9** V-T If something or someone **guides** you, they influence your actions or decisions. □ *Let your thoughts and feelings guide you.* [from Old French]

| **Thesaurus** | *guide* | Also look up : |
| --- | --- | --- |
| N. | directory, handbook, information **1** **2** | |
| V. | accompany, direct, instruct, lead, navigate; (*ant.*) follow **4** **7** | |

**guide|line** /gaɪdlaɪn/ (**guidelines**) N-COUNT If an organization issues **guidelines on** something, it issues official advice about how to do it. □ *The government has issued new guidelines on religious education.*

**guild** /gɪld/ (**guilds**) N-COUNT A **guild** is an organization of people who do the same job. □ ...*the Writers' Guild of America.* [of Scandinavian origin]

**guilt** /gɪlt/ **1** N-UNCOUNT **Guilt** is an unhappy feeling that you have because you have done something wrong or think that you have done something wrong. □ *She felt a lot of guilt about her children's unhappiness.* **2** N-UNCOUNT **Guilt** is the fact that you have done something wrong or illegal. □ *The jury was convinced of his guilt.* [from Old English]

| **Word Partnership** | Use *guilt* with : |
| --- | --- |
| N. | **burden of** guilt, **feelings of** guilt, **sense of** guilt, guilt **trip** **1** |
| V. | **admit** guilt **2** |

**guilty** /gɪlti/ (**guiltier, guiltiest**) **1** ADJ If you feel **guilty**, you feel unhappy because you think that you have done something wrong or have failed to do something which you should have done. □ *I feel so guilty, leaving all this work to you.* • **guilt|i|ly** ADV □ *He looked up guiltily when I walked in.* **2** ADJ You use **guilty** to describe an action or fact that you feel guilty about. □ *He discovered her guilty secret.* **3 guilty conscience** → see **conscience**

**4** ADJ If someone is **guilty of** doing something wrong or of committing a crime or offense, they have done that thing or committed that crime. □ *They were found guilty of murder.* □ *He was guilty of making some serious mistakes.* [from Old English] → see **trial**

| **Word Partnership** | Use *guilty* with : |
| --- | --- |
| V. | **feel** guilty, **look** guilty **1** **find** *someone* guilty, **plead (not)** guilty, **prove** *someone* guilty **4** |
| N. | guilty **conscience**, guilty **secret** **2** guilty **party**, guilty **plea**, guilty **verdict** **4** |
| PREP. | guilty **of** *something* **4** |

**guinea pig** (**guinea pigs**) **1** N-COUNT If someone is used as a **guinea pig** in an experiment, something is tested on them that has not been tested on people before. □ *The doctor used himself as a guinea pig in his research.* **2** N-COUNT A **guinea pig** is a small, furry animal without a tail. Guinea pigs are often kept as pets.

**guise** /gaɪz/ (**guises**) N-COUNT You use **guise** to refer to the outward appearance or form of someone or something, which is often temporary or different from their real nature. □ *In the guise of concern for his health, she asked more questions.* [from Old French]

**gui|tar** /gɪtɑr/ (**guitars**) N-VAR A **guitar** is a musical instrument with six strings that are plucked or strummed. • **gui|tar|ist** /gɪtɑrɪst/ (**guitarists**) N-COUNT □ ...*the world's best jazz guitarists.* [from Spanish] → see **string**

**gulch** /gʌltʃ/ (**gulches**) N-COUNT A **gulch** is a long narrow valley with steep sides which has been made by a stream flowing through it. □ ...*California Gulch.*

**gulf** /gʌlf/ (**gulfs**) **1** N-COUNT A **gulf** is an important or significant difference between two people, things, or groups. □ *There is a growing gulf between rich and poor.* **2** N-COUNT A **gulf** is a large area of sea which extends a long way into the surrounding land. □ ...*the Gulf of Mexico.* [from Old French]

**gul|lible** /gʌlɪbəl/ ADJ If you describe someone as **gullible**, you mean they are easily tricked because they are too trusting. □ *How can you be so gullible?* • **gul|li|bil|ity** /gʌləbɪlɪti/ N-UNCOUNT □ *I was ashamed of my gullibility.*

**gul|ly** /gʌli/ (**gullies**) also **gulley** N-COUNT A **gully** is a long, narrow valley with steep sides. □ *They fell down a steep gully.* [from French] → see **erosion**

**gulp** /gʌlp/ (**gulps, gulping, gulped**) **1** V-T If you **gulp** something, you eat or drink it very quickly by swallowing large quantities of it at once. □ *She gulped her soda.* **2** V-T/V-I If you **gulp** or **gulp** air, you swallow air, often making a noise in your throat as you do so, because you are nervous or excited. [WRITTEN] □ *I gulped nervously, then started to speak.* **3** N-COUNT A **gulp** of air, food, or drink, is a large amount of it that you swallow at once. □ *I took in a large gulp of air.* [from Middle Dutch]

**gum** /gʌm/ (**gums**) **1** N-UNCOUNT **Gum** is a flavored substance, which you chew for a long time but do not swallow. □ *I do not chew gum in* public. **2** N-COUNT Your **gums** are the areas of firm, pink flesh inside your mouth, which your teeth grow out of. ❑ *Gently brush your teeth and gums.* [Sense 1 from Old French. Sense 2 from Old English] → see **teeth**

**gum|ball** /gʌmbɔːl/ (**gumballs**) N-COUNT **Gumballs** are round, brightly coloured balls of chewing gum.

**gun** /gʌn/ (**guns, gunning, gunned**) **1** N-COUNT A **gun** is a weapon from which bullets or other things are fired. ❑ *He pointed the gun at officers as they chased him.* **2** → see also **shotgun** **3** PHRASE If you **stick to** your **guns**, you continue to have your own opinion about something even though other people are trying to tell you that you are wrong. [INFORMAL] ❑ *He stuck to his guns and refused to meet her.* [of Scandinavian origin]

▶ **gun down** PHR-VERB If someone **is gunned down**, they are shot and severely injured or killed. ❑ *He had been gunned down and killed.*

**gun|fire** /gʌnfaɪər/ N-UNCOUNT **Gunfire** is the repeated shooting of guns. ❑ *The sound of gunfire....*

**gun|man** /gʌnmən/ (**gunmen**) N-COUNT A **gunman** is a man who uses a gun to commit a crime. ❑ *A gunman fired at police.*

**gun|point** /gʌnpɔɪnt/ PHRASE If you are held **at gunpoint**, someone threatens to shoot and kill you if you do not obey them. ❑ *They were held at gunpoint by a thief.*

**gun|shot** /gʌnʃɒt/ (**gunshots**) **1** N-UNCOUNT **Gunshot** is used to refer to bullets that are fired from a gun. ❑ *He was brought to the hospital with gunshot wounds.* **2** N-COUNT A **gunshot** is the firing of a gun or the sound of a gun being fired. ❑ *They heard thousands of gunshots.*

**gur|gle** /gɜrgəl/ (**gurgles, gurgling, gurgled**) **1** V-I If water **gurgles**, it makes a bubbling sound. ❑ *Water gurgled in the pipes.* ● **Gurgle** is also a noun. ❑ *We could hear the gurgle of water against the boat.* **2** V-I If someone, especially a baby, **gurgles**, they make a bubbling sound in their throat. ❑ *Henry gurgles happily in his baby chair.* ● **Gurgle** is also a noun. ❑ *The baby gave a gurgle of laughter.* [from Vulgar Latin]

**gur|ney** /gɜrni/ (**gurneys**) N-COUNT A **gurney** is a bed on wheels that is used in hospitals for moving sick or injured people.

**guru** /guːruː/ (**gurus**) **1** N-COUNT A **guru** is a person whom some people regard as an expert or leader. ❑ *...fashion gurus.* **2** N-COUNT; N-TITLE A **guru** is a religious and spiritual leader and teacher, especially in Hinduism. [from Hindi]

**gush** /gʌʃ/ (**gushes, gushing, gushed**) **1** V-T/V-I When liquid **gushes** out of something, or when something **gushes** a liquid, the liquid flows out very quickly and in large quantities. ❑ *Hot water gushed out.* **2** N-SING A **gush of** liquid is a sudden, rapid flow of liquid, or a quantity of it that suddenly flows out. ❑ *I heard a gush of water.* **3** V-T/V-I If someone **gushes**, they express their admiration or pleasure in an exaggerated way. ❑ *"Oh, it was brilliant," he gushes.* ● **gush|ing** ADJ ❑ *She sent Hassan a gushing letter.* [from Old Norse]

**gust** /gʌst/ (**gusts, gusting, gusted**) **1** N-COUNT A **gust** is a short, strong, sudden rush of wind. ❑ *A gust of wind came down the valley.* **2** V-I When the wind **gusts**, it blows with short, strong, sudden rushes. ❑ *The wind gusted, blowing off his hat.* [from

Old Norse]

**gut** /gʌt/ (**guts, gutting, gutted**) **1** N-PLURAL A person's or animal's **guts** are all the organs inside them. ❑ *She cleaned out all the fish guts.* **2** V-T When someone **guts** a dead animal or fish, they prepare it for cooking by removing all the organs from inside it. ❑ *We gut the fish and then freeze them.* **3** N-SING The **gut** is the tube inside the body of a person or animal through which food passes while it is being digested. ❑ *The food then passes into the gut.* **4** N-UNCOUNT **Guts** is the will and courage to do something that is difficult or unpleasant, or which might have unpleasant results. [INFORMAL] ❑ *She has the guts to say what she thinks.* **5** ADJ A **gut** feeling is based on instinct or emotion rather than reason. ❑ *My gut reaction was not to believe him.* **6** V-T To **gut** a building means to destroy the inside of it so that only its outside walls remain. ❑ *Fire gutted a building where 60 people lived.* [from Old English]

**gut|ter** /gʌtər/ (**gutters**) **1** N-COUNT The **gutter** is the edge of a road next to the pavement, where rainwater collects and flows away. ❑ *His hat fell into the gutter.* **2** N-COUNT A **gutter** is a plastic or metal channel attached to the lower edge of the roof of a building, which rainwater drains into. ❑ *We need to fix the gutters.* [from Old French]

**guy** /gaɪ/ (**guys**) **1** N-COUNT A **guy** is a man. [INFORMAL] ❑ *I was working with a guy from Milwaukee.* **2** N-VOC; N-PLURAL You can address a group of people, whether they are male or female, as **guys** or **you guys**. [INFORMAL] ❑ *Hi, guys. How are you doing?* [after Guy Fawkes (1570–1606), an English conspirator in the Gunpowder Plot]

**gym** /dʒɪm/ (**gyms**) **1** N-COUNT A **gym** is a club, building, or large room, usually containing special equipment, where people go to do physical exercise and get fit. ❑ *Twice a week, I go to the gym.* **2** N-UNCOUNT **Gym** is the activity of doing physical exercises in a gym, especially at school. ❑ *...gym classes.*

**gym|na|sium** /dʒɪmneɪziəm/ (**gymnasiums** or **gymnasia** /dʒɪmneɪziə/) N-COUNT A **gymnasium** is the same as a **gym**. [FORMAL] [from Latin]

**gym|no|sperm** /dʒɪmnəspɜrm/ (**gymnosperms**) N-PLURAL A **gymnosperm** is a plant that produces seeds but does not produce flowers. [TECHNICAL]

---

**Word Link** gyn ≈ female, woman : andro**gyn**y, **gyn**ecology, miso**gyn**ist

---

**gy|ne|col|ogy** /gaɪnɪkɒlədʒi/ N-UNCOUNT **Gynecology** is the branch of medical science that deals with women's diseases and medical conditions. ● **gy|ne|colo|gist** (**gynecologists**) N-COUNT ❑ *She went to see her gynecologist.* ● **gy|ne|co|logi|cal** /gaɪnɪkəlɒdʒɪkəl/ ADJ ❑ *...a gynecological examination.* [from Greek]

**gyro** /dʒaɪroʊ/ (**gyros**) N-COUNT A **gyro** is the same as a **gyroscope**. [INFORMAL] ❑ *We have six gyros on board.* [from Greek]

**gyro|scope** /dʒaɪrəskoʊp/ (**gyroscopes**) N-COUNT A **gyroscope** is a device that contains a disc turning on an axis that can turn freely in any direction, so that the disc maintains the same position whatever the position or movement of the surrounding structure. ❑ *Crewmen inspected the gyroscope.* [from French]

G

# Hh

**H** On a weather map, **H** is an abbreviation for "high pressure."

**hab|it** /hǽbɪt/ (**habits**) **1** N-VAR A **habit** is something that you do often or regularly. ▢ *He has a habit of licking his lips.* ▢ *He had a habit of taking a 30-minute bath each morning.* **2** N-COUNT A drug **habit** is an addiction to a drug such as heroin or cocaine. **3** PHRASE If you **are in the habit of** doing something or **make a habit of** doing it, you do it regularly or often. If you **get into the habit of** doing something, you begin to do it regularly or often. ▢ *They were in the habit of watching TV every night.* ▢ *Make a habit of hanging your clothes up each night.* [from Latin]

**habi|tat** /hǽbɪtæt/ (**habitats**) N-VAR The **habitat** of an animal or plant is the natural environment in which it normally lives or grows. ▢ *In its natural habitat, the plant will grow up to 25 feet.* [from Latin]
→ see Word Web: **habitat**

**ha|bitu|al** /həbɪ́tʃuəl/ ADJ A **habitual** action, state, or way of behaving is one that someone usually does or has, especially one that is considered to be typical or characteristic of them. ▢ *With her habitual honesty, she talked about being a mother.* ● **ha|bitu|al|ly** ADV ▢ *He habitually shouted at them.* [from Latin]

**hack** /hǽk/ (**hacks, hacking, hacked**) **1** V-T/V-I If you **hack** something or **hack away at** it, you cut it with strong, rough strokes using a sharp tool such as an ax or a knife. ▢ *He hacked the wood with an ax.* ▢ *He started to hack away at the tree bark.* **2** V-I If someone **hacks into** a computer system, they break into it, especially in order to get secret information. ▢ *Criminals hacked into websites owned by the bank.* ● **hack|er** (**hackers**) N-COUNT ▢ *...a hacker who steals credit card numbers.*

● **hack|ing** N-UNCOUNT ▢ *...the common crime of computer hacking.* **3** N-COUNT If you refer to a professional writer, such as a journalist, as a **hack**, you disapprove of them because they write for money and do not worry very much about the quality of their writing. ▢ *...newspaper hacks, always eager to find something to write about.* [Senses 1 and 2 from Old English.]
→ see **Internet**

**had**

| |
|---|
| The auxiliary verb is pronounced /həd/, STRONG hǽd/. For the main verb, the pronunciation is /hǽd/. |

**Had** is the past tense and past participle of **have**. [from Old English]

**had|dock** /hǽdək/ (**haddock**) N-VAR **Haddock** is a type of sea fish. ▢ *...fishing boats which normally catch a mix of cod and haddock.*

**hadn't** /hǽdᵊnt/ **Hadn't** is the usual spoken form of "had not." [from Old English]

**hag|gle** /hǽgᵊl/ (**haggles, haggling, haggled**) V-RECIP If you **haggle**, you argue about something before reaching an agreement, especially about the cost of something. ▢ *He haggled with the jeweler and got a $80 discount on the ring.* ▢ *He always haggles over the price.* ● **hag|gling** N-UNCOUNT ▢ *After months of haggling, they got some of their money back.* [of Scandinavian origin]

**hail** /héɪl/ (**hails, hailing, hailed**) **1** V-T If a person, event, or achievement **is hailed as** important or successful, they are praised publicly. ▢ *He was hailed as a hero after rescuing a boy from the fire.* **2** N-UNCOUNT **Hail** consists of small balls of ice that fall like rain from the sky. ▢ *...a storm with hail.* **3** V-T If you **hail** a taxi, you wave at it in order to stop it because you want the driver to take you

**h**

## Word Web    habitat

The **environment** where a plant or animal lives is its **habitat**. The habitat provides **food**, **water**, and **shelter**. Each habitat has different **temperatures**, **rainfall**, and amounts of **sunlight**. A **desert** is a sunny, dry habitat where few plants and animals can live. The **tropical** rainforest gets heavy rain every day and has many types of **vegetation** and animal life. **Grasslands** or **prairies** get little rain but are home to many **grass**-eating animals. The boreal **forest** is the largest biome in the world. Its winters are cold and snowy, and summers are warm, rainy, and humid.

desert

boreal forest

rainforest

grassland

## Picture Dictionary hair

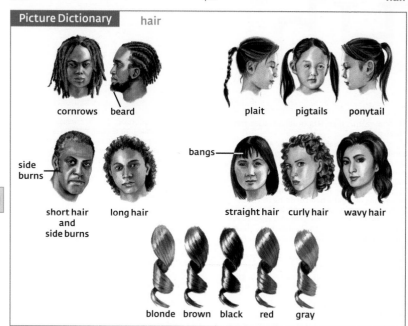

cornrows    beard

plait    pigtails    ponytail

side burns

bangs

short hair and side burns    long hair

straight hair    curly hair    wavy hair

blonde    brown    black    red    gray

somewhere. ❑ *We tried to hail a taxi after the movie.* [Senses 1 and 3 from Old Norse. Sense 2 from Old English.]
→ see **precipitation, storm**

**hair** /hɛər/ (**hairs**) **1** N-VAR Your **hair** is the fine threads that grow on your head. ❑ *I wash my hair every night.* ❑ *My Mom gets some gray hairs but she pulls them out.* **2** N-VAR **Hair** is the short, fine threads that grow on different parts of your body. ❑ *Most men have hair on their chest.* **3** N-VAR **Hair** is the threads that cover the body of an animal such as a dog, or make up a horse's mane and tail. ❑ *She had dog hair on her clothes.* [from Old English]
→ see Picture Dictionary: **hair**

### Word Partnership Use *hair* with :

| | |
|---|---|
| ADJ. | **black/blonde/brown/gray** hair, **curly/ straight/wavy** hair **1** |
| V. | **bleach** *your* hair, **brush/comb** *your* hair, **color** hair, **cut** *your* hair, **do** *your* hair, **dry** *your* hair, **fix** *your* hair, **lose** *your* hair, **pull** *someone's* hair, **wash** *your* hair **1** |
| N. | **lock of** hair **1** |

**hair|cut** /hɛərkʌt/ (**haircuts**) **1** N-COUNT If you get a **haircut**, someone cuts your hair for you. ❑ *You need a haircut.* **2** N-COUNT A **haircut** is the style in which your hair has been cut. ❑ *Who's that guy with the funny haircut?*

**hair|dresser** /hɛərdrɛsər/ (**hairdressers**) **1** N-COUNT A **hairdresser** is a person who cuts, colors, and styles people's hair. ● **hair|dressing** N-UNCOUNT ❑ *She makes a living from hairdressing.*

**2** N-COUNT A **hairdresser** or a **hairdresser's** is a place where a hairdresser works. ❑ *I work in this new hairdresser's.*

**hair|style** /hɛərstaɪl/ (**hairstyles**) N-COUNT Your **hairstyle** is the style in which your hair has been cut or arranged. ❑ *Her new hairstyle looks great.*

**hairy** /hɛəri/ (**hairier, hairiest**) **1** ADJ Someone or something that is **hairy** is covered with hairs. ❑ *He was wearing shorts which showed his hairy legs.* **2** ADJ If you describe a situation as **hairy**, you mean that it is exciting, worrying, and somewhat frightening. [INFORMAL] ❑ *His driving was slightly hairy.* [from Old English]

**halal** /həlɑl/ N-UNCOUNT **Halal** meat is meat from animals that have been killed according to Muslim law. ❑ *...a halal butcher's shop.* [from Arabic]

**half** /hæf/ (**halves** /hævz/) **1** ORD **Half** of a number, an amount, or an object is one of two equal parts that together make up the whole number, amount, or object. ❑ *More than half of all U.S. houses are heated with gas.* ● **Half** is also a predeterminer. ❑ *We sat and talked for half an hour.* ❑ *They only received half the money that they were expecting.* ● **Half** is also an adjective. ❑ *I'll stay with you for the first half hour.* **2** ADV You use **half** to say that something is only partly true or only partly happens. ❑ *His eyes were half closed.* ❑ *The glass was half empty.* **3** N-COUNT In games such as football, soccer, rugby, and basketball, games are divided into two equal periods of time which are called **halves**. ❑ *Jakobsen scored a goal early in the second half.* **4** ADV You use **half** to say that someone has parents of different nationalities. For example, if you are **half** German, one of your parents is German. ❏ *She was half Italian and half American.* [from Old English]

**half|heart|ed** /hǽfhɑrtɪd/ ADJ If someone does something in a **halfhearted** way, they do it without any real effort, interest, or enthusiasm. ❏ *...a halfhearted apology.* ● **half|heart|ed|ly** ADV ❏ *I can't do anything halfheartedly. I have to do everything 100 percent.*

**half-hour** (**half-hours**) N-COUNT A **half-hour** is a period of thirty minutes. ❏ *...a talk followed by a half-hour of discussion.*

**half-life** (**half-lives**) also **half life** N-COUNT The **half-life** of a radioactive substance is the amount of time that it takes to lose half its radioactivity.

**half note** (**half notes**) N-COUNT A **half note** is a musical note that has a time value equal to two quarter notes.

**half|time** /hǽftaɪm/ N-UNCOUNT **Halftime** is the short period of time between the two parts of a sports event such as a football, hockey, or basketball game, when the players take a short rest. ❏ *We bought something to eat during halftime.*

**half|way** /hǽfweɪ/ ◼ ADV **Halfway** means in the middle of a place or between two points, at an equal distance from each of them. ❏ *He was halfway up the ladder.* ◻ ADV **Halfway** means in the middle of a period of time or of an event. ❏ *We were more than halfway through our tour.* ● **Halfway** is also an adjective. ❏ *Cleveland was winning at the halfway point in the game.* [from Old English]

**hall** /hɔl/ (**halls**) ◼ N-COUNT The **hall** in a house or an apartment is the area just inside the front door, into which some of the other rooms open. ❏ *The lights were on in the hall.* ◻ N-COUNT A **hall** in a building is a long passage with doors into rooms on both sides of it. ❏ *There are 10 rooms along each hall.* ◾ N-COUNT A **hall** is a large room or building which is used for public events such as concerts and meetings. ❏ *We went into the lecture hall.* [from Old English] ◿ → see also **town hall**
→ see **house**

**Hal|ley's com|et** /hǽliz kɒmɪt, heɪ-/ N-PROPER **Halley's comet** is a comet that is visible from the Earth every 76 years.

**Hal|low|een** /hǽloʊwin/ also **Hallowe'en** N-UNCOUNT **Halloween** is the night of October 31st and is traditionally said to be the time when ghosts and witches can be seen.

**hal|lu|ci|na|tion** /həlusɪneɪ°n/ (**hallucinations**) N-VAR A **hallucination** is the experience of seeing something that is not really there because you are ill or have taken a drug. ❏ *She had hallucinations and couldn't sleep or eat.*

**hall|way** /hɔlweɪ/ (**hallways**) ◼ N-COUNT A **hallway** in a building is a long passage with doors into rooms on both sides of it. ❏ *They walked along the quiet hallway.* ◻ → see also **hall** ◾ N-COUNT A

**hallway** in a house or an apartment is the area just inside the front door, into which some of the other rooms open. ❏ *...the coats hanging in the hallway.* [from Old English]

**halo** /heɪloʊ/ (**haloes** or **halos**) N-COUNT A **halo** is a circle of light that is shown in pictures around the head of a holy figure such as a saint or angel. [from Medieval Latin]

**halo|gen** /hǽlədʒən/ (**halogens**) N-VAR A **halogen** is one of a group of chemical elements that includes chlorine, fluorine, and iodine. Halogens are often used in lighting and heating devices. ❏ *...a halogen lamp.* [from Swedish]

**halo|phile** /hǽləfaɪl/ (**halophiles**) N-COUNT **Halophiles** are bacteria that need salt in order to grow. [TECHNICAL]

**halt** /hɔlt/ (**halts, halting, halted**) ◼ V-T/ V-I When a person or a vehicle **halts** or when something **halts** them, they stop moving in the direction they were going and stand still. ❏ *Judges halted the race at 5:30 p.m. yesterday.* ◻ V-T/V-I When something such as growth, development, or activity **halts** or when you **halt** it, it stops completely. ❏ *Last week's storm halted business.* ◾ PHRASE If someone or something comes **to a halt**, they stop moving. ❏ *The elevator came to a halt at the first floor.* ◿ PHRASE If something such as growth, development, or activity **comes** or **grinds to a halt** or **is brought to a halt**, it stops completely. ❏ *Her career came to a halt in 2005.* [from German]

**halve** /hǽv/ (**halves, halving, halved**) ◼ V-T/V-I When you **halve** something or when it **halves**, it is reduced to half its previous size or amount. ❏ *People who exercise may halve their risk of getting heart disease.* ◻ V-T If you **halve** something, you divide it into two equal parts. ❏ *Halve the peppers and remove the seeds.* ◾ **Halves** is the plural of **half**. [from Old English]

**ham** /hǽm/ (**hams**) N-VAR **Ham** is meat from the top of the back leg of a pig, specially treated so that it can be kept for a long period of time. ❏ *...ham sandwiches.* [from Old English]

**ham|burg|er** /hǽmbɜrgər/ (**hamburgers**) N-COUNT A **hamburger** is ground meat which has been shaped into a flat circle. Hamburgers are fried or grilled and often eaten on a bun.

**ham|mer** /hǽmər/ (**hammers, hammering, hammered**) ◼ N-COUNT A **hammer** is a tool that consists of a heavy piece of metal at the end of a handle. It is used, for example, to hit nails into something, or to break things into pieces. ❏ *He used a hammer to knock the nail in.* ◻ V-T If you **hammer** an object such as a nail, you hit it with a hammer. ❏ *She hammered a nail into the window frame.* ◾ V-I If you **hammer on** a surface, you hit it several times in order to make a noise, or to emphasize something you are saying when you are angry. ❏ *We had to hammer on the door before they opened it.* ◿ V-T If you say that someone **hammers** another person, you mean that they attack, criticize, or punish the other person severely. ❏ *Sports officials hammered him with a 15-day ban.* [from Old English]
→ see **tools**

▶ **hammer out** PHR-VERB If people **hammer out** an agreement or treaty, they succeed in producing it after a long or difficult discussion. ❏ *I think we can hammer out a solution.*

**ham|per** /hæmpər/ (**hampers, hampering, hampered**) **1** V-T If someone or something **hampers** you, they make it difficult for you to do what you are trying to do. ❑ *The bad weather hampered rescue operations.* **2** N-COUNT A **hamper** is a large basket with a lid, used especially for carrying food. ❑ *...a picnic hamper.* **3** N-COUNT A **hamper** is a storage container for soiled laundry. ❑ *He threw his wet towel into the laundry hamper.* [Sense 1 from Old English. Senses 2 and 3 from Old French.]

**ham|string** /hæmstrɪŋ/ (**hamstrings, hamstringing, hamstrung**) **1** N-COUNT A **hamstring** is a length of tissue or tendon behind your knee which joins the muscles of your thigh to the bones of your lower leg. ❑ *Webster has not played since suffering a hamstring injury.* **2** V-T If you are **hamstrung** by a person, problem, or difficulty, they make it very difficult for you to take any action. ❑ *The country is hamstrung by lack of money.*

---
**hand**
---
**1** NOUN USES AND PHRASES
**2** VERB USES
---

**1 hand** /hænd/ (**hands**) **1** N-COUNT Your **hands** are the parts of your body at the end of your arms. ❑ *I put my hand into my pocket and pulled out the letter.* **2** N-SING If you ask someone for **a hand** with something, you are asking them to help you in what you are doing. ❑ *Come and give me a hand in the kitchen.* **3** N-COUNT In a game of cards, your **hand** is the set of cards that you are holding in your hand at a particular time or the cards that are dealt to you at the beginning of the game. ❑ *He carefully looked at his hand.* **4** N-COUNT The **hands** of a clock or watch are the thin pieces of metal, plastic, or other material that indicate what time it is. ❑ *The hands of the clock on the wall moved with a slight click.* **5** PHRASE If something is **at hand**, **near at hand**, or **close at hand**, it is very near in place or time. ❑ *She sat down, with the phone close at hand.* **6** PHRASE If you do something **by hand**, you do it using your hands rather than a machine. ❑ *...a dress made entirely by hand.* **7** PHRASE When something **changes hands**, its ownership changes, usually because it is sold to someone else. ❑ *The firm has changed hands many times.* **8** PHRASE If someone gives you **a free hand**, they give you the freedom to use your own judgment and to do exactly as you wish. ❑ *He gave Stephanie a free hand in the decoration of the house.* **9** PHRASE If two things **go hand in hand**, they are closely connected and cannot be considered separately from each other. ❑ *Research and teaching go hand in hand.* **10** PHRASE If you **have a hand in** something such as an event or activity, you are involved in it. ❑ *He thanked everyone who had a hand in the event.* **11** PHRASE If a situation is **in hand**, it is under control. ❑ *The Olympic organizers say that plans are well in hand.* **12** PHRASE If someone **lives hand to mouth** or **lives from hand to mouth**, they have hardly enough food or money to live on. ❑ *I have a wife and two children and we live from hand to mouth on what I earn.* **13** PHRASE If someone or something is **on hand**, they are near and able to be used if they are needed. ❑ *There are experts on hand to give you all the help you need.* **14** PHRASE You use **on the one hand** to introduce the first of two contrasting points, facts, or ways of looking at something. It is always followed by "on the other hand" or "on the other." ❑ *On the one hand, the body cannot survive without fat. On the other hand, if the body has too much fat, our health starts to suffer.* **15** PHRASE You use **on the other hand** to introduce the second of two contrasting points, facts, or ways of looking at something. You do not need to use **on the one hand** before it. ❑ *The movie lost money; reviews, on the other hand, were mostly favorable.* **16** PHRASE If a person or a situation gets **out of hand**, you are no longer able to control them. ❑ *Officials tried to stop the demonstration from getting out of hand.* **17** PHRASE If you **try your hand at** an activity, you attempt to do it, usually for the first time. ❑ *He tried his hand at fishing, but he wasn't very good at it.* **18** PHRASE If you **wash your hands of** someone or something, you refuse to be involved with them any more or to take responsibility for them. ❑ *He has washed his hands of the job.* [from Old English] **19** with one's **bare hands** → see **bare** **20** to **shake** someone's **hand** → see **shake** **21** to **shake hands** → see **shake** → see Picture Dictionary: hand → see **body, time**

**2 hand** /hænd/ (**hands, handing, handed**) V-T If you **hand** something **to** someone, you pass it to them. ❑ *He handed me a piece of paper.*
▸ **hand down** PHR-VERB If you **hand down** something such as knowledge, a possession, or a skill, you give or leave it to people who belong to a younger generation. ❑ *The idea of handing down knowledge to your children is important.*
▸ **hand in** PHR-VERB If you **hand in** something such as homework or something that you have found, you give it to a teacher, police officer, or other person in authority. ❑ *I need to hand in my homework today.*
▸ **hand on** → see **hand down**
▸ **hand out** **1** PHR-VERB If you **hand** things **out** to people, you give one or more to each person in a group. ❑ *My job was to hand out the prizes.* **2** → see also **handout**
▸ **hand over** PHR-VERB If you **hand over** to someone or **hand** something **over to** them, you give them the responsibility for dealing with a particular situation or problem. ❑ *The chairman handed over control to someone younger.*

**hand|bag** /hændbæg/ (**handbags**) N-COUNT A **handbag** is a small bag which a woman uses to carry things such as her money and keys in when she goes out.

**hand|book** /hændbʊk/ (**handbooks**) N-COUNT A **handbook** is a book that gives you advice and instructions about a particular subject, tool, or machine. ❑ *...a handbook on growing vegetables.*

**hand|cuff** /hændkʌf/ (**handcuffs, handcuffing, handcuffed**) **1** N-PLURAL **Handcuffs** are two metal rings which are joined together and can be locked around someone's wrists. ❑ *He was taken to jail in handcuffs.* **2** V-T If you **handcuff** someone, you put handcuffs around their wrists. ❑ *Police tried to handcuff him but he ran away.*

**hand|ful** /hændfʊl/ (**handfuls**) **1** N-SING A **handful** of people or things is a small number of them. ❑ *Only a handful of people knew his secret.* **2** N-COUNT A **handful** of something is the amount of it that you can hold in your hand. ❑ *...a handful of sand.* **3** N-SING If you say that someone, especially a child, is a **handful**, you mean that they

## Picture Dictionary hand

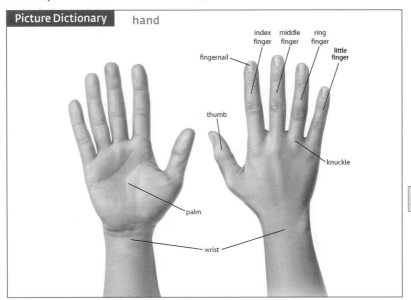

- index finger
- middle finger
- ring finger
- little finger
- fingernail
- thumb
- knuckle
- palm
- wrist

are difficult to control. [INFORMAL] ❑ *Sarah is a handful sometimes.* [from Old English]

**handi|cap** /hǽndikæp/ (**handicaps, handicapping, handicapped**) **1** N-COUNT A **handicap** is a physical or mental disability. ❑ *He lost his leg when he was ten, but learned to live with his handicap.* **2** N-COUNT A **handicap** is an event or situation that makes it harder for you to do something. ❑ *Being a foreigner was not a handicap.* **3** V-T If an event or a situation **handicaps** someone or something, it makes it harder for them to do something. ❑ *Their nationality handicaps them in the job market.*

**handi|capped** /hǽndikæpt/ ADJ Someone who is **handicapped** has a physical or mental disability. Some people find this term offensive and prefer to use **disabled**. ❑ *She teaches handicapped kids to fish.*

**hand|ker|chief** /hǽŋkərtʃɪf/ (**handkerchiefs**) N-COUNT A **handkerchief** is a small square piece of fabric which you use for blowing your nose.

**han|dle** /hǽndᵊl/ (**handles, handling, handled**)

handle

**1** N-COUNT A **handle** is a small round object or a lever that is attached to a door and is used for opening and closing it. ❑ *I turned the handle and the door opened.* **2** N-COUNT A **handle** is the part of an object such as a tool, bag, or cup that you hold in order to be able to pick up and use the object. ❑ *...a knife handle.* **3** V-T If you **handle** a problem or situation, you deal with it. ❑ *I don't know if I can handle the job.* ❑ *I think I handled the meeting very badly.* ● **han|dling** N-UNCOUNT ❑ *He questioned them*

*about their handling of the case.* **4** V-T If you **handle** a particular area of work, you have responsibility for it. ❑ *She handles travel plans for the company's managers.* **5** V-T When you **handle** something, you hold it or move it with your hands. ❑ *Wash your hands before handling food.* [from Old English]

### Word Partnership Use *handle* with :

| | |
|---|---|
| N. | handle **a job/problem/situation**, handle **pressure/responsibility 3 4** **ability to** handle *something* **3 – 5** |
| ADJ. | **difficult/easy/hard to** handle **3 – 5** |

**han|dler** /hǽndlər/ (**handlers**) **1** N-COUNT A **handler** is someone whose job is to be in charge of and control an animal. ❑ *...dog handlers.* **2** N-COUNT A **handler** is someone whose job is to deal with a particular type of object. ❑ *...baggage handlers at the airport.* [from Old English]

**hand|made** /hǽndmeɪd/ also **hand-made** ADJ **Handmade** objects have been made by someone using their hands or using tools rather than by machines. ❑ *...handmade jewelry.*

**hand-me-down** (**hand-me-downs**) **1** N-COUNT **Hand-me-downs** are things, usually clothes, which someone else has already used and which are given to you to use. ❑ *Edward wore Andrew's hand-me-downs.* **2** ADJ **Hand-me-down** is used to describe things, usually clothes, which someone else has already used and which are given to you to use. ❑ *Most of the boys wore hand-me-down shirts from their fathers.*

**hand|out** /hǽndaʊt/ (**handouts**) **1** N-COUNT A **handout** is a gift of money, clothing, or food, which is given free to poor people. ❑ *Each family got a cash handout of six thousand rupees after the fire.* **2** N-COUNT A **handout** is a document which contains news or information about something. ❏ *Turn to the first page of the handout.*

**hands-free** ADJ A **hands-free** telephone or other device can be used without being held in your hand. ❏ *...laws to ban handheld and hands-free cellphones in moving cars.*

**hand|shake** /hændʃeɪk/ (**handshakes**) ■ N-COUNT If you give someone a **handshake**, you take their right hand with your own right hand and hold it firmly or move it up and down, as a sign of greeting or to show that you have agreed about something. ❏ *He has a strong handshake.*

**hands-off** ADJ A **hands-off** policy or approach to something consists of not being personally or directly involved in it. ❏ *...the government's hands-off attitude toward large businesses.*

**hand|some** /hænsəm/ ■ ADJ A **handsome** man has an attractive face with regular features. ❏ *...a tall, handsome farmer.* ② ADJ A **handsome** sum of money is a large or generous amount. [FORMAL] ❏ *They will make a handsome profit when they sell the house.* [from Dutch]

**hands-on** ADJ **Hands-on** experience or work involves actually doing a particular thing, rather than just talking about it or getting someone else to do it. ❏ *Her hands-on management style often means she works from 6 a.m. to 11 p.m.*

**hand|writing** /hændraɪtɪŋ/ N-UNCOUNT Your **handwriting** is your style of writing with a pen or pencil. ❏ *The address was in Anna's handwriting.*

**hand|written** /hændrɪtᵊn/ ADJ A piece of writing that is **handwritten** is one that someone has written using a pen or pencil rather than by typing it. ❏ *...a handwritten note.*

**handy** /hændi/ (**handier, handiest**) ■ ADJ Something that is **handy** is useful. ❏ *The book gives handy hints on growing plants.* ② ADJ A thing or place that is **handy** is nearby and therefore easy to get or reach. ❏ *Make sure you have a pencil and paper handy.* [from Old English]

**hang** /hæŋ/ (**hangs, hanging, hung** or **hanged**)

> The form **hanged** is used as the past tense and past participle for meaning ③.

■ V-T/V-I If something **hangs** in a high place or position, or if you **hang** it there, it is attached there so it does not touch the ground. ❏ *Posters advertising the show hang at every entrance.* • **Hang up** means the same as **hang**. ❏ *I found his jacket hanging up in the hallway.* ② V-I If something **hangs** in a particular way or position, that is how it is worn or arranged. ❏ *She always wore a coat that hung down to her ankles.* ❏ *Her long hair hung loose about her shoulders.* ③ V-T/V-I If someone **is hanged** or if they **hang**, they are killed by having a rope tied around their neck and the support taken away from under their feet. ❏ *The five men were hanged on Tuesday.* ❏ *He hanged himself in prison.* ④ V-I If a possibility **hangs over** you, it worries you and makes your life unpleasant or difficult because you think it might happen. ❏ *The threat of unemployment hangs over many workers.* ⑤ → see also **hung** ⑥ PHRASE If you **get the hang of** something such as a skill or activity, you begin to understand or realize how to do it. [INFORMAL] ❏ *Driving is difficult at first until you get the hang of it.* [from Old English]

▸ **hang back** PHR-VERB If you **hang back**, you move or stay slightly behind a person or group,

usually because you are shy or nervous about something. ❏ *He hung back while the others moved forward.*

▸ **hang on** ■ PHR-VERB If you ask someone to **hang on**, you ask them to wait or stop what they are doing or saying for a moment. [INFORMAL] ❏ *Can you hang on for a minute?* ② PHR-VERB If you **hang on**, you manage to survive, achieve success, or avoid failure in spite of great difficulties or opposition. ❏ *He hung on to finish second in the race.* ③ PHR-VERB If you **hang on to** or **hang onto** something that gives you an advantage, you succeed in keeping it for yourself. ❏ *The tennis player was unable to hang on to his lead and lost the game.* ④ PHR-VERB If you **hang on to** or **hang onto** something, you hold it very tightly. ❏ *He hung on to the rail as he went downstairs.* ❏ *The child hung onto his legs.* ⑤ PHR-VERB If one thing **hangs on** another, it depends on it in order to be successful. ❏ *The success of the agreement hangs on this meeting.*

▸ **hang out** ■ PHR-VERB If you **hang out** clothes that you have washed, you hang them on a clothes line to dry. ❏ *I hung my laundry out.* ② PHR-VERB If you **hang out** in a particular place or area, you go and stay there for no particular reason, or spend a lot of time there. [INFORMAL] ❏ *I often hang out at the mall.*

▸ **hang up** ■ → see **hang** ① ② PHR-VERB If you **hang up** or you **hang up** the phone, you end a phone call. If you **hang up on** someone you are speaking to on the phone, you end the phone call suddenly and unexpectedly. ❏ *Mom hung up the phone.* ❏ *Don't hang up on me!*

**hang|ar** /hæŋər/ (**hangars**) N-COUNT A **hangar** is a large building in which aircraft are kept. [from French]

**hang|er** /hæŋər/ (**hangers**) N-COUNT A **hanger** is the same as a **coat hanger**. [from Old English]

**hang|ing val|ley** (**hanging valleys**) N-COUNT A **hanging valley** is a type of valley associated with glaciers. It is smaller and higher than the main glacial valley, to which it is connected. [TECHNICAL]

**hang|ing wall** (**hanging walls**) N-COUNT A **hanging wall** is the rock above a geological fault. Compare **footwall**. [TECHNICAL]

**hap|haz|ard** /hæphæzərd/ ADJ If you describe something as **haphazard**, you are critical of it because it is not at all organized or is not arranged according to a plan. ❏ *The investigation seemed haphazard.* • **hap|haz|ard|ly** ADV ❏ *The books were arranged haphazardly, so it was difficult to find anything.*

**hap|less** /hæplɪs/ ADJ A **hapless** person is unlucky. [FORMAL] ❏ *...his hapless victim.* [from Late Middle English]

**hap|pen** /hæpən/ (**happens, happening, happened**) ■ V-I Something that **happens** occurs or is done without being planned. ❏ *We don't know what will happen.* ② V-I When something **happens to** you, it takes place and affects you. ❏ *What's the worst thing that has ever happened to you?* ③ V-T If you **happen to** do something, you do it by chance. ❏ *We happened to be there at the same time.* ④ PHRASE You use **as it happens** in order to introduce a statement, especially one that is rather surprising. ❏ *As it happened, I was the first to arrive.*

**hap|pen|ing** /hæpənɪŋ/ (**happenings**) N-COUNT

**Happenings** are things that happen, often in a way that is unexpected or hard to explain. ❑ *The North End News told people about the latest happenings in the city.*

**hap|pi|ly** /hǽpɪli/ **1** ADV You can add **happily** to a statement to indicate that you are glad that something happened. ❑ *Happily, most kittens are adopted within days of arriving at the shelter.* **2** → see also **happy**

**hap|py** /hǽpi/ (**happier, happiest**) **1** ADJ Someone who is **happy** has feelings of pleasure. ❑ *Marina was a happy child.* ● **hap|pi|ly** ADV ❑ *Albert leaned back happily and drank his coffee.* ● **hap|pi|ness** N-UNCOUNT ❑ *I think she was looking for happiness.* **2** ADJ A **happy** time, place, or relationship is full of happy feelings and pleasant experiences, or has an atmosphere in which people feel happy. ❑ *She had a happy childhood.* ❑ *It was always a happy place.* **3** ADJ If you are **happy about** or **with** a situation or arrangement, you are satisfied with it. ❑ *I'm not happy with what I've written.* **4** ADJ If you say you are **happy to** do something, you mean that you are very willing to do it. ❑ *I'm happy to answer any questions.* ● **hap|pi|ly** ADV ❑ *I will happily apologize if I've upset anyone.* **5** ADJ **Happy** is used in greetings and other conventional expressions to say that you hope someone will enjoy a special occasion. ❑ *Happy Birthday!*
→ see **emotion**

| **Thesaurus** | *happy* | Also look up : |
| --- | --- | --- |
| ADJ. | cheerful, content, delighted, glad, pleased, upbeat; (*ant.*) sad, unhappy **1** | |

| **Word Partnership** | Use *happy* with : |
| --- | --- |
| ADV. | **extremely/perfectly/very** happy **1** |
| V. | **feel** happy, **make** *someone* happy, **seem** happy **1** |
| N. | happy **ending**, happy **family**, happy **marriage 2** |

**har|ass** /hərǽs, hǽrəs/ (**harasses, harassing, harassed**) V-T If someone **harasses** you, they trouble or annoy you. ❑ *Players harassed the referee throughout the game.* ● **har|ass|ment** /hərǽsmənt, hǽrəs-/ N-UNCOUNT ❑ *...rules to prevent harassment at work.* [from French]

**har|assed** /hərǽst, hǽrəst/ ADJ If you are **harassed**, you are anxious and tense because you have too much to do or too many problems to cope with. ❑ *He looked harassed and tired.* [from French]

**har|bor** /hɑ́rbər/ (**harbors, harboring, harbored**) **1** N-COUNT A **harbor** is an area of water which is partly enclosed by land or strong walls, so that boats can be left there safely. ❑ *The fishing boats left the harbor and motored out to sea.* **2** V-T If you **harbor** an emotion, thought, or secret, you have it in your mind over a long period of time. ❑ *She harbored a lot of anger about her childhood.* **3** V-T If a person or country **harbors** someone who is wanted by the police, they let them stay in their house or country and offer them protection. ❑ *...states that harbored terrorists.* [from Old English]

**har|bor|mas|ter** /hɑ́rbərmæstər/ (**harbormasters**) also **harbor master** N-COUNT A **harbormaster** is the official in charge of a harbor. [from Old English]

**hard** /hɑ́rd/ (**harder, hardest**) **1** ADJ Something that is **hard** is very firm and stiff to touch and is not easily bent, cut, or broken. ❑ *...the hard wooden floor.* ● **hard|ness** N-UNCOUNT ❑ *...the hardness of the iron railing.* **2** ADJ Something that is **hard** is very difficult to do or deal with. ❑ *That's a very hard question.* ❑ *She had a hard life.* **3** ADV If you work **hard** doing something, you are very active or work intensely, with a lot of effort. ❑ *If I work hard, I'll finish the work by tomorrow.* ● **Hard** is also an adjective. ❑ *I admired him as a hard worker.* ❑ *...a hard day's work.* **4** ADV If you strike or take hold of something **hard**, you strike or take hold of it with a lot of force. ❑ *I kicked a trash can very hard and broke my toe.* ● **Hard** is also an adjective. ❑ *She gave me a hard push and I fell over.* **5** ADJ If a person or their expression is **hard**, they show no kindness or sympathy. ❑ *His father was a hard man.* **6** ADJ **Hard** evidence or facts are definitely true and do not need to be questioned. ❑ *You should base your decision on hard facts.* **7** PHRASE If you say that something is **hard going**, you mean it is difficult and requires a lot of effort. ❑ *The job was hard going at the start.* [from Latin] [from Old English]

| **Thesaurus** | *hard* | Also look up : |
| --- | --- | --- |
| ADJ. | firm, solid, tough; (*ant.*) gentle, soft **1** complicated, difficult, tough; (*ant.*) easy **2** | |

**hard|ball** /hɑ́rdbɔl/ PHRASE If someone **plays hardball**, they will do anything that is necessary to achieve or get what they want, even if this involves being harsh or unfair. ❑ *She is playing hardball in a difficult business.*

**hard ci|der** (**hard ciders**) N-UNCOUNT **Hard cider** is an alcoholic drink that is made from apples.

**hard core** also **hard-core** N-SING You can refer to the members of a group who are the most committed to its activities or who are the most involved in them as a **hard core of** members or as the **hard-core** members. ❑ *The violence was started by a hard core of troublemakers.* ❑ *Hard-core Harry Potter fans criticized the film for changing important parts of the book.*

**hard|cover** /hɑ́rdkʌvər/ (**hardcovers**) N-COUNT A **hardcover** is a book which has a stiff hard cover. Compare **softcover**. ❑ *The book was published in hardcover last October.*

**hard cur|ren|cy** (**hard currencies**) N-VAR A **hard currency** is one which is unlikely to lose its value and so is considered to be a good one to have or to invest in. ❑ *The country does not have enough hard currency to pay for imports.*

**hard disk** (**hard disks**) N-COUNT A computer's **hard disk** is a stiff magnetic disk on which data and programs can be stored.

**hard drive** (**hard drives**) N-COUNT The **hard drive** on a computer is the part that contains the computer's hard disk. ❑ *You can play music from the PC's hard drive.*

**hard-earned** ADJ A **hard-earned** victory or **hard-earned** cash is a victory or money that someone deserves because they have worked hard for it. ❑ *Don't waste any more of your hard-earned money on that dress!*

**hard|en** /hɑ́rdᵊn/ (**hardens, hardening, hardened**) **1** V-T/V-I When something **hardens** or when you **harden** it, it becomes stiff or firm.

h

❏ *Mold the mixture before it hardens.* **2** V-T/V-I When an attitude or opinion **hardens** or **is hardened**, it becomes harsher, stronger, or fixed. ❏ *Their actions will harden the government's attitude.* ● **hard|en|ing** N-SING ❏ *...a hardening of public opinion.* **3** V-T/V-I When events **harden** people or when people **harden**, they become less easily affected emotionally and less sympathetic and gentle than they were before. ❏ *Nina's heart hardened against her father.* [from Old English]

**hard la|bor** N-UNCOUNT **Hard labor** is hard physical work which people have to do as punishment for a crime. ❏ *The sentence of the court was twelve years' hard labor.*

**hard-line** also **hardline** ADJ If you describe someone's policy or attitude as **hard-line**, you mean that it is strict or extreme, and they refuse to change it. ❏ *...the country's hard-line government.*

**hard|ly** /ˈhɑrdli/ **1** ADV You use **hardly** to say that something is only just true. ❏ *I hardly know you.* ❏ *I've hardly slept for three days.* **2** ADV You use **hardly** in expressions such as **hardly ever**, **hardly any**, and **hardly anyone** to mean almost never, almost none, or almost no one. ❏ *We hardly ever eat fish.* ❏ *...young workers with hardly any experience.* **3** ADV You use **hardly** to mean "not" when you want to suggest that you are expecting your listener or reader to agree with your comment. ❏ *It's hardly surprising his ideas didn't work.* [from Old English]

> **Usage** **hardly** and **hard**
>
> *Hardly* is not the adverb form of *hard. Hard* is used for both the adjective: *The test was very hard.* and the adverb: *The staff worked hard.* However, to say: "*The staff hardly worked.*" means that they did not work hard. The adverbs *hardly* and *hard* means just about the opposite of each other.

**hard-pressed** also **hard pressed** **1** ADJ If someone is **hard-pressed**, they are under a lot of strain and worry. ❏ *...hard-pressed families who can't afford to buy food.* **2** ADJ If you will be **hard-pressed to** do something, you will have great difficulty doing it. ❏ *You'd be hard-pressed to find anyone better.*

**hard|ship** /ˈhɑrdʃɪp/ (**hardships**) N-VAR **Hardship** is a situation in which your life is difficult or unpleasant. ❏ *Higher bus fares are a hardship on elderly people.* [from Old English]

> **Word Link** **ware ≈ merchandise : hard**ware, **soft**ware, **ware**house

**hard|ware** /ˈhɑrdwɛər/ **1** N-UNCOUNT In computer systems, **hardware** refers to the machines themselves as opposed to the programs which tell the machines what to do. Compare **software**. ❏ *The hardware costs about $200.* **2** N-UNCOUNT **Hardware** refers to tools and equipment that are used in the home and garden, for example nuts and bolts, screwdrivers, and hinges. ❏ *...a hardware store.*

**har|dy** /ˈhɑrdi/ (**hardier, hardiest**) ADJ People, animals and plants that are **hardy** are strong and able to survive difficult conditions. ❏ *The plant is hardy and easy to grow.* [from Old French]

**hare** /hɛər/ (**hares**) N-VAR A **hare** is an animal like a rabbit but larger with long ears, long legs, and a small tail. [from Old English]

**hark** /hɑrk/ (**harks, harking, harked**) [from Old English]
▶ **hark back to** PHR-VERB If you say that one thing **harks back to** another thing in the past, you mean it is similar to it or takes it as a model. ❏ *The design harks back to the 1800s.*

**harm** /hɑrm/ (**harms, harming, harmed**)
**1** V-T To **harm** someone or something means to injure or damage them. ❏ *They didn't mean to harm anyone.* ❏ *...a warning that the product may harm the environment.* **2** N-UNCOUNT **Harm** is injury or damage to a person or thing. ❏ *All dogs are capable of doing harm to people.* **3** PHRASE If you say **it does no harm to** do something or **there is no harm in** doing something, you mean that it might be worth doing, and you will not be blamed for doing it. ❏ *I don't think he'll help, but there's no harm in asking.* [from Old English]

> **Thesaurus** **harm** Also look up :
>
> v. abuse, damage, hurt, injure, ruin, wreck; (ant.) benefit **1**
> n. abuse, damage, hurt, injury, ruin, violence **2**

> **Word Partnership** Use *harm* with :
>
> ADJ. **bodily** harm **2**
> v. **cause** harm, **not mean any** harm **2**
> n. harm **the environment 2**

**harm|ful** /ˈhɑrmfəl/ ADJ Something that is **harmful** has a bad effect on someone or something. ❏ *...the harmful effects of the sun.* [from Old English]

**harm|less** /ˈhɑrmlɪs/ **1** ADJ Something that is **harmless** does not have any bad effects. ❏ *These bugs don't bite and are harmless.* **2** ADJ If you describe someone or something as **harmless**, you mean that they are unlikely to annoy other people or cause trouble. ❏ *He seemed harmless.* [from Old English]

**har|mon|ic** /hɑrˈmɒnɪk/ ADJ **Harmonic** means composed, played, or sung using two or more notes which sound right and pleasing together. ❏ *...the harmonic structure of the music.* [from Latin]

**har|mon|ic pro|gres|sion** (**harmonic progressions**) N-COUNT A **harmonic progression** is a series of chords or harmonies within a piece of music. [TECHNICAL]

**har|mo|nize** /ˈhɑrmənaɪz/ (**harmonizes, harmonizing, harmonized**) V-RECIP If two or more people or things **harmonize with** each other, they fit in well with each other. ❏ *If we understand people, it is easier to harmonize with them.* [from Latin]

**har|mo|ny** /ˈhɑrməni/ (**harmonies**)
**1** N-UNCOUNT If people are living **in harmony** with each other, they are living together peacefully rather than fighting or arguing. ❏ *People should live in harmony with each other and with nature.* **2** N-VAR **Harmony** is the pleasant combination of different notes of music played at the same time. ❏ *...singing in harmony.* **3** N-UNCOUNT The **harmony** of something is the way in which its parts are combined into a pleasant arrangement. ❏ *...the beauty and harmony of the design.* [from Latin]

H

**Picture Dictionary**

hats

cowboy hat

top hat

beret

baseball cap

cycle helmet

fedora

balaclava

stocking cap

hard hat

Panama hat

bonnet

mortarboard

h

**har|ness** /hɑrnɪs/ (**harnesses, harnessing, harnessed**) ■ V-T If you **harness** something such as an emotion or natural source of energy, you bring it under your control and use it. □ *Turkey plans to harness the waters of the Tigris and Euphrates rivers.* ■ N-COUNT A **harness** is a set of straps which fit under a person's arms and fasten around their body in order to keep a piece of equipment in place or to prevent the person moving from a place. ■ N-COUNT A **harness** is a set of leather straps and metal links fastened around a horse's head or body so that the horse can have a carriage, cart, or plow fastened to it. ■ V-T If a horse or other animal **is harnessed**, a harness is put on it, especially so that it can pull a carriage, cart, or plow. □ *The horses were harnessed to a heavy wagon.* [from Old French]

**harp** /hɑrp/ (**harps, harping, harped**) N-VAR A **harp** is a large musical instrument consisting of a row of strings stretched from the top to the bottom of a frame. You play the harp by plucking the strings with your fingers. [from Old English] → see **string**

▶ **harp on** PHR-VERB If someone **harps on** a subject, or **harps on about** it, they keep on talking about it in a way that other people find annoying. □ *Jones harps on this subject more than on any other.*

**har|row|ing** /hærouɪŋ/ ADJ A **harrowing** experience is extremely upsetting or disturbing. □ *...their harrowing experiences during Word War II.* [of Scandinavian origin]

**harsh** /hɑrʃ/ (**harsher, harshest**) ■ ADJ **Harsh** climates or conditions are very difficult for people, animals, and plants to live in. □ *...the harsh desert climate.* ● **harsh|ness** N-UNCOUNT □ *...the harshness of their living conditions.* ■ ADJ **Harsh** actions or speech are unkind and show no understanding

or sympathy. □ *He said many harsh things about his opponents.* ● **harsh|ly** ADV □ *He was harshly treated in prison.* ● **harsh|ness** N-UNCOUNT □ *...the harshness of her words.* ■ ADJ Something that is **harsh** is so hard, bright, or rough that it seems unpleasant or harmful. □ *The harsh light made the room look very unattractive.* [of Scandinavian origin]

**har|vest** /hɑrvɪst/ (**harvests, harvesting, harvested**) ■ N-SING **The harvest** is the gathering of a crop. □ *The bean harvest starts in January.* ■ N-COUNT A **harvest** is the crop that is gathered in. □ *...the potato harvest.* ■ V-T When you **harvest** a crop, you gather it in. □ *Farmers here still plant and harvest their crops by hand.* [from Old English] → see **farm, grain**

**has**

The auxiliary verb is pronounced /həz, STRONG hæz/. The main verb is usually pronounced /hæz/.

**Has** is the third person singular of the present tense of **have**. [from Old English]

**hash** /hæʃ/ (**hashes, hashing, hashed**) N-VAR **Hash** is a dish made from meat cut into small pieces and fried with other ingredients such as onions or potato. □ *...potato hash.* [from Old French]

▶ **hash out** PHR-VERB If people **hash out** something such as a plan or a problem, they discuss it thoroughly until they reach an agreement. □ *The two sides are hashing out the details of the agreeement.*

**hasn't** /hæzªnt/ **Hasn't** is the usual spoken form of "has not." [from Old English]

**has|sle** /hæsªl/ (**hassles, hassling, hassled**) ■ N-VAR A **hassle** is a situation that is difficult and involves problems, effort, or arguments with people. [INFORMAL] ❑ *Moving to a new house is a lot of hassle.* **2** V-T If someone **hassles** you, they cause problems for you, often by repeatedly telling you or asking you to do something, usually in an annoying way. [INFORMAL] ❑ *The kids started hassling me about going to the movies.*

**haste** /heɪst/ **1** N-UNCOUNT **Haste** is the quality of doing something quickly, sometimes too quickly so that you are careless and make mistakes. ❑ *Why did they marry with such haste?* **2** PHRASE If you do something **in haste**, you do it quickly and hurriedly, and sometimes carelessly. ❑ *If you act in haste, you might regret it.* [from Old French]

**has|ten** /heɪsˀn/ (**hastens, hastening, hastened**) **1** V-T If you **hasten** an event or process, you make it happen faster or sooner. ❑ *It was part of a plan to hasten his departure.* **2** V-T If you **hasten to** do something, you are quick to do it. ❑ *She hastened to sign the contract.* [from Old French]

**has|ty** /heɪsti/ (**hastier, hastiest**) **1** ADJ A **hasty** movement, action, or statement is sudden, and often done in reaction to something that has just happened. ❑ *Donald knocked over a chair in his hasty departure.* ● **hasti|ly** /heɪstɪli/ ADV ❑ *A meeting was hastily arranged to discuss the problem.* **2** ADJ If you describe a person or their behavior as **hasty**, you are critical of them because they act too quickly, without thinking carefully. ❑ *Don't make a hasty decision.* ● **hasti|ly** ADV ❑ *I decided that I wouldn't do anything hastily.* [from Old French]

**hat** /hæt/ (**hats**) N-COUNT A **hat** is a head covering. ❑ *...a red hat.* [from Old English]
→ see Picture Dictionary: **hats**

**hatch** /hætʃ/ (**hatches, hatching, hatched**) **1** V-T/V-I When a baby bird, insect, or other animal **hatches**, or when it **is hatched**, it comes out of its egg by breaking the shell. You can also say that an egg **hatches**. ❑ *The young birds died soon after they were hatched.* ❑ *The eggs hatch after a week.* **2** V-T If you **hatch** a plot or a scheme, you think of it and work it out. ❑ *He hatched a plot to embarrass the president.* **3** N-COUNT A **hatch** is an opening in the deck of a ship, through which people or cargo can go. ❑ *He moved through the hatch to the passageway.* [Senses 1 and 2 of Germanic origin. Sense 3 from Old English.]

**hatch|et** /hætʃɪt/ (**hatchets**) N-COUNT A **hatchet** is a small ax. [from Old French]

**hate** /heɪt/ (**hates, hating, hated**) **1** V-T If you **hate** someone or something, you have an extremely strong feeling of dislike for them. ❑ *Most people hate him.* ❑ *He hates to lose.* ● **Hate** is also a noun. ❑ *I was 17 and full of hate.* **2** V-T You can use **hate** in expressions such as "**I hate to say it**" or "**I hate to tell you**" when you want to express regret about what you are about to say, because you think it is unpleasant or should not be the case. ❑ *I hate to say it but I think he's too old for the job.* [from Old English] **3** to **hate** someone's **guts** → see **gut**
→ see **emotion**

**ha|tred** /heɪtrɪd/ (**hatreds**) N-UNCOUNT **Hatred** is an extremely strong feeling of dislike for someone or something. ❑ *...her hatred of her daughter's killer.* [from Old English]

**haul** /hɔl/ (**hauls, hauling, hauled**) **1** V-T If you **haul** something which is heavy or difficult to move, you move it using a lot of effort. ❑ *They used a crane to haul the car out of the water.* **2** PHRASE If you say that a task or a journey is a **long haul**, you mean that it takes a long time and a lot of effort. ❑ *It's been a long haul since leaving Miami at 7 a.m.* [from Old French]

**haunt** /hɔnt/ (**haunts, haunting, haunted**) **1** V-T If something unpleasant **haunts** you, you keep thinking or worrying about it over a long period of time. ❑ *The memory of the accident haunted him for a long time.* **2** N-COUNT A place that is the **haunt** of a particular person is one which they often visit because they enjoy going there. ❑ *The islands are a favorite summer haunt for tourists.* **3** V-T A ghost or spirit that **haunts** a place or a person regularly appears in the place, or is seen by the person and frightens them. ❑ *His ghost is believed to haunt the room.* [from Old French]

**haunt|ed** /hɔntɪd/ **1** ADJ A **haunted** building or other place is one where a ghost regularly appears. ❑ *Tracy said the cabin was haunted.* **2** ADJ Someone who has a **haunted** expression looks very worried or troubled. ❑ *She looked so haunted, I almost didn't recognize her.* [from Old French]

**haunt|ing** /hɔntɪŋ/ ADJ **Haunting** sounds, images, or words remain in your thoughts because they are very beautiful or sad. ❑ *...the haunting calls of wild birds.* ● **haunt|ing|ly** ADV ❑ *Each one of these old towns is hauntingly beautiful.* [from Old French]

---

| **have** |
|---|
| **❶** AUXILIARY VERB USES |
| **❷** USED WITH NOUNS DESCRIBING ACTIONS |
| **❸** OTHER VERB USES AND PHRASES |
| **❹** MODAL PHRASES |

**❶ have** /həv, STRONG hæv/ (**has, having, had**)

In spoken English, forms of **have** are often shortened, for example **I have** is shortened to **I've** and **has not** is shortened to **hasn't**.

**1** AUX You use the forms **have** and **has** with a past participle to form the present perfect tense of verbs. ❑ *Alex has already gone.* ❑ *What have you found?* ❑ *Frankie hasn't been feeling well for a long time.* **2** AUX You use the form **had** with a past participle to form the past perfect tense of verbs. ❑ *When I met her, she had just returned from a job interview.* **3** AUX **Have** is used in question tags. ❑ *You haven't seen her, have you?* **4** AUX You use **have** when you are confirming or contradicting a statement containing "have," "has," or "had," or answering a question. ❑ *"You've never seen the Marilyn Monroe film?" — "No I haven't."* [from Old English]

**❷ have** /hæv/ (**has, having, had**)

**Have** is used in combination with a wide range of nouns, where the meaning of the combination is mostly given by the noun.

**1** V-T You can use **have** followed by a noun to talk about an action or event, when it would be possible to use the same word as a verb. For example, you can say "**I had a look at the photos**" instead of "I looked at the photos." ❑ *I went out and had a walk around.* **2** V-T In normal spoken or written English, people use **have** with a wide range of nouns to talk about actions and events, often instead of a more specific verb. For example people are more likely to say "**we had ice cream**" or "**he's had a shock**" than "we ate ice cream," or "he's suffered a shock." □ *Come and have a meal with us tonight.* □ *We are having a meeting to decide what to do.* [from Old English]

❸ **have** /hæv/ (**has, having, had**) ■ V-T You use **have** to say that someone or something owns a particular thing, or when you are mentioning one of their qualities or characteristics. □ *Billy has a new bicycle.* □ *She had a good job.* □ *You have beautiful eyes.* □ *Do you have any brothers and sisters?* ❷ V-T If you **have** something **to** do, you are responsible for doing it or must do it. □ *He had plenty of work to do.* ❸ V-T If you **have** something such as a part of your body in a particular position or state, it is in that position or state. □ *Mary had her eyes closed.* □ *They had the windows open.* ❹ V-T If you **have** something done, someone does it for you or you arrange for it to be done. □ *I had your room cleaned.* □ *He had his hair cut.* ❺ V-T If someone **has** something unpleasant happen to them, it happens to them. □ *We had our money stolen.* ❻ V-T If someone **has** you **by** a part of your body, they are holding you there and they are trying to hurt you or force you to go somewhere. □ *She had the child by the arm and was pulling him along.* ❼ V-T If a woman **has** a baby, she gives birth to it. If she is **having** a baby, she is pregnant. □ *My wife has just had a baby.* ❽ PHRASE You can use **has it** in expressions such as "**rumor has it that**" or "**as legend has it**" when you are quoting something that you have heard, but you do not necessarily think it is true. □ *Rumor has it that tickets were being sold for $300.* [from Old English]

> ### Usage   have
> In speech, when *have* follows verbs such as *could, should, would, might,* and *must,* contracting *have* makes it sound like *of: could've* sounds like "could of"; *might've* sounds like "might of"; and so on. Be sure to say (and write) *have* when you dont use contractions: *could have; might have;* and so on.

❹ **have** /hæv, hæf/ (**has, having, had**) PHRASE You use **have to** when you are saying that something is necessary or required, or must happen. If you do not **have to** do something, it is not necessary or required. □ *He had to go to work.* □ *You have to be careful what you say on TV.* [from Old English]

**ha|ven** /heɪvᵊn/ (**havens**) ■ N-COUNT A **haven** is a place where people or animals feel safe, secure, and happy. □ *...Lake Baringo, a haven for birds.* [from Old English] ❷ → see also **safe haven**

**haven't** /hævᵊnt/ **Haven't** is the usual spoken form of "have not." [from Old English]

hawk

**hav|oc** /hævək/ ■ N-UNCOUNT **Havoc** is great disorder and confusion. □ *Protestors caused havoc in the center of the town.* ❷ PHRASE If one thing **wreaks havoc on** another, it prevents it from continuing or functioning as normal, or damages it. □ *Snow and ice wreaked havoc on bus and train services.* [from Old French]

**hawk** /hɔk/ (**hawks**) N-COUNT A **hawk** is a large bird that catches and eats small birds and animals. [from Old English]

**hay** /heɪ/ N-UNCOUNT **Hay** is grass which has been cut and dried so that it can be used to feed animals. [from Old English]
→ see **barn**

**hay fe|ver** N-UNCOUNT If someone is suffering from **hay fever**, they sneeze and their eyes itch, because they are allergic to certain kinds of grass, trees, or flowers.

**haz|ard** /hæzərd/ (**hazards, hazarding, hazarded**) ■ N-COUNT A **hazard** is something which could be dangerous to you, your health or safety, or your plans or reputation. □ *A report says that chewing gum may be a health hazard.* ❷ V-T If you **hazard** a **guess**, you make a suggestion about something which is only a guess and which you know might be wrong. □ *We can only hazard a guess at the reasons for this.* [from Old French]

**haz|ard|ous** /hæzərdəs/ ADJ Something that is **hazardous** is dangerous, especially to people's health or safety. □ *Some people think cell phones are hazardous to health.* [from Old French]

**haze** /heɪz/ (**hazes**) ■ N-VAR **Haze** is light mist, caused by particles of water or dust in the air. □ *...a heat haze.* ❷ N-SING If there is a **haze of** something such as smoke or steam, you cannot see clearly through it. [LITERARY] □ *...a haze of smoke.*

**ha|zel** /heɪzᵊl/ (**hazels**) ■ N-VAR A **hazel** is a small tree which produces nuts that you can eat. ❷ COLOR **Hazel** eyes are greenish brown in color. [from Old English]

**haz|ing** /heɪzɪŋ/ (**hazings**) N-VAR **Hazing** is a ritual practiced in some universities and other institutions, in which a new member of a club or organization is forced to do something embarrassing or dangerous. □ *She was a victim of hazing but escaped serious injury.* □ *...a vicious hazing ritual.*

**hazy** /heɪzi/ (**hazier, haziest**) ■ ADJ **Hazy** weather makes things difficult to see, because of light mist, hot air, or dust. □ *Tomorrow's weather will be hazy sunshine.* ❷ ADJ If you are **hazy about** ideas or details, or if they are **hazy**, you are uncertain or confused about them. □ *I have only a hazy memory of what he was like.*

**HDTV** /eɪtʃdi ti vi/ N-UNCOUNT **HDTV** is a television system that provides a clearer image than conventional television systems. **HDTV** is an abbreviation for "high-definition television." □ *The quality of digital TV is better, especially HDTV.*

**he** /hi, i, STRONG hi/

> **He** is a third person singular pronoun. **He** is used as the subject of a verb.

PRON You use **he** to refer to a man, boy, or male animal. □ *He couldn't remember my name.* [from Old English]

## head

❶ NOUN USES
❷ VERB USES
❸ PHRASES

❶ **head** /hɛd/ (**heads**) ■ N-COUNT Your **head** is the top part of your body, which has your eyes, mouth, and brain in it. □ *She turned her head away*

h

from him. **2** N-COUNT You can use **head** to refer to your mind and your mental abilities. ▫ *He could do difficult math in his head.* **3** N-COUNT The **head** of a company or organization is the person in charge of it and in charge of the people in it. ▫ *Heads of government from more than 100 countries will meet in Geneva tomorrow.* **4** N-COUNT The **head** of something is the top, start, or most important end of it. ▫ *She sat at the head of the table.* ▫ *He went to the head of the line.* **5** ADV If you flip a coin and it comes down **heads**, you can see the side of the coin which has a picture of a head on it. ▫ *Let's flip a coin for it. If it's heads, then we'll talk.* [from Old English] → see **body**

❷ **head** /hɛd/ (**heads, heading, headed**) **1** V-T If someone or something **heads** a line or procession, they are at the front of it. ▫ *I headed the line walking down the sidewalk.* **2** V-T If something **heads** a list or group, it is at the top of it. ▫ *She heads the list of the most popular actors in the U.S.* **3** V-T If you **head** a department, company, or organization, you are the person in charge of it. ▫ *Michael Williams heads the department's Office of Civil Rights.* **4** V-T If you **are heading** or **are headed** for a particular place, you are going toward that place. ▫ *He headed for the bus stop.* ▫ *Many people are heading back to Washington tomorrow.* **5** V-T/V-I If something or someone **is heading for** or **is headed for** a particular result, it means that the result is very likely. ▫ *The talks seem to be heading for failure.* **6** V-T If you **head** a ball in soccer, you hit it with your head in order to make it go in a particular direction. ▫ *He headed the ball into the goal.* [from Old English] **7** → see also **heading**

❸ **head** /hɛd/ (**heads**) **1** EXCLAM If someone shouts "**Heads up!**" to you, they are warning you to move out of the way, usually because something is falling on you from above, or because something is coming towards you very quickly. ▫ *Heads up! Watch out for the baseball!* **2** PHRASE The cost or amount **a head** or **per head** is the cost or amount for one person. ▫ *This simple meal costs less than $3 a head.* **3** PHRASE If a problem or disagreement **comes to a head** or **is brought to a head**, it becomes so bad that something must be done about it. ▫ *Things came to a head on Saturday when they had a fight.* **4** PHRASE If you **get** a fact or idea **into your head**, you suddenly realize or think that it is true and you usually do not change your opinion about it. ▫ *Once they get an idea into their heads, they never give up.* **5** PHRASE If something such as praise or success **goes to** someone's **head**, they start to believe that they are better than they really are. ▫ *Ford is not the type of man to let success go to his head.* **6** PHRASE If you **keep** your **head**, you remain calm in a difficult situation. If you **lose** your **head**, you panic or do not remain calm in a difficult situation. ▫ *She kept her head and didn't panic.* **7** PHRASE If something such as an idea, joke, or comment goes **over** someone's **head**, it is too difficult for them to understand. ▫ *A lot of the ideas at the meeting went over my head.* [from Old English]

head|ache /hɛdeɪk/ (**headaches**) **1** N-COUNT If you have a **headache**, you have a pain in your head. ▫ *I have a terrible headache.* **2** N-COUNT If you say that something is a **headache**, you mean that it causes you difficulty or worry. ▫ *The biggest headache for mothers who want to return to work is childcare.*

head|er /hɛdər/ (**headers**) N-COUNT A **header** is text such as a name or a page number that can be automatically displayed at the top of each page of a printed document. Compare **footer**. [COMPUTING] ▫ *…page formatting like headers, footers, and page numbers.* [from Old English]

head|first /hɛdfɜrst/ also **head-first** ADV If you move **headfirst** in a particular direction, your head is the part of your body that is furthest forward as you are moving. ▫ *He fell headfirst down the stairs.*

head|ing /hɛdɪŋ/ (**headings**) **1** N-COUNT A **heading** is the title of a piece of writing, which is written or printed at the top of the page. ▫ *…chapter headings.* [from Old English] **2** → see also **head**

| **Word Link** | light ≈ shining : daylight, enlighten, headlight |
|---|---|

head|light /hɛdlaɪt/ (**headlights**) N-COUNT A vehicle's **headlights** are the large powerful lights at the front. ▫ *He turned on the car's headlights in the tunnel.*

head|line /hɛdlaɪn/ (**headlines, headlining, headlined**) **1** N-COUNT A **headline** is the title of a newspaper story, printed in large letters at the top of it. ▫ *The headline said: "New government plans."* **2** N-PLURAL The **headlines** are the main points of the news which are read on radio or television. ▫ *Claudia Polley read the news headlines.* **3** PHRASE Someone or something that **hits the headlines** or **grabs the headlines** gets a lot of publicity from the media. ▫ *Johnson first hit the world headlines last year.*

head|long /hɛdlɔŋ/ **1** ADV If you fall or move **headlong**, you fall or move with your head furthest forward. ▫ *She fell headlong down the stairs.* **2** ADV If you rush **headlong into** something, you do it quickly without thinking carefully about it. ▫ *Do not leap headlong into decisions.* ● **Headlong** is also an adjective. ▫ *…the headlong rush toward Christmas.* **3** ADV If you move **headlong** in a particular direction, you move there very quickly. ▫ *He ran headlong for the door.* **4** → see also **headfirst**

head|master /hɛdmæstər/ (**headmasters**) N-COUNT A **headmaster** is the principal of a private school. [from Old English]

head of state (**heads of state**) N-COUNT A **head of state** is the leader of a country, for example a president, king, or queen. ▫ *…the Algerian head of state.*

head-on **1** ADV If two vehicles hit each other **head-on**, they hit each other with their fronts pointing toward each other. ▫ *The car crashed head-on into a truck.* ● **Head-on** is also an adjective. ▫ *There was a serious head-on crash.* **2** ADJ A **head-on** conflict or approach is direct, without any attempt to compromise or avoid the issue. ▫ *…a head-on clash between the president and the government.* ● **Head-on** is also an adverb. ▫ *I dealt with the issue head-on.*

headphones

head|phones /hɛdfoʊnz/ N-PLURAL **Headphones** are small speakers which you wear over your ears in order to listen to music or other sounds without other people hearing it. ❑ *I listened to the program on headphones.*

**head|quarters** /hɛdkwɔrtərz/ N-SING The **headquarters** of an organization are its main offices. ❑ *…Chicago's police headquarters.*

**head start** (**head starts**) N-COUNT If you have a **head start on** other people, you have an advantage over them in something such as a competition or race. ❑ *A good education gives a child a head start in life.*

**heads-up** N-SING If you give someone a **heads-up** about something that is going to happen, you tell them about it before it happens. ❑ *They changed the rules without giving anyone a heads-up.*

**head|waters** /hɛdwɔtərz/ also **head-waters** or **head waters** N-PLURAL The **headwaters** of a river are smaller streams which flow into the river near its source. ❑ *…the headwaters of the Amazon River.*

**head|way** /hɛdweɪ/ PHRASE If you **make headway**, you progress toward achieving something. ❑ *Police are making headway in the investigation.* [from Old English]

**heady** /hɛdi/ (**headier, headiest**) ADJ A **heady** drink, atmosphere, or experience strongly affects your senses, by making you feel excited. ❑ *I remember the heady days just after graduation.* [from Old English]

**heal** /hil/ (**heals, healing, healed**) 1 V-I When a broken bone or other injury **heals**, it becomes healthy and normal again. ❑ *It took six months for her injuries to heal.* 2 V-T/V-I If you **heal** something such as a disagreement, or if it **heals**, the situation is put right so that people are friendly or happy again. ❑ *When you remember the other person is your friend, you can begin to heal the disagreement.* [from Old English]

**heal|er** /hilər/ (**healers**) N-COUNT A **healer** is a person who treats sick people, especially a person who claims to heal through prayer and religious faith. [from Old English]

**health** /hɛlθ/ 1 N-UNCOUNT A person's **health** is the condition of their body. ❑ *Too much fatty food is bad for your health.* 2 N-UNCOUNT **Health** is a state in which a person is fit and well. ❑ *In the hospital they nursed me back to health.* 3 N-UNCOUNT The **health** of something such as an organization or a system is its success and the fact that it is working well. ❑ *…the health of the banking industry.* [from Old English]

**health care** also **healthcare** N-UNCOUNT **Health care** is the various services for the prevention or treatment of illness and injuries. ❑ *Nobody wants to pay more for health care.* ❑ *…the nation's health care system.*

**health cen|ter** (**health centers**) N-COUNT A **health center** is a building in which a group of doctors have offices where their patients can visit them.

**health main|te|nance or|gani|za|tion** (**health maintenance organizations**) N-COUNT A **health maintenance organization** is an organization to which you pay a fee and that allows you to use only doctors and hospitals which belong to the organization. The abbreviation **HMO** is often used. ❑ *…a health maintenance organization for retired workers in northern California.*

**healthy** /hɛlθi/ (**healthier, healthiest**) 1 ADJ Someone who is **healthy** is well and is not suffering from any illness. ❑ *Most of us need to exercise more to be healthy.* ● **healthi|ly** /hɛlθɪli/ ADV ❑ *I want to live healthily for as long as possible.* 2 ADJ Something that is **healthy** is good for your health. ❑ *He always tried to eat a healthy diet.* 3 ADJ A **healthy** organization or system is successful. ❑ *…an economically healthy country.* 4 ADJ A **healthy** amount of something is a large amount that shows success. ❑ *…healthy profits.* [from Old English]

**heap** /hip/ (**heaps, heaping, heaped**) 1 N-COUNT A **heap** of things is an untidy pile of them. ❑ *…a heap of clothes.* 2 V-T If you **heap** things in a pile, you arrange them in a large pile. ❑ *His mother heaped more carrots onto Michael's plate.* ● **Heap up** means the same as **heap**. ❑ *He was heaping up wood for the fire.* 3 V-T If you **heap** praise or criticism **on** someone or something, you give them a lot of praise or criticism. ❑ *They heaped praise on the president for his efforts.* 4 QUANT **Heaps of** something or a **heap of** something is a large quantity of it. [INFORMAL] ❑ *You have heaps of time.* [from Old English]

**heap|ing** /hipɪŋ/ ADJ A **heaping** spoonful has the contents of the spoon piled up above the edge. ❑ *Add one heaping tablespoon of salt.* [from Old English]

**hear** /hɪər/ (**hears, hearing, heard** /hɜrd/) 1 V-T/V-I When you **hear** a sound, you become aware of it through your ears. ❑ *She heard no further sounds.* ❑ *I heard him say, "Thanks."* ❑ *He doesn't hear very well.* 2 V-T When a judge or a court of law **hears** a case, or evidence in a case, they listen to it officially in order to make a decision about it. [FORMAL] ❑ *The court will hear the case next week.* 3 V-I If you **hear from** someone, you receive a letter or telephone call from them. ❑ *It's always great to hear from you.* 4 V-T/V-I If you **hear** some news or information about something, you find out about it by someone telling you, or from the radio or television. ❑ *My mother heard of the school from Karen.* ❑ *He heard that the house was sold.* 5 V-I If you **have heard of** something or someone, you know about them, but not in great detail. ❑ *I've heard of him, but never met him.* 6 PHRASE If you say that you **won't hear of** someone doing something, you mean that you refuse to let them do it. ❑ *I wanted to be an actor but Dad wouldn't hear of it.* [from Old English]

**hear|ing** /hɪərɪŋ/ (**hearings**) 1 N-UNCOUNT **Hearing** is the sense which makes it possible for you to be aware of sounds. ❑ *His hearing was excellent.* 2 N-COUNT A **hearing** is an official meeting which is held in order to collect facts about an incident or problem. ❑ *The hearing will last about two weeks.* 3 PHRASE If someone gives you **a fair hearing** or **a hearing**, they listen to you when you give your opinion about something. ❑ *Weber* *gave a fair hearing to anyone who had a different opinion.* [from Old English]

→ see **disability**

| **Word Partnership** | Use *hearing* with : |
|---|---|
| N. | hearing **impairment/loss** 🔢 |
| | **court** hearing 🔢 |
| V. | **hold** a hearing, **testify at/before** a hearing 🔢 |

---

**heart**

❶ NOUN USES
❷ PHRASES

---

**❶ heart** /hɑrt/ (**hearts**) 🔢 N-COUNT Your **heart** is the organ in your chest that pumps the blood around your body. People also use **heart** to refer to the area of their chest that is closest to their heart. ▢ *…the beating of his heart.* 🔢 N-COUNT You can refer to your **heart** when you are talking about your deep feelings and beliefs. [LITERARY] ▢ *Alik's words filled her heart with joy.* 🔢 N-VAR You use **heart** when you are talking about someone's character and attitude toward other people, especially when they are kind and generous. ▢ *She's got a good heart.* 🔢 N-SING The **heart of** something is the most central and important part of it. ▢ *The heart of the problem is money.* 🔢 N-SING The **heart of** a place is its center. ▢ *…a busy hotel in the heart of the city.* 🔢 N-COUNT A **heart** is a shape that is used as a symbol of love: ♥. ▢ *…heart-shaped chocolates.* 🔢 N-UNCOUNT **Hearts** is one of the four suits in a deck of playing cards. Each card in the suit is marked with one or more symbols in the shape of a heart. ● A **heart** is a playing card of this suit. ▢ *West decided to play a heart.* [from Old English]

**❷ heart** /hɑrt/ (**hearts**) 🔢 PHRASE If you say that someone is a particular kind of person **at heart**, you mean that that is what they are really like, even though they may seem very different. ▢ *He was a gentle boy at heart.* 🔢 PHRASE If someone or something **breaks** your **heart**, they make you very unhappy. [LITERARY] ▢ *I fell in love on vacation but the girl broke my heart.* 🔢 PHRASE If you know something such as a poem **by heart**, you have learned it so well that you can remember it without having to read it. ▢ *Mike knew this song by heart.* 🔢 PHRASE If someone has a **change of heart**, their attitude toward something changes. ▢ *She was surprised by David's change of heart.* 🔢 PHRASE If something such as a subject or project is **close to** your **heart** or **near to** your **heart**, it is very important to you and you are very interested in it and concerned about it. ▢ *This is a subject very close to my heart.* 🔢 PHRASE If you say something **from the heart** or **from the bottom of** your **heart**, you sincerely mean what you say. ▢ *He spoke from the heart.* 🔢 PHRASE If you **take heart from** something, you are encouraged and made to feel optimistic by it. ▢ *He should take heart from our success.* 🔢 PHRASE If you **take** something **to heart**, you are deeply affected and upset by it. ▢ *If someone says something unpleasant, I take it to heart.* 🔢 PHRASE If you feel or believe something **with all** your **heart**, you feel or believe it very strongly. ▢ *I loved him with all my heart.* [from Old English]

→ see **cardiovascular system, donor**

**heart|ache** /hɑrteɪk/ (**heartaches**) N-VAR **Heartache** is very great sadness and emotional

suffering. ▢ *…the heartache of her divorce.*

**heart at|tack** (**heart attacks**) N-COUNT If someone has a **heart attack**, their heart begins to beat very irregularly or stops completely. ▢ *He died of a heart attack.*

**heart|beat** /hɑrtbit/ (**heartbeats**) N-SING Your **heartbeat** is the regular movement of your heart as it pumps blood around your body. ▢ *The doctor listened to her heartbeat.*

**heart|break** /hɑrtbreɪk/ (**heartbreaks**) N-VAR **Heartbreak** is very great sadness and emotional suffering. ▢ *…the heartbreak of learning that she couldn't have children.*

**heart|breaking** /hɑrtbreɪkɪŋ/ ADJ Something that is **heartbreaking** makes you feel extremely sad and upset. ▢ *He told her the heartbreaking news that her son was dead.*

**heart|broken** /hɑrtbroʊkən/ ADJ Someone who is **heartbroken** is very sad and emotionally upset. ▢ *We are heartbroken over the death of our dog.*

**heart|en** /hɑrtᵊn/ (**heartens, heartening, heartened**) V-T If someone **is heartened by** something, it encourages them and makes them cheerful. ▢ *The news heartened everybody.* ● **heart|ened** ADJ ▢ *I feel heartened by her progress.* ● **heart|en|ing** ADJ ▢ *This is heartening news.* [from Old English]

**heart fail|ure** N-UNCOUNT **Heart failure** is a serious medical condition in which someone's heart does not work as well as it should, or stops completely. ▢ *He suffered heart failure.*

**heart|felt** /hɑrtfɛlt/ ADJ **Heartfelt** is used to describe a deep or sincere feeling or wish. ▢ *My heartfelt sympathy goes to everyone involved in the accident.*

**hearth** /hɑrθ/ (**hearths**) N-COUNT The **hearth** is the floor of a fireplace, which sometimes extends into the room. ▢ *There was a huge fire in the hearth.* [from Old English]

**heart|land** /hɑrtlænd/ (**heartlands**) N-COUNT **Heartland** or **heartlands** is used to refer to the area or region where a particular set of activities or beliefs is most significant. ▢ *…the industrial heartland of America.*

**heart-stopping** also **heartstopping** 🔢 ADJ A **heart-stopping** moment is one that makes you anxious or frightened because it seems that something bad is likely to happen. ▢ *There was a heart-stopping moment when she fell backward.* 🔢 ADJ A **heart-stopping** event or sight is very impressive or exciting. ▢ *The restaurant has a heart-stopping sea view.*

**heart|worm** /hɑrtwɜrm/ (**heartworms**) N-VAR **Heartworms** are parasitic worms that are spread through mosquito bites and affect cats, dogs, foxes and some other animals. You can also use **heartworm** to mean the disease caused by heartworms.

**hearty** /hɑrti/ (**heartier, heartiest**) 🔢 ADJ **Hearty** people or actions are loud, cheerful, and energetic. ▢ *Wade was a hearty, athletic sort of guy.* ● **heart|i|ly** ADV ▢ *He laughed heartily.* 🔢 ADJ **Hearty** feelings or opinions are strongly felt or strongly held. ▢ *Arnold was in hearty agreement with her.* ● **heart|i|ly** ADV ▢ *I'm heartily sick of him.* 🔢 ADJ A **hearty** meal is large and very satisfying. ▢ *The men ate a hearty breakfast.* ● **heart|i|ly** ADV ▢ *He ate heartily but drank only water.* [from Old English]

**heat** /hit/ (**heats, heating, heated**) ◼ V-T When you **heat** something, you raise its temperature. ❑ *Heat the tomatoes and oil in a pan.* ◼ N-UNCOUNT **Heat** is warmth or the quality of being hot. ❑ *...the strong heat of the sun.* ◼ N-UNCOUNT The **heat** of something that is warm or being heated is its temperature. ❑ *...the heat of the oven.* ◼ N-SING You use **heat** to refer to a source of heat, for example a burner on a stove or the heating system of a house. ❑ *Remove the pan from the heat.* ◼ N-SING The **heat of** a particular activity is the point when there is the greatest activity or excitement. ❑ *People say all kinds of things in the heat of an argument.* [from Old English]
→ see **cooking, fire, pan, petroleum, weather**
▶ **heat up** ◼ PHR-VERB When you **heat** something **up**, especially food which has already been cooked and allowed to go cold, you make it hot. ❑ *Freda heated up a pie for me.* ◼ PHR-VERB When something **heats up**, it gradually becomes hotter. ❑ *In the summer her house heats up like an oven.*

**heat|ed** /hitɪd/ ◼ ADJ A **heated** discussion or quarrel is one where the people involved are angry and excited. ❑ *It was a heated argument.* ◼ ADJ If someone gets **heated about** something, they get angry and excited about it. ❑ *People get heated about issues such as these.* ● **heat|ed|ly** ADV ❑ *The crowd continued to argue heatedly.* [from Old English]

**heat en|gine** (**heat engines**) N-COUNT A **heat engine** is a machine that uses energy from heat to do work. [TECHNICAL]

**heat|er** /hitər/ (**heaters**) N-COUNT A **heater** is a piece of equipment or a machine which is used to raise the temperature of something. ❑ *There's an electric heater in the bedroom.* [from Old English]
→ see **aquarium**

**heave** /hiv/ (**heaves, heaving, heaved**) ◼ V-T If you **heave** something heavy or difficult to move somewhere, you push, pull, or lift it using a lot of effort. ❑ *Five strong men to heaved it up the hill.* ● **Heave** is also a noun. ❑ *It took one heave to throw him into the river.* ◼ V-I If something **heaves**, it moves up and down with large regular movements. ❑ *His chest heaved as he took a deep breath.* [from Old English] ◼ to heave **a sigh of relief** → see **sigh**

**heav|en** /hɛvən/ (**heavens**) ◼ N-PROPER In some religions, **heaven** is said to be the place where God lives, where good people go when they die. ❑ *I believe that when I die I will go to heaven.* ◼ EXCLAM You say "**Good heavens!**" or "**Heavens!**" to express surprise or to emphasize that you agree or disagree with someone. [SPOKEN] ❑ *Good Heavens! That explains a lot!* ◼ PHRASE You can say "**Heaven knows**" to emphasize that you do not know something, or that you find something very surprising. [SPOKEN] ❑ *Heaven knows what he'll do next!* ◼ PHRASE You can say "**Heaven knows**" to emphasize something that you feel or believe very strongly. [SPOKEN] ❑ *Heaven knows they have enough money.* [from Old English] ◼ **thank heavens** → see **thank**

**heav|en|ly** /hɛvənli/ ◼ ADJ **Heavenly** things are things that are connected with the religious idea of heaven. ❑ *...heavenly beings who serve God.* ◼ ADJ Something that is **heavenly** is very pleasant and enjoyable. [INFORMAL] ❑ *She makes heavenly chocolates.* [from Old English]

**heav|i|ly** /hɛvɪli/ ◼ ADV If someone says

something **heavily**, they say it in a slow way which shows a feeling such as sadness, tiredness, or annoyance. ❑ *"I didn't think about her," he said heavily.* [from Old English] ◼ → see also **heavy**

**heavy** /hɛvi/ (**heavier, heaviest**) ◼ ADJ Something that is **heavy** weighs a lot. ❑ *The bag is very heavy.* ● **heavi|ness** N-UNCOUNT ❑ *...the heaviness of lead.* ◼ ADJ You use **heavy** to ask or talk about how much someone or something weighs. ❑ *How heavy are you?* ◼ ADJ **Heavy** means great in amount, degree, or intensity. ❑ *There was heavy fighting in the area.* ● **heavi|ly** ADV ❑ *It rained heavily all day.* ● **heavi|ness** N-UNCOUNT ❑ *...the heaviness of his blood loss.* ◼ ADJ If a person's breathing is **heavy**, it is very loud and deep. ❑ *Her breathing was slow and heavy.* ● **heavi|ly** ADV ❑ *She was breathing heavily as if asleep.* ◼ ADJ A **heavy** movement or action is done with a lot of force or pressure. ❑ *...a heavy blow on the back of the head.* ● **heavi|ly** ADV ❑ *I sat down heavily on the ground.* ◼ ADJ If you describe a period of time or a schedule as **heavy**, you mean it involves a lot of work. ❑ *It's been a heavy day and I'm tired.* ◼ ADJ **Heavy** work requires a lot of strength or energy. ❑ *John does all the heavy work.* ◼ ADJ Air or weather that is **heavy** is unpleasantly still, hot, and damp. ❑ *The outside air was heavy and damp.* ◼ ADJ A situation that is **heavy** is serious and difficult to cope with. [INFORMAL] ❑ *It was a heavy conversation when I told her I didn't love her any more.* [from Old English]

| **Thesaurus** | *heavy* | Also look up : |
|---|---|---|
| ADJ. | hefty, overweight; (*ant.*) light ◼ | |
| | forceful, powerful ◼ | |
| | complex, difficult, tough ◼ | |

**heavy cream** N-UNCOUNT **Heavy cream** is very thick cream.

**heavy-duty** ADJ A **heavy-duty** piece of equipment is very strong and can be used a lot. ❑ *...a heavy-duty plastic bag.*

**heavy-handed** ADJ If you say that someone's behavior is **heavy-handed**, you are criticizing them for being too forceful or too rough. ❑ *The police were heavy-handed.*

**heavy|weight** /hɛviweɪt/ (**heavyweights**) ◼ N-COUNT A **heavyweight** is a boxer weighing more than 175 pounds and therefore in the heaviest class. ◼ N-COUNT If you refer to a person or organization as a **heavyweight**, you mean that they have a lot of influence, experience, and importance in a particular field. ❑ *He was a political heavyweight.*

**He|brew** /hibru/ N-UNCOUNT **Hebrew** is a language spoken by Jews. ❑ *He speaks Hebrew very well.* [from Old French]

**heck** /hɛk/ ◼ EXCLAM People sometimes say "**heck!**" when they are slightly irritated or surprised. [INFORMAL] ❑ *Heck, if you don't like him, don't talk to him.* ❑ *What the heck's that?* ◼ PHRASE People use **a heck of** to emphasize how big something is or how much of it there is. [INFORMAL] ❑ *They're spending a heck of a lot of money.*

**heck|le** /hɛkºl/ (**heckles, heckling, heckled**) V-T/V-I If people in an audience **heckle** public speakers or performers, they interrupt them by making rude remarks. ❑ *The crowd heckled him.* ● **Heckle** is also a noun. ❑ *...a heckle from the back of the room.*

h

● **heck|ling** N-UNCOUNT ❑ ...*the heckling of the audience.* ● **heck|ler** /hˈɛklər/ (**hecklers**) N-COUNT ❑ *He tried to silence the hecklers.* [from Northern English and East Anglian dialect]

**hec|tare** /hˈɛktɛər/ (**hectares**) N-COUNT A **hectare** is a measurement of an area of land which is equal to 10,000 square meters, or 2.471 acres. [from French]

**hec|tic** /hˈɛktɪk/ ADJ A **hectic** situation is one that is very busy and involves a lot of rushed activity. ❑ *Ben had a hectic work schedule.* [from Late Latin]

**he'd** /hid, id, STRONG hˈid/ **1** **He'd** is the usual spoken form of "he had," especially when "had" is an auxiliary verb. ❑ *He'd seen her before.* **2** **He'd** is a spoken form of "he would." ❑ *He'd like to come with us.*

**hedge** /hˈɛdʒ/ (**hedges, hedging, hedged**) **1** N-COUNT A **hedge** is a row of bushes or small trees, usually along the edge of a lawn, garden, field, or road. **2** V-I If you **hedge against** something unpleasant or unwanted that might affect you, especially losing money, you do something which will protect you from it. ❑ *You can hedge against illness with insurance.* **3** PHRASE If you **hedge** your **bets**, you reduce your chances of losing by supporting more than one person or thing. ❑ *The organization may support one candidate, or hedge its bets by supporting several candidates.* [from Old English]

**hedge|hog** /hˈɛdʒhɔɡ/ (**hedgehogs**) N-COUNT A **hedgehog** is a small brown animal with sharp spikes covering its back. [from Late Middle English]

**hedge|hog cac|tus** (**hedgehog cacti**) N-VAR **Hedgehog cactus** is a name given to several types of cactus with short prickly spines, especially a type that has edible fruit.

**heed** /hˈid/ (**heeds, heeding, heeded**) **1** V-T If you **heed** someone's advice or warning, you pay attention to it and do what they suggest. [FORMAL] ❑ *Few people heeded his warning about the weather.* **2** PHRASE If you **take heed of** what someone says or if you **pay heed to** them, you pay attention to them and consider carefully what they say. [FORMAL] ❑ *The government must take heed of what they say.* [from Old English]

**heel** /hˈil/ (**heels**) **1** N-COUNT Your **heel** is the back part of your foot, just below your ankle. ❑ *He hurt his heel.* **2** N-COUNT The **heel** of a shoe is the raised part on the bottom at the back. ❑ ...*shoes with high heels.* [from Old English] **3** to **drag** your **heels** → see **drag**
→ see **foot**

**hefty** /hˈɛfti/ (**heftier, heftiest**) ADJ **Hefty** means large in size, weight, or amount. [INFORMAL] ❑ *My mother was quite a hefty woman.* [from Late Middle English]

**height** /hˈaɪt/ (**heights**) **1** N-VAR The **height** of a person or thing is their size or length from the bottom to the top. ❑ *Her weight is normal for her height.* ❑ *I am five feet six inches in height.* **2** N-UNCOUNT **Height** is the quality of being tall. ❑ *He is almost her height.* **3** N-VAR A particular **height** is the distance that something is above the ground. ❑ ...*the speed and height at which the plane was moving.* **4** N-COUNT A **height** is a high position or place above the ground. ❑ *I'm not afraid*

of heights. **5** N-SING When an activity, situation, or organization is **at** its **height**, it is at its most successful, powerful, or intense. ❑ ...*the time when his career was at its height.* **6** N-SING If you say that something is **the height of** a particular quality, you are emphasizing that it is that quality to the greatest degree possible. ❑ *The dress was the height of fashion.* [from Old English]
→ see **area**

**height|en** /hˈaɪtᵊn/ (**heightens, heightening, heightened**) V-T/V-I If something **heightens** a feeling or if the feeling **heightens**, the feeling increases in degree or intensity. ❑ *It heightened awareness of the differences between them.* ❑ *Chris's interest in Katherine heightened.* [from Old English]

**heir** /ɛər/ (**heirs**) N-COUNT An **heir** is someone who has the right to inherit a person's money, property, or title when that person dies. ❑ *He is the heir to a fortune.* [from Old French]

**heir|ess** /ɛˈərɪs/ (**heiresses**) N-COUNT An **heiress** is a woman or girl who has the right to inherit property or a title, or who has inherited it, especially when this involves great wealth. ❑ *She became the heiress to a jewelry empire.* [from Old French]

**held** /hˈɛld/ **Held** is the past tense and past participle of **hold**. [from Old English]

helicopter

**heli|cop|ter** /hˈɛlɪkɒptər/ (**helicopters**) N-COUNT A **helicopter** is an aircraft with long blades on top that go around very fast. It is able to stay still in the air and to move straight upward or downward. [from French]
→ see **fly**

**hell** /hˈɛl/ (**hells**) **1** N-PROPER; N-COUNT In some religions, **hell** is the place where the Devil lives, and where bad people are sent when they die. ❑ *I don't believe in heaven or hell.* **2** N-VAR If you say that a particular situation or place is **hell**, you are emphasizing that it is extremely unpleasant. ❑ ...*the hell of prison.* [from Old English]

**he'll** /hˈil, il, STRONG hˈil/ **He'll** is the usual spoken form of "he will." ❑ *He'll be very successful, I'm sure.*

**hel|lo** /hˈɛloʊ/ (**hellos**) also **hullo**
**1** CONVENTION You say "**Hello**" to someone when you meet them. ❑ *Hello, Trish. How are you?* ● **Hello** is also a noun. ❑ *The salesperson greeted me with a warm hello.* **2** CONVENTION You say "**Hello**" to someone at the beginning of a telephone conversation, either when you answer the phone or before you give your name or say why you are phoning. ❑ *Cohen picked up the phone. "Hello?"*

helmet

**hel|met** /hɛlmɪt/ (**helmets**) N-COUNT A **helmet** is a hat made of a strong material which you wear to protect your head. [from Old French]
→ see **army, football, hat**

**help** /hɛlp/ (**helps, helping, helped**) ■ V-T/V-I If you **help** someone, you make it easier for them to do something, for example by doing part of the work for them or by giving them advice or money. ❑ *He helped to raise money.* ❑ *You can help by giving them some money.* ● **Help** is also a noun. ❑ *Thanks very much for your help.* ② V-T/V-I If you say that something **helps**, you mean that it makes something easier to do or get, or that it improves a situation. ❑ *The right clothes can help to make you look slim.* ❑ *I'm happy to help.* ● **Help** is also a noun. N-SING ❑ *Thank you. You've been a great help.* ❸ N-UNCOUNT **Help** is action taken to rescue a person who is in danger. You shout "help!" when you are in danger in order to attract someone's attention so that they can come and rescue you. ❑ *He shouted for help.* ④ V-T If you **help yourself to** something, you serve yourself or you take it for yourself. If someone tells you to **help yourself**, they are telling you politely to serve yourself anything you want or to take anything you want. ❑ *There's bread on the table. Help yourself.* ❺ PHRASE If you **can't help** the way you feel or behave, you cannot control it or stop it from happening. You can also say that you **can't help yourself**. ❑ *I can't help feeling sorry for the poor man.* ❻ PHRASE If someone or something **is of help**, they make a situation easier or better. ❑ *Can I be of help to you?* [from Old English]
→ see **donor**

▶ **help out** PHR-VERB If you **help** someone **out**, you help them by doing some work for them or by lending them some money. ❑ *I help out with the secretarial work.* ❑ *I didn't have enough money so my mother helped me out.*

---

**Usage** help

After *help*, you can use the infinitive with or without *to*: *Budi helped Lastri study for the exam; then he asked her to help him to write an e-mail to the professor.*

---

**Thesaurus** help Also look up :

V. aid, assist, support; (*ant.*) hinder ■
N. aid, assistance, guidance, support ■

---

**Word Partnership** Use *help* with :

ADJ. **financial** help, **professional** help ■
V. **ask for** help, **get** help, **need** help, **try to** help, **want to** help ■
**cry/scream/shout for** help ❸
**can't** help **thinking/feeling** *something* ❺

---

**help desk** (**help desks**) N-COUNT A **help desk** is a special service that you can telephone or e-mail in order to get information about a particular product or subject. ❑ *Our help desk can solve any kind of problem.*

**help|er** /hɛlpər/ (**helpers**) N-COUNT A **helper** is a person who helps another person or group with a job they are doing. ❑ *Phyllis and her helpers gave us some food.* [from Old English]

**help|ful** /hɛlpfəl/ ■ ADJ If someone is **helpful**, they help you by doing part of your job for you or by giving you advice or information. ❑ *The staff in the hotel are helpful.* ● **help|ful|ly** ADV ❑ *They helpfully told us how to find the house.* ② ADJ Something that is **helpful** makes a situation more pleasant or more easy to tolerate. ❑ *It is helpful to have someone with you when you go to the doctor.* [from Old English]

**help|less** /hɛlpləs/ ADJ If you are **helpless**, you do not have the strength or power to do anything useful or to control or protect yourself. ❑ *Parents often feel helpless when their kids are sick.* ● **help|less|ly** ADV ❑ *They watched helplessly as the house burned to the ground.* ● **help|less|ness** N-UNCOUNT ❑ *I remember my feelings of helplessness.* [from Old English]

**hem** /hɛm/ (**hems, hemming, hemmed**) N-COUNT A **hem** on a piece of cloth is an edge that is folded over and stitched down to prevent threads coming loose. The **hem** of a skirt or dress is the bottom edge. ❑ *She lifted the hem of her dress and brushed her knees.* [from Old English]
▶ **hem in** ■ PHR-VERB If a place is **hemmed in by** something tall such as mountains or walls, it is surrounded by them. ❑ *The canyon is hemmed in by walls of rock.* ② PHR-VERB If someone is **hemmed in** or if someone **hems** them **in**, they are prevented from moving or changing. ❑ *The company complains that it is hemmed in by the new laws.*

**hema|tol|ogy** /himətɒlədʒi/ N-UNCOUNT **Hematology** is the branch of medicine that is concerned with diseases of the blood. ❑ *...the American Society of Hematology.* [from Greek]

---

**Word Link** sphere ≈ ball : atmosphere, blogosphere, hemisphere

---

**hemi|sphere** /hɛmɪsfɪər/ (**hemispheres**) N-COUNT A **hemisphere** is one half of the earth. ❑ *...the northern hemisphere.*
→ see **globe, solid**

**hem|or|rhage** /hɛmərɪdʒ/ (**hemorrhages, hemorrhaging, hemorrhaged**) ■ N-VAR A **hemorrhage** is serious bleeding inside a person's body. ❑ *He died of a brain hemorrhage.* ② V-I If someone **is hemorrhaging**, there is serious bleeding inside their body. ❑ *She hemorrhaged badly after the birth of the baby.* ● **hem|or|rhag|ing** N-UNCOUNT ❑ *Tests showed he died from hemorrhaging.* [from Latin]

**hen** /hɛn/ (**hens**) N-COUNT A **hen** is a female chicken. [from Old English]

**hence** /hɛns/ ADV You use **hence** to indicate that the statement you are about to make is a consequence of what you have just said. [FORMAL] ❑ *This problem is likely to happen again. Hence we need a new plan.* [from Old English]

**hence|forth** /hɛnsfɔrθ/ ADV **Henceforth** means from this or that time onward. [FORMAL] ❑ *Henceforth all groups were equal to one another.*

---

**Word Link** itis ≈ inflammation : arthritis, hepatitis, meningitis

---

**hepa|ti|tis** /hɛpətaɪtɪs/ N-UNCOUNT **Hepatitis** is a serious disease which affects the liver. [from Greek]

**her** /hər, ər, STRONG hɜr/

> **Her** is a third person singular pronoun. **Her** is used as the object of a verb or a preposition. **Her** is also a possessive determiner.

**1** PRON You use **her** to refer to a woman, girl, or female animal. ❑ *I told her that dinner was ready.* ● **Her** is also a possessive determiner. ❑ *Liz traveled around the world with her husband, James.* **2** PRON **Her** is sometimes used to refer to a country or nation. [FORMAL OR WRITTEN] ● **Her** is also a possessive determiner. ❑ *America and her partners are helping to rebuild roads and buildings.* **3** PRON People sometimes use **her** to refer to a car, machine, or ship. ❑ *The ship had her sides painted white.* ● **Her** is also a possessive determiner. ❑ *This photograph of the ship was taken by one of her passengers.* [from Old English]

**her|ald** /hɛrəld/ (**heralds, heralding, heralded**) **1** V-T Something that **heralds** a future event or situation is a sign that it is going to happen or appear. [FORMAL] ❑ *This discovery could herald a cure for cancer.* **2** N-COUNT Something that is a **herald of** a future event or situation is a sign that it is going to happen or appear. [FORMAL] ❑ *These cool mornings are a herald of fall.* [from Old French]

**herb** /ɜrb/ (**herbs**) N-COUNT An **herb** is a plant whose leaves are used in cooking to add flavor to food, or as a medicine. ❑ *…herbs such as basil and coriander.* ● **herb|al** ADJ ❑ *…herbal remedies for colds.* [from Old French]

**her|bi|vore** /hɜrbɪvɔr, ɜr-/ (**herbivores**) N-COUNT A **herbivore** is an animal that only eats plants. [from New Latin]
→ see Word Web: **herbivore**
→ see **carnivore**

**herbivorous** /hɜrbɪvərəs, ɜr-/ ADJ **Herbivorous** animals only eat plants. [from New Latin]

**herd** /hɜrd/ (**herds, herding, herded**) **1** N-COUNT A **herd** is a large group of animals of one kind that live together. ❑ *…herds of elephants.* **2** V-T If you **herd** people or animals somewhere, you make them move there in a group. ❑ *Stefano used a dog to herd the sheep.* [from Old English]

**here** /hɪər/ **1** ADV You use **here** when you are referring to the place where you are. ❑ *I can't stand here talking all day.* **2** ADV You use **here** when you are pointing toward a place that is near you, in order to draw someone else's attention to it. ❑ *Come and sit here.* **3** ADV You use **here** in order to draw attention to something or someone who has just arrived in the place where you are, or to draw attention to the place you have just arrived at. ❑ *"Here's the taxi," she said.* **4** ADV You use **here**

to refer to a particular point or stage of a situation or subject that you have come to or that you are dealing with. ❑ *It's here that our problems started.* **5** ADV You use **here** when you are offering or giving something to someone. ❑ *Here's your coffee.* [from Old English]

**he|redi|tary** /hɪrɛdɪtɛri/ **1** ADJ A **hereditary** characteristic or illness is passed on to a child from its parents before it is born. ❑ *I know my illness is hereditary.* **2** ADJ A title or position in society that is **hereditary** is one that is passed on as a right from parent to child. ❑ *The title of head of state is hereditary.* [from Old French]

**he|red|ity** /hɪrɛdɪti/ N-UNCOUNT **Heredity** is the process by which features and characteristics are passed on from parents to their children before the children are born. [from Old French]

**her|esy** /hɛrɪsi/ (**heresies**) N-VAR **Heresy** is a belief or action that most people think is wrong, because it disagrees with the principles of a particular religion. ❑ *He said it was heresy to suggest that women should not be priests.* [from Old French]

**her|it|age** /hɛrɪtɪdʒ/ (**heritages**) N-VAR A country's **heritage** is all the qualities, traditions, or features of life there that have continued over many years and have been passed on from one generation to another. ❑ *Old buildings are part of our heritage.* [from Old French]

**her|mit** /hɜrmɪt/ (**hermits**) N-COUNT A **hermit** is a person who lives alone, away from people and society. ❑ *He lived like a hermit.* [from Old French]

**her|nia** /hɜrniə/ (**hernias**) N-VAR A **hernia** is a medical condition in which one of your internal organs sticks through a weak point in the surrounding tissue. [from Latin]

**hero** /hɪəroʊ/ (**heroes**) **1** N-COUNT The **hero** of a book, play, movie, or story is the main male character, who usually has good qualities. ❑ *The actor Daniel Radcliffe plays the hero in the Harry Potter movies.* **2** N-COUNT A **hero** is someone who has done something brave, new, or good, and who is admired by a lot of people. ❑ *He called Mr. Mandela a hero who had inspired millions.* [from Latin]
→ see Word Web: **hero**
→ see **myth**

**he|ro|ic** /hɪroʊɪk/ (**heroics**) **1** ADJ If you describe a person or their actions as **heroic**, you admire them because they show extreme bravery. ❑ *People praised his heroic deeds.* ● **he|roi|cal|ly** /hɪroʊɪkli/ ADV ❑ *He acted heroically when the boat started to sink.* **2** ADJ If you describe an action or event as **heroic**, you admire it because it involves great effort or determination to succeed. ❑ *The company made heroic efforts to reduce costs.*

---

## Word Web    herbivore

**Herbivores** come in all shapes and sizes. The tiny **aphid** lives on the juices found in **plants**. The **elephant** eats 100 to 1,000 pounds of **vegetation** a day. Some herbivores prefer a single plant. For example, the **koala** eats only eucalyptus **leaves**. **Cattle graze** on grass all day long. In the evening they regurgitate food from their stomachs and chew it again. **Rodents** have two pairs of long teeth in the front of their mouths. These teeth never stop growing. They use them to gnaw on hard **seeds**.

## Word Web    hero

Odysseus is a **hero** from Greek **mythology**. He is a warrior. He is brave in battle. He faces many **dangers**. However, he knows he must return home after the Trojan War*. During his **epic** journey home, Odysseus faces many trials. He must survive wild storms at sea and fight a monster. He must also resist the temptations of sirens and outsmart the goddess Circe*. At home Penelope, Odysseus' wife, **defends** their home and **protects** their son. She remains **loyal** and **brave** through many trials. She is the **heroine** of the story.

*Trojan War: a legendary war between Greece and Troy.*

*Circe: a Greek goddess.*

*Odysseus saves his men from the Cyclops.*

● he|roi|cal|ly ADV ❑ *Single parents manage heroically in doing the job of two people.* [from Latin]

hero|in /hɛroʊɪn/ N-UNCOUNT **Heroin** is a powerful illegal drug which people can become addicted to. [from German]

hero|ine /hɛroʊɪn/ (**heroines**) **1** N-COUNT The **heroine** of a book, play, movie, or story is the main female character, who usually has good qualities. ❑ *The heroine is a young doctor.* **2** N-COUNT A **heroine** is a woman who has done something brave, new, or good, and is admired by a lot of people. ❑ *China's first gold medal winner became a national heroine.* [from Latin]
→ see hero

hero|ism /hɛroʊɪzəm/ N-UNCOUNT **Heroism** is great courage and bravery. ❑ *...acts of heroism.* [from Latin]

her|pes /hɑrpiz/ N-UNCOUNT **Herpes** is a disease which causes painful red spots to appear on the skin. [from Latin]

her|ring /hɛrɪŋ/ (**herring, herrings**) N-VAR A **herring** is a long silver-colored fish. ● **Herring** is a piece of this fish eaten as food. ❑ *...a can of herring.* [from Old English]

hers /hɜrz/

**Hers** is a third person possessive pronoun.

PRON You use **hers** to indicate that something belongs or relates to a woman, girl, or female animal. ❑ *His hand as it shook hers was warm and firm.*

her|self /hərsɛlf/

**Herself** is a third person singular reflexive pronoun. **Herself** is used when the object of a verb or preposition refers to the same person as the subject of the verb.

**1** PRON You use **herself** to refer to a woman, girl, or female animal. ❑ *She made herself a sandwich.* ❑ *Jennifer didn't feel good about herself.* **2** PRON You use **herself** to emphasize the person or thing that you are referring to. ❑ *She herself was not hungry.*

Hertz|sprung-Rus|sell dia|gram /hɛərtsprʊŋrʌsᵊl daɪəgræm/ (**Hertzsprung-Russell diagrams**) N-COUNT The **Hertzsprung-Russell diagram** is a chart used in astronomy to show the relationships between different types of stars. The abbreviations *H-R diagram* and *HRD* are also used. [from Danish]

he's /hiz, iz, STRONG hiz/ **He's** is the usual spoken form of "he is" or "he has," especially when "has" is an auxiliary verb. ❑ *He's leaving.*

hesi|tant /hɛzɪtᵊnt/ ADJ If you are **hesitant** about doing something, you do not do it quickly or immediately, usually because you are uncertain, embarrassed, or worried. ❑ *She was hesitant about meeting him.* ● hesi|tan|cy /hɛzɪtənsi/ N-UNCOUNT ❑ *Hesitancy can cause mistakes.* ● hesi|tant|ly ADV ❑ *"Can you help?" she asked hesitantly.* [from Latin]

hesi|tate /hɛzɪteɪt/ (**hesitates, hesitating, hesitated**) **1** V-I If you **hesitate**, you do not speak or act for a short time, usually because you are uncertain, embarrassed, or worried about what you are going to say or do. ❑ *Catherine hesitated before answering.* ● hesi|ta|tion /hɛzɪteɪʃᵊn/ (**hesitations**) N-VAR ❑ *After some hesitation, she replied, "I'll have to think about that."* **2** V-T If you **hesitate to** do something, you are unwilling to do it, usually because you are not certain it would be right. ❑ *Don't hesitate to ask if you have any questions.* ● hesi|ta|tion N-VAR **Hesitation** is an unwillingness to do something, or a delay in doing it, because you are uncertain, worried, or embarrassed about it. ❑ *He said there would be no more hesitation in making changes.* [from Latin]

## Thesaurus    hesitate    Also look up :

v.    falter, pause, wait **1** **2**

hetero|gene|ous /hɛtərədʒiniəs, -dʒinyəs/ ADJ A **heterogeneous** group consists of different types of things or people. [FORMAL] [from Medieval Latin]

hetero|gene|ous mix|ture (**heterogeneous mixtures**) N-COUNT In chemistry, a **heterogeneous mixture** is a mixture of two or more substances that remain separate, for example oil and water.

hetero|sex|ual /hɛtəroʊsɛkʃuəl/ (**heterosexuals**) ADJ Someone who is **heterosexual** is sexually attracted to people of the opposite sex. ❑ *...heterosexual couples.* ● **Heterosexual** is also a noun. ❑ *...unmarried heterosexuals.* ● hetero|sex|ual|ity /hɛtəroʊsɛkʃuælɪti/ N-UNCOUNT ❑ *He is proud of his heterosexuality.*

hey /heɪ/ **1** CONVENTION In informal situations, you say or shout "**hey**" to attract someone's attention, or to show surprise, interest,

or annoyance. ❑ *"Hey! Look out!" shouted Patty.*
**2** CONVENTION In informal situations, you can
say "**hey**" to greet someone. ❑ *He smiled and said
"Hey, Kate." [from Old French]*

**hey|day** /ˈheɪdeɪ/ N-SING Someone's **heyday** is
the time when they are most powerful, successful,
or popular. ❑ *In their heyday, they performed several
shows a day.*

**hi** /haɪ/ CONVENTION In informal situations, you
say "**hi**" to greet someone. ❑ *"Hi, Liz," she said.*

**hi|ber|nate** /ˈhaɪbərneɪt/ (**hibernates,
hibernating, hibernated**) V-I Animals that
**hibernate** spend the winter in a state like a deep
sleep. [from Latin]

**hi|ber|na|tion** /ˌhaɪbərˈneɪʃ³n/ N-UNCOUNT
**Hibernation** is the act or state of hibernating.
[from Latin]

**hic|cup** /ˈhɪkʌp/ (**hiccups, hiccuping** or
**hiccupping, hiccuped** or **hiccupped**) also
**hiccough** **1** N-COUNT You can refer to a small
problem or difficulty as a **hiccup**. ❑ *A recent sales
hiccup is nothing to panic about.* **2** N-UNCOUNT
When you have **hiccups**, you make repeated sharp
sounds in your throat, often because you have
been eating or drinking too quickly. ❑ *Babies
sometimes get hiccups when they are feeding.* **3** V-I
When you **hiccup**, you make repeated sharp
sounds in your throat. ❑ *She was still hiccuping.*

**hick|o|ry** /ˈhɪkəri/ (**hickories**) N-VAR A **hickory**
is a tree which has large leaves, greenish flowers,
and nuts with smooth shells. ❑ *They cut down many
hickories.* ● **Hickory** is the wood of this tree. ❑ *The
first skis were made of hickory.* [from Algonquian]

**hid** /hɪd/ **Hid** is the past tense of **hide**. [from Old
English]

**hid|den** /ˈhɪd³n/ **1** **Hidden** is the past participle
of **hide**. **2** ADJ **Hidden** facts, feelings, activities, or
problems are not easy to notice or discover. ❑ *There
are hidden dangers on the beach.* **3** ADJ A **hidden**
place is difficult to find. ❑ *He suddenly saw the
hidden waterfall.* [from Old English]

**hide** /haɪd/ (**hides, hiding, hid, hidden**) **1** V-T If
you **hide** something or someone, you put them in
a place where they cannot easily be seen or found.
❑ *He hid the bicycle behind the wall.* **2** V-T/V-I If you
**hide** or if you **hide yourself**, you go somewhere
where you cannot easily be seen or found. ❑ *The
little boy ran and hid.* **3** V-T To **hide** something
means to cover it so that people cannot see it.
❑ *She hid her face in her hands.* **4** V-T If you **hide** what
you feel or know, you keep it a secret, so that no
one knows about it. ❑ *Lee tried to hide his excitement.*
**5** N-VAR A **hide** is the skin of a large animal which
can be used for making leather. ❑ *...cow hides.*
[from Old English] **6** → see also **hidden, hiding**

**Thesaurus**    *hide*    Also look up :

| | |
|---|---|
| v. | camouflage, cover, lock up **1** **3** |

**Word Partnership**    Use *hide* with :

| | |
|---|---|
| ADV. | **nowhere to** hide **1** **2** |
| v. | **attempt/try to** hide **1** – **4** |
| | **run and** hide **2** |
| N. | hide **your face** **3** |
| | hide **a fact/secret**, hide **your fear/
feelings/tears/** **4** |

**hid|eous** /ˈhɪdiəs/ ADJ If you say that someone or
something is **hideous**, you mean that they are very
ugly or unpleasant. ❑ *He was the victim of a hideous
attack.* ● **hid|eous|ly** ADV ❑ *He was hideously ugly.*
[from Old French]

**hid|ing** /ˈhaɪdɪŋ/ N-UNCOUNT If someone is in
**hiding**, they have secretly gone somewhere where
they cannot be seen or found. ❑ *Cohen is in hiding
with his wife.* [from Old English]

**Word Link**    *arch ≈ rule : an*arch*y, hier*arch*y,
mon*arch

**hi|er|ar|chy** /ˈhaɪərɑrki/ (**hierarchies**) **1** N-VAR
A **hierarchy** is a system of organizing people
into different ranks or levels of importance, for
example in society or in a company. ❑ *Workers
and managers did not mix in the company hierarchy.*
● **hi|er|ar|chi|cal** /ˌhaɪəˈrɑrkɪk³l/ ADJ ❑ *...a
hierarchical society.* **2** N-COUNT The **hierarchy** of an
organization is the group of people who manage
and control it. ❑ *The church hierarchy feels that the
church needs to modernize.* [from Medieval Latin]

**high** /haɪ/ (**higher, highest, highs**) **1** ADJ
Something that is **high** extends a long way from
the bottom to the top when it is upright. You do
not use **high** to describe people, animals, or plants.
❑ *...a house with a high wall around it.* ❑ *Mount Marcy
is the highest mountain in the Adirondacks.* ● **High** is
also an adverb. ❑ *...wagons packed high with goods.*
**2** ADJ You use **high** to talk or ask about how much
something upright measures from the bottom
to the top. ❑ *How high is the door?* ❑ *The grass in the
yard was a foot high.* **3** ADJ If something is **high**, it
is a long way above the ground, above sea level,
or above a person or thing. ❑ *I looked down from the
high window.* ❑ *The sun was high in the sky.* ● **High**
is also an adverb. ❑ *She can jump higher than other
people.* **4** PHRASE If something is **high up**, it is
a long way above the ground, above sea level, or
above a person or thing. ❑ *His farm was high up in the
hills.* **5** ADJ **High** means great in amount, degree,
or intensity. ❑ *High winds knocked down trees.* ❑ *The
number of people injured was high.* ● **High** is also an
adverb. ❑ *Unemployment rose even higher last year.*
**6** ● You can use phrases such as "**in the high 80s**"
to indicate that a number or level is, for example,
more than 85 but not as much as 90. **7** ADJ If a
food or other substance is **high in** a particular
ingredient, it contains a large amount of that
ingredient. ❑ *Foods such as ice cream and pizza are
high in fat.* **8** N-COUNT If something reaches a
**high of** a particular amount or degree, that is the
greatest it has ever been. ❑ *Sales have reached an all-
time high.* **9** ADJ If you say that something is a **high**
priority or is **high on** your list, you mean that you
consider it to be one of the most important things
you have to do or deal with. ❑ *The government made
education a high priority.* **10** ADJ Someone who is
**high in** a particular profession or society, or has
a **high** position, has a very important position
and has great authority and influence. ❑ *He was
very high in the administration.* **11** PHRASE Someone
who is **high up in** a profession or society has a very
important position. ❑ *He is quite high up in the navy.*
**12** ADJ If the quality or standard of something is
**high**, it is extremely good. ❑ *This is high quality stuff.*
**13** ADJ A **high** sound or voice is close to the top of a
particular range of notes. ❑ *She spoke in a high voice.*
**14** ADJ If your spirits are **high**, you feel happy and

excited. ❑ *Her spirits were high with the hope of seeing Nick.* [from Old English]

| **Thesaurus** | *high* | Also look up : |
| --- | --- | --- |

ADJ. tall **1** **2**
elevated, lofty, tall; (*ant.*) low **3**

**high beams** N-PLURAL A car's or truck's **high beams** are its headlights when they are set to shine their brightest. ❑ *He switched on his high beams.*

**high-class** ADJ If you describe something as **high-class**, you mean that it is of very good quality or of superior social status. ❑ *...a high-class jeweler.*

**high|er edu|ca|tion** N-UNCOUNT **Higher education** is education at universities and colleges. ❑ *...students in higher education.*

**high fi|del|ity** also **high-fidelity** N-UNCOUNT **High fidelity** is the use of electronic equipment to reproduce a sound or image with very little distortion or loss of quality. ❑ *...a digital, high-fidelity audio system.*

**high-flying** ADJ A **high-flying** person is successful or is likely to be successful in their career. ❑ *...a high-flying newspaper editor.*

**high-frequency word** (**high-frequency words**) N-COUNT **High-frequency words** are words that occur much more often than most other words in written or spoken language.

**high-impact** ADJ **High-impact** exercise puts a lot of stress on your body.

**high|lands** /ha͟ɪləndz/ N-PLURAL **Highlands** are mountainous areas of land.

**high|light** /ha͟ɪlaɪt/ (**highlights, highlighting, highlighted**) **1** V-T If someone or something **highlights** a point or problem, they emphasize it or make you think about it. ❑ *Collins wrote a song which highlighted the problems of homeless people.* **2** N-COUNT The **highlights of** an event, activity, or period of time are the most interesting or exciting parts of it. ❑ *...the highlights of the game.*

**high|ly** /ha͟ɪli/ **1** ADV **Highly** is used before some adjectives to mean "very." ❑ *Mr. Singh was a highly successful salesman.* ❑ *It seems highly unlikely that she will win.* **2** ADV You use **highly** to indicate that someone has an important position in an organization or set of people. ❑ *...a highly placed government advisor.* **3** ADV If you think **highly** of something or someone, you think they are extremely good. ❑ *Michael thought highly of the school.* [from Old English]

| **Word Partnership** | Use *highly* with : |
| --- | --- |

ADJ. highly **addictive**, highly **competitive**, highly **controversial**, highly **critical**, highly **educated**, highly **intelligent**, highly **qualified**, highly **skilled**, highly **successful**, highly **technical**, highly **trained**, highly **unlikely**, highly **visible 1**
V. highly **recommended**, highly **respected 1**

**high-maintenance** also **high maintenance** ADJ If you describe something or someone as **high-maintenance**, you mean that they require a lot of time, money, or effort. ❑ *Small gardens can be high maintenance.* ❑ *She was a high-maintenance girl.*

**High|ness** /ha͟ɪnɪs/ (**Highnesses**) N-VOC Expressions such as "**Your Highness**" or "**His Highness**" are used to address or refer to a member of a royal family other than a king or queen. ❑ *Certainly, Your Highness.* [from Old English]

**high-pitched** ADJ A **high-pitched** sound is high and unpleasant. ❑ *She cried in a high-pitched voice.*

**high-powered** ADJ Someone who is **high-powered** or has a **high-powered** job has a very responsible job. ❑ *...a high-powered attorney.*

**high power lens** (**high power lenses**) N-COUNT A **high power lens** is a very powerful lens on an instrument such as a microscope.

**high-profile** ADJ A **high-profile** person or a **high-profile** event attracts a lot of attention or publicity. ❑ *She was a high-profile businesswoman.*

**high-rise** (**high-rises**) ADJ **High-rise** buildings are modern buildings which are very tall and have many levels or floors. ❑ *...high-rise office buildings.* ● A **high-rise** is a high-rise building. ❑ *That big high-rise is where Brian lives.*

**high road** N-SING If you say that someone is taking the **high road** in a situation, you mean that they are taking the most positive and careful course of action. ❑ *He tried to start an argument with her, but she took the high road and ignored him.*

**high school** (**high schools**) N-VAR; N-COUNT A **high school** is a school for children usually aged between fourteen and eighteen. ❑ *My daughter has just started high school.*
→ see **graduation**

**high-stakes** ADJ A **high-stakes** game or contest is one in which the people involved can gain or lose a lot. ❑ *...the high-stakes television debate.*

**high-strung** ADJ If someone is **high-strung**, they are very nervous and easily upset. ❑ *The pressure of his work was making the high-strung man sick.*

**high-tech** /ha͟ɪ te͟k/ also **high tech** or **hi tech** ADJ **High-tech** activities or equipment involve or use high technology. ❑ *...high-tech industries such as computers and telecommunications.*

**high tech|nol|ogy** N-UNCOUNT **High technology** is the development and use of advanced electronics and computers. ❑ *...the high technology section of the newspaper.*

**high tide** N-UNCOUNT At the coast, **high tide** is the time when the sea is at its highest level because the tide is in.

**high|way** /ha͟ɪweɪ/ (**highways**) N-COUNT A **highway** is a main road, especially one that connects towns or cities. ❑ *I crossed the highway.* [from Old English]
→ see **traffic**

**high|way pa|trol** (**highway patrols**) N-COUNT In the United States, the **highway patrol** is the part of the police force within a particular state that is responsible for making sure that the roads are safe and for dealing with drivers who break the law. ❑ *...highway patrol officers.*

**hijack** /ha͟ɪdʒæk/ (**hijacks, hijacking, hijacked**) V-T If someone **hijacks** a plane or other vehicle, they illegally take control of it by force while it is traveling from one place to another. ❑ *Two men hijacked the plane.* ● **Hijack** is also a noun. ❑ *Finally, six months after the hijack, he was arrested.* ● **hijack|er** (**hijackers**) N-COUNT ❑ *There was a fight between the hijackers and the pilots.* ● **hijack|ing** (**hijackings**)

N-COUNT ❏ *There are nearly fifty car hijackings a day.*

**hike** /haɪk/ (**hikes, hiking, hiked**) **1** N-COUNT
A **hike** is a long walk in the country, especially
one that you go on for pleasure. ❏ *We went for a
30-minute hike through a forest.* **2** V-I If you **hike**,
you go for a long walk in the country. ❏ *You can
hike through the Fish River Canyon.* • **hik|er** (**hikers**)
N-COUNT ❏ *The hikers spent the night in the mountains.*
• **hik|ing** N-UNCOUNT ❏ *I love hiking and horseback
riding in the mountains.* **3** V-T To **hike** prices, rates,
taxes, or quantities means to increase them
suddenly or by a large amount. [INFORMAL] ❏ *The
company hiked its prices by 5 percent.* • **Hike up** means
the same as **hike**. ❏ *The government hiked up the tax.*

**hi|lari|ous** /hɪlɛəriəs/ ADJ If something is
**hilarious**, it is extremely funny. ❏ *He told me a
hilarious story.* • **hi|lari|ous|ly** ADV ❏ *She found it
hilariously funny.* [from Latin]

**hill** /hɪl/ (**hills**) N-COUNT A **hill** is an area of land
that is higher than the land that surrounds it. ❏ *I
walked up the hill.* [from Old English]

**hilly** /hɪli/ (**hillier, hilliest**) ADJ A **hilly** area has
many hills. ❏ *The area is hilly and densely wooded.*
[from Old English]

**him** /hɪm/

> **Him** is a third person singular pronoun. **Him** is
> used as the object of a verb or a preposition.

**1** PRON You use **him** to refer to a man, boy, or male
animal. ❏ *Elaine met him at the railroad station.* ❏ *Is
Sam there? Let me talk to him.* **2** PRON In written
English, **him** is sometimes used to refer to a person
without saying whether that person is a man or a
woman. Some people dislike this use and prefer to
use "him or her" or "them." ❏ *If I see a person who is
new, I ask him why he is here.* [from Old English]

**him|self** /hɪmsɛlf/

> **Himself** is a third person singular reflexive
> pronoun. **Himself** is used when the object of a
> verb or preposition refers to the same person as
> the subject of the verb.

**1** PRON You use **himself** to refer to a man, boy,
or male animal. ❏ *He poured himself a cup of coffee.*
❏ *He was talking to himself.* **2** PRON You use **himself**
to emphasize the person or thing that you are
referring to. ❏ *The president himself is on a visit to
Beijing.* [from Old English]

**hind** /haɪnd/ ADJ An animal's **hind** legs are at
the back of its body. ❏ *Suddenly the cow kicked up its
hind legs.* [from Old English]

**hin|der** /hɪndər/ (**hinders, hindering, hindered**)
V-T If something **hinders** you, it makes it more
difficult for you to do something. ❏ *Alan was
hindered by money problems.* ❏ *A thigh injury hindered
him last month.* [from Old English]

**hin|drance** /hɪndrəns/ (**hindrances**) N-COUNT
A **hindrance** is a person or thing that makes it
more difficult for you to do something. ❏ *He was
no help. In fact he was a hindrance.* [from Old English]

**hind|sight** /haɪndsaɪt/ N-UNCOUNT **Hindsight**
is the ability to understand and realize something
about an event after it has happened, although
you did not understand or realize it at the time.
❏ *With hindsight, we'd all do things differently.*

**Hin|du** /hɪndu/ (**Hindus**) **1** N-COUNT A **Hindu** is
a person who believes in Hinduism. **2** ADJ **Hindu**
is used to describe things that belong or relate to
Hinduism. ❏ *...a Hindu temple.* [from Persian]

**Hin|du|ism** /hɪnduɪzəm/ N-UNCOUNT
**Hinduism** is an Indian religion. It has many gods
and teaches that people have another life on earth
after they die. [from Persian]

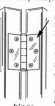

**hinge** /hɪndʒ/ (**hinges, hinging,
hinged**) N-COUNT A **hinge** is a
piece of metal, wood, or plastic
that is used to join a door to
its frame or to join two things
together so that one of them can
swing freely. ❏ *Heavy doors opened
on oiled hinges.* [from Old English]
▶ **hinge on** PHR-VERB Something
that **hinges on** one thing or event
depends entirely on it. ❏ *The plan
hinges on this agreement.*

hinge

**hint** /hɪnt/ (**hints, hinting, hinted**) **1** N-COUNT
A **hint** is a suggestion about something that is
made in an indirect way. ❏ *I gave him a hint about
coming to visit me.* **2** V-I If you **hint at** something,
you suggest it in an indirect way. ❏ *She hinted
at a trip to her favorite store.* **3** N-COUNT A **hint**
is a helpful piece of advice. ❏ *Here are some
helpful hints to make your trip easier.* **4** N-SING A
**hint** of something is a very small amount of it.
❏ *...pancakes with a hint of vanilla.*

| Word Partnership | Use *hint* with : | |
|---|---|---|
| v. | **take a** hint **1** | |
| | **drop a** hint, **give a** hint **1** **3** | |
| ADJ. | **slight** hint **1** | |
| | **helpful** hint **3** | |

**hip** /hɪp/ (**hips**) **1** N-COUNT Your **hips** are
the two areas or bones at the sides of your body
between the tops of your legs and your waist.
❏ *Tracey put her hands on her hips and laughed.*
❏ *Surgeons replaced both hips.* **2** ADJ If you say
that someone is **hip**, you mean that they are very
modern and follow all the latest fashions, for
example in clothes and ideas. [INFORMAL] ❏ *...a hip
young man.* [Sense 1 from Old English.]

**hip|pie** /hɪpi/ (**hippies**) also **hippy** N-COUNT
**Hippies** were young people in the 1960s and
1970s who rejected conventional ways of living,
dressing, and behaving, and tried to live a life
based on peace and love.

**hire** /haɪər/ (**hires, hiring, hired**) V-T If you
**hire** someone, you employ them or pay them to
do a particular job for you. ❏ *He just hired a new
secretary.* [from Old English]
▶ **hire out** PHR-VERB If you **hire out** a person's
services, you allow them to be used in return for
payment. ❏ *His agency hires out bodyguards.*

**his**

> The determiner is pronounced /hɪz/. The
> pronoun is pronounced /hɪz/.

> **His** is a third person singular possessive
> determiner. **His** is also a possessive pronoun.

DET You use **his** to indicate that something
belongs or relates to a man, boy, or male animal.
❏ *He spent part of his career in Hollywood.* • **His** is also
a possessive pronoun. ❏ *Staff say the decision was
his.* [from Old English]

**His|pan|ic** /hɪspænɪk/ (**Hispanics**) ADJ A
**Hispanic** person is a citizen of the United States
of America who originally came from Latin

America, or whose family originally came from Latin America. ❑ *...a group of Hispanic doctors.* ● A **Hispanic** is someone who is Hispanic. ❑ *About 80 percent of Hispanics here are U.S. citizens.* [from Latin]

**hiss** /hɪs/ (**hisses, hissing, hissed**) v-ɪ To **hiss** means to make a sound like a long "s." ❑ *My cat hissed when I stepped on its tail.* ● **Hiss** is also a noun. ❑ *...the hiss of water running into the hot pan.* ● **hiss|ing** N-UNCOUNT ❑ *I could hear a steady hissing.*

**his|to|gram** /hɪstəgræm/ (**histograms**) N-COUNT A **histogram** is a graph that uses vertical bars with no spaces between them to represent the distribution of a set of data. [TECHNICAL]

**his|to|rian** /hɪstɔriən/ (**historians**) N-COUNT A **historian** is a person who specializes in the study of history, and who writes books and articles about it. [from Latin]
→ see **history**

**his|tor|ic** /hɪstɔrɪk/ ADJ Something that is **historic** is important in history, or likely to be considered important at some time in the future. ❑ *...the historic changes in Europe.* [from Latin]

**his|tori|cal** /hɪstɔrɪkᵊl/ **1** ADJ **Historical** people, situations, or things existed in the past and are considered to be a part of history. ❑ *...an important historical figure.* ● **his|tori|cal|ly** ADV ❑ *Historically, royal marriages have been unhappy.* **2** ADJ **Historical** books, works of art, or studies are concerned with people, situations, or things that existed in the past. ❑ *...a historical novel about nineteenth-century France.* [from Latin]

**his|to|ry** /hɪstəri, -tri/ (**histories**) **1** N-UNCOUNT You can refer to the events of the past as **history**. You can also refer to the past events which concern a particular topic or place as its **history**. ❑ *He studied history at Indiana*

University. ❑ *...great moments in football history.* **2** N-COUNT A **history** is an account of events that have happened in the past. ❑ *...the history of the modern world.* **3** N-COUNT If a person or a place has **a history of** something, it has been very common or has happened frequently in their past. ❑ *He had a history of health problems.* **4** N-COUNT Someone's **history** is the set of facts that are known about their past. ❑ *He couldn't get a new job because of his medical history.* **5** PHRASE Someone who **makes history** does something that is thought to be important and significant in the development of the world or of a particular society. ❑ *Willy Brandt made history by visiting East Germany in 1970.* **6** PHRASE If someone or something **goes down in history**, people in the future remember them because of a particular thing they have done or because of particular events that have happened. ❑ *John Paul will go down in history as the most important leader of the 20th century.* [from Latin]
→ see Word Web: **history**

**hit** /hɪt/ (**hits, hitting**)

The form **hit** is used in the present tense and is the past and present participle.

**1** V-T If you **hit** someone or something, you deliberately touch them with a lot of force, with your hand or an object held in your hand. ❑ *She hit the ball hard.* **2** V-T When one thing **hits** another, it touches it with a lot of force. ❑ *The car hit a traffic sign.* ● **Hit** is also a noun. ❑ *The building took a direct hit from the bomb.* **3** V-T If something **hits** a person, place, or thing, it affects them very badly. ❑ *The earthquake hit Peru.* **4** V-T When a feeling or an idea **hits** you, it suddenly affects you or comes into your mind. ❑ *It hit me that I had a choice.* **5** N-COUNT If a CD, movie, or play is a **hit**, it is very popular

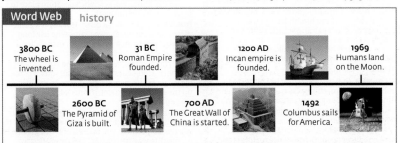

and successful. ❏ *The song was a big hit.* **6** N-COUNT A **hit** is a single visit to a website. [COMPUTING] ❏ *The company has had 78,000 hits on its webpages.* **7** N-COUNT If someone who is searching for information on the Internet gets a **hit**, they find a website where there is that information. **8** PHRASE If two people **hit it off**, they like each other and become friendly as soon as they meet. [INFORMAL] ❏ *Dad and Walter hit it off straight away.* [from Old English] **9** to **hit the headlines** → see **headline** **10** to **hit the roof** → see **roof**

▶ **hit on** or **hit upon** PHR-VERB If you **hit on an** idea or a solution to a problem, or **hit upon** it, you think of it. ❏ *We finally hit on a solution.*

▶ **hit up** PHR-VERB If you **hit** somebody **up** for something, especially for money, you ask them for it. [INFORMAL] ❏ *They hit up Harry for the last $250.*

| Thesaurus | hit | Also look up : |
|---|---|---|
| v. | bang, beat, knock, pound, slap, smack, strike **1** | |
| N. | smash, success, triumph; *(ant.)* failure **5** | |

| Word Partnership | Use *hit* with : |
|---|---|
| N. | hit **a ball**, hit **a button**, hit **the brakes 1** earthquakes/famine/storms hit someplace **3** a hit movie/show/song **5** |

**hit-and-miss** also **hit and miss** ADJ If something is **hit-and-miss** or **hit-or-miss**, it is sometimes successful and sometimes not. ❏ *Their new album is a hit-and-miss collection of songs.*

**hit-and-run** ADJ A **hit-and-run** accident is an accident in which the driver of a vehicle hits someone and then drives away without stopping. ❏ *He was the victim of a hit-and-run accident.*

**hitch** /hɪtʃ/ (**hitches, hitching, hitched**) **1** N-COUNT A **hitch** is a slight problem. ❏ *After some hitches the show finally started.* **2** V-T/V-I If you **hitch, hitch** a lift, or **hitch** a ride, you hitchhike. [INFORMAL] ❏ *I hitched a ride into town.* **3** V-T If you **hitch** something to something else, you hook it or fasten it there. ❏ *We hitched the horse to the cart.*

**hitch|hike** /hɪtʃhaɪk/ (**hitchhikes, hitchhiking, hitchhiked**) V-I If you **hitchhike**, you travel by getting rides from passing vehicles without paying. ❏ *Neil hitchhiked to New York during his vacation.* ● **hitch|hiker** (**hitchhikers**) N-COUNT ❏ *On my way to Vancouver I picked up a hitchhiker.*

**hi tech** → see **high-tech**

**hither|to** /hɪðərtu/ ADV You use **hitherto** to indicate that something was true up until the time you are talking about, although it may no longer be true. [FORMAL] ❏ *…a hitherto unknown movie he made eight years ago.*

**HIV** /eɪtʃaɪ vi/ **1** N-UNCOUNT **HIV** is a virus which reduces people's resistance to illness and can cause AIDS. **HIV** is an abbreviation for "human immunodeficiency virus." **2** PHRASE If someone is **HIV positive**, they are infected with the HIV virus, and may develop AIDS. If someone is **HIV negative**, they are not infected with the virus.

**hive** /haɪv/ (**hives**) **1** N-COUNT A **hive** is a structure in which bees are kept. **2** N-COUNT If you describe a place as a **hive of** activity, you are saying that there is a lot of activity there or that

people are busy working there, and that you think this is a good thing. ❏ *The house was a hive of activity.* [from Old English]

**HMO** /eɪtʃem oʊ/ (**HMOs**) N-COUNT An **HMO** is an organization to which you pay a fee and that allows you to use only doctors and hospitals which belong to the organization. **HMO** is an abbreviation for **health maintenance organization**.

**hoard** /hɔrd/ (**hoards, hoarding, hoarded**) **1** V-T If you **hoard** things such as food or money, you save or store them, often in secret, because they are valuable or important to you. ❏ *They began to hoard food and gasoline.* **2** N-COUNT A **hoard** is a store of things that you have saved and that are valuable or important to you or you do not want other people to have. ❏ *…a hoard of silver and jewels valued at up to $40m.* [from Old English]

**hoarse** /hɔrs/ (**hoarser, hoarsest**) ADJ If your voice is **hoarse** or if you are **hoarse**, your voice sounds rough and unclear, for example because your throat is sore. ❏ *"What do you think?" she said in a hoarse whisper.* ● **hoarse|ly** ADV ❏ *"Thank you," Maria said hoarsely.* [of Scandinavian origin]

**hoax** /hoʊks/ (**hoaxes**) N-COUNT A **hoax** is a trick in which someone tells people a lie, for example that there is a bomb somewhere. ❏ *Police say the letter may be a hoax.*

**hob|ble** /hɒbəl/ (**hobbles, hobbling, hobbled**) V-I If you **hobble**, you walk in an awkward way with small steps, for example because your foot is injured. ❏ *He got up slowly and hobbled over to the table.* [from Low German]

**hob|by** /hɒbi/ (**hobbies**) N-COUNT A **hobby** is an activity that you enjoy doing in your spare time. ❏ *My hobbies are music and tennis.*

| Thesaurus | hobby | Also look up : |
|---|---|---|
| N. | activity, craft, interest, pastime | |

**hobo** /hoʊboʊ/ or **hoboes** **1** N-COUNT A **hobo** is a person who has no home, especially one who travels from place to place and gets money by begging. **2** N-COUNT A **hobo** is a worker, especially a farm worker, who goes from place to place in order to find work.

**hock|ey** /hɒki/ N-UNCOUNT **Hockey** is a game played on ice between two teams who use long curved sticks to hit a small rubber disk, called a puck, and try to score goals. ❏ *…a new hockey rink.*

**hoe** /hoʊ/ (**hoes**) N-COUNT A **hoe** is a gardening tool with a long handle and a small square blade, which you use to remove small weeds and break up the surface of the soil. [from Old French] → see **garden**

**hog** /hɒg/ (**hogs, hogging, hogged**) **1** N-COUNT A **hog** is a pig. ❏ *We fed the corn to the hogs.* **2** V-T If you **hog** something, you take all of it in a greedy or impolite way. [INFORMAL] ❏ *Have you finished hogging the bathroom?* [from Old English]

**hoist** /hɔɪst/ (**hoists, hoisting, hoisted**) **1** V-T If you **hoist** something heavy somewhere, you lift it or pull it up there. ❏ *I hoisted my bag on to my shoulder.* **2** V-T If something heavy **is hoisted** somewhere, it is lifted there using a machine such as a crane. ❏ *The hut was hoisted onto a truck.* **3** N-COUNT A **hoist** is a machine for lifting heavy things or people. ❏ *It takes three nurses and a hoist* *to get me from bed into the chair.* **4** V-T If you **hoist** a flag or a sail, you pull it up to its correct position by using ropes. ❑ *They hoisted the flag on top of the building.* [from Low German]

---

### hold

**①** PHYSICALLY TOUCHING, SUPPORTING, OR CONTAINING
**②** HAVING OR DOING
**③** CONTROLLING OR REMAINING
**④** PHRASES
**⑤** PHRASAL VERBS

---

**① hold** /hoʊld/ (**holds, holding, held**) **1** V-T When you **hold** something, you carry or support it, using your hands or your arms. ❑ *I held the baby in my arms.* ● **Hold** is also a noun. ❑ *He let go his hold on the door.* **2** N-UNCOUNT **Hold** is used in expressions such as **grab hold of**, **catch hold of**, and **get hold of**, to indicate that you close your hand tightly around something. ❑ *I woke up when someone grabbed hold of my sleeping bag.* ❑ *A doctor and a nurse caught hold of his arms.* **3** V-T When you **hold** a part of your body in a particular position, you put it into that position and keep it there. ❑ *Hold your hands in front of your face.* **4** V-T If one thing **holds** another in a particular position, it keeps it in that position. ❑ *The doorstop held the door open.* **5** V-T If one thing is used to **hold** another, it is used to store it. ❑ *Two drawers hold her favorite T-shirts.* **6** N-COUNT In a ship or airplane, a **hold** is a place where cargo or luggage is stored. ❑ *A fire started in the hold.* **7** V-T If something **holds** a particular amount of something, it can contain that amount. ❑ *One CD-ROM disk can hold over 100,000 pages of text.* [from Old English]

| **Thesaurus** | *hold* | Also look up : |
|---|---|---|
| v. | carry, support **①** **1** | |

**② hold** /hoʊld/ (**holds, holding, held**)

**Hold** is often used to indicate that someone or something has the particular thing, characteristic, or attitude that is mentioned. Therefore it takes most of its meaning from the word that follows it.

**1** V-T If you **hold** an opinion or belief, that is your opinion or belief. ❑ *He held opinions which were usually different from mine.* **2** V-T **Hold** is used with words such as "fear" or "mystery" to say that something has a particular quality or characteristic. ❑ *Death doesn't hold any fear for me.* **3** V-T **Hold** is used with nouns such as "office," "power," and "responsibility" to indicate that someone has a particular position of power or authority. ❑ *She has never held an elected office.* **4** V-T **Hold** is used with nouns such as "permit," "degree," or "ticket" to indicate that someone has a particular document that allows them to do something. ❑ *He did not hold a driver's license.* ● **holder** (**holders**) N-COUNT ❑ *...season-ticket holders.* **5** V-T **Hold** is used with nouns such as "party," "meeting," "talks," "election," and "trial" to indicate that people are organizing a particular activity. ❑ *The country will hold elections within a year.* **6** V-RECIP **Hold** is used with nouns such as "conversation," "interview," and "talks" to indicate that two or more people meet and

discuss something. ❑ *The prime minister is holding talks to finalize the agreement.* **7** V-T **Hold** is used with nouns such as "attention" or "interest" to indicate that what you do or say keeps someone interested or listening to you. ❑ *If you want to hold someone's attention, look straight into their eyes.* [from Old English]

**③ hold** /hoʊld/ (**holds, holding, held**) **1** V-T If someone **holds** you in a place, they keep you there as a prisoner and do not allow you to leave. ❑ *Two angry motorists held a man prisoner in his own car.* **2** N-SING If you have a **hold over** someone, you have power or control over them. ❑ *Because he once loved her, she still has a hold on him.* **3** V-T/V-I If you ask someone to **hold**, or to **hold the line**, when you are answering a telephone call, you are asking them to wait for a short time, for example so that you can find the person they want to speak to. ❑ *Could you hold on? I'll just get a pen.* **4** V-I If something **holds**, it remains the same. ❑ *Will the weather hold?* [from Old English]

**④ hold** /hoʊld/ (**holds, holding, held**) **1** PHRASE If you **get hold of** an object or information, you obtain it, usually after some difficulty. ❑ *It is hard to get hold of medicines in poor countries.* **2** PHRASE If you **get hold of** someone, you succeed in contacting them. ❑ *I tried to call him but I couldn't get hold of him.* **3** CONVENTION If you say "**Hold it**," you are telling someone to stop what they are doing and to wait. ❑ *Hold it! Don't move!* **4** PHRASE If you can do something well enough to **hold your own**, you do not appear foolish when you are compared with someone who is generally thought to be very good at it. ❑ *She can hold her own against almost any player.* **5** PHRASE If you put something **on hold**, you decide not to do it, deal with it, or change it now, but to leave it until later. ❑ *He put his retirement on hold to help to find a solution.* **6** PHRASE If something **takes hold**, it gains complete control or influence over a person or thing. ❑ *Excitement took hold of her.* [from Old English] **7** to **hold** something **at bay** → see **bay** **8** to **hold** something **in check** → see **check** **9** to **hold fast** → see **fast** **10** to **hold your ground** → see **ground** **11** to **hold** someone **ransom** → see **ransom** **12** to **hold sway** → see **sway**

**⑤ hold** /hoʊld/ (**holds, holding, held**)
▶ **hold against** PHR-VERB If you **hold** something **against** someone, you dislike them because of something they did in the past. ❑ *Bernstein lost the case, but didn't hold it against Grundy.*
▶ **hold back** **1** PHR-VERB If you **hold back** or if something **holds** you **back**, you hesitate before you do something because you are not sure whether it is the right thing to do. ❑ *I was holding back a little.* **2** PHR-VERB To **hold** someone or something **back** means to prevent someone from doing something, or to prevent something from happening. ❑ *He wanted to help but something held him back.* **3** PHR-VERB If you **hold** something **back**, you do not include it in the information you are giving about something.
▶ **hold down** PHR-VERB If you **hold down** a job or a place on a team, you manage to keep it. ❑ *He couldn't hold down a job.*
▶ **hold off** PHR-VERB If you **hold off** doing something, you delay doing it or delay making a decision about it. ❑ *I held off buying for a while.*
▶ **hold on** or **hold onto** **1** PHR-VERB If you **hold**

h

**on**, or **hold onto** something, you keep your hand on it or around it. ❑ *He held on to a coffee cup.* ❑ *He was holding onto a rock on the cliff.* ☑ PHR-VERB If you **hold on**, you manage to achieve success or avoid failure in spite of great difficulties or opposition. ❑ *The Rams held on to defeat the Nevada Wolf Pack, 32–28.*
▸ **hold out** ☐ PHR-VERB If you **hold out** your hand or something you have in your hand, you move your hand away from your body, for example to shake hands with someone. ❑ *"I'm Nancy," she said, holding out her hand.* ☑ PHR-VERB If you **hold out for** something, you refuse to accept something inferior or you refuse to surrender. ❑ *He held out for a better deal.* ❑ *The soldiers held out for two weeks until they were rescued.*
▸ **hold up** ☐ PHR-VERB To **hold up** a person or process means to make them late or delay them. ❑ *Why were you holding everyone up?* ☑ PHR-VERB If someone **holds up** a place such as a bank or a store, they point a weapon at someone there to make them give them money or valuable goods. ❑ *He held up a gas station with a toy gun.* ☒ → see also **holdup**

**hold|er** /hoʊldər/ (**holders**) N-COUNT A **holder** is a container in which you put an object. ❑ *...a toothbrush holder.* [from Old English]

**hold|ing** /hoʊldɪŋ/ (**holdings**) N-COUNT If you have a **holding** in a company, you own shares in it. [BUSINESS] ❑ *Their holdings grew by 40 percent.* [from Old English]

**hold|ing pat|tern** (**holding patterns**) ☐ N-COUNT If an aircraft is put **in a holding pattern**, it is instructed to continue flying while waiting for permission to land. ❑ *Planes were kept in a holding pattern until they were allowed to land.* ☑ N-COUNT If something or someone is **in a holding pattern**, they remain in the same state or continue to do the same thing while waiting for something to happen. ❑ *The computer market is in a kind of holding pattern.*

**hold|over** /hoʊldoʊvər/ (**holdovers**) N-COUNT A **holdover from** an earlier time is a person or thing which existed or occurred at that time and which still exists or occurs today. ❑ *There are only four holdovers from last season's football team.*

**holdup** /hoʊldʌp/ (**holdups**) also **hold-up** ☐ N-COUNT A **holdup** is a situation in which someone is threatened with a weapon in order to make them hand over money or valuables. ❑ *Police are looking for a man after an armed hold-up.* ☑ N-COUNT A **holdup** is a delay. ❑ *There was a four-minute hold-up during the game.*

**hole** /hoʊl/ (**holes**) ☐ N-COUNT A **hole** is an opening or hollow space in something. ❑ *He dug a hole 45 feet wide and 15 feet deep.* ❑ *...kids with holes in the knees of their jeans.* ☑ PHRASE If a person or organization is **in the hole**, they owe money to someone else. [INFORMAL] ❑ *The business is $14,000 in the hole.* [from Old English]
→ see **golf**

**holi|day** /hɒlɪdeɪ/ (**holidays**) N-COUNT A **holiday** is a day when people do not go to work or school because of a religious or national celebration. ❑ *New Year's Day is a public holiday.* [from Old English]

**holi|ness** /hoʊlinɪs/ ☐ N-UNCOUNT **Holiness** is the state or quality of being holy. ❑ *We immediately noticed this city's holiness.* ☑ N-VOC You say **Your Holiness** or **His Holiness** when you address or refer respectfully to the Pope or to leaders of some other religions. ❑ *The president invited His Holiness to the White House.* [from Old English]

**ho|lis|tic** /hoʊlɪstɪk/ ADJ A **holistic** approach to something treats it as a whole rather than as a number of different parts. ❑ *He believed stongly in holistic medicine.*

**hol|ler** /hɒlər/ (**hollers, hollering, hollered**) V-T/V-I If you **holler**, you shout loudly. [INFORMAL] ❑ *He'll be hollering at me for being late.* ❑ *"Watch out!" he hollered.* [from French]

**hol|low** /hɒloʊ/ (**hollows**) ☐ ADJ Something that is **hollow** has a space inside it. ❑ *...a hollow tree.* ☑ ADJ A surface that is **hollow** curves inward. ❑ *He was young, with hollow cheeks.* ☒ N-COUNT A **hollow** is an area that is lower than the surrounding surface. ❑ *Below him the town lay in the hollow of the hill.* ☓ ADJ If you describe a statement, situation, or person as **hollow**, you mean they have no real value, worth, or effectiveness. ❑ *Any threat to tell the police is a hollow one.* ● **hol|low|ness** N-UNCOUNT ❑ *I saw the hollowness of his promises.* ☕ ADJ A **hollow** sound is dull and echoing. ❑ *...the hollow sound of a baseball bat on the road.* [from Old English]

**hol|ly** /hɒli/ (**hollies**) N-VAR **Holly** is an evergreen tree or shrub which has hard, shiny leaves with sharp points, and red berries in winter. [from Old English]

**holo|caust** /hɒləkɔst, hoʊlə-/ (**holocausts**) ☐ N-VAR A **holocaust** is an event in which there is a lot of destruction and many people are killed, especially one caused by war. ❑ *...fear of a nuclear holocaust.* ☑ N-SING **The Holocaust** is used to refer to the killing by the Nazis of millions of Jews during the Second World War. ❑ *Their family and friends died in the Holocaust.* [from Late Latin]

**holy** /hoʊli/ (**holier, holiest**) ADJ Something that is **holy** is considered to be special because it is connected with God or a particular religion. ❑ *This is a holy place.* [from Old English]

**Holy Land** N-SING People sometimes refer to the part of the Middle East where most of the Bible is set as **the Holy Land**. ❑ *We went on a trip to the Holy Land.*

**holy war** (**holy wars**) N-COUNT A **holy war** is a war that people fight in order to defend or support their religion. ❑ *More than 1,000 young men have joined the holy war.*

**hom|age** /hɒmɪdʒ, ɒm-/ N-UNCOUNT **Homage** is respect shown toward someone or something you admire, or to a person in authority. ❑ *They paid homage to their leader.* [from Old French]

**home** /hoʊm/ (**homes**) ☐ N-COUNT Someone's **home** is the house or apartment where they live. ❑ *Last night she stayed home and watched TV.* ❑ *Hi, Mom, I'm home!* ☑ N-UNCOUNT You can use **home** to refer in a general way to the house, town, or country where someone lives now or where they were born. ❏ *Ms. Highsmith has made Switzerland her home.* ❏ *His father worked away from home most of the time.* ❸ ADV **Home** means to or at the place where you live. ❏ *She wasn't feeling well and she wanted to go home.* ❏ *I'll call you as soon as I get home.* ❹ N-COUNT A **home** is a building where people who cannot care for themselves live and are cared for. ❏ *It's a home for elderly people.* ❺ N-SING If you refer to the **home** of something, you mean the place where it began or where it is most typically found. ❏ *Greece is the home of the Olympics.* ❻ ADV If you drive, or hammer something **home**, you explain it to people as forcefully as possible. ❏ *I want to drive home the point that exercise is as important as eating healthily.* ❼ N-UNCOUNT When a sports team plays **at home**, they play a game on their own field, rather than on the opposing team's field. ❏ *I scored in both games; we lost at home and won away.* ● **Home** is also an adjective. ❏ *They see all home games together.* ❽ PHRASE If you feel **at home**, you feel comfortable in the place or situation that you are in. ❏ *We soon felt at home.* [from Old English]

### Thesaurus          home     Also look up :

N.    dwelling, house, residence ❶
      birthplace ❷

### Word Partnership     Use *home* with :

V.    **bring/take** *someone/something* home,
      **build** a home, **buy** a home, **call/phone**
      home, **come** home, **drive** home, **feel at**
      home, **fly** home, **get** home, **go** home,
      **head for** home, **leave** home, **return**
      home, **ride** home, **sit** *at* home, **stay** *at*
      home, **walk** home,
      **work at** home ❶ – ❸
ADJ.  **new** home ❶ ❷
      **close to** home ❶ – ❸

**home|body** /hoʊmbɒdi/ (**homebodies**) N-COUNT If you describe someone as a **homebody**, you mean that they enjoy being at home and spend most of their time there. ❏ *We're both homebodies. We don't like going to parties.*

**home|coming** /hoʊmkʌmɪŋ/ (**homecomings**) ❶ N-VAR Your **homecoming** is your return to your home or your country after being away for a long time. ❏ *"What a wonderful homecoming. It's nice to see so many people," she said.* ❷ N-UNCOUNT **Homecoming** is a day or weekend each year when former students of a particular school, college, or university go back to it to meet each other again and go to parties and sports events. ❏ *…a Penn State graduate who was back for Homecoming weekend.*

**home field** (**home fields**) N-COUNT A sports team's **home field** is their own playing field, as opposed to that of other teams.

**home front** N-SING If something is happening on **the home front**, it is happening within the country where you live. ❏ *I wanted to find out what was happening on the home front.*

**home|grown** /hoʊmgroʊn/ ADJ **Homegrown** fruit and vegetables have been grown in your garden, rather than on a farm, or in your country rather than abroad. ❏ *…homegrown fruit from California's Bajaro Valley.*

**home|land** /hoʊmlænd/ (**homelands**) N-COUNT Your **homeland** is your native country. [mainly WRITTEN] ❏ *Many people are planning to return to their homeland.*

**home|less** /hoʊmlɪs/ ADJ **Homeless** people have nowhere to live. ❏ *…the growing number of homeless families.* ● **The homeless** are people who are homeless. ❏ *…raising money for the homeless.* ● **home|less|ness** N-UNCOUNT ❏ *The only way to solve homelessness is to build more homes.* [from Old English]

**home|ly** /hoʊmli/ ADJ If you say that someone is **homely**, you mean that they are not very attractive to look at. ❏ *John was homely and overweight.* [from Old English]

**home|made** /hoʊmmeɪd/ ADJ Something that is **homemade** has been made in someone's home, rather than in a store or factory. ❏ *…homemade bread.*

**home|maker** /hoʊmmeɪkər/ (**homemakers**) ❶ N-COUNT A **homemaker** is a woman who spends a lot of time taking care of her home and family. A **homemaker** usually does not have another job. ❷ → see also **housewife**

**homeopa|thy** /hoʊmiɒpəθi/ N-UNCOUNT **Homeopathy** is a way of treating an illness in which the patient is given very small amounts of a drug that produces signs of the illness in healthy people. ● **homeo|path|ic** /hoʊmioʊpæθɪk/ ADJ ❏ *…homeopathic remedies.*

**homeo|sta|sis** /hoʊmiəsteɪsɪs/ N-UNCOUNT An organism or a system that is capable of **homeostasis** is able to regulate processes such as its temperature so that it can function normally when external conditions change. [TECHNICAL] ● **homeo|stat|ic** /hoʊmiəstætɪk/ ADJ ❏ *…a homeostatic mechanism.*

**home plate** N-UNCOUNT In baseball, **home plate** is the piece of rubber or other material that the batter stands beside. It is the last of the four bases that a runner must touch in order to score a run. ❏ *He broke his ankle in a fall at home plate.*

**home|room** /hoʊmrum, -rʊm/ (**homerooms**) N-VAR In a school, **homeroom** is the class or room where students in the same grade meet to get general information and where their homeroom teacher checks attendance. ❏ *Twice a week in homeroom, teachers help students work through a math problem.*

**home run** (**home runs**) N-COUNT In baseball, a **home run** is a hit that allows the batter to run around all four bases and score a run. ❏ *Ruth hit sixty home runs that year.*

**home school|ing** also **home-schooling** N-UNCOUNT **Home schooling** is the practice of educating your child at home rather than in a school. ❏ *All fifty American states allow home schooling.*

**home|sick** /hoʊmsɪk/ ADJ If you are **homesick**, you feel unhappy because you are away from home and are missing your family and friends. ❏ *He was homesick for his family.* ● **home|sick|ness** N-UNCOUNT ❏ *…feelings of homesickness.*

### Word Link     stead ≈ place, stand : home*stead*, in*stead*, *stead*y

**home|stead** /hoʊmstɛd/ (**homesteads**) N-COUNT A **homestead** is a farmhouse, together with the land around it.

**home|work** /ˈhoʊmwɜrk/ **1** N-UNCOUNT
**Homework** is schoolwork that teachers give to students to do at home in the evening or on the weekend. ❑ *Have you done your homework, Gemma?* **2** N-UNCOUNT If you **do** your **homework**, you find out what you need to know in preparation for something. ❑ *Before you buy a new computer, do your homework on the best prices.*

**homey** /ˈhoʊmi/ ADJ If you describe a room or house as **homey**, you like it because you feel comfortable and relaxed there. [INFORMAL] ❑ *...a large, homey dining room.* [from Old English]

**homi|ci|dal** /ˌhɒmɪˈsaɪdəl, ˌhoʊmɪ-/ ADJ
**Homicidal** is used to describe someone who is dangerous because they are likely to kill someone. ❑ *Some drugs can make people homicidal.* [from Old French]

> **Word Link** cide ≈ killing : geno*cide*, homi*cide*, pesti*cide*

**homi|cide** /ˈhɒmɪsaɪd, ˈhoʊmɪ-/ **(homicides)**
N-VAR **Homicide** is the illegal killing of a person. ❑ *The police arrived at the scene of the homicide.* [from Old French]

**homi|nid** /ˈhɒmɪnɪd/ **(hominids)** N-COUNT
**Hominids** are members of a group of animals that includes human beings and early ancestors of human beings. [TECHNICAL] [from New Latin]

**homo|geneous** /ˌhɒməˈdʒiniəs, ˌhoʊ-/
also **homogenous** /həˈmɒdʒənəs/ ADJ
**Homogeneous** is used to describe a group or thing which has members or parts that are all the same. [FORMAL] ❑ *Scotland seems one of the most traditional and homogenous places in Britain.*

**homo|geneous mixture (homogeneous mixtures)** N-COUNT In chemistry, a **homogeneous mixture** is a mixture of two or more substances that have mixed completely, for example salt and water.

**homo|graph** /ˈhɒməgræf/ **(homographs)**
N-COUNT **Homographs** are words that are spelled the same but have different meanings and are sometimes pronounced differently. For example, "bow" (a weapon) and "bow" (the front of a ship) are homographs. [TECHNICAL]

**ho|molo|gous** /həˈmɒləgəs/ ADJ **Homologous** chromosomes are pairs of chromosomes that contain the same genetic information but come from different parents. [TECHNICAL]

**homo|pho|bia** /ˌhɒməˈfoʊbiə/ N-UNCOUNT
**Homophobia** is a strong and unreasonable dislike of gay people, especially gay men.
● **ho|mo|pho|bic** /ˌhɒməˈfoʊbɪk/ ADJ ❑ *I'm not homophobic in any way.*

**homo|phone** /ˈhɒməfoʊn/ **(homophones)**
N-COUNT In linguistics, **homophones** are words with different meanings which are pronounced in the same way but are spelled differently. For example, "write" and "right" are homophones.

**homo|sex|ual** /ˌhoʊmoʊˈsɛkʃuəl/
**(homosexuals)** ADJ Someone who is **homosexual** is sexually attracted to people of the same sex. ❑ *I knew from an early age that I was homosexual.*
● **Homosexual** is also a noun. ❑ *The organization wants equality for homosexuals in South African society.* ● **homo|sex|ual|ity** /ˌhoʊmoʊsɛkʃuˈælɪti/
N-UNCOUNT ❑ *...a place where they could openly discuss homosexuality.*

**hone** /ˈhoʊn/ **(hones, honing, honed)** V-T If you **hone** something, for example a skill, technique, idea, or product, you carefully develop it so that it is exactly right for your purpose. ❑ *Companies spend time and money on honing the skills of managers.* [from Old English]

**hon|est** /ˈɒnɪst/ **1** ADJ If you describe someone as **honest**, you mean that they always tell the truth, and do not try to deceive people or break the law. ❑ *She's honest and reliable.* ● **hon|est|ly** ADV ❑ *Lawrence acted fairly and honestly.* **2** ADJ If you are **honest** in a particular situation, you tell the complete truth or give your sincere opinion, even if this is not very pleasant. ❑ *I was honest about what I was doing.* ● **hon|est|ly** ADV ❑ *She answered the question honestly.* **3** ADV You say "**honest**" before or after a statement to emphasize that you are telling the truth and that you want people to believe you. [INFORMAL] ❑ *I'm not sure, honest.*
● **hon|est|ly** ADV ❑ *Honestly, I don't know anything about it.* [from Old French]

> **Thesaurus** honest Also look up :
>
> ADJ. fair, genuine, sincere, true, truthful, upright **1**
> candid, frank, straight, truthful **2**

**hon|est|ly** /ˈɒnɪstli/ **1** ADV You use **honestly** to indicate that you are annoyed or impatient. [SPOKEN] ❑ *Honestly, Brian! I wish you weren't so rude to him.* [from Old French] **2** → see also **honest**

**hon|es|ty** /ˈɒnɪsti/ N-UNCOUNT **Honesty** is the quality of being honest. ❑ *I can answer you with complete honesty.* [from Old French]

**hon|ey** /ˈhʌni/ **(honeys)** **1** N-VAR **Honey** is a sweet, sticky, yellowish substance that is made by bees. **2** N-VOC You call someone **honey** as a sign of affection. ❑ *Honey, I don't think that's a good idea.* [from Old English]

**honey|moon** /ˈhʌnimun/ **(honeymoons, honeymooning, honeymooned)** **1** N-COUNT A **honeymoon** is a vacation taken by a man and a woman who have just gotten married. ❑ *We went to Florida on our honeymoon.* **2** V-I When a recently married couple **honeymoon** somewhere, they go there on their honeymoon. ❑ *They honeymooned in Venice.*

→ see **wedding**

**hon|or** /ˈɒnər/ **(honors, honoring, honored)**
**1** N-UNCOUNT **Honor** means doing what you believe to be right and being confident that you have done what is right. ❑ *He behaved with honor.* **2** N-COUNT An **honor** is a special award that is given to someone, usually because they have done something good or because they are greatly respected. ❑ *He won many honors — among them an Oscar.* **3** V-T If someone **is honored**, they are given public praise or an award for something they have done. ❑ *Maradona was honored with an award presented by Argentina's soccer association.* **4** N-SING If you describe doing or experiencing something as an **honor**, you mean you think it is something special and desirable. ❑ *...the honor of hosting the Olympic Games.* **5** V-T PASSIVE If you say that you **would be honored to** do something, you are saying very politely and formally that you would be pleased to do it. If you say that you **are honored by** something, you are saying that you are grateful for it and pleased about it. ❑ *Ms. Payne said she was*

*honored to accept the job.* ◻ v-t If you **honor** an arrangement or promise, you do what you said you would do. ◻ *I wanted to see if he was ready to honor the agreement.* ◻ N-VOC Judges and mayors are sometimes called **your honor** or referred to as **his honor** or **her honor.** ◻ *I say this, your honor, because I think it is important.* ◻ PHRASE If something is arranged **in honor of** a particular event, it is arranged in order to celebrate that event. ◻ *They're holding a dinner in honor of the president's visit.* [from Old French]

| **Thesaurus** | *honor* | Also look up : |
| --- | --- | --- |
| N. | award, distinction, recognition ◻ | |
| V. | commend, praise, recognize ◻ | |

| **Word Partnership** | Use *honor* with : |
| --- | --- |
| N. | code of honor, sense of honor ◻ honor a ceasefire ◻ |
| ADJ. | great/highest honor ◻ ◻ |

**hon|or|able** /ɒnərəbəl/ ADJ If you describe people or actions as **honorable,** you mean that they are good and deserve to be respected and admired. ◻ *...patient, friendly and honorable priests.* ● **hon|or|ably** /ɒnərəbli/ ADV ◻ *She behaved honorably.* [from Old French]

**hon|or|able men|tion** (honorable mentions) N-VAR If something that you do in a competition is given an **honorable mention,** it receives special praise from the judges although it does not actually win a prize. ◻ *His designs received an honorable mention.*

**hon|or|ary** /ɒnərɛri/ ◻ ADJ An **honorary** title or membership of a group is given as a sign of respect to someone who does not qualify for it in the normal way. ◻ *Harvard awarded him an honorary degree.* ◻ ADJ **Honorary** is used to describe an official job that is done without payment. ◻ *She acted as the honorary secretary of the club.* [from Old French]

**hon|or roll** (honor rolls) N-COUNT An **honor roll** is a list of the names of people who are admired or respected for something they have done, such as doing very well in a sport or in school. ◻ *If you study hard, you can be on the honor roll.*

**hon|or sys|tem** N-SING If a service such as an arrangement for buying something is based on an **honor system,** people are trusted to use the service honestly and without cheating or lying. ◻ *Readers can borrow or buy on the honor system.*

**hood** /hʊd/ (hoods) ◻ N-COUNT A **hood** is a part of a coat or other garment which you can pull up to cover your head. ◻ *She pushed back the hood of her coat.* ◻ N-COUNT The **hood** of a car is the metal cover over the engine at the front. ◻ *He raised the hood of the truck.* ◻ N-COUNT A **hood** is a covering on a vehicle or a piece of equipment, which is usually curved and can be removed. [from Old English]

**hood|ed** /hʊdɪd/ ◻ ADJ A **hooded** piece of clothing or furniture has a hood. ◻ *...a blue hooded sweatshirt.* ◻ ADJ A **hooded** person is wearing a hood or a piece of clothing pulled down over their face, so they are difficult to recognize. ◻ *Police were looking for a hooded man.* [from Old English]

**hoof** /hʊf, huf/ (hoofs or hooves) N-COUNT The

**hooves** of an animal such as a horse are the hard lower parts of its feet. ◻ *He heard the sound of horses' hooves.* [from Old English]
→ see **horse**

**hook** /hʊk/ (hooks, hooking, hooked) ◻ N-COUNT A **hook** is a bent piece of metal or plastic that is used for catching or holding things, or for hanging things up. ◻ *His jacket hung from a hook.* ◻ v-t/v-i If you **hook** one thing **to** another, you attach it there using a hook. If something **hooks** somewhere, it can be hooked there. ◻ *Paul hooked his tractor to the car and pulled it to safety.* ◻ N-COUNT A **hook** is a short sharp blow with your fist that you make with your elbow bent. ◻ *Lewis tried to stay away from Ruddock's big left hook.* ◻ PHRASE If someone gets **off the hook** or is let **off the hook,** they manage to get out of the awkward or unpleasant situation that they are in. [INFORMAL] ◻ *You're not getting off the hook that easily!* ◻ PHRASE If you take a phone **off the hook,** you take the receiver off the part that it normally rests on, so that the phone will not ring. ◻ *I took my phone off the hook to try to get some sleep.* ◻ PHRASE If your phone **is ringing off the hook,** so many people are trying to telephone you that it is ringing constantly. ◻ *After the earthquake, the phones at donation centers were ringing off the hook.* [from Old English]

▸ **hook up** ◻ PHR-VERB If someone **hooks up with** another person, they begin a sexual or romantic relationship with that person. You can also say that two people **hook up.** [INFORMAL] ◻ *I hooked up with an intelligent, beautiful girl.* ◻ *We haven't hooked up yet.* ◻ PHR-VERB If you **hook up with** someone, you meet them and spend time with them. You can also say that two people **hook up.** [INFORMAL] ◻ *He hooked up with other cyclists and joined a club.* ◻ *This afternoon Jude and Chris hooked up.* ◻ PHR-VERB When someone **hooks up** a computer or other electronic machine, they connect it to other similar machines or to a central power supply. ◻ *...technicians who hook up computer systems and networks.* ◻ *He hooked the machine up and we got it to work.*

**hooked** /hʊkt/ ◻ ADJ A **hooked** object is shaped like a hook. ◻ *He picked up the sack using a long, hooked stick.* ◻ ADJ If you are **hooked on** something, you enjoy it so much that it takes up a lot of your interest and attention. [INFORMAL] ◻ *I've been hooked on sailing since I was eight.* [from Old English]

**hoo|li|gan** /huligən/ (hooligans) N-COUNT If you describe young people as **hooligans,** you are critical of them because they behave in a noisy and violent way in a public place. ◻ *...the problem of soccer hooligans.* [from Irish]

**hoop** /hʊp/ (hoops) ◻ N-COUNT A **hoop** is a ring made of wood, metal, or plastic. ◻ *She wears jeans, sneakers and gold hoop earrings.* ◻ N-COUNT A basketball **hoop** is the ring that players try to throw the ball into in order to score points for their team. [from Old English]

**hoop|la** /hʊplɑ/ N-UNCOUNT **Hoopla** is great fuss or excitement. [INFORMAL] ◻ *He didn't want a lot of hoopla.*

**hoot** /hut/ (hoots, hooting, hooted) v-i If you **hoot,** you make a loud high-pitched noise when you are laughing or showing disapproval. ◻ *The men hooted angrily at them.* ● **Hoot** is also a noun.

❏ *He was greeted with hoots of laughter.*

**hooves** /hʊvz/ **Hooves** is a plural of **hoof**. [from Old English]

**hop** /hɒp/ (**hops, hopping, hopped**) **1** V-I If you **hop**, you move along by jumping on one foot. ❏ *I hopped down three steps.* ● **Hop** is also a noun. ❏ *"This is a great tune," he said, with a few little hops.* **2** V-I When birds and some small animals **hop**, they move along by jumping on both feet or all four feet together. ❏ *A small brown bird hopped in front of them.* ❏ *The rabbit took four hops.* **3** V-I If you **hop** somewhere, you move there quickly or suddenly. [INFORMAL] ❏ *We hopped on the train.* **4** N-COUNT A **hop** is a short, quick trip, usually by plane. [INFORMAL] ❏ *They went for a short hop in the plane.* [from Old English]

**hope** /hoʊp/ (**hopes, hoping, hoped**) **1** V-T/V-I If you **hope** that something is true, or if you **hope** for something, you want it to be true or to happen, and you usually believe that it is possible or likely. ❏ *I hope that's OK.* ❏ *He waited and looked as if he was hoping for an answer.* **2** N-UNCOUNT **Hope** is a feeling of desire and expectation that things will go well in the future. ❏ *Many people have hope for genuine changes in the system.* ❏ *Kevin hasn't given up hope of losing weight.* **3** N-COUNT If someone wants something to happen, and considers it likely or possible, you can refer to their **hopes of** that thing, or to their **hope that** it will happen. ❏ *They have hopes of reaching the final.* ❏ *My hope is that, in the future, I will move to Australia.* **4** PHRASE If you are in a difficult situation and do something and **hope for the best**, you hope that everything will happen in the way you want, although you know that it may not. ❏ *Some companies are cutting costs and hoping for the best.* **5** PHRASE If you do one thing **in the hope of** another thing happening, you do it because you think it might cause or help the other thing to happen, which is what you want. ❏ *He was studying in the hope of going to college.* [from Old English]

| **Thesaurus** | | *hope* | Also look up : |
|---|---|---|---|
| V. | aspire, desire, dream, wish **1** | | |
| N. | ambition, aspiration, desire, dream, wish **3** | | |

| **Word Partnership** | Use *hope* with : |
|---|---|
| V. | give *someone* hope, give up *all* hope, hold out hope, lose *all* hope **2** **3** |
| ADJ. | faint hope, false hope, little hope **2** **3** |
| N. | glimmer of hope **3** |

**hope|ful** /hoʊpfəl/ (**hopefuls**) **1** ADJ If you are **hopeful**, you are fairly confident that something that you want to happen will happen. ❏ *I am hopeful that with help she will recover.* **2** ADJ If something such as a sign or event is **hopeful**, it makes you feel that what you want to happen will happen. ❏ *He welcomed the news as a hopeful sign.* [from Old English]

**hope|ful|ly** /hoʊpfəli/ ADV You say **hopefully** when mentioning something that you hope will happen. Some careful speakers of English think that this use of **hopefully** is not correct, but it is very frequently used. ❏ *Hopefully, you won't have any more problems.* [from Old English]

| **Word Link** | *less ≈ without : end*less, *hope*less, *wire*less |
|---|---|

**hope|less** /hoʊplɪs/ **1** ADJ If you feel **hopeless**, you feel very unhappy because there seems to be no possibility of a better situation or success. ❏ *He had not heard her cry before in this uncontrolled, hopeless way.* ● **hope|less|ly** ADV ❏ *I looked around hopelessly.* ● **hope|less|ness** N-UNCOUNT ❏ *She had a feeling of hopelessness about the future.* **2** ADJ Someone or something that is **hopeless** is certain to fail or be unsuccessful. ❏ *I don't believe your situation is as hopeless as you think it is.* **3** ADJ You use **hopeless** to emphasize how bad or inadequate something or someone is. ❏ *He's hopeless without her.* ● **hope|less|ly** ADV ❏ *Harry was hopelessly lost.* [from Old English]

**horde** /hɔrd/ (**hordes**) N-COUNT A **horde** is a very large number of people. ❏ *Hordes of tourists come to Las Vegas every year.* [from Polish]

**ho|ri|zon** /həraɪzᵊn/ (**horizons**) **1** N-SING The **horizon** is the line in the far distance where the sky seems to meet the land or the sea. ❏ *A small boat appeared on the horizon.* **2** N-COUNT Your **horizons** are the limits of what you want to do or of what you are interested or involved in. ❏ *Children's horizons open up when they start school.* **3** PHRASE If something is **on the horizon**, it is almost certainly going to happen or be done quite soon. ❏ *There is more bad news on the horizon.* [from Latin]

**hori|zon|tal** /hɒrɪzɒntᵊl/ ADJ Something that is **horizontal** is flat and level with the ground, rather than at an angle to it. ❏ *...vertical and horizontal lines.* ● **Horizontal** is also a noun. ❏ *Do not raise your left arm above the horizontal.* ● **hori|zon|tal|ly** ADV ❏ *The wind blew the snow almost horizontally.* [from Latin]
→ see **graph**

**hor|mone** /hɔrmoʊn/ (**hormones**) N-COUNT A **hormone** is a chemical, usually occurring naturally in your body, that makes an organ of your body do something. ❏ *...female hormones.* ● **hor|mo|nal** /hɔrmoʊnᵊl/ ADJ ❏ *...a hormonal weight problem.* [from Greek]
→ see **emotion**

**horn** /hɔrn/ (**horns**) **1** N-COUNT On a vehicle such as a car, the **horn** is the device that makes a loud noise, and is used as a signal or warning. ❏ *He sounded the car horn.* **2** N-COUNT The **horns** of an animal such as a cow or deer are the hard pointed things that grow from its head. ❏ *A mature cow has horns.* **3** N-COUNT A **horn** is a musical instrument, which is part of the brass section in an orchestra or band. It is a long circular metal tube, wide at one end, which you play by blowing. ❏ *He started playing the horn when he was eight.* **4** N-COUNT A **horn** is a musical instrument consisting of a metal tube that is wide at one end and narrow at the other. ❏ *...a hunting horn.* **5** N-COUNT In geology, a **horn** is a sharp peak that forms when the sides of a mountain are eroded. [TECHNICAL] [from Old English]

| **Word Link** | *scope ≈ looking : horo*scope, *micro*scope, *tele*scope |
|---|---|

**horo|scope** /hɔrəskoʊp/ (**horoscopes**) N-COUNT Your **horoscope** is a prediction of events which some people believe will happen to you in the future. Horoscopes are based on the position of the stars when you were born. ❑ *I always read my horoscope and follow the advice.* [from Old English]

**hor|ren|dous** /hɔrɛndəs, hɒ-, hə-/ ADJ Something that is **horrendous** is very bad or unpleasant. ❑ *...a horrendous accident.* ● **hor|ren|dous|ly** ADV ❑ *The man was horrendously fat.* [from Latin]

**hor|ri|ble** /hɔrɪbªl, hɒr-/ ADJ If you describe something or someone as **horrible**, you mean that they are very unpleasant. [INFORMAL] ❑ *Her voice sounds horrible.* ❑ *The situation was a horrible mess.* ● **hor|ri|bly** /hɔrɪbli, hɒr-/ ADV ❑ *When trouble comes they behave selfishly and horribly.* ❑ *Our plans have gone horribly wrong.* [from Old French]

**hor|rid** /hɔrɪd, hɒr-/ ADJ If you describe someone or something as **horrid**, you mean that they are very unpleasant. [INFORMAL] ❑ *What a horrid smell!* [from Latin]

**hor|rif|ic** /hɔrɪfɪk, hɒ-, hə-/ ADJ If you describe a physical attack, accident, or injury as **horrific**, you mean that it is very bad, so that people are shocked by it. ❑ *I have never seen such horrific injuries.* ● **hor|rifi|cal|ly** ADV ❑ *He was horrifically burned.* [from Latin]

**hor|ri|fy** /hɔrɪfaɪ, hɒr-/ (**horrifies, horrifying, horrified**) V-T If someone **is horrified**, they feel shocked or disgusted. ❑ *His family was horrified by the news.* ● **hor|ri|fy|ing** ADJ ❑ *It was a horrifying sight.* [from Latin]

**hor|ror** /hɔrər, hɒr-/ (**horrors**) ■ N-UNCOUNT **Horror** is a feeling of great shock, fear, and worry caused by something extremely unpleasant. ❑ *I felt sick with horror.* ■ N-SING If you have a horror **of** something, you are afraid of it or dislike it very much. ❑ *...his horror of death.* ■ N-COUNT You can refer to extremely unpleasant or frightening experiences as **horrors**. ❑ *...the horrors of war.* ■ ADJ A **horror** film or story is intended to be very frightening. [from Latin]
→ see **genre**

**horse** /hɔrs/ (**horses**) N-COUNT A **horse** is a large animal which people can ride. ❑ *...a man on a gray horse.* [from Old English]
→ see Picture Dictionary: **horse**

**horse|back** /hɔrsbæk/ ■ N-UNCOUNT If you do something **on horseback**, you do it while riding a horse. ❑ *Many people traveled on horseback.* ■ ADJ A **horseback** ride is a ride on a horse. ❑ *...a horseback ride into the mountains.* ● **Horseback** is also an adverb. ❑ *Many people here ride horseback.*

**horse|back rid|ing** N-UNCOUNT **Horseback riding** is the activity of riding a horse.

**horse|power** /hɔrspaʊər/ N-UNCOUNT **Horsepower** is a unit of power used for measuring how powerful an engine is. ❑ *...a 300-horsepower engine.*

**horse|shoe** /hɔrsʃu/ (**horseshoes**) N-COUNT A **horseshoe** is a piece of metal shaped like a U, which is fixed with nails to a horse's hoof.

**hor|ti|cul|ture** /hɔrtɪkʌltʃər/ N-UNCOUNT **Horticulture** is the study and practice of growing plants. ● **hor|ti|cul|tur|al** /hɔrtɪkʌltʃərªl/ ADJ ❑ *...horticultural workers.* [from Latin]

**hose** /hoʊz/ (**hoses, hosing, hosed**) ■ N-COUNT A **hose** is a long, flexible pipe made of rubber or plastic. Water is directed through a hose in order to do things such as put out fires, clean cars, or water gardens. ❑ *You've left the garden hose on.* ■ V-T If you **hose** something, you wash or water it using a hose. ❑ *We hose our gardens without thinking about how much water we use.* [from Old English]
→ see **garden**

**hos|pice** /hɒspɪs/ (**hospices**) N-COUNT A **hospice** is a special hospital for people who are dying. ❑ *...a hospice for cancer patients.* [from French]

**hos|pi|table** /hɒspɪtəbªl, hɒspɪt-/ ADJ A **hospitable** person is friendly, generous, and welcoming to guests or people they have just met. ❑ *The local people are hospitable and welcoming.* [from Medieval Latin]

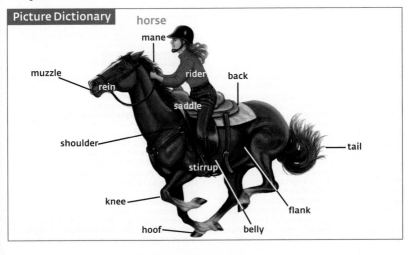

**Picture Dictionary**

**horse**

mane
muzzle
rein
rider
back
saddle
shoulder
tail
stirrup
knee
flank
hoof
belly

## Word Web hospital

Children's **Hospital** in Boston has one of the best pediatric **wards** in the country. Its Advanced Fetal Care Center can even treat babies before they are born. The hospital records about 18,000 inpatient **admissions** every year. It also has over 150 outpatient programs and takes care of more than 300,000 **emergency cases**. The staff includes 700 **residents** and **fellows**, who are studying to be doctors. Many of the **physicians** teach at nearby Harvard University. The hospital also has excellent **researchers**. Their work helped find **vaccines** for **polio** and **measles**. The hospital has also led the way in liver, heart, and lung **transplants** in children.

## Word Link hosp, host ≈ guest : hospital, hospitality, hostage

**hos|pi|tal** /hɒspɪtəl/ (**hospitals**) N-VAR A **hospital** is a place where people who are ill are cared for by nurses and doctors. ▢ ...a children's hospital. [from Medieval Latin]
→ see Word Web: **hospital**

## Word Partnership Use hospital with :

V. admit *someone* to a hospital, **bring/ rush/take** *someone* to a hospital, **end up in** a hospital, **go to** a hospital, **visit** *someone* **in** a hospital

**hos|pi|tal|ity** /hɒspɪtælɪti/ N-UNCOUNT **Hospitality** is friendly, welcoming behavior toward guests or people you have just met. ▢ Every visitor to Georgia notices the kindness and hospitality of the people. [from Medieval Latin]

**hos|pi|tal|ize** /hɒspɪtəlaɪz/ (**hospitalizes, hospitalizing, hospitalized**) V-T If someone **is hospitalized**, they are sent or admitted to a hospital. ▢ He was hospitalized after a heart attack. ● **hos|pi|tali|za|tion** /hɒspɪtələzeɪʃən/ N-UNCOUNT ▢ Her hospitalization lasted several months. [from Medieval Latin]

**host** /hoʊst/ (**hosts, hosting, hosted**)
**1** N-COUNT The **host** at a party is the person who has invited the guests and provides the food, drink, or entertainment. ▢ Apart from my host, I didn't know anyone at the party. **2** V-T If someone **hosts** a party, dinner, or other function, they have invited the guests and provide the food, drink, or entertainment. ▢ She hosted a party for 300 guests. **3** N-COUNT A country, city, or organization that is the **host** of an event provides the facilities for that event to take place. ▢ Atlanta was the host of the 1996 Olympic games. **4** V-T If a country, city, or organization **hosts** an event, they provide the facilities for the event to take place. ▢ New Bedford hosts several festivals in the summer. **5** N-COUNT The **host** of a radio or television show is the person who introduces it and talks to the people who appear in it. ▢ I am the host of a live radio program. **6** V-T The person who **hosts** a radio or television show introduces it and talks to the people who appear in it. ▢ She hosts a show on St. Petersburg Radio. **7** QUANT A **host** of things is a lot of them. ▢ A host of problems delayed the opening of the new

bridge. **8** N-COUNT The **host** of a parasite is the plant or animal which it lives on or inside and from which it gets its food. [TECHNICAL] [Senses 1–6 and 8 from French. Sense 7 from Old French.]

**hos|tage** /hɒstɪdʒ/ (**hostages**) **1** N-COUNT A **hostage** is someone who has been captured by a person or organization and who may be killed or injured if people do not do what that person or organization demands. ▢ The two hostages were freed yesterday. **2** PHRASE If someone **is taken hostage** or **is held hostage**, they are captured and kept as a hostage. ▢ He was taken hostage on his first trip to the country. [from Old French]

**host|ess** /hoʊstɪs/ (**hostesses**) N-COUNT The **hostess** at a party is the woman who has invited the guests and provides the food, drink, or entertainment. ▢ The hostess introduced them. [from French]

**hos|tile** /hɒstəl/ **1** ADJ If you are **hostile** to another person or an idea, you disagree with them or disapprove of them. ▢ The governor faced hostile crowds. ● **hos|til|ity** /hɒstɪlɪti/ N-UNCOUNT ▢ There's a lot of hostility in the city. **2** ADJ Someone who is **hostile** is unfriendly and aggressive. ▢ He was angry, hostile and had a bad attitude toward his boss. ● **hos|til|ity** N-UNCOUNT ▢ He felt the hostility toward him from other players. **3** ADJ **Hostile** situations and conditions make it difficult for you to achieve something. ▢ ...some of the most hostile weather conditions in the world. [from Latin]

## Word Partnership Use hostile with :

N. hostile **attitude/feelings/intentions 1** hostile **act/action**, hostile **environment 3** hostile **takeover 4**
ADV. **increasingly** hostile **1 – 3**

**hos|til|ities** /hɒstɪlɪtiz/ N-PLURAL You can refer to fighting between two countries or groups who are at war as **hostilities**. [FORMAL] ▢ Hostilities broke out in many areas of the country. [from Latin]

**hot** /hɒt/ (**hotter, hottest**) **1** ADJ Something that is **hot** has a high temperature. ▢ When the oil is hot, add the sliced onion. ▢ He needed a hot bath and a good sleep. **2** ADJ **Hot** is used to describe the weather or the air in a room or building when the temperature is high. ▢ It was too hot even for a gentle walk. **3** ADJ If you are **hot**, you feel as if your body is at an unpleasantly high temperature. ▢ I was *too hot and tired to eat much.* **4** ADJ You can say that food is **hot** when it has a strong, burning taste caused by spices. □ *...hot curries.* **5** ADJ You can use **hot** to describe an issue or event that is very important, exciting, or popular at the present time. [INFORMAL] □ *...the hottest movie of the summer.* □ *The magazine contains hot news about TV celebrities.* [from Old English]

→ see **weather**

| Thesaurus | hot | Also look up : |
|---|---|---|

ADJ.   sweltering; (ant.) chilly, cold **1**
     spicy; (ant.) bland, mild **4**
     cool, popular; (ant.) unpopular **5**

**hot but|ton** (**hot buttons**) N-COUNT A **hot button** is a subject or problem that people have very strong feelings about. □ *Health care is a political hot button.*

**hot dog** (**hot dogs**) N-COUNT A **hot dog** is a long bun with a hot sausage inside it.

**ho|tel** /hoʊtɛl/ (**hotels**) N-COUNT A **hotel** is a building where people stay, paying for their rooms and meals. [from French]
→ see Word Web: **hotel**

| Word Partnership | Use *hotel* with : |
|---|---|

V.   **check into a** hotel, **check out of a** hotel,
     **stay at a** hotel
N.   hotel **guest**, hotel **reservation**, hotel
     **room**
ADJ.   **luxury** hotel, **new** hotel

**hot|line** /hɒtlaɪn/ (**hotlines**) also **hot line**
**1** N-COUNT A **hotline** is a telephone line that the public can use to contact an organization about a particular subject. □ *...a telephone hotline for parents needing advice on childcare.* **2** N-COUNT A **hotline** is a special, direct telephone line between the heads of government in different countries. □ *They set up a hotline between London and Moscow.*

**hot|ly** /hɒtli/ **1** ADV If people discuss, argue, or say something **hotly**, they speak in a lively or angry way, because they feel strongly. □ *The bank hotly denies any wrongdoing.* **2** ADV If you are being **hotly** pursued, someone is trying hard to catch you and is close behind you. □ *He left the U.S. hotly pursued by detectives.* [from Old English]

**hot spot** (**hot spots**) also **hotspot** N-COUNT In geology, **hot spots** are areas beneath the Earth's surface where lava rises and often forms volcanoes. [TECHNICAL]

**hound** /haʊnd/ (**hounds, hounding, hounded**)
**1** N-COUNT A **hound** is a type of dog that is often used for hunting or racing. □ *Rainey's main interest is hunting with hounds.* **2** V-T If someone **hounds** you, they constantly disturb or speak to you in an annoying or upsetting way. □ *People were always hounding him for advice.* [from Old English]

**hour** /aʊər/ (**hours**) **1** N-COUNT An **hour** is a period of sixty minutes. □ *They waited for about two hours.* □ *I only slept about half an hour last night.* **2** N-PLURAL You can refer to the period of time during which something happens or operates each day as the **hours** during which it happens or operates. □ *...the hours of darkness.* □ *Call us on this number during office hours.* **3** → see also **rush hour**
**4** PHRASE If something happens **on the hour**, it happens every hour at, for example, nine o'clock, ten o'clock, and so on. □ *There are newscasts every hour on the hour.* [from Old French]
→ see **time**

**hour|ly** /aʊərli/ **1** ADJ An **hourly** event happens once every hour. □ *He turned on the radio to hear the hourly news program.* ● **Hourly** is also an adverb. □ *The buses run hourly between the two cities.* **2** ADJ Your **hourly** earnings are the money that you earn in one hour. □ *...jobs with the same hourly pay.* [from Old French]

**house** (**houses, housing, housed**)

The noun is pronounced /haʊs/. The verb is pronounced /haʊz/. The form **houses** is pronounced /haʊzɪz/.

**1** N-COUNT A **house** is a building in which people live. □ *She has moved to a small house.* **2** N-SING You can refer to all the people who live together in a house as **the house**. □ *He set his alarm clock for midnight, and it woke the whole house.* **3** N-COUNT **House** is used in the names of types of places where people go to eat and drink. □ *...a steak house.* **4** N-COUNT **House** is used in the names of types of companies, especially ones which publish books, lend money, or design clothes. □ *The clothes came from the world's top fashion houses.* **5** N-COUNT You can refer to one of the two bodies of the U.S. Congress as a **House**. The House of Representatives is sometimes referred to as the **House**. □ *Some members of the House and Senate worked all day yesterday.* **6** V-T To **house** someone means to provide a house or apartment for them to live in. □ *...homes that house up to nine people.* **7** V-T A building or container that **houses** something is the place where it is located or from where it operates. □ *The building houses a museum*

| Word Web | hotel |
|---|---|

When making **reservations** at a **hotel**, most people request a **single** or a **double** room. Sometimes the **clerk** invites the person to **upgrade** to a **suite**. When arriving at the hotel, the first person to greet the **guest** is the **bellhop**. He will put the person's suitcases on a **luggage cart** and later deliver them to their room. The guest then goes to the **front desk** and **checks in**. The clerk often describes **amenities** such as a **fitness club** or **spa**. Most hotels provide **room service** for late night snacks. There is often a concierge to help arrange dinners and other entertainment outside of the hotel.

## Picture Dictionary house

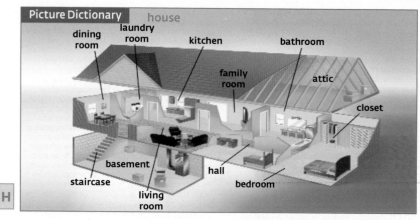

dining room
laundry room
kitchen
bathroom
family room
attic
closet
basement
staircase
hall
bedroom
living room

H

and a restaurant. [from Old English] **8** → see also **White House**
→ see Picture Dictionary: **house**

| Thesaurus | house | Also look up : |
|---|---|---|
| N. | dwelling, home, place, residence **1** | |

| Word Partnership | Use *house* with : |
|---|---|
| V. | **break into** a house, **build** a house, **buy** a house, **find** a house, **live in** a house, **own** a house, **rent** a house **1** |
| ADJ. | **empty** house, **expensive** house, **little** house, **new/old** house **1** |
| N. | house **prices**, a **room in** a house **1** |

**house ar|rest** N-UNCOUNT If someone is **under house arrest**, they are officially ordered not to leave their home, because they are suspected of being involved in an illegal activity. ❑ *The government officials were under house arrest.*

**house|hold** /ha͟ʊsho͟ʊld/ (**households**)
**1** N-COUNT A **household** is all the people in a family or group who live together in a house. ❑ *...growing up in a large household.* **2** N-SING The **household** is your home and everything that is connected with taking care of it. ❑ *...household duties.* **3** ADJ Someone or something that is a **household** name or word is very well known. ❑ *Today, fashion designers are household names.*

**house|keep|er** /ha͟ʊski͟pər/ (**housekeepers**)
N-COUNT A **housekeeper** is a person whose job is to cook, clean, and take care of a house for its owner.

**house|keep|ing** /ha͟ʊski͟pɪŋ/ N-UNCOUNT **Housekeeping** is the work and organization involved in running a home, including the shopping and cleaning. ❑ *I thought that cooking and housekeeping were easy.*

**house-sit** (**house-sits, house-sitting, house-sat**)
V-I If someone **house-sits** for you, they stay at your house and look after it while you are away. ❑ *Bill was house-sitting for me.*

**house|wife** /ha͟ʊswaɪf/ (**housewives**)
**1** N-COUNT A **housewife** is a woman who does not have a paid job, but instead takes care of her home

and children. ❑ *She was a housewife and mother of four children.* **2** → see also **homemaker**

**house|work** /ha͟ʊswɜrk/ N-UNCOUNT **Housework** is the work such as cleaning, washing, and ironing that you do in your home. ❑ *Men are doing more housework nowadays.*

**hous|ing** /ha͟ʊzɪŋ/ N-UNCOUNT **Housing** is the buildings that people live in. ❑ *...a housing shortage.* [from Old English]

**hous|ing proj|ect** (**housing projects**) N-COUNT A **housing project** is a group of homes for poorer families which is funded and controlled by the local government.

**hov|er** /hʌ͟vər/ (**hovers, hovering, hovered**)
**1** V-I To **hover** means to stay in the same position in the air without moving forward or backward. ❑ *Butterflies hovered above the flowers.* **2** V-I If you **hover**, you stay in one place and move slightly in a nervous way, for example because you cannot decide what to do. ❑ *Judith was hovering in the doorway.*

**how** /ha͟ʊ/

The conjunction is pronounced /haʊ/.

**1** ADV You use **how** to ask about the way in which something happens or is done. ❑ *How do you manage to keep the place so neat?* ● **How** is also a conjunction. ❑ *I don't want to know how he died.* **2** ADV You use **how** to ask questions about the quantity or degree of something. ❑ *How much money do you have?* ❑ *How many people work there?* ❑ *How long will you stay?* ❑ *How old is your son now?* **3** ADV You use **how** when you are asking someone whether something was successful or enjoyable. ❑ *How was your trip to Orlando?* ❑ *How did your meeting go?* **4** ADV You use **how** to ask about someone's health or to find out their news. ❑ *Hi! How are you doing?* ❑ *How's Rosie?* **5** ADV You use **how** to emphasize the degree to which something is true. ❑ *I didn't know how heavy the bag was.*
**6** ADV You use **how** in expressions such as "**How about...**" or "**How would you like...**" when you are making an offer or a suggestion. ❑ *How about a cup of coffee?* **7** CONVENTION If you ask someone "**How about you?**" you are asking them what they think or want. ❑ *Well, I enjoyed that. How about you two?* [from Old English]

**how|dy** /haʊdi/ CONVENTION "Howdy" is an informal way of saying "Hello." [DIALECT]

**how|ever** /haʊɛvər/ **1** ADV You use **however** when you are adding a comment which is surprising or which contrasts with what has just been said. ❑ *This is not an easy decision. It is, however, a decision that we have to make.* **2** ADV You use **however** before an adjective or adverb to say that the degree or extent of something cannot change a situation. ❑ *You should try to achieve more, however well you have done before.* ❑ *However hard she tried, nothing seemed to work.* **3** CONJ You use **however** when you want to say that it makes no difference how something is done. ❑ *Wear your hair however you want.* **4** ADV You can use **however** to ask in an emphatic way how something has happened which you are very surprised about. Some speakers of English think that this form is incorrect and prefer to use "how ever." ❑ *However did you find this place in such bad weather?*

> **Usage** **however**
>
> Be sure to punctuate sentences with *however* correctly. When *however* expresses contrast, it is followed by a comma (and preceded by a period or a semicolon): *Dae's parents sent her a new computer; however, she can't figure out how to set it up.* In other uses, *however* isn't followed by a comma: *I'm surprised — Dae can usually figure anything out, however difficult it seems to be.*

**howl** /haʊl/ (**howls, howling, howled**) **1** V-I If an animal such as a wolf or a dog **howls**, it makes a long, loud, crying sound. ❑ *A dog suddenly howled.* ● **Howl** is also a noun. ❑ *The dog let out a long howl.* **2** V-I If a person **howls**, they make a long, loud cry expressing pain, anger, or unhappiness. ❑ *He howled like a wounded animal.* ● **Howl** is also a noun. ❑ *He gave a howl of pain.* **3** V-I When the wind **howls**, it blows hard and makes a loud noise. ❑ *The wind howled all night.* **4** V-I If you **howl** with laughter, you laugh very loudly. ❑ *Joe and Tom howled with delight.* ● **Howl** is also a noun. ❑ *His stories caused howls of laughter.* [from Middle High German]
→ see **laugh**

**how-to** ADJ A **how-to** book provides instructions on how to do or make a particular thing, especially something that you do or make as a hobby. ❑ *...a simple how-to book that explains each step in taking a photo.*

**HQ** /eɪtʃkyu/ (**HQs**) N-VAR **HQ** is an abbreviation for **headquarters**. ❑ *The HQ is a large office in downtown Seattle.*

**hr** (**hrs**) **hr** is a written abbreviation for **hour**. ❑ *Cook the meat for another 1 hr 15 mins.*

**H-R dia|gram** also **HRD** (**H-R diagrams**) N-COUNT An **H-R diagram** or **HRD** is the same as a **Hertzsprung-Russell diagram**.

**HTML** /eɪtʃti ɛm ɛl/ N-UNCOUNT **HTML** is a system of codes for producing documents for the Internet. **HTML** is an abbreviation for "hypertext markup language." [COMPUTING] ❑ *...HTML documents.*

**hub** /hʌb/ (**hubs**) **1** N-COUNT You can describe a place as a **hub** of an activity when it is a very important center for that activity. ❑ *He said that New York is the hub of the art world.* **2** N-COUNT The **hub** of a wheel is the part at the center.

**3** N-COUNT A **hub** or a **hub airport** is a large airport from which you can travel to many other airports. ❑ *The airport is Europe's main international hub.*

**hud|dle** /hʌdəl/ (**huddles, huddling, huddled**) **1** V-I If you **huddle** somewhere, you sit, stand, or lie there holding your arms and legs close to your body, usually because you are cold or frightened. ❑ *Mr. Pell huddled in a corner.* **2** V-I If people **huddle together** or **huddle around** something, they stand, sit, or lie close to each other, usually because they all feel cold or frightened. ❑ *Tired and lost, we huddled together.* **3** V-RECIP If people **huddle** in a group, they gather together to discuss something quietly or secretly. ❑ *Jordan and Kreps huddled to discuss something.* ❑ *The president is huddling with his most senior aides.* **4** N-COUNT A **huddle** is a small group of people or things standing or sitting very close together. ❑ *...a huddle of stone buildings.* [from Middle English]

**hue** /hyu/ (**hues**) N-COUNT A **hue** is a color. [LITERARY] ❑ *The same hue will look different in different light.* [from Old English]

**huff** /hʌf/ (**huffs, huffing, huffed**) **1** V-T If you **huff**, you indicate that you are annoyed or offended about something, usually by the way that you say something. ❑ *"This is not what I asked for," she huffed.* **2** PHRASE If someone is **in a huff**, they are behaving in a bad-tempered way because they are annoyed and offended. [INFORMAL] ❑ *He was very disappointed and walked off in a huff.*

**hug** /hʌg/ (**hugs, hugging, hugged**) **1** V-T When you **hug** someone, you put your arms around them and hold them tightly, for example because you like them or are pleased to see them. ❑ *She hugged him and invited him to dinner the next day.* ● **Hug** is also a noun. ❑ *She leapt out of the car, and gave him a hug.* **2** V-T If you **hug** something, you hold it close to your body with your arms tightly around it. ❑ *He walked toward them, hugging a large box.* **3** V-T Something that **hugs** the ground or a stretch of land or water stays very close to it. [WRITTEN] ❑ *The road hugs the coast for hundreds of miles.* [of Scandinavian origin]

**huge** /hyudʒ/ (**huger, hugest**) ADJ Something or someone that is **huge** is extremely large in size, amount or degree. ❑ *...a tall woman with huge black glasses.* ❑ *I have a huge number of ties because I never throw them away.* ● **huge|ly** ADV ❑ *This hotel is hugely popular.* [from Old French]

**hull** /hʌl/ (**hulls**) N-COUNT The **hull** of a boat or tank is the main body of it. ❑ *The ship is new, with a steel hull.* [from Old English]

**hul|lo** /hʌloʊ/ → see **hello**

**hum** /hʌm/ (**hums, humming, hummed**) **1** V-I If something **hums**, it makes a low continuous noise. ❑ *The birds sang and the bees hummed.* ● **Hum** is also a noun. ❑ *...the hum of traffic.* **2** V-T/V-I When you **hum**, or **hum** a tune, you sing a tune with your lips closed. ❑ *She was humming a tune.* [from Dutch]

**hu|man** /hyumən/ (**humans**) **1** ADJ **Human** means relating to or concerning people. ❑ *...the human body.* **2** N-COUNT You can refer to people as **humans**, especially when you are comparing them with animals or machines. ❑ *Like humans, cats and dogs can eat meat and plants.* [from Latin]
→ see **evolution, primate**

**Word Partnership**   Use *human* with :

N.    human **behavior**, human **body**, human **brain**, human **dignity**, human **life** 1

**hu|man be|ing** (human beings) N-COUNT A **human being** is a man, woman, or child. ❑ *Can't we discuss this like sensible human beings?*

**Word Link**   man ≈ human being : fore*man*, hu*man*e, wo*man*

**hu|mane** /hyuˈmeɪn/ ADJ **Humane** people act in a kind, sympathetic way toward other people and animals. ❑ *...a humane society.* • **hu|mane|ly** ADV ❑ *We should treat all animals humanely.*

**Hu|man Ge|nome Proj|ect** /hyuˈmən dʒiˈnoʊm prɒdʒɛkt/ N-SING **The Human Genome Project** is an international research program that is designed to provide a complete set of information about human DNA.

**hu|man|ism** /hyuˈmənɪzəm/ N-UNCOUNT **Humanism** is the belief that people can achieve happiness and live well without religion. • **hu|man|ist** (humanists) N-COUNT ❑ *He is a humanist thinker.*

**Word Link**   arian ≈ believing in, having : human*itarian*, totalit*arian*, veget*arian*

**hu|mani|tar|ian** /hyuˌmænɪˈtɛəriən/ ADJ If a person or society has **humanitarian** ideas or behavior, they try to avoid making people suffer or they help people who are suffering. ❑ *The soldiers were there for humanitarian reasons, to give out food and medicines.* [from Latin]

**hu|man|ity** /hyuˈmænɪti/ (humanities) 1 N-UNCOUNT All the people in the world can be referred to as **humanity**. ❑ *...an act of humanity* 2 N-UNCOUNT A person's **humanity** is their state of being a human being. [FORMAL] ❑ *He was in prison and it made him feel he had lost his humanity.* 3 N-UNCOUNT **Humanity** is the quality of being kind, thoughtful, and sympathetic. ❑ *Her speech showed great humanity.* 4 N-PLURAL The **humanities** are the subjects such as history, philosophy, and literature which are concerned with human ideas and behavior. ❑ *The number of students studying the humanities has fallen by more than 50%.*

**hu|man na|ture** N-UNCOUNT **Human nature** is the natural qualities and ways of behavior that most people have. ❑ *It is human nature to worry.*

**hu|man race** N-SING **The human race** is the same as **mankind**. ❑ *Can the human race carry on increasing in the same way that it is now?*

**hu|man rights** N-PLURAL **Human rights** are basic rights which many societies believe that all people should have. ❑ *Both sides promised to respect human rights.*

**hum|ble** /hʌmbᵊl/ (humbler, humblest, humbles, humbling, humbled) 1 ADJ A **humble** person is not proud and does not believe that they are better than other people. ❑ *He gave a great performance, but he was very humble.* • **hum|bly** ADV ❑ *"I'm a lucky man, and I don't deserve it," he said humbly.* 2 ADJ People with low social status are sometimes described as **humble**. ❑ *He started his career as a humble fisherman.* 3 ADJ A **humble** person, place,

or thing is ordinary and not special in any way. ❑ *This is our humble home.* 4 V-T If something or someone **humbles** you, they make you realize that you are not as important or good as you thought you were. ❑ *Ted's words humbled me.* • **hum|bling** ADJ ❑ *It's humbling to know that so many people care.* [from Old French]

**hu|mid** /hyuˈmɪd/ ADJ You use **humid** to describe an atmosphere or climate that is very damp, and usually very hot. ❑ *We can expect hot and humid conditions.* [from Latin]
→ see **weather**

**hu|mid|ity** /hyuˈmɪdɪti/ N-UNCOUNT **Humidity** is the amount of water in the air. ❑ *The humidity is relatively low.* [from Latin]
→ see **forecast**

**Word Link**   ate ≈ causing to be : compli*cate*, humili*ate*, moti*vate*

**hu|mili|ate** /hyuˈmɪlieɪt/ (humiliates, humiliating, humiliated) V-T To **humiliate** someone means to say or do something which makes them feel ashamed or stupid. ❑ *He enjoyed humiliating me.* • **hu|mili|at|ed** ADJ ❑ *I have never felt so humiliated in my life.* • **hu|mili|at|ing** ADJ ❑ *...a humiliating defeat.* [from Late Latin]

**hu|milia|tion** /hyuˌmɪliˈeɪʃⁿn/ (humiliations) 1 N-UNCOUNT **Humiliation** is the embarrassment and shame you feel when someone makes you appear stupid, or when you make a mistake in public. ❑ *He faced the humiliation of forgetting his wife's birthday.* 2 N-COUNT A **humiliation** is an occasion or situation in which you feel embarrassed and ashamed. ❑ *The result is a humiliation for the president.* [from Late Latin]

**hu|mil|ity** /hyuˈmɪlɪti/ N-UNCOUNT Someone who has **humility** is not proud and does not believe they are better than other people. ❑ *Bernal knows that there are other actors who are more talented than him, and this humility is unusual in Hollywood.* [from Old French]

**hu|mor** /hyuˈmər/ (humors, humoring, humored) 1 N-UNCOUNT You can refer to the amusing things that people say as their **humor**. ❑ *He told his story with humor.* 2 → see also **sense of humor** 3 N-UNCOUNT **Humor** is a quality in something that makes you laugh, for example in a situation, in someone's words or actions, or in a book or movie. ❑ *She felt sorry for the man but she couldn't ignore the humor of the situation.* 4 N-VAR If you are **in a good humor**, you feel cheerful and happy, and are pleasant to people. If you are **in a bad humor**, you feel bad tempered and unhappy, and are unpleasant to people. ❑ *She wondered why he was in such bad humor.* 5 V-T If you **humor** someone who is behaving strangely, you try to please them or pretend to agree with them, so that they will not become upset. ❑ *I agreed, partly to humour him.* [from Latin]
→ see **laugh**

**Word Partnership**   Use *humor* with :

N.    **brand of** humor, **sense of** humor 1
ADJ.   **good** humor 3

**hu|mor|less** /hyuˈmərlɪs/ ADJ Someone who is **humorless** is very serious about everything and does not find things amusing. ❑ *This man was as* humorless as a dictionary. [from Latin]

**hu|mor|ous** /hyumərəs/ ADJ If someone or something is **humorous**, they are amusing, especially in a clever or witty way. ❑ *He was quite humorous, and I liked that.* ● **hu|mor|ous|ly** ADV ❑ *He looked at me humorously.* [from Latin]

**hump** /hʌmp/ (**humps**) **1** N-COUNT A **hump** is a small hill or raised area. ❑ *The path goes over a large hump by a tree.* **2** N-COUNT A camel's **hump** is the large lump on its back. ❑ *Camels store water in their hump.*

**hump|back whale** /hʌmpbæk weɪl/ (**humpback whales**) N-COUNT A **humpback whale** is a large whale with long front fins.

**hu|mus** /hyuməs/ N-UNCOUNT **Humus** is the part of soil which consists of dead plants that have begun to decay. [from Latin]

**hunch** /hʌntʃ/ (**hunches, hunching, hunched**) **1** N-COUNT If you have a **hunch** about something, you are sure that it is correct or true, even though you do not have any proof. ❑ *I had a hunch that Susan and I would work well together.* **2** V-I If you **hunch** forward or **hunch** your shoulders, you raise your shoulders, put your head down, and lean forward. ❑ *He got out his map and hunched over it.* ❑ *Wes hunched his shoulders and leaned forward on the counter.*

**hun|dred** /hʌndrɪd/ (**hundreds**)

The plural form is **hundred** after a number, or after a word or expression referring to a number, such as "several" or "a few."

**1** NUM A **hundred** or **one hundred** is the number 100. ❑ *More than a hundred people were there.* **2** QUANT You can use **hundreds** to mean an extremely large number of things or people. ❑ *He received hundreds of letters.* ● You can also use **hundreds** as a pronoun. ❑ *Hundreds were killed in the fighting.* **3** PHRASE You can use **a hundred percent** or **one hundred percent** to emphasize that you agree completely with something or that it is completely right or wrong. [INFORMAL] ❑ *I'm a hundred percent sure that's what I saw.* [from Old English]

**hun|dredth** /hʌndrɪdθ, -drɪtθ/ (**hundredths**) **1** ORD The **hundredth** item in a series is the one that you count as number one hundred. ❑ *The bank's hundredth anniversary is in December.* **2** ORD A **hundredth** of something is one of a hundred equal parts of it. ❑ *Mitchell beat Lewis by three-hundredths of a second.* [from Old English]

**hung** /hʌŋ/ **1** **Hung** is the past tense and past participle of most of the senses of **hang**. **2** ADJ A **hung** jury is the situation that occurs when a jury is unable to reach a decision. ❑ *His trial ended in a hung jury.* [from Old English]

**hun|ger** /hʌŋgər/ (**hungers, hungering, hungered**) **1** N-UNCOUNT **Hunger** is the feeling of weakness or discomfort that you get when you need something to eat. ❑ *Hunger is the body's signal that you need to eat.* **2** N-UNCOUNT **Hunger** is a severe lack of food which causes suffering or death. ❑ *Three hundred people in this town are dying of hunger every day.* **3** N-SING If you have a **hunger for** something, you want or need it very much. [WRITTEN] ❑ *Geffen has a hunger for success.* **4** V-I If you **hunger for** something or **hunger after** it, you want it very much. [FORMAL] ❑ *Jules hungered for*

adventure. [from Old English]

**hun|ger strike** (**hunger strikes**) N-VAR If someone goes **on hunger strike** or goes **on a hunger strike**, they refuse to eat as a way of protesting about something. ❑ *She ended a weeklong hunger strike.*

**hun|gry** /hʌŋgri/ (**hungrier, hungriest**) **1** ADJ When you are **hungry**, you want some food. ❑ *My friend was hungry, so we drove to a shopping mall to get some food.* ● **hun|gri|ly** /hʌŋgrɪli/ ADV ❑ *James ate hungrily.* **2** PHRASE If people **go hungry**, they do not have enough food to eat. ❑ *Nobody went hungry, even for a day.* **3** ADJ If you are **hungry** for something, you want it very much. [LITERARY] ❑ *He's hungry for power.* ● **hun|gri|ly** ADV ❑ *They were hungrily waiting for news.* [from Old English]

| **Thesaurus** | *hungry* | Also look up : |
|---|---|---|
| ADJ. | starving; (*ant.*) full **1** | |
| | eager **3** | |

**hunk** /hʌŋk/ (**hunks**) N-COUNT A **hunk of** something is a large piece of it. ❑ *…a thick hunk of bread.* [from Flemish]

**hunker** /hʌŋkər/ (**hunkers, hunkering, hunkered**) [from Flemish]
▶ **hunker down** **1** PHR-VERB If you **hunker down**, you bend your knees so that you are in a low position, balancing on your feet. ❑ *Betty hunkered down on the floor.* ❑ *He hunkered down beside her.* **2** PHR-VERB If you say that someone **hunkers down**, you mean that they are trying to avoid doing things that will make them noticed or put them in danger. ❑ *They hunkered down until the situation became calmer.*

**hunt** /hʌnt/ (**hunts, hunting, hunted**) **1** V-I If you **hunt for** something or someone, you try to find them by searching carefully or thoroughly. ❑ *He hunted for an apartment.* ● **Hunt** is also a noun. ❑ *Several people helped in the hunt for the missing children.* ● **hunt|ing** N-UNCOUNT ❑ *Job hunting is not easy.* **2** V-T If you **hunt** a criminal or an enemy, you search for them in order to catch or harm them. ❑ *Detectives have been hunting him for more than seven months.* ● **Hunt** is also a noun. ❑ *More than 70 police officers are involved in the hunt for her killer.* **3** V-T/V-I When people or animals **hunt**, or **hunt** something, they chase and kill wild animals for food or as a sport. ❑ *I learned to hunt and fish when I was a child.* ● **Hunt** is also a noun. ❑ *He went on a nineteen-day moose hunt.* ● **hunt|ing** N-UNCOUNT ❑ *He went deer hunting with his cousins.* [from Old English]
▶ **hunt down** PHR-VERB If you **hunt down** a criminal or an enemy, you find them after searching for them. ❑ *They hunted down and killed one of the gang members.*

**hunt|er** /hʌntər/ (**hunters**) **1** N-COUNT A **hunter** is a person who hunts wild animals for food or as a sport. ❑ *…deer hunters.* **2** N-COUNT People who are searching for things of a particular kind are often referred to as **hunters**. ❑ *…job-hunters.* [from Old English]

**hur|dle** /hɜrd°l/ (**hurdles**) **1** N-COUNT A **hurdle** is a problem, difficulty, or part of a process that may prevent you from achieving something. ❑ *Writing a résumé is the first hurdle in a job search.* **2** N-COUNT **Hurdles** is a race in which people have to jump over a number of obstacles that are also

h

## Word Web hurricane

A **hurricane** is a violent **storm** or tropical **cyclone** that develops in the Atlantic Ocean or Caribbean Sea. When a hurricane develops in the Pacific Ocean it is known as a typhoon. A hurricane begins as a **tropical depression**. It becomes a **tropical storm** when its winds reach 39 miles per hour (mph). When wind speeds reach 74 mph, a distinct **eye** forms in the center. Then the storm is officially a hurricane. It has heavy **rains** and very high **winds**. When a hurricane makes landfall or moves over cool water, it loses some of its power.

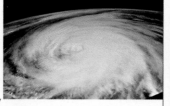

called hurdles. ❑ ...*the 400 meter hurdles*. [from Old English]

**hur|dler** /hɜrdlər/ (**hurdlers**) N-COUNT A **hurdler** is an athlete who runs in hurdles races. [from Old English]

**hurl** /hɜrl/ (**hurls, hurling, hurled**) **1** V-T If you **hurl** something, you throw it violently and with a lot of force. ❑ *Groups of boys hurled stones at police.* ❑ *Simon caught the book and hurled it back.* **2** V-T If you **hurl** abuse or insults **at** someone, you shout insults at them aggressively. ❑ *The driver of the other car hurled abuse at him.*

**hur|ri|cane** /hɜrɪkeɪn, hʌr-/ (**hurricanes**) N-COUNT A **hurricane** is an extremely violent storm that begins over ocean water. [from Spanish]
→ see Word Web: **hurricane**
→ see **disaster**

**hur|ried** /hɜrid, hʌr-/ ADJ A **hurried** action is done quickly. ❑ ...*a hurried breakfast.* ● **hur|ried|ly** ADV ❑ *She hurriedly left the room.* [from Middle High German]

**hur|ry** /hɜri, hʌr-/ (**hurries, hurrying, hurried**) **1** V-I If you **hurry** somewhere, you go there as quickly as you can. ❑ *Claire hurried along the road.* **2** V-T If you **hurry to** do something, you start doing it as soon as you can, or try to do it quickly. ❑ *Latecomers hurried to find a seat.* **3** N-SING If you are **in a hurry to** do something, you need or want to do something quickly. If you do something **in a hurry**, you do it quickly. ❑ *Mike was in a hurry to get back to work.* **4** V-T To **hurry** something or someone means to try to make something happen more quickly. ❑ *Sorry to hurry you, John.* **5** V-T If you **hurry** someone to a place or into a situation, you try to make them go to that place or get into that situation quickly. ❑ *I won't hurry you into a decision.* [from Middle High German]
▸ **hurry along** → see **hurry up 2**
▸ **hurry up 1** PHR-VERB If you tell someone to **hurry up**, you are telling them to do something more quickly than they were doing. ❑ *Hurry up and get ready.* **2** PHR-VERB If you **hurry** something **up** or **hurry** it **along**, you make it happen faster or sooner than it would otherwise have done. ❑ *We could hurry the wedding plans along if you want to.*

### Thesaurus hurry Also look up :

V. rush, run; (*ant.*) slow down, relax **1**

**hurt** /hɜrt/ (**hurts, hurting, hurt**) **1** V-T If you **hurt yourself** or **hurt** a part of your body, you feel pain because you have injured yourself. ❑ *Yasin*

hurt himself while trying to escape. **2** V-I If a part of your body **hurts**, you feel pain there. ❑ *His arm hurt.* **3** ADJ If you are **hurt**, you have been injured. ❑ *His friends asked him if he was hurt.* **4** V-T/V-I If you **hurt** someone, you cause them to feel pain. ❑ *I didn't mean to hurt her.* ❑ *That hurts!* **5** V-T/V-I If someone or something **hurts**, or **hurts** you, they say or do something that makes you unhappy. ❑ *He is afraid of hurting Bessy's feelings.* ❑ *What hurts most is that I had to find out for myself.* **6** ADJ If you are **hurt**, you are upset because of something that someone has said or done. ❑ *She was deeply hurt by what Smith said.* **7** V-T To **hurt** someone or something means to have a bad effect on them. ❑ *The hot weather is hurting many businesses.* [from Old French]

### Thesaurus hurt Also look up :

| | |
|---|---|
| V. | ache, smart, sting **2** harm, injure, wound **3** |
| ADJ. | injured, wounded **3** saddened, upset **6** |

### Word Partnership Use hurt with :

| | |
|---|---|
| ADV. | **badly/seriously** hurt **1 3** |
| V. | **get** hurt **3** **feel** hurt **6** |
| N. | hurt *someone's* **chances**, hurt **the economy**, hurt *someone's* **feelings**, hurt **sales 7** |

**hurt|le** /hɜrtᵊl/ (**hurtles, hurtling, hurtled**) V-I If someone or something **hurtles** somewhere, they move there very quickly, often in a rough or violent way. ❑ *A woman hurtled down the stairs.*

**hus|band** /hʌzbənd/ (**husbands**) N-COUNT A woman's **husband** is the man she is married to. ❑ *Eva married her husband in 1957.* [from Old English]
→ see **family, love**

**hush** /hʌʃ/ (**hushes, hushing, hushed**) **1** CONVENTION You say "**Hush!**" to someone when you are asking or telling them to be quiet. ❑ *Hush, my love, it's all right.* **2** N-SING You say there is a **hush** in a place when everything is quiet and peaceful, or suddenly becomes quiet. ❑ *A hush fell over the crowd.*
▸ **hush up** PHR-VERB If someone **hushes** something **up**, they prevent other people from knowing about it. ❑ *I tried to hush the whole thing up.*

**hushed** /hʌʃt/ ADJ **Hushed** means quiet and calm. ❑ *We spoke in hushed voices.*

**hus|tle** /hʌsᵊl/ (**hustles, hustling, hustled**) **1** V-T If you **hustle** someone, you try to make them go somewhere or do something quickly, for example by pulling or pushing them along. ❑ *The guards hustled Harry out of the car.* **2** V-I If you **hustle**, you go somewhere or do something as quickly as you can. ❑ *You'll have to hustle if you're going to get home for supper.* **3** V-I If someone **hustles**, they try hard to earn money or to gain an advantage from a situation. ❑ *I like it here. It forces you to hustle and you can earn money.* ❑ *Hustling for business doesn't just happen. You have to make it happen.* **4** V-T If someone **hustles** you, or if they **hustle** something, they try hard to get something, often by using dishonest or illegal means. ❑ *Two teenage boys asked us for money, and were hustling us.* [from Dutch]

**hut** /hʌt/ (**huts**) N-COUNT A **hut** is a small simple building, especially one made of wood, mud, grass, or stones. [from French]

**hy|brid** /haɪbrɪd/ (**hybrids**) **1** N-COUNT A **hybrid** is an animal or plant that has been bred from two different species of animal or plant. [TECHNICAL] ❑ *These brightly colored hybrids are so lovely in the garden.* ● **Hybrid** is also an adjective. ❑ *…the hybrid corn seed.* **2** N-COUNT A **hybrid** or a **hybrid car** is a car that can be powered by either gasoline or electricity. ❑ *Hybrid cars can go almost 600 miles between refueling.* **3** N-COUNT You can use **hybrid** to refer to anything that is a mixture of other things, especially two other things. ❑ *…a hybrid of solid and liquid fuel.* ● **Hybrid** is also an adjective. ❑ *…a hybrid system.* [from Latin]
→ see **car**

Word Link **Word Link** hydr ≈ water : carbo**hydr**ate, de**hydr**ate, **hydr**aulic

**hy|drau|lic** /haɪdrɔlɪk, -drɒl-/ ADJ **Hydraulic** equipment or machinery involves or is operated by a fluid that is under pressure, such as water or oil. ❑ *The boat has five hydraulic pumps.* [from Latin]

**hydro|car|bon** /haɪdroʊkɑrb³n/ (**hydrocarbons**) N-COUNT A **hydrocarbon** is a chemical compound that is a mixture of hydrogen and carbon.

**hydro|elec|tric** /haɪdroʊɪlɛktrɪk/ also hydro-electric ADJ **Hydroelectric** means relating to or involving electricity made from the energy of running water.

**hydro|elec|tric|ity** /haɪdroʊɪlɛktrɪsɪti/ N-UNCOUNT **Hydroelectricity** is electricity made from the energy of running water.

**hydro|gen** /haɪdrədʒ³n/ N-UNCOUNT **Hydrogen** is a colorless gas that is the lightest and most common element in the universe. [from French]
→ see **sun**

**hydro|log|ic cy|cle** /haɪdrəlɒdʒɪk saɪk³l/ N-SING The **hydrologic cycle** is the process by which the earth's water is circulated from the surface to the atmosphere through evaporation and back to the surface through rainfall. [TECHNICAL]

**hydro|pon|ics** /haɪdrəpɒnɪks/ N-UNCOUNT **Hydroponics** is a method of growing plants without the use of soil, by using water through which nutrients are pumped. ❑ *Is hydroponics a cheaper way of producing food?* ● **hydro|pon|ic** ADJ ❑ *…hydroponic strawberries.* ● **hydro|poni|cal|ly** ADV ❑ *…hydroponically grown plants.*

**hydro|power** /haɪdrəpoʊər/ N-UNCOUNT **Hydropower** is the use of energy from running

water, especially in hydroelectricity.

**hy|giene** /haɪdʒin/ N-UNCOUNT **Hygiene** is the practice of keeping yourself and your surroundings clean, especially in order to prevent the spread of disease. ❑ *Be careful about personal hygiene.* ● **hy|gien|ic** /haɪdʒɛnɪk/ ADJ ❑ *…a white kitchen that was easy to keep clean and hygienic.* [from New Latin]

**hymn** /hɪm/ (**hymns**) N-COUNT A **hymn** is a religious song that Christians sing in church. ❑ *I like singing hymns.* [from Latin]

**hype** /haɪp/ (**hypes, hyping, hyped**) **1** N-UNCOUNT **Hype** is the use of a lot of publicity and advertising to make people interested in something such as a product. ❑ *There's been a lot of hype about her new book.* **2** V-T To **hype** a product means to advertise or praise it a lot. ❑ *We hyped the film to raise money.* ● **Hype up** means the same as **hype**. ❑ *…hyping up famous people.*

**hyper|link** /haɪpərlɪŋk/ (**hyperlinks**) N-COUNT In an HTML document, a **hyperlink** is a link to another part of the document or to another document. Hyperlinks are shown as words with a line under them. [COMPUTING] ❑ *…Web pages full of hyperlinks.*

**hyper|son|ic** /haɪpərsɒnɪk/ ADJ A **hypersonic** rocket or missile travels at five times the speed of sound or faster. ❑ *…hypersonic aircraft.*

**hy|phen** /haɪf³n/ (**hyphens**) N-COUNT A **hyphen** is the punctuation sign used to join words together to make a compound, as in "left-handed." [from Late Latin]
→ see **punctuation**

**Word Link** osis ≈ state or condition : hypn**osis**, metamorph**osis**, neur**osis**

**hyp|no|sis** /hɪpnoʊsɪs/ **1** N-UNCOUNT **Hypnosis** is a state in which a person seems to be asleep but can still see, hear, or respond to things said to them. ❑ *Bevin talked about her childhood under hypnosis.* **2** N-UNCOUNT **Hypnosis** is the art or practice of hypnotizing people. [from Late Latin]

**hyp|not|ic** /hɪpnɒtɪk/ **1** ADJ If someone is in a **hypnotic** state, they have been hypnotized. ❑ *The hypnotic state is somewhere between being awake and being asleep.* **2** ADJ Something that is **hypnotic** holds your attention completely or makes you feel sleepy. ❑ *His songs are hypnotic and pleasant.* [from Late Latin]

**hyp|no|tize** /hɪpnətaɪz/ (**hypnotizes, hypnotizing, hypnotized**) **1** V-T If someone **hypnotizes** you, they put you into a state in which you seem to be asleep but can still see, hear, or respond to things said to you. ❑ *He hypnotized me and cured my fear of flying.* ● **hyp|no|tism** /hɪpnətɪzəm/ N-UNCOUNT ❑ *The doctor used hypnotism to help her deal with her fear.* ● **hyp|no|tist** (**hypnotists**) N-COUNT ❑ *…regular visits to a hypnotist.* **2** V-T If you **are hypnotized by** someone or something, you are so fascinated by them that you cannot think of anything else. ❑ *He's hypnotized by her beautiful hair.* [from Late Latin]

**hy|poc|ri|sy** /hɪpɒkrɪsi/ (**hypocrisies**) N-VAR If you accuse someone of **hypocrisy**, you mean that they pretend to have qualities, beliefs, or feelings that they do not really have. ❑ *He accused newspapers of hypocrisy in the way they reported the story.* [from Old French]

**hypo|crite** /hɪpəkrɪt/ (**hypocrites**) N-COUNT
If you accuse someone of being a **hypocrite**, you
mean that they pretend to have qualities, beliefs,
or feelings that they do not really have. ❑ *She said
he was a liar and a hypocrite.* [from Old French]

**hypo|criti|cal** /hɪpəkrɪtɪkᵊl/ ADJ If you accuse
someone of being **hypocritical**, you mean that
they pretend to have qualities, beliefs, or feelings
that they do not really have. ❑ *It's hypocritical of
vegetarians to wear leather shoes.* [from Old French]

**hypo|thala|mus** /haɪpoʊθæləməs/
(**hypothalami**) N-COUNT The **hypothalamus** is the
part of the brain that controls functions such as
hunger and thirst. [MEDICAL]

**hy|poth|esis** /haɪpɒθɪsɪs/ (**hypotheses**) N-VAR
A **hypothesis** is an idea which is suggested as a
possible explanation for a particular situation or
condition, but which has not yet been proved to
be correct. [FORMAL] ❑ *Work will now begin to test the
hypothesis in rats.* [from Greek]
→ see **experiment**, **science**

**hypo|theti|cal** /haɪpəθɛtɪkᵊl/ ADJ If something
is **hypothetical**, it is based on possible ideas
or situations rather than actual ones. ❑ *...a
hypothetical situation.* ● **hypo|theti|cal|ly**
/haɪpəθɛtɪkli/ ADV ❑ *He was willing to discuss the
idea hypothetically.* [from Greek]

**hys|ter|ec|to|my** /hɪstərɛktəmi/
(**hysterectomies**) N-COUNT A **hysterectomy** is a
surgical operation to remove a woman's uterus.
❑ *My sister had a hysterectomy.* [from Greek]

**hys|te|ria** /hɪstɛriə/ N-UNCOUNT **Hysteria**
among a group of people is a state of uncontrolled
excitement, anger, or panic. ❑ *There was hysteria
in the station when part of the roof fell in.* [from New
Latin]

**hys|teri|cal** /hɪstɛrɪkᵊl/ ■ ADJ Someone who is
**hysterical** is in a state of uncontrolled excitement,
anger, or panic. ❑ *Calm down. Don't get hysterical.*
● **hys|teri|cal|ly** /hɪstɛrɪkli/ ADV ❑ *The woman
screamed hysterically.* ■ ADJ **Hysterical** laughter is
loud and uncontrolled. [INFORMAL] ❑ *He burst into
hysterical laughter.* ● **hys|teri|cal|ly** ADV ❑ *Everyone
was laughing hysterically.* ■ ADJ If you describe
something or someone as **hysterical**, you think
that they are very funny. [INFORMAL] ❑ *His stories
were hysterical.* ● **hys|teri|cal|ly** ADV ❑ *His new play is
hysterically funny.* [from Latin]

**hys|ter|ics** /hɪstɛrɪks/ ■ N-PLURAL If someone
is **in hysterics** or is having **hysterics**, they are
in a state of uncontrolled excitement, anger,
or panic. [INFORMAL] ❑ *I'm sick of you having
hysterics.* ■ N-PLURAL You can say that someone
is **in hysterics** or is having **hysterics** when they
are laughing loudly in an uncontrolled way.
[INFORMAL] ❑ *We were all in hysterics when we saw his
silly hat.* [from New Latin]

H

# I i

**I** /aɪ/ PRON A speaker or writer uses **I** to refer to himself or herself. **I** is used as the subject of a verb. ❑ *Jim and I are getting married.* [from Latin]

**ice** /aɪs/ (**ices, icing, iced**) **1** N-UNCOUNT **Ice** is frozen water. ❑ *The ground was covered with ice.* **2** → see also **iced** **3** PHRASE If you **break the ice** at a party or meeting, or in a new situation, you say or do something to make people feel relaxed and comfortable. ❑ *Her friendly manner helped break the ice.* [from Old English]
→ see **climate, crystal, glacier, precipitation, snow**

**Ice Age** N-PROPER **The Ice Age** was a period of time lasting many thousands of years, during which a lot of the earth's surface was covered with ice.

**ice|berg** /aɪsbɜrg/ (**icebergs**) **1** N-COUNT An **iceberg** is a large tall mass of ice floating in the sea. [from Middle Dutch] **2 the tip of the iceberg** → see **tip**

**ice cream** (**ice creams**) **1** N-VAR **Ice cream** is a very cold sweet food made from frozen cream or a substance like cream and has a flavor such as vanilla, chocolate, or strawberry. ❑ *I'll get you some ice cream.* **2** N-COUNT An **ice cream** is a portion of ice cream. ❑ *Do you want an ice cream?*
→ see **dessert**

**iced** /aɪst/ ADJ An **iced** drink has been made very cold, often by putting ice in it. ❑ *...iced tea.* [from Old English]

**ice hock|ey** N-UNCOUNT **Ice hockey** is a game played on ice between two teams of 11 players who use long curved sticks to hit a small rubber disk, called a puck, and try to score goals. [AM usually **hockey**]

**ice wa|ter** N-UNCOUNT **Ice water** is very cold water served as a drink.

**ice wedg|ing** /aɪs wedʒɪŋ/ N-UNCOUNT **Ice wedging** is a geological process in which rocks are broken because water freezes in gaps or cracks in the rocks. [TECHNICAL]

**ici|cle** /aɪsɪkəl/ (**icicles**) N-COUNT An **icicle** is a long pointed piece of ice hanging down from a surface. [from Old English]

**icky** /ɪki/ **1** ADJ If you describe something as **icky**, you dislike it because it is very emotional or sentimental. [INFORMAL] ❑ *...an icky photo of the loving couple.* **2** ADJ If you describe a substance as **icky**, you mean that it is disgustingly sticky. [INFORMAL] ❑ *She felt something icky on her fingers.*

**icon** /aɪkɒn/ (**icons**) **1** N-COUNT If you describe something or someone as an **icon**, you mean that they are important as a symbol of a particular thing. ❑ *Mohammed Ali was a boxing icon.* **2** N-COUNT An **icon** is a picture of Christ, his mother, or a saint painted on a wooden panel. ❑ *He is a painter of religious icons.* **3** N-COUNT

An **icon** is a picture on a computer screen representing a particular computer function. If you want to use it, you move the cursor onto the icon using a mouse. [COMPUTING] ❑ *Kate clicked on the mail icon on her computer screen.* [from Latin]

**icy** /aɪsi/ (**icier, iciest**) **1** ADJ Something that is **icy** or **icy cold** is extremely cold. ❑ *An icy wind blew.* **2** ADJ An **icy** road has ice on it. ❑ *The roads were icy.* [from Old English]

**ID** /aɪ di/ (**IDs**) N-VAR If you have **ID** or an **ID**, you are carrying a document such as an identity card or driver's license that tells who you are. ❑ *I had no ID so I couldn't prove that it was my car.*

**I'd** /aɪd/ **1** **I'd** is the usual spoken form of "I had," especially when "had" is an auxiliary verb. ❑ *I was sure I'd seen her before.* **2** **I'd** is the usual spoken form of "I would." ❑ *There are some questions I'd like to ask.*

**ID card** (**ID cards**) N-COUNT An **ID card** is the same as an **identity card, identification card**. ❑ *You have to carry an ID card.*

**idea** /aɪdiə/ (**ideas**) **1** N-COUNT An **idea** is a plan, suggestion, or possible course of action. ❑ *I really like the idea of helping people.* **2** N-COUNT An **idea** is an opinion or belief about what something is like or should be like. ❑ *Everyone has different ideas about how to raise children.* **3** N-SING If you have an **idea** of something, you have some knowledge or information about it. ❑ *We had no idea what was happening.* **4** N-SING **The idea** of an action or activity is its aim or purpose. ❑ *The idea is to have fun.* [from Late Latin]

| **Word Partnership** | Use *idea* with : |
|---|---|
| ADJ. | **bad** idea, **bright** idea, **brilliant** idea, **great** idea **1** |
| | **crazy** idea, **different** idea, **dumb** idea, **interesting** idea, **new** idea, **original** idea **1 2** |
| | **the main** idea, **the whole** idea **1 4** |
| V. | **get an** idea, **have an** idea **1 3** |

| **Word Link** | *ide, ideo ≈ idea : idea, idealize, ideology* |
|---|---|

**ideal** /aɪdiəl/ (**ideals**) **1** N-COUNT An **ideal** is a principle, idea, or standard that seems very good and worth trying to achieve. ❑ *He stayed true to his ideals.* **2** N-SING Your **ideal of** something is the person or thing that seems to you to be the best possible example of it. ❑ *...the American ideal of equality.* **3** ADJ The **ideal** person or thing for a particular task or purpose is the best possible person or thing for it. ❑ *You are the ideal person to do the job.* ● **ideal|ly** ADV ❑ *They were a happy couple, ideally matched.* **4** ADJ An **ideal** society or world is the best possible one that you can imagine.

❏ *We do not live in an ideal world.* [from Late Middle English]

**ideal|ism** /aɪdiəlɪzəm/ N-UNCOUNT **Idealism** is the beliefs and behavior of someone who has ideals and who tries to base their behavior on these ideals. ❏ *...the idealism of the 1960s.* ● **ideal|ist** (**idealists**) N-COUNT ❏ *He is such an idealist that he cannot see the problems.* [from Late Middle English]

**ideal|is|tic** /aɪdiəlɪstɪk, aɪdiə-/ ADJ If you describe someone as **idealistic**, you mean that they have ideals, and base their behavior on these ideals, even though this may be impractical. ❏ *Idealistic young people died for the cause.* [from Late Middle English]

| **Word Link** | *ide, ideo ≈ idea : ideal, idealize, ideology* |

**ideal|ize** /aɪdiəlaɪz/ (**idealizes, idealizing, idealized**) V-T If you **idealize** something or someone, you think of them as being perfect or much better than they really are. ❏ *People idealize the past.* [from Late Middle English]

**ideal|ly** /aɪdiəli/ ADV If you say that **ideally** a particular thing should happen or be done, you mean that this is what you would like to happen or be done, but you know that it may not be possible or practical. ❏ *Ideally, you should drink every 10–15 minutes during exercise.* [from Late Middle English]

**ideal ma|chine** (**ideal machines**) N-COUNT An **ideal machine** is a machine that is a hundred percent efficient but cannot exist in reality because of forces such as friction. [TECHNICAL]

| **Word Link** | *ident ≈ same : identical, identification, unidentified* |

**iden|ti|cal** /aɪdɛntɪkᵊl/ ADJ Things that are **identical** are exactly the same. ❏ *The houses were almost identical.* ● **iden|ti|cal|ly** /aɪdɛntɪkli/ ADV ❏ *...nine identically dressed dancers.* [from Late Latin]
→ see **clone**

**iden|ti|fi|able** /aɪdɛntɪfaɪəbᵊl/ ADJ Something or someone that is **identifiable** can be recognized. ❏ *The building is easily identifiable as a hospital.* [from Late Latin]

**iden|ti|fi|ca|tion** /aɪdɛntɪfɪkeɪʃᵊn/ N-UNCOUNT If someone asks you for some **identification**, they want to see something such as a driver's license that proves who you are. ❏ *The police asked him to show some identification.* [from Late Latin]

**iden|ti|fi|ca|tion card** (**identification cards**) N-COUNT An **identification card** is the same as an **identity card**. The abbreviation **ID card** is also used.

**iden|ti|fy** /aɪdɛntɪfaɪ/ (**identifies, identifying, identified**) **1** V-T If you can **identify** someone or something, you are able to recognize them or distinguish them from others. ❏ *Now we have identified the problem, we must decide how to fix it.* ● **iden|ti|fi|ca|tion** /aɪdɛntɪfɪkeɪʃᵊn/ (**identifications**) N-VAR ❏ *Early identification of the disease is important.* **2** V-T If you **identify** someone or something, you name them and say who or what they are. ❏ *Police have already identified 10 murder suspects.* ● **iden|ti|fi|ca|tion** (**identifications**) N-VAR ❏ *He made a formal identification of the body.* **3** V-T If you **identify** something, you discover or notice its existence. ❏ *Scientists have identified drugs which are able to*

fight cancer. **4** V-T If a particular thing **identifies** someone or something, it makes them easy to recognize, by making them different in some way. ❏ *She wore a nurse's hat to identify her.* **5** V-T If you **identify** one person or thing **with** another, you think that they are closely associated or involved in some way. ❏ *He identified himself with modern Russian composers.* ● **iden|ti|fi|ca|tion** N-VAR ❏ *...the identification of Spain with Catholicism.* [from Late Latin]

**iden|tity** /aɪdɛntɪti/ (**identities**) **1** N-COUNT Your **identity** is who you are. ❏ *He uses the name Abu to hide his identity.* **2** N-VAR The **identity** of a person or place is the characteristics that distinguish them from others. ❏ *I wanted a sense of my own identity.* [from Late Latin]

| **Word Partnership** | Use *identity* with : |
|---|---|
| N. | identity **theft** **1** |
| | identity **crisis**, **sense of** identity **2** |
| ADJ. | **ethnic** identity, **national** identity, **personal** identity **2** |

**iden|tity card** (**identity cards**) N-COUNT An **identity card** is a card with a person's name, photograph, date of birth, and other information on it. In some countries, people are required to carry identity cards in order to prove who they are. The abbreviation **ID card** is also used.

**iden|tity cri|sis** (**identity crises**) N-COUNT If someone or something is having an **identity crisis**, it is not clear what kind of person or thing they are, or what kind of person or thing they would like to be. ❏ *Halfway through his career he suffered an identity crisis.*

**iden|tity theft** N-UNCOUNT **Identity theft** is the crime of getting personal information about another person without their knowledge, for example, in order to gain access to their bank account. ❏ *...how to protect yourself from identity theft.*

**ideol|ogy** /aɪdiɒlədʒi, ɪdi-/ (**ideologies**) N-VAR An **ideology** is a set of beliefs, especially the political beliefs on which people, parties, or countries base their actions. ❏ *...capitalist ideology.* ● **ideo|logi|cal** /aɪdiəlɒdʒɪkᵊl, ɪdi-/ ADJ ❏ *Others left the party for ideological reasons.* ● **ideo|logi|cal|ly** /aɪdiəlɒdʒɪkli, ɪdi-/ ADV ❏ *He was ideologically opposed to the plan.* [from French]

**idi|om** /ɪdiəm/ (**idioms**) N-COUNT An **idiom** is a group of words that have a different meaning when used together from the one they would have if you took the meaning of each word separately. For example, "to live from hand to mouth" is an idiom meaning to have very little food or money to live on. [TECHNICAL] [from Latin]

**idio|phone** /ɪdiəfoʊn/ (**idiophones**) N-COUNT An **idiophone** is any musical instrument that produces its sound by being hit or shaken.

**id|iot** /ɪdiət/ (**idiots**) N-COUNT If you call someone an **idiot**, you are showing that you think they are very stupid or have done something very stupid. ❏ *You were an idiot to stay there.* [from Latin]

**idle** /aɪdᵊl/ (**idles, idling, idled**) **1** ADJ If people who were working are **idle**, they have no jobs or work. ❏ *4,000 workers have been idle for 12 weeks.* **2** ADJ If machines or factories are **idle**, they are not working or being used. ❏ *The machine is lying* *idle*. **3** ADJ If you say that someone is **idle**, you disapprove of them because they are not doing anything and you think they should be. ❏ *...idle men who spent the day reading newspapers.* ● **idly** ADV ❏ *We were idly sitting around.* **4** ADJ **Idle** is used to describe something that you do for no particular reason. ❏ *We filled the time with idle talk.* ● **idly** ADV ❏ *We talked idly about baseball.* [from Old English]

**idol** /ˈaɪdᵊl/ (**idols**) N-COUNT If you refer to someone such as a movie, pop, or sports star as an **idol**, you mean that they are greatly admired or loved by their fans. ❏ *The crowd cheered as they caught sight of their idol.* [from Late Latin]

**idol|ize** /ˈaɪdəlaɪz/ (**idolizes, idolizing, idolized**) V-T If you **idolize** someone, you admire them very much. ❏ *Naomi idolized her father when she was young.* [from Late Latin]

**idyl|lic** /aɪˈdɪlɪk/ ADJ Something that is **idyllic** is extremely pleasant, simple, and peaceful without any difficulties. ❏ *...an idyllic setting for a summer romance.* [from Latin]

**if** /ɪf/

Often pronounced /ɪf/ at the beginning of the sentence.

**1** CONJ You use **if** in conditional sentences to introduce the circumstances in which an event or situation might happen, might be happening, or might have happened. ❏ *She gets very upset if I disagree with her.* ❏ *You can go if you want.* **2** CONJ You use **if** in indirect questions where the answer is either "yes" or "no." ❏ *He asked if I wanted some water.* **3** CONJ You use **if** to suggest that something might be slightly different from what you are stating in the main part of the sentence, for example, that there might be slightly more or less of a particular quality. ❏ *That standard is quite difficult, if not impossible, to achieve.* ❏ *What one quality, if any, do you dislike about your partner?* **4** PHRASE You use **if only** with past tenses to introduce what you think is a fairly good reason for doing something, although you realize it may not be a very good one. ❏ *She writes me once a month, if only to remind me that I haven't answered her last letter.* **5** PHRASE You use **if only** to express a wish or desire, especially one that cannot be fulfilled. ❏ *If only you had told me that earlier.* **6** PHRASE You use **as if** to describe something or someone by comparing them with another thing or person. ❏ *He made a movement with his hand, as if he were writing something.* [from Old English]
→ see also **whether**

**ig|ne|ous** /ˈɪgniəs/ ADJ In geology, **igneous** rocks are rocks that were once so hot that they were liquid. [TECHNICAL] [from Latin]

**ig|nite** /ɪgˈnaɪt/ (**ignites, igniting, ignited**) V-T/V-I When you **ignite** something or when it **ignites**, it starts burning or explodes. ❏ *The bombs ignited a fire which destroyed 60 houses.* [from Latin]

**ig|ni|tion** /ɪgˈnɪʃᵊn/ (**ignitions**) **1** N-SING Inside a car, the **ignition** is the part where you turn the key so that the engine starts. ❏ *She put the key in the ignition.* **2** N-UNCOUNT **Ignition** is the process of something starting to burn. ❏ *The ignition of gas killed eight men.* [from Latin]

**ig|no|rant** /ˈɪgnərənt/ **1** ADJ If you describe someone as **ignorant**, you mean that they do not know things they should know. If someone is **ignorant of** a fact, they do not know it. ❏ *People*

don't want to appear ignorant.* ● **ig|no|rance** /ˈɪgnərəns/ N-UNCOUNT ❏ *I feel embarrassed by my ignorance of world history.* **2** ADJ People are sometimes described as **ignorant** when they do something that is not polite or kind. ❏ *Some ignorant people called me names.* [from Latin]
→ see also **stupid**

**ig|nore** /ɪgˈnɔr/ (**ignores, ignoring, ignored**) V-T If you **ignore** someone or something, you pay no attention to them. ❏ *Her husband ignored her.* [from Latin]

**ill** /ɪl/ (**ills**) **1** ADJ Someone who is **ill** is suffering from a disease or a health problem. ❏ *He was ill with pneumonia.* ● People who are ill in some way can be referred to as, for example, **the** mentally **ill**. ❏ *She visits the seriously ill.* **2** N-COUNT Difficulties and problems are sometimes referred to as **ills**. [FORMAL] ❏ *He's responsible for many of the country's ills.* **3** ADJ You can use **ill** in front of some nouns to indicate that you are referring to something harmful or unpleasant. [FORMAL] ❏ *She brought ill luck into her family.* **4** N-UNCOUNT **Ill** is evil or harm. [LITERARY] ❏ *I don't wish them any ill.* [from Old Norse] **5** to **speak ill of** someone → see **speak**

### Word Partnership   Use *ill* with :

| | |
|---|---|
| V. | **become** ill, **feel** ill, **look** ill **1** |
| ADV. | **critically** ill, **mentally** ill, **physically** ill, **seriously** ill, **very** ill **1** |

**I'll** /aɪl/ **I'll** is the usual spoken form of "I will" or "I shall." ❏ *I'll go there tomorrow.*

### Word Link   il ≈ not : illegal, illiterate, illogical

**il|le|gal** /ɪˈligᵊl/ (**illegals**) ADJ If something is **illegal**, the law says that it is not allowed. ❏ *It is illegal for the governor to take gifts of more than $10 in value.* ❏ *...illegal activities.* ● **il|le|gal|ly** ADV ❏ *He was fined for parking illegally.*

**il|le|giti|mate** /ˌɪlɪˈdʒɪtɪmɪt/ **1** ADJ A person who is **illegitimate** was born to parents who were not married to each other. ❏ *He learned that he had an illegitimate child.* **2** ADJ **Illegitimate** is used to describe activities and institutions that are not allowed by law or are not acceptable according to standards of what is right. ❏ *He called the new government illegitimate.*

**ill-fated** ADJ If you describe something as **ill-fated**, you mean that it ended or will end in an unsuccessful or unfortunate way. ❏ *...an ill-fated expedition to Antarctica.*

**ill health** N-UNCOUNT Someone who suffers from **ill health** has an illness or is not healthy. ❏ *He left his job because of ill health.*

**il|lic|it** /ɪˈlɪsɪt/ ADJ An **illicit** activity or substance is not allowed by law or the social customs of a country. ❏ *Illicit business practices meant that the store had to be closed down.* [from French]

**il|lit|er|ate** /ɪˈlɪtərɪt/ ADJ Someone who is **illiterate** does not know how to read or write. ❏ *Many people are illiterate.*

**ill|ness** /ˈɪlnɪs/ (**illnesses**) **1** N-UNCOUNT **Illness** is the fact or experience of being ill. ❏ *He was away from school because of illness.* **2** N-COUNT An **illness** is a particular disease such as measles or pneumonia. ❏ *She is recovering from a serious illness.* [from Old Norse]
→ see Word Web: **illness**

## Word Web illness

Most **infectious diseases** pass from person to person. However, some people have caught **viruses** from animals. During the 2002 SARS **epidemic**, doctors discovered that the disease came from birds. SARS caused more than 800 deaths in 32 countries. The disease had to be stopped quickly. Hospitals **quarantined** SARS patients so they would not make other people sick. Medical workers used **symptoms** such as **fever, chills**, and a **cough** to help **diagnose** the disease. **Treatment** was not easy. By the time the symptoms appeared, the disease had already caused a lot of damage. **Patients** received oxygen and **physical therapy** to help clear the lungs.

## Thesaurus illness Also look up:

N. sickness; (*ant.*) health **1**
ailment, disease **2**

## Word Partnership Use *illness* with:

N. **signs/symptoms of an** illness **2**
ADJ. **long/short** illness, **mental** illness, **mysterious** illness, **serious** illness, **sudden** illness, **terminal** illness **1**
V. **suffer from an** illness, **treat an** illness **2**
**diagnose an** illness, **have an** illness **2**

## Word Link *il ≈ not : illegal, illiterate, illogical*

il|logi|cal /ɪlɒdʒɪkəl/ ADJ If you describe an action, feeling, or belief as **illogical**, you are critical of it because you think that it does not result from a logical and ordered way of thinking. ❑ *It is illogical to blame her.*

il|lu|mi|nate /ɪlu:mɪneɪt/ (**illuminates, illuminating, illuminated**) **1** V-T To **illuminate** something means to shine light on it and to make it brighter. [FORMAL] ❑ *Streetlights illuminated the street.* ● il|lu|mi|na|tion /ɪlu:mɪneɪʃən/ N-UNCOUNT ❑ *The only illumination came from a small candle in the window.* **2** V-T If you **illuminate** something that is unclear or difficult to understand, you make it clearer by explaining it carefully or giving information about it. [FORMAL] ❑ *They use games and drawings to illuminate their subject.* ● il|lu|mi|nat|ing ADJ ❑ *This is a very illuminating book.* [from Latin]

il|lu|sion /ɪlu:ʒən/ (**illusions**) **1** N-COUNT An **illusion** is something that appears to exist or be a particular thing but does not actually exist or is in reality something else. ❑ *Large windows can give the illusion of more space.* **2** N-VAR An **illusion** is a false idea or belief. ❑ *He's under the illusion that money automatically makes people happy.* [from Latin]

## Word Partnership Use *illusion* with:

V. **create an** illusion, **give an** illusion **about/of/that** *something* **1 2**
PREP. **be under an** illusion **2**

il|lus|trate /ɪləstreɪt/ (**illustrates, illustrating, illustrated**) **1** V-T If something **illustrates** a situation or point, it makes it clearer or shows that it exists or is right. ❑ *Let me give an example*
to illustrate my point. ❑ *The accident illustrates how difficult it is to design a safe system.* ● il|lus|tra|tion /ɪləstreɪʃən/ (**illustrations**) N-VAR ❑ *This is a good illustration of how an essay should be written.* **2** V-T If you **illustrate** a book, you put pictures, photographs or diagrams into it. ❑ *She illustrates children's books.* ● il|lus|tra|tion (**illustrations**) N-VAR ❑ *...a book with beautiful illustrations.* [from Latin]
→ see **animation**

il|lus|tri|ous /ɪlʌstriəs/ ADJ An **illustrious** person is well known because they have a high position in society or they have done something impressive or important. ❑ *...the most illustrious scientists in the world.* [from Latin]

IM /aɪ ɛm/ (**IMs**) **1** N-VAR **IM** is an abbreviation for **instant messaging**. ❑ *The device lets you chat via IM.* **2** N-VAR **IM** is an abbreviation for **instant message**.

I'm /aɪm/ **I'm** is the usual spoken form of "I am." ❑ *I'm sorry.*

im|age /ɪmɪdʒ/ (**images**) **1** N-COUNT If you have an **image** of something or someone, you have a picture or idea of them in your mind. ❑ *If you talk about California, people have an image of sunny blue skies.* **2** N-COUNT The **image** of a person, group, or organization is the way that they appear to other people. ❑ *The government does not have a good public image.* **3** N-COUNT An **image** is a picture of someone or something. [FORMAL] ❑ *...photographic images of children.* **4** N-COUNT An **image** is a poetic description of something. [FORMAL] ❑ *He uses a lot of images from nature in his poetry.* [from Old French]
→ see **eye, photography, telescope, television**

## Word Partnership Use *image* with:

N. **body** image, **self-**image **1** image **on a screen** **3**
ADJ. **corporate** image, **negative/positive** image, **public** image **2**
V. **project an** image **2 3** **display an** image **3**

im|age|ry /ɪmɪdʒri/ N-UNCOUNT You can refer to the descriptions or symbols in something such as a poem, song, or movie and the pictures they create in your mind, as its **imagery**. [FORMAL] ❑ *...the nature imagery in the poem.* [from Old French]

im|agi|nable /ɪmædʒɪnəbəl/ ADJ You use **imaginable** after a superlative such as "best" or "worst" to emphasize that something is extreme in some way. ❑ *He had the worst imaginable day.* [from Latin]

**im|agi|nary** /ɪmædʒɪnɛri/ ADJ An **imaginary** person, place, or thing exists only in your mind or in a story, and not in real life. ❑ *Lots of children have imaginary friends.* [from Latin]
→ see **fantasy**

**im|agi|na|tion** /ɪmædʒɪneɪʃⁿn/ (**imaginations**) N-VAR Your **imagination** is the ability that you have to form pictures or ideas in your mind of new, exciting, or imaginary things. ❑ *Children have lively imaginations.* [from Latin]
→ see **fantasy**

**Word Partnership** Use *imagination* with :

| | |
|---|---|
| ADJ. | **active** imagination, **lively** imagination, **vivid** imagination |
| PREP. | **beyond** (*someone's*) imagination |
| N. | **lack of** imagination |

**im|agi|na|tive** /ɪmædʒɪnətɪv/ ADJ If you describe someone or their ideas as **imaginative**, you are praising them because they are easily able to think of or create new or exciting things. ❑ *...an imaginative writer.* • **im|agi|na|tive|ly** ADV ❑ *The hotel is decorated imaginatively.* [from Latin]

**im|ag|ine** /ɪmædʒɪn/ (**imagines, imagining, imagined**) ■ V-T If you **imagine** something, you think about it and your mind forms a picture or idea of it. ❑ *He could not imagine a more peaceful scene.* ■ V-T If you **imagine** that something is true, you think that it is true. ❑ *I imagine that you're hungry.* ■ V-T If you **imagine** something, you think that you have seen, heard, or experienced that thing, although actually you have not. ❑ *I realize that I imagined the whole thing.* [from Latin]

**Thesaurus** *imagine* Also look up :

| | |
|---|---|
| V. | picture, see, visualize ■ |
| | believe, guess, think ■ |

**Word Partnership** Use *imagine* with :

| | |
|---|---|
| V. | **can/can't/could/couldn't** imagine *something*, **try to** imagine ■ ■ |
| ADJ. | **difficult/easy/hard/impossible to** imagine ■ ■ |

**Word Link** *im ≈ not : imbalance, immature, impossible*

**im|bal|ance** /ɪmbæləns/ (**imbalances**) N-VAR If there is an **imbalance** in a situation, the things involved are not the same size, or are not the right size in relation to each other. ❑ *There is an imbalance between people and water resources in the east of the country.* [from Old French]

**im|bue** /ɪmbyu/ (**imbues, imbuing, imbued**) V-T If someone or something **is imbued** with an idea, feeling, or quality, they are filled with it. [FORMAL] ❑ *The movie is imbued with charm and humor.* [from Latin]

**imi|tate** /ɪmɪteɪt/ (**imitates, imitating, imitated**) ■ V-T If you **imitate** someone, you copy what they do or produce. ❑ *Birds are starting to imitate the ringtones of cellphones.* • **imi|ta|tor** /ɪmɪteɪtər/ (**imitators**) N-COUNT ❑ *He has had many imitators but no equals.* ■ V-T If you **imitate** a person or animal, you copy the way they speak or behave, usually because you are trying to be

funny. ❑ *I didn't like the way he imitated my voice.* [from Latin]

**imi|ta|tion** /ɪmɪteɪʃⁿn/ (**imitations**) ■ N-COUNT An **imitation** of something is a copy of it. ❑ *...a European imitation of Chinese art.* ■ N-UNCOUNT **Imitation** means copying someone else's actions. ❑ *She learned to dance by imitation.* ■ ADJ **Imitation** things are not genuine but are made to look as if they are. ❑ *...books covered in imitation leather.* ■ N-COUNT If someone does an **imitation** of another person, they copy the way they speak or behave, sometimes in order to be funny. ❑ *One boy did an imitation of the teacher.* [from Latin]

**im|macu|late** /ɪmækyʊlɪt/ ■ ADJ If something is **immaculate**, it is extremely clean, or neat. ❑ *Her kitchen was immaculate.* • **im|macu|late|ly** ADV ❑ *He was always immaculately dressed.* ■ ADJ If you say that something is **immaculate**, you are emphasizing that it is perfect, without any mistakes or bad parts at all. ❑ *The player's performance was immaculate.* • **im|macu|late|ly** ADV ❑ *The orchestra plays immaculately.* [from Latin]

**im|ma|teri|al** /ɪmətɪəriəl/ ADJ If something is **immaterial**, it is not important or not relevant. ❑ *It is immaterial whether you go.* [from French]

**im|ma|ture** /ɪmətʃʊər, -tʊər/ ■ ADJ Something or someone that is **immature** is not yet completely grown or fully developed. ❑ *She is emotionally immature.* ■ ADJ If you describe someone as **immature**, you are being critical of them because they do not behave in a sensible or responsible way. ❑ *You're being silly and immature.* [from Latin]

**Thesaurus** *immature* Also look up :

| | |
|---|---|
| ADJ. | underdeveloped, unripe ■ |
| | childish, foolish, juvenile ■ |

**im|medi|ate** /ɪmidiɪt/ ■ ADJ An **immediate** result, action, or reaction happens or is done without any delay. ❑ *The changes in the law had an immediate effect.* • **im|medi|ate|ly** ADV ❑ *He immediately fell to the floor.* ■ ADJ **Immediate** needs and concerns must be dealt with quickly. ❑ *The immediate problem is that people have no clean water.* ■ ADJ The **immediate** person or thing comes just before or just after another person or thing in a sequence. ❑ *Her immediate boss refused to help, so she went to his boss.* • **im|medi|ate|ly** ADV ❑ *...the weeks immediately before the war.* ■ ADJ You use **immediate** to describe an area or position that is next to or very near a particular place or person. ❑ *People had to leave the immediate area.* ■ ADJ Your **immediate** family are your parents, children, brothers, and sisters. ❑ *Only their immediate family came to the wedding.* [from Medieval Latin]

**Word Partnership** Use *immediate* with :

| | |
|---|---|
| N. | immediate **action**, immediate **plans**, immediate **reaction**, immediate **response**, immediate **results** ■ |
| | immediate **future** ■ |
| | immediate **surroundings** ■ |
| | immediate **family** ■ |

**im|medi|ate|ly** /ɪmidiɪtli/ ■ ADV If something is **immediately** obvious, it can be seen or understood without any delay. ❑ *The cause of the accident was not immediately clear.* ■ ADV

**Immediately** is used to emphasize that something comes next, or is next to something else. ❑ *The speeches began immediately after dinner.* [from Medieval Latin]

**im|mense** /ɪmɛns/ ADJ If you describe something as **immense**, you mean that it is extremely large or great. ❑ *...an immense cloud of smoke.* [from Latin]

**im|mense|ly** /ɪmɛnsli/ ADV You use **immensely** to emphasize the degree or extent of a quality, feeling, or process. ❑ *I enjoyed the movie immensely.* [from Latin]

**im|merse** /ɪmɜrs/ (**immerses, immersing, immersed**) ◼ V-T If you **immerse** yourself in something that you are doing, you become completely involved in it. ❑ *She immersed herself in her studies.* ● **im|mersed** ADJ ❑ *He was immersed in his work.* ◼ V-T If you **immerse** something in a liquid, you put it into the liquid so that it is completely covered. ❑ *His whole body was immersed in the water.* [from Latin]

> **Word Link** migr ≈ moving, changing : emigrant, immigrant, migrant

**im|mi|grant** /ɪmɪgrənt/ (**immigrants**) N-COUNT An **immigrant** is a person who has come to live in a country from some other country. Compare **emigrant.** ❑ *...immigrant workers.* [from Latin]
→ see **culture**

**im|mi|gra|tion** /ɪmɪgreɪʃⁿn/ ◼ N-UNCOUNT **Immigration** is the fact or process of people coming into a country in order to live and work there. ❑ *...laws controlling immigration.* ◼ N-UNCOUNT **Immigration** or **immigration control** is the place at a port, airport, or international border where officials check the passports of people who wish to come into the country. ❑ *You have to go through immigration and customs when you enter the country.* [from Latin]

**im|mi|nent** /ɪmɪnənt/ ADJ If something is **imminent**, it is almost certain to happen very soon. ❑ *We are not in any imminent danger.* [from Latin]

**im|mor|al** /ɪmɔrᵊl/ ADJ If you describe someone or their behavior as **immoral**, you believe that their behavior is morally wrong. ❑ *Some people think that earning a lot of money is immoral.* [from Latin]

**im|mor|tal** /ɪmɔrtᵊl/ (**immortals**) ◼ ADJ Someone or something that is **immortal** is famous and likely to be remembered for a long time. ❑ *He wrote the immortal book "The Adventures of Huckleberry Finn."* ● An **immortal** is someone who will be remembered for a long time. ❑ *These players are the immortals of baseball.* ● **im|mor|tal|ity** /ɪmɔrtælɪti/ N-UNCOUNT ❑ *Artists want to gain immortality through their work.* ◼ ADJ Someone or something that is **immortal** will live or last forever and never die or be destroyed. ❑ *...the immortal gods.* ● **im|mor|tal|ity** N-UNCOUNT ❑ *...belief in the immortality of the soul.* [from Latin]

**im|mor|tal|ize** /ɪmɔrtᵊlaɪz/ (**immortalizes, immortalizing, immortalized**) V-T If someone or something **is immortalized** in a story, movie, or work of art, they appear in it, and will be remembered for it. [WRITTEN] ❑ *Ths story is immortalized in several movies.* [from Latin]

**im|mune** /ɪmyun/ ◼ ADJ If you are **immune**

to a particular disease, you cannot be affected by it. ❑ *Some people are naturally immune to measles.* ● **im|mun|ity** /ɪmyunɪti/ N-UNCOUNT ❑ *Immunity to the common cold increases with age.* ◼ ADJ If you are **immune to** something that happens or is done, you are not affected by it. ❑ *She is immune to criticism.* ◼ ADJ Someone or something that is **immune from** a particular process or situation is able to avoid it. ❑ *Nobody's life is immune from pain.* ● **im|mun|ity** N-UNCOUNT ❑ *His official status gave him immunity from inspection at the airport.* [from Latin]

**im|mune sys|tem** (**immune systems**) N-COUNT Your **immune system** consists of all the organs and processes in your body that protect you from illness and infection. ❑ *The disease affects the immune system.*

**im|mun|ize** /ɪmyənaɪz/ (**immunizes, immunizing, immunized**) V-T If people or animals **are immunized**, they are made immune to a particular disease, often by being given an injection. ❑ *Every student is immunized against hepatitis B.* ● **im|mun|iza|tion** /ɪmyənɪzeɪʃⁿn/ (**immunizations**) N-VAR ❑ *...immunization against childhood diseases.* [from Latin]

**im|mu|no|de|fi|cien|cy** /ɪmyənoʊdɪfɪʃⁿnsi/ N-UNCOUNT **Immunodeficiency** is a weakness in a person's immune system or the failure of a person's immune system to work properly. [MEDICAL] ❑ *...a type of immunodeficiency disease.*

**im|pact** (**impacts, impacting, impacted**)

> The noun is pronounced /ɪmpækt/. The verb is pronounced /ɪmpækt/ or /ɪmpækt/.

◼ N-COUNT If something has an **impact on** a situation, process, or person, it has a strong effect on them. ❑ *The experience had a strong impact on him.* ◼ N-VAR An **impact** is the action of one object hitting another, or the force with which one object hits another. ❑ *The impact of the crash threw the truck off the roadway.* ◼ V-T To **impact** a situation, process, or person means to affect them. ❑ *The new law has impacted small businesses.* [from Latin]
→ see **crash**

> **Word Partnership** Use *impact* with :
>
> ADJ. **historical** impact, **important** impact ◼
> V. **have an** impact, **make an** impact ◼
> **die on** impact ◼
> PREP. **on** impact ◼

**im|pair** /ɪmpɛər/ (**impairs, impairing, impaired**) V-T To **impair** something such as an ability or the way something works means to damage it or make it worse. [FORMAL] ❑ *Worry never helps; it impairs your health.* ● **im|paired** ADJ ❑ *The blast left him with impaired hearing.* [from Old French]

**im|pair|ment** /ɪmpɛərmənt/ (**impairments**) N-VAR If someone has an **impairment**, they have a condition that prevents their eyes, ears, limbs, or brain from working properly. ❑ *He has a visual impairment.* [from Old French]

**im|part** /ɪmpɑrt/ (**imparts, imparting, imparted**) V-T If you **impart** information to people, you give it to them. [FORMAL] ❑ *...a teacher's ability to impart knowledge.* [from Old French]

**im|par|tial** /ɪmpɑrʃ°l/ ADJ Someone who is
**impartial** is not directly involved in a particular
situation, and is therefore able to give a fair
opinion or decision about it. ❑ *A counselor can give
you impartial advice.* ● **im|par|tial|ity** /ɪmpɑrʃiælɪti/
N-UNCOUNT ❑ …*the fairness or impartiality of the
trial.* ● **im|par|tial|ly** ADV ❑ *He promised to judge the
contest impartially.* [from Old French]

**im|passe** /ɪmpæs/ N-SING An **impasse** is a
difficult situation in which it is impossible to
make any progress. ❑ *The talks are once again at an
impasse.* [from French]

**im|pas|sioned** /ɪmpæʃ°nd/ ADJ An
**impassioned** speech or piece of writing is one in
which someone expresses their strong feelings
about an issue in a forceful way. [WRITTEN] ❑ *He
made an impassioned speech.*

**im|pas|sive** /ɪmpæsɪv/ ADJ If someone is
**impassive** or their face is **impassive**, they are not
showing any emotion. ● **im|pas|sive|ly** ADV ❑ *The lawyer
looked impassively at him and said nothing.* [from
Latin]

**im|pa|tient** /ɪmpeɪʃ°nt/ **1** ADJ If you are
**impatient**, you are annoyed because you have
to wait too long for something. ❑ *People are
impatient for the war to be over.* ● **im|pa|tient|ly**
ADV ❑ *She waited impatiently for the mail to arrive.*
● **im|pa|tience** /ɪmpeɪʃ°ns/ N-UNCOUNT ❑ *I
remember his impatience with long speeches.* **2** ADJ
If you are **impatient**, you are easily irritated by
things. ❑ *Try not to be impatient with your kids.*
● **im|pa|tient|ly** ADV ❑ *"Come on, David," Harry said
impatiently.* ● **im|pa|tience** N-UNCOUNT ❑ *She tried
to hide her growing impatience with him.* **3** ADJ If you
are **impatient to** do something or **impatient for**
something to happen, you are eager to do it or for
it to happen and do not want to wait. ❑ *He was
impatient to get home.* ● **im|pa|tience** N-UNCOUNT
❑ *He didn't hide his impatience to leave.*

**im|pec|cable** /ɪmpɛkəb°l/ ADJ If you describe
something such as someone's behavior or
appearance as **impeccable**, you are emphasizing
that it is perfect and has no faults. ❑ *She
had impeccable taste in clothes.* ● **im|pec|cably**
/ɪmpɛkəbli/ ADV ❑ *He was impeccably dressed.* [from
Late Latin]

**im|pede** /ɪmpid/ (**impedes, impeding, impeded**)
V-T If you **impede** someone or something, you
make their movement, development, or progress
difficult. [FORMAL] ❑ *Bad weather conditions are
impeding the progress of rescue workers.* [from Latin]

**im|pedi|ment** /ɪmpɛdɪmənt/ (**impediments**)
**1** N-COUNT An **impediment to** a person or thing
makes their movement, development, or progress
difficult. [FORMAL] ❑ *There is no legal impediment
to the marriage.* **2** N-COUNT Someone who has a
speech **impediment** has a disability that makes
speaking difficult. ❑ *John's speech impediment made
it difficult for people to understand him.* [from Latin]

**im|pend|ing** /ɪmpɛndɪŋ/ ADJ An **impending**
event is one that is going to happen very soon.
[FORMAL] ❑ *I had a feeling of impending disaster.* [from
Latin]

**im|pen|etrable** /ɪmpɛnɪtrəb°l/ **1** ADJ An
**impenetrable** barrier or forest is impossible or
very difficult to get through. ❑ *The mountains
form an almost impenetrable barrier between the two*

*countries.* **2** ADJ If you describe something such
as a book or a theory as **impenetrable**, you are
emphasizing that it is impossible or very difficult
to understand. ❑ *His writing is impenetrable.*

**im|pera|tive** /ɪmpɛrətɪv/ (**imperatives**) **1** ADJ
If it is **imperative** that something be done, that
thing is extremely important and must be done.
[FORMAL] ❑ *It is imperative that we do something
quickly.* **2** N-COUNT An **imperative** is something
that is extremely important and must be done.
[FORMAL] ❑ *Our imperative is to reduce the number of
deaths.* **3** N-SING In grammar, a clause that is in
**the imperative** contains the base form of a verb
and usually has no subject. Imperative clauses are
used to tell someone to do something. Examples
are "Go away" and "Please be careful." **4** ADJ
An **imperative** sentence is a sentence that tells
someone to do something, for example "Go home."
[from Late Latin]

**im|per|fect** /ɪmpɜrfɪkt/ **1** ADJ Something that
is **imperfect** has faults and is not exactly as you
would like it to be. [FORMAL] ❑ *We live in an imperfect
world.* **2** N-SING In grammar, **the imperfect** or
**the imperfect** tense of a verb is used to describe
continuous situations or repeated actions in the
past. Examples are "I was reading" and "they were
eating." [from Latin]

**im|per|fec|tion** /ɪmpərfɛkʃ°n/ (**imperfections**)
N-VAR An **imperfection** in someone or something
is a fault or weakness. ❑ *He admits that there are
imperfections in the system.* [from Latin]

**im|pe|rial** /ɪmpɪəriəl/ **1** ADJ **Imperial** is used
to refer to things or people that are or were
connected with an empire. ❑ …*the Imperial
Palace in Tokyo.* **2** ADJ The **imperial** system of
measurement uses inches, feet, yards, and miles
to measure length, ounces and pounds to measure
weight, and pints, quarts, and gallons to measure
volume. [from Late Latin]

**im|peri|al|ism** /ɪmpɪəriəlɪzəm/ N-UNCOUNT
**Imperialism** is a system in which a rich and
powerful country controls other countries.
❑ …*nations which have been victims of imperialism.*
● **im|peri|al|ist** (**imperialists**) N-COUNT ❑ *He called
his enemies "imperialists."* [from Late Latin]

**im|per|son|al** /ɪmpɜrsən°l/ **1** ADJ If you
describe a place, organization, or activity as
**impersonal**, you dislike it because it is not very
friendly and makes you feel unimportant.
❑ …*expensive impersonal hotels.* **2** ADJ If you
describe someone's behavior as **impersonal**, you
mean that they do not show any emotion about
the person they are dealing with. ❑ *Doctors must
often make decisions in an impersonal way.*

**im|per|son|ate** /ɪmpɜrsəneɪt/ (**impersonates,
impersonating, impersonated**) V-T If someone
**impersonates** a person, they pretend to be that
person, either to deceive people or to make people
laugh. ❑ *As a child I was always impersonating family
and friends.* ● **im|per|sona|tion** /ɪmpɜrsəneɪʃ°n/
(**impersonations**) N-VAR ❑ *His classmates liked his*

*impersonations of their teachers.*

**im|pe|tus** /ɪmpɪtəs/ N-UNCOUNT Something that gives a process **impetus** or an **impetus** makes it happen or progress more quickly. ❑ *His speech created new impetus for political change.* [from Latin]

**im|plac|able** /ɪmplækəbəl/ ADJ If you say that someone is **implacable**, you mean that their attitude or feelings about something are firm and will not be changed by other people's opinions. ❑ *He now had three implacable enemies against him.* ● **im|plac|ably** ADV ❑ *His mother was implacably against the marriage.* [from Late Middle English]

**im|plant** (**implants, implanting, implanted**)

> The verb is pronounced /ɪmplænt/. The noun is pronounced /ɪmplænt/.

**1** V-T To **implant** something into a person's body means to put it there, usually by means of a medical operation. ❑ *Doctors implanted a new heart a year ago.* **2** N-COUNT An **implant** is something that is implanted into a person's body. ❑ *We can replace your knee with an artificial implant.* **3** V-I When an egg or embryo **implants** in the womb, it becomes established there and can then develop. ● **im|plan|ta|tion** /ɪmplænteɪʃən/ N-UNCOUNT ❑ *The hormone may prevent implantation of the embryo.* [from Old English]

**im|ple|ment** (**implements, implementing, implemented**)

> The verb is pronounced /ɪmplɪmɛnt/ or /ɪmplɪmənt/. The noun is pronounced /ɪmplɪmənt/.

**1** V-T If you **implement** a plan, system, or law, you carry it out. ❑ *The government implemented a new system for inspecting schools.* ● **im|ple|men|ta|tion** /ɪmplɪmənteɪʃən, -mɛn-/ N-UNCOUNT ❑ *...the implementation of the peace agreement.* **2** N-COUNT An **implement** is a tool or other piece of equipment. [FORMAL] ❑ *...kitchen implements.* [from Late Latin]

**im|pli|cate** /ɪmplɪkeɪt/ (**implicates, implicating, implicated**) V-T To **implicate** someone means to show or claim that they were involved in something wrong or criminal. ❑ *A newspaper article implicated him in the killings.* ● **im|pli|ca|tion** N-UNCOUNT ❑ *...his implication in a murder.* [from Latin]

**im|pli|ca|tion** /ɪmplɪkeɪʃən/ (**implications**) **1** N-COUNT The **implications of** something are the things that are likely to happen as a result. ❑ *What are the implications of his decision?* [from Latin] **2** → see also **implicate**

**Word Partnership** Use *implication* with :

ADJ. **clear** implication, **important** implication, **obvious** implication **1**

**im|plic|it** /ɪmplɪsɪt/ **1** ADJ Something that is **implicit** is expressed in an indirect way. ❑ *Some people laughed at the implicit joke.* ● **im|plic|it|ly** ADV ❑ *He implicitly agreed.* **2** ADJ If you have an **implicit** belief or faith in something, you have complete faith in it and no doubts at all. ❑ *He had implicit faith in the democratic system.* ● **im|plic|it|ly** ADV ❑ *I trust him implicitly.* [from Latin]

**im|plore** /ɪmplɔr/ (**implores, imploring, implored**) V-T If you **implore** someone **to** do something, you ask them to do it in a forceful,

emotional way. ❑ *We implore both sides to continue the discussions.* [from Latin]

**im|ply** /ɪmplaɪ/ (**implies, implying, implied**) **1** V-T If you **imply that** something is true, you say something that indicates in an indirect way that it is true. ❑ *Are you implying that this is my fault?* **2** V-T If an event or situation **implies** that something is true, it makes you think that it is true. ❑ *The news article implies that he is guilty.* [from Old French]

**Usage** **imply** and **infer**

*Imply* and *infer* are often confused. When you *imply* something, you say or suggest it indirectly, but when you *infer* something, you figure it out: *Xian-li smiled to imply that she thought Dun was nice, but Dun inferred that she thought he was silly.*

**Thesaurus** *imply* Also look up :

v. hint, insinuate, point to, suggest **1** **2**

**Word Link** port ≈ carrying : export, import, portable

**im|port** (**imports, importing, imported**)

> The verb is pronounced /ɪmpɔrt/ or /ɪmpɔrt/. The noun is pronounced /ɪmpɔrt/.

**1** V-T To **import** products or raw materials means to buy them from another country for use in your own country. ❑ *The U.S. imports over half of its oil.* ● **Import** is also a noun. ❑ *Pizza is an import from Italy.* ● **im|por|ta|tion** /ɪmpɔrteɪʃən/ N-UNCOUNT ❑ *...rules about the importation of birds.* ● **im|port|er** (**importers**) N-COUNT ❑ *Japan is the biggest importer of U.S. beef.* **2** N-COUNT **Imports** are products or raw materials bought from another country for use in your own country. ❑ *...cheap imports from other countries.* [from Latin]

**im|por|tant** /ɪmpɔrtᵊnt/ **1** ADJ Something that is **important** is very significant, is highly valued, or is necessary. ❑ *The most important thing in my life is my career.* ❑ *It's important to answer her questions honestly.* ● **im|por|tance** N-UNCOUNT ❑ *The teacher stressed the importance of doing our homework.* ● **im|por|tant|ly** ADV ❑ *I was hungry, and, more importantly, my children were hungry.* **2** ADJ Someone who is **important** has influence or power within a society or a particular group. ❑ *She's an important person in the world of television.* ● **im|por|tance** N-UNCOUNT ❑ *I didn't realize his importance in the company.* [from Old Italian]

**Thesaurus** *important* Also look up :

ADJ. critical, essential, principal, significant; (*ant.*) unimportant **1** distinguished **2**

**Word Partnership** Use *importance* with :

ADJ. **critical** importance, **enormous** importance, **growing/increasing** importance, **utmost** importance **1**
V. **place less/more** importance **on something**, **recognize the** importance, **understand the** importance **1**
N. **self**-importance, **sense of** importance **2**

**im|pose** /ɪmpoʊz/ (**imposes, imposing, imposed**) **1** V-T If you **impose** something on people, you force them to accept it. ❑ *We impose fines on drivers who break the speed limit.* ● **im|po|si|tion** /ɪmpəzɪʃ<sup>ə</sup>n/ N-UNCOUNT ❑ ...*the imposition of a new property tax.* **2** V-T If you **impose** your opinions or beliefs **on** other people, you try to make people accept them as a rule or as a model to copy. ❑ *He tries to impose his own taste on all of us.* **3** V-I If someone **imposes on** you, they unreasonably expect you to do something for them which you do not want to do. ❑ *I won't stay overnight because I don't want to impose on you.* ● **im|po|si|tion** N-COUNT ❑ *He brought all his friends with him, which was a real imposition.* [from Old French]

**im|pos|ing** /ɪmpoʊzɪŋ/ ADJ If you describe someone or something as **imposing**, you mean that they have an impressive appearance or manner. ❑ *He was an imposing man.* [from Old French]

---

**Word Link** | im ≈ not : imbalance, immature, impossible

---

**im|pos|sible** /ɪmpɒsɪb<sup>ə</sup>l/ **1** ADJ Something that is **impossible** cannot be done or cannot happen. ❑ *It was impossible for anyone to get in because no one knew the password.* ❑ *Heavy snow in New York made it impossible to play the game.* ● **The impossible** is something that is impossible. ❑ *They expected us to do the impossible.* ● **im|pos|sibly** ADV ❑ *Mathematical physics is an almost impossibly difficult subject.* ● **im|pos|sibil|ity** /ɪmpɒsɪbɪlɪti/ (**impossibilities**) N-VAR ❑ ...*the impossibility of knowing the whole truth.* **2** ADJ An **impossible** situation or an **impossible** position is one that is very difficult to deal with. ❑ *He was in an impossible position.* **3** ADJ If you describe someone as **impossible**, you are annoyed that their bad behavior or strong views make them difficult to deal with. ❑ *You are an impossible man!* [from Latin]

---

**Word Partnership** Use *impossible* with :

| | |
|---|---|
| V. | impossible **to describe**, impossible **to find**, impossible **to prove**, impossible **to say/tell 1** |
| ADV. | **absolutely** impossible, **almost** impossible, **nearly** impossible **1 2** |
| N. | **an** impossible **task 1 2** |

---

**Word Link** | potent ≈ ability, power : impotent, potent, potential

---

**im|po|tent** /ɪmpətənt/ **1** ADJ If someone feels **impotent**, they feel that they have no power to influence people or events. ❑ *Bullying makes children feel depressed and impotent.* ● **im|po|tence** /ɪmpətəns/ N-UNCOUNT ❑ ...*a sense of national impotence.* **2** ADJ If a man is **impotent**, he is unable to get an erection. ● **im|po|tence** N-UNCOUNT ❑ *Impotence affects 10 million men in the U.S.* [from Latin]

**im|pound** /ɪmpaʊnd/ (**impounds, impounding, impounded**) V-T If something **is impounded** by police officers, customs officers, or other officials, they officially take it away from the owner because a law or rule has been broken. ❑ *The ship was impounded by customs officers.* [from Old English]

**im|pov|er|ish** /ɪmpɒvərɪʃ/ (**impoverishes, impoverishing, impoverished**) V-T Something that **impoverishes** a person or a country makes them poor. ❑ *Years of war have impoverished the country.* ● **im|pov|er|ished** ADJ ❑ *They put on a play for children in impoverished areas.* [from Old French]

**im|prac|ti|cal** /ɪmpræktɪk<sup>ə</sup>l/ ADJ If you describe an object, idea, or course of action as **impractical**, you mean that it is not sensible or realistic. ❑ *It is impractical to get there by train.* [from French]

**im|press** /ɪmprɛs/ (**impresses, impressing, impressed**) **1** V-T If something **impresses** you, you feel great admiration for it. ❑ *Their speed impressed everyone.* ● **im|pressed** ADJ ❑ *I was very impressed by his lecture.* **2** V-T If you **impress** something **on** someone, you make them understand its importance or degree. ❑ *I impressed the importance of hard work on the children.* [from Latin]

**im|pres|sion** /ɪmprɛʃ<sup>ə</sup>n/ (**impressions**)
**1** N-COUNT Your **impression** of a person or thing is what you think they are like. Your **impression** of a situation is what you think is going on. ❑ *What were your first impressions of college?* ❑ *My impression is that the kids are totally out of control.* **2** N-SING If someone gives you a particular **impression**, they cause you to believe that something is true, often when it is not. ❑ *I don't want to give the impression that I'm running away.* **3** N-COUNT An **impression** is an amusing imitation of someone's behavior or way of talking, usually someone well-known. ❑ ...*a great impression of the teacher.* **4** N-COUNT An **impression** of an object is a mark or outline that it has left after being pressed hard onto a surface. ❑ ...*impressions of dinosaur bones in the rock.* **5** PHRASE If someone or something **makes an impression**, they have a strong effect on people or a situation. ❑ *It's her first day at work and she has already made an impression.* **6** PHRASE If you are **under the impression that** something is true, you believe that it is true. ❑ *I was under the impression that you were angry.* [from Latin]

**im|pres|sive** /ɪmprɛsɪv/ ADJ Something that is **impressive** impresses you, for example, because it is great in size or degree, or is done with a lot of skill. ❑ ...*an impressive amount of cash: $390.8 million.* ● **im|pres|sive|ly** ADV ❑ ...*an impressively bright woman.* [from Latin]

**im|print** (**imprints, imprinting, imprinted**)

The noun is pronounced /ɪmprɪnt/. The verb is pronounced /ɪmprɪnt/.

**1** N-COUNT If something leaves an **imprint** on a place or on your mind, it has a strong and lasting effect on it. ❑ *The experience left a strong imprint on my mind.* **2** V-T When something **is imprinted on** your memory, it is firmly fixed in your memory so that you will not forget it. ❑ *The beautiful view was imprinted on my memory.* **3** N-COUNT An **imprint** is a mark or outline made by the pressure of one object on another. ❑ *She could see the imprint of his shoes in the earth.* **4** V-T If a surface **is imprinted with** a mark or design, that mark or design is printed on the surface or pressed into it. ❑ *The paper can be imprinted with your name and address.* [from Old French]

**im|pris|on** /ɪmprɪz<sup>ə</sup>n/ (**imprisons, imprisoning, imprisoned**) V-T If someone **is imprisoned**, they are locked up or kept somewhere. ❑ *He* *was imprisoned for 18 months.* • **im|pris|on|ment** /ɪmˈprɪzᵊnmənt/ N-UNCOUNT ❑ *She was sentenced to seven years' imprisonment.* [from Old French]

**im|prob|able** /ɪmˈprɒbəbᵊl/ ■ ADJ Something that is **improbable** is unlikely to be true or to happen. ❑ *It's improbable that he will come back.* • **im|prob|abil|ity** /ɪmˌprɒbəˈbɪlɪti/ (**improbabilities**) N-VAR ❑ *...the improbability of his explanation.* ■ ADJ If you describe something as **improbable**, you mean it is strange, unusual, or ridiculous. ❑ *They seem an improbable couple.* • **im|prob|ably** ADV ❑ *The sea is improbably pale.* [from Old French]

**im|promp|tu** /ɪmˈprɒmptu/ ADJ An **impromptu** action is one that you do without planning or organizing it in advance. ❑ *...an impromptu party.* [from French]

**im|prop|er** /ɪmˈprɒpər/ ■ ADJ **Improper** activities are illegal or dishonest. [FORMAL] ❑ *The two men were arrested for improper use of a computer.* • **im|prop|er|ly** ADV ❑ *I did not act improperly.* ■ ADJ **Improper** conditions or methods of treatment are not suitable or good enough for a particular purpose. [FORMAL] ❑ *The improper use of medicine could be dangerous.* • **im|prop|er|ly** ADV ❑ *Many doctors were improperly trained.* ■ ADJ If you describe someone's behavior as **improper**, you mean it is offensive or shocking. ❑ *He considered it improper for a young lady to go out alone.* • **im|prop|er|ly** ADV ❑ *He showed up at his job interview improperly dressed.* [from Old French]

**im|prove** /ɪmˈpruv/ (**improves, improving, improved**) ■ V-T/V-I If something **improves** or if you **improve** it, it gets better. ❑ *Your general health will improve if you drink more water.* ❑ *Their French has improved enormously.* • **im|prove|ment** /ɪmˈpruvmənt/ (**improvements**) N-VAR ❑ *...the dramatic improvements in technology in recent years.* ■ V-I If you **improve on** a previous achievement of your own or of someone else, you achieve a better standard or result. ❑ *We need to improve on our successes.* • **im|prove|ment** (**improvements**) N-COUNT ❑ *The new governor is an improvement on the previous one.* [from Late Latin]

**im|pro|vise** /ˈɪmprəvaɪz/ (**improvises, improvising, improvised**) ■ V-T/V-I If you **improvise**, you make or do something using whatever you have or without having planned it in advance. ❑ *If children don't have toys to play with, they improvise.* ❑ *I used socks to improvise a pair of gloves.* ■ V-T/V-I When performers **improvise**, they invent music or words as they

play, sing, or speak. ❑ *The jazz band improvised on well-known tunes.* ❑ *Richard improvised a prayer.* • **im|provi|sa|tion** /ɪmˌprɒvɪˈzeɪʃᵊn/ N-UNCOUNT [from French]

**im|pulse** /ˈɪmpʌls/ (**impulses**) ■ N-VAR An **impulse** is a sudden desire to do something. ❑ *She couldn't resist the impulse to look at him.* ■ N-COUNT An **impulse** is a short electrical signal that is sent along a wire or nerve or through the air, usually as one of a series. ❑ *The machine reads the electrical impulses and turns them into messages.* ■ PHRASE If you do something **on impulse**, you suddenly decide to do it, without planning it. ❑ *Sean usually acts on impulse.* [from Latin]

**im|pul|sive** /ɪmˈpʌlsɪv/ ADJ If you describe someone as **impulsive**, you mean that they do things suddenly without thinking about them carefully first. ❑ *He is too impulsive to be a parent.* • **im|pul|sive|ly** ADV ❑ *He said impulsively: "Let's get married."* [from Latin]

**im|pure** /ɪmˈpyʊər/ ADJ A substance that is **impure** is not of good quality because it has other substances mixed with it. ❑ *...impure water.* [from Old French]

**im|pu|rity** /ɪmˈpyʊərɪti/ (**impurities**) N-COUNT **Impurities** are substances that are present in small quantities in another substance and make it dirty or of an unacceptable quality. ❑ *The air is filtered to remove impurities.* [from Old French]

## in

| | |
|---|---|
| ❶ | POSITION OR MOVEMENT |
| ❷ | INCLUSION OR INVOLVEMENT |
| ❸ | TIME AND NUMBERS |
| ❹ | STATES AND QUALITIES |
| ❺ | OTHER USES AND PHRASES |

**❶ in**

The preposition is pronounced /ɪn/. The adverb is pronounced /ɪn/.

In addition to the uses shown below, **in** is used after some verbs, nouns, and adjectives in order to introduce extra information. **In** is also used with verbs of movement such as "walk" and "push," and in phrasal verbs such as "give in" and "dig in."

■ PREP Someone or something that is **in** something else is enclosed by it or surrounded by it. If you put something **in** a container, you move it so that it is enclosed by the container. ❑ *He was in his car.* ■ PREP If something happens **in** a place, it happens there. ❑ *We spent a few days in a hotel.* ■ ADV If you **are in**, you are present at your home or place of work. ❑ *My mother was in at the time.* ■ ADV When someone comes **in**, they enter a room or building. ❑ *She looked up as he came in.*

**5** ADV If a train, boat, or plane has come **in** or is **in**, it has arrived at a station, port, or airport. □ *A plane was coming in from Los Angeles.* **6** ADV When the ocean or tide comes **in**, the ocean moves toward the shore rather than away from it. □ *The tide rushed in, covering the sand.* **7** PREP Something that is **in** a window, especially a store window, is just behind the window so that you can see it from outside. □ *There was a camera for sale in the window.* **8** PREP When you see something **in** a mirror, the mirror shows an image of it. □ *I looked at my reflection in the mirror.* **9** PREP If you are dressed **in** a piece of clothing, you are wearing it. □ *He was in a suit and tie.* [from Old English]
→ see **location**

❷ **in** /ɪn/ **1** PREP If something is **in** a book, movie, play, or picture, you can read it or see it there. □ *I'll read you what it says in the book.* **2** PREP If you are **in** something such as a play or a race, you are one of the people involved with it. □ *Alfredo offered her a part in his play.* **3** PREP Something that is **in** a group or collection is a member of it or part of it. □ *The New England team is the worst in the country.* **4** PREP You use **in** to specify a general subject or field of activity. □ *He works in the music industry.* [from Old English]

❸ **in** /ɪn/ **1** PREP If something happens **in** a particular year, month, or other period of time, it happens during that time. □ *He was born in April 1996.* □ *Sales improved in the last month.* **2** PREP If you do something **in** a particular period of time, that is how long it takes you to do it. □ *He walked two hundred miles in eight days.* **3** PREP If something will happen **in** a particular length of time, it will happen after that length of time. □ *Breakfast will be ready in a few minutes.* **4** PREP You use **in** to indicate roughly how old someone is. For example, if someone is **in** their fifties, they are between 50 and 59 years old. □ *...young people in their twenties.* **5** PREP You use **in** to indicate roughly how many people or things do something. □ *People came in their thousands to hear him speak.* **6** PREP You use **in** to express a relationship between numbers. □ *One in three children can't find the U.S. on a map.* [from Old English]

❹ **in** /ɪn/ **1** PREP If something or someone is **in** a particular state or situation, that is their present state or situation. □ *The economy was in trouble.* □ *Dave was in a hurry to get back to work.* **2** PREP You use **in** to indicate the feeling or desire that someone has when they do something, or which causes them to do it. □ *Simpson looked at them in surprise.* **3** PREP You use **in** to indicate how someone is expressing something. □ *Can you give me the information in writing?* **4** PREP You use **in** in expressions such as **in a row** or **in a ball** to describe the arrangement or shape of something. □ *She put her shoes in a row on the floor.* **5** PREP You use **in** to specify which feature or aspect of something you are talking about. □ *The movie is nearly two hours in length.* [from Old English]

❺ **in** (ins)

Pronounced /ɪn/ for meanings **1** and **3** to **5**, and /ɪn/ for meaning **2**.

**1** ADJ If you say that something is **in**, or is the **in** thing, you mean it is fashionable or popular. [INFORMAL] □ *A few years ago jogging was the in thing.* **2** PHRASE If you say that someone **is in**

for a shock or a surprise, you mean they are going to experience it. □ *You might be in for a shock at how hard you have to work.* **3** PHRASE If someone **has it in for** you, they dislike you and try to cause problems for you. [INFORMAL] □ *The other kids had it in for me.* **4** PHRASE If you are **in on** something, you are involved in it or know about it. □ *She suspected him of being in on the plan.* **5** PHRASE You use **in that** to introduce an explanation of a statement you have just made. □ *I'm lucky in that I've got four sisters.* [from Old English]

<table><tr><td>**Word Link**</td><td>in ≈ not : **in**ability, **in**accurate, **in**adequate</td></tr></table>

**in·abil·ity** /ɪnəbɪlɪti/ N-UNCOUNT Someone's **inability to** do something is the fact that they are unable to do it. □ *Her inability to concentrate could cause an accident.* [from Old French]

**in·ac·ces·sible** /ɪnəksɛsɪbᵊl/ **1** ADJ An **inaccessible** place is very difficult or impossible to reach. □ *...people living in inaccessible parts of China.* **2** ADJ Someone or something that is **inaccessible** is difficult or impossible to understand or appreciate. □ *The language in the book is inaccessible to ordinary people.* [from Old French]

**in·ac·cu·rate** /ɪnækyərɪt/ ADJ If a statement or measurement is **inaccurate**, it is not accurate or correct. □ *The book is inaccurate and untrue.* ● **in·ac·cu·ra·cy** /ɪnækyərəsi/ (**inaccuracies**) N-VAR □ *...the inaccuracy of the answers.* [from Latin]

**in·ac·tion** /ɪnækʃᵊn/ N-UNCOUNT If you refer to someone's **inaction**, you disapprove of the fact that they are doing nothing. □ *The problem has been caused by the government's inaction.* [from Latin]

**in·ac·tive** /ɪnæktɪv/ ADJ Someone or something that is **inactive** is not doing anything or is not working. □ *He has always been politically inactive.* ● **in·ac·tiv·ity** /ɪnæktɪvɪti/ N-UNCOUNT □ *Long periods of inactivity are bad for you.* [from Latin]

**in·ad·equate** /ɪnædɪkwɪt/ **1** ADJ If something is **inadequate**, there is not enough of it or it is not good enough. □ *Supplies of food are inadequate.* ● **in·ad·equa·cy** /ɪnædɪkwəsi/ (**inadequacies**) N-VAR □ *...the inadequacy of the water supply.* ● **in·ad·equate·ly** ADV □ *The schools were inadequately funded.* **2** ADJ If someone feels **inadequate**, they feel that they do not have the qualities and abilities necessary to do something or to cope with life in general. □ *Many people are inadequately prepared for old age.* ● **in·ad·equa·cy** N-UNCOUNT □ *I had a feeling of inadequacy.* [from Latin]

**in·ad·vert·ent** /ɪnədvɜrtᵊnt/ ADJ An **inadvertent** action is one that you do without realizing what you are doing. □ *The army said it was an inadvertent mistake.* ● **in·ad·vert·ent·ly** ADV □ *You inadvertently pressed the wrong button.*

**in·ap·pro·pri·ate** /ɪnəproʊpriɪt/ ADJ Something that is **inappropriate** is not suitable for a particular situation or purpose. □ *The movie is inappropriate for young children.* [from Late Latin]

**in·as·much as** /ɪnəzmʌtʃæz/ PHRASE You use **inasmuch as** to introduce a statement that explains something you have just said, and adds to it. [FORMAL] □ *We were lucky inasmuch as my friend spoke Greek well.*

**in|augu|ral** /ɪnɔ̩gyərəl/ ADJ An **inaugural** meeting or speech is the first meeting of a new organization or the first speech by the new leader of an organization or a country. ❑ *The president gave his inaugural address.* [from French]

**in|augu|rate** /ɪnɔ̩gyʊreɪt/ (**inaugurates, inaugurating, inaugurated**) ◼ V-T When a new leader **is inaugurated,** they are formally given their new position at an official ceremony. ❑ *The new president will be inaugurated on January 20th.* • **in|augu|ra|tion** /ɪnɔ̩gyʊreɪᵊn/ (**inaugurations**) N-VAR ❑ *…the inauguration of the new governor.* ◼ V-T If you **inaugurate** a new system or service, you start it. [FORMAL] ❑ *Pan Am inaugurated the first scheduled international flight.* [from Latin]

**in|box** /ɪnbɒks/ also in-box ◼ N-COUNT An **inbox** is a shallow container used in offices to put letters and documents in before they are dealt with. ◼ N-COUNT On a computer, your **inbox** is the part of your mailbox which stores e-mails that have arrived for you. ❑ *I went home and checked my inbox.* [from Old English]

**Inc.** Inc. is an abbreviation for **Incorporated** when it is used after a company's name. [BUSINESS] ❑ *…BP America Inc.*

**in|ca|pable** /ɪnkeɪpəᵇl/ ADJ Someone who is **incapable of** doing something is unable to do it. ❑ *She seemed incapable of deciding what to do.* [from French]

**in|car|cer|ate** /ɪnkɑrsəreɪt/ (**incarcerates, incarcerating, incarcerated**) V-T If people **are incarcerated,** they are kept in a prison or other place. [FORMAL] ❑ *They were incarcerated for ten years.* • **in|car|cera|tion** N-UNCOUNT ❑ *…her incarceration in a psychiatric hospital.* [from Medieval Latin]

| Word Link | *carn ≈ flesh : carnage, carnation, incarnation* |

**in|car|na|tion** /ɪnkɑrneɪᵊn/ (**incarnations**) ◼ N-COUNT If you say that someone is the **incarnation of** a particular quality, you mean that they represent that quality or are typical of it in an extreme form. ❑ *The regime was an incarnation of evil.* ◼ N-COUNT An **incarnation** is one of the lives that a person has, according to some beliefs. ❑ *She believed she was a queen in a previous incarnation.* [from French]

**in|cen|di|ary** /ɪnsɛndieri/ ADJ **Incendiary** weapons or attacks are ones that cause large fires. ❑ *Five incendiary devices were found in her house.* [from Latin]

**in|cense** (**incenses, incensing, incensed**)

The noun is pronounced /ɪnsɛns/. The verb is pronounced /ɪnsɛns/.

◼ N-UNCOUNT **Incense** is a substance that is burned for its sweet smell, often as part of a religious ceremony. ◼ V-T If something **incenses** you, it makes you extremely angry. ❑ *This proposal will incense teachers.* • **in|censed** ADJ ❑ *Mom was incensed at his lack of compassion.* [Sense 1 from Old French. Sense 2 from Latin.]

**in|cen|tive** /ɪnsɛntɪv/ (**incentives**) N-VAR An **incentive** is something that encourages you to do something. ❑ *We want to give our employees an incentive to work hard.* [from Late Latin]

**in|ces|sant** /ɪnsɛsᵊnt/ ADJ An **incessant** process or activity is one that continues without stopping.

❑ *She hated the incessant rain.* • **in|ces|sant|ly** ADV ❑ *Dee talked incessantly about herself.* [from Late Latin]

**in|cest** /ɪnsɛst/ N-UNCOUNT **Incest** is the crime of two members of the same family having sexual intercourse. [from Latin]

**inch** /ɪntʃ/ (**inches, inching, inched**) ◼ N-COUNT An **inch** is a unit of length, approximately equal to 2.54 centimeters. There are twelve inches in a foot. ❑ *Dig a hole 18 inches deep.* ◼ V-T/V-I To **inch** somewhere or to **inch** something somewhere means to move there very slowly and carefully, or to make something do this. ❑ *A climber was inching up the wall of rock.* ❑ *He inched the van forward.* [from Old English]
→ see **measurement**

**in|ci|dence** /ɪnsɪdəns/ (**incidences**) N-VAR The **incidence of** something, especially something bad, is the frequency with which it occurs, or the occasions when it occurs. ❑ *…the high incidence of cancer within the same family.* [from Medieval Latin]

**in|ci|dent** /ɪnsɪdənt/ (**incidents**) N-COUNT An **incident** is something that happens, often something that is unpleasant. [FORMAL] ❑ *He was furious about the whole incident.* [from Medieval Latin]

| Thesaurus | *incident* Also look up : |
| N. | episode, event, fact, happening, occasion, occurrence |

**in|ci|den|tal** /ɪnsɪdɛntᵊl/ ADJ If one thing is **incidental** to another, it is less important than the other thing or is not a major part of it. ❑ *…scenes in the movie that are incidental to the plot.* [from Medieval Latin]

**in|ci|den|tal|ly** /ɪnsɪdɛntli/ ADV You use **incidentally** to introduce a point that is not directly relevant to what you are saying, often a question or extra information that you have just thought of. ❑ *She introduced me to her boyfriend (who, incidentally, doesn't speak a word of English).* [from Medieval Latin]

**in|cin|er|ate** /ɪnsɪnəreɪt/ (**incinerates, incinerating, incinerated**) V-T When authorities **incinerate** garbage or waste material, they burn it in a special container. ❑ *They were incinerating leaves.* • **in|cin|era|tion** /ɪnsɪnəreɪᵊn/ N-UNCOUNT ❑ *…the incineration of the weapons.* [from Medieval Latin]
→ see **dump**

**in|cin|era|tor** /ɪnsɪnəreɪtər/ (**incinerators**) N-COUNT An **incinerator** is a special large container for burning garbage at a very high temperature. [from Medieval Latin]

**in|ci|sive** /ɪnsaɪsɪv/ ADJ You use **incisive** to describe a person, their thoughts, or their speech when you approve of their ability to think and express their ideas clearly, briefly, and forcefully. ❑ *He has an incisive mind.* [from Latin]

**in|cite** /ɪnsaɪt/ (**incites, inciting, incited**) V-T If someone **incites** people to behave in a violent or illegal way, they encourage people to behave in that way. ❑ *The witness was incited to lie in court.* ❑ *The party agreed not to incite its supporters to violence.* • **in|cite|ment** (**incitements**) N-VAR ❑ *Insults can lead to the incitement of violence.* [from Latin]

**in|cli|na|tion** /ɪnklɪneɪ°n/ (**inclinations**) N-VAR
An **inclination** is a feeling that makes you want to
act in a particular way. ❑ *She showed no inclination to
go.* [from Latin]

| Word Link | clin ≈ leaning : decline, incline, recline |
|---|---|

**in|cline** (**inclines, inclining, inclined**)

> The noun is pronounced /ɪnklaɪn/. The verb is
> pronounced /ɪnklaɪn/.

■ N-COUNT An **incline** is land that slopes at an
angle. [FORMAL] ❑ *He stopped at the edge of a steep
incline.* ◻ V-T If you **incline to** think or act in a
particular way, or if something **inclines** you **to** it,
you are likely to think or act in that way. [FORMAL]
❑ *...factors that incline us toward particular beliefs.*
[from Latin]

**in|clined** /ɪnklaɪnd/ ■ ADJ If you say that you
are **inclined to** have a particular opinion, you
mean that you hold this opinion but you are not
expressing it strongly. ❑ *I am inclined to agree with
Alan.* ◻ ADJ Someone who is mathematically
**inclined** or artistically **inclined**, for example, has a
natural talent for mathematics or art. ❑ *...students
who are musically inclined.* [from Latin] ◻ → see also
**incline**

**in|clined plane** (**inclined planes**) N-COUNT An
**inclined plane** is a flat surface that is sloping at a
particular angle.

**in|clude** /ɪnklud/ (**includes, including,
included**) V-T If one thing **includes** another thing,
it has it as one of its parts. ❑ *The trip will include a
day at the beach.* [from Latin]

| Usage | include |
|---|---|

> Saying that a group *includes* one or more people
> or things implies that the group has additional
> people or things in it also. For instance, the
> sentence: *Cities in Japan include Tokyo and Kyoto*
> implies that Japan has additional cities.

**in|clud|ing** /ɪnkludɪŋ/ PREP You use **including**
to introduce examples of people or things that
are part of the group of people or things that you
are talking about. ❑ *Thousands were killed, including
many women and children.* [from Latin]

**in|clu|sion** /ɪnkluʒ°n/ (**inclusions**) N-VAR
**Inclusion** is the act of making a person or thing
part of a group or collection. ❑ *...his inclusion on the
baseball team.* [from Latin]

**in|clu|sive** /ɪnklusɪv/ ■ ADJ If you describe a
group or organization as **inclusive**, you mean that
it allows all kinds of people to belong to it, rather
than just one kind of person. ❑ *The college is far
more inclusive now than it used to be.* ◻ ADJ After
stating the first and last item in a set of things,
you can add **inclusive** to make it clear that the
items stated are included in the set. ❑ *I will be
away on vacation from June 6 to June 14 inclusive.* ◻ ADJ
If a price is **inclusive**, it includes all the charges
connected with the goods or services offered. If
a price is **inclusive of** shipping and handling, it
includes the charge for this. ❑ *All prices are inclusive
of delivery.* ● **Inclusive** is also an adverb. ❑ *The trip
costs $105 per day, all inclusive.* [from Latin]

**in|co|her|ent** /ɪnkoʊhɪərənt/ ADJ If someone
is **incoherent**, they are talking in a confused and
unclear way. ❑ *The man was incoherent with fear.*

**in|come** /ɪnkʌm/ (**incomes**) N-VAR A person's
or organization's **income** is the money that they
earn or receive. [BUSINESS] ❑ *...families on low
incomes.* [from Old English]

| Word Partnership | Use *income* with : |
|---|---|
| ADJ. | **average** income, **fixed** income, **large/ small** income, **a second** income, **steady** income, **taxable** income |
| V. | **earn** *an* income, **supplement** *your* income |
| N. | **loss of** income, **source of** income |

**in|come tax** (**income taxes**) N-VAR **Income
tax** is a part of your income that you have to pay
regularly to the government. [BUSINESS] ❑ *You pay
income tax every month.*

**in|com|ing** /ɪnkʌmɪŋ/ ■ ADJ An **incoming**
message or phone call is one that you receive. ❑ *We
keep a record of incoming calls.* ◻ ADJ An **incoming**
plane or passenger is one that is arriving at a
place. ❑ *The airport was closed to incoming flights.*
[from Old English]

**in|com|pat|ible** /ɪnkəmpætɪb°l/ ADJ If one
thing or person is **incompatible with** another,
they are very different in important ways, and
do not suit each other or agree with each other.
❑ *She feels that this work is incompatible with her
beliefs.* ● **in|com|pat|ibil|ity** /ɪnkəmpætɪbɪlɪti/
N-UNCOUNT ❑ *...the incompatibility of these two ideas.*
[from Medieval Latin]

**in|com|pe|tent** /ɪnkɒmpɪtənt/ ADJ If you
describe someone as **incompetent**, you are
criticizing them because they are unable to do
their job or a task properly. ❑ *He threatened to
fire incompetent employees.* ● **in|com|pe|tence**
N-UNCOUNT ❑ *The incompetence of government
officials is shocking.* [from Latin]

**in|com|plete** /ɪnkəmplit/ ADJ Something that
is **incomplete** is not yet finished, or does not have
all the parts or details that it needs. ❑ *The data we
have is incomplete.* [from Latin]

**in|com|pre|hen|sible** /ɪnkɒmprɪhɛnsɪb°l/ ADJ
Something that is **incomprehensible** is impossible
to understand. ❑ *...incomprehensible mathematics
puzzles.*

**in|con|ceiv|able** /ɪnkənsivəb°l/ ADJ If you
describe something as **inconceivable**, you think
it is very unlikely to happen or be true. ❑ *It was
inconceivable to me that Toby could lie.* [from Old
French]

**in|con|clu|sive** /ɪnkənklusɪv/ ADJ If something
is **inconclusive**, it does not provide any clear
answer or result. ❑ *Research has so far proved
inconclusive.* [from Old French]

**in|con|gru|ous** /ɪnkɒŋgruəs/ ADJ Someone
or something that is **incongruous** seems strange
when considered together with other aspects
of a situation. [FORMAL] ❑ *She was small and
fragile and looked incongruous in an army uniform.*
● **in|con|gru|ous|ly** ADV ❑ *He wore a dark suit and an
incongruously bright tie.*

**in|con|sid|er|ate** /ɪnkənsɪdərɪt/ ADJ If you
accuse someone of being **inconsiderate**, you are
critical of them because they do not take enough
care over how their words or actions will affect
other people. ❑ *It was inconsiderate of her not to tell
you she was coming.* [from Latin]

**in|con|sist|ent** /ɪnkənsɪ́stənt/ **1** ADJ If you describe someone as **inconsistent**, you are criticizing them for not behaving in the same way every time a similar situation occurs. ❑ *You are inconsistent and unpredictable.* ● **in|con|sist|en|cy** N-UNCOUNT ❑ *His worst fault was his inconsistency.* **2** ADJ If something is **inconsistent with** a set of ideas or values, it does not fit in well with them or match them. ❑ *This new law is inconsistent with the idea of freedom of speech.*

**in|con|ti|nent** /ɪnkɒ́ntɪnənt/ ADJ Someone who is **incontinent** is unable to prevent urine or feces from coming out of their body. ❑ *His disease made him incontinent.* ● **in|con|ti|nence** N-UNCOUNT ❑ *Incontinence is not just a condition of old age.* [from Old French]

**in|con|ven|ience** /ɪnkənvíːnyəns/ (**inconveniences, inconveniencing, inconvenienced**) **1** N-VAR If someone or something causes **inconvenience**, they cause problems or difficulties. ❑ *We apologize for any inconvenience caused during the repairs.* **2** V-T If someone **inconveniences** you, they cause problems or difficulties for you. ❑ *He apologized and promised not to inconvenience them any further.* [from Latin]

**in|con|ven|ient** /ɪnkənvíːnyənt/ ADJ Something that is **inconvenient** causes problems or difficulties for someone. ❑ *Can you come at 10.30? I know it's inconvenient, but I have to see you now.* [from Latin]

**in|cor|po|rate** /ɪnkɔ́ːpəreɪt/ (**incorporates, incorporating, incorporated**) V-T If one thing **incorporates** another thing, it includes the other thing. [FORMAL] ❑ *The new cars will incorporate a number of major changes.* [from Late Latin]

**In|cor|po|rated** /ɪnkɔ́ːpəreɪtɪd/ ADJ **Incorporated** is used after a corporation's name to show that it is a legally established company in the United States. [BUSINESS] ❑ *...MCA Incorporated.* [from Late Latin]

**in|cor|rect** /ɪnkərékt/ ADJ Something that is **incorrect** is wrong or untrue. ❑ *The answer he gave was incorrect.* ● **in|cor|rect|ly** ADV ❑ *The article suggested, incorrectly, that he was planning to retire.* [from Latin]

> **Word Link** cresc, creas ≈ growing : crescent, decrease, increase

**in|crease** (**increases, increasing, increased**)

> The verb is pronounced /ɪnkríːs/. The noun is pronounced /ɪ́nkriːs/.

increase

**1** V-T/V-I If something **increases** or you **increase** it, it becomes greater in number, level, or amount. ❑ *The population continues to increase.* ❑ *Japanese exports increased by 2% last year.* **2** N-COUNT If there is an **increase** in the number, level, or amount of something, it becomes greater. ❑ *...a sharp increase in cost.* **3** PHRASE If something is **on the increase**, it is happening more often or becoming greater in number or intensity. ❑ *Crime is on the increase.* [from Old French]

> **Thesaurus** *increase* Also look up :
>
> V. expand, extend, raise; (ant.) decrease, reduce **1**
> N. gain, hike, raise, rise; (ant.) decrease, reduction **2**

> **Word Partnership** Use *increase* with :
>
> ADV. increase **dramatically**, increase **rapidly 1**
> N. **population** increase, **price** increase, **salary** increase **1**
> increase **in crime**, increase **in demand**, increase **in spending**, increase **in temperature**, increase **in value 2**
> ADJ. **big** increase, **marked** increase, **sharp** increase **1 2**

**in|creas|ing|ly** /ɪnkríːsɪŋli/ ADV You can use **increasingly** to indicate that a situation or quality is becoming greater in intensity or more common. ❑ *He was finding it increasingly difficult to make decisions.* [from Old French]

> **Word Link** cred ≈ to believe : credentials, credibility, incredible

**in|cred|ible** /ɪnkrédɪbəl/ **1** ADJ If you describe something or someone as **incredible**, you like them very much or are impressed by them, because they are extremely or unusually good. ❑ *The food was incredible.* ● **in|cred|ibly** ADV ❑ *Their father was incredibly good-looking.* **2** ADJ If you say that something is **incredible**, you mean that it is very unusual or surprising, and you cannot believe it is really true, although it may be. ❑ *It seemed incredible that people still wanted to play football during a war.* ● **in|cred|ibly** ADV ❑ *Incredibly, some people don't like the name.* **3** ADJ You use **incredible** to emphasize the degree, amount, or intensity of something. ❑ *I work an incredible number of hours.* ● **in|cred|ibly** ADV ❑ *It was incredibly hard work.* [from Latin]

> **Word Partnership** Use *incredible* with :
>
> N. incredible **discovery**, incredible **prices 1** incredible **experience 1 – 3**
> ADV. **absolutely** incredible **1 – 3**

**in|credu|lous** /ɪnkrédʒələs/ ADJ If someone is **incredulous**, they are unable to believe something because it is very surprising or shocking. ❑ *Her voice was incredulous.* ● **in|credu|lous|ly** ADV ❑ *"You told Pete?" Rachel said incredulously.* [from Latin]

**in|crimi|nate** /ɪnkrɪ́mɪneɪt/ (**incriminates, incriminating, incriminated**) V-T If something **incriminates** you, it suggests that you are responsible for something bad, especially a crime. ❑ *They are afraid of incriminating themselves.* ● **in|crimi|nat|ing** ADJ ❑ *...incriminating evidence.* [from Late Latin]

**in|cum|bent** /ɪnkʌ́mbənt/ (**incumbents**) N-COUNT An **incumbent** is someone who holds an official post at a particular time. [FORMAL] ❑ *Incumbents usually have a high chance of being re-elected.* ● **Incumbent** is also an adjective. ❑ *...the only candidate who defeated an incumbent senator.* [from Latin]

**in|cur** /ɪnkɜ̱r/ (**incurs, incurring, incurred**) V-T If you **incur** something unpleasant, it happens to you because of something you have done. [WRITTEN] ☐ *The government incurred huge debts.* [from Latin]

**in|cur|able** /ɪnkyʊ̱ərəbᵊl/ **1** ADJ An **incurable** disease cannot be cured. ☐ *He is suffering from an incurable skin disease.* ● **in|cur|ably** /ɪnkyʊ̱ərəbli/ ADV ☐ *...youngsters who are incurably ill.* **2** ADJ You can use **incurable** to indicate that someone has a particular quality or attitude and will not change. ☐ *Bill is an incurable romantic.* ● **in|cur|ably** ADV ☐ *I know you think I'm incurably nosy, but I'm worried about you.* [from Old French]

**in|debt|ed** /ɪnde̱tɪd/ ADJ If you say that you are **indebted to** someone, you mean that you are very grateful to them for something. ☐ *I am indebted to him for his help.*

**in|de|cent** /ɪndi̱sᵊnt/ ADJ If you describe something as **indecent**, you mean that it is shocking and offensive, usually because it relates to sex or nakedness. ☐ *...indecent material on the Internet.* ● **in|de|cen|cy** /ɪndi̱sᵊnsi/ N-UNCOUNT ☐ *...the indecency of their language.* ● **in|de|cent|ly** ADV ☐ *...an indecently short skirt.* [from Latin]

**in|de|ci|sion** /ɪndɪsɪ̱ʒᵊn/ N-UNCOUNT If someone suffers from **indecision**, they find it very difficult to make decisions. ☐ *After months of indecision, the government agreed to the plan.* [from Old French]

**in|de|ci|sive** /ɪndɪsa̱ɪsɪv/ ADJ If someone is **indecisive**, they find it very difficult to make decisions. ☐ *He was criticized as a weak and indecisive leader.* [from Old French]

**in|deed** /ɪndi̱d/ **1** ADV You use **indeed** to confirm or agree with something that has just been said. ☐ *He admitted that he had indeed paid him.* ☐ *"Did you know him?" — "I did indeed."* **2** ADV You use **indeed** to introduce a further comment or statement that strengthens the point you have already made. ☐ *We have nothing against change; indeed, we encourage it.* **3** ADV You use **indeed** at the end of a clause to give extra force to the word "very," or to emphasize a particular word. ☐ *The results were very strange indeed.* [from Old English]

**in|defi|nite** /ɪnde̱fɪnɪt/ **1** ADJ If a situation or period is **indefinite**, people have not decided when it will end. ☐ *He was sent to jail for an indefinite period.* ● **in|defi|nite|ly** ADV ☐ *The visit has been postponed indefinitely.* **2** ADJ Something that is **indefinite** is not exact or clear. ☐ *...indefinite fears about the future.* [from Latin]

**in|defi|nite ar|ti|cle** (**indefinite articles**) N-COUNT The words "a" and "an" are sometimes called the **indefinite article**.

**in|defi|nite pro|noun** (**indefinite pronouns**) N-COUNT An **indefinite pronoun** is a pronoun such as "someone," "anything," or "nobody" that you use to refer in a general way to a person or thing.

**in|de|pend|ent** /ɪndɪpɛ̱ndənt/ (**independents**) **1** ADJ If one thing or person is **independent of** another, they are separate and not connected,

so the first one is not affected or influenced by the second. ☐ *The two organizations are completely independent of one another.* ● We need an independent review. ● **in|de|pen|dent|ly** ADV ☐ *...people working independently in different parts of the world.* **2** ADJ If someone is **independent**, they do not need help or money from anyone else. ☐ *Children become more independent as they grow.* ● **in|de|pend|ence** N-UNCOUNT ☐ *Her financial independence was very important to her.* ● **in|de|pen|dent|ly** ADV ☐ *We want to help disabled students to live independently.* **3** ADJ **Independent** countries and states are not ruled by other countries but have their own government. ☐ *Papua New Guinea became independent from Australia in 1975.* ● **in|de|pend|ence** N-UNCOUNT ☐ *Argentina declared its independence from Spain in 1816.*

**in-depth** ADJ An **in-depth** analysis or study of something is a very detailed and complete study of it. ☐ *...an in-depth look at film-making.*

**in|dex** /ɪ̱ndɛks/ (**indices, indexes, indexing, indexed**)

The usual plural is **indexes**, but the form **indices** can be used for meaning **1**.

**1** N-COUNT An **index** is a system by which changes in the value of something can be recorded, measured, or interpreted. ☐ *...a change in the consumer price index.* **2** N-COUNT An **index** is an alphabetical list that is printed at the back of a book and tells you on which pages important topics are referred to. ☐ *There's a subject index at the back of the book.* **3** V-T If you **index** a book or a collection of information, you make an alphabetical list of the items in it. ☐ *Songs are indexed alphabetically by title.* **4** V-T If a quantity or value **is indexed to** another, a system is arranged so that it increases or decreases whenever the other one increases or decreases. ☐ *My bonus is indexed to the company's profits.* [from Latin]

**in|dex con|tour** (**index contours**) also **index contour line** N-COUNT An **index contour** is a thick contour line on a map which shows the height of the area marked by the line. [TECHNICAL]

**in|di|cate** /ɪ̱ndɪkeɪt/ (**indicates, indicating, indicated**) **1** V-T If one thing **indicates** another, the first thing shows that the second is true or exists. ☐ *The survey indicates that most people agree.* **2** V-T If you **indicate** an opinion, an intention, or a fact, you mention it in an indirect way. ☐ *Mr. Rivers indicated that he might leave the company.* **3** V-T If you **indicate** something to someone, you show them where it is. [FORMAL] ☐ *He indicated a chair. "Sit down."* [from Latin]

**in|di|ca|tion** /ɪ̱ndɪkeɪ̱ʃᵊn/ (**indications**) N-VAR An **indication** is a sign that suggests, for example, what people are thinking or feeling. ☐ *We have no* *indication of where he is.* [from Latin]

**in|dica|tive** /ɪndɪkətɪv/ ADJ If one thing is **indicative** of another, it suggests what the other thing is likely to be. [FORMAL] ❑ *Often a person's appearance is indicative of how they feel.* [from Latin]

**in|di|ca|tor** /ɪndɪkeɪtər/ (**indicators**)
■ N-COUNT An **indicator** is a measurement or value that gives you an idea of what something is like. ❑ *The phone has a low battery indicator.* ■ [from Latin]

**in|di|ces** /ɪndɪsiz/ **Indices** is a plural form of **index.** [from Latin]

**in|dict** /ɪndaɪt/ (**indicts, indicting, indicted**)
V-T If someone **is indicted for** a crime, they are officially charged with it. [LEGAL] ❑ *He was indicted and arrested yesterday.* ● **in|dict|ment** /ɪndaɪtmənt/ (**indictments**) N-VAR [LEGAL] ❑ *Steele said the indictment came as a surprise to him.*

**in|dict|ment** /ɪndaɪtmənt/ (**indictments**)
■ N-COUNT If you say that one thing is **an indictment of** another thing, you mean that it shows how bad the other thing is. ❑ *The movie is an indictment of Hollywood.* ■ → see also **indict**

**in|dif|fer|ent** /ɪndɪfərənt/ ■ ADJ If you accuse someone of being **indifferent to** something, you mean that they have a complete lack of interest in it. ❑ *People have become indifferent to the suffering of others.* ● **in|dif|fer|ence** N-UNCOUNT ❑ *...his cruel indifference to his son.* ● **in|dif|fer|ent|ly** ADV ❑ *"It doesn't really matter," said Tom indifferently.* ■ ADJ If you describe something or someone as **indifferent,** you mean that their standard or quality is not very good, and often quite bad. ❑ *She starred in several very indifferent movies.* [from Latin]

**in|dig|enous** /ɪndɪdʒɪnəs/ ADJ **Indigenous** people or things belong to the country in which they are found, rather than coming there or being brought there from another country. [FORMAL] ❑ *...the country's indigenous population.* [from Latin]

**in|di|ges|tion** /ɪndɪdʒɛstʃⁿn, -daɪ-/ N-UNCOUNT If you have **indigestion,** you have pains in your stomach and chest that are caused by difficulties in digesting food.

---

**Word Link** **dign ≈ proper, worthy : dignified, dignitary, indignant**

**in|dig|nant** /ɪndɪgnənt/ ADJ If you are **indignant,** you are shocked and angry, because you think that something is unjust or unfair. ❑ *He is indignant at suggestions that they were spies.* ● **in|dig|nant|ly** ADV ❑ *"That is not true," Erica said indignantly.* [from Latin]

**in|dig|na|tion** /ɪndɪgneɪʃⁿn/ N-UNCOUNT **Indignation** is a feeling of shock and anger when you think that something is unjust or unfair. ❑ *The story filled me with indignation.* [from Old French]

**in|dig|nity** /ɪndɪgnɪti/ (**indignities**) N-VAR If you talk about **the indignity of** doing something, you mean that it makes you feel embarrassed or unimportant. [FORMAL] ❑ *He suffered the indignity of having to clean the floor.* [from Old French]

**in|di|rect** /ɪndaɪrɛkt, -dɪr-/ ■ ADJ An **indirect** result or effect is not caused immediately and obviously by a thing or person, but happens because of something else that they have done. ❑ *Millions could die of hunger as an indirect result of the war.* ● **in|di|rect|ly** ADV ❑ *The government is indirectly*

---

*responsible for the violence.* ■ ADJ An **indirect** route or journey does not use the shortest or easiest way between two places. ❑ *He took an indirect route back home.* ■ ADJ **Indirect** remarks and information suggest something or refer to it, without actually mentioning it or stating it clearly. ❑ *...an indirect criticism of the president.* ● **in|di|rect|ly** ADV ❑ *He referred indirectly to their divorce.* [from Latin]

**in|di|rect dis|course** N-UNCOUNT **Indirect discourse** tells you what someone said but does not use the person's actual words: for example, "They said you didn't like it," "I asked him what his plans were," and "People complained about the smoke."

**in|di|rect ob|ject** (**indirect objects**) N-COUNT An **indirect object** is an object that is used with a transitive verb to indicate who benefits from an action or gets something as a result. For example, in "She gave him her address", "him" is the indirect object. Compare **direct object.**

**in|di|rect speech** N-UNCOUNT **Indirect speech** is the same as **indirect discourse.**

**in|dis|crimi|nate** /ɪndɪskrɪmɪnɪt/ ADJ If you describe an action as **indiscriminate,** you are critical of it because it does not involve any careful thought or choice. ❑ *Indiscriminate use of chemicals is dangerous.* ● **in|dis|crimi|nate|ly** ADV ❑ *The disease kills indiscriminately.* [from Latin]

**in|dis|pen|sable** /ɪndɪspɛnsəbⁿl/ ADJ If you say that someone or something is **indispensable,** you mean that they are absolutely essential and other people or things cannot function without them. ❑ *She was indispensable to the company.*

**in|dis|put|able** /ɪndɪspyutəbⁿl/ ADJ If you say that something is **indisputable,** you are emphasizing that it is true and cannot be shown to be untrue. ❑ *It is indisputable that the firefighters are heroes.*

**in|dis|tin|guish|able** /ɪndɪstɪŋgwɪʃəbⁿl/ ADJ If one thing is **indistinguishable from** another, the two things are so similar that it is difficult to know which is which. ❑ *Fake passports are often indistinguishable from real ones.*

**in|di|vid|ual** /ɪndɪvɪdʒuⁿl/ (**individuals**) ■ ADJ **Individual** means relating to one person or thing, rather than to a large group. ❑ *You should decide as a group rather than making individual decisions.* ● **in|di|vid|ual|ly** ADV ❑ *...individually made pies.* ■ N-COUNT An **individual** is a person. ❑ *We want to reward individuals who do good within our community.* [from Medieval Latin]

---

**Thesaurus** **individual** Also look up :

N. human being, person ■
PRON. somebody, someone ■

---

**in|di|vidu|al|ity** /ɪndɪvɪdʒuælɪti/ N-UNCOUNT The **individuality** of a person or thing consists of the qualities that make them different from other people or things. ❑ *People should be free to express their individuality.* [from Medieval Latin]

**in|door** /ɪndɔr/ ADJ **Indoor** activities or things are ones that happen or are used inside a building and not outside. ❑ *The matches were moved to an indoor tennis club 40 miles away.* [from Old English]

**in|doors** /ɪndɔrz/ ADV If something happens **indoors,** it happens inside a building. ❑ *I think we should go indoors.* [from Old English]

## Word Web · industry

There are three general categories of **industry**. Primary industry means **extracting raw materials** from the environment. Examples include **agriculture, forestry,** and **mining**. In secondary industry people **refine** raw materials to make new **products**. It also includes **assembling** parts made by other **manufacturers**. There are two types of secondary industry—**light industry** (such as **textile weaving**) and **heavy industry** (such as shipbuilding). The third industry, tertiary industry, is **service**, which does not produce a product. Some examples are **banking, tourism,** and education. Recently, computers have created millions of jobs in the **information technology** field. Some researchers describe this as a fourth type of industry.

**in|duce** /ɪndjuːs/ (**induces, inducing, induced**)
◼ V-T To **induce** a state or condition means to cause it. ❑ *Doctors said surgery could induce a heart attack.* ◼ V-T If you **induce** someone to do something, you persuade or influence them to do it. ❑ *More than 4,000 teachers were induced to retire early.* [from Latin]

**in|duce|ment** /ɪndjuːsmənt/ (**inducements**)
N-COUNT An **inducement** is something that might persuade someone to do a particular thing. ❑ *They offer inducements to foreign businesses to open up in their country.* [from Latin]

**in|duct** /ɪndʌkt/ (**inducts, inducting, inducted**)
V-T If someone **is inducted into** the army, they are officially made to join the army. ❑ *He was inducted into the army.* [from Latin]

**in|duc|tion** /ɪndʌkʃⁿn/ (**inductions**) ◼ N-VAR **Induction** is a procedure or ceremony for introducing someone to a new job, organization, or way of life. ❑ ...*his induction as president.* ◼ N-UNCOUNT **Induction** is the process by which electricity or magnetism is passed between two objects or circuits without them touching each other. [TECHNICAL] [from Latin]

**in|dulge** /ɪndʌldʒ/ (**indulges, indulging, indulged**) ◼ V-T/V-I If you **indulge in** something or if you **indulge yourself**, you allow yourself to have or do something that you know you will enjoy. ❑ *She occasionally indulges in a candy bar.* ❑ *In New York you can indulge your passion for art.* ◼ V-T If you **indulge** someone, you let them have or do what they want, even if this is not good for them. ❑ *He did not agree with indulging children.* [from Latin]

**in|dul|gent** /ɪndʌldʒⁿnt/ ADJ If you are **indulgent**, you treat a person with special kindness, often in a way that is not good for them. ❑ *His indulgent mother gave him anything he wanted.* ● **in|dul|gence** (**indulgences**) N-VAR ❑ *A teacher should not show too much indulgence.* ● **in|dul|gent|ly** ADV ❑ *Najib smiled at him indulgently.* [from Latin]

**in|dus|trial** /ɪndʌstriəl/ ◼ ADJ You use **industrial** to describe things that relate to or are used in industry. ❑ ...*industrial machinery and equipment.* ◼ ADJ An **industrial** city or country is one in which industry is important or highly developed. ❑ ...*Western industrial countries.* [from Latin]

### Word Partnership    Use *industrial* with :

| | |
|---|---|
| N. | industrial **machinery**, industrial **production**, industrial **products** ◼ industrial **area**, industrial **city**, industrial **country** ◼ |

**in|dus|tri|al|ist** /ɪndʌstriəlɪst/ (**industrialists**)
N-COUNT An **industrialist** is a person who owns or controls large industrial companies or factories. ❑ *They contacted well-known Japanese industrialists.* [from Latin]

**in|dus|tri|al|ize** /ɪndʌstriəlaɪz/ (**industrializes, industrializing, industrialized**) V-T/V-I When a country **industrializes** or **is industrialized**, it develops a lot of industries. ❑ *By the late nineteenth century, both Russia and Japan had begun to industrialize.* ● **in|dus|tri|ali|za|tion** /ɪndʌstriəlaɪzeɪʃⁿn/ N-UNCOUNT ❑ *Industrialization began early in Spain.* [from Latin]

**in|dus|trial park** (**industrial parks**) N-COUNT An **industrial park** is an area which has been specially planned for a lot of factories.

**in|dus|trial re|la|tions** N-PLURAL **Industrial relations** refers to the relationship between employers and employees in industry, and the political decisions and laws that affect it. [BUSINESS] ❑ ...*an attempt to make industrial relations better.*

**in|dus|try** /ɪndəstri/ (**industries**)
◼ N-UNCOUNT **Industry** is the work and processes involved in making things in factories. ❑ *Industry needs to carry out more research.* ◼ N-COUNT A particular **industry** consists of all the people and activities involved in making a particular product or providing a particular service. ❑ ...*the tourism industry in this area has been flourishing for some years.* [from Latin]
→ see Word Web: **industry**

**in|ed|ible** /ɪnɛdɪbⁿl/ ADJ If something is **inedible**, you cannot eat it, for example, because it tastes bad or is poisonous. ❑ *The food was so bad it was inedible.* [from Late Latin]
→ see **cooking**

**in|ef|fec|tive** /ɪnɪfɛktɪv/ ADJ If you say that something is **ineffective**, you mean that it has no effect on a process or situation. ❑ *The new rules are ineffective.* [from Latin]

**in|ef|fec|tual** /ɪnɪfɛktʃuəl/ ADJ If someone or something is **ineffectual**, they fail to do what they are expected to do or are trying to do. ❏ *…a weak and ineffectual president.* • **in|ef|fec|tu|al|ly** ADV ❏ *Her voice trailed off ineffectually.*

**in|ef|fi|cient** /ɪnɪfɪʃ⁰nt/ ADJ **Inefficient** people, organizations, systems, or machines do not use time, energy, or other resources in the best way. ❏ *Their communication systems are inefficient.* • **in|ef|fi|cien|cy** (**inefficiencies**) N-VAR ❏ *The inefficiency of the sales department has lost millions of dollars for the company.* • **in|ef|fi|cient|ly** ADV ❏ *Many of us use energy inefficiently.* [from Latin]

**in|ept** /ɪnɛpt/ ADJ If you say that someone is **inept**, you are criticizing them because they do something with a complete lack of skill. ❏ *Plimpton was the most inept player ever to play for the team.* [from Latin]

**in|equal|ity** /ɪnɪkwɒlɪti/ (**inequalities**) **1** N-VAR **Inequality** is the difference in social status, wealth, or opportunity between people or groups. ❏ *People are worried about social inequality.* **2** N-VAR In mathematics, an **inequality** is the relationship between two quantities that are not equal. Sometimes **inequality** is also used to mean that one quantity is either greater than or equal to another quantity. [TECHNICAL] [from Latin]

| Word Partnership | Use *inequality* with : |
| --- | --- |
| ADJ. | **economic** inequality, **growing/ increasing** inequality, **racial** inequality, **social** inequality **1** |
| N. | **gender** inequality, **income** inequality **1** |

**in|ert** /ɪnɜrt/ ADJ Someone or something that is **inert** does not move at all. ❏ *He covered the inert body with a blanket.* [from Latin]

**in|er|tia** /ɪnɜrʃə/ **1** N-UNCOUNT If you have a feeling of **inertia**, you feel very lazy and unwilling to move or be active. ❏ *He was annoyed by her inertia, her lack of energy.* **2** N-UNCOUNT **Inertia** is the tendency of a physical object to remain still or to continue moving, unless a force is applied to it. [TECHNICAL] [from Latin]

**in|es|cap|able** /ɪnɪskeɪpəb⁰l/ ADJ If you describe a fact, situation, or activity as **inescapable**, you mean that it is difficult not to notice it or be affected by it. ❏ *The inescapable conclusion is that the accident was his fault.*

**in|evi|table** /ɪnɛvɪtəb⁰l/ ADJ If something is **inevitable**, it is certain to happen and cannot be prevented or avoided. ❏ *Suffering is an inevitable part of life.* • **The inevitable** is something that is inevitable. ❏ *Prepare yourself for the inevitable.* • **in|evi|tabil|ity** /ɪnɛvɪtəbɪlɪti/ N-VAR ❏ *…the inevitability of death.* • **in|evi|tably** /ɪnɛvɪtəbli/ ADV ❏ *Technological changes will inevitably lead to unemployment.* [from Latin]

**in|exo|rable** /ɪnɛksərəb⁰l/ ADJ You use **inexorable** to describe a process that cannot be prevented from continuing or progressing. [FORMAL] ❏ *…the inexorable rise in unemployment.* • **in|exo|rably** /ɪnɛksərəbli/ ADV ❏ *Spending on health is growing inexorably.* [from Latin]

**in|ex|pen|sive** /ɪnɪkspɛnsɪv/ ADJ Something that is **inexpensive** does not cost very much. ❏ *There are a number of good, inexpensive restaurants.* [from Late Latin]

**in|ex|pe|ri|ence** /ɪnɪkspɪəriəns/ N-UNCOUNT If you refer to someone's **inexperience**, you mean that they have little knowledge or experience of a particular situation or activity. ❏ *Critics attacked the inexperience of his staff.* [from Latin]

**in|ex|pe|ri|enced** /ɪnɪkspɪəriənst/ ADJ If you are **inexperienced**, you have little knowledge or experience of a particular situation or activity. ❏ *…inexperienced young doctors.* [from Latin]

**in|ex|pli|cable** /ɪnɛksplɪkəb⁰l, ɪnɪksplɪk-/ ADJ If something is **inexplicable**, you cannot explain why it happens or why it is true. ❏ *His behavior was inexplicable.* • **in|ex|pli|cably** /ɪnɛksplɪkəbli, ɪnɪksplɪk-/ ADV ❏ *She suddenly and inexplicably said she was leaving.*

**in|ex|tri|cably** /ɪnɛkstrɪkəbli, ɪnɪkstrɪk-/ ADV If two or more things are **inextricably** linked, they cannot be considered separately. [FORMAL] ❏ *Our survival is inextricably linked to the survival of the rainforest.*

**in|fa|mous** /ɪnfəməs/ ADJ **Infamous** people or things are well-known because of something bad. [FORMAL] ❏ *He was infamous for his part in a racist attack.* [from Latin]

**in|fan|cy** /ɪnfənsi/ **1** N-UNCOUNT **Infancy** is the period of your life when you are a baby or very young child. ❏ *…the way our brains develop during infancy.* **2** N-UNCOUNT If something is in its **infancy**, it is new and has not developed very much. ❏ *Computing science was still in its infancy.*

**in|fant** /ɪnfənt/ (**infants**) N-COUNT An **infant** is a baby or very young child. [FORMAL] ❏ *He held the infant in his arms.* ❏ *…their infant son.* [from Latin]
→ see **age**, **child**

**in|fan|try** /ɪnfəntri/ N-UNCOUNT **Infantry** are soldiers who fight on foot. ❏ *…an infantry division.* [from Italian]

**in|fect** /ɪnfɛkt/ (**infects, infecting, infected**) **1** V-T To **infect** people, animals, or plants means to cause them to have a disease or illness. ❏ *A single mosquito can infect a large number of people.* ❏ *You can't catch the disease just by touching an infected person.* • **in|fec|tion** /ɪnfɛkʃ⁰n/ N-UNCOUNT ❏ *Any form of cut can lead to infection.* **2** V-T If a virus **infects** a computer, it damages or destroys files or programs. [COMPUTING] ❏ *This virus infected thousands of computers across the world.* [from Latin]

| Word Partnership | Use *infect* with : |
| --- | --- |
| PRON. | **infect others 1** |
| N. | **bacteria** infect, infect **cells**, infect **people 1** **viruses** infect, infect **with a virus 1 2** |

**in|fec|tion** /ɪnfɛkʃ⁰n/ (**infections**) **1** N-COUNT An **infection** is a disease caused by germs or bacteria. ❏ *Ear infections are common in young children.* [from Latin] **2** → see also **infect**
→ see **diagnosis**

| Word Partnership | Use *infection* with : |
| --- | --- |
| N. | **cases of** infection, **rates of** infection, **risk of** infection, **symptoms of** infection **1** |
| V. | **cause an** infection, **have an** infection, **prevent** infection, **spread an** infection **1** |

**in|fec|tious** /ɪnfɛkʃəs/ ■ ADJ A disease that is **infectious** can be caught by being near a person who has it. Compare **contagious**. ❑ ...*infectious diseases such as measles.* ■ ADJ If a feeling is **infectious**, it spreads to other people. ❑ *She has an infectious enthusiasm for everything she does.* [from Latin]
→ see **illness**

**in|fer** /ɪnfɜr/ (**infers, inferring, inferred**) V-T If you **infer** that something is true, you decide that it is true on the basis of information that you already have. ❑ *I inferred from what she said that you were sick.* [from Latin]
→ see also **imply**

**in|fer|ence** /ɪnfərəns/ (**inferences**) N-COUNT An **inference** is a conclusion that something is true. ❑ *What inferences did you draw from her letter?* [from Latin]

**in|fe|ri|or** /ɪnfɪəriər/ (**inferiors**) ■ ADJ Something that is **inferior** is not as good as something else. ❑ *The fruit was of inferior quality.* ■ ADJ If one person is regarded as **inferior to** another, they are regarded as less important because they have less status or ability. ❑ *Successful people made him feel inferior.* ● **Inferior** is also a noun. ❑ *The general was always polite, even to his inferiors.* ● **in|fe|ri|or|ity** /ɪnfɪriɒrɪti/ N-UNCOUNT ❑ *I felt a sense of social inferiority.* [from Latin]

**in|fer|tile** /ɪnfɜrtˀl/ ■ ADJ A person or animal that is **infertile** is unable to produce babies. ❑ *One woman in eight is infertile.* ● **in|fer|til|ity** /ɪnfɜrtɪlɪti/ N-UNCOUNT ❑ *Male infertility is becoming more common.* ■ ADJ **Infertile** soil is of poor quality because it lacks substances that plants need. ❑ *The land was poor and infertile.* [from Latin]

**in|fi|del|ity** /ɪnfɪdɛlɪti/ (**infidelities**) N-VAR **Infidelity** occurs when a person who is married or in a steady relationship has sex with another person. ❑ *George ignored his partner's infidelities.* [from Latin]

**in|field** /ɪnfild/ (**infields**) ■ N-COUNT In baseball, the **infield** is the part of the playing field that is inside the area marked by the four bases. ❑ ...*the right side of the infield.* ■ ADV In sports such as soccer and rugby, if players move **infield**, they move toward the center of the playing field. ❑ *Farrell threw himself infield and caught the ball.* [from Old English]

**in|fil|trate** /ɪnfɪltreɪt/ (**infiltrates, infiltrating, infiltrated**) V-T If people **infiltrate** a place or organization, they enter it secretly in order to spy on it or influence it. ❑ *Spies infiltrated the organization.* ● **in|fil|tra|tion** /ɪnfɪltreɪʃˀn/ (**infiltrations**) N-VAR ❑ ...*the recent infiltration by a terrorist group.*

**in|fi|nite** /ɪnfɪnɪt/ ■ ADJ If you describe something as **infinite**, you are emphasizing that it is extremely great in amount or degree. ❑ ...*an infinite variety of plants.* ❑ *With infinite care, John laid down the baby.* ● **in|fi|nite|ly** ADV ❑ *His design was infinitely better than anything I could have done.* ■ ADJ Something that is **infinite** has no limit, end, or edge. ❑ ...*an infinite number of stars.* ● **in|fi|nite|ly** ADV ❑ *A centimeter can be infinitely divided into smaller units.* [from Latin]

**in|fini|tive** /ɪnfɪnɪtɪv/ (**infinitives**) N-COUNT The **infinitive** of a verb is the basic form, for example, "do," "be," "take," and "eat." The

infinitive is often used with "to" in front of it. [from Latin]

**in|fin|ity** /ɪnfɪnɪti/ ■ N-UNCOUNT **Infinity** is a number that is larger than any other number and can never be given an exact value. ■ N-UNCOUNT **Infinity** is a point that is further away than any other point and can never be reached. ❑ ...*job applicants whose experience ranged from zero to infinity.* [from Latin]

**in|fir|ma|ry** /ɪnfɜrməri/ (**infirmaries**) N-COUNT An **infirmary** is a place in a school or other institution that is used to take care of people who are sick or injured. [from Late Middle English]

**in|flame** /ɪnfleɪm/ (**inflames, inflaming, inflamed**) V-T If something **inflames** a situation or **inflames** people's feelings, it makes people feel even more strongly about something. ❑ *His comments have just inflamed the situation.* [from Old French]

**in|flamed** /ɪnfleɪmd/ ADJ If part of your body is **inflamed**, it is red or swollen, usually as a result of an infection, injury, or illness. ❑ *The infection causes painful and inflamed skin.* [from Old French]

**in|flam|ma|tion** /ɪnfləmeɪʃˀn/ (**inflammations**) N-VAR An **inflammation** is a painful redness or swelling of a part of your body that results from an infection, injury, or illness. ❑ *The drug can cause inflammation of the heart.* [from Old French]

**in|flam|ma|tory** /ɪnflæmətɔri/ ADJ **Inflammatory** words or actions are likely to make people react very angrily. ❑ *He made inflammatory comments about immigrants.* [from Old French]

**in|flat|able** /ɪnfleɪtəbˀl/ ADJ An **inflatable** object is one that you fill with air when you want to use it. ❑ *The children were playing on the inflatable castle.* [from Latin]

**in|flate** /ɪnfleɪt/ (**inflates, inflating, inflated**) V-T/V-I If you **inflate** something such as a balloon or tire, or if it **inflates**, it becomes bigger as it is filled with air or a gas. ❑ *The children's parents inflated the balloons.* [from Latin]

inflate

**in|fla|tion** /ɪnfleɪʃˀn/ N-UNCOUNT **Inflation** is a general increase in the prices of goods and services in a country. [BUSINESS] ❑ ...*rising unemployment and high inflation.* [from Latin]

**in|fla|tion|ary** /ɪnfleɪʃəneri/ ADJ **Inflationary** means causing or relating to inflation. [BUSINESS] ❑ ...*the government's inflationary policies.* [from Latin]

**in|flect** /ɪnflɛkt/ (**inflects, inflecting, inflected**) V-I If a word **inflects**, its ending or form changes in order to show its grammatical function. If a language **inflects**, it has words in it that inflect.

● in|flect|ed ADJ ❑ *German is a highly inflected language.* [from Latin]

in|flec|tion /ɪnflɛkʃ°n/ (**inflections**) N-VAR An **inflection** in your voice is a change in its tone or pitch as you are speaking. [WRITTEN] ❑ *A question has an upward inflection.* [from Latin]

in|flex|ible /ɪnflɛksɪb°l/ **1** ADJ Something that is **inflexible** cannot be altered in any way, even if the situation changes. ❑ *Workers said the new system was too inflexible.* ● in|flex|ibil|ity /ɪnflɛksɪbɪlɪti/ N-UNCOUNT ❑ *Marvin's father was known for the inflexibility of his rules.* **2** ADJ If you say that someone is **inflexible**, you are criticizing them because they refuse to change their mind or alter their way of doing things. ❑ *He is stubborn and inflexible.* ● in|flex|ibil|ity N-UNCOUNT ❑ *Joyce was angry at the inflexibility of her colleagues.* [from Latin]

---

**Word Link** flict ≈ striking : af*flict*ion, con*flict*, in*flict*

---

in|flict /ɪnflɪkt/ (**inflicts, inflicting, inflicted**) V-T To **inflict** harm or damage **on** someone or something means to make them suffer it. ❑ *...sports which inflict pain on animals.* [from Latin]

in|flu|ence /ɪnfluəns/ (**influences, influencing, influenced**) **1** N-UNCOUNT **Influence** is the power to make other people agree with your opinions or do what you want. ❑ *He used his influence to get his son into medical school.* **2** V-T If you **influence** someone, you use your power to make them agree with you or do what you want. ❑ *He tried to influence a witness.* **3** N-COUNT To have an **influence on** people or situations means to affect what they do or what happens. ❑ *Van Gogh had a big influence on the development of modern painting.* **4** V-T If someone or something **influences** a person or situation, they have an effect on that person's behavior or that situation. ❑ *We became the best of friends and he influenced me deeply.* **5** N-COUNT Someone or something that is a good or bad **influence on** people has a good or bad effect on them. ❑ *I thought Sonny would be a good influence on you.* [from Medieval Latin]

in|flu|en|tial /ɪnfluɛnʃ°l/ ADJ Someone or something that is **influential** has a lot of influence over people or events. ❑ *It helps to have influential friends.* ❑ *He was influential in changing the law.* [from Medieval Latin]

in|flux /ɪnflʌks/ (**influxes**) N-COUNT An **influx of** people or things into a place is their arrival there in large numbers. ❑ *...problems caused by the influx of refugees.* [from Late Latin]

info /ɪnfoʊ/ N-UNCOUNT **Info** is information. [INFORMAL] ❑ *For more info call 414-3935.*

in|form /ɪnfɔrm/ (**informs, informing, informed**) V-T If you **inform** someone **of** something, you tell them about it. ❑ *We will inform you of any changes.* ❑ *My daughter informed me that she was pregnant.* [from Latin]

in|for|mal /ɪnfɔrm°l/ ADJ **Informal** speech, behavior, or situations are relaxed and friendly rather than serious, very correct, or official. ❑ *Her style of teaching is very informal.* ❑ *The house has an informal atmosphere.* ● in|for|mal|ly ADV ❑ *She was chatting informally to the children.* [from Latin]

---

**Thesaurus** informal Also look up :

| N. | casual, natural, relaxed, unofficial; *(ant.)* formal |
|----|-------------------------------------------------------|

---

in|for|mal thea|ter N-UNCOUNT **Informal theater** is drama that is performed in somewhere such as a classroom or workshop and is not usually intended to be seen by the general public.

in|form|ant /ɪnfɔrmənt/ (**informants**) N-COUNT An **informant** is someone who gives information to another person, especially to the police. [FORMAL] ❑ *He was a informant for the government.* [from Latin]

in|for|ma|tion /ɪnfɔrmeɪʃ°n/ **1** N-UNCOUNT **Information** about someone or something consists of facts about them. ❑ *Pat did not give her any information about Sarah.* ❑ *We can provide information on training.* **2** N-UNCOUNT **Information** is a service that you can telephone to find out someone's telephone number. ❑ *He called information, and they gave him the number.* [from French]

---

**Word Partnership** Use *information* with :

| ADJ. | **additional** information, **background** information, **important** information, **personal** information **1** |
|------|--------------------------------------------------------|
| V. | **find** information, **get** information, **have** information, **provide** information, **retrieve** information, **want** information **1** |

---

in|for|ma|tion tech|nol|ogy N-UNCOUNT **Information technology** is the theory and practice of using computers to store and analyze information. The abbreviation **IT** is often used. ❑ *...the information technology industry.* → see **industry**

in|forma|tive /ɪnfɔrmətɪv/ ADJ Something that is **informative** gives you useful information. ❑ *The meeting was friendly and informative.* [from French]

in|formed /ɪnfɔrmd/ **1** ADJ Someone who is **informed** knows about a subject or what is happening in the world. ❑ *Informed people know the company is in trouble.* **2** → see also **well-informed** **3** ADJ An **informed** guess or decision is one that is likely to be good, because it is based on definite knowledge or information. ❑ *We can now make informed choices about medical treatment.* [from Latin] **4** → see also **inform**

in|form|er /ɪnfɔrmər/ (**informers**) N-COUNT An **informer** is a person who tells the police that someone has done something illegal. ❑ *The two men are police informers.* [from Old French]

in|frac|tion /ɪnfrækʃ°n/ (**infractions**) N-COUNT An **infraction** of a rule or law is an instance of breaking it. ❑ *...an infraction of school rules.* [from Late Latin]

infra|red /ɪnfrərɛd/ **1** ADJ **Infrared** radiation is similar to light but has a longer wavelength, so you cannot see it without special equipment. **2** ADJ **Infrared** equipment detects infrared radiation. ❑ *...infrared scanners.* → see **sun**

infra|struc|ture /ɪnfrəstrʌktʃər/ (**infrastructures**) N-VAR The **infrastructure** of a country, society, or organization consists of the basic facilities such as transportation, communications, power supplies, and buildings, which enable it to function. ❑ ...*improvements in the country's infrastructure.*

in|fringe /ɪnfrɪndʒ/ (**infringes, infringing, infringed**) ◼ V-T If someone **infringes** a law or a rule, they break it. ❑ *The article infringed his copyright by quoting from his book without asking him first.* • in|fringe|ment /ɪnfrɪndʒmənt/ (**infringements**) N-VAR ❑ *There has been an infringement of the rules.* ◻ V-T/V-I If something **infringes** people's rights, or **infringes** on them, it interferes with these rights and does not allow people the freedom they are entitled to. ❑ *This would infringe freedom of the press.* • in|fringe|ment (**infringements**) N-VAR ❑ ...*infringement of privacy.* [from Latin]

in|furi|ate /ɪnfyʊərieɪt/ (**infuriates, infuriating, infuriated**) V-T If something or someone **infuriates** you, they make you extremely angry. ❑ *His behavior infuriated her.* • in|furi|at|ing ADJ ❑ *It's infuriating to watch them play so badly.* [from Medieval Latin]

in|fuse /ɪnfyuz/ (**infuses, infusing, infused**) V-T To **infuse** a quality into someone or something, or to **infuse** them **with** a quality, means to fill them with it. [FORMAL] ❑ *Their relationship was infused with tension.* [from Latin]

in|gen|ious /ɪndʒinyəs/ ADJ Something that is **ingenious** is very clever and involves new ideas, methods, or equipment. ❑ ...*an ingenious invention.* [from Latin]

in|genu|ity /ɪndʒənuɪti/ N-UNCOUNT **Ingenuity** is skill at working out how to achieve things or skill at inventing new things. ❑ *Solving this problem will take ingenuity.* [from Latin]

in|grained /ɪngreɪnd/ ADJ **Ingrained** habits and beliefs are difficult to change or remove. ❑ *People's beliefs about right and wrong are often deeply ingrained.*

in|gre|di|ent /ɪngridiənt/ (**ingredients**) ◼ N-COUNT **Ingredients** are the things that are used to make something, especially all the different foods you use when you are cooking a particular meal. ❑ *Mix together all the ingredients.* ◻ N-COUNT An **ingredient** of a situation is one of the essential parts of it. ❑ *The movie has all the ingredients of a Hollywood success.* [from Latin]

| Word Partnership | Use *ingredient* with : |
| --- | --- |
| ADJ. | **active** ingredient, **a common** ingredient, **secret** ingredient ◼ **important** ingredient, **key** ingredient, **main** ingredient ◼ ◻ |

in|hab|it /ɪnhæbɪt/ (**inhabits, inhabiting, inhabited**) V-T If a place or region **is inhabited** by a group of people or a species of animal, those people or animals live there. ❑ *The house next to mine is inhabited by a 90-year-old.* ❑ ...*the people who inhabit these islands.* [from Latin]

in|hab|it|ant /ɪnhæbɪtənt/ (**inhabitants**) N-COUNT The **inhabitants** of a place are the people who live there. ❑ ...*the inhabitants of the town.* [from Latin]

in|hale /ɪnheɪl/ (**inhales, inhaling, inhaled**) V-T/V-I When you **inhale**, you breathe in. When you **inhale** something such as smoke, you take it into your lungs when you breathe in. ❑ *He took a long*

slow breath, inhaling deeply. [from Latin]
→ see **respiration**

inhale

in|her|ent /ɪnhɛrənt, -hɪər-/ ADJ The **inherent** qualities of something are the necessary and natural parts of it. ❑ *Stress is an inherent part of life.* • in|her|ent|ly ADV ❑ *Airplanes are not inherently dangerous.* [from Latin]

in|her|it /ɪnhɛrɪt/ (**inherits, inheriting, inherited**) ◼ V-T If you **inherit** money or property, you receive it from someone who has died. ❑ *He has no child to inherit his house.* ◻ V-T If you **inherit** something such as a task, problem, or attitude, you get it from the people who used to have it. ❑ *The government has inherited a difficult situation.* ◼ V-T If you **inherit** a characteristic or quality, you are born with it, because your parents or ancestors also had it. ❑ *We inherit a lot of our behavior from our parents.* ❑ *Her children have inherited her love of sports.* [from Old French]

in|her|it|ance /ɪnhɛrɪtᵊns/ (**inheritances**) ◼ N-VAR An **inheritance** is money or property that you receive from someone who has died. ❑ *She used her inheritance to buy a house.* ◻ N-COUNT If you get something such as job, problem, or attitude from someone who used to have it, you can refer to this as an **inheritance**. ❑ *The new president's inheritance was high unemployment.* [from Old French]

in|hib|it /ɪnhɪbɪt/ (**inhibits, inhibiting, inhibited**) V-T If something **inhibits** an event or process, it prevents it or slows it down. ❑ *This law inhibits freedom of speech.* [from Latin]

in|hib|it|ed /ɪnhɪbɪtɪd/ ADJ If you say that someone is **inhibited**, you mean that they find it difficult to behave naturally and show their feelings, and that you think this is a bad thing. ❑ *He was too inhibited to join in the singing.* [from Latin]

in|hi|bi|tion /ɪnɪbɪʃᵊn/ (**inhibitions**) N-VAR **Inhibitions** are feelings of fear or embarrassment that make it difficult for you to behave naturally. ❑ *When you dance you can lose all your inhibitions.* [from Latin]

in|hib|i|tor /ɪnhɪbɪtər/ (**inhibitors**) N-COUNT An **inhibitor** is a substance that slows down or stops a chemical reaction. [TECHNICAL] [from Latin]

in|hu|man /ɪnhyumən/ ◼ ADJ If you describe treatment or an action as **inhuman**, you mean that it is extremely cruel. ❑ *The prisoners are held in inhuman conditions.* ◻ ADJ If you describe someone or something as **inhuman**, you mean that they are strange or bad because they do not seem human in some way. ❑ ...*inhuman screams and moans.* [from Latin]

ini|tial /ɪnɪʃᵊl/ (**initials, initialing, initialed**) ◼ ADJ You use **initial** to describe something that happens at the beginning of a process. ❑ *The initial reaction has been excellent.* ◻ N-COUNT **Initials** are the capital letters that begin each word of a name. ❑ ...*a silver car with her initials JB on the side.* ◼ V-T If someone **initials** an official document, they write their initials on it, to show that they have seen it or that they accept or agree with it. ❑ *Would you mind initialing this check?* [from Latin]

**ini|tial con|so|nant** (**initial consonants**) also
**initial blend** N-COUNT In linguistics, **initial
consonants** are two or more letters that begin a
word and are pronounced in their normal way
when they are joined, for example the letters "b"
and "l" in "blue". [TECHNICAL]

**ini|tial|ly** /ɪnɪʃəli/ ADV **Initially** means soon
after the beginning of a process or situation,
rather than in the middle or at the end of it. ◻ *The
storms are not as bad as we initially thought.* [from
Latin]

**ini|ti|ate** /ɪnɪʃieɪt/ (**initiates, initiating,
initiated**) **1** V-T If you **initiate** something, you
start it or cause it to happen. ◻ *He wanted to initiate
a discussion on education.* • **ini|tia|tion** /ɪnɪʃieɪʃⁿn/
N-UNCOUNT ◻ *...the initiation of a program of changes.*
**2** V-T If someone **is initiated into** something
such as a religion, secret society, or social group,
they become a member of it during a special
ceremony. ◻ *In many societies, young people are
formally initiated into their adult roles.* • **ini|tia|tion**
(**initiations**) N-VAR ◻ *This was my initiation into the
peace movement.* [from Latin]

**ini|tia|tive** /ɪnɪʃiətɪv, -ʃətɪv/ (**initiatives**)
**1** N-COUNT An **initiative** is an important act or
statement that is intended to solve a problem.
◻ *...new initiatives to help young people.* **2** N-SING
If you have **the initiative**, you are in a stronger
position than your opponents because you are able
to do something first. ◻ *We'll make sure we don't lose
the initiative.* **3** N-UNCOUNT If you have **initiative**,
you have the ability to decide what to do next and
to do it, without needing other people to tell you
what to do. ◻ *Don't keep asking me for help — use your
initiative.* **4** N-COUNT An **initiative** is a political
procedure in which a group of citizens propose a
new law or a change to the law, which all voters
can then vote on. ◻ *The public will vote on the
initiative in May.* **5** PHRASE If you **take the initiative**
in a situation, you are the first person to act, and
are therefore able to control the situation. ◻ *We
must take the initiative and end the war.* [from Latin]

**in|ject** /ɪndʒɛkt/ (**injects, injecting, injected**)
**1** V-T To **inject** a substance such as a medicine
into someone means to put it into their body
using a device with a needle called a syringe.
◻ *She was injected with painkillers.* ◻ *The doctor
injected morphine into him.* **2** V-T If you **inject** a new,
exciting, or interesting quality **into** a situation,
you add it. ◻ *She tried to inject a little fun into their
relationship.* **3** V-T If you **inject** money or resources
**into** a business or organization, you provide more
money or resources for it. [BUSINESS] ◻ *We need to
inject money into the economy.* [from Latin]

**in|jec|tion** /ɪndʒɛkʃⁿn/ (**injections**) **1** N-COUNT
If you have an **injection**, a doctor or nurse puts
a medicine into your body using a device with a
needle called a syringe. ◻ *They gave me an injection
to help me sleep.* **2** N-COUNT An **injection of** money
or resources into an organization is the act of
providing it with more money or resources,
to help it become more efficient or profitable.
[BUSINESS] ◻ *An injection of cash is needed to fund
these projects.* [from Latin]

**in|junc|tion** /ɪndʒʌŋkʃⁿn/ (**injunctions**)
N-COUNT An **injunction** is a court order, usually
one telling someone not to do something. [LEGAL]
◻ *He got an injunction which stopped the newspaper
from printing the story.* [from Late Latin]

**in|jure** /ɪndʒər/ (**injures, injuring, injured**) V-T If
you **injure** a person or animal, you damage some
part of their body. ◻ *The bomb seriously injured at
least five people.*
→ see **war**

| Word Partnership | Use *injure* with : |
| --- | --- |
| V. | **kill or** injure |
| ADV. | **seriously** injure |
| PRON. | injure *someone*, injure *yourself* |

**in|jured** /ɪndʒərd/ **1** ADJ An **injured** person
or animal has physical damage to part of their
body, usually as a result of an accident or fighting.
◻ *Nurses helped the injured man.* • **The injured** are
people who are injured. ◻ *Army helicopters moved
the injured.* **2** ADJ If you have **injured** feelings, you
feel upset because you believe someone has been
unfair or unkind to you. ◻ *...a look of injured pride.*

| Word Partnership | Use *injured* with : |
| --- | --- |
| N. | injured **in an accident/attack**, injured **people 1** |
| ADV. | **badly** injured, **critically** injured, **seriously** injured **1** |
| ADJ. | **dead/killed and** injured **1** |
| V. | **get** injured, **rescue the** injured **1** |

**in|ju|ry** /ɪndʒəri/ (**injuries**) **1** N-VAR An **injury**
is damage done to a person's or an animal's body.
◻ *He died from his injuries at Hope Hospital.* [from
Latin] **2** to **add insult to injury** → see **insult**

| Word Partnership | Use *injury* with : |
| --- | --- |
| ADJ. | **bodily** injury, **internal** injury, **minor** injury, **personal** injury, **serious** injury, **severe** injury **1** |
| V. | **escape** injury, **suffer an** injury **1** |

**in|jus|tice** /ɪndʒʌstɪs/ (**injustices**) N-VAR
**Injustice** is a lack of fairness in a situation.
◻ *They'll continue to fight injustice.* [from Old French]

**ink** /ɪŋk/ (**inks**) N-VAR **Ink** is the colored liquid
used for writing or printing. ◻ *She wrote in black
ink.* [from Old French]

**in|land**

The adverb is pronounced /ɪnlænd, -lənd/. The
adjective is pronounced /ɪnlənd/.

**1** ADV If something is situated **inland**, it is away
from the coast, toward or near the middle of a
country. ◻ *Most of the population live inland.* ◻ *It's
about 15 minutes' drive inland from Pensacola.* **2** ADJ
**Inland** areas, lakes, and places are not on the coast,
but in or near the middle of a country. ◻ *...a quiet
inland town.* [from Old English]

**in-laws** N-PLURAL Your **in-laws** are the parents
and close relatives of your husband or wife. ◻ *He
spent Thanksgiving with his in-laws.*

| Word Link | let ≈ little : book*let*, drop*let*, in*let* |
| --- | --- |

**in|let** /ɪnlɛt, -lɪt/ (**inlets**) N-COUNT An **inlet** is
a narrow strip of water that goes from an ocean
or lake into the land. ◻ *...a fishing village by a rocky
inlet.* [from Old English]

**in-line skate** (**in-line skates**) N-COUNT **In-line
skates** are a type of roller skates with a single line
of wheels along the bottom.

**in|mate** /ɪnmeɪt/ (**inmates**) N-COUNT The **inmates** of a prison or mental hospital are the prisoners or patients who live there. □ …*a programme of education for prison inmates.* [from Middle Low German]

**inn** /ɪn/ (**inns**) N-COUNT An **inn** is a hotel, or restaurant, often one in the country. □ …*the Waterside Inn.* [from Old English]

**in|nate** /ɪneɪt/ ADJ An **innate** quality or ability is one that a person is born with. □ *The men had an innate sense of style and good taste.* ● **in|nate|ly** ADV □ *Kids are innately curious.* [from Latin]

**in|ner** /ɪnər/ **1** ADJ The **inner** parts of something are the parts contained or enclosed inside the other parts, closest to the center. □ *The room opened onto an inner courtyard.* **2** ADJ Your **inner** feelings are feelings that you have but do not show to other people. □ *Loving relationships give a child an inner sense of security.* [from Old English]

**in|ner cir|cle** (**inner circles**) N-COUNT An **inner circle** is a small group of people within a larger group who have a lot of power, influence, or special information. □ …*my inner circle of friends.*

**in|ner city** (**inner cities**) N-COUNT You use **inner city** to refer to the areas in or near the center of a large city where people live and where there are often social and economic problems. □ …*problems of crime in the inner city.*
→ see **city**

**in|ner core** (**inner cores**) N-COUNT The **inner core** of the Earth is the central part of the Earth's interior. It is solid and made of nickel and iron.

**in|no|cence** /ɪnəsəns/ **1** N-UNCOUNT **Innocence** is the quality of having no experience or knowledge of the more complex or unpleasant aspects of life. □ …*the sweet innocence of youth.* **2** N-UNCOUNT If someone proves their **innocence**, they prove that they are not guilty of a crime. □ *She has information which could prove his innocence.* [from Latin]

**in|no|cent** /ɪnəsənt/ (**innocents**) **1** ADJ If someone is **innocent**, they did not commit a crime that they have been accused of. □ *He was sure that the man was innocent.* **2** ADJ If someone is **innocent**, they have no experience or knowledge of the more complex or unpleasant aspects of life. □ *They seemed so young and innocent.* ● An **innocent** is someone who is innocent. □ *Greg was a complete innocent regarding women.* ● **in|no|cent|ly** ADV □ *She smiled innocently.* **3** ADJ **Innocent** people are those who are not involved in a crime or conflict, but are injured or killed as a result of it. □ *The bombing had many innocent victims.* **4** ADJ An **innocent** question, remark, or comment is not intended to offend or upset people, even if it does so. □ *It was an innocent question, I didn't mean to upset her.* [from Latin]

### Word Partnership    Use *innocent* with :

| | |
|---|---|
| v. | **plead** innocent, **presumed** innocent, **proven** innocent **1** |
| N. | innocent **man/woman 1** innocent **children 2** innocent **bystander**, innocent **civilians**, innocent **people**, innocent **victim 3** |

**in|nocu|ous** /ɪnɒkyuəs/ ADJ Something that is **innocuous** is not at all harmful or offensive.

[FORMAL] □ *The mushrooms look innocuous but are in fact deadly.* [from Latin]

### Word Link    nov = new : in*nov*ation, *nov*el, re*nov*ate

**in|no|va|tion** /ɪnəveɪʃ°n/ (**innovations**) **1** N-COUNT An **innovation** is a new thing or a new method of doing something. □ *Vegetarian burgers were an innovation which quickly spread across the world.* **2** N-UNCOUNT **Innovation** is the introduction of new ideas, methods, or things. □ *Technological innovation is very important to business.* [from Latin]

**in|no|va|tive** /ɪnəveɪtɪv/ **1** ADJ Something that is **innovative** is new and original. □ …*innovative products.* **2** ADJ An **innovative** person introduces changes and new ideas. □ *He was one of the most creative and innovative engineers of his generation.* [from Latin]
→ see **technology**

**in|no|va|tor** /ɪnəveɪtər/ (**innovators**) N-COUNT An **innovator** is someone who introduces changes and new ideas. □ *He is an innovator in fashion.* [from Latin]

**in|nu|en|do** /ɪnyuɛndoʊ/ (**innuendoes** or **innuendos**) N-VAR **Innuendo** is indirect reference to something offensive or unpleasant. □ *The report was based on rumors and innuendo.* [from Latin]

### Word Link    numer ≈ number : in*numer*able, *numer*ous, *numer*ical

**in|nu|mer|able** /ɪnumərəb°l/ ADJ **Innumerable** means very many, or too many to be counted. □ *She had innumerable medical tests.*

**in|or|di|nate** /ɪnɔrd°nɪt/ ADJ If you describe something as **inordinate**, you are emphasizing that it is unusually or excessively great in amount or degree. [FORMAL] □ *They spend an inordinate amount of time talking.* ● **in|or|di|nate|ly** ADV □ *He is inordinately proud of his wife.* [from Latin]

**in|put** /ɪnpʊt/ (**inputs, inputting, input**) **1** N-VAR **Input** consists of information or resources that someone receives. □ *We value the students' input in planning the class.* **2** N-UNCOUNT **Input** is information that is put into a computer. [COMPUTING] □ *The computer processes input to produce reports.* **3** V-T If you **input** information into a computer, you put it in, for example, by typing it on a keyboard. [COMPUTING] □ *We need more keyboarders to input the data.* [from Old English]

**in|put force** (**input forces**) N-VAR In physics, the **input force** is the effort that is applied to a machine such as a lever or pulley in order to do work. Compare **output force**. [TECHNICAL]

**in|quest** /ɪnkwɛst/ (**inquests**) N-COUNT An **inquest** is an official inquiry into the cause of someone's death. □ *The inquest into their deaths began yesterday.* [from Medieval Latin]

**in|quire** /ɪnkwaɪər/ (**inquires, inquiring, inquired**) **1** V-T/V-I If you **inquire** about something, you ask for information about it. [FORMAL] □ *"What are you doing here?" she inquired.* □ *He called them to inquire about job possibilities.* **2** V-I If you **inquire into** something, you investigate it carefully. □ *Inspectors will inquire into the company's affairs.* [from Latin]

## Thesaurus  inquire  Also look up :

v.   ask, question, quiz ■

**in|quir|ing** /ɪnkwaɪərɪŋ/ ■ ADJ If you have an **inquiring** mind, you have a great interest in learning new things. ❏ *He has a very active and inquiring mind.* ■ ADJ If someone has an **inquiring** expression on their face, they are showing that they want to know something. [WRITTEN] ❏ *She gave an inquiring look at his dirty clothes.* [from Latin]

**in|quiry** /ɪnkwaɪəri, ɪŋkwɪri/ (**inquiries**) ■ N-COUNT An **inquiry** is a question you ask in order to get some information. ❏ *He made some inquiries and discovered she had gone to Connecticut.* ■ N-COUNT An **inquiry** is an official investigation. ❏ *...an official murder inquiry.* [from Latin]

**in|quisi|tive** /ɪnkwɪzɪtɪv/ ADJ An **inquisitive** person likes finding out about things, especially secret things. ❏ *Barrow has an inquisitive nature.* [from Latin]

**in|roads** /ɪnroʊdz/ PHRASE If one thing **makes inroads into** another, the first thing starts affecting or destroying the second. ❏ *Television has made inroads into movie audiences.*

### Word Link  san ≈ health : insane, sane, sanitation

**in|sane** /ɪnseɪn/ ■ ADJ Someone who is **insane** is severely mentally ill. ❏ *Some people cannot cope and just go insane.* ● **in|san|ity** /ɪnsænɪti/ N-UNCOUNT ❏ *...a psychiatrist who specialized in diagnosing insanity.* ■ ADJ If you describe a decision or action as **insane**, you think it is very foolish or excessive. ❏ *I thought the idea was completely insane.* ● **in|sane|ly** ADV ❏ *Try to arrive early during the*

insanely busy months of July and August. ● **in|san|ity** N-UNCOUNT ❏ *...the insanity of war.* [from Latin]

### Word Link  sat, satis ≈ enough : dissatisfaction, insatiable, satisfy

**in|sa|tiable** /ɪnseɪʃəb°l, -ʃiə-/ ADJ If someone has an **insatiable** desire for something, they want as much of it as they can possibly get. ❏ *The public has an insatiable appetite for stories about famous people.*

### Word Link  scrib ≈ writing : inscribe, scribble, transcribe

**in|scribe** /ɪnskraɪb/ (**inscribes, inscribing, inscribed**) V-T If you **inscribe** words on an object, you write or carve the words on the object. ❏ *She inscribed her name on the wall.* [from Latin]

**in|scrip|tion** /ɪnskrɪpʃ°n/ (**inscriptions**) N-COUNT An **inscription** is writing carved into something, or written on a book or photograph. ❏ *The inscription in the book reads "for Frankie."* [from Latin]

**in|sect** /ɪnsɛkt/ (**insects**) N-COUNT An **insect** is a very small animal that has six legs. Most insects have wings. [from Latin]
→ see Picture Dictionary: insect

**in|sec|ti|cide** /ɪnsɛktɪsaɪd/ (**insecticides**) N-VAR **Insecticide** is a chemical substance that is used to kill insects. ❏ *Spray the plants with insecticide.* [from Latin]
→ see farm

**in|secure** /ɪnsɪkyʊər/ ■ ADJ If you are **insecure**, you lack confidence because you think that you are not good enough or are not loved. ❏ *Most people are a little insecure about their looks.* ● **in|secu|rity** /ɪnsɪkyʊərɪti/ (**insecurities**) N-VAR ❏ *She is full*

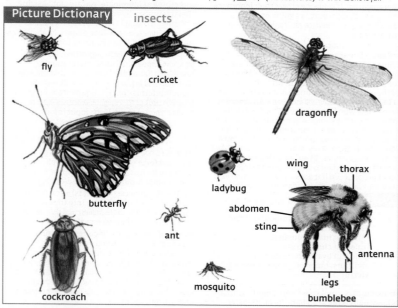

**Picture Dictionary** insects

fly
cricket
dragonfly
wing
thorax
ladybug
abdomen
butterfly
sting
ant
antenna
cockroach
mosquito
legs
bumblebee

*of emotional insecurity.* **2** ADJ Something that is **insecure** is not safe or protected. □ *...low-paid, insecure jobs.* ● **in|secu|rity** N-UNCOUNT □ *Crime creates feelings of insecurity in the population.* [from Latin]

**in|sen|si|tive** /ɪnsɛnsɪtɪv/ ADJ If you describe someone as **insensitive**, you are criticizing them for being unaware of or unsympathetic to other people's feelings. □ *My husband is very insensitive to my problem.* ● **in|sen|si|tiv|ity** /ɪnsɛnsɪtɪvɪti/ N-UNCOUNT □ *I was sorry about my insensitivity toward her.* [from Medieval Latin]

**in|sepa|rable** /ɪnsɛpərəbəl/ **1** ADJ If one thing is **inseparable from** another, the two things cannot be considered separately. □ *Olive oil is inseparable from any well-made salad.* **2** ADJ If two people are **inseparable**, they are very good friends and spend a lot of time together. □ *She and her best friend were inseparable.*

**in|sert** (**inserts, inserting, inserted**)

> The verb is pronounced /ɪnsɜrt/. The noun is pronounced /ɪnsɜrt/.

**1** V-T If you **insert** an object **into** something, you put the object inside it. □ *He took a key from his pocket and inserted it into the lock.* ● **in|ser|tion** /ɪnsɜrʃ°n/ (**insertions**) N-VAR □ *...an experiment involving the insertion of chemicals into a human being.* **2** V-T If you **insert** a comment into a piece of writing or a speech, you add it. □ *He inserted a paragraph about the recent accident.* ● **in|ser|tion** N-VAR □ *Here are two more names for insertion in the list.* [from Latin]

**in|side** /ɪnsaɪd/ (**insides**)

> The preposition is usually pronounced /ɪnsaɪd/.

**1** PREP Something or someone that is **inside** or **inside of** a place, container, or object is in it or is surrounded by it. □ *Inside the envelope was a photograph.* □ *Have you ever looked inside of a piano?* ● **Inside** is also an adverb. □ *The couple chatted on the doorstep before going inside.* ● **Inside** is also an adjective. □ *...an inside wall.* **2** N-COUNT The **inside** of something is the part or area that its sides surround or contain. □ *The doors were locked from the inside.* □ *The paper has a photo feature on its inside pages.* **3** ADJ **Inside** information is obtained from someone who is involved in a situation and therefore knows a lot about it. □ *I have no inside knowledge.* **4** N-PLURAL Your **insides** are your internal organs, especially your stomach. [INFORMAL] □ *The pill made my insides hurt.* **5** PHRASE If something such as a piece of clothing is **inside out**, the part that is normally inside now faces outward. □ *The wind blew her umbrella inside out.* [from Old English]

| Thesaurus | inside | Also look up : |
|---|---|---|
| PREP. | in; (*ant.*) outside **1** | |
| N. | interior, middle **2** | |
| ADV. | indoors **2** | |

**in|sid|er** /ɪnsaɪdər/ (**insiders**) N-COUNT An **insider** is someone who is involved in a situation and who knows more about it than other people. □ *An insider told the newspaper that the couple were getting married.* [from Old English]

**in|sidi|ous** /ɪnsɪdiəs/ ADJ Something that is **insidious** is unpleasant or dangerous and develops gradually without being noticed. □ *The changes are insidious.* [from Latin]

**in|sight** /ɪnsaɪt/ (**insights**) N-VAR If you gain **insight into** a complex situation or problem, you gain an accurate and deep understanding of it. □ *...new insights into what is happening to the Earth.* [from Old English]

**in|sig|nifi|cant** /ɪnsɪgnɪfɪkənt/ ADJ Something that is **insignificant** is unimportant, especially because it is very small. □ *In 1949 Bonn was a small, insignificant city.* ● **in|sig|nifi|cance** N-UNCOUNT □ *With this book, he went from insignificance to worldwide fame.* [from Latin]

**in|sist** /ɪnsɪst/ (**insists, insisting, insisted**) **1** V-T/V-I If you **insist that** something should be done, you say so very firmly. □ *He insisted that I should stay for dinner.* □ *She insisted on being present.* ● **in|sist|ence** N-UNCOUNT □ *...her insistence on personal privacy.* **2** V-T/V-I If you **insist** that something is true, you say so very firmly and refuse to change your mind. □ *He insisted that he never accepted any gifts.* □ *He insisted on his innocence.* [from Latin]

**in|sist|ent** /ɪnsɪstənt/ **1** ADJ Someone who is **insistent** keeps insisting that a particular thing should be done or is true. □ *She is insistent that she has done nothing wrong.* ● **in|sist|ent|ly** ADV □ *"What is it?" she asked insistently.* **2** ADJ An **insistent** noise or rhythm keeps going on for a long time and holds your attention. □ *...the insistent rhythms of American rock music.* [from Latin]

**in|so|far as** /ɪnsoʊfɑr æz, ɪnsoʊ-/ PHRASE You use **insofar as** to introduce a statement that explains and adds to something you have just said. [FORMAL] □ *Thinking about the past helps, insofar as it helps you learn from your mistakes.*

**in|som|nia** /ɪnsɒmniə/ N-UNCOUNT Someone who suffers from **insomnia** finds it difficult to sleep. [from Latin]
→ see **sleep**

**in|spect** /ɪnspɛkt/ (**inspects, inspecting, inspected**) V-T If you **inspect** something, you examine it or check it carefully. □ *He inspected the car carefully before he bought it.* ● **in|spec|tion** /ɪnspɛkʃ°n/ (**inspections**) N-VAR □ *Officials will make an inspection of the site.* [from Latin]

**in|spec|tor** /ɪnspɛktər/ (**inspectors**) **1** N-COUNT An **inspector** is a person whose job is to find out whether people are obeying official regulations. □ *Health and safety inspectors are still examining the incident.* **2** N-COUNT; N-TITLE; N-VOC An **inspector** is an officer in the police who is next in rank to a superintendent or police chief. □ *...a San Francisco police inspector.* [from Latin]

**in|spi|ra|tion** /ɪnspɪreɪʃ°n/ **1** N-UNCOUNT **Inspiration** is a feeling of enthusiasm you get from someone or something, that gives you new ideas. □ *My inspiration comes from poets like Walt Whitman.* **2** N-SING If something or someone is **the inspiration for** a particular book, work of art, or action, they are the source of the ideas in it or act as a model for it. □ *The garden was the inspiration for a series of flower paintings.* [from Latin]

**Word Link**  spir ≈ breath : aspire, inspire, respiratory

**in|spire** /ɪnspaɪər/ (**inspires, inspiring, inspired**) **1** V-T If someone or something **inspires** you, they give you new ideas and a strong feeling of enthusiasm. ❑ *Guitarist Jimi Hendrix inspired a generation.* ● **in|spir|ing** ADJ ❑ *She was one of the most inspiring people I ever met.* **2** V-T If a book, work of art, or action **is inspired by** something, that thing is the source of the idea for it. ❑ *The book was inspired by a real person.* **3** V-T Someone or something that **inspires** a particular emotion or reaction in people makes them feel that emotion or reaction. ❑ *The way he manages people certainly inspires confidence.* [from Latin]

**Word Link**  stab ≈ steady : de**stab**ilize, e**stab**lish, in**stab**ility

**in|stabil|ity** /ɪnstəbɪlɪti/ (**instabilities**) N-VAR **Instability** is a lack of stability in a place, situation, or person. ❑ *...political instability.*

**in|stall** /ɪnstɔl/ (**installs, installing, installed**) **1** V-T If you **install** a piece of equipment, you put it somewhere so that it is ready to be used. ❑ *They installed a new phone line in the apartment.* ● **in|stal|la|tion** N-UNCOUNT ❑ *The installation of smoke alarms could save hundreds of lives.* **2** V-T If someone **is installed** in a new job or important position, they are officially given the job or position. ❑ *A temporary government was installed.* ❑ *He was installed as defense secretary yesterday.* [from Medieval Latin]

**Word Partnership**  Use install with :

ADJ.   **easy to** install **1**
N.     install **equipment**, install **machines**, install **software** **1**

**in|stal|la|tion art** N-UNCOUNT **Installation art** is art that uses a variety of materials such as everyday objects, video, and sound to create an artistic work.

**in|stall|ment** /ɪnstɔlmənt/ (**installments**) **1** N-COUNT If you pay for something in **installments**, you pay small sums of money at regular intervals over a period of time. ❑ *You can choose to pay your tax in installments.* **2** N-COUNT An **installment** of a story or plan is one of its parts that are published or carried out separately one after the other. ❑ *The next installment of this four-part series is about Africa.* [from Old French]

**in|stall|ment plan** (**installment plans**) N-COUNT An **installment plan** is a way of buying goods gradually. You make regular payments to the seller until you have paid the full price and the goods belong to you.

**in|stance** /ɪnstəns/ (**instances**) **1** PHRASE You use **for instance** to introduce a particular event, situation, or person that is an example of what you are talking about. ❑ *...We held a debate on the important issues that face us all, for instance, global warming.* **2** N-COUNT An **instance** is a particular example or occurrence of something. ❑ *This was an instance of bad timing.* **3** PHRASE You say **in the first instance** to mention something that is the first step in a series of actions. [INFORMAL] ❑ *In the first instance you should visit your doctor.* [from Medieval Latin]

**in|stant** /ɪnstənt/ (**instants**) **1** N-COUNT An **instant** is an extremely short period of time or a point in time. ❑ *For an instant, I wanted to cry.* ❑ *At that instant all the lights went out.* **2** PHRASE To do

something **the instant** something else happens means to do it immediately. ❑ *I knew who he was the instant I saw him.* **3** ADJ You use **instant** to describe something that happens immediately. ❑ *Her book was an instant hit.* ● **in|stant|ly** ADV ❑ *The man was killed instantly.* **4** ADJ **Instant** food is food that you can prepare very quickly, for example, by just adding water. ❑ *He stirred instant coffee into a mug of hot water.* [from Latin]

**Thesaurus**      *instant*      Also look up :

N.    minute, second **1**

**Word Partnership**  Use *instant* with :

PREP.  **for an** instant, **in an** instant **1**
ADJ.   **the next** instant **1** **2**
N.     instant **access**, instant **messaging**, instant **success** **3**

**in|stan|ta|neous** /ɪnstənteɪniəs/ ADJ Something that is **instantaneous** happens immediately and very quickly. ❑ *Medical experts said his death was probably instantaneous.* ● **in|stan|ta|neous|ly** ADV ❑ *The Internet allows you to communicate with others instantaneously.* [from Latin]

**in|stant mes|sage** (**instant messages, instant messaging, instant messaged**) **1** N-VAR An **instant message** is a written message that is sent from one computer to another. The message appears immediately on the screen of the computer you send it to, provided the computer is using the service. The abbreviation **IM** is also used. ❑ *Instructors answer student questions by e-mail, instant message, phone or fax.* **2** V-T If you **instant message** someone, you send them an **instant message.** ❑ *You can instant message your friends whenever you like.*

**in|stant mes|sag|ing** N-UNCOUNT **Instant messaging** is the sending of written messages from one computer to another. The message appears immediately on the screen of the computer you send it to, provided the computer is using the service. The abbreviation **IM** is also used. ❑ *...instant-messaging services.*

**in|stant re|play** (**instant replays**) N-COUNT An **instant replay** is a repeated showing, usually in slow motion, of an event that has just been on television.

**Word Link**  stead ≈ place, stand : home**stead**, in**stead**, **stead**y

**in|stead** /ɪnstɛd/ **1** PHRASE If you do one thing **instead of** another, you do the first thing and not the second thing, as the result of a choice or a change of behavior. ❑ *Why don't you try to help, instead of complaining?* **2** ADV If you do not do something, but do something else **instead**, you do the second thing and not the first thing. ❑ *I'm going to forget about dieting and eat normally instead.*

**in|sti|gate** /ɪnstɪɡeɪt/ (**instigates, instigating, instigated**) V-T Someone who **instigates** an event causes it to happen. ❑ *He did not instigate the violence.* ● **in|sti|ga|tion** /ɪnstɪɡeɪʃ°n/ N-UNCOUNT ❑ *The talks are taking place at the instigation of Germany.* ● **in|sti|ga|tor** /ɪnstɪɡeɪtər/ (**instigators**)

N-COUNT ❑ *He was the main instigator of the trouble.* [from Latin]

**in|still** /ɪnstɪl/ (**instills, instilling, instilled**) V-T If you **instill** an idea or feeling in someone, especially over a period of time, you make them think it or feel it. ❑ *We're trying to instill a positive attitude in the kids.* [from Latin]

**in|stinct** /ɪnstɪŋkt/ (**instincts**) **1** N-VAR **Instinct** is the natural tendency that a person or animal has to behave or react in a particular way. ❑ *She had a strong maternal instinct.* **2** N-VAR **Instinct** is a feeling, rather than an opinion or idea based on facts, that something is true. ❑ *I have an instinct that he may be right.* [from Latin]

| Word Partnership | Use *instinct* with : |
| --- | --- |
| ADJ. | **basic** instinct, **maternal** instinct, **natural** instinct **1** |
| N. | **survival** instinct **1** |

**in|stinc|tive** /ɪnstɪŋktɪv/ ADJ An **instinctive** feeling, idea, or action is one that you have or do without thinking or reasoning. ❑ *It's an instinctive reaction — if a child falls you pick him or her up.* ● **in|stinc|tive|ly** ADV ❑ *Jane instinctively knew something was wrong.* [from Latin]

**in|sti|tute** /ɪnstɪtut/ (**institutes, instituting, instituted**) **1** N-COUNT An **institute** is an organization or building where a particular type of work is done, especially about research or teaching. ❑ *...the National Cancer Institute.* **2** V-T If you **institute** a system, rule, or course of action, you start it. [FORMAL] ❑ *We will institute a number of changes to improve public safety.* [from Latin]

**in|sti|tu|tion** /ɪnstɪtuʃn/ (**institutions**) **1** N-COUNT An **institution** is a large important organization such as a university, church, or bank. ❑ *...financial institutions.* **2** N-COUNT An **institution** is a building where certain people are cared for, such as people who are mentally ill. ❑ *Larry has been in an institution since he was four.* **3** N-COUNT An **institution** is a custom or system that is considered an important or typical feature of a particular society or group, usually because it has existed for a long time. ❑ *I believe in the institution of marriage.* [from Latin]

**in-store** ADJ **In-store** facilities are facilities that are available within a department store, supermarket or other large store. ❑ *...an in-store bakery.* ● **In-store** is also an adverb. ❑ *Ask in-store for details.*

| Word Link | struct ≈ building : construct, destructive, instruct |
| --- | --- |

**in|struct** /ɪnstrʌkt/ (**instructs, instructing, instructed**) **1** V-T If you **instruct** someone to do something, you formally tell them to do it. [FORMAL] ❑ *A doctor will often instruct patients to exercise.* ❑ *"Go and speak to her," Ken instructed.* **2** V-T Someone who **instructs** people in a subject or skill teaches it to them. ❑ *He instructed us in nursing techniques.* [from Latin]

**in|struc|tion** /ɪnstrʌkʃn/ (**instructions**) **1** N-COUNT An **instruction** is something that someone tells you to do. ❑ *We had instructions not to leave the building.* **2** N-UNCOUNT If someone gives you **instruction** in a subject or skill, they teach it to you. [FORMAL] ❑ *Each new member is given*

instruction in safety. **3** N-PLURAL **Instructions** are detailed information on how to do something. ❑ *The instructions that come with the software are easy to understand.* [from Latin]

| Thesaurus | instruction | Also look up : |
| --- | --- | --- |
| N. | direction, order **1** education, learning **2** | |

| Word Partnership | Use *instruction* with : |
| --- | --- |
| ADJ. | **explicit** instruction **1 2** |
| N. | **classroom** instruction, instruction **manual 2** |
| V. | **give** instruction, **provide** instruction, **receive** instruction **2** |

**in|struc|tive** /ɪnstrʌktɪv/ ADJ Something that is **instructive** gives useful information. ❑ *...an entertaining and instructive program.* [from Latin]

**in|struc|tor** /ɪnstrʌktər/ (**instructors**) N-COUNT An **instructor** is someone who teaches a skill such as driving or skiing. An **instructor** can also be used to refer to a schoolteacher or to a college teacher of low rank. ❑ *...a swimming instructor.* [from Latin]

| Thesaurus | instructor | Also look up : |
| --- | --- | --- |
| N. | educator, leader, professor, teacher | |

**in|stru|ment** /ɪnstrəmənt/ (**instruments**) **1** N-COUNT An **instrument** is a tool or device that is used to do a particular task. ❑ *...instruments for cleaning and polishing teeth.* **2** N-COUNT A musical **instrument** is an object such as a piano, guitar, or flute, which you play in order to produce music. ❑ *Learning a musical instrument helps a child to understand music.* [from Latin]
→ see **concert, orchestra**

**in|stru|men|tal** /ɪnstrəmɛntl/ (**instrumentals**) **1** ADJ Someone or something that is **instrumental in** a process or event helps to make it happen. ❑ *He was instrumental in the company's success.* **2** ADJ **Instrumental** music is performed by instruments and not by voices. ❑ *...a CD of vocal and instrumental music.* ● **Instrumentals** are pieces of instrumental music. ❑ *There's a short instrumental after each of the songs.* [from Latin]

**in|suf|fi|cient** /ɪnsəfɪʃnt/ ADJ Something that is **insufficient** is not large enough in amount or degree for a particular purpose. [FORMAL] ❑ *There was insufficient evidence to charge him with murder.* ● **in|suf|fi|cient|ly** ADV ❑ *Food that is insufficiently cooked can cause food poisoning.* [from Latin]

| Word Link | insula ≈ island : insular, insulate, insulation |
| --- | --- |

**in|su|lar** /ɪnsələr/ ADJ If you describe someone as **insular**, you are critical of them because they are unwilling to meet new people or to consider new ideas. ❑ *They were an insular family.* ● **in|su|lar|ity** /ɪnsəlærɪti/ N-UNCOUNT ❑ *Small communities can sometimes have a feeling of insularity.* [from Late Latin]

**in|su|late** /ɪnsəleɪt/ (**insulates, insulating, insulated**) **1** V-T To **insulate** something such as a building means to protect it from cold, heat, or noise by placing a layer of other material around it or inside it. ❑ *People should insulate their homes* to save energy. **2** V-T If a piece of equipment **is insulated**, it is covered with rubber or plastic to prevent electricity from passing through it and giving the person using it an electric shock. ❑ *In order to make it safe, the equipment is electrically insulated.* **3** V-T If a person or group **is insulated from** the rest of society or from outside influences, they are protected from them. ❑ *Small towns are no longer insulated from the problems of big cities.* [from Late Latin]

> **Word Link**    insula ≈ island : insular, insulate, insulation

insulation

in|su|la|tion /ˌɪnsəleɪʃ°n/ **1** N-UNCOUNT **Insulation** is a thick layer of a substance that keeps something warm, especially a building. ❑ *Better insulation could cut your heating bills.* [from Late Latin] **2** → see also **insulate**

in|su|la|tor /ˈɪnsəleɪtər/ (**insulators**) N-COUNT An **insulator** is a material that insulates something. [from Late Latin]

in|su|lin /ˈɪnsəlɪn/ N-UNCOUNT **Insulin** is a substance that most people produce naturally in their body and that controls the level of sugar in their blood. ❑ *...cells that produce insulin.* [from New Latin]

in|sult (**insults, insulting, insulted**)

> The verb is pronounced /ɪnsʌlt/. The noun is pronounced /ˈɪnsʌlt/.

**1** V-T If someone **insults** you, they say or do something that is rude or offensive. ❑ *I didn't intend to insult you.* ● in|sult|ed ADJ ❑ *I was really insulted by the way he spoke to me.* ● in|sult|ing ADJ ❑ *...insulting language.* **2** N-COUNT An **insult** is a rude remark, or something a person says or does which insults you. ❑ *They shouted insults at each other.* **3** PHRASE You say **to add insult to injury** when mentioning an action or fact that makes an unfair or unacceptable situation even worse. ❑ *To add insult to injury, when the package finally arrived the contents were damaged.* [from Latin]

> **Word Link**    ance ≈ quality, state : insurance, performance, resistance

in|sur|ance /ɪnˈʃʊərəns/ **1** N-UNCOUNT **Insurance** is an arrangement in which you pay money to a company, and they pay you if something bad happens to you, for example, if your property is stolen. ❑ *His employer provided health insurance.* **2** N-SING If you do something as **insurance against** something bad happening, you do it to protect yourself in case the bad thing happens. ❑ *Farmers grow a mixture of crops as insurance against crop failure.* [from Old French]

> **Word Partnership**    Use *insurance* with :
>
> | | |
> |---|---|
> | N. | insurance **claim**, insurance **company**, insurance **coverage**, insurance **payments**, insurance **policy 1** |
> | V. | **buy/purchase** insurance, **carry** insurance, **sell** insurance **1** |

in|sure /ɪnˈʃʊər/ (**insures, insuring, insured**) V-T/V-I If you **insure** yourself or your property, you pay money to an insurance company so that, if

you become ill or if your property is damaged or stolen, the company will pay you a sum of money. ❑ *It costs a lot of money to insure your car.* ❑ *Many people insure against death or long-term sickness.* [from Old French]
→ see also **ensure**

> **Word Partnership**    Use *insure* with :
>
> | | |
> |---|---|
> | N. | insure **your** car/health/house/ property, insure **your** safety |
> | ADJ. | **difficult to** insure, **necessary to** insure |

in|sur|er /ɪnˈʃʊərər/ (**insurers**) N-COUNT An **insurer** is a company that sells insurance. [BUSINESS] [from Old French]

in|sur|gen|cy /ɪnˈsɜrdʒ°nsi/ (**insurgencies**) N-VAR An **insurgency** is a violent attempt to remove a country's government carried out by citizens of that country. [FORMAL] ❑ *He believed there could be a communist insurgency.* [from Latin]

in|sur|rec|tion /ˌɪnsərɛkʃ°n/ (**insurrections**) N-VAR An **insurrection** is violent action by a group of people against the rulers of their country. [FORMAL] ❑ *...an armed insurrection.* [from Late Latin]

in|tact /ɪnˈtækt/ ADJ Something that is **intact** is complete and has not been damaged or changed. ❑ *The roof was still intact.* [from Latin]

in|take /ˈɪnteɪk/ N-SING Your **intake** of a particular kind of food or drink is the amount that you eat or drink. ❑ *Your intake of salt should be no more than a few grams per day.* [from Old English]
→ see **engine**

in|tan|gible /ɪnˈtændʒɪb°l/ (**intangibles**) ADJ Something that is **intangible** is abstract or is hard to define or measure. ❑ *Friendship brings many intangible rewards.* ● You can refer to intangible things as **intangibles**. ❑ *It's important to consider intangibles such as how happy workers are.* [from Late Latin]

in|te|ger /ˈɪntɪdʒər/ (**integers**) N-COUNT In mathematics, an **integer** is an exact whole number such as 1, 7, or 24 as opposed to a number with fractions or decimals. [TECHNICAL] [from Latin]

in|te|gral /ˈɪntɪgrəl/ ADJ Something that is an **integral** part of something is an essential part of that thing. ❑ *Technology is an integral part of our society.* [from Latin]

in|te|grate /ˈɪntɪgreɪt/ (**integrates, integrating, integrated**) **1** V-T/V-I If someone **integrates** into a social group, or **is integrated** into it, they behave in such a way that they become part of the group or are accepted into it. When different races **integrate**, they begin to live and work together, instead of separately. ❑ *He didn't integrate successfully into the Italian way of life.* ❑ *Integrating the kids with the community is essential.* ● in|te|grat|ed ADJ ❑ *...a fully integrated, supportive society.* ● in|te|gra|tion /ˌɪntɪgreɪʃ°n/ N-UNCOUNT ❑ *...the integration of robots into the daily lives of humans.* **2** V-RECIP If you **integrate** things, you combine them so that they become closely linked or so that they form one thing. ❑ *The two airlines will integrate their services.* ● in|te|grat|ed ADJ ❑ *...integrated computer systems.* [from Latin]

| **Thesaurus** | *integrate* Also look up : |

| v. | assimilate, combine, consolidate, incorporate, synthesize, unite; (*ant.*) separate **2** |

in|teg|rity /ɪntɛgrɪti/ N-UNCOUNT If you have **integrity**, you are honest and firm in your moral principles. □ *I regard him as a man of integrity.* [from Latin]

in|tegu|men|tary sys|tem /ɪntɛgyəmɛntəri sɪstəm/ (**integumentary systems**) N-COUNT The **integumentary system** of animals and people is a group of body parts which includes the skin, hair, and nails. [TECHNICAL]

in|tel|lect /ɪntɪlɛkt/ (**intellects**) **1** N-VAR **Intellect** is the ability to understand or deal with ideas and information. □ *Puzzles and games can help develop the intellect.* **2** N-VAR **Intellect** is the quality of being intelligent. □ *She is famous for her intellect.* [from Latin]

in|tel|lec|tual /ɪntɪlɛktʃuəl/ (**intellectuals**) **1** ADJ **Intellectual** means involving a person's ability to think and to understand ideas and information. □ *...the intellectual development of children.* • in|tel|lec|tual|ly ADV □ *...intellectually satisfying work.* **2** N-COUNT An **intellectual** is someone who spends a lot of time studying and thinking about complicated ideas. □ *...teachers, artists and other intellectuals.* • **Intellectual** is also an adjective. □ *They were very intellectual and witty.* [from Latin]

in|tel|lec|tual prop|er|ty N-UNCOUNT **Intellectual property** is something such as an invention or a copyright which is officially owned by someone. [LEGAL] □ *...music and movies that are defined as intellectual property.*

in|tel|li|gence /ɪntɛlɪdʒᵊns/ **1** N-UNCOUNT **Intelligence** is the ability to understand and learn things. □ *She's a woman of great intelligence.* **2** N-UNCOUNT **Intelligence** is the ability to think, reason, and understand instead of doing things by instinct. □ *Your intelligence can help you solve your problems.* **3** N-UNCOUNT **Intelligence** is information that is gathered by the government or the army about their country's enemies and their activities. □ *...the need for better military intelligence.* [from Latin]

| **Word Partnership** | Use *intelligence* with : |

| ADJ. | **human** intelligence **2** |
| | **secret** intelligence **3** |
| N. | intelligence **agent**, intelligence **expert**, **military** intelligence **3** |

in|tel|li|gent /ɪntɛlɪdʒᵊnt/ **1** ADJ A person or animal that is **intelligent** has the ability to think, understand, and learn things quickly and well. □ *Susan's a very intelligent woman.* • in|tel|li|gent|ly ADV □ *They don't think intelligently about politics.* **2** ADJ Something that is **intelligent** can think and understand instead of doing things automatically or by instinct. □ *Intelligent computers will soon be an important tool for every doctor.* [from Latin]

| **Thesaurus** | *intelligent* Also look up : |

| ADJ. | bright, clever, sharp, smart; (*ant.*) dumb, stupid **1** **2** |

in|tel|li|gi|ble /ɪntɛlɪdʒɪbᵊl/ ADJ Something that is **intelligible** can be understood. □ *Darwin wrote in a way that was intelligible to non-experts.* [from Latin]

in|tend /ɪntɛnd/ (**intends, intending, intended**) **1** V-T If you **intend** to do something, you have decided or planned to do it. □ *Maybe he intends to resign.* □ *What do you intend to do when you leave college?* **2** V-T If something **is intended** for a particular purpose, it has been planned to fulfill that purpose. If something **is intended** for a particular person, it has been planned to be used by that person or to affect them in some way. □ *This money is intended for schools.* □ *The big windows were intended to make the room brighter.* [from Latin]

in|tense /ɪntɛns/ **1** ADJ **Intense** is used to describe something that is very great or extreme in strength or degree. □ *He was sweating from the intense heat.* □ *...intense hatred.* • in|tense|ly ADV □ *The fast-food business is intensely competitive.* • in|ten|si|ty /ɪntɛnsɪti/ N-UNCOUNT □ *The intensity of the attack was a shock.* **2** ADJ An **intense** person is very serious. □ *He's a very intense player who loves to win.* [from Latin]

| **Word Link** | *ify* ≈ making : cla*ify*, diver*sify*, *intensify* |

in|ten|si|fy /ɪntɛnsɪfaɪ/ (**intensifies, intensifying, intensified**) V-T/V-I If you **intensify** something or if it **intensifies**, it becomes greater in strength, amount, or degree. □ *We must intensify our efforts to find a solution.* □ *As he ran, the pain intensified.* [from Latin]

in|ten|si|ty /ɪntɛnsɪti/ (**intensities**) **1** N-COUNT The **intensity** of a color is how bright or dull it is. [from Latin] **2** → see also **intense**

in|ten|sive /ɪntɛnsɪv/ **1** ADJ **Intensive** activity involves concentrating a lot of effort or people on one particular task. □ *...several days of intensive negotiations.* • in|ten|sive|ly ADV □ *He is working intensively on his book.* **2** ADJ **Intensive** farming involves producing as many crops or animals as possible from your land, usually with the aid of chemicals. □ *...intensive methods of growing larger tomatoes.* [from Latin]

in|ten|sive care N-UNCOUNT If someone is **in intensive care**, they are being given extremely thorough care in a hospital because they are very ill or very badly injured. □ *She spent the night in intensive care.*

in|tent /ɪntɛnt/ (**intents**) **1** ADJ If you are **intent on** doing something, you are eager and determined to do it. □ *We are intent on winning this competition.* **2** ADJ If someone does something in an **intent** way, they pay great attention to what they are doing. [WRITTEN] □ *There was an intent expression of concentration on her face.* • in|tent|ly ADV □ *He listened intently.* **3** N-UNCOUNT, N-SING A person's **intent** is their intention to do something. [FORMAL] □ *It was our intent to keep the wedding as private as possible.* □ *...an intent to frighten us.* **4** PHRASE You say **for all intents and purposes** to suggest that a situation is not exactly as you describe it but the effect is the same as if it were. ❑ *He sees me as his second son, which I am, for all intents and purposes.* [from Late Latin]

**in|ten|tion** /ɪntɛnʃⁿn/ (**intentions**) **1** N-VAR An **intention** is an idea or plan of what you are going to do. ❑ *The company has every intention of keeping the share price high.* ❑ *It is my intention to retire later this year.* **2** PHRASE If you say that you **have no intention of** doing something, you are emphasizing that you are not going to do it. If you say that you **have every intention of** doing something, you are emphasizing that you intend to do it. ❑ *I have no intention of going without you.* [from Late Latin]

**in|ten|tion|al** /ɪntɛnʃənⁿl/ ADJ Something that is **intentional** is deliberate. ❑ *She was a victim of intentional discrimination.* ● **in|ten|tion|al|ly** ADV ❑ *I've never intentionally hurt anyone.* [from Late Latin]

**inter|act** /ɪntərækt/ (**interacts, interacting, interacted**) **1** V-RECIP When people **interact with** each other or **interact**, they communicate as they work or spend time together. ❑ *The other children interacted and played together.* ● **inter|ac|tion** /ɪntəræk ʃⁿn/ (**interactions**) N-VAR ❑ *...social interactions with other people.* **2** V-RECIP When one thing **interacts with** another or two things **interact**, the two things affect each other's behavior or condition. ❑ *You have to understand how cells interact.* ● **inter|ac|tion** N-VAR ❑ *...the interaction between physical and emotional illness.* [from Latin]

**inter|ac|tive** /ɪntəræktɪv/ ADJ An **interactive** computer program or electronic device is one that allows direct communication between the user and the machine. ❑ *This will make computer games more interactive than ever.* ● **inter|ac|tiv|ity** /ɪntəræktɪvɪti/ N-UNCOUNT ❑ *...digital television, with more channels and interactivity.* [from Latin]

**inter|cept** /ɪntərsɛpt/ (**intercepts, intercepting, intercepted**) V-T If you **intercept** someone or something that is traveling from one place to another, you stop them before they get to their destination. ❑ *We can easily intercept emails on non-secure Web sites.* ● **inter|cep|tion** /ɪntərsɛpʃⁿn/ (**interceptions**) N-VAR ❑ *...the interception of a ship off the coast of Oregon.* [from Latin]

| Word Link | inter ≈ between : interchange, interconnect, internal |
|---|---|

**inter|change** (**interchanges, interchanging, interchanged**)

The noun is pronounced /ɪntərtʃeɪndʒ/. The verb is pronounced /ɪntərtʃeɪndʒ/.

**1** N-COUNT An **interchange** on a road is a place where it joins another main road. ❑ *...the Highway 167/Interstate 105 interchange.* **2** V-RECIP If you **interchange** things, you exchange one thing for the other. ❑ *Your task is to interchange words so that the sentence makes sense.* ● **Interchange** is also a noun. ❑ *...ways to facilitate the interchange of information.* [from Old French]

**inter|change|able** /ɪntərtʃeɪndʒəbⁿl/ ADJ Things that are **interchangeable** can be exchanged with each other without it making any difference. ❑ *In most recipes, chicken and turkey are almost interchangeable.* ● **inter|change|ably** ADV ❑ *These expressions are often used interchangeably, but they have*

different meanings. [from Old French]

**inter|col|legi|ate** /ɪntərkəlidʒɪt, -dʒiɪt/ ADJ **Intercollegiate** means involving or related to more than one college or university. ❑ *...an intercollegiate basketball team championship.*

**inter|con|nect** /ɪntərkənɛkt/ (**interconnects, interconnecting, interconnected**) V-RECIP Things that **interconnect** or **are interconnected** are connected to or with each other. ❑ *The two bedrooms and the bathroom interconnect.* [from Latin]

**inter|con|nec|tion** /ɪntərkənɛkʃⁿn/ (**interconnections**) N-VAR If you say that there is an **interconnection** between two or more things, you mean that they are very closely connected. [FORMAL] ❑ *...the interconnection between environmental destruction and poverty.* [from Latin]

**inter|con|ti|nen|tal** /ɪntərkɒntɪnɛntⁿl/ ADJ **Intercontinental** is used to describe something that exists or happens between continents. ❑ *...intercontinental flights.* [from Latin]

**inter|course** /ɪntərkɔrs/ N-UNCOUNT **Intercourse** is the act of having sex. [FORMAL] [from Medieval Latin]

**inter|de|pend|ent** /ɪntərdɪpɛndənt/ ADJ People or things that are **interdependent** all depend on each other. ❑ *We live in an increasingly interdependent world.* ● **inter|de|pend|ence** N-UNCOUNT ❑ *...the interdependence of nations.*

**in|ter|est** /ɪntrɪst, -tərɪst/ (**interests, interesting, interested**) **1** N-UNCOUNT; N-SING If you have an **interest in** something, you want to learn or hear more about it. ❑ *There has been a lot of interest in the elections in the last two weeks.* ❑ *She liked him at first, but soon lost interest.* **2** N-COUNT Your **interests** are the things that you enjoy doing. ❑ *Encourage your child in her interests and hobbies.* **3** V-T If something **interests** you, you want to learn or hear more about it or continue doing it. ❑ *Your financial problems do not interest me.* **4** N-COUNT If something is in the **interests** of a particular person or group, it will benefit them in some way. ❑ *He has a duty to act in the best interests of the company.* **5** N-COUNT A person or organization that has an **interest** in an area, a company, a property, or in a particular type of business owns stock in it. [BUSINESS] ❑ *My father had many business interests in Vietnam.* **6** N-COUNT If a person, country, or organization has an **interest** in a possible event or situation, they want that event or situation to happen because they are likely to benefit from it. ❑ *The West has an interest in promoting democracy.* **7** N-UNCOUNT **Interest** is extra money that you receive if you have invested a sum of money. **Interest** is also the extra money that you pay if you have borrowed money. ❑ *Does your checking account pay interest?* **8** → see also **interested, interesting, self-interest, vested interest** **9** PHRASE If you do something **in the interests of** a particular result or situation, you do it in order to achieve that result or maintain that situation. ❑ *The president agreed to meet with the country's leader in the interests of peace.* [from Latin] **10** to have someone's **interests at heart** → see **heart**

**Word Partnership** Use *interest* with :

| ADJ. | **great** interest, **little** interest, **strong** interest ◼ |
| N. | **level of** interest, **places of** interest, **self-** interest ◼ |
| | **conflict of** interest ◼ ◼ ◼ |
| | interest **charges**, interest **expenses** ◼ |
| V. | **attract** interest, **express** interest, **lose** interest ◼ |
| | **earn** interest, **pay** interest ◼ |

**in|ter|est|ed** /ɪntərɛstɪd, -trɪstɪd/ ◼ ADJ If you are **interested in** something, you think it is important and want to learn more about it or spend time doing it. ❑ *I thought you might be interested in this article.* ◼ ADJ An **interested** party or group of people is affected by or involved in a particular event or situation. ❑ *All the interested parties eventually agreed to the idea.* [from Latin]

**Word Partnership** Use *interested* with :

| V. | **become** interested, interested **in buying**, **get** interested, interested **in getting**, interested **in helping**, interested **in learning**, interested **in making**, **seem** interested ◼ |
| ADV. | **really** interested, **very** interested ◼ |

**in|ter|est|ing** /ɪntərɛstɪŋ, -trɪstɪŋ/ ADJ If you find something **interesting**, it attracts you or holds your attention. ❑ *It was interesting to be in a new town.* ● **in|ter|est|ing|ly** /ɪntərɛstɪŋli, -trɪstɪŋli/ ADV ❑ *Interestingly, a few weeks later, he married again.* [from Latin]

**Word Partnership** Use *interesting* with :

| ADV. | **especially** interesting, **really** interesting, **very** interesting |
| N. | interesting **idea**, interesting **people**, interesting **point**, interesting **question**, interesting **story**, interesting **things** |

**inter|face** /ɪntərfeɪs/ (**interfaces**) ◼ N-COUNT The **interface** between two subjects or systems is the area in which they affect each other or have links with each other. ❑ *...a funny story about the interface between bureaucracy and the working world.* ◼ N-COUNT The user **interface** of a piece of computer software is its presentation on the screen and how easy it is to operate. [COMPUTING] ❑ *...the development of better user interfaces.* [from Old French]

**inter|fere** /ɪntərfɪər/ (**interferes, interfering, interfered**) ◼ V-I If someone **interferes in** a situation, they get involved in it although it does not concern them and their involvement is not wanted. ❑ *I wish everyone would stop interfering and just leave me alone.* ◼ V-I Something that **interferes with** a situation, activity, or process has a damaging effect on it. ❑ *Many things can interfere with a good night's sleep.* [from Old French]

**inter|fer|ence** /ɪntərfɪərəns/ ◼ N-UNCOUNT **Interference** is unwanted or unnecessary involvement in something. ❑ *She didn't appreciate her mother's interference in her life.* ◼ N-UNCOUNT When there is **interference**, a radio signal is affected by other radio waves or electrical activity so that it cannot be received properly. ❑ *There was too much interference and we couldn't hear the broadcast.* [from Old French]

**in|ter|im** /ɪntərɪm/ ◼ ADJ **Interim** is used to describe something that is intended to be used until something permanent is done or established. ❑ *...an interim government.* ◼ PHRASE **In the interim** means until a particular thing happens or until a particular thing happened. [FORMAL] ❑ *She will return in the fall, and in the interim we have hired a temporary teacher.* [from Latin]

**in|te|ri|or** /ɪntɪəriər/ (**interiors**) ◼ N-COUNT The **interior** of something is the inside part of it. ❑ *The interior of the house was dark and old-fashioned.* ◼ N-SING The **interior** of a country or continent is the central area of it. ❑ *The country's interior is very mountainous.* [from Latin]

**Thesaurus** *interior* Also look up :

| N. | inside; (*ant.*) exterior, outside ◼ |

**inter|lude** /ɪntərlud/ (**interludes**) N-COUNT An **interlude** is a short period of time when an activity or situation stops and something else happens. [from Medieval Latin]

**Word Link** *med ≈ middle : inter*med*iary, * media, * medium*

**inter|medi|ary** /ɪntərmidiɛri/ (**intermediaries**) N-COUNT An **intermediary** is a person who passes messages or proposals between two people or groups. ❑ *He acted as an intermediary in the dispute.* [from Medieval Latin]

**inter|medi|ate** /ɪntərmidiɪt/ ◼ ADJ An **intermediate** stage, level, or position is one that occurs between two other stages, levels, or positions. ❑ *Do you make any intermediate stops between your home and work?* ◼ ADJ **Intermediate** learners of something have some knowledge or skill but are not yet advanced. ❑ *We teach beginner, intermediate, and advanced level students.* [from Medieval Latin]

**in|ter|mi|nable** /ɪntɜrmɪnəbᵊl/ ADJ If you describe something as **interminable**, you mean that it continues for a very long time and that you wish it would stop. ❑ *...an interminable meeting.* ● **in|ter|mi|nably** ADV ❑ *He talked to me interminably about his first wife.*

**inter|mit|tent** /ɪntərmɪtᵊnt/ ADJ Something that is **intermittent** happens occasionally rather than continuously. ❑ *After three hours of intermittent rain, the game was abandoned.* ● **inter|mit|tent|ly** ADV ❑ *The talks went on intermittently for years.* [from Latin]

**in|tern** (**interns, interning, interned**)

The verb is pronounced /ɪntɜrn/. The noun is pronounced /ɪntɜrn/.

◼ V-T If someone **is interned**, they are put in prison or in a prison camp for political reasons. ❑ *He was interned as a prisoner of war.* ◼ N-COUNT An **intern** is an advanced student or a recent graduate, especially in medicine, who is being given practical training under supervision. ❑ *...a medical intern.* [from Latin]

---

**Word Link** *inter ≈ between : interchange, interconnect, internal*

**in|ter|nal** /ɪntɜrnᵊl/ **1** ADJ **Internal** is used to describe things that exist or happen inside a country or organization. ❑ *The country improved its internal security.* ❑ *…Russia's Ministry of Internal Affairs.* ● **in|ter|nal|ly** ADV ❑ *We need to fight terrorism both internally and abroad.* **2** ADJ **Internal** is used to describe things that exist or happen inside a particular person, object, or place. ❑ *He suffered internal bleeding.* ● **in|ter|nal|ly** ADV ❑ *The herb has calming effects when taken internally.* [from Medieval Latin]
→ see **engine**

**in|ter|nal com|bus|tion en|gine** (**internal combustion engines**) N-COUNT An **internal combustion engine** is an engine that creates its energy by burning fuel inside itself. Most cars have internal combustion engines.

**in|ter|nal fer|ti|li|za|tion** N-UNCOUNT **Internal fertilization** is a method of reproduction in which the egg and sperm join together inside the female's body. Compare **external fertilization**. [TECHNICAL]

**In|ter|nal Rev|enue Ser|vice** N-PROPER The **Internal Revenue Service** is the U.S. government authority that collects taxes. The abbreviation **IRS** is often used.

**inter|na|tion|al** /ɪntərnæʃənᵊl/ ADJ **International** means between or involving different countries. ❑ *…an international organization that brings fun and games to children in refugee camps.* ● **inter|na|tion|al|ly** ADV ❑ *…rules that have been internationally agreed upon.*

**In|ter|net** /ɪntərnɛt/ also **internet** N-PROPER The **Internet** is the network that allows computer users to connect with computers all over the world, and that carries e-mail.
→ see Word Web: **internet**

**In|ter|net café** (**Internet cafés**) N-COUNT An **Internet café** is a café with computers where people can pay to use the Internet.

**in|tern|ist** /ɪntɜrnɪst/ (**internists**) N-COUNT An **internist** is a doctor who specializes in the nonsurgical treatment of disorders occurring inside people's bodies. ❑ *I've been to see an internist.* [from Latin]

**in|tern|ship** /ɪntɜrnʃɪp/ (**internships**) N-COUNT An **internship** is the position held by an intern,

or the period of time when someone is an intern. [from Latin]

**inter|per|son|al** /ɪntərpɜrsənᵊl/ ADJ **Interpersonal** means relating to relationships between people. ❑ *You need good interpersonal skills in my job.*

**in|ter|pret** /ɪntɜrprɪt/ (**interprets, interpreting, interpreted**) **1** V-T If you **interpret** something in a particular way, you decide that this is its meaning or significance. ❑ *I interpreted her look as a sign she didn't approve.* ❑ *The judge has to interpret the law.* **2** V-T/V-I If you **interpret** what someone is saying, you translate it immediately into another language. ❑ *She spoke little English, so her husband came with her to interpret.* ● **in|ter|pret|er** /ɪntɜrprɪtər/ (**interpreters**) N-COUNT ❑ *Speaking through an interpreter, he said that he was very pleased with the result.* [from Latin]
→ see **dream**

**in|ter|pre|ta|tion** /ɪntɜrprɪteɪʃᵊn/ (**interpretations**) **1** N-VAR An **interpretation** of something is an opinion about what it means. ❑ *Professor Wolfgang gives the data a very different interpretation.* **2** N-COUNT A performer's **interpretation** of something such as a piece of music or a role in a play is the particular way in which they choose to perform it. ❑ *…the pianist's interpretation of Chopin.* [from Latin]
→ see **art**

**in|ter|ro|gate** /ɪntɛrəgeɪt/ (**interrogates, interrogating, interrogated**) V-T If someone, especially a police officer, **interrogates** someone, they question them thoroughly for a long time in order to get some information from them. ❑ *The police interrogated him for 90 minutes.* ● **in|ter|ro|ga|tion** /ɪntɛrəgeɪʃᵊn/ (**interrogations**) N-VAR ❑ *…rules controlling the interrogation of prisoners.* [from Latin]

**in|ter|roga|tive** /ɪntərɒgətɪv/ **1** N-SING In grammar, a clause that is in **the interrogative** is in the form of a question. Examples are "When did he get back?" and "Are you all right?" **2** ADJ An **interrogative** sentence is a sentence that asks a question, for example "Who are you?" [from Latin]

---

**Word Link** *rupt ≈ breaking : disrupt, erupt, interrupt*

**in|ter|rupt** /ɪntərʌpt/ (**interrupts, interrupting, interrupted**) **1** V-T/V-I If you **interrupt** someone who is speaking, you say or do something that

---

**Word Web** Internet

The **Internet** allows information to be shared by users around the world. The **World-Wide Web** allows users to access **servers** anywhere. **User names** and **passwords** give access and protect information. **E-mail** travels through **networks**. **Websites** are created by companies and individuals to share information. **Web pages** can include images, words, sound, and video. Some organizations have built private **intranets**. These groups have to guard the **gateway** between their system and the larger Internet. **Hackers** can break into computer networks. They sometimes steal information or damage the system. **Webmasters** usually build firewalls for protection.

The Internet
World Wide Web
servers
computer
Internet provider

causes them to stop. ❑ *I'm sorry to interrupt, but there's a phone call for you.* ❑ *Don't interrupt the teacher when she's speaking.* ● **in|ter|rup|tion** /ɪntərʌpʃ⁰n/ **(interruptions)** N-VAR ❑ *The sudden interruption stopped Justin in the middle of a sentence.* **2** V-T If someone or something **interrupts** a process or activity, they stop it for a period of time. ❑ *She kept coming into the room, interrupting my work.* ● **in|ter|rup|tion** N-VAR ❑ *...telephone interruptions.* [from Latin]

**inter|sec|tion** /ɪntərsɛkʃ⁰n/ **(intersections)** N-COUNT An **intersection** is a place where roads or other lines meet or cross. ❑ *We crossed at a busy intersection.* [from Latin]

**inter|spersed** /ɪntərspɜrst/ ADJ If one group of things are **with** another or **interspersed among** another, the second things occur between or among the first things. ❑ *I could hear the sound of the waves interspersed with the cry of sea birds.* [from Latin]

**inter|state** /ɪntərsteɪt/ **(interstates)** **1** ADJ **Interstate** means between states, especially the states of the United States. ❑ *...interstate commerce.* **2** N-COUNT An **interstate** or **interstate highway** is a major road linking states. ❑ *We were traveling on Interstate 75.* [from Old French]

**in|ter|val** /ɪntərv⁰l/ **(intervals)** **1** N-COUNT An **interval** between two events or dates is the period of time between them. ❑ *After an interval of six months, doctors repeat the test.* **2** N-COUNT An **interval** in music is the distance in pitch between two tones. **3** PHRASE If something happens **at intervals**, it happens several times with gaps or pauses in between. ❑ *She woke him for his medication at intervals throughout the night.* **4** PHRASE If things are placed **at** particular **intervals**, there are spaces of a particular size between them. ❑ *White barriers marked the road at intervals of about a mile.* [from Latin]

**inter|vene** /ɪntərvin/ **(intervenes, intervening, intervened)** V-I If you **intervene** in a situation, you become involved in it and try to change it. ❑ *The situation calmed down when police intervened.* ● **inter|ven|tion** /ɪntərvɛnʃ⁰n/ **(interventions)** N-VAR ❑ *...the intervention of the U.S. in the affairs of other countries.* [from Latin]

**inter|ven|ing** /ɪntərvinɪŋ/ ADJ An **intervening** period of time is one that separates two events or points in time. ❑ *I spent the intervening time in London.* [from Latin]

**inter|view** /ɪntərvyu/ **(interviews, interviewing, interviewed)** **1** N-VAR An **interview** is a formal meeting at which someone is asked questions in order to find out if they are suitable for a job. ❑ *The interview went well.* **2** V-T If you **are interviewed** for a particular job, someone asks you questions about yourself to find out if you suitable for it. ❑ *She was interviewed for a management job.* **3** N-COUNT An **interview** is a conversation in which a journalist asks a famous person a series of questions. ❑ *Allan gave an interview to the Chicago Tribune last month.* **4** V-T When a journalist **interviews** someone such as a famous person, they ask them a series of questions. ❑ *She has interviewed many famous actors.* ● **inter|view|er** **(interviewers)** N-COUNT ❑ *Being a good interviewer requires preparation and skill.* [from Old French]

| Word Partnership | Use *interview* with : |
| --- | --- |
| N. | job interview **1** |
| | (tele)phone interview **1** **3** |
| | radio/magazine/newspaper/ television interview **3** |
| V. | conduct an interview, give an interview, request an interview **1** **3** |

**inter|viewee** /ɪntərvyui/ **(interviewees)** N-COUNT An **interviewee** is a person who is being interviewed. ❑ *The interviewee was asked some questions about his interests.* [from Old French]

**in|tes|tine** /ɪntɛstɪn/ **(intestines)** N-COUNT Your **intestines** are the tubes in your body through which food passes when it has left your stomach. ❑ *He has a problem with his intestines.* ● **in|tes|ti|nal** /ɪntɛstɪn⁰l/ ADJ [FORMAL] ❑ *...the intestinal wall.* [from Latin]

**in|ti|ma|cy** /ɪntɪməsi/ N-UNCOUNT **Intimacy** between two people is a very close personal relationship between them. ❑ *I need friendship, intimacy, and honesty.* [from Latin]

**in|ti|mate** **(intimates, intimating, intimated)**

The adjective is pronounced /ɪntɪmɪt/. The verb is pronounced /ɪntɪmeɪt/.

**1** ADJ If you have an **intimate** friendship with someone, you know them very well and like them a lot. ❑ *I told my intimate friends I wanted to have a baby.* ● **in|ti|mate|ly** ADV ❑ *He knew them quite well, but not intimately.* **2** ADJ If two people are in an **intimate** relationship, they are involved with each other in a loving or sexual way. ❑ *...a private and intimate moment between two people.* **3** ADJ If you use **intimate** to describe an occasion or the atmosphere of a place, you like it because it is quiet and pleasant, and seems suitable for close conversations between friends. ❑ *...an intimate dinner for two.* **4** ADJ An **intimate** knowledge of something is a deep and detailed knowledge of it. ❑ *She surprised me with her intimate knowledge of football.* ● **in|ti|mate|ly** ADV ❑ *...musicians whose work she knew intimately.* **5** V-T If you **intimate** something, you say it in an indirect way. [FORMAL] ❑ *He intimated that things were going to change dramatically.* [Senses 1–4 from Latin. Sense 5 from Late Latin.]

**in|timi|date** /ɪntɪmɪdeɪt/ **(intimidates, intimidating, intimidated)** V-T If you **intimidate** someone, you frighten them, often deliberately in order to make them do what you want them to do. ❑ *My new boss tried to intimidate me.* ● **in|timi|dat|ed** /ɪntɪmɪdeɪtɪd/ ADJ ❑ *Children often feel intimidated starting in a new school.* ● **in|timi|dat|ing** /ɪntɪmɪdeɪtɪŋ/ ADJ ❑ *He was a huge, intimidating man.* ● **in|timi|da|tion** /ɪntɪmɪdeɪʃ⁰n/ N-UNCOUNT ❑ *Witnesses may not give evidence because they are afraid of intimidation.* [from Medieval Latin]

**into** /ɪntu/

Pronounced /ɪntu/ or /ɪntu/, particularly before pronouns.

In addition to the uses shown below, **into** is used after some verbs and nouns in order to introduce extra information. **Into** is also used with verbs of movement, such as "walk" and "push," and in phrasal verbs such as "enter into" and "talk into."

**1** PREP If you put one thing **into** another, you put the first thing inside the second. ❑ *Put the apples into a dish.* **2** PREP If you go **into** a place or vehicle, you move from being outside it to being inside it. ❑ *She got into the car and started the engine.* **3** PREP If you bump **into** something or crash **into** something, you hit it accidentally. ❑ *A train crashed into the barrier at the end of the track.* **4** PREP When you get **into** a piece of clothing, you put it on. ❑ *I'll change into some warmer clothes.* **5** PREP If someone or something gets **into** a particular state, they start being in that state. ❑ *He got into a panic.* **6** PREP If you talk someone **into** doing something, you persuade them to do it. ❑ *They talked him into selling the farm.* **7** PREP If something changes **into** something else, it then has a new form, shape, or nature. ❑ *Malmsten turned her hobby into a business.* **8** PREP If something is cut or split **into** a number of pieces or sections, it is divided so that it becomes several smaller pieces or sections. ❑ *Sixteen teams are taking part, divided into four groups.* **9** PREP An investigation **into** a subject or event is concerned with that subject or event. ❑ *...research into AIDS.*

**in|tol|er|able** /ɪntɒlərəbᵊl/ ADJ If something is **intolerable**, it is so bad or extreme that no one can bear it or tolerate it. ❑ *His job put intolerable pressure on him.* ● **in|tol|er|ably** /ɪntɒlərəbli/ ADV ❑ *...intolerably crowded conditions.*

**in|tol|er|ant** /ɪntɒlərənt/ ADJ If you describe someone as **intolerant**, you dislike them because they do not accept behavior and opinions that are different from their own. ❑ *He was intolerant of any advice.* ● **in|tol|er|ance** N-UNCOUNT ❑ *...his intolerance of any opinion other than his own.*

**in|toxi|cat|ed** /ɪntɒksɪkeɪtɪd/ **1** ADJ Someone who is **intoxicated** is drunk. [FORMAL] ❑ *He appeared to be intoxicated, police said.* **2** ADJ If you are **intoxicated by** or **with** something such as a feeling or an event, you are so excited by it that you find it hard to think clearly and sensibly. [LITERARY] ❑ *They seem to have become intoxicated by their success.* [from Medieval Latin]

**in|trac|table** /ɪntræktəbᵊl/ **1** ADJ **Intractable** people are very difficult to control or influence. [FORMAL] ❑ *...an intractable child.* **2** ADJ **Intractable** problems or situations are very difficult to deal with. [FORMAL] ❑ *The economy still faces intractable problems.*

| **Word Link** | *intra ≈ inside, within : intramural, intranet, intravenous* |

**in|tra|mu|ral** /ɪntrəmyʊərəl/ ADJ **Intramural** activities happen within one college or university, rather than between different colleges or universities. ❑ *...a program of intramural sports.* [from Latin]

**in|tra|net** /ɪntrənɛt/ (**intranets**) N-COUNT An **intranet** is a network of computers, similar to the Internet, within a particular company or organization.
→ see **Internet**

**in|tran|si|gent** /ɪntrænsɪdʒᵊnt/ ADJ If you describe someone as **intransigent**, you are criticizing them for their refusal to behave differently or to change their attitude to something. [FORMAL] ❑ *Sami's father was intransigent and would not listen to her.* ● **in|tran|si|gence** N-UNCOUNT ❑ *He was often*

*frustrated by the intransigence of both sides.* [from Spanish]

**in|tran|si|tive** /ɪntrænsɪtɪv/ ADJ An **intransitive** verb does not have an object.

**intra|venous** /ɪntrəvinəs/ ADJ **Intravenous** foods or drugs are put into people's bodies through their veins, rather than their mouths. [MEDICAL] ❑ *...intravenous fluids.* ● **intra|venous|ly** ADV ❑ *Premature babies have to be fed intravenously.*

**in|trep|id** /ɪntrɛpɪd/ ADJ An **intrepid** person acts in a brave way. ❑ *...an intrepid space traveler.* [from Latin]

**in|tri|cate** /ɪntrɪkɪt/ ADJ You use **intricate** to describe something that has many small parts or details. ❑ *...carpets with very intricate patterns.* ● **in|tri|ca|cy** /ɪntrɪkəsi/ N-UNCOUNT ❑ *The price depends on the intricacy of the work.* ● **in|tri|cate|ly** ADV ❑ *...intricately carved sculptures.* [from Latin]

**in|trigue** (**intrigues, intriguing, intrigued**)

The noun is pronounced /ɪntrig/. The verb is pronounced /ɪntrig/.

**1** N-VAR **Intrigue** is the making of secret plans to harm or deceive people. ❑ *...political intrigue.* **2** V-T If something, especially something strange, **intrigues** you, it interests you and you want to know more about it. ❑ *Her remark intrigued him.* ● **in|trigued** ADJ ❑ *I would be intrigued to hear his views.* [from French]

**in|tri|guing** /ɪntrigɪŋ/ **1** ADJ If you describe something as **intriguing**, you mean that it is interesting or strange. ❑ *This is an intriguing story.* ● **in|tri|guing|ly** ADV ❑ *The results are intriguingly different each time.* [from French] **2** → see also **intrigue**

**in|trin|sic** /ɪntrɪnsɪk/ ADJ If something has **intrinsic** value or **intrinsic** interest, it is valuable or interesting because of its basic nature or character, and not because of its connection with other things. [FORMAL] ❑ *Diamonds have little intrinsic value.* ● **in|trin|si|cal|ly** /ɪntrɪnsɪkli/ ADV ❑ *The sounds of speech are intrinsically interesting to babies.* [from Late Latin]

**intro|duce** /ɪntrədus/ (**introduces, introducing, introduced**) **1** V-T To **introduce** something means to cause it to enter a place or exist in a system for the first time. ❑ *They are introducing new rules for student visas.* ● **intro|duc|tion** /ɪntrədʌkʃᵊn/ N-UNCOUNT ❑ *...the introduction of a computerized payment system.* **2** V-T If you **introduce** one person to another, or you **introduce** two people, you tell them each other's names, so that they can get to know each other. If you **introduce yourself** to someone, you tell them your name. ❑ *Tim, may I introduce you to my wife?* ❑ *We haven't been introduced. My name is Ned Taylor.* ● **intro|duc|tion** (**introductions**) N-VAR ❑ *Elaine, the hostess, performed the introductions.* **3** V-T If you **introduce** someone to something, you cause them to learn about it or experience it for the first time. ❑ *He introduced us to the delights of Spanish food.* ● **intro|duc|tion** N-SING ❑ *The vacation was a gentle introduction to camping.* **4** V-T The person who **introduces** a television or radio program speaks at the beginning of it, and often between the different items in it, in order to explain what the program or the items are about. ❑ *The show is introduced by Abby Clarke.* [from Latin]

| **Word Partnership** | Use *introduce* with : |
|---|---|
| N. | introduce **a bill**, introduce **changes**, introduce **legislation**, introduce **reform** 1 |
| V. | **allow me to** introduce, **let me** introduce, **want to** introduce 2 |

**intro|duc|tion** /ɪntrədʌkʃ°n/ (**introductions**)
**1** N-COUNT The **introduction** to a book or talk is the part that comes at the beginning and tells you what the rest of the book or talk is about. □ *Ellen Malos wrote the introduction to the book.* **2** N-COUNT If you refer to a book as an **introduction to** a particular subject, you mean that it explains the basic facts about that subject. □ *The book is a simple introduction to physics.* [from Latin] **3** → see also **introduce**

**intro|duc|tory** /ɪntrədʌktəri/ **1** ADJ An **introductory** remark, talk, or part of a book gives a small amount of general information about a particular subject, often before a more detailed explanation. □ *...an introductory course in information technology.* **2** ADJ An **introductory** offer or price on a new product is something such as a free gift or a low price that is meant to attract new customers. [BUSINESS] □ *...a special introductory offer.* [from Latin]

**in|trude** /ɪntrud/ (**intrudes, intruding, intruded**) V-I If you say that someone **is intruding into** a particular place or situation, you mean that they are not wanted or welcome there. □ *The press should not intrude into people's personal lives.* [from Latin]

**in|trud|er** /ɪntrudər/ (**intruders**) N-COUNT An **intruder** is a person who goes into a place where they are not supposed to be. □ *Windows and lighting help homeowners see intruders.* [from Latin]

**in|tru|sion** /ɪntruʒ°n/ (**intrusions**) N-VAR An **intrusion** is something that disturbs you when you are in a private place or in a private situation. □ *I felt it was an intrusion into our lives.* [from Latin]

**in|tru|sive** /ɪntrusɪv/ **1** ADJ Something that is **intrusive** disturbs your mood or your life in a way you do not like. □ *The cameras were an intrusive presence.* **2** ADJ **Intrusive** rock is rock that forms when lava from inside the Earth cools and becomes solid just below the Earth's surface. Compare **extrusive**. [TECHNICAL] [from Latin]

**in|tui|tion** /ɪntuɪʃ°n/ (**intuitions**) N-VAR Your **intuition** or your **intuitions** are unexplained feelings that something is true even when you have no evidence or proof of it. □ *Her intuition told her that something was wrong.* [from Late Latin]

**in|tui|tive** /ɪntuɪtɪv/ ADJ If you have an **intuitive** idea or feeling about something, you feel that it is true although you have no evidence or proof of it. □ *He has an intuitive understanding of art.* ● **in|tui|tive|ly** ADV □ *She knew intuitively that I missed my mother.* [from Late Latin]

**in|un|date** /ɪnʌndeɪt/ (**inundates, inundating, inundated**) V-T If you **are inundated with** things such as letters, demands, or requests, you receive so many of them that you cannot deal with them all. □ *We were inundated with letters of complaint.* [from Latin]

**in|vade** /ɪnveɪd/ (**invades, invading, invaded**) **1** V-T/V-I To **invade** a country means to enter it by force with an army. □ *In autumn 1944 the Allies invaded the Italian mainland.* □ *...invading armies.* ● **in|vad|er** (**invaders**) N-COUNT **Invaders** are soldiers who are invading a country. □ *The city was destroyed by foreign invaders.* **2** V-T If you say that people or animals **invade** a place, you mean that they enter it in large numbers, often in a way that is unpleasant or difficult to deal with. □ *Every so often ants invaded the kitchen.* [from Latin]

**in|va|lid** (**invalids**)

> The noun is pronounced /ɪnvəlɪd/. The adjective is pronounced /ɪnvælɪd/ and is hyphenated in|val|id.

**1** N-COUNT An **invalid** is someone who needs to be cared for because they have an illness or disability. □ *I hate being called an invalid.* **2** ADJ If an action, procedure, or document is **invalid**, it cannot be accepted, because it breaks the law or some official rule. □ *The trial was stopped and the results were declared invalid.* **3** ADJ An **invalid** argument or conclusion is wrong because it is based on a mistake. □ *The facts show that this argument is invalid.* [Sense 1 from Latin. Senses 2 and 3 from Medieval Latin.]

**in|valu|able** /ɪnvælyuəb°l/ ADJ If you describe something as **invaluable**, you mean that it is extremely useful. □ *I gained invaluable experience during that year.*

**in|vari|ably** /ɪnvɛəriəbli/ ADV If something **invariably** happens or is **invariably** true, it always happens or is always true. □ *He is invariably late.*

**in|va|sion** /ɪnveɪʒ°n/ (**invasions**) **1** N-VAR If there is an **invasion** of a country, a foreign army enters it by force. □ *...the German invasion of Poland in 1939.* **2** N-VAR If you refer to the arrival of a large number of people or things as an **invasion**, you are emphasizing that they are unpleasant or difficult to deal with. □ *...the annual summer invasion of flies.* **3** N-VAR If you describe an action as an **invasion**, you disapprove of it because it affects someone or something in a way that is not wanted. □ *Reading someone's diary is an invasion of privacy.* [from Latin]

**in|va|sive** /ɪnveɪsɪv/ ADJ You use **invasive** to describe something undesirable that spreads very quickly and that is very difficult to stop from spreading. □ *...invasive plants.* [from Latin]

**in|vent** /ɪnvɛnt/ (**invents, inventing, invented**) **1** V-T If you **invent** something such as a machine or process, you are the first person to think of it or make it. □ *He invented the first electric clock.* ● **in|ven|tor** (**inventors**) N-COUNT □ *...Alexander Graham Bell, the inventor of the telephone.* **2** V-T If you **invent** a story or excuse, you try to make other people believe that it is true when in fact it is not. □ *I tried to invent a good excuse.* [from Latin]

**in|ven|tion** /ɪnvɛnʃ°n/ (**inventions**) **1** N-COUNT An **invention** is a machine, device, or system that has been invented by someone. □ *Paper was a Chinese invention.* **2** N-UNCOUNT **Invention** is the act of inventing something that has never been made or used before. □ *...the invention of the telephone.* **3** N-VAR If you refer to someone's account of something as an **invention**, you think that it is untrue and that they have made it up. □ *His story was an invention from start to finish.* [from Latin]

**in|ven|tive** /ɪnvɛntɪv/ ADJ An **inventive** person is good at inventing things or has clever and original ideas. □ *I'm trying to be more inventive with* my cooking. ● in|ven|tive|ness N-UNCOUNT ❑ He surprised us with his inventiveness. [from Latin]

in|ven|tory /ˈɪnvəntɔri/ (inventories) ■ N-VAR An **inventory** is a supply or stock of something. ❑ ...an inventory of ten items at $15 each. ☑ N-COUNT An **inventory** is a written list of all the objects in a particular place such as all the merchandise in a store. ❑ He made an inventory of everything that was in the apartment. [from Medieval Latin]

in|vert /ɪnˈvɜrt/ (inverts, inverting, inverted) V-T If you **invert** something, you turn it upside down or back to front. [FORMAL] ❑ Invert the cake onto a serving plate. [from Latin]

in|ver|te|brate /ɪnˈvɜrtɪbrɪt/ (invertebrates) N-COUNT An **invertebrate** is a creature that does not have a spine such as an insect, a worm, or an octopus. [TECHNICAL] ● **Invertebrate** is also an adjective. ❑ ...invertebrate creatures.

in|vest /ɪnˈvɛst/ (invests, investing, invested) ■ V-T/V-I If you **invest** in something, or if you **invest** a sum of money, you use your money in a way that you hope will increase its value, for example, by buying securities or property. ❑ Many people don't like to invest in stocks. ❑ He invested millions of dollars in the business. ● in|ves|tor (investors) N-COUNT ❑ The main investor in the project is the French bank Crédit National. ☑ V-T/V-I If you **invest in** something useful, you buy it, because it will help you to do something more efficiently or more cheaply. ❑ We decided to invest in new computers. ☒ V-T If you **invest** time or energy in something, you spend a lot of time or energy on it because you think it will be useful or successful. ❑ I would rather invest time in my children than in my work. ☓ V-T To **invest** someone **with** rights or responsibilities means to give them those rights or responsibilities legally or officially. [FORMAL] [from Medieval Latin]

in|ves|ti|gate /ɪnˈvɛstɪgeɪt/ (investigates, investigating, investigated) V-T/V-I If someone, especially an official, **investigates** an event, situation, or claim, they try to find out what happened or what is the truth. ❑ Officials are still investigating the cause of the explosion. ❑ Police are investigating how the accident happened. ● in|ves|ti|ga|tion /ɪnˌvɛstɪˈgeɪʃən/ (investigations) N-VAR ❑ He ordered an investigation into the affair. [from Latin]

in|ves|ti|ga|tive /ɪnˈvɛstɪgeɪtɪv/ ADJ **Investigative** work, especially journalism, involves investigating things. ❑ ...an investigative reporter. [from Latin]

in|ves|ti|ga|tor /ɪnˈvɛstɪgeɪtər/ (investigators) N-COUNT An **investigator** is someone who carries out investigations, especially as part of their job. ❑ ...a private investigator. [from Latin]

in|vest|ment /ɪnˈvɛstmənt/ (investments) ■ N-UNCOUNT **Investment** is the activity of investing money. ❑ ...rules on investment. ☑ N-VAR An **investment** is an amount of money that you invest, or the thing that you invest in it. ❑ ...an investment of twenty-eight million dollars. ☒ N-COUNT If you describe something you buy as an **investment**, you mean that it will be useful, especially because it will help you to do a task more cheaply or efficiently. ❑ Buying good quality leather boots is a wise investment. [from Medieval Latin]

in|vig|or|at|ing /ɪnˈvɪgəreɪtɪŋ/ ADJ Something that is **invigorating** makes you feel more energetic. ❑ ...the invigorating northern air of the Canadian lakes.

in|vin|ci|ble /ɪnˈvɪnsɪbəl/ ADJ If you describe an army or sports team as **invincible**, you believe that they cannot be defeated. ❑ The players began to feel like they were invincible. [from Late Latin]

in|vis|ible /ɪnˈvɪzɪbəl/ ■ ADJ If something is **invisible**, you cannot see it, for example, because it is transparent, hidden, or very small. ❑ The mark is invisible from a distance. ☑ ADJ If you say that a person, problem, or situation is **invisible**, you are complaining that they are being ignored. ❑ He felt completely invisible in the room. ● in|vis|ibil|ity /ɪnˌvɪzɪˈbɪlɪti/ N-UNCOUNT ❑ She talked about the invisibility of women in society. [from Latin] → see sun

in|vi|ta|tion /ɪnvɪˈteɪʃən/ (invitations) ■ N-COUNT An **invitation** is a written or spoken request to come to an event such as a party, a meal, or a meeting. ❑ I accepted her invitation to lunch. ☑ N-COUNT An **invitation** is the card or paper on which an invitation is written or printed. ❑ Hundreds of invitations are being sent out this week. ☒ N-SING If you believe that someone's action is likely to have a particular result, especially a bad one, you can refer to the action as an **invitation to** that result. ❑ Don't leave your purse in your car — it's an invitation to theft. [from Latin]

**Word Partnership** Use invitation with :

V. accept an invitation, decline an invitation, extend an invitation ■ get/receive an invitation ■ ☑

in|vi|ta|tion|al /ɪnvɪˈteɪʃənəl/ (invitationals) ADJ An **invitational** tournament or event is a sports competition in which only players who have been asked to take part can compete. ❑ The golf tournament in Spain is an invitational tournament. ● **Invitational** is also a noun. ❑ ...a 59-team invitational. [from Latin]

in|vite (invites, inviting, invited)

The verb is pronounced /ɪnˈvaɪt/. The noun is pronounced /ˈɪnvaɪt/.

■ V-T If you **invite** someone to something such as a party or a meal, you ask them to come to it. ❑ She invited him to her 26th birthday party. ❑ Barron invited her to go with him to the theater. ☑ V-T If you **are invited to** do something, you are formally asked or given permission to do it. ❑ Managers were invited to buy stocks in the company. ❑ He invited me to go into partnership with him. ☒ V-T If something you say or do **invites** trouble or criticism, it makes trouble or criticism more likely. ❑ Their refusal to compromise will invite more criticism. ☓ N-COUNT An **invite** is an invitation to something such as a party or a meal. [INFORMAL] ❑ She tried to get an invite to the party. [from Latin]

| Word Partnership | Use *invite* with : |
| --- | --- |
| N. | invite *someone* to dinner, invite **friends**, invite **people** ■ |
| | invite **criticism**, invite **questions** ■ |

**in|vit|ing** /ɪnvaɪtɪŋ/ ■ ADJ If you say that something is **inviting**, you mean that it has good qualities that attract you or make you want to experience it. ❑ *The February air was soft, cool, and inviting.* ● **in|vit|ing|ly** ADV ❑ *The water is invitingly warm and clear.* [from Latin] ■ → see also **invite**

**in|vo|ca|tion** /ɪnvoʊkeɪʃⁿn/ N-COUNT An **invocation** is a prayer at a public meeting, usually at the beginning. ❑ *Dr. Jerome Taylor will give the invocation.* [from Latin]

**in|voice** /ɪnvɔɪs/ (**invoices, invoicing, invoiced**) ■ N-COUNT An **invoice** is a document that lists goods that have been supplied or services that have been done, and says how much money you owe for them. ❑ *We will send you an invoice for the course fees.* ■ V-T If you **invoice** someone, you send them a bill for goods or services you have provided them with. ❑ *The agency invoiced the client.* [from Old French]

**in|voke** /ɪnvoʊk/ (**invokes, invoking, invoked**) ■ V-T If you **invoke** a law, you state that you are taking a particular action because that law allows or tells you to. ❑ *The judge invoked an international law that protects refugees.* ■ V-T If you **invoke** something such as a principle, a saying, or a famous person, you refer to them in order to support your argument. ❑ *He invoked the name of Dr. Martin Luther King in his speech.* [from Latin]

| Word Link | *vol* ≈ will : bene**vol**ent, in**vol**untary, **vol**ition |
| --- | --- |

**in|vol|un|tary** /ɪnvɒlənteri/ ADJ If you make an **involuntary** movement or sound, you make it suddenly and without intending to because you are unable to control yourself. ❑ *Pain in my ankle caused me to give an involuntary scream.* ● **in|vol|un|tari|ly** /ɪnvɒləntɛərɪli/ ADV ❑ *I smiled involuntarily.* [from Latin] → see **muscle**

**in|volve** /ɪnvɒlv/ (**involves, involving, involved**) ■ V-T If a situation or activity **involves** something, that thing is a necessary part or consequence of it. ❑ *Running a household involves lots of organizational skills.* ■ V-T If a situation or activity **involves** someone, they are taking part in it. ❑ *The case involved people at the highest levels of government.* ■ V-T If you **involve** someone in something, you get them to take part in it. ❑ *We involve the children in everything.* [from Latin]

**in|volved** /ɪnvɒlvd/ ■ ADJ If you are **involved** in a situation or activity, you are taking part in it or have a strong connection with it. ❑ *She has been involved in business since she was a young woman.* ■ ADJ If you are **involved** in something, you give a lot of time, effort, or attention to it. ❑ *The family was deeply involved in their local church.* ■ ADJ The things **involved** in something such as a job or system are the necessary parts or consequences of it. ❑ *There is a lot of hard work involved in the job.* ■ ADJ If a situation or activity is **involved**, it is very complicated. ❑ *The surgery can be quite involved.* [from Latin]

**in|volve|ment** /ɪnvɒlvmənt/ N-UNCOUNT Your **involvement in** or **with** something is the fact that you are taking part in it. ❑ *His parents didn't like his involvement with the group.* [from Latin]

| Word Link | *ward* ≈ in the direction of : back**ward**, for**ward**, in**ward** |
| --- | --- |

**in|ward** /ɪnwərd/ ■ ADJ Your **inward** thoughts or feelings are the ones that you do not express or show to other people. ❑ *I felt inward relief.* ● **in|ward|ly** ADV ❑ *Sara was inwardly furious.* ■ ADJ An **inward** movement is one toward the inside or center of something. ■ ADV If something moves or faces **inward**, it moves or faces toward the inside or center of something. ❑ *He pushed the front door, which swung inward.* [from Old English]

**iodine** /aɪədaɪn/ N-UNCOUNT **Iodine** is a dark-colored substance used in medicine and photography. [from French]

**ion** /aɪən, aɪɒn/ (**ions**) N-COUNT **Ions** are electrically charged atoms. [TECHNICAL] [from Greek]

**ion|ic bond** /aɪɒnɪk bɒnd/ (**ionic bonds**) N-COUNT An **ionic bond** is a force that holds together two atoms with opposite electric charges. [TECHNICAL]

**ion|ic com|pound** (**ionic compounds**) N-COUNT An **ionic compound** is a chemical compound, consisting of a metal and a nonmetal, in which the atoms are held together by ionic bonds. [TECHNICAL]

**IP ad|dress** /aɪ pi ædrɛs/ (**IP addresses**) N-COUNT An **IP address** is a series of numbers that identify which particular computer or network is connected to the Internet. **IP** is an abbreviation for "Internet Protocol." [COMPUTING] ❑ *Every computer on the Internet has an unique IP address.*

**IQ** /aɪ kyu/ (**IQs**) N-VAR Your **IQ** is your level of intelligence, as indicated by a special test that you take. **IQ** is an abbreviation for "intelligence quotient." ❑ *His IQ is above average.*

**irate** /aɪreɪt/ ADJ If someone is **irate**, they are very angry about something. ❑ *He was so irate he started throwing things.* [from Latin]

**iris** /aɪrɪs/ (**irises**) N-COUNT The **iris** is the round colored part of a person's eye. [from Latin] → see **eye, muscle**

**iron** /aɪ_rɒd/ (**irons, ironing, ironed**) ■ N-UNCOUNT **Iron** is an element that usually takes the form of a hard, dark gray metal. ❑ *...a gate made of iron.* ■ N-COUNT An **iron** is an electrical device with a flat metal base. You heat it until the base is hot, then rub it over clothes to remove creases. ■ V-T If you **iron** clothes, you remove the creases from them using an iron. ❑ *She used to iron his shirts.* ● **iron|ing** N-UNCOUNT ❑ *I did all the ironing this morning.* ■ ADJ You can use **iron** to describe the character or behavior of someone who is very firm in their decisions and actions, or who can control their feelings well. ❑ *He has an iron will.* ❑ *...a man*

iron

of iron determination. [from Old English]

▶ **iron out** PHR-VERB If you **iron out** difficulties, you resolve them and bring them to an end. ❑ *We had to iron out a lot of problems.*

| Word Partnership | Use *iron* with : |
| --- | --- |
| N. | iron **bar**, iron **gate** 1 |
| | iron **a shirt** 3 |
| | **an** iron **fist/hand** 4 |
| ADJ. | **cast** iron, **wrought** iron 1 |
| | **a hot** iron 2 |

**iron|ic** /aɪrɒnɪk/ also **ironical** /aɪrɒnɪkᵊl/
1 ADJ When you make an **ironic** remark, you say the opposite of what you really mean, as a joke. ❑ *The comment was meant to be ironic.* ● **ironi|cal|ly** /aɪrɒnɪkli/ ADV ❑ *His enormous dog is ironically called "Tiny."* 2 ADJ An **ironic** situation is odd or amusing because it involves a contrast. ❑ *It is ironic that so many women are anti-feminist.* ● **ironi|cal|ly** ADV ❑ *Ironically, many people who drown know how to swim.* [from Latin]

**iro|ny** /aɪrəni, aɪər-/ (**ironies**) 1 N-UNCOUNT **Irony** is a subtle form of humor that involves saying things that are the opposite of what you really mean. ❑ *His tone was full of irony.* 2 N-VAR If you talk about the **irony** of a situation, you mean that it is odd or amusing because it involves a contrast. ❑ *The irony is that although we all know we should save money for the future, few of us do.* [from Latin]

| Word Link | ir ≈ not : i*r*rational, i*r*regular, i*r*responsible |
| --- | --- |

| Word Link | ratio ≈ reasoning : ir*ratio*nal, *ratio*nal, *ratio*nale |
| --- | --- |

**ir|ra|tion|al** /ɪræʃənᵊl/ ADJ **Irrational** feelings and behavior are not based on logical reasons or clear thinking. ❑ *...an irrational fear of science.* ● **ir|ra|tion|al|ly** ADV ❑ *My husband is irrationally jealous of my ex-boyfriends.* ● **ir|ra|tion|al|ity** /ɪræʃᵊnælɪti/ N-UNCOUNT ❑ *...the irrationality of his behavior.* [from Latin]

**ir|ra|tion|al num|ber** (**irrational numbers**) N-COUNT An **irrational number** is a number that cannot be written as a simple fraction, for example the square root of 2. [TECHNICAL]

**ir|rec|on|cil|able** /ɪrɛkənsaɪləbᵊl/ 1 ADJ If two things such as opinions or proposals are **irreconcilable**, they are so different from each other that it is not possible to believe or have both of them. [FORMAL] ❑ *These beliefs are irreconcilable with modern life.* 2 ADJ An **irreconcilable** disagreement or conflict is so serious that it cannot be settled. [FORMAL] ❑ *He said he had "irreconcilable differences" with the club.*

**ir|regu|lar** /ɪrɛgyələr/ (**irregulars**) 1 ADJ If events or actions occur at **irregular** intervals, the periods of time between them are of different lengths. ❑ *Cars passed at irregular intervals.* ❑ *Two years of irregular rainfall have brought problems for farmers.* ● **ir|regu|lar|ly** ADV ❑ *He was eating irregularly and losing weight.* ● **ir|regu|lar|ity** /ɪrɛgyəlærɪti/ (**irregularities**) N-VAR ❑ *...a dangerous irregularity in her heartbeat.* 2 ADJ Something that is **irregular** is not smooth or straight, or does not form a regular pattern. ❑ *The*

irregular surface makes it difficult for plants to grow. ● **ir|regu|lar|ly** ADV ❑ *The lake was irregularly shaped.* 3 ADJ **Irregular** behavior is dishonest or not in accordance with the normal rules. ❑ *...irregular business practices.* ● **ir|regu|lar|ity** N-VAR ❑ *We are investigating financial irregularities in the company.* 4 ADJ An **irregular** verb, noun, or adjective has different forms from most other verbs, nouns, or adjectives in the language. For example, "break" is an irregular verb because its past form is "broke," not "breaked." ● **ir|regu|lar|ity** (**irregularities**) N-VAR ❑ *...irregularities such as irregular plurals (sheep, oxen, phenomena).* [TECHNICAL] [from Old French]

**ir|regu|lar gal|axy** (**irregular galaxies**) N-COUNT A **irregular galaxy** is a galaxy with an irregular shape that does not belong to the other main types of galaxy such as spiral or elliptical galaxies. [TECHNICAL]

**ir|rel|evant** /ɪrɛlɪvᵊnt/ ADJ If you describe something as **irrelevant**, you mean that it is not important to or connected with what you are discussing or dealing with. ❑ *...irrelevant details.* ❑ *Your age is irrelevant — what matters is whether you can do your job.* ● **ir|rel|evance** N-UNCOUNT ❑ *...the irrelevance of the debate.* [from Medieval Latin]

**ir|re|sist|ible** /ɪrɪzɪstɪbᵊl/ 1 ADJ If a desire or force is **irresistible**, it is so powerful that it makes you act in a certain way, and there is nothing you can do to prevent this. ❑ *He had an irresistible urge to yawn.* ● **ir|re|sist|ibly** /ɪrɪzɪstɪbli/ ADV ❑ *I found myself irresistibly drawn to Steve.* 2 ADJ If you describe something or someone as **irresistible**, you mean that they are so good or attractive that you cannot stop yourself from liking them or wanting them. [INFORMAL] ❑ *The music is irresistible.* ● **ir|re|sist|ibly** ADV ❑ *She had a charm that men found irresistibly attractive.*

**ir|re|spec|tive** /ɪrɪspɛktɪv/ PHRASE If something happens **irrespective** of other things, those things do not affect it. [FORMAL] ❑ *We are all one people irrespective of religious and political beliefs.*

**ir|re|spon|sible** /ɪrɪspɒnsɪbᵊl/ ADJ If you describe someone as **irresponsible**, you are criticizing them because they do things without properly considering their possible consequences. ❑ *It is irresponsible to leave such a young child alone.* ● **ir|re|spon|sibly** /ɪrɪspɒnsɪbli/ ADV ❑ *They behaved irresponsibly.* ● **ir|re|spon|sibil|ity** /ɪrɪspɒnsɪbɪlɪti/ N-UNCOUNT ❑ *I am surprised at the irresponsibility of their behavior.* [from Latin]

| Word Link | vere ≈ fear, awe : ir*rever*ent, *reve*re, *reve*rence |
| --- | --- |

**ir|rev|er|ent** /ɪrɛvərənt/ ADJ If you describe someone as **irreverent**, you mean that they do not show respect for people or things that are generally respected. ❑ *He had an irreverent attitude to history.* ● **ir|rev|er|ence** N-UNCOUNT ❑ *...her irreverence for authority.*

**ir|re|vers|ible** /ɪrɪvɜrsɪbᵊl/ ADJ If a change is **irreversible**, things cannot be changed back to the way they were before. ❑ *He suffered irreversible brain damage.*

**ir|revo|cable** /ɪrɛvəkəbᵊl/ ADJ If a decision, action, or change is **irrevocable**, it cannot be changed or reversed. [FORMAL] ❑ *She said the decision was irrevocable.* ● **ir|revo|cably** /ɪrɛvəkəbli/ ADV ❑ *A serious illness can irrevocably change your* *relationships with friends and family.*

**ir|ri|gate** /ɪrɪgeɪt/ (**irrigates, irrigating, irrigated**) v-t To **irrigate** land means to supply it with water in order to help crops grow. □ *Water from Lake Powell is used to irrigate the area.* ● **ir|ri|ga|tion** /ɪrɪgeɪʃ°n/ N-UNCOUNT □ *The irrigation of the surrounding agricultural land is poor.* [from Latin]
→ see **dam**

**ir|ri|table** /ɪrɪtəb°l/ ADJ If you are **irritable**, you are easily annoyed. □ *After waiting for over an hour, she was feeling irritable.* ● **ir|ri|tably** /ɪrɪtəbli/ ADV □ *"Why are you whispering?" he asked irritably.* ● **ir|ri|tabil|ity** /ɪrɪtəbɪlɪti/ N-UNCOUNT □ *Patients can suffer from personality changes and irritability.* [from Latin]

**ir|ri|tant** /ɪrɪtənt/ (**irritants**) **1** N-COUNT If you describe something as an **irritant**, you mean that it keeps annoying you. [FORMAL] □ *The problem is a major irritant to the government.* **2** N-COUNT An **irritant** is a substance that causes a part of your body to itch or become sore. [FORMAL] □ *Many pesticides are irritants.* [from Latin]

**ir|ri|tate** /ɪrɪteɪt/ (**irritates, irritating, irritated**) **1** v-t If something **irritates** you, it keeps annoying you. □ *Their attitude irritates me.* ● **ir|ri|tat|ed** ADJ □ *Her teacher got irritated with her.* ● **ir|ri|tat|ing** ADJ □ *They have an irritating habit of interrupting.* ● **ir|ri|tat|ing|ly** ADV □ *He is irritatingly indecisive.* **2** v-t If something **irritates** a part of your body, it causes it to itch or become sore. □ *Chilies can irritate the skin.* [from Latin]

**ir|ri|ta|tion** /ɪrɪteɪʃ°n/ (**irritations**) **1** N-UNCOUNT **Irritation** is a feeling of annoyance. □ *He tried not show his irritation.* **2** N-COUNT An **irritation** is something that keeps annoying you. □ *Don't let a minor irritation at work make you unhappy.* **3** N-VAR **Irritation** in a part of your body is a feeling of slight pain and discomfort there. □ *These oils may cause irritation to sensitive skins.* [from Latin]

**is** /ɪz/ **Is** is the third person singular of the present tense of **be**. [from Old English]

**Is|lam** /ɪslɑm/ N-UNCOUNT **Islam** is the religion of the Muslims, which was started by Mohammed. □ *He converted to Islam at the age of 16.* ● **Is|lam|ic** /ɪslæmɪk, -lɑ-/ ADJ □ *...Islamic law.* [from Arabic]

**is|land** /aɪlənd/ (**islands**) N-COUNT An **island** is a piece of land that is completely surrounded by water. □ *...the Canary Islands.* [from Old English]

**is|land|er** /aɪləndər/ (**islanders**) N-COUNT **Islanders** are people who live on an island. □ *Tourism is very important to the islanders.* [from Old English]

**isle** /aɪl/ (**isles**) N-COUNT An **isle** is an island; often used as part of an island's name, or in literary English. □ *...the Isle of Pines.* [from Old French]

**isn't** /ɪz°nt/ **Isn't** is the usual spoken form of "is not." [from Old English]

**iso|bar** /aɪsəbɑr/ (**isobars**) N-COUNT An **isobar** is a line on a weather map that connects points of equal atmospheric pressure. [from Greek]

**iso|late** /aɪsəleɪt/ (**isolates, isolating, isolated**) v-t To **isolate** someone or something means to make them become separate from other people or things of the same kind, either physically or socially. □ *His difficult behavior isolated him from other children.* ● **iso|lat|ed** ADJ □ *She was completely isolated, living alone in a big house.* ● **iso|la|tion** /aɪsəleɪʃ°n/ N-UNCOUNT □ *Boredom and isolation were enough to upset her.* [from Italian]

**iso|lat|ed** /aɪsəleɪtɪd/ **1** ADJ An **isolated** place is a long way away from large towns and is difficult to reach. □ *Their village is in an isolated area.* **2** ADJ An **isolated** example is an example of something that is not very common. □ *There was one isolated case of cheating.* [from Italian]

**iso|la|tion** /aɪsəleɪʃ°n/ (**isolations**) **1** N-VAR In dance, an **isolation** is a movement or exercise that involves only one part of your body, for example shrugging your shoulders or rolling your head. [TECHNICAL] **2** → see also **isolate** **3** PHRASE If someone does something **in isolation**, they do it without other people present or without their help. □ *She is good at working in isolation.* [from Italian]

**iso|tope** /aɪsətoʊp/ (**isotopes**) N-COUNT **Isotopes** are atoms that have the same number of protons and electrons but different numbers of neutrons and therefore have different physical properties. [TECHNICAL] [from Greek]

**ISP** /aɪ ɛs pi/ (**ISPs**) N-COUNT An **ISP** is a company that provides Internet and e-mail services. **ISP** is an abbreviation for "Internet service provider."

**is|sue** /ɪʃu/ (**issues, issuing, issued**) **1** N-COUNT An **issue** is an important subject that people are arguing about or discussing. □ *She raised the issue of money with her boss.* **2** N-SING If something is **the issue**, it is the thing you consider to be the most important part of a situation or discussion. □ *Job satisfaction is the issue for me, not money.* **3** N-COUNT An **issue** of something such as a magazine or newspaper is the version of it that is published, for example, in a particular month or on a particular day. □ *...the latest issue of the "Scientific American."* **4** v-t If you **issue** a statement or a warning, you make it known formally or publicly. □ *The government issued a warning of possible terrorist attacks.* **5** v-t If you **are issued with** something, it is officially given to you. □ *He was issued with a new passport.* ● **Issue** is also a noun. □ *...a pair of army issue boots.* **6** PHRASE The question or point **at issue** is the question or point that is being argued about or discussed. □ *The point at issue is who controls the company.* [from Old French]
→ see **philosophy**

**it** /ɪt/

It is a third person singular pronoun. **It** is used as the subject or object of a verb, or as the object of a preposition.

**1** PRON You use **it** to refer to an object, animal, or other thing that has already been mentioned, or to a situation that you have just described. □ *It's a wonderful city. I'll show it to you.* □ *She has a health problem but is embarrassed to ask the doctor about it.* □ *He quit sports, not because of injury but because he wanted it that way.* **2** PRON You use **it** before certain nouns, adjectives, and verbs to introduce your feelings or point of view about a situation. □ *It was nice to see Steve again.* □ *It's a pity you can't come, Sarah.* **3** PRON You use **it** in passive clauses that report a situation or event. □ *It is said that stress can cause cancer.* **4** PRON You use **it** as the subject of "be" to say what the time, day, or date is. ❑ *It's three o'clock in the morning.* ❑ *It was a Monday, so she was at home.* ◻ PRON You use **it** as the subject of a linking verb to describe the weather, the light, or the temperature. ❑ *It was very wet and windy.* ◻ PRON You use **it** when you are telling someone who you are, or asking them who they are, especially at the beginning of a phone call. You also use **it** in statements and questions about the identity of other people. ❑ *"Who is it?" he called. — "It's your neighbor."* ◻ PRON When you are emphasizing or drawing attention to something, you can put that thing immediately after **it** and a form of the verb "be." ❑ *It's my father they're talking about.* [from Old English]

**ital|ic** /ɪtǽlɪk/ (**italics**) ◻ N-PLURAL **Italics** are letters that slope to the right. Italics are often used to emphasize a particular word or sentence. The examples in this dictionary are printed in italics. ❑ *The title is printed in italics.* ◻ ADJ **Italic** letters slope to the right. ❑ *She wrote to them in her beautiful italic handwriting.* [from Venice]

**itch** /ɪtʃ/ (**itches, itching, itched**) ◻ V-I When a part of your body **itches**, you have an unpleasant feeling on your skin that makes you want to scratch. ❑ *Her perfume made my eyes itch.* ● **Itch** is also a noun. ❑ *Scratch my back — I've got an itch.* ● **itch|ing** N-UNCOUNT ❑ *The disease can cause severe itching.* ● **itchy** ADJ ❑ *...itchy, sore eyes.* ◻ V-T If you **are itching** to do something, you are very eager or impatient to do it. [INFORMAL] ❑ *I was itching to start.* ● **Itch** is also a noun. ❑ *...TV viewers with an itch to switch from channel to channel.* [from Old English]

**it'd** /ɪtəd/ ◻ **It'd** is a spoken form of "it would." ❑ *It'd be better to keep quiet.* ◻ **It'd** is a spoken form of "it had," especially when "had" is an auxiliary verb. ❑ *Marcie was watching a movie. It'd just started.* [from Old English]

**item** /áɪtəm/ (**items**) ◻ N-COUNT An **item** is one of a collection or list of objects. ❑ *The most valuable item on show was a Picasso drawing.* ◻ N-COUNT An **item** is one of a list of things for someone to do, deal with, or talk about. ❑ *The other item on the agenda is sales.* ◻ N-COUNT An **item** is a report or article in a newspaper or magazine, or on television or radio. ❑ *There was an item in the paper about him.* [from Latin]

| Thesaurus | *item* | Also look up : |
|---|---|---|
| N. | issue, subject, task ◻ | |
| | article, story ◻ | |

**itin|er|ary** /aɪtɪnəˈrɛri/ (**itineraries**) N-COUNT An **itinerary** is a plan of a trip, including the route and the places that you will visit. ❑ *The next place on our itinerary was Sedona.* [from Late Latin]

**it'll** /ɪt°l/ ◻ **It'll** is a spoken form of "it will." ❑ *It'll be nice to see them next weekend.* [from Old English]

**its** /ɪts/

| Its is a third person singular possessive determiner. |
|---|

DET You use **its** to indicate that something belongs or relates to a thing, place, or animal that has just been mentioned or whose identity is known. ❑ *He held the knife by its handle.* [from Old English]

**Usage** **its** and **it's**

Its is the possessive form of *it*, and *it's* is the contraction of *it is* or *it has*. They are often confused because they are pronounced the same and because the possessive *its* doesn't have an apostrophe: *It's been a month since Maricel's store lost its license, but it's still doing business.*

**it's** /ɪts/ **It's** is the usual spoken form of "it is" or "it has," when "has" is an auxiliary verb. [from Old English]

**it|self** /ɪtsɛlf/ ◻ PRON **Itself** is used as the object of a verb or preposition when it refers to something that is the same thing as the subject of the verb. ❑ *The body refreshes itself while we sleep.* ◻ PRON You use **itself** to emphasize the thing you are referring to. ❑ *Life itself is a learning process.* ◻ PRON If you say that someone is, for example, politeness **itself** or kindness **itself**, you are emphasizing that they are extremely polite or extremely kind. ❑ *I wasn't really happy there, though the people were kindness itself.*

**IV** /áɪ víː/ (**IVs**) ◻ N-COUNT An **IV** or an **IV drip** is a piece of medical equipment by which a liquid is slowly passed through a tube into a patient's blood. ❑ *She was attached to an IV.* ◻ ADJ **IV** is an abbreviation for **intravenous.** ❑ *...a plastic bottle of IV fluids.*

**I've** /aɪv/ **I've** is the usual spoken form of "I have," especially when "have" is an auxiliary verb. ❑ *I've been invited to a party.* [from Old English]

**IVF** /áɪ viː ɛf/ N-UNCOUNT **IVF** is a method of helping a woman to have a baby in which an egg is removed from one of her ovaries, fertilized outside her body, and then replaced in her womb. **IVF** is an abbreviation for "in vitro fertilization." ❑ *After years of trying for a baby she had IVF.*

**ivo|ry** /áɪvəri/ N-UNCOUNT **Ivory** is a hard cream-colored substance that forms the tusks of elephants. ❑ *...the international ban on the sale of ivory.* [from Old French]

**ivy** /áɪvi/ (**ivies**) N-VAR **Ivy** is an evergreen plant that grows up walls or along the ground. [from Old English]

**Ivy League** ◻ N-PROPER **The Ivy League** is a group of eight colleges in the northeastern United States, which have high academic and social status. ❑ *...an Ivy League college.* ◻ ADJ You use **Ivy League** to describe fashions and attitudes typical of students at Ivy League colleges. ❑ *...Ivy League shirts.*

# Jj

**jab** /dʒæb/ (**jabs, jabbing, jabbed**) V-T/V-I If you **jab** something, you push it with a quick, sudden movement. ❑ *She jabbed her thumb on a red button.* ❑ *Stern jabbed at me with his glasses.* [from Scottish]

**jack** /dʒæk/ (**jacks**)
◻ N-COUNT A **jack** is a piece of equipment for lifting a heavy object, such as a car, off the ground. ◻ N-COUNT A **jack** is a playing card whose value is between a ten and a queen. ❑ *...the jack of spades.*

jack

**jack|et** /dʒækɪt/ (**jackets**)
◻ N-COUNT A **jacket** is a short coat with long sleeves. ❑ *...a black leather jacket.* ◻ N-COUNT The **jacket** of a book is the paper cover that protects the book. ❑ *There's a picture of a beautiful girl on the jacket of this book.* ❑ *The back cover of the book's jacket* [from Old French]
→ see **clothing**

**jack|ham|mer** /dʒækhæmər/ (**jackhammers**) N-COUNT A **jackhammer** is a large powerful hammer that is used for breaking up rocks and other hard material.

**jack-o'-lantern** /dʒæk əlæntərn/ (**jack-o'-lanterns**) also **jack o'lantern** N-COUNT A **jack-o'-lantern** is a lantern made from a hollow pumpkin that has been carved to look like a face.

**jack|pot** /dʒækpɒt/ (**jackpots**) N-COUNT A **jackpot** is a large sum of money that is the most valuable prize in a game or lottery. ❑ *She won the jackpot of $5 million.*

**jade** /dʒeɪd/ N-UNCOUNT **Jade** is a hard green type of stone used for making jewelry and ornaments. [from French]

**jad|ed** /dʒeɪdɪd/ ADJ If you are **jaded**, you feel bored, tired, and not enthusiastic. ❑ *He can sound jaded at times.* [from French]

**jag|ged** /dʒægɪd/ ADJ Something that is **jagged** has a rough, uneven shape or edge with lots of sharp points. ❑ *...jagged black cliffs.*

**jail** /dʒeɪl/ (**jails, jailing, jailed**) ◻ N-VAR A **jail** is a place where criminals are kept in order to punish them. ❑ *Three prisoners escaped from a jail.* ◻ V-T If someone **is jailed**, they are put into jail. ❑ *He was jailed for twenty years.* [from Old French]

**jail|house** /dʒeɪlhaʊs/ (**jailhouses**) N-COUNT A **jailhouse** is a small prison.

**jam** /dʒæm/ (**jams, jamming, jammed**) ◻ V-T If you **jam** something somewhere, you push it there roughly. ❑ *Pete jammed his hands into his pockets.* ◻ V-T/V-I If something **jams**, or if you **jam** it, it becomes fixed in position and is unable to move freely or work properly. ❑ *When he tried to open the door, it jammed.* ❑ *He jammed the key in the lock.*

◻ V-T/V-I If a lot of people **jam** a place, or **jam into** a place, they are pressed tightly together so that they can hardly move. ❑ *Hundreds of people jammed the streets.* ● **jammed** ADJ ❑ *The stadium was jammed and they had to turn away hundreds of disappointed fans.* ◻ N-COUNT If there is a traffic **jam** on a road, there are so many vehicles there that they cannot move. ❑ *Trucks sat in a jam for ten hours.* ◻ V-T To **jam** a radio or electronic signal means to interfere with it and prevent it from being received or heard clearly. ❑ *The plane is used to jam radar equipment.* ● **jam|ming** N-UNCOUNT ❑ *...electronic signal jamming equipment.*
→ see **traffic**

**Jane Doe** /dʒeɪn doʊ/ (**Jane Does**) N-COUNT **Jane Doe** is used to refer to a woman whose real name is not known or cannot be revealed, for example, for legal reasons. ❑ *The patient, known as "Jane Doe," knew about Mr. Jackson's secret plan.*

**jan|gle** /dʒæŋg°l/ (**jangles, jangling, jangled**) V-T/V-I When objects strike against each other and make a ringing noise, you can say that they **jangle** or **are jangled**. ❑ *Her bracelets jangled.* [from Old French]

**jani|tor** /dʒænɪtər/ (**janitors**) N-COUNT A **janitor** is a person whose job is to take care of a building. ❑ *Ed Roberts had been a school janitor for a long time.* [from Latin]

**Janu|ary** /dʒænyuɛri/ (**Januaries**) N-VAR **January** is the first month of the year in the Western calendar. ❑ *We always have snow in January.* [from Latin]

**jar** /dʒɑr/ (**jars, jarring, jarred**) ◻ N-COUNT A **jar** is a glass container with a lid that is used for storing food. ❑ *...candy in glass jars.* ◻ V-T/V-I If

jar

something **jars**, or **jars** you, you find it unpleasant or shocking. ❑ *The question jarred her a little.* ● **jar|ring** ADJ ❑ *...the jarring sound of the machine.* ◻ V-T/V-I If an object **jars**, or if something **jars** it, the object moves with a fairly hard shaking movement. ❑ *The ship jarred a little.* ❑ *The sudden movement jarred the box.* [Sense 1 from Old French. Senses 2 and 3 from Old English.]
→ see **container**

**jar|gon** /dʒɑrgən/ N-UNCOUNT You use **jargon** to refer to words and expressions that are used in special or technical ways, often making the language difficult to understand. ❑ *The report was full of technical jargon.* [from Old French]

**jaun|ty** /dʒɔnti/ (**jauntier, jauntiest**) ADJ If you

describe someone or something as **jaunty**, you mean that they are full of confidence and energy. ❑ *…a jaunty little man.* ● **jaun|ti|ly** /dʒɔntɪli/ ADV ❑ *He walked jauntily into the café.* [from French]

**java** /dʒɑvə/ N-UNCOUNT **Java** is coffee. [INFORMAL] ❑ *…a cup of hot java.*

**jave|lin** /dʒævlɪn/ (**javelins**) ■ N-COUNT A **javelin** is a long spear that is thrown in sports competitions. ■ N-SING You can refer to the competition in which the javelin is thrown as **the javelin.** ❑ *Steve Backley won the javelin.* [from Old French]

**jaw** /dʒɔ/ (**jaws**) ■ N-COUNT Your **jaw** is the lower part of your face ❑ *Andrew broke his jaw in two places.* ■ N-COUNT A person's or animal's **jaws** are the two bones in their head that their teeth are attached to. ❑ *…an animal with powerful jaws.* [from Old French]

**jazz** /dʒæz/ N-UNCOUNT **Jazz** is a style of music that was invented by African American musicians in the early part of the twentieth century. Jazz music has very strong rhythms and often involves improvisation. ❑ *The club plays live jazz on Sundays.* → see **genre**

**jazz dance** N-UNCOUNT **Jazz dance** is a form of dance that developed in America in the twentieth century, based on jazz-influenced music and complex rhythmic movements.

**jeal|ous** /dʒɛləs/ ■ ADJ If someone is **jealous**, they feel angry or bitter because they think that another person is trying to take a lover or friend, or a possession, away from them. ❑ *She got jealous and there was a fight.* ● **jeal|ous|ly** ADV ❑ *Her recipe for chocolate cake was a jealously guarded secret.* ■ ADJ If you are **jealous** of another person's possessions or qualities, you feel angry or bitter because you do not have them. ❑ *She was jealous of his wealth.* ● **jeal|ous|ly** ADV ❑ *Gloria looked jealously at the red sports car.* [from Old French]

**jeal|ousy** /dʒɛləsi/ ■ N-UNCOUNT **Jealousy** is the feeling of anger or bitterness that someone has when they think that another person is trying to take a lover or friend, or a possession, away from them. ❑ *He could not control his jealousy when he saw her new husband.* ■ N-UNCOUNT **Jealousy** is the feeling of anger or bitterness that someone has when they wish that they could have the qualities or possessions that another person has. ❑ *…jealousy of her beauty.* [from Old French]

**jeans** /dʒinz/ N-PLURAL **Jeans** are casual pants that are usually made of strong cotton cloth called denim. ❑ *…a young man in jeans and a T-shirt.* → see **clothing**

**jeer** /dʒɪər/ (**jeers, jeering, jeered**) ■ V-T/V-I To **jeer** at someone means to say or shout rude and insulting things to them to show that you do not respect them. ❑ *The crowds jeered at the referee.* ❑ *They jeered the president.* ● **jeer|ing** N-UNCOUNT ❑ *There was constant jeering from the audience.* ■ N-COUNT **Jeers** are rude and insulting things that people shout to show they do not respect someone. ❑ *…jeers from the crowd.*

**jell** /dʒɛl/ (**jells, jelling, jelled**) also **gel** V-I If people, things, or ideas **jell**, they or their different parts begin to work well together to form a successful whole. ❑ *It takes a while for a team to jell.*

**jel|ly** /dʒɛli/ (**jellies**) N-VAR **Jelly** is a sweet food made by cooking fruit with a large amount of sugar, that is usually spread on bread. ❑ *…peanut butter and jelly sandwiches.* [from Old French]

**jel|ly|fish** /dʒɛlifɪs/ (**jellyfish**) N-COUNT A **jellyfish** is a sea creature that has a clear soft body and can sting you.

**jel|ly roll** (**jelly rolls**) N-VAR **Jelly roll** is a long cake made from a thin, flat cake which is covered with jam or cream on one side, then rolled up.

**jeop|ard|ize** /dʒɛpərdaɪz/ (**jeopardizes, jeopardizing, jeopardized**) V-T To **jeopardize** a situation or activity means to do something that may destroy it or cause it to fail. ❑ *He has jeopardized his future career.* [from Old French]

**jeop|ardy** /dʒɛpərdi/ PHRASE If someone or something is **in jeopardy**, they are in danger of being harmed or lost. ❑ *His job was in jeopardy.* [from Old French]

**jerk** /dʒɜrk/ (**jerks, jerking, jerked**) ■ V-T/V-I If you **jerk** something or someone in a particular direction, or they **jerk** in a particular direction, they move a short distance very suddenly and quickly. ❑ *Mr. Griffin jerked forward in his chair.* ❑ *"This is Brady," said Sam, jerking his head in my direction.* ● **Jerk** is also a noun. ❑ *He gave a jerk of his head to the other two men.* ■ N-COUNT If you call someone a **jerk**, you are insulting them because you think they are stupid or you do not like them. [INFORMAL] [from Old English]

**jerky** /dʒɜrki/ (**jerkier, jerkiest**) ADJ **Jerky** movements are very sudden and quick, and do not flow smoothly. ❑ *Avoid any sudden or jerky movements.* ● **jerk|i|ly** /dʒɜrkɪli/ ADV ❑ *He moved jerkily toward the car.* [from Old English]

**jer|sey** /dʒɜrzi/ (**jerseys**) N-VAR **Jersey** is a knitted, slightly stretchy fabric used especially to make women's clothing. ❑ *…a black jersey top.*

**Jesus** /dʒizəs/ N-PROPER **Jesus** or **Jesus Christ** is the name of the man who Christians believe was the son of God, and whose teachings are the basis of Christianity. [from Latin]

**jet** /dʒɛt/ (**jets, jetting, jetted**) ■ N-COUNT A **jet** is an aircraft that is powered by jet engines. ❑ *…her private jet.* ❑ *He arrived from Key West by jet.* ■ V-I If you **jet** somewhere, you travel there in a fast plane. ❑ *The president will jet off to Germany today.* ■ N-COUNT A **jet** of liquid or gas is a strong, fast, thin stream of it. ❑ *A jet of water poured through the windows.* [from Old French] → see **fly**

**jet en|gine** (**jet engines**) N-COUNT A **jet engine** is an engine in which hot air and gases are forced out at the back.

**jet lag** N-UNCOUNT If you are suffering from **jet lag**, you feel tired after a long trip by airplane. ❑ *…the best way to avoid jet lag.*

**jet|liner** /dʒɛtlaɪnər/ (**jetliners**) N-COUNT A **jetliner** is a large aircraft, especially one which carries passengers.

**jet stream** (**jet streams**) N-COUNT The **jet stream** is a very strong wind that blows high in the Earth's atmosphere and has an important influence on the weather.

**jet|ti|son** /dʒɛtɪsən, -zən/ (**jettisons, jettisoning, jettisoned**) V-T If you **jettison** something that is not needed, you throw it away or get rid of it. ❑ *The governor has jettisoned the plan.* [from Old French]

## Picture Dictionary — jewelry

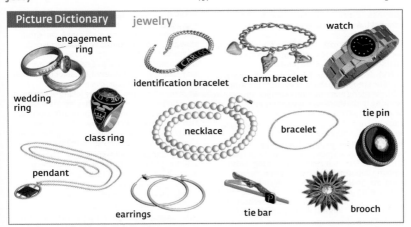

engagement ring

watch

identification bracelet

charm bracelet

wedding ring

tie pin

class ring

necklace

bracelet

pendant

earrings

tie bar

brooch

**jet|ty** /dʒɛti/ (**jetties**) N-COUNT A **jetty** is a wide stone wall or wooden platform where boats stop to let people get on or off, or to load or unload goods. [from Old French]

**Jew** /dʒu/ (**Jews**) N-COUNT A **Jew** is a person who believes in and practices the religion of Judaism. [from Old French]

**jew|el** /dʒuəl/ (**jewels**) N-COUNT A **jewel** is a precious stone used to decorate valuable things, such as rings or necklaces. ❏ ...precious jewels. [from Old French]

**jew|el|er** /dʒuələr/ (**jewelers**) ◼ N-COUNT A **jeweler** is a person who makes, sells, and repairs jewelry and watches. ◼ N-COUNT A **jeweler** is a store where jewelry and watches are made, sold, and repaired. ❏ ...a jeweler on Fifth Avenue. [from Old French]

**jew|el|ry** /dʒuəlri/ N-UNCOUNT **Jewelry** is ornaments that people wear, such as rings and bracelets. ❏ ...a selection of expensive watches and jewelry. [from Old French]
→ see Picture Dictionary: **jewelery**

**Jew|ish** /dʒuɪʃ/ ADJ **Jewish** means belonging or relating to the religion of Judaism, or to Jews as an ethnic group. ❏ ...the Jewish festival of Passover. [from Old French]

**jibe** /dʒaɪb/ (**jibes, jibing, jibed**)

> The spelling **gibe** is also used for meanings ◼ and ◼.

◼ N-COUNT A **jibe** is a rude or insulting remark about someone that is intended to make them look foolish. ❏ ...a cruel jibe about his loss of hair. ◼ V-T To **jibe** means to say something rude or insulting that is intended to make another person look foolish. [WRITTEN] ❏ "No doubt he'll give me the chance to fight him again," he jibed. [from Old French]

**jig** /dʒɪg/ (**jigs, jigging, jigged**) ◼ N-COUNT A **jig** is a lively dance. ❏ She danced an Irish jig. ◼ V-I To **jig** means to dance or move energetically. ❏ Louis jigged around to the music.

**jig|saw** /dʒɪgsɔ/ (**jigsaws**) N-COUNT A **jigsaw** or **jigsaw puzzle** is a picture on cardboard or wood that has been cut up into odd shapes that have

jigsaw puzzle

to be put back together again. ❏ The children were doing a jigsaw puzzle.

**jin|gle** /dʒɪŋgəl/ (**jingles, jingling, jingled**) ◼ V-T/ V-I When something **jingles** or when you **jingle** it, it makes a gentle ringing noise, like small bells. ❏ Brian put his hands in his pockets and jingled some coins. ◼ N-COUNT A **jingle** is a short, simple tune, often with words, that is used to advertise a product or program on radio or television. ❏ ...advertising jingles. [from Dutch]

**jit|ters** /dʒɪtərz/ N-PLURAL If you have the **jitters**, you feel nervous, for example because you have to do something important or because you are expecting important news. [INFORMAL] ❏ Amanda suffered pre-wedding jitters before marrying her boyfriend.

**jit|tery** /dʒɪtəri/ ADJ If someone is **jittery**, they feel nervous or are behaving nervously. [INFORMAL] ❏ She felt weak and a little jittery.

**jive** /dʒaɪv/ ◼ N-UNCOUNT **Jive** is rock and roll or swing music that you dance to. ◼ N-UNCOUNT **Jive** or **jive talk** is a kind of informal language used by some African Americans.

**job** /dʒɒb/ (**jobs**) ◼ N-COUNT A **job** is the work that someone does to earn money. ❏ I want to get a job. ❏ Terry was looking for a new job. ◼ N-COUNT A **job** is a particular task. ❏ I'm glad I don't have the job of replacing him. ◼ N-COUNT The **job** of a particular person or thing is their duty or function. ❏ Drinking a lot of water helps the kidneys do their job. ◼ N-SING If you say that someone is doing a good job, you mean that they are doing something well. ❏ He did a far better job of managing the project than I did. ◼ **the job in hand** → see **hand**

| Thesaurus | job | Also look up : |
|---|---|---|
| N. | employment, occupation, profession, vocation; (ant.) work ◼ | |

**job|less** /dʒɒblɪs/ ADJ Someone who is **jobless** does not have a job, but would like one. ❑ ...*millions of jobless Americans.*

**job sat|is|fac|tion** N-UNCOUNT **Job satisfaction** is the pleasure that you get from doing your job. ❑ *I'll never be rich, but I get job satisfaction.*

**job share** (**job shares, job sharing, job shared**) V-I If two people **job share**, they share the same job by working part-time, for example, one person working in the mornings and the other in the afternoons. ❑ *They both want to job share.*

**jock|ey** /dʒɒki/ (**jockeys**) N-COUNT A **jockey** is someone who rides a horse in a race.

**jog** /dʒɒg/ (**jogs, jogging, jogged**) ■ V-I If you **jog**, you run slowly, often as a form of exercise. ❑ *I got up early the next morning to jog.* ● **Jog** is also a noun. ❑ *He went for another early morning jog.* ● **jog|ger** (**joggers**) N-COUNT ❑ *The park was full of joggers.* ● **jog|ging** N-UNCOUNT ❑ *The jogging helped him to lose weight.* ■ V-T If you **jog** something, you push or bump it slightly so that it moves. ❑ *Avoid jogging the camera.*

**John Doe** /dʒɒn doʊ/ (**John Does**) N-COUNT **John Doe** is used to refer to a man whose real name is not known or cannot be revealed, for example, for legal reasons. ❑ *...a letter from someone who signed himself "John Doe."*

**join** /dʒɔɪn/ (**joins, joining, joined**) ■ V-T If one person or vehicle **joins** another, they move or go to the same place. ❑ *She joined him in a trip to France.* ■ V-T If you **join** an organization, you become a member of it. ❑ *He joined the Army five years ago.* ■ V-T/V-I If you **join** an activity, or **join in** an activity, you take part in it or become involved with it. ❑ *The United States joined the war in April 1917.* ❑ *Thousands of people will join in the celebrations.* ■ V-T If you **join** a line, you stand at the end of it so that you are part of it. ❑ *He joined the line of people waiting to board the plane.* ■ V-T To **join** two things means to attach or fasten them together. ❑ *"And" is often used to join two sentences.* [from Old French] ■ **join forces** → see **force**
▸ **join in** PHR-VERB If you **join in** an activity, you take part in it or become involved in it. ❑ *I hope everyone will join in the fun.*
▸ **join up** PHR-VERB If someone **joins up**, they become a member of the army, the navy, or the air force. ❑ *When the war started, he joined up.*

**joint** /dʒɔɪnt/ (**joints**) ■ ADJ **Joint** means shared by or belonging to two or more people. ❑ *...a joint bank account.* ● **joint|ly** ADV ❑ *They jointly write and direct every film themselves.* ■ N-COUNT A **joint** is a part of your body such as your elbow or knee where two bones meet and are able to move together. ❑ *Her joints ache if she exercises.* ■ N-COUNT A **joint** is the place where two things are fastened or joined together. ❑ *...the joint between two layers of wood.* [from Old French]

**joint ven|ture** (**joint ventures**) N-COUNT A **joint venture** is a business or project in which two or more companies or individuals have invested, with the intention of working together. [BUSINESS] ❑ *...a joint venture between Dow Jones and Westinghouse Broadcasting.*

**joke** /dʒoʊk/ (**jokes, joking, joked**) ■ N-COUNT A **joke** is something that is said or done to make you laugh, such as a funny story. ❑ *He made a joke about it.* ■ V-I If you **joke**, you tell funny stories

or say amusing things. ❑ *She often joked about her appearance.* ❑ *I was only joking!* ■ N-SING If you say that something or someone is **a joke**, you think they are ridiculous and do not deserve respect. [INFORMAL] ❑ *The whole idea is a joke.* ■ PHRASE If you describe a situation as **no joke**, you are emphasizing that it is very difficult or unpleasant. [INFORMAL] ❑ *Eight hours on a bus is no joke.* ■ CONVENTION You say **you're joking** or **you must be joking** to someone when they have just told you something that is so surprising or unreasonable that you find it difficult to believe. [SPOKEN] ❑ *You're joking. Are you serious?* ❑ *You've got to be joking if you choose him instead of me.* [from Latin]

**jok|er** /dʒoʊkər/ (**jokers**) N-COUNT The **joker** in a deck of playing cards is the card that does not belong to any of the four suits. [from Latin]

**jol|ly** /dʒɒli/ (**jollier, jolliest**) ADJ Someone who is **jolly** is happy and cheerful. ❑ *She was a jolly, kindhearted woman.* [from Old French]

**jolt** /dʒoʊlt/ (**jolts, jolting, jolted**) ■ V-T/V-I If something **jolts** or if something **jolts** it, it moves suddenly and quite violently. ❑ *An earthquake jolted the Philippines early Wednesday.* ❑ *The train jolted again.* ● **Jolt** is also a noun. ❑ *One tiny jolt could kill her.* ■ V-T If something **jolts** someone, it gives them an unpleasant surprise or shock. ❑ *It jolted me when I realized how old they were.* ● **Jolt** is also a noun. ❑ *A jolt of pain went through his finger.*

**jos|tle** /dʒɒsᵊl/ (**jostles, jostling, jostled**) ■ V-T/V-I If people **jostle** you, they bump against you or push you in a crowd. ❑ *There were 2,000 people jostling each other.* ❑ *We jostled with the crowds as we did our shopping.* ■ V-I If people **are jostling for** something such as attention or a reward, they are competing with each other for it. ❑ *...the people who have been jostling for the top job.*

**jot** /dʒɒt/ (**jots, jotting, jotted**) V-T If you **jot** something somewhere, you write it down so that you will remember it. ❑ *Could you jot his name on this piece of paper?* ● **jot down** means the same as **jot.** ❑ *Listen carefully to the instructions and jot them down.* [from Latin]

**joule** /dʒuːl/ (**joules**) N-COUNT In physics, a **joule** is a unit of energy or work. [TECHNICAL] [after James Prescott Joule (1818–89), an English physicist]

**jour|nal** /dʒɜrnᵊl/ (**journals**) ■ N-COUNT A **journal** is a magazine or newspaper, especially one that deals with a specialized subject. ❑ *The results were published in scientific journals.* ■ N-COUNT A **journal** is a notebook or diary. ❑ *Sara wrote her private thoughts in her journal.* [from Old French]

**jour|nal|ist** /dʒɜrnəlɪst/ (**journalists**) N-COUNT A **journalist** is a person whose job is to collect news and write about it for newspapers, magazines, television, or radio. ● **jour|nal|ism** N-UNCOUNT ❑ *He began a career in journalism.* [from Old French]

**jour|ney** /dʒɜrni/ (**journeys, journeying, journeyed**) ■ N-COUNT When you make a **journey**, you travel from one place to another. [FORMAL] ❑ *...the 3,000-mile journey from New York to San Francisco.* ■ V-I If you **journey** somewhere, you travel there. [FORMAL] ❑ *Naomi journeyed to the United States for the first time.* [from Old French]

## Thesaurus — *journey* Also look up :

| | |
|---|---|
| N. | adventure, trip, visit, voyage **1** |
| V. | cruise, fly, go, travel **2** |

## Word Partnership — Use *journey* with :

| | |
|---|---|
| V. | **begin a** journey, **complete a** journey, **make a** journey **1** |
| N. | journey **of discovery, end of a** journey, **first/last leg of a** journey **1** |

**joy** /dʒɔɪ/ (**joys**) **1** N-UNCOUNT **Joy** is a feeling of great happiness. ◻ *She shouted with joy.* **2** N-COUNT A **joy** is something or someone that makes you feel happy or gives you great pleasure. ◻ *Spending evenings outside is one of the joys of summer.* [from Old French]
→ see **emotion**

## Word Partnership — Use *joy* with :

| | |
|---|---|
| V. | **bring** *someone* joy, **cry/weep for** joy, **feel** joy **1** |
| ADJ. | **filled with** joy, **great** joy, **pure** joy, **sheer** joy **1** |
| N. | **tears of** joy **1** |

## Word Link — *joy ≈ being glad : enjoy, joyful, joyous*

**joy|ful** /dʒɔɪfəl/ **1** ADJ Something that is **joyful** causes happiness and pleasure. [FORMAL] ◻ *A wedding is a joyful occasion.* **2** ADJ Someone who is **joyful** is extremely happy. [FORMAL] ◻ *...crowds of joyful students.* ● **joy|ful|ly** ADV ◻ *They greeted him joyfully.* [from Old French]

**joy|ous** /dʒɔɪəs/ ADJ **Joyous** means extremely happy. [LITERARY] ◻ *She made their childhood joyous and exciting.* ● **joy|ous|ly** ADV ◻ *Sarah accepted joyously.* [from Old French]

**joy|rider** /dʒɔɪraɪdər/ (**joyriders**) N-COUNT A **joyrider** is someone who steals cars in order to drive around in them at high speed. ◻ *...a car crash caused by joyriders.*

**ju|bi|lant** /dʒubɪlənt/ ADJ If you are **jubilant**, you feel extremely happy because of a success. ◻ *Thousands of jubilant supporters greeted the team.* [from Latin]

**ju|bi|lee** /dʒubɪli/ (**jubilees**) N-COUNT A **jubilee** is a special anniversary of an event, especially the 25th or 50th anniversary. ◻ *...Queen Victoria's jubilee.* [from Old French]

**Ju|da|ism** /dʒudiɪzəm, -deɪ-/ N-UNCOUNT **Judaism** is the religion of the Jewish people. It is based on the Old Testament of the Bible and the Talmud. [from Late Latin]

**judge** /dʒʌdʒ/ (**judges, judging, judged**)
**1** N-COUNT; N-TITLE A **judge** is the person in a court of law who decides how the law should be applied, for example how criminals should be punished. ◻ *A state judge sent him to jail for 100 days.* **2** N-COUNT A **judge** is a person who decides who will be the winner of a competition. ◻ *A panel of judges is now choosing the winner.* **3** V-T If you **judge** a competition, you decide who or what is the winner. ◻ *He was asked to judge the competition.* **4** V-T If you **judge** something or someone, you form an opinion about them based on the evidence or information that you have. ◻ *People should judge his music for themselves.* ◻ *I want to judge myself on how I play.* ◻ *Other people can judge how much I have improved.* **5** N-COUNT If someone is a good **judge of** something, they understand it and can make sensible decisions about it. ◻ *I'm a pretty good judge of character.* [from Old French]
→ see **trial**

**judg|ment** /dʒʌdʒmənt/ (**judgments**) **1** N-VAR A **judgment** is an opinion that you have or express after thinking carefully about something. ◻ *In your judgment, what has changed?* **2** N-UNCOUNT **Judgment** is the ability to make sensible guesses about a situation or sensible decisions about what to do. ◻ *I respect his judgment and I'll follow any advice he gives me.* **3** N-VAR A **judgment** is a decision made by a judge or by a court of law. ◻ *We are waiting for a judgment from the Supreme Court.* [from Old French]

**ju|di|cial** /dʒudɪʃəl/ ADJ **Judicial** means relating to the legal system and to judgments made in a court of law. ◻ *...our judicial system.* [from Latin]

**ju|di|ci|ary** /dʒudɪʃieri/ N-SING The **judiciary** is the branch of authority in a country that is concerned with law and the legal system. [FORMAL] ◻ *...the head of the judiciary committee.* [from Latin]

**ju|di|cious** /dʒudɪʃəs/ ADJ If you describe an action or decision as **judicious**, you approve of it because you think that it shows good judgment and sense. [FORMAL] ◻ *Her judicious comments made her easy to talk with.* ● **ju|di|cious|ly** ADV ◻ *He chose his words judiciously.* [from Latin]

**jug** /dʒʌg/ (**jugs**) N-COUNT A **jug** is a container with a handle used for holding and pouring liquids.

**jug|gle** /dʒʌgəl/ (**juggles, juggling, juggled**) **1** V-T If you **juggle** lots of different things, you try to give enough time or attention to all of them. ◻ *He was finding it hard to juggle both careers.*
jug
**2** V-T/V-I If you **juggle**, you entertain people by throwing things into the air, catching each one, and throwing it up again so that there are several of them in the air at the same time. ◻ *She was juggling five eggs.* ● **jug|gler** (**jugglers**) N-COUNT ◻ *...a professional juggler.* ● **jug|gling** N-UNCOUNT ◻ *...a children's show with juggling and comedy.* [from Old French]

**juice** /dʒus/ (**juices**) **1** N-VAR **Juice** is the liquid that can be obtained from a fruit or vegetable. ◻ *...fresh orange juice.* **2** N-PLURAL The **juices** of a piece of meat are the liquid that comes out of it when you cook it. ◻ *Pour off the juices and put the meat in a frying pan.* [from Old French]

## Word Partnership — Use *juice* with :

| | |
|---|---|
| N. | **bottle of** juice, **fruit** juice, **glass of** juice **1** |
| ADJ. | **fresh-squeezed** juice **1** |

**juicy** /dʒusi/ (**juicier, juiciest**) **1** ADJ If food is **juicy**, it has a lot of juice in it and is very enjoyable to eat. ◻ *...a thick, juicy steak.* **2** ADJ **Juicy** gossip or stories contain exciting or scandalous details. [INFORMAL] [from Old French]

j

**July** /dʒʊlaɪ/ (**Julys**) N-VAR **July** is the seventh month of the year in the Western calendar. ◻ *In July 1969, Neil Armstrong walked on the moon.* [from Latin]

**jum|ble** /dʒʌmbəl/ (**jumbles, jumbling, jumbled**) ◼ N-COUNT A **jumble** of things is a lot of different things that are all mixed together in a disorganized or confused way. ◻ *...a jumble of huge stones.* ◻ *...a meaningless jumble of words.* ◼ V-T/V-I If you **jumble** things, they become mixed together so that they are untidy or are not in the correct order. ◻ *He's making a new film by jumbling together parts of his other movies.* ● To **jumble up** means the same as to **jumble**. ◻ *My thoughts are jumbled up in my head.*

**jum|bo** /dʒʌmboʊ/ (**jumbos**) ◼ ADJ **Jumbo** means very large. ◻ *...a jumbo box of tissues.* ◼ N-COUNT A **jumbo** or a **jumbo jet** is a very large jet aircraft. [from Swahili]

**jump** /dʒʌmp/ (**jumps, jumping, jumped**) ◼ V-T/V-I If you **jump**, you bend your knees, push against the ground with your feet, and move quickly upward into the air. ◻ *I jumped over the fence.* ◻ *He jumped out of a first-floor window.* ◻ *I jumped seventeen feet in the long jump.* ● **Jump** is also a noun. ◻ *...the longest jump by a man.* ◼ V-T If you **jump** something such as a fence, you move quickly up and through the air over or across it. ◻ *He jumped the first fence beautifully.* ◼ V-I If you **jump** somewhere, you move there quickly and suddenly. ◻ *Adam jumped from his seat when he heard the girl's cry.* ◼ V-I If something **makes** you **jump**, it makes you make a sudden movement because you are frightened or surprised. ◻ *The phone rang and made her jump.* ◼ V-T/V-I If an amount or level **jumps**, it suddenly increases by a large amount in a short time. ◻ *Sales jumped from $94 million to $101 million.* ◻ *The number of crimes jumped by ten percent.* ◻ *The company's shares jumped $2.50 in value.* ● **Jump** is also a noun. ◻ *...a big jump in sales.* ◼ V-I If you **jump at** an offer or opportunity, you accept it quickly and eagerly. ◻ *She'd jump at the chance to be on TV.* [from Swedish]

| **Thesaurus** | *jump* | Also look up : |
|---|---|---|
| V. | bound, hop, leap, lunge ◼ | |
| | hurdle ◼ | |
| | startle ◼ | |
| | increase, rise, shoot up ◼ | |

| **Word Partnership** | Use *jump* with : |
|---|---|
| ADJ. | **big** jump ◼ ◼ |
| N. | jump **to your feet** ◼ |
| | jump **in prices**, jump **in sales** ◼ |

**jump|er** /dʒʌmpər/ (**jumpers**) N-COUNT A **jumper** is a sleeveless dress that is worn over a blouse or sweater. ◻ *She wore a blue jumper.* [from Old French]

**jump|er ca|bles** N-PLURAL **Jumper cables** are thick wires that can be used to start a car when its battery does not have enough power.

**jump rope** (**jump ropes**) N-COUNT A **jump rope** is a piece of rope, usually with handles at each end, that you use for exercising by jumping over it as you turn it round and round.

**June** /dʒun/ (**Junes**) N-VAR **June** is the sixth

month of the year in the Western calendar. ◻ *We last saw him in June 2006.* [from Old English]

**jun|gle** /dʒʌŋgəl/ (**jungles**) ◼ N-VAR A **jungle** is a forest in a tropical country where large numbers of tall trees and plants grow very close together. ◻ *...the mountains and jungles of Papua New Guinea.* ◼ N-SING If you describe a situation as **a jungle**, you dislike it because it is complicated and difficult to get what you want from it. ◻ *...a jungle of complex rules.* [from Hindi]

**jun|ior** /dʒunyər/ (**juniors**) ◼ ADJ A **junior** official or employee holds a low-ranking position in an organization or profession. ◻ *His father was a junior officer in the army.* ● **Junior** is also a noun. ◻ *...a job as an office junior.* ◼ N-SING If you are someone's **junior**, you are younger than they are. ◻ *She lives with actor Denis Lawson who is 10 years her junior.* ◼ N-COUNT In the United States, a student in the third year of high school or college is called a **junior**. ◻ *Amy is a junior at the University of Evansville.* [from Latin]

**jun|ior col|lege** (**junior colleges**) N-COUNT In the United States, a **junior college** is a college that provides a two-year course that is usually equivalent to the first two years of a 4-year undergraduate course of study. ◻ *He went to a junior college and majored in computer programming.*

**jun|ior high school** (**junior high schools**) also **junior high** N-VAR; N-COUNT A **junior high school** or a **junior high** is a school for students from 7th through 9th or 10th grade. ◻ *I teach junior high school and I love it.* ◻ *...Benjamin Franklin Junior High.*

**junk** /dʒʌŋk/ ◼ N-UNCOUNT **Junk** is old and useless things that you do not want or need. [INFORMAL] ◻ *What are you going to do with all that junk, Larry?* ◼ N-UNCOUNT **Junk** is old and used goods that people buy and collect. ◻ *Rose buys her furniture in junk shops.*

**junkie** /dʒʌŋki/ (**junkies**) N-COUNT A **junkie** is a drug addict. [INFORMAL] ◻ *Your mother is the last person to believe you're a junkie.* [from Late Middle English]

**jun|ta** /dʒʌntə, hʊntə/ (**juntas**) N-COUNT A **junta** is a military government that has taken power by force. [from Spanish]

**Ju|pi|ter** /dʒupɪtər/ N-PROPER **Jupiter** is the fifth planet from the sun and the largest in our solar system. [from Latin]

**ju|ris|dic|tion** /dʒʊərɪsdɪkʃən/ (**jurisdictions**) N-UNCOUNT **Jurisdiction** is the power that a court of law or an official has to carry out legal judgments or to enforce laws. [FORMAL] ◻ *The police have no jurisdiction over foreign bank accounts.* [from Latin]

**ju|ror** /dʒʊərər/ (**jurors**) N-COUNT A **juror** is a member of a jury. ◻ *The jurors reached a verdict.* [from Old French]
→ see **citizenship**

**jury** /dʒʊəri/ (**juries**) ◼ N-COUNT In a court of law, the **jury** is the group of people who have been chosen from the general public to listen to the facts about a crime and to decide whether the person accused is guilty or not. ◻ *I sat on a jury two years ago.* ◼ N-COUNT A **jury** is a group of people who choose the winner of a competition. ◻ *The jury chose to award the prize to this novel.* [from Old French]
→ see **trial**

J

**Word Partnership**  Use *jury* with :

| N. | jury **duty**, **trial by** jury **1** |
| V. | jury **convicts** **1** |
|  | jury **announces** **1** **2** |
| ADJ. | **hung** jury **1** |
|  | **unbiased** jury **1** **2** |

**just**

❶ ADVERB USES
❷ ADJECTIVE USE

❶ **just** /dʒʌst/ **1** ADV If you say that something **just happened** or **has just happened**, you mean that it happened a very short time ago. ❑ *I just had the most awful dream.* **2** ADV If you say that you are **just** doing something, you mean that you will finish doing it soon. If you say that you are **just about to** do something, or **just going to** do it, you mean that you will do it very soon. ❑ *I'm just making the sauce for the cauliflower.* ❑ *I'm just going to go mail a letter.* **3** ADV You use **just** to indicate that something is no more important, interesting, or difficult, for example, than you say it is. ❑ *It's just a thought.* **4** ADV You use **just** to indicate that what you are saying is true, but only by a very small degree or amount. ❑ *I arrived just in time for my flight.* **5** ADV You use **just** to put emphasis on the word that follows, in order to express feelings such as annoyance, admiration, or certainty. ❑ *She just won't relax.* **6** ADV You can use **just** with instructions or polite requests to make your request seem less difficult than someone might think. ❑ *I'm just going to ask you a bit more about your father's business.* **7** ADV You use **just** to mean exactly or precisely. ❑ *They are just like the rest of us.* ❑ *My arm hurts too, just here.* **8** PHRASE You use **just about** to indicate that what you are talking about is so close to being true that it can be accepted as being true. ❑ *He is just about the best golfer in the world.* **9** **just my luck** → see luck [from Latin] **10** **not just** → see not **11** **just now** → see now **12** it **just goes to show** → see show

❷ **just** /dʒʌst/ ADJ If you describe a situation, action, or idea as **just**, you mean that it is right or acceptable according to moral principles. [FORMAL] ❑ *They believe that they are fighting a just war.* ● **just|ly** ADV ❑ *They were not treated justly in the past.* [from Latin]

**jus|tice** /dʒʌstɪs/ (**justices**) **1** N-UNCOUNT **Justice** is fairness in the way that people are treated. ❑ *We want freedom, justice and equality.* **2** N-UNCOUNT The **justice of** a cause, claim, or argument is its quality of being reasonable, fair, or right. ❑ *We must convince people of the justice of our cause.* **3** N-UNCOUNT **Justice** is the system that a country uses in order to deal with people who break the law. ❑ *Many young people feel that the justice system does not treat them fairly.* **4** N-COUNT A **justice** is a judge. ❑ *He is a justice on the Supreme Court.* **5** N-TITLE **Justice** is used before the names of judges. ❑ *...Justice Hutchison.* **6** PHRASE If a criminal is **brought to justice**, he or she is punished for a crime by being arrested and tried in a court of law. ❑ *The people responsible for the crime should be brought to justice.* **7** PHRASE If you **do justice to** someone or something, you deal with them properly and completely. ❑ *This article doesn't do the topic justice.* [from Old French]

**Word Partnership**  Use *justice* with :

| V. | **seek** justice **1** |
| ADJ. | **racial** justice, **social** justice **1** |
|  | **criminal** justice, **equal** justice **3** |
| N. | **obstruction of** justice, justice **system** **3** |

**jus|ti|fi|able** /dʒʌstɪfaɪəbªl/ ADJ An action, situation, emotion, or idea that is **justifiable** is acceptable or correct because there is a good reason for it. ❑ *Sometimes there is a justifiable reason for our anger.* ● **jus|ti|fi|ably** /dʒʌstɪfaɪəbli/ ADV ❑ *He was justifiably proud of his achievements.* [from Old French]

**jus|ti|fi|ca|tion** /dʒʌstɪfɪkeɪʃªn/ (**justifications**) N-VAR A **justification** for something is an acceptable reason or explanation for it. ❑ *There is no justification for this huge price rise.* [from Old French]

**jus|ti|fied** /dʒʌstɪfaɪd/ ADJ A decision, action, or idea that is **justified** is reasonable and acceptable. ❑ *In my opinion, the decision was justified.* ❑ *We felt justified in blaming him.* [from Old French]

**jus|ti|fy** /dʒʌstɪfaɪ/ (**justifies, justifying, justified**) V-T To **justify** a decision, action, or idea means to show or prove that it is reasonable or necessary. ❑ *Is there anything that can justify a war?* [from Old French]

**jut** /dʒʌt/ (**juts, jutting, jutted**) V-I If something **juts out**, it sticks out above or beyond a surface. ❑ *The northern end of the island juts out into the sea.*

**ju|venile** /dʒuvənªl, -naɪl/ (**juveniles**) N-COUNT A **juvenile** is a child or young person who is not yet old enough to be treated as an adult. [FORMAL] ❑ *...the number of juveniles in the general population.* [from Latin]

**jux|ta|pose** /dʒʌkstəpoʊz/ (**juxtaposes, juxtaposing, juxtaposed**) V-T If you **juxtapose** two contrasting objects, images, or ideas, you place them together or describe them together, so that the differences between them are emphasized. [FORMAL] ❑ *Modern photos are juxtaposed with a sixteenth-century mirror.* ● **jux|ta|po|si|tion** /dʒʌkstəpəzɪʃªn/ (**juxtapositions**) N-VAR [FORMAL] ❑ *...the juxtaposition of the old and the new.* [from Latin]

j

# Kk

**K-12** /keɪ twɛlv/ ADJ **K-12** education is education for children from kindergarten through twelfth grade. ❑ *...all of the state's 11,000 K-12 schools.*

**Ka|bu|ki** /kəbuki/ N-UNCOUNT **Kabuki** is a form of traditional Japanese theater that uses dance and music as well as acting.

**kan|ga|roo** /kæŋgəru/ (**kangaroos**) N-COUNT A **kangaroo** is a large Australian animal. Female kangaroos carry their babies in a pocket on their

kangaroo

stomach. [from a native Australian language]

**kan|ga|roo rat** (**kangaroo rats**) N-COUNT A **kangaroo rat** is a small rodent that lives in North and Central America. It has long back legs, which it uses in order to hop.

**kar|at** /kærət/ N-COUNT A **karat** is a unit for measuring the purity of gold. The purest gold is 24-karat gold. ❑ *...a twenty-four-karat gold necklace.* [from Old French]

**ka|ra|te** /kərɑti/ N-UNCOUNT **Karate** is a martial art in which people fight using their hands, elbows, feet, and legs. [from Japanese]

**karst to|pog|r|aphy** /kɑrst təpɒgrəfi/ N-UNCOUNT **Karst topography** is land where rainwater has dissolved the rock, and features such as caves and underground streams have formed. [TECHNICAL]

**Kb** also **kb** **Kb** or **kb** is a written abbreviation for **kilobit** or **kilobits**. [COMPUTING]

**KB** also **K** **KB** or **K** is a written abbreviation for **kilobyte** or **kilobytes**. [COMPUTING]

**Kbps** also **kbps** **Kbps** or **kbps** is a written abbreviation for "kilobits per second." ❑ *...a 28.8 Kbps modem.*

**keel** /kil/ (**keels, keeling, keeled**) PHRASE If something is **on an even keel**, it is working or progressing smoothly and steadily, without any sudden changes. ❑ *There is enough money to keep the family on an even keel.* [from Old Norse]
▸ **keel over** PHR-VERB If someone **keels over**, they fall down because they are tired or sick. [INFORMAL] ❑ *He keeled over and fell flat on his back.*

**keen** /kin/ (**keener, keenest**) **1** ADJ If you have a **keen** eye or ear, you are able to notice things that are difficult to detect. ❑ *...an artist with a keen eye for detail.* ● **keen|ly** ADV ❑ *Charles listened keenly.* **2** ADJ If someone has a **keen** mind, they are very clever and aware of what is happening around them. ❑ *...a man of keen intelligence.* ● **keen|ly** ADV ❑ *I am keenly aware of the things that we share as Americans.* [from Old English]

---

## keep

**1** REMAIN, STAY, OR CONTINUE TO HAVE/DO
**2** STOP OR PREVENT
**3** COST OF LIVING
**4** PHRASAL VERBS

**1 keep** /kip/ (**keeps, keeping, kept**) **1** V-LINK If someone **keeps** or **is kept** in a particular state, they remain in it. ❑ *The noise kept him awake.* ❑ *People had to burn wood to keep warm.* **2** V-T/V-I If you **keep** or you **are kept** in a particular position or place, you remain in it. ❑ *Keep away from the doors while the train is moving.* ❑ *He kept his head down, hiding his face.* **3** V-T If you **keep** doing something, you do it repeatedly or continue to do it. ❑ *I keep forgetting it's December.* ❑ *She forced herself to keep going.* ● **keep on** means the same as **keep**. ❑ *Did he give up or keep on trying?* **4** V-T If you **keep** something, you continue to have it. If you **keep** it somewhere, you store it there. ❑ *We must decide what to keep and what to give away.* ❑ *She kept her money under the bed.* **5** V-T **Keep** is used with some nouns to indicate that someone does something for a period of time or continues to do it. For example, if you **keep a grip on** something, you continue to hold or control it. ❑ *One of them would keep watch on the road.* **6** V-T When you **keep** something such as a promise or an appointment, you do what you said you would do. ❑ *I'm hoping you'll keep your promise to come.* **7** V-T If you **keep** a record of a series of events, you write down details of it so that they can be referred to later. ❑ *Eleanor began to keep a diary.* **8** PHRASE If one thing is **in keeping with** another, it is suitable because of that thing. ❑ *This job is in keeping with his experience.* **9** PHRASE If you **keep** something **to yourself**, you do not tell anyone else about it. ❑ *I have to tell someone. I can't keep it to myself.* **10** PHRASE If you **keep to yourself**, you stay on your own most of the time and do not mix socially with other people. ❑ *He was a quiet man who always kept to himself.* [from Old English] **11** to **keep** someone **company** → see **company** **12** to **keep a straight face** → see **face** **13** to **keep** your **head** → see **head** **14** to **keep pace** → see **pace** **15** to **keep the peace** → see **peace** **16** to **keep quiet** → see **quiet** **17** to **keep a secret** → see **secret** **18** to **keep time** → see **time** **19** to **keep track** → see **track**

**2 keep** /kip/ (**keeps, keeping, kept**) **1** V-T If someone or something **keeps** you **from** doing something, they prevent you from doing it. ❑ *Embarrassment has kept me from doing all sorts of things.* **2** V-T If someone or something **keeps** you, they delay you and make you late. ❑ *Sorry to keep you, Jack.* **3** V-T If you **keep** something **from** someone, you do not tell them about it. ❑ *She knew* that Gabriel was keeping something from her. [from Old English]

❸ **keep** /kip/ N-SING Someone's **keep** is the cost of food and other things that they need in their daily life. ❏ Ray will earn his keep on local farms while he is a student. [from Old English]

❹ **keep** /kip/ (keeps, keeping, kept)
▶ **keep down** PHR-VERB If you **keep** the amount of something **down**, you do not let it increase. ❏ The aim is to keep prices down.
▶ **keep on** ■ → see keep ❶ 3 ❷ PHR-VERB If you **keep** someone **on**, you continue to employ them, for example after other employees have lost their jobs. ❏ Firing him would be more damaging than keeping him on.
▶ **keep to** ■ PHR-VERB If you **keep to** a rule, plan, or agreement, you do exactly what you are expected or supposed to do. ❏ You've got to keep to the speed limit. ❷ PHR-VERB If you **keep** something **to** a particular number or quantity, you limit it to that number or quantity. ❏ Keep costs to a minimum.
▶ **keep up** ■ PHR-VERB If you **keep up with** someone or something, you move at the same speed or progress at the same rate. ❏ He walked faster to keep up with his father. ❏ Cell phones are changing so fast it's hard to keep up. ❷ PHR-VERB If you **keep** something **up**, you continue to do it or provide it. ❏ I could not keep the diet up for longer than a month.

**keep|er** /kipər/ (keepers) N-COUNT A **keeper** is a person who takes card of something; a **keeper** at a zoo is a person who takes care of the animals. [from Old English]

**ken|nel** /kɛnᵊl/ (kennels) N-COUNT A **kennel** is a place where dogs are bred and trained, or cared for when their owners are away. ❏ Mrs Wray said the dogs would stay at the kennels until tomorrow. [from Old French]

**kept** /kɛpt/ **Kept** is the past tense and past participle of **keep**. [from Old English]

**kero|sene** /kɛrəsin/ N-UNCOUNT **Kerosene** is a strong-smelling liquid which is used as a fuel in heaters and lamps. ❏ ...a kerosene lamp. [from Greek]

**ket|tle** /kɛtᵊl/ (kettles) ■ N-COUNT A **kettle** is a covered container that you use for boiling water. ❏ I'll put the kettle on and make us some tea. ❷ N-COUNT A **kettle** is a metal pot for boiling or cooking things in. ❏ Put the meat into a small kettle. [from Old Norse]

**key** /ki/ (keys, keying, keyed) ■ N-COUNT A **key** is a specially shaped piece of metal that fits in a lock and is turned in order to open something, or start an engine. ❏ They put the key in the door and entered. ❷ N-COUNT The **keys** on a computer keyboard or typewriter are the buttons that you press in order to operate it. ❏ Finally, press the "Delete" key. ❸ N-COUNT The **keys** of a piano or organ are the white and black bars that you press in order to play it. ❹ N-VAR In music, a **key** is a scale of musical notes that starts on one specific note. ❏ ...the key of A minor. ❺ ADJ The **key** person or thing in a group is the most important one. ❏ He is expected to be the key witness at the trial. ❻ N-COUNT The **key to** something good is the things that help you achieve it. ❏ The key to getting good grades is to concentrate in class and work hard. [from Old English]
→ see **graph**

| **Thesaurus** | key | Also look up : |
| --- | --- | --- |
| ADJ. | critical, important, major, vital ❺ | |

| **Word Partnership** | Use key with : |
| --- | --- |
| V. | turn a key ■ |
| ADJ. | key component, key decision, key factor, key figure, key ingredient, key issue, key official, key player, key point, key question, key role, key word ❺<br>key to success ❻ |

**key|board** /kibɔrd/ (keyboards) ■ N-COUNT The **keyboard** of a typewriter or computer is the set of keys that you press in order to operate it. ❏ Ryan sat down at the keyboard and wrote a message. ❷ N-COUNT The **keyboard** of a piano or organ is the set of black and white keys that you press in order to play it. [from Old English]
→ see Picture Dictionary: **keyboard**
→ see **computer**

k

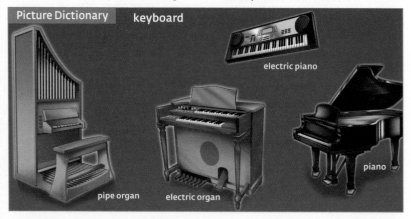

**Picture Dictionary** — keyboard

electric piano

piano

pipe organ

electric organ

**key card** (**key cards**) N-COUNT A **key card** is a small plastic card which you can use instead of a key to open a door or barrier, for example in some hotels and parking lots. ❑ *The electronic key card to Julie's room didn't work.*

**key|word** /kíwɜrd/ (**keywords**) also **key word**
**1** N-COUNT A **keyword** is a word or phrase that is associated with a particular document in Internet searches. ❑ *Users can search by title, by author, and by keyword.* **2** N-COUNT The **keyword** in a situation is a word or phrase that is very important in that situation. ❑ *Compromise is the keyword.*

**kg** **kg** is a written abbreviation for **kilogram** or **kilograms**.

**kha|ki** /kǽki/ COLOR Something that is **khaki** is greenish brown or yellowish brown in color. ❑ *He was dressed in khaki trousers.* [from Urdu]

**kick** /kík/ (**kicks, kicking, kicked**) **1** V-T/V-I If you **kick** someone or something, you hit them

kick

with your foot. ❑ *He kicked the door hard.* ❑ *He kicked the ball away.* ❑ *He threw the ball on the ground and started to kick.* ● **Kick** is also a noun. ❑ *He suffered a kick to the knee.* **2** V-T/V-I If you **kick** or if you **kick** your legs, you move your legs with very quick, small, and forceful movements, once or repeatedly. ❑ *They were dragged away struggling and kicking.* ❑ *The baby smiled and kicked her*

*legs.* **3** V-T If you **kick** a bad habit, you stop having it. [INFORMAL] ❑ *Nail-biting is a difficult habit to kick.* **4** N-SING If something gives you **a kick**, it gives you pleasure or excitement. [INFORMAL] ❑ *I got a kick out of seeing my name in print.* **5** to **kick up a fuss** → see **fuss**

▶ **kick in** **1** PHR-VERB If something **kicks in**, it begins to take effect. ❑ *I hoped the aspirin would kick in soon.* **2** PHR-VERB If someone **kicks in** a particular amount of money, they provide that amount of money to help pay for something. ❑ *Kansas City churches kicked in $35,000 to support the event.*

▶ **kick off** PHR-VERB If an event, game, series, or discussion **kicks off**, or **is kicked off**, it begins. ❑ *The show kicks off on October 24th.* ❑ *The mayor kicked off the party.*

▶ **kick out** PHR-VERB To **kick** someone **out of** a place or an organization means to force them to leave it. [INFORMAL] ❑ *They kicked five foreign journalists out of the country.*

| **Thesaurus** | kick | Also look up : |
| --- | --- | --- |
| V. | abandon, give up, quit, stop; *(ant.)* start, take up **3** | |
| N. | enjoyment, excitement, fun, thrill **4** | |

| **Word Partnership** | Use *kick* with : |
| --- | --- |
| N. | kick **a ball**, kick **a door**, **penalty** kick **1** kick **a habit 3** |

**kick|er** /kíkər/ (**kickers**) N-COUNT In sports such as football and rugby, the **kicker** is a player whose role includes kicking the ball. ❑ *...Broncos kicker Jason Elam.* [of Scandinavian origin]

**kick|off** /kíkɔf/ (**kickoffs**) **1** N-VAR In football or

soccer, the **kickoff** is the time at which a particular game starts. ❑ *Officials expect about 65,000 fans for the 7:30 kickoff.* **2** N-COUNT In football, a **kickoff** is the kick that begins play, for example at the beginning of a half or after a touchdown or goal has been scored.

**kick|stand** /kíkstænd/ (**kickstands**) N-COUNT A **kickstand** is a metal bar attached to a bicycle or motorcycle that holds it upright when it is not being used. ❑ *He put down the kickstand and took off his helmet.*

**kick-start** (**kick-starts, kick-starting, kick-started**) also **kickstart** V-T To **kick-start** a process that has stopped working or progressing is to take a course of action that will quickly start it going again. ❑ *He's rasing money to kick-start a youth basketball league.*

**kid** /kíd/ (**kids, kidding, kidded**) **1** N-COUNT You can refer to a child as a **kid**. [INFORMAL] ❑ *They have three kids.* **2** V-I If you **are kidding**, you are saying something that is not really true, as a joke. [INFORMAL] ❑ *I thought he was kidding but he was serious.* ❑ *I'm just kidding.* **3** V-T If people **kid themselves**, they allow themselves to believe something that is not true because they wish that it was true. ❑ *We're kidding ourselves, Bill. We're not winning, we're not even doing well.* **4** N-COUNT A **kid** is a young goat. [of Scandinavian origin]

| **Word Partnership** | Use *kid* with : |
| --- | --- |
| ADJ. | **fat** kid, **friendly** kid, **good** kid, **little** kid, **new** kid, **nice** kid, **poor** kid, **skinny** kid, **smart** kid, **tough** kid, **young** kid **1** |
| N. | **school** kid, kid **stuff 1** |
| V. | **raise a** kid **1** |

**kid|do** /kídoʊ/ (**kiddos**) N-VOC You can call someone **kiddo**, especially someone who is younger than you, as a sign of affection. [INFORMAL] ❑ *I'll miss you, kiddo.* [of Scandinavian origin]

**kid|nap** /kídnæp/ (**kidnaps, kidnapping** or **kidnaping, kidnapped** or **kidnaped**) **1** V-T To **kidnap** someone is to take them away illegally and by force, and usually to hold them prisoner in order to demand something from their family, employer, or government. ❑ *The police uncovered a plot to kidnap him.* ● **kid|nap|per** (**kidnappers**) N-COUNT ❑ *His kidnappers have threatened to kill him.* ● **kid|nap|ping** (**kidnappings**) N-VAR ❑ *Two men have been arrested and charged with kidnapping.* **2** N-VAR **Kidnap** or a **kidnap** is the crime of taking someone away by force. ❑ *He was charged with the kidnap of a 25-year-old woman.*

**kid|ney** /kídni/ (**kidneys**) N-COUNT Your **kidneys** are the two organs in your body that take waste matter from your blood and send it out of your body as urine. ❑ *...a kidney transplant.*
→ see **donor**

**kid|ney bean** (**kidney beans**) N-COUNT **Kidney beans** are small, reddish-brown beans that are eaten as a vegetable. They are the seeds of a bean plant.

**kill** /kíl/ (**kills, killing, killed**) **1** V-T/V-I If a person, animal, or other living thing **is killed**, something or someone causes them to die. ❑ *More than 1,000 people have been killed by the armed forces.* ❑ *Drugs can kill.* ● **kill|ing** N-UNCOUNT ❑ *...the killing*

K

of seven civilians. **2** V-T If something or someone **kills** an activity, process, or feeling, they prevent it from continuing. ❑ *His objective was to kill the project altogether.* ● **Kill off** means the same as **kill.** ❑ *Global warming might kill off polar bears.* **3** V-T If you **are killing** time, you are doing something because you have some time available, not because you really want to do it. ❑ *To kill the hours while she waited, Anna worked in the yard.* [from Old English] **4 dressed to kill** → see **dressed** **5** **to be killed outright** → see **outright** → see **war**

▶ **kill off** **1** → see **kill 3** **2** PHR-VERB If you **kill** things **off,** you destroy or kill all of them. ❑ *Author J K Rowling is going to kill off a character in her next book.* ❑ *...poison to kill off the rats.*

| **Thesaurus** | *kill* | Also look up : |
| --- | --- | --- |
| V. | execute, murder, put down, slay, wipe out **1** | |

**kill|er** /kɪlər/ (**killers**) **1** N-COUNT A **killer** is a person who has killed someone. ❑ *The police are searching for the killers.* **2** N-COUNT You can refer to anything that causes death as a **killer.** ❑ *Heart disease is the biggest killer of men in some countries.* [from Old English]

**kilo** /kiloʊ/ (**kilos**) N-COUNT A **kilo** is the same as a **kilogram.** ❑ *He went on diet and lost ten kilos in weight.*

**kilo|bit** /kɪləbɪt/ (**kilobits**) N-COUNT In computing, a **kilobit** is 1,024 bits of data. ❑ *...a 256-kilobit chip.* [COMPUTING]

| **Word Link** | *kilo ≈ thousand : kilobyte, kilogram, kilometer* |
| --- | --- |

**kilo|byte** /kɪləbaɪt/ (**kilobytes**) N-COUNT In computing, a **kilobyte** is 1,024 bytes of data. [COMPUTING]

**kilo|calo|rie** /kɪləkæləri/ (**kilocalories**) N-COUNT A **kilocalorie** is a unit of energy that is equal to one thousand calories. [TECHNICAL]

**kilo|gram** /kɪləgræm/ (**kilograms**) N-COUNT A **kilogram** is a metric unit of mass. One kilogram is a thousand grams, and is equal to 2.2 pounds. ❑ *...a box weighing around 4.5 kilograms.*

| **Word Link** | *meter ≈ measuring : kilometer, meter, perimeter* |
| --- | --- |

**kilo|meter** /kɪləmitər, kɪlɒmɪtər/ (**kilometers**) N-COUNT A **kilometer** is a metric unit of distance or length. One kilometer is a thousand meters, and is equal to 0.62 miles. ❑ *...only one kilometer from the border.* → see **measurement**

**kin** /kɪn/ PHRASE Your **next of kin** is your closest relative, especially in official or legal documents. [FORMAL] ❑ *We have notified the next of kin.* [from Old English]

## kind

**❶** NOUN USES AND PHRASES
**❷** ADJECTIVE USES

**❶ kind** /kaɪnd/ (**kinds**) **1** N-COUNT If you talk about a particular **kind of** thing, you are talking about one of the types or sorts of that thing. ❑ *The party needs a different kind of leadership.* ❑ *Has Jamie* ever been in any kind of trouble? **2** PHRASE You use **kind of** when you want to say that something or someone can be roughly described in a particular way. [SPOKEN] ❑ *It was kind of sad, really.* **3** PHRASE Payment **in kind** is payment in the form of goods or services and not money. ❑ *...gifts in kind.* [from Old English]

| **Word Link** | *est ≈ most : greatest, kindest, loudest* |
| --- | --- |

| **Word Link** | *ness ≈ state, condition : awareness, consciousness, kindness* |
| --- | --- |

**❷ kind** /kaɪnd/ (**kinder, kindest**) ADJ Someone who is **kind** behaves in a gentle, caring, and helpful way toward other people. ❑ *I must thank you for being so kind to me.* ● **kind|ly** ADV ❑ *"You seem tired this morning, Jenny," she said kindly.* ● **kind|ness** N-UNCOUNT ❑ *We have been treated with such kindness by everybody.* [from Old English]

| **Thesaurus** | *kind* | Also look up : |
| --- | --- | --- |
| N. | sort, type **❶** **1** | |
| ADJ. | affectionate, considerate, gentle **❷** **1** | |

**kin|der|gar|ten** /kɪndərgɑrtᵊn/ (**kindergartens**) N-VAR A **kindergarten** is a school for children aged 4 to 6 years old, that prepares them to go into the first grade. ❑ *She's in kindergarten now.* [from German]

**kind|ly** /kaɪndli/ **1** ADJ A **kindly** person is kind, caring, and sympathetic. ❑ *He was an extremely kindly man.* **2** ADV If someone asks you to **kindly** do something, they are asking you in a way which shows that they have authority over you, or that they are angry with you. [FORMAL] ❑ *Will you kindly obey the instructions?* [from Old English] **3** → see also **kind**

**kin|es|thet|ic** /kɪnɪsθɛtɪk/ also **kinaesthetic** ADJ **Kinesthetic** means relating to sensations caused by movement of the body. [TECHNICAL] [from New Latin]

**ki|net|ic en|er|gy** N-UNCOUNT In physics, **kinetic energy** is the energy that is produced when something moves. [TECHNICAL]

**king** /kɪŋ/ (**kings**) **1** N-TITLE; N-COUNT A **king** is a man who a member of the royal family of his country, and who is the head of state of that country. ❑ *...the king and queen of Spain.* **2** N-COUNT A **king** is a playing card with a picture of a king on it. ❑ *...the king of diamonds.* **3** N-COUNT In chess, the **king** is the piece which each player must try to capture. [from Old English] → see **chess**

**king|dom** /kɪŋdəm/ (**kingdoms**) **1** N-COUNT A **kingdom** is a country or region that is ruled by a king or queen. ❑ *The kingdom's power grew.* **2** N-SING All the animals, birds, and insects in the world can be referred to together as the animal **kingdom.** All the plants can be referred to as the plant **kingdom.** ❑ *The animal kingdom is full of wonderful creatures.* [from Old English]

**ki|osk** /kiɒsk/ (**kiosks**) N-COUNT A **kiosk** is a small structure with an open window at which people can buy things like newspapers, pay an attendant at a parking lot, or get information about something. ❑ *I was getting a newspaper at the kiosk.* ❑ *You can pick up a brochure at the information desk.* [from French]

**k**

## Word Web    kiss

Some anthropologists believe mothers invented the **kiss**. They chewed a bit of food and then used their lips to place it in their child's mouth. Others believe that kissing started with primates. There are many types of kisses. Kisses express affection or accompany a greeting or a goodbye. Friends and family members exchange **social kisses** on the **lips** or sometimes on the **cheek**. When people are about to kiss they pucker their lips. In European countries, friends kiss each other lightly on both cheeks. And in the Middle East, a kiss between two leaders shows support for each other.

**kiss** /kɪs/ (**kisses, kissing, kissed**) v-RECIP If you **kiss** someone, you touch them with your lips to show affection or to greet them. ❑ *She leaned up and kissed him on the cheek.* ❑ *Her parents kissed her goodbye as she set off from their home.* ❑ *They kissed for almost half a minute.* ● **Kiss** is also a noun. ❑ *I put my arms around her and gave her a kiss.* [from Old English]
→ see Word Web: **kiss**

**kit** /kɪt/ (**kits, kitting, kitted**) **1** N-COUNT A **kit** is a group of items that are kept together because they are used for a similar purpose. ❑ *...a first aid kit.* **2** N-COUNT A **kit** is a set of parts that can be put together in order to make something. ❑ *...model airplane kits.* [from Middle Dutch]

**kitch|en** /kɪtʃⁿn/ (**kitchens**) N-COUNT A **kitchen** is a room that is used for cooking and for household jobs such as washing dishes. [from Old English]
→ see Picture Dictionary: **kitchen utensils**
→ see **house**

**kite** /kaɪt/ (**kites**) N-COUNT A **kite** is an object consisting of a light frame covered with paper or cloth, which you fly in the air at the end of a long string. [from Old English]

**kitsch** /kɪtʃ/ N-UNCOUNT You can refer to a work of art or an object as **kitsch** if it is showy and in bad taste. ❑ *...an embarrassing piece of kitsch.* ● **Kitsch** is also an adjective. ❑ *She was wearing kitsch green eyeshadow.* [from German]

**kit|ten** /kɪtⁿn/ (**kittens**) N-COUNT A **kitten** is a very young cat. [from Old Northern French]

**kit|ty** /kɪti/ (**kitties**) **1** N-COUNT A **kitty** is an amount of money gathered from several people, which is used to buy things that they will share or use together. ❑ *You haven't put any money in the kitty.* **2** N-COUNT A **kitty** is a cat, especially a young one. [INFORMAL]

**kitty-corner** ADJ → see **catty-corner**

**kiwi** /kiwi/ (**kiwis**) A **kiwi** is the same as a **kiwi fruit**.
→ see **fruit**

**kiwi fruit** (**kiwi fruits**)

Kiwi fruit can also be used as the plural form.

N-VAR A **kiwi fruit** is a fruit with a brown hairy skin and green flesh.

**klutz** /klʌts/ (**klutzes**) N-COUNT You can refer to someone who is very clumsy as a **klutz**. [INFORMAL] [from German]

**km** (**kms**) **km** is a written abbreviation for **kilometer**.

**knack** /næk/ (**knacks**) N-COUNT If you have the **knack** of doing something difficult or skillful, you are able to do it easily. ❑ *He's got the knack of getting people to listen.*

## Picture Dictionary    kitchen utensils

**knead** /niːd/ (**kneads, kneading, kneaded**) v-t
When you **knead** dough, you press and squeeze it
with your hands to make it smooth. ❑ *Knead the
dough for a few minutes.* [from Old English]

**knee** /niː/ (**knees**) ■ N-COUNT Your **knee** is the
place where your leg bends. ❑ *He will receive physical
therapy on his left knee.* ■ N-COUNT If something
or someone is **on** your **knee** or **on** your **knees**, they
are resting or sitting on the upper part of your
legs when you are sitting down. ❑ *He sat with
the package on his knees.* ■ N-PLURAL If you are **on**
your **knees**, your legs are bent and your knees are
on the ground. ❑ *She fell to the ground on her knees
and prayed for forgiveness.* ■ PHRASE If a country or
organization **is brought to its knees**, it is almost
completely destroyed by someone or something.
❑ *The country was being brought to its knees by the
loss of 2.4 million manufacturing jobs.* [from Old
English]
→ see **body, horse**

| Word Partnership | Use *knee* with : |
| --- | --- |
| N. | knee **injury** ■ |
| ADJ. | **left/right** knee, **weak-**kneed ■ |
| V. | **bend** *your* knees, knees **buckle** ■ |
| | **fall on** *your* knees ■ |

**kneel** /niːl/ (**kneels, kneeling, kneeled** or **knelt**)
v-i When you **kneel**, you bend your legs so that
your knees are touching the ground. ❑ *She knelt by
the bed and prayed.* ❑ *Other people were kneeling, but
she just sat.* ● **Kneel down** means the same as **kneel**.
❑ *She kneeled down beside him.* [from Old English]

**knew** /njuː/ **Knew** is the past tense of **know**.
[from Old English]

**knife** /naɪf/ (**knives, knifes, knifing, knifed**)

**Knives** is the plural form of the noun and **knifes**
is the third person singular of the present tense
of the verb.

■ N-COUNT A **knife** is a tool consisting of a sharp
flat piece of metal attached to a handle, used to cut
things or as a weapon. ❑ *...a knife and fork.* ■ V-T
To **knife** someone means to attack and injure them
with a knife. ❑ *Julius Caesar was knifed to death.*
[from Old English]
→ see **tools, painting**

**knight** /naɪt/ (**knights, knighting, knighted**)
■ N-COUNT In medieval times, a **knight** was a
man of noble birth, who served his king or lord
in battle. ❑ *...King Arthur's faithful knight, Gawain.*
■ V-T If someone **is knighted**, they are given
a knighthood. ❑ *He was knighted in June 1988.*
■ N-COUNT In chess, a **knight** is a piece which is
shaped like a horse's head. [from Old English]
→ see **chess**

**knight|hood** /naɪthʊd/ (**knighthoods**)
N-COUNT A **knighthood** is a title that is given
to a man by a British king or queen for his
achievements or his service to his country. A man
who has been given a knighthood can put "Sir"
in front of his name. ❑ *When he finally received his
knighthood in 1975 Chaplin was 85.* [from Old English]

**knit** /nɪt/ (**knits, knitting, knitted**) v-t/v-i If you
**knit** something, especially an article of clothing,
you make it from wool or a similar thread by using
two long needles or a machine. ❑ *I had endless hours
to knit and sew.* ❑ *I have already started knitting baby
clothes.* ● **knit|ting** N-UNCOUNT ❑ *...a relaxing hobby,*

such as knitting. [from Old English]

**knit|ting** /nɪtɪŋ/ N-UNCOUNT **Knitting** is
something, such as an article of clothing, that
is being knitted. ❑ *She had been sitting with her
knitting.* [from Old English]

**knives** /naɪvz/ **Knives** is the plural of **knife**.
[from Old English]

**knob** /nɒb/ (**knobs**) N-COUNT A **knob** is a round
handle or switch. ❑ *He turned the knob and pushed
against the door.* ❑ *...the volume knob.* [from Middle
Low German]

**knock** /nɒk/ (**knocks, knocking, knocked**)
■ V-I If you **knock on** something such as a door or
window, you hit it, usually several times, to attract
someone's attention. ❑ *She went directly to Simon's
apartment and knocked on the door.* ● **Knock** is also

knock

a noun. ❑ *They heard a knock
at the front door.* ● **knock|ing**
N-SING ❑ *...a loud knocking at
the door.* ■ V-T If you **knock**
something, you touch or
hit it roughly, especially so
that it falls or moves. ❑ *She
accidentally knocked the glass
off the shelf.* ❑ *The raccoons
knock over the garbage cans in
search of food.* ● **Knock** is also
a noun. ❑ *...tough materials
to protect against knocks.* ■ V-T To **knock** someone
into a particular position, state, or condition
means to hit them very hard so that they fall over
or become unconscious. ❑ *The third wave was so
strong it knocked me backward.* ❑ *He nearly knocked me
over.* ■ V-T If you **knock** something or someone,
you criticize them. [INFORMAL] ❑ *I'm not knocking
them: if they want to do it, it's up to them.* [from Old
English] ■ to **knock** someone or something **into
shape** → see **shape**
▶ **knock down** ■ PHR-VERB To **knock down** a
building or part of a building means to demolish
or destroy it. ❑ *Why doesn't he just knock the wall
down?* ■ PHR-VERB To **knock down** a price or
amount means to decrease it. ❑ *The market might
knock down its price.*
▶ **knock off** PHR-VERB To **knock off** an amount
from a price, time, or level means to reduce it by
that amount. ❑ *We have knocked 10% off admission
prices.*
▶ **knock out** ■ PHR-VERB To **knock** someone **out**
means to cause them to become unconscious.
❑ *He was knocked out in a fight.* ■ PHR-VERB If a
person or team **is knocked out** of a competition,
they are defeated in a game, so that they take no
more part in the competition. ❑ *He got knocked out
in the first inning.* ■ → see also **knockout**

| Word Partnership | Use *knock* with : |
| --- | --- |
| V. | **answer** a knock, **hear** a knock ■ |
| N. | knock **on/at a door** ■ |
| ADJ. | **loud** knock ■ |
| | knock *someone* **out cold**, knock *someone*
**unconscious** ■ |

**knock|out** /nɒkaʊt/ (**knockouts**) also
**knock-out** ■ N-COUNT In boxing, a **knockout**
is a situation in which a boxer wins the fight by
making his opponent fall to the ground and be
unable to stand up before the referee has counted
to ten. ❑ *Lewis ended the fight with a knockout in the*

k

*eighth round.* **2** ADJ A **knockout** blow is an action or event that completely defeats an opponent. ❑ *He delivered a knockout blow to all of his enemies.*

**knot** /nɒt/ (**knots, knotting, knotted**) **1** V-T If you **knot** a piece of string, rope, cloth, or other

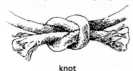

knot

material, you pass one end or part of it through a loop and pull it tight. ❑ *He knotted the laces securely together.* ❑ *He knotted the scarf around his neck.* • **Knot** is also a noun. ❑ *One lace had broken and been tied in a knot.* **2** V-T/V-I If your stomach **knots** or if something **knots** it, it feels tight because you are afraid or excited. ❑ *My stomach knotted with fear.* • **Knot** is also a noun. ❑ *There was a knot of tension in his stomach.* **3** N-COUNT A **knot** is a unit used for measuring the speed of ships, aircraft, and wind. ❑ *They travel at speeds of up to 30 knots.* [from Old English]

---

**know**

**❶** VERB USES
**❷** PHRASES

---

**❶ know** /noʊ/ (**knows, knowing, knew, known**) **1** V-T If you **know** a fact, a piece of information, or an answer, you have it correctly in your mind. ❑ *I don't know the name of the place.* ❑ *"People like doing things for nothing." — "I know they do."* ❑ *I don't know what happened to her husband.* ❑ *"How did he meet your mother?" — "I don't know."* **2** V-T If you **know** a person or place, you are familiar with them. ❑ *I'd known him for nine years.* ❑ *No matter how well you know this city, it is easy to get lost.* **3** V-I If you **know of** something, you have heard about it but you do not necessarily have a lot of information about it. ❑ *We know of the accident but have no further details.* **4** V-T/V-I If you **know about** something or **know** it, you understand it, or have the necessary skills and understanding to do it. ❑ *Hire someone with experience, someone who knows about real estate.* ❑ *She didn't know anything about music.* ❑ *It helps to know French.* ❑ *The health authorities now know how to deal with the disease.* **5** V-T If someone or something **is known as** a particular name, they are called by that name. ❑ *Rubella is more commonly known as German measles.* ❑ *Everyone knew him as Dizzy.* [from Old English] **6** → see also **known**

**Thesaurus** *know* Also look up :

V. comprehend, recognize, understand **❶** **1**

**❷ know** /noʊ/ (**knows, knowing, knew, known**) **1** PHRASE If you **get to know** someone, you find out what they are like by spending time with them. ❑ *The new neighbors were getting to know each other.* **2** CONVENTION You say **"I know"** to show that you agree with what has just been said. ❑ *"This country is so awful." — "I know, I know."* **3** PHRASE Someone who is **in the know** has information about something that only a few people have. ❑ *It was good to be in the know about important people.* **4** CONVENTION You say **"You never know"** or **"One never knows"** to indicate

that it is not definite or certain what will happen in the future, and to suggest that there is some hope that things will turn out well. ❑ *You never know, I might get lucky.* **5** CONVENTION You use **you know** to emphasize or to draw attention to what you are saying. [SPOKEN] ❑ *The conditions in there are awful, you know.* [from Old English] **6** to **know best** → see **best** **7** to **know better** → see **better** **8** to **know** something **for a fact** → see **fact** **9** as **far as I know** → see **far** **10** not **to know the first thing about** something → see **first** **11** to **know full well** → see **full** **12** to **let** someone **know** → see **let** **13** to **know** your **own mind** → see **mind** **14** to **know the ropes** → see **rope**

**know-how** N-UNCOUNT **Know-how** is knowledge of the methods or techniques of doing something. [INFORMAL] ❑ *He doesn't have the know-how to run a farm.*

**know|ing|ly** /noʊɪŋli/ ADV If you **knowingly** do something wrong, you do it even though you know it is wrong. ❑ *The company is knowingly breaking the law.* [from Old English]

**know-it-all** (**know-it-alls**) N-COUNT If you say that someone is a **know-it-all**, you are critical of them because they think that they know a lot more than other people. [INFORMAL]

**knowl|edge** /nɒlɪdʒ/ **1** N-UNCOUNT **Knowledge** is information and understanding about a subject which a person has, or which all people have. ❑ *He has a wide knowledge of sports.* **2** PHRASE If you say that something is true **to** your **knowledge** or **to the best of** your **knowledge**, you mean that you believe it to be true but it is possible that you do not know all the facts. ❑ *The president, to my knowledge, hasn't commented on it.* [from Old English]

**Word Partnership** Use *knowledge* with :

| | |
|---|---|
| V. | **acquire** knowledge, **gain** knowledge, **have** knowledge, **require** knowledge, **test your** knowledge, **use your** knowledge **1** |
| ADJ. | **background** knowledge, **common** knowledge, **prior** knowledge, **scientific** knowledge, **useful** knowledge, **vast** knowledge **1** |
| N. | knowledge **base 1** |

**knowl|edge|able** /nɒlɪdʒəbəl/ also **knowledgable** ADJ Someone who is **knowledgeable** knows about many different things or a lot about a particular subject. ❑ *Do you think you are more knowledgeable about life than your parents are at your age?* [from Old English]

**known** /noʊn/ **1** **Known** is the past participle of **know**. **2** ADJ You use **known** to describe someone or something that is clearly recognized by or familiar to all people or to a particular group of people. ❑ *He was a known face at the cafés along Broadway.* **3** PHRASE If you **let it be known that** something is true, or **let** something **be known**, you make sure that people know it or can find out about it. ❑ *The president has let it be known that he is against it.* [from Old English]

**knuck|le** /nʌkəl/ (**knuckles**) **1** N-COUNT Your **knuckles** are the rounded pieces of bone where your fingers join your hands, and where your fingers bend. ❑ *Brenda's knuckles were white as she gripped the arms of the chair.* [from Middle High

K

German] **2** a **rap on the knuckles** → see **rap** → see **hand**

**kook** /ku̲k/ (**kooks**) N-COUNT You can refer to someone who you think is slightly strange or eccentric as a **kook**. [INFORMAL]

**Ko|ran** /kɔra̲n, -ræn/ N-PROPER The **Koran** is the sacred book on which the religion of Islam is based. [from Arabic]

**Kuiper belt** /ka̲ɪpər bɛlt/ N-SING The **Kuiper belt** is a region of the solar system beyond Neptune where there are many small, icy comets. [TECHNICAL] [from Dutch American]

**Kurd** /ka̲rd/ (**Kurds**) N-COUNT A **Kurd** is a member of a race of people who live mainly in parts of Turkey, Iran, and Iraq. ❑ *...a group of Iraqi Kurds.* [from Kurdish]

**Kur|dish** /ka̲rdɪʃ/ **1** ADJ **Kurdish** means belonging or relating to the Kurds, or to their language or culture. ❑ *...Kurdish villages.* **2** N-UNCOUNT **Kurdish** is the language spoken by Kurds. ❑ *...schoolchildren speaking Kurdish.*

**kvetch** /kvɛtʃ/ (**kvetches, kvetching, kvetched**) V-I If someone **kvetches** about something, they complain about it constantly or in a bad-tempered way. [INFORMAL] ❑ *The woman kept kvetching about how he should change into something nicer.* ❑ *I just really love to kvetch.* [from Yiddish]

**kW** also **KW** **kW** or **KW** is a written abbreviation for **kilowatt**.

**k**

# L1

**L** On a weather map, **L** is an abbreviation for "low pressure."

**lab** /læb/ (**labs**) N-COUNT A **lab** is the same as a **laboratory**.

**laba|no|ta|tion** /lɑbənoʊteɪʃ³n, leɪb-/ N-UNCOUNT **Labanotation** is a system for recording dance movements that uses symbols to represent points on the dancer's body. [TECHNICAL]

**lab apron** (**lab aprons**) N-COUNT A **lab apron** is a piece of clothing that you wear when you are working in a laboratory, in order to prevent your clothes from getting dirty.

**la|bel** /leɪb³l/ (**labels, labeling** or **labelling, labeled** or **labelled**) ◼ N-COUNT A **label** is a piece of paper or plastic that is attached to an object in order to give information about it. ❑ ...the label on the bottle. ◻ V-T If something **is labeled**, a label is attached to it giving information about it. ❑ All foods must be clearly labeled. ❑ The radio was labeled "Made in China." ◼ V-T If you say that someone or something **is labeled as** a particular thing, you mean they generally describe them that way and you think that this is unfair. ❑ He was labeled as a difficult child. [from Old French]
→ see **graph**

**la|bor** /leɪbər/ (**labors, laboring, labored**) ◼ N-VAR **Labor** is very hard work, usually physical work. ❑ ...the labor of moving heavy rocks. ◻ V-I Someone who **labors** works hard using their hands. ❑ The miners labored 1400 yards below ground. ◼ V-T/V-I If you **labor to** do something, you do it with difficulty. ❑ The police labored for months to try to solve the case. ❑ He could feel his heart laboring in his chest. ◼ N-UNCOUNT **Labor** is used to refer to the workers of a country or industry. ❑ Employers want cheap labor. ◼ N-UNCOUNT **Labor** is the last stage of pregnancy, in which the mother gradually pushes the baby out. ❑ Her labor was long and difficult. [from Old French]
→ see **factory**

**la|bora|tory** /læbrətɔri/ (**laboratories**) N-COUNT A **laboratory** is a building or a room where scientific experiments and research are carried out. ❑ ...a research laboratory at Columbia University. [from Medieval Latin]
→ see Picture Dictionary: **laboratory equipment**
→ see Word Web: **laboratory**

**la|bor camp** (**labor camps**) N-COUNT A **labor camp** is a kind of prison, where the prisoners are forced to do hard, physical work, usually outdoors.

**la|bored** /leɪbərd/ ◼ ADJ If your breathing is **labored**, it is slow and seems to take a lot of effort. ❑ ...harsh, labored breathing. ◻ ADJ If something such as someone's writing or speech is **labored**, they have put too much effort into it so it seems awkward and unnatural. [from Old French]

**la|bor|er** /leɪbərər/ (**laborers**) N-COUNT A **laborer** is a person who does a job which involves a lot of hard physical work. ❑ ...a farm laborer. [from Old French]
→ see **union**

**la|bor force** (**labor forces**) N-COUNT The **labor force** consists of all the people who are able to work in a country or area, or all the people who work for a particular company. [BUSINESS] ❑ At least 20% of the labor force is unemployed.

## Word Web    laboratory

The discovery of the life-saving drug penicillin was a lucky accident. While cleaning his **laboratory**, a **researcher** named Alexander Fleming* noticed that the bacteria in one **Petri dish** had been killed by some kind of **mold**. He took a **sample** and found that it was a form of penicillin. Fleming and others did further **research** and **published** their **findings** in 1928, but few people took notice. However, ten years later a team at Oxford University in England read Fleming's **study** and began animal and human **experiments**. Within ten years, drug companies were manufacturing 650 billion units of penicillin a month!

*Alexander Fleming (1881-1955): a Scottish biologist and pharmacologist.*

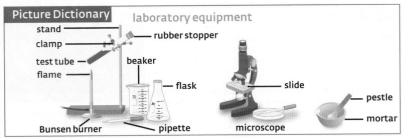

### Picture Dictionary — laboratory equipment

stand — rubber stopper
clamp
test tube — beaker
flame
— flask — slide
— pestle
— mortar
Bunsen burner — pipette — microscope

**labor-intensive** ADJ **Labor-intensive** industries or methods of making things involve a lot of workers. Compare **capital-intensive**. [BUSINESS] □ *Making clothing is very labor-intensive.*

**la|bo|ri|ous** /ləbɔ̱riəs/ ADJ If you describe a task or job as **laborious**, you mean that it takes a lot of time and effort. □ *Keeping the yard neat in the fall is a laborious task.* ● **la|bo|ri|ous|ly** ADV □ *He sat behind a desk laboriously writing.* [from Old French]

**la|bor mar|ket** (**labor markets**) N-COUNT When you talk about **the labor market**, you are referring to all the people who are able to work and want jobs in a country or area, in relation to the number of jobs there are available. [BUSINESS] □ *Women's wages are still less than men's in today's labor market.*

**la|bor re|la|tions** N-PLURAL **Labor relations** refers to the relationship between employers and employees in industry, and the political decisions and laws that affect it. □ *We have to balance good labor relations against the need to cut costs.*

**labor-saving** ADJ A **labor-saving** device or idea makes it possible for you to do something with less effort than usual. □ *...labor-saving devices such as washing machines.*

**la|bor un|ion** (**labor unions**) N-COUNT A **labor union** is an organization that represents the rights and interests of workers to their employers.

**laby|rinth** /læ̱bɪrɪnθ/ (**labyrinths**) **1** N-COUNT If you describe a place as a **labyrinth**, you mean that it is made up of a complicated series of paths or passages, through which it is difficult to find your way. [LITERARY] □ *...the labyrinth of tunnels.* **2** N-COUNT If you describe a situation, process, or area of knowledge as a **labyrinth**, you mean that it is very complicated. [FORMAL] □ *...a labyrinth of different opinions.* [from Latin]

**lace** /le̱ɪs/ (**laces, lacing, laced**) **1** N-UNCOUNT **Lace** is a very delicate cloth which is made by twisting together very fine threads leaving holes in between. □ *...a dress made of lace.* **2** N-COUNT **Laces** are thin pieces of material that are used to fasten some types of clothing, especially shoes. □ *Barry tied the laces on his shoes.* **3** V-T If you **lace** something such as a pair of shoes, you tighten the laces of your shoes by pulling the laces through the holes, and tying them together. □ *I laced my ice-skates tightly.* ● **Lace up** means the same as **lace**. □ *He laced up his boots.* **4** V-T To **lace** food or drink with something

lace

harmful means to put a small amount of the substance into the food or drink. □ *She laced his food with poison.* [from Old French]

**lack** /læ̱k/ (**lacks, lacking, lacked**) **1** N-UNCOUNT; N-SING If there is a **lack of** something, there is not enough of it or it does not exist at all. □ *Despite his lack of experience, he got the job.* □ *The police dropped the charges for lack of evidence.* **2** V-T/V-I If you say that someone or something **lacks** a particular quality or that a particular quality is **lacking** in them, you mean that they do not have any or enough of it. □ *The meal lacked flavor.* ● **lack|ing** /læ̱kɪŋ/ ADJ □ *She felt nervous and lacking in confidence.* **3** PHRASE If you say there is **no lack of** something, you are emphasizing that there is a great deal of it. □ *There was no lack of things for them to talk about.* [from Middle Dutch]

### Word Partnership Use *lack* with :

| | |
|---|---|
| N. | lack *of* confidence, lack *of* control, lack *of* enthusiasm, lack *of* evidence, lack *of* exercise, lack *of* experience, lack *of* food, lack *of* information, lack *of* knowledge, lack *of* money, lack *of* progress, lack *of* resources, lack *of* skills, lack *of* sleep, lack *of* support, lack *of* trust, lack *of* understanding **1** |

**lack|luster** /læ̱klʌstər/ ADJ If you describe something or someone as **lackluster**, you mean that they are not exciting or energetic. □ *He gave a lackluster speech at the conference.*

**lac|quer** /læ̱kər/ (**lacquers**) N-VAR **Lacquer** is a special liquid which is painted on wood or metal in order to protect it and to make it shiny. □ *We put on the second coating of lacquer.* [from French]

**lacy** /le̱ɪsi/ (**lacier, laciest**) ADJ **Lacy** things are made from lace or have pieces of lace attached to them. □ *...lacy nightgowns.* [from Old French]

ladder

**lad|der** /læ̱dər/ (**ladders**) N-COUNT A **ladder** is a piece of equipment used for climbing up something or down from something. It consists of two long pieces of wood, metal, or rope with steps fixed between them. □ *He climbed the ladder so he could see over the wall.* [from Old English]

**lad|en** /le̱ɪdən/ **1** ADJ If someone or something is **laden** with a lot of heavy things, they are holding or carrying them. [LITERARY] □ *I came home laden with cardboard boxes.* □ *The peach tree was laden with fruit.* **2** ADJ If you describe a person or thing as **laden**

## Word Web    lake

Several forces create **lakes**. The movement of a glacier can carve out a deep **basin** in the soil. The Great Lakes between the U.S. and Canada are **glacial** lakes. Very deep lakes appear when large pieces of the earth's crust suddenly shift. Lake Baikal in Russia is more than a mile deep. When a volcano erupts, it creates a **crater**. Crater Lake in Oregon is the perfectly round remains of a volcanic cone. The **water** comes from melted snow and rain.
Erosion also creates lakes. When the wind blows away sand, the hole left behind forms a natural lake **bed**.

with something, particularly something bad, you mean that they have a lot of it. □ *We're laden with guilt.* [from Old English]

**lady** /leɪdi/ (**ladies**) **1** N-COUNT You can use **lady** when you are referring to a woman, especially when you are showing politeness or respect. □ *She's a very sweet old lady.* □ *Here's the lady's purse.* **2** N-VOC "**Lady**" is sometimes used by men as a form of address when they are talking to a woman that they do not know, especially in stores and on the street. [INFORMAL] □ *What seems to be the trouble, lady?* [from Old English]

**lag** /læg/ (**lags, lagging, lagged**) **1** V-I If you **lag behind** someone or something, you make slower progress than them. □ *She's lagging behind the others.* **2** N-COUNT A time **lag** or a **lag** of a particular length of time is a period of time between one event and another related event. □ *There's a time lag between exposure and getting sick.*

**la|goon** /ləgun/ (**lagoons**) N-COUNT A **lagoon** is an area of calm sea water that is separated from the ocean by a line of rock or sand. [from Italian]

**laid** /leɪd/ **Laid** is the past tense and past participle of **lay**. [from Old French]

**laid-back** ADJ If you describe someone as **laid-back**, you mean that they behave in a calm, relaxed way as if nothing will ever worry them. [INFORMAL] □ *He has a really laid-back attitude.*

**lain** /leɪn/ **Lain** is the past participle of **lie**. [from Old English]

**lake** /leɪk/ (**lakes**) N-COUNT A **lake** is a large area of fresh water, surrounded by land. □ *They went fishing in the lake.* [from Old French]
→ see Word Web: **lake**
→ see **river**

**lake|front** /leɪkfrʌnt/ also **lake front** or **lake-front** N-SING The **lakefront** is the area of land around the edge of a lake. □ *...a cabin down on the lakefront.*

**lamb** /læm/ (**lambs**) N-COUNT A **lamb** is a young sheep. ● **Lamb** is the flesh of a lamb eaten as food. □ *For supper she served lamb.* [from Old English]

**lame** /leɪm/ (**lamer, lamest**) **1** ADJ If someone is **lame**, they are unable to walk properly because of damage to one or both of their legs. □ *She was lame in one leg.* ● The **lame** are people who are lame. □ *...the wounded and the lame of the last war.* **2** ADJ If you describe an excuse, argument, or remark as **lame**, you mean that it is poor or weak. □ *He gave me some lame excuse about being too busy to call me.* ● **lame|ly** ADV □ *"I've forgotten my phone number," I said lamely.* [from Old English]

**la|ment** /ləmɛnt/ (**laments, lamenting, lamented**) **1** V-T/V-I If you **lament** something, you express your sadness, regret, or disappointment about it. [mainly FORMAL OR WRITTEN] □ *He laments that he never went to college.* □ *Mama's always lamenting because she does all the cleaning herself.* **2** N-COUNT Someone's **lament** is an expression of their sadness, regret, or disappointment about something. [mainly FORMAL OR WRITTEN] □ *You hear the same lament at every golf club about not having younger members.* [from Latin]

**lamp** /læmp/ (**lamps**) N-COUNT A **lamp** is a light that works by using electricity or by burning oil or gas. □ *She switched on her lamp.* [from Old French]

**land** /lænd/ (**lands, landing, landed**) **1** N-UNCOUNT **Land** is an area of ground, especially one that is used for a particular purpose such as farming or building. □ *There is not enough good agricultural land.* □ *...160 acres of land.* □ *It isn't clear whether the plane crashed on land or in the ocean.* **2** N-COUNT You can use **land** to refer to a country in a poetic or emotional way. [LITERARY] □ *...America, land of opportunity.* **3** V-I When someone or something **lands**, they come down to the ground after moving through the air or falling. □ *He was sent flying into the air and landed 20 feet away.* **4** V-T/V-I When someone **lands** a plane, ship, or spacecraft, or when it **lands**, it arrives somewhere after a journey. □ *The plane landed after a flight of three hours.* □ *He landed his boat on the western shore.* ● **land|ing** (**landings**) N-VAR □ *The pilot made a controlled landing.* **5** V-T/V-I If you **land in** an unpleasant situation or place or if something **lands** you in it, something causes you to be in it. [INFORMAL] □ *His big ideas have landed him in trouble.* [from Old English] **6** to **land on** your **feet** → see **foot**
→ see **biosphere, continent, earth**

### Thesaurus    land    Also look up :

| | |
|---|---|
| N. | area, country, real estate **1** |
| V. | arrive, touch down; *(ant.)* take off **3 4** |

### Word Partnership    Use *land* with :

| | |
|---|---|
| N. | **acres of** land, **area of** land, **desert** land, land **management**, land **ownership**, land **use**, **piece of** land, **plot of** land, **strip of** land, **tract of** land **1** |
| ADJ. | **agricultural** land, **fertile** land, **flat** land, **grazing** land, **private** land, **public** land, **undeveloped** land, **vast** land **1** |
| V. | **buy** land, **own** land, **sell** land **1** |

**land|fill** /lændfɪl/ (**landfills**) **1** N-UNCOUNT

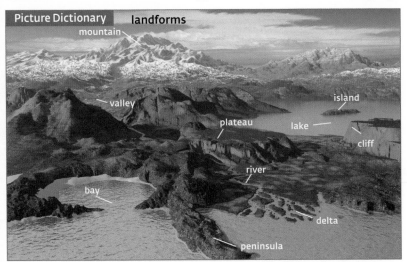

**Picture Dictionary** landforms

mountain

valley

plateau

island

lake

cliff

river

bay

delta

peninsula

**Landfill** is a method of getting rid of very large amounts of garbage by burying it in a large deep hole. ❑ ...*the high cost of landfill.* **2** N-COUNT A **landfill** is a large deep hole in which very large amounts of garbage are buried. ❑ *The trash in modern landfills does not decompose easily.*
→ see **dump**

**land|form** /lǽndfɔrm/ (**landforms**) also **land form** N-COUNT A **landform** is any natural feature of the Earth's surface, such as a hill, a lake, or a beach. ❑ *This country has a huge variety of landforms.*
→ see Picture Dictionary: **landforms**

**land|ing** /lǽndɪŋ/ (**landings**) N-COUNT In a house or other building, the **landing** is the area at the top of the staircase which has rooms leading off it. [from Old English]

**land|lady** /lǽndleɪdi/ (**landladies**) N-COUNT Someone's **landlady** is the woman who allows them to live or work in a building which she owns, in return for rent. ❑ ... *a note from my landlady.*

**land|lord** /lǽndlɔrd/ (**landlords**) N-COUNT Someone's **landlord** is the man who allows them to live or work in a building which he owns, in return for rent. ❑ *His landlord doubled the rent.*

> **Word Link** mark ≈ boundary, sign : **book**mark, **ear**mark, **land**mark

**land|mark** /lǽndmɑrk/ (**landmarks**)
**1** N-COUNT A **landmark** is a building or feature which is easily noticed and can be used to judge your position or the position of other buildings or features. ❑ *The Empire State Building is a New York landmark.* **2** N-COUNT You can refer to an important stage in the development of something as a **landmark**. ❑ *The baby was a landmark in our lives.*

**land|scape** /lǽndskeɪp/ (**landscapes, landscaping, landscaped**) **1** N-VAR The **landscape** is everything you can see when you look across an area of land, including hills, rivers, buildings, trees, and plants. ❑ ...*Arizona's desert landscape.*

**2** N-COUNT A **landscape** is a painting which shows a scene in the countryside. **3** V-T If an area of land **is landscaped**, it is changed to make it more attractive. ❑ *The back garden was landscaped.* ● **land|scap|ing** N-UNCOUNT ❑ *The house and the landscaping are lovely.* [from Middle Dutch]
→ see **art, painting**

**land|slide** /lǽndslaɪd/ (**landslides**) **1** N-COUNT A **landslide** is a victory in an election in which a person or political party gets far more votes or seats than their opponents. ❑ *He won the election by a landslide.* **2** N-COUNT A **landslide** is a large amount of earth and rocks falling down a cliff or the side of a mountain. ❑ *The storm caused landslides and flooding.*
→ see **disaster, tsunami**

**lane** /leɪn/ (**lanes**) **1** N-COUNT A **lane** is a narrow road, especially in the country. ❑ ...*a quiet country lane.* ❑ *They had a house on Spring Park Lane in East Hampton.* **2** N-COUNT A **lane** is a part of a main road which is marked by the edge of the road and a painted line, or by two painted lines. ❑ *The truck was traveling at 20 mph in the slow lane.* **3** N-COUNT At a swimming pool, athletics track, or bowling alley, a **lane** is a long narrow section which is separated from other sections, for example by lines or ropes. ❑ *Who is the runner in the inside lane?* **4** N-COUNT A **lane** is a route that is frequently used by aircraft or ships. ❑ ...*one of the busiest shipping lanes in the world.* [from Old English]
→ see **traffic**

**lan|guage** /lǽŋgwɪdʒ/ (**languages**) **1** N-COUNT A **language** is a system of communication which consists of a set of sounds and written symbols which are used by the people of a particular country or region for talking or writing. ❑ ...*the English language.* ❑ *Students must learn to speak a second language.* **2** N-UNCOUNT **Language** is the use of a system of communication which consists of a set of sounds or written symbols. ❑ *Students studied how children develop language.* **3** N-UNCOUNT You can refer to the words used in connection

with a particular subject as **the language of** that subject. ❑ ...*the language of business.* **4** N-UNCOUNT The **language** of a piece of writing or speech is the style in which it is written or spoken. ❑ *Why can't they explain things in plain language?* ❑ *The tone of his language was polite.* [from Old French]
→ see **culture, English**

N.   communication, dialect **1** **2** **4**
     jargon, slang, terminology **4**

**Word Partnership**   Use *language* with :

V.   **know** a language, **learn** a language,
     **speak** a language, **teach** a language,
     **understand** a language,
     **use** a language **1**
ADJ. **a different** language, **foreign** language,
     **native** language, **official** language,
     **second** language **1**
     **bad** language, **foul** language, **plain**
     language, **simple** language, **technical**
     language, **vulgar** language **4**
N.   language **acquisition**, language
     **barrier**, language **of children**,
     language **classes**, language
     **comprehension**, language
     **development**, language **skills** **1** **2**

**lan|guid** /lǽŋgwɪd/ ADJ If you describe someone as **languid**, you mean that they show little energy or interest and are very slow and casual in their movements. [LITERARY] ❑ *He's a large, languid man.* ● **lan|guid|ly** ADV ❑ *We sat about languidly.* [from Latin]

**lan|guish** /lǽŋgwɪʃ/ (**languishes, languishing, languished**) V-I If someone **languishes** somewhere, they are forced to remain and suffer in an unpleasant situation. ❑ *Pollard continues to languish in prison.* [from Old French]

lantern

**lan|tern** /lǽntərn/ (**lanterns**) N-COUNT A **lantern** is a lamp in a metal frame with glass sides. [from Latin]

**lap** /lǽp/ (**laps, lapping, lapped**) **1** N-COUNT Your **lap** is the flat area formed by your thighs when you are sitting down. ❑ *She waited quietly with her hands in her lap.* **2** N-COUNT In a race, a competitor completes a **lap** when they have gone around a course once. ❑ ...*the last lap of the race.* **3** V-T In a race, if you **lap** another competitor, you go past them while they are still on the previous lap. ❑ *Schumacher lapped every other driver in the race.* **4** V-T/V-I When water **laps** against something such as the shore or the side of a boat, it touches it gently and makes a soft sound. [WRITTEN] ❑ *Water lapped against the shore.* ❑ ...*white beaches lapped by warm blue seas.* ● **lap|ping** N-UNCOUNT ❑ *The only sound was the lapping of the waves.* **5** V-T When an animal **laps** a drink, it uses short quick movements of its tongue to take liquid up into its mouth. ❑ *The cat lapped milk from a dish.* ● **Lap up** means the same as **lap.** ❑ *She poured some water into a bowl and the dog lapped it up eagerly.* [from Old English]

▶ **lap up** PHR-VERB If someone **laps up** something such as information or attention, they accept it eagerly. ❑ *Children lap up adult attention.*

lapel

**la|pel** /ləpɛ́l/ (**lapels**) N-COUNT The **lapels** of a jacket or coat are the two top parts at the front that are folded back on each side and join on to the collar. ❑ *He wore a flower in his lapel.*

**Word Link**   *lapse* ≈ *falling* : **col**lapse, **e**lapse, **lapse**

**lapse** /lǽps/ (**lapses, lapsing, lapsed**) **1** N-COUNT A **lapse** is a moment or instance of bad behavior by someone who usually behaves well. ❑ ...*a lapse in his usual calm behavior.* **2** N-COUNT A **lapse of** something such as concentration or judgment is a temporary lack of that thing, which can often cause you to make a mistake. ❑ *I had a little lapse of concentration in the middle of the race.* **3** V-I If someone **lapses into** a particular way of speaking, or behaving, they start speaking or behaving in that way ❑ *They all lapsed into silence.* ● **Lapse** is also a noun. ❑ *Her lapse didn't seem strange to her friend.* **4** N-SING A **lapse of** time is a period that is long enough for a situation to change. ❑ *I started playing the flute again after a lapse of five years.* **5** V-I If a period of time **lapses**, it passes. ❑ *A few days had lapsed since Grace's death.* **6** V-I If a situation or legal contract **lapses**, it ends rather than being continued, renewed, or extended. ❑ *The terms of the treaty lapsed in 1987.* [from Latin]

**lap|top** /lǽptɒp/ (**laptops**) N-COUNT A **laptop** or a **laptop computer** is a small portable computer. ❑ *She was working at her laptop.*
→ see **computer**

**large** /lɑ́rdʒ/ (**larger, largest**) **1** ADJ A **large** thing or person is greater in size than usual or average. ❑ *This fish lives mainly in large rivers and lakes.* **2** ADJ A **large** amount or number of people or things is more than the average amount or number. ❑ *The gang got away with a large amount of cash.* ❑ *There are a large number of places where you can take full-time courses.* **3** ADJ **Large** is used to indicate that a problem or issue is very important or serious. ❑ *One large problem remains.* **4** PHRASE You use **at large** to indicate that you are talking in a general way about most of the people mentioned. ❑ *He wanted to get the public at large interested in modern art.* [from Old French]

**Thesaurus**   *large*   Also look up :

ADJ.   big, sizable, spacious, substantial; *(ant.)* small **1**

**large|ly** /lɑ́rdʒli/ **1** ADV You use **largely** to say that a statement is not completely true but is mostly true. ❑ *The project is largely funded by donations.* ❑ *The government is largely to blame for this.* **2** ADV **Largely** is used to introduce the main reason for a particular event or situation. ❑ *She failed her exams, largely because she did no work.* [from Old French]

**large-scale** also **large scale** **1** ADJ A **large-scale** action or event happens over a very wide area or involves a lot of people or things. ❑ ...*a large-scale military operation.* **2** ADJ A **large-scale**

Lasers are an amazing form of technology. Laser **beams** read **CDs** and **DVDs**. They can create three-dimensional holograms. Laser **light shows** add excitement at concerts. **Fiber optic cables** carry intense flashes of laser light. This allows a single cable to transmit thousands of e-mail and phone messages at the same time. Laser **scanners** read prices from bar codes. Lasers are also used as scalpels in **surgery**, and to remove hair, birthmarks and tattoos. Dentists use lasers to remove cavities. Laser eye surgery has become very popular. In manufacturing, lasers make precise cuts in everything from fabric to steel.

map or diagram represents a small area of land or a building or machine in a way that allows small details to be shown.

**lark** /lɑrk/ (**larks**) N-COUNT A **lark** is a small brown bird which has a pleasant song. [from Old English]

**lar|va** /lɑrvə/ (**larvae** /lɑrvi/) N-COUNT A **larva** is an insect at the stage of its life after it has developed from an egg and before it changes into its adult form. □ *The eggs quickly hatch into larvae.* [from Latin] → see **amphibian**

**lar|ynx** /lærɪŋks/ (**larynxes**) N-COUNT Your **larynx** is the top part of the passage that leads from your throat to your lungs and contains your vocal cords. [MEDICAL] [from New Latin]

**la|ser** /leɪzər/ (**lasers**) N-COUNT A **laser** is a narrow beam of concentrated light produced by a special machine. □ *…new laser technology.* → see Word Web: **laser**

**lash** /læʃ/ (**lashes, lashing, lashed**) ◼ N-COUNT Your **lashes** are the hairs that grow on the edge of your eyelids. □ *His eyes had very long lashes.* ◼ V-T If you **lash** two or more things together, you tie one of them firmly to the other. □ *We built the shelter by lashing poles together.* ◼ V-T/V-I If wind, rain, or water **lashes** someone or something, it hits them violently. [WRITTEN] □ *Storms lashed the east coast of North America.* □ *Rain lashed against the windows.* ◼ N-COUNT A **lash** is a blow with a whip, especially a blow on someone's back as a punishment. □ *The villagers sentenced one man to five lashes for stealing.* [Sense 2 from Old French]
▸ **lash out** ◼ PHR-VERB If you **lash out**, you attempt to hit someone quickly and violently with a weapon or with your hands or feet. □ *They held his arms to stop him from lashing out.* ◼ PHR-VERB If you **lash out** at someone or something, you speak to them or about them very angrily or critically. □ *His laughter made her angry and she lashed out at him.*

**Lasik** /leɪsɪk/ also LASIK N-UNCOUNT **Lasik** is a form of eye surgery that uses lasers to improve or correct people's eyesight. **Lasik** is an abbreviation for "laser-assisted in situ keratomileusis."

**last** /læst/ (**lasts, lasting, lasted**) ◼ DET You use **last** in expressions such as **last Friday, last night,** and **last year** to refer, for example, to the most recent Friday, night, or year. □ *I got married last July.* □ *He didn't come home last night.* ◼ ADJ The **last** event, person, thing, or period of time is the most recent one. □ *Much has changed since my last visit.* □ *I split up with my last boyfriend three years ago.* ● **Last** is also a pronoun. □ *Each song was better than the last.* ◼ ADV If something **last** happened on a particular occasion, that is the most recent occasion on which it happened. □ *When were you there last?* □ *He is a lot taller than when I last saw him.*

◼ ORD The **last** thing, person, event, or period of time is the one that happens or comes after all the others of the same kind. □ *…the last three pages of the chapter.* ● **Last** is also a pronoun. □ *It wasn't the first time he had cried and it wouldn't be the last.* ◼ ADV If you do something **last**, you do it after everyone else does, or after you do everything else. □ *I arrived home last.* □ *I was always picked last for the football team at school.* ◼ PRON If you are **the last to** do or know something, everyone else does or knows it before you. □ *She was the last to go to bed.* ◼ ADJ **Last** is used to refer to the only thing, person, or part of something that remains. □ *Can I have the last piece of pizza?* ● **Last** is also a noun. □ *He finished off the last of the coffee.* ◼ ADJ You can use **last** to indicate that something is extremely undesirable or unlikely. □ *The last thing I wanted to do was teach.* ● **Last** is also a pronoun. □ *I'm the last to say that science explains everything.* ◼ V-T/V-I If an event, situation, or problem **lasts** for a particular length of time, it continues to exist or happen for that length of time. □ *The marriage lasted for less than two years.* □ *The games lasted only half the normal time.* ◼ V-T/V-I If something **lasts** for a particular length of time, it continues to be able to be used for that time, for example, because there is some of it left or because it is in good enough condition. □ *This battery lasts twice as long as the smaller size.* ◼ → see also **lasting** ◼ PHRASE If you say that something has happened **at last** or **at long last**, you mean it has happened after you have been hoping for it for a long time. □ *I'm so glad that we've found you at last!* □ *Here, at long last, was the moment he was waiting for.* ◼ PHRASE You use expressions such as **the night before last, the election before last** and **the leader before last** to refer to the period of time, event, or person that came immediately before the most recent one in a series. □ *I went out with Helen the night before last.* ◼ PHRASE You can use expressions such as **the last I heard** and **the last she heard** to introduce a piece of information that is the most recent that you have on a particular subject. □ *The last I heard, they were still happily married.* [from Old English] ◼ **the last straw** → see **straw** ◼ **last thing** → see **thing**

**last-ditch** ADJ A **last-ditch** action is done only because there are no other ways left to achieve something or to prevent something from happening. ❏ *…a last-ditch attempt to prevent war.*

**last|ing** /lɑːstɪŋ/ ◼ ADJ You can use **lasting** to describe a situation, result, or agreement that continues to exist or have an effect for a very long time. ❏ *Everyone wants a lasting peace.* [from Old English] ◻ → see also **last**

**last|ly** /lɑːstli/ ◼ ADV You use **lastly** when you want to make a final point, ask a final question, or mention a final item that is connected with the other ones you have already asked or mentioned. ❏ *Lastly, can I ask about your future plans?* ◼ ADV You use **lastly** when you are saying what happens after everything else in a series of actions or events. ❏ *They wash their hands and faces, and lastly, they wash their feet.* [from Old English]

**last-minute** → see **minute**

**latch** /lætʃ/ (**latches, latching, latched**)
◼ N-COUNT A **latch** is a fastening on a door or gate. It consists of a metal bar which you lift in order to open the door. ❏ *She lifted up the latch and pushed the door open.* ◼ N-COUNT A **latch** is a lock on a door which locks automatically when you shut the door, so that you need a key in order to open it from the outside. ❏ *He heard a key click in the latch of the front door.* [from Old English]

▸ **latch onto** or **latch on** ◼ PHR-VERB If someone **latches onto** a person or an idea or **latches on**, they become very interested in the person or idea, often finding them so useful that they do not want to leave them. [INFORMAL] ❏ *Rob latched onto me and followed me around everywhere.* ◼ PHR-VERB If one thing **latches onto** another, or if it **latches on**, it attaches itself to it and becomes part of it. ❏ *Bedbugs latch onto the skin to feed.*

**late** /leɪt/ (**later, latest**) ◼ ADJ **Late** means near the end of a day, week, year, or other period of time. ❏ *It was late in the afternoon.* ❏ *He married late in life.* ● **Late** is also an adjective. ❏ *We went on vacation in late spring.* ❏ *He was in his late 20s.* ◼ ADJ If it is **late**, it is near the end of the day or it is past the time that you feel something should have been done. ❏ *It was very late and the streets were empty.* ● **late|ness** N-UNCOUNT ❏ *A crowd gathered despite the lateness of the hour.* ◼ ADV **Late** means after the time that was arranged or expected. ❏ *Steve arrived late.* ❏ *The talks began fifteen minutes late.* ● **Late** is also an adjective. ❏ *His campaign got off to a late start.* ❏ *The train was 40 minutes late.* ● **late|ness** N-UNCOUNT ❏ *He apologized for his lateness.* ◼ ADV **Late** means after the usual time that a particular event or activity happens. ❏ *We went to bed very late.* ● **Late** is also an adjective. ❏ *They had a late lunch.* ◼ ADJ You use **late** when you are talking about someone who is dead, especially someone who has died recently. ❏ *…my late husband.* ◼ → see also **later, latest** ◼ PHRASE If an action or event is **too late**, it is useless or ineffective because it occurs after the best time for it. ❏ *It was too late to change her mind.* [from Old English] ◼ **a late night** → see **night**

**late|ly** /leɪtli/ ADV You use **lately** to describe events in the recent past, or situations that started a short time ago. ❏ *Dad hasn't been well lately.* ❏ *Have you seen her lately?* [from Old English] → see also **recently**

**la|tent** /leɪtᵊnt/ ADJ **Latent** is used to describe something which is hidden and not obvious at the moment, but which may develop further in the future. ❏ *He had latent feelings of anger toward his parents.* [from Latin]

**lat|er** /leɪtər/ ◼ **Later** is the comparative of **late**. ◼ ADV You use **later** to refer to a time or situation that is after the one that you have been talking about or after the present one. ❏ *He left ten years later.* ◼ PHRASE You use **later on** to refer to a time or situation that is after the one that you have been talking about or after the present one. ❏ *Later on I'll be speaking to her.* ◼ ADJ You use **later** to refer to an event, period of time, or other thing which comes after the one that you have been talking about or after the present one. ❏ *The race was re-scheduled for a later date.* ◼ ADJ You use **later** to refer to the last part of someone's life or career or the last part of a period of history. ❏ *He found happiness in later life.* ❏ *…the later part of the 20th century.* [from Old English] ◼ → see also **late**

**lat|er|al** /lætərəl/ ADJ **Lateral** means relating to the sides of something, or moving in a sideways direction. ❏ *…the lateral movement of the bridge.* [from Latin]

**lat|er|al line sys|tem** (**lateral line systems**)
N-COUNT A **lateral line system** is a row of sense organs along each side of a fish's body that helps it to detect movement in the water. [TECHNICAL]

**lat|est** /leɪtɪst/ ◼ **Latest** is the superlative of **late**. ◼ ADJ You use **latest** to describe something that is the most recent thing of its kind. ❏ *…her latest book.* ◼ ADJ You can use **latest** to describe something that is very new and modern and is better than older things of a similar kind. ❏ *Criminals are using the latest laser photocopiers to produce fake dollars.* ◼ → see also **late** ◼ PHRASE You use **at the latest** in order to indicate that something must happen at or before a particular time and not after that time. ❏ *She'll be back by ten o'clock at the latest.* [from Old English]

**La|ti|na** /lætiːnə/ (**Latinas**) N-COUNT A **Latina** is a female citizen of the United States who originally came from Latin America, or whose family originally came from Latin America. ❏ *He married a Latina.* [from Latin American Spanish]

**Lat|in Ameri|can** /lætɪn əmɛrɪkən/ ADJ **Latin American** means belonging or relating to the countries of South America, Central America, and Mexico. **Latin American** also means belonging or relating to the people or culture of these countries. ❏ *…Latin American writers.*

**La|ti|no** /lætiːnoʊ/ (**Latinos**) also **latino**
N-COUNT A **Latino** is a citizen of the United States who originally came from Latin America, or whose family originally came from Latin America. ❏ *…Emilio Estevez and other famous Latinos.*

**lati|tude** /lætɪtuːd/ (**latitudes**) ◼ N-VAR The **latitude** of a place is its distance from the equator. Compare **longitude**. ❏ *In the middle to high latitudes rainfall has risen over the last 20–30 years.* ● **Latitude** is also an adjective. ❏ *…places above 36° latitude north.* ◼ N-UNCOUNT **Latitude** is freedom to choose the way in which you do something. [FORMAL] ❏ *He was given every latitude in forming a new government.* [from Latin] → see **globe**

**lat|ter** /lætər/ ◼ PRON When two people, things, or groups have just been mentioned, you can refer to the second of them as **the latter**. You can refer to the first of them as **the former**. ❑ *He found his cousin and uncle. The latter was sick.* ● **Latter** is also an adjective. ❑ *Some people like public speaking and some don't. Mike belongs in the latter group.* ◻ ADJ You use **latter** to describe the later part of a period of time or event. ❑ *…in the latter years of his career.* ◻ → see also **last** [from Old English]

**latter-day** ADJ **Latter-day** is used to describe someone or something that is a modern equivalent of a person or thing in the past. ❑ *He sees himself as a latter-day Teddy Roosevelt.*

**lat|tice** /lǽtɪs/ (**lattices**) N-COUNT A **lattice** is a pattern or structure made of strips of wood or another material which cross over each other diagonally leaving holes in between. ❑ *…the narrow steel lattice of the bridge.* [from Old French]

**laugh** /lǽf/ (**laughs, laughing, laughed**) ◻ V-T/ V-I When you **laugh**, you make a sound with your throat while smiling and show that you are happy or amused. People also sometimes laugh when they feel nervous or are being unfriendly. ❑ *When I saw what he was wearing, I started to laugh.* ❑ *"We need some help," he laughed.* ● **Laugh** is also a noun. ❑ *Lysenko gave a deep laugh at his own joke.* ◻ V-I If people **laugh at** someone or something, they mock them or make jokes about them. ❑ *People used to laugh at me because I was so small.* [from Old English]
▶ **laugh off** PHR-VERB If you **laugh off** a difficult or serious situation, you try to suggest that it is amusing and unimportant. ❑ *He laughed off reports that he is to be replaced as the team manager.*
→ see Word Web: **laugh**

| Thesaurus | laugh | Also look up : |
|---|---|---|
| v. | chuckle, crack up, giggle, howl; (*ant.*) cry ◻ | |

| Word Partnership | Use *laugh* with : |
|---|---|
| v. | **begin/start to** laugh, **hear** *someone* laugh, **make** *someone* laugh, **try to** laugh ◻ |
| ADJ. | **big** laugh, **good** laugh, **hearty** laugh, **little** laugh ◻ |

**laugh|ter** /lǽftər/ N-UNCOUNT **Laughter** is the sound of people laughing. ❑ *Their laughter filled the room.* [from Old English]
→ see **laugh**

| Word Partnership | Use *laughter* with : |
|---|---|
| v. | **burst into** laughter, **hear** laughter, **roar with** laughter |
| N. | **burst of** laughter, **sound of** laughter |
| ADJ. | **hysterical** laughter, **loud** laughter, **nervous** laughter |

**launch** /lɔ́ntʃ/ (**launches, launching, launched**) ◻ V-T To **launch** a rocket, missile, or satellite means to send it into the air or into space. ❑ *NASA plans to launch a new satellite.* ● **Launch** is also a noun. ❑ *…the launch of a space shuttle.* ◻ V-T To **launch** a ship or a boat means to put it into water, often for the first time after it has been built. ❑ *The "Titanic" was launched in 1911.* ● **Launch** is also a noun. ❑ *The launch of a ship was a big occasion.* ◻ V-T To **launch** a large and important activity means to start it. ❑ *The police have launched an investigation into the crime.* ● **Launch** is also a noun. ❑ *…the launch of a campaign for healthy eating.* ◻ V-T If a company **launches** a new product, it makes it available to the public. ❑ *The company launched a low-cost computer.* ● **Launch** is also a noun. ❑ *…the launch of a new magazine.* [from Anglo-French]
→ see **satellite**
▶ **launch into** PHR-VERB If you **launch into** something such as a speech, task, or fight, you enthusiastically start it. ❑ *Horrigan launched into a speech about the importance of new projects.*

**launch|er** /lɔ́ntʃər/ (**launchers**) N-COUNT A missile **launcher** or a grenade **launcher** is a device that is used for firing missiles or grenades. [from Late Latin]

**launch pad** (**launch pads**) N-COUNT A **launch pad** or **launching pad** is a platform from which rockets, missiles, or satellites are launched.

**launch ve|hi|cle** (**launch vehicles**) N-COUNT A **launch vehicle** is a rocket that is used to launch a satellite or spacecraft.

**laun|der** /lɔ́ndər/ (**launders, laundering, laundered**) ◻ V-T To **launder** money that has been obtained illegally means to move it into a legal business or a foreign bank, so that nobody knows where the money came from. ❑ *How they launder the money is unclear.* ● **laun|der|er** (**launderers**) N-COUNT ❑ *…a money launderer.* ◻ V-T When you **launder** clothes, sheets, and towels, you wash and iron them. [FORMAL] ❑ *Hotels launder towels and sheets every day.* [from Old French]

**laun|dro|mat** /lɔ́ndrəmæt/ (**laundromats**) N-COUNT A **laundromat** is a place where people can pay to use machines to wash and dry their clothes.

| Word Web | laugh |
|---|---|

There is an old saying, "**Laughter** is the best medicine." New scientific research supports the idea that **humor** really is good for your health. For example, laughing 100 times provides the same exercise benefits as a 15-minute bike ride. When a person **bursts out laughing**, levels of stress hormones in the bloodstream immediately drop. And laughter is more than just a sound. **Howling with laughter** gives face, stomach, leg, and back muscles a good workout. From polite **giggles** to noisy guffaws, laughter allows the release of anger, sadness, and fear. And that has to be good for you.

**laun|dry** /lɔndri/ (**laundries**) ◼ N-UNCOUNT
**Laundry** is used to refer to clothes, sheets, and
towels that are about to be washed, are being
washed, or have just been washed. ❑ *I'll do your
laundry.* ❑ *…the room where I hang the laundry.*
◻ N-COUNT A **laundry** is a business that washes
and irons clothes, sheets, and towels for people.
❑ *He gets his washing done at the laundry.* ◼ N-COUNT
A **laundry** or a **laundry room** is a room in a house,
hotel, or institution where clothes, sheets, and
towels are washed. ❑ *…the prison laundry.*
→ see **house, soap**

**lau|rel** /lɔrᵊl/ (**laurels**) N-VAR A **laurel** or a
**laurel tree** is a small evergreen tree with shiny
leaves. The leaves are sometimes used to make
decorations such as wreaths. [from Old French]

**lava** /lɑvə, lævə/ N-UNCOUNT **Lava** is the very
hot liquid rock that comes out of a volcano. ❑ *…the
lava and ash that came out of Mexico's Mount Colima.*
[from Italian Neapolitan]
→ see **rock, volcano**

**lav|en|der** /lævɪndər/ (**lavenders**) N-VAR
**Lavender** is a garden plant with sweet-smelling,
bluish-purple flowers. [from French]

**lav|ish** /lævɪʃ/ (**lavishes, lavishing, lavished**)
◼ ADJ If you describe something as **lavish**, you
mean that it is very elaborate and impressive and
a lot of money has been spent on it. ❑ *…a lavish
party.* ● **lav|ish|ly** ADV ❑ *The apartment was lavishly
decorated.* ◻ ADJ If you say that spending, praise,
or the use of something is **lavish**, you mean that
someone spends a lot or that something is praised
or used a lot. ❑ *Some people disapprove of his lavish
spending.* ◼ V-T If you **lavish** money, affection, or
praise on someone or something, you spend a lot
of money on them or give them a lot of affection or
praise. ❑ *Walmsley lavished gifts on family and friends.*
[from Old French]

**law** /lɔ/ (**laws**) ◼ N-SING The **law** is a system
of rules that a society or government develops in
order to deal with crime, business agreements,
and social relationships. You can also use **the law**
to refer to the people who work in this system.
❑ *Threatening phone calls are against the law.* ❑ *We
will punish those who break the law.* ❑ *The book looks
at how the law treats young people who commit crimes.*
◻ N-COUNT A **law** is one of the rules in a system
of law which deals with a particular type of
agreement, relationship, or crime. ❑ *…a new law
to protect young people.* ◼ N-PLURAL The **laws** of an
organization or activity are its rules, which are
used to organize and control it. ❑ *…the laws of the
Catholic Church.* ◼ N-COUNT A **law** is a rule or set
of rules for good behavior which is considered
right and important by the majority of people for
moral, religious, or emotional reasons. ❑ *…laws of
morality.* ◼ N-COUNT A **law** is a natural process in
which a particular event or thing always leads to a
particular result, or a scientific rule that someone
has invented to explain such a process. ❑ *A falling
apple led Isaac Newton to discover the law of gravity.*
◼ N-UNCOUNT **Law** or **the law** is all the professions
which deal with advising people about the law,
representing people in court, or giving decisions
and punishments. ❑ *He is interested in a career in
law.* ◼ N-UNCOUNT **Law** is the study of systems
of law and how laws work. ❑ *He studied law.* [from
Old English]

**law-abiding** ADJ A **law-abiding** person always
obeys the law and is considered to be good and
honest because of this. ❑ *…decent, law-abiding
citizens.*

**law and or|der** N-UNCOUNT When there is
**law and order** in a country, the laws are generally
accepted and obeyed, so that society there
functions normally. ❑ *…the breakdown of law and
order.*

**law enforcement** N-UNCOUNT Agencies
or officials whose job is **law enforcement** are
responsible for catching people who break the
law. ❑ *…increased funding for prisons and local law
enforcement.* ❑ *…law enforcement agencies such as
the police.*

**law|ful** /lɔfəl/ ADJ If an activity, organization,
or product is **lawful**, it is allowed by law. [FORMAL]
❑ *…fair and lawful treatment of prisoners.* ● **law|ful|ly**
ADV ❑ *Did the police act lawfully in shooting him?* [from
Old English]

**law|less** /lɔlɪs/ ADJ **Lawless** actions break the
law, especially in a wild and violent way. ❑ *There
were problems in urban areas and this led to lawless
behavior.* ● **law|less|ness** N-UNCOUNT ❑ *Lawlessness
is a major problem.* [from Old English]

**law|maker** /lɔmeɪkər/ (**lawmakers**) N-COUNT A
**lawmaker** is someone such as a politician who is
responsible for proposing and passing new laws.

**lawn** /lɔn/ (**lawns**) N-VAR A **lawn** is an area of
grass that is kept cut short and is usually part
of someone's yard, or part of a park. ❑ *They were
sitting on the lawn.* [from Old French]

**lawn bowl|ing** N-UNCOUNT **Lawn bowling** is
a game in which players try to roll large wooden
balls as near as possible to a small wooden ball.
Lawn bowling is usually played outdoors on grass.
❑ *…a revival of lawn bowling in the U.S.*

**lawn chair** (**lawn chairs**) N-COUNT A **lawn chair**
is a simple chair with a folding frame. Lawn
chairs are usually used outdoors.

**lawn|mow|er** /lɔnmoʊər/ (**lawnmowers**)
N-COUNT A **lawnmower** is a machine for cutting
grass on lawns.
→ see **garden**

**law|suit** /lɔsut/ (**lawsuits**) N-COUNT A **lawsuit**
is a case in a court of law which concerns a dispute
between two people or organizations. [FORMAL]
❑ *Some of the dead soldiers' families filed a million-dollar
lawsuit against the army.*

**law|yer** /lɔɪər, lɔyər/ (**lawyers**) N-COUNT A
**lawyer** is a person who is qualified to advise people
about the law and represent them in court. ❑ *His
lawyers say that he is innocent.*
→ see **trial**

| **Word Link** | lax ≈ allowing, loosening : lax, laxative, relax |
|---|---|

**lax** /læks/ (**laxer, laxest**) ADJ If you say that a
person's behavior or a system is **lax**, you mean
they are not careful or strict about maintaining
high standards. ❑ *One of the problems is lax security
in the airport.* ● **lax|ity** N-UNCOUNT ❑ *…police laxity
in the murder investigation.* [from Latin]

**laxa|tive** /læksətɪv/ (**laxatives**) N-VAR A
**laxative** is something you eat or drink that makes
you go to the toilet to empty your bowel. [from
Medieval Latin]

## lay

**❶ VERB AND NOUN USES**
**❷ ADJECTIVE USES**

**❶ lay** /leɪ/ (**lays, laying, laid**)

In standard English, the form **lay** is also the past tense of the verb **lie** in some meanings. In informal English, people sometimes use the word **lay** instead of **lie** in those meanings.

**1** V-T If you **lay** something somewhere, you put it there in a careful, gentle, or neat way. □ *Lay a sheet of newspaper on the floor.* □ *Mothers usually lay babies on their backs to sleep.* **2** V-T If you **lay** something such as carpets, cables, or foundations, you put them into their permanent position. □ *Workmen are currently laying new drains.* **3** V-T/V-I When a female bird **lays** or **lays** an egg, it produces an egg by pushing it out of its body. **4** V-T **Lay** is used with some nouns to talk about making official preparations for something. For example, if you **lay the basis** for something or **lay plans** for it, you prepare it carefully. □ *We have already laid plans for our next trip.* **5** V-T **Lay** is used with some nouns in expressions about accusing or blaming someone. For example, if you **lay the blame** for a mistake on someone, you say it is their fault. □ *She refused to lay the blame on any one person.* [from Old English]
**6** → see also **lie**

▸ **lay aside** PHR-VERB If you **lay aside** a feeling or belief, you reject it or give it up in order to progress with something. □ *We laid aside our differences, and got on with the job.*

▸ **lay down** PHR-VERB If rules or people in authority **lay down** what people should do or must do, they officially state what they should or must do. □ *Not all companies lay down written guidelines.*

▸ **lay off** PHR-VERB If workers **are laid off**, they are told by their employers to leave their job, usually because there is no more work for them to do. [BUSINESS] □ *100,000 employees will be laid off to cut costs.*

▸ **lay out** **1** PHR-VERB If you **lay out** a group of things, you spread them out and arrange them neatly, for example, so that they can all be seen clearly. □ *We spread the blanket and laid out the food.* **2** PHR-VERB To **lay out** ideas, principles, or plans means to explain or present them clearly, for example, in a document or a meeting. □ *Bob listened as Ted laid out his plan.* **3** → see also **layout**

**❷ lay** /leɪ/ **1** ADJ You use **lay** to describe people who are involved with a Christian church but are not members of the clergy or are not monks or nuns. □ *Edwards is a Methodist lay preacher.* **2** ADJ You use **lay** to describe people who are not experts or professionals in a particular subject or activity. □ *He was able to understand the science and explain it to a lay person.* [from Old French]

**lay|er** /leɪər/ (**layers, layering, layered**)
**1** N-COUNT A **layer** of a material or substance is a quantity or piece of it that covers a surface or that is between two other things. □ *A fresh layer of snow covered the street.* **2** N-COUNT If something such as a system or an idea has many **layers**, it has many different levels or parts. □ *…the layers of meaning in the artist's paintings.* **3** V-T If you **layer** something, you arrange it in layers. □ *Layer the onion slices on top of the potatoes.*
→ see **ozone**

**Word Partnership** Use *layer* with :

| | |
|---|---|
| ADJ. | **bottom/top** layer, **lower/upper** layer, **outer** layer, **protective** layer, **single** layer, **thick/thin** layer **1** |
| N. | layer **cake**, layer **of dust**, layer **of fat**, **ozone** layer, layer **of skin**, **surface** layer |

**lay|man** /leɪmən/ (**laymen**) N-COUNT A **layman** is a person who is not trained, qualified, or experienced in a particular subject or activity. □ *The book contains information that a layman can understand.*

**lay|out** /leɪaʊt/ (**layouts**) N-COUNT The **layout** of a park, building, or piece of writing is the way in which the parts of it are arranged. □ *He tried to remember the layout of the farmhouse.*

**lay|over** /leɪoʊvər/ (**layovers**) N-COUNT A **layover** is a short stay in a place in between parts of a journey, especially a plane journey. □ *She booked a plane for Denver with a layover in Dallas.*

**lazy** /leɪzi/ (**lazier, laziest**) **1** ADJ If someone is **lazy**, they do not want to work or make any effort to do anything. □ *I'm not lazy: I hate lounging about, doing nothing.* ● **la|zi|ness** N-UNCOUNT □ *Through laziness, he didn't bother to learn our names.* **2** ADJ You can use **lazy** to describe an activity or event in which you are very relaxed and which you do or take part in without making much effort. □ *Her novel is perfect for a lazy summer's afternoon reading.* ● **la|zi|ly** /leɪzɪli/ ADV □ *Liz yawned and stretched lazily.*

**lb.**

The plural is **lbs.** or **lb.**.

**lb.** is a written abbreviation for **pound**, when it refers to weight. □ *The baby weighed 8 lbs. 5 oz.* [from Latin]

## lead

**❶ BEING AHEAD OR TAKING SOMEONE SOMEWHERE**
**❷ SUBSTANCES**

**❶ lead** /liːd/ (**leads, leading, led**) **1** V-T If you **lead** a group of people, you walk or ride in front of them. □ *A brass band led the parade.* □ *He led his soldiers into battle.* **2** V-T If you **lead** someone to a particular place or thing, you take them there. □ *He took Dick's hand and led him into the house.* **3** V-I If a road, gate, or door **leads** somewhere, you can get there by following the road or going through the gate or door. □ *The door led to the yard.* □ *A hallway leads to a living room.* **4** V-T/V-I If you **are leading** at a particular point in a race or competition, you are winning at that point. □ *He's leading the presidential race.* □ *So far Fischer leads by five wins to two.* □ *Drury led 49 – 41 at halftime.* **5** N-SING If you have **the lead** or are **in the lead** in a race or competition, you are winning. □ *Harvard took the lead early in the game.* **6** V-T If you **lead** a group of people, an organization, or an activity, you are in control or in charge of the people or the activity. □ *He led the country between 1949 and 1984.* **7** V-T You can use **lead** when you are saying what kind of life someone has. For example, if you **lead** a busy life, your life is busy. □ *She led a normal, happy life.* **8** V-I If something **leads to** a

situation or event, usually an unpleasant one, it begins a process which causes that situation or event to happen. ❑ *Every time we talk about money it leads to an argument.* **9** V-T If something **leads** you **to** do something, it influences or affects you in such a way that you do it. ❑*What led you to write this book?* **10** V-T You can say that one point or topic in a discussion or piece of writing **leads** you **to** another in order to introduce a new point or topic that is linked with the previous one. ❑ *That leads me to the real point.* **11** N-COUNT A **lead** is a piece of information or an idea which may help people to discover the facts in a situation where many facts are not yet known, for example, in the investigation of a crime or in a scientific experiment. ❑ *The police are following up possible leads after receiving 400 calls from the public.* **12** N-COUNT A **lead** in a piece of equipment is a piece of wire covered in plastic which supplies electricity to the equipment or carries it from one part of the equipment to another. ❑ *This lead plugs into the camcorder.* **13** N-COUNT The **lead** in a play, film, or show is the most important part in it. The person who plays this part can also be called the **lead**. ❑ *Neve Campbell is the lead, playing one of the dancers.* [from Old English] **14** → see also **leading** **15** to **lead** someone **astray** → see **astray**
▶ **lead up to** **1** PHR-VERB The events that **lead up to** a particular event happen one after the other until that event occurs. ❑ *...the events that led up to his death.* **2** PHR-VERB If someone **leads up to** a particular subject, they gradually guide a conversation to a point where they can introduce it. ❑ *I wondered what he was leading up to.*

| **Thesaurus** | lead | Also look up : |
|---|---|---|
| v. | escort, guide, precede; (ant.) follow **1** **2** govern, head, manage **9** **6** | |

**❷ lead** /lɛd/ (**leads**) **1** N-UNCOUNT **Lead** is a soft, gray, heavy metal. ❑*...old-fashioned lead pipes.* **2** N-COUNT The **lead** in a pencil is the center part of it which makes a mark on paper. ❑*He started writing with pencil, but the lead immediately broke.* [from Old English]
→ see **mineral**

**lead|er** /lidər/ (**leaders**) **1** N-COUNT The **leader** of a group of people or an organization is the person who is in charge of it. ❑ *Illinois Republicans met Monday to elect a new leader.* **2** N-COUNT The **leader** at a particular point in a race or competition is the person who is winning at that point. ❑ *The leader came in two minutes before the other runners.* [from Old English]

**lead|er|ship** /lidərʃɪp/ (**leaderships**) **1** N-COUNT You refer to people who are in control of a group or organization as the **leadership**. ❑ *He held talks with the Croatian and Slovenian leaderships.* **2** N-UNCOUNT Someone's **leadership** is their position or state of being in control of a group of people. ❑ *The company doubled in size under her leadership.* [from Old English]

**lead|ing** /lidɪŋ/ **1** ADJ The **leading** person or thing in a particular area is the one which is most important or successful. ❑ *...a leading member of the city's Sikh community.* **2** ADJ The **leading** role in a play or movie is the main role. A **leading** lady or man is an actor who plays this role. ❑ *He played the leading role in a Mamet play.* [from Old English]

**leaf** /lif/ (**leaves, leafs, leafing, leafed**) N-COUNT

The **leaves** of a tree or plant are the parts that are flat, thin, and usually green. ❑ *The leaves of the tree moved gently in the wind.* [from Old English] → see **flower, herbivore, tea**

leaf

▶ **leaf through** PHR-VERB If you **leaf through** something such as a book or magazine, you turn the pages without reading or looking at them very carefully. ❑ *She enjoyed leafing through old photo albums.*

**leaf|let** /liflɪt/ (**leaflets**) N-COUNT A **leaflet** is a little book or a piece of paper containing information about a particular subject. ❑ *Officials handed out leaflets to workers.*

**leafy** /lifi/ **1** ADJ **Leafy** trees and plants have lots of leaves on them. ❑ *...tall, leafy trees.* **2** ADJ You say that a place is **leafy** when there are lots of trees and plants there. ❑ *...the narrow leafy streets at the top of the hill.* [from Old English]

**league** /lig/ (**leagues**) **1** N-COUNT A **league** is a group of people, clubs, or countries that have joined together for a particular purpose, or because they share a common interest. ❑ *...the League of Nations.* **2** N-COUNT A **league** is a group of teams that play the same sport or activity against each other. ❑ *...the American League series between the Boston Red Sox and World Champion Oakland Athletics.* **3** N-COUNT You use **league** to make comparisons between different people or things, especially in terms of their quality. ❑ *Her success has taken her out of my league.* **4** PHRASE If you say that someone is **in league with** another person to do something bad, you mean that they are working together to do that thing. ❑ *They stole billions of dollars in league with the mafia.* [from Old French]

**leak** /lik/ (**leaks, leaking, leaked**) **1** V-I If a container **leaks**, there is a hole or crack in it which

lets a substance such as liquid or gas escape. You can also say that liquid or gas **leaks** from a container. ❑ *The roof leaked.* ❑ *The swimming pool's sides cracked and the water leaked out.* ● **Leak** is also a noun. ❑*A gas leak may have caused the explosion.* **2** N-COUNT A **leak** is a crack, hole, or other gap that a substance such as a liquid or gas can pass through. ❑ *...a leak in the radiator.* **3** V-T/V-I If a secret document or piece of information **leaks** or is **leaked**, someone lets the public know about it. ❑ *The police were leaking information to a newspaper.* ❑ *We don't know how the story leaked.* ● **Leak** is also a noun. ❑*A leak to a newspaper made the story public.* [of Scandinavian origin]

leak

| **Thesaurus** | leak | Also look up : |
|---|---|---|
| v. | drip, ooze, seep, trickle **1** come out, divulge, pass on **3** | |
| N. | crack, hole, opening **2** | |

**leak|age** /líːkɪdʒ/ (**leakages**) N-VAR **Leakage** is the escape of liquid or gas from a pipe or container through a crack or hole. ❑ *A leakage of kerosene has polluted the water.* [of Scandinavian origin]

**lean** /liːn/ (**leans, leaning, leaned, leaner, leanest**) ■ V-I When you **lean** in a particular

lean

direction, you bend your body in that direction. ❑ *The driver leaned across and opened the passenger door.* ■ V-T/V-I If you **lean on** or **against** someone or something, you rest against them so that they partly support your weight. If you **lean** an object **on** or **against** something, you place the object so that it is partly supported by that thing. ❑ *She was feeling tired and leaned against him.* ❑ *Lean the plants against a wall.* ■ ADJ If you describe someone as **lean**, you mean that they are thin but look strong and healthy. ❑ *Like most athletes, she was lean and muscular.* ■ ADJ If meat is **lean**, it does not have very much fat. ■ ADJ If you describe periods of time as **lean**, you mean that people have less of something, such as money, than they used to have, or are less successful than they used to be. ❑ *My parents lived through the lean years of the 1930s.* [from Old English]

▸ **lean on** or **lean upon** PHR-VERB If you **lean on** someone or **lean upon** them, you depend on them for support and encouragement. ❑ *She leaned on him to help her to solve her problems.*

**leap** /liːp/ (**leaps, leaping, leaped** or **leapt**) ■ V-I If you **leap**, you jump high in the air or jump a long distance. ❑ *He leaped in the air and waved his hands.* ● **Leap** is also a noun. ❑ *Phillips won the long jump with a leap of 27 feet, 5 inches.* ■ V-I To **leap** somewhere means to move there suddenly and quickly. ❑ *The two men leaped into the car and sped off.* ❑ *The dog leapt forward again.* ■ N-COUNT A **leap** is a large and important change, increase, or advance. ❑ *There was a giant leap in productivity at the factory.* ❑ *...a further leap in prices.* ■ V-I If you **leap to** a particular place or position, you make a large and important change, increase, or advance. ❑ *The song leapt to the top of the charts.* [from Old English]

**learn** /lɜːrn/ (**learns, learning, learned** or **learnt**) ■ V-T/V-I If you **learn** something, you obtain knowledge or a skill through studying or training. ❑ *Where did you learn English?* ❑ *He is learning to play the piano.* ❑ *These guys learn quickly.* ● **learn|er** (**learners**) N-COUNT ❑ *Clint was a quick learner and soon settled into the job.* ● **learn|ing** N-UNCOUNT ❑ *...the learning of English.* ■ V-T/V-I If you **learn**, or **learn** of, something, you find out about it. ❑ *We first learned of her plans in a newspaper report.* ❑ *She wasn't surprised to learn that he was involved.* ■ V-T If people **learn to** behave or react in a particular way, they gradually start to behave in that way as a result of a change in their attitude. ❑ *She's learning to talk about her problems.* ■ V-T/V-I If you **learn from** an unpleasant experience, you change the way you behave so that it does not happen again or so that, if it happens again, you can deal with it better. ❑ *It's important to learn from your mistakes.* ❑ *I hope we all learn some lessons from this.* ■ V-T If you **learn** something such as a poem or a role in a play, you study or repeat the words so that you can remember them. ❑ *He learned this song as a child.* [from Old English] ■ → see also **learned** → see **brain**

**learn|ed** /lɜːrnɪd/ ADJ A **learned** person has gained a lot of knowledge by studying. [from Old English]

**learned be|hav|ior** (**learned behaviors**) N-VAR **Learned behavior** is a way of behaving that someone has learned through experience or observation rather than because it is a natural instinct.

**learn|er's per|mit** (**learner's permits**) N-COUNT A **learner's permit** is a license that allows you to drive a vehicle before you have passed your driving test. ❑ *She's still too young to get a learner's permit.*

**lease** /liːs/ (**leases, leasing, leased**) ■ N-COUNT A **lease** is a legal agreement by which the owner of a building, a piece of land, or something such as a car allows someone else to use it for a period of time in return for money. ❑ *He took up a 10-year lease on the house.* ■ V-T If you **lease** property or something such as a car from someone or if they **lease** it to you, they allow you to use it in return for regular payments of money. ❑ *He leased an apartment in Toronto.* ❑ *She's going to lease the building to students.* [from Old French]

**least** /liːst/

**Least** is often considered to be the superlative form of **little**.

■ PHRASE You use **at least** to say that a number or amount is the minimum that is possible or likely and that more may be possible. The forms **at the least** and **at the very least** are also used. ❑ *Drink at* *least half a pint of milk each day.* ❑ *You could at least say thank you.* **2** PHRASE You use **at least** to indicate an advantage that exists in a bad situation. ❑ *At least we know he is still alive.* **3** ADJ You use **the least** to mean a smaller amount than anyone or anything else, or the smallest amount possible. ❑ *He wants to save money and to spend the least amount of money on a car.* ● **Least** is also a pronoun. ❑ *On education, Japan performs best but spends the least per student.* ● **Least** is also an adverb. ❑ *The extra money may benefit those who need it the least.* ❑ *He is one of the least friendly people I have ever met.* **4** ADJ You use **least** when you are emphasizing that a particular situation or event is much less important or serious than other possible or actual ones. ❑ *Getting up at three o'clock every morning was the least of her worries.* **5** PHRASE You can use **in the least** and **the least bit** to emphasize a negative. ❑ *I'm not like that at all. Not in the least.* ❑ *Alice wasn't the least bit frightened.* **6** PHRASE You can use **not least** to emphasize an important example or reason. ❑ *Everyone is more worried about traveling these days, not least Americans.* **7** PHRASE You can use **to say the least** to suggest that a situation is actually much more extreme or serious than you say it is. ❑ *The experience was interesting, to say the least.* [from Old English]

| **Thesaurus** | *least* | Also look up : |
|---|---|---|

ADJ. fewest, lowest, minimum, smallest **3**

**leath|er** /lɛðər/ (**leathers**) N-VAR **Leather** is treated animal skin which is used for making shoes, clothes, bags, and furniture. ❑ *...a leather jacket.* [from Old English]

---

## leave

**❶** VERB USES
**❷** NOUN USE
**❸** PHRASAL VERBS

---

**❶ leave** /liv/ (**leaves, leaving, left**) **1** V-T/V-I If you **leave** a place or person, you go away from that place or person. ❑ *He couldn't leave the country.* ❑ *My flight leaves in less than an hour.* **2** V-T/V-I If you **leave** an institution, group, or job, you permanently stop attending that institution, being a member of that group, or doing that job. ❑ *He left school before graduating.* ❑ *I am leaving to spend more time with my family.* **3** V-T If you **leave** your husband, wife, or some other person with whom you have had a close relationship, you stop living with them or you end the relationship. ❑ *He'll never leave you. You needn't worry.* **4** V-T If you **leave** something or someone in a particular place, you let them remain there when you go away. If you **leave** something or someone with a person, you let them remain with that person so they are safe while you are away. ❑ *I left my bags in the car.* ❑ *Leave your key with a neighbor.* **5** V-T If you **leave** someone **to** do something, you go away from them so that they do it on their own. If you **leave** someone **to** himself or herself, you go away from them and allow them to be alone. ❑ *I'll leave you to get to know each other.* ❑ *I can see you're busy — I'll leave you to it.* **6** V-T To **leave** an amount of something means to keep it available after the rest has been used or taken away. ❑ *He always left a little food for the next day.* **7** V-T If an event **leaves**

people or things in a particular state, they are in that state when the event has finished. ❑ *An auto accident left him unable to walk.* **8** V-T If something **leaves** a mark, effect, or sign, it causes that mark, effect, or sign to remain as a result. ❑ *The wound healed well and only left a small scar.* **9** V-T If you **leave** something **until** a particular time, you delay doing it or dealing with it until then. ❑ *Don't leave it all until the last minute.* **10** PHRASE If you **leave** something **too late**, you delay doing it so that when you eventually do it, it is useless or ineffective. **11** V-T If you **leave** property or money **to** someone, you arrange for it to be given to them after you have died. ❑ *He left everything to his wife when he died.* **12** V-T If you **leave** something somewhere, you forget to bring it with you. ❑ *I left my purse back there in the gas station.* [from Old English] **13** → see also **left**

| **Thesaurus** | *leave* | Also look up : |
|---|---|---|

V. abandon, depart, go away; (*ant.*) arrive, come, stay **❶ 1**
give up, quit, resign; (*ant.*) remain, stay **❶ 2**
abandon, desert, ditch, take off **❶ 3**

**❷ leave** /liv/ N-UNCOUNT **Leave** is a period of time when you are not working at your job, because you are on vacation, or for some other reason. If you are **on leave**, you are not working at your job. ❑ *Why don't you take a few days' leave?* ❑ *...maternity leave.* [from Old English]

**❸ leave** /liv/ (**leaves, leaving, left**)
▶ **leave behind** **1** PHR-VERB If you **leave** someone or something **behind**, you go away permanently from them. ❑ *He left his friends and family behind in Canada.* **2** PHR-VERB If you **leave behind** an object or a situation, it remains after you have left a place. ❑ *He left his glasses behind in his office.* **3** PHR-VERB If a person, country, or organization **is left behind**, they remain at a lower level than others because they are not as quick at understanding things or developing. ❑ *We're going to be left behind by the rest of the world.* ❑ *I'm slow at reading, so I got left behind at school.*
▶ **leave off** PHR-VERB If someone or something **is left off** a list, they are not included on that list. ❑ *She was left off the guest list.*
▶ **leave out** PHR-VERB If you **leave** someone or something **out** of an activity, collection, discussion, or group, you do not include them in it. ❑ *They shouldn't have left her out of the team.* ❑ *If you like mild flavors, leave out the chili.*

**leav|ened** /lɛvənd/ ADJ **Leavened** bread or dough is made with yeast. [from Old French]

**leaves** /livz/ **Leaves** is the plural form of **leaf**, and the third person singular form of **leave**. [from Old English]

**lec|ture** /lɛktʃər/ (**lectures, lecturing, lectured**) **1** N-COUNT A **lecture** is a talk someone gives in order to teach people about a particular subject, usually at a university or college. ❑ *...a lecture by Professor Eric Robinson.* **2** V-I If you **lecture on** a particular subject, you give a lecture or a series of lectures about it. ❑ *She invited him to Atlanta to lecture on the history of art.* **3** V-T If someone **lectures** you about something, they criticize you or tell you how they think you should behave. ❑ *They lectured us about our eating habits.* ❑ *Chuck*

L

lectured me about getting a haircut. ● **Lecture** is also a noun. ❑ *We had a lecture on safety.* [from Medieval Latin]

**lec|tur|er** /lɛktʃərər/ (**lecturers**) N-COUNT A **lecturer** is a teacher at a university or college. ❑ *…a lecturer in law.* [from Medieval Latin]

**led** /lɛd/ **Led** is the past tense and past participle of **lead.** [from Old English]

**ledge** /lɛdʒ/ (**ledges**) ◼ N-COUNT A **ledge** is a piece of rock on the side of a cliff or mountain, which is in the shape of a narrow shelf. ❑ *The bird landed on a mountain ledge.* ◼ N-COUNT A **ledge** is a narrow shelf along the bottom edge of a window. ❑ *Dorothy climbed onto the ledge outside his window.*

**ledg|er** /lɛdʒər/ (**ledgers**) N-COUNT A **ledger** is a book in which a company or organization writes down the amounts of money it spends and receives. [BUSINESS]

**leek** /lik/ (**leeks**) N-VAR **Leeks** are long, thin vegetables that are white at one end and have long green leaves. [from Old English]

**leer** /lɪər/ (**leers, leering, leered**) V-I If someone **leers** at you, they smile in an unpleasant way, usually because they are sexually interested in you. ❑ *Men were standing around, leering at passing females.* [from Old English]

---

**left**

❶ REMAINING
❷ DIRECTION AND POLITICAL GROUPINGS

---

❶ **left** /lɛft/ ◼ **Left** is the past tense and past participle of **leave.** ◼ ADJ If there is a certain amount of something **left**, or if you have a certain amount of it **left**, it remains when the rest has gone or been used. ❑ *Is there any milk left?* ❑ *They still have six games left to play.* ◼ PHRASE If there is a certain amount of something **left over**, or if you have it **left over**, it remains when the rest has gone or been used. ❑ *She spends so much money on clothes, there's never any left over to buy books.* [from Old English]

❷ **left** /lɛft/

The spelling **Left** is also used for meanings ◼ and ◼.

◼ N-SING The **left** is one of two opposite directions, sides, or positions. If you are facing north and you turn to the left, you will be facing west. In the word "to," the "t" is to the left of the "o." ❑ *Take a left at the end of the road.* ❑ *…the brick wall to the left of the building.* ● **Left** is also an adverb. ❑ *Turn left at the corner.* ◼ ADJ Your **left** arm, leg, or ear, for example, is the one which is on the left side of your body. Your **left** shoe or glove is the one which is intended to be worn on your left foot or hand. ❑ *Fred fell and twisted his left leg.* ◼ N-SING In the U.S., the **left** refers to people who want to use legislation and the tax system to improve social conditions. In most other countries, the **left** refers to people who support the ideas of socialism. ❑ *…the political parties of the left.* ◼ N-SING If you say that a person or political party has moved **to the left,** you mean that their political beliefs have become more left-wing. [from Old English]

**left-hand** ADJ If something is on the **left-hand** side of something, it is positioned on the left of it.

❑ *The Japanese drive on the left-hand side of the road.*

**left-handed** ADJ Someone who is **left-handed** uses their left hand rather than their right hand for activities such as writing and sports and for picking things up. ❑ *…a store that sells everything for left-handed people.*

**left|ist** /lɛftɪst/ (**leftists**) N-COUNT A **leftist** is someone who supports the ideas of the political left. ❑ *Two of the men were leftists and two were centrists.* [from Old English]

**left-of-center** ADJ **Left-of-center** people or political parties support the ideals of the political left.

**left|over** /lɛftoʊvər/ (**leftovers**) ◼ N-PLURAL You can refer to food that has not been eaten after a meal as **leftovers.** ❑ *Put any leftovers in the refrigerator.* ◼ ADJ You use **leftover** to describe an amount of something that remains after the rest of it has been used or eaten. ❑ *…leftover pieces of wallpaper.*

**left-wing** also **left wing** ◼ ADJ **Left-wing** people support the ideas of the political left. ❑ *They will not be voting for him because he is too left-wing.* ◼ N-SING The **left wing** of a group of people, especially a political party, consists of the members of it whose beliefs are closer to those of the political left than are those of its other members. ❑ *She belongs on the left wing of the Democratic Party.*

**lefty** /lɛfti/ (**lefties**) N-COUNT A **lefty** is someone, especially a sports player, who is left-handed. [INFORMAL] [from Old English]

**leg** /lɛg/ (**legs**) ◼ N-COUNT A person's or animal's **legs** are the long parts of their body that they use to stand on. ❑ *He broke his right leg in a motorcycle accident.* ◼ N-COUNT The **legs** of a pair of pants are the parts that cover your legs. ❑ *Anthony dried his hands on the legs of his jeans.* ◼ N-COUNT A **leg** of lamb, pork, chicken, or other meat is a piece of meat that consists of the animal's or bird's leg, especially the thigh. ❑ *…a chicken leg.* ◼ N-COUNT The **legs** of a table, chair, or other piece of furniture are the parts that rest on the floor and support the furniture's weight. ❑ *She sat on his knee. Then the chair legs broke.* ◼ N-COUNT A **leg** of a long journey is one part of it, usually between two points where you stop. ❑ *The first leg of the journey was by boat to Lake Naivasha in Kenya.* [from Old Norse]

→ see **body, insect, shellfish**

**lega|cy** /lɛgəsi/ (**legacies**) ◼ N-COUNT A **legacy** is money or property which someone leaves to you when they die. ❑ *His father left him a generous legacy.* ◼ N-COUNT A **legacy of** an event or period of history is something which is a direct result of it and which continues to exist after it is over. ❑ *…the legacy of slavery.* [from Medieval Latin]

**le|gal** /ligᵊl/ ◼ ADJ **Legal** is used to describe things that relate to the law. ❑ *He promised to take legal action.* ❑ *…the legal system.* ● **le|gal|ly** ADV ❑ *It could be difficult, legally speaking.* ◼ ADJ An action or situation that is **legal** is allowed or required by law. ❑ *What I did was perfectly legal.* ● **le|gal|ity** /ligælɪti/ N-UNCOUNT ❑ *Some people question the legality of the contracts.* [from Latin]

## Word Partnership   Use *legal* with :

N.   legal **action**, legal **advice**, legal **battle**,
     legal **bills**, legal **costs/expenses**,
     legal **defense**, legal **department**,
     legal **documents**, legal **expert**, legal
     **fees**, legal **guardian**, legal **issue**,
     legal **liability**, legal **matters**, legal
     **obligation**, legal **opinion**, legal
     **problems/troubles**, legal **procedures**,
     legal **profession**, legal **responsibility**,
     legal **rights**, legal **services**, legal **status**,
     legal **system** ∎

**le|gal|ize** /líɡəlaɪz/ (**legalizes, legalizing,
legalized**) V-T If something **is legalized**, a law is
passed that makes it legal. ❑ *Divorce was legalized in
1981.* [from Latin]

**leg|end** /lɛdʒⁿnd/ (**legends**) ∎ N-VAR A **legend**
is a very old and popular story that may be true.
❑ *...the legends of ancient Greece.* ∎ N-COUNT If you
refer to someone as a **legend**, you mean that they
are very famous and admired by a lot of people.
❑ *...singing legend Frank Sinatra.* [from Medieval
Latin]
→ see **fantasy**

**leg|end|ary** /lɛdʒⁿndɛri/ ∎ ADJ If you describe
someone or something as **legendary**, you mean
that they are very famous and that many stories
are told about them. ❑ *...the legendary jazz singer
Adelaide Hall.* ∎ ADJ A **legendary** person, place, or
event is mentioned or described in an old legend.
❑ *...the legendary King Arthur.* [from Medieval Latin]

**leg|gings** /lɛɡɪŋz/ N-PLURAL **Leggings** are
close-fitting pants, usually made out of a stretchy
fabric, that are worn by women and girls. [from
Old Norse]

**le|gion** /lídʒⁿn/ (**legions**) N-COUNT A **legion** is
a large group of soldiers who form one section of
an army. ❑ *...the French Foreign Legion.* [from Old
French]

**leg|is|late** /lɛdʒɪsleɪt/ (**legislates, legislating,
legislated**) V-T/V-I When a government or state
**legislates**, it passes a new law. [FORMAL] ❑ *Some
countries have legislated against too much overtime
work.* ❑ *You cannot legislate to change attitudes.*

**leg|is|la|tion** /lɛdʒɪsleɪʃⁿn/ N-UNCOUNT
**Legislation** consists of a law or laws passed by a
government. [FORMAL] ❑ *...legislation to protect
women's rights.*

## Word Partnership   Use *legislation* with :

V.   **draft** legislation, **enact** legislation,
     **introduce** legislation, **oppose**
     legislation, **pass** legislation,
     **veto** legislation
ADJ.  **federal** legislation, **new** legislation,
     **proposed** legislation

**leg|is|la|tive** /lɛdʒɪsleɪtɪv/ ADJ **Legislative**
means involving or relating to the process of
making and passing laws. [FORMAL] ❑ *Today's
hearing was just the first step in the legislative process.*

**leg|is|la|tor** /lɛdʒɪsleɪtər/ (**legislators**) N-COUNT
A **legislator** is a person who is involved in making
or passing laws. [FORMAL] ❑ *The agency made an
attempt to get U.S. legislators to change the system.*
[from Latin]

**leg|is|la|ture** /lɛdʒɪsleɪtʃər/ (**legislatures**)
N-COUNT The **legislature** of a particular state or
country is the group of people in it who have the
power to make and pass laws. ❑ *...members of the
legislature.* [FORMAL]

**le|giti|mate** /lɪdʒɪtɪmɪt/ ∎ ADJ Something that
is **legitimate** is acceptable according to the law.
❑ *...a legitimate driver's license with my picture on it.*
● **le|giti|ma|cy** /lɪdʒɪtɪməsi/ N-UNCOUNT ❑ *...the
political legitimacy of his government.* ● **le|giti|mate|ly**
ADV ❑ *The government was legitimately elected by the
people.* ∎ ADJ If you say that something such as
a feeling or claim is **legitimate**, you think that
it is reasonable and justified. ❑ *That's a perfectly
legitimate fear.* ● **le|giti|ma|cy** N-UNCOUNT ❑ *He
refused to accept the legitimacy of Helen's anger.*
● **le|giti|mate|ly** ADV ❑ *They argued quite legitimately
with some of my choices.* [from Medieval Latin]

**leg|work** /lɛɡwɜrk/ N-UNCOUNT You use
**legwork** to refer to work that involves physical
activity such as interviewing people or gathering
information, especially when this work forms the
basis of other, more intellectual work. ❑ *He helped
with the routine legwork in the investigation.*

**lei|sure** /líʒər, lɛʒ-/ ∎ N-UNCOUNT **Leisure** is
the time when you are not working and you can
relax and do things that you enjoy. ❑ *They spend
their leisure time painting or drawing.* ∎ PHRASE If
someone does something **at leisure** or **at** their
**leisure**, they enjoy themselves by doing it when
they want to, without hurrying. ❑ *You can walk at
leisure through the gardens.* [from Old French]

**lei|sure|ly** /líʒərli, lɛʒ-/ ADJ A **leisurely** action is
done in a relaxed and unhurried way. ❑ *Lunch was
a leisurely affair.* ● **Leisurely** is also an adverb. ❑ *We
walked leisurely around the hotel.* [from Old French]

**lem|on** /lɛmən/ (**lemons**) N-VAR A **lemon** is a
bright yellow fruit with very sour juice. Lemons
grow on trees in warm countries. ❑ *...a slice of
lemon.* [from Medieval Latin]
→ see **fruit**

**lem|on|ade** /lɛməneɪd/ (**lemonades**) N-VAR
**Lemonade** is a drink that is made from lemons,
sugar, and water. ❑ *He was pouring ice and lemonade
into tall glasses.* ❑ *They ordered two lemonades.* [from
French]

**lend** /lɛnd/ (**lends, lending, lent**) ∎ V-T/V-I
When people or organizations such as banks
**lend** you money, they give it to you and you
agree to pay it back at a future date, often with
an extra amount as interest. ❑ *Banks are not the
only institutions that lend money.* ❑ *The government
will lend you money at very good rates, between zero
percent and 3 percent.* ❑ *Banks have never been more
ready to lend.* ● **lend|er** (**lenders**) N-COUNT ❑ *...the
six leading mortgage lenders.* ● **lend|ing** N-UNCOUNT
❑ *...a financial institution that specializes in lending
money.* ∎ V-T If you **lend** something that you
own, you allow someone to have it or use it for a
period of time. ❑ *Will you lend me your pen?* ∎ V-T If
you **lend** your support **to** someone or something,
you help them with what they are doing or with
a problem that they have. ❑ *He was asked to lend
support to a charity.* ∎ V-T If something **lends itself
to** a particular activity or result, it is easy for it to
be used for that activity or to achieve that result.
❑ *The piano lends itself to all styles of music.* [from Old
English] ∎ → see also **borrow, lent**

**length** /lɛŋθ/ (**lengths**) ◼ N-VAR The **length** of something is the amount that it measures from one end to the other. ❑ *It is about a meter in length.* ❑ *...the length of the fish.*

◼ N-VAR The **length** of something such as a piece of writing is the amount of writing that is contained in it. ❑ *...a book of at least 100 pages in length.* ◼ N-VAR The **length** of an event, activity, or situation is the period of time from beginning to end for which something lasts or during which something happens. ❑ *The length of each class may vary.* ◼ N-COUNT A **length** of rope, cloth, wood, or other material is a piece of it that is intended to be used for a particular purpose or that exists in a particular situation. ❑ *...a three-foot length of rope.* ◼ N-UNCOUNT The **length of** something is its quality of being long. ❑ *We were surprised at the length of time it took him to make up his mind.* ◼ PHRASE If someone does something **at length**, they do it for a long time or in great detail. ❑ *They spoke at length.* ◼ PHRASE If someone **goes to great lengths** to achieve something, they try very hard and perhaps do extreme things in order to achieve it. ❑ *She went to great lengths to hide from reporters.* [from Old English] ◼ → see also **full-length**

| **Word Partnership** | Use *length* with : |
| --- | --- |
| ADJ. | **average** length, **entire** length ◼ – ◼ |
| N. | length **and width** ◼ ◼ |
| | length **of** *your* **stay**, length **of time**, length **of** ◼ ◼ |

**length|en** /lɛŋθən/ (**lengthens, lengthening, lengthened**) V-T/V-I When something **lengthens** or when you **lengthen** it, it becomes longer. ❑ *The evening shadows were lengthening.* ❑ *The judge lengthened the prison sentence.* [from Old English]

**lengthy** /lɛŋθi/ (**lengthier, lengthiest**) ◼ ADJ You use **lengthy** to describe an event or process which lasts for a long time. ❑ *There was a lengthy meeting to decide the company's future.* ◼ ADJ A **lengthy** report, article, book, or document contains a lot of speech, writing, or other material. ❑ *The U.N. issued a lengthy report on the subject.* [from Old English]

| **Word Partnership** | Use *lengthy* with : |
| --- | --- |
| N. | lengthy **period** ◼ |
| | lengthy **description**, lengthy **discourse**, lengthy **discussion**, lengthy **report** ◼ |

**le|ni|ent** /liniənt, linyənt/ ADJ When someone in authority is **lenient**, they are not as strict or severe as expected. ❑ *He says parents are often too lenient with their children.* ● **le|ni|ent|ly** ADV ❑ *Many people believe careless drivers are treated too leniently.* [from Latin]

**lens** /lɛnz/ (**lenses**) ◼ N-COUNT A **lens** is a thin, curved piece of glass or plastic used in things such as cameras, telescopes, and pairs of glasses. You look through a lens in order to make things look larger, smaller, or clearer. ❑ *...a powerful lens for my camera.* ◼ N-COUNT In your eye, the **lens** is

the part behind the pupil that focuses light and helps you to see clearly. [from Latin] ◼ → see also **contact lens**
→ see **eye**

**lent** /lɛnt/ **Lent** is the past tense and past participle of **lend**. [from Old English]

**len|til** /lɛntɪl, -tᵊl/ (**lentils**) N-COUNT **Lentils** are the seeds of a lentil plant. They are usually dried and are used to make soups and stews. [from Old French]

**leop|ard** /lɛpərd/ (**leopards**) N-COUNT A **leopard** is a type of large, wild cat. Leopards have yellow fur and black spots, and live in Africa and Asia. [from Old French]

**lep|re|chaun** /lɛprəkɒn/ (**leprechauns**) N-COUNT In Irish folklore, a **leprechaun** is an imaginary creature that looks like a little old man. [from Irish Gaelic]

**les|bian** /lɛzbiən/ (**lesbians**) ADJ **Lesbian** is used to describe homosexual women. ❑ *...in the lesbian community.* ● **lesbian** is also a noun. ❑ *...a group for lesbians, gays and bisexuals.* [from Greek]

**less** /lɛs/

**Less** is often considered to be the comparative form of **little**.

◼ DET You use **less** to indicate that there is a smaller amount of something than before or than average. ❑ *People should eat less fat.* ❑ *This dishwasher uses less water than older machines.* ● **Less** is also a pronoun. ❑ *He thinks people should spend less and save more.* ● **Less** is also a quantifier. ❑ *I see less of my cousins now that they've moved out of town.* ◼ PHRASE You use **less than** before a number or amount to say that the actual number or amount is smaller than this. ❑ *The population of the country is less than 12 million.* ◼ PREP When you are referring to amounts, you use **less** in front of a number or quantity to indicate that it is to be subtracted from another number or quantity already mentioned. ❑ *You will pay between ten and twenty five percent, less tax.* ◼ PHRASE You use **less than** to say that something does not have a particular quality. For example, if you describe something as **less than** perfect, you mean that it is not perfect at all. ❑ *Her greeting was less than welcoming.* [from Old English] ◼ **more or less** → see **more**

| **Usage** | **less** and **fewer** |
| --- | --- |

*Less* is used to describe general amounts (or uncount nouns). *Less snow fell in December than in January. Fewer* is used to describe amounts of countable items. *Maria is working fewer hours this semester.*

**less|en** /lɛsᵊn/ (**lessens, lessening, lessened**) V-T/V-I If something **lessens** or you **lessen** it, it becomes smaller in size, amount, degree, or importance. ❑ *A change in lifestyle would lessen the risk of heart disease.* ● **less|en|ing** N-UNCOUNT ❑ *...a lessening of support for the United States.* [from Old English]

**less|er** /lɛsər/ ADJ You use **lesser** in order to indicate that something is smaller in extent, degree, or amount than another thing that has been mentioned. ❑ *He watches sports to a lesser degree than he did five years ago.* ● **Lesser** is also an adverb. ❑ *...lesser-known works by famous artists.* [from Old English] les|son /lɛsˀn/ (lessons) ■ N-COUNT A **lesson** is a fixed period of time when people are taught about a particular subject or taught how to do something. ❑ *Johanna took piano lessons.* ■ N-COUNT You use **lesson** to refer to an experience which acts as a warning to you or an example from which you should learn. ❑ *I learned an important lesson: never think you know everything.* ■ PHRASE If you say that you are going to **teach** someone **a lesson**, you mean that you are going to punish them for something that they have done so that they do not do it again. [from Old French]

| **Thesaurus** | *lesson* | Also look up : |
|---|---|---|
| N. | class, course, instruction, session ■ | |

| **Word Partnership** | Use *lesson* with : |
|---|---|
| ADJ. | **private** lesson ■<br>**hard** lesson, **important** lesson, **painful** lesson, **valuable** lesson ■ |
| V. | **get** a lesson, **give** a lesson ■ ■<br>**learn** a lesson, **teach** *someone* a lesson ■ |

lest /lɛst/ CONJ If you do something **lest** something unpleasant should happen, you do it to try to prevent the unpleasant thing from happening. [FORMAL] ❑ *She didn't tell anyone, lest the news got around her small town.* [from Old English]

let /lɛt/ (lets, letting, let)

The form **let** is used in the present tense and is the past tense and past participle.

■ V-T If you **let** something happen, you allow it to happen without doing anything to stop or prevent it. ❑ *Thorpe let him talk.* ❑ *I couldn't let myself cry.* ■ V-T If you **let** someone do something, you give them your permission to do it. ❑ *I love candy but Mom doesn't let me have it very often.* ■ V-T If you **let** someone into, out of, or through a place, you allow them to enter, leave, or go through it, for example, by opening a door or making room for them. ❑ *I had to let them into the building because they had lost their keys.* ■ V-T You use **let me** when you are introducing something you want to say. ❑ *Let me tell you what I saw.* ❑ *Let me explain why.* ■ V-T You use **let me** when you are offering politely to do something. ❑ *Let me take your coat.* ■ V-T You say **let's** or, in formal English, **let us**, when you are making a suggestion. ❑ *I'm bored. Let's go home.* ■ PHRASE **Let alone** is used after a statement, usually a negative one, to indicate that the statement is even more true of the person, thing, or situation that you are going to mention next. ❑ *It is amazing that the child could reach the pedals, let alone drive the car.* ■ PHRASE If you **let go of** someone or something, you stop holding them. ❑ *She let go of Mona's hand.* ■ PHRASE If you **let** someone **know** something, you tell them about it or make sure that they know about it. ❑ *I want to let them know that I'm safe.* [from Old English]
▸ **let down** PHR-VERB If you **let** someone **down**, you disappoint them, by not doing something that you have said you will do or that they expected you to do. ❑ *I didn't want to let him down by not going out with him.*
▸ **let in** PHR-VERB If an object **lets in** something such as air, light, or water, it allows air, light, or water to get into it. ❑ *These materials let in air but not light.*

▸ **let off** ■ PHR-VERB If a situation, or someone in authority, **lets** you **off** a task or duty, they make it possible for you, or give you permission, not to do it. ❑ *The teachers let us off afternoon classes to watch the game.* ■ PHR-VERB If you **let** someone **off**, you give them a lighter punishment than they expect or no punishment at all. ❑ *He thought that if he said he was sorry, the judge would let him off.* ■ PHR-VERB If you **let off** an explosive or a gun, you explode or fire it. ❑ *They let off fireworks to celebrate New Year's at midnight.*
▸ **let out** PHR-VERB If something or someone **lets** water, air, or breath **out**, they allow it to flow out or escape. ❑ *The large windows let in light and give views across the countryside.*
▸ **let up** PHR-VERB If an unpleasant, continuous process **lets up**, it stops or becomes less intense. ❑ *The traffic in this city never lets up.*

| **Thesaurus** | *let* | Also look up : |
|---|---|---|
| V. | allow, approve, permit; (*ant.*) prevent, stop ■ ■ | |

le|thal /liθˀl/ ADJ A substance that is **lethal** can kill people or animals. ❑ *…a lethal dose of sleeping pills.* [from Latin]

le|thar|gic /lɪθɑrdʒɪk/ ADJ If you are **lethargic**, you do not have much energy or enthusiasm. ❑ *He felt too miserable and lethargic to get dressed.* [from Late Latin]

leth|ar|gy /lɛθərdʒi/ N-UNCOUNT **Lethargy** is the condition or state of being lethargic. ❑ *Symptoms include paleness and lethargy.* [from Late Latin]

let's /lɛts/ **Let's** is the usual spoken form of "let us." [from Old English]

**Usage** **let's**

Be sure to include the apostrophe when you write *let's* (the contraction of *let us*), in order to avoid confusing it with *lets*: Nisim sometimes lets his workers go home early, and when he does, he always laughs and says, "Let's stop now. We've done enough damage for one day!"

let|ter /lɛtər/ (letters) ■ N-COUNT If you write a **letter** to someone, you write a message on paper and send it to them. ❑ *I received a letter from a friend.* ❑ *…a letter offering me the job.* ■ N-COUNT **Letters** are written symbols which represent one of the sounds in a language. ❑ *…the letters of the alphabet.* ■ V-I If a student **letters** in sports or athletics by being part of the high school, university, or college team, they are entitled to wear on their jacket the initial letter of the name of their high school, university, or college. ❑ *Burkoth lettered in soccer.* ■ N-COUNT If a student earns a **letter** in sports or athletics by being part of the high school, university, or college team, they are entitled to wear on their jacket the initial letter of the name of their high school, university, or college. ❑ *Valerie earned letters in volleyball and basketball.* [from Old French] ■ → see also **newsletter**

let|ter car|ri|er (letter carriers) N-COUNT A **letter carrier** is a person whose job is to collect and deliver letters and parcels that are sent by mail.

let|ter|ing /lɛtərɪŋ/ N-UNCOUNT **Lettering** is writing, especially when you are describing the type of letters used. ❑ ...*a small blue sign with white lettering.* [from Old French]

**let|tuce** /lɛtɪs/ (**lettuces**) N-VAR A **lettuce** is a plant with large green leaves that is the basic ingredient of many salads. [from Old French]

**leu|ke|mia** /lukimiə/ N-UNCOUNT **Leukemia** is a disease of the blood in which the body produces too many white blood cells. [from Greek]

**levee** /lɛvi/ (**levees**) N-COUNT A **levee** is a raised bank alongside a river. ❑ *Water poured over a levee and flooded about 75 percent of Montegut.* [from French]

**lev|el** /lɛvᵊl/ (**levels, leveling** or **levelling, leveled** or **levelled**) ◼ N-COUNT A **level** is a point on a scale, for example, a scale of amount, quality, or difficulty. ❑ *We have the lowest level of inflation for some years.* ◻ N-SING The **level** of something is its height or the height of its surface. ❑ *The water level of the Mississippi River is 6.5 feet below normal.* ❑ *Liz sank down in the tub until the water came up to her chin and the bubbles were at eye level.* ◼ → see also **sea level** ◹ N-COUNT A **level** of a building is one of its different stories, which is situated above or below other stories. ❑ *Thurlow's rooms were on the second level.* ◿ N-COUNT A **level** is a device for testing to see if a surface is level. It consists of a plastic, wood, or metal frame containing a glass tube of liquid with an air bubble in it. ❒ ADJ If one thing is **level** with another thing, it is at the same height as it. ❑ *He leaned over the counter so his face was level with the boy's.* ◻ ADJ When something is **level**, it is completely flat. ❑ *The floor was level, but the ceiling sloped.* ❒ ADV If you draw **level** with someone or something, you get closer to them until you are by their side. ❑ *Courtney walked past me but I drew level with a few quick steps.* ● **Level** is also an adjective. ❑ *He waited until they were level with the door.* ❒ V-T If someone or something such as a violent storm **levels** a building or area of land, they destroy it completely or make it completely flat. ❑ *The storm leveled areas of forest and destroyed homes.* ◻ V-T If an accusation or criticism **is leveled at** someone, they are accused of doing wrong or they are criticized for something they have done. ❑ *Many criticisms have been leveled at the president.* ◼ a **level playing field** → see **playing field** ◻ N-COUNT In the theater, an actor's **level** is their height above the stage at a particular time, for example when they are sitting or lying down. [from Old French]

▸ **level off** or **level out** PHR-VERB If a changing number or amount **levels off** or **levels out**, it stops increasing or decreasing at such a fast speed. ❑ *The rate of unemployment is beginning to level off.*

| Word Partnership | Use *level* with : |
|---|---|
| ADJ. | **basic** level, **increased** level, **intermediate** level, **top** level, **upper** level ◼ **high/low** level ◼ ◻ |
| N. | level **of activity**, level **of awareness**, **cholesterol** level, **college** level, **comfort** level, level **of difficulty**, **energy** level, **noise** level, **reading** level, **skill** level, **stress** level, level **of violence** ◼ **eye** level, **ground** level, **street** level ◻ |

**lev|el|er** /lɛvələr/ (**levelers**) also **leveller** N-COUNT If you describe something as a **leveler**, you mean that it makes all people seem the same, in spite of their differences in, for example, age or social status. ❑ *War is a great leveler — everyone helps each other, whoever they are.* [from Old French]

**lev|er** /livər, lɛv-/ (**levers**) ◼ N-COUNT A **lever** is a handle or bar that is attached to a piece of machinery and which you push or pull in order to operate the machinery. ❑ *Push the lever to switch the machine on.* ◻ N-COUNT A **lever** is a long bar, one end of which is placed under a heavy object so that when you press down on the other end you can move the object. ❑ *He worked a lever that lifted the lid of the box.* [from Old French]

**lev|er|age** /lɛvərɪdʒ/ N-UNCOUNT **Leverage** is the ability to influence situations or people so that you can control what happens. ❑ *His senior position gives him leverage to get things done.* [from Old French]

**levy** /lɛvi/ (**levies, levying, levied**) ◼ N-COUNT A **levy** is a sum of money that you have to pay, for example, as a tax to the government. ❑ ...*an annual levy on all drivers.* ◻ V-T If a government or organization **levies** a tax or other sum of money, it demands it from people or organizations. ❑ *States levy their own taxes.* [from Old French]

**lia|bil|ity** /laɪəbɪlɪti/ (**liabilities**) ◼ N-COUNT If you say that someone or something is a **liability**, you mean that they cause a lot of problems or embarrassment. ❑ *We want to be an asset to the city, not a liability.* ◻ N-COUNT A company's or organization's **liabilities** are the sums of money which it owes. [BUSINESS OR LEGAL] ❑ *The company had assets of $138 million and liabilities of $120.5 million.* [from Old French] ◼ → see also **liable**

**lia|ble** /laɪəbᵊl/ ◼ PHRASE When something **is liable to** happen, it is very likely to happen. ❑ ...*equipment that is liable to break.* ◻ ADJ If people or things are **liable to** something unpleasant, they are likely to experience it or do it. ❑ ...*a woman liable to depression.* ◼ ADJ If you are **liable for** something such as a debt, you are legally responsible for it. ❑ *Companies who pollute the river are liable for damages to wildlife.* ● **lia|bil|ity** N-UNCOUNT ❑ *The delivery company does not accept liability for breakages.* [from Old French]

**liai|son** /lieɪzɒn/ N-UNCOUNT **Liaison** is cooperation and the exchange of information between different organizations or between different sections of an organization. ❑ *He was in charge of liaison between the press and the president.* [from French]

| Word Link | *ar, er* ≈ *one who acts as :* buy*er*, li*ar*, sell*er* |
|---|---|

**liar** /laɪər/ (**liars**) N-COUNT A **liar** is someone who tells lies. ❑ *He was a liar and a cheat.* [from Old English]

**li|bel** /laɪbᵊl/ (**libels, libeling** or **libelling, libeled** or **libelled**) ◼ N-VAR **Libel** is a written statement which wrongly accuses someone of something, and which is therefore against the law. Compare **slander**. [LEGAL] ❑ *Warren sued him for libel over the remarks in the newspaper.* ◻ V-T To **libel** someone means to write or print something in a book, newspaper, or magazine which wrongly damages that person's reputation and is therefore against the law. [LEGAL] ❑ *The newspaper which libeled him offered him a large amount of money.* [from Old French]

## Word Web library

**Public libraries** are changing. Many new **services** are now available. Websites often allow you to search the library's **catalog** of books and **periodicals** from your own computer. Many libraries have computers with Internet access for the public. Some offer literacy classes, tutoring, and homework assistance. Of course, you can still **borrow** and **return books, magazines**, DVDs, CDs, and other **media** free of charge. You can still go to the **fiction** section to find a good **novel**. You can also search the nonfiction bookshelves for an interesting **biography**. And if you need help, the **librarian** is still there to answer your questions.

li|bel|ous /laɪbələs/ also **libellous** ADJ If a statement in a book, newspaper, or magazine is **libelous**, it wrongly accuses someone of something, and is therefore against the law. ❑ *The stories were libelous.* [from Old French]

### Word Link liber ≈ free : liberal, liberate, liberty

lib|er|al /lɪbərəl, lɪbrəl/ (liberals) **1** ADJ Someone who has **liberal** views believes people should have a lot of freedom in deciding how to behave and think. ❑ *She has liberal views on divorce.* ● **Liberal** is also a noun. ❑ *...a nation of liberals.* **2** ADJ A **liberal** system allows people or organizations a lot of political or economic freedom. ❑ *...a liberal democracy.* ● **Liberal** is also a noun. ❑ *...the free-market liberals.* **3** ADJ A **Liberal** politician or voter is a member of a Liberal Party or votes for a Liberal Party. ❑ *My father was always a Liberal voter.* ● **Liberal** is also a noun. ❑ *The Liberals did well in the election.* **4** ADJ **Liberal** means giving, using, or taking a lot of something, or existing in large quantities. ❑ *He is liberal with his jokes.* ● **lib|er|al|ly** ADV ❑ *Season the steaks liberally with salt and pepper.* [from Latin]

lib|er|al arts N-PLURAL At a university or college, **liberal arts** courses are on subjects such as history or literature rather than science, law, medicine, or business.

lib|er|al|ize /lɪbərəlaɪz, lɪbrəl-/ (liberalizes, liberalizing, liberalized) V-T/V-I When a country or government **liberalizes**, or **liberalizes** its laws or its attitudes, it allows people more freedom in their actions. ❑ *Some states are only beginning to liberalize.* ● **lib|er|ali|za|tion** /lɪbərəlɪzeɪʃən, lɪbrəl-/ N-UNCOUNT ❑ *...the liberalization of divorce laws.* [from Latin]

lib|er|ate /lɪbəreɪt/ (liberates, liberating, liberated) **1** V-T To **liberate** a place or the people in it means to free them from the political or military control of another country, area, or group of people. ❑ *They planned to liberate the city.* ● **lib|era|tion** /lɪbəreɪʃən/ N-UNCOUNT ❑ *...a mass liberation movement.* **2** V-T To **liberate** someone **from** something means to help them escape from it or overcome it, and lead a better way of life. ❑ *The leadership is committed to liberating its people from poverty.* ● **lib|er|at|ing** ADJ ❑ *Talking to a therapist can be a very liberating experience.* ● **lib|era|tion** N-UNCOUNT ❑ *...the women's liberation movement.* [from Latin]

### Thesaurus liberate Also look up :

v. free, let out, release; (ant.) confine **1**

lib|er|at|ed /lɪbəreɪtɪd/ ADJ If you describe someone as **liberated**, you approve of them because they do not accept their society's traditional values or restrictions on behavior. ❑ *...a liberated businesswoman.* [from Latin]

lib|er|ty /lɪbərti/ (liberties) **1** N-VAR **Liberty** is the freedom to live your life in the way that you want and go where you want to. ❑ *We are united because the attack on America was an attack on the liberty of us all.* **2** PHRASE If someone is **at liberty to** do something, they have been given permission to do it. ❑ *I'm not at liberty to tell you where he lives.* [from Old French]

### Thesaurus liberty Also look up :

N. freedom, independence, privilege **1**

### Word Partnership Use liberty with :

ADJ. **human** liberty, **individual** liberty, **personal** liberty, **religious** liberty **1**

li|brar|ian /laɪbrɛəriən/ (librarians) N-COUNT A **librarian** is a person who is in charge of a library or who has been specially trained to work in a library. [from Old French]
→ see **library**

li|brary /laɪbrɛri/ (libraries) N-COUNT A public **library** is a building where things such as books, newspapers, videos, and music are kept for people to read, use, or borrow. ❑ *...the local library.* [from Old French]
→ see Word Web: **library**

lice /laɪs/ N-PLURAL **Lice** are small insects that live on the bodies of people or animals. **Lice** is the plural of **louse**. [from Old English]

li|cense /laɪsᵊns/ (licenses, licensing, licensed) **1** N-COUNT A **license** is an official document which gives you permission to do, use, or own something. ❑ *You need a license to teach foreign students.* **2** V-T To **license** a person or activity means to give official permission for the person to do something or for the activity to take place. ❑ *...to license songs for films or video games.* [from Old French]

### Word Partnership Use license with :

N. **driver's** license, license **fees, hunting** license, **liquor** license, **marriage** license, **pilot's** license, **software** license **1**
V. **get/obtain a** license, **renew a** license, **revoke a** license **1**
ADJ. **suspended** license, **valid** license **1**

**li|censed** /laɪsᵊnst/ **1** ADJ If you are **licensed to** do something, you have official permission from the government or from the authorities to do it. ❑ *There were about 250 people on board, 100 more than the ferry was licensed to carry.* **2** ADJ If something that you own or use is **licensed**, you have official permission to own it or use it. ❑ *...a licensed rifle.* [from Old French]

**li|cense num|ber** (**license numbers**) N-COUNT The **license number** of a car or other road vehicle is the series of letters and numbers that are shown at the front and back of it.

**li|cense plate** (**license plates**) N-COUNT A **license plate** is a sign on the back, and in some places also on the front, of a vehicle that shows its license number. ❑ *...a car with Austrian license plates.*

**lick** /lɪk/ (**licks, licking, licked**) V-T When people or animals **lick** something, they move their tongue across its surface. ❑ *She licked the stamp and pressed it onto the envelope.* ● **Lick** is also a noun. ❑ *The cat took a lick of milk.* [from Old English]

**lickety-split** /lɪkətisplɪt/ ADV If you do something **lickety-split**, you do it very quickly. [INFORMAL] ❑ *The waiter returned lickety-split with our meal.*

**lid** /lɪd/ (**lids**) N-COUNT A **lid** is the top of a box or other container which can be removed or raised when you want to open the container. ❑ *She lifted the lid of the box.* [from Old English]

---

**lie**

**❶** POSITION OR SITUATION
**❷** THINGS THAT ARE NOT TRUE

---

**❶ lie** /laɪ/ (**lies, lying, lay, lain**) **1** V-I If you **are lying** somewhere, you are in a horizontal position and are not standing or sitting. ❑ *There was a man lying on the ground.* **2** V-I If an object **lies** in a particular place, it is in a flat position in that place. ❑ *The newspaper was lying on a chair.* **3** V-I If you say that a place **lies** in a particular position or direction, you mean that it is situated there. ❑ *The islands lie at the southern end of Florida.* **4** V-LINK You can use **lie** to say that something is or remains in a particular state or condition. For example, if something **lies forgotten**, it has been and remains forgotten. ❑ *The picture lay hidden in the library for over 40 years.* **5** V-I You can talk about where something such as a problem, solution, or fault **lies** to say what you think it consists of, involves, or is caused by. ❑ *Some of the blame lies with the president.* **6** V-I You use **lie** in expressions such as **lie ahead**, **lie in store**, and **lie in wait** when you are talking about what someone is going to experience in the future, especially when it is something unpleasant or difficult. ❑ *You'll need all her strength to cope with what lies ahead.* [from Old English]
▸ **lie around** PHR-VERB If things are left **lying around**, they are not put away but left casually somewhere where they can be seen. ❑ *People should not leave their possessions lying around.*
▸ **lie behind** PHR-VERB If you refer to what **lies behind** a situation or event, you are referring to the reason the situation exists or the event happened. ❑ *Worries about money lay behind their problems.*
▸ **lie down** PHR-VERB When you **lie down**, you move into a horizontal position, usually in order to rest or sleep. ❑ *Why don't you go upstairs and lie down?*

---

**Usage** **lie and lay**

*Lie* and *lay* are often confused. *Lie* is generally used without an object: *Please lie down.* Lay usually requires an object: *Lay your head on the pillow.*

---

**❷ lie** /laɪ/ (**lies, lying, lied**) **1** N-COUNT A **lie** is something that someone says or writes which they know is untrue. ❑ *"Who else do you work for?" —"No one."—"That's a lie."* **2** V-I If someone **is lying**, they are saying something which they know is not true. ❑ *I know he's lying.* ● **lying** N-UNCOUNT ❑ *Lying is something that I hate.* [from Old English]

---

**Thesaurus** *lie* Also look up :

| | |
|---|---|
| v. | recline, rest; (*ant.*) stand ❶ **1** **2** |
| | deceive, distort, fake, falsify, mislead ❷ **2** |
| N. | dishonesty ❷ **1** |

---

**lieu|ten|ant** /lutɛnənt/ (**lieutenants**) N-COUNT; N-TITLE; N-VOC A **lieutenant** is a junior officer in the army, navy, marines, or air force, or in the U.S. police force. ❑ *Lieutenant Campbell ordered the man to stop.* [from Old French]

**lieu|ten|ant gov|er|nor** (**lieutenant governors**) **1** N-COUNT A **lieutenant governor** is an elected official who acts as the deputy of a state governor in the United States. **2** N-COUNT A **lieutenant governor** is an official elected by the Canadian government to act as a representative of the British king or queen in a province of Canada.

**life** /laɪf/ (**lives** /laɪvz/) **1** N-UNCOUNT **Life** is the quality which people, animals, and plants have when they are not dead. ❑ *...a baby's first minutes of life.* **2** N-UNCOUNT You can use **life** to refer to things or groups of things which are alive. ❑ *Is there life on Mars?* **3** N-COUNT Someone's **life** is their state of being alive, or the period of time during which they are alive. ❑ *A nurse tried to save his life.* ❑ *He spent the last fourteen years of his life in France.* **4** N-COUNT You can use **life** to refer to particular activities which people regularly do during their lives. ❑ *My personal life has suffered because of my career.* **5** N-UNCOUNT You can use **life** to refer to the things that people do and experience that are characteristic of a particular place, group, or activity. ❑ *How do you like college life?* ❑ *He loves the challenges of political life.* **6** N-UNCOUNT If you say that someone or something is full of **life**, you like them because they give an impression of excitement, energy, or cheerfulness. ❑ *The town was full of life and character.* **7** N-UNCOUNT If someone is sentenced to **life**, they are sentenced to stay in prison for the rest of their life or for a very long time. [INFORMAL] ❑ *He could get life in prison, if he is found guilty.* **8** N-COUNT The **life** of something such as a machine, organization, or project is the period of time that it lasts for. ❑ *The repairs did not increase the value or the life of the equipment.* **9** PHRASE If you say that someone **is fighting for** their **life**, you mean that they are in a very serious condition and may die as a result of an accident or illness. ❑ *The robbery left a man fighting for his life.* [from Old English]
→ see **biosphere, earth**

**life|boat** /ˈlaɪfboʊt/ (**lifeboats**) N-COUNT A **lifeboat** is a boat that is used to rescue people who are in danger at sea.

**life ex|pec|tan|cy** (**life expectancies**) N-VAR The **life expectancy** of a person, animal, or plant is the length of time that they are normally likely to live. ❑ *The average life expectancy used to be 40.*

**life|guard** /ˈlaɪfɡɑrd/ (**lifeguards**) N-COUNT A **lifeguard** is a person who works at a beach or swimming pool and rescues people who are in danger of drowning.

**life|less** /ˈlaɪflɪs/ ◼ ADJ If a person or animal is **lifeless**, they are dead, or are so still that they appear to be dead. ❑ *She looked almost lifeless, lying there on the floor.* ◼ ADJ If you describe an object or a machine as **lifeless**, you mean that they are not living things, even though they may resemble living things. ❑ *The statue was made of plaster, hard and white and lifeless.* ◼ ADJ A **lifeless** place or area does not have anything living or growing there at all. ❑ *Dry stone walls may look lifeless, but they are a home for plants and animals.* [from Old English]

**life|line** /ˈlaɪflaɪn/ (**lifelines**) N-COUNT A **lifeline** is something that enables an organization or group to survive or to continue with an activity. ❑ *Information about the job market is a lifeline for those who are out of work.*

**life|long** /ˈlaɪflɔŋ/ ADJ **Lifelong** means existing or happening for the whole of a person's life. ❑ *...her lifelong friendship with Naomi.*

**life pre|serv|er** (**life preservers**) N-COUNT A **life preserver** is something such as a ring or a jacket, which helps you to float when you have fallen into deep water.

**life sci|ence** (**life sciences**) N-COUNT The **life sciences** are sciences such as zoology, botany, and anthropology which are concerned with human beings, animals, and plants.

**life|span** /ˈlaɪfspæn/ (**lifespans**) also **life span** N-VAR The **lifespan** of a person, animal, or plant is the period of time for which they live or are normally expected to live. ❑ *A 15-year lifespan is quite normal for a dog.*

**life|style** /ˈlaɪfstaɪl/ (**lifestyles**) also **life-style**, **life style** ◼ N-VAR The **lifestyle** of a particular person or group is the living conditions, behavior, and habits that are typical of them or are chosen by them. ❑ *They had a lifestyle that many people would envy.* ◼ ADJ **Lifestyle** magazines, television programs, and products are aimed at people who are interested in glamorous and successful lifestyles. ❑ *The footwear ads will appear this fall in fashion and lifestyle magazines.*

**life support** N-UNCOUNT **Life support** is a system that is used to keep a person alive when they are very ill and cannot breathe without help. ❑ *She was on life support for several weeks.*

**life-threatening** ADJ If someone has a **life-threatening** illness or is in a **life-threatening** situation, there is a strong possibility that the illness or the situation will kill them. ❑ *Caitlin was born with a life-threatening heart problem.*

**life|time** /ˈlaɪftaɪm/ (**lifetimes**) N-COUNT A **lifetime** is the length of time that someone is alive. ❑ *He traveled a lot during his lifetime.*

**lift** /lɪft/ (**lifts, lifting, lifted**) ◼ V-T If you **lift** something, you move it to another position, especially upward. ❑ *He lifted the bag onto his shoulder.* ● **Lift up** means the same as **lift**. ❑ *She lifted the baby up and gave him to me.* ◼ V-T If people in authority **lift** a law or rule that prevents people from doing something, they end it. ❑ *France finally lifted its ban on importing British beef.* ◼ N-COUNT If you give someone a **lift** somewhere, you take them there in your car as a favor to them. ❑ *He had a car and often gave me a lift home.* ◼ N-UNCOUNT **Lift** is the force that makes an aircraft leave the ground and stay in the air. [of Scandinavian origin] ◼ to **lift a finger** → see **finger**

| **Thesaurus** | *lift* | Also look up: |
|---|---|---|
| v. | boost, hoist, pick up; (ant.) drop, lower, put down ◼ | |

**liga|ment** /ˈlɪɡəmənt/ (**ligaments**) N-COUNT A **ligament** is a band of strong tissue in a person's body which connects bones. ❑ *He suffered torn ligaments in his knee.* [from Medieval Latin]

## light

❶ BRIGHTNESS OR ILLUMINATION
❷ NOT GREAT IN WEIGHT, AMOUNT, OR INTENSITY
❸ UNIMPORTANT OR NOT SERIOUS

❶ **light** /laɪt/ (**lights, lighting, lit** or **lighted, lighter, lightest**) ◼ N-UNCOUNT **Light** is the brightness that lets you see things. Light comes from sources such as the sun, moon, lamps, and fire. ❑ *Cracks of light came through the dirty window.* ❑ *...ultraviolet light.* ◼ N-COUNT A **light** is something such as an electric lamp which produces light. ❑ *The janitor comes around to turn the lights out.* ◼ V-T If a place or object **is lit by** something, it has light shining on it. ❑ *The moon lit the road brightly.* ❑ *The room was lit by only one light.* ◼ ADJ If it is **light**, the sun is providing light at the beginning or end of the day. ❑ *It was still light when we arrived at Lalong Creek.* ◼ ADJ If a room or building is **light**, it has a lot of natural light in it. ❑ *It is a light room with tall windows.* ● **light|ness** N-UNCOUNT ❑ *...the lightness of the bedroom.* ◼ V-T/V-I If you **light** something such as a candle or a fire, or if it **lights**, it starts burning. ❑ *Stephen leaned forward to light the candle.* ❑ *The fire wouldn't light.* ◼ N-COUNT If something is presented in a particular **light**, it is presented so that you think about it in a particular way or so that it appears to be of a particular nature. ❑ *He worked hard to show New York in a better light.* ◼ → see also **lighter, lighting** ◼ PHRASE If something **comes to light** or **is brought to light**, it becomes obvious or is made known to a lot of people. ❑ *Nothing about this money has come to light.* ◼ PHRASE If something is possible **in the light of** particular information, it is only possible because you have this information. ❑ *People often change their opinions in the light of new information.* ◼ PHRASE To **shed light on**, **throw light on**, or **cast light on** something means to make it easier to understand, because more information is known about it. ❑ *No one could shed light on her secret past.* [from Old English] → see **color, eye, laser, light bulb, ozone, telescope, wave**

▶ **light up** ◼ PHR-VERB If you **light** something **up** or if it **lights up**, it becomes bright. ❑ *The coffee*

## Word Web    light bulb

The incandescent **light bulb** has changed little since the 1870s. It consists of a **glass** globe containing an inert gas, such as argon, some wires, and a filament. **Electricity** flows through the wires and the tungsten filament. The filament heats up and **glows**. Light bulbs aren't very efficient. They give off more heat than **light**. **Fluorescent** lights are much more efficient. They contain liquid mercury and argon gas. A layer of phosphorus covers the inside of the tube. When electricity begins to flow, the mercury becomes a gas and **emits** ultraviolet light. This causes the phosphor coating to **shine**.

*maker lights up when you switch it on.* **2** PHR-VERB If your face or your eyes **light up**, you suddenly look very surprised or happy. □ *Sue's face lit up with surprise.*

### Thesaurus    light    Also look up :

| N. | brightness, glow, radiance, shine **1** **1** |
| ADJ. | bright, sunny **1** **4** **5** |

**2 light** /laɪt/ (lighter, lightest) **1** ADJ Something that is **light** does not weigh very much. □ *I'm about 30 pounds lighter than I was.* □ *...weight training with light weights.* • **light|ness** N-UNCOUNT □ *It is made of steel for lightness and strength.* **2** ADJ Something that is **light** is not very great in amount, degree, or intensity. □ *It's a Sunday, with the usual light traffic in the city.* □ *Trading on the stock exchange was very light.* • **light|ly** ADV □ *Cook the onions until they are lightly browned.* **3** ADJ Something that is **light** is pale in color. □ *He is light haired with gray eyes.* □ *...a light green van.* **4** ADJ **Light** work does not involve much physical effort. [from Old English]

**3 light** /laɪt/ (lighter, lightest) **1** ADJ If you describe things such as books, music, and movies as **light**, you mean that they entertain you without making you think. □ *He doesn't like reading light novels.* □ *...light classical music.* **2** ADJ If you say something in a **light** way, you sound as if you think that something is not important or serious. □ *Talk to him in a friendly, light way about the relationship.* • **light|ly** ADV □ *"Sure," he said lightly.* [from Old English]

**light bulb** (light bulbs) N-COUNT A **light bulb** is the round glass part of an electric light or lamp which light shines from.
→ see Word Web: light bulb

**light cream** N-UNCOUNT **Light cream** is thin cream that does not have a lot of fat in it.

### Word Link    light = not heavy : lighten, lighthearted, lightweight

**light|en** /laɪtᵊn/ (lightens, lightening, lightened) **1** V-T/V-I When something **lightens** or when you **lighten** it, it becomes less dark in color. □ *The sky began to lighten.* **2** V-T/V-I If your attitude or mood **lightens**, or if someone or something **lightens** it, they make you feel more cheerful, happy, and relaxed. □ *As they approached the city, Ella's mood lightened.* [from Old English]

**light en|er|gy** N-UNCOUNT **Light energy** is energy in the form of electromagnetic waves.

**light|er** /laɪtər/ (lighters) N-COUNT A **lighter** is a small device that produces a flame which you can

use to light cigarettes. [from Old English]

**light|heart|ed** /laɪthɑrtɪd/ **1** ADJ Someone who is **lighthearted** is cheerful and happy. □ *Kelly was at first lighthearted, but turned serious.* **2** ADJ Something that is **lighthearted** is intended to be entertaining or amusing, and not at all serious. □ *...a lighthearted movie.*

lighthouse

**light|house** /laɪthaʊs/ (lighthouses) N-COUNT A **lighthouse** is a tower built on rocks, near or in the sea. Lighthouses have a powerful flashing lamp and are used to guide ships or to warn them of danger.

**light|ing** /laɪtɪŋ/ N-UNCOUNT The **lighting** in a place is the way that it is lit, or the quality of the light in it. □ *...bright fluorescent lighting.* □ *The whole room has soft lighting.* [from Old English]
→ see concert, drama , photography, theater

**light min|ute** (light minutes) N-COUNT A **light minute** is the distance that light travels in one minute. [TECHNICAL]

**light|ning** /laɪtnɪŋ/ **1** N-UNCOUNT **Lightning** is the very bright flashes of light in the sky that happen during thunderstorms. □ *One man died when he was struck by lightning.* □ *Another flash of lightning lit up the cave.* **2** ADJ **Lightning** describes things that happen very quickly or last for only a short time. □ *He drove off at lightning speed.*
→ see Word Web: lightning
→ see storm

**light|ning rod** (lightning rods) **1** N-COUNT A **lightning rod** is a long thin piece of metal on top of a building that attracts lightning and allows it to reach the ground safely. **2** PHRASE If you say that someone **is a lightning rod for** something, you mean that they attract that thing to themselves. □ *He is a lightning rod for trouble.*

**light source** (light sources) N-COUNT A **light source** is any object or device that gives off light, such as the sun or an electric light bulb.

**light|weight** /laɪtweɪt/ (lightweights) also **light-weight** **1** ADJ Something that is **lightweight** weighs less than most other things of the same type. □ *...lightweight denim.* **2** N-UNCOUNT **Lightweight** is a category in some sports, such as boxing, judo, or rowing, based on the weight of the athlete. □ *...the junior lightweight champion.* **3** N-COUNT If you describe someone as

## Word Web    lightning

**Lightning** forms in storm clouds. Strong winds cause tiny **particles** within the clouds to rub together violently. This creates **positive charges** on some particles and **negative charges** on others. The negatively charged particles sink to the bottom of the cloud. There they are attracted by the positively charged surface of the earth. Gradually a large negative charge accumulates in a cloud. When it is large enough, a **bolt** of lightning strikes the earth. When a bolt branches out in several directions, the result is called **forked lightning**. Sheet lightning occurs when the bolt **discharges** within a cloud, instead of on the earth.

a **lightweight**, you are critical of them because you think that they are not very important or skillful in a particular area of activity. ❑ *Critics say that she is an intellectual lightweight.* ● **Lightweight** is also an adjective. ❑ *Some of the discussion in the book is lightweight and unconvincing.*

**light year** (light years) **1** N-COUNT A **light year** is the distance that light travels in a year. ❑ *...a star system millions of light years away.* **2** N-COUNT You can say that two things are **light years** apart to emphasize a very great difference or a very long distance or period of time between them. [INFORMAL] ❑ *Our computer system is light years ahead of anyone else's.*
→ see **galaxy**

**lik|able** /ˈlaɪkəbəl/ also **likeable** ADJ Someone or something that is **likable** is pleasant and easy to like. ❑ *He was a clever and likable guy.* [from Old English]

### like

❶ PREPOSITION AND
    CONJUNCTION USES
❷ VERB USES
❸ NOUN USES AND PHRASES

❶ **like** /laɪk, lɑɪk/ **1** PREP If you say that one person or thing is **like** another, you mean that they share some of the same qualities or features. ❑ *He looks like Father Christmas.* ❑ *When I was in New York City, I kept thinking, "This is just like the movies."* ❑ *It's nothing like what happened last year.* **2** PREP If you talk about what something or someone is **like**, you are talking about their qualities or features. ❑ *What was Bulgaria like?* ❑ *What did she look like?* **3** PREP You can use **like** to introduce an example of the set of things or people that you have just mentioned. ❑ *...large cities like New York.* **4** PREP If you say that someone is behaving **like** something or someone else, you mean that they are behaving in a way that is typical of that kind of thing or person. **Like** is used in this way in many fixed expressions, for example, **to cry like a baby** and **to watch someone like a hawk**. ❑ *I was shaking all over, trembling like a leaf.* **5** CONJ **Like** is sometimes used as a conjunction in order to say that something appears to be true when it is not. Some people consider this use to be incorrect. ❑ *His arms are so thin that they look like they might break.* **6** CONJ **Like** is sometimes used as a conjunction in order to indicate that something happens or is done in the same way as something else. Some people consider this use to be incorrect. ❑ *People are*

walking around the park, just like they do every Sunday. ❑ *He spoke exactly like I did.* **7** PREP You can use **like** in expressions such as **nothing like** to make an emphatic negative statement. ❑ *Three hundred million dollars will be nothing like enough.* [from Old English]

❷ **like** /laɪk/ (likes, liking, liked) **1** V-T If you **like** something or someone, you think they are interesting, enjoyable, or attractive. ❑ *He likes baseball.* ❑ *I don't like being in crowds.* ❑ *Do you like to go swimming?* **2** V-T If you say that you **would like** something or **would like** to do something, you are indicating a wish or desire that you have. ❑ *I'd like a bath.* ❑ *Would you like to have some coffee?* [from Old English]

### Thesaurus    like    Also look up :

| | |
|---|---|
| ADJ. | alike, comparable, similar ❶ **1** |
| V. | admire, appreciate, enjoy;<br>(ant.) dislike ❷ **1** |

❸ **like** /laɪk/ (likes) **1** N-PLURAL Someone's **likes** are the things that they enjoy or find pleasant. ❑ *I knew all Jemma's likes and dislikes.* **2** → see also **liking** **3** PHRASE You say **if you like** when you are making or agreeing to an offer or suggestion in a casual way. ❑ *You can stay here if you like.* **4** PHRASE You say **like this, like that,** or **like so** when you are showing someone how something is done. ❑ *It opens and closes, like this.* **5** PHRASE You use the expression **something like** with an amount, number, or description to indicate that it is approximately accurate. ❑ *They can get something like $3,000 a year.* [from Old English]

**like|able** /ˈlaɪkəbəl/ → see **likable**

**like|li|hood** /ˈlaɪklihʊd/ N-UNCOUNT The **likelihood** of something happening is how likely it is to happen. ❑ *The likelihood of getting the disease is small.* [from Old Norse]

**like|ly** /ˈlaɪkli/ (likelier, likeliest) **1** ADJ You use **likely** to indicate that something is probably true or will probably happen in a particular situation. ❑ *Experts say a "yes" vote is still the likely outcome.* ● **Likely** is also an adverb. ❑ *Profit will most likely rise by about $25 million.* **2** ADJ If someone or something is **likely** to do a particular thing, they will very probably do it. ❑ *The problem seems likely to continue.* [from Old Norse]

**like-minded** ADJ **Like-minded** people have similar opinions, ideas, attitudes, or interests. ❑ *...the opportunity to meet like-minded people.*

**lik|en** /ˈlaɪkən/ (likens, likening, likened) V-T If you **liken** one thing or person **to** another thing or person, you say that they are similar. ◻ *Benjamin Franklin likened the game of chess to life itself.*

**like|ness** /ˈlaɪknɪs/ (**likenesses**) **1** N-SING If two things or people have a **likeness** to each other, they are similar to each other. ◻ *These stories have a surprising likeness to one another.* **2** N-COUNT If you say that a picture of someone is a good **likeness**, you mean that it looks just like them. ◻ *The artist's drawing is an excellent likeness of her sister.* [from Old English]

> **Word Link** wise ≈ in the direction or manner of : clockwise, likewise, otherwise

**like|wise** /ˈlaɪkwaɪz/ **1** ADV You use **likewise** when you are comparing two methods, states, or situations and saying that they are similar. ◻ *What is fair for you likewise should be fair to me.* **2** ADV If you do something and someone else does **likewise**, they do the same or a similar thing. ◻ *He gave money to charity and encouraged others to do likewise.* [from Old English]

**lik|ing** /ˈlaɪkɪŋ/ **1** N-SING If you have **a liking for** something or someone, you like them. ◻ *She had a liking for good clothes.* **2** PHRASE If something is, for example, too fast **for** your **liking**, you would prefer it to be slower. If it is not fast enough **for** your **liking**, you would prefer it to be faster. ◻ *He was too powerful for their liking.* **3** PHRASE If something is **to** your **liking**, it suits your interests, tastes, or wishes. ◻ *London was more to his liking than Rome.* [from Old English]

**li|lac** /ˈlaɪlək, -læk, -lək/ (**lilacs**)

> Lilac can also be used as the plural form.

**1** N-VAR A **lilac** or a **lilac tree** is a small tree which has sweet-smelling purple, pink, or white flowers. ◻ *Lilacs grew against the side wall.* **2** COLOR Something that is **lilac** is pale pinkish-purple in color. ◻ *The bride wore a lilac dress.* [from French]

**lily** /ˈlɪli/ (**lilies**) N-VAR A **lily** is a plant with large sweet-smelling flowers. [from Old English]

**limb** /lɪm/ (**limbs**) **1** N-COUNT Your **limbs** are your arms and legs. ◻ *She stretched out her aching limbs.* **2** PHRASE If someone goes **out on a limb**, they do something they strongly believe in even though it is risky or extreme. ◻ *I'm going to go out on a limb here and say this is good news.* [from Old English]

→ see **mammal**

**lim|bo** /ˈlɪmboʊ/ N-UNCOUNT If someone or something is **in limbo**, they are in a situation where they seem to be caught between two stages and it is unclear what will happen next. ◻ *The discussions have been in limbo since December.* [from Medieval Latin]

**lime** /laɪm/ (**limes**) **1** N-VAR A **lime** is a round, green fruit that tastes like a lemon. ◻ *...slices of lime.* **2** N-UNCOUNT **Lime** is a substance containing calcium. It is found in soil and water. ◻ *If your soil is very acidic, add lime.* [Sense 1 from French. Sense 2 from Old English.]

**lime|light** /ˈlaɪmlaɪt/ N-UNCOUNT If someone is in the **limelight**, a lot of attention is being paid to them, because they are famous or because they have done something very unusual or exciting. ◻ *Tony is in the limelight, with a high-profile job.*

**lime|stone** /ˈlaɪmstoʊn/ (**limestones**) N-VAR **Limestone** is a whitish-colored rock which is used

for building and for making cement. ◻ *...limestone cliffs.* [from Old English]

**lim|it** /ˈlɪmɪt/ (**limits, limiting, limited**) **1** N-COUNT A **limit** is the greatest amount, extent, or degree of something that is possible. ◻ *Her love for him was tested to its limits.* ◻ *There is no limit to how much fresh fruit you can eat in a day.* **2** N-COUNT A **limit** of a particular kind is the largest or smallest amount of something such as time or money that is allowed because of a rule, law, or decision. ◻ *The three-month time limit will be over in June.* **3** V-T If you **limit** something, you prevent it from becoming greater than a particular amount or degree. ◻ *Residents must limit water use to 15,000 gallons per month.* • **lim|i|ta|tion** /ˌlɪmɪˈteɪʃ°n/ N-UNCOUNT ◻ *...the limitation of nuclear weapons.* **4** V-T If you **limit yourself** to something, or if someone or something **limits** you, the number of things that you have or do is reduced. ◻ *Limit yourself to three meals and a snack each day.* • **lim|it|ing** ADJ ◻ *I found the conditions very limiting.* **5** V-T If something **is limited to** a particular place or group of people, it exists only in that place, or is had or done only by that group. ◻ *The protests were not limited to New York.* **6** → see also **limited** **7** PHRASE If an area or a place is **off limits**, you are not allowed to go there. ◻ *Parts of the church are off limits to visitors.* [from Latin]

**lim|i|ta|tion** /ˌlɪmɪˈteɪʃ°n/ (**limitations**) **1** N-VAR A **limitation on** something is a rule or decision which prevents that thing from growing or extending beyond certain limits. ◻ *...a limitation on the amount of tax you pay in a year.* **2** N-PLURAL The **limitations** of someone or something are the things that they cannot do, or the things that they do badly. ◻ *Parents often blame schools for the limitations of their children.* **3** N-VAR A **limitation** is a fact or situation that allows only some actions and makes others impossible. ◻ *She has ongoing pain and limitation of movement in her arm.* [from Latin] **4** → see also **limit**

**lim|it|ed** /ˈlɪmɪtɪd/ ADJ Something that is **limited** is not very great in amount, range, or degree. ◻ *They had only a limited amount of time to talk.* [from Latin]

**lim|it|ed edi|tion** (**limited editions**) N-COUNT A **limited edition** is something such as a book which is only produced in very small numbers, so that each one will be valuable in the future. ◻ *The limited edition of 300 copies was published yesterday.*

**lim|it|ing fac|tor** (**limiting factors**) N-COUNT A **limiting factor** is a feature of the environment, such as space, sunlight or water, which is only available in small amounts and therefore limits the size of a population of animals or plants.

**lim|it|less** /ˈlɪmɪtlɪs/ ADJ If you describe something as **limitless**, you mean that there is or appears to be so much of it that it will never be exhausted. ◻ *...her limitless energy in working for the homeless.* [from Latin]

**lim|ou|sine** /ˈlɪməzin/ (**limousines**) N-COUNT A **limousine** is a large and very comfortable car. Limousines are usually driven by a chauffeur and often hired for important occasions. [from French]

**limp** /lɪmp/ (**limps, limping, limped, limper, limpest**) **1** V-I If a person or animal **limps**, they walk with difficulty or in an uneven way because one of their legs or feet is hurt. ◻ *James limps because of a hip injury.* • **Limp** is also a noun. ◻ *Anne* *walks with a limp.* **2** ADJ If something is **limp**, it is soft or weak when it should be firm or strong. ❑ *...people with limp handshakes.* ● **limp|ly** ADV ❑ *Flags hung limply in the still air.* [Sense 1 from Old English. Sense 2 of Scandinavian origin.]

---
**line**
---

❶ NOUN USES
❷ PHRASES
❸ VERB USES
❹ PHRASAL VERB

---

❶ **line** /laɪn/ (**lines**) **1** N-COUNT A **line** is a long, thin mark which is drawn or painted on a surface. ❑ *Draw a line at the bottom of the page.* ❑ *...a dotted line.* **2** N-COUNT The **lines** on your skin, especially on your face, are long thin marks that appear there as you grow older. ❑ *He has a large round face with deep lines.* **3** N-COUNT A **line** of people or vehicles is a number of them that are waiting one behind another or side by side. ❑ *I saw a line of people waiting to get into the building.* **4** N-COUNT An actor's **lines** are the words they speak in a play or movie. ❑ *He is having trouble memorizing his lines.* **5** N-VAR You can refer to a long piece of wire, string, or cable as a **line** when it is used for a particular purpose. ❑ *She put her washing on the line.* ❑ *...a piece of fishing-line.* **6** N-COUNT A **line** is a route along which people or things move or are sent. ❑ *The telephone lines went dead.* ❑ *They've got to stay on the train all the way to the end of the line.* **7** N-COUNT A state or county **line** is a boundary between two states or counties. ❑ *...the California state line.* **8** N-COUNT The particular **line** that a person has toward a problem is the attitude that they have toward it. ❑ *The official company line is that we will continue as planned.* **9** N-COUNT Your **line** of business or work is the kind of work that you do. [BUSINESS] ❑ *So what was your father's line of business?* [from Latin] **10** → see also **bottom line, front line, production line**
→ see **chart, football, graph, mathematics, soccer, train**

| **Thesaurus** | line | Also look up : |
|---|---|---|
| N. | cable, rope, wire ❶ **5** | |

❷ **line** /laɪn/ (**lines**) **1** PHRASE If you **draw the line at** a particular activity, you refuse to do it, because you disapprove of it or because it is more extreme than what you normally do. ❑ *They decided to draw the line at raising taxes.* **2** PHRASE If one thing is **in line with** another, or is brought **into line with** it, the first thing is, or becomes, similar to the second, especially in a way that has been planned or expected. ❑ *Prices go up in line with people's incomes.* ❑ *This brings the law into line with most medical opinion.* **3** PHRASE If you do something **on line**, you do it using a computer or a computer network. ❑ *They can order their books on line.* **4** → see also **online 5** PHRASE When people **stand in line** or **wait in line**, they stand one behind the other in a line, waiting their turn for something. ❑ *For the homeless, standing in line for meals is part of the daily routine.* [from Latin] **6** to **sign on the dotted line** → see **dotted**

❸ **line** /laɪn/ (**lines, lining, lined**) **1** V-T If people or things **line** a road, room, or other place, they are present in large numbers along its edges or sides.

❑ *Thousands of local people lined the streets.* **2** V-T If you **line** a wall, container, or other object, you put a layer of something such as leaves or paper on the inside surface of it in order to make it stronger, warmer, or cleaner. ❑ *Line the basket with a napkin before adding the cookies.* [from Latin] **3** → see also **lining**

❹ **line** /laɪn/ (**lines, lining, lined**)
▶ **line up 1** PHR-VERB If people **line up** or if you **line** them **up**, they move so that they are standing in a line. ❑ *The leaders lined up behind him in rows.* ❑ *The gym teachers lined us up against the walls.* **2** PHR-VERB If you **line** things **up**, you move them into a straight row. ❑ *I would line up my toys and play.* **3** PHR-VERB If you **line up** an event or activity, you arrange for it to happen. If you **line** someone **up** for an event or activity, you arrange for them to be available for that event or activity. ❑ *She lined up all her friends to be on the committee.* **4** → see also **lineup**

**lin|ear** /lɪniər/ **1** ADJ A **linear** process or development is one in which something changes or progresses straight from one stage to another. ❑ *Life is a series of events, progressing in a linear way from beginning to end.* **2** ADJ A **linear** shape or form consists of straight lines. ❑ *...sharp, linear designs.* [from Latin]

**lin|ear equa|tion** (**linear equations**) N-COUNT A **linear equation** is a mathematical equation that contains linear expressions. [TECHNICAL]

**lin|ear ex|pres|sion** (**linear expressions**) N-COUNT A **linear expression** is a mathematical expression that contains a variable and does not contain any exponents such as squared or cubed numbers. [TECHNICAL]

**lin|ear per|spec|tive** (**linear perspectives**) N-VAR **Linear perspective** is a technique that is used in painting and drawing to create the appearance of three dimensions on a flat surface. [TECHNICAL]

**line di|rec|tion** (**line directions**) N-VAR **Line direction** is the direction in which a line is drawn or painted, for example vertically or horizontally.

**line drive** (**line drives**) N-COUNT In baseball, a **line drive** is a ball that is hit hard and travels straight and close to the ground. ❑ *...a line drive into the left-field corner.*

**line graph** (**line graphs**) N-COUNT A **line graph** is a graph in which the data are represented by points connected by one or more lines.

**line|man** /laɪnmən/ (**linemen**) N-COUNT In football, a **lineman** is one of the players on the line of scrimmage at the start of each play. ❑ *He is a defensive lineman for the Atlanta Falcons.*

**lin|en** /lɪnɪn/ (**linens**) N-VAR **Linen** is a kind of cloth that is made from a plant called flax. ❑ *...a white linen suit.* [from Old English]

**line of cred|it** (**lines of credit**) N-COUNT A **line of credit** is the same as a **credit line**.

**line of scrim|mage** N-SING In football, **the line of scrimmage** is an imaginary line on either side of which the offense and defense line up. ❑ *The Bears stacked the line of scrimmage with extra defenders to stop the run.*

**line qual|ity** (**line qualities**) N-VAR **Line quality** is all the characteristics of a drawn or painted line, such as its direction, darkness, and thickness.

**lin|er** /ˈlaɪnər/ (liners) N-COUNT A **liner** is a large ship in which people travel long distances, especially on vacation. ❑ ...luxury ocean liners.
→ see **ship**

**lin|er note** (liner notes) N-COUNT The **liner notes** on CD jackets are short pieces of writing that tell you something about the CD or the musicians playing on the CD.

**lines|man** /ˈlaɪnzmən/ (linesmen) N-COUNT A **linesman** is an official who assists the referee or umpire in games such as football and tennis by indicating when the ball goes over the lines around the edge of the field or court.

**line|up** /ˈlaɪnʌp/ (lineups) N-COUNT A **lineup** is a group of people or a series of things that have been gathered together to be part of a particular event. ❑ ...a new show with a great lineup of musicians.

**lin|ger** /ˈlɪŋgər/ (lingers, lingering, lingered)
■ V-I When something such as an idea, feeling, or illness **lingers**, it continues to exist for a long time. ❑ The scent of her perfume lingered on in the room. ❑ He was ashamed. That feeling lingered for some time.
■ V-I If you **linger** somewhere, you stay there for a longer time than is necessary. ❑ Customers are welcome to linger over coffee until around midnight. [from Old English]

**lin|ge|rie** /ˈlɑnʒəreɪ, læn-/ N-UNCOUNT **Lingerie** is women's underwear and nightclothes. ❑ She put it into her drawer, next to her lingerie. [from French]

**lin|gui|ne** /lɪŋˈwini/ also linguini N-UNCOUNT **Linguine** is a kind of pasta in the shape of thin, flat strands. [from Italian]

---

**Word Link**    *lingu ≈ language : bilingual, linguist, linguistics*

---

**lin|guist** /ˈlɪŋgwɪst/ (linguists) ■ N-COUNT A **linguist** is someone who is good at speaking or learning foreign languages. ❑ He was a very able linguist, able to speak eight or nine languages.
■ N-COUNT A **linguist** is someone who studies or teaches linguistics. ❑ ...Professor Noam Chomsky, linguist and political activist. [from Latin]

**lin|guis|tics** /lɪŋˈgwɪstɪks/ (linguistic)
■ N-PLURAL **Linguistics** is the study of the way in which language works. ❑ ...courses in linguistics.
■ ADJ **Linguistic** abilities or ideas relate to language or linguistics. ❑ ...linguistic skills. [from Latin]

**lin|ing** /ˈlaɪnɪŋ/ (linings) ■ N-VAR The **lining** of something such as a piece of clothing or a curtain is a layer of cloth attached to the inside of it in order to make it thicker or warmer, or in order to make it hang better. ❑ ...a black jacket with a red lining. ■ N-COUNT The **lining** of your stomach or other organ is a layer of tissue on the inside of it. [from Old French] ■ → see also **line**

**link** /ˈlɪŋk/ (links, linking, linked) ■ N-COUNT If there is a **link between** two things or situations, there is a relationship between them, for example, because one thing causes or affects the other. ❑ ...the link between fast food and being overweight. ● **Link** is also a verb. ❑ Studies have linked television violence with aggressive behavior in children. ■ N-COUNT A **link between** two things or places is a physical connection between them. ❑ ...the railroad link between Boston and New York. ● **Link** is also a verb. ❑ The Rama Road links the capital, Managua, with the Caribbean coast. ■ N-COUNT A **link** between people, organizations, or places

is a connection between them. ❑ Kiev hopes to develop close links with Bonn. ❑ She was my only link with the past. ❑ The Red Cross was created to provide a link between soldiers in battle and their families at home. ■ V-T If you **link** one person or thing to another, you claim that there is a relationship or connection between them. ❑ The DNA evidence linked him to the crime. ■ N-COUNT In computing, a **link** is a connection between different documents, or between different parts of the same document, using hypertext. ❑ The website has links to other tourism sites. ● **Link** is also a verb. ❑ Hypertext is used to link Internet documents. ■ N-COUNT A **link** is one of the rings in a chain. ❑ ...a chain of heavy gold

links. ■ V-T If you **link** one thing with another, you join them by putting one thing through the other. ❑ She linked her arm through his. [of Scandinavian origin]
■ → see also **linkup**
▶ **link up** ■ PHR-VERB If you **link up with** someone, you join them for a particular purpose. ❑ I linked up with them on the walk. ■ PHR-VERB If one thing is **linked up to** another, the two things are connected to

**link**

each other. ❑ The machine was linked up to a computer.

---

**Word Partnership**    Use **link** with :

| | |
|---|---|
| ADJ. | **direct** link, **possible** link, **vital** link ■ ■ ■, **strong/weak** link ■ – ■ ■ |
| V. | **establish** a link, **find** a link ■ – ■ **attempt to** link ■ – ■ ■ |

---

**link|up** /ˈlɪŋkʌp/ (linkups) N-COUNT A **linkup** is a relationship or partnership between two organizations. ❑ ...new linkups between schools and businesses.

**lint** /ˈlɪnt/ N-UNCOUNT **Lint** is small unwanted threads or fibers that collect on clothes. [from Latin]

**lion** /ˈlaɪən/ (lions) N-COUNT A **lion** is a large wild member of the cat family that is found in Africa. Lions have yellowish fur, and male lions have long hair on their head and neck. [from Old English]
→ see **carnivore**

**lion's share** N-SING If a person, group, or project gets **the lion's share** of something, they get the largest part of it. ❑ The lion's share of the work will go to American companies.

**lip** /ˈlɪp/ (lips) N-COUNT Your **lips** are the two outer parts of the edge of your mouth. ❑ He kissed her gently on the lips. [from Old English]
→ see **face, kiss**

**lip|id** /ˈlɪpɪd, laɪp-/ (lipids) N-COUNT **Lipids** are fatty substances that do not dissolve in water and are found in living cells. [TECHNICAL] [from French]

**lip|stick** /ˈlɪpstɪk/ (lipsticks) N-VAR **Lipstick** is a colored substance in the form of a stick which women put on their lips. ❑ She was wearing red lipstick.
→ see **makeup**

**li|queur** /lɪˈkɜr, -kyʊər/ (liqueurs) N-VAR A **liqueur** is a strong alcoholic drink with a sweet

taste. ❑ ...*liqueurs such as Grand Marnier and Kirsch.*
[from French]

**liq|uid** /lɪkwɪd/ (**liquids**) N-VAR A **liquid** is a
substance which is not solid but which flows and
can be poured, for example, water. ❑ *Drink plenty of
liquid.* [from Old French]
→ see **matter**

**liq|ui|date** /lɪkwɪdeɪt/ (**liquidates, liquidating,
liquidated**) V-T To **liquidate** a company is to
close it down and sell all its assets, usually
because it is in debt. [BUSINESS] ❑ *They decided to
liquidate the business.* ● **liq|ui|da|tion** /lɪkwɪdeɪʃⁿn/
(**liquidations**) N-VAR ❑ *The company went
into liquidation.* ● **liq|ui|da|tor** /lɪkwɪdeɪtər/
(**liquidators**) N-COUNT [BUSINESS] ❑ ...*the failed
company's liquidators.* [from Old French]

**liq|uor** /lɪkər/ (**liquors**) N-VAR Strong alcoholic
drinks such as whiskey, vodka, and gin can be
referred to as **liquor**. ❑ *The room was filled with cases
of liquor.* [from Old French]

**liq|uor store** (**liquor stores**) N-COUNT A **liquor
store** is a store which sells beer, wine, and other
alcoholic drinks.

**list** /lɪst/ (**lists, listing, listed**) ◼ N-COUNT A **list**
of things such as names or addresses is a set of
them which all belong to a particular category,
written down one below the other. ❑ ...*a shopping
list.* ❑ *There were six names on the list.* ◼ → see also
**mailing list** ◼ V-T To **list** several things such as
reasons or names means to write or say them one
after another, usually in a particular order. ❑ *The
students were asked to list the sports they liked best.*
[from Old French]

**Word Partnership** Use *list* with :

| | |
|---|---|
| V. | **add** someone/something **to** a list, list **includes** |
| N. | list **of candidates**, list **of demands, guest** list, list **of ingredients**, list **of items**, list **of names, price** list, list **of questions, reading** list, list **of things, wine** list, list **of words** ◼ |
| ADJ. | **complete** list, **disabled** list, **injured** list, **short** list ◼ |

**lis|ten** /lɪsⁿn/ (**listens, listening, listened**)
◼ V-I If you **listen to** someone who is talking or
to a sound, you give your attention to them or it.
❑ *He spent his time listening to the radio.* ● **lis|ten|er**
(**listeners**) N-COUNT ❑ *A few listeners fell asleep while
the president was speaking.* ◼ V-I If you **listen for** a
sound, you keep alert and are ready to hear it if
it occurs. ❑ *We listened for footsteps.* ◼ V-I If you
**listen to** someone, you do what they advise you to
do, or you believe them. ❑ *Anne, please listen to me
this time.* ◼ CONVENTION You say **listen** when you
want someone to pay attention to you because
you are going to say something. ❑ *Listen, there's
something I should warn you about.* ◼ CONVENTION
You say **listen up** when you want someone to
listen to what you are going to say. [SPOKEN]
❑ *Okay, listen up, guys. We've got to talk a little about
how you look.* [from Old English]
▸ **listen in** PHR-VERB If you **listen in** to a private
conversation, you secretly listen to it. ❑ *He was sure
that someone was listening in on his phone calls.*

**Thesaurus**     *listen*     Also look up :

| | |
|---|---|
| V. | catch, pick up, tune in; (*ant.*) ignore ◼ heed, mind ◼ |

**Word Partnership** Use *listen* with :

| | |
|---|---|
| V. | listen **to** someone's **voice** ◼ **sit up** and listen, **willing to** listen ◼ – ◼ |
| ADV. | listen **carefully**, listen **closely** ◼ – ◼ |

**lis|ten|er** /lɪsənər, lɪsnər/ (**listeners**)
◼ N-COUNT A **listener** is a person who listens to
the radio or to a particular radio program. ❑ *I'm
a regular listener to her show.* [from Old English]
◼ → see also **listen**
→ see **radio**

**list|less** /lɪstlɪs/ ADJ Someone who is **listless**
has no energy or enthusiasm. ❑ *He was listless and
pale and wouldn't eat much.* ● **list|less|ly** ADV ❑ *He sat
listlessly, too hot to do anything else.*

**list|serv** /lɪstsɜrv/ (**listservs**) N-COUNT A
**listserv** is a computerized list of names and e-mail
addresses that a company or organization keeps,
so that they can send people e-mails containing
information or advertisements.

**lit** /lɪt/ **Lit** is a past tense and past participle of
**light.** [from Old English]

**li|ter** /lɪtər/ (**liters**) N-COUNT A **liter** is a
metric unit of volume that is a thousand cubic
centimeters. It is equal to 2.11 pints. ❑ ...*a
13-thousand liter water tank.* ❑ *It costs eight cents a
liter.* [from French]
→ see **measurement**

**lit|era|cy** /lɪtərəsi/ N-UNCOUNT **Literacy** is
the ability to read and write. ❑ *Many adults have
problems with literacy.* [from Latin]

**Word Link** liter ≈ letter : il*liter*ate, *liter*al, *liter*ature

**lit|er|al** /lɪtərəl/ ◼ ADJ The **literal** sense of a
word or phrase is its most basic sense. ❑ *The people
there are fighting, in a literal sense, for their homes.*
◼ ADJ A **literal** translation is one in which you
translate each word of the original work rather
than giving the meaning of each expression
or sentence using words that sound natural.
❑ *A literal translation of the name Tapies is "walls."*
● **lit|er|al|ly** ADV ❑ *The word "volk" translates literally
as "folk."* [from Late Latin]

**lit|er|al|ly** /lɪtərəli/ ADV You can use **literally**
to emphasize an exaggeration. Some careful
speakers of English think that this use is
incorrect. ❑ *The view is literally breathtaking.* [from
Late Latin]

**lit|er|ary** /lɪtəreri/ ◼ ADJ **Literary** means
connected with literature. ❑ ...*literary criticism.*
❑ *She's the literary editor of the "Sunday Review."* ◼ ADJ
**Literary** words and expressions are often unusual
in some way and are used to create a special effect
in a piece of writing such as a poem, speech, or
novel. [from Latin]

**lit|er|ary analy|sis** N-UNCOUNT **Literary
analysis** is the academic study of the techniques
used in the creation of literature.

**lit|er|ary criti|cism** N-UNCOUNT **Literary
criticism** is the analysis and judgment of works of
literature.

**lit|er|ate** /lɪtərɪt/ ADJ Someone who is **literate** is able to read and write. □ *Over one-quarter of the population are not fully literate.* [from Latin]

**lit|era|ture** /lɪtərətʃər, -tʃʊər/ ■ N-UNCOUNT Novels, plays, and poetry are referred to as **literature**, especially when they are considered to be good or important. □ ...*classic works of literature.* ■ N-UNCOUNT **Literature** is written information produced by people who want to sell you something or give you advice. □ *I am sending you literature from two other companies.* [from Latin]
→ see **genre**

**litho|sphere** /lɪθəsfɪər/ N-SING The **lithosphere** is the outer layer of the Earth's surface, consisting of the crust and the outer mantle. [TECHNICAL]

**liti|ga|tion** /lɪtɪɡeɪʃən/ N-UNCOUNT **Litigation** is the process of fighting or defending a case in a civil court of law. □ *The settlement ends more than four years of litigation.* [from Latin]

**lit|ter** /lɪtər/ (**litters, littering, littered**) ■ N-UNCOUNT **Litter** is garbage or trash that is left lying around. □ *If you see litter in the corridor, pick it up.* ■ V-T If a number of things **litter** a place, they are scattered around it or over it. □ *Broken glass and paper bags litter the sidewalk.* ● **lit|tered** ADJ □ *The room was littered with toys.* ■ ADJ If something is
litter **littered with** things, it contains many examples of it. □ *History is littered with war plans that went wrong.* [from Latin]

**litter|bug** /lɪtərbʌɡ/ (**litterbugs**) N-COUNT If you refer to someone as a **litterbug**, you disapprove of the fact that they drop litter in public places. □ ...*a city full of litterbugs.*

## little

❶ DETERMINER, QUANTIFIER, AND ADVERB USES
❷ ADJECTIVE USES

❶ **lit|tle** /lɪtəl/ ■ DET You use **little** to indicate that there is only a very small amount of something. □ *I had little money and little free time.* □ *I get very little sleep these days.* ● **Little** is also a quantifier. □ *Little of the existing housing is of good enough quality.* ● **Little** is also a pronoun. □ *He ate little, and drank less.* □ *In general, employers do little to help the single working mother.* ■ ADV **Little** means not very often or to only a small extent. □ *They spoke very little.* ■ DET **A little** of something is a small amount of it. □ *Mrs. Patel needs a little help getting her groceries home.* □ *A little sugar in your diet does no harm.* ● **Little** is also a pronoun. □ *They get paid for it. Not much. Just a little.* ● **Little** is also a quantifier. □ *Pour a little of the sauce over the chicken.* ■ ADV If you do something **a little**, you do it for

a short time. □ *He walked a little by himself.* ■ ADV **A little** or **a little bit** means to a small extent or degree. □ *He complained a little of a pain between his shoulders.* □ *He was a little bit afraid of the dog.* [from Old English]

❷ **lit|tle** /lɪtəl/ (**littler, littlest**)

The comparative **littler** and the superlative **littlest** are sometimes used in spoken English for meanings ■ and ■, but otherwise the comparative and superlative forms of the adjective **little** are not used.

■ ADJ **Little** things are small in size. **Little** is slightly more informal than **small**. □ *We sat around a little table, eating.* ■ ADJ **A little** distance, period of time, or event is short in length. □ *Go down the road a little way, turn left, and cross the bridge.* □ *Why don't we walk a little while and see what happens?* ■ ADJ You use **little** to indicate that something is not serious or important. □ ...*annoying little habits.* [from Old English]

**lit|to|ral zone** /lɪtərəl zoʊn/ (**littoral zones**) N-COUNT The **littoral zone** is the area along the edge of a pond, lake or sea. [TECHNICAL]

## live

❶ VERB USES
❷ ADJECTIVE USES

❶ **live** /lɪv/ (**lives, living, lived**) ■ V-I If someone **lives** in a particular place or with a particular person, their home is in that place or with that person. □ *She lived there for 10 years.* □ *Where do you live?* ■ V-T/V-I If you say that someone **lives** in particular circumstances or that they **live** a particular kind of life, you mean that they are in those circumstances or that they have that kind of life. □ *We live very well.* □ *She lived a life of luxury in Paris.* □ ...*people living a hundred years ago.* ■ V-I If you say that someone **lives for** a particular thing, you mean that it is the most important thing in their life. □ *He lived for his work.* ■ V-T/V-I To **live** means to be alive. If someone **lives** to a particular age, they stay alive until they are that age. □ *He's very ill and will not live long.* □ *He lived to be 103.* ■ V-I If people **live by** doing a particular activity, they get the money, food, or clothing they need by doing that activity. □ ...*the last people to live by hunting.* ■ → see also **living** ■ PHRASE If you **live it up**, you have a very enjoyable and exciting time. [INFORMAL] □ *There is no reason why you shouldn't live it up sometimes.* [from Old English] ■ to **live hand to mouth** → see **hand**
▶ **live down** PHR-VERB If you are unable to **live down** a mistake, failure, or bad reputation, you are unable to make people forget about it. □ *You can't live down a mistake like this.*
▶ **live off** PHR-VERB If you **live off** another person, you rely on them to provide you with money. □ *He lived off his father.*
▶ **live on** or **live off** ■ PHR-VERB If you **live on** or **live off** a particular amount of money, you have

that amount of money to buy things. ❑ *They are trying to live on $100 a week.* **2** PHR-VERB If an animal **lives on** or **lives off** a particular food, this is the kind of food that it eats. ❑ *The fish live on smaller fish.*

▶ **live up to** PHR-VERB If someone or something **lives up to** what they were expected to be, they are as good as they were expected to be. ❑ *Sales have not lived up to expectations this year.*

❷ **live** /laɪv/ **1** ADJ **Live** animals or plants are alive, rather than being dead or artificial. ❑ *…a protest against the company's tests on live animals.* **2** ADJ A **live** television or radio program is one in which an event or performance is broadcast at the time that it happens. ❑ *They watch all the live games.* ● **Live** is also an adverb. ❑ *The game was broadcast live in 50 countries.* **3** ADJ A **live** performance is given in front of an audience, rather than being recorded. ❑ *…live music.* ❑ *A live audience will ask the questions.* ● **Live** is also an adverb. ❑ *Kat Johnson has been playing live with her new band.* **4** ADJ A **live** wire or piece of electrical equipment is directly connected to a source of electricity. ❑ *The plug broke, showing live wires.* [from Old English]

| Thesaurus | live | Also look up : |
|---|---|---|
| v. | dwell, inhabit, occupy, reside ❶ **1** manage, subsist, survive ❶ **2** **5** exist ❶ **4** | |
| ADJ. | active, alive, living, vigorous ❷ **1** | |

**live·li·hood** /laɪvlihʊd/ (**livelihoods**) N-VAR Your **livelihood** is the job or other source of income that gives you the money to buy the things you need. ❑ *These fishermen depend on the seas for their livelihood.* [from Old English]

**live·ly** /laɪvli/ (**livelier, liveliest**) **1** ADJ You can describe someone as **lively** when they behave in an enthusiastic and cheerful way. ❑ *She has a lively personality.* ● **live·li·ness** N-UNCOUNT ❑ *The first thing you notice about him is his liveliness.* **2** ADJ A **lively** event or a **lively** discussion, for example, has lots of interesting and exciting things happening or being said in it. ❑ *…a lively debate.* **3** ADJ Someone who has a **lively** mind is intelligent and interested in a lot of different things. ❑ *She was an intelligent girl with a lively mind.* [from Old English]

| Word Partnership | Use *lively* with : |
|---|---|
| ADV. | **very** lively **1** – **3** |
| N. | lively **atmosphere**, lively **conversation**, lively **debate**, lively **discussion**, lively **music**, lively **performance** **2** lively **imagination**, lively **interest** **3** |

**liv·en** /laɪvᵊn/ (**livens, livening, livened**) [from Old English]
▶ **liven up** **1** PHR-VERB If a place or event **livens up**, or if something **livens** it **up**, it becomes more interesting and exciting. ❑ *What can we do to the room to liven it up?* ❑ *That should liven up the party a bit.* **2** PHR-VERB If people **liven up**, or if something **livens** them **up**, they become more cheerful and energetic. ❑ *Talking about her daughters livens her up.*

**liv·er** /lɪvər/ (**livers**) **1** N-COUNT Your **liver** is a large organ in your body which processes your blood and helps to clean unwanted substances out of it. **2** N-VAR **Liver** is the liver of some

animals, especially lambs, pigs, and cows, which is cooked and eaten. ❑ *…grilled calves' liver.* [from Old English]
→ see **donor**

**liv·er·wort** /lɪvərwɜrt, -wɔrt/ (**liverworts**) N-COUNT A **liverwort** is a plant with no leaves or stem that grows in wet places and resembles seaweed or moss. [from Old English]

**lives**

Pronounced /laɪvz/ for meaning **1**, and /lɪvz/ for meaning **2**.

**1 Lives** is the plural of **life**. **2 Lives** is the third person singular form of **live**. [from Old English]

**live·stock** /laɪvstɒk/ N-UNCOUNT Animals such as cattle and sheep which are kept on a farm are referred to as **livestock**. ❑ *The heavy rains killed a lot of livestock.*
→ see **barn**

**liv·id** /lɪvɪd/ ADJ Someone who is **livid** is extremely angry. [INFORMAL] ❑ *When Spyros heard about the incident, he was livid.* [from French]

**liv·ing** /lɪvɪŋ/ (**livings**) **1** N-COUNT The work that you do for a **living** is the work that you do in order to earn the money that you need. ❑ *Dad never talked about what he did for a living.* **2** N-UNCOUNT You use **living** when you are talking about the quality of people's daily lives. ❑ *She believes in healthy living.* [from Old English]

**liv·ing room** (**living rooms**) also **living-room** N-COUNT The **living room** in a house is the room where people sit and relax. ❑ *We were sitting on the couch in the living room watching TV.*
→ see **house**

**liz·ard** /lɪzərd/ (**lizards**) N-COUNT A **lizard** is a reptile with short legs and a long tail. [from Old French]
→ see **desert**

**load** /loʊd/ (**loads, loading, loaded**) **1** V-T If you **load** a vehicle or a container, you put a large quantity of things into it. ❑ *The men finished loading the truck.* ❑ *Mr. Dambar loaded his plate with food.* **2** N-COUNT A **load** is something, usually a large quantity or heavy object, which is being carried. ❑ *This car is easy to drive and takes a big load.* **3** QUANT If you refer to **a load of** people or things or **loads of** them, you are emphasizing that there are a lot of them. [INFORMAL] ❑ *I've got loads of money.* ❑ *…a load of kids.* **4** V-T When someone **loads** a weapon such as a gun, they put a bullet or missile in it so that it is ready to use. ❑ *I knew how to load and handle a gun.* ❑ *He carried a loaded gun.* **5** V-T To **load** a camera or other piece of equipment means to put film, tape, or data into it so that it is ready to use. ❑ *A photographer from the newspaper was loading his camera with film.* **6** N-COUNT A **load** is any electrical device that is connected to a source of electricity such as a generator or circuit. [TECHNICAL] **7** N-VAR A river's **load** is the sediment and other material that it carries with it. [TECHNICAL] [from Old English] **8** → see also **loaded** **9 a load off** your **mind** → see **mind**
→ see **photography**

| Thesaurus | load | Also look up : |
|---|---|---|
| v. | arrange, fill, pack, pile up, stack **1** |
| N. | bundle, cargo, freight, haul, shipment **2** |

**load|ed** /lóʊdɪd/ 1 ADJ A **loaded** question or word has more meaning or purpose than it appears to have, because the person who uses it hopes it will cause people to respond in a particular way. ❑ *That's a loaded question.* 2 ADJ If a place or object is **loaded with** things, it has very many of them in it or it is full of them. ❑ *...a tray loaded with cups.* ❑ *The store was loaded with jewelry.* 3 ADJ If you say that something is **loaded in favor of** someone, you mean it works unfairly to their advantage. If you say it is **loaded against** them, you mean it works unfairly to their disadvantage. ❑ *The education system is loaded in favor of the rich.* [from Old English]

**loaf** /lóʊf/ (**loaves**) N-COUNT A **loaf** of bread is bread which has been shaped and baked in one piece and can be cut into slices. [from Old English]
→ see **bread**

**loam** /lóʊm/ N-UNCOUNT **Loam** is soil that is good for growing crops and plants in because it contains a lot of decayed vegetable matter and does not contain too much sand or clay. [from Old English]

**loan** /lóʊn/ (**loans, loaning, loaned**) 1 N-COUNT A **loan** is a sum of money that you borrow. ❑ *She didn't have enough money to buy the car, so she got a loan.* 2 → see also **bridge loan** 3 N-SING If someone gives you a **loan of** something, you borrow it from them. ❑ *I need a loan of a bike for a few weeks.* 4 V-T If you **loan** something to someone, you lend it to them. ❑ *He offered to loan us his car.* 5 PHRASE If something is **on loan**, it has been borrowed. ❑ *...paintings on loan from the Metropolitan Museum.* [from Old Norse]

**loath** /lóʊθ/ also **loth** ADJ If you are **loath** to do something, you do not want to do it. ❑ *We were doing so well we were loath to change our system.* [from Old English]

**loathe** /lóʊð/ (**loathes, loathing, loathed**) V-T If you **loathe** something or someone, you dislike them very much. [FORMAL] ❑ *The two men loathe each other.* ● **loath|ing** N-UNCOUNT ❑ *She looked at him with loathing.* [from Old English]

**loaves** /lóʊvz/ **Loaves** is the plural of **loaf**. [from Old English]

**lob** /lɒb/ (**lobs, lobbing, lobbed**) V-T If you **lob** something, you throw it so that it goes quite high in the air. ❑ *I lobbed the ball back over the net.* [from Low German]

**lob|by** /lɒbi/ (**lobbies, lobbying, lobbied**) 1 V-T/V-I If you **lobby** someone such as a member of a government or council, you try to persuade them that a particular law should be changed or that a particular thing should be done. ❑ *Mr. Bass lobbied city officials for money to build a community center.* ❑ *The group lobbies for women's rights.* 2 N-COUNT A **lobby** is a group of people who represent a particular organization or campaign, and try to persuade a government or council to help or support them. ❑ *The American Association of Retired Persons is one of the most powerful lobbies in the United States.* 3 N-COUNT In a hotel or other large building, the **lobby** is the area near the entrance that usually has corridors and staircases leading off it. ❑ *I met her in the lobby of the museum.* [from Medieval Latin]

**lobe** /lóʊb/ (**lobes**) N-COUNT The **lobe** of your ear is the soft, fleshy part at the bottom. [from Late Latin]

lobster

**lob|ster** /lɒbstər/ (**lobsters**) N-VAR A **lobster** is a sea creature that has a hard shell, two large claws, and eight legs. ❑ *She sold me two live lobsters.* ● **Lobster** is the flesh of a lobster eaten as food. ❑ *...lobster on a bed of fresh vegetables.* [from Old English]
→ see **shellfish**

**lo|cal** /lóʊkªl/ (**locals**) ADJ **Local** means existing in or belonging to the area where you live, or to the area that you are talking about. ❑ *...the local paper.* ❑ *Some local residents joined the students' protest.* ● The **locals** are local people. ❑ *Camping is a great way to meet the locals.* ● **lo|cal|ly** ADV ❑ *She bought her clothes locally.* [from Old French]

**lo|cal col|or** N-UNCOUNT **Local color** is used to refer to customs, traditions, dress, and other things which give a place or period of history its own particular character. ❑ *There's plenty of local color in the book.*

**lo|cal gov|ern|ment** N-UNCOUNT **Local government** is the system of electing representatives to be responsible for the administration of public services and facilities in a particular area.

**lo|cal|ity** /loʊkælɪti/ (**localities**) N-COUNT A **locality** is a small area of a country or city. [FORMAL] ❑ *Find out what is available in your locality.* [from Old French]

**lo|cate** /lóʊkeɪt/ (**locates, locating, located**) 1 V-T If you **locate** something or someone, you find out where they are. [FORMAL] ❑ *They couldn't locate the missing ship.* 2 V-T If you **locate** something in a particular place, you put it there or build it there. [FORMAL] ❑ *Business people voted Atlanta the best city in which to locate a business.* ● **lo|cat|ed** ADJ ❑ *A shop and beauty salon are located in the hotel.* 3 V-I If you **locate** in a particular place, you move there or open a business there.

**Picture Dictionary** location

The squirrel is above/over the bench.

The squirrel is in the tree.

The squirrel is on the bench.

The squirrel is between the bench and the tree.

The squirrel is behind the bench.

The squirrel is under/underneath the bench.

The squirrel is in front of the bench.

[BUSINESS] ❏ ...businesses that locate in poor neighborhoods. [from Latin]

**lo|ca|tion** /loʊkeɪʃªn/ (**locations**) **1** N-COUNT A **location** is the place where something happens or is situated. ❏ Rand pointed out the location of the different school buildings. **2** N-VAR A **location** is a place away from a studio where a movie or part of a movie is made. ❏ ...a movie with many locations. [from Latin]
→ see Picture Dictionary: **location**

| Word Partnership | Use *location* with : |
| --- | --- |
| ADJ. | **central** location, **convenient** location, **exact** location, **geographic** location, **present** location, **secret** location, **specific** location **1** |
| V. | **pinpoint** a location **1** |

**loch** /lɒx, lɒk/ (**lochs**) N-COUNT A **loch** is a large area of water in Scotland that is completely or almost completely surrounded by land. ❏ ...twenty miles north of Loch Ness. [from Gaelic]

**lock** /lɒk/ (**locks, locking, locked**) **1** V-T When you **lock** something, you fasten it with a key. ❏ Are you sure you locked the front door? **2** N-COUNT The **lock** on something such as a door or a drawer is the device which is used to keep it shut. Locks are opened with a key. ❏ He heard Gill's key turning in the lock. **3** V-T If you **lock** something or someone in a place, room, or container, you put them there and fasten the lock. ❏ She locked the case in the closet. **4** V-T/V-I If you **lock** something in a particular position, or if it **locks** there, it is held or fitted firmly in that position. ❏ He locked his fingers behind his head. **5** N-COUNT On a canal or river, a **lock** is a place where walls have been built with gates at each end so that boats can move to a higher or lower section of the canal or river, by gradually changing the water level inside the gates. ❏ The lock slowly filled with water. **6** N-COUNT A **lock of**

hair is a small bunch of hairs on your head that grow together in the same direction. [from Old English]

▶ **lock away 1** PHR-VERB If you **lock** something **away** in a place or container, you put or hide it there and fasten the lock. ❏ She carefully cleaned her jewelry and locked it away in a case. **2** PHR-VERB To **lock** someone **away** means to put them in prison. ❏ You can't lock someone away because they are mentally ill.

▶ **lock up 1** PHR-VERB To **lock** someone **up** means to put them in prison. ❏ He is a criminal: they should lock him up. **2** PHR-VERB When you **lock up** a building or car, or **lock up**, you make sure that all the doors and windows are locked so that nobody can get in. ❏ Don't forget to lock up.

| Word Partnership | Use *lock* with : |
| --- | --- |
| N. | lock **a car**, lock **a door**, lock **a room 1** **combination** lock, **door** lock, lock **and key, key in a** lock **2** |
| V. | **change a** lock, **open a** lock, **pick a** lock **2** |

locker

**lock|er** /lɒkər/ (**lockers**) N-COUNT A **locker** is a small metal or wooden cabinet with a lock, where you can put your personal possessions, for example in a school, place of work, or sports club. [from Old English]

**lock|smith** /lɒksmɪθ/ (**locksmiths**) N-COUNT A **locksmith** is a person whose job is to make or repair locks.

**lock-up** (**lock-ups**) also **lockup** N-COUNT A **lock-up** is the same as a **jail**. [INFORMAL] ❏ ...the 450 prisoners at the lock-up in Lucasville.

**lo|co|mo|tive** /loʊkəmoʊtɪv/ (**locomotives**) N-COUNT A **locomotive** is a large vehicle that pulls a train. [FORMAL] [from Modern Latin]

**lo|co|mo|tor** /loʊkəmoʊtər/ ADJ **Locomotor** movements are actions such as walking or running, which involve moving from one place to another. [from Latin]

**lo|cust** /loʊkəst/ (**locusts**) N-COUNT **Locusts** are large insects, similar to grasshoppers, that live mainly in hot areas and often cause serious damage to crops. [from Latin]

**lodge** /lɒdʒ/ (**lodges, lodging, lodged**) ◼ N-COUNT A **lodge** is a house or hotel in the country or in the mountains where people stay on vacation. ❑ *...a hunting lodge.* ◻ V-T If you **lodge** a complaint, protest, accusation, or claim, you officially make it. ❑ *Customers pay to log on and speak to other users.* ◻ V-T/V-I If you **lodge** somewhere, such as in someone else's house or if you **are lodged** there, you live there, usually paying rent. ❑ *She is lodging with a farming family.* ● **lodg|er** (**lodgers**) N-COUNT ❑ *Jennie took in a lodger to help pay the mortgage.* ◻ V-T/V-I If an object **lodges** or **is lodged** somewhere, it becomes stuck there. ❑ *The bullet lodged in his leg.* [from Old French] ◻ → see also **lodging**

**lodg|ing** /lɒdʒɪŋ/ (**lodgings**) N-UNCOUNT If you are provided with **lodging** or **lodgings**, you are provided with a place to stay for a period of time. ❑ *He was given free lodging.* [from Old French]

**lo|ess** /loʊɪs, lɛs, lɜrs/ N-UNCOUNT **Loess** is a mixture of sand, soil, and other material that has been deposited by the wind. [TECHNICAL] [from German]

**Word Link** loft ≈ air : aloft, loft, lofty

**loft** /lɔft/ (**lofts**) ◼ N-COUNT A **loft** is the space inside the sloping roof of a house or other building, where things are sometimes stored. ❑ *They took the holiday decorations out of the loft.* ◻ N-COUNT A **loft** is an apartment in the upper part of a building, especially a building such as a warehouse or factory that has been converted for people to live in. Lofts are usually large and not divided into separate rooms. ❑ *...Andy Warhol's New York loft.* [from Late Old English]

**lofty** /lɔfti/ (**loftier, loftiest**) ◼ ADJ A **lofty** ideal or ambition is noble, important, and admirable. ❑ *Martin made lofty promises of change that will "make history."* ◻ ADJ A **lofty** building or room is very high. [FORMAL] ❑ *...a light, lofty apartment.* ◻ ADJ If you say that someone behaves in a **lofty** way, you are critical of them for behaving in a proud and somewhat overbearing way, as if they think they are very important. ❑ *...a lofty speech about Imtiaz's genius and greatness.* [from Late Old English]

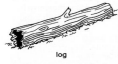

**log** /lɔg/ (**logs, logging, logged**) ◼ N-COUNT A **log** is a thick piece of wood cut from a branch or the trunk of a tree.

log

❑ *He put the logs near the fireplace.* ◻ N-COUNT A **log** is an official written account of what happens each day, for example, on board a ship. ❑ *He wrote about his experience in his ship's log.* ◻ V-T If you **log** an event or fact, you record it officially in writing or on a computer. ❑ *They log everything that comes in and out of here.*

→ see **blog, forest**

▶ **log in** or **log on** PHR-VERB When someone **logs in**, **logs on**, or **logs into** a computer system, they start using the system, usually by typing their name and a password. ❑ *Customers pay to log on and speak to other users.*

▶ **log out** or **log off** PHR-VERB When someone who is using a computer system **logs out** or **logs off**, they finish using the system by typing a particular command. ❑ *Remember to log off when you have finished.*

**loga|rithm** /lɔgərɪðəm/ (**logarithms**) N-COUNT In mathematics, the **logarithm** of a number is a number that it can be represented by in order to make a difficult multiplication or division sum simpler. [from New Latin]

**log|ger** /lɔgər/ (**loggers**) N-COUNT A **logger** is a man whose job is to cut down trees.

**log|ger|head tur|tle** /lɔgərhɛd tɜrtᵊl/ (**loggerhead turtles**) N-COUNT A **loggerhead turtle** is a large, carnivorous sea turtle.

**Word Link** log ≈ reason, speech : apology, dialogue, logic

**log|ic** /lɒdʒɪk/ N-UNCOUNT **Logic** is a method of reasoning that involves a series of statements, each of which must be true if the statement before it is true. ❑ *Students study philosophy and logic.* [from Old French]

→ see **philosophy**

**logi|cal** /lɒdʒɪkᵊl/ ◼ ADJ In a **logical** argument or method of reasoning, each step must be true if the step before it is true. ❑ *Each logical step is checked by other mathematicians.* ● **logi|cal|ly** /lɒdʒɪkli/ ADV ❑ *I have learned to think about things logically.* ◻ ADJ The **logical** conclusion or result of a series of facts or events is the only one which can come from it, according to the rules of logic. ❑ *Brown and Harris lost their jobs and the logical conclusion is that I'll be next.* ● **logi|cal|ly** ADV ❑ *We worked it all out logically.* ◻ ADJ Something that is **logical** seems reasonable or sensible in the circumstances. ❑ *Connie seemed the logical person to go with her.* ❑ *There was a logical explanation.* [from Old French]

**lo|gis|tics** /loʊdʒɪstɪks/ N-UNCOUNT If you refer to the **logistics** of doing something complicated that involves a lot of people or equipment, you are referring to the skillful organization of it so that it can be done successfully and efficiently. ❑ *...the logistics of getting such a big show on the road.* [from French]

**logo** /loʊgoʊ/ (**logos**) N-COUNT The **logo** of a company or organization is the special design or way of writing its name that it puts on all its products, stationery, or advertisements. ❑ *Everyone recognized the famous MGM logo of the roaring lion.* [from Greek]

**loi|ter** /lɔɪtər/ (**loiters, loitering, loitered**) V-I If you **loiter** somewhere, you remain there or walk up and down without any real purpose. ❑ *Young men loiter at the entrance of the factory.* [from Middle Dutch]

**LOL** **LOL** is a written abbreviation for "laughing out loud" or "lots of love," often used in e-mail and text messages.

**lone** /loʊn/ ADJ A **lone** person or thing is alone. ❑ *A lone walker disappeared over the top of the hill into the mist.*

**lone|ly** /lóunli/ (**lonelier, loneliest**) ■ ADJ Someone who is **lonely** is unhappy because they are alone or do not have anyone they can talk to. ❑ *He has been lonely since his wife died.* ● **lone|li|ness** N-UNCOUNT ❑ *I have a fear of loneliness.* ■ ADJ A **lonely** place is one where very few people come. ❑ *It felt like the loneliest place in the world.*

**lon|er** /lóunər/ (**loners**) N-COUNT A **loner** is someone who prefers to be alone. ❑ *I'm a loner — I never go out.*

**lone|some** /lóunsəm/ ■ ADJ Someone who is **lonesome** is unhappy because they do not have any friends or do not have anyone to talk to. ❑ *I get lonesome without anybody to talk to.* ■ ADJ A **lonesome** place is one which very few people come to and which is a long way from places where people live. ❑ *...lonesome little towns like Acorn and Hatfield.*

---

**long**

❶ TIME
❷ DISTANCE AND SIZE
❸ PHRASES
❹ VERB USES

---

**❶ long** /lɔ́ŋ/ (**longer** /lɔ́ŋgər/, **longest** /lɔ́ŋgɪst/) ■ ADV **Long** means a great amount of time or for a great amount of time. ❑ *The repairs did not take too long.* ❑ *Have you known her parents long?* ❑ *It all happened so long ago.* ■ PHRASE The expression **for long** is used to mean "for a great amount of time." ❑ *"Did you live there?" — "Not for long."* ■ ADJ A **long** event or period of time lasts for a great amount of time or takes a great amount of time. ❑ *We had a long meeting.* ❑ *She is planning a long vacation in Europe.* ■ ADV You use **long** to ask or talk about amounts of time. ❑ *How long have you lived around here?* ● **Long** is also an adjective. ❑ *So how long is the movie?* ■ ADJ A **long** speech, book, movie, or list contains a lot of information or a lot of items and takes a lot of time to listen to, read, watch, or deal with. ❑ *He made a long speech.* [from Old English]

**❷ long** /lɔ́ŋ/ (**longer** /lɔ́ŋgər/, **longest** /lɔ́ŋgɪst/) ■ ADJ Something that is **long** measures a great distance from one end to the other. ❑ *...a long table.* ❑ *Lucy had long dark hair.* ■ ADJ A **long** distance is a great distance. A **long** journey or route covers a great distance. ❑ *These people were a long way from home.* ❑ *The long journey made him tired.* ■ ADJ You use **long** to talk or ask about the distance something measures from one end to the other. ❑ *The cut on his arm was an inch long.* ❑ *How long is the tunnel?* ❑ *...a three-foot-long hole in the ship's side.* [from Old English]
→ see **hair**

**❸ long** /lɔ́ŋ/ (**longer** /lɔ́ŋgər/) ■ PHRASE If you say that something is true **as long as** or **so long as** something else is true, you mean that it is only true if the second thing is true. ❑ *They can do what they want as long as they are not breaking the law.* ■ PHRASE If you say that something will happen or happened **before long**, you mean that it happened or will happen soon. ❑ *Prices will fall before long.* ■ PHRASE Something that is **no longer** the case used to be the case but is not the case now. You can also say that something is not

the case **any longer**. ❑ *Food shortages are no longer a problem.* ❑ *She couldn't afford to pay the rent any longer.* ■ PHRASE If you say that someone **won't be long**, you mean that you think they will arrive or be back soon. If you say that it **won't be long** before something happens, you mean that you think it will happen soon. ❑ *"What's happened to her?" — "I'm sure she won't be long."* [from Old English] ■ **at long last** → see **last** ■ **in the long run** → see **run** ■ **a long shot** → see **shot** ■ **in the long term** → see **term** ■ **to go a long way** → see **way**

**❹ long** /lɔ́ŋ/ (**longs, longing, longed**) V-T/V-I If you **long for** something, you want it very much. ❑ *Steve longed for his old life.* ❑ *I'm longing to meet her.* ● **long|ing** (**longings**) N-VAR ❑ *She never lost the longing for her own home and country.* [from Old English]

**long-distance** ■ ADJ **Long-distance** is used to describe travel between places that are far apart. ❑ *Trains are best for long-distance travel.* ■ ADJ **Long-distance** is used to describe communication that takes place between people who are far apart. ❑ *...a long-distance phone call.*

**lon|gev|ity** /lɒndʒévɪti/ N-UNCOUNT **Longevity** is long life. [FORMAL] ❑ *I asked him what was the secret of his longevity.* [from Late Latin]

**lon|gi|tude** /lɒndʒɪtud/ (**longitudes**) N-VAR The **longitude** of a place is its distance to the west or east of a line passing through Greenwich, England. Compare **latitude**. [from Latin]
→ see **globe**

**lon|gi|tu|di|nal wave** /lɒndʒɪtudᵊnᵊl wéɪv/ (**longitudinal waves**) N-COUNT **Longitudinal waves** are waves such as sound waves in which the material that the waves are passing through moves in the same direction as the waves. Compare **transverse wave**. [TECHNICAL]

**long-lasting** (**longer-lasting**) also **long-lasting** ADJ Something that is **long-lasting** lasts for a long time. ❑ *...the long-lasting effects of the infection.*

**long-lost** ADJ You use **long-lost** to describe someone or something that you have not seen for a long time. ❑ *...a reunion with her long-lost sister.*

**long-range** ADJ A **long-range** plan or prediction relates to a period extending a long time into the future. ❑ *...the need for long-range planning.*

**long|shore cur|rent** /lɔ́ŋʃɔr kɜ́rənt/ (**longshore currents**) N-COUNT A **longshore current** is an ocean current that flows close to, and parallel to, the shore. [TECHNICAL]

**long|shore|man** /lɔ́ŋʃɔrmən/ (**longshoremen**) N-COUNT A **longshoreman** is a person who works in the docks, loading and unloading ships.

**long-standing** ADJ A **long-standing** situation has existed for a long time. ❑ *They resolved their long-standing dispute over money.*

**long-suffering** ADJ Someone who is **long-suffering** patiently puts up with a lot of trouble or unhappiness. ❑ *He went back to his loyal, long-suffering wife.*

**long-time** ADJ You use **long-time** to describe something that has existed or been a particular thing for a long time. ❑ *...long-time sweethearts.*

## look

**❶ USING YOUR EYES OR YOUR MIND**
**❷ APPEARANCE**

**❶ look** /lʊk/ (**looks, looking, looked**) **1** V-I If you **look** in a particular direction, you direct your eyes there in order to see what is there. ❑ *I looked down the hallway.* ❑ *If you look, you'll see a lake.* ● **Look** is also a noun. ❑ *Lucille took a last look in the mirror.* **2** V-I If you **look for** something or someone, you try to find them. ❑ *I'm looking for a child.* ❑ *I looked everywhere for ideas.* ● **Look** is also a noun. ❑ *Go and have another look.* **3** V-I If you **look at** a subject, problem, or situation, you examine it, consider it, or judge it. ❑ *Next term we'll be looking at the Second World War.* ❑ *Anne Holker looks at ways of making changes to your home.* ❑ *Brian learned to look at her with new respect.* ● **Look** is also a noun. ❑ *...a quick look at the morning newspapers.* **4** CONVENTION You say **look** when you want someone to pay attention to you because you are going to say something important. ❑ *Look, I'm sorry. I didn't mean it.* **5** V-T/V-I You can use **look** to draw attention to a particular situation, person, or thing, for example because you find it very surprising, significant, or annoying. ❑ *Look at the time! We've got to go.* ❑ *Look at how many people watch television and how few read books.* ❑ *Look what you've done!* **6** V-I If something such as a building or window **looks** somewhere, it has a view of a particular place. ❑ *The apartment looks over a park.* **7** EXCLAM If you say or shout **"look out!"** to someone, you are warning them that they are in danger. ❑ *"Look out!" somebody shouted, as the truck started to roll toward the sea.* [from Old English] **8** to **look** someone **in the eye** → see **eye**

▶ **look after 1** PHR-VERB If you **look after** someone or something, you do what is necessary to keep them healthy, safe, or in good condition. ❑ *I love looking after the children.* **2** PHR-VERB If you **look after** something, you are responsible for it and deal with it. ❑ *The farm manager looks after the day-to-day business.*

▶ **look around** PHR-VERB If you **look around** or **look round** a building or place, you walk round it and look at the different parts of it. ❑ *She left Annie looking around the store.*

▶ **look back** PHR-VERB If you **look back**, you think about things that happened in the past. ❑ *Looking back, I am surprised how easy it was.*

▶ **look down on** PHR-VERB To **look down on** someone means to consider that person to be inferior or unimportant, usually when this is not true. ❑ *They looked down on me because I wasn't successful.*

▶ **look forward to** PHR-VERB If you **look forward to** something that is going to happen, you want it to happen because you think you will enjoy it. ❑ *He was looking forward to working with the new manager.*

▶ **look into** PHR-VERB If you **look into** something, you find out about it. ❑ *He once looked into buying his own island.*

▶ **look on** PHR-VERB If you **look on** while something happens, you watch it happening without taking part yourself. ❑ *Local people looked on in silence as he walked past.*

▶ **look on** or **look upon** PHR-VERB If you **look on** or **look upon** someone or something in a particular way, you think of them in that way. ❑ *I looked upon him as a friend.* ❑ *A lot of people look on it like that.*

▶ **look out** → see **look ❶7**

▶ **look out for** PHR-VERB If you **look out for** something, you pay attention so that you notice it if or when it occurs. ❑ *Look out for special deals.*

▶ **look round** → see **look around**

▶ **look through** PHR-VERB If you **look through** a book, a magazine, or a group of things, you get an idea of what is in it by examining a lot of the items in it. ❑ *Peter started looking through the mail at once.*

▶ **look to** PHR-VERB If you **look to** someone or something for a particular thing, you expect or hope that they will provide it. ❑ *The nation looks to them for help.*

▶ **look up 1** PHR-VERB If you **look up** a fact or a piece of information, you find it out by looking in something such as a reference book or a list. ❑ *I looked your address up in the phone book.* **2** PHR-VERB If you **look** someone **up**, you visit them after not having seen them for a long time. ❑ *I'll look him up when I'm in New York.*

▶ **look up to** PHR-VERB If you **look up to** someone, especially someone older than you, you respect and admire them. ❑ *A lot of the younger girls look up to you.*

**❷ look** /lʊk/ (**looks, looking, looked**) **1** V-LINK You use **look** when describing the appearance of a person or thing or the impression that they give. ❑ *Sheila was looking sad.* ❑ *In time, owners begin to look like their dogs.* ❑ *He looked as if he was going to smile.* **2** N-SING If someone or something has a particular **look**, they have a particular appearance or expression. ❑ *She had the look of someone with a secret.* ❑ *The kitchen has a country look.* **3** N-PLURAL When you refer to someone's **looks**, you are referring to how beautiful or ugly they are. ❑ *I never chose friends just because of their looks.* **4** V-LINK You use **look** when indicating what you think will happen in the future or how a situation seems to you. ❑ *He had lots of time to think about the future, and it didn't look good.* ❑ *It looks like we're going to win.* ❑ *The 90 degree heat looks like it will return for the weekend.* **5** PHRASE You use expressions such as **by the look of him** and **by the looks of it** when you want to indicate that you are giving an opinion based on the appearance of someone or something. ❑ *He was not a well man by the look of him.* **6** PHRASE If you **don't like the look of** something or someone, you feel that they may be dangerous or cause problems. ❑ *I don't like the look of those clouds.* [from Old English]

**look|out** /lʊkaʊt/ (**lookouts**) **1** N-COUNT A **lookout** is a place from which you can see clearly in all directions. ❑ *Soldiers looked down from their lookout post.* **2** N-COUNT A **lookout** is someone who is watching for danger in order to warn other people about it. ❏ *One of them acted as a lookout.*

**loom** /lum/ (**looms, looming, loomed**) **1** V-I If something **looms over** you, it appears as a large or unclear shape, often in a frightening way. ❏ *She loomed over me, pale and gray.* **2** V-I If a worrying or threatening situation or event **is looming**, it seems likely to happen soon. ❏ *Another economic crisis is looming.* ❏ *The threat of war looms ahead.* **3** N-COUNT A **loom** is a machine that is used for weaving thread into cloth. [Senses 1 and 2 from East Frisian. Sense 3 from Old English.]

**loom**

**loony** /luni/ (**loonies**) **1** N-COUNT If you refer to someone as a **loony**, you mean that they behave in a way that seems crazy, strange, or eccentric. Some people consider this use offensive. [INFORMAL] ❏ *At first they all thought I was a loony.* **2** ADJ If you describe someone's behavior or ideas as **loony**, you mean that they seem mad, strange, or eccentric. Some people consider this use offensive. [INFORMAL] ❏ *She's as loony as her brother!* [from Old French]

**loop** /lup/ (**loops, looping, looped**) **1** N-COUNT A **loop** is a curved or circular shape in something long, for example, in a piece of string. ❏ *...a loop of garden hose.* **2** V-T If you **loop** something such as a piece of rope around an object, you tie a length of it in a loop around the object, for example, in order to fasten it to the object. ❏ *He looped the rope over the wood.* **3** V-I If something **loops** somewhere, it goes there in a circular direction that makes the shape of a loop. ❏ *The enemy was looping around the south side.* **4** PHRASE If someone is **in the loop**, they are part of a group of people who make decisions about important things, or they know about these decisions. If they are **out of the loop**, they do not make or know about important decisions. [INFORMAL] ❏ *I think that the vice president was in the loop.*

**loop|hole** /luphoul/ (**loopholes**) N-COUNT A **loophole** in the law is a small mistake which allows people to do something that would otherwise be illegal. ❏ *A loophole in the law meant that many businesses were not paying enough tax.*

**loose** /lus/ (**looser, loosest**) **1** ADJ Something that is **loose** is not firmly held or fixed in place. ❏ *If a tooth feels very loose, your dentist may recommend that it be taken out.* ❏ *Two wooden beams came loose from the ceiling.* ● **loose|ly** ADV ❏ *Tim held his hands loosely in front of his belly.* **2** ADJ If people or animals break **loose** or are set **loose**, they are no longer held, tied, or kept somewhere and can move around freely. ❏ *They tried to stop her but she broke loose.* **3** ADJ Clothes that are **loose** are somewhat large and do not fit closely. ❏ *...a loose shirt.* ● **loose|ly** ADV ❏ *A scarf hung loosely round his neck.* **4** ADJ A **loose** grouping, arrangement, or organization is flexible rather than strictly controlled or organized. ❏ *Murray and Alison came to some sort of loose arrangement.* ● **loose|ly** ADV ❏ *...a loosely-organized group of criminals.* **5** PHRASE If a person or an animal is **on the loose**, they are free because they have escaped from a person or place. ❏ *A dangerous criminal is on the loose after escaping from jail.* [from Old Norse] **6** → see also **lose**

**Thesaurus** *loose* Also look up :

ADJ. slack, wobbly **1**
free **2**
baggy **3**

**loose end** (**loose ends**) N-COUNT A **loose end** is part of a story, situation, or crime that has not yet been explained. ❏ *There are some annoying loose ends in the movie.*

**loose-fitting** also **loose fitting** ADJ **Loose-fitting** clothes are somewhat large and do not fit tightly on your body. ❏ *...a pair of loose-fitting black pants.*

**loos|en** /lusᵊn/ (**loosens, loosening, loosened**) **1** V-T If someone **loosens** restrictions or laws, for example, they make them less strict or severe. ❏ *It looks like the government will loosen controls on the newspapers.* ● **loos|en|ing** N-SING ❏ *...the loosening of trade restrictions.* **2** V-T/V-I If your clothing or something that is tied or fastened **loosens**, or you **loosen** it, you undo it slightly so that it is less tight or less firmly held in place. ❏ *He reached up to loosen the scarf around his neck.*
▸ **loosen up** **1** PHR-VERB If a person or situation **loosens up**, they become more relaxed and less tense. ❏ *Relax, smile; loosen up.* **2** PHR-VERB If you **loosen up** your body, or if it **loosens up**, you do simple exercises to get your muscles ready for a difficult physical activity, such as running or playing sports. ❏ *Squeeze your foot with both hands to loosen up tight muscles.*

**loot** /lut/ (**loots, looting, looted**) V-T/V-I If people **loot** stores or houses, or if they **loot** things from them, they steal things from them, for example, during a war or riot. ❏ *People started breaking windows and looting shops.* ❏ *The men looted food supplies.* ❏ *People came into the city to look for food and to loot.* ● **loot|ing** N-UNCOUNT ❏ *There has been rioting and looting.* ● **loot|er** (**looters**) N-COUNT ❏ *Looters took thousands of dollars' worth of food.* [from Hindi]

**lop|sided** /lɒpsaɪdɪd/ ADJ Something that is **lopsided** is uneven because one side is lower or heavier than the other. ❏ *His suit had shoulders that made him look lopsided.*

**lord** /lɔrd/ (**lords**) **1** N-COUNT; N-TITLE A **lord** is a man who has a high rank in the nobility, for example, an earl, a viscount, or a marquis. ❏ *She married a lord.* **2** N-PROPER In the Christian church, people refer to God and to Jesus Christ as the **Lord**. ❏ *She prayed now. "Lord, help me to find courage."* [from Old English]

**lore** /lɔr/ N-UNCOUNT The **lore** of a particular country or culture is its traditional stories and history. ❏ *The Book of the Sea was full of sailors' lore.* [from Old English]

**lose** /luz/ (**loses, losing, lost**) **1** V-T/V-I If you **lose** a contest, a fight, or an argument, someone defeats you. ❏ *The Golden Bears lost three games this season.* ❏ *The government lost the argument.* ❏ *No one likes to lose.* **2** V-T If you **lose** something, you do not know where it is, for example, because you have forgotten where you put it. ❏ *I lost my keys.* **3** V-T You say that you **lose** something when you no longer have it because it has been taken away from you. ❏ *I lost my job when the company moved to another state.* ❏ *He lost his license for six months.*

**4** V-T If someone **loses** a quality, characteristic, attitude, or belief, they no longer have it. ❑ *He lost all sense of reason.* **5** V-T If someone or something **loses** heat, their temperature becomes lower. ❑ *Babies lose heat much faster than adults.* **6** V-T If you **lose** blood or fluid from your body, it leaves your body so that you have less of it. ❑ *The victim lost a lot of blood.* **7** V-T If you **lose** weight, you become less heavy, and usually look thinner. ❑ *I lost a lot of weight.* **8** V-T If someone **loses** their life, they die. ❑ *192 people lost their lives in the disaster.* **9** V-T If you **lose** a close relative or friend, they die. ❑ *My Grandma lost her brother in the war.* **10** V-T If you **lose** time, something slows you down so that you do not make as much progress as you hoped. ❑ *Police lost time in the early part of the investigation.* **11** V-T If you **lose** an opportunity, you do not take advantage of it. ❑ *If you don't do it soon, you're going to lose your opportunity.* ❑ *They did not lose the opportunity to say what they thought.* **12** V-T If a business **loses** money, it earns less money than it spends, and is therefore in debt. [BUSINESS] ❑ *His stores might lose millions of dollars.* **13** → see also **lost** **14** PHRASE If you **lose** your **way**, you become lost when you are trying to go somewhere. ❑ *The men lost their way in a storm.* [from Old English] **15** to **lose face** → see **face** **16** to **lose** your **head** → see **head** **17** to **lose sight of** → see **sight** **18** to **lose** your **temper** → see **temper** **19** to **lose track of** → see **track** **20** → see also **miss**

▶ **lose out** PHR-VERB If you **lose out**, you suffer a loss or disadvantage because you have not succeeded in what you were doing. ❑ *We both lost out.* ❑ *Laura lost out to Tom.*

> **Usage** lose and loose
>
> Be careful not to write *loose* when you mean *lose*. *Lose* means that you no longer have something, and *loose* describes something that is not held firmly or attached. *Loose* rhymes with *goose*, while *lose* rhymes with *shoes*: *You might lose your dog if you let him run loose.*

los|er /lúzər/ (losers) **1** N-COUNT The **losers** of a game, contest, or struggle are the people who are defeated or beaten. ❑ *...the losers of this year's Super Bowl.* **2** PHRASE If someone is a **good loser**, they accept that they have lost a game or contest without complaining. If someone is a **bad loser**, they hate losing and complain about it. ❑ *I try to be a good loser.* [from Old English]

loss /lɔs/ (losses) **1** N-VAR **Loss** is the fact of no longer having something or having less of it than before. ❑ *...loss of sight.* ❑ *...hair loss.* **2** N-UNCOUNT The **loss** of a relative or friend is their death. ❑ *They talked about the loss of Thomas.* **3** N-UNCOUNT **Loss** is the feeling of sadness you experience when someone or something you like is taken away from you. ❑ *...feelings of loss and grief.* **4** N-COUNT A **loss** is the disadvantage you suffer when a valuable and useful person or thing leaves or is taken away. ❑ *His death was a great loss to his family.* ❑ *...a terrible loss of human life.* **5** N-VAR If a business makes a **loss**, it earns less than it spends. ❑ *...the company's continuing losses.* **6** PHRASE If you say that you are **at a loss**, you mean that you do not know what to do in a particular situation. ❑ *I was at a loss for what to do next.* [from Old English] → see **diet, disaster**

> **Word Partnership** Use *loss* with :
>
> N. loss **of appetite**, **blood** loss, loss **of control**, **hair** loss, **hearing** loss, loss **of income**, loss **of a job**, **memory** loss, **weight** loss **1**
>
> ADJ. **great/huge/substantial** loss **1** – **4** **tragic** loss **2** **3** **net** loss **5**

lost /lɔst/ **1** **Lost** is the past tense and past participle of **lose**. **2** ADJ If you are **lost** or if you get **lost**, you do not know where you are or are unable to find your way. ❑ *I realized I was lost.* **3** ADJ If something is **lost**, or you cannot find it. ❑ *...a lost book.* ❑ *His pen was lost under the sheets of paper.* **4** ADJ If you feel **lost**, you feel very uncomfortable because you are in an unfamiliar situation. ❑ *He remembered feeling very lost at the funeral.* [from Old English]

> **Thesaurus** lost Also look up :
>
> ADJ. adrift **2** missing **3**

lost and found **1** N-SING **Lost and found** is the place where lost property is kept. **2** ADJ **Lost-and-found** things are things which someone has lost and which someone else has found.

lot /lɒt/ (lots) **1** QUANT **A lot of** something or **lots of** it is a large amount of it. ❑ *A lot of our land is used to grow crops.* ❑ *He drank lots of milk.* ● **Lot** is also a pronoun. ❑ *I like to be in a town where there's lots going on.* ❑ *I learned a lot from him.* **2** ADV **A lot** means to a great extent or degree. ❑ *Matthew goes out quite a lot.* ❑ *I like you, a lot.* **3** N-COUNT You can use **lot** to refer to a set or group of things or people. ❑ *He bought two lots of shares in the company.* **4** N-SING You can refer to a specific group of people as a particular **lot**. [INFORMAL] ❑ *Our grandchildren will think that we were a boring lot.* **5** N-COUNT A **lot** is a small area of land that belongs to a person or company. ❑ *Oil was discovered under their lot.* **6** → see also **parking lot** **7** N-COUNT A **lot** in an auction is one of the objects or groups of objects that are being sold. ❑ *They want to sell the furniture as one lot.* **8** PHRASE If people **draw lots** to decide who will do something, they each take a piece of paper from a container. One or more pieces of paper is marked, and the people who take marked pieces are chosen. ❑ *They drew lots to decide who would finish second and third.* [from Old English]

> **Usage** lot
>
> Both *a lot* and *lots* mean "very many," "a large number," or "a large amount," and both can be followed by a singular or plural verb, depending on what is being talked about: *Lots/A lot of people are here. A lot* is also an adverb: *I like him a lot.*

loth /loʊθ/ → see **loath**

lo|tion /loʊʃ³n/ (lotions) N-VAR A **lotion** is a liquid that you use to clean, improve, or protect your skin or hair. ❑ *...suntan lotion.* [from Old French]

lot|tery /lɒtəri/ (lotteries) **1** N-COUNT A **lottery** is a type of gambling game in which people buy numbered tickets. Several numbers are then chosen, and the people who have those numbers on their tickets win a prize. ❑ ...the national lottery. **2** N-SING If you describe something as **a lottery**, you mean that what happens depends entirely on luck or chance. ❑ The stockmarket is a lottery. [from Old French]

| Word Link | er ≈ more : bigger, louder, taller |
|---|---|

| Word Link | est ≈ most : greatest, kindest, loudest |
|---|---|

**loud** /laʊd/ (**louder, loudest**) **1** ADJ If a noise is **loud**, the level of sound is very high and it can be easily heard. Someone or something that is **loud** produces a lot of noise. ❑ There was a loud bang. ❑ His voice was harsh and loud. ● **Loud** is also an adverb. ❑ He turned the volume on the television up very loud. ● **loud|ly** ADV ❑ His footsteps sounded loudly in the hall. **2** ADJ If you describe something, especially a piece of clothing, as **loud**, you dislike it because it has very bright colors or very large, bold patterns which look unpleasant. ❑ He wore gold chains and loud clothes. **3** PHRASE If you say or read something **out loud**, you say it or read it so that it can be heard, rather than just thinking it. ❑ Parts of the book made me laugh out loud. [from Old English]

**Word Partnership** Use *loud* with :

| N. | loud **bang**, loud **crash**, loud **explosion**, loud **music**, loud **noise**, loud **voice 1** |
|---|---|
| ADJ. | loud **and clear 1** |
| V. | **laugh out** loud, **read out** loud, **say** something **out** loud, **think out** loud |

**lounge** /laʊndʒ/ (**lounges, lounging, lounged**) **1** N-COUNT In a hotel, club, or other public place, a **lounge** is a room where people can sit and relax. ❑ Afternoon tea is served in the hotel lounge. **2** N-COUNT In an airport, a **lounge** is a very large room where people can sit and wait for aircraft to arrive or leave. ❑ ...the departure lounge. **3** V-I If you **lounge** somewhere, you sit or lie there in a relaxed or lazy way. ❑ They ate and drank and lounged in the shade.

**louse** /laʊs/ (**lice**) N-COUNT **Lice** are small insects that live on the bodies of people or animals. [from Old English]

**lousy** /laʊzi/ (**lousier, lousiest**) **1** ADJ If you describe something as **lousy**, you mean that it is of very bad quality or that you do not like it. [INFORMAL] ❑ He blamed Fiona for a lousy weekend. ❑ At Billy's Café, the food is lousy. **2** ADJ If you describe someone as **lousy**, you mean that they are very bad at something they do. [INFORMAL] ❑ I was a lousy secretary. **3** ADJ If you feel **lousy**, you feel very ill. [INFORMAL] ❑ I wasn't actually sick but I felt lousy. [from Old English]

**lout** /laʊt/ (**louts**) N-COUNT If you describe a man or boy as a **lout**, you are critical of them because they behave in an impolite or aggressive way. ❑ Louts shouted at the visiting players. [from Old English]

**lov|able** /lʌvəbʰl/ ADJ If you describe someone as **lovable**, you mean that they have attractive qualities, and are easy to like. ❑ His shyness makes him even more lovable. [from Old English]

**love** /lʌv/ (**loves, loving, loved**) **1** V-T If you **love** someone, you feel romantically or sexually attracted to them, and they are very important to you. ❑ Oh, Amy, I love you. **2** N-UNCOUNT **Love** is a very strong feeling of affection toward someone who you are romantically or sexually attracted to. ❑ In the four years since we married, our love has grown stronger. ❑ ...a old-fashioned love story. **3** V-T You say that you **love** someone when their happiness is very important to you, so that you behave in a kind and caring way toward them. ❑ You'll never love anyone the way you love your baby. **4** N-UNCOUNT **Love** is the feeling that a person's happiness is very important to you, and the way you show this feeling in your behavior toward them. ❑ ...my love for my children. **5** V-T If you **love** something, you like it very much. ❑ I love food, I love cooking and I love eating. ❑ They love to be in the outdoors. **6** V-T You can say that you **love** something when you consider that it is important and want to protect or support it. ❑ I love my country. **7** N-UNCOUNT **Love** is a strong liking for something, or a belief that it is important. ❑ I love taking photographs. ❑ a love of literature. **8** V-T If you **would love to** have or do something, you very much want to have it or do it. ❑ I would love to be thinner. ❑ I would love a hot bath. **9** NUM In tennis, **love** is a score of zero. ❑ He beat Thomas Muster three sets to love. **10** CONVENTION You can use expressions such as **love**, **love from**, and **all my love**, followed by your name, as an informal way of ending a letter to a friend or relative. ❑ ...with love from Grandma. **11** → see also **loving 12** PHRASE If you **fall in love with** someone, you start to be in love with them. ❑ I fell in love with him because he was so kind. [from Old English]

→ see Word Web: **love**
→ see **emotion**

**Word Web** love

Until the Middle Ages, **romance** was not an important part of **marriage**. Parents decided who their children would marry. The social class and political connections of a future **spouse** were very important. No one expected a couple to **fall in love**. However, during the Middle Ages, poets and musicians began to write about love in a new way. These **romantic** poems and songs describe a new type of courtship. In them, the man **woos** a woman for her **affection**. This is the basis for the modern idea of a romantic **bond** between **husband** and **wife**.

**love af|fair** (**love affairs**) N-COUNT A **love affair** is a romantic and usually sexual relationship between two people who love each other but who are not married or living together. ❏ *The love affair lasted almost five years.*

**love life** (**love lives**) N-COUNT Someone's **love life** is the part of their life that consists of their romantic and sexual relationships. ❏ *His love life was complicated.*

**love|ly** /lʌvli/ (**lovelier, loveliest**) ADJ If you describe someone or something as **lovely**, you mean that they are very beautiful and therefore pleasing to look at or to listen to. ❏ *You look lovely, Marcia.* ❏ *He had a lovely voice.* [from Old English]

**love|making** /lʌvmeɪkɪŋ/ N-UNCOUNT **Lovemaking** refers to sexual activities that take place between two people, especially between people who love each other.

**lov|er** /lʌvər/ (**lovers**) **1** N-COUNT Someone's **lover** is someone who they are having a sexual relationship with but are not married to. ❏ *Every Thursday she met her lover Leon.* **2** N-COUNT If you are a **lover** of something such as animals or the arts, you enjoy them very much and take great pleasure in them. ❏ *She is a great lover of horses.* [from Old English]

**lov|ing** /lʌvɪŋ/ **1** ADJ Someone who is **loving** feels or shows love to other people. ❏ *...a loving husband.* ● **lov|ing|ly** ADV ❏ *Brian gazed lovingly at Mary.* **2** ADJ **Loving** actions are done with great enjoyment and care. ❏ *The house has been decorated with loving care.* ● **lov|ing|ly** ADV ❏ *...lovingly-prepared food.* [from Old English]

**low** /loʊ/ (**lower, lowest, lows**) **1** ADJ Something that is **low** measures only a short distance from the bottom to the top, or from the ground to the top. ❏ *...the low garden wall.* ❏ *...the low hills of the country.* **2** ADJ If something is **low**, it is close to the ground, to sea level, or to the bottom of something. ❏ *He bumped his head on the low beams.* ❏ *It was late afternoon and the sun was low in the sky.* **3** ADJ You can use **low** to indicate that something is small in amount or that it is at the bottom of a particular scale. You can use phrases such as **in the low 80s** to indicate that a number or level is less than 85 but not as little as 80. ❏ *...low incomes.* ❏ *They are still living on very low incomes.* **4** ADJ **Low** is used to describe people who are not considered to be very important or who are near the bottom of a particular scale or system. ❏ *...a soldier of low rank.* **5** N-COUNT If something reaches a **low** of a particular amount or degree, that is the smallest it has ever been. ❏ *Prices dropped to a low of about $1.12.* **6** ADJ If the quality or standard of something is **low**, it is very poor. ❏ *...low-quality work.* ❏ *The hospital was criticized for its low standard of care.* **7** ADJ If you have a **low** opinion of someone or something, you disapprove of them or dislike them. ❏ *...his low opinion of rap music.* **8** ADJ A **low** sound or noise is deep and quiet. ❏ *Her voice was so low he couldn't hear it.* **9** ADJ A light that is **low** is not bright or strong. ❏ *Their*

eyesight is poor in low light. **10** ADJ If a radio, oven, or light is on **low**, it has been adjusted so that only a small amount of power, heat, or light is produced. ❏ *She turned her radio on low.* ❏ *We keep the light on low beside her bed.* **11** ADJ If you are **low**, you are depressed. [INFORMAL] ❏ *She tried to make him smile when he was feeling low.* [from Old Norse] **12** → see also **lower 13** **low profile** → see **profile**

**low-end** ADJ **Low-end** products, especially electronic products, are the least expensive of their kind. ❏ *...a low-end laser printer.*

**low|er** /loʊər/ (**lowers, lowering, lowered**) **1** ADJ You can use **lower** to refer to the bottom one of a pair of things. ❏ *She bit her lower lip.* ❏ *...the lower of the two holes.* **2** V-T If you **lower** something, you move it slowly downward. ❏ *They lowered the coffin into the grave.* ❏ *Chris lowered himself into the chair.* **3** V-T If you **lower** something, you make it less in amount, degree, value, or quality. ❏ *The Central Bank lowered interest rates.* ● **low|er|ing** N-UNCOUNT ❏ *...the lowering of the retirement age.* [from Old Norse] **4** → see also **low**

**low|er class** (**lower classes**) also **lower-class** N-COUNT Some people use **the lower class** or **the lower classes** to refer to the division of society that they consider to have the lowest social status. ❏ *Education offers the lower classes better job opportunities.* ● **Lower class** is also an adjective. ❏ *...lower-class families.*

**low|er man|tle** N-SING The **lower mantle** is the part of the Earth's interior that lies between the upper mantle and the outer core.

**low-impact** ADJ **Low-impact** exercise does not put a lot of stress on your body.

**low-key** ADJ If you say that something is **low-key**, you mean that it is on a small scale rather than involving a lot of activity or being made to seem impressive or important. ❏ *...a low-key wedding.*

**low|ly** /loʊli/ (**lowlier, lowliest**) ADJ If you describe someone or something as **lowly**, you mean that they are low in rank, status, or importance. ❏ *...lowly officials pretending to be important.* [from Old Norse]

**low-maintenance** also **low maintenance** ADJ If you describe something or someone as **low-maintenance**, you mean that they require very little time, money, or effort. ❏ *...a small, low-maintenance yard.*

**low-rise** (**low-rises**) ADJ **Low-rise** buildings are modern buildings which have only a few stories. ❏ *...low-rise apartment buildings.* ● **Low-rise** is also a noun. ❏ *...a mix of low-rises and town houses.*

**low tide** (**low tides**) N-VAR At the coast, **low tide** is the time when the sea is at its lowest level because the tide is out.

**loy|al** /lɔɪəl/ ADJ Someone who is **loyal** remains firm in their friendship or support for a person or thing. ❏ *They stayed loyal to the Republican party.* ● **loy|al|ly** ADV ❏ *They loyally supported their leader.* [from Old French] → see **hero**

**loy|al|ty** /lɔɪəlti/ (**loyalties**) **1** N-UNCOUNT **Loyalty** is the quality of staying firm in your friendship or support for someone or something. ❏ *I believe in family loyalty.* **2** N-COUNT **Loyalties** are feelings of friendship, support, or duty toward someone or something. ❏ *She had developed strong* *loyalties to the Manet family.* [from Old French]

**LP** /ɛl piː/ (**LPs**) N-COUNT An **LP** is a vinyl disk which usually has about 25 minutes of music or speech on each side. **LP** is an abbreviation for "long-playing record."

**LPN** /ɛl pi ɛn/ (**LPNs**) N-COUNT An **LPN** is a nurse who is trained to provide patients with basic care under the supervision of a doctor or a registered nurse. **LPN** is an abbreviation for "licensed practical nurse." □ *She'll become an LPN after graduating next March.*

**LSAT** /ɛlsæt/ (**LSATs**) N-PROPER The **LSAT** is an examination which is often taken by students who wish to enter a law school. **LSAT** is an abbreviation for "Law School Admission Test." □ *These students are preparing to take their LSAT.*

**lub|ri|cant** /luːbrɪkənt/ (**lubricants**) N-COUNT A **lubricant** is a substance which you put on the surfaces or parts of something, especially something mechanical, to make the parts move smoothly. [from Latin]

**lu|bri|cate** /luːbrɪkeɪt/ (**lubricates, lubricating, lubricated**) V-T If you **lubricate** something such as a part of a machine, you put a substance such as oil on it so that it moves smoothly. [FORMAL] □ *Paint the front door and lubricate the handle.*
● **lu|bri|ca|tion** /luːbrɪkeɪʃən/ N-UNCOUNT □ *Use a small amount of oil for lubrication.* [from Latin]

**Word Link** luc ≈ light : hallucination, lucid, translucent

**lu|cid** /luːsɪd/ ■ ADJ **Lucid** writing or speech is clear and easy to understand. □ *...his lucid explanation of the work.* ● **lu|cid|ly** ADV □ *He can present difficult subjects lucidly.* ● **lu|cid|ity** /lusɪdɪti/ N-UNCOUNT □ *His writing has great lucidity.* ■ ADJ If someone is **lucid**, they are thinking clearly again after a period of illness or confusion. [FORMAL] □ *He wasn't very lucid and didn't quite know where he was.* ● **lu|cid|ity** N-UNCOUNT □ *The pain lessened in the night, but so did his lucidity.* [from Latin]

**luck** /lʌk/ (**lucks, lucking, lucked**) ■ N-UNCOUNT **Luck** or **good luck** is success or good things that happen to you, that do not come from your own abilities or efforts. □ *I knew I needed a bit of luck to win.* □ *We are having no luck with the weather.* ■ N-UNCOUNT **Bad luck** is lack of success or bad things that happen to you, that have not been caused by yourself or other people. □ *I had a lot of bad luck during the first half of this season.* ■ CONVENTION You can say "**Bad luck**" or "**Hard luck**" to someone when you want to express sympathy to them. [INFORMAL] □ *Bad luck, man, just bad luck.* ■ CONVENTION If you say "**Good luck**" or "**Best of luck**" to someone, you are telling them that you hope they will be successful in something they are trying to do. [INFORMAL] □ *He kissed her on the cheek. "Best of luck!"* ■ PHRASE You can say someone **is in luck** when they are in a situation where they can have what they want or need. □ *You're in luck. The doctor's still here.* [from Middle Dutch]

▸ **luck out** PHR-VERB If you **luck out**, you get some advantage or are successful because you have good luck. □ *Was he born to be successful, or did he just luck out?*

**Word Partnership** Use *luck* with :

V. **bring** *someone* luck, **need a little** luck, **need some** luck, **push** *your* luck, **try** *your* luck, **wish** *someone* luck ■ **have any/bad/better/good/no** luck ■ ■

ADJ. **dumb** luck, **good** luck, **just** luck, **pure** luck, **sheer** luck ■

**luck|i|ly** /lʌkɪli/ ADV You add **luckily** to a statement to indicate that it is good that a particular thing happened or is true. □ *Luckily, we both love football.* [from Middle Dutch]

**lucky** /lʌki/ (**luckier, luckiest**) ■ ADJ You say that someone is **lucky** when they have something that is very desirable or when they are in a very desirable situation. □ *I am luckier than most people round here. I have a job.* □ *He is very lucky to be alive.* ■ ADJ Someone who is **lucky** seems to always have good luck. □ *Some people are born lucky, aren't they?* ■ ADJ If you describe an action or experience as **lucky**, you mean that it was good or successful, and that it happened by chance and not as a result of planning or preparation. □ *I got the answer right, but it was just a lucky guess.* ■ ADJ A **lucky** object is something that people believe helps them to be successful. □ *He says this pair of green socks is lucky.* ■ PHRASE If you say that someone **will be lucky to** do or get something, you mean that they are very unlikely to do or get it. □ *You'll be lucky if you get any breakfast.* □ *Those remaining in work will be lucky to get a pay increase.* [from Middle Dutch]

**Word Partnership** Use *lucky* with :

V. **be** lucky, **feel** lucky, **get** lucky, **lucky to get** *something*, **lucky to have** *something* ■

ADV. **lucky enough**, **pretty** lucky, **really** lucky, **so** lucky ■

N. **lucky break**, **lucky guess** ■

**lu|cra|tive** /luːkrətɪv/ ADJ A **lucrative** activity, job, or business deal is very profitable. □ *...his lucrative career as a filmmaker.* [from Old French]

**lu|di|crous** /luːdɪkrəs/ ADJ If you describe something as **ludicrous**, you are emphasizing that you think it is foolish, unreasonable, or unsuitable. □ *It was ludicrous to think that we could keep the visit a secret.* ● **lu|di|crous|ly** ADV □ *The prices are ludicrously low.* [from Latin]

**lug** /lʌg/ (**lugs, lugging, lugged**) V-T If you **lug** a heavy or awkward object somewhere, you carry it with difficulty. [INFORMAL] □ *Nobody wants to lug around cases full of clothes.* [of Scandinavian origin]

**lug|gage** /lʌgɪdʒ/ (**luggage racks**) N-UNCOUNT **Luggage** is the suitcases and bags that you take with you when you travel. □ *Leave your luggage in the hotel.* → see **hotel**

**lug|gage rack** N-COUNT A **luggage rack** is a shelf for putting luggage on, in a vehicle such as a train or bus.

**luke|warm** /luːkwɔrm/ ■ ADJ Something, especially a liquid, that is **lukewarm** is only slightly warm. □ *Wash your face with lukewarm water.*

luggage

**2** ADJ If you describe a person or their attitude as **lukewarm**, you mean that they are not showing much enthusiasm or interest. ❑ *Their offer received a lukewarm response.* [from Old English]

**lull** /lʌl/ (**lulls, lulling, lulled**) **1** N-COUNT A **lull** is a period of quiet or calm in a longer period of activity or excitement. ❑ *There was a lull in the excitement.* **2** V-T If you **are lulled into** feeling safe, someone or something causes you to feel safe at a time when you are not safe. ❑ *It is easy to be lulled into a false sense of security.* ❑ *I was lulled into thinking no one would notice.* [from Middle Low German]

**lum|ber** /lʌmbər/ (**lumbers, lumbering, lumbered**) **1** N-UNCOUNT **Lumber** consists of trees and large pieces of wood that have been roughly cut up. **2** V-I If someone or something **lumbers** from one place to another, they move there very slowly and clumsily. ❑ *He lumbered back to his chair.* [from Swedish dialect]
→ see **forest**

**lumber|man** /lʌmbərmən/ (**lumbermen**) N-COUNT A **lumberman** is a man who sells timber.

**lumber|yard** /lʌmbəryɑrd/ (**lumberyards**) also **lumber yard** N-COUNT A **lumberyard** is a place where wood is stored and sold.

**lu|mi|nous** /lumɪnəs/ ADJ Something that is **luminous** shines or glows in the dark. ❑ *...the luminous dial on the clock.* [from Latin]

**lump** /lʌmp/ (**lumps, lumping, lumped**) **1** N-COUNT A **lump** of something is a solid piece of it. ❑ *...a lump of wood.* **2** N-COUNT A **lump** on or in your body is a small, hard swelling that has been caused by an injury or an illness. ❑ *I've got a lump on my shoulder.* [from Early Dutch] **3** → see also **lump sum**

▸ **lump together** PHR-VERB If a number of different people or things **are lumped together**, they are considered as a group rather than separately. ❑ *Policemen, bankers and butchers are all lumped together in one group.*

**lump sum** (**lump sums**) N-COUNT A **lump sum** is an amount of money that is paid as a large amount on a single occasion rather than as smaller amounts on several separate occasions. ❑ *...a tax-free lump sum of $50,000.*

**lumpy** /lʌmpi/ (**lumpier, lumpiest**) ADJ Something that is **lumpy** contains lumps or is covered with lumps. ❑ *When rice isn't cooked properly it is lumpy.* [from Dutch]

**lu|nar** /lunər/ ADJ **Lunar** means relating to the moon. ❑ *...the lunar landscape.* [from Latin]
→ see **eclipse**

**lu|nar eclipse** (**lunar eclipses**) N-COUNT A **lunar eclipse** is an occasion when the Earth is between the sun and the moon, so that for a short time you cannot see part or all of the moon. Compare **solar eclipse**.

**lu|nar mod|ule** (**lunar modules**) N-COUNT A **lunar module** is a part of a spacecraft that is designed to separate from the rest of the spacecraft and land on the moon.

**lu|na|tic** /lunətɪk/ (**lunatics**) **1** N-COUNT If you describe someone as a **lunatic**, you think they behave in a dangerous, stupid, or annoying way. [INFORMAL] ❑ *Her friends think she's a lunatic.* **2** ADJ If you describe someone's behavior or ideas as **lunatic**, you think they are very foolish and possibly dangerous. ❑ *By now, I knew this was a lunatic plan.* [from Old French]

**lunch** /lʌntʃ/ (**lunches, lunching, lunched**) **1** N-VAR **Lunch** is the meal that you have in the middle of the day. ❑ *Shall we meet somewhere for lunch?* ❑ *He did not enjoy business lunches.* **2** V-I When you **lunch**, you have lunch, especially at a restaurant. [FORMAL] ❑ *Only very rich people can afford to lunch at the Mirabelle.*
→ see **meal**

---

**Word Partnership** Use *lunch* with :

| | |
|---|---|
| V. | **bring your** lunch, **break for** lunch, **buy** *someone* lunch, **eat** lunch, **go** *somewhere* **for** lunch, **go to have** lunch, **have** lunch, **pack** a lunch, **serve** lunch **1** |
| ADJ. | **free** lunch, **good** lunch, **hot** lunch, **late** lunch **1** |

---

**lunch|eon** /lʌntʃən/ (**luncheons**) N-COUNT A **luncheon** is a formal lunch, for example, to celebrate an important event or to raise money for charity. ❑ *A luncheon for former U.N. staff was held in Vienna.* [from Middle English]

**lunch meat** (**lunch meats**) N-VAR **Lunch meat** is meat that you eat in a sandwich or salad, and that is usually cold and either sliced or formed into rolls.

**lunch|room** /lʌntʃrum/ (**lunchrooms**) also **lunch room** N-COUNT A **lunchroom** is the room in a school or at work where you buy and eat your lunch.

**lunch|time** /lʌntʃtaɪm/ (**lunchtimes**) also **lunch time** N-VAR **Lunchtime** is the period of the day when people have their lunch. ❑ *Could we meet at lunchtime?*

**lung** /lʌŋ/ (**lungs**) N-COUNT Your **lungs** are the two organs inside your chest which fill with air when you breathe in. ❑ *...lung disease.* [from Old English]
→ see **amphibian, cardiovascular system, donor, respiration**

**lunge** /lʌndʒ/ (**lunges, lunging, lunged**) V-I If you **lunge** in a particular direction, you move in that direction suddenly and clumsily. ❑ *She lunged at me, grabbing my arms.* ● **Lunge** is also a noun. ❑ *The attacker made a lunge for Tom when he answered the door.* [from French]

**lurch** /lɜrtʃ/ (**lurches, lurching, lurched**) V-I If you **lurch**, you make a sudden movement, especially forward, in an uncontrolled way. ❑ *Henry lurched across the room and tripped over a chair.* ● **Lurch** is also a noun. ❑ *The car took a lurch forward.*

**lure** /lʊər/ (**lures, luring, lured**) **1** V-T To **lure** someone means to trick them into a particular place or to trick them into doing something that they should not do. ❑ *They lured him into a trap.* **2** N-COUNT A **lure** is an attractive quality that something has, or something that you find attractive. ❑ *The lure of country life is as strong as ever.* [from Old French]

**lu|rid** /lʊərɪd/ **1** ADJ If you say that something is **lurid**, you are critical of it because it involves a lot of violence or shocking detail. ❑ *...lurid tales of spy networks.* **2** ADJ If you describe something as **lurid**, you do not like it because it is very brightly colored. ❑ *She painted her toe nails a lurid red.* [from Latin]

**lurk** /lɜrk/ (**lurks, lurking, lurked**) **1** V-I If someone **lurks** somewhere, they hide there, usually because they intend to do something bad. ❏ *He thought he saw someone lurking outside.* **2** V-I If something such as a danger, doubt, or fear **lurks** somewhere, it exists but is not obvious or easily recognized. ❏ *Hidden dangers lurk everywhere.* [from Middle Dutch]

**lus|cious** /lʌʃəs/ ADJ **Luscious** food is juicy and very good to eat. ❏ *…a small tree with luscious fruit.*

**lush** /lʌʃ/ (**lusher, lushest**) ADJ **Lush** fields or gardens have a lot of very healthy grass or plants. ❏ *…Ohio's lush lawns.* [from Old French]

**lust** /lʌst/ N-UNCOUNT **Lust** is a feeling of strong sexual desire for someone. ❏ *Their relationship was a mixture of lust and friendship.* **2** N-UNCOUNT A **lust** for something is a very strong and eager desire to have it. ❏ *…his lust for life* [from Old English]

**lus|ter** /lʌstər/ N-UNCOUNT **Luster** is gentle shining light that is reflected from a surface, for example from polished metal. [from Old French]

**Lu|ther|an** /luθərən/ (**Lutherans**) **1** ADJ **Lutheran** means belonging or relating to a Protestant church, founded on the teachings of Martin Luther, which emphasizes the importance of faith and the authority of the Bible. ❏ *…the Lutheran church.* ❏ *…a Lutheran hymn.* **2** N-COUNT A **Lutheran** is a member of the Lutheran church. ❏ *…a school run by Lutherans.* [after Martin Luther (1483–1546), the German leader of the Protestant Reformation]

**luxu|ri|ous** /lʌgʒʊəriəs/ **1** ADJ If you describe something as **luxurious**, you mean that it is very comfortable and expensive. ❏ *…a luxurious hotel.* ● **luxu|ri|ous|ly** ADV ❏ *The dining-room is luxuriously furnished.* **2** ADJ **Luxurious** means feeling or expressing great pleasure and comfort. ❏ *She lay back in the hot bath with a luxurious sigh.* ● **luxu|ri|ous|ly** ADV ❏ *Liz laughed, stretching luxuriously.* [from Old French]

**luxu|ry** /lʌkʃəri, lʌgʒə-/ (**luxuries**) **1** N-UNCOUNT **Luxury** is very great comfort, especially among beautiful and expensive surroundings. ❏ *He leads a life of luxury.* **2** N-COUNT A **luxury** is something expensive which is not necessary but which gives you pleasure. ❏ *A week by the sea is a luxury they can no longer afford.* **3** ADJ A **luxury** item is something expensive which is not necessary but which gives you pleasure. ❏ *…luxury leather goods.* **4** N-SING A **luxury** is a pleasure which you do not often have the opportunity to

enjoy. ❏ *Hot baths are my favorite luxury.* [from Old French]

| **Thesaurus** | *luxury* | Also look up : |
|---|---|---|
| N. | comfort, splendor **1** | |
| | extra, extravagance, nonessential, treat **2** **3** | |

**ly|ing** /laɪɪŋ/ **Lying** is the present participle of **lie**. [from Old English]

**lymph** /lɪmf/ N-UNCOUNT **Lymph** is a liquid that flows through your body and contains cells that help your body to fight infection. [TECHNICAL] [from Latin]

**lym|phat|ic sys|tem** /lɪmfætɪk sɪstəm/ (**lymphatic systems**) N-COUNT The **lymphatic system** is the network of tissues and organs in your body that produces white blood cells and carries lymph. [TECHNICAL]

**lym|phat|ic ves|sel** (**lymphatic vessels**) N-COUNT **Lymphatic vessels** are thin tubes that carry lymph through your body. [TECHNICAL]

**lymph ca|pil|lary** (**lymph capillaries**) N-COUNT **Lymph capillaries** are tiny tubes that join together to form lymphatic vessels. [TECHNICAL]

**lymph node** /lɪmf noʊd/ (**lymph nodes**) N-COUNT **Lymph nodes** are small bean-shaped masses of tissue that help to protect the body against infection by killing bacteria. [TECHNICAL]

**lym|pho|cyte** /lɪmfəsaɪt/ (**lymphocytes**) N-COUNT **Lymphocytes** are white blood cells that are involved in fighting infection and disease. [TECHNICAL] [from Latin]

**lynch** /lɪntʃ/ (**lynches, lynching, lynched**) V-T If an angry crowd of people **lynch** someone, they kill that person by hanging them, without letting them have a trial, because they believe that that person has committed a crime. ❏ *They broke into his house and threatened to lynch him.* [from Virginia]

**lyr|ic** /lɪrɪk/ (**lyrics**) **1** ADJ **Lyric** poetry is written in a simple and direct style, and usually expresses personal emotions such as love. **2** N-COUNT The **lyrics** of a song are its words. ❏ *…a Broadway opera with lyrics by Langston Hughes.* [from Latin]

**lyri|cal** /lɪrɪkəl/ ADJ Something that is **lyrical** is poetic and romantic. ❏ *Wilson's writing is lyrical and passionate.* [from Latin]

**lyso|some** /laɪsəsoʊm/ (**lysosomes**) N-COUNT A **lysosome** is a part of a cell that contains enzymes which can break down many different substances. [TECHNICAL] [from Greek]

# Mm

**ma'am** /mæm/ N-VOC People sometimes say **ma'am** as a polite way of addressing a woman whose name they do not know, especially in the American South. ❑ *Would you repeat that please, ma'am?*

**ma|ca|bre** /məkɑbrə/ ADJ You describe something such as an event or story as **macabre** when it is strange and horrible or upsetting, usually because it involves death or injury. ❑ *Police have made a macabre discovery.* [from Old French]

**maca|ro|ni and cheese** /mækərouni ən tʃiz/ N-UNCOUNT **Macaroni and cheese** is a dish made from macaroni pasta and a cheese sauce.

**ma|chete** /məʃɛti/ (**machetes**) N-COUNT A **machete** is a large knife with a broad blade. [from Spanish]

**ma|chine** /məʃin/ (**machines**) **1** N-COUNT A **machine** is a piece of equipment that uses electricity or an engine in order to do a particular kind of work. ❑ *I put the coin in the machine.* **2** N-COUNT You can use **machine** to refer to a large and well-controlled system or organization. ❑ *...the New York political machine.* [from French] → see **dairy**

**ma|chine gun** (**machine guns**) N-COUNT A **machine gun** is a gun which fires a lot of bullets one after the other very quickly. ❑ *Attackers fired machine guns at the car.*

**ma|chin|ery** /məʃinəri/ **1** N-UNCOUNT You can use **machinery** to refer to machines in general, or machines that are used in a factory or on a farm. ❑ *...machinery for making cars.* **2** N-SING The **machinery** of a government or organization is the system that it uses to deal with things. ❑ *...the machinery of the legal system.* [from French]

**ma|chin|ist** /məʃinɪst/ (**machinists**) N-COUNT A **machinist** is a person whose job is to operate a machine, especially in a factory. ❑ *His father is a machinist in a car factory.* [from French]

**macho** /mɑtʃou/ ADJ You use **macho** to describe men who are very conscious and proud of their masculinity. [INFORMAL] ❑ *He tried to be macho by opening the bottle with his teeth.* [from Spanish]

**mack|er|el** /mækərəl, mækrəl/ (**mackerel**) N-VAR A **mackerel** is a sea fish with a dark, patterned back. ❑ *The boat was fishing for mackerel.* ● **Mackerel** is this fish eaten as food. ❑ *...piles of smoked mackerel.* [from Old French]

**macro|eco|nom|ics** /mækrouɛkənɒmɪks, -ik-/ also **macro-economics** N-UNCOUNT **Macroeconomics** is the branch of economics that is concerned with the major, general features of a country's economy, such as the level of inflation, employment, or interest rates. ❑ *He teaches macroeconomics.* ● **macro|eco|nom|ic** ADJ ❑ *The goal of macroeconomic policy is a growing economy.*

**mad** /mæd/ (**madder, maddest**) **1** ADJ If you say that someone is **mad**, you mean that they are very angry. [INFORMAL] ❑ *You're just mad at me because I'm late.* **2** ADJ You use **mad** to describe people or things that you think are very foolish. ❑ *You'd be mad to work with him again.* ● **mad|ness** N-UNCOUNT ❑ *It is madness to spend $1,000 on a dress.* **3** ADJ Someone who is **mad** has a mental illness which makes them behave in a strange way. ❑ *She was afraid of going mad.* ● **mad|ness** N-UNCOUNT ❑ *What or who caused his madness?* **4** ADJ If you are **mad about** something or someone, you like them very much. [INFORMAL] ❑ *I'm mad about sports.* ❑ *He's mad about you.* **5** ADJ **Mad** behavior is wild and uncontrolled. ❑ *There was a mad rush to get out of the building.* ● **mad|ly** ADV ❑ *People on the streets were waving madly.* **6** PHRASE If you say that someone or something **drives** you **mad**, you mean that you find them extremely annoying. [INFORMAL] ❑ *The noise was driving me mad.* **7** PHRASE If you do something **like mad**, you do it very energetically or enthusiastically. [INFORMAL] ❑ *He was training for the competition like mad.* [from Old English] **8** → see also **madly**

**mad|am** /mædəm/ also **Madam** N-VOC **Madam** is a very formal and polite way of addressing a woman whose name you do not know. ❑ *Good morning, madam.* [from Old French]

**mad|den** /mæd³n/ (**maddens, maddening, maddened**) V-T To **madden** a person or animal means to make them very angry. ❑ *The animals were maddening farmers by eating their crops.* ● **mad|den|ing** /mæd³nɪŋ/ ADJ ❑ *He treats me like a child, which is maddening.* ● **mad|den|ing|ly** ADV ❑ *The computer is maddeningly slow.* [from Old English]

m

**made** /meɪd/ **1** Made is the past tense and past participle of **make**. **2** ADJ If something is **made of** or **made out of** a particular substance, that substance was used to build it. ☐ *The top of the table is made of glass.* [from Old English]

**made to or|der** also **made-to-order** ADJ If something is **made to order**, it is made according to your special requirements. ☐ *The dining room table was made to order.* ☐ *...a maker of made-to-order jewelry.*

**mad|ly** /mædli/ ADV You can use **madly** to indicate that one person loves another a great deal. ☐ *She is madly in love with him.* [from Old English]

**Ma|fia** /mɑfiə/ (**Mafias**) also **mafia** **1** N-PROPER The **Mafia** is a criminal organization that makes money illegally, especially by threatening people and dealing in drugs. ☐ *Italian television does not ignore the Mafia.* **2** N-COUNT You can use **mafia** to refer to an organized group of people who you disapprove of because they use unfair or illegal means in order to get what they want. ☐ *I will not let the fashion mafia tell me what to wear.* [from Sicilian]

**maf|ic** /mæfɪk/ ADJ **Mafic** rocks are igneous rocks that contain a lot of heavier elements such as magnesium and iron. Compare **felsic**. [TECHNICAL]

**mag** /mæg/ (**mags**) N-COUNT A **mag** is the same as a magazine. [INFORMAL] ☐ *...a music mag for girls.*

**maga|zine** /mægəzin, -zin/ (**magazines**) **1** N-COUNT A **magazine** is a monthly or weekly publication which contains articles, stories, photographs, and advertisements. ☐ *Her face is often on the cover of magazines.* **2** N-COUNT In an automatic gun, the **magazine** is the part that contains the bullets. ☐ *The took the empty magazine out of his gun.* [from French]
→ see **library**

**mag|got** /mægət/ (**maggots**) N-COUNT **Maggots** are creatures that look like very small worms and turn into flies. [from Old Norse]

**mag|ic** /mædʒɪk/ **1** N-UNCOUNT **Magic** is the power to use supernatural forces to make impossible things happen, such as making people disappear or controlling events in nature. ☐ *They believe in magic.* **2** ADJ You use **magic** to describe something that does things, or appears to do things, by magic. ☐ *...the magic ingredient in the face cream that helps to keep skin looking smooth.* **3** N-UNCOUNT **Magic** is the art and skill of performing tricks to entertain people, for example by making things appear and disappear. ☐ *He loves performing magic tricks.* **4** N-UNCOUNT The **magic**

of something is a special mysterious quality which makes it seem wonderful and exciting. ☐ *Children love the magic of the movies.* ● **Magic** is also an adjective. ☐ *We had some magic moments together.* [from Old French]

| **Thesaurus** | *magic* | Also look up : |
|---|---|---|
| N. | enchantment, illusion, sorcery, witchcraft **1** <br> appeal, beauty, charm **4** | |

**magi|cal** /mædʒɪkəl/ **1** ADJ Something that is **magical** seems to use magic or to be able to produce magic. ☐ *...the story of a little boy who has magical powers.* ● **magi|cal|ly** /mædʒɪkli/ ADV ☐ *You can't magically turn back the clock to a happier time.* **2** ADJ You can say that a place or object is **magical** when it has a special mysterious quality that makes it seem wonderful and exciting. ☐ *Bermuda is a magical place to get married.* [from Old French]

**ma|gi|cian** /mədʒɪʃ³n/ (**magicians**) N-COUNT A **magician** is a person who entertains people by doing magic tricks. [from Old French]

**mag|is|trate** /mædʒɪstreɪt/ (**magistrates**) N-COUNT A **magistrate** is an official who acts as a judge in law courts which deal with minor crimes or disputes. ☐ *The magistrate did not believe our story.* [from Latin]

**mag|ma** /mægmə/ N-UNCOUNT **Magma** is molten rock that is formed in very hot conditions inside the earth. [TECHNICAL] ☐ *The volcano threw magma and ash into the air.* [from Latin]
→ see **volcano**

| **Word Link** | *magn ≈ great :* magnate, magnificent, magnitude |
|---|---|

**mag|nate** /mægneɪt, -nɪt/ (**magnates**) N-COUNT A **magnate** is someone who has earned a lot of money from a particular business or industry. ☐ *...a shipping magnate.* [from Late Latin]

**mag|net** /mægnɪt/ (**magnets**) N-COUNT A **magnet** is a piece of iron or other material which attracts iron toward it. ☐ *The children used a magnet to find objects made of iron.* [from Latin]
→ see Word Web: **magnet**

**mag|net|ic** /mægnɛtɪk/ **1** ADJ If something metal is **magnetic**, it acts like a magnet. ☐ *...iron-rich magnetic minerals.* **2** ADJ You use **magnetic** to describe tapes and other objects which have a coating of a magnetic substance and contain coded information that can be read by computers or other machines. ☐ *...an ID card with a magnetic strip.* **3** ADJ If you describe something or someone as **magnetic**, you mean that they are very

| **Word Web** | magnet |
|---|---|

**Magnets** have a north **pole** and a south pole. One side has a **negative charge** and the other side has a **positive** charge. The negative side of a magnet **attracts** the positive side of another magnet. Two sides that have the same charge will **repel** each other. The earth itself is a huge magnet, with a North Pole and a South Pole. A **compass** uses a **magnetized** needle to indicate direction. The "north" end of the needle always points toward the earth's North Pole.

M

attractive to people because they have unusual, powerful, and exciting qualities. ❑ *The park has a beauty that is magnetic.* [from Latin]

**mag|net|ic dec|li|na|tion** /mægnɛtɪk dɛklɪneɪʃ°n/ (**magnetic declinations**) N-VAR **Magnetic declination** is the angle between the magnetic North Pole of the Earth and the geographic North Pole. [TECHNICAL]

**mag|net|ic field** (**magnetic fields**) N-COUNT A **magnetic field** is an area around a magnet, or something functioning as a magnet, in which the magnet's power to attract things is felt.

**mag|net|ic pole** (**magnetic poles**) N-COUNT The **magnetic poles** of a magnet are the two areas at opposite ends of the magnet where the magnetic field is strongest. The **magnetic poles** of the Earth are the two areas near the North and South Poles where the Earth's magnetic field is strongest.

**mag|net|ic re|ver|sal** (**magnetic reversals**) N-VAR **Magnetic reversal** is the process which causes the Earth's magnetic North Pole and its magnetic South Pole to reverse their positions. [TECHNICAL]

**mag|net|ism** /mægnɪtɪzəm/ ■ N-UNCOUNT **Magnetism** is the natural power of some objects and substances, especially iron, to attract other objects toward them. ❑ *...his research in electricity and magnetism.* ■ N-UNCOUNT Someone or something that has **magnetism** has unusual, powerful, and exciting qualities which attract people to them. ❑ *Her personal magnetism makes people want to work with her.* [from Latin]

**Word Link** *magn ≈ great : magnate, magnificent, magnitude*

**mag|nifi|cent** /mægnɪfɪsənt/ ADJ Something or someone that is **magnificent** is extremely good, beautiful, or impressive. ❑ *...a magnificent country house.* ● **mag|nifi|cence** N-UNCOUNT ❑ *...the magnificence of the Swiss mountains.* ● **mag|nifi|cent|ly** ADV ❑ *The team played magnificently.* [from Latin]

**mag|ni|fy** /mægnɪfaɪ/ (**magnifies, magnifying, magnified**) ■ V-T To **magnify** an object means to make it appear larger than it really is, by means of a special lens or mirror. ❑ *This telescope magnifies images 11 times.* ❑ *A lens magnified the picture so it was like looking at a large TV screen.* ● **mag|ni|fi|ca|tion** /mægnɪfɪkeɪʃ°n/ N-UNCOUNT ❑ *Some creatures are too small to see without magnification.* ■ V-T To **magnify** something means to increase its effect, size, loudness, or intensity. ❑ *The space in the church seemed to magnify every sound.* [from Old French]

**mag|ni|tude** /mægnɪtud/ (**magnitudes**) ■ N-UNCOUNT The **magnitude** of something is its great size, scale, or importance. ❑ *An operation of this magnitude is going to be difficult.* ■ N-COUNT A star's **magnitude** is its brightness. [from Latin] ■ → see also **absolute magnitude, apparent magnitude**

**mag|pie** /mægpaɪ/ (**magpies**) N-COUNT A **magpie** is a large black and white bird with a long tail.

**ma|hoga|ny** /məhɒɡəni/ N-UNCOUNT **Mahogany** is a dark reddish-brown wood that is used to make furniture. ❑ *...mahogany tables and chairs.*

**maid** /meɪd/ (**maids**) N-COUNT A **maid** is a woman who cleans rooms in a hotel or private house. ❑ *A maid brought me breakfast.*

**maid|en** /meɪd°n/ (**maidens**) ■ N-COUNT A **maiden** is a young girl or woman. [LITERARY] ❑ *...beautiful maidens.* ■ ADJ The **maiden** voyage or flight of a ship or aircraft is the first official journey that it makes. ❑ *In 1912, the Titanic sank on her maiden voyage.* [from Old English]

**maid of hon|or** (**maids of honor**) N-COUNT A **maid of honor** is the chief bridesmaid at a wedding.

**mail** /meɪl/ (**mails, mailing, mailed**) ■ N-SING The **mail** is the public service or system by which letters and packages are collected and delivered. ❑ *Your check is in the mail.* ■ N-UNCOUNT You can refer to letters and packages that are delivered to you as **mail**. ❑ *There was no mail this morning.* ■ V-T If you **mail** something to someone, you send it to them by mail. ❑ *He mailed the documents to journalists.* ❑ *He mailed me the contract.* ■ V-T To **mail** a message to someone means to send it to them by means of e-mail or a computer network. ● **Mail** is also a noun. ❑ *If you have any problems then send me a mail.* [from Old French] ■ → see also **e-mail**

▸ **mail out** PHR-VERB If someone **mails out** things such as letters, leaflets, or bills, they send them to a large number of people at the same time. ❑ *We have mailed out our wedding invitations.*

**Word Partnership** Use *mail* with :

PREP. **by** mail, **in the** mail, **through the** mail ■
N. mail **carrier, fan** mail ■
V. **deliver** mail, **get** mail, **open** mail, **read** mail, **receive** mail, **send** mail ■

**mail|box** /meɪlbɒks/ (**mailboxes**) ■ N-COUNT A **mailbox** is a box outside your house where your letters are delivered. ❑ *The next day there was a letter in her mailbox.* ■ N-COUNT A **mailbox** is a metal box in a public place, where you put letters and small packages to be collected. ❑ *He dropped the letters into the mailbox.* ■ N-COUNT On a computer, your **mailbox** is the file where your e-mail is stored. ❑ *There were 30 new messages in his mailbox.*

**mail|er** /meɪlər/ (**mailers**) ■ N-COUNT A **mailer** is a box, large envelope, or other container for mailing things. ❑ *Put the CD in this mailer and send it back to us.* ■ N-COUNT A **mailer** is a letter advertising something or appealing for money for a particular charity. Mailers are sent out to a large number of people at once. ❑ *Thousands of mailers go straight into the trash.* ■ N-COUNT A **mailer** is a company that sends out mail. ❑ *The group represents mailers who send only a small volume of mail.* [from Old French]

**mail|man** /meɪlmæn/ (**mailmen**) N-COUNT A **mailman** is a man whose job is to collect and deliver letters and packages that are sent by mail.

**mail or|der** N-UNCOUNT **Mail order** is a system of buying and selling goods. You choose them from a catalog, and the company sends them to you by mail. ❑ *The toys are available by mail order.*

**maim** /meɪm/ (**maims, maiming, maimed**) V-T To **maim** someone means to injure them so badly that part of their body is permanently damaged. ❑ *Bombs have maimed and killed many civilians.* [from Old French]

m

**main** /meɪn/ (**mains**) **1** ADJ The **main** thing is the most important one of several similar things in a particular situation. ❑ *The main reason I came was to say sorry.* **2** PHRASE If you say that something is true **in the main**, you mean that it is generally true, although there may be exceptions. ❑ *Nurses are, in the main, women.* **3** N-COUNT The **mains** are the pipes which supply gas or water to buildings, or which take sewage away from them. ❑ *…the water supply from the mains.* [from Old English]

| Thesaurus | main | Also look up : |
|---|---|---|

| ADJ. | chief, major, primary, principal **1** |
|---|---|

**main clause** (**main clauses**) N-COUNT A **main clause** is a clause that can stand alone as a complete sentence. Compare **subordinate clause**.

**main drag** N-SING **The main drag** in a town is its main street. [INFORMAL] ❑ *Michigan Avenue is the town's main drag.*

**main|frame** /meɪnfreɪm/ (**mainframes**) N-COUNT A **mainframe** or **mainframe computer** is a large, powerful computer which can be used by many people at the same time. ❑ *The names of all patients are on the hospital mainframe.*

**main idea** (**main ideas**) N-COUNT The **main idea** of a piece of writing is the most important subject or point of view that it discusses or expresses.

**main|land** /meɪnlænd/ N-SING You can refer to the largest part of a country or continent as **the mainland** when contrasting it with the islands around it. ❑ *She caught a boat to the mainland.*

**main|ly** /meɪnli/ ADV You use **mainly** to say that a statement is true in most cases or to a large extent. ❑ *The African people there were mainly from Senegal.* [from Old English]

**main road** (**main roads**) N-COUNT A **main road** is an important road that leads from one town or city to another. ❑ *Troops had blocked the main road from the airport.*

**main-sequence star** (**main-sequence stars**) N-COUNT A **main-sequence star** is the most common type of star, which gets its energy by converting hydrogen into helium. [TECHNICAL]

**main|stay** /meɪnsteɪ/ (**mainstays**) N-COUNT If you describe something as **the mainstay of** a particular thing, you mean that it is the most basic part of it. ❑ *Fish and rice are the mainstays of the country's diet.*

**main|stream** /meɪnstrim/ (**mainstreams**) N-COUNT People, activities, or ideas that are part of the **mainstream** are regarded as typical, normal, and conventional. ❑ *Some people like to live outside the mainstream.*
→ see **culture**

**Main Street** **1** N-PROPER In small towns in the United States, the street where most of the stores are is often called **Main Street**. **2** N-UNCOUNT **Main Street** is used by journalists to refer to the ordinary people of America who live in small towns rather than big cities or are not very rich. ❑ *This financial crisis had a big impact on Main Street.*

**main|tain** /meɪnteɪn/ (**maintains, maintaining, maintained**) **1** V-T If you **maintain** something, you continue to have it, and do not let it stop or grow weaker. ❑ *France maintained close contacts with Jordan during the Gulf War.* **2** V-T If

you **maintain that** something is true, you state your opinion strongly. ❑ *He maintained that he had not stolen the money.* ❑ *"Not all women want to have children," Jo maintains.* **3** V-T If you **maintain** something **at** a particular rate or level, you keep it at that rate or level. ❑ *She maintained her weight at 150 pounds.* **4** V-T If you **maintain** a road, building, vehicle, or machine, you keep it in good condition by regularly checking it and repairing it when necessary. ❑ *The house costs a lot to maintain.* **5** V-T If you **maintain** someone, you provide them with money and other things that they need. ❑ *…the costs of maintaining a child in college.* [from Old French]

| Thesaurus | maintain | Also look up : |
|---|---|---|

| V. | carry on, continue; (ant.) neglect **1** keep up, look after, protect, repair **4** |
|---|---|

**main|te|nance** /meɪntɪnəns/ **1** N-UNCOUNT The **maintenance** of a building, vehicle, road, or machine is the process of keeping it in good condition by regularly checking it and repairing it when necessary. ❑ *…maintenance work on government buildings.* ❑ *They replaced the window during routine maintenance.* **2** N-UNCOUNT If you ensure the **maintenance of** a state or process, you make sure that it continues. ❑ *…the maintenance of peace in Asia.* **3** N-UNCOUNT **Maintenance** is money that someone gives regularly to another person to pay for the things that the person needs. ❑ *He pays a lot in maintenance for his children.* [from Old French]

**maî|tre d'** /meɪtrədi, meɪtər-/ (**maitre d's, maitres d'**) N-COUNT At a restaurant, the **maitre d'** is the head waiter. ❑ *We found a table and the maitre d' told us that we would be served quickly.*

**ma|jes|tic** /mədʒɛstɪk/ ADJ If you describe something or someone as **majestic**, you think they are very beautiful, dignified, and impressive. ❑ *…a majestic country home.* ● **ma|jes|ti|cal|ly** /mədʒɛstɪkli/ ADV ❑ *The ship sailed majestically in from the Atlantic Ocean.* [from Old French]

**ma|jes|ty** /mædʒɪsti/ (**majesties**) **1** N-VOC; PRON You use majesty in expressions such as **Your Majesty** or **Her Majesty** when you are addressing or referring to a king or queen. ❑ *His Majesty will see you now.* **2** N-UNCOUNT **Majesty** is the quality of being beautiful, dignified, and impressive. ❑ *…the majesty of the mountains.* [from Old French]

| Word Link | major ≈ larger : major, majority, major league |
|---|---|

**ma|jor** /meɪdʒər/ (**majors, majoring, majored**) **1** ADJ You use **major** when you want to describe something that is more important, serious, or significant than other things in a group or situation. ❑ *His family was a major factor in his decision to leave his job.* ❑ *Homelessness is a major problem in some cities.* **2** N-COUNT; N-TITLE; N-VOC A **major** is an officer who is one rank above captain in the United States Army, Air Force, or Marines. ❑ *I was a major in the war, you know.* **3** N-COUNT At a university or college, a student's **major** is the main subject that they are studying. ❑ *"What's your major?" — "Chemistry."* **4** N-COUNT At a university or college, if a student is, for example, a geology **major**, geology is the main subject they are studying. ❑ *She was a history major at the University* of Oklahoma. **5** V-I If a student at a university or college **majors in** a particular subject, that subject is the main one they study. ❑ *He majored in finance at Claremont Men's College in California.* **6** N-PLURAL The **majors** are groups of professional sports teams that compete against each other, especially in baseball. ❑ *I just wanted a chance to play in the majors.* [from Latin]

| Thesaurus | major | Also look up : |
|---|---|---|
| ADJ. | chief, critical, crucial, key, main, principal; (*ant.*) little, minor, unimportant **1** | |

| Word Link | major ≈ larger : major, majority, major league |
|---|---|

**majority** /mədʒɒrɪti/ (**majorities**) **1** N-SING The **majority** of people or things in a group is more than half of them. ❑ *The majority of my patients are women.* **2** PHRASE If a group is **in a majority** or **in the majority**, they form more than half of a larger group. ❑ *Supporters of the proposal are still in the majority.* **3** N-COUNT A **majority** is the difference between the number of votes or seats in a legislature or parliament that the winner gets in an election, and the number of votes or seats that the next person or party gets. ❑ *After the November elections, the Democrats had a majority of 32 seats.* [from Medieval Latin]

| Word Partnership | Use *majority* with : |
|---|---|
| ADJ. | **overwhelming** majority, **vast** majority **1 3** |
| N. | majority **of people**, majority **of the population** **1** majority **leader** **3** |

**major key** N-COUNT In music, the **major key** is based on the major scale, in which the third note is two tones higher than the first.

**major league** (**major leagues**) **1** N-PLURAL The **major leagues** are groups of professional sports teams that compete against each other, especially in baseball. ❑ *At 47, he was the oldest player in the major leagues last season.* **2** ADJ **Major league** means connected with the major leagues in baseball. ❑ *I live in a town with no major league baseball.* **3** ADJ **Major-league** people or institutions are important or successful. ❑ *His first film has major-league stars.*

---

**make**

❶ CARRYING OUT AN ACTION
❷ CAUSING OR CHANGING
❸ CREATING OR PRODUCING
❹ LINK VERB USES
❺ ACHIEVING OR REACHING
❻ PHRASAL VERBS

---

❶ **make** /meɪk/ (**makes, making, made**)

**Make** is used in a large number of expressions which are explained under other words in this dictionary. For example, the expression "to make sense" is explained at "sense."

**1** V-T You can use **make** with a wide range of nouns to indicate that someone performs an action or says something. ❑ *I'd just like to make a comment.* ❑ *I made a few phone calls.* **2** PHRASE If you **make do with** something, you use or have it instead of something else that you do not have, although it is not as good. ❑ *Why make do with a copy if you can afford the real thing?* [from Old English]

❷ **make** /meɪk/ (**makes, making, made**) **1** V-T If something **makes** you do something, it causes you to do it. ❑ *Dirt from the highway made him cough.* ❑ *Her long dress made her look like a movie star.* **2** V-T If you **make** someone do something, you force them to do it. ❑ *You can't make me do anything.* **3** V-T You use **make** to talk about causing someone or something to be a particular thing or to have a particular quality. For example, to **make** someone a star means to cause them to become a star, and to **make** someone angry means to cause them to become angry. ❑ *Home-schooling made me a better person.* ❑ *She made life very difficult for me.* **4** V-T If you **make yourself** understood, heard, or known, you succeed in getting people to understand you, hear you, or know that you are there. ❑ *He was able to make himself understood in Spanish.* **5** V-T If you **make** something **into** something else, you change it in some way so that it becomes that other thing. ❑ *We made our house into a beautiful home.* [from Old English] **6** to **make friends** → see **friend**

❸ **make** /meɪk/ (**makes, making, made**) **1** V-T To **make** something means to produce, construct, or create it. ❑ *She made her own bread every day.* ❑ *Having curtains made can be expensive.* **2** V-T If you **make** a note or list, you write something down in that form. ❑ *Mr. Perry made a note in his book.* **3** V-T If you **make** rules or laws, you decide what these should be. ❑ *The police don't make the laws.* **4** V-T If you **make** money, you get it by working for it, by selling something, or by winning it. ❑ *I think every business's goal is to make money.* **5** N-COUNT The **make** of something such as a car or radio is the name of the company that made it. ❑ *What make of car do you drive?* [from Old English]

| Thesaurus | make | Also look up : |
|---|---|---|
| V. | build, compose, create, fabricate, produce; (*ant.*) destroy ❸ **1** | |

❹ **make** /meɪk/ (**makes, making, made**) **1** V-LINK You can use **make** to say that someone or something has the right qualities for a particular task or role. ❑ *She'll make a good actress, if she gets the right training.* ❑ *You've a very good idea there. It will make a good book.* **2** V-LINK You can use **make** to say what two numbers add up to. ❑ *Four twos make eight.* [from Old English]

❺ **make** /meɪk/ (**makes, making, made**) **1** V-T If someone **makes** a particular team or **makes** a particular high position, they do so well that they are put on that team or get that position. ❑ *The athletes are just happy to make the team.* **2** PHRASE If you **make it** somewhere, you succeed in getting there, especially in time to do something. ❑ *So you did make it to America, after all.* **3** PHRASE If you **make it**, you are successful in achieving something difficult, or in surviving through a very difficult period. ❑ *I believe I have the talent to make it.* [from Old English]

m

**❻ make** /meɪk/ (**makes, making, made**)
▶ **make for** PHR-VERB If you **make for** a place, you move toward it. □ *He made for the door.*
▶ **make of** PHR-VERB If you ask a person what they **make of** something, you want to know what their impression, opinion, or understanding of it is. □ *Nancy wasn't sure what to make of Alexander's apology.*
▶ **make off** PHR-VERB If you **make off**, you leave somewhere as quickly as possible, often in order to escape. □ *They made off in a stolen car.*
▶ **make out** ◼ PHR-VERB If you **make** something **out**, you can see, hear or understand it. □ *I could just make out a tall figure of a man.* □ *She thought she heard a name. She couldn't make it out, though.* □ *I couldn't make out what he was saying.* ◻ PHR-VERB If you **make out that** something is true or **make** something **out to** be true, you try to cause people to believe that it is the case. □ *They were trying to make out that I stole the money.* □ *They made him out to be an awful guy.* ◼ PHR-VERB When you **make out** a check, receipt, or order form, you write all the necessary information on it. □ *I'll make the check out to you and put it in the mail later this afternoon.*
▶ **make up** ◼ PHR-VERB The people or things that **make up** something are the members or parts that form that thing. □ *Women officers make up 13 percent of the police force.* ◻ PHR-VERB If you **make up** something such as a story or excuse, you invent it. □ *It's very unkind of you to make up stories about him.* ◼ PHR-VERB If two people **make up** after a quarrel or disagreement, they become friends again. □ *She came back and they made up.*

**mak|er** /meɪkər/ (**makers**) N-COUNT The **maker** of a something is the person or company that makes it. □ *...Japan's two largest car makers.* [from Old English]

**make|shift** /meɪkʃɪft/ ADJ **Makeshift** things are temporary and usually of poor quality, but they are used because there is nothing better available. □ *Homeless people lived in makeshift shelters.*

**make|up** /meɪkʌp/ ◼ N-UNCOUNT **Makeup** consists of things such as lipstick, eye shadow, and powder which some women put on their faces to make themselves look more attractive. □ *Normally she wore little makeup.* ◻ N-UNCOUNT The **makeup** of something consists of its different parts and the way these parts are arranged. □ *The makeup of the unions has changed a lot.* ◼ N-UNCOUNT **Makeup** consists of things such as lipstick, eye shadow, and powder, and sometimes hairstyles,

which an actor wears on stage.
→ see Word Web: **makeup**
→ see **theater**

**mak|ing** /meɪkɪŋ/ (**makings**) ◼ N-UNCOUNT The **making** of something is the act or process of producing or creating it. □ *...Salamon's book about the making of the movie.* ◻ PHRASE If you describe a person or thing as something **in the making**, you mean that they are going to become known or recognized as that thing. □ *Her drama teacher thinks Julie is a star in the making.* ◼ PHRASE If something **is the making of** a person or thing, it is the reason that they become successful or become very much better than they used to be. □ *This new school might be the making of him.* ◼ PHRASE If you say that a person or thing **has the makings of** something, you mean it seems possible or likely that they will become that thing, as they have the necessary qualities. □ *Godfrey had the makings of a successful journalist.* ◼ PHRASE If you say that something such as a problem you have is **of** your **own making**, you mean you have caused or created it yourself. □ *Some of his problems are of his own making.* [from Old English]

> **Word Link**    **mal ≈ bad : malaria, malfunction, malicious**

**ma|laria** /məlɛəriə/ N-UNCOUNT **Malaria** is a serious disease carried by mosquitoes, which causes periods of fever. [from Italian]

**male** /meɪl/ (**males**) ◼ N-COUNT A **male** is a person or animal that belongs to the sex that cannot lay eggs or have babies. □ *...males and females of all ages.* ● **Male** is also an adjective. □ *...male dancers.* □ *...male cows.* ◻ ADJ **Male** means relating to, belonging to, or affecting men rather than women. □ *...male unemployment.* [from Old French]
→ see **reproduction**

**mal|func|tion** /mælfʌŋkʃən/ (**malfunctions, malfunctioning, malfunctioned**) V-I If a machine or part of the body **malfunctions**, it fails to work properly. [FORMAL] □ *Something made the dishwasher malfunction.* ● **Malfunction** is also a noun. □ *There was a computer malfunction.*

**mal|ice** /mælɪs/ N-UNCOUNT **Malice** is behavior that is intended to harm people or their reputations, or cause them embarrassment and upset. □ *His voice was full of malice.* [from Old French]

---

**Word Web**    makeup

The women of ancient Egypt were among the first to **wear makeup**. They **applied foundation** to lighten their skin and used kohl as **eye shadow** to darken their eyelids. Greek women used charcoal as an **eyeliner** and rouge on their cheeks. In 14th century Europe, the most popular **cosmetic** was a **powder** made from wheat flour. Women whitened their faces to show their high social class. A light **complexion** meant the woman didn't have to work outdoors. **Cosmetics** containing poisons, such as lead and arsenic, sometimes caused illness and death. Makeup use grew in the early 1900s. For the first time many women could afford to buy mass-produced **lipstick**, **mascara**, and **face powder**.

| **Word Link** | mal ≈ bad : *malaria*, *malfunction*, *malicious* |
|---|---|

**ma|li|cious** /məlɪʃəs/ ADJ **Malicious** words or actions are intended to harm people or their reputation, or to embarrass or upset them. ❑ *They have been spreading malicious lies about us.* ● **ma|li|cious|ly** ADV ❑ *He made jokes about her, but not maliciously.* [from Old French]

**ma|lig|nant** /məlɪgnənt/ ADJ A **malignant** tumor or disease is out of control and likely to cause death. [MEDICAL] ❑ *The lump in her breast was not malignant.* [from Late Latin]

**mall** /mɔl/ (**malls**) N-COUNT A **mall** is a very large, enclosed shopping area. [after The Mall, in St. James's Park, London, England]

**mal|le|able** /mæliəbəl/ **1** ADJ Someone who is **malleable** is easily influenced or controlled by other people. [WRITTEN] ❑ *She was young enough to be malleable.* **2** ADJ A substance that is **malleable** is soft and can easily be made into different shapes. ❑ *Silver is the most malleable of all metals.* ● **mal|le|abil|ity** /mæliəbɪlɪti/ N-UNCOUNT ❑ *Red-hot metals rapidly lose their malleability as they cool.* [from Old French]

**mal|let** /mælɪt/ (**mallets**) N-COUNT A **mallet** is a wooden hammer with a square head. [from Old French]

**mal|nu|tri|tion** /mælnutrɪʃən/ N-UNCOUNT If someone is suffering from **malnutrition**, they are physically weak and extremely thin because they have not eaten enough food. ❑ *Infections are more likely in people suffering from malnutrition.*

**mal|prac|tice** /mælpræktɪs/ (**malpractices**) N-VAR If you accuse someone of **malpractice**, you are accusing them of breaking the law or the rules of their profession. [FORMAL] ❑ *They accused the doctor of malpractice.*

**malt** /mɔlt/ (**malts**) **1** N-UNCOUNT **Malt** is a substance made from grain that is used to make alcoholic drinks. ❑ *When malt is mixed with water it turns into alcohol.* **2** N-COUNT A **malt** is a drink made from malt, milk, ice cream, and other flavorings. ❑ *...a chocolate malt.* [from Old English]

**mama** /mɑmə, məmɑ/ (**mamas**) also **mamma** N-COUNT; N-VOC **Mama** means the same as **mother**. [INFORMAL]

**mam|bo** /mɑmboʊ/ (**mambos**) N-COUNT The **mambo** is a lively dance that comes from Cuba. ❑ *The mambo was very popular in the 1940s and 1950s.* ❑ *...mambo music.* [from American Spanish]

**mam|mal** /mæməl/ (**mammals**) N-COUNT **Mammals** are animals such as humans, dogs, lions, and whales. In general, female mammals give birth to babies rather than laying eggs, and feed their young with milk. [from New Latin]
→ see Word Web: **mammal**
→ see **bat, pet, whale**

**mam|ma|ry** /mæməri/ ADJ **Mammary** means relating to the breasts. [TECHNICAL] [from Latin]

**mam|ma|ry glands** N-COUNT **Mammary glands** are milk-producing glands in mammals. [TECHNICAL]

**mam|mog|ra|phy** /məmɑgrəfi/ N-UNCOUNT **Mammography** is the use of X-rays to examine women's breasts in order to detect cancer. ❑ *Mammography is not always available in poor countries.*

**mam|moth** /mæməθ/ (**mammoths**) **1** ADJ You can use **mammoth** to emphasize that a task or change is very large and needs a lot of effort to achieve. ❑ *...the mammoth task of moving the library.* **2** N-COUNT A **mammoth** was an animal like an elephant, with very large tusks and long hair, that lived a long time ago but no longer exists. [from Russian]

**man** /mæn/ (**men, mans, manning, manned**) **1** N-COUNT A **man** is an adult male human being. ❑ *A young man walked into the room.* ❑ *Both men and women will enjoy this movie.* **2** N-VAR **Man** and **men** are sometimes used to refer to all human beings, including both males and females. Some people dislike this use. ❑ *...when man first arrived in the Americas.* **3** CONVENTION Some people address a man as **my man**. [INFORMAL] ❑ *"Get the guy in the purple shirt." — "All right, my man."* **4** V-T If you **man** something such as a place or machine, you operate it or are in charge of it. ❑ *Two officers manned the aircraft.* ❑ *...the person manning the phone.* [from Old Norse] **5** → see also **manned, no-man's land**
→ see **age, horse**

**man|age** /mænɪdʒ/ (**manages, managing, managed**) **1** V-T If you **manage** an organization, business, or system, or the people who work in it, you are responsible for controlling them. ❑ *Within two years he was managing the store.* **2** V-T If you **manage** time, money, or other resources, you deal with them carefully and do not waste them. ❑ *In a busy world, managing your time is very important.* **3** V-T If you **manage to** do something, especially something difficult, you succeed in doing it. ❑ *Somehow, he managed to persuade Kay to buy a*

---

**Word Web** mammal

Elephants, dogs, mice, and humans all belong to the class of animals called **mammals**. Mammals have live babies rather than laying eggs. The females also feed their **young** with milk from their bodies. Mammals are **warm-blooded** and usually have hair on their bodies. Some, such as the brown bear and the raccoon, are omnivorous—they eat meat and plants. Deer and zebras are herbivorous, living mostly on grass and leaves. Lions and tigers are carnivorous—they eat meat. They must have a supply of large **game** to survive. Mammals have a variety of different types of **limbs**. Monkeys have long arms for climbing. Seals have flippers for swimming.

computer for him. ❑ I managed to pull myself out of the water. **4** V-I If you **manage**, you succeed in coping with a difficult situation. ❑ She managed without medication for three years. [from Italian]

**man|age|able** /ˈmænɪdʒəbᵊl/ ADJ Something that is **manageable** is of a size, quantity, or level of difficulty that people are able to deal with. ❑ We need to reduce the classes to a more manageable size. [from Italian]

**man|aged care** N-UNCOUNT **Managed care** is a method of controlling the cost of medical care by fixing a doctor's fees and limiting a patient's choice of doctors and hospitals.

| Word Link | ment ≈ state, condition : agreement, management, movement |
| --- | --- |

**man|age|ment** /ˈmænɪdʒmənt/ (**managements**) **1** N-UNCOUNT **Management** is the control and organizing of a business or other organization. ❑ The zoo needed better management rather than more money. **2** N-VAR You can refer to the people who control and organize a business or other organization as the **management**. [BUSINESS] ❑ The management is trying hard to keep employees happy. ❑ We need to get more women into top management. [from Italian]

| Word Partnership | Use management with : |
| --- | --- |
| N. | **business** management, **crisis** management, management **skills**, management **style**, **waste** management **1** management **team**, management **training 2** |
| ADJ. | **new** management, **senior** management **2** |

**man|ag|er** /ˈmænɪdʒər/ (**managers**) N-COUNT A **manager** is a person who is responsible for running part of or the whole of a business organization. ❑ The chef, staff, and managers are all Chinese. [from Italian]
→ see **concert**

**mana|ge|rial** /ˌmænɪdʒɪəriəl/ ADJ **Managerial** means relating to the work of a manager. ❑ ...his managerial skills. ❑ ...a managerial career. [from Italian]

**mana|tee** /ˈmænəti/ (**manatees**) N-COUNT A **manatee** is a mammal which lives in the sea and looks like a small whale with a broad, flat tail. [from Spanish]

**man|date** /ˈmændeɪt/ (**mandates, mandating, mandated**) **1** N-COUNT A government's **mandate** is the authority it has to carry out a particular policy or task as a result of winning an election or vote. ❑ The election result gave the new leader a mandate for change. **2** N-COUNT If someone is given a **mandate** to carry out a particular policy or task, they are given the official authority to do it. ❑ The company has a mandate to help their clients. **3** V-T When someone **is mandated to** carry out a particular policy or task, they are given the official authority to do it. [FORMAL] ❑ The organization was mandated to look after the country's blood supplies. **4** V-T To **mandate** something means to make it mandatory. ❑ The law mandates a 40-hour work week. ❑ Congress mandated that all 4th graders take the reading test. [from Latin]

**man|da|tory** /ˈmændətɔri/ ADJ If an action or procedure is **mandatory**, people have to do it, because it is a rule or a law. [FORMAL] ❑ ...the mandatory retirement age of 65. ❑ ...mandatory safety tests. [from Latin]

**man|di|ble** /ˈmændɪbᵊl/ (**mandibles**) N-COUNT A **mandible** is the bone in the lower jaw of a person or animal. [TECHNICAL] [from Old French]

**mane** /meɪn/ (**manes**) N-COUNT The **mane** on a horse or lion is the long, thick hair that grows from its neck. ❑ You can wash the horse's mane at the same time as his body. [from Old English]

**ma|neu|ver** /məˈnuvər/ (**maneuvers, maneuvering, maneuvered**) **1** V-T/V-I If you **maneuver** something into or out of an awkward position, you skillfully move it there. ❑ He maneuvered the car through the narrow gate. ❑ I maneuvered my way among the tables to the back of the restaurant. ● **Maneuver** is also a noun. ❑ The airplanes performed some difficult maneuvers. **2** N-COUNT A **maneuver** is something clever which you do to change a situation to your advantage. ❑ ...dishonest maneuvers to make him sell his house. **3** N-PLURAL Military **maneuvers** are training exercises which involve the movement of soldiers and equipment over a large area. ❑ The army begins maneuvers tomorrow. [from French]

**man|gle** /ˈmæŋgᵊl/ (**mangles, mangling, mangled**) V-T If something **is mangled**, it is crushed or twisted very forcefully, so that it is difficult to see what its original shape was. ❑ My book was mangled when I drove the car over it. [from Norman French]

**man|go** /ˈmæŋgoʊ/ (**mangoes** or **mangos**) N-VAR A **mango** is a large, sweet, yellowish fruit which grows on a tree in hot areas. [from Portuguese]

| Word Link | hood ≈ state, condition : adulthood, childhood, manhood |
| --- | --- |

**man|hood** /ˈmænhʊd/ N-UNCOUNT **Manhood** is the state of being a man rather than a boy. ❑ Fathers must help their sons grow from boyhood to manhood. [from Old English]

**ma|nia** /ˈmeɪniə/ (**manias**) N-COUNT If you say that a person or group has a **mania for** something, you mean that they enjoy it very much or spend a lot of time on it. ❑ The mania for dinosaurs began in the 1800s. [from Late Latin]

**ma|ni|ac** /ˈmeɪniæk/ (**maniacs**) N-COUNT A **maniac** is a crazy person who is violent and dangerous. ❑ The room looked as if a maniac had been in there. [from Late Latin]

**man|ic** /ˈmænɪk/ ADJ If you describe someone as **manic**, you mean that they do things extremely quickly or energetically, often because they are very excited or anxious about something. ❑ He was really manic. ● **man|ic|al|ly** /ˈmænɪkli/ ADV ❑ We cleaned the house manically. [from Greek]

| Word Link | man ≈ hand : emancipate, manacle, manicure |
| --- | --- |

**mani|cure** /ˈmænɪkyʊər/ (**manicures, manicuring, manicured**) V-T If you **manicure** your hands or nails, you care for them by softening your skin and cutting and polishing your nails. ❑ She carefully manicured her long nails. ● **Manicure** is also a noun. ❑ I sometimes have a manicure. [from French]

**mani|fest** /mǽnɪfɛst/ (**manifests, manifesting, manifested**) **1** ADJ If you say that something is **manifest**, you mean that it is clearly true and that nobody would disagree with it if they saw it or considered it. [FORMAL] ❑ ...*the manifest power of prayer.* ● **mani|fest|ly** ADV ❑ *It is manifestly clear that she hates me.* **2** V-T If you **manifest** a particular quality, feeling, or illness, or if it **manifests itself**, it becomes visible or obvious. [FORMAL] ❑ *He manifested health problems when he was a child.* ❑ *The virus needs two weeks to manifest itself.* ● **Manifest** is also an adjective. ❑ *Fear is manifest everywhere.* [from Latin]

**mani|fes|ta|tion** /mǽnɪfɛsteɪʃ°n/ (**manifestations**) N-COUNT A **manifestation of** something is one of the different ways in which it can appear. [FORMAL] ❑ *Different animals have different manifestations of the disease.* [from Latin]

**mani|fes|to** /mǽnɪfɛstoʊ/ (**manifestos** or **manifestoes**) N-COUNT A **manifesto** is a statement published by a person or group of people, especially a political party or a government, in which they say what their aims and policies are. ❑ *The Republicans are preparing their election manifesto.* [from Italian]

**ma|nipu|late** /mənɪpyəleɪt/ (**manipulates, manipulating, manipulated**) **1** V-T If you say that someone **manipulates** people or events, you disapprove of them because they use or control them for their own benefit. ❑ *She was unable to control and manipulate events.* ❑ *She's always manipulating me to give her money.* ● **ma|nipu|la|tion** /mənɪpyəleɪʃ°n/ N-VAR ❑ *Crying can be a form of emotional manipulation.* **2** V-T If you **manipulate** something that requires skill, such as a complicated piece of equipment or a difficult idea, you operate it or process it. ❑ *The technology uses a pen to manipulate a computer.* ● **ma|nipu|la|tion** N-VAR ❑ ...*mathematical manipulations.* [from Latin]

**ma|nipu|la|tive** /mənɪpyəleɪtɪv, -lətɪv/ ADJ If you describe someone as **manipulative**, you disapprove of them because they manipulate people. ❑ *He was cold and manipulative.* [from Latin]

**man|kind** /mǽnkaɪnd/ N-UNCOUNT You can refer to all human beings as **mankind** when considering them as a group. Some people dislike this use. ❑ ...*a better future for all mankind.*

**man|ly** /mǽnli/ (**manlier, manliest**) ADJ If you describe a man's behavior or appearance as **manly**, you approve of it because it shows qualities that are considered typical of a man, such as strength or courage. ❑ *He had strong manly shoulders.* ● **man|li|ness** N-UNCOUNT ❑ *He has no doubts about his manliness.* [from Old English]

**man-made** also **manmade** ADJ **Man-made** things are created or caused by people, rather than occurring naturally. ❑ *Some of the world's problems are man-made.* ❑ ...*man-made lakes.*

**manned** /mǽnd/ ADJ A **manned** vehicle such as a spacecraft has people in it who are operating its controls. ❑ *In thirty years from now, the United States should have a manned spacecraft on Mars.* [from Old English]

**man|ner** /mǽnər/ (**manners**) **1** N-SING The **manner** in which you do something is the way that you do it. ❑ *She smiled again in a friendly manner.* **2** N-SING Someone's **manner** is the way in which they behave and talk when they are

with other people. ❑ *He has a very confident manner.* ● **-mannered** ADJ ❑ ...*a quiet-mannered woman.* **3** N-PLURAL If someone has **good manners**, they are polite and observe social customs. If someone has **bad manners**, they are impolite and do not observe these customs. ❑ *He dressed well and had perfect manners.* [from Norman French]

| **Word Partnership** | Use *manner* with : |
|---|---|
| ADJ. | **effective** manner, **efficient** manner **1** **abrasive** manner, **abrupt** manner, **appropriate** manner, **businesslike** manner, **different** manner, **friendly** manner, **usual** manner **1 2** |

**man|power** /mǽnpaʊər/ N-UNCOUNT Workers are sometimes referred to as **manpower** when they are being considered as a part of the process of producing goods or providing services. ❑ *We need more money and more manpower.*

**man|sion** /mǽnʃ°n/ (**mansions**) N-COUNT A **mansion** is a very large, impressive house. ❑ ...*an eighteenth-century mansion in New Hampshire.* [from Old French]

**man|slaughter** /mǽnslɔtər/ N-UNCOUNT **Manslaughter** is the illegal killing of a person by someone who did not intend to kill them. [LEGAL] ❑ *She was guilty of manslaughter.*

**mantel|piece** /mǽnt°lpis/ (**mantelpieces**) also **mantlepiece** N-COUNT A **mantelpiece** is a shelf over a fireplace. ❑ *There is a glass vase on the mantelpiece.*

**man|tle** /mǽnt°l/ (**mantles**) N-SING In geology, **the mantle** is the part of the earth that lies between the crust and the core. It is divided into the upper mantle and the lower mantle. [TECHNICAL] [from Old French]

**man|tra** /mǽntrə/ (**mantras**) N-COUNT A **mantra** is a word or phrase repeated by Buddhists and Hindus when they meditate, or to help them feel calm. [from Sanskrit]

**manu|al** /mǽnyuəl/ (**manuals**) **1** ADJ **Manual** work is work in which you use your hands or your physical strength. ❑ ...*manual workers.* **2** ADJ **Manual** means operated by hand, rather than by electricity or a motor. ❑ *We used a manual pump to get the water out of the hole.* ● **manu|al|ly** ADV ❑ *We cut the weeds down manually.* **3** N-COUNT A **manual** is a book which tells you how to do something or how a piece of machinery works. ❑ ...*the instruction manual.* [from Old French]

**manu|fac|ture** /mǽnyəfæktʃər/ (**manufactures, manufacturing, manufactured**) **1** V-T To **manufacture** something means to make it in a factory. [BUSINESS] ❑ *The company manufactures plastics.* ● **Manufacture** is also a noun. ❑ ...*the manufacture of steel.* ● **manu|fac|tur|ing** N-UNCOUNT ❑ *Manufacturing in China has increased dramatically.* **2** V-T If you say that someone **manufactures** information, you are criticizing them because they invent information that is not true. ❑ *The criminals had manufactured their story completely.* [from Late Latin]

**manu|fac|tured home** (**manufactured homes**) N-COUNT A **manufactured home** is a house built with parts which have been made in a factory and then quickly put together at the place where the house is located.

**manu|fac|tur|er** /mǽnyəfæktʃərər/ (**manufacturers**) N-COUNT A **manufacturer** is a business or company which makes goods in large quantities. [BUSINESS] ❑ ...the world's largest doll manufacturer. [from Late Latin]
→ see **industry**

**ma|nure** /mənuər/ (**manures**) N-UNCOUNT **Manure** is animal feces that is spread on the ground in order to make plants grow healthy and strong. ❑ We used bags of manure. [from Medieval Latin]

| Word Link | script ≈ writing : manuscript, scripture, transcript |
|---|---|

**manu|script** /mǽnyəskrɪpt/ (**manuscripts**) N-COUNT A **manuscript** is a handwritten or typed document, especially a writer's first version of a book before it is published. ❑ He has seen a manuscript of the book. [from Medieval Latin]

**many** /mɛni/ ❶ DET You use **many** to indicate a large number of people or things. ❑ I don't think many people would argue with that. ❑ Not many films are made in Finland. ● **Many** is also a pronoun. ❑ He made a list of his friends. There weren't many. ● **Many** is also a quantifier. ❑ Why do many of us feel the need to get married? ● **Many** is also an adjective. ❑ His many hobbies include swimming and reading. ❷ ADV You use **many** in expressions such as "not many," "not very many," and "too many" when replying to questions about numbers of things or people. ❑ "How many of their songs were hits?" — "Not very many." ❸ DET You use **many** after "how" to talk and ask questions about numbers or quantities. ❑ How many years have you been here? ● **Many** is also a pronoun. ❑ There were some mistakes, but I'm not sure how many. ❹ PHRASE You use **as many as** before a number to suggest that it is surprisingly large. ❑ As many as 4 million people watched today's parade. [from Old English]

**map** /mǽp/ (**maps, mapping, mapped**) ❶ N-COUNT A **map** is a drawing of a particular area such as a city, a country, or a continent, showing its main features as they would appear if you looked at them from above. ❑ He unfolded the map and put it on the floor. ❷ N-COUNT A **map** is a model or representation of the Earth's surface. [from Medieval Latin]
▶ **map out** PHR-VERB If you **map out** something that you are intending to do, you work out in detail how you will do it. ❑ I went home and mapped out my plan. ❑ Before writing a play he sits down and maps it out.

| Word Partnership | Use map with : |
|---|---|
| ADJ. | **detailed** map ❶ |
| V. | **draw a** map, **look at a** map, **open a** map, **read a** map ❶ |

**map key** (**map keys**) N-COUNT A **map key** is a list which explains the meaning of the symbols and abbreviations used on a map.

**ma|ple** /meɪpəl/ (**maples**) N-VAR A **maple** or a **maple tree** is a tree with five-pointed leaves which turn bright red or gold in the fall. ● **Maple** is the wood of this tree. ❑ ...a solid maple table. [from Old English]

**ma|quette** /mǽkɛt/ (**maquettes**) N-COUNT A **maquette** is a small model of a sculpture.

Sculptors often use maquettes as a preparation for a larger sculpture. [TECHNICAL] [from French]

**mar** /mɑr/ (**mars, marring, marred**) V-T To **mar** something means to spoil or damage it. ❑ A number of problems marred the event. [from Old English]

**mara|thon** /mǽrəθɒn/ (**marathons**) ❶ N-COUNT A **marathon** is a race in which people run a distance of 26 miles, which is about 42 km. ❑ He is running in his first marathon. ❷ ADJ A **marathon** event or task takes a long time and is very tiring. ❑ People make marathon journeys to buy glass ware. [from Greek]

**mar|ble** /mɑrbəl/ (**marbles**) ❶ N-UNCOUNT **Marble** is a type of very hard rock which feels cold when you touch it. Statues and parts of buildings are sometimes made of marble. ❷ N-UNCOUNT **Marbles** is a children's game played with small balls made of colored glass. You roll a ball along the ground and try to hit an opponent's ball with it. ❑ Two boys were playing marbles. ❸ N-COUNT A **marble** is one of the small balls used in the game of marbles. ❑ ...a glass marble. [from Old French]

**march** /mɑrtʃ/ (**marches, marching, marched**) ❶ V-T/V-I When soldiers **march** somewhere, or when a commanding officer **marches** them somewhere, they walk there with very regular steps, as a group. ❑ Some soldiers were marching down the street. ❑ Captain Ramirez marched them off to the main camp. ● **March** is also a noun. ❑ After a short march, the soldiers entered the village. ❷ V-I When a large group of people **march** for a cause, they walk somewhere together in order to express their ideas or to protest about something. ❑ The demonstrators marched through the capital city. ● **March** is also a noun. ❑ Organizers expect 300,000 protesters to join the march. ● **march|er** (**marchers**) N-COUNT ❑ The police arrested several marchers. ❸ V-I If someone **marches** somewhere, they walk there quickly and in a determined way, for example because they are angry. ❑ He marched into the kitchen without knocking. ❹ V-T If you **march** someone somewhere, you force them to walk there with you, for example by holding their arm tightly. ❑ The teacher marched me into the principal's office. ❺ N-SING The **march of** something is its steady development or progress. ❑ The march of technology brings more and more new products. [from Old French]

**March** /mɑrtʃ/ (**Marches**) N-VAR **March** is the third month of the year in the Western calendar. ❑ I flew to Milwaukee in March. ❑ She was born on March 6, 1920. [from Old French]

**mare** /mɛər/ (**mares**) N-COUNT A **mare** is an adult female horse. [from Old English]

**mar|ga|rine** /mɑrdʒərɪn/ (**margarines**) N-VAR **Margarine** is a yellow substance similar to butter that is made from vegetable oil.

**mar|gin** /mɑrdʒɪn/ (**margins**) ❶ N-COUNT A **margin** is the difference between two amounts, especially the difference in the number of votes or points between the winner and the loser in an election or other contest. ❑ They won with a 50-point margin. ❷ N-COUNT The **margin** of a written or printed page is the empty space at the side of the page. ❑ She added her comments in the margin. ❸ N-VAR If there is a **margin** for something in a situation, there is some freedom to choose what to do or decide how to do it. ❑ *There is no margin for error in dangerous sports.* [from Latin]

---

**Word Partnership**    Use *margin* with :

| | |
|---|---|
| ADJ. | **comfortable** margin, **large** margin, **slim** margin ■<br>**narrow** margin, **wide** margin ■ ■ |
| N. | margin **for error** ■ |

---

**mar|gin|al** /mɑrdʒɪnªl/ ADJ If you describe something as **marginal**, you mean that it is small or not very important. ❑ *This is a marginal improvement.* ● **mar|gin|al|ly** /mɑrdʒɪnªli/ ADV ❑ *Sales last year were marginally higher.* [from Latin]

**mari|achi** /mæriɑtʃi/ N-UNCOUNT In Mexico, a **mariachi** band is a small group of musicians who play music in the street. ❑ *My father was a singer in a mariachi band.* ❑ *...joyous mariachi music.* [from Mexican Spanish]

**ma|ri|jua|na** /mæriwɑnə/ N-UNCOUNT **Marijuana** is an illegal drug which can be smoked. [from Mexican Spanish]

**ma|ri|na** /mərinə/ (**marinas**) N-COUNT A **marina** is a small harbor for small boats that are used for leisure. [from Italian]

**mari|nade** /mærineɪd/ (**marinades, marinading, marinaded**) ■ N-COUNT A **marinade** is a sauce of oil, vinegar, spices, and herbs, which you pour over meat or fish before you cook it, in order to add flavor, or to make the meat or fish softer. ❑ *I added a marinade to the fish to give it flavor.* ■ V-T/V-I To **marinade** means the same as to **marinate**. ❑ *Leave the meat to marinade for 24 hours.* [from French]

**mari|nate** /mærineɪt/ (**marinates, marinating, marinated**) V-T/V-I If you **marinate** meat or fish, or if it **marinates**, you soak it in oil, vinegar, spices, and herbs before cooking it, so that it develops a special flavor. ❑ *Marinate the chicken for 4 hours.* [from Italian]

---

**Word Link**    *mar ≈ sea : marine, maritime, submarine*

---

**ma|rine** /mərin/ (**marines**) ■ N-COUNT; N-PROPER A **marine** is a soldier, for example in the U.S. Marine Corps or the Royal Marines, who is specially trained for military duties at sea as well as on land. ❑ *A small number of Marines were wounded.* ■ ADJ **Marine** is used to describe things relating to the sea. ❑ *...the colorful marine life in the Indian Ocean.* [from Old French] → see **ship**

**mari|tal** /mærɪtªl/ ADJ **Marital** means relating to marriage. ❑ *Their marital home was in Pittsburgh.* [from Latin]

**mari|time** /mærɪtaɪm/ ADJ **Maritime** means relating to the sea and to ships. ❑ *...a maritime museum.* [from Latin]

**mark** /mɑrk/ (**marks, marking, marked**) ■ N-COUNT A **mark** is a small area of something such as dirt that has accidentally gotten onto a surface or piece of clothing. ❑ *There was a red paint mark on the wall.* ■ V-T/V-I If something **marks** a surface, or if the surface **marks**, the surface is damaged by marks or a mark. ❑ *His shoes marked the carpet.* ■ N-COUNT A **mark** is a written or printed symbol, for example a letter of the alphabet. ❑ *He made marks with a pencil.*

■ V-T If you **mark** something with a particular word or symbol, you write that word or symbol on it. ❑ *She marked the letter "sent."* ❑ *Each farmer marks his sheep with a different symbol.* ■ N-COUNT A **mark** is a point that is given for a correct answer or for doing something well in an exam or competition. A mark can also be a written symbol such as a letter that indicates how good a student's work is. ❑ *He scored 9 marks out of 10.* ■ V-T When a teacher **marks** a student's work, the teacher decides how good it is and writes a number or letter on it to indicate this opinion. ❑ *He was marking essays in his small study.* ● **mark|ing** N-UNCOUNT ❑ *Marking students' work can take a long time.* ■ N-COUNT A particular **mark** is a particular number, point, or stage which has been reached or might be reached, especially a significant one. ❑ *Unemployment is almost at the one million mark.* ■ N-SING If you say that a type of behavior or an event is **a mark of** a particular quality, feeling, or situation, you mean it shows that that quality, feeling, or situation exists. ❑ *She put her arm around him: a mark of how caring she was.* ■ V-T If something **marks** a place or position, it shows where a particular thing is or was. ❑ *A big hole in the road marks the place where the bomb landed.* ● **mark|er** (**markers**) N-COUNT ❑ *He put a marker in his book.* ■ V-T An event that **marks** a particular stage or point is a sign that something different is about to happen. ❑ *The announcement marks the end of an extraordinary period in European history.* ■ → see also **marked, marking** ■ → see also **punctuation mark, question mark** ■ PHRASE If someone or something **leaves** their **mark** or **leaves a mark**, they have a lasting effect on another person or thing. ❑ *Her parents' unhappy marriage left its mark on her.* ■ PHRASE If you **make** your **mark** or **make a mark**, you become noticed or famous by doing something impressive or unusual. ❑ *She made her mark in the movie business in the 1960s.* ■ PHRASE If something such as a claim or estimate is **wide of the mark**, it is incorrect or inaccurate. ❑ *His answer was wide of the mark.* [from Old English]

▶ **mark down** ■ PHR-VERB To **mark** an item **down** or **mark** its price **down** means to reduce its price. ❑ *The toy store marked down many computer games.* ■ PHR-VERB If you **mark** something **down**, you write it down. ❑ *I forget things unless I mark them down.*

▶ **mark up** PHR-VERB If you **mark** something **up**, you increase its price. ❑ *We sell goods to stores at one price, then the stores mark them up.*

**marked** /mɑrkt/ ADJ A **marked** change or difference is very obvious and easily noticed. ❑ *There has been a marked increase in traffic on the roads.* ● **mark|ed|ly** /mɑrkɪdli/ ADV ❑ *The movie is markedly different from the play.* [from Old English]

**mar|ket** /mɑrkɪt/ (**markets, marketing, marketed**) ■ N-COUNT A **market** is a place where goods are bought and sold, usually outdoors. ❑ *They usually buy fruit and vegetables at the market.* ■ N-COUNT The **market** for a particular type of thing is the number of people who want to buy it, or the area of the world in which it is sold. [BUSINESS] ❑ *The foreign market is very important.* ■ N-SING The **market** refers to the total amount of a product that is sold each year, especially when you are talking about the competition between the companies who sell that product. [BUSINESS] ❑ *The two big companies control 72% of the market.*

m

**4** V-T To **market** a product means to organize its sale, by deciding on its price, where it should be sold, and how it should be advertised. [BUSINESS] ❏ They market our music in a very different way than pop music. • **mar|ket|ing** N-UNCOUNT ❏ ...the marketing department. **5** → see also **black market 6** PHRASE If something is **on the market**, it is available for people to buy. If it comes **onto the market**, it becomes available for people to buy. [BUSINESS] ❏ There are many empty offices on the market. [from Latin]

**market|place** /mɑrkɪtpleɪs/ (**marketplaces**) **1** N-COUNT The **marketplace** refers to the activity of buying and selling products. [BUSINESS] ❏ This company has a very important role in the marketplace. **2** N-COUNT A **marketplace** is a small area in a city or town where goods are bought and sold, often outdoors. ❏ The marketplace was full of people buying and selling things.

**mark|ing** /mɑrkɪŋ/ (**markings**) **1** N-COUNT **Markings** are colored lines, shapes, or patterns on the surface of something, which help to identify it. ❏ The plane had British markings. [from Old English] **2** → see also **mark**

**mar|ma|lade** /mɑrməleɪd/ (**marmalades**) N-VAR **Marmalade** is a food like jam made from oranges, lemons, or grapefruit. [from French]

**ma|roon** /mərun/ (**maroons, marooning, marooned**) **1** COLOR Something that is **maroon** is dark reddish purple in color. ❏ ...maroon velvet curtains. **2** V-T If someone **is marooned** somewhere, they are left in a place that is difficult for them to escape from. ❏ He was marooned for a year in Jamaica. [Sesne 1 from French. Sense 2 from American Spanish.]

**mar|quee** /mɑrki/ (**marquees**) **1** N-COUNT A **marquee** is a large tent which is used at a fair, garden party, or other outdoor event, usually for eating and drinking in. **2** N-COUNT A **marquee** is a cover over the entrance of a building, for example a hotel or a theater, that has a sign with the name of the film or play on it. ❏ ...the marquees of Broadway.

**mar|quis** /mɑrkwɪs/ (**marquises**) also **marquess** N-COUNT; N-TITLE A **marquis** is a male member of the nobility who has a rank between duke and earl. [from Old French]

---

**Word Link** | age ≈ state of, related to : cour*age*, marri*age*, percent*age*

---

**mar|riage** /mærɪdʒ/ (**marriages**) **1** N-COUNT A **marriage** is the relationship between a husband and wife, or the state of being married. ❏ In a good marriage, both husband and wife are happy. ❏ When I was 35 my marriage ended. **2** N-VAR A **marriage** is the act of marrying someone, or the ceremony at which this is done. ❏ Her marriage to Darryl was a mistake. [from Old French]
→ see **love, wedding**

**mar|riage li|cense** (**marriage licenses**) N-COUNT A **marriage license** is an official document that you need in order to get married. ❏ They got the marriage license before the ceremony, which was held in Los Angeles.

**mar|ried** /mærɪd/ **1** ADJ If you are **married**, you have a husband or wife. ❏ We have been married for 14 years. ❏ She is married to an Englishman. **2** ADJ **Married** means relating to marriage or to people

who are married. ❏ For the first ten years of our married life we lived in a farmhouse. [from Old French]

**mar|ry** /mæri/ (**marries, marrying, married**) **1** V-RECIP When two people **get married** or **marry**, they legally become husband and wife in a special ceremony. ❏ I thought he would change after we got married. ❏ They married a month after they met. ❏ He wants to marry her. **2** V-T When a priest or official **marries** two people, he or she conducts the ceremony in which the two people legally become husband and wife. ❏ The minister has agreed to marry us next week. [from Old French]

**Mars** /mɑrz/ N-PROPER **Mars** is the fourth planet from the sun, between the Earth and Jupiter. [from Latin]

**marsh** /mɑrʃ/ (**marshes**) N-VAR A **marsh** is a wet, muddy area of land. [from Old English]

**mar|shal** /mɑrʃ°l/ (**marshals, marshaling** or **marshalling, marshaled** or **marshalled**) **1** V-T If you **marshal** people or things, you gather them together and arrange them for a particular purpose. ❏ Napoleon marshalled his troops. **2** N-COUNT A **marshal** is an official who helps to supervise a public event, especially a sports event. ❏ Several marshals control the race. **3** N-COUNT In the United States and some other countries, a **marshal** is a police officer, often one who is responsible for a particular area. ❏ A federal marshal arrested him. **4** N-COUNT A **marshal** is an officer in a fire department. ❏ A fire marshal told her there was a gas leak. [from Old French]

**mar|su|pial** /mɑrsupiəl/ (**marsupials**) N-COUNT A **marsupial** is an animal such as a kangaroo or an opossum. Female marsupials carry their babies in a pouch on their stomach.

**mar|tial** /mɑrʃ°l/ ADJ **Martial** is used to describe things relating to soldiers or war. [FORMAL] ❏ ...a martial court. [from Latin]

**mar|tial art** (**martial arts**) N-COUNT A **martial art** is one of the methods of fighting, often without weapons, that come from the Far East, for example kung fu or karate.

**mar|tyr** /mɑrtər/ (**martyrs, martyring, martyred**) **1** N-COUNT A **martyr** is someone who is killed or made to suffer greatly because of their religious or political beliefs. ❏ If he dies, his followers will think of him as a martyr. **2** V-T If someone **is martyred**, they are killed or made to suffer greatly because of their religious or political beliefs. ❏ St. Pancras was martyred in A.D. 304. [from Old English]

**mar|vel** /mɑrv°l/ (**marvels, marveling** or **marvelling, marveled** or **marvelled**) **1** V-T/V-I If you **marvel** at something, you express your great surprise, wonder, or admiration. ❏ Her friends marveled at her great energy. ❏ Sara and I read the story and marveled. **2** N-COUNT You can describe something or someone as a **marvel** to indicate that you think that they are wonderful. ❏ The whale is one of the marvels of nature. [from French]

**mar|vel|ous** /mɑrvələs/ ADJ If you describe someone or something as **marvelous**, you are emphasizing that they are very good. ❏ It's a marvelous piece of music. • **mar|vel|ous|ly** ADV ❏ We want people to think he's doing marvelously. [from Old French]

**Marx|ism** /mɑrksɪzəm/ N-UNCOUNT **Marxism** is a political philosophy based on the writings of Karl Marx which stresses the importance of the struggle between different social classes. [after Karl Marx (1818–83), a German political philosopher]

**Marx|ist** /mɑːksɪst/ (**Marxists**) **1** ADJ **Marxist** means based on Marxism or relating to Marxism. ❑ ...*a Marxist state*. **2** N-COUNT A **Marxist** is a person who believes in Marxism or who is a member of a Marxist party. ❑ ...*a 78-year-old former Marxist*. [after Karl Marx (1818–83), a German political philosopher]

**mas|cara** /mæskærə/ (**mascaras**) N-UNCOUNT **Mascara** is a substance used to make eyelashes darker. [from Spanish]
→ see **makeup**

**mas|cot** /mæskɒt/ (**mascots**) N-COUNT A **mascot** is an animal, toy, or symbol which is associated with a particular organization or event, and which is thought to bring good luck. ❑ ...*the official mascot of the Detroit Tigers*. [from French]

**mas|cu|line** /mæskyəlɪn/ ADJ **Masculine** qualities and things relate to or are considered typical of men, in contrast to women. ❑ ...*masculine characteristics like a deep voice and hair on the face*. ● **mas|cu|lin|ity** /mæskyəlɪnɪti/ N-UNCOUNT ❑ *Some men think doing dangerous things is a sign of masculinity*. [from French]

**mash** /mæʃ/ (**mashes, mashing, mashed**) V-T If you **mash** food that is solid but soft, you crush it so that it forms a soft mass. ❑ *Mash the bananas with a fork*. [from Old English]

**mask** /mæsk/ (**masks, masking, masked**) **1** N-COUNT A **mask** is something which you wear over your face for protection or to disguise yourself. ❑ *The gunman's mask slipped so we could see his face*. ❑ *You must wear goggles and a mask that will protect you against the smoke*. **2** N-COUNT If you describe someone's behavior as a **mask**, you mean that they do not show their real feelings or character. ❑ *Her happy face is just a mask*. **3** V-T If you **mask** your feelings, you deliberately do not show them in your behavior, so that people cannot know what you really feel. ❑ *She tried to mask her anger by laughing*. **4** V-T If one thing **masks** another, it prevents people from noticing or recognizing the other thing. ❑ *The smoke masked their faces*. [from Italian] **5** → see also **gas mask**
→ see **football**

mask

**masked** /mæskt/ ADJ If someone is **masked**, they are wearing a mask. ❑ *I looked directly into his masked face*. [from Italian]

**maso|chism** /mæsəkɪzəm/ N-UNCOUNT **Masochism** is behavior in which someone gets sexual pleasure from their own pain or suffering. ● **maso|chist** (**masochists**) N-COUNT ❑ ...*sexual masochists*. ● **maso|chis|tic** /mæsəkɪstɪk/ ADJ ❑ ...*masochistic behavior*.

**ma|son** /meɪsᵊn/ (**masons**) N-COUNT A **mason** is a person who is skilled at making things or building things with stone or bricks. [from Old French]

**ma|son jar** (**mason jars**) also **Mason jar** N-COUNT A **mason jar** is a glass jar with a lid that you screw on, which is used for preserving food.

**ma|son|ry** /meɪsənri/ N-UNCOUNT **Masonry** is bricks or pieces of stone which have been stuck together with cement as part of a wall or building. ❑ *A piece of masonry fell from the top of the building*. [from Old French]

**mas|quer|ade** /mæskəreɪd/ (**masquerades, masquerading, masqueraded**) V-I To **masquerade as** someone or something means to pretend to be that person or thing. ❑ *He masqueraded as a doctor and fooled everyone*. [from Spanish]

**mass** /mæs/ (**masses, massing, massed**) **1** N-SING A **mass** of things is a large number of them grouped together. ❑ *On his desk is a mass of books and papers*. **2** N-SING A **mass of** something is a large amount of it. ❑ *She had a mass of black hair*. **3** QUANT **Masses of** something means a large amount of it. [INFORMAL] ❑ *She has masses of work to do*. **4** ADJ **Mass** is used to describe something which involves or affects a very large number of people. ❑ *Mass unemployment is a big problem*. **5** N-PLURAL **The masses** are the ordinary people in society. ❑ *His music is aimed at the masses*. **6** V-T/V-I When people or things **mass**, or when you **mass** them, they gather together into a large crowd or group. ❑ *Police began to mass outside the football stadium*. ● **massed** ADJ ❑ *The massed crowd began to shout*. **7** N-VAR In physics, the **mass** of an object is the amount of physical matter that it has. [TECHNICAL] ❑ ...*the mass of a single atom*. **8** N-VAR **Mass** is a Christian church ceremony, especially in a Roman Catholic or Orthodox church, during which people eat bread and drink wine in order to remember the last meal of Jesus Christ. ❑ *She went to Mass each day*. [from Old French]
→ see **continent, transportation**

**mas|sa|cre** /mæsəkər/ (**massacres, massacring, massacred**) **1** N-VAR A **massacre** is the killing of a large number of people at the same time in a violent and cruel way. ❑ *Her mother died in the massacre*. **2** V-T If people **are massacred**, a large number of them are attacked and killed in a violent and cruel way. ❑ *300 people were massacred by the soldiers*. [from Old French]

**mas|sage** /məsɑːʒ/ (**massages, massaging, massaged**) **1** N-VAR **Massage** is the action of rubbing someone's body, as a way of making them relax or reducing their pain. ❑ *Alex asked me if I wanted a massage*. **2** V-T If you **massage** someone or a part of their body, you rub their body, in order to make them relax or reduce their pain. ❑ *She continued massaging her right foot*. [from French]

**masse** /mæs/ → see **en masse**

**mass ex|tinc|tion** (**mass extinctions**) N-VAR A **mass extinction** is a period of time when many different species of animals and plants become extinct.

**mas|sive** /mæsɪv/ ADJ Something that is **massive** is very large in size, quantity, or extent. ❑ *They borrowed massive amounts of money*. ❑ ...*a massive new store*. ● **mas|sive|ly** ADV ❑ ...*a massively popular game*. [from French]

**mass me|dia** N-SING

> **Mass media** can take the singular or plural form of the verb.

The **mass media** are television, radio, newspapers, and magazines. ❑ *Reports in the mass media*.

**mass move|ment** (**mass movements**) N-VAR
In geology, **mass movement** is the downhill
movement of rocks and soil as a result of gravity.
Compare **creep**. [TECHNICAL]

**mass num|ber** (**mass numbers**) N-VAR The
**mass number** of a chemical element is the total
number of protons and neutrons in the atomic
nucleus of that element. [TECHNICAL]

**mass-produce** (**mass-produces, mass-
producing, mass-produced**) V-T To **mass-produce**
something means to make it in large quantities,
usually by machine. [BUSINESS] ❑ ...*machines to
mass-produce shoes.* ● **mass-produced** ADJ ❑ ...*the
first mass-produced bike.*

**mass trans|it** N-UNCOUNT **Mass transit** is the
transportation of people by means of buses, trains,
or other vehicles running on fixed routes within
a city or town. ❑ *The president wants to spend $105
billion to improve the nation's mass transit systems.*

**mast** /mæst/ (**masts**) ◼ N-COUNT The **masts**
of a boat are the tall, upright poles that support
its sails. ◼ N-COUNT A radio **mast** is a tall
upright structure that is used to transmit radio or
television signals. [from Old English]

**mas|ter** /mæstər/ (**masters, mastering,
mastered**) ◼ N-COUNT A servant's **master** is the
man that he or she works for. ❑ *My master ordered
me to deliver a message.* ◼ N-COUNT If you say that
someone is a **master** of a particular activity, you
mean that they are extremely skilled at it. ❑ *She
was a master of the English language.* ● **Master** is also
an adjective. ❑ ...*a master craftsman.* ◼ N-VAR If
you are **master** of a situation, you have complete
control over it. ❑ *Sometimes he didn't feel master of
his own thoughts.* ◼ V-T If you **master** something,
you learn how to do it properly or you succeed in
understanding it completely. ❑ *David soon mastered
the skills of soccer.* [from Old English]

### Thesaurus     *master*     Also look up :

| | |
|---|---|
| N. | owner; (*ant.*) servant, slave ◼ |
| | artist, expert, professional ◼ |
| V. | learn, study, understand ◼ |

**master|mind** /mæstərmaɪnd/ (**masterminds,
masterminding, masterminded**) ◼ V-T If you
**mastermind** a difficult or complicated activity,
you plan and organize it. ❑ *No one knows who
masterminded the attacks.* ◼ N-COUNT The
**mastermind behind** a difficult or complicated
plan, often a criminal one, is the person who
is responsible for planning and organizing it.
❑ *He was the mastermind behind the plan to steal the
painting.*

**master|piece** /mæstərpis/ (**masterpieces**)
N-COUNT A **masterpiece** is an extremely good
painting, novel, movie, or other work of art. ❑ *His
book is a masterpiece.* [from Dutch]

**mas|tery** /mæstəri/ N-UNCOUNT If you show
**mastery of** a particular skill or language, you
show that you have learned or understood it
completely and have no difficulty using it. ❑ *He
doesn't have mastery of the basic rules of grammar.*
[from Old English]

**mat** /mæt/ (**mats**) ◼ N-COUNT A **mat** is a small
piece of something such as cloth, wood, or plastic
which you put on a table to protect it from plates
or cups. ❑ *The food is served on big tables with mats.*

◼ N-COUNT A **mat** is a small piece of carpet or
other thick material which is put on the floor.
❑ *There was a letter on the mat.* [from Old English]
◼ → see also **matte**

**match** /mætʃ/ (**matches, matching, matched**)
◼ N-COUNT A **match** is an organized game of
tennis, soccer, cricket, or some other sport. ❑ *He
was watching
a soccer match.*
◼ N-COUNT A
**match** is a small
wooden or paper
stick with a
substance on
one end that

match

produces a flame
when you rub it
along a rough surface. ◼ V-RECIP If something
of a particular color or design **matches** another
thing, they have the same color or design, or
have a pleasing appearance when they are used
together. ❑ *Your shoes match your dress.* ❑ *All the
chairs matched.* ● **match|ing** ADJ ❑ ...*a hat and a
matching scarf.* ◼ V-RECIP If something such as
an amount or a quality **matches with** another
amount or quality, they are both the same or
equal. ❑ *Their skills in basketball matched.* ◼ V-T If
your opinion does not match with their opinion. ◼ V-T If you
**match** something, you are as good as it or equal to
it, for example in speed, size, or quality. ❑ *They're
a good team, but I think we matched them in that game.*
[Senses 1, 3, 4 and 5 from Old English. Sense 2 from
Old French.] ◼ → see also **matched**
→ see **fire**

### Word Partnership     Use *match* with :

| | |
|---|---|
| N. | **boxing** match, **chess** match, **tennis** match, **wrestling** match ◼ |
| V. | **strike** a match ◼ |

**match|book** /mætʃbʊk/ (**matchbooks**)
N-COUNT A **matchbook** is a folded piece of
cardboard with paper
matches inside.

matchbook

**matched** /mætʃt/ ◼ ADJ If
two people are well **matched**,
they have qualities that
will enable them to have
a good relationship. ❑ *My
parents were not very well
matched.* ◼ ADJ In sports and
other competitions, if the
opponents or teams are well **matched**, they are
both of the same standard in strength or ability.
❑ *The two teams were pretty well-matched.* [from Old
English]

**mate** /meɪt/ (**mates, mating, mated**)
◼ N-COUNT An animal's **mate** is its sexual
partner. ❑ *The male shows its colorful feathers to
attract a mate.* ◼ V-RECIP When animals **mate**, a
male and a female have sex in order to produce
young. ❑ *Some females eat the males after they mate.*
❑ *They want the males to mate with wild females.* [from
Middle Low German] ◼ → see also **classmate,
roommate, running mate**

**ma|terial** /mətɪəriəl/ (**materials**) ◼ N-VAR A
**material** is a solid substance. ❑ ...*a material such
as a metal.* ◼ N-VAR **Material** is cloth. ❑ ...*the thick
material of her skirt.* ◼ N-PLURAL **Materials** are

## Word Web — mathematics

During prehistoric times people **counted** things they could see—for example, four sheep. Later they began to use **numbers** with abstract **quantities** like time—for example, two days. This led to the development of basic **arithmetic**—**addition**, **subtraction**, **multiplication**, and **division**. When people discovered how to use write numerals, they could do more complex **mathematical calculations**. **Mathematicians** developed new types of **math** to **measure** land and keep financial records. **Algebra** and **geometry** developed in the Middle East between 2,000 and 3,000 years ago. Algebra uses letters to represent possible quantities. Geometry deals with the relationships among **lines**, **angles**, and **shapes**.

the things that you need for a particular activity. ❑ *The builders needed some more materials.* ◳ ADJ **Material** things are related to possessions or money, rather than to more abstract things such as ideas or values. ❑ *Every room was full of material things.* • **ma|teri|al|ly** ADV ❑ *He tried to help the child materially and spiritually.* [from French]
→ see **industry**

### Word Partnership — Use *material* with :

ADJ. **genetic** material, **hazardous** material ◳
**new** material, **original** material ◲ ◳
**raw** materials ◳

**ma|teri|al|ism** /mətɪəriəlɪzəm/ N-UNCOUNT **Materialism** is the attitude of someone who attaches a lot of importance to money and wants to possess a lot of material things. ❑ *A lot of the world's problems are because of materialism.* [from French]

**ma|teri|al|ize** /mətɪəriəlaɪz/ (**materializes, materializing, materialized**) V-I If a possible or expected event does not **materialize**, it does not happen. ❑ *An invitation to dinner did not materialize.* [from French]

**ma|ter|nal** /mətɜrn³l/ ADJ **Maternal** is used to describe feelings or actions which are typical of those of a kind mother toward her child. ❑ *...maternal love.* [from Medieval Latin]

**ma|ter|nity** /mətɜrnɪti/ ADJ **Maternity** is used to describe things relating to the help and medical care given to a woman when she is pregnant and when she gives birth. ❑ *Sam was born in the maternity hospital.* [from Medieval Latin]

**math** /mæθ/ N-UNCOUNT **Math** is the same as **mathematics**. ❑ *He studied math in college.*
→ see **mathematics**

**math|emati|cal** /mæθəmætɪk³l/ ADJ Something that is **mathematical** involves numbers and calculations. ❑ *...mathematical calculations.* • **math|emati|cal|ly** /mæθəmætɪkli/ ADV ❑ *...a mathematically complicated problem.* [from Latin]
→ see **mathematics**

**math|ema|ti|cian** /mæθəmətɪʃ³n/ (**mathematicians**) N-COUNT A **mathematician** is a person who is trained in the study of mathematics. [from Latin]
→ see **mathematics**

**math|emat|ics** /mæθəmætɪks/ N-UNCOUNT **Mathematics** is the study of numbers, quantities, or shapes. ❑ *...a professor of mathematics at Boston College.* [from Latin]
→ see Word Web: **mathematics**

**mati|nee** /mæt³neɪ/ (**matinees**) N-COUNT A **matinee** is a performance of a play or a showing of a movie which takes place in the afternoon. [from French]

**ma|trix** /meɪtrɪks/ (**matrices**) N-COUNT A **matrix** is the environment or context in which something such as a society develops and grows. [FORMAL] ❑ *...the matrix of their culture.* [from Latin]

**ma|tron of hon|or** /meɪtrən əv hɒnər/ (**matrons of honor**) N-COUNT A **matron of honor** is a married woman who serves as the chief bridesmaid at a wedding. ❑ *My sister was the matron of honor at our wedding.*

**matte** /mæt/ also **matt** or **mat** ADJ A **matte** color, paint, or surface is dull rather than shiny. ❑ *...a white matte paint.* [from French]

**mat|ter** /mætər/ (**matters, mattering, mattered**) ◳ N-COUNT A **matter** is a task, situation, or event which you have to deal with or think about. ❑ *She wanted to discuss some private matter.* ❑ *Business matters took him to Louisville.* ◲ N-PLURAL You use **matters** to refer to the situation you are talking about. ❑ *We are hoping that this change will improve matters.* ❑ *If it would make matters easier, I will come to New York.* ◳ N-UNCOUNT Printed **matter** consists of books, newspapers, and other texts that are printed. Reading **matter** consists of things that are suitable for reading, such as books and newspapers. ❑ *The government plans to put a tax on printed matter.* ◴ N-UNCOUNT **Matter** is the physical part of the universe consisting of solids, liquids, and gases. ❑ *The universe is made up of matter and energy.* ◵ N-SING You use **matter** in expressions such as **"What's the matter?"** or **"Is anything the matter?"** when you think that someone has a problem and you want to know what it is. ❑ *Carole, what's the matter? You don't seem happy.* ◶ N-SING You use **matter** in expressions such as **"a matter of weeks"** when you are emphasizing how small an amount is or how short a period of time is. ❑ *Within a matter of days she was back at work.* ◷ V-T/V-I If you say that something does not **matter**, you mean that it is not important to you because it does not have an effect on you or on a particular situation.

m

---

**Word Web**    matter

Matter exists in three states—**solid**, **liquid**, and **gas**. Changes in the state of matter happen frequently. For example, when a solid becomes hot enough, it **melts** and becomes a liquid. When a liquid is hot enough, it **evaporates** into a gas. The process also works the other way around. A gas which becomes very cool will **condense** into a liquid. And a liquid that is cooled enough will freeze and become a solid. Other changes in **state** are possible. Sublimation describes what happens when a solid, dry ice, turns directly into a gas, carbon dioxide. And did you know that glass is actually a liquid, not a solid?

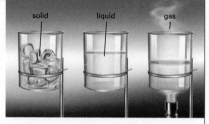

---

❑ *A lot of the food goes on the floor but that doesn't matter.* ❑ *It does not matter how long your essay is.* ❑ → see also **subject matter** ❑ PHRASE If you say that something is **another matter** or **a different matter**, you mean that it is very different from the situation that you have just discussed. ❑ *Taking care of yourself is one thing, but taking care of someone else is a different matter.* ❑ PHRASE If you are going to do something **as a matter of** urgency or priority, you are going to do it as soon as possible, because it is important. ❑ *You need to go to your doctor as a matter of urgency.* ❑ CONVENTION You say **"it doesn't matter"** to tell someone who is apologizing to you that you are not angry or upset, and that they should not worry. ❑ *"Did I wake you?"* — *"Yes, but it doesn't matter."* ❑ PHRASE You use **no matter** in expressions such as **"no matter how"** and **"no matter what"** to say that something is true or happens in all circumstances. ❑ *Anyone can learn to swim, no matter what their age.* [from Latin] ❑ a matter of **life and death** → see **death** ❑ **as a matter of fact** → see **fact**
→ see Word Web: **matter**

**matter-of-fact** ADJ If you describe a person as **matter-of-fact**, you mean that they show no emotions such as enthusiasm, anger, or surprise, especially in a tense or difficult situation. ❑ *John gave Francis the news in a matter-of-fact way.* • **matter-of-factly** ADV ❑ *"She thinks you're lying,"* Scott said matter-of-factly.

**mat|tress** /mǽtrɪs/ (**mattresses**) N-COUNT A **mattress** is the large, flat object which is put on a bed to make it comfortable to sleep on. [from Old French]
→ see **bed**

**ma|ture** /mətyʊ́ər, -tʊ́ər, -tʃʊ́ər/ (**matures, maturing, matured, maturer, maturest**) ❑ V-I When a child or young animal **matures**, it becomes an adult. ❑ *You will learn what to expect as your child matures physically.* ❑ ADJ A **mature** person or animal is fully grown. • **maturity** /mətyʊ́ərɪti, -tʊ́ər-, -tʃʊ́ər-/ N-UNCOUNT ❑ *We stop growing at maturity.* ❑ V-I When something **matures**, it reaches a state of complete development. ❑ *When the trees matured they cut them down.* ❑ ADJ If you describe someone as **mature**, you think that their behavior is responsible and sensible. ❑ *Fiona was mature for her age.* • **ma|tur|ity** N-UNCOUNT ❑ *Her speech showed great maturity.* [from Latin]

**maul** /mɔ́l/ (**mauls, mauling, mauled**) V-T If someone **is mauled** by an animal, they are violently attacked by it and badly injured. ❑ *He was mauled by a bear.* [from Old French]

**ma|ven** /mēɪvᵊn/ (**mavens**) N-COUNT A **maven** is a person who is an expert on a particular subject. ❑ *...style maven Andre Leon Talley.* [from Yiddish]

**mav|er|ick** /mǽvərɪk/ (**mavericks**) N-COUNT If you describe someone as a **maverick**, you mean that they are unconventional and independent, and do not think or behave in the same way as other people. ❑ *He was too much of a maverick ever to be president.* • **Maverick** is also an adjective. ❑ *...a maverick group of scientists.*

---

**Word Link**    maxim ≈ greatest : maxim, maximize, maximum

---

**max|im** /mǽksɪm/ (**maxims**) N-COUNT A **maxim** is a rule for good or sensible behavior, especially one in the form of a saying. ❑ *I believe in the maxim "if it isn't broken, don't fix it".* [from French]

**max|im|ize** /mǽksɪmaɪz/ (**maximizes, maximizing, maximized**) V-T If you **maximize** something, you make it as great in amount or importance as you can. ❑ *In order to maximize profit, the firm produces as many goods as possible.* [from Latin]

**maxi|mum** /mǽksɪməm/ ❑ ADJ You use **maximum** to describe an amount which is the largest that is possible, allowed, or required. ❑ *The maximum height for a garden fence is 6 feet.* • **Maximum** is also a noun. ❑ *...a maximum of two years in prison.* ❑ ADJ You use **maximum** to indicate how great an amount is. ❑ *I need the maximum amount of information you can give me.* ❑ ADV If you say that something is a particular amount **maximum**, you mean that this is the greatest amount it should be or could possibly be, although a smaller amount is acceptable or very possible. ❑ *We need 6 grams of salt a day maximum.* [from Latin]

---

**Thesaurus**    maximum    Also look up :

ADJ.    biggest, greatest, highest, most; (ant.) lowest, minimum ❑ ❑

### Word Partnership    Use *maximum* with :

N.    maximum **benefit**, maximum **charge**, maximum **efficiency**, maximum **fine**, maximum **flexibility**, maximum **height**, maximum **penalty**, maximum **rate**, maximum **sentence**, maximum **speed** ◼

**may** /meɪ/

May is a modal verb. It is used with the base form of a verb.

◼ MODAL You use **may** to indicate that there is a possibility that something will happen or is true. ❑ *We may have some rain today.* ❑ *I may be back next year.* ◻ MODAL You use **may** in statements where you are accepting the truth of a situation, but contrasting it with something that is more important. ❑ *I may be almost 50, but I can remember most things.* ◼ MODAL You use **may** to indicate that someone is allowed to do something. ❑ *If you will be away on election day, you may vote by mail.* ❑ *May we come in?* [from Old English] ◼ **may as well** → see **well**
→ see also **can**

**May** /meɪ/ (**Mays**) N-VAR **May** is the fifth month of the year in the Western calendar. ❑ *We went on vacation in early May.* [from Old French]

**may|be** /meɪbi/ ◼ ADV You use **maybe** to express uncertainty, for example when you do not know that something is definitely true. ❑ *Maybe she is in love.* ❑ *I do think about having children, maybe when I'm 40.* ❑ *"Is she coming back?" — "Maybe."* ◻ ADV You use **maybe** when you are making suggestions or giving advice. ❑ *Maybe we can go to the movies or something.* ❑ *Maybe you should go there and look at it.* ◼ ADV You use **maybe** when you are making a rough guess at a number, quantity, or value, rather than stating it exactly. ❑ *The men were maybe a hundred feet away and coming closer.*

### Usage    maybe

*Maybe* is often confused with *may be*. *Maybe* is an adverb: *Maybe we'll be a little late. May be* is a verb form that means the same thing as *might be*: *We may be a little late.*

**may|hem** /meɪhɛm/ N-UNCOUNT You use **mayhem** to refer to a situation that is not controlled or ordered, when people are behaving in a disorganized, confused, and often violent way. ❑ *Their arrival caused mayhem as crowds of people*

rushed towards them. [from Anglo-French]

**may|on|naise** /meɪəneɪz/ N-UNCOUNT **Mayonnaise** is a thick, pale sauce made from egg yolks and oil. [from French]

**mayor** /meɪər, mɛər/ (**mayors**) N-COUNT The **mayor** of a city or town is the person who has been elected for a fixed period of time to run its government. ❑ *...the mayor of New York.* [from Old French]

**maze** /meɪz/ (**mazes**) N-COUNT A **maze** is a complex system of passages or paths between walls or hedges. It is designed to confuse people who try to find their way through it. ❑ *The palace has large gardens, a maze, and tennis courts.*

maze

**me** /mi, STRONG mi/ PRON A speaker or writer uses **me** to refer to himself or herself. **Me** is a first person singular pronoun. **Me** is used as the object of a verb or a preposition. ❑ *I had to make decisions that would affect me for the rest of my life.* ❑ *He asked me to go to California with him.* [from Old English]

**mead|ow** /mɛdoʊ/ (**meadows**) N-COUNT A **meadow** is a field which has grass and flowers growing in it. [from Old English]

**mea|ger** /migər/ ADJ A **meager** amount of something is very small or not enough. ❑ *They ate their meager meal in silence.* [from Old French]

**meal** /mil/ (**meals**) ◼ N-COUNT A **meal** is an occasion when people sit down and eat. ❑ *She sat next to him throughout the meal.* ◻ N-COUNT A **meal** is the food you eat during a meal. ❑ *Steil finished his meal in silence.* [from Old English]
→ see Word Web: **meal**

### Thesaurus    meal    Also look up :

N.    breakfast, dinner, lunch, supper ◼

### Word Partnership    Use *meal* with :

V.    **enjoy** a meal, **miss** a meal, **skip** a meal ◼
    **cook** a meal, **eat** a meal, **have** a meal, **order** a meal, **prepare** a meal, **serve** a meal ◻

ADJ.    **big** meal, **delicious** meal, **good** meal, **hot** meal, **large** meal, **simple** meal, **well-balanced** meal ◻

m

### Word Web    meal

Customs for eating meals are very different around the world. In the Middle East, popular **breakfast** foods include pita bread, olives and white cheese. In China, favourite **fast food** breakfast items are steamed buns and fried breadsticks. The **continental breakfast** in Europe consists of bread, butter, jam, and a hot drink. In many places **lunch** is a light **meal**, like a **sandwich**. But in Germany, lunch is the main meal of the day. In most places, **dinner** is the name of the meal eaten in the evening. However, some people say they eat dinner at noon and supper at night.

**mealtime** /míltaɪm/ (**mealtimes**) N-VAR
**Mealtimes** are occasions when you eat breakfast, lunch, or dinner. ❑ *At mealtimes he would watch her eat.*

**mealy** /míli/ ADJ Food that is dry and powdery can be described as **mealy**. ❑ *The boiled potato was mealy.*

---
**mean**
---

❶ VERB USES
❷ ADJECTIVE USES
❸ NOUN USE

❶ **mean** /mín/ (**means, meaning, meant**) ◼ V-T If you want to know what a word, code, signal, or gesture **means**, you want to know what it refers to or what its message is. ❑ *"Unable" means "not able."* ❑ *What does "disapproving" mean?* ◻ V-T If something **means** something **to** you, it is important to you in some way. ❑ *Her feelings meant nothing to him.* ◻ V-T If one thing **means** another, it shows that the second thing is true or makes it certain that it will happen. ❑ *The new factory means more jobs for people who live here.* ◻ V-T If you **mean** what you are saying, you are serious about it and are not joking. ❑ *He said he loves her. And I think he meant it.* ◻ V-T If someone **meant to** do something, they did it deliberately. ❑ *I didn't mean to hurt you.* ◻ PHRASE You can use **"I mean"** to introduce a statement, when you are explaining, justifying, or correcting something that you have just said. [SPOKEN] ❑ *I'm sure he wouldn't mind. I mean, I was the one who asked him.* ❑ *It was English or Spanish — I mean French or Spanish.* [from Old English] ◻ → see also **meaning, means, meant**

❷ **mean** /mín/ (**meaner, meanest**) ◼ ADJ If someone is being **mean**, they are being unkind to another person, for example by not allowing them to do something. ❑ *Their older brother was being mean to them.* ● **mean|ness** N-UNCOUNT ❑ *You took his toys out of meanness.* ◻ ADJ If you describe a person or animal as **mean**, you are saying that they are very bad-tempered and cruel. ❑ *...the meanest fighter in the world.* ◻ [AM **cheap, stingy**] [from Old English]

❸ **mean** /mín/ ◼ N-SING The **mean** is a number that is the average of a set of numbers. ❑ *Take a hundred numbers and calculate the mean.* [from Old French] ◻ → see also **means**

**me|ander** /miǽndər/ (**meanders, meandering, meandered**) V-I If a river or road **meanders**, it has a lot of bends in it. ❑ *The road meandered through farmland.* ❑ *We crossed a bridge that went over a meandering stream.* [from Latin]

**mean|ing** /mínɪŋ/ (**meanings**) ◼ N-VAR The **meaning** of a word, expression, or gesture is the thing or idea that it refers to or represents and which can be explained using other words. ❑ *What is the meaning of the word "disgusting" ?* ◻ N-UNCOUNT If an activity or action has **meaning**, it has a purpose and is worthwhile. ❑ *Art has real meaning when it helps people to understand themselves.* [from Old English]

**mean|ing|ful** /mínɪŋfəl/ ◼ ADJ If you describe something as **meaningful**, you mean that it is serious, important, or useful in some way. ❑ *He does meaningful work, working with children with AIDS.* ● **mean|ing|ful|ly** ADV ❑ *We need to talk meaningfully about these problems.* ◻ ADJ A **meaningful** look or gesture is one that is intended to express something, usually to a particular person. ❑ *She gave Jane a meaningful look.* ● **mean|ing|ful|ly** ADV ❑ *He glanced meaningfully at the other policeman.* [from Old English]

**mean|ing|less** /mínɪŋlɪs/ ADJ Something that is **meaningless** has no meaning or purpose. ❑ *The sentence "kicked the ball the man" is meaningless.* ❑ *...meaningless life.* [from Old English]

**means** /mínz/ ◼ N-COUNT A **means** of doing something is a method, instrument, or process which can be used to do it. **Means** is both the singular and the plural form for this use. ❑ *She used tears as a means to get his attention.* ❑ *The army used terror as a means of controlling the people.* ◻ N-PLURAL You can refer to the money that someone has as their **means**. [FORMAL] ❑ *...a person of means.* ◻ PHRASE If you do something **by means of** a particular method, instrument, or process, you do it using that method, instrument, or process. ❑ *This course is taught by means of lectures and seminars.* ◻ CONVENTION You can say **"by all means"** to tell someone that you are very willing to allow them to do something. ❑ *"Can I come to your house?" — "Yes, by all means."* [from Old English]

**meant** /mɛnt/ ◼ **Meant** is the past tense and past participle of **mean**. ◻ ADJ You use **meant to** to say that something or someone was intended to be or do a particular thing, especially when they have failed to be or do it. ❑ *I can't say any more, it's meant to be a big secret.* ❑ *Everything is meant to be informal.* ◻ ADJ If something **is meant for** particular people or for a particular situation, it is intended for those people or for that situation. ❑ *These stories aren't just meant for children.* ◻ PHRASE If you say that something **is meant to** have a particular quality or characteristic, you mean that it has a reputation for being like that. ❑ *They're are meant to be one of the best teams in the league.* [from Old English]

**mean|time** /míntaɪm/ PHRASE **In the meantime** or **meantime** means in the period of time between two events. ❑ *Elizabeth wants to go to college but in the meantime she has to work.*

**mean|while** /mínwaɪl/ ADV **Meanwhile** means in the period of time between two events or while a particular thing is happening. ❑ *I'll be ready to meet them. Meanwhile, I'm going to talk to Karen.*

**mea|sles** /míz°lz/ N-UNCOUNT **Measles** is an infectious illness that gives you a high temperature and red spots. [from Middle Low German] → see **hospital**

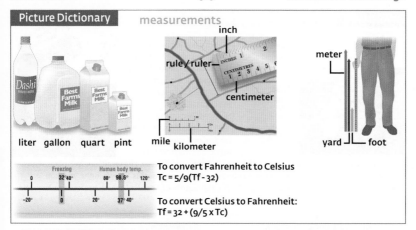

**Picture Dictionary** measurements

inch

rule / ruler — INCHES 1 2
CENTIMETRES 1 2 3 4 5 6

centimeter

meter

liter gallon quart pint mile kilometer

yard foot

| Freezing | Human body temp. |
| 32° 40° | 80° 98.6° 120° |
| 0 | |
| -20° 0 20° 37° 40° | |

**To convert Fahrenheit to Celsius**
$Tc = 5/9(Tf - 32)$

**To convert Celsius to Fahrenheit:**
$Tf = 32 + (9/5 \times Tc)$

**meas|ur|able** /mɛʒərəbᵊl/ ADJ If you describe something as **measurable**, you mean that it is large enough to be noticed or to be significant. [FORMAL] ❑ *Both leaders expected measurable progress.* [from Old French]

**meas|ure** /mɛʒər/ (**measures, measuring, measured**) ◻ V-T If you **measure** the quality, quantity, or value of something, you find out or judge how great it is. ❑ *Measure the length of the table.* ◻ *I measured his height against the chart in the doctor's office.* ◻ V-T If something **measures** a particular length, width, or amount, that is its size or intensity, expressed in numbers. ❑ *The football field measures 400 feet.* ◻ N-SING A **measure of** a particular quality, feeling, or activity is a fairly large amount of it. [FORMAL] ❑ *Everyone achieved a measure of success.* ◻ N-SING If something is a **measure of** a situation, it shows that the situation is very serious or has developed to a very great extent. ❑ *That is a measure of how bad things have become at the bank.* ◻ N-COUNT When someone takes **measures** to do something, they carry out particular actions in order to achieve a particular result. [FORMAL] ❑ *The police are taking measures to deal with the problem.* ◻ N-COUNT In music, a **measure** is one of the several short parts of the same length into which a piece of music is divided. ❑ *The music changes style for a few measures.* [from Old French] ◻ → see also **tape measure**
→ see **mathematics, thermometer**
▶ **measure up** PHR-VERB If you do not **measure up** to a standard or to someone's expectations, you are not good enough to achieve the standard or fulfill the person's expectations. ❑ *I was trying to measure up to her high standards.*

**Word Partnership** Use *measure* with :

N. measure **intelligence**, measure **performance**, measure **progress**, **tests** measure ◻

**meas|ure|ment** /mɛʒərmənt/ (**measurements**) ◻ N-COUNT A **measurement** is a result that you obtain by measuring something. ❑ *We took lots of measurements.* ◻ N-VAR **Measurement** of something is the process of measuring it. ❑ *Tests include measurement of height and weight.* ◻ N-PLURAL Your **measurements** are the size of your waist, chest, hips, and other parts of your body, which you need to know when you are buying clothes. ❑ *I know all her measurements and find it easy to buy clothes she likes.* [from Old French]
→ see Picture Dictionary: **measurements**

**meat** /mit/ (**meats**) N-VAR **Meat** is flesh taken from a dead animal that people cook and eat. ❑ *I don't eat meat or fish.* ❑ *...imported meat products.* [from Old English]
→ see Word Web: **meat**
→ see **carnivore, vegetarian**

**meat|pack|ing** /mitpækɪŋ/ also meat-packing or meat packing N-UNCOUNT **Meatpacking** is the processing and packaging of meat for sale. ❑ *He works at the local meatpacking plant.*

**me|chan|ic** /mɪkænɪk/ (**mechanics**) ◻ N-COUNT A **mechanic** is someone whose job is to repair and maintain machines and engines, especially car engines. ❑ *If you smell burning in your car, take it to your mechanic.* ◻ N-PLURAL The **mechanics** of a process, system, or activity are the way in which it works or the way in which it is done. ❑ *What are the mechanics of this new process?* [from Latin]

**me|chani|cal** /mɪkænɪkᵊl/ ◻ ADJ A **mechanical** device has parts that move when it is working, often using power from an engine or from electricity. ❑ *...mechanical parts for trains.* ❑ *...a working mechanical clock.* ● **me|chani|cal|ly** /mɪkænɪkli/ ADV ❑ *The machine is mechanically operated.* ◻ ADJ A **mechanical** action is done automatically, without thinking about it. ❑ *He reacted in a mechanical way.* ● **me|chani|cal|ly** ADV ❑ *He nodded his head mechanically.* [from Latin]

**me|chani|cal ad|van|tage** (**mechanical advantages**) N-VAR The **mechanical advantage** of a machine such as a lever or pulley is a measure of the difference between the force applied to the machine and the force exerted by the machine. [TECHNICAL]

m

## Word Web    meat

The English language has different words for animals and the **meat** that comes from those animals. This is because of influences from other languages. In the

year 1066 AD the Anglo-Saxons of England lost a major battle to the French-speaking Normans. As a result, the Normans became the ruling class and the Anglo-Saxons worked on farms. The Anglo-Saxons tended the

animals. They tended **sheep**, **cows**, **chickens**, and **pigs** in the fields. The wealthier Normans, who purchased and ate the meat from these animals, used different words. They bought "mouton," which became the word **mutton**, "bouef," which became **beef**, "poulet," which became **poultry**, and "porc," which became **pork**.

**me|chani|cal en|er|gy** N-UNCOUNT
**Mechanical energy** is the energy that an object such as a machine has because of its movement or position.

**me|chani|cal weath|er|ing** N-UNCOUNT
**Mechanical weathering** is a geological process in which rock is broken down into smaller pieces, for example because of frost. [TECHNICAL]

**mecha|nism** /mɛkənɪzəm/ (**mechanisms**)
**1** N-COUNT In a machine or piece of equipment, a **mechanism** is a part which performs a particular function. □ ...locking mechanism. **2** N-COUNT A **mechanism** is a special way of getting something done within a particular system. □ There's no mechanism for making changes. [from Latin]

**mecha|nize** /mɛkənaɪz/ (**mechanizes, mechanizing, mechanized**) V-T If someone **mechanizes** a process, they cause it to be done by a machine or machines. □ Technologies are developing to mechanize the job. ● **mecha|ni|za|tion** /mɛkənɪzeɪʃᵊn/ N-UNCOUNT □ Mechanization happened years ago. [from Latin]

**med|al** /mɛdᵊl/ (**medals**) N-COUNT A **medal** is a small metal disk which is given as an award for

medal

bravery or as a prize in a sports event. □ ...the country's highest medal for bravery. [from French]

**med|al|ist** /mɛdᵊlɪst/ (**medalists**) N-COUNT A **medalist** is a person who has won a medal in sports. □ ...the Olympic gold medalists. [from French]

**Med|al of Hon|or** (**Medals of Honor**) N-COUNT The **Medal of Honor** is a medal that is given to members of the U.S. armed forces who have shown special courage or bravery in battle. □ He won the Medal of Honor for his actions in 1943.

**med|dle** /mɛdᵊl/ (**meddles, meddling, meddled**) V-I If you say that someone **meddles** in something, you are criticizing the fact that they try to influence or change it without being asked. □ Do scientists have any right to meddle in such matters? □ You should not have meddled. [from Old French]

**Word Link**    med ≈ middle : inter**med**iary, **med**ia, **med**ium

**me|dia** /midiə/ **1** N-SING

**Media** can take the singular or plural form of the verb.

You can refer to television, radio, newspapers, and magazines as **the media**. □ A lot of people in the media have written bad things about him. □ They told their story to the news media. **2** → see also **mass media, multimedia 3** Media is a plural of **medium**. [from Latin]
→ see **library**

**me|dia cir|cus** (**media circuses**) N-COUNT If an event is described as a **media circus**, a large group of people from the media are there to report on it and take photographs. □ The couple married in the Caribbean to avoid a media circus.

**me|dian** /midiən/ (**medians**) ADJ The **median** value of a set of values is the middle one when they are arranged in order. For example, if a group of five students take a test and their scores are 5, 7, 7, 8, and 10, the median score is 7. [TECHNICAL] [from Latin]

**me|dian strip** (**median strips**) N-COUNT The **median strip** is the strip of ground, often covered with grass, that separates the two sides of a major road.

**me|dia source** (**media sources**) N-COUNT You can refer to television, radio, newspapers, the Internet, and other forms of mass communication as **media sources**.

**me|di|ate** /midieɪt/ (**mediates, mediating, mediated**) V-T/V-I If someone **mediates** between two groups of people, or **mediates** an agreement **between** them, they try to settle an argument between them. □ My mom mediated between Zelda and her mom. □ United Nations officials have mediated a series of peace meetings between the two sides. ● **me|dia|tion** /midieɪʃᵊn/ N-UNCOUNT □ ...to solve disputes informally through mediation. ● **me|dia|tor** (**mediators**) N-COUNT □ A cleric acted as mediator between the rebels and the government. [from Late Latin]
→ see **war**

**med|ic** /mɛdɪk/ (**medics**) **1** N-COUNT A **medic** is a doctor who works with the armed forces, as part

of a medical corps. □ ...an army medic. **2** N-COUNT
A **medic** is a doctor or medical student. □ She was
treated by medics at the scene.

**Medi|caid** /mɛdɪkeɪd/ N-PROPER In the United
States, **Medicaid** is a government program that
helps to pay medical costs for poor people. □ For her
medical care, the family used Medicaid. □ Some doctors
won't accept Medicaid patients.

**medi|cal** /mɛdɪkᵊl/ (**medicals**) ADJ **Medical**
means relating to illness and injuries and to
their treatment or prevention. □ Several police
officers received medical treatment for cuts and bruises.
● **medi|cal|ly** /mɛdɪkli/ ADV □ Most teachers are not
medically trained. [from Medieval Latin]

**Word Partnership**    Use *medical* with :

N.    medical **advice**, medical **attention**,
      medical **bills**, medical **care**, medical
      **center**, medical **doctor**, medical
      **emergency**, medical **practice**, medical
      **problems**, medical **research**, medical
      **science**, medical **supplies**, medical
      **tests**, medical **treatment**

**medi|cal ex|am|in|er** (**medical examiners**)
N-COUNT A **medical examiner** is a medical expert
who is responsible for investigating the deaths
of people who have died in a sudden, violent, or
unusual way.

**Medi|care** /mɛdɪkeər/ N-PROPER In the United
States, **Medicare** is a government program that
provides health insurance to cover medical costs
for people aged 65 and older.

**medi|ca|tion** /mɛdɪkeɪ∫ᵊn/ (**medications**)
N-VAR **Medication** is medicine that is used to treat
and cure illness. □ Are you taking any medication?

**me|dici|nal** /mədɪsənᵊl/ ADJ **Medicinal**
substances are used to treat and cure illnesses.
□ We cultivate medicinal plants in the garden. [from
Old French]

**medi|cine** /mɛdɪsɪn/ (**medicines**)
**1** N-UNCOUNT **Medicine** is the treatment of
illness and injuries by doctors and nurses. □ He

decided on a career in medicine. **2** N-VAR **Medicine** is
a substance that you drink or swallow in order to
treat or cure an illness. □ The medicine saved his life.
[from Old French]
→ see Word Web: medicine

**Word Partnership**    Use *medicine* with :

V.    **practice** medicine, **study** medicine **1**
      **give** *someone* medicine, **take** medicine,
      **use** medicine **2**

**me|di|eval** /mɪdiivᵊl, mɪdivᵊl/ ADJ Something
that is **medieval** relates to or was made in the
period of European history between the end of the
Roman Empire in A.D. 476 and about A.D. 1500.
□ ...a medieval castle. [from New Latin]

**me|dio|cre** /midioukər/ ADJ If you describe
something as **mediocre**, you mean that it is of
average quality but you think it should be better.
□ His school test results were mediocre. ● **me|di|oc|rity**
/midiɒkriti/ N-UNCOUNT □ ...the mediocrity of her
work. [from French]

**medi|tate** /mɛdɪteɪt/ (**meditates, meditating,
meditated**) **1** V-I If you **meditate on** something,
you think about it very carefully and deeply
for a long time. □ She meditated on how to be a
good mother. **2** V-I If you **meditate**, you remain
in a silent and calm state for a period of time,
often as part of a religious training. □ When you
meditate, you think about nothing. ● **medi|ta|tion**
/mɛdɪteɪ∫ᵊn/ N-UNCOUNT □ I enjoy yoga and
meditation. [from Latin]

**Word Link**    med ≈ middle : inter**med**iary, **med**ia,
**med**ium

**me|dium** /midiəm/ (**mediums** or **media**) **1** ADJ
If something is of **medium** size, it is neither
large nor small, but approximately halfway
between the two. □ Mix the cream and eggs in a
medium bowl. **2** ADJ You use **medium** to describe
something that is average in degree or amount,
or approximately halfway along a scale between
two extremes. □ Bread and cakes contain only medium

m

**Word Web**    medicine

**Medicine** began in the Western Hemisphere
in ancient Greece. The Greek philosopher
Hippocrates separated medicine from
religion and **disease** from supernatural
explanations. He created the Hippocratic
**oath** which describes a **physician's** duties.
During the Middle Ages, Andreas Vesalius
helped to advance medicine through his
**research** on **anatomy**. Another major step
forward was Friedrich Henle's development
of **germ** theory. An understanding of germs
led to Joseph Lister's demonstrations of the
effective use of **antiseptics**, and Alexander
Fleming's discovery of the **antibiotic** penicillin.

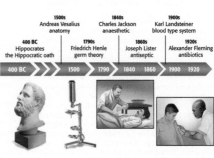

| 400 BC | 1500s | 1790s | 1840s | 1860s | 1900s | 1920s |

| 400 BC | | 1500 | 1790 | 1840 | 1860 | 1900 | 1920 |

*Important Medical Advances*

*levels of salt.* ● **Medium** is also an adverb. ❑ *Andrea has medium brown hair.* **3** N-COUNT A **medium** is a way or means of expressing your ideas or of communicating with people. ❑ *English is a medium of communication in many countries.* **4** N-COUNT A **medium** is a substance or material which is used for a particular purpose or in order to produce a particular effect. [from Latin] **5** → see also **media**

**medley** /mɛdli/ (**medleys**) **1** N-COUNT In music, a **medley** is a collection of different songs that are played one after the other as a single piece of music. ❑ *...a medley of traditional songs.* **2** N-COUNT In sports, a **medley** is a swimming race in which the four main strokes are used one after the other. ❑ *Japan won the Men's 200 meter individual medley.*

**me|dul|la** /mədʌlə/ (**medullas** or **medullae** /mədʌli/) N-COUNT The **medulla** is a part of the brain in humans and other animals that connects the brain to the spinal cord. It controls functions such as breathing and swallowing. The form **medulla oblongata** is also used. [TECHNICAL] [from Latin]

**me|du|sa** /mədusə/ (**medusas** or **medusae**) N-COUNT A **medusa** is a type of jellyfish. [TECHNICAL]

**meek** /mik/ (**meeker, meekest**) ADJ If you describe a person as **meek**, you think that they are gentle and quiet, and likely to do what other people say. ❑ *He was a quiet meek boy.* ● **meek|ly** ADV ❑ *Most people meekly accepted the advice.* [from Old Norse]

**meet** /mit/ (**meets, meeting, met**) **1** V-RECIP If you **meet** someone, you happen to be in the same place as them and start talking to them. ❑ *I have just met an amazing man.* ❑ *He's the kindest person I've ever met.* ● **Meet up** means the same as **meet.** ❑ *Last night he met up with a friend from school.* **2** V-RECIP If two or more people **meet,** they go to the same place, which they have earlier arranged to do, so that they can talk or do something together. ❑ *We could meet for a game of tennis after work.* ● **Meet up** means the same as **meet.** ❑ *We meet up for lunch once a week.* **3** V-T If you **meet** someone at their train, plane, or bus, you go to the station, airport, or bus stop in order to be there when they arrive. ❑ *Mama met me at the station.* **4** V-I If you **meet with** someone, you have a meeting with them. ❑ *A group of lawyers met with the president yesterday.* **5** V-T/V-I If something such as a suggestion, proposal, or new book **meets with** or is **met with** a particular reaction, it gets that reaction from people. ❑ *We hope today's offer will meet with your approval.* **6** V-T If something **meets** a need, requirement, or condition, it is good enough to do what is required. ❑ *This hospital does not meet some patients' needs.* **7** V-T If you **meet** something such as a problem or challenge, you deal with it satisfactorily or do what is required. ❑ *Some people can't meet the problems of daily life.* **8** V-T If you **meet** the cost of something, you provide the money that is needed for it. ❑ *The government will meet some of the cost of the damage.* **9** V-RECIP If two areas **meet,** they are next to one another. ❑ *...where the desert meets the sea.* **10** V-RECIP The place where two lines **meet** is the place where they join together. ❑ *Parallel lines will never meet.* [from Old English] **11** to **make ends meet** → see **end**
▶ **meet up** → see **meet 1, 2**

**meet|ing** /mitɪŋ/ (**meetings**) **1** N-COUNT A **meeting** is an event in which a group of people come together to discuss things or make decisions. ❑ *Can we have a meeting to discuss that?* ● You can also refer to the people at a meeting as **the meeting.** ❑ *The meeting decided that more work was necessary.* **2** N-COUNT A **meeting** is an occasion when you meet someone. ❑ *In January, 37 years after our first meeting, I was back in the studio with Dennis.* [from Old English]

**mega|byte** /mɛgəbaɪt/ (**megabytes**) N-COUNT In computing, a **megabyte** is one million bytes of data. ❑ *...256 megabytes of memory.*

**meio|sis** /maɪoʊsɪs/ N-UNCOUNT **Meiosis** is a type of cell division that results in egg and sperm cells with only half the usual number of chromosomes. [TECHNICAL] [from New Latin]

**mel|an|choly** /mɛlənkɒli/ ADJ Something that is **melancholy** gives you an intense feeling of sadness. ❑ *...the melancholy cries of the sheep.* [from Old French]

**mela|nin** /mɛlənɪn/ N-UNCOUNT **Melanin** is a dark substance in the skin, eyes, and hair of people and animals, which gives them color and can protect them against strong sunlight. [from Greek]

**meld** /mɛld/ (**melds, melding, melded**) **1** V-T/V-I If several things **meld,** or if something **melds** them, they combine or blend in a pleasant or useful way. [FORMAL] ❑ *She listened to the way the words melded with the music.* ❑ *Leave the sauce for 30 minutes for the flavors to meld.* **2** V-T/V-I If several things **meld into** another thing, or if they **are melded into** another thing, they combine and become the other thing. [FORMAL] ❑ *Fact and fiction seemed to meld into a familiar legend.* ❑ *Two unions were melded into one group.* **3** N-COUNT A **meld** of things is a mixture or combination of them that is useful or pleasant. [FORMAL] ❑ *...a perfect meld of art and news.*

**mel|low** /mɛloʊ/ (**mellower, mellowest, mellows, mellowing, mellowed**) **1** ADJ **Mellow** is used to describe things that have a pleasant, soft, rich color, usually red, orange, yellow, or brown. ❑ *...the softer, mellow light of evening.* **2** ADJ A **mellow** sound or flavor is pleasant, smooth, and rich. ❑ *His voice was deep and mellow.* **3** V-T/V-I If someone **mellows** or if something **mellows** them, they become kinder or less extreme in their behavior, especially as a result of growing older. ❑ *When the children married and had children* *of their own, he mellowed a little.* ● **Mellow** is also an adjective. ❑ *Is she more mellow than she was?* [from Old English]

▶ **mellow out** PHR-VERB If someone **mellows out**, they become very relaxed. [INFORMAL] ❑ *Everyone started telling me to mellow out.*

**melo|dra|ma** /mɛlədrɑmə/ (**melodramas**) N-VAR A **melodrama** is a story or play in which there are a lot of exciting or sad events and in which people's emotions are very exaggerated. [from French]

**melo|dra|mat|ic** /mɛlədrəmætɪk/ ADJ **Melodramatic** behavior is behavior in which someone treats a situation as much more serious than it really is. ❑ *Stop being so melodramatic!* [from French]

**melo|dy** /mɛlədi/ (**melodies**) N-COUNT A **melody** is a tune. ❑ *I whistle melodies from my favorite TV shows.* [from Old French]

**mel|on** /mɛlən/ (**melons**) N-VAR A **melon** is a large fruit which is sweet and juicy inside and has a hard green or yellow skin. ❑ *…some juicy slices of melon.* [from Old French]

**melt** /mɛlt/ (**melts, melting, melted**) **1** V-T/V-I When a solid substance **melts** or when you **melt** it, it changes to a liquid, usually because it has been heated. ❑ *The snow melted.* ❑ *Melt the chocolate in a bowl.* ● **melting** N-UNCOUNT ❑ *This experiment investigates if mass also changes during melting.* **2** V-I If something **melts**, it suddenly disappears. [LITERARY] ❑ *His feelings of worry melted, but returned later.* ● **Melt away** means the same as **melt**. ❑ *Scot felt his doubts melt away.* **3** V-I If a person or thing **melts into** something such as darkness or a crowd of people, they become difficult to see. [LITERARY] ❑ *He turned and melted into the darkness.* **4** N-COUNT A **melt** is a piece of bread which has meat or fish on it, and melted cheese on top. ❑ *…a tuna melt.* [from Old English]
→ see **glacier, matter**

**melt|ing point** (**melting points**) N-COUNT The **melting point** of a substance is the temperature at which it melts when you heat it.

**mem|ber** /mɛmbər/ (**members**) N-COUNT A **member** of a group or organization is one of the people, animals, or things belonging to that group. ❑ *Britain is a full member of NATO.* ❑ *A member of the public saw the accident.* ❑ *The support of our members is very important to the organization.* [from Latin]

**Mem|ber of Par|lia|ment** (**Members of Parliament**) N-COUNT A **Member of Parliament** is a person who has been elected by the people in a particular area to represent them in a country's parliament. The abbreviation **MP** is often used.

**mem|ber|ship** /mɛmbərʃɪp/ (**memberships**) **1** N-UNCOUNT **Membership** in an organization is the state of being a member of it. ❑ *…his membership in the Communist Party.* **2** N-VAR The **membership** of an organization is the people who belong to it, or the number of people who belong to it. ❑ *By 1890 the organization had a membership of 409,000.* [from Latin]

**mem|brane** /mɛmbreɪn/ (**membranes**) N-COUNT A **membrane** is a thin piece of skin that connects or covers parts of a person's or animal's body. ❑ *…the thin membrane on the edge of the heart.* [from Latin]

**mem|bra|no|phone** /mɛmbreɪnəfoʊn/ (**membranophones**) N-COUNT A **membranophone** is any musical instrument that produces its sound by the vibration of a stretched skin, for example a drum. [TECHNICAL] [from Latin]

**memo** /mɛmoʊ/ (**memos**) N-COUNT A **memo** is a short official note that is sent by one person to another within the same company or organization. ❑ *He sent a memo to all staff.* [from Latin]

**mem|oirs** /mɛmwɑrz/ N-PLURAL A person's **memoirs** are a written account of the people who they have known and events that they remember. ❑ *He published his memoirs after he retired from work.* [from French]

**memo|ra|bilia** /mɛmərəbɪliə/ N-PLURAL **Memorabilia** are things that you collect because they are connected with a person or organization in which you are interested. ❑ *He collects Elvis memorabilia.* [from Latin]

**memo|rable** /mɛmərəbᵊl/ ADJ Something that is **memorable** is worth remembering or likely to be remembered, because it is special or very enjoyable. ❑ *Our wedding was a very memorable day.* [from Latin]

**memo|ran|dum** /mɛmərændəm/ (**memoranda** or **memorandums**) N-COUNT A **memorandum** is a memo. ❑ *…a memorandum sent to all senior UN personnel.* [FORMAL] [from Latin]

| **Word Link** | *memor ≈ memory : com**memor**ate, **memor**ial, **memor**y* |
| --- | --- |

**me|mo|rial** /mɪmɔriəl/ (**memorials**) **1** N-COUNT A **memorial** is a structure built in order to remind people of a famous person or event. ❑ *He wanted to build a memorial to Columbus.* **2** ADJ A **memorial** event, object, or prize is in honor of someone who has died, so that they will be remembered. ❑ *A memorial service was held for her at St. Paul's Church.* [from Late Latin]

memorial

**memo|rize** /mɛməraɪz/ (**memorizes, memorizing, memorized**) V-T If you **memorize** something, you learn it so that you can remember it exactly. ❑ *He tried to memorize the way to Rose's street.* [from Old French]

**memo|ry** /mɛməri/ (**memories**) **1** N-VAR Your **memory** is your ability to remember things. ❑ *All the details of the meeting are fresh in my memory.* ❑ *He had a good memory for faces.* **2** N-COUNT A **memory** is something that you remember from the past. ❑ *She doesn't like to watch the film because of the bad memories it brings back.* **3** N-COUNT A computer's **memory** is the part of the computer where information is stored, especially for a short time before it is transferred to disks or magnetic tapes. [COMPUTING] ❑ *The data are stored in the computer's memory.* **4** N-SING If you talk about the **memory** of someone who has died, especially someone who was loved or respected, you are referring to the thoughts, actions, and ceremonies by which they are remembered. ❑ *I planted a tree in memory of my grandmother.* **5** PHRASE If you do something **from memory**, for example speak the words of a poem or play a piece of music, you do it without looking at it, because you know it very well. □ *Many members of the church sang from memory.* [from Old French]

---

### Word Partnership    Use *memory* with :

ADJ.   **conscious** memory, **failing** memory, **fresh in your** memory, **long-/short-term** memory, **poor** memory, **in recent** memory **1**
     **bad** memory, **good** memory **1 2**
     **happy** memory, **painful** memory, **sad** memory, **vivid** memory **2**

N.     **computer** memory, **random access** memory, memory **storage 3**

---

**memo|ry card** (**memory cards**) N-COUNT A **memory card** is a type of card containing computer memory that is used in digital cameras and other devices. [COMPUTING]

**men** /mɛn/ **Men** is the plural of **man**. [from Old English]

**men|ace** /mɛnɪs/ (**menaces, menacing, menaced**) **1** N-COUNT Someone or something that is a **menace** is likely to cause serious harm. □ *You are a menace to the public.* **2** N-UNCOUNT **Menace** is a quality or atmosphere that gives you the feeling that you are in danger or that someone wants to harm you. □ *His voice was full of menace.* **3** V-T If you say that one thing **menaces** another, you mean that the first thing is likely to cause the second thing serious harm. □ *No foreign army menaced the country.* ● **men|ac|ing** /mɛnɪsɪŋ/ ADJ □ *His strong dark eyes gave his face a menacing look.* ● **men|ac|ing|ly** ADV □ *A group of men moved menacingly forward to block her way.* [from Latin]

**mend** /mɛnd/ (**mends, mending, mended**) **1** V-T If you **mend** a tear or a hole in a piece of clothing, you repair it by sewing it. □ *He earns money by mending clothes.* **2** V-T/V-I If a person or a part of their body **mends** or **is mended**, they get better after they have been ill or have had an injury. □ *I'm feeling a lot better. The cut aches, but it's mending.* **3** PHRASE If you are **on the mend** after an illness or injury, you are recovering from it. [INFORMAL] □ *The baby has been ill, but is on the mend now.*

---

### Word Link    *itis ≈ inflammation : arthritis, hepatitis, meningitis*

**men|in|gi|tis** /mɛnɪndʒaɪtɪs/ N-UNCOUNT **Meningitis** is a serious infectious illness which affects your brain and spinal cord. [from Greek]

**me|nis|cus** /mɪnɪskəs/ (**menisci**) N-COUNT A **meniscus** is the curved surface of a liquid in a narrow tube. [TECHNICAL] [from New Latin]

**Men|no|nite** /mɛnənaɪt/ (**Mennonites**) **1** N-COUNT **Mennonites** are members of a Protestant sect who do not baptize their children and who are opposed to military service. **2** ADJ **Mennonite** means relating to the religious beliefs or practices of Mennonites. □ *...Pennsylvania's Mennonite communities.* [from German]

**meno|pause** /mɛnəpɔz/ N-SING **Menopause** is the time during which a woman gradually stops menstruating, usually when she is about fifty. ● **meno|pau|sal** ADJ □ *...a menopausal woman.* [from French]

**me|no|rah** /mənɔrə, -nourə/ (**menorahs**) N-COUNT A **menorah** is a candelabra consisting of seven or sometimes eight branches. It is a symbol

of Judaism. □ *We lit the menorah.* [from Hebrew]

**men's room** (**men's rooms**) N-COUNT The **men's room** is a bathroom for men in a public building.

**men|strual** /mɛnstruəl/ ADJ **Menstrual** means relating to menstruation. □ *...the menstrual cycle.* [from Latin]

**men|stru|ate** /mɛnstrueɪt/ (**menstruates, menstruating, menstruated**) V-I When a woman **menstruates**, a flow of blood comes from her uterus. [FORMAL] □ *Women athletes may menstruate less frequently.* ● **men|strua|tion** /mɛnstrueɪʃ°n/ N-UNCOUNT □ *Menstruation stops when a woman is between forty-five and fifty.* [from Latin]

**mens|wear** /mɛnzwɛər/ N-UNCOUNT **Menswear** is clothing for men. □ *...the menswear industry.*

---

### Word Link    *ment ≈ mind : demented, mental, mentality*

**men|tal** /mɛnt°l/ **1** ADJ **Mental** means relating to the process of thinking. □ *...the mental development of the children.* ● **men|tal|ly** ADV □ *I think you are mentally tired.* **2** ADJ A **mental** act is one that involves only thinking and not physical action. □ *Allen did a quick mental calculation.* ● **men|tal|ly** ADV □ *This technique will help people mentally organize information.* [from Late Latin]

**men|tal|ity** /mɛntælɪti/ (**mentalities**) N-COUNT Your **mentality** is your attitudes and your way of thinking. □ *...a criminal mentality.* [from Late Latin]

**men|tion** /mɛnʃ°n/ (**mentions, mentioning, mentioned**) V-T If you **mention** something, you say something about it, usually briefly. □ *She did not mention her name.* □ *I may not have mentioned it to her.* □ *I mentioned that I didn't really like pop music.* [from Old French]

---

### Word Partnership    Use *mention* with :

V.    **fail to** mention, **forget to** mention, **neglect to** mention

---

**men|tor** /mɛntɔr/ (**mentors**) N-COUNT A person's **mentor** is someone who gives them help and advice over a period of time. □ *Leon Sullivan was my mentor and my friend.*

**menu** /mɛnyu/ (**menus**) **1** N-COUNT In a restaurant or café, the **menu** is a list of the meals and drinks that are available. □ *A waiter offered him the menu.* **2** N-COUNT On a computer screen, a **menu** is a list of choices of things that you can do using the computer. □ *Press F7 to show the print menu.* [from French]

**MEP** /ɛm i pi/ (**MEPs**) N-COUNT An **MEP** is a person who has been elected to the European Parliament. **MEP** is an abbreviation for "Member of the European Parliament."

**Mercator pro|jec|tion** /mərkeɪtər prəjɛkʃ°n/ (**Mercator projections**) N-VAR A **Mercator projection** is an image of a map that is made by projecting the map on a globe onto a cylindrical surface. Compare **azimuthal projection, conic projection**. [TECHNICAL] [from Flemish]

**mer|ce|nary** /mɜrsənɛri/ (**mercenaries**) **1** N-COUNT A **mercenary** is a soldier who is paid to fight by a country or group that they do not belong to. □ *The war has brought in foreign mercenaries.* **2** ADJ If you describe someone as **mercenary**, you are criticizing them because you think that they are only interested in the money that they can get from a particular person or situation. ❑ *"I hate to sound mercenary," Labane said, "but am I getting paid to act in your play?"* [from Latin]

---

**Word Link** | merc ≈ trading : commerce, merchandise, merchant

---

**mer|chan|dise** /mɜrtʃəndaɪz, -daɪs/ N-UNCOUNT **Merchandise** is products that are bought, sold, or traded. [FORMAL] ❑ *The company provides merchandise for elderly people.* [from Old French]

**mer|chan|dis|er** /mɜrtʃəndaɪzər/ (**merchandisers**) N-COUNT A **merchandiser** is a person or company that sells goods to the public. [BUSINESS] ❑ *...a fashion merchandiser.* [from Old French]

**mer|chan|dis|ing** /mɜrtʃəndaɪzɪŋ/ N-UNCOUNT **Merchandising** is the way stores and businesses organize the sale of their products, for example the way they are displayed and the prices that are chosen. [BUSINESS] ❑ *The band earns a lot of money through merchandising.* [from Old French]

**mer|chant** /mɜrtʃənt/ (**merchants**) ◼ N-COUNT A **merchant** is a person who buys or sells goods in large quantities. ❑ *His father was a successful wool merchant.* ◼ N-COUNT A **merchant** is a person who owns or runs a store or shop. ❑ *The family buys most of the things it needs from local merchants.* ◼ ADJ **Merchant** seamen or ships are involved in carrying goods for trade. ❑ *...the merchant navy.* [from Old French]

**mer|ci|ful|ly** /mɜrsɪfəli/ ADV You can use **mercifully** to show that you are glad that something good has happened, or that something bad has not happened or has stopped. ❑ *Mercifully, a friend saw what was happening and came to help.* [from Old French]

**mer|ci|less** /mɜrsɪlɪs/ ADJ If you describe someone as **merciless**, you mean that they are very cruel or determined and do not show any concern for the effect their actions have on other people. ❑ *Their merciless laughter made her very upset.* ● **mer|ci|less|ly** ADV ❑ *We teased him mercilessly.* [from Old French]

**mer|cu|ry** /mɜrkyəri/ N-UNCOUNT **Mercury** is a silver-colored liquid metal that is used especially in thermometers and barometers. [from Latin] → see **thermometer**

**Mer|cu|ry** /mɜrkyəri/ N-PROPER **Mercury** is the planet that is closest to the sun. [from Latin]

**mer|cy** /mɜrsi/ (**mercies**) ◼ N-UNCOUNT If someone in authority shows **mercy**, they choose not to harm or punish someone they have power over. ❑ *His attacker showed no mercy.* ◼ PHRASE If one person or thing is **at the mercy of** another, the first person or thing is in a situation where they cannot prevent themselves from being harmed or affected by the second. ❑ *We slept outside, at the mercy of the mosquitoes.* [from Old French]

**mere** /mɪər/ (**merest**)

**Mere** does not have a comparative form. The superlative form **merest** is used to emphasize how small something is, rather than in comparisons.

ADJ You use **mere** to emphasize how unimportant, insufficient, or small something is. ❑ *Sixty percent of teachers are women, but a mere five percent of women are principals.* ❑ *Some people are terrified at the mere sight of a spider.* ● **mere|ly** ADV ❑ *The brain accounts for merely three percent of body weight.* [from Latin]

**mere|ly** /mɪərli/ ◼ ADV You use **merely** to emphasize that something is only what you say and not better, more important, or more exciting. ❑ *Michael is now merely a good friend.* ◼ PHRASE You use **not merely** before the less important of two contrasting statements, as a way of emphasizing the more important statement. ❑ *The team needs players who want to play for Canada, not merely any country that will have them.* [from Latin]

---

**Word Link** | merg ≈ sinking : emerge, merge, submerge

---

**merge** /mɜrdʒ/ (**merges, merging, merged**) V-RECIP If one thing **merges with** another, or is **merged with** another, they combine or come together to make one whole thing. ❑ *Bank of America merged with another bank.* ❑ *The rivers merge just north of here.* ❑ *The two countries merged into one.* [from Latin]

**mer|ger** /mɜrdʒər/ (**mergers**) N-COUNT A **merger** is the joining together of two separate companies or organizations so that they become one. [BUSINESS] ❑ *...a merger between two of America's biggest companies.* [from Latin]

**mer|it** /mɛrɪt/ (**merits, meriting, merited**) ◼ N-UNCOUNT If something has **merit**, it has good or worthwhile qualities. ❑ *The argument had considerable merit.* ◼ N-PLURAL The **merits** of something are its advantages or other good points. ❑ *We need to persuade them of the merits of peace.* ◼ V-T If someone or something **merits** a particular action or treatment, they deserve it. [FORMAL] ❑ *He made a mistake, but that does not merit going to jail.* [from Old French]

**mer|maid** /mɜrmeɪd/ (**mermaids**) N-COUNT In fairy tales and legends, a **mermaid** is a woman with a fish's tail, who lives in the sea.

**mer|ry** /mɛri/ (**merrier, merriest**) ADJ **Merry** means happy and cheerful. ❑ *...a merry little tune.* ❑ *Merry Christmas, everyone.* ● **mer|ri|ly** ADV ❑ *Chris laughed merrily.* [from Old English]

**me|sa** /meɪsə/ (**mesas**) N-COUNT A **mesa** is a large hill with a flat top and steep sides, especially in the southwestern United States. [from Spanish]

**mesh** /mɛʃ/ (**meshes, meshing, meshed**) ◼ N-VAR **Mesh** is material like a net made from wire, thread, or plastic. ❑ *...wire mesh.* ◼ V-RECIP If two things or ideas **mesh** or **are meshed**, they go together well or fit together closely. ❑ *Their senses of humor meshed perfectly.* ❑ *How do the new players mesh with the old ones?* [from Dutch]

**mes|mer|ize** /mɛzməraɪz/ (**mesmerizes, mesmerizing, mesmerized**) V-T If you **are mesmerized** by something or someone, you are so interested in them or so attracted to them that you cannot think about anything else. ❑ *He was absolutely mesmerized by Pavarotti on television.* [after F. A. Mesmer (1734–1815), an Austrian physician]

**meso|sphere** /mɛzəsfɪər/ ◼ N-SING The **mesosphere** is the layer of the Earth's atmosphere that is directly above the stratosphere. [TECHNICAL] ◼ N-SING The **mesosphere** is the part of the Earth's interior that lies between the upper

**m**

mantle and the outer core. [TECHNICAL]

**Meso|zo|ic era** /mɛzəzouɪk ɪərə/ N-SING The **Mesozoic era** is a period in the history of the Earth that began around 250 million years ago and ended around 65 million years ago. [TECHNICAL]

**mess** /mɛs/ (**messes, messing, messed**)
**1** N-SING If something is **a mess** or **in a mess**, it is not neat. ❑ *The house is a mess.* **2** N-VAR If you say that a situation is **a mess**, you mean that it is full of trouble or problems. You can also say that something is **in a mess**. ❑ *I've made such a mess of my life.* ❑ *...the reasons why the economy is in such a mess.* [from Old French]
▶ **mess around 1** PHR-VERB If you **mess around**, you spend time doing things without any particular purpose or without achieving anything. ❑ *We were just messing around playing with paint.* **2** PHR-VERB If you say that someone **is messing around with** something, you mean that they are interfering with it in a harmful way. ❑ *You don't want to go messing around with bears.*
▶ **mess up 1** PHR-VERB If you **mess** something **up** or if you **mess up**, you cause something to fail or be spoiled. [INFORMAL] ❑ *When politicians mess things up, it is the people who suffer.* ❑ *He has messed up one career.* **2** PHR-VERB If you **mess up** a place or a thing, you make it dirty or not neat. [INFORMAL] ❑ *I hope they haven't messed up your video tapes.*

### Word Partnership    Use mess with :

| | |
|---|---|
| V. | **clean up** a mess, **leave** a mess, **make a** mess **1** **2** |
| | **get into** a mess **2** |

**mes|sage** /mɛsɪdʒ/ (**messages, messaging, messaged**) **1** N-COUNT A **message** is a piece of information or a request that you send to someone or leave for them when you cannot speak to them directly. ❑ *I got a message you were trying to find me.* **2** N-COUNT The **message** that someone is trying to communicate is the idea or point that they are trying to communicate. ❑ *The report's message was clear.* ❑ *We've been getting the message from you that we're useless.* **3** V-T/V-I If you **message** someone, you send them a message electronically using a computer or another device such as a cellphone. ❑ *People who message a lot feel unpopular if they don't get many back.* [from Old French]

### Word Partnership    Use message with :

| | |
|---|---|
| V. | **give** *someone* **a** message, **leave** a message, **read** a message, **take** a message **1** |
| | **deliver** a message, **get** a message, **hear** a message, message **1** **2** |
| | **get** a message **across**, |
| | **spread** a message **2** |
| ADJ. | **clear** message, **important** message, **urgent** message **1** **2** |
| | **powerful** message, **simple** message, **strong** message, **wrong** message **2** |

**mes|sage board** (**message boards**) N-COUNT A **message board** is a bulletin board, especially on the Internet.

**mes|sen|ger** /mɛsɪndʒər/ (**messengers**) N-COUNT A **messenger** takes a message or package to someone, or takes them regularly as their job. ❑ *There will be a messenger at the airport to collect the*

photographs. [from Old French]

**Messiah** /mɪsaɪə/ N-PROPER For Jews, **the Messiah** is a king or leader who will be sent to them by God. For Christians, **the Messiah** is Jesus Christ. [from Old French]

**messy** /mɛsi/ (**messier, messiest**) **1** ADJ A **messy** person or activity makes things dirty or not neat. ❑ *She was a messy cook.* **2** ADJ Something that is **messy** is dirty or not neat. ❑ *His writing is very messy.* **3** ADJ If you describe a situation as **messy**, you are emphasizing that it is confused or complicated, and therefore unsatisfactory. ❑ *John's divorce was very messy.* [from Old French]

**met** /mɛt/ **Met** is the past tense and past participle of **meet**.

**meta|bol|ic** /mɛtəbɒlɪk/ ADJ **Metabolic** means relating to a person's or animal's metabolism. ❑ *People who have a low metabolic rate will gain weight.* [from Greek]

### Word Link    meta ≈ beyond, change : metabolism, metamorphosis, metaphor

**me|tabo|lism** /mɪtæbəlɪzəm/ (**metabolisms**) N-VAR Your **metabolism** is the way that chemical processes in your body cause food to be used in an efficient way, for example to make new cells and to give you energy. ❑ *If you don't eat breakfast, your metabolism slows down.* [from Greek]

**met|al** /mɛtᵊl/ (**metals**) N-VAR **Metal** is a hard substance such as iron, steel, gold, or lead. ❑ *...a table with metal legs.* [from Latin]
→ see Word Web: **metal**
→ see **mineral**

**me|tal|lic** /mətælɪk/ ADJ **Metallic** things are made of metal, or look or sound like metal. ❑ *There was a metallic click and the gates swung open.* ❑ *...metallic silver paint.* [from Latin]

**me|tal|lic bond** (**metallic bonds**) N-COUNT A **metallic bond** is the kind of chemical bond that occurs in metals. [TECHNICAL]

**met|al|loid** /mɛtᵊlɔɪd/ (**metalloids**) N-COUNT **Metalloids** are chemical elements that have some of the properties of metals and some of the properties of nonmetals. [TECHNICAL] ● **metalloid** is also an adjective ADJ ❑ *...metalloid elements.*

**meta|mor|phic** /mɛtəmɔrfɪk/ ADJ **Metamorphic** rock is rock that is formed from other rock as a result of heat or pressure beneath the surface of the Earth. Compare **igneous**, **sedimentary**.

### Word Link    osis ≈ state or condition : hypnosis, metamorphosis, neurosis

**meta|mor|pho|sis** /mɛtəmɔrfəsɪs/ (**metamorphoses**) N-VAR When a **metamorphosis** occurs, a person or thing develops and changes into something completely different. [FORMAL] ❑ *...his metamorphosis from a Republican to a Democrat.* ❑ *It undergoes its metamorphosis from a caterpillar to a butterfly.* [from Latin]
→ see **amphibian**

**meta|phase** /mɛtəfeɪz/ (**metaphases**) N-VAR **Metaphase** is a stage in the process of cell division in which the chromosomes line up before they separate. [TECHNICAL]

## Word Web   metal

In their natural state, most **metals** are not pure. They are usually combined with other materials in mixtures known as **ores**. Almost all metals are shiny. Many metals share these special properties. They are ductile, meaning that they can be made into

**copper**    **aluminium**    **gold**

**wire**. They are malleable and can be formed into thin, flat sheets. And they are also good **conductors** of heat and electricity. Except for **copper** and **gold**, metals are generally gray or silver in color.

---

**Word Link**   meta ≈ beyond, change : metabolism, metamorphosis, metaphor

**meta|phor** /mɛtəfɔr/ (**metaphors**) N-VAR A **metaphor** is an imaginative way of describing something by referring to something else which is the same in a particular way. ❑ She uses a lot of religious metaphors in her writing. [from Latin]

**meta|phori|cal** /mɛtəfɔrɪkᵊl/ ADJ You use the word **metaphorical** to indicate that you are not using words with their ordinary meaning, but are describing something by means of an image or symbol. ❑ ...the metaphorical language used in poetry. ● **meta|phori|cal|ly** ADV ❑ You're speaking metaphorically, I hope. [from Latin]

**me|tas|ta|size** /mətæstəsaɪz/ (**metastasizes, metastasizing, metastasized**) V-I If cancer cells **metastasize**, they spread to another part of the body. [MEDICAL] ❑ A small tumor on his left lung has started to metastasize. [from Latin]

**me|teor** /mitiər/ (**meteors**) N-COUNT A **meteor** is a piece of rock or metal that burns very brightly when it enters the Earth's atmosphere from space. [from Medieval Latin]
→ see Word Web: **meteor**

---

**Word Link**   ite ≈ mineral, rock : granite, graphite, meteorite

**me|teor|ite** /mitiəraɪt/ (**meteorites**) N-COUNT A **meteorite** is a large piece of rock or metal from space that has landed on Earth. [from Medieval Latin]
→ see **meteor**

**me|teor|oid** /mitiərɔɪd/ (**meteoroids**) N-COUNT A **meteoroid** is a piece of rock or dust that travels around the sun. [TECHNICAL] [from Medieval Latin]

**me|teoro|logi|cal** /mitiərəlɒdʒɪkᵊl/ ADJ **Meteorological** means relating to the weather or to weather forecasting. ❑ ...bad meteorological conditions. [from Greek]

**me|teor|ol|ogy** /mitiərɒlədʒi/ N-UNCOUNT **Meteorology** is the study of the processes in the Earth's atmosphere that cause particular weather conditions, especially in order to predict the weather. [from Greek]

---

**Word Link**   meter ≈ measuring : kilometer, meter, perimeter

**me|ter** /mitər/ (**meters**) **1** N-COUNT A **meter** is a device that measures and records something such as the amount of gas or electricity that you have used. ❑ He was there to read the electricity meter. **2** N-COUNT A **meter** is a metric unit of length equal to 100 centimeters. ❑ She's running the 1,500 meters race. **3** N-VAR In music, **meter** is the rhythmic arrangement of beats according to particular patterns. [TECHNICAL] **4** PHRASE **Meters per second** is a unit of speed in physics. An object that is moving at a particular number of **meters per second** travels that number of meters in one second. The abbreviation m/s is also used. [Sense 1 from Old English. Sense 2 from French. Sense 3 from Latin.]
→ see **measurement**

**metha|done** /mɛθədoʊn/ N-UNCOUNT **Methadone** is a drug that is sometimes prescribed to heroin addicts as a substitute for heroin.

**me|thane** /mɛθeɪn/ N-UNCOUNT **Methane** is a colorless gas that has no smell.

**metha|no|gen** /məθænədʒən/ (**methanogens**) N-COUNT **Methanogens** are bacteria that produce methane. [TECHNICAL]

**metha|nol** /mɛθənɔl/ N-UNCOUNT **Methanol** is a colorless, poisonous liquid, used as a solvent and fuel. ❑ Methanol is a cleaner fuel than oil.

**meth|od** /mɛθəd/ (**methods**) N-COUNT A **method** is a particular way of doing something. ❑ ...new teaching methods. [from French]
→ see **experiment, science**

m

---

## Word Web   meteor

As an asteroid flies through **space**, small pieces called meteoroids sometimes break off. When a meteoroid enters the earth's **atmosphere**, we call it a **meteor**. As the earth passes through asteroid belts we see spectacular **meteor** showers. Meteors that reach the earth are called meteorites. Scientists believe a huge **meteorite** struck the earth about

65 million years ago. It left a pit in Mexico called the Chicxulub **Crater**. It's about 150 miles wide. The crash caused earthquakes and tsunamis. It may also have produced a change in the earth's environment. Some believe this event caused the dinosaurs to die out.

| **Thesaurus** | *method* | Also look up : |

| N. | manner, procedure, process, system, technique |

| **Word Partnership** | Use *method* with : |

| ADJ. | **alternative/traditional** method, **best** method, **new** method, **preferred** method |
| V. | **develop a** method, **use a** method |
| N. | method **of payment**, **teaching** method |

**me|thod|i|cal** /məθɒdɪkᵊl/ ADJ If you describe someone as **methodical**, you mean that they do things carefully, thoroughly, and in order. ❑ *Da Vinci was methodical in his research.* ● **me|thod|i|cal|ly** /məθɒdɪkli/ ADV ❑ *She methodically put her things into her suitcase.* [from French]

**meth|od|ol|ogy** /mɛθədɒlədʒi/ (**methodologies**) N-VAR A **methodology** is a system of methods and principles for doing something. [FORMAL] ❑ *Teachers use different teaching methodologies in different subjects.* ● **meth|odo|logi|cal** /mɛθədəlɒdʒɪkᵊl/ ADJ ❑ *We had serious methodological difficulties.* [from French]

**me|ticu|lous** /mətɪkyələs/ ADJ Someone who is **meticulous** does things very carefully and with great attention to detail. ❑ *He was so meticulous about everything.* ● **me|ticu|lous|ly** ADV ❑ *They cleaned the apartment meticulously every week.* [from Latin]

**met|ric** /mɛtrɪk/ ADJ **Metric** means relating to the metric system. ❑ *...80,000 metric tons of food.* [from French]

**met|ric sys|tem** N-SING The **metric system** is the system of measurement that uses meters, grams, and liters.

**met|ric ton** (**metric tons**) N-COUNT A **metric ton** is 1,000 kilograms. ❑ *The Wall Street Journal uses 220,000 metric tons of paper each year.*

**met|ro** /mɛtroʊ/ (**metros**) also **Metro** N-COUNT The **metro** is the subway system in some cities, for example in Washington or Paris. ❑ *A new metro runs under the square.* [from French]
→ see **transportation**

| **Word Link** | *poli* ≈ *city* : *cosmopolitan, metropolis, politics* |

**me|tropo|lis** /mətrɒpəlɪs/ (**metropolises**) N-COUNT A **metropolis** is the largest, busiest, and most important city in a country or region. ❑ *He lives in the metropolis of Chengdu.* [from Late Latin]

**met|ro|poli|tan** /mɛtrəpɒlɪtᵊn/ ADJ **Metropolitan** means belonging to or typical of a large, busy city. ❑ *...the metropolitan district of Miami.* ❑ *...major metropolitan hospitals.* [from Late Latin]

**mez|za|nine** /mɛzənin/ (**mezzanines**) **1** N-COUNT A **mezzanine** is a small floor which is built between two main floors of a building. ❑ *...the mezzanine floor.* **2** N-COUNT The **mezzanine** is the lowest balcony in a theater, or the front rows in the lowest balcony. [from French]

**mg mg** is a written abbreviation for **milligram** or **milligrams**. ❑ *...300 mg of calcium.*

**MIA** /ɛm aɪ eɪ/ (**MIAs**) ADJ **MIA** is used to describe members of the armed forces who do not return from a military operation but who are not known to have been killed or captured. **MIA** is an abbreviation for "missing in action." ❑ *Hundreds of soldiers were MIA.* ● An **MIA** is a member of the armed forces who is missing in action. ❑ *...the families of MIAs.*

**mice** /maɪs/ **Mice** is the plural of **mouse**. [from Old English]

**mi|crobe** /maɪkroʊb/ (**microbes**) N-COUNT A **microbe** is a very small living thing, which you can only see if you use a microscope. ❑ *...the microbes that cause food poisoning.* [from French]

| **Word Link** | *micro* ≈ *small* : *microchip, microeconomics, microscope* |

**micro|chip** /maɪkroʊtʃɪp/ (**microchips**) N-COUNT A **microchip** is a very small piece of silicon inside a computer that has electronic circuits on it.

**micro|cli|mate** /maɪkroʊklaɪmɪt/ (**microclimates**) also **micro-climate** N-COUNT A **microclimate** is the climate that exists in a particular small area, which may be different from the climate of the surrounding area.

**micro|cosm** /maɪkrəkɒzəm/ (**microcosms**) N-COUNT A **microcosm** is a small society, place, or activity which has all the typical features of a much larger one and so seems like a smaller version of it. [FORMAL] ❑ *The city was a microcosm of all American culture during the 1960s.* [from Medieval Latin]

**micro|eco|nom|ics** /maɪkroʊkɛnɒmɪks, -ik-/ also **micro-economics** N-UNCOUNT **Microeconomics** is the branch of economics that is concerned with individual areas of economic activity, such as those within a particular company or relating to a particular market. ❑ *...a theory based on microeconomics.* ● **micro|eco|nom|ic** /maɪkroʊkɛnɒmɪk, -ik-/ ADJ ❑ *...microeconomic theory.*

**micro|fiber** /maɪkroʊfaɪbər/ (**microfibers**) N-VAR **Microfibers** are extremely light artificial fibers that are used to make cloth. ❑ *...microfiber fabric.*

**micro|organism** /maɪkroʊɔrgənɪzəm/ (**microorganisms**) N-COUNT A **microorganism** is a very small living thing which you can only see if you use a microscope.
→ see **fungus**

| **Word Link** | *phon* ≈ *sound* : *microphone, symphony, telephone* |

**micro|phone** /maɪkrəfoʊn/ (**microphones**) N-COUNT A **microphone** is a device that is used to make sounds louder or to record them on a tape recorder.
→ see **concert**

**micro|proc|es|sor** /maɪkroʊprɒsɛsər/ (**microprocessors**) N-COUNT In a computer, the **microprocessor** is the main microchip, which controls its most important functions. [COMPUTING]

microphone

**Word Link** | micro ≈ small : microchip, microeconomics, microscope

**Word Link** | scope ≈ looking : horoscope, microscope, telescope

**micro|scope** /maɪkrəskoʊp/ (**microscopes**)
N-COUNT A **microscope** is a scientific instrument which makes very small objects look bigger so that more detail can be seen.

**micro|scop|ic** /maɪkrəskɒpɪk/ ADJ **Microscopic** objects are extremely small, and usually can be seen only through a microscope. ❑ ...microscopic cells.

**micro|wave** /maɪkroʊweɪv/ (**microwaves, microwaving, microwaved**) ◼ N-COUNT A **microwave** or a **microwave oven** is an oven which cooks food very quickly by electromagnetic radiation rather than by heat. ◻ V-T To **microwave** food or drink means to cook or heat it in a microwave oven. ❑ Microwave the vegetables first.
→ see **cook, wave**

**mid|air** /mɪdeər/ N-UNCOUNT If something happens in **midair**, it happens in the air, rather than on the ground. ❑ The bird stopped in midair.

**mid-Atlantic** ADJ A **mid-Atlantic** accent is a mixture of British and American accents. ❑ He had a mid-Atlantic accent.

**mid|day** /mɪddeɪ/ N-UNCOUNT **Midday** is twelve o'clock in the middle of the day. ❑ At midday everyone had lunch.

**mid|dle** /mɪdᵊl/ (**middles**) ◼ N-COUNT The **middle of** something is the part of it that is farthest from its edges, ends, or outside surface. ❑ Howard stood in the middle of the room. ❑ They had a tennis court in the middle of the garden. ◻ **the middle of nowhere** → see **nowhere** ◼ ADJ The **middle** object in a row of objects is the one that has an equal number of objects on each side. ❑ ...the middle button of his uniform jacket. ◼ N-SING The **middle of** an event or period of time is the part that comes after the first part and before the last part. ❑ I woke up in the middle of the night and could hear a noise outside. ● **Middle** is also an adjective. ❑ He was now in his middle years, and looked even better than before. ◼ PHRASE If you are **in the middle of** doing something, you are busy doing it. ❑ I'm in the middle of cooking for nine people. [from Old English]

**mid|dle age** N-UNCOUNT **Middle age** is the period in your life when you are between the ages of about 40 and 60. ❑ Men often gain weight in middle age.

**middle-aged** ADJ A **middle-aged** person is between the ages of about 40 and 60. ❑ ...middle-aged, married businessmen
→ see **age**

**mid|dle class** (**middle classes**) N-COUNT The **middle class** or **middle classes** are the people in a society who are not lower class or upper class, for example business people, managers, doctors, lawyers, and teachers. ❑ The middle class is leaving the cities. ● **Middle class** is also an adjective. ❑ ...middle-class families.

**Mid|dle East** N-PROPER The **Middle East** is the area around the eastern Mediterranean that includes Iran and all the countries in Asia to the west and southwest of Iran. ❑ ...the two great rivers

of the Middle East.

**middle|man** /mɪdᵊlmæn/ (**middlemen**)
◼ N-COUNT A **middleman** is a person or company which buys things from the people who produce them and sells them to the people who want to buy them. [BUSINESS] ❑ Brian bought his sofas from a middleman who wouldn't tell him where they came from. ◻ N-COUNT A **middleman** is a person who helps in negotiations between people who are unwilling to meet each other directly. ❑ The two sides would only meet indirectly, through middlemen.

**mid|field** /mɪdfild/ N-UNCOUNT In football and soccer, the **midfield** is the central area of the playing field between the two goals, or the players whose usual position is in this area. ❑ In the last two years, I played a lot of games in midfield. ❑ ...the best midfield player in the world.

**mid|field|er** /mɪdfildər/ (**midfielders**) N-COUNT In soccer, a **midfielder** is a player whose usual position is in the midfield. ❑ The young French midfielder scored a goal.

**Word Link** | mid ≈ middle : midnight, midterm, midtown

**mid|night** /mɪdnaɪt/ N-UNCOUNT **Midnight** is twelve o'clock in the middle of the night. ❑ It was well after midnight.
→ see **time**

**mid-ocean ridge** (**mid-ocean ridges**) also mid-oceanic ridge N-COUNT A **mid-ocean ridge** is a range of mountains beneath the ocean.

**mid|ship|man** /mɪdʃɪpmən/ (**midshipmen**)
N-COUNT; N-TITLE A **midshipman** is a cadet who is training to become a junior officer in the navy. ❑ He became a midshipman at age sixteen. ❑ ...midshipman Edward Brooke of the U.S. Navy.

**midst** /mɪdst/ ◼ PHRASE If you are **in the midst** of doing something, you are doing it at the moment. ❑ We are in the midst of one of the worst wars for many, many years. ◻ PHRASE If something happens **in the midst of** an event, it happens during it. ❑ Eleanor arrived in the midst of a storm. ◼ PHRASE If someone or something is **in the midst of** a group of people or things, they are among them or surrounded by them. ❑ I was surprised to see him in the midst of a large crowd.

**mid|term** /mɪdtɜrm/ (**midterms**) ◼ ADJ A **midterm** election is an election that takes place approximately halfway through a president's or a government's term of office. ❑ ...midterm congressional elections in November. ◻ N-COUNT A **midterm** or a **midterm exam** is a test which a student takes in the middle of a school or college term. ❑ She walked into a midterm exam for a subject she knew very little about.

**mid|town** /mɪdtaʊn/ ADJ **Midtown** places are in the center of a city. ❑ ...a midtown Manhattan hotel. ● **Midtown** is also a noun. ❑ He drove around midtown.

**mid|way** /mɪdweɪ/ ◼ ADV If something is **midway between** two places, it is between them and the same distance from each of them. ❑ The studio is midway between his office and his home. ● **Midway** is also an adjective. ❑ Fresno is close to the midway point between Los Angeles and San Francisco. ◻ ADV If something happens **midway through** a period of time, it happens during the middle part of it. ❑ He crashed midway through the race. ● **Midway**

is also an adjective. ❑ *They scored before the midway point of the first half.*

**mid|week** /mɪdwik/ ADJ **Midweek** describes something that happens in the middle of the week. ❑ *I enjoyed our midweek walks in the park.*
● **Midweek** is also an adverb. ❑ *They'll be able to go up to Washington midweek.*

**mid|wife** /mɪdwaɪf/ (**midwives**) N-COUNT A **midwife** is a nurse who is trained to deliver babies and to advise pregnant women. ❑ *The midwife placed the baby in his mother's arms.* [from Old English]

---
**might**

❶ MODAL USES
❷ NOUN USES
---

❶ **might** /maɪt/

**Might** is a modal verb. It is used with the base form of a verb.

**1** MODAL You use **might** to indicate that something will possibly happen or be true in the future. ❑ *The baby might be born early.* ❑ *I might regret it later.* **2** MODAL You use **might** to indicate that there is a possibility that something is true. ❑ *They still hope that he might be alive.* ❑ *You might be right.* **3** MODAL You use **might** to make a suggestion or to give advice in a very polite way. ❑ *Next time you see them you might thank them for their help.* **4** MODAL You use **might** as a polite way of interrupting someone, asking a question, making a request, or introducing what you are going to say next. [FORMAL, SPOKEN] ❑ *Might I make a suggestion?* ❑ *Might I ask what you're doing here?* [from Old English]

❷ **might** /maɪt/ N-UNCOUNT **Might** is power or strength. [FORMAL] ❑ *They were powerless against the might of the army.* [from Old English]

**mightn't** /maɪtᵊnt/ **Mightn't** is a spoken form of "might not." [from Old English]

**might've** /maɪtəv/ **Might've** is the usual spoken form of "might have," especially when "have" is an auxiliary verb. [from Old English]

**mighty** /maɪti/ (**mightier, mightiest**) **1** ADJ **Mighty** is used to describe something that is very large or powerful. [LITERARY] ❑ *There was a flash and a mighty bang.* **2** ADV **Mighty** is used in front of adjectives and adverbs to emphasize the quality that they are describing. [INFORMAL] ❑ *I'm mighty proud of my son.* [from Old English]

**mi|graine** /maɪɡreɪn/ (**migraines**) N-VAR A **migraine** is an extremely painful headache that makes you feel very ill. ❑ *Her mother suffered from migraines.* [from French]

**Word Link** migr ≈ moving, changing : emigrant, immigrant, migrant

**mi|grant** /maɪɡrənt/ (**migrants**) N-COUNT A **migrant** is a person who moves from one place to another, especially in order to find work. ❑ *Most of his workers were migrants from the South.* [from Latin]

**mi|grate** /maɪɡreɪt/ (**migrates, migrating, migrated**) **1** V-I If people **migrate**, they move from one place to another, especially in order to find work. ❑ *People migrate to cities like Jakarta searching for work.* ● **mi|gra|tion** /maɪɡreɪʃᵊn/ (**migrations**) N-VAR ❑ *...the migration of Jews to*

Israel. **2** V-I When birds, fish, or animals **migrate**, they move at a particular season from one part of the world or from one part of a country to another, usually in order to breed or to find food. ❑ *Most birds have to fly long distances to migrate.* ● **mi|gra|tion** N-VAR ❑ *...the migration of animals in the Serengeti.* [from Latin]

**mike** /maɪk/ (**mikes**) N-COUNT A **mike** is the same as a **microphone**. [INFORMAL]

**mild** /maɪld/ (**milder, mildest**) **1** ADJ **Mild** is used to describe something that is not very strong or severe. ❑ *Teddy turned to Mona with a look of mild confusion.* ❑ *This cheese has a soft, mild flavor.* ● **mild|ly** ADV ❑ *She had the disease very mildly because she felt fine.* **2** ADJ **Mild** weather is pleasant because it is neither extremely hot nor extremely cold. ❑ *The area has very mild winters.* [from Old English]

**mile** /maɪl/ (**miles**) **1** N-COUNT A **mile** is a unit of distance equal to 1760 yards or approximately 1.6 kilometers. ❑ *They drove 600 miles across the desert.* ❑ *She lives just half a mile away.* **2** N-PLURAL **Miles** is used, especially in the expression **miles away**, to refer to a long distance. ❑ *The gym is miles away from her home.* [from Old English]
→ see **measurement**

**Word Partnership** Use *mile* with :

ADJ. mile **high**, mile **long, nautical** mile, **square** mile, mile **wide** **1**

**mile|age** /maɪlɪdʒ/ (**mileages**) **1** N-VAR **Mileage** refers to the distance that you have traveled, measured in miles. ❑ *Most of their mileage is in and around town.* **2** N-UNCOUNT The **mileage** in a particular course of action is its usefulness in getting you what you want. ❑ *It's important to get as much mileage out of the meeting as possible.* [from Old English]

**mile|stone** /maɪlstoʊn/ (**milestones**) N-COUNT A **milestone** is an important event in the history or development of something or someone. ❑ *This new job represents a milestone in my life.* [from Old English]

**mili|tant** /mɪlɪtənt/ (**militants**) ADJ You use **militant** to describe people who believe in something very strongly and are active in trying to bring about political or social change, often in extreme ways that other people find unacceptable. ❑ *Militant workers voted to go on strike.* ● **Militant** is also a noun. ❑ *...terrorist acts committed by militants.* ● **mili|tan|cy** N-UNCOUNT ❑ *...the rise of militancy in the labor unions.* [from Latin]

**Word Link** milit ≈ soldier : demilitarize, military, militia

**mili|tary** /mɪlɪteri/ (**militaries**) **1** ADJ **Military** means relating to the armed forces of a country. ❑ *Military action may become necessary.* ❑ *...a meeting of military leaders.* ● **mili|tari|ly** /mɪlɪteərɪli/ ADV ❑ *...militarily useful weapons.* **2** N-COUNT The **military** are the armed forces of a country, especially officers of high rank. **Military** can take the singular or plural form of the verb. ❑ *The military have said little about the attacks.* [from French]
→ see **army**

| Word Link | milit ≈ soldier : demilitarize, military, militia |
|---|---|

**mi|li|tia** /mɪlɪʃə/ (**militias**) N-COUNT A **militia** is an organization that operates like an army but whose members are not professional soldiers. ❑ *Young men formed their own militias.* [from Latin] → see **army**

**milk** /mɪlk/ (**milks, milking, milked**) **1** N-VAR **Milk** is the white liquid produced by cows, goats, and some other animals, which people drink and use to make butter, cheese, and yogurt. ❑ *He went out to buy a quart of milk.* **2** V-T If someone **milks** a cow or goat, they get milk from it, using either their hands or a machine. ❑ *Farm workers milked cows by hand.* ● **milk|ing** N-UNCOUNT ❑ *...helping to bring the cows in for milking.* **3** N-UNCOUNT **Milk** is the white liquid produced by women to feed their babies. ❑ *Milk from the mother's breast is a perfect food for the human baby.* **4** V-T If you say that someone **milks** something, you are critical of them for getting as much benefit or profit as they can from it, without caring about the effects this has on other people. ❑ *A few people tried to milk the insurance companies.* [from Old English] → see **dairy**

**milky** /mɪlki/ (**milkier, milkiest**) **1** ADJ If you describe something as **milky**, you mean that it is pale white in color. ❑ *A milky mist filled the valley.* **2** ADJ Drinks or food that are **milky** contain a lot of milk. ❑ *...a big cup of milky coffee.* [from Old English]

**mill** /mɪl/ (**mills, milling, milled**) **1** N-COUNT A **mill** is a building in which grain is crushed to make flour. ❑ *The old mill is now a restaurant.* **2** N-COUNT A **mill** is a small device used for grinding something such as coffee or pepper. ❑ *...a pepper mill.* **3** N-COUNT A **mill** is a factory used for making and processing materials such as steel, wool, or cotton. ❑ *...a steel mill.* [from Old English]

▶ **mill around** PHR-VERB When a crowd of people **mill around**, they move around in a disorganized way. ❑ *Quite a few people were milling around.*

| Word Link | enn ≈ year : centennial, millennium, perennial |
|---|---|

| Word Link | mill ≈ thousand : millennium, million, millionaire |
|---|---|

**mil|len|nium** /mɪlɛniəm/ (**millenniums** or **millennia**) N-COUNT A **millennium** is a period of one thousand years. [FORMAL] ❑ *...the beginning of a new millennium.* [from New Latin]

| Word Link | milli ≈ thousandth : milligram, milliliter, millimeter |
|---|---|

**mil|li|gram** /mɪlɪgræm/ (**milligrams**) N-COUNT A **milligram** is a metric unit of weight that is equal to a thousandth of a gram. ❑ *...0.5 milligrams of sodium.* [from French]

**mil|li|li|ter** /mɪlɪlitər/ (**milliliters**) N-COUNT A **milliliter** is a metric unit of volume for liquids and gases that is equal to a thousandth of a liter. ❑ *...100 milliliters of blood.*

**mil|li|meter** /mɪlɪmitər/ (**millimeters**) N-COUNT A **millimeter** is a metric unit of length that is equal to a tenth of a centimeter or a thousandth of a meter. ❑ *The creature is tiny, just 10 millimeters long.*

**mil|lion** /mɪlyən/ (**millions**)

The plural form is **million** after a number, or after a word or expression referring to a number, such as "several" or "a few."

**1** NUM A **million** or one **million** is the number 1,000,000. ❑ *Five million people visit the county each year.* **2** QUANT If you talk about **millions of** people or things, you mean that there is a very large number of them. ❑ *The program was watched on television in millions of homes.* [from Old French]

**mil|lion|aire** /mɪlyənɛər/ (**millionaires**) N-COUNT A **millionaire** is a person who has money or property worth at least a million dollars. ❑ *By the time he died, he was a millionaire.* [from Old French]

**mil|lionth** /mɪlyənθ/ (**millionths**) ORD The **millionth** item in a series is the one you count as number one million. ❑ *It seemed like the millionth time she asked the question.* [from Old French]

**mime** /maɪm/ (**mimes, miming, mimed**) **1** N-VAR **Mime** is the use of movements and gestures in order to express something or tell a story without using speech. ❑ *...a story told with music and mime.* **2** V-T/V-I If you **mime** something, you describe or express it using mime rather than speech. ❑ *In the dance a woman mimed a lot of housework.* [from Old English]

**mim|ic** /mɪmɪk/ (**mimics, mimicking, mimicked**) **1** V-T If you **mimic** the actions or voice of a person or animal, you imitate them, usually in a way that is meant to be amusing or entertaining. ❑ *He could mimic anybody, and often made Isabel laugh.* **2** N-COUNT A **mimic** is a person who is able to mimic people or animals. ❑ *At school I was a good mimic.* [from Latin]

**mince** /mɪns/ (**minces, mincing, minced**) **1** V-T If you **mince** food such as meat or vegetables, you cut or chop it up into very small pieces. ❑ *Mince the onions and mix in well.* **2** [from Old French] → see **cut**

---

**mind**

**❶** NOUN USES
**❷** VERB USES

**❶ mind** /maɪnd/ (**minds**) **1** N-COUNT You refer to someone's **mind** when talking about their thoughts. ❑ *I'm trying to clear my mind of bad thoughts.* ❑ *There was no doubt in his mind that the man was serious.* **2** N-COUNT Your **mind** is your ability to think and reason. ❑ *You have a good mind.* ❑ *Studying improved my mind and got me thinking about things.* **3** N-COUNT If you have a particular type of **mind**, you have a particular way of thinking which is part of your character, or a result of your education or professional training. ❑ *Andrew, you have a very suspicious mind.* ❑ *You need a logical mind to solve this problem.* **4** → see also **frame of mind, state of mind 5** PHRASE If you tell someone to **bear** something **in mind** or to **keep** something **in mind**, you are reminding or warning them about something important which they should remember. ❑ *Bear in mind that there aren't many gas stations out of town.* **6** PHRASE If you **change** your **mind**, or if someone or something **changes** your **mind**, you change a decision you have made

## Word Web    mineral

The **extraction** of **minerals** from ore is an ancient process. Neolithic people discovered **copper** around 8000 BC. Using fire and charcoal, they **reduced** the ore to its pure **metal** form. About 4,000 years later, Egyptians learned to pour molten copper into molds. **Silver** ore often contains large amounts of copper and **lead**. Silver **refineries** often use the smelting process to remove these other metals from the silver. Most **gold** does not exist as an ore. Instead, veins of gold run through the earth. Refiners use chemicals such as cyanide to get pure gold.

or an opinion that you had. ❏ *I was going to vote for him, but I changed my mind.* **7** PHRASE If you say that an idea or possibility never **crossed** your **mind**, you mean that you did not think of it. ❏ *It didn't cross his mind that there might be a problem.* **8** PHRASE If you see something **in your mind's eye**, you imagine it and have a clear picture of it in your mind. ❏ *In his mind's eye, he can imagine the effect he's having.* **9** PHRASE If you **make up** your **mind** or **make** your **mind up**, you decide which of a number of possible things you will have or do. ❏ *He made up his mind to call Kathy.* **10** PHRASE If something is **on** your **mind**, you are worried or concerned about it and think about it a lot. ❏ *The game was on my mind all week.* **11** PHRASE If your **mind is on** something or you **have** your **mind on** something, you are thinking about that thing. ❏ *At school my mind was never on my work.* **12** PHRASE If you have an **open mind**, you avoid forming an opinion or making a decision until you know all the facts. ❏ *Try to keep an open mind until you have all the facts.* **13** PHRASE If you say that someone is **out of their mind**, you mean that they are crazy or very foolish. [INFORMAL] ❏ *What are you doing? Are you out of your mind?* **14** PHRASE If something **takes** your **mind off** a problem or unpleasant situation, it helps you to forget about it for a while. ❏ *I thought a game of tennis might take his mind off his problems.* **15** PHRASE You say or write **to my mind** to indicate that the statement you are making is your own opinion. ❏ *To my mind, this play is too violent.* [from Old English]

**❷ mind** /maɪnd/ (**minds, minding, minded**) **1** V-T/V-I If you do not **mind** something, you are not annoyed or bothered by it. ❏ *I don't mind the noise during the day.* ❏ *I hope you don't mind me calling you so late.* ❏ *I opened a window and nobody seemed to mind.* **2** V-T If someone does not **mind** what happens or what something is like, they do not have a strong preference for any particular thing. ❏ *I don't mind what we play, really.* **3** V-T If you **mind** something such as a store or luggage, you take care of it, usually while the person who owns it or is usually responsible for it is somewhere else. ❏ *Jim Coulters will mind the store while I'm away.* **4** PHRASE You use **never mind** to tell someone that they do not have to do something or worry about something, because it is not important or because you will do it yourself. ❏ *"Was his name David?" — "No I don't think it was, but never mind, go on."* ❏ *Dorothy, come on. Never mind your coat. We'll drive.* **5** PHRASE You use **never mind** after a statement, often a negative one, to indicate that

the statement is even more true of the person, thing, or situation that you are going to mention next. ❏ *He's too shy even to look at her, never mind talk to her!* **6** PHRASE If you say that you **wouldn't mind** something, you mean that you would like it. ❏ *I wouldn't mind a cup of coffee.* **7** [from Old English]

**mind|ful** /maɪndfəl/ ADJ If you are **mindful of** something, you think about it and consider it when taking action. [FORMAL] ❏ *We must be mindful of the results of our actions.* [from Old English]

**mind|less** /maɪndlɪs/ **1** ADJ If you describe a violent action as **mindless**, you mean that it is done without thought and will achieve nothing. ❏ *...mindless violence.* **2** ADJ If you describe an activity as **mindless**, you mean that it is so dull or boring that people do it or take part in it without thinking. ❏ *It was mindless work, but it gave me something to do.* ● **mind|less|ly** ADV ❏ *I spent many hours mindlessly hitting a tennis ball against the wall.* [from Old English]

### mine

**❶** PRONOUN USE
**❷** NOUN AND VERB USES

**❶ mine** /maɪn/ PRON **Mine** is the first person singular possessive pronoun. A speaker or writer uses **mine** to refer to something that belongs or relates to himself or herself. ❏ *Her right hand was close to mine.* [from Old English]

**❷ mine** /maɪn/ (**mines, mining, mined**) **1** N-COUNT A **mine** is a place where deep holes and tunnels are dug under the ground in order to obtain minerals such as coal, diamonds, or gold. ❏ *...coal mines.* **2** V-T When a mineral **is mined**, it is obtained from the ground by digging deep holes and tunnels. ❏ *Diamonds are mined in South Africa.* ● **min|er** (**miners**) N-COUNT ❏ *My father was a miner.* ● **min|ing** N-UNCOUNT ❏ *...industries such as coal mining and steel making.* **3** N-COUNT A **mine** is a bomb which is hidden in the ground or in water and which explodes when people or things touch it. [from Old French]
→ see **industry, tunnel**

**mine|field** /maɪnfild/ (**minefields**) N-COUNT A **minefield** is an area of land or water where explosive mines have been hidden.

**min|er|al** /mɪnərəl/ (**minerals**) N-COUNT A **mineral** is a substance such as tin, salt, or sulfur that is formed naturally in rocks and in the earth. [from Medieval Latin]
→ see Word Web: **mineral**
→ see **photosynthesis, rock**

**min|er|al wa|ter** (**mineral waters**) N-VAR
**Mineral water** is water that comes out of the
ground naturally and is considered healthy to
drink.

**min|gle** /mɪŋgᵊl/ (**mingles, mingling, mingled**)

mingle

**1** V-RECIP If things such as sounds, smells, or
feelings **mingle**, they become
mixed together but are
usually still recognizable.
◻ The smell of flowers and fresh
bread mingled. **2** V-RECIP At a
party, if you **mingle with** the
other people there, you move
around and talk to them.
◻ They mingled with other people
at the wedding. ◻ Guests ate and
mingled. [from Old English]

---

**Word Link**    mini ≈ very small : miniature,
minibus, minimum

---

**minia|ture** /mɪniətʃər, -tʃʊər/ (**miniatures**)
**1** ADJ **Miniature** is used to describe something
that is very small, especially a smaller version
of something which is normally much bigger.
◻ ...miniature roses. **2** PHRASE If you describe
one thing as another thing **in miniature**, you
mean that it is much smaller in size or scale than
the other thing, but is otherwise exactly the
same. ◻ Ecuador is like the whole of South America in
miniature. **3** N-COUNT A **miniature** is a very small,
detailed painting, often of a person. [from Italian]
**mini|bus** /mɪnibʌs/ (**minibuses**) also **mini-bus**
N-COUNT A **minibus** is a large van which has seats
in the back for passengers, and windows along its
sides. ◻ A minibus drove them to the airport.

---

**Word Link**    minim ≈ smallest : minimal,
minimize, minimum

---

**mini|mal** /mɪnɪmᵊl/ ADJ Something that
is **minimal** is very small in quantity, value, or
degree. ◻ The difference between the two computers is
minimal. ● **mini|mal|ly** ADV ◻ They paid him, but only
minimally. [from Latin]
**mini|mal|ism** /mɪnɪməlɪzəm/ N-UNCOUNT
**Minimalism** is a style in which a small number of
very simple things are used to create a particular
effect. ◻ ...the minimalism of her home. [from Latin]
**minimalist** /mɪnɪməlɪst/ (**minimalists**)
**1** N-COUNT A **minimalist** is an artist or designer
who uses minimalism. ◻ ...the minimalists in
the 1970s. **2** ADJ **Minimalist** is used to describe
ideas, artists, or designers that are influenced by
minimalism. ◻ The two designers used a minimalist
approach. [from Latin]
**mini|mize** /mɪnɪmaɪz/ (**minimizes, minimizing,
minimized**) **1** V-T If you **minimize** a risk, problem,
or unpleasant situation, you reduce it to the
lowest possible level, or prevent it from increasing
beyond that level. ◻ People want to minimize the risk
of getting cancer. **2** V-T If you **minimize** something,
you make it seem smaller or less significant than
it really is. ◻ Do not minimize the danger. [from Latin]
**mini|mum** /mɪnɪməm/ **1** ADJ You use
**minimum** to describe an amount which is the
smallest that is possible, allowed, or required.
◻ He was only five feet nine, the minimum height for a
policeman. ● **Minimum** is also a noun. ◻ This will
take a minimum of one hour. **2** ADJ You use **minimum**

to state how small an amount is. ◻ This book tells
you how to get through college with minimum work
and maximum fun. ● **Minimum** is also a noun. ◻ It
is better to travel with a minimum of baggage. [from
Latin]
→ see **factory**

---

**Word Partnership**   Use minimum with :

| | |
|---|---|
| N. | minimum **age**, minimum **balance**, minimum **purchase**, minimum **salary 1** |
| ADJ. | **absolute** minimum, **bare** minimum **1** |

---

**mini|mum se|cu|ri|ty pris|on** (**minimum
security prisons**) N-COUNT A **minimum security
prison** is a prison where there are fewer
restrictions on prisoners than in a normal prison.
**min|is|ter** /mɪnɪstər/ (**ministers**) **1** N-COUNT
A **minister** is a member of the clergy, especially
in Protestant churches. ◻ His father was a Baptist
minister. **2** N-COUNT A **minister** is a person who
officially represents their government in a
foreign country and has a lower rank than an
ambassador. ◻ ...the Danish minister in Washington.
**3** N-COUNT In some countries outside the United
States, a **minister** is a person who is in charge of
a particular government department. ◻ He was
named minister of culture. [from Old French]
**min|is|te|ri|al** /mɪnɪstɪəriəl/ ADJ You use
**ministerial** to refer to people, events, or jobs that
are connected with government ministers. ◻ ...a
series of ministerial meetings in Brussels. [from Old
French]
**min|is|try** /mɪnɪstri/ (**ministries**) **1** N-COUNT
The **ministry** of a religious person is the work that
they do that is inspired by their religious beliefs.
◻ His ministry is among poor people. **2** N-SING
Members of the clergy belonging to some
branches of the Christian church are referred to
as **the ministry**. ◻ What made him enter the ministry?
**3** N-COUNT In many countries, a **ministry** is a
government department which deals with a
particular thing or area of activity, for example
trade, defense, or transportation. ◻ ...the Ministry
of Justice. [from Latin]
**mini|van** /mɪnivæn/ (**minivans**) N-COUNT A
**minivan** is a large, tall car whose seats can be
moved or removed, for example, so that it can
carry large loads. ◻ A minivan drove by with five faces
looking out of the window.

**mink** /mɪŋk/ (**minks**)

| |
|---|
| **Mink** can also be used as the plural form. |

**1** N-COUNT A **mink** is a small animal with highly
valued fur. ◻ The hunting of mink is not allowed.
● **Mink** is the fur of a mink. ◻ ...a mink coat.
**2** N-COUNT A **mink** is a coat or other garment
made from the fur of a mink. ◻ Some people like to
dress in minks and diamonds. [from Scandinavian]
**mi|nor** /maɪnər/ (**minors**) **1** ADJ You use **minor**
when you want to describe something that is
less important, serious, or significant than other
things in a group or situation. ◻ She had a number
of minor roles in films. **2** N-COUNT A **minor** is a
person who is still legally a child. In most states
in the United States, people are minors until they
reach the age of eighteen. ◻ Minors are not allowed
to vote. [from Latin]

**m**

## Thesaurus    *minor*    Also look up :

ADJ.    insignificant, lesser, small, unimportant; (*ant.*) important, major, significant ◼

## Word Partnership    Use *minor* with :

N.    minor **adjustment**, minor **damage**, minor **detail**, minor **illness**, minor **injury**, minor **operation**, minor **problem**, minor **surgery** ◼

ADV.    **relatively** minor ◼

**mi|nor|ity** /mɪnɔ̱rɪti, maɪ-/ (**minorities**)
◼ N-SING If you talk about a **minority** of people or things in a larger group, you are referring to a number of them that forms less than half of the larger group, usually much less than half. ❑ *A minority of mothers go out to work.* ◼ PHRASE If people are **in a minority** or **in the minority**, they belong to a group of people or things that form less than half of a larger group. ❑ *Male nurses are in a minority.* ◼ N-COUNT A **minority** is a group of people of the same race, culture, or religion who live in a place where most of the people around them are of a different race, culture, or religion. ❑ *...the region's ethnic minorities.* [from Medieval Latin]

## Word Partnership    Use *minority* with :

N.    minority **leader**, minority **party** ◼
minority **applicants**, minority **community**, minority **group**, minority **population**, minority **students**, minority **voters**, minority **women** ◼

**mi|nor key** N-COUNT In music, the **minor key** is based on the minor scale, in which the third note is three semitones higher than the first.

**mi|nor league** (**minor leagues**) ◼ N-COUNT In baseball, a **minor league** is a professional league that is not one of the major leagues. ❑ *In 1952, there were 43 minor leagues.* ◼ ADJ **Minor-league** people are not very important or not very successful. ❑ *...minor-league actors.*

**min|strel show** /mɪ̱nstrəl ʃoʊ/ (**minstrel shows**) N-COUNT In the past, a **minstrel show** was a form of entertainment consisting of songs, dances, and comedy performed by actors wearing black face make-up.

**mint** /mɪ̱nt/ (**mints, minting, minted**)
◼ N-UNCOUNT **Mint** is an herb with fresh-tasting leaves. ❑ *The lamb was served with mint.* ◼ N-COUNT A **mint** is a candy with a peppermint flavor. Some people suck mints in order to make their breath smell fresher. ❑ *She put a mint into her mouth before the meeting.* ◼ N-COUNT The **mint** is the place where the official coins of a country are made. ❑ *In 1965 the mint stopped putting silver in dimes.* ◼ V-T To **mint** coins or medals means to make them in a mint. ❑ *...the right to mint coins.* ● **mint|ing** N-UNCOUNT ❑ *...the minting of new gold coins.* [from Old English]
→ see **money**

## Word Link    *min ≈ small, lessen : diminish, minus, minute*

**mi|nus** /ma̱ɪnəs/ (**minuses**) ◼ CONJ You use **minus** to show that one number or quantity is being subtracted from another. ❑ *One minus one is zero.* ◼ ADJ **Minus** before a number or quantity means that the number or quantity is less than zero. ❑ *...temperatures of minus 65 degrees.* ◼ PREP To be **minus** something means not to have that thing. [INFORMAL] ❑ *The company closed, leaving Chris minus a job.* ◼ N-COUNT A **minus** is a disadvantage. [INFORMAL] ❑ *The idea had a lot more pluses than minuses.* [from Latin]

## Thesaurus    *minus*    Also look up :

PREP.    without ◼
N.    deficiency, disadvantage, drawback ◼

## Word Link    *cule ≈ small : minuscule, molecule, ridicule*

**mi|nus|cule** /mɪ̱nɪskyul/ ADJ If you describe something as **minuscule**, you mean that it is very small. ❑ *They filmed the movie in 17 days, a minuscule amount of time.* [from French]

---

## minute
❶ NOUN AND VERB USES
❷ ADJECTIVE USE

❶ **mi|nute** /mɪ̱nɪt/ (**minutes**) ◼ N-COUNT A **minute** is one of the sixty parts that an hour is divided into. People often say "**a minute**" or "**minutes**" when they mean a short length of time. ❑ *The pizza will take twenty minutes to cook.* ❑ *Bye Mom, see you in a minute.* ◼ N-PLURAL The **minutes** of a meeting are the written records of the things that are discussed or decided at it. ❑ *He read the minutes of the last meeting.* ◼ PHRASE If you say that something will or may happen **at any minute** or **any minute now**, you are emphasizing that it is likely to happen very soon. ❑ *It looks as though it might rain at any minute.* ◼ PHRASE A **last-minute** action is one that is done at the latest time possible. ❑ *He made a last-minute decision to stay at home.* ◼ PHRASE If you say that something happens **the minute** something else happens, you are emphasizing that it happens immediately after the other thing. ❑ *The minute he lay down on his bed, he fell asleep.* ◼ CONVENTION People often use expressions such as **wait a minute** or **just a minute** when they want to stop you from doing or saying something. ❑ *Wait a minute, something is wrong here.* [from Old French]
→ see **time**

❷ **mi|nute** /maɪnu̱t/ (**minutest**) ADJ If something is **minute**, it is very small. ❑ *Only a minute amount of glue is needed.* ● **mi|nute|ly** /maɪnu̱tli/ ADV ❑ *Then the pain changed minutely.* [from Latin]

## Word Partnership    Use *minute* with :

DET.    a minute **or two**, **another** minute, **each** minute, **half** a minute ❶ ◼
V.    **take** a minute ❶ ◼
**wait** a minute ❶ ◼
N.    minute **detail**, minute **quantity of something** ❷

**mira|cle** /mɪ̱rək²l/ (**miracles**) ◼ N-COUNT If you say that something is a **miracle**, you mean that it is very surprising and fortunate. ❑ *It's a miracle that he survived the accident.* ◼ ADJ A **miracle** drug or product does something that was thought almost impossible. ❑ ...the miracle drugs that keep him alive. **3** N-COUNT A **miracle** is a wonderful and surprising event that is believed to be caused by God. ❑ ...Jesus's ability to perform miracles. [from Latin]

**mi|racu|lous** /mɪrækyələs/ **1** ADJ If you describe a good event as **miraculous**, you mean that it is very surprising and unexpected. ❑ The sick horse made a miraculous recovery. ● **mi|racu|lous|ly** ADV ❑ Miraculously, no one got hurt. **2** ADJ If someone describes a wonderful event as **miraculous**, they believe that the event was caused by God. ❑ ...miraculous healing. ● **mi|racu|lous|ly** ADV ❑ He miraculously appeared to walk on water. [from Latin]

**mir|ror** /mɪrər/ (**mirrors, mirroring, mirrored**) **1** N-COUNT A **mirror** is a flat piece of glass in which you can see your reflection. ❑ He looked at himself in the mirror. **2** V-T If something **mirrors** something else, it has similar features to it, and therefore seems like a copy or representation of it. ❑ The book mirrors the author's own experiences. **3** V-T If you see something reflected in water, you can say that the water **mirrors** it. [LITERARY] ❑ The river mirrors the sky. [from Old French]
→ see **telescope**

---

**Word Partnership** Use *mirror* with :

| | |
|---|---|
| V. | **glance in** a mirror, **look in** a mirror, **reflect in** a mirror **1** |
| PREP. | **in front of** a mirror **1** |
| N. | **reflection in** a mirror **1** |

---

**mis|be|hav|ior** /mɪsbɪheɪvyər/ N-UNCOUNT **Misbehavior** is behavior that is not acceptable to other people. [FORMAL] ❑ What was causing their son's misbehavior? [from Middle English]

**mis|cal|cu|late** /mɪskælkyəleɪt/ (**miscalculates, miscalculating, miscalculated**) V-T/V-I If you **miscalculate**, you make a mistake in judging a situation or in making a calculation. ❑ He badly miscalculated the mood of the people. ● **mis|cal|cu|la|tion** /mɪskælkyəleɪʃ°n/ (**miscalculations**) N-VAR ❑ The windows were too small because of miscalculations by the builders. [from Late Latin]

**mis|car|riage** /mɪskærɪdʒ, -kær-/ (**miscarriages**) N-COUNT If a pregnant woman has a **miscarriage**, she gives birth to her baby before it is properly formed, and it dies. [from Old Northern French]

**mis|cel|la|neous** /mɪsəleɪniəs/ ADJ A **miscellaneous** group consists of many different kinds of things or people that are difficult to put into a particular category. ❑ ...a box of miscellaneous junk. [from Latin]

**mis|chief** /mɪstʃɪf/ **1** N-UNCOUNT **Mischief** is playing harmless tricks on people or doing things you are not supposed to do. It can also refer to the desire to do this. ❑ He's a typical little boy — full of mischief. **2** N-UNCOUNT **Mischief** is behavior that is intended to cause trouble for people. It can also refer to the trouble that is caused. ❑ Brandi loves to cause mischief. [from Old French]

**mis|chie|vous** /mɪstʃɪvəs/ **1** ADJ A **mischievous** person likes to have fun by playing harmless tricks on people or doing things

they are not supposed to do. ❑ She behaves like a mischievous child. ● **mis|chie|vous|ly** ADV ❑ Kathryn smiled mischievously. **2** ADJ **mischievous** act or suggestion is intended to cause trouble. ❑ "I have a few mischievous plans," says Zevon. [from Old French]

**mis|con|cep|tion** /mɪskənsɛpʃ°n/ (**misconceptions**) N-COUNT A **misconception** is an idea that is not correct. ❑ It is a misconception that Peggy was rich. [from Latin]

**mis|con|duct** /mɪskɒndʌkt/ N-UNCOUNT **Misconduct** is bad or unacceptable behavior, especially by a professional person. ❑ A doctor was found guilty of serious misconduct yesterday. [from Medieval Latin]

**mis|de|mean|or** /mɪsdɪminər/ (**misdemeanors**) **1** N-COUNT A **misdemeanor** is an act that some people consider to be wrong or unacceptable. [FORMAL] ❑ Paul had to explain his various misdemeanors. **2** N-COUNT In the United States and other countries where the legal system distinguishes between very serious crimes and less serious ones, a **misdemeanor** is a less serious crime. [LEGAL] ❑ It is a misdemeanor to use a fake degree to get a job.

**mis|er|able** /mɪzərəb°l/ **1** ADJ If you are **miserable**, you are very unhappy. ❑ I had a job which made me really miserable. ● **mis|er|ably** /mɪzərəbli/ ADV ❑ He looked miserably down at his plate. **2** ADJ A **miserable** place or **miserable** weather makes you feel unhappy or depressed. ❑ There was nothing in this miserable place to enjoy. ❑ It was a gray, wet, miserable day. [from Old French]

---

**Thesaurus** *miserable* Also look up :

| | |
|---|---|
| ADJ. | unhappy **1** |
| | unfortunate, wretched **2** |

---

**mis|ery** /mɪzəri/ (**miseries**) **1** N-VAR **Misery** is great unhappiness. ❑ All that money brought nothing but sadness and misery. **2** N-UNCOUNT **Misery** is the way of life and unpleasant living conditions of people who are very poor. ❑ ...the misery of some African people. [from Old French]

**mis|fit** /mɪsfɪt/ (**misfits**) N-COUNT A **misfit** is a person who is not easily accepted by other people, often because their behavior is very different from that of everyone else. ❑ I feel like a misfit because I don't want children. [from Middle Dutch]

**mis|for|tune** /mɪsfɔrtʃən/ (**misfortunes**) N-VAR A **misfortune** is something unpleasant or unlucky that happens to someone. ❑ She seemed to enjoy the misfortunes of other people. [from Old French]

**mis|giv|ing** /mɪsgɪvɪŋ/ (**misgivings**) N-VAR If you have **misgivings** about something that is being suggested or done, you feel that it is not quite right, and are worried that it may have unwanted results. ❑ She had some misgivings about what she was going to do.

**mis|guid|ed** /mɪsgaɪdɪd/ ADJ If you describe an opinion or plan as **misguided**, you are critical of it because you think it is based on a mistake or misunderstanding. ❑ I think that decision was misguided.

**mis|hap** /mɪshæp/ (**mishaps**) N-VAR A **mishap** is an unfortunate but not very serious event that happens to someone. ❑ After a number of mishaps, she managed to get back to Germany.

m

## Word Link
mis ≈ bad : misinterpret, misleading, mismanage

**mis|in|ter|pret** /mɪsɪntɜrprɪt/ (**misinterprets, misinterpreting, misinterpreted**) v-T If you **misinterpret** something, you understand it wrongly. ❑ He misinterpreted the situation completely.
● **mis|in|ter|pre|ta|tion** /mɪsɪntɜrprɪteɪʃⁿn/ (**misinterpretations**) N-VAR ❑ ...a misinterpretation of the facts. [from Latin]

**mis|judge** /mɪsdʒʌdʒ/ (**misjudges, misjudging, misjudged**) v-T If someone **has misjudged** a person or situation, they have formed an incorrect idea or opinion about them. ❑ I have misjudged her. I thought she was only interested in Joe's money. [from Old French]

**mis|lead** /mɪslid/ (**misleads, misleading, misled**) v-T If you say that someone or something **has misled** you, you mean that they have made you believe something that is not true. ❑ ...government lawyers who have misled the court. [from Old English]

**mis|lead|ing** /mɪslidɪŋ/ ADJ If you describe something as **misleading**, you mean that it gives you a wrong idea or impression. ❑ It would be misleading to say that we were friends.
● **mis|lead|ing|ly** ADV ❑ The facts have been presented misleadingly. [from Old English]

**mis|led** /mɪslɛd/ **Misled** is the past tense and past participle of **mislead**. [from Old English]

**mis|man|age** /mɪsmænɪdʒ/ (**mismanages, mismanaging, mismanaged**) v-T To **mismanage** something means to manage it badly. ❑ A lot of people think the president mismanaged the economy. ● **mis|man|age|ment** N-UNCOUNT ❑ His mismanagement caused many problems for the company. [from Italian]

**mis|per|cep|tion** /mɪspərsɛpʃⁿn/ (**misperceptions**) N-COUNT A **misperception** is an idea or impression that is not correct. ❑ There's a misperception that all women want to have children. [from Latin]

**mis|placed** /mɪspleɪst/ ADJ If you describe a feeling or action as **misplaced**, you are critical of it because you think it is inappropriate, or directed toward the wrong thing or person. ❑ We believed that she would be honest with us; that trust was misplaced.

**mis|read** /mɪsrid/ (**misreads, misreading**)

The form **misread** is used in the present tense, and is the past tense and past participle, when it is pronounced /mɪsrɛd/.

**1** v-T If you **misread** a situation or someone's behavior, you do not understand it properly. ❑ I misread the signals, and thought she wanted me to kiss her. ● **mis|read|ing** (**misreadings**) N-COUNT ❑ ...a misreading of public opinion in France. **2** v-T If you **misread** something that has been written or printed, you look at it and think that it says something that it does not say. ❑ He misread his route and took a wrong turn. [from Old English]

**mis|rep|re|sent** /mɪsrɛprɪzɛnt/ (**misrepresents, misrepresenting, misrepresented**) v-T If someone **misrepresents** a person or situation, they give a wrong or inaccurate account of what the person or situation is like. ❑ The newspapers misrepresented him as selfish. ❑ Hollywood films misrepresented us as stupid people.

● **mis|rep|re|sen|ta|tion** /mɪsrɛprɪzɛnteɪʃⁿn/ (**misrepresentations**) N-VAR ❑ ...your misrepresentation of the facts. [from Latin]

### miss

❶ USED AS A TITLE OR A FORM OF ADDRESS
❷ VERB AND NOUN USES

❶ **Miss** /mɪs/ (**Misses**) N-TITLE You use **Miss** in front of the name of a girl or unmarried woman when you are speaking to her or referring to her. [FORMAL] ❑ It was nice talking to you, Miss Ellis.

❷ **miss** /mɪs/ (**misses, missing, missed**)
**1** v-T/v-I If you **miss** something you are trying to hit, you fail to hit it. ❑ She threw her glass across the room, and it missed my head by an inch. ❑ His first shot missed the goal completely. ● **Miss** is also a noun. ❑ After more misses, they finally put two arrows into the lion's chest. **2** v-T If you **miss** something, you fail to notice it. ❑ He watched, never missing a detail. **3** v-T If you **miss** the meaning or importance of something, you fail to understand or appreciate it. ❑ He totally missed the point of the question. **4** v-T If you **miss** someone who is no longer with you or who has died, you feel sad and wish that they were still with you. ❑ Your mama and I are going to miss you at Thanksgiving. **5** v-T If you **miss** something, you feel sad because you no longer have it or are no longer doing or experiencing it. ❑ If I moved into an apartment I'd miss my garden. **6** v-T If you **miss** something such as a plane or train, you arrive too late to catch it. ❑ He missed the last bus home and had to stay with a friend. **7** v-T If you **miss** something such as a meeting or an activity, you do not go to it or take part in it. ❑ Martha and I had to miss our class last week. [from Old English] **8** → see also **missing**
▶ **miss out** PHR-VERB If you **miss out on** something that would be enjoyable or useful to you, you are not involved in it or do not take part in it. ❑ We're missing out on a great opportunity.

### Usage    miss and lose
Miss and lose have similar meanings. Miss is used to express something you didn't do: I missed class yesterday. Lose is used when you can't find something you once had. Cancel your ATM card if you lose your wallet.

## Word Link
miss ≈ sending : dismiss, missile, missionary

**mis|sile** /mɪsⁿl/ (**missiles**) **1** N-COUNT A **missile** is a tube-shaped weapon that travels long distances through the air and explodes when it reaches its target. ❑ They fired missiles all night. **2** N-COUNT Anything that is thrown as a weapon can be called a **missile**. ❑ The football fans threw missiles onto the field. [from Latin]

**miss|ing** /mɪsɪŋ/ **1** ADJ If something is **missing** or has **gone missing**, it is not in its usual place, and you cannot find it. ❑ I discovered that my cellphone was missing. **2** ADJ If a part of something is **missing**, it has been removed or has come off, and has not been replaced. ❑ Three buttons were missing from his shirt. **3** ADJ Someone who is **missing** cannot be found, and it is not known whether they are alive or dead. ❑ Five people died in the explosion and one person is still missing. **4** PHRASE If a member of the armed forces is **missing in action**, they have not returned from a battle, their body has not been found, and they are not thought to have been captured. [from Old English] **5** → see also **MIA**

### Word Partnership Use *missing* with :

ADV. **still** missing **1** **3**
N. missing **piece** **1** **2**
missing **information**, missing **ingredient** **2**
missing **children**, missing **girl**, missing **people**, missing **soldiers** **3**

**mis|sion** /mɪʃ°n/ (**missions**) **1** N-COUNT A **mission** is an important task that people are given to do, especially one that involves traveling to another country. ❏ *His government sent him on a mission to North America.* **2** N-COUNT A **mission** is a group of people who have been sent to a foreign country to carry out an official task. ❏ *...the head of the trade mission to Zimbabwe.* **3** N-COUNT A **mission** is a special journey made by a military airplane or spacecraft. ❏ *The plane crashed during a training mission in the mountains.* **4** N-SING If you have a **mission**, you have a strong commitment and sense of duty to do or achieve something. ❏ *His mission in life was to tell people about Jesus.* [from Latin]

### Word Partnership Use *mission* with :

ADJ. **dangerous** mission, **secret** mission, **successful** mission **1**
N. **peacekeeping** mission **1** **2**
**combat** mission, **rescue** mission, **training** mission **1** **3**
V. **accomplish a** mission, **carry out a** mission **1** **3** **4**

### Word Link miss ≈ sending : dismiss, missile, missionary

**mis|sion|ary** /mɪʃəneri/ (**missionaries**) N-COUNT A **missionary** is a Christian who has been sent to a foreign country to teach people about Christianity. ❏ *My mother would like me to be a missionary in Africa.* [from Latin]

**mis|state** /mɪssteɪt/ (**misstates, misstating, misstated**) V-T If you **misstate** something, you state it incorrectly or give false information about it. ❏ *The report misstated important facts.* [from Old French]

**mis|state|ment** /mɪssteɪtmənt/ (**misstatements**) N-COUNT A **misstatement** is an incorrect statement, or the giving of false information. ❏ *He finally corrected his misstatement.* ❏ *This book is filled with misstatements of fact.* [from Old French]

**mis|step** /mɪsstɛp/ (**missteps**) N-COUNT A **misstep** is a mistake. ❏ *A single misstep could make him lose his job.* [from Old English]

**mist** /mɪst/ (**mists, misting, misted**) **1** N-VAR **Mist** consists of a large number of tiny drops of water in the air, which make it difficult to see very far. ❏ *Thick mist made flying impossible.* **2** V-T/V-I If a piece of glass **mists** or **is misted**, it becomes covered with tiny drops of moisture, so that you cannot see through it easily. ❏ *The windows misted, and I couldn't see out.* ● **Mist over** means the same as

**mist**. ❏ *The front windshield was misting over.* [from Old English]

**mis|take** /mɪsteɪk/ (**mistakes, mistaking, mistook, mistaken**) **1** N-COUNT If you make a **mistake**, you do something which you did not intend to do, or which produces a result that you do not want. ❏ *They made the big mistake of thinking they would win easily.* ❏ *There must be some mistake.* **2** N-COUNT A **mistake** is something or part of something that is incorrect or not right. ❏ *Her mother erased a mistake in her letter.* **3** V-T If you **mistake** one person or thing **for** another, you wrongly think that they are the other person or thing. ❏ *People are always mistaking her for her sister.* **4** PHRASE You can say **there is no mistaking** something when you are emphasizing that you cannot fail to recognize or understand it. ❏ *There's no mistaking he comes from Mexico.* [from Old Norse]

### Word Partnership Use *mistake* with :

ADJ. **fatal** mistake, **honest** mistake, **tragic** mistake **1**
**big** mistake, **common** mistake, **costly** mistake, **huge** mistake, **serious** mistake, **terrible** mistake **1** **2**
V. **admit a** mistake, **correct a** mistake, **fix a** mistake, **make a** mistake, **realize a** mistake **1** **2**

**mis|tak|en** /mɪsteɪkən/ **1** ADJ If you are **mistaken about** something, you are wrong about it. ❏ *I was mistaken about you.* **2** ADJ A **mistaken** belief or opinion is incorrect. ❏ *I had a mistaken view of what was happening.* ● **mis|tak|en|ly** ADV ❏ *They mistakenly believed there was no one in the house.* [from Old Norse]

**mis|ter** /mɪstər/ N-VOC Men are sometimes addressed as **mister**, especially by children and especially when the person talking to them does not know their name. [INFORMAL] ❏ *Look, Mister, don't try to tell us what to do.*

**mis|took** /mɪstʊk/ **Mistook** is the past tense and past participle of **mistake**. [from Old Norse]

**mis|tri|al** /mɪstraɪəl/ (**mistrials**) N-COUNT A **mistrial** is a legal trial which ends without a verdict, for example because the jury cannot agree on one. ❏ *The judge refused to declare a mistrial.*

**mis|trust** /mɪstrʌst/ (**mistrusts, mistrusting, mistrusted**) **1** N-UNCOUNT **Mistrust** is the feeling that you have toward someone who you do not trust. ❏ *There was a lot of mistrust between the two men.* **2** V-T If you **mistrust** someone or something, you do not trust them. ❏ *He mistrusts all journalists.* [from Old Norse]

**misty** /mɪsti/ ADJ On a **misty** day, there is a lot of mist in the air. ❏ *It's a little misty this morning.* [from Old English]

**mis|under|stand** /mɪsʌndərstænd/ (**misunderstands, misunderstanding, misunderstood**) **1** V-T/V-I If you **misunderstand** someone or something, you do not understand them properly. ❏ *I misunderstood you.* **2** *They have misunderstood what rock and roll is.* [from Old English] **3** → see also **misunderstood**

**mis|under|stand|ing** /mɪsʌndərstændɪŋ/ (**misunderstandings**) **1** N-VAR A **misunderstanding** is a failure to understand something properly, for example a situation

m

or a person's remarks. ❑ *There has been some misunderstanding of what we are trying to do.* **2** N-COUNT You can refer to a disagreement or slight quarrel as a **misunderstanding**. [FORMAL] ❑ *There was a little misunderstanding with the police and they arrested him.* [from Old English]

**mis|under|stood** /mɪsʌndərstʊd/ **1** **Misunderstood** is the past tense and past participle of **misunderstand**. **2** ADJ If you describe someone or something as **misunderstood**, you mean that people do not understand them and have a wrong impression or idea of them. ❑ *Eric is very badly misunderstood.* [from Old English]

**mis|use** (**misuses, misusing, misused**)

The noun is pronounced /mɪsyus/. The verb is pronounced /mɪsyuz/.

**1** N-VAR The **misuse** of something is incorrect, careless, or dishonest use of it. ❑ *…the misuse of power.* **2** V-T If someone **misuses** something, they use it incorrectly, carelessly, or dishonestly. ❑ *She misused her position by giving her son a job in the organization.* ❑ *That word is often misused.* [from Old French]

**mite** /maɪt/ (**mites**) N-COUNT **Mites** are very tiny creatures that live on plants, for example, or in animals' fur. ❑ *…a problem caused by tiny mites on the skin.* [from Old English]

**miti|gate** /mɪtɪgeɪt/ (**mitigates, mitigating, mitigated**) V-T To **mitigate** something means to make it less unpleasant, serious, or painful. [FORMAL] ❑ *…ways of mitigating the effects of an explosion.* [from Latin]

**miti|gat|ing** /mɪtɪgeɪtɪŋ/ ADJ **Mitigating** circumstances or factors make a bad action, especially a crime, easier to understand and excuse. [LEGAL] ❑ *The judge found that there were mitigating facts.* [from Latin]

**mito|chon|drion** /maɪtəkɒndriən/ (**mitochondria**) N-COUNT **Mitochondria** are the parts of a cell that convert nutrients into energy. [TECHNICAL] [from New Latin]

**mi|to|sis** /maɪtoʊsɪs/ N-UNCOUNT **Mitosis** is the process by which a cell divides into two identical halves. [TECHNICAL] [from New Latin]

**mix** /mɪks/ (**mixes, mixing, mixed**) **1** V-RECIP If two substances **mix** or if you **mix** one substance **with** another, they combine to become a single substance. ❑ *Oil and water don't mix.* ❑ *A quick stir will mix them thoroughly.* ❑ *Mix the sugar with the butter.* **2** V-T If you **mix** something, you prepare it by mixing other things together. ❑ *He spent several hours mixing cement.* **3** N-VAR A **mix** is a powder containing all the substances that you need in order to make something. When you want to use it, you add liquid. ❑ *…a package of cake mix.* **4** N-COUNT A **mix of** different things or people is two or more of them together. ❑ *The story is a mix of fact and fiction.* **5** V-RECIP If you **mix with** other people, you meet them and talk to them. ❑ *He loved to mix with the rich and famous.* ❑ *The meeting gave younger and older students the chance to mix.* [from Old French]

▶ **mix up** **1** PHR-VERB If you **mix up** two things or people, you confuse them, so that you think that one of them is the other one. ❑ *People often mix me up with other actors.* ❑ *Children often mix up their words.* **2** → see also **mixed up**

| | |
|---|---|
| N. | mix **ingredients**, mix **with water** **1** **2** |
| ADV. | mix **thoroughly**, mix **together** **1** **2** |

**mixed** /mɪkst/ **1** ADJ If you have **mixed** feelings about something or someone, you feel uncertain about them because you can see both good and bad points about them. ❑ *I came home from the meeting with mixed feelings.* **2** ADJ You use **mixed** to describe something which includes or consists of different things or people of the same general kind. ❑ *…a teaspoon of mixed herbs.* **3** ADJ **Mixed** is used to describe something that involves people from two or more different races. ❑ *I went to a racially mixed school.* **4** ADJ **Mixed** education or accommodations are intended for both males and females. ❑ *Girls who go to a mixed school know how to speak to boys.* [from Old French]

**mixed me|dia** N-UNCOUNT **Mixed media** is the use of more than one medium or material in a work of art, for example the use of both painting and collage. [TECHNICAL]

**mixed me|ter** (**mixed meters**) N-VAR Music that is written in **mixed meter** combines two or more meters, for example duple and triple meters. [TECHNICAL]

**mixed up** **1** ADJ If you are **mixed up**, you are confused. ❑ *He's a rather mixed-up kid.* **2** ADJ To be **mixed up in** something bad, or **with** someone you disapprove of, means to be involved in it or with them. ❑ *Why did I ever get mixed up with you?*

**mix|er** /mɪksər/ (**mixers**) N-COUNT A **mixer** is a machine used for mixing things together. ❑ *Using an electric mixer, beat the butter for 45 seconds.* [from Old French]

→ see **utensil**

**mix|ture** /mɪkstʃər/ (**mixtures**) **1** N-SING A **mixture** of things consists of several different things together. ❑ *They looked at him with a mixture of horror and surprise.* **2** N-COUNT A **mixture** is a substance that consists of other substances which have been stirred or shaken together. ❑ *…a mixture of water and sugar and salt.* [from Latin]

| | |
|---|---|
| N. | blend, collection, variety **1** |
| | blend, compound **2** |

**ml** **ml** is a written abbreviation for **milliliter** or **milliliters**. ❑ *Boil the sugar and 100 ml of water.*

**mm** **mm** is a written abbreviation for **millimeter** or **millimeters**. ❑ *…a 135 mm lens.*

**moan** /moʊn/ (**moans, moaning, moaned**) **1** V-I/V-I If you **moan**, you make a low sound, usually because you are unhappy or in pain. ❑ *Tony moaned in his sleep.* ● **Moan** is also a noun. ❑ *A moan came from the crowd.* **2** V-I To **moan** means to complain or speak in a way which shows that you are very unhappy. ❑ *She moans if she doesn't get more than six hours' sleep at night.* ❑ *…moaning about the weather.* [from Old English]

**mob** /mɒb/ (**mobs, mobbing, mobbed**) **1** N-COUNT A **mob** is a large, disorganized, and often violent crowd of people. ❑ *…a mob of angry men.* **2** V-T If you say that someone **is being mobbed by** a crowd of people, you mean that the people are trying to talk to them or get near them in an enthusiastic or threatening way. ❑ *Her car was mobbed by reporters.* [from Latin]

**Word Link** mobil ≈ moving : auto**mobil**e, **mobil**e, **mobil**ize

**mo|bile** /moʊbᵊl/ (**mobiles**) **1** ADJ You use **mobile** to describe something large that can be moved easily from place to place. ❑ *...a mobile theater.* **2** ADJ If you are **mobile**, you can move or travel easily from place to place. ❑ *I'm still very mobile.* ● **mo|bil|ity** /moʊbɪlɪti/ N-UNCOUNT ❑ *The car gave him much more mobility.* **3** ADJ In a **mobile** society, people move easily from one job, home, or social class to another. ❑ *We are a very mobile society and like to take everything with us.* ● **mo|bil|ity** N-UNCOUNT ❑ *Before the nineteenth century, there was little mobility among the classes.* [from Old French] → see **cellphone**

**Word Partnership** Use mobile with :

N. mobile **device**, mobile **service** **1**

**mo|bi|lize** /moʊbɪlaɪz/ (**mobilizes, mobilizing, mobilized**) **1** V-T/V-I If you **mobilize** support or **mobilize** people to do something, you succeed in encouraging people to take action. ❑ *The government could not mobilize public support.* ● **mo|bi|li|za|tion** /moʊbɪlɪzeɪʃᵊn/ N-UNCOUNT ❑ *...the mobilization of opinion in support of the revolution.* **2** V-T/V-I If a country **mobilizes**, or **mobilizes** its armed forces, or if its armed forces **mobilize**, orders are given to prepare for a conflict. ❑ *Sudan threatened to mobilize.* ● **mo|bi|li|za|tion** N-UNCOUNT ❑ *...mobilization to defend the republic.* [from Old French]

**mo|cha** /moʊkə/ (**mochas**) **1** N-VAR **Mocha** is a drink that is a mixture of coffee and chocolate. A **mocha** is a cup of mocha. ❑ *...a cup of mocha.* **2** N-UNCOUNT **Mocha** is a type of strong coffee. [after Mocha, a port in Yemen]

**mock** /mɒk/ (**mocks, mocking, mocked**) **1** V-T If you **mock** someone, you laugh at them, tease them, or try to make them look foolish. ❑ *I thought you were mocking me.* ● **mock|ing** /mɒkɪŋ/ ADJ ❑ *She gave a mocking smile.* **2** ADJ You use **mock** to describe something which is not real or genuine, but which is intended to be very similar to the real thing. ❑ *"It's tragic!" said Jeffrey in mock horror.* [from Old French]

**mock|ery** /mɒkəri/ **1** N-UNCOUNT If someone mocks you, you can refer to their behavior or attitude as **mockery**. ❑ *His eyes were full of mockery.* **2** N-SING If something makes **a mockery of** something, it makes it appear worthless and foolish. ❑ *His 16 years in jail for a crime he didn't commit makes a mockery of the law.* [from Old French]

**mod|al** /moʊdᵊl/ (**modals**) N-COUNT In grammar, a **modal** or a **modal auxiliary** is a word such as "can" or "would" which is used with a main verb to express ideas such as possibility, intention, or necessity. [TECHNICAL] [from Latin]

**Word Link** mod ≈ measure, manner : **mod**e, **mod**el, **mod**ern

**mode** /moʊd/ (**modes**) **1** N-COUNT A **mode** of life or behavior is a particular way of living or behaving. [FORMAL] ❑ *He decided to completely*

change his mode of life. **2** N-COUNT A **mode** is a particular style in art, literature, or dress. ❑ *...a formal mode of dress.* **3** N-COUNT In statistics, the **mode** of a set of numbers is the number that occurs most often. [TECHNICAL] **4** N-COUNT In music, a **mode** is a scale with a particular arrangement of intervals. [TECHNICAL] [from Latin]

**mod|el** /mɒdᵊl/ (**models, modeling, modelling, modeled, modelled**) **1** N-COUNT A **model** of an object is a physical representation that shows what it looks like or how it works. The model is often smaller than the object it represents. ❑ *...a model of a house.* ❑ *I made a model out of paper and glue.* ● **Model** is also an adjective. ❑ *...model trains.* **2** N-COUNT A **model** is a system that is being used and that people might want to copy in order to achieve similar results. [FORMAL] ❑ *...the old-fashioned model of teaching.* **3** N-COUNT If you say that someone or something is **a model of** a particular quality, you approve of them because they have that quality to a large degree. ❑ *He is a model of good manners.* **4** ADJ You use **model** to express approval of someone when you think that they perform their role or duties extremely well. ❑ *She was a model student.* **5** V-T If one thing **is modeled on** another, the first thing is made so that it is like the second thing in some way. ❑ *The system was modeled on the one used in Europe.* **6** N-COUNT A particular **model** of a machine is a particular version of it. ❑ *You don't need an expensive computer, just a basic model.* **7** N-COUNT An artist's **model** is a person who is drawn, painted or sculpted by them. ❑ *The model for his painting was his sister.* **8** N-COUNT A fashion **model** is a person whose job is to display clothes by wearing them. ❑ *...Paris's top fashion model.* **9** V-T/V-I If someone **models** clothes, they display them by wearing them. ❑ *She began modeling at age 15.* ● **mod|el|ing** N-UNCOUNT ❑ *Modeling is not an easy job.* [from Old French] **10** → see also **role model** → see **forecast**

**Word Partnership** Use model with :

| | |
|---|---|
| V. | **build a** model, **make a** model **1** **base something on a** model, **follow a** model, **serve as a** model **1** – **3** |
| N. | **business** model **2** |
| ADJ. | **basic** model, **current** model, **latest** model, **new** model, **standard** model **6** |

**mod|er|ate** (**moderates, moderating, moderated**)

The adjective and noun are pronounced /mɒdərɪt/. The verb is pronounced /mɒdəreɪt/.

**1** ADJ **Moderate** political opinions or policies are not extreme. ❑ *He has very moderate views.* **2** ADJ You use **moderate** to describe people or groups who have moderate political opinions or policies. ❑ *...a moderate Democrat.* ● A **moderate** is someone with moderate political opinions. ❑ *He needs the moderates on his side.* **3** ADJ You use **moderate** to describe something that is neither large nor small in amount or degree. ❑ *A moderate amount of stress can be good for you.* ● **mod|er|ate|ly** ADV ❑ *...a moderately large animal.* **4** V-T/V-I If you **moderate** something or if it **moderates**, it becomes less extreme or violent and easier to deal with or accept. ❑ *Will he ever moderate his views?*

m

● mod|era|tion /mɒdəreɪʃ°n/ N-UNCOUNT □ ...a moderation in food prices. [from Latin]

### Word Partnership   Use moderate with :

N.   moderate **approach**, moderate **position**, moderate **view** 🔢
moderate **amount**, moderate **exercise**, moderate **growth**, moderate **heat**, moderate **improvement**, moderate **prices**, moderate **speed** 🔢

mod|era|tion /mɒdəreɪʃ°n/ 🔢 N-UNCOUNT If you say that someone's behavior shows **moderation**, you approve of them because they act in a way that is reasonable and not extreme. □ He asked everyone to show moderation. 🔢 PHRASE If someone does something such as eat, drink, or smoke **in moderation**, they do not eat, drink, or smoke too much or more than is reasonable. [from Latin] 🔢 → see also **moderate**

### Word Link   mod ≈ measure, manner : mode, model, modern

mod|ern /mɒdərn/ 🔢 ADJ **Modern** means relating to the present time, for example the present decade or present century. □ ...the problems in modern society. 🔢 ADJ Something that is **modern** is new and involves the latest ideas or equipment. □ It was a very modern school for its time. [from Old French]
→ see **dance**

### Thesaurus   modern   Also look up :

ADJ.   contemporary, current, present 🔢
state-of-the-art, up-to-date 🔢

### Word Partnership   Use modern with :

N.   modern **civilization**, modern **culture**, modern **era**, modern **life**, modern **science**, modern **society**, modern **times**, modern **warfare** 🔢
modern **conveniences**, modern **equipment**, modern **methods**, modern **techniques**, modern **technology** 🔢

mod|ern dance N-UNCOUNT **Modern dance** is a form of dance that developed in the twentieth century and uses movement to express emotion and abstract ideas.

### Word Link   ize ≈ making : finalize, modernize, normalize

mod|ern|ize /mɒdərnaɪz/ (modernizes, modernizing, modernized) V-T To **modernize** something such as a system or a factory means to change it by replacing old equipment or methods with new ones. □ ...to modernize our schools.
● mod|erni|za|tion /mɒdərnɪzeɪʃ°n/ N-UNCOUNT □ ...a five-year modernization program. [from Old French]

mod|est /mɒdɪst/ 🔢 ADJ A **modest** house or other building is not large or expensive. □ They spent the night at a modest hotel. 🔢 ADJ You use **modest** to describe something such as an amount, rate, or improvement which is fairly small. □ Unemployment rose to the still modest rate of 0.7%.
● mod|est|ly ADV □ The results improved modestly.

🔢 ADJ If you say that someone is **modest**, you approve of them because they do not talk much about their abilities or achievements. □ He's modest, as well as being a great player. ● mod|est|ly ADV □ "You really must be very good at what you do." — "I suppose I am," Kate said modestly. [from Old French]

mod|es|ty /mɒdɪsti/ N-UNCOUNT Someone who shows **modesty** does not talk much about their abilities or achievements. □ He speaks about his achievements with modesty. [from Old French]

modi|fi|er /mɒdɪfaɪər/ (modifiers) N-COUNT A **modifier** is a word or group of words that modifies another word or group. In some descriptions of grammar, only words that are used before a noun are called **modifiers**. [from Old French]

modi|fy /mɒdɪfaɪ/ (modifies, modifying, modified) V-T If you **modify** something, you change it slightly, usually in order to improve it. □ We all modify our behavior in different situations.
● modi|fi|ca|tion /mɒdɪfɪkeɪʃ°n/ (modifications) N-VAR □ A few small modifications were needed. [from Old French]

mod|ule /mɒdʒul/ (modules) 🔢 N-COUNT A **module** is a part of a spacecraft which can operate by itself, often away from the rest of the spacecraft. □ This module is where the crew lives. 🔢 N-COUNT A **module** is a part of a machine, especially a computer, which performs a particular function. [from Latin]

Moho /moʊhoʊ/ also Mohorovicic Discontinuity N-SING **The Moho** is the boundary between the Earth's crust and its mantle. [TECHNICAL]

moist /mɔɪst/ (moister, moistest) ADJ Something that is **moist** is slightly wet. □ The soil is moist after the September rain. [from Old French]

mois|ture /mɔɪstʃər/ N-UNCOUNT **Moisture** is tiny drops of water in the air, on a surface, or in the ground. □ When the soil is dry, more moisture is lost from the plant. [from Old French]

mold /moʊld/ (molds, molding, molded) 🔢 N-COUNT A **mold** is a hollow container that you pour liquid into. When the liquid becomes solid, it takes the same shape as the mold. □ ...a plastic jelly mold. 🔢 V-T If you **mold** a soft substance such as plastic or clay, you make it into a particular shape or into an object. □ He began to mold the clay into a different shape. 🔢 V-T To **mold** someone or something means to change or influence them over a period of time so that they develop in a particular way. □ My mother molded my ideas a lot. 🔢 N-UNCOUNT **Mold** is a soft gray, green, or blue substance that sometimes forms in spots on old food or on damp walls or clothes. □ She discovered black and green mold growing in her closet. [from Old English]
→ see **fungus, laboratory**

mole /moʊl/ (moles) 🔢 N-COUNT A **mole** is a natural dark spot or small dark lump on your skin. □ She has a mole on the side of her nose. 🔢 N-COUNT A **mole** is a small animal with black fur that lives underground. 🔢 N-COUNT A **mole** is a member of a government or other organization who gives secret information to the press or to a rival organization. □ After returning to London in 1951, Philby continued his career as a mole. [Sense 1 from Old English. Senses 2 and 3 from Middle Dutch.]

M

**mo|lecu|lar** /məlɛkyələr/ ADJ **Molecular** means relating to or involving molecules. ❏ ...the molecular structure of oil. [from French]

| **Word Link** | cule ≈ small : minuscule, molecule, ridicule |
|---|---|

**mol|ecule** /mɒlɪkyul/ (**molecules**) N-COUNT A **molecule** is the smallest amount of a chemical substance which can exist by itself. ❏ ...water molecules. [from French]
→ see **element**

**mo|lest** /məlɛst/ (**molests, molesting, molested**) V-T A person who **molests** someone touches them in a sexual way against their will. [from Latin]

**mol|ten** /moʊltⁿn/ ADJ **Molten** rock, metal, or glass has been heated to a very high temperature and has become a hot, thick liquid. ❏ The molten metal is extremely hot. [from Old English]
→ see **volcano**

**molt|ing** /moʊltɪŋ/ N-UNCOUNT **Molting** is a process in which an animal or bird gradually loses its coat or feathers so that a new coat or feathers can grow. [from Old English]

**mom** /mɒm/ (**moms**) N-COUNT; N-VOC Your **mom** is your mother. [INFORMAL] ❏ We waited for Mom and Dad to get home.

**mo|ment** /moʊmənt/ (**moments**) **1** N-COUNT You can refer to a very short period of time, for example a few seconds, as a **moment** or **moments**. ❏ In a moment he was gone. ❏ In moments, I was asleep again. **2** N-COUNT A particular **moment** is the point in time at which something happens. ❏ At that moment a car stopped at the house. **3** PHRASE You use expressions such as **at the moment, at this moment,** and **at the present moment** to indicate that a particular situation exists at the time when you are speaking. ❏ At the moment, no one is talking to me. ❏ He's in South America at this moment in time. **4** PHRASE You use **for the moment** to indicate that something is true now, even if it will not be true in the future. ❏ For the moment, everything is fine. **5** PHRASE If you say that something happens **the moment** something else happens, you are emphasizing that it happens immediately after the other thing. ❏ The moment I closed my eyes, I fell asleep. [from Old French] **6** **spur of the moment** → see **spur**

| **Word Partnership** | Use moment with : |
|---|---|
| ADV. | a moment **ago, just** a moment **1** |
| N. | moment **of silence,** moment **of thought 1** |
| V. | **stop for** a moment, **take a** moment, **think for** a moment, **wait a** moment **1** |
| ADJ. | an **awkward** moment, a **critical** moment, **the right** moment **2** |

**mo|men|tari|ly** /moʊməntɛərɪli/ ADV **Momentarily** means very soon. ❏ My husband will be here momentarily. [from Old French]

**mo|men|tary** /moʊmənteri/ ADJ Something that is **momentary** lasts for a very short period of time, for example for a few seconds or less. ❏ ...a momentary silence. ● **mo|men|tari|ly** /moʊməntɛərɪli/ ADV ❏ She paused momentarily when she saw them. [from Old French]

**mo|men|tous** /moʊmɛntəs/ ADJ A **momentous** decision, event, or change is very important. ❏ ...the momentous decision to get married. [from Old French]

**mo|men|tum** /moʊmɛntəm/ **1** N-UNCOUNT If a process or movement gains **momentum**, it keeps developing or happening more quickly and keeps becoming less likely to stop. ❏ This campaign is really gaining momentum. **2** N-UNCOUNT In physics, **momentum** is the mass of a moving object multiplied by its speed in a particular direction. [TECHNICAL] [from Latin]
→ see **motion**

| **Word Partnership** | Use momentum with : |
|---|---|
| V. | **build** momentum, **gain** momentum, **gather** momentum, **have** momentum, **lose** momentum, **maintain** momentum **1** **2** |

**mom|ma** /mɒmə/ (**mommas**) N-COUNT; N-VOC **Momma** means the same as **mommy**. [INFORMAL]

**mom|my** /mɒmi/ (**mommies**) N-COUNT; N-VOC Some people, especially young children, call their mother **mommy**. [INFORMAL] ❏ Mommy and I went in an airplane.

| **Word Link** | arch ≈ rule : anarchy, hierarchy, monarch |
|---|---|

**mon|arch** /mɒnərk, -ɑrk/ (**monarchs**) N-COUNT The **monarch** of a country is the king, queen, emperor, or empress. [from Late Latin]

**mon|ar|chist** /mɒnərkɪst/ (**monarchists**) ADJ If someone has **monarchist** views, they believe that their country should have a monarch, such as a king or queen. ❏ ...a monarchist political party. ● A **monarchist** is someone with monarchist views. ❏ Monarchists are interested in what he has to say. [from Late Latin]

**mon|ar|chy** /mɒnərki/ (**monarchies**) N-VAR A **monarchy** is a system in which a country has a monarch. ❏ ...a discussion about the future of the monarchy. [from Late Latin]

**mon|as|tery** /mɒnəsteri/ (**monasteries**) N-COUNT A **monastery** is a building in which monks live. [from Church Latin]

**Mon|day** /mʌndeɪ, -di/ (**Mondays**) N-VAR **Monday** is the day after Sunday and before Tuesday. ❏ I went back to work on Monday. ❏ The first meeting was last Monday. [from Old English]

**mon|etary** /mɒnɪteri/ ADJ **Monetary** means relating to money, especially the total amount of money in a country. [BUSINESS] ❏ The U.S. monetary system is a decimal system, with 100 cents in one dollar. [from Late Latin]

**mon|ey** /mʌni/ (**monies** or **moneys**) **1** N-UNCOUNT **Money** is the coins or banknotes that you use to buy things, or the sum that you have in an account. ❏ Cars cost a lot of money. ❏ A lot of football players earn money from advertising. ❏ Companies have to make money. **2** PHRASE If you **get** your **money's worth**, you get something which is worth the money that it costs or the effort you have put in. ❏ The team's fans get their money's worth. [from Old French]
→ see Word Web: **money**
→ see **donor**

m

## Word Web    money

Early traders used a system of **barter** which didn't involve **money**. For example, a farmer might trade a cow for a

wooden cart. In China, India, and Africa, cowrie shells* became a form of **currency**. The first **coins** were crude lumps of metal. Uniform circular coins appeared in China around 1500 BC. In 1150 AD, the Chinese started using paper bills for money. In 560 BC, the Lydians (living in what is now Turkey) **minted** three types of coins—a **gold** coin, a **silver** coin, and a mixed metal coin. Their use quickly spread through Asia Minor and Greece.

*cowrie shell: a small, shiny, oval shell.*

## Thesaurus    *money*    Also look up :

N.    capital, cash, currency, funds, wealth **1**

**mon|ey or|der** (**money orders**) N-COUNT A **money order** is a piece of paper representing a sum of money which you can buy at a post office and send to someone as a way of sending them money by mail.

**moni|tor** /mɒnɪtər/ (**monitors, monitoring, monitored**) **1** V-T If you **monitor** something, you regularly check its development or progress. ❑ *Officials monitored the voting.* **2** N-COUNT A **monitor** is a machine that is used to check or record things. ❑ *The monitor shows his heartbeat.* **3** N-COUNT A **monitor** is a screen which is used to display certain kinds of information. ❑ *He was watching a game of tennis on a television monitor.* [from Latin]
→ see **computer, tsunami**

## Word Partnership    Use *monitor* with :

| | |
|---|---|
| ADV. | **carefully** monitor, **closely** monitor **1** |
| N. | monitor **activity**, monitor **elections**, monitor **performance**, monitor **progress** **1**<br>**color** monitor, **computer** monitor, **video** monitor **3** |

**monk** /mʌŋk/ (**monks**) N-COUNT A **monk** is a member of a male religious community. ❑ *...Buddhist monks.* [from Old English]

**mon|key** /mʌŋki/ (**monkeys**) N-COUNT A **monkey** is an animal with a long tail which lives in hot countries and climbs trees. [from Low German]
→ see **primate**

**mon|key bars** N-PLURAL **Monkey bars** are metal or wooden bars that are joined together to form a structure for children to climb and play on.

**mono** /mɒnoʊ/ N-UNCOUNT **Mono** is the same as **mononucleosis**. [INFORMAL] [from Greek]

**mono|chro|mat|ic** /mɒnəkrəmætɪk/ ADJ **Monochromatic** pictures use only one color in various shades.

**mono|cline** /mɒnoʊklaɪn/ (**monoclines**) N-COUNT A **monocline** is a rock formation in which layers of rock are folded so that they are horizontal on both sides of the fold. [TECHNICAL] [from Greek]

## Word Link    mono ≈ one : monogamous, monologue, monopoly

**mo|noga|my** /mənɒgəmi/ N-UNCOUNT **Monogamy** is the state or custom of having a sexual relationship with only one partner or being married to only one person. ❑ *People still choose monogamy and marriage.* ● **mo|noga|mous** /mənɒgəməs/ ADJ ❑ *Do you believe that men are not naturally monogamous?* [from French]

**mono|lith|ic** /mɒnˈlɪθɪk/ ADJ If you refer to an organization or system as **monolithic**, you are critical of it because it is very large and very slow to change. ❑ *...a monolithic system.*

**mono|logue** /mɒnˈlɔg/ (**monologues**) also **monolog** **1** N-COUNT If you refer to a long speech by one person during a conversation as a **monologue**, you mean it prevents other people from talking or expressing their opinions. ❑ *Morris continued his monologue.* **2** N-VAR A **monologue** is a long speech which is spoken by one person as an entertainment, or as part of an entertainment such as a play. [from French]

**mo|no|mial** /mɒnoʊmiəl/ (**monomials**) N-COUNT A **monomial** is an expression in algebra that consists of just one term, for example "5xy." Compare **binomial, polynomial**. [TECHNICAL] ● **monomial** is also an adjective ADJ ❑ *...monomial expressions.*

**mono|nu|cleo|sis** /mɒnoʊnuklioʊsɪs/ N-UNCOUNT **Mononucleosis** is a disease which causes swollen glands, fever, and a sore throat.

**mo|nopo|lize** /mənɒpəlaɪz/ (**monopolizes, monopolizing, monopolized**) V-T If someone **monopolizes** something, they have a very large share of it and prevent other people from having a share. ❑ *One company is monopolizing the market.* [from Late Latin]

**mo|nopo|ly** /mənɒpəli/ (**monopolies**) **1** N-VAR If a company, person, or state has a **monopoly** on something such as an industry, they have complete control over it. [BUSINESS] ❑ *The company has a monopoly on trade with India.* **2** N-COUNT A **monopoly** is a company which is the only one providing a particular product or service. [BUSINESS] ❑ *The two companies joined together, creating a monopoly.* [from Late Latin]

**mono|theism** /mɒnəθiɪzəm/ N-UNCOUNT **Monotheism** is the belief that there is only one God. ❑ *...the monotheism of the Christian religion.*

**mono|theis|tic** /mɒnəθiɪstɪk/ ADJ **Monotheistic** religions believe that there is only one God. ❑ *...all the major monotheistic religions.*

**mo|noto|nous** /mənɒtᵊnəs/ ADJ Something that is **monotonous** is very boring because it has a regular, repeated pattern which never changes. ❑ *It's monotonous work, like most factory jobs.*

**mono|treme** /mɒnətrim/ (**monotremes**) N-COUNT A **monotreme** is a mammal that gives birth by laying eggs. [TECHNICAL] [from New Latin]

**mon|soon** /mɒnsun/ (**monsoons**) N-COUNT The **monsoon** is the season in southern Asia when there is a lot of very heavy rain. ❑ *...the end of the monsoon.* [from Dutch]
→ see **disaster**

**mon|ster** /mɒnstər/ (**monsters**) **1** N-COUNT A **monster** is a large imaginary creature that looks very ugly and frightening. ❑ *The movie is about a monster in the bedroom closet.* **2** ADJ **Monster** means extremely and surprisingly large. [INFORMAL] ❑ *...a monster weapon.* [from Old French]

**mon|strous** /mɒnstrəs/ **1** ADJ If you describe a situation or event as **monstrous**, you mean that it is extremely shocking or unfair. ❑ *His monstrous behavior lasted for years.* ● **mon|strous|ly** ADV ❑ *Your husband's family has behaved monstrously.* **2** ADJ If you describe an unpleasant thing as **monstrous**, you mean that it is extremely large in size or extent. ❑ *...a monstrous building.* ● **mon|strous|ly** ADV ❑ *It would be monstrously unfair.* [from Old French]

**month** /mʌnθ/ (**months**) N-COUNT A **month** is one of the twelve periods of time that a year is divided into, for example January or February. ❑ *The trial will begin next month.* [from Old English]
→ see **year**

**month|ly** /mʌnθli/ ADJ A **monthly** event or publication happens or appears every month. ❑ *Many people are now having trouble making their monthly payments.* ● **Monthly** is also an adverb. ❑ *The magazine is published monthly.* [from Old English]

**monu|ment** /mɒnyəmənt/ (**monuments**) N-COUNT A **monument** is a large structure, usually made of stone, which is built to remind people of an event in history or of a famous person. ❑ *This monument was built in memory of the 90,000 Indian soldiers who died in World War I.* [from Latin]

**monu|men|tal** /mɒnyəmɛntᵊl/ ADJ You can use **monumental** to emphasize the large size or extent of something. ❑ *It was a monumental mistake to give him the job.* ❑ *...his monumental work on AIDS.* [from Latin]

**mood** /mud/ (**moods**) **1** N-COUNT Your **mood** is the way you are feeling at a particular time. ❑ *He is in a good mood today.* ❑ *Lily was in one of her aggressive moods.* **2** N-COUNT If someone is **in a mood**, the way they are behaving shows that they are feeling angry and impatient. ❑ *She was obviously in a mood.* **3** N-SING The **mood** of a group of people is the way that they think and feel about an idea, event, or question at a particular time. ❑ *The mood of the people changed.* [from Old English]

| | Word Partnership | Use *mood* with : |
|---|---|---|
| ADJ. | bad/good mood, depressed mood, foul mood, positive mood, tense mood **1** | |
| N. | mood change, mood disorder, mood swings **1** | |
| V. | create a mood, set a mood **3** | |

**moody** /mudi/ (**moodier, moodiest**) ADJ A **moody** person often becomes depressed or angry without any warning. ❑ *David's mother was very moody.* ● **moodi|ly** /mudɪli/ ADV ❑ *He sat and stared moodily out the window.* ● **moodi|ness** N-UNCOUNT ❑ *His poor health probably caused his moodiness.* [from Old English]

**moon** /mun/ (**moons**) **1** N-SING The **moon** is the object in the sky that goes around the earth once every four weeks. You often see it at night as a circle or part of a circle. ❑ *...the first man on the moon.* **2** N-COUNT A **moon** is an object similar to a small planet that travels around a planet. ❑ *...Neptune's large moon.* [from Old English]
→ see Word Web: **moon**
→ see **astronomer, eclipse, satellite, solar system, tide**

**moon|light** /munlaɪt/ (**moonlights, moonlighting, moonlighted**) **1** N-UNCOUNT **Moonlight** is the light that comes from the moon at night. ❑ *They walked along the road in the moonlight.* **2** V-I If someone **moonlights**, they have a second job in addition to their main job. ❑ *He was a builder moonlighting as a taxi driver.*

**moon|shine** /munʃaɪn/ **1** N-UNCOUNT **Moonshine** is whiskey that is made illegally. **2** N-UNCOUNT If you say that someone's thoughts, ideas, or comments are **moonshine**, you think they are foolish and not based on reality.

**moor** /mʊər/ (**moors, mooring, moored**) **1** V-T/V-I If you **moor**, or **moor** a boat somewhere, you stop and tie the boat to the land with a rope

m

**Word Web** moon

Scientists believe the **moon** is about five billion years old. They think a large asteroid hit the earth. A big piece of the earth broke off. It went flying into **space**. However, the earth's **gravity** caught it. It began to circle the earth. This piece became our moon. The moon orbits the earth once a month. It also **rotates** on its **axis** every thirty days. The moon has no **atmosphere**, so meteoroids crash into it. When a meteoroid hits the moon, it makes a **crater**. Craters cover the surface of the moon.

or chain so that it cannot move away. ☐ *She had moored her boat on the right bank of the river.* ☐ *I decided to moor near some small boats.* [of Germanic origin]
**2** → see also **mooring**

**moor|ing** /mʊ̯ərɪŋ/ (**moorings**) N-COUNT A **mooring** is a place where a boat can be tied so that it cannot move away, or the object it is tied to. ☐ *Free moorings will be available.* [from Old English]

**moose** /mu̯s/ (**moose**) N-COUNT A **moose** is a large type of deer with big flat horns called antlers. [from Algonquian]

**mop** /mɒp/ (**mops, mopping, mopped**)
**1** N-COUNT A **mop** is a piece of equipment for washing floors. It consists of a sponge or many pieces of string attached to a long handle. **2** V-T If you **mop** a surface such as a floor, you clean it with a mop. ☐ *There was a woman mopping the stairs.* **3** V-T If you **mop** sweat from your forehead or **mop** your forehead, you wipe it with a piece of cloth. ☐ *He mopped sweat from his forehead.* [from Medieval Latin]
▶ **mop up** PHR-VERB If you **mop up** a liquid, you clean it with a cloth so that the liquid is absorbed. ☐ *A waiter mopped up the mess as well as he could.* ☐ *If the washing machine leaks water we can mop it up.*

**mope** /mo̯ʊp/ (**mopes, moping, moped**) V-I If you **mope**, you feel miserable and do not feel interested in doing anything. ☐ *Get on with life and don't sit back and mope.*

**mo|ped** /mo̯ʊpɛd/ (**mopeds**) N-COUNT A **moped** is a small motorcycle which you can also pedal like a bicycle.

**mo|raine** /mərei̯n/ (**moraines**) N-COUNT A **moraine** is a pile of rocks and soil left behind by a glacier. [TECHNICAL] [from French]

**mor|al** /mɔr¹l/ (**morals**) **1** N-PLURAL **Morals** are principles and beliefs concerning right and wrong behavior. ☐ *...Western ideas and morals.* **2** ADJ **Moral** means relating to beliefs about what is right or wrong. ☐ *She had to make a moral judgment about what was the right thing to do.* ● **mor|al|ly** ADV ☐ *It is morally wrong to kill a person?* **3** ADJ A **moral** person behaves in a way that is believed by most people to be good and right. ☐ *The minister was a very moral man.* ● **mor|al|ly** ADV ☐ *Art is not there to improve you morally.* **4** ADJ If you give someone **moral** support, you encourage them in what they are doing by expressing approval. ☐ *I'm just there to give her moral support.* **5** N-COUNT The **moral** of a story or event is what you learn from it about how you should or should not behave. ☐ *The moral of the story is do not trust anyone.* [from Latin]
→ see **philosophy**

**mo|rale** /mərǽl/ N-UNCOUNT **Morale** is the amount of confidence and cheerfulness that a group of people have. ☐ *Many teachers are suffering from low morale.* [from French]

**mor|al fi|ber** N-UNCOUNT **Moral fiber** is the quality of being determined to do what you think is right. ☐ *He was a man of strong moral fiber.*

**mo|ral|ity** /mərǽlɪti/ **1** N-UNCOUNT **Morality** is the belief that some behavior is right and acceptable and that other behavior is wrong. ☐ *...standards of morality in society.* **2** N-UNCOUNT The **morality** of something is how right or acceptable it is. ☐ *...arguments about the morality of nuclear weapons.* [from French]

**mora|to|rium** /mɔrətɔri̯əm/ (**moratoriums or**

**moratoria**) N-COUNT If there is a **moratorium on** a particular activity or process, it is stopped for a fixed period of time. ☐ *They voted on a one-year moratorium on missile tests.* [from New Latin]

**mor|bid** /mɔrbɪd/ ADJ If someone has a **morbid** interest in something unpleasant, especially death, they are very interested in it. ☐ *Some people have a morbid interest in crime.* ● **mor|bid|ly** ADV ☐ *There's something morbidly exciting about the idea.* [from Latin]

**more** /mɔr/

> **More** is often considered to be the comparative form of **much** and **many**.

**1** DET You use **more** to indicate that there is a greater amount of something than before or than average, or than something else. You can use "a little," "a lot," "a bit," "far," and "much" in front of **more**. ☐ *More and more people are surviving heart attacks.* ☐ *He spent more time going out with his friends.* ● **More** is also a pronoun. ☐ *As the workers worked harder, they ate more.* ● **More** is also a quantifier. ☐ *They're doing more of their own work.* **2** PHRASE You use **more than** before a number or amount to say that the actual number or amount is even greater. ☐ *The airport had been closed for more than a year.* **3** ADV You can use **more** or **some more** to indicate that something continues to happen for a further period of time. ☐ *You should talk about your problems a bit more.* **4** ADV You use **more** to indicate that something is repeated. ☐ *This train will stop twice more before we arrive in Baltimore.* **5** DET You use **more** to refer to an additional thing or amount. ☐ *They needed more time to think about what to do.* ● **More** is also an adjective. ☐ *We stayed in Danville two more days.* ● **More** is also a pronoun. ☐ *We should be doing more to help people with AIDS.* **6** PHRASE You can use **more and more** to indicate that something is becoming greater in amount, extent, or degree all the time. ☐ *She began eating more and more.* **7** PHRASE You use **more than** to say that something is true to a greater degree than is necessary or than average. ☐ *The company has more than enough money to pay what it owes.* **8** PHRASE You can use **what is more** or **what's more** to introduce an extra piece of information which supports or emphasizes the point you are making. ☐ *I am able to help you, and what is more, I want to.* [from Old English] **9** **all the more** → see **all** **10** **any more** → see **any**

**more|over** /mɔrou̯vər/ ADV You use **moreover** to introduce a piece of information that adds to or supports the previous statement. [FORMAL] ☐ *She saw that there was a man behind her. Moreover, he was looking at her.*

**morgue** /mɔrg/ (**morgues**) N-COUNT A **morgue** is a building or a room in a hospital where dead bodies are kept before they are buried or cremated, or before they are identified or examined. [from French]

**morn|ing** /mɔrnɪŋ/ (**mornings**) **1** N-VAR The **morning** is the part of each day between the time that people usually wake up and 12 o'clock noon or lunchtime. ☐ *Tomorrow morning your guide will take you around the city.* ☐ *On Sunday morning the telephone woke Bill.* **2** N-SING If you refer to a particular time in the **morning**, you mean a time between 12 o'clock midnight and 12 o'clock noon. ☐ *I often stayed up until two or three in the morning.* **3** PHRASE If you say that something will happen **in the**

**morning**, you mean that it will happen during the morning of the following day. ❑ *I'll fly to St. Louis in the morning.*
→ see **time**

| **Thesaurus** | *morning* | Also look up : |
|---|---|---|
| N. | dawn, light, sunrise ❶ | |

**mo|rose** /mərous/ ADJ Someone who is **morose** is miserable, bad-tempered, and not willing to talk very much to other people. ❑ *She was morose, pale, and quiet.* ● **mo|rose|ly** ADV ❑ *One old man sat morosely at a table.* [from Latin]

**mor|phine** /mɔrfin/ N-UNCOUNT **Morphine** is a drug used to relieve pain. [from French]

**mor|sel** /mɔrsᵊl/ (**morsels**) N-COUNT A **morsel** is a very small amount of something, especially a very small piece of food. ❑ *...a delicious little morsel of meat.* [from Old French]

**mor|tal** /mɔrtᵊl/ (**mortals**) ❶ ADJ If you refer to the fact that people are **mortal**, you mean that they have to die and cannot live forever. ❑ *A man is mortal. He grows, he becomes old, and he dies.* ● **mor|tal|ity** /mɔrtæliti/ N-UNCOUNT ❑ *...fears about our own mortality.* ❷ N-COUNT You can describe someone as a **mortal** when you want to say that they are an ordinary person. ❑ *We are all mere mortals and we make mistakes.* ❸ ADJ You can use **mortal** to show that something is very serious or may cause death. ❑ *The police were defending people against mortal danger.* ● **mor|tal|ly** ADV ❑ *He falls, mortally wounded.* [from Latin]

**mor|tal|ity** /mɔrtæliti/ N-UNCOUNT The **mortality** in a particular place or situation is the number of people who die. ❑ *Infant mortality in some African countries is very high.* [from Latin]

**mor|tar** /mɔrtər/ (**mortars**) ❶ N-COUNT A **mortar** is a big gun that fires missiles high into the air over a short distance. ❑ *Mortars were still exploding.* ❷ N-UNCOUNT **Mortar** is a mixture of sand, water, and cement or lime which is put between bricks to hold them together. ❑ *Bricks and mortar are basic building materials.* [from Latin]

**mort|gage** /mɔrgɪdʒ/ (**mortgages, mortgaging, mortgaged**) ❶ N-COUNT A **mortgage** is a loan of money which you get from a bank or savings and loan association in order to buy a house. ❑ *We go to work each day to pay the mortgage.* ❷ V-T If you **mortgage** your house or land, you use it as a guarantee to a company in order to borrow money from them. ❑ *They had to mortgage their home to pay the bills.* [from Old French]

**mor|ti|cian** /mɔrtɪʃᵊn/ (**morticians**) N-COUNT A **mortician** is a person whose job is to deal with the bodies of people who have died and to arrange funerals.

**mor|tu|ary** /mɔrtʃuɛri/ (**mortuaries**) ❶ N-COUNT A **mortuary** is a building or a room in a hospital where dead bodies are kept before they are buried or cremated, or before they are identified or examined. ❷ N-COUNT A **mortuary** is the same as a **funeral home**. [from Medieval Latin]

**mo|sa|ic** /mouzeɪɪk/ (**mosaics**) N-VAR A **mosaic** is a design which consists of small pieces of colored glass, pottery, or stone set in concrete or plaster. ❑ *The Roman house has a beautiful mosaic floor.* [from French]

**Mos|lem** /mɑzlɪm, mʊs-/ → see **Muslim**

**mosque** /mɒsk/ (**mosques**) N-COUNT A **mosque** is a building where Muslims go to worship. [from Old French]

**mos|qui|to** /məskitou/ (**mosquitoes** or **mosquitos**) N-COUNT **Mosquitos** are small flying insects which bite people and animals in order to suck their blood. [from Spanish]
→ see **insect**

**moss** /mɔs/ (**mosses**) N-VAR **Moss** is a very small, soft, green plant which grows on damp soil, or on wood or stone. ❑ *...ground covered with moss.* [from Old English]

**most** /moust/

> **Most** is often considered to be the superlative form of **much** and **many**.

❶ QUANT You use **most** to refer to the majority of a group of things or people, or the largest part of something. ❑ *Most of the houses here are very old.* ❑ *I was away from home most of the time.* ● **Most** is also a determiner. ❑ *Most people think he is younger than he is.* ● **Most** is also a pronoun. ❑ *Seventeen people were hurt. Most are students.* ❷ ADJ You use **the most** to mean a larger amount than anyone or anything else, or the largest amount possible. ❑ *The president won the most votes.* ● **Most** is also a pronoun. ❑ *The most they earn in a day is fifty dollars.* ❸ ADV You use **most** to indicate that something is true or happens to a greater degree or extent than anything else. ❑ *What she feared most was becoming like her mother.* ❑ *...Professor Morris, the teacher he most disliked.* ❹ PHRASE You use **most of all** to indicate that something happens or is true to a greater extent than anything else. ❺ ADV You use **most** to indicate that someone or something has a greater amount of a particular quality than most other things of its kind. ❑ *Her children had the most unusual birthday parties in the neighborhood.* ❑ *He was one of the most kind men I have ever met.* ❻ ADV If you do something **the most**, you do it to the greatest extent possible or with the greatest frequency. ❑ *What question are you asked the most?* ❼ PHRASE You use **at most** or **at the most** to say that a number or amount is the maximum that is possible and that the actual number or amount may be smaller. ❑ *Heat the sauce for ten minutes at most.* ❽ PHRASE If you **make the most of** something, you get the maximum use or advantage from it. ❑ *Happiness is the ability to make the most of what you have.* [from Old English]
❾ → see also **almost**

**most|ly** /moustli/ ADV You use **mostly** to indicate that a statement is generally true, for example true about the majority of a group of things or people, true most of the time, or true in most respects. ❑ *My friends are mostly students.* ❑ *Cars are mostly metal.* [from Old English]

**mo|tel** /moutɛl/ (**motels**) N-COUNT A **motel** is a hotel intended for people who are traveling by car.

**moth** /mɔθ/ (**moths**) N-COUNT A **moth** is an insect like a butterfly which usually flies around at night. [from Old English]

**moth|er** /mʌðər/ (**mothers, mothering, mothered**) ❶ N-COUNT Your **mother** is your female parent. ❑ *She's a mother of two children.* ❷ V-T If you **mother** someone, you treat them with great care and affection, as if they were a small child. ❑ *Stop mothering me.* [from Old English]
→ see **family**

m

## Word Web   motion

Newton's three laws of **motion** describe how **forces** affect the movement of objects. This is the first law: an object at **rest** won't move unless a force makes it move. Also, a moving object keeps its **momentum** unless something stops it. The second law is about **acceleration**. The **rate** of acceleration depends on two things: how strong the push on the object is, and how much the object weighs. The third law says that for every **action** there is an equal and opposite **reaction**. When one object **exerts** a force on another, the second object pushes back with an equal force.

**moth|er coun|try** (**mother countries**) N-COUNT Someone's **mother country** is the country in which they or their ancestors were born and to which they still feel emotionally linked, even if they live somewhere else. ❑ *He thinks of Turkey as his mother country.*

**moth|er|hood** /mˈʌðərhʊd/ N-UNCOUNT **Motherhood** is the state of being a mother. ❑ *A lot of women try to combine work and motherhood.* [from Old English]

**mother-in-law** (**mothers-in-law**) N-COUNT Someone's **mother-in-law** is the mother of their husband or wife.
→ see **family**

**moth|er|ly** /mˈʌðərli/ ADJ **Motherly** feelings or actions are like those of a kind mother. ❑ *...motherly love.* [from Old English]

**mo|tif** /moʊtˈiːf/ (**motifs**) **1** N-COUNT A **motif** is a design which is used as a decoration or as part of an artistic pattern. ❑ *...a rose motif.* **2** N-COUNT A **motif** is a distinctive idea which is repeated over and over again to create a theme, especially in music or literature. [from French]

### Word Link   mot ≈ moving : motion, motivate, promote

**mo|tion** /mˈoʊʃ³n/ (**motions, motioning, motioned**) **1** N-UNCOUNT **Motion** is the activity or process of continually changing position or moving from one place to another. ❑ *...Newton's three laws of motion.* ❑ *The doors will not open when the elevator is in motion.* **2** N-COUNT A **motion** is an action, gesture, or movement. ❑ *He made a motion toward the door with his hand.* **3** N-COUNT A **motion** is a formal proposal or statement in a meeting, debate, or trial, which is discussed and then voted on or decided on. ❑ *The committee debated the motion all day.* **4** V-T/V-I If you **motion** to someone, you move your hand or head as a way of telling them to do something or telling them where to go. ❑ *She motioned for my father to come in.* ❑ *He motioned Don to the door.* **5** → see also **slow motion** **6** PHRASE If you say that someone **is going through the motions**, you think they are only saying or doing something because it is expected of them without being interested, enthusiastic, or sympathetic. ❑ *"You really don't care, do you?" she said quietly. "You're just going through the motions."* **7** PHRASE If a process or event is set **in motion**, it is happening or beginning to happen. ❑ *Big changes can be set in motion by small things.* **8** PHRASE If someone **sets the wheels in motion**, they take the necessary action to make something start happening.

❑ *They have set the wheels in motion to sell their Arizona home.* [from Latin]
→ see Word Web: **motion**

### Word Partnership   Use *motion* with :

| | |
|---|---|
| ADJ. | **constant** motion, **full** motion, **perpetual** motion **1** |
| | **circular** motion, **smooth** motion **1 2** |
| | **quick** motion **2** |
| V. | **set** *something* **in** motion **1 7 8** |

**mo|tion|less** /mˈoʊʃ³nlɪs/ ADJ Someone or something that is **motionless** is not moving at all. ❑ *He stayed as motionless as a statue.* [from Latin]

**mo|tion pic|ture** (**motion pictures**) N-COUNT A **motion picture** is a movie made for movie theaters. [FORMAL] ❑ *...the motion picture industry.*

### Word Link   ate ≈ causing to be : complicate, humiliate, motivate

**mo|ti|vate** /mˈoʊtɪveɪt/ (**motivates, motivating, motivated**) **1** V-T If you **are motivated** by something, especially an emotion, it causes you to behave in a particular way. ❑ *They are motivated by greed.* ● **mo|ti|vat|ed** ADJ ❑ *...highly motivated employees.* ● **mo|ti|va|tion** /mˈoʊtɪvˈeɪʃ³n/ N-UNCOUNT ❑ *His poor performance is caused by lack of motivation.* **2** V-T If someone **motivates** you to do something, they make you feel determined to do it. ❑ *How do you motivate people to work hard?* ● **mo|ti|va|tion** N-UNCOUNT ❑ *Students are more likely to succeed if they have parental motivation.* [from Old French]

**mo|ti|va|tion** /mˈoʊtɪvˈeɪʃ³n/ (**motivations**) N-COUNT Your **motivation** for doing something is what causes you to want to do it. ❑ *Money is my motivation.* [from Old French]

**mo|tive** /mˈoʊtɪv/ (**motives**) N-COUNT Your **motive** for doing something is your reason for doing it. ❑ *Police do not think robbery was a motive for the killing.* [from Old French]

**mo|tor** /mˈoʊtər/ (**motors**) **1** N-COUNT The **motor** in a machine, vehicle, or boat is the part that uses electricity or fuel to produce movement, so that the machine, vehicle, or boat can work. ❑ *She got in the boat and started the motor.* **2** ADJ **Motor** vehicles and boats have a gasoline or diesel engine. ❑ *Motor vehicles use a lot of fuel.* [from Latin]

**motor|bike** /mˈoʊtərbaɪk/ (**motorbikes**) N-COUNT A **motorbike** is a lighter, less powerful motorcycle.

**motor|cycle**
/mo͞utərsaɪkᵊl/
(**motorcycles**) N-COUNT A
**motorcycle** is a vehicle with
two wheels and an engine.

**motor|cyclist**
/mo͞utərsaɪklɪst/
(**motorcyclists**) N-COUNT
A **motorcyclist** is a person
who rides a motorcycle.

motorcycle

**mo|tor|ist** /mo͞utərɪst/ (**motorists**) N-COUNT A
**motorist** is a person who drives a car. ❑ *Motorists should take extra care on the roads when it is raining.* [from Latin]

**mo|tor|ized** /mo͞utəraɪzd/ ADJ A **motorized** vehicle has an engine. ❑ *...a motorized cart.* [from Latin]

**mo|tor neu|ron** (**motor neurons**) N-COUNT **Motor neurons** are nerve cells that carry information from the brain and spinal cord to the muscles in your body. [TECHNICAL]

**mot|to** /mɒto͞u/ (**mottoes** or **mottos**) N-COUNT A **motto** is a short sentence or phrase that expresses a rule for sensible behavior, especially a way of behaving in a particular situation. ❑ *My motto is "Don't start what you can't finish."* [from Italian]

**mound** /maʊnd/ (**mounds**) **1** N-COUNT A **mound** of something is a large, rounded pile of it. ❑ *...huge mounds of dirt.* **2** N-COUNT In baseball, the **mound** is the raised area where the pitcher stands when he or she throws the ball. ❑ *He went to the mound to talk with the pitcher.* [from Old English] → see **baseball**

**mount** /maʊnt/ (**mounts, mounting, mounted**) **1** V-T If you **mount** a campaign or event, you organize it and make it take place. ❑ *The police mounted a search of the area.* **2** V-I If something **mounts**, it increases in intensity. ❑ *The pressure was mounting.* **3** V-I If something **mounts**, it increases in quantity. ❑ *The garbage mounts in*

*city streets.* ● To **mount up** means the same as to **mount.** ❑ *Her medical bills mounted up.* **4** V-T If you **mount** the stairs or a platform, you go up the stairs or go up onto the platform. [FORMAL] ❑ *I mounted the steps to my room.* **5** V-T If you **mount** a horse or motorcycle, you climb onto it so that you can ride it. ❑ *A man was mounting a motorcycle.* **6** V-T If you **mount** an object **on** something, you fix it there firmly. ❑ *Her husband mounts the work on colored paper.* ● **-mounted** ADJ ❑ *...a wall-mounted electric fan.* **7** N-COUNT **Mount** is used as part of the name of a mountain. ❑ *...Mount Everest.* [Senses 1–6 from Old French. Sense 7 from Old English.] **8** → see also **mounted**

**moun|tain** /maʊntᵊn/ (**mountains**) **1** N-COUNT A **mountain** is a very high area of land with steep sides. ❑ *Mt. McKinley is the highest mountain in North America.* **2** QUANT A **mountain of** something is a very large amount of it. [INFORMAL] ❑ *He has a mountain of homework.* [from Old French] → see Picture Dictionary: **mountain**

**moun|tain bike** (**mountain bikes**) N-COUNT A **mountain bike** is a type of bicycle that is suitable for riding over rough ground. It has a strong frame and thick tires.

**moun|tain|eer** /maʊntᵊnɪər/ (**mountaineers**) N-COUNT A **mountaineer** is a person who is skillful at climbing the steep sides of mountains. [from Old French]

**moun|tain go|ril|la** (**mountain gorillas**) N-COUNT A **mountain gorilla** is a type of gorilla that has long, dark hair and lives in central Africa.

**moun|tain lion** (**mountain lions**) N-COUNT A **mountain lion** is a wild animal that is a member of the cat family. Mountain lions have brownish-gray fur and live in mountain regions of North and South America.

m

**Picture Dictionary**   mountain

ridge   pass   peak   cliff   summit

glacier

**moun|tain|ous** /ma͟ʊntᵊnəs/ ADJ A **mountainous** place has a lot of mountains. ❑ ...the mountainous region of New Mexico. [from French]

**moun|tain|side** /ma͟ʊntᵊnsaɪd/ (**mountainsides**) N-COUNT A **mountainside** is one of the steep sides of a mountain. ❑ He climbed up the mountainside.

**mount|ed** /ma͟ʊntɪd/ ■ ADJ **Mounted** police or soldiers ride horses when they are on duty. ❑ A group of mounted police rode forward. [from Old French] ■ → see also **mount**

**mourn** /mɔ͟rn/ (**mourns, mourning, mourned**) ■ V-T/V-I If you **mourn** someone who has died or **mourn for** them, you are very sad that they have died and show your sorrow in the way that you behave. ❑ Joan still mourns her father. ❑ He mourned for his dead son. ■ V-T/V-I If you **mourn** something or **mourn for** it, you regret that you no longer have it and show your regret in the way that you behave. ❑ We mourned the loss of open space and parks in our cities. [from Old English]

**mourn|er** /mɔ͟rnər/ (**mourners**) N-COUNT A **mourner** is a person who attends a funeral. ❑ Weeks after his death, mourners still gather outside his house. [from Old English]

**mourn|ful** /mɔ͟rnfəl/ ADJ If you are **mournful**, you are very sad. ❑ He looked mournful, as though he was going to cry. ● **mourn|ful|ly** ADV ❑ He stood mournfully at the gate waving goodbye. [from Old English]

**mouse** /ma͟ʊs/ (**mice**) ■ N-COUNT A **mouse** is a small, furry animal with a long tail. ❑ ...a mouse in a cage. ■ N-COUNT A **mouse** is a device that you use to do things on a computer without using the keyboard. ❑ She clicked the mouse twice. [from Old English]
→ see **computer**

**mouse pad** (**mouse pads**) also **mousepad** N-COUNT A **mouse pad** is a flat piece of plastic or some other material that you rest the mouse on while using a computer.
→ see **computer**

**mousse** /mu͟s/ (**mousses**) N-VAR **Mousse** is a sweet, light food made from eggs and cream. ❑ ...chocolate mousse. [from French]
→ see **dessert**

**mouth** (**mouths, mouthing, mouthed**)

The noun is pronounced /ma͟ʊθ/. The verb is pronounced /ma͟ʊð/. The plural of the noun and the third person singular of the verb are both pronounced /ma͟ʊðz/.

■ N-COUNT Your **mouth** is the area of your face where your lips are, or the space behind your lips where your teeth and tongue are. ❑ She covered her mouth with her hand. ● -**mouthed** /-ma͟ʊðd/ ADJ ❑ He looked at me, open-mouthed. ■ N-COUNT The **mouth** of a cave, hole, or bottle is its entrance or opening. ❑ He stopped at the mouth of the tunnel. ■ N-COUNT The **mouth** of a river is the place where it flows into the sea. ❑ ...the town at the mouth of the River Fox. ■ V-T If you **mouth** something, you form words with your lips without making any sound. ❑ I mouthed a goodbye and hurried in the house. [from Old English] ■ to **live hand to mouth** → see **hand**
→ see **face, respiration**

**mouth|ful** /ma͟ʊθfʊl/ (**mouthfuls**) N-COUNT A **mouthful of** drink or food is the amount that you put or have in your mouth. ❑ She drank a mouthful of coffee. [from Old English]

**mouth|piece** /ma͟ʊθpis/ (**mouthpieces**) ■ N-COUNT The **mouthpiece** of a telephone is the part that you speak into. ❑ He shouted into the mouthpiece. ■ N-COUNT The **mouthpiece** of a musical instrument or other device is the part that you put into your mouth. ❑ He showed him how to blow into the trumpet's mouthpiece. ■ N-COUNT The **mouthpiece** of an organization or person is someone who informs other people of the opinions and policies of that organization or person. ❑ The organization's mouthpiece is the vice president.

**mov|able** /mu͟vəbᵊl/ also **moveable** ADJ Something that is **movable** can be moved from one place or position to another. ❑ It's a doll with movable arms and legs. [from Latin]
→ see **printing**

**mov|able pul|ley** (**movable pulleys**) also **moveable pulley** N-COUNT A **movable pulley** is a pulley in which the axle is not attached to anything and can therefore move freely. Compare **fixed pulley**. [TECHNICAL]

┌─────────────────────────────┐
│ **move**                        │
│ ❶ VERB AND NOUN USES            │
│ ❷ PHRASES                       │
│ ❸ PHRASAL VERBS                 │
└─────────────────────────────┘

❶ **move** /mu͟v/ (**moves, moving, moved**) ■ V-T/V-I When you **move** something or when it **moves**, its position changes. ❑ She moved her clothes off the bed. ❑ A policeman asked him to move his car. ❑ The train began to move. ■ V-I When you **move**, you change your position or go to a different place. ❑ She waited for him to get up, but he didn't move. ❑ He moved around the room, putting things in a bag. ● **Move** is also a noun. ❑ The doctor made a move toward the door. ■ N-COUNT A **move** is an action that you take in order to achieve something. ❑ Going to bed early was a sensible move. ❑ It may be a good move to talk to someone about your problems. ■ V-I If a person or company **moves**, they leave the building where they have been living or working, and they go to live or work in a different place, taking their possessions with them. ❑ The children don't want to move. ❑ She often considered moving to Seattle. ● **Move** is also a noun. ❑ After his move to New York, he got a job as an actor. ■ V-I If you **move from** one job or interest **to** another, you change to it. ❑ He moved from a teacher to a college vice president. ● **Move** is also a noun. ❑ His move to the chairmanship means he will have a lot more work. ■ V-I If you **move** toward a particular state, activity, or opinion, you start to be in that state, do that activity, or have that opinion. ❑ Many countries are now moving toward democracy. ● **Move** is also a noun. ❑ ...the politician's move to the left. ■ V-I If a situation or process **is moving**, it is developing or progressing, rather than staying still. ❑ Events are moving fast. ■ V-T If something **moves** you **to** do something, it influences you and causes you to do it. ❑ What moved you to join a band? ■ V-T If something **moves** you, it causes you to feel sadness or sympathy for another person. ❑ These stories surprised and moved me. ● **moved** ADJ ❑ We were moved when we heard his story. [from Latin]

❷ **move** /muːv/ PHRASE If you are **on the move**, you are going from one place to another. ❑ *Jack never wanted to stay in one place for very long, so they were always on the move.* [from Latin]

❸ **move** /muːv/ (**moves, moving, moved**) [from Latin]

▸ **move in** ❶ PHR-VERB When you **move in** somewhere, you begin to live there as your home. ❑ *Her house was perfect when she moved in.* ❑ *After college, Woody moved back in with Mom.* ❷ PHR-VERB If police, soldiers, or attackers **move in**, they go toward a place or person in order to deal with or attack them. ❑ *Police moved in to stop the fighting.*

▸ **move off** PHR-VERB When you **move off**, you start moving away from a place. ❑ *The car moved off.*

▸ **move on** PHR-VERB When you **move on** somewhere, you leave the place where you have been staying or waiting and go there. ❑ *Mr. Brooke moved on from Los Angeles to Phoenix.*

▸ **move out** PHR-VERB If you **move out**, you stop living in a particular house or place and go to live somewhere else. ❑ *I had a fight with my roommate and decided to move out.*

▸ **move up** PHR-VERB If you **move up**, you change your position, especially in order to be nearer someone or to make room for someone else. ❑ *Move up, John, and let the lady sit down.*

**move|able** /muːvəbəl/ → see **movable**

| Word Link | ment ≈ state, condition : agreement, management, movement |
|---|---|

| Word Link | mov ≈ moving : movement, movie, remove |
|---|---|

**move|ment** /muːvmənt/ (**movements**)
❶ N-COUNT A **movement** is a group of people who share the same beliefs, ideas, or aims. ❑ *...an Islamic political movement.* ❷ N-VAR **Movement** involves changing position or going from one place to another. ❑ *...the movement of the fish going up the river.* ❑ *There was movement behind the window in the back door.* ❸ N-VAR **Movement** is a gradual development or change of an attitude, opinion, or policy. ❑ *...the movement toward democracy in Latin America.* ❹ N-PLURAL Your **movements** are everything that you do or plan to do during a period of time. ❑ *What were your movements the night Mr. Gower was killed?* [from Latin]
→ see **brain**

**move|ment pat|tern** (**movement patterns**) N-COUNT A **movement pattern** is a series of movements that involve a particular part of the body, for example the neck or head. [TECHNICAL]

**mov|er** /muːvər/ (**movers**) N-COUNT **Movers** are people whose job is to move furniture or equipment from one building to another. [from Latin]

**mov|ie** /muːvi/ (**movies**) ❶ N-COUNT A **movie** is a series of moving pictures that have been recorded so that they can be shown in a theater or on television. A movie tells a story, or shows a real situation. ❑ *...the first movie Tony Curtis ever made.* ❷ N-PLURAL You can talk about the **movies** when you are talking about seeing a movie in a movie theater. ❑ *He took her to the movies.*
→ see **genre**

| Word Partnership | Use *movie* with : |
|---|---|
| ADJ. | **bad/good** movie, **favorite** movie, **new/old** movie ❶ |
| V. | **go to a** movie, **see a** movie, **watch a** movie ❶ |
| N. | **scene in a** movie, movie **screen**, movie **set, television/TV** movie ❶ |

**mov|ie star** (**movie stars**) N-COUNT A **movie star** is a famous actor or actress who appears in movies.

**mov|ie thea|ter** (**movie theaters**) N-COUNT A **movie theater** is a place where people go to watch movies for entertainment.

**mov|ing** /muːvɪŋ/ ❶ ADJ If something is **moving**, it makes you feel a strong emotion such as sadness, pity, or sympathy. ❑ *It is very moving to see how much she loves her mother.* ● **mov|ing|ly** ADV ❑ *You write very movingly about your family.* ❷ ADJ A **moving** model or part of a machine moves or is able to move. ❑ *...a tape recorder with no moving parts.* [from Latin]

**mow** /moʊ/ (**mows, mowing, mowed, mown**)

The past participle can be either **mowed** or **mown**.

V-T/V-I If you **mow** an area of grass, you cut it using a machine called a lawn mower. ❑ *He was mowing the lawn.* [from Old English]

▸ **mow down** PHR-VERB If someone is **mowed down**, they are killed violently by a vehicle or gunfire. ❑ *She was mowed down on a busy road.*

**mow|er** /moʊər/ (**mowers**) N-COUNT A **mower** is a machine for cutting something such as grass, corn, or wheat. [from Old English]

**moz|za|rel|la** /mɑtsərɛlə, moʊt-/ (**mozzarellas**) N-UNCOUNT **Mozzarella** is a type of white Italian cheese, often used as a topping for pizzas. ❑ *...layers of fresh mozzarella.* [from Italian]

**MP3** /ɛm pi θriː/ N-UNCOUNT **MP3** is a kind of technology that enables you to download and play music from the Internet.

**MP3 play|er** (**MP3 players**) N-COUNT An **MP3 player** is a machine on which you can play music downloaded from the Internet.

**mph** also **m.p.h.** **mph** is written after a number to indicate the speed of something such as a vehicle. **mph** is an abbreviation for "miles per hour." ❑ *On this road, you must not drive faster than 20 mph.*

**Mr.** /mɪstər/ N-TITLE **Mr.** is used before a man's name when you are speaking or referring to him. ❑ *...Mr. Grant.* ❑ *...Mr. Bob Price.*

**Mrs.** /mɪsɪz/ N-TITLE **Mrs.** is used before the name of a married woman when you are speaking or referring to her. ❑ *Hello, Mrs. Miles.* ❑ *...Mrs. Anne Pritchard.*

**Ms.** /mɪz/ N-TITLE **Ms.** is used, especially in written English, before a woman's name when you are speaking to her or referring to her. If you use **Ms.**, you are not specifying if the woman is married or not. ❑ *...Ms. Brown.*

**MS** /ɛm ɛs/ N-UNCOUNT **MS** is a serious disease of the nervous system, which gradually makes a person weaker, and sometimes affects their sight or speech. **MS** is an abbreviation for "multiple sclerosis."

m

**m/s** m/s is an abbreviation for **meters per second**.

**m/s/s** m/s/s or m/s **per second** is a unit of acceleration in physics. **m/s/s** is an abbreviation for "meters per second per second." [TECHNICAL]

**much** /mʌtʃ/ **1** ADV You use **much** to indicate the great intensity, extent, or degree of something such as an action, feeling, or change. **Much** is usually used with "so," "too," and "very," and in negative clauses with this meaning. □ *She laughs too much.* □ *Thank you very much.* **2** ADV If something does not happen **much**, it does not happen very often. □ *He said that his father never talked much about the war.* □ *Gwen did not see her father all that much.* **3** ADV If one thing is **much** the same as another thing, it is very similar to it. □ *The day ended much as it began.* **4** DET You use **much** to indicate that you are referring to a large amount of a substance or thing. □ *These plants do not need much water.* □ *He doesn't earn much money.* ● **Much** is also a pronoun. □ *You eat too much.* ● **Much** is also a quantifier. □ *Much of the time we do not notice that we are solving problems.* **5** DET You use **much** in the expression **how much** to ask questions about amounts or degrees, and also in reported clauses and statements to give information about the amount or degree of something. □ *How much money can I spend?* ● **Much** is also an adverb. □ *She knows how much this upsets me.* ● **Much** is also a pronoun. □ *How much do you earn?* **6** PHRASE If you say that something is not **so much** one thing **as** another, you mean that it is more like the second thing than the first. □ *I don't really think of her as a daughter so much as a very good friend.* **7** PHRASE If a situation or action is **too much for** you, it is so difficult, tiring, or upsetting that you cannot cope with it. □ *All the traveling got too much for her.* [from Old English] **8 a bit much → see bit**

**muck** /mʌk/ N-UNCOUNT **Muck** is dirt or some other unpleasant substance. [INFORMAL] □ *He's always covered in muck.* [from Scandinavian]

**mu|cus** /myuːkəs/ N-UNCOUNT **Mucus** is a thick liquid that is produced in some parts of your body, for example the inside of your nose. [from Latin]

**mud** /mʌd/ N-UNCOUNT **Mud** is a sticky mixture of earth and water. □ *His clothes were covered with mud.* [from Middle Low German]

**mud|dle** /mʌdəl/ (muddles, muddling, muddled) **1** N-VAR If people or things are **in a muddle**, they are in a state of confusion or disorder. □ *My thoughts are all in a muddle.* □ *We are going to get into a muddle.* **2** V-T If you **muddle** things or people, you get them mixed up, so that you do not know which is which. □ *People often muddle the two names.* ● **Muddle up** means the same as **muddle**. □ *The question muddles up three separate issues.* ● **mud|dled up** ADJ □ *I know that I am getting my words muddled up.* [from Middle Dutch]
▶ **muddle through** PHR-VERB If you **muddle through**, you manage to do something even though you do not have the proper equipment or do not really know how to do it. □ *We will muddle through until we get the right equipment.* □ *They may be able to muddle through the next five years like this.*
▶ **muddle up → see muddle 2**

**mud|dled** /mʌdəld/ ADJ If someone is **muddled**, they are confused about something. □ *I'm afraid I'm a little muddled. I'm not exactly sure where to begin.* [from Middle Dutch]

**mud|dy** /mʌdi/ (muddier, muddiest, muddies, muddying, muddied) **1** ADJ Something that is **muddy** contains mud or is covered in mud. □ *...a muddy track.* **2** V-T If you **muddy** something, you cause it to be muddy. □ *The ground was wet and they muddied their shoes.* **3** V-T If someone or something **muddies** a situation or issue, they cause it to seem less clear and less easy to understand. □ *Don't muddy the issue with religion.* [from Middle Low German]

**mud|flow** /mʌdfloʊ/ (mudflows) N-COUNT A **mudflow** is the same as a **mudslide**.

**mud|slide** /mʌdslaɪd/ (mudslides) N-COUNT A **mudslide** is a large amount of mud sliding down a mountain, usually causing damage or destruction.

**muf|fin** /mʌfɪn/ (muffins) N-COUNT **Muffins** are small, round, sweet cakes, often with fruit inside. They are usually eaten for breakfast. □ *...blueberry muffins.* [from Low German]

**muf|fle** /mʌfəl/ (muffles, muffling, muffled) V-T If something **muffles** a sound, it makes it quieter and more difficult to hear. □ *Blake held his hand over the telephone to muffle his voice.* [from Old French]

**mug** /mʌg/ (mugs, mugging, mugged) **1** N-COUNT A **mug** is a large, deep cup with straight sides. □ *He put sugar into two of the mugs.* **2** V-T If someone **mugs** you, they attack you in order to steal your money. □ *I was walking to my car when this guy tried to mug me.* ● **mug|ging** (muggings) N-VAR □ *Muggings are unusual in this neighborhood.* ● **mug|ger** (muggers) N-COUNT □ *...hiding places for muggers and thieves.* [of Scandinavian origin]
**→ see crime**

**mule** /myuːl/ (mules) N-COUNT A **mule** is an animal whose parents are a horse and a donkey. [from Old French]

**mull** /mʌl/ (mulls, mulling, mulled) V-T If you **mull** something, you think about it for a long time before deciding what to do. □ *She mulled the offer for several days before accepting the job.* [from Middle Dutch]
▶ **mull over** PHR-VERB **Mull over** means the same as **mull**. □ *McLaren had been mulling over an idea to make a movie.*

**multi|cel|lu|lar** /mʌltisɛlyələr/ ADJ **Multicellular** organisms are organisms such as animals and plants that consist of more than one cell.

| Word Link | multi ≈ many : multicolored, multimedia, multinational |
| --- | --- |

**multi|col|ored** /mʌltikʌlərd/ ADJ A **multicolored** object has many different colors. □ *...a multicolored shirt.*

**multi|lat|er|al** /mʌltilætərəl/ ADJ **Multilateral** means involving at least three different groups of people or nations. □ *...multilateral trade talks.*

**multi|media** /mʌltimiːdiə/ **1** N-UNCOUNT You use **multimedia** to refer to computer programs and products which involve sound, pictures, and film, as well as text. □ *...teachers who use multimedia in the classroom.* **2** N-UNCOUNT In education, **multimedia** is the use of television and other different media in a lesson, as well as books. □ *I am making a multimedia presentation for my science project.*

---

**Word Link**    multi ≈ many : multicolored, multimedia, multi**national**

**multi|na|tion|al** /mʌltɪnæʃənᵊl/
(**multinationals**) **1** ADJ A **multinational** company has branches or owns companies in many different countries. ● **Multinational** is also a noun. ❑ …multinationals such as Ford and IBM. **2** ADJ **Multinational** armies, organizations, or other groups involve people from several different countries. ❑ The U.S. soldiers will be part of a multinational force.

**multi|ple** /mʌltɪpᵊl/ (**multiples**) **1** ADJ You use **multiple** to describe things that consist of many parts, involve many people, or have many uses. ❑ He died of multiple injuries. **2** N-COUNT If one number is a **multiple of** a smaller number, it can be exactly divided by that smaller number. ❑ Our system of numbers is based on multiples of the number ten. [from French]

**multi|ple scle|ro|sis** /mʌltɪpᵊl skləroʊsɪs/
N-UNCOUNT **Multiple sclerosis** is a serious disease of the nervous system, which gradually makes a person weaker, and sometimes affects their sight or speech. The abbreviation **MS** is also used.

**multi|plic|ity** /mʌltɪplɪsɪti/ QUANT A **multiplicity of** things is a large number or a large variety of them. [FORMAL] ❑ …a writer who uses a multiplicity of styles.

**multi|pli|er** /mʌltɪplaɪər/ (**multipliers**)
N-COUNT When you multiply a number by another number, the second number is the **multiplier**. [TECHNICAL] [from Old French]

**multi|ply** /mʌltɪplaɪ/ (**multiplies, multiplying, multiplied**) **1** V-T/V-I When something **multiplies** or when you **multiply** it, it increases greatly in number or amount. ❑ Such arguments multiplied in the eighteenth and nineteenth centuries. ● **multi|pli|ca|tion** /mʌltɪplɪkeɪʃᵊn/ N-UNCOUNT ❑ …the multiplication of cells. **2** V-T If you **multiply** one number by another, you add the first number to itself as many times as is indicated by the second number. ❑ What do you get if you multiply six by nine? ● **multi|pli|ca|tion** N-UNCOUNT ❑ There will be simple tests in multiplication. [from Old French]
→ see **mathematics**

**multi|pur|pose** /mʌltɪpɜrpəs/ ADJ A **multipurpose** object can be used for several different purposes. ❑ …a multipurpose tool.

**multi|story** /mʌltɪstɔri/ also **multistoried**
ADJ A **multistory** building has several floors at different levels above the ground. ❑ The store is a big multistory building. ❑ …a multistory parking garage.

**multi|tude** /mʌltɪtud/ (**multitudes**) QUANT A **multitude of** things or people is a very large number of them. ❑ There is a multitude of quiet roads to cycle along. [from Old French]

**multi|vita|min** /mʌltɪvaɪtəmɪn/
(**multivitamins**) also **multi-vitamin** N-COUNT **Multivitamins** are pills that contain several different vitamins.

**mum|ble** /mʌmbᵊl/ (**mumbles, mumbling, mumbled**) V-T/V-I If you **mumble**, you speak very quietly and not at all clearly, with the result that the words are difficult to understand. ❑ Her grandmother mumbled in her sleep. ❑ He mumbled a few words. ● **Mumble** is also a noun. ❑ …the low mumble of his voice.

**mum|my** /mʌmi/ (**mummies**) N-COUNT A **mummy** is a dead body which was preserved long ago by being rubbed with special oils and wrapped in cloth. ❑ …an Egyptian mummy. [from Old French]

**munch** /mʌntʃ/ (**munches, munching, munched**) V-T/V-I If you **munch** food, you eat it by chewing it slowly and thoroughly. ❑ Luke munched the chicken sandwiches. ❑ She munched at her spaghetti.

**mun|dane** /mʌndeɪn/ ADJ Something that is **mundane** is very ordinary and not at all interesting or unusual. ❑ …mundane tasks. [from French]

**mu|nici|pal** /myunɪsɪpᵊl/ ADJ **Municipal** means associated with or belonging to a city or town that has its own local government. ❑ …next month's municipal elections. [from Latin]

**mu|nici|pal|ity** /myunɪsɪpælɪti/
(**municipalities**) N-COUNT A **municipality** is a city or town that is incorporated and can elect its own government, which is also called a **municipality**. [from Latin]

**mu|ni|tions** /myunɪʃᵊnz/ N-PLURAL **Munitions** are military equipment and supplies, especially bombs, shells, and guns. ❑ There are not enough men and munitions. [from French]

**mu|ral** /myʊərəl/ (**murals**) N-COUNT A **mural** is a picture painted on a wall. ❑ …a mural of San Francisco Bay. [from Latin]

**mur|der** /mɜrdər/ (**murders, murdering, murdered**) **1** N-VAR **Murder** is the crime of deliberately killing a person. ❑ The jury found him guilty of murder. ❑ The detective has worked on hundreds of murder cases. **2** V-T To **murder** someone means to commit the crime of killing them deliberately. ❑ …a movie about a woman who murders her husband. ● **mur|der|er** /mɜrdərər/ (**murderers**) N-COUNT ❑ One of these men is the murderer. [from Old English]

**mur|der|ous** /mɜrdərəs/ **1** ADJ Someone who is **murderous** is likely to murder someone. ❑ What will happen to this murderous man? **2** ADJ A **murderous** attack is very violent and intended to result in someone's death. [from Old English]

**murky** /mɜrki/ (**murkier, murkiest**) **1** ADJ A **murky** place or time of day is dark and rather unpleasant because there is not enough light. ❑ …a cold murky room. **2** ADJ **Murky** water or fog is so dark and dirty that you cannot see through it. ❑ …the deep, murky waters of the lake. **3** ADJ If you describe something as **murky**, you mean that it is difficult to understand. ❑ The law here is a little bit murky. [probably from Old Norse]

**mur|mur** /mɜrmər/ (**murmurs, murmuring, murmured**) **1** V-T If you **murmur** something, you say it very quietly, so that not many people can hear what you are saying. ❑ He turned and murmured something to Karen. ❑ "How lovely," she murmured. **2** N-COUNT A **murmur** is something that is said but can hardly be heard. ❑ They spoke in low murmurs. **3** N-SING A **murmur** is a continuous low sound, like the noise of a river or of voices far away. ❑ The music mixes with the murmur of conversation. [from Latin]

**mus|cle** /mʌsᵊl/ (**muscles, muscling, muscled**)
**1** N-VAR A **muscle** is a piece of tissue inside your body that connects two bones and which you use

m

## Word Web  muscle

There are three types of **muscles** in the body. **Voluntary** or **skeletal** muscles make external movements. **Involuntary** or **smooth** muscles move within the body. For example, the smooth muscles in the **iris** of the eye adjust the size of the pupil. This controls how much light enters the eye. **Cardiac** muscles are in the heart. They work constantly but never get tired. When we **exercise**, voluntary muscles **contract** and then **relax**. Repeated **workouts** can **build** these muscles and increase their **strength**. If we don't exercise, these muscles can atrophy and become **weak**.

when you make a movement. ❏ *Exercise helps to keep your muscles strong.* **2** N-UNCOUNT If you say that someone has **muscle**, you mean that they have power and influence, which enables them to do difficult things. ❏ *The president used his muscle to change the law.* **3** PHRASE If a group, organization, or country **flexes** its **muscles**, it does something to impress or frighten people, in order to show them that it has power and is considering using it. ❏ *The government began to flex its muscles.* [from Latin]
→ see **nervous system**
▸ **muscle in** PHR-VERB If someone **muscles in on** something, they force their way into a situation where they have no right to be and where they are not welcome. ❏ *Cohen complained that Kravis was muscling in on his deal.*
→ see Word Web: **muscle**

### Word Partnership  Use *muscle* with :

| | |
|---|---|
| N. | muscle **aches**, muscle **mass**, muscle **pain**, muscle **tone** **1** |
| V. | **contract** a muscle, **flex** a muscle, **pull** a muscle **1** |

**mus|cle tis|sue** (muscle tissues) N-VAR **Muscle tissue** is tissue in animals and plants which is made of cells that can become shorter or longer.

**mus|cu|lar** /mʌ́skyələr/ **1** ADJ **Muscular** means involving or affecting your muscles. ❏ *..exercises to improve muscular strength.* **2** ADJ If a person or their body is **muscular**, they have strong, firm muscles. ❏ *He was tall and muscular.* [from New Latin]

**mus|cu|lar sys|tem** (muscular systems) N-COUNT The **muscular system** is the muscles and other parts of the body that control movement.

**muse** /myuz/ (muses, musing, mused) V-T/V-I If you **muse** on something, you think about it, usually saying or writing what you are thinking at the same time. [WRITTEN] ❏ *Many of the papers muse on what will happen to the president.* ❏ *"I like most of his work," she muses.* ● **mus|ing** (musings) N-COUNT ❏ *His mother interrupted his musings.* [from Old French]

**mu|seum** /myuzíəm/ (museums) N-COUNT A **museum** is a building where a large number of interesting and valuable objects, such as works of art or historical items, are kept, studied, and displayed to the public. ❏ *Malcolm wanted to visit the New York art museums.* [from Latin]

**mush|room** /mʌ́ʃrum/ (mushrooms, mushrooming, mushroomed) **1** N-VAR **Mushrooms** are fungi with short stems and round tops that you can eat. ❏ *There are many types of*

wild mushrooms. **2** V-I If something such as an industry or a place **mushrooms**, it grows or comes into existence very quickly. ❏ *Internet companies mushroomed very quickly.* [from Old French]
→ see **fungus**

**mu|sic** /myúzɪk/ **1** N-UNCOUNT **Music** is the pattern of sounds produced by people singing or playing instruments. ❏ *classical music.* **2** N-UNCOUNT **Music** is the symbols written on paper which represent musical sounds. ❏ *He can't read music.* [from Old French]
→ see Word Web: **music**
→ see **concert, genre**

### Word Partnership  Use *music* with :

| | |
|---|---|
| ADJ. | **live** music, **loud** music, **new** music, **pop(ular)** music **1** |
| N. | **background** music, music **critic**, music **festival** **1** <br> music **business**, music **industry**, music **lesson** **2** |
| V. | **download** music, **hear** music, **listen to** music, **play** music **1** <br> **compose** music, **study** music, **write** music **2** |

**mu|si|cal** /myúzɪk³l/ (musicals) **1** ADJ You use **musical** to indicate that something is connected with playing or studying music. ❏ *...a series of musical notes.* ● **mu|si|cal|ly** /myúzɪkli/ ADV ❏ *Musically there is a lot to enjoy.* **2** N-COUNT A **musical** is a play or movie that uses singing and dancing in the story. ❏ *...the musical, "Miss Saigon."* **3** ADJ Someone who is **musical** has a natural ability and interest in music. ❏ *I came from a musical family.* [from Old French]
→ see **theater**

**mu|si|cal in|stru|ment** (musical instruments) N-COUNT A **musical instrument** is an object such as a piano, guitar, or violin which you play in order to produce music. ❏ *The drum is one of the oldest musical instruments.*

**mu|si|cal|ity** /myuzɪkǽlɪti/ N-UNCOUNT In dance, **musicality** is the ability to interpret music artistically by dancing in a way that is appropriate for the music. [from Old French]

**mu|si|cal thea|ter** N-UNCOUNT **Musical theater** is a form of entertainment that contains music, song, and dance, as well as spoken dialogue.

### Word Link  ician ≈ person who works at : electrician, musician, physician

**mu|si|cian** /myuzɪ́ʃ³n/ (musicians) N-COUNT

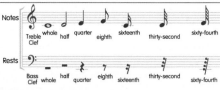

**Word Web** music

Wolfgang Amadeus Mozart lived only 35 years (1756-1791). However, he is one of the most important **musicians** in history. Mozart began playing the **piano** when he was four years old. A year later he **composed** his first **song**. Since he hadn't learned musical notation yet, his father wrote out the **score** for him. Mozart played for royalty across Europe. Soon Mozart became known as a gifted **composer**. He wrote more than 50 **symphonies**. He also composed **operas**, **concertos**, arias, and other musical works.

A **musician** is a person who plays a musical instrument as their job or hobby. ❑ *He was a brilliant musician.* [from Old French]
→ see concert, music, orchestra

**Mus|lim** /mʌzlɪm/ (**Muslims**) **1** N-COUNT A **Muslim** is someone who believes in Islam and lives according to its rules. **2** ADJ **Muslim** means relating to Islam or Muslims. ❑ *...Iran and other Muslim countries.* [from Arabic]

**mus|lin** /mʌzlɪn/ (**muslins**) N-VAR **Muslin** is very thin cotton cloth. ❑ *...white muslin curtains.* [from French]

**muss** /mʌs/ (**musses, mussing, mussed**) V-T To **muss** something, especially someone's hair, or to **muss** it **up**, means to make it messy. ❑ *He reached out and mussed my hair.* ❑ *His clothes were all mussed up.*

**mus|sel** /mʌsəl/ (**mussels**) N-COUNT **Mussels** are a kind of shellfish that you can eat from their shells. [from Old English]
→ see shellfish

**must** /məst, STRONG mʌst/ (**musts**)

The noun is pronounced /mʌst/.

**Must** is a modal verb. It is followed by the base form of a verb.

**1** MODAL You use **must** to indicate that you think it is very important or necessary for something to happen. ❑ *Your clothes must fit well.* ❑ *You must tell me everything you know.* **2** MODAL You use **must** to indicate that you are fairly sure that something is true. ❑ *At 20 years old, Russell must be one of the youngest company directors.* ❑ *Claire's car wasn't there, so she must have gone to her mother's.* **3** MODAL You use **must** to express your intention to do something. ❑ *I must go home now.* ❑ *I must telephone my parents.* **4** MODAL You use **must** to make suggestions or invitations very forcefully. ❑ *You must see a doctor, Frederick.* **5** MODAL You use **must** in questions to express your anger or irritation about something that someone has done, usually because you do not understand their behavior. ❑ *Why must she interrupt?* **6** N-COUNT If you refer to something as **a must**, you mean that it is absolutely necessary. [INFORMAL] ❑ *When you go walking, a pair of good shoes is a must.* **7** PHRASE You say **"if you must"** when you know that you cannot stop someone from doing something that you think is wrong or stupid. ❑ *If you must be in the sun, use the strongest sunscreen you can get.* [from old English]

**mus|tache** /mʌstæʃ/ (**mustaches**) N-COUNT A man's **mustache** is the hair that grows on his upper lip. ❑ *He has a black mustache.* [from French]

**mus|tard** /mʌstərd/ (**mustards**) N-VAR **Mustard** is a yellow or brown paste usually eaten with meat. It tastes hot and spicy. ❑ *...a jar of mustard.* [from Old French]

**mus|ter** /mʌstər/ (**musters, mustering, mustered**) **1** V-T If you **muster** something such as support, strength, or energy, you gather as much of it as you can in order to do something. ❑ *He traveled around Africa trying to muster support for his organization.* **2** V-T/V-I When soldiers **muster** or **are mustered**, they gather together in one place in order to take part in a military action. ❑ *The men mustered in front of their chiefs.* [from French]

**mustn't** /mʌsənt/ **Mustn't** is the usual spoken form of "must not." [from Old English]

**must've** /mʌstəv/ **Must've** is the usual spoken form of "must have," especially when "have" is an auxiliary verb. [from Old English]

**mu|ta|gen** /myutədʒən, -dʒɛn/ (**mutagens**) N-COUNT **Mutagens** are processes or substances, for example x-rays or certain chemicals, that can cause genetic changes in cells. [TECHNICAL]

**mu|tant** /myutənt/ (**mutants**) N-COUNT A **mutant** is an animal or plant that is physically different from others of the same species because of a change in its genes. ❑ *New species are mutants of earlier ones.* [from Latin]

**mu|tate** /myuteɪt/ (**mutates, mutating, mutated**) V-T/V-I If an animal or plant **mutates**, or something **mutates** it, it develops different characteristics as the result of a change in its genes. ❑ *The virus mutates in your body.* ❑ *In the movie, the creature mutates into a human.* ● **mu|ta|tion** /myuteɪʃən/ (**mutations**) N-VAR ❑ *...mutations in animal cells.* [from Latin]

**mute** /myut/ (**mutes, muting, muted**) **1** ADJ Someone who is **mute** does not speak. ❑ *Alexander was mute for a few minutes.* ● **Mute** is also an adverb. ❑ *He could watch her standing mute by the phone.* **2** V-T If someone **mutes** something such as their feelings or their activities, they reduce the strength or intensity of them. ❑ *The problems have not muted the country's economic success.* ● **mut|ed** ADJ ❑ *...muted criticism.* **3** V-T If you **mute** a noise or sound, you lower its volume or make it less distinct. ❑ *They begin to mute their voices.* ● **mut|ed** ADJ ❑ *His voice was so muted that I couldn't hear his reply.* [from Old French]

**mu|ti|late** /myutəleɪt/ (**mutilates, mutilating, mutilated**) V-T If a person or animal is **mutilated**, their body is severely damaged, usually by someone who physically attacks them. ❑ *More*

m

than 30 horses were mutilated. ❑ He mutilated six young men. • mu|ti|la|tion /myut³leɪʃ°n/ (mutilations) N-VAR ❑ ...mutilation of a part of the body. [from Latin]

mu|ti|ny /myut³ni/ (mutinies) N-VAR A mutiny is a refusal by people, usually soldiers or sailors, to continue obeying a person in authority. ❑ There was a series of mutinies within the army. [from Old French]

mut|ter /mʌtər/ (mutters, muttering, muttered) V-T/V-I If you mutter, you speak very quietly so that you cannot easily be heard, often because you are complaining about something. ❑ "He's crazy," she muttered. ❑ She can hear the old woman muttering about politeness. • Mutter is also a noun. ❑ ...a mutter of protest. • mut|ter|ing (mutterings) N-VAR ❑ He heard muttering from the front of the crowd. [from Norwegian]

mut|ton /mʌt°n/ N-UNCOUNT Mutton is meat from an adult sheep. ❑ ...a leg of mutton. [from Old French]
→ see meat

mu|tu|al /myutʃuəl/ ADJ You use mutual to describe a situation, feeling, or action that is experienced, felt, or done by both of two people mentioned. ❑ The East and the West can work together for their mutual benefit. • mu|tu|al|ly ADV ❑ They tried to reach a mutually acceptable solution. [from Old French] → see exclusive

mu|tu|al fund (mutual funds) N-COUNT A mutual fund is an organization which invests money in many different kinds of businesses and which offers units for sale to the public as an investment. [BUSINESS]

mu|tu|al|ism /myutʃuəlɪzəm/ (mutualisms) N-VAR Mutualism is a relationship between two species of animals or plants from which both species benefit. [TECHNICAL] [from Old French]

muz|zle /mʌz°l/ (muzzles, muzzling, muzzled) ❶ N-COUNT The muzzle of an animal such as a dog is its nose and mouth. ❑ The dog wanted me to scratch its muzzle. ❷ N-COUNT A muzzle is an object that is put over a dog's nose and mouth so that it cannot bite people or make a noise. ❑ Some dogs have to wear a muzzle. ❸ V-T If you muzzle a dog or other animal, you put a muzzle over its nose and mouth. ❑ He refused to muzzle his dog. ❹ N-COUNT The muzzle of a gun is the end where the bullets come out when it is fired. ❑ Mickey felt the muzzle of a gun press against his neck. [from Old French]
→ see horse

MVP /ɛm vi pi/ (MVPs) N-COUNT Journalists sometimes use MVP to talk about the player on a sports team who has performed best in a particular game or series of games. MVP is an abbreviation for "most valuable player." ❑ Brondello won the MVP award by scoring 357 points.

my /maɪ/

My is the first person singular possessive determiner.

DET A speaker or writer uses my to indicate that something belongs or relates to himself or herself. ❑ I invited him back to my apartment. [from Old English]

myr|i|ad /mɪriəd/ (myriads) QUANT A myriad or myriads of people or things is a very large number or great variety of them. ❑ They face a myriad of

problems. [from Late Latin]

my|self /maɪsɛlf/

Myself is the first person singular reflexive pronoun.

❶ PRON A speaker or writer uses myself to refer to himself or herself. Myself is used as the object of a verb or preposition when the subject refers to the same person. ❑ I asked myself what I should do. ❷ PRON You use myself to emphasize a first person singular subject. In more formal English, myself is sometimes used instead of "me" as the object of a verb or preposition, for emphasis. ❑ I myself enjoy movies and long walks. ❸ PRON If you say something such as "I did it myself," you are emphasizing that you did it, rather than anyone else. ❑ "Where did you get that dress?" — "I made it myself."

mys|te|ri|ous /mɪstɪəriəs/ ❶ ADJ Someone or something that is mysterious is strange and is not known about or understood. ❑ He died in mysterious circumstances. ❑ A mysterious illness made him sick. • mys|te|ri|ous|ly ADV ❑ Two messages mysteriously disappeared. ❷ ADJ If someone is mysterious about something, they deliberately do not talk much about it, sometimes because they want to make people more interested in it. ❑ He was very mysterious about his job. • mys|te|ri|ous|ly ADV ❑ When I asked her what she meant, she just smiled mysteriously. [from Medieval Latin]

mys|tery /mɪstri, mɪstri/ (mysteries) ❶ N-COUNT A mystery is something that is not understood or known about. ❑ Who took the painting is still a mystery. ❷ N-UNCOUNT If you talk about the mystery of someone or something, you are talking about how difficult they are to understand or know about, especially when this gives them a rather strange or magical quality. ❑ She's a lady of mystery. ❸ ADJ A mystery person or thing is one whose identity or nature is not known. ❑ The mystery hero immediately called the police after seeing a bomb. ❹ N-COUNT A mystery is a story in which strange things happen that are not explained until the end. ❑ His fourth novel is a mystery set in London. [from Latin]

| Word Partnership | Use mystery with : |
|---|---|
| V. | remain a mystery, unravel a mystery ❶ solve a mystery ❶ ❹ |
| N. | murder mystery, mystery novel, mystery readers ❹ |

mys|tic /mɪstɪk/ (mystics) ❶ N-COUNT A mystic is a person who practices or believes in religious mysticism. ❑ ...an Indian mystic known as Bhagwan Shree Rajneesh. • mys|ti|cism /mɪstɪsɪzəm/ N-UNCOUNT ❑ Harrison was interested in Indian mysticism. ❷ ADJ Mystic means the same as mystical. ❑ ...mystic union with God. [from Latin]

mys|ti|cal /mɪstɪk°l/ ADJ Something that is mystical involves spiritual powers and influences that most people do not understand. ❑ That was a mystical experience. [from Latin]

mys|ti|fy /mɪstɪfaɪ/ (mystifies, mystifying, mystified) V-T If you are mystified by something, you find it impossible to explain or understand. ❑ The audience was mystified by the story. • mys|ti|fy|ing ADJ ❑ Your attitude is mystifying, Marilyn. [from French]

**mys|tique** /mɪstiːk/ N-VAR If there is a **mystique** about someone or something, they are thought to be special and people do not know much about them. ❑ *His book destroyed the mystique of the British royal family.* [from French]

**myth** /mɪθ/ (**myths**) ■ N-VAR A **myth** is a well-known story which was made up in the past to explain natural events or to justify religious beliefs or social customs. ❑ *...a famous Greek myth.* ● **mythi|cal** ADJ Something or someone that is **mythical** exists only in myths and is therefore imaginary. ❑ *The Hydra is a mythical beast that had seven or more heads.* ■ N-VAR If you describe a belief or explanation as a **myth**, you mean that many people believe it but it is actually untrue. ❑ *It is a myth that all women love spending money.*

[from Late Latin]
→ see Word Web: **myth**
→ see **fantasy, myth**

| **Word Partnership** | Use *myth* with : |
|---|---|
| ADJ. | **ancient** myth, **Greek** myth ■ |
| | **popular** myth ■ |

**my|thol|ogy** /mɪθɒlədʒi/ (**mythologies**) N-VAR **Mythology** is a group of myths, especially all the myths from a particular country, religion, or culture. ❑ *...Greek mythology.* ● **mytho|logi|cal** /mɪθəlɒdʒɪkəl/ ADJ ❑ *...mythological creatures.* [from Late Latin]
→ see **hero, myth**

## Word Web    myth

The scholar Joseph Campbell* believed that **mythologies** explain how a **culture** understands its world. **Stories, symbols, rituals,** and **myths** explain the **psychological, social,** cosmological, and **spiritual** parts of life. Campbell also believed that artists and thinkers are a culture's mythmakers. He explored **archetypal themes** in myths from many different cultures. He showed that themes are repeated in many different cultures. For example, the **hero's** journey appears in ancient Greece in *The Odyssey*. The hero's journey also appeared later in England in a story about King Arthur's* search for the Holy Grail*. The film *Star Wars* is a 20th century version of the hero's journey.

*Joseph Campbell (1904–1987): an American professor and author.*

*The Odyssey: an epic poem from ancient Greece.*

*King Arthur: a legendary king of Great Britain.*

*Holy Grail: a cup that legends say Jesus used.*

m

# Nn

**na|cho** /nɑtʃoʊ/ (**nachos**) N-COUNT **Nachos** are a snack, originally from Mexico, consisting of pieces of fried tortilla, usually with a topping of cheese, salsa, and chili peppers. □ *…a plate of nachos.* [perhaps from Mexican Spanish]

**nag** /næg/ (**nags, nagging, nagged**) **1** V-T/V-I If someone **nags** you, or if they **nag**, they keep asking you to do something you have not done yet or do not want to do. □ *My girlfriend nagged me to cut my hair.* ● **nag|ging** N-UNCOUNT □ *Her nagging never stops.* **2** V-T/V-I If something such as a doubt or worry **nags at** you, or **nags** you, it keeps worrying you. □ *The feeling that he could be wrong nagged at him.* □ *The problem nagged Amy all through lunch.* [of Scandinavian origin]

**nail** /neɪl/ (**nails, nailing, nailed**) **1** N-COUNT A **nail** is a thin piece of metal with one pointed

nails

end and one flat end. You hit the flat end with a hammer in order to push the nail into something such as a wall. □ *A mirror hung on a nail above the sink.* **2** V-T If you **nail** something somewhere, you fasten it there using one or more nails. □ *Frank put the first board down and nailed it in place.* □ *They nailed the window shut.*

**3** N-COUNT Your **nails** are the thin hard parts that grow at the ends of your fingers and toes. □ *Keep your nails short.* [from Old English]

▶ **nail down 1** PHR-VERB If you **nail down** something unknown or uncertain, you find out exactly what it is. □ *Try to nail down the date of the meeting.* **2** PHR-VERB If you **nail down** an agreement, you manage to reach a firm agreement with a definite result. □ *The two men tried to nail down the contract.*

**na|ive** /nɑɪiv/ also **naïve** ADJ If you describe someone as **naive**, you think they lack experience and so expect things to be easy or people to be honest or kind. □ *I was naive to think they would agree.* ● **na|ive|ly** ADV □ *I naively thought that everything would be fine once we were married.* ● **na|ive|té** /nɑɪiviteɪ, -ɪvteɪ/ N-UNCOUNT □ *I was alarmed by his naiveté.* [from French]

**na|ked** /neɪkɪd/ **1** ADJ Someone who is **naked** is not wearing any clothes. □ *She held the naked baby in her arms.* ● **na|ked|ness** N-UNCOUNT □ *He pulled the blanket over his body to hide his nakedness.* **2** ADJ You can describe an object as **naked** when it does not have its normal covering. □ *…a naked light bulb.* **3** ADJ **Naked** emotions are easily recognized because they are very strongly felt and cannot be hidden. [WRITTEN] □ *I could see the naked hatred in her face.* ● **nakedly** ADV □ *He nakedly desired success.*

**4** PHRASE If you say that something cannot be seen by **the naked eye**, you mean that it cannot be seen without the help of equipment such as a telescope or microscope. [from Old English]

**name** /neɪm/ (**names, naming, named**) **1** N-COUNT The **name** of a person, place, or thing is the word or words that you use to identify them. □ *"What's his name?" — "Peter."* □ *They changed the name of the street.* **2** V-T When you **name** someone or something, you give them a name, usually at the beginning of their life. If you **name** someone or something **after** a person or thing, you give them the same name as that person or thing. □ *…a man named John T. Benson.* □ *He named his first child after his brother.* **3** V-T If you **name** someone, you identify them by stating their name. □ *The victim was named as twenty-year-old John Barr.* **4** V-T If you **name** something such as a price, time, or place, you say what you want it to be. □ *Call Marty, and tell him to name his price.* **5** N-COUNT You can refer to the reputation of a person or thing as their **name**. □ *…the good name of the vice-president.* **6** N-COUNT You can refer to someone as, for example, a famous **name** or a great **name** when they are well known. □ *…some of the most famous names in show business.* **7** → see also **brand name, Christian name, first name, maiden name** **8** PHRASE You can use **by name** or **by the name of** when you are saying what someone is called. [FORMAL] □ *He met a young Australian by the name of Harry Busteed.* **9** PHRASE If someone **calls** you **names**, they insult you by saying unpleasant things to you or about you. □ *At school they called me names because I was fat.* **10** PHRASE If something is **in** someone's **name**, it officially belongs to them or is reserved for them. □ *The house is in my name.* **11** PHRASE If you do something **in the name of** an ideal or an abstract thing, you do it in order to preserve or promote that thing. □ *We all do crazy things in the name of love.* **12** PHRASE If you **make a name for yourself** or make your **name as** something, you become well known for that thing. □ *She is making a name for herself as a photographer.* **13** If you say that something is **the name of the game**, you mean that it is the most important aspect of a situation. [INFORMAL] □ *Survival is the name of the game.* [from Old English]
→ see **Internet**

**name|ly** /neɪmli/ ADV You use **namely** to introduce detailed information about the subject you are discussing, or a particular aspect of it. ❑ ...*the starting point of business, namely money.* [from Old English]

**nan|ny** /nǽni/ (**nannies**) N-COUNT A **nanny** is a woman who is paid by parents to take care of their child or children.

**nap** /nǽp/ (**naps, napping, napped**) **1** N-COUNT If you take or have a **nap**, you have a short sleep, usually during the day. ❑ *We had a nap after lunch.* **2** V-I If you **nap**, you sleep for a short period of time, usually during the day. ❑ *Many elderly people nap during the day.* [from Old English]
→ see **sleep**

**nap|kin** /nǽpkɪn/ (**napkins**) N-COUNT A **napkin** is a square of cloth or paper that you use when you are eating to protect your clothes, or to wipe your mouth or hands. ❑ *I took a bite of a hot dog and wiped my lips with a napkin.* [from Old French]

**nar|cot|ic** /nɑrkɒ́tɪk/ (**narcotics**) **1** N-COUNT **Narcotics** are drugs such as opium or heroin which make you sleepy and stop you from feeling pain. You can also use **narcotics** to mean any kind of illegal drugs. **2** ADJ If something, especially a drug, has a **narcotic** effect, it makes the person who uses it feel sleepy. ❑ ...*a narcotic painkiller.* [from Medieval Latin]

**Word Link** *ator ≈ one who does : creator, narrator, translator*

**nar|rate** /nǽreɪt/ (**narrates, narrating, narrated**) V-T If you **narrate** a story, you tell it from your own point of view. [FORMAL] ❑ *He narrated the story in his own words.* ● **nar|ra|tion** /nǽreɪʃ⁰n/ N-UNCOUNT ❑ ...*Jim Dale's narration of the Harry Potter books.* ● **nar|ra|tor** /nǽreɪtər/ (**narrators**) N-COUNT ❑ *The story's narrator is a famous actress.* [from Latin]

**nar|ra|tive** /nǽrətɪv/ (**narratives**) N-COUNT A **narrative** is a story or an account of a series of events. ❑ ...*a fast-moving narrative.* [from Latin]

**nar|row** /nǽroʊ/ (**narrower, narrowest, narrows, narrowing, narrowed**) **1** ADJ Something that is **narrow** measures a very small distance from one side to the other, especially compared to its length or height. ❑ ...*the town's narrow streets.* ❑ *She had long, narrow feet.* ● **nar|row|ness** N-UNCOUNT ❑ ...*the narrowness of her waist.* **2** V-I If something **narrows**, it becomes less wide. ❑ *The wide track narrows before crossing a stream.* **3** ADJ If you describe someone's ideas, attitudes, or beliefs as **narrow**, you disapprove of them because they are restricted in some way, and often ignore the more important aspects of an argument or situation. ● **nar|row|ness** N-UNCOUNT ❑ ...*the narrowness of their opinions.* **4** V-T/V-I If something **narrows** or if you **narrow** it, its extent or range becomes smaller. ❑ *The EU and America narrowed their political differences.* ● **nar|row|ing** N-SING ❑ ...*a narrowing of the gap between rich and poor people.* **5** ADJ If you have a **narrow** victory, you succeed in winning but only by a small amount. ❑ *Mr Kerry won the debate by a narrow margin.* ● **nar|row|ly** ADV ❑ *She narrowly failed to win enough votes.* **6** ADJ If you have a **narrow** escape, something unpleasant nearly happens to you. ● **nar|row|ly** ADV ❑ *Five firefighters narrowly escaped death when a staircase fell on them.* [from Old English]

▶ **narrow down** PHR-VERB If you **narrow down** a range of things, you reduce the number of things included in it. ❑ *The committee has narrowed down the list to the best candidates.*

**Thesaurus** narrow Also look up :

ADJ. close, cramped, restricted, tight; (*ant.*) broad, wide **1** **3**

**Word Partnership** Use *narrow* with :

N. narrow **band**, narrow **hallway**, narrow **opening**, narrow **path** **1**
narrow **definition**, narrow **focus**, narrow **mind**, narrow **view** **3**
ADV. **relatively** narrow, **too** narrow **1**

**na|sal** /néɪz⁰l/ **1** ADJ **Nasal** is used to describe things relating to the nose. ❑ *Nasal sprays are sometimes used to treat asthma.* **2** ADJ If someone's voice is **nasal**, it sounds as if air is passing through their nose as well as their mouth while they are speaking. ❑ *He had a nasal voice.* [from French]
→ see **smell**

**nas|ty** /nǽsti/ (**nastier, nastiest**) **1** ADJ Something that is **nasty** is very unpleasant or unattractive. ❑ ...*a very nasty murder.* ● **nas|ti|ness** N-UNCOUNT ❑ ...*the nastiness of war.* **2** ADJ If you describe a person or their behavior as **nasty**, you mean that they behave in an unkind and unpleasant way. ❑ *She is so nasty to me.* ❑ *The guards looked really nasty.* ● **nas|ti|ly** ADV ❑ *Mr. Saunders looked at him nastily.* **3** ADJ A **nasty** problem or situation is very worrisome and difficult to deal with. ❑ *It was a nasty problem but we solved it.* **4** ADJ If you describe an injury or a disease as **nasty**, you mean that it is serious or looks unpleasant. ❑ *Alison cut her knee — it was a nasty wound.* ❑ *She had a nasty infection.* [from Swedish]

**na|tion** /néɪʃ⁰n/ (**nations**) N-COUNT A **nation** is an individual country considered together with its social and political structures. ❑ ...*the United States and other nations.* [from Old French]
→ see **country**

**Thesaurus** nation Also look up :

N. country, democracy, population, republic, society **1**

**na|tion|al** /nǽʃən⁰l/ (**nationals**) **1** ADJ **National** means relating to the whole of a country or nation rather than to part of it or to other nations. ❑ ...*major national and international issues.* ● **na|tion|al|ly** ADV ❑ ...*a nationally-televised speech.* **2** ADJ **National** means typical of the people or customs of a particular country or nation. ❑ *Baseball is the national pastime.* **3** N-COUNT You can refer to someone who is legally a citizen of a country as a **national** of that country. ❑ ...*a French national.* [from Old French]

**na|tion|al debt** (**national debts**) N-COUNT A country's **national debt** is all the money that the government of the country has borrowed and still owes. ❑ ...*the importance of reducing the national debt.*

**na|tion|al holi|day** (**national holidays**) N-COUNT A **national holiday** is a day when people do not go to work or school and celebrate some special event, often a national or religious event. ❑ *Today is a national holiday in Japan.*

n

**na|tion|al|ist** /nǽʃənᵊlɪst/ (**nationalists**)
**1** ADJ **Nationalist** means connected with the desire of a group of people within a country for political independence. ❑ *She has nationalist views.* ● A **nationalist** is someone with nationalist views. ❑ *...demands by nationalists for an independent state.* **2** ADJ **Nationalist** means connected with a person's great love for their nation, or their belief that their nation is better than others. ❑ *...nationalist beliefs.* ● A **nationalist** is someone with nationalist views. ❑ *...the late African-American nationalist, Malcolm X.* ● **nationalism** N-UNCOUNT ❑ *...extreme nationalism.* [from Old French]

**na|tion|al|ity** /nǽʃənǽlɪti/ (**nationalities**)
N-VAR If you have the **nationality** of a particular country, you were born there or have the legal right to be a citizen. ❑ *Mr Harris has joint British and Australian nationality.* [from Old French]

**na|tion|al|ize** /nǽʃənᵊlaɪz/ (**nationalizes, nationalizing, nationalized**) V-T If a government **nationalizes** a private company or industry, that company or industry becomes owned by the state and controlled by the government. [BUSINESS] ❑ *His government nationalized the banks.* ● **na|tion|ali|za|tion** /nǽʃənᵊlɪzeɪʃᵊn/ N-UNCOUNT ❑ *...the nationalization of the coal mines.* [from Old French]

**na|tion|al se|cu|rity** N-UNCOUNT A country's **national security** is its ability to protect itself from the threat of violence or attack. ❑ *We must deal with threats to our national security.*

| Word Link | wide ≈ extending throughout : citywide, nationwide, worldwide |

**nation|wide** /neɪʃᵊnwaɪd/ ADJ **Nationwide** activities or situations happen or exist in all parts of a country. ❑ *Car crime is a nationwide problem.* ● **Nationwide** is also an adverb. ❑ *Unemployment fell nationwide last month.*

**na|tive** /neɪtɪv/ (**natives**) **1** ADJ Your **native** country or area is the country or area where you were born and brought up. ❑ *It was his first visit to his native country since 1948.* **2** N-COUNT A **native of** a particular country, region or town is someone who was born in that country, region or town. ❑ *Dr. Aubin is a native of St. Louis.* ● **Native** is also an adjective. ❑ *Joshua Halpern is a native Northern Californian.* **3** ADJ Your **native** language or tongue is the first language that you learned to speak when you were a child. ❑ *Her native language was Swedish.* **4** ADJ Plants or animals that are **native to** a particular region live or grow there naturally and were not brought there. ❑ *Many of the plants are native to Brazil.* ● **Native** is also a noun. ❑ *The coconut palm is a native of Malaysia.* [from Latin]

| Word Partnership | Use *native* with : |
|---|---|
| N. | native **country**, native **land** **1** native **language**, native **tongue** **3** |

**natu|ral** /nǽtʃərəl, nǽtʃrəl/ (**naturals**) **1** ADJ If you say that it is **natural** for someone to act in a particular way or for something to happen in that way, you mean that it is reasonable in the circumstances. ❑ *It is only natural for youngsters to want excitement.* **2** ADJ **Natural** behavior is shared by all people or all animals of a particular type. ❑ *...the insect's natural instinct to feed.* **3** ADJ

Someone with a **natural** ability or skill was born with that ability and did not have to learn it. ❑ *Alan is a natural musician.* **4** N-COUNT If you say that someone is a **natural**, you mean that they do something very well and very easily. ❑ *He's a natural with children.* **5** ADJ If someone's behavior is **natural**, they appear to be relaxed and are not trying to hide anything. ❑ *Mary's sister is as friendly and natural as the rest of the family.* ● **natu|ral|ly** ADV ❑ *It's important to act naturally if you can.* ● **natu|ral|ness** N-UNCOUNT ❑ *The critics praised the naturalness of the acting.* **6** ADJ **Natural** things exist in nature and were not created by people. ❑ *...a natural harbor.* ● **natu|ral|ly** ADV ❑ *Gas is naturally odorless.* [from Old French]
→ see **energy**

| Thesaurus | natural | Also look up : |
|---|---|---|
| ADJ. | normal **1** | |
| | innate, instinctive **2** **3** | |
| | genuine, sincere, unaffected **5** | |
| | wild; (ant.) artificial **6** | |

| Word Partnership | Use *natural* with : |
|---|---|
| ADV. | **perfectly** natural **1** **2** **5** |
| N. | natural **reaction**, natural **tendency** **2** natural **beauty**, natural **disaster**, natural **food** **6** |

**natu|ral food** (**natural foods**) N-VAR **Natural food** is food which has not been processed much and has not had artificial ingredients added to it. ❑ *Olive oil is a natural food.*

**natu|ral gas** N-UNCOUNT **Natural gas** is gas which is found underground or under the sea. It is collected and stored, and piped into people's homes to be used for cooking and heating

**natu|ral|ist** /nǽtʃərəlɪst, nǽtʃrəl-/ (**naturalists**) N-COUNT A **naturalist** is a person who studies plants, animals, insects, and other living things. [from Old French]
→ see **aquarium**

**natu|ral light** N-UNCOUNT **Natural light** is light from the sun rather than from an artificial source such as an electric light.

**natu|ral|ly** /nǽtʃərəli, nǽtʃrəli/ **1** ADV You use **naturally** to indicate that something is very obvious and not surprising under the circumstances. ❑ *When things go wrong, all of us naturally feel disappointed.* **2** ADV If one thing develops **naturally** from another, it develops as a normal result of it. ❑ *His love of machines led naturally to a career in engineering.* **3** PHRASE If something **comes naturally to** you, you find it easy to do and quickly become good at it. ❑ *Biking comes naturally to kids.* [from Old French] **4** → see also **natural**

**natu|ral re|sources** N-PLURAL **Natural resources** are all the land, forests, energy sources and minerals existing naturally in a place that can be used by people.

**natu|ral se|lec|tion** N-UNCOUNT **Natural selection** is a process by which species of animals and plants that are best adapted to their environment survive and reproduce, while those that are less well adapted die out.

**na|ture** /neɪtʃər/ **1** N-UNCOUNT **Nature** is all

the animals, plants, and other things in the world that are not made by people, and all the events and processes that are not caused by people. ❑ *...the relationship between man and nature.* **2** N-SING The **nature** of something is its basic quality or character. ❑ *The police would not comment on the nature of the investigation.* ❑ *He is quiet by nature.* **3** N-SING Someone's **nature** is their character, which they show by the way they behave. ❑ *Her nickname was "Sunny" because of her friendly nature.* ❑ *She trusted people. That was her nature.* **4** → see also **human nature** **5** PHRASE If you say that something has a particular characteristic **by its nature** or **by its very nature**, you mean that things of that type always have that characteristic. ❑ *Hockey is by its nature a violent game.* **6** PHRASE If a way of behaving is **second nature to** you, you do it almost without thinking because it is easy for you or obvious to you. ❑ *Planning ahead came as second nature to her.* [from Old French]

Word Partnership   Use *nature* with :

| | |
|---|---|
| V. | love nature, **preserve** nature **1** |
| N. | love of nature, **wonders of** nature **1** nature **of life**, nature **of society**, nature **of work 2** |

**naugh|ty** /nɔti/ (**naughtier, naughtiest**) ADJ A **naughty** child behaves badly or does not do what they are told. ❑ *Girls, you're being very naughty.*

**nau|sea** /nɔziə, -ʒə, -siə, -ʃə/ N-UNCOUNT **Nausea** is a feeling that you are going to vomit. ❑ *The symptoms include headaches and nausea.* [from Latin]

**nau|ti|cal** /nɔtɪkəl/ ADJ **Nautical** means relating to ships and sailing. ❑ *...a nautical chart of the region.* [from Latin]

Word Link   nav ≈ ship : naval, navigate, navy

**na|val** /neɪvəl/ ADJ **Naval** means belonging to, relating to, or involving a country's navy. ❑ *He was a senior naval officer.* [from Latin]

**na|vel** /neɪvəl/ (**navels**) N-COUNT Your **navel** is the small hollow just below your waist at the front of your body. ❑ *...a pain slightly above the navel and below the rib cage.* [from Old English]

**navi|gate** /nævɪgeɪt/ (**navigates, navigating, navigated**) **1** V-T/V-I When someone **navigates** a ship or an aircraft somewhere, they decide which course to follow and steer it there. ❑ *Captain Cook navigated his ship without accident for 100 voyages.* ❑ *I navigated for 12 or 14 hours a day on the boat.*

● **navi|ga|tion** /nævɪgeɪʃⁿn/ (**navigations**) N-VAR ❑ *The planes had their navigation lights on.* **2** V-T/V-I When a ship or boat **navigates** an area of water, it sails on or across it. ❑ *Every year they navigate the Greek islands in a sailboat.* ❑ *Such boats can navigate on the Hudson.* [from Latin]
→ see Word Web: **navigation**
→ see **star**

**navy** /neɪvi/ (**navies**) **1** N-COUNT A country's **navy** consists of the people it employs to fight at sea, and the ships they use. ❑ *The operation was organized by the U.S. Navy.* ❑ *Her own son was also in the navy.* **2** COLOR Something that is **navy** or **navy-blue** is very dark blue. ❑ *I mostly wore white shirts and black or navy pants.* [from Old French]

**NBA** /ɛn bi eɪ/ N-PROPER In the United States, the **NBA** is the organization responsible for professional basketball. **NBA** is an abbreviation for "National Basketball Association." ❑ *The Portland Trail Blazers had the best record in the NBA last year.* ❑ *...the new NBA champions.*

**Ne|an|der|thal** /niændərθɔl, -tɔl/ (**Neanderthals**) ADJ **Neanderthal** people lived in Europe between 35,000 and 70,000 years ago. ● You can refer to people from the Neanderthal period as **Neanderthals**. [after Neandertal, a valley near Düsseldorf, Germany]

**neap tide** /nip taɪd/ (**neap tides**) N-COUNT A **neap tide** is a tide with a smaller rise and fall than normal, which occurs when the moon is halfway between a new moon and a full moon.

**near** /nɪər/ (**nearer, nearest, nears, nearing, neared**) **1** PREP If something is **near** a place, thing, or person, it is a short distance from them. ❑ *Don't come near me.* ● **Near** is also an adverb. ❑ *He stood as near to the door as he could.* ● **Near** is also an adjective. ❑ *He sat in the nearest chair.* ❑ *The nearer of the two cars was half a mile away.* **2** PHRASE If someone or something is **near to** a particular state, they have almost reached it. ❑ *They are near to reaching agreement.* ● **Near** means the same as **near to.** ❑ *He was near tears.* **3** PHRASE If something is similar to something else, you can say that it is **near to** it. ❑ *...a feeling that was near to panic.* ● **Near** means the same as **near to.** ❑ *Her feelings were nearer hatred than love.* **4** PREP If something happens **near** a particular time, it happens just before or just after that time. ❑ *They stopped for lunch near midday.* **5** PREP You use **near** to say that something is a little more or less than an amount or number stated. ❑ *Temperatures dropped to near zero.* **6** ADJ You use **near** to indicate

Word Web   navigation

Early explorers used the **sun** and **stars** to navigate the seas. The **sextant** allowed later navigators to use these celestial objects to accurately calculate their **position**. By sighting or measuring their position at noon, sailors could determine their latitude. The **compass** helped sailors determine their position at any time of night or day. It also worked in all weather. Today all sorts of travelers use the **global positioning system (GPS)** to guide their journeys. A **GPS receiver** is connected to a system of 24 **satellites** that can establish a location within a few feet.

**compass**     **sextant**     **GPS**

that something is almost the thing mentioned. ❑ *They sat in near darkness.* • **Near** is also an adverb. ❑ *She had near perfect eyesight.* **7** V-T When someone or something **nears** a particular place, stage or point, they will soon reach that stage or point. ❑ *His age is hard to guess — he must be nearing fifty.* **8** PHRASE If you say that something will happen **in the near future**, you mean that it will happen quite soon. ❑ *We're going to New York in the near future.* **9** PHRASE You use **nowhere near** and **not anywhere near** to say that something is not the case. ❑ *They are nowhere near good enough to win.* ❑ *It was not anywhere near as bad as David expected.* [from Old English]

**near|by** /nɪɑrbaɪ/ ADV If something is **nearby**, it is only a short distance away. ❑ *Her sister lived nearby.* ❑ *The helicopter crashed to earth nearby.* • **Nearby** is also an adjective. ❑ *...a nearby table.*

**near|ly** /nɪɑrli/ **1** ADV If something is **nearly** a quantity, it is very close to that quantity but slightly less than it. If something is **nearly** a certain state, it is very close to that state but has not quite reached it. ❑ *We waited nearly half an hour for the bus.* ❑ *It was already nearly eight o'clock.* ❑ *I've nearly finished.* **2** PHRASE You use **not nearly** to emphasize that something is not the case. For example, if something is **not nearly** big enough, it is much too small. ❑ *My father's apartment isn't nearly as large as this.* [from Old English]

**near-sighted** ADJ Someone who is **near-sighted** cannot see distant things clearly. ❑ *She was near-sighted, which made it necessary for her to wear glasses.*

**neat** /nit/ (**neater, neatest**) **1** ADJ A **neat** place, thing, or person is organized and clean, and has everything in the correct place. ❑ *She put her clothes down in a neat pile.* • **neat|ly** ADV ❑ *He folded his paper neatly.* • **neat|ness** N-UNCOUNT ❑ *...the neatness of her appearance.* **2** ADJ If you say that something is **neat**, you mean that it is very good. [INFORMAL] ❑ *He thought Mike was a really neat guy.* **3** ADJ A **neat** explanation or method is clever and convenient. ❑ *It was such a neat, clever plan.* • **neat|ly** ADV ❑ *Real people do not fit neatly into these categories.* [from Old English]

**nebu|la** /nɛbyələ/ (**nebulae**) N-COUNT A **nebula** is a cloud of dust and gas in space. New stars are produced from nebulae. [from Latin]

**nec|es|sari|ly** /nɛsɪsɛərɪli/ ADV If you say that something is **not necessarily** true, you mean that it may not be true or is not always true. ❑ *Women do not necessarily have to act like men to be successful.* • CONVENTION If you reply "**Not necessarily**," you mean that what has just been said or suggested may not be true. ❑ *"He was lying, of course." — "Not necessarily."* [from Latin]

**nec|es|sary** /nɛsɪsɛri/ **1** ADJ Something that is **necessary** is needed in order for something else to happen. ❑ *It might be necessary to leave fast.* **2** PHRASE A **necessary evil** is something unpleasant or which you do not like but which must happen in order to achieve the result you

want. ❑ *For most of us, work is a necessary evil.* [from Latin]

**ne|ces|si|tate** /nɪsɛsɪteɪt/ (**necessitates, necessitating, necessitated**) V-T If something **necessitates** an event, action, or situation, it makes it necessary. [FORMAL] ❑ *Having more students will necessitate a new building.* [from Latin]

**ne|ces|sity** /nɪsɛsɪti/ (**necessities**) **1** N-UNCOUNT The **necessity** of something is the fact that it must happen or exist. ❑ *He learned the necessity of hiding his feelings.* **2** PHRASE If you say that something is **of necessity** true, you mean that it is true because nothing else is possible or practical under the circumstances. [FORMAL] ❑ *In large families, children, of necessity, shared a bed.* **3** N-COUNT **Necessities** are things that you must have to live. ❑ *Water is a necessity of life.* [from Latin]

**neck** /nɛk/ (**necks**) **1** N-COUNT Your **neck** is the part of your body which joins your head to the rest of your body. ❑ *She was wearing a red scarf around her neck.* **2** N-COUNT The **neck** of a shirt or a dress is the part which surrounds your neck. ❑ *...the low neck of her dress.* **3** N-COUNT The **neck** of something such as a bottle or a guitar is the long narrow part at one end of it. ❑ *The neck of the bottle broke.* **4** PHRASE In a competition, especially an election, if two or more competitors are **neck and neck**, they are level with each other and have an equal chance of winning. ❑ *The Democrats and the Republicans are neck and neck.* [from Old English]
→ see **body**

**neck|lace** /nɛklɪs/ (**necklaces**) N-COUNT A **necklace** is a piece of jewelry such as a chain or a string of beads which someone, usually a woman, wears around their neck. ❑ *...a diamond necklace.*
→ see **jewelry**

**nec|tar** /nɛktər/ N-UNCOUNT **Nectar** is a sweet liquid produced by flowers, which bees and other insects collect. [from Latin]

**nec|tar|ine** /nɛktərin/ (**nectarines**) N-COUNT A **nectarine** is a fruit which is similar to a peach but has a smooth skin.

**need** /nid/ (**needs, needing, needed**) **1** V-T If you **need** something, or **need** to do something, you cannot successfully achieve what you want or live properly without it. ❑ *He desperately needed money.* ❑ *I need to make a phone call.* ❑ *I need you to do something for me.* • **Need** is also a noun. ❑ *Charles has never felt the need to compete with anyone.* **2** V-T If an object or place **needs** something done to it, that action should be done to improve the object or place. If a task **needs** doing, it should be done to improve a particular situation. ❑ *The building needs quite a few repairs.* ❑ *My house needs cleaning.* **3** N-SING If there is a **need for** something, that thing would improve a situation. ❑ *"I think you* *should see a doctor." — "I don't think there's any need for that.* **4** V-T If you say that someone does not **need to** do something, you are telling them not to do it, or advising or suggesting that they should not do it. ❑ *You don't need to apologize.* **5** V-T If someone **didn't need to** do something, it wasn't necessary or useful for them to do it, although they did it. ❑ *You didn't need to give me any more money, but thank you.* **6** PHRASE People **in need** do not have enough of essential things such as money, food, or good health. ❑ *Leiter's Landing is a charity that helps children in need.* **7** PHRASE If you are **in need of** something, you need it or ought to have it. ❑ *I was all right but in need of rest.* ❑ *He was badly in need of a shave.* [from Old English]

| Thesaurus | *need* | Also look up : |
|---|---|---|
| v. | demand, require **1** | |

**nee|dle** /niːd<sup>ə</sup>l/ (**needles**) **1** N-COUNT A **needle**

is a small, very thin piece of polished metal which is used for sewing. It has a sharp point at one end and a hole in the other for a thread to go through. ❑ *...a needle and thread.* **2** N-COUNT A **needle** is a thin hollow metal tube with a sharp point. It is used to give injections. ❑ *Dirty needles spread disease.* **3** N-COUNT Knitting **needles** are thin metal or plastic sticks that are used for knitting.

**needle**

❑ *...a pair of knitting needles.* **4** N-COUNT On an instrument which measures something such as speed or weight, the **needle** is the long strip of metal or plastic on the dial that moves backward and forward, showing the measurement. ❑ *The needle on the boiler had reached 200 degrees.* **5** N-COUNT The **needles** of a fir or pine tree are its thin, hard, pointed leaves. ❑ *Pine needles lay thickly on the ground.* [from Old English]

**need|less** /niːdlɪs/ **1** ADJ Something that is **needless** is completely unnecessary. ❑ *His death was so needless.* ● **need|less|ly** ADV ❑ *Children are dying needlessly.* **2** PHRASE You say **needless to say** to emphasize that what you are saying is obvious. ❑ *Needless to say, I'm delighted.* [from Old English]

**needy** /niːdi/ (**needier, neediest**) ADJ **Needy** people do not have enough food, medicine, or clothing, or good enough houses. ❑ *They provide housing for needy families.* ● **The needy** are people who are needy. ❑ *We are trying to get food to the needy.* [from Old English]

**ne|gate** /nɪɡeɪt/ (**negates, negating, negated**) V-T If one thing **negates** another, it causes that other thing to lose the effect or value that it had. [FORMAL] ❑ *A poor diet can negate the effects of an athlete's training.* [from Latin]

**nega|tive** /nɛɡətɪv/ (**negatives**) **1** ADJ A fact, situation, or experience that is **negative** is unpleasant, depressing, or harmful. ❑ *The news from overseas is very negative.* **2** ADJ If someone is **negative** or has a **negative** attitude, they consider only the bad aspects of a situation, rather than the good ones. ❑ *When someone asks for your views, don't be negative.* ● **nega|tive|ly** ADV ❑ *Why do so many people think negatively?* ● **nega|tiv|ity** /nɛɡətɪvɪti/

N-UNCOUNT ❑ *I hate negativity. I can't stand people who complain.* **3** ADJ A **negative** reply or decision indicates the answer "no." ❑ *Dr. Velayati gave a negative response.* ● **nega|tive|ly** ADV ❑ *Sixty percent of people answered negatively.* **4** N-COUNT A **negative** is a word, expression, or gesture that means "no" or "not." ❑ *He used five negatives in 53 words.* **5** ADJ In grammar, a **negative** clause contains a word such as "not," "never," or "no one." ❑ *...using negatives such as "no one."* **6** ADJ If a medical test or scientific test is **negative**, it shows that the medical condition or substance that you are looking for is not there. ❑ *So far all the tests have been negative.* **7** ADJ A **negative** number, quantity, or measurement is less than zero. ❑ *...negative numbers such as -1.* **8** ADJ In painting and sculpture, **negative** space is the empty space that surrounds an object or form. [TECHNICAL] [from Latin]
→ see **lightning, magnet**

| Word Partnership | Use *negative* with : |
|---|---|
| N. | negative **effect**, negative **experience**, negative **image**, negative **publicity** **1** negative **attitude**, negative **thoughts** **1 2** negative **comment**, negative **reaction**, negative **response** **3** |

**nega|tive ac|cel|era|tion** N-UNCOUNT **Negative acceleration** is a decrease in speed or velocity. [TECHNICAL]

**ne|glect** /nɪɡlɛkt/ (**neglects, neglecting, neglected**) **1** V-T If you **neglect** someone or something, you do not take care of them properly. ❑ *The woman denied neglecting her child.* ● **Neglect** is also a noun. ❑ *The house has suffered years of neglect.* **2** V-T If you **neglect** someone or something, you fail to give them the amount of attention that they deserve. ❑ *He worked long hours and neglected her.* ● **ne|glect|ed** ADJ ❑ *She feels lonely and neglected.* ❑ *...a neglected period of the city's history.* **3** V-T If you **neglect** to do something, you fail to do it. ❑ *We often neglect to eat a healthy diet.* [from Latin]

**neg|li|gent** /nɛɡlɪdʒ<sup>ə</sup>nt/ ADJ If someone in a position of responsibility is **negligent**, they fail to do something which they should do. ❑ *The jury decided that the airline was negligent.* ● **neg|li|gent|ly** ADV ❑ *The physician acted negligently and harmed his patient.* ● **neg|li|gence** N-UNCOUNT ❑ *His negligence caused the accident.* [from Latin]

**neg|li|gible** /nɛɡlɪdʒɪb<sup>ə</sup>l/ ADJ An amount or effect that is **negligible** is so small that it is not worth considering or worrying about. ❑ *The soldiers' pay was negligible.* [from Latin]

**ne|go|tiable** /nɪɡoʊʃiəb<sup>ə</sup>l, -ʃəb<sup>ə</sup>l/ ADJ Something that is **negotiable** can be changed or agreed upon when people discuss it. ❑ *My fee is negotiable.* [from Latin]

**ne|go|ti|ate** /nɪɡoʊʃieɪt/ (**negotiates, negotiating, negotiated**) V-RECIP If people **negotiate with** each other or **negotiate** an agreement, they talk about a problem or a situation such as a business arrangement in order to solve the problem or complete the arrangement. ❑ *The president is willing to negotiate with the Democrats.* ❑ *The government and the army negotiated an agreement.* [from Latin]

**ne|go|tia|tion** /nɪɡoʊʃieɪʃ<sup>ə</sup>n/ (**negotiations**) N-VAR **Negotiations** are discussions between people with different aims, during which they

**n**

try to reach an agreement. ❑ *The negotiations were successful.* [from Latin]

**neigh|bor** /nˈeɪbər/ (**neighbors**) **1** N-COUNT Your **neighbor** is someone who lives near you. ❑ *My neighbor is a teacher.* **2** N-COUNT You can refer to the person who is standing or sitting next to you as your **neighbor**. ❑ *The woman spoke to her neighbor.* **3** N-COUNT You can refer to something which stands next to something else of the same kind as its **neighbor**. ❑ *Consider each plant in your garden in relation to its neighbors.* [from Old English]

**neigh|bor|hood** /nˈeɪbərhʊd/ (**neighborhoods**) N-COUNT A **neighborhood** is one of the parts of a town where people live. ❑ *...a wealthy Los Angeles neighborhood.* [from Old English]

---

**Word Partnership** Use *neighborhood* with :

ADJ. **poor** neighborhood, **residential** neighborhood, **run-down**

---

**neigh|bor|ing** /nˈeɪbərɪŋ/ ADJ **Neighboring** places or things are near other things of the same kind. ❑ *...Thailand and its neighboring countries.* [from Old English]

**neigh|bor|ly** /nˈeɪbərli/ ADJ If the people who live near you are **neighborly**, they are friendly and helpful. ❑ *They welcomed us in a very neighborly way.* [from Old English]

**nei|ther** /nˈiðər, nˈaɪ-/ **1** CONJ You use **neither** in front of the first of two or more words or expressions when you are linking two or more things which are not true or do not happen. The other thing is introduced by "nor." ❑ *Professor Hisamatsu spoke neither English nor German.* **2** DET You use **neither** to refer to each of two things or people, when you are making a negative statement that includes both of them. ❑ *At first, neither man could speak.* ● **Neither** is also a quantifier. ❑ *Neither of us felt like going out.* ● **Neither** is also a pronoun. ❑ *Neither noticed him leave the room.* **3** CONJ If you say that one person or thing does not do something and **neither** does another, what you say is true of all the people or things that you are talking about. ❑ *I never learned to swim and neither did they.* [from Old English]

**nek|ton** /nˈɛktɒn/ N-PLURAL **Nekton** are animals such as fish and whales that are capable of swimming against a current. [TECHNICAL] [from German]

**neon** /nˈiɒn/ **1** ADJ **Neon** lights or signs are made from glass tubes filled with neon gas which produce a bright electric light. ❑ *In the city squares the neon lights flashed.* **2** N-UNCOUNT **Neon** is a gas which occurs in very small amounts in the atmosphere. [from New Latin]

**neph|ew** /nˈɛfyu/ (**nephews**) N-COUNT Someone's **nephew** is the son of their sister or brother. [from Old French]

**Nep|tune** /nˈɛptun/ N-PROPER **Neptune** is the eighth planet from the sun. [from Latin]

**nerve** /nˈɜrv/ (**nerves**) **1** N-COUNT **Nerves** are long thin fibers that send messages between your brain and other parts of your body. ❑ *...pain from a damaged nerve.* **2** N-PLURAL If you refer to someone's **nerves**, you mean their ability to cope with problems such as stress, worry, and danger. ❑ *His nerves are bad — he has a lot of depression.* **3** N-UNCOUNT You can refer to someone's feelings of worry or stress as **nerves**. ❑ *It wasn't nerves — I just played badly.* **4** N-UNCOUNT **Nerve** is the courage that you need in order to do something difficult or dangerous. ❑ *I don't know why he lost his nerve.* **5** PHRASE If someone or something **gets on** your **nerves**, they annoy or irritate you. [INFORMAL] ❑ *The children's constant demands get on his nerves.* **6** PHRASE If you say that someone **has a nerve** or **has the nerve** to do something, you are criticizing them for doing something which you feel they had no right to do. [INFORMAL] ❑ *I can't believe you have the nerve to tell unkind stories about him.* [from Latin]

→ see **ear**, **eye**, **nervous system**, **smell**

**nerv|ous** /nˈɜrvəs/ **1** ADJ If someone is **nervous**, they are frightened or worried, and show this in their behavior. ❑ *I was very nervous during the job interview.* ● **nerv|ous|ly** ADV ❑ *Beth stood up nervously as the men came into the room.* ● **nerv|ous|ness** N-UNCOUNT ❑ *I smiled warmly so he wouldn't see my nervousness.* **2** ADJ A **nervous** person is very tense and easily upset. ❑ *She was a nervous person, easily startled.* **3** ADJ A **nervous** illness or condition is one that affects your mental state. ❑ *Abel has just been released from hospital where he was treated for a nervous disorder.* [from Latin]

---

**Word Partnership** Use *nervous* with :

PREP. nervous **about** *something* **1**
V. **become** nervous, **feel** nervous, **get** nervous, **look** nervous, **make** *someone* nervous **1**
ADV. **increasingly** nervous, **a little** nervous, **too** nervous, **very** nervous **1** **2**

---

**nerv|ous sys|tem** (**nervous systems**) N-COUNT Your **nervous system** consists of all the nerves in your body together with your brain and spinal cord. ❑ *...a disease of the nervous system.*
→ see Word Web: **nervous system**

**nerv|ous tis|sue** (**nervous tissues**) N-VAR **Nervous tissue** is tissue in the bodies of animals that consists of neurons. [TECHNICAL]

---

**Word Web** nervous system

The body's **nervous system** is a two-way road which carries electrochemical messages to and from different parts of the body. **Sensory** neurons carry information from both inside and outside the body to the **central nervous system** (CNS). The CNS is made of both the **brain** and the **spinal cord**. Motor neurons carry impulses from the CNS to **organs** and to **muscles** such as the muscles in the hand, telling them how to move. **Nerves** are made of sensory and motor neurons. **Nerves** run through the whole body.

**nervy** /nˈɜrvi/ (**nervier, nerviest**) If you say that someone is **nervy**, you mean that their behavior is bold or daring. ADJ ❑ *John liked him because he was a nervy guy.* [from Latin]

**nest** /nɛst/ (**nests, nesting, nested**) **1** N-COUNT A bird's **nest** is the home that it makes to lay its

eggs in. ❑ *...the cuckoo's habit of laying its eggs in the nests of other birds.* **2** V-I When a bird **nests** somewhere, it builds a nest and settles there to lay its eggs. ❑ *There are birds nesting on the cliffs.* **3** N-COUNT A **nest** is a home that a group of insects or small animals make in order to live in and give birth to their

**nest**

young in. ❑ *Some bees make their nests in the ground.* [from Old English]
→ see **bird**

**nestle** /nˈɛsᵊl/ (**nestles, nestling, nestled**) **1** V-I If you **nestle** somewhere, you move into a comfortable position, usually by pressing against someone or against something soft. ❑ *The two little girls nestled against their mother.* **2** V-I If something such as a building **nestles** somewhere, it is in that place and seems safe or sheltered. ❑ *Nestling in the hills was the children's home.* [from Old English]

**net**

**❶** NOUN AND VERB USES
**❷** ADJECTIVE AND ADVERB USES

**❶ net** /nɛt/ (**nets, netting, netted**) **1** N-UNCOUNT **Net** is a kind of material made of threads, strings or wires woven together so that there are small equal spaces between them. ❑ *...net curtains.* **2** N-COUNT A **net** is a piece of net which is used, for example, to cover something or to catch fish. ❑ *...a mosquito net.* ❑ *The fishermen sat fixing their nets.* **3** V-T If you **net** something, you manage to get it, especially by using skill. ❑ *Their first movie netted them an Oscar.* **4** V-T If you **net** a particular amount of money, you gain it as profit after all expenses have been paid. ❑ *He netted a profit of $1.85 billion.* **5** N-SING **The Net** is the same as the **Internet**. ❑ *We've been on the Net since 1993.* [from Old English] **6** → see also **safety net**
→ see **tennis**

**❷ net** /nɛt/ **1** ADJ A **net** amount is the amount that remains when everything that should be subtracted from it has been subtracted. ❑ *...a rise in sales and net profit.* ● **Net** is also an adverb. ❑ *They pay him around $2 million net.* **2** ADJ The **net** weight of something is its weight without its container or the material that has been used to wrap it. ❑ *...the finest candies, net weight 1 pound.* **3** ADJ A **net** result is a final result after all the details have been considered or included. ❑ *...a net increase in jobs.* [from French]

**Word Partnership** Use *net* with :

| | |
|---|---|
| N. | **fishing** net **❶ 2** |
| | Net **users ❶ 5** |
| V. | **access the** Net, **surf the** Net **❶ 5** |
| N. | net **earnings**, net **gain**, net **income/loss**, net **increase**, net **proceeds**, net **profit**, net **result**, net **revenue ❷ 1** |

**net force** (**net forces**) N-COUNT A **net force** is the overall force that is acting upon an object, after all the individual forces acting on the object have been added together. [TECHNICAL]

**nettle** /nˈɛtᵊl/ (**nettles**) N-COUNT **Nettles** are wild plants which have leaves covered with fine hairs that sting you when you touch them. ❑ *The nettles stung their legs.* [from Old English]

**network** /nˈɛtwɜrk/ (**networks, networking, networked**) **1** N-COUNT A radio or television **network** is a company or group of companies that broadcast radio or television programs throughout an area. ❑ *...a Spanish-language television network.* **2** N-COUNT A **network of** people or institutions is a large number of them that have a connection with each other and work together as a system. ❑ *She has a strong network of friends and family to help her.* **3** N-COUNT A particular **network** is a system of things which are connected and which operate together. For example, a **computer network** consists of a number of computers that are part of the same system. ❑ *...a computer network with 54 machines.* **4** N-COUNT A **network of** lines, roads, veins, or other long thin things is a large number of them which cross each other or meet at many points. ❑ *Strasbourg has a network of old streets.* **5** V-I If you **network**, you try to meet new people who might be useful to you in your job. [BUSINESS] ❑ *In business, it is important to network with as many people as possible.*
→ see **Internet**

**Word Partnership** Use *network* with :

| | |
|---|---|
| N. | **broadcast** network, **cable** network, **radio** network **1** |
| | network **administrator**, **computer** network, network **support 3** |
| ADJ. | **extensive** network, **nationwide** network, **vast** network, **worldwide** network **1** – **4** |
| | **wireless** network **3** |

**network card** (**network cards**) also **network interface card** N-COUNT A **network card** or a **network interface card** is a card that connects a computer to a network. [COMPUTING]

**networking** /nˈɛtwɜrkɪŋ/ **1** N-UNCOUNT **Networking** is the process of trying to meet new people who might be useful to you in your job, often through social activities. [BUSINESS] ❑ *Shy people find networking difficult.* **2** N-UNCOUNT You can refer to the things associated with a computer system or the process of establishing such a system as **networking**. ❑ *The government aims to fund computer networking in every school.*

**neuron** /nˈʊərɒn/ (**neurons**) N-COUNT A **neuron** is a cell which is part of the nervous system. Neurons send messages to and from the brain. [TECHNICAL] ❑ *Information is transferred along each neuron by means of an electrical impulse.* [from Greek]

**Word Link** *osis ≈ state or condition : hypnosis, metamorphosis, neurosis*

**neurosis** /nʊərˈoʊsɪs/ (**neuroses** /nʊərˈoʊsiːz/) N-VAR **Neurosis** is a mental condition which causes people to have unreasonable fears and worries over a long period of time. ❑ *I have a neurosis about being cold.* [from Modern Latin]

| Word Link | otic ≈ affecting, causing : cha*otic*, neur*otic*, patri*otic* |
|---|---|

**neu|rot|ic** /nʊərɒtɪk/ (**neurotics**) ADJ If someone is **neurotic**, they are always frightened or worried about things that you consider unimportant. ❑ *These Hollywood actresses are neurotic about reaching the age of 40.* ● A **neurotic** is someone who is neurotic. ❑ *...the film director Woody Allen's obsession with New York neurotics.* [from Modern Latin]

**neu|tral** /nutrəl/ ■ ADJ A **neutral** person or country does not support anyone in a disagreement, war, or contest. ❑ *Let's meet on neutral territory.* ● **neu|tral|ity** /nutrælɪti/ N-UNCOUNT ❑ *...the loss of political neutrality.* ■ ADJ If someone's facial expression or language is **neutral**, they do not show what they are thinking or feeling. ❑ *Isabel said in a neutral voice, "You're very late, darling."* ■ N-UNCOUNT **Neutral** is the position between the gears of a vehicle, in which the gears are not connected to the engine. ❑ *She put the truck in neutral and started it again.* ■ ADJ **Neutral** colors are colors such as black, white, and gray that are considered to combine well with other colors. [from Latin]
→ see **war**

**neu|tral|ize** /nutrəlaɪz/ (**neutralizes, neutralizing, neutralized**) V-T To **neutralize** something means to prevent it from having any effect or from working properly. ❑ *The burglars neutralized the alarm system.* [from Latin]

**neu|tron** /nutrɒn/ (**neutrons**) N-COUNT A **neutron** is an atomic particle that has no electrical charge.

**neu|tron star** (**neutron stars**) N-COUNT A **neutron star** is a star that has collapsed under the weight of its own gravity.

**nev|er** /nɛvər/ ■ ADV **Never** means at no time in the past or future. ❑ *I have never lost the weight I put on in my teens.* ❑ *Never say that!* ■ ADV **Never** means not in any circumstances. ❑ *I would never do anything to hurt him.* ❑ *Losing is never easy.* ■ PHRASE **Never ever** is a strong way of saying "never." ❑ *I never, ever sit around thinking, "What shall I do next?"* ■ ADV **Never** is used to refer to the past and means "not." ❑ *He never did anything to hurt anyone.* ❑ *I never knew him.* [from Old English] ■ **never mind** → see **mind**

**never-ending** ADJ If you describe something bad or unpleasant as **never-ending**, you are emphasizing that it seems to last a very long time. ❑ *...a never-ending series of problems.*

**never|the|less** /nɛvərðəlɛs/ ADV You use **nevertheless** when saying something that contrasts with what has just been said. [FORMAL] ❑ *Leon had problems, but nevertheless managed to finish his most famous painting.*

**new** /nu/ (**newer, newest**) ■ ADJ Something that is **new** has been recently created or invented. ❑ *They've just opened a new hotel.* ❑ *These ideas are nothing new.* ■ ADJ Something that is **new** has not been used or owned by anyone. ❑ *That afternoon she went out and bought a new dress.* ■ ADJ You use **new** to describe something which has replaced another thing, for example because you no longer have the old one, or it no longer exists, or it is no longer useful. ❑ *I had to find somewhere new to live.* ❑ *Rachel*

has a new boyfriend. ■ ADJ **New** is used to describe something that has only recently been discovered or noticed. ❑ *The new planet is about ten times the size of the earth.* ■ ADJ If you are **new to** a situation or place, or if the situation or place is **new to** you, you have not seen it or had any experience of it before. ❑ *She is new to the company.* ❑ *His name was new to me.* [from Old English] ■ → see also **brand-new** ■ as **good as new** → see **good**

| Thesaurus | new | Also look up : |
|---|---|---|
| ADJ. | contemporary, current, latest, modern, novel; (*ant.*) existing, old, past ■ | |

**new|born** /nubɔrn/ (**newborns**) ADJ A **newborn** baby or animal is one that has just been born. ❑ *...a mother and her newborn child.* ● The **newborn** are babies or animals who are newborn. ❑ *...the daily care of the newborn.*

**new|com|er** /nukʌmər/ (**newcomers**) N-COUNT A **newcomer** is a person who has recently arrived in a place, joined an organization, or started a new activity. ❑ *...a newcomer to Salt Lake City.*

**new|ly** /nuli/ ADV **Newly** is used before a past participle or an adjective to indicate that an action or situation is very recent. ❑ *She was young at the time, and newly married.* [from Old English]

**news** /nuz/ ■ N-UNCOUNT **News** is information about a recently-changed situation or a recent event. ❑ *We waited and waited for news of him.* ❑ *They still haven't had any news about when they'll be able to go home.* ■ N-UNCOUNT **News** is information that is published in newspapers and broadcast on radio and television about recent events in the country or world or in a particular area of activity. ❑ *Foreign News is on page 16.* ❑ *Those are some of the top stories in the news.* ■ N-SING **The news** is a television or radio broadcast which consists of information about recent events. ❑ *I heard all about the bombs on the news.* ■ PHRASE If you say that something is **bad news**, you mean that it will cause you trouble or problems. If you say that something is **good news**, you mean that it will be useful or helpful to you. ❑ *The agreement is good news for U.S. firms.* ■ PHRASE If you say that something **is news to** you, you mean that you did not already know what you have just been told, especially when you are surprised or annoyed about it. ❑ *This is news to me. I haven't heard about it.* [from Middle English]

| Word Partnership | Use *news* with : |
|---|---|
| ADJ. | **big** news, **grim** news, **sad** news ■ **latest** news ■ ■ |
| V. | **spread** the news, **tell** *someone* the news ■ **hear** the news ■ – ■ **listen to** the news, **watch** the news ■ |
| N. | news **headlines**, news **media**, news **report**, news **update** ■ |

**news agen|cy** (**news agencies**) N-COUNT A **news agency** is an organization that collects news stories from a particular country or from all over the world and supplies them to journalists. ❑ *...a correspondent for Reuters news agency.*

**news|cast** /nuzkæst/ (**newscasts**) N-COUNT A **newscast** is a news program that is broadcast on the radio or on television. ❑ *Coming up after the newscast, a review of the week's news.*

**news|caster** /n<u>u</u>zkæstər/ (**newscasters**) N-COUNT A **newscaster** is a person who reads the news on the radio or on television. ❑ ...TV newscaster Barbara Walters.

**news con|fer|ence** (**news conferences**) N-COUNT A **news conference** is a meeting held by a famous or important person in which they answer journalists' questions. ❑ He is due to hold a news conference in about an hour.

**news|group** /n<u>u</u>zgrup/ (**newsgroups**) N-COUNT A **newsgroup** is an Internet site where people can put information and opinions about a particular subject so they can be read by everyone who looks at the site. [COMPUTING] ❑ You can exchange information with others in newsgroups.

**news|letter** /n<u>u</u>zlɛtər/ (**newsletters**) N-COUNT A **newsletter** is one or more printed sheets of paper containing information about an organization that is sent regularly to its members. ❑ ...a monthly newsletter.

**news|paper** /n<u>u</u>zpeɪpər, n<u>u</u>s-/ (**newspapers**) **1** N-COUNT A **newspaper** is a publication consisting of a number of large sheets of folded paper, on which news, advertisements, and other information is printed. ❑ They read about it in the newspaper. **2** N-COUNT A **newspaper** is an organization that produces a newspaper. ❑ It is the nation's fastest-growing national daily newspaper. **3** N-UNCOUNT **Newspaper** consists of pieces of old newspapers, especially when they are being used for another purpose such as wrapping things up. ❑ He found two pots, each wrapped in newspaper.

**news re|lease** (**news releases**) N-COUNT A **news release** is a written statement about a matter of public interest which is given to the press by an organization concerned with the matter. ❑ The company made the announcement in a news release.

**new|ton** /n<u>u</u>t<sup>ə</sup>n/ (**newtons**) N-COUNT In physics, a **newton** is a unit of force. The abbreviation **N** is also used. [TECHNICAL] [after Sir Isaac Newton (1642–1727), an English physicist, mathematician, astronomer, and philosopher]

**New Year's** N-UNCOUNT **New Year's** is the time when people celebrate the start of a year.

**next** /nɛkst/ **1** ORD The **next** period of time, event, person, or thing is the one that comes immediately after the present one or after the previous one. ❑ I got up early the next morning. ❑ Who will be the next mayor? **2** DET You use **next** in expressions such as **next Friday**, **next day**, and **next year** to refer, for example, to the first Friday, day, or year that comes after the present or previous one. ❑ He retires next January. ● **Next** is also an adjective. ❑ I'll be 26 years old next Friday. ● **Next** is also a pronoun. ❑ John is coming the week after next. **3** ADJ The **next** place or person is the one that is nearest to you or that is the first one that you come to. ❑ There was a party going on in the next room. **4** ADV The thing that happens **next** is the thing that happens immediately after something else. ❑ Next, close your eyes. ❑ I don't know what to do next. **5** ADV When you **next** do something, you do it for the first time since you last did it. ❑ I next saw him at his house in Vermont. **6** ADV You use **next** to say that something has more of a particular quality than all other things except one. For example, the thing that is **next** best is the one that is the best except for one other thing. ❑ I think he feels that a grandson is the next best thing to a son. **7** PHRASE If one thing is **next to** another, it is at the side of it. ❑ She sat down next to him on the sofa. **8** PHRASE You use **next to** before a negative, or a word that suggests something negative, to mean almost, but not completely. ❑ Johnson still knew next to nothing about politics. [from Old English]

**Word Partnership** Use *next* with :

| | |
|---|---|
| N. | next **election**, next **generation**, next **level**, next **move**, next **question**, next **step**, next **time**, next **train** **1** next **day/hour/month/week/year** **1** **2** |
| V. | **come** next, **go** next, **happen** next **4** |

**NFL** /ɛn ɛf ɛl/ N-PROPER In the United States, the **NFL** is the organization responsible for professional football. **NFL** is an abbreviation for "National Football League." ❑ ...one of the best teams in the NFL. ❑ ...an NFL player.

**NHL** /ɛn eɪtʃɛl/ N-PROPER In the United States, the **NHL** is the organization responsible for professional ice hockey. **NHL** is an abbreviation for "National Hockey League." ❑ ...the best goalkeeper in the NHL.

**nib|ble** /n<u>ɪ</u>b<sup>ə</sup>l/ (**nibbles, nibbling, nibbled**) **1** V-T/V-I If you **nibble** food, you eat it by biting very small pieces of it. ❑ Linda lay on the couch, nibbling popcorn. ❑ She nibbled at a piece of bread. ● **Nibble** is also a noun. ❑ We each took a nibble. **2** V-T/V-I When an animal **nibbles** something or **nibbles away** at it, it takes small bites of it quickly and repeatedly. ❑ A herd of goats was nibbling the grass. [from Low German]

**nice** /n<u>aɪ</u>s/ (**nicer, nicest**) **1** ADJ If you say that something is **nice**, you mean that it is attractive, pleasant, or enjoyable. ❑ The chocolate-chip cookies were nice. ❑ It's nice to be here together again. ● **nice|ly** ADV ❑ The book is nicely illustrated. **2** ADJ If someone is **nice**, they are friendly and pleasant. ❑ I've met your father and he's very nice. ● **nice|ly** ADV ❑ He treated you nicely. **3** ADJ If you say that it is **nice of** someone to say or do something, you are saying that they are being kind and thoughtful. This is often used as a way of thanking someone. ❑ It's nice of you to come all this way to see me. ❑ "How are you?" — "How nice of you to ask." [from Old French] **4** → see also **nicely**

**Thesaurus** *nice* Also look up :

| | |
|---|---|
| ADJ. | friendly, kind, likable, pleasant, polite; (*ant.*) mean, unpleasant **2** **3** |

**Word Partnership** Use *nice* with :

| | |
|---|---|
| ADJ. | nice **and clean** **1** |
| V. | **look** nice, nice **to see** *someone/something* **1** |
| N. | nice **clothes**, nice **guy**, nice **people**, nice **place**, nice **smile** **1** **2** |

**nice|ly** /n<u>aɪ</u>sli/ **1** ADV If something is happening or working **nicely**, it is happening or working in a satisfactory way or in the way that you want it to. ❑ The computer system is now working nicely. [from Old French] **2** → see also **nice**

**niche** /n<u>ɪ</u>tʃ, niʃ/ (**niches**) **1** N-COUNT A **niche** in the market is a specific area of marketing which has its own particular requirements, customers, and products. [BUSINESS] ❑ *I think we have found a niche in the toy market.* ◼ N-COUNT A **niche** is a hollow area in a wall, which has been made to hold a statue, or a natural hollow part in a hill or cliff. ❑ *They hid the gold in a niche in a cave.* ◼ N-COUNT Your **niche** is the job or activity which is exactly suitable for you. ❑ *Steve found his niche as a Web designer.* ◼ N-COUNT The **niche** of a species of animal or plant is the particular position that the species occupies in its environment and the way it interacts with that environment. [from French]

**nick** /nɪk/ (**nicks, nicking, nicked**) ◼ V-T If you **nick** something or **nick** yourself, you accidentally make a small cut in the surface of the object or your skin. ❑ *A bullet nicked the edge of the wall.* ❑ *He nicked himself on the chin when he was shaving.* ◼ N-COUNT A **nick** is a small cut made in the surface of something, usually in someone's skin. ❑ *I had a nick just below my eye.* ◼ PHRASE If something is achieved **in the nick of time**, it is achieved successfully, at the last possible moment. [INFORMAL] ❑ *We got here in the nick of time.*

**nick|el** /nɪkəl/ (**nickels**) ◼ N-UNCOUNT **Nickel** is a silver-colored metal that is used in making steel. ◼ N-COUNT In the United States and Canada, a **nickel** is a coin worth five cents. ❑ *The jar was filled with nickels, dimes, and quarters.* [from German]

**nick|name** /nɪkneɪm/ (**nicknames, nicknaming, nicknamed**) ◼ N-COUNT A **nickname** is an informal name for someone or something. ❑ *Red got his nickname for his red hair.* ◼ V-T If you **nickname** someone or something, you give them an informal name. ❑ *When he got older, I nicknamed him Little Alf.*

**niece** /nis/ (**nieces**) N-COUNT Someone's **niece** is the daughter of their sister or brother. ❑ *...his niece, the daughter of his eldest sister.* [from Old French]

**night** /naɪt/ (**nights**) ◼ N-VAR The **night** is the part of each period of twenty-four hours when the sun has set and it is dark outside, especially the time when people are sleeping. ❑ *The fighting continued all night.* ❑ *It was one of the darkest nights I'd ever seen.* ◼ N-COUNT The **night** is the period of time between the end of the afternoon and the time that you go to bed, especially the time when you relax before going to bed. ❑ *Whose party did you go to last night?* ◼ PHRASE If it is a particular time **at night**, it is during the time when it is dark and is before midnight. ❑ *It's eleven o'clock at night in Moscow.* ◼ PHRASE If something happens **day and night** or **night and day**, it happens all the time without stopping. ❑ *The doctors and nurses have been working day and night for weeks.* ◼ PHRASE If you have **an early night**, you go to bed early. If you have **a late night**, you go to bed late. ❑ *All I want is an early night.* [from Old English] ◼ **morning, noon, and night** → see **morning**
→ see **star, time**

| Word Partnership | Use *night* with : |
| --- | --- |
| ADJ. | **cold** night, **cool** night, **dark** night, **rainy** night, **warm** night ◼ |
| V. | **spend a/the** night ◼ |
| | **sleep at** night, **stay out at** night, **stay the** night ◼ ◼ |

**night|club** /naɪtklʌb/ (**nightclubs**) N-COUNT A **nightclub** is a place where people go late in the evening to drink and dance.

**night|gown** /naɪtgaʊn/ (**nightgowns**) N-COUNT A **nightgown** is a sort of loose dress that a woman or girl wears in bed.

**night|life** /naɪtlaɪf/ N-UNCOUNT **Nightlife** is all the entertainment and social activities that are available at night in cities and towns, such as nightclubs and theaters. ❑ *There's plenty of nightlife.*

**night|ly** /naɪtli/ ADJ A **nightly** event happens every night. ❑ *We watched the nightly news.*
● **Nightly** is also an adverb. ❑ *She appears nightly on the television news.* [from Old English]

**night|mare** /naɪtmɛər/ (**nightmares**) ◼ N-COUNT A **nightmare** is a very frightening dream. ❑ *She woke up during the night with a nightmare.* ◼ N-COUNT If you refer to a situation as a **nightmare**, you mean that it is very unpleasant. ❑ *The years in prison were a nightmare.* ◼ N-COUNT If you refer to a situation as a **nightmare**, you are saying strongly that it causes you a lot of trouble. ❑ *New York traffic is a nightmare.* [from Old English]

**night|stick** /naɪtstɪk/ (**nightsticks**) N-COUNT A **nightstick** is a short thick club that is carried by police officers in the United States.

**nil** /nɪl/ N-UNCOUNT If you say that something is **nil**, you mean that it does not exist at all. ❑ *Their legal rights are almost nil.* [from Latin]

**nim|ble** /nɪmbəl/ (**nimbler, nimblest**) ADJ Someone who is **nimble** is able to move their fingers, hands, or legs quickly and easily. ❑ *...nimble dancers.* [from Old English]

**NIMBY** /nɪmbi/ also **Nimby** ADJ If you say that someone has a **NIMBY** attitude, you are criticizing them because they do not want something such as a new road, housing development, or prison built near where they live. **NIMBY** is an abbreviation for "not in my backyard." [INFORMAL] ❑ *...the usual NIMBY protests from local residents.*

**nine** /naɪn/ (**nines**) NUM **Nine** is the number 9. ❑ *...nine hundred dollars.* [from Old English]

**nine-eleven** /naɪn ɪlɛvən/ also **nine eleven** also **9/11** N-PROPER **9/11** or **nine-eleven** is used to refer to the events that took place in the United States on September 11, 2001, when terrorists attacked the World Trade Center in New York and the Pentagon in Washington. ❑ *...the victims of 9/11.* ❑ *Everything changed after nine-eleven.*

**nine|teen** /naɪntin/ (**nineteens**) NUM **Nineteen** is the number 19. ❑ *He was in prison for nineteen years.* [from Old English]

**nine|teenth** /naɪntinθ/ ORD The **nineteenth** item in a series is the one that you count as number nineteen. ❑ *...my nineteenth birthday.* [from Old English]

**nine|ti|eth** /naɪntiɪθ/ ORD The **ninetieth** item in a series is the one that you count as number ninety. ❑ *He celebrates his ninetieth birthday on Friday.* [from Old English]

**nine-to-five** ADJ A **nine-to-five** job is one that you do during normal office hours, for example a job in a factory or an office. ❑ *She works a nine-to-five job.* ● **Nine to five** is also an adverb. ❑ *I wish I could go to work in a factory, nine to five.*

**nine|ty** /naɪnti/ (**nineties**) ◼ NUM **Ninety** is the number 90. ❑ *Ninety people were hurt in the accident.* ◼ N-PLURAL When you talk about the **nineties**, you are referring to numbers between 90 and 99.

For example, if you are **in your nineties**, you are aged between 90 and 99. If the temperature is **in the nineties**, the temperature is between 90 and 99 degrees. □ *Now in his nineties, Compay Segundo shows no sign of retiring.* ◆ N-PLURAL **The nineties** is the decade between 1990 and 1999. □ *...British art in the nineties.* [from Old English]

**ninth** /naɪnθ/ (**ninths**) ◆ ORD The **ninth** item in a series is the one that you count as number nine. □ *...January the ninth.* □ *...students in the ninth grade.* ◆ FRACTION A **ninth** is one of nine equal parts of something. □ *The area covers one-ninth of the Earth's surface.* [from Old English]

**nip** /nɪp/ (**nips, nipping, nipped**) ◆ V-T If an animal or person **nips** you, they bite or pinch you lightly. □ *Rebecca's dog nipped her ankle.* ● **Nip** is also a noun. □ *A kitten can give you a nasty nip.* [of Scandinavian origin] ◆ to **nip** something **in the bud** → see **bud**

**nip|ple** /nɪpəl/ (**nipples**) N-COUNT The **nipples** on someone's body are the two small round pieces of slightly hard flesh on their chest. Babies suck milk through their mothers' nipples.

**nite** /naɪt/ (**nites**) N-VAR **Nite** is another spelling of **night**, used in less formal written English. □ *...$50 per nite, $350 weekly.*

**ni|trate** /naɪtreɪt/ (**nitrates**) N-COUNT A **nitrate** is a chemical compound that includes nitrogen and oxygen. Nitrates are used as fertilizers in agriculture. □ *...high levels of nitrates.* [from French] → see **firework**

**ni|tro|gen** /naɪtrədʒən/ N-UNCOUNT **Nitrogen** is a colorless element that has no smell and is usually found as a gas. It forms about 78 percent of the Earth's atmosphere, and is found in all living things. [from French] → see **air**

**nix** /nɪks/ (**nixes, nixing, nixed**) V-T If you **nix** a plan or suggestion, you reject or forbid it. [INFORMAL] □ *It only took a few minutes for me to nix this proposal.* [from German]

**no** /noʊ/ (**noes** or **no's**) ◆ CONVENTION You use **no** to give a negative response to a question, to say that something is not true, to refuse an offer or a request, or to refuse permission. □ *"Any problems?" — "No, I'm O.K."* □ *"We thought you were sick." — "No, no."* □ *"Here, have mine." — "No, this is fine."* □ *No. I forbid it.* ◆ CONVENTION You use **no** to acknowledge a negative statement or to show that you accept and understand it. □ *"We're not on the main campus." — "No."* □ *"It's not my favorite kind of music." — "No."* ◆ CONVENTION You use **no** before correcting what you have just said. □ *I was twenty-two — no, twenty-one.* ◆ EXCLAM You use **no** to express shock or disappointment at something you have just been told. □ *Oh no, not again.* ◆ DET You use **no** to mean not any or not one person or thing. □ *He had no intention of paying.* □ *No letters survive from the early part of his life.* ◆ DET You use **no** to emphasize that someone or something is not the type of thing mentioned. □ *He is no singer.* □ *It's no secret that people were very upset.* ◆ ADV You can use **no** to make the negative form of a comparative. □ *...no later than the end of 2014.* ◆ DET **No** is used in notices or instructions to say that a particular activity or thing is forbidden. □ *The door was marked "NO ENTRY."* ◆ N-COUNT A **no** is a person who has answered "no" to a question or who has voted against something. **No** is also

used to refer to their answer or vote. □ *According to the latest opinion polls, the noes have 50 percent, the yeses 35 percent.* ◆ PHRASE If you say **there is no** doing a particular thing, you mean that it is very difficult or impossible to do that thing. □ *There is no going back to the life she had.* [from Old English] ◆ not to **take no for an answer** → see **answer** ◆ **no doubt** → see **doubt** ◆ **no longer** → see **long** ◆ **in no way** → see **way** ◆ **there's no way** → see **way** ◆ **no way** → see **way**

**No.** (**Nos**) **No.** is a written abbreviation for **number**. □ *That year he was named the nation's No. 1 college football star.*

**no|bil|ity** /noʊbɪlɪti/ ◆ N-SING The **nobility** of a society are all the people who have titles and belong to a high social class. □ *...the grand homes of the nobility.* ◆ N-UNCOUNT A person's **nobility** is their noble character and behavior. [FORMAL] □ *He has great nobility of spirit.* [from Old French]

**no|ble** /noʊbəl/ (**nobler, noblest**) ◆ ADJ If you say that someone is a **noble** person, you admire and respect them because they are unselfish and morally good. □ *He was a generous and noble man who was willing to help.* ● **no|bly** ADV □ *Eric's sister nobly offered to help with the gardening.* ◆ ADJ **Noble** means belonging to a high social class and having a title. □ *...rich and noble families.* [from Old French]

**no|ble gas** (**noble gases**) N-COUNT The **noble gases** are chemical elements such as helium, neon, and argon, which do not generally react when mixed with other substances. [TECHNICAL]

**no|body** /noʊbɒdi, -bʌdi/ (**nobodies**) ◆ PRON **Nobody** means not a single person. □ *For a long time nobody spoke.* □ *Nobody realizes how bad things are.* ◆ N-COUNT If someone says that a person is a **nobody**, they are saying in an unkind way that the person is not at all important. □ *A man in my position has nothing to fear from a nobody like you.*

**no-brain|er** (**no-brainers**) N-COUNT If you describe a question or decision as a **no-brainer**, you mean that it is a very easy one to answer or make. [INFORMAL] □ *It's a no-brainer that music is part of a well-rounded education.*

**noc|tur|nal** /nɒktɜrnəl/ ◆ ADJ **Nocturnal** means occurring at night. □ *...long nocturnal walks.* ◆ ADJ **Nocturnal** animals are active mainly at night. □ *Rats are nocturnal creatures.* [from Late Latin] → see **bat**

**nod** /nɒd/ (**nods, nodding, nodded**) ◆ V-T/V-I If you **nod**, you move your head downward and upward to show that you are answering "yes" to a question, or to show agreement, understanding, or approval. □ *"Are you okay?" I asked. She nodded and smiled.* □ *Jacques tasted a cookie and nodded his approval.* ● **Nod** is also a noun. □ *She gave a nod and said, "I see."* ◆ V-I If you **nod** in a particular direction, you bend your head once in that direction in order to indicate something or to give someone a signal. □ *"Does it work?" he asked, nodding at the piano.* □ *She nodded toward the dining room. "He's in there."* ◆ V-T/V-I If you **nod**, you bend your head once, as a way of saying hello or goodbye. □ *All the girls nodded and said "Hi."* □ *Both of them smiled and nodded at friends.* □ *Tom nodded a greeting.*

▶ **nod off** PHR-VERB If you **nod off**, you fall asleep, especially when you did not intend to. [INFORMAL] □ *The judge appeared to nod off.*

n

**Noh** /noʊ/ N-UNCOUNT **Noh** is a traditional form of Japanese theater which combines dance, music, and poetry, and in which the actors wear masks. [from Japanese]

**noise** /nɔɪz/ (**noises**) ◼ N-UNCOUNT **Noise** is a loud or unpleasant sound. □ *The noise from the crowd became deafening.* ◼ N-COUNT **A noise** is a sound that someone or something makes. □ *A noise came from behind the tent.* □ *…animal noises.* [from Old French]

---

**Word Partnership** Use *noise* with :

| N. | **background** noise, noise **level**, noise **pollution**, **traffic** noise ◼ |
|---|---|
| ADJ. | **loud** noise ◼ ◼ |
| V. | **hear a** noise, **make a** noise ◼ |

---

**noisy** /nɔɪzi/ (**noisier, noisiest**) ◼ ADJ A **noisy** person or thing makes a lot of loud or unpleasant noise. □ *…my noisy old car.* ● **noisi**|**ly** ADV □ *The students cheered noisily.* ◼ ADJ A **noisy** place is full of a lot of loud or unpleasant noise. □ *The café is a noisy place.* □ *The airport was crowded and noisy.* [from Old French]

**no**|**mad** /noʊmæd/ (**nomads**) N-COUNT A **nomad** is a member of a group of people who travel from place to place rather than living in one place all the time. □ *…a country of nomads who raise cattle and camels.* ● **no**|**mad**|**ic** /noʊmædɪk/ ADJ □ *…the nomadic tribes of the Western Sahara.* [from French]

**no-man's land** N-UNCOUNT **No-man's land** is an area of land that is not owned or controlled by anyone, for example the area of land between two opposing armies. □ *…the no-man's land between the two countries.*

**nomi**|**nal** /nɒmɪnᵊl/ ◼ ADJ You use **nominal** to indicate that someone or something is supposed to have a particular identity or status, but in reality does not have it. □ *His wife became the nominal head of the company.* ● **nomi**|**nal**|**ly** ADV □ *Both countries are nominally equal.* ◼ ADJ A **nominal** price or sum of money is very small in comparison with the real cost or value of the thing that is being bought or sold. □ *I sold my car at a nominal price.* [from Latin]

**nomi**|**nate** /nɒmɪneɪt/ (**nominates, nominating, nominated**) V-T If someone is **nominated** for a job, a position, or a prize, their name is formally suggested for it. □ *He was nominated by the Democratic Party for the presidency of the United States.* □ *This year a panel of writers nominated six novels for the Booker Prize.* [from Latin]

**nomi**|**na**|**tion** /nɒmɪneɪʃᵊn/ (**nominations**) N-COUNT A **nomination** is an official suggestion of someone as a candidate for a job, position, or prize. □ *…his candidacy for the Republican presidential nomination.* □ *He's certain to get an Oscar nomination for best actor.* [from Latin]

**nomi**|**nee** /nɒmɪni/ (**nominees**) N-COUNT A **nominee** is someone who is nominated for a job, position, or award. □ *…his nominee for vice president.*

---

**Word Link** *non* ≈ *not :* **non**chalant, **non**prescription, **non**sense

---

**non**|**cha**|**lant** /nɒnʃəlɒnt/ ADJ Someone who is **nonchalant** seems very calm and appears not to worry or care about things. □ *Perrin is remarkably nonchalant about his new-found wealth.* □ *Denis tried to look nonchalant.* ● **non**|**cha**|**lance** /nɒnʃəlɒns/ N-UNCOUNT □ *He played with such nonchalance that they started calling him "Cool."* ● **non**|**cha**|**lant**|**ly** ADV □ *"I meant to ask you," he said, as nonchalantly as possible. "How was your lunch with Burke yesterday?"* [from French]

**none** /nʌn/ ◼ QUANT **None of** something means not even a small amount of it. **None of** a group of people or things means not even one of them. □ *None of us knew her.* ● **None** is also a pronoun. □ *I searched bookstores and libraries for information, but found none.* ◼ PHRASE You use **none the** to say that someone or something does not have any more of a particular quality than they did before. □ *Three months after the event, police are still none the wiser as to the motive for the attack.* ◼ PHRASE You use **none too** in front of an adjective or adverb in order to emphasize that the quality mentioned is not present. [FORMAL] □ *He was none too pleased to hear from me.* [from Old English] ◼ **second to none →** see **second**

**none**|**the**|**less** /nʌnðəlɛs/ ADV **Nonetheless** means the same as **nevertheless**. [FORMAL] □ *There is still a long way to go. Nonetheless, some progress has been made.*

**non**|**fo**|**li**|**at**|**ed** /nɒnfoʊlieɪtɪd/ ADJ **Nonfoliated** rock is rock that does not consist of regular, thin layers. [TECHNICAL]

**non**|**liv**|**ing** /nɒnlɪvɪŋ/ also **non-living** ADJ **Nonliving** objects are objects that are not alive, such as rocks and minerals. [from Old English]

**non**|**met**|**al** /nɒnmɛtᵊl/ also **non-metal** (**nonmetals**) N-COUNT **Nonmetals** are chemical elements that are not metals. [from Latin]

**non**|**ob**|**jec**|**tive** /nɒnəbjɛktɪv/ ADJ **Nonobjective** art makes use of shapes and patterns rather than showing people or things. [TECHNICAL]

**no-nonsense** ◼ ADJ If you describe someone as a **no-nonsense** person, you approve of the fact that they are efficient, direct, and quite tough. □ *…a no-nonsense, modern woman.* ◼ ADJ If you describe something as a **no-nonsense** thing, you approve of the fact that it is plain and does not have unnecessary parts. □ *She wore her hair in a short, no-nonsense cut.*

**nonpoint-source pol**|**lu**|**tion** /nɒnpɔɪnt sɔrs pəluʃᵊn/ N-UNCOUNT **Nonpoint-source pollution** is pollution that comes from many different sources, for example chemicals from farmland and factories that are carried into rivers by rain. [TECHNICAL]

**non**|**pre**|**scrip**|**tion** /nɒnprɪskrɪpʃᵊn/ ADJ **Nonprescription** drugs are medicines that you can buy without the need for a doctor's prescription. □ *Aspirin is the most popular nonprescription drug on the market.* [from Latin]

**non**|**profit** /nɒnprɒfɪt/ also **not-for-profit** ADJ A **nonprofit** organization is one which is not run with the aim of making a profit. [BUSINESS] □ *…a nonprofit foundation that brings technology into public schools.* [from Latin]

**non**|**re**|**new**|**able** /nɒnrɪnuəbᵊl/ also **non-renewable** (**nonrenewables**) ◼ ADJ **Nonrenewable** resources are natural materials such as coal, oil and gas that exist in limited amounts and take a very long time to replace.

**2** N-PLURAL You can refer to nonrenewable resources as **nonrenewables**.

---
**Word Link** non = not : non**chalant**, non**prescription**, non**sense**
---

**non|sense** /nɒnsɛns, -səns/ **1** N-UNCOUNT If you say that something spoken or written is **nonsense**, you think it is untrue or silly. ▫ *Most doctors say this is complete nonsense.* ▫ *...all that poetic nonsense about love.* **2** N-UNCOUNT; N-SING You can use **nonsense** to refer to behavior that you think is foolish or that you disapprove of. ▫ *I don't think people can take much more of this nonsense.* [from Latin] **3** → see also **no-nonsense**

**non|sense syl|la|ble** (**nonsense syllables**) N-COUNT A **nonsense syllable** is a combination of letters, for example "kak" or "mek", that does not form a proper word. Nonsense syllables are used in the teaching of reading skills. [TECHNICAL]

**non|sili|cate min|er|al** /nɒnsɪlɪkɪt mɪnərəl/ (**nonsilicate minerals**) N-COUNT A **nonsilicate mineral** is a mineral that does not contain a compound of silicone and oxygen. [TECHNICAL]

**non|stand|ard unit** (**nonstandard units**) N-COUNT **Nonstandard units** are units of measurement consisting of objects which are not normally used to measure things, for example matchsticks or paper clips. [TECHNICAL]

**non|vas|cu|lar plant** /nɒnvæskyələr plænt/ also **non-vascular plant** (**nonvascular plants**) N-COUNT **Nonvascular plants** are plants such as mosses and algae that are unable to move water or nutrients through themselves. [TECHNICAL]

**non|ver|bal** /nɒnvɜrbªl/ ADJ **Nonverbal** communication consists of things such as the expression on your face, your arm movements, or your tone of voice, which show how you feel about something without using words.

**noo|dle** /nudªl/ (**noodles**) N-COUNT **Noodles** are long, thin strips of pasta. They are used especially in Chinese and Italian cooking. [from German]

**noon** /nun/ **1** N-UNCOUNT **Noon** is twelve o'clock in the middle of the day. ▫ *The meetings started at noon.* [from Old English] **2** morning, noon, and night → see morning → see time

**no one** PRON **No one** means not a single person, or not a single member of a particular group or set. ▫ *Everyone wants to be a hero, but no one wants to die.*

**noon|time** /nuntaɪm/ also **noon-time** or **noon time** N-UNCOUNT **Noontime** is the middle part of the day. ▫ *There was a demonstration at noontime yesterday at the Chinese Embassy.* ▫ *...their noontime meal.*

**noose** /nus/ (**nooses**) N-COUNT A **noose** is a loop at the end of a piece of rope or wire that is used to trap animals or hang people. [from Provençal]

**nope** /noʊp/ CONVENTION **Nope** is sometimes used instead of "no" as a negative response. [INFORMAL, SPOKEN] ▫ *"Is she supposed to work today?" — "Nope, tomorrow."*

**nor** /nɔr/ **1** CONJ You use **nor** after "neither" to introduce the second thing that a negative statement applies to. ▫ *Neither Mr. Reese nor Mr. Woodhouse was available for comment.* ▫ *I can give you neither an opinion nor any advice.* **2** CONJ You use **nor** after a negative statement in order to

introduce another negative statement which adds information to the previous one. ▫ *Cooking a quick meal doesn't mean you have to sacrifice flavor. Nor does fast food have to be junk food.* **3** CONJ You use **nor** after a negative statement in order to indicate that the negative statement also applies to you or to someone or something else. ▫ *"None of us has any idea how long we're going to be here." — "Nor do I."* ▫ *"If my husband has no future," she said, "then nor do my children."* [from Old English]

**norm** /nɔrm/ (**norms**) **1** N-COUNT **Norms** are ways of behaving that are considered normal in a particular society. ▫ *...the professional norms of journalism.* **2** N-SING If you say that a situation is **the norm**, you mean that it is usual and expected. ▫ *Families of six or seven are the norm in Borough Park.* [from Latin]

**nor|mal** /nɔrmªl/ **1** ADJ Something that is **normal** is usual and ordinary, and is what people expect. ▫ *The situation has returned to normal.* ▫ *Her height and weight are normal for her age.* **2** ADJ A **normal** person has no serious physical or mental health problems. ▫ *She gave birth to a normal, healthy baby.* [from Latin]

---
**Thesaurus** normal Also look up :

ADJ. ordinary, regular, typical, usual **1**
---

---
**Word Partnership** Use *normal* with :

N. normal **conditions**, normal **development**, normal **routine** **1**
V. **return to** normal **1**
ADV. **back to** normal **1**
   **completely** normal, **perfectly** normal **1** **2**
---

**nor|mal fault** (**normal faults**) N-COUNT A **normal fault** is a fault in the surface of the Earth where the rock above the fault has moved down. [TECHNICAL]

**nor|mal|ity** /nɔrmælɪti/ N-UNCOUNT **Normality** is a situation in which everything is normal. ▫ *We want the country to return to normality.* [from Latin]

---
**Word Link** ize = making : final**ize**, modern**ize**, normal**ize**
---

**nor|mal|ize** /nɔrməlaɪz/ (**normalizes, normalizing, normalized**) V-T/V-I When you **normalize** a situation or when it **normalizes**, it becomes normal. ▫ *The two governments were close to normalizing relations.* ● **nor|mali|za|tion** /nɔrməlɪzeɪʃªn/ N-UNCOUNT ▫ *...a first step toward normalization.* [from Latin]

**nor|mal|ly** /nɔrməli/ **1** ADV If you say that something **normally** happens or that you **normally** do a particular thing, you mean that it is what usually happens or what you usually do. ▫ *All airports in the country are working normally today.* ▫ *Normally the bill is less than $30 a month.* **2** ADV If you do something **normally**, you do it in the usual or conventional way. ▫ *She's getting better and beginning to eat normally again.* [from Latin]

**north** /nɔrθ/ also **North** **1** N-UNCOUNT The **north** is the direction which is on your left when you are looking toward the direction where the sun rises. ▫ *In the north snow and ice cover the ground.* ▫ *Birds usually migrate from north to south.*

**2** N-SING **The north** of a place, country, or region is the part which is in the north. ❑ *He lives in the north of England.* **3** ADV If you go **north**, you travel toward the north. ❑ *Anita drove north up Pacific Highway.* **4** ADV Something that is **north** of a place is positioned to the north of it. ❑ *She lives in a village a few miles north of Portland.* **5** ADJ **The north** edge, corner, or part of a place or country is the part which is toward the north. ❑ *...the north side of the mountain.* ❑ *...North America.* **6** ADJ A **north** wind is a wind that blows from the north. ❑ *...a bitterly cold north wind.* [from Old English]

**north|east** /nɔrθist/ **1** N-UNCOUNT The **northeast** is the direction which is halfway between north and east. ❑ *The earthquake was felt in Jerusalem, more than 250 miles to the northeast.* **2** N-SING **The northeast** of a place, country, or region is the part which is in the northeast. ❑ *Kruger Park, located in the northeast of South Africa, is the size of a small European country.* **3** ADV If you go **northeast**, you travel toward the northeast. ❑ *I think we need to go northeast.* **4** ADV Something that is **northeast** of a place is positioned to the northeast of it. ❑ *Payson is a small town about 70 miles northeast of Phoenix.* **5** ADJ The **northeast** part of a place, country, or region is the part which is toward the northeast. ❑ *...rural northeast Louisiana.* ❑ *...Northeast Asia.* **6** ADJ A **northeast** wind is a wind that blows from the northeast. ❑ *...a light northeast wind.*

**north|eastern** /nɔrθistərn/ ADJ **Northeastern** means in or from the northeast of a region or country. ❑ *Smith had three children and came from northeastern England.*

**nor|ther|ly** /nɔrðərli/ ADJ A **northerly** point, area, or direction is to the north or toward the north. ❑ *The storm is headed on a northerly path.* [from Old English]

**north|ern** /nɔrðərn/ also **Northern** ADJ **Northern** means in or from the north of a region, state, or country. ❑ *...Northern Ireland.* [from Old English]

**north|ern|er** /nɔrðərnər/ (**northerners**) N-COUNT A **northerner** is a person who was born in or lives in the north of a country. ❑ *He was a northerner, born in New York City.* [from Old English]

**north|ward** /nɔrθwərd/ also **northwards** ADV **Northward** or **northwards** means toward the north. ❑ *The storm is pushing northward up Florida's coast.* ● **Northward** is also an adjective. ❑ *The northward journey from Jalalabad was no more than 120 miles.* [from Old English]

**nose** /noʊz/ (**noses**) **1** N-COUNT Your **nose** is the part of your face which sticks out above your mouth. You use it for smelling and breathing. ❑ *She wiped her nose with a tissue.* **2** N-COUNT The **nose** of a vehicle such as an airplane or a boat is the front part of it. **3** PHRASE If you do something **under** someone's **nose**, you do it right in front of them, without trying to hide it from them. ❑ *She stole items from right under the noses of the staff.* [from Old English] **4** to put someone's **nose out of joint** → see **joint**
→ see **face, respiration, smell**

---

| **Word Partnership** | Use *nose* with : |
| --- | --- |
| ADJ. | **big** nose, **bloody** nose, **broken** nose, **long** nose, **red** nose, **runny** nose, **straight** nose **1** |

---

**nosh** /nɒʃ/ N-SING A **nosh** is a snack or light meal. [INFORMAL] [from Yiddish]

**no-show** (**no-shows**) N-COUNT If someone who is expected to go somewhere fails to go there, you can say that they are a **no-show**. ❑ *John Henry Williams was a no-show at last week's game in Milwaukee.*

**nos|tal|gia** /nɒstældʒə/ N-UNCOUNT **Nostalgia** is an affectionate feeling you have for the past. ❑ *...nostalgia for his happy youth.* [from New Latin]

**nos|tal|gic** /nɒstældʒɪk/ **1** ADJ **Nostalgic** things cause you to think affectionately about the past. ❑ *...nostalgic snow scenes on Christmas cards.* **2** ADJ If you feel **nostalgic**, you think affectionately about experiences you had in the past. ❑ *Many people were nostalgic for the good old days.* ● **nos|tal|gi|cal|ly** /nɒstældʒɪkli/ ADV ❑ *She loved to talk nostalgically about old times.* [from New Latin]

**nos|tril** /nɒstrɪl/ (**nostrils**) N-COUNT Your **nostrils** are the two openings at the end of your nose. ❑ *Keeping your mouth closed, breathe in through your nostrils.* [from Old English]

**not** /nɒt/

> **Not** is often shortened to **n't** in spoken English, and added to the auxiliary or modal verb. For example, "did not" is often shortened to "didn't."

**1** NEG You use **not** with verbs to form negative statements. ❑ *Their plan was not working.* ❑ *I don't trust my father anymore.* **2** NEG You use **not** to form questions to which you expect the answer "yes." ❑ *Haven't they got enough problems there already?* ❑ *Didn't I see you at the party last week?* **3** NEG You use **not**, usually in the form **n't**, in questions which imply that someone should have done something, or to express surprise that something is not the case. ❑ *Why didn't you do it months ago?* ❑ *Why couldn't he listen to her?* **4** NEG You use **not**, usually in the form **n't**, when you want to change a positive statement into a question. ❑ *It's crazy, isn't it?* ❑ *I've been a great husband, haven't I?* **5** NEG You use **not**, usually in the form **n't**, in polite suggestions. ❑ *Why don't you fill out the application?* **6** NEG You use **not** to represent the negative of a word, group, or clause that has just been used. ❑ *"Have you found Paula?" — "I'm afraid not."* **7** NEG You can use **not** in front of "all" or "every" when you want to say something that applies only to some members of the group that you are talking about. ❑ *Not all the money has been spent.* **8** NEG You can use **not** or **not even** in front of "a" or "one" to emphasize that there is none at all of what is being mentioned. ❑ *I sent report after report. But not one word was published.* **9** NEG You use **not** when you are contrasting something that is true with something that people might wrongly believe to be true. ❑ *People are working very hard, not because they have to, but because they want to.* ❑ *Training is an investment not a cost.* **10** NEG You use **not** in expressions such as "not only," "not just," and "not simply" to emphasize that something is true, but it is not the whole truth. ❑ *These movies* were not only making money; they were also very good. ❑ *Not every applicant has a degree.* **11** PHRASE You use **not that** to introduce a negative clause that contradicts something in the previous statement. ❑ *He only had four hours' sleep. Not that he's complaining.* **12** CONVENTION **Not at all** is a strong way of saying "No" or of agreeing that the answer to a question is "No." ❑ *"Sorry. I sound like Abby, don't I?" — "No. Not at all."* [from Old English] **13 not half →** see **half 14 if not →** see **if 15 more often than not →** see **often**

**no|ta|ble** /no͟ʊtəbᵊl/ ADJ Someone or something that is **notable** is important or interesting. ❑ *The town is notable for its church.* [from Old French]

**no|ta|bly** /no͟ʊtəbli/ ADV You use **notably** to specify an important or typical example of something that you are talking about. ❑ *He has apologized many times, most notably in the newspapers.* [from Old French]

**no|ta|tion** /no͟ʊte͟ɪʃᵊn/ (**notations**) N-VAR A system of **notation** is a set of written symbols that are used to represent something such as music or mathematics. [from Latin]

**notch** /nɒtʃ/ (**notches, notching, notched**) **1** N-COUNT You can refer to a level on a scale of measurement or achievement as a **notch**. ❑ *Average earnings moved up another notch in August.* **2** N-COUNT A **notch** is a small V-shaped or circular cut in the surface or edge of something. [from Old French]

▶ **notch up** PHR-VERB If you **notch up** something such as a score or total, you achieve it. ❑ *He has notched up more than 25 victories worldwide.*

**note** /no͟ʊt/ (**notes, noting, noted**) **1** N-COUNT A **note** is a short letter. ❑ *Steven wrote him a note asking him to come to his apartment.* **2** N-COUNT A **note** is something that you write down to remind yourself of something. ❑ *She didn't take notes on the lecture.* **3** N-COUNT In a book or article, a **note** is a short piece of additional information. ❑ *See Note 16 on p. 223.* **4** N-COUNT In music, a **note** is the sound of a particular pitch, or a written symbol representing this sound. ❑ *She has a deep voice and can't sing high notes.* **5** N-SING You can use **note** to refer to a particular feeling, impression, or atmosphere. ❑ *The movie ends on a positive note.* ❑ *There was a note of surprise in his voice.* **6** V-T If you **note** a fact, you become aware of it. ❑ *We noted his absence an hour ago.* ❑ *Suddenly, I noted that the rain had stopped.* **7** V-T When you **note** something, you write it down as a record of what has happened. ❑ *"He has been very ill," she noted in her diary.* ❑ *An off-duty police officer noted the license plate of the car.* **8** → see also **noted, promissory note** **9** PHRASE If you **compare notes with** someone or if the two of you **compare notes,** you talk to them and find out whether they have the same opinion, information, or experiences as yourself. ❑ *...the chance to compare notes with other mothers.* **10** PHRASE Someone or something that is **of note** is important, worth mentioning, or well known. ❑ *...politicians of note.* **11** PHRASE If you **take note of** something, you pay attention to it because you think that it is important or significant. ❑ *Take note of the weather conditions.* [from Old French]

▶ **note down** PHR-VERB If you **note down** something, you write it down quickly, so that you have a record of it. ❑ *She noted down the names.* ❑ *If you find a name that's on the list, note it down.*

**note|book** /no͟ʊtbʊk/ (**notebooks**) **1** N-COUNT A **notebook** is a small book for writing notes in. ❑ *He took a notebook and pen from his pocket.* **2** N-COUNT A **notebook** computer is a small personal computer. ❑ *...a new range of notebook computers.*

notebook

**not|ed** /no͟ʊtɪd/ ADJ To be **noted for** something you do or have means to be well known and admired for it. ❑ *Sanders was a man noted for his leadership skills.* [from Old French]

**noth|ing** /nʌ̱θɪŋ/ (**nothings**) **1** PRON **Nothing** means not a single thing, or not a single part of something. ❑ *I've done nothing much since this morning.* ❑ *There is nothing wrong with the car.* **2** PRON You use **nothing** to indicate that something or someone is not important or significant. ❑ *Because he has always had money, it means nothing to him.* ❑ *Do our years together mean nothing?* **3** PHRASE You use **nothing but** in front of a noun, an infinitive without "to," or an "-ing" form to mean "only." ❑ *All that money brought nothing but misery.* ❑ *He is focused on nothing but winning.* **4** PHRASE If you say about an activity that **there is nothing to it,** you mean that it is extremely easy. ❑ *Don't be scared — there's really nothing to it!* [from Old English] **5 nothing to write home about →** see **home 6 to stop at nothing →** see **stop 7 to think nothing of →** see **think**

**no|tice** /no͟ʊtɪs/ (**notices, noticing, noticed**) **1** V-T/V-I If you **notice** something or someone, you become aware of them. ❑ *Didn't you notice anything special about him?* ❑ *She noticed he was acting strangely.* ❑ *Luckily, I noticed where you left the car.* ❑ *If he thought no one would notice, he's wrong.* **2** N-COUNT A **notice** is a written announcement in a place where everyone can read it. ❑ *A few guest houses had "No Vacancies" notices in their windows.* **3** N-UNCOUNT If you give **notice** about something that is going to happen, you give a warning in advance that it is going to happen. ❑ *She was moved to a different office without notice.* ❑ *You have to give three months' notice if you want to leave.* **4** PHRASE **Notice** is used in expressions such as "on short notice," "at a moment's notice," or "at twenty-four hours' notice," to indicate that something can or must be done within a short period of time. ❑ *There's no one available on such short notice to take her class.* ❑ *I live just a mile away, so I can usually be available on short notice.* **5** PHRASE If a situation will exist **until further notice,** it will continue until someone changes it. ❑ *All flights were canceled until further notice.* **6** PHRASE If an employer **gives** an employee **notice,** the employer tells the employee that they must leave their job within a short fixed period of time. [BUSINESS] ❑ *The next morning I gave him his notice.* **7** PHRASE If you **give**

n

**notice** or **hand in notice** you tell your employer that you intend to leave your job soon, within a set period of time. You can also **hand in** your **notice.** [BUSINESS] ❑ *He handed in his notice at the bank.* **8** PHRASE If you **take notice of** a particular fact or situation, you behave in a way that shows that you are aware of it. ❑ *We want the government to take notice of what we say.* **9** PHRASE If you **take no notice of** someone or something, you do not consider them to be important enough to affect what you think or what you do. ❑ *For years, society took no notice of the needs of the disabled.* [from Old French]

<table>
<tr><td colspan="3">Thesaurus    notice    Also look up :</td></tr>
<tr><td>v.</td><td colspan="2">note, observe, perceive, see 1</td></tr>
<tr><td>N.</td><td colspan="2">advertisement, announcement 2</td></tr>
</table>

<table>
<tr><td colspan="2">Word Partnership   Use notice with :</td></tr>
<tr><td>N.</td><td>notice a change, notice a difference 1</td></tr>
<tr><td>v.</td><td>begin to notice, fail to notice, pretend not to notice 1<br>receive notice, serve notice 3<br>give notice 3 6 7</td></tr>
</table>

**no|tice|able** /nˈoʊtɪsəbəl/ ADJ Something that is **noticeable** is very obvious, so that it is easy to see, hear, or recognize. ❑ *It was noticeable that his face and arms were red.* ● **no|tice|ably** ADV ❑ *The traffic has gotten noticeably worse.* [from Old French]

**no|ti|fy** /nˈoʊtɪfaɪ/ (**notifies, notifying, notified**) V-T If you **notify** someone of something, you officially inform them about it. [FORMAL] ❑ *We have notified the police.* ❑ *They were notified that they had to leave.* ● **no|ti|fi|ca|tion** /nˌoʊtɪfɪkˈeɪʃən/ (**notifications**) N-VAR ❑ *We gave them notification that we would end the agreement September 15.* [from Old French]

**no|tion** /nˈoʊʃən/ (**notions**) **1** N-COUNT A **notion** is an idea or belief about something. ❑ *We each have a notion of what kind of person we'd like to be.* **2** N-PLURAL **Notions** are small articles for sewing, such as buttons, zippers, and thread. [from Latin]

<table>
<tr><td colspan="2">Thesaurus    notion    Also look up :</td></tr>
<tr><td>N.</td><td>concept, idea, opinion, thought 1</td></tr>
</table>

**no|to|ri|ety** /nˌoʊtərˈaɪɪti/ N-UNCOUNT To achieve **notoriety** means to become well known for something bad. ❑ *She achieved notoriety through the murder.* [from Medieval Latin]

**no|to|ri|ous** /nˌoʊtˈɔriəs/ ADJ To be **notorious** means to be well known for something bad. ❑ *...an area notorious for crime and violence.* ● **no|to|ri|ous|ly** ADV ❑ *Living space in New York City is notoriously expensive.* [from Medieval Latin]

**not|with|stand|ing** /nˌɒtwɪθstˈændɪŋ, -wɪð-/ PREP If something is true **notwithstanding** something else, it is true in spite of that other thing. [FORMAL] ❑ *He despised Paul, notwithstanding the similar views they both held.* ● **Notwithstanding** is also an adverb. ❑ *Differences of opinion notwithstanding, they generally got along well.* [from Old English]

**noun** /nˈaʊn/ (**nouns**) **1** N-COUNT A **noun** is a word such as "car," "love," or "Anne" which is used to refer to a person or thing. [from Latin] **2** → see also **count noun, proper noun**

**nour|ish** /nˈɜrɪʃ/ (**nourishes, nourishing, nourished**) V-T To **nourish** a person, animal, or plant means to provide them with the food that is necessary for life, growth, and good health. ❑ *The food she eats nourishes both her and the baby.* ● **nour|ish|ing** ADJ ❑ *...nourishing home-cooked food.* ● **nour|ish|ment** N-UNCOUNT ❑ *He was unable to take nourishment for several days.* [from Old French]

<table>
<tr><td colspan="2">Word Link   nov ≈ new : innovation, novel, renovate</td></tr>
</table>

**nov|el** /nˈɒvəl/ (**novels**) **1** N-COUNT A **novel** is a long written story about imaginary people and events. ❑ *...a novel by Herman Hesse.* **2** ADJ **Novel** things are new and different from anything that has been done, experienced, or made before. ❑ *...a novel way of raising money.* [Sense 1 from Old French. Sense 2 from Latin.]
→ see **library**

**nov|el|ist** /nˈɒvəlɪst/ (**novelists**) N-COUNT A **novelist** is a person who writes novels. ❑ *...a successful novelist.* [from Old French]
→ see **fantasy**

**nov|el|ty** /nˈɒvəlti/ (**novelties**) **1** N-UNCOUNT **Novelty** is the quality of being different, new, and unusual. ❑ *People are eager for novelty.* **2** N-COUNT A **novelty** is something that is new and therefore interesting. ❑ *Camera phones are no longer a novelty.* **3** N-COUNT **Novelties** are cheap toys, ornaments, or other objects that are sold as presents or souvenirs. ❑ *...plastic eggs filled with small toys, novelties, and coins.* [from Old French]

**No|vem|ber** /nˌoʊvˈɛmbər/ (**Novembers**) N-VAR **November** is the eleventh month of the year in the Western calendar. ❑ *He arrived in London in November 1939.* [from Old French]

**nov|ice** /nˈɒvɪs/ (**novices**) N-COUNT A **novice** is someone who has been doing a job or other activity for only a short time and so is not experienced at it. ❑ *I'm a novice at these things. You're the professional.* [from Old French]

**now** /nˈaʊ/ **1** ADV You use **now** to refer to the present time, often in contrast to a time in the past or the future. ❑ *She should know that by now.* ❑ *I must go now.* ● **Now** is also a pronoun. ❑ *Now is your chance to talk to him.* **2** CONJ You use **now** or **now that** to indicate that an event has occurred and as a result something else may or will happen. ❑ *Now our children are grown, I have time to help other people.* **3** ADV You use **now** in statements which specify the length of time up to the present that something has lasted. ❑ *They've been married now for 30 years.* ❑ *They have been missing for a long time now.* **4** ADV You say "**Now**" or "**Now then**" to indicate to the person or people you are with that you want their attention, or that you are about to change the subject. [SPOKEN] ❑ *"Now then," Max said, "to get back to the point." ❑ Now then, what's the trouble?* **5** ADV You can say "**Now**" to introduce new information into a story or account. [SPOKEN] ❑ *Now I didn't tell him that, so he must have found out on his own.* **6** PHRASE If you say that something will happen **any day now, any moment now,** or **any time now,** you mean that it will happen very soon. ❑ *We are expecting him home any day now.* **7** PHRASE **Just now** means a very short time ago. [SPOKEN] ❑ *You looked pretty upset just now.* **8** PHRASE If you say that something happens **now and then** or **every now and again,** you mean that it happens sometimes but not very often or regularly. ❑ *Now and then they heard the roar of a heavy truck.* [from Old English]

**nowa|days** /n<u>au</u>ədeɪz/ ADV **Nowadays** means at the present time, in contrast with the past. ❑ *Nowadays we have more career choices when we leave school.* [from Old English]

**no|where** /n<u>ou</u>wɛər/ ■ ADV You use **nowhere** to emphasize that a place has more of a particular quality than any other place, or that it is the only place where something happens or exists. ❑ *Nowhere is the problem worse than in Asia.* ❑ *This kind of forest exists nowhere else in the world.* ❷ ADV You use **nowhere** when making negative statements to say that a suitable place of the specified kind does not exist. ❑ *There was nowhere to hide and nowhere to run.* ❑ *I have nowhere else to go, nowhere in the world.* ❸ ADV If you say that something or someone appears **from nowhere** or **out of nowhere**, you mean that they appear suddenly and unexpectedly. ❑ *A car came from nowhere, and I had to jump back off the road.* ❹ PHRASE If you say that you **are getting nowhere** or that something **is getting** you **nowhere**, you mean that you are not achieving anything or having any success. ❑ *Oh, stop arguing! This is getting us nowhere.* ❺ PHRASE If you say that a place is **in the middle of nowhere**, you mean that it is a long way from other places. ❑ *We put up our tent in the middle of nowhere.* ❻ PHRASE If you use **nowhere near** in front of a word or expression, you are emphasizing that the real situation is very different from, or has not reached, the state which that word or expression suggests. ❑ *He's nowhere near finished yet.*

| Word Partnership | Use *nowhere* with : |
| --- | --- |
| v. | nowhere **to be found**, nowhere **to be seen**, *have* nowhere **to go**, *have* nowhere **to hide**, *have* nowhere **to run** ❷ <br> **go** nowhere ❹ |

**no-win situa|tion (no-win situations)** N-COUNT If you are in a **no-win situation**, any action you take will fail to benefit you in any way. ❑ *They are in a no-win situation. Whatever they do, they are going to get criticized for it.*

**nu|ance** /n<u>u</u>ɑns/ (**nuances**) N-VAR A **nuance** is a small difference in sound, feeling, appearance, or meaning. ❑ *They talked for hours about him, analyzing every nuance of his behavior.* [from French]

**nu|clear** /n<u>u</u>kliər/ ADJ **Nuclear** means relating to the nuclei of atoms, or to the energy released when these nuclei are split or combined. ❑ *...a nuclear power station.* ❑ *...nuclear weapons.* [from Latin]
→ see **energy**

**nu|clear en|er|gy** N-UNCOUNT **Nuclear energy** is energy that is released when the nuclei of atoms are split or combined.

**nu|clear fis|sion** N-UNCOUNT **Nuclear fission** is the same as **fission**.

**nu|clear fu|sion** N-UNCOUNT → see **fusion**

**nu|cleic acid** /nukl<u>i</u>ɪk <u>æ</u>sɪd, -kl<u>eɪ</u>-/ (**nucleic acids**) N-COUNT **Nucleic acids** are complex chemical substances, such as DNA, which are found in living cells. [TECHNICAL]

**nu|cleo|tide** /n<u>u</u>kliətaɪd/ (**nucleotides**) N-COUNT **Nucleotides** are molecules that join

together to form DNA and RNA. [TECHNICAL]

**nu|cleus** /n<u>u</u>kliəs/ (**nuclei** /n<u>u</u>kliaɪ/) ■ N-COUNT The **nucleus** of an atom or cell is the central part of it. ❷ N-COUNT The **nucleus of** a group of people or things is the small number of members which form the most important part of the group. ❑ *Matt Cummings and Liko Soules-Ono form the nucleus of the team.* [from Latin]

**nude** /n<u>u</u>d/ (**nudes**) ■ ADJ A **nude** person is not wearing any clothes. ❑ *Students draw the human form from nude models.* PHRASE ● If you do something **in the nude**, you are not wearing any clothes. If you paint or draw someone **in the nude**, they are not wearing any clothes. ❑ *He sleeps in the nude regardless of how cold it is.* ❷ N-COUNT A **nude** is a picture or statue of a person who is not wearing any clothes. ❑ *...Matisse's nudes.* [from Latin]

**nudge** /n<u>ʌ</u>dʒ/ (**nudges, nudging, nudged**) V-T If you **nudge** someone, you push them gently, usually with your elbow. ❑ *I nudged Stan and pointed again.* ● **Nudge** is also a noun. ❑ *She gave him a nudge.* [of Scandinavian origin]

**nui|sance** /n<u>u</u>sᵊns/ (**nuisances**) ■ N-COUNT If you say that someone or something is a **nuisance**, you mean that they annoy you or cause you a lot of problems. ❑ *He can be a bit of a nuisance sometimes.* ❑ *Sorry to be a nuisance.* ❷ PHRASE If someone **makes a nuisance of** themselves, they behave in a way that annoys other people. ❑ *The children were hanging around and making a nuisance of themselves.* [from Old French]

**numb** /n<u>ʌ</u>m/ (**numbs, numbing, numbed, number, numbest**) ■ ADJ If a part of your body is **numb**, you cannot feel anything there. ❑ *He could feel his fingers growing numb.* ● **numb|ness** N-UNCOUNT ❑ *I'm suffering from pain and numbness in my hands.* ❷ ADJ If you are **numb with** shock, fear, or grief, you are so shocked, frightened, or upset that you cannot think clearly or feel any emotion. ❑ *He looked at the price label and went numb with surprise.* ❸ V-T If an event or experience **numbs** you, you can no longer think clearly or feel any emotion. ❑ *For a while the shock of Philippe's letter numbed her.* ● **numbed** ADJ ❑ *We were numbed by the terrible news.* ❹ V-T If cold weather, a drug, or a blow **numbs** a part of your body, you can no longer feel anything in it. ❑ *The cold numbed my fingers.* [from Old English]

**num|ber** /n<u>ʌ</u>mbər/ (**numbers, numbering, numbered**) ■ N-COUNT A **number** is a word such as "two," "nine," or "twelve," or a symbol such as 1, 3, or 47, which is used in counting something. ❑ *I don't know the room number.* ❑ *...number 3, Argyll Street.* ❷ N-COUNT You use **number** with words such as "large" or "small" to say approximately how many things or people there are. ❑ *We're holding a large number of interviews for this job.* ❑ *I have received an enormous number of letters.* ❸ N-SING If there are **a number of** things or people, there are several of them. If there are **any number of** things or people, there is a large quantity of them. ❑ *Sam told a number of lies.* ❹ V-T If a group of people or things **numbers** a particular total, that is how many there are. ❑ *Their village numbered 100 houses.* ❺ N-COUNT A **number** is the series of numbers that you dial when you are making a telephone call. ❑ *...a list of names and telephone numbers.* ❑ *My number is 414-3925.* ❻ V-T If you **number** something, you mark it with a number, usually

n

starting at 1. ❑ *He cut the paper up into tiny squares, and he numbered each one.* [from Old French]
→ see also **amount**
→ see **mathematics, zero**

**nu|meri|cal** /nuˈmɛrɪkᵊl/ ADJ **Numerical** means expressed in numbers or relating to numbers. ❑ *The page numbers aren't in numerical order.* • **nu|meri|cal|ly** ADV ❑ *The price is written both numerically and in words.* [from Medieval Latin]

**nu|mer|ous** /ˈnuːmərəs/ ADJ If people or things are **numerous**, they exist or are present in large numbers. ❑ *He made numerous attempts to lose weight.* [from Late Middle English]

**nun** /nʌn/ (**nuns**) N-COUNT A **nun** is a member of a female religious community. ❑ *She is studying to become a nun.* [from Old English]

**nurse** /nɜrs/ (**nurses, nursing, nursed**)
**1** N-COUNT; N-TITLE; N-VOC A **nurse** is a person whose job is to care for people who are ill. ❑ *She spent 29 years as a nurse.* **2** V-T If you **nurse** someone, you care for them when they are ill. ❑ *All the years he was sick my mother nursed him.* **3** V-T If you **nurse** an illness or injury, you allow it to get better by resting as much as possible. ❑ *We're going to go home and nurse our colds.* **4** V-T If you **nurse** an emotion or desire, you feel it strongly for a long time. ❑ *Jane still nurses the pain of rejection.* [from Old French]

**nurse prac|ti|tion|er** (**nurse practitioners**) N-COUNT A **nurse practitioner** is a nurse with advanced training who provides some of the medical care usually provided by a doctor. ❑ *California law allows nurse practitioners to write prescriptions.*

**nurse|ry** /ˈnɜrsəri/ (**nurseries**) N-COUNT A **nursery** is a place where plants are grown in order to be sold. ❑ *The garden, developed over the past 35 years, includes a nursery.* [from Old French]

**nurse|ry rhyme** (**nursery rhymes**) N-COUNT A **nursery rhyme** is a poem or song for young children, especially one that is old or well known.

**nurs|ing home** (**nursing homes**) N-COUNT A **nursing home** is a residence for old or sick people. ❑ *Isaac Binger died in a nursing home in Florida at the age of 87.*

**nur|ture** /ˈnɜrtʃər/ (**nurtures, nurturing, nurtured**) **1** V-T If you **nurture** something such as a young child or a young plant, you care for

it while it is growing and developing. [FORMAL] ❑ *Parents want to know the best way to nurture and raise their child.* **2** V-T If you **nurture** plans, ideas, or people, you encourage them or help them to develop. [FORMAL] ❑ *She always nurtured the talent of others.* [from Old French]

**nut** /nʌt/ (**nuts**) **1** N-COUNT The firm shelled fruit of some trees and bushes are called **nuts**. ❑ *Nuts and seeds are very good for you.* → see also **peanut 3** N-COUNT A **nut** is a thick metal ring which you screw onto a metal rod called a bolt. Nuts and bolts are used to hold things such as

pieces of machinery together. ❑ *If you want to repair the wheels, you must undo the four nuts.* **4** N-COUNT If you describe someone as, for example, a baseball **nut** or a health **nut**, you mean that they are extremely enthusiastic about the thing mentioned.

**nuts and bolts**

[INFORMAL] ❑ *I'm a football nut.* **5** ADJ If you are **nuts about** something or someone, you like them very much. [INFORMAL] ❑ *She's nuts about you and you're in love with her.* **6** ADJ If you say that someone goes **nuts** or is **nuts**, you mean that they go crazy or are very foolish. [INFORMAL] ❑ *You guys are nuts.* **7** PHRASE If someone **goes nuts**, they become extremely angry. [INFORMAL] ❑ *My father would go nuts if I told him.* [from Old English]
→ see **peanut**

**nu|tri|ent** /ˈnuːtriənt/ (**nutrients**) N-COUNT **Nutrients** are substances that help plants and animals to grow. ❑ *...vitamins, minerals, and other essential nutrients.* [from Latin]
→ see **cardiovascular system, food**

**nu|tri|tion** /nuˈtrɪʃᵊn/ N-UNCOUNT **Nutrition** is the process of taking and absorbing nutrients from food. ❑ *He offers nutrition advice to families.* [from Late Latin]

**nu|tri|tion|al** /nuˈtrɪʃənᵊl/ ADJ The **nutritional** content of food is all the substances that are in it which help you to remain healthy. ❑ *All the recipes include complete nutritional information.* • **nu|tri|tion|al|ly** ADV ❑ *...a nutritionally-balanced diet.* [from Late Latin]

**nu|tri|tious** /nuˈtrɪʃəs/ ADJ **Nutritious** food contains substances which help your body to be healthy. ❑ *It is important to eat enjoyable, nutritious foods.* [from Latin]

**ny|lon** /ˈnaɪlɒn/ N-UNCOUNT **Nylon** is a strong, flexible artificial fiber. ❑ *The chair is made of lightweight nylon.*

N

# Oo

**oak** /oʊk/ (**oaks**) N-VAR An **oak** or an **oak tree** is a large tree with strong, hard wood. ● **Oak** is the wood of this tree. [from Old English]

**oar** /ɔr/ (**oars**) N-COUNT Oars are long poles with a wide, flat blade at one end which are used for rowing a boat. [from Old English]
→ see **boat**

oar

**oasis** /oʊeɪsɪs/ (**oases** /oʊeɪsiz/) **1** N-COUNT An **oasis** is a small area in a desert where water and plants are found. **2** N-COUNT You can refer to a pleasant place or situation as an **oasis** when it is surrounded by unpleasant ones. ❑ *Gardens are an oasis in a busy city.* [from Latin]
→ see **desert**

**oath** /oʊθ/ (**oaths**) **1** N-COUNT An **oath** is a formal promise. ❑ *The soldiers take an oath to defend the country.* **2** N-SING In a court of law, when someone takes **the oath**, they make a formal promise to tell the truth. You can say that someone is **under oath** when they have made this promise. [from Old English]

**oat|meal** /oʊtmil/ N-UNCOUNT Oatmeal is a thick sticky food made from oats cooked in water or milk and eaten hot, especially for breakfast.

**oats** /oʊts/ N-PLURAL Oats are a cereal crop or its grains, used for making cookies or oatmeal, or for feeding animals. [from Old English]
→ see **grain**

**obe|di|ent** /oʊbidiənt/ ADJ A person or animal who is **obedient** does what they are told to do. ❑ *He was always obedient to his parents.* ● **obedi|ence** /oʊbidiəns/ N-UNCOUNT ❑ *...complete obedience to the law.* ● **obedi|ent|ly** ADV ❑ *The dog sat beside him obediently.* [from Old French]

**obese** /oʊbis/ ADJ If someone is **obese**, they are extremely fat. ❑ *Obese people often have more health problems than thinner people.* ● **obesity** /oʊbisiti/ N-UNCOUNT ❑ *Eating too much sugar can lead to obesity.* [from Latin]
→ see **diet, sugar**

**obey** /oʊbeɪ/ (**obeys, obeying, obeyed**) V-T/V-I If you **obey** a person, a command, or an instruction, you do what you are told to do. ❑ *Most people obey the law.* ❑ *It was his duty to obey.* [from Old French]

| **Word Partnership** | Use *obey* with : |
| --- | --- |
| N. | obey **a command**, obey **the law**, obey **orders**, obey **the rules** |
| V. | **refuse to** obey |

**ob/gyn** /oʊ bi dʒi waɪ ɛn/ (**ob/gyns**)
**1** N-UNCOUNT **Ob/gyn** is the branch of medicine that deals with women's medical conditions, pregnancy, and birth. **Ob/gyn** is an abbreviation for "obstetrics/gynecology." [INFORMAL]
**2** N-COUNT An **ob/gyn** is a doctor who specializes in women's medical conditions, pregnancy, and birth. **Ob/gyn** is an abbreviation for "obstetrician/gynecologist." [INFORMAL]

**obi|tu|ary** /oʊbɪtʃuɛri/ (**obituaries**) N-COUNT Someone's **obituary** is an account of their life and achievements which is published soon after they die. ❑ *I read his obituary in the newspaper.* [from Medieval Latin]

**ob|ject** (**objects, objecting, objected**)

> The noun is pronounced /ɒbdʒɪkt/. The verb is pronounced /əbdʒɛkt/.

**1** N-COUNT An **object** is anything that has a fixed shape or form, and that is not alive. ❑ *...everyday objects such as wooden spoons.* ❑ *...an object the shape of an orange.* **2** N-COUNT The **object** of what someone is doing is their aim or purpose. ❑ *The object of the event is to raise money.* **3** N-COUNT The **object** of a particular feeling or reaction is the person or thing that is directed toward or that causes it. ❑ *The object of her love was Bob Andrews.* **4** N-COUNT In grammar, the **object** of a verb or a preposition is the word or phrase which completes the structure begun by the verb or preposition. **5** → see also **direct object, indirect object** **6** V-T/V-I If you **object** to something, you express your dislike or disapproval of it. ❑ *A lot of people objected to the book.* ❑ *Cullen objected that he had too much work.* **7** PHRASE If you say that **money is no object** or **distance is no object**, you are emphasizing that you will spend as much money as necessary or travel whatever distance is required. ❑ *If money was no object, would you buy this car?* [Senses 1–5 and 7 from Late Latin. Sense 6 from Latin.]

| **Thesaurus** | *object* | Also look up : |
| --- | --- | --- |
| N. | item, thing **1** | |
| | aim, goal, intent **2** | |
| V. | argue, disagree, oppose, protest against **6** | |

| **Word Partnership** | Use *object* with : |
| --- | --- |
| ADJ. | **foreign** object, **inanimate** object, **moving** object, **solid** object **1** |
| N. | object **to** *someone/something* **6** |

**ob|jec|tion** /əbdʒɛkʃ°n/ (**objections**) N-VAR If you express or raise an **objection** to something, you say that you do not like it or agree with it. ❑ *I don't have any objection to banks making money.* [from Late Latin]

O

**ob|jec|tive** /əbdʒɛktɪv/ (**objectives**)
■ N-COUNT Your **objective** is what you are trying to achieve. ❑ *Our main objective was to find the child.* ■ ADJ **Objective** information is based on facts. ❑ *Give me some objective evidence and I'll believe it.* ● **ob|jec|tive|ly** ADV ❑ *We want to inform people objectively about events.* ● **ob|jec|tiv|ity** /ˌɒbdʒɛktɪvɪti/ N-UNCOUNT ❑ *Most people worry about the objectivity of research.* ■ ADJ If someone is **objective**, they base their opinions on facts rather than on their personal feelings. ❑ *A journalist should be completely objective.* ● **ob|jec|tive|ly** ADV ❑ *Try to see things more objectively.* ● **ob|jec|tiv|ity** N-UNCOUNT ❑ *Doctors must maintain objectivity.* [from Late Latin]

**ob|jec|tive lens** (**objective lenses**) N-COUNT The **objective lens** of a microscope is the lens that is closest to the object being observed and furthest from the eyepiece.

**ob|li|ga|tion** /ˌɒblɪɡeɪʃⁿn/ (**obligations**) ■ N-VAR If you have an **obligation to** do something, it is your duty to do it. ❑ *The judge has an obligation to find out the truth.* ■ N-VAR If you have an **obligation to** a person, it is your duty to take care of them. ❑ *...the United States' obligations to its own citizens.* [from Old French]

| **Thesaurus** | *obligation* Also look up : |
| --- | --- |
| N. | duty, responsibility ■ ■ |

| **Word Partnership** | Use *obligation* with : |
| --- | --- |
| V. | obligation **to pay** ■ |
| | **feel an** obligation, **fulfill an** obligation, |
| | **meet an** obligation ■ ■ |
| ADJ. | **legal** obligation, **moral** obligation ■ ■ |
| N. | **sense of** obligation ■ ■ |

**ob|liga|tory** /əblɪɡətɔri/ ADJ If something is **obligatory**, you must do it because of a rule or a law. ❑ *Medical tests are usually not obligatory.* [from Old French]

**oblige** /əblaɪdʒ/ (**obliges, obliging, obliged**) ■ V-T If you **are obliged to** do something, a situation, rule, or law makes it necessary for you to do it. ❑ *My family needed the money so I was obliged to work.* ■ V-T/V-I To **oblige** someone means to be helpful to them by doing what they have asked you to do. ❑ *If you ever need help, I'd be happy to oblige.* ❑ *They obliged with very simple answers.* [from Old French]

**oblig|ing** /əblaɪdʒɪŋ/ ADJ If you describe someone as **obliging**, you think that they are willing and eager to be helpful and you approve of this. [WRITTEN] ❑ *...a pleasant and obliging man.* ● **oblig|ing|ly** ADV ❑ *Ben obligingly held the door open.* [from Old French]

**oblique** /oublik/ ADJ An **oblique** statement is not expressed directly or openly, making it difficult to understand. ❑ *He made an oblique criticism of the president in his speech.* ● **oblique|ly** ADV ❑ *He obliquely referred to the U.S.* [from Old French]

**oblit|erate** /əblɪtəreɪt/ (**obliterates, obliterating, obliterated**) ■ V-T If something **obliterates** an object or place, it destroys it completely. ❑ *These weapons are powerful enough to obliterate the world.* ● **oblit|era|tion** /əblɪtəreɪʃⁿn/

N-UNCOUNT ❑ *...the obliteration of three rainforests.* ■ V-T If you **obliterate** a memory, emotion, or thought, you remove it completely from your mind. ❑ *She obliterated memories of her unhappy childhood.* [from Latin]

**obliv|ion** /əblɪviən/ ■ N-UNCOUNT **Oblivion** is the state of not being aware of what is happening around you. ❑ *She was so unhappy that she welcomed the oblivion of sleep.* ■ N-UNCOUNT **Oblivion** is the state of having been forgotten or of no longer being considered important. ❑ *The theory is likely to disappear into oblivion.* [from Old French]

**oblivi|ous** /əblɪviəs/ ADJ If you are **oblivious** to something or **oblivious** of it, you are not aware of it. ❑ *Tourists walked about, oblivious to the dangers around them.* [from Old French]

**ob|nox|ious** /əbnɒkʃəs/ ADJ If you describe someone as **obnoxious**, you think that he or she is very unpleasant or offensive. ❑ *John was obnoxious and so I left early.* [from Latin]

**obo** In advertisements, **obo** is used after a price to indicate that the person who is selling something is willing to accept slightly less money than the sum they have mentioned. **Obo** is a written abbreviation for "or best offer." ❑ *Family boat. $6,000 obo.*

**ob|scene** /əbsin/ ADJ If you describe something as **obscene**, you mean it offends you because it relates to sex or violence in an unpleasant and shocking way. ❑ *...obscene photographs.* [from Latin]

**ob|scen|ity** /əbsɛnɪti/ (**obscenities**) ■ N-UNCOUNT **Obscenity** is behavior, art, or language that is sexual and offends or shocks people. ❑ *These photos were obscenity not art.* ■ N-VAR An **obscenity** is a very offensive word or expression. ❑ *They shouted obscenities at us.* [from Latin]

**ob|scure** /əbskyʊər/ (**obscurer, obscurest, obscures, obscuring, obscured**) ■ ADJ If something or someone is **obscure**, they are unknown, or are known by only a few people. ❑ *The origin of the word is obscure.* ● **ob|scu|rity** N-UNCOUNT ❑ *She came from obscurity into the world of television.* ■ ADJ Something that is **obscure** is difficult to understand and deal with, usually because it involves so many parts or details. ❑ *The contracts are written in obscure language.* ● **ob|scu|rity** N-UNCOUNT ❑ *He was irritated by the obscurity of Henry's reply.* ■ V-T If one thing **obscures** another, it prevents it from being seen or heard properly. ❑ *Trees obscured his view of the scene.* [from Old French]

**ob|ser|va|tion** /ˌɒbzərveɪʃⁿn/ (**observations**) ■ N-UNCOUNT **Observation** is the action or process of carefully watching someone or something. ❑ *In the hospital she'll be under observation all the time.* ● **ob|ser|va|tion|al** ADJ ❑ *...observational studies of children.* ■ N-COUNT An **observation** is something that you have learned by seeing or watching something and thinking about it. ❑ *...observations about the causes of heart disease.* ■ N-COUNT If a person makes an **observation**, they make a comment about something or someone after watching how they behave. ❑ *He made the observation that life is full of difficulty.* ■ N-UNCOUNT **Observation** is the ability to notice things that are not usually noticed. ❑ *She*

*has good powers of observation.* [from Old French]
→ see **experiment, forecast, science**

### Word Partnership    Use *observation* with :

| | |
|---|---|
| PREP. | **by** observation, **through** observation, **under** observation ∎ |
| ADJ. | **careful** observation ∎ **direct** observation ∎ ∎ |
| V. | **make an** observation ∎ |

**ob|ser|va|tory** /əbzɜrvətɔri/ (**observatories**)
N-COUNT An **observatory** is a building with a large telescope from which you can study the stars and planets. [from French]

### Word Link    serv ≈ keeping : conserve, observe, preserve

**ob|serve** /əbzɜrv/ (**observes, observing, observed**) ∎ V-T If you **observe** a person or thing, you watch them carefully, especially in order to learn something about them. ▢ *Olson studied and observed the behavior of babies.* ∎ V-T If you **observe** someone or something, you see or notice them. [FORMAL] ▢ *He observed a red spot on his skin.* ∎ V-T If you **observe** something such as a law or custom, you obey it or follow it. ▢ *Drivers should observe speed limits.* ● **ob|ser|vance** (**observances**) N-VAR ▢ *...strict observance of laws.* [from Old French]

### Thesaurus    observe    Also look up :

| | |
|---|---|
| V. | study, watch ∎ detect, notice, spot ∎ |

### Word Partnership    Use *observe* with :

| | |
|---|---|
| N. | observe **behavior**, **opportunity to** observe ∎ ∎ observe **guidelines**, observe **rules** ∎ |

**ob|serv|er** /əbzɜrvər/ (**observers**) ∎ N-COUNT You can refer to someone who sees or notices something as an **observer**. ▢ *Observers say the woman stabbed him.* ∎ N-COUNT An **observer** is someone who studies current events and situations. ▢ *Observers say the president's decision will affect his popularity .* [from Old French]

**ob|sess** /əbsɛs/ (**obsesses, obsessing, obsessed**) V-T/V-I If something **obsesses** you or if you **obsess about** something, you keep thinking about it and find it difficult to think about anything else. ▢ *The idea of space travel has obsessed me all my life.* ▢ *She was obsessing about her weight.* ● **ob|sessed** ADJ ▢ *He was obsessed with crime movies.* [from Latin]

**ob|ses|sion** /əbsɛʃ°n/ (**obsessions**) N-VAR If you say that someone has an **obsession** with a person or thing, you think they are spending too much time thinking about them. ▢ *She tried to forget her obsession with Christopher.* [from Latin]

**ob|ses|sive** /əbsɛsɪv/ ADJ If your behavior is **obsessive**, you cannot stop doing a particular thing or behaving in a particular way. ▢ *Williams is obsessive about car racing.* ● **ob|ses|sive|ly** ADV ▢ *He worried obsessively about the future.* [from Latin]

**ob|so|lete** /ɒbsəlit/ ADJ Something that is **obsolete** is no longer needed because something better has been invented. ▢ *A lot of equipment becomes obsolete almost as soon as it's made.* [from Latin]

**ob|sta|cle** /ɒbstək°l/ (**obstacles**) N-COUNT An **obstacle** is an object that makes it difficult for you to go where you want to go, or to do something. ▢ *We came to our first major obstacle, a fallen tree across the road.* ▢ *The most difficult obstacle to overcome was the heavy rain.* [from Old French]

### Word Partnership    Use *obstacle* with :

| | |
|---|---|
| V. | **be an** obstacle, **hit an** obstacle, **overcome an** obstacle |
| ADJ. | **big/biggest** obstacle, **main** obstacle, **major** obstacle, **serious** obstacle |
| N. | obstacle **course**, obstacle **to peace** |

**ob|ste|tri|cian** /ɒbstətrɪʃ°n/ (**obstetricians**) N-COUNT An **obstetrician** is a doctor who is specially trained to deal with pregnancy and birth. [MEDICAL] → see **gynecologist** [from New Latin]

**ob|sti|nate** /ɒbstɪnɪt/ ADJ If you describe someone as **obstinate**, you are criticizing them because they are determined to do what they want, and cannot be persuaded to do something else. ▢ *When she says "no," nothing can make her change, and she can be very obstinate.* ● **ob|sti|nate|ly** ADV ▢ *Smith obstinately refused to carry out the order.* ● **ob|sti|na|cy** N-UNCOUNT ▢ *He, with his usual obstinacy, was determined to continue the conversation.* [from Latin]

**ob|struct** /əbstrʌkt/ (**obstructs, obstructing, obstructed**) ∎ V-T If something **obstructs** someone or something, it blocks their path, making it difficult for them to get past. ▢ *A group of cars obstructed the road.* ∎ V-T To **obstruct** progress or a process means to prevent it from happening properly. ▢ *The government is obstructing the investigation.* [from Latin]

**ob|struc|tion** /əbstrʌkʃ°n/ (**obstructions**) ∎ N-COUNT An **obstruction** is something that blocks a road or path. ▢ *The cars parked outside his house were causing an obstruction.* ∎ N-UNCOUNT **Obstruction** is the act of deliberately delaying something or preventing something from happening. ▢ *...the obstruction of government business.* [from Latin]

**ob|tain** /əbteɪn/ (**obtains, obtaining, obtained**) V-T To **obtain** something means to get it. [FORMAL] ▢ *Evans tried to obtain a false passport.* [from Old French]

### Word Partnership    Use *obtain* with :

| | |
|---|---|
| ADJ. | **able to** obtain, **difficult to** obtain, **easy to** obtain, **unable to** obtain |
| N. | obtain **approval**, obtain **a copy**, obtain **financing**, obtain **help**, obtain **information**, obtain **insurance**, obtain **permission**, obtain **weapons** |

**ob|vi|ous** /ɒbviəs/ ADJ If something is **obvious**, it is easy to see or understand. ▢ *It's obvious he's worried about us.* [from Latin]

### Thesaurus    obvious    Also look up :

| | |
|---|---|
| ADJ. | noticeable, plain, unmistakable |

O

## Word Partnership Use *obvious* with :

| | |
|---|---|
| N. | obvious **answer**, obvious **choice**, obvious **differences**, obvious **example**, obvious **question**, obvious **reasons**, obvious **solution** |
| ADV. | **fairly** obvious, **immediately** obvious, **less** obvious, **most** obvious, **painfully** obvious, **quite** obvious, **so** obvious |

**ob|vi|ous|ly** /ɒbviəsli/ **1** ADV You use **obviously** when you are stating something that you expect the person who is listening to know already. ◻ *Obviously I'll be disappointed if they don't come, but it wouldn't be a disaster.* **2** ADV You use **obviously** to indicate that something is easily noticed, seen, or recognized. ◻ *He obviously likes you very much.* [from Latin]

**oc|ca|sion** /əkeɪʒən/ (**occasions**) **1** N-COUNT An **occasion** is a time when something happens. ◻ *On one occasion he looked so sick that we took him to the hospital.* **2** N-COUNT An **occasion** is an important event, ceremony, or celebration. ◻ *The wedding was a happy occasion.* **3** N-COUNT An **occasion for** doing something is an opportunity for doing it. [FORMAL] ◻ *It is an occasion for all the family to celebrate.* [from Latin]

## Word Partnership Use *occasion* with :

| | |
|---|---|
| ADJ. | **festive** occasion, **historic** occasion, **rare** occasion, **solemn** occasion, **special** occasion **2** |
| V. | **mark an** occasion **2** |

**oc|ca|sion|al** /əkeɪʒənᵊl/ ADJ **Occasional** means happening sometimes, but not regularly or often. ◻ *I get occasional headaches.*
● **oc|ca|sion|al|ly** ADV ◻ *He misbehaves occasionally.* [from Latin]

**oc|cult** /əkʌlt, ɒkʌlt/ N-SING The **occult** is the knowledge and study of supernatural or magical forces. ◻ *He is interested in the occult.* [from Latin]

**oc|cu|pan|cy** /ɒkyəpənsi/ N-UNCOUNT **Occupancy** is the act of using a room, building, or area of land, usually for a fixed period of time. [FORMAL] ◻ *Hotel occupancy was as low as 40% in winter.* [from Old French]

## Word Link ant ≈ one who does, has : *defendant, dependant, occupant*

**oc|cu|pant** /ɒkyəpənt/ (**occupants**) N-COUNT The **occupants** of a building or room are the people who live or work there. ◻ *Almost all of the occupants left the building before the fire spread.* [from Old French]

**oc|cu|pa|tion** /ɒkyəpeɪʃən/ (**occupations**) **1** N-COUNT Your **occupation** is your job or profession. ◻ *I was looking for an occupation which was enjoyable.* ● **oc|cu|pa|tion|al** ADJ ◻ *...advertising people and other occupational groups.* **2** N-COUNT An **occupation** is something that you spend time doing, either for pleasure or because it needs to be done. ◻ *Mining is a dangerous occupation.* **3** N-UNCOUNT The **occupation** of a country happens when it is entered and controlled by a foreign army. ◻ *...the occupation of Poland from 1939 to 1945.* [from Old French]

**oc|cu|py** /ɒkyəpaɪ/ (**occupies, occupying, occupied**) **1** V-T The people who **occupy** a building or a place are the people who live or work there. ◻ *The company occupies the top floor of the building.* **2** V-T PASSIVE If a room or something such as a seat **is occupied**, someone is using it, so that it is not available for anyone else. ◻ *The armchair was occupied by his wife.* **3** V-T If an army **occupies** a place, they move into it, using force in order to gain control of it. ◻ *U.S. forces occupy a part of the country.* **4** V-T If someone or something **occupies** a particular place in a system, process, or plan, they have that place. ◻ *Managers occupy a position of power.* **5** V-T If something **occupies** you, or if you **occupy** yourself, your time, or your mind with it, you are busy doing it or thinking about it. ◻ *Her career occupies all of her time.* ◻ *He occupied himself all morning carefully loading the car.* ● **oc|cu|pied** ADJ ◻ *Keep your brain occupied.* [from Old French]

## Word Partnership Use *occupy* with :

| | |
|---|---|
| N. | occupy **a house**, occupy **land** **1** occupy **a place** **1** **3** **4** occupy **a position** **3** **4** occupy **an area**, **forces** occupy someplace, occupy **space**, **troops** occupy someplace **3** |

**oc|cur** /əkɜr/ (**occurs, occurring, occurred**) **1** V-I When something **occurs**, it happens. ◻ *The car crash occurred at night.* **2** V-I When something **occurs** in a particular place, it exists or is present there. ◻ *Snow showers will occur in the mountains today.* **3** V-I If a thought or idea **occurs to** you, you suddenly think of it or realize it. ◻ *Suddenly it occurred to her that the door might be open.* [from Latin]

## Thesaurus occur Also look up :

| | |
|---|---|
| V. | come about, develop, happen **1** dawn on, strike **3** |

## Word Partnership Use *occur* with :

| | |
|---|---|
| N. | **accidents** occur, **changes** occur, **deaths** occur, **diseases** occur, **events** occur, **injuries** occur, **problems** occur **1** |
| ADV. | **frequently** occur, **naturally** occur, **normally** occur, **often** occur, **usually** occur **1** – **3** |

**oc|cur|rence** /əkɜrəns/ (**occurrences**) N-COUNT An **occurrence** is something that happens. [FORMAL] ◻ *Complaints against the company were an everyday occurrence.* [from Latin]

**ocean** /oʊʃᵊn/ (**oceans**) **1** N-SING The **ocean** is the salty water that covers much of the Earth's surface. ◻ *...the beautiful sight of the ocean.* **2** N-COUNT An **ocean** is one of the five very large areas of salt water on the Earth's surface. ◻ *...the Pacific Ocean.* [from Old French]
→ see Word Web: **ocean**
→ see **beach, earth, river, ship, tide, whale**

**ocean|og|ra|phy** /oʊʃənɒgrəfi/ N-UNCOUNT **Oceanography** is the scientific study of sea currents, the ocean floor, and the fish and animals that live in the sea. [from Old French]

## Word Web ocean

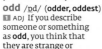

**Oceans** cover more than seventy-five percent of the earth. These huge bodies of **saltwater** are always moving. On the surface, the wind pushes the water into **waves**. At the same time, **currents** under the surface flow like rivers through the oceans. These currents are affected by the earth's rotation. It shifts them to the right in the northern hemisphere and to the left in the southern hemisphere. Other forces affect the oceans as well. For example, the gravitational pull of the moon and sun cause the **ebb** and **flow** of ocean **tides**.

---

**ocean trench** (**ocean trenches**) N-COUNT An **ocean trench** is a deep crack in the sea floor that forms when one section of the sea floor slides under another section. [TECHNICAL]

**o'clock** /əklɒk/ ADV You use **o'clock** after numbers from one to twelve to say what time it is. ❑ *I went to bed at ten o'clock last night so I didn't hear anything.*

### Usage o'clock

Use *o'clock* for times that are exactly on the hour: *"Is it four o'clock yet?" "Not quite, it's three forty-five."*

**Oc|to|ber** /ɒktoubər/ (**Octobers**) N-VAR **October** is the tenth month of the year in the Western calendar. ❑ *My sister got married in early October.* ❑ *They left on October 2.* [from Old English]

octopus

**oc|to|pus** /ɒktəpəs/ (**octopuses**) N-VAR An **octopus** is a soft sea creature with eight long arms called tentacles. [from New Latin]

**odd** /ɒd/ (**odder, oddest**) **1** ADJ If you describe someone or something as **odd**, you think that they are strange or unusual. ❑ *His behavior was odd.* ● **odd|ly** ADV ❑ *...an oddly shaped hill.* **2** ADJ You use **odd** before a noun to indicate that the type, size, or quality of something is not important. ❑ *We hear the odd car going by.* **3** ADV You use **odd** after a number to indicate that it is only approximate. [INFORMAL] ❑ *He appeared in sixty odd movies.* **4** ADJ **Odd** numbers, such as 3 and 17, are those which cannot be divided exactly by the number two. **5** ADJ You say that two things are **odd** when they do not belong to the same set or pair. ❑ *I'm wearing odd socks.* **6** PHRASE **The odd man out,** or **the odd one out** in a particular situation is the one that is different from the others. ❑ *Martin is becoming the odd man out in the company.* [from Old Norse] **7** → see also **odds**

### Thesaurus odd Also look up:

ADJ. bizarre, different, eccentric, peculiar, strange, unusual, weird; (*ant.*) normal, regular **1**

### Word Partnership Use *odd* with:

V. feel odd, look odd, seem odd, sound odd, **strike** *someone* as odd, think *something* odd **1**
N. odd **combination,** odd **thing 1** odd **job 2**
ADJ. odd **numbered 4**

**odd|ity** /ɒdɪti/ (**oddities**) N-COUNT An **oddity** is someone or something that is very strange. ❑ *After dinner there was another oddity: green lemonade.* [from Old Norse]

**odd jobs** N-PLURAL **Odd jobs** are various small jobs that have to be done in your home, such as cleaning or repairing things.

**odds** /ɒdz/ **1** N-PLURAL You refer to how likely something is to happen as the **odds** that it will happen. ❑ *What are the odds of finding a parking space right outside the door?* **2** PHRASE If someone is **at odds** with someone else, or if two people are **at odds,** they are disagreeing or arguing with each other. **3** PHRASE If something happens **against all odds,** it happens or succeeds although it seemed impossible or very unlikely. ❑ *...families who have stayed together against all odds.* [from Old Norse]

### Word Partnership Use *odds* with:

V. beat the odds **1**
N. odds **in** *someone's/something's* **favor,** odds **of winning 1**
PREP. the odds **of** *something* **1** at odds (**with** *someone*) **2** against all odds **3**

**odom|eter** /oudɒmɪtər/ (**odometers**) N-COUNT An **odometer** is a device in a vehicle which shows how far the vehicle has traveled. [from Greek]

**odor** /oudər/ (**odors**) N-VAR An **odor** is a smell. ❑ *...the odor of rotting fish.* [from Old French] → see **smell, taste**

**odor|less** /oudərlɪs/ ADJ An **odorless** substance has no smell. ❑ *...an odorless gas.* [from Old French]

**od|ys|sey** /ɒdɪsi/ (**odysseys**) N-COUNT An **odyssey** is a long, exciting journey on which a lot of things happen. [LITERARY] [from Latin]

**of** /əv, STRONG AV/ **1** PREP You use **of** to say who or what someone or something belongs to or is connected with. ❑ *...the luxury homes of rich people.* ❑ *...the new mayor of Los Angeles.* **2** PREP You use

O

**of** to say what something relates to or concerns. ❑ ...*her feelings of anger.* ❑ ...*a fracture of the skull.* **3** PREP You use **of** to say who or what a feeling or quality relates to. ❑ *I am very fond of Alec.* ❑ *She was guilty of lying to her mother.* **4** PREP You use **of** to talk about someone or something else who is involved in an action. ❑ *He was dreaming of her.* ❑ *People accused him of ignoring the problem.* **5** PREP You use **of** to show that someone or something is part of a larger group. ❑ *She is the youngest child of three.* **6** PREP You use **of** to talk about amounts or contents. ❑ ...*a rise of 13.8%.* ❑ ...*a glass of milk.* **7** PREP You use **of** to say how old someone or something is. ❑ *She is a young woman of twenty-six.* **8** PREP You use **of** to say the date when talking about what day of the month it is. ❑ ...*the 4th of July.* **9** PREP You use **of** to say when something happened. ❑ ...*the mistakes of the past.* ❑ *Rene is retiring at the end of the month.* **10** PREP You use **of** to say what substance or materials something is formed from. ❑ ...*a mixture of flour and water.* **11** PREP You use **of** to say what caused or is causing a person's or animal's death. ❑ *He died of a heart attack.* **12** PREP You use **of** to talk about someone's qualities or characteristics. ❑ *Andrew is a man of great intelligence.* **13** PREP You use **of** to describe someone's behavior. ❑ *It's very kind of you to help.* **14** PREP You can use **of** to say what time it is by indicating how many minutes there are before the hour mentioned. ❑ *It's a quarter of eight.* [from Old English]

**of course** **1** ADV You say **of course** to suggest that something is not surprising because it is normal, obvious, or well-known. [SPOKEN] ❑ *Of course there were lots of interesting things to see.* **2** CONVENTION You use **of course** as a polite way of giving permission. [SPOKEN] ❑ *"Can I ask you something?" — "Yes, of course."* **3** ADV You use **of course** in order to emphasize a statement that you are making. [SPOKEN] ❑ *Of course I'm not afraid!* **4** CONVENTION **Of course not** is an emphatic way of saying no. [SPOKEN] ❑ *"You're not going to go, are you?" — "No, of course not."*

---

**off**

① AWAY FROM
② OTHER USES

---

In addition to the uses shown below, **off** is used after some verbs and nouns in order to introduce extra information. **Off** is also used in phrasal verbs such as "get off," "pair off," and "sleep off."

**① off**

The preposition is pronounced /ɔf/. The adverb is pronounced /ɔf/.

**1** PREP If something is taken **off** something else or moves **off** it, it is no longer touching that thing. ❑ *He took his feet off the desk.* ● **Off** is also an adverb. ❑ *I broke off a piece of chocolate and ate it.* **2** PREP When you get **off** a bus, train, or plane, you come out of it. ❑ *Don't get on or off a moving train!* ● **Off** is also an adverb. ❑ *At the next station the man got off.* **3** PREP If you keep **off** a street or piece of land, you do not go there. ❑ *The police told visitors to keep off the beach.* ● **Off** is also an adverb. ❑ *A sign on the grass said "Keep Off."* **4** PREP If something is situated **off** a place such as a coast, room, or road, it is near to it or next to it, but not exactly in it. ❑ *The boat*

*was sailing off the northern coast.* ❑ ...*a house just off Park Avenue.* **5** ADV If you go **off**, you leave a place. ❑ *He was just about to drive off.* ❑ *She is off to Spain tomorrow.* **6** ADV If you have time **off** or a particular day **off**, you do not go to work or school, for example, because you are sick or it is a day when you do not usually work. ❑ *She had the day off.* ❑ *I'm off tomorrow.* ● **Off** is also a preposition. ❑ *He could not get time off work to go on vacation.* **7** ADV If something is a long time **off**, it will not happen for a long time. ❑ *An end to the war seems a long way off.*

**② off**

The preposition is pronounced /ɔf/. The adverb is pronounced /ɔf/.

**1** ADV If something such as an agreement or a sports event is **off**, it is canceled. ❑ *The deal's off.* **2** PREP If you are **off** something, you have stopped using it or liking it. ❑ *I'm off coffee at the moment.* ❑ *The doctor took her off the medicine.* **3** ADV When something such as a machine or electric light is **off**, it is not functioning or in use. ❑ *Her bedroom light was off.* ❑ *We turned the engine off to save fuel.* **4** PHRASE If something happens **on and off**, or **off and on**, it happens occasionally, or only for part of a period of time, not in a regular or continuous way. ❑ *I work on and off as a waitress.*

**of|fal** /ɔfᵊl/ N-UNCOUNT **Offal** is the liver, kidneys, and other internal organs of animals, used for food. [from German]

**off-balance** also **off balance** ADJ If someone or something is **off-balance**, they can easily fall or be knocked over because they are not standing firmly.

**off-center** **1** ADJ If something is **off-center**, it is not exactly in the middle of a space or surface. ❑ ...*an off-center smile.* **2** ADJ If you describe someone or something as **off-center**, you mean that they are less conventional than other people or things. ❑ *David's writing is too off-center to be popular.*

**off-color** ADJ An **off-color** joke or remark is rude or offensive.

---

**Word Link** *fend ≈ striking : de*fend, *fender,* off*end*

---

**of|fend** /əfɛnd/ (**offends, offending, offended**) **1** V-T/V-I If you **offend** someone, you say or do something which upsets or embarrasses them. ❑ *I'm sorry if I offended you.* ❑ *Do not use words that are likely to offend.* ● **of|fend|ed** ADJ ❑ *He was very offended by her comments.* **2** V-I If someone **offends**, they commit a crime. [FORMAL] ❑ *Women are less likely to offend than men.* ● **of|fend|er** (**offenders**) N-COUNT ❑ *Should the public be told when an offender leaves prison?* [from Old French]

**of|fense** /əfɛns/ (**offenses**)

Pronounced /ɔfɛns/ for meaning **3**.

**1** N-COUNT An **offense** is a crime that breaks a particular law. ❑ *There is a fine of $1,000 for a first offense.* **2** N-VAR **Offense** or an **offense** is behavior that causes people to be upset or embarrassed. ❑ *He didn't mean to cause offense.* **3** N-SING In sports such as football or basketball, **the offense** is the team which has possession of the ball and is trying to score. **4** PHRASE If you **take offense**, you are upset by something that someone says or does. ❑ *Instead of taking offense, the woman smiled.*

## Picture Dictionary office

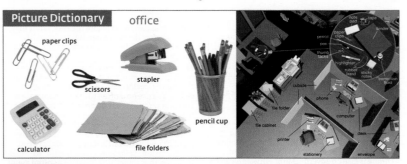

paper clips

stapler

scissors

pencil cup

calculator

file folders

### Thesaurus    offense    Also look up :

N.  crime, infraction, violation, wrongdoing **1**
    assault, attack, insult, snub **2**

### Word Partnership    Use *offense* with :

ADJ.  **criminal** offense **1**
      **serious** offense **1** **2**
V.    **commit an** offense **1** **2**
      **take** offense **4**

**of|fen|sive** /əfɛnsɪv/ (**offensives**) **1** ADJ Something that is **offensive** upsets or embarrasses people because it is rude or insulting. ❑ *Some people thought the play was offensive.* **2** N-COUNT A military **offensive** is a carefully planned attack made by a large group of soldiers. **3** ADJ In sports such as football or basketball, the **offensive** team is the team which has possession of the ball and is trying to score. **4** PHRASE If you **go on the offensive**, or **take the offensive**, you begin to take strong action against people who have been attacking you.

### Word Partnership    Use *offensive* with :

N.  offensive **language** **1**
V.  **launch an** offensive,
    **mount an** offensive **2**
    **take the** offensive **4**

**of|fer** /ɔfər/ (**offers, offering, offered**) **1** V-T If you **offer** something to someone, you ask them if they would like to have it or use it. ❑ *He offered his seat to the young woman.* ❑ *She offered him a cup of tea.* **2** V-T If you **offer to** do something, you say that you are willing to do it. ❑ *Peter offered to teach me to drive.* **3** N-COUNT An **offer** is something that someone says they will give you or do for you. ❑ *I hope you will accept my offer of help.* **4** N-COUNT An **offer** in a store is a specially low price for something or something extra that you get if you buy a certain product. ❑ *There's a special offer on computers.* **5** V-T If you **offer** a particular amount of money for something, you say that you will pay that much to buy it. ❑ *He offered $5,000 for the car.* **6** [from Old English]

**of|fer|ing** /ɔfərɪŋ/ (**offerings**) N-COUNT An **offering** is something that is being sold. ❑ *The meal was much better than offerings in many other restaurants.* [from Old English]

**of|fice** /ɔfɪs/ (**offices**) **1** N-COUNT An **office** is a room or a part of a building where people work sitting at desks. ❑ *Flynn arrived at his office.* **2** N-COUNT An **office** is a department of an organization, especially the government, where people deal with a particular kind of administrative work. ❑ *...the Congressional Budget Office.* **3** N-COUNT An **office** is a small building or room where people can go for information, tickets, or a service of some kind. ❑ *...the tourist office.* **4** N-COUNT A doctor's or dentist's **office** is a place where a doctor or dentist sees their patients. **5** N-UNCOUNT If someone holds **office** in a government, they have an important job or position of authority. ❑ *The events marked the president's four years in office.* [from Old French] **6** → see also **box office, post office**
→ see Picture Dictionary: **office**

**of|fice build|ing** (**office buildings**) N-COUNT An **office building** is a large building that contains offices.

**of|fic|er** /ɔfɪsər/ (**officers**) **1** N-COUNT In the armed forces, an **officer** is a person in a position of authority. ❑ *...an army officer.* **2** N-COUNT; N-VOC Members of the police force can be referred to as **officers**. ❑ *The officer saw no sign of a robbery.* ❑ *Officer Montoya was the first on the scene.* **3** N-COUNT An **officer** is a person who has a responsible position in an organization, especially a government organization. ❑ *...chief executive officer of Boeing Commercial Airplanes.* [from Old French] **4** → see also **police officer, probation officer**

**of|fi|cial** /əfɪʃᵊl/ (**officials**) **1** ADJ **Official** means approved by the government or by someone in authority. ❑ *...the official unemployment figures.* ● **of|fi|cial|ly** ADV ❑ *The election results have not yet been officially announced.* **2** ADJ **Official** activities are carried out by a person in authority as part of their job. ❑ *The president is in Brazil for an official visit.* **3** ADJ **Official** things are used by a person in authority as part of their job. ❑ *...the White House, the official residence of the U.S. president.* **4** N-COUNT An **official** is a person who holds a position of authority in an organization. ❑ *...a senior United Nations official.* [from Middle English]

### Thesaurus    official    Also look up :

ADJ.  authentic, formal, legitimate, valid; (*ant.*) unauthorized, unofficial **1**
N.    administrator, director, executive, manager **4**

### Word Partnership  Use *official* with :

N.  official **documents**, official **language**, official **report**, official **sources**, official **statement** ◼
administration official, **city** official, **government** official ◼

ADJ.  **elected** official, **federal** official, **local** official, **military** official, **senior** official, **top** official ◼

**off|line** /ˈɒflaɪn/ ADJ If a computer is **offline**, it is not connected to the Internet. Compare **online**. [COMPUTING] ❑ *The system was offline for a few days.* ● **Offline** is also an adverb. ❑ *Most software programs allow you to write e-mails offline.*

**off-peak** ADJ You use **off-peak** to describe something that happens or that is used at times when there is the least demand for it. Prices at off-peak times are often lower than at other times. ● **Off-peak** is also an adverb. ❑ *Calls cost 36 cents per minute off-peak.*

**off-ramp** (**off-ramps**) N-COUNT An **off-ramp** is a road which cars use to drive off a highway.

**off|set** /ˈɒfsɛt/ (**offsets, offsetting**)

The form **offset** is used in the present tense and is the past tense and past participle of the verb.

V-T If one thing **is offset** by another, the effect of the first thing is reduced by the second, so that any advantage or disadvantage is canceled out. ❑ *The increase in costs was offset by higher sales.*

**off|shoot** /ˈɒfʃuːt/ (**offshoots**) N-COUNT If one thing is an **offshoot** of another, it has developed from that other thing. ❑ *The magazine is an offshoot of "People" magazine.*

**off|shore** /ɒfˈʃɔːr/ ADJ **Offshore** means situated or happening in the ocean, near the coast. ❑ *...the offshore oil industry.* ● **Offshore** is also an adverb. ❑ *A ship anchored offshore.*

**off|side** /ɒfˈsaɪd/ also **off-side** ◼ ADJ In football, a player is **offside** if they cross the line of scrimmage before a play begins. ◼ ADJ In games such as soccer or hockey, when an attacking player is **offside**, they have broken the rules by moving too far forward. ● **Offside** is also an adverb. ❑ *Yoon was standing at least ten yards offside.*

**off|spring** /ˈɒfsprɪŋ/

**Offspring** is both the singular and the plural form.

N-COUNT You can refer to a person's children or to an animal's young as their **offspring**. [FORMAL] ❑ *Eleanor was worried about her offspring.*

**of|ten** /ˈɒfⁿn/

**Often** is usually used before the verb, but it may be used after the verb when it has a word like "less" or "more" before it, or when the clause is negative.

◼ ADV If something **often** happens, it happens many times or much of the time. ❑ *They often spend the weekend together.* ❑ *That doesn't happen very often.* ◼ ADV You use **how often** to ask questions about frequency. You also use **often** in statements to give information about the frequency of something. ❑ *How often do you brush your teeth?* ◼ PHRASE If something happens **every so often**, it happens regularly, but with fairly long periods between each occasion. ❑ *She visited every so often.* ◼ PHRASE If you say that something happens **as often as not**, or **more often than not**, you mean that it happens fairly frequently, and that this can be considered as typical. ❑ *As often as not, they argue.*

### Thesaurus  often  Also look up :

ADV.  regularly, repeatedly, usually; (*ant.*) never, rarely, seldom ◼

**often|times** /ˈɒfⁿntaɪmz/ ADV If something **oftentimes** happens, it happens many times or much of the time. ❑ *Oftentimes, I didn't even return his calls.*

**oh** /oʊ/ ◼ CONVENTION You use **oh** to introduce a response or a comment on something that has just been said. [SPOKEN] ❑ *"Have you spoken to her about it?"* — *"Oh yes."* ◼ EXCLAM You use **oh** to express a feeling such as surprise, pain, annoyance, or happiness. [SPOKEN] ❑ *"Oh!" Kenny said. "Has everyone gone?"* ◼ CONVENTION You use **oh** when you are hesitating while speaking, for example, because you are trying to estimate something, or because you are searching for the right word. [SPOKEN] ❑ *I've been here, oh, since the end of June.*

**oil** /ɔɪl/ ◼ N-VAR **Oil** is a smooth, thick liquid that is used as a fuel and for making the parts of machines move smoothly. Oil is found underground. ❑ *The company buys and sells 600,000 barrels of oil a day.* ◼ V-T If you **oil** something, you put oil onto or into it, for example, to make it work smoothly or to protect it. ❑ *He oiled the lock on the door.* ◼ N-VAR **Oil** is a smooth, thick liquid made from plants and is often used for cooking. ❑ *...olive oil.* [from Old French] ◼ → see also **crude oil, olive oil** ◼ to **burn the midnight oil** → see **midnight**
→ see **petroleum, ship**
→ see Word Web: **oil**

### Word Web  oil

There is a great demand for **petroleum** in the world today. Companies are always **drilling oil wells** in **oilfields** on land and on the ocean floor. In the ocean, drilling **rigs** or **oil platforms** sit on concrete or metal foundations on man-made islands. Others float on ships. The **crude oil** from these wells goes to **refineries** through **pipelines** or in huge **tanker** ships. At the refinery, the crude oil is processed into a variety of products including **gasoline, aviation fuel**, and **plastics**.

**oil paint** (**oil paints**) N-VAR **Oil paint** is a thick paint used by artists.

**oil paint|ing** (**oil paintings**) N-COUNT An **oil painting** is a picture which has been painted using oil paints.

**oil slick** (**oil slicks**) N-COUNT An **oil slick** is a layer of oil that is floating on the ocean or on a lake because it has accidentally come out of a ship or container.

**oily** /ˈɔɪli/ (**oilier, oiliest**) ADJ Something that is **oily** is covered with oil, contains oil, or looks, feels, or tastes like oil. ❑ He wiped his hands on an oily rag. ❑ Paul thought the sauce was too oily. [from Old French]

**oint|ment** /ˈɔɪntmənt/ (**ointments**) N-VAR An **ointment** is a smooth, thick substance that is put on sore skin or a wound to help it heal. ❑ Ointments are available for the treatment of skin problems. [from Old French]

**OJ** /ˌoʊ ˈdʒeɪ/ N-UNCOUNT **OJ** is the same as **orange juice**. [INFORMAL]

**okay** /ˌoʊˈkeɪ/ (**okays**) also **OK, O.K., ok** **1** ADJ If you say that something is **okay**, you find it acceptable. [INFORMAL] ❑ …Is it OK to talk now? ❑ Is it okay if I go by myself? ● **Okay** is also an adverb. ❑ We seemed to manage okay. **2** ADJ If you say that someone is **okay**, you mean that they are safe and well. [INFORMAL] ❑ Check that the baby's okay. **3** CONVENTION You can say **"Okay"** to show that you agree to something. [INFORMAL] ❑ "Just tell him I'm here." — "OK." **4** CONVENTION You can say **"Okay?"** to check whether the person you are talking to understands what you have said and accepts it. [INFORMAL] ❑ We'll meet next week, OK?

**okey do|key** /ˌoʊki ˈdoʊki/ also **okey doke** CONVENTION **Okey dokey** is used in the same way as **"OK"** to show that you agree to something, or that you want to start talking about something else or doing something else. [INFORMAL, SPOKEN] ❑ Okey dokey. I'll call you tomorrow.

**old** /oʊld/ (**older, oldest**) **1** ADJ Someone who is **old** has lived for many years and is no longer young. ❑ …an old man. ● **The old** are people who are old. ❑ …the needs of the old. **2** ADJ You use **old** to talk or ask about the age of someone or something. ❑ He is three months old. ❑ How old are you now? **3** ADJ Something that is **old** has existed for a long time. ❑ …the big old house. ❑ These books look very old. **4** ADJ Something that is **old** is no longer in good condition because of its age or because it has been used a lot. ❑ …his old jeans. **5** ADJ You use **old** to refer to something that is no longer used, that no longer exists, or that has been replaced by something else. ❑ Grass covered the old road. **6** ADJ You use **old** to refer to something that used to belong to you, or to a person or thing that used to have a particular role in your life. ❑ You can stay in your old room. ❑ I still remember my old school. **7** ADJ An **old** friend, enemy, or rival is someone who has been your friend, enemy, or rival for a long time. ❑ I called my old friend John Horner. **8** PHRASE You use **any old** to emphasize that the quality or type of something is not important. [INFORMAL] ❑ On Sundays I wear any old thing that's comfortable. ❑ But not any old peanut butter is good enough for U.S. troops — it's made specially for them in Georgia. [from Old English] **9** **good old** → see **good** **10** to **settle an old score** → see **score**

**old age** N-UNCOUNT Your **old age** is the period of years toward the end of your life. ❑ They didn't have much money in their old age.

**old-fashioned** ADJ Something that is **old-fashioned** is no longer used, done, or believed by most people, because it has been replaced by something more modern. ❑ The house was old-fashioned and in bad condition.

**Old Glo|ry** N-UNCOUNT People sometimes refer to the flag of the United States as **Old Glory**.

**old-timer** (**old-timers**) N-COUNT An old man is sometimes referred to as an **old-timer**. [INFORMAL] ❑ The old-timers used to talk about their early childhoods.

**old world** also **Old World, old-world** ADJ **Old world** is used to describe places and things that are or seem to be from an earlier period of history, and that look interesting or attractive. ❑ The village's Old World charm attracted many visitors.

**ol|ive** /ˈɒlɪv/ (**olives**) **1** N-VAR **Olives** are small green or black fruits with a bitter taste. **2** N-COUNT An **olive tree** or an **olive** is a tree on which olives grow. **3** COLOR Something that is **olive** is yellowish-green in color. [from Old French]

**ol|ive oil** (**olive oils**) N-VAR **Olive oil** is oil used in cooking that is obtained by pressing olives.

**Olym|pic** /əˈlɪmpɪk/ (**Olympics**) **1** ADJ **Olympic** means relating to the Olympic Games. ❑ …the Olympic champion. **2** N-PROPER **The Olympics** are the Olympic Games. [from Latin]

**Olym|pic Games** N-PROPER **The Olympic Games** are a set of international sports competitions which take place every four years, each time in a different city.

**ome|let** /ˈɒmlɪt, ˈɒmələt/ (**omelets**) also **omelette** N-COUNT An **omelet** is a type of food made by beating eggs and cooking them in a frying pan. ❑ I had a cheese omelet for lunch. [from French]
→ see **egg**

**omen** /ˈoʊmən/ (**omens**) N-COUNT If you say that something is an **omen**, you think it indicates what is likely to happen in the future and whether it will be good or bad. ❑ He told himself that his dream was a good omen. [from Latin]

**omi|nous** /ˈɒmɪnəs/ ADJ If you describe something as **ominous**, you mean that it worries you because it makes you think that something bad is going to happen. ❑ There was an ominous silence after he spoke. ● **omi|nous|ly** ADV ❑ The house was ominously quiet in the middle of the night. [from Latin]

**omis|sion** /oʊˈmɪʃᵊn/ (**omissions**) N-VAR **Omission** is the act of not including something or not doing something. ❑ …the omission of information from the list. [from Latin]

**omit** /oʊˈmɪt/ (**omits, omitting, omitted**) **1** V-T If you **omit** something, you do not include it in an activity or piece of work. ❑ Omit the salt in this recipe. **2** V-T If you **omit to** do something, you do not do it. [FORMAL] ❑ *He omitted to mention his friend's name.* [from Latin]

| **Thesaurus** | *omit* | Also look up : |
| --- | --- | --- |
| v. | forget, leave out, miss; *(ant.)* add, include ◼ | |

**om|ni|vore** /ɒmnɪvɔr/ (**omnivores**) N-COUNT An **omnivore** is an animal that eats all kinds of food, including both meat and plants. Compare **carnivore**, **herbivore**. [TECHNICAL] [from Latin]

---
on
---

❶ DESCRIBING POSITIONS AND LOCATIONS
❷ TALKING ABOUT HOW OR WHEN SOMETHING HAPPENS
❸ OTHER USES
❹ PHRASES

In addition to the uses shown below, **on** is used after some verbs, nouns, and adjectives in order to introduce extra information. **On** is also used in phrasal verbs such as "keep on" and "sign on."

❶ **on**

The preposition is pronounced /ɒn/. The adverb and the adjective are pronounced /ɒn/.

◼ PREP If someone or something is **on** a surface or object, the surface or object is immediately below them and is supporting their weight. ❑ *He sat beside her on the sofa.* ❑ *On top of the cupboard was a basket.* ◼ PREP If something is **on** a surface or object, it is stuck to it or attached to it. ❑ *…the paint on the door.* ❑ *…the clock on the wall.* ◼ ADV When you put a piece of clothing **on**, you place it over part of your body in order to wear it. If you have it **on**, you are wearing it. ❑ *He put his coat on.* ◼ PREP You can say that you have something **on** you if you are carrying it in your pocket or in a purse. ❑ *I didn't have any money on me.* ◼ PREP If you get **on** a bus, train, or plane, you go into it in order to travel somewhere. If you are **on** it, you are traveling in it. ❑ *We got on the plane.* [from Old English] → see **location**

❷ **on**

The preposition is pronounced /ɒn/. The adverb and the adjective are pronounced /ɒn/.

◼ PREP If something is done **on** an instrument or a machine, it is done using that instrument or machine. ❑ *I played these songs on the piano.* ◼ PREP If something is being broadcast, you can say that it is **on** the radio or television. ❑ *What's on TV?* ◼ ADJ When an activity is taking place, you can say that it is **on**. ❑ *There's an exciting game on right now.* ◼ ADV You use **on** in expressions such as **"have a lot going on"** and **"not have very much on"** to indicate how busy someone is. [SPOKEN] ❑ *I have a lot going on next week.* ◼ PREP If something happens **on** a particular day or date, that is when it happens. ❑ *This year's event will be on June 19th.* ❑ *We'll see you on Tuesday.* ◼ PREP You use **on** when mentioning an event that was followed by another one. ❑ *She waited to welcome her children on their arrival from Vancouver.* ◼ ADV You use **on** to say that someone is continuing to do something. ❑ *They walked on for a while.* ❑ *We worked on into the night.* [from Old English]

❸ **on**

The preposition is pronounced /ɒn/. The adverb and the adjective are pronounced /ɒn/.

◼ PREP Books, discussions, or ideas **on** a particular subject are concerned with that subject. ❑ *…advice on health.* ❑ *There was no information on the cause of the crash.* ◼ ADV When something such as a machine or an electric light is **on**, it is functioning or in use. ❑ *The light was on.* ❑ *The heat was turned off. I've turned it on again.* ◼ PREP If you are **on** a committee or council, you are a member of it. ❑ *Claire and Alita were on the organizing committee.* ◼ PREP Someone who is **on** a drug takes it regularly. ❑ *She was on antibiotics for an eye infection.* ◼ PREP When you spend time or energy **on** a particular activity, you spend time or energy doing it. ❑ *Some children spend a lot of time on computer games.* ❑ *I won't waste time on guys like him.* [from Old English]

❹ **on** /ɒn/ ◼ **on behalf of** → see **behalf** ◼ **on and off** → see **off** ◼ **and so on** → see **so** ◼ **on top of** → see **top**

**on board** also **onboard**, **on-board** ADJ If a person or group of people is **on board**, they support you and agree with what you are doing. ❑ *We want everyone to be on board for making changes.*

**once** /wʌns/ ◼ ADV If something happens **once**, it happens one time only. ❑ *I met Miquela once, briefly.* ❑ *The baby hasn't once slept through the night.* ◼ ADV If something was **once** true, it was true at some time in the past, but is no longer true. ❑ *Her parents once owned a store.* ❑ *I lived in Paris once.* ◼ CONJ If something happens **once** another thing has happened, it happens immediately afterward. ❑ *The decision was easy once he read the letter.* ◼ PHRASE If you do something **at once**, you do it immediately. ❑ *I have to go at once.* ◼ PHRASE If a number of different things happen **at once** or **all at once**, they all happen at the same time. ❑ *You can't do both things at once.* ◼ PHRASE **For once** is used to emphasize that something happens on this particular occasion, that it has never happened before, and may never happen again. ❑ *For once, Dad is not complaining.* ◼ PHRASE If something happens **once and for all**, it happens completely or finally. ❑ *We must solve the problem once and for all.* ◼ PHRASE If something happens **once in a while**, it happens sometimes, but not very often. ❑ *Everyone feels sad once in a while.*

---
one
---

❶ NUMBER
❷ PRONOUN AND DETERMINER USES
❸ PHRASES

❶ **one** /wʌn/ (**ones**) NUM **One** is the number 1. ❑ *They have one daughter.* ❑ *…one thousand years ago.* [from Old English]

❷ **one** /wʌn/ (**ones**) ◼ DET You can use **one** to refer to the first of two or more things that you are comparing. ❑ *Prices vary from one store to another.* ● **One** is also a pronoun. ❑ *The twins wore different clothes and one was thinner than the other.* ◼ PRON You can use **one** or **ones** instead of a noun when it is clear what type of thing or person you are referring to and you are describing them or giving more information about them. ❑ *They are selling* their house and moving to a smaller one. **3** DET You can use **one** when referring to a time in the past or in the future. For example, if you say that you did something **one day**, you mean that you did it on a day in the past. ❑ *Would you like to go out one night?* **4** one day → see day **5** PRON Speakers and writers sometimes use **one** to make statements about people in general which also apply to themselves. **One** can be used as the subject or object of a sentence. [FORMAL] ❑ *If one thinks about it, a lot of good things are happening in the world.* [from Old English]

**❸ one** /wʌn/ **1** PHRASE You use **one or other** to refer to one or more things or people in a group, when it does not matter which particular one or ones are thought of or chosen. ❑ *One or other of the two women was wrong.* **2** PHRASE **One or two** means a few. ❑ *We made one or two changes.* [from Old English] **3** one another → see another **4** one thing after another → see another **5** of one mind → see mind **6** in one piece → see piece

**one-of-a-kind** ADJ You use **one-of-a-kind** to describe something that is unique because there is nothing else exactly like it. ❑ *…a small one-of-a-kind publisher.*

**one-on-one** ADJ In a **one-on-one** relationship, one person deals directly with only one other person. ❑ *…one-on-one training.* ● **One-on-one** is also an adverb. ❑ *She wanted to talk to people one-on-one.*

**one-point per|spec|tive** (**one-point perspectives**) N-COUNT A **one-point perspective** is a method of drawing or painting something in which you create the appearance of three dimensions by using slanting lines that appear to meet at a point on the horizon. [TECHNICAL]

**on|er|ous** /ɒnərəs, oʊnər-/ ADJ If you describe a task as **onerous**, you dislike having to do it because you find it difficult or unpleasant. [FORMAL] ❑ *…the onerous work of caring for a child.* [from Latin]

**one's** /wʌnz/ **1** DET Speakers and writers use **one's** to indicate that something belongs or relates to people in general, or to themselves in particular. [FORMAL] ❑ *It is natural to care for one's family and one's children.* **2** **One's** can be used as a spoken form of "one is" or "one has," especially when "has" is an auxiliary verb. ❑ *No one's going to hurt you.* → see one [from Old English]

**one|self** /wʌnsɛlf/

**Oneself** is a third person singular reflexive pronoun.

PRON A speaker or writer uses **oneself** to refer to themselves, or to any person in general. [FORMAL] ❑ *To work one must have time to oneself.*

**one-shot** ADJ A **one-shot** thing is made or happens only once. ❑ *This is not a one-shot deal.*

**one-sided** **1** ADJ If you say that an activity or relationship is **one-sided**, you think that one of the people or groups involved does much more than the other or is much stronger than the other. ❑ *The conversation was completely one-sided.* **2** ADJ If you describe someone as **one-sided**, you are critical of what they say or do because you think it shows that they have considered only one side of an issue or event. ❑ *The government is being one-sided.*

**one-time** also **onetime** **1** ADJ **One-time** is used to describe something which happened in the past, or something such as a job or position which someone used to have. ❑ *…Al Gore, the one-time presidential candidate.* **2** ADJ A **one-time** thing is made or happens only once. ❑ *…a one-time charge.*

**one-way** **1** ADJ In **one-way** streets or traffic systems, vehicles can only travel along in one direction. **2** ADJ A **one-way** ticket or fare is for a trip from one place to another, but not back again. ❑ *…a one-way ticket from New York to Los Angeles.* ● **One-way** is also an adverb. ❑ *The fare is $80 one-way.*

**on|going** /ɒngoʊɪŋ/ ADJ An **ongoing** situation has been happening for quite a long time and seems likely to continue. ❑ *There is an ongoing debate on the issue.*

**on|ion** /ʌnyən/ (**onions**) N-VAR An **onion** is a round vegetable with a light brown skin. It has a strong, sharp smell and taste. [from Old French] → see spice, vegetable

**on|line** /ɒnlaɪn/ also **on-line** **1** ADV If a company goes **online**, its services become available on the Internet. [BUSINESS, COMPUTING] ● **Online** is also an adjective. ❑ *…an online shopping center.* **2** ADJ If you are **online**, your computer is connected to the Internet. Compare **offline**. [COMPUTING] ❑ *You can chat to other people who are online.* ● **Online** is also an adverb. ❑ *…the things you can buy online.* **3** on line → see line

**on|look|er** /ɒnlʊkər/ (**onlookers**) N-COUNT An **onlooker** is someone who watches an event but does not take part in it. ❑ *A group of onlookers stood and watched the fight.*

---

**only**

❶ ADVERB AND ADJECTIVE USES
❷ CONJUNCTION
❸ PHRASES

**❶ only** /oʊnli/

In written English, **only** is usually placed immediately before the word it qualifies. In spoken English, however, you can use stress to indicate what **only** qualifies, so its position is not so important.

**1** ADV You use **only** to indicate the one thing that is true, appropriate, or necessary in a particular situation, in contrast to all the other things that are not. ❑ *It's a decision only the president can make.* ❑ *You can only start a business if you have enough money.* **2** ADV You use **only** to introduce the thing which must happen before the thing mentioned in the main part of the sentence can happen. ❑ *The lawyer is paid only if he wins.* **3** ADJ If you talk about **the only** person or thing involved in a particular situation, you mean there are no others involved in it. ❑ *She was the only woman in the department.* **4** ADJ An **only** child is a child who has no brothers or sisters. **5** ADV You use **only** to

O

indicate that something is unimportant. ❑ *It's only an idea.* ❑ *I'm only a sergeant.* **6** ADV You use **only** to emphasize how small an amount is or how short a length of time is. ❑ *The movie only cost $3.99 to rent.* **7** ADV You can use **only** in the expressions **I only wish** or **I only hope** in order to emphasize what you are hoping or wishing. ❑ *I only hope he knows what he's doing.* **8** ADV You can use **only** before an infinitive to introduce an event which happens immediately after one you have just mentioned, and which is surprising or unfortunate. ❑ *Ron called her office, only to learn that she was in a meeting.* **9** ADV You can use **only** to emphasize how appropriate a certain course of action or type of behavior is. ❑ *It's only fair to tell her you're coming.* [from Old English]

| **Thesaurus** | *only* | Also look up : |
|---|---|---|
| ADJ. | alone, individual, single, solitary, unique ❶ 🔳 ❸ | |

❷ **only** /oʊnli/ **1** CONJ **Only** can be used to add a comment which slightly changes or limits what you have just said. [INFORMAL] ❑ *The situation is as dramatic as a movie, only it's real.* ❑ *It's like my house, only nicer.* **2** CONJ **Only** can be used after a clause with "would" to indicate why something is not done. [SPOKEN] ❑ *I'd ask you to come with me, only it's such a long way.* [from Old English]

❸ **only** /oʊnli/ **1** PHRASE You can say that something has **only just** happened when you want to emphasize that it happened a very short time ago. ❑ *I've only just arrived.* **2** PHRASE You use **only just** to emphasize that something is true, but by such a small degree that it is almost not true at all. ❑ *We only just managed to get to the airport in time for the flight.* ❑ *I am old enough to remember the war, but only just.* [from Old English] **3** **if only** → see **if** **4** **not only** → see **not**

**ono|mato|poeia** /ɒnəmætəpiːə, -mɑːtə-/ N-UNCOUNT **Onomatopoeia** refers to the use of words which sound like the noise they refer to. "Hiss," "buzz," and "rat-a-tat-tat" are examples of onomatopoeia. [TECHNICAL] [from Late Latin]

**on-ramp** (**on-ramps**) N-COUNT An **on-ramp** is a road which cars use to drive onto a highway.

**on-screen** also **onscreen** **1** ADJ **On-screen** means appearing on the screen of a television, movie theater, or computer. ❑ *Read the on-screen instructions.* **2** ADJ **On-screen** means relating to the roles played by movie or television actors, in contrast with their real lives. ❑ *She had her first on-screen kiss in that movie.* ● **On-screen** is also an adverb. ❑ *He was attractive to women, on-screen and off-screen.*

**on|set** /ɒnsɛt/ N-SING **The onset of** something, especially something unpleasant, is the beginning of it. ❑ *...the onset of winter.*

**on|slaught** /ɒnslɔt/ (**onslaughts**) **1** N-COUNT An **onslaught** on someone or something is a very violent, forceful attack against them. ❑ *The media launched another onslaught on the president.* **2** N-COUNT If you refer to an **onslaught of** something, you mean that there is a large amount of it, often so that it is very difficult to deal with. ❑ *...the constant onslaught of ads on TV.* [from Middle Dutch]

**onto** /ɒntu/

The spelling **on to** is also used, when **on** is part of a phrasal verb.

**1** PREP If something moves **onto** or is put **onto** an object or surface, it is then on that object or surface. ❑ *I lowered myself onto the floor.* **2** PREP When you get **onto** a bus, train, or plane, you enter it. ❑ *He got onto the plane.* **3** PREP **Onto** is used after verbs such as "hold," "hang," and "cling" to indicate what someone is holding firmly or where something is being held firmly. ❑ *Nick smiled and held onto her hand tightly.* **4** PREP If people who are talking get **onto** a different subject, they begin talking about it. ❑ *Let's get on to more important things.* **5** PREP If someone **is onto** something, they are about to discover something important. [INFORMAL] ❑ *We knew we were onto something exciting when we started digging.* **6** PREP If someone **is onto** you, they have discovered that you are doing something illegal or wrong. [INFORMAL] ❑ *The police were onto him.*

**onus** /oʊnəs/ N-SING If you say that **the onus is on** someone **to** do something, you mean it is their responsibility to do it. [FORMAL] ❑ *The onus is on me to find the answer.* [from Latin]

**on|ward** /ɒnwərd/

The form **onwards** can also be used as an adverb.

**1** ADJ **Onward** means moving forward or continuing a journey. ❑ *American Airlines flies to Bangkok, and there are onward flights to Phnom Penh.* ● **Onward** is also an adverb. ❑ *The bus continued onward.* **2** ADJ **Onward** means developing, progressing, or becoming more important over a period of time. ❑ *...the onward march of progress in the aircraft industry.* ● **Onward** is also an adverb. ❑ *It was onward and upward all the way.* **3** ADV If something happens from a particular time **onward**, it begins to happen at that time and continues to happen afterward. ❑ *From the age of six months onward, you should start to give babies solid food.* [from Old English]

**Oort cloud** /ɔrt klaʊd/ (**Oort clouds**) N-COUNT The **Oort cloud** is a region of rocks, dust, and comets that surrounds our solar system. [TECHNICAL]

**ooze** /uz/ (**oozes, oozing, oozed**) **1** V-T/V-I When a thick or sticky liquid **oozes** from something or when something **oozes** it, the liquid flows slowly and in small quantities. ❑ *...sweets oozing with honey and nuts.* **2** V-T/V-I If you say that someone or something **oozes** a quality or characteristic, or **oozes** with it, you mean that they show it very strongly. ❑ *The house oozes charm.* [from Old English]

**opaque** /oʊpeɪk/ **1** ADJ If an object or substance is **opaque**, you cannot see through it. ❑ *...opaque glass.* **2** ADJ If you say that something is **opaque**, you mean that it is difficult to understand. ❑ *...the opaque language of the report.* [from Latin]

**op-ed** ADJ In a newspaper, the **op-ed** page is a page containing articles in which people express their opinions about things. [INFORMAL]

## open

❶ DESCRIBING A POSITION OR MOVEMENT
❷ ACCESSIBLE OR AVAILABLE; NOT HIDDEN, BLOCKED, ETC.
❸ BEGIN, START
❹ PHRASES AND PHRASAL VERBS

**❶ open** /ˈoʊpən/ (**opens, opening, opened**)
**1** V-T/V-I If you **open** something such as a door, window, or lid, or if it **opens**, its position is changed so that it no longer covers a hole or gap. ❑ *He opened the window.* ● **Open** is also an adjective. ❑ *…an open door.* **2** V-T If you **open** something such as a container or a letter, you move, remove, or cut part of it so you can take out what is inside. ❑ *He opened the pack of cards.* ● **Open** is also an adjective. ❑ *…an open bottle.* ● **Open up** means the same as **open**. ❑ *He opened up the boxes of food.* **3** V-T/V-I If you **open** something such as a book, an umbrella, or your hand, or if it **opens**, the different parts of it move away from each other so that the inside of it can be seen. ❑ *He opened the book.* ❑ *The flower opened and there was a bee inside.* ● **Open** is also an adjective. ❑ *Barbara put the book into her open hand.* ● **Open out** means the same as **open**. ❑ *Keith took a map and opened it out on his knees.* **4** V-T If you **open** a computer file, you give the computer an instruction to display it on the screen. [COMPUTING] **5** V-T/V-I When you **open** your eyes or your eyes **open**, you move your eyelids upward, for example, when you wake up, so that you can see. ● **Open** is also an adjective. ❑ *His eyes were open and he was smiling.* **6** V-T If you **open** your shirt or coat, you undo the buttons or pull down the zipper. ❑ *I opened my jacket to put away my pen.* ● **Open** is also an adjective. ❑ *You can wear the shirt open over a T-shirt.* [from Old English]

**❷ open** /ˈoʊpən/ (**opens, opening, opened**)
**1** V-T/V-I If people **open** something such as a blocked road or a border, or if it **opens**, people can then pass along it or through it. ❑ *Police opened the road two hours after the accident.* ● **Open** is also an adjective. ❑ *We want to keep the highway open.* ● **Open up** means the same as **open**. ❑ *Workers opened up roads today, after the floods.* **2** ADJ An **open** area is a large area that does not have many buildings or trees in it. ❑ *Police officers continued their search of open ground.* **3** ADJ An **open** structure or object is not covered or enclosed. ❑ *…a room with an open fire.* **4** V-T/V-I When a store, office, or public building **opens** or is **opened**, its doors are unlocked and people can go in. ❑ *Banks don't open again until Monday morning.* ● **Open** is also an adjective. ❑ *The store is open Monday through Friday, 9 a.m. to 6 p.m.* **5** V-T/V-I When a public building, factory, or company **opens** or when someone **opens** it, it starts operating for the first time. ❑ *The station opened in 1955.* **6** ADJ If you describe a person or their character as **open**, you mean they are honest and do not want or try to hide anything or to deceive anyone. ❑ *He was always open with her.* ● **open|ness** N-UNCOUNT ❑ *Our relationship is based on honesty and openness.* **7** ADJ If you are **open** to suggestions or ideas, you are ready and willing to consider or accept them. ❑ *They are open to suggestions on how working conditions could be improved.* **8** ADJ If you say that a system, person,

or idea is **open to** something such as abuse or criticism, you mean they might receive abuse or criticism because of their qualities, effects, or actions. ❑ *Their behavior is open to question.* [from Old English]

**❸ open** /ˈoʊpən/ (**opens, opening, opened**)
**1** V-T/V-I When an event such as a conference **opens**, or is **opened**, it begins. ❑ *The conference will open tomorrow.* ● **open|ing** N-SING ❑ *…the opening of the talks.* **2** V-I When a movie, play, or other public event **opens**, it begins to be shown, be performed, or to take place for a limited time. ❑ *A photographic exhibition opens at the museum on Wednesday.* ● **open|ing** N-SING ❑ *…the opening of the Olympic Games.* **3** V-T If you **open** an account with a bank or a commercial organization, you begin to use their services. [from Old English]

**❹ open** /ˈoʊpən/ (**opens, opening, opened**)
**1** PHRASE If you do something **in the open** or **out in the open**, you do it outdoors. ❑ *Many people sleep in the open because they are homeless.* **2** PHRASE If an attitude or situation is **in the open** or **out in the open**, people know about it and it is no longer kept secret. ❑ *We wanted the secret to be out in the open.* **3** with open arms → see arm **4** to keep your eyes open → see eye **5** with your eyes open → see eye **6** to open your eyes → see eye **7** to open fire → see fire **8** to open your heart → see heart **9** the heavens open → see heaven [from Old English] **10** an open mind → see mind **11** to open your mind → see mind **12** to keep your options open → see option
▸ **open out** → see open ❶3
▸ **open up 1** → see open ❶2, ❷1 **2** PHR-VERB If a place, economy, or area of interest **opens up**, or if someone **opens** it **up**, more people can go there or become involved in it. ❑ *As the market opens up, more goods will be available.* ❑ *He wanted to see how Albania was opening up to the world.* **3** PHR-VERB If something **opens up** opportunities or possibilities, or if they **open up**, they are created. ❑ *The changes have opened up new opportunities for the company.* **4** PHR-VERB When you **open up** a building, you unlock and open the door so that people can get in. ❑ *Several customers were waiting when I arrived to open up the store.*

**open-air** also **open air**

Only the form **open air** is used in meaning **2**.

**1** ADJ An **open-air** place or event is outside rather than in a building. ❑ *…an open-air concert.* **2** N-SING If you are **in the open air**, you are outside rather than in a building. ❑ *We ate our meals in the open air.*

**open cir|cu|la|tory sys|tem** (**open circulatory systems**) N-COUNT In animals that have an **open circulatory system**, the heart pumps blood into spaces around the body. [TECHNICAL]

**open clus|ter** (**open clusters**) N-COUNT An **open cluster** is a group of stars that were all formed at the same time and are held together by gravity. [TECHNICAL]

**open-ended** ADJ When people begin an **open-ended** discussion or activity, they do not start with any intention of achieving a particular decision or result. ❑ *Ken and I have a very open-ended approach to our work.*

**open|er** /ˈoʊpənər/ (**openers**) N-COUNT An **opener** is a tool which is used to open containers

O

such as cans or bottles. ❏ ...a can opener. [from Old English]

→ see **utensil**

**open|ing** /ouʊpənɪŋ/ (openings) **1** ADJ The **opening** event, item, day, or week in a series is the first one. ❏ ...the competition's opening game. **2** N-COUNT The **opening of** something such as a book, play, or concert is the first part of it. ❏ They waited for the opening of the musical. **3** N-COUNT An **opening** is a hole or empty space through which things or people can pass. ❏ He pushed through a narrow opening in the fence. **4** N-COUNT An **opening** in a forest is a small area where there are no trees or bushes. ❏ I looked down at the beach as we passed an opening in the trees. **5** N-COUNT An **opening** is a good opportunity to do something. ❏ All she needed was an opening to show what she could do. **6** N-COUNT An **opening** is a job that is available. ❏ We don't have any openings now. [from Old English] **7** → see also **open**

| **Thesaurus** | | opening | Also look up : |
|---|---|---|---|
| N. | cut, door, gap, slot, space, window **3** | | |
| | clearing **4** | | |
| | job, position **6** | | |

**open|ly** /ouʊpənli/ ADV If you do something **openly**, you do it without hiding any facts or your feelings. ❏ She openly talked with friends about it. [from Old English]

**open-minded** ADJ If you describe someone as **open-minded**, you approve of them because they are willing to listen to and consider other people's ideas. ❏ He says that he is open-minded about tomorrow's talks. ● **open-mindedness** N-UNCOUNT ❏ He shows open-mindedness and willingness to learn.

**open-source** also **open source** ADJ **Open-source** software is software that anyone is allowed to modify without asking permission from the company that developed it. [COMPUTING]

**open-water zone** (open-water zones) N-COUNT The **open-water zone** of a lake or pond is the area closest to the surface, where sunlight can reach. [TECHNICAL]

**Word Link** oper ≈ work : cooperate, opera, operation

**op|era** /ɒpərə, ɒprə/ (operas) **1** N-VAR An **opera** is a play with music in which all the words are sung. ❏ ...an opera singer. **2** → see also **soap opera** ● **op|er|at|ic** /ɒpərætɪk/ ADJ ❏ ...the local amateur operatic society. [from Italian]

→ see **music**

**op|er|ate** /ɒpəreɪt/ (operates, operating, operated) **1** V-T/V-I If you **operate** a business or organization, or if it **operates**, it does the work it is supposed to. ❏ Greenwood owned and operated a truck rental company. ❏ ...the first overseas bank to operate in Cambodia for more than 15 years. ● **op|era|tion** /ɒpəreɪʃⁿn/ N-UNCOUNT ❏ ...the day-to-day operation of the company. **2** V-I The way that something **operates** is the way that it works or has a particular effect. ❏ Ceiling and wall lights can operate independently. ● **op|era|tion** N-UNCOUNT ❏ ...the operation of government. **3** V-T/V-I When you **operate** a machine or device, or when it **operates**, you make it work. ❏ He used to sing as he was operating the machine. ● **op|era|tion** N-UNCOUNT ❏ ...the operation of the engine. **4** V-I When

surgeons **operate on** a patient, they cut open the patient's body in order to remove, replace, or repair a diseased or damaged part. ❏ Surgeons operated on Max to remove a brain tumor. [from Latin] **5** → see also **operation**

**Word Partnership** Use operate with :

| N. | operate **a business/company, schools** |
|---|---|
| | operate **1** |
| | **forces** operate **1 2** |
| V. | **be allowed to** operate, **continue to** operate **1 – 3** |
| ADV. | operate **efficiently 1 2** |
| | operate **independently 2** |

**op|er|at|ing room** (operating rooms) N-COUNT An **operating room** is a room in a hospital where surgeons carry out medical operations.

**op|era|tion** /ɒpəreɪʃⁿn/ (operations) **1** N-COUNT An **operation** is a highly-organized activity that involves many people doing different things. ❏ The rescue operation began on Friday. **2** N-COUNT A business or company can be referred to as an **operation**. [BUSINESS] ❏ ...an electronics operation. **3** N-COUNT When a patient has an **operation**, a surgeon cuts open their body in order to remove, replace, or repair a diseased or damaged part. ❏ Bob had an operation on his arm. **4** N-UNCOUNT If a system is **in operation**, it is being used. ❏ This banking system is currently in operation. **5** N-UNCOUNT If a machine or device is **in operation**, it is working. ❏ There are three ski lifts in operation today. [from Latin] **6** → see also **operative**

**Word Partnership** Use operation with :

| N. | **relief** operation, **rescue** operation **1** |
|---|---|
| V. | **carry out an** operation, **plan an** operation **1** |
| | **perform an** operation **1 3** |
| ADJ. | **covert** operation, **massive** operation, **military** operation, **undercover** operation **1** |
| | **major** operation, |
| | **successful** operation **1 – 3** |
| | **emergency** operation **1 3** |

**op|era|tion|al** /ɒpəreɪʃənⁿl/ **1** ADJ A machine or piece of equipment that is **operational** is in use or is ready for use. ❏ The new system will be fully operational by December. **2** ADJ **Operational** factors or problems relate to the working of a system, device, or plan. ❏ ...high operational costs. ● **op|era|tion|al|ly** ADV ❏ Operationally, the company is performing well. [from Latin]

**op|era|tive** /ɒpərətɪv, -əreɪtɪv/ (operatives) **1** ADJ A system or service that is **operative** is working or having an effect. [FORMAL] ❏ The service was no longer operative. **2** N-COUNT An **operative** is a worker, especially one who does work with their hands. [FORMAL] ❏ In an automated car factory, you can't see any human operatives. **3** N-COUNT An **operative** is someone who works for a government agency such as the intelligence service. ❏ The CIA wants to protect its operatives. **4** PHRASE If you describe a word as the **operative word**, you want to draw attention to it because you think it is important or exactly true in a particular situation. ❏ This is a good little company, but the *operative word is "little."* [from Latin]

**op|era|tor** /ɒpəreɪtər/ (**operators**) **1** N-COUNT
An **operator** is a person who connects telephone
calls at a telephone exchange or in a place such
as an office or hotel. ❑ *He called the operator.*
**2** N-COUNT An **operator** is a person who is
employed to operate or control a machine.
❑ *...computer operators.* **3** N-COUNT An **operator**
is a person or a company that operates a business.
[BUSINESS] ❑ *...the nation's largest cable TV operator.*
[from Latin]

**opin|ion** /əpɪnyən/ (**opinions**) **1** N-COUNT
Your **opinion** about something is what you think
or believe about it. ❑ *I didn't ask for your opinion.*
**2** N-SING Your **opinion of** someone is your
judgment of their character or ability. ❑ *Thomas
has a high opinion of himself.* ❑ *She held the opinion that
he was a fool.* **3** N-UNCOUNT You can refer to the
beliefs or views that people have as **opinion.** ❑ *The
president understands the importance of world opinion.*
[from Old French]

| **Thesaurus** | *opinion* | Also look up : |
| --- | --- | --- |
| N. | feeling, judgment, thought, viewpoint **1** – **3** | |

| **Word Partnership** | Use *opinion* with : |
| --- | --- |
| V. | **ask for an** opinion, **express an** opinion, opinion, **share an** opinion **1 2** |
| ADJ. | **favorable** opinion **1** – **3** **expert** opinion, **legal** opinion, **majority** opinion, **medical** opinion **3** |

**opin|ion poll** (**opinion polls**) N-COUNT An
**opinion poll** involves asking people's opinions on
a particular subject, especially one concerning
politics. ❑ *75% of people questioned in an opinion poll
agreed with the committee's decision.*

**opium** /oʊpiəm/ N-UNCOUNT **Opium** is a
powerful drug made from the seeds of a type of
poppy. [from Latin]

**op|po|nent** /əpoʊnənt/ (**opponents**)
**1** N-COUNT A politician's **opponents** are other
politicians who belong to a different party or
who have different aims or policies. ❑ *...Mr.
Kennedy's opponent in the contest.* **2** N-COUNT In
a sports contest, your **opponent** is the person
who is playing against you. ❑ *Los Angeles will be
the team's first-round opponent.* **3** N-COUNT The
**opponents of** an idea or policy do not agree with
it. ❑ *...opponents of the increase in nuclear weapons.*
[from Latin]
→ see **chess**

**op|por|tun|ist** /ɒpərtunɪst/ (**opportunists**)
N-COUNT An **opportunist** is someone who takes
advantage of any situation in order to gain money
or power. ❑ *He's a real opportunist and doesn't
care about what happens to his business partners.*
● **op|por|tun|ism** N-UNCOUNT ❑ *Personal gain
and opportunism are Mr. Lanctt's real motivations.*
❑ *...political opportunism.* [from Late Middle English]

**op|por|tun|is|tic** /ɒpərtunɪstɪk/ ADJ If you
describe someone's behavior as **opportunistic**, you
are critical of them because they take advantage of
situations in order to gain money or power. ❑ *A lot
of people support him for opportunistic reasons.* [from
Late Middle English]

**op|por|tu|nity** /ɒpərtunɪti/ (**opportunities**)
N-VAR An **opportunity** is a situation in which it is
possible for you to do something that you want to
do. ❑ *I had an opportunity to go to New York and study.*
❑ *We provide opportunities for people to meet each other.*
[from Late Middle English]

| **Word Partnership** | Use *opportunity* with : |
| --- | --- |
| N. | **business** opportunity, **employment** opportunity, **investment** opportunity |
| ADJ. | **economic** opportunity, **educational** opportunity, **equal** opportunity, **golden** opportunity, **great** opportunity, **lost** opportunity, **rare** opportunity, **unique** opportunity |
| V. | **have an** opportunity, **miss an** opportunity, **see an** opportunity, **seize an** opportunity, opportunity **to speak**, **take advantage of an** opportunity |

**op|pose** /əpoʊz/ (**opposes, opposing, opposed**)
V-T If you **oppose** someone or **oppose** their plans
or ideas, you disagree with what they want to
do and try to prevent them from doing it. ❑ *He
said that he would oppose any tax increase.* [from Old
French]

**op|posed** /əpoʊzd/ **1** ADJ If you **are opposed to**
something, you disagree with it or disapprove of
it. ❑ *I am opposed to any form of terrorism.* **2** ADJ You
say that two ideas or systems are **opposed** when
they are opposite to each other or very different
from each other. ❑ *...people with policies opposed to
his own.* **3** PHRASE You use **as opposed to** when
you want to make it clear that you are talking
about one particular thing and not something
else. ❑ *We ate in the restaurant, as opposed to the café.*
[from Old French]

**op|pos|ing** /əpoʊzɪŋ/ **1** ADJ **Opposing** ideas
or tendencies are totally different from each
other. ❑ *My friends have opposing views on the
war.* **2** ADJ **Opposing** groups of people disagree
about something or are in competition with
one another. ❑ *He hoped for discussion between the
opposing sides.* [from Old French]

**op|po|site** /ɒpəzɪt/ (**opposites**) **1** PREP If one
thing is **opposite** another, it is facing it. ❑ *Jennie
sat opposite her at breakfast.* ● **Opposite** is also
an adverb. ❑ *He looked at the buildings opposite.*
**2** ADJ The **opposite** side or part of something is
the side or part that is furthest away from you.
❑ *...the opposite corner of the room.* **3** ADJ **Opposite**
is used to describe things of the same kind
which are completely different in a particular
way. ❑ *We watched the cars driving in the opposite
direction.* **4** N-COUNT The **opposite of** someone
or something is the person or thing that is most
different from them. ❑ *Whatever he says, he's
probably thinking the opposite.* [from Old French]

| **Word Partnership** | Use *opposite* with : |
| --- | --- |
| ADV. | **directly** opposite **1** **exactly (the)** opposite, **precisely (the)** opposite, **quite the** opposite **1 3 4** |
| N. | opposite **corner**, opposite **end**, opposite **side 2** opposite **direction**, opposite **effect 3** |
| ADJ. | **complete** opposite, **exact** opposite **3 4** |
| PREP. | **the** opposite **of** *someone/something* **4** |

O

**op|po|site sex** N-SING If you are talking about men and refer to **the opposite sex**, you mean women. If you are talking about women and refer to **the opposite sex**, you mean men. □ ...*ways to attract members of the opposite sex.*

**opos|sum** /əpɒsəm/ (**opossums**) N-VAR An **opossum** is a small animal that lives in America and Australia. It carries its young in a pouch on its body, and has thick fur and a long hairless tail. [from Algonquian]

**op|po|si|tion** /ɒpəzɪʃⁿn/ (**oppositions**)
■ N-UNCOUNT **Opposition** is strong, angry, or violent disagreement and disapproval. □ *There is bitter opposition to the plan from local people.*
■ N-COUNT In countries with a parliament, such as Britain, **the opposition** refers to the politicians or political parties that form part of the parliament, but are not the government. □ ...*the Leader of the Opposition.* [from Old French]

**op|press** /əprɛs/ (**oppresses, oppressing, oppressed**) V-T To **oppress** people means to treat them cruelly or to prevent them from having the same opportunities and freedom as others. □ ...*people who are oppressed by their governments.*
● **op|pressed** ADJ □ *The country's oppressed people became even poorer.* ● **op|pres|sion** N-UNCOUNT □ ...*political oppression.* ● **op|pres|sor** (**oppressors**) N-COUNT □ *They had no defense against their oppressors.* [from Old French]

**op|pres|sive** /əprɛsɪv/ ■ ADJ **Oppressive** laws, societies, and customs treat people cruelly and unfairly. □ *The new laws were as oppressive as the old ones.* ■ ADJ If you describe the weather or the atmosphere in a room as **oppressive**, you mean that it is unpleasantly hot and damp. □ ...*the oppressive heat of last summer.* ■ ADJ An **oppressive** situation makes you feel depressed and uncomfortable. □ ...*the oppressive sadness that he felt.* [from Old French]

**opt** /ɒpt/ (**opts, opting, opted**) V-T/V-I If you **opt for** something, or **opt to** do something, you choose it or decide to do it in preference to anything else. □ *Many students opt for private schools.* [from French]
▸ **opt out** PHR-VERB If you **opt out of** something, you choose to be no longer involved in it. □ *Rich people can opt out of the public school system.*

**op|tic** /ɒptɪk/ ADJ **Optic** means relating to the eyes or to sight. □ ...*the optic nerve.* [from Medieval Latin]
→ see **eye**

| Word Link | op ≈ eye : optical, optician, optometrist |
|---|---|

**op|ti|cal** /ɒptɪkⁿl/ ADJ **Optical** devices, processes, and effects involve or relate to vision, light, or images. □ ...*optical telescopes.* □ ...*an optical scanner.* [from Medieval Latin]

**op|ti|cal fi|ber** (**optical fibers**) N-VAR An **optical fiber** is a very thin thread of glass inside a protective coating. Optical fibers are used to carry information in the form of light.

**op|ti|cian** /ɒptɪʃⁿn/ (**opticians**) N-COUNT An **optician** is someone whose job is to make and sell eyeglasses and contact lenses. [from Medieval Latin]

**op|tic nerve** N-COUNT The **Optic nerve** is the nerve that transfers electrical impulses from the eye to the brain.

| Word Link | ism ≈ action or state : communism, optimism, patriotism |
|---|---|

| Word Link | optim ≈ the best : optimism, optimistic, optimum |
|---|---|

**op|ti|mism** /ɒptɪmɪzəm/ N-UNCOUNT **Optimism** is the feeling of being hopeful about the future or about the success of something. □ *There is optimism about the possibility of peace.* ● **op|ti|mist** (**optimists**) N-COUNT □ *He is an optimist about the country's future.* [from French]

**op|ti|mis|tic** /ɒptɪmɪstɪk/ ADJ Someone who is **optimistic** is hopeful about the future or the success of something. □ *She is optimistic that they can reach an agreement.* ● **op|ti|mis|ti|cal|ly** ADV □ *Both sides spoke optimistically about the talks.* [from French]

**op|ti|mum** /ɒptɪməm/ also **optimal** ADJ The **optimum** or **optimal** level or state of something is the best level or state that it could achieve. [FORMAL] □ *Try to do some exercise three times a week for optimum health.* [from Latin]

| Word Link | opt ≈ choosing : adopt, option, optional |
|---|---|

**op|tion** /ɒpʃⁿn/ (**options**) ■ N-COUNT An **option** is a choice between two or more things. □ *The cost of that option will be $8.8 billion.* ■ N-SING If you have the **option** of doing something, you can choose whether to do it or not. □ *Some criminals are given the option of going to jail or doing a training program.* ■ PHRASE If you **keep** your **options open** or **leave** your **options open**, you delay making a decision about something. □ *I am keeping my options open; I can decide in a few months.* [from Latin]

| Thesaurus | option | Also look up : |
|---|---|---|

N.    alternative, choice, opportunity, preference; (ant.) selection ■ ■

**op|tion|al** /ɒpʃənⁿl/ ADJ If something is **optional**, you can choose whether or not you do it or have it. □ *The service offers many optional extras.* [from Latin]

**op|tom|etrist** /ɒptɒmətrɪst/ (**optometrists**) N-COUNT An **optometrist** is someone whose job is to test people's eyesight. [from Greek]

| Word Link | ulent ≈ full of : opulent, succulent, turbulent |
|---|---|

**opu|lent** /ɒpyələnt/ ADJ **Opulent** things or places look grand and expensive. [FORMAL] □ ...*opulent furnishings.* ● **opu|lence** N-UNCOUNT □ ...*the elegant opulence of the hotel.* [from Latin]

**opus** /oupəs/ (**opuses** or **opera**) N-COUNT An **opus** is a piece of classical music by a particular composer. □ ...*Beethoven's Piano Sonata in E minor, Opus 90.* [from Latin]

**or** /ər, STRONG ɔr/ ■ CONJ You use **or** to link alternatives. □ "*Tea or coffee?*" *John asked.* □ *He said he would write or call.* ■ CONJ You use **or** to give another alternative, when the first alternative is introduced by "either" or "whether." □ *Either you talk to him, or I will.* ■ CONJ You use **or** between two numbers to indicate that you are giving an approximate amount. □ *You should only drink one*

## Word Web   orchestra

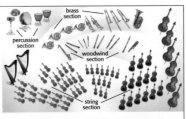

The modern **symphony orchestra** usually has between 60 and 100 **musicians**. The largest group of musicians are in the **string** section. It gives the orchestra its rich, flowing sound. String **instruments** include **violins, violas, cellos,** and usually **double basses. Flutes,** oboes, **clarinets,** and bassoons make up the woodwind section. The **brass** section is usually quite small. Too much of this sound could overwhelm the quieter strings. Brass **instruments** include the French horn, **trumpet, trombone** and tuba. The size of the **percussion** section depends on the **composition** being performed. However, there is almost always a timpani player.

*or two cups of coffee a day.* **4** CONJ You use **or** to introduce a comment which corrects or modifies what you have just said. ❑ *The man was a fool, he thought, or at least careless.* **5** CONJ If you say that someone should do something **or** something bad will happen, you are warning them that if they do not do it, the bad thing will happen. ❑ *She had to have the operation, or she would die.* **6** CONJ You use **or** to introduce something which is evidence for the truth of a statement you have just made. ❑ *He must think Jane is special or he wouldn't have asked her for a date.* [from Old English] **7 or else** → see **else 8 or so** → see **so 9 or something** → see **something**

**oral** /ɔ́rəl/ (orals) **1** ADJ **Oral** communication is spoken rather than written. ❑ *...the written and oral traditions of ancient cultures.* ● **oral|ly** ADV ❑ *Your success depends largely on how well you communicate orally and in writing.* **2** N-COUNT An **oral** is an examination, especially in a foreign language, that is spoken rather than written. **3** ADJ **Oral** means relating to a person's mouth. ❑ *...good oral hygiene.* ● **oral|ly** ADV ❑ *...tablets taken orally.* [from Late Latin]

**oral his|to|ry** (oral histories) N-VAR **Oral history** consists of spoken memories, stories, and songs, and the study of these, as a way of communicating and discovering information about the past.

**or|ange** /ɔ́rɪndʒ/ (oranges) **1** COLOR Something that is **orange** is of a color between red and yellow. **2** N-VAR An **orange** is a round, juicy fruit with a thick, orange-colored skin. [from Old French]
→ see **color, fruit, rainbow**

**ora|to|rio** /ɔ̀rətɔ́riou/ (oratorios) N-COUNT An **oratorio** is a long piece of music with a religious theme which is written for singers and an orchestra. [from Italian]

**ora|tory** /ɔ́rətɔri/ N-UNCOUNT **Oratory** is the art of making formal speeches. [FORMAL] ❑ *Martin Luther King, Jr. had a gift for oratory.* [from Latin]

orbit

**or|bit** /ɔ́rbɪt/ (orbits, orbiting, orbited) **1** N-COUNT An **orbit** is the curved path in space that is followed by an object going around and around a planet, moon, or the sun. ❑ *Mars and Earth have orbits which* change over time. **2** V-T If something such as a satellite **orbits** a planet, moon, or sun, it moves around it in a continuous, curving path. ❑ *The moon orbits the Earth.* [from Latin]
→ see **satellite, solar system**

**or|bit|al** /ɔ́rbɪtᵊl/ ADJ **Orbital** means relating to the orbit of an object in space. ❑ *...the Earth's orbital path.* [from Latin]

**or|chard** /ɔ́rtʃərd/ (orchards) N-COUNT An **orchard** is an area of land on which fruit trees are grown. [from Old English]
→ see **barn**

**or|ches|tra** /ɔ́rkɪstrə/ (orchestras) **1** N-COUNT An **orchestra** is a large group of musicians who play a variety of different instruments together. ❑ *the Los Angeles Philharmonic Orchestra.* **2** → see also **symphony orchestra** ● **or|ches|tral** /ɔrkɛ́strəl/ ADJ ❑ *...an orchestral concert.* **3** N-SING **The orchestra** or **the orchestra seats** in a theater or concert hall are the seats on the first floor directly in front of the stage. ❑ *People filled most of the orchestra seats.* [from Latin]
→ see Word Web: **orchestra**
→ see **theater**

**or|ches|trate** /ɔ́rkɪstreɪt/ (orchestrates, orchestrating, orchestrated) V-T If you say that someone **orchestrates** an event or situation, you mean that they carefully organize it in a way that will produce the result that they want. ❑ *He helped to orchestrate the deal.* ● **or|ches|tra|tion** N-UNCOUNT ❑ *It takes careful orchestration to get the meat, fish, and vegetables ready at exactly the same time.* [from Latin]

**or|ches|tra|tion** /ɔ̀rkɪstreɪ́ʃᵊn/ (orchestrations) N-COUNT An **orchestration** is a piece of music that has been rewritten so that it can be played by an orchestra. [from Latin]

**or|chid** /ɔ́rkɪd/ (orchids) N-COUNT **Orchids** are plants with brightly colored, unusually shaped flowers. [from New Latin]

**or|dain** /ɔrdeɪ́n/ (ordains, ordaining, ordained) V-T When someone **is ordained**, they are made a member of the clergy in a religious ceremony. ❑ *He was ordained a Catholic priest in 1982.* [from Late Latin]

**or|deal** /ɔrdíl/ (ordeals) N-COUNT If you describe an experience or situation as an **ordeal**, you think it is difficult and stressful. ❑ *He said the trip was an ordeal.* [from Old English]

## order

**❶** CONJUNCTION USES
**❷** COMMANDS AND REQUESTS
**❸** ARRANGEMENTS, SITUATIONS, AND GROUPINGS

**❶ or|der** /ɔrdər/ **1** PHRASE If you do something **in order to** achieve a particular thing or **in order that** something can happen, you do it because you want to achieve that thing. ❑ *Some schools are having to reduce the number of staff in order to cut costs.* **2** PHRASE If something must happen **in order for** something else to happen, the second thing cannot happen if the first thing does not happen. ❑ *In order for the computer to find someone's records, we need the person's name and address.* [from Old French]

**❷ or|der** /ɔrdər/ (**orders, ordering, ordered**) **1** V-T If a person in authority **orders** someone **to** do something, they tell them to do it. ❑ *Williams ordered him to leave.* **2** V-T If someone in authority **orders** something, they give instructions that it should be done. ❑ *The president ordered a full report of what happened.* **3** N-COUNT If someone in authority gives you an **order**, they tell you to do something. ❑ *The commander gave orders to move out in a few minutes.* **4** V-T/V-I When you **order** something that you are going to pay for, you ask for it to be brought to you or sent to you. ❑ *They ordered a new washing machine.* ❑ *The waitress asked, "Are you ready to order?"* **5** N-COUNT Someone's **order** is what they have asked to be brought, made, or obtained for them in return for money. ❑ *The waiter returned with their order.* **6** → see also **mail order** **7** PHRASE If you are **under orders to** do something, you have been told to do it by someone in authority. ❑ *I am under orders not to discuss his location with anyone.* [from Old French] **8 a tall order** → see **tall**

▶ **order around** PHR-VERB If you say that someone **is ordering** you **around**, you mean they are telling you what to do as if they have authority over you, and you dislike this. ❑ *He started ordering me around.*

| **Thesaurus** | order | Also look up : |
|---|---|---|
| V. | charge, command, direct, tell ❷ **1** | |
| | buy, request ❷ **4** | |
| N. | command, direction, instruction ❷ **3** | |

**❸ or|der** /ɔrdər/ (**orders**) **1** N-UNCOUNT If things are arranged or done in a particular **order**, one thing is put first or done first, another thing second, another thing third, and so on. ❑ *Bookstores should arrange the books in alphabetical order.* **2** N-UNCOUNT **Order** is the situation that exists when everything is in the correct or expected place, or happens at the correct time. ❑ *I love rules. I love order.* **3** N-UNCOUNT **Order** is the situation that exists when people obey the law and do not fight or riot. ❑ *Troops were sent to the islands to restore order.* **4** N-SING When people talk about a particular **order**, they mean the way society is organized at a particular time. ❑ *He and his followers want to create a better social order.* **5** N-COUNT A religious **order** is a group of monks or nuns who live according to a particular set of rules. ❑ *...the Benedictine order of monks.* **6** N-COUNT In biology, an **order** of animals or plants is a

group of related species. Compare **class, family**. **7** → see also **law and order** **8** PHRASE You use **in the order of** or **on the order of** when mentioning an approximate figure. ❑ *They borrowed something in the order of $10 million.* **9** PHRASE A machine or device that is **in working order** is functioning properly and is not broken. ❑ *...a ten-year-old car that is in perfect working order.* **10** PHRASE A machine or device that is **out of order** is broken and does not work. ❑ *Their phone's out of order.* [from Old French] **11 to put your house in order** → see **house** **12 order of magnitude** → see **magnitude**

**or|der|ly** /ɔrdərli/ (**orderlies**) **1** ADJ Something that is **orderly** is neat or arranged in a neat way. ❑ *It's a beautiful, clean and orderly city.* ● **or|der|li|ness** N-UNCOUNT ❑ *I loved the orderliness of their house.* **2** N-COUNT An **orderly** is a person who works in a hospital and does not have special medical training. [from Old French]

**or|di|nance** /ɔrdⁿnəns/ (**ordinances**) N-COUNT An **ordinance** is an official rule or order. [FORMAL] ❑ *The new ordinance allows buildings to be as tall as 55 feet.* [from Old French]

**or|di|nari|ly** /ɔrdⁿnɛərɪli/ ADV If you say what is **ordinarily** true, you are saying what is normally true. ❑ *The streets were ordinarily full of people.* [from Latin]

**or|di|nary** /ɔrdⁿnɛri/ **1** ADJ **Ordinary** people or things are normal and not special or different in any way. ❑ *Most ordinary people would agree with me.* ❑ *It has 25 calories fewer than ordinary ice cream.* **2** PHRASE Something that is **out of the ordinary** is unusual or different. ❑ *The police chief asked the public to report anything out of the ordinary.* [from Latin]

| **Thesaurus** | ordinary | Also look up : |
|---|---|---|
| ADJ. | common, everyday, normal, regular, standard, typical, usual; (ant.) abnormal, unusual **1** | |

| **Word Partnership** | Use *ordinary* with : |
|---|---|
| N. | ordinary **Americans**, ordinary **circumstances**, ordinary **citizens**, ordinary **day**, ordinary **expenses**, ordinary **folk**, ordinary **life**, ordinary **people**, ordinary **person** **1** |
| PREP. | **out of the** ordinary **2** |

**or|di|na|tion** /ɔrdⁿneɪʃⁿn/ (**ordinations**) N-VAR Someone's **ordination** is when they are made a minister, priest, or rabbi. ❑ *...supporters of the ordination of women.* [from Late Latin]

**ore** /ɔr/ (**ores**) N-VAR **Ore** is rock or earth from which metal can be obtained. ❑ *...iron ore.* [from Old English]
→ see **metal**

**or|gan** /ɔrgən/ (**organs**) **1** N-COUNT An **organ** is a part of your body that has a particular purpose or function, for example, your heart or lungs. ❑ *...damage to the muscles and internal organs.* ❑ *...human organs.* **2** N-COUNT An **organ** is a large musical instrument with pipes of different lengths through which air is forced. It has keys and pedals like a piano. ● **or|gan|ist** (**organists**) N-COUNT ❑ *...the church organist.* [from Old French]
→ see **donor, keyboard, nervous system**

**or|gan|elle** /ɔrgənɛl/ (**organelles**) N-COUNT
**Organelles** are structures within cells that have a
specialized function, such as mitochondria or the
nucleus. [TECHNICAL] [from New Latin]

**or|gan|ic** /ɔrgænɪk/ **1** ADJ **Organic** farming
or gardening uses only natural animal and plant
products and does not use artificial fertilizers or
pesticides. ● **or|gani|cal|ly** ADV □ ...*organically
grown vegetables.* **2** ADJ **Organic** substances are
produced by or found in living things. □ ...*organic
waste such as unwanted food.* **3** ADJ In art, **organic**
shapes or designs use curved lines rather than
straight lines and resemble shapes that exist in
nature. [from Old French]

**or|gan|ic com|pound** (**organic compounds**)
N-COUNT An **organic compound** is a chemical
compound that contains carbon. [TECHNICAL]

**or|gan|ism** /ɔrgənɪzəm/ (**organisms**) N-COUNT
An **organism** is an animal or plant, especially one
that is so small that you cannot see it without
using a microscope. □ ...*tiny organisms such as
bacteria.* [from Old French]

**or|gani|za|tion** /ɔrgənɪzeɪʃⁿn/ (**organizations**)
**1** N-COUNT An **organization** is an official group of
people, for example, a political party, a business, a
charity, or a club. □ *She worked for the organization for
six years.* ● **or|gani|za|tion|al** ADJ □ ...*organizational
change.* **2** N-UNCOUNT The **organization** of an
event or activity involves making all the necessary
arrangements for it. □ *I helped in the organization
of the concert.* ● **or|gani|za|tion|al** ADJ □ ...*Evelyn's
excellent organizational skills.* **3** N-UNCOUNT The
**organization** of something is the way in which
its different parts are arranged or relate to each
other. □ *Is the general organization of your report clear?*
● **or|gani|za|tion|al** ADJ □ *Big organizational changes
are needed.* [from Medieval Latin]

**or|gan|ize** /ɔrgənaɪz/ (**organizes, organizing,
organized**) **1** V-T If you **organize** an event or
activity, you make all the arrangements for it.
□ *We decided to organize a concert.* ● **or|gan|iz|er**
(**organizers**) N-COUNT □ *He was a great organizer
and leader.* **2** V-T If you **organize** something that
someone wants or needs, you make sure that it
is provided. □ *I will organize transportation.* **3** V-T
If you **organize** things, you arrange them in an
ordered way or give them a structure. □ *He began to
organize his papers.* [from Medieval Latin]
→ see **union**

**or|gan|ized** /ɔrgənaɪzd/ **1** ADJ An **organized**
activity or group involves a number of people
doing something together in a structured way,
rather than doing it by themselves. □ ...*organized
groups of art thieves.* □ ...*organized religion.* **2** ADJ
Someone who is **organized** plans their work and
activities efficiently. □ *Managers need to be very
organized.* [from Medieval Latin]

**or|gan sys|tem** (**organ systems**) N-COUNT An
**organ system** is a group of related organs within
an organism, for example the nervous system.

**ori|ent** /ɔriɛnt, -ɛnt/ (**orients, orienting,
oriented**) **1** V-T When you **orient yourself to** a
new situation or course of action, you learn about

it and prepare to deal with it. [FORMAL] □ *You will
need to orient yourself to eating different types of food.*
[from French] **2** → see also **oriented**

**ori|en|tal** /ɔriɛntⁿl/ ADJ **Oriental** means coming
from or associated with eastern Asia, especially
China and Japan. □ ...*oriental carpets.* [from
French]

**ori|en|tat|ed** /ɔriənteɪtɪd/ ADJ **Orientated**
means the same as **oriented**. [from French]

**ori|en|ta|tion** /ɔriənteɪʃⁿn/ (**orientations**)
**1** N-VAR If you talk about the **orientation** of an
organization or country, you are talking about its
aims and interests. □ *Society has lost its orientation.*
**2** N-VAR Someone's **orientation** is their basic
beliefs or preferences. □ ...*the religious orientation of
the school.* [from French]

**ori|ent|ed** /ɔriɛntɪd/

The form **orientated** is also used.

ADJ If someone **is oriented toward** or **oriented
to** a particular thing or person, they are mainly
concerned with that thing or person. □ *The town
has lots of family-oriented things to do.* [from French]

**ori|gin** /ɔrɪdʒɪn/ (**origins**) **1** N-COUNT You
can refer to the beginning, cause, or source of
something as its **origin** or **origins**. □ ...*theories
about the origin of life.* □ *The names "Gullah" and
"Geechee" are African in origin.* **2** N-COUNT Your
**origin** or **origins** is the country, race, or living
conditions of your parents or ancestors. □ *Thomas
has not forgotten his humble origins.* □ ...*people of Asian
origin.* [from French]

**origi|nal** /ərɪdʒɪnⁿl/ (**originals**) **1** ADJ You
use **original** when referring to something that
existed at the beginning of a process or activity, or
the characteristics that something had when it
began or was made. □ *The original plan was to go by
bus.* ● **origi|nal|ly** ADV □ *They stayed longer than they
originally intended.* **2** N-COUNT If something such
as a document, a work of art, or a piece of writing
is an **original**, it is not a copy or a later version.
□ *Photocopy the document and send the original to
your employer.* **3** ADJ An **original** piece of writing
or music was written recently and has not been
published or performed before. □ ...*with original
songs by Richard Warner.* **4** ADJ If you describe
someone or their work as **original**, you approve
of them because they are very imaginative and
have new ideas. □ *Kandinsky is arguably the most
original painter of the past 100 years.* ● **origi|nal|ity**
/ərɪdʒɪnælɪti/ N-UNCOUNT □ ...*a musical work of
great originality.* [from French]

| Thesaurus | | *original* | Also look up : |
|---|---|---|---|
| ADJ. | early, first, initial **1** **2** | | |
| | authentic, genuine **2** | | |
| | creative, unique **4** | | |
| N. | master; (*ant.*) copy **2** | | |

**origi|nate** /ərɪdʒɪneɪt/ (**originates, originating, originated**) V-I If something **originated** at a particular time or in a particular place, it began to happen or exist at that time or in that place. [FORMAL] ❑ *The disease originated in Africa.* [from French]

**ori|ole** /ɔrioʊl/ (**orioles**) N-COUNT An **oriole** is a bird which has black and yellow or orange feathers. [from Medieval Latin]

**or|na|ment** /ɔrnəmənt/ (**ornaments**)
**1** N-COUNT An **ornament** is an attractive object that you display in your home or in your garden. ❑ *The shelf contained a few ornaments.* **2** N-UNCOUNT Decorations and patterns on a building or a piece of furniture can be referred to as **ornament**. [FORMAL] ❑ *...the building's heavy 19th century ornament.* [from Latin]

**or|na|men|tal** /ɔrnəmɛntəl/ ADJ Something that is **ornamental** is attractive and decorative. ❑ *...an ornamental lake.* [from Latin]

**or|nate** /ɔrneɪt/ ADJ An **ornate** building, piece of furniture, or object has a lot of decoration on it. ❑ *...an ornate iron staircase.* [from Latin]

**or|nery** /ɔrnəri/ ADJ If you describe someone as **ornery**, you mean that they are bad-tempered, difficult, and often do things that are mean. [INFORMAL] ❑ *The old lady was still being ornery, but she agreed to his visit.*

**or|phan** /ɔrfən/ (**orphans, orphaned**)
**1** N-COUNT An **orphan** is a child whose parents are dead. **2** V-T PASSIVE If a child **is orphaned**, their parents die, or their remaining parent dies. [from Late Latin]

**or|phan|age** /ɔrfənɪdʒ/ (**orphanages**) N-COUNT An **orphanage** is a place where orphans live and are cared for. [from Late Latin]

**ortho|dox** /ɔrθədɒks/

The spelling **Orthodox** is also used for meaning **2**.

**1** ADJ **Orthodox** beliefs, methods, or systems are ones which are accepted or used by most people. ❑ *...orthodox medical treatment.* **2** ADJ If you describe someone as **orthodox**, you mean that they hold the older and more traditional ideas of their religion or party. ❑ *...Orthodox Jews.* [from Church Latin]

**ortho|doxy** /ɔrθədɒksi/ (**orthodoxies**)
**1** N-VAR An **orthodoxy** is an accepted view about something. ❑ *These ideas became the new orthodoxy in teaching.* **2** N-UNCOUNT The old, traditional beliefs of a religion, political party, or philosophy can be referred to as **orthodoxy**. ❑ *...his religious orthodoxy.* [from Church Latin]

**or|thog|ra|phy** /ɔrθɒɡrəfi/ (**orthographies**) N-VAR The **orthography** of a language is the set of rules about how to spell words in the language correctly. [TECHNICAL] [from Late Middle English]

**ortho|pedic** /ɔrθəpidɪk/ ADJ **Orthopedic** means relating to problems affecting people's joints and spines. [MEDICAL] ❑ *...an orthopedic surgeon.* ❑ *...orthopedic shoes.* [from French]

**OS** /oʊ ɛs/ (**OS's**) N-COUNT **OS** is an abbreviation for **operating system**. [COMPUTING]

**OSHA** /oʊʃə/ N-PROPER **OSHA** is a government agency in the United States which is responsible for maintaining standards of health and safety in workplaces. **OSHA** is an abbreviation for "Occupational Safety and Health Administration."

**os|ten|ta|tious** /ɒstɛnteɪʃəs/ **1** ADJ If you describe something as **ostentatious**, you disapprove of it because it is expensive and is intended to impress people. ❑ *...very large, ostentatious houses.* **2** ADJ If you describe someone as **ostentatious**, you disapprove of them because they want to impress people with their wealth or importance. ❑ *He was generous with his money, without being ostentatious.* ● **os|ten|ta|tious|ly** ADV ❑ *...ostentatiously dressed.* [from Late Middle English]

**os|ti|na|to** /ɒstɪnɑtoʊ/ (**ostinatos**) N-COUNT An **ostinato** is a short melody or rhythm that is repeated continually throughout a piece of music. [TECHNICAL] [from Italian]

**os|trich** /ɔstrɪtʃ/ (**ostriches**) N-COUNT An **ostrich** is a very large, long-necked African bird that cannot fly. [from Old French]

ostrich

**OT** /oʊ ti/ (**OTs**) N-VAR In sports, **OT** is an abbreviation for **overtime**. ❑ *Mullin's team got a one-point victory in OT.*

**oth|er** /ʌðər/ (**others**)

When **other** follows the determiner **an**, it is written as one word: see **another**.

**1** ADJ You use **other** to refer to an additional thing or person of the same type as one that has been mentioned or is known about. ❑ *They were just like any other young couple.* ● **Other** is also a pronoun. ❑ *Four people were killed, one other was injured.* **2** ADJ You use **other** to indicate that a thing or person is not the one already mentioned, but a different one. ❑ *Johnson and other teachers at the school are very worried.* ❑ *He would have to accept it; there was no other way.* ● **Other** is also a pronoun. ❑ *This issue, more than any other, has upset local people.* **3** ADJ You use the **other** to refer to the second of two things or people when the identity of the first is already known or understood, or has already been mentioned. ❑ *William was at the other end of the room.* ● **The other** is also a pronoun. ❑ *He had a pen in one hand and a book in the other.* **4** ADJ You use the **other** to refer to the rest of the people or things in a group, when you are talking about one particular person or thing. ❑ *The other kids went to the park but he stayed home.* ● **The others** is also a pronoun. ❑ *Alison is coming here with the others.* **5** ADJ **Other** people are people in general, as opposed to yourself or a person you have already mentioned. ❑ *The suffering of other people upsets me.* ● **Others** means the same as **other people**. ❑ *...his hate for others.* **6** ADJ You use **other** in expressions of time such as **the other day**, **the other evening**, or **the other week** to refer to a day, evening, or week in the recent past. ❑ *I called her the other day.* **7** PHRASE If something happens, for example, **every other day** or **every other month**, there is a day or month when it does not happen between each day or month when it happens. ❑ *I wash my hair every other day.* **8** PHRASE You use **nothing other than** and **no other than** to talk about a course of action, decision, or description that is the only one possible in the situation. ❑ *His success was due to nothing other than hard work.* **9** PHRASE You use **other than** after a negative in order to introduce an exception to what you have said. ❑ *She did not talk about any work other than her own.* [from Old English] **10** each other → see each **11** one after the other → see one **12** one or other → see one **13** this, that and the other → see this **14** in other words → see word

> **Word Link** wise ≈ *in the direction or manner of* : clock**wise**, like**wise**, other**wise**

**other|wise** /ˈ∆ðərwaɪz/ **1** ADV You use **otherwise** after mentioning a situation or fact, to say what the result would be if the situation or fact was not true. ❑ *I'm lucky that I enjoy school, otherwise I'd go crazy.* **2** ADV You use **otherwise** to state the general condition or quality of something, when you are also mentioning an exception to this. ❑ *He woke at about 7 a.m., very hungry but otherwise happy.* **3** ADV You use **otherwise** to refer to actions or ways of doing something that are different from the one mentioned in your main statement. [WRITTEN] ❑ *Take one pill three times a day, unless told otherwise by a doctor.* [from Old English]

**ot|to|man** /ˈɒtəmən/ (**ottomans**) **1** N-COUNT An **ottoman** is a low, padded seat similar to a couch but without a back or arms. **2** N-COUNT An **ottoman** is a low, padded stool that you can rest your feet on when you are sitting in a chair. [from French]

**ought** /ɔt/

> **Ought** is a phrasal modal verb. It is used with the base form of a verb.

**1** PHRASE If you say that someone **ought to** do something, you mean that it is the right or sensible thing to do. ❑ *You ought to read the book.* ❑ *He ought to say sorry.* **2** PHRASE You use **ought to** to indicate that you expect something to be true or to happen. ❑ *"This party ought to be fun," he told Alex.* **3** PHRASE You use **ought to** to indicate that you expect something to have happened. ❑ *He ought to be home by now.* **4** PHRASE If you say that someone **ought to have** done something, you mean that it would have been the right or sensible thing to do, but they did not do it. ❑ *She ought to have told him about it.* ❑ *I ought not to have asked you. I'm sorry.* [from Old English]

> **Usage** ought
> *Ought* is generally used with *to*: *We ought to go home soon. You ought to tell her the good news right away!*

**oughtn't** /ˈɔtⁿnt/ **Oughtn't** is a spoken form of "ought not." [from Old English]

**ounce** /aʊns/ (**ounces**) **1** N-COUNT An **ounce** is a unit of weight used in the U.S. and Britain. There are sixteen ounces in a pound and one ounce is equal to 28.35 grams. **2** N-SING You can refer to a

very small amount of something, such as a quality or characteristic, as an **ounce**. ❑ *He didn't have an ounce of business sense.* [from Old French]

**our** /aʊər/

> **Our** is the first person plural possessive determiner.

**1** DET A speaker or writer uses **our** to indicate that something belongs or relates both to himself or herself and to one or more other people. ❑ *We're expecting our first baby.* **2** DET A speaker or writer sometimes uses **our** to indicate that something belongs or relates to people in general. ❑ *We are responsible for our actions.* [from Old English]

**ours** /aʊərz/

> **Ours** is the first person plural possessive pronoun.

PRON A speaker or writer uses **ours** to refer to something that belongs or relates both to himself or herself and to one or more other people. ❑ *That car is ours.* [from Old English]

**our|selves** /aʊərsɛlvz/

> **Ourselves** is the first person plural reflexive pronoun.

**1** PRON You use **ourselves** to refer to yourself and one or more other people as a group. ❑ *We sat by the fire to keep ourselves warm.* **2** PRON A speaker or writer sometimes uses **ourselves** to refer to people in general. ❑ *We all worry about ourselves and the situation we're in.* **3** PRON You use **ourselves** to emphasize a first person plural subject. ❑ *Other people think the same as we ourselves think.* **4** PRON If you say something such as "We did it **ourselves**," you are indicating that the people you are referring to did it, rather than anyone else. ❑ *We built the house ourselves.*

**oust** /aʊst/ (**ousts, ousting, ousted**) V-T If someone **is ousted** from a position of power, job, or place, they are forced to leave it. ❑ *The leaders were ousted from power.* ❑ *The Republicans may oust him in November.* ● **oust|er** (**ousters**) N-COUNT ❑ *Some groups called for the ouster of the police chief.* ● **oust|ing** N-UNCOUNT ❑ *...the ousting of his boss.* [from Latin]

> **out**
> **1** ADVERB USES
> **2** ADJECTIVE AND ADVERB USES
> **3** PREPOSITION USES

**1 out** /aʊt/

> **Out** is often used with verbs of movement, such as "walk" and "pull," and also in phrasal verbs such as "give out" and "run out."

**1** ADV When something is in a particular place and you take it **out**, you remove it from that place. ❑ *He took out his notebook.* **2** ADV If you are **out**, you are not at home or not at your usual place of work. ❑ *I called you yesterday, but you were out.* [from Old English]

**2 out** /aʊt/ **1** ADJ If a light or fire is **out** or goes **out**, it is no longer shining or burning. ❑ *All the lights were out in the house.* **2** ADJ If flowers are **out**, their petals have opened. ● **Out** is also an adverb. ❑ *I love it when I see the spring flowers coming out.* **3** ADJ If something such as a book or CD is **out**, it is available for people to buy. ❑ *Their new* *album is out now.* ● **Out** is also an adverb. ❑ *The book came out in 2006.* **4** ADJ In a game or sport, if someone is **out**, they can no longer take part either because they are unable to or because they have been defeated. **5** ADJ In baseball, a player is **out** if they do not reach a base safely. When three players on a team are out in an inning, then the team is **out**. **6** ADJ If you say that a calculation or measurement is **out**, you mean that it is incorrect. ❑ *It was only a few inches out.* **7** ADJ If someone is **out** to do something, they intend to do it. [INFORMAL] ❑ *Most companies are just out to make money.* [from Old English]

**❸ out** /aʊt/

> **Out of** is used with verbs of movement, such as "walk" and "pull," and also in phrasal verbs such as "get out of" and "grow out of." **Out** is often used instead of **out of**, for example in "He looked out the window."

**1** PHRASE If you go **out of** a place, you leave it. ❑ *She let him out of the house.* **2** PHRASE If you take

out

something **out of** the container or place where it has been, you remove it so that it is no longer there. ❑ *I took the key out of my purse.* **3** PHRASE If you look or shout **out of** a window, you look or shout from the room where you are toward the outside. ❑ *He was looking out of the window.* **4** PHRASE If you are **out of** the sun, the rain, or the wind, you are sheltered from it. ❑ *Keep babies out of the sun.* **5** PHRASE If someone or something gets **out of** a situation, especially an unpleasant one, they are then no longer in it. If they keep **out of** it, they do not start being in it. ❑ *He needed his brother to get him out of trouble.* **6** PHRASE You use **out of** to say what feeling or reason causes someone to do something. ❑ *He visited her out of a sense of duty.* **7** PHRASE If you get something such as information or work **out of** someone, you manage to make them give it to you. ❑ *I asked him where she was, but I couldn't get anything out of him.* **8** PHRASE If you get pleasure or an advantage **out of** something, you get it as a result of being involved with that thing or making use of it. ❑ *I wasn't getting any fun out of tennis anymore.* **9** PHRASE If you are **out of** something, you no longer have any of it. ❑ *We're out of milk.* **10** PHRASE If something is made **out of** a particular material, it has been formed or constructed from it. ❑ *...buildings made out of wood.* **11** PHRASE You use **out of** to indicate what proportion of a group of things something is true of. ❑ *Three out of four people say there's too much violence on TV.* [from Old English]

**out|age** /aʊtɪdʒ/ (outages) N-COUNT An **outage** is a period of time when the electricity supply to a building or area is interrupted, for example because of damage to the cables. ❑ *A windstorm caused power outages throughout the region.* [from Old English]

**out|back** /aʊtbæk/ N-SING The parts of Australia that are far away from towns are referred to as **the outback**.

**out|box** /aʊtbɒks/ (outboxes) also out-box **1** N-COUNT An **outbox** is a shallow container used in offices to put letters and documents in when

they have been dealt with. ❑ *He put the letter in his outbox.* **2** N-COUNT On a computer, your **outbox** is the part of your mailbox which stores e-mails that you have not yet sent.

**out|break** /aʊtbreɪk/ (outbreaks) N-COUNT If there is an **outbreak of** something unpleasant, such as violence or a disease, it suddenly starts to happen. ❑ *The outbreak of violence involved hundreds of youths.* ❑ *...an outbreak of flu.*

**out|burst** /aʊtbɜrst/ (outbursts) **1** N-COUNT An **outburst** of an emotion, especially anger, is a sudden strong expression of that emotion. ❑ *...an outburst of grief.* **2** N-COUNT An **outburst of** violent activity is a sudden period of this activity. ❑ *Five people were killed in an outburst of violence.*

**out|cast** /aʊtkæst/ (outcasts) N-COUNT An **outcast** is someone who is not accepted by a group of people or by society. ❑ *He was an outcast, unwanted and alone.*

**out|come** /aʊtkʌm/ (outcomes) N-COUNT The **outcome** of an activity, process, or situation is the situation that exists at the end of it. ❑ *He was pleased with the outcome of the meeting.* ❑ *It's too early to know the outcome of her illness.*

**out|cry** /aʊtkraɪ/ (outcries) N-VAR An **outcry** is a reaction of strong disapproval and anger shown by the public or media about a recent event. ❑ *The killing caused an international outcry.*

**out|dat|ed** /aʊtdeɪtɪd/ ADJ If you describe something as **outdated**, you mean that you think it is old-fashioned and no longer useful or relevant to modern life. ❑ *...outdated and inefficient factories.* ❑ *...outdated attitudes.*

**out|do** /aʊtduː/ (outdoes, outdoing, outdid, outdone) V-T If you **outdo** someone, you are a lot more successful than they are at a particular activity. ❑ *His cousin outdid him in everything.*

**out|door** /aʊtdɔr/ ADJ **Outdoor** activities or things happen or are used outside and not in a building. ❑ *If you enjoy outdoor activities, you should try rock climbing.*

**out|doors** /aʊtdɔrz/ **1** ADV If something happens **outdoors**, it happens outside rather than in a building. ❑ *It was warm enough to be outdoors all afternoon.* **2** N-SING You refer to **the outdoors** when talking about activities that take place outside away from buildings. ❑ *I love the outdoors.*

**out|doors|man** /aʊtdɔrzmən/ (outdoorsmen) N-COUNT An **outdoorsman** is a man who spends a lot of time outdoors, doing things such as camping, hunting, or fishing.

**out|er** /aʊtər/ ADJ The **outer** parts of something are the parts which contain or enclose the other parts, and which are furthest from the center. ❑ *He heard a voice in the outer room.* [from Old English]

**out|er core** N-SING The **outer core** of the Earth is the layer of the Earth's interior between the mantle and the inner core.

**out|er space** N-UNCOUNT **Outer space** is the area outside the Earth's atmosphere where the other planets and stars are.
→ see **satellite**

**out|fit** /aʊtfɪt/ (outfits, outfitting, outfitted) **1** N-COUNT An **outfit** is a set of clothes. ❑ *William wore a green outfit with brown shoes.* **2** N-COUNT You can refer to an organization as an **outfit**.

❑ *We are a professional outfit.* **3** V-T To **outfit** someone or something means to provide them with equipment for a particular purpose. ❑ *They outfitted me with a talking computer.*

**out|flow** /ˈaʊtfloʊ/ (**outflows**) N-COUNT When there is an **outflow of** money or people, a large amount of money or people move from one place to another. ❑ *There was an outflow of about $650 million.*

**out|going** /ˈaʊtgoʊɪŋ/ **1** ADJ **Outgoing** things such as planes, mail, and passengers are leaving or being sent somewhere. ❑ *All outgoing flights were canceled.* **2** ADJ Someone who is **outgoing** is very friendly and likes meeting and talking to people. ❑ *He was an outgoing, fun-loving guy.* **3** ADJ You use **outgoing** to describe a person in charge of something who is soon going to leave that position. ❑ *...the outgoing director of the International Music Festival.*

**out|grow** /ˌaʊtˈgroʊ/ (**outgrows, outgrowing, outgrew, outgrown**) V-T If a child **outgrows** a piece of clothing, they grow bigger, so that it no longer fits them. ❑ *She has outgrown her clothes, so her mother is buying her new ones.*

**out|house** /ˈaʊthaʊs/ (**outhouses**) N-COUNT An **outhouse** is an outside toilet.

**out|ing** /ˈaʊtɪŋ/ (**outings**) N-COUNT An **outing** is a short trip, usually with a group of people, away from your home, school, or place of work. ❑ *She went on an outing to the local movie theater.* [from Old English]

**out|law** /ˈaʊtlɔ/ (**outlaws, outlawing, outlawed**) V-T When you **outlaw** something, or it is **outlawed**, it is made illegal. ❑ *Should using a cellphone while driving be outlawed?* ❑ *The government has outlawed some political groups.*

**out|lay** /ˈaʊtleɪ/ (**outlays**) N-VAR **Outlay** is the amount of money that you have to spend in order to buy something or start a project. ❑ *...the financial outlay for equipment.*

**out|let** /ˈaʊtlɛt, -lɪt/ (**outlets**) **1** N-COUNT An **outlet** is a store or organization which sells the goods made by a particular manufacturer at a discount price, often direct from the manufacturer. ❑ *...the largest retail outlet in the city.* ❑ *At the factory outlet you'll find items costing 75% less than regular prices.* **2** N-COUNT If someone has an **outlet for** their feelings or ideas, they have a means of expressing and releasing them. ❑ *Trevor found an outlet for his talent when he got a part in the school play.* **3** N-COUNT An **outlet** is a hole or pipe through which liquid or air can flow away. ❑ *...a warm air outlet.* **4** N-COUNT An **outlet** is a place, usually in a wall, where you can connect electrical devices to the electricity supply. ❑ *Just plug it into any electric outlet.*

**out|line** /ˈaʊtlaɪn/ (**outlines, outlining, outlined**) **1** V-T If you **outline** an idea or a plan, you explain it in a general way. ❑ *The governor outlined his plan to improve the state's image.* **2** N-COUNT An **outline** is a general explanation or description of something. ❑ *...an outline of the results of the study.* **3** V-T PASSIVE You say that an object **is outlined** when you can see its general shape because there is light behind it. ❑ *The hotel was outlined against the lights.*

**out|live** /ˌaʊtˈlɪv/ (**outlives, outliving, outlived**) V-T If one person **outlives** another, they are still alive after the second person has died. If one thing **outlives** another thing, it still exists after the second thing has disappeared. ❑ *I'm sure Rose will outlive many of us.*

**out|look** /ˈaʊtlʊk/ (**outlooks**) **1** N-COUNT Your **outlook** is your general attitude toward life. ❑ *He had a positive outlook on life.* **2** N-SING The **outlook** for something is whether or not it is going to be positive, successful, or safe. ❑ *The economic outlook is not good.*

**out|ly|ing** /ˈaʊtlaɪɪŋ/ ADJ **Outlying** places are far away from the main cities of a country. ❑ *Tourists can visit outlying areas like the Napa Valley.*

**out|ma|neu|ver** /ˌaʊtməˈnuvər/ (**outmaneuvers, outmaneuvering, outmaneuvered**) V-T If you **outmaneuver** someone, you gain an advantage over them in a particular situation by behaving in a clever and skillful way. ❑ *Murphy quietly outmaneuvered him in the competition.*

**out|num|ber** /ˌaʊtˈnʌmbər/ (**outnumbers, outnumbering, outnumbered**) V-T If one group of people or things **outnumbers** another, the first group has more people or things in it than the second group. ❑ *In this town, men outnumber women four to one.*

**out-of-court** → see court

**out of date** also **out-of-date** ADJ Something that is **out of date** is old-fashioned and no longer useful. ❑ *The rules were out of date and confusing.*

**out-of-state** **1** ADJ **Out-of-state** is used to describe people who do not live permanently in a particular state within a country, but have traveled there from somewhere else. ❑ *95% of our students are out-of-state students.* **2** ADJ **Out-of-state** companies are based outside a particular state but conduct business within that state. ❑ *...competition from out-of-state banks.*

**out of work** ADJ Someone who is **out of work** does not have a job. ❑ *Many people are out of work in this town.*

**out|post** /ˈaʊtpoʊst/ (**outposts**) N-COUNT An **outpost** is a small settlement or community that is far away from the main cities and towns of a country. ❑ *This rural outpost has only a few houses.*

**out|put** /ˈaʊtpʊt/ (**outputs**) **1** N-VAR **Output** is used to refer to the amount of something that a person or thing produces. ❑ *...a large fall in industrial output.* **2** N-VAR The **output** of a computer is the information that it displays on a screen or prints on paper as a result of a particular program. ❑ *You run the software, then look at the output.*

**out|put force** (**output forces**) N-VAR The **output force** is the force that is applied to an object by a machine. [TECHNICAL]

O

**out|rage** (outrages, outraging, outraged)

The verb is pronounced /aʊtreɪdʒ/. The noun is pronounced /aʊtreɪdʒ/.

**1** V-T If you **are outraged** by something, it makes you extremely angry and shocked. ◻ *Many people were outraged by his comments.* ● **out|raged** ADJ ◻ *...outraged readers.* **2** N-UNCOUNT **Outrage** is an intense feeling of anger and shock. ◻ *Several teachers wrote to the newspapers to express their outrage.* **3** N-COUNT You can refer to an act or event that angers and shocks you as an **outrage**. ◻ *It is an outrage that he is being let out of prison so soon.* [from French]

**out|ra|geous** /aʊtreɪdʒəs/ ADJ If you describe something as **outrageous**, you are emphasizing that it is unacceptable or very shocking. ◻ *It was outrageous behavior.* ● **out|ra|geous|ly** ADV ◻ *...outrageously expensive skincare items.* [from French]

**out|right**

The adjective is pronounced /aʊtraɪt/. The adverb is pronounced /aʊtraɪt/.

**1** ADJ You use **outright** to describe behavior and actions that are open and direct, rather than indirect. ◻ *He told an outright lie.* ● **Outright** is also an adverb. ◻ *Why don't you tell me outright?* **2** ADJ **Outright** means complete and total. ◻ *She failed to win an outright victory.* ● **Outright** is also an adverb. ◻ *The offer wasn't rejected outright.* **3** PHRASE If someone **is killed outright**, they die immediately, for example, in an accident.

**out|set** /aʊtsɛt/ PHRASE If something happens **at the outset** of an event, process, or period of time, it happens at the beginning of it. If something happens **from the outset**, it happens from the beginning and continues to happen. ◻ *You must decide at the outset which courses you want to take.*

**out|side** /aʊtsaɪd/ (outsides)

The form **outside of** can also be used as a preposition.

**1** N-COUNT The **outside** of something is the part which surrounds or encloses the rest of it. ◻ *...the outside of the building.* ● **Outside** is also an adjective. ◻ *...the outside wall.* **2** ADV If you are **outside**, you are not inside a building but are quite close to it. ◻ *She went outside to look for Sam.* ● **Outside** is also a preposition. ◻ *The victim was outside a store when he was attacked.* ● **Outside** is also an adjective. ◻ *...the outside temperature.* **3** PREP If you are **outside** a room, you are not in it but are in the passage or area next to it. ◻ *She sent him outside the classroom.* ● **Outside** is also an adverb. ◻ *They heard voices coming from outside in the hall.* **4** ADJ When you talk about the **outside** world, you are referring to things that happen or exist in places other than your own home or community. ◻ *The soldiers had no radios and no news of the outside world.* **5** PREP People or things **outside** a country, city, or region are not in it. ◻ *...a castle outside Budapest.* ● **Outside** is also a noun. ◻ *We can only look at this society from the outside.* **6** ADJ **Outside** people or organizations are not part of a particular organization or group. ◻ *...outside consultants.* ● **Outside** is also a preposition. ◻ *He hired someone from outside the company.* **7** PREP Something that happens **outside** a particular period of time happens at a different

time from the one mentioned. ◻ *The bank is open outside normal banking hours.*

**Thesaurus** *outside* Also look up :

ADJ. exterior, outdoor; (ant.) inside, interior **1**
PREP. beyond, near; (ant.) inside **3**

**Word Partnership** Use *outside* with :

N. the outside **of a building** **1**
outside **a building**, outside **a car**,
outside **a room**, outside **a store** **3**
the outside **world** **4**
outside **a city/town**, outside **a country** **5**
outside **sources** **6**
ADJ. **cold** outside, **dark** outside **2**
V. **gather** outside, **go** outside, **park**
outside, **sit** outside, **stand** outside, **step**
outside, **wait** outside **2 3**

**out|sid|er** /aʊtsaɪdər/ (outsiders) **1** N-COUNT An **outsider** is someone who does not belong to a particular group or organization. ◻ *A lot of the work went to outsiders.* **2** N-COUNT An **outsider** is someone who is not accepted by a particular group, or who feels that they do not belong in it. ◻ *Malone felt very much an outsider.* **3** N-COUNT In a competition, an **outsider** is a competitor who is unlikely to win. ◻ *He was an outsider in the race.*

**out|skirts** /aʊtskɜrts/ N-PLURAL The **outskirts** of a city or town are the parts of it that are farthest away from its center. ◻ *...the outskirts of New York.*

**out|spo|ken** /aʊtspoʊkən/ ADJ Someone who is **outspoken** gives their opinions about things openly and honestly, even if they are likely to shock or offend people. ◻ *He was outspoken in his support for political change.* ● **out|spo|ken|ness** N-UNCOUNT ◻ *The company fired her because of her outspokenness.*

**out|stand|ing** /aʊtstændɪŋ/ **1** ADJ If you describe someone or something as **outstanding**, you think that they are very remarkable and impressive. ◻ *Derartu is an outstanding athlete.* ● **out|stand|ing|ly** ADV ◻ *Guatemala is an outstandingly beautiful place.* **2** ADJ Money that is **outstanding** has not yet been paid and is still owed to someone. ◻ *The total debt outstanding is $70 billion.* **3** ADJ **Outstanding** issues or problems have not yet been resolved. ◻ *There are still outstanding matters to resolve.* **4** ADJ **Outstanding** means very important or obvious. ◻ *...an outstanding example of a small business that became a big one.*

**out|stretched** /aʊtstrɛtʃt/ ADJ If a part of the body of a person or animal is **outstretched**, it is stretched out as far as possible. ◻ *She held his outstretched hand.*

**out|strip** /aʊtstrɪp/ (outstrips, outstripping, outstripped) V-T If one thing outstrips another, the first thing becomes larger in amount, or more successful or important, than the second thing. ◻ *Sales of digital cameras have outstripped those of film cameras for the last two years.*

**outta** /aʊtə/ **Outta** is used in written English to represent the words "out of" when they are pronounced informally. ◻ *Get outta here!*

**out|ward** /aʊtwərd/

The form **outwards** can also be used for meaning **3**.

**1** ADJ The **outward** feelings, qualities, or attitudes of someone or something are the ones they appear to have rather than the ones that they actually have. ❑ *In spite of my outward calm, I was scared.*
● **out|ward|ly** ADV ❑ *He was outwardly friendly.*
**2** ADJ The **outward** features of something are the ones that you can see from the outside. ❑ *Mark had no outward sign of injury.* **3** ADV If something moves or faces **outward**, it moves or faces away from the place you are in or the place you are talking about. ❑ *The top door opened outward.* **4** ADJ An **outward** flight or journey is one that you make away from a place that you are intending to return to later. [from Old English]

**out|wards** /aʊtwərdz/ → see **outward**

**out|weigh** /aʊtweɪ/ (**outweighs, outweighing, outweighed**) V-T If one thing **outweighs** another, the first thing is of greater importance, benefit, or significance than the second thing. [FORMAL] ❑ *The advantages of this deal outweigh the disadvantages.*

**out|wit** /aʊtwɪt/ (**outwits, outwitting, outwitted**) V-T If you **outwit** someone, you use your intelligence or a trick to defeat them or to gain an advantage over them. ❑ *He needs to outwit the others in the competition.*

**oval** /oʊvəl/ (**ovals**) ADJ **Oval** things have a shape that is like a circle but is wider in one direction than the other. ● **Oval** is also a noun. ❑ *Cut the cheese into ovals.* [from Medieval Latin] → see **circle, shape**

**Oval Of|fice** N-UNCOUNT The **Oval Office** is the American president's private office in the White House. You can also use **the Oval Office** to refer to the American presidency itself.

**ova|ry** /oʊvəri/ (**ovaries**) N-COUNT A woman's **ovaries** are the two organs in her body that produce eggs. [from New Latin]

**ova|tion** /oʊveɪʃən/ (**ovations**) N-COUNT An **ovation** is a large amount of applause from an audience for a particular performer. [FORMAL] ❑ *The band received an ovation on their appearance in New York City.* [from Latin]

**oven** /ʌvən/ (**ovens**) N-COUNT An **oven** is a device for cooking that is like a large box with a door. [from Old English]

---
**over**
**1** POSITION AND MOVEMENT
**2** AMOUNTS AND OCCURRENCES
**3** OTHER USES
---

**1 over** /oʊvər/

In addition to the uses shown below, **over** is used after some verbs, nouns, and adjectives in order to introduce extra information. **Over** is also used in phrasal verbs such as "hand over" and "glaze over."

**1** PREP If one thing is **over** another thing or is moving **over** it, the first thing is directly above the second, either resting on it, or with a space between them. ❑ *He looked at himself in the mirror over the table.* ● **Over** is also an adverb. ❑ *…planes*

flying over. **2** PREP If one thing is **over** another thing, it covers part or all of it. ❑ *Pour the sauce over the mushrooms.* ❑ *He was wearing a gray suit over a shirt.* ● **Over** is also an adverb. ❑ *Heat the milk and pour it over.* **3** PREP If you lean **over** an object, you bend your body so that the top part of it is above the object. ❑ *They stopped to lean over a gate.* ● **Over** is also an adverb. ❑ *Sam leaned over, and opened the door of the car.* **4** PREP If you look **over** or talk **over** an object, you look or talk across the top of it. ❑ *I looked over his shoulder.* **5** PREP If a window has a view **over** an area of land or water, you can see the land or water through the window. ❑ *The restaurant has a wonderful view over the river.* **6** PREP If someone or something goes **over** a barrier, obstacle, or boundary, they get to the other side of it by going across it, or across the top of it. ❑ *I stepped over a piece of wood.* ● **Over** is also an adverb. ❑ *I climbed over into the back seat of the car.* **7** PREP If something is on the opposite side of a road or river, you can say that it is **over** the road or river. ❑ *…a fashionable neighborhood, just over the river from Manhattan.* **8** ADV You can use **over** to indicate a particular position or place a short distance away from you. ❑ *He saw Rolfe standing over by the window.* **9** ADV If something rolls **over** or is turned **over**, its position changes so that the part that was facing upward is now facing downward. ❑ *His car rolled over on an icy road.* **10** PHRASE **Over here** means near you, or in the country you are in. ❑ *Why don't you come over here tomorrow?* **11** PHRASE **Over there** means in a place a short distance away from you, or in another country. ❑ *The café is just over there.* ❑ *Ray asked me about France. He's going over there for a while.* [from Old English]
→ see **location**

**2 over** /oʊvər/ **1** PREP If something is **over** a particular amount, measurement, or age, it is more than that amount, measurement, or age. ❑ *The disease killed over 4 million people last year.* ❑ *The house is worth well over $1 million.* ● **Over** is also an adverb. ❑ *…people aged 65 and over.* **2** PHRASE **Over and above** an amount, especially a normal amount, means more than that amount or in addition to it. ❑ *We grew vegetables in the garden over and above our own needs.* **3** PREP If you do something **over**, you do it again or start doing it again from the beginning. ❑ *He wanted a chance to come back and do it over.* [from Old English]

**3 over** /oʊvər/ **1** ADJ If an activity is **over** or **all over**, it is completely finished. ❑ *The war is over.* ❑ *I am glad it's all over.* **2** PREP If you are **over** an illness or an experience, it has finished and you have recovered from its effects. ❑ *I'm glad that you're over the flu.* **3** PREP If you have control or influence **over** someone or something, you are able to control them or influence them. ❑ *He never had any influence over her.* **4** PREP You use **over** to indicate what a disagreement or feeling relates to or is caused by. ❑ *Staff are protesting over pay.* **5** PREP If something happens **over** a particular period of time or **over** something such as a meal, it happens during that time or during the meal. ❑ *The number of attacks has gone down over the past week.* [from Old English]

**over|all** (**overalls**)

The adjective and adverb are pronounced /oʊvərɔl/. The noun is pronounced /oʊvərɔl/.

**1** ADJ You use **overall** to indicate that you are

talking about a situation in general or about the whole of something. ❑ ...*the overall rise in unemployment.* ● **Overall** is also an adverb. ❑ *Overall I was disappointed.* **2** N-PLURAL **Overalls** are pants that are attached to a piece of cloth which covers your chest and which has straps going over your shoulders. [from Old English]

**over|board** /**oʊ**vərbɔrd/ ADV If you fall **overboard**, you fall over the side of a boat into the water.

**over|came** /**oʊ**vərkeɪm/ **Overcame** is the past tense of **overcome**.

**over|charge** /**oʊ**vərtʃɑrdʒ/ (**overcharges, overcharging, overcharged**) V-T If someone **overcharges** you, they charge you too much for their goods or services. ❑ *The taxi driver overcharged him.*

**over|coat** /**oʊ**vərkoʊt/ (**overcoats**) N-COUNT An **overcoat** is a thick warm coat.

**over|come** /**oʊ**vərk**ʌ**m/ (**overcomes, overcoming, overcame**)

> The form **overcome** is used in the present tense and is also the past participle.

**1** V-T If you **overcome** a problem or a feeling, you successfully deal with it and control it. ❑ *Molly finally overcame her fear of flying.* **2** V-T If you **are overcome by** a feeling, you feel it very strongly. ❑ *The night before the test I was overcome by fear.* **3** V-T If you **are overcome by** smoke or a poisonous gas, you become very ill or die from breathing it in. ❑ *People tried to escape from the fire but were overcome by smoke.*

---

**Word Partnership** Use *overcome* with :

| | |
|---|---|
| ADJ. | **difficult to** overcome, **hard to** overcome **1** |
| N. | overcome **difficulties**, overcome a **fear**, overcome **an obstacle/problem**, overcome **opposition 1** overcome **by emotion**, overcome **by fear 2** |

---

**over|crowd|ed** /**oʊ**vərkraʊdɪd/ ADJ An **overcrowded** place has too many things or people in it. ❑ ...*an overcrowded beach.*

**over|crowd|ing** /**oʊ**vərkraʊdɪŋ/ N-UNCOUNT If there is a problem of **overcrowding**, there are more people living in a place than it was designed for. ❑ *Students are protesting at overcrowding in the dorms.*

**over|do** /**oʊ**vərdu/ (**overdoes, overdoing, overdid, overdone**) **1** V-T If someone **overdoes** something, they behave in an exaggerated or extreme way. ❑ *Don't overdo the praise.* **2** V-T If you **overdo** an activity, you try to do more than you can physically manage. ❑ *It is important not to overdo new exercises.* ❑ *It's important to study hard, but don't overdo it.*

**over|dose** /**oʊ**vərdoʊs/ (**overdoses, overdosing, overdosed**) **1** N-COUNT If someone takes an **overdose** of a drug, they take more of it than is safe. ❑ *He died of an overdose of sleeping pills.* **2** V-I If someone **overdoses on** a drug, they take more of it than is safe. ❑ *He overdosed on painkillers.*

**over|draft** /**oʊ**vərdræft/ (**overdrafts**) N-COUNT If you have an **overdraft**, you have spent more money than you have in your bank account, and so you are in debt to the bank.

**over|due** /**oʊ**vərdu/ **1** ADJ If you say that a change or an event is **overdue**, you mean that you think it should have happened before now. ❑ *This discussion is long overdue.* **2** ADJ **Overdue** sums of money have not been paid, even though it is later than the date on which they should have been paid. ❑ ...*a 2% interest charge on overdue accounts.*

**over easy** also **over-easy** PHRASE If a fried egg is served **over easy**, it is cooked on both sides.

**over|eat** /**oʊ**vərit/ (**overeats, overeating, overate, overeaten**) V-I If someone **overeats**, he or she eats more than is necessary to be healthy. ❑ *Some people overeat because they're unhappy.*

**over|es|ti|mate** (**overestimates, overestimating, overestimated**)

> The verb is pronounced /**oʊ**vər**ɛ**stimeɪt/. The noun is pronounced /**oʊ**vər**ɛ**stimit/.

**1** V-T If you **overestimate** something, you think it is greater in amount or importance than it really is. ❑ *He overestimated their desire for peace.* ❑ *You should overestimate the amount of money you need, as things usually cost more than you expect.* **2** V-T If you **overestimate** someone, you think that they have more of a skill or quality than they really have. ❑ *I think you're overestimating me.*

**over|flow** (**overflows, overflowing, overflowed**)

> The verb is pronounced /**oʊ**vərfloʊ/. The noun is pronounced /**oʊ**vərfloʊ/.

**1** V-T/V-I If a liquid or a river **overflows**, it flows over the edges of the container or place it is in. ❑ *The rivers overflowed their banks.* ❑ *The bath overflowed.* **2** V-I If a place or container **is overflowing with** people or things, it is too full of them. ❑ ...*a room overflowing with journalists.*

**over|grown** /**oʊ**vərgroʊn/ ADJ If a garden or other place is **overgrown**, it is covered with a lot of weeds and wild plants because it has not been cared for. ❑ *The yard was overgrown with weeds.*

**over|hang** (**overhangs, overhanging, overhung** /**oʊ**vərhæŋ/) V-T If one thing **overhangs** another, it sticks out over and above it. ❑ *Part of the roof overhung the path.*

**over|haul** (**overhauls, overhauling, overhauled**)

> The verb is pronounced /**oʊ**vərhɔl/. The noun is pronounced /**oʊ**vərhɔl/.

**1** V-T If a piece of equipment **is overhauled**, it is cleaned, checked thoroughly, and repaired if necessary. ❑ *The heating system was overhauled a year ago.* ● **Overhaul** is also a noun. ❑ ...*the overhaul of a ship.* **2** V-T If you **overhaul** a system or method, you examine it carefully and make many changes in it in order to improve it. ❑ ...*plans to overhaul the banking laws.* ● **Overhaul** is also a noun. ❑ *We really need an overhaul of the legal system.*

**over|head**

> The adjective is pronounced /**oʊ**vərh**ɛ**d/. The adverb is pronounced /**oʊ**vərh**ɛ**d/.

ADJ You use **overhead** to indicate that something is above you or above the place that you are talking about. ❑ *She turned on the overhead light.* ● **Overhead** is also an adverb. ❑ *Planes passed overhead.*

**over|hear** /**oʊ**vərhɪər/ (**overhears, overhearing, overheard**) V-T If you **overhear** someone, you hear what they are saying when they are not talking to you and they do not know that you are listening. ❑ *I overheard two doctors discussing my case.*

**over|heat** /o͞uvərhi̱t/ (**overheats, overheating, overheated**) v-t/v-i If something **overheats** or if you **overheat** it, it becomes hotter than is necessary or desirable. ❑ *The car's engine was overheating.* • **over|heat|ed** ADJ ❑ *...a stuffy, overheated apartment.*

**over|hung** /o͞uvərhʌ̱ŋ/ **Overhung** is the past tense and past participle of **overhang.**

**over|joyed** /o͞uvərdʒɔ̱ɪd/ ADJ If you are **overjoyed**, you are extremely happy about something. ❑ *Shelley was overjoyed to see me.*

**over|land** /o͞uvərlænd/ ADJ An **overland** journey is made across land rather than by ship or airplane. • **Overland** is also an adverb. ❑ *They're traveling to Baghdad overland.*

**over|lap** (**overlaps, overlapping, overlapped**)

The verb is pronounced /o͞uvərlæ̱p/. The noun is pronounced /o͞uvərlæp/.

**1** v-recip If one thing **overlaps** another, or if you **overlap** them, a part of the first thing covers a part of the other. You can also say that two things **overlap**. ❑ *When the bag is folded, the bottom overlaps one side.* ❑ *Overlap the tomato slices.* **2** v-recip If one idea or activity **overlaps** another, or **overlaps** with another, they involve some of the same subjects, people, or periods of time. ❑ *The baseball season overlapped with the Olympics.* • **Overlap** is also a noun. ❑ *...the overlap between the policies of the two political parties.*

**over|load** (**overloads, overloading, overloaded**)

The verb is pronounced /o͞uvərlo͞u̱d/. The noun is pronounced /o͞uvərlo͞ud/.

**1** v-t If you **overload** something such as a vehicle, you put more things or people into it than it was designed to carry. ❑ *Don't overload the boat or it will sink.* • **over|load|ed** ADJ ❑ *...overloaded trucks.* **2** v-t To **overload** someone **with** work, problems, or information means to give them more work, problems, or information than they can cope with. ❑ *We're trying not to overload staff with too much paperwork.* • **Overload** is also a noun. ❑ *57 percent of people complained of work overload.* • **over|load|ed** ADJ ❑ *The waiter was already overloaded with orders.*

**over|look** /o͞uvərlʊ̱k/ (**overlooks, overlooking, overlooked**) **1** v-t If a building or window **overlooks** a place, you can see the place clearly from the building or window. ❑ *The hotel's rooms overlook a beautiful garden.* **2** v-t If you **overlook** a fact or problem, you do not notice it, or do not realize how important it is. ❑ *We overlook all sorts of warning signals about our own health.* **3** v-t If you **overlook** someone's faults or bad behavior, you forgive them and take no action. ❑ *They're a close family who overlook each other's faults.*

**over|ly** /o͞uvərli/ ADV **Overly** means more than is normal, necessary, or reasonable. ❑ *Employers were overly cautious about hiring new staff.*

**over|night** /o͞uvərna̱ɪt/ **1** ADV **Overnight** means throughout the night or at some point during the night. ❑ *The decision was reached overnight.* • **Overnight** is also an adjective. ❑ *Travel and overnight accommodations are included in the price.* **2** ADV You can say that something happens **overnight** when it happens very quickly and unexpectedly. ❑ *The rules are not going to change overnight.* • **Overnight** is also an adjective. ❑ *He became an overnight success.* [from Old English]

**over|pass** /o͞uvərpæs/ (**overpasses**) N-count An **overpass** is a structure which carries one road over the top of another one. [from Old French]

**over|popu|la|tion** /o͞uvərpɒpyəleɪ̯ʃ°n/ N-uncount If there is a problem of **overpopulation** in an area, there are more people living there than can be supported properly.

**over|pow|er** /o͞uvərpaʊ̯ər/ (**overpowers, overpowering, overpowered**) **1** v-t If you **overpower** someone, you manage to take hold of and keep hold of them, although they struggle a lot. ❑ *It took ten men to overpower him.* **2** v-t If a feeling **overpowers** you, it suddenly affects you very strongly. ❑ *A sudden weakness overpowered him.* • **over|pow|ering** ADJ ❑ *Jealousy can be overpowering.* [from vulgar Latin]

**over|pow|er|ing** /o͞uvərpaʊ̯ərɪŋ/ ADJ An **overpowering** person makes other people feel uncomfortable because they have such a strong personality. ❑ *Mrs. Winter was large and overpowering.* [from vulgar Latin]

**over|ran** /o͞uvərræ̱n/ **Overran** is the past tense of **overrun.**

**over|rate** /o͞uvərreɪ̱t/ (**overrates, overrating, overrated**) v-t If you say that something or someone **is overrated**, you mean that people have a higher opinion of them than they deserve. ❑ *The joys of work are overrated.* • **over|rat|ed** ADJ ❑ *Life in the city is very overrated.* [from Old French]

**over|ride** (**overrides, overriding, overrode, overridden**)

The verb is pronounced /o͞uvərraɪ̱d/. The noun is pronounced /o͞uvərraɪd/.

**1** v-t If one thing in a situation **overrides** other things, it is more important than they are. ❑ *A child's needs should always override those of its parents.* • **over|rid|ing** ADJ ❑ *My overriding concern is to raise the standards of education.* **2** v-t If someone in authority **overrides** a person or their decisions, they cancel their decisions. ❑ *The senate failed to override his decision.* **3** N-count An **override** is an attempt to cancel a decision by using your authority over someone or by gaining more votes than they do in an election or contest. ❑ *...the override of a decision of the Supreme Court.* [from Old English]

**over|rule** /o͞uvərru̱l/ (**overrules, overruling, overruled**) v-t If someone in authority **overrules** a person or their decision, they officially decide that the decision is incorrect or not valid. ❑ *The court overruled his decision.* [from Old French]

**over|run** /o͞uvərrʌ̱n/ (**overruns, overrunning, overran**) **1** v-t If an army **overruns** a place, it succeeds in occupying it very quickly. ❑ *A group of soldiers overran the area.* **2** ADJ If you say that a place **is overrun with** things that you consider undesirable, you mean that there are a large number of them there. ❑ *The hotel closed because it was overrun by mice and rats.* **3**

**over|seas** /o͞uvərsi̱z/ **1** ADJ You use **overseas** to describe things that involve or are in foreign countries. ❑ *...his overseas trip.* • **Overseas** is also an adverb. ❑ *He's currently working overseas.* **2** ADJ An **overseas** student or visitor comes from a foreign country. ❑ *Every year nine million overseas visitors come to the city.*

**over|see** /o͞uvərsi̱/ (**oversees, overseeing,**

O

**oversaw, overseen**) V-T If someone in authority **oversees** a job or an activity, they make sure that it is done properly. ❏ *As program manager, she oversaw a team of engineers working on a new line of cars.*

**over|shad|ow** /oʊvərʃædoʊ/ (**overshadows, overshadowing, overshadowed**) ■ V-T If an unpleasant event or feeling **overshadows** something, it makes it less happy or enjoyable. ❏ *Gordon's early life was overshadowed by the death of his father.* ■ V-T If you **are overshadowed by** a person or thing, you are less successful, important, or impressive than they are. ❏ *Helen is overshadowed by her younger and more attractive sister.*

**over|sight** /oʊvərsaɪt/ (**oversights**) N-COUNT If there has been an **oversight**, someone has forgotten to do something which they should have done. ❏ *He apologized for the oversight.*

**over|state** /oʊvərsteɪt/ (**overstates, overstating, overstated**) V-T If you say that someone **is overstating** something, you mean they are describing it in a way that makes it seem more important or serious than it really is. ❏ *It's impossible to overstate the importance of his work.*

**overt** /oʊvɜrt/ ADJ An **overt** action or attitude is done or shown in an open and obvious way. ❏ *...overt criticism.* ● **overt|ly** ADV ❏ *He wrote a few overtly political songs.*

**over|take** /oʊvərteɪk/ (**overtakes, overtaking, overtook, overtaken**) ■ V-T If a feeling **overtakes** you, it affects you very strongly. [LITERARY] ❏ *A feeling of panic overtook me.* ■

**over|throw** (**overthrows, overthrowing, overthrew, overthrown**)

> The verb is pronounced /oʊvərθroʊ/. The noun is pronounced /oʊvərθroʊ/.

V-T When a government or leader **is overthrown**, they are removed from power by force. ❏ *The government was overthrown by the army.* ● **Overthrow** is also a noun. ❏ *...the overthrow of the dictator last April.*

**over|time** /oʊvərtaɪm/ ■ N-UNCOUNT **Overtime** is time that you spend doing your job in addition to your normal working hours. ❏ *He worked overtime to finish the job.* ■ N-UNCOUNT **Overtime** is an additional period of time that is added to the end of a sports game in which the score is tied, so that one team can score and win the game. ❏ *Denver won the championship in overtime.*

**over|tone** /oʊvərtoʊn/ (**overtones**) N-COUNT If something has **overtones of** a particular thing or quality, it suggests that thing or quality but does not openly express it. ❏ *The photographs have overtones of 17th-century Dutch paintings.*

**over|took** /oʊvərtʊk/ **Overtook** is the past tense of **overtake**. [from Old English]

**over|ture** /oʊvərtʃər, -tʃʊər/ (**overtures**) N-COUNT An **overture** is a piece of music, often one that is the introduction to an opera or play.

**over|turn** /oʊvərtɜrn/ (**overturns, overturning, overturned**) ■ V-T/V-I If something **overturns** or if you **overturn** it, it turns upside down or on its side. ❏ *The car went out of control and overturned.* ❏ *Alex jumped up so quickly that he overturned his glass of water.* ■ V-T If someone in authority **overturns** a legal decision, they officially decide that that decision is incorrect or not valid. ❏ *The courts overturned his decision.*

**over|view** /oʊvərvyu/ (**overviews**) N-COUNT An **overview of** a situation is a general understanding or description of it as a whole. ❏ *...an historical overview of the subject.*

**over|weight** /oʊvərweɪt/ ADJ Someone who is **overweight** weighs more than is considered healthy or attractive.
→ see **diet**

**over|whelm** /oʊvərwɛlm/ (**overwhelms, overwhelming, overwhelmed**) ■ V-T If you **are overwhelmed by** a feeling or event, it affects you very strongly, and you do not know how to deal with it. ❏ *They were overwhelmed by the kindness of the local people.* ● **over|whelmed** ADJ *She felt a little overwhelmed by the crowds.* ■ V-T If a group of people **overwhelm** a place or another group, they gain control over them. ❏ *The attack overwhelmed the weakened enemy.*

**over|whelm|ing** /oʊvərwɛlmɪŋ/ ■ ADJ If something is **overwhelming**, it affects you very strongly, and you do not know how to deal with it. ❏ *She had an overwhelming feeling of guilt.* ● **over|whelm|ing|ly** ADV ❏ *The others all seemed overwhelmingly confident.* ■ ADJ You can use **overwhelming** to emphasize that an amount or quantity is much greater than other amounts or quantities. ❏ *The overwhelming majority of small businesses go bankrupt within the first twenty-four months.* ● **over|whelm|ing|ly** ADV ❏ *The people voted overwhelmingly for change.*

**over|work** /oʊvərwɜrk/ (**overworks, overworking, overworked**) V-T/V-I If you **overwork** or if someone **overworks** you, you work too hard, and are likely to become very tired or sick. ● **Overwork** is also a noun. ❏ *His heart attack was caused by overwork.* ● **over|worked** ADJ ❏ *...an overworked doctor.*

**ovu|late** /ɒvyəleɪt, oʊv-/ (**ovulates, ovulating, ovulated**) V-I When a woman or female animal **ovulates**, an egg is produced from one of her ovaries. ● **ovu|la|tion** /ɒvyəleɪʃᵊn, oʊv-/ N-UNCOUNT ❏ *...normal patterns of ovulation.*

**ovule** /ɒvyul, oʊv-/ (**ovules**) N-COUNT An **ovule** is the part of a plant that develops into a seed. [TECHNICAL] [from French]

**owe** /oʊ/ (**owes, owing, owed**) ■ V-T If you **owe** money to someone, they have lent it to you and you have not yet paid it back. ❏ *The company owes money to more than 60 banks.* ❏ *Blake owed him nearly $50.* ■ V-T If someone or something **owes** a particular quality or their success **to** a person or thing, they only have it because of that person or thing. ❏ *I owe him my life.* ■ V-T If you say that you **owe** someone gratitude, respect, or loyalty, you mean that they deserve it from you. ❏ *We owe him respect and gratitude for his work.* ❏ *I owe you an apology.* ■ V-T If you say that you **owe it to** someone to do something, you mean that you should do that thing because they deserve it. ❏ *I owe it to him to stay.* ■ PHRASE You use **owing to** when you are introducing the reason for something. ❏ *Owing to staff shortages, there was no food on the plane.* [from Old English]

| Word Partnership | Use *owe* with : |
|---|---|
| N. | owe **a debt**, owe **money**, owe **taxes** ■ owe **a great deal to** *someone* ■ |

**owl** /aʊl/ (**owls**) N-COUNT An **owl** is a bird with a flat face, large eyes, and a small sharp beak. [from Old English]

**own** /oʊn/ (**owns, owning, owned**) **1** ADJ You use **own** to indicate that something belongs to a particular person or thing. ❑ *I wanted to have my own business.* ❑ *He didn't trust his own judgment anymore.* ● **Own** is also a pronoun. ❑ *The man's face was a few inches from his own.* **2** ADJ You use **own** to indicate that something is used by, or is characteristic of, only one person, thing, or group. ❑ *Jennifer wanted her own room.* ❑ *Everyone has their own way of doing things.* ● **Own** is also a pronoun. ❑ *She has a style that is very much her own.* **3** ADJ You use **own** to indicate that someone does something without any help from other people. ❑ *They enjoy making their own decisions.* ● **Own** is also a pronoun. ❑ *There's no career structure; you have to create your own.* **4** V-T If you **own** something, it is your property. ❑ *His father owns a local computer store.* **5** PHRASE If someone or something **comes into their own**, they become very successful or start to perform very well because the circumstances are right. ❑ *Many women come into their own as teachers.* **6** PHRASE When you are **on** your **own**, you are alone. ❑ *He lives on his own.* ❑ *I felt pretty lonely on my own.* **7** PHRASE If you do something **on** your **own**, you do it without any help from other people. ❑ *I work best on my own.* [from Old English] **8** to **hold** your **own** → see **hold**

▶ **own up** PHR-VERB If you **own up** to something wrong that you have done, you admit that you did it. ❑ *The teacher is waiting for someone to own up to breaking the window.*

**own|er** /oʊnər/ (**owners**) N-COUNT If you are the **owner** of something, it belongs to you. ❑ *...the owner of the store.* [from Old English]

**own|er|ship** /oʊnərʃɪp/ N-UNCOUNT **Ownership** of something is the state of owning it. ❑ *...the increase in home ownership.* [from Old English]

**ox** /ɒks/ (**oxen** /ɒksən/) N-COUNT An **ox** is a bull that has been castrated. [from Old English]

**ox|ford** /ɑksfərd/ (**oxfords**) also **Oxford** **1** N-PLURAL **Oxfords** are low shoes with laces at the front. **2** N-UNCOUNT **Oxford** or **oxford cloth** is a type of cotton fabric, used especially for men's shirts. [after Oxford, a city in England]

**oxy|gen** /ɒksɪdʒən/ N-UNCOUNT **Oxygen** is a colorless gas in the air which is needed by all plants and animals. [from French]
→ see **air, cardiovascular system, earth, ozone, photosynthesis, respiration**

**oys|ter** /ɔɪstər/ (**oysters**) N-COUNT An **oyster** is a large flat shellfish. [from Old French]
→ see **shellfish**

**oz.** **Oz.** is a written abbreviation for **ounce**. ❑ *...1 oz. of butter.*

**ozone** /oʊzoʊn/ N-UNCOUNT **Ozone** is a colorless gas which is a form of oxygen. There is a layer of ozone high above the Earth's surface, that protects us from harmful radiation from the sun. [from German]

**ozone-friendly** ADJ **Ozone-friendly** chemicals, products, or technology do not cause harm to the ozone layer.

**ozone lay|er** N-SING The **ozone layer** is the part of the Earth's atmosphere that has the most ozone in it and protects living things from the harmful radiation of the sun. ❑ *...the hole in the ozone layer.*
→ see **air**
→ see Word Web: **ozone**

O

## Word Web    ozone

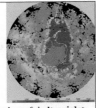

In the Earth's **atmosphere** there are small amounts of **ozone**. Ozone is a molecule that is made up of three **oxygen** atoms. Too much ozone can cause problems. Near the ground, it can be a **pollutant**. Cars and factories produce **carbon monoxide** and **carbon dioxide**. These gases mix with ozone and make **smog**. Too little ozone can also cause problems. The **ozone layer** in the upper **atmosphere** stops harmful **ultraviolet light** from reaching the Earth. Some scientists say a large hole is opening in the ozone layer. This may add to the **greenhouse effect** and **global warming**.

# Pp

**PAC** /pæk/ (**PACs**) N-COUNT A **PAC** is an organization that campaigns for particular political policies, and that gives money to political parties or candidates who support those policies. **PAC** is an abbreviation for **political action committee**. ❑ ...$2 million of PAC money.

**pace** /peɪs/ (**paces, pacing, paced**) **1** N-SING The **pace** of something is the speed at which it happens or is done. ❑ Many people were not satisfied with the pace of change. **2** N-SING Your **pace** is the speed at which you walk. ❑ He moved at a fast pace. **3** N-COUNT A **pace** is the distance that you move when you take one step. ❑ Peter walked a few paces behind me. **4** V-T/V-I If you **pace** a small area, you keep walking up and down it, because you are anxious or impatient. ❑ As they waited, Kravis paced the room nervously. ❑ He found John pacing around the house. **5** PHRASE To **keep pace with** something that is changing means to change quickly in response to it. ❑ We need 32,000 new homes a year to keep pace with population growth. **6** PHRASE If you do something **at** your **own pace**, you do it at a speed that is comfortable for you. ❑ The computer will allow students to learn at their own pace. [from Old French]

---

### Word Partnership  Use *pace* with :

| | |
|---|---|
| N. | pace **of change 1** |
| ADJ. | **brisk** pace, **fast** pace, **record** pace, **slow** pace **1 2** |
| V. | **pick up** the pace, **set a** pace **1 2** keep pace **with** *something* **5** |

---

**Pa·cif·ic Rim** N-SING The **Pacific Rim** is the area on the western shores of the Pacific Ocean, including Japan, China, Korea, Thailand, and Malaysia. ❑ ...the growing need for energy in Asia and the Pacific Rim.

**paci·fi·er** /pæsɪfaɪər/ (**pacifiers**) N-COUNT A **pacifier** is a rubber or plastic object that you give to a baby to suck so that he or she feels comforted. [from Old French]

**paci·fist** /pæsɪfɪst/ (**pacifists**) N-COUNT A **pacifist** is someone who believes that violence is wrong and refuses to take part in wars. ❑ Many protesters are pacifists, opposed to war. ● **Pacifist** is also an adjective. ❑ ...his mother's pacifist views. ● **paci·fism** /pæsɪfɪzəm/ N-UNCOUNT ❑ ...a long tradition of pacifism. [from Old French]

**pac·ing** N-UNCOUNT The **pacing** of something such as a play, movie, or novel is the speed at which the story develops. [from Old French]

**pack** /pæk/ (**packs, packing, packed**) **1** V-T/V-I When you **pack** a bag, you put clothes and other things into it, because you are leaving. ❑ When I was 17, I packed my bags and left home. ❑ I began to pack for the trip. ● **pack·ing** N-UNCOUNT ❑ She left

pack

Frances to finish her packing. **2** V-T To **pack** things, for example, in a factory, means to put them into containers or boxes so that they can be shipped and sold. ❑ They offered me a job packing boxes in a warehouse. ❑ Machines pack the olives in jars. **3** V-T/V-I If people **pack into** a place or if they **pack** a place, there are so many of them that the place is full. ❑ Hundreds of people packed into the temple. ● **packed** ADJ ❑ The place is packed at lunchtime. ❑ ...a packed meeting. **4** N-COUNT A **pack of** things is a collection of them that is sold or given together in a container, box or bag. ❑ ...a free information pack with road travel advice. ❑ ...a pack of gum. **5** N-COUNT A **pack of** wolves or dogs is a group of them that hunt together. ❑ ...a pack of wild dogs. **6** [from Middle Low German]

**pack·age** /pækɪdʒ/ (**packages, packaging, packaged**) **1** N-COUNT A **package** is something wrapped in paper so that it can be sent to someone by mail. ❑ I tore open the package. **2** N-COUNT A **package** is a small bag, box, or envelope in which a quantity of something is sold. ❑ ...a package of doughnuts. **3** N-COUNT A **package** is a set of proposals that are made by a government or organization. ❑ Congress passed a package of new rules for the financial markets. **4** V-T When a product is **packaged**, it is put into containers to be sold. ❑ The coffee beans are ground and packaged for sale. [from Middle Low German]

---

### Thesaurus  *package*  Also look up :

| | |
|---|---|
| N. | batch, bundle, container, pack **2** |

---

**pack·ag·ing** /pækɪdʒɪŋ/ N-UNCOUNT **Packaging** is the container or covering that something is sold in. ❑ It is selling very well because the packaging is so attractive. [from Middle Low German]

**pack·et** /pækɪt/ (**packets**) **1** N-COUNT A **packet** is a set of information about a particular subject that is given to people who are interested in it. ❑ Call us for a free information packet. **2** N-COUNT A **packet** is a small box, bag, or envelope in which a quantity of something is sold. ❑ ...a packet of sugar. [from Old French]
→ see **container**

**pact** /pækt/ (**pacts**) N-COUNT A **pact** is a formal agreement between two or more people, organizations, or governments. ❑ He signed a new pact with Germany. [from Old French]

**pad** /pæd/ (**pads**) **1** N-COUNT A **pad** is a fairly thick, flat piece of a material such as cloth or rubber. Pads are used, for example, to clean things

P

or for protection. ❑ *He placed a pad of cotton over the spot.* ❑ *...an oven-cleaning pad.* **2** N-COUNT A **pad of** paper is a number of pieces of paper attached together along the top or the side, so that each piece can be torn off when it has been used. ❑ *Have a pad ready and write down the information.*

**pad|ded** /pǽdɪd/ ADJ Something that is **padded** has soft material on it or inside it which makes it less hard, protects it, or changes its shape. ❑ *...a padded jacket.* [from Low German]

**pad|ding** /pǽdɪŋ/ N-UNCOUNT **Padding** is soft material on the outside or inside of something which makes it less hard, protects it, or changes its shape. ❑ *...the foam rubber padding on the headphones.* ❑ *Players must wear padding to protect them from injury.* [from Low German]

**pad|dle** /pǽd³l/ (**paddles**) **1** N-COUNT A **paddle** is a short pole with a wide flat part at one end or at both ends, used to move a small boat through water. ❑ *We were able to push ourselves across with the paddle.* **2** N-COUNT A **paddle** is a specially shaped piece of wood that is used for hitting the ball in table tennis.
→ see **boat**

**pad|dock** /pǽdək/ (**paddocks**) N-COUNT A **paddock** is a small field where horses are kept. [from Old English]

**pad|dy** /pǽdi/ (**paddies**) N-COUNT A **paddy** or a **paddy field** is a flooded field that is used for growing rice. [from Malay]

**pad|lock** /pǽdlɒk/ (**padlocks, padlocking, padlocked**) **1** N-COUNT A **padlock** is a metal lock that is used for fastening two things together. ❑ *They had put a padlock on the door of his house.* **2** V-T If you **padlock** something, you lock it or fasten it to something else using a padlock. ❑ *Eddie parked his bicycle against a fence and padlocked it.*

**padlock**

**pa|gan** /péɪgən/ ADJ **Pagan** beliefs are ones that do not belong to any of the main religions of the world, often ancient beliefs that existed before these religions developed. ❑ *...the pagan festival of Yule.* [from Church Latin]

**page** /péɪdʒ/ (**pages**) **1** N-COUNT A **page** is one side of one of the pieces of paper in a book, magazine, or newspaper. ❑ *Turn to page 4.* ❑ *...the front page of USA Today.* **2** N-COUNT The **pages** of a book, magazine, or newspaper are the pieces of paper it consists of. ❑ *He turned the pages of his notebook.* **3** N-COUNT A **page** is a young person who takes messages or does small jobs for members of the United States Congress or state legislatures. [from Old French]
→ see **printing**

**pag|eant** /pǽdʒənt/ (**pageants**) **1** N-COUNT A **pageant** or a **beauty pageant** is a competition in which young women are judged to decide which one is the most beautiful. **2** N-COUNT A **pageant** is a colorful public procession, show, or ceremony, often held to celebrate events or people from history. ❑ *...a historical pageant of kings and queens.* [from Medieval Latin]

**paid** /péɪd/ **1 Paid** is the past tense and past participle of **pay**. **2** ADJ **Paid** means given money

in exchange for working for an employer. ❑ *...a small team of paid staff.* ❑ *...two weeks' paid vacation.* ❑ *...a well-paid accountant.* [from Old French]

**pail** /péɪl/ (**pails**) N-COUNT A **pail** is a bucket, usually made of metal or wood. [from Old English]

**pain** /péɪn/ (**pains, pained**) **1** N-VAR **Pain** is a feeling of great discomfort in part of your body, because of illness or an injury. ❑ *...a bone disease that caused terrible pain.* ❑ *I felt a sharp pain in my lower back.* **2** PHRASE If you are **in pain**, you feel pain. ❑ *She was obviously in pain.* **3** N-UNCOUNT **Pain** is the unhappiness that you feel when something very upsetting happens. ❑ *...gray eyes that seemed filled with pain.* **4** V-T If something **pains** you, it makes you feel upset or unhappy. ❑ *Sylvia shook her head as if the memory pained her.* ● **pained** ADJ ❑ *...a pained look.* **5** PHRASE If you call someone or something **a pain** or **a pain in the neck**, you mean that they are very annoying or irritating. [INFORMAL] ❑ *It was a real pain having to get up at 4 a.m.* **6** PHRASE If you **take pains to** do something, you try hard to do it successfully. ❑ *He took great pains to see that he did it right.* [from Old French]

<table>
<tr><td colspan="3">**Thesaurus** *pain* Also look up :</td></tr>
<tr><td>N.</td><td colspan="2">ache, agony, discomfort **1**<br>anguish, distress, heartache, suffering **2**</td></tr>
<tr><td>V.</td><td colspan="2">bother, distress, grieve, hurt, upset, wound **3**</td></tr>
</table>

**pain|ful** /péɪnfəl/ **1** ADJ If a part of your body is **painful**, it hurts. ❑ *Her toe was swollen and painful.* ● **pain|ful|ly** ADV ❑ *His tooth started to throb painfully.* **2** ADJ If something such as an illness, injury, or operation is **painful**, it causes you a lot of physical pain. ❑ *...a painful back injury.* ● **pain|ful|ly** ADV ❑ *He knocked his head painfully against the cupboard.* **3** ADJ Situations, memories, or experiences that are **painful** are difficult and unpleasant to deal with, and often make you feel sad and upset. ❑ *His unkind remarks brought back painful memories.* [from Old French]

<table>
<tr><td colspan="2">**Word Partnership** Use *painful* with :</td></tr>
<tr><td>ADV.</td><td>**extremely** painful, **less/more** painful, **often** painful, **too** painful, **very** painful **1 – 3**</td></tr>
<tr><td>N.</td><td>painful **death**, painful **process 2 3**<br>painful **experience**, painful **feelings**, painful **lesson**, painful **memory 3**</td></tr>
</table>

**pain|ful|ly** /péɪnfəli/ **1** ADV You use **painfully** to emphasize a quality or situation that is undesirable. ❑ *Things are moving painfully slowly.* ❑ *...a painfully shy young man.* [from Old French]
**2** → see also **painful**

**pain|killer** /péɪnkɪlər/ (**painkillers**) N-COUNT A **painkiller** is a drug that reduces or stops physical pain.

**pain|less** /péɪnlɪs/ **1** ADJ If something such as a treatment is **painless** it causes no physical pain. ❑ *The operation itself is a quick, painless procedure.* ● **pain|less|ly** ADV ❑ *She died quietly and painlessly at the age of 101.* **2** ADJ If a process or activity is **painless**, you do not have to make a great effort or suffer in any way. ❑ *The trip was relatively painless, even with the children.* ● **pain|less|ly** ADV ❑ *...a game for children that painlessly teaches basic reading skills.* [from Old French]

**P**

**pains|taking** /ˈpeɪnzteɪkɪŋ, peɪnsteɪ-/ ADJ A **painstaking** search, examination, or investigation is done extremely carefully and thoroughly. □ *...a painstaking search for information.* ● **pains|taking|ly** ADV □ *Broken bones were painstakingly pieced together.*

**paint** /peɪnt/ (**paints, painting, painted**)
■ N-VAR **Paint** is a colored liquid that you put onto a surface with a brush in order to protect the surface or to make it look nice, or that you use to produce a picture. □ *...a can of red paint.* □ *They saw some large letters in white paint.* □ *The paint was peeling on the window frames.* ② V-T If you **paint** a wall or an object, you cover it with paint. □ *They started to paint the walls.* ③ V-T/V-I If you **paint** something or **paint** a picture of it, you produce a picture of it using paint. □ *He is painting a huge volcano.* □ *Why do people paint pictures?* □ *I came here to paint.* [from Old French] ④ → see also **painting, oil paint**
→ see **draw, painting, petroleum**

### Word Partnership    Use *paint* with :

| | |
|---|---|
| ADJ. | **blue/green/red/white/yellow** paint, **fresh** paint, **peeling** paint ■ |
| N. | **can of** paint, **coat of** paint ■ paint **a picture**, paint **a portrait** ③ |

**paint|brush** /ˈpeɪntbrʌʃ/ (**paintbrushes**) N-COUNT A **paintbrush** is a brush that you use for painting.
→ see **painting**

**paint|er** /ˈpeɪntər/ (**painters**) ■ N-COUNT A **painter** is an artist who paints pictures. □ *...the French painter Claude Monet.* ② N-COUNT A **painter** is someone who paints walls, doors, and some other parts of buildings as their job. □ *I've worked as a house painter.* [from Old French]

**paint|ing** /ˈpeɪntɪŋ/ (**paintings**) ■ N-COUNT A **painting** is a picture that someone has painted. □ *...a large painting of Dwight Eisenhower.* ② N-UNCOUNT **Painting** is the activity of painting pictures or covering surfaces with paint. □ *She enjoyed painting and gardening.* [from Old French]
→ see **art**
→ see Word Web: **painting**

**pair** /peər/ (**pairs**) ■ N-COUNT A **pair of** things are two things of the same size and shape that are used together. □ *...a pair of socks.* □ *...earrings that cost $142.50 a pair.* ② N-COUNT Some objects that have two main parts of the same size and shape are referred to as a **pair**, for example, **a pair of pants** or **a pair of scissors.** □ *...a pair of faded jeans.* ③ N-SING You can refer to two people as a **pair** when they are standing or walking together.

□ *...a pair of teenage boys in private school uniforms.* [from Old French] ④ → see also **au pair**

### Thesaurus    *pair*    Also look up :

| | |
|---|---|
| N. | combination, couple, duo, match, two ■ ③ |

**pa|jam|as** /pəˈdʒɑːməz, -dʒæm-/ N-PLURAL A pair of **pajamas** consists of loose pants and a top that people wear to bed. □ *I don't want to get out of my pajamas in the morning.* [from Persian]

**pal** /pæl/ (**pals**) N-COUNT Your **pals** are your friends. [INFORMAL] □ *They talked like old pals.* [from Romany]

**pal|ace** /ˈpælɪs/ (**palaces**) N-COUNT A **palace** is a very large impressive house, especially the official home of a king, queen, or president. □ *...Buckingham Palace.* [from Old French]

**pal|at|able** /ˈpælətəbəl/ ■ ADJ If you describe food or drink as **palatable**, you mean that it tastes pleasant. [FORMAL] □ *There are several ways of making the rice more palatable.* ② ADJ If you describe an idea or method as **palatable**, you mean that people are willing to accept it. □ *...a palatable way of firing employees.* [from Latin]

**pal|ate** /ˈpælɪt/ (**palates**) ■ N-COUNT Your **palate** is the top part of the inside of your mouth. ② N-COUNT You can refer to someone's **palate** as a way of talking about their ability to judge good food or drink. □ *This is food for young palates.* [from Latin]

**pale** /peɪl/ (**paler, palest**) ■ ADJ Something that is **pale** is not strong or bright in color. □ *...a pale blue dress.* □ *Birds filled the pale sky.* ② ADJ If someone looks **pale**, their face looks a lighter color than usual, usually because they are ill, frightened, or shocked. □ *She looked pale and tired.* [from Old French]

**pale|on|tol|ogy** /ˌpeɪliənˈtɒlədʒi/ N-UNCOUNT **Paleontology** is the study of fossils as a guide to the history of life on earth. ● **pale|on|tolo|gist** (**paleontologists**) N-COUNT [from Greek]

**Paleo|zo|ic era** /ˌpeɪliəˈzoʊɪk ɪərə/ N-SING The **Paleozoic era** is a period in the history of the Earth that began around 550 million years ago and ended around 230 million years ago. [TECHNICAL]

### Word Link    *ette ≈ small : cas**ette**, gaz**ette**, pal**ette***

**pal|ette** /ˈpælɪt/ (**palettes**) N-COUNT A **palette** is a flat piece of wood or plastic on which an artist mixes paints. [from French]
→ see **painting**

### Word Web    painting

Oil **painting** uses special tools and techniques. First, artists stretch a piece of **canvas** over a wooden **frame**. Then they cover the canvas with a **coat** of white **paint**. When it dries, they put it on an **easel**. Most painters use a **palette knife** on a **palette** to mix **colors** together. They paint the canvas with soft bristle **paintbrushes**. When they are finished, they use turpentine to clean the brushes and the palette. Three common oil painting **genres** are the **still life**, the **landscape**, and the **portrait**.

**pall** /pɔl/ (**palls, palled**) ■ V-I If something **palls**, it becomes less interesting or less enjoyable. □ *The frequent business trips overseas began to pall.* ② N-COUNT A **pall of** smoke is a thick cloud of it. □ *A pall of black smoke drifted over the town.* [Sense 1 from Old French. Sense 2 from Old English.]

**palm** /pɑm/ (**palms**) ■ N-VAR A **palm** or a **palm tree** is a tree that grows in hot countries. It has long leaves at the top, and no branches. □ *...golden sands and swaying palms.* ② N-COUNT The **palm of** your hand is the inside part of your hand, between your fingers and your wrist. □ *Dornberg slapped the table with the palm of his hand.* [Sense 1 from Old English. Sense 2 from Old French.]
→ see **desert, hand**

**pal|pable** /pælpəbəl/ ADJ Something that is **palpable** is very obvious. □ *The tension between Amy and Jim is palpable.* ● **pal|pably** /pælpəbli/ ADV □ *The man was palpably nervous.* [from Late Latin]

**pal|try** /pɔltri/ ADJ A **paltry** amount of money or of something else is very small. □ *...a paltry fine of $150.*

**pam|per** /pæmpər/ (**pampers, pampering, pampered**) V-T If you **pamper** someone, you do everything for them and give them everything that they want. □ *Why don't you let your mother pamper you for a while?* ● **pam|pered** ADJ □ *...today's pampered superstars.* [from Germanic]

**pam|phlet** /pæmflɪt/ (**pamphlets**) N-COUNT A **pamphlet** is a very thin book with a paper cover that gives information about something. □ *I gave her a pamphlet about parenting.* [from Medieval Latin]

**pan** /pæn/ (**pans**) ■ N-COUNT A **pan** is a round metal container with a long handle, that is used for cooking things in, usually on top of a stove. □ *Heat the butter and oil in a large pan.* ② N-COUNT A **pan** is a shallow metal container used for baking foods. [from Old English]
→ see Word Web: **pan**

**pana|cea** /pænəsiə/ (**panaceas**) N-COUNT If you say that something is a **panacea for** a set of problems, you mean that it will solve all those problems. □ *This measure is not a panacea; it will not solve all of our problems.* [from Latin]

**pa|nache** /pənæʃ/ N-UNCOUNT If you do something **with panache**, you do it in a confident and stylish way. □ *The orchestra played with great panache.* [from French]

**pan|cake** /pænkeɪk/ (**pancakes**) N-COUNT A **pancake** is a thin, flat, circular piece of cooked batter made from milk, flour, and eggs. Pancakes

pancakes

are usually eaten for breakfast, with butter and syrup.

**pan|da** /pændə/ (**pandas**) N-COUNT A **panda** is a large animal with black and white fur that lives in China. [from French]
→ see **zoo**

**pan|der** /pændər/ (**panders, pandering, pandered**) V-I If you **pander to** someone, you do everything that they want even when this is wrong, often to get some advantage for yourself. □ *...politicians who pander to millionaires.*

**pane** /peɪn/ (**panes**) N-COUNT A **pane** of glass is a flat sheet of glass in a window or door. □ *I watched my reflection in a pane of glass.* [from Old French]

**pan|el** /pænəl/ (**panels**) ■ N-COUNT A **panel** is a small group of people who are chosen to do something, for example, to discuss something in public or to make a decision. □ *He assembled a panel of scholars to advise him.* ② N-COUNT A **panel** is a flat rectangular piece of wood or other material that forms part of a larger object such as a door. □ *...the glass panel set in the center of the door.* ③ N-COUNT A control **panel** or instrument **panel** is a board containing switches and controls. □ *The equipment was monitored from a central control panel.* [from Old French]

**pan|eled** /pænəld/ also **panelled** ADJ A **paneled** room or door has decorative wooden panels on its surface. □ *...a large paneled library.* [from Old French]

**pan|el|ist** /pænəlɪst/ (**panelists**) N-COUNT A **panelist** is a person who is a member of a panel and speaks in public, especially on a radio or television program. [from Old French]

**pan|el truck** (**panel trucks**) N-COUNT A **panel truck** is a small van, used especially for delivering goods.

**pang** /pæŋ/ (**pangs**) N-COUNT A **pang** is a sudden strong feeling, for example, of sadness or pain. □ *Ruth felt a pang of guilt.* [from Germanic]

**Pan|gaea** /pændʒiə/ N-PROPER **Pangaea** is the name given by scientists to the huge landmass that existed on the Earth millions of years ago, before it split into separate continents. [TECHNICAL] [from Greek]

**pan|han|dle** /pænhændəl/ (**panhandles, panhandling, panhandled**) ■ N-COUNT A **panhandle** is a narrow strip of land joined to a larger area of land. □ *...the Texas panhandle.* ② V-I

**P**

---

### Word Web pan

No **saucepan** or **frying pan** is perfect. **Copper pans** conduct heat well. This makes them good for cooking on the stove. However, copper also reacts with the acid in some foods. For this reason, the best pans have a thin layer of **tin** covering the copper. **Cast iron** pans are very heavy and **heat up** slowly. But they stay hot for a long time. Some people like **stainless steel** pans because they heat up quickly and don't react with chemicals in food. However, the bottom of a stainless pan may not heat up evenly.

If someone **panhandles**, they stop people in the street and ask them for food or money. [INFORMAL] ❑ *These people support themselves by panhandling.*
● **pan|han|dler** (**panhandlers**) N-COUNT [INFORMAL] ❑ *You can't walk downtown without a panhandler asking you for money.*

**pan|ic** /pǽnɪk/ (**panics, panicking, panicked**)
**1** N-VAR **Panic** is a strong feeling of anxiety or fear that makes you act without thinking carefully. ❑ *An earthquake caused panic among the population.* ❑ *I'm in a panic about getting everything done in time.*
**2** V-T/V-I If you **panic** or if someone **panics** you, you suddenly feel anxious or afraid, and act without thinking carefully. ❑ *Guests panicked and screamed when the bomb exploded.* ❑ *The sudden memory panicked her.* [from French]

| **Thesaurus** | | *panic* | Also look up : |
|---|---|---|---|
| N. | agitation, alarm, dread, fear, fright; (*ant.*) calm **1** | | |
| V. | alarm, fear, terrify, unnerve; (*ant.*) relax **2** | | |

**pano|ra|ma** /pænərǽmə, -rάːmə/ (**panoramas**) N-COUNT A **panorama** is a view in which you can see a long way over a wide area of land. ❑ *Horton looked out over a panorama of green valleys and gentle hills.* ● **pano|ram|ic** /pænərǽmɪk/ ADJ ❑ *...a panoramic view of Los Angeles.* [from Greek]

**pant** /pǽnt/ (**pants, panting, panted**) **1** V-I If you **pant**, you breathe quickly and loudly, because you have been doing something energetic. ❑ *She was panting with the effort.* [from Old French]
**2** → see also **pants**

**panties** /pǽntiz/ N-PLURAL **Panties** are short, close-fitting underpants worn by women or girls.

**pan|to|mime** /pǽntəmaɪm/ (**pantomimes**) N-COUNT A **pantomime** is a performance involving acting without words through facial expression, gesture, and movement. [from Latin]

**pants** /pǽnts/ N-PLURAL **Pants** are a piece of clothing that covers the lower part of your body and each leg. ❑ *He wore brown corduroy pants and a white cotton shirt.*
→ see **clothing**

**pant|suit** /pǽntsut/ (**pantsuits**) also **pants suit** N-COUNT A **pantsuit** is women's clothing consisting of a pair of pants and a jacket which are made from the same material. ❑ *She wore a red pantsuit that fit very well.*

**pan|ty|hose** /pǽntihoʊz/ also **panty hose** N-PLURAL **Pantyhose** are a piece of thin nylon clothing worn by women, that cover the body from the waist downward and cover each leg separately.

**pa|pal** /peɪpᵊl/ ADJ **Papal** is used to describe things relating to the Pope. ❑ *...a papal visit to Mexico.* [from Late Middle English]

**pa|pa|raz|zi** /pɑpərɑtsi/ N-PLURAL The **paparazzi** are photographers who follow famous people around, hoping to take interesting or shocking photographs of them. ❑ *The paparazzi pursue Armani wherever he goes.* [from Italian]

**pa|per** /peɪpər/ (**papers, papering, papered**)
**1** N-UNCOUNT **Paper** is a material that you write on or wrap things with. ❑ *He wrote his name on a piece of paper.* ❑ *...a paper bag.* **2** N-COUNT A **paper** is a newspaper. ❑ *I might get a paper in the town.* **3** N-PLURAL **Papers** are sheets of paper with information on them. ❑ *...papers including letters and legal documents.* **4** N-PLURAL Your **papers** are your official documents, such as your passport or identity card. ❑ *The young man refused to show his papers to the police.* **5** N-COUNT A **paper** is a long piece of writing on an academic subject. ❑ *He just published a paper in the journal "Nature."* ❑ *...the ten errors that appear most frequently in student papers.* **6** N-COUNT A **paper** prepared by a government or a committee is a report on a question they have been considering or a set of proposals for changes in the law. ❑ *...a new government paper on education.* **7** V-T If you **paper** a wall, you put wallpaper on it. ❑ *We papered all four bedrooms.* [from Latin]
→ see Word Web: **paper**

| **Word Partnership** | | Use *paper* with : |
|---|---|---|
| ADJ. | blank paper, brown paper, colored paper, recycled paper **1** daily paper **2** | |
| V. | fold paper **1** read the paper **2** present a paper, publish a paper **5** draft a paper, write a paper **5 6** | |
| N. | morning paper **2** research paper **5 6** | |

**paper|back** /peɪpərbæk/ (**paperbacks**) N-COUNT A **paperback** is a book with a thin cardboard or paper cover. ❑ *She will buy the book when it comes out in paperback.*

**pa|per route** (**paper routes**) N-COUNT A **paper route** is the job of delivering newspapers to particular houses, often done by children.

**pa|per trail** N-SING Documents which provide evidence of someone's activities can be referred to as a **paper trail**. ❑ *We are not certain of the amounts lost, as there is no paper trail.*

**paper|work** /peɪpərwɜrk/ N-UNCOUNT **Paperwork** is the routine part of a job that involves

**Word Web**    paper

Around 3000 BC, Egyptians began to make **paper** from the papyrus plant. They cut the stems of the plant into thin slices and pressed them into **sheets**. A very different Chinese technique developed about the same time. It was more like today's paper-making process. Chinese paper makers cooked **fiber** made of tree bark. Then they pressed it into molds and let it dry. Around 200 BC, a third paper-making process began in the Middle East. Craftsmen started using animal skins to make parchment. Today, paper manufacturing destroys millions of trees every year. This has led to **recycling** programs and paperless offices.

dealing with letters, reports, and records. ❑ *There will be paperwork — forms to fill in, letters to write.*

**par** /pɑr/ **1** PHRASE If you say that two people or things are **on a par with** each other, you mean that they are equally good or bad, or equally important. ❑ *The coffee was on a par with the one he had in Paris.* **2** PHRASE If you say that someone or something is **below par**, they are below the standard you expected. ❑ *Duffy's guitar playing is well below par.* [from Latin]

**para|ble** /pærəbᵊl/ (**parables**) N-COUNT A **parable** is a short story that makes a moral or religious point. ❑ *...the parable of the lost sheep.* [from Old French]

**para|chute** /pærəʃut/ (**parachutes, parachuting, parachuted**) **1** N-COUNT A **parachute** is a device that enables a person to jump from an aircraft and float safely to the ground. It consists of a large piece of thin cloth attached to your body by strings. ❑ *They fell 41,000 feet before opening their parachutes.* **2** V-T/V-I If a person **parachutes** or someone **parachutes** them somewhere, they jump from an aircraft using a parachute. ❑ *He parachuted into Warsaw.* [from French]
→ see **fly**

*parachute*

**pa|rade** /pəreɪd/ (**parades, parading, paraded**) **1** N-COUNT A **parade** is a line of people or vehicles moving through a public place in order to celebrate an important day or event. ❑ *A military parade marched down Pennsylvania Avenue.*

**2** V-I When people **parade** somewhere, they walk together in a formal group or a line, usually with other people watching them. ❑ *Soldiers*

*parade*

*paraded down the Champs Élysées.* **3** N-VAR **Parade** is a formal occasion when soldiers stand in lines to be seen by an important person, or march in a group. ❑ *They were already on parade at six o'clock in the morning.* **4** V-T If someone **parades** a person or thing, they show them in public, often in order to impress people or gain some advantage. ❑ *She refused to parade her problems on TV.* ❑ *Captured prisoners were paraded before television cameras.* [from French]

**para|dise** /pærədaɪs/ (**paradises**) **1** N-PROPER According to some religions, **paradise** is a wonderful place where people go after they die, if they have led good lives. ❑ *The Koran describes paradise as a garden of delight.* **2** N-VAR You can refer to a place or situation that seems beautiful or perfect as **paradise** or **a paradise**. ❑ *Bali is one of the world's natural paradises.* [from Old English]

| **Word Link** | *para ≈ beside : paradox, paralegal, parallel* |

**para|dox** /pærədɒks/ (**paradoxes**) **1** N-COUNT You describe a situation as a **paradox** when it involves two or more facts or qualities that seem to contradict each other. ❑ *The paradox is that the more you exercise, the more energy you have.* ● **para|doxi|cal** /pærədɒksɪkᵊl/ ADJ ❑ *Low-fat diets have the paradoxical effect of making some people gain weight.* ● **para|doxi|cal|ly** ADV ❑ *The second method is more complicated, but paradoxically, less expensive.* **2** N-VAR A **paradox** is a statement in which it seems that if one part of it is true, the other part of it cannot be true. ❑ *The story contains many levels of paradox.* [from Late Latin]

**par|af|fin** /pærəfɪn/ N-UNCOUNT **Paraffin** is a white wax obtained from petroleum or coal. It is used to make candles, to form seals, and in beauty treatments. [from German]

**para|gon** /pærəgɒn/ (**paragons**) N-COUNT A **paragon** is someone who appears to be perfect or to have a lot of a good qualities. ❑ *Her paragon of a husband gets up early to bring her breakfast in bed.* [from French]

**para|graph** /pærəgræf/ (**paragraphs**) N-COUNT A **paragraph** is a section of a piece of writing. A paragraph always begins on a new line and contains at least one sentence. ❑ *His story was only one paragraph long.* [from Medieval Latin]

**para|le|gal** /pærəligᵊl/ (**paralegals**) N-COUNT A **paralegal** is someone who helps lawyers with their work but is not completely qualified as a lawyer.

**par|al|lax** /pærəlæks/ (**parallaxes**) N-VAR **Parallax** is when an object appears to change its position because the person or instrument observing it has changed their position. [TECHNICAL] [from French]

**par|al|lel** /pærəlɛl/ (**parallels, paralleling, paralleled**) **1** N-COUNT If something has a **parallel**, it is similar to something else in some way. ❑ *It is impossible to draw parallels between the UK and New Zealand, a country with a population of four million.* ❑ *It's a disaster with no parallel anywhere else in the world.* **2** V-T If one thing **parallels** another, they happen at the same time or are similar, and often seem to be connected. ❑ *His remarks paralleled those of the president.* **3** ADJ **Parallel** events or situations happen at the same time, or are similar to one another. ❑ *...parallel talks between the two countries' foreign ministers.* **4** ADJ If two lines, two objects, or two lines of movement are **parallel**, they are the same distance apart along their whole length. ❑ *...seventy-two ships, drawn up in two parallel lines.* ❑ *Remsen Street is parallel with Montague Street.* [from French]

**par|al|lel cir|cuit** (**parallel circuits**) N-COUNT A **parallel circuit** is an electrical circuit in which the current travels along more than one path so that it can power several devices at the same time. [TECHNICAL]

**par|al|lel|ism** /pærəlɛlɪzəm/ N-UNCOUNT **Parallelism** is the use of similar grammatical structures within a piece of writing so that ideas which are closely related are expressed in a similar way. The phrase "government of the people, by the people, for the people" is an example of parallelism. [TECHNICAL] [from French]

**pa|raly|sis** /pərælɪsɪs/ N-UNCOUNT **Paralysis** is the loss of the ability to move and feel in all or part of your body. ❑ *...paralysis of the leg.* [from Latin]

**para|lyze** /pærəlaɪz/ (**paralyzes, paralyzing, paralyzed**) **1** V-T If someone **is paralyzed** by

P

an accident or an illness, they have no feeling in their body, or in part of their body, and are unable to move. ❑ *She is paralyzed from the waist down.* ● **para|lyzed** ADJ ❑ *...a guy with paralyzed legs.* 🄲 V-T If a person, place, or organization **is paralyzed by** something, they become unable to act or function properly. ❑ *She was paralyzed by fear.* [from French]
→ see **disability**

**para|mecium** /pærəmiʃiəm, -si-/ (**paramecia**) N-COUNT **Paramecia** are a type of protozoa that are found in fresh water. [from New Latin]

**pa|ram|eter** /pəræmɪtər/ (**parameters**) N-COUNT **Parameters** are factors or limits that affect the way something can be done or the way it happens. [FORMAL] ❑ *I will do my best to work within these parameters.* [from New Latin]

**para|mili|tary** /pærəmɪlɪteri/ (**paramilitaries**) ADJ A **paramilitary** organization is a group that is organized like an army but is not part of an official army. ❑ *...paramilitary forces.* ● **Paramilitaries** are members of a paramilitary organization. ❑ *Paramilitaries patrolled the village.*

**para|mount** /pærəmaʊnt/ ADJ Something that is **paramount** or of **paramount** importance is more important than anything else. ❑ *The children's happiness must be seen as paramount.* [from Old French]

**para|noia** /pærənɔɪə/ 🄸 N-UNCOUNT If you say that someone suffers from **paranoia**, you think that they are too suspicious or afraid of other people. ❑ *...a mood of paranoia and expectation of war.* 🄲 N-UNCOUNT In psychology, if someone suffers from **paranoia**, they wrongly believe that other people are trying to harm them. [from New Latin]

**para|noid** /pærənɔɪd/ 🄸 ADJ If you say that someone is **paranoid**, you mean that they are extremely suspicious and afraid of other people. ❑ *I'm not going to get paranoid about it.* ❑ *...a paranoid politician who saw enemies all around him.* 🄲 ADJ Someone who is **paranoid** suffers from the mental illness of paranoia. ❑ *...paranoid feelings.* [from New Latin]

**para|pher|na|lia** /pærəfərneɪlyə, -fəneɪl-/ N-UNCOUNT You can refer to a large number of objects that someone has with them or that are connected with a particular activity as **paraphernalia**. ❑ *...a yard full of builders' paraphernalia.* [from Medieval Latin]

**para|phrase** /pærəfreɪz/ (**paraphrases, paraphrasing, paraphrased**) 🄸 V-T If you **paraphrase** someone or something **paraphrase** something that they have said or written, you express what they have said or written in a different way. ❑ *To paraphrase Oscar Wilde, acting is so much more real than life.* ❑ *...a paraphrased edition of the Bible.* 🄲 N-COUNT A **paraphrase** of something written or spoken is the same thing expressed in a different way. ❑ *The last two sentences were an exact quote rather than a paraphrase.* [from French]

**para|site** /pærəsaɪt/ (**parasites**) 🄸 N-COUNT A **parasite** is a small animal or plant that lives on or inside a larger animal or plant, and gets its food from it. ❑ *Very small parasites live in the stomach of some insects.* ● **para|sit|ic** /pærəsɪtɪk/ ADJ ❑ *...tiny parasitic insects.* 🄲 N-COUNT If you call someone a **parasite**, you disapprove of them because you

think that they get money or other things from people but do not do anything in return. ❑ *He was a parasite, who produced nothing, but lived on the work of others.* [from Latin]

**para|sit|ism** /pærəsaɪtɪzəm/ N-UNCOUNT In biology, **parasitism** is the state of being a parasite. [from Latin]

**para|troop|er** /pærətrupər/ (**paratroopers**) N-COUNT **Paratroopers** are soldiers who are trained to be dropped by parachute into battle or into enemy territory.

**par|cel** /pɑrs⁰l/ (**parcels**) 🄸 N-COUNT A **parcel** is something wrapped in paper, usually so that it can be sent by mail. ❑ *They sent parcels of food and clothing.* 🄲 PHRASE If you say that something is **part and parcel of** something else, you are emphasizing that it is involved or included in it. ❑ *Learning about a new culture is part and parcel of going to live abroad.* [from Old French]

**par|cel post** N-UNCOUNT **Parcel post** is a mail service for the delivery of packages. ❑ *It is much quicker than sending them by parcel post.*

**parched** /pɑrtʃt/ 🄸 ADJ If the ground or a plant is **parched**, it is very dry because there has been no rain. ❑ *Rain poured down on the parched earth.* 🄲 ADJ If your mouth, throat, or lips are **parched**, they are unpleasantly dry. ❑ *Her throat was parched.* 🄳 ADJ If you say that you are **parched**, you mean that you are very thirsty. [INFORMAL]

| Word Link | don ≈ giving : donate, donor, pardon |
|---|---|

**par|don** /pɑrd⁰n/ (**pardons, pardoning, pardoned**) 🄸 CONVENTION You say "**Pardon?,**" "**I beg your pardon?,**" or "**Pardon me?**" when you want someone to repeat what they have just said, either because you have not heard or understood it or because you are surprised by it. [SPOKEN] ❑ *"Will you let me open it?" — "Pardon?" — "Can I open it?"* 🄲 CONVENTION You say "**I beg your pardon**" as a way of apologizing for accidentally doing something wrong, such as disturbing someone or making a mistake. [SPOKEN] ❑ *I beg your pardon. I thought you were someone else.* 🄳 V-T If someone who has been found guilty of a crime **is pardoned**, they are officially allowed to go free and are not punished. ❑ *Hundreds of political prisoners were pardoned and released.* ● **Pardon** is also a noun. ❑ *He received a pardon from the president.* [from Old French]

**pare** /pɛər/ (**pares, paring, pared**) 🄸 V-T When you **pare** something, or **pare** part of it **off** or **away**, you cut off its skin or its outer layer. ❑ *Pare the carrots and slice them thinly.* ❑ *He took out a piece of cheese and pared off a slice.* 🄲 V-T If you **pare** something **down** or **back**, or if you **pare** it, you reduce it. ❑ *The governor's campaign fund could be pared down to $500.* ❑ *The bank is trying to pare back its costs at this difficult time.* [from Old French]

**par|ent** /pɛərənt, pær-/ (**parents**) 🄸 N-COUNT Your **parents** are your mother and father. ❑ *Children need their parents.* 🄲 → see also **single parent** ● **pa|ren|tal** /pərɛnt⁰l/ ADJ ❑ *Children must have parental permission to attend the party.* [from Old French]
→ see **child**

**par|ent cell** (**parent cells**) N-COUNT A **parent cell** is a cell in an organism which divides to produce other cells. Compare **daughter cell**. [TECHNICAL]

## Word Web park

Central Park* was the first planned urban **park** in the United States. When it opened in 1858 only a few wealthy families lived close enough to enjoy it. Today more than 20 million visitors use the park for **recreation** each year. Children enjoy the **playgrounds**, the carousel, and the petting **zoo**. Families have **picnics** on the grass. Couples rent rowboats and row around the lake. Seniors **stroll** through the **gardens**. Players use the **tennis courts** and

**baseball diamonds** all summer. **Cyclists** and **runners** use Central Park Drive* on weekends when it is closed to car traffic.

*Central Park: an 843-acre park in New York City.*
*Central Park Drive: a road in Central Park.*

---

**par|ent|hood** /pɛərənthʊd, pær-/ N-UNCOUNT **Parenthood** is the state of being a parent. ❑ *...the responsibilities of parenthood.* [from Old French]

**par|ent|ing** /pɛərəntɪŋ, pær-/ N-UNCOUNT **Parenting** is the activity of bringing up and taking care of your child. ❑ *...parenting classes.* [from Old French]

**par|ish** /pærɪʃ/ (**parishes**) **1** N-COUNT A **parish** is part of a city or town that has its own church and priest. **2** N-COUNT In some parts of the United States, a **parish** is a small region within a state which has its own local government. [from Old French]

**pa|rish|ion|er** /pərɪʃənər/ (**parishioners**) N-COUNT A priest's **parishioners** are the people in his or her parish. [from Old French]

**par|ity** /pærɪti/ N-UNCOUNT If there is **parity** between two things, they are equal. [FORMAL] ❑ *New York police wanted pay parity with officers in Newark.* [from Late Latin]

**park** /pɑrk/ (**parks, parking, parked**) **1** N-COUNT A **park** is a public area of land with grass and trees, usually in a town, where people go in order to relax and enjoy themselves. ❑ *...Central Park.* ❑ *...a walk with the dog around the park.* **2** N-COUNT A **park** is a place where baseball is played. ❑ *Jack hit the ball out of the park.* **3** V-T/V-I When you **park** a vehicle or **park** somewhere, you drive the vehicle into a position where it can stay for a period of time and you leave it. ❑ *They parked in the street outside the house.* ❑ *He found a place to park the car.* ● **parked** ADJ ❑ *We're parked over there.* ● **parking** N-UNCOUNT ❑ *Parking is allowed only on one side of the street.* [from Old French]
→ see Word Web: **park**

**park|ing gar|age** (**parking garages**) N-COUNT A **parking garage** is a building where people can leave their cars.

**park|ing lot** (**parking lots**) N-COUNT A **parking lot** is an area of ground where people can leave their cars. ❑ *I found a parking lot one block away.*

**park|way** /pɑrkweɪ/ (**parkways**) N-COUNT A **parkway** is a wide road with trees and grass on both sides. [from Old French]

**par|lia|ment** /pɑrləmənt/ (**parliaments**) also **Parliament** **1** N-COUNT; N-PROPER The **parliament** of some countries is the group of people who make or change its laws. ❑ *The Bangladesh Parliament today approved the policy.* [from Old French] **2** → see also **Member of Parliament**

**par|lia|men|ta|ry** /pɑrləmɛntəri/ ADJ **Parliamentary** is used to describe things that are connected with a parliament. ❑ *...a parliamentary debate.* [from Old French]

**par|lor** /pɑrlər/ (**parlors**) N-COUNT **Parlor** is used in the names of some types of stores or businesses that provide a service. ❑ *...a funeral parlor.* [from Old French]

**pa|ro|chial** /pəroʊkiəl/ ADJ If you describe someone as **parochial**, you are critical of them because you think they are too concerned with unimportant local affairs and their own interests. ❑ *She wanted to escape from her parochial life.* [from Old French]

**pa|ro|chial school** (**parochial schools**) N-COUNT A **parochial school** is a private school that is funded and controlled by a particular branch of the Christian church.

**paro|dy** /pærədi/ (**parodies, parodying, parodied**) **1** N-VAR A **parody** is a humorous piece of writing, drama, or music that imitates the style of a well-known person or represents a familiar situation in an exaggerated way. ❑ *...a parody of the "Star Wars" movies.* **2** V-T To **parody** a particular work, thing, or person means to imitate it in an amusing or exaggerated way. ❑ *...an article parodying the views of the president.* [from Latin]

**pa|role** /pəroʊl/ (**paroles, paroling, paroled**) **1** N-UNCOUNT If a prisoner is given **parole**, he or she is released before the official end of their prison sentence on condition that they behave well. ❑ *He will be considered for parole after 10 years.* **2** PHRASE Someone who is **on parole** will stay out of prison if they behave well. **3** V-T If a prisoner **is paroled**, he or she is given parole. ❑ *He could be paroled after eight years.* [from Old French]

**par|rot** /pærət/ (**parrots, parroting, parroted**) **1** N-COUNT A **parrot** is a tropical bird with a

**p**

curved beak and brightly-colored or gray feathers. Parrots can be kept as pets. **2** V-T If you **parrot** what someone else says, you repeat it without really understanding what it means. □ *Students have learned to parrot the standard answers.* [from French]

**pars|ley** /pɑrsli/ N-UNCOUNT **Parsley** is a small plant whose leaves are used for flavoring or decorating food. [from Old English]

**pars|nip** /pɑrsnɪp/ (**parsnips**) N-COUNT A **parsnip** is a long cream-colored root vegetable. [from Old French]

---

### part
**❶** NOUN USES AND PHRASES
**❷** VERB USES

**❶ part** /pɑrt/ (**parts**) **1** N-VAR **Part of** something or a **part** of it is one of the pieces, sections, or elements that it consists of. □ *I like that part of Cape Town.* □ *Perry spent part of his childhood in Canada.* **2** N-COUNT A **part** for a machine or vehicle is one of the smaller pieces that is used to make it. □ *...spare parts for military equipment.* **3** N-COUNT A **part** in a play or movie is one of the roles in it which an actor or actress can perform. □ *Alf offered her a part in the play he was directing.* **4** N-SING Your **part** in something that happens is your involvement in it. □ *He tried to conceal his part in the accident.* **5** N-COUNT A **part** in your hair is a line running from the front to the back of your head where your hair lies in different directions. **6** PHRASE If something or someone **plays a** large or important **part in** an event or situation, they are very involved in it and have an important effect on what happens. □ *Work plays an important part in our lives.* **7** PHRASE If you **take part in** an activity, you do it together with other people. □ *Thousands of students have taken part in demonstrations.* **8** PHRASE You can say, for example, that **for** your **part** you thought or did something, to introduce what you thought or did. [FORMAL] □ *For my part, I feel close to tears.* **9** PHRASE If you talk about a feeling or action **on** your **part**, you are referring to something that you feel or do. □ *There is no need for any further instructions on my part.* **10** PHRASE You use **in part** to indicate that something exists or happens to some extent but not completely. [FORMAL] □ *They're getting more visitors than before, thanks in part to the weather.* [from Old French] **11 part and parcel** → see **parcel**

**❷ part** /pɑrt/ (**parts, parting, parted**) **1** V-T/V-I If things that are next to each other **part** or if you **part** them, they move away from each other. □ *Her lips parted in a smile.* □ *Livy parted the curtains.* **2** V-T If you **part** your hair, you comb it in two different directions so that there is a straight line from the front of your head to the back. □ *Picking up a brush, Joanna parted her hair.* **3** V-RECIP When two people **part**, or if one person **parts from** another, they leave each other. [FORMAL] □ *He gave me the envelope and we parted.* ● **part|ing** (**partings**) N-VAR □ *After their parting, she lived in France.* [from Old French] ▶ **part with** PHR-VERB If you **part with** something that is valuable or that you would prefer to keep, you give it or sell it to someone else. □ *Think carefully before parting with money.*

N.    component, fraction, half, ingredient, piece, portion, section; (ant.) entirety, whole **❶ 1**
      role, share **❶ 4**
V.    break up, separate, split **❷ 3**

**par|tial** /pɑrʃ°l/ **1** ADJ You use **partial** to refer to something that is not complete or whole. □ *Partial agreement was all they could manage.* □ *The plant enjoys partial shade.* ● **par|tial|ly** ADV □ *Lisa is partially blind.* **2** ADJ If you are **partial to** something, you like it. □ *Mollie is partial to pink.* [from Old French]

**par|tial eclipse** (**partial eclipses**) N-COUNT A **partial eclipse of** the sun is an occasion when the moon is between the earth and the sun, so that for a short time you cannot see part of the sun. A **partial eclipse of** the moon is an occasion when the earth is between the sun and the moon, so that for a short time you cannot see part of the moon. Compare **total eclipse**.

**par|tici|pant** /pɑrtɪsɪpənt/ (**participants**) N-COUNT The **participants** in an activity are the people who take part in it. □ *40 of the course participants were offered employment.* [from Latin]

**par|tici|pate** /pɑrtɪsɪpeɪt/ (**participates, participating, participated**) V-I If you **participate** in an activity, you take part in it. □ *Most sufferers can drive a car, participate in sports, etc.* ● **par|tici|pa|tion** /pɑrtɪsɪpeɪʃ°n/ N-UNCOUNT □ *...participation in religious activities.* [from Latin]

**par|tici|ple** /pɑrtɪsɪp°l/ (**participles**) N-COUNT In grammar, a **participle** is a form of a verb that can be used in compound tenses of the verb. English verbs have a past participle, which usually ends in "-ed," and a present participle, which ends in "-ing." [from Old French]

**par|ti|cle** /pɑrtɪk°l/ (**particles**) N-COUNT A **particle** of something is a very small piece or amount of it. □ *...a particle of hot metal.* □ *There is a particle of truth in his statement.* [from Latin] → see **lightning**

**par|ticu|lar** /pərtɪkyələr/ **1** ADJ You use **particular** to emphasize that you are talking about one thing or one kind of thing rather than other similar ones. □ *Where and when did you hear that particular story?* □ *I have to know exactly why I'm doing a particular job.* **2** ADJ If a person or thing has a **particular** quality or possession, it is distinct and belongs only to them. □ *I have a particular responsibility to make the right decision.* **3** ADJ You can use **particular** to emphasize that something is greater or more intense than usual. □ *Particular emphasis will be placed on language training.* **4** ADJ Someone who is **particular** chooses and does things very carefully, and is not easily satisfied. □ *Ted was very particular about the colors he wore.* **5** → see also **particulars** **6** PHRASE You use **in particular** to indicate that what you are saying applies especially to one thing or person. □ *Why should he notice her car in particular?* [from Old French]

**par|ticu|lar|ly** /pərtɪkyələrli/ ADV You use **particularly** to indicate that what you are saying applies especially to one thing or situation. ❑ *Keep your office space looking good, particularly your desk.* ❑ *I particularly liked the wooden chairs.* [from Old French]

**par|ticu|lars** /pərtɪkyələrz/ N-PLURAL The **particulars** of something or someone are facts or details about them that are kept as a record. ❑ *You will find all the particulars in Chapter 9.* [from Old French]

**par|ti|san** /pɑrtɪzən/ (**partisans**) ADJ Someone who is **partisan** strongly supports a particular person or cause, often without thinking carefully about the matter. ❑ *It was an extremely partisan crowd, and they were very enthusiastic.* [from French]

**par|ti|tion** /pɑrtɪʃ°n/ (**partitions, partitioning, partitioned**) ◼ N-COUNT A **partition** is a wall or screen that separates one part of a room or vehicle from another. ❑ *...new offices divided only by glass partitions.* ◻ V-T If you **partition** a room, you separate one part of it from another by means of a partition. ❑ *Bedrooms have been created by partitioning a single larger room.* ◼ V-T If a country **is partitioned**, it is divided into two or more independent countries. ❑ *Ireland was partitioned in 1920.* ● **Partition** is also a noun. ❑ *...the partition of India.* [from Old French]

**part|ly** /pɑrtli/ ADV You use **partly** to indicate that something happens or exists to some extent, but not completely. ❑ *It's partly my fault.* ❑ *I have not worried so much this year, partly because I have had other things to think about.* [from Old French]

**part|ner** /pɑrtnər/ (**partners, partnering, partnered**) ◼ N-COUNT Your **partner** is the person you are married to or are having a long-term sexual relationship with. ❑ *Wanting other friends doesn't mean you don't love your partner.* ◻ N-COUNT Your **partner** in an activity such as a game or dance is the person you are playing or dancing with. ❑ *Her partner for the doubles game was Venus Williams.* ◼ N-COUNT The **partners** in a firm or business are the people who share the ownership of it. [BUSINESS] ❑ *He's a partner in a Chicago law firm.* ◼ N-COUNT The **partner** of a country or organization is another country or organization with which they work or do business. ❑ *Spain has been one of Cuba's major trading partners.* ◼ V-T If you **partner** someone, you are their partner in a game or in a dance. ❑ *He partnered a Russian ballerina.*

**part|ner and group skills** N-PLURAL **Partner and group skills** are skills that require people to work together as a team.

**part|ner|ship** /pɑrtnərʃɪp/ (**partnerships**) N-VAR **Partnership** or a **partnership** is a relationship in which two or more people, organizations, or countries work together as partners. ❑ *...the partnership between Germany's banks and its businesses.*

**part-time**

Also pronounced /bɪˈlʌvd/ when used after a noun or after the verb 'be'.

The adverb is also spelled **part time**. ADJ If someone is a **part-time** worker or has a **part-time** job, they work for only part of each day or week. ❑ *...lower-paid part-time workers.* ● **Part-time** is also an adverb. ❑ *I want to work part-time.*

**par|ty** /pɑrti/ (**parties, partying, partied**) ◼ N-COUNT A **party** is a political organization whose members have similar aims and beliefs,

that tries to get its members elected to the legislature of a country. ❑ *...a member of the Republican Party.* ◻ N-COUNT A **party** is a social event at which people enjoy themselves doing things such as eating or dancing. ❑ *The couple met at a party.* ❑ *We organized a huge birthday party.* ◼ V-I If you **party**, you enjoy yourself doing things such as going out to parties and dancing. ❑ *He partied a little just like all teenagers.* ◼ N-COUNT A **party** of people is a group of them doing something together, for example, traveling. ❑ *They became separated from their party.* ❑ *I was watching a party of tourists.* ◼ N-COUNT One of the people involved in a legal agreement or dispute can be referred to as a particular **party**. [LEGAL] ❑ *They must prove that we are the guilty party.* ◼ PHRASE Someone who **is a party to** or **is party to** an action or agreement is involved in it, and therefore partly responsible for it. ❑ *I would never be a party to such a terrible thing.* [from Old French]

**pas|cal** /pæskæl, pɑskɑl/ (**pascals**) N-COUNT In physics, a **pascal** is a unit of pressure. The abbreviation "Pa" is also used. [TECHNICAL] [from French]

**Pascal's prin|ci|ple** also Pascal's law N-UNCOUNT **Pascal's principle** or **Pascal's law** is a rule in physics which states that, when pressure is applied to a fluid in a container, the pressure is distributed equally throughout all parts of the fluid. [TECHNICAL]

| pass |
| --- |
| ❶ VERB USES |
| ❷ NOUN USES |
| ❸ PHRASAL VERBS |

**❶ pass** /pæs/ (**passes, passing, passed**) ◼ V-T/V-I To **pass** someone or something means to go past them. ❑ *As she passed the library door, the telephone began to ring.* ❑ *Jane stood aside to let her pass.* ◻ V-I When someone or something **passes** in a particular direction, they move in that direction. ❑ *He passed through the doorway into the kitchen.* ❑ *A dirt road passes through the town.* ◼ V-T If you **pass** something through, over, or around something else, you move or push it through, over, or around that thing. ❑ *He passed a hand through his hair.* ◼ V-T If you **pass** an object to someone, you give it to them either from your hand or by kicking or throwing it to them. ❑ *Ken passed the books to Dr Wong.* ❑ *Your partner should then pass the ball back to you.* ◼ V-T/V-I If something **passes** or **is passed** from one person to another, the first person gives it to the second. ❑ *His mother's property passed to him after her death.* ❑ *Officials failed to pass important information to their bosses.* ● **Pass on** means the same as **pass.** ❑ *I passed on the information.* ◼ V-I When a period of time **passes**, it happens and finishes. ❑ *He has let so much time pass without contacting her.* ❑ *As the years passed he felt trapped by marriage.* ● **pass|ing** N-SING ❑ *...the passing of time.* ◼ V-T If you **pass** a period of time in a particular way, you spend it in that way. ❑ *The children passed the time playing in the streets.* ◼ V-T If an amount **passes** a particular total or level, it becomes greater than that total or level. ❑ *...the first company to pass the $2 billion mark.* ◼ V-T/V-I If someone or something **passes** a test or **is passed**, they are considered to be of an acceptable standard. ❑ *Kevin has just passed*

**p**

his driving test. ❑ I didn't pass. ⑩ V-T When people in authority **pass** a new law or a proposal, they formally agree to it or approve it. ❑ Congress may pass a law that allows banks to sell insurance. ⑪ V-I To **pass for** or **pass as** a particular thing means to be accepted as that thing, in spite of not having all the right qualities. ❑ You could pass for a high school senior. ❑ Ted, with his fluent French, passed as one of the locals. [from Old French] ⑫ to **pass the buck** → see **buck** ⑬ to **pass judgment** → see **judgment** → see also **past**

❷ **pass** /pæs/ (**passes**) ① N-COUNT A **pass** in an examination, test, or course is a successful result in it. ❑ He's been allowed to re-take the exam, and he'll probably pass. ② N-COUNT A **pass** is a document that allows you to do something. ❑ He used his journalist's pass to enter the White House. ③ N-COUNT A **pass** in a game such as football or basketball is an act of throwing the ball to someone on your team. ❑ Bryan Randall threw a short pass to Ernest Wilford. ④ N-COUNT A **pass** is a narrow path or route between mountains. ❑ The village is in a mountain pass. [from Old French]
→ see **mountain**

❸ **pass** /pæs/ (**passes, passing, passed**)
▶ **pass away** PHR-VERB You can say that someone **passed away** to mean that they died, if you want to avoid using the word "die" because it might upset people. ❑ He passed away last year.
▶ **pass off as** PHR-VERB If you **pass** something **off as** something that it is not, you convince people that it is that thing. ❑ He passed himself off as a doctor. ❑ Some bad writers try to pass off their gossiping as reporting.
▶ **pass on** ① PHR-VERB **Passed on** means the same as **pass away**. ❑ He passed on at the age of 72. ② → see also **pass** ❶ 5
▶ **pass out** PHR-VERB If you **pass out**, you faint or collapse. ❑ He felt sick and dizzy and then passed out.
▶ **pass over** PHR-VERB If someone **is passed over** for a job, they do not get the job and someone younger or less experienced is chosen instead. ❑ She was repeatedly passed over for promotion.
▶ **pass up** PHR-VERB If you **pass up** an opportunity, you do not take advantage of it. ❑ We can't pass up a chance like this.

**pas|sage** /pæsɪdʒ/ (**passages**) ① N-COUNT A **passage** is a long narrow space with walls or fences on both sides, that connects one place or room with another. ❑ Harry stepped into the passage. ② N-COUNT A **passage** in a book, speech, or piece of music is a section of it. ❑ He read a passage from Emerson. ③ N-UNCOUNT The **passage** of someone or something is their movement or progress from one place or stage to another. ❑ ...the passage of troops through Spain. ❑ ...Russia's passage to democracy. ④ N-SING The **passage of** a period of time is its passing. ❑ The painting will increase in value with the passage of time. [from Old French]

**passage|way** /pæsɪdʒweɪ/ (**passageways**) N-COUNT A **passageway** is a long narrow space between walls or fences, that connects one place or room with another. ❑ Outside, in the passageway, I could hear people moving around. [from Old French]

**pas|sen|ger** /pæsɪndʒər/ (**passengers**) N-COUNT A **passenger** in a vehicle such as a bus, boat, or plane is a person who is traveling in it, but who is not driving it or working on it. ❑ Mr. Smith

was a passenger in the car when it crashed. [from Old French]
→ see **fly, train**

**pass|ing** /pæsɪŋ/ ① ADJ A **passing** feeling or action is brief and not very serious or important. ❑ ...a passing remark in a television interview. ② N-SING The **passing** of a person or thing is the fact of their dying or coming to an end. ❑ We celebrated the passing of the century. ❑ His passing will be mourned by many people. ③ → see also **pass** ④ PHRASE If you mention something **in passing**, you mention it briefly while you are talking or writing about something else. ❑ He mentioned the army in passing. [from Old French]

**pas|sion** /pæʃ°n/ (**passions**) ① N-UNCOUNT **Passion** is a very strong feeling of love and sexual attraction for someone. ❑ I can't feel any passion for George. ② N-UNCOUNT **Passion** is a very strong feeling about something or a strong belief in something. ❑ He spoke with great passion. ③ N-COUNT If you have a **passion for** something, you have a very strong interest in it and like it very much. ❑ She had a passion for gardening. [from French]

| **Thesaurus** | passion | Also look up : |
|---|---|---|
| N. | affection, desire, love ① | |
| | enthusiasm, fondness, interest ② ③ | |

**pas|sion|ate** /pæʃənɪt/ ADJ A **passionate** person has very strong feelings about something or a strong belief in something. ❑ ...his passionate commitment to peace. ❑ He is very passionate about the project. ● **pas|sion|ate|ly** ADV ❑ I am passionately opposed to the plans. [from French]

**pas|sive** /pæsɪv/ ① ADJ If you describe someone as **passive**, you disapprove of the fact that they do not take action, but instead let things happen to them. ❑ ...his passive attitude. ● **pas|sive|ly** ADV ❑ He sat there passively, waiting for his father to say something. ② N-SING In grammar, **the passive** or **the passive voice** is formed using "be" and the past participle of a verb. The subject of a passive clause does not perform the action expressed by the verb but is affected by it. For example, in "He's been murdered," the verb is in the passive. Compare **active**. [from Latin]

**pas|sive so|lar heat|ing** N-UNCOUNT **Passive solar heating** is a method of heating a building by using the materials or design of the building to collect sunlight directly, for example by the use of thick walls or large windows.

**pas|sive trans|port** N-UNCOUNT In biology, **passive transport** is the movement of chemicals and other substances through the membranes of cells by a process called diffusion, which does not require the cells to use energy. Compare **active transport**. [TECHNICAL]

**Pass|over** /pæsoʊvər/ N-UNCOUNT **Passover** is a Jewish festival that begins in March or April and lasts for seven or eight days. [from Hebrew]

**pass|port** /pæsport/ (**passports**) N-COUNT Your **passport** is an official document which you have to show when you enter or leave a country. ❑ You should take your passport with you when changing money. [from French]

**pass|word** /pæswɜrd/ (**passwords**) N-COUNT A **password** is a secret word or phrase that enables

you to enter a place or use a computer system. ❏ *They were only allowed in if they could give the password.*
→ see **Internet**

**past** /pæst/ (**pasts**)

In addition to the uses shown below, **past** is used in phrasal verbs such as "run past."

**1** N-SING The **past** is the time before the present, and the things that have happened. ❏ *In the past, most babies with the disease died.* **2** N-COUNT Your **past** consists of all the things that you have done or that have happened to you. ❏ *He was honest about his past.* **3** ADJ **Past** events and things happened or existed before the present time. ❏ *I knew from past experience that this treatment could help.* ❏ *...scenes from life in past centuries.* **4** ADJ You use **past** to talk about a period of time that has just finished. ❏ *Most stores have remained closed for the past three days.* **5** PREP You use **past** when you are stating a time that is thirty minutes or less after a particular hour. ❏ *It's ten past eleven.* ● **Past** is also an adverb. ❏ *I have my lunch at half past.* **6** PREP If you go **past** someone or something, you go near them and keep moving, so that they are then behind you. ❏ *I walked past him.* ● **Past** is also an adverb. ❏ *An ambulance drove past.* **7** PREP If something is **past** a place, it is on the other side of it. ❏ *Go north on Route I-15 to the exit just past Barstow.*
→ see **history**

**Usage** **past** and **passed**

The adverb or adjective *past* and the verb *passed* (past tense of *pass*) are often confused. They are pronounced the same and can have similar meanings: *Jack passed Jill by rolling past her down the hill. This past week, Shaya passed his history exam and his driving test!*

**pasta**

**pas|ta** /pɑstə/ (**pastas**) N-VAR **Pasta** is a type of food made from a mixture of flour, eggs, and water that is formed into different shapes and then boiled. Spaghetti and macaroni are types of pasta. [from Italian]

**paste** /peɪst/ (**pastes, pasting, pasted**) **1** N-UNCOUNT **Paste** is a soft, wet, sticky mixture that can be spread easily. Some types of paste are used to stick things together. ❏ *Mix a little milk with the powder to form a paste.* ❏ *...tomato paste.* **2** V-T If you **paste** something on a surface, you put glue or paste on it and stick it on the surface. ❏ *...pasting labels on bottles.* [from Old French]

**pas|tel** /pæstɛl/ (**pastels**) ADJ **Pastel** colors are pale rather than dark or bright. ❏ *...delicate pastel shades.* ❏ *...pastel pink, blue, and green.* ● **Pastel** is also a noun. ❏ *The bathroom is decorated in pastels.* [from French]

**pas|time** /pæstaɪm/ (**pastimes**) N-COUNT A **pastime** is something that you enjoy doing in your spare time. ❏ *His favorite pastime is golf.* [from French]

**pas|to|ral** /pæstərəl, pæstɔr-/ **1** ADJ The **pastoral** duties of a priest or other religious leader involve looking after the people he or she has responsibility for, especially by helping them

with their personal problems. ❏ *...the pastoral care of the sick.* **2** ADJ **Pastoral** means characteristic of peaceful country life. ❏ *...a pretty pastoral scene.* [from Latin]

**pas|try** /peɪstri/ (**pastries**) **1** N-UNCOUNT **Pastry** is a food made from flour, fat, and water that is used, for example, for making pies. **2** N-COUNT A **pastry** is a small cake made with sweet pastry. ❏ *...a wide range of cakes and pastries.*

**pas|ture** /pæstʃər/ (**pastures**) N-VAR **Pasture** is land with grass growing on it for farm animals to eat. ❏ *The cows are out now, grazing in the pasture.* [from Old French]
→ see **barn**

**pat** /pæt/ (**pats, patting, patted**) **1** V-T If you **pat** something or someone, you tap them lightly, usually with your hand held flat. ❏ *"Don't you worry about this," she said patting me on the knee.* ❏ *The lady patted her hair nervously.* ● **Pat** is also a noun. ❏ *He gave her an encouraging pat on the shoulder.* **2** PHRASE If you **stand pat**, you refuse to change your mind about something. ❏ *He seems to think that the right thing in this situation is to stand pat.*

**patch** /pætʃ/ (**patches, patching, patched**) **1** N-COUNT A **patch** on a surface is a part of it that is different in appearance from the area around it. ❏ *...the bald patch on the top of his head.* ❏ *There was a small patch of blue in the gray clouds.* **2** N-COUNT A **patch of** land is a small area of land where a particular plant or crop grows. ❏ *...a patch of land covered with trees.* ❏ *...the little vegetable patch in her backyard.* **3** N-COUNT A **patch** is a piece of material that you use to cover a hole in something. ❏ *...jackets with patches on the elbows.* **4** V-T If you **patch** something that has a hole in it, you repair it by fastening a patch over the hole. ❏ *He and Williams patched the barn roof.* **5** N-COUNT A **patch** is a piece of computer program code written as a temporary solution for dealing with a problem. [COMPUTING] ❏ *Older machines will need a software patch to correct the date.* **6** PHRASE If you have or go through **a rough patch**, you have a lot of problems for a time. ❏ *He went through a rough patch after he lost his job.* [from French]
▶ **patch up** **1** PHR-VERB If you **patch up** an argument or relationship, you try to be friendly again and not to argue anymore. ❏ *They soon patched up their friendship.* ❏ *Robbie has patched things up with his mom.* **2** PHR-VERB If you **patch up** something that is damaged, you repair it. ❏ *We can patch up those holes.*

**patch|work** /pætʃwɜrk/ ADJ A **patchwork** quilt or piece of clothing is made by sewing together small pieces of material.

**patchy** /pætʃi/ **1** ADJ A **patchy** substance or color exists in some places but not in others, or is thick in some places and thin in others. ❏ *...thick patchy fog.* ❏ *...the brown, patchy grass.* **2** ADJ If something is **patchy**, it is not completely reliable or satisfactory because it is not always good. ❏ *Her knowledge of the case was patchy.* [from French]

**pa|tent** /pæt³nt/ (**patents, patenting, patented**) **1** N-COUNT A **patent** is an official right to be the only person or company allowed to make or sell a new product for a certain period of time. ❏ *P&G applied for a patent on its cookies.* ❏ *He held a number of patents for his many inventions.* **2** V-T If you **patent** something, you obtain a patent for it. ❏ *He patented the idea that the atom could be split.* ❏ *The*

**p**

invention has been patented by the university. **3** ADJ You use **patent** to emphasize that something, especially something bad, is obvious. ❑ *This was patent nonsense.* ● **pa|tent|ly** ADV ❑ *He made his anger patently obvious.* [from Old French]

**pa|ter|nal** /pətɜrn°l/ ADJ **Paternal** is used to describe feelings or actions that are typical of those of a kind father toward his child. ❑ *…paternal love.* [from Late Latin]

**path** /pæθ/ (**paths**) **1** N-COUNT A **path** is a strip of ground that people walk along. ❑ *We followed the path along the cliff.* ❑ *Feet had worn a path in the rock.* **2** N-COUNT Your **path** is the space ahead of you as you move along. ❑ *A group of reporters blocked his path.* **3** N-COUNT The **path** of something is the line that it moves along in a particular direction. ❑ *He stepped into the path of a moving car.* ❑ *…people who live under the flight path of airplanes.* **4** N-COUNT A **path** that you take is a particular course of action or way of achieving something. ❑ *He chose the path of rock stardom.* [from Old English]
→ see **golf**

**pa|thet|ic** /pəθɛtɪk/ **1** ADJ If you describe a person or animal as **pathetic**, you mean that they are sad and weak or helpless, and they make you feel very sorry for them. ❑ *…a pathetic little dog with a curly tail.* ❑ *The small group of onlookers were a pathetic sight.* ● **pa|thet|i|cal|ly** /pəθɛtɪkli/ ADV ❑ *She was pathetically thin.* **2** ADJ If you describe someone or something as **pathetic**, you mean that they make you feel impatient or angry, often because they are weak or not very good. ❑ *What pathetic excuses.* ❑ *Don't be so pathetic.* ● **pa|thet|i|cal|ly** ADV ❑ *Five women in a group of 18 people is a pathetically small number.* [from French]

**patho|logi|cal** /pæθəlɒdʒɪk°l/ **1** ADJ You describe a person as **pathological** when they behave in an extreme and unacceptable way, and have very powerful feelings that they cannot control. ❑ *He experiences almost pathological jealousy.* ❑ *He's a pathological liar.* **2** ADJ **Pathological** means relating to pathology or illness. [MEDICAL] ❑ *…pathological conditions in animals.* [from Latin]

**pa|thol|ogy** /pəθɒlədʒi/ N-UNCOUNT **Pathology** is the study of the way illnesses develop, and the examination of dead bodies in order to find out the cause of death. [MEDICAL] ● **pa|tholo|gist** /pəθɒlədʒɪst/ (**pathologists**) N-COUNT ❑ *The pathologist told the court that Mrs Snook died of old age.* [from Latin]

**pa|thos** /peɪθɒs/ N-UNCOUNT **Pathos** is a quality in a situation that makes people feel sadness and pity. ❑ *…the pathos of his situation.* [from Greek]

**path|way** /pæθweɪ/ (**pathways**) **1** N-COUNT A **pathway** is the same as a **path**. ❑ *Richard was coming up the pathway.* ❑ *…the pathway to success.* **2** N-COUNT The **pathway** of something is the line which it moves along in a particular direction. [from Old English]

**pa|tience** /peɪʃ°ns/ N-UNCOUNT If you have **patience**, you are able to stay calm and not get annoyed, for example, when something takes a long time. ❑ *He doesn't have the patience to wait.* [from French]

**pa|tient** /peɪʃ°nt/ (**patients**) **1** N-COUNT A **patient** is a person who receives medical treatment from a doctor or hospital. ❑ *45,000 patients have been waiting more than six months for operations.* ❑ *She was tough but wonderful with her patients.* **2** ADJ If you are **patient**, you stay calm and do not get annoyed, for example, when something takes a long time. ❑ *Please be patient — your check will arrive.* ● **pa|tient|ly** ADV ❑ *She waited patiently for Frances to finish.* **2** → see also **customer**
→ see **diagnosis, illness**

**pa|tio** /pætioʊ/ (**patios**) N-COUNT A **patio** is an area of flat stones of stone or concrete next to a house, where people can sit and relax or eat. [from Spanish]

**pa|tri|ot** /peɪtriət/ (**patriots**) N-COUNT A **patriot** is someone who loves their country and feels very loyal toward it. ❑ *…true patriots.* [from French]

| Word Link | *otic* ≈ *affecting, causing* : *chaotic,* *neurotic, patriotic* |
|---|---|

| Word Link | *ism* ≈ *action or state* : *communism,* *optimism, patriotism* |
|---|---|

**pat|ri|ot|ic** /peɪtriɒtɪk/ ADJ Someone who is **patriotic** loves their country and feels very loyal toward it. ❑ *They are very patriotic guys who give everything for their country..* ● **pat|ri|ot|ism** /peɪtriətɪzəm/ N-UNCOUNT ❑ *…a boy who joined the army out of a sense of patriotism.* [from French]

**pa|trol** /pətroʊl/ (**patrols, patrolling, patrolled**) **1** V-T When soldiers, police, or guards **patrol** an area or building, they move around it in order to make sure that there is no trouble there. ❑ *Prison officers continued to patrol the grounds.* ● **Patrol** is also a noun. ❑ *He failed to return from a patrol.* ❑ *The army is now on patrol.* **2** N-COUNT A **patrol** is a group of soldiers or vehicles that are patrolling an area. ❑ *Police are searching for three men who attacked a patrol last night.* [from French]

**patrol|man** /pətroʊlmən/ (**patrolmen**) N-COUNT A **patrolman** is a policeman who patrols a particular area.

**pa|tron** /peɪtrən/ (**patrons**) **1** N-COUNT A **patron** is a person who supports and gives money to artists, writers, or musicians. ❑ *…a patron of the arts.* **2** N-COUNT The **patron** of a charity, group, or campaign is an important person who allows his or her name to be used for publicity. ❑ *He has now become one of the patrons of the association.* **3** N-COUNT The **patrons** of a place such as a restaurant or hotel are its customers. ❑ *…patrons of a high-priced hotel.* [from Old French]

**pat|ron|age** /peɪtrənɪdʒ, pæt-/ N-UNCOUNT **Patronage** is the support and money given by someone to a person or a group such as a charity. ❑ *…government patronage of the arts.* [from Old French]

**pat|ron|ize** /peɪtrənaɪz/ (**patronizes, patronizing, patronized**) V-T If someone **patronizes** you, they speak or behave toward you in a way that seems friendly, but that shows that they think that they are superior to you. ❑ *Don't patronize me!* ● **pat|ron|iz|ing** ADJ ❑ *The tone of the interview was patronizing.* [from Old French]

**pat|ter** /pætər/ (**patters, pattering, pattered**) V-I If something **patters** on a surface, it hits it quickly several times, making quiet, tapping sounds. ❑ *Rain pattered gently outside.* ● **Patter** is also a noun. N-SING ❑ *…the patter of the rain on the roof.*

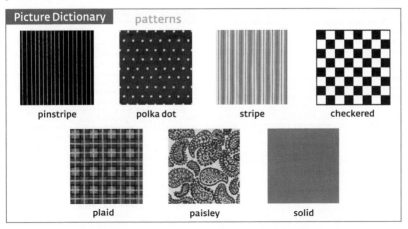

**Picture Dictionary** patterns

pinstripe  polka dot  stripe  checkered

plaid  paisley  solid

**pat|tern** /pǽtərn/ (**patterns**) **1** N-COUNT A **pattern** is the repeated or regular way in which something happens or is done. ❑ *All three attacks followed the same pattern.* **2** N-COUNT A **pattern** is an arrangement of lines or shapes repeated at regular intervals. ❑ ...*a pattern of light and dark stripes.* **3** N-COUNT A **pattern** is a diagram or shape that you can use as a guide when you are making something such as a model or a piece of clothing. ❑ *Send for our free knitting patterns.* [from Medieval Latin]
→ see Picture Dictionary: **pattern**
→ see **quilt**

**pat|terned** /pǽtərnd/ ADJ Something that is **patterned** is covered with a pattern or design. ❑ ...*a plain carpet with a patterned border.* [from Medieval Latin]

**pat|ty** /pǽti/ (**patties**) N-COUNT A **patty** is an amount of ground beef formed into a flat, round shape. ❑ ...*the beef patties frying on the grill.* [from French]

**pause** /pɔz/ (**pauses, pausing, paused**) **1** V-I If you **pause** while you are doing something, you stop for a short period and then continue. ❑ *"It's rather embarrassing," he began, and paused.* ❑ *He talked for two hours, hardly pausing for breath.* **2** N-COUNT A **pause** is a short period when you stop doing something before continuing. ❑ *After a pause Al said: "I'm sorry if I upset you."* [from Latin]

**pave** /peɪv/ (**paves, paving, paved**) V-T If a road

or an area of ground **has been paved**, it has been covered with asphalt or concrete, so that it is easy to walk or drive on. ❑ *The avenue has never been paved.* [from Old French]

**pave|ment** /peɪvmənt/ (**pavements**) N-COUNT The **pavement** is the hard surface of a road. ❑ ...*the wet pavement.* [from Latin]

**pa|vil|ion** /pəvɪlyən/ (**pavilions**) **1** N-COUNT A **pavilion** is a large temporary structure such as a tent that is used at outdoor public events. **2** N-COUNT A **pavilion** is an ornamental building in a garden or park. [from Old French]

**paw** /pɔ/ (**paws, pawing, pawed**) **1** N-COUNT The **paws** of an animal such as a cat, dog, or bear are its feet. ❑ *The kitten was black with white front paws.* **2** V-T If an animal **paws** something, it draws its paw or hoof over it. ❑ *Madigan's horse pawed the ground.* [from Old French]

**pawn** /pɔn/ (**pawns, pawning, pawned**) **1** V-T If you **pawn** something that you own, you leave it with a pawnbroker, who gives you money for it and who can sell it if you do not pay back the money before a certain time. ❑ *He is thinking about pawning his watch.* **2** N-COUNT In chess, a **pawn** is the smallest and least valuable playing piece. Each player has eight pawns at the start of the game. **3** N-COUNT If you say that someone is using you as a **pawn**, you mean that they are using you for their own advantage. ❑ *He is being used as a political pawn by the president.* [Sense 1 from Old French. Senses 2 and 3 from Anglo–Norman.]
→ see **chess**

**pawn|broker** /pɔnbroʊkər/ (**pawnbrokers**) N-COUNT A **pawnbroker** is a person who lends people money. People give the pawnbroker something they own, which can be sold if they do not pay back the money before a certain time.

**pay** /peɪ/ (**pays, paying, paid**) **1** V-T/V-I When you **pay** an amount of money to someone, you give it to them because you are buying something from them or because you owe it to them. When you **pay** something such as a bill or a debt, you pay the amount that you owe. ❑ *You've already paid for the call.* ❑ *The wealthier people may have to pay a little more in taxes.* **2** V-T When you **are paid**, you get

p

your wages or salary from your employer. ❑ *The lawyer was paid a huge salary.* ❑ *I get paid monthly.*
● **Pay** is also a noun. N-UNCOUNT ❑ *...complaints about their pay and working conditions.* **3** If a course of action **pays**, it results in some advantage or benefit for you. ❑ *As always, it pays to do some research.* ❑ *We must show that crime does not pay.* **4** V-T/V-I If you **pay for** something that you do or have, you suffer as a result of it. ❑ *Lakoto paid for his beliefs with years in prison.* ❑ *Why should I pay the penalty for somebody else's mistake?* **5** V-T You use **pay** with some nouns, such as in the expressions **pay a visit** and **pay attention**, to indicate that something is given or done. ❑ *Pay us a visit next time you're in Portland.* ❑ *He felt a heavy bump, but paid no attention to it.* [from Old French] **6** → see also **paid** **7** **to pay dividends** → see **dividend** **8** **to pay through the nose** → see **nose**

▸ **pay back** PHR-VERB If you **pay back** money that you have borrowed or taken from someone, you give them an equal amount at a later time. ❑ *He will have to pay back everything he has stolen.*
▸ **pay off** **1** PHR-VERB If you **pay off** a debt, you give back all the money that you owe. ❑ *It will take him the rest of his life to pay off that loan.* **2** PHR-VERB If an action **pays off**, it is successful. ❑ *It looks like all their hard work finally paid off.* **3** → see also **payoff**
▸ **pay out** PHR-VERB If you **pay out** money, usually a large amount, you spend it on something. ❑ *The insurance industry will pay out billions of dollars for damage caused by Hurricane Katrina.*
▸ **pay up** PHR-VERB If you **pay up**, you give someone money that they say you owe them. ❑ *We asked for a refund, but they would not pay up.*

**pay|able** /ˈpeɪəbəl/ **1** ADJ If an amount of money is **payable**, it has to be paid or it can be paid. ❑ *The money is not payable until January 31.* **2** ADJ If a check or money order is made **payable to** you, it has your name written on it to indicate that you are the person who will receive the money. ❑ *Make your check payable to "Stanford Alumni Association."* [from Old French]

**pay|back** /ˈpeɪbæk/ N-SING A **payback** is the profit or benefit that you obtain from something that you have spent money, time, or effort on. ❑ *With such high costs, there would be no payback from the program.*

**pay|check** /ˈpeɪtʃɛk/ (**paychecks**) N-COUNT Your **paycheck** is the money that your employer gives you as your wages or salary. ❑ *I just get a small paycheck every month.*

**pay|dirt** /ˈpeɪdɜrt/ also pay dirt PHRASE If you say that someone **has struck paydirt** or **has hit paydirt**, you mean that they have achieved sudden success or gained a lot of money very quickly. [INFORMAL] ❑ *Howard Hawks hit paydirt with "Rio Bravo."*

**pay|er** /ˈpeɪər/ (**payers**) N-COUNT You can refer to someone as a **payer** if they pay a particular kind of bill or fee. For example, a tax**payer** is someone who pays tax. ❑ *Lower interest rates pleased millions of mortgage payers.* [from Old French] **2** → see also **taxpayer**

**pay|ment** /ˈpeɪmənt/ (**payments**) **1** N-COUNT A **payment** is an amount of money that is paid to someone. ❑ *...mortgage payments.* **2** N-UNCOUNT **Payment** is the act of paying money to someone or of being paid. ❑ *Players now expect payment for interviews.* [from Old French] **3** → see also **down payment**

| | Word Partnership | Use *payment* with : |
|---|---|---|
| V. | **accept** payment, **make a** payment, **receive** payment **1** | |
| ADJ. | **late** payment, **minimum** payment, **monthly** payment **1** | |
| N. | payment **in cash**, payment **by check**, **mortgage** payment **1** payment **date 1 2** payment **method**, payment **plan 2** | |

**pay|off** /ˈpeɪɔf/ (**payoffs**) also pay-off **1** N-COUNT The **payoff from** an action is the advantage or benefit that you get from it. ❑ *The payoffs from this approach are huge.* **2** N-COUNT A **payoff** is a payment made to someone, often secretly or illegally, so that they will not cause trouble. ❑ *At that time, payoffs to public officials were quite usual.*

**pay|roll** /ˈpeɪroʊl/ (**payrolls**) N-COUNT The people **on** the **payroll** of a company or an organization are the people who work for it and are paid by it. [BUSINESS] ❑ *They have 87,000 employees on the payroll.*

**PBS** /ˈpi bi ɛs/ N-PROPER In the United States, **PBS** is an organization that broadcasts television programs and is not financed by advertising. **PBS** is an abbreviation for "Public Broadcasting Service."

**PC** /ˈpi si/ (**PCs**) N-COUNT A **PC** is a computer that is used by one person at a time in a business, a school, or at home. **PC** is an abbreviation for **personal computer**. ❑ *The price of a PC has fallen.*

**PDA** /ˈpi di eɪ/ (**PDAs**) N-COUNT A **PDA** is a handheld computer, used mainly for storing and accessing personal information such as addresses, telephone numbers, and memos. **PDA** is an abbreviation for **personal digital assistant**. ❑ *A typical PDA can function as a cell phone and a personal organizer.*

**PDF** /ˈpi di ɛf/ N-UNCOUNT **PDF** files are computer documents which look exactly like the original documents, regardless of which software or operating system was used to create them. **PDF** is an abbreviation for "Portable Document Format." [COMPUTING]

**pea** /ˈpi/ (**peas**) N-COUNT **Peas** are small, round, green seeds that are eaten as a vegetable.

**peace** /ˈpis/ **1** N-UNCOUNT When there is **peace** in a country, it is not involved in a war. ❑ *...a shared commitment to world peace.* ❑ *...a peace agreement.* **2** N-UNCOUNT **Peace** is a state of undisturbed quiet and calm. ❑ *All I want is to have some peace and quiet.* **3** N-UNCOUNT If there is **peace** among a group of people, they live or work together in a friendly way and do not argue. ❑ *Mandela called for peace among people of different races and cultures.* [from Old French]

**peace|ful** /ˈpisfəl/ **1** ADJ **Peaceful** means not involving war or violence. ❑ *He has attempted to find a peaceful solution to the conflict.* ● **peace|ful|ly** ADV ❑ *The governor asked the protestors to leave peacefully.* **2** ADJ A **peaceful** place or time is quiet, calm, and free from disturbance. ❑ *...a peaceful house in the Ozarks.* ● **peace|ful|ly** ADV ❑ *Except for traffic noise, the night passed peacefully.* **3** ADJ

Someone who feels or looks **peaceful** feels or looks calm and free from worry or pain. ● **peace|ful|ly** ADV ❑ *He was sleeping peacefully at her side.* [from Old French] **4** → see also **peaceful**

**peach** /piːtʃ/ (**peaches**) **1** N-COUNT A **peach** is a soft, round, slightly furry fruit with sweet yellow flesh and pinky-orange skin. **2** COLOR Something that is **peach** is pale pinky-orange in color. ❑ *...a peach silk blouse.* [from Old French]

**peachy** /piːtʃi/ ADJ If you say that something is **peachy** or **peachy keen**, you mean that it is very nice. [INFORMAL] ❑ *Everything in her life is just peachy.* [from Old French]

**peak** /piːk/ (**peaks, peaking, peaked**) **1** N-COUNT The **peak** of a process or an activity is the point at which it is at its strongest, most successful, or most fully developed. ❑ *His career was at its peak when he died.* **2** V-I When something **peaks**, it reaches its highest value or its highest level. ❑ *Temperatures have peaked at over 90 degrees.* **3** ADJ The **peak** level or value of something is its highest level or value. ❑ *Today's price is 59% lower than the peak level of $1.5 million.* **4** N-COUNT A **peak** is a mountain or the top of a mountain. ❑ *...the snow-covered peaks.* [from Spanish]
→ see **mountain**

**peal** /piːl/ (**peals, pealing, pealed**) **1** V-I When bells **peal**, they ring one after another, making a musical sound. ❑ *Church bells pealed at the stroke of midnight.* ● **Peal** is also a noun. ❑ *...the peal of the cathedral bells.* **2** N-COUNT A **peal of** laughter or thunder consists of a long, loud series of sounds. ❑ *I heard a peal of laughter.*

**pea|nut** /piːnʌt, -nət/ (**peanuts**) N-COUNT **Peanuts** are small nuts often eaten as a snack.
→ see Word Web: **peanut**

**pear** /pɛər/ (**pears**) N-COUNT A **pear** is a juicy fruit that is narrow at the top and wider at the bottom. Pears have white flesh and green, yellow, or brown skin. [from Old English]
→ see **fruit, vegetable**

**pearl** /pɜrl/ (**pearls**) N-COUNT A **pearl** is a hard, white, shiny, round object that grows inside the shell of an oyster and is used for making jewelry. ❑ *She wore a string of pearls.* [from Old French]

**peas|ant** /pɛzənt/ (**peasants**) N-COUNT People refer to small farmers or farm workers in poor countries as **peasants**. ❑ *The film describes the customs and habits of peasants in Peru.* [from Old French]

**peat** /piːt/ N-UNCOUNT **Peat** is decaying plant material that is found in some cool, wet regions. ❑ *A peat fire burned smokily in the large fireplace.* [from Anglo-Latin]

**peb|ble** /pɛbəl/ (**pebbles**) N-COUNT A **pebble** is a small, smooth stone. [from Old English]
→ see **beach**

**peck** /pɛk/ (**pecks, pecking, pecked**) **1** V-T/V-I If a bird **pecks at** something or **pecks** something, it moves its beak forward quickly and bites at it. ❑ *The sparrows were pecking at whatever they could find.* ❑ *Chickens pecked in the dust.* ❑ *It pecked his leg.* **2** V-T If you **peck** someone **on** the cheek, you give them a quick, light kiss. ❑ *Elizabeth walked up to him and pecked him on the cheek.* ● **Peck** is also a noun. ❑ *He gave me a little peck on the cheek.*

**pe|cu|liar** /pɪkjuːlyər/ **1** ADJ If you describe someone or something as **peculiar**, you think that they are strange or unusual, sometimes in an unpleasant way. ❑ *Mr. Kennet has a rather peculiar sense of humor.* ● **pe|cu|liar|ly** ADV ❑ *His face became peculiarly expressionless.* **2** ADJ If something is **peculiar to** a particular thing, person, or situation, it belongs or relates only to that thing, person, or situation. ❑ *This expression is peculiar to British English.* ● **pe|cu|liar|ly** ADV ❑ *...the peculiarly American business of making Hollywood movies.* [from Latin]

**pe|cu|li|ar|ity** /pɪkjuːliæriti/ (**peculiarities**) **1** N-COUNT A **peculiarity** that someone or something has is a strange or unusual characteristic or habit. ❑ *Joe's peculiarity was that he was constantly munching hard candy.* **2** N-COUNT A **peculiarity** is a characteristic or quality that belongs or relates only to one person or thing. ❑ *...a strange peculiarity of the U.S. system.* [from Latin]

**Word Link** ped ≈ foot : *pedal*, *pedestal*, *pedestrian*

**ped|al** /pɛdəl/ (**pedals, pedaling** or **pedalling, pedaled** or **pedalled**) **1** N-COUNT The **pedals** on a bicycle are the two parts that you push with your feet in order to make the bicycle move. **2** V-T/V-I When you **pedal** a bicycle, you push the pedals around with your feet to make it move. ❑ *She pedaled the five miles home.* ❑ *We pedalled slowly through the city streets.* **3** N-COUNT A **pedal** in a car or on a machine is a lever that you press with your foot in order to control the car or machine. ❑ *...the brake and the gas pedal.* [from Latin]
→ see **bicycle**

**ped|dle** /pɛdəl/ (**peddles, peddling, peddled**) **1** V-T Someone who **peddles** things, especially things which are inexpensive or illegal, goes from place to place trying to sell them. ❑ *He peddled juice and coffee from a cart.* ● **ped|dler** N-COUNT ❑ *Harry worked as a peddler and junk dealer.* **2** V-T If you

P

**Word Web** peanut

The **peanut** is not really a **nut**. It is a legume and grows under the ground. Peanuts originated in South America about 3,500 years ago. Explorers took them to Africa. Later, African slaves introduced the peanut into North America. Only poor people ate them at first. But they were a popular **snack** by 1900. You could buy **roasted** peanuts on city streets and at baseball games and circuses. Some scientists believe that roasted peanuts cause more **allergic** reactions than boiled peanuts. George Washington Carver, an African-American scientist, found 325 different uses for peanuts—including **peanut butter**.

say that someone **peddles** an idea or a piece of information, you disapprove of the fact that they are trying to get people to accept it. ❑ *He peddled a story about needing money.*

**ped|es|tal** /pɛdɪstəl/ (**pedestals**) N-COUNT A **pedestal** is the base on which something such as a statue stands. ❑ *The statue stood on a stone pedestal.* [from French]

> **Word Link** an, ian ≈ one of, relating to : Christ*ian*, Europe*an*, pedestr*ian*

**pe|des|trian** /pɪdɛstriən/ (**pedestrians**) ◼ N-COUNT A **pedestrian** is a person who is walking, especially in a town. ❑ *...Los Angeles, where a pedestrian is a rare sight.* ◻ ADJ If you describe something as **pedestrian**, you mean that it is ordinary and not at all interesting. ❑ *His writing style is so pedestrian that the book becomes boring.* [from Latin]

**pe|dia|tri|cian** /pidiətrɪʃən/ (**pediatricians**) N-COUNT A **pediatrician** is a doctor who specializes in treating children.

> **Word Link** iatr ≈ healing : ger*iatr*ic, ped*iatr*ics, psych*iatr*y

**pe|di|at|rics** /pidiætrɪks/

> The form **pediatric** is used as a modifier.

N-UNCOUNT **Pediatrics** is the area of medicine that is concerned with the treatment of children. ❑ *...a career in pediatrics.* ❑ *...pediatric medicine.*

**pedi|gree** /pɛdɪgri/ (**pedigrees**) ◼ N-COUNT If a dog, cat, or other animal has a **pedigree**, its ancestors are known and recorded. ❑ *60 percent of dogs and ten percent of cats have pedigrees.* ◻ N-COUNT Someone's **pedigree** is their background or their ancestors. ❑ *...his noble pedigree.* [from Old French]

**pe|dom|eter** /pɪdɒmɪtər/ (**pedometers**) N-COUNT A **pedometer** is a device that measures the distance that someone has walked.

**peek** /pik/ (**peeks, peeking, peeked**) V-I If

peek

you **peek at** something or someone, you take a quick look at them, often secretly. ❑ *She peeked at him through a crack in the wall.* ● **Peek** is also a noun. ❑ *Companies have been paying huge amounts of money for a peek at the information.* [from Middle Dutch]

**peel** /pil/ (**peels, peeling, peeled**) ◼ N-VAR The **peel** of a fruit such as a lemon or an apple is its skin. ❑ *...grated lemon peel.* ❑ *...a banana peel.* ◻ V-T When you **peel** fruit or vegetables, you remove their skins. ❑ *She began peeling potatoes.* ◼ V-T/V-I If you **peel** something **off** a surface or if it **peels off**, it comes away from the surface. ❑ *One of the kids was peeling plaster off the wall.* ❑ *It took me two days to peel off the labels.* ❑ *Paint was peeling off the walls.* [from Old English]
→ see **cut, fruit**

**peep** /pip/ (**peeps, peeping, peeped**) ◼ V-I If you **peep**, or **peep at** something, you take a quick look at it, often secretly and quietly. ❑ *Children came to peep at him around the doorway.* ● **Peep** is also

a noun. ❑ *"Fourteen minutes," Chris said, taking a peep at his watch.* ◻ V-I If something **peeps** out from behind or under something, a small part of it is visible. ❑ *Purple and yellow flowers peeped out from between rocks.* ◼ V-I If you say that you **don't hear a peep from** someone, you mean that they do not say anything or make any noise. [INFORMAL] ❑ *You don't hear a peep from her once she's gone to bed.*

**peer** /pɪər/ (**peers, peering, peered**) ◼ V-I If you **peer at** something, you look at it very hard, usually because it is difficult to see clearly. ❑ *He found her peering at a computer print-out.* ◻ N-COUNT Your **peers** are the people who are the same age as you or who have the same status as you. ❑ *He is popular with his peers.* [Sense 1 from Flemish. Sense 2 from Old French.]

**peer press|ure** N-UNCOUNT If someone does something because of **peer pressure**, they do it because other people in their social group do it. ❑ *...peer pressure to be cool.*

**peeve** /piv/ (**peeves**) N-COUNT If something is your **peeve** or your **pet peeve**, it makes you particularly irritated or angry. ❑ *Ads on the computer screen are a pet peeve for many users.*

**peg** /pɛg/ (**pegs, pegging, pegged**) ◼ N-COUNT A **peg** is a small piece of wood or metal that is used for fastening something to something else. ❑ *He builds furniture using wooden pegs instead of nails.* ◻ N-COUNT A **peg** is a small hook or knob that is attached to a wall or door and is used for hanging things on. ❑ *His work jacket hung on the peg in the kitchen.* ◼ V-T If a price or amount of something **is pegged at** a particular level, it is fixed at that level. ❑ *The peso is pegged to the dollar.* ❑ *The bank wants to peg rates at 9%.*

**pe|lag|ic en|vi|ron|ment** /pəlædʒɪk ɛnvaɪrənmənt, -vaɪərn-/ also **pelagic zone** N-SING The **pelagic environment** or **pelagic zone** is the parts of the ocean that are away from the coast and above the ocean floor, and all the organisms that live there. Compare **benthic**. [TECHNICAL]

**pel|let** /pɛlɪt/ (**pellets**) N-COUNT A **pellet** is a small ball of food, mud, lead, or other material. ❑ *The bird could collect food pellets from a feeder.* [from Old French]

**pelt** /pɛlt/ (**pelts, pelting, pelted**) ◼ N-COUNT The **pelt** of an animal is its skin, which can be used to make clothing or rugs. ❑ *...a bed covered with beaver pelts.* ◻ V-T If you **pelt** someone **with** things, you throw things at them. ❑ *The men began to pelt one another with snowballs.* ◼ V-I If it is **pelting down**, it is raining very hard. [INFORMAL] ❑ *The rain now was pelting down.*

**pel|vic** /pɛlvɪk/ ADJ **Pelvic** means near or relating to your pelvis. ❑ *Place the hands on the pelvic bones.* [from Latin]

**pel|vis** /pɛlvɪs/ (**pelvises**) N-COUNT Your **pelvis** is the wide, curved group of bones at the level of your hips. [from Latin]

**pen** /pɛn/ (**pens, penning, penned**) ◼ N-COUNT A **pen** is a long thin object which you use to write in ink. ◻ V-T If someone **pens** a letter, article, or book, they write it. [FORMAL] ❑ *I really intended to pen this letter to you early this morning.* ◼ N-COUNT A **pen** is also a small area with a fence around it in which farm animals are kept for a short time. ❑ *...a holding pen for sheep.* ◼ V-T If people

or animals **are penned** somewhere or **are penned up**, they are forced to remain in a very small area. ❑ *The cattle were penned for the night.* ❑ *The animals were penned up in cages.* **5** N-COUNT People sometimes refer to a prison as **the pen**. [INFORMAL] [from Old English]
→ see **office**

**pe|nal** /piːnˀl/ ADJ **Penal** means relating to the punishment of criminals. ❑ *...penal and legal systems.* [from Late Latin]

**pe|nal|ize** /piːnəlaɪz/ (penalizes, penalizing, penalized) V-T If a person or group **is penalized** for something, they are made to suffer some disadvantage because of it. ❑ *Some of the players may break the rules and be penalized.* [from Late Latin]

**pen|al|ty** /pɛnˀlti/ (penalties) **1** N-COUNT A **penalty** is a punishment for doing something which is against a law or rule. ❑ *He faces a penalty of 10 years in prison and a $500,000 fine.* **2** N-COUNT In sports such as soccer, football, and hockey, a **penalty** is a disadvantage forced on the team that breaks a rule. ❑ *The team needs to work hard to avoid bad penalties.* [from Medieval Latin]

**pen|chant** /pɛntʃənt/ N-SING If someone has a **penchant for** something, they have a special liking for it or a tendency to do it. [FORMAL] ❑ *...a stylish woman with a penchant for dark glasses.* [from French]

**pen|cil** /pɛnsˀl/ (pencils) N-COUNT A **pencil** is a thin wooden rod with a black or colored substance through the middle that you write or draw with. ❑ *I found a pencil and some blank paper.* [from Old French]
→ see **office**

**pen|cil push|er** (pencil pushers) N-COUNT If you call someone a **pencil pusher**, you disapprove of them because you think that their work consists of writing documents rather than dealing with real people or real situations. ❑ *That's a job for a pencil pusher.*

**pen|dant** /pɛndənt/ (pendants) N-COUNT A **pendant** is an ornament on a chain that you wear around your neck. [from Old French]
→ see **jewelry**

**pend|ing** /pɛndɪŋ/ **1** ADJ If something such as a legal procedure is **pending**, it is waiting to be dealt with or settled. [FORMAL] ❑ *He will not be available while the case is pending.* **2** PREP If something is done **pending** a future event, it is done until that event happens. [FORMAL] ❑ *The police released him pending a further investigation.* [from French]

**pen|du|lum** /pɛndʒələm/ (pendulums) **1** N-COUNT The **pendulum** of a clock is a rod with a weight at the end which swings from side to side in order to make the clock work. **2** N-SING People use the word **pendulum** as a way of talking about regular changes in a situation or in people's opinions. ❑ *The political pendulum has swung in favor of the liberals.* [from Latin]

**pen|etrate** /pɛnɪtreɪt/ (penetrates, penetrating, penetrated) **1** V-T If something or someone **penetrates** a physical object or an area, they succeed in getting into it or passing through it. ❑ *X-rays can penetrate many objects.* ● **pen|etra|tion** /pɛnɪtreɪʃˀn/ (penetrations) N-UNCOUNT ❑ *The thick walls prevented penetration by rainwater.* **2** V-T If someone **penetrates** an organization, a group, or a profession, they

succeed in entering it although it is difficult to do so. ❑ *We need people who can speak foreign languages to penetrate these organizations.* **3** V-T If someone **penetrates** an enemy group, they succeed in joining it in order to get information or to cause trouble. ❑ *It is not normally possible to penetrate a terrorist organization from the outside.* ● **pen|etra|tion** N-UNCOUNT ❑ *...the penetration of foreign companies to gather business information.* [from Latin]

**pen|etrat|ing** /pɛnɪtreɪtɪŋ/ **1** ADJ A **penetrating** sound is loud and clear. ❑ *...the penetrating siren of an ambulance.* **2** ADJ If someone gives you a **penetrating** look, it makes you think that they know what you are thinking. ❑ *He gazed at me with a sharp, penetrating look.* [from Latin]

penguin

**pen|guin** /pɛŋgwɪn/ (penguins) N-COUNT A **penguin** is a black and white sea bird found mainly in the Antarctic. Penguins cannot fly. [from Welsh]

**pen|in|su|la** /pənɪnsələ, -nɪnsyə-/ (peninsulas) N-COUNT A **peninsula** is a long narrow piece of land that sticks out from a larger piece of land and is almost completely surrounded by water. ❑ *...the Iberian peninsula.* [from Latin]

**pe|nis** /piːnɪs/ (penises) N-COUNT A man's **penis** is the part of his body that he uses when he urinates and when he has sex. [from Latin]

**peni|ten|tia|ry** /pɛnɪtɛnʃəri/ (penitentiaries) N-COUNT A **penitentiary** is a prison for criminals who have committed serious crimes. [FORMAL] [from Medieval Latin]

**pen|nant** /pɛnənt/ (pennants) N-COUNT In baseball, a **pennant** is a flag that is given each year to the top team in a league. ❑ *The Red Sox lost the pennant to Detroit by a single game.*

**pen|ni|less** /pɛnɪlɪs/ ADJ Someone who is **penniless** has almost no money. ❑ *They would soon be penniless and homeless.* [from Old English]

**pen|ny** /pɛni/ (pennies) N-COUNT A **penny** is one cent, or a coin worth one cent. [INFORMAL] ❑ *The price of gasoline rose by more than a penny a gallon.* [from Old English]

**pen|sion** /pɛnʃˀn/ (pensions) N-COUNT A **pension** is a sum of money that a retired, widowed, or disabled person regularly receives from a former employer. ❑ *He gets a $35,000 a year pension.* [from Old French]

**Pen|ta|gon** N-PROPER The **Pentagon** is the main building of the U.S. Defense Department, in Washington DC. ❑ *...a news conference at the Pentagon.* [from Latin]

**pen|ta|ton|ic scale** /pɛntətɒnɪk skeɪl/ (pentatonic scales) N-COUNT A **pentatonic scale** is a musical scale that has five notes in each octave. [TECHNICAL]

**pent|house** /pɛnthaʊs/ (penthouses) N-COUNT A **penthouse** or a **penthouse** apartment or suite is a luxurious apartment or set of rooms at the top of a tall building. ❑ *...her elegant Manhattan penthouse.* [from Old French]

**pent-up** /pɛnt ʌp/ ADJ **Pent-up** emotions have been held back and not expressed. ❑ *He still had a lot of pent-up anger.*

**Word Link** ultim ≈ end, last : *penultim*ate, *ultim*ate, *ultim*atum

**pe|nul|ti|mate** /pɪnʌltɪmɪt/ ADJ The **penultimate** thing in a series of things is the second to the last. [FORMAL] ❑ ...*on the penultimate day of the Asian Games.* [from Latin]

**peo|ple** /pip°l/ (**peoples, peopling, peopled**)
■ N-PLURAL **People** are men, women, and children. **People** is normally used as the plural of **person**, instead of "persons." ❑ *Millions of people have lost their homes.* ❑ ...*the people of Angola.*
■ N-PLURAL **The people** is sometimes used to refer to ordinary men and women, in contrast to the government or the military. ❑ ...*the will of the people.* ■ N-COUNT A **people** is all the men, women, and children of a particular country or race. ❑ ...*the native peoples of Central and South America.* ■ V-T If a place or country **is peopled by** a particular group of people, that group of people live there. ❑ *It was a country peopled by proud men and women.* [from Old French]

**pep|per** /pɛpər/ (**peppers, peppering, peppered**)
■ N-UNCOUNT **Pepper** or **black pepper** is a hot-tasting spice used to flavor food. ❑ *Season with salt and pepper.* ■ N-COUNT A **pepper**, or a **bell pepper**, is a hollow green, red, or yellow vegetable with seeds inside it. ❑ ...*2 red or green peppers, sliced.*
■ V-T If something **is peppered with** things, there are a lot of those things in it. ❑ *Readers' letters on the subject were peppered with words like "horrible" and "ugly."* ■ V-T If something **is peppered with** small objects, a lot of those objects hit it. ❑ *Houses were peppered with machine gun fire.* [from Old English]
→ see **spice, vegetable**

**pepper|mint** /pɛpərmɪnt/ (**peppermints**)
■ N-UNCOUNT **Peppermint** is a strong, sharp flavoring from the peppermint plant. ■ N-COUNT A **peppermint** is a peppermint-flavored piece of candy.

**pep|per shak|er** (**pepper shakers**) N-COUNT A **pepper shaker** is a small container with holes at one end, used for shaking pepper onto food.
→ see **dish**

**pep|per spray** (**pepper sprays**) N-VAR A **pepper spray** is a device that releases a substance which stings the skin, used as a defense against rioters or attackers. ❑ *The officers blasted him with pepper spray.*

**pep ral|ly** (**pep rallies**) N-COUNT A **pep rally** at a school, college, or university is a gathering to support a sports team.

**per** /pər, STRONG pɜr/ ■ PREP You use **per** to express rates and ratios. For example, if a vehicle is traveling at 40 miles **per** hour, it travels 40 miles each hour. ❑ ...*$16 per week for lunch.* [from Latin]
■ **per head** → see **head**

**per an|num** /pər ænəm/ ADV A particular amount **per annum** means that amount each year. ❑ ...*a fee of $35 per annum.*

**per capi|ta** /pər kæpɪtə/ ADJ The **per capita** amount of something is the total amount of it in a country or area divided by the number of people in that country or area. ❑ *They have the world's largest per capita income.* ● **Per capita** is also an adverb. ❑ ...*the lowest oil consumption per capita in the world.* [from Latin]

**Word Link** per ≈ through, thoroughly : *per*ceive, *per*fect, *per*mit

**per|ceive** /pərsiv/ (**perceives, perceiving, perceived**) ■ V-T If you **perceive** something, you see, notice, or realize it, especially when it is not obvious. ❑ *A great artist teaches us to perceive life in a different way.* ■ V-T If you **perceive** someone or something **as** doing or being a particular thing, it is your opinion that they do this thing or that they are that thing. ❑ *Stress is widely perceived as a cause of heart disease.* [from Old French]

**Word Link** age ≈ state of, related to : cour*age*, marri*age*, percent*age*

**Word Link** cent ≈ hundred : *cent*s, *cent*ury, per*cent*age

**per|cent|age** /pərsɛntɪdʒ/ (**percentages**) N-COUNT A **percentage** is a fraction of an amount expressed as a particular number of hundredths. ❑ ...*a high percentage of fat.* [from Medieval Latin]
→ see **fraction**

**per|cent|age point** (**percentage points**) N-COUNT A **percentage point** is one percent of something. ❑ *New home sales fell by a full percentage point in September.*

**per|cen|tile** /pərsɛntaɪl/ (**percentiles**) N-COUNT A **percentile** is one of the equal divisions of an amount, expressed on a scale from 0 to 100. The 90th percentile of an amount is all amounts between zero percent and ninety percent. [from Medieval Latin]

**per|cep|tion** /pərsɛpʃ°n/ (**perceptions**)
■ N-COUNT Your **perception of** something is the way that you think about it or the impression you have of it. ❑ *Our perceptions of death affect the way we live.* ■ N-UNCOUNT Someone who has **perception** realizes or notices things that are not obvious. ❑ *It did not require a lot of perception to realize the interview was over.* ■ N-COUNT **Perception** is the recognition of things using your senses, especially the sense of sight. [from Latin]

**per|cep|tive** /pərsɛptɪv/ ADJ A **perceptive** person realizes or notices things that are not obvious. ❑ ...*one of the finest and most perceptive sports writers.* [from Latin]

**perch** /pɜrtʃ/ (**perches, perching, perched**) ■ V-I If you **perch on** something, you sit down lightly on the very edge of it. ❑ *He perched on the corner of the desk.* ■ V-I To **perch** somewhere means to be on the top or edge of something. ❑ *The big mansion perches high on a hill.* ■ V-T If you **perch** something **on** something else, you put or balance it on the top or edge of that thing. ❑ *He perched a pair of reading glasses low on his nose.* ■ V-I When a bird **perches on** a branch or a wall, it lands on it and stands there. ❑ *Two doves perched on a nearby fence.* [from Old French]

**per|cus|sion** /pərkʌʃ°n/ N-UNCOUNT **Percussion** instruments are musical instruments that you

P

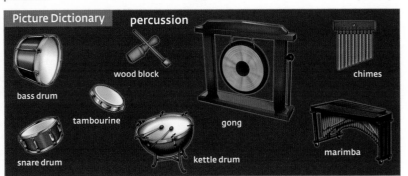

**Picture Dictionary** percussion

bass drum

wood block

tambourine

snare drum

kettle drum

gong

chimes

marimba

hit, such as drums. ❑ ...*the orchestra's powerful percussion section.* [from Latin]
→ see Picture Dictionary: **percussion**
→ see **orchestra**

**per diem** /pɜr diəm, pər/ N-SING A **per diem** is an amount of money that someone is given to cover their daily expenses while they are working. ❑ *He received a per diem allowance for his travel expenses.* [from Latin]

**per|en|nial** /pərɛniəl/ ADJ You use **perennial** to describe situations or problems that keep occurring or that seem to exist all the time. ❑ ...*the perennial problem of homelessness.* [from Latin]

**per|fect** (**perfects, perfecting, perfected**)

| The adjective is pronounced /pɜrfɪkt/. The verb is pronounced /pərfɛkt/. |

**1** ADJ Something that is **perfect** is as good as it could possibly be. ❑ *He spoke perfect English.* ❑ *Nobody is perfect.* ● **per|fect|ly** ADV ❑ *The system worked perfectly.* **2** ADJ If you say that something is **perfect** for a particular person, thing, or activity, you are emphasizing that it is very suitable for them or for that activity. ❑ *The pool area is perfect for entertaining.* **3** ADJ You can use **perfect** for emphasis. ❑ *She felt a perfect fool.* ● **per|fect|ly** ADV ❑ *They made it perfectly clear that they didn't want us to continue.* **4** V-T If you **perfect** something, you improve it so that it becomes as good as it can possibly be. ❑ *We perfected our recipe for vegetable stew.* [from Latin]

**Thesaurus**   *perfect*   Also look up :

ADJ.   flawless, ideal; (*ant.*) defective, faulty **1**

**per|fec|tion** /pərfɛkʃn/ N-UNCOUNT **Perfection** is the quality of being as good as it is possible for something of a particular kind to be. ❑ *The meat was cooked to perfection.* [from Latin]

**per|fec|tion|ist** /pərfɛkʃənɪst/ (**perfectionists**) N-COUNT Someone who is a **perfectionist** refuses to do or accept anything that is not as good as it could possibly be. ❑ *He was such a perfectionist.* [from Latin]

**per|form** /pərfɔrm/ (**performs, performing, performed**) **1** V-T When you **perform** a task or action, you do it. ❑ ...*people who have performed outstanding acts of bravery.* ❑ *You must perform this exercise correctly to avoid back pain.* **2** V-T/V-I To **perform** a play, a piece of music, or a dance means to do it in front of an audience. ❑ *They will be performing works by Bach and Scarlatti.* ❑ *He began performing regularly in the early fifties.* ● **per|form|er** (**performers**) N-COUNT ❑ *She was one of the top jazz performers in New York City.* **3** V-I If someone or something **performs well**, they work well or achieve a good result. ❑ *He has not performed well on his exams.* ❑ *Those industries will always perform poorly.* ● **per|form|er** N-COUNT ❑ ...*the stock-market's star performers.* [from Old French]

**Word Partnership**   Use *perform* with :

| N. | perform **miracles**, perform **tasks** **1** |
| ADJ. | **able to** perform **1 2** |
| V. | **continue to** perform **1 2** |
| ADV. | perform **well** **3** |

**per|for|mance** /pərfɔrməns/ (**performances**) **1** N-COUNT A **performance** involves entertaining an audience by singing, dancing, or acting. ❑ *They were giving a performance of Bizet's "Carmen."* **2** N-VAR Someone's or something's **performance** is how successful they are or how well they do something. ❑ *The study looked at the performance of 18 surgeons.* ❑ ...*the poor performance of the U.S. economy.* [from Old French]
→ see **concert**

**per|for|mance art** N-UNCOUNT **Performance art** is a theatrical presentation that includes various art forms such as dance, music, painting, and sculpture.

**per|fume** /pɜrfyum, pərfyum/ (**perfumes**) N-VAR **Perfume** is a pleasant-smelling liquid that women put on their skin to make themselves smell nice. ❑ *The hall smelled of her mother's perfume.* [from French]

**per|haps** /pərhæps, præps/ ADV You use **perhaps** to indicate that you are not sure whether something is true, possible, or likely. ❑ *In the end they lost millions, perhaps billions.* ❑ *Perhaps, in time, they will understand.*

P

## Word Web · periodic table

### The Periodic Table of Elements

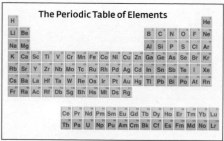

Scientists started finding **elements** thousands of years ago. But it was not until 1869 that anyone understood how one element related to another. In that year, the Russian scientist Dmitri Mendeleyev created the **periodic table**. The vertical columns are called **groups**. Each group contains elements with similar **chemical** and **physical properties**. The horizontal rows are called **periods**.

The elements in each row increase in **atomic mass** from left to right. Mendeleyev's original chart had may gaps. He predicted that scientists would find elements to fill these spaces. He was correct. He also predicted the properties of these new elements quite accurately.

**peri|he|lion** /pɛrɪhiːliən, -hiːlyən/ (**perihelia**) N-COUNT The **perihelion** of a planet is the point in its orbit at which it is closest to the sun. Compare **aphelion**. [TECHNICAL] [from New Latin]

**per|il** /pɛrɪl/ (**perils**) N-VAR **Perils** are great dangers. [FORMAL] ❑ ...*the perils of the sea.* ❑ *In spite of great peril, I survived the earthquake.* [from Old French]

**peri|lous** /pɛrɪləs/ ADJ Something that is **perilous** is very dangerous. [LITERARY] ❑ ...*a perilous journey across the war zone.* ● **peri|lous|ly** ADV ❑ *One of their swimmers came perilously close to drowning.* [from Old French]

> **Word Link**  meter ≈ measuring : kilometer, meter, perimeter

> **Word Link**  peri ≈ around : perimeter, periodic, periphery

**pe|rim|eter** /pərɪmɪtər/ (**perimeters**) N-COUNT The **perimeter** of an area of land is the whole of its outer edge or boundary. ❑ ...*the perimeter of the airport.* [from French]
→ see **area**

**pe|ri|od** /pɪəriəd/ (**periods**) 1 N-COUNT A **period** is a length of time. ❑ *He couldn't work for a long period of time.* ❑ *I lived in New York for a period of a few months.* ❑ ...*a period of economic health.* 2 ADJ **Period** costumes, furniture, and instruments were made at an earlier time in history, or look as if they were made then. ❑ *The characters were dressed in full period costume.* 3 N-COUNT A **period** is the punctuation mark (.) that you use at the end of a sentence when it is not a question or an exclamation. 4 N-COUNT When a woman has her **period**, she bleeds from her uterus. This usually happens once a month, unless she is pregnant. 5 N-COUNT In chemistry, a **period** is one of the horizontal rows of substances in the periodic table of elements. [TECHNICAL] 6 PHRASE The **period of revolution** of an object such as a planet is the time it takes to orbit another object such as a star. The Earth's period of revolution is one year. 7 PHRASE The **period of rotation** of an object such as a planet is the time it takes to turn once on its axis. The Earth's period of rotation is one day. [from Latin]
→ see **periodic table, punctuation**

**pe|ri|od|ic** /pɪəriɒdɪk/ ADJ **Periodic** events or situations happen occasionally, at fairly regular intervals. ❑ *Periodic checks ensure that high standards are maintained.* [from Latin]

**pe|ri|od|ical** /pɪəriɒdɪkəl/ (**periodicals**) 1 N-COUNT A **periodical** is a magazine. ❑ ...*a large selection of books and periodicals.* 2 ADJ **Periodical** means the same as **periodic**. ❑ *She made periodical visits to her dentist.* ● **pe|ri|od|ical|ly** /pɪəriɒdɪkli/ ADV ❑ *Meetings are held periodically.* [from Latin]
→ see **library**

**pe|ri|od|ic law** N-SING The **periodic law** is a law in chemistry which describes the relationship between the chemical properties of elements and their atomic numbers. [TECHNICAL]

**pe|ri|od|ic ta|ble** N-SING In chemistry, **the periodic table** is a table showing the chemical elements arranged according to their atomic numbers.
→ see Word Web: **periodic table**

**pe|riph|er|al** /pərɪfərəl/ (**peripherals**) 1 ADJ A **peripheral** activity or issue is not very important compared with other activities or issues. ❑ *The peripheral events were sometimes even more dramatic.* 2 ADJ **Peripheral** areas of land are ones that are on the edge of a larger area. ❑ ...*development in the peripheral areas of large towns.* 3 N-COUNT **Peripherals** are devices such as printers that can be attached to computers. [COMPUTING] [from Late Latin]

**pe|riph|er|al ner|vous sys|tem** (**peripheral nervous system**) N-COUNT Your **peripheral nervous system** is all the nerves in your body that are outside your brain and spinal cord. Compare **central nervous system**. [TECHNICAL]

**pe|riph|ery** /pərɪfəri/ (**peripheries**) N-COUNT If something is on the **periphery** of an area, place, or thing, it is on the edge of it. [FORMAL] ❑ ...*a well-kept garden with flowers around its periphery.* [from Late Latin]

**per|ish** /pɛrɪʃ/ (**perishes, perishing, perished**) V-I To **perish** means to die or be destroyed. [WRITTEN] ❑ *Most of the butterflies perish in the fall.* [from Old French]

**per|jury** /pɜrdʒəri/ N-UNCOUNT If someone who is giving evidence in a court of law commits **perjury**, they lie. [LEGAL] [from Latin]

**perk** /pɜrk/ (**perks, perking, perked**) N-COUNT
**Perks** are benefits that are given to people who have a particular job or belong to a particular group. ❑ *...health insurance and other perks.*
▸ **perk up** PHR-VERB If something **perks** you **up** or if you **perk up**, you become cheerful and lively, after feeling tired, bored, or depressed. ❑ *He perked up and started to make jokes with them.*

**perm** /pɜrm/ (**perms, perming, permed**)
**1** N-COUNT If you have a **perm**, your hair is curled and treated with chemicals so that it stays curly for several months. ❑ *...a middle-aged lady with a perm.* **2** V-T When a hairstylist **perms** your hair, he or she gives you a perm. ❑ *She had her hair permed.*

**per|ma|frost** /pɜrməfrɔst/ N-UNCOUNT
**Permafrost** is land that is permanently frozen to a great depth.

**per|ma|nent** /pɜrmənənt/ (**permanents**) ADJ
**Permanent** means lasting forever or occurring all the time. ❑ *Some ear infections can cause permanent damage..* ❑ *...a permanent state of tension.* ● **per|ma|nent|ly** ADV ❑ *His confidence has been permanently affected.* ❑ *...the heavy, permanently locked gate.* ● **per|ma|nence** N-UNCOUNT ❑ *...the permanence of the treaty.* [from Latin]

**per|me|able** /pɜrmiəbᵊl/ ADJ If a substance is **permeable**, something such as water or gas can pass through it or soak into it. ● **permeability** /pɜrmiəbɪliti/ N-UNCOUNT ❑ *...the permeability of the rock.* [from Late Latin]
→ see **amphibian**

**per|me|ate** /pɜrmieɪt/ (**permeates, permeating, permeated**) **1** V-T If an idea, feeling, or attitude **permeates** society or a system, it affects every part of it or is present throughout it. ❑ *Parents' attitudes permeate every part of a child's life.* **2** V-T If something **permeates** a place, it spreads throughout the place. ❑ *The smell of roast beef permeated the air.* [from Latin]

**per|mis|sible** /pərmɪsəbᵊl/ ADJ If something is **permissible**, it is allowed because it does not break any laws or rules. ❑ *There are times when this sort of behavior is perfectly permissible.* [from Latin]

**per|mis|sion** /pərmɪʃᵊn/ N-UNCOUNT If you give someone **permission to** do something, you tell them that they can do it. ❑ *He asked permission to leave the room.* ❑ *They cannot leave the country without permission.* [from Latin]

**per|mis|sive** /pərmɪsɪv/ ADJ A **permissive** person or society allows or tolerates things that other people disapprove of. ❑ *...the permissive tolerance of the 1960s.* ● **per|mis|sive|ness** N-UNCOUNT ❑ *Permissiveness and democracy go together.* [from Latin]

**per|mit** (**permits, permitting, permitted**)

The verb is pronounced /pərmɪt/. The noun is pronounced /pɜrmɪt/.

**1** V-T If someone **permits** you **to** do something, they allow you to do it. [FORMAL] ❑ *The guards permitted me to bring my camera.* **2** N-COUNT A **permit** is an official document allowing you to do something. ❑ *...a work permit.* **3** V-T/V-I If a situation **permits** something, it makes it possible for that thing to exist, happen, or be done. [FORMAL] ❑ *Go out for a walk at lunchtime, if the weather permits.* ❑ *This job permits me to arrange my hours around my family.* [from Latin]

**per|mu|ta|tion** /pɜrmyʊteɪʃᵊn/ (**permutations**) N-COUNT A **permutation** is one of the ways in which a number of things can be ordered or arranged. [from Latin]

**per|ni|cious** /pərnɪʃəs/ ADJ If you describe something as **pernicious**, you mean that it is very harmful. [FORMAL] ❑ *Her mother's influence was pernicious.* [from Latin]

**per|pe|trate** /pɜrpɪtreɪt/ (**perpetrates, perpetrating, perpetrated**) V-T If someone **perpetrates** a crime or any other immoral or harmful act, they do it. [FORMAL] ❑ *A high proportion of crime is perpetrated by young males.* ● **per|pe|tra|tor** (**perpetrators**) N-COUNT ❑ *...perpetrators of terrorist acts.* [from Latin]

**per|pet|ual** /pərpɛtʃuəl/ ADJ A **perpetual** feeling, state, or quality never ends or changes. ❑ *He's got a perpetual smile on his face.* ● **per|pet|ual|ly** ADV ❑ *They were all perpetually starving.* [from Latin]

**per|pet|ual mo|tion ma|chine** (**perpetual motion machines**) N-COUNT A **perpetual motion machine** is an imaginary machine which, if it existed, would be able to continue working forever because it does not need energy from anything else.

**per|petu|ate** /pərpɛtʃueɪt/ (**perpetuates, perpetuating, perpetuated**) V-T To **perpetuate** a situation, system, or belief, especially a bad one, means to cause it to continue. ❑ *People everywhere want to perpetuate their own culture.* [from Latin]

**per|plexed** /pərplɛkst/ ADJ If you are **perplexed**, you are puzzled or do not know what to do. ❑ *She is perplexed about what to do for her daughter.* [from Latin]

**per|secute** /pɜrsɪkyut/ (**persecutes, persecuting, persecuted**) V-T If someone **is persecuted**, they are treated cruelly and unfairly, often because of their race or beliefs. ❑ *They have been persecuted because of their beliefs.* ❑ *They began persecuting the Catholic Church.* ● **per|secu|tion** N-UNCOUNT ❑ *...victims of political persecution.* ● **per|secu|tor** (**persecutors**) N-COUNT ❑ *How could he forgive his persecutors?* [from Old French]

**per|severe** /pɜrsɪvɪər/ (**perseveres, persevering, persevered**) V-I If you **persevere with** something difficult, you continue doing it and do not give up. ❑ *...his ability to persevere despite difficulties.* ❑ *...a school with a reputation for persevering with difficult children.* ● **per|sever|ance** N-UNCOUNT ❑ *He has never stopped trying, and shows great perseverance.* [from Old French]

p

**per|sist** /pərsɪst/ (**persists, persisting, persisted**) **1** V-I If something undesirable **persists**, it continues to exist. ❑ *Contact your doctor if the cough persists.* **2** V-I If you **persist in** doing something, you continue to do it, even though it is difficult or other people oppose you. ❑ *Why do people persist in ignoring the problem?* ❑ *He urged them to persist with their efforts to bring peace.* [from Latin]

**per|sis|tent** /pərsɪstənt/ **1** ADJ Something undesirable that is **persistent** continues to exist or happen for a long time. ❑ *...persistent fears.* ❑ *His cough grew more persistent.* ● **per|sis|tence** N-UNCOUNT ❑ *...the persistence of the same problems year after year.* ● **per|sis|tent|ly** ADV ❑ *...persistently high unemployment.* **2** ADJ Someone who is **persistent** continues trying to do something, even though it is difficult or other people are against it. ❑ *...a persistent critic of the president.* ● **per|sis|tence** N-UNCOUNT ❑ *Skill comes only with practice, patience, and persistence.* ● **per|sis|tent|ly** ADV ❑ *He persistently refused to see a doctor.* [from Latin]

**per|snick|ety** /pərsnɪkɪti/ ADJ If you describe someone as **persnickety**, you disapprove of the fact that they pay too much attention to small, unimportant details. [INFORMAL] ❑ *He has a persnickety housekeeper and never has parties.* [from Scottish]

**per|son** /pɜrsᵊn/ (**people** or **persons**)

> The usual plural of person is **people**. The form **persons** is used as the plural in formal or legal language.

**1** N-COUNT A **person** is a man, woman, or child. ❑ *At least one person died and several others were injured.* ❑ *They were both lovely, friendly people.* **2** PHRASE If you do something **in person**, you do it yourself rather than letting someone else do it for you. ❑ *You must collect the mail in person.* **3** PHRASE If you meet, hear, or see someone **in person**, you are in the same place as them, rather than speaking to them on the telephone or writing to them. ❑ *She saw him in person for the first time last night.* **4** N-COUNT In grammar, we use the term **first person** when referring to "I" and "we," **second person** when referring to "you," and **third person** when referring to "he," "she," "it," "they," and all other noun groups. **Person** is also used like this when referring to the verb forms that go with these pronouns and noun groups. [from Old French]

**per|so|na** /pərsoʊnə/ (**personas** or **personae** /pərsoʊni/) N-COUNT Someone's **persona** is the aspect of their character or nature that they present to other people. [FORMAL] ❑ *...the differences between her private life and her public persona.* [from Latin]

**per|son|al** /pɜrsᵊnᵊl/ **1** ADJ A **personal** opinion, quality, or thing belongs or relates to a particular person. ❑ *He learned this lesson the hard way — from his own personal experience.* ❑ *That's my personal opinion.* **2** ADJ If you give something your **personal** care or attention, you deal with it yourself rather than letting someone else deal with it. ❑ *...a personal letter from the president's secretary.* **3** ADJ **Personal** matters relate to your feelings, relationships, and health. ❑ *You never allow personal problems to affect your performance.* **4** ADJ **Personal** comments refer to your appearance or character in an offensive way. ❑ *I*

have had to face a lot of personal criticism. [from Old French] **5** → see also **personals**

**per|son|al com|put|er** (**personal computers**) N-COUNT A **personal computer** is a computer that is used by one person at a time in a business, a school, or at home. The abbreviation **PC** is also used.

**per|son|al ex|emp|tion** (**personal exemptions**) N-COUNT Your **personal exemption** is the amount of money that is deducted from your gross income before you have to start paying income tax. ❑ *Changes for this year include an increase in the personal exemption.*

**per|son|al|ity** /pɜrsənælɪti/ (**personalities**) **1** N-VAR Your **personality** is your whole character and nature. ❑ *She has such a kind, friendly personality.* ❑ *The contest was as much about personalities as it was about politics.* **2** N-COUNT You can refer to a famous person, especially in entertainment, broadcasting, or sports, as a **personality**. ❑ *...the radio and television personality, Johnny Carson.* [from Old French]

> **Word Partnership** Use *personality* with:
>
> | ADJ. | **strong** personality, **unique** personality **1** |
> |---|---|
> | N. | personality **trait 1** |
> | | **radio** personality, **television/TV** personality **2** |

**per|son|al|ly** /pɜrsənəli/ **1** ADV You use **personally** to emphasize that you are giving your own opinion. ❑ *Personally I think it's a waste of time.* **2** ADV If you do something **personally**, you do it yourself rather than letting someone else do it. ❑ *We will personally inspect the apartment with you when you arrive.* **3** ADV If you meet or know someone **personally**, you meet or know them in real life, rather than knowing about them or knowing their work. ❑ *He did not know them personally, but he was familiar with their reputation.* [from Old French]

**per|son|al pro|noun** (**personal pronouns**) N-COUNT A **personal pronoun** is a pronoun such as "I," "you," "she," or "they" which is used to refer to the speaker or the person spoken to, or to a person or thing whose identity is clear.

**per|son|als** /pɜrsənᵊlz/ N-PLURAL The section in a newspaper or magazine which contains messages or advertisements from individual people rather than businesses is called the **personals**. [from Old French]

**per|soni|fy** /pərsɒnɪfaɪ/ (**personifies, personifying, personified**) V-T If you say that someone **personifies** a particular thing or quality, you mean that they are a perfect example of that thing, or they have a lot of that quality. ❑ *She seemed to personify goodness.* ● **per|soni|fi|ca|tion** /pərsɒnɪfɪkeɪʃᵊn/ N-SING ❑ *Joplin was the personification of the '60s female rock singer.* [from Old French]

**per|son|nel** /pɜrsənɛl/ N-PLURAL The **personnel** of an organization are the people who work for it. ❑ *...military personnel.* [from French]

**per|spec|tive** /pərspɛktɪv/ (**perspectives**) **1** N-COUNT A particular **perspective** is a particular way of thinking about something. ❑ *The death of his father has given him a new perspective on life.* ❑ *...two different perspectives on child* development. **2** N-UNCOUNT **Perspective** is the theory of representing three dimensions on a two-dimensional surface, in order to recreate the appearance of objects that are further away as smaller than those that are nearer. **3** PHRASE If you get something **in perspective** or **into perspective**, you judge its real importance by considering it in relation to everything else. If you get something **out of perspective**, you fail to do this. ❏ *Remember to keep things in perspective.* ❏ *I think I've let things get out of perspective.* [from Medieval Latin]

| **Thesaurus** | *perspective* | Also look up : |
|---|---|---|
| N. | attitude, outlook, viewpoint **1** | |

**per|spi|ra|tion** /pɜrspɪreɪʃⁿn/ N-UNCOUNT **Perspiration** is the liquid that comes out on the surface of your skin when you are hot or frightened. [FORMAL] ❏ *His hands were wet with perspiration.* [from Latin]

| **Word Link** | *suad, suas ≈ urging : dissuade, persuade, persuasive* |
|---|---|

**per|suade** /pərsweɪd/ (**persuades, persuading, persuaded**) **1** V-T If you **persuade** someone **to** do something, you cause them to do it by giving them good reasons for doing it. ❏ *My husband persuaded me to come.* **2** V-T If you **persuade** someone that something is true, you say things that eventually make them believe that it is true. ❏ *I've persuaded her to talk to you.* [from Latin]

| **Thesaurus** | *persuade* | Also look up : |
|---|---|---|
| V. | cajole, convince, influence, sway, talk into, win over; (*ant.*) discourage, dissuade **1** **2** | |

| **Word Partnership** | Use *persuade* with : |
|---|---|
| V. | **attempt to** persuade, **be able to** persuade, **fail to** persuade, **try to** persuade **1** **2** |

**per|sua|sion** /pərsweɪʒⁿn/ (**persuasions**) **1** N-UNCOUNT **Persuasion** is the act of persuading someone to do something or to believe that something is true. ❏ *After much persuasion from Ellis, she agreed to perform.* **2** N-COUNT If you are **of** a particular **persuasion**, you have a particular belief or set of beliefs. [FORMAL] ❏ *...people of all political persuasions.* [from Latin]

**per|sua|sive** /pərsweɪsɪv/ ADJ Someone or something that is **persuasive** is likely to persuade a person to believe or do a particular thing. ❏ *...persuasive arguments.* ❏ *I can be very persuasive.* ● **per|sua|sive|ly** ADV ❏ *...a trained lawyer who can present arguments persuasively.* [from Latin]

**per|tain** /pərteɪn/ (**pertains, pertaining, pertained**) V-I If one thing **pertains to** another, it relates or belongs to it. [FORMAL] ❏ *...matters pertaining to the environment.* [from Latin]

**per|ti|nent** /pɜrtⁿnənt/ ADJ Something that is **pertinent** is relevant to a particular subject. [FORMAL] ❏ *She asked some pertinent questions.* [from Latin]

**per|vade** /pərveɪd/ (**pervades, pervading, pervaded**) V-T If something **pervades** a place or

thing, it is a noticeable feature throughout it. [FORMAL] ❏ *The smell of glue pervaded the factory.* [from Latin]

**per|va|sive** /pərveɪsɪv/ ADJ Something that is **pervasive** is present or felt throughout a place or thing. [FORMAL] ❏ *Technology has become more pervasive in our lives.* [from Latin]

**per|verse** /pərvɜrs/ ADJ Someone who is **perverse** deliberately does things that are unreasonable. ❏ *It's perverse to complain about it.* ❏ *He took a perverse pleasure in being disagreeable.* ● **per|verse|ly** ADV ❏ *She was perversely pleased to be causing trouble.* [from Old French]

**per|ver|sion** /pərvɜrʒⁿn, -ʃⁿn/ (**perversions**) **1** N-VAR A **perversion** is a sexual desire or action that you consider to be abnormal and unacceptable. **2** N-VAR The **perversion of** something is the changing of it so that it is no longer what it should be. ❏ *The film is clearly a perversion of the truth.* [from Old French]

**per|vert** (**perverts, perverting, perverted**)

The verb is pronounced /pərvɜrt/. The noun is pronounced /pɜrvɜrt/.

**1** V-T If you **pervert** something such as a process or society, you interfere with it so that it is not as good as it used to be or as it should be. [FORMAL] ❏ *He was attempting to pervert the course of justice.* **2** N-COUNT If you refer to someone as a **pervert**, you consider their sexual behavior or desires to be immoral or unacceptable. ❏ *I hope the police catch these perverts.* [from Old French]

**per|vert|ed** /pərvɜrtɪd/ ADJ If you say that someone is **perverted**, you mean that you consider their sexual behavior or desires to be immoral or unacceptable. ❏ *...sick and perverted men.* [from Old French]

**pes|si|mism** /pɛsɪmɪzəm/ N-UNCOUNT **Pessimism** is the belief that bad things are going to happen. ❏ *...general pessimism about the economy.* ● **pes|si|mist** (**pessimists**) N-COUNT ❏ *I'm a natural pessimist; I usually expect the worst.* ● **pes|si|mis|tic** /pɛsɪmɪstɪk/ ADJ ❏ *She is so pessimistic about the future.* [from Latin]

**pest** /pɛst/ (**pests**) **1** N-COUNT **Pests** are insects or small animals that damage crops or food supplies. ❏ *There are very few insect pests or diseases in this country.* **2** N-COUNT You can describe someone, especially a child, as a **pest** if they keep bothering you. [INFORMAL] ❏ *He climbed on the table, pulled my hair, and was generally a pest.* [from Latin] → see **farm**

**pes|ter** /pɛstər/ (**pesters, pestering, pestered**) V-T If you say that someone is **pestering** you, you mean that they keep asking you to do something, or keep talking to you, and you find this annoying. ❏ *I wish she would stop pestering me.* [from Old French]

| **Word Link** | *cide ≈ killing : genocide, homicide, pesticide* |
|---|---|

**pes|ti|cide** /pɛstɪsaɪd/ (**pesticides**) N-VAR **Pesticides** are chemicals that farmers put on their crops to kill harmful insects. [from Latin] → see **pollution**

**pet** /pɛt/ (**pets, petting, petted**) **1** N-COUNT A **pet** is an animal that you keep in your home to give you company and pleasure. ❏ *It is cruel to keep turtles as pets.* ❏ *...his pet dog.* **2** ADJ Someone's **pet**

p

## Word Web    pet

Americans love **pets**. They own more than 51 million **dogs**, 56 million **cats**, and 45 million **birds**. They also have more than 75 million small **mammals** and **reptiles**, and millions of **fish**. Recent studies suggest that adult pet owners are healthier than adults who don't have **companion animals**. One study (Katcher, 1982) suggests that pet owners have lower blood pressure. In 2001 the German Socio-Economic Panel Survey studied a group of people. Some of the people owned pets and some did not. The survey showed that people with pets went to the doctor less often than people without pets. And a study in the *American Journal of Cardiology* found that male dog owners were less likely to die within a year after a heart attack than people who didn't own dogs.

---

subject is one that they particularly like. ❑ *Her pet subject is education.* ❸ V-T If you **pet** an animal, you pat or stroke it in an affectionate way. ❑ *He reached down and petted the dog.*
→ see Word Web: **pet**

**pet|al** /pɛtᵊl/ (**petals**) N-COUNT The **petals** of a flower are the thin colored or white parts that together form the flower. ❑ *...bowls of dried rose petals.* [from New Latin]
→ see **flower**

**pe|ter** /pitər/ (**peters, petering, petered**)
▶ **peter out** PHR-VERB If something **peters out**, it gradually comes to an end. ❑ *The strike seems to be petering out.*

**pe|tite** /pətit/ ADJ A **petite** woman is small and slim. ❑ *...catalogs that supply clothes for the petite female customer.* [from French]

**pe|ti|tion** /pətɪʃᵊn/ (**petitions, petitioning, petitioned**) ❶ N-COUNT A **petition** is a document signed by a lot of people that asks a government or other official group to do a particular thing. ❑ *...a petition signed by 4,500 people.* ❷ V-T/V-I If you **petition** someone in authority, you make a formal request to them. [LEGAL] ❑ *...couples petitioning for divorce.* ❑ *All the attempts to petition Congress have failed.* [from Latin]

**Petri dish** /pitri dɪʃ/ (**Petri dishes**) N-COUNT A **Petri dish** is a shallow circular dish that is used in laboratories for producing groups of microorganisms. [TECHNICAL] [from German]

**pet|ri|fied** /pɛtrɪfaɪd/ ADJ If you are **petrified**,

you are extremely frightened. ❑ *I've always been petrified of being alone.* [from French]

**pe|tro|leum** /pətrouliəm/ N-UNCOUNT **Petroleum** is oil that is found under the surface of the earth or under the sea bed. Gasoline and kerosene are obtained from petroleum. [from Medieval Latin]
→ see **energy, oil, petroleum**
→ see Word Web: **petroleum**

**pet|ty** /pɛti/ (**pettier, pettiest**) ❶ ADJ You can use **petty** to describe things such as problems, rules, or arguments that you think are unimportant. ❑ *Fights would start over petty things.* ❑ *...endless rules and petty regulations.* ❷ ADJ If you describe someone as **petty**, you disapprove of them because they are willing to be unpleasant to other people because of small, unimportant things. ❑ *Always give your best, never be petty.*
● **pet|ti|ness** N-UNCOUNT ❑ *...nasty pettiness.*
❸ ADJ **Petty** is used of people or actions that are less important, serious, or great than others. ❑ *...petty crime, such as purse-snatching.* [from Old French]

**petu|lant** /pɛtʃələnt/ ADJ Someone who is **petulant** is unreasonably angry and upset in a childish way. ❑ *He's just being silly and petulant.*
● **petu|lance** N-UNCOUNT ❑ *His petulance made her impatient.* [from Old French]

**pew** /pyu/ (**pews**) N-COUNT A **pew** is a long wooden seat with a back that people sit on in church. ❑ *Charlene sat in the front pew.* [from Old French]

## Word Web    petroleum

Most **petroleum** is used as **fuel**. We use **petrol** to power our cars and **heating oil** to warm our homes. About 20% of **crude oil** becomes **gas** and 10% becomes heating oil. Today 90% of the **energy** used in transportation comes from petroleum. Other petroleum products include household items such as **paint**, **deodorant**, and **shampoo**. Some of our clothes are also made using petroleum. These include **shoes**, **sweaters**, and **polyester shirts** and **dresses**. Petroleum products are also important for building new houses. They are used to make water **pipes**, **shower** doors, and even **toilet** seats.

**pew|ter** /pyutər/ N-UNCOUNT **Pewter** is a grey metal that is made by mixing tin and lead. [from Old French]

**pH** /pi eɪtʃ/ N-UNCOUNT The **pH of** a solution indicates how acid or alkaline the solution is. A pH of less than 7 indicates that it is an acid, and a pH of more than 7 indicates that it is an alkali.

**phan|tom** /fæntəm/ (**phantoms**) **1** N-COUNT A **phantom** is a ghost. ❑ *They vanished down the stairs like two phantoms.* **2** ADJ You use **phantom** to describe something that does not really exist, but that someone believes or pretends exist. ❑ *He invented a phantom life.* [from Old French]

| Word Link | *pharma ≈ drug : pharmaceutical, pharmacist, pharmacy* |
|---|---|

**phar|ma|ceu|ti|cal** /fɑrməsutɪkªl/ (**pharmaceuticals**) **1** ADJ **Pharmaceutical** means connected with the industrial production of medicines. ❑ *...a Swiss pharmaceutical company.* **2** N-PLURAL **Pharmaceuticals** are medicines. [from Late Latin]

| Word Link | *ist ≈ one who practices : archaeologist, biologist, pharmacist* |
|---|---|

**phar|ma|cist** /fɑrməsɪst/ (**pharmacists**) N-COUNT A **pharmacist** is a person who is qualified to prepare and sell medicines. ❑ *Ask your pharmacist for advice.* [from Medieval Latin]

**phar|ma|cy** /fɑrməsi/ (**pharmacies**) **1** N-COUNT A **pharmacy** is a place where medicines are sold or given out. ❑ *Pick up the medicine from the pharmacy.* **2** N-UNCOUNT **Pharmacy** is the job or the science of preparing medicines. ❑ *He spent four years studying pharmacy.* [from Medieval Latin]

**phar|ynx** /færɪŋks/ (**pharynges** /fərɪndʒiz/ or **phar+ynxes** /færɪŋksɪz/) N-COUNT Your **pharynx** is the area at the back of your throat, which connects your mouth and nose to your windpipe. [TECHNICAL] [from New Latin]

**phase** /feɪz/ (**phases, phasing, phased**) N-COUNT A **phase** is a particular stage in a process or in the development of something. ❑ *6000 women will take part in the first phase of the project.* ❑ *The crisis is entering a critical phase.* N-COUNT The **phases** of the moon are the different stages of the moon's appearance, for example a new moon or a full moon. [from New Latin]
▶ **phase in** PHR-VERB If a new way of doing something **is phased in**, it is introduced gradually. ❑ *The reforms will be phased in over three years.*
▶ **phase out** PHR-VERB If something **is phased out**, people gradually stop using it. ❑ *They think that the present system should be phased out.*

**Ph.D.** /pi eɪtʃdi/ (**Ph.D.s**) also **PhD** N-COUNT A **Ph.D.** is a degree awarded to people who have done advanced research into a particular subject. **Ph.D.** is an abbreviation for **Doctor of Philosophy**. ❑ *He is highly educated and has a Ph.D.in chemistry.*

**pheas|ant** /fɛzªnt/ (**pheasants**)

| Pheasant can also be used as the plural form. |
|---|

N-COUNT A **pheasant** is a bird with a long tail. Pheasants are often shot as a sport and then eaten. [from Old French]

**phe|nom|enal** /fɪnɒmɪnªl/ ADJ Something that is **phenomenal** is unusually great or good.

❑ *We're talking about a phenomenal amount of money.*
● **phe|nom|enal|ly** ADV ❑ *...her phenomenally successful singing career.* [from Late Latin]

**phe|nom|enon** /fɪnɒmɪnɒn/ (**phenomena**) N-COUNT A **phenomenon** is something that is observed to happen or exist. [FORMAL] ❑ *...a natural phenomenon such as thunder.* [from Late Latin]
→ see **experiment, science**

**phe|no|type** /finətaɪp/ (**phenotypes**) N-VAR The **phenotype** of an animal or plant is all the physical characteristics it has as a result of the interaction between its genes and the environment. Compare **phenotype**. [TECHNICAL] [from Greek]

**phero|mone** /fɛrəmoʊn/ (**pheromones**) N-COUNT Some animals and insects produce chemicals called **pheromones** that affect the behavior of other animals and insects of the same type, for example, by attracting them sexually. [TECHNICAL] [from Greek]

**phi|loso|pher** /fɪlɒsəfər/ (**philosophers**) N-COUNT A **philosopher** is a person who studies or writes about philosophy. ❑ *...the Greek philosopher Plato.* [from Old French]
→ see **philosophy**

**philo|soph|ic** /fɪləsɒfɪk/ ADJ **Philosophic** means the same as **philosophical**. [from Old French]

**philo|sophi|cal** /fɪləsɒfɪkªl/ **1** ADJ **Philosophical** means concerned with or relating to philosophy. ❑ *...philosophical discussions.*
● **philo|sophi|cal|ly** ADV ❑ *He's philosophically opposed to war.* **2** ADJ Someone who is **philosophical** does not get upset when disappointing or disturbing things happen; used to show approval. ❑ *Lewis grew philosophical about life.* ● **philo|sophi|cal|ly** ADV ❑ *She says philosophically: "It could have been far worse."* [from Old French]

**phi|loso|phy** /fɪlɒsəfi/ (**philosophies**) **1** N-UNCOUNT **Philosophy** is the study or creation of theories about basic things such as the nature of existence or how people should live. ❑ *...traditional Chinese philosophy.* **2** N-COUNT A **philosophy** is a particular theory or belief. ❑ *The best philosophy is to change to a low-sugar diet.* [from Old French]
→ see Word Web: **philosophy**

**phloem** /floʊɛm/ (**phloems**) N-VAR **Phloem** is the layer of material in plants that carries food from the leaves to the rest of the plant. Compare **xylem▸**. [TECHNICAL] [from German]

**pho|bia** /foʊbiə/ (**phobias**) N-COUNT A **phobia** is a strong irrational fear or hatred of something. ❑ *The man had a phobia about flying.* [from Greek]

**phone** /foʊn/ (**phones, phoning, phoned**) **1** N-SING The **phone** is an electrical system that you use to talk to someone else in another place, by dialing a number on a piece of equipment and speaking into it. ❑ *I told you over the phone.* ❑ *She talked to her daughter by phone.* **2** N-COUNT The **phone** is the piece of equipment that you use when you dial a phone number and talk to someone. ❑ *Two minutes later the phone rang.* **3** → see also **cellular phone** **4** V-T/V-I When you **phone** someone or when you **phone** them **up**, you dial their phone number and speak to them by phone. ❑ *He phoned Laura to see how she was.* ❑ *"Did*

## Word Web  philosophy

**Philosophy** helps us **understand** ourselves and the purpose of our lives. **Philosophers** have studied the same **issues** for thousands of years. The Chinese philosopher Confucius* wrote about personal and **political morals**. He taught that people should love others and honor their parents. They should do what is right, not what is best for themselves. He thought that a ruler who had to use force had failed. The Greek philosopher Plato* wrote about politics and science. Later, Aristotle* created a system of **logic** and **reasoning**. He wanted to be absolutely sure of what is true and what is not.

Plato            Aristotle            Confucius

Confucius (551-479 BC)
Plato (427-347 BC)
Aristotle (384-322 BC)

anybody phone?" asked Alberg. **5** PHRASE If someone is **on the phone**, they are speaking to someone by phone. □ She's always on the phone. [from Greek]
→ see **office**

**phone booth** (**phone booths**) N-COUNT A **phone booth** is a small shelter outdoors or in a building in which there is a public telephone.

**phone call** (**phone calls**) N-COUNT If you make a **phone call**, you dial a phone number and speak to someone by phone. □ I have to make a phone call.

**phone|card** /fo͟ʊnkɑrd/ (**phonecards**) also **phone card** N-COUNT A **phonecard** is a plastic card that you can use instead of money in some telephones.

**pho|neme** /fo͟ʊnim/ (**phonemes**) N-COUNT A **phoneme** is the smallest unit of significant sound in a language. [TECHNICAL] [from French]

**pho|ne|mic aware|ness** /fəni͟mɪk/ N-UNCOUNT **Phonemic awareness** is the ability to distinguish the small, separate sounds that spoken words consist of. [TECHNICAL]

**phon|ics** /fɒ͟nɪks/ N-UNCOUNT **Phonics** is a method of teaching people to read by training them to associate written letters with their sounds. [TECHNICAL] [from Greek]

**pho|no|gram** /fo͟ʊnəgræm/ (**phonograms**) N-COUNT A **phonogram** is a written letter or symbol, or a series of written letters or symbols, that represents a word or part of a word. For example, the symbol "@" is a phonogram that represents the word "at," and the letters "ake" are a phonogram that appears in words such as "make" and "take." [TECHNICAL]

**pho|ny** /fo͟ʊni/ also **phoney** (**phonier, phoniest, phonies**) **1** ADJ If you describe something as **phony**, you disapprove of it because it is not genuine. [INFORMAL] □ He had a phony excuse. **2** ADJ If you describe someone as **phony**, you disapprove of them because they are pretending to be something they are not. [INFORMAL] ● **Phony** is also a noun. □ He's such a phony.

**phos|phate** /fɒ͟sfeɪt/ (**phosphates**) N-VAR A **phosphate** is a chemical compound containing phosphorus that is used in fertilizers. [from French]

**phos|pho|lip|id** /fɒ͟sfoʊlɪpɪd, -laɪp-/ (**phospholipids**) N-COUNT **Phospholipids** are fats

that form an important part of the structure of cell membranes. [TECHNICAL]

**pho|to** /fo͟ʊtoʊ/ (**photos**) N-COUNT A **photo** is the same as a **photograph**. [from Greek]
→ see **photography**

**photo|cell** /fo͟ʊtoʊsɛl/ (**photocells**) also **photoelectric cell** N-COUNT A **photocell** or a **photoelectric cell** is a device that measures the amount of light that is present and converts it into electricity. [TECHNICAL]

**pho|to|cop|i|er** /fo͟ʊtəkɒpiər/ (**photocopiers**) N-COUNT A **photocopier** is a machine that quickly copies documents by photographing them.

photocopier

**photo|copy** /fo͟ʊtəkɒpi/ (**photocopies, photocopying, photocopied**) **1** N-COUNT A **photocopy** is a copy of a document made using a photocopier. □ He was shown a photocopy of the letter. **2** V-T If you **photocopy** a document, you make a copy of it using a photocopier. □ Staff photocopied the check before cashing it.

**photo|graph** /fo͟ʊtəgræf/ (**photographs, photographing, photographed**) **1** N-COUNT A **photograph** is a picture that is made using a camera. □ He wants to take some photographs of the house. **2** V-T When you **photograph** someone or something, you use a camera to obtain a picture of them. [FORMAL] □ She photographed the children.

**pho|tog|ra|pher** /fəto͟grəfər/ (**photographers**) N-COUNT A **photographer** is someone who takes photographs as a job or hobby. □ ...a professional photographer.
→ see **photography**

**photo|graph|ic** /fo͟ʊtəgræ͟fɪk/ ADJ **Photographic** means connected with photographs or photography. □ ...photographic equipment.

**pho|tog|ra|phy** /fəto͟grəfi/ N-UNCOUNT **Photography** is the skill, job, or process of producing photographs. □ Her hobby is photography.
→ see Word Web: **photography**

**photo|recep|tor** /fo͟ʊtoʊrɪsɛptər/ (**photoreceptors**) N-COUNT **Photoreceptors** are

| Word Web | photography |
|---|---|

It's easy to **take a picture** with a digital **camera**. You just look through the viewfinder and push the **shutter button**. But professional **photographers** need to produce high quality **photos**. So their job is harder. First they choose the right **film** and **load** the camera. Then they check the **lighting** and carefully **focus** the camera. They usually take several **shots**, one after another. Then it's time to **develop** the film and make **prints**. Sometimes a photographer will **crop** a photo or **enlarge** it to create a more striking **image**.

very small structures in the eye which can detect and respond to light. [TECHNICAL]

**pho|to shoot** (photo shoots) also **photo-shoot** N-COUNT A **photo shoot** is an occasion when a photographer takes pictures, especially of models or famous people, to be used in a newspaper or magazine. □ *...a long day of interviews and photo-shoots.*

**photo|sphere** /foʊtəsfɪər/ N-COUNT The **photosphere** is the surface of the sun, where the sun's gases appear solid. [TECHNICAL]

**photo|syn|the|sis** /foʊtoʊsɪnθəsɪs/ N-UNCOUNT **Photosynthesis** is the way that green plants make their food using sunlight. [TECHNICAL]
→ see Word Web: photosynthesis

**pho|tot|ro|pism** /foʊtɒtrəpɪzəm/ (phototropisms) N-VAR **Phototropism** is the tendency of a plant to grow in the direction of a light source. [TECHNICAL]

**photovoltaic** /foʊtoʊvɒlteɪɪk/ A **photovoltaic** cell or panel is a device that uses sunlight to cause a chemical reaction which produces electricity. [TECHNICAL] ADJ

**phras|al verb** /freɪzᵊl vɜrb/ (phrasal verbs) N-COUNT A **phrasal verb** is a combination of a verb and an adverb or preposition, for example, "get over" or "knock back," which together have a particular meaning.

**phrase** /freɪz/ (phrases, phrasing, phrased) **1** N-COUNT A **phrase** is a short group of words that are used as a unit and whose meaning may not be obvious from the words contained in it. □ *I hate the phrase: "You have to be cruel to be kind."* **2** V-T If you **phrase** something in a particular way, you say or write it in that way. □ *I would have phrased it quite differently.* □ *The speech was carefully phrased.*

**3** N-COUNT A **phrase** is a short section of a piece of music which expresses a musical idea. **4** PHRASE If someone has a particular **turn of phrase**, they have a particular way of expressing themselves in words. □ *...an entertaining person with a delightful turn of phrase.* [from Latin] **5** to **coin a phrase** → see **coin**

**phras|ing** /freɪzɪŋ/ N-UNCOUNT The **phrasing** of someone who is singing, playing a piece of music, acting, dancing, or reading something aloud is the way in which they divide up the work by pausing slightly in appropriate places. [from Latin]

**phy|lum** /faɪləm/ (phyla) N-COUNT A **phylum** is a group of related species of animals or plants. Compare **kingdom, class.** [TECHNICAL] [from New Latin]

**phys ed** /fɪz ɛd/ N-UNCOUNT **Phys ed** is the same as **physical education.** [INFORMAL] □ *...Don, who taught phys ed at a junior high school.*

| Word Link | physi ≈ of nature : physical, physician, physics |
|---|---|

**physi|cal** /fɪzɪkᵊl/ **1** ADJ **Physical** means connected with a person's body, rather than with their mind. □ *...physical and mental problems.* □ *Physical activity promotes good health.* ● **physi|cal|ly** ADV □ *You may be physically and mentally exhausted after a long flight.* **2** ADJ **Physical** things are real things that can be touched and seen. □ *There is no physical barrier to prevent escape.* □ *...physical evidence to support the story.* [from Latin]
→ see **diagnosis, periodic table**

**physi|cal change** (physical changes) N-VAR When there is a **physical change** to a substance, its form or appearance changes but it does not become a different substance.

| Word Web | photosynthesis |
|---|---|

**Plants** make their own food from **sunlight, water,** and **soil.** They get water and **minerals** from the ground through their roots. They also absorb **carbon dioxide** from the air through tiny holes in their leaves. The green pigment in plant leaves is called **chlorophyll.** It combines **solar energy** with water and carbon dioxide to produce **glucose.** This process is called **photosynthesis.** During the process, the plant releases **oxygen** into the atmosphere. It uses some of the glucose to grow larger. When humans and other animals eat plants, they also make use of this stored **energy.**

**phys|i|cal ed|u|ca|tion** N-UNCOUNT **Physical education** is the school subject in which students do physical exercises or take part in physical games and sports.

**phys|i|cal prop|er|ty** (**physical properties**) N-COUNT The **physical properties** of a substance are qualities such as its size and shape, which can be measured without changing what the substance is.

**phys|i|cal sci|ence** (**physical sciences**) N-COUNT The **physical sciences** are branches of science such as physics, chemistry, and geology that are concerned with natural forces and with things that do not have life.

**phys|i|cal ther|a|py** N-UNCOUNT **Physical therapy** is medical treatment given to people who have injured part of their body that involves exercise, massage, or heat treatment.

→ see **illness**

| Word Link | ician ≈ person who works at : electrician, musician, physician |
|---|---|

| Word Link | physi ≈ of nature : physical, physician, physics |
|---|---|

**phy|si|cian** /fɪzɪʃⁿn/ (**physicians**) N-COUNT A **physician** is a medical doctor. [FORMAL] □ ...*your family physician*. [from Old French]
→ see **diagnosis, hospital, medicine**

**phy|si|cian's as|sis|tant** (**physician's assistants**) N-COUNT A **physician's assistant** is a person who is trained to do some of the same work that a doctor does but who is not a doctor.

**physi|cist** /fɪzɪsɪst/ (**physicists**) N-COUNT A **physicist** is a person who studies physics. □ ...*a nuclear physicist*. [from Latin]

**phys|ics** /fɪzɪks/ N-UNCOUNT **Physics** is the scientific study of forces such as heat, light, sound, pressure, gravity, and electricity. □ ...*the laws of physics*. [from Latin]

**physi|ol|ogy** /fɪziɒlədʒi/ ◼ N-UNCOUNT **Physiology** is the scientific study of how people, animals, and plants grow and function. □ ...*the Nobel Prize for Medicine and Physiology*. ◼ N-UNCOUNT The **physiology** of an animal or plant is the way that it functions. □ ...*the physiology of pain*. ● **physio|logi|cal** /fɪziəlɒdʒɪkⁿl/ ADJ □ ...*the physiological effects of stress*. [from Latin]

**phy|sique** /fɪzik/ (**physiques**) N-COUNT Someone's **physique** is the shape and size of their body. □ *He has the physique of a man half his age.* [from French]

**phyto|plank|ton** /faɪtoʊplæŋktən/ N-PLURAL **Phytoplankton** are tiny plants such as algae that are found in plankton. [TECHNICAL]

**pia|nist** /piænɪst, piɑnɪst/ (**pianists**) N-COUNT A **pianist** is a person who plays the **piano**. □ ...*a concert pianist*. [from Italian]

**pi|ano** /piænoʊ, pyænoʊ/ (**pianos**) N-VAR A **piano** is a large musical instrument with a row of black and white keys, which you strike with your fingers. □ *I taught myself how to play the piano.* [from Italian]
→ see **keyboard, music**

**pick** /pɪk/ (**picks, picking, picked**) ◼ V-T If you **pick** a particular person or thing, you choose that one. □ *Mr. Nowell picked ten people to interview.*

◼ N-SING You can refer to the best things or people in a particular group as **the pick of** that group. □ *The boys here are the pick of the high school's soccer players.* ◼ V-T When you **pick** flowers, fruit, or leaves, you break them off the plant or tree and collect them. □ *I've picked some flowers from the garden.* ◼ V-T If you **pick** something from a place, you remove it from there with your fingers or your hand. □ *He picked the napkin from his lap.* ◼ V-T If you **pick** a fight **with** someone, you deliberately cause one. □ *He picked a fight with a waiter.* ◼ V-T If someone such as a thief **picks** a lock, they open it without a key, for example, by using a piece of wire. □ *She picked the lock on his door and stepped inside.* [from French] ◼ to **pick holes in** something → see **hole** ◼ to **pick** someone's **pocket** → see **pocket**

▶ **pick on** PHR-VERB If someone **picks on** you, they repeatedly criticize you unfairly or treat you unkindly. [INFORMAL] □ *Bullies often pick on younger children.*

▶ **pick out** ◼ PHR-VERB If you **pick out** someone or something, you recognize them when it is difficult to see them. □ *I had trouble picking out the words, even with my glasses on.* ◼ PHR-VERB If you **pick out** someone or something, you choose them from a group of people or things. □ *I have been picked out to represent the whole team.*

▶ **pick up** ◼ PHR-VERB When you **pick** something **up**, you lift it up. □ *He picked his cap up from the floor.* ◼ PHR-VERB When you **pick up** someone or something, you collect them from somewhere, often in a car. □ *She was going over to her parents' house to pick up some clean clothes.* ◼ PHR-VERB If you **pick up** a skill or an idea, you acquire it without effort over a period of time. [INFORMAL] □ *Where did you pick up your English?* ◼ PHR-VERB If you **pick up** an illness, you get it from somewhere or something. □ *They've picked up an infection from something they've eaten.* ◼ PHR-VERB If a piece of equipment **picks up** a signal or sound, it receives it or detects it. □ *We can pick up Mexican television.* ◼ PHR-VERB If trade or the economy of a country **picks up**, it improves. □ *Industrial production is beginning to pick up.*

| Thesaurus | pick | Also look up : |
|---|---|---|
| v. | choose, decide on, elect, select ◼ collect, gather, harvest, pull ◼ | |

**pick|ax** /pɪkæks/ (**pickaxes**) also **pickaxe** N-COUNT A **pickax** is a large tool consisting of a curved, pointed piece of metal with a long handle attached to the middle. Pickaxes are used for breaking up rocks or the ground. [from Old French]

**pick|et** /pɪkɪt/ (**pickets, picketing, picketed**) ◼ V-T/V-I When people **picket** a place, they stand outside it in order to make a protest, to prevent people from going in, or to persuade the workers to join a strike. □ *A group of employees picketed the company's headquarters.* □ *They were picketing outside the school.* ● **Picket** is also a noun. □ *Forty demonstrators have set up a twenty-four hour picket.* ◼ N-COUNT **Pickets** are people who are picketing a place of work. □ *The strikers agreed to remove their pickets.* [from French]

**pick|le** /pɪkⁿl/ (**pickles**) ◼ N-PLURAL **Pickles** are vegetables or fruit which have been kept in vinegar or salt water for a long time to give them a strong, sharp taste. ❑ *...a hamburger with pickles, ketchup, and mustard.* **2** N-VAR **Pickle** is a cold spicy sauce with pieces of vegetables and fruit in it. ❑ *...jars of pickle.* [from Middle Dutch]

**pick|led** /pɪkˀld/ ADJ **Pickled** food has been kept in vinegar or salt water to preserve it. ❑ *...a jar of pickled fruit.* [from Middle Dutch]

**pic|nic** /pɪknɪk/ (**picnics, picnicking, picnicked**) **1** N-COUNT When people have a **picnic**, they eat a meal outdoors, usually in a park or a forest, or at the beach. ❑ *We're going on a picnic tomorrow.* **2** V-I When people **picnic** somewhere, they have a picnic. ❑ *We picnicked by the river.* [from French] → see **park**

**pic|to|rial** /pɪktɔriəl/ ADJ **Pictorial** means using or relating to pictures. ❑ *...a pictorial history of the Jewish people.* [from Late Latin]

**Word Link** *pict ≈ painting : depict, picture, picturesque*

**pic|ture** /pɪktʃər/ (**pictures, picturing, pictured**) **1** N-COUNT A **picture** consists of lines and shapes that are drawn, painted, or printed on a surface and show a person, thing, or scene. ❑ *...a small picture drawn with colored chalk.* **2** N-COUNT A **picture** is a photograph. ❑ *The tourists have nothing to do but take pictures of each other.* **3** N-COUNT Television **pictures** are the scenes that you see on a television screen. ❑ *...television pictures of human suffering.* **4** V-T If someone or something **is pictured** in a newspaper or magazine, they appear in a photograph in it. ❑ *The golfer is pictured on many of the front pages.* **5** N-COUNT You can refer to a movie as a **picture**. ❑ *...a director of action pictures.* **6** V-T If you **picture** something in your mind, you think of it and have such a clear memory or idea of it that you seem to be able to see it. ❑ *He pictured her with long black hair.* ❑ *He pictured Carrie sitting out in the car.* ● **Picture** is also a noun. ❑ *We do have a picture of how we'd like things to be.* **7** N-COUNT A **picture** of something is a description of it or an indication of what it is like. ❑ *I'll try and give you a better picture of what the boys do.* **8** N-SING When you refer to the **picture** in a particular place, you are referring to the situation there. ❑ *It's a similar picture across the border in Ethiopia.* **9** PHRASE If you **put** someone **in the picture**, you tell them about a situation which they need to know about. ❑ *Has anyone put you in the picture?* [from Latin] → see **photography**

**Thesaurus** *picture* Also look up :

N. drawing, illustration, image, painting **1** photograph **2**
V. envision, imagine, visualize **6**

**Word Partnership** Use *picture* with :

ADJ. **pretty as a** picture **1** **mental** picture **6** **accurate** picture, **clear** picture, **complete** picture, **different** picture, **larger** picture, **overall** picture, **vivid** picture, **whole** picture **6** – **8**

**pic|ture mes|sag|ing** N-UNCOUNT **Picture messaging** is the sending of photographs or pictures from one cellphone to another.

**pic|tur|esque** /pɪktʃərɛsk/ ADJ A **picturesque** place is attractive and interesting, and has no ugly modern buildings. ❑ *...a picturesque mountain village.* [from French]

**pie** /paɪ/ (**pies**) **1** N-VAR A **pie** consists of fruit, meat, or vegetables baked in pastry. ❑ *...a slice of apple pie.* **2** to **eat humble pie** → see **humble** → see **chart, dessert**

**piece** /pis/ (**pieces, piecing, pieced**) **1** N-COUNT A **piece of** something is an amount of it that has been broken off, torn off, or cut off. ❑ *...a piece of cake.* ❑ *Cut the ham into pieces.* **2** N-COUNT A **piece of** something of a particular kind is an individual item of it. For example, you can refer to some advice as a **piece of advice**. ❑ *This is his finest piece of work yet.* ❑ *...an interesting piece of information.* **3** N-COUNT A **piece** is something that is written or created, such as an article, work of art, or musical composition. [FORMAL] ❑ *She wrote a piece on Gwyneth Paltrow for the "New Yorker".* ❑ *Each piece is painted by an artist according to your design.* **4** N-COUNT A **piece of** something is part of it or a share of it. ❑ *They got a small piece of the profits.* **5** PHRASE If someone or something is still **in one piece** after a dangerous journey or experience, they are safe and not damaged or hurt. ❑ *The main thing is that my brother gets back in one piece.* **6** PHRASE If you **go to pieces**, you are so upset or nervous that you lose control of yourself and cannot do what you should do. [INFORMAL] ❑ *She nearly went to pieces when Arnie died.* [from Old French] **7** **a piece of the action** → see **action** **8** **bits and pieces** → see **bit** → see **chess**

▸ **piece together** **1** PHR-VERB If you **piece together** the truth about something, you gradually discover it. ❑ *They've pieced together his movements for the last few days.* ❑ *I've been trying to piece together what happened.* **2** PHR-VERB If you **piece** something **together**, you gradually make it by joining several things or parts together. ❑ *This process is like piecing together a jigsaw puzzle.*

**piece|meal** /pismil/ ADJ A **piecemeal** process happens gradually and in irregular or unconnected stages, usually in a way that is unsatisfactory. ❑ *These piecemeal solutions won't work.* ● **Piecemeal** is also an adverb. ❑ *It was built piecemeal over 130 years.* [from Old English]

**pie chart** (**pie charts**) N-COUNT A **pie chart** is a circle divided into sections to show the relative proportions of a set of things.

**pier** /pɪər/ (**piers**) N-COUNT A **pier** is a platform sticking out into water that people walk along or use when getting onto or off boats. ❑ *...Chicago's Navy Pier.*

**pierce** /pɪərs/ (**pierces, piercing, pierced**) **1** V-T If a sharp object **pierces** something, or if you **pierce** something **with** a sharp object, the object goes into it and makes a hole in it. ❑ *Pierce the chicken with a knife to check that it is cooked.* **2** V-T If you have your ears or another part of your body **pierced**, you have a small hole made through them so that you can wear a piece of jewelry in them. ❑ *I'm having my ears pierced on Saturday.* ● **pierc|ing** N-VAR ❑ *...health risks from needles used in piercing.* ❑ *...girls with braids and piercings.* [from Old French]

**pierc|ing** /pɪərsɪŋ/ **1** ADJ A **piercing** sound or voice is high-pitched and very sharp and clear in an unpleasant way. ❑ *...a piercing scream.* **2** ADJ

If someone has **piercing** eyes or a **piercing** stare, they seem to look at you very intensely. [WRITTEN] ❑ …his blond hair and piercing blue eyes. [from Old French]

**pig** /pɪg/ (**pigs**) **1** N-COUNT A **pig** is a farm animal with pink, white, or black skin. Pigs are kept for their meat, which is called pork, ham, or bacon. ❑ Kids can help feed the pigs. **2** → see also **guinea pig 3** N-COUNT If you call someone a **pig**, you are insulting them, usually because you think that they are greedy or unkind. [INFORMAL] ❑ These guys destroyed the company. They're a bunch of greedy pigs.
→ see **meat**

**pi|geon** /pɪdʒɪn/ (**pigeons**) N-COUNT A **pigeon** is a gray bird that is often seen in cities. [from Old French]

**pig|ment** /pɪgmənt/ (**pigments**) N-VAR A **pigment** is a substance that gives something a particular color. [FORMAL] ❑ The Romans used natural pigments on their fabrics. [from Latin]

**pig|pen** /pɪgpɛn/ (**pigpens**) also pig pen N-COUNT A **pigpen** is an enclosed place where pigs are kept on a farm.

**pike** /paɪk/ (**pike**)

| The plural can also be **pikes**. |

**1** N-VAR A **pike** is a large fish that lives in rivers and lakes and eats other fish. **2** PHRASE When something **comes down the pike**, it happens or occurs. [INFORMAL] ❑ …every news story that comes down the pike. [from Old English]

**Pilates** /pɪlɑtiz/ N-UNCOUNT **Pilates** is a type of exercise similar to yoga. ❑ She's never done Pilates before. [from German]

**pile** /paɪl/ (**piles, piling, piled**) **1** N-COUNT A **pile of** things is a quantity of them lying on top of one another. ❑ …a pile of boxes. ❑ The leaves have been swept into huge piles. **2** V-T If you **pile** things somewhere, you put them there so that they form a pile. ❑ He was piling clothes into the suitcase. **3** V-T If something **is piled with** things, it is covered or filled with piles of things. ❑ Tables were piled with food. **4** V-I If a group of people **pile into** or **out of** a place, they all get into it or out of it in a disorganized way. ❑ They all piled into Jerry's car. **5** N-SING The **pile** of a carpet or of a fabric such as velvet is its soft surface. It consists of a lot of little threads standing on end. ❑ …the carpet's thick pile. **6** PHRASE Someone who is **at the bottom of the pile** is low down in society or low down in an organization. Someone who is **at the top of the pile** is high up in society or high up in an organization. [INFORMAL] ❑ These workers are at the bottom of the pile when it comes to pay. [Senses 1–4 from Old French. Sense 5 from Anglo–Norman.]
▶ **pile up 1** PHR-VERB If you **pile up** a quantity of things or if they **pile up**, they gradually form a pile. ❑ They piled up rocks to build a wall. **2** PHR-VERB If you **pile up** work, problems, or losses or if they **pile up**, you get more and more of them. ❑ Problems were piling up at work.

**pil|grim** /pɪlgrɪm/ (**pilgrims**) N-COUNT **Pilgrims** are people who journey to a holy place for a religious reason. ❑ …tourists and pilgrims visiting Rome. [from Provençal]

**pil|grim|age** /pɪlgrɪmɪdʒ/ (**pilgrimages**) N-COUNT If you make a **pilgrimage** to a place,

you make a trip there because the place is holy according to your religion, or very important to you personally. ❑ …the pilgrimage to Mecca. ❑ …a private pilgrimage to family graves. [from Provençal]

**pill** /pɪl/ (**pills**) **1** N-COUNT **Pills** are small solid round masses of medicine or vitamins that you swallow. ❑ Why do I have to take all these pills? **2** N-SING If a woman is **on the pill**, she takes a special pill that prevents her from becoming pregnant. ❑ She has been on the pill for three years. [from Middle Flemish]

**pil|lar** /pɪlər/ (**pillars**) **1** N-COUNT A **pillar** is a tall solid structure that is usually used to support part of a building. ❑ …the pillars supporting the roof. **2** N-COUNT If you describe someone as a **pillar of** the community, you approve of them because they play an important and active part in the community. [from Old French]

**pil|low** /pɪloʊ/ (**pillows**) N-COUNT A **pillow** is a rectangular cushion that you rest your head on when you are in bed. [from Old English]
→ see **sleep**

**pi|lot** /paɪlət/ (**pilots, piloting, piloted**) **1** N-COUNT A **pilot** is a person who is trained to fly an aircraft. ❑ He spent ten years as an airline pilot. **2** V-T If someone **pilots** an aircraft or ship, they act as its pilot. ❑ He piloted his own plane to Washington. **3** N-COUNT A **pilot** plan or a **pilot** project is one that is used to test an idea before deciding whether to introduce it on a larger scale. ❑ We are running a pilot study funded by the government. **4** V-T If a government or organization **pilots** a program or project, they test it, before deciding whether to introduce it on a larger scale. ❑ Teachers are piloting a reading program. [from French]

**pin** /pɪn/ (**pins, pinning, pinned**) **1** N-COUNT **Pins** are very small thin pointed pieces of metal which are used to fasten things together. ❑ …a box of needles and pins. **2** V-T If you **pin** something **on** or **to** something, you attach it there with a pin. ❑ They pinned a notice to the door. ❑ Everyone was supposed to pin money on the bride's dress. **3** V-T If someone **pins** you in a particular position, they press you against a surface so that you cannot move. ❑ I pinned him against the wall. ❑ I pinned him down until the police arrived. **4** N-COUNT A **pin** is any long narrow piece of metal or wood that is not sharp, especially one that is used to fasten two things together. ❑ …the 18-inch steel pin holding his left leg together. **5** V-T If someone tries to **pin** something bad **on** you, they say that you were responsible for it. ❑ They couldn't pin the blame on anyone. **6** V-T If you **pin** your hopes **on** someone or something, your future success or happiness depends on them. ❑ The Democrats are pinning their hopes on the next election. **7** N-COUNT A **pin** is a decorative object worn on your clothing which is fastened with a pointed piece of metal. ❑ …necklaces, bracelets, and pins.
[from Old English]
→ see **jewelry**
▶ **pin down 1** PHR-VERB If you try to **pin** something **down**, you try to discover exactly what, where, or when it is. ❑ I'm trying to pin down the location of the building. ❑ I can pin the event down to some time between 1936 and 1942. **2** PHR-VERB If you **pin** someone **down**, you force them to make a definite statement. ❑ She couldn't pin him down to a date.

**pin|cer** /pɪnsər/ (**pincers**) **1** N-PLURAL **Pincers** consist of two pieces of metal that are hinged in the middle. They are used as a tool for gripping things or for pulling things out. ❑ *His surgical instruments were a knife and a pair of pincers.* **2** N-COUNT The **pincers** of an animal such as a crab or a lobster are its front claws. [from Old French]

**pinch** /pɪntʃ/ (**pinches, pinching, pinched**) **1** V-T If you **pinch** someone, you squeeze a part of their body between your thumb and first finger. ❑ *She pinched his arm as hard as she could.* ● **Pinch** is also a noun. ❑ *She gave him a little pinch.* **2** N-COUNT A **pinch** of an ingredient such as salt is the amount of it that you can hold between your thumb and your first finger. ❑ *...a pinch of cinnamon.* **3** to **take** something **with a pinch of salt** → see **salt** **4** V-T To **pinch** something, especially something of little value, means to steal it. [INFORMAL] ❑ *Do you remember when I pinched your glasses?* **5** PHRASE If a person or company **is feeling the pinch**, they do not have as much money as they used to, and so they cannot buy the things they would like to buy. ❑ *American small businesses are feeling the pinch from rising gas prices.* [from Old Norman French]

**pinch-hit** /pɪntʃhɪt/ also **pinch hit** **1** V-I If you **pinch-hit for** someone, you do something for them because they are unexpectedly unable to do it. ❑ *The staff here can pinch hit for each other when the hotel is busy.* **2** V-I In a game of baseball, if you **pinch-hit** for another player, you hit the ball instead of them. ❑ *Davalillo goes up to pinch-hit.*

**pine** /paɪn/ (**pines, pining, pined**) **1** N-VAR A **pine tree** or a **pine** is a tall tree with long, thin leaves that it keeps all year round. ❑ *...high mountains covered in pine trees.* ● **Pine** is the wood of this tree. ❑ *...a big pine table.* **2** V-I If you **pine for** something or someone, you feel sad because you cannot have them or cannot be with them. ❑ *I pine for the countryside.* [from Old English]

**pine|apple** /paɪnæpᵊl/ (**pineapples**) N-VAR A **pineapple** is a large oval fruit with sweet, juicy, yellow flesh and thick brown skin.
→ see **fruit**

**pink** /pɪŋk/ (**pinks, pinker, pinkest**) COLOR Something that is **pink** is the color between red and white. ❑ *...pink lipstick.* ❑ *...white flowers edged with pink.* [from Dutch]

**pink slip** (**pink slips**) N-COUNT If employees are given their **pink slips**, they are informed that they are no longer needed to do the job that they have been doing. [INFORMAL] ❑ *It was his fourth pink slip in two years.*

**pin|na|cle** /pɪnɪkəl/ (**pinnacles**) **1** N-COUNT A **pinnacle** is a pointed piece of stone or rock that is high above the ground. ❑ *A walker fell 80 feet from a rocky pinnacle.* **2** N-COUNT The **pinnacle of** something is the best or highest level of it. ❑ *She was still at the pinnacle of her career.* [from Old French]

**pin|point** /pɪnpɔɪnt/ (**pinpoints, pinpointing, pinpointed**) V-T If you **pinpoint** something, you discover or describe exactly what or where it is. ❑ *It was almost impossible to pinpoint the cause of death.* ❑ *I could pinpoint his precise location on a map.*

**pint** /paɪnt/ (**pints**) N-COUNT A **pint** is a unit of measurement for liquids equal to 473 cubic centimeters or one eighth of a gallon. ❑ *...a pint of ice cream.* [from Old French]

→ see **measurement**

**pin|to bean** /pɪntoʊ bin/ (**pinto beans**) N-COUNT **Pinto beans** are a type of bean, similar to kidney beans, that are eaten as a vegetable.

**pio|neer** /paɪənɪər/ (**pioneers, pioneering, pioneered**) **1** N-COUNT A **pioneer** in a particular area of activity is one of the first people to be involved in it. ❑ *...one of the leading pioneers of the Internet.* **2** V-T Someone who **pioneers** a new activity, invention, or process is one of the first people to do it. ❑ *...Professor Alec Jeffreys, who invented and pioneered DNA tests.* ● **pio|neer|ing** ADJ ❑ *The school has won awards for its pioneering work with the community.* **3** N-COUNT **Pioneers** are people who leave their own country and go and live in a place that has not been lived in before. [from Old French]

**pi|ous** /paɪəs/ ADJ Someone who is **pious** is very religious and moral. ❑ *He was brought up by pious female relatives.* ● **pi|ous|ly** ADV ❑ *Conti kneeled and crossed himself piously.* [from Latin]

**pipe** /paɪp/ (**pipes, piping, piped**) **1** N-COUNT A **pipe** is a long, round, hollow object through

pipe

which a liquid or gas can flow. ❑ *...water pipes.* **2** N-COUNT A **pipe** is an object that is used for smoking tobacco. ❑ *Do you smoke a pipe?* **3** N-COUNT **Organ pipes** are the long hollow tubes which produce musical notes from an organ. **4** V-T If liquid or gas **is piped** somewhere, it is transferred from one place to another through a pipe. ❑ *Clean water is piped into our homes.* [from Old English] **5** → see also **piping**
→ see **keyboard, petroleum**

**pipe|line** /paɪplaɪn/ (**pipelines**) **1** N-COUNT A **pipeline** is a large pipe that is used for carrying oil or gas over a long distance, often underground. ❑ *...a natural-gas pipeline.* **2** PHRASE If something is **in the pipeline**, it has been planned or begun. ❑ *A 2.9 percent pay increase is in the pipeline for teachers.*
→ see **oil**

**pipe or|gan** (**pipe organs**) N-COUNT A **pipe organ** is a large musical instrument with pipes of different lengths through which air is forced. It has keys and pedals like a piano.

**pip|ing** /paɪpɪŋ/ N-UNCOUNT **Piping** is metal, plastic, or another substance made in the shape of a pipe or tube. ❑ *...bright yellow plastic piping.* [from Old English]

**pi|ra|cy** /paɪrəsi/ **1** N-UNCOUNT **Piracy** is robbery at sea carried out by pirates. ❑ *Seven of the men were charged with piracy.* **2** N-UNCOUNT You can refer to the illegal copying of things such as DVDs and computer programs as **piracy**. ❑ *...protection against piracy of books and films.* [from Late Greek]

**pi|rate** /paɪrɪt/ (**pirates, pirating, pirated**) **1** N-COUNT **Pirates** are sailors who attack other ships and steal property from them. ❑ *In the nineteenth century, pirates sailed the seas.* **2** V-T Someone who **pirates** CDs, DVDs, books, or computer programs copies and sells them when they have no right to do so. ❑ *Computer crimes include data theft and pirating software.* ● **pi|rated** ADJ ❑ *...pirated copies of music and movies.* [from Latin]

**pis|til** /pɪstᵊl/ (**pistils**) N-COUNT The **pistil** is the female part of a flower, which produces seeds. [TECHNICAL] [from Latin]

**pis|tol** /pɪstᵊl/ (**pistols**) N-COUNT A **pistol** is a small gun. [from French]

**pis|ton** /pɪstᵊn/ (**pistons**) N-COUNT A **piston** is a cylinder or metal disk that is part of an engine. [from French]

**pit** /pɪt/ (**pits, pitting, pitted**) **1** N-COUNT A **pit** is the underground part of a mine, especially a coal mine. **2** V-T If two opposing things or people **are pitted against** one another, they are in conflict or in competition. ❏ *You will be pitted against people who are as good as you are.* **3** N-COUNT A **pit** is a large hole that is dug in the ground. ❏ *Eric lost his footing and began to slide into the pit.* **4** N-PLURAL In auto racing, **the pits** are the areas at the side of the track where drivers go for fuel and repairs during races. **5** N-COUNT A **pit** is the large hard seed of a fruit or vegetable. ❏ *…cherry pits.* [Senses 1–4 from Old English. Sense 5 from Dutch.] **6** → see also **pitted**

**pitch** /pɪtʃ/ (**pitches, pitching, pitched**) **1** V-T If you **pitch** something somewhere, you throw it with some force. ❏ *Simon pitched the empty bottle into the lake.* **2** V-I To **pitch** somewhere means to fall forward suddenly and with a lot of force. ❏ *The movement took him by surprise, and he pitched forward.* **3** N-UNCOUNT The **pitch** of a sound is how high or low it is. ❏ *He raised his voice to an even higher pitch.* **4** V-T If something **is pitched at** a particular level, it is set at that level. ❏ *The level of the course is pitched too high for our students.* **5** N-SING If something such as a feeling or a situation rises to a high **pitch**, it rises to a high level. ❏ *The game ended on a high pitch of excitement.* [from Old French]

▸ **pitch in** PHR-VERB If you **pitch in**, you join in and help with an activity. [INFORMAL] ❏ *International agencies also have pitched in.*

**pitch|er** /pɪtʃər/ (**pitchers**) **1** N-COUNT A **pitcher** is a cylindrical container with a handle, used for holding and pouring liquids. ❏ *…a pitcher of iced water.* **2** N-COUNT In baseball, the **pitcher** is the person who throws the ball to the batter, who tries to hit it. [Sense 1 from Old French. Sense 2 from French.]

pitcher

→ see **baseball**

**pit|fall** /pɪtfɔl/ (**pitfalls**) N-COUNT The **pitfalls** involved in a particular activity or situation are the things that may go wrong or may cause problems. ❏ *The pitfalls of working abroad are numerous.* [from Old English]

**piti|ful** /pɪtɪfəl/ **1** ADJ Someone or something that is **pitiful** is so sad, weak, or small that you feel pity for them. ❏ *The children were a pitiful sight.* ● **piti|ful|ly** ADV ❏ *His legs were pitifully thin.* **2** ADJ If you describe something as **pitiful**, you mean that it is completely inadequate. ❏ *The choice is pitiful.* ● **piti|ful|ly** ADV ❏ *Government help for the homeless is pitifully inadequate.* [from Old French]

**pit|ted** /pɪtɪd/ **1** ADJ **Pitted** fruits have had their pits removed. ❏ *…pitted olives.* **2** ADJ If the surface of something is **pitted**, it is covered with a lot of small, shallow holes. ❏ *The walls are pitted with bullet holes.* [from Old English]

**pity** /pɪti/ (**pities, pitying, pitied**) **1** V-T If you **pity** someone, you feel very sorry for them. ❏ *I don't know whether to hate or pity him.* ● **Pity** is also a noun. ❏ *He felt a sudden tender pity for her.* **2** → see also **self-pity** **3** N-SING If you say that it is a **pity** that something is true, you mean that you feel disappointment or regret about it. ❏ *It is a great pity that all students cannot have the same chances.* ❏ *It's a pity you arrived so late.* **4** PHRASE If you **take pity on** someone, you feel sorry for them and help them. ❏ *Nobody took pity on him.* [from Old French]

**piv|ot** /pɪvət/ (**pivots, pivoting, pivoted**) **1** N-COUNT The **pivot** in a situation is the most important thing that everything else is based on or arranged around. ❏ *This year's Senate race may pivot on one central question.* **2** V-I If something or someone **pivots**, they balance or turn on a central point. ❏ *The wheels pivot for easy turning.* ❏ *He pivoted on his heels and walked down the hall.* **3** N-COUNT A **pivot** is the pin or the central point on which something balances or turns. ❏ *…the pivot from which the ladder operates..* [from Old French]

**piv|ot|al** /pɪvətᵊl/ ADJ A **pivotal** role, point, or figure in something is one that is very important and affects the success of that thing. ❏ *The elections may be pivotal in Colombia's political history.* [from Old French]

**piz|za** /piːtsə/ (**pizzas**) N-VAR A **pizza** is a flat, round piece of dough covered with tomatoes, cheese, and other toppings, and then baked in an oven. ❏ *…the last piece of pizza.* [from Italian]

**pjs** /piːdʒeɪz/ also **pj's** N-PLURAL **Pjs** are the same as **pajamas**. [INFORMAL] ❏ *I work from home and live in my pjs most of the time.*

**pkg.** **Pkg.** is a written abbreviation for **package**.

**plac|ard** /plækɑrd, -kərd/ (**placards**) N-COUNT A **placard** is a large notice that is carried or displayed in a public place. ❏ *The protesters sang songs and waved placards.* [from Old French]

Word Link    *plac* ≈ *pleasing* : *complacent, placate, placid*

**pla|cate** /pleɪkeɪt/ (**placates, placating, placated**) V-T If you **placate** someone, you do or say something to make them stop feeling angry. [FORMAL] ❏ *He smiled, and made a gesture intended to placate me.* [from Latin]

**place**

❶ NOUN USES
❷ VERB USES
❸ PHRASES

❶ **place** /pleɪs/ (**places**) **1** N-COUNT A **place** is any point, building, area, town, or country. ❏ *…a list of museums and places of interest.* ❏ *We're going to a place called Plataro.* ❏ *The pain is always in the same place.* **2** N-SING **Place** can be used after "any," "no," "some," or "every" to mean "anywhere," "nowhere," "somewhere," or "everywhere." [INFORMAL] ❏ *The poor guy didn't have any place to go for Easter.* **3** N-COUNT You can refer to the position where something belongs, or where it is supposed to be, as its **place**. ❏ *He returned the album to its place on the shelf.* **4** N-COUNT A **place** is a seat or position that is available for someone to

occupy. □ *He sat at the nearest of two empty places.*
**5** N-COUNT Someone's or something's **place** in a society, system, or situation is their position in relation to other people or things. □ *...educating the children so they can take their place in adult society..*
**6** N-COUNT Your **place** in a race or competition is your position in relation to the other competitors. If you are in first place, you are ahead of all the other competitors. □ *He has risen to second place in the opinion polls.* **7** N-COUNT If you get a **place** on a team, on a committee, or in an institution, for example, you are accepted as a member of the team or committee or as a resident of the institution. □ *Derek has lost his place on the team.*
**8** N-COUNT Your **place** is the house or apartment where you live. [INFORMAL] □ *Let's all go back to my place!* [from Old French]
→ see **zero**

**❷ place** /pleɪs/ (**places, placing, placed**) **1** V-T If you **place** something somewhere, you put it in a particular position. □ *Brand placed the letter in his pocket.* **2** V-T You can use **place** instead of "put" or "lay" in certain expressions where the meaning is carried by the following noun. For example, if you **place emphasis** on something, you emphasize it, and if you **place the blame on** someone, you blame them. □ *He placed great importance on family life.* **3** V-T If you **place** someone or something in a particular class or group, you label or judge them in that way. □ *We are placed second among the state's most successful firms.* **4** V-T If you **place an order for** a product or **for** a meal, you ask for it to be sent or brought to you. □ *It is a good idea to place your order early.* **5** V-T If you **place an advertisement in** a newspaper, you arrange for the advertisement to appear in the newspaper. □ *They placed an advertisement in the paper for a secretary.* [from Old French]

**❸ place** /pleɪs/ (**places, placing, placed**) **1** PHRASE If you have been trying to understand something puzzling and then everything **falls into place** or **clicks into place**, you suddenly understand how different pieces of information are connected and everything becomes clearer. □ *When the reasons for the decision were explained, it all fell into place.* **2** PHRASE If things **fall into place**, events happen naturally to produce a situation you want. □ *Once the decision was made, things fell into place.* **3** PHRASE If something such as a law, a policy, or system is **in place**, it is working or able to be used. □ *A similar program is already in place in Utah.* **4** PHRASE If one thing or person is used or does something **in place of** another, they replace the other thing or person. □ *Cooked kidney beans can be used in place of green beans.* **5** PHRASE You say **in the first place** when you are talking about the beginning of a situation or about the situation as it was before a series of events. □ *What brought you here in the first place?* **6** PHRASE If you **put** someone **in their place**, you show them that they are less important or clever than they think they are. □ *In a few words she put him in his place.* **7** PHRASE When something **takes place**, it happens, especially in a controlled or organized way. □ *The discussions took place in Paris.* [from Old French]

**place|ment** /pleɪsmənt/ (**placements**) **1** N-UNCOUNT The **placement of** something is the act of putting it in a particular place. □ *...the placement of the rooms and elevators in the building.*

**2** N-UNCOUNT The **placement** of someone in a job, home, or school is the act or process of finding them a job, home, or school. □ *The children were waiting for placement with a family.* **3** N-COUNT If someone gets a **placement**, they get a job for a short period of time to gain experience. □ *...a six-month work placement with the government.* [from Old French]

**place|ment test** (**placement tests**) N-COUNT A **placement test** is a test given by a school to determine the academic or skill level of a student in order to place them in the correct class. □ *Students are required to take placement tests.*

**pla|cen|ta** /pləsɛntə/ (**placentas**) N-COUNT The **placenta** is the mass of veins and tissue inside the uterus of a pregnant woman or animal, which the unborn baby is attached to. [from Latin]

**pla|cen|tal mam|mal** /pləsɛntᵊl mæməl/ (**placental mammals**) N-COUNT A **placental mammal** is an animal that has a placenta. [TECHNICAL]

**Word Link**   *plac = pleasing : com*plac*ent, plac*ate, plac*id*

**plac|id** /plæsɪd/ ADJ A **placid** person or animal is calm and does not easily become excited, angry, or upset. □ *She was a placid child.* [from Latin]

**plague** /pleɪg/ (**plagues, plaguing, plagued**) **1** N-COUNT A **plague** is an infectious disease that spreads quickly and kills large numbers of people. □ *A cough or a sneeze could spread the plague.* **2** N-COUNT A **plague of** unpleasant things is a large number of them that arrive or happen at the same time. □ *...a plague of rats.* **3** V-T If you **are plagued by** unpleasant things, they continually cause you a lot of trouble or suffering. □ *She was plagued by weakness and dizziness.* [from Late Latin]

**plaice** /pleɪs/ (**plaice**) N-VAR A **plaice** is a type of flat sea fish. ● **Plaice** is this fish eaten as food. [from Old French]

**plain** /pleɪn/ (**plainer, plainest, plains**) **1** ADJ A **plain** object, surface, or fabric is entirely in one color and has no pattern, design, or writing on it. □ *A plain carpet makes a room look bigger.* **2** ADJ Something that is **plain** is very simple in style. □ *It was a plain, gray stone house.* ● **plain|ly** ADV □ *He was very tall and plainly dressed.* **3** ADJ If a fact, situation, or statement is **plain**, it is easy to recognize or understand. □ *It was plain to him what had to be done.* **4** ADJ If you describe someone as **plain**, you think they look ordinary and not at all beautiful. □ *...a shy, rather plain girl.* **5** N-COUNT A **plain** is a large flat area of land with very few trees on it. □ *Once there were 70 million buffalo on the plains.* [from Old French] **6 plain sailing** → see **sailing**

**Thesaurus**   *plain*   Also look up :

ADJ.   bare, modest, simple; (*ant.*) elaborate, fancy **1**
       common, everyday, modest, ordinary, simple, usual; (*ant.*) elaborate, fancy **2**
       clear, distinct, evident, transparent **3**

**Word Partnership**   Use *plain* with :

N.   plain **style 2**
     plain **English**, plain **language**, plain **speech**, plain **truth 3**

P

**plain|ly** /pleɪnli/ **1** ADV If something is **plainly** true, it is obviously true. ❑ *The judge's conclusion was plainly wrong.* ❑ *Plainly, the end was near.* **2** ADV You use **plainly** to indicate that something is easily seen, noticed, or recognized. ❑ *I could plainly see him turning his head.* [from Old French] **3** → see also **plain**

**plain|tiff** /pleɪntɪf/ (**plaintiffs**) N-COUNT A **plaintiff** is a person who brings a legal case against someone in a court of law. ❑ *The government was ordered to pay $83,000 to each plaintiff.* [from French] → see **trial**

**plain|tive** /pleɪntɪv/ ADJ A **plaintive** sound or voice sounds sad. [LITERARY] ❑ *...the plaintive cry of the seagulls.* [from Old French]

**plan** /plæn/ (**plans, planning, planned**) **1** N-COUNT A **plan** is a method of achieving something that you have worked out in detail beforehand. ❑ *He says that everything is going according to plan.* **2** V-T/V-I If you **plan** what you are going to do, you decide in detail what you are going to do. ❑ *Plan what you're going to eat.* ❑ *He plans to leave Baghdad on Monday.* **3** N-PLURAL If you have **plans**, you are intending to do a particular thing. ❑ *"I'm sorry," she said. "I have plans for tonight."* **4** N-COUNT A **plan of** something that is going to be built or made is a detailed diagram or drawing of it. ❑ *...a plan of the garden.* [from French] **5** → see also **planning**
▸ **plan on** PHR-VERB If you **plan on** doing something, you intend to do it. ❑ *They were planning on getting married.*

**plane** /pleɪn/ (**planes, planing, planed**) **1** N-COUNT A **plane** is a vehicle with wings and engines that can fly. ❑ *He had plenty of time to catch his plane.* **2** N-COUNT A **plane** is a flat, level surface that may be sloping at a particular angle. ❑ *...the angled plane of the propeller.* **3** N-COUNT A **plane** is a tool that has a flat bottom with a sharp blade in it, used for shaping and smoothing wood. **4** V-T If you **plane** a piece of wood, you make it smaller or smoother by using a plane. ❑ *He found his father planing wood in the shed.* [Senses 1 and 2 from Latin. Senses 3 and 4 from Old French.]

| Thesaurus | | *plane* | Also look up : |
| --- | --- | --- | --- |
| N. | aircraft, airplane, craft, jet **1** | | |
| | horizontal, level, surface **2** | | |

**plan|et** /plænɪt/ (**planets**) N-COUNT A **planet** is a large, round object in space that moves around a star. The Earth is a planet. ❑ *...the planets in the solar system.* [from French]
→ see **astronomer, galaxy, satellite, solar system**

**plan|etary** /plænɪteri/ ADJ **Planetary** means relating to or belonging to planets. ❑ *...planetary systems.* [from Old French]

**plan|etesi|mal** /plænɪtɛsɪməl/ (**planetesimals**) N-COUNT **Planetesimals** are small pieces of rock in space that combine to form planets. [TECHNICAL]

**plank** /plæŋk/ (**planks**) N-COUNT A **plank** is a long, flat, rectangular piece of wood. ❑ *...three solid planks of wood.* [from Old Norman French]

**plank|ton** /plæŋktən/ N-UNCOUNT **Plankton** is a mass of tiny animals and plants that live in the surface layer of the sea. [from German]

**plan|ner** /plænər/ (**planners**) N-COUNT **Planners** are people whose job is to make decisions

about what is going to be done in the future. ❑ *...city planners.* [from French]

**plan|ning** /plænɪŋ/ **1** N-UNCOUNT **Planning** is the process of deciding in detail how to do something before you actually start to do it. ❑ *The trip needs careful planning.* **2** → see also **family planning** **3** N-UNCOUNT **Planning** is control by the local government of the way that land is used in an area and of what new buildings are built there. ❑ *He is a town-planning expert.* [from French]

**plant** /plænt/ (**plants, planting, planted**) **1** N-COUNT A **plant** is a living thing that grows in the earth and has a stem, leaves, and roots. ❑ *Water each plant as often as required.* **2** V-T When you **plant** a seed, plant, or young tree, you put it into the ground so that it will grow. ❑ *He plans to plant fruit trees.* • **plant|ing** N-UNCOUNT ❑ *Bad weather has delayed planting.* **3** V-T When someone **plants** land, they put plants, seeds, or young trees into the land to grow. ❑ *We've been planting a vegetable garden.* **4** N-COUNT A **plant** is a factory or a place where power is produced. ❑ *...Ford's car assembly plants.* **5** N-UNCOUNT **Plant** is large machinery that is used in industrial processes. ❑ *The company is planning to invest in plant and equipment abroad.* **6** V-T If you **plant** something somewhere, you put it there firmly. ❑ *She planted her feet wide apart.* **7** V-T To **plant** a bomb means to hide it somewhere so that it explodes there. ❑ *So far no one has admitted planting the bomb.* **8** V-T If something such as a weapon or drugs is **planted** on someone, it is put among their possessions or in their house so that they will be wrongly accused of a crime. ❑ *Alexia says that she is innocent, and that the gun was planted.* [from Old English]
→ see Picture Dictionary: **plants**
→ see **earth, farm, food, herbivore, photosynthesis, tree**

**Plan|tae** /plænti/ N-PLURAL All the plants in the world can be referred to together as **Plantae.** [TECHNICAL] [from Latin]

**plan|ta|tion** /plænteɪʃən/ (**plantations**) **1** N-COUNT A **plantation** is a large piece of land, where crops such as rubber, tea, or sugar are grown. ❑ *...banana plantations in Costa Rica.* **2** N-COUNT A **plantation** is a large number of trees that have been planted together. ❑ *...a plantation of young trees.* [from Old English]

**plaque** /plæk/ (**plaques**) **1** N-COUNT A **plaque** is a flat piece of metal or stone with writing on it which is fixed to a wall or monument to remind people of a person or event. ❑ *A plaque was placed at the scene of the accident.* **2** N-UNCOUNT **Plaque** is a substance containing bacteria that forms on the surface of your teeth. ❑ *The main point of cleaning teeth is to remove plaque.* [from French]
→ see **teeth**

**plas|ma** /plæzmə/ (**plasmas**) **1** N-UNCOUNT **Plasma** is the clear liquid part of blood that contains the blood cells. **2** N-VAR A **plasma** is a very hot substance similar to a gas that contains electrically charged particles such as ions and electrons. **Plasma** is often considered to be a fourth state of matter because it is neither a solid nor a liquid nor a gas. [TECHNICAL] [from Late Latin]

**plas|ma screen** (**plasma screens**) also **plasma display** N-COUNT A **plasma screen** is a type of thin television screen or computer screen that produces high-quality images.

**Picture Dictionary: plants**

(deciduous) tree
crop
flower
(evergreen) tree / conifer
grass
weed
bush/shrub

**plas|ter** /plǽstər/ (plasters, plastering, plastered) **1** N-UNCOUNT **Plaster** is a smooth paste made of sand, lime, and water that dries and forms a hard layer. Plaster is used to cover walls and ceilings. □ *There were huge cracks in the plaster.* **2** V-T If you **plaster** a wall or ceiling, you cover it with a layer of plaster. □ *He has just plastered the ceiling.* [from Old English] **3** → see also **plastered**

**plas|tered** /plǽstərd/ **1** ADJ If something is **plastered to** a surface, it is sticking to the surface. □ *His hair was plastered down to his head.* **2** ADJ If a surface is **plastered with** something, it is covered with it. □ *My hands, boots, and pants were plastered with mud.* [from Old English]

**plas|tic** /plǽstɪk/ (plastics) N-VAR **Plastic** is a light but strong material produced by a chemical process. □ *...sheets of plastic.* □ *...the plastics that carmakers use.* [from Latin] → see **oil**

**plas|tic sur|gery** N-UNCOUNT **Plastic surgery** is the practice of performing operations to repair or replace skin that has been damaged, or to improve people's appearance. □ *She had plastic surgery to change the shape of her nose.*

**plas|tic wrap** N-UNCOUNT **Plastic wrap** is a thin, clear, stretchy plastic which you use to cover food to keep it fresh.

**plate** /pleɪt/ (plates) **1** N-COUNT A **plate** is a round or oval flat dish that is used to hold food. □ *Anita pushed her plate away.* □ *...a huge plate of bacon and eggs.* **2** N-COUNT A **plate** is a flat piece of metal, for example on part of a machine. □ *He has had a metal plate inserted into his broken jaw.* **3** N-PLURAL On a road vehicle, the **plates** are the panels on the front and back that display the license number. □ *...cars with New Jersey plates.* **4** → see also **license plate 5** N-COUNT A **plate** in a book is a picture or photograph that takes up a whole page. □ *The book has 55 color plates.* **6** N-COUNT In baseball, **the plate** is the same as the **home plate. 7** N-COUNT In geology, a **plate** is a large piece of the Earth's surface, perhaps as large as a continent, which moves very slowly. [TECHNICAL] [from Old French] → see **baseball, continent, dish, earthquake, rock**

**plat|eau** /plætoʊ/ (plateaus or plateaux) **1** N-COUNT A **plateau** is a large area of high and fairly flat land. □ *...a high, flat plateau of cultivated land.* **2** N-COUNT If an activity or process has reached a **plateau**, it is at a stage where there is no change or development. □ *Sales have now reached a plateau.* [from French]

**plate bound|a|ry** (plate boundaries) N-COUNT A **plate boundary** is a place on the Earth's surface where two or more tectonic plates meet. [TECHNICAL]

**plat|ed** /pleɪtɪd/ ADJ If something made of metal is **plated with** a thin layer of another type of metal, it is covered with it. □ *...a range of jewelry, plated with 22-carat gold.* [from Old French]

**plate|let** /pleɪtlɪt/ (platelets) N-COUNT **Platelets** are a kind of blood cell. If you cut yourself and you are bleeding, platelets help to stop the bleeding. [TECHNICAL] → see **cardiovascular system**

**plate tec|ton|ics** N-UNCOUNT **Plate tectonics** is the way that large pieces of the Earth's surface move slowly around. [TECHNICAL]

**plat|form** /plǽtfɔrm/ (platforms) **1** N-COUNT A **platform** is a flat raised structure or area on which someone or something can stand. □ *He walked toward the platform to begin his speech.* □ *They found a rocky platform where they could put up their tents.* **2** N-COUNT A **platform** in a train or subway station is the area beside the tracks where you wait for or get off a train. □ *The train was about to leave and I was not even on the platform.* **3** N-COUNT The **platform** of a political party is what they say they will do if they are elected. □ *...a platform of political and economic reforms.* [from French] → see **oil**

**plati|num** /plætɪnəm, plætnəm/ N-UNCOUNT **Platinum** is a very valuable, silvery-gray metal. [from New Latin]

**plati|tude** /plætɪtud/ (platitudes) N-COUNT A **platitude** is a statement that is considered meaningless because it has been made many times before in similar situations. □ *Why couldn't he say something original instead of just repeating the same old platitudes?* [from French]

P

**pla|ton|ic** /plətɒnɪk/ ADJ **Platonic** relationships or feelings of affection do not involve sex. ❑ *She values her platonic friendship with Chris.* [from Latin]

**plat|ter** /plætər/ (**platters**) ■ N-COUNT A **platter** is a large flat plate used for serving food. ❑ *The food was served on silver platters.* ② PHRASE If you say that someone has things **handed to** them **on a platter**, you disapprove of them because they get good things easily. ❑ *The job was handed to him on a platter.* [from Old French]
→ see **dish**

**plau|sible** /plɔzɪbªl/ ADJ An explanation or statement that is **plausible** seems likely to be true or valid. ❑ *This is a plausible explanation of what might have happened.* ● **plau|sibly** /plɔzɪbli/ ADV ❑ *Since he has gotten in without paying, he cannot plausibly demand his money back.* ● **plau|sibil|ity** /plɔzɪbɪlɪti/ N-UNCOUNT ❑ *...the plausibility of the theory.* [from Latin]

**play** /pleɪ/ (**plays, playing, played**) ■ V-I When children or animals **play**, they spend time doing enjoyable things, such as using toys and taking part in games. ❑ *They played in the little garden.* ❑ *Polly was playing with her dolls.* ● **Play** is also a noun. ❑ *I said they could have a few hours of play until the babysitter puts them to bed.* ② V-T When you **play** a sport, game, or match, you take part in it. ❑ *The twins played cards.* ❑ *I used to play basketball.* ● **Play** is also a noun. ❑ *This team has a more exciting style of play.* ③ V-T/V-I When one person or team **plays** another or **plays against** them, they compete against them in a sport or game. ❑ *Dallas will play Green Bay.* ④ V-T If you **play** a joke or a trick on someone, you deceive them or give them a surprise in a way that you think is funny, but may cause problems for them or annoy them. ❑ *Someone played a trick on her, and stretched a piece of string across the top of those steps.* ⑤ N-COUNT A **play** is a piece of writing performed in a theater, on the radio, or on television. ❑ *"Hamlet" is my favorite play.* ⑥ V-T If an actor **plays** a role or character in a play or movie, he or she performs the part of that character. ❑ *...a production of Dr. Jekyll and Mr. Hyde, in which he played Hyde.* ⑦ V-T/V-I If you **play** a musical instrument or **play** a tune on it, you produce music from it. ❑ *Nina was playing the piano.* ❑ *He played for me.* ⑧ V-T/V-I If you **play** a record, a CD, or a DVD, you put it into a machine, and sound and sometimes pictures are produced. ❑ *She played her CDs too loudly.* ❑ *There is classical music playing in the background.* ⑨ PHRASE If something or someone **plays a part** or **plays a role** in a situation, they are involved in it and have an effect on it. ❑ *It appears that the weather played a role in the crash.* ⑩ **to play ball** → see **ball** ⑪ **to play the fool** → see **fool** ⑫ **to play to the gallery** → see **gallery** ⑬ **to play hard to get** → see **hard** ⑭ **to play havoc** → see **havoc** ⑮ **to play host** → see **host** ⑯ **to play safe** → see **safe** [from Old English]
→ see **theater**

▸ **play around** ■ PHR-VERB If you **play around**, you behave in a silly way to amuse yourself or other people. [INFORMAL] ❑ *Stop playing around and eat!* ② PHR-VERB If you **play around with** a problem or an arrangement of objects, you try different ways of organizing it in order to find the best solution or arrangement. [INFORMAL] ❑ *I can play around with the pictures to make them more appealing.*

▸ **play at** ■ PHR-VERB If you say that someone **is playing at** something, you disapprove of the fact that they are doing it casually and not very seriously. ❑ *It was a terrible piece of work; now I see that I was just playing at being a writer.* ② PHR-VERB If you ask what someone **is playing at**, you are angry because you do not understand what they are doing or why they are doing it. [INFORMAL] ❑ *She began to wonder what he was playing at.*

▸ **play back** PHR-VERB When you **play back** a tape or film, you listen to the sounds or watch the pictures after recording them. ❑ *If you press this button, the machine plays back your messages.*

▸ **play down** PHR-VERB If you **play down** something, you try to make people believe that it is not particularly important. ❑ *Politicians have played down the significance of the reports.*

▸ **play on** PHR-VERB If you **play on** someone's fears, weaknesses, or faults, you deliberately use them in order to achieve what you want. ❑ *...new laws which play on the population's fear of change.*

**play-by-play** N-SING A **play-by-play** is a commentary on a sports game or other event that describes every part of it in great detail. ❑ *Gene Deckerhoff does radio play-by-play for Florida State.*

**play|er** /pleɪər/ (**players**) ■ N-COUNT A **player** in a sport or game is a person who takes part. ❑ *She was a good tennis player.* ② N-COUNT You can use **player** to refer to a musician. ❑ *...a professional trumpet player.* ③ N-COUNT If a person, country, or organization is a **player in** something, they are involved in it and important in it. ❑ *The company is a major player in the film world.* [from Old English] ④ → see also **CD player, record player**
→ see **chess, football, soccer**

**play|ful** /pleɪfəl/ ADJ A **playful** gesture or person is friendly or humorous. ❑ *...a playful kiss.* ❑ *...a playful fight.* ● **play|ful|ly** ADV ❑ *She pushed him away playfully.* ● **play|ful|ness** N-UNCOUNT ❑ *...the child's natural playfulness.* [from Old English]

**play|ground** /pleɪgraʊnd/ (**playgrounds**) N-COUNT A **playground** is a piece of land where children can play. ❑ *...a seven-year-old boy playing in a school playground.*
→ see **park**

**play|group** /pleɪgrup/ (**playgroups**) also **play group** N-COUNT A **playgroup** is an informal school for very young children, where they learn by playing.

**play|ing card** (**playing cards**) N-COUNT **Playing cards** are thin pieces of cardboard with numbers or pictures printed on them that are used to play games. ❑ *...a deck of playing cards.*

**play|ing field** (**playing fields**) ■ N-COUNT A **playing field** is a large area of grass where people play sports.

playing card

❑ *The town has three grass playing fields and 18 football teams.* ② PHRASE You talk about **a level playing field** to mean a situation that is fair, because no competitor or opponent in it has an advantage over another. ❑ *Students are not working on a level playing field: some have quiet homes, some do not.*

**play|off** /pleɪɔf/ (**playoffs**) ■ N-COUNT A

**playoff** is an extra game that is played to decide the winner of a sports competition when two or more people have the same score. ❑ *Nick Faldo was beaten by Peter Baker in a playoff.* ◻ N-COUNT You use **playoffs** to refer to a series of games that are played to decide the winner of a championship. ❑ *The two teams faced each other in the playoffs.*

**play|wright** /pleɪraɪt/ (**playwrights**) N-COUNT A **playwright** is a person who writes plays.
→ see **theater**

**pla|za** /plɑzə, plæzə/ (**plazas**) ◻ N-COUNT A **plaza** is an open square in a city. ❑ *Across the busy plaza, vendors sell hot dogs.* ◻ N-COUNT A **plaza** is a group of stores or buildings that are joined together or share common areas. ❑ *...a new retail plaza.* [from Spanish]

**plea** /pli/ (**pleas**) ◻ N-COUNT A **plea** is an appeal or request for something, made in an intense or emotional way. ❑ *...an emotional plea for help.* ◻ N-COUNT In a court of law, a person's **plea** is the answer that they give when they have been charged with a crime. ❑ *We will enter a plea of not guilty.* [from Old French]

**plead** /plid/ (**pleads, pleading, pleaded, pled**) ◻ V-I If you **plead with** someone to do something, you ask them in an intense, emotional way to do it. ❑ *The lady pleaded with her daughter to come back home.* ❑ *He was kneeling on the floor pleading for mercy.* ◻ V-I When someone charged with a crime **pleads guilty** or **not guilty** in a court of law, they officially state that they are guilty or not guilty of the crime. ❑ *Morris pleaded guilty to robbery.* ◻ V-T If you **plead the case** or **cause** of someone or something, you speak out in their support or defense. ❑ *He appeared before the committee to plead his case.* ◻ V-T If you **plead** a particular thing as the reason for doing or not doing something, you give it as your excuse. ❑ *Mr. Giles pleads ignorance as his excuse.* [from Old French]
→ see **trial**

**plead|ing** /plidɪŋ/ (**pleadings**) ◻ ADJ A **pleading** expression or gesture shows someone that you want something very much. ❑ *...his pleading eyes.* ◻ N-VAR **Pleading** is asking someone for something you want very much, in an intense or emotional way. ❑ *He simply ignored Sid's pleading.* [from Old French]

**pleas|ant** /plɛzªnt/ (**pleasanter, pleasantest**) ◻ ADJ Something that is **pleasant** is enjoyable or attractive. ❑ *I've got a pleasant little apartment.* ● **pleas|ant|ly** ADV ❑ *We talked pleasantly of old times.* ◻ ADJ Someone who is **pleasant** is friendly and likeable. ❑ *The woman had a pleasant face.* [from Old French]

| Thesaurus | *pleasant* | Also look up : |
| --- | --- | --- |

ADJ. agreeable, cheerful, delightful, likable, friendly, nice; (ant.) unpleasant ◻

**please** /pliz/ (**pleases, pleasing, pleased**) ◻ ADV You say **please** when you are politely asking or inviting someone to do something. ❑ *Can you help us, please?* ❑ *Please come in.* ❑ *Can we have the bill, please?* ◻ ADV You say **please** when you are accepting something politely. ❑ *"Tea?" — "Yes, please."* ◻ V-T/V-I If someone or something **pleases** you, they make you feel happy and satisfied. ❑ *More than anything, I want to please you.* ❑ *It pleased him to talk to her.* ❑ *He was anxious to please.*

◻ PHRASE You use **please** in expressions such as **as she pleases, whatever you please,** and **anything he pleases** to indicate that someone can do or have whatever they want. ❑ *Women should be free to dress as they please.* ❑ *He does whatever he pleases.* [from Old French]

**pleased** /plizd/ ◻ ADJ If you are **pleased**, you are happy about something or satisfied with something. ❑ *Felicity seemed pleased at the suggestion.* ❑ *I think he's going to be pleased that we solved the problem.* ❑ *I'm pleased with the way things have been going.* ❑ *I am very pleased about the result.* ◻ CONVENTION You can say **"Pleased to meet you"** as a polite way of greeting someone who you are meeting for the first time. [from Old French]

**pleas|ing** /plizɪŋ/ ADJ Something that is **pleasing** gives you pleasure and satisfaction. ❑ *This area of France has a pleasing climate.* ● **pleas|ing|ly** ADV ❑ *The design is pleasingly simple.* [from Old French]

**pleas|ur|able** /plɛʒərəbªl/ ADJ **Pleasurable** experiences or sensations are pleasant and enjoyable. ❑ *The most pleasurable experience of the evening was the fireworks display.* [from Old French]

**pleas|ure** /plɛʒər/ (**pleasures**) ◻ N-UNCOUNT If something gives you **pleasure**, you get a feeling of happiness, satisfaction, or enjoyment from it. ❑ *Watching sports gave him great pleasure.* ❑ *Everybody takes pleasure in eating.* ◻ N-UNCOUNT **Pleasure** is the activity of enjoying yourself, especially rather than working. ❑ *He mixes business and pleasure.* ◻ N-COUNT A **pleasure** is an activity or experience that you find enjoyable and satisfying. ❑ *Watching TV is our only pleasure.* ❑ *...the pleasure of seeing a smiling face.* ◻ CONVENTION You can say **"It's a pleasure"** or **"My pleasure"** as a polite way of replying to someone who has just thanked you for doing something. ❑ *"Thanks very much anyhow." — "It's a pleasure."* [from Old French]

**pleat** /plit/ (**pleats**) N-COUNT A **pleat** in a piece of clothing is a permanent fold made in the cloth. ❑ *Her skirt hangs in perfect wide pleats.*

**pleat|ed** /plitɪd/ ADJ A **pleated** piece of clothing has pleats in it. ❑ *...a short white pleated skirt.*

**pledge** /plɛdʒ/ (**pledges, pledging, pledged**) ◻ V-T When someone **pledges** to do something, they promise in a serious way to do it. When they **pledge** something, they promise to give it. ❑ *He pledged to support the group.* ❑ *The French president is pledging $150 million in aid next year.* ● **Pledge** is also a noun. ❑ *...a pledge to improve relations between the six states.* ◻ V-T If you **pledge yourself to** something, you commit yourself to following a particular course of action or to supporting a particular person, group, or idea. ❑ *The president pledged himself to protect the poor.* [from Old French]

| Word Link | *plen* ≈ full : plentiful, plenty, replenish |
| --- | --- |

**plen|ti|ful** /plɛntɪfəl/ ADJ Things that are **plentiful** exist in such large amounts or numbers that there is enough for people's wants or needs. ❑ *Fish are plentiful in the lake.* [from Old French]

**plen|ty** /plɛnti/ QUANT If there is **plenty of** something, there is a large amount of it, often more than is needed. ❑ *There was still plenty of time to take Jill out for pizza.* ❑ *Most businesses face plenty of competition.* ● **Plenty** is also a pronoun. ❑ *I don't*

p

*believe in long interviews. Fifteen minutes is plenty.*
[from Old French]

| **Thesaurus** | *plenty* | Also look up : |
|---|---|---|
| N. | abundance, capacity, quantity; *(ant.)* scarcity | |

**pli|ers** /ˈplaɪərz/ N-PLURAL **Pliers** are a tool with two handles at one end and two hard, flat, metal parts at the other. Pliers are used for holding or pulling out things such as nails, or for bending or cutting wire.
→ see **tools**

**plight** /plaɪt/ (**plights**) N-COUNT Someone's **plight** is the difficult or dangerous situation that they are in. ❑ ...*the plight of children living in war zones.* [from Old French]

**plod** /plɒd/ (**plods, plodding, plodded**) **1** V-I If someone **plods**, they walk slowly and heavily. ❑ *Crowds of people plodded around in plastic raincoats.* **2** V-I If you **plod on** or **plod along** with a job, you keep doing it, although it is taking a long time or is not progressing quickly. ❑ *He is plodding on with negotiations.*

**plot** /plɒt/ (**plots, plotting, plotted**) **1** V-T/V-I If people **plot to** do something or **plot** something illegal or wrong, they plan secretly to do it. ❑ *They plotted to overthrow the government.* ❑ ...*They were accused of plotting against the state.* ● **Plot** is also a noun. ❑ ...*a plot to pass secrets to the Russians.* ● **plot|ter** (**plotters**) N-COUNT ❑ *The plotters used the Internet to communicate.* **2** N-VAR The **plot** of a movie, novel, or play is the connected series of events which make up the story. ❑ *He told me the plot of his new book.* **3** N-COUNT A **plot** is a small piece of land, especially one that is intended for a purpose, such as building houses or growing vegetables. ❑ *I bought a small plot of land and built a house on it.* **4** V-T When people **plot** a strategy or a course of action, they carefully plan each step of it. ❑ *The aim of the meeting was to plot a strategy for the party.* **5** V-T When someone **plots** something on a graph, they mark certain points on it and then join the points up. ❑ *We plotted about eight points on the graph.* **6** V-T When someone **plots** the position or progress of something, they follow its position or progress and show it on a map or diagram. ❑ *We were trying to plot the course of the submarine.* [from Old English]

**plot|line** /ˈplɒtlaɪn/ (**plotlines**) N-COUNT The **plotline** of a book, movie, or play is its plot and the way in which it develops.

**plow** /plaʊ/ (**plows, plowing, plowed**)
**1** N-COUNT A **plow** is a large farming tool with sharp blades that is pulled across the soil to turn it over, usually before seeds are planted. **2** → see also **snowplow** **3** V-T When someone **plows** an area of land, they turn over the soil using a plow. ❑ *They were using horses to plow their fields.* [from Old English]

**plow**

→ see **barn**

**ploy** /plɔɪ/ (**ploys**) N-COUNT A **ploy** is a way of behaving that someone plans carefully and secretly in order to gain an advantage for themselves. ❑ *Christmas should be a time of*

*excitement and wonder, not a marketing ploy.* [from Scots]

**pluck** /plʌk/ (**plucks, plucking, plucked**) **1** V-T If you **pluck** a fruit, flower, or leaf, you take it between your fingers and pull it from its stalk. [WRITTEN] ❑ *I plucked a lemon from the tree.* **2** V-T If you **pluck** something from somewhere, you take it between your fingers and pull it sharply from where it is. [WRITTEN] ❑ *He quickly plucked the coin from Marlette's hand.* **3** V-T If you **pluck** a guitar or other musical instrument, you pull the strings with your fingers and let them go, so that they make a sound. ❑ *Nell was plucking a harp.* **4** V-T If you **pluck** a chicken or other dead bird, you pull its feathers out to prepare it for cooking. ❑ *She looked relaxed as she plucked a chicken.* **5** V-T If you **pluck** your **eyebrows**, you shape them by pulling out some of the hairs. ❑ *You've plucked your eyebrows!* **6** PHRASE If you **pluck up the courage** to do something, you make an effort to be brave enough to do it. ❑ *It took me two hours to pluck up the courage to call.* [from Old English]

**plug** /plʌg/ (**plugs, plugging, plugged**)
**1** N-COUNT A **plug** on a piece of electrical

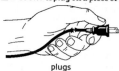

**plugs**

equipment is a small plastic object with two or three metal pins that fit into the holes of an electric outlet and connect the equipment to the electricity supply. ❑ *I used to go around and take every plug out at night.* **2** N-COUNT A **plug** is a thick, circular piece of rubber or plastic that you use to block the hole in a bathtub or sink when it is filled with water. ❑ *She put in the plug and filled the sink with cold water.* **3** V-T If you **plug** a hole or a leak, you block it with something.

❑ *Crews are working to plug a major oil leak.* **4** V-T If someone **plugs** a product such as a book or a movie, they talk about it in order to encourage people to buy it or see it. ❑ *Most people on the show are only interested in plugging a book or movie.* ● **Plug** is also a noun. ❑ *They managed to put in a plug for the store's new website.* **5** PHRASE If someone in a position of power **pulls the plug on** a project or on someone's activities, they use their power to stop them from continuing. ❑ *The banks have the power to pull the plug on the project.* [from Middle Dutch]
▶ **plug in** or **plug into** PHR-VERB If you **plug** a piece of electrical equipment **into** an electricity supply or if you **plug** it **in**, you push its plug into an electric outlet so that it can work. ❑ *They plugged in their tape-recorders.* ❑ *I had a TV set but there was no place to plug it in.*

**plugged** /plʌgd/ also **plugged up** ADJ If something is **plugged** or **plugged up**, it is completely blocked so that nothing can get through it. ❑ ...*a plugged toilet.* ❑ *His ears and nose were plugged up.* [from Middle Dutch]

**plum** /plʌm/ (**plums**) N-COUNT A **plum** is a small, sweet fruit with a smooth purple, red, or yellow skin and a pit in the middle. [from Old English]

**plumb|er** /plʌmər/ (**plumbers**) N-COUNT A **plumber** is a person whose job is to connect and repair things such as water and drainage pipes, bathtubs, and toilets. [from Old French]

**plumb|ing** /plʌmɪŋ/ **1** N-UNCOUNT The **plumbing** in a building consists of the water and drainage pipes, bathtubs, and toilets in it. ❑ *The entire building was in need of new plumbing.* **2** N-UNCOUNT **Plumbing** is the work of connecting and repairing water and drainage pipes, bathtubs, and toilets. ❑ *They run a small plumbing business.* [from Old French]

**plume** /plum/ (**plumes**) N-COUNT A **plume of** smoke, dust, fire, or water is a large quantity of it that rises into the air in a column. ❑ *...a plume of black smoke.* [from Old French]

**plum|met** /plʌmɪt/ (**plummets, plummeting, plummeted**) V-I If an amount, rate, or price **plummets**, it decreases quickly by a large amount. ❑ *The president's popularity plummeted to an all-time low.* [from Old French]

**plump** /plʌmp/ (**plumper, plumpest**) ADJ A **plump** person is somewhat fat. ❑ *Maria was small and plump.* [from Middle Dutch]

**plun|der** /plʌndər/ (**plunders, plundering, plundered**) V-T If someone **plunders** a place, they steal things from it. [LITERARY] ❑ *They plundered the palaces.* ● **Plunder** is also a noun. ❑ *...robbery and plunder.* [from Dutch]

**plunge** /plʌndʒ/ (**plunges, plunging, plunged**) **1** V-I If something or someone **plunges** in a particular direction, especially into water, they fall, rush, or throw themselves in that direction. ❑ *The bus plunged into a river.* **2** V-T If you **plunge** an object **into** something, you push it quickly or violently into it. ❑ *He plunged a fork into his dinner.* **3** V-T/V-I If a person or thing **is plunged into** a particular state or situation, or if they **plunge into** it, they are suddenly in that state or situation. ❑ *Reforms threaten to plunge the country into violence.* ❑ *...a country plunging into poverty.* **4** V-T/V-I If you **plunge into** an activity or **are plunged into** it, you suddenly get very involved in it. ❑ *The two men plunged into discussion.* **5** V-I If an amount or rate **plunges**, it decreases quickly and suddenly. ❑ *His weight began to plunge.* ● **Plunge** is also a noun. ❑ *...the stock market plunge.* **6** PHRASE If you **take the plunge**, you decide to do something that you consider difficult or risky. ❑ *She took the plunge and invited him back.* [from Old French]

**plunk** /plʌŋk/ (**plunks, plunking, plunked**) **1** V-T If you **plunk** something somewhere, you put it there without great care. [INFORMAL] ❑ *Melanie plunked her case down on a chair.* **2** V-I If you **plunk yourself** somewhere, or **plunk down**, you sit down heavily and clumsily. [INFORMAL] ❑ *I plunked down on one of the small chairs.*

**plu|ral** /plʊərəl/ (**plurals**) N-COUNT The **plural** of a noun is the form of it that is used to refer to more than one person or thing. ❑ *What is the plural of "person?"* ● **Plural** is also an adjective. ❑ *"Men" is the plural form of "man."* [from Old French]

**plu|ral|ism** /plʊərəlɪzəm/ N-UNCOUNT If there is **pluralism** within a society, it has many different groups and political parties. [FORMAL] ❑ *...as the country moves toward political pluralism.* [from Old French]

**plus** /plʌs/ (**pluses** or **plusses**) **1** CONJ You say **plus** to show that one number or quantity is being added to another. ❑ *...$5 for a small locker, plus a $3 deposit.* **2** ADJ **Plus** before a number or quantity means that the number or quantity is greater than zero. ❑ *...temperatures from minus 65 degrees to plus 120 degrees.* **3** CONJ You can use **plus** when mentioning an additional item or fact. [INFORMAL] ❑ *It's just the original story plus a lot of extra photographs.* **4** ADJ You use **plus** after a number or quantity to indicate that the actual number or quantity is greater than the one mentioned. ❑ *There are only 35 staff to serve 30,000-plus customers.* **5** ADJ Teachers use **plus** in grading work. "B plus" is a better grade than "B," but it is not as good as "A." **6** N-COUNT A **plus** is an advantage or benefit. [INFORMAL] ❑ *Experience in sales is a big plus.* [from Latin]

**plush** /plʌʃ/ (**plusher, plushest**) ADJ If you describe something as **plush**, you mean that it is very comfortable and expensive. ❑ *...their plush new training facility.* [from French]

**Pluto** /plutoʊ/ N-PROPER **Pluto** is the second largest dwarf planet in the Solar System. [from Latin]

**plu|to|nium** /plutoʊniəm/ N-UNCOUNT **Plutonium** is a radioactive element used especially in nuclear weapons and as a fuel in nuclear power stations.

**ply** /plaɪ/ (**plies, plying, plied**) V-T If you **ply** someone **with** food or drink, you keep giving them more of it. ❑ *Elsie plied me with food.* [from Old French]

**ply|wood** /plaɪwʊd/ N-UNCOUNT **Plywood** is wood that consists of thin layers of wood stuck together. ❑ *...a sheet of plywood.*

**p.m.** /pi ɛm/ also **pm** ADV **p.m.** is used after a number to show that you are referring to a particular time between 12 noon and 12 midnight. Compare **a.m.** ❑ *The pool is open from 7:00 a.m. to 9:00 p.m. every day.* [from Latin]

**pneu|mo|nia** /numoʊnyə, -moʊniə/ N-UNCOUNT **Pneumonia** is a serious disease that affects your lungs and makes it difficult for you to breathe. ❑ *She nearly died of pneumonia.* [from New Latin]

**poach** /poʊtʃ/ (**poaches, poaching, poached**) **1** V-T/V-I If someone **poaches**, or **poaches** fish, animals, or birds, they illegally catch them on someone else's property. ❑ *...a boy who poached rabbits.* ● **poach|er** (**poachers**) N-COUNT ❑ *We have security cameras to guard against poachers.* ● **poach|ing** N-UNCOUNT ❑ *...the poaching of elephants for their tusks.* **2** V-T If an organization **poaches** members or customers **from** another organization, they secretly or dishonestly persuade them to join them or become their customers. ❑ *Companies sometimes poach employees from one another.* ● **poach|ing** N-UNCOUNT ❑ *The union was accused of poaching.* **3** V-T If you **poach** food such as fish, you cook it gently in boiling water, milk, or other liquid. ❑ *Poach the chicken until it is just cooked.* [from Old French]

**pock|et** /pɒkɪt/ (**pockets, pocketing, pocketed**) **1** N-COUNT A **pocket** is a small bag or pouch that forms part of a piece of clothing. ❑ *...his jacket pocket.* **2** N-COUNT You can use

**pocket** in expressions that refer to money that people have, get, or spend. For example, if someone gives or pays a lot of money, you can say that they **dig deep into** their **pocket.** ❑ ...ladies' fashions to suit all shapes, sizes, and pockets. **3** ADJ You use **pocket** to describe something that is small enough to fit into a pocket. ❑ ...a pocket calculator. **4** V-T If someone **pockets** something that does not belong to them, they keep it or steal it. ❑ Banks have passed some of the savings on to customers and pocketed the rest. **5** PHRASE If you are **out of pocket,** you have less money than you should have or than you intended. ❑ Make sure you claim back the money; I don't want you to be out of pocket. [from Middle Dutch]

**pocket|book** /pɒkɪtbʊk/ (**pocketbooks**) N-COUNT A **pocketbook** is a small bag which a woman uses to carry things such as her money and keys.

**pock|et mon|ey** N-UNCOUNT **Pocket money** is money for buying small things that you want or need. ❑ They earned themselves a little pocket money by selling magazines.

**pod** /pɒd/ (**pods**) N-COUNT A **pod** is a seed container that grows on plants such as peas. ❑ ...fresh peas in the pod.

**pod|cast** /pɒdkæst/ (**podcasts**) N-COUNT A **podcast** is an audio file similar to a radio broadcast, that can be downloaded and listened to on a computer or **MP3 player.** ❑ There are thousands of new podcasts available every day.

**po|dium** /poʊdiəm/ (**podiums**) N-COUNT A **podium** is a small platform on which someone stands in order to give a lecture or conduct an orchestra. ❑ He stood on the podium and spoke into the microphone. [from Latin]

**poem** /poʊəm/ (**poems**) N-COUNT A **poem** is a piece of writing in which the words are chosen for their beauty and sound and are carefully arranged, often in short lines. ❑ ...a book of love poems. [from Latin]

**poet** /poʊɪt/ (**poets**) N-COUNT A **poet** is a person who writes poems. ❑ He was a painter and poet. [from Latin]

**po|et|ic** /poʊɛtɪk/ **1** ADJ Something that is **poetic** is very beautiful and expresses emotions in a sensitive or moving way. ❑ I think Italian is a very poetic language. **2** ADJ **Poetic** means relating to poetry. ❑ ...Keats' famous poetic lines. [from Latin]

**po|et|ic li|cense** N-UNCOUNT If someone such as a writer or movie director uses **poetic license,** they break the usual rules of language or style, or they change the facts, in order to create a particular effect. ❑ Memory takes a lot of poetic license: it leaves out some details and focuses on others.

**po|et|ry** /poʊɪtri/ N-UNCOUNT Poems, considered as a form of literature, are referred to as **poetry.** ❑ ...Russian poetry. [from Medieval Latin]
→ see **genre**

**poign|ant** /pɔɪnyənt/ ADJ Something that is **poignant** affects you deeply and makes you feel sadness or regret. ❑ Some of his new songs are very poignant. [from Old French]

---

**point**

❶ NOUN USES
❷ VERB USES
❸ PHRASES

**❶ point** /pɔɪnt/ (**points**) **1** N-COUNT A **point** is an opinion or fact expressed by someone. ❑ We disagree with every point she makes. **2** N-SING If you say that someone **has a point,** or if you **take** their **point,** you mean that you accept that what they have said should be considered. ❑ "You have a point there," Dave agreed. **3** N-SING **The point** of what you are saying or discussing is the most important part. ❑ "Did I ask you to talk to me?" — "That's not the point." ❑ He came to the point at once. "You did a splendid job." **4** N-SING If you ask what **the point** **of** something is, or say that there is **no point in** it, you are indicating that a particular action has no purpose or would not be useful. ❑ What was the point of thinking about him? **5** N-COUNT A **point** is an aspect or quality of something or someone. ❑ The most interesting point about the village was its religion. **6** N-COUNT A **point** is a particular position or time. ❑ The pain was coming from a point in his right thigh. ❑ We're all going to die at some point. **7** N-COUNT The **point** of something such as a needle or knife is the thin, sharp end of it. ❑ ...the point of a knife. **8** In spoken English, you use **point** to refer to the dot or mark in a decimal number that separates the whole numbers from the fractions. ❑ The earthquake measured five-point-two on the Richter scale. **9** N-COUNT In some sports and games, a **point** is one of the single marks that are added together to give the total score. ❑ Chamberlain scored 50 points in the match. **10** N-COUNT The **points of the compass** are directions such as North, South, East, and West. ❑ People came
to visit from all points of the compass. [from Old French] **11** → see also **breaking point, focal point, point of sale, vantage point**

| Thesaurus | point | Also look up : |
|---|---|---|
| N. | argument, gist, topic **❶** **3** | |
| | location, place, position, spot **❶** **6** | |

**❷ point** /pɔɪnt/ (**points, pointing, pointed**) **1** V-I If you **point at** a person or thing, you hold out your finger or an object toward them in order to make someone notice them. ❑ I pointed at the boy sitting nearest me. **2** V-T If you **point** something **at** someone, you aim the tip or end of it toward them. ❑ A man pointed a gun at them. **3** V-I If something **points to** a place or **points** in a particular direction, it shows where that place is or it faces in that direction. ❑ An arrow pointed to the restrooms. **4** V-I If something **points to** a particular situation, it suggests that the situation exists or is likely to occur. ❑ Earlier reports pointed to improved results. [from Old French] **5** → see also **pointed**

**❸ point** /pɔɪnt/ **1** PHRASE If you **make a point** **of** doing something, you do it in a deliberate or obvious way. ❑ She made a point of spending as much time as possible away from Oklahoma. **2** PHRASE If you are **on the point of** doing something, you are about to do it. ❑ He was on the point of saying something when the phone rang. **3** PHRASE If you say that something is true **up to a point,** you mean that it is partly but not completely true. □ *It worked up to a point.* [from Old French] **4 in point of fact →** see **fact 5 to point the finger at** someone **→** see **finger 6 a sore point →** see **sore** ▸ **point out 1** PHR-VERB If you **point out** an object or place to someone, you direct their attention to it. □ *Encourage your baby to lift his head by calling to him and pointing things out.* **2** PHR-VERB If you **point out** a fact or mistake, you tell someone about it. □ *I should point out that he was joking, of course.*

**point-blank 1** ADV If you say something **point-blank**, you say it very directly or rudely, without explaining or apologizing. □ *The army refused point blank to do what was required.* ● **Point-blank** is also an adjective. □ *...a point-blank question.* **2** ADV If someone or something is shot **point-blank**, they are shot when the gun is touching them or extremely close to them. □ *He fired point-blank at the target.* ● **Point-blank** is also an adjective. □ *He was shot at point-blank range.*

**point|ed** /ˈpɔɪntɪd/ **1** ADJ Something that is **pointed** has a point at one end. □ *...a pointed roof.* **2** ADJ **Pointed** comments or behavior express criticism in a clear and direct way. □ *...her mother's criticisms and pointed remarks.* ● **point|ed|ly** ADV □ *They were pointedly absent from the news conference.* [from Old French]

**point|er** /ˈpɔɪntər/ (**pointers**) N-COUNT A **pointer** is a piece of advice or information that helps you to understand a situation or solve a problem. □ *Here are a few pointers to help you make a choice.* [from Old French]

**point|less** /ˈpɔɪntlɪs/ ADJ Something that is **pointless** has no sense or purpose. □ *Violence is always pointless.* □ *Without an audience the performance is pointless.* ● **point|less|ly** ADV □ *The movie is pointlessly long, with a weak ending.* [from Old French]

**point of view** (**points of view**) **1** N-COUNT You can refer to the opinions that you have about something as your **point of view.** □ *Thanks for your point of view, John.* **2** N-COUNT If you consider something **from** a particular **point of view**, you use one aspect of a situation in order to judge it. □ *This is enormously important from the point of view of protecting citizens.* **3** N-COUNT The **point of view** of someone who is looking at a painting or other object is the angle or position from which they are viewing it.
**→** see **history**

**point-source pol|lu|tion** N-UNCOUNT **Point-source pollution** is pollution that comes from one particular source, for example from a particular factory. [TECHNICAL]

**poise** /ˈpɔɪz/ N-UNCOUNT If someone has **poise**, they are calm, dignified, and self-controlled. □ *What amazed him even more than her appearance was her poise.* [from Old French]

**poised** /ˈpɔɪzd/ **1** ADJ If a part of your body is **poised**, it is completely still but ready to move at any moment. □ *He studied the keyboard carefully, one finger poised.* **2** ADJ If someone is **poised** to do something, they are ready to take action at any moment. □ *Foster looked poised to win the match when he won the first game 6 – 2.* **3** ADJ If you are **poised**, you are calm, dignified, and self-controlled. □ *She was self-assured, poised.* [from Old French]

**poi|son** /ˈpɔɪzᵊn/ (**poisons, poisoning, poisoned**) **1** N-VAR **Poison** is a substance that harms or kills people or animals if they swallow it or absorb it. □ *Poison from the fish causes swelling and nausea.* **2** V-T To **poison** someone or something means to harm or damage them by giving them poison or putting poison into them. □ *...rumors that she had poisoned him.* □ *The land was poisoned by chemicals.* ● **poi|son|ing** N-UNCOUNT □ *...imprisonment for poisoning and attempted murder.* **3** V-T Something that **poisons** a good situation or relationship spoils it or destroys it. □ *The letter poisoned her relationship with her family forever.* [from Old French]

**poi|son oak** N-UNCOUNT **Poison oak** is a plant that causes a rash or skin problems if you touch it.

**poi|son|ous** /ˈpɔɪzᵊnəs/ **1** ADJ Something that is **poisonous** will kill you or harm you if you swallow or absorb it. □ *All parts of the yew tree are poisonous.* **2** ADJ An animal that is **poisonous** produces a poison that will kill you or make you ill if the animal bites you. □ *...poisonous spiders and snakes.* [from Old French]

**poke** /ˈpoʊk/ (**pokes, poking, poked**) **1** V-T If you **poke** someone or something, you quickly push them with your finger or with a sharp object. □ *Lindy poked him in the ribs.* ● **Poke** is also a noun. □ *John gave Richard a playful poke.* **2** V-T If you **poke** one thing **into** another, you push the first thing into the second thing. □ *He poked his finger into the hole.* **3** V-I If something **pokes out of** or **through** another thing, or if someone **pokes** it there, you can see part of it appearing from behind or underneath the other thing. □ *He saw the dog's nose poke out of the basket.* □ *Julie tapped on my door and poked her head in.* [from Low German and Middle Dutch] **4 to poke fun at →** see **fun 5 to poke** your **nose into** something **→** see **nose**

**pok|er** /ˈpoʊkər/ (**pokers**) N-UNCOUNT **Poker** is a card game, usually played in order to win money. □ *Lon and I play in the same weekly poker game.* [from French]

**po|lar** /ˈpoʊlər/ ADJ **Polar** means near the North Pole or South Pole. □ *...the polar regions.* [from Latin] **→** see **glacier**

**po|lar co|or|di|nate** (**polar coordinates**) N-COUNT **Polar coordinates** are a set of two numbers that are used in mathematics to describe the position of something by measuring its distance and angle from a particular point. [TECHNICAL]

**po|lar east|er|lies** N-PLURAL The **polar easterlies** are winds that blow from the north and south poles towards the equator. [TECHNICAL]

**po|lar equa|tion** (**polar equations**) N-COUNT A **polar equation** is a mathematical equation that uses polar coordinates. [TECHNICAL]

**po|lar|ize** /ˈpoʊləraɪz/ (**polarizes, polarizing, polarized**) V-T If something **polarizes** people, it causes them to form two separate groups with opposite opinions or positions. □ *The issue of free trade was polarizing the country.* ● **po|lari|za|tion** /ˌpoʊlərɪˈzeɪʃᵊn/ N-UNCOUNT □ *...the increasing polarization between the rich and the poor.* [from Latin]

**po|lar zone** (**polar zones**) N-COUNT The **polar zones** are the areas of the Earth around the north and south poles.

**pole** /ˈpoʊl/ (**poles**) **1** N-COUNT A **pole** is a long thin piece of wood or metal, used especially

for supporting things. □ *…a telephone pole.*
**2** N-COUNT The Earth's **poles** are the two opposite ends of its axis, its most northern and southern points. □ *For six months of the year, there is hardly any light at the poles.* [Sense 1 from Old English. Sense 2 from Latin.]

→ see **globe, magnet**

**po|lem|ic** /pəlɛmɪk/ (**polemics**) N-VAR A **polemic** is a very strong written or spoken attack on, or defense of, a particular belief or opinion. □ *…a polemic against the danger of secret societies.* [from Medieval Latin]

**po|lice** /pəliːs/ (**polices, policing, policed**)
**1** N-PLURAL The **police** are the official organization that is responsible for making sure that people obey the law. □ *The police are looking for the car.* □ *Police say they have arrested twenty people.*
**2** N-PLURAL **Police** are men and women who are members of the police. □ *More than one hundred police are in the area.* **3** V-T To **police** an area, event, or activity means to make sure that the law or rules are followed within it. □ *…It is difficult to police the border effectively.* [from French] **4** → see also **secret police**

**po|lice de|part|ment** (**police departments**)
N-COUNT A **police department** is an official organization which is responsible for making sure that people obey the law. □ *…the Los Angeles Police Department.*

**po|lice force** (**police forces**) N-COUNT A **police force** is the police organization in a particular country or area. □ *…the Wichita police force.*

**police|man** /pəliːsmən/ (**policemen**) N-COUNT A **policeman** is a man who is a member of the police force.

**po|lice of|fic|er** (**police officers**) N-COUNT A **police officer** is a member of the police force. □ *…a meeting of senior police officers.*

**po|lice sta|tion** (**police stations**) N-COUNT A **police station** is the local office of a police force in a particular area. □ *Two police officers arrested him and took him to Gettysburg police station.*

**police|woman** /pəliːswʊmən/ (**policewomen**)
N-COUNT A **policewoman** is a woman who is a member of the police force.

**poli|cy** /pɒlɪsi/ (**policies**) **1** N-VAR A **policy** is a set of ideas or plans that is used as a basis for making decisions, especially in politics, economics, or business. □ *…changes in foreign policy.* □ *…the government's policy on housing.*
**2** N-COUNT An insurance **policy** is a document that shows an agreement that you have made with an insurance company. [BUSINESS] □ *…car insurance policies.* [from Old French]

**po|lio** /poʊlioʊ/ N-UNCOUNT **Polio** is a serious infectious disease that can cause paralysis. □ *Their first child died of polio at the age of 3.*

→ see **hospital**

**pol|ish** /pɒlɪʃ/ (**polishes, polishing, polished**)

**1** N-VAR **Polish** is a substance that you put on the surface of an object in order to clean it, protect it, and make it shine. □ *…furniture polish.* **2** V-T If you **polish** something, you put polish on it or rub

polish

it with a cloth to make it shine. □ *He polished his shoes.* ● **pol|ished** ADJ □ *…a highly polished floor.*
**3** N-UNCOUNT If you say that a performance or piece of work has **polish**, you mean that it is of a very high standard. □ *The opera lacks the polish of his later work.* ● **pol|ished** ADJ □ *…a very polished performance.* **4** V-T If you **polish** your technique, performance, or skill at doing something, you work on improving it. □ *They need to polish their technique.* ● **Polish up** means the same as **polish**. □ *Polish up your writing skills.* [from Old French]

**po|lite** /pəlaɪt/ (**politer, politest**) ADJ A **polite** person has good manners and is not rude to other people. □ *…a quiet and very polite young man.*
● **po|lite|ly** ADV □ *"Your home is beautiful," I said politely.* ● **po|lite|ness** N-UNCOUNT □ *She listened to him, but only out of politeness.* [from Latin]

**po|liti|cal** /pəlɪtɪkəl/ **1** ADJ **Political** means relating to the way power is achieved and used in a country or society. □ *All other political parties there have been completely banned.* ● **po|liti|cal|ly** /pəlɪtɪkli/ ADV □ *The news was politically damaging for the Republicans.* **2** ADJ Someone who is **political** is interested in politics and holds strong beliefs about it. □ *I'm not political, I take no interest in politics.* [from Old French]

→ see **philosophy, empire**

**po|liti|cal ac|tion com|mit|tee** (**political action committees**) N-COUNT A **political action committee** is an organization which campaigns for particular political policies, and that gives money to political parties or candidates who support those policies. The abbreviation **PAC** is also used.

**poli|ti|cian** /pɒlɪtɪʃən/ (**politicians**) N-COUNT A **politician** is a person whose job is in politics, especially a member of the government. □ *They have arrested a number of politicians.* [from Old French]

**poli|tics** /pɒlɪtɪks/ **1** N-UNCOUNT **Politics** is the actions or activities concerned with achieving and using power in a country or organization. □ *He was involved in local politics.* **2** N-PLURAL Your **politics** are your beliefs about how a country ought to be governed. □ *His politics are extreme and often confused.* [from Old French]

**poll** /poʊl/ (**polls**) **1** N-COUNT A **poll** is a survey in which people are asked their opinions about something. □ *Polls show that 70% of the time it is women who decide which movie to see on a date.*
**2** → see **opinion poll** **3** N-PLURAL The **polls** means an election for a country's government, or the place where people go to vote in an election. □ *Voters go to the polls on Sunday to elect a new president.* [from Middle Low German] **4** → see also **polling**

→ see **election, vote**

**pol|len** /pɒlən/ (**pollens**) N-VAR **Pollen** is a powder produced by flowers that fertilizes other flowers. [from Latin]

**pol|li|nate** /pɒlmeɪt/ (**pollinates, pollinating, pollinated**) v-t To **pollinate** a plant or tree means to fertilize it with pollen. This is often done by insects. ❏ *Many of the indigenous insects are needed to pollinate the local plants.* ● **pol|li|na|tion** /pɒlɪneɪʃᵊn/ N-UNCOUNT ❏ *Without sufficient pollination, the growth of the corn is stunted.* [from Latin]

**poll|ing** /poʊlɪŋ/ N-UNCOUNT **Polling** is the act of voting in an election. ❏ *There has been a busy start to polling in today's local elections.* [from Middle Low German]

**poll|ing place** (**polling places**) N-COUNT A **polling place** is a place where people go to vote in an election. ❏ *Voters were lining up at polling places as early as 6:00 this morning.*

**pol|lu|tant** /pəlutᵊnt/ N-VAR **Pollutants** are substances that pollute the environment, especially poisonous chemicals produced as waste by vehicles and by industry. [from Latin]
→ see **ozone**

**pol|lute** /pəlut/ (**pollutes, polluting, polluted**) v-t To **pollute** water, air, or land means to make it dirty and dangerous to live in or to use, especially with poisonous chemicals or sewage. ❏ *Industry pollutes our rivers with chemicals.* ● **pol|lut|ed** ADJ ❏ *...the polluted river.* [from Latin]

**pol|lu|tion** /pəluʃᵊn/ **1** N-UNCOUNT **Pollution** is the process of polluting water, air, or land. ❏ *...measures to stop pollution of the air, sea, rivers, and soil.* **2** N-UNCOUNT **Pollution** is poisonous substances that are polluting water, air, or land. ❏ *The level of pollution in the river was falling.* [from Latin]
→ see Word Web: **pollution**
→ see **air, factory, solar**

**polo** /poʊloʊ/ N-UNCOUNT **Polo** is a ball game played between two teams of players riding on horses. [from Tibetan]

**poly|es|ter** /pɒliɛstər/ (**polyesters**) N-UNCOUNT **Polyester** is a type of synthetic cloth used especially to make clothes. ❏ *...a green polyester shirt.*
→ see **petroleum**

**poly|no|mial** /pɒlɪnoʊmiəl/ (**polynomials**) N-COUNT A **polynomial** is an expression in algebra that is the sum of several terms. Compare **binomial, monomial.** [TECHNICAL] ● **Polynomial** is also an adjective. ADJ ❏ *...a polynomial expression*

**pol|yp** /pɒlɪp/ (**polyps**) N-COUNT A **polyp** is a small animal that lives in the sea. It has a hollow body like a tube and long parts called tentacles around its mouth. [from French]

**pom|mel horse** (**pommel horses**) N-COUNT A **pommel horse** is a tall piece of gymnastic equipment for jumping over.

**pomp** /pɒmp/ N-UNCOUNT **Pomp** is the use of a lot of fine clothes, decorations, and formal words or actions. ❏ *I hate all this pomp and ceremony.* [from Old French]

**pomp|ous** /pɒmpəs/ ADJ If you describe someone as **pompous**, you disapprove of the fact that they speak or behave in a very serious way that suggests that they think they are very important. ❏ *He was rather pompous and had a high opinion of himself.* ● **pom|pos|ity** /pɒmpɒsɪti/ N-UNCOUNT ❏ *She hated pomposity and did not like talking about her achievements.* ● **pomp|ous|ly** ADV ❏ *Robin told me pompously that he had an important business appointment.* [from Old French]

**pond** /pɒnd/ (**ponds**) N-COUNT A **pond** is a small, usually artificially made, area of water. ❏ *We sat on a bench beside the duck pond.*

**pon|der** /pɒndər/ (**ponders, pondering, pondered**) v-t If you **ponder** something, you think about it carefully. ❏ *I found myself constantly pondering the question.* [from Old French]

**pon|der|ous** /pɒndərəs/ ADJ **Ponderous** writing or speech is very serious and dull. ❏ *He had a heavy, ponderous style.* [from Latin]

**pony** /poʊni/ (**ponies, ponying, ponied**) N-COUNT A **pony** is a small or young horse. [from Scottish]
▸ **pony up** PHR-VERB If you **pony up** a sum of money, you pay the money that is needed for something, often unwillingly. [INFORMAL] ❏ *They are not prepared to pony up the $4 billion that we need.*

**pony|tail** /poʊniteɪl/ (**ponytails**) N-COUNT A **ponytail** is a hairstyle in which your hair is tied up at the back of your head and hangs down like a tail. ❏ *Her long, fine hair was tied back in a ponytail.*
→ see **hair**

**poo|dle** /pudᵊl/ (**poodles**) N-COUNT A **poodle** is a type of dog with thick curly hair. [from German]

**pool** /pul/ (**pools, pooling, pooled**) **1** N-COUNT A **pool** is the same as a **swimming pool.** ❏ *...a heated indoor pool.* **2** N-COUNT A **pool** is a small area of still water. ❏ *The pool has dried up.* **3** N-COUNT A **pool of** liquid or light is a small area of it. ❏ *...the pool of light cast from his desk lamp.* **4** N-COUNT A **pool of** people, money, or things is a quantity or number of them that is available for use. ❏ *The population is quite small and the available pool of talent is limited.* **5** → see also **carpool** **6** v-t If people **pool** their money, knowledge, or equipment, they share it or put it together so that it can be used for a particular purpose. ❏ *We pooled*

**Word Web** pollution

**Pollution** affects the whole **environment. Airborne emissions** from factories and car **exhaust** cause air pollution. These smoky **emissions** combine with fog and make **smog.** Pollutants in the air can travel long distances. **Acid rain** caused by factories in the Midwest falls on states to the east. There it damages trees and kills fish in lakes. Chemicals from factories, **sewage,** and **garbage** pollute the water and land in many areas. Too many **pesticides** and **fertilizers** make the problem worse. These chemicals build up in the soil and poison the earth.

*ideas and information.* ◼ N-UNCOUNT **Pool** is a game played on a special table. Players use a long stick called a cue to hit a white ball so that it knocks colored balls into six holes around the edge of the table. [Senses 1–3 from Old English. Senses 4–7 from French.]

**pool hall** (**pool halls**) N-COUNT A **pool hall** is a building where you can play pool.

**pooped** /pupt/ ADJ If you are **pooped**, you are very tired. [INFORMAL]

**poor** /pʊər/ (**poorer, poorest**) ◼ ADJ Someone who is **poor** has very little money and few possessions. ❑ *"We were very poor in those days," he says.* ● **The poor** are people who are poor. ❑ *...huge differences between the rich and the poor.* ◻ ADJ A **poor** country or area is inhabited by people who are poor. ❑ *The country is poor, and many people are unemployed.* ◻ ADJ You use **poor** to express your sympathy for someone. ❑ *I feel sorry for that poor child.* ◻ ADJ If you describe something as **poor**, you mean that it is of a low quality or standard. ❑ *...the poor state of the economy.* ● **poor|ly** ADV ❑ *They are living in poorly built apartments.* ◻ ADJ If you describe an amount, rate, or number as **poor**, you mean that it is less than expected or less than is considered reasonable. ❑ *...poor wages and working conditions.* ● **poor|ly** ADV ❑ *The evening meetings were poorly attended.* ◻ ADJ You use **poor** to describe someone who is not very skillful in a particular activity. ❑ *He was a poor actor.* ● **poor|ly** ADV ❑ *"We played poorly in the first game," Mendez said.* ◻ ADJ If something is **poor in** a particular quality or substance, it contains very little of the quality or substance. ❑ *Fat and sugar are very rich in energy, but poor in vitamins.* [from Old French]

| **Thesaurus** | *poor* | Also look up : |
|---|---|---|
| ADJ. | impoverished, penniless; *(ant.)* rich, wealthy ◼ ◻ inferior ◻ | |

**pop** /pɒp/ (**pops, popping, popped**)
◼ N-UNCOUNT **Pop** is modern music that usually has a strong rhythm and uses electronic equipment. ❑ *...the perfect combination of Caribbean rhythms and European pop.* ❑ *...a poster of a pop star.* ◻ V-I If something **pops**, it makes a short sharp sound. ❑ *He heard a balloon pop behind his head.* ● **Pop** is also a noun. ❑ *Each corn kernel will make a loud pop when cooked.* ◻ V-I If your eyes **pop**, you look very surprised or excited when you see something. [INFORMAL] ❑ *My eyes popped at the sight of the food.* ◻ V-T If you **pop** something somewhere, you put it there quickly. [INFORMAL] ❑ *He popped some gum into his mouth.* ◻ N-COUNT Some people call their father **pop**. [INFORMAL] ❑ *I looked at Pop and he had big tears in his eyes.*
▸ **pop off** PHR-VERB If someone **pops off**, they say or write something very angrily or in a very emotional way. [INFORMAL] ❑ *He made the mistake of popping off about his boss to one of his colleagues.*
▸ **pop up** PHR-VERB If someone or something **pops up**, they appear in a place or situation unexpectedly. [INFORMAL] ❑ *She was startled when Lisa popped up.*

**pop|corn** /pɒpkɔrn/ N-UNCOUNT **Popcorn** is a snack that consists of grains of corn that have been heated until they have burst and become large and light.

**pop|over** /pɒpoʊvər/ (**popovers**) N-COUNT A **popover** is a light, hollow muffin. ❑ *...blueberry popovers.*

**pop|per** /pɒpər/ N-COUNT A **popper** is a pan or basket that you use when making popcorn. [from Old English]

**pop|py** /pɒpi/ (**poppies**) N-COUNT A **poppy** is a plant with a large, delicate, red flower. ❑ *...a field of poppies.* [from Old English]

| **Word Link** | popul ≈ people : *popul*ace, *popul*ar, *popul*ation |
|---|---|

**popu|lace** /pɒpyələs/ N-UNCOUNT The **populace** of a country is its people. [FORMAL] ❑ *...a large section of the populace.* [from French]

**popu|lar** /pɒpyələr/ ◼ ADJ Something or someone that is **popular** is liked by a lot of people. ❑ *He was the most popular politician in Arkansas.* ❑ *Chocolate sauce is always popular with youngsters.* ● **popu|lar|ity** /pɒpyəlærɪti/ N-UNCOUNT ❑ *...the growing popularity of Polish sausage among consumers.* ❑ *...his popularity with ordinary people.* ◻ ADJ **Popular** newspapers, television programs, or forms of art are aimed at ordinary people and not at experts or intellectuals. ❑ *...the popular press in Britain.* ❑ *...one of the classics of modern popular music.* ◻ ADJ **Popular** ideas or attitudes are approved of or held by most people. ❑ *...the popular belief that unemployment causes crime.* ● **popu|lar|ity** N-UNCOUNT ❑ *Over time, Watson's views gained in popularity.* ◻ ADJ **Popular** is used to describe political activities that involve the ordinary people of a country. ❑ *The government is trying to build popular support for military action.* [from Latin]
→ see **genre**

**Word Partnership** Use *popular* with :

| ADV. | **extremely** popular, **increasingly** popular, **most** popular, **wildly** popular ◼ |
|---|---|
| N. | popular **movie**, popular **restaurant**, popular **show**, popular **song** ◼ popular **magazine**, popular **novel** ◼ ◻ popular **culture**, popular **music** ◻ |

**popu|lar|ize** /pɒpyələraɪz/ (**popularizes, popularizing, popularized**) V-T To **popularize** something means to make a lot of people interested in it and able to enjoy it. ❑ *Irving Brokaw popularized the sport of figure skating in the U.S.* ● **popu|lari|za|tion** /pɒpyʊlərɪzeɪʃⁿn/ N-UNCOUNT ❑ *...the popularization of sports through television.* [from Latin]

**popu|lar|ly** /pɒpyələrli/ ◼ ADV If something or someone is **popularly** known as something, most people call them that, although it is not their official name or title. ❑ *...an infection popularly called mad cow disease.* ◻ ADV If something is **popularly** believed or supposed to be the case, most people believe or suppose it to be the case, although it may not be true. ❑ *His mother was popularly believed to be a witch.* [from Latin]

**popu|late** /pɒpyəleɪt/ (**populates, populating, populated**) V-T If an area is **populated by** certain people or animals, those people or animals live there, often in large numbers. ❑ *The island was originally populated by native American Arawaks.*

• **popu|lat|ed** ADJ ❑ *The southeast is the most densely populated area.* [from Medieval Latin]

**Word Link** *popul ≈ people : populace, popular, population*

**popu|la|tion** /pɒpyəleɪʃᵊn/ (**populations**) **1** N-COUNT The **population** of a country or area is all the people who live in it. ❑ *Bangladesh now has a population of about 110 million.* ❑ *...the annual rate of population growth.* **2** N-COUNT If you refer to a particular type of **population** in a country or area, you are referring to all the people or animals of that type there. [FORMAL] ❑ *...75.6 percent of the male population.* [from Medieval Latin]
→ see **country**

**porce|lain** /pɔrsəlɪn, pɔrslɪn/ N-UNCOUNT **Porcelain** is a hard, shiny substance made by heating clay. It is used to make cups, plates, and ornaments. ❑ *...tall white porcelain vases.* [from French]
→ see **pottery**

**porch** /pɔrtʃ/ (**porches**) N-COUNT A **porch** is a raised platform built along the outside wall of a house and often covered with a roof. ❑ *He was standing on the porch, waving as we drove away.* [from French]

porch

**pore** /pɔr/ (**pores, poring, pored**) **1** N-COUNT Your **pores** are the tiny holes in your skin. ❑ *Use hot water to clear blocked pores.* **2** V-I If you **pore over** or **through** information, you look at it and study it very carefully. ❑ *We spent hours poring over travel brochures.* [Sense 1 from Late Latin. Sense 2 from Flemish.]

**pork** /pɔrk/ N-UNCOUNT **Pork** is meat from a pig, usually fresh and not smoked or salted. ❑ *...fried pork chops.* [from Old French]
→ see **meat**

**pork bar|rel** also **pork-barrel** N-SING If you say that someone is using **pork barrel** politics, you disapprove of the fact that they are spending a lot of government money on a local project in order to win the votes of the people who live in that area. ❑ *...useless billion dollar pork barrel projects.*

**po|ros|ity** /pɔrɒsɪti/ N-UNCOUNT **Porosity** is the amount of open space between individual rock particles. [from Medieval Latin]

**po|rous** /pɔrəs/ ADJ Something that is **porous** has many small holes in it that water and air can pass through. ❑ *...a porous material like sand.* [from Medieval Latin]
→ see **pottery**

**port** /pɔrt/ (**ports**) **1** N-COUNT A **port** is a town or a harbor area where ships load and unload goods or passengers. ❑ *...the Mediterranean port of Marseilles.* **2** N-COUNT A **port** on a computer is a place where you can attach another piece of equipment such as a printer. [COMPUTING] ❑ *The scanner plugs into the printer port of your computer.* **3** ADJ The **port** side of a ship is the left side when you are on it and facing toward the front. [TECHNICAL] • **Port** is also a noun. ❑ *The ship turned to port.* **4** N-VAR **Port** is a type of strong, sweet red wine. ❑ *...a glass of port.* [Senses 1 and 2 from Old English. Sense 4 after Oporto, a city in Portugal.]
→ see **ship**

**Word Link** *able ≈ able to be : acceptable, incurable, portable*

**Word Link** *port ≈ carrying : export, import, portable*

**port|able** /pɔrtəbᵊl/ (**portables**) **1** ADJ A **portable** machine or device is designed to be easily carried or moved. ❑ *...a little portable television.* **2** N-COUNT A **portable** is something such as a television, radio, or computer that can be easily carried or moved. ❑ *We bought a portable for the bedroom.* [from Late Latin]

**por|ter** /pɔrtər/ (**porters**) N-COUNT A **porter** is a person whose job is to carry things, for example, people's luggage at a train station or in a hotel. ❑ *Our taxi arrived at the station and a porter came to the door.* [from Old French]

**port|fo|lio** /pɔrtfoʊlioʊ/ (**portfolios**) **1** N-COUNT A **portfolio** is a set of pictures or photographs of someone's work, which they show when they are trying to get a job. ❑ *Edith showed them a portfolio of her drawings.* **2** N-COUNT A **portfolio** is an organized collection of student work. [from Italian]

**por|tion** /pɔrʃᵊn/ (**portions**) **1** N-COUNT A **portion of** something is a part of it. ❑ *Only a small portion of the castle was damaged.* ❑ *I have spent a large portion of my life here.* **2** N-COUNT A **portion** is the amount of food that is given to one person at a meal. ❑ *The portions were generous.* [from Old French]

**por|trait** /pɔrtrɪt, -treɪt/ (**portraits**) N-COUNT A **portrait** is a painting, drawing, or photograph of a particular person. ❑ *...family portraits.* [from Old French]
→ see **painting**

**por|tray** /pɔrtreɪ/ (**portrays, portraying, portrayed**) **1** V-T When an actor or actress **portrays** someone, he or she plays that person in a play or movie. ❑ *He portrayed the king in "Camelot."* **2** V-T To **portray** someone or something means to represent them, for example in a book or movie. ❑ *The film portrays a group of young people who live in lower Manhattan.* [from Old French]

**por|tray|al** /pɔrtreɪəl/ (**portrayals**) N-COUNT A **portrayal of** someone or something is a representation of them in a book, movie, or play. ❑ *...his portrayal of a prison officer in the film "The Last Emperor."* ❑ *...a truthful portrayal of family life.* [from Old French]

**pose** /poʊz/ (**poses, posing, posed**) **1** V-T If something **poses** a problem or a danger, it is the cause of that problem or danger. ❑ *New shopping malls pose a threat to independent stores.* **2** V-T If you **pose** a question, you ask it. [FORMAL] ❑ *I finally posed the question, "Why?"* **3** V-I If you **pose as** someone, you pretend to be that person in order to deceive people. ❑ *...people employed to pose as customers.* **4** V-I If you **pose for** a photograph or painting, you stay in a particular position so that someone can photograph you or paint you. ❑ *The six foreign ministers posed for photographs.* **5** N-COUNT A **pose** is a particular position that you stay in when you are being photographed or painted. ❑ *We tried various poses.* [from Old French]

**posh** /pɒʃ/ (**posher, poshest**) **1** ADJ If you describe something as **posh**, you mean that it is elegant, fashionable, and expensive. [INFORMAL] □ …*a posh hotel.* **2** [from British slang]

**po|si|tion** /pəzɪʃ*ə*n/ (**positions, positioning, positioned**) **1** N-COUNT The **position** of someone or something is the place where they are in relation to other things. □ …*a device for planning your route and locating your position.* **2** N-COUNT When someone or something is in a particular **position**, they are sitting, lying, or arranged in that way. □ *Mr. Dambar raised himself to a sitting position.* **3** V-T If you **position** something somewhere, you put it there carefully, so that it is in the right place or position. □ *Position the table in an open area where a cat can't jump onto it.* **4** N-COUNT Your **position** in society is the role and the importance that you have in it. □ …*their changing role and position in society.* **5** N-COUNT A **position** in a company or organization is a job. [FORMAL] □ *He left a career in teaching to take a position with IBM.* **6** N-COUNT Your **position** in a race or competition is how well you did in relation to the other competitors or how well you are doing. □ *The car was running in eighth position.* **7** N-COUNT You can describe your situation at a particular time by saying that you are in a particular **position**. □ *He's going to be in a very difficult position if things go badly.* □ *The club's financial position is still uncertain.* **8** N-COUNT Your **position on** a particular matter is your attitude toward it or your opinion of it. [FORMAL] □ *What is your position on this issue?* **9** N-SING If you are **in a position to** do something, you are able to do it. □ *I am not in a position to comment.* [from Late Latin]
→ see **navigation**

**posi|tive** /pɒzɪtɪv/ **1** ADJ If you are **positive**, you are hopeful and confident, and think of the good aspects of a situation rather than the bad ones. □ *Be positive about your future.* ● **posi|tive|ly** ADV □ *You really must try to start thinking positively.* **2** ADJ A **positive** situation or experience is pleasant and helpful to you in some way. □ *I've got two grandchildren now, and I want to have a positive effect on their lives.* ● **The positive** in a situation is the good and pleasant aspects of it. □ *He prefers to focus on the positive.* **3** ADJ If you make a **positive** decision or take **positive** action, you do something definite in order to deal with a task or problem. □ *I wanted to do something positive and creative, for myself and the country.* **4** ADJ A **positive** response to something indicates agreement, approval, or encouragement. □ *There's been a positive response to the UN's recent peace efforts.* ● **posi|tive|ly** ADV □ *He responded positively and accepted the idea.* **5** ADJ If you are **positive** about something, you are completely sure about it. □ *"Judith's never late. You sure she said eight?" — "Positive."* **6** ADJ **Positive** evidence gives definite proof of something. □ *There is some positive evidence that the economy is improving.* ● **posi|tive|ly** ADV □ *He has positively identified the body as that of his wife.* **7** ADJ If a medical or scientific test is **positive**, it shows that something has happened or is present. □ *If the test is positive, treatment will start immediately.* **8** **HIV positive** → see **HIV** **9** ADJ In art and sculpture, **positive** space is the parts of a painting that represent solid objects or the parts of a sculpture that are made of solid material. Compare **negative**. [TECHNICAL] [from Late Latin]
→ see **magnet, lightning**

**posi|tive ac|cel|era|tion** N-UNCOUNT **Positive acceleration** is an increase in speed or velocity. Compare **negative acceleration**. [TECHNICAL]

**posi|tive|ly** /pɒzɪtɪvli/ ADV You use **positively** to emphasize that something really is true. □ *This is positively the last chance.* [from Late Latin]

**pos|sess** /pəzɛs/ (**possesses, possessing, possessed**) V-T If you **possess** something, you have it or own it. □ *He possessed charm and diplomatic skills.* [from Old French]

**pos|sessed** /pəzɛst/ **1** ADJ If someone is described as being **possessed by** an evil spirit, it is believed that their mind and spirit are controlled by an evil spirit. □ *She even claimed that the couple's daughter was possessed by the devil.* **2** → see also **possess**

**pos|ses|sion** /pəzɛʃ*ə*n/ (**possessions**) **1** N-UNCOUNT If you are **in possession of** something, you have it, because you have obtained it or because it belongs to you. [FORMAL] □ *Those documents are now in the possession of the Washington Post.* □ …*the possession of private property.* **2** N-COUNT Your **possessions** are the things that you own or have with you at a particular time. □ *People have lost their homes and all their possessions.* [from Old French]

**pos|ses|sive** /pəzɛsɪv/ **1** ADJ Someone who is **possessive about** another person wants all that person's love and attention. □ *Danny could be very jealous and possessive about me.* ● **pos|ses|sive|ness** N-UNCOUNT □ *I've ruined every relationship with my possessiveness.* **2** ADJ In grammar, a **possessive determiner** or **possessive adjective** is a word such as "my" or "his" that shows who or what something belongs to or is connected with. The **possessive** form of a name or noun has 's added to it, as in "Jenny's" or "cat's." [from Old French]

**pos|sibil|ity** /pɒsɪbɪlɪti/ (**possibilities**) **1** N-COUNT If you say there is a **possibility that** something is true or **that** something will happen, you mean that it might be true or it might happen. □ *Be prepared for the possibility that he may never answer.* **2** N-COUNT A **possibility** is one of several different things that could be done. □ *There were several possibilities open to us.* [from Latin]

**pos|sible** /pɒsɪb*ə*l/ (**possibles**) **1** ADJ If it is **possible** to do something, it can be done. □ *If it is possible to find out where your brother is, we will.* □ *Anything is possible if you want it enough.* **2** ADJ A **possible** event is one that might happen. □ *The army is prepared for possible military action.* **3** ADJ If you say that it is **possible that** something is true or correct, you mean that although you do not know whether it is true or correct, you accept that it might be. □ *It is possible that he's telling the truth.* **4** ADJ If you do something **as soon as possible**,

P

you do it as soon as you can. If you get **as** much **as possible** of something, you get as much of it as you can. ☐ *Please make your decision as soon as possible.* ☐ *Mrs. Pollard decided to learn as much as possible about the country before going there.* **5** ADJ You use **possible** with superlative adjectives to emphasize that something has more or less of a quality than anything else of its kind. ☐ *They joined the company at the worst possible time.* ☐ *He is doing the best job possible.* **6** N-SING **The possible** is everything that can be done in a situation. ☐ *Politics is the art of the possible.* [from Latin]

| **Thesaurus** | *possible* | Also look up : |

ADJ. feasible, likely; (ant.) impossible, unlikely **1**

**pos|sibly** /pɒsɪbli/ **1** ADV You use **possibly** to indicate that you are not sure whether something is true or might happen. ☐ *Exercise will possibly protect against heart attacks.* ☐ *They were casually dressed; possibly students.* **2** ADV You use **possibly** to emphasize that you are surprised or puzzled. ☐ *How could they possibly eat that stuff?* **3** ADV You use **possibly** to emphasize that something is possible, or with a negative to emphasize that it is not possible. ☐ *They've done everything they can possibly think of.* ☐ *I can't possibly answer that!* [from Latin]

### post

❶ INFORMATION AND COMMUNICATION
❷ JOBS AND PLACES
❸ POLE

❶ **post** /poʊst/ (**posts, posting, posted**) **1** V-T If you **post** notices, signs, or other pieces of information somewhere, you attach them to a wall or board so that everyone can see them. ☐ *Officials began posting warning notices.* ● **Post up** means the same as **post.** ☐ *He has posted a sign up that says "No Fishing."* **2** V-T If you **post** information on the Internet, you make the information available to other people on the Internet. [COMPUTING] ☐ *...a statement posted on the Internet.* [from Old English]

❷ **post** /poʊst/ (**posts, posting, posted**) **1** N-COUNT A **post** in a company or organization is a job or official position in it. [FORMAL] ☐ *She took up a post as President Menem's assistant.* **2** V-T If you **are posted** somewhere, you are sent there by your employers to work. ☐ *After her training she was posted to Biloxi.* [from French] **3** → see also **posting**

❸ **post** /poʊst/ (**posts**) N-COUNT A **post** is a strong upright pole fixed into the ground. ☐ *The device is fixed to a post.* [from Old English]

**post|age** /poʊstɪdʒ/ N-UNCOUNT **Postage** is the money that you pay for sending letters and packages by mail. ☐ *All prices include postage.* [from Old French]

**post|card** /poʊstkɑrd/ (**postcards**) also **post card** N-COUNT A **postcard** is a thin card, often with a picture on one side, which you can write on and mail to someone without using an envelope. [from Old French]

**post|er** /poʊstər/ (**posters**) N-COUNT A **poster** is a large notice or picture that you stick on a wall

or board, often in order to advertise something. ☐ *...a poster for the jazz festival in Monterey.* [from Old English]

**post|er child** also **poster boy** also **poster girl** N-COUNT If someone or something is a **poster child for** a particular cause, characteristic, or activity, they are seen as a very good or typical example of it. ☐ *He called Coleman a "poster child for what is wrong in politics."*

| **Word Link** | *post ≈ after : posterity, postpone, postwar* |

**pos|ter|ity** /pɒstɛrɪti/ N-UNCOUNT You can refer to everyone who will be alive in the future as **posterity**. [FORMAL] ☐ *A photographer recorded the scene on video for posterity.* [from French]

**post|ing** /poʊstɪŋ/ (**postings**) **1** N-COUNT If you get a **posting to** a particular place, you are sent to live and work there for a period. ☐ *...his posting to Berlin in 1960.* **2** N-COUNT A **posting** is a message that is placed on the Internet. [COMPUTING] ☐ *Postings on the Internet can be accessed from anywhere in the world.* [Sense 1 from French. Sense 2 from Old English.]

**post|mod|ern dance** also **post-modern dance** N-UNCOUNT **Postmodern dance** is a form of dance that began in the 1960s as a reaction against modern dance.

**post|mor|tem** /poʊstmɔrtəm/ (**postmortems**) **1** N-COUNT A **postmortem** is a medical examination of a dead person's body to find out how they died. ☐ *The body was taken to hospital for a postmortem.* **2** N-COUNT A **postmortem** is an examination of something that has recently happened, especially something that has failed or gone wrong. ☐ *The postmortem on the presidential campaign is under way.* [from Latin]

**post of|fice** (**post offices**) **1** N-COUNT A **post office** is a building where you can buy stamps, mail letters and packages, and use other services provided by the national postal service. ☐ *She needed to get to the post office before it closed.* **2** N-SING **The Post Office** is sometimes used to refer to the U.S. Postal Service.

**post|par|tum de|pres|sion** /poʊstpɑrtəm dɪprɛʃ°n/ N-UNCOUNT **Postpartum depression** is a mental state involving feelings of anxiety and sudden mood swings which some women experience after they have given birth.

**post|pone** /poʊstpoʊn, poʊspoʊn/ (**postpones, postponing, postponed**) V-T If you **postpone** an event, you delay it or arrange for it to take place at a later time than was originally planned. ☐ *He decided to postpone the trip until the following day.* ● **post|pone|ment** (**postponements**) N-VAR ☐ *...the postponement of yesterday's match.* [from Latin]

**pos|tu|late** /pɒstʃəleɪt/ (**postulates, postulating, postulated**) V-T If you **postulate** something, you suggest it as the basis for a theory, argument, or calculation. [FORMAL] ☐ *Scientists have postulated that modern birds are linked to dinosaurs.* [from Latin]

**pos|ture** /pɒstʃər/ (**postures**) **1** N-VAR Your **posture** is the position in which you stand or sit. ☐ *You can make your stomach look flatter by improving your posture.* **2** N-COUNT A **posture** is an attitude that you have or a way that you behave toward a

| **Word Web** | pottery |

There are three basic types of **pottery**. Earthenware **dishes** are made from **clay** and **fired** at a relatively low temperature. They are **porous** and must be **glazed** in order to hold water. Potters first created earthenware objects about 15,000 years ago. Stoneware pieces are heavier and are fired at a higher temperature. They are impermeable even without a glaze. **Porcelain ceramics** are fragile. They have thin walls and are **translucent**. Stoneware and porcelain are not as old as earthenware. They appeared about 2,000 years ago when the Chinese started building high-temperature kilns. Another name for porcelain is **china**.

person or thing. [FORMAL] ❑ *Mr Bush's new posture helped open the way for the next proposal.* [from French]
→ see **brain**

**post|war** /poʊstwɔr/ ADJ **Postwar** is used to describe things that happened, existed, or were made in the period immediately after a war, especially World War II, 1939 – 45. ❑ *Bottle feeding babies was popular in the early postwar years.* [from Old Northern French]

**pot** /pɒt/ (**pots, potting, potted**) ■ N-COUNT A **pot** is a deep round container used for cooking food. ❑ *...metal cooking pots.* ❷ N-COUNT A **pot** is a teapot or coffee pot. ❑ *There's tea in the pot.* ❸ V-T If you **pot** a plant, you put it into a container filled with soil. ❑ *Pot the plants individually.* N-SING ❹ N-SING You can refer to a fund consisting of money from several people as **the pot.** ❑ *I've taken some money from the pot to buy wrapping paper.* ❺ N-COUNT Someone who has a **pot** has a round, fat stomach which sticks out. [from Late Old English]

**po|table** /poʊtəbᵊl/ ADJ **Potable** water is clean and safe for drinking. [from Late Latin]

**po|ta|to** /pəteɪtoʊ/ (**potatoes**) N-VAR **Potatoes** are round vegetables with brown or red skins and white insides. They grow under the ground. [from Spanish]
→ see **vegetable**

**po|ta|to chip** (**potato chips**) N-COUNT **Potato chips** are very thin slices of potato that have been fried until they are hard, dry, and crisp.

| **Word Link** | potent ≈ ability, power : im*potent*, *potent*, *potent*ial |

**po|tent** /poʊtᵊnt/ ADJ Something that is **potent** is very effective and powerful. ❑ *Their most potent weapon was the Exocet missile.* ● **po|ten|cy** /poʊtᵊnsi/ N-UNCOUNT ❑ *Sunscreen can lose its potency if left over winter in the bathroom cabinet.* [from Latin]

**po|ten|tial** /pətɛnʃᵊl/ ■ ADJ You use **potential** to say that someone or something is capable of developing in a particular kind of person or thing. ❑ *The company has identified 60 potential customers.* ❑ *We are aware of the potential problems.* ● **po|ten|tial|ly** ADV ❑ *This is a potentially dangerous situation.* ❷ N-UNCOUNT If you say that someone or something has **potential**, you mean that they have the necessary abilities or qualities to become successful or useful in the future. ❑ *The boy has great potential.* ❸ N-UNCOUNT If you say that someone or something has **potential for** doing a

particular thing, you mean that it is possible they may do it. If there is **the potential for** something, it may happen. ❑ *The potential for conflict is great.* [from Old French]

**po|ten|tial dif|fer|ence** /pətɛnʃᵊl dɪfərəns, dɪfrəns/ N-VAR **Potential difference** is the difference in voltage between two points in an electrical circuit. [TECHNICAL]

**po|ten|tial en|er|gy** N-UNCOUNT **Potential energy** is the energy that an object has because of its position or condition, for example because it is raised above the ground. Compare **kinetic energy**.

**po|tion** /poʊʃᵊn/ (**potions**) N-COUNT A **potion** is a drink that contains medicine, poison, or something that is supposed to have magic powers. ❑ *...a magic potion that will make him fall in love.* [from Old French]

**pot|tery** /pɒtəri/ (**potteries**) ■ N-UNCOUNT **Pottery** is pots, dishes, and other objects made from clay. ❑ *...a fine range of pottery.* ❷ N-UNCOUNT **Pottery** is the craft or activity of making objects out of clay. ❑ *He became interested in sculpting and pottery.* [from Old French]
→ see Word Web: **pottery**

**pot|ty** /pɒti/ (**potties**) N-COUNT A **potty** is a deep bowl that a small child uses instead of a toilet.

**pouch** /paʊtʃ/ (**pouches**) ■ N-COUNT A **pouch** is a flexible container like a small bag. ❑ *...a pouch of silver coins.* ❷ N-COUNT The **pouch** of an animal such as a kangaroo or a koala bear is the pocket of skin on its stomach in which its baby grows. ❑ *...a kangaroo with a baby in its pouch.* [from Old Norman French]

**poul|try** /poʊltri/ N-PLURAL You can refer to chickens, ducks, and other birds that are kept for their eggs and meat as **poultry**. ❑ *...methods of raising poultry.* ● Meat from these birds is also referred to as **poultry**. ❑ *The menu offers roast meats and poultry.* [from Old French]
→ see **meat**

**pounce** /paʊns/ (**pounces, pouncing, pounced**) ■ V-I If a person or animal **pounces on** another person or animal, they jump toward them and try to take hold of them or attack them. ❑ *He pounced on the photographer and smashed his camera.* ❑ *Before I could get the pigeon, the cat pounced.* ❷ V-I If someone **pounces on** something such as a mistake, they draw attention to it, usually in order to gain an advantage. ❑ *The Democrats were ready to pounce on any Republican mistakes.* [from Middle English]

P

**pound** /paʊnd/ (**pounds, pounding, pounded**)
**1** N-COUNT A **pound** is a unit of weight used mainly in the U.S., Britain, and other countries where English is spoken. One pound is equal to 0.454 kilograms. ❑ *Her weight was under ninety pounds.* ❑ *...a pound of cheese.* **2** N-COUNT The **pound** is the unit of money which is used in Britain. It is represented by the symbol £. Some other countries, for example, Egypt, also have a unit of money called a **pound**. **3** V-T/V-I If you **pound** something or **pound on** it, you hit it with great force, usually loudly and repeatedly. ❑ *He pounded the table with his fist.* ❑ *Somebody began pounding on the front door.* **4** V-I If your heart is **pounding**, it is beating with an unusually strong and fast rhythm, usually because you are afraid. ❑ *I'm sweating, my heart is pounding.* [from Old English]

**pound cake** (**pound cakes**) N-VAR A **pound cake** is a very rich cake, originally made using a pound of butter, a pound of sugar, and a pound of flour.

**pour** /pɔr/ (**pours, pouring, poured**) **1** V-T If you **pour** a liquid or other substance, you make it flow steadily out of a container by holding the container at an angle. ❑ *She poured some water into a bowl.* **2** V-T If you **pour** someone a drink, you put some of the drink in a cup or glass so that they can drink it. ❑ *She asked Tillie to pour her a cup of coffee.* **3** V-I When a liquid or other substance **pours** somewhere, it flows there quickly and in large quantities. ❑ *Blood was pouring from his broken nose.* ❑ *Tears poured down our faces.* **4** V-I When it rains very heavily, you can say that **it is pouring**. ❑ *It was still pouring outside.* ❑ *The rain was pouring down.* **5** V-I If people **pour** into or out of a place, they go there quickly and in large numbers. ❑ *At six p.m. workers poured from the offices.* **6** V-I If something such as information **pours** into a place, a lot of it is obtained or given. ❑ *Thousands of get-well messages poured in from all over the world.* **7** to **pour cold water on** something → see **water**

▶ **pour out** PHR-VERB If you **pour out** a drink, you put some of it in a cup or glass. ❑ *Larry poured out four glasses of water.*

| **Word Partnership** | Use *pour* with : |
|---|---|
| N. | pour **a liquid**, pour **a mixture**, pour **water** **1** pour **coffee**, pour **a drink** **2** |

**pout** /paʊt/ (**pouts, pouting, pouted**) V-I If you **pout**, you stick out your lips, usually as a way of showing that you are annoyed. ❑ *He pouted when he did not get what he wanted.*

**pov|er|ty** /pɒvərti/ N-UNCOUNT **Poverty** is the state of being very poor. ❑ *...people living in poverty.* [from Old French]

**pow|der** /paʊdər/ (**powders**) N-VAR **Powder** consists of many tiny particles of a solid substance. ❑ *Put a small amount of the powder into a container and mix with water.* ❑ *...cocoa powder.* [from Old French]
→ see **makeup**

**pow|dered** /paʊdərd/ ADJ A **powdered** substance is one that is in the form of a powder although it can come in a different form. ❑ *...powdered milk.* [from Old French]

**pow|er** /paʊər/ (**powers, powering, powered**)
**1** N-UNCOUNT If someone has **power**, they have a lot of control over people and activities. ❑ *When your children are young you still have a lot of power; you shape your child's world.* **2** N-UNCOUNT Your **power** to do something is your ability to do it. ❑ *She has the power to charm anyone.* **3** N-UNCOUNT If it is **in** or **within** your **power** to do something, you are able to do it or you have the resources to deal with it. ❑ *It is within your power to change your life if you are not happy.* **4** N-UNCOUNT If someone in authority has the **power** to do something, they have the legal right to do it. ❑ *The police have the power to arrest people carrying knives.* **5** N-UNCOUNT If people take **power** or come to **power**, they take charge of a country's affairs. If a group of people are **in power**, they are in charge of a country's affairs. ❑ *Amin came into power several years later.* **6** N-UNCOUNT The **power** of something is its physical strength or the ability that it has to move or affect things. ❑ *The vehicle had better power and better brakes.* **7** N-UNCOUNT **Power** is energy, especially electricity, that is obtained in large quantities from a fuel source. ❑ *Nuclear power is cleaner than coal.* ❑ *Power has been restored to most areas that were affected by the high winds.* **8** V-T The device or fuel that **powers** a machine provides the energy that the machine needs in order to work. ❑ *The battery could power an electric car.* **9** N-UNCOUNT In physics, **power** is a measure of the amount of work that is done in a particular time. [TECHNICAL] [from Vulgar Latin]
→ see **electricity, energy, solar**

**pow|er|ful** /paʊərfəl/ **1** ADJ A **powerful** person or organization is able to control or influence people and events. ❑ *You're a powerful man — people will listen to you.* ❑ *...Russia and India, two large, powerful countries.* **2** ADJ You say that someone's body is **powerful** when it is physically strong. ❑ *...his powerful muscles.* ● **pow|er|ful|ly** ADV ❑ *...a strong, powerfully built man of 60.* **3** ADJ A **powerful** machine or substance is effective because it is very strong. ❑ *The more powerful the car the more difficult it is to control.* ❑ *...powerful computer systems.* ● **pow|er|ful|ly** ADV ❑ *The SC430 model has a powerfully smooth engine.* **4** ADJ A **powerful** smell is very strong. ❑ *There's a powerful smell of cooking.* **5** ADJ A **powerful** voice is loud and can be heard from a long way away. ❑ *Mrs. Jones's powerful voice interrupted them.* **6** ADJ You describe a piece of writing, speech, or work of art as **powerful** when it has a strong effect on people's feelings or beliefs. ❑ *...a powerful drama about the effects of racism.* ● **pow|er|ful|ly** ADV ❑ *The play is painful, funny, and powerfully acted.* [from Vulgar Latin]

**pow|er|less** /paʊrlɪs/ **1** ADJ Someone who is **powerless** is unable to control or influence events. ❑ *If you don't have money, you're powerless.* ● **pow|er|less|ness** N-UNCOUNT ❑ *...feelings of powerlessness.* **2** ADJ If you are **powerless to** do something, you are completely unable to do it. ❑ *Security guards were powerless to stop the crowd throwing bottles.* [from Vulgar Latin]

**pow|er line** (**power lines**) N-COUNT A **power line** is a cable, especially above ground, along which

p

electricity is passed to an area or building.

**pow|er plant** (**power plants**) N-COUNT A **power plant** is the same as a **power station**.

**pow|er sta|tion** (**power stations**) N-COUNT A **power station** is a place where electricity is produced.

→ see **electricity**

**pow|er walk|ing** also power-walking N-UNCOUNT **Power walking** is the activity of walking very fast, as a means of keeping fit.

**PPO** /pi pi <u>ou</u>/ (**PPOs**) N-COUNT A **PPO** is an organization whose members receive medical care at a greatly reduced cost only if they use doctors and hospitals which belong to the organization. **PPO** is an abbreviation for **Preferred Provider Organization**.

**PR** /pi <u>a</u>r/ N-UNCOUNT **PR** is an abbreviation for **public relations**. ❑ …*a PR firm.*

**prac|ti|cable** /pr<u>æ</u>ktɪkəbᵊl/ ADJ If a task, plan, or idea is **practicable**, people are able to carry it out. [FORMAL] ❑ *It is not practicable to offer her the job back.* [from French]

**prac|ti|cal** /pr<u>æ</u>ktɪkᵊl/ **1** ADJ **Practical** means involving real situations and events, rather than ideas and theories. ❑ …*practical suggestions on how to eat more fiber.* **2** ADJ You describe people as **practical** when they make sensible decisions and deal effectively with problems. ❑ *You were always so practical, Maria.* **3** ADJ **Practical** ideas and methods are likely to be effective or successful in a real situation. ❑ *Our system is the most practical way of preventing crime.* **4** ADJ You can describe clothes and things in your house as **practical** when they are useful rather than just being fashionable or attractive. ❑ …*lightweight, practical clothes.* [from French]

| **Thesaurus** | *practical* | Also look up : |
| --- | --- | --- |
| ADJ. | businesslike, pragmatic, reasonable, sensible, systematic; (*ant.*) impractical **2** **3** | |

**prac|ti|cal|ity** /pr<u>æ</u>ktɪk<u>æ</u>lɪti/ (**practicalities**) N-VAR The **practicalities of** a situation are the practical aspects of it, as opposed to its theoretical aspects. ❑ …*the practicalities of everyday life.* [from French]

**prac|ti|cal|ly** /pr<u>æ</u>ktɪkli/ **1** ADV **Practically** means almost. ❑ *He's known the old man practically all his life.* **2** ADV You use **practically** to describe something that involves real actions or events rather than ideas or theories. ❑ *The course is practically based.* [from French]

**prac|tice** /pr<u>æ</u>ktɪs/ (**practices, practicing, practiced**) **1** N-COUNT You can refer to something that people do regularly as a **practice**. ❑ …*the practice of using chemicals to color the hair.* **2** N-VAR **Practice** means doing something regularly in order to be able to do it better. A **practice** is one of these periods of doing something. ❑ …*the hard practice necessary to become a good musician.* ❑ …*a basketball practice.* **3** N-UNCOUNT The work done by doctors and lawyers is referred to as the **practice** of medicine and law. People's religious activities are referred to as the **practice** of a religion. ❑ …*the practice of modern medicine.* **4** N-COUNT A doctor's or lawyer's **practice** is his or her business, often shared with other

doctors or lawyers. ❑ *The new doctor's practice was miles away from where I lived.* **5** V-T/V-I If you **practice** something, you keep doing it regularly in order to do it better. ❑ *She practiced the piano in the school basement.* ❑ *Keep practicing, and maybe next time you'll do better* **6** → see also **practiced** **7** V-T When people **practice** something such as a custom, craft, or religion, they take part in the activities associated with it. ❑ …*a family that practiced traditional Judaism.* ● **prac|tic|ing** ADJ ❑ *He was a practicing Muslim throughout his life.* **8** V-T/V-I Someone who **practices** medicine or law works as a doctor or a lawyer. ❑ *He doesn't practice medicine for the money.* ❑ …*my license to practice as a lawyer.* **9** PHRASE What happens **in practice** is what actually happens, in contrast to what is supposed to happen. ❑ *Let's review the plan when we've seen how it works in practice.* **10** PHRASE If you **put** a belief or method **into practice**, you behave or act in accordance with it. ❑ *The mayor has another chance to put his new ideas into practice.* [from Medieval Latin]

| **Thesaurus** | *practice* | Also look up : |
| --- | --- | --- |
| N. | custom, habit, method, procedure, system, way **1** exercise, rehearsal, training, workout **2** | |

**prac|ticed** /pr<u>æ</u>ktɪst/ ADJ Someone who is **practiced at** doing something is good at it because they have had experience and have developed their skill at it. ❑ *She's well practiced at appearing happy.* ❑ …*a practiced and experienced surgeon.* [from Medieval Latin]

**prac|ti|tion|er** /pr<u>æ</u>ktɪʃənər/ (**practitioners**) N-COUNT Doctors are sometimes referred to as **practitioners**. [FORMAL] [from Old French]

**prag|mat|ic** /pr<u>æ</u>gm<u>æ</u>tɪk/ ADJ A **pragmatic** way of dealing with something is based on practical considerations, rather than theoretical ones. A **pragmatic** person deals with things in a practical way. ❑ *Robin took a pragmatic look at her situation.* ● **prag|mati|cal|ly** /pr<u>æ</u>gm<u>æ</u>tɪkli/ ADV ❑ *"I can't imagine us doing anything else," stated Brian pragmatically.* [from Late Latin]

**prag|ma|tism** /pr<u>æ</u>gmətɪzəm/ N-UNCOUNT **Pragmatism** means thinking of or dealing with problems in a practical way, rather than by using theory or abstract principles. [FORMAL] ❑ *She had a reputation for clear thinking and pragmatism.* ● **prag|ma|tist** (**pragmatists**) N-COUNT ❑ *He is a political pragmatist, not an idealist.* [from Late Latin]

**prai|rie** /pr<u>ɛ</u>əri/ (**prairies**) N-VAR A **prairie** is a large area of flat, grassy land in North America where very few trees grow. [from French] → see **grassland, habitat**

**praise** /pr<u>eɪ</u>z/ (**praises, praising, praised**) V-T If you **praise** someone or something, you express approval for their achievements or qualities. ❑ *The American president praised Turkey for its courage.* ❑ *The passengers praised John for saving their lives.* ● **Praise** is also a noun. ❑ *The ladies are full of praise for the staff.* ❑ *I have nothing but praise for the police.* [from Old French]

**pray** /pr<u>eɪ</u>/ (**prays, praying, prayed**) **1** V-T/V-I When people **pray**, they speak to God in order to give thanks or to ask for help. ❑ *He spent his time in prison praying and studying.* ❑ *Now all we can do is to pray to God.* ❑ *We pray that Billy's family will now find* *peace.* **2** V-T/V-I When someone is hoping very much that something will happen, you can say that they **are praying** that it will happen. ❑ *I'm praying for good weather.* ❑ *I'm praying that somebody in Congress will do something before it's too late.* [from Old French]

**prayer** /prɛər/ (**prayers**) **1** N-UNCOUNT **Prayer** is the activity of speaking to God. ❑ *They dedicated their lives to prayer.* **2** N-COUNT A **prayer** is the words a person says when they speak to God. ❑ *They should say a prayer for the people on both sides.* **3** N-COUNT You can refer to a strong hope that you have as your **prayer.** ❑ *This new drug could be the answer to our prayers.* **4** N-PLURAL A short religious service at which people gather to pray can be referred to as **prayers.** ❑ ...*evening prayers.* [from Old French]

**preach** /pritʃ/ (**preaches, preaching, preached**) **1** V-T/V-I When a member of the clergy **preaches** a sermon, he or she gives a talk on a religious or moral subject during a religious service. ❑ *The priest preached a sermon on the devil.* ❑ *The bishop will preach to a crowd of several hundred people.* • **preacher** (**preachers**) N-COUNT ❑ ...*acceptance of women preachers.* **2** V-T/V-I When people **preach,** or **preach** a belief or a course of action, they try to persuade other people to accept the belief or to take the course of action. ❑ *He was trying to preach peace.* ❑ *Experts are preaching that even a little exercise is better than none at all.* [from Old French]

**Pre|cam|brian** /prikæmbriən/ also **Pre-Cambrian** ADJ **Precambrian** time is the period of the Earth's history from the time the Earth formed until around 600 million years ago. [TECHNICAL]

**pre|cari|ous** /prikɛəriəs/ **1** ADJ If your situation is **precarious,** you are not in complete control of events and might fail in what you are doing at any moment. ❑ *Our financial situation has become precarious.* • **pre|cari|ous|ly** ADV ❑ *This left him clinging precariously to his job.* **2** ADJ Something that is **precarious** is not securely held in place and seems likely to fall or collapse at any moment. ❑ *They crawled up precarious ladders.* • **pre|cari|ous|ly** ADV ❑ *One of my grocery bags was precariously balanced on the car trunk.* [from Latin]

> **Word Link** **caut ≈ taking care : caution, cautious, precaution**

> **Word Link** **pre ≈ before : precaution, precede, predict**

**pre|cau|tion** /prɪkɔʃⁿn/ (**precautions**) N-COUNT A **precaution** is an action that is intended to prevent something dangerous or unpleasant from happening. ❑ *Just as a precaution, couldn't he move to a place of safety?* [from French]

**pre|cede** /prɪsid/ (**precedes, preceding, preceded**) V-T If one event or period of time **precedes** another, it happens before it. [FORMAL] ❑ *Discussions between the main parties preceded the vote.* ❑ *The earthquake was preceded by a loud roar.* [from Old French]

**prec|edence** /prɛsɪdəns/ N-UNCOUNT If one thing takes **precedence over** another, it is regarded as more important than the other thing. ❑ *Have fun at college, but don't let it take precedence over work.* [from Old French]

**prec|edent** /prɛsɪdənt/ (**precedents**) N-VAR If there is a **precedent for** an action or event, it has happened before, and this can be regarded as an argument for doing it again. [FORMAL] ❑ *The trial could set an important precedent for dealing with similar cases.* [from Old French]

**pre|cept** /prisɛpt/ (**precepts**) N-COUNT A **precept** is a general rule that helps you to decide how you should behave in particular circumstances. [FORMAL] ❑ ...*the central precept that all people are born equal.* [from Latin]

**pre|cinct** /prisɪŋkt/ (**precincts**) N-COUNT A **precinct** is a part of a city or town that has its own police force. ❑ *The robbery occurred in the 34th Precinct.* [from Medieval Latin]

**pre|cious** /prɛʃəs/ **1** ADJ If something such as a resource is **precious,** it is valuable and should not be wasted or used badly. ❑ *After four months of being abroad, every hour at home was precious.* **2** ADJ **Precious** objects and materials are worth a lot of money because they are rare. ❑ ...*precious metals.* **3** ADJ If something is **precious** to you, you regard it as important and do not want to lose it. ❑ *Her family's support is particularly precious to Josie.* [from Old French]

**pre|cipi|tate** (**precipitates, precipitating, precipitated**)

> The verb is pronounced /prisipəteit/. The adjective is pronounced /prisipitit/.

**1** V-T If something **precipitates** an event or situation, usually a bad one, it causes it to happen suddenly or sooner than normal. [FORMAL] ❑ ...*the events that precipitated the current crisis.* **2** ADJ A **precipitate** action or decision happens or is made more quickly or suddenly than most people think is sensible. [FORMAL] ❑ *I don't think we should make precipitate decisions.* [from Latin]

**pre|cipi|ta|tion** /prisipɪteiʃⁿn/ **1** N-UNCOUNT **Precipitation** is rain, snow, or hail. [TECHNICAL] **2** N-UNCOUNT **Precipitation** is a process in a chemical reaction that causes solid particles to become separated from a liquid. [TECHNICAL] [from Latin]
→ see Word Web: **precipitation**

**pre|cise** /prisais/ **1** ADJ You use **precise** to emphasize that you are referring to an exact thing, rather than something vague. ❑ *I can remember the precise moment when my daughter came to see me.* ❑ *The equipment sent back information on the precise distance between the moon and the Earth.* **2** ADJ Something that is **precise** is exact and accurate in all its details. ❑ *They speak very precise English.* [from French]

**pre|cise|ly** /prisaisli/ **1** ADV **Precisely** means accurately and exactly. ❑ *Nobody knows precisely how many people are still living there.* ❑ *The first bell rang at precisely 10:29 a.m.* **2** ADV You can use **precisely** to emphasize that a reason or fact is the only important one there is, or that it is obvious. ❑ *Children come to zoos precisely to see captive animals.* [from French]

**pre|ci|sion** /prisiʒⁿn/ N-UNCOUNT If you do something **with precision,** you do it exactly as it should be done. ❑ *The choir sang with precision.* [from Latin]

**pre|clude** /prɪklud/ (**precludes, precluding, precluded**) V-T If something **precludes** an event

P

## Word Web    precipitation

Clouds are made of tiny **droplets** of **water vapor**. When the droplets fall to earth, they are called **precipitation**. Tiny droplets fall as **drizzle**. Larger droplets fall as **rain**. **Snow** is falling **ice crystals**. **Freezing rain** begins as snow. The **snowflakes** melt and then freeze again when they hit an object. **Sleet** is frozen **raindrops** that bounce when they hit the ground. **Hail** is made of frozen raindrops that travel up and down within a cloud. Each time they move downward, more water freezes on their surfaces. Finally they strike the earth as balls of ice.

or action, it prevents the event or action from happening. [FORMAL] ❑ *At 84, John feels his age precludes too much travel.* ❑ *The constitution precludes them from becoming a single state.* [from Latin]

**pre|co|cial** /prɪkoʊʃ°l/ ADJ A **precocial** chick is a young bird that is relatively well-developed when it is born and requires little parental care. Compare **altricial**. [TECHNICAL]

**pre|co|cious** /prɪkoʊʃəs/ ADJ A **precocious** child is very clever, mature, or good at something, often in a way that you usually only expect to find in an adult. ❑ *...a precocious 14-year-old.* [from Latin]

**pre|con|cep|tion** /prɪkənsɛpʃ°n/ (preconceptions) N-COUNT Your **preconceptions** about something are beliefs formed about it before you have enough information or experience. ❑ *Did you have any preconceptions about the sort of people who did computing?*

**pre|con|di|tion** /prɪkəndɪʃ°n/ (preconditions) N-COUNT If one thing is a **precondition for** another, it must happen or be done before the second thing can happen or exist. [FORMAL] ❑ *They demanded the release of three prisoners as a precondition for negotiation.*

**pre|cur|sor** /prɪkɜrsər/ (precursors) N-COUNT A **precursor** of something is a similar thing that happened or existed before it, often something that led to its existence. ❑ *...the HIV virus, the precursor to AIDS.* [from Latin]

**preda|tor** /prɛdətər/ (predators) N-COUNT A **predator** is an animal that kills and eats other animals. ❑ *With no natural predators on the island, the herd increased rapidly.* [from Latin]
→ see **carnivore, food, shark**

**preda|tory** /prɛdətɔri/ ADJ **Predatory** animals live by killing other animals for food. ❑ *...predatory birds like the eagle.* [from Latin]

**pre|de|ces|sor** /prɛdɪsɛsər/ (predecessors) **1** N-COUNT Your **predecessor** is the person who had your job before you. ❑ *He learned everything he knew from his predecessor.* **2** N-COUNT The **predecessor** of an object or machine is the object or machine that came before it in a sequence or process of development. ❑ *The car is 2 inches shorter than its predecessor.* [from Old French]

**pre|dica|ment** /prɪdɪkəmənt/ (predicaments) N-COUNT If you are in a **predicament**, you are in a difficult situation. ❑ *Hank explained our predicament.* [from Late Latin]

**Word Link**   dict ≈ speaking : contra**dict**, **dict**ate, pre**dict**

**Word Link**   pre ≈ before : **pre**caution, **pre**cede, **pre**dict

**pre|dict** /prɪdɪkt/ (predicts, predicting, predicted) V-T If you **predict** an event, you say that it will happen. ❑ *The latest opinion polls are predicting a very close contest.* ❑ *He predicted that my hair would grow back quickly.* [from Latin]
→ see **experiment, forecast**

**pre|dict|able** /prɪdɪktəb°l/ ADJ If you say that an event is **predictable**, you mean that it is obvious in advance that it will happen. ❑ *This was a predictable reaction.* ● **pre|dict|ably** ADV ❑ *His article is, predictably, an attack on capitalism.* ● **pre|dict|abil|ity** /prɪdɪktəbɪlɪti/ N-UNCOUNT ❑ *Your mother values the predictability of your Sunday calls.* [from Latin]

**pre|dic|tion** /prɪdɪkʃ°n/ (predictions) N-VAR If you make a **prediction**, you say what you think will happen. ❑ *Weather prediction has never been a perfect science.* [from Latin]
→ see **science**

**pre|dis|pose** /prɪdɪspoʊz/ (predisposes, predisposing, predisposed) **1** V-T If something **predisposes** you **to** think or behave in a particular way, it makes it likely that you will think or behave in that way. [FORMAL] ❑ *...people whose personalities predispose them to serve customers well.* ● **pre|dis|posed** ADJ ❑ *...people who are predisposed to crime.* **2** V-T If something **predisposes** you **to** a disease or illness, it makes it likely that you will suffer from that disease or illness. [FORMAL] ❑ *...a gene that predisposes people to cancer.* ● **pre|dis|posed** ADJ ❑ *Some people are genetically predisposed to diabetes.*

**pre|dis|po|si|tion** /prɪdɪspəzɪʃ°n/ (predispositions) N-COUNT If you have a **predisposition to** a particular disease, condition, or way of behaving, you are likely to suffer from that disease or condition, or to behave in that way. [FORMAL] ❑ *...a predisposition to panic.* ❑ *...a genetic predisposition to lung cancer.*

**Word Link**   dom, domin ≈ rule, master : **domin**ate, **domain**, pre**domin**ant

**pre|domi|nant** /prɪdɒmɪnənt/ ADJ If

something is **predominant**, it is more important or noticeable than anything else in a set of people or things. ❑ *Mandy's predominant emotion was confusion.* ● **pre|domi|nance** N-SING ❑ *...the predominance of women in teaching.* ● **pre|domi|nant|ly** ADV ❑ *Scotland is a predominantly rural country.* [from Medieval Latin]

**pre|domi|nate** /prɪdɒmɪneɪt/ (**predominates, predominating, predominated**) V-I If one type of person or thing **predominates** in a group, there is more of that type of person or thing in the group than of any other. [FORMAL] ❑ *Although girls predominate, more and more boys are joining in the fun.* [from Medieval Latin]

**pre|emi|nent** /priɛmɪnənt/ also **pre-eminent** ADJ The **preeminent** person in a group is the most important or powerful one. [FORMAL] ❑ *...one of the preeminent child psychologists of the twentieth century.* ● **pre|emi|nence** /priɛmɪnəns/ N-UNCOUNT ❑ *...the nation's preeminence in science and technology.*

**pre|empt** /priɛmpt/ (**preempts, preempting, preempted**) also **pre-empt** V-T If you **preempt** an action, you prevent it from happening by doing something before it can happen. ❑ *The army will tighten security to preempt future attacks.*

**pre|emp|tive** /priɛmptɪv/ also **pre-emptive** ADJ A **preemptive** attack or strike is intended to weaken or damage an enemy or opponent, for example, by destroying their weapons before they can do any harm. ❑ *A preemptive strike raises moral issues.*

**preen** /prin/ (**preens, preening, preened**) V-T When birds **preen** their feathers, they clean them and arrange them neatly using their beaks. ● **preening** N-UNCOUNT ❑ *Preening of the feathers keeps them waterproof and in good condition.* [from Old English]

**pref|ace** /prɛfɪs/ (**prefaces, prefacing, prefaced**) ◼ N-COUNT A **preface** is an introduction at the beginning of a book. ❑ *...the preface to Kelman's novel.* ◻ V-T If you **preface** an action or speech **with** something else, you do or say this other thing first. ❑ *I will preface what I am going to say with a few lines from Shakespeare.* [from Medieval Latin]

**pre|fer** /prɪfɜr/ (**prefers, preferring, preferred**) V-T If you **prefer** someone or something, you like that person or thing better than another. ❑ *Does he prefer a particular sort of music?* ❑ *I preferred books and people to politics.* ❑ *I prefer to think of peace not war.* ❑ *He would prefer to be in Philadelphia.* [from Latin]

**prefer|able** /prɛfərəbəl, prɛfrə-, prɪfɜrə-/ ADJ If you say that one thing is **preferable to** another, you mean that it is more desirable or suitable. ❑ *A big earthquake a long way off is preferable to a smaller one nearby.* ❑ *Prevention of a problem is preferable to trying to cure it.* ● **prefer|ably** /prɛfərəbli,, prɛfrə-, prɪfɜrə-/ ADV ❑ *Get exercise, preferably in the fresh air.* [from Latin]

**prefer|ence** /prɛfərəns/ (**preferences**) ◼ N-VAR If you have a **preference for** something, you would like to have or do that thing rather than something else. ❑ *...a preference for salty snacks over cookies.* ◻ N-UNCOUNT If you **give preference to** someone with a particular qualification or feature, you choose them rather than someone else. ❑ *The university will give preference to students from poorer backgrounds.* [from Latin]

**prefer|en|tial** /prɛfərɛnʃəl/ ADJ If you get **preferential** treatment, you are treated better than other people. ❑ *Those aged over 60 received preferential treatment.* [from Latin]

---

**Word Link** *fix ≈ fastening : fixture, prefix, suffix*

---

**pre|fix** /prifɪks/ (**prefixes**) N-COUNT A **prefix** is a letter or group of letters that is added to the beginning of a word in order to form a different word. For example, the prefix "un-" is added to "happy" to form "unhappy."

**pre|game** /prigeɪm/ also **pre-game** ADJ **Pregame** activities take place before a sports game. ❑ *...pregame ceremonies.*

**preg|nant** /prɛgnənt/ ADJ If a woman or female animal is **pregnant**, she has a baby or babies developing in her body. ❑ *I'm seven months pregnant.* ● **preg|nan|cy** /prɛgnənsi/ (**pregnancies**) N-VAR ❑ *...weight gain during pregnancy.* [from Latin] → see **reproduction**

---

**Word Partnership** Use *pregnant* with :

| N. | pregnant **with a baby/child**, pregnant **mother**, pregnant **wife**, pregnant **woman** |
|---|---|
| V. | be pregnant, **become** pregnant, **get** pregnant |

---

**pre|heat** /prihit/ (**preheats, preheating, preheated**) V-T If you **preheat** an oven, you switch it on and allow it to reach a certain temperature before you put food inside it. ❑ *Preheat the oven to 400 degrees.*

**pre|his|tor|ic** /prihɪstɔrɪk/ ADJ **Prehistoric** people and things existed at a time before information was written down. ❑ *...the prehistoric cave paintings of Lascaux.*

**preju|dice** /prɛdʒədɪs/ (**prejudices, prejudicing, prejudiced**) ◼ N-VAR **Prejudice** is an unreasonable dislike of a particular group of people or things, or an unreasonable preference for one group over another. ❑ *...racial prejudice.* ❑ *There seems to be some prejudice against workers over 45.* ◻ V-T If you **prejudice** someone or something, you influence them so that they are unfair in some way. ❑ *Words like "mankind" and "manpower" may prejudice us against women.* ❑ *The report was held back for fear of prejudicing his trial.* ◾ V-T If someone **prejudices** another person's situation, they do something that makes it worse than it should be. [FORMAL] ❑ *Her report was not intended to prejudice the future of the college.* [from Old French]

---

**Thesaurus** *prejudice* Also look up :

| N. | bias, bigotry, disapproval, intolerance; (*ant.*) tolerance ◼ |
|---|---|

---

**preju|diced** /prɛdʒədɪst/ ADJ A person who is **prejudiced** against someone from a different racial group has an unreasonable dislike of them. ❑ *They complained that the police were racially prejudiced.* [from Old French]

**pre|limi|nary** /prɪlɪmɪnɛri/ ADJ **Preliminary** activities or discussions take place at the beginning of an event, often as a form of preparation. ❑ *Preliminary results show the Republican Party with 11 percent of the vote.* [from New Latin]

p

**prel|ude** /prɛlyud, preɪlud/ (**preludes**) N-COUNT
You can describe an event as a **prelude to** another
event or activity when it happens before it and
acts as an introduction to it. □ *For him, reading was a*
*necessary prelude to sleep.* [from Medieval Latin]

**prema|ture** /primətʃʊər/ **1** ADJ Something
that is **premature** happens too early or earlier
than people expect. □ …*the commonest cause*
*of premature death.* □ *His career was brought to a*
*premature end.* ● **prema|ture|ly** ADV □ *The years in*
*the harsh mountains has prematurely aged him.* **2** ADJ
A **premature** baby is one that was born before
the date when it was expected to be born. □ *Even*
*very young premature babies respond to their mother's*
*presence.* ● **prema|ture|ly** ADV □ *Danny was born*
*prematurely, weighing only 3 lb 3 oz.* [from Latin]

**pre|med** /primɛd/ also **pre-med** ADJ A **premed**
student is a student who is taking courses that
are required in order for the student to study
at medical school. [INFORMAL] □ *Tim is a premed*
*student at MSU.*

**prem|ier** /prɪmɪər/ (**premiers**) **1** N-COUNT
The leader of the government of a country is
sometimes referred to as the country's **premier**.
□ …*Australian premier John Howard.* **2** ADJ **Premier**
is used to describe something that is considered to
be the best or most important thing of a particular
type. □ …*the country's premier opera company.* [from
Old French]

**premi|ere** /prɪmɪər, prɪmyɛər/ (**premieres**)
N-COUNT The **premiere** of a new play or movie is
the first public performance of it. □ …*last week's*
*premiere of his new movie.* [from French]

**prem|ier|ship** /prɪmɪərʃɪp/ N-SING
**Premiership** is the position of being the leader
of a government. □ …*the final years of Margaret*
*Thatcher's premiership.* [from Old French]

**prem|ise** /prɛmɪs/ (**premises**) **1** N-PLURAL The
**premises** of a business or an institution are all
the buildings and land that it occupies. □ *There is*
*a kitchen on the premises.* **2** N-COUNT A **premise** is
something that you suppose is true and that you
use as a basis for developing an idea. [FORMAL]
□ *The premise is that schools will work harder to improve*
*if they must compete.* [from Old French]

**pre|mium** /primiəm/ (**premiums**) **1** N-COUNT
A **premium** is a sum of money that you pay
regularly to an insurance company for an
insurance policy. □ …*insurance premiums.*
**2** N-COUNT A **premium** is a sum of money that
you have to pay for something in addition to the
normal cost. □ *People will normally pay a premium for*
*a good house in a good area.* **3** PHRASE If something
is **at a premium**, it is wanted or needed, but is
difficult to get or achieve. □ *If space is at a premium,*
*choose furniture that folds away.* [from Latin]

**premo|ni|tion**
/priːmənɪʃ°n, prɛm-/ (**premonitions**) N-COUNT If
you have a **premonition**, you have a feeling that
something is going to happen, often something
unpleasant. □ *He had a premonition that he would die.*
[from Late Latin]

**pre|na|tal** /prineɪt°l/ ADJ **Prenatal** is used to
describe things relating to the medical care of
women during pregnancy. □ *I met her briefly in a*
*prenatal class.*

**pre|nup** /priːnʌp/ (**prenups**) also **pre-nup**
N-COUNT A **prenup** is the same as a **prenuptial**

agreement. [INFORMAL]

**pre|nup|tial agree|ment**
/prinʌpʃ°l əgriːmənt, -nʌptʃ°l/ (**prenuptial**
**agreements**) also **pre-nuptial agreement**
N-COUNT A **prenuptial agreement** is a written
contract made between a man and a woman
before they marry, in which they state how their
assets such as property and money should be
divided if they get divorced. □ *We signed a prenuptial*
*agreement.*

**pre|oc|cu|py** /priɒkyəpaɪ/ (**preoccupies,**
**preoccupying, preoccupied**) V-T If something **is**
**preoccupying** you, you are thinking about it a lot.
□ *Crime and the fear of crime preoccupy the community.*
● **pre|oc|cu|pied** ADJ □ *Tom Banbury was preoccupied*
*with the missing child.* ● **pre|oc|cu|pa|tion**
(**preoccupations**) N-VAR □ *In our society we have a*
*preoccupation with trying to be thin.* [from Latin]

**pre-owned** ADJ Something that is **pre-owned**
has been owned by someone else and is now for
sale. □ …*pre-owned vehicles.*

**prep** /prɛp/ (**prepping, prepped**) **1** V-T If you
**prep** something, you prepare it. [INFORMAL] □ *After*
*prepping the boat, they sailed it down to Carloforte.*
**2** V-T If a doctor or nurse **preps** a patient, they
get them ready for surgery or another procedure.
[INFORMAL] □ *I was already prepped for surgery.*

**prepa|ra|tion** /prɛpəreɪʃ°n/ (**preparations**)
**1** N-UNCOUNT **Preparation** is the process of
getting something ready for use or for a particular
purpose. □ *Todd put the papers in his briefcase in*
*preparation for the meeting.* □ …*the preparation of*
*his weekly sermons.* **2** N-PLURAL **Preparations** are
all the arrangements that are made for a future
event. □ *We were making preparations for our wedding.*
[from Latin]

**pre|para|tory** /prɪpærətɔri, prɛpərə-/ ADJ
**Preparatory** actions are done before doing
something else as a form of preparation or as an
introduction. □ *A year's preparatory work will be*
*necessary before building can start.* [from Latin]

**pre|pare** /prɪpɛər/ (**prepares, preparing,**
**prepared**) **1** V-T If you **prepare** something, you
make it ready for something that is going to
happen. □ *They were preparing a recording of last*
*week's program.* □ *We will need 1,000 hours to prepare*
*the report.* **2** V-T/V-I If you **prepare for** an event
or action that will happen soon, you get yourself
ready for it or make the necessary arrangements.
□ …*to prepare for the cost of your child's education.*
□ *He went back to his hotel and prepared to catch a train.*
**3** V-T When you **prepare** food, you get it ready
to be eaten. □ *She entered the kitchen, hoping to find*
*someone preparing dinner.* [from Latin]

| Word Partnership | Use *prepare* with : |
|---|---|
| N. | prepare **a list**, prepare **a plan**, prepare **a** **report** **1** |
| | prepare **for battle/war**, prepare **for the** **future**, prepare **for the worst** **2** |
| | prepare **dinner**, prepare **food**, prepare **a meal** **3** |

**pre|pared** /prɪpɛərd/ **1** ADJ If you are **prepared**
**to** do something, you are willing to do it if
necessary. □ *Are you prepared to take action?* **2** ADJ
If you are **prepared for** something that you think
is going to happen, you are ready for it. □ *Police*

P

*are prepared for large numbers of demonstrators.*
● **pre|par|ed|ness** /prɪpɛ̱ərɪdnɪs/ N-UNCOUNT
❑ *...the need for military preparedness.* **3** ADJ You can describe something as **prepared** when it has been done or made beforehand, so that it is ready when it is needed. ❑ *He ended his prepared statement by thanking the police.* [from Latin]

**pre-pay** (pre-pays, pre-paying, pre-paid) also **prepay** V-T/V-I If you **pre-pay** something or **pre-pay for** it, you pay for it before you receive it or use it. ❑ *...electricity customers who prepay for their energy.*

**Word Link** *pos ≈ placing : de**pos**it, pre**pos**ition, re**pos**itory*

**prepo|si|tion** /prɛ̱pəzɪ̱ʃ<sup>ə</sup>n/ (**prepositions**) N-COUNT A **preposition** is a word such as "by," "for," "into," or "with" that usually has a noun group as its object. [from Latin]

**pre|pos|ter|ous** /prɪpɒ̱stərəs, -trəs/ ADJ If you describe something as **preposterous**, you mean that it is extremely unreasonable and foolish. ❑ *The whole idea was preposterous.*
● **pre|pos|ter|ous|ly** ADV ❑ *Some prices are preposterously high.* [from Latin]

**prep|py** /prɛ̱pi/ (**preppies**) **1** N-COUNT In the United States, **preppies** are young people who are conventional and conservative in their attitudes and dress, usually young people who have been to an expensive private school. **2** ADJ If you describe someone or their clothes, attitudes, or behavior as **preppy**, you mean that they are like a preppy. ❑ *...preppy students.* ❑ *...a preppy shirt and tie.*

**pre|requi|site** /prɪrɛ̱kwɪzɪt/ (**prerequisites**) N-COUNT If one thing is a **prerequisite for** another, it must happen or exist before the other thing is possible. ❑ *Knowledge of computing is not a prerequisite for the course.*

**pre|roga|tive** /prɪrɒ̱gətɪv/ (**prerogatives**) N-COUNT Something that is the **prerogative** of a particular person or group is a privilege or a power that they have. [FORMAL] ❑ *He considered it his prerogative to go wherever he liked, when he liked.* [from Latin]

**pre|scribe** /prɪskra̱ɪb/ (**prescribes, prescribing, prescribed**) **1** V-T If a doctor **prescribes** medicine or treatment for you, he or she tells you what medicine or treatment to have. ❑ *The physician examines the patient and prescribes medication.* ❑ *...the prescribed dose of sleeping tablets.* **2** V-T If a person or set of laws or rules **prescribes** an action or duty, they state that it must be carried out. [FORMAL] ❑ *...Article II of the Constitution, which prescribes the method of electing a president.* [from Latin]

**pre|scrip|tion** /prɪskrɪ̱pʃ<sup>ə</sup>n/ (**prescriptions**) **1** N-COUNT A **prescription** is a medicine that a doctor has told you to take, or the piece of paper on which the doctor writes an order for the prescription. ❑ *He gave me a prescription for some cream.* **2** PHRASE If a medicine is available **by prescription**, you can only get it from a pharmacist if a doctor gives you a prescription for it. [from Latin]

**pre|sea|son** /prɪsi̱z<sup>ə</sup>n/ also **pre-season** ADJ **Preseason** activities take place before the start of a sports season. ❑ *...a preseason game against Phoenix.*

**pres|ence** /prɛ̱z<sup>ə</sup>ns/ (**presences**) **1** N-SING Someone's **presence** in a place is the fact that they are there. ❑ *His presence causes too much trouble.* **2** N-UNCOUNT If you say that someone has

**presence**, you mean that they impress people by their appearance and manner. ❑ *...the authoritative presence of those great men.* **3** PHRASE If you are **in** someone's **presence**, you are in the same place as that person, and are close enough to them to be seen or heard. ❑ *Doing homework in the presence of parents was related to higher achievement in school.* [from Old French]

---

**present**

❶ EXISTING OR HAPPENING NOW
❷ BEING SOMEWHERE
❸ GIFT
❹ VERB USES

---

❶ **pres|ent** /prɛ̱z<sup>ə</sup>nt/ **1** ADJ You use **present** to describe things and people that exist now, rather than those that existed in the past or those that may exist in the future. ❑ *...the present crisis.* ❑ *...the present owners of the property.* **2** N-SING The **present** is the period of time that we are in now and the things that are happening now. ❑ *...the story of my life from my childhood up to the present.* **3** PHRASE A situation that exists **at present** exists now, although it may change. ❑ *At present, there is no way of knowing which people will develop the disease.* **4** PHRASE **The present day** is the period of history that we are in now. ❑ *...Western European art from the period of Giotto to the present day.* [from Latin]

❷ **pres|ent** /prɛ̱z<sup>ə</sup>nt/ **1** ADJ If someone is **present at** an event, they are there. ❑ *Nearly 85 percent of men are present at the birth of their children.* **2** ADJ If something, especially a substance or disease, is **present in** something else, it exists within that thing. ❑ *Vitamin D is naturally present in breast milk.* [from Latin]

❸ **pre|sent** /prɛ̱z<sup>ə</sup>nt/ (**presents**) N-COUNT A **present** is something that you give to someone, for example, on their birthday or when you visit them. ❑ *The carpet was a wedding present from Jack's parents.* ❑ *She bought a birthday present for her mother.* [from Old French]

❹ **pre|sent** /prɪzɛ̱nt/ (**presents, presenting, presented**) **1** V-T If you **present** someone **with** something such as a prize or document, or if you **present** it to them, you formally give it to them. ❑ *The mayor presented him with a gold medal.* ❑ *Betty will present the prizes to the winners.* ● **pres|en|ta|tion** N-UNCOUNT ❑ *Then came the presentation of the awards.* **2** V-T If something **presents** a difficulty or challenge, it causes or provides it. ❑ *This presents a problem for many customers.* ❑ *The future presents many challenges.* **3** V-T If you **present** someone or something in a particular way, you describe them in that way. ❑ *Many false statements were presented as facts.* ❑ *...tricks to help him present himself in a more confident way.* [from Old French]

**Usage** **present**

Make sure you pronounce *present* correctly — the noun or adjective has stress on the first syllable, while the verb has stress on the second syllable: *At the present moment, Timmy has two birthday presents hidden in his closet, ready to present to Abby when she comes home.*

**pres|en|ta|tion** /prɪ̱zɛnte̱ɪʃ<sup>ə</sup>n/ (**presentations**) **1** N-UNCOUNT **Presentation** is the appearance of something that someone has worked to create.

❏ *Keep the presentation of food attractive but simple.*
**2** N-COUNT A **presentation** is a formal event at which someone is given a prize or award. ❏ *He received his award at a presentation in Kansas City.*
**3** N-COUNT When someone gives a **presentation**, they give a formal talk. ❏ *Philip and I gave a video presentation.* [from Latin] **4** → see also **present**

**present-day** ADJ **Present-day** things, situations, and people exist at the time in history we are now in. ❏ *Even by present-day standards these were large aircraft.* ❏ *...an area of northern India, stretching from present-day Afghanistan to Bengal.*

**pres|ent|ly** /prɛzⁿntli/ **1** ADV If you say that something is **presently** happening, you mean that it is happening now. ❏ *She is presently developing a number of projects.* ❏ *These items are presently only available by mail.* **2** ADV You use **presently** to indicate that something happened a short time after the time or event that you have just mentioned. [WRITTEN] ❏ *He could smell coffee from the room where they would presently eat the food.* [from Latin]

**pre|serva|tive** /prɪzɜrvətɪv/ (**preservatives**) N-VAR A **preservative** is a chemical that prevents things from decaying. ❏ *...preservatives used in food processing.* [from Old French]

| Word Link | ation ≈ state of : dehydr**ation**, elev**ation**, preserv**ation** |
|---|---|

| Word Link | serv ≈ keeping : con**serv**e, ob**serv**e, pre**serv**e |
|---|---|

**pre|serve** /prɪzɜrv/ (**preserves, preserving, preserved**) **1** V-T If you **preserve** a situation or condition, you make sure that it remains as it is, and does not change or end. ❏ *We will do everything to preserve peace.* ● **pres|er|va|tion** /prɛzərveɪʃⁿn/ N-UNCOUNT ❏ *...the preservation of political freedom.* **2** V-T If you **preserve** something, you take action to save it or protect it. ❏ *We need to preserve the forest.* ● **pres|er|va|tion** N-UNCOUNT ❏ *...the preservation of historic buildings.* **3** V-T If you **preserve** food, you treat it in order to prevent it from decaying. ❏ *Use only enough sugar to preserve the plums.* **4** N-COUNT A nature **preserve** is an area of land or water where animals are protected from hunters. ❏ *...Pantanal, one of the world's great wildlife preserves.* [from Old French]

| Word Link | sid ≈ sitting : pre**sid**e, pre**sid**ent, re**sid**e |
|---|---|

**pre|side** /prɪzaɪd/ (**presides, presiding, presided**) V-I If you **preside over** a meeting or an event, you are in charge. ❏ *Rumsfeld presided over a ceremony at the Pentagon.* [from French]

**presi|den|cy** /prɛzɪdənsi/ (**presidencies**) N-COUNT The **presidency** of a country or organization is the position of being the president or the period of time during which someone is president. ❏ *He was offered the presidency of the University of Saskatchewan.* [from Old French]

**presi|dent** /prɛzɪdənt/ (**presidents**) **1** N-TITLE; N-COUNT The **president** of a country that has no king or queen is the person who is the head of state of that country. ❏ *...President Mubarak.* ❏ *...the president's ability to act quickly.* **2** N-COUNT The **president** of an organization is the person who has the highest position in it. ❏ *...the*

*president of the medical commission.* [from Old French]
→ see **election**

**presi|den|tial** /prɛzɪdɛnʃⁿl/ ADJ **Presidential** activities or things relate or belong to a president. ❏ *...Peru's presidential election.* [from Old French]
→ see **election**

**Presi|dents' Day** N-UNCOUNT In the United States, **Presidents' Day** is a public holiday held in commemoration of the birthdays of George Washington and Abraham Lincoln. It is the third Monday in February. ❏ *Today is Presidents' Day, a federal holiday.*

**press** /prɛs/ (**presses, pressing, pressed**) **1** V-T If you **press** something somewhere, you push it firmly against something else. ❏ *He pressed his back against the door.* **2** V-T If you **press** a button or switch, you push it with your finger in order to make a machine or device work. ❏ *Drago pressed a button and the door closed.* ● **Press** is also a noun. ❏ *...a TV that rises from a table at the press of a button.* **3** V-T/V-I If you **press** something or **press down** on it, you push hard against it with your foot or hand. ❏ *He pressed the gas pedal hard.* **4** V-I If you **press for** something, you try hard to persuade someone to give it to you or to agree to it. ❏ *Police might now press for changes in the law.* **5** V-T If you **press** someone, you try hard to persuade them to do something. ❏ *They pressed him to have something to eat.* ❏ *It is certain they will press Mr. King for more details.* **6** V-T If you **press** clothes, you iron them. ❏ *Vera pressed his shirt.* **7** N-SING Newspapers and the journalists and reporters who write for them are referred to as **the press**. ❏ *...interviews in the local and foreign press.* ❏ *Christie looked relaxed and calm as she faced the press.* **8** N-COUNT A **press** or a **printing press** is a machine used for printing things such as books and newspapers. **9** → see also **pressing** **10** PHRASE If you **press charges against** someone, you make an official accusation against them that has to be decided in a court of law. ❏ *I could have pressed charges against him.* **11** PHRASE When substances such as sand or gravel **press together** or when they **are pressed together**, they are pushed hard against each other so that they form a single layer. [from Old French]
→ see **printing**

| Word Partnership | Use *press* with : |
|---|---|
| N. | press **a button**, at the press **of a button** **2** press **accounts**, press **coverage**, **freedom of the** press, press **reports** **7** press **charges** **10** |

**press con|fer|ence** (**press conferences**) N-COUNT A **press conference** is a meeting held by a famous or important person in which they answer reporters' questions. ❏ *She gave her reaction at a press conference.*

**press|ing** /prɛsɪŋ/ **1** ADJ A **pressing** problem, need, or issue has to be dealt with immediately. ❏ *It is one of the most pressing problems facing this country.* [from Old French] **2** → see also **press**

**press re|lease** (**press releases**) N-COUNT A **press release** is a written statement about a matter of public interest that is given to the press by an organization concerned with the matter. ❏ *The company sent out a press release announcing some more bad news.*

**pres|sure** /prɛʃər/ (**pressures, pressuring, pressured**) ■ N-UNCOUNT **Pressure** is force that you produce when you press hard on something. ❑ *She pushed the door with her foot, and the pressure was enough to open it.* ❑ *The pressure of his fingers on her arm relaxed.* ■ N-UNCOUNT The **pressure** in a place or container is the force produced by the quantity of gas or liquid in that place or container. ❑ *If the pressure falls in the cabin, an oxygen mask will drop in front of you.* ■ N-UNCOUNT If there is **pressure on** a person, someone is trying to persuade or force them to do something. ❑ *He may have put pressure on her to agree.* ❑ *The director was under pressure to leave the company.* ■ N-UNCOUNT If you are experiencing **pressure**, you feel that you must do a lot of tasks or make a lot of decisions in very little time, or that people expect a lot from you. ❑ *Can you work under pressure?* ❑ *Even if I had the talent to play tennis professionally, I couldn't stand the pressure.* ■ V-T If you **pressure** someone **to** do something, you try forcefully to persuade them to do it. ❑ *He will never pressure you to get married.* ❑ *He was pressured into making a decision.* ● **pres|sured** ADJ ❑ *You're likely to feel anxious and pressured.* [from Late Latin] ■ → see also **blood pressure**
→ see **forecast, weather**

**pres|sure group** (**pressure groups**) N-COUNT A **pressure group** is an organization that campaigns to try to persuade a government to do something. ❑ *...the environmental pressure group Greenpeace.*

**pres|sur|ized** /prɛʃəraɪzd/ ADJ In a **pressurized** container or area, the pressure inside is different from the pressure outside. ❑ *...a pipe carrying highly pressurized gas.* [from Late Latin]

**pres|tige** /prɛstiʒ, -stidʒ/ N-UNCOUNT If a person, a country, or an organization has **prestige**, they are admired and respected because they are important or successful. ❑ *...efforts to build up the prestige of the United Nations.* ❑ *His position in the company brought him prestige.* [from French]

**pres|tig|ious** /prɛstidʒəs, -stidʒəs/ ADJ A **prestigious** institution, job, or activity is respected and admired by people. ❑ *...one of the most prestigious schools in the country.* [from French]

**pre|sum|ably** /prizuməbli/ ADV If you say that something is **presumably** the case, you mean that you think it is very likely to be the case, although you are not certain. ❑ *He's not going this year, presumably because of his age.* [from Old French]

**pre|sume** /prizum/ (**presumes, presuming, presumed**) ■ V-T If you **presume that** something is the case, you think that it is the case, although you are not certain. ❑ *I presume that you're here on business.* ❑ *"Has he been home all week?" — "I presume so."* ■ V-T If you say that someone **presumes to** do something, you mean that they do it even though they have no right to do it. [FORMAL] ❑ *I would not presume to advise you on such matters.* [from Old French]

**pre|sump|tion** /prizʌmpʃən/ (**presumptions**) N-COUNT A **presumption** is something that is accepted as true but is not certain to be true.

❑ *...the presumption that a person is innocent until proved guilty.* [from Old French]

**pre|sump|tu|ous** /prizʌmptʃuəs/ ADJ If you describe someone or their behavior as **presumptuous**, you disapprove of them because they are doing something that they have no right or authority to do. ❑ *It would be presumptuous to guess what the result will be.* [from Old French]

**pre|tend** /pritɛnd/ (**pretends, pretending, pretended**) ■ V-T If you **pretend that** something is true, you try to make people believe that it is true, although in fact it is not. ❑ *I pretend that things are really okay when they're not.* ❑ *He pretended to be asleep.* ■ V-T If you **pretend** that you are doing something, you imagine that you are doing it, for example, as part of a game. ❑ *She can sunbathe and pretend she's in Cancun.* [from Latin]

**pre|tense** /pritɛns, pritɛns/ (**pretenses**) ■ N-VAR A **pretense** is an action or way of behaving that is intended to make people believe something that is not true. ❑ *He found it difficult to keep up the pretense of happiness.* ■ PHRASE If you do something **under false pretenses**, you do it when people do not know the truth about you and your intentions. ❑ *This interview was conducted under false pretenses.* [from Latin]

**pre|ten|sion** /pritɛnʃən/ (**pretensions**) N-VAR If you say that someone has **pretensions**, you disapprove of them because they pretend they are more important than they really are. ❑ *...the pretensions of artists.* [from Latin]

**pre|ten|tious** /pritɛnʃəs/ ADJ If you say that someone or something is **pretentious**, you mean that they try to seem important or significant, but you do not think that they are. ❑ *His speech was full of pretentious nonsense.* [from Latin]

**pre|text** /pritɛkst/ (**pretexts**) N-COUNT A **pretext** is a reason that you pretend has caused you to do something. ❑ *They wanted a pretext for taking control of the region.* [from Latin]

**pret|ty** /priti/ (**prettier, prettiest**) ■ ADJ If you describe someone, especially a girl, as **pretty**, you mean that they look nice and are attractive in a delicate way. ❑ *She's a very charming and very pretty girl.* ● **pret|ti|ly** /pritili/ ADV ❑ *She smiled again, prettily.* ■ ADJ A place or a thing that is **pretty** is attractive and pleasant, in a charming way but not particularly unusual way. ❑ *...a very pretty little town.* ● **pret|ti|ly** ADV ❑ *The living-room was prettily decorated.* ■ ADV You can use **pretty** before an adjective or adverb to mean 'fairly' or 'quite'. [INFORMAL] ❑ *I had a pretty good idea what she was going to do.* [from Old English]

**pre|vail** /priveɪl/ (**prevails, prevailing, prevailed**) ■ V-I If a proposal, principle, or opinion **prevails**, it gains influence or is accepted. ❑ *We hoped that common sense would prevail.* ❑ *Rick still believes that justice will prevail.* ■ V-I If a situation or attitude **prevails** in a particular place at a particular time, it is normal or most common in that place at that time. ❑ *A similar situation prevails in Canada.* ❑ *...the confusion which prevailed at the time of the revolution.* [from Latin]

**pre|vail|ing** /prɪveɪlɪŋ/ ADJ The **prevailing** wind in an area is the type of wind that blows over that area most of the time. [from Latin]

**preva|lent** /prɛvələnt/ ADJ A condition, practice, or belief that is **prevalent** is common. ❑ Single-parent households are becoming increasingly prevalent. ● **preva|lence** N-UNCOUNT ❑ ...the prevalence of heart disease in this country. [from Latin]

**pre|vent** /prɪvɛnt/ (**prevents, preventing, prevented**) V-T To **prevent** something means to ensure that it does not happen. ❑ The best way to prevent injury is to wear a seat belt. ❑ The new law may prevent companies from creating new jobs. ● **pre|ven|tion** N-UNCOUNT ❑ ...the prevention of heart disease. [from Latin]

| **Word Partnership** | Use prevent with : |
|---|---|
| N. | prevent **attacks**, prevent **cancer**, prevent **damage**, prevent **disease**, prevent **infection**, prevent **injuries**, prevent **loss**, prevent **pregnancy**, prevent **problems**, prevent **violence**, prevent **war** |

**pre|ven|ta|tive** /prɪvɛntətɪv/ ADJ **Preventative** means the same as **preventive**. [from Latin]

**pre|ven|tive** /prɪvɛntɪv/ ADJ **Preventive** actions are intended to help prevent things such as disease or crime. ❑ ...clinics providing preventive health care. [from Latin]

**pre|view** /prɪvyu/ (**previews**) N-COUNT A **preview** is an opportunity to see something such as a movie or invention before it is open or available to the public. ❑ He went to a preview of the play.

**pre|vi|ous** /prɪviəs/ ADJ A **previous** event or thing is one that happened or existed before the one that you are talking about. ❑ She has a teenage daughter from a previous marriage. [from Latin]

**pre|vi|ous|ly** /prɪviəsli/ ■ ADV **Previously** means at some time before the period that you are talking about. ❑ Guyana's railroads were previously owned by private companies. ❑ They gave the contract to a previously unknown company. ■ ADV You can use **previously** to say how much earlier one event was than another event. ❑ Ingrid had moved to San Diego two weeks previously. [from Latin]

**pre|war** /prɪwɔr/ also **pre-war** ADJ **Prewar** is used to describe things that happened, existed, or were made in the period immediately before a war, especially World War II, 1939 – 45. ❑ ...Poland's prewar leader.

**pre|writ|ing** /prɪraɪtɪŋ/ also **pre-writing** N-UNCOUNT **Prewriting** is the thinking and planning that a writer does before beginning to write something.

**prey** /preɪ/ (**preys, preying, preyed**) ■ N-UNCOUNT A creature's **prey** are the creatures that it hunts and eats in order to live. ❑ They may not eat their prey until much later. ■ V-I A creature that **preys on** other creatures lives by catching and eating them. ❑ ...mountain lions and bears that prey on sheep. [from Old French]
→ see **carnivore, shark**

**price** /praɪs/ (**prices, pricing, priced**) ■ N-COUNT The **price** of something is the amount of money that you have to pay in order to buy it. ❑ The price of gas has risen 30 percent. ❑ They expect home

prices to rise. ■ N-SING The **price** that you pay for something that you want is an unpleasant thing that you have to do or suffer in order to get it. ❑ These stars often pay a high price for their success. ■ V-T If something **is priced at** a particular amount, the price is set at that amount. ❑ The software is priced at $90. ● **pric|ing** N-UNCOUNT ❑ We need a change in the rules on car pricing. ■ PHRASE If you want something **at any price**, you are determined to get it, even if unpleasant things happen as a result. ❑ They wanted fame at any price. [from Old French]

**price|less** /praɪslɪs/ ■ ADJ Something that is **priceless** is worth a very large amount of money. ❑ I live among priceless and beautiful things. ■ ADJ If you say that something is **priceless**, you mean that it is extremely useful or valuable. ❑ Our national parks are priceless treasures. [from Old French]

**pricey** /praɪsi/ (**pricier, priciest**) also **pricy** ADJ If something is **pricey**, it is expensive. [INFORMAL] ❑ Medical insurance is very pricey. [from Old French]

**prick** /prɪk/ (**pricks, pricking, pricked**) ■ V-T If you **prick** something or **prick** holes in it, you make small holes in it with a sharp object such as a pin. ❑ Prick the potatoes and rub the skins with salt. ■ V-T If something sharp **pricks** you or if you **prick yourself with** something sharp, it sticks into you or presses your skin and causes you pain. ❑ She pricked her finger with the needle. ● **Prick** is also a noun. ❑ She felt a prick on her neck. [from Old English]

**prick|ly** /prɪkli/ ■ ADJ Something that is **prickly** feels rough and uncomfortable, as if it has a lot of sharp points. ❑ The mattress was hard and the blankets were prickly. ■ ADJ Someone who is **prickly** loses their temper or gets upset very easily. ❑ You know how prickly she is. [from Old English]

**pride** /praɪd/ (**prides, priding, prided**) ■ N-UNCOUNT **Pride** is a feeling of satisfaction that you have because you or people close to you have done something good or possess something good. ❑ ...the sense of pride in a job well done. ❑ We take pride in offering you the highest standards. ■ N-UNCOUNT **Pride** is a sense of dignity and self-respect. ❑ His pride wouldn't allow him to ask for help. ■ N-UNCOUNT Someone's **pride** is the feeling that they have that they are better or more important than other people. ❑ His pride may still be his downfall. ■ V-T If you **pride** yourself **on** a quality or skill that you have, you are very proud of it. ❑ He prides himself on being a good listener. [from Old English]

**priest** /prist/ (**priests**) ■ N-COUNT A **priest** is a member of the Christian clergy in the Catholic, Anglican, or Orthodox church. ❑ He trained to be a Catholic priest. ■ N-COUNT In many non-Christian religions a **priest** is a man who has particular duties and responsibilities in a place where people worship. ❑ ...a New Age priest or priestess. [from Old English]

**priest|ess** /pristɪs/ (**priestesses**) N-COUNT A **priestess** is a woman in a non-Christian religion who has particular duties and responsibilities in a place where people worship. ❑ ...the priestess of the temple. [from Old English]

**priest|hood** /pristhʊd/ ■ N-UNCOUNT **Priesthood** is the position of being a priest or the period of time during which someone is a

## Word Web — primate

Monkeys, **apes**, and **humans** are all primates. Humans and other primates are alike in surprising ways. We used to believe that only humans were right-handed or left-handed. But when researchers studied a group of 66 **chimpanzees**, they found that chimps are also right-handed and left-handed. Other researchers learned that chimpanzee groups have different cultures. In 1972 a female **gorilla** named Koko began to learn sign language from a college student. Today Koko understands about 2,000 words and can sign about 500 of them. She makes up sentences using three to six words.

priest. ❑ ...the demands of priesthood. **2** N-SING The **priesthood** is all the members of the Christian clergy, especially in a particular church. ❑ He spent 16 years in the priesthood. [from Old English]

**prim** /prɪm/ ADJ If you describe someone as **prim**, you disapprove of them because they behave very correctly and are too easily shocked by anything vulgar. ❑ We imagine that the Victorians were very prim and proper. ● **prim|ly** ADV ❑ We sat primly at either end of a long bench.

**pri|mal** /praɪmᵊl/ ADJ **Primal** is used to describe something that relates to the origins of things or that is very basic. [FORMAL] ❑ Jealousy is a primal emotion. [from Medieval Latin]

**pri|mari|ly** /praɪmɛrɪli/ ADV You use **primarily** to say what is mainly true in a particular situation. ❑ These reports come primarily from passengers on the plane. [from Latin]

Word Link | prim ≈ first : primary, primate, prime

**pri|ma|ry** /praɪmeri, -məri/ (**primaries**) **1** ADJ You use **primary** to describe something that is very important or most important for someone or something. [FORMAL] ❑ His difficulty with language was the primary cause of his problems. **2** ADJ **Primary** education is the first few years of formal education for children. ❑ Ninety-nine percent of primary students now have experience with computers. **3** N-COUNT A **primary** or a **primary election** is an election in an American state in which people vote for someone to become a candidate for a political office. ❑ ...the 1968 New Hampshire primary. [from Latin]
→ see color

**pri|ma|ry col|or** (**primary colors**) N-COUNT **Primary colors** are basic colors that can be mixed together to produce other colors. They are usually considered to be red, yellow, and blue. ❑ ...bright primary colors that kids will love.

**pri|ma|ry pol|lu|tant** (**primary pollutants**) N-COUNT **Primary pollutants** are substances that are released into the atmosphere and cause pollution. Compare **secondary pollutant**. [TECHNICAL]

**pri|mate** /praɪmeɪt/ (**primates**) N-COUNT A **primate** is a member of the group of mammals that includes humans, monkeys, and apes. ❑ The woolly spider monkey is the largest primate in the Americas. [from New Latin]
→ see Word Web: primate

**prime** /praɪm/ (**primes, priming, primed**) **1** ADJ You use **prime** to describe something that is most

important in a situation. ❑ Your happiness is my prime concern. ❑ It could be a prime target for attack. **2** ADJ You use **prime** to describe something that is of the best possible quality. ❑ These beaches are prime sites for development. **3** ADJ You use **prime** to describe an example of a particular kind of thing that is absolutely typical. ❑ Jodie Foster: the prime example of a child actor who became a respected adult star. **4** N-UNCOUNT Your **prime** is the stage in your life when you are strongest, most active, or most successful. ❑ I'm just coming into my prime now. ❑ Some of these athletes are well past their prime. **5** V-T If you **prime** someone to do something, you prepare them to do it, for example, by giving them information about it beforehand. ❑ Arnold primed her for her duties. **6** N-COUNT A **prime** is the same as a **prime number**. [TECHNICAL] [from Latin]

**prime me|rid|ian** N-SING The **prime meridian** is the line of longitude, corresponding to zero degrees and passing through Greenwich, England, from which all the other lines of longitude are calculated. [TECHNICAL]

**prime min|is|ter** (**prime ministers**) N-COUNT; N-TITLE The leader of the government in some countries is called the **prime minister**. ❑ ...the former prime minister of Pakistan, Miss Benazir Bhutto.

**primi|tive** /prɪmɪtɪv/ **1** ADJ **Primitive** means belonging to a society in which people live in a very simple way, usually without industries or a writing system. ❑ ...studies of primitive societies. **2** ADJ **Primitive** means belonging to a very early period in the development of an animal or plant. ❑ ...primitive whales. **3** ADJ If you describe something as **primitive**, you mean that it is very simple in style or very old-fashioned. ❑ The conditions are primitive. [from Latin]

**prim|rose** /prɪmrouz/ (**primroses**) N-VAR A **primrose** is a wild plant that has pale yellow flowers in the spring. [from Old French]

**prince** /prɪns/ (**princes**) N-TITLE; N-COUNT A **prince** is a male member of a royal family, especially the son of the king or queen of a country. [from Old French]

**prin|cess** /prɪnsɪs, -sɛs/ (**princesses**) N-TITLE; N-COUNT A **princess** is a female member of a royal family, usually the daughter of a king or queen or the wife of a prince. [from Old French]

**prin|ci|pal** /prɪnsɪpᵊl/ (**principals**) **1** ADJ **Principal** means first in order of importance. ❑ Money was not the principal reason for his action. ❑ Newspapers were the principal source of information. **2** N-COUNT The **principal** of a school is the person in charge of the school. ❑ *Donald King is the principal of Dartmouth High School*. [from Old French]

**prin|ci|pal|ly** /prɪnsɪpli/ ADV **Principally** means more than anything else. ❑ *Williams is principally a popular science writer*. [from Old French]

**prin|ci|pal parts** N-PLURAL In grammar, the **principal parts** of a verb are the main inflected forms of the verb. The principal parts of the verb "to sing" are "sings", "singing", "sang", and "sung". [TECHNICAL]

**prin|ci|ple** /prɪnsɪpᵊl/ (**principles**) 🞱 N-VAR A **principle** is a belief that you have about the way you should behave. ❑ *These changes go against my principles*. ❑ *...a matter of principle*. 🞲 N-COUNT The **principles of** a particular theory or philosophy are its basic rules or laws. ❑ *...the basic principles of democracy*. 🞳 PHRASE If you agree with something **in principle**, you agree in general terms to the idea of it, although you do not yet know the details or know if it will be possible. ❑ *I agree with it in principle but I doubt if it will happen in practice*. 🞴 PHRASE If you refuse to do something **on principle**, you refuse to do it because of your beliefs. ❑ *He would vote against the proposal on principle*. 🞵 PHRASE The **principles of composition** are the rules used by choreographers, writers, and other artists to produce good dance, writing, and other art forms. 🞶 PHRASE The **principles of design** are the rules used by painters and other visual artists to create a work of art, involving concepts such as balance, contrast, and emphasis. [from Latin]

**prin|ci|pled** /prɪnsɪpᵊld/ ADJ If you describe someone as **principled**, you approve of them because they have strong moral principles. ❑ *She was a strong, principled woman*. [from Latin]

**print** /prɪnt/ (**prints, printing, printed**) 🞱 V-T If someone **prints** something such as a book or newspaper, they produce it in large quantities using a machine. ❑ *He started to print his own posters*. ❑ *The new calendar is printed on high quality paper*. ● **Print up** means the same as **print**. ❑ *We're printing up shirts and caps, trying to get everybody involved*. ● **print|ing** N-UNCOUNT ❑ *...a printing and publishing company*. 🞲 V-T If a newspaper or

magazine **prints** a piece of writing, it includes it or publishes it. ❑ *We can only print letters that have the writer's name and address on them*. 🞳 V-T If numbers, letters, or designs **are printed on** a surface, they appear on it. ❑ *...the number printed on the receipt*. ❑ *The company prints its phone number on all of its products*. 🞴 N-UNCOUNT **Print** is used to refer to letters and numbers as they appear on the pages of a printed document. ❑ *...columns of tiny print*. 🞵 V-T If you **print** words, you write in letters that are not joined together. ❑ *Print your name and address on a postcard and send it to us*. 🞶 → see also **printing** 🞷 PHRASE If you appear **in print**, or get **into print**, what you say or write is published in a book or newspaper. ❑ *These poets appeared in print long after their deaths*. [from Old French]
→ see **photography**

▶ **print out** PHR-VERB If a computer or a machine attached to a computer **prints** something **out**, it produces a copy of it on paper. ❑ *You enter measurements and the computer will print out the pattern*. → see also **printout**
→ see Word Web: **printing**

**print|er** /prɪntər/ (**printers**) 🞱 N-COUNT A **printer** is a machine that can be connected to a computer in order to make copies on paper of information held by the computer. ❑ *Can you send that to the printer*. 🞲 N-COUNT A **printer** is a person or company whose job is printing things such as books. ❑ *The manuscript has been sent off to the printer*. [from Old French]
→ see **computer, office, printing**

**print|mak|ing** /prɪntmeɪkɪŋ/ N-UNCOUNT **Printmaking** is an artistic technique that consists of making a series of pictures from an original, or from a specially prepared surface.

**print|out** /prɪntaʊt/ (**printouts**) also **print-out** N-COUNT A **printout** is a piece of paper on which information from a computer has been printed. ❑ *...a computer printout of the report*.

**pri|or** /praɪər/ 🞱 ADJ You use **prior** to indicate that something has already happened, or must happen, before another event takes place. ❑ *He claimed he had no prior knowledge of the protest*. 🞲 PHRASE If something happens **prior to** a particular time or event, it happens before that time or event. [FORMAL] ❑ *Prior to his trip to Japan, he went to New York*. [from Latin]

**pri|or|ity** /praɪɔrɪti/ (**priorities**) 🞱 N-COUNT If something is a **priority**, it is the most important thing you have to achieve or deal with before everything else. ❑ *Being a parent is her first priority*. ❑ *The government's priority is to build more schools*. 🞲 PHRASE If you **give priority to** something or

---

**Word Web**      printing

Before **printing** was invented scribes wrote **documents** by hand. The first **printers** were the Chinese. They used pieces of wood with rows of **characters** carved into them. Later, they started using **movable type** made of baked clay. They created full **pages** by lining up rows of type. A German named Gutenberg made the first metal type. He also invented the **printing press**. The idea came from the wine press, which was hundreds of years old. In the 1500s, printed advertisements were handbills. The earliest newspapers were **published** in the 1600s.

someone, you treat them as more important than anything or anyone else. ❑ *Most schools give priority to children who live nearby.* ◼ PHRASE If something **takes priority** or **has priority over** other things, it is regarded as being more important than them and is dealt with first. ❑ *The needs of the poor must take priority over the desires of the rich.* [from Latin]

**pri|ory** /prɑɪəri/ (**priories**) N-COUNT A **priory** is a place where a small group of monks live and work together. [from Medieval Latin]

**prism** /prɪzəm/ (**prisms**) N-COUNT A **prism** is a block of clear glass or plastic that separates the light passing through it into different colors. [from Medieval Latin]

**pris|on** /prɪzᵊn/ (**prisons**) N-VAR A **prison** is a building where criminals are kept as punishment. ❑ *He went to prison for robbery.* [from Old French]

---

### Word Partnership    Use *prison* with :

| | |
|---|---|
| V. | **die in** prison, **escape from** prison, **face** prison, **go to** prison, **release** *someone* **from** prison, **send** *someone* **to** prison, **serve/spend time in** prison |
| N. | **life in** prison, prison **officials**, prison **population**, prison **reform**, prison **sentence**, prison **time** |

---

**pris|on|er** /prɪzənər/ (**prisoners**) N-COUNT A **prisoner** is a person who is kept in a prison as a punishment or because they have been captured by an enemy. ❑ *...the large number of prisoners sharing cells.* ❑ *...a former Vietnam war prisoner.* [from Old French]
→ see **war**

**pris|tine** /prɪstin, prɪstin/ ADJ **Pristine** things are extremely clean or new. [FORMAL] ❑ *The house is in pristine condition.* [from Latin]

**pri|va|cy** /prɑɪvəsi/ N-UNCOUNT If you have **privacy**, you are in a private place or situation where you can do things without being seen or disturbed. ❑ *...exercises you can do in the privacy of your own home.* ❑ *...relaxing and reading in privacy.* [from Latin]

**pri|vate** /prɑɪvɪt/ (**privates**) ◼ ADJ **Private** companies, industries, and services are owned or controlled by individuals or stockholders, rather than by the government or an official organization. [BUSINESS] ❑ *...research facilities in private industry.* ❑ *...the cost of private education.* ● **pri|vate|ly** ADV ❑ *...privately owned businesses.* ◼ ADJ If something is **private**, it is for the use of one person or group, and not for the general public. ❑ *...private golf clubs.* ❑ *The door is marked "Private."* ◼ ADJ **Private** meetings, discussions, and other activities involve only a small number of people, who do not discuss them with other people. ❑ *...private conversations.* ● **pri|vate|ly** ADV ❑ *Privately her resignation has been welcomed.* ◼ ADJ Your **private life** is that part of your life that is concerned with your personal relationships and activities, rather than with your work or business. ❑ *I've always kept my private and professional life separate.* ◼ ADJ Your **private** thoughts or feelings are ones that you do not talk about to other people. ❑ *...his private grief.* ● **pri|vate|ly** ADV ❑ *Privately, she worries about whether she's really good enough.* ◼ ADJ If you describe a place as **private**, you mean that it is a quiet place and you can be alone there without being disturbed. ❑ *It was the only private*

place they could find. ◼ N-COUNT; N-TITLE; N-VOC A **private** is a soldier of the lowest rank in an army or the marines. ❑ *He was a private in the U.S. Army.* ◼ PHRASE If you do something **in private**, you do it without other people being present, often because it is something that you want to keep secret. ❑ *This should be discussed in private.* [from Latin]

**privately held corporation** (**privately held corporations**) N-COUNT A **privately held corporation** is a company whose shares cannot be bought by the general public.

**pri|vate school** (**private schools**) N-VAR A **private school** is a school that is not supported financially by the government and that parents have to pay for their children to go to. ❑ *...a fancy private school.*

**pri|vat|ize** /prɑɪvətɑɪz/ (**privatizes, privatizing, privatized**) V-T If a company, industry, or service that is owned by the state **is privatized**, the government sells it and makes it a private company. [BUSINESS] ❑ *Many state-owned companies were privatized.* ● **pri|vati|za|tion** /prɑɪvətɪzeɪʃᵊn/ (**privatizations**) N-VAR ❑ *...the privatization of government services.* [from Latin]

**privi|lege** /prɪvɪlɪdʒ, prɪvlɪdʒ/ (**privileges**) ◼ N-COUNT A **privilege** is a special right or advantage that only one person or group has. ❑ *...special privileges for government officials.* ◼ N-UNCOUNT **Privilege** is the power and advantages that belong to a small group of people, usually because of their wealth or their connections with powerful people. ❑ *...a life of privilege.* [from Old French]

---

### Word Partnership    Use *privilege* with :

| | |
|---|---|
| ADJ. | **executive** privilege, **special** privilege ◼ |
| N. | **attorney-client** privilege ◼ **power** and privilege ◼ |

---

**privi|leged** /prɪvɪlɪdʒd, prɪvlɪdʒd/ ADJ Someone who is **privileged** has an advantage or opportunity that most other people do not have, often because of their wealth or connections with powerful people. ❑ *...wealthy, privileged young women.* [from Old French]

**prize** /prɑɪz/ (**prizes, prizing, prized**) ◼ N-COUNT A **prize** is money or something valuable, such as money or a trophy, that is given to the winner of a game or competition. ❑ *He won first prize.* ❑ *He was awarded the Nobel Prize for Physics.* ◼ ADJ You use **prize** to describe things that are of such good quality that they win prizes or deserve to win prizes. ❑ *...a prize bull.* ◼ V-T Something that **is prized** is wanted and admired because it is considered to be very valuable or very good quality. ❑ *These colorful baskets are prized by collectors.* ◼ V-T If you **prize** something **open** or **prize** it away from a surface, you force it open or away from a surface. ❑ *The drawer has been prized open with a screwdriver.* [from Old French]

---

### Word Partnership    Use *prize* with :

| | |
|---|---|
| V. | **award a** prize, **claim a** prize, **receive a** prize, **share a** prize, **win a** prize ◼ |
| ORD. | **first** prize ◼ |
| ADJ. | **grand** prize, **top** prize ◼ |

---

**pro** /proʊ/ (**pros**) ◼ N-COUNT A **pro** is a

P

professional, especially a professional athlete. [INFORMAL] ❑ *Langer was a pro for 29 years, and competed in nearly 80 championships.* ❑ *...a former college and pro basketball player.* **2** PHRASE The **pros and cons** of something are its advantages and disadvantages. ❑ *Motherhood has its pros and cons.* [Sense 2 from Latin]

### Word Link
prob ≈ testing : probability, probably, probation

**prob|abil|ity** /prɒbəbɪlɪti/ (**probabilities**) **1** N-VAR The **probability of** something happening is how likely it is to occur, sometimes expressed as a fraction or a percentage. ❑ *The victim's probability of dying was 100%.* ❑ *Every day, the probabilities of being shot or injured increase.* **2** N-VAR You say that there is a **probability that** something will happen when it is likely to happen. ❑ *If you've owned property for several years, the probability is that values have increased.* **3** PHRASE If you say that something will happen **in all probability,** you mean that you think it is very likely to happen. ❑ *In all probability, they are going to lose.* [from Old French]

**prob|able** /prɒbəb³l/ **1** ADJ If you say that something is **probable,** you mean that it is likely to be true or likely to happen. ❑ *It is probable that he never really understood the system.* **2** ADJ You can use **probable** to describe a role or function that someone or something is likely to have. ❑ *...their probable presidential candidate.* [from Old French]

**prob|ably** /prɒbəbli/ ADV If you say that something is **probably** the case, you think that it is likely to be the case, although you are not sure. ❑ *The White House probably won't make this plan public until July.* ❑ *Van Gogh is probably the best-known painter in the world.* [from Old French]

**pro|ba|tion** /proʊbeɪʃ³n/ N-UNCOUNT **Probation** is a period of time during which a person who has committed a crime has to obey the law and be supervised by a probation officer, rather than being sent to prison. ❑ *She admitted theft and was put on probation for two years.* [from Medieval Latin]

**pro|ba|tion of|fic|er** (**probation officers**) N-COUNT A **probation officer** is a person whose job is to supervise and help people who have committed crimes and been put on probation.

**probe** /proʊb/ (**probes, probing, probed**) **1** V-I If you **probe into** something, you ask questions or try to discover facts about it. ❑ *The more they probed into his background, the more suspicious they became.* ● **Probe** is also a noun. ❑ *Officials have opened a probe into Monday's crash.* **2** V-T If you **probe** a place, you search it in order to find someone or something that you are looking for. ❑ *A flashlight beam probed the bushes.* [from Medieval Latin]

**prob|lem** /prɒbləm/ (**problems**) **1** N-COUNT A **problem** is a situation that is unsatisfactory and causes difficulties for people. ❑ *...the economic problems of the city.* ❑ *I do not have a simple solution to the garbage problem.* **2** N-COUNT A **problem** is a puzzle that requires logical thought or mathematics to solve it. ❑ *...geometry problems.* [from Late Latin]
→ see **fraction**

### Thesaurus
problem    Also look up :

| | |
|---|---|
| N. | complication, difficulty, hitch **1** puzzle, question, riddle **2** |

**prob|lem|at|ic** /prɒbləmætɪk/ ADJ Something that is **problematic** involves problems and difficulties. ❑ *Parents may need help in dealing with a child's problematic behavior.* [from Late Latin]

**pro|ce|dur|al** /prəsidʒərəl/ ADJ **Procedural** means involving a formal procedure. ❑ *A procedural rule states that the votes of 60 senators are needed.* [from Latin]

**pro|ce|dure** /prəsidʒər/ (**procedures**) N-VAR A **procedure** is a way of doing something, especially the usual or correct way. ❑ *...a minor surgical procedure.* ❑ *...the correct procedure in applying for a visa.* [from Latin]

### Word Partnership
Use *procedure* with :

| | |
|---|---|
| V. | **follow a** procedure, **perform a** procedure, **use a** procedure |
| ADJ. | **simple** procedure, **standard (operating)** procedure, **surgical** procedure |

### Word Link
pro ≈ in front, before : proceed, produce, prologue

**pro|ceed** (**proceeds, proceeding, proceeded**)

The verb is pronounced /prəsid/. The plural noun in meaning **3** is pronounced /proʊsidz/.

**1** V-T If you **proceed to** do something, you do it after doing something else. ❑ *He proceeded to tell me the real story.* **2** V-I To **proceed** means to continue. [FORMAL] ❑ *The group proceeded with a march despite the warning.* ❑ *Their development has proceeded steadily since the war.* **3** N-PLURAL The **proceeds** of an event or activity are the money that has been obtained from it. ❑ *The proceeds of the concert went to charity.* [from Latin]

**pro|cess** /prɒsɛs/ (**processes, processing, processed**) **1** N-COUNT A **process** is a series of actions or events which have a particular result. ❑ *...agreement to start the peace process as soon as possible.* ❑ *It occurs as part of the aging process.* **2** V-T When raw materials or foods **are processed,** they are prepared in factories before they are used or sold. ❑ *The fish are processed by freezing, canning, and smoking.* ❑ *The material will be processed into plastic pellets.* ● **pro|cess|ing** N-UNCOUNT ❑ *America sent cotton to England for processing.* **3** V-T When people **process** information, they put it through a system or into a computer in order to deal with it. ❑ *...facilities to process the data.* ● **pro|cess|ing** N-UNCOUNT ❑ *...data processing.* **4** → see also **word processing** **5** N-COUNT A **process** is a series of things that happen naturally and result in a biological or chemical change. **6** PHRASE If you are **in the process of** doing something, you have started to do it and are still doing it. ❑ *We are in the process of working out the details.* **7** PHRASE If you are doing something and you do something else **in the process,** you do the second thing as part of doing the first thing. ❑ *We attend the meetings and in the process, we learn new words and phrases.* [from Old French]

**pro|ces|sion** /prəsɛʃ³n/ (**processions**) N-COUNT A **procession** is a group of people who are walking, riding, or driving in a line as part of a public event. ❏ *...a funeral procession.* [from Old French]

**pro|ces|sor** /prɒsɛsər/ (**processors**)

**1** N-COUNT A **processor** is the part of a computer that interprets commands and performs the processes the user has requested. [COMPUTING] [from Old French] **2** → see also **word processor**

**pro|claim** /proʊkleɪm/ (**proclaims, proclaiming, proclaimed**) V-T If people **proclaim** something, they formally make it known. ❏ *The new government proclaimed its independence.* ❏ *Britain proudly proclaims that it is a nation of animal lovers.* [from Latin]

**proc|la|ma|tion** /prɒkləmeɪʃᵊn/ (**proclamations**) N-COUNT A **proclamation** is a public announcement about something important. ❏ *...the proclamation of independence.* [from Latin]

**pro|cure** /prəkyʊər/ (**procures, procuring, procured**) V-T If you **procure** something, especially something that is difficult to get, you obtain it. [FORMAL] ❏ *It was very difficult to procure food.* [from Latin]

**pro|cure|ment** /prəkyʊərmənt/ N-UNCOUNT **Procurement** is the act of obtaining something such as supplies for an army or other organization. [FORMAL] ❏ *...procurement of new weapons.* [from Latin]

**prod** /prɒd/ (**prods, prodding, prodded**) **1** V-T If you **prod** someone or something, you give them a quick push with your finger or with a pointed object. ❏ *He prodded Murray with the shotgun.* ❏ *He found nothing but continued to prod the ground.* ● **Prod** is also a noun. ❏ *He gave the donkey a prod.* **2** V-T If you **prod** someone **into** doing something, you remind or persuade them to do it. ❏ *The question is intended to prod students into examining the concept of freedom.*

**pro|di|gious** /prədɪdʒəs/ ADJ Something that is **prodigious** is very large or impressive. [LITERARY] ❏ *This business generates cash in prodigious amounts.* ● **pro|di|gious|ly** ADV ❏ *She ate prodigiously.* [from Latin]

**prod|i|gy** /prɒdɪdʒi/ (**prodigies**) N-COUNT A **prodigy** is someone who has a great natural ability for something which shows itself at an early age. sports. ❏ *...a Russian tennis prodigy.* [from Latin]

> **Word Link**    pro ≈ in front, before : *proceed, produce, prologue*

**pro|duce** (**produces, producing, produced**)

The verb is pronounced /prədus/. The noun is pronounced /prɒdus/ or /proʊdus/.

**1** V-T To **produce** something means to cause it to happen. ❏ *The drug can produce side-effects.* **2** V-T If you **produce** something, you make or create it. ❏ *The company produced nearly 200,000 tons of coal last year.* ● **pro|duc|er** (**producers**) N-COUNT ❏ *...Saudi Arabia, the world's leading oil producer.* **3** V-T If you **produce** evidence or an argument, you show it or explain it to people. ❏ *He had to produce evidence of where he would be staying.* **4** V-T If you **produce** an object from somewhere, you show it or bring it out so that it can be seen. ❏ *To rent a car you must produce a passport.* **5** V-T If someone **produces** something such as a movie, a magazine, or a CD, they organize it and decide

how it should be made. ❏ *He has produced his own sports magazine.* ● **pro|duc|er** (**producers**) N-COUNT ❏ *...a film producer.* **6** N-UNCOUNT **Produce** is fruit and vegetables that are grown in large quantities to be sold. ❏ *We manage to get most of our produce in farmers' markets.* [from Latin]

**pro|duc|er** /prədusər/ (**producers**) N-COUNT In biology, **producers** are plants or bacteria that can produce their own food, especially by means of photosynthesis. [TECHNICAL] [from Latin]
→ see **theater**

**prod|uct** /prɒdʌkt/ (**products**) **1** N-COUNT A **product** is something that is produced and sold in large quantities. ❏ *Try to get the best product at the lowest price.* **2** N-COUNT If you say that someone or something is a **product of** a situation or process, you mean that the situation or process has had a significant effect in making them what they are. ❏ *We are all products of our time.* **3** N-COUNT The **product** of a chemical reaction is the substance that is formed as a result of the chemical reaction. [from Latin]
→ see **industry**

**pro|duc|tion** /prədʌkʃᵊn/ (**productions**) **1** N-UNCOUNT **Production** is the process of manufacturing or growing something in large quantities, or the amount of goods manufactured or grown. ❏ *That model won't go into production before late 2007.* ❏ *We needed to increase production.* **2** N-UNCOUNT The **production of** something is its creation as the result of a natural process. ❏ *These proteins stimulate the production of blood cells.* **3** N-UNCOUNT **Production** is the process of organizing and preparing a play, movie, program, or CD, in order to present it to the public. ❏ *She is head of the production company.* **4** N-COUNT A **production** is a play, opera, or other show that is performed in a theater. ❏ *...a production of "Othello."* [from Latin]
→ see **theater**

**pro|duc|tion line** (**production lines**) N-COUNT A **production line** is an arrangement of machines in a factory where the products pass from machine to machine until they are finished. ❏ *A new production line has been installed at the factory in Solihull.*

**pro|duc|tion val|ues** N-PLURAL The **production values** of a movie or play are the quality of its technical aspects, such as the lighting, sets, makeup, and special effects.

**pro|duc|tive** /prədʌktɪv/ **1** ADJ Someone or something that is **productive** produces or does a lot for the amount of resources used. ❏ *Training makes workers more productive.* ❏ *The more productive farmers can provide cheaper food.* **2** ADJ If you say that a relationship between people is **productive**, you mean that a lot of good or useful things happen as a result of it. ❏ *He was hopeful that the talks would be productive.* [from Latin]

**prod|uc|tiv|ity** /prɒdʌktɪvɪti/ N-UNCOUNT **Productivity** is the rate at which goods are produced. ❏ *...continued improvements in productivity.* [from Latin]

**pro|fess** /prəfɛs/ (**professes, professing, professed**) **1** V-T If you **profess to** do or have something, you claim that you do it or have it, often when you do not. [FORMAL] ❏ *She professed to hate her name.* ❏ *Why do organizations profess that they* care? **2** V-T If you **profess** a feeling, opinion, or belief, you express it. [FORMAL] ❑ *He professed to be content.* ❑ *Miller professed himself "very happy" with the decision.* [from Latin]

**pro|fes|sion** /prəfɛʃⁿn/ (**professions**)
**1** N-COUNT A **profession** is a type of job that requires advanced education or training. ❑ *Harper was a teacher by profession.* **2** N-COUNT You can use **profession** to refer to all the people who have the same profession. ❑ *...the medical profession.* [from Medieval Latin]

**pro|fes|sion|al** /prəfɛʃənᵊl/ (**professionals**)
**1** ADJ **Professional** means relating to a person's work, especially work that requires special training. ❑ *His professional career started at Colgate University.* ● **pro|fes|sion|al|ly** ADV ❑ *...a professionally qualified architect.* **2** ADJ **Professional** people have jobs that require advanced education or training. ❑ *...highly qualified professional people like doctors and engineers.* ● **Professional** is also a noun. ❑ *My father wanted me to become a professional.* **3** ADJ You use **professional** to describe people who do a particular thing to earn money rather than as a hobby. ❑ *...a professional athlete.* ● **Professional** is also a noun. ❑ *He has been a professional since March 1985.* ● **pro|fes|sion|al|ly** ADV ❑ *By age 16 he was playing professionally with bands.* **4** ADJ If you say something that someone does or produces is **professional**, you approve of it because you think that it is of a very high standard. ❑ *They run it with a truly professional but personal touch.* ● **Professional** is also a noun. ❑ *...a dedicated professional who worked well with others.* ● **pro|fes|sion|al|ism** N-UNCOUNT ❑ *She did her job with supreme professionalism.* ● **pro|fes|sion|al|ly** ADV ❑ *...very professionally designed invitations.* [from Medieval Latin]

**pro|fes|sor** /prəfɛsər/ (**professors**) **1** N-COUNT; N-TITLE; N-VOC A **professor** in an American or Canadian university or college is a teacher of the highest rank. ❑ *...a professor of economics at George Washington University.* **2** N-TITLE; N-COUNT; N-VOC A **professor** in a British university is the most senior teacher in a department. ❑ *...Professor Cameron.* [from Medieval Latin]
→ see **graduation**

**prof|fer** /prɒfər/ (**proffers, proffering, proffered**) V-T If you **proffer** something to someone, you offer it to them. [FORMAL] ❑ *The army has not yet proffered an explanation.* [from Old French]

**pro|fi|cient** /prəfɪʃənt/ ADJ If you are **proficient** in something, you can do it well. ❑ *Many of them are proficient in foreign languages.* ● **pro|fi|cien|cy** N-UNCOUNT ❑ *...basic proficiency in English.* [from Latin]

**pro|file** /proʊfaɪl/ (**profiles**) **1** N-COUNT Your **profile** is the outline of your face seen from the side. ❑ *He was young and slim, with black hair and a handsome profile.* **2** PHRASE If someone has a **high profile**, people notice them and what they do. If you **keep a low profile**, you avoid doing things that will make people notice you. ❑ *Indians make up only 2% of South Africa's population but they have a high profile.* [from Italian] **3** → see also

profile

**high-profile**

**prof|it** /prɒfɪt/ (**profits, profiting, profited**)
**1** N-VAR A **profit** is an amount of money that you gain when you are paid more for something than it cost you. ❑ *The bank made profits of $6.5 million.* **2** V-I If you **profit from** something, you earn a profit or gain some advantage from it. ❑ *No one was profiting from the war effort.* ❑ *She would profit from a more relaxed lifestyle.* [from Latin]

**prof|it|able** /prɒfɪtəbᵊl/ **1** ADJ A **profitable** organization or practice makes a profit. ❑ *...the most profitable business in the U.S.* ● **prof|it|ably** /prɒfɪtəbli/ ADV ❑ *The 28 French stores are trading profitably.* ● **prof|it|abil|ity** /prɒfɪtəbɪlɪti/ N-UNCOUNT ❑ *Changes were made to increase profitability.* **2** ADJ Something that is **profitable** results in some benefit for you. ❑ *...a profitable exchange of ideas.* ● **prof|it|ably** ADV ❑ *He could have spent his time more profitably.* [from Latin]

**pro|found** /prəfaʊnd/ (**profounder, profoundest**) **1** ADJ You use **profound** to emphasize that something is very great or intense. ❑ *...discoveries which had a profound effect on many areas of medicine.* ❑ *...profound disagreement.* ● **pro|found|ly** ADV ❑ *This has profoundly affected my life.* **2** ADJ A **profound** idea, work, or person shows great intellectual depth and understanding. ❑ *...this tender and profound love poem.* [from Old French]

**pro|fuse** /prəfyus/ ADJ **Profuse** means doing something or happening a lot. [FORMAL] ❑ *...profuse sweating.* ❑ *...profuse apologies.* ● **pro|fuse|ly** ADV ❑ *He was bleeding profusely.* [from Latin]

**pro|fu|sion** /prəfyuʒⁿn/ If there is a **profusion of** something or if it occurs **in profusion**, there is a very large quantity or variety of it. [FORMAL] ❑ *...a profusion of wild flowers.* [from Latin]

**prog|no|sis** /prɒgnoʊsɪs/ (**prognoses** /prɒgnoʊsiz/) N-COUNT A **prognosis** is an estimate of the future of someone or something, especially about whether a patient will recover from an illness. [FORMAL] ❑ *The doctor's prognosis was that Laurence might walk within 12 months.* [from Latin]

**pro|grade ro|ta|tion** /proʊgreɪd roʊteɪʃⁿn/ N-UNCOUNT Planets that have **prograde rotation** spin on their axis in the same direction that they orbit the sun. Compare **retrograde rotation**. [TECHNICAL]

---

**Word Link**    *gram ≈ writing : diagram, program, telegram*

---

**pro|gram** /proʊgræm, -grəm/ (**programs, programming, programmed**) **1** N-COUNT A **program** of actions or events is a series of actions or events that are planned to be done. ❑ *...the nation's largest training and education program for adults.* **2** N-COUNT A television or radio **program** is something that is broadcast on television or radio. ❑ *...a network television program.* **3** N-COUNT A theater or concert **program** is a small book or sheet of paper that gives information about the play or concert. ❑ *When you go to concerts, it's helpful to read the program.* **4** V-T When you **program** a machine or system, you set its controls so that it will work in a particular way. ❑ *Parents can program the machine not to turn on at certain times.* **5** N-COUNT A **program** is a set of instructions that a computer follows in order to perform a particular task. [COMPUTING] ❑ *...an error in a computer program.*

**6** V-T When you **program** a computer, you give it a set of instructions to make it able to perform a particular task. [COMPUTING] ❑ He programmed his computer to compare the 1,431 possible combinations. ● pro|gram|ming N-UNCOUNT ❑ ...programming skills. ● pro|gram|mer (**programmers**) N-COUNT ❑ ...a computer programmer. [from Late Latin]
→ see radio

### Word Partnership    Use *program* with :

| | |
|---|---|
| V. | **create** a program, **expand** a program, **implement** a program, **launch** a program, **run** a program **1 5** |
| | program **a computer 6** |
| N. | **computer** program, **software** program **5** |

**pro|gress** (**progresses, progressing, progressed**)

The noun is pronounced /prɒgrɛs/. The verb is pronounced /prəgrɛs/.

**1** N-UNCOUNT **Progress** is the process of gradually improving or getting nearer to achieving or completing something. ❑ We are making progress in the fight against cancer. **2** N-SING The **progress** of a situation or action is the way in which it develops. ❑ The president was delighted with the progress of the first day's talks. **3** V-I To **progress** means to improve or to become more advanced or successful. ❑ He will visit regularly to see how his new employees are progressing. **4** V-I If events **progress**, they continue to happen gradually over a period of time. ❑ As the evening progressed, sadness turned to anger. **5** PHRASE If something is **in progress**, it has started and is still continuing. ❑ The game was already in progress when we arrived. [from Latin]

**pro|gres|sion** /prəgrɛʃ°n/ (**progressions**) N-COUNT A **progression** is a gradual development from one state to another. ❑ ...treatment to slow the progression of the disease. [from Latin]

**pro|gres|sive** /prəgrɛsɪv/ (**progressives**) **1** ADJ Someone who is **progressive** has modern ideas about how things should be done, rather than traditional ones. ❑ ...a progressive businessman who fought for the rights of consumers. ● A **progressive** is someone who is progressive. ❑ The Republicans were split between progressives and conservatives. **2** ADJ A **progressive** change happens gradually over a period of time. ❑ One symptom of the disease is progressive loss of memory. ● pro|gres|sive|ly ADV ❑ Her symptoms became progressively worse. [from Latin]

**pro|hib|it** /proʊhɪbɪt/ (**prohibits, prohibiting, prohibited**) V-T If a law or someone in authority **prohibits** something, they forbid it or make it illegal. [FORMAL] ❑ ...a school that prohibits calculators. ❑ Fishing is prohibited. ● pro|hi|bi|tion /proʊɪbɪʃ°n/ N-UNCOUNT ❑ ...the prohibition of slavery. [from Latin]

**pro|hibi|tive** /proʊhɪbɪtɪv/ ADJ If the cost of something is **prohibitive**, it is so high that many people cannot afford it. [FORMAL] ❑ The cost of private treatment can be prohibitive. ● pro|hibi|tive|ly ADV ❑ Meat and butter were prohibitively expensive. [from Latin]

**proj|ect** (**projects, projecting, projected**)

The noun is pronounced /prɒdʒɛkt/. The verb is pronounced /prədʒɛkt/.

**1** N-COUNT A **project** is a task that requires a lot of time and effort. ❑ Money will go into local development projects. ❑ ...an international science project. **2** N-COUNT A **project** is a detailed study of a subject by a student. ❑ The kids in my class have just finished a project on ancient Greece. **3** V-T If something **is projected**, it is planned or expected. ❑ 13% of Americans are over 65; this number is projected to reach 22% by the year 2030. ❑ The government has projected a 5% price increase for the year. **4** V-T If you **project** a particular feeling or quality, you show it in your behavior. If you **project** yourself in a particular way, you try to make people see you in that way. ❑ Bradley projects a natural warmth and sincerity. ❑ He hasn't been able to project himself as a strong leader. **5** V-T If you **project** a film or picture onto a screen or wall, you make it appear there. ❑ We tried projecting the maps onto the screen. **6** V-I If something **projects**, it sticks out above or beyond a surface or edge. [FORMAL] ❑ ...a narrow ledge that projected out from the bank of the river. [from Latin]

### Word Partnership    Use *project* with :

| | |
|---|---|
| V. | **approve** a project, **launch** a project **1** **complete** a project, **start** a project **1 2** |
| N. | **construction** project, **development** project, project **director/manager 1** **research** project, **writing** project **1 2** **science** project **1 2** |
| ADJ. | **involved in** a project, **latest** project, **new** project, **special** project **1 2** |

**pro|jec|tile mo|tion** N-UNCOUNT **Projectile motion** is the curved path of an object which has been propelled into the air at an angle, for example a ball that is kicked or thrown. [TECHNICAL]

**pro|jec|tion** /prədʒɛkʃ°n/ (**projections**) **1** N-COUNT A **projection** is an estimate of a future amount. ❑ ...the company's projection of 11 million visitors for the first year. **2** N-UNCOUNT The **projection** of a film or picture is the act of projecting it onto a screen or wall. ❑ They took me into a projection room to see the movie they had made. **3** N-UNCOUNT A speaker or performer who has good **projection** is skillful at speaking to an audience or communicating with an audience in a clear and confident way. [from Latin]

**pro|jec|tor** /prədʒɛktər/ (**projectors**) N-COUNT A **projector** is a machine that projects films or slides onto a screen or wall. ❑ ...a slide projector. [from Latin]

**pro|karyo|tic cell** /proʊkæriɒtɪk/ (**prokaryotic cells**) also **prokaryote** /proʊkærioʊt/ N-COUNT **Prokaryotic cells** or **prokaryotes** are cells or organisms such as bacteria that do not have a nucleus. Compare **eukaryotic cell** [TECHNICAL]

**pro|lif|er|ate** /prəlɪfəreɪt/ (**proliferates, proliferating, proliferated**) V-I If things **proliferate**, they increase in number very quickly. [FORMAL] ❑ Computerized databases are proliferating fast. ● pro|lif|era|tion /prəlɪfəreɪ°n/ N-UNCOUNT ❑ ...the proliferation of nuclear weapons. [from Medieval Latin]

**pro|lif|ic** /prəlɪfɪk/ ADJ A **prolific** writer, artist, or composer produces a large number of works. ❑ She is a prolific writer of novels and short stories. [from Medieval Latin]

p

**Word Link** pro ≈ in front, before : proceed, produce, prologue

**pro|logue** /proʊlɔg/ (**prologues**) also **prolog**
N-COUNT A **prologue** is a speech or section of text
that introduces a play or book. ❑ ...the prologue to
the novel. [from Latin]

**pro|long** /prəlɔŋ/ (**prolongs, prolonging,
prolonged**) V-T To **prolong** something means
to make it last longer. ❑ Foreign military aid was
prolonging the war. [from Late Latin]

**pro|longed** /prəlɔŋd/ ADJ A **prolonged** event or
situation continues for a long time, or for longer
than expected. ❑ ...a prolonged period of peace. [from
Late Latin]

**prom** /prɒm/ (**proms**) N-COUNT A **prom** is a
formal dance at a school or college which usually
takes place at the end of the academic year. ❑ I
didn't want to go to the prom with Craig. ❑ ...my senior
prom.

**promi|nent** /prɒmɪnənt/ **1** ADJ Someone
who is **prominent** is important and well-known.
❑ ...the children of very prominent or successful parents.
● **promi|nence** N-UNCOUNT ❑ Crime prevention
needs to have more prominence. **2** ADJ Something
that is **prominent** is very noticeable. ❑ ...a
prominent nose. ● **promi|nent|ly** ADV ❑ The poster is
prominently displayed in the hall. [from Latin]

**pro|mis|cu|ous** /prəmɪskyuəs/ ADJ If you
describe someone as **promiscuous**, you disapprove
of the fact that they have sex with many different
people. ❑ The new law could encourage promiscuous
behavior. ● **promis|cu|ity** /prɒmɪskyuɪti/
N-UNCOUNT ❑ ...sexual promiscuity. [from Latin]

**prom|ise** /prɒmɪs/ (**promises, promising,
promised**) **1** V-T/V-I If you **promise that** you will
do something, you say to someone that you will
definitely do it. ❑ The post office has promised to
resume mail delivery to the area on Friday. ❑ He promised
that the rich would no longer get special treatment.
❑ Promise me you will not waste my time. ● **Promise** is
also a noun. ❑ If you make a promise, you should keep
it. **2** V-T If you **promise** someone something, you
tell them that you will definitely give it to them
or make sure that they have it. ❑ I've promised them
a house in the country. **3** V-T If a situation or event
**promises to** have a particular quality or **to** be a
particular thing, it shows signs that it will have
that quality or be that thing. ❑ Thursday promises
to be a busy day. **4** N-UNCOUNT If someone or
something shows **promise**, they seem likely to be
very good or successful. ❑ The boy showed promise as
an athlete. [from Latin]

**Word Partnership** Use promise with :

| | |
|---|---|
| N. | **campaign** promise **1** |
| V. | **break a** promise, **deliver on a** promise,<br>**keep a** promise, **make a** promise **1**<br>**hold** promise, **show** promise **4** |
| ADJ. | **broken** promise, **empty** promise, **false**<br>promise **1**<br>**enormous** promise, **great** promise, **real**<br>promise **4** |

**prom|is|ing** /prɒmɪsɪŋ/ ADJ Someone or
something that is **promising** seems likely to
be very good or successful. ❑ ...one of the most
promising poets of his generation. [from Latin]

**prom|is|sory note** /prɒmɪsɔri noʊt/
(**promissory notes**) N-COUNT A **promissory note** is
a written promise to pay a specific sum of money
to a particular person. [BUSINESS] ❑ ...a $36.4
million, five-year promissory note.

**Word Link** mot ≈ moving : motion, motivate,
promote

**pro|mote** /prəmoʊt/ (**promotes, promoting,
promoted**) **1** V-T If people **promote** something,
they help it to happen, increase, or become
more popular. ❑ ...trying to promote the idea that
war is a bad thing. ● **pro|mo|tion** (**promotions**)
N-VAR ❑ ...the promotion of democracy. ❑ ...TV
commercials and other promotions. **2** V-T If someone
**is promoted**, they are given a more important job
or rank in the organization that they work for.
❑ He was promoted to general manager. ● **pro|mo|tion**
N-VAR ❑ Consider changing jobs or trying for promotion.
[from Latin]
→ see **concert**

**pro|mot|er** /prəmoʊtər/ (**promoters**)
**1** N-COUNT A **promoter** is a person who helps
organize and finance an event, especially a sports
event. ❑ ...one of the top boxing promoters in Las
Vegas. **2** N-COUNT The **promoter** of a cause or idea
tries to make it become popular. ❑ His father is a
publisher and promoter of classical music. [from Latin]

**pro|mo|tion|al** /prəmoʊʃənəl/ ADJ **Promotional**
material, events, or ideas are designed to increase
the sales of a product or service. ❑ The hotel's
promotional shows a couple in the pool. [from Latin]

**prompt** /prɒmpt/ (**prompts, prompting,
prompted**) **1** V-T To **prompt** someone **to** do
something means to make them decide to do it.
❑ The article prompted readers to complain. **2** V-T If
you **prompt** someone, you encourage or remind
them to do something or to continue doing
something. ❑ "Well, Daniel?" Wilson prompted.
● **prompt|ing** (**promptings**) N-VAR ❑ The team
needed little prompting from their coach. **3** ADJ A
**prompt** action is done without any delay. ❑ It is not
too late, but prompt action is needed. [from Latin]

**prompt|ly** /prɒmptli/ **1** ADV If you do
something **promptly**, you do it immediately.
❑ She entered the room, took her seat, and promptly fell
asleep. **2** ADV If you do something **promptly at**
a particular time, you do it at exactly that time.
❑ Promptly at a quarter past seven, we left the hotel.
[from Latin]

**prone** /proʊn/ ADJ To be **prone to** something,
usually something bad, means to have a tendency
to be affected by it or to do it. ❑ They are prone to
errors and accidents. ● **Prone** combines with nouns
to make adjectives that describe people who are
frequently affected by something bad. ❑ ...the
most injury-prone rider. [from Latin]

**pro|noun** /proʊnaʊn/ (**pronouns**) N-COUNT A
**pronoun** is a word that you use instead of a noun
group to refer to someone or something. "It,"
"she," "something," and "myself" are pronouns.
[from Latin]

**Word Link** nounce ≈ reporting : announce,
denounce, pronounce

**pro|nounce** /prənaʊns/ (**pronounces,
pronouncing, pronounced**) **1** V-T To **pronounce**
a word means to say it using particular sounds.

❏ *Have I pronounced your name correctly?* **2** v-т If you **pronounce** something, you state it formally or publicly. [FORMAL] ❏ *A specialist has pronounced him fully fit.* [from Latin]
→ see **trial**

**pro|nounced** /prənaʊnst/ ADJ Something that is **pronounced** is very noticeable. ❏ *She speaks with a pronounced Dublin accent.* [from Latin]

**pro|nounce|ment** /prənaʊnsmənt/ (**pronouncements**) N-COUNT **Pronouncements** are public or official statements on an important subject. ❏ …*the director's latest pronouncements.* [from Latin]

**pro|nun|cia|tion** /prənʌnsieɪʃⁿn/ (**pronunciations**) N-VAR The **pronunciation** of a word or language is the way it is pronounced. ❏ *She gave the word its French pronunciation.* [from Latin]

**proof** /pruf/ (**proofs**) N-VAR **Proof** is a fact, argument, or piece of evidence showing that something is true or exists. ❏ *You have to have proof of residence in the state.* ❏ *This is proof that he is wrong.* [from Old French]

---

**Word Partnership**    Use *proof* with :

| | |
|---|---|
| ADJ. | **convincing** proof, **final** proof, **living** proof, proof **positive** |
| V. | **have** proof, **need** proof, **offer** proof, **provide** proof, **require** proof, **show** proof |

---

**prop** /prɒp/ (**props, propping, propped**) **1** v-т If you **prop** an object **on** or **against** something, you support it by putting something underneath it or by resting it somewhere. ❏ *He propped his feet on the desk.* ● **Prop up** means the same as **prop.** ❏ *Sam propped his elbows up on the bench behind him.* **2** N-COUNT A **prop** is a stick or other object that you use to support something. ❏ *Using the table as a prop, he dragged himself to his feet.* **3** N-COUNT The **props** in a play or movie are the objects and pieces of furniture that are used in it. ❏ …*the props for a stage show.* [Senses 1 and 2 from Middle Dutch. Sense 3 from Old French.]
→ see **theater**

▸ **prop up** PHR-VERB To **prop up** something means to support it or help it to survive. ❏ *Investments in the U.S. money market have propped up the dollar.*
→ see **prop 1**

**propa|gan|da** /prɒpəgændə/ N-UNCOUNT **Propaganda** is information, often inaccurate information, that a political organization publishes or broadcasts in order to influence people. ❏ *A huge propaganda campaign was mounted by the state media.* [from Italian]

**propa|gate** /prɒpəgeɪt/ (**propagates, propagating, propagated**) v-т If people **propagate** an idea or piece of information, they spread it and try to make people believe it or support it. [FORMAL] ❏ *He returned to Poland to propagate his new theory.* ● **propa|ga|tion** /prɒpəgeɪʃⁿn/ N-UNCOUNT ❏ …*the propagation of true Buddhism.* [from Latin]

---

**Word Link**    *pel ≈ driving, forcing : com***pel**, ex***pel***, **prop***el*

---

**pro|pel** /prəpɛl/ (**propels, propelling, propelled**) v-т To **propel** something in a particular direction means to cause it to move in that direction. ❏ *The tiny rocket is designed to propel the spacecraft toward*

*Mars.* [from Latin]

**pro|pel|ler** /prəpɛlər/ (**propellers**) N-COUNT A **propeller** is a device with blades attached to a boat or aircraft, that spins around and causes the boat or aircraft to move. ❏ …*a three-bladed propeller.* [from Latin]

**pro|pen|sity** /prəpɛnsiti/ (**propensities**) N-COUNT A **propensity to** do something or a **propensity for** something is a natural tendency to behave in a particular way. [FORMAL] ❏ …*those who have a propensity for violence.* [from Latin]

**prop|er** /prɒpər/ **1** ADJ You use **proper** to describe things that you consider to be real and satisfactory rather than inadequate in some way. ❏ *Two out of five people lack a proper job.* ● **prop|er|ly** ADV ❏ *You're not eating properly.* **2** ADJ The **proper** thing is the one that is correct or most suitable. ❏ *The proper procedures have been followed.* **3** ADJ If you say that a way of behaving is **proper**, you mean that it is considered socially acceptable and right. ❏ *It was not thought proper for a woman to be on the stage.* ● **prop|er|ly** ADV ❏ *It's about time he learned to behave properly.* [from Old French]

**prop|er noun** (**proper nouns**) N-COUNT A **proper noun** is the name of a particular person, place, organization, or thing. Proper nouns begin with a capital letter.

---

**Word Link**    *propr ≈ owning :* **propr***ty,* **propr***ietary,* **propr***ietor*

---

**prop|er|ty** /prɒpərti/ (**properties**) **1** N-UNCOUNT Someone's **property** is all the things that belong to them or something that belongs to them. [FORMAL] ❏ …*her personal property.* **2** N-VAR A **property** is a building and the land belonging to it. [FORMAL] ❏ *Get out of here — this is a private property!* **3** N-COUNT The **properties** of a substance or object are the ways in which it behaves in particular conditions. ❏ *A radio signal has both electrical and magnetic properties.* [from Old French]
→ see **element, periodic table**

**prop|er|ty tax** (**property taxes**) N-VAR **Property tax** is tax that you pay on buildings and land that you own. ❏ *We've got the highest property taxes in the United States.*

**pro|phase** /proʊfeɪz/ (**prophases**) N-VAR **Prophase** is the first stage of cell division, in which the DNA inside a cell forms into chromosomes. [TECHNICAL]

**proph|ecy** /prɒfɪsi/ (**prophecies**) N-VAR A **prophecy** is a statement in which someone says they strongly believe that a particular thing will happen. ❏ *Will the teacher's prophecy be fulfilled?* [from Greek]

**proph|esy** /prɒfɪsaɪ/ (**prophesies, prophesying, prophesied**) v-т If you **prophesy** that something will happen, you say that you strongly believe that it will happen. ❏ *He prophesied that within five years his opponent would be dead.*

**proph|et** /prɒfɪt/ (**prophets**) N-COUNT A **prophet** is a person who is believed to be chosen by God to say the things that God wants to tell people. ❏ …*the Holy Prophet of Islam.* [from Old French]

**pro|phet|ic** /prəfɛtɪk/ ADJ If something was **prophetic**, it described or suggested something that did actually happen later. ❏ …*George Orwell's prophetic novel, "1984."* [from Greek]

**pro|po|nent** /prəpoʊnənt/ (**proponents**)
N-COUNT If you are a **proponent** of a particular idea or course of action, you actively support it. [FORMAL] ❑ ...*a leading proponent of the theory.* [from Latin]

**pro|por|tion** /prəpɔrʃən/ (**proportions**)
◼ N-COUNT A **proportion** of a group or an amount is a part of it. [FORMAL] ❑ *A large proportion of the dolphins in that area will die.* ◼ N-COUNT The **proportion** of one kind of person or thing in a group is the number of people or things of that kind compared to the total number of people or things in the group. ❑ *The proportion of women in the profession is now 17.3%.* ◼ N-PLURAL If you refer to the **proportions** of something, you are referring to its size, usually when this is extremely large. [WRITTEN] ❑ *In the tropics plants grow to huge proportions.* ◼ N-PLURAL If you refer to the **proportions** in a work of art or design, you are referring to the relative sizes of its different parts. ❑ *This computer program lets you change the proportions of things in your picture very simply.* ◼ PHRASE If one thing increases or decreases **in proportion to** another thing, it increases or decreases to the same degree as that thing. ❑ *They have agreed to increase wages in proportion to price increases.* ◼ PHRASE If something is small or large **in proportion to** something else, it is small or large when compared with that thing. ❑ *His head was large in proportion to the rest of his body.* ◼ PHRASE If you say that something is **out of proportion** to something else, you think that it is far greater or more serious than it should be. ❑ *The punishment was out of all proportion to the crime.* [from Latin]

**pro|por|tion|al** /prəpɔrʃənªl/ ADJ If one amount is **proportional to** another, the two amounts increase and decrease at the same rate so there is always the same relationship between them. [FORMAL] ❑ *Loss of weight is directly proportional to taking more exercise and eating carefully.* [from Latin]

**pro|por|tion|ate** /prəpɔrʃənɪt/ ADJ **Proportionate** means the same as **proportional**. ❑ *They decided that punishment must be proportionate to the crime.* ● **pro|por|tion|ate|ly** ADV ❑ *We have increased the number of teachers but the size of the classes hasn't changed proportionately.* [from Latin]

**pro|pos|al** /prəpoʊzªl/ (**proposals**) ◼ N-COUNT A **proposal** is a suggestion or plan, often a formal or written one. ❑ ...*the details of their new proposals.* ❑ ...*a UN proposal to grant the colony independence.* ◼ N-COUNT A **proposal** is the act of asking someone to marry you. ❑ *Pam accepted Randy's proposal of marriage.* [from Old French]

| ADJ. | new proposal, original proposal ◼ |
|---|---|
| V. | adopt a proposal, approve a proposal, support a proposal, vote on a proposal ◼ accept a proposal, make a proposal, reject a proposal ◼ ◼ |
| N. | budget proposal, peace proposal ◼ marriage proposal ◼ |

**pro|pose** /prəpoʊz/ (**proposes, proposing, proposed**) ◼ V-T If you **propose** a plan or an idea, you suggest it. ❑ *Morris proposed a change in the law.* ◼ V-T If you **propose** to do something, you intend to do it. ❑ *Congress is proposing a change to the*

law. ◼ V-I If you **propose to** someone, or **propose marriage to** them, you ask them to marry you. ❑ *He proposed to his girlfriend.* [from Old French]

| Word Partnership | Use *propose* with : |
|---|---|
| N. | propose **changes**, propose **legislation**, propose **a plan**, propose **a solution**, propose **a tax**, propose **a theory**, propose **a toast** ◼ ◼ propose **marriage** ◼ |

**propo|si|tion** /prɒpəzɪʃən/ (**propositions**) ◼ N-COUNT If you describe something such as a task or an activity as, for example, a difficult **proposition** or an attractive **proposition**, you mean that it is difficult or pleasant to do. ❑ *Making money easily has always been an attractive proposition.* ◼ N-COUNT A **proposition** is a statement or an idea that people can consider or discuss to decide whether it is true. [FORMAL] ❑ ...*the proposition that democracies do not fight each other.* ◼ N-COUNT A **proposition** is an offer or a suggestion. ❑ *I went to see him at his office the other day with a business proposition.* [from Latin]

**pro|pri|etary** /prəpraɪəteri/ ADJ **Proprietary** substances or products are sold under a brand name. [FORMAL] ❑ ...*some proprietary brands of dog food.* [from Late Latin]

**pro|pri|etor** /prəpraɪətər/ (**proprietors**) N-COUNT The **proprietor** of a hotel, store, newspaper, or other business is the person who owns it. [FORMAL] ❑ ...*the proprietor of a local restaurant.* [from Late Latin]

**pro|rate** /proʊreɪt/ (**prorates, prorating, prorated**) also pro-rate V-T If a cost **is prorated**, it is divided or assessed in a proportional way. ❑ *If sea conditions cause your trip to return early, the boat fare will be prorated.*

**pro|sa|ic** /proʊzeɪɪk/ ADJ Something that is **prosaic** is dull and uninteresting. [FORMAL] ❑ *His instructor offered a more prosaic explanation.* [from Late Latin]

**pro|sce|nium** /proʊsiniəm, prə-/ (**prosceniums**) N-COUNT A **proscenium** or a **proscenium arch** is an arch in a theater that separates the stage from the audience. [from Latin]

**prose** /proʊz/ N-UNCOUNT **Prose** is ordinary written language, in contrast to poetry. ❑ *She wrote both poetry and prose.* [from Old French]

**pros|ecute** /prɒsɪkyut/ (**prosecutes, prosecuting, prosecuted**) V-T/V-I If the authorities **prosecute** someone, they charge them with a crime and put them on trial. ❑ *The police have decided not to prosecute.* ❑ *Photographs taken by roadside cameras are used to prosecute drivers for speeding.* ● **pros|ecu|tion** (**prosecutions**) N-VAR ❑ *The government called for the prosecution of those responsible.* [from Latin]

**pros|ecu|tion** /prɒsɪkyuʃən/ N-SING The lawyers who try to prove that a person on trial is guilty are called **the prosecution**. ❑ ...*a witness for the prosecution.* [from Latin]

**pros|ecu|tor** /prɒsɪkyutər/ (**prosecutors**) N-COUNT In some countries, a **prosecutor** is a lawyer or official who brings charges against someone or tries to prove in a trial that they are guilty. [from Latin]

**pro|sim|ian** /proʊsɪmiən/ (**prosimians**) also **pro-simian** N-COUNT **Prosimians** are animals such as lemurs and other primates who resemble the early ancestors of apes and humans. [TECHNICAL] ● **prosimian** is also an adjective. ADJ ❑ *...a prosimian species.* [from New Latin]

**pros|pect** /prɒspɛkt/ (**prospects, prospecting, prospected**) **1** N-VAR A **prospect** is a possibility or possible event. ❑ *There is little prospect of getting an answer to these questions.* ❑ *The prospects for peace are becoming brighter.* **2** N-PLURAL Someone's **prospects** are their chances of being successful. ❑ *I chose to work abroad to improve my career prospects.* **3** V-I To **prospect for** a substance such as oil or gold means to look for it in the ground or under the sea. ❑ *He has prospected for minerals everywhere.* [from Latin]

**pro|spec|tive** /prəspɛktɪv/ ADJ You use **prospective** to describe someone who wants to be the thing mentioned or who is likely to be the thing mentioned. ❑ *The story should act as a warning to prospective buyers.* [from Latin]

**pro|spec|tus** /prəspɛktəs/ (**prospectuses**) N-COUNT A **prospectus** is a detailed document, giving information about the financial situation of a company. ❑ *The prospectus contains information on the company's previous performance.* [from Latin]

**pros|per** /prɒspər/ (**prospers, prospering, prospered**) V-I If people or businesses **prosper**, they are financially successful. [FORMAL] ❑ *His business continued to prosper.* [from Latin]

> **Word Link** sper ≈ hope : desperate, exasperate, prosperity

**pros|per|ity** /prɒspɛrɪti/ N-UNCOUNT **Prosperity** is a condition in which a person or community is doing well financially. ❑ *...a long period of peace and prosperity.* [from Latin]

**pros|per|ous** /prɒspərəs/ ADJ **Prosperous** people, places, and economies are rich and successful. [FORMAL] ❑ *...a relatively prosperous family.* [from Latin]

**pros|ti|tute** /prɒstɪtut/ (**prostitutes**) N-COUNT A **prostitute** is a person, usually a woman, who has sex with men in exchange for money. [from Latin]

**pros|ti|tu|tion** /prɒstɪtuʃⁿn/ N-UNCOUNT **Prostitution** means having sex with people in exchange for money. [from Latin]

> **Word Link** agon ≈ struggling : agonize, agony, protagonist

**pro|tago|nist** /proʊtægənɪst/ (**protagonists**) **1** N-COUNT A **protagonist of** an idea or movement is a supporter of it. [FORMAL] ❑ *The Greeks were the protagonists of this philosophy.* **2** N-COUNT A **protagonist** in a play, novel, or real event is one of the main people in it. [FORMAL] ❑ *...the protagonist of J. D. Salinger's novel "The Catcher in the Rye."* [from Greek]

> **Word Link** tect ≈ covering : detect, protect, protective

**pro|tect** /prətɛkt/ (**protects, protecting, protected**) V-T To **protect** someone or something

means to prevent them from being harmed or damaged. ❑ *What can women do to protect themselves from heart disease?* ❑ *We are committed to protecting the interests of children.* ● **pro|tec|tor** (**protectors**) N-COUNT ❑ *I always saw my father as a protector.* [from Latin]
→ see **hero**

> **Word Partnership** Use *protect* with :
>
> N. protect **against attacks**, protect **children**, protect **citizens, duty to** protect, **efforts to** protect, protect **the environment, laws** protect, protect **people**, protect **privacy**, protect **property**, protect **women**, protect **workers**
>
> ADJ. **designed to** protect, **necessary to** protect, **supposed to** protect

**pro|tec|tion** /prətɛkʃⁿn/ (**protections**) N-VAR If something gives **protection** against something unpleasant, it prevents people or things from being harmed or damaged by it. ❑ *The diet is believed to offer protection against cancer.* ❑ *The primary duty of parents is to provide protection for our children.* [from Latin]

**pro|tec|tive** /prətɛktɪv/ **1** ADJ **Protective** means designed or intended to protect something or someone from harm. ❑ *You should wear protective gloves.* **2** ADJ If someone is **protective toward** you, they look after you and show a strong desire to keep you safe. ❑ *He is very protective toward his mother.* [from Latin]

**pro|té|gé** /proʊtɪʒeɪ, -ʒeɪ/ (**protégés**)

> The spelling **protégée** is often used when referring to a girl or a woman.

N-COUNT The **protégé** of an older and more experienced person is a young person who is helped and guided by them over a period of time. ❑ *...Kelley, a former lawyer and protégé of Steven Bochco.* [from French]

**pro|tein** /proʊtin/ (**proteins**) N-VAR **Protein** is a substance which the body needs and which is found in meat, eggs, and milk. ❑ *Fish is a major source of protein.* [from German]
→ see **calorie, diet**

**pro|test** (**protests, protesting, protested**)

> The verb is usually pronounced /prətɛst/. The noun, and sometimes the verb, is pronounced /proʊtɛst/.

**1** V-T/V-I To **protest** means to say or show publicly that you object to something. ❑ *They were protesting high prices.* ❑ *...demonstrators protesting against food price rises.* ● **pro|test|er** (**protesters**) also **protestor** N-COUNT ❑ *The protesters say the government is corrupt.* **2** N-VAR A **protest** is the act of saying or showing publicly that you object to something. ❑ *...the start of protests against the war.* ❑ *The Mexican president canceled a trip to Texas in protest.* **3** V-T If you **protest** that something is the case, you insist that it is the case, when other people think that it may not be. ❑ *We tried to protest that Mo was beaten up.* ❑ *"I never said any of that to her," he protested.* [from Latin]

P

### Word Partnership   Use *protest* with :

| | |
|---|---|
| N. | **workers** protest **1** |
| | protest **demonstrations**, protest |
| | **groups**, protest, protest **rally 2** |
| ADJ. | **anti-government** protest, **anti-war** |
| | protest, **organized** protest, **peaceful** |
| | protest, **political** protest **2** |

**Prot|es|tant** /prɒtɪstənt/ (**Protestants**)
N-COUNT A **Protestant** is a Christian who
belongs to the branch of the Christian church
that separated from the Catholic church in the
sixteenth century. [from Latin]

**pro|tist** /proʊtɪst/ (**protists**) N-COUNT **Protists**
are organisms such as algae and molds that are
not animals, plants or fungi. [TECHNICAL] [from
New Latin]

**Pro|tis|ta** /proʊtɪstə/ N-UNCOUNT **Protista** is
the biological group to which organisms called
protists belong. [TECHNICAL] [from New
Latin]

**proto|col** /proʊtəkɔl/ (**protocols**) N-VAR
**Protocol** is a system of rules or agreements about
the correct way to act in a particular situation or
to do a particular thing. ❑ *Protocol required him to
shake hands with the new minister.* [from Medieval
Latin]

**pro|ton** /proʊtɒn/ (**protons**) N-COUNT A **proton**
is an atomic particle that has a positive electrical
charge. [TECHNICAL] [from Greek]

**proto|type** /proʊtətaɪp/ (**prototypes**) N-COUNT
A **prototype** is the first model or example of a new
type of thing. ❑ *...a prototype of a pollution-free car.*
[from Greek]

**proto|zoan** /proʊtəzoʊən/ (**protozoa** or
**protozoans**) N-COUNT **Protozoa** are very small
organisms that often live inside larger animals.
[TECHNICAL] [from New Latin]

**pro|tract|ed** /proʊtræktɪd/ ADJ Something
that is **protracted** lasts longer than usual or
longer than you hoped. [FORMAL] ❑ *After protracted
discussions Ogden got what he wanted.* ❑ *...a protracted
civil war.* [from Latin]

**pro|trude** /proʊtrud, prə-/ (**protrudes**,
**protruding**, **protruded**) V-I If something
**protrudes from** somewhere, it sticks out. [FORMAL]
❑ *...a huge mass of rock protruding from the water.*
[from Latin]

**proud** /praʊd/ (**prouder, proudest**) **1** ADJ If
you feel **proud**, you feel
pleased and satisfied about
something good that you
own, have done, or are
connected with. ❑ *I felt
proud of his efforts.* ❑ *They
are proud that she is doing
well at school.* ● **proud|ly**
ADV ❑ *"That's the first part
finished," he said proudly.*
**2** ADJ Someone who is
**proud** has a lot of dignity
and self-respect. ❑ *He was
too proud to ask his family for help and support.* **3** ADJ
Someone who is **proud** feels that they are better or
more important than other people. ❑ *He described
Sir Terence as "vain, proud and selfish."* [from Late Old
English]

proud

**prove** /pruv/ (**proves, proving, proved, proven**)

> The forms **proved** and **proven** can both be used as
> a past participle.

**1** V-LINK If something **proves to** be true or **to** have
a particular quality, it becomes clear after a period
of time that it is true or has that quality. ❑ *All
our reports proved to be true.* ❑ *This process has often
proven difficult.* **2** V-T If you **prove that** something
is true, you show by means of argument or
evidence that it is definitely true. ❑ *My theory has
been proved!* ❑ *These results prove that we were right.*
❑ *I was determined to prove him wrong.* **3** V-T If you
**prove yourself**, you show by your actions that you
have a certain good quality. ❑ *I had two injuries, but
I felt I had to come back and prove myself.* [from Old
French]
→ see **science**

### Word Partnership   Use *prove* with :

| | |
|---|---|
| ADJ. | prove **(to be) difficult**, prove **helpful**, |
| | prove **useful**, prove **worthy 1** |
| V. | **difficult to** prove, **hard to** prove **2** |
| | **be able to** prove, **have to** prove, |
| | **have *something* to** prove, **try to** |
| | prove **2** |

### Word Link   verb ≈ word : adverb, proverb, verbal

**prov|erb** /prɒvɜrb/ (**proverbs**) N-COUNT A
**proverb** is a short sentence that people often
quote, because it gives advice or tells you
something about life. ❑ *An old Arab proverb says,
"The enemy of my enemy is my friend."* [from Old
French]

**pro|ver|bial** /prəvɜrbiəl/ ADJ You use **proverbial**
to show that you know the way you are describing
something is one that is often used or is part of
a popular saying. ❑ *The limousine sped off down the
road in the proverbial cloud of dust.* [from Old French]

**pro|vide** /prəvaɪd/ (**provides, providing,
provided**) **1** V-T If you **provide** something that
someone needs or wants, or if you **provide** them
**with** it, you give it to them or make it available to
them. ❑ *They would not provide any details.* ❑ *They
provided him with a car and a driver.* **2** V-T If a law or
agreement **provides that** something will happen,
it states that it will happen. [FORMAL] ❑ *Muslim law
provides that women must dress modestly.* [from Latin]
**3** → see also **provided, providing**
▶ **provide for 1** PHR-VERB If you **provide for**
someone, you support them financially and make
sure that they have the things that they need.
❑ *Elaine wouldn't let him provide for her.* **2** PHR-VERB
If you **provide for** something that might happen
or that might need to be done, you make
arrangements to deal with it. ❑ *Jim has provided for
just such an emergency.*

**pro|vid|ed** /prəvaɪdɪd/ CONJ If you say that
something will happen **provided** or **providing** that
something else happens, you mean that the first
thing will happen only if the second thing also
happens. ❑ *The banks are prepared to help, provided
that he has a specific plan.* [from Latin]

**provi|dence** /prɒvɪdəns/ N-UNCOUNT
**Providence** is God, or a force that is believed by
some people to arrange the things that happen to
us. [LITERARY] ❑ *These women regard his death as an
act of providence.* [from Latin]

P

**pro|vid|ing** /prəvaɪdɪŋ/ CONJ → see **provided**

**prov|ince** /prɒvɪns/ (**provinces**) **1** N-COUNT A **province** is a large section of a country that has its own administration. ❑ …*the Algarve, Portugal's southernmost province.* **2** N-PLURAL **The provinces** are all the parts of a country except the part where the capital is situated. ❑ …*plans to transfer 30,000 government jobs from Paris to the provinces.* [from Old French]

**pro|vin|cial** /prəvɪnʃᵊl/ **1** ADJ **Provincial** means connected with the parts of a country away from the capital city. ❑ …*the Quebec and Ontario provincial police.* **2** ADJ If you describe someone or something as **provincial**, you disapprove of them because you think that they are old-fashioned and boring. ❑ …*the company's provincial image.* [from Old French]

**pro|vi|sion** /prəvɪʒᵊn/ (**provisions**) **1** N-UNCOUNT The **provision of** something is the act of giving it or making it available to people who want or need it. ❑ *The department is responsible for the provision of services.* **2** N-VAR If you make **provision for** something that might happen or that might need to be done, you make arrangements to deal with it. ❑ *Has she made provision for her retirement?* **3** N-COUNT A **provision** in a law or an agreement is an arrangement which is included in it. ❑ …*a provision that allows the president to decide how to spend the money.* [from Latin]

**pro|vi|sion|al** /prəvɪʒənᵊl/ ADJ You use **provisional** to describe something that has been arranged or appointed for the present, but may be changed in the future. ❑ …*a provisional government.* ● **pro|vi|sion|al|ly** ADV ❑ *We've provisionally booked seats for Thursday.* [from French]

**provo|ca|tion** /prɒvəkeɪʃᵊn/ (**provocations**) N-VAR **Provocation** is a deliberate attempt to make someone react angrily. ❑ *They say they were attacked without provocation.* [from Latin]

**pro|voca|tive** /prəvɒkətɪv/ **1** ADJ Something that is **provocative** is intended to make people react angrily. ❑ …*outspoken and sometimes provocative speeches.* **2** ADJ **Provocative** behavior or dress is intended to make someone feel sexual desire. ❑ *She returned wearing a much less provocative dress.* [from Latin]

**pro|voke** /prəvoʊk/ (**provokes, provoking, provoked**) **1** V-T If you **provoke** someone, you deliberately annoy them and try to make them behave aggressively. ❑ *I didn't do anything to provoke him.* **2** V-T If something **provokes** a reaction, it causes it. ❑ *The election result provoked an angry reaction from some students.* [from Latin]

**pro|vo|lo|ne** /proʊvəloʊni/ also **provolone cheese** N-UNCOUNT **Provolone** is a type of cream-colored, smoked cheese, originally made in Italy. ❑ …*a slice of provolone.* [from Italian]

**prow|ess** /praʊɪs/ N-UNCOUNT Someone's **prowess** is their great skill at doing something. [FORMAL] ❑ …*his prowess as a hunter.* [from Old French]

**prowl** /praʊl/ (**prowls, prowling, prowled**) V-I If an animal or a person **prowls around**, they move around quietly, for example, when they are hunting. ❑ *He prowled around the room, not sure what he was looking for.*

**prox|im|ity** /prɒksɪmɪti/ N-UNCOUNT **Proximity** to a place or person is nearness to that place or person. [FORMAL] ❑ *Part of the attraction of Darwin is its proximity to Asia.* [from Latin]

**proxy** /prɒksi/ N-UNCOUNT If you do something **by proxy**, you arrange for someone else to do it for you. ❑ *Those not attending the meeting may vote by proxy.* [from Latin]

**prude** /pruːd/ (**prudes**) N-COUNT If you call someone a **prude**, you mean that they are too easily shocked by things relating to sex. [from French]

**pru|dent** /pruːdᵊnt/ ADJ Someone who is **prudent** is sensible and careful. ❑ *It is clearly prudent to take all precautions.* ● **pru|dent|ly** ADV ❑ *I believe it is essential that we act prudently.* ● **pru|dence** N-UNCOUNT [FORMAL] ❑ *Businessmen are showing great prudence in investing in the region.* [from Latin]

**prune** /pruːn/ (**prunes, pruning, pruned**) **1** N-COUNT A **prune** is a dried plum. **2** V-T When you **prune** a tree or bush, you cut off some of the branches so that it will grow better the next year. ❑ *You have to prune a bush if you want fruit.* ● **Prune back** means the same as **prune**. ❑ *Cherry trees can be pruned back when they've lost their leaves.* [from Old French]

**prun|ing shears** N-PLURAL **Pruning shears** are a gardening tool that look like a pair of strong, heavy scissors, used for cutting the stems of plants.

**pry** /praɪ/ (**pries, prying, pried**) **1** V-I If someone **pries**, they try to find out about someone else's private affairs, or look at their personal possessions. ❑ *We do not want people prying into our affairs.* ❑ *She worried that Imelda might think she was prying.* **2** V-T If you **pry** something **open** or **pry** it away from a surface, you force it open or away from a surface. ❑ *They pried open a can of blue paint.* ❑ *They pried the bars apart to free the dog.* **3** V-T If you **pry** something such as information **out of** someone, you persuade them to tell you although they may be very unwilling to. ❑ *She finally managed to pry the news out of me.*

**P.S.** /piː ɛs/ also **PS** You write **P.S.** to introduce something that you add at the end of a letter after you have signed it. ❑ *P.S. Please show your friends this letter.*

**pseudo|nym** /suːdənɪm/ (**pseudonyms**) N-COUNT A **pseudonym** is a name that someone, usually a writer, uses instead of his or her real name. ❑ *Both plays were published under the pseudonym of Philip Dayre.* [from French]

**pseudo|pod** /suːdəpɒd/ (**pseudopods** or **pseudopodia**) N-COUNT **Pseudopods** are the tiny extensions of cells within some microorganisms that are used for movement and feeding. [TECHNICAL]

**psy|che** /saɪki/ (**psyches**) N-COUNT In psychology, your **psyche** is your mind and your deepest feelings and attitudes. [TECHNICAL] ❑ *The book had a strong influence on the American psyche.* [from Latin]

**psychedel|ic** /saɪkədɛlɪk/ **1** ADJ **Psychedelic** means relating to drugs such as LSD that have a strong effect on your mind, often making you see things that are not there. ❑ ...*his first real psychedelic experience.* **2** ADJ **Psychedelic** art has bright colors and strange patterns. ❑ ...*psychedelic artwork.* [from Greek]

**Word Link** *iatr ≈ healing : geriatric, pediatrics, psychiatry*

**Word Link** *psych ≈ mind : psyche, psychiatrist, psychic*

**psy|chia|try** /sɪkaɪətri/ N-UNCOUNT **Psychiatry** is the branch of medicine concerned with the treatment of mental illness. ● **psy|chi|at|ric** /saɪkiætrɪk/ ADJ ❑ ...*psychiatric illnesses.* ● **psy|chia|trist** /sɪkaɪətrɪst/ (**psychiatrists**) N-COUNT ❑ *A colleague urged him to see a psychiatrist.* [from Greek]

**psy|chic** /saɪkɪk/ (**psychics**) **1** ADJ If you believe that someone is **psychic**, you believe that they have strange mental powers, such as being able to read the minds of other people or to see into the future. ❑ *The woman helped police by using her psychic powers.* ● A **psychic** is someone who seems to be psychic. ❑ ...*a psychic who can see the future.* **2** ADJ **Psychic** means relating to ghosts and the spirits of the dead. ❑ ...*his total disbelief in psychic phenomena.* [from Greek]

**psycho|analy|sis** /saɪkoʊənælɪsɪs/ N-UNCOUNT **Psychoanalysis** is the treatment of someone who has mental problems by asking them about their feelings and their past in order to try to discover what may be causing their condition. ● **psycho|ana|lyst** /saɪkoʊænəlɪst/ (**psychoanalysts**) N-COUNT ❑ *Jane is seeing a psychoanalyst.*

**psycho|logi|cal** /saɪkəlɒdʒɪkəl/ ADJ **Psychological** means concerned with a person's mind and thoughts. ❑ ...*physical and psychological abuse.* ● **psycho|logi|cal|ly** /saɪkəlɒdʒɪkli/ ADV ❑ *It was very important psychologically for us to succeed.* [from Modern Latin]
→ see **myth**

**psy|chol|ogy** /saɪkɒlədʒi/ **1** N-UNCOUNT **Psychology** is the scientific study of the human mind and the reasons for people's behavior. ❑ ...*Professor of Psychology at Haverford College.* ● **psy|cholo|gist** (**psychologists**) N-COUNT ❑ *She is seeing a psychologist.* **2** N-UNCOUNT The **psychology of** a person is the kind of mind that they have, which makes them think or behave in the way that they do. ❑ ...*the psychology of murderers.* [from Modern Latin]

**psycho|path** /saɪkəpæθ/ (**psychopaths**) N-COUNT A **psychopath** is someone who has serious mental problems and who may act in a violent way without feeling sorry for what they have done. ❑ ...*a dangerous psychopath.*

**psy|cho|sis** /saɪkoʊsɪs/ (**psychoses**) N-VAR **Psychosis** is mental illness of a severe kind that can make people lose contact with reality. [MEDICAL] ❑ *He may have some kind of psychosis.* ● **psy|chot|ic** /saɪkɒtɪk/ ADJ ❑ *Police believe that the attacker may be psychotic.* [from New Latin]

**psycho|thera|py** /saɪkoʊθɛrəpi/ N-UNCOUNT **Psychotherapy** is the use of psychological methods in treating people who are mentally ill. ❑ *For milder depressions, certain forms of psychotherapy work well.* ● **psycho|thera|pist** (**psychotherapists**) N-COUNT ❑ *He arranged for Jim to see a psychotherapist.*

**psy|chrom|eter** /saɪkrɒmɪtər/ (**psychrometers**) N-COUNT A **psychrometer** is an instrument that is used to measure the amount of water vapor in the air. [TECHNICAL]

**pu|ber|ty** /pyubərti/ N-UNCOUNT **Puberty** is the stage in your life when your body starts to become physically mature. ❑ *Moesha reached puberty when she was 11.* [from Latin]

**pub|lic** /pʌblɪk/ **1** N-SING You can refer to people in general as **the public**. ❑ *The park is now open to the public.* ❑ *The car is not yet for sale to the general public.* **2** ADJ **Public** means relating to all the people in a country or community. ❑ *Their policies enjoy strong public support.* **3** ADJ **Public** means relating to the government or state, or things that are done for the people by the state. ❑ *More public spending cuts were announced this week.* ● **pub|lic|ly** ADV ❑ ...*publicly funded legal services.* **4** ADJ **Public** buildings and services are provided for everyone to use. ❑ ...*the New York Public Library.* ❑ ...*public transportation.* **5** ADJ If someone is a **public figure** or in **public life**, many people know who they are because they are often mentioned in newspapers and on television. ❑ ...*politicians and other public figures.* **6** ADJ **Public** is used to describe statements, actions, and events that are made or done in such a way that any member of the public can see them or be aware of them. ❑ ...*a public inquiry.* ❑ ...*the governor's first public statement on the subject.* ● **pub|lic|ly** ADV ❑ *He never spoke publicly about the incident.* **7** ADJ If a fact is made **public** or becomes **public**, it becomes known to everyone rather than being kept secret. ❑ *The news finally became public.* **8** PHRASE If you say or do something **in public**, you say or do it when a group of people are present. ❑ *He hasn't performed in public in more than 40 years.* [from Latin]
→ see **library**

**pub|lic as|sis|tance** N-UNCOUNT In the United States, **public assistance** is money that is paid by the government to people who are poor, unemployed, or sick. ❑ *More than 70 percent of the citizens are on public assistance.*

**pub|li|ca|tion** /pʌblɪkeɪʃən/ (**publications**) **1** N-UNCOUNT The **publication** of a book or magazine is the act of printing it and sending it to stores to be sold. ❑ *The guide will be ready for publication near Christmas.* **2** N-COUNT A **publication** is a book or magazine that has been published. ❑ *He has written for several local New York publications.* [from Old French]

**pub|lic de|fend|er** (**public defenders**) N-COUNT A **public defender** is a lawyer who is employed by a city or county to represent people who are accused of crimes but cannot afford to pay for a lawyer themselves.

**pub|lic hous|ing** N-UNCOUNT **Public housing** is apartments or houses that are rented to poor people, usually at a low cost, by the government. ❑ ...*the construction of more public housing.*

**pub|li|cist** /pʌblɪsɪst/ (**publicists**) N-COUNT A **publicist** is a person whose job involves getting publicity for people, events, or things such as movies or books. ❑ ...*Larry Kaplan, a publicist for the movie "Cold Mountain."* [from Latin]

**pub|lic|ity** /pʌblɪsiti/ **1** N-UNCOUNT **Publicity** is information or actions that are intended to attract the public's attention to someone or something. ❑ *A lot of publicity was given to the talks.* ❑ *…government publicity campaigns.* **2** N-UNCOUNT When the news media and the public show a lot of interest in something, you can say that it is receiving **publicity**. ❑ *The case has generated enormous publicity in Brazil.* [from French]

**pub|li|cize** /pʌblɪsaɪz/ (**publicizes, publicizing, publicized**) V-T If you **publicize** a fact or event, you make it widely known to the public. ❑ *The author appeared on television to publicize her latest book.* [from Latin]

**pub|lic of|fice** N-UNCOUNT Someone who is in **public office** is in a job that they have been elected to do by the public. ❑ *He has held public office for twenty years.*

**pub|lic re|la|tions** **1** N-UNCOUNT **Public relations** is the part of an organization's work that is concerned with obtaining the public's approval for what it does. The abbreviation **PR** is often used. [BUSINESS] ❑ *Mr. MacGregor runs a public relations firm in London.* **2** N-PLURAL You can refer to the opinion that the public has of an organization as **public relations**. ❑ *Cutting costs is important for public relations.*

**pub|lic school** (**public schools**) **1** N-VAR In the United States, Australia, and many other countries, a **public school** is a school that is supported financially by the government and usually provides free education. ❑ *…Milwaukee's public school system.* **2** N-VAR In Britain, a **public school** is a private school that provides secondary education that parents have to pay for. The students often live at the school during the school term. ❑ *He was headmaster of a public school in the West of England.*

**pub|lic sec|tor** N-SING The **public sector** is the part of a country's economy which is controlled or supported financially by the government. [BUSINESS] ❑ *…Menem's policy of reducing the public sector.*

**pub|lic tele|vi|sion** also **public TV** N-UNCOUNT **Public television** is television that is funded by the government, businesses, and viewers, rather than by advertising. ❑ *…the kind of program you only find on public television.*

**pub|lic trans|por|ta|tion** N-UNCOUNT **Public transportation** is a system for taking people from one place to another, for example, using buses or trains. ❑ *There is no electricity, no water, no public transportation.*

**pub|lish** /pʌblɪʃ/ (**publishes, publishing, published**) **1** V-T When a company **publishes** a book or magazine, it prints copies of it, which are sent to stores to be sold. ❑ *They publish reference books.* **2** V-T When the people in charge of a newspaper or magazine **publish** a piece of writing or a photograph, they print it in their newspaper or magazine. ❑ *The magazine no longer publishes articles about losing weight.* **3** V-T If someone **publishes** a book or an article that they have written, they arrange to have it published. ❑ *Walker has published four books of her poetry.* [from Old French]
→ see **laboratory, printing**

**pub|lish|er** /pʌblɪʃər/ (**publishers**) N-COUNT A **publisher** is a person or a company that publishes books, newspapers, or magazines. ❑ *The publishers plan to produce a new weekly journal.* [from Old French]

**pub|lish|ing** /pʌblɪʃɪŋ/ N-UNCOUNT **Publishing** is the profession of publishing books. ❑ *I had a job in publishing.* [from Old French]

**pub|lish|ing house** (**publishing houses**) N-COUNT A **publishing house** is a company that publishes books.

**pud|ding** /pʊdɪŋ/ (**puddings**) N-VAR A **pudding** is a cooked sweet food made from ingredients such as milk, sugar, flour, and eggs, and is served either hot or cold. ❑ *…a banana vanilla pudding.* [from Old English]
→ see **dessert**

**pud|dle** /pʌdᵊl/ (**puddles**) N-COUNT A **puddle** is a small, shallow pool of liquid on the ground. ❑ *The road was shiny with puddles.* [from Old English]

**pudgy** /pʌdʒi/ ADJ If you describe someone as **pudgy**, you mean that they are rather fat in an unattractive way. ❑ *He put a pudgy arm around Harry's shoulder.* [from Scottish]

**pueb|lo** /pwɛblu/ (**pueblos**) N-COUNT A **pueblo** is a village, especially in the southwestern United States. ❑ *There are several Indian pueblos near Santa Fe.* [from Spanish]

**puff** /pʌf/ (**puffs, puffing, puffed**) **1** V-T If someone **puffs on** or **at** a cigarette, cigar, or pipe, they smoke it. ❑ *He lit his pipe and puffed on it twice.* ● **Puff** is also a noun. ❑ *I took a puff on the cigarette and started coughing.* **2** N-COUNT A **puff of** air or smoke is a small amount of it that is blown out from somewhere. ❑ *The wind caught a sudden puff of dust.* **3** V-I If you **are puffing**, you are breathing loudly and quickly with your mouth open because you are out of breath after a lot of physical effort. ❑ *I could see he was unfit, because he was puffing.* **4** N-COUNT A **puff for** a book, movie, or product is something that is done or said in order to attract people's attention and tell them how good it is. [INFORMAL] ❑ *The interview was just a puff for his latest work.* [from Old English]

**Pu|lit|zer Prize** /pʊlɪtsər praɪz/ (**Pulitzer Prizes**) N-COUNT A **Pulitzer Prize** is one of a series of prizes awarded each year in the United States for outstanding achievement in the fields of journalism, literature, and music. ❑ *He won the Pulitzer Prize for Poetry.*

**pull** /pʊl/ (**pulls, pulling, pulled**) **1** V-T/V-I When you **pull** something, you hold it firmly and use force in order to move it toward you or away from its previous position. ❑ *The dentist pulled out all his teeth.* ❑ *Erica was pulling at her blonde curls.* ❑ *I helped pull him out of the water.* ❑ *Someone pulled her hair.* ● **Pull** is also a noun.

**pull**

P

❏ *The feather must be removed with a straight, firm pull.*
**2** V-T When a vehicle, animal, or person **pulls** a cart or piece of machinery, they are attached to it or hold it, so that it moves along behind them when they move forward. ❏ *The beast pulled the cart.* **3** V-T When you **pull yourself** or **pull** a part of your body in a particular direction, you move your body or a part of your body with effort or force. ❏ *Hughes pulled himself slowly to his feet.* ❏ *He pulled his arms out of the sleeves.* **4** N-COUNT A **pull** is a strong physical force that causes things to move in a particular direction. ❏ *…the pull of gravity.* **5** to **pull a face** → see **face** [from Old English] **6** to **pull** someone's **leg** → see **leg** **7** to **pull strings** → see **string** **8** to **pull** your **weight** → see **weight**

▶ **pull away** **1** PHR-VERB When a vehicle or driver **pulls away**, the vehicle starts moving forward. ❏ *I watched him back out of the driveway and pull away.* **2** PHR-VERB If you **pull away from** someone that you have had close links with, you deliberately become less close to them. ❏ *The Soviet Union began to pull away from Cuba.*

▶ **pull back** **1** PHR-VERB If someone **pulls back from** an action, they decide not to do it or continue with it, because it could have bad consequences. ❏ *He encouraged both sides to pull back from the violence.*

▶ **pull down** PHR-VERB To **pull down** a building or statue means to deliberately destroy it. ❏ *They pulled the offices down, leaving a large open space.*

▶ **pull in** PHR-VERB When a vehicle or driver **pulls in** somewhere, the vehicle stops there. ❏ *He pulled in at the side of the road.*

▶ **pull into** PHR-VERB When a vehicle or driver **pulls into** a place, the vehicle moves into the place and stops there. ❏ *He pulled into the driveway in front of her garage.*

▶ **pull off** PHR-VERB If you **pull off** something very difficult, you succeed in achieving it. ❏ *The National League for Democracy pulled off a victory.*

▶ **pull out** **1** PHR-VERB When a vehicle or driver **pulls out**, the vehicle moves out into the road or nearer the center of the road. ❏ *She pulled out into the street.* **2** PHR-VERB If you **pull out of** an agreement, a contest, or an organization, you withdraw from it. ❏ *The World Bank should pull out of the project.* **3** PHR-VERB If troops **pull out of** a place, they leave it. ❏ *Israeli forces agreed to pull out of Ramallah last night.*

▶ **pull over** PHR-VERB When a vehicle or driver **pulls over**, the vehicle moves closer to the side of the road and stops there. ❏ *I had to pull over and force him to get out.*

▶ **pull through** PHR-VERB If someone with a serious illness or someone in a very difficult situation **pulls through**, they recover. ❏ *Everyone was very concerned whether he would pull through or not.*

▶ **pull together** **1** PHR-VERB If people **pull together**, they cooperate with each other. ❏ *The nation was urged to pull together to avoid complete chaos.* **2** PHR-VERB If you are upset or depressed and someone tells you to **pull yourself together**, they are telling you to control your feelings and behave calmly again. ❏ *Pull yourself together, boy!*

▶ **pull up** PHR-VERB When a vehicle or driver **pulls up**, the vehicle slows down and stops. ❏ *The cab pulled up and the driver jumped out.*

**pul|ley** /pʊli/ (**pulleys**) N-COUNT A **pulley** is a device consisting of a wheel over which a rope or

chain is pulled in order to lift heavy objects. [from Old French]

**Pull|man** /pʊlmən/ N-COUNT A **Pullman** or a **Pullman car** on a train is a railway car that has beds for passengers to sleep in.

**pull|over** /pʊloʊvər/ (**pullovers**) N-COUNT A **pullover** is a piece of clothing that covers the upper part of your body and your arms.

**pul|mo|nary cir|cu|la|tion** N-UNCOUNT **Pulmonary circulation** is the flow of blood between the heart and lungs.
→ see **cardiovascular system**

**pulp** /pʌlp/ (**pulps, pulping, pulped**) **1** N-SING If an object is pressed into a **pulp**, it is crushed or beaten until it is soft, smooth, and wet. ❏ *The olives are crushed to a pulp by stone rollers.* **2** N-SING In fruit or vegetables, **the pulp** is the soft part inside the skin. ❏ *Use the whole fruit, including the pulp.* [from Latin]

**pul|pit** /pʊlpɪt, pʌl-/ (**pulpits**) N-COUNT A **pulpit** is a small raised platform in a church, where a member of the clergy stands to speak. [from Latin]

**pul|sar** /pʌlsɑr/ (**pulsars**) N-COUNT A **pulsar** is a star that spins very fast and cannot be seen but produces regular radio signals.

**pul|sate** /pʌlseɪt/ (**pulsates, pulsating, pulsated**) V-I If something **pulsates**, it beats, moves in and out, or shakes with strong, regular movements. ❏ *…a star that pulsates.* [from Latin]

**pulse** /pʌls/ (**pulses**) **1** N-COUNT Your **pulse** is the regular beating of blood through your body, which you can feel when you touch particular parts of your body, especially your wrist. ❏ *Mahoney's pulse was racing, and he felt confused.* **2** N-COUNT A **pulse of** electrical current, light, or sound is a temporary increase in its level. ❏ *…a pulse of radio waves.* [from Latin]

**pump** /pʌmp/ (**pumps, pumping, pumped**) **1** N-COUNT A **pump** is a machine that is used to force a liquid or gas to flow in a particular direction. ❏ *…pumps that circulate the fuel around the engine.* ❏ *…a gas pump.* **2** V-T To **pump** a liquid or gas in a particular direction means to force it to flow in that direction using a pump. ❏ *They've been getting rid of sewage by pumping it out to sea.* **3** V-T If someone **has** their stomach **pumped**, doctors remove the contents of their stomach, for example, because they have swallowed poison or drugs. ❏ *One woman was rushed to the emergency room to have her stomach pumped.* **4** N-COUNT **Pumps** are women's shoes that do not cover the top part of the foot and are usually made of plain leather. [Senses 1–3 from Middle Dutch.]
→ see **shoe**

▶ **pump out** PHR-VERB To **pump out** something means to produce or supply it continually and in large amounts. ❏ *Japanese companies have been pumping out plenty of new products.*

▶ **pump up** PHR-VERB If you **pump up** something such as a tire, you fill it with air using a pump. ❏ *Pump all the tires up.*

**pump|kin** /pʌmpkɪn/ (**pumpkins**) N-VAR A **pumpkin** is a large, round, orange vegetable with a thick skin. ❏ *Cut the pumpkin into four and remove the seeds.* [from Old French]

**pun** /pʌn/ (**puns**) N-COUNT A **pun** is a clever and amusing use of a word or phrase with two meanings, or of words with the same sound but

## Picture Dictionary — punctuation

**A: I want to learn to drive; however, cars scare me.**
semi-colon                                                        period

**B: Why not take a driver-training course?**
hyphen                                    question mark

**A: I'm not ready.**
apostrophe

**B: I know! If you want, I'll teach you to drive.**
exclamation mark        comma

**A: OK, but remember this: it was your idea, not mine.**
colon

different meanings. ❑ *The name 7C is a pun on "seven seas."* [from Italian]

**punch** /pʌntʃ/ (**punches, punching, punched**)
**1** v-т If you **punch** someone or something, you

punch

hit them hard with your fist. ❑ *After punching him on the chin she hit him over the head.* ● **Punch** is also a noun. ❑ *He was hurting Johansson with body punches in the fourth round.* ● **Punch out** means the same as **punch**. ❑ *I punched out this guy.* **2** v-т If you **punch** something such as the

buttons on a keyboard, you press them in order to store information on a machine such as a computer or to give the machine a command to do something. ❑ *Lianne punched the button to call the elevator.* **3** v-т If you **punch** holes in something, you make holes in it by pushing or pressing it with something sharp. ❑ *I took a pen and punched a hole in the box.* **4** N-COUNT A **punch** is a tool that you use for making holes in something. ❑ *...a three-hole punch.* **5** N-VAR **Punch** is a drink made from wine, spirits, or fruit juice, mixed with things such as sugar and spices. ❑ *...a bowl of punch.* [Senses 1–4 from Old French. Sense 5 from Hindi.]
▸ **punch in** PHR-VERB If you **punch in** a number on a machine or **punch** numbers **into** it, you push the machine's buttons or keys in order to give it a command to do something. ❑ *Punch in your account number on the phone.*

**punch|ing bag** (**punching bags**) N-COUNT A **punching bag** is a heavy leather bag, filled with firm material, that hangs on a rope and is used for training by boxers and other athletes.

**punc|tu|al** /pʌŋktʃuəl/ ADJ If you are **punctual**, you do something or arrive somewhere at the right time and are not late. ❑ *He's always very punctual.* ● **punc|tu|al|ly** ADV ❑ *My guest arrived punctually.* [from Medieval Latin]

**punc|tu|ate** /pʌŋktʃueɪt/ (**punctuates, punctuating, punctuated**) v-т If an activity or situation **is punctuated by** particular things, it is interrupted by them at intervals. [WRITTEN] ❑ *The game was punctuated by a series of injuries.* [from Medieval Latin]

**punc|tua|tion** /pʌŋktʃueɪʃ°n/ N-UNCOUNT **Punctuation** is the system of signs such as periods, commas, or question marks that you use in writing to divide words into sentences and

clauses. ❑ *He was known for his poor grammar and punctuation.* [from Medieval Latin]
→ see Picture Dictionary: **punctuation**

**punc|tua|tion mark** (**punctuation marks**) N-COUNT A **punctuation mark** is a symbol such as a period, comma, or question mark.

**punc|ture** /pʌŋktʃər/ (**punctures, puncturing, punctured**) **1** N-COUNT A **puncture** is a small hole in a car tire or bicycle tire that has been made by a sharp object. ❑ *Somebody helped me to fix the puncture.* **2** v-т If a sharp object **punctures** something, it makes a hole in it. ❑ *The bullet punctured the skull.* [from Latin]

**pun|dit** /pʌndɪt/ (**pundits**) N-COUNT A **pundit** is a person who knows a lot about a subject and is often asked to give information or opinions about it to the public. ❑ *...a well-known political pundit.* [from Hindi]

**pun|gent** /pʌndʒ°nt/ ADJ Something that is **pungent** has a strong, bitter smell or taste. ❑ *The more herbs you use, the more pungent the sauce will be.* [from Latin]

**pun|ish** /pʌnɪʃ/ (**punishes, punishing, punished**) **1** v-т To **punish** someone means to make them suffer in some way because they have done something wrong. ❑ *I don't think George ever had to punish the children.* **2** v-т To **punish** a crime means to punish anyone who commits that crime. ❑ *...federal laws to punish crimes such as murder.* [from Old French]

**pun|ish|ing** /pʌnɪʃɪŋ/ ADJ A **punishing** schedule, activity, or experience requires a lot of physical effort and makes you very tired or weak. ❑ *Her punishing work schedule gave her little time for her family.* [from Old French]

**pun|ish|ment** /pʌnɪʃmənt/ (**punishments**) **1** N-UNCOUNT **Punishment** is the act of punishing someone or of being punished. ❑ *...the physical punishment of children.* **2** N-VAR A **punishment** is a particular way of punishing someone. ❑ *There will be tougher punishments for crimes of violence.* [from Old French] **3** → see also **capital punishment, corporal punishment**

**pu|ni|tive** /pyuːnɪtɪv/ ADJ **Punitive** actions are intended to punish people. [FORMAL] ❑ *The company has been ordered to pay punitive costs.* [from Medieval Latin]

**punk** /pʌŋk/ (**punks**) **1** N-UNCOUNT **Punk** or

**punk rock** is rock music that is played in a fast, loud, and aggressive way and is often a protest against conventional attitudes and behavior. Punk rock was particularly popular in the late 1970s. **2** N-COUNT A **punk** or a **punk rocker** is a young person who likes punk music and dresses in a very noticeable and unconventional way, for example, by having brightly colored hair and wearing metal chains. ❑ *In the 1970s, punks wore safety pins through their cheeks.* **3** N-COUNT A **punk** is a young person who behaves in a rude, aggressive, or violent way. [INFORMAL] ❑ *Brad Pitt stars as a young punk living in New York's Lower East Side.* [from Spanish]

**Pun|nett square** /pʌnɪt skweər/ (**Punnett squares**) N-COUNT A **Punnett square** is a diagram used by biologists to predict the genetic makeup of an organism. [TECHNICAL]

**pup** /pʌp/ (**pups**) **1** N-COUNT A **pup** is a young dog. ❑ *I'll get you an Alsatian pup for Christmas.* **2** N-COUNT The young of some other animals, for example, seals, are called **pups**. ❑ *...gray seal pups.*

**pu|pil** /pyupɪl/ (**pupils**) **1** N-COUNT A **pupil** of a painter, musician, or other expert is someone who studies under that expert and learns his or her skills. ❑ *Goldschmidt became a pupil of the composer Franz Schreker.* **2** N-COUNT The **pupils** of a school are the children who go to it. ❑ *...schools with over 1,000 pupils.* **3** N-COUNT The **pupils** of your eyes are the small, round, black holes in the center of them. ❑ *The pupils of her eyes widened.* [from Latin]
→ see **eye**

**pup|pet** /pʌpɪt/ (**puppets**) **1** N-COUNT A **puppet** is a doll that you can move, either by pulling strings that are attached to it or by putting your hand inside its body and moving your fingers. **2** N-COUNT You can refer to a person or country as a **puppet** when you mean that their actions are controlled by a more powerful person or government, even though they may appear to be independent. ❑ *They accused his government of being a puppet of Moscow.* [from Old French]

**pup|pet|ry** /pʌpɪtri/ N-UNCOUNT **Puppetry** is the art of entertaining people with puppets. [from Old French]

**pup|py** /pʌpi/ (**puppies**) N-COUNT A **puppy** is a young dog. [from Old French]

**pur|chase** /pɜrtʃɪs/ (**purchases, purchasing, purchased**) **1** V-T When you **purchase** something, you buy it. [FORMAL] ❑ *He purchased a ticket.* ● **pur|chas|er** (**purchasers**) N-COUNT ❑ *The broker will get 5% if he finds a purchaser.* **2** N-UNCOUNT The **purchase of** something is the act of buying it. [FORMAL] ❑ *The company will today announce the purchase of two radio stations.* **3** N-COUNT A **purchase** is something that you buy. [FORMAL] ❑ *She opened the box and looked at her purchase.* [from Old French]

**pure** /pyʊər/ (**purer, purest**) **1** ADJ A **pure** substance is not mixed with anything else. ❑ *...a carton of pure orange juice.* ● **pu|ri|ty** /pyʊərɪti/ N-UNCOUNT ❑ *...their obsession with moral purity.* **2** ADJ Something that is **pure** is clean and does not contain any harmful substances. ❑ *The air is pure and the crops are free of chemicals.* ● **pu|ri|ty** N-UNCOUNT ❑ *They worried about the purity of the tap water.* **3** ADJ **Pure** science or **pure** research is concerned only with theory and not with how this theory can be used in practical ways. ❑ *Physics isn't just pure science; it has uses.* **4** ADJ **Pure** means complete and total. ❑ *...a look of pure surprise.* [from Old French]
→ see **science**

**pu|ree** /pyʊreɪ, -ri/ (**purees**) N-VAR **Puree** is food that has been crushed or beaten so that it forms a thick, smooth liquid. ❑ *...a can of tomato puree.* [from Hindi]

**pure|ly** /pyʊərli/ ADV You use **purely** to emphasize that the thing you are mentioning is the most important feature or that it is the only thing which should be considered. ❑ *It is a racing machine, designed purely for speed.* [from Old French]

**purge** /pɜrdʒ/ (**purges, purging, purged**) **1** V-T To **purge** an organization **of** its unacceptable members means to remove them from it. You can also talk about **purging** people **from** an organization. ❑ *The plan was to purge the country of its internal enemies.* ● **Purge** is also a noun. ❑ *...the terror of the purges of the 1930s.* **2** V-T If you **purge** something **of** undesirable things, you get rid of them. ❑ *He closed his eyes, trying to purge his mind of anxiety.* [from Old French]

**pu|ri|fy** /pyʊərɪfaɪ/ (**purifies, purifying, purified**) V-T If you **purify** a substance, you make it pure by removing any harmful, dirty, or inferior substances from it. ❑ *The ability to purify dirty water could solve the world's water crisis.* ● **pu|ri|fi|ca|tion** /pyʊərɪfɪkeɪʃⁿn/ N-UNCOUNT ❑ *...a water purification plant.* [from Old French]

**pur|ist** /pyʊərɪst/ (**purists**) N-COUNT A **purist** is a person who believes in absolute correctness, especially in something they know a lot about. ❑ *Purists say the language is under threat.* [from Old French]

**pu|ri|tan** /pyʊərɪtⁿn/ (**puritans**) N-COUNT You describe someone as a **puritan** when they live according to strict moral or religious principles, especially ones that forbid physical pleasures, and you do not agree with this. ❑ *Malinin was rather a puritan.* ● **Puritan** is also an adjective. ❑ *...a puritan tradition.* [from Late Latin]

**pu|ri|tani|cal** /pyʊərɪtænɪkⁿl/ ADJ If you describe someone as **puritanical**, you mean that they disapprove of pleasure, for example because they are strictly religious, and you do not agree with this. ❑ *...their puritanical values of hard work.* [from Late Latin]

**pu|rity** /pyʊərɪti/ → see **pure**

**pur|ple** /pɜrpⁿl/ (**purples**) COLOR Something that is **purple** is of a reddish-blue color. ❑ *She wore purple and green silk.* [from Old English]

**pur|port** /pərpɔrt/ (**purports, purporting, purported**) V-T If someone or something **purports** to do or be a particular thing, they claim to do or be that thing. [FORMAL] ❑ *...a book that purports to tell the whole truth.* [from Old French]

**pur|pose** /pɜrpəs/ (**purposes**) **1** N-COUNT The **purpose** of something is the reason for which it is made or done. ❑ *The purpose of the occasion was to raise money for medical supplies.* ❑ *...the use of nuclear energy for military purposes.* **2** N-COUNT Your **purpose** is the thing that you want to achieve. ❑ *They might be prepared to harm you in order to achieve their purpose.* **3** N-UNCOUNT **Purpose** is the feeling of having a definite aim and of being determined to achieve it. ❑ *Our teachers have a sense of purpose.* **4** PHRASE If you do something **on purpose**, you do it intentionally. ❑ *Was it an accident or did David do it on purpose?* [from Old French]

**pur|pose|ful** /pɜ́rpəsfəl/ ADJ If someone is **purposeful**, they show that they have a definite aim and a strong desire to achieve it. ❑ *...a purposeful journey.* ● **pur|pose|ful|ly** ADV ❑ *They walked purposefully out of the rain to the shelter of the platform.* [from Old French]

**purr** /pɜ́r/ (**purrs, purring, purred**) **1** V-I When a cat **purrs**, it makes a low vibrating sound with its throat because it is contented. ❑ *The kitten settled comfortably in her arms and was purring enthusiastically.* **2** V-I When the engine of a machine such as a car **purrs**, it is working and making a quiet, continuous, vibrating sound. ❑ *Both boats purred out of the cave and into open water.* ● **Purr** is also a noun. ❑ *Carmela heard the purr of a motorcycle coming up the drive.* [from French]

**purse** /pɜ́rs/ (**purses, pursing, pursed**) **1** N-COUNT A **purse** is a small bag or a handbag that women carry. ❑ *She reached in her purse for her keys.* **2** V-T If you **purse** your **lips**, you move them into a small, rounded shape. ❑ *She pursed her lips in disapproval.* [from Old English]

**pur|sue** /pərsú/ (**pursues, pursuing, pursued**) **1** V-T If you **pursue** a particular aim or result, you make efforts to achieve it, often over a long period of time. [FORMAL] ❑ *He will pursue a trade policy that protects American workers.* **2** V-T If you **pursue** a particular topic, you try to find out more about it by asking questions. [FORMAL] ❑ *If there has been a mistake, you should pursue the matter with our customer service department.* **3** V-T If you **pursue** a person, vehicle, or animal, you follow them, usually in order to catch them. [FORMAL] ❑ *She pursued the man who stole the woman's bag.* ● **pur|su|er** (**pursuers**) N-COUNT ❑ *They could hear the voices of their pursuers.* [from Old French]

**pur|suit** /pərsút/ (**pursuits**) **1** N-UNCOUNT Your **pursuit of** something is your attempts at achieving it. ❑ *...his pursuit of excellence.* ❑ *They frequently move around the country in pursuit of a medical career.* **2** N-UNCOUNT If you are **in pursuit** of a person, vehicle, or animal, you are chasing them. ❑ *...a police patrol car in pursuit of a motorcycle.* **3** N-COUNT Your **pursuits** are your activities, usually activities that you enjoy when you are not working. ❑ *They both love outdoor pursuits.* [from Old French]

**pur|vey|or** /pərvéɪər/ (**purveyors**) N-COUNT A **purveyor of** goods or services is a person or company that provides them. [FORMAL] ❑ *...purveyors of gourmet foods.* [from Old French]

**push** /pʊʃ/ (**pushes, pushing, pushed**) **1** V-T/V-I When you **push** something, you use force to make it move away from you or away from its previous position. ❑ *The woman pushed back her chair and stood up.* ❑ *They pushed him into the car.* ❑ *...a pregnant woman pushing a stroller.* ❑ *He put both hands on the*

door and pushed as hard as he could. ● **Push** is also a noun. ❑ *He gave me a sharp push.* **2** V-T/V-I If you **push through** things that are blocking your way or **push** your **way through** them, you use force in order to move past them. ❑ *I pushed through the crowds and on to the escalator.* ❑ *He pushed his way toward her, laughing.* **3** V-T To **push** a value or amount **up** or **down** means to cause it to increase or decrease. ❑ *Any shortage could push up grain prices.* **4** V-T If you **push** someone **to** do something or **push** them **into** doing it, you encourage or force them to do it. ❑ *She thanked her parents for pushing her to study.* ❑ *Jason did not push her into stealing the money.* ● **Push** is also a noun. ❑ *We need a push to take the first step.* **5** V-I If you **push for** something, you try very hard to achieve it or to persuade someone to do it. ❑ *Consumer groups are pushing for health care changes.* ● **Push** is also a noun. ❑ *...a push for economic growth.* **6** V-T If someone **pushes** an idea, a point, or a product, they try in a forceful way to convince people to accept it or buy it. ❑ *...an advertising campaign to push a product.* **7** V-T When someone **pushes** drugs, they sell them illegally. [INFORMAL] **8** if **push comes to shove** → see **shove** [from Old French]

▸ **push ahead** or **push forward** PHR-VERB If you **push ahead** or **push forward with** something, you make progress with it. ❑ *The government intends to push ahead with the changes.*

▸ **push on** PHR-VERB When you **push on**, you continue with a trip or task. ❑ *Although the journey was a long and lonely one, Tumalo pushed on.*

▸ **push over** PHR-VERB If you **push** someone or something **over**, you push them so that they fall onto the ground. ❑ *...people damaging hedges, uprooting trees and pushing over walls.*

▸ **push through** PHR-VERB If someone **pushes through** a law, they succeed in getting it accepted although some people oppose it. ❑ *He tried to push the law through.*

**push|cart** /pʊ́ʃkɑrt/ (**pushcarts**) N-COUNT A **pushcart** is a cart from which fruit or other goods are sold in the street.

**push-up** (**push-ups**) N-COUNT **Push-ups** are exercises to strengthen your arms and chest muscles. They are done by lying with your face towards the floor and pushing with your hands to raise your body until your arms are straight.

**put** /pʊ́t/ (**puts, putting**)

The form **put** is used in the present tense and is the past tense and past participle.

p

**Put** is used in a large number of expressions that are explained under other words in this dictionary. For example, the expression **to put someone in the picture** is explained at **picture**.

**1** V-T When you **put** something in a particular place or position, you move it into that place or position. ❑ *Leaphorn put the photograph on the desk.* ❑ *She put her hand on Grace's arm.* **2** V-T If you **put** someone somewhere, you cause them to go there and to stay there for a period of time. ❑ *Rather than put him in the hospital, she is caring for him at home.* **3** V-T To **put** someone or something in a particular state or situation means to cause them to be in that state or situation. ❑ *This is going to put them out of business.* ❑ *He was putting himself at risk.* **4** V-T If you **put** your trust, faith, or confidence in someone or something, you trust them or have faith or confidence in them. ❑ *Are we right to put our confidence in computers?* **5** V-T If you **put** time, strength, or energy **into** an activity, you use it in doing that activity. ❑ *She did not put much energy into the discussion.* **6** V-T When you **put** an idea or remark in a particular way, you express it in that way. You can use expressions like **to put it simply** and **to put it bluntly** before saying something when you want to explain how you are going to express it. ❑ *You can't put that sort of fear into words.* ❑ *He admitted the security forces might have made some mistakes, as he put it.* **7** V-T When you **put a question** to someone, you ask them the question. ❑ *Is this fair? Well, I put that question today to the mayor.* **8** V-T If you **put** something **at** a particular value or in a particular category, you consider that it has that value or that it belongs in that category. ❑ *I would put her age at about 50.* ❑ *The more technically advanced countries put a high value on science.* **9** V-T If you **put** written information somewhere, you write, type, or print it there. ❑ *They put an announcement in the local paper.* [from Old English]

▶ **put across** or put over PHR-VERB When you **put** something **across** or **put** it **over**, you succeed in describing or explaining it to someone. ❑ *If you don't put your point across, you can't expect people to understand.*

▶ **put aside** PHR-VERB If you **put** something **aside**, you keep it to be dealt with or used at a later time. ❑ *Encourage children to put aside some money to buy Christmas presents.*

▶ **put away** PHR-VERB If you **put** something **away**, you put it into the place where it is normally kept when it is not being used. ❑ *She finished putting the milk away.* ❑ *She slowly put away her doll.*

▶ **put back** PHR-VERB To **put** something **back** means to delay it or arrange for it to happen later than you previously planned. ❑ *There are always problems which put the opening date back further.*

▶ **put down** **1** PHR-VERB If you **put** something **down** somewhere, you write or type it there. ❑ *Never put anything down on paper which might be used against you.* ❑ *The journalists simply put down what they thought they heard.* **2** PHR-VERB If you **put down** some money, you pay part of the price of something, and will pay the rest later. ❑ *He bought a property for $100,000 and put down $20,000.* **3** PHR-VERB When soldiers, police, or the government **put down** a riot or rebellion, they stop it by using force. ❑ *Soldiers went in to put down a riot.* **4** PHR-VERB If someone **puts** you **down**, they treat

you in an unpleasant way by criticizing you in front of other people or making you appear foolish. ❑ *I know that I sometimes put people down.* **5** PHR-VERB When an animal **is put down**, it is killed because it is dangerous or very ill. ❑ *The judge ordered the dog to be put down immediately.*

▶ **put down to** PHR-VERB If you **put** something **down to** a particular thing, you believe that it is caused by that thing. ❑ *He first felt the pain in January, but put it down to tiredness.*

▶ **put forward** PHR-VERB If you **put forward** a plan, proposal, or name, you suggest that it should be considered for a particular purpose or job. ❑ *He has put forward new peace proposals.*

▶ **put in** **1** PHR-VERB If you **put in** time or effort doing something, you spend that time or effort doing it. ❑ *They've put in time and effort to keep the strike going.* **2** PHR-VERB If you **put in** a request or **put in for** something, you make a formal request or application. ❑ *I put in a request for some overtime.*

▶ **put off** **1** PHR-VERB If you **put** something **off**, you delay doing it. ❑ *He frequently puts off making difficult decisions.* **2** PHR-VERB If you **put** someone **off**, you make them wait for something that they want. ❑ *He tried to put them off, saying that it was late.* **3** PHR-VERB To **put** someone **off** something means to cause them to dislike it or not want it. ❑ *That cake put me off chocolate for life.* ❑ *His personal habits put them off.* **4** PHR-VERB If someone or something **puts** you **off**, they take your attention from what you are trying to do and make it more difficult for you to do it. ❑ *She said it put her off if I laughed.*

▶ **put on** **1** PHR-VERB When you **put on** clothing or makeup, you place it on your body in order to wear it. ❑ *She put her coat on and went out.* ❑ *Maximo put on a pair of glasses.* **2** PHR-VERB When people **put on** a show, exhibition, or service, they perform it or organize it. ❑ *The band is hoping to put on a show before the end of the year.* **3** PHR-VERB If someone **puts on** weight, they become heavier. ❑ *I can eat what I want but I never put on weight.* **4** PHR-VERB If you **put on** a piece of equipment or a device, you make it start working, for example, by pressing a switch or turning a knob. ❑ *I put the radio on.* **5** PHR-VERB If you **put on** a record, tape, or CD on, you place it in a record, tape, or CD player and listen to it. ❑ *Why not just put a CD on, or a tape, and listen to music that way?*

▶ **put out** **1** PHR-VERB If you **put out** an announcement or story, you make it known to a lot of people. ❑ *Thomson put out a statement saying there was no problem between the two men.* **2** PHR-VERB If you **put out** a fire, candle, or cigarette, you make it stop burning. ❑ *Firemen tried to put out the blaze.* **3** PHR-VERB If you **put out** an electric light, you make it stop shining by pressing a switch. ❑ *He went to the table and put out the light.* **4** PHR-VERB If you **put out** things that will be needed, you place them somewhere ready to be used. ❑ *Paula put out her luggage for the bus.* **5** PHR-VERB If you **put out** your **hand**, you move it forward, away from your body. ❑ *He put out his hand to Alfred.* **6** PHR-VERB If you **put** someone **out**, you cause them trouble because they have to do something for you. ❑ *"I can give you a lift." — "No, no. I can't put you out like that."*

▶ **put over** → see **put across**

▶ **put through** **1** PHR-VERB When someone **puts through** someone who is making a telephone call, they make the connection that allows the telephone call to take place. ❑ *The operator will put you through.* ◻ PHR-VERB If someone **puts** you **through** an unpleasant experience, they make you experience it. ❑ *We've put them through a lot. Now it's time we let them have a rest.*

▶ **put together** ◻ PHR-VERB If you **put** something **together**, you join its different parts to each other so that it can be used. ❑ *He took it apart brick by brick, and put it back together again.* ◻ PHR-VERB If you **put together** a group of people or things, you form them into a team or collection. ❑ *I put together a group of 125 volunteers.* ◻ PHR-VERB If you **put together** an agreement, plan, or product, you design and create it. ❑ *We wouldn't have time to put together an agreement.*

▶ **put up** ◻ PHR-VERB If people **put up** a wall, building, tent, or other structure, they construct it. ❑ *He put up a new office building.* ◻ PHR-VERB If you **put up** a poster or notice, you attach it to a wall or board. ❑ *They're putting new street signs up.* ◻ PHR-VERB To **put up** resistance to something means to resist it. ❑ *The man put up no resistance as they took him from his car.* ◻ PHR-VERB If you **put up** money for something, you provide the money that is needed to pay for it. ❑ *The state agreed to put up $69,000 to start his company.* ◻ PHR-VERB To **put up** the price of something means to cause it to increase. ❑ *Their friends told them they should put up their prices.* ◻ PHR-VERB If a person or hotel **puts** you **up**, you stay there for one or more nights. ❑ *I wanted to know if she could put me up for a few days.*

▶ **put up with** PHR-VERB If you **put up with** something, you tolerate or accept it, even though you find it unpleasant or unsatisfactory. ❑ *They put up with terrible behavior from their son.*

**putt** /pʌt/ (**putts, putting, putted**) V-T/V-I In golf, when you **putt**, or **putt** the ball, you hit it a short distance on the green. ❑ *Turner putted superbly.* [from Scottish]

**putt|er** /pʌtər/ (**putters, puttering, puttered**) ◻ N-COUNT A **putter** is a club used for hitting a golf ball a short distance on the green. ◻ V-I If you **putter around**, you do unimportant but quite enjoyable things, without hurrying. ❑ *I started puttering around outside.* [Sense 1 of Scottish origin. Sense 2 from Old English.]

**puz|zle** /pʌzəl/ (**puzzles**) ◻ V-T If something **puzzles** you, you do not understand it and feel confused. ❑ *My sister puzzles me.* ● **puz|zled**

/pʌzəld/ ADJ ❑ *Critics remain puzzled by the election results.* ● **puz|zling** ADJ ❑ *His letter poses a number of puzzling questions.* ◻ V-I If you **puzzle over** something, you try hard to think of the answer to it or the explanation for it. ❑ *In reading Shakespeare, I puzzle over his verse and prose.*

puzzle

◻ N-COUNT A **puzzle** is a question, game, or toy that you have to think about carefully in order to answer it correctly or put it together properly. ❑ *...a word puzzle.* ◻ → see also **crossword, jigsaw** ◻ N-SING You can describe a person or thing that is hard to understand as **a puzzle**. ❑ *The rise in accidents remains a puzzle.*

**P wave** /pi weɪv/ also **P-wave** (**P waves**) N-COUNT **P waves** are rapid waves of energy that are released in an earthquake. **P wave** is an abbreviation for "pressure wave" or "primary wave". [TECHNICAL]

**pyra|mid** /pɪrəmɪd/ (**pyramids**) N-COUNT A **pyramid** is a three-dimensional shape with a flat base and flat triangular sides that slope upward to a point. [from Latin] → see **solid, volume**

**pyro|clas|tic ma|terial** /paɪrəklæstɪk mətɪəriəl/ N-UNCOUNT **Pyroclastic material** is fragments of rock and other substances that are released into the air when a volcano erupts. [TECHNICAL]

**py|thon** /paɪθɒn, -θən/ (**pythons**) N-COUNT A **python** is a type of large snake. [from New Latin]

P

# Qq

**qt. qt.** is a written abbreviation for **quart**.

**quad|rat|ic func|tion** /kwɒdrætɪk fʌŋkʃⁿn/ (**quadratic functions**) N-COUNT A **quadratic function** is a mathematical expression that is used in calculating the area within a square. [TECHNICAL]

**quad|ru|ple** /kwɒdrʌpəl, -drupⁿl, kwɒdrupⁿl/ (**quadruples, quadrupling, quadrupled**) ◻ V-T/ V-I If someone **quadruples** an amount or if it **quadruples**, it becomes four times bigger. ◻ *The new system will quadruple the number of phone lines.* ◻ PREDET If one amount is **quadruple** another amount, it is four times bigger. ◻ *There are about 60 cases of the disease a year; that's quadruple the number we had five years ago.* ◻ ADJ You use **quadruple** to indicate that something has four parts or happens four times. ◻ *She's a quadruple gold medal winner.* [from Old French]

**quad|ru|plet** /kwɒdrʌplɪt, -druplɪt, kwɒdruplɪt/ (**quadruplets**) N-COUNT **Quadruplets** are four children who are born to the same mother at the same time.

**quag|ga** /kwægə/ (**quaggas**) N-COUNT A **quagga** was a type of zebra that is now extinct. [from Afrikaans]

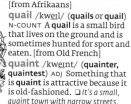

**quail** /kweɪl/ (**quails** or **quail**) N-COUNT A **quail** is a small bird that lives on the ground and is sometimes hunted for sport and eaten. [from Old French]

**quaint** /kweɪnt/ (**quainter, quaintest**) ADJ Something that is **quaint** is attractive because it is old-fashioned. ◻ *It's a small, quaint town with narrow streets.* [from Old French]

quail

**quake** /kweɪk/ (**quakes, quaking, quaked**) ◻ N-COUNT A **quake** is the same as an **earthquake**. [INFORMAL] ◻ V-I If you **quake**, you shake, usually because you are very afraid. ◻ *I stood there, quaking with fear.* [from Old English]

**quali|fi|ca|tion** /kwɒlɪfɪkeɪʃⁿn/ (**qualifications**) ◻ N-COUNT The **qualifications** you need for an activity or task are the qualities and skills that you need to be able to do it. ◻ *I believe I have all the qualifications to be a good teacher.* ◻ N-VAR A **qualification** is a detail or explanation that you add to a statement to make it less strong or less general. ◻ *The president accepted the peace plan without qualification.* [from Old French]

### Word Partnership  Use *qualification* with :

| | |
|---|---|
| N. | qualification **for a job, standards for** qualification ◻ |
| ADJ. | **necessary** qualification ◻ |
| PREP. | **without** qualification ◻ |

**quali|fied** /kwɒlɪfaɪd/ ADJ If you give someone or something **qualified** support or approval, your support or approval is not total because you have some doubts. ◻ *William answered the question with a qualified "yes."* [from Old French]

**quali|fi|er** /kwɒlɪfaɪər/ (**qualifiers**) ◻ N-COUNT A **qualifier** is an early round or stage in some competitions. ◻ *Wang quickly won her three qualifiers.* [from Old French] ◻ → see also **qualify**

**quali|fy** /kwɒlɪfaɪ/ (**qualifies, qualifying, qualified**) ◻ V-I If you **qualify** in a competition, you are successful in one part of it and go on to the next stage. ◻ *We qualified for the final by beating Stanford.* ● **quali|fi|er** (**qualifiers**) N-COUNT ◻ *Kenya's Robert Kibe was the fastest qualifier for the 800 meters final.* ◻ V-T If you **qualify** a statement, you make it less strong or less general by adding a detail or explanation to it. ◻ *He later qualified his remarks by agreeing that the movie was successful.* ◻ V-T/V-I If you **qualify** for something or if something **qualifies** you for it, you have the right to do it or have it. ◻ *This course does not qualify you to practice as a therapist.* ◻ V-I When someone **qualifies**, they receive the certificate or license that they need to be able to work in a particular profession. ◻ *I qualified and started teaching last year.* [from Old French] ◻ → see also **qualified**

### Word Partnership  Use *qualify* with :

| | |
|---|---|
| PREP. | qualify **as something** ◻ |
| | qualify **for something** ◻ |
| V. | **chance to** qualify, **fail to** qualify ◻ ◻ ◻ |

**quali|ta|tive** /kwɒlɪteɪtɪv/ ADJ **Qualitative** means relating to the quality of things. [FORMAL] ◻ *It is impossible to make qualitative choices about the best movies of the year.* [from Old French]

**qual|ity** /kwɒlɪti/ (**qualities**) ◻ N-UNCOUNT The **quality** of something is how good or bad it is. ◻ *The quality of the food here is excellent.* ◻ N-UNCOUNT Something of **quality** is of a high standard. ◻ *This is a college of quality.* ◻ N-COUNT Someone's **qualities** are their good characteristics. ◻ *Where do your kids get their lovable qualities from?* ◻ N-COUNT You can describe a particular characteristic of a person or thing as a **quality**. ◻ *He has a childlike quality.* [from Old French]

### Word Partnership  Use *quality* with :

| | |
|---|---|
| N. | **air** quality, quality **of life**, quality **of service, water** quality, quality **of work** ◻ |
| ADJ. | **best/better/good** quality, **high/ higher/highest** quality, **low** quality, **poor** quality, **top** quality ◻ ◻ |

**qual|ity of life** N-SING Someone's **quality of life**

is the extent to which their life is comfortable or satisfying. ❑ *Before the operation, the patient did not have a very high quality of life.*

**qualm** /kwɑm/ (**qualms**) N-COUNT If you have no **qualms** about doing something, you are not worried that it may be wrong. ❑ *She had no qualms about taking the money.* [from Old English]

| Word Link | quant ≈ how much : *quantifier*, *quantitative*, *quantity* |

**quan|ti|fi|er** /kwɒntɪfaɪər/ (**quantifiers**) N-COUNT In grammar, a **quantifier** is a word or phrase such as "plenty" or "a lot" which you use to refer to a quantity of something without being exact. It is often followed by "of," as in "a lot of money." [from Old French]

**quan|ti|ta|tive** /kwɒntɪteɪtɪv/ ADJ **Quantitative** means relating to different sizes or amounts of things. [FORMAL] ❑ *The database gives quantitative information.* [from Old French]

**quan|tity** /kwɒntɪti/ (**quantities**) ◼ N-VAR A **quantity** is an amount. ❑ *Pour a small quantity of water into a pan.* ◻ N-UNCOUNT Things that are produced or available in **quantity** are produced or available in large amounts. ❑ *These toys are sold in quantity and the quality doesn't seem to matter.* [from Old French]

→ see **mathematics**

**quan|tum** /kwɒntəm/ ◼ ADJ In physics, **quantum** theory and **quantum** mechanics are concerned with the behavior of atomic particles. ◻ ADJ A **quantum leap** or **quantum jump** in something is a very great and sudden increase in its size, amount, or quality. ❑ *We haven't had a quantum leap in aircraft technology for a few years.* [from Latin]

**quar|an|tine** /kwɒrəntin/ N-UNCOUNT If a person or animal is in **quarantine**, they are kept separate from other people or animals for a period of time, because they have or may have a disease that could spread. [from Italian]

→ see **illness**

**quar|rel** /kwɒrəl/ (**quarrels, quarreling, quarreled**) ◼ N-COUNT A **quarrel** is an angry argument between two or more friends or family members. ❑ *I had a terrible quarrel with my brothers.* ◻ V-RECIP When two or more people **quarrel**, they have an angry argument. ❑ *Yes, we quarreled over something again.* ◼ N-SING If you say that you have no **quarrel** with someone or something, you mean that you do not disagree with them. [from Old French]

**quar|ry** /kwɒri/ (**quarries, quarrying, quarried**) ◼ N-COUNT A **quarry** is an area that is dug out from a piece of land or the side of a mountain in order to get stone or minerals. ❑ *...the biggest stone quarry in Britain.* ◻ V-T When stone or minerals **are quarried** or when an area **is quarried** for them, they are removed from the area by digging, drilling, or using explosives. ❑ *Stone for the Pentagon was quarried in Bedford.* [from Old French]

| Word Link | quart ≈ four : *quart*, *quarter*, *quarterback* |

**quart** /kwɔrt/ (**quarts**) N-COUNT A **quart** is a unit of volume that is equal to two pints. ❑ *Use a quart of milk.* [from Old French]

→ see **measurement**

**quar|ter** /kwɔrtər/ (**quarters**) ◼ ORD A **quarter** is one of four equal parts of something. ❑ *A quarter of the residents are over 55 years old.* ❑ *Prices have fallen by a quarter since January.* ● **Quarter** is also a predeterminer. ❑ *The planet is about a quarter the size of the moon.* ● **Quarter** is also an adjective. ❑ *...the past quarter century.* ◻ N-COUNT A **quarter** is an American or Canadian coin that is worth 25 cents. ◼ N-COUNT A **quarter** is a fixed period of three months. ❑ *Results for the third quarter are due on October 31.* ◼ N-UNCOUNT; N-SING When you are telling the time, you use **quarter** to talk about the fifteen minutes before or after an hour. For example, 8:15 is **quarter after** eight and 8:45 is a **quarter of** nine. You can also say that 8:15 is **quarter past** eight, and 8:45 is **quarter to** nine. ◼ N-COUNT A particular **quarter** of a town is a part of the town where a particular group of people traditionally live or work. ❑ *I work in the Chinese quarter.* ◼ PHRASE If you do something **at close quarters**, you do it very near to a particular person or thing. ❑ *You can watch aircraft take off or land at close quarters.* [from Old French]

| Word Partnership | Use *quarter* with : |
|---|---|
| N. | quarter (**of a**) **century**, quarter (**of a**) **pound** ◼ |
| ADJ. | **first/fourth/second/third** quarter ◼ |
| PREP. | **for the** quarter, **in the** quarter ◼ quarter **after**, quarter **of**, quarter **past**, quarter **to** ◼ |

**quarter|back** /kwɔrtərbæk/ (**quarterbacks**) N-COUNT In football, a **quarterback** is the player on the attacking team who begins each play and who decides which play to use.

**quarter|final** /kwɔrtərfaɪnªl/ (**quarterfinals**) N-COUNT A **quarterfinal** is one of the four games in a competition which decides which four players or teams will compete in the semifinals.

**quar|ter|ly** /kwɔrtərli/ ADJ A **quarterly** event happens four times a year, at intervals of three months. ❑ *...the latest Bank of Japan quarterly report.* ● **Quarterly** is also an adverb. ❑ *Your money can be paid quarterly or annually.* [from Old French]

**quar|ter note** (**quarter notes**) N-COUNT A **quarter note** is a musical note that has a time value equal to two eighth notes.

**quar|tet** /kwɔrtɛt/ (**quartets**) ◼ N-COUNT A **quartet** is a group of four people who play musical instruments or sing together. ◻ N-COUNT A **quartet** is a piece of music for four instruments or four singers. [from Italian]

**quartz** /kwɔrts/ N-UNCOUNT **Quartz** is a hard, shiny crystal used in making electronic equipment and very accurate watches and clocks. [from German]

**qua|sar** /kweɪzɑr/ (**quasars**) N-COUNT A **quasar** is an object far away in space that produces bright light and radio waves.

**quash** /kwɒʃ/ (**quashes, quashing, quashed**) V-T If a court or someone in authority **quashes** a decision or judgment, they officially reject it. ❑ *The mayor quashed the deal after critics complained.* [from Old French]

**quay** /ki/ (**quays**) N-COUNT A **quay** is a long platform beside the ocean or a river where boats can be tied. [from Old French]

**q**

**queen** /kwi̱n/ (**queens**) ◼ N-TITLE; N-COUNT A **queen** is a woman who rules a country as its monarch. ❑ *...Queen Elizabeth.* ◾ N-COUNT In chess, the **queen** is the most powerful piece, which can be moved in any direction. ◼ N-COUNT A **queen** is a playing card with a picture of a queen on it. ❑ *...the queen of spades.* [from Old English] → see **chess**

**quell** /kwe̱l/ (**quells, quelling, quelled**) ◼ V-T To **quell** opposition or violent behavior means to stop it. ❑ *Troops eventually quelled the disturbance.* ◾ V-T If you **quell** an unpleasant feeling such as fear or anger, you stop yourself or other people from having that feeling. ❑ *Dawn tried everything she could think of to quell her son's fears.* [from Old English]

**quench** /kwe̱ntʃ/ (**quenches, quenching, quenched**) V-T If someone who is thirsty **quenches** their **thirst**, they satisfy their thirst by having a drink. ❑ *We drank lots of water to quench our thirst.* [from Old English]

**que|ry** /kwi̱əri/ (**queries, querying, queried**) ◼ N-COUNT A **query** is a question, especially one that you ask an organization, publication, or expert. ❑ *If you have any queries, please do not hesitate to contact us.* ◾ V-T If you **query** something, you check it by asking about it because you are not sure if it is correct. ❑ *There's a number you can call to query your bill.* ◼ V-T To **query** means to ask a question. ❑ *"Is there something else?" Ray queried.* [from Latin]

**quest** /kwe̱st/ (**quests**) N-COUNT A **quest** is a long and difficult search for something. [LITERARY] ❑ *My quest for a better bank continues.* [from Old French]

**ques|tion** /kwe̱stʃ°n/ (**questions, questioning, questioned**) ◼ N-COUNT A **question** is something that you say or write in order to ask a person about something. ❑ *They asked a lot of questions about her health.* ◾ V-T If you **question** someone, you ask them a lot of questions about something. ❑ *The doctor questioned Jim about his parents.* ● **ques|tion|er** (**questioners**) N-COUNT ❑ *He agreed with the questioner.* ● **ques|tion|ing** N-UNCOUNT ❑ *The police want thirty-two people for questioning.* ◼ V-T If you **question** something, you have or express doubts about it. ❑ *They never question the doctor's decisions.* ◢ N-SING If you say that there is some **question** about something, you mean that there is doubt or uncertainty about it. If something is **in question** or has been **called into question**, doubt or uncertainty has been expressed about it. ❑ *There's no question about their success.* ◼ N-COUNT A **question** is a problem, matter, or point which needs to be considered. ❑ *The question of nuclear energy is complex.* ◼ N-COUNT The **questions** on an examination are the problems that test your knowledge or ability. ❑ *That question came up on the test.* ◼ → see also **questioning** ◼ PHRASE The person, thing, or time **in question** is one which you have just been talking about. ❑ *Add up all your income over the time in question.* ◼ PHRASE If you say that something is **out of the question**, it is completely impossible or unacceptable. ❑ *An expensive vacation is out of the question for him.* ◼ PHRASE If you say that **there is no question of** something happening, you are emphasizing that it is not going to happen. ❑ *There was no question of visiting her school friends.* [from Old French]

**Word Partnership** Use *question* with :

| | |
|---|---|
| V. | **answer a** question, **ask a** question, **beg the** question, **pose a** question, **raise a** question ◼ |
| N. | **answer/response to a** question ◼ |
| ADJ. | **difficult** question, **good** question, **important** question ◼ |

**ques|tion|able** /kwe̱stʃənəb°l/ ADJ If you say that something is **questionable**, you mean that it is not completely honest or reasonable. [FORMAL] ❑ *These are questionable business practices.* [from Old French]

**ques|tion|ing** /kwe̱stʃənɪŋ/ ◼ ADJ If someone has a **questioning** expression on their face, they look as if they want to know the answer to a question. [WRITTEN] ❑ *He raised a questioning eyebrow.* [from Old French] ◾ → see also **question**

**ques|tion mark** (**question marks**) N-COUNT A **question mark** is the punctuation mark ? which is used in writing at the end of a question. ❑ *Why does the title of the show "Who Wants To Be A Millionaire" not have a question mark at the end?* → see **punctuation**

**ques|tion|naire** /kwe̱stʃənɛ̱ər/ (**questionnaires**) N-COUNT A **questionnaire** is a written list of questions which are answered by a lot of people in order to provide information for a report or a survey. ❑ *Each person will fill out a five-minute questionnaire.* [from French]

**quib|ble** /kwɪ̱b°l/ (**quibbles, quibbling, quibbled**) ◼ V-RECIP When people **quibble over** a small matter, they argue about it even though it is not important. ❑ *The senate is quibbling over how much money each state receives.* ◾ N-COUNT A **quibble** is a small and unimportant complaint about something. ❑ *These are minor quibbles.* [from Latin]

**quick** /kwɪ̱k/ (**quicker, quickest**) ◼ ADJ Someone or something that is **quick** moves or does things with great speed. ❑ *You'll have to be quick the flight leaves in three hours.* ● **quick|ly** ADV ❑ *Cussane worked quickly.* ● **quick|ness** N-UNCOUNT ❑ *The program is for athletes who want to improve their speed, agility, and quickness.* ◾ ADJ Something that is **quick** takes or lasts only a short time. ❑ *He took a quick look around the room.* ● **quick|ly** ADV ❑ *You can get fit quite quickly if you exercise.* ◼ ADJ **Quick** means happening with very little delay. ❑ *We are hoping for a quick end to the strike.* ● **quick|ly** ADV ❑ *We need to get it back as quickly as possible.* [from Old English] ◢ **quick as a flash** → see **flash**

**Thesaurus** *quick* Also look up :

| | |
|---|---|
| ADJ. | brisk, fast, rapid, speedy, swift; (*ant.*) slow ◼ |

**Word Partnership** Use *quick* with :

| | |
|---|---|
| N. | quick **learner** ◼ |
| | quick **glance**, quick **kiss**, quick **look**, quick **question**, quick **smile** ◾ |
| | quick **action**, quick **profit**, quick **response**, quick **start**, quick **thinking** ◼ |

**quick|en** /kwɪ̱kən/ (**quickens, quickening, quickened**) V-T/V-I If something **quickens** or if

## Word Web   quilt

The Hmong* tribes are famous for their colorful **quilts**. Many people think of a quilt as a bed covering. But these **textiles** feature pictures that tell stories about the people who made them. A favorite story shows how the Hmong fled from China to southeast Asia in the early 1800s. The story sometimes shows the quiltmaker arriving in a new country. The seamstress **sews** small pieces of colourful **fabric** together to make the **design**. The needlework is very complicated. It includes cross-stitching, **embroidery**, and appliqué. A common border **pattern** is a design that represents mountains—the Hmong's original home.

*Hmong: a group of people who live in the mountains of China, Vietnam, Laos, and Thailand.*

you **quicken** it, it becomes faster or moves at a greater speed. ❑ *Ann's heartbeat quickened.* [from Old English]

**quick study** (**quick studies**) N-COUNT If you describe someone as a **quick study**, you mean that they are able to learn or memorize things very quickly. ❑ *She's a quick study. She sees a thing once and remembers it.*

**qui|et** /kwaɪɪt/ (**quieter, quietest, quiets, quieting, quieted**) **1** ADJ Someone or something that is **quiet** makes only a small amount of noise. ❑ *Tania kept the children reasonably quiet.* ● **qui|et|ly** ADV ❑ *The officers spoke so quietly that we couldn't hear anything they said.* ● **qui|et|ness** N-UNCOUNT ❑ *I liked the smoothness and quietness of the flight.* **2** ADJ If a place, situation, or time is **quiet**, there is no excitement, activity, or trouble. ❑ *It's in a quiet little village.* ● **qui|et|ly** ADV ❑ *He spends his free time quietly on his farm.* ● **qui|et|ness** N-UNCOUNT ❑ *He read the letter in the quietness of the morning.* **3** ADJ If you are **quiet**, you are not saying anything. ❑ *I told them to be quiet and go to sleep.* ● **qui|et|ly** ADV ❑ *Amy stood quietly in the doorway.* **4** V-T/V-I If someone or something **quiets** or if you **quiet** them, they become less noisy, less active, or silent. ❑ *The group of people quieted as Derek and Billy walked past.* **5** V-T To **quiet** fears or complaints means to persuade people that there is no good reason for them. ❑ *Music seemed to quiet her worries.* **6** PHRASE If you **keep quiet about** something or **keep** something **quiet**, you do not say anything about it. ❑ *I told her to keep quiet about it.* [from Latin]

## Word Partnership   Use *quiet* with :

| | |
|---|---|
| V. | be quiet, keep quiet **1** |
| ADV. | really quiet, relatively quiet, too quiet, quiet **1** – **3** |
| N. | quiet day/evening/night, quiet life, quiet neighborhood/street, peace and quiet, quiet place/spot **2** |

**quilt** /kwɪlt/ (**quilts**) **1** N-COUNT A **quilt** is a bed cover made by sewing layers of cloth together, usually with different colors sewn together to make a design. ❑ *An old quilt was on the bed.* **2** N-COUNT A **quilt** is the same as a **comforter**. [from Old French] → see Word Web: **quilt**

**quilt|ing** /kwɪltɪŋ/ N-UNCOUNT **Quilting** is the activity of making a quilt. ❑ *She does a lot of quilting.* [from Old French]

**quin|tu|plet** /kwɪntʌplɪt, -tuplɪt, kwɪntʊplɪt/ (**quintuplets**) N-COUNT **Quintuplets** are five children who are born to the same mother at the same time.

**quip** /kwɪp/ (**quips**) N-COUNT A **quip** is a remark that is intended to be amusing or clever. [WRITTEN] ❑ *On the way to class, we joked and made quips about our professors.* [from Latin]

**quirk** /kwɜrk/ (**quirks**) **1** N-COUNT A **quirk** is something unusual or interesting that happens by chance. ❑ *The successes of the 1980s may be explained by a quirk of history.* **2** N-COUNT A **quirk** is a habit or aspect of a person's character which is odd or unusual. ❑ *Brown was fascinated by the quirks of people in everyday situations.*

**quirky** /kwɜrki/ (**quirkier, quirkiest**) ADJ Something or someone that is **quirky** is odd or unpredictable in their appearance, character, or behavior. ❑ *...her quirky and original style.* ● **quirki|ness** N-UNCOUNT ❑ *You might notice a quirkiness in his behavior.*

**quit** /kwɪt/ (**quits, quitting**)

The form **quit** is used in the present tense and is the past tense and past participle.

**1** V-T/V-I If you **quit**, or **quit** your job, you choose to leave it. [INFORMAL] ❑ *Christina quit her job last year to stay home with her young son.* **2** V-T If you **quit** an activity or **quit** doing something, you stop doing it. ❑ *Quit acting like you don't know.* **3** V-T If you **quit** a place, you leave it completely and do not go back to it. ❑ *He quit school at the age of 16.* **4** PHRASE If you say that you are going to **call it quits**, you mean that you have decided to stop doing something or being involved in something. ❑ *They raised $630,000 from supporters, and then called it quits.* [from Old French]

**quite** /kwaɪt/ **1** ADV You use **quite** to indicate that something is true to a fairly great extent. **Quite** is not as strong as "very." ❑ *I felt quite bad about it at the time.* ❑ *You need to do quite a bit of work.* **2** ADV You use **quite** to emphasize what you are saying. ❑ *I made it quite clear again and again.* ❑ *My position is quite different.* **3** ADV You use **quite** after a negative to make what you are saying weaker or less definite. ❑ *Something here is not quite right.* **4** PREDET You use **quite** in front of a noun

**q**

group to emphasize that a person or thing is very impressive or unusual. ❑ *He's quite a character.*

**quiv|er** /kwɪvər/ (**quivers, quivering, quivered**)
■ V-I If something **quivers**, it shakes with very small movements. ❑ *Her lip quivered and tears filled her eyes.* ■ V-I If you say that someone or their voice **is quivering with** an emotion such as rage or excitement, you mean that they are strongly affected by this emotion and show it in their appearance or voice. ❑ *Cooper arrived, quivering with rage.* ● **Quiver** is also a noun. ❑ *I felt a quiver of panic.*

**quiz** /kwɪz/ (**quizzes, quizzing, quizzed**)
■ N-COUNT A **quiz** is a test, game, or competition in which someone tests your knowledge by asking you questions. ❑ *We'll have a quiz after we visit the museum.* ■ N-COUNT A **quiz** is a short test that a teacher gives to a class. ❑ *We had a vocabulary quiz today in English class.* ■ V-T If you **are quizzed** by someone about something, they ask you questions about it. ❑ *I quizzed him about his income.*

**quo|ta** /kwoʊtə/ (**quotas**) ■ N-COUNT A **quota** is the limited number or quantity of something which is officially allowed. ❑ *There's a quota of four tickets per person.* ■ N-COUNT Someone's **quota of** something is their expected or deserved share of it. ❑ *She's had the usual quota of teenage problems.* [from Latin]

**quo|ta|tion** /kwoʊteɪʃⁿn/ (**quotations**)
■ N-COUNT A **quotation** is a sentence or phrase taken from a book, poem, speech, or play, which is repeated by someone else. ❑ *He used quotations from Martin Luther King Jr. in his lecture.* ■ N-COUNT When someone gives you a **quotation**, they tell

you how much they will charge to do a particular piece of work. ❑ *Get several written quotations before you agree on a price.* [from Medieval Latin]

**quo|ta|tion mark** (**quotation marks**) N-COUNT **Quotation marks** are punctuation marks that are used in writing to show where speech or a quotation begins and ends. They are usually written or printed as "...".

**quote** /kwoʊt/ (**quotes, quoting, quoted**)
■ V-T/V-I If you **quote** someone as saying something or **quote** from something, you repeat what someone has written or said. ❑ *I gave the letter to the reporter and he quoted from it.* ■ N-COUNT A **quote from** a book, poem, play, or speech is a passage or phrase from it. ■ V-T If you **quote** something such as a law or a fact, you state it because it supports what you are saying. ❑ *The congresswoman quoted figures to prove her point.* ■ V-T If someone **quotes** a price **for** doing something, they say how much money they would charge you for it. ❑ *A travel agent quoted her $260 for a flight from Boston to New Jersey.* ■ N-COUNT A **quote for** a piece of work is the price that someone says they will charge you for it. ❑ *Always get a written quote for any repairs needed.* ■ N-PLURAL **Quotes** are the same as **quotation marks.** [INFORMAL] ❑ *The word "remembered" is in quotes.* [from Medieval Latin]

| **Thesaurus** | *quote* | Also look up : |
|---|---|---|
| V. | cite, recite, repeat ■ ■ | |
| N. | estimate, price ■ | |

Q

# Rr

**rab|bi** /ˈræbaɪ/ (**rabbis**) N-COUNT; N-TITLE A **rabbi** is a Jewish religious leader. [from Hebrew]

**rab|bit** /ˈræbɪt/ (**rabbits**) N-COUNT A **rabbit** is a small, furry animal with long ears. Rabbits are sometimes kept as pets, or live wild in holes in the ground. [from Flemish]

**rab|ble** /ˈræbəl/ N-SING A **rabble** is a crowd of noisy people who seem likely to cause trouble. ◻ ...a rabble of supporters.

*rabbit*

**ra|bies** /ˈreɪbiz/ N-UNCOUNT **Rabies** is a serious disease that humans can get from the bite of an animal such as a dog that has the disease. [from Latin]

**race** /ˈreɪs/ (**races, racing, raced**) **1** N-COUNT A **race** is a competition to see who is the fastest, for example in running, swimming, or driving. **2** V-T/V-I If you **race**, you take part in a race. ◻ In the 10 years I raced in Europe, 30 drivers were killed. ◻ We raced them to the top of the hill. **3** N-COUNT A **race** is a situation in which people or organizations compete with each other for power or control. ◻ He's in the race for the governor of Oregon. **4** N-VAR A **race** is one of the major groups which human beings can be divided into according to their physical features, such as the color of their skin. ◻ The college welcomes students of all races. **5** → see also **human race, race relations 6** V-I If you **race** somewhere, you go there as quickly as possible. ◻ He raced across town to the hospital. **7** V-I If your mind **races**, or if thoughts **race** through your mind, you think very fast about something, especially when you are in a difficult or dangerous situation. ◻ I sounded calm but my mind was racing. **8** V-I If your heart **races**, it beats very quickly because you are excited or afraid. ◻ Kate felt her heart racing when she heard the news. **9** → see also **racing 10** PHRASE You describe a situation as a **race against time** when you have to work very fast in order to do something before a particular time. ◻ The rescue operation was a race against time. [Senses 1 to 3 and 7 to 9 from Old Norse. Sense 5 from French.]

**race|horse** /ˈreɪshɔrs/ (**racehorses**) N-COUNT A **racehorse** is a horse that is trained to run in races.

**rac|er** /ˈreɪsər/ (**racers**) **1** N-COUNT A **racer** is a person or animal that takes part in races. ◻ He is an international sports car racer. **2** N-COUNT A **racer** is a vehicle such as a car or bicycle that is designed to be used in races and therefore travels fast. ◻ The winner flew the racer from California to Ohio in 9 hours. [from Old Norse]

**race re|la|tions** N-PLURAL **Race relations** are

the ways in which people of different races living together in the same community behave toward one another. ◻ ...a breakdown in race relations.

**race|track** /ˈreɪstræk/ (**racetracks**) also **race track 1** N-COUNT A **racetrack** is a track on which horses race. **2** N-COUNT A **racetrack** is a track for races, for example car or bicycle races.

**race|way** /ˈreɪsweɪ/ (**raceways**) N-COUNT A **raceway** is a racetrack. [from Old Norse]

**ra|cial** /ˈreɪʃəl/ ADJ **Racial** describes things relating to people's race. ◻ ...the protection of racial minorities. ● **ra|cial|ly** ADV ◻ ...children of racially mixed marriages. [from French]

---

**Word Partnership**    Use *racial* with:

N.    racial **differences**, racial **discrimination**, racial **diversity**, racial **equality**, racial **groups**, racial **minorities**, racial **prejudice**, racial **tensions**

---

**rac|ing** /ˈreɪsɪŋ/ N-UNCOUNT **Racing** refers to races between animals, especially horses, or between vehicles. [from Old Norse]
→ see **bicycle**

**rac|ist** /ˈreɪsɪst/ (**racists**) ADJ If you describe people, things, attitudes, or behavior as **racist**, you disapprove of them because they are influenced by the belief that some people are inferior because they belong to a particular culture. ◻ We live in a racist society. ● A **racist** is someone who is racist. ◻ ...white racists. ● **rac|ism** N-UNCOUNT ◻ The level of racism is increasing. [from Old Norse]

**rack** /ˈræk/ (**racks, racking, racked**)

The spelling **wrack** is also used for meaning **2**.

**1** N-COUNT A **rack** is a frame or shelf, usually with bars or hooks, that is used for holding things or for hanging things on. ◻ ...a luggage rack. **2** V-T If someone **is racked by** something such as illness or anxiety, it causes them great suffering or pain. ◻ His body was racked by pain. **3** PHRASE **Off-the-rack** clothes or goods are made in large numbers, rather than being made specially for a particular person. ◻ ...an off-the-rack dress. [from Middle Dutch]

**rack|et** /ˈrækɪt/ (**rackets**)

The spelling **racquet** is also used for meaning **3**.

**1** N-SING A **racket** is a loud, unpleasant noise. ◻ The children were making a racket. **2** N-COUNT You can refer to an illegal activity used to make money as a **racket**. [INFORMAL] ◻ ...an international smuggling racket. **3** N-COUNT A **racket** is an oval-shaped bat with

*racket*

*r*

strings across it, which is used in games such as tennis.

**rac|quet|ball** /ˈrækɪtbɔl/ N-UNCOUNT
**Racquetball** is a game which is similar to squash but which uses a different ball, racket, and court size.

**racy** /ˈreɪsi/ (**racier, raciest**) ADJ **Racy** writing or behavior is lively, amusing, and slightly shocking. ❑ ...racy stories about her life as an actor. [from Old Norse]

| Word Link | rad ≈ ray : radar, radiant, radiation |

**ra|dar** /ˈreɪdɑr/ (**radars**) N-VAR **Radar** is a way of discovering the position or speed of objects such as aircraft or ships when they cannot be seen, by using radio signals. ❑ ...a ship's radar screen.
→ see **bat, forecast**

**ra|dial sym|me|try** N-UNCOUNT An organism that has **radial symmetry** has a body that resembles the pattern you get when straight lines are drawn from the center of a circle to a number of points around the edge. Compare **bilateral symmetry**. [TECHNICAL]

**ra|di|ant** /ˈreɪdiənt/ **1** ADJ Someone who is **radiant** is so happy that their happiness shows in their face. ❑ The bride looked radiant. ● **ra|di|ance** N-UNCOUNT ❑ She had started to lose her radiance. **2** ADJ Something that is **radiant** glows brightly. ❑ ...the radiant glow of the fire. ● **radiance** N-UNCOUNT ❑ ...the radiance of the candles. [from Latin]

**ra|di|ate** /ˈreɪdieɪt/ (**radiates, radiating, radiated**) **1** V-I If things **radiate from** a place, they spread out like lines drawn from the center of a circle to various points on its edge. ❑ Paths radiate from a central area. **2** V-T/V-I If you **radiate** an emotion or quality or if it **radiates from** you, people can see it very clearly in your face and in your behavior. ❑ She radiates happiness. [from Latin]

**ra|dia|tion** /ˌreɪdiˈeɪʃⁿn/ **1** N-UNCOUNT **Radiation** consists of very small particles of a radioactive substance. Large amounts of radiation can cause illness and death. ❑ They suffer from health problems and the long term effects of radiation. **2** N-UNCOUNT **Radiation** is energy, especially heat, that comes from a particular source. ❑ ...energy radiation from the stars. [from Latin]
→ see **greenhouse effect, wave, cancer**

**ra|dia|tion sick|ness** N-UNCOUNT **Radiation sickness** is an illness that people get when they are exposed to too much radiation.

| Word Partnership | Use radiation with : |

| ADJ. | **nuclear** radiation **1** |
| N. | radiation **levels**, radiation **therapy/treatment 1** |
| | radiation **damage, effects of** radiation, **exposure** radiation **1 2** |

**ra|dia|tive zone** /ˈreɪdieɪtɪv zoʊn/ (**radiative zones**) N-COUNT The **radiative zone** is the area of the sun around the core, where energy travels in the form of radiation. [TECHNICAL]

**ra|dia|tor** /ˈreɪdieɪtər/ (**radiators**) **1** N-COUNT A **radiator** is a hollow metal device, usually connected by pipes to a central heating system, that is used to heat a room. **2** N-COUNT The **radiator** in a car is the part of the engine that is filled with water in order to cool the engine. [from Latin]

radiator

**radi|cal** /ˈrædɪkⁿl/ (**radicals**) **1** ADJ **Radical** changes and differences are very important and great in degree. ❑ ...radical economic reforms. ● **radi|cal|ly** /ˈrædɪkli/ ADV ❑ ...people with radically different beliefs. **2** ADJ **Radical** people believe that there should be great changes in society and try to bring about these changes. ❑ ...a radical leader. ● A **radical** is someone who has radical views. ❑ ...student radicals. [from Late Latin]

**ra|dii** /ˈreɪdiaɪ/ **Radii** is the plural of **radius**. [from Latin]

**ra|dio** /ˈreɪdioʊ/ (**radios, radioing, radioed**) **1** N-UNCOUNT **Radio** is the broadcasting of programs for the public to listen to, by sending out signals from a transmitter. ❑ The event was broadcast on local radio. **2** N-SING You can refer to the programs broadcast by radio stations as **the radio**. ❑ A lot of people listen to the radio. **3** N-COUNT A **radio** is the piece of equipment that you use in order to listen to radio programs. ❑ He turned on the radio. **4** N-UNCOUNT **Radio** is a system of sending and receiving sound using electronic signals. ❑ They are in radio contact with the leader. **5** N-COUNT A **radio** is a piece of equipment that is used for sending and receiving spoken messages. ❑ The policeman called for extra officers on his radio. **6** V-T/V-I If you **radio** someone, you send a spoken message to them by radio. ❑ The officer radioed for advice. ❑ Martin radioed his team to tell them he was OK.
→ see Word Web: **radio**
→ see **telescope, wave**

**Word Web**    radio

**Radio's** first use was for **communication** between ships. Ships also radioed **stations** on land. In 1912, the *Titanic* sank in the North Atlantic with more than 2,000 people on board. A radio call to a nearby ship helped save a third of the passengers. What we call a radio is actually a **receiver**. The **waves** it receives come from a **transmitter**. Radio is an important source of **entertainment**. **AM** radio carries all kinds of radio **programs**. **Listeners** often prefer musical programs on the FM waveband or from **satellites** because the sound quality is better.

**radio|ac|tive** /ˌreɪdioʊˈæktɪv/ ADJ Something that is **radioactive** contains a substance that produces energy in the form of powerful and harmful rays. ❑ ...*radioactive waste.*
● **radio|ac|tiv|ity** /ˌreɪdioʊækˈtɪvɪti/ N-UNCOUNT ❑ ...*a harmful release of radioactivity.*

**radio|act|ive sym|bol** (**radioactive symbols**) N-COUNT A **radioactive symbol** is a printed sign which shows that a place or an object contains dangerous amounts of radiation.

**ra|dio tele|scope** (**radio telescopes**) N-COUNT A **radio telescope** is an instrument that receives radio waves from space and finds the position of stars and other objects in space.

**ra|dio wave** (**radio waves**) N-COUNT **Radio waves** are the form in which radio signals travel.

**ra|dius** /ˈreɪdiəs/ (**radii** /ˈreɪdiaɪ/) **1** N-SING The **radius** around a particular point is the distance from it in any direction. ❑ *Nick searched for work in a ten-mile radius around his home.* **2** N-COUNT The **radius** of a circle is the distance from its center to its outside edge. ❑ ...*a circle with a radius of about thirty miles.* [from Latin]
→ see **area**

**raf|fle** /ˈræfᵊl/ (**raffles**) N-COUNT A **raffle** is a competition in which you buy tickets with numbers on them. If your ticket is chosen, you win a prize. ❑ ...*raffle tickets.* [from Old French]

**raft** /ræft/ (**rafts**) **1** N-COUNT A **raft** is a floating platform made from large pieces of wood or other materials tied together. ❑ ...*a river trip on bamboo rafts.* **2** N-COUNT A **raft** is a small rubber or plastic boat that you blow air into to make it float. ❑ *The crew spent two days and nights in their raft.* [from Old Norse]
→ see **boat**

**raft|er** /ˈræftər/ (**rafters**) N-COUNT **Rafters** are the sloping pieces of wood that support a roof. [from Old English]

**rag** /ræg/ (**rags**) **1** N-VAR A **rag** is a piece of old cloth which you can use to clean or wipe things. ❑ *He was wiping his hands on an oily rag.* **2** N-PLURAL **Rags** are old torn clothes. ❑ ...*children dressed in rags.* [from Old English]

**rage** /reɪdʒ/ (**rages, raging, raged**) **1** N-VAR **Rage** is strong anger that is difficult to control. ❑ *His face was red with rage.* **2** V-I You say that something powerful or unpleasant **rages** when it continues with great force or violence. ❑ *The fire raged for four hours.* ● **rag|ing** ADJ ❑ *The raging river flooded many villages.* **3** V-I If you **rage** about something, you speak or think very angrily about it. ❑ *She was raging about her unfair treatment.* [from Old French]
→ see **anger**

| **Thesaurus** | *rage* | Also look up : |
|---|---|---|
| N. | anger, frenzy, madness, tantrum **1** | |
| V. | fume, scream, yell **3** | |

**rag|ged** /ˈrægɪd/ **1** ADJ Someone who is **ragged** looks messy and is wearing clothes that are old and torn. ❑ ...*a thin ragged man.* **2** ADJ **Ragged** clothes are old and torn. **3** ADJ You can say that something is **ragged** when it is rough or uneven. ❑ *Her breath came in ragged gasps.*

**raid** /reɪd/ (**raids, raiding, raided**) **1** V-T When soldiers **raid** a place, they make a sudden armed

attack against it, with the aim of causing damage. ● **Raid** is also a noun. ❑ *The soldiers attempted a raid on the camp.* **2** → see also **air raid 3** V-T If the police **raid** a building, they enter it suddenly and by force in order to look for someone or something. ❑ *Police raided the company's offices.* ● **Raid** is also a noun. ❑ *They were arrested after a raid on a house by police.* [from Scots]

**rail** /reɪl/ (**rails**) **1** N-COUNT A **rail** is a horizontal bar around or along something that you hold on to for support. ❑ *She gripped the hand rail.* **2** N-COUNT A **rail** is a horizontal bar that you hang things on. ❑ *These curtains will fit a rail that is 6 feet wide.* **3** N-COUNT **Rails** are the steel bars which trains run on. ❑ *The train left the rails.* **4** N-UNCOUNT If you travel or send something **by rail**, you travel or send it on a train. ❑ *The president traveled by rail.* [from Old French]
→ see **train, transportation**

**rail|ing** /ˈreɪlɪŋ/ (**railings**) N-COUNT A fence made from metal bars is called a **railing** or **railings**. ❑ *He rested his arms on the railing of the balcony.* [from Old French]

**rail|road** /ˈreɪlroʊd/ (**railroads**) **1** N-COUNT A **railroad** is a route between two places along which trains travel on steel rails. ❑ ...*railroad tracks.* **2** N-COUNT A **railroad** is a company or organization that operates railroad routes. ❑ ...*the Chicago and Northwestern Railroad.*

**rail|road cross|ing** (**railroad crossings**) N-COUNT A **railroad crossing** is a place where a railroad track crosses a road at the same level. ❑ *His van was hit by a train at a railroad crossing.*

**rain** /reɪn/ (**rains, raining, rained**) **1** N-UNCOUNT **Rain** is water that falls from the clouds in small drops. ❑ *We got very wet in the rain.* **2** V-I When rain falls, you can say that **it is raining**. ❑ *It was raining hard.* [from Old English]
→ see **disaster, hurricane, precipitation, storm, water**
▸ **rain out** PHR-VERB If a sports game **is rained out**, it has to stop, or it is not able to start, because of rain.

| **Thesaurus** | *rain* | Also look up : |
|---|---|---|
| N. | drizzle, shower, sleet **1** | |

**rain|bow** /ˈreɪnboʊ/ (**rainbows**) N-COUNT A **rainbow** is an arch of different colors that you can sometimes see in the sky when it rains or after it rains.
→ see Word Web: **rainbow**

**rain check** (**rain checks**) N-COUNT A **rain check** is a free ticket that is given to people when an outdoor game or event is stopped because of rain or bad weather, so that they can go to it when it is held again.

**rain|coat** /ˈreɪnkoʊt/ (**raincoats**) N-COUNT A **raincoat** is a waterproof coat.

**rain|drop** /ˈreɪndrɒp/ (**raindrops**) N-COUNT A **raindrop** is a single drop of rain.
→ see **precipitation**

**rain|fall** /ˈreɪnfɔl/ N-UNCOUNT **Rainfall** is the amount of rain that falls in a place during a particular period. ❑ ...*below average rainfall.*
→ see **erosion, storm, habitat**

**rain for|est** (**rain forests**) also **rainforest** N-VAR A **rain forest** is a thick forest of tall trees which is

r

## Word Web    rainbow

**Sunlight** contains all colors. When a **ray** of sunlight passes through a prism, it splits into different colors. This is also what happens when light passes through the drops of water in the air. The light is refracted, and we see a **rainbow**. The colors of the rainbow are **red**, **orange**, **yellow**, **green**, **blue**, indigo, and **violet**. One tradition says that there is a pot of gold at the end of the rainbow. Other myths say that the rainbow is a bridge between Earth and the land of the gods.

found mainly in tropical areas where there is a lot of rain. ❑ *…the destruction of the Amazon rain forest.* → see **habitat**

**rainy** /reɪni/ (**rainier, rainiest**) ADJ If it is **rainy** it is raining a lot. ❑ *…a rainy day.* [from Old English]

**raise** /reɪz/ (**raises, raising, raised**) ◾ V-T If you **raise** something, you move it so that it is in a higher position. ❑ *He raised his hand to wave.* ❑ *Milton raised the glass to his lips.* ◾ V-T If you **raise** the rate or level of something, you increase it. ❑ *Many stores have raised their prices.* ◾ V-T To **raise** the standard of something means to improve it. ❑ *…a new program to raise standards in schools.* ◾ V-T If you **raise** your **voice**, you speak more loudly. ◾ N-COUNT A **raise** is an increase in your wages or salary. ❑ *Kelly got a raise.* ◾ V-T If you **raise** money **for** a charity or an institution, you ask people for money which you collect on its behalf. ❑ *The event is to raise money for the school.* ◾ V-T If an event **raises** a particular emotion or question, it makes people feel the emotion or consider the question. ❑ *The agreement raised hopes that the war would end soon.* ◾ V-T If you **raise** a subject, an objection, or a question, you mention it or bring it to someone's attention. ❑ *They asked him to help and he raised no objections.* ◾ V-T To **raise** children means to takes care of them until they are grown up. ❑ *She raised four children on her own.* ◾ V-T To **raise** a particular type of animal or crop means to breed that animal or grow that crop. [from Old Norse] ◾ to **raise the alarm** → see **alarm** ◾ to **raise** your **eyebrows** → see **eyebrow** ◾ to **raise a finger** → see **finger** → see **union**

### Usage    raise and rise

*Raise* is often confused with *rise*, but it has a different meaning. *Raise* means "to move something to a higher position": *Students raise their hand when they want to speak in class. Rise* means that something moves upward: *When steam rises from the pot, add the pasta.*

**rai|sin** /reɪzⁿn/ (**raisins**) N-COUNT **Raisins** are dried grapes. [from Old French]

**rake** /reɪk/ (**rakes, raking, raked**) ◾ N-COUNT A **rake** is a garden tool consisting of a row of metal or wooden teeth attached to a long handle. ◾ V-T If you **rake** a surface, you move a rake across it in order to make it smooth and level. ❑ *Rake the soil and plant the seeds.* ◾ V-T If you **rake** leaves or ashes, you move them somewhere using a rake. ❑ *The men raked the leaves into piles.* [from Old English] → see **garden**

rake

▶ **rake in** PHR-VERB If you say that someone **is raking in** money, you mean that they are making a lot of money. [INFORMAL] ❑ *The company raked in more than $500 million last year.*

**ral|ly** /ræli/ (**rallies, rallying, rallied**) ◾ N-COUNT A **rally** is a large public meeting that is held in order to show support for something such as a political party. ❑ *…a rally to demand better working conditions.* ◾ V-T/V-I When people **rally to** something or when something **rallies** them, they unite to support it. ❑ *Her colleagues rallied to her support.* ◾ V-I When someone or something **rallies**, they begin to recover or improve after having been weak. ❑ *He rallied enough to thank his doctors.* ◾ N-COUNT A **rally** is a competition in which vehicles are driven over public roads. ❑ *Rally driver John Crawford won titles from '82 to '87.* [from Old French]

▶ **rally around** PHR-VERB When people **rally around**, they work as a group in order to support someone or something at a difficult time. ❑ *Many people rallied around the family to help them.*

### Word Partnership    Use *rally* with :

| | |
|---|---|
| ADJ. | **political** rally ◾ |
| N. | **campaign** rally, **protest** rally, rally **in support of** *someone/something* ◾ **prices/stocks** rally ◾ |
| PREP. | rally **behind** *someone/something* ◾ |

**rallying cry** (**rallying cries**) N-COUNT A **rallying cry** or **rallying call** is something such as a word or phrase, an event, or a belief which encourages people to unite and to act in support of a particular group or idea. ❑ *…an issue that is fast becoming a rallying cry for many Democrats.*

**ram** /ræm/ (**rams, ramming, rammed**) ◾ V-T If a vehicle **rams** something such as another vehicle, it crashes into it with a lot of force. ❑ *The truck rammed a car.* ◾ V-T If you **ram** something somewhere, you push it there with great force. ❑ *He rammed the key into the lock.* ◾ N-COUNT A **ram** is an adult male sheep. [from Old English] ◾ to **ram** something **down** someone's **throat** → see **throat**

**ram|ble** /ræmbᵊl/ (**rambles, rambling, rambled**) ◾ N-COUNT A **ramble** is a long walk in the countryside. ❑ *…a ramble through the forest.*

**2** V-I If you **ramble**, you go on a long walk in the countryside. □ ...*freedom to ramble across the hills.* **3** V-I If someone **rambles** in their speech or writing, they do not make much sense because they keep going off the subject in a confused way. □ *Sometimes she spoke sensibly; sometimes she rambled.* [from Middle Dutch]

**ram|bunc|tious** /ræmbʌŋkʃəs/ ADJ A **rambunctious** person is energetic in a cheerful, noisy way. □ ...*a very rambunctious and energetic class.* [from Icelandic]

**rami|fi|ca|tion** /ræmɪfɪkeɪʃ⁰n/ (**ramifications**) N-COUNT The **ramifications** of a decision, plan, or event are all of its consequences and effects, especially ones that are not obvious at first. □ ...*the political ramifications of the decision.* [from French]

**ramp** /ræmp/ (**ramps**) **1** N-COUNT A **ramp** is a sloping surface between two places that are at different levels. □ *Lillian was coming down the ramp from the museum.* **2** N-COUNT An entrance **ramp** is a road which cars use to drive onto a major road, and an exit **ramp** is a road which cars use to drive off a major road. [from Old French]
→ see **traffic**

**ram|page** (**rampages, rampaging, rampaged**)

> Pronounced /ræmpeɪdʒ/ for meaning **1**, and /ræmpeɪdʒ/ for meaning **2**.

**1** V-I When people or animals **rampage** through a place, they rush around there in a wild or violent way, causing damage or destruction. □ *People rampaged through the town, smashing store windows.* **2** PHRASE If people go **on a rampage**, they rush around in a wild or violent way, causing damage or destruction. [from Scottish]

**ram|pant** /ræmpənt/ ADJ If something bad is **rampant**, it is very common and is increasing in an uncontrolled way. □ ...*rampant crime.* [from Old French]

**ram|shack|le** /ræmʃæk⁰l/ ADJ A **ramshackle** building is badly made or in bad condition, and looks as if it is likely to fall down. □ *They entered the store, which was a strange ramshackle building.*

**ran** /ræn/ **Ran** is the past tense of **run**. [from Old English]

**ranch** /ræntʃ/ (**ranches**) N-COUNT A **ranch** is a large farm used for raising animals. □ ...*a cattle ranch in Texas.* [from Mexican Spanish]

**ranch house** (**ranch houses**) **1** N-COUNT A **ranch house** is a single-story house, usually with a low roof. □ ...*streets full of treeless lawns and one-story ranch houses.* **2** N-COUNT A **ranch house** is the main house on a ranch.

**ran|dom** /rændəm/ **1** ADJ A **random** sample or method is one in which all the people or things involved have an equal chance of being chosen. □ *The survey used a random sample of two thousand people.* ● **ran|dom|ly** ADV □ ...*interviews with a randomly chosen sample of 30 girls.* **2** ADJ If you describe events as **random**, you mean that they do not seem to follow a definite plan or pattern. □ ...*random violence against innocent victims.* ● **ran|dom|ly** ADV □ *Pictures were placed randomly on the walls.* **3** PHRASE If something happens **at random**, it happens without a definite plan or pattern. □ *The gunman fired at random.* [from Old French]

**ran|dom vari|able** (**random variables**) N-COUNT In statistics, a **random variable** is a quantity whose value depends on a set of probabilities. [TECHNICAL]

**R&R** /ɑr ən ɑr/ also **R and R** N-UNCOUNT **R&R** refers to time that you spend relaxing, when you are not working. **R&R** is an abbreviation for "rest and relaxation." □ *Our vacation homes are just the thing for serious R&R.*

**rang** /ræŋ/ **Rang** is the past tense of **ring**. [from Old English]

**range** /reɪndʒ/ (**ranges, ranging, ranged**) **1** N-COUNT A **range of** things is a number of different things of the same general kind. □ ...*a wide range of colors.* **2** N-COUNT A **range** is the complete group that is included between two points on a scale of measurement or quality. □ *The average age range is between 35 and 55.* **3** N-COUNT The **range of** something is the maximum area in which it can reach things or detect things. □ *The weapon has a range of 18,000 yards.* **4** V-I If things **range between** two points or **range from** one point **to** another, they vary within these points on a scale of measurement or quality. □ *They range in price from $3 to $15.* **5** N-COUNT A **range** of mountains or hills is a line of them. □ ...*snowy mountain ranges.* **6** N-COUNT A rifle **range** or a shooting **range** is a place where people can practice shooting at targets. **7** N-COUNT The **range** of a set of numbers is the difference between the biggest number and the smallest number. [from Old French]
→ see **graph**

| Word Partnership | Use *range* with : |
|---|---|
| ADJ. | broad range, limited range, narrow range, wide range **1** full range, normal range, whole range **2** |
| N. | range of emotions, range of possibilities **1** age range, price range, temperature range **2** |

**rang|er** /reɪndʒər/ (**rangers**) N-COUNT A **ranger** is a person whose job is to take care of a forest or large park. □ ...*a park ranger at the National Park.* [from Old French]

**rank** /ræŋk/ (**ranks, ranking, ranked**) **1** N-VAR Someone's **rank** is the position or grade that they have in an organization. □ *He rose to the rank of captain.* **2** V-T/V-I If an official organization **ranks** someone or something 1st, 5th, or 50th, for example, they calculate that the person or thing has that position on a scale. You can also say that someone or something **ranks** 1st, 5th, or 50th, for example. □ *The report ranks the U.S. 20th out of 22 countries.* □ *She doesn't even rank in the world's top ten.* **3** N-PLURAL The **ranks** are the ordinary members of an organization, especially of the armed forces. □ *He rose through the ranks from researcher to professor.* **4** PHRASE If a member of a group or organization **breaks rank**, they disobey the instructions of their group or organization. □ *The senator broke ranks with the rest of his party.* **5** PHRASE If the members of a group **close ranks**, they are supporting each other only because their group is being criticized. □ *The party closed ranks to support their leader.* [from Old French]

**r**

---

**Word Partnership** Use *rank* with :

ADJ. **high** rank, **top** rank ◼
PREP. rank **above**, rank **below** ◼

---

**rank and file** N-SING **The rank and file** are the ordinary members of an organization or the ordinary workers in a company. ❑ *He had a lot of support from the rank and file.*

**rank|ing** /rǽŋkɪŋ/ ADJ The **ranking** member of a group, usually a political group, is the most senior person in it. ❑ *...the ranking American diplomat in Baghdad.* [from Old French]

**ran|sack** /rǽnsæk/ (**ransacks, ransacking, ransacked**) V-T If people **ransack** a building, they damage things in it or make it very messy, often because they are looking for something. ❑ *He ransacked the apartment and stole some money.* [from Old Norse]

**ran|som** /rǽnsəm/ (**ransoms**) ◼ N-VAR A **ransom** is the money that has to be paid to someone so that they will set free a person they have kidnapped. ❑ *Her kidnapper asked for a $250,000 ransom.* ◼ PHRASE If a kidnapper **is holding** a person **for ransom**, they keep that person prisoner until they are given what they want. [from Old French]

**rant** /rǽnt/ (**rants, ranting, ranted**) V-I If someone **rants**, they talk loudly or angrily, and exaggerate or say foolish things. ❑ *The boss began to rant.* ● *He ranted for hours.* ● **Rant** is also a noun. ❑ *...a rant against religion.* ● **rant|ing** (**rantings**) N-VAR ❑ *He listened to Goldstone's rantings all night.* [from Dutch]

**rap** /rǽp/ (**raps, rapping, rapped**) ◼ N-UNCOUNT **Rap** is a type of music in which the words are not sung but are spoken in a rapid, rhythmic way. ❑ *...a rap group.* ● **rap|per** (**rappers**) N-COUNT ❑ *...a talented rapper.* ◼ V-I Someone who **raps** performs rap music. ◼ V-T/V-I If you **rap on** something or **rap** it, you hit it with a series of quick blows. ❑ *Mary rapped on Charlie's door.* ● **Rap** is also a noun. ❑ *There was a loud rap on the door.* ◼ N-COUNT A **rap** is a statement in a court of law that someone has committed a particular crime, or the punishment for committing it. [INFORMAL] ❑ *...you're facing a murder rap.* [of Scandinavian origin]

**rape** /rǽp/ (**rapes, raping, raped**) ◼ V-T If someone **is raped**, they are forced to have sex, usually by violence. ❑ *A young woman was raped yesterday evening.* ● **rapist** (**rapists**) N-COUNT ❑ *...information that led to the rapist's arrest.* ◼ N-VAR **Rape** is the crime of forcing someone to have sex. [from Latin]

**rap|id** /rǽpɪd/ ◼ ADJ A **rapid** change is one that happens very quickly. ❑ *...the country's rapid economic growth.* ● **rap|id|ly** ADV ❑ *...countries with rapidly growing populations.* ● **ra|pid|ity** /rəpɪdɪti/ N-UNCOUNT ❑ *...the rapidity with which the weather can change.* ◼ ADJ A **rapid** movement is one that is very fast. ❑ *He walked at a rapid pace.* ● **rap|id|ly** ADV ❑ *He was moving rapidly around the room.* ● **ra|pid|ity** N-UNCOUNT ❑ *The water rushed through the tunnel with great rapidity.* [from Latin]

---

**Thesaurus** *rapid* Also look up :

ADJ. fast, speedy, swift; (*ant.*) slow ◼ ◼

---

**Word Partnership** Use *rapid* with :

N. rapid **change**, rapid **decline**, rapid **development**, rapid **expansion**, rapid **growth**, rapid **increase**, rapid **progress** ◼
rapid **pace**, rapid **pulse** ◼

---

**rapid-fire** ADJ A **rapid-fire** economic activity or development is one that takes place very quickly. [JOURNALISM] ❑ *...the rapid-fire buying and selling of shares.*

**rap|ids** /rǽpɪdz/ N-PLURAL **Rapids** are a section of a river where the water moves very fast. [from Latin]

**rap|pel** /rǽpɛl, rə-/ (**rappels, rappelling, rappelled**) V-I To **rappel** down a cliff or rock face means to slide down it in a controlled way using a rope, with your feet against the cliff or rock. [from French]

**rap|port** /rǽpɔr/ N-UNCOUNT; N-SING **Rapport** is a feeling of understanding and sympathy between two or more people. ❑ *He has a good rapport with all his colleagues.* ❑ *Her rapport with the children is amazing.* [from French]

**rap sheet** (**rap sheets**) N-COUNT A **rap sheet** is a legal document which records someone's arrests and crimes.

**rap|ture** /rǽptʃər/ N-UNCOUNT **Rapture** is a feeling of extreme happiness or pleasure. [LITERARY] ❑ *She was filled with rapture.* [from Medieval Latin]

**rap|tur|ous** /rǽptʃərəs/ ADJ A **rapturous** feeling or reaction is one of extreme happiness or enthusiasm. ❑ *The students gave him a rapturous welcome.* [from Medieval Latin]

**rare** /rɛər/ (**rarer, rarest**) ◼ ADJ Something that is **rare** is not common and is therefore interesting or valuable. ❑ *...one of the rarest birds in the world.* ◼ ADJ An event or situation that is **rare** does not occur very often. ❑ *...on the rare occasions when he sees her.* ◼ ADJ Meat that is **rare** is cooked very lightly so that the inside is still red. [from Old English]

**rar|efac|tion** /rɛərɪfǽkʃn/ N-UNCOUNT **Rarefaction** is a reduction in the density of something, especially the density of the atmosphere. [TECHNICAL] [from Old French]

**rare|ly** /rɛərli/ ADV If something **rarely** happens, it does not happen very often. [from Latin]

**rar|ity** /rɛərɪti/ (**rarities**) ◼ N-COUNT If someone or something is a **rarity**, they are interesting or valuable because they are so unusual. ❑ *Heated swimming pools were a rarity in the past.* ◼ N-UNCOUNT The **rarity** of something is the fact that it is very uncommon. ❑ *The jewel was valuable because of its rarity.* [from Latin]

**rash** /rǽʃ/ (**rashes**) ◼ ADJ If someone is **rash** or does **rash** things, they act without thinking carefully first. ❑ *You might regret a rash decision like that for years.* ● **rash|ly** ADV ❑ *I made a lot of money, but I rashly spent most of it.* ◼ N-COUNT A **rash** is an area of red spots that appears on your skin when you are ill or have a bad reaction to something that you have eaten or touched. ❑ *I always get a rash when I've eaten nuts.* ◼ N-SING A **rash of** events or things is a large number of them that all happen or appear within a short period of time. ❑ *...a rash of burglaries.* [Sense 1 from Old High German. Sense 2 and 3 from Old French.]

**rasp** /ræsp/ (**rasps, rasping, rasped**) v-ι If someone **rasps**, their voice or breathing is harsh and unpleasant to listen to. ❑ *His breath was rasping in his chest.* ● **Rasp** is also a noun. ❑ *...the rasp of Rennie's voice.* [from Old French]

**rasp|berry** /ræzbɛri/ (**raspberries**) N-COUNT **Raspberries** are small, soft, red fruit that grow on bushes.

**rat** /ræt/ (**rats**) N-COUNT A **rat** is an animal which has a long tail and looks like a large mouse. ❑ *...experiments with rats.* [from Old English]

**rate** /reɪt/ (**rates, rating, rated**) **1** N-COUNT The **rate** at which something happens is the speed with which it happens. ❑ *...the rate at which hair grows.* **2** N-COUNT The **rate** at which something happens is the number of times it happens over a period of time. ❑ *New diet books appear at a rate of one a week.* **3** N-COUNT A **rate** is the amount of money that is charged for goods or services. ❑ *The hotel offers a special weekend rate.* **4** → see also **exchange rate 5** N-COUNT The **rate** of taxation or interest is the amount of tax or interest that needs to be paid, expressed as a percentage. [BUSINESS] ❑ *...interest rate cuts.* **6** V-T/V-I If you **rate** someone or something as good or bad, you consider them to be good or bad. ❑ *We rate him as one of the best.* ❑ *This small shop rated well in our survey.* **7** → see also **rating 8** PHRASE You use **at any rate** to indicate that what you have just said might be incorrect or unclear in some way, and that you are now being more precise. ❑ *His friends liked her — well, most of them at any rate.* **9** PHRASE If you say that **at this rate** something bad or extreme will happen, you mean that it will happen if things continue to develop as they have been doing. ❑ *At this rate we'll never get home.* → see **motion**

| | |
|---|---|
| N. | rate **of change 1** |
| | **birth** rate, **crime** rate, **dropout** rate, **heart** rate, **pulse** rate, **survival** rate, **unemployment** rate **2** |
| | **interest** rate **4** |
| ADJ. | **average** rate, **faster** rate, **slow** rate, **steady** rate **1 2** |
| | **high** rate, **low** rate **1** – **3 5** |

**ra|ther** /ræðər/ **1** PHRASE You use **rather than** when you are contrasting two things or situations. **Rather than** introduces the thing or situation that is not true or that you do not want. ❑ *I use the bike when I can rather than the car.* ● **Rather than** is also a conjunction. ❑ *Use glass bottles again rather than throw them away.* **2** ADV You use **rather** when you are correcting something that you have just said, especially when you are describing a particular situation after saying what it is not. ❑ *This is not a solution, but rather will create new problems.* **3** PHRASE If you **would rather** do something, you would prefer to do it. ❑ *Kids would rather play than study.* **4** ADV You use **rather** to indicate that something is true to a fairly great extent. ❑ *...rather unusual circumstances.* [from Old English]

**rati|fy** /rætɪfaɪ/ (**ratifies, ratifying, ratified**) V-T When national leaders or organizations **ratify** a treaty or written agreement, they make it official by giving their formal approval to it, usually by signing it or voting for it. ● **rati|fi|ca|tion** /rætɪfɪkeɪʃ³n/ (**ratifications**) N-VAR ❑ *We hope for early ratification of the treaty.* [from Old French]

**rat|ing** /reɪtɪŋ/ (**ratings**) N-COUNT A **rating** of something is a score or measurement of how good or popular it is. ❑ *The president's popularity rating is at its lowest point.* [from Old French]

| | |
|---|---|
| N. | **approval** rating **1** |
| ADJ. | **high** rating, **low** rating, **poor** rating, **top** rating **1 2** |

**ra|tio** /reɪʃoʊ, -ʃioʊ/ (**ratios**) N-COUNT A **ratio** is a relationship between two things when it is expressed in numbers or amounts. ❑ *The adult to child ratio is one to six.* [from Latin]

**ra|tion** /ræʃ³n, reɪ-/ (**rations, rationing, rationed**) **1** N-COUNT When there is not enough of something, your **ration** of it is the amount that you are allowed to have. ❑ *The meat ration was one pound per person per week.* **2** V-T When something **is rationed**, you are only allowed to have a limited amount of it. ❑ *Food such as bread and rice was rationed.* ● **ra|tion|ing** N-UNCOUNT ❑ *...food rationing.* **3** N-PLURAL **Rations** are the food that is given to soldiers or to people who do not have enough food. [from French]

**ra|tion|al** /ræʃən³l/ **1** ADJ **Rational** decisions and thoughts are based on reason rather than on emotion. ❑ *They discussed it in a rational manner.* ● **ra|tion|al|ly** ADV ❑ *It is difficult to think rationally when you're worried.* ● **ra|tion|al|ity** /ræʃənælɪti/ N-UNCOUNT ❑ *We live in a time of rationality.* **2** ADJ A **rational** person is someone who is sensible and is able to make decisions based on intelligent thinking rather than on emotion. ❑ *Rachel looked calmer and more rational now.* [from Latin]

| | |
|---|---|
| N. | rational **approach**, rational **choice**, rational **decision**, rational **explanation 1** |
| | rational **human being**, rational **person 2** |

**ra|tion|ale** /ræʃənæl, -nɑl/ (**rationales**) N-COUNT The **rationale** for a course of action, practice, or belief is the set of reasons on which it is based. [FORMAL] ❑ *The rationale for the decision is not only economic.* [from New Latin]

**ra|tion|al|ist** /ræʃən³lɪst/ (**rationalists**) **1** ADJ Someone who is **rationalist** has beliefs that are based on reason and logic rather than emotion or religion. ❑ *...a rationalist philosopher.* ● **ra|tion|al|ism** N-UNCOUNT ❑ *...the rationalism of Western culture.* **2** N-COUNT A **rationalist** bases his or her life on rationalist beliefs. ❑ *...the rationalists and scientists of the nineteenth century.* [from New Latin]

r

**ra|tion|al|ize** /rǽʃənªlaɪz/ (**rationalizes, rationalizing, rationalized**) V-T If you try to **rationalize** attitudes or actions that are difficult to accept, you think of reasons to justify or explain them. ❏ *He rationalized her behavior by the fact that she was not well.* [from Latin]

**ra|tion|al num|ber** (**rational numbers**) N-COUNT **Rational numbers** are numbers that can be expressed as whole numbers, fractions, or decimals. [TECHNICAL]

**rat|tle** /rǽtªl/ (**rattles, rattling, rattled**) ■ V-T/V-I When something **rattles** or when you **rattle** it, it makes short, sharp, knocking sounds because it is being shaken or it keeps hitting against something hard. ❏ *A train rattled by.* ● **Rattle** is also a noun. ❏ *…a rattle of the door handle.* ■ N-COUNT A **rattle** is a baby's toy with small, loose objects inside which make a noise when the baby shakes it. ■ V-T If something or someone **rattles** you, they make you nervous. ❏ *The meeting with her boss rattled her.* ● **rat|tled** ADJ ❏ *His expression showed that he was rattled.* [from Middle Dutch]

**rat|ty** /rǽti/ (**rattier, rattiest**) ADJ **Ratty** clothes and objects are torn or in bad condition, especially because they are old. ❏ *…my ratty old pajamas.* [from Old English]

**rau|cous** /rɔ́kəs/ ADJ A **raucous** sound is loud, harsh, and rather unpleasant. ❏ *…raucous laughter.* ● **rau|cous|ly** ADV ❏ *They laughed raucously.* [from Latin]

**rav|age** /rǽvɪdʒ/ (**ravages, ravaging, ravaged**) V-T A city, country, or economy that **has been ravaged** has been damaged so much that it is almost completely destroyed. ❏ *The country has been ravaged by war.* [from French]

**rav|ages** /rǽvɪdʒɪz/ N-PLURAL The **ravages of** time, war, or the weather are the damaging effects that they have. ❏ *…the ravages of two wars.* [from French]

**rave** /reɪv/ (**raves, raving, raved**) ■ V-T/V-I If someone **raves**, they talk in an excited and uncontrolled way. ❏ *"What is wrong with you?" she raved.* ❏ *She cried and raved for hours.* ■ V-T/V-I If you **rave about** something, you speak or write about it with great enthusiasm. ❏ *Rachel raved about the movie.* ❏ *"I didn't know Italy was so beautiful!" she raved.* ■ N-COUNT A **rave** is a big event at which young people dance to electronic music in a large building or in the open air. ❏ *…an all-night rave.* [from Old French] ■ → see also **raving**

**ra|ven** /reɪvªn/ (**ravens**) N-COUNT A **raven** is a large bird with shiny black feathers and a deep harsh call. [from Old English]

**ra|vine** /rəvín/ (**ravines**) N-COUNT A **ravine** is a very deep, narrow valley with steep sides. ❏ *The bus overturned and fell into a ravine.* [from Old French]

**rav|ing** /reɪvɪŋ/ ■ ADJ You use **raving** to describe someone who you think is completely mad. [INFORMAL] ❏ *…a raving idiot.* ● **Raving** is also an adverb. ❏ *Have you gone raving mad?* [from Old French] ■ → see also **rave**

**raw** /rɔ́/ (**rawer, rawest**) ■ ADJ **Raw** materials or substances are in their natural state before being processed. ❏ *We import raw materials.* ■ ADJ **Raw** food is eaten uncooked, has not yet been cooked, or has not been cooked enough. ❏ *…a dish made of raw fish.* ■ ADJ If a part of your body is **raw**, it is red and painful, perhaps because the skin has come

off or has been burned. ❏ *Her skin was raw where the ropes had rubbed it.* ■ ADJ If you describe someone in a new job as **raw**, or as a **raw** recruit, you mean that they lack experience in that job. ■ PHRASE If you say that you are getting **a raw deal**, you mean that you are being treated unfairly. [INFORMAL] ❏ *I think the man who lost his job got a raw deal.* [from Old English]

| **Thesaurus** | *raw* | Also look up : |
|---|---|---|
| ADJ. | natural ■ | |
| | fresh; (*ant.*) cooked ■ | |

**raw|hide** /rɔ́haɪd/ N-UNCOUNT **Rawhide** is leather that comes from cattle, and has not been treated or tanned.

**ray** /reɪ/ (**rays**) ■ N-COUNT **Rays** of light are narrow beams of light. ❏ *…the sun's rays.* ■ → see also **X-ray** ■ N-COUNT A **ray of** hope, comfort, or other positive quality is a small amount of it that makes a bad situation seem less bad. ❏ *The research provides a ray of hope for sufferers of the disease.* [from Old French]

→ see **rainbow, telescope**

**ra|zor** /reɪzər/ (**razors**) N-COUNT A **razor** is a tool that people use for shaving. [from Old French]

**razz** /rǽz/ (**razzes, razzing, razzed**) V-T To **razz** someone means to tease them, especially in an unkind way. [INFORMAL] ❏ *Molly razzed me about dropping the ball.*

**r-controlled sound** /ɑ́rkəntroʊld saʊnd/ (**r-controlled sounds**) N-COUNT In language teaching, an **r-controlled sound** is a vowel that is pronounced differently when it comes before the letter "r," such as the vowel sound represented by the letters "ai" in "air." [TECHNICAL]

**reach** /rítʃ/ (**reaches, reaching, reached**) ■ V-T When someone or something **reaches** a place, they arrive there. ❏ *He did not stop until he reached the door.* ■ V-T If someone or something has **reached** a certain stage, level, or amount, they are at that stage, level, or amount. ❏ *The figure could reach 100,000 next year.* ■ V-I If you **reach** somewhere, you move your arm and hand to take or touch something. ❏ *Judy reached into her bag.* ■ V-T If you can **reach** something, you are able to touch it by stretching out your arm or leg. ❏ *Can you reach your toes with your fingertips?* ■ V-T If you try to **reach** someone, you try to contact them, usually by telephone. ❏ *You can reach me at this phone number.* ■ V-T/V-I If something **reaches** a place, point, or level, it extends as far as that place, point, or level. ❏ *…a shirt that reached to his knees.* ■ V-T When people **reach** an agreement or a decision, they succeed in achieving it. ❏ *They failed to reach agreement over the issue.* [from Old English]

| **Word Partnership** | Use *reach* with : |
|---|---|
| N. | reach **a destination** ■ |
| | reach **a goal**, reach *one's* **potential** ■ |
| | reach **(an) agreement**, reach **a** |
| | **compromise**, reach **a consensus**, reach |
| | **a decision** ■ |

**re|act** /riǽkt/ (**reacts, reacting, reacted**) ■ V-I When you **react to** something that has happened to you, you behave in a particular way because of it. ❑ *They reacted violently to the news.* **2** V-I If you **react against** someone's way of behaving, you deliberately behave in a different way because you do not like the way he or she behaves. ❑ *My father never saved money and I reacted against that.* **3** V-I If you **react to** a substance such as a drug, or **to** something you have touched, you are affected unpleasantly or made ill by it. ❑ *Someone who is allergic to milk will also react to cheese.* **4** V-RECIP When one chemical substance **reacts with** another, or when two chemical substances **react**, they combine chemically to form another substance. ❑ *Calcium reacts with water.* [from Late Latin]

### Word Partnership Use *react* with :

| | |
|---|---|
| ADJ. | **slow to** react **1** |
| N. | react **to news**, react **to a situation 1** |
| ADV. | react **differently**, react **emotionally**, **how to** react, react **negatively**, react **positively**, react **quickly 1** react **strongly**, react **violently 1** – **4** |

**re|ac|tant** /riˈæktənt/ (**reactants**) N-COUNT In a chemical reaction, the **reactants** are the substances that are present at the start of the reaction. [TECHNICAL] [from Late Latin]

**re|ac|tion** /riˈækʃ⁽ə⁾n/ (**reactions**) **1** N-VAR Your **reaction to** something that has happened or something that you have experienced is what you feel, say, or do because of it. ❑ *He showed no reaction to the news.* **2** N-COUNT A **reaction against** something is a way of behaving or doing something that is deliberately different from what has been done before. ❑ *...a reaction against this type of progress.* **3** N-PLURAL Your **reactions** are your ability to move quickly in response to something. ❑ *The sport requires very fast reactions.* **4** N-COUNT A chemical **reaction** is a process in which two substances combine together chemically to form another substance. ❑ *...a chemical reaction between oxygen and hydrogen.* **5** N-COUNT If you have a **reaction to** a substance such as a drug, or **to** something you have touched, you are affected unpleasantly or made ill by it. ❑ *He suffered a serious reaction to the drug.* [from Latin]
→ see **motion**

### Word Partnership Use *reaction* with :

| | |
|---|---|
| ADJ. | **mixed** reaction, **negative** reaction, **positive** reaction **1** **emotional** reaction, **initial** reaction **1 2** **chemical** reaction **4** **allergic** reaction **5** |

**re|ac|tion|ary** /riˈækʃənɛri/ (**reactionaries**) ADJ You describe someone as **reactionary** when he or she tries to prevent changes in the political or social system of his or her country, and you disapprove of this. ❑ *The chairman was too reactionary.* ● A **reactionary** is someone with reactionary views. ❑ *Critics viewed him as a reactionary.* [from Latin]

**re|ac|tor** /riˈæktər/ (**reactors**) N-COUNT A **reactor** is the same as a **nuclear reactor**. [from Late Latin]

**read** (**reads, reading, read**)

> The form **read** is pronounced /riːd/ when it is the present tense, and /rɛd/ when it is the past tense and past participle.

**1** V-T/V-I When you **read** something such as a book or article, you look at and understand the words that are written there. ❑ *Have you read this book?* ❑ *She spends all her time reading.* ● **Read** is also a noun. ❑ *I sat down to have a good read.* **2** V-T If you can **read** music, you have the ability to look at and understand the symbols that are used in written music to represent musical sounds. **3** V-T You can use **read** when saying what is written on something or in something. ❑ *The sign on the door read "Private."* **4** V-I If you refer to how a piece of writing **reads**, you are referring to its style. ❑ *The book reads very awkwardly.* **5** N-COUNT If you say that a book or magazine is a good **read**, you mean that it is very enjoyable to read. ❑ *Ben Okri's novel is a good read.* **6** V-T If someone **reads** your mind or thoughts, he or she knows exactly what you are thinking without you telling him or her. **7** V-T When you **read** a measuring device, you look at it to see what the figure or measurement on it is. ❑ *He was able to read a thermometer.* [from Old English] **8** → see also **reading**

▸ **read into** PHR-VERB If you **read** a meaning **into** something, you think it is there although it may not actually be there. ❑ *Don't read too much into his comments.*
▸ **read out** PHR-VERB If you **read out** a piece of writing, you say it aloud. ❑ *The evidence was read out in court.*
▸ **read up on** PHR-VERB If you **read up on** a subject, you read a lot about it so that you become informed about it. ❑ *I've read up on the subject.*

### Thesaurus read Also look up :

| | |
|---|---|
| V. | scan, skim, study **1** comprehend; (*ant.*) sense **1 2** |

### Word Partnership Use *read* with :

| | |
|---|---|
| N. | **ability to** read, read **a book/magazine/(news)paper**, read **a sentence**, read **a sign**, read **a statement 1** |
| ADV. | read **carefully**, read **silently 1** |
| V. | **learn (how) to** read, **like to** read, *someone* read, **want to** read **1** |

**read|able** /ˈriːdəb⁽ə⁾l/ ADJ If you say that a book or article is **readable**, you mean that it is enjoyable and easy to read. ❑ *...a very readable book.* [from Old English]

**read|er** /ˈriːdər/ (**readers**) N-COUNT The **readers** of a newspaper, magazine, or book are the people who read it. ❑ *The book gives the reader an interesting view of life in Spain.* [from Old English]

**read|er|ship** /ˈriːdərʃɪp/ (**readerships**) N-COUNT The **readership** of a book, newspaper, or magazine is the number or type of people who read it. ❑ *...articles which will appeal to our readership.* [from Old English]

**read|er's thea|ter** N-UNCOUNT **Reader's theater** is a form of theater, used especially in teaching, in which the performers read from scripts and which does not involve costumes, stage sets, or special lighting.

r

**read|ily** /rɛdɪli/ ■ ADV If you do something **readily**, you do it in a way which shows that you are very willing to do it. ❑ *I asked her to help, and she readily agreed.* ■ ADV You also use **readily** to say that something can be done or obtained quickly and easily. For example, if you say that something can be readily understood, you mean that people can understand it quickly and easily. ❑ *The parts are readily available in hardware stores.* [from Old English]

**read|ing** /rɪdɪŋ/ (**readings**) ■ N-UNCOUNT **Reading** is the activity of reading books. ❑ *I love reading.* ■ N-COUNT A **reading** is an event at which poetry or extracts from books are read to an audience. ❑ *I asked him to come to a poetry reading.* ■ N-COUNT The **reading** on a measuring device is the figure or measurement that it shows. ❑ *The thermometer gave a faulty reading.* [from Old English]

**re|adjust** /rɪədʒʌst/ (**readjusts, readjusting, readjusted**) ■ V-I When you **readjust to** a new situation, you adapt to it. ❑ *I lived abroad for many years and it was difficult to readjust to life in the U.S.* ● **re|adjust|ment** N-UNCOUNT ❑ *...a period of readjustment.* ■ V-T If you **readjust** something, you change it to make it more effective or appropriate. ❑ *Serious illness forced me to readjust my thinking.* [from Old French]

**ready** /rɛdi/ (**readier, readiest, readies, readying, readied**) ■ ADJ If someone is **ready**, they are properly prepared for something. If something is **ready**, it has been properly prepared and is now able to be used. ❑ *It took her a long time to get ready for school.* ● **readi|ness** N-UNCOUNT ❑ *We keep the room neat and clean in readiness for visitors.* ■ ADJ If you are **ready to** do something, you are willing to do it. ❑ *They were ready to help.* ● **readiness** N-UNCOUNT ❑ *...their readiness to cooperate.* ■ ADJ If you are **ready for** something, you need it or want it. ❑ *I'm ready for bed.* ■ ADJ To be **ready to** do something means to be about to do it or likely to do it. ❑ *She looked ready to cry.* ■ ADJ You use **ready** to describe things that are able to be used very quickly and easily. ❑ *I didn't have a ready answer for this question.* ■ V-T When you **ready** something, you prepare it for a particular purpose. [FORMAL] ❑ *Soldiers were readying themselves for the attack.* [from Old English]

**ready-made** ■ ADJ If something that you buy is **ready-made**, you can use it immediately. ❑ *...ready-made meals.* ■ ADJ **Ready-made** means extremely convenient or useful for a particular purpose. ❑ *...a ready-made topic of conversation.*

**re|affirm** /rɪəfɜrm/ (**reaffirms, reaffirming, reaffirmed**) V-T If you **reaffirm** something, you state it again clearly and firmly. [FORMAL] ❑ *He reaffirmed his support for the project.* [from Old French]

**real** /rɪl/ ■ ADJ Something that is **real** actually exists and is not imagined or theoretical. ❑ *No, it wasn't a dream. It was real.* ■ ADJ A material or object that is **real** is natural or functioning, and not artificial or an imitation. ❑ *...the smell of real leather.* ■ ADJ You can use **real** to describe someone or something that has all the characteristics or qualities that such a person or thing typically has. ❑ *...his first real girlfriend.* ■ ADJ You can use **real** to describe something that is the true or original thing of its kind, rather than what someone wants you to believe. ❑ *This was the real reason for her call.* ■ ADV You can use **real** to emphasize an adjective or adverb. [INFORMAL] ❑ *He is finding prison life "real tough."* ■ PHRASE If you say that someone does something **for real**, you mean that they actually do it and do not just pretend to do it. [INFORMAL] ❑ *I dreamed about becoming an actor but I never thought I'd do it for real.* [from Old French]

**real es|tate** ■ N-UNCOUNT **Real estate** is property in the form of land and buildings. ❑ *...investing in real estate.* ■ N-UNCOUNT **Real estate** businesses or **real estate** agents sell houses, buildings, and land.

**re|al|ism** /rɪəlɪzəm/ ■ N-UNCOUNT When people show **realism** in their behavior, they recognize and accept the true nature of a situation and try to deal with it in a practical way. ● **re|al|ist** (**realists**) N-COUNT ❑ *I'm a realist.* ■ N-UNCOUNT If things and people are presented with **realism** in paintings, stories, or movies, they are presented in a way that is like real life. ● **realist** ADJ ❑ *...a realist painter.* [from Old French]
→ see **genre**

**re|al|is|tic** /rɪəlɪstɪk/ ■ ADJ If you are **realistic** about a situation, you recognize and accept its true nature and try to deal with it in a practical way. ❑ *Police must be realistic about violent crime.* ● **re|al|is|ti|cal|ly** ADV ❑ *As an adult, you can think about the situation realistically.* ■ ADJ You say that a painting, story, or movie is **realistic** when the people and things in it are like people and things in real life. ● **re|al|is|ti|cal|ly** ADV ❑ *The movie begins realistically and then turns into a fantasy.* [from Old French]
→ see **art, fantasy**

**re|al|ity** /riˈæliti/ (**realities**) **1** N-UNCOUNT
You use **reality** to refer to real things or the real
nature of things rather than imagined, invented,
or theoretical ideas. ❑ *Her dream ended and she
had to return to reality.* **2** → see also **virtual reality**
**3** N-COUNT **The reality of** a situation is the
truth about it, especially when it is unpleasant.
❑ *...the harsh reality of life.* **4** N-SING If something
becomes a **reality**, it actually exists or is actually
happening. ❑ *The reality is that they are poor.*
**5** PHRASE You can use **in reality** to introduce a
statement about the real nature of something,
when it contrasts with something incorrect that
has just been described. ❑ *He promised a lot, but in
reality nothing changed.* [from Old French]
→ see **fantasy**

**re|al|ity check** (**reality checks**) N-COUNT If you
say that something is a **reality check** for someone,
you mean that it makes them recognize the truth
about a situation, especially about the difficulties
involved. ❑ *It's time for a reality check.*

**re|al|ity show** (**reality shows**) N-COUNT A
**reality show** is a type of television program that
aims to show how ordinary people behave in
everyday life or in situations which are intended
to represent everyday life.

**re|al|ity TV** N-UNCOUNT **Reality TV** is a type
of television programming that aims to show
how ordinary people behave in everyday life or
in situations which are intended to represent
everyday life.

**re|al|ize** /riˈəlaɪz/ (**realizes, realizing, realized**)
**1** V-T/V-I If you **realize** that something is true,
you become aware of that fact or understand
it. ❑ *As soon as we realized that something was
wrong, we rushed to help.* ❑ *People don't realize how
serious the situation is.* ● **re|al|iza|tion** /riˌəlaɪˈzeɪʃᵊn/
(**realizations**) N-VAR ❑ *There was a growing
realization that something must change.* **2** V-T If your
hopes, desires, or fears **are realized**, the things
that you hope for, desire, or fear actually happen.
❑ *All his worst fears were realized.* ● **re|al|iza|tion**
N-UNCOUNT ❑ *...the realization of his hopes.* **3** V-T
When someone **realizes** a design or an idea, they
make or organize something based on that design
or idea. [FORMAL] ❑ *...the method that I used in order
to realize the sculpture.* [from Old French]

**re|al|ly** /ˈriəli/ **1** ADV You can use **really** to
emphasize a statement. [SPOKEN] ❑ *I'm very sorry.
I really am.* **2** ADV You use **really** when you are
discussing the real facts about something, in
contrast to the ones someone wants you to believe.
❑ *My father didn't really have a wooden leg.* **3** ADV
People sometimes use **really** to slightly reduce the
force of a negative statement. [SPOKEN] ❑ *I'm not
really surprised.* **4** CONVENTION You can say **really**
to express surprise or disbelief at what someone
has said. [SPOKEN] ❑ *"I once met the president."*
— *"Really?"* [from Old French]

**realm** /rɛlm/ (**realms**) N-COUNT You can use
**realm** to refer to any area of activity, interest, or
thought. [FORMAL] [from Old French]

**real num|ber** (**real numbers**) N-COUNT In
mathematics, rational numbers and irrational
numbers can be referred to collectively as **real
numbers**. [TECHNICAL]

**real prop|er|ty** N-UNCOUNT **Real property** is
property in the form of land and buildings, rather
than personal possessions.

**real world** N-SING If you talk about **the real
world**, you are referring to the world and life in
general, in contrast to a particular person's own
life, experience, and ideas. ❑ *I'm not sure whether
the plan will work in the real world.*

**reap** /rip/ (**reaps, reaping, reaped**) V-T If you
**reap** the benefits or the rewards of something, you
enjoy the good things that happen as a result of
it. ❑ *You'll soon begin to reap the benefits of exercising
more.* [from Old English]

**re|appear** /ˌriəˈpɪər/ (**reappears, reappearing,
reappeared**) V-I When people or things **reappear**,
they return again after they have been away or
out of sight. ● **re|appear|ance** (**reappearances**)
N-COUNT ❑ *His sudden reappearance was a shock.*
[from Old French]

**rear** /rɪər/ (**rears, rearing, reared**) **1** N-SING The
**rear** of something is the back part of it. ❑ *He settled
back in the rear of the taxi.* ● **Rear** is also an adjective.
❑ *...rear seat belts.* **2** V-T If you **rear** children, you
take care of them until they are old enough to take
care of themselves. ❑ *I was reared in Texas.* **3** V-T If
you **rear** a young animal, you keep and take care of
it until it is old enough to be used for work or food,
or until it can look after itself. ❑ *She spends a lot of
time rearing animals.* **4** V-I When a horse **rears**, it
moves the front part of its body upward, so that its
front legs are high in the air and it is standing on
its back legs. ❑ *The horse reared and threw off its rider.*
[from Old English]

**re|arrange** /ˌriəˈreɪndʒ/ (**rearranges,
rearranging, rearranged**) V-T If you **rearrange**
things, you change the way in which they are
organized or ordered. ❑ *Malcolm rearranged all the
furniture.* ● **re|arrange|ment** (**rearrangements**)
N-VAR ❑ *...a rearrangement of the company structure.*
[from Old French]

**rea|son** /ˈrizᵊn/ (**reasons, reasoning, reasoned**)
**1** N-COUNT The **reason for** something is a fact or
situation which explains why it happens. ❑ *There
is a reason for every important thing that happens.*
**2** N-UNCOUNT If you say that you have **reason
to** believe something or **to** have a particular
emotion, you mean that you have evidence for
your belief or there is a definite cause of your
feeling. ❑ *They had reason to believe that he was*

**r**

not telling the truth. **3** N-UNCOUNT The ability that people have to think and to make sensible judgments can be referred to as **reason**. ❑ *...a conflict between emotion and reason.* **4** V-T If you **reason that** something is true, you decide that it is true after thinking carefully about all the facts. ❑ *I reasoned that if he could do it, so could I.* **5** → see also **reasoned, reasoning** **6** PHRASE If one thing happens **by reason of** another, it happens because of it. [FORMAL] ❑ *The boss has enormous influence by reason of his position.* [from Old French] **7** to **see reason** → see **see** **8** it **stands to reason** → see **stand** ▶ **reason with** PHR-VERB If you try to **reason with** someone, you try to persuade them to do or accept something by using sensible arguments. ❑ *He never listens. I can't reason with him.*

---

**Word Partnership**   Use *reason* with :

ADJ.    **main** reason, **major** reason, **obvious** reason, **only** reason, **primary** reason, **real** reason, **same** reason, **simple** reason **1**
        **compelling** reason, **good** reason, **sufficient** reason **1** **2**

---

**rea|son|able** /ríːzənəbᵊl/ **1** ADJ If you think that someone is fair and sensible you can say that they are **reasonable**. ❑ *He's a reasonable person.* ● **rea|son|ably** /ríːzənəbli/ ADV ❑ *"Can I think about it?" she asked reasonably.* ● **rea|son|able|ness** N-UNCOUNT ❑ *"I can understand how you feel," Dan said with great reasonableness.* **2** ADJ If you say that a decision or action is **reasonable**, you mean that it is fair and sensible. ❑ *...a perfectly reasonable decision.* **3** ADJ If you say that an expectation or explanation is **reasonable**, you mean that there are good reasons why it may be correct. ❑ *It seems reasonable to think that cities will increase in size.* ● **rea|son|ably** ADV ❑ *You can reasonably expect your goods to arrive within six weeks.* **4** ADJ If you say that the price of something is **reasonable**, you mean that it is fair and not too high. ● **rea|son|ably** ADV ❑ *...reasonably priced hotels.* **5** ADJ You can use **reasonable** to describe something that is fairly good, but not very good. ❑ *The boy spoke reasonable French.* ● **rea|son|ably** ADV ❑ *I can dance reasonably well.* **6** ADJ A **reasonable** amount of something is a fairly large amount of it. ❑ *They will need a reasonable amount of space.* ● **rea|son|ably** ADV ❑ *Things happened reasonably quickly.* [from Old French]

---

**Thesaurus**    *reasonable* Also look up :

ADJ.    **rational** **1**
        acceptable, fair, sensible; (ant.)
        unreasonable **2**
        likely, probable, right **3**
        fair, inexpensive **4**

---

**Word Partnership**   Use *reasonable* with :

N.    reasonable **person** **1**
      **beyond a** reasonable **doubt**, reasonable **expectation**, reasonable **explanation** **3**
      reasonable **cost**, reasonable **price**, reasonable **rates** **4**
      reasonable **amount** **6**

---

**rea|soned** /ríːzᵊnd/ ADJ A **reasoned** discussion or argument is based on sensible reasons, rather than on feelings. ❑ *Their opinions are not based on reasoned argument.* [from Old French]

**rea|son|ing** /ríːzənɪŋ/ (**reasonings**) N-VAR **Reasoning** is the process by which you reach a conclusion after thinking about all the facts. ❑ *...the reasoning behind the decision.* [from Old French]
→ see **philosophy**

**re|as|sert** /ríːəsɜ́rt/ (**reasserts, reasserting, reasserted**) **1** V-T If you **reassert** your control or authority, you make it clear that you are still in a position of power, or you strengthen the power that you had. ❑ *...the government's effort to reassert its control.* **2** V-T If something such as an idea or habit **reasserts itself**, it becomes noticeable again. ❑ *His sense of humor was beginning to reassert itself.* [from Latin]

**re|as|sess** /ríːəsɛ́s/ (**reassesses, reassessing, reassessed**) V-T If you **reassess** a situation, you think about it and decide whether you need to change your opinion about it. ● **re|as|sess|ment** (**reassessments**) N-VAR ❑ *...a total reassessment of what he wanted.* [from Old French]

**re|assure** /ríːəʃʊ́ər/ (**reassures, reassuring, reassured**) V-T If you **reassure** someone, you say or do things to make them stop worrying about something. ● **re|assur|ance** N-UNCOUNT ❑ *He needed reassurance that she loved him.* [from Old French]

---

**Word Partnership**   Use *reassure* with :

N.    reassure **citizens**, reassure **customers**, reassure **investors**, reassure **the public**
V.    **seek to** reassure, **try to** reassure

---

**re|assured** /ríːəʃʊ́ərd/ ADJ If you feel **reassured**, you feel less worried about something, because you have received help or advice. ❑ *I felt reassured after I had spoken to the doctor.* [from Old French]

**re|assur|ing** /ríːəʃʊ́ərɪŋ/ ADJ If you find someone's words or actions **reassuring**, they make you feel less worried about something. ❑ *It was reassuring to hear John's voice.* ● **re|assur|ing|ly** ADV ❑ *"It's okay," he said reassuringly.* [from Old French]

**re|bate** /ríːbeɪt/ (**rebates**) N-COUNT A **rebate** is an amount of money which is returned to you after you have paid for goods or services or after you have paid tax or rent. [from Old French]

**re|bel** (**rebels, rebelling, rebelled**)

---

The noun is pronounced /rɛ́bᵊl/. The verb is pronounced /rɪbɛ́l/.

---

**1** N-COUNT **Rebels** are people who are fighting against their own country's army in order to change the political system there. ❑ *...fighting between rebels and government forces.* **2** N-COUNT You can say that someone is a **rebel** if you think that they behave differently from other people and have rejected the values of society or of their parents. ❑ *She was a rebel at school.* **3** V-I When someone **rebels**, they start to behave differently from other people and reject the values of society or of their parents. ❑ *Teenagers often rebel.* [from Old French]

**re|bel|lion** /rɪbɛ́lyən/ (**rebellions**) N-VAR A **rebellion** is a violent organized action by a large group of people who are trying to change their country's political system. ❑ *...the government's response to the rebellion.* [from Old French]

**re|bel|lious** /rɪbɛlyəs/ ADJ A **rebellious** person behaves in an unacceptable way and does not do what he or she is told. ❑ ...a rebellious teenager. ● **re|bel|lious|ness** N-UNCOUNT ❑ ...the normal rebelliousness of youth. [from Old French]

**re|birth** /ribȝrθ/ N-UNCOUNT You can refer to a change that leads to a new period of growth and improvement in something as its **rebirth**. ❑ ...the rebirth of democracy in the country. [from Old Norse]

**re|boot** /ribut/ (reboots, rebooting, rebooted) V-T/V-I If you **reboot** a computer, or if you **reboot**, you shut it down and start it again. [COMPUTING] ❑ When you reboot your computer, the software is ready to use. ● **Reboot** is also a noun. ❑ ...the time spent waiting for a reboot. [from Old French]

**re|bound** /rɪbaund/ (rebounds, rebounding, rebounded) **1** V-I If something **rebounds** from a solid surface, it bounces or springs back from it. ❑ The ball rebounded from a post. **2** V-I If an action or situation **rebounds on** you, it has an unpleasant effect on you, especially when this effect was intended for someone else. ❑ Her trick rebounded on her. [from Old French]

**re|buff** /rɪbʌf/ (rebuffs, rebuffing, rebuffed) V-T If you **rebuff** someone or **rebuff** a suggestion that they make, you refuse to do what they suggest. ● **Rebuff** is also a noun. ❑ The election results were an embarrassing rebuff for the president. [from Old French]

**re|build** /ribɪld/ (rebuilds, rebuilding, rebuilt) **1** V-T When people **rebuild** something such as a building, they build it again after it has been damaged or destroyed. ❑ The house must be rebuilt. **2** V-T When people **rebuild** something such as an institution, a system, or an aspect of their lives, they take action to bring it back to its previous condition. ❑ Everyone worked hard to rebuild the economy. [from Old English]

**re|buke** /rɪbyuk/ (rebukes, rebuking, rebuked) V-T If you **rebuke** someone, you speak severely to them because they have said or done something that you do not approve of. [FORMAL] ● **Rebuke** is also a noun. ❑ ...a public rebuke from the chairman. [from Old Norman French]

**re|call** (recalls, recalling, recalled)

> The verb is pronounced /rɪkɔl/. The noun is pronounced /rikɔl/.

**1** V-T/V-I When you **recall** something, you remember it. ❑ He recalled that he met Pollard during a business trip. ❑ "What was his name?" — "I don't recall." **2** V-T If you **are recalled** to your home, country, or the place where you work, you are ordered to return there. ❑ The U.S. representative was recalled to Washington. [from Old English]

**re|cap|ture** /rikæptʃər/ (recaptures, recapturing, recaptured) **1** V-T When soldiers **recapture** an area of land or a place, they gain control of it again from an opposing army who took it from them. ● **Recapture** is also a noun. ❑ ...the recapture of the city. **2** V-T To **recapture** a person or animal which has escaped from somewhere means to catch them again. ● **Recapture** is also a noun. ❑ ...the recapture of the prisoner. [from Latin]

**re|cede** /rɪsid/ (recedes, receding, receded) **1** V-I If something **recedes** from you, it moves away into the distance. ❑ Luke's footsteps receded. **2** V-I When something such as a quality, problem, or illness **recedes**, it becomes weaker, smaller, or less intense. **3** V-I If a man's hair starts to **recede**, it no longer grows on the front of his head. [from Latin]

**re|ceipt** /rɪsit/ (receipts) **1** N-COUNT A **receipt** is a piece of paper that you get from someone as proof that they have received money or goods from you. ❑ I gave her a receipt for the money. **2** N-PLURAL **Receipts** are the amount of money received during a particular period, for example by a store or theater. ❑ He was adding up the day's receipts. **3** N-UNCOUNT The **receipt** of something is the act of receiving it. [FORMAL] ❑ Goods are sent within 28 days after the receipt of your order. [from Old Norman French]

**re|ceive** /rɪsiv/ (receives, receiving, received) **1** V-T When you **receive** something, you get it after someone gives it to you or sends it to you. ❑ They received their awards at a ceremony in San Francisco. **2** V-T You can use **receive** to say that certain kinds of things happen to someone. ❑ He received most of the blame. **3** V-T If you say that something **is received** in a particular way, you mean that people react to it in that way. ❑ The decision was received with great disappointment. [from Old French]

**re|ceiv|er** /rɪsivər/ (receivers) **1** N-COUNT A telephone's **receiver** is the part that you hold near to your ear and speak into. ❑ She picked up the receiver and started to dial. **2** N-COUNT A **receiver** is the part of a radio or television that picks up signals and converts them into sound or pictures. **3** N-COUNT The **receiver** is someone who is appointed by a court of law to manage the affairs of a business, usually when it is facing financial failure. [BUSINESS] [from Old French]
→ see **tennis, navigation, radio, television**

**re|cent** /risᵊnt/ ADJ A **recent** event or period of time happened only a short while ago. ❑ ...the recent murder of an American journalist. [from Latin]

**re|cent|ly** /risᵊntli/ ADV If something happened **recently**, it happened only a short time ago. ❑ The bank recently opened a branch in Miami. [from Latin]

**Usage** recently

Recently and lately can both be used to express that something began in the past and continues into the present: Recently/Lately I've been considering going back to school to get a master's degree. Recently, but not lately, is also used to describe a completed action: I recently graduated from high school.

**re|cep|tion** /rɪsɛpʃᵊn/ (receptions) **1** N-COUNT A **reception** is a formal party which is given to welcome someone or to celebrate a special event. ❑ ...a wedding reception. **2** N-UNCOUNT **Reception** in a hotel is the desk or office that books rooms for people and answers their questions. ❑ She was waiting at reception. **3** N-COUNT If someone or something has a particular kind of **reception**, that is the way that people react to them. ❑ They gave Mr. Mandela a friendly reception. **4** N-UNCOUNT If you get good **reception** from your radio or television, the sound or picture is clear because the signal is strong. If the **reception** is poor, the sound or picture is unclear because the signal is weak. [from Latin]
→ see **wedding**

r

**re|cep|tion|ist** /rɪsɛpʃənɪst/ (**receptionists**)
■ N-COUNT In an office or hospital, the **receptionist** is the person whose job is to answer the telephone, arrange appointments, and deal with people when they first arrive. ■ N-COUNT In a hotel, the **receptionist** is the person whose job is to reserve rooms for people and answer their questions. [from Latin]

**re|cep|tive** /rɪsɛptɪv/ ADJ Someone who is **receptive to** new ideas or suggestions is prepared to consider them or accept them. ❑ *The voters were receptive to his ideas.* [from Latin]

**re|cep|tor** /rɪsɛptər/ (**receptors**) N-COUNT **Receptors** are nerve endings in your body which react to changes and stimuli and make your body respond in a particular way. [TECHNICAL] [from Latin]

**re|cess** /rɪsɛs, rɪsɛs/ (**recesses, recessing, recessed**) ■ N-COUNT A **recess** is a break between the periods of work of an official body such as a committee, a court of law, or a government. ❑ *…the court's summer recess.* ■ N-VAR In a school, **recess** is the period of time between classes when the children are allowed to play. ❑ *She visited the school library during recess.* ■ V-I When formal meetings or court cases **recess**, they stop temporarily. [FORMAL] ❑ *The hearings have recessed for dinner.* ■ N-COUNT In a room, a **recess** is part of a wall which is built further back than the rest of the wall. ■ N-COUNT The **recesses of** something or somewhere are the deep or hidden parts. ❑ *He came out of the dark recesses of the garage.* [from Latin]

**re|ces|sion** /rɪsɛʃᵊn/ (**recessions**) N-VAR A **recession** is a period when the economy of a country is doing badly. ❑ *The oil price increases sent Europe into recession.* [from Latin]

**re|ces|sive** /rɪsɛsɪv/ ADJ A **recessive** gene produces a particular characteristic only if a person has two of these genes, one from each parent. Compare **dominant**. [TECHNICAL] [from Latin]

**reci|pe** /rɛsɪpi/ (**recipes**) ■ N-COUNT A **recipe** is a list of ingredients and a set of instructions that tell you how to cook something. ❑ *…a recipe for chocolate cake.* ■ N-SING If you say that something is a **recipe for** a particular situation, you mean that it is likely to result in that situation. ❑ *Having no smoke alarm is a recipe for disaster.* [from Latin]

**re|cipi|ent** /rɪsɪpiənt/ (**recipients**) N-COUNT The **recipient** of something is the person who receives it. [FORMAL] ❑ *…the recipient of the prize.* [from French]
→ see **donor**

**re|cip|ro|cal** /rɪsɪprəkᵊl/ ■ ADJ A **reciprocal** action or agreement involves two people or groups who do the same thing to each other or agree to help each other in a similar way. [FORMAL] ❑ *…a reciprocal loving relationship between a man and a woman.* ■ N-COUNT A **reciprocal** is a pair of numbers whose product is one. For example, the reciprocal of 3 is 1/3. [TECHNICAL] [from Latin]

**re|cip|ro|cate** /rɪsɪprəkeɪt/ (**reciprocates, reciprocating, reciprocated**) V-T/V-I If your feelings or actions toward someone **are reciprocated**, the other person feels or behaves in the same way toward you as you have felt or behaved toward them. ❑ *Her feelings of love were not*

reciprocated. ❑ *You smile and the baby reciprocates by smiling back.* [from Latin]

**re|cit|al** /rɪsaɪtᵊl/ (**recitals**) N-COUNT A **recital** is a performance of music or poetry, usually given by one person. [from Latin]

**re|cite** /rɪsaɪt/ (**recites, reciting, recited**) ■ V-T When someone **recites** a poem or other piece of writing, they say it aloud after they have learned it. ❑ *They recited poetry.* ■ V-T If you **recite** something such as a list, you say it aloud. ❑ *He recited a list of government failings.* [from Latin]

**reck|less** /rɛklɪs/ ADJ A **reckless** person shows a lack of care about danger or the results of his or her actions. ❑ *…reckless driving.* ● **reck|less|ly** ADV ❑ *He was leaning recklessly out of the open window.* ● **reck|less|ness** N-UNCOUNT ❑ *…an act of recklessness.* [from Old English]

**reck|on** /rɛkən/ (**reckons, reckoning, reckoned**) ■ V-T If you **reckon** that something is true, you think that it is true. [INFORMAL] ❑ *I reckon it's about three o'clock.* ■ V-T If something **is reckoned** to be a particular figure, it is calculated to be roughly that amount. ❑ *The business is reckoned to be worth $1.4 billion.* [from Old English]
▶ **reckon with** ■ PHR-VERB If you say that you had not **reckoned with** something, you mean that you had not expected it and so were not prepared for it. ❑ *Gary had not reckoned with the strength of Sally's feelings.* ■ PHRASE If you say that there is someone or something **to be reckoned with**, you mean that they must be dealt with and it will be difficult. ❑ *He was someone to be reckoned with.*

**reck|on|ing** /rɛkənɪŋ/ (**reckonings**) N-VAR Someone's **reckoning** is a calculation they make about something. ❑ *By my reckoning the trip will take about two hours.* [from Old English]

**re|claim** /rɪkleɪm/ (**reclaims, reclaiming, reclaimed**) ■ V-T If you **reclaim** something that you have lost or that has been taken away from you, you succeed in getting it back. ❑ *It was difficult for him to reclaim his authority.* ■ V-T When people **reclaim** land, they make it suitable for a purpose such as farming or building, for example by draining it or by building a barrier against the sea. ❑ *They are reclaiming farmland from water.* [from Old French]

**rec|la|ma|tion** /rɛkləmeɪʃᵊn/ N-UNCOUNT **Reclamation** is the process of changing land that is unsuitable for farming or building into land that can be used. [from Old French]

| Word Link | clin ≈ *leaning* : *decline*, *incline*, *recline* |
|---|---|

**re|cline** /rɪklaɪn/ (**reclines, reclining, reclined**) ■ V-I If you **recline on** something, you sit or lie on it with the upper part of your body supported at an angle. ❑ *She was reclining on the sofa.* ■ V-T/V-I When a seat **reclines** or when you **recline** it, you lower the back so that it is more comfortable to sit in. ❑ *First-class seats on the plane recline almost like beds.* [from Old French]

**re|clin|er** /rɪklaɪnər/ (**recliners**) N-COUNT A **recliner** is a type of armchair with a back which can be adjusted to slope at different angles. [from Old French]

**re|cluse** /rɪklus, rɛklus/ (**recluses**) N-COUNT A **recluse** is a person who lives alone and deliberately avoids other people. ❑ *Jean became a* *recluse in the seaside town of Carmel, California.* [from Old French]

**re|clu|sive** /rɪklúsɪv/ ADJ A **reclusive** person or animal lives alone and deliberately avoids the company of others. [from Old French]

**rec|og|ni|tion** /rɛkəgníʃ°n/ **1** N-UNCOUNT **Recognition** is the act of recognizing someone or identifying something when you see it. □ *There was no sign of recognition on her face.* **2** N-UNCOUNT **Recognition of** something is an understanding and acceptance of it. □ *...recognition of the importance of exercise.* **3** N-UNCOUNT When a person receives **recognition** for the things that they have done, people acknowledge the value or skill of their work. □ *His work received public recognition.* **4** PHRASE If something is done **in recognition of** someone's achievements, it is done as a way of showing official appreciation of him or her. □ *...a small gift in recognition of her contribution to the university.* [from Latin]

**rec|og|niz|able** /rɛkəgnáɪzəbᵊl/ ADJ Something that is **recognizable** can be recognized or identified. □ *It's one of the most recognizable buildings in New York.* [from Latin]

**rec|og|nize** /rɛkəgnaɪz/ (**recognizes, recognizing, recognized**) **1** V-T If you **recognize** someone or something, you know who that person is or what that thing is because you have seen or heard them before. □ *She recognized him immediately.* **2** V-T If someone says that they **recognize** something, they acknowledge that it exists or that it is true. □ *I recognize my own faults.* **3** V-T If people or organizations **recognize** something as valid, they officially accept it or approve of it. □ *They recognized the independence of Slovenia.* **4** V-T When people **recognize** the work that someone has done, they show their appreciation of it, often by giving that person an award. [from Latin]

**re|coil** (**recoils, recoiling, recoiled**)

| The verb is pronounced /rɪkɔ́ɪl/. The noun is pronounced /ríkɔɪl/. |
| --- |

**1** V-I If something makes you **recoil**, you move your body quickly away from it because it frightens, offends, or hurts you. □ *She recoiled from the smell when she opened the door.* **2** V-I If you **recoil from** doing something or **recoil at** the idea of something, you refuse to do it or accept it because you dislike it so much. □ *Voters recoiled from the government's action.* [from Old French]

**rec|ol|lec|tion** /rɛkəlɛ́kʃ°n/ (**recollections**) N-VAR If you have a **recollection of** something, you remember it. □ *Pat has few recollections of the trip.* [from Latin]

**re|com|bi|nant DNA** /rikɒ́mbɪnənt diː ɛn eɪ/ N-UNCOUNT **Recombinant DNA** is DNA that contains genes from different sources, which have been combined using genetic engineering. [TECHNICAL]

**rec|om|mend** /rɛkəmɛ́nd/ (**recommends, recommending, recommended**) **1** V-T If someone **recommends** a person or thing to you, they suggest that you would find that person or thing good or useful. □ *I recommend Barbados as a place for a vacation.* □ *I'll recommend you for the job.* ● **rec|om|mend|ed** ADJ □ *This book is highly recommended.* ● **rec|om|men|da|tion** N-COUNT (**recommendations**) □ *The best way of*

*finding a lawyer is through personal recommendation.* **2** V-T If you **recommend** that something is done, you suggest that it should be done. □ *The doctor recommended that I lose some weight.* ● **recommendation** N-COUNT □ *...the committee's recommendations.* **3** V-T If something or someone has a particular quality to **recommend** them, that quality makes them attractive or gives them an advantage over similar things or people. □ *The restaurant has much to recommend it.* [from Medieval Latin]

| **Word Partnership** | Use *recommend* with : |
| --- | --- |
| N. | **doctors** recommend, **experts** recommend **1** **2** recommend **changes** **2** |
| ADV. | **highly** recommend, **strongly** recommend **1** **2** |

**rec|on|cile** /rɛ́kənsaɪl/ (**reconciles, reconciling, reconciled**) **1** V-T If you **reconcile** two beliefs, facts, or demands that seem to be opposed or completely different, you find a way in which they can both be true or both be successful. □ *It's difficult to reconcile the demands of my job and the wish to be a good father.* **2** V-I/V-RECIP-PASSIVE If you **reconcile** or **are reconciled with** someone, you become friendly with them again after a disagreement. □ *I don't think Susan and I will be reconciled.* □ *You must reconcile with your partner.* ● **rec|on|cilia|tion** /rɛkənsɪliéɪʃ°n/ (**reconciliations**) N-VAR □ *...an appeal for reconciliation between the two religious groups.* **3** V-T If you **reconcile yourself to** an unpleasant situation, you accept it. □ *She reconciled herself to never seeing him again.* ● **rec|on|ciled** ADJ □ *He seemed reconciled to defeat.* [from Latin]

**re|con|nais|sance** /rɪkɒ́nɪsəns/ N-UNCOUNT **Reconnaissance** is the activity of obtaining military information about a place using soldiers, planes, or satellites. □ *The plane was returning from a reconnaissance mission.* [from French]

**re|con|sid|er** /rikənsɪ́dər/ (**reconsiders, reconsidering, reconsidered**) V-T/V-I If you **reconsider** a decision or opinion, you think about it and try to decide whether it should be changed. □ *We want you to reconsider your decision to resign.* □ *He made his decision and said he wouldn't reconsider.* [from Latin]

**re|con|struct** /rikənstrʌ́kt/ (**reconstructs, reconstructing, reconstructed**) **1** V-T If you **reconstruct** something that has been destroyed or badly damaged, you build it and make it work again. □ *We need to rebuild roads and reconstruct bridges.* **2** V-T To **reconstruct** a system or policy means to change it so that it works in a different way. □ *She wanted to reconstruct the state and change society.* **3** V-T If you **reconstruct** an event that happened in the past, you try to get a complete understanding of it by combining a lot of small pieces of information. □ *They reconstructed his journey home using information from his friends.* ● **re|con|struc|tion** N-COUNT (**reconstructions**) □ *She was too upset to take part in a reconstruction of the crime.* [from Latin]

**rec|ord** (**records, recording, recorded**)

| The noun is pronounced /rɛ́kərd/. The verb is pronounced /rɪkɔ́rd/. |
| --- |

**record** N-COUNT If you keep a **record of** something, you keep a written account or photographs of it so that it can be referred to later. ◻ *Keep a record of all the payments.* ◼ V-T If you **record** a piece of information or an event, you write it down, photograph it, or put it into a computer so that in the future people can refer to it. ◻ *Her letters record the details of her life in China.* ◼ V-T If you **record** something such as a speech or performance, you put it on tape or film so that it can be heard or seen again later. ◻ *Viewers can record the films.* ◼ N-COUNT A **record** is a round, flat piece of black plastic on which sound, especially music, is stored, and which can be played on a record player. ◼ N-COUNT A **record** is the best result that has ever been achieved in a particular sport or activity, for example the fastest time or the farthest distance. ◻ *He set the world record of 12.92 seconds.* ◼ → see also **recording, track record** ◼ PHRASE If something that you say is **off the record**, you do not intend it to be considered as official, or published with your name attached to it. ◼ PHRASE If you keep information **on record**, you write it down or store it in a computer so that it can be used later. [from Old French]
→ see **diary, history**

| Word Partnership | Use *record* with : |
| --- | --- |
| N. | record **a song** ◼ |
| | record **album**, record **club**, record **company**, **hit** record, record **industry**, record **label**, record **producer**, record **store** ◼ |
| | record **earnings**, record **high**, record **low**, record **numbers**, record **temperatures**, record **time**, **world** record ◼ |
| V. | **break** a record, **set** a record ◼ |

**re|cord|er** /rɪkɔrdər/ (**recorders**) N-VAR A **recorder** is a wooden or plastic musical instrument in the shape of a pipe that you play by blowing down one end and covering holes with your fingers.

**re|cord|ing** /rɪkɔrdɪŋ/ (**recordings**) ◼ N-COUNT A **recording** of something is a record, CD, tape, video, or DVD of it. ◻ *...a video recording of a police interview.* ◼ N-UNCOUNT **Recording** is the process of making records, CDs, tapes, videos, or DVDs. ◻ *...the recording industry.* [from Old French]

**rec|ord play|er** (**record players**) N-COUNT A **record player** is a machine on which you play records.

**re|count** (**recounts, recounting, recounted**)

The verb is pronounced /rɪkaʊnt/. The noun is pronounced /rɪkaʊnt/.

◼ V-T If you **recount** a story or event, you tell or describe it to people. [FORMAL] ◻ *He recounted the story of his first day at work.* ◼ N-COUNT A **recount** is a second count of votes in an election when the result is very close. [from Old French]

**re|coup** /rɪkup/ (**recoups, recouping, recouped**) V-T If you **recoup** a sum of money that you have spent or lost, you get it back. ◻ *Insurance companies are trying to recoup their losses.* [from Old French]

**re|course** /rɪkɔrs/ N-UNCOUNT If you have **recourse to** something, you use it to help you in a difficult situation. [FORMAL] ◻ *The countries reached an agreement without recourse to war.* [from Old French]

**re|cov|er** /rɪkʌvər/ (**recovers, recovering, recovered**) ◼ V-I When you **recover from** an illness or an injury, you become well again. ◻ *He is recovering from a knee injury.* ◼ V-I If you **recover from** an unhappy or unpleasant experience, you stop being upset by it. ◻ *...a tragedy from which he never fully recovered.* ◼ V-T If you **recover** something that has been lost or stolen, you find it or get it back. ◻ *Police raided five houses and recovered stolen goods.* ◼ V-T If you **recover** your former mental or physical state, it comes back again. ◻ *She never recovered consciousness.* [from Old French]

**re|cov|ery** /rɪkʌvəri/ (**recoveries**) ◼ N-VAR If a sick person makes a **recovery**, he or she becomes well again. ◻ *He made a remarkable recovery from his injuries.* ◼ N-VAR When there is a **recovery** in a country's economy, it improves. ◻ *The measures have failed to bring about economic recovery.* ◼ N-UNCOUNT You talk about the **recovery of** something when you get it back after it has been lost or stolen. ◻ *The museum is offering a reward for the recovery of the painting.* ◼ N-UNCOUNT You talk about the **recovery of** someone's physical or mental state when he or she returns to this state. ◻ *...the sudden loss and recovery of consciousness.* [from Old French]

**re|cov|ery room** (**recovery rooms**) N-COUNT A **recovery room** is a room where patients who have just had an operation are placed, so that they can be watched while they recover.

| Word Link | *creat ≈ making* : **creation, creature, recreate** |
| --- | --- |

**re|cre|ate** /rikrieɪt/ (**recreates, recreating, recreated**) V-T If you **recreate** something, you succeed in making it exist or seem to exist again. ◻ *You can't recreate the past.* ● **rec|re|ation** /rikrieɪʃⁿn/ (**recreations**) N-COUNT ◻ *The museum has a recreation of a castle.* [from Latin]

**rec|rea|tion** /rɛkrieɪʃⁿn/ (**recreations**) N-VAR **Recreation** consists of things that you do in your spare time to relax. ◻ *Saturday afternoon is for recreation.* ● **rec|rea|tion|al** ADJ ◻ *...parks and other recreational facilities.* [from Latin]
→ see **park**

**rec|rea|tion|al ve|hi|cle** (**recreational vehicles**) N-COUNT A **recreational vehicle** is a large vehicle that you can live in. The abbreviation **RV** is also used.

**re|crimi|na|tion** /rɪkrɪmɪneɪʃⁿn/ (**recriminations**) N-VAR **Recriminations** are accusations that two people or groups make about each other. ◻ *...angry arguments and recriminations.* [from Medieval Latin]

**re|cruit** /rɪkrut/ (**recruits, recruiting, recruited**) ◼ V-T If you **recruit** people for an organization, you select them and persuade them to join it or work for it. ◻ *We need to recruit and train more teachers.* ● **re|cruit|ing** N-UNCOUNT ◻ *...an army recruiting office.* ● **re|cruit|ment** N-UNCOUNT ◻ *...the recruitment of soldiers.* ◼ N-COUNT A **recruit** is a person who has recently joined an organization or an army. ◻ *...a new recruit to the police department.* [from French]

**rec|tan|gle** /rɛktæŋgᵊl/ (**rectangles**) N-COUNT A **rectangle** is a four-sided shape whose corners are all ninety-degree angles. Each side of a rectangle is the same length as the one opposite to it. [from Medieval Latin]
→ see **shape, volume**

**rec|tan|gu|lar** /rɛktæŋgyələr/ ADJ Something that is **rectangular** is shaped like a rectangle. ❑ ...a rectangular table. [from Medieval Latin]

**rec|ti|fy** /rɛktɪfaɪ/ (**rectifies, rectifying, rectified**) V-T If you **rectify** something that is wrong, you change it so that it becomes correct or satisfactory. ❑ Only a new law will rectify the situation. [from Old French]

**rec|ti|lin|ear** /rɛktɪlɪniər/ ADJ A **rectilinear** shape has straight lines. Compare **curvilinear**.

**re|cu|per|ate** /rɪkupəreɪt/ (**recuperates, recuperating, recuperated**) V-I When you **recuperate**, you recover your health or strength after you have been ill or injured. ❑ I went away to the country to recuperate. ● **re|cu|pera|tion** /rɪkupəreɪʃᵊn/ N-UNCOUNT ❑ Sleep is necessary for recuperation. [from Latin]

**re|cur** /rɪkɜr/ (**recurs, recurring, recurred**) V-I If something **recurs**, it happens more than once. ❑ ...a theme that recurs frequently in his work. ● **re|cur|rence** /rɪkɜrəns/ N-VAR ❑ Police want to prevent a recurrence of the violence. [from Latin]

**re|cur|rent** /rɪkɜrənt/ ADJ A **recurrent** event or feeling happens or is experienced more than once. ❑ ...a recurrent problem. [from Old French]

**re|cuse** /rɪkyuz/ (**recuses, recusing, recused**) V-T If a judge **recuses** himself or herself from a legal case, they state that they will not be involved in making decisions about the case, for example because they think they are biased. ❑ The judge himself must decide which cases to recuse himself from.

**re|cy|cle** /risaɪkᵊl/ (**recycles, recycling, recycled**) V-T If you **recycle** things that have already been used, such as bottles or sheets of paper, you process them so that they can be used again. [from Late Latin]
→ see **dump, paper**

**red** /rɛd/ (**reds, redder, reddest**) **1** COLOR Something that is **red** is the color of blood or a tomato. ❑ ...a bunch of red roses. ❑ She was dressed in red. **2** COLOR **Red** hair is between red and brown in color. **3** PHRASE If a person or company is **in the red** or if their bank account is **in the red**, they have spent more money than they have in their account and therefore they owe money to the bank. **4** PHRASE If you **see red**, you suddenly become very angry. ❑ I didn't mean to hit him. I just saw red. [from Old English]
→ see **color, hair, rainbow**

**red blood cell** (**red blood cells**) N-COUNT Your **red blood cells** are the cells in your blood which carry oxygen around your body. Compare **white blood cell**.
→ see **cardiovascular system**

**red card** (**red cards**) N-COUNT In soccer, if a player is shown the **red card**, the referee holds up a red card to indicate that the player must leave the field for breaking the rules. ❑ He received a red card

for arguing with the referee.

**red|dish** /rɛdɪʃ/ ADJ **Reddish** means slightly red in color. ❑ ...reddish brown hair. [from Old English]

**re|deem** /rɪdim/ (**redeems, redeeming, redeemed**) **1** V-T If you **redeem yourself** or your reputation, you do something that makes people have a good opinion of you again after you have behaved or performed badly. ❑ He realized his mistake and wanted to redeem himself. **2** V-T When something **redeems** an unpleasant thing or situation, it prevents it from being completely bad. ❑ Nothing can redeem our relationship now. **3** V-T If you **redeem** a debt or money that you have promised to someone, you pay money that you owe or that you promised to pay. [FORMAL] ❑ They needed $358,587 to redeem the debt. [from Old French]

**re|demp|tion** /rɪdɛmpʃᵊn/ (**redemptions**) N-VAR **Redemption** is the act of redeeming something or of being redeemed by something. [FORMAL] ❑ ...redemption for his sins. ❑ ...redemption of the loan. [from Old French]

**re|devel|op|ment** /ridɪvɛləpmənt/ N-UNCOUNT When **redevelopment** takes place, the buildings in one area of a town are knocked down and new ones are built in their place. ❑ The intention is to clear the site for redevelopment. [from Old French]

**red gi|ant** (**red giants**) N-COUNT A **red giant** is a very large, relatively cool star that is in the final stages of its life.

**red her|ring** (**red herrings**) N-COUNT If you say that something is a **red herring**, you mean that it is not important and it takes your attention away from the main subject or problem you are considering.

**red-hot** ADJ Something that is **red-hot** is extremely hot. ❑ ...red-hot radiators.

**re|di|rect** /ridɪrɛkt, -daɪ-/ (**redirects, redirecting, redirected**) **1** V-T If you **redirect** your energy, resources, or ability, you begin doing something different or trying to achieve something different. ❑ We need to redirect resources. **2** V-T If you **redirect** someone or something, you change their course. ❑ She redirected them to the fourth floor of the store. [from Latin]

**re|dis|trib|ute** /ridɪstrɪbyut/ (**redistributes, redistributing, redistributed**) V-T If money or property **is redistributed**, it is shared among people or organizations in a different way from the way that it was previously shared. ❑ Money was redistributed more fairly. ● **re|dis|tri|bu|tion** /ridɪstrɪbyuʃᵊn/ N-UNCOUNT ❑ ...the redistribution of income. [from Latin]

**re|dis|trict|ing** /ridɪstrɪktɪŋ/ N-UNCOUNT **Redistricting** is the division of an area into new administrative or election districts. ❑ A redistricting committee will redraw the City Council district lines.

**re|dress** /rɪdrɛs/ (**redresses, redressing, redressed**)

The noun is also pronounced /rɪdrɛs/ in American English.

**1** V-T If you **redress** something such as a wrong or a complaint, you do something to correct it or to improve things for the person who has been badly treated. [FORMAL] ❑ ...attempts to redress wrongs done to them. **2** V-T If you **redress** the balance or the imbalance between two things that have become unfair or unequal, you make them fair and equal again. [FORMAL] □ *We need to redress the economic imbalance between rich and poor countries.* ◼ N-UNCOUNT **Redress** is money that someone pays you because they have caused you harm or loss. [FORMAL] □ *...their legal battle to seek some redress from the government.* [from Old French]

**red tape** N-UNCOUNT You refer to official rules and procedures as **red tape** when they seem unnecessary and cause delay. □ *...promises to reduce educational red tape in their states.*

**re|duce** /rɪdu̱s/ (**reduces, reducing, reduced**) ◼ V-T If you **reduce** something, you make it smaller. □ *Exercise reduces the risks of heart disease.* ◻ V-T If someone **is reduced to** a weaker or inferior state, they become weaker or inferior as a result of something that happens to them. □ *They were reduced to extreme poverty.* ◼ V-T If you say that someone **is reduced to** doing something, you mean that they have to do it, although it is unpleasant or embarrassing. □ *He was reduced to begging on the streets.* ◼ V-T If something is changed to a different or less complicated form, you can say that it **is reduced to** that form. □ *The buildings were reduced to rubble by the earthquake.* [from Latin]
→ see **dump, mineral**

**re|duc|tion** /rɪdʌkʃⁿn/ (**reductions**) N-VAR When there is a **reduction in** something, it is made smaller. □ *...a reduction in prices.* [from Latin]

**re|dun|dant** /rɪdʌndənt/ ADJ Something that is **redundant** is unnecessary, for example, because it has been replaced by something else. □ *Changes in technology mean that many skills are now redundant.* [from Latin]

**reed** /ri̱d/ (**reeds**) N-COUNT **Reeds** are tall plants that grow in large groups in shallow water or on wet ground. [from Old English]

**reef** /ri̱f/ (**reefs**) N-COUNT A **reef** is a long line of rocks or sand, the top of which is just above or just below the surface of the sea. □ *...an ocean reef.* [from Middle Dutch]

**reek** /ri̱k/ (**reeks, reeking, reeked**) ◼ V-I To reek of something, usually something unpleasant, means to smell very strongly of it. □ *Your breath reeks of garlic.* ● **Reek** is also a noun. □ *...the reek of dead fish.* ◻ V-I If you say that something **reeks** of unpleasant ideas, feelings, or practices, you disapprove of it because it involves those ideas, feelings, or practices. □ *The whole thing reeks of stupidity.* [from Old English]

**reel** /ri̱l/ (**reels, reeling, reeled**) ◼ N-COUNT A **reel** is a cylindrical object around which you wrap something such as movie film, magnetic tape, or fishing line. □ *...a 30-meter reel of cable.*

◻ V-I If someone **reels**, they move about in an unsteady way as if they are going to fall. □ *She was reeling with tiredness.* ◼ V-I If you **are reeling** from a shock, you are feeling extremely surprised or upset because of it. □ *I'm still reeling from the shock of his death.* ◼ V-I If you say that your brain or your mind **is reeling**, you mean that you are very confused because you have too many things to think about. [from Old English]
▸ **reel off** PHR-VERB If you **reel off** information, you repeat it from memory quickly and easily. □ *She reeled off a list of things she was going to do.*

**re|elect** /ri̱ɪlɛkt/ (**reelects, reelecting, reelected**) also **re-elect** V-T When someone such as a politician or an official who has been elected **is reelected**, they win another election and are therefore able to continue in their position. □ *He was reelected five times.* ● **re|elec|tion** /ri̱ɪlɛkʃⁿn/ N-UNCOUNT □ *He will run for reelection next year.* [from Latin]

**re|evalu|ate** /ri̱ɪvæljueɪt/ (**reevaluates, reevaluating, reevaluated**) V-T If you **reevaluate** something or someone, you consider them again in order to reassess your opinion of them. □ *This is the time to reevaluate the whole issue.* ● **re|evalu|ation** /ri̱ɪvæljueɪʃⁿn/ (**reevaluations**) N-VAR □ *...a period of reevaluation.* [from French]

**re|ex|am|ine** /ri̱ɪgzæmɪn/ (**reexamines, reexamining, reexamined**) also **re-examine** V-T If a person or group of people **reexamine** their ideas, beliefs, or attitudes, they think about them carefully because they are no longer sure if they are correct. □ *My illness made me reexamine my life.* ● **re|ex|ami|na|tion** /ri̱ɪgzæmɪneɪʃⁿn/ (**reexaminations**) N-VAR □ *...a reexamination of the rules.* [from Old French]

**re|fer** /rɪfɜr/ (**refers, referring, referred**) ◼ V-I If you **refer to** a particular subject or person, you mention them. □ *He referred to his trip to Canada.* ● **refer|ence** /rɛfərəns, rɛfrəns/ N-VAR □ *He made no reference to any agreement.* ◻ V-I If a word **refers to** a particular thing, situation, or idea, it describes it. □ *The word "man" refers most clearly to an adult male.* ◼ V-T If a person who is ill **is referred to** a hospital or a specialist, they are sent there by a doctor in order to be treated. □ *She was referred to the hospital by her doctor.* ◼ V-T If you **refer** a task or a problem **to** a person or an organization, you formally tell them about it, so that they can deal with it. □ *He could refer the matter to the high court.* ◼ V-I If you **refer to** a book or other source of information, you look at it in order to find something out. □ *He referred briefly to his notebook.* ● **refer|ence** N-UNCOUNT □ *Keep this book in a safe place for reference.* [from Latin]

**ref|eree** /rɛfəri̱/ (**referees, refereeing, refereed**) ◼ N-COUNT The **referee** is the official who controls a sports event such as a football game or a boxing match. ◻ V-I When someone **referees** a sports event, they act as referee. □ *Vautrot refereed in two soccer games.* [from Latin]
→ see **basketball, football, tennis**

referee

**ref|er|ence** /rɛfərəns, rɛfrəns/ (**references**) ◼ ADJ **Reference** books are ones that you look at when you need specific information or facts about a subject. **2** N-COUNT A **reference** is something such as a number or a name that tells you where you can obtain the information. □ ...*the reference number on the form.* **3** N-COUNT A **reference** is a letter that is written by someone who knows you and which describes your character and abilities. □ *The firm gave her a reference.* **4** PHRASE You use **with reference to** or **in reference to** in order to indicate what something relates to. □ *I am writing with reference to your article on trees.* [from Latin]

**ref|er|ence point** (**reference points**) N-COUNT A **reference point** is a fixed point, for example on the surface of the Earth, that is used in order to measure the motion of a moving object.

**ref|er|en|dum** /rɛfərɛndəm/ (**referendums** or **referenda** /rɛfərɛndə/) N-COUNT A **referendum** is a vote in which all the people in a country are asked whether they agree or disagree with a particular policy. □ *The country held a referendum on independence.* [from Latin]

**re|fer|ral** /rɪfɜrəl/ (**referrals**) N-VAR **Referral** is the act of officially sending someone to a person or authority that is qualified to deal with them. □ ...*an increase in referrals to the hospital.* [from Latin]

**re|fill** (**refills, refilling, refilled**)

The verb is pronounced /rifɪl/. The noun is pronounced /rifɪl/.

V-T If you **refill** something, you fill it again after it has been emptied. □ *I refilled our glasses.* ● **Refill** is also a noun. [INFORMAL] □ *Max held out his cup for a refill.* [from Old English]

**re|fine** /rɪfaɪn/ (**refines, refining, refined**) **1** V-T When a substance **is refined**, it is made pure by having all other substances removed from it. □ *Oil is refined to remove impurities.* ● **re|fin|ing** N-UNCOUNT □ ...*oil refining.* **2** V-T If something such as a process, theory, or machine **is refined**, it is improved by having small changes made to it. □ *Medical techniques are constantly being refined.* ● **re|fine|ment** (**refinements**) N-VAR □ *Older cars lack the latest safety refinements.*
→ see **industry, sugar**

**re|fined** /rɪfaɪnd/ ADJ If you say that someone is **refined**, you mean that they are very polite and have good manners and good taste.

**re|fin|ery** /rɪfaɪnəri/ (**refineries**) N-COUNT A **refinery** is a factory where a substance such as oil or sugar is refined. □ ...*an oil refinery.*
→ see **mineral, oil**

**re|fit** (**refits, refitting, refitted**)

The verb is pronounced /rifɪt/. The noun is pronounced /rifɪt/.

V-T When a ship **is refitted**, it is repaired or is given new parts, equipment, or furniture. ● **Refit** is also a noun. □ *The ship finished a refit last year.* [from Middle Dutch]

**re|flect** /rɪflɛkt/ (**reflects, reflecting, reflected**) **1** V-T If something **reflects** an attitude or situation, it shows that the attitude or situation exists. □ *The agreement was changed to reflect the views of Russia and France.* **2** V-T/V-I When light, heat, or other rays **reflect** off a surface or when a surface **reflects** them, they are sent back from the surface and do not pass through it. □ *The sun reflected off the snow-covered mountains.* **3** V-T When something **is reflected** in a mirror or in water, you can see its image in the mirror or in the water. □ *His face was reflected in the mirror.* **4** V-I When you **reflect on** something, you think deeply about it. □ *We need some time to reflect.* **5** V-I If an action or situation **reflects** in a particular way on someone or something, it gives people a good or bad impression of them. □ *It will reflect badly on me if I don't tell the police.* [from Latin]
→ see **echo, telescope**

**re|flec|tion** /rɪflɛkʃən/ (**reflections**) **1** N-COUNT A **reflection** is an image that you can see in a mirror or in glass or water. □ *Meg stared at her reflection in the mirror.*

**2** N-COUNT If you say that something is a **reflection of** a particular person's attitude or of a situation, you mean that it shows that attitude or situation exists. □ *His drawings are a reflection of his own unhappiness.* **3** N-SING If something is a **reflection** or a **sad reflection on** a

reflection

person or thing, it gives a bad impression of them. □ *The increase in crime is a sad reflection on society.* **4** N-UNCOUNT **Reflection** is careful thought about a particular subject. □ *After days of reflection she decided to write to him.* **5** N-COUNT A **reflection** produces a mirror image of a geometric figure. For example, a **reflection** of the letter "d" would look like the letter "b." **6** N-UNCOUNT **Reflection** is the process by which light and heat are sent back from a surface and do not pass through it. **7** N-SING The **law of reflection** is a principle in physics which states that, when a light wave strikes a flat surface, it is returned at the same angle at which it struck the surface. [TECHNICAL] [from Latin]
→ see **echo**

**re|flec|tive** /rɪflɛktɪv/ **1** ADJ If you are **reflective**, you are thinking deeply about something. [WRITTEN] □ *I was in a reflective mood.* **2** ADJ If something is **reflective of** a particular situation or attitude, it shows that situation or attitude exists. □ *The government's attitude is not reflective of public opinion.* **3** ADJ A **reflective** surface or material sends back light or heat. [FORMAL] □ *The pans have a reflective base.* [from Latin]

**re|flex** /riflɛks/ (**reflexes**) **1** N-COUNT A **reflex** or a **reflex action** is a normal, uncontrollable reaction of your body to something that you feel, see, or experience. □ *Blushing is a reflex action.* **2** N-PLURAL Your **reflexes** refer to your ability to react quickly

r

with your body when something unexpected happens. □ …the reflexes of an athlete. [from Latin]

**re|flex|ive pro|noun** (reflexive pronouns) N-COUNT A **reflexive pronoun** is a pronoun such as "myself" which refers back to the subject of a sentence or clause.

**re|flex|ive verb** (reflexive verbs) N-COUNT A **reflexive verb** is a transitive verb whose subject and object always refer to the same person or thing, so the object is always a reflexive pronoun. An example is "to enjoy yourself."

**re|form** /rɪfɔrm/ (reforms, reforming, reformed) **1** N-VAR **Reform** consists of changes and improvements to a law, social system, or institution. A **reform** is an instance of such a change or improvement. □ …a program of economic reform. **2** V-T If someone **reforms** something such as a law, social system, or institution, they change or improve it. □ …his plans to reform the country's economy. ● **re|form|er** (reformers) N-COUNT □ …prison reformers. **3** V-T/V-I When someone **reforms** or when something **reforms** them, they stop doing things that society does not approve of. □ After his time in prison, James promised to reform. ● **re|formed** ADJ □ …a reformed criminal. [from Old French]

---

**Word Partnership** Use *reform* with :

| | |
|---|---|
| ADJ. | **economic** reform, **political** reform **1** |
| N. | **education** reform, **election** reform, **health care** reform, reform **movement**, **party** reform, **prison** reform, **tax** reform **1** |

---

**re|form school** (reform schools) N-VAR A **reform school** is a prison for young criminals who are not old enough to be sent to ordinary prisons.

**re|fract** /rɪfrækt/ (refracts, refracting, refracted) V-T/V-I When a ray of light or a sound wave **refracts** or **is refracted**, the path it follows bends at a particular point, for example when it enters water or glass. □ As we age, the lenses of the eyes thicken, and thus refract light differently. □ …surfaces that cause the light to reflect and refract. ● **re|frac|tion** /rɪfrækʃⁿn/ N-UNCOUNT □ …the refraction of the light on the dancing waves. [from Latin]

**re|fract|ing tele|scope** (refracting telescopes) N-COUNT A **refracting telescope** is a telescope that uses lenses to focus light rays and produce a clear image.

**re|frain** /rɪfreɪn/ (refrains, refraining, refrained) **1** V-I If you **refrain from** doing something, you deliberately do not do it. □ Mrs. Hardie refrained from making any comment. **2** N-COUNT A **refrain** is a short, simple part of a song, which is repeated many times. □ …a refrain from an old song. [from Latin]

**re|fresh** /rɪfrɛʃ/ (refreshes, refreshing, refreshed) **1** V-T If something **refreshes** you when you are hot, tired, or thirsty, it makes you feel cooler or more energetic. □ The lotion cools and refreshes the skin. ● **re|freshed** ADJ □ He awoke feeling completely refreshed. ● **re|fresh|ing** ADJ □ …refreshing drinks. **2** V-T If someone **refreshes** your memory, they tell you something that you had forgotten. □ Can you refresh my memory and tell me what I need to do? [from Old French]

**re|fresh|ing** /rɪfrɛʃɪŋ/ ADJ You say that something is **refreshing** when it is pleasantly different from what you are used to. □ It's refreshing to hear somebody speaking so honestly. ● **re|fresh|ing|ly** ADV □ He was refreshingly honest. [from Old French]

**re|fresh|ment** /rɪfrɛʃmənt/ (refreshments) **1** N-PLURAL **Refreshments** are drinks and small amounts of food that are provided, for example, during a meeting or a trip. □ Refreshments will be provided. **2** N-UNCOUNT You can refer to food and drink as **refreshment**. [FORMAL] □ May I offer you some refreshment? [from Old French]

**re|fried beans** /rifraɪd binz/ N-PLURAL **Refried beans** are beans that have been boiled and crushed before being fried, used especially in Mexican cooking.

**re|frig|er|ate** /rɪfrɪdʒəreɪt/ (refrigerates, refrigerating, refrigerated) V-T If you **refrigerate** food, you make it cold by putting it in a refrigerator. □ Refrigerate the bread dough overnight. [from Latin]
→ see **dairy**

**re|frig|era|tor** /rɪfrɪdʒəreɪtər/ (refrigerators) N-COUNT A **refrigerator** is a large container which is kept cool inside, usually by electricity, so that the food and drink in it stays fresh. [from Latin]

---

**Word Link** re ≈ back, again : reflect, refuel, restate

---

**re|fu|el** /rifyuəl/ (refuels, refueling or refuelling, refueled or refuelled) V-T/V-I When an aircraft or other vehicle **refuels** or when someone **refuels** it, it is filled with more fuel so that it can continue its journey. ● **re|fu|el|ing** N-UNCOUNT □ …refueling of vehicles. [from Old French]

**ref|uge** /rɛfyudʒ/ (refuges) **1** N-UNCOUNT If you take **refuge** somewhere, you try to protect yourself from physical harm by going there. □ They took refuge in a shelter. **2** N-COUNT A **refuge** is a place where you go for safety and protection. □ …a refuge for homeless people. [from Old French]

**refu|gee** /rɛfyudʒi/ (refugees) N-COUNT **Refugees** are people who have been forced to leave their homes or their country, either because there is a war there or because of their political or religious beliefs. [from Old French]

**re|fund** /rifʌnd/ (refunds, refunding, refunded)

The noun is pronounced /rifʌnd/. The verb is pronounced /rɪfʌnd/.

**1** N-COUNT A **refund** is a sum of money that is returned to you, for example because you have paid too much or because you have returned goods to a store. □ He took the boots back to the store and asked for a refund. **2** V-T If someone **refunds** your money, they return it to you, for example because you have paid too much or because you have returned goods to a store. [from Latin]

---

**Thesaurus** refund Also look up :

| | |
|---|---|
| N. | payment, reimbursement **1** |
| V. | give back, pay back, reimburse **2** |

---

**re|fur|bish** /rifɜrbɪʃ/ (refurbishes, refurbishing, refurbished) V-T To **refurbish** a building or room means to clean it and decorate it and make it more attractive or better equipped. □ We refurbished the offices. • re|fur|bish|ment (refurbishments) N-VAR ❑ The restaurant is closed for refurbishment.

re|fus|al /rɪfyuˈzᵊl/ (refusals) N-VAR Someone's refusal to do something is the fact of them showing or saying that they will not do it, allow it, or accept it. ❑ …her refusal to accept change. [from Old French]

re|fuse (refuses, refusing, refused)

> The verb is pronounced /rɪfyuz/. The noun is pronounced /rɛfyus/ and is hyphenated ref|use.

■ V-I If you refuse to do something, you deliberately do not do it, or you say firmly that you will not do it. ❑ He refused to comment. ❑ I couldn't refuse, could I? ■ V-T If someone refuses you something, they do not give it to you or do not allow you to have it. ❑ The United States has refused him a visa. ■ V-T If you refuse something that is offered to you, you do not accept it. ❑ The patient has the right to refuse treatment. ■ N-UNCOUNT Refuse consists of the trash and all the things that are not wanted in a house, store, or factory, and that are regularly thrown away. ❑ …a weekly collection of refuse. [from Old French]
→ see dump

**Thesaurus** refuse Also look up :

v. decline, reject, turn down;
(ant.) accept ■ ■
N. garbage, rubbish, trash ■

**Word Partnership** Use refuse with :

v. refuse to answer, refuse to cooperate,
refuse to go, refuse to participate,
refuse to pay ■
refuse to allow, refuse to give ■ ■
refuse to accept ■ ■

re|fute /rɪfyut/ (refutes, refuting, refuted) ■ V-T If you refute an argument, accusation, or theory, you prove that it is wrong. [FORMAL] ❑ It was the kind of rumor that is impossible to refute. ■ V-T If you refute an argument or accusation, you say that it is not true. [FORMAL] ❑ He angrily refuted the accusation. [from Latin]

re|gain /rɪgeɪn/ (regains, regaining, regained) V-T If you regain something that you have lost, you get it back again. ❑ Troops have regained control of the city. [from Old French]

re|gal /rigᵊl/ ADJ If you describe something as regal, you mean that it is suitable for a king or queen, because it is very impressive or beautiful. ❑ …regal style. [from Latin]

re|gard /rɪgɑrd/ (regards, regarding, regarded) ■ V-T If you regard someone or something as being a particular thing or as having a particular quality, you believe that they are that thing or have that quality. ❑ He was regarded as the most successful president of modern times. ■ V-T If you regard something or someone with a feeling such as dislike or respect, you have that feeling about them. ❑ He regarded her with suspicion. ■ N-UNCOUNT If you have regard for someone or something, you respect them. ❑ I have a very high regard for him and his achievements. ■ N-PLURAL Regards are greetings. You use regards in expressions such as best regards and with kind regards as a way of expressing friendly feelings

toward someone. ❑ Give my regards to your family. ■ PHRASE You can use as regards to indicate the subject that is being talked or written about. ❑ As regards the future of the business, we are discussing a deal. ■ PHRASE You can use with regard to or in regard to to indicate the subject that is being talked or written about. ❑ …his opinions with regard to the law. [from Old French]

re|gard|ing /rɪgɑrdɪŋ/ PREP You can use regarding to indicate the subject that is being talked or written about. ❑ He refused to give any information regarding the man's financial situation. [from Old French]

re|gard|less /rɪgɑrdlɪs/ ■ PHRASE If something happens regardless of something else, it is not affected or influenced at all by that other thing. ❑ The organization helps anyone regardless of their age. ■ ADV If you say that someone did something regardless, you mean that they did it even though there were problems or factors that could have stopped them. ❑ Her knee was painful but she continued walking regardless. [from Old French]

re|gat|ta /rɪgætə, -gɑtə/ (regattas) N-COUNT A regatta is a sports event consisting of races between yachts or other boats. [from Italian Venetian]

re|gen|er|ate /rɪdʒɛnəreɪt/ (regenerates, regenerating, regenerated) V-T To regenerate something that has been declining means to develop and improve it to make it more active or successful. ❑ The government is trying to regenerate inner-city areas. • re|gen|era|tion /rɪdʒɛnəreɪʃᵊn/ N-UNCOUNT ❑ …the economic regeneration of the area. [from Latin]

reg|gae /rɛgeɪ/ N-UNCOUNT Reggae is a kind of West Indian popular music with a very strong beat. [from West Indian]

re|gime /reʒim, reɪ-/ (regimes) N-COUNT If you refer to a government or system of running a country as a regime, you are critical of it because you think it is not democratic and uses unacceptable methods. ❑ …the collapse of the regime. [from French]

regi|ment /rɛdʒɪmənt/ (regiments) N-COUNT A regiment is a large group of soldiers that is commanded by a colonel. • regi|men|tal /rɛdʒɪmɛntᵊl/ ADJ ❑ …a regimental commander. [from Old French]

re|gion /ridʒᵊn/ (regions) ■ N-COUNT A region is an area of a country or of the world. ❑ …the coastal region of South Carolina. • re|gion|al ADJ ❑ …Hawaiian regional cooking. ■ PHRASE You say in the region of to indicate that an amount that you are stating is approximate. ❑ The plan will cost in the region of six million dollars. [from Latin]

reg|is|ter /rɛdʒɪstər/ (registers, registering, registered) ■ N-COUNT A register is an official list or record of people or things. ❑ …registers of births, deaths, and marriages. ■ V-T/V-I If you register, or register to do something, you put your name on an official list, in order to be able to do that thing. ❑ Thousands of people registered to vote. ❑ He is not registered to practice law in Virginia. ■ V-T If you register something, you have it recorded on an official list. ❑ The boy's mother never registered his birth. ■ V-T/V-I When something registers on a scale or measuring instrument, it shows a particular value. You can also say that something

r

registers a certain amount **on** a scale or measuring instrument. ❏ *The earthquake registered 5.7 on the Richter scale.* **5** V-T If you **register** your feelings or opinions about something, you do something that makes them clear to other people. ❏ *Voters registered their dissatisfaction with the government.* [from Medieval Latin]

| Word Partnership | Use *register* with : |
|---|---|
| N. | **voters** register **2** |
| V. | register **to vote 2** |

**reg|is|tered nurse** (**registered nurses**) N-COUNT A **registered nurse** is someone who is qualified to work as a nurse.

**reg|is|trar** /rέdʒɪstrɑr/ (**registrars**) N-COUNT A **registrar** is an administrative official in a college or university who is responsible for student records. [from Medieval Latin]

**reg|is|tra|tion** /rὲdʒɪstreɪʃᵊn/ N-UNCOUNT The **registration** of something is the recording of it in an official list. ❏ *...voter registration.* [from Medieval Latin]

**reg|is|try** /rέdʒɪstri/ (**registries**) N-COUNT A **registry** is a collection of all the official records relating to something, or the place where they are kept. ❏ *...the official registry of prisoners.* [from Medieval Latin]

**re|gress** /rɪgrέs/ (**regresses, regressing, regressed**) V-I When people or things **regress**, they return to an earlier and less advanced stage of development. [FORMAL] ❏ *...if your child regresses to babyish behavior.* ● **re|gres|sion** /rɪgrέʃᵊn/ (**regressions**) N-VAR ❏ *...regression in a student's learning process.* [from Latin]

**re|gret** /rɪgrέt/ (**regrets, regretting, regretted**) **1** V-T If you **regret** something that you have done, you wish that you had not done it. ❏ *I lied to him, and I've regretted it ever since.* ❏ *Ellis regretted that he had asked the question.* **2** N-VAR **Regret** is a feeling of sadness or disappointment, which is caused by something that has happened or something that you have done or not done. ❏ *He had no regrets about leaving.* **3** V-T You use **regret** in expressions such as **I regret to say** or **I regret to inform you** to show that you are sorry about something. [from Old French]

| Word Partnership | Use *regret* with : |
|---|---|
| N. | regret **a decision**, regret **a loss 1** |
| V. | **come to** regret **1** |
| | **express** regret **2** |

**re|gret|table** /rɪgrέtəbᵊl/ ADJ You describe something as **regrettable** when you think that it is bad and that it should not happen or have happened. [FORMAL] ❏ *...a regrettable mistake.* ● **re|gret|tably** ADV ❏ *Regrettably we couldn't find the man.* [from Old French]

**re|group** /rigrʌ́p/ (**regroups, regrouping, regrouped**) V-T/V-I When people, especially soldiers, **regroup**, or when someone **regroups** them, they form an organized group again, in order to continue fighting. ❏ *The rebel army has regrouped and reorganized.* [from French]

**regu|lar** /rέgyələr/ (**regulars**) **1** ADJ **Regular** events have equal amounts of time between them, so that they happen, for example, at the same time each day or each week. ❏ *Get regular exercise.* ● **regu|lar|ly** ADV ❏ *He writes regularly for the magazine.* ● **regu|lar|ity** N-UNCOUNT ❏ *...the regularity of the payments.* **2** ADJ **Regular** events happen often. ❏ *We meet on a regular basis.* ● **regu|lar|ly** ADV ❏ *...if you regularly take snacks instead of eating properly.* ● **regu|lar|ity** N-UNCOUNT ❏ *Job losses were announced with regularity.* **3** ADJ If you are, for example, a **regular** customer at a store or a **regular** visitor to a place, you go there often. ❏ *She was a regular visitor to the museum.* **4** N-COUNT The **regulars** at a place or on a team are the people who often go to the place or are often on the team. ❏ *...regulars at the club.* **5** ADJ **Regular** means normal or ordinary. ❏ *They were just regular trucks.* **6** ADJ If something has a **regular** shape, both halves are the same and it has straight edges or a smooth outline. ❏ *...a man of average height with regular features.* **7** ADJ In grammar, a **regular** verb, noun, or adjective inflects in the same way as most verbs, nouns, or adjectives in the language. [from Old French]

| Word Partnership | Use *regular* with : |
|---|---|
| N. | regular **basis**, regular **checkups**, regular **exercise**, regular **meetings**, regular **schedule**, regular **visits 1 2** regular **customer**, regular **visitor 3** regular **coffee**, regular **guy**, regular **hours**, regular, regular **season 5** regular **verbs 7** |

**regu|late** /rέgyəleɪt/ (**regulates, regulating, regulated**) V-T To **regulate** an activity or process means to control it, especially by means of rules. ❏ *The plan will regulate competition among insurance companies.* [from Late Latin]

**regu|la|tion** /rέgyəleɪʃᵊn/ (**regulations**) N-COUNT **Regulations** are rules made by a government or other authority in order to control the way something is done or the way people behave. ❏ *...new safety regulations.* [from Late Latin]
→ see **factory**

**regu|la|tor** /rέgyəleɪtər/ (**regulators**) N-COUNT A **regulator** is a person or organization appointed by a government to regulate an area of activity such as banking or industry. ❏ *Regulators took control of the $22 billion banking company on Sunday.* ● **regu|la|tory** /rέgyələtɔri/ ADJ ❏ *...the U.S.'s financial regulatory system.* [from Late Latin]

**re|ha|bili|tate** /rihəbɪlɪteɪt/ (**rehabilitates, rehabilitating, rehabilitated**) V-T To **rehabilitate** someone who has been ill or in prison means to help them to live a normal life again. ● **re|ha|bili|ta|tion** /rihəbɪlɪteɪʃᵊn/ N-UNCOUNT ❏ *...the rehabilitation of prisoners.* [from Medieval Latin]

**re|hears|al** /rɪhɜ́rsᵊl/ (**rehearsals**) **1** N-VAR A **rehearsal** of a play, dance, or piece of music is a practice of it in preparation for a performance. ❏ *...rehearsals for the concert.* [from Old French] **2** → see also **dress rehearsal**
→ see **theater**

**re|hearse** /rɪhɜ́rs/ (**rehearses, rehearsing, rehearsed**) V-T/V-I When people **rehearse** a play, dance, or piece of music, they practice it. ❏ *The actors are rehearsing a play.* ❏ *Thousands of people are rehearsing for the ceremony.* [from Old French]

R

**reign** /reɪn/ (**reigns, reigning, reigned**) ◼ V-I If you say, for example, that silence **reigns** in a place or confusion **reigns** in a situation, you mean that the place is silent or the situation is confused. [WRITTEN] ◼ V-I When a king or queen **reigns**, he or she rules a country. ❑ ...*Henry II, who reigned in England from 1154 to 1189.* ● **Reign** is also a noun. ❑ ...*Queen Victoria's reign.* [from Old French]

**re|im|burse** /riːɪmbɜrs/ (**reimburses, reimbursing, reimbursed**) V-T If you **reimburse** someone **for** something, you pay them back the money that they have spent or lost because of it. [FORMAL] ❑ *I'll reimburse you for any expenses you have.* ● **re|im|burse|ment** (**reimbursements**) N-VAR ❑ *She wants reimbursement for medical expenses.* [from Medieval Latin]

**rein** /reɪn/ (**reins, reining, reined**) ◼ N-PLURAL **Reins** are the thin leather straps attached around a horse's neck which are used to control the horse. ❑ *She held the reins while the horse pulled.* ◼ PHRASE If you **give free rein to** someone, you give them a lot of freedom to do what they want. ❑ *Horrigan was given free rein to run the company.* [from Old French] → see **horse**

▸ **rein in** PHR-VERB To **rein in** something means to control it. ❑ *We need to rein in spending.*

**re|incar|na|tion** /riːɪŋkɑrneɪʃⁿn/ (**reincarnations**) ◼ N-UNCOUNT If you believe in **reincarnation**, you believe that people are born again as different people or animals after they die. ◼ N-COUNT A **reincarnation** is a person or animal who is believed to be the spirit of a dead person. ❑ *People believed the little girl was the reincarnation of her grandmother.* [from French]

**rein|deer** /reɪndɪər/ (**reindeer**) N-COUNT A **reindeer** is a deer with large horns that lives in northern areas of Europe, Asia, and America. [from Old Norse]

**re|inforce** /riːɪnfɔrs/ (**reinforces, reinforcing, reinforced**) ◼ V-T If something **reinforces** a feeling, situation, or process, it makes it stronger. ❑ *This reinforced our determination to deal with the problem.* ● **re|inforce|ment** (**reinforcements**) N-VAR ❑ ...*the reinforcement of peace.* ◼ V-T To **reinforce** an object means to make it stronger and harder. ❑ *They had to reinforce the floor with concrete.* [from French]

**re|inforce|ments** /riːɪnfɔrsmənts/ N-PLURAL **Reinforcements** are soldiers or police officers who are sent to join an army or group of police in order to make it stronger. ❑ *The police received 1,700 reinforcements from around the country.* [from French]

**re|install** /riːɪnstɔl/ (**reinstalls, reinstalling, reinstalled**) V-T If you **reinstall** something such as software on your computer, you set it up again, usually because you have been having problems with it. ❑ *You need to reinstall all the software.* [from Medieval Latin]

**re|instate** /riːɪnsteɪt/ (**reinstates, reinstating, reinstated**) V-T If you **reinstate** someone, you give them back a job or position that was taken away from them. ❑ *The governor will reinstate the five workers who were fired.* ● **re|instate|ment** N-UNCOUNT ❑ *The former officers will now apply for reinstatement.*

**re|it|er|ate** /riːɪtəreɪt/ (**reiterates, reiterating, reiterated**) V-T If you **reiterate** something, you say it again to emphasize it. [FORMAL] ❑ *He reiterated his opposition to the plan.* [from Latin]

**re|ject** (**rejects, rejecting, rejected**)

> The verb is pronounced /rɪdʒɛkt/. The noun is pronounced /riːdʒɛkt/.

◼ V-T If you **reject** something such as a proposal or a request, you do not accept it or agree to it. ❑ *The president rejected the offer.* ● **re|jec|tion** /rɪdʒɛkʃⁿn/ (**rejections**) N-VAR ❑ ...*his rejection of our values.* ◼ V-T If someone **is rejected** for a job or course of study, it is not offered to them. ❑ *He was rejected by another university.* ● **re|jec|tion** N-COUNT ❑ *Be prepared for lots of rejections before you get a job.* ◼ V-T If someone **rejects** another person who expects affection from them, they are cold and unfriendly toward them. ❑ ...*people who were rejected by their parents.* ● **re|jec|tion** N-VAR ❑ ...*feelings of rejection and hurt.* ◼ N-COUNT A **reject** is a product that has not been accepted for use or sale, because there is something wrong with it. ❑ *The shirt is a reject — all the buttons are missing.* [from Latin]

| Word Partnership | Use *reject* with : |
| --- | --- |
| N. | reject **an application**, reject **an idea**, reject **an offer**, reject **a plan**, reject **a proposal**, **voters** reject ◼ |
| V. | **vote to** reject ◼ |

**re|joice** /rɪdʒɔɪs/ (**rejoices, rejoicing, rejoiced**) V-I If you **rejoice**, you are very pleased about something and you show it in your behavior. ❑ *We rejoiced in the victory.* ● **re|joic|ing** N-UNCOUNT ❑ *There was much rejoicing at the news.* [from Old French]

**re|ju|venate** /rɪdʒuvəneɪt/ (**rejuvenates, rejuvenating, rejuvenated**) V-T If something **rejuvenates** you, it makes you feel or look young again. ❑ *The Italian climate rejuvenated him.* [from Latin]

**re|kin|dle** /riːkɪndⁿl/ (**rekindles, rekindling, rekindled**) V-T If something **rekindles** an interest, feeling, or thought that you used to have, it makes you think about it or feel it again. ❑ *The article rekindled many memories.*

**re|lapse** /rɪlæps/ (**relapses, relapsing, relapsed**)

> The noun can be pronounced /rɪlæps/ or /riːlæps/.

◼ V-I If you say that someone **relapses into** a way of behaving that is undesirable, you mean that they start to behave in that way again. ❑ *"I wish I could do it," said Phil, relapsing into his usual misery.* ● **Relapse** is also a noun. ❑ ...*a relapse into the problems of the last century.* ◼ V-I If a sick person **relapses**, their health suddenly gets worse after it had been improving. ● **Relapse** is also a noun. ❑ *She was well for two years but had a relapse in January.* [from Latin]

**re|late** /rɪleɪt/ (**relates, relating, related**) ◼ V-I If something **relates to** a particular subject, it concerns that subject. ❑ ...*information relating to the crime.* ◼ V-RECIP The way that two things **relate**, or the way that one thing **relates to** another, is the sort of connection that exists between them. ❑ *He tried to relate new ideas to his past experiences.* ● **re|lat|ed** ADJ ❑ *Crime and poverty are closely related.* ◼ V-RECIP If you can **relate to** someone, you can understand how they feel or behave so that you

**r**

are able to communicate with them or deal with them easily. ❏ *He is unable to relate to other people.* [from Latin]

**re|lat|ed** /rɪleɪtɪd/ ADJ People who are **related** belong to the same family. ❏ *The boys have the same last name but are not related.* [from Latin]

**re|la|tion** /rɪleɪʃ°n/ (**relations**) **1** N-COUNT **Relations** between people, groups, or countries are contacts between them and the way in which they behave toward each other. ❏ *The country has good relations with Israel.* **2** → see also **industrial relations, public relations, race relations** **3** N-COUNT The **relation** of one thing to another is the connection between them. ❏ *…the relation of his job to his lifestyle.* **4** N-COUNT Your **relations** are the members of your family. ❏ *…visits to friends and relations.* **5** PHRASE You can talk about something **in relation to** something else when you want to compare the size, condition, or position of the two things. ❏ *The cost was small in relation to his salary.* [from Latin]

**re|la|tion|ship** /rɪleɪʃ°nʃɪp/ (**relationships**) **1** N-COUNT The **relationship** between two people or groups is the way in which they feel and behave toward each other. ❏ *…the friendly relationship between France and Britain.* **2** N-COUNT A **relationship** is a close friendship between two people, especially one involving romantic or sexual feelings. ❏ *She felt their relationship was developing too quickly.* **3** N-COUNT The **relationship** between two things is the way in which they are connected. ❏ *…a relationship between diet and cancer.* **4** N-COUNT The **relationship** between an organism and its environment is the way that the organism and its environment interact and the effect they have on each other. [from Latin]

**rela|tive** /rɛlətɪv/ (**relatives**) **1** N-COUNT Your **relatives** are the members of your family. ❏ *Ask a relative to look after the children.* **2** ADJ You use **relative** to say that something is true to a certain degree, especially when compared with other things of the same kind. ❏ *The fighting started again after a period of relative calm.* **3** ADJ You use **relative** when you are comparing the quality or size of two things. ❏ *…the relative advantages of New York and Washington as places to live.* ● **rela|tive|ly** ADV ❏ *The amount of money that you need is relatively small.* **4** PHRASE **Relative to** something means with reference to it or in comparison with it. ❏ *Japanese interest rates rose relative to France's.* [from Late Latin]

**Word Partnership** Use *relative* with :

| | |
|---|---|
| ADJ. | **close** relative, **distant** relative **1** |
| N. | **friend and** relative **1** |
| | relative **calm**, relative **ease**, relative **safety**, relative **stability** **2** |

**rela|tive clause** (**relative clauses**) N-COUNT A **relative clause** is a subordinate clause that gives information about a person or thing. Relative clauses come after a noun or pronoun and often begin with "who," "which," or "that."

**rela|tive dat|ing** N-UNCOUNT **Relative dating** is a technique used by archaeologists to determine whether an object such as a fossil is older or younger than other objects.

**rela|tive hu|mid|ity** (**relative humidities**) N-VAR **Relative humidity** is a measure of the amount of water vapor contained in the air,

compared with the maximum amount of water vapor that the air is able to hold.

**rela|tive pro|noun** (**relative pronouns**) N-COUNT A **relative pronoun** is a word such as "who," "that," or "which" that is used to introduce a relative clause.

**Word Link** *lax ≈ allowing, loosening : lax, laxative, relax*

**re|lax** /rɪlæks/ (**relaxes, relaxing, relaxed**) **1** V-T/V-I If you **relax** or if something **relaxes** you, you feel more calm and less worried or tense. ❏ *I should relax and stop worrying.* ● **re|laxa|tion** /rɪlækseɪ°ʃn/ N-UNCOUNT ❏ *…relaxation techniques.* ● **re|laxed** ADJ ❏ *The atmosphere at lunch was relaxed.* ● **re|lax|ing** ADJ ❏ *I find cooking very relaxing.* **2** V-T/V-I When a part of your body **relaxes**, or when you **relax** it, it becomes less stiff or firm. ❏ *Have a massage to relax your muscles.* **3** V-T If you **relax** your grip or hold on something, you hold it less tightly than before. **4** V-T/V-I If you **relax** a rule or your control over something, or if it **relaxes**, it becomes less firm or strong. ❏ *The rules have relaxed in recent years.* [from Latin] **5** → see also **relaxed, relaxing** → see **muscle**

**Thesaurus** *relax* Also look up :

| | |
|---|---|
| V. | calm down, rest; (*ant.*) easy, unwind **2** loosen **3** **4** |

**Word Partnership** Use *relax* with :

| | |
|---|---|
| V. | **sit back and** relax **1** **begin to** relax, **try to** relax **1** **2** |
| N. | **time to** relax **1** relax *your* **body, muscles** relax **2** |

**re|lay** (**relays, relaying, relayed**)

The noun is pronounced /riːleɪ/. The verb is pronounced /rɪleɪ/.

**1** N-COUNT A **relay** or a **relay race** is a race between two or more teams in which each member of the team runs or swims one section of the race. ❏ *Britain's chances of winning the relay were good.* **2** V-T To **relay** television or radio signals means to send them or broadcast them. ❏ *The satellite relays television programs.* [from Old French]

**re|lease** /rɪliːs/ (**releases, releasing, released**) **1** V-T If a person or animal **is released**, they are set free. ❏ *He was released from prison the next day.* **2** V-T If someone or something **releases** you **from** a duty, task, or feeling, they free you from it. [FORMAL] ❏ *Finally the record company released him from his contract.* ● **Release** is also a noun. ❏ *…release from stress.* **3** V-T If someone in authority **releases** something such as a document or information, they make it available. ❏ *Police are not releasing any more details yet.* ● **Release** is also a noun. ❏ *…the release of the names of those who died.* **4** V-T If you **release** someone or something, you stop holding them. [FORMAL] ❏ *He released her hand and they walked on in silence.* **5** V-T When a form of energy or a substance such as a gas **is released** from something, it enters the surrounding atmosphere or area. ❏ *…a weapon that releases poisonous gas.* ● **Release** is also a noun. ❏ *…the release of radioactive materials into the environment.* **6** V-T When an entertainer or company **releases**

a new CD, DVD, or movie, it becomes available so that people can buy it or see it. ❑ *He is releasing a CD of love songs.* ☑ N-COUNT A new **release** is a new CD, DVD, or movie that has just become available for people to buy or see. ❑ *A movie — generally a new release — is shown each night.* [from Old French]
☐ → see also **press release**

**re|le|gate** /rɛlɪgeɪt/ (**relegates, relegating, relegated**) V-T If you **relegate** someone or something to a less important position, you give them this position. ❑ *The coach relegated him to a place on the second team.* [from Latin]

**re|lent** /rɪlɛnt/ (**relents, relenting, relented**) V-I If you **relent**, you allow someone to do something that you had previously refused to allow them to do. ❑ *His mother relented and allowed him to marry.* [from Latin]

**re|lent|less** /rɪlɛntlɪs/ ADJ Something bad that is **relentless** never stops or never becomes less intense. ❑ *The pressure was relentless.*
● **re|lent|less|ly** ADV ❑ *It rained relentlessly.* [from Latin]

**rel|evant** /rɛləvᵊnt/ ADJ Something that is **relevant to** a situation or person is important or significant in that situation or to that person. ❑ *Is religion still relevant to people's lives?* ● **rel|evance** /rɛləvᵊns/ N-UNCOUNT ❑ *Politicians' private lives have no relevance to their public roles.* [from Medieval Latin]

**re|li|able** /rɪlaɪəbᵊl/ ☐ ADJ People or things that are **reliable** can be trusted to work well or to behave in the way that you want them to. ❑ *She was efficient and reliable.* ● **re|li|ably** /rɪlaɪəbli/ ADV ❑ *The washing machine worked reliably for years.* ● **re|li|abil|ity** /rɪlaɪəbɪlɪti/ N-UNCOUNT ❑ *He's worried about his car's reliability.* ☑ ADJ Information that is **reliable** or that is from a **reliable** source is very likely to be correct. ❑ *There is no reliable information about how many people have died.* ● **re|li|ably** ADV ❑ *We are reliably informed that he is here.* ● **re|li|abil|ity** N-UNCOUNT ❑ *We questioned the reliability of the research.* [from Old French]

**re|li|ant** /rɪlaɪənt/ ADJ A person or thing that is **reliant on** something needs it and often cannot live or work without it. ❑ *Young children are reliant on their parents.* ● **re|li|ance** /rɪlaɪəns/ N-UNCOUNT ❑ *...the organization's reliance on money from the government.* [from Old French]

**rel|ic** /rɛlɪk/ (**relics**) ☐ N-COUNT If you refer to something or someone as a **relic of** an earlier period, you mean that they belonged to that period but have survived into the present. ❑ *The law is a relic of a past age.* ☑ N-COUNT A **relic** is something which was made or used a long time ago and which is kept for its historical significance. ❑ *...a museum of war relics.* [from Old French]

**re|lief** /rɪlif/ ☐ N-UNCOUNT; N-SING If you feel a sense of **relief**, you feel happy because

something unpleasant has not happened or is no longer happening. ❑ *I breathed a sigh of relief.* ☑ N-UNCOUNT If something provides **relief from** pain or distress, it stops the pain or distress. ❑ *...relief from the pain.* ☒ N-UNCOUNT **Relief** is money, food, or clothing that is provided for people who are very poor, or who have been affected by war or a natural disaster. ❑ *Relief agencies are increasing efforts to provide food and shelter.* ☐ N-UNCOUNT The **relief** on a map is the difference in height between the highest area on the map and the lowest area. [from Old French]

**re|lief map** (**relief maps**) N-COUNT A **relief map** is a map that shows the height of the land, usually by using different colors or by raising some parts.

**re|lieve** /rɪliv/ (**relieves, relieving, relieved**) ☐ V-T If something **relieves** an unpleasant feeling or situation, it makes it less unpleasant or causes it to disappear completely. ❑ *Drugs can relieve the pain.* ☑ V-T If someone or something **relieves** you **of** an unpleasant feeling or difficult task, they take it from you. ❑ *Receiving the check relieved me of a lot of worry.* ☒ V-T If you **relieve** someone, you take their place and continue to do the job or duty that they have been doing. ❑ *At seven o'clock another nurse arrived to relieve her.* [from Old French]

**re|lieved** /rɪlivd/ ADJ If you are **relieved**, you feel happy because something unpleasant has not happened or is no longer happening. ❑ *We are relieved to be back home.* [from Old French]

**re|li|gion** /rɪlɪdʒᵊn/ (**religions**) ☐ N-UNCOUNT **Religion** is belief in a god or gods and the activities that are connected with this belief. ❑ *...Indian philosophy and religion.* ☑ N-COUNT A **religion** is a particular system of belief in a god or gods and the activities that are connected with this system. ❑ *...the Christian religion.* [from Old French]

**re|li|gious** /rɪlɪdʒəs/ ☐ ADJ **Religious** means connected with religion or with one particular religion. ❑ *Religious groups are able to meet quite freely.* ☑ ADJ Someone who is **religious** has a strong belief in a god or gods. [from Old French]

**re|lin|quish** /rɪlɪŋkwɪʃ/ (**relinquishes, relinquishing, relinquished**) V-T If you **relinquish** something such as power or control, you give it up. [FORMAL] [from French]

**rel|ish** /rɛlɪʃ/ (**relishes, relishing, relished**) ☐ V-T If you **relish** something, you get a lot of enjoyment from it. ❑ *I relish the challenge of doing the job.* ● **Relish** is also a noun. ❑ *The men ate with relish.* ☑ N-VAR **Relish** is a thick sauce made from fruit or vegetables that is eaten with meat, often with hot dogs. [from Old French]

**re|live** /rɪlɪv/ (**relives, reliving, relived**) V-T If you **relive** something that has happened to you in the past, you remember it and imagine that

r

you are experiencing it again. ❑ *There is no point in reliving the past.* [from Old English]

**re|lo|cate** /rɪˈloʊkeɪt/ (**relocates, relocating, relocated**) V-T/V-I If people or businesses **relocate** or if someone **relocates** them, they move to a different place. ❑ *The company relocated, and many employees were forced to move.* ● **re|lo|ca|tion** /rɪˌloʊˈkeɪʃ⁰n/ (**relocations**) N-VAR ❑ *...the cost of relocation.*

**re|luc|tant** /rɪˈlʌktənt/ ADJ If you are **reluctant to** do something, you are unwilling to do it and hesitate before doing it, or do it slowly and without enthusiasm. ❑ *Mr. Spero was reluctant to ask for help.* ● **re|luc|tant|ly** ADV ❑ *We have reluctantly agreed to let him go.* ● **re|luc|tance** N-UNCOUNT ❑ *Frank boarded his train with great reluctance.* [from Latin]

**rely** /rɪˈlaɪ/ (**relies, relying, relied**) **1** V-I If you **rely on** someone or something, you need them and depend on them in order to live or work properly. ❑ *They relied heavily on the advice of their professional advisers.* **2** V-I If you can **rely on** someone to work well or to behave as you want them to, you can trust them to do this. ❑ *I know I can rely on you to deal with the problem.* [from Old French]

**re|main** /rɪˈmeɪn/ (**remains, remaining, remained**) **1** V-LINK To **remain** in a particular state or condition means to stay in that state or condition and not change. ❑ *The men remained silent.* ❑ *The government remained in control.* **2** V-I If you **remain** in a place, you stay there and do not move away. ❑ *Police asked people to remain in their homes.* **3** V-I You can say that something **remains** when it still exists. ❑ *The wider problem remains.* **4** V-LINK If something **remains to be** done, it still needs to be done. ❑ *Questions remain to be answered about his work.* **5** N-PLURAL The **remains** of something are the parts of it that are left after most of it has been taken away or destroyed. ❑ *They were cleaning up the remains of their picnic.* **6** N-PLURAL The **remains** of a person or animal are the parts of their body that are left after they have died, sometimes after they have been dead for a long time. ❑ *...human remains.* [from Old French] **7** → see also **remaining**

**re|main|der** /rɪˈmeɪndər/ QUANT The **remainder** of a group are the things or people that still remain after the other things or people have gone or have been dealt with. ❑ *He drank the remainder of his coffee.* [from Old French]

**re|main|ing** /rɪˈmeɪnɪŋ/ **1** ADJ The **remaining** things or people out of a group are the things or people that still exist, are still present, or have not yet been dealt with. ❑ *...his few remaining supporters.* [from Old French] **2** → see also **remain**

**re|make** (**remakes, remaking, remade**)

The noun is pronounced /ˈriːmeɪk/. The verb is pronounced /riːˈmeɪk/.

**1** N-COUNT A **remake** is a movie that has the same story, and often the same title, as a movie that was made earlier. ❑ *...a 1953 remake of the musical "Roberta."* **2** V-T If a movie **is remade**, a new movie is made that has the same story, and often the same title, as a movie that was made earlier. ❑ *The movie was remade as "The Magnificent Seven."* [from Old English]

**re|mand** /rɪˈmænd/ (**remands, remanding, remanded**) **1** V-T If a person who is accused of a crime **is remanded** in custody, they are kept in prison until their trial begins. **2** N-UNCOUNT **Remand** is used to refer to the process of remanding someone in custody or on bail, or to the period of time until their trial begins. ❑ *He was on remand for murder.* [from Medieval Latin]

**re|mark** /rɪˈmɑrk/ (**remarks, remarking, remarked**) **1** V-T/V-I If you **remark** that something is true, you say that it is true. ❑ *Many people remarked that the president had not been tough enough.* ❑ *She remarked on how tired I looked.* **2** N-COUNT If you make a **remark** about something, you say something about it. ❑ *She made rude remarks about his weight.* [from French]

| Word Partnership | Use *remark* with : |
|---|---|
| ADJ. | **casual** remark, **offhand** remark **2** |
| V. | **hear a** remark, **make a** remark **2** |

**re|mark|able** /rɪˈmɑrkəb⁰l/ ADJ Someone or something that is **remarkable** is very impressive or unusual. ❑ *He was a remarkable man.* ● **re|mark|ably** /rɪˈmɑrkəbli/ ADV ❑ *The book was remarkably successful.* [from Old French]

**re|match** /ˈriːmætʃ/ (**rematches**) N-COUNT A **rematch** is a second game or contest between two people or teams who have already faced each other. ❑ *Stanford will play in a rematch.* [from Old English]

**re|me|dial** /rɪˈmiːdiəl/ ADJ **Remedial** action is intended to correct something that has been done wrong or that has not been successful. [FORMAL] ❑ *Some organizations are taking remedial action.* [from Latin]

**rem|edy** /ˈrɛmədi/ (**remedies, remedying, remedied**) **1** N-COUNT A **remedy** is a successful way of dealing with a problem. ❑ *The government's remedy involved tax increases.* **2** N-COUNT A **remedy** is something that is intended to cure you when you are ill or in pain. ❑ *...natural remedies for infections.* **3** V-T If you **remedy** something that is wrong or harmful, you correct it or improve it. ❑ *They worked hard to remedy the situation.* [from Latin]

**re|mem|ber** /rɪˈmɛmbər/ (**remembers, remembering, remembered**) **1** V-T/V-I If you **remember** people or events from the past, you still have an idea of them in your mind and you are able to think about them. ❑ *I remember the first time I met him.* ❑ *I remember that we went to his wedding.* ❑ *The weather was terrible, do you remember?* **2** V-T If you **remember** that something is true, you become aware of it again after a time when you did not think about it. ❑ *She remembered that she was going to the club that evening.* **3** V-T If you **remember to** do something, you do it when you intend to. ❑ *Please remember to mail the letter.* [from Old French]

| Thesaurus | *remember* Also look up : |
|---|---|
| V. | look back, recall, think back; *(ant.)* forget **1 3** |

## Word Partnership Use *remember* with :

ADV. remember **clearly**, remember **correctly**, remember, **still** remember, remember **vividly** ■
ADJ. **easy to** remember, **important to** remember ■ ■
CONJ. remember **what**, remember **when**, remember **where**, remember **why** ■ – ■

**re|mem|brance** /rɪmɛmbrəns/ N-UNCOUNT
If you do something **in remembrance of** a dead person, you do it as a way of showing that you want to remember them and that you respect them. [FORMAL] ❑ *They wore black in remembrance of the people who died.* [from Old French]

**re|mind** /rɪmaɪnd/ (**reminds, reminding, reminded**) ■ V-T If someone **reminds** you **of** a fact or event that you already know about, they say something which makes you think about it. ❑ *She reminded Tim of the last time they met.* ■ V-T If someone **reminds** you **to** do a particular thing, they say something which makes you remember to do it. ❑ *Can you remind me to buy some milk?* ■ V-T If you say that someone or something **reminds** you **of** another person or thing, you mean that they are similar to the other person or thing and that they make you think about them. ❑ *She reminds me of your sister.* [from Old English]

## Word Partnership Use *remind* with :

PREP. remind *someone* **of** *something* ■
remind *you* **of** *someone/something* ■

**re|mind|er** /rɪmaɪndər/ (**reminders**)
■ N-COUNT Something that serves as a **reminder of** another thing makes you think about the other thing. [WRITTEN] ❑ *...a constant reminder of a bad experience.* ■ N-COUNT A **reminder** is a letter or note that is sent to tell you that you have not done something such as pay a bill or return library books. ❑ *...the final reminder for the gas bill.* [from Old English]

**rem|i|nisce** /rɛmɪnɪs/ (**reminisces, reminiscing, reminisced**) V-I If you **reminisce** about something from your past, you write or talk about it, often with pleasure. [FORMAL] ❑ *I don't like reminiscing because it makes me feel old.* [from Latin]

**rem|i|nis|cence** /rɛmɪnɪsəns/
N-VAR Someone's **reminiscences** are things that they remember from the past, and which they talk or write about. [FORMAL] ❑ *Am I boring you with my reminiscences?* [from Latin]

**rem|i|nis|cent** /rɛmɪnɪsənt/ ADJ If you say that one thing is **reminiscent of** another, you mean that it reminds you of it. [FORMAL] ❑ *His voice was reminiscent of her son's.* [from Latin]

**re|mis|sion** /rɪmɪʃ°n/ (**remissions**) N-VAR If someone who has had a serious disease such as cancer is **in remission** or if the disease is **in remission**, the disease has been controlled so that they are not as ill as they were. [from Latin]

**rem|nant** /rɛmnənt/ (**remnants**) N-COUNT The **remnants of** something are small parts of it that are left over when the main part has disappeared or has been used or destroyed. ❑ *Under the church there were remnants of an older building.* [from Old French]

**re|mold** /rɪmoʊld/ (**remolds, remolding, remolded**) V-T To **remold** something such as an idea or an economy means to change it so that it has a new structure or is based on new principles. ❑ *...our ability to remold our lives after a severe loss.* [from Old French]

**re|morse** /rɪmɔrs/ N-UNCOUNT **Remorse** is a strong feeling of sadness and regret about something wrong that you have done. ❑ *He was full of remorse and asked Beatrice what he could do to make her feel better.* [from Medieval Latin]

**re|mote** /rɪmoʊt/ (**remoter, remotest**) ■ ADJ **Remote** areas are far away from cities and places where most people live. ❑ *...villages in remote areas.* ■ ADJ If something is **remote from** what people want or need, it is not relevant to it because it is so different from it or has no connection with it. ❑ *Teenagers have to study subjects that seem remote from their daily lives.* ■ ADJ If there is a **remote** possibility that something will happen, there is only a very small chance that it will happen. ❑ *I use sunscreen when there is a remote possibility that I will be in the sun.* ■ ADJ If you describe someone as **remote**, you mean that they behave as if they do not want to be friendly or closely involved with other people. [from Latin]

**re|mote con|trol** (**remote controls**)
■ N-UNCOUNT **Remote control** is a system of controlling a machine or a vehicle from a distance by using radio or electronic signals. ❑ *The bomb was exploded by remote control.* ■ N-COUNT The **remote control** for a television or other equipment is the device that you use to control the machine from a distance, by pressing the buttons on it. ❑ *Richard picked up the remote control and turned on the television.*

**re|mote|ly** /rɪmoʊtli/ ADV You use **remotely** with a negative statement to emphasize the statement. ❑ *He wasn't remotely interested in her.* [from Latin]

**re|mote sens|ing** N-UNCOUNT **Remote sensing** is the gathering of information about something by observing it from space or from the air.

**re|mov|al** /rɪmuv°l/ (**removals**) N-UNCOUNT The **removal** of something is the act of removing it. ❑ *...the removal of a tumor.* [from Old French]

## Word Link mov ≈ moving : movement, movie, remove

**re|move** /rɪmuv/ (**removes, removing, removed**) ■ V-T If you **remove** something from a place, you take it away. [WRITTEN] ❑ *Remove the cake from the oven when it is cooked.* ■ V-T If you **remove** clothing, you take it off. [WRITTEN] ❑ *He removed his jacket.* ■ V-T If you **remove** an obstacle, a restriction, or a problem, you get rid of it. ❑ *Yesterday they removed the last remaining obstacle for peace.* [from Old French]

## Thesaurus remove Also look up :

V. take away, take out ■
take off, undress ■

**re|moved** /rɪmuvd/ ADJ If you say that an idea or situation is far **removed from** something, you mean that it is very different from it. ❑ *The story was far removed from the truth.* [from Old French]

**re|nais|sance** /rɛnɪsɑns/ N-SING If something experiences a **renaissance**, it becomes popular or successful again after a time when people were not interested in it. ❑ *The jazz trumpet is experiencing a renaissance.* [from French]

**ren|der** /rɛndər/ (**renders, rendering, rendered**) V-T You can use **render** to say that something is changed into a different state. ❑ *...a problem with the phone which rendered it unusable.* [from Old French]

**ren|der|ing** /rɛndərɪŋ/ (**renderings**) **1** N-COUNT A **rendering of** a play, poem, or piece of music is a performance of it. ❑ *...a rendering of the U.S. national anthem.* **2** N-COUNT A **rendering** of an expression or piece of writing or speech is a translation of it. ❑ *The phrase was a rendering of an Arabic expression.* [from Old French]

**ren|dez|vous** /rɒndeɪvu/ (**rendezvous, rendezvousing, rendezvoused**)

> The form **rendezvous** is pronounced /rɒndeɪvuz/ when it is the plural of the noun or the third person singular of the verb.

**1** N-COUNT A **rendezvous** is a meeting, often a secret one, that you have arranged with someone for a particular time and place. ❑ *I had a rendezvous with Tony.* **2** V-RECIP If you **rendezvous with** someone or if the two of you **rendezvous**, you meet them at a time and place that you have arranged. ❑ *The plan was to rendezvous with him on Sunday afternoon.* [from French]

**ren|egade** /rɛnɪgeɪd/ (**renegades**) N-COUNT A **renegade** is a person who abandons the religious, political, or philosophical beliefs that he or she used to have, and accepts opposing or different beliefs. ❑ *These are renegade groups who will not take orders from the govenment.* [from Spanish]

**re|new** /rɪnu/ (**renews, renewing, renewed**) **1** V-T If you **renew** an activity, you begin it again. ❑ *He renewed his attack on government policy.* **2** V-T If you **renew** a relationship **with** someone, you start it again after you have not seen them or have not been friendly with them for some time. ❑ *When the men met again after the war they renewed their friendship.* **3** V-T When you **renew** something such as a license or a contract, you extend the period of time for which it is valid. ❑ *Larry's landlord refused to renew his lease.* **4** V-T You can say that something **is renewed** when it grows again or is replaced after it has been destroyed or lost. ❑ *Cells in the body are being constantly renewed.* [from Old English]

**Thesaurus** renew Also look up :

V.   continue, resume, revive **1** – **3**

**re|new|able** /rɪnuəbəl/ **1** ADJ **Renewable** resources are natural ones such as wind, water, and sunlight which are always available. ❑ *...renewable energy sources.* **2** N-PLURAL You can refer to renewable resources as **renewables**. **3** ADJ If a contract or agreement is **renewable**, it can be extended when it reaches the end of a fixed period of time. [from Old English]

**re|new|al** /rɪnuəl/ (**renewals**) **1** N-SING If there is a **renewal of** an activity or a situation, it starts again. ❑ *...the renewal of fighting in the area.* **2** N-VAR The **renewal** of a document such as a license or a contract is an official extension of the period of time for which it remains valid. ❑ *His contract is due for renewal.* [from Old English]

**re|nounce** /rɪnaʊns/ (**renounces, renouncing, renounced**) V-T If you **renounce** a belief or a way of behaving, you decide and declare publicly that you no longer have that belief or will no longer behave in that way. ❑ *He renounced violence and war.* [from Old French]

**reno|vate** /rɛnəveɪt/ (**renovates, renovating, renovated**) V-T If someone **renovates** an old building, they repair and improve it and get it back into good condition. ❑ *They spent a lot of money renovating the house.* ● **reno|va|tion** /rɛnəveɪʃən/ (**renovations**) N-VAR ❑ *...a house which needs extensive renovation.* [from Latin]

**re|nown** /rɪnaʊn/ N-UNCOUNT A person **of renown** is well-known, usually because they do or have done something good. ❑ *She used to be a singer of some renown.* [from Old French]

**re|nowned** /rɪnaʊnd/ ADJ A person or place that is **renowned for** something, usually something good, is well known because of it. ❑ *The area is renowned for its beautiful churches.* [from Old French]

**rent** /rɛnt/ (**rents, renting, rented**) **1** V-T If you **rent** something, such as a car or property, you regularly pay its owner a sum of money in order to be able to have it or use it yourself. ❑ *She rents a house with three other women.* **2** V-T If you **rent** something **to** someone, you let them have it and use it in exchange for a sum of money which they pay you regularly. ❑ *She rented rooms to university students.* ● **Rent out** means the same as **rent**. ❑ *Last summer Brian Williams rented out his house and went camping.* **3** N-VAR **Rent** is the amount of money that you pay regularly to use a house, apartment, or piece of land. ❑ *She worked to pay the rent.* [from Old French]

**rent|al** /rɛntəl/ (**rentals**) **1** N-UNCOUNT The **rental** of something such as a car or piece of equipment is the activity or process of renting it. ❑ *We can arrange car rental from the airport.* **2** N-COUNT The **rental** is the amount of money that you pay when you rent something such as a car, property, or piece of equipment. ❑ *We pay a yearly rental of $393,000.* **3** ADJ You use **rental** to describe things that are connected with the renting of goods, properties, and services. ❑ *...a rental car.* [from Old French]

**re|or|gan|ize** /riɔrgənaɪz/ (**reorganizes, reorganizing, reorganized**) V-T/V-I To **reorganize** something means to change the way in which it is organized, arranged, or done. ❑ *She wanted to reorganize her life.* ● **re|or|gani|za|tion** /riɔrgənaɪzeɪʃən/ (**reorganizations**) N-VAR ❑ *...the reorganization of the legal system.* [from Medieval Latin]

**rep** /rɛp/ (**reps**) **1** N-COUNT A **rep** is a person whose job is to sell a company's products or services, especially by traveling around and visiting other companies. ❑ *...a sales rep for a photographic company.* **2** N-COUNT A **rep** is a person who acts as a representative for a group of people, usually a group of people who work together. ❑ *...a labor union rep.* [from French]

**Rep.** Rep. is a written abbreviation for **Representative**.

re|paid /rɪpeɪd/ **Repaid** is the past tense and past participle of **repay**.

re|pair /rɪpɛər/ (**repairs, repairing, repaired**) ◼ V-T If you **repair** something that has been damaged or is not working properly, you fix it. □ *Goldman has repaired the roof.* ◼ N-VAR A **repair** is something that you do to mend a machine, building, piece of clothing, or other thing that has been damaged or is not working properly. □ *Many people do not know how to make repairs on their cars.* [from Old French]

### Word Partnership    Use *repair* with :

N.    repair **a chimney**, repair **damage**, repair **equipment**, repair **a roof** ◼ auto repair, car repair, home repair, repair **parts**, road repair, repair **service**, repair **shop** ◼

re|pair|man /rɪpɛərmæn/ (**repairmen**) N-COUNT A **repairman** is a man who fixes broken machines such as televisions and telephones.

re|pat|ri|ate /ripeɪtrieɪt/ (**repatriates, repatriating, repatriated**) V-T If a country **repatriates** someone, it sends them back to their home country. □ *The government does not repatriate genuine refugees.* ● re|pat|ri|a|tion /ripeɪtrieɪʃ⁰n/ (**repatriations**) N-VAR □ *...the forced repatriation of immigrants.* [from Late Latin]

re|pay /rɪpeɪ/ (**repays, repaying, repaid**) ◼ V-T If you **repay** a debt, you pay back the money that you owe to someone. ◼ V-T If you **repay** a favor that someone did for you, you do something for them in return. □ *It was very kind. I don't know how I can ever repay you.* [from Old French]

re|pay|ment /rɪpeɪmənt/ (**repayments**) N-UNCOUNT The **repayment of** money is the act or process of paying it back to the person you owe it to. □ *...the repayment of a $114 million loan.* [from Old French]

re|peal /rɪpil/ (**repeals, repealing, repealed**) V-T If the government **repeals** a law, it officially ends it, so that it is no longer valid. ● **Repeal** is also a noun. □ *...the repeal of the law.* [from Old French]

re|peat /rɪpit/ (**repeats, repeating, repeated**) ◼ V-T If you **repeat** something, you say or write it again. □ *He repeated that he was innocent.* □ *She repeated her request for more money.* ◼ V-T If you **repeat** something that someone else has said or written, you say or write the same thing. □ *She had a habit of repeating everything I said to her.* ◼ V-T If you **repeat** an action, you do it again. □ *The next day I repeated the task.* ◼ V-T If an event or series of events **repeats itself**, it happens again. □ *They say sometimes history repeats itself.* ◼ N-COUNT If there is a **repeat of** an event, usually an undesirable event, it happens again. □ *...a repeat of last year's strikes.* ◼ N-COUNT A **repeat** is a television or radio program that has been broadcast before. [from Old French]

### Thesaurus    *repeat*    Also look up :

V.    reiterate, restate ◼ ◼
N.    encore ◼

re|peat|ed /rɪpitɪd/ ADJ **Repeated** actions or events are ones that happen many times. □ *He did not return the money, despite repeated reminders.* ● re|peat|ed|ly ADV □ *Both men have repeatedly denied doing anything wrong.* [from Old French]

re|pel /rɪpɛl/ (**repels, repelling, repelled**) ◼ V-T When an army **repels** an attack, they successfully fight and drive back soldiers from another army who have attacked them. [FORMAL] ◼ V-T If something **repels** you, you find it horrible and disgusting. □ *Politics both fascinated and repelled him.* ● re|pelled ADJ □ *She was very beautiful but in some way I felt repelled.* [from Latin]
→ see **magnet**

re|pel|lent /rɪpɛlənt/ (**repellents**) ◼ ADJ If you think that something is horrible and disgusting you can say that it is **repellent**. [FORMAL] □ *...a very large, very repellent snake.* ◼ N-VAR Insect **repellent** is a chemical substance that is used to keep insects away. □ *...mosquito repellent.* [from Latin]

re|pent /rɪpɛnt/ (**repents, repenting, repented**) V-I If you **repent**, you show or say that you are sorry for something wrong you have done. □ *People who refuse to repent will be punished.* ● re|pent|ance N-UNCOUNT □ *He showed no repentance during his trial.* ● re|pent|ant ADJ □ *...a repentant criminal.* [from Old French]

rep|er|toire /rɛpərtwɑr/ (**repertoires**) N-COUNT A performer's **repertoire** is all the plays or pieces of music that he or she has learned and can perform. □ *She has thousands of songs in her repertoire.* [from French]

rep|er|tory /rɛpərtɔri/ N-UNCOUNT A **repertory** company is a group of actors and actresses who perform a small number of plays for just a few weeks at a time. □ *...a well-known repertory company in Boston.* [from Late Latin]

rep|eti|tion /rɛpɪtɪʃ⁰n/ (**repetitions**) ◼ N-VAR If there is a **repetition** of an event, usually an undesirable event, it happens again. □ *The city government wants to prevent a repetition of last year's violence.* ◼ N-VAR In dance, **repetition** means performing the same movement again or doing it several times. [from Latin]

re|peti|tive /rɪpɛtɪtɪv/ ADJ Something that is **repetitive** involves actions or elements that are repeated many times and is therefore boring. □ *...factory workers who do repetitive jobs.* [from Latin]

re|place /rɪpleɪs/ (**replaces, replacing, replaced**) ◼ V-T To **replace** a person or thing means to put another person or thing in their place. □ *...the lawyer who replaced Robert as chairman.* ◼ V-T If you **replace** something that is broken, damaged, or lost, you get a new one to use instead. □ *The shower has broken and we cannot afford to replace it.* ● re|place|ment N-UNCOUNT □ *...the replacement of damaged books.* ◼ V-T If you **replace** something, you put it back where it was before. □ *Replace the caps on the bottles.* [from Old French]

re|place|ment /rɪpleɪsmənt/ (**replacements**) N-COUNT One thing or person that replaces another can be referred to as their **replacement**. □ *Taylor has suggested Adams as his replacement.* [from Old French]

re|play (**replays, replaying, replayed**)

The verb is pronounced /ripleɪ/. The noun is pronounced /ripleɪ/.

**1** V-T If a game or match between two sports teams **is replayed**, the two teams play it again, because neither team won the first time, or because the game was stopped because of bad weather. **2** N-COUNT ❏ *They won the replay 2 – 1.* **3** N-COUNT A **replay** of something which has been recorded on film or tape is another showing of it. ❏ *…a slow-motion replay of his fall.* [from Old English]

**Word Link** plen ≈ full : plentiful, plenty, replenish

**re|plen|ish** /rɪplɛnɪʃ/ (**replenishes, replenishing, replenished**) V-T If you **replenish** something, you make it full or complete again. [FORMAL] ❏ *The waitress came to replenish their coffee cups.*
● **re|plen|ish|ment** N-UNCOUNT ❏ *There is a concern about replenishment of the population.* [from Old French]

**rep|li|ca** /rɛplɪkə/ (**replicas**) N-COUNT A **replica** of something such as a statue, building, or weapon is an accurate copy of it. ❏ *…a replica of the ship.* [from Italian]

**re|ply** /rɪplaɪ/ (**replies, replying, replied**)
**1** V-T/V-I When you **reply to** something that someone has said or written to you, you say or write an answer to them. ❏ *"That's a nice dress,"said Michael. "Thanks," she replied.* ❏ *He replied that this was absolutely impossible.* ❏ *He never replied to the letters.* **2** N-COUNT A **reply** is something that you say or write when you answer someone or answer a letter or advertisement. ❏ *I called out, but there was no reply.* **3** V-I If you **reply to** something such as an attack **with** violence or **with** another action, you do something in response. ❏ *The soldiers replied with an offer of peace.* [from Old French]

**Thesaurus** *reply* Also look up :

| | |
|---|---|
| V. | acknowledge, answer, respond, return **1** |
| N. | acknowledgement, answer, response **2** |

**Word Partnership** Use *reply* with :

| | |
|---|---|
| N. | reply **card**, reply **envelope**, reply **form 2** |
| V. | **make** a reply, **receive** a reply **2** |

**re|port** /rɪpɔrt/ (**reports, reporting, reported**)
**1** V-T If you **report** something that has happened, you tell people about it. ❏ *I reported the theft to the police.* ❏ *Officials reported that the ships were heading for Malta.* ❏ *"He seems to be all right now,"he reported.* ❏ *She reported him missing the next day.* **2** V-I If you **report on** an event or subject, you tell people about it, because it is your job or duty to do so. ❏ *…journalists reporting on politics.* **3** N-COUNT A **report** is a news article or broadcast which gives information about something that has just happened. ❏ *According to a newspaper report, the couple are getting married.* **4** N-COUNT If you give someone a **report** on something, you tell them what has been happening. ❏ *She gave us a progress report on the project.* **5** V-T If someone **reports** you **to** a person in authority, they tell that person about something wrong that you have done. ❏ *His boss reported him to police.* **6** V-I If you **report to** a person or place, you go to them and say that you are ready to start work. [from Old French] **7** → see also **reporting**

**re|port card** (**report cards**) N-COUNT A **report**

**card** is an official written account of how well or how badly a student has done during the term or year that has just finished. ❏ *I brought home straight "A"s on my report card.*

**re|port|ed|ly** /rɪpɔrtɪdli/ ADV If you say that something is **reportedly** true, you mean that someone has said that it is true, but you have no direct evidence of it. [FORMAL] ❏ *More than two hundred people were reportedly killed.* [from Old French]

**re|port|ed speech** N-UNCOUNT **Reported speech** is speech which tells you what someone said, but does not use the person's actual words: for example, "They said you didn't like it," and "I asked him what his plans were."

**re|port|er** /rɪpɔrtər/ (**reporters**) N-COUNT A **reporter** is someone who writes news articles or who broadcasts news reports. ❏ *…a TV reporter.* [from Old French]

**re|port|ing** /rɪpɔrtɪŋ/ N-UNCOUNT **Reporting** is the presenting of news in newspapers, on radio, and on television. ❏ *…political reporting.* [from Old French]

**Word Link** pos ≈ placing : deposit, preposition, repository

**re|posi|tory** /rɪpɒzitɔri/ (**repositories**) N-COUNT A **repository** is a place where something is kept safely. [FORMAL] ❏ *The nation's giant historical repository is called the Smithsonian Institution.* [from Latin]

**re|pos|sess** /ripəzɛs/ (**repossesses, repossessing, repossessed**) V-T If your car or house **is repossessed**, it is taken away from you because you have not paid what you owe for it. [from Old French]

**re|pos|ses|sion** /ripəzɛʃ°n/ (**repossessions**) N-VAR The **repossession** of your house or car is the act of repossessing it. ❏ *The sherriff also does car repossessions now.* [from Old French]

**rep|re|sent** /rɛprɪzɛnt/ (**represents, representing, represented**) **1** V-T If someone such as a lawyer or a politician **represents** a person, a group of people, or a place, they act on behalf of that person, group, or place. ❏ *…the politicians we elect to represent us.* **2** V-T If a sign or symbol **represents** something, it is accepted as meaning that thing. ❏ *A cross on the map represents a church.* **3** V-T To **represent** an idea or quality means to be a symbol or an expression of that idea or quality. ❏ *New York represents everything that's great about America.* **4** V-T If you **represent** a person or thing **as** a particular thing, you describe them as being that thing. ❏ *The newspaper represented him as a hero.* [from Latin]

**rep|re|sen|ta|tion** /rɛprɪzɛnteɪʃ°n/ (**representations**) **1** N-UNCOUNT If a group or person has **representation** in a legislature or on a committee, someone in the legislature or on the committee supports them and makes decisions on their behalf. ❏ *Puerto Ricans are U.S. citizens but they have no representation in Congress.* **2** N-COUNT You can describe a picture, model, or statue of a person or thing as a **representation** of them. [FORMAL] ❏ *…a lifelike representation of Bill Clinton.* [from Latin]

**rep|re|senta|tive** /rɛprɪzɛntətɪv/ (**representatives**) **1** N-COUNT A **representative** is a person who has been chosen to act or make

## Word Web    reproduction

Human **reproduction** requires a **sperm** from the **male** and an **egg** from the **female**. These two cells come together to begin the new life. This process is called **fertilization**. It is the beginning of the woman's **pregnancy**. From fertilization to eight weeks of development, we call the fertilized egg a **zygote**. From eight to twelve weeks, it is called an **embryo**. After three months of development, we call it a **fetus**. **Birth** usually takes place after nine months of pregnancy.

**egg and sperm**

**zygote**

**embryo**

**fetus**

**mother, father, and baby**

decisions on behalf of another person or a group of people. ❑ ...*labor union representatives.* ◻ N-COUNT In the United States, a **representative** is a member of the House of Representatives, the less powerful of the two parts of Congress. ❑ ...*a Republican representative from Wyoming.* ◻ ADJ A **representative** group consists of a small number of people who have been chosen to make decisions on behalf of a larger group. ❑ *The new chairman was chosen by a representative council.* ◻ ADJ If someone or something is **representative** of a group, he, she or it is typical of it. ❑ *He was in no way representative of teachers in general.* [from Latin]

re|press /rɪprɛs/ (**represses, repressing, repressed**) ◻ V-T If you **repress** a feeling, you make a deliberate effort not to show or have this feeling. ❑ *Anger that is repressed leads to violence.* ● re|pres|sion /rɪprɛʃ°n/ N-UNCOUNT ❑ ...*the repression of his feelings.* ◻ V-T If you say that a section of society **is repressed**, you disapprove of the fact that their freedom is restricted by the people who have authority over them. ❑ ...*a government that represses its people.* ● re|pres|sion N-UNCOUNT ❑ ...*a society that is ruined by violence and repression.* [from Latin]

re|pressed /rɪprɛst/ ADJ A **repressed** person does not allow themselves to have natural feelings and desires. ❑ *She was shy and repressed.* [from Latin]

re|pres|sive /rɪprɛsɪv/ ADJ If you describe a government as **repressive**, you disapprove of it because it restricts people's freedom and controls them by using force. ❑ *The government was unpopular and repressive.* [from Latin]

re|prieve /rɪpriv/ (**reprieves, reprieving, reprieved**) ◻ V-T If someone who has been sentenced in a court **is reprieved**, their punishment is officially delayed or canceled. ● **Reprieve** is also a noun. ❑ *He was saved by a last-minute reprieve.* ◻ N-COUNT A **reprieve** is a delay before a very unpleasant or difficult situation which may or may not take place. ❑ *The college got a reprieve just days before it was supposed to close.* [from Old French]

rep|ri|mand /rɛprɪmænd/ (**reprimands, reprimanding, reprimanded**) V-T If someone **is reprimanded**, they are spoken to angrily or seriously for doing something wrong, usually by a

person in authority. [FORMAL] ❑ *He was reprimanded by a teacher for talking in the library.* ● **Reprimand** is also a noun. ❑ *He received a fine of five thousand dollars and a severe reprimand.* [from French]

re|print (**reprints, reprinting, reprinted**)

The verb is pronounced /riprɪnt/. The noun is pronounced /riprɪnt/.

◻ V-T If a book **is reprinted**, further copies of it are printed when all the other ones have been sold. ◻ N-COUNT A **reprint** is a new copy of a book or article, printed because all the other ones have been sold or because minor changes have been made to the original. ❑ ...*a reprint of a novel.* [from Old French]

re|pris|al /rɪpraɪz°l/ (**reprisals**) N-VAR If you do something to a person **in reprisal**, you hurt or punish them because they have done something violent or unpleasant to you. ❑ *Some people were killed in reprisal.* [from Old French]

re|proach /rɪproʊtʃ/ (**reproaches, reproaching, reproached**) ◻ V-T If you **reproach** someone, you say or show that you are disappointed, upset, or angry because they have done something wrong. ❑ *He publicly reproached his daughter.* ◻ N-VAR If you look at or speak to someone with **reproach**, you show or say that you are disappointed, upset, or angry because they have done something wrong. ❑ *He looked at her with reproach.* [from Old French]

re|pro|duce /riprədus/ (**reproduces, reproducing, reproduced**) ◻ V-T If you try to **reproduce** something, you copy it. ❑ *The effect was hard to reproduce.* ◻ V-I When people, animals, or plants **reproduce**, they produce young. ❑ ...*people's ability to reproduce.* ● re|pro|duc|tion /riprədʌkʃ°n/ N-UNCOUNT ❑ ...*human reproduction.* [from Latin]
→ see Word Web: **reproduction**

re|pro|duc|tion /riprədʌkʃ°n/ (**reproductions**) ◻ N-COUNT A **reproduction** is a copy of something such as a piece of furniture or a work of art. ❑ ...*a reproduction of a religious painting.* [from Latin] ◻ → see also **reproduce**

re|pro|duc|tive /riprədʌktɪv/ ADJ **Reproductive** processes and organs are concerned with the reproduction of living things. ❑ ...*the female reproductive system.* [from Latin]

rep|tile /rɛptaɪl, -tɪl/ (**reptiles**) N-COUNT

r

**Reptiles** are a group of cold-blooded animals which lay eggs and have skins covered with small, hard plates called scales. Snakes, lizards, and crocodiles are reptiles. [from Late Latin]
→ see **pet**

re|pub|lic /rɪpʌblɪk/ (**republics**) N-COUNT A **republic** is a country that has a president or whose system of government is based on the idea that every citizen has equal status. ❑ In 1918, Austria became a republic. ❑ ...the Baltic republics. [from French]

re|pub|li|can /rɪpʌblɪkən/ (**republicans**) **1** ADJ A **republican** government has a president or is based on the idea that every citizen has equal status. You can also say that someone has **republican** views. ❑ ...the republican side in the Spanish Civil War. **2** ADJ If someone is **Republican**, they belong to or support the Republican Party. ❑ Lower taxes made Republican voters happier with their party. ● A **Republican** is someone who supports or belongs to the Republican Party. ❑ What made you decide to become a Republican? [from French]

re|pu|di|ate /rɪpyudieɪt/ (**repudiates, repudiating, repudiated**) V-T If you **repudiate** something or someone, you show that you strongly disagree with them and do not want to be connected with them in any way. [FORMAL OR WRITTEN] ❑ She repudiated most of what he wrote. ● re|pu|dia|tion /rɪpyudieɪ ʃ°n/ (**repudiations**) N-VAR ❑ ...his public repudiation of the decision. [from Latin]

re|pul|sive /rɪpʌlsɪv/ ADJ **Repulsive** means horrible and disgusting. ❑ Some people found the movie repulsive. [from Latin]

repu|table /rɛpyətəbəl/ ADJ A **reputable** company or person is reliable and can be trusted. ❑ Buy your car through a reputable dealer. [from Old French]

repu|ta|tion /rɛpyəteɪʃ°n/ (**reputations**) **1** N-COUNT To have a **reputation for** something means to be known or remembered for it. ❑ ...his reputation for honesty. **2** N-COUNT Your **reputation** is the opinion that people have about you. ❑ This college has a good reputation. [from Latin]

| Word Partnership | Use *reputation* with : |
|---|---|
| ADJ. | **bad** reputation, **good** reputation **1 2** |
| V. | **acquire** a reputation, **build** a reputation, **damage** *someone's* reputation, **earn** a reputation, **establish** a reputation, **gain** a reputation, **have** a reputation, **ruin** *someone's* reputation, **tarnish** *someone's* reputation **1 2** |

re|put|ed /rɪpyutɪd/ V-T PASSIVE If you say that something **is reputed to** be true, you mean that people say it is true, but you do not know if it is definitely true. [FORMAL] ❑ He was reputed to be a good cook. ● re|put|ed|ly /rɪpyutɪdli/ ADV ❑ He reputedly earns two million dollars a year. [from Old French]

re|quest /rɪkwɛst/ (**requests, requesting, requested**) **1** V-T If you **request** something, you ask for it politely or formally. [FORMAL] ❑ He requested the use of a telephone. **2** N-COUNT If you make a **request**, you politely or formally ask someone to do something. ❑ They agreed to his request for more money. **3** PHRASE If you

do something **at** someone's **request**, you do it because he or she has asked you to. ❑ No one sent flowers for his funeral at the request of his family. **4** PHRASE If something is given or done **on request**, it is given or done whenever you ask for it. ❑ Details are available on request. [from Old French]

re|quire /rɪkwaɪər/ (**requires, requiring, required**) **1** V-T To **require** something means to need it. [FORMAL] ❑ If you require further information, please write to this address. ❑ ...the kind of problem that requires us to act immediately. **2** V-T If a law or rule **requires** you **to** do something, you have to do it. [FORMAL] ❑ The rules require employers to provide safety training. ❑ ...a law requiring immediate reporting of faults. [from Old French]

re|quire|ment /rɪkwaɪərmənt/ (**requirements**) **1** N-COUNT A **requirement** is a quality or qualification that you must have in order to be allowed to do something or to be suitable for something. ❑ Its products met all legal requirements. **2** N-COUNT Your **requirements** are the things that you need. [FORMAL] ❑ We can provide various programs to suit your requirements. [from Old French]

| Word Partnership | Use *requirement* with : |
|---|---|
| ADJ. | **legal** requirement, **minimum** requirement **1** |
| V. | **meet** a requirement **1** |

requi|site /rɛkwɪzɪt/ ADJ **Requisite** means necessary for a particular purpose. [FORMAL] ❑ He lacked the requisite knowledge for the job. [from Latin]

res|cue /rɛskyu/ (**rescues, rescuing, rescued**) **1** V-T If you **rescue** someone, you get them out of a dangerous or unpleasant situation. ❑ Helicopters rescued 20 people from the roof of the building. ● res|cu|er (**rescuers**) N-COUNT ❑ It took rescuers 90 minutes to reach the trapped men. **2** N-VAR A **rescue** is an attempt to save someone from a dangerous or unpleasant situation. ❑ A major rescue is taking place. ❑ ...a big rescue operation. **3** PHRASE If someone **goes to** your **rescue** or **comes to** your **rescue**, he or she helps you when you are in danger or difficulty. ❑ Her screams were heard by a neighbor who went to her rescue. [from Old French]

| Word Partnership | Use *rescue* with : |
|---|---|
| N. | **firefighters** rescue, rescue **a hostage**, rescue **miners**, rescue **people**, **police** rescue, **volunteers** rescue, rescue **wildlife 1** |
| | rescue **attempt**, rescue **crews**, rescue **effort**, rescue **mission**, rescue **operation**, rescue **teams**, rescue **workers 2** |

re|search /rɪsɜrtʃ, rɪsɜrtʃ/ (**researches, researching, researched**) **1** N-UNCOUNT **Research** is work that involves studying something and trying to discover facts about it. ❑ ...scientific research. **2** V-T If you **research** something, you try to discover facts about it. ❑ She spent two years in Florida researching her book. ● re|search|er (**researchers**) N-COUNT ❑ ...a market researcher. [from Old French]
→ see **laboratory, medicine, science, zoo, hospital, laboratory**

R

**Word Partnership** Use *research* with :

ADJ. **biological** research, **clinical** research, **current** research, **experimental** research, **medical** research, **recent** research, **scientific** research ■

N. **animal** research, **cancer** research, research **facility**, research **findings**, **laboratory** research, research **methods**, research **paper**, research **project**, research **report**, research **results**, research **scientist** ■

**re|sem|blance** /rɪzɛmbləns/ (**resemblances**)
N-VAR If there is a **resemblance** between two people or things, they are similar to each other. □ *There was a remarkable resemblance between him and Pete.* [from Old French]

**re|sem|ble** /rɪzɛmbᵊl/ (**resembles, resembling, resembled**) V-T If one thing or person **resembles** another, they are similar to each other. □ *She resembles her mother.* [from Old French]

**re|sent** /rɪzɛnt/ (**resents, resenting, resented**) V-T If you **resent** someone or something, you feel bitter and angry about them. □ *She resents her mother for leaving.* [from French]

**re|sent|ful** /rɪzɛntfəl/ ADJ If you are **resentful**, you feel resentment. □ *I felt resentful and angry about losing my job.* [from French]

**re|sent|ment** /rɪzɛntmənt/ (**resentments**) N-VAR **Resentment** is bitterness and anger that someone feels about something. □ *She felt resentment at his behavior.* [from French]

**res|er|va|tion** /rɛzərveɪʃⁿn/ (**reservations**)
■ N-VAR If you have **reservations about** something, you are not sure that it is entirely good or right. □ *He had no reservations at all about leaving home.* ■ N-COUNT If you make a **reservation**, you arrange for something such as a table in a restaurant or a room in a hotel to be kept for you. □ *He went to the desk to make a reservation.* [from Old French]
→ see **hotel**

**re|serve** /rɪzɜrv/ (**reserves, reserving, reserved**)
■ V-T If something **is reserved for** a particular person or purpose, it is kept specially for that person or purpose. □ *A room was reserved for him.* ■ N-COUNT A **reserve** is a supply of something that is available for use when it is needed. □ *...the world's oil reserves.* ■ N-UNCOUNT If someone shows **reserve**, they keep their feelings hidden. □ *He lost his reserve and told her what he thought.* ■ PHRASE If you have something **in reserve**, you have it available for use when it is needed. □ *...the money that he kept in reserve.* [from Old French] ■ to **reserve judgment** → see **judgment**

**re|served** /rɪzɜrvd/ ADJ Someone who is **reserved** keeps their feelings hidden. □ *He was quiet and reserved.* [from Old French]

**res|er|voir** /rɛzərvwɑr/ (**reservoirs**) ■ N-COUNT A **reservoir** is a lake that is used for storing water before it is supplied to people. ■ N-COUNT A **reservoir of** something is a large quantity of it that is available for use when needed. □ *...the huge oil reservoir beneath the desert.* [from French]
→ see **dam**

**Word Link** sid ≈ sitting : preside, president, reside

**re|side** /rɪzaɪd/ (**resides, residing, resided**) V-I If someone **resides** somewhere, they live there or are staying there. [FORMAL] □ *Margaret resides with her mother.* [from Latin]

**resi|dence** /rɛzɪdəns/ (**residences**) ■ N-COUNT A **residence** is a house where people live. [FORMAL] □ *...a private residence.* ■ N-UNCOUNT Your place of **residence** is the place where you live. [FORMAL] ■ PHRASE If someone is **in residence** in a particular place, they are living there. [from Latin]

**resi|dence hall** (**residence halls**) N-COUNT **Residence halls** are buildings with rooms or apartments, usually built by universities or colleges, in which students live during the school year. □ *A freshman adviser lives in each residence hall.*

**resi|den|cy** /rɛzɪdənsi/ (**residencies**) N-COUNT A doctor's **residency** is the period of specialized training in a hospital that he or she receives after completing an internship. □ *He completed his residency at Stanford University Hospital.* [from Latin]

**Word Link** ent ≈ one who does, has : dependent, resident, superintendent

**resi|dent** /rɛzɪdənt/ (**residents**) ■ N-COUNT The **residents** of a house or area are the people who live there. □ *Local residents complained that the road was dangerous.* ■ N-COUNT Someone who is a **resident of** a country or a city lives there. □ *He has been a resident of Baltimore since 1967.* ■ N-COUNT A **resident** or a **resident** doctor is a doctor who is receiving a period of specialized training in a hospital after completing his or her internship. [from Latin]
→ see **country**

**resi|dent alien** (**resident aliens**) N-COUNT A **resident alien** is a person who was born in one country but has moved to another country and has official permission to live there.

**resi|den|tial** /rɛzɪdɛnʃⁿl/ ■ ADJ A **residential** area contains houses rather than offices or factories. □ *...a residential area of Maryland.* ■ ADJ A **residential** institution is one where people live while they are studying there or being cared for there. □ *...a two-year residential college.* [from Latin]

**re|sid|ual** /rɪzɪdʒuəl/ ADJ **Residual** is used to describe what remains of something when most of it has gone. □ *She had a slight residual headache after bumping her head.* [from Old French]

**resi|due** /rɛzɪdu, -dyu/ (**residues**) N-COUNT A **residue** of something is a small amount that remains after most of it has gone. □ *A residue can build up on the hair if you always use the same shampoo.* [from Old French]

**re|sign** /rɪzaɪn/ (**resigns, resigning, resigned**)
■ V-T/V-I If you **resign** from a job or position, you formally announce that you are leaving it. □ *He was forced to resign.* □ *Mr. Robb resigned his position last month.* ■ V-T If you **resign yourself to** an unpleasant situation or fact, you accept it because you realize that you cannot change it. □ *Pat and I resigned ourselves to another summer without a boat.* [from Old French] ■ → see also **resigned**

r

| **Thesaurus** | *resign* | Also look up : |

| v. | leave, quit, step down ◼ |

**res|ig|na|tion** /rɛzɪgneɪʃ°n/ (**resignations**)
◼ N-VAR Your **resignation** is a formal statement of your intention to leave a job or position. ❑ *Bob Morgan offered his resignation and it was accepted.*
◻ N-UNCOUNT **Resignation** is the acceptance of an unpleasant situation or fact because you realize that you cannot change it. ❑ *He sighed with resignation.* [from Old French]

**re|signed** /rɪzaɪnd/ ADJ If you are **resigned to** an unpleasant situation or fact, you accept it without complaining because you realize that you cannot change it. ❑ *He is resigned to the noise and the mess.* [from Old French]

**re|sili|ent** /rɪzɪlyənt/ ADJ People and things that are **resilient** are able to recover easily and quickly from unpleasant or damaging events. ❑ *The Japanese stock market was the most resilient.*
● **re|sili|ence** N-UNCOUNT; N-SING ❑ *...the resilience of human beings.* [from Latin]

**res|in** /rɛzɪn/ (**resins**) ◼ N-VAR Resin is a sticky substance produced by some trees. ◻ N-VAR **Resin** is a substance that is produced chemically and used to make plastics. [from Old French]

**re|sist** /rɪzɪst/ (**resists, resisting, resisted**)
◼ V-T If you **resist** something such as a change, you refuse to accept it and try to prevent it. ❑ *They resisted our attempts to change things.* ◻ V-T/V-I If you **resist** someone or **resist** an attack by them, you fight back against them. ❑ *The man tried to resist arrest.* ❑ *When she attempted to cut his nails he resisted.* ◼ V-T If you **resist** doing something, or **resist** the temptation to do it, you stop yourself from doing it although you would like to do it. ❑ *She resisted the urge to laugh.* ◼ V-T If someone or something **resists** damage, they are not damaged. ❑ *This leather resists water, oil, grease and even acids.* [from Latin]

| **Word Link** | *ance ≈ quality, state : insurance, performance, resistance* |

**re|sist|ance** /rɪzɪstəns/ (**resistances**)
◼ N-UNCOUNT **Resistance** to something such as a change or a new idea is a refusal to accept it. ❑ *...his resistance to anything new.* ◻ N-UNCOUNT **Resistance** to an attack consists of fighting back against the people who have attacked you. ❑ *The soldiers are facing strong resistance.* ◼ N-UNCOUNT The **resistance** of your body **to** germs or diseases is its power to remain unharmed or unaffected by them. ❑ *Most people have a natural resistance to the disease.* ◼ N-VAR In electrical engineering or physics, **resistance** is the ability of a substance or an electrical circuit to stop the flow of an electrical current through it. [from Latin]
→ see **bicycle**

**re|sist|ant** /rɪzɪstənt/ ◼ ADJ Someone who is **resistant to** something is opposed to it and wants to prevent it. ❑ *Some people are very resistant to the idea of exercise.* ◻ ADJ If something is **resistant to** a particular thing, it is not harmed by it. ❑ *...how to make plants more resistant to disease.* [from Latin]

**reso|lute** /rɛzəlut/ ADJ Someone who is **resolute** is determined not to change their mind or not to give up a course of action. [FORMAL] ❑ *...a*

decisive and resolute leader. ● **reso|lute|ly** ADV ❑ *He resolutely refused to speak English.* [from Latin]

**reso|lu|tion** /rɛzəluʃ°n/ (**resolutions**)
◼ N-COUNT A **resolution** is a formal decision made at a meeting by means of a vote. ❑ *He was not satisfied with the resolution.* ◻ N-COUNT If you make a **resolution**, you decide to try very hard to do something. ❑ *They made a resolution to get more exercise.* ◼ N-UNCOUNT **Resolution** is determination to do something or not do something. ❑ *"I think I'll look for a new job," I said with sudden resolution.* ◼ N-SING The **resolution** of a problem or difficulty is the final solving of it. [FORMAL] ❑ *...the successful resolution of an argument.* [from Latin]

**re|solve** /rɪzɒlv/ (**resolves, resolving, resolved**)
◼ V-T To **resolve** a problem, argument, or difficulty means to find a solution to it. [FORMAL] ❑ *We must resolve these problems.* ◻ V-T If you **resolve to** do something, you make a firm decision to do it. [FORMAL] ❑ *Judy resolved to be a better mother.* ◼ N-VAR **Resolve** is determination to do what you have decided to do. [FORMAL] ❑ *...the American public's resolve to go to war if necessary.* [from Latin]

**re|solved** /rɪzɒlvd/ ADJ If you are **resolved to** do something, you are determined to do it. [FORMAL] ❑ *He was resolved to stay until the end.* [from Latin]

**reso|nance** /rɛzənəns/ (**resonances**) N-VAR A **resonance** is the sound that is produced by an object when it vibrates at the same rate as the sound waves from another object. [TECHNICAL] [from Latin]

**reso|nant** /rɛzənənt/ ADJ A sound that is **resonant** is deep and strong. ❑ *His voice sounded resonant in the empty room.* ● **reso|nance** /rɛzənəns/ N-UNCOUNT ❑ *Her voice has lost its resonance.* [from Latin]

**reso|nate** /rɛzəneɪt/ (**resonates, resonating, resonated**) V-I If something **resonates**, it vibrates and produces a deep, strong sound. ❑ *Traffic noise resonated in the room.* [from Latin]

**re|sort** /rɪzɔrt/ (**resorts, resorting, resorted**)
◼ V-I If you **resort to** a course of action that you do not really approve of, you adopt it because you cannot see any other way of achieving what you want. ❑ *The two men resorted to shouting.* ◻ PHRASE If you do something **as a last resort**, you do it because you can find no other way of getting out of a difficult situation or of solving a problem. ❑ *As a last resort, we hired a private detective.* ◼ N-COUNT A **resort** is a place where a lot of people spend their vacation. ❑ *...ski resorts.* [from Old French]

**re|sound|ing** /rɪzaundɪŋ/ ◼ ADJ A **resounding** sound is loud and clear. ❑ *...a resounding cheer from the crowd.* ◻ ADJ You can refer to a very great success as a **resounding** success. ❑ *The good weather made the vacation a resounding success.* [from Old French]

**re|source** /rɪsɔrs/ (**resources**) N-COUNT The **resources** of a country, organization, or person are the materials, money, and other things that they have and can use. ❑ *Some families don't even have the resources to feed themselves.* [from Old French]

**re|source|ful** /rɪsɔrsfəl/ ADJ Someone who is **resourceful** is good at finding ways of dealing with problems. ❑ *He was very resourceful.*

R

## Word Web   respiratory system

**Respiration** moves **air** into and out of the **lungs**. Air enters through the **nose** or **mouth**. Then it travels down the windpipe and into the **lungs**. In the lungs **oxygen** absorbs into the bloodstream. Blood carries oxygen to the heart and other organs. The lungs also remove **carbon dioxide** from the blood. This gas is then **exhaled** through the mouth. During **inhalation** the **diaphragm** moves downward and the lungs fill with air. During exhalation the diaphragm relaxes and air flows out. Adult humans **breathe** about six liters of air each minute.

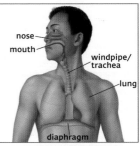

nose
mouth
windpipe/trachea
lung
diaphragm

● re|source|ful|ness N-UNCOUNT ❑ *He showed resourcefulness in emergencies.* [from Old French]
re|source re|cov|ery N-UNCOUNT **Resource recovery** is the process of obtaining useful materials or energy from things that are thrown away, such as paper or glass.

re|spect /rɪspɛkt/ (**respects, respecting, respected**) **1** V-T If you **respect** someone, you have a good opinion of their character or ideas. ❑ *I want her to respect me for my work.* **2** N-UNCOUNT If you have **respect for** someone, you have a good opinion of them. ❑ *I have tremendous respect for Dean.* **3** → see also **self-respect 4** V-T If someone **respects** your wishes, rights, or customs, he or she avoids doing things that you would dislike or regard as wrong. ❑ *I tried to respect her wishes.* **5** N-UNCOUNT If someone shows **respect for** your wishes, rights, or customs, he or she avoids doing anything you would dislike or regard as wrong. ❑ *...respect for people's rights and customs.* **6** PHRASE If you **pay** your **respects to** someone, you go to see them or speak to them in order to be polite. [FORMAL] ❑ *I have come to pay my respects to the princess.* **7** PHRASE You use expressions like **in this respect** and **in many respects** to indicate that what you are saying applies to the thing or things you have just mentioned. ❑ *The brothers were different from each other in many respects.* **8** PHRASE You use **with respect to** to say what something relates to. [FORMAL] ❑ *The decision was legal with respect to Swiss law.* [from Latin] **9** → see also **respected**

### Thesaurus    *respect*    Also look up :

| | |
|---|---|
| V. | admire **1** |
| N. | consideration, courtesy, esteem **4** |

re|spect|able /rɪspɛktəbªl/ **1** ADJ Someone or something that is **respectable** is approved of by society and considered to be morally correct. ❑ *...a respectable family.* ● re|spect|abil|ity /rɪspɛktəbɪlɪti/ N-UNCOUNT ❑ *A single house with a yard became the sign of respectability.* **2** ADJ **Respectable** means good enough or acceptable. ❑ *The team scored a respectable 68.* [from Latin]
re|spect|ed /rɪspɛktɪd/ ADJ Someone or something that is **respected** is admired and considered important by many people. ❑ *He is highly respected for his art.* [from Latin]
re|spect|ful /rɪspɛktfəl/ ADJ If you are **respectful**, you show respect for someone. ❑ *The children were always respectful to older people.* ● re|spect|ful|ly ADV ❑ *"You are an artist," she said respectfully.* [from Latin]

re|spec|tive /rɪspɛktɪv/ ADJ **Respective** means relating or belonging separately to the individual people you have just mentioned. ❑ *Steve and I were at very different stages in our respective careers.* [from Latin]
re|spec|tive|ly /rɪspɛktɪvli/ ADV **Respectively** means in the same order as the items that you have just mentioned. ❑ *Their sons, Ben and Jonathan, were three and six respectively.* [from Latin]
res|pi|ra|tion /rɛspɪreɪʃªn/ N-UNCOUNT **Respiration** is the exchange of gases between living cells and their environment. In humans and animals, **respiration** is breathing. [MEDICAL] [from Latin]

### Word Link   spir ≈ breath : a*spir*e, in*spir*e, *respir*atory

res|pi|ra|tory /rɛspərətɔri/ ADJ **Respiratory** means relating to breathing. [MEDICAL] ❑ *...people with respiratory problems.* [from Latin]
res|pi|ra|tory sys|tem (**respiratory systems**) N-COUNT Your body's **respiratory system** is the group of organs that are involved in breathing, including the nose, mouth, and lungs.
→ see Word Web: **respiratory system**
res|pite /rɛspɪt/ N-SING A **respite** is a short period of rest from something unpleasant. [FORMAL] ❑ *He was enjoying a respite from his job.* [from Old French]
re|spond /rɪspɒnd/ (**responds, responding, responded**) V-T/V-I When you **respond** to something that is done or said, you react to it by doing or saying something yourself. ❑ *They responded positively to the president's request for financial help.* ❑ *The army responded with gunfire.* ❑ *"I have no idea," she responded.* [from Old French]
re|sponse /rɪspɒns/ (**responses**) **1** N-COUNT Your **response** to an event or to something that is said is your reply or reaction to it. ❑ *There has been no response to his remarks.* **2** N-COUNT The **response** of an organism to a stimulus is the way that the organism reacts to it. [from Latin]

### Word Partnership   Use *response* with :

| | |
|---|---|
| ADJ. | **correct** response, **enthusiastic** response, **immediate** response, **military** response, **negative/positive** response, **overwhelming** response, **quick** response, **written** response |

re|spon|sibil|ity /rɪspɒnsɪbɪlɪti/ (**responsibilities**) **1** N-UNCOUNT If you have

r

**responsibility** for something or someone, or if they are your **responsibility**, it is your job or duty to deal with them. ❑ *Each manager had responsibility for ten people.* ❷ N-UNCOUNT If you accept **responsibility for** something that has happened, you agree that you were to blame for it. ❑ *No one admitted responsibility for the attacks.* ❸ N-PLURAL Your **responsibilities** are the duties that you have because of your job or position. ❑ *...work and family responsibilities.* ❹ N-SING If you think that you have a **responsibility to** do something, you feel that you ought to do it because it is morally right to do it. ❑ *We have a responsibility to help older people in our community.* [from Latin]
→ see **citizenship**

| Word Partnership | Use *responsibility* with : |
|---|---|
| v. | **be given** responsibility ❶ |
| | **assume** responsibility, **bear** responsibility, **take** responsibility ❶ ❷ ❹ |
| | **have (a)** responsibility ❶ ❹ |
| | **accept** responsibility, **claim** responsibility ❷ |
| ADJ. | **financial** responsibility, **moral** responsibility, **personal** responsibility ❶ ❷ ❹ |

re|spon|sible /rɪspɒnsɪbªl/ ❶ ADJ If someone or something is **responsible for** a particular event or situation, they are the cause of it or they can be blamed for it. ❑ *He still felt responsible for her death.* ❷ ADJ If you are **responsible for** something, it is your job or duty to deal with it. ❑ *...the people responsible for sales and marketing.* ❸ ADJ If you are **responsible to** a person or group, they have authority over you and you have to report to them about what you do. ❑ *The President of the Republic is responsible to the French people.* ❹ ADJ **Responsible** people behave properly and sensibly, without needing to be supervised. ❑ *The media should be more responsible in what they report.* ● re|spon|sibly ADV ❑ *He urged her to behave responsibly.* [from Latin]

re|spon|sive /rɪspɒnsɪv/ A **responsive** person is quick to react to people or events and to show emotions such as pleasure and affection. ❑ *Harriet was a responsive little girl.* ● re|spon|sive|ness N-UNCOUNT ❑ *...the mother's responsiveness to the child's needs.* [from Latin]

rest
❶ QUANTIFIER USES
❷ VERB AND NOUN USES

❶ rest /rɛst/ ❶ QUANT The **rest** is used to refer to all the parts of something or all the things in a group that remain or that you have not already mentioned. ❑ *...an experience I will remember for the rest of my life.* ● **Rest** is also a pronoun. ❑ *I ate two cakes and saved the rest.* ❷ PHRASE You can add **and the rest** or **all the rest of it** to the end of a statement or list when you want to refer in a vague way to other things that are associated with the ones you have already mentioned. [SPOKEN] ❑ *...a man with nice clothes, a nice car and the rest.* [from Old French]

❷ rest /rɛst/ (rests, resting, rested) ❶ V-T/V-I If you **rest** or if you **rest** your body, you do not do anything active for a time. ❑ *He's tired and the doctor advised him to rest.* ● rest|ed ADJ ❑ *He looked well rested after his vacation.* ❷ N-VAR If you get some **rest** or have a **rest**, you do not do anything active for a time. ❑ *You're exhausted — go home and get some rest.* ❸ V-I If something such as a theory or your success **rests on** a particular thing, it depends on that thing. [FORMAL] ❑ *My whole future rests on his decision.* ❹ V-T If you **rest** something somewhere, you put it there so that its weight is supported. ❑ *He rested his arms on the back of the chair.* ❺ V-T/V-I If something **is resting** somewhere, or if you **are resting** it there, it is in a position where its weight is supported. ❑ *His head was resting on her shoulder.* ❻ V-I If you **rest** on or against someone or something, you lean on them so that they support the weight of your body. ❑ *He rested on his shovel.* ❼ PHRASE When an object that has been moving **comes to rest**, it finally stops. [FORMAL] ❑ *The car skidded off the road and came to rest in a field.* [from Old English] ❽ **rest assured** → see **assured** ❾ **to rest on** your **laurels** → see **laurel**
→ see **motion, sleep**

| Thesaurus | rest | Also look up : |
|---|---|---|
| v. | lie down, relax ❷ ❶ | |

**rest area** (rest areas) N-COUNT A **rest area** is a place beside a highway where you can buy gasoline and other things, or have a meal.

| Word Link | re ≈ back, again : reflect, refuel, restate |
|---|---|

re|state /risteɪt/ (restates, restating, restated) V-T If you **restate** something, you say it again in words or writing, usually in a slightly different way. [FORMAL] ❑ *He continued to restate his opposition to violence.* [from Old French]

res|tau|rant /rɛstərənt, -tərɑnt, -trɑnt/ (restaurants) N-COUNT A **restaurant** is a place where you can buy and eat a meal and pay for it. In restaurants, your food is usually served to you at your table by a waiter or waitress. ❑ *...an Italian restaurant.* [from French]
→ see **city**

rest|less /rɛstlɪs/ ❶ ADJ If you are **restless**, you are bored, impatient, or dissatisfied, and you want to do something else. ❑ *I got restless and moved to San Francisco.* ● rest|less|ness N-UNCOUNT ❑ *Many fears and anxieties cause a feeling of restlessness.* ❷ ADJ If someone is **restless**, they keep moving around because they find it difficult to keep still. ❑ *My father seemed very restless and excited.* ● rest|less|ly ADV ❑ *He walked up and down restlessly.* [from Old English]

re|store /rɪstɔr/ (restores, restoring, restored) ❶ V-T To **restore** something means to cause it to exist again. ❑ *The army was brought in to restore order.* ● res|to|ra|tion /rɛstəreɪʃªn/ N-UNCOUNT ❑ *...the restoration of law and order.* ❷ V-T To **restore** someone or something **to** a previous condition or place means to cause them to be in that condition or place again. ❑ *We will restore her to health.* ❸ V-T To **restore** an old building, painting, or piece of furniture means to repair and clean it, so that it looks like it did when it was new. ❑ *...experts who specialize in restoring old buildings.* ● res|to|ra|tion (restorations) N-VAR ❑ *...the restoration of old houses.* [from Old French]

R

**re|strain** /rɪstreɪn/ (restrains, restraining, restrained) **1** V-T If you **restrain** someone, you stop them from doing what they intended or wanted to do, usually by using your physical strength. ❑ *Wally gripped my arm to restrain me.* **2** V-T If you **restrain** an emotion or you **restrain yourself from** doing something, you prevent yourself from showing that emotion or doing what you wanted or intended to do. ❑ *She was unable to restrain her anger.* ● **re|strained** ADJ ❑ *He was very restrained in the circumstances.* **3** V-T To **restrain** something that is growing or increasing means to prevent it from getting too large. ❑ *The speech is about economic growth and restrained spending.* [from Old French]

**re|strain|ing or|der** (restraining orders) N-COUNT A **restraining order** is an order by a court of law that someone should stop doing something until a court decides whether they are legally allowed to continue doing it. [LEGAL] ❑ *She took out a restraining order against him.*

**re|straint** /rɪstreɪnt/ (restraints) **1** N-VAR **Restraints** are rules or conditions that limit or restrict someone or something. ❑ *...the need for spending restraints in some areas.* **2** N-UNCOUNT **Restraint** is calm, controlled, and unemotional behavior. ❑ *They behaved with great restraint.* [from Old French]

**re|strict** /rɪstrɪkt/ (restricts, restricting, restricted) **1** V-T If you **restrict** something, you put a limit on it to prevent it from becoming too great. ❑ *...restricting the number of students.* ● **re|strict|ed** ADJ ❑ *...a carefully restricted diet.* ● **re|stric|tion** /rɪstrɪkʃ<sup>ə</sup>n/ (restrictions) N-VAR ❑ *...restrictions on spending.* **2** V-T To **restrict** the movement or actions of someone or something means to prevent them from moving or acting freely. ❑ *The government restricted the media.* ● **re|strict|ed** ADJ ❑ *...a highly restricted area.* ● **re|stric|tion** N-VAR ❑ *...this restriction of individual freedom.* ❑ *...the restrictions of city living.* **3** V-T If you **restrict** someone or their activities **to** one thing, they can only do, have, or deal with that thing. If you **restrict** them **to** one place, they cannot go anywhere else. ❑ *Patients are restricted to the grounds of the hospital.* **4** V-T If you **restrict** something **to** a particular group, only that group can do it or have it. If you **restrict** something to a particular place, it is allowed only in that place. ❑ *They decided to restrict acceptance to 30 percent of applicants.* [from Latin]

**re|stric|tive** /rɪstrɪktɪv/ ADJ Something that is **restrictive** prevents people from doing what they want to do. ❑ *...restrictive immigration laws.* [from Latin]

**restroom** (restrooms) also **rest room** N-COUNT In a restaurant, theater, or other public place, a **restroom** is a room with a toilet for people to use.

**re|struc|ture** /ristrʌktʃər/ (restructures, restructuring, restructured) V-T To **restructure** an organization or system means to change the way it is organized, usually in order to make it work more effectively. ❑ *...plans to restructure American education.* ● **re|struc|tur|ing** (restructurings) N-VAR ❑ *The company got rid of 1,520 workers as part of a restructuring.* [from Latin]

**rest stop** (rest stops) N-COUNT On a long journey by road, a **rest stop** is a short period when you stop and leave your vehicle, for example to eat

or use the restroom.

**re|sult** /rɪzʌlt/ (results, resulting, resulted) **1** N-COUNT A **result** is something that happens or exists because of something else that has happened. ❑ *...people who developed the disease as a direct result of their work.* **2** V-I If something **results in** a particular situation or event, it causes that situation or event to happen. ❑ *Fifty percent of road accidents result in head injuries.* **3** V-I If something **results from** a particular event or action, it is caused by that event or action. ❑ *Many hair problems result from what you eat.* **4** N-COUNT A **result** is the situation that exists at the end of a contest. ❑ *...election results.* **5** N-COUNT A **result** is the number that you get when you do a calculation. ❑ *Our computers made the same calculation but got different results.* [from Latin]

**re|sult|ant** /rɪzʌltənt/ ADJ **Resultant** means caused by the event just mentioned. [FORMAL] ❑ *...the operation and the resultant pain.* [from Latin]

**re|sult|ant ve|loc|ity** (resultant velocities) N-COUNT The **resultant velocity** of a moving object is its total speed in a particular direction once all the different forces acting on it have been taken into account. [TECHNICAL]

**re|sume** /rɪzum/ (resumes, resuming, resumed) V-T/V-I If you **resume** an activity or if it **resumes**, it begins again. [FORMAL] ❑ *After the war he resumed his job at Wellesley College.* ● **re|sump|tion** /rɪzʌmpʃ<sup>ə</sup>n/ N-UNCOUNT ❑ *...the resumption of discussions.* [from Latin]

**ré|su|mé** /rɛzumeɪ/ (résumés) also **resume** **1** N-COUNT A **résumé** is a short account, either spoken or written, of something that has happened or that someone has said or written. ❑ *...a résumé of his speech.* **2** N-COUNT Your **résumé** is a brief account of your personal information, your education, and the jobs you have had. [from French]

**re|sur|gence** /rɪsɜrdʒ<sup>ə</sup>ns/ N-SING If there is a **resurgence** of an attitude or activity, it reappears and grows. [FORMAL] ❑ *...the resurgence of violence.* [from Latin]

**res|ur|rect** /rɛzərɛkt/ (resurrects, resurrecting, resurrected) V-T If you **resurrect** something, you cause it to exist again after it had disappeared or ended. ❑ *The company decided to resurrect old advertisements.* ● **res|ur|rec|tion** /rɛzərɛkʃ<sup>ə</sup>n/ N-UNCOUNT ❑ *...a resurrection of an old story from the mid-70s.* [from Old French]

**re|sus|ci|tate** /rɪsʌsɪteɪt/ (resuscitates, resuscitating, resuscitated) V-T If you **resuscitate** someone who has stopped breathing, you cause them to start breathing again. ❑ *They rushed her to the hospital for resuscitation and treatment.* [from Latin]

**re|tail** /riteɪl/ (retails, retailing, retailed) **1** N-UNCOUNT **Retail** is the activity of selling products directly to the public. [BUSINESS] ❑ *...retail stores.* **2** V-I If an item in a store **retails at** or **for** a particular price, it is for sale at that price. [BUSINESS] ❑ *It originally retailed for $23.50.* [from Old French] **3** → see also **retailing**

**re|tail|er** /riteɪlər/ (retailers) N-COUNT A **retailer** is a person or business that sells goods to the public. [BUSINESS] ❑ *...carpet retailers.* [from Old French]

r

**re|tail|ing** /rɪ́teɪlɪŋ/ N-UNCOUNT **Retailing** is the activity of selling products directly to the public. [BUSINESS] ❑ *She spent fourteen years in retailing.* [from Old French]

**re|tain** /rɪteɪn/ (**retains, retaining, retained**) V-T To **retain** something means to continue to have that thing. [FORMAL] ❑ *The inside of the shop still retains a nineteenth-century atmosphere.* [from Old French]

| Thesaurus | retain | Also look up : |
|---|---|---|
| v. | hold, keep, maintain, remember, save; (*ant.*) give up, lose | |

**re|tali|ate** /rɪtǽlieɪt/ (**retaliates, retaliating, retaliated**) V-I If you **retaliate** when someone harms or annoys you, you do something which harms or annoys them in return. ❑ *I was tempted to retaliate.* ❑ *...actions designed to retaliate against the government.* **re|talia|tion** /rɪtælieɪʃ°n/ N-UNCOUNT ❑ *The attack was in retaliation for his death.* [from Late Latin]

**re|ten|tion** /rɪtɛnʃ°n/ N-UNCOUNT The **retention** of something is the keeping of it. [FORMAL] ❑ *They argued for the retention of a strong central government.* [from Latin]

**re|think** /riθɪŋk/ (**rethinks, rethinking, rethought**) ◼ V-T If you **rethink** something such as a problem, a plan, or a policy, you think about it again and change it. ❑ *Both political parties are rethinking their policies.* ❑ *Several of his friends are also rethinking their career plans.* ◼ N-SING If you have a **rethink** of a problem, a plan, or a policy, you think about it again and change it. ❑ *This is part of a rethink in foreign policy.* [from Old English]

**reti|cent** /rɛ́tɪsənt/ ADJ Someone who is **reticent** does not tell people about things. ❑ *She is so reticent about her achievements.* **reti|cence** N-UNCOUNT ❑ *Pauline liked his reticence.* [from Latin]

**reti|na** /rɛ́tɪnə/ (**retinas**) N-COUNT Your **retina** is the area at the back of your eye that sends images to your brain. [from Medieval Latin]
→ see **eye**

**re|tire** /rɪtaɪər/ (**retires, retiring, retired**) V-I When older people **retire**, they leave their job and usually stop working completely. ❑ *He planned to retire at 65.* **re|tired** ADJ ❑ *...a seventy-three-year-old retired teacher.* [from French]

**re|tiree** /rɪtaɪəri/ (**retirees**) N-COUNT A **retiree** is a retired person. ❑ *...a city suitable for retirees and young families.* [from French]

**re|tire|ment** /rɪtaɪərmənt/ (**retirements**) ◼ N-VAR **Retirement** is the time when a worker retires. ❑ *...the proportion of people who are over retirement age.* ◼ N-UNCOUNT A person's **retirement** is the period in their life after they have retired. ❑ *...financial support during retirement.* [from French]

**re|tire|ment fund** (**retirement funds**) N-COUNT A **retirement fund** is a special fund which people pay money into so that, when they retire from their job, they will receive money regularly as a pension.

**re|tire|ment plan** (**retirement plans**) N-COUNT A **retirement plan** is a savings plan in which part of the money that you earn is invested in the plan for you to use when you retire. [BUSINESS]

**re|tort** /rɪtɔ́rt/ (**retorts, retorting, retorted**) V-T To **retort** means to reply angrily to someone. [WRITTEN] ❑ *"I did not!" Sherrie retorted.* **Retort** is also a noun. ❑ *She was trying to think of some smart retort.* [from Latin]

**re|trace** /rɪtreɪs/ (**retraces, retracing, retraced**) V-T If you **retrace** your steps or **retrace** your way, you return to the place you started from by going back along the same route. ❑ *He retraced his steps to the place where he started.* [from French]

**re|tract** /rɪtrǽkt/ (**retracts, retracting, retracted**) V-T/V-I If you **retract** something that you have said or written, you say that you did not mean it. [FORMAL] ❑ *Mr. Smith tried to retract the statement.* ❑ *He's hoping that if he makes me feel guilty, I'll retract.* **re|trac|tion** /rɪtrǽkʃ°n/ (**retractions**) N-COUNT ❑ *Miss Pearce said she expected a retraction of his comments.* [from Latin]

**re|treat** /rɪtrit/ (**retreats, retreating, retreated**) ◼ V-I If you **retreat**, you move away from something or someone. ❑ *I retreated from the room.* ◼ V-I When an army **retreats**, it moves away from enemy forces in order to avoid fighting them. ❑ *The French were forced to retreat.* **Retreat** is also a noun. ❑ *The British Army was in full retreat.* ◼ N-COUNT A **retreat** is a quiet, isolated place that you go to in order to rest or to do things in private. ❑ *He spent yesterday hidden away in his country retreat.* [from Old French]

**ret|ri|bu|tion** /rɛtrɪbyuʃ°n/ N-UNCOUNT **Retribution** is punishment for a crime, especially punishment that is carried out by someone other than the official authorities. [FORMAL] ❑ *The attack was retribution for the U.S. bombings.* [from Old French]

**re|triev|al** /rɪtriv³l/ N-UNCOUNT The **retrieval** of something is the process of getting it back from a particular place. ❑ *Data is stored in a computer so that retrieval is very easy.* [from Old French]

**re|trieve** /rɪtriv/ (**retrieves, retrieving, retrieved**) V-T If you **retrieve** something, you get it back from the place where you left it. ❑ *Alexander went into the bedroom to retrieve his hat.* [from French]

**ret|ro** /rɛ́troʊ/ ADJ **Retro** clothes, music, and objects are based on the styles of the past. ❑ *...1950s retro dresses.* [from Latin]

**retro|grade** /rɛ́trəgreɪd/ (**retrogrades**) N-VAR A **retrograde** is a section of dance or music in which the usual order is reversed, by beginning at the end and ending at the beginning. [TECHNICAL] [from Latin]

**retro|grade or|bit** (**retrograde orbits**) N-VAR Planets that have a **retrograde orbit** move around the sun in the opposite direction to the direction in which they spin on their own axis. [TECHNICAL]

**retro|grade ro|ta|tion** N-UNCOUNT Planets that have **retrograde rotation** spin on their axis in the opposite direction to the direction that they move around the sun. Compare **prograde rotation**. [TECHNICAL]

**retro|spect** /rɛ́trəspɛkt/ PHRASE When you consider something **in retrospect**, you think about it afterward, and often have a different opinion about it from the one that you had at the time. ❑ *The decision was not a very good one in retrospect.* [from Latin]

**retro|spec|tive** /rɛtrəspɛktɪv/ (**retrospectives**)
N-COUNT A **retrospective** is an exhibition or
showing of work done by an artist over many
years, rather than his or her most recent work.
❑ ...a retrospective of the movies of Judy Garland. [from
Latin]

**re|turn** /rɪtɜrn/ (**returns, returning, returned**)
**1** V-I When you **return to** a place, you go back
there after you have been away. ❑ He will return to
Moscow tomorrow. **2** N-SING Your **return** is your
arrival back at a place where you were before.
❑ Kenny explained the reason for his sudden return to
Dallas. **3** V-T If you **return** something that you
have borrowed or taken, you give it back or put it
back. ❑ I enjoyed the book and said so when I returned
it. ● **Return** is also a noun. ❑ ...Japan's demand
for the return of the islands. **4** V-T If you **return**
someone's action, you do the same thing to him
or her as he or she has just done to you. If you
**return** someone's feelings, you feel the same way
toward him or her as he or she feels toward you.
❑ Harry returned my phone call. **5** V-I If you **return to**
a state that you were in before, you start being in
that state again. ❑ Life has improved and returned to
normal. ● **Return** is also a noun. ❑ He made a return
to normal health. **6** V-I If you **return to** a subject
that you have mentioned before, you begin talking
about it again. ❑ Reporters returned to the subject of
baseball. **7** V-I If you **return to** an activity that you
were doing before, you start doing it again. ❑ At
52, he is young enough to return to politics. ● **Return**
is also a noun. ❑ He has not ruled out the possibility
of a return to football. **8** V-T When a judge or jury
**returns** a verdict, they announce whether they
think the person on trial is guilty or not. ❑ They
returned a verdict of not guilty. **9** N-COUNT The
**return on** an investment is the profit that you get
from it. [BUSINESS] ❑ The return on the money remains
tiny. **10** PHRASE If you do something **in return for**
what someone else has done for you, you do it
because they did that thing for you. ❑ He nodded
at Alison and she nodded in return. [from Old French]
**11** to return fire → see fire
→ see library

**re|uni|fi|ca|tion** /riyunɪfɪkeɪ∫ən/ N-UNCOUNT
The **reunification** of a country or city that has been
divided into two or more parts for some time is the
joining of it together again. ❑ ...the reunification of
East and West Beirut in 1991.

**re|union** /riyunɪən/ (**reunions**) **1** N-COUNT A
**reunion** is a party attended by members of the
same family, school, or other group who have not
seen each other for a long time. ❑ The school holds
an annual reunion. **2** N-VAR A **reunion** is a meeting

between people who have been separated for some
time. ❑ It was a very emotional reunion. [from Church
Latin]

**re|unite** /riyunaɪt/ (**reunites, reuniting,
reunited**) **1** V-T If people **are reunited**, they meet
each other again after they have been separated
for some time. ❑ She was finally reunited with her
family. **2** V-T/V-I If a divided organization or
country **is reunited**, or if it **reunites**, it becomes
one united organization or country again. ❑ His
first job was to reunite the army. [from Late Latin]

**re|use** (**reuses, reusing, reused**)

> The verb is pronounced /riyuz/. The noun is
> pronounced /riyus/.

V-T When you **reuse** something, you use it again
instead of throwing it away. ❑ Try where possible to
reuse paper. ● **Reuse** is also a noun. ❑ Copper, brass,
and aluminium are separated and remelted for reuse.
[from Old French]
→ see dump

**rev** /rɛv/ (**revs, revving, revved**) **1** V-T/V-I When
the engine of a vehicle **revs**, or when you **rev** it,
the engine speed is increased as the accelerator is
pressed. ❑ The engine revved, and the car jerked away.
❑ The bus was revving its engine. ● **Rev up** means
the same as **rev**. ❑ ...the sound of a car revving up.
**2** N-PLURAL An engine's **revs** are its speed, which
is measured in revolutions per minute.

**re|vamp** /rivæmp/ (**revamps, revamping,
revamped**) V-T If someone **revamps** something,
they make changes to it in order to try and
improve it. ❑ It is time to revamp the system.
● **Revamping** is also a noun. ❑ The revamping
includes replacing the old uniform.

**re|veal** /rɪvil/ (**reveals, revealing, revealed**)
**1** V-T To **reveal** something means to make
people aware of it. ❑ She has refused to reveal any
more details. ❑ A survey revealed that a growing
number of people are overweight. **2** V-T If you **reveal**
something that has been out of sight, you uncover
it so that people can see it. ❑ We removed the carpet
to reveal the wooden floor beneath. [from Old French]

**re|veal|ing** /rɪvilɪŋ/ ADJ A **revealing** statement,
account, or action tells you something that you
did not know, especially about the person doing
it or making it. ❑ ...a revealing interview. [from Old
French]

**rev|el** /rɛvəl/ (**revels, reveling** or **revelling,
reveled** or **revelled**) V-I If you **revel in** a situation
or experience, you enjoy it very much. ❑ Annie was
smiling and laughing, clearly reveling in the attention.
[from Old French]

**rev|ela|tion** /rɛvəleɪ∫ən/ (**revelations**)
**1** N-COUNT A **revelation** is a surprising or
interesting fact that is made known to people.
❑ ...revelations about his private life. **2** N-VAR The
**revelation of** something is the act of making
it known. ❑ ...the revelation of his true identity.
**3** N-SING If you say that something you
experienced was **a revelation**, you are saying that
it was very surprising or very good. ❑ Degas's work
was a revelation to her. [from Church Latin]

**rev|el|er** /rɛvələr/ (**revelers**) also **reveller**
N-COUNT **Revelers** are people who are enjoying
themselves in a noisy way. [LITERARY] ❑ ...a crowd
of revelers. [from Old French]

**re|venge** /rɪvɛndʒ/ N-UNCOUNT **Revenge**
involves hurting or punishing someone who has

r

hurt or harmed you. ❑ *The attackers took revenge on the boy, claiming he was a school bully.* [from Old French]

**rev|enue** /rɛvənyu/ (**revenues**) ◼ N-VAR **Revenue** is money that a company, organization, or government receives from people. [BUSINESS] ❑ *One butcher shop saw a 50 percent drop in revenue.* [from Old French] ◻ → see also **Internal Revenue Service**

**rev|enue stream** (**revenue streams**) N-COUNT A company's **revenue stream** is the amount of money that it receives from selling a particular product or service. [BUSINESS] ❑ *This unexpected revenue stream provided them with cash.*

**re|ver|ber|ate** /rɪvɜrbəreɪt/ (**reverberates, reverberating, reverberated**) V-I When a loud sound **reverberates** through a place, it echoes through it. ❑ *The noise reverberated through the house.* [from Latin]

**Word Link** vere ≈ fear, awe : irre**vere**nt, re**vere**, re**vere**nce

**re|vere** /rɪvɪər/ (**reveres, revering, revered**) V-T If you **revere** someone or something, you respect and admire them greatly. [FORMAL] ❑ *The Chinese revered corn as a gift from heaven.* ● **re|vered** ADJ ❑ *...some of the country's most revered organizations.* ● **rev|er|ence** /rɛvərəns/ N-UNCOUNT ❑ *We stand together at this ceremony in reverence for the dead.* [from Latin]

**Rev|er|end** /rɛvərənd/ N-TITLE **Reverend** is a title used before the name or rank of an officially appointed Christian religious leader. ❑ *...the Reverend Jim Simons.*

**re|ver|sal** /rɪvɜrsᵊl/ (**reversals**) N-COUNT A **reversal** of a process, policy, or trend is a complete change in it. ❑ *This is a complete reversal of previous U.S. policy.* [from Old French]

**re|verse** /rɪvɜrs/ (**reverses, reversing, reversed**) ◼ V-T To **reverse** a decision, policy, or trend means to change it to the opposite decision, policy, or trend. ❑ *They will not reverse the decision to increase prices.* ◻ V-T If you **reverse** the order of a set of things, you arrange them in the opposite order, so that the first thing comes last. ❑ *In German, you sometimes have to reverse the normal word order.* ◾ N-UNCOUNT If your car is **in reverse**, you have changed gears so that you can drive it backward. ◹ ADJ **Reverse** means opposite from what you expect or to what has just been described. ❑ *The wrong attitude will have exactly the reverse effect.* ◺ N-SING If you say that one thing is **the reverse** of another, you are emphasizing that the first thing is the complete opposite of the second thing. ❑ *He was not at all happy. Quite the reverse.* ◻ PHRASE If something happens **in reverse** or goes **into reverse**, things happen in the opposite way from what usually happens or from what has been happening. ❑ *Amis tells the story in reverse, from the moment the man dies.* [from Old French]

**re|verse fault** (**reverse faults**) N-COUNT A **reverse fault** is a fault in the surface of the Earth where the rock above the fault has moved up. Compare **normal fault**. [TECHNICAL]

**re|verse psy|chol|ogy** N-UNCOUNT If you use **reverse psychology** on someone, you try to get them to do something by saying or doing the opposite of what they expect. ❑ *He was trying some*

reverse psychology, pretending he wasn't interested, when really he was.

**re|vert** /rɪvɜrt/ (**reverts, reverting, reverted**) V-I When people or things **revert to** a previous state, system, or type of behavior, they go back to it. ❑ *He made a few comments and then reverted to silence.* [from Latin]

**re|view** /rɪvyu/ (**reviews, reviewing, reviewed**) ◼ N-COUNT A **review of** a situation or system is an examination of it by people in authority, to see if changes are needed. ❑ *The president ordered a review of the situation.* ◻ V-T If you **review** a situation or system, you consider it carefully to see if changes are needed. ❑ *The new proposal will be reviewed by the city council on Monday.* ◾ N-COUNT A **review** is a report in the media in which someone gives their opinion of something such as a new book or movie. ❑ *The movie had a good review in the magazine.* ◹ V-T If someone **reviews** something such as a new book or movie, they write a report or give a talk on television or radio in which they express their opinion of it. ❑ *Richard Coles reviews all the latest DVD releases.* ● **re|view|er** (**reviewers**) N-COUNT ❑ *...the reviewer for Atlantic Monthly.* ◻ V-T/V-I When you **review for** an exam, or when you **review** your work, you read things again and make notes in order to be prepared for the exam. ❑ *Review all the notes for each course.* ● **Review** is also a noun. ❑ *...three two-hour reviews.* [from French]

**Word Partnership** Use *review* with :

N. **performance** review ◼
review **a case**, review **evidence** ◻
**book** review, **film/movie** review,
**restaurant** review ◹
review **questions** ◻

**re|vise** /rɪvaɪz/ (**revises, revising, revised**) V-T If you **revise** something, you alter it in order to make it better or more accurate. ❑ *He revised his opinion of the professor.* ❑ *They revised their prices to make them equal with their competitors' prices.* ● **re|vi|sion** /rɪvɪʒᵊn/ (**revisions**) N-VAR ❑ *The phase of writing that is most important is revision.* [from Latin]

**re|vis|it** /rɪvɪzɪt/ (**revisits, revisiting, revisited**) V-T If you **revisit** a place, you return there for a visit after you have been away for a long time. ❑ *When we returned to Canada, we revisited this lake.* [from Latin]

**Word Link** vita ≈ life : re**vita**lize, **vita**l, **vita**lity

**re|vi|tal|ize** /rɪvaɪtᵊlaɪz/ (**revitalizes, revitalizing, revitalized**) V-T To **revitalize** something that is no longer active or healthy means to make it active or healthy again. ❑ *This hair conditioner is excellent for revitalizing hair.*

**Word Link** viv ≈ living : re**viv**al, sur**viv**e, **viv**id

**re|viv|al** /rɪvaɪvᵊl/ (**revivals**) ◼ N-COUNT When there is a **revival of** something, it becomes active or popular again. ❑ *...a revival of interest in a number of artists.* ◻ N-COUNT A **revival** is a new production of a play, an opera, or a ballet. ❑ *...John Clement's revival of Chekhov's "The Seagull."* [from Old French]

**re|vive** /rɪvaɪv/ (**revives, reviving, revived**) ◼ V-T/V-I When something such as the economy, a business, a trend, or a feeling **is revived** or when it **revives**, it becomes active, popular, or successful again. ❑ …*an attempt to revive the economy.* **2** V-T When someone **revives** a play, opera, or ballet, they present a new production of it. ❑ *His plays were revived both here and abroad.* **3** V-T/V-I If you **revive** someone who has fainted or if they **revive**, they become conscious again. ❑ *She tried to revive him.* [from Old French]

re|**voke** /rɪvoʊk/ (**revokes, revoking, revoked**) V-T When people in authority **revoke** something such as a license, a law, or an agreement, they cancel it. [FORMAL] ❑ *Police revoked his driver's license.* [from Latin]

re|**volt** /rɪvoʊlt/ (**revolts, revolting, revolted**)
**1** N-VAR A **revolt** is an illegal and often violent attempt by a group of people to change their country's political system. ❑ …*a revolt by ordinary people against their leaders.* **2** V-I When people **revolt**, they make an illegal and often violent attempt to change their country's political system. ❑ *In 1375 the people revolted.* **3** N-VAR A **revolt** by a person or group against someone or something is a refusal to accept the authority of that person or thing. ❑ *Conservative Republicans led the revolt against the policy.* **4** V-I When people **revolt against** someone or something, they reject the authority of that person or reject that thing. ❑ *California taxpayers revolted against higher taxes.* [from French]

re|**volt**|ing /rɪvoʊltɪŋ/ ADJ **Revolting** means horrible and disgusting. ❑ *The smell was revolting.* [from French]

revo|**lu**|tion /rɛvəluʃᵊn/ (**revolutions**)
**1** N-COUNT A **revolution** is a successful attempt by a large group of people to change the political system of their country by force. ❑ *The period since the revolution has been very unsettled.* **2** N-COUNT A **revolution** in a particular area of human activity is an important change in that area. ❑ *There was a revolution in ship design in the nineteenth century.* **3** N-COUNT A **revolution** of an object such as a planet is one complete circle that it makes around a central point such as a star. [from Old French]

revo|**lu**|tion|ary /rɛvəluʃənɛri/
(**revolutionaries**) **1** ADJ **Revolutionary** activities, organizations, or people have the aim of causing a political revolution. ❑ *Do you know anything about the revolutionary movement?* **2** N-COUNT A **revolutionary** is a person who tries to cause a revolution or who takes an active part in one. **3** ADJ **Revolutionary** ideas and developments involve great changes in the way that something is done or made. ❑ …*a revolutionary new product.* [from Old French]

revo|**lu**|tion|ize /rɛvəluʃənaɪz/ (**revolutionizes, revolutionizing, revolutionized**) V-T When something **revolutionizes** an activity, it causes great changes in the way that it is done. ❑ *Plastics have revolutionized the way we live.* [from Old French]

re|**volve** /rɪvɒlv/ (**revolves, revolving, revolved**)
**1** V-I If one thing **revolves around** another thing, the second thing is the main feature or focus of the first thing. ❑ *Since childhood, her life has revolved around tennis.* **2** V-I If a discussion or conversation **revolves around** a particular topic, it is mainly about that topic. ❑ *Most of the conversation revolved around Daniel's trip to New York.* **3** V-T/V-I When something **revolves** or when you **revolve** it, it moves or turns in a circle around a central point or

line. ❑ *The fan revolved slowly.* [from Latin]

re|**volv**|er /rɪvɒlvər/ (**revolvers**) N-COUNT A **revolver** is a kind of hand gun. [from Latin]

re|**vue** /rɪvyu/ (**revues**) N-COUNT A **revue** is a theatrical performance consisting of songs, dances, and jokes about recent events. [from French]

re|**vul**|sion /rɪvʌlʃᵊn/ N-UNCOUNT **Revulsion** is a strong feeling of disgust or disapproval. ❑ *Victoria looked about with revulsion at the dirty apartment.* [from Latin]

re|**ward** /rɪwɔrd/ (**rewards, rewarding, rewarded**) **1** N-COUNT A **reward** is something that you are given, for example because you have behaved well, worked hard, or provided a service to the community. ❑ *The school gives rewards for good behavior.* **2** N-COUNT A **reward** is a sum of money offered to anyone who can give information about lost or stolen property, a missing person, or someone who is wanted by the police. ❑ *The firm offered a $10,000 reward for information leading to the arrest of the killer.* **3** V-T If you do something and **are rewarded** with a particular benefit, you receive that benefit as a result of doing that thing. ❑ *He thanked her and was rewarded with a smile.* [from Old Norman French]

| **Thesaurus** | *reward* | Also look up : |
|---|---|---|
| N. | bonus, prize; (*ant.*) punishment **1** | |

re|**ward**|ing /rɪwɔrdɪŋ/ ADJ An experience or action that is **rewarding** gives you satisfaction or brings you benefits. ❑ …*a career that is very rewarding.* [from Old Norman French]

re|**writ**|able /rɪraɪtəbᵊl/ also **rewriteable** ADJ A **rewritable** CD or DVD is a CD or DVD that you can record onto more than once. [from Old English]

re|**write** /rɪraɪt/ (**rewrites, rewriting, rewrote, rewritten**) V-T If someone **rewrites** a piece of writing such as a book, an article, or a law, they write it in a different way in order to improve it. ❑ *She decided to rewrite her will.* [from Old English]

rheto|**ric** /rɛtərɪk/ N-UNCOUNT If you refer to speech or writing as **rhetoric**, you disapprove of it because it is intended to convince and impress people but may not be sincere or honest. ❑ …*political rhetoric rather than reality.* [from Latin]

rhe|**tori**|cal /rɪtɔrɪkᵊl/ **1** ADJ A **rhetorical** question is one that is asked in order to make a statement rather than to get an answer. ● rhe|**tori**|cal|ly /rɪtɔrɪkli/ ADV ❑ *"Do these kids know how lucky they are?" Jackson asked rhetorically.* **2** ADJ **Rhetorical** language is intended to be grand and impressive. [FORMAL] [from Latin]

rhe|**tori**|cal strat|egy (**rhetorical strategies**) N-COUNT A **rhetorical strategy** is one of the traditional methods used to communicate meaning in a speech or piece of writing, for example exposition or description.

**rhi**|no /raɪnoʊ/ (**rhinos**) N-COUNT A **rhino** is the same as a **rhinoceros**. [INFORMAL]

rhi|**noc**|er|os /raɪnɒsərəs/ (**rhinoceroses**) N-COUNT A **rhinoceros** is a large Asian or African animal with thick, gray skin and a horn, or two horns, on its nose. [from Latin]

**rhi**|zoid /raɪzɔɪd/ (**rhizoids**) N-COUNT **Rhizoids** are thin structures that grow downward from plants such as mosses and fungi and have a

r

similar function to roots. [TECHNICAL] [from Greek]

**rhi|zome** /ráɪzoʊm/ (**rhizomes**) N-COUNT **Rhizomes** are the horizontal stems from which some plants, such as irises, grow. Rhizomes are found on or just under the surface of the earth. [from New Latin]

**rhyme** /ráɪm/ (**rhymes, rhyming, rhymed**)
◼ V-RECIP If one word **rhymes with** another or if two words **rhyme**, they have a very similar sound. ❑ *June rhymes with moon.* ❑ *...names that rhyme: Donnie, Ronnie, Connie.* ◻ N-COUNT A **rhyme** is a short poem which has rhyming words at the ends of its lines. ❑ *He was teaching Helen a rhyme.* ◻ N-UNCOUNT **Rhyme** is the use of rhyming words as a technique in poetry. ❑ *The plays are in rhyme.* [from Old French]

**rhythm** /ríðəm/ (**rhythms**) ◼ N-VAR A **rhythm** is a regular series of sounds or movements. ❑ *...the rhythms of jazz.* ◻ N-COUNT A **rhythm** is a regular pattern of changes, for example changes in your body, in the seasons, or in the tides. ◻ N-COUNT A **rhythm** is a regular repetition of lines or shapes to achieve a specific effect or pattern. [from Latin]

**rhyth|mic** /ríðmɪk/ also **rhythmical** /ríðmɪkᵊl/ ADJ A **rhythmic** movement or sound is repeated at regular intervals. ❑ *Good breathing is slow, rhythmic and deep.* ● **rhyth|mi|cal|ly** /ríðmɪkli/ ADV ❑ *They all stood, moving rhythmically to the music.* [from Latin]

**rib** /ríb/ (**ribs**) N-COUNT Your **ribs** are the 12 pairs of curved bones that surround your chest. ❑ *Her heart was thumping against her ribs.* [from Old English]

**rib|bon** /ríbən/ (**ribbons**) N-VAR A **ribbon** is a long, narrow piece of cloth that you use for tying things together or as a decoration. ❑ *She tied back her hair with a ribbon.* [from Old French]

**ribo|some** /ráɪbəsoʊm/ (**ribosomes**) N-COUNT **Ribosomes** are structures within the cells of an organism that produce proteins.

**rice** /ráɪs/ (**rices**) N-VAR **Rice** consists of white or brown grains taken from a cereal plant. ❑ *...a meal consisting of chicken, rice, and vegetables.* [from French]
→ see Word Web: **rice**
→ see **grain**

**rich** /rítʃ/ (**richer, richest, riches**) ◼ ADJ A **rich** person has a lot of money or valuable possessions. ❑ *He was a very rich man.* ● **The rich** are rich people. ❑ *Only the rich can afford to live there.* ◻ N-PLURAL **Riches** are valuable possessions or large amounts of money. ❑ *He starred in a movie that led to success*

and riches. ◻ ADJ If something is **rich in** a useful or valuable substance or is a **rich source of** it, it contains a lot of it. ❑ *Oranges are rich in vitamin C.* ◻ ADJ **Rich** food contains a lot of fat or oil. ❑ *More cream would make it too rich.* ◻ ADJ A **rich** life or history is one that is interesting because it is full of different events and activities. ❑ *...a rich and interesting life.* ● **rich|ness** N-UNCOUNT ❑ *...the richness of human life.* [from Old English]

**rich|ly** /rítʃli/ ◼ ADV If something is **richly** colored, flavored, or perfumed, it has a pleasantly strong color, flavor, or perfume. ❑ *...richly colored paintings.* ◻ ADV If something is **richly** decorated, patterned, or furnished, it has a lot of elaborate and beautiful decoration, patterns, or furniture. ❑ *...a richly decorated silver pot.* ◻ ADV If you say that someone **richly** deserves an award, success, or victory, you approve of what they have done and feel very strongly that they deserve it. ❑ *He achieved the success he so richly deserved.* [from Old English]

**rick|ety** /ríkɪti/ ADJ A **rickety** structure or piece of furniture is not very strong or well made, and seems likely to collapse or break. ❑ *...rickety wooden stairs.*

**ri|cot|ta** /rɪkɒtə/ also **ricotta cheese** N-UNCOUNT **Ricotta** is a soft, white, unsalted cheese made from sheep's milk. [from Italian]

**rid** /ríd/ (**rids, ridding**)

The form **rid** is used in the present tense and is the past tense and past participle of the verb.

◼ PHRASE When you **get rid of** something that you do not want or do not like, you take action so that you no longer have it. ❑ *The owner needs to get rid of the car for financial reasons.* ◻ PHRASE If you **get rid of** someone who is causing problems for you or who you do not like, you make them

R

leave. □ *He believed that his manager wanted to get rid of him.* **3** V-T If you **rid** a place or person **of** something undesirable, you succeed in removing it completely from that place or person. □ *...an attempt to rid the country of political corruption.* **4** ADJ If you **are rid of** someone or something that you did not want or that caused problems for you, they are no longer with you or causing problems for you. □ *The family wanted a way to be rid of her.* [from Old Norse]

**rid|den** /rɪd³n/ **Ridden** is the past participle of **ride**. [from Old English]

**rid|dle** /rɪd³l/ (**riddles**) **1** N-COUNT A **riddle** is a puzzle or joke in which you ask a question that seems to be nonsense but which has a clever or amusing answer. **2** N-COUNT You can describe something that is puzzling as a **riddle**. □ *Police are trying to solve the riddle of Tina's murder.* [from Old English]

**rid|dled** /rɪd³ld/ **1** ADJ If something is **riddled with** bullets or bullet holes, it is full of bullet holes. **2** ADJ If something is **riddled with** undesirable qualities or features, it is full of them. □ *...a bank riddled with corruption.* [from Old English]

**ride** /raɪd/ (**rides, riding, rode, ridden**) **1** V-T/V-I When you **ride** a horse, you sit on it and control its movements. □ *I saw a girl riding a horse.* □ *Can you ride?* **2** V-T/V-I When you **ride** a bicycle or a motorcycle, you sit on it, control it, and travel along on it. □ *Riding a bike is great exercise.* □ *...men riding on motorcycles.* **3** V-I When you **ride in** a vehicle such as a car, you travel in it. □ *He prefers traveling on the subway to riding in a car.* **4** N-COUNT A **ride** is a trip on a horse or bicycle, or in a vehicle. □ *She took some friends for a ride in the car.* **5** → see also **riding** **6** PHRASE If you say that someone faces **a rough ride**, you mean that things are going to be difficult for them because people will criticize them a lot or treat them badly. [INFORMAL] □ *The president will face a rough ride unless the plan works.* **7** PHRASE If someone **rides herd on** other people or their actions, they supervise them or watch them closely. □ *Hank often stayed late at the office, riding herd on the day-to-day business of the magazine.* [from Old English]

**Word Partnership** Use *ride* with :

| | |
|---|---|
| N. | **bus/car/train/subway** ride **4** |
| V. | **give** *someone* **a** ride, **go for a** ride, **offer** *someone* **a** ride **4** |
| ADV. | ride **home 4** |
| ADJ. | **long** ride, **scenic** ride, **short** ride, **smooth** ride **4** |

**rid|er** /raɪdər/ (**riders**) N-COUNT A **rider** is someone who rides a horse, a bicycle, or a motorcycle. □ *She is a very good rider.* [from Old English]

→ see **horse**

**ridge** /rɪdʒ/ (**ridges**) **1** N-COUNT A **ridge** is a long, narrow piece of raised land. □ *...a high road along a mountain ridge.* **2** N-COUNT A **ridge** is a raised line on a flat surface. □ *...the bony ridge of his nose.* [from Old English]

→ see **mountain**

**Word Link** cule ≈ small : minuscule, molecule, ridicule

**Word Link** rid, ris ≈ laughing : deride, derision, ridicule

**ridi|cule** /rɪdɪkyul/ (**ridicules, ridiculing, ridiculed**) **1** V-T If you **ridicule** someone or **ridicule** their ideas or beliefs, you make fun of them in an unkind way. □ *They ridiculed him because of the way he spoke.* **2** N-UNCOUNT If someone or something is an object of **ridicule** or is held up to **ridicule**, someone makes fun of them in an unkind way. □ *As a child, she was the object of ridicule from classmates.* [from French]

**ri|dicu|lous** /rɪdɪkyələs/ ADJ If you say that something or someone is **ridiculous**, you mean that they are very foolish. □ *It is ridiculous to suggest we are having a romance.* [from Latin]

**ri|dicu|lous|ly** /rɪdɪkyələsli/ ADV You use **ridiculously** to emphasize the fact that you think something is unreasonable or very surprising. □ *...rolls of silk that were ridiculously cheap.* [from Latin]

**rid|ing** /raɪdɪŋ/ N-UNCOUNT **Riding** is the activity or sport of riding horses. □ *The next morning we went riding across the sands together.* [from Old English]

**rife** /raɪf/ ADJ If you say that something, usually something bad, is **rife** in a place or that the place is **rife with** it, you mean that it is very common. □ *Disease was rife in the prison.* [from Old English]

**ri|fle** /raɪf³l/ (**rifles, rifling, rifled**) **1** N-COUNT A **rifle** is a gun with a long barrel. □ *They shot him with an automatic rifle.* **2** V-T/V-I If you **rifle through** things or **rifle** them, you make a quick search among them in order to find something or steal something. □ *She was rifling though her files.* [from Old French]

**rift** /rɪft/ (**rifts**) **1** N-COUNT A **rift** between people or countries is a serious quarrel or disagreement that stops them from having a good relationship. □ *...a growing rift between the president and congress.* **2** N-COUNT A **rift** is a split that appears in something solid, especially in the ground. **3** N-COUNT In geology, a **rift** occurs when the tectonic plates of the Earth separate. [from Old Norse]

**rift val|ley** (**rift valleys**) N-COUNT A **rift valley** is a valley formed as the result of a crack in the Earth's surface.

**rig** /rɪg/ (**rigs, rigging, rigged**) **1** V-T If someone **rigs** an election, a job appointment, or a game, they dishonestly arrange it to get the result they want or to give someone an unfair advantage. □ *She accused her opponents of rigging the vote.* ● **rig|ging** N-UNCOUNT □ *...vote rigging.* **2** N-COUNT A **rig** is a large structure that is used for looking for oil or gas and for taking it out of the ground or the bottom of the ocean. □ *...oil rigs.* **3** N-COUNT A **rig** is a truck that is made in two or more sections which are jointed together by metal bars, so that the vehicle can turn more easily. [of Scandinavian origin]

→ see **oil**

r

---

**right**

❶ CORRECT, APPROPRIATE, OR ACCEPTABLE

❷ DIRECTION AND POLITICAL GROUPINGS

❸ ENTITLEMENT

❹ DISCOURSE USES

❺ USED FOR EMPHASIS

---

❶ **right** /raɪt/ (**rights, righting, righted**) ◼ ADJ If something is **right**, it is correct and agrees with the facts. ❏ *That's absolutely right.* ❏ *That clock never told the right time.* ● **Right** is also an adverb. ❏ *He guessed right about some things.* ◻ ADJ If you do something in the **right** way or in the **right** place, you do it as or where it should be done or was planned to be done. ❏ *Walking, done in the right way, is a good form of exercise.* ❏ *...delivery of the right pizza to the right place.* ● **Right** is also an adverb. ❏ *To make sure I did everything right, I bought an instruction book.* ◼ ADJ If you say that someone is seen in **all the right** places or knows **all the right** people, you mean that they go to places that are socially acceptable or know people who are socially acceptable. ◼ ADJ If someone is **right about** something, they are correct in what they say or think about it. ❏ *Ron was right about the result of the election.* ◼ ADJ If something such as a choice, action, or decision is the **right** one, it is the best or most suitable one. ❏ *She made the right choice in leaving New York.* ◼ ADJ **Right** is used to refer to activities or actions that are considered to be morally good and acceptable. ❏ *It's not right, leaving her like this.* ● **Right** is also a noun. ❏ *He knew right from wrong.* ● **right|ness** N-UNCOUNT ❏ *...an offense against rightness.* ◼ V-T If you **right** a wrong, you do something to make up for a mistake or something bad that you did in the past. ◼ V-T If you **right** something that has fallen or rolled over, or if it **rights itself**, it returns to its normal upright position. ❏ *He righted the boat and continued the race.* ◼ ADJ The **right** side of a material is the side that is intended to be seen and that faces outward when it is made into something. ❏ *Turn the pants right side out.* [from Old English] ◼ **heart in the right place** → see **heart** ◼ **it serves** you **right** → see **serve**

❷ **right** /raɪt/

The spelling **Right** is also used for meaning ◼.

◼ N-SING The **right** is one of two opposite directions, sides, or positions. If you are facing north and you turn to the right, you will be facing east. ❏ *On the right is a lovely garden.* ● **Right** is also an adverb. ❏ *Turn right into the street.* ◻ ADJ Your **right** arm, leg, or ear, for example, is the one which is on the right side of your body. ◼ N-SING You can refer to people who support the political ideals of capitalism and conservatism as the **right**. ❏ *This man is the best hope of the Republican Right.* [from Old English]

❸ **right** /raɪt/ (**rights**) ◼ N-PLURAL Your **rights** are what you are morally or legally entitled to do or to have. ❏ *They don't know their rights.* ◻ N-SING If you have a **right** to do or to have something, you are morally or legally entitled to do it or to have it. ❏ *We have the right to protest.* ◼ PHRASE If something is not true but you think that it

should be, you can say that **by rights** it should be true. ❏ *She did work which by rights should be done by someone else.* ◼ PHRASE If someone is a successful or respected person **in** their **own right**, they are successful or respected because of their own efforts and talents rather than those of the people they are connected with. ❏ *The president's daughter is famous in her own right.* [from Old English]
→ see **citizenship**

❹ **right** /raɪt/ CONVENTION You can use **right** to check whether what you have just said is correct. [SPOKEN] ❏ *They have a small plane, right?* [from Old English]
→ see also **all right**

❺ **right** /raɪt/ ◼ ADV You can use **right** to emphasize the exact place, position, or time of something. ❏ *A car appeared right in front of him.* ◻ ADV If you say that something happened **right after** a particular time or event or **right before** it, you mean that it happened immediately after or before it. ❏ *All of a sudden, right after the summer, Mother got married.* ◼ ADV If you say **I'll be right there** or **I'll be right back**, you mean that you will get to a place or get back to it in a very short time. ❏ *I'm going to get some water. I'll be right back.* ◼ PHRASE If you do something **right away**, you do it immediately. [INFORMAL] ❏ *He wants to see you right away.* ◼ PHRASE You can use **right now** to emphasize that you are referring to the present moment. [INFORMAL] ❏ *Right now I'm feeling very excited.* [from Old English]

**right an|gle** (**right angles**) ◼ N-COUNT A **right angle** is an angle of ninety degrees. ◻ PHRASE If two things are **at right angles**, they form an angle of 90° where they touch each other. You can also say that one thing is **at right angles** to another. ❏ *...two lines at right angles.*

**right|eous** /raɪtʃəs/ ADJ Someone who is **righteous** is morally good, especially according to the rules of a religion. [FORMAL] ❏ *He was young and righteous.* [from Old English]

**right|ful** /raɪtfəl/ ADJ If you say that someone or something has returned to its **rightful** place or position, they have returned to the place or position that you think they should have. ❏ *The stolen goods were returned to their rightful owner.*
● **right|ful|ly** ADV ❏ *Jealousy is the feeling that someone else has something that rightfully belongs to you.* [from Old English]

**right-hand** ADJ If something is on the **right-hand** side of something, it is positioned on the right of it. ❏ *...a church on the right-hand side of the road.*

**right-handed** ADJ Someone who is **right-handed** uses their right hand rather than their left hand for activities such as writing and sports, and for picking things up. ● **Right-handed** is also an adverb. ❏ *I batted left-handed and bowled right-handed.*

**right-of-center** ADJ A **right-of-center** person or political party has political views which are closer to capitalism and conservatism than to socialism but which are not very extreme. ❏ *...the right-of-center candidate.*

**right of way** (**rights of way**) N-COUNT A **right of way** is a public path across private land.

**right tri|an|gle** (**right triangles**) N-COUNT A **right triangle** has one angle that is a right angle.

## right-wing

The spelling **right wing** is used for meaning **2**.

**1** ADJ A **right-wing** person or group has conservative or capitalist views. ❑ *...a right-wing government.* ● **right-winger** (**right-wingers**) N-COUNT ❑ *Across Europe, right-wingers are gaining power.* **2** N-SING **The right wing** of a political party consists of the members who have the most conservative or the most capitalist views. ❑ *...the right wing of the Republican Party.*

**rig|id** /rɪdʒɪd/ **1** ADJ Laws, rules, or systems that are **rigid** cannot be changed or varied, and are therefore considered to be rather severe. ❑ *...rigid rules about student behavior.* ● **ri|gid|ity** /rɪdʒɪdɪti/ N-UNCOUNT ❑ *...the rigidity of government policy.* ● **rig|id|ly** ADV ❑ *The law was rigidly enforced.* **2** ADJ A **rigid** substance or object is stiff and does not bend, stretch, or twist easily. ❑ *...rigid plastic containers.* ● **ri|gid|ity** N-UNCOUNT ❑ *...the strength and rigidity of glass.* [from Latin]

**rig|id mo|tion** (**rigid motions**) N-VAR **Rigid motion** is a change to the position of a geometric figure such as a triangle in which the distances and angles between points in the figure remain the same. [TECHNICAL]

**rig|or** /rɪgər/ (**rigors**) **1** N-PLURAL **The rigors of** an activity or job are the difficult or unpleasant things that are associated with it. ❑ *...the rigors of army life.* **2** N-UNCOUNT If something is done with **rigor**, it is done in a strict, thorough way. ❑ *The prince behaved with professional rigor.* [from Latin]

**rig|or|ous** /rɪgərəs/ ADJ A test, system, or procedure that is **rigorous** is very thorough and strict. ❑ *...rigorous tests.* ● **rig|or|ous|ly** ADV ❑ *...rigorously conducted research.*

**rim** /rɪm/ (**rims**) N-COUNT The **rim** of a container or a circular object is the edge that goes all the way around the top or around the outside. ❑ *She looked at him over the rim of her glass.* [from Old English]

**rind** /raɪnd/ (**rinds**) **1** N-VAR The **rind** of a fruit such as a lemon or orange is its thick outer skin. **2** N-VAR The **rind** of cheese or bacon is the hard outer edge which you do not usually eat. [from Old English]

**rind**

---

### ring

**1** TELEPHONING OR MAKING A SOUND
**2** SHAPES AND GROUPS

**1 ring** /rɪŋ/ (**rings, ringing, rang, rung**) **1** V-I When a telephone **rings**, it makes a sound to let you know that someone is phoning you. ● **Ring** is also a noun. ❑ *After eight rings, someone answered the phone.* **2** V-T/V-I When you **ring** a bell or when a bell **rings**, it makes a sound. ❑ *He heard the school bell ring.* ● **Ring** is also a noun. ❑ *There was a ring of the bell.* **3** N-SING You can use **ring** to describe a quality that something such as a statement, discussion, or argument seems to have. For example, if an argument **has a familiar ring**, it seems familiar. **4** PHRASE If a statement **rings true**, it seems to be true or genuine. If it **rings hollow**, it does not seem to be true or genuine. [from Old English] **5** to **ring a bell** → see **bell**
▸ **ring up** → see **ring 1 2**

**2 ring** /rɪŋ/ (**rings, ringing, ringed**) **1** N-COUNT A **ring** is a small circle of metal that you wear on your finger. ❑ *...a gold wedding ring.* **2** N-COUNT An object or substance that is in the shape of a circle can be described as a **ring**. ❑ *...a large ring of keys.* **3** N-COUNT At a boxing or wrestling match or a circus, the **ring** is the place where the contest or performance takes place. ❑ *...a boxing ring.* **4** N-COUNT You can refer to an organized group of people who are involved in an illegal activity as a **ring**. ❑ *...an art theft ring.* **5** V-T If a building or place **is ringed with** or **by** something, it is surrounded by it. ❑ *The areas are ringed by soldiers.* [from Old English]
→ see **jewelry, circle**

**ring|tone** (**ringtones**) N-COUNT The **ringtone** is the sound made by a telephone, especially a cellphone, when it rings.

**rink** /rɪŋk/ (**rinks**) N-COUNT A **rink** is a large area covered with ice where people go to ice-skate. ❑ *The other skaters left the rink.* [from Scots]

**rinky-dink** /rɪŋkidɪŋk/ ADJ **Rinky-dink** things are small or unimportant. [INFORMAL] ❑ *I moved to this rinky-dink little place in Massachusetts.*

**rinse** /rɪns/ (**rinses, rinsing, rinsed**) V-T When you **rinse** something, you wash it in clean water in order to remove dirt or soap from it. ❑ *Rinse the rice.* ● **Rinse** is also a noun. ❑ *...a rinse with water.* [from Old French]

**riot** /raɪət/ (**riots, rioting, rioted**) **1** N-COUNT When there is a **riot**, a crowd of people behave violently in a public place. ❑ *Twelve people were killed during a riot at the prison.* **2** V-I If people **riot**, they behave violently in a public place. ❑ *They rioted in protest against the government.* ● **ri|ot|er** (**rioters**) N-COUNT ❑ *The police held the rioters back.* ● **ri|ot|ing** N-UNCOUNT ❑ *...three days of rioting.* [from Old French]

**rip** /rɪp/ (**rips, ripping, ripped**) **1** V-T/V-I When something **rips** or when you **rip** it, you tear it forcefully with your hands or with a tool such as a knife. ❑ *She ripped the photographs to pieces.* **2** N-COUNT A **rip** is a long cut or split in something made of cloth or paper. ❑ *...the rip in her new dress.* **3** V-T If you **rip** something away, you remove it quickly and forcefully. ❑ *Tatiana ripped the ring off her finger.* [from Flemish]
→ see **cut**

**rip**

▸ **rip off** PHR-VERB If someone **rips** you **off**, they cheat you by charging you too much money for something. [INFORMAL] ❑ *Make sure the taxi driver doesn't rip you off.*
▸ **rip up** PHR-VERB If you **rip** something **up**, you tear it into small pieces. ❑ *He ripped up the letter.*

**ripe** /raɪp/ (**riper, ripest**) **1** ADJ **Ripe** fruit or grain is fully grown and ready to eat. ❑ *...firm, but ripe fruit.* **2** ADJ If a situation is **ripe for** a particular development or event, that development or event is likely to happen soon. ❑ *The time was ripe for change.* [from Old English]

r

**rip|en** /ˈraɪpən/ (ripens, ripening, ripened)
v-T/v-I When crops **ripen** or when the sun **ripens** them, they become ripe. □ *I'm waiting for the apples to ripen.* [from Old English]

ripple

**rip|ple** /ˈrɪpəl/ (ripples, rippling, rippled)
■ N-COUNT **Ripples** are little waves on the surface of water caused by the wind or by something moving in or on the water. ■ v-T/v-I When the surface of an area of water **ripples** or when something **ripples** it, a number of little waves appear on it. □ *You throw a stone in a pool and it ripples.* [from Germanic]

**rise** /raɪz/ (rises, rising, rose, risen) ■ v-I If something **rises**, it moves upward. □ *Wilson watched the smoke rise from the chimney.* ● **Rise up** means the same as **rise**. □ *The bubbles rose up to the surface of the water.* ■ v-I When you **rise**, you stand up. [FORMAL] □ *Luther rose slowly from the chair.* ■ v-I When you **rise**, you get out of bed. [FORMAL] □ *Tony rose early.* ■ v-I When the sun or moon **rises**, it appears in the sky. ■ v-I If land **rises**, it slopes upward. □ *...the slope of land that rose from the house.* ■ v-T/v-I If an amount **rises**, it increases. □ *Interest rates rose from 4% to 5%.* □ *Exports rose 23%.* ■ N-COUNT A **rise in** the amount of something is an increase in it. □ *...another rise in interest rates.* ■ v-I If a sound **rises** or if your voice **rises**, it becomes louder or higher. □ *Her voice rose angrily.* ■ v-I If someone **rises to** a higher position or status, they become more important, successful, or powerful. □ *She was an intelligent woman who rose to the top of the organization.* ■ N-SING The **rise** of someone is the process by which they become more important, successful, or powerful. □ *His rise at the company was very quick.* ■ PHRASE If something **gives rise to** an event or situation, it causes that event or situation to happen. □ *...problems in communities which give rise to crime.* [from Old English] ■ to **rise to the challenge** → see **challenge** ■ to **rise to the occasion** → see **occasion** → see also **raise**

▶ **rise above** PHR-VERB If you **rise above** a difficulty or problem, you manage not to let it affect you. □ *You must rise above personal feeling.*

▶ **rise up** PHR-VERB When the people in a country **rise up**, they rebel against the people in authority and start fighting them. □ *People have risen up against their leader.*

**ris|ing ac|tion** N-UNCOUNT The **rising action** in the plot of a play or story is the events that lead to the climax of the plot. [TECHNICAL]

**risk** /rɪsk/ (risks, risking, risked) ■ N-VAR If there is a **risk** of something unpleasant, there is a possibility that it will happen. □ *There is a small risk of brain damage from the operation.* ■ N-COUNT If something that you do is a **risk**, it might have unpleasant or undesirable results. □ *You're taking a big risk showing this to Kravis.* ■ N-COUNT If you say that something or someone is a **risk**, you mean they are likely to cause harm. □ *Being very fat is a health risk.* ■ v-T If you **risk** something unpleasant, you do something knowing that

the unpleasant thing might happen as a result. □ *He risked breaking his leg when he jumped.* ■ v-T If you **risk** doing something, you do it, even though you know that it might have undesirable consequences. □ *I risked going back.* ■ v-T If you **risk** your life or something else important, you behave in a way that might result in it being lost or harmed. □ *She risked her own life to help him.* ■ PHRASE To be **at risk** means to be in a situation where something unpleasant might happen. □ *Overweight people are more at risk from heart disease.* ■ PHRASE If you tell someone that they are doing something **at their own risk**, you are warning them that, if they are harmed, it will be their own responsibility. □ *People who wish to come here do so at their own risk.* ■ PHRASE If you **run the risk of** doing or experiencing something undesirable, you do something knowing that the undesirable thing might happen as a result. □ *The officers ran the risk of losing their jobs.* [from French]

| **Thesaurus** | | risk | Also look up : |
|---|---|---|
| N. | accident, danger, gamble, hazard; (ant.) safety ■ ■ | | |
| V. | chance, endanger, gamble, jeopardize ■ ■ | | |

**risky** /ˈrɪski/ (riskier, riskiest) ADJ If an activity or action is **risky**, it is dangerous or likely to fail. □ *...risky projects.* [from French]

**rite** /raɪt/ (rites) N-COUNT A **rite** is a traditional ceremony that is carried out by a particular group or society. □ *...a religious rite.* [from Latin]

**rit|u|al** /ˈrɪtʃuəl/ (rituals) ■ N-VAR A **ritual** is a religious service or other ceremony which involves a series of actions performed in a fixed order. □ *...the holiest of their rituals.* ■ ADJ **Ritual** activities happen as part of a ritual or tradition. □ *...ritual dancing.* ■ N-VAR A **ritual** is a way of behaving or a series of actions that people regularly carry out in a particular situation. □ *It was a ritual that Lisa and Sarah had lunch together once a week.* [from Latin]
→ see **myth**

**ri|val** /ˈraɪvəl/ (rivals, rivaling or rivalling, rivaled or rivalled) ■ N-COUNT If people or groups are **rivals**, they are competing against each other for the same thing. □ *He is well ahead of his nearest rival.* ■ v-T If you say that one thing **rivals** another, you mean that they are both of the same standard or quality. □ *In my opinion, Chinese cooking rivals that of the French.* [from Latin]

**ri|val|ry** /ˈraɪvəlri/ (rivalries) N-VAR **Rivalry** is competition or conflict between people or groups who want the same things. □ *What causes rivalry between brothers?* [from Latin]

**riv|er** /ˈrɪvər/ (rivers) N-COUNT A **river** is a large amount of fresh water flowing continuously in a long line across the land. [from Old French]
→ see Picture Dictionary: **river**

**river|side** /ˈrɪvərsaɪd/ N-SING The **riverside** is the area of land by the side of a river. □ *They walked along the riverside.*

**riv|et** /ˈrɪvɪt/ (rivets, riveting, riveted) v-T If you **are riveted** by something, it fascinates you and holds your interest completely. □ *As a child I was riveted by my grandfather's appearance.* ● **riv|et|ing** ADJ □ *...Jeffrey Wolf's riveting book.* [from Old French]

Picture Dictionary
river
spring
lake
stream
gorge
valley
river
ocean
delta

**RNA** /ɑr ɛn eɪ/ N-UNCOUNT **RNA** is an acid in the chromosomes of the cells of living things which plays an important part in passing information about protein structure between different cells. **RNA** is an abbreviation for "ribonucleic acid." [TECHNICAL]

**roach** /roʊtʃ/ (**roaches**) N-COUNT A **roach** is the same as a **cockroach**. ❑ …a damp, roach-infested apartment. [from Old French]

**road** /roʊd/ (**roads**) N-COUNT A **road** is a long piece of hard ground that is built between two places so that people can drive or ride easily from one place to the other. ❑ There was very little traffic on the roads. [from Old English]
→ see **traffic**

**road|kill** /roʊdkɪl/ also **road kill** N-UNCOUNT **Roadkill** refers to the remains of animals that have been killed on the road by vehicles. ❑ I hate to see roadkill.

**road rage** N-UNCOUNT **Road rage** is anger or violent behavior by a driver toward another driver. ❑ …a road rage attack on a motorist.

**road|runner** /roʊdrʌnər/ (**roadrunners**) N-COUNT A **roadrunner** is a bird with a long tail, found mainly in the southwestern United States, that is able to run very quickly.

**road|side** /roʊdsaɪd/ (**roadsides**) N-COUNT The **roadside** is the area at the edge of a road. ❑ Bob left the car at the roadside and ran for help.

**road test** (**road tests, road testing, road tested**) also **road-test** ■ V-T If you **road test** a car or other vehicle, you drive it on roads in order to make sure that it is working properly. ● **Road test** is also a noun. ❑ …a road test of the car. ■ N-COUNT A **road test** is a driving test that you must pass in order to get a driver's license. ■ V-T If someone **road tests** a new product, they use it in order to make sure that it works properly. ❑ Catherine Young road tests waterproof jackets. ● **Road test** is also a noun. ❑ The kids gave all three toys thorough road tests.

**road|work** /roʊdwɜrk/ N-UNCOUNT **Roadwork** refers to repairs or other work being done on a road. ❑ The traffic was not moving due to roadwork.

**roam** /roʊm/ (**roams, roaming, roamed**) V-T/V-I If you **roam** an area or **roam around** it, you wander around it without having a particular purpose. ❑ Children roamed the streets.

**roar** /rɔr/ (**roars, roaring, roared**) ■ V-I If something, usually a vehicle, **roars** somewhere, it goes there very fast, making a loud noise. [WRITTEN] ❑ A police car roared past. ■ V-I If something **roars**, it makes a very loud noise. [WRITTEN] ❑ The engine roared, and the vehicle moved forward. ● **Roar** is also a noun. ❑ …the roar of traffic. ■ V-I If someone **roars** with laughter, they laugh in a very noisy way. ■ V-T/V-I If someone **roars**, they shout something in a very loud voice. [WRITTEN] ❑ "I'll kill you for that," he roared. ■ V-I When a lion **roars**, it makes the loud sound that lions typically make. ● **Roar** is also a noun. ❑ …the roar of lions. [from Old English]

**roar|ing** /rɔrɪŋ/ ■ ADJ A **roaring** fire has large flames and sends out a lot of heat. ❑ …nighttime beach parties, with a roaring fire. ■ ADJ If something is a **roaring** success, it is extremely successful. ❑ The book was a roaring success. [from Old English]
■ → see also **roar**

**roast** /roʊst/ (**roasts, roasting, roasted**) ■ V-T When you **roast** meat or other food, you cook it by dry heat in an oven or over a fire. ❑ He roasted the chicken. ■ ADJ **Roast** meat has been cooked by roasting. ❑ …roast beef. [from Old French]
→ see **cook, peanut**

**rob** /rɒb/ (**robs, robbing, robbed**) ■ V-T If someone **is robbed**, they have money or property stolen from them. ❑ Mrs. Yacoub was robbed of her watch. ● **rob|ber** (**robbers**) N-COUNT ❑ Armed robbers broke into a jeweler's. ■ V-T If someone **is robbed of** something that they deserve, have, or need, it is taken away from them. ❑ A knee injury robbed him of his place on the football team. [from Old French]

**rob|bery** /rɒbəri/ (**robberies**) N-VAR **Robbery** is the crime of stealing money or property from a place, often by using force. ❑ The gang committed several armed robberies. [from Old French]

**robe** /roʊb/ (**robes**) ■ N-COUNT A **robe** is a loose piece of clothing, usually worn in official or

r

> ## Word Web · rock
>
> **Rocks** are made of **minerals**.
> Sometimes they may contain only
> one **element**. Usually they contain
>
>
>
> igneous      sedimentary      metamorphic
>
> **compounds** of several elements. Each type of rock also has a unique **crystal** structure. Rock is
> always changing. When **lava erupts** from a **volcano**, it forms igneous rock. Wind, water, and ice
> **erode** this type of rock. The resulting **sediment** collects in rivers. Layers of sediment build up and
> form sedimentary rock. When tectonic **plates** move around, they create heat and pressure. This
> melting and crushing changes sedimentary rock into metamorphic rock.

religious ceremonies. [FORMAL] ❑ ...*the Pope's white robes.* ② N-COUNT A **robe** is a piece of clothing, often made of toweling, which people wear in the house, especially when they have just gotten up or taken a bath or shower. ❑ *Kyle put on a robe and went down to the kitchen.* [from Old French]

**rob|in** /rɒbɪn/ (**robins**) N-COUNT A **robin** is a brown bird with an orangey red neck and breast. European robins are smaller than North American ones, and are a completely different species of bird.

**ro|bot** /roʊbɒt, -bɒt/ (**robots**) N-COUNT A **robot** is a machine that is programmed to move and perform tasks automatically. ❑ ...*very lightweight robots that we could send to the moon.* [from Czech]

**ro|bust** /roʊbʌst, roʊbʌst/ ADJ Someone or something that is **robust** is very strong or healthy. ❑ *He was young and physically robust.* [from Latin]

**rock** /rɒk/ (**rocks, rocking, rocked**)
① N-UNCOUNT **Rock** is the hard substance which the Earth is made of. ❑ *The hills above the valley are bare rock.* ② N-COUNT A **rock** is a large piece of rock that sticks up out of the ground or the sea, or that has broken away from a mountain or a cliff. ❑ *She sat on the rock.* ③ N-COUNT A **rock** is a piece of rock that is small enough for you to pick up. ❑ *She picked up a rock and threw it into the water.* ④ V-T/V-I When something **rocks** or when you **rock** it, it moves slowly and regularly backward and forward or from side to side. ❑ *His body rocked from side to side with the train.* ⑤ V-T If an event or a piece of news **rocks** a group or society, it shocks them or makes them feel less secure. ❑ *His death rocked the fashion business.* ⑥ N-UNCOUNT **Rock** is loud music with a strong beat that is usually played and sung by a small group of people using instruments such as electric guitars and drums. ❑ ...*a rock concert.* [Senses 1 to 3 from Old French. Senses 4 to 6 from Old English.]
→ see Word Web: **rock**
→ see **earth, fossil, genre, crystal**

**rock and roll** also **rock'n'roll** N-UNCOUNT **Rock and roll** is a kind of popular music developed in the 1950s which has a strong beat and is played on electrical instruments. ❑ ...*Elvis Presley — the King of Rock and Roll.*

**rock cy|cle** (**rock cycles**) N-COUNT The **rock cycle** is the continuous process in which a particular type of rock, such as igneous rock, slowly changes into other types of rock, such as sedimentary or metamorphic rock. [TECHNICAL]

**rock|et** /rɒkɪt/ (**rockets, rocketing, rocketed**)
① N-COUNT A **rocket** is a space vehicle that is

shaped like a long tube. ❑ ...*the rocket that took astronauts to the moon.* ② N-COUNT A **rocket** is a missile containing explosives that is powered by gas. ❑ *There was another rocket attack on the city.* ③ V-I If things such as prices or social problems **rocket**, they increase very quickly and suddenly. ❑ *Prices for fresh food have rocketed.* [from Old French]

**rock fall** (**rock falls**) N-COUNT A **rock fall** is the movement of a group of loose rocks down a steep slope such as the side of a mountain.

**rocky** /rɒki/ (**rockier, rockiest**) ADJ A **rocky** place is covered with rocks or consists of large areas of bare rock. ❑ *The paths are very rocky.* [from Old English]

**rod** /rɒd/ (**rods**) ① N-COUNT A **rod** is a long, thin, metal or wooden bar. ❑ *The roof was strengthened with steel rods.* ② N-COUNT **Rods** are cells in the retina of the eye that help you to see in dim light. Compare **cone**. [TECHNICAL] [from Old English]

**rode** /roʊd/ **Rode** is the past tense of **ride**.

**ro|dent** /roʊdⁿnt/ (**rodents**) N-COUNT **Rodents** are small mammals which have sharp front teeth. Rats, mice, and squirrels are rodents. [from Latin]
→ see **herbivore**

**ro|deo** /roʊdioʊ, roʊdeɪoʊ/ (**rodeos**) N-COUNT A **rodeo** is a public entertainment event in which cowboys show different skills, including riding wild horses and catching cattle with ropes. [from Spanish]

**rogue** /roʊg/ (**rogues**) N-COUNT A **rogue** is a man who behaves in a dishonest or criminal way. [from Latin]

**rogue state** (**rogue states**) N-COUNT When politicians or journalists talk about a **rogue state**, they mean a country that they regard as a threat to their own country's security, for example, because it supports terrorism. ❑ ...*possible attacks from rogue states and terrorists.*

**roil** /rɔɪl/ (**roils, roiling, roiled**) V-I If water **roils**, it is rough and disturbed. ❑ *The water roiled as he climbed at the edge of the waterfall.*

**role** /roʊl/ (**roles**) ① N-COUNT The **role** of someone or something in a situation is their position and function in it. ❑ ...*the role of parents in raising their children.* ② N-COUNT A **role** is one of the characters that an actor or singer can play in a movie, play, or opera. ❑ *She got the lead role in the movie.* [from French]
→ see **theater**

| **Word Partnership** | Use *role* with : |
| --- | --- |
| ADJ. | **active** role, **key** role, **parental** role, **positive** role, role, **traditional** role, **vital** role **1** |
| | **bigger/larger** role, **leading** role, **major** role **1 2** |
| | **starring** role **2** |
| N. | **leadership** role, role **reversal 1** |
| | **lead** role **1** |
| V. | **play** a role, **take on** a role **1 2** |

**role mod|el** (**role models**) N-COUNT A **role model** is someone you admire and try to imitate. ❑ *Anne is my role model, who I look up to.*

**roll** /roʊl/ (**rolls, rolling, rolled**) **1** V-T/V-I When something **rolls** or when you **roll** it, it moves along a surface, turning over many times. ❑ *The ball rolled into the net.* **2** V-I When vehicles **roll** along, they move along slowly. ❑ *The truck rolled forward.* **3** V-I If drops of liquid **roll** down a surface, they move quickly down it. ❑ *Tears rolled down her cheeks.* **4** V-T If you **roll** something flexible **into** a cylinder or a ball, you form it into a cylinder or a ball by wrapping it several times around itself or by shaping it between your hands. ❑ *He took off his sweater, rolled it into a pillow, and lay down.* ● **Roll up** means the same as **roll**. ❑ *Stein rolled up the paper bag.* **5** N-COUNT A **roll of** paper, plastic, cloth, or wire is a long piece of it that has been wrapped many times around itself or around a tube. ❑ *...twelve rolls of film.* **6** N-COUNT A **roll** is a small piece of bread that is round or long and is made to be eaten by one person. ❑ *He spread butter on a roll.* **7** N-COUNT A **roll** is an official list of people's names. ❑ *...a roll of people who can vote.* **8** → see also **rolling, rock and roll** **9** PHRASE If something is several things **rolled into one**, it combines the main features or qualities of those things. ❑ *This is our kitchen, living room, and dining room all rolled into one.* [from Old French] **10** **heads will roll** → see **head** → see **bread**

▶ **roll in** PHR-VERB If something such as money **is rolling in**, it is appearing or being received in large quantities. [INFORMAL] ❑ *The money was rolling in.*
▶ **roll up 1** PHR-VERB If you **roll up** your sleeves or pant legs, you fold the ends back several times, making them shorter. ❑ *The jacket was too big so he*

*rolled up the cuffs.* **2** → see also **roll 4**

**roll|back** /roʊlbæk/ (**rollbacks**) N-COUNT A **rollback** is a reduction in price or some other change that makes something like it was before. ❑ *The tax rollback would destroy basic services.*

**roll|er** /roʊlər/ (**rollers**) N-COUNT A **roller** is a cylinder that turns around in a machine or device. [from Old French]

**roll|ing** /roʊlɪŋ/ ADJ **Rolling** hills are small hills with gentle slopes that extend a long way into the distance. ❑ *...the rolling countryside of southwestern France.* [from Old French]

**ROM** /rɒm/ **1** N-UNCOUNT **ROM** is the permanent part of a computer's memory. The information stored there can be read but not changed. **ROM** is an abbreviation for "read-only memory." [COMPUTING] **2** → see also **CD-ROM**

**Ro|man** /roʊmən/ (**Romans**) **1** ADJ **Roman** means related to or connected with ancient Rome and its empire. ❑ *...the Roman Empire.* ● A **Roman** was a citizen of ancient Rome or its empire. ❑ *The Romans brought this custom to Britain.* **2** ADJ **Roman** means related to or connected with modern Rome. ❑ *...a Roman hotel room.* ● A **Roman** is someone who lives in or comes from Rome. ❑ *...soccer-mad Romans.* [from Middle English]
→ see Picture Dictionary: **Roman numeral**

**Ro|man Catho|lic** (**Roman Catholics**) **1** ADJ The **Roman Catholic** Church is the same as the **Catholic** Church. ❑ *...a Roman Catholic priest.* **2** N-COUNT A **Roman Catholic** is the same as a **Catholic**. ❑ *Maria was a Roman Catholic.*

**ro|mance** /roʊmæns, roʊmæns/ (**romances**) **1** N-COUNT A **romance** is a relationship between two people who are in love with each other but who are not married to each other. ❑ *After a short romance they got married.* **2** N-UNCOUNT **Romance** refers to the actions and feelings of people who are in love, especially behavior that is very caring or affectionate. ❑ *He still finds time for romance by cooking for his girlfriend.* **3** N-UNCOUNT You can refer to the pleasure and excitement of doing something new or exciting as **romance**. ❑ *...the romance that used to be part of travel.* **4** N-COUNT A **romance** is a novel or movie about a love affair. ❑ *...historical romances.* [from Old French]
→ see **love**

r

| **Picture Dictionary** | Roman numerals |
| --- | --- |

| | | | | | | | |
| --- | --- | --- | --- | --- | --- | --- | --- |
| I | 1 | XI | 11 | XXI | 21 | XL | 40 |
| II | 2 | XII | 12 | XXII | 22 | L | 50 |
| III | 3 | XIII | 13 | XXIII | 23 | LX | 60 |
| IV | 4 | XIV | 14 | XXIV | 24 | LXX | 70 |
| V | 5 | XV | 15 | XXV | 25 | LXXX | 80 |
| VI | 6 | XVI | 16 | XXVI | 26 | XC | 90 |
| VII | 7 | XVII | 17 | XXVII | 27 | C | 100 |
| VIII | 8 | XVIII | 18 | XXVIII | 28 | D | 500 |
| IX | 9 | XIX | 19 | XXIX | 29 | M | 1000 |
| X | 10 | XX | 20 | XXX | 30 | MMVII | 2007 |

**ro|man|tic** /roʊmæntɪk/ (**romantics**) **1** ADJ Someone who is **romantic** or does **romantic** things says and does things that make their partner feel special and loved. □ ...*a romantic dinner for two people*. **2** ADJ **Romantic** means connected with sexual love. □ *He was not interested in a romantic relationship with Ingrid*. ● **ro|man|ti|cal|ly** ADV □ *We are not romantically involved*. **3** ADJ A **romantic** play, movie, or story describes or represents a love affair. □ ...*a lovely romantic comedy*. **4** ADJ If you say that someone has a **romantic** view or idea of something, you are critical of them because they think that thing is better or more exciting than it really is. □ *He has a romantic view of society*. ● A **romantic** is a person who has romantic views. □ *You're a romantic*. [from French]
→ see **love**

**romp** /rɒmp/ (**romps, romping, romped**) V-I When children or animals **romp**, they play noisily and happily. □ *Little children romped happily in the yard*. [from Old French]

**ron|do** /rɒndoʊ/ (**rondos**) N-COUNT A **rondo** is a piece of music in which the main theme is repeated several times, with other themes or sections between each repetition. [from Italian]

**roof** /ruf/ (**roofs**)

The plural can be pronounced /rufs/ or /ruvz/.

**1** N-COUNT The **roof** of a building is the covering on top of it. □ ...*a cottage with a red roof*. **2** N-COUNT

The **roof** of a car or other vehicle is the top part of it. □ *The car rolled onto its roof, trapping him*. **3** N-COUNT The **roof** of your mouth is the highest part of the inside of your mouth. □ *She put her tongue against the roof of her mouth*. **4** PHRASE If the level or price of something **goes through the roof**, it suddenly increases very rapidly. [INFORMAL] □ *Prices have gone through the roof*. **5** PHRASE If you **hit the roof** or **go through the roof**, you become very angry, and usually show your anger by shouting at someone. [INFORMAL] □ *Dad will hit the roof when I tell him what you did*. [from Old English]

**roof**

| | |
|---|---|
| **Word Partnership** | Use *roof* with : |

| | |
|---|---|
| N. | roof **of a building/house**, **metal** roof, **rain on a** roof, **slate** roof, **tin** roof **1** |
| V. | roof **collapses**, roof **leaks**, **repair a** roof **1** |
| ADJ. | **retractable** roof **1 2** |

**roof|top** /ruftɒp/ (**rooftops**) N-COUNT A **rooftop** is the outside part of the roof of a building. □ *Below us we could see the rooftops of small villages*.

**rookie** /rʊki/ (**rookies**) N-COUNT A **rookie** is someone who has just started doing a job and does not have much experience, especially someone who has just joined a professional sports team or the police force. [INFORMAL] □ *I don't want another rookie to train*.

**room** /rum/ (**rooms**) **1** N-COUNT A **room** is one of the separate parts of the inside of a building. Rooms have their own walls, ceilings, floors, and doors. □ *A minute later he left the room*. □ *The largest conference room seats 5,000 people*. **2** N-COUNT If you talk about your **room**, you are referring to the room that you alone use, especially your bedroom at home. □ *Go to my room and bring down my sweater, please*. **3** N-UNCOUNT If there is **room** somewhere, there is enough empty space there for people or things to be fitted in. □ *There is room for 80 visitors*. **4** N-UNCOUNT There is **room for** a particular kind of behavior or action, people are able to behave in that way or to take that action. □ *The amount of work left little room for worrying*. [from Old English] **5** → see also **chat room, dining room, emergency room, living room, restroom**
→ see **hotel**

**room and board** N-UNCOUNT If you are provided with **room and board**, you are provided with food and a place to sleep, especially as part of the conditions of a job or a course of study. □ *Students receive free room and board*.

**room|ing house** (**rooming houses**) N-COUNT A **rooming house** is a building that is divided into small apartments or single rooms which people rent to live in.

**room|mate** /rummeɪt/ (**roommates**) N-COUNT Your **roommate** is the person you share a room, apartment, or house with, for example when you are in college. □ *Derek and I were roommates for two years*.

**roomy** /rumi/ (**roomier, roomiest**) ADJ If you describe a place as **roomy**, you mean that you like it because it is large inside and you can move around freely and comfortably. □ *The car is roomy and a good choice for families*. [from Old English]

**roost** /rust/ (**roosts, roosting, roosted**) **1** N-COUNT A **roost** is a place where birds or bats rest or sleep. **2** V-I When birds or bats **roost** somewhere, they rest or sleep there. □ *The birds roost in nearby bushes*. [from Old English]
→ see **bat**

**roost|er** /rustər/ (**roosters**) N-COUNT A **rooster** is an adult male chicken. [from Old English]

**rooster**

**root** /rut/ (**roots, rooting, rooted**) **1** N-COUNT The **roots** of a plant are the parts of it that grow under the ground. □ ...*the twisted roots of an apple tree*. **2** N-COUNT The **root** of a hair or tooth is the part of it that is underneath the skin. **3** N-PLURAL You can refer to the place or culture that a person or their family comes from as their **roots**. □ *I am proud of my Brazilian roots*. **4** N-COUNT You can refer to the cause of a problem or of an unpleasant situation as **the root of** it or **the roots of** it. □ *We got to the root of the problem*. **5** V-I If you **root through** or **in** something, you search for something by moving other things around. □ *She rooted through the bag and found what she wanted*. **6** → see also **rooted, grassroots, square root** **7** PHRASE If an idea, belief, or custom **takes root**, it becomes established among a group of people. □ *Time was needed for democracy to take root*. [from Old English]
→ see **flower**

▶ **root out** **1** PHR-VERB If you **root out** a person,

you find them and force them from the place they are in, usually in order to punish them. ❑ *They tried to root out corrupt officials.* **2** PHR-VERB If you **root out** a problem or an unpleasant situation, you find out who or what is the cause of it and put an end to it. ❑ *There was a campaign to root out corruption.*

| Word Partnership | Use *root* with : |
| --- | --- |
| N. | **tree** root **1**<br>root **cause of** *something*, root **of a problem** **4** |
| V. | **take** root **7** |

**root|ed** /ruːtɪd/ **1** ADJ If one thing is **rooted in** another, it is strongly influenced by it or has developed from it. ❑ *...ideas rooted in his understanding of Japan.* **2** ADJ If someone has deeply **rooted** opinions or feelings, they believe or feel something extremely strongly and are unlikely to change. ❑ *Racism is a deeply rooted prejudice.* [from Old English]

**root ex|trac|tion** (root extractions) N-VAR In mathematics, **root extraction** is a method of using a particular number to find another number which, when it is multiplied by itself a certain number of times, produces the original number.

**root hair** (root hairs) N-COUNT A plant's **root hairs** are the thin extensions that grow from its roots and take in water and minerals from the soil.

**root sys|tem** (root systems) N-COUNT A plant's **root system** is the part of the plant that contains the roots. Compare **shoot system**.

**root word** (root words) N-COUNT A **root word** is a word or part of a word to which other letters can be added in order to form new words. [TECHNICAL]

**rope** /roʊp/ (ropes, roping, roped) **1** N-VAR A **rope** is a thick cord or wire that is made by

rope

twisting together several thinner cords or wires. ❑ *He tied the rope around his waist.* **2** V-T If you **rope** one thing **to** another, you tie the two things together with a rope. ❑ *They roped their horses to a branch of the tree.* [from Old English] ▶ **rope in** PHR-VERB If you say that you **were roped in to** do a particular task, you mean that someone persuaded you to help them do that task. [INFORMAL] ❑ *Visitors were roped in to help pick tomatoes.*

**rose** /roʊz/ (roses) **1** **Rose** is the past tense of **rise.** **2** N-COUNT A **rose** is a flower with a pleasant smell, which grows on a bush with thorns. [from Old English]

**rosé** /roʊzeɪ/ (rosés) N-VAR **Rosé** is wine that is pink in color. ❑ *Most wines from this area are rosés.* [from French]

**rose-colored** PHRASE If you look at a person or situation through **rose-colored glasses** or **rose-tinted glasses**, you see only their good points and therefore your view of them is unrealistic. ❑ *She looks at the world through rose-colored glasses.*

**ros|ter** /rɒstər/ (rosters) **1** N-COUNT A **roster** is a list of names which gives details of the order in which different people have to do a particular job. ❑ *He put himself on the roster for cleaning.* **2** N-COUNT A **roster** is a list of names, especially of the people who work for a particular organization or are available to do a particular job. ❑ *...the Amateur Softball Association's roster of umpires.* [from Dutch]

**rosy** /roʊzi/ (rosier, rosiest) **1** ADJ If you say that someone has a **rosy** face, you mean that they have pink cheeks and look very healthy. **2** ADJ If you say that a situation looks **rosy** or that the picture looks **rosy**, you mean that the situation seems likely to be good or successful. ❑ *The job prospects for engineers are less rosy now than they used to be.* [from Old English]

**rot** /rɒt/ (rots, rotting, rotted) **1** V-T/V-I When food, wood, or another substance **rots**, or when something **rots** it, it becomes softer and is gradually destroyed. ❑ *The grain will start to rot after the rain.* **2** N-UNCOUNT If there is **rot** in something, especially something that is made of wood, parts of it have decayed and fallen apart. ❑ *Investigations showed extensive rot in the doors.* **3** N-SING You can use **the rot** to refer to the way something gradually gets worse. ❑ *The newspaper said "Don't wait until the next election to stop the rot."* [from Old English]

| Word Link | rot ≈ turning : rotary, rotate, rotation |
| --- | --- |

**ro|ta|ry** /roʊtəri/ (rotaries) **1** ADJ **Rotary** means turning or able to turn around a fixed point. ❑ *...rotary motion.* **2** N-COUNT A **rotary** is a circular structure in the road at a place where several roads meet. You drive around it until you come to the road that you want. [from Medieval Latin]

**ro|tate** /roʊteɪt/ (rotates, rotating, rotated) **1** V-T/V-I When something **rotates** or when you **rotate** it, it turns with a circular movement. ❑ *The earth rotates around the sun.* ● **ro|ta|tion** /roʊteɪʃⁿn/ (rotations) N-COUNT ❑ *...the daily rotation of the earth.* **2** V-T/V-I If people or things **rotate**, or if someone **rotates** them, they take turns to do something. ❑ *The men rotated frequently.* ● **ro|ta|tion** N-COUNT ❑ *The men will play in rotation.* [from Old English] → see **moon**

**ro|ta|tion** /roʊteɪʃⁿn/ (rotations) **1** N-VAR **Rotation** is circular movement. A **rotation** is the movement of something through one complete circle. **2** N-VAR In geometry, a **rotation** is a transformation in which the coordinate axes are rotated by a fixed angle about the origin. [from Old English]

**ROTC** /ɑr oʊ ti si/ N-PROPER **The ROTC** is a military organization that trains college students to become officers in the armed forces, so that they are ready to join a military operation if they are needed. **ROTC** is an abbreviation for "Reserve Officers Training Corps." ❑ *...the Army ROTC program at Fresno State University.*

**rot|ten** /rɒtⁿn/ **1** ADJ If food, wood, or another substance is **rotten**, it has decayed and can no longer be used. ❑ *The smell was very strong — like rotten eggs.* **2** ADJ If you describe something as **rotten**, you think it is very unpleasant or of very poor quality. [INFORMAL] ❑ *I think it's a rotten idea.* [from Old Norse]

r

**rott|wei|ler** /ˈrɒtwaɪlər/ (**rottweilers**) also **Rottweiler** N-COUNT A **rottweiler** is a large black and brown breed of dog which is often used as a guard dog.

**rough** /rʌf/ (**rougher, roughest**) **1** ADJ If a surface is **rough**, it is uneven and not smooth. ❑ *His hands were rough.* ● **rough|ness** N-UNCOUNT ❑ *...the roughness of his jacket.* **2** ADJ You say that people or their actions are **rough** when they use too much force and not enough care or gentleness. ❑ *Football's a rough game.* ● **rough|ly** ADV ❑ *They roughly pushed past him.* **3** ADJ A **rough** area, city, school, or other place is unpleasant and dangerous because there is a lot of violence or crime there. ❑ *It was a rough part of town.* **4** ADJ If you say that someone has had a **rough** time, you mean that they have had some difficult or unpleasant experiences. ❑ *Old people have a rough time in our society.* **5** ADJ A **rough** calculation or guess is approximately correct, but not exact. ❑ *...a rough estimate of how much fuel we need.* ● **rough|ly** ADV ❑ *Cancer was killing roughly half a million people a year.* [from Old English] **6** **rough justice** → see **justice**

**rou|lette** /ruːˈlɛt/ N-UNCOUNT **Roulette** is a gambling game in which a ball is dropped onto a wheel with numbered holes in it while the wheel is spinning around. The players bet on which hole the ball will be in when the wheel stops spinning. [from French]

---
### round

**①** PREPOSITION AND ADVERB USES
**②** NOUN USES
**③** ADJECTIVE USES
**④** VERB USES
---

**① round** /raʊnd/

> **Round** is used mainly in British English. See **around**.

PHRASE If something happens **all year round**, it happens throughout the year. ❑ *Many of these plants are evergreen, so you can enjoy them all year round.* [from Old French]

**② round** /raʊnd/ (**rounds**) **1** N-COUNT A **round** of events is a series of related events, especially one which comes after or before a similar series of events. ❑ *They held another round of talks.* **2** N-COUNT In sports, a **round** is a series of games in a competition in which the winners go on to play in the next round. ❑ *...in the third round of the competition.* **3** N-COUNT In a boxing or wrestling match, a **round** is one of the periods during which the boxers or wrestlers fight. **4** N-COUNT A **round** of golf is one game, usually including half a million people 18 holes. **5** N-COUNT A person's **rounds** are a series of visits he or she makes as part of his or her job. ❑ *The doctors did their morning rounds.* **6** N-COUNT If you buy a **round** of drinks, you buy a drink for each member of the group of people that you are with. **7** N-COUNT A **round** of ammunition is the bullet or bullets released when a gun is fired. [from Old French]

**③ round** /raʊnd/ (**rounder, roundest**) ADJ Something that is **round** is shaped like a circle or ball. ❑ *She had a round face.* [from Old French]

**④ round** /raʊnd/ (**rounds, rounding, rounded**) **1** V-T If you **round** a place or obstacle, you move

in a curve past the edge or corner of it. ❑ *The house disappeared from sight as we rounded a corner.* **2** V-T If you **round** an amount **up** or **down**, or if you **round** it **off**, you change it to the nearest whole number or nearest multiple of 10, 100, 1000, and so on. ❑ *We needed to round up and round down numbers.* [from Old French] **3** → see also **rounded**

▶ **round up** **1** PHR-VERB If the police or army **round up** a number of people, they arrest or capture them. ❑ *The police rounded up a number of suspects.* **2** PHR-VERB If you **round up** animals or things, you gather them together. ❑ *He wanted a job as a cowboy, rounding up cattle.* **3** → see also **round ④ 2, roundup**

**round|about** /ˈraʊndəbaʊt/ **1** ADJ If you go somewhere by a **roundabout** route, you do not go there by the shortest and quickest route. ❑ *He left today on a roundabout route for Jordan.* **2** ADJ If you do or say something in a **roundabout** way, you do not do or say it in a simple, clear, and direct way. ❑ *She was telling him in a roundabout way that she was getting married.*

**round|ed** /ˈraʊndɪd/ ADJ Something that is **rounded** is curved in shape, without any points or sharp edges. ❑ *...a low, rounded hill.* [from Old French]

**round trip** (**round trips**) N-COUNT If you make a **round trip**, you travel to a place and then back again. ❑ *The train makes the 2,400-mile round trip every week.*

**round|up** /ˈraʊndʌp/ (**roundups**) N-COUNT A **roundup** is an occasion when cattle, horses, or other animals are collected together so that they can be counted or sold.

**rouse** /raʊz/ (**rouses, rousing, roused**) **1** V-T/V-I If someone **rouses** you when you are sleeping or if you **rouse**, you wake up. [LITERARY] ❑ *Hilton roused him at eight-thirty by knocking on the door.* **2** V-T If you **rouse yourself**, you stop being inactive and start doing something. ❑ *She was unable to rouse herself to do anything.* **3** V-T If something or someone **rouses** you, they make you very emotional or excited. ❑ *He did more to rouse the crowd there than anybody else.* ● **rous|ing** ADJ ❑ *...a rousing speech.*
→ see **dream**

**roust** /raʊst/ (**rousts, rousting, rousted**) V-T If you **roust** someone, you disturb, upset, or hit them, or make them move from their place. ❑ *We're not trying to roust you. We just want some information.*

**rout** /raʊt/ (**routs, routing, routed**) V-T If an army, sports team, or other group **routs** its opponents, it defeats them completely and easily. ❑ *The army routed the English.* ● **Rout** is also a noun. ❑ *He rode forward to stop the rout.* [from Old French]

**route** /ruːt, raʊt/ (**routes, routing, routed**) **1** N-COUNT A **route** is a way from one place to another. ❑ *...the most direct route to the center of town.* **2** N-COUNT In the United States, **Route** is used in front of a number in the names of main roads between major cities. ❑ *...the next exit on Route 580.* **3** N-COUNT You can refer to a way of achieving something as a **route**. ❑ *Researchers are trying to get the information through an indirect route.* **4** V-T If vehicles, goods, or passengers are **routed** in a particular direction, they are made to travel in that direction. **5** PHRASE **En route to** a place means on the way to that place. ❑ *They* *arrived in London en route to the United States.* [from Old French]

**Word Partnership**   Use *route* with :

| | |
|---|---|
| N. | **escape** route, **parade** route **1** |
| ADJ. | **main** route, **scenic** route **1** |
| | **alternative** route, **different** route, |
| | **direct** route, **shortest** route **1 3** |

**rou|tine** /rutin/ (**routines**) **1** N-VAR A **routine** is the usual series of things that you do at a particular time in a particular order. ❑ *The players changed their daily routine.* **2** ADJ You use **routine** to describe activities that are done as a normal part of a job or process. ❑ ...*a series of routine medical tests.* ● **rou|tine|ly** ADV ❑ *Doctors routinely wash their hands before examining a patient.* [from Old French]

**Word Partnership**   Use *routine* with :

| | |
|---|---|
| ADJ. | **daily** routine, **normal** routine, **regular** routine, **usual** routine **1** |
| N. | **exercise** routine, **morning** routine, routine **1** |
| | routine **maintenance**, routine **tests** **2** |

**rov|ing** /roʊvɪŋ/ ADJ You use **roving** to describe a person who travels around, rather than staying in a fixed place. ❑ ...*a roving reporter.* [of Scandinavian origin]

---

**row**

❶ ARRANGEMENT OR SEQUENCE
❷ MAKING A BOAT MOVE

---

❶ **row** /roʊ/ (**rows**) **1** N-COUNT A **row** of things or people is a number of them arranged in a line. ❑ ...*a row of pretty little cottages.* **2** → see also **death row** **3** PHRASE If something happens several times **in a row**, it happens that number of times without a break. If something happens several days **in a row**, it happens on each of those days. ❑ *They won five championships in a row.* [from Old English]

❷ **row** /roʊ/ (**rows, rowing, rowed**) V-T/V-I When you **row**, you sit in a boat and make it move through the water by using oars. ❑ *He rowed as quickly as he could to the shore.* ❑ *The boatman refused to row him back.* ● **row|ing** N-UNCOUNT ❑ ...*competitions in rowing and swimming.* [from Old English]

**row|boat** /roʊboʊt/ (**rowboats**) N-COUNT A **rowboat** is a small boat that you move through the water by using oars.

**row|dy** /raʊdi/ (**rowdier, rowdiest**) ADJ When people are **rowdy**, they are noisy, rough, and likely to cause trouble. ❑ *He complained to the police about rowdy neighbors.*

**row house** (**row houses**) also **rowhouse** N-COUNT A **row house** is one of a row of similar houses that are joined together by both of their side walls.

**roy|al** /rɔɪəl/ ADJ **Royal** means connected with a king, queen, or emperor, or their family. ❑ ...*an invitation to a royal garden party.* [from Old French]

**roy|al|ist** /rɔɪəlɪst/ (**royalists**) N-COUNT A **royalist** is someone who supports their country's royal family or who believes that their country should have a king or queen. [from Old French]

**roy|al|ty** /rɔɪəlti/ (**royalties**) **1** N-UNCOUNT The members of royal families are sometimes referred to as **royalty**. ❑ ...*royalty and government leaders from around the world.* **2** N-PLURAL **Royalties** are payments made to authors and musicians when their work is sold or performed. [from Old French]

**Rte.** **Rte.** is used in front of a number in the names of main roads between major cities. **Rte.** is a written abbreviation for **route**. ❑ *Winterthur is on Rte. 52 in Delaware.*

**rub** /rʌb/ (**rubs, rubbing, rubbed**) **1** V-T/V-I If you **rub** a part of your body or if you **rub at** it, you move your hand or fingers backward and forward over it while pressing firmly. ❑ *He rubbed his arms and stiff legs.* **2** V-T/V-I If you **rub against** a surface or **rub** a part of your body **against** a surface, you move it backward and forward while pressing it against the surface. ❑ *A cat was rubbing against my leg.* **3** V-T/V-I If you **rub** something or you **rub at** it, you move a cloth backward and forward over it in order to clean or dry it. ❑ *She took off her glasses and rubbed them hard.* **4** V-T If you **rub** a substance **into** a surface or **rub** something such as dirt **from** a surface, you spread it over the surface or remove it from the surface using your hand or a cloth. ❑ *He rubbed oil into my back.* **5** V-T/V-I If you **rub** two things **together** or if they **rub together**, they move backward and forward, pressing against each other. ❑ *He rubbed his hands together.* **6** PHRASE If you **rub shoulders with** famous people, you meet them and talk to them. You can also say that you **rub elbows with** someone. ❑ *He regularly rubbed shoulders with famous people.* [from Low German] **7** to **rub** someone's **nose in** it → see **nose**

**Word Partnership**   Use *rub* with :

| | |
|---|---|
| PREP. | **rub against** **2** |
| | **rub off**, rub **with** **4** |
| ADV. | **rub together** **5** |

**rub|ber** /rʌbər/ (**rubbers**) N-UNCOUNT **Rubber** is a strong, waterproof, elastic substance used for making tires, boots, and other products. ❑ ...*the smell of burning rubber.*

**rub|ber boot** (**rubber boots**) N-COUNT **Rubber boots** are long boots made of rubber that you wear to keep your feet dry.

**rub|ber stamp** (**rubber stamps, rubber stamping, rubber stamped**) also **rubber-stamp** V-T When someone in authority **rubber-stamps** a decision, plan, or law, they agree to it. ❑ *The committee's job is to rubber-stamp his decisions.*

**rub|bing al|co|hol** N-UNCOUNT **Rubbing alcohol** is a liquid which is used to clean wounds or surgical instruments.

**rub|ble** /rʌbəl/ N-UNCOUNT **Rubble** consists of the pieces of brick, stone, or other materials that remain when a building is destroyed. ❑ ...*bodies are still buried in the rubble.* [from Middle English]

**rub|down** /rʌbdaʊn/ (**rubdowns**) N-COUNT If you give someone a **rubdown**, you dry them or massage them with something such as a towel or cloth. ❑ *He found a towel and gave his body a rubdown.*

**ru|bric** /rubrɪk/ (**rubrics**) **1** N-COUNT A **rubric** is a title or heading under which something operates or is studied. [FORMAL] **2** N-COUNT A **rubric** is a set of rules or instructions, for example the rules at the beginning of an examination paper. [FORMAL] [from Latin]

r

**ruby** /ˈruːbi/ (**rubies**) N-COUNT A **ruby** is a dark red jewel. ❑ ...a ruby ring. [from Old French]

**ruck|us** /ˈrʌkəs/ N-SING If someone or something causes a **ruckus**, they cause a great deal of noise, argument, or confusion. [INFORMAL] ❑ This caused such a ruckus that they had to change their mind.

**rud|der** /ˈrʌdər/ (**rudders**) N-COUNT A **rudder** is a device for steering a boat or airplane. [from Old English]

**rud|dy** /ˈrʌdi/ (**ruddier, ruddiest**) ADJ If someone's face is **ruddy**, it is a reddish color, usually because he or she is healthy or has been working hard. ❑ He had a naturally ruddy face. [from Old English]

**rude** /ˈruːd/ (**ruder, rudest**) ◼ ADJ When people are **rude**, they behave in an impolite way. ❑ He's rude to her friends. ● **rude|ly** ADV ❑ ...hotel guests who treat staff rudely. ● **rude|ness** N-UNCOUNT ❑ Mother is annoyed at Caleb's rudeness. ◼ ADJ **Rude** words and behavior are likely to embarrass or offend people because they relate to sex or to body functions. ❑ Fred keeps telling rude jokes. ◼ ADJ If someone receives a **rude** shock, something unpleasant happens unexpectedly. ❑ My first day at work was a rude shock. ● **rude|ly** ADV ❑ People were rudely awakened by a siren. [from Old French] ◼ rude awakening → see awakening

| Thesaurus | rude | Also look up : |
|---|---|---|
| ADJ. | vulgar; (ant.) polite ◼ | |

**ru|di|men|ta|ry** /ˌruːdɪˈmɛntəri, -tri/ ◼ ADJ **Rudimentary** things are very basic or simple and are therefore unsatisfactory. [FORMAL] ❑ There was a rudimentary kitchen. ◼ ADJ **Rudimentary** knowledge includes only the simplest and most basic facts. [FORMAL] ❑ He had only a rudimentary knowledge of French. [from Latin]

**rue|ful** /ˈruːfəl/ ADJ If someone is **rueful**, they feel or express regret or sorrow in a quiet and gentle way. [LITERARY] ❑ ...a rueful smile. ● **rue|ful|ly** ADV ❑ He smiled at her ruefully. [from Old English]

**ruf|fle** /ˈrʌfəl/ (**ruffles, ruffling, ruffled**) ◼ V-T If you **ruffle** someone's hair, you move your hand backward and forward through it as a way of showing your affection toward him or her. ❑ "Don't be upset," he said, ruffling Ben's dark hair. ◼ V-T/V-I If a bird **ruffles** its feathers or if its feathers **ruffle**, they stand out on its body, for example when it is cleaning itself. ◼ N-COUNT **Ruffles** are folds of cloth at the neck or the ends of the arms of a piece of clothing. [of Germanic origin]

**ruf|fled** /ˈrʌfəld/ ADJ Something that is **ruffled** is no longer smooth or neat. ❑ Her short hair was ruffled. [of Germanic origin]

**rug** /ˈrʌɡ/ (**rugs**) N-COUNT A **rug** is a piece of thick material that you put on a floor. It is like a carpet but covers a smaller area. ❑ ...a Persian rug. [of Scandinavian origin]

**rug|by** /ˈrʌɡbi/ N-UNCOUNT **Rugby** or **rugby football** is a game played by two teams, who try to get an oval ball past a line at their opponents' end of the field.

**rug|ged** /ˈrʌɡɪd/ ◼ ADJ A **rugged** area of land is uneven and covered with rocks. [LITERARY] ❑ ...a rugged coastline. ◼ ADJ If you describe a man as

**rugged**, you mean that he has strong, masculine features and this makes him attractive. [LITERARY] ◼ ADJ A **rugged** piece of equipment is strong and is designed to last a long time. ❑ ...rugged cameras. [of Scandinavian origin]

**ruin** /ˈruːɪn/ (**ruins, ruining, ruined**) ◼ V-T To **ruin** something means to severely harm, damage, or spoil it. ❑ My wife was ruining her health through worry. ◼ V-T To **ruin** someone means to cause them to no longer have any money. ❑ He ruined her financially with his love of expensive things. ◼ N-UNCOUNT **Ruin** is the state of no longer having any money. ❑ ...a country on the edge of ruin. ◼ N-PLURAL The **ruins of** something are the parts of it that remain after it has been severely damaged or weakened. ❑ He bought the ruins of other people's failed businesses. ◼ N-PLURAL The **ruins of** a building are the parts of it that remain after the rest has fallen down or been destroyed. ❑ Police found two bodies in the ruins of the house. ◼ → see also **ruined** ◼ PHRASE If something is **in ruins**, it is completely spoiled. ❑ The economy is in ruins. ◼ PHRASE If a building or place is **in ruins**, most of it has been destroyed and only parts of it remain. ❑ The church was in ruins. [from Old French]

**ruined** /ˈruːɪnd/ ADJ A **ruined** building or place has been very badly damaged or has fallen apart. ❑ ...a ruined church. [from Old French]

**rule** /ˈruːl/ (**rules, ruling, ruled**) ◼ N-COUNT **Rules** are instructions that tell you what you are allowed to do and what you are not allowed to do. ❑ ...a book explaining the rules of basketball. ◼ N-COUNT The **rules of** something such as a language or a science are statements that describe the way that things usually happen in a particular situation. ❑ ...the rules of the language. ◼ N-SING If something is **the rule**, it is normal or usual. ❑ For many Americans, weekend work has become the rule. ◼ V-T/V-I The person or group that **rules** a country controls its affairs. ❑ For four centuries, foreigners have ruled Angola. ❑ He ruled for eight months. ◼ → see also **ground rule, ruling** ◼ PHRASE If you say that something happens **as a rule**, you mean that it usually happens. ❑ As a rule, I walk to work rather than drive. ◼ PHRASE If someone in authority **bends the rules** or **stretches the rules**, they do something even though it is against the rules. ❑ Surely you can bend the rules in this case? [from Old French]

▶ **rule out** ◼ PHR-VERB If you **rule out** a course of action, an idea, or a solution, you decide that it is impossible or unsuitable. ◼ PHR-VERB If something **rules out** a situation, it prevents it from happening or from being possible. ❑ A serious car accident ruled out a career in soccer.

| Thesaurus | rule | Also look up : |
|---|---|---|
| N. | guideline, law, standard ◼ ◼ | |
| V. | command, dictate, govern ◼ | |

| Word Partnership | Use rule with : |
|---|---|
| V. | **break a** rule, **change a** rule, **follow a** rule ◼ |
| N. | **gag** rule ◼ **exception to a** rule ◼ – ◼ |
| PREP. | **against a** rule, **under a** rule ◼ ◼ |

R

**rul|er** /ˈruːlər/ (rulers) **1** N-COUNT The **ruler** of a country is the person who rules the country. □ ...the ruler of Lesotho. **2** N-COUNT A **ruler** is a long, flat object with straight edges, for measuring things and drawing straight lines. [from Old French]
→ see **measurement**

ruler

**rul|ing** /ˈruːlɪŋ/ (rulings) **1** ADJ The **ruling** group of people in a country or organization is the group that controls its affairs. □ ...a ruling party politician. **2** N-COUNT A **ruling** is an official decision made by a judge or court. □ He was angry at the court's ruling. [from Old French]

**rum** /rʌm/ (rums) N-VAR **Rum** is an alcoholic drink made from sugar cane juice.

**rum|ble** /ˈrʌmbəl/ (rumbles, rumbling, rumbled) **1** N-COUNT A **rumble** is a low, continuous noise. □ ...the distant rumble of traffic. **2** V-I If something **rumbles**, it makes a low, continuous noise. □ Her stomach was rumbling because she missed breakfast. [from Middle Dutch]

**rum|bling** /ˈrʌmblɪŋ/ (rumblings) **1** N-COUNT A **rumbling** is a low, continuous noise. □ ...the rumbling of an empty stomach. **2** N-COUNT **Rumblings** are signs that a bad situation is developing or that people are becoming annoyed or unhappy. □ There were rumblings of discontent in the office. [from Middle Dutch]

**rum|mage** /ˈrʌmɪdʒ/ (rummages, rummaging, rummaged) V-I If you **rummage through** something, you search for something you want by moving things around in a careless or hurried way. □ They rummage through clothes for something that fits. ● **Rummage** is also a noun. □ She found the right coins after a rummage in her purse. ● **Rummage around** means the same as **rummage**. □ I opened the fridge and rummaged around. [from Old French]

**rum|mage sale** (rummage sales) N-COUNT A **rummage sale** is a sale of cheap used goods that is usually held to raise money for charity.

**ru|mor** /ˈruːmər/ (rumors) N-VAR A **rumor** is a story or piece of information that may or may not be true, but that people are talking about. □ U.S. officials denied the rumor. [from Old French]

| Word Partnership | Use *rumor* with : |
| --- | --- |
| ADJ. | **false** rumor |
| V. | **hear** a rumor, **spread** a rumor, **start** a rumor |

**ru|mored** /ˈruːmərd/ V-T PASSIVE If something **is rumored** to be true, people are suggesting that it is true, but they do not know for certain. □ The company is rumored to be in financial trouble. [from Old French]

**ru|mor mill** (rumor mills) N-COUNT You can refer to the people in a particular place or profession who spread rumors as the **rumor mill**. □ The Hollywood rumor mill is already talking about a marriage between the two stars.

**rumor|monger** /ˈruːmərmʌŋgər, -mɒŋgər/ (rumormongers) N-COUNT If you call someone a **rumormonger**, you disapprove of the fact that they spread rumors.

**rump** /rʌmp/ (rumps) N-COUNT An animal's **rump** is the part at its back end, above its back legs. □ The cows' rumps were marked with their owner's name. [of Scandinavian origin]

**run**

**1** VERB USES
**2** NOUN USES
**3** PHRASES
**4** PHRASAL VERBS

**❶ run** /rʌn/ (runs, running, ran)

The form **run** is used in the present tense and is also the past participle of the verb.

**1** V-T/V-I When you **run**, you move quickly, leaving the ground during each stride. □ I ran back to the telephone. □ He ran the last block. ● **run|ning** N-UNCOUNT □ We did some running. **2** V-I If you say that something long, such as a road, **runs** in a particular direction, you are describing its course or position. □ ...the path which ran through the forest. **3** V-T If you **run** your hand or an object **through** something, you move your hand or the object through it. □ He ran his fingers through his hair. **4** V-I If someone **runs for** office in an election, they take part as a candidate. □ He announced he was running for president. □ I intend to run against him in the next election. **5** V-T If you **run** something such as a business or an activity, you are in charge of it or you organize it. □ His father ran a paint business. □ ...a well-run, successful organization. ● **run|ning** N-UNCOUNT □ ...the day-to-day running of the business. **6** V-I If you talk about how a system, an organization, or your life **is running**, you are saying how well it is operating or progressing. □ The system is now running smoothly. **7** V-T/V-I If you **run** an experiment, computer program, or other process, or start it **running**, you start it and let it continue. □ The doctor ran some tests and found that I had an infection. **8** V-T/V-I When a machine **is running** or when you **are running** it, it is switched on and is working. □ We told him to wait outside the house with the engine running. **9** V-I A machine or equipment that **runs on** or **off** a particular source of energy functions by using that source of energy. □ The buses run on diesel. **10** V-I When vehicles such as trains and buses **run** from one place to another, they regularly travel along that route. □ A bus runs frequently between the station and downtown. **11** V-T If you **run** someone somewhere in a car, you drive them there. [INFORMAL] □ Could you run me up to Baltimore? **12** V-I If you **run** over or down to a place that is quite near, you drive there. [INFORMAL] □ I'll run over to the village and check on Mrs. Adams. **13** V-I If a liquid **runs** in a particular direction, it flows in that direction. □ Tears were running down her cheeks. **14** V-T If you **run** water, or if you **run** a faucet or a bath, you cause water to flow from a faucet. □ She went to the sink and ran water into her empty glass. ● **run|ning** ADJ □ ...the sound of running water. **15** V-I If the dye in some cloth or the ink on some paper **runs**, it comes off or spreads when the cloth or paper gets wet. **16** V-I If a play, event, or legal contract **runs** for a particular period of time, it lasts for that period of time. □ The play ran for only three months. □ The contract runs from 1992 to 2020. **17** V-I If someone or something **is running** late, they have taken more time than was planned. If they **are running** on time or ahead of time, they have taken the time planned or less than the time

r

planned. ❑ *I'll call you back later, I'm running late.* [from Old English] **18** → see also **running**

---

| **Thesaurus** | *run* | Also look up : |
|---|---|---|
| v. | dash, jog, sprint **❶ 1** | |
| | follow, go **❶ 2** | |
| | administer, conduct, manage **❶ 5** | |

---

**❷ run** /rʌn/ (**runs**) **1** N-COUNT A **run** is a time when you move quickly, leaving the ground with each stride, usually for exercise. ❑ *After a six-mile run, Jackie went home for breakfast.* **2** N-COUNT A **run** of a play or television program is the period of time during which performances are given or programs are shown. ❑ *The show had a month's run in Philadelphia.* [from Old English]

**❸ run** /rʌn/ (**runs, running, ran**)

The form **run** is used in the present tense and is also the past participle of the verb.

**1** PHRASE If you talk about what will happen **in the long run**, you are saying what you think will happen over a long period of time in the future. If you talk about what will happen **in the short run**, you are saying what you think will happen in the near future. ❑ *Spending more on education will save money in the long run.* **2** PHRASE If someone is **on the run**, they are trying to escape or hide from someone such as the police or an enemy. [from Old English] **3** to **run deep** → see **deep** **4** to **run an errand** → see **errand** **5** to **run the gauntlet** → see **gauntlet** **6** to **run a risk** → see **risk** **7** to **run wild** → see **wild**

**❹ run** /rʌn/ (**runs, running, ran**)

The form **run** is used in the present tense and is also the past participle of the verb.

▶ **run across** PHR-VERB If you **run across** someone or something, you meet them or find them unexpectedly. ❑ *We ran across some old friends.*
▶ **run away 1** PHR-VERB If you **run away** from a place, you leave it because you are unhappy there. ❑ *I ran away from home when I was sixteen.* ❑ *After the attack, Stewart ran away.* **2** → see also **runaway**
▶ **run away with** PHR-VERB If you let your imagination or your emotions **run away with** you, you fail to control them and cannot think sensibly. ❑ *You're letting your imagination run away with you.*
▶ **run down 1** PHR-VERB If you **run** people or things **down**, you criticize them strongly. ❑ *I'm always running myself down.* **2** PHR-VERB If a vehicle or its driver **runs** someone **down**, the vehicle hits them and injures them. ❑ *The motorcycle driver tried to run him down.* **3** → see also **run-down**
▶ **run into 1** PHR-VERB If you **run into** problems or difficulties, you unexpectedly begin to experience them. ❑ *...companies that have run into trouble.* **2** PHR-VERB If you **run into** someone, you meet them unexpectedly. ❑ *He ran into Krettner in the hall.* **3** PHR-VERB If a vehicle **runs into** something, it accidentally hits it. ❑ *The driver was going too fast and ran into a tree.* **4** PHR-VERB You use **run into** when indicating that the cost or amount of something is very great. ❑ *...costs running into millions of dollars.*
▶ **run off 1** PHR-VERB If you **run off** with someone, you secretly go away with them in order to live with them or marry them. ❑ *His secretary just ran off with the mailman.* **2** PHR-VERB If you **run**

off copies of a piece of writing, you produce them using a machine.
▶ **run out 1** PHR-VERB If you **run out of** something, you have no more of it left. ❑ *They have run out of ideas.* **2** to **run out of steam** → see **steam** **3** PHR-VERB If something **runs out**, it becomes used up so that there is no more left. ❑ *Supplies are running out.* **4** PHR-VERB When a legal document **runs out**, it stops being valid. ❑ *When the lease ran out the family moved to Cleveland.*
▶ **run over** PHR-VERB If a vehicle or its driver **runs** a person or animal **over**, it knocks them down and drives over them. ❑ *He nearly ran me over.*
▶ **run through 1** PHR-VERB If you **run through** a list of items, you read or mention all the items quickly. ❑ *I ran through the choices with him.* **2** PHR-VERB If you **run through** a performance or a series of actions, you practice it. ❑ *The dance instructor ran through a few moves.*
▶ **run up** PHR-VERB If someone **runs up** bills or debts, they acquire them by buying a lot of things or borrowing money. ❑ *She managed to run up a debt of $60,000.*
▶ **run up against** PHR-VERB If you **run up against** problems, you suddenly begin to experience them. ❑ *I ran up against several problems.*

**run|away** /rʌnəweɪ/ (**runaways**) **1** ADJ You use **runaway** to describe a situation in which something increases or develops very quickly and cannot be controlled. ❑ *Our sale was a runaway success.* **2** N-COUNT A **runaway** is someone, especially a child, who leaves home without telling anyone or without permission. ❑ *...a teenage runaway.* **3** ADJ A **runaway** vehicle or animal is moving forward quickly, and its driver or rider has lost control of it. ❑ *The runaway car hit a tree.* [from Old English]

**run-down**

The spelling **rundown** is also used. The adjective is pronounced /rʌn daʊn/. The noun is pronounced /rʌn daʊn/.

**1** ADJ If someone is **run-down**, they are tired or slightly ill. [INFORMAL] **2** ADJ A **run-down** building or area is in very poor condition. ❑ *...run-down areas of town.* **3** N-SING If you give someone a **rundown of** a group of things or a **rundown on** something, you give them details about it. [INFORMAL] ❑ *Here's a rundown of the choices we have.*

**rung** /rʌŋ/ (**rungs**) **1** Rung is the past participle of **ring**. **2** N-COUNT The **rungs** on a ladder are the wooden or metal bars that form the steps. ❑ *I swung myself onto the ladder and felt for the next rung.* **3** N-COUNT If you reach a particular **rung** in your career, in an organization, or in a process, you reach that level in it. ❑ *We were both on the lowest rung of our careers.* [from Old English]

rung

**run-in** (**run-ins**) N-COUNT A **run-in** is an argument or quarrel with someone. [INFORMAL] ❑ *I had a run-in with him.*

**run|ner** /rʌnər/ (**runners**) **1** N-COUNT A **runner** is a person who runs, especially for sport or pleasure. ❑ *...a marathon runner.* **2** N-COUNT

**Runners** are thin strips of wood or metal underneath something which help it to move smoothly. ❑ *…the runners of his sled.* ❸ N-COUNT On a plant, **runners** are long shoots that grow from the main stem and put down roots to form a new plant. [from Old English]
→ see **park**

**runner-up** (**runners-up**) N-COUNT A **runner-up** is someone who has finished in second place in a race or competition. ❑ *The runner-up will receive $500.*

**run|ning** /rʌnɪŋ/ ❶ ADJ You use **running** to describe things that continue or keep occurring over a period of time. ❑ *He began a running argument with Dean.* ❷ ADJ A **running** total is a total which changes because numbers keep being added to it as something progresses. ❑ *He kept a running total of who called him.* ❸ ADV You can use **running** when indicating that something keeps happening. ❑ *A lack of rain caused crop failure for the second year running.* ❹ PHRASE If someone is **in the running for** something, they have a good chance of winning or obtaining it. If they are **out of the running for** something, they have no chance of winning or obtaining it. ❑ *Four people are in the running for managing director.* [from Old English] ❺ → see also **run**

**run|ning mate** (**running mates**) N-COUNT In an election campaign, a candidate's **running mate** is the person that they have chosen to help them in the election. If the candidate wins, the running mate will become the second most important person after the winner. ❑ *…Clinton's selection of Al Gore as his running mate.*

**run|ny** /rʌni/ ❶ ADJ Something that is **runny** is more liquid than usual or than was intended. ❑ *Warm the honey until it is runny.* ❷ ADJ If someone has a **runny** nose or **runny** eyes, liquid is flowing from their nose or eyes. [from Old English]

**run|off** /rʌnɔf/ N-UNCOUNT **Runoff** is rainwater that forms a stream rather than being absorbed by the ground.

**run-through** (**run-throughs**) N-COUNT A **run-through** for a show or event is a practice for it.

**run|way** /rʌnweɪ/ (**runways**) N-COUNT At an airport, the **runway** is the long strip of ground with a hard surface which an airplane takes off from or lands on. [from Old English]

**rup|ture** /rʌptʃər/ (**ruptures, rupturing, ruptured**) ❶ N-COUNT A **rupture** is a severe injury in which an internal part of your body tears or bursts open. ❑ *He died after a rupture in a blood vessel in his head.* ❷ V-T/V-I If a person or animal **ruptures** a part of their body or if it **ruptures**, it tears or bursts open. ❑ *His stomach might rupture.* ❑ *I ruptured a tendon in my knee.* ❸ N-COUNT If there is a **rupture** between people, relations between them get much worse or end completely. ❑ *…a rupture in the political relations between countries.* ❹ V-T If someone or something **ruptures** relations between people, they damage them, causing them to become worse or to end. ❑ *Fights between protesters and police ruptured the city's government.* [from Latin]
→ see **crash**

**ru|ral** /rʊərəl/ ❶ ADJ **Rural** places are in the country, away from cities or large towns. ❑ *…rural areas.* ❷ ADJ **Rural** means having features which

are typical of country areas away from cities or large towns. ❑ *…the old rural way of life.* [from Old French]

**ruse** /ruz, rus/ (**ruses**) N-COUNT A **ruse** is an action or plan which is intended to deceive someone. [FORMAL] ❑ *a ruse to avoid paying taxes.* [from Old French]

**rush** /rʌʃ/ (**rushes, rushing, rushed**) ❶ V-I If you **rush** somewhere, you go there quickly. ❑ *Emma rushed into the room.* ❑ *I've got to rush. I have a meeting in a few minutes.* ❑ *I rushed for the 7:00 a.m. train.* ❷ V-T If people **rush to** do something, they do it as soon as they can, because they are very eager to do it. ❑ *Russian banks rushed to buy as many dollars as they could.* ❸ N-SING A **rush** is a situation in which you need to go somewhere or do something very quickly. ❑ *The men left in a rush.* ❹ N-SING If there is a **rush for** something, many people suddenly try to get it or do it. ❑ *Record stores are expecting a huge rush for the CD.* ❺ V-T/V-I If you **rush** something, or if you **rush** at it, you do it in a hurry, often too quickly. ❑ *You can't rush a search.* ● **rushed** ADJ ❑ *…a rushed job.* ❻ V-T If you **rush** someone or something to a place, you take them there quickly. ❑ *They rushed him to a hospital.* ❼ V-T/V-I If you **rush into** something or **are rushed into** it, you do it without thinking about it for long enough. ❑ *He will not rush into any decisions.* ❑ *They rushed in without knowing enough about the task.* ● **rushed** ADJ ❑ *I didn't feel rushed or under pressure.* ❽ N-COUNT If you experience a **rush of** a feeling, you suddenly experience it very strongly. ❑ *A rush of love swept over him.* [from Old French]

| **Word Partnership** | Use *rush* with : |
|---|---|
| N. | **evening** rush, **morning** rush ❸ |
| | rush **of adrenaline** ❽ |
| ADJ. | **mad** rush ❸ ❹ |
| | **sudden** rush ❸ ❹ ❽ |

**rush hour** (**rush hours**) N-COUNT The **rush hour** is one of the periods of the day when most people are traveling to or from work. ❑ *During the evening rush hour there was a lot of traffic.*

**Rus|sian dress|ing** N-UNCOUNT **Russian dressing** is a salad dressing made from mayonnaise mixed with a spicy sauce and chopped pickles.

**rust** /rʌst/ (**rusts, rusting, rusted**) ❶ N-UNCOUNT **Rust** is a reddish-brown substance that forms on iron or steel when it comes into contact with water. ❑ *The old car was red with rust.* ❷ V-I When a metal object **rusts**, it becomes covered in rust. ❑ *Iron rusts.* [from Old English]

**rus|tic** /rʌstɪk/ ADJ You can use **rustic** to describe things or people that you approve of because they are simple or unsophisticated in a way that is typical of the countryside. ❑ *…the rustic charm of a country lifestyle.* [from Old French]

**rus|tle** /rʌsⁿl/ (**rustles, rustling, rustled**) V-T/V-I When something thin and dry **rustles** or when you **rustle** it, it makes soft sounds as it moves. ❑ *The leaves rustled in the wind.* ❑ *She rustled her papers impatiently.* ● **Rustle** is also a noun. ❑ *…a rustle of her dress.* ● **rus|tling** (**rustlings**) N-VAR ❑ *…the rustling of papers.* [from Old English]

**rus|tler** /rʌslər/ (**rustlers**) N-COUNT **Rustlers** are people who steal farm animals, especially cattle, horses, and sheep. ❑ ...*cattle rustlers.* [from Old English]

**rusty** /rʌsti/ (**rustier, rustiest**) ◼ ADJ A **rusty** metal object is covered with rust. ❑ ...*a rusty iron gate.* ◼ ADJ If a skill that you have or your knowledge of something is **rusty**, it is not as good as it used to be, because you have not used it for a long time. ❑ ...*her rusty shooting skills.* [from Old English]

**rut** /rʌt/ (**ruts**) ◼ N-COUNT If someone is **in a rut**, he or she has become fixed in a particular way of thinking and doing things, and finds it difficult to change. ❑ *I don't like being in a rut — I like to keep doing new things.* ◼ N-COUNT A **rut** is a deep, narrow mark made in the ground by the wheels of a vehicle. ❑ *Our driver slowed the car as we went over the ruts in the road.* [from French]

**ru|ta|ba|ga** /rutəbeɪgə/ (**rutabagas**) N-VAR A **rutabaga** is a round yellow root vegetable with a pale yellow or purple skin. [from Swedish]

**ruth|less** /ruθlɪs/ ADJ If you say that someone is **ruthless**, you mean that you disapprove of them because they are very harsh or cruel, and will do anything that is necessary to achieve what they want. ❑ *Was she a ruthless murderer or an innocent woman?* ● **ruth|less|ly** ADV ❑ *The party has ruthlessly crushed any opposition.* ● **ruth|less|ness** N-UNCOUNT ❑ ...*a mixture of ambition and ruthlessness.* [from Middle English]

**RV** /ɑr vi/ (**RVs**) N-COUNT An **RV** is a van which is equipped with such things as beds and cooking equipment, so that people can live in it, usually while they are on vacation. **RV** is an abbreviation for "recreational vehicle."

**Rx** /ɑr ɛks/ (**Rxs**) ◼ N-COUNT An **Rx** is a doctor's prescription. ❑ ...*an Rx for a painkiller.* ◼ N-COUNT An **Rx** is a solution to a problem. ❑ ...*an Rx for America's health-care problems.*

**rye** /raɪ/ ◼ N-UNCOUNT **Rye** is a cereal grown in cold countries. Its grains can be used to make flour, bread, or other foods. ◼ N-UNCOUNT **Rye** is bread made from rye. ❑ ...*Swiss cheese on rye.* [from Old English]
→ see **bread**

R

# Ss

**Sab|bath** /sǽbəθ/ N-PROPER **The Sabbath** is the day of the week when members of some religious groups do not work. The Jewish Sabbath is on Saturday and the Christian Sabbath is on Sunday. ❑ *He's a religious man and will not discuss politics on the Sabbath.* [from Old English]

**sa|ber** /séɪbər/ (**sabers**) N-COUNT A **saber** is a heavy sword with a curved blade that was used in the past by soldiers on horseback. [from French]

**saber-rattling** N-UNCOUNT If you describe a threat, especially a threat of military action, as **saber-rattling**, you do not believe that the threat will actually be carried out. ❑ *We can't say if these threats are just saber-rattling.*

**sabo|tage** /sǽbətɑʒ/ (**sabotages, sabotaging, sabotaged**) **1** V-T If a machine, railroad line, or bridge **is sabotaged**, it is deliberately damaged or destroyed, for example, in a war. ❑ *The main water pipeline was sabotaged in the night.* ● **Sabotage** is also a noun. ❑ *The bombing was an act of sabotage.* **2** V-T If someone **sabotages** a plan or a meeting, they deliberately prevent it from being successful. ❑ *They tried to sabotage the peace talks.* [from French]

**sack** /sǽk/ (**sacks**) N-COUNT A **sack** is a large bag made of thick paper or rough material. ❑ *...a sack of potatoes.* [from Old English]

**sa|cred** /séɪkrɪd/ **1** ADJ Something that is **sacred** is believed to be holy and to have a special connection with God. ❑ *The eagle is sacred to Native Americans.* ● **sac|red|ness** N-UNCOUNT ❑ *...the sacredness of the place.* **2** ADJ You can describe something as **sacred** when it is regarded as too important to be changed or interfered with. ❑ *My memories are sacred to me.* ● **sac|red|ness** N-UNCOUNT ❑ *...the sacredness of life.* [from Latin]

**sac|ri|fice** /sǽkrɪfaɪs/ (**sacrifices, sacrificing, sacrificed**) **1** V-T To **sacrifice** an animal or person means to kill them in a special religious ceremony as an offering to a god. ❑ *The priest sacrificed a chicken.* ● **Sacrifice** is also a noun. ❑ *...animal sacrifices to the gods.* ● **sac|ri|fi|cial** /sǽkrɪfɪʃᵊl/ ADJ ❑ *...a sacrificial lamb.* **2** V-T If you **sacrifice** something that is valuable or important, you give it up, usually to obtain something else for yourself or for other people. ❑ *She sacrificed family life to her career.* ❑ *Kitty Aldridge sacrificed everything for her movie.* ● **Sacrifice** is also a noun. ❑ *She made many sacrifices for Anita's education.* [from Old French]

**sad** /sǽd/ (**sadder, saddest**) **1** ADJ If you are **sad**, you feel unhappy, usually because something has happened that you do not like. ❑ *The end of the relationship made me feel sad and empty.* ❑ *I'm sad that Julie's going away.* ● **sad|ly** ADV ❑ *This man will be sadly missed by all his friends.* ❑ *I left with a mixture of sadness and joy.* **2** ADJ **Sad** stories and **sad** news make you feel sad. ❑ *It's a terribly sad novel.* **3** ADJ A **sad** event or situation is

unfortunate or undesirable. ❑ *The sad truth is that I never opened that present.* ● **sad|ly** ADV ❑ *Sadly, these plants die after they flower.* [from Old English]
→ see **cry, emotion**

<table>
<tr><td colspan="3">Thesaurus    sad    Also look up :</td></tr>
<tr><td>ADJ.</td><td colspan="2">depressed, down, gloomy, unhappy; (ant.) cheerful, happy 1<br>miserable, tragic, unhappy 3</td></tr>
</table>

<table>
<tr><td colspan="3">Word Partnership    Use sad with :</td></tr>
<tr><td>V.</td><td colspan="2">feel sad, look sad, seem sad 1</td></tr>
<tr><td>N.</td><td colspan="2">sad eyes 1<br>sad news, sad story 2<br>sad day, sad fact, sad truth 3</td></tr>
<tr><td>ADV.</td><td colspan="2">kind of sad, a little sad, really sad, so sad, too sad, very sad 1 – 3</td></tr>
</table>

**sad|den** /sǽdᵊn/ (**saddens, saddened**) V-T If something **saddens** you, it makes you feel sad. ❑ *The news saddened me greatly.* ● **sad|dened** ADJ ❑ *He was disappointed and saddened that the trial was stopped.* [from Old English]

**sad|dle** /sǽdᵊl/ (**saddles, saddling, saddled**) **1** N-COUNT A **saddle** is a leather seat that you put on the back of an animal so that you can ride the animal. **2** V-T If you **saddle** a horse, you put a saddle on it so that you can ride it. ❑ *Let's saddle some horses and go for a ride!* ● **Saddle up** means the same as **saddle**. ❑ *I want to leave as soon as we can saddle up.* **3** N-COUNT A **saddle** is a seat on a bicycle or motorcycle. [from Old English]
→ see **horse**

**sa|fa|ri** /səfɑri/ (**safaris**) N-COUNT A **safari** is a trip to observe or hunt wild animals, especially in East Africa. ❑ *Most visitors arrive at the park the night before their safari.* [from Swahili]

**safe** /séɪf/ (**safer, safest, safes**) **1** ADJ Something that is **safe** does not cause physical harm or danger. ❑ *Is it safe yet to bring emergency food supplies into the city?* ● **safe|ly** ADV ❑ *The smashed car was safely moved to one side of the road.* ❑ *"Drive safely," he said, waving goodbye.* **2** ADJ If a person or thing is **safe from** something, they cannot be harmed or damaged by it. ❑ *They are safe from the fighting here.* **3** ADJ If you are **safe**, you have not been harmed, or you are not in danger of being harmed. ❑ *Where is Sophy? Is she safe?* ● **safe|ly** ADV ❑ *All 140 guests were brought out of the building safely.* **4** ADJ A **safe** place is one where it is unlikely that any harm, damage, or unpleasant things will happen to the people or things that are there. ❑ *This plan will make the workplace safer for everyone.* ● **safe|ly** ADV ❑ *The manager keeps the money safely under his bed.* **5** ADJ If people or things have a **safe** trip, they reach their destination

S

without harm, damage, or unpleasant things happening to them. ❑ *I hope you have a safe trip home.* ● **safe|ly** ADV ❑ *The space shuttle returned safely today.* ❻ ADJ If **it is safe to** say or assume something, you can say it with very little risk of being wrong. ❑ *It's probably safe to say that it will be difficult for everyone.* ● **safe|ly** ADV ❑ *I think you can safely say she will not appear in another of my movies.* ❼ N-COUNT A **safe** is a strong metal cabinet with special locks, in which you keep money, jewelry, or other valuable things. ❑ *He's the only one with a key to the safe.* ❽ → see also **safely** ❾ PHRASE If you say that a person or thing is **in safe hands**, you mean that they are being taken care of by a reliable person and will not be harmed. ❑ *I made sure the package remained in safe hands.* ❿ PHRASE If you say you are doing something **to be on the safe side**, you mean that you are doing it in case something undesirable happens, even though this may be unnecessary. ❑ *Do you still want to go for an X-ray, just to be on the safe side?* [from Old French]

**safe|guard** /seɪfgɑrd/ (**safeguards, safeguarding, safeguarded**) ❶ V-T To **safeguard** something or someone means to protect them from being harmed, lost, or badly treated. [FORMAL] ❑ *We must act now to safeguard the planet's future.* ❷ N-COUNT A **safeguard** is a law, rule, or measure intended to prevent someone or something from being harmed. ❑ *There are no safeguards to protect people from harm.* ❑ *As an additional safeguard against weeds, you can use a plastic sheet.*

**safe ha|ven** N-UNCOUNT If a country provides **safe haven** for people from another country who have been in danger, it allows them to stay there under its official protection. ❑ *Should these people have temporary safe haven in the U.S.?*

**safe sex** N-UNCOUNT **Safe sex** is sexual activity in which people protect themselves against the risk of AIDS and other diseases, usually by using condoms.

**safe|ty** /seɪfti/ ❶ N-UNCOUNT **Safety** is the state of being safe from harm or danger. ❑ *The report recommends improving safety on aircraft.* ❷ N-SING If you are concerned about the **safety** of something, you are concerned that it might be harmful or dangerous. ❑ *We're worried about the safety of the food we buy.* ❸ N-SING If you are concerned for someone's **safety**, you are concerned that they might be in danger. ❑ *There is serious concern for their safety.* ❹ ADJ **Safety** features or measures are intended to make something less dangerous. ❑ *A smoke alarm is an important safety feature of any home.* [from Old French]
→ see **glass**

**safe|ty net** (**safety nets**) N-COUNT A **safety net** is something that you can rely on to help you if you get into a difficult situation. ❑ *Welfare is the only safety net for low-income workers.*

**sag** /sæg/ (**sags, sagging, sagged**) V-I When something **sags**, it hangs down loosely or sinks downward in the middle. ❑ *The dress won't sag or lose its shape after washing.* [of Scandinavian origin]

**saga** /sɑgə/ (**sagas**) N-COUNT A **saga** is a long story, account, or sequence of events. ❑ *...a 600 page saga about China.* [from Old Norse]

**sage** /seɪdʒ/ (**sages**) N-VAR **Sage** is an herb used in cooking. [from Old French]

**said** /sɛd/ **Said** is the past tense and past participle of **say**. [from Old English]

**sail** /seɪl/ (**sails, sailing, sailed**) ❶ N-COUNT **Sails** are large pieces of material attached to the mast

sail

of a ship. ❑ *I watched the sails disappear in the distance.* ❷ V-I You say a ship **sails** when it moves over the sea. ❑ *The ferry sailed from the port of Zeebrugge.* ❸ V-T/V-I If you **sail** a boat or if a boat **sails**, it moves across water using its sails. ❑ *The crew's job is to sail the boat.* ❑ *I'd buy a big boat and sail around the world.* ❹ → see also **sailing** ❺ PHRASE When a ship **sets sail**, it leaves a port. ❑ *Some ship captains won't set sail on Friday the 13th.* [from Old English]

▶ **sail through** PHR-VERB If someone or something **sails through** a difficult situation or experience, they deal with it easily and successfully. ❑ *She sailed through her exams, but he didn't.*

**sail|boat** /seɪlboʊt/ (**sailboats**) N-COUNT A **sailboat** is a boat with sails.

**sail|ing** /seɪlɪŋ/ (**sailings**) ❶ N-UNCOUNT **Sailing** is the activity or sport of sailing boats. ❑ *There was swimming and sailing on the lake.* ❷ N-COUNT **Sailings** are trips made by a ship carrying passengers. ❑ *Ferry companies are providing extra sailings.* [from Old English]
→ see **boat**

**sail|or** /seɪlər/ (**sailors**) N-COUNT A **sailor** is someone who works on a ship or sails a boat. [from Old English]

**saint** /seɪnt/ (**saints**) ❶ N-COUNT; N-TITLE A **saint** is someone who has died and been officially recognized and honored by the Christian church because his or her life was a perfect example of the way Christians should live. ❑ *Every church here was named after a saint.* ❷ N-COUNT If you refer to a living person as a **saint**, you mean that they are extremely kind, patient, and unselfish. ❑ *My girlfriend is a saint to stay with me.* ● **saint|ly** ADJ ❑ *The main story is about a saintly priest.* [from Old French]

**sake** /seɪk/ (**sakes**) **1** PHRASE If you do something **for the sake of** something, you do it for that purpose or in order to achieve that result. You can also say that you do it **for** something's **sake.** ❑ *Let's say for argument's sake that we manage to build the database.* ❑ *For the sake of peace, I am willing to forgive them.* **2** PHRASE If you do something **for** its **own sake**, you do it because you want to, or because you enjoy it, and not for any other reason. ❑ *Change for its own sake cannot be good.* **3** PHRASE When you do something **for** someone's **sake**, you do it in order to help them or make them happy. ❑ *Please do a good job, for Stan's sake.* [from Old English]

**sal|ad** /sæləd/ (**salads**) N-VAR A **salad** is a mixture of cold foods such as lettuce, tomatoes, or cold cooked potatoes, cut up and mixed with a dressing. It is often served with other food as part of a meal. ❑ *…a salad of tomato, onion, and cucumber.* [from Old French]

**sala|man|der** /sæləmændər/ (**salamanders**) N-COUNT A **salamander** is an animal that looks rather like a lizard, and that can live both on land and in water. [from Old French]

**sala|ry** /sæləri/ (**salaries**) N-VAR A **salary** is the money that someone earns each month or year from their employer. [BUSINESS] ❑ *The lawyer was paid a huge salary.* [from Latin]

**sale** /seɪl/ (**sales**) **1** N-SING The **sale** of goods is the act of selling them for money. ❑ *Their advice was to stop the sale of milk from these cows.* ❑ *He is learning the best way to make a sale.* **2** N-PLURAL The **sales** of a product are the quantity of it that is sold. ❑ *The newspaper has sales of 1.72 million.* ❑ *…huge Christmas sales of computer games.* **3** N-PLURAL The part of a company that deals with **sales** deals with selling the company's products. ❑ *Until 1983 he worked in sales and marketing.* **4** N-COUNT A **sale** is an occasion when a store sells things at less than their normal price. ❑ *I got my jeans half-price in a sale.* **5** PHRASE If something is **for sale**, it is being offered to people to buy. ❑ *The yacht is for sale for 1.7 million dollars.* **6** PHRASE Products that are **on sale** can be bought. ❑ *Tickets go on sale this week.* **7** PHRASE Products that are **on sale** are for sale at a reduced price. ❑ *At many stores, everything is on sale.* **8** PHRASE If a property or company is **up for sale**, its owner is trying to sell it. ❑ *The house has been put up for sale.* [from Old English]

**sales clerk** (**sales clerks**) also **salesclerk** N-COUNT A **sales clerk** is a person who works in a store selling things to customers.

**sales|man** /seɪlzmən/ (**salesmen**) N-COUNT A **salesman** is a man whose job is to sell things, especially directly to stores or other businesses on behalf of a company. ❑ *He's an insurance salesman.*

**sales|person** /seɪlzpɜrsⁿn/ (**salespeople** or **salespersons**) N-COUNT A **salesperson** is a person who sells things, either in a store or directly to customers on behalf of a company. [BUSINESS] ❑ *We'll send a salesperson out to measure your bathroom.*

**sales slip** (**sales slips**) N-COUNT A **sales slip** is a piece of paper that you are given when you buy something in a store, which shows when you bought it and how much you paid.

**sa|lin|ity** /səlɪnɪti/ N-UNCOUNT The **salinity** of water is the amount of salt it contains. [from Late Latin]

**sa|li|va** /səlaɪvə/ N-UNCOUNT **Saliva** is the watery liquid that forms in your mouth. [from Latin]

**salm|on** /sæmən/ (**salmon**) N-COUNT A **salmon** is a large silver-colored fish. ● **Salmon** is the flesh of this fish eaten as food. ❑ *He gave them a plate of salmon.* [from Old French]

**sa|lon** /səlɒn/ (**salons**) N-COUNT A **salon** is a place where people have their hair cut or colored, or have beauty treatments. ❑ *…a new hair salon.* [from French]

**salt** /sɔlt/ (**salts, salting, salted**) **1** N-UNCOUNT **Salt** is a strong-tasting substance, in the form of white powder or crystals, which is used to improve the flavor of food or to preserve it. ❑ *Now add salt and pepper.* **2** V-T When you **salt** food, you add salt to it. ❑ *Salt the soup and cook it very gently.* ● **salt|ed** ADJ ❑ *Boil a pan of salted water.* **3** N-COUNT **Salts** are substances that are formed when an acid reacts with an alkali. ❑ *The rock is rich in mineral salts.* [from Old English]

→ see **crystal**

**sal|ta|tion** /sælteɪʃⁿn/ N-UNCOUNT **Saltation** is the movement of sand and other particles as a result of being blown by the wind. [TECHNICAL] [from Latin]

**salt|ine** /sɔltin/ (**saltines**) N-COUNT A **saltine** is a thin square cracker with salt baked into its surface. [from Old English]

**salt shak|er** (**salt shakers**) N-COUNT A **salt shaker** is a small container for salt with a hole or holes in the top.

→ see **dish**

**salt|water** /sɔltwɔtər/ also **salt water** **1** N-UNCOUNT **Saltwater** is water, especially from the ocean, which has salt in it. **2** ADJ **Saltwater** fish live in water which is salty. **Saltwater** lakes contain salty water. ❑ *…useful information for owners of saltwater fish.*

**salty** /sɔlti/ (**saltier, saltiest**) ADJ Something that is **salty** contains salt or tastes of salt. ❑ *Ham and bacon are salty foods.* [from Old English]

→ see **taste**

**sa|lute** /səlut/ (**salutes, saluting, saluted**) **1** V-T/V-I If you **salute** someone, you greet them or show your respect with a formal sign. Soldiers usually salute officers by raising their right hand so that their fingers touch their forehead. ❑ *I saluted as the captain entered the room.* ❑ *I stood to attention and saluted.* ● **Salute** is also a noun. ❑ *He gave his salute and left.* **2** V-T To **salute** a person or their achievements means to publicly show or state your admiration for them. ❑ *I salute the governor for his strong leadership.* [from Latin]

**sal|vage** /sælvɪdʒ/ (**salvages, salvaging, salvaged**) **1** V-T If something **is salvaged**, someone manages to save it, for example, from a ship that has sunk, or from a building that has been damaged. ❑ *The team had to decide what equipment could be salvaged.* **2** N-UNCOUNT **Salvage** is the act of salvaging things from somewhere such as a damaged ship or building. ❑ *The salvage operation went on.* **3** N-UNCOUNT The **salvage** from

S

somewhere such as a damaged ship or building is the things that are saved from it. ❑ *They climbed up the hill with their salvage.* ◳ V-T If you manage to **salvage** a difficult situation, you manage to get something useful from it so that it is not a complete failure. ❑ *We tried hard to salvage the situation.* [from Old French]

**sal|va|tion** /sælˈveɪʃ°n/ ◰ N-UNCOUNT In Christianity, **salvation** is the fact that Christ has saved a person from evil. ❑ *The church's message of salvation has changed many lives.* ◳ N-UNCOUNT The **salvation** of someone or something is the act of saving them from harm, destruction, or an unpleasant situation. ❑ *She felt that writing was her salvation.* [from Old French]

**same** /seɪm/ ◰ ADJ If two or more things, actions, or qualities are **the same**, or if one is **the same as** another, they are very like each other in some way. ❑ *The houses are all the same.* ❑ *All these people have the same experience in the job.* ◳ ADJ You use **same** to indicate that you are referring to only one place, time, or thing, and not to different ones. ❑ *Bernard works at the same institute as Arlette.* ❑ *Can we get everybody together at the same time?* ◴ ADJ Something that is still **the same** has not changed in any way. ❑ *If prices rise and your income stays the same, you have to buy less.* ◵ PRON You use **the same** to refer to something that has previously been mentioned or suggested. ❑ *I breathed deeply and watched Terry do the same.* ❑ *We made the decision which was right for us. Other parents must do the same.* ● **Same** is also an adjective. ❑ *He's so brave. I admire Ginny for the same reason.* ◶ PHRASE You can say **all the same** or **just the same** to introduce a statement which indicates that a situation or your opinion has not changed, in spite of what has happened or what has just been said. ❑ *It was a private arrangement. All the same, it was illegal.* [from Old Norse] ◷ **at the same time** → see **time**

| Thesaurus | *same* | Also look up : |
|---|---|---|

| ADJ. | alike, equal, identical; (ant.) different ◰ |
|---|---|

**sam|ple** /sæmp°l/ (**samples, sampling, sampled**) ◰ N-COUNT A **sample** of a substance or product is a small quantity of it that shows you what it is like. ❑ *You'll receive samples of paint on cards.* ❑ *We're giving away 2,000 free samples.* ◳ N-COUNT A **sample** of a substance is a small amount of it that is examined and analyzed scientifically. ❑ *They took samples of my blood.* ◴ N-COUNT A **sample** of people or things is a number of them chosen out of a larger group and then used in tests or used to provide information about the whole group. ❑ *We tested a sample of more than 200 males.* ◵ V-T If you **sample** food or drink, you taste a small amount of it in order to find out if you like it. ❑ *We sampled several different bottled waters.* ◶ V-T If you **sample** a place or situation, you experience it for a short time in order to find out about it. ❑ *It was a chance to sample a different way of life.* [from Old French] → see **laboratory**

| Thesaurus | *sample* | Also look up : |
|---|---|---|

| N. | bit, piece, portion ◰ ◳ |
|---|---|
| V. | experience, taste, try ◵ ◶ |

**sanc|tion** /sæŋkʃ°n/ (**sanctions, sanctioning,**

**sanctioned**) ◰ V-T If someone in authority **sanctions** an action or practice, they officially approve of it and allow it to be done. ❑ *He may now sanction the use of force.* ● **Sanction** is also a noun. ❑ *The newspaper is run by citizens without the sanction of the government.* ◳ N-PLURAL **Sanctions** are measures taken by countries to restrict trade and official contact with a country that has broken international law. ❑ *Unfortunately, they have no power to impose sanctions on countries that break the rules.* [from Latin]

| Word Partnership | Use *sanction* with : |
|---|---|

| PREP. | **without** sanction ◰ <br> sanction **against** ◳ |
|---|---|
| ADJ. | **legal** sanction, **official** sanction, <br> **proposed** sanction ◰ ◳ |
| V. | **impose a** sanction, **lift a** sanction ◳ |

**sanc|tity** /sæŋktɪti/ N-UNCOUNT If you talk about **the sanctity of** something, you mean that it is very important and must be treated with respect. ❑ *...the sanctity of human life.* [from Old French]

**sanc|tu|ary** /sæŋktʃuɛri/ (**sanctuaries**) ◰ N-VAR A **sanctuary** is a place where people who are in danger from other people can go to be safe. ❑ *His church became a sanctuary for homeless people.* ◳ N-COUNT A **sanctuary** is a place where birds or animals are protected and allowed to live freely. ❑ *...a bird sanctuary.* [from Old French]

**sand** /sænd/ (**sands, sanding, sanded**) ◰ N-UNCOUNT **Sand** is a substance that looks like powder, and consists of extremely small pieces of stone. Some deserts and most beaches are made up of sand. ❑ *They walked across the sand to the water's edge.* ◳ N-PLURAL **Sands** are a large area of sand, for example, a beach. ❑ *There are miles of golden sands.* ◴ V-T If you **sand** a wood or metal surface, you rub sandpaper over it in order to make it smooth or clean. ❑ *Sand the surface carefully.* [from Old English] → see **beach, desert, erosion, glass**

**san|dal** /sænd°l/ (**sandals**) N-COUNT **Sandals** are light shoes that you wear in warm weather, which have straps instead of a solid part over the top of your foot. ❑ *...a pair of old sandals.* [from Medieval Latin] → see **shoe**

**sand|box** /sændbɒks/ (**sandboxes**) N-COUNT A **sandbox** is a shallow hole or box in the ground with sand in it where children can play.

**sand dune** (**sand dunes**) N-COUNT A **sand dune** is a hill of sand near the sea or in a sand desert.

**sand|stone** /sændstoʊn/ (**sandstones**) N-VAR **Sandstone** is a type of rock which contains a lot of sand. ❑ *...the red sandstone walls.* [from Old English]

**sand trap** (**sand traps**) N-COUNT On a golf course, a **sand trap** is a hollow area filled with sand, which is put there as an obstacle that players must try to avoid. → see **golf**

**sand|wich** /sænwɪtʃ, sænd-/ (**sandwiches, sandwiching, sandwiched**) ◰ N-COUNT A **sandwich** usually consists of two slices of bread with a layer of food such as cheese or meat between them. ❑ *...a ham sandwich.* ◳ V-T If you

**sandwich** two things **together** with something else, you put that other thing between them. If one thing is **sandwiched** between two other things, it is in a narrow space between them. ❑ *Cut the cake open, then sandwich the two halves together with cream.*
→ see **meal**

**sandy** /sǽndi/ (**sandier, sandiest**) ADJ A **sandy** area is covered with sand. ❑ …*long, sandy beaches.* [from Old English]

| Word Link | *san ≈ health* : *insane, sane, sanitation* |

**sane** /seɪn/ (**saner, sanest**) **1** ADJ Someone who is **sane** is able to think and behave normally and reasonably, and is not mentally ill. ❑ *He seemed perfectly sane.* **2** ADJ A **sane** action or idea is reasonable and sensible. ❑ …*extremely sane advice.* [from Latin]

**sang** /sæŋ/ **Sang** is the past tense of **sing**. [from Old English]

**sani|tary** /sǽniteri/ ADJ **Sanitary** means concerned with keeping things clean and healthy. ❑ *Sanitary conditions in the camp are very bad.* [from French]

**sani|tary nap|kin** (**sanitary napkins**) N-COUNT A **sanitary napkin** is a pad of thick soft material which women wear to absorb the blood during their period.

**sani|ta|tion** /sæniteɪʃⁿn/ N-UNCOUNT **Sanitation** is the process of keeping places clean and healthy, especially by providing a sewage system and a clean water supply. ❑ *There is now a serious sanitation problem in the city.* [from French]

**san|ity** /sǽniti/ N-UNCOUNT A person's **sanity** is their ability to think and behave normally and reasonably. ❑ *Nobody with any sanity wants this job.* [from Latin]

**sank** /sæŋk/ **Sank** is the past tense of **sink**.

**sap** /sæp/ (**saps, sapping, sapped**) **1** V-T If something **saps** your strength or confidence, it gradually weakens or destroys it. ❑ *The sickness sapped my strength.* **2** N-UNCOUNT **Sap** is the watery liquid in plants and trees. ❑ *The leaves and sap are made into herbal medicines.* [from Old English]

**sap|py** /sǽpi/ ADJ If you describe someone or something as **sappy**, you think they are foolish. [INFORMAL] ❑ *I wrote this sappy love song.* [from Old English]

**sar|casm** /sɑ́rkæzəm/ N-UNCOUNT **Sarcasm** is speech or writing which actually means the opposite of what it seems to say. Sarcasm is usually intended to mock or insult someone. ❑ *"How nice of you to join us," he said with heavy sarcasm.* [from Late Latin]

**sar|cas|tic** /sɑrkǽstɪk/ ADJ Someone who is **sarcastic** says or does the opposite of what they really mean in order to mock or insult someone. ❑ …*sarcastic remarks.* ● **sar|cas|ti|cal|ly** /sɑrkǽstɪkli/ ADV ❑ *"What a surprise!" Caroline said sarcastically.* [from Late Latin]

**sar|dine** /sɑrdín/ (**sardines**) N-COUNT **Sardines** are a kind of small sea fish, often eaten as food. ❑ *They opened a can of sardines.* [from Old French]

**sar|don|ic** /sɑrdɒ́nɪk/ ADJ If you describe someone as **sardonic**, you mean their attitude to

people or things is humorous but rather critical. ❑ *She saw the look of surprise before his usual sardonic expression returned.* ● **sar|don|i|cal|ly** /sɑrdɒ́nɪkli/ ADV ❑ *He grinned sardonically.* [from French]

**sar|gas|sum** /sɑrgǽsəm/ N-UNCOUNT **Sargassum** is seaweed and other plant material that has formed into a large floating mass. [TECHNICAL] [from New Latin]

**SASE** /ɛs eɪ ɛs i/ (**SASEs**) N-SING An **SASE** is an envelope on which you have stuck a stamp and written your own name and address. You send it to a person or an organization so they can reply to you. **SASE** is an abbreviation for "self-addressed stamped envelope."

**sass** /sæs/ (**sasses, sassing, sassed**) **1** N-UNCOUNT **Sass** is disrespectful talk. [INFORMAL] ❑ *We're going, and I want no sass from you.* **2** V-T If someone **sasses** you, they speak to you in a disrespectful way. [INFORMAL] ❑ *The girl sassed the teacher all day.*

**sas|sa|fras** /sǽsəfræs/ (**sassafras**) **1** N-VAR **Sassafras** is an herb which is produced from the dried roots of the sassafras tree. **2** N-COUNT A **sassafras** or a **sassafras tree** is a tree, found mainly in North America, the roots of which are used to make the herb sassafras. [from Spanish]

**sas|sy** /sǽsi/ **1** ADJ If an older person describes a younger person as **sassy**, they mean that they are disrespectful in a lively, confident way. [INFORMAL] ❑ *Are you that sassy with your parents, young lady?* **2** ADJ **Sassy** is used to describe things that are smart and stylish. [INFORMAL] ❑ …*his sassy hairstyle.* ❑ *We sell colorful and sassy fashion accessories.*

**sat** /sæt/ **Sat** is the past tense and past participle of **sit**. [from Old English]

**SAT** /ɛs eɪ ti/ (**SATs**) N-PROPER The **SAT** is an examination which is often taken by students who wish to enter a college or university. **SAT** is an abbreviation for "Scholastic Aptitude Test."

**Satan** /seɪtⁿn/ N-PROPER In religions such as Christianity and Islam, **Satan** is the Devil, a powerful evil being who is the chief opponent of God. ● **sa|tan|ic** /sətǽnɪk, seɪ–/ ADJ ❑ …*satanic power.* [from Old English]

**sat|el|lite** /sǽtⁿlaɪt/ (**satellites**) **1** N-COUNT A **satellite** is an object which has been sent into space in order to collect information or to be part of a communications system. ❑ *The rocket carried two communications satellites.* **2** ADJ **Satellite** television is broadcast using a satellite. ❑ *They have four satellite channels.* **3** N-COUNT A **satellite** is a natural object in space that moves around a planet or star. ❑ …*the satellites of Jupiter.* [from Latin]
→ see Word Web: **satellite**
→ see **astronomer, forecast, navigation, radio, television**

**sat|el|lite dish** (**satellite dishes**) N-COUNT A **satellite dish** is a piece of equipment which people have on their house in order to receive satellite television.

**sat|in** /sǽtⁿn/ (**satins**) N-VAR **Satin** is a smooth, shiny kind of cloth, usually made from silk. ❑ …*a satin dress.* [from Old French]

**sat|ire** /sǽtaɪər/ (**satires**) **1** N-UNCOUNT **Satire** is the use of humor or exaggeration in order to mock or criticize people's behavior or ideas.

S

### Word Web    satellite

The **moon** is the earth's best-known **satellite**. In 1957 humans began **launching** objects into **space**. That's when the first man-made satellite, Sputnik, began to **orbit** the earth. Today, hundreds of satellites circle the **planet**. The largest satellite is the International **Space Station**. It completes an orbit about every 90 minutes and sometimes can be seen from the earth. Others, such as the Hubble Telescope, help us learn more about **outer space**. The NOAA 12 measures the earth's climate. TV weather forecasts often use pictures taken from satellites. Today, many TV programs are also broadcast by satellite.

❑ *Politicians are an easy target for satire.* **2** N-COUNT A **satire** is a play, movie, or novel in which humor or exaggeration is used to criticize something. ❑ *...a satire on the American political process.* [from Latin]

**sa|tiri|cal** /sətɪrɪkəl/ ADJ A **satirical** drawing, piece of writing, or comedy show is one in which humor or exaggeration is used to criticize something. ❑ *It's a satirical novel about New York life.* [from Latin]

**sat|is|fac|tion** /sætɪsfækʃən/ **1** N-UNCOUNT **Satisfaction** is the pleasure that you feel when you do something or get something that you wanted or needed to do or get. ❑ *She felt a sense of satisfaction.* **2** N-UNCOUNT If you get **satisfaction** from someone, you get money or an apology from them because you have been treated badly. ❑ *If you can't get any satisfaction, complain to the park owner.* [from French]

**sat|is|fac|tory** /sætɪsfæktəri/ ADJ Something that is **satisfactory** is acceptable to you or fulfills a particular need or purpose. ❑ *I never got a satisfactory answer.* • **sat|is|fac|to|ri|ly** /sætɪsfæktərɪli/ ADV ❑ *How she died was never satisfactorily explained.* [from French]

**sat|is|fied** /sætɪsfaɪd/ ADJ If you are **satisfied with** something, you are happy because you have gotten what you wanted or needed. ❑ *We are not satisfied with these results.* [from Old French]

### Word Link    sat, satis ≈ enough : dis*satis*faction, in*satia*ble, *satis*fy

**sat|is|fy** /sætɪsfaɪ/ (**satisfies, satisfying, satisfied**) **1** V-T If someone or something **satisfies** you, they give you enough of what you want or need to make you pleased or contented. ❑ *He will satisfy all his fans with this CD.* **2** V-T To **satisfy** someone **that** something is true or has been done properly means to convince them by giving them more information or by showing them what has been done. ❑ *He has to satisfy the public that he is making real progress.* **3** V-T If you **satisfy** the requirements for something, you are good enough or have the right qualities to fulfill these requirements. ❑ *Private companies have to satisfy the needs of their workers.* [from Old French]

### Word Partnership    Use *satisfy* with :

N.   satisfy **an appetite**, satisfy **demands**, satisfy **a desire** **1**
satisfy **a need** **1** **3**
satisfy **critics**, satisfy *someone's curiosity* **2**

**sat|is|fy|ing** /sætɪsfaɪɪŋ/ ADJ Something that is **satisfying** makes you feel happy, especially because you feel you have achieved something. ❑ *It was a very satisfying experience.* [from Old French]

**satu|rate** /sætʃəreɪt/ (**saturates, saturating, saturated**) **1** V-T If people or things **saturate** a place or object, they fill it completely so that no more can be added. ❑ *No one wants to saturate the city with car parking.* • **satu|ra|tion** /sætʃəreɪʃən/ N-UNCOUNT ❑ *We actually want to see the saturation of the market with goods.* **2** V-T If someone or something **is saturated**, they become extremely wet. ❑ *The ground seemed to be saturated with water.* [from Latin]

**satu|rat|ed hydro|car|bon** /sætʃəreɪtɪd haɪdroʊkarbən/ (**saturated hydrocarbons**) N-COUNT A **saturated hydrocarbon** is a compound of hydrogen and carbon which contains the maximum number of hydrogen atoms. [TECHNICAL]

**satu|rat|ed so|lu|tion** (**saturated solutions**) N-COUNT A **saturated solution** is a liquid that contains so much of a dissolved substance that it is unable to contain any more of it.

**Sat|ur|day** /sætərdeɪ, -di/ (**Saturdays**) N-VAR **Saturday** is the day after Friday and before Sunday. ❑ *He called her on Saturday morning.* ❑ *Every Saturday, Dad made soup.* [from Old English]

**Sat|urn** /sætərn/ N-PROPER **Saturn** is the sixth planet from the sun. It is surrounded by rings made of ice and dust. [from Latin]

**sauce** /sɔs/ (**sauces**) N-VAR A **sauce** is a thick liquid which is served with other food. ❑ *This pasta is cooked in a tomato sauce.* [from Old French]

**sauce|pan** /sɔspæn/ (**saucepans**) N-COUNT A **saucepan** is a deep metal cooking pot, usually with a long handle and a lid. ❑ *Place the potatoes in a saucepan and boil them.*
→ see **pan**

**S**

**sau|cer** /sɔsər/ (**saucers**) N-COUNT A **saucer** is a small curved plate on which you stand a cup. □ *Rae's coffee splashed in the saucer as she picked it up.* [from Old French]
→ see **dish**

**sau|na** /sɔnə/ (**saunas**) ◼ N-COUNT If you have a **sauna**, you sit or lie in a room that is so hot that it makes you sweat. □ *Every month I have a sauna.* ◼ N-COUNT A **sauna** is a room or building where you can have a sauna. □ *The hotel has a sauna and a swimming pool.* [from Finnish]

**saun|ter** /sɔntər/ (**saunters, sauntering, sauntered**) V-I If you **saunter** somewhere, you walk there in a slow, casual way. □ *We watched the students saunter into the building.*

**sau|sage** /sɔsɪdʒ/ (**sausages**) N-VAR A **sausage** consists of minced meat, usually pork, mixed with other ingredients, inside a long thin skin. □ *Tonight we're having sausages and fries.* [from Old Norman French]

**sau|té** /soʊteɪ/ (**sautés, sautéing, sautéed**) V-T When you **sauté** food, you fry it quickly in hot oil or butter. □ *Sauté the chicken until it's golden.* [from French]

**sav|age** /sævɪdʒ/ (**savages, savaging, savaged**) ◼ ADJ Someone or something that is **savage** is extremely cruel, violent, and uncontrolled. □ *This was a savage attack on a young girl.* ● **sav|age|ly** ADV □ *He was savagely beaten.* ◼ N-COUNT If you refer to people as **savages**, you dislike them because you think that they do not have an advanced society and are violent. □ *The Dutch and British who settled there thought the people were savages.* ◼ V-T If someone is **savaged** by a dog or other animal, the animal attacks them violently. □ *The animal then turned on him and he was badly savaged.* [from Old French]

**sav|age|ry** /sævɪdʒri/ N-UNCOUNT **Savagery** is extremely cruel and violent behavior. □ *...the savagery of war.* [from Old French]

**sa|van|na** /səvænə/ (**savannas**) also **savannah** N-VAR A **savanna** is a large area of flat, grassy land, usually in Africa. [from Spanish]

**save** /seɪv/ (**saves, saving, saved**) ◼ V-T If you **save** someone or something, you help them to avoid harm or to escape from a dangerous or unpleasant situation. □ *The program will save the country's failing economy.* □ *We must save these children from disease and death.* ◼ V-T/V-I If you **save**, you gradually collect money by spending less than you get, usually in order to buy something that you want. □ *Most people intend to save, but find it difficult.* □ *Tim and Barbara are now saving for a house.* □ *I was saving money to go to college.* ● **Save up** means the same as **save**. □ *Julie was saving up for something special.* ● **sav|er** (**savers**) N-COUNT □ *They aren't big savers and don't have bank accounts.* ◼ V-T/V-I If you **save** something such as time or money, you prevent the loss or waste of it. □ *The drivers believe going through the city saves time.* □ *I'll try to save him the cost of a flight from Perth.* □ *Families move in together to save on rent.* ◼ V-T If you **save** something, you keep it because it will be needed later. □ *Don't tell her now. Save the news for later.* ◼ V-T If someone or something **saves** you **from** an unpleasant action or experience, they change the situation so that you do not have to do it or experience it. □ *This information will save you many* hours of searching later. □ *We must act to save people from starvation.* ◼ V-T/V-I If you **save** data in a computer, you give the computer an instruction to store the data on a tape or disk. [COMPUTING] □ *Save your work regularly.* □ *It's important to save frequently when you are working on a document.* ◼ V-T/V-I If a goalkeeper **saves**, or **saves** a shot, they succeed in preventing the ball from going into the goal. □ *He saved one shot when the ball hit him on the head.* ● **Save** is also a noun. □ *The goalkeeper made some great saves.* [from Old French]
▶ **save up** → see **save 2**

**sav|ings** /seɪvɪŋz/ N-PLURAL Your **savings** are the money that you have saved, especially in a bank. □ *Her savings were in the First National Bank.* [from Old French]

**sav|ings and loan** also **savings and loans** N-COUNT A **savings and loan** is a business where people save money to earn interest, and which lends money to savers to buy houses. [BUSINESS]

**sav|ior** /seɪvyər/ (**saviors**) N-COUNT A **savior** is a person who saves someone or something from danger, ruin, or defeat. □ *...the savior of his country.* [from Old French]

**sa|vor** /seɪvər/ (**savors, savoring, savored**) V-T If you **savor** something pleasant, you enjoy it as much as you can. □ *She savored this new freedom.* □ *Just relax and savor the full flavor of your food.* [from Old French]

**sa|vory** /seɪvəri/ ADJ **Savory** food has a salty or spicy flavor rather than a sweet one. □ *We had all sorts of sweet and savory breads.* [from Old French]

**saw** /sɔ/ (**saws, sawing, sawed, sawed** or **sawn**) ◼ **Saw** is the past tense of **see**. ◼ N-COUNT A **saw** is a tool for cutting wood, which has a blade with sharp teeth along one edge. ◼ V-T/V-I If you **saw** something, you cut it with a saw. □ *He escaped by sawing through the bars of his jail cell.* □ *Father sawed the dead branches off the tree.* [from Old English]
→ see **cut, tools**

**saw|dust** /sɔdʌst/ N-UNCOUNT **Sawdust** is dust and very small pieces of wood which are produced when you saw wood.

**sax** /sæks/ (**saxes**) N-COUNT A **sax** is the same as a **saxophone**. [INFORMAL]

**saxo|phone** /sæksəfoʊn/ (**saxophones**) N-VAR A **saxophone** is a musical instrument in the shape of a curved metal tube with a narrower part that you blow into and keys that you press. ● **sax|opho|nist** /sæksəfoʊnɪst/ (**saxophonists**) N-COUNT □ *...the great jazz saxophonist Sonny Rollins.*

| **say** |
|---|
| ❶ VERB AND NOUN USES |
| ❷ PHRASES AND CONVENTIONS |

❶ **say** /seɪ/ (**says** /sɛz/, **saying, said** /sɛd/) ◼ V-T When you **say** something, you speak words. □ *"I'm sorry," he said.* □ *She said that they were very pleased.* □ *Forty people are said to have died.* □ *I packed and said goodbye to Charlie.* ◼ V-T You use **say** to show that you are expressing an opinion or stating a fact. □ *I would say this is probably illegal.* □ *I must say that rather shocked me, too.* ◼ V-T You can mention the contents of a piece of writing by mentioning what it **says** or what someone **says** in it. □ *Our report says six people were injured.* □ *As the song says, "You can't have one without the other."*

**4** V-T If you **say** something **to yourself**, you think it. □ *"I'm still dreaming," I said to myself.* **5** N-SING If you have **a say in** something, you have the right to give your opinion and influence decisions relating to it. □ *We want to have a say in the decision.* **6** V-T You understand the information given by something such as a clock, dial, or map by mentioning what it **says**. □ *The clock said four minutes past eleven.* **7** V-T If something **says** something **about** a person, situation, or thing, it gives important information about them. □ *The fact that he is still popular says a lot about his music.* **8** PHRASE You can use **say** or **let's say** when you mention something as an example. □ *…a painting by, say, Picasso.* [from Old English]

**②** say /seɪ/ (**says** /sɛz/, **saying, said** /sɛd/) **1** EXCLAM **Say** is used to attract someone's attention or to express surprise, pleasure, or admiration. [INFORMAL] □ *Say, Leo, how would you like to have dinner one night?* **2** PHRASE If you say that something **says it all**, you mean that it shows you very clearly the truth about a situation or someone's feelings. □ *This is my third visit in a week, which says it all.* **3** PHRASE If you say there is a lot **to be said for** something, you mean you think it has a lot of good qualities or aspects. □ *There's a lot to be said for working in the country.* **4** PHRASE If something **goes without saying**, it is obvious. □ *It goes without saying that the spices must be fresh.* **5** PHRASE You use **that is to say** or **that's to say** to indicate that you are about to express the same idea more clearly or precisely. [FORMAL] □ *They work with world music, that is to say, non-American, non-European music.* **6** CONVENTION You can use **"You can say that again"** to express strong agreement with what someone has just said. [INFORMAL] □ *"You are in trouble already." — "You can say that again,"* sighed Richard. [from Old English]

**say|ing** /seɪɪŋ/ (**sayings**) N-COUNT A **saying** is a sentence that people often say and that gives advice or information about human life and experience. □ *The saying goes, "Be careful what you ask for, you might just get it."* [from Old English]

**scaf|fold|ing** /skæfəldɪŋ/ N-UNCOUNT **Scaffolding** consists of poles and boards made into a temporary framework that is used by workers when they are working on the outside of a building. □ *Workers have put up scaffolding around the tower.* [from Old French]

**sca|lar ma|trix** /skeɪlər meɪtrɪks/ (**scalar matrices**) N-COUNT A **scalar matrix** is a mathematical arrangement of numbers, symbols, or letters in which all of the diagonal elements are equal. [TECHNICAL]

**scald** /skɔld/ (**scalds, scalding, scalded**) **1** V-T If you **scald yourself**, you burn yourself with very hot liquid or steam. □ *A patient scalded herself in the bath.* **2** N-COUNT A **scald** is a burn caused by very hot liquid or steam. □ *Do not apply ointments or creams to burns and scalds.* [from Old Norman French]

> **Word Link**    scal, scala ≈ ladder, stairs : escalate, escalator, scale

**scale** /skeɪl/ (**scales, scaling, scaled**) **1** N-SING If you refer to the **scale** of something, you are referring to its size or extent, especially when it is very big. □ *He doesn't realize the scale of the problem.* □ *Our business now operates on a greatly reduced scale.* **2** → see also **full-scale, large-scale,**

**small-scale 3** N-COUNT A **scale** is a set of levels or numbers which are used in a particular system of measuring things or are used when comparing things. □ *The earthquake measured 5.5 on the Richter scale.* □ *He's on the high end of the pay scale.* **4** N-COUNT The **scale** of a map, plan, or model is the relationship between the size of something in the map, plan, or model and its size in the real world. □ *The map is on a scale of 1:10,000.* **5** → see also **full-scale, large-scale 6** ADJ A **scale** model or **scale** replica of a building or object is a model of it which is smaller than the real thing but has all the same parts and features. □ *Frank made his mother a scale model of the house.* **7** N-COUNT In music, a **scale** is a fixed sequence of musical notes, each one higher than the next, which begins at a particular note. □ *Play a scale of C major.* **8** N-COUNT The **scales** of a fish or reptile are the small, flat pieces of hard skin that cover its body. □ *Remove the scales from the fish skin.* **9** N-COUNT A **scale** is a piece of equipment used for weighing things, for example, for weighing amounts of food that you need in order to make a particular meal. □ *I have new kitchen scales.* □ *…a bathroom scale.* **10** V-T If you **scale** something such as a mountain or a wall, you climb up it or over it. [WRITTEN] □ *Rebecca Stephens was the first British woman to scale Everest.* [Senses 1 to 5 and 8 from Italian. Sense 6 from Old French. Sense 7 from Old Norse.]
→ see **fish, graph, shellfish, thermometer, utensil**
▶ **scale back** PHR-VERB To **scale back** means the same as to **scale down**. □ *Manufacturers are scaling back production.*
▶ **scale down** PHR-VERB If you **scale down** something, you make it smaller in size, amount, or extent that it used to be. □ *One factory scaled down its workforce from six hundred to only six.*

**scal|lion** /skælyən/ (**scallions**) N-COUNT A **scallion** is a small onion with long green leaves. [from Latin]

**scal|lop** /skɒləp, skæl-/ (**scallops**) N-COUNT **Scallops** are large shellfish with two flat fan-shaped shells. Scallops can be eaten. [from Old French]
→ see **shellfish**

**scalp** /skælp/ (**scalps, scalping, scalped**) **1** N-COUNT Your **scalp** is the skin under the hair on your head. □ *He smoothed his hair back over his scalp.* **2** V-T If someone **scalps** tickets, they sell them outside a sports stadium or theater, usually for more than their original value. □ *He made some cash scalping tickets.* [of Scandinavian origin]

**scalp|er** /skælpər/ (**scalpers**) N-COUNT A **scalper** is someone who sells tickets outside a sports stadium or theater, usually for more than their original value. □ *A scalper charged $1000 for a $125 ticket.* [of Scandinavian origin]

**scamp|er** /skæmpər/ (**scampers, scampering, scampered**) V-I When people or small animals **scamper** somewhere, they move there quickly with small, light steps. □ *Children scampered off the bus and into the playground.*

**scan** /skæn/ (**scans, scanning, scanned**) **1** V-T/V-I When you **scan** written material, you look through it quickly in order to find important or interesting information. □ *She scanned the front page of the newspaper.* ● **Scan** is also a noun. □ *I had a quick scan through your book again.* **2** V-T/V-I

When you **scan** a place or group of people, you look at it carefully, usually because you are looking for something or someone. ❑ *The officer scanned the room.* ❑ *She nervously scanned the crowd for Paul.* ❸ V-T If people **scan** something such as luggage, they examine it using a machine that can show or find things inside it that cannot be seen from the outside. ❑ *They scan every bag with an X-ray machine.* ❹ N-COUNT A **scan** is a medical test in which a machine sends a beam of X-rays over a part of your body in order to check that it is healthy. ❑ *A brain scan showed a strange shadow.* [from Late Latin]

**scan|dal** /skǽndˀl/ (**scandals**) ❶ N-COUNT A **scandal** is a situation or event that is thought to be shocking and immoral and that everyone knows about. ❑ *It was a financial scandal.* ❷ N-UNCOUNT **Scandal** is talk about the shocking and immoral aspects of someone's behavior or something that has happened. ❑ *He loved gossip and scandal.* [from Late Latin]

**scan|dal|ous** /skǽndˀləs/ ADJ **Scandalous** behavior or activity is considered immoral and shocking. ❑ *Stories of their scandalous behavior were in all the newspapers.* ● **scan|dal|ous|ly** ADV ❑ *He asked Ingrid to stop behaving so scandalously.* [from Late Latin]

**scan|ner** /skǽnər/ (**scanners**) N-COUNT A **scanner** is a machine which is used to examine, identify, or record things, for example by using a beam of light, sound, or X-rays. ❑ *... brain scanners.* [from Late Latin]
→ see **laser**

**scant** /skǽnt/ ADJ You use **scant** to indicate that there is very little of something or not as much of something as there should be. ❑ *The administration paid scant attention to these issues.* [from Old Norse]

**scape|goat** /skéɪpgoʊt/ (**scapegoats**) N-COUNT If someone is made a **scapegoat for** something bad that has happened, people blame them and may punish them for it although it may not be their fault. ❑ *Don't make me a scapegoat because of a couple of bad results.* [from Biblical Hebrew]

**scar** /skɑr/ (**scars, scarring, scarred**) ❶ N-COUNT A **scar** is a mark on the skin which is left after a wound has healed. ❑ *He had a scar on his forehead.* ❷ V-T If your skin **is scarred**, it is badly marked as a result of a wound. ❑ *He was scarred for life during a fight.* ❸ V-T If a surface **is scarred**, it is damaged and there are ugly marks on it. ❑ *The land is scarred by huge holes.* ❹ N-COUNT If an unpleasant physical or emotional experience leaves a **scar** on someone, it has a permanent effect on their mind. ❑ *The years of fear left a deep scar on the young boy.* ❺ V-T If an unpleasant physical or emotional experience **scars** you, it has a permanent effect on your mind. ❑ *This will scar him forever.* [from Late Latin]

**scarce** /skɛ́ərs/ (**scarcer, scarcest**) ADJ If something is **scarce**, there is not enough of it. ❑ *Food was scarce and expensive.* ❑ *Jobs are becoming scarce.* [from Old Norman French]

**scarce|ly** /skɛ́ərsli/ ❶ ADV You use **scarcely** to emphasize that something is only just true. ❑ *He could scarcely breathe.* ❑ *I scarcely knew him.* ❷ ADV You can use **scarcely** to say that something is not true, in a humorous or critical way. ❑ *I would scarcely expect them to say anything else.* ❸ ADV If you say **scarcely had** one thing happened when

something else happened, you mean that the first event was followed immediately by the second. ❑ *Scarcely had they counted the votes when the telephone rang.* [from Old Norman French]

**scar|city** /skɛ́ərsɪti/ (**scarcities**) N-VAR If there is a **scarcity of** something, there is not enough of it for the people who need it or want it. [FORMAL] ❑ *The scarcity of water is worrying.* [from Old Norman French]

**scare** /skɛ́ər/ (**scares, scaring, scared**) ❶ V-T If something **scares** you, it frightens or worries you. ❑ *You're scaring me.* ❑ *The thought of failure scares me.* ❷ N-SING If a sudden unpleasant experience gives you a **scare**, it frightens you. ❑ *Don't you realize what a scare you gave us?* ❸ N-COUNT A **scare** is a situation in which many people are afraid or worried because they think something dangerous is happening which will affect them all. ❑ *The airport has reopened after a natural gas scare this morning.* ❹ N-COUNT A bomb **scare** or a security **scare** is a situation in which there is believed to be a bomb in a place. ❑ *There have been many bomb scares, but no one has yet been hurt.* [from Old Norse] ❺ → see also **scared**
▸ **scare away** → see **scare off**
▸ **scare off** PHR-VERB If you **scare off** or **scare away** a person or animal, you frighten them so that they go away. ❑ *The alarm will scare off an attacker.*

**scared** /skɛ́ərd/ ❶ ADJ If you are **scared of** someone or something, you are frightened of them. ❑ *I'm not scared of him.* ❑ *I was too scared to move.* ❷ ADJ If you are **scared that** something unpleasant might happen, you are nervous and worried because you think that it might happen. ❑ *I was scared that I might be sick.* [from Old Norse]

**scarf** /skɑrf/ (**scarfs** or **scarves**) N-COUNT A **scarf** is a piece of cloth that you wear around your neck or head, usually to keep yourself warm. ❑ *He loosened the scarf around his neck.*

**scar|let** /skɑrlɪt/ (**scarlets**) COLOR Something that is **scarlet** is bright red. ❑ *She wore scarlet lipstick.* [from Old French]

**scary** /skɛ́əri/ (**scarier, scariest**) ADJ Something that is **scary** is rather frightening. [INFORMAL] ❑ *I think prison will be scary for Harry.* ❑ *There's something very scary about him.* [from Late Latin]

**scath|ing** /skéɪðɪŋ/ ADJ If you say that someone is being **scathing** about something, you mean that they are being very critical of it. ❑ *He made some scathing comments about the design.* ● **scath|ing|ly** ADV ❑ *"Here, let me do it," she said scathingly.* [from Old English]

**scat|ter** /skǽtər/ (**scatters, scattering, scattered**) ❶ V-T If you **scatter** things over an area, you throw or drop them so that they spread all over the area. ❑ *She scattered the flowers over the grave.* ❑ *They've scattered toys everywhere.* ❷ V-T/V-I If a group of people **scatter** or if you **scatter** them, they suddenly separate and move in different directions. ❑ *After dinner, everyone scattered.* ❸ → see also **scattered, scattering**

**scat|tered** /skǽtərd/ ❶ ADJ **Scattered** things are spread over an area in a messy or irregular way. ❑ *Tomorrow there will be a few scattered showers.* ❷ ADJ If something is **scattered with** a lot of small things, they are spread all over it. ❑ *Every surface is scattered with photographs.*

S

**scat|ter|ing** /skǽtərɪŋ/ (**scatterings**)
**1** N-COUNT A **scattering of** things or people is a small number of them spread over an area. □ *There's a scattering of houses east of the village.* **2** N-UNCOUNT In physics, **scattering** is a process in which light waves are spread out in a disorganized way as a result of hitting a surface or hitting particles in the atmosphere. [TECHNICAL]

**scatter|plot** /skǽtərplɒt/ (**scatterplots**)
N-COUNT A **scatterplot** is a type of graph used in statistics to compare two sets of data. [TECHNICAL]

**scav|enge** /skǽvɪndʒ/ (**scavenges, scavenging, scavenged**) V-T/V-I If people or animals **scavenge for** things, they collect them by searching among waste or unwanted objects. □ *Children had to scavenge for food to survive.* [from Old Norman French]

**scav|en|ger** /skǽvɪndʒər/ (**scavengers**)
N-COUNT A **scavenger** is an animal that feeds on the bodies of dead animals. [TECHNICAL] □ *...scavengers such as rats.* [from Old Norman French]

**scav|en|ger hunt** (**scavenger hunts**) N-COUNT A **scavenger hunt** is a game, usually played outdoors, in which the players must collect various objects from a list of things they have been given. □ *On scavenger hunts I always asked Mrs. Martin for empty coffee cans.*

**sce|nario** /sɪnǽrioʊ/ (**scenarios**) N-COUNT If you talk about a likely or possible **scenario**, you are talking about the way in which a situation may develop. □ *The only reasonable scenario is that he will resign.* [from Italian]

**scene** /siːn/ (**scenes**) **1** N-COUNT A **scene** in a play, movie, or book is part of it in which a series of events happens in the same place. □ *This is the opening scene of "Tom Sawyer."* □ *...Act 1, scene 1.* **2** N-COUNT You refer to a place as a **scene** when you are describing its appearance and indicating what impression it makes on you. □ *It's a scene of complete horror.* **3** N-COUNT The **scene of** an event is the place where it happened. □ *The area has been the scene of fierce fighting for three months.* **4** N-SING You can refer to an area of activity as a particular type of **scene**. □ *...the local music scene.* **5** N-COUNT If you make a **scene**, you embarrass people by publicly showing your anger about something. □ *I'm sorry I made such a scene.* **6** PHRASE If something is done **behind the scenes**, it is done secretly rather than publicly. □ *Mr. Cain worked quietly behind the scenes to get a deal done.* [from Latin] **7** to **set the scene for** something → see **set** → see **animation**

**scen|ery** /siːnəri/ **1** N-UNCOUNT The **scenery** in a country area is the land, water, or plants that you can see around you. □ *...the island's beautiful scenery.* **2** N-UNCOUNT In a theater, the **scenery** consists of the structures and painted backgrounds that show where the action in the play takes place. □ *The actors will move the scenery themselves.* [from Italian]

**sce|nic** /siːnɪk/ ADJ A **scenic** place has attractive scenery. □ *This is an extremely scenic part of America.* [from Latin]

**scent** /sɛnt/ (**scents, scenting, scented**)
**1** N-COUNT The **scent** of something is the pleasant smell that it has. □ *Flowers are chosen for their scent.* **2** N-UNCOUNT **Scent** is a liquid which

women put on their necks and wrists to make themselves smell nice. □ *She opened her bottle of scent.* **3** N-VAR The **scent** of a person or animal is the smell that they leave and that other people sometimes follow when looking for them. □ *A police dog picked up the murderer's scent.* **4** V-T When an animal **scents** something, it becomes aware of it by smelling it. □ *The dogs scent the hidden birds.* [from Old French]

**scent|ed** /sɛntɪd/ ADJ **Scented** things have a pleasant smell, either naturally or because perfume has been added to them. □ *The white flowers are pleasantly scented.* [from Old French]

**sched|ule** /skɛdʒul, -uəl/ (**schedules, scheduling, scheduled**) **1** N-COUNT A **schedule** is a plan that gives a list of events or tasks and the times at which each one should happen or be done. □ *He had to adjust his schedule.* **2** N-UNCOUNT You can use **schedule** to refer to the time or way something is planned to be done. For example, if something is completed **on schedule**, it is completed at the time planned. □ *The plane arrived two minutes ahead of schedule.* □ *Everything went according to schedule.* **3** V-T If something **is scheduled** to happen at a particular time, arrangements are made for it to happen at that time. □ *The space shuttle was scheduled to lift off at 04:38.* □ *The next meeting is scheduled for tomorrow morning.* **4** N-COUNT A **schedule** is a written list of things, for example, a list of prices, details, or conditions. □ *We will issue a pricing schedule for tickets later this year.* **5** N-COUNT A **schedule** is a list of all the times when trains, boats, buses, or aircraft are supposed to arrive at or leave a particular place. □ *...a bus schedule.* [from Old French]

| **Word Partnership** | Use *schedule* with: |
| --- | --- |
| ADJ. | **busy** schedule, **hectic** schedule **1** **regular** schedule **1** **5** |
| N. | **change of** schedule, schedule **of events**, **payment** schedule, **playoff** schedule, **work** schedule **1** **4** **bus** schedule, **train** schedule **5** |
| PREP. | **according to** schedule, **ahead of** schedule, **behind** schedule, **on** schedule **2** |

**scheme** /skiːm/ (**schemes, scheming, schemed**) **1** N-COUNT A **scheme** is a plan for achieving something, especially something that will bring you some benefit. □ *...a quick money-making scheme.* □ *First they had to work out some scheme for breaking the lock.* **2** V-T/V-I If you say that people **are scheming**, you disapprove of the fact that they are making secret plans in order to gain something for themselves. □ *Everyone's always scheming.* □ *The family was scheming to prevent the wedding.* **3** PHRASE When people talk about **the scheme of things** or **the grand scheme of things**, they are referring to the way that everything in the world seems to be organized. □ *When you look at the sea, you realize how small you are in the scheme of things.* [from Latin]

| **Thesaurus** | *scheme* | Also look up : |
| --- | --- | --- |
| N. | design, plan, strategy **1** | |

**schizo|phre|nia** /skɪtsəfriːniə/ N-UNCOUNT **Schizophrenia** is a serious mental illness. People who suffer from it are unable to relate their thoughts and feelings to what is happening around them. [from Greek]

**schizo|phren|ic** /skɪtsəfrɛnɪk/ (**schizophrenics**) N-COUNT A **schizophrenic** is a person who is suffering from schizophrenia. □ *He remained a schizophrenic until his death.* ● **Schizophrenic** is also an adjective. □ *...a schizophrenic patient.* [from Greek]

**schlep** /ʃlɛp/ (**schleps, schlepping, schlepped**) also **schlepp** ■ V-T If you **schlep** something somewhere, you take it there although this is difficult or inconvenient. [INFORMAL] □ *You didn't just schlep your guitar around from club to club.* ■ V-I If you **schlep** somewhere, you go there. [INFORMAL] □ *It's too cold to schlep around looking at property.* [from Yiddish]

**schmooze** /ʃmuz/ (**schmoozes, schmoozing, schmoozed**) V-I If you **schmooze**, you talk casually and socially with someone. [INFORMAL] □ *There are coffee houses where you can schmooze for hours.* [from Yiddish]

**schmuck** /ʃmʌk/ (**schmucks**) N-COUNT If you call someone a **schmuck**, you mean that they are stupid or you do not like them. [INFORMAL] □ *I played like a schmuck.* [from Yiddish]

**schol|ar** /skɒlər/ (**scholars**) N-COUNT A **scholar** is a person who studies an academic subject and knows a lot about it. [FORMAL] □ *The library is full of scholars and researchers from all over the world.* [from Old French]
→ see **history**

**schol|ar|ly** /skɒlərli/ ■ ADJ A **scholarly** person spends a lot of time studying and knows a lot about academic subjects. □ *He was a quiet, scholarly man.* ■ ADJ A **scholarly** book or article contains a lot of academic information and is intended for academic readers. □ *A few scholarly works about Jesus have appeared recently.* [from Old French]

**schol|ar|ship** /skɒlərʃɪp/ (**scholarships**) ■ N-COUNT If you get a **scholarship** to a school or university, your studies are paid for by the school or university or by some other organization. □ *He got a scholarship to the Pratt Institute of Art.* ■ N-UNCOUNT **Scholarship** is serious academic study and the knowledge that is obtained from it. □ *Can I ask you about your lifetime of scholarship?* [from Old French]

**school** /skul/ (**schools**) ■ N-VAR A **school** is a place where children are educated. You usually refer to this place as **school** when you are talking about the time that children spend there. □ *That boy was in my class at school.* □ *Homework is what we all disliked about school.* □ *The school was built in the 1960s.* ■ N-COUNT A **school** is the students or staff at a school. □ *Deirdre, the whole school will hate you.* ■ N-COUNT A privately-run place where a particular skill or subject is taught can be referred to as a **school**. □ *He owns a riding school.* ■ N-VAR A university, college, or university department specializing in a particular subject can be referred to as a **school**. □ *She's a professor in the school of medicine at the University of Pennsylvania.* ■ N-UNCOUNT **School** is used to refer to college. □ *Jack eventually graduated from school in 1998.* [from Old English] ■ → see also **boarding school, grammar school, high school, private school, public school, schooling, state school**

**school board** (**school boards**) N-COUNT A **school board** is a committee in charge of education in a particular city or area, or in a particular school, especially in the United States. □ *Mr. Nelson served on the school board.*

**school|boy** /skulbɔɪ/ (**schoolboys**) N-COUNT A **schoolboy** is a boy who goes to school. □ *There was a group of about ten schoolboys.*

**school|child** /skultʃaɪld/ (**schoolchildren**) N-COUNT **Schoolchildren** are children who go to school. □ *I had an audience of schoolchildren and they laughed at everything.*

**school|days** /skuldeɪz/ also **school days** N-PLURAL Your **schooldays** are the period of your life when you are at school. □ *His wife was a girl he had known since his schooldays.*

**school dis|trict** (**school districts**) N-COUNT A **school district** is an area which includes all the schools that are situated within that area and are governed by a particular authority. □ *The San Francisco school district is one of the largest in the state.*

**school|girl** /skulgɜrl/ (**schoolgirls**) N-COUNT A **schoolgirl** is a girl who goes to school. □ *There were half a dozen laughing schoolgirls.*

**school|house** /skulhaʊs/ (**schoolhouses**) N-COUNT A **schoolhouse** is a small building used as a school.

**school|ing** /skulɪŋ/ N-UNCOUNT **Schooling** is education that children receive at school. □ *His formal schooling continued only until he was eleven.* [from Old English]

**school|teach|er** /skultitʃər/ (**schoolteachers**) N-COUNT A **schoolteacher** is a teacher in a school.

**schtick** /ʃtɪk/ (**schticks**) N-VAR An entertainer's **schtick** is a series of funny or entertaining things that they say or do. [INFORMAL] □ *His schtick is perfect for the show.* [from Yiddish]

| **Word Link** | *sci* ≈ knowing : *conscience, conscious, science* |
|---|---|

**sci|ence** /saɪəns/ (**sciences**) ■ N-UNCOUNT **Science** is the study of the nature and behavior of natural things and the knowledge that we obtain about them. □ *The best discoveries in science are very simple.* ■ N-COUNT A **science** is a particular branch of science such as physics, chemistry, or biology. □ *He taught music as if it were a science.* ■ N-COUNT A **science** is the study of some aspect of human behavior, for example, sociology or anthropology. □ *Psychology is a modern science.* [from Old French] ■ → see also **social science**
→ see Word Web: **science**

**sci|ence fic|tion** N-UNCOUNT **Science fiction** consists of stories in books, magazines, and movies about events that take place in the future or in other parts of the universe.

**sci|en|tif|ic** /saɪəntɪfɪk/ ■ ADJ **Scientific** is used to describe things that relate to science or to a particular science. □ *This is scientific research.* ● **sci|en|tifi|cal|ly** /saɪəntɪfɪkli/ ADV □ *...scientifically advanced countries.* ■ ADJ If you do something in a **scientific** way, you do it carefully and thoroughly, using experiments or tests. □ *It's not a scientific way to test their opinions.* ● **sci|en|tifi|cal|ly** ADV □ *It must be researched scientifically.* [from Old French]
→ see **experiment, science**

S

**Word Web** science

**Science** is the study of physical laws. These laws govern the natural world. Science uses **research** and **experiments** to explain various **phenomena**. Scientists follow the **scientific method** which begins with **observation** and measurement. Then they state a **hypothesis**, which is a possible explanation for the observations and measurements. Next, scientists make a **prediction**, which is a logical **deduction** based on the hypothesis. The last step is to conduct experiments which **prove** or **disprove** the hypothesis. Scientists construct and modify **theories** based on **empirical findings**. **Pure** science deals with theories only. When people use science to do something, that is **applied** science.

**sci|en|tif|ic meth|od** N-SING The **scientific method** is the set of rules and procedures followed by scientists, especially the use of experiments to test hypotheses.

**sci|en|tif|ic no|ta|tion** (**scientific notations**) N-VAR **Scientific notation** is a method of writing very large or very small numbers by expressing them as numbers multiplied by a power of ten. [TECHNICAL]

**sci|en|tist** /sาɪəntɪst/ (**scientists**) N-COUNT A **scientist** is someone who has studied science and whose job is to teach or do research in science. ❏ *Scientists say they've already collected more data than they expected.* [from Old French]
→ see **evolution**, **experiment**

**sci-fi** /saɪ faɪ/ N-UNCOUNT **Sci-fi** is short for **science fiction**. [INFORMAL] ❏ *It's a two hour sci-fi movie.*

**scis|sors** /sɪzərz/ N-PLURAL **Scissors** are a small cutting tool with two sharp blades that are screwed together. You use scissors for cutting things such as paper and cloth. ❏ *He told me to get some scissors.* [from Old French]
→ see **office**

**scoff** /skɒf/ (**scoffs, scoffing, scoffed**) V-I If you **scoff at** something, you speak about it in a way that shows you think it is ridiculous or inadequate. ❏ *At first I scoffed at the idea.* [of Scandinavian origin]

**scold** /skoʊld/ (**scolds, scolding, scolded**) V-T If you **scold** someone, you speak angrily to them because they have done something wrong. [FORMAL] ❏ *If he finds out, he'll scold me.* ❏ *I scolded myself for talking so much.* [from Old Norse]

**scoop** /skup/ (**scoops, scooping, scooped**)
1 V-T If you **scoop** something from a container, you remove it with something such as a spoon. ❏ *I heard him scooping dog food out of a can.* 2 N-COUNT A **scoop** is an object like a spoon which is used for picking up a quantity of a food such as ice cream or an ingredient such as flour. ❏ *Here, use the ice-cream scoop.* 3 N-COUNT You can use **scoop** to refer to an exciting news story which is reported in one newspaper or on one television program before it appears anywhere else. ❏ *It was one of the biggest scoops in the history of newspapers.* 4 V-T If you **scoop** a person or thing somewhere, you put your hands or arms under or around them and quickly move them there. ❏ *Michael scooped her into*

his arms. [from Middle Dutch]
▶ **scoop up** PHR-VERB If you **scoop** something **up**, you put your hands or arms under it and lift it in a quick movement. ❏ *Use both hands to scoop up the leaves.*

**scoot|er** /skutər/ (**scooters**) 1 N-COUNT A **scooter** is a small light motorcycle which has a low seat. 2 N-COUNT A **scooter** is a type of child's bicycle which has two wheels joined by a wooden board and a handle on a long pole attached to the front wheel. [of Scandinavian origin]

**scope** /skoʊp/ 1 N-UNCOUNT If there is **scope for** a particular kind of behavior or activity, people have the opportunity to behave in this way or do that activity. ❏ *There's not a lot of scope for change here.* 2 N-SING The **scope of** an activity, topic, or piece of work is the whole area which it deals with or includes. ❏ *The scope of the project is too large for us to manage alone.* [from Italian]

**scorch** /skɔrtʃ/ (**scorches, scorching, scorched**) V-T To **scorch** something means to burn it slightly. ❏ *The bomb scorched the side of the building.* ● **scorched** ADJ ❏ *...scorched black earth.* [from Old Norse]

**scorch|ing** /skɔrtʃɪŋ/ ADJ **Scorching** or **scorching hot** weather or temperatures are very hot indeed. [INFORMAL] ❏ *That race took place in scorching weather.* [from Old Norse]

**score** /skɔr/ (**scores, scoring, scored**) 1 V-T/V-I In a sport or game, if a player **scores** a goal or a point, they gain a goal or point. ❏ *Patten scored his second touchdown of the game.* ❏ *He scored late in the third quarter.* ● **scor|er** (**scorers**) N-COUNT ❏ *David Hirst is the scorer of 11 goals this season.* 2 V-T/V-I If you **score** a particular number or amount, for example, as a mark on a test, you achieve that number or amount. ❏ *Kelly scored 147 on the test.* ❏ *Congress scores low in public opinion polls.* 3 N-COUNT Someone's **score** in a game or on a test is a number, for example, a number of points or runs, which shows what they have achieved or what level they have reached. ❏ *The U.S. Open golf tournament was won by Ben Hogan, with a score of 287.* 4 N-COUNT The **score** in a game is the result of it up to a particular time, as indicated by the number of goals, runs, or points obtained by the two teams or players. ❏ *4 – 1 was the final score.* 5 V-T If you **score** a success, a victory, or a hit, you are successful in what you are doing. [WRITTEN] ❏ *The play scored a success on Broadway,*

*winning a couple of awards.* **6** N-COUNT The **score** of a piece of music is the written version of it. ❑ *He knows enough music to be able to follow a score.* **7** QUANT If you refer to **scores of** things or people, you are emphasizing that there are very many of them. [WRITTEN] ❑ *Scores of buses transported the elderly from a nearby hospital.* **8** V-T If you **score** a surface with something sharp, you cut a line or number of lines in it. ❑ *Score the surface of the steaks with a sharp knife.* **9** PHRASE You can use **on that score** or **on this score** to refer to something that has just been mentioned, especially an area of difficulty or concern. ❑ *On that score I can say very little.* **10** PHRASE If you **settle a score** or **settle an old score with** someone, you take revenge on them for something they have done in the past. ❑ *The groups had old scores to settle with each other.* [from Old English]
→ see **music**

**scorn** /skɔrn/ (**scorns, scorning, scorned**) **1** N-UNCOUNT If you treat someone or something **with scorn**, you show that you do not respect them. ❑ *Her words were met with scorn.* **2** V-T If you **scorn** someone or something, you feel or show contempt for them. ❑ *Several officers have openly scorned the peace talks.* **3** V-T If you **scorn** something, you refuse to have it or accept it because you think it is not good enough or suitable for you. ❑ *People still scorn traditional methods.* [from Old French]

**scorn|ful** /skɔrnfəl/ ADJ If you are **scornful of** someone or something, you show that you do not respect them. ❑ *He is deeply scornful of politicians.* ● **scorn|ful|ly** ADV ❑ *They laughed scornfully.* [from Old French]

**scour** /skaʊər/ (**scours, scouring, scoured**) **1** V-T If you **scour** something such as a place or a book, you make a thorough search of it to try to find what you are looking for. ❑ *Rescue teams scoured an area of 30 square miles.* **2** V-T If you **scour** something such as a sink, floor, or pan, you clean its surface by rubbing it hard with something rough. ❑ *He decided to scour the pots.* [from Middle Low German]

**scourge** /skɜrdʒ/ (**scourges**) N-COUNT A **scourge** is something that causes a lot of trouble or suffering to a group of people. ❑ *This is a chance to end the scourge of terrorism.* [from Old French]

**scout** /skaʊt/ (**scouts, scouting, scouted**) **1** N-COUNT A **scout** is someone who is sent to an area of countryside to find out the position of an enemy army. ❑ *They set off, with two men out in front as scouts.* **2** V-T/V-I If you **scout** somewhere **for** something, you go through that area searching for it. ❑ *The girls scouted the site for materials people had left behind.* ❑ *A team was sent to scout for a nuclear test site.* [from Old French]

**scowl** /skaʊl/ (**scowls, scowling, scowled**) V-I When someone **scowls**, an angry expression appears on their face. ❑ *He scowled, and slammed the door.* ● **Scowl** is also a noun. ❑ *Brodie answered with a scowl.* [of Scandinavian origin]

**scrag|gly** /skrægli/ (**scragglier, scraggliest**) ADJ **Scraggly** hair or plants are thin and messy. ❑ *He had a scraggly mustache.*

**scram|ble** /skræmbəl/ (**scrambles, scrambling, scrambled**) **1** V-I If you **scramble** over rocks or up a hill, you move quickly over them or up it using

your hands to help you. ❑ *Tourists were scrambling over the rocks to the beach.* **2** V-I If you **scramble** to a different place or position, you move there in a hurried, awkward way. ❑ *Ann scrambled out of bed.* **3** V-T/V-I If a number of people **scramble for** something, they compete energetically with each other for it. ❑ *More than a million fans scrambled for tickets.* ● **Scramble** is also a noun. ❑ *Then it's a scramble for jobs.* **4** V-T If you **scramble** eggs, you break them, mix them together, and then cook them in butter. ❑ *Make the toast and scramble the eggs.* ● **scram|bled** ADJ ❑ *It's just scrambled eggs and bacon.*
→ see **egg**

**scrap** /skræp/ (**scraps, scrapping, scrapped**) **1** N-COUNT A **scrap** of something is a very small piece or amount of it. ❑ *A scrap of red paper was found in her handbag.* **2** N-PLURAL **Scraps** are pieces of unwanted food which are thrown away or given to animals. **3** V-T If you **scrap** something, you get rid of it or cancel it. ❑ *The president called on Middle Eastern countries to scrap nuclear weapons.* **4** N-UNCOUNT **Scrap** is metal from old or damaged machinery or cars. ❑ *...a truck piled with scrap metal.* [from Old Norse]

**scrape** /skreɪp/ (**scrapes, scraping, scraped**) **1** V-T If you **scrape** something from a surface, you remove it, especially by pulling a sharp object over the surface. ❑ *She scraped the frost off the car windows.* **2** V-T/V-I If something **scrapes** against something else, it rubs against it, making a noise or causing slight damage. ❑ *The only sound is knives and forks scraping against plates.* ❑ *The car passed us, scraping the wall as it went.* ● **scrap|ing** N-SING ❑ *...the scraping of a chair across the floor.* **3** V-T If you **scrape** a part of your body, you accidentally rub it against something hard and rough, and damage it slightly. ❑ *She fell, scraping her hands and knees.* [from Old English]
▶ **scrape through** PHR-VERB If you **scrape through** an examination, you just succeed in passing it. ❑ *He only just scraped through his final year.*
▶ **scrape together** PHR-VERB If you **scrape together** an amount of money or a number of things, you succeed in obtaining it with difficulty. ❑ *They just managed to scrape the money together.*

**scratch** /skrætʃ/ (**scratches, scratching, scratched**) **1** V-T/V-I If you **scratch yourself**, you

scratch

rub your fingernails against your skin because it is itching. ❑ *He scratched himself under his arm.* ❑ *She scratched her nose.* **2** V-T If a sharp object **scratches** someone or something, it makes small shallow cuts on their skin or surface. ❑ *The branches scratched my face.* **3** N-COUNT **Scratches** on someone or something are small shallow cuts. ❑ *He was found with scratches on his face and neck.* **4** PHRASE If you do something **from scratch**, you do it without making use of anything that has been done before. ❑ *Building a home from scratch can be very exciting.* [from Old French]

**scratch card** (**scratch cards**) also **scratchcard** N-COUNT A **scratch card** is a card with hidden words or symbols on it. You scratch the surface off to reveal the words or symbols and find out if you have won a prize.

**scrawl** /skrɔl/ (**scrawls, scrawling, scrawled**) ■ V-T If you **scrawl** something, you write it in a careless and messy way. ❑ *He scrawled a note to his wife.* ❑ *Someone scrawled "pig" on his car.* ■ N-VAR You can refer to writing that looks careless and messy as a **scrawl**. ❑ *The letter was written in a terrible scrawl.*

**scream** /skrim/ (**screams, screaming, screamed**) ■ V-I When someone **screams**, they make a very loud, high-pitched cry, for example, because they are in pain or are very frightened. ❑ *Women were screaming in the houses nearest the fire.* ● **Scream** is also a noun. ❑ *Hilda let out a scream.* ■ V-T If you **scream** something, you shout it in a loud, high-pitched voice. ❑ *"Brigid!" she screamed.* [from Germanic]

**screech** /skritʃ/ (**screeches, screeching, screeched**) ■ V-I If a vehicle **screeches** somewhere or if its tires **screech**, its tires make an unpleasant high-pitched noise on the road. ❑ *A car screeched to a halt beside the helicopter.* ■ V-T/V-I When you **screech** something, you shout it in a loud, unpleasant, high-pitched voice. ❑ *"Get me some water!" I screeched.* ● **Screech** is also a noun. ❑ *The child gave a screech.*

**screen** /skrin/ (**screens, screening, screened**) ■ N-COUNT A **screen** is a flat vertical surface on which pictures or words are shown. Television sets and computers have screens, and movies are shown on a screen in movie theaters. ■ → see also **widescreen** ■ V-T When a movie or a television program **is screened**, it is shown in the movie theater or broadcast on television. ❑ *The series will be screened in January.* ● **screening** (**screenings**) N-COUNT ❑ *The movie-makers will be at the screenings to introduce their works.* ■ N-COUNT A **screen** is a vertical panel which can be used to separate different parts of a room. ❑ *There was a screen in front of me so I couldn't see what was going on.* ■ V-T If something **is screened by** another thing, it is behind it and hidden by it. ❑ *The road was screened by an apartment building.* ■ V-T/V-I To **screen** people **for** a disease means to examine people to make sure that they do not have it. ❑ *All states now screen for the condition.* ● **screening** N-VAR ❑ *...cancer-screening tests.* [from Old French]
→ see **television**

**screen|play** /skrinpleɪ/ (**screenplays**) N-COUNT A **screenplay** is the words to be spoken in a movie, and instructions about what will be seen in it.

**screen|writer** /skrinraɪtər/ (**screenwriters**) N-COUNT A **screenwriter** is a person who writes screenplays.

**screw** /skru/ (**screws, screwing, screwed**) ■ N-COUNT A **screw** is a metal object similar to a nail, with a raised spiral line around it. You turn a screw using a screwdriver so that it goes through two things, for example, two pieces of wood, and fastens them together. ❑ *Each shelf is fixed to the wall with screws.* ■ V-T/V-I If you **screw** something somewhere or if it **screws** somewhere, you fix it in place by means of a screw or screws. ❑ *I screwed the shelf on the wall myself.* ❑ *Screw down any loose floorboards.* ■ V-T/V-I If you **screw** something somewhere or if it **screws** somewhere, you fix it in place by twisting it around and around. ❑ *"Ready?" asked Kelly, screwing the lens on the camera.* ❑ *Screw*

down the lid tightly. ■ V-T If you **screw** your face or your eyes **into** a particular expression, you tighten the muscles of your face to form that expression, for example, because you are in pain or because the light is too bright. ❑ *He screwed his face into an expression of pain.* [from French]
▶ **screw up** PHR-VERB To **screw** something **up**, or to **screw up**, means to cause something to fail or be spoiled. [INFORMAL] ❑ *Don't open the window because it screws up the air conditioning.* ❑ *Get out! You've screwed things up enough already!*

**screw|driver** /skrudraɪvər/ (**screwdrivers**) N-COUNT A **screwdriver** is a tool that is used for turning screws.
→ see **tools**

┌─────────────────────────────────────────┐
│ **Word Link**   scrib ≈ writing : in*scrib*e, *scrib*ble, │
│                 tran*scrib*e             │
└─────────────────────────────────────────┘

**scrib|ble** /skrɪbªl/ (**scribbles, scribbling, scribbled**) ■ V-T/V-I If you **scribble** something, you write it quickly and roughly. ❑ *She scribbled a note to Mom.* ■ V-I To **scribble** means to make meaningless marks or rough drawings using a pencil or pen. ❑ *When Caroline was five she scribbled on a wall.* ■ N-VAR **Scribble** is something that has been written or drawn quickly and roughly. ❑ *I'm sorry my letter was such a scribble.* [from Medieval Latin]

**scrim|mage** /skrɪmɪdʒ/ (**scrimmages**) ■ N-COUNT In football, **scrimmage** is the action during a single period of play. ❑ *Bloom scored two touchdowns Saturday in a scrimmage.* ■ N-COUNT In sports such as football and hockey, a **scrimmage** is a session of practice that consists of an actual game. ❑ *It was the first full scrimmage in Flyers training camp.*

**script** /skrɪpt/ (**scripts**) ■ N-COUNT The **script** of a play, movie, or television program is the written version of it. ❑ *Jenny's writing a movie script.* ■ N-VAR You can refer to a particular system of writing as a particular **script**. ❑ *The text is in Arabic script.* [from Latin]
→ see **animation**

┌─────────────────────────────────────────┐
│ **Word Link**   script ≈ writing : manu*script*, │
│                 *script*ure, tran*script* │
└─────────────────────────────────────────┘

**scrip|ture** /skrɪptʃər/ (**scriptures**) N-VAR **Scripture** or the **scriptures** refers to writings that are regarded as holy in a particular religion, for example, the Bible in Christianity. ❑ *It's a quote from scripture.* [from Latin]

**scroll** /skroul/ (**scrolls, scrolling, scrolled**) ■ N-COUNT A **scroll** is a long roll of paper or a similar material with writing on it. ❑ *They found ancient scrolls near the Dead Sea.* ■ V-I If you **scroll** through text on a computer screen, you move the text up or down to find the information that you need. [COMPUTING] ❑ *I scrolled down to find "United States of America."* [from Old French]

**scroll bar** (**scroll bars**) N-COUNT On a computer screen, a **scroll bar** is a long thin box along one edge of a window, which you click on with the mouse to move the text up, down, or across the window. [COMPUTING]

**scro|tum** /skroutəm/ (**scrotums**) N-COUNT A man's **scrotum** is the bag of skin that contains his testicles. [from Latin]

**scrub** /skrʌb/ (**scrubs, scrubbing, scrubbed**)

**scrub** ◼ V-T If you **scrub** something, you rub it hard in order to clean it, using a stiff brush and water. ❑ *Surgeons must scrub their hands and arms with soap and water.* ● **Scrub** is also a noun. ❑ *The walls needed a good scrub.* ◼ N-UNCOUNT **Scrub** consists of low trees and bushes, especially in an area that has very little rain. ❑ *There is an area of scrub beside the railroad.* ◼ N-PLURAL **Scrubs** are the protective clothes that surgeons and other hospital staff wear in operating rooms. [INFORMAL] ❑ *The men wore blue hospital scrubs.* [Senses 1 and 3 from Middle Low German. Sense 2 from Old English.]

**scrub|ber** /skrʌbər/ (**scrubbers**) N-COUNT A **scrubber** is a device that removes pollution from gases that are released into the atmosphere, for example from a factory furnace.

**scruffy** /skrʌfi/ (**scruffier, scruffiest**) ADJ Someone or something that is **scruffy** is dirty and messy. ❑ *The man was pale, scruffy and unshaven.*

**scrunchie** /skrʌntʃi/ (**scrunchies**) also **scrunchy** N-COUNT A **scrunchie** is an elastic band that is covered with material and is used to tie back your hair, for example in a ponytail.

**scru|pu|lous** /skrupyələs/ ◼ ADJ Someone who is **scrupulous** takes great care to do what is fair, honest, or morally right. ❑ *You are always more scrupulous than other people.* ❑ *The officials are scrupulous about protecting all students.* ● **scru|pu|lous|ly** ADV ❑ *He is scrupulously fair.* ◼ ADJ **Scrupulous** means thorough, exact, and careful about details. ❑ *They admire Knutson's scrupulous attention to detail.* ● **scru|pu|lous|ly** ADV ❑ *The streets were scrupulously clean.* [from Latin]

**scru|ti|nize** /skrutⁿnaɪz/ (**scrutinizes, scrutinizing, scrutinized**) V-T If you **scrutinize** something, you examine it very carefully. ❑ *She scrutinized his face to see if he was an honest man.* [from Late Latin]

**scru|ti|ny** /skrutⁿni/ N-UNCOUNT If a person or thing is under **scrutiny**, they are being studied or observed very carefully. ❑ *His private life came under public scrutiny.* [from Late Latin]

**scuf|fle** /skʌfⁿl/ (**scuffles, scuffling, scuffled**) ◼ N-COUNT A **scuffle** is a short, disorganized fight or struggle. ❑ *Violent scuffles broke out in the crowd.* ◼ V-RECIP If people **scuffle**, they fight for a short time in a disorganized way. ❑ *Police scuffled with some of the protesters.* [of Scandinavian origin]

**sculpt** /skʌlpt/ (**sculpts, sculpting, sculpted**) V-T/V-I When an artist **sculpts** something, they carve or shape it out of a material such as stone or clay. ❑ *An artist sculpted a copy of her head.* ● **sculp|tor** (**sculptors**) N-COUNT ❑ *No sculptor has been chosen yet.* [from French]

**sculp|ture** /skʌlptʃər/ (**sculptures**) ◼ N-VAR A **sculpture** is a three-dimensional work of art that is produced by carving or shaping stone, wood, clay, or other materials. ❑ *There were stone sculptures of different animals.* ◼ N-UNCOUNT **Sculpture** is the art of creating sculptures. ❑ *Both of them studied sculpture.* [from Latin]

**scum** /skʌm/ N-UNCOUNT **Scum** is a layer of a dirty or unpleasant-looking substance on the surface of a liquid. [of Germanic origin]

**scur|ry** /skɜri/ (**scurries, scurrying, scurried**) V-I When people or small animals **scurry** somewhere, they move there quickly and hurriedly, especially because they are frightened. [WRITTEN] ❑ *The*

*attack began, and people scurried off the street.*

**scut|tle** /skʌtⁿl/ (**scuttles, scuttling, scuttled**) V-I When people or small animals **scuttle** somewhere, they run there with short quick steps. ❑ *Two small children scuttled away in front of them.*

**sea** /si/ (**seas**) ◼ N-SING The **sea** is the salty water that covers about three-quarters of the Earth's surface. ❑ *The kids have never seen the sea.* ◼ N-PLURAL You use **seas** when you are describing the sea at a particular time or in a particular area. [LITERARY] ❑ *The seas are warm further south.* ◼ N-COUNT A **sea** is a large area of salty water that is part of an ocean or is surrounded by land. ❑ *...the North Sea.* ◼ PHRASE **At sea** means on or under the sea, far away from land. ❑ *The boats are at sea for ten days at a time.* [from Old English]

> **Word Partnership** Use *sea* with :
>
> PREP. **above the** sea, **across the** sea, **below the** sea, **beneath the** sea, **by** sea, **from the** sea, **into the** sea, **near the** sea, **over the** sea ◼
>
> N. sea **air**, sea **coast**, **land and** sea, sea **voyage** ◼
>
> ADJ. **calm** sea, **deep** sea ◼

**sea-floor spread|ing** N-UNCOUNT **Sea-floor spreading** is the expansion of the ocean floor that occurs when two tectonic plates move apart and new rock is formed. [TECHNICAL]

**sea|food** /sifud/ (**seafoods**) N-VAR **Seafood** is shellfish and other sea creatures that you can eat. ❑ *Let's find a seafood restaurant.*

**sea|gull** /sigʌl/ (**seagulls**) N-COUNT A **seagull** is a common kind of bird with white or gray feathers that lives near the ocean.

**sea|horse** /sihɔrs/ (**seahorses**) also **sea horse** N-COUNT A **seahorse** is a type of small fish which appears to swim in a vertical position and whose head looks a little like the head of a horse.

| seal |
| --- |
| ❶ CLOSING |
| ❷ ANIMAL |

❶ **seal** /sil/ (**seals, sealing, sealed**) ◼ V-T When you **seal** an envelope, you close it by folding part of it over and sticking it down. ❑ *He sealed the envelope and put on a stamp.* ❑ *Write your letter and seal it in a new envelope.* ◼ V-T If you **seal** a container or an opening, you cover it with something in order to prevent air, liquid, or other material from getting in or out. If you **seal** something **in** a container, you put it inside and then close the container tightly. ❑ *She filled the containers, sealed them, and stuck on labels.* ❑ *A woman picks the parts up and seals them in plastic bags.* ◼ N-COUNT The **seal** on a container or opening is the part where it has been sealed. ❑ *Wet the edges of the pie and join them to form a seal.* ◼ N-COUNT A **seal** is a device or a piece of material, for example, in a machine, which closes an opening tightly so that air, liquid, or other substances cannot get in or out. ❑ *Check the seal on the fridge regularly.* ◼ N-COUNT A **seal** is a special mark or design, for example, on a document, representing someone or something. It may be used to show that something is genuine or officially approved. ❑ *The notepaper carries the presidential seal.* ◼ V-T If someone in authority

S

**seals** an area, they stop people from entering or passing through it, for example, by placing barriers in the way. ❑ *The soldiers were told to seal the border.* ● **Seal off** means the same as **seal**. ❑ *Police sealed off the area after the attack.* [from Old French]

❷ **seal** /sil/ (**seals**) N-COUNT A **seal** is a large animal with a rounded body and flat legs called flippers. Seals eat fish and live in and near the ocean. [from Old English]

**sea level** also **sea-level** N-UNCOUNT **Sea level** is the average level of the ocean with respect to the land. The height of mountains or other areas is calculated in relation to **sea level**. ❑ *The stadium was 5,000 feet above sea level.* ❑ *The whole place is at sea level.*
→ see **glacier**

**seam** /sim/ (**seams**) ▪ N-COUNT A **seam** is a line of stitches which joins two pieces of cloth together. ❑ *The skirt tore open along a seam.* ❷ N-COUNT A **seam** of coal is a long, narrow layer of it underneath the ground. ❑ *The average coal seam here is three feet thick.* ❸ PHRASE If a place is very full, you can say that it **is bursting at the seams**. ❑ *The hotels of Warsaw were bursting at the seams.* [from Old English]

**sea|man** /simən/ (**seamen**) N-COUNT A **seaman** is a sailor, especially one who is not an officer. ❑ *The men all work as seamen.*

**seam|less** /simlɪs/ ADJ You use **seamless** to describe something that has no breaks or gaps in it or which continues without stopping. ❑ *The links between the songs turn the record into a single, seamless whole.* ● **seam|less|ly** ADV ❑ *The dialogue moves seamlessly between English and Spanish.* [from Old English]

**sea|mount** /simaʊnt/ (**seamounts**) N-COUNT A **seamount** is a mountain that lies beneath the surface of the ocean. [TECHNICAL]

**search** /sɜrtʃ/ (**searches, searching, searched**) ▪ V-I If you **search for** something or someone, you look carefully for them. ❑ *Police are already searching for the men.* ❑ *They searched for a space to sit on the floor.* ❷ V-T/V-I If you **search** a place, you look carefully for something or someone there. ❑ *The police are searching for the missing men.* ❑ *She searched for the papers but couldn't find them.* ❸ N-COUNT A **search** is an attempt to find something or someone by looking for them carefully. ❑ *The search is being stopped because of the heavy snow.* ❹ V-T If a police officer or someone else in authority **searches** you, they look carefully to see whether you have something hidden on you. ❑ *Of course the police searched her.* ❺ → see also **searching** ❻ PHRASE If you go **in search of** something or someone, you try to find them. ❑ *She went in search of Jean-Paul.* [from Old French]

| Word Partnership | Use *search* with : |
|---|---|
| N. | search **for clues, police** search ▪ – ❹ |
| | search **for information** ▪ ❸ |
| | **investigators** search ▪ ❷ ❹ |
| | search **for a job,** search **for** |
| | **the truth** ▪ ❸ |
| | search **an area** ❷ |
| | **talent** search ❸ |
| | search **suspects** ❹ |
| V. | **conduct a** search ❸ |

**search and res|cue** also **search-and-rescue** N-UNCOUNT **Search and rescue** operations involve looking for people who are lost or in danger and bringing them back safely. ❑ *A search and rescue team found the man about 12:30 p.m.*

**search en|gine** (**search engines**) N-COUNT A **search engine** is a computer program that searches for documents containing a particular word or words on the Internet. [COMPUTING]

**search|ing** /sɜrtʃɪŋ/ ADJ A **searching** question or look is intended to discover the truth about something. ❑ *They asked her some searching questions at the interview.* [from Old French]

**sear|ing** /sɪərɪŋ/ ▪ ADJ **Searing** is used to indicate that something such as pain or heat is very intense. ❑ *She woke with a searing pain in her feet.* ❷ ADJ A **searing** speech or piece of writing is very critical. ❑ *There's a searing article in the paper about the president's decision.* [from Old English]

**sea|side** /sisaɪd/ N-SING You can refer to an area that is close to the ocean, especially one where people go for their vacation, as **the seaside**. ❑ *I spent a few days at the seaside.*

**sea|son** /sizᵊn/ (**seasons, seasoning, seasoned**) ▪ N-COUNT The **seasons** are the periods into which a year can be divided and which each have their own typical weather conditions. ❑ *Fall is my favorite season.* ❷ N-COUNT You can use **season** to refer to the period during each year when something happens. ❑ *Then the birds arrive for the nesting season.* ❑ *...the baseball season.* ❸ V-T If you **season** food with salt, pepper, or spices, you add them to it in order to improve its flavor. ❑ *Season the meat with salt and pepper.* [from Old French] ❹ → see also **seasoned, seasoning**
→ see Word Web: **seasons**

**sea|son|al** /sizənᵊl/ ADJ A **seasonal** factor, event, or change occurs during one particular time of the year. ❑ *The seasonal workers will return from Mexico in the next few months.* ● **sea|son|al|ly** ADV ❑ *Restaurant menus change seasonally here.* [from Old French]

**sea|soned** /sizᵊnd/ ADJ You can use **seasoned** to describe a person who has a lot of experience of something. ❑ *The author is a seasoned academic.* [from Old French]

**sea|son|ing** /sizənɪŋ/ (**seasonings**) N-VAR **Seasoning** is salt, pepper, or other spices that are added to food to improve its flavor. ❑ *Mix the meat with the onion and some seasoning.* [from Old French]

**sea|son tick|et** (**season tickets**) N-COUNT A **season ticket** is a ticket that you can use repeatedly during a certain period, without having to pay each time. ❑ *We have a monthly season ticket.*

**sea star** also **seastar** (**sea stars**) N-COUNT A **sea star** is a flat, star-shaped creature, usually with five arms, that lives in the sea.

**seat** /sit/ (**seats, seating, seated**) ▪ N-COUNT A **seat** is an object that you can sit on, for example, a chair. ❑ *Stephen returned to his seat.* ❷ N-COUNT The **seat** of a chair is the part that you sit on. ❑ *The sofa had a red plastic seat.* ❸ V-T If you **seat yourself** somewhere, you sit down. [WRITTEN] ❑ *He seated himself at his desk.* ❹ V-T A building or vehicle that **seats** a particular number of people has enough seats for that number. ❑ *The theater seats 570 people.* ❺ N-COUNT When someone is elected to

---

   seasons

The ancient Mayans* built a pyramid at Chichen Itza*. One use of this structure was to predict the **seasons** of the **year**. As the sun shone on the pyramid, it created distinct shadows. These shadows moved during the year. Trained leaders observed these changing patterns of light throughout the year. The shadows fell in specific places at the time of the **solstices** and equinoxes. They showed the leaders the best times to plant and harvest crops. The shadows also told them when to hold special religious ceremonies. Thousands of tourists visit Chichen Itza each spring to observe the arrival of the vernal* equinox.

*Mayans (250-900 AD): Indians who lived in Mexico and Central America.*

*Chichen Itza (700-900 AD): a Mayan city in Mexico.*

*vernal: spring*

---

a legislature you can say that they, or their party, have won a **seat**. ❑ *Men won the majority of seats on the council.* **6** N-COUNT If someone has a **seat** on the board of a company or on a committee, they are a member of it. ❑ *He has been trying to win a seat on the board of the company.* **7** → see also **deep-seated** **8** PHRASE If you **take a back seat**, you allow other people to have all the power and to make all the decisions. ❑ *You need to take a back seat and think about the future.* **9** PHRASE If you **take a seat**, you sit down. [FORMAL] ❑ *"Take a seat," he said.* [from Old English]

   Use *seat* with :

| | |
|---|---|
| ADJ. | **back** seat, **empty** seat, **front** seat **1** **vacant** seat, **vacated** seat **1 6** **congressional** seat **5** |
| N. | **car** seat, **child** seat, **driver's** seat, **passenger** seat, seat **at a table**, **theater** seat, **toilet** seat **1** seat **in the House/Senate 5** seat **on the board 6** |

**seat belt** (**seat belts**) N-COUNT A **seat belt** is a strap attached to a seat in a car or airplane. You fasten it around your body and it stops you from being thrown forward if there is an accident. ❑ *Please fasten your seat belts.*

seat belt

**seat|ing** /siːtɪŋ/ N-UNCOUNT You can refer to the seats in a place as the **seating**. ❑ *The stadium has seating for over eighty thousand fans.* [from Old English]

**sea tur|tle** (**sea turtles**) N-COUNT A **sea turtle** is a large reptile which has a thick shell covering its body and which lives in the ocean most of the time.

**sea|weed** /siːwiːd/ (**seaweeds**) N-VAR **Seaweed** is a plant that grows in the ocean. ❑ *Seaweed is washed up on the beach.*

**SEC** /ɛs i siː/ N-PROPER In the United States, **the SEC** is a government agency that regulates the buying and selling of stocks and bonds. **SEC** is an abbreviation for "Securities and Exchange Commission." ❑ *The President believes the SEC is doing an excellent job.*

**se|clud|ed** /sɪkluːdɪd/ ADJ A **secluded** place is quiet and private. ❑ *We ate in a secluded corner of the room.* [from Medieval Latin]

**se|clu|sion** /sɪkluːʒ³n/ N-UNCOUNT If you are living **in seclusion**, you are in a quiet place away from other people. ❑ *She lived in seclusion on their farm in Panama.* [from Medieval Latin]

---

**second**

❶ PART OF A MINUTE
❷ COMING AFTER SOMETHING ELSE

---

❶ **sec|ond** /sɛkənd/ (**seconds**) N-COUNT A **second** is one of the sixty parts that a minute is divided into. People often say "**a second**" or "**seconds**" when they simply mean a very short time. ❑ *For a few seconds nobody spoke.* ❑ *It only takes forty seconds.* [from Old French]
→ see **time**

❷ **sec|ond** /sɛkənd/ (**seconds, seconding, seconded**) **1** ORD The **second** item in a series is the one that you count as number two. ❑ *It was the second day of his visit to Florida.* ❑ *He is their second child.* ❑ *...the Second World War.* ❑ *The party is the second strongest in Italy.* ❑ *First, all children must start school ready to learn; and second, the high school graduation rate must increase.* **2** N-COUNT **Seconds** are goods that are sold cheaply in stores because they have slight faults. ❑ *These are not seconds, but first-quality products.* **3** V-T If you **second** a proposal in a meeting or debate, you formally express your agreement with it so that it can then be discussed or voted on. ❑ *The members proposed*

S

*and seconded his nomination.* **4** V-T If you **second** what someone has said, you say that you agree with them or say the same thing yourself. *□ All the other girls seconded her idea.* **5** PHRASE If you say that something is **second to none**, you are emphasizing that it is very good indeed or the best that there is. *□ Our scientific research is second to none.* **6** PHRASE If you say that something is **second only to** something else, you mean than that only that thing is better or greater than it. *□ India is second only to China with a population of 1.1 billion.* [from Old French] **7 second nature** → see **nature**

**sec|ond|ary** /sɛkəndɛri/ **1** ADJ If you describe something as **secondary**, you mean that it is less important than something else. *□ After the bomb fell there were secondary explosions in other buildings. □ Money is of secondary importance to them.* **2** ADJ **Secondary** education is given to students between the ages of 11 or 12 and 17 or 18. *□ They take examinations after five years of secondary education.* [from Old French]
→ see **color**

**sec|ond|ary col|or** (**secondary colors**) N-COUNT **Secondary colors** are colors such as orange and violet that are a mixture of two primary colors.

**sec|ond|ary pol|lu|tant** (**secondary pollutants**) N-COUNT **Secondary pollutants** are pollutants that are created by chemical reactions in the atmosphere. Compare **primary pollutant**. [TECHNICAL]

**sec|ond best** also **second-best** ADJ **Second best** is used to describe something that is not as good as the best thing of its kind but is better than all the other things of that kind. *□ He put on his second best suit.* ● **Second best** is also a noun. *□ Water is a good second best.*

**second-class** also **second class** ADJ **Second-class** things are regarded as less valuable and less important than others of the same kind. *□ The airlines treat children as second-class citizens. □ …a second-class education.*

**second|hand** /sɛkəndhænd/ also **second-hand** **1** ADJ **Secondhand** things are not new and have been owned by someone else. *□ They could just afford a secondhand car.* ● **Secondhand** is also an adverb. *□ They bought the furniture secondhand.* **2** ADJ A **secondhand** store sells secondhand goods. *□ These are old pieces bought from a secondhand store.* **3** ADJ **Secondhand** stories, information, or opinions are those you learn about from other people rather than directly or from your own experience. *□ The progress reports are based on secondhand information.* ● **Secondhand** is also an adverb. *□ I heard about it secondhand.*

**second|hand smoke** also **second-hand smoke** N-UNCOUNT **Secondhand smoke** is tobacco smoke that people breathe in because other people around them are smoking.

**sec|ond|ly** /sɛkəndli/ ADV You say **secondly** when you want to make a second point or give a second reason for something. *□ Think firstly how you're treated and secondly how you treat everybody else.* [from Old French]

**second-rate** ADJ If you describe something as **second-rate**, you mean that it is of poor quality. *□ …second-rate restaurants.*

**se|cre|cy** /sikrəsi/ N-UNCOUNT **Secrecy** is the act of keeping something secret, or the state of

being kept secret. *□ They met in complete secrecy.* [from Old French]

**se|cret** /sikrɪt/ (**secrets**) **1** ADJ If something is **secret**, it is known about by only a small number of people, and is not told or shown to anyone else. *□ They tried to keep their marriage secret.* **2** → see also **top secret** ● **se|cret|ly** ADV *□ He wore a microphone to secretly record conversations.* **3** N-COUNT A **secret** is a fact that is known by only a small number of people, and is not told to anyone else. *□ I think he enjoyed keeping our secret.* **4** N-SING If a particular way of doing things is **the secret of** achieving something, it is the best or only way to achieve it. *□ The secret of success is honesty.* **5** PHRASE If you do something **in secret**, you do it without anyone else knowing. *□ Dan found out that we were meeting in secret.* [from Old French]

| **Thesaurus** | *secret* | Also look up : |
|---|---|---|
| ADJ. | hidden, private, unknown; (*ant.*) known | |

**sec|re|tar|ial** /sɛkrɪtɛəriəl/ ADJ **Secretarial** work is the work done by a secretary in an office. *□ I was doing temporary secretarial work.* [from Medieval Latin]

**sec|re|tary** /sɛkrɪteri/ (**secretaries**) **1** N-COUNT A **secretary** is a person who is employed to do office work, such as typing letters, answering phone calls, and arranging meetings. **2** N-COUNT The **secretary** of a company is the person who has the legal duty of keeping the company's records. **3** N-COUNT; N-TITLE **Secretary** is used in the titles of high officials who are in charge of main government departments. *□ …the Venezuelan foreign secretary.* [from Medieval Latin]

**Sec|re|tary of State** (**Secretaries of State**) N-COUNT In the United States, **the Secretary of State** is the head of the government department which deals with foreign affairs.

**se|crete** /sikrit/ (**secretes, secreting, secreted**) V-T If part of a plant, animal, or human **secretes** a liquid, it produces it. *□ The skin begins to secrete an oily substance.* ● **se|cre|tion** /sikriʃⁿn/ N-UNCOUNT **Secretion** is the process by which certain liquid substances are produced by parts of plants or from the bodies of people or animals. *□ The amount of natural oil secretion begins to decrease.*

**se|cre|tive** /sikrətɪv, sikrit-/ ADJ If you are **secretive**, you like to have secrets and to keep your knowledge, feelings, or intentions hidden. *□ The very rich are often secretive about exactly how much money they have.*

**se|cret po|lice** N-UNCOUNT **The secret police** is a police force in some countries that works secretly and deals with political crimes committed against the government. *□ They were all members of the secret police.*

**se|cret ser|vice** (**secret services**) **1** N-COUNT A country's **secret service** is a secret government department whose job is to find out enemy secrets and to prevent its own government's secrets from being discovered. *□ …French secret service agents.* **2** N-COUNT **The Secret Service** is the government department in the United States which protects the president, the vice president, and their families. *□ The Secret Service arrested 19 people outside the White House today.*

**sect** /sɛkt/ (**sects**) N-COUNT A **sect** is a group of people that has separated from a larger group and has a particular set of religious or political beliefs. [from Latin]

**sec|tar|ian** /sɛktɛəriən/ ADJ **Sectarian** means resulting from the differences between different religions. ❑ *He was killed in sectarian violence.* ❑ *The police said the murder was sectarian.* [from Latin]

**sec|tion** /sɛkʃ°n/ (**sections**) **1** N-COUNT A **section** of something is one of the parts into which it is divided or from which it is formed. ❑ *He said it was wrong to blame one section of society.* ❑ *...the Georgetown section of Washington, D.C.* [from Latin] **2** → see also **cross-section**

**Word Partnership** Use *section* with :

ADJ. **main** section, **new** section, **special** section, **thin** section **1**
N. section **of a city**, section **of a coast**, **rhythm** section, **sports** section **1**

**sec|tor** /sɛktər/ (**sectors**) N-COUNT A **sector** of something, especially a country's economy, is one of the parts that it is divided into. ❑ *...the nation's manufacturing sector.* ❑ *These workers came from the poorest sectors of society.* [from Late Latin]

**Word Partnership** Use *sector* with :

N. **banking** sector, **business** sector, **government** sector, **growth in a** sector, **job in a** sector, **manufacturing** sector, **technology** sector, **telecommunications** sector

**secu|lar** /sɛkyələr/ ADJ You use **secular** to describe things that have no connection with religion. ❑ *He spoke about keeping the country as a secular state.* [from Old French]

**se|cure** /sɪkyʊər/ (**secures, securing, secured**) **1** V-T If you **secure** something that you want or need, you obtain it, often after a lot of effort. [FORMAL] ❑ *Western lawyers are trying to secure his release.* **2** V-T If you **secure** a place, you make it safe from harm or attack. [FORMAL] ❑ *Their mission is to secure the city's airport.* **3** ADJ A **secure** place is tightly locked or well protected, so that people cannot enter it or leave it. ❑ *We'll make our home as secure as possible.* ● **se|cure|ly** ADV ❑ *He locked the heavy door securely.* **4** V-T If you **secure** an object, you fasten it firmly to another object. ❑ *He secured the rope to the front of the boat.* **5** ADJ If an object is **secure**, it is fixed firmly in position. ❑ *Check that the wooden joints are secure.* ● **se|cure|ly** ADV ❑ *He fastened his belt securely.* **6** ADJ If you describe something such as a job as **secure**, it is certain not to change or end. ❑ *For the moment, his job is secure.* **7** ADJ If you feel **secure**, you feel safe and happy and are not worried about life. ❑ *She felt secure when she was with him.* [from Latin]

**Thesaurus** secure Also look up :

V. catch, get, obtain; (*ant.*) lose **1** attach, fasten **4**
ADJ. safe, sheltered **3** locked, tight **5**

**Word Partnership** Use *secure* with :

N. secure **a job/place/position**, secure **a loan**, secure **peace**, secure **your rights 1** secure **borders 3** secure **future**, secure **jobs 6**
ADV. **less** secure, **more** secure **3 5 7** **financially** secure **6**

**se|cu|ri|ty** /sɪkyʊəriti/ (**securities**) **1** N-UNCOUNT **Security** refers to all the measures that are taken to protect a place. ❑ *They are tightening their airport security.* ❑ *Strict security measures are in force in the capital.* **2** N-UNCOUNT A feeling of **security** is a feeling of being safe and free from worry. ❑ *He loves the security of a happy home life.* **3** N-UNCOUNT If something is **security** for a loan, you promise to give that thing to the person who lends you money, if you fail to pay the money back. [BUSINESS] ❑ *She's using her own home as security for a business loan.* [from Latin] **4** → see also **Social Security**

**se|cu|ri|ty cam|era** (**security cameras**) N-COUNT A **security camera** is a video camera that records people's activities in order to detect and prevent crime.

**se|dan** /sɪdæn/ (**sedans**) N-COUNT A **sedan** is a car with seats for four or more people, a fixed roof, and a trunk that is separate from the part of the car that you sit in. [from Latin]

**se|date** /sɪdeɪt/ (**sedates, sedating, sedated**) **1** ADJ If you describe someone or something as **sedate**, you mean that they are quiet and rather dignified, though perhaps a bit dull. ❑ *She visited her sedate, elderly cousins.* ❑ *Her life was quiet and sedate.* **2** V-T If someone **is sedated**, they are given a drug to calm them or to make them sleep. ❑ *The patient is sedated with strong drugs.* [from Latin]

**se|da|tion** /sɪdeɪʃ°n/ N-UNCOUNT If someone is **under sedation**, they have been given medicine or drugs in order to calm them or make them sleep. ❑ *His mother was under sedation after the shock of the attack.* [from Latin]

**seda|tive** /sɛdətɪv/ (**sedatives**) N-COUNT A **sedative** is a medicine or drug that calms you or makes you sleep. ❑ *He will have a sedative before the operation.* [from Medieval Latin]

**sed|en|tary** /sɛd°ntɛri/ ADJ Someone who has a **sedentary** lifestyle or job sits down a lot of the time and does not do much exercise. ❑ *A sedentary lifestyle can increase your risk of getting heart disease.* [from Latin]

**sedi|ment** /sɛdɪmənt/ (**sediments**) N-VAR **Sediment** is solid material that settles at the bottom of a liquid. ❑ *At the bottom of the ocean, over time, the sediment forms into rock.* [from Latin] → see **rock**

**sedi|men|tary** /sɛdɪmɛntəri/ ADJ **Sedimentary** rocks are formed from sediment left by water, ice, or wind. [from Latin]

**se|duce** /sɪdus/ (**seduces, seducing, seduced**) V-T If something **seduces** you, it is so attractive that it makes you do something that you would not otherwise do. ❑ *The fabulous view always seduces visitors.* ● **se|duc|tion** /sɪdʌkʃ°n/ (**seductions**) N-VAR ❑ *...the seduction of words.* [from Latin]

**se|duc|tive** /sɪdʌktɪv/ ADJ Something that is **seductive** is very attractive or makes you want to

S

do something that you would not otherwise do. ❑ *It's a seductive argument.* [from Latin]

## see

❶ VERB USES
❷ EXPRESSIONS, PHRASES AND CONVENTIONS
❸ PHR-VERBS

❶ **see** /siː/ (**sees, seeing, saw, seen**) **1** V-T/V-I When you **see** something, you notice it using your eyes. ❑ *You can't see colors at night.* ❑ *She can see, hear, touch, smell, and taste.* **2** V-T If you **see** someone, you visit them or meet them. ❑ *I saw him yesterday.* ❑ *Mick wants to see you in his office now.* **3** V-T If you **see** an entertainment such as a play, movie, concert, or sports game, you watch it. ❑ *I haven't seen a movie for ages.* **4** V-T/V-I If you **see** that something is true or exists, you realize by observing it that it is true or exists. ❑ *I could see she was lonely.* ❑ *A lot of people saw what happened.* ❑ *My taste has changed a bit, as you can see.* **5** V-T If you **see** what someone means or **see** why something happened, you understand what they mean or understand why it happened. ❑ *Oh, I see what you're saying.* ❑ *I really don't see any reason for changing it.* ❑ *"He came home in my car." — "I see."* **6** V-T If you **see** someone or something **as** a certain thing, you have the opinion that they are that thing. ❑ *They saw him as a boy, not a man.* ❑ *He saw it as an opportunity.* ❑ *As I see it, Steve has three choices.* **7** V-T If you **see** a particular quality **in** someone, you believe they have that quality. If you ask what someone **sees in** a particular person or thing, you want to know what they find attractive about that person or thing. ❑ *Frankly, I don't know what Paul sees in her.* **8** V-T If you **see** something happening in the future, you imagine it, or predict that it will happen. ❑ *It's a good idea, but can you see Taylor trying it?* **9** V-T If a period of time or a person **sees** a particular change or event, it takes place during that period of time or while that person is alive. ❑ *Yesterday saw heavy fighting in the city.* ❑ *He worked well with the general and was sorry to see him go.* **10** V-T If you **see that** something is done or if you **see to it that** it is done, you make sure that it is done. ❑ *See that you take care of him.* **11** V-T If you **see** someone to a particular place, you accompany them to make sure that they get there safely, or to show politeness. ❑ *He didn't offer to see her to her car.* **12** V-T **See** is used in books to indicate to readers that they should look at another part of the book, or at another book, because more information is given there. ❑ *See chapter 7 for more information.* [from Old English] → see also **look**

| Thesaurus | *see* | Also look up : |
|---|---|---|
| v. | glimpse, look, observe, watch ❶ **1** | |
| | grasp, observe, understand ❶ **5** | |

❷ **see** /siː/ (**sees, seeing, saw, seen**) **1** CONVENTION People say **"I'll see"** or **"We'll see"** to indicate that they do not intend to make a decision immediately, and will decide later. ❑ *We'll see. It's a possibility.* **2** CONVENTION People say **"let me see"** or **"let's see"** when they are trying to remember something, or are trying to find

something. ❑ *Let's see, they're six — no, five hours ahead of us.* **3** PHRASE You can use **seeing that** or **seeing as** to introduce a reason for what you are saying. [INFORMAL, SPOKEN] ❑ *Seeing as you're part of the family, I'll let you borrow it.* **4** CONVENTION **"See you," "be seeing you,"** and **"see you later"** are ways of saying goodbye to someone when you expect to meet them again soon. [INFORMAL, SPOKEN] ❑ *"Talk to you later." — "All right. See you."* [from Old English] **5** to **see fit** → see **fit** **6** to **see red** → see **red**

❸ **see** /siː/ (**sees, seeing, saw, seen**)
▸ **see about** PHR-VERB When you **see about** something, you arrange for it to be done or provided. ❑ *It was time to see about lunch.*
▸ **see off** PHR-VERB When you **see** someone **off**, you go with them to the station, airport, or port that they are leaving from, and say goodbye to them there. ❑ *Ben had an early night after seeing Jackie off on her plane.*
▸ **see through** PHR-VERB If you **see through** someone or their behavior, you realize what their intentions are, even though they are trying to hide them. ❑ *I saw through your plan from the start.* → see also **see-through**
▸ **see to** PHR-VERB If you **see to** something that needs attention, you deal with it. ❑ *While Frank saw to the luggage, Sara took Ellie home.*

**seed** /siːd/ (**seeds**) **1** N-VAR A **seed** is the small, hard part of a plant from which a new plant grows. ❑ *I planted the seeds in small plastic pots.* **2** N-PLURAL You can refer to the **seeds of** something when you want to talk about the beginning of a feeling or process that gradually develops and becomes stronger or more important. [LITERARY] ❑ *His questions planted seeds of doubt in my mind.* [from Old English] → see **fruit, herbivore, rice**

**seed fern** (**seed ferns**) N-COUNT A **seed fern** was a plant, with leaves resembling those of a fern, that is now extinct.

**seed|less** /siːdlɪs/ ADJ A **seedless** fruit has no seeds in it. ❑ *...seedless grapes.* [from Old English]

**seed|ling** /siːdlɪŋ/ (**seedlings**) N-COUNT A **seedling** is a young plant that has been grown from a seed. [from Old English]

**seedy** /siːdi/ (**seedier, seediest**) ADJ If you describe a person or place as **seedy**, you disapprove of them because they look dirty and messy, or they have a bad reputation. ❑ *They wondered if this seedy individual lived in the van.* ❑ *It was a seedy hotel.* [from Old English]

**seek** /siːk/ (**seeks, seeking, sought**) **1** V-T If you **seek** something, you try to find it or obtain it. [FORMAL] ❑ *The students are seeking work in hotels and bars during their summer vacation.* ❑ *The Baltic states sought help from the United Nations.* ● **seek|er** (**seekers**) N-COUNT ❑ *I am a seeker after truth.* **2** V-T If you **seek to** do something, you try to do it. [FORMAL] ❑ *The U.S. should not seek to be the world's policeman.* [from Old English]
▸ **seek out** PHR-VERB If you **seek out** someone or something or **seek** them **out**, you keep looking for them until you find them. ❑ *Local companies are seeking out business opportunities in Europe.*

## Word Partnership    Use *seek* with :

N.    seek **advice**, seek **approval**, seek
**assistance/help**, seek **asylum**, seek
**counseling**, seek **election**, seek
**employment**, seek **justice**, seek
**permission**, seek **protection**, seek
**revenge**, seek **shelter**, seek **support** ▣

**seem** /sim/ (**seems, seeming, seemed**) ▣ V-LINK
You use **seem** to say that someone or something
gives the impression of having a particular
quality, or of happening in the way you describe.
❏ *The thunder seemed quite close.* ❏ *They seemed an
ideal couple to everyone who knew them.* ❏ *The calming
effect seemed to last for about ten minutes.* ❏ *It seems
that the attack was carefully planned.* ❏ *It seems as if
she's never coming back.* ▤ V-LINK You use **seem**
when you are describing your own feelings or
thoughts, or describing something that has
happened to you, in order to make your statement
less forceful. ❏ *I seem to have lost all my self-
confidence.* ❏ *I seem to remember giving you very clear
instructions.* ▥ PHRASE If you say that you **cannot
seem** or **could not seem to** do something, you
mean that you have tried to do it and were unable
to. ❏ *As a society, we cannot seem to look honestly at
ourselves.* [from Old Norse]

**seem|ing** /simɪŋ/ ADJ **Seeming** means
appearing to be true, but not necessarily true.
[FORMAL] ❏ *A seeming coldness existed between us.*
● **seem|ing|ly** ADV ❏ *He moved to Spain, seemingly to
enjoy a slower style of life.* [from Old Norse]

**seen** /sin/ **Seen** is the past participle of **see**.
[from Old English]

**seep** /sip/ (**seeps, seeping, seeped**) V-I If liquid
or gas **seeps** somewhere, it flows slowly and in
small amounts into a place where it should not go.
❏ *Polluted water seeped into the soil.* ❏ *Gas is seeping
out of the pipes.* ● **Seep** is also a noun. ❏ *...an oil seep.*
[from Old English]

**seethe** /sið/ (**seethes, seething, seethed**) V-I
When you **are seething**, you are very angry about
something but do not express your feelings
about it. ❏ *She looked calm but under the surface she
was seething.* ❏ *I was seething with anger.* [from Old
English]

**see-through** ADJ **See-through** clothes are made
of thin cloth, so that you can see a person's body
or underwear through them. ❏ *She wore a white,
see-through blouse.*

**seg|ment** /segmənt/ (**segments**) ▣ N-COUNT
A **segment** of something is one part of it. ❏ *They
come from the poorer segments of society.* ▤ N-COUNT
The **segments** of an animal's body are its different
sections, especially the sections between two
joints. [from Latin]
→ see **fruit**

**seg|re|gate** /segrɪgeɪt/ (**segregates,
segregating, segregated**) V-T To **segregate** two
groups of people or things means to keep them
physically apart from each other. ❏ *It was decided to
segregate the two groups of protesters.* ● **seg|re|gat|ed**
/segrɪgeɪtɪd/ ADJ ❏ *Men and women once led fairly
segregated lives in Japanese society.* ● **seg|re|ga|tion**
/segrɪgeɪ°n/ N-UNCOUNT ❏ *In 1948 there were still
laws about segregation of the races.* [from Latin]

**seis|mic** /saɪzmɪk/ ▣ ADJ **Seismic** means caused

by or relating to an earthquake. ❏ *Earthquakes
produce two types of seismic waves.* ▤ ADJ A **seismic**
shift or change is a very sudden or dramatic
change. ❏ *I have never seen such a seismic shift in
public opinion in such a short period of time.* [from
Greek]

**seis|mic gap** (**seismic gaps**) N-COUNT A **seismic
gap** is a section of a geological fault where there
has not been an earthquake for a relatively long
time. [TECHNICAL]

**seis|mo|gram** /saɪzməgræm/ (**seismograms**)
N-COUNT A **seismogram** is a graph produced by
a seismograph which shows the strength of an
earthquake. [TECHNICAL]

**seis|mo|graph** /saɪzməgræf/ (**seismographs**)
N-COUNT A **seismograph** is an instrument
for recording and measuring the strength of
earthquakes.
→ see **tsunami**

**seis|mol|ogy** /saɪzmɒlədʒi/ N-UNCOUNT
**Seismology** is the scientific study of
earthquakes.

**seize** /siz/ (**seizes, seizing, seized**) ▣ V-T If
you **seize** something, you take hold of it quickly,
firmly, and forcefully. ❏ *He seized my arm to hold me
back.* ▤ V-T When a group of people **seize** a place
or **seize** control of it, they take control of it quickly
and suddenly, using force. ❏ *Guards were ordered to
seize him.* ▥ V-T When someone is **seized**, they are
arrested or captured. ❏ *U.N. officials say two military
observers were seized yesterday.* ▦ V-T When you
**seize** an opportunity, you take advantage of it and
do something that you want to do. ❏ *They seized
the opportunity to study his pictures during their visits.*
[from Old French]
▸ **seize on** PHR-VERB If you **seize on** something or
**seize upon** it, you show great interest in it, often
because it is useful to you. ❏ *Steve seized on the idea
and I was interested too.*
▸ **seize up** PHR-VERB If an engine or a part of
your body **seizes up**, it stops working. ❏ *After that
exercise, it's your arms that seize up, not your legs.*

**sei|zure** /siʒər/ (**seizures**) ▣ N-COUNT If
someone has a **seizure**, they have a sudden violent
attack of an illness, especially one that affects
their heart or brain. ❏ *His mother had a seizure and
collapsed.* ▤ N-COUNT If there is a **seizure of** power
or a **seizure of** an area of land, a group of people
suddenly take control of the place, using force.
❏ *...the seizure of territory through force.* [from Old
French]

**sel|dom** /seldəm/ ADV If something **seldom**
happens, it happens only occasionally. ❏ *They
seldom speak.* ❏ *I've seldom felt so happy.* [from Old
English]

**se|lect** /sɪlekt/ (**selects, selecting, selected**)
▣ V-T If you **select** something, you choose it from
a number of things of the same kind. ❏ *Please
select 5 out of the 10 events.* ❏ *You can select a 6th
book for only $4.95.* ● **se|lec|tion** N-UNCOUNT ❏ *Dr.
Sullivan's selection was very popular.* ▤ ADJ A **select**
group is a small group of some of the best people
or things of their kind. ❏ *Then select voters got a
letter from the Commissioner.* ❏ *It was a select party.*
[from Latin]

S

| **Thesaurus** | *select* | Also look up : |
|---|---|---|
| V. | choose, pick out, take **1** | |
| ADJ. | best, exclusive **2** | |

**se|lec|tion** /sɪlɛkʃ°n/ (**selections**) **1** N-COUNT A **selection of** people or things is a set of them that has been selected from a larger group. ❑ ...*this selection of popular songs.* **2** N-COUNT The **selection of** goods in a store is the particular range of goods that it has available and from which you can choose what you want. ❑ *It offers the widest selection of antiques in a one day market.* [from Latin]

**se|lec|tive** /sɪlɛktɪv/ **1** ADJ A **selective** process applies only to a few things or people. ❑ *They put together a selective list of people to invite to the party.* ● **se|lec|tive|ly** ADV ❑ *Within the project, trees are selectively cut down.* **2** ADJ When someone is **selective**, they choose things carefully, for example, the things that they buy or do. ❑ *Sales still happen, but buyers are more selective.* ● **se|lec|tive|ly** ADV ❑ *People on small incomes want to shop selectively.* [from Latin]

**se|lec|tive breed|ing** N-UNCOUNT **Selective breeding** is the process of breeding certain traits in animals in preference to others.

**self** /sɛlf/ (**selves**) N-COUNT Your **self** is your basic personality or nature. ❑ *You're looking like your usual self again.* [from Old English]

**self-centered** ADJ Someone who is **self-centered** is only concerned with their own wants and needs and never thinks about other people. ❑ *It's very self-centered to think that people are talking about you.*

**self-confident** ADJ Someone who is **self-confident** behaves confidently because they feel sure of their abilities or value. ❑ *She's become a very self-confident young woman.* ● **self-confidence** N-UNCOUNT ❑ *I lost all my self-confidence.*

**self-conscious** ADJ Someone who is **self-conscious** is easily embarrassed and nervous because they feel that everyone is looking at them and judging them. ❑ *I felt a bit self-conscious in my bikini.*

**self-contained** **1** ADJ You can describe someone or something as **self-contained** when they are complete and separate and do not need help or resources from outside. ❑ *He seems completely self-contained and doesn't miss you at all.* **2** ADJ **Self-contained** accommodations such as an apartment have all their own facilities, so that a person living there does not have to share rooms such as a kitchen or bathroom with other people. ❑ *They live in a self-contained three-bedroom suite in the back of the main house.*

**self-control** N-UNCOUNT **Self-control** is the ability to not show your feelings or not do the things that your feelings make you want to do. ❑ *She was told she must learn self-control.*

**self-defense** N-UNCOUNT **Self-defense** is the use of force to protect yourself against someone who is attacking you. ❑ *The women acted in self-defense.*

**self-determination** N-UNCOUNT **Self-determination** is the right of a country to be independent, instead of being controlled by a foreign country, and to choose its own form of government. ❑ ...*Lithuania's right to self-determination.*

**self-employed** ADJ If you are **self-employed**, you organize your own work and taxes and are paid by people for a service you provide, rather than being paid a regular salary by a person or a company. [BUSINESS] ❑ *You can change the time you start work easily if you are self-employed.* ● The **self-employed** are people who are self-employed. ❑ *We want more support for the self-employed.*

**self-esteem** N-UNCOUNT Your **self-esteem** is how you feel about yourself and whether you have a good opinion of yourself. ❑ *Harry was a man of low self-esteem.*

**self-evident** ADJ A fact or situation that is **self-evident** is so obvious that there is no need for proof or explanation. ❑ *It is self-evident that we will never have enough money.*

**self-help** N-UNCOUNT **Self-help** consists of people providing support and help for each other in an informal way, rather than relying on official organizations. ❑ *She set up a self-help group for parents with overweight children.*

**self-image** (**self-images**) N-COUNT Your **self-image** is the set of ideas you have about your own qualities and abilities. ❑ *He seems to have a very healthy self-image right now.*

**self-imposed** ADJ A **self-imposed** restriction, task, or situation is one that you have deliberately created or accepted for yourself. ❑ *He ended his self-imposed silence with an interview last week.*

**self-indulgent** ADJ If you say that someone is **self-indulgent**, you mean that they allow themselves to have or do the things that they enjoy very much. ❑ *We live in a world full of self-indulgent people.* ● **self-indulgence** (**self-indulgences**) N-VAR ❑ *He prayed to be saved from self-indulgence.*

**self-interest** N-UNCOUNT If you accuse someone of **self-interest**, you disapprove of them because they always want to do what is best for themselves rather than for anyone else. ❑ *It's good to find people who have no self-interest.*

**self|ish** /sɛlfɪʃ/ ADJ If you say that someone is **selfish**, you disapprove of them because they care only about themselves, and not about other people. ❑ *I think I've been very selfish.* ● **self|ish|ly** ADV ❑ *Someone has selfishly emptied the cookie jar.* ● **self|ish|ness** N-UNCOUNT ❑ *Julie's selfishness made us sad.* [from Old English]

**self|less** /sɛlflɪs/ ADJ If you say that someone is **selfless**, you approve of them because they care about other people more than themselves. ❑ *Her kindness was entirely selfless.* [from Old English]

**self-pity** N-UNCOUNT **Self-pity** is a feeling of unhappiness that you have about yourself and your problems, especially when this is unnecessary or greatly exaggerated. ❑ *I was unable to get over my self-pity.*

**self-pollinating** ADJ If a plant is **self-pollinating**, the female part of the plant is fertilized by pollen from the male part of the same plant.

**self-promotion** N-UNCOUNT If you accuse someone of **self-promotion**, you disapprove of them because they are trying to make themselves seem more important than they actually are. ❑ *His self-promotion has not made him popular among his co-workers.*

**self-respect** N-UNCOUNT **Self-respect** is a feeling of confidence and pride in your own ability and worth. ❑ *They have lost their jobs, their homes and their self-respect.*

**self-righteous** ADJ If you describe someone as **self-righteous**, you disapprove of them because they are convinced that they are right in their beliefs, attitudes, and behavior and that other people are wrong. ❑ *He thinks they are narrow-minded and self-righteous.* ● **self-righteousness** N-UNCOUNT ❑ *Her self-righteousness made him very angry.*

**self-rising flour** N-UNCOUNT **Self-rising flour** is flour that makes cakes rise as you bake them because it has chemicals added to it.

**self-study** N-UNCOUNT **Self-study** is study that you do on your own, without a teacher. ❑ *...self-study courses.*

**self-styled** ADJ If you describe someone as a **self-styled** leader or expert, you disapprove of them because they claim to be a leader or expert but they do not actually have the right to call themselves this. ❑ *He's a self-styled "expert."*

**self-sufficient** ADJ If a country or group is **self-sufficient**, it is able to produce or make everything that it needs. ❑ *Now the country is self-sufficient in sugar.* ● **self-sufficiency** /sɛlf səfɪʃ°nsi/ N-UNCOUNT ❑ *We dreamed of self-sufficiency.*

**sell** /sɛl/ (**sells, selling, sold**) ◼ V-T/V-I If you **sell** something that you own, you let someone have it in return for money. ❑ *Catlin sold the paintings to Joseph Harrison.* ❑ *The directors sold the business for $14.8 million.* ❑ *When is the best time to sell?* ◻ V-T If a store **sells** a particular thing, it is available for people to buy there. ❑ *It sells everything from hair ribbons to carpets.* ◼ V-I If something **sells for** a particular price, that price is paid for it. ❑ *The candy usually sells for $5.* ◼ V-I If something **sells**, it is bought by the public, usually in fairly large quantities. ❑ *Even if this album doesn't sell, we won't change our style.* [from Old English]
▶ **sell out** ◼ PHR-VERB If a store **sells out** of something, it sells all its supply of it. ❑ *The supermarket sold out of flour in a single day.* ◻ PHR-VERB If a performance, sports event, or other entertainment **sells out**, all the tickets for it are sold. ❑ *Football games often sell out fast.* ◼ PHR-VERB If you accuse someone of **selling out**, you disapprove of the fact that they do something which used to be against their principles, or give in to an opposing group. ❑ *You don't have to sell out and work for some corporation.* ◻ → see also **sell-out**

**sell|er** /sɛlər/ (**sellers**) ◼ N-COUNT A **seller** of a type of thing is a person or company that sells that type of thing. ❑ *She's a flower seller.* ◻ N-COUNT In a business deal, the **seller** is the person who is selling something to someone else. ❑ *The seller is responsible for collecting the tax.* ◼ N-COUNT If you describe a product as, for example, a big **seller**, you mean that large numbers of it are being sold. ❑ *I think our new phone is going to be a big seller.* [from Old English] ◻ → see also **bestseller**

**sell-off** (**sell-offs**) also **selloff** N-COUNT The **sell-off** of something, for example, an industry owned by the state, is the selling of it. [BUSINESS] ❑ *The*

value of the company fell during the sell-off.

**sell-out** (**sell-outs**) also **sellout** ◼ N-COUNT If a play, sports event, or other entertainment is a **sell-out**, all the tickets for it are sold. ❑ *Their concert there was a sell-out.* ◻ N-COUNT If you describe someone's behavior as a **sell-out**, you disapprove of the fact that they have done something which used to be against their principles. ❑ *For some, his decision to become a Socialist was simply a sell-out.*

**selt|zer** /sɛltsər/ (**seltzers**) also **seltzer water** N-VAR **Seltzer** is carbonated water with a lot of minerals in. ❑ *...a bottle of seltzer.*

**selves** /sɛlvz/ **Selves** is the plural of **self**. [from Old English]

**sem|blance** /sɛmbləns/ N-UNCOUNT If there is a **semblance of** a particular condition or quality, it appears to exist, even though this may be a false impression. [FORMAL] ❑ *All semblance of law and order has disappeared.* [from Old French]

**se|men** /siːmən/ N-UNCOUNT **Semen** is the liquid containing sperm that is produced by the sex organs of men and male animals. [from Latin]

**se|mes|ter** /sɪmɛstər/ (**semesters**) N-COUNT In colleges and universities in some countries, a **semester** is one of the two main periods into which the year is divided. ❑ *February 22nd is when most of their students begin their spring semester.* [from German]

**semiannual** ADJ A **semiannual** event happens twice a year. ❑ *We hold our semiannual meeting in September.*

**semi|co|lon** /sɛmikoʊlən/ (**semicolons**) N-COUNT A **semicolon** is the punctuation mark ; which is used in writing to separate different parts of a sentence or list or to indicate a pause. [from Latin]
→ see **punctuation**

**semi|con|duc|tor** /sɛmikəndʌktər, sɛmaɪ-/ (**semiconductors**) N-COUNT A **semiconductor** is a substance used in electronics whose ability to conduct electricity increases with greater heat.
→ see **solar**

**semi|fi|nal** /sɛmifaɪn°l, sɛmaɪ-/ (**semifinals**) N-COUNT A **semifinal** is one of the two games or races in a competition that are held to decide who will compete in the final. ❑ *The basketball team lost in their semifinal yesterday.* [from Latin]

**semi|nal** /sɛmɪn°l/ ADJ **Seminal** is used to describe things such as books, works, events, and experiences that have had a great influence in a particular field. [FORMAL] ❑ *He wrote a seminal book on the subject.* [from Late Latin]

**semi|nar** /sɛmɪnɑr/ (**seminars**) N-COUNT A **seminar** is a class at a college or university in which the teacher and a small group of students discuss a topic. ❑ *Students are asked to prepare material for the weekly seminars.* [from German]

**semi|nif|er|ous tu|bule** /sɛmɪnɪfərəs tuːbyul/ (**seminiferous tubules**) N-COUNT **Seminiferous tubules** are tubes inside the testes of male animals where sperm is produced. [TECHNICAL]

**Se|mit|ic** /sɪmɪtɪk/ ◼ ADJ **Semitic** languages are a group of languages that include Arabic and Hebrew. ◻ ADJ **Semitic** people belong to one of the

S

groups of people who speak a Semitic language. ❏ *…an ancient Semitic religion.* ❸ ADJ **Semitic** is sometimes used to mean Jewish. [from Modern Latin]

**Sen|ate** /sɛnɪt/ (**Senates**) N-PROPER **The Senate** is the smaller and more important of the two parts of the legislature in some U.S. states and in some countries, for example, the United States and Australia. ❏ *That year the Republicans gained two Senate seats.*

---

> **Word Link**    sen ≈ old : sen**a**tor, sen**i**le, sen**i**or

**sena|tor** /sɛnɪtər/ (**senators**) N-COUNT; N-TITLE A **senator** is a member of a Senate, for example, in the United States or Australia. [from Latin]

**send** /sɛnd/ (**sends, sending, sent**) ❶ V-T When you **send** someone something, you arrange for it to be taken and delivered to them, for example, by mail. ❏ *Myra Cunningham sent me a note thanking me for dinner.* ❏ *I sent a copy to the school principal.* ● **send|er** (**senders**) N-COUNT ❏ *The sender of the best letter will win a check for $50.* ❷ V-T If you **send** someone somewhere, you arrange for them to go there or stay there. ❏ *The Inspector came to see her, but she sent him away.* ❏ *The government has decided to send troops to the region.* ❏ *I sent him for an X-ray.* ❏ *His parents have chosen to send him to a boarding school.* ❸ V-T To **send** a signal means to cause it to go to a place by means of radio waves or electricity. ❏ *The transmitters will send a signal to a local base station.* ❹ V-T If something **sends** things or people in a particular direction, it causes them to move in that direction. ❏ *The explosion sent bits of metal flying across the crowded highway.* ❏ *The gunshot sent him running off through the woods.* ❺ V-T To **send** someone or something **into** a particular state means to cause them to go into or be in that state. ❏ *Something about the men sent him into a panic.* ❏ *Civil war sent the country plunging into chaos.* [from Old English]

▶ **send for** ❶ PHR-VERB If you **send for** someone, you send them a message asking them to come and see you. ❏ *I've sent for the doctor.* ❷ PHR-VERB If you **send for** something, or **send away for** it, or **send off for** it, you write and ask for it to be sent to you. ❏ *Send for your free catalog today.*

▶ **send off** PHR-VERB When you **send off** a letter or package, you send it somewhere by mail. ❏ *He sent off copies to various people.*

▶ **send off for** → see **send for** 2

▶ **send out** ❶ PHR-VERB If you **send out** things such as letters or bills, you send them to a large number of people at the same time. ❏ *She sent out four hundred invitations that afternoon.* ❷ PHR-VERB To **send out** a signal, sound, light, or heat means to produce it. ❏ *The crew did not send out any emergency signals.*

▶ **send out for** PHR-VERB If you **send out for** food, for example, pizza or sandwiches, you phone and ask for it to be delivered to you. ❏ *Let's send out for a pizza.*

**se|nile** /sinaɪl/ ADJ If old people become **senile**, they become confused, can no longer remember things, and are unable to take care of themselves. ❏ *He's ninety years old and a bit senile.* ● **se|nil|ity** /sɪnɪlɪti/ N-UNCOUNT ❏ *The old man was showing signs of senility.* [from Latin]

**sen|ior** /sinyər/ (**seniors**) ❶ ADJ The **senior** people in an organization or profession have the highest and most important jobs. ❏ *These were senior officials in the Israeli government.* ❏ *…the company's senior management.* ❷ ADJ If someone is **senior to** you, they have a higher and more important job than you. ❏ *The job had to be done by an officer senior to Haig.* ● Your **seniors** are the people who are senior to you. ❏ *His seniors described him as an excellent officer.* ❸ N-SING **Senior** is used when indicating how much older one person is than another. ❏ *Her brother was in fact many years her senior.* ❹ N-COUNT **Seniors** are students in a high school, university, or college who are in their fourth year of study. ❏ *How many high school seniors go on to college?* [from Latin]

**sen|ior citi|zen** (**senior citizens**) N-COUNT A **senior citizen** is an older person, especially someone over 65. **Senior citizens** have often retired and often receive social security benefits. ❏ *…services for senior citizens.*
→ see **age**

**sen|ior high school** (**senior highs schools**) also **senior high** N-VAR A **senior high school** or a **senior high** is a school for students between the ages of 14 or 15 and 17 or 18. ❏ *Our children are in senior high school.* ❏ *This is a daily news program for middle and senior high schools.* ❏ *…Mount Pearl Senior High.*

**sen|ior mo|ment** (**senior moments**) N-COUNT If an elderly person has a **senior moment**, he or she forgets something or makes a mistake. [INFORMAL] ❏ *He is 69 in February and sometimes has a senior moment.*

---

> **Word Link**    sens ≈ feeling : sen**s**ation, sen**s**eless, sen**s**itive

**sen|sa|tion** /sɛnseɪʃən/ (**sensations**) ❶ N-COUNT A **sensation** is a physical feeling. ❏ *Floating can be a pleasant sensation.* ❷ N-UNCOUNT **Sensation** is your ability to feel things physically. ❏ *The pain was so bad that she lost all sensation.* ❸ N-COUNT You can use **sensation** to refer to the general feeling or impression caused by a particular experience. ❏ *It's a funny sensation to know someone's talking about you in another language.* ❹ N-COUNT If a person, event, or situation is a **sensation**, it causes great excitement or interest. ❏ *This movie turned her into an overnight sensation.* [from Medieval Latin]
→ see **taste**

**sen|sa|tion|al** /sɛnseɪʃənᵊl/ ❶ ADJ A **sensational** result, event, or situation is so remarkable that it causes great excitement and interest. ❏ *The world champions suffered a sensational defeat.* ● **sen|sa|tion|al|ly** ADV ❏ *The judge sensationally stopped the trial yesterday.* ❷ ADJ You can describe something as **sensational** when you think that it is extremely good. ❏ *Her voice is sensational.* ● **sen|sa|tion|al|ly** ADV ❏ *This is sensationally good food.* [from Medieval Latin]

**sense** /sɛns/ (**senses, sensing, sensed**) ❶ N-COUNT Your **senses** are the physical abilities of sight, smell, hearing, touch, and taste. ❏ *She stared at him, unable to believe her senses.* ❷ V-T If you **sense** something, you become aware of it or you realize it, although it is not very obvious. ❏ *She probably sensed that I wasn't telling the truth.* ❏ *He looked around him, sensing danger.* ❸ N-SING If you have a **sense of** guilt or relief, for example, you feel guilty or relieved. ❏ *When your child is unhappy, you*

feel this terrible sense of guilt. ◢ N-UNCOUNT **Sense** is the ability to make good judgments and to behave sensibly. ❑ *When he was younger, he had a bit more sense.* ❑ *If that doesn't work, they sometimes have the sense to ask for help.* ◳ → see also **common sense** ◳ N-COUNT A **sense** of a word or expression is one of its possible meanings. ❑ *This noun has four senses.* ◱ PHRASE If you say that someone **has come to their senses** or **has been brought to their senses**, you mean that they have stopped being foolish and are being sensible again. ❑ *Eventually the world will come to its senses.* ◳ PHRASE If something **makes sense**, you can understand it. ❑ *He sat there saying, "Yes, the figures make sense."* ◳ PHRASE When you **make sense** of something, you succeed in understanding it. ❑ *If you don't try to make sense of it, it sounds beautiful.* ◰ PHRASE If a course of action **makes sense**, it seems sensible. ❑ *It makes sense to take care of yourself.* ❑ *Does this project make good economic sense?* [from Latin]
→ see **smell**

**Word Link**    sens ≈ feeling : sensation, senseless, sensitive

**sense|less** /sɛnslɪs/ ◱ ADJ A **senseless** action seems to have no purpose and produce no benefit. ❑ *People's lives are destroyed by acts of senseless violence.* ◲ ADJ If someone is **senseless**, they are unconscious. ❑ *They knocked him to the ground and beat him senseless.* [from Latin]

**sense memo|ry** (**sense memories**) N-VAR **Sense memory** is the memory of physical sensations such as sounds and smells, which actors sometimes use in order to gain a better understanding of the character they are playing.

**sense of hu|mor** N-SING Someone who has a **sense of humor** often finds things amusing, rather than being serious all the time. ❑ *She has a good sense of humor.*

**sen|sibil|ity** /sɛnsɪbɪlɪti/ (**sensibilities**) N-VAR **Sensibility** is the ability to experience deep feelings. ❑ *He was a man of deep sensibility.* [from Old French]

**sen|sible** /sɛnsɪbᵊl/ ◱ ADJ **Sensible** actions or decisions are good because they are based on reasons rather than emotions. ❑ *It might be sensible to get a lawyer.* ❑ *The sensible thing is to leave them alone.* ● **sen|sibly** /sɛnsɪbli/ ADV ❑ *He sensibly decided to hide for a while.* ◲ ADJ **Sensible** people behave in a sensible way. ❑ *She was a sensible girl and did not panic.* ❑ *Oh come on, let's be sensible about this.* [from Old French]

**sen|si|tive** /sɛnsɪtɪv/ ◱ ADJ If you are **sensitive to** other people's needs, problems, or feelings, you show understanding and awareness of them. ❑ *The classroom teacher must be sensitive to a child's needs.* ● **sen|si|tive|ly** ADV ❑ *The investigation should be done carefully and sensitively.* ● **sen|si|tiv|ity** /sɛnsɪtɪviti/ N-UNCOUNT ❑ *A good relationship involves sensitivity for each other's feelings.* ◲ ADJ If you are **sensitive about** something, you are easily worried and offended when people talk about it. ❑ *Young people are sensitive about their appearance.* ● **sen|si|tiv|ity** (**sensitivities**) N-VAR ❑ *Some people suffer extreme sensitivity about what others think.* ◳ ADJ A **sensitive** subject or issue needs to be dealt with carefully because it is likely to cause disagreement or make people angry or upset. ❑ *Employment is a very sensitive issue.* ● **sen|si|tiv|ity**

N-UNCOUNT ❑ *He could not give any details because of the sensitivity of the subject.* ◢ ADJ Something that is **sensitive to** a physical force, substance, or treatment is easily affected by it and often harmed by it. ❑ *This chemical is sensitive to light.* ● **sen|si|tiv|ity** N-UNCOUNT ❑ *We measure the sensitivity of cells to damage.* ◳ ADJ A **sensitive** piece of scientific equipment is capable of measuring or recording very small changes. ❑ *We need an extremely sensitive microscope.* [from Medieval Latin]

**Word Partnership**    Use *sensitive* with :

| | |
|---|---|
| ADV. | **overly** sensitive, **so** sensitive, **too** sensitive ◱ ◲ |
| | **highly** sensitive, **very** sensitive ◱ – ◳ |
| | **politically** sensitive ◳ |
| | **environmentally** sensitive ◢ |
| N. | sensitive **areas**, sensitive **information**, sensitive **issue**, sensitive **material** ◳ |
| | **heat** sensitive, **light** sensitive, sensitive **skin** ◢ |
| | sensitive **equipment** ◳ |

**sen|sor** /sɛnsər/ (**sensors**) N-COUNT A **sensor** is an instrument which reacts to certain physical conditions such as heat or light. ❑ *This data was collected from sensors aboard the space shuttle.* [from Latin]

**Word Link**    ory ≈ relating to : advisory, contradictory, sensory

**sen|so|ry** /sɛnsəri/ ADJ **Sensory** means relating to the physical senses. [FORMAL] ❑ *A number of sensory changes can be expected with age.* [from Latin]
→ see **nervous system, smell**

**sen|so|ry neu|ron** (**sensory neurons**) N-COUNT **Sensory neurons** are nerve cells that respond to stimuli such as light or sound and send the information to the central nervous system. [TECHNICAL]

**sen|sual** /sɛnʃuəl/ ◱ ADJ Someone or something that is **sensual** shows or suggests a great liking for physical pleasures. ❑ *He was a very sensual person.* ❑ *There was a sensual curve to her lips.* ● **sen|su|al|ity** /sɛnʃuæliti/ N-UNCOUNT ❑ *Her blonde curls gave her sensuality and youth.* ◲ ADJ Something that is **sensual** gives pleasure to your physical senses rather than to your mind. ❑ *It was an opera, very glamorous and very sensual.* ● **sen|su|al|ity** N-UNCOUNT ❑ *These perfumes have warmth and sensuality.* [from Late Latin]

**sen|su|ous** /sɛnʃuəs/ ADJ Something that is **sensuous** gives pleasure to the mind or body through the senses. ❑ *The movie has a sensuous musical score.* ● **sen|su|ous|ly** ADV ❑ *She lay in the bath, enjoying its sensuously perfumed water.* [from Latin]

**sent** /sɛnt/ **Sent** is the past tense and past participle of **send**. [from Old English]

**sen|tence** /sɛntəns/ (**sentences, sentencing, sentenced**) ◱ N-COUNT A **sentence** is a group of words which, when they are written down, begin with a capital letter and end with a period, question mark, or exclamation mark. Most sentences contain a subject and a verb. ❑ *Here we have several sentences wrongly joined by commas.* ◲ N-VAR In a law court, a **sentence** is the

S

punishment that a person receives after they have been found guilty of a crime. ❑ *They are already serving prison sentences for their crimes.* ❑ *He was given a four-year sentence.* **3** V-T When a judge **sentences** someone, he or she states in court what their punishment will be. ❑ *The court sentenced him to five years in prison.* [from Old French]
→ see **trial**

**sen|ti|ment** /sɛntɪmənt/ (**sentiments**)
**1** N-VAR A **sentiment** is an attitude, feeling, or opinion. ❑ *Public sentiment was turning against him.* **2** N-UNCOUNT **Sentiment** is feelings such as pity or love, especially for things in the past, and may be considered exaggerated and foolish. ❑ *Laura kept that letter out of sentiment.* [from Medieval Latin]

**sen|ti|men|tal** /sɛntɪmɛntᵊl/ **1** ADJ Someone or something that is **sentimental** feels or shows pity or love, sometimes to an extent that is considered exaggerated and foolish. ❑ *I'm trying not to be sentimental about the past.* ● **sen|ti|men|tal|ly** ADV ❑ *We look back sentimentally to our childhood.* ● **sen|ti|men|tal|ity** /sɛntɪmɛntælɪti/ N-UNCOUNT ❑ *In this book there is no sentimentality.* **2** ADJ **Sentimental** means relating to or involving feelings such as pity or love, especially for things in the past. ❑ *Our photographs are only of sentimental value.* [from Medieval Latin]

**sen|try** /sɛntri/ (**sentries**) N-COUNT A **sentry** is a soldier who guards a camp or a building. ❑ *The sentry would not let her enter.*

**se|pal** /sipəl/ (**sepals**) N-COUNT **Sepals** are a part of the outer structure of a flower, which resemble leaves and protect the bud while it is growing. [TECHNICAL] [from New Latin]

**sepa|rate** (**separates, separating, separated**)

The adjective and noun are pronounced /sɛpərɪt/. The verb is pronounced /sɛpəreɪt/.

**1** ADJ If one thing is **separate from** another, the two things are apart and are not connected. ❑ *They are now making plans to form their own separate organization.* ❑ *Use separate surfaces for cutting raw meats and cooked meats.* ❑ *Men and women have separate exercise rooms.* ● **sepa|rate|ly** /sɛpərɪtli/ ADV ❑ *Cook each vegetable separately.* **2** V-T/V-I If you **separate** people or things that are together, or if they **separate**, they move apart. ❑ *Police moved in to separate the two groups.* ❑ *They separated and Stephen went home.* ● **sepa|ra|tion** /sɛpəreɪʃᵊn/ (**separations**) N-VAR ❑ *She wondered if Harry would remember her after this long separation.* **3** V-T/V-I If you **separate** people or things that have been connected, or if one **separates from** another, the connection between them is ended. ❑ *We want to separate teaching from research.* **4** V-RECIP If a couple who are married or living together **separate**, they decide to live apart. ❑ *Her parents separated when she was very young.* ● **sepa|rat|ed** /sɛpəreɪtɪd/ ADJ ❑ *Most single parents are either divorced or separated.* ● **sepa|ra|tion** /sɛpəreɪʃᵊn/ (**separations**) N-VAR ❑ *They agreed to try a separation.* **5** V-T An object, obstacle, distance, or period of time which **separates** two people, groups, or things exists between them. ❑ *The white fence separated the yard from the field.* ❑ *Six years separated these two important events.* **6** V-T If you **separate** one idea or fact **from** another, you clearly see or show the difference

between them. ❑ *It is difficult to separate these two aims.* ❑ *We learn how to separate real problems from imaginary illnesses.* ● **Separate out** means the same as **separate**. ❑ *In adult speech it is often difficult to separate out individual words.* ● **sepa|ra|tion** /sɛpəreɪʃᵊn/ (**separations**) N-VAR ❑ *...the separation of the body and the soul.* **7** V-T A quality or factor that **separates** one thing **from** another is the reason why the two things are different from each other. ❑ *It is the lighting that separates ordinary photographs from good photographs.* **8** V-T/V-I If you **separate** a group of people or things **into** smaller elements, or if a group **separates**, it is divided into smaller elements. ❑ *The police wanted to separate them into smaller groups.* ❑ *Let's separate into small groups.* ● **Separate out** means the same as **separate**. ❑ *If you do it too soon, the mixture may separate out.* **9** N-PLURAL **Separates** are clothes such as skirts, pants, and shirts which cover just the top half or the bottom half of your body. ❑ *She wears matching separates instead of a suit.* **10** PHRASE When two or more people who have been together for some time **go** their **separate ways**, they go to different places or end their relationship. ❑ *Sue and her husband decided to go their separate ways.* [from Latin]

▶ **separate out** PHR-VERB If you **separate out** something from the other things it is with, you take it out. ❑ *If you beat it too much, the mixture may separate out.*

| **Thesaurus** | separate | Also look up : |
|---|---|---|
| ADJ. | disconnected, divided **1** | |
| V. | divide, split **2** **5** | |

**sepa|ra|tist** /sɛpərətɪst/ (**separatists**) N-COUNT **Separatists** are people of an ethnic or cultural group within a country who want their own separate government. ❑ *A group of separatists wants independence from the government.* ● **sepa|ra|tism** N-UNCOUNT ❑ *He promised to fight separatism.* [from Latin]

**Sep|tem|ber** /sɛptɛmbər/ (**Septembers**) N-VAR **September** is the ninth month of the year in the Western calendar. ❑ *Her son was born in September.* ❑ *We didn't meet the September 30 deadline.* [from Old English]

**sep|tic tank** (**septic tanks**) N-COUNT A **septic tank** is an underground tank where feces, urine, and other waste matter is made harmless using bacteria.

| **Word Link** | sequ ≈ following : consequence, sequel, sequence |
|---|---|

**se|quel** /sikwᵊl/ (**sequels**) N-COUNT A **book** or movie which is a **sequel to** an earlier one continues the story of the earlier one. ❑ *She is writing a sequel to Daphne du Maurier's "Rebecca."* [from Late Latin]

**se|quence** /sikwəns/ (**sequences**) **1** N-COUNT A **sequence of** events or things is a number of events or things that come one after another in a particular order. ❑ *This is the sequence of events which led to the murder.* **2** N-COUNT A particular **sequence** is a particular order in which things happen or are arranged. ❑ *The color sequence is yellow, orange, purple, blue, green, and white.* [from Medieval Latin]

**se|quin** /sikwɪn/ (**sequins**) N-COUNT **Sequins**

are small, shiny disks that are sewn on clothes to decorate them. ❑ *The costumes are covered in thousands of sequins.* [from French]

**se|quined** /sˈiːkwɪnd/ also **sequinned** ADJ A **sequined** piece of clothing is decorated or covered with sequins. ❑ *She wore a sequined evening gown.* [from French]

**se|quoia** /sɪˈkwɔɪə/ (**sequoias**) N-COUNT A **sequoia** is a very tall tree which grows in California. [from New Latin]

**se|rene** /sɪˈriːn/ ADJ Someone or something that is **serene** is calm and quiet. ❑ *She looked as calm and serene as she always did.* ❑ *We sailed serenely down the river.* ● **se|rene|ly** ADV ❑ *I had a wonderful feeling of peace and serenity.* [from Latin]

**ser|geant** /sˈɑːrdʒənt/ (**sergeants**) ◼ N-COUNT; N-TITLE; N-VOC A **sergeant** is an officer of low rank in the army, marines, or air force. ❑ *A sergeant with four men came into view.* ◼ N-COUNT; N-TITLE; N-VOC A **sergeant** is a police officer with the rank immediately below a captain. ❑ *A police sergeant patrolling the area noticed the fire.* [from Old French]

**ser|geant ma|jor** (**sergeant majors**) also **sergeant-major** N-COUNT; N-TITLE; N-VOC A **sergeant major** is an officer of the middle rank in the army or the marines.

**se|rial** /sˈɪəriəl/ (**serials**) ◼ N-COUNT A **serial** is a story which is broadcast on television or radio or is published in a magazine or newspaper in a number of parts over a period of time. ❑ *This is one of television's most popular serials.* ◼ ADJ **Serial** killings or attacks are a series of killings or attacks committed by the same person. This person is known as a **serial** killer or attacker. ❑ *...serial murders.* [from New Latin]

**se|rial mu|sic** N-UNCOUNT **Serial music** is a type of music that uses a particular set of notes, usually twelve, and organizes them in a particular way. [TECHNICAL]

**se|ries** /sˈɪəriz/ (**series**) ◼ N-COUNT A **series** of things or events is a number of them that come one after the other. ❑ *There will be a series of meetings with political leaders.* ◼ N-COUNT A radio or television **series** is a set of programs of a particular kind which have the same title. ❑ *I love the TV series "Star Trek."* [from Latin]

**se|ries cir|cuit** (**series circuits**) N-COUNT A **series circuit** is an electrical circuit in which there is only one possible path that the electricity can follow. [TECHNICAL]

**se|ri|ous** /sˈɪəriəs/ ◼ ADJ **Serious** problems or situations are very bad and cause people to be worried or afraid. ❑ *Crime is a serious problem in Russian society.* ❑ *The government faces very serious difficulties.* ● **se|ri|ous|ly** ADV ❑ *This law could seriously damage my business.* ● **se|ri|ous|ness** N-UNCOUNT ❑ *They don't realize the seriousness of the crisis.* ◼ ADJ **Serious** matters are important and deserve careful thought. ❑ *I regard this as a serious matter.* ❑ *It is a question that deserves serious consideration.* ● **se|ri|ous|ly** ADV ❑ *The management will have to think seriously about their positions.* ◼ ADJ If you are **serious** about something, you are sincere about it. ❑ *You really are serious about this, aren't you?* ● **se|ri|ous|ly** ADV ❑ *Are you seriously jealous of Erica?* ● **se|ri|ous|ness** N-UNCOUNT ❑ *In all seriousness, what else can I do?* ◼ ADJ **Serious** people

are thoughtful and quiet, and do not laugh very often. ❑ *He's quite a serious person.* ● **se|ri|ous|ly** ADV ❑ *They spoke to me very seriously.* [from Late Latin]

**se|ri|ous|ly** /sˈɪəriəsli/ ◼ ADV You use **seriously** to indicate that you really mean what you say, or to ask someone if they really mean what they have said. ❑ *Seriously, I only watch TV in the evenings.* ❑ *"I followed him home," he said. "Seriously?"* ◼ → see also **serious** ◼ PHRASE If you **take** someone or something **seriously**, you believe that they are important and deserve attention. ❑ *It's hard to take them seriously in their pretty uniforms.* [from Late Latin]

**ser|mon** /sˈɜːrmən/ (**sermons**) N-COUNT A **sermon** is a talk on a religious or moral subject that is given by a member of the clergy as part of a religious service. ❑ *Cardinal Murphy will deliver the sermon on Sunday.* [from Old French]

**ser|pent** /sˈɜːrpənt/ (**serpents**) N-COUNT A **serpent** is a snake. [LITERARY] [from Old French]

**se|rum** /sˈɪərəm/ (**serums**) N-VAR A **serum** is a liquid that is injected into your blood to protect you against a poison or disease. ❑ *Is there an anti-cancer serum?* [from Latin]

**serv|ant** /sˈɜːrvənt/ (**servants**) ◼ N-COUNT A **servant** is someone who is employed to work at another person's home, for example, as a cleaner or a gardener. ❑ *It was a large Victorian family with several servants.* [from Old French] ◼ → see also **civil servant**

**serve** /sˈɜːrv/ (**serves, serving, served**) ◼ V-T If you **serve** your country, an organization, or a person, you do useful work for them. ❑ *This decision is unfair to soldiers who have served their country well.* ❑ *During the second world war he served with the army.* ❑ *They have both served on the school board.* ◼ V-T/V-I If something **serves as** a particular thing or **serves** a particular purpose, it performs a particular function, which is often not its intended function. ❑ *She showed me into the front room, which served as her office.* ❑ *I do not think an investigation would serve any useful purpose.* ◼ V-T If something **serves** people or an area, it provides them with something that they need. ❑ *There are thousands of small businesses which serve the community.* ◼ V-T/V-I When you **serve** food and drinks, you give people food and drinks. ❑ *Serve the cakes warm.* ❑ *Refrigerate until ready to serve.* ● **Serve up** means the same as **serve.** ❑ *It is no use serving up delicious meals if the kids won't eat them.* ◼ V-T/V-I Someone who **serves** customers in a store or a bar helps them and provides them with what they want to buy. ❑ *Maggie served me coffee and pie.* ◼ V-T If you **serve** something such as a prison sentence or an apprenticeship, you spend a period of time doing it. ❑ *Leo is serving a life sentence for murder.* ◼ V-T/V-I When you **serve** in games such as tennis and badminton, you throw up the ball or shuttlecock and hit it to start play. ❑ *She served again and eventually won the game.* ● **Serve** is also a noun. ❑ *His second serve hit the net.* ◼ → see also **serving** ◼ PHRASE If you say **it serves** someone **right** when something unpleasant happens to them, you mean that it is their own fault and you have no sympathy for them. ❑ *It serves her right for being so difficult.* [from Old French]

▸ **serve up** → see **serve 4**

**S**

**Word Partnership** Use *serve* with :

| | |
|---|---|
| N. | serve **a community**, serve **the public** ❶ ❸<br>serve **a purpose** ❷<br>serve **cake**, serve **food** ❹ |

**serv|er** /sɜrvər/ (**servers**) ❶ N-COUNT In computing, a **server** is part of a computer network which does a particular task, such as storing or processing information, for all or part of the network. [COMPUTING] ❷ N-COUNT A **server** is a person who works in a restaurant, serving people with food and drink. ❑ *A server came by with a tray of coffee cups.* [from Old French] → see **tennis, Internet**

**service**

❶ NOUN AND ADJECTIVE USES
❷ VERB USES
❸ PHRASES

❶ **ser|vice** /sɜrvɪs/ (**services**) ❶ N-COUNT A **service** is something that the public needs, such as transportation, communications facilities, hospitals, or energy supplies. ❑ *The postal service has been trying to cut costs.* ❷ N-COUNT A **service** is a job that an organization or business can do for you. ❑ *The hotel kitchen has a twenty-four hour service.* ❸ N-UNCOUNT The level or standard of **service** provided by an organization or company is the amount or quality of the work it can do for you. ❑ *We try to provide effective and efficient customer service.* ❹ N-UNCOUNT **Service** is the state or activity of working for a particular person or organization. ❑ *He's given a lifetime of service to athletics.* ❑ *Most employees had long service with the company.* ❺ N-COUNT **The services** are the army, the navy, the air force, and the marines. ❑ *Some of the money should be spent on training in the services.* ❻ N-UNCOUNT When you receive **service** in a restaurant, hotel, or store, an employee asks you what you want or gives you what you have ordered. ❑ *The service was fast and polite.* ❼ N-COUNT A **service** is a religious ceremony that takes place in a church or synagogue. ❑ *After the service, his body was taken to a cemetery.* ❽ N-COUNT If a vehicle or machine has a **service**, it is examined, adjusted, and cleaned so that it will keep working efficiently and safely. ❑ *The car needs a service.* [from Old French] ❾ → see also **civil service, community service** → see **industry, library**

❷ **ser|vice** /sɜrvɪs/ (**services, servicing, serviced**) V-T If you have a vehicle or machine **serviced**, you arrange for someone to examine, adjust, and clean it so that it will keep working efficiently and safely. ❑ *I have my car serviced at the local garage.* [from Old French]

❸ **ser|vice** /sɜrvɪs/ PHRASE If a piece of equipment or type of vehicle is **in service**, it is being used or is able to be used. If it is **out of service**, it is not being used, usually because it is not working properly. ❑ *Most of the planes should be back in service by the end of the week.* ❑ *The elevator was out of service so she took the stairs.* [from Old French]

**ser|vice|man** /sɜrvɪsmən/ (**servicemen**) N-COUNT A **serviceman** is a man who is in the army, navy, air force, or marines. ❑ *He was an American serviceman in Vietnam.*

**ser|vice pro|vid|er** (**service providers**) N-COUNT A **service provider** is a company that provides a service, especially an Internet service. [COMPUTING]

**serv|ing** /sɜrvɪŋ/ (**servings**) N-COUNT A **serving** is an amount of food that is given to one person at a meal. ❑ *How many servings do you want to prepare?* [from Old French]

**ses|sion** /sɛʃən/ (**sessions**) ❶ N-COUNT A **session** is a meeting or series of meetings of a court, legislature, or other official group. ❑ *After two late night sessions, they failed to reach agreement.* ❑ *The Arab League is meeting in emergency session today.* ❑ *Congress remained in session from September until December.* ❷ N-COUNT A **session** of a particular activity is a period of that activity. ❑ *The two leaders arrived for a photo session.* [from Latin]

**set**

❶ NOUN USES
❷ VERB AND ADJECTIVE USES

❶ **set** /sɛt/ (**sets**) ❶ N-COUNT A **set of** things is a number of things that belong together or that are thought of as a group. ❑ *There must be one set of laws for the whole country.* ❑ *The table and chairs are normally bought as a set.* ❑ *...a chess set.* ❷ N-COUNT In tennis, a **set** is one of the groups of six or more games that form part of a match. ❑ *Williams was leading 5 – 1 in the first set.* ❸ N-COUNT The **set** for a play, movie, or television show is the furniture and scenery that is on the stage when the play is being performed or in the studio where filming takes place. ❑ *From the moment he got on the set, he wanted to be a director.* ❑ *Across the street, the buildings look like stage sets.* ❹ N-COUNT A television **set** is a television. ❑ *Children spend too much time in front of the television set.* [from Old French] → see **drama, theater**

❷ **set** /sɛt/ (**sets, setting**)

The form **set** is used in the present tense and is the past tense and past participle of the verb.

❶ V-T If you **set** something somewhere, you put it there, especially in a careful or deliberate way. ❑ *He set the case carefully on the floor.* ❷ ADJ If something is **set** in a particular place or position, it is in that place or position. ❑ *The castle is set in 25 acres of park land.* ❸ ADJ If something is **set into** a surface, it is fixed there and does not stick out. ❑ *The man unlocked a gate set in a high wall.* ❹ V-T You can use **set** to say that a person or thing causes another person or thing to be in a particular condition or situation. For example, to **set** someone free means to cause them to be free. ❑ *His words set my mind wandering.* ❑ *Many vehicles were set on fire.* ❺ V-T When you **set** a clock or control, you adjust it to a particular point or level. ❑ *Set the volume as high as possible.* ❻ V-T If you **set** a date, price, goal, or level, you decide what it will be. ❑ *The conference chairman has set a deadline of noon tomorrow.* ❑ *A date will be set for a future meeting.* ❼ V-T If you **set** something such as a record, or an example, you do something that people will want to copy or try to achieve. ❑ *The new world record was set by Stephen Jones of Great Britain.* ❽ V-T If someone **sets** you a task or aim or if you **set** yourself a task or goal, you need to succeed in doing it. ❑ *I have to plan my work and set myself clear targets.* **9** ADJ You use **set** to describe something which is fixed and cannot be changed. ❑ *I wrote music during a set period every morning.* **10** ADJ If a play, movie, or story is **set** in a particular place or period of time, the events in it take place in that place or period. ❑ *The play is set in a small Midwestern town.* **11** ADJ If you are **set to** do something, you are ready to do it or are likely to do it. If something is **set to** happen, it is about to happen or likely to happen. ❑ *Roberto Baggio was set to become one of the greatest players of all time.* **12** ADJ If you are **set on** something, you are strongly determined to do or have it. ❑ *She was set on going to an all-girls school.* **13** V-I When something such as jelly, glue, or cement **sets**, it becomes firm or hard. ❑ *You can add fruit to these desserts as they begin to set.* **14** V-I When the sun **sets**, it goes below the horizon. ❑ *They watched the sun set behind the distant hills.* **15** → see also **setting** **16** PHRASE If someone **sets the scene** or **sets the stage for** an event to take place, they make preparations so that it can take place. ❑ *Today's opening will set the scene for next week's meeting of world leaders.* [from Old English] **17** to **set fire to** something → see **fire** **18** to **set foot** somewhere → see **foot** **19** to **set sail** → see **sail** → see also **sit**

▶ **set aside** **1** PHR-VERB If you **set** something **aside for** a special use or purpose, you keep it available for that use or purpose. ❑ *Try to set aside time each day to relax.* **2** PHR-VERB If you **set aside** a belief, principle, or feeling, you decide that you will not be influenced by it. ❑ *At this dinner party, politics are set aside.*

▶ **set back** **1** PHR-VERB If something **sets** you **back** or **sets back** a project or plan, it causes a delay. ❑ *We have been set so far back that I'm not sure how long it will take for us to catch up.* **2** PHR-VERB If something **sets** you **back** a certain amount of money, it costs you that much money. [INFORMAL] ❑ *A bottle of olive oil could set you back $7.* **3** → see also **setback**

▶ **set down** PHR-VERB If a committee or organization **sets down** rules for doing something, it decides what they should be and officially records them. ❑ *I like to make suggestions rather than setting down laws.*

▶ **set in** PHR-VERB If something unpleasant **sets in**, it begins and seems likely to continue or develop. ❑ *Winter is setting in and the population is facing food shortages.*

▶ **set off** **1** PHR-VERB When you **set off**, you start a journey. ❑ *Nick set off for his farmhouse in Connecticut.* **2** PHR-VERB If something **sets off** something such as an alarm or a bomb, it makes it start working so that the alarm rings or the bomb explodes. ❑ *Any escape sets off the alarm.*

▶ **set out** **1** PHR-VERB When you **set out**, you start a journey. ❑ *When setting out on a long walk, always wear suitable shoes.* **2** PHR-VERB If you **set out to** do something, you start trying to do it. ❑ *He did what he set out to do.* **3** PHR-VERB If you **set** things **out**, you arrange or display them somewhere. ❑ *Set out the cakes attractively.* **4** PHR-VERB If you **set out** a number of facts, beliefs, or arguments, you explain them in writing or speech in a clear, organized way. ❑ *He has written a letter to The New York Times setting out his views.*

▶ **set up** **1** PHR-VERB If you **set** something **up**, you create or arrange it. ❑ *The two sides agreed to set up an investigation.* ❑ *We set up meetings about issues of interest to women.* ● **setting up** N-UNCOUNT ❑ *The government announced the setting up of a special fund.* **2** PHR-VERB If you **set up** a temporary structure, you place it or build it somewhere. ❑ *Brian set up a tent on the lawn.* **3** PHR-VERB If you **set up** somewhere or **set yourself up** somewhere, you establish yourself in a new business or new area. ❑ *The mayor offered to help companies setting up in lower Manhattan.* **4** → see also **setup**

**set|back** /sɛtbæk/ (**setbacks**) N-COUNT A **setback** is an event that delays your progress or reverses some of the progress that you have made. ❑ *He suffered a serious setback in his career.*

**set|tee** /sɛti/ (**settees**) N-COUNT A **settee** is a long comfortable seat with a back and arms, which two or more people can sit on.

**set|ting** /sɛtɪŋ/ (**settings**) **1** N-COUNT A particular **setting** is a particular place or type of surroundings where something is or takes place. ❑ *Rome is the perfect setting for romance.* **2** N-COUNT A **setting** is one of the positions to which the controls of a device such as a stove or heater can be adjusted. ❑ *Bake the fish on a high setting.* [from Old English]

**set|tle** /sɛtᵊl/ (**settles, settling, settled**) **1** V-T If people **settle** an argument or problem, or if something **settles** it, they solve it by making a decision about who is right or about what to do. ❑ *They agreed to try again to settle the dispute.* **2** V-T/V-I If you **settle** a bill or debt, you pay the amount that you owe. ❑ *I settled the bill for my coffee and left.* **3** V-T If something **is settled**, it has all been decided and arranged. ❑ *We feel the matter is now settled.* **4** V-I When people **settle** a place or in a place, they start living there permanently. ❑ *He visited Paris and eventually settled there.* **5** V-T/V-I If you **settle yourself** somewhere or **settle** somewhere, you sit down or make yourself comfortable. ❑ *Albert settled himself on the sofa.* **6** V-I If something **settles**, it sinks slowly down and becomes still. ❑ *A fly settled on the wall.* ❑ *The fog blows over the mountains and settles in the valley.* [from Old English] **7** → see also **settled** **8** **when the dust settles** → see **dust** **9** to **settle a score** → see **score**

▶ **settle down** **1** PHR-VERB When someone **settles down**, they start living a quiet life in one place, especially when they get married or buy a house. ❑ *One day I'll settle down and have a family.* **2** PHR-VERB If a situation or a person that has been going through a lot of problems or changes **settles down**, they become calm. ❑ *The situation in Europe will soon settle down.* **3** PHR-VERB If you **settle down to** do something or **to** something, you prepare to do it and concentrate on it. ❑ *He settled down to listen to the music.*

▶ **settle for** PHR-VERB If you **settle for** something, you choose or accept it, especially when it is not what you really want but there is nothing else available. ❑ *Virginia would never settle for anything less than perfection.*

▶ **settle in** PHR-VERB If you **settle in**, you become used to living in a new place, doing a new job, or going to a new school. ❑ *I enjoyed school once I settled in.*

▶ **settle on** PHR-VERB If you **settle on** a particular

S

thing, you choose it after considering other possible choices. ❑ *I finally settled on a Mercedes.*
▶ **settle up** PHR-VERB When you **settle up**, you pay a bill or a debt. ❑ *I'll have to settle up before I leave.*

### Word Partnership    Use *settle* with :

| | |
|---|---|
| N. | settle **differences**, settle **things** ■ |
| | settle **a dispute**, settle **a matter** ■ ◨ |
| V. | **agree to** settle, **decide to** settle ■ ◨ |

**set|tled** /sɛtᵊld/ ■ ADJ If you have a **settled** way of life, you stay in one place, in one job, or with one person, rather than moving around or changing. ❑ *He decided to lead a more settled life.* ◨ ADJ A **settled** situation or system stays the same all the time. ❑ *The weather will be more settled tomorrow.* [from Old English]

**set|tle|ment** /sɛtᵊlmənt/ (**settlements**) ■ N-COUNT A **settlement** is an official agreement between two sides who were involved in a conflict or argument. ❑ *Officials are hoping for a peaceful settlement of the crisis.* ◨ N-COUNT A **settlement** is a place where people have come to live and have built homes. ❑ *The village is a settlement of just fifty houses.* [from Old English]

**set|tler** /sɛtlər, sɛtᵊl-/ (**settlers**) N-COUNT **Settlers** are people who go to live in a new country. ❑ *...the early settlers in North America.* [from Old English]

**set|up** /sɛtʌp/ (**setups**) also set-up N-COUNT A particular **setup** is a particular system or way of organizing something. [INFORMAL] ❑ *It appears to be the ideal domestic setup.*

**sev|en** /sɛvᵊn/ (**sevens**) NUM **Seven** is the number 7. ❑ *Sarah and Ella have been friends for seven years.* [from Old English]

### Word Link    teen ≈ plus ten, from 13-19 : eighteen, seventeen, teenager

**sev|en|teen** /sɛvᵊntin/ (**seventeens**) NUM **Seventeen** is the number 17. ❑ *Jenny is seventeen years old.* [from Old English]

**sev|en|teenth** /sɛvᵊntinθ/ (**seventeenths**) ORD The **seventeenth** item in a series is the one that you count as number seventeen. ❑ *She got the job just after her seventeenth birthday.* [from Old English]

**sev|enth** /sɛvᵊnθ/ (**sevenths**) ■ ORD The **seventh** item in a series is the one that you count as number seven. ❑ *I was the seventh child in the family.* ◨ N-COUNT A **seventh** is one of seven equal parts of something. ❑ *A million people died, a seventh of the population.* [from Old English]

**sev|en|ti|eth** /sɛvᵊntiəθ/ (**seventieths**) ORD The **seventieth** item in a series is the one that you count as number seventy. ❑ *It was my grandmother's seventieth birthday last week.* [from Old English]

**sev|en|ty** /sɛvᵊnti/ (**seventies**) ■ NUM **Seventy** is the number 70. ❑ *Seventy people were killed in the fire.* ◨ N-PLURAL The **seventies** is the decade between 1970 and 1979. ❑ *In the early Seventies, he wanted to direct.* [from Old English]

**sev|er** /sɛvər/ (**severs, severing, severed**) ■ V-T To **sever** something means to cut completely through it or to cut it completely off. [FORMAL] ❑ *Richardson severed his foot in a motorcycle accident.*

◨ V-T If you **sever** a relationship or connection that you have with someone, you end it suddenly and completely. [FORMAL] ❑ *She severed her ties with her family.* [from Old French]

**sev|er|al** /sɛvrəl/ DET **Several** is used to refer to a number of people or things that is not large but is greater than two. ❑ *I lived two doors away from this family for several years.* ❑ *There were several blue plastic boxes under the window.* ● **Several** is also a quantifier. ❑ *He was with his sons, several of whom work in the business with him.* ● **Several** is also a pronoun. ❑ *Sometimes several different treatments have to be tried.* [from Medieval Latin]

**se|vere** /sɪvɪər/ (**severer, severest**) ■ ADJ You use **severe** to indicate that something bad or undesirable is great or intense. ❑ *The business has severe financial problems.* ● **se|vere|ly** ADV ❑ *An aircraft crashed on the runway and was severely damaged.* ● **se|ver|ity** /sɪvɛrɪti/ N-UNCOUNT ❑ *Not everyone agrees about the severity of the problem.* ◨ ADJ **Severe** punishments or criticisms are very strong or harsh. ❑ *A severe sentence is necessary for such a crime.* ● **se|vere|ly** ADV ❑ *They want to change the law and punish dangerous drivers more severely.* ● **se|ver|ity** N-UNCOUNT ❑ *They were surprised by the severity of the criticism.* [from Latin]

### Thesaurus    severe    Also look up :

| | |
|---|---|
| ADJ. | critical, extreme, intense, tough ■ ◨ |

### Word Partnership    Use *severe* with :

| | |
|---|---|
| N. | severe **consequences**, severe **depression**, severe **disease/illness**, severe **drought**, severe **flooding**, severe **injuries**, severe **pain**, severe **problem**, severe **symptoms**, severe **weather** ■ severe **penalty**, severe **punishment** ◨ |
| ADV. | **less/more/most** severe, **very** severe ■ ◨ |

**sew** /soʊ/ (**sews, sewing, sewed, sewn**) V-T/V-I When you **sew** something such as clothes, you make it or repair it by joining pieces of cloth together by passing thread through them with a needle. ❑ *She sewed the dresses on the sewing machine.* ❑ *Anyone can sew on a button.* ● **sew|ing** N-UNCOUNT ❑ *Her mother always did all the sewing.* [from Old English]
→ see **quilt**

**sew|age** /suɪdʒ/ N-UNCOUNT **Sewage** is waste matter such as feces or dirty water from homes and factories, which flows away through sewers. ❑ *...treatment of raw sewage.*
→ see **pollution**

**sew|age treat|ment plant** (**sewage treatment plants**) N-COUNT A **sewage treatment plant** is a factory that removes waste materials from water that comes from sewers and drains.

**sew|er** /suər/ (**sewers**) N-COUNT A **sewer** is a large underground channel that carries waste matter and rain water away. ❑ *...the city's sewer system.* [from Old French]

**sew|ing** /soʊɪŋ/ N-UNCOUNT **Sewing** is clothes or other things that are being sewn. ❑ *We all sat down in front of the fire with our sewing.* [from Old English]

**sewn** /soʊn/ **Sewn** is the past participle of **sew**. [from Old English]

**sex** /sɛks/ (**sexes, sexing, sexed**) **1** N-COUNT The two **sexes** are the two groups, male and female, into which people and animals are divided. ❑ *This movie appeals to both sexes.* **2** → see also **opposite sex 3** N-COUNT The **sex** of a person or animal is their characteristic of being either male or female. ❑ *We can identify the sex of your unborn baby.* **4** N-UNCOUNT **Sex** is the physical activity by which people can produce children. ❑ *He was very open in his attitudes about sex.* **5** PHRASE If two people **have sex**, they perform the act of sex. [from Latin]

**sex cell** (**sex cells**) N-COUNT **Sex cells** are the two types of male and female cells that join together to make a new creature.

**sex chro|mo|some** (**sex chromosomes**) N-COUNT **Sex chromosomes** are the chromosomes that carry the genes which determine whether an individual will be male or female. [TECHNICAL]

**sex|ist** /sɛksɪst/ (**sexists**) ADJ If you describe people or their behavior as **sexist**, you disapprove of them because they show prejudice and discrimination against the members of one sex, usually women. ❑ *Old-fashioned sexist attitudes are still common.* ● A **sexist** is someone with sexist views or behavior. ❑ *You know I'm not a sexist.* ● **sex|ism** /sɛksɪzəm/ N-UNCOUNT ❑ *Students here can live in a community free of sexism.* [from Latin]

**sex of|fend|er** (**sex offenders**) N-COUNT A **sex offender** is a person who has been found guilty of a sexual crime such as rape or sexual assault.

**sex|ual** /sɛkʃuəl/ **1** ADJ **Sexual** feelings or activities are connected with the act of sex or with people's desire for sex. ❑ *The use of sexual images in advertising is not new.* **2** ADJ **Sexual** means relating to the differences between male and female people. ❑ *...sexual discrimination.* **3** ADJ **Sexual** means relating to the biological process by which people and animals produce young. ❑ *Girls usually reach sexual maturity earlier than boys.* ● **sex|ual|ly** ADV ❑ *...organisms that reproduce sexually.* [from Late Latin]

**sex|ual inter|course** N-UNCOUNT **Sexual intercourse** is the physical act of sex between two people. [FORMAL]

**sexu|al|ity** /sɛkʃuælɪti/ **1** N-UNCOUNT A person's **sexuality** is their sexual feelings. ❑ *The program focuses on the scientific aspects of sexuality.* **2** N-UNCOUNT You can refer to a person's **sexuality** when you are talking about whether they are sexually attracted to people of the same sex or a different sex. ❑ *...information about sexuality, reproduction, and the human body.* [from Late Latin]

**sex|ual|ly trans|mit|ted dis|ease** (**sexually transmitted diseases**) N-COUNT A **sexually transmitted disease** is a disease such as syphilis or herpes that can be passed from one person to another as a result of sexual activity. The abbreviation **STD** is also used.

**sex|ual re|pro|duc|tion** N-UNCOUNT **Sexual reproduction** is the creation of new people, animals, or plants as a result of sexual activity.

**sexy** /sɛksi/ (**sexier, sexiest**) ADJ You can describe people and things as **sexy** if you think they are sexually exciting or sexually attractive. ❑ *She is the sexiest woman I have ever seen.* [from Latin]

**shab|by** /ʃæbi/ (**shabbier, shabbiest**) ADJ **Shabby** things or places look old and in bad condition. ❑ *His clothes were old and shabby.* [from Old English]

**shack** /ʃæk/ (**shacks**) N-COUNT A **shack** is a simple hut built from tin, wood, or other materials.

**shade** /ʃeɪd/ (**shades, shading, shaded**) **1** N-COUNT A **shade of** a particular color is one of its different forms. ❑ *The sky was a heavy shade of gray.* ❑ *The walls were painted in two shades of green.* **2** N-UNCOUNT **Shade** is an area of darkness under or next to an object such as a tree, where sunlight does not reach. ❑ *Temperatures in the shade can reach eighty degrees Fahrenheit here.* ❑ *Alexis was reading in the shade of a high cliff.* **3** V-T If a place **is shaded** by something, that thing prevents light from falling on it. ❑ *The beach was shaded by palm trees.* **4** N-UNCOUNT **Shade** is darkness or shadows as they are shown in a picture. ❑ *...Rembrandt's skillful use of light and shade.* **5** N-COUNT The **shades of** something abstract are its many, slightly different forms. ❑ *In this poem we find many shades of meaning.* **6** N-COUNT A **shade** is a piece of stiff cloth or heavy paper that you can pull down over a window as a covering. ❑ *Nancy left the shades down.* **7** N-COUNT A **shade** is color with black added to it. [from Old English]

**shad|ow** /ʃædoʊ/ (**shadows, shadowing, shadowed**) **1** N-COUNT A **shadow** is a dark shape on a surface that is made when something stands between a light and the surface. ❑ *A tree threw its shadow over the pool.* **2** N-UNCOUNT **Shadow** is darkness in a place caused by something preventing light from reaching it. ❑ *Most of the lake was in shadow.* **3** V-T If something **shadows** a thing or place, it covers it with a shadow. ❑ *The hat shadowed her face.* **4** V-T If someone **shadows** you, they follow you very closely wherever you go. ❑ *The president is shadowed by bodyguards.* [from Old English]

**shad|owy** /ʃædoʊi/ **1** ADJ A **shadowy** place is dark or full of shadows. ❑ *I watched him from a shadowy corner.* **2** ADJ You describe activities and people as **shadowy** when very little is known about them. ❑ *...the shadowy world of spies.* [from Old English]

**shad|ow zone** (**shadow zones**) N-COUNT A **shadow zone** is an area on the Earth's surface where seismic waves from an earthquake cannot be detected because they are unable to pass through the Earth's core. [TECHNICAL]

**shady** /ʃeɪdi/ (**shadier, shadiest**) **1** ADJ A **shady** place is pleasant because it is sheltered from bright sunlight. ❑ *Place the pot in a shady corner of the garden.* **2** ADJ You can describe people or activities as **shady** when you think that they might be dishonest or illegal. ❑ *In the 1990s, the company was involved in some shady deals.* [from Old English]

**shaft** /ʃæft/ (**shafts**) **1** N-COUNT A **shaft** is a long vertical passage, for example, for an elevator. ❑ *The fire began in an elevator shaft.* **2** N-COUNT In a machine, a **shaft** is a rod that turns around continually in order to transfer movement in the machine. ❑ *...a drive shaft.* **3** N-COUNT A **shaft of** light is a beam of light, for example, sunlight shining through an opening. ❑ *A shaft of sunlight fell through the doorway.* [from Old English]

S

**shag|gy** /ʃægi/ (**shaggier, shaggiest**) ADJ
**Shaggy** hair or fur is long and messy. ❏ *Tim still has shaggy hair.* [from Old English]

**shake** /ʃeɪk/ (**shakes, shaking, shook, shaken**)
**1** V-T If you **shake** something or someone, you hold them and move them quickly backward and forward or up and down. ❏ *The nurse took the thermometer and shook it.* ● **Shake** is also a noun. ❏ *She picked up the bag and gave it a shake.* **2** V-T If you **shake** your **head**, you turn it from side to side in order to say "no" or to show disbelief or sadness. ❏ *Kathryn shook her head wearily.* ● **Shake** is also a noun. ❏ *"The trees are dying," said Palmer, with a sad shake of his head.* **3** V-T/V-I If a force **shakes** something, or if something **shakes**, it moves from side to side or up and down with quick, small, but sometimes violent movements. ❏ *An explosion shook buildings several miles away.* **4** V-T If an event or a piece of news **shakes** you, it makes you feel upset and unable to think calmly. ❏ *The news of Tandy's escape shook them all.* **5** PHRASE If you **shake hands with** someone, you take their right hand in your own for a few moments, often moving it up and down slightly, when you are saying hello or goodbye to them, congratulating them, or agreeing on something. You can also say that two people **shake hands**. ❏ *Michael shook hands with Burke.* [from Old English]
▸ **shake off** PHR-VERB If you **shake off** someone or something that you do not want, you manage to get rid of them. ❏ *Jimmy still could not shake off his doubts.* ❏ *I could not shake him off.*
▸ **shake out** PHR-VERB If you wonder how something will **shake out**, you wonder how it will develop and what the outcome will be. ❏ *We don't know how this situation will shake out.*

**shake|up** /ʃeɪkʌp/ (**shakeups**) N-COUNT
A **shakeup** is a major set of changes in an organization or a system. ❏ *A spy scandal has led to a shakeup in the government.*

**shaky** /ʃeɪki/ (**shakier, shakiest**) **1** ADJ If you describe a situation as **shaky**, you mean that it is weak or unstable, and seems unlikely to last long or be successful. ❏ *The president's position became increasingly shaky.* **2** ADJ If your body or your voice is **shaky**, you cannot control it properly and it shakes, for example, because you are ill or nervous. ❏ *Even small operations can leave you feeling a bit shaky.* ● **shak|ily** ADV ❏ *"I'm OK," she said shakily.* [from Old English]

**shall** /ʃəl, STRONG ʃæl/

Shall is a modal verb. It is used with the base form of a verb.

**1** MODAL You use **shall** with "I" and "we" in questions in order to make offers or suggestions, or to ask for advice. ❏ *Shall I get the keys?* ❏ *Well, shall we go?* ❏ *Let's go for a walk, shall we?* **2** MODAL You use **shall**, usually with "I" and "we," when you are referring to something that you intend to do, or when you are referring to something that you are sure will happen to you in the future. [FORMAL] ❏ *We shall be landing in Paris in sixteen minutes.* ❏ *I shall know more next month.* **3** MODAL You use **shall** to indicate that something must happen, usually because of a rule or law. You use **shall not** to indicate that something must not happen. ❏ *The president shall hold office for five years.* [from Old English]

**Usage** shall *and* will

*Shall* is mainly used in the most formal writing and speech; in everyday English, use *will*. *We shall overcome all obstacles to achieve victory. We will be home later.*

**shal|low** /ʃæloʊ/ (**shallower, shallowest**)
**1** ADJ A **shallow** container, hole, or area of water measures only a short distance from the top to the bottom. ❏ *The water is quite shallow.* **2** ADJ If you describe a person, piece of work, or idea as **shallow**, you disapprove of them because they do not show or involve any serious or careful thought. ❏ *I think he is shallow and dishonest.* **3** ADJ If your breathing is **shallow**, you take only a very small amount of air into your lungs at each breath. ❏ *She could hear her own shallow breathing.* [from Old English]

**shal|lows** /ʃæloʊz/ N-PLURAL The **shallows** are the shallow part of an area of water. ❏ *At nightfall more fish come into the shallows.* [from Old English]

**sham** /ʃæm/ (**shams**) N-COUNT Something that is a **sham** is not real or is not really what it seems to be. ❏ *Their marriage was a sham.* [from Northern English]

**sham|bles** /ʃæmbᵊlz/ N-SING If a place, event, or situation is a **shambles** or is **in a shambles**, everything is in disorder. ❏ *Inside the house was a complete shambles.* [from Old English]

**shame** /ʃeɪm/ (**shames, shaming, shamed**)
**1** N-UNCOUNT **Shame** is an uncomfortable feeling that you get when you have done something wrong or embarrassing, or when someone close to you has. ❏ *She felt a deep sense of shame.* ❏ *At first, to my shame, I thought it was a joke.* **2** N-UNCOUNT If someone brings **shame on** you, they make other people lose their respect for them. ❏ *I don't want to bring shame on the family name.* **3** V-T If something **shames** you, it causes you to feel shame. ❏ *Her son's behavior shamed her.* **4** V-T If you **shame** someone **into** doing something, you force them to do it by making them feel ashamed not to. ❏ *He would not let neighbors shame him into silence.* **5** N-SING If you say that something is a **shame**, you are expressing your regret about it and indicating that you wish it had happened differently. ❏ *What a shame the weather is so bad.* [from Old English]
→ see **emotion**

**Word Partnership** Use *shame* with :

| | |
|---|---|
| V. | **experience** shame, **feel** shame **1** |
| N. | **feelings of** shame, **sense of** shame **1** |

**shame|ful** /ʃeɪmfəl/ ADJ If you describe a person's action or attitude as **shameful**, you think that it is so bad that the person ought to be ashamed. ❏ *They said it was shameful that a hospital had been attacked.* ● **shame|ful|ly** ADV ❏ *Shamefully, officials did not do anything about it.* [from Old English]

**shame|less** /ʃeɪmlɪs/ ADJ If you describe someone as **shameless**, you mean that they should be ashamed of their behavior, which is unacceptable to other people. ❏ *He is totally shameless about telling lies.* ● **shame|less|ly** ADV ❏ *Shamelessly, we opened their letters and read them.* [from Old English]

**sham|poo** /ʃæmpu/ (**shampoos, shampooing,**

## Picture Dictionary   shapes

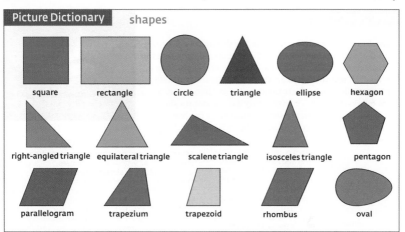

square    rectangle    circle    triangle    ellipse    hexagon

right-angled triangle    equilateral triangle    scalene triangle    isosceles triangle    pentagon

parallelogram    trapezium    trapezoid    rhombus    oval

shampooed) **1** N-VAR **Shampoo** is a soapy liquid that you use for washing your hair. ❑ ...*a bottle of shampoo.* **2** V-T When you **shampoo** your hair, you wash it using shampoo. ❑ *Shampoo your hair and dry it.* [from Hindi]

**shan't** /ʃænt/ **Shan't** is the usual spoken form of "shall not."

**shape** /ʃeɪp/ (**shapes, shaping, shaped**)
**1** N-COUNT The **shape of** an object, a person, or an area is the appearance of their outside edges or surfaces. ❑ *Each mirror can be designed to almost any shape or size.* ❑ *They sold little pens in the shape of baseball bats.* ❑ *We had sofas and chairs of different shapes and colors.* **2** N-COUNT A **shape** is a space enclosed by an outline, for example, a circle, a square, or a triangle. ❑ *Imagine a sort of a heart shape.* **3** N-SING The **shape of** something that is planned or organized is its structure and character. ❑ *The article outlines the shape of the changes we are planning.* **4** V-T Someone or something that **shapes** a situation or an activity has a very great influence on the way it develops. ❑ *Our families shape our lives and make us what we are.* **5** V-T If you **shape** an object, you give it a particular shape, using your hands or a tool. ❑ *Shape the mixture into 24 meatballs.* **6** → see also **shaped** **7** PHRASE If someone or something is **in shape**, or **in good shape**, they are in a good state of health or in a good condition. If they are **in bad shape**, they are in a bad state of health or in a bad condition. ❑ *He was in better shape than many young men.* **8** PHRASE If you are **out of shape**, you are unhealthy and unable to do a lot of physical activity without getting tired. ❑ *I weighed 245 pounds and was out of shape.* [from Old English]
→ see Picture Dictionary: **shape**
→ see **circle, mathematics**

▶ **shape up** PHR-VERB If something **is shaping up**, it is starting to develop or seems likely to happen. ❑ *A real battle is shaping up for tonight.* ❑ *The accident is already shaping up as a major disaster.*

**shaped** /ʃeɪpt/ ADJ Something that is **shaped** like a particular object or in a particular way has the shape of that object or a shape of that type. ❑ *The perfume was in a bottle shaped like a flower.* ❑ *...large heart-shaped leaves.* [from Old English]

**share** /ʃɛər/ (**shares, sharing, shared**)
**1** N-COUNT A company's **shares** are the many equal parts into which its ownership is divided. Shares can be bought by people as an investment. [BUSINESS] ❑ *People in China want to buy shares in new businesses.* **2** V-RECIP If you **share** something **with** another person, you both have it, use it, do it, or experience it. ❑ *He shared his food with the family.* ❑ *Two Americans will share this year's Nobel Prize for Medicine.* **3** N-COUNT If you have or do your **share of** something, you have or do an amount that seems reasonable to you, or to other people. ❑ *Women must receive their fair share of job training.* [from Old English] **4** → see also **lion's share**
▶ **share out** PHR-VERB If you **share out** an amount of something, you give each person in a group an equal or fair part of it.

**share|holder** /ʃɛərhoʊldər/ (**shareholders**)
N-COUNT A **shareholder** is a person who owns shares in a company. [BUSINESS] ❑ *...a shareholders' meeting.*

**shark** /ʃɑrk/ (**sharks**)
N-COUNT A **shark** is a very large fish. Some sharks have very sharp teeth and may attack people.
→ see Word Web: **shark**

shark

**sharp** /ʃɑrp/ (**sharps, sharper, sharpest**) **1** ADJ A

S

## Word Web    shark

**Sharks** are different from other **fish**. The **skeleton** of a shark is made of **cartilage**, not bone. The flexibility of cartilage allows this **predator** to maneuver around its **prey** easily. Sharks also have several gill **slits** with no flap covering them. Its **scales** are also much smaller and harder than fish scales. And its teeth are special too. Sharks grow new teeth when they lose old ones. It's almost impossible to escape from a shark. Some of them can swim up to 44 miles per hour. But sharks only kill 50 to 75 people each year worldwide.

sharp

**sharp** point or edge is very thin and can cut through things very easily. ❑ *With a sharp knife, cut the skin off the chicken breast.* **2** ADJ A **sharp** bend or turn is one that changes direction suddenly. ❑ *I came to a sharp bend in the road to the left.* ● **Sharp** is also an adverb. ❑ *Do not cross the bridge but turn sharp left instead.* ● **sharp|ly** ADV ❑ *Room nine was at the end of the hall where it turned sharply to the right.* **3** ADJ If you describe someone as **sharp**, you are praising them because they are quick to notice, hear, understand, or react to things. ❑ *He is very sharp, a quick thinker.* ● **sharp|ness** N-UNCOUNT ❑ *I liked their sharpness of mind.* **4** ADJ If someone says something in a **sharp** way, they say it suddenly and rather firmly or angrily, for example, because they are warning or criticizing you. ❑ *His sharp reply clearly surprised her.* ● **sharp|ly** ADV ❑ *"You knew," she said sharply, "and you didn't tell me?"* ● **sharp|ness** N-UNCOUNT ❑ *Malone was surprised at the sharpness in his voice.* **5** ADJ A **sharp** change, movement, or feeling occurs suddenly, and is great in amount, force, or degree. ❑ *There's been a sharp rise in the rate of inflation.* ● **sharp|ly** ADV ❑ *Unemployment rose sharply last year.* **6** ADJ A **sharp** difference, image, or sound is very easy to see, hear, or distinguish. ❑ *There are sharp differences between the two governments.* ❑ *All the footprints are quite sharp and clear.* ● **sharp|ly** ADV ❑ *Opinions on this subject are sharply divided.* ● **sharp|ness** N-UNCOUNT ❑ *They were amazed at the sharpness of the first picture.* **7** ADJ A **sharp** taste or smell is rather strong or bitter, but is often also clear and fresh. ❑ *The apple tasted sharp, yet sweet.* **8** ADV **Sharp** is used after stating a particular time to show that something happens at exactly the time stated. ❑ *She unlocked the store at 8:00 sharp this morning.* **9** N-COUNT **Sharp** is used after a letter representing a musical note to show that the note should be played or sung half a tone higher. **Sharp** is often represented by the symbol ♯. ❑ *The viola played a soft F sharp.* [from Old English]

## Word Partnership    Use *sharp* with :

N.  sharp **edge**, sharp **point**, sharp **teeth** **1**
    sharp **eyes**, sharp **mind** **3**
    sharp **criticism** **4**
    sharp **decline**, sharp **increase**,
    sharp **pain** **5**
    sharp **contrast** **6**
ADV.  **very** sharp **1** – **7**

**sharp|en** /ˈʃɑrpən/ (**sharpens, sharpening, sharpened**) **1** V-T/V-I If your senses, understanding, or skills **sharpen** or are **sharpened**, you become better at noticing things, thinking, or doing something. ❑ *Her look sharpened, as if she had seen something unusual.* ❑ *To prepare for the test, students are sharpening their writing skills.* **2** V-T If you **sharpen** an object, you make its edge very thin or you make its end pointed. ❑ *He started to sharpen his knife.* [from Old English]

**sharp-tongued** ADJ If you describe someone as **sharp-tongued**, you are being critical of them for speaking in a way which is unkind though often clever. [DISAPPROVAL] ❑ *Julia was a tough sharp-tongued woman.*

**shat|ter** /ˈʃætər/ (**shatters, shattering, shattered**) **1** V-T/V-I If something **shatters** or **is shattered**, it breaks into a lot of small pieces. ❑ *Safety glass won't shatter if it's broken.* ❑ *The car shattered into a thousand burning pieces.* ● **shat|ter|ing** N-UNCOUNT ❑ *...the shattering of glass.* **2** V-T If something **shatters** your dreams, hopes, or beliefs, it completely destroys them. ❑ *Just one incident can shatter the trust of the people.* ❑ *Our dreams were shattered by the news.* **3** V-T If someone **is shattered** by an event, it shocks and upsets them very much. ❑ *He was shattered by his son's death.* ● **shat|ter|ing** ADJ ❑ *Yesterday's decision was shattering.* **4** → see also **shattered**
→ see **crash, glass**

**shat|tered** /ˈʃætərd/ ADJ If you are **shattered**, you are extremely shocked and upset. ❑ *I was shattered to hear the news.*

**shave** /ʃeɪv/ (**shaves, shaving, shaved**) **1** V-T/V-I To **shave** means to remove hair from your face or body using a razor or shaver. ❑ *He took a bath and shaved.* ❑ *Many women shave their legs.* ● **Shave** is also a noun. ❑ *He never seemed to need a shave.* ● **shav|ing** N-UNCOUNT ❑ *We sell a range of shaving products.* **2** V-T If you **shave off** part of a piece of wood or other material, you cut very thin pieces from it. ❑ *I put the log on the ground and shaved off the bark.* [from Old English]
**3** → see also **shaving**

**shav|er** /ˈʃeɪvər/ (**shavers**) N-COUNT A **shaver** is an electric device, used for shaving hair from the face and body. ❑ *...men's electric shavers.* [from Old English]

**shav|ing** /ˈʃeɪvɪŋ/ (**shavings**) **1** N-COUNT **Shavings** are small very thin pieces of wood or other material which have been cut from a larger piece. ❑ *The floor was covered with wood shavings.* [from Old English] **2** → see also **shave**

S

**shawl** /ʃɔl/ (**shawls**) N-COUNT A **shawl** is a large piece of woolen cloth which a woman wears over her shoulders or head, or which is wrapped around a baby to keep it warm. [from Persian]
→ see **clothing**

**she** /ʃi, STRONG ʃi/

> **She** is a third person singular pronoun. **She** is used as the subject of a verb.

PRON You use **she** to refer to a woman, girl, or female animal who has already been mentioned or whose identity is clear. ❑ *When Ann arrived home she found Brian watching TV.* ❑ *She's seventeen years old.* [from Old English]

**shear** /ʃɪər/ (**shears, shearing, sheared, sheared** or **shorn**) ◼ V-T To **shear** a sheep means to cut its wool off. ❑ *Competitors have six minutes to shear four sheep.* ● **shearing** N-UNCOUNT ❑ *There's a display of sheep shearing tomorrow.* ◼ N-PLURAL A pair of **shears** is a garden tool like a very large pair of scissors. ❑ *Trim the grass with shears.* [from Old English]

**sheath** /ʃiθ/ (**sheaths**) N-COUNT A **sheath** is a covering for the blade of a knife. [from Old English]

**shed** /ʃɛd/ (**sheds, shedding**)

> The form **shed** is used in the present tense and in the past tense and past participle of the verb.

◼ N-COUNT A **shed** is a small building that is used for storing things such as garden tools. ❑ *It's in the garden shed.* ◼ V-T When a tree **sheds** its leaves, its leaves fall off in the fall. When an animal **sheds** hair or skin, some of its hair or skin drops off. ❑ *The trees were beginning to shed their leaves.* ◼ V-T To **shed** something means to get rid of it. [FORMAL] ❑ *The firm is going to shed 700 jobs.* ◼ V-T If you **shed** tears, you cry. ❑ *They will shed a few tears at their daughter's wedding.* ◼ V-T To **shed** blood means to kill people in a violent way. If someone **sheds** their blood, they are killed in a violent way, usually when they are fighting in a war. [FORMAL] ❑ *Britain was prepared to shed blood in support of the United States.* [from Old English] ◼ to **shed light on** something → see **light**
→ see **cry**

**she'd** /ʃid, ʃid/ ◼ **She'd** is the usual spoken form of "she had," especially when "had" is an auxiliary verb. ❑ *She'd been all over the world.* ◼ **She'd** is a spoken form of "she would." ❑ *She'd do anything for a bit of money.*

**sheen** /ʃin/ N-SING If something has a **sheen**, it has a smooth and gentle brightness on its surface. ❑ *The carpet had a silver sheen.* [from Old English]

**sheep** /ʃip/ (**sheep**) N-COUNT A **sheep** is a farm animal which is covered with thick hair called wool. Sheep are kept for their wool or for their meat. [from Old English]
→ see **meat**

**sheepish** /ʃipɪʃ/ ADJ If you look **sheepish**, you look slightly embarrassed because you feel foolish. ❑ *I asked him why he was leaving and he looked a little sheepish.* ● **sheepishly** ADV ❑ *He grinned sheepishly.* [from Old English]

**sheer** /ʃɪər/ (**sheerer, sheerest**) ◼ ADJ You can use **sheer** to emphasize that a state or situation is complete and does not involve or is not mixed with anything else. ❑ *His music is sheer delight.* ❑ *By sheer chance he was there.* ◼ ADJ A **sheer** cliff or drop is extremely steep or completely vertical. ❑ *There was a sheer drop just outside my window.* ◼ ADJ **Sheer** material is very thin, light, and delicate. ❑ *She wore sheer black stockings.* [from Old English]

**sheet** /ʃit/ (**sheets**) ◼ N-COUNT A **sheet** is a large rectangular piece of cotton or other cloth that you sleep on or cover yourself with in a bed. ❑ *Once a week, we change the sheets.* ◼ N-COUNT A **sheet** of paper is a rectangular piece of paper. ❑ *Use a sheet of newspaper.* ◼ N-COUNT A **sheet of** glass, metal, or wood is a large, flat, thin piece of it. ❑ *The cranes were lifting giant sheets of steel.* [from Old English]
→ see **bed, glass, paper**

**sheikh** /ʃik, ʃeɪk/ (**sheikhs**) also **sheik** N-TITLE; N-COUNT A **sheikh** is a male Arab chief or ruler. ❑ *...Sheikh Khalifa.* [from Arabic]

**shelf** /ʃɛlf/ (**shelves**) N-COUNT A **shelf** is a flat piece of wood, metal, or glass which is attached to a wall or to the sides of a cabinet. Shelves are used for keeping things on. ❑ *He took a book from the shelf.* [from Old English]

**shell** /ʃɛl/ (**shells, shelling, shelled**) ◼ N-COUNT The **shell** of a nut or egg is the hard covering which surrounds it. ❑ *They cracked the nuts and removed their shells.* ● **Shell** is the substance that a shell is made of. ❑ *It was a necklace made from bits of walnut shell.* ◼ N-COUNT The **shell** of an animal such as a tortoise, snail, or crab is the hard protective covering that it has around its body or on its back. ❑ *The snail's shell forms a spiral.* ◼ N-COUNT **Shells** are hard objects found on beaches. They are usually pink, white, or brown and are the coverings which used to surround small sea creatures. ❑ *I collect shells and interesting seaside items.* ◼ V-T If you **shell** nuts, peas, shrimp, or other food, you remove their natural outer covering. ❑ *She shelled and ate a few nuts.* ◼ N-COUNT A **shell** is a weapon consisting of a metal container filled with explosives that can be fired from a large gun over long distances. ❑ *Tanks fired shells at the house.* ◼ V-T To **shell** a place means to fire explosive shells at it. ❑ *The army shelled the port.* ● **shelling** (**shellings**) N-VAR ❑ *Out on the streets, the shelling continued.* [from Old English]
→ see **shellfish**

▸ **shell out** PHR-VERB If you **shell out for** something, you spend a lot of money on it. [INFORMAL] ❑ *He shelled out $950 for his trip.* ❑ *We didn't have to shell out for taxis because we had our own driver.*

**S**

## Picture Dictionary shellfish

shrimp

claw

leg

crab

lobster

crayfish

mussel

oyster

shell

clam

scallop

**she'll** /ʃil, ʃɪl/ **She'll** is the usual spoken form of "she will." ❏ *Sharon was wonderful; I know she'll be greatly missed.*

**shell|fish** /ʃɛlfɪʃ/ (**shellfish**) N-VAR **Shellfish** are small creatures that live in the sea and have a shell. ❏ *Fish and shellfish are our specialties.*
→ see Picture Dictionary: **shellfish**

**shel|ter** /ʃɛltər/ (**shelters, sheltering, sheltered**) ◼ N-COUNT A **shelter** is a small building or covered place which is made to protect people from bad weather or danger. ❏ *...a bus shelter.* ◼ N-UNCOUNT If a place provides **shelter**, it provides you with a place to stay or live, especially when you need protection from bad weather and danger. ❏ *The number of families needing shelter rose by 17 percent.* ❏ *Horses don't mind the cold but shelter from rain and wind is important.* ◼ V-I If you **shelter** in a place, you stay there and are protected from bad weather or danger. ❏ *A man sheltered in a doorway.* ◼ V-T If a place or thing **is sheltered** by something, it is protected by that thing from wind and rain. ❏ *The house was sheltered from the sun by huge trees.* ◼ V-T If you **shelter** someone, usually someone who is being hunted by police or other people, you provide them with a place to stay or live. ❏ *A neighbor sheltered the boy for seven days.*
→ see **habitat**

## Word Partnership Use *shelter* with:

| | |
|---|---|
| N. | **bomb** shelter ◼<br>**emergency** shelter ◼ ◼<br>shelter **and clothing, food and** shelter ◼ |
| ADJ. | **temporary** shelter ◼ ◼ |
| V. | **find** shelter, **provide** shelter, **seek** shelter ◼ |

**shel|tered** /ʃɛltərd/ ◼ ADJ A **sheltered** place is protected from wind and rain. ❏ *The beach is next to a sheltered bay.* ◼ ADJ If you say that someone has led a **sheltered** life, you mean that they have been protected from difficult or unpleasant experiences. ❏ *Perhaps I've just led a really sheltered life.* ◼ → see also **shelter**

**shelve** /ʃɛlv/ (**shelves, shelving, shelved**) ◼ V-T If someone **shelves** a plan or project, they decide

not to continue with it, either for a while or permanently. ❏ *He has shelved plans for a hotel and club.* ◼ **Shelves** is the plural of **shelf**.

**shep|herd** /ʃɛpərd/ (**shepherds, shepherding, shepherded**) ◼ N-COUNT A **shepherd** is a person, especially a man, whose job is to take care of sheep. ◼ V-T If you **are shepherded** somewhere, someone takes you there to make sure that you arrive at the right place safely. ❏ *She was shepherded up the steps of the aircraft.* [from Old English]

**sher|bet** /ʃɜrbɪt/ (**sherbets**) N-VAR **Sherbet** is like ice cream but made with fruit juice, sugar, and water. ❏ *...lemon sherbet.* [from Turkish]

**sher|iff** /ʃɛrɪf/ (**sheriffs**) N-COUNT; N-TITLE In the United States, a **sheriff** is a person who is elected to make sure that the law is obeyed in a particular county. ❏ *He's the local sheriff.* [from Old English]

**she's** /ʃiz, ʃɪz/ ◼ **She's** is the usual spoken form of "she is." ❏ *She's a really good cook.* ◼ **She's** is a spoken form of "she has," especially when "has" is an auxiliary verb. ❏ *She's been married for seven years.*

**shield** /ʃild/ (**shields, shielding, shielded**) ◼ V-T If something or someone **shields** you from a danger or risk, they protect you from it. ❏ *He shielded his eyes from the sun.* ◼ N-COUNT A **shield** is a large piece of metal or leather which soldiers used to carry to protect their bodies while they were fighting. [from Old English]
→ see **army**

**shield vol|ca|no** (**shield volcanoes**) N-COUNT A **shield volcano** is a broad volcano with low, sloping sides that is formed from lava that has erupted and become solid. [TECHNICAL]

**shift** /ʃɪft/ (**shifts, shifting, shifted**) ◼ V-T/V-I If you **shift** something or if it **shifts**, it moves slightly. ❏ *He stopped, shifting his bag to his left hand.* ❏ *He shifted from foot to foot.* ◼ V-T/V-I If your opinion, a situation, or a policy **shifts** or **is shifted**, it changes slightly. ❏ *Attitudes to mental illness have shifted in recent years.* ● **Shift** is also a noun. ❏ *There's been a shift in government policy.* ◼ V-T If you **shift** gears in a car, you put the car into a different gear. ❏ *He shifted gears and pulled away slowly.* ◼ N-COUNT A **shift** is a set period of work in a place like a

## Word Web    ship

Large **ocean-going vessels** are an important way of carrying people and **cargo**. **Oil tankers** and **container ships** are common in many **ports**. **Ocean liners** carry tourists and give them a place to stay. Some of these **ships** are several stories tall. The **captain** steers a **cruise ship** from the bridge, while passengers enjoy themselves on the promenade **deck**. Huge **warships** carry thousands of soldiers to battlefields around the world. **Aircraft carriers** include a **flight deck** where planes can take off and land. **Ferries**, **barges**, fishing **craft**, and research **boats** are also an important part of the **marine** industry.

factory or a hospital. ❏ *His father worked shifts in a steel mill.*
[from Old English]

## Word Partnership    Use *shift* with :

| | |
|---|---|
| N. | shift *your* **weight** ■ |
| | shift *your* **position** ■ ■ |
| | shift *your* **attention**, shift **in focus**, **policy** shift, shift **in/of power**, shift **in priorities** ■ |
| | shift **gears** ■ |
| | shift **change**, **night** shift ■ |
| ADJ. | **dramatic** shift, **major** shift, **significant** shift ■ |

**Shi|ite** /ʃiaɪt/ (**Shiites**) also **Shi'ite** ■ N-COUNT
**Shiites** are members of a branch of Islam which regards Mohammed's cousin Ali and his successors, rather than Mohammed himself, as the final authority on religious matters. ❏ *...the Shiites in southern Iraq.* ■ ADJ **Shiite** means relating to Shiites and their religious beliefs or practises. ❏ *Iraq's population is roughly half Shiite Muslims.* [from Arabic]

**shim|mer** /ʃɪmər/ (**shimmers, shimmering, shimmered**) V-I If something **shimmers**, it shines with a faint, unsteady light. ❏ *The lights shimmered on the water.* ● **Shimmer** is also a noun. ❏ *There was a shimmer of starlight.* [from Old English]

**shin** /ʃɪn/ (**shins**) N-COUNT Your **shins** are the front parts of your legs between your knees and your ankles. ❏ *She kicked him in the shins.* [from Old English]

**shine** /ʃaɪn/ (**shines, shining, shined** or **shone**) ■ V-I When the sun or a light **shines**, it gives out bright light. ❏ *It is warm and the sun is shining.* ■ V-T If you **shine** a flashlight or other light somewhere, you point it there. ❏ *A man shone a light in his face.* ❏ *The man walked toward her, shining a flashlight.* ■ V-I Something that **shines** is very bright and clear because it is reflecting light. ❏ *Her blue eyes shone.* ■ N-SING Something that has a **shine** is bright and clear because it is reflecting light. ❏ *This gel gives a beautiful shine to the hair.* ■ V-I Someone who **shines** at a skill or activity does it extremely well. ❏ *Did you shine at school?* [from Old English] ■ → see also **shining**
→ see **light bulb**

## Thesaurus    shine    Also look up :

| | |
|---|---|
| V. | glare, gleam, illuminate, shimmer ■ ■ |
| N. | light, radiance, sheen ■ |

**shin|gle** /ʃɪŋgᵊl/ (**shingles**) ■ N-UNCOUNT
**Shingle** is a mass of small rough pieces of stone on the shore of a sea or a river. ❏ *The beach is both sand and shingle.* ■ N-COUNT **Shingles** are thin pieces of wood or another material which are fixed in rows to cover a roof or wall. ❏ *The roofs had shingles missing.* ■ N-COUNT A **shingle** is a small sign that is hung outside a building, such as the place where a doctor or lawyer works. ■ PHRASE If you **hang out** your **shingle** or **hang out** a **shingle**, you start your own business. ❏ *She hung out her shingle under the name "Designs by Pamela."* [Sense 1 of Scandinavian origin. Senses 2 to 4 from Late Latin.]

**shin|ing** /ʃaɪnɪŋ/ ■ ADJ A **shining** achievement or quality is a very good one which should be greatly admired. ❏ *She is a shining example to us all.* [from Old English] ■ → see also **shine**

**shiny** /ʃaɪni/ (**shinier, shiniest**) ADJ **Shiny** things are bright and reflect light. ❏ *Her blonde hair was shiny and clean.* [from Old English]
→ see **metal**

**ship** /ʃɪp/ (**ships, shipping, shipped**) ■ N-COUNT A **ship** is a large boat which carries passengers or cargo. ❏ *The ship was ready for departure.* ❏ *We went by ship over to Europe.* ■ V-T If people, supplies, or goods **are shipped** somewhere, they are sent there on a ship or by some other means of transportation. ❏ *We'll ship your order to the address on your checks.* ❏ *Food is being shipped to Southern Africa.* ● **ship|ment** N-UNCOUNT ❏ *We ask for payment before shipment of the goods.* [from Old English] ■ → see also **shipping**
→ see Word Web: **ship**

## Word Partnership    Use *ship* with :

| | |
|---|---|
| V. | **board** a ship, **build** a ship, ship **docks**, **jump** ship, ship ■ |
| N. | **bow** of a ship, **captain** of a ship, **cargo** ship, **ship's crew** ■ |

**ship|ment** /ʃɪpmənt/ (**shipments**) N-COUNT
A **shipment** is an amount of a particular kind of cargo that is sent to another country on a ship, train, airplane, or other vehicle. ❏ *Food shipments*

S

to the port could begin in a few weeks. [from Old English]

**ship|ping** /ʃɪpɪŋ/ N-UNCOUNT **Shipping** is the transportation of cargo or goods as a business, especially on ships. ❑ ...the international shipping industry. ❑ Here's a coupon for free shipping of your catalog order. [from Old English]

**ship|wreck** /ʃɪprɛk/ (**shipwrecks, shipwrecked**) **1** N-VAR If there is a **shipwreck**, a ship is destroyed in an accident at sea. ❑ He was drowned in a shipwreck off the coast of Spain. **2** N-COUNT A **shipwreck** is a ship which has been destroyed in an accident at sea. ❑ More than 1,000 shipwrecks lie in the seas around the islands. **3** V-T PASSIVE If someone **is shipwrecked**, their ship is destroyed in an accident at sea but they survive and manage to reach land. ❑ He was shipwrecked after visiting the island. [from Old English]

**ship|yard** /ʃɪpyɑrd/ (**shipyards**) N-COUNT A **shipyard** is a place where ships are built and repaired. ❑ The Queen Mary 2 is docked at the shipyard. [from Old English]

**shirt** /ʃɜrt/ (**shirts**) **1** N-COUNT A **shirt** is a piece of clothing that you wear on the upper part of your body. Shirts have a collar, sleeves, and buttons down the front. [from Old English] **2** → see also **sweatshirt, T-shirt**
→ see **clothing**

<table><tr><td>Usage</td><td>shirt and blouse</td></tr></table>

Be careful not to use *blouse* when you should use *shirt*. Both men and women wear shirts, but only women wear blouses, which are usually thought of as more loose fitting and a little fancier than shirts: *Reynaldo put on a fancy shirt to go to the party, but Alma was afraid she'd get her new blouse dirty, so she put on one of the shirts she often wore to work.*

**shiv|er** /ʃɪvər/ (**shivers, shivering, shivered**) V-I When you **shiver**, your body shakes slightly because you are cold or frightened. ❑ He shivered in the cold. ● **Shiver** is also a noun. ❑ The emptiness here sent shivers down my spine. [from Old English]

**Word Partnership** Use *shiver* with :

V.     feel a shiver, shiver **goes/runs down**
        *your* spine, *something* **makes** *you* shiver,
        *something* **sends** a shiver **down** *your* **spine**

**shoal** /ʃoʊl/ (**shoals**) N-COUNT A **shoal of** fish is a large group of them swimming together. ❑ The fish swam in shoals around them. [from Old English]

**shock** /ʃɒk/ (**shocks, shocking, shocked**) **1** N-COUNT If you have a **shock**, something suddenly happens which is unpleasant, upsetting, or very surprising. ❑ The city violence came as a shock. ❑ He never recovered from the shock of his brother's death. **2** N-UNCOUNT **Shock** is a person's emotional and physical condition when something very frightening or upsetting has happened to them. ❑ The boy was speechless with shock. **3** N-UNCOUNT If someone is **in shock**, they are suffering from a serious physical condition in which their blood is not flowing around their body properly, for example, because they have had a bad injury. ❑ He was in shock when we found him. **4** V-T If something **shocks** you, it makes you feel very upset, because it involves death or suffering

and because you did not expect it. ❑ After forty years in the police, nothing much shocks me. ● **shocked** ADJ ❑ It was a bad attack and the woman is still very shocked. **5** V-T/V-I If someone or something **shocks** you, it upsets or offends you because you think it is vulgar or morally wrong. ❑ You can't shock me. ❑ We were easily shocked in those days. ❑ Their story still has the power to shock. ● **shocked** ADJ ❑ Don't look so shocked. **6** N-VAR A **shock** is the force of something suddenly hitting or pulling something else. ❑ The steel bars will absorb the shock. **7** N-COUNT A **shock** is the same as an **electric shock**. [from Old French]

**Word Partnership** Use *shock* with :

V.     come as a shock **1**
        send a shock **1 6 7**
        express shock, feel shock **2**
N.     in a state of shock, shock value **2**

**shock|ing** /ʃɒkɪŋ/ **1** ADJ You can say that something is **shocking** if you think that it is very bad. [INFORMAL] ❑ The newspaper story was shocking. ● **shock|ing|ly** ADV ❑ His memory became shockingly bad. **2** ADJ You can say that something is **shocking** if you think that it is morally wrong. ❑ It is shocking that nothing was said. ● **shock|ing|ly** ADV ❑ Shockingly, this dangerous treatment did not end until the 1930s. [from Old French] **3** → see also **shock**

**shock wave** (**shock waves**) also **shockwave** **1** N-COUNT A **shock wave** is an area of very high pressure moving through the air, earth, or water. It is caused by an explosion or an earthquake, or by an object traveling faster than sound. ❑ The shock waves were felt from Las Vegas to San Diego. **2** N-COUNT A **shock wave** is the effect of something surprising, such as a piece of unpleasant news, that causes strong reactions when it spreads through a place. ❑ The crime sent shock waves through the country.
→ see **sound**

**shod** /ʃɒd/ **1** ADJ You can use **shod** when you are describing the kind of shoes that a person is wearing. [FORMAL] ❑ He was shod in running shoes. **2** **Shod** is a past tense and past participle of **shoe**. [from Old English]

**shod|dy** /ʃɒdi/ (**shoddier, shoddiest**) ADJ **Shoddy** work or a **shoddy** product has been done or made carelessly or badly. ❑ I'm normally quick to complain about shoddy service. ● **shod|di|ly** ADV ❑ These products are shoddily produced.

**shoe** /ʃu/ (**shoes, shoeing, shoed** or **shod**) **1** N-COUNT **Shoes** are objects which you wear on your feet. They cover most of your foot but not your ankles. ❑ ...a pair of shoes. ❑ Low-heeled comfortable shoes are best. **2** V-T When a blacksmith **shoes** a horse, they attach horseshoes onto their feet. ❑ Blacksmiths spent most of their time shoeing horses. **3** PHRASE If you talk about being in someone's **shoes**, you talk about what you would do or how you would feel if you were in their situation. ❑ I wouldn't like to be in his shoes. [from Old English]
→ see Picture Dictionary: **shoe**
→ see **clothing**

**shoe|string** /ʃustrɪŋ/ (**shoestrings**) **1** N-COUNT **Shoestrings** are long, narrow pieces of material like pieces of string that you use to fasten your shoes. **2** PHRASE If you do something or make

## Picture Dictionary — shoe

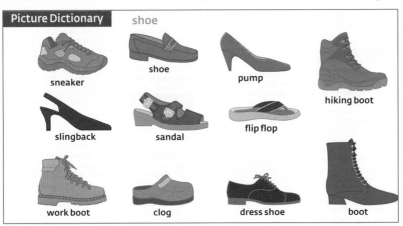

sneaker

shoe

pump

hiking boot

slingback

sandal

flip flop

work boot

clog

dress shoe

boot

something **on a shoestring**, you do it using very little money. ❑ *We run the theater on a shoestring.*

**shone** /ʃoʊn/ **Shone** is the past tense and past participle of **shine**. [from Old English]

**shoo-in** /ʃu ɪn/ (**shoo-ins**) N-COUNT A **shoo-in** is a person who seems sure to win. [INFORMAL] ❑ *He's a shoo-in to win the award this season.*

**shook** /ʃʊk/ **Shook** is the past tense of **shake**. [from Old English]

**shoot** /ʃut/ (**shoots, shooting, shot**) **1** V-T If someone **shoots** a person or an animal, they kill them or injure them by firing a bullet or arrow at them. ❑ *The police had orders to shoot anyone who attacked them.* ❑ *A man was shot dead during the robbery.* ● **shoot|ing** (**shootings**) N-COUNT ❑ *Two bodies were found after the shooting.* **2** V-I To **shoot** means to fire a bullet from a weapon such as a gun. ❑ *He raised his arms above his head, shouting, "Don't shoot!"* ❑ *The police started shooting at us.* **3** V-I If someone or something **shoots** in a particular direction, they move in that direction quickly and suddenly. ❑ *A car shot out of the driveway and crashed into them.* **4** V-T When people **shoot** a movie or **shoot** photographs, they make a movie or take photographs using a camera. ❑ *He wants to shoot his movie in Mexico.* ● **Shoot** is also a noun. ❑ *The farm is being used for a video shoot.* **5** V-T When someone **shoots** pool or **shoots** craps, they play a game of pool or the dice game called craps. ❑ *People are still here shooting pool.* **6** N-COUNT **Shoots** are plants that are beginning to grow, or new parts growing from a plant or tree. ❑ *New shoots appear every year.* **7** V-I In sports such as soccer or basketball, when someone **shoots**, they try to score by kicking or throwing the ball toward the goal or hoop. ❑ *Spencer shot wide when he should have scored.* [from Old English] **8** → see also **shooting, shot** **9** to **shoot from the hip** → see **hip**
▸ **shoot down** PHR-VERB If someone **shoots down** an airplane, a helicopter, or a missile, they make it fall to the ground by hitting it with a bullet or missile. ❑ *They claim they shot down a missile.*
▸ **shoot up** PHR-VERB If something **shoots up**, it grows or increases very quickly. ❑ *Sales shot up by*

9% *last month.*

**shoot sys|tem** (**shoot systems**) N-COUNT A plant's **shoot system** is the part of the plant that is above the ground, including the stem and leaves. Compare **root system.**

**shop** /ʃɒp/ (**shops, shopping, shopped**) **1** N-COUNT A **shop** is a small store that sells one type of merchandise. ❑ *Try the gift shop.* ❑ *He and his wife run a flower shop.* **2** V-I When you **shop**, you go to stores or shops and buy things. ❑ *He always shopped on Saturday mornings.* ❑ *Here's some advice for when you're shopping for a new carpet.* ● **shop|per** (**shoppers**) N-COUNT ❑ *There were crowds of shoppers on the streets.* [from Old English] **3** → see also **coffee shop, shopping**
▸ **shop around** PHR-VERB If you **shop around**, you go to different stores or companies in order to compare the prices and quality of goods or services before you decide to buy them. ❑ *Prices vary so it's worth shopping around.*

| **Word Partnership** | Use *shop* with : |
|---|---|
| N. | antique shop, pet shop, souvenir shop **1** |
| | auto shop, barber shop, beauty shop, shop owner, repair shop **1 2** |

**shop floor** also **shop-floor** or **shopfloor** N-SING The **shop floor** is used to refer to all the ordinary workers in a factory or the area where they work, especially in contrast to the people who are in charge. ❑ *A sign at the entrance to the shop floor says "Employees Only."*

**shop|keep|er** /ʃɒpkipər/ (**shopkeepers**) N-COUNT A **shopkeeper** is a person who owns or manages a shop.

**shop|lift** /ʃɒplɪft/ (**shoplifts, shoplifting, shoplifted**) V-T/V-I If someone **shoplifts**, they steal goods from a store by hiding them in a bag or in their clothes. ❑ *He openly shoplifted from a supermarket.* ● **shop|lifter** (**shoplifters**) N-COUNT ❑ *He began watching her as a possible shoplifter.* ● **shop|lifting** /ʃɒplɪftɪŋ/ N-UNCOUNT ❑ *He accused her of shoplifting.*
→ see **crime**

S

**shop|ping** /ʃɒpɪŋ/ N-UNCOUNT When you do **the shopping**, you go to the stores or shops and buy things. ❑ *I'll do the shopping this afternoon.* [from Old English]

| Word Partnership | Use *shopping* with : |
|---|---|
| N. | shopping **bag**, shopping **district**, **food** shopping, **grocery** shopping, **holiday** shopping, **online** shopping, shopping **spree** |

**shop|ping cart** (**shopping carts**) N-COUNT A **shopping cart** is a large metal basket on wheels which is provided by stores such as supermarkets for customers to use while they are in the store.

**shop|ping cen|ter** (**shopping centers**) N-COUNT A **shopping center** is a specially built area containing a lot of different stores. ❑ *They met in the parking lot at the shopping center.*

**shop|ping mall** (**shopping malls**) N-COUNT A **shopping mall** is a specially built covered area containing stores and restaurants.

**shore** /ʃɔr/ (**shores, shoring, shored**) N-COUNT The **shores** or the **shore** of an ocean, lake, or wide river is the land along the edge of it. Someone who is **on shore** is on the land rather than on a ship. ❑ *They walked down to the shore.* [from Middle Low German]

▸ **shore up** PHR-VERB If you **shore up** something that is weak or about to fail, you do something in order to strengthen it or support it. ❑ *We need to shore up public confidence in this process.*

**shore|line** /ʃɔrlaɪn/ (**shorelines**) N-COUNT A **shoreline** is the edge of an ocean, lake, or wide river. ❑ *We sat on rocks along the shoreline.*

**shorn** /ʃɔrn/ **Shorn** is the past participle of **shear**. [from Old English]

---
**short**

❶ ADJECTIVE AND ADVERB USES
❷ NOUN USES

---

❶ **short** /ʃɔrt/ (**shorter, shortest**) ◼ ADJ If something is **short** or lasts for a **short** time, it does not last very long. ❑ *The announcement was made a short time ago.* ❑ *Kemp gave a short laugh.* ◢ ADJ Someone who is **short** is not as tall as most people are. ❑ *I'm tall and thin and he's short and fat.* ❑ *She's a short woman with gray hair.* ◣ ADJ Something that is **short** measures only a small amount from one end to the other. ❑ *The restaurant is only a short distance away.* ❑ *A short staircase led to a grand doorway.* ◤ ADJ If you are **short of** something or if it is **short**, you do not have enough of it. ❑ *Now the family is short of money.* ❑ *Government forces are running short of fuel.* ◥ ADJ If someone or something is or stops **short of** a place, they have not quite reached it. If they are or fall **short of** an amount, they have not quite achieved it. ❑ *He stopped a hundred yards short of the building.* ◧ ADV If something is **cut short** or **stops short**, it is stopped before people expect it to or before it has finished. ❑ *His career was cut short by a heart attack.* ◨ ADJ If a name or abbreviation is **short for** another name, it is the short version of that name. ❑ *Her friend Kes (short for Kesewa) was in tears.* ◩ ADJ If you have a **short** temper, you get angry very easily. ❑ *She was an impatient woman with a short temper.* ◪ PHRASE You use **in short** when

you have been giving a lot of details and you want to give a conclusion or summary. ❑ *Try running or swimming. In short, anything active.* ◉ PHRASE If someone **stops short of** doing something, they come close to doing it but do not actually do it. ❑ *She stopped short of calling me a liar.* [from Old English] ◫ **in short supply** → see **supply** ◬ **in the short term** → see **term** → see **hair**

| Thesaurus | | *short* | Also look up : |
|---|---|---|---|
| ADJ. | brief, quick; (*ant.*) long ◼ | | |
| | petite, slight, small; (*ant.*) tall ◢ | | |

❷ **short** /ʃɔrt/ (**shorts**) ◼ N-PLURAL **Shorts** are pants with very short legs. ❑ *Two women arrived in bright cotton shorts.* ◢ N-PLURAL **Shorts** are men's underpants with short legs. [from Old English]

**short|age** /ʃɔrtɪdʒ/ (**shortages**) N-VAR If there is a **shortage of** something, there is not enough of it. ❑ *Officials are worried about the shortage of cheap housing.* ❑ *Vietnam is suffering from food shortages.* [from Old English]

**short|cake** /ʃɔrtkeɪk/ (**shortcakes**) N-VAR **Shortcake** is a cake or dessert which consists of a biscuit or cake with layers of fruit and whipped cream. ❑ *It's strawberry shortcake for dessert.*

**short|com|ing** /ʃɔrtkʌmɪŋ/ (**shortcomings**) N-COUNT Someone's or something's **shortcomings** are the faults or weaknesses which they have. ❑ *The only shortcoming with Cooperstown is that it's full of tourists.*

**short|en** /ʃɔrtᵊn/ (**shortens, shortening, shortened**) ◼ V-T/V-I If you **shorten** an event or the length of time that something lasts, or if it **shortens**, it does not last as long as it would usually last. ❑ *Eating too much can shorten your life.* ❑ *The days shorten in winter.* ◢ V-T/V-I If you **shorten** an object or if it **shortens**, it becomes smaller in length. ❑ *She paid $5,000 for an operation to shorten her nose.* [from Old English]

**short|en|ing** /ʃɔrtnɪŋ/ (**shortenings**) N-VAR **Shortening** is cooking fat that you use with flour in order to make pastry or dough. [from Old English]

**short|fall** /ʃɔrtfɔl/ (**shortfalls**) N-COUNT If there is a **shortfall in** something, there is less of it than you need. ❑ *The government refused to make up the $50,000 shortfall.*

**short|hand** /ʃɔrthænd/ N-UNCOUNT **Shorthand** is a quick way of writing and uses signs to represent words or syllables. ❑ *Ben took notes in shorthand.*

**short|list** /ʃɔrtlɪst/ (**shortlists, shortlisting, shortlisted**) also **short list** ◼ N-COUNT A **shortlist** is a list of people or things that have been chosen from a larger group, for example, for a job or a prize. The successful person is then chosen from the small group. ❑ *You are on a shortlist of six applicants.* ◢ V-T If someone or something **is shortlisted for** a job or a prize, they are put on a shortlist. ❑ *He was shortlisted for the Nobel Prize for literature.*

**short-lived** ADJ Something that is **short-lived** does not last very long. ❑ *The excitement was short-lived.*

**short|ly** /ʃɔrtli/ ADV If something happens **shortly** after or before something else, it happens not long after or before it. If something is going to happen **shortly**, it is going to happen soon. ❑ *Their* *trial will shortly begin.* ❑ *Shortly after moving into her apartment, she found a job.* [from Old English]

**short-order** ADJ A **short-order** cook is a person who is employed in a small restaurant such as a diner to cook food that is easily and quickly prepared. ❑ *They employed short-order cooks to make the burgers.*

**short|sighted** /ʃɔrtsaɪtɪd/ also **short-sighted** ADJ If someone is **shortsighted** about something, or if their ideas are **shortsighted**, they do not make proper or careful judgments about the future. ❑ *Today we're paying the price of previous shortsighted solutions.*

**short-term** ADJ **Short-term** is used to describe things that will last for a short time, or things that will have an effect soon rather than in the distant future. ❑ *We have a short-term oil crisis facing us.* ❑ *The company has 90 staff on short-term contracts.*

**shot** /ʃɒt/ (**shots**) **1** **Shot** is the past tense and past participle of **shoot**. **2** N-COUNT A **shot** is an act of firing a gun. ❑ *He murdered Perceval with a single shot.* **3** N-COUNT Someone who is a good **shot** can shoot well. Someone who is a bad **shot** cannot shoot well. ❑ *He was not a very good shot.* **4** N-COUNT In sports, a **shot** is an act of kicking, hitting, or throwing the ball, especially in an attempt to score a point. ❑ *He had only one shot at the goal.* **5** N-COUNT A **shot** is a photograph or a particular sequence of pictures in a movie. ❑ *A film crew was taking shots of the street.* **6** N-COUNT If you have a **shot at** something, you attempt to do it. [INFORMAL] ❑ *The Olympic champion will get a shot at the world title.* **7** N-COUNT A **shot of** a drug is an injection of it. ❑ *The doctor gave me a shot of Nembutal.* **8** PHRASE If you **give** something your **best shot**, you do it as well as you possibly can. [INFORMAL] ❑ *I don't expect to win, but I'm going to give it my best shot.* **9** PHRASE The person who **calls the shots** is in a position to tell others what to do. ❑ *The directors here call the shots.* **10** PHRASE If you describe something as a **long shot**, you mean that it is unlikely to succeed, but is worth trying. ❑ *It was a long shot that she'd find him in the park, but it wasn't impossible.* [from Old English]
→ see **photography**

| Word Partnership | Use *shot* with : |
|---|---|
| V. | **fire** a shot, **hear** a shot **2** |
| | **miss** a shot **2 4** |
| | **take** a shot **2 4 5** |
| | **block** a shot, **hit** a shot **4** |
| | **get** a shot, **give** *someone* a shot **7** |
| ADJ. | **single** shot, **warning** shot **2** |
| | **good** shot **2** – **5** |
| | **winning** shot **4** |

**shot|gun** /ʃɒtgʌn/ (**shotguns**) N-COUNT A **shotgun** is a gun used for shooting birds and animals which fires a lot of small metal balls at one time.

**should** /ʃəd, STRONG ʃʊd/

**Should** is a modal verb. It is used with the base form of a verb.

**1** MODAL You use **should** when you are saying what would be the right thing to do or the right state for something to be in. ❑ *I should exercise more.* ❑ *I don't think he should ever forget this.* **2** MODAL You use **should** to give someone an order to do

something, or to report an official order. ❑ *18-year-olds should remember to register to vote.* **3** MODAL If you say that something **should have** happened, you mean that it did not happen, but that you wish it had. ❑ *I should have gone this morning but I was feeling ill.* ❑ *You shouldn't have said what you did.* **4** MODAL You use **should** when you are saying that something is probably true or will probably happen in the way you are describing. If you say that something **should have** happened by a particular time, you mean that it will probably have happened by that time. ❑ *You should have no problem reading this.* ❑ *The doctor said I should be fine by next week.* **5** MODAL You use **should** in questions when you are asking someone for advice, permission, or information. ❑ *Should I ask for more help?* ❑ *What should I do?* **6** MODAL You use **should** in "that" clauses after certain verbs, nouns, and adjectives when you are talking about a future event or situation. ❑ *He suggested that I should take a break.* ❑ *I thought that we should look at every car.* **7** MODAL You use **should** in expressions such as **I should think** and **I should imagine** to indicate that you think something is true but you are not sure. ❑ *I should think it will rain soon.* [from Old English]

**shoul|der** /ʃoʊldər/ (**shoulders, shouldering, shouldered**) **1** N-COUNT Your **shoulders** are between your neck and the tops of your arms. ❑ *She put her arm round his shoulders.* **2** N-PLURAL When you talk about someone's problems or responsibilities, you can say that they carry them **on** their **shoulders**. ❑ *No one understood how much he carried on his shoulders.* **3** V-T If you **shoulder** the responsibility or the blame for something, you accept it. ❑ *After Theresa died, John shouldered the full responsibility of continuing his work.* **4** N-COUNT On a busy road such as a highway, the **shoulder** is the area at the side of the road where vehicles are allowed to stop in an emergency. [from Old English] **5** to **rub shoulders with** → see **rub**
→ see **body, horse**

| Word Partnership | Use *shoulder* with : |
|---|---|
| ADJ. | **bare** shoulder, **broken** shoulder, **dislocated** shoulder, shoulder **1** |
| V. | **look over** *your* shoulder, **tap** *someone* on the shoulder **1** |
| N. | **head on** *someone's* shoulder **1** |
| | shoulder **a burden 3** |

**shouldn't** /ʃʊdənt/ **Shouldn't** is the usual spoken form of "should not."

**should've** /ʃʊdəv/ **Should've** is the usual spoken form of "should have," especially when "have" is an auxiliary verb.

**shout** /ʃaʊt/ (**shouts, shouting, shouted**) V-T/V-I If you **shout**, you say something very loudly. ❑ *He had to shout over the noise of the wind.* ❑ *"She's alive!" he shouted.* ❑ *Andrew ran out of the house, shouting for help.* ● **Shout** is also a noun. ❑ *There were shouts from the crowd.* ● **shout|ing** N-UNCOUNT ❑ *My grandchildren heard the shouting first.* [from Old Norse] ▶ **shout out** PHR-VERB If you **shout** something **out**, you say it very loudly so that people can hear you clearly. ❑ *They shouted out the names of the winners.* ❑ *I shouted out "I'm OK!"*

**shove** /ʃʌv/ (**shoves, shoving, shoved**) V-T/V-I If you **shove** someone or something, you push them with a quick, violent movement. ❑ *She shoved the other customers out of the way.* ❑ *He's the one who shoved me.* • **Shove** is also a noun. ❑ *She gave Gracie a shove toward the house.* [from Old English]

**shov|el** /ʃʌvᵊl/ (**shovels, shoveling** or **shovelling, shoveled** or **shovelled**) ◼ N-COUNT A **shovel** is a tool with a long handle that is used for lifting and moving earth, coal, or snow. ❑ *I'll need the snow shovel.* ◼ V-T If you **shovel** earth, coal, or snow, you lift and move it with a shovel. ❑ *He has to go and shovel snow.* [from Old English]
→ see **garden**

---

### show

❶ VERB USES
❷ NOUN AND ADJECTIVE USES
❸ PHR-VERBS

---

❶ **show** /ʃoʊ/ (**shows, showing, showed, shown**) ◼ V-T If something **shows that** a situation exists, it gives information that proves it or makes it clear to people. ❑ *Research shows that certain foods can help prevent headaches.* ❑ *These figures show an increase of over one million in unemployment.* ◼ V-T If a picture, chart, movie, or piece of writing **shows** something, it represents it or gives information about it. ❑ *Figure 4.1 shows the lower leg.* ❑ *The mirror, shown left, measures 20 x 12 inches.* ❑ *The movie shows a boy trying to become a ballet dancer.* ◼ V-T If you **show** someone something, you give it to them, take them to it, or point to it, so that they can see it or know what you are referring to. ❑ *Go and show this to your boss.* ❑ *He showed me the apartment he shares with Esther.* ◼ V-T If you **show** someone to a room or seat, you lead them there. ❑ *Let me show you to your seat.* ❑ *Milton was shown into the office.* ◼ V-T If you **show** someone how to do something, you do it yourself so that they can watch you and learn how to do it. ❑ *Claire showed us how to make a cake.* ◼ V-T/V-I If something **shows** or if you **show** it, it is visible or noticeable. ❑ *He smiled and showed a row of strong white teeth.* ❑ *The sky was showing through the light cloud.* ◼ V-T If something **shows** a quality or characteristic or if that quality or characteristic **shows itself**, that quality or characteristic can be noticed or observed. ❑ *The story shows a strong imagination and plenty of humor too.* ❑ *Rouse's career shows no sign of slowing down.* ◼ V-I If a person you are expecting to meet does not **show**, they do not arrive at the place where you expect to meet them. ❑ *There was a possibility he wouldn't show.* • **Show up** means the same as **show**. ❑ *We waited until five, but he didn't show up.* ◼ V-T/V-I If someone **shows** a movie or television program, it is broadcast or appears on television or in the movie theater. ❑ *The TV news showed the same bit of film all day.* ❑ *The movie is now showing at theaters around the country.* ◼ PHRASE If you **have** something **to show for** your efforts, you have achieved something as a result of what you have done. ❑ *I wish I had something to show for my time in my job.* [from Old English] ◼ **to show** someone **the door** → see **door** ◼ **to show** your **face** → see **face**

❷ **show** /ʃoʊ/ (**shows**) ◼ N-COUNT A **show of** a feeling or quality is an attempt by someone to make it clear that they have that feeling or quality. ❑ *Workers gathered in the city center in a show of support for the government.* ◼ N-UNCOUNT If you say that something is **for show**, you mean

that it has no real purpose and is done just to give a good impression. ❑ *Is this all for show or are you serious?* ◼ N-COUNT A television or radio **show** is a program on television or radio. ❑ *I had my own TV show.* ❑ *It's a popular talk show on a Cuban radio station.* ◼ N-COUNT A **show** in a theater is an entertainment or concert, especially one that includes different items such as music, dancing, and comedy. ❑ *How about going to see a show?* ◼ N-COUNT A **show** is a public exhibition of things. ❑ *The show is in Boston now.* ❑ *About 30 fashion shows are planned for this fall.* [from Old English]
→ see **concert, laser**

❸ **show** /ʃoʊ/ (**shows, showing, showed, shown**) ▶ **show off** ◼ PHR-VERB If you say that someone **is showing off**, you are criticizing them for trying to impress people by showing in a very obvious way what they can do or what they own. ❑ *All right, there's no need to show off.* ◼ PHR-VERB If you **show off** something that you have, you show it to a lot of people or make it obvious that you have it, because you are proud of it. ❑ *Naomi was showing off her engagement ring.* ◼ → see also **show-off**

**show and tell** also **show-and-tell** N-UNCOUNT **Show and tell** is a school activity in which children present an object to their class and talk about it. ❑ *She can bring her dog to school for show-and-tell.*

**show busi|ness** N-UNCOUNT **Show business** is the entertainment industry of movies, theater, and television. ❑ *He started his career in show business by playing the piano.*

**show|down** /ʃoʊdaʊn/ (**showdowns**) N-COUNT A **showdown** is a big argument or conflict which is intended to settle a dispute that has lasted for a long time. ❑ *They were pushing the president toward a final showdown with his party.*

**show|er** /ʃaʊər/ (**showers, showering, showered**) ◼ N-COUNT A **shower** is a device which sprays you with water so you can wash yourself. ❑ *She heard him turn on the shower.* ◼ N-COUNT If you take a **shower**, you wash yourself by standing under a spray of water from a shower. ❑ *I think I'll take a shower.* ◼ V-I If you **shower**, you wash yourself by standing under a spray of water from a shower. ❑ *There wasn't time to shower.* ◼ N-COUNT A **shower** is a short period of rain, especially light rain. ❑ *There'll be scattered showers this afternoon.* ◼ N-COUNT You can refer to a lot of things that are falling as a **shower** of them. ❑ *The suitcase fell open and a shower of banknotes fell out.* ◼ V-T If you **are showered with** a lot of small objects or pieces, they are scattered over you. ❑ *The bride and groom were showered with rice in the traditional manner.* ◼ N-COUNT A **shower** is a party, usually for a woman who is getting married or having a baby, at which the guests bring gifts. ❑ *...a baby shower.* [from Old English]
→ see **bathroom, meteor, soap, wedding**

**show|er gel** (**shower gels**) N-VAR **Shower gel** is a type of liquid soap designed for use in the shower.

**shown** /ʃoʊn/ **Shown** is the past participle of **show**. [from Old English]

**show-off** (**show-offs**) also **showoff** N-COUNT If you say that someone is a **show-off**, you are criticizing them for trying to impress people by showing in a very obvious way what they can do or what they own. [INFORMAL] ❑ *I was a show-off as a child.*

**show|piece** /ʃoʊpis/ (**showpieces**) also show-piece N-COUNT A **showpiece** is something that is admired because it is the best thing of its type, especially something that is intended to be impressive. ❑ *I don't want my home to be a showpiece. I want it to be comfortable.*

**show|room** /ʃoʊrum/ (**showrooms**) N-COUNT A **showroom** is a store in which goods are displayed for sale, especially goods such as cars or electrical or gas appliances. ❑ *He's in the car showroom.*

**shrank** /ʃræŋk/ **Shrank** is a past tense of **shrink**. [from Old English]

**shrap|nel** /ʃræpnªl/ N-UNCOUNT **Shrapnel** consists of small pieces of metal which are scattered from exploding bombs and shells. ❑ *He was hit by shrapnel in the explosion.* [after H. Shrapnel (1761-1842), an English army officer]

**shred** /ʃrɛd/ (**shreds, shredding, shredded**) ■ V-T If you **shred** something such as food or paper, you cut it or tear it into very small, narrow pieces. ❑ *They are shredding documents.* ■ N-COUNT If you cut or tear food or paper **into shreds**, you cut or tear it into small, narrow pieces. ❑ *Cut the cabbage into long shreds.* [from Old English]

**shrewd** /ʃrud/ (**shrewder, shrewdest**) ADJ A **shrewd** person is able to understand and judge a situation quickly and to use this understanding to their own advantage. ❑ *She's a shrewd businesswoman.* ● **shrewd|ly** ADV ❑ *She looked at him shrewdly.* ● **shrewd|ness** N-UNCOUNT ❑ *She never really liked him but she respected his shrewdness.*

**shriek** /ʃrik/ (**shrieks, shrieking, shrieked**) V-I When someone **shrieks**, they make a short, very loud cry. ❑ *She shrieked and jumped off the bed.* ● **Shriek** is also a noun. ❑ *Sue let out a terrific shriek.* [from Old Norse]

**shrill** /ʃrɪl/ (**shriller, shrillest**) ADJ A **shrill** sound is high-pitched and unpleasant. ❑ *Shrill cries came from inside.* ❑ *...the shrill whistle of the engine.* [from Old English]

**shrimp** /ʃrɪmp/ (**shrimp**)

The plural can also be **shrimps**.

N-COUNT **Shrimp** are small shellfish with long tails and many legs. ❑ *Add the shrimp and cook for 30 seconds.* [from Germanic]
→ see **shellfish**

**shrimp cock|tail** (**shrimp cocktails**) N-VAR A **shrimp cocktail** is a dish that consists of shrimp, and a sauce. It is usually eaten at the beginning of a meal.

**shrine** /ʃraɪn/ (**shrines**) N-COUNT A **shrine** is a place of worship which is associated with a particular holy person or object. ❑ *They visited the holy shrine of Mecca.* [from Old English]

**shrink** /ʃrɪŋk/ (**shrinks, shrinking, shrank** or **shrunk**) ■ V-I If cloth or clothing **shrinks**, it becomes smaller in size, usually as a result of being washed. ❑ *A cotton shirt shrank so much after one wash that she couldn't wear it.* ■ V-T/V-I If something **shrinks** or something else **shrinks** it, it becomes smaller. ❑ *The forests of West Africa have shrunk.* ■ V-I If you **shrink away from** someone or something, you move away from them because you are frightened, shocked, or disgusted with them. ❑ *One child shrinks away from me when I try to talk to him.* ■ N-COUNT A **shrink** is a psychiatrist. [INFORMAL] ❑ *I've seen a shrink already.* [from Old

English]

**shriv|el** /ʃrɪvªl/ (**shrivels, shriveling** or **shrivelling, shriveled** or **shrivelled**) V-T/V-I When something **shrivels** or when something **shrivels** it, it becomes dryer and smaller. ❑ *The plant shrivels and dies.* ● **Shrivel up** means the same as **shrivel**. ❑ *The leaves started to shrivel up.* ● **shriv|eled** ADJ ❑ *...a shriveled onion.* [of Scandinavian origin]

**shroud** /ʃraʊd/ (**shrouds, shrouding, shrouded**) ■ N-COUNT A **shroud** is a cloth which is used for wrapping a dead body. ❑ *This was the burial shroud.* ■ V-T If something **has been shrouded in** mystery or secrecy, very little information about it has been made available. ❑ *So much of history is shrouded in mystery.* ■ V-T If darkness, fog, or smoke **shrouds** an area, it covers it so that it is difficult to see. ❑ *Clouds shrouded the hilltops.* [from Old English]

**shrub** /ʃrʌb/ (**shrubs**) N-COUNT **Shrubs** are plants that have several woody stems. ❑ *...flowering shrubs.* [from Old English]
→ see **plant**

**shrug** /ʃrʌg/ (**shrugs, shrugging, shrugged**) V-I If you **shrug**, you raise your shoulders to show that you are not interested in something or that you do not know or care about something. ❑ *I shrugged, as if to say, "Why not?"* ● **Shrug** is also a noun. ❑ *"I suppose so," said Anna with a shrug.*
▶ **shrug off** PHR-VERB If you **shrug** something **off**, you ignore it or treat it as if it is not really important or serious. ❑ *He shrugged off the criticism.*

**shrunk** /ʃrʌŋk/ **Shrunk** is the past participle of **shrink**. [from Old English]

**shuck** /ʃʌk/ (**shucks, shucking, shucked**) ■ V-T If you **shuck** something such as corn or shellfish, you remove it from its outer covering. ❑ *She went outside to pick peas and to shuck them in the sunlight.* ■ EXCLAM **Shucks** is an exclamation that is used to express embarrassment, disappointment, or annoyance. [INFORMAL] ❑ *Terry said "Oh, shucks!" when they complimented her on her singing.* [from American English]

**shud|der** /ʃʌdər/ (**shudders, shuddering, shuddered**) ■ V-I If you **shudder**, you shake with fear, horror, or disgust, or because you are cold. ❑ *She shuddered at the memory of it.* ● **Shudder** is also a noun. ❑ *She gave a violent shudder.* ■ V-I If something such as a machine or vehicle **shudders**, it shakes suddenly and violently. ❑ *The train began to move forward, then shuddered to a halt.* [from Middle Low German]

**shuf|fle** /ʃʌfªl/ (**shuffles, shuffling, shuffled**) ■ V-I If you **shuffle** somewhere, you walk there without lifting your feet properly off the ground. ❑ *Moira shuffled across the kitchen.* ● **Shuffle** is also a noun. ❑ *Her walk has become a shuffle.* ■ V-T/V-I If you **shuffle around**, you move your feet about while standing or you move your bottom about while sitting, often because you feel uncomfortable or embarrassed. ❑ *He shuffled around in his chair.* ❑ *He smiled and shuffled his feet.* ■ V-T If you **shuffle** playing cards, you mix them up before you begin a game. ❑ *There are different ways of shuffling the cards.* ■ V-T If you **shuffle** things such as pieces of paper, you move them around so that they are in a different order. [from Low German]

**shun** /ʃʌn/ (**shuns, shunning, shunned**) V-T If you **shun** someone or something, you deliberately

S

avoid them or keep away from them. ❑ *From that moment everybody shunned him.* [from Old English]

**shunt** /ʃʌnt/ (**shunts, shunting, shunted**) V-T If a person or thing **is shunted** somewhere, they are moved or sent there, usually because someone finds them inconvenient. ❑ *He was always being shunted between his mother and his father.*

**shut** /ʃʌt/ (**shuts, shutting**)

The form **shut** is used in the present tense and is the past tense and past participle.

**1** V-T/V-I If you **shut** something such as a door or if it **shuts**, it moves so that it fills a hole or a space. ❑ *Please shut the gate.* ❑ *The door shut gently.* • **Shut** is also an adjective. ❑ *They have warned us to keep our doors and windows shut.* **2** V-T If you **shut** your eyes, you lower your eyelids so that you cannot see anything. ❑ *Lucy shut her eyes so she wouldn't see it happen.* • **Shut** is also an adjective. ❑ *His eyes were shut and he seemed to be asleep.* **3** V-T/V-I If your mouth **shuts** or if you **shut** your mouth, you place your lips firmly together. ❑ *Daniel's mouth opened, and then shut again.* • **Shut** is also an adjective. ❑ *She was silent for a moment, her lips tight shut.* **4** V-T/V-I When a store or other public building **shuts** or when someone **shuts** it, it is closed and you cannot use it until it is open again. ❑ *They shut the museum without giving any notice.* ❑ *Stores usually shut from noon to 3 p.m.* • **Shut** is also an adjective. ❑ *Make sure you have food when the local store may be shut.* [from Old English]

▸ **shut down** PHR-VERB If a factory or business **shuts down** or if someone **shuts** it **down**, work there stops or it is no longer in business. ❑ *The factory is shutting down for two weeks.*

▸ **shut in** PHR-VERB If you **shut** a person or animal **in** a room, you close the door so that they cannot leave it. ❑ *We shut the animals in the shelter in bad weather.*

▸ **shut off** PHR-VERB If you **shut off** something such as an engine or an electrical appliance, you turn it off to stop it from working. ❑ *He shut off the car engine.*

▸ **shut out** **1** PHR-VERB If you **shut** something or someone **out**, you prevent them from getting into a place. ❑ *"I shut him out of the house," said Maureen.* **2** PHR-VERB If you **shut out** a thought or a feeling, you prevent yourself from thinking or feeling it. ❑ *I tried to shut out the memory.* **3** PHR-VERB In sports such as football and hockey, if one team **shuts out** the team they are playing against, they win and prevent the opposing team from scoring. ❑ *Harvard shut out Yale, 14 – 0.* **4** → see also **shutout**

▸ **shut up** PHR-VERB If someone **shuts up** or if someone **shuts** them **up**, they stop talking. You can say **"shut up"** as an impolite way to tell a person to stop talking. ❑ *Just shut up, will you?*

**Word Partnership**     Use *shut* with :

| N. | shut **a door**, shut **a gate**, shut **a window** **1** |
| V. | **force** *something* shut, **pull** *something* shut, **push** *something* shut, **slam** *something* shut **1** |
| ADV. | shut **tight/tightly** **1** – **3** shut **temporarily** **4** |

**shut|down** /ʃʌtdaʊn/ (**shutdowns**) N-COUNT A **shutdown** is the closing of a factory, store, or other business. ❑ *People had to walk home during the*

*shutdown of subways and trains.*

**shut|out** /ʃʌtaʊt/ (**shutouts**) also **shut-out** N-COUNT In sports such as football and hockey, a **shutout** is a game or part of a game in which one of the teams wins and prevents the opposing team from scoring. ❑ *It was the Mariners' 10th shutout.*

**shut|ter** /ʃʌtər/ (**shutters**) **1** N-COUNT **Shutters** are wooden or metal covers fitted on the outside of a window. They can be opened to let in the light, or closed to keep out the sun or the cold. ❑ *She opened the shutters and looked out of the window.* **2** N-COUNT The **shutter** in a camera is the part which opens to allow light through the lens when a photograph is taken. ❑ *He pointed the camera at them and pressed the shutter.* [from Old English]
→ see **photography**

**shut|tle** /ʃʌtəl/ (**shuttles, shuttling, shuttled**) **1** N-COUNT A **shuttle** is the same as a **space shuttle**. **2** N-COUNT A **shuttle** is a plane, bus, or train which makes frequent trips between two places. ❑ *There is a free shuttle between the airport terminals.* **3** V-T/V-I If someone or something **shuttles** or **is shuttled** from one place to another place, they frequently go from one place to the other. ❑ *He has to shuttle between Boston and New York for his work.* [from Old English]

**shut|tle|cock** /ʃʌtəlkɒk/ (**shuttlecocks**) N-COUNT A **shuttlecock** is the small object that you hit over the net in a game of badminton.

**shy** /ʃaɪ/ (**shyer, shyest, shies, shying, shied**) **1** ADJ A **shy** person is nervous and uncomfortable in the company of other people. ❑ *She was a shy, quiet girl.* ❑ *I was too shy to say anything.* • **shy|ly** ADV ❑ *The children smiled shyly.* • **shy|ness** N-UNCOUNT ❑ *His shyness made it difficult for him to make friends.* **2** ADJ If you are **shy about** or **shy of** doing something, you are unwilling to do it because you are afraid of what might happen. ❑ *They feel shy about showing their feelings.* [from Old English]

▸ **shy away from** PHR-VERB If you **shy away from** doing something, you avoid doing it, often because you are afraid or not confident enough. ❑ *We shy away from making decisions.*

**Thesaurus**     *shy*          Also look up :

| ADJ. | nervous, quiet, sheepish, uncomfortable; *(ant.)* confident **1** |

**Si|be|rian ti|ger** (**Siberian tigers**) N-COUNT A **Siberian tiger** is a species of large tiger that lives in parts of Russia.

**sib|ling** /sɪblɪŋ/ (**siblings**) N-COUNT Your **siblings** are your brothers and sisters. [FORMAL] ❑ *His siblings are older than him.* [from Old English]

**sick** /sɪk/ (**sicker, sickest**) **1** ADJ If you are **sick**, you are ill. ❑ *He's very sick. He needs a doctor.* ❑ *She had two small children, a sick husband, and no money.* • **The sick** are people who are sick. ❑ *There are no doctors to treat the sick.* **2** ADJ If you are **sick**, the food that you have eaten comes up from your stomach and out of your mouth. If you **feel sick**, you feel as if you are going to be sick. ❑ *She was sick over the side of the ship.* ❑ *The smell of food made him feel sick.* **3** ADJ If you are **sick of** something, you are very annoyed by it and want it to stop. [INFORMAL] ❑ *I am sick of hearing these people complain.* **4** ADJ If you describe something such as a joke or story as **sick**, you mean that it deals with death or suffering in an unpleasantly humorous way. ❑ *He told a sick joke about a cat.* ⑤ PHRASE If you say that something or someone **makes** you **sick**, you mean that they make you feel angry or disgusted. [INFORMAL] ❑ *It makes me sick that he lied like that.* ⑥ PHRASE If you are **out sick**, you are not at work because you are sick. ❑ *Tom is out sick today.* [from Old English]

| **Word Partnership** | Use *sick* with : |
| --- | --- |
| v. | **care for the** sick ① |
| | **become** sick, **feel** sick, **get** sick ① ② |
| N. | sick **children**, sick **mother**, sick **patients**, sick **people**, sick **person** ① |
| ADV. | **really** sick, **very** sick ① ② |

**sick|en** /sɪkən/ (**sickens, sickening, sickened**) V-T If something **sickens** you, it makes you feel disgusted. ❑ *The way they behaved sickened him.* ● **sick|en|ing** ADJ ❑ *...the sickening way we treat older people in our society.* [from Old English]

**sick|ly** /sɪkli/ (**sicklier, sickliest**) ① ADJ A **sickly** person or animal is weak, unhealthy, and often ill. ❑ *He was a sickly child.* ② ADJ A **sickly** smell or taste is unpleasant and makes you feel slightly sick, often because it is extremely sweet. ❑ *The flowers had a strong, sickly smell.* [from Old English]

**sick|ness** /sɪknɪs/ (**sicknesses**) ① N-UNCOUNT **Sickness** is the state of being ill or unhealthy. ❑ *He had one week of sickness in fifty-two years of working.* ② N-UNCOUNT **Sickness** is the uncomfortable feeling that you are going to vomit. ❑ *She suffered terribly with sickness when she was pregnant.* ③ N-VAR A **sickness** is a particular illness. ❑ *She became ill with a mysterious sickness.* [from Old English]

---

**side**

① A SURFACE, POSITION, OR PLACE
② ONE ASPECT OR ONE POINT OF VIEW
③ PHRASES

---

**① side** /saɪd/ (**sides**) ① N-COUNT The **side of** something is a position to the left or right of it, rather than in front of it, behind it, or on it. ❑ *On the left side of the door there's a door bell.* ❑ *Joe and Ken stood one on each side of me.* ② N-COUNT The **side** of an object, building, or vehicle is any of its flat surfaces which is not considered to be its front, its back, its top, or its bottom. ❑ *We put a label on the side of the box.* ❑ *The carton of milk lay on its side.* ③ N-COUNT The **sides** of a hollow place or a container are its inside vertical surfaces. ❑ *The sides of the valley are very steep.* ❑ *Grease the bottom and sides of the dish.* ④ N-COUNT The **sides of** an area or surface are its edges. ❑ *We parked on the side of the road.* ❑ *...a beach on the north side of the island.* ⑤ N-COUNT The two **sides of** an area, surface, or object are its two halves or surfaces. ❑ *She lay on the other side of the bed.* ❑ *You should only write on one side of the paper.* ⑥ N-COUNT Your **sides** are the parts of your body between your front and your back, from under your arms to your hips. ❑ *His arms were hanging by his sides.* ⑦ N-COUNT If someone is **by** your **side** or **at** your **side**, they stay near you and give you comfort or support. ❑ *He was at his wife's side the whole time she was sick.* ⑧ ADJ **Side** is used to describe things that are not the main or most

important ones of their kind. ❑ *She left the theater by a side door.* ⑨ N-COUNT A **side** is a small plate of food, such as French fries or salad, that you eat at the same time as the main course of a meal. [from Old English]

**② side** /saɪd/ (**sides, siding, sided**) ① N-COUNT The different **sides** in a war, argument, or negotiation are the groups of people who are opposing each other. ❑ *Both sides want the war to end.* ❑ *We have to find a solution that all sides agree with.* ② N-COUNT The different **sides of** an argument or deal are the different points of view or positions involved in it. ❑ *People on both sides of the issue are angry.* ③ V-I If one person or country **sides with** another, they support them in an argument or a war. If one person or countries **side against** another person or country, they support each other against them. ❑ *Kentucky eventually sided with the Union.* ④ N-COUNT A particular **side** of something such as a situation or someone's character is one aspect of it. ❑ *He showed a kind, gentle side of his character.* [from Old English]

**③ side** /saɪd/ (**sides**) ① PHRASE If something moves **from side to side**, it moves repeatedly to the left and to the right. ❑ *She shook her head from side to side.* ② PHRASE If you are **on** someone's **side**, you are supporting them in an argument or a war. ❑ *He has his manager on his side.* ③ PHRASE If someone does something **on the side**, they do it in addition to their main work. ❑ *She babysits to make a little money on the side.* ④ PHRASE If you have one type of food with another food **on the side**, you have an amount of the second food served with the first. ❑ *Serve a bowl of warm tomato sauce on the side.* ⑤ PHRASE If you **put** something **to one side** or **put** it **on one side**, you temporarily ignore it in order to concentrate on something else. ❑ *He put the project to one side so he could spend more time with his family.* ⑥ PHRASE If two people or things are **side by side**, they are next to each other. ❑ *We sat side by side on the beach.* [from Old English] ⑦ to **err on the side of** something → see **err** ⑧ to **be on the safe side** → see **safe** ⑨ someone's **side of the story** → see **story**

**side effect** (**side effects**) also **side-effect** N-COUNT The **side effects** of a drug are the effects, usually bad ones, that the drug has on you in addition to its function of curing illness or pain. ❑ *The main side effect of the drug is tiredness.*

**side|line** /saɪdlaɪn/ (**sidelines**) ① N-COUNT A **sideline** is something that you do in addition to your main job in order to earn extra money. ❑ *Many musicians teach music as a sideline.* ② N-PLURAL The **sidelines** are the lines marking the long sides of the playing area, for example, on a football field or tennis court. ③ N-PLURAL If you are **on the sidelines** in a situation, you do not influence events at all, either because you have chosen not to be involved, or because other people have not involved you. ❑ *They always leave me on the sidelines when important decisions are made.* → see **basketball, football, soccer, tennis**

**side road** (**side roads**) N-COUNT A **side road** is a road which leads off a busier, more important road.

**side sal|ad** (**side salads**) N-COUNT A **side salad** is a bowl of salad for one person which is served with a main meal.

S

**side|step** /sáɪdstɛp/ (**sidesteps, sidestepping, sidestepped**) also side-step v-т If you **sidestep** a problem, you avoid discussing it or dealing with it. ❑ *The mayor sidestepped the question.*

**side street** (**side streets**) N-COUNT A **side street** is a quiet, often narrow street which leads off a busier street.

**side|walk** /sáɪdwɔk/ (**sidewalks**) N-COUNT A **sidewalk** is a path with a hard surface by the side of a road. ❑ *She was walking down the sidewalk toward him.*

**side|ways** /sáɪdweɪz/ ADV **Sideways** means from or toward the side of something or someone. ❑ *Pete looked sideways at her.* ● **Sideways** is also an adjective. ❑ *Alfred gave him a sideways glance.*

**siege** /sídʒ/ (**sieges**) N-COUNT A **siege** is a military or police operation in which soldiers or police surround a place in order to force the people there to come out or give up control of the place. ❑ *The siege has been going on for three days.* [from Old French]

### Word Partnership  Use *siege* with :

| | |
|---|---|
| PREP. | **after a** siege, **during a** siege, **under** siege |
| V. | **end a** siege, **lift a** siege |

**si|er|ra** /siɛrə/ (**sierras**) N-COUNT A **sierra** is a range of mountains with jagged peaks.❑ *...the remote sierras of the south.* [from Spanish]

**sieve** /sív/ (**sieves, sieving, sieved**) ◼ N-COUNT A **sieve** is a tool used for separating solids from liquids or larger pieces of something from smaller pieces. It consists of a ring with a net underneath, which the liquid or smaller pieces pass through. ❑ *Press the soup through a sieve into a bowl.* ◻ V-T When you **sieve** a substance, you put it through a sieve. ❑ *Sieve the flour into a bowl.* [from Old English]

**sift** /síft/ (**sifts, sifting, sifted**) ◼ V-T If you **sift** a powder such as flour or sand, you put it through a sieve in order to remove large pieces or lumps. ❑ *Sift the flour into a bowl.* ◻ V-I If you **sift through** something such as evidence, you examine it thoroughly. ❑ *Police are still sifting through the remains of the building.* [from Old English]

**sigh** /sáɪ/ (**sighs, sighing, sighed**) V-I When you **sigh**, you let out a deep breath, as a way of expressing feelings such as disappointment, tiredness, or pleasure. ❑ *Michael sighed and sat down slowly.* ❑ *Roberta sighed with relief.* ● **Sigh** is also a noun. ❑ *She kicked off her shoes with a sigh.* [from Old English]

### Word Partnership  Use *sigh* with :

| | |
|---|---|
| ADJ. | **collective** sigh, **deep** sigh, **long** sigh |
| V. | **breathe a** sigh, **give a** sigh, **hear a** sigh, **heave a** sigh, **let out a** sigh |

**sight** /sáɪt/ (**sights, sighting, sighted**) ◼ N-UNCOUNT Your **sight** is your ability to see. ❑ *My sight is not as good as my son's.* ◻ N-SING The **sight** of something is the act of seeing it or an occasion on which you see it. ❑ *I feel ill at the sight of blood.* ◼ V-T If you **sight** someone or something, you suddenly see them, often briefly. ❑ *Police sighted a man entering the building.* ◼ N-PLURAL The

**sights** are the places that are interesting to see and that are often visited by tourists. ❑ *We saw the sights of Paris.* ◼ → see also **sighting** ◼ PHRASE If you **catch sight** of someone, you suddenly see them, often briefly. ❑ *He caught sight of her in the crowd.* ◼ PHRASE If something is **in sight** or **within sight**, you can see it. If it is **out of sight**, you cannot see it. ❑ *At last the beach was in sight.* ◼ PHRASE If a result or a decision is **in sight** or **within sight**, it is likely to happen within a short time. ❑ *An agreement was in sight.* ◼ PHRASE If you **lose sight of** an important aspect of something, you no longer pay attention to it because you are worrying about less important things. ❑ *It is important not to lose sight of what really matters: your family.* ◼ PHRASE If someone does something **on sight**, they do it without delay, as soon as a person or thing is seen. ❑ *He disliked her on sight.* ◼ PHRASE If you **set** your **sights on** something, you decide that you want it and try hard to get it. ❑ *They set their sights on the world record.* [from Old English]

### Word Partnership  Use *sight* with :

| | |
|---|---|
| V. | **catch** sight of *someone/something* ◼ **come into** sight, **keep** *someone/something* **in** sight ◼ |
| N. | **the end is in** sight ◼ |

**sight|ing** /sáɪtɪŋ/ (**sightings**) N-COUNT A **sighting of** something, especially something unusual or unexpected is an occasion on which it is seen. ❑ *...the sighting of a rare sea bird.* [from Old English]

**sight|see|ing** /sáɪtsiɪŋ/ N-UNCOUNT If you go **sightseeing** or do some **sightseeing**, you travel around visiting the interesting places that tourists usually visit. ❑ *...a day's sightseeing in Venice.*
→ see **city**

**sight word** (**sight words**) N-COUNT A **sight word** is a word that most readers of a language can recognize immediately without needing to analyze its separate parts. [TECHNICAL]

**sign** /sáɪn/ (**signs, signing, signed**) ◼ N-COUNT A **sign** is a mark or shape that always has a particular meaning, for example, in mathematics or music. ❑ *This = is an equals sign.* ◻ N-COUNT A **sign** is a movement of your arms, hands, or head which is intended to have a particular meaning. ❑ *They gave me a thumbs-up sign to show that everything was OK.* ◼ N-COUNT A **sign** is a piece of wood, metal, or plastic with words or pictures on it. Signs give you information about something, or give you a warning or an instruction. ❑ *There was a sign saying that the highway was closed because of snow.* ◼ N-VAR If there is a **sign of** something, there is something which shows that it exists or is happening. ❑ *Some people see crying as a sign of weakness.* ❑ *His face rarely showed any sign of fear.* ◼ V-T When you **sign** a document, you write your name on it. ❑ *World leaders have signed an agreement to protect the environment.* ● **sign|ing** N-UNCOUNT ❑ *The signing of the treaty will take place today.* ◼ V-T/V-I If an organization **signs** someone or if someone **signs** for an organization, they sign a contract agreeing to work for that organization for a specified period of time. ❑ *The Minnesota Vikings signed Walker to play for them for the next three years.* ◼ N-COUNT In astrology, a **sign** or a **sign of**

## Picture Dictionary    sign language

### The American Manual Alphabet

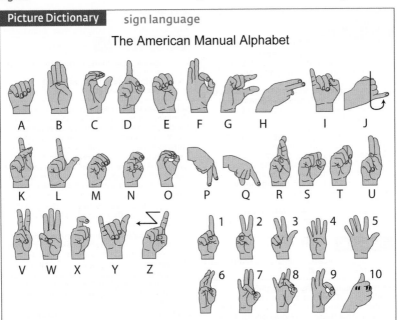

A B C D E F G H I J

K L M N O P Q R S T U

V W X Y Z

1 2 3 4 5

6 7 8 9 10

---

the **zodiac** is one of the twelve areas into which the heavens are divided. □ *She was born under the sign of Libra.* **8** PHRASE If you say that there is **no sign of** someone, you mean that they have not yet arrived, although you are expecting them to come. □ *I arrived at the meeting place, but there was no sign of Laura.* [from Old French]

▶ **sign for** PHR-VERB If you **sign for** something, you officially state that you have received it, by signing a form or book. □ *A package arrived and I signed for it.*

▶ **sign in** PHR-VERB If you **sign in**, you officially indicate that you have arrived at a hotel or club by signing a book or form. □ *I signed in and went straight to my room.*

▶ **sign up** PHR-VERB If you **sign up** for an organization or if an organization **signs** you **up**, you sign a contract officially agreeing to do a job or course of study. □ *He signed up as a flight attendant with American Airlines.*

→ see Picture Dictionary: **sign language**

| Thesaurus | sign | Also look up : |
|---|---|---|
| N. | nod, signal, wave **2** | |
| V. | authorize, autograph, endorse **5** | |

**sig|nal** /sɪgnəl/ (**signals, signaling** or **signalling, signaled** or **signalled**) **1** N-COUNT A **signal** is a gesture, sound, or action which is intended to give a particular message to the person who sees or hears it. □ *The captain gave the signal to attack.* **2** V-T/V-I If you **signal to** someone, you make a gesture or sound in order to send them a particular message. □ *Mandy signaled to Jesse to follow her.* □ *She signaled that she was leaving.* **3** N-COUNT If an event

or action is a **signal of** something, it suggests that this thing exists or is going to happen. □ *His visit seemed to be a signal of support.* **4** V-T If someone or something **signals** an event, they suggest that the event is happening or likely to happen. □ *In her speech, she signaled important changes in government policy.* **5** N-COUNT A **signal** is a piece of equipment beside a railroad, which indicates to engineers whether they should stop the train or not. □ *The crash was caused by a broken signal.* **6** N-COUNT A **signal** is a series of radio waves, light waves, or changes in electrical current which may carry information. □ *...high-frequency radio signals.* [from Old French]

→ see **cellphone, television**

| Word Partnership | Use *signal* with : |
|---|---|
| V. | give a signal **1 3** |
| | send a signal **1 3 6** |
| ADJ. | wrong signal **1 3** |
| | clear signal, strong signal **1 3 6** |
| | important signal **3** |

**sig|na|tory** /sɪgnətɔri/ (**signatories**) N-COUNT The **signatories** of an official document are the people, organizations, or countries that have signed it. [FORMAL] □ *Both countries are signatories to the treaty.* [from Latin]

**sig|na|ture** /sɪgnətʃər, -tʃʊər/ (**signatures**) N-COUNT Your **signature** is your name, written in your own characteristic way. □ *I put my signature at the bottom of the page.* [from Old French]

**sig|nifi|cance** /sɪgnɪfɪkəns/ N-UNCOUNT The **significance** of something is the importance that

S

it has. ❑ *What do you think is the significance of this event?* [from Latin]

**sig|nifi|cant** /sɪgnɪfɪkənt/ **1** ADJ A **significant** amount or effect is large enough to be important or noticeable. ❑ *A small but significant number of 11-year-olds cannot read.* ● **sig|nifi|cant|ly** ADV ❑ *The number of Senators who agreed with him increased significantly.* **2** ADJ A **significant** fact, event, or thing is one that is important or shows something. ❑ *I think it was significant that he never knew his own father.* ● **sig|nifi|cant|ly** ADV ❑ *Significantly, the company recently opened a huge store in Atlanta.* [from Latin]

**sig|ni|fy** /sɪgnɪfaɪ/ (**signifies, signifying, signified**) V-T If an event, a sign, or a symbol **signifies** something, it is a sign of that thing or represents that thing. ❑ *These changes signify the end of childhood.* [from Old French]

**Sikh** /siːk/ (**Sikhs**) N-COUNT A **Sikh** is a person who follows the Indian religion of Sikhism. Sihkism is an Indian religion which separated from Hinduism in the sixteenth century and which teaches that there is only one God. ❑ *Her husband is a Sikh.* ❑ *...a Sikh temple.* [from Hindi]

**si|lence** /saɪləns/ (**silences, silencing, silenced**) **1** N-VAR If there is **silence**, nobody is speaking. ❑ *They stood in silence.* ❑ *There was a long silence.* **2** N-UNCOUNT Someone's **silence** about something is their failure or refusal to speak to other people about it. ❑ *His silence on the subject doesn't mean he is guilty.* **3** PHRASE If someone **breaks** their **silence** about something, they talk about something that they have not talked about before for a long time. **4** V-T If someone **silences** you, they stop you from expressing opinions that they do not agree with. ❑ *He tried to silence anyone who spoke out against him.* [from Old French]

**si|lent** /saɪlənt/ **1** ADJ Someone who is **silent** is not speaking. ❑ *Trish was silent because she did not know what to say.* ❑ *He spoke no English and stayed completely silent.* ● **si|lent|ly** ADV ❑ *She and Ned sat silently, enjoying the peace of the lake.* **2** ADJ A place that is **silent** is completely quiet, with no sound

at all. Something that is **silent** makes no sound at all. ❑ *The room was silent except for the TV.* ● **si|lent|ly** ADV ❑ *He moved silently across the room.* [from Latin]

**si|lent part|ner** (**silent partners**) N-COUNT A **silent partner** is a person who provides some of the capital for a business but who does not take an active part in managing the business. [BUSINESS]

**sil|hou|ette** /sɪluːɛt/ (**silhouettes**) N-COUNT A **silhouette** is the solid dark shape that you see when someone or something has a bright light or pale background behind them. ❑ *The silhouette of the castle stood out against the sky.* [from French]

**sili|ca** /sɪlɪkə/ N-UNCOUNT **Silica** is silicon dioxide, a compound of silicon which is found in sand, quartz, and flint, and which is used to make glass [from New Latin]

**sili|cate min|er|al** /sɪlɪkɪt mɪnərəl/ (**silicate minerals**) N-COUNT **Silicate minerals** are minerals that are made mostly of a substance called silica.

**sili|con** /sɪlɪkən, -kɒn/ N-UNCOUNT **Silicon** is an element that is found in sand and in minerals such as quartz and granite. Silicon is used to make parts of computers and other electronic equipment. ❑ *...a silicon chip.*

**sili|cone** /sɪlɪkoʊn/ N-UNCOUNT **Silicone** is a tough artificial substance made from silicon, which is used to make polishes, and also used in cosmetic surgery and plastic surgery. ❑ *Regular silicone treatments will keep these boots waterproof.*

**silk** /sɪlk/ (**silks**) N-VAR **Silk** is a substance which is made into smooth fine cloth and sewing thread. You can also refer to this cloth or thread as **silk**. ❑ *They bought silks from China.* ❑ *Pauline wore a silk dress.* [from Old English]

**silky** /sɪlki/ (**silkier, silkiest**) ADJ If something has a **silky** texture, it is smooth, soft, and shiny, like silk. ❑ *...dresses in silky fabrics.* [from Old English]

**sill** /sɪl/ (**sills**) N-COUNT A **sill** is a shelf along the bottom edge of a window, either inside or outside a building. ❑ *Whitlock sat on the sill by the desk.* [from Old English]

**sil|ly** /sɪli/ (**sillier, silliest**) ADJ If you say that someone or something is **silly**, you mean that they are foolish, childish, or ridiculous. ❑ *She thinks that I am silly.* ❑ *I thought it would be silly to say no.* ● **sil|li|ness** N-UNCOUNT ❑ *Let's stop this silliness.* [from Old English]

**silt** /sɪlt/ N-UNCOUNT **Silt** is fine sand, soil, or mud which is carried along by a river. ❑ *The lake was full of silt.* [of Scandinavian origin] → see **erosion**

**sil|ver** /sɪlvər/ **1** N-UNCOUNT **Silver** is a valuable pale gray metal that is used for making jewelry and ornaments. ❑ *...a bracelet made from silver.* **2** N-UNCOUNT **Silver** consists of coins that are made from silver or that look like silver. ❑ *The thieves took $150,000 in silver.* **3** N-UNCOUNT You can use **silver** to refer to all the things in a house that are made of silver, especially the flatware and dishes. ❑ *He polished the silver.* **4** COLOR **Silver**

is used to describe things that are shiny and pale gray in color. ❑ *He had thick silver hair.* [from Old English]
→ see **mineral, money, silverware**

**sil|ver med|al** (**silver medals**) N-COUNT If you win a **silver medal**, you come second in a competition. ❑ *Gillingham won the silver medal in the 200 meters.*

**sil|very** /sɪlvəri/ ADJ **Silvery** things look like silver or are the color of silver. ❑ *My father is a small man with silvery hair.* [from Old English]

**SIM card** /sɪm kɑrd/ (**SIM cards**) N-COUNT A **SIM card** is a microchip in a cell phone that connects it to a particular phone network. **SIM** is an abbreviation for "Subscriber Identity Module."

**simi|lar** /sɪmɪlər/ **1** ADJ If one thing is **similar to** another, or if two things are **similar**, they have features that are the same. ❑ *The cake tastes similar to carrot cake.* ❑ *The accident was similar to one that happened in 2003.* **2** ADJ In geometry, two figures, such as triangles, are **similar** if they have the same shape, although they may not be the same size. [TECHNICAL] [from Old French]

**simi|lar|ity** /sɪmɪlærɪti/ (**similarities**) **1** N-UNCOUNT If there is a **similarity between** two or more things, they are similar to each other. ❑ *I was amazed at the similarity between the brothers.* **2** N-COUNT **Similarities** are features that things have which make them similar to each other. ❑ *There are some similarities between the two machines.* **3** N-UNCOUNT In geometry, **similarity** is the relationship between two figures such as triangles that have the same shape, although they may not be the same size. [TECHNICAL] [from Old French]

**simi|lar|ly** /sɪmɪlərli/ **1** ADV You use **similarly** to say that something is similar to something else. ❑ *Most of the men were similarly dressed.* **2** ADV You use **similarly** when mentioning a fact or situation that is similar to the one you have just mentioned. ❑ *Young babies prefer faces to other shapes. Similarly, they prefer familiar faces to ones they don't know.* [from Old French]

**sim|mer** /sɪmər/ (**simmers, simmering, simmered**) V-T/V-I When you **simmer** food or when it **simmers**, you cook it by keeping it at boiling point or just below boiling point. ❑ *Simmer the fruit and sugar together.* [from German]

**sim|ple** /sɪmpᵊl/ (**simpler, simplest**) **1** ADJ If something is **simple**, it is not complicated, and is therefore easy to understand. ❑ *...simple pictures and diagrams.* ❑ *...some simple advice on filling in forms.* ● **simp|ly** ADV ❑ *He explained his views simply and clearly.* **2** ADJ If you describe people or things as **simple**, you mean that they have all the basic or necessary things they require, but nothing extra. ❑ *He ate a simple dinner of rice and beans.* ❑ *...the simple pleasures of childhood.* ● **simp|ly** ADV ❑ *She decorated her house simply.* **3** ADJ You use **simple** to emphasize that the thing you are referring to is the only important or relevant reason for something. ❑ *One reason why he found his new life difficult was simple boredom.* **4** ADJ In grammar, **simple** tenses are ones which are formed without an auxiliary verb "be," for example, "I dressed and went for a walk" and "This tastes nice." Compare **continuous.** [from Old French] **5** → see also **simply**

**Thesaurus** *simple* Also look up :

ADJ. clear, easy, understandable; (*ant.*) complicated **1** **3** plain **2**

**Word Partnership** Use *simple* with :

N. simple **concept**, simple **explanation**, simple simple **language**, simple **message**, simple **procedure**, simple **steps** **1**
simple **life**, simple **pleasure** **2**
simple **answer**, simple **matter**, simple **question**, simple **task**, simple **test** **3**
ADV. simple **enough**, so simple **1** **3**
**fairly** simple, **quite** simple, **pretty** simple, **really** simple, **relatively** simple, **very** simple **1** – **3**

**sim|ple ma|chine** (**simple machines**) N-COUNT A **simple machine** is a device such as a lever, wheel, or screw that forms a part of other, more complex machines. Compare **compound machine**.

**sim|plic|ity** /sɪmplɪsɪti/ N-UNCOUNT The **simplicity** of something is the fact that it is not complicated and can be understood or done easily. ❑ *The simplicity of the story makes it popular with children.* [from Old French]

**sim|pli|fy** /sɪmplɪfaɪ/ (**simplifies, simplifying, simplified**) V-T If you **simplify** something, you make it easier to understand. ❑ *We want to simplify the education system.* ● **sim|pli|fied** ADJ ❑ *...a short, simplified version of his speech.* ● **sim|pli|fi|ca|tion** /sɪmplɪfɪkeɪʃᵊn/ (**simplifications**) N-VAR ❑ *...the simplification of legal language.* [from French]

**sim|plis|tic** /sɪmplɪstɪk/ ADJ A **simplistic** view or interpretation of something makes it seem much simpler than it really is. ❑ *He has a simplistic view of how society works.* [from Old French]

**sim|ply** /sɪmpli/ **1** ADV You use **simply** to emphasize that something consists of only one thing, happens for only one reason, or is done in only one way. ❑ *The table is simply a circle of wood.* ❑ *Most of the damage was simply caused by falling trees.* **2** ADV You use **simply** to emphasize what you are saying. ❑ *This behavior is simply unacceptable.* [from Old French] **3** → see also **simple**

**simu|late** /sɪmyəleɪt/ (**simulates, simulating, simulated**) V-T If you **simulate** an action or a feeling, you pretend to do it. If you **simulate** a set of conditions, you create them artificially. ❑ *He tried to simulate confidence.* ❑ *Scientists developed a model to simulate the globe's climate.* ● **simu|la|tion** /sɪmyəleɪʃᵊn/ (**simulations**) N-VAR ❑ *Training includes a simulation of an accident.* [from Latin]

**sim|ul|ta|neous** /saɪmᵊlteɪniəs/ ADJ Things which are **simultaneous** happen or exist at the same time. ❑ *...the simultaneous release of the book and the CD.* ● **sim|ul|ta|neous|ly** ADV ❑ *They began to speak simultaneously.* [from Latin]

**sin** /sɪn/ (**sins, sinning, sinned**) **1** N-VAR **Sin** or a **sin** is an action or type of behavior which is believed to break the laws of God. ❑ *Lying is a sin.* **2** V-I If you **sin**, you do something that is believed to break the laws of God. ❑ *She believes she has sinned.* ● **sin|ner** /sɪnər/ (**sinners**) N-COUNT ❑ *Her mother thinks she's a sinner.* [from Old English]

**S**

**since** /sɪns/ ■ PREP You use **since** when you are mentioning a time or event in the past and indicating that a situation has continued from then until now. ❑ *He's lived in India since 1995.* ❑ *They met ten years ago, and since then they have had three children.* ● **Since** is also an adverb. ❑ *They worked together in the 1980s, and have kept in contact ever since.* ● **Since** is also a conjunction. ❑ *I've earned my own living since I was seventeen.* ❷ PREP You use **since** to mention a time or event in the past when you are describing an event or situation that has happened after that time. ❑ *I haven't seen him since the war.* ● **Since** is also a conjunction. ❑ *So much has changed since I was a teenager.* ❸ ADV When you are talking about an event or situation in the past, you use **since** to indicate that another event happened at some point later in time. ❑ *Five people were arrested, but have since been released.* ❹ CONJ You use **since** to introduce reasons or explanations. ❑ *I'm always on a diet, since I put on weight easily.* [from Old English]

**sin|cere** /sɪnsɪər/ ADJ If you say that someone is **sincere**, you approve of them because they really mean the things they say. ❑ *He's sincere in his views.* ● **sin|cer|ity** /sɪnsɛrɪti/ N-UNCOUNT ❑ *I like his sincerity.* [from Latin]

**sin|cere|ly** /sɪnsɪərli/ ❶ ADV If you say or feel something **sincerely**, you really mean or feel it, and are not pretending. ❑ *"Congratulations," he said sincerely.* ❷ CONVENTION People write "**Sincerely yours**" or "**Sincerely**" before their signature at the end of a formal letter when they have addressed it to someone by name. People sometimes write "**Yours sincerely**" instead. ❑ *Sincerely yours, Robbie Weinz.* [from Latin]

**sine** /saɪn/ (**sines**) N-COUNT A **sine** is a mathematical calculation that is used especially in the study of triangles. In a right triangle, the sine is the ratio between the hypotenuse and the side opposite a particular angle. The abbreviation **sin** is also used. [TECHNICAL] [from Latin]

**sinew** /sɪnyu/ (**sinew**) N-COUNT A **sinew** is a cord in your body that connects a muscle to a bone. ❑ *...the sinews of the neck.*

**sin|ful** /sɪnfəl/ ADJ If you describe someone or something as **sinful**, you mean that they are wicked or immoral. ❑ *This is a sinful world.* [from Old English]

**sing** /sɪŋ/ (**sings, singing, sang, sung**) V-T/V-I When you **sing**, you make musical sounds with your voice, usually producing words that fit a tune. ❑ *I love singing.* ❑ *He sings about love most of the time.* ❑ *They were all singing the same song.* ● **sing|ing** N-UNCOUNT ❑ *...a carnival, with singing and dancing in the streets.* ❑ *...the singing of a traditional hymn.* [from Old English]

▸ **sing along** PHR-VERB If you **sing along with** a piece of music, you sing it while you are listening to someone else perform it. ❑ *The children can sing along with all the tunes.* ❑ *Fifteen hundred people all sang along.*

**sing|er** /sɪŋər/ (**singers**) N-COUNT A **singer** is a person who sings, especially as a job. ❑ *My mother was a singer in a band.* [from Old English]
→ see **concert**

**sin|gle** /sɪŋgᵊl/ (**singles, singling, singled**) ■ ADJ You use **single** to emphasize that you are referring to one thing, and no more than one thing. ❑ *She hasn't said a single word.* ❑ *We sold over two hundred pizzas in a single day.* ❷ ADJ You use **single** to indicate that you are considering something on its own and separately from other things like it. ❑ *It is the single most important decision I have ever made.* ❸ ADJ Someone who is **single** is not married. ❑ *When I was single, I never worried about money.* ❹ ADJ A **single** room is a room intended for one person to stay or live in. ❑ *Each guest has her own single room.* ❺ ADJ A **single** bed is wide enough for one person to sleep in. ❑ *...his bedroom with its single bed.* ❻ N-COUNT A **single** is a CD which has one main song or a few songs on it. ❑ *...the band's new single.* ❼ N-UNCOUNT **Singles** is a game of tennis or badminton in which one player plays another. The plural **singles** can be used to refer to one or more of these matches. ❑ *Roger Federer won the men's singles.* [from Old French] ❽ **in single file** → see **file**
→ see **hotel, tennis**

▸ **single out** PHR-VERB If you **single** someone **out** from a group, you choose them and give them special attention or treatment. ❑ *She always singles me out and criticizes me.* ❑ *His boss singled him out for special praise.*

**single-handed** also **single-handedly** ADV If you do something **single-handed**, you do it on your own, without help from anyone else. ❑ *I brought up my seven children single-handed.*

**single-minded** ADJ Someone who is **single-minded** has only one aim or purpose and is determined to achieve it. ❑ *They were single-minded in their desire to win.* ● **single-mindedness** N-UNCOUNT ❑ *...the single-mindedness of the athletes as they train.*

**sin|gle par|ent** (**single parents**) N-COUNT A **single parent** is someone who is bringing up a child on their own, because the other parent is not living with them. ❑ *I raised my three children as a single parent.* ❑ *...single-parent families.*

**sin|gle-re|place|ment re|ac|tion** (**single-replacement reactions**) N-COUNT A **single-replacement reaction** is a chemical reaction between an element and a compound in which the atoms of the element switch places with some of the atoms of the compound. Compare **double-replacement reaction**. [TECHNICAL]

**sin|gu|lar** /sɪŋgyələr/ ■ ADJ The **singular** form of a word is the form that is used when referring to one person or thing. ❑ *The singular form of "mice" is "mouse."* ❷ N-SING The **singular** of a noun is the form of it that is used to refer to one person or thing. ❑ *What is the singular of "geese?"* [from Latin]

**sin|is|ter** /sɪnɪstər/ ADJ Something that is **sinister** seems evil or harmful. ❑ *There was* *something sinister about him.* [from Latin]

**sink** /sɪŋk/ (**sinks, sinking, sank, sunk**)

**1** N-COUNT A **sink** is a large fixed container in a kitchen or bathroom, with faucets to supply water. □ *There were dirty dishes in the sink.* □ *The bathroom has a toilet, a shower, and a sink.* **2** V-T/V-I If a boat **sinks** or if someone or something **sinks** it, it disappears below the surface of a mass of water. □ *The boat was beginning to sink.* □ *A torpedo from a submarine sank the ship.* **3** V-I If something **sinks**, it disappears below the surface of a mass of water. □ *A fresh egg will sink and an old egg will float.* **4** V-I If something **sinks**, it moves slowly downward. □ *In the west the sun was sinking.* **5** V-I If something **sinks to** a lower level or standard, it falls to that level or standard. □ *Pay increases have sunk to around three percent.* **6** V-I If your heart or your spirits **sink**, you become depressed or lose hope. □ *My heart sank because I thought he didn't like me.* **7** V-T/V-I If something sharp **sinks** or is **sunk into** something solid, it goes deeply into it. □ *I sank my teeth into an apple.* [from Old English] **8** → see also **sunk**

→ see **bathroom**

▸ **sink in** PHR-VERB When a statement or fact **sinks in**, you finally understand or realize it fully. □ *The news took a while to sink in.*

---

**Word Partnership** Use *sink* with :

| | |
|---|---|
| N. | **bathroom** sink, **dishes in a** sink, **kitchen** sink **1** sink **a ship 2** |

---

**sip** /sɪp/ (**sips, sipping, sipped**) **1** V-T/V-I If you **sip** a drink or **sip at** it, you drink by taking just a small amount at a time. □ *Jessica sipped her drink slowly.* □ *He sipped at the lemonade.* **2** N-COUNT A **sip** is a small amount of drink that you take into your mouth. □ *Harry took a sip of tea.* [from Low German]

**si|phon** /saɪfᵊn/ (**siphons, siphoning, siphoned**) also **syphon** **1** V-T If you **siphon** liquid from a container, you make it come out through a tube by enabling the pressure of the air on it to push it out. □ *Someone tried to siphon gas from his car.* **2** N-COUNT A **siphon** is a tube that you use for siphoning liquid. [from Latin]

**sir** /sɜr/ (**sirs**) **1** N-VOC People sometimes say **sir** as a polite way of addressing a man whose name they do not know, or an older man. □ *Excuse me sir, is this your car?* **2** N-TITLE **Sir** is the title used in front of the name of a knight. □ *She introduced me to Sir Tobias and Lady Clarke.* **3** CONVENTION You use the expression **Dear Sir** at the beginning of a formal letter or a business letter when you are writing to a man. □ *Dear Sir, Enclosed is a copy of my résumé for your consideration.*

**si|ren** /saɪrən/ (**sirens**) N-COUNT A **siren** is a warning device which makes a long, loud noise. Most fire engines, ambulances, and police cars have sirens. □ *We heard a police siren.* [from Old French]

**sis|ter** /sɪstər/ (**sisters**) **1** N-COUNT Your **sister** is a girl or woman who has the same parents as you. □ *This is my sister Sarah.* □ *...Vanessa Bell, the sister of Virginia Woolf.* **2** N-TITLE; N-COUNT; N-VOC **Sister** is a title given to a woman who belongs to a religious community, such as a nun. □ *Sister Francesca went into the chapel.* **3** N-COUNT You can describe a woman as your **sister** if you feel a

connection with her, for example, because she belongs to the same race, religion, country, or profession. □ *...our Jewish brothers and sisters.* [from Old English]

→ see **family**

**sister-in-law** (**sisters-in-law**) N-COUNT Your **sister-in-law** is the sister of your husband or wife, or the woman who is married to your brother.

→ see **family**

**sit** /sɪt/ (**sits, sitting, sat**) **1** V-I If you **are sitting** somewhere, for example, in a chair, your bottom is resting on the chair and the upper part of your body is upright. □ *Mother was sitting in her chair in the kitchen.* □ *They sat watching television.* **2** V-I When you **sit** somewhere, you lower your body until you are sitting on something. □ *He put down the box and sat on it.* □ *Eva got a chair and sat beside her husband.* ● **Sit down** means the same as **sit**. □ *I sat down, shocked.* **3** V-T If you **sit** someone somewhere, you tell them to sit there or put them in a sitting position. □ *Dad sat me on his lap.* ● To **sit** someone **down** somewhere means to **sit** them there. □ *She sat the baby down on the floor.* **4** V-I If you **sit on** a committee or other official group, you are a member of it. □ *They asked him to sit on the committee.* **5** V-I When a legislature, court, or other official body **sits**, it officially carries out its work. [FORMAL] □ *We will discuss this next time the Parliament sits.* **6** PHRASE If you **sit tight**, you remain in the same place or situation and do not take any action, usually because you are waiting for something to happen. □ *Sit tight. I'll be right back.* [from Old English] **7** to **sit on the fence** → see **fence**

▸ **sit back** PHR-VERB If you **sit back** while something is happening, you relax and do not become involved in it. [INFORMAL] □ *Just sit back and enjoy the show.*

▸ **sit in on** PHR-VERB If you **sit in on** a lesson, meeting, or discussion, you are present while it is taking place but do not take part in it. □ *I sat in on a few classes.*

▸ **sit on** PHR-VERB If you say that someone **is sitting on** something, you mean that they are delaying dealing with it. [INFORMAL] □ *He sat on my job application for weeks.*

▸ **sit out** PHR-VERB If you **sit** something **out**, you wait for it to finish, without taking any action. □ *I decided to keep quiet and sit the argument out.*

▸ **sit through** PHR-VERB If you **sit through** something such as a movie, lecture, or meeting, you stay until it is finished although you are not enjoying it. □ *The movie was so bad I couldn't sit through it.*

▸ **sit up** **1** PHR-VERB If you **sit up**, you move into a sitting position when you have been leaning back or lying down. □ *She felt dizzy when she sat up.* **2** PHR-VERB If you **sit up**, you do not go to bed although it is very late. □ *We sat up talking.* **3** → see also **sit-up**

---

**Usage** **sit and set**

Be careful not to confuse the verbs *sit* and *set*. *Sit* means "to be seated," and is generally used intransitively: *Sit down and let's get started. Set* means "to place something down somewhere," and is generally used transitively: *Terence took off his glasses and set them on the table.*

S

## Word Partnership  Use *sit* with :

| | |
|---|---|
| ADV. | sit **alone**, sit **back**, sit **comfortably**, sit **quietly**, sit **still** 🔟 |
| PREP. | sit **in a circle**, sit **on the porch**, sit **on the sidelines** 🔟 |
| | sit **on a bench**, sit **in a chair**, sit **down to dinner**, sit **on the floor**, sit **on** *someone's* **lap**, sit **around/at a table** 🔟 🔞 |
| V. | sit **and eat**, sit **and enjoy**, sit **and listen**, sit **and talk**, sit **and wait**, sit **and watch** (or sit **watching**) 🔟 |
| | sit **down to eat**, sit **down and relax** 🔟 🔞 |

**site** /saɪt/ (**sites**, **siting**, **sited**) 🔟 N-COUNT A **site** is a piece of ground that is used for a particular purpose or where a particular thing happens. ❑ *I worked on a building site.* ❑ *This city was the site of a terrible earthquake.* 🔞 N-COUNT A **site** is the same as a **website**. ❑ *Here are some of the best sites for online shopping.* 🔟 V-T If something **is sited** in a particular place or position, it is put there or built there. ❑ *These weapons have never been sited in Germany.* ● **sit|ing** N-SING ❑ *...the siting of a new power plant.* [from Latin]

**situ|at|ed** /sɪtʃueɪtɪd/ ADJ If something is **situated** in a particular place or position, it is in that place or position. ❑ *His hotel is situated in the Loire Valley.* [from Late Latin]

## Word Link  site, situ ≈ position, location : campsite, situation, website

**situa|tion** /sɪtʃueɪʃən/ (**situations**) N-COUNT You use **situation** to refer generally to what is happening in a particular place at a particular time, or to refer to what is happening to you. ❑ *His situation is very difficult, because he has no job or home.* ❑ *Army officers said the situation was under control.* [from Late Latin]

## Word Partnership  Use *situation* with :

| | |
|---|---|
| ADJ. | **bad** situation, **complicated** situation, **current** situation, **dangerous** situation, **difficult** situation, **economic** situation, **financial** situation, **political** situation, **present** situation, **same** situation, **tense** situation, **terrible** situation, **unique** situation, **unusual** situation, **whole** situation |
| V. | **describe a** situation, **discuss a** situation, **handle a** situation, **improve a** situation, **understand a** situation |

**sit-up** (**sit-ups**) also **situp** N-COUNT **Sit-ups** are exercises that you do to strengthen your stomach muscles. They involve sitting up from a lying position while keeping your knees slightly bent and your feet flat on the floor. ❑ *He does 100 sit-ups each day.*

**six** /sɪks/ (**sixes**) NUM **Six** is the number 6. [from Old English]

**six king|doms** N-PLURAL The **six kingdoms** are the six general types of organism that make up all living things: Animalia, Plantae, Fungi, Protista, Archaebacteria and Eubacteria. [TECHNICAL]

**six|teen** /sɪkstin/ (**sixteens**) NUM **Sixteen** is the number 16. [from Old English]

**six|teenth** /sɪkstinθ/ (**sixteenths**) 🔟 ORD The sixteenth item in a series is the one that you count as number sixteen. ❑ *...the sixteenth century AD.* 🔞 N-COUNT A **sixteenth** is one of sixteen equal parts of something. ❑ *...a sixteenth of a second.* [from Old English]

**sixth** /sɪksθ/ (**sixths**) 🔟 ORD The **sixth** item in a series is the one that you count as number six. ❑ *...the sixth round of the competition.* 🔞 N-COUNT A **sixth** is one of six equal parts of something. ❑ *A sixth of the workforce lost their jobs.* [from Old English]

**sixth form** (**sixth forms**) also **sixth-form** N-COUNT The **sixth form** in a British school consists of students aged 16 to 18.

**six|ti|eth** /sɪkstiəθ/ (**sixtieths**) ORD The **sixtieth** item in a series is the one that you count as number sixty. ❑ *...his sixtieth birthday.* [from Old English]

**six|ty** /sɪksti/ (**sixties**) 🔟 NUM **Sixty** is the number 60. 🔞 N-PLURAL The **sixties** is the decade between 1960 and 1969. ❑ *He came to Britain in the sixties to work as a doctor.* [from Old English]

**siz|able** /saɪzəbªl/ also **sizeable** ADJ **Sizable** means fairly large. ❑ *Harry bought a sizable piece of land.* [from Old French]

**size** /saɪz/ (**sizes**, **sizing**, **sized**) 🔟 N-VAR The **size** of something is how big or small it is. ❑ *The size of the room was about 10 feet by 15 feet.* ❑ *...shelves containing books of various sizes.* ● **-sized** ADJ ❑ *...a medium-sized company.* 🔞 N-UNCOUNT The **size** of something is the fact that it is very large. ❑ *He understands the size of the task.* 🔟 N-COUNT A **size** is one of a series of graded measurements, especially for things such as clothes or shoes. ❑ *My sister is a size 8.* ❑ *What size are your feet?* [from Old French] ▸ **size up** PHR-VERB If you **size up** a person or situation, you carefully look at the person or think about the situation, so that you can decide how to act. [INFORMAL] ❑ *The two groups of men looked at each other, sizing one another up.*

## Word Partnership  Use *size* with :

| | |
|---|---|
| ADJ. | **average** size, **full** size 🔟 **sheer** size 🔞 size **large/medium/small**, **mid** size, **right** size, 🔟 |
| N. | **bite** size, **class** size, **family** size, **life** size, **pocket** size 🔟 size **chart**, **king/queen** size 🔟 |
| V. | **double in** size, **increase in** size, **vary in** size 🔟 a size **fits** 🔟 |

**siz|zle** /sɪzªl/ (**sizzles**, **sizzling**, **sizzled**) V-I If something such as hot oil or fat **sizzles**, it makes hissing sounds. ❑ *The sausages sizzled on the barbecue.* [from West Frisian]

**skate** /skeɪt/ (**skates**, **skating**, **skated**) 🔟 N-COUNT **Skates** are ice-skates. 🔞 N-COUNT **Skates** are roller-skates. 🔟 V-I If you **skate**, you move around wearing ice-skates or roller-skates. ❑ *When the pond freezes you can skate on it.* ● **skat|ing** N-UNCOUNT ❑ *They all went skating together in the winter.* ● **skat|er** (**skaters**) N-COUNT ❑ *The ice-rink was full of skaters.* [from Dutch]

**ske|dad|dle** /skɪdædªl/ (**skedaddles**, **skedaddling**, **skedaddled**) V-I If you tell someone to **skedaddle**, you are telling them to run away or to leave a place quickly. [INFORMAL] ❑ *Now you children skedaddle. Go outside and play.*

**skel|etal** /skɛlɪt³l/ ADJ **Skeletal** means relating to the bones in your body. ❑ *...the skeletal remains of a large animal.* [from New Latin]
→ see **muscle**

**skel|etal mus|cle** (**skeletal muscles**) N-VAR **Skeletal muscle** is muscle that is attached to a bone and can therefore move parts of your body. [TECHNICAL]

**skel|eton** /skɛlɪt³n/ (**skeletons**) **1** N-COUNT Your **skeleton** is the framework of bones in your body. ❑ *...a human skeleton.* **2** ADJ A **skeleton** staff is the smallest number of staff necessary in order to run an organization or service. ❑ *We have just a skeleton staff working here over the holiday period.* [from New Latin]
→ see **shark**

**skep|tic** /skɛptɪk/ (**skeptics**) N-COUNT A **skeptic** is a person who has doubts about things that other people believe. ❑ *He is a skeptic who tries to keep an open mind.* [from Latin]

**skep|ti|cal** /skɛptɪk³l/ ADJ If you are **skeptical about** something, you have doubts about it. ❑ *We are skeptical about whether he has made the right decision.* [from Latin]

**skep|ti|cism** /skɛptɪsɪzəm/ N-UNCOUNT **Skepticism** is great doubt about whether something is true or useful. ❑ *People feel a lot of skepticism about the president's plans.* [from Latin]

**sketch** /skɛtʃ/ (**sketches, sketching, sketched**) **1** N-COUNT A **sketch** is a drawing that is done quickly without a lot of details. ❑ *He did a quick sketch of the building.* **2** V-T/V-I If you **sketch** something, you make a quick, rough drawing of it. ❑ *I always sketch with a pen.* ❑ *She sketched a view of the hills.* **3** N-COUNT A **sketch of** a situation, person, or incident is a brief description of it without many details. ❑ *He writes amusing sketches about politicians.* **4** V-T If you **sketch** a situation or incident, you give a short description of it, including only the most important facts. ❑ *Smith sketched the story briefly.* ● **Sketch out** means the same as **sketch**. ❑ *He sketched out his plans for the future.* **5** N-COUNT A **sketch** is a short humorous piece of acting, usually forming part of a comedy show. ❑ *They performed a very funny sketch about the president.* [from Dutch]
→ see **animation, draw**

**sketchy** /skɛtʃi/ (**sketchier, sketchiest**) ADJ **Sketchy** information about something does not include many details and is therefore incomplete or inadequate. ❑ *Details of what actually happened are sketchy.* [from Dutch]

**skew|er** /skyuər/ (**skewers**) N-COUNT A **skewer** is a long pin made of wood or metal that is used to hold pieces of food together during cooking.

**ski** /ski/ (**skis, skiing, skied**) **1** N-COUNT **Skis** are long, flat, narrow pieces of wood, metal, or plastic that are fastened to boots so that you can move easily on snow or water. ❑ *...a pair of skis.* **2** V-I When people **ski**, they move over snow or water on skis. ❑ *They love to ski.* ● **ski|er** /skiər/ (**skiers**) N-COUNT ❑ *He is a good skier.* ● **ski|ing** N-UNCOUNT ❑ *My hobbies are skiing and swimming.* **3** ADJ You use **ski** to refer to things that are concerned with skiing. ❑ *...a Canadian ski resort.* ❑ *...a ski instructor.* [from Norwegian]

**skid** /skɪd/ (**skids, skidding, skidded**) V-I If a vehicle **skids**, it slides sideways or forward while moving, for example, when you are trying to stop it suddenly on a wet road. ❑ *The car skidded on the dusty road.* ● **Skid** is also a noun. ❑ *I braked too suddenly and went into a skid.* [of Scandinavian origin]

**skill** /skɪl/ (**skills**) **1** N-COUNT A **skill** is a type of work or activity which requires special training and knowledge. ❑ *It's good to learn new skills, whatever your age.* **2** N-UNCOUNT **Skill** is the knowledge and ability that enables you to do something well. ❑ *He showed great skill on the football field.* [from Old Norse]

| **Thesaurus** | *skill* | Also look up : |
|---|---|---|
| N. | ability, proficiency, talent **1** **2** | |

**skilled** /skɪld/ **1** ADJ Someone who is **skilled** has the knowledge and ability to do something well. ❑ *She is skilled in explaining difficult ideas to her students.* **2** ADJ **Skilled** work can only be done by people who have had some training. ❑ *There was a shortage of skilled labor in the area.* [from Old Norse]

**skill|ful** /skɪlfəl/ ADJ Someone who is **skillful** at something does it very well. ❑ *He is a skillful craftsman.* ● **skill|ful|ly** ADV ❑ *The story is skillfully written from a child's point of view.* [from Old Norse]

**skim** /skɪm/ (**skims, skimming, skimmed**) **1** V-T If you **skim** something **from** the surface of a liquid, you remove it. ❑ *Skim the fat off the gravy.* **2** V-T/V-I If something **skims** a surface, it moves quickly along just above it. ❑ *We watched seagulls skimming the waves.* ❑ *We threw stones, making them skim across the water.* **3** V-T/V-I If you **skim** a piece of writing or **skim through** it, you read through it quickly. ❑ *I didn't read the report carefully — I just skimmed it.*

**skim milk** N-UNCOUNT **Skim milk** is milk from which the cream has been removed.

**skimpy** /skɪmpi/ (**skimpier, skimpiest**) ADJ Something that is **skimpy** is too small in size or quantity. ❑ *...skimpy underwear.*

**skin** /skɪn/ (**skins, skinning, skinned**) **1** N-VAR Your **skin** is the natural covering of your body. ❑ *His skin is smooth.* **2** N-VAR An animal skin is skin which has been removed from a dead animal. ❑ *Is that real crocodile skin?* **3** N-VAR The **skin** of a fruit or vegetable is its outer layer or covering. ❑ *...banana skins.* **4** N-SING If a **skin** forms on the surface of a liquid, a thin, fairly solid layer forms on it. ❑ *Stir the sauce to stop a skin from forming.* **5** V-T If you **skin** a dead animal, you remove its skin. ❑ *The chef showed her how to skin a rabbit.* [from Old English]
→ see **Word Web: skin**
→ see **fruit**

| **Word Partnership** | Use *skin* with : |
|---|---|
| ADJ. | **dark** skin, **dry** skin, **fair** skin, **oily** skin, **pale** skin, skin, **smooth** skin, **soft** skin **1** |
| N. | skin **and bones**, skin **cancer**, skin **cells**, skin **color** (or color of *someone's* skin), skin **cream**, skin **problems**, skin **type** **1** **leopard** skin **2** |

**skip** /skɪp/ (**skips, skipping, skipped**) **1** V-I If you **skip** along, you move with a series of little

S

## Word Web   skin

What is the best thing you can do for your **skin**? Stay out of the sun. When skin **cells** grow normally, the skin remains smooth and firm. However, the sun's **ultraviolet** rays sometimes cause damage. This can lead to **sunburn**, **wrinkles**, and skin cancer. The damage may not be apparent for several years. However, doctors have discovered that even a light **suntan** can be dangerous. **Sunlight** makes the melanin in skin turn dark. This is the body's attempt to protect itself from the ultraviolet radiation. **Dermatologists** recommend limiting exposure to the sun and always using a **sunscreen**.

jumps from one foot to the other. ❑ *They saw a little girl skipping along.* ❑ *We skipped down the street.* ● **Skip** is also a noun. ❑ *He gave a little skip as he left the room.* ◼ V-T When someone **skips rope**, they jump up and down over a rope which they or two other people are holding at each end and turning around and around. ❑ *They skip rope in the school yard.* ● **skip|ping** N-UNCOUNT ❑ *We did rope skipping and things like that.* ◼ V-T If you **skip** something that you usually do or something that most people do, you decide not to do it. ❑ *It is important not to skip meals.* ◼ V-T/V-I If you **skip** or **skip over** a part of something you are reading or a story you are telling, you omit it or skim over it and move on to something else. ❑ *You might want to skip this chapter.* [of Scandinavian origin]

**skip|per** /skɪpər/ (**skippers**) N-COUNT; N-VOC You can use **skipper** to refer to the captain of a ship or boat. ❑ *...the skipper of a fishing boat.* [from Middle Low German]

**skip rope** (**skip ropes**) N-COUNT A **skip rope** is a piece of rope, usually with handles at each end. You exercise or play with it by turning it around and around and jumping over it.

**skir|mish** /skɜrmɪʃ/ (**skirmishes**) N-COUNT A **skirmish** is a minor battle. ❑ *Skirmishes on the border are common.* [from Old French]

**skirt** /skɜrt/ (**skirts, skirting, skirted**)
◼ N-COUNT A **skirt** is a piece of clothing worn by women and girls. It fastens at the waist and hangs down around the legs. ❑ *She was wearing a pretty green skirt.* ◼ V-T Something that **skirts** an area is situated around the edge of it. ❑ *The path skirted the main lawn.* ◼ V-T/V-I If you **skirt** a problem or question, you avoid dealing with it. ❑ *They skirted around the problem.* ❑ *He skirted the most difficult issues.* [from Old Norse]
→ see **clothing**

**skull** /skʌl/ (**skulls**) N-COUNT Your **skull** is the bony part of your head which encloses your brain. ❑ *They X-rayed his skull after he fell.* [of Scandinavian origin]

**sky** /skaɪ/ (**skies**) N-VAR The **sky** is the space around the Earth which you can see when you stand outside and look upward. ❑ *The sun was shining in the sky.* ❑ *Today we have clear blue skies.* [from Old Norse]
→ see **star**

## Word Partnership   Use *sky* with :

| | |
|---|---|
| ADV. | sky **above**, the sky **overhead**, **up in the** sky |
| ADJ. | **black** sky, **blue** sky, **bright** sky, **clear** sky, **cloudless** sky, **dark** sky, **empty** sky, **high in the** sky |

**sky|line** /skaɪlaɪn/ (**skylines**) N-COUNT The **skyline** is the line or shape that is formed where the sky meets buildings or the land. ❑ *The church is clear on the skyline.*

**sky|scraper** /skaɪskreɪpər/ (**skyscrapers**) N-COUNT A **skyscraper** is a very tall building in a city.
→ see **city**

**slab** /slæb/ (**slabs**) N-COUNT A **slab of** something is a thick, flat piece of it. ❑ *...slabs of stone.*

**slack** /slæk/ (**slacker, slackest**) ◼ ADJ Something that is **slack** is loose and not firmly stretched or tightly in position. ❑ *Her grip went slack and she let go.* ◼ ADJ A **slack** period is one in which there is not much work or activity. ❑ *The shop has busy times and slack periods.* ◼ ADJ Someone who is **slack** does not do their work properly, or does not make other people do their work properly. ❑ *Many teachers are far too slack.* [from Old English]

**slack|en** /slækən/ (**slackens, slackening, slackened**) ◼ V-T/V-I If something **slackens** or if you **slacken** it, it becomes slower, less active, or less intense. ❑ *The wind slackened.* ◼ V-T/V-I If your grip or a part of your body **slackens** or if you **slacken** your grip, it becomes looser or more relaxed. ❑ *Her grip slackened on Arnold's arm.* [from Old English]

**slain** /sleɪn/ **Slain** is the past participle of **slay**. [from Old English]

**slam** /slæm/ (**slams, slamming, slammed**)
◼ V-T/V-I If you **slam** a door or window or if it **slams**, it shuts noisily and with great force. ❑ *She slammed the door behind her.* ❑ *I heard the front door slam.* ◼ V-T If you **slam** something **down**, you put it there quickly and with great force. ❑ *She slammed the phone down angrily.* ◼ V-T/V-I If one thing **slams** into or against another, it crashes into it with great force. ❑ *He slammed his fist against the wall.* ❑ *The car slammed into a tree.* [of Scandinavian origin]

**Word Partnership** Use *slam* with :

N.   slam **a door** 🔳
V.   **hear** *something* slam 🔳
ADJ. slam (*something*) **shut** 🔳

**slam dunk** (**slam dunks**) also **slam-dunk**
🔳 N-COUNT If you say that something is a **slam dunk**, you mean that a success or victory will be easily achieved. [INFORMAL] ❏ *The movie was a financial slam dunk.* 🔳 N-COUNT In basketball, a **slam dunk** is a shot in which a player jumps up and forces the ball through the basket. ❏ *He is famous for his slam dunks.*

**slan|der** /slǽndər/ (**slanders, slandering, slandered**) 🔳 N-VAR **Slander** is an untrue spoken statement about someone which is intended to damage their reputation. Compare **libel**. ❏ *Dr. Bach is suing the company for slander.* 🔳 V-T To **slander** someone means to say untrue things about them in order to damage their reputation. ❏ *He accused me of slandering him.* [from Old French]

**slang** /slǽŋ/ N-UNCOUNT **Slang** consists of words, expressions, and meanings that are very informal and are used by people who know each other very well or who have the same interests. ❏ *Soldiers have their own slang.*

**slant** /slǽnt/ (**slants, slanting, slanted**) 🔳 V-I Something that **slants** is sloping, rather than horizontal or vertical. ❏ *The morning sun slanted through the glass roof.* 🔳 N-SING If something is **on a slant**, it is in a slanting position. ❏ *Her hair was cut on a slant.* 🔳 V-T If information or a system is **slanted**, it is made to show favor toward a particular group or opinion. ❏ *The program was slanted to make the home team look good.* 🔳 N-SING A particular **slant** on a subject is a particular way of thinking about it, especially one that is unfair. ❏ *The political slant of the newspaper is liberal.* [of Scandinavian origin]

**slap** /slǽp/ (**slaps, slapping, slapped**) 🔳 V-T If you **slap** someone, you hit them with the palm of your hand. ❏ *I slapped him hard across the face.* ● **Slap** is also a noun. ❏ *She gave him a slap.* 🔳 V-T If you **slap** something **onto** a surface, you put it there quickly, roughly, or carelessly. ❏ *He slapped some money on the table.* [from Low German]

**Word Partnership** Use *slap* with :

N.   a slap **on the back**, a slap **on the wrist**, a slap **in the face** 🔳

**slash** /slǽʃ/ (**slashes, slashing, slashed**) 🔳 V-T If you **slash** something, you make a long, deep cut in it. ❏ *Four cars had their tires slashed.* ● **Slash** is also a noun. ❏ *Make deep slashes in the fish and push in the herbs.* 🔳 V-I If you **slash at** a person or thing, you quickly hit at them with something such as a knife. ❏ *He slashed wildly at them.* 🔳 V-T To **slash** something such as costs or jobs means to reduce them by a large amount. ❏ *Car makers are slashing prices.* [from Old French]

**slate** /sléɪt/ (**slates**) 🔳 N-UNCOUNT **Slate** is a dark gray rock that can be easily split into thin layers. Slate is often used for covering roofs. ❏ *They lived in a cottage with a traditional slate roof.* 🔳 N-COUNT A **slate** is one of the small flat pieces of slate that are used for covering roofs. ❏ *Thieves also*

stole the slates from the roof. [from Old French]

**slaugh|ter** /slɔ́tər/ (**slaughters, slaughtering, slaughtered**) 🔳 V-T If large numbers of people or animals **are slaughtered**, they are killed in a way that is cruel or unnecessary. ❏ *Innocent people have been slaughtered.* ● **Slaughter** is also a noun. ❏ *In this war the slaughter of civilians was common.* 🔳 V-T To **slaughter** animals such as cows and sheep means to kill them for their meat. ❏ *The farmers slaughter their own cows.* ● **Slaughter** is also a noun. ❏ *The sheep were taken away for slaughter.* [from Old English]

**slave** /sléɪv/ (**slaves**) 🔳 N-COUNT A **slave** is someone who is the property of another person and has to work for that person. ❏ *They had to work as slaves.* 🔳 N-COUNT You can describe someone as a **slave** when they are completely under the control of another person or of a powerful influence. ❏ *She is a slave to her job.* [from Old French]

**slave la|bor** 🔳 N-UNCOUNT **Slave labor** refers to slaves or to work done by slaves. ❏ *...a campaign to end slave labor.* 🔳 N-UNCOUNT If people work very hard for long hours for very little money, you can refer to it as **slave labor**. ❏ *Working in the kitchen here is slave labor.*

**slav|ery** /sléɪvəri, sléɪvri/ N-UNCOUNT **Slavery** is the system by which people are owned by other people as slaves. ❏ *My people survived 400 years of slavery.* [from Old French]

**slaw** /slɔ́/ N-UNCOUNT **Slaw** is a salad of chopped raw carrot and cabbage in mayonnaise. [from Dutch]

**slay** /sléɪ/ (**slays, slaying, slew, slayed, slain**) 🔳 V-T If someone **slays** an animal, they kill it in a violent way. [FORMAL] ❏ *The story is about a knight who slays a dragon.* 🔳 V-T PASSIVE If someone **has been slain**, they have been murdered. ❏ *Innocent people were slain.* [from Old English]

**slay|ing** /sléɪɪŋ/ (**slayings**) N-COUNT A **slaying** is a murder. ❏ *...the slaying of nine people.* [from Old English]

**slea|zy** /slízi/ (**sleazier, sleaziest**) 🔳 ADJ If you describe a place as **sleazy**, you dislike it because it looks dirty and badly cared for, and not respectable. [INFORMAL] ❏ *...sleazy bars.* 🔳 ADJ If you describe something or someone as **sleazy**, you disapprove of them because you think they are not respectable or honest. [INFORMAL] ❏ *...a sleazy salesman.*

**sled** /sléd/ (**sleds, sledding, sledded**) 🔳 N-COUNT A **sled** is an object used for traveling over snow. It consists of a framework which slides on two strips of wood or metal. ❏ *We pulled the children across the snow on a sled.* 🔳 V-I If you **sled** or go **sledding**, you ride on a sled. ❏ *We went sledding on the small hill near our house.* [from Middle Dutch]

**sleek** /slík/ (**sleeker, sleekest**) 🔳 ADJ **Sleek** hair or fur is smooth and shiny and looks healthy. ❏ *...sleek black hair.* 🔳 ADJ If you describe someone as **sleek**, you mean that they look rich and stylish. ❏ *His wife is sleek and elegant.* 🔳 ADJ **Sleek** vehicles, furniture, or other objects look smooth, shiny, and expensive. ❏ *...a sleek white car.*

**sleep** /slíp/ (**sleeps, sleeping, slept**) 🔳 N-UNCOUNT **Sleep** is the natural state of rest in which your eyes are closed, your body is inactive, and your mind does not think. ❏ *They*

S

were exhausted from lack of sleep. ❑ Be quiet and go to sleep. **2** V-I When you **sleep**, you rest with your eyes closed and your mind and body inactive. ❑ I couldn't sleep last night. **3** N-COUNT A **sleep** is a period of sleeping. ❑ I think he needs a sleep. **4** V-T If a building or room **sleeps** a particular number of people, it has beds for that number of people. ❑ The house sleeps 10. **5** PHRASE If you say that you didn't **lose** any **sleep over** something, you mean that you did not worry about it at all. ❑ I didn't lose much sleep over his criticism. **6** PHRASE If a sick or injured animal **is put to sleep**, it is killed by a vet in a way that does not cause it pain. ❑ We had to have the dog put to sleep. [from Old English] **7** to **sleep rough** → see **rough**

→ see Word Web: **sleep**

→ see **dream**

▶ **sleep off** PHR-VERB If you **sleep off** the effects of too much traveling, drink, or food, you recover from it by sleeping. ❑ She needs to sleep off her jet lag.

| **Thesaurus** | sleep | Also look up : |
|---|---|---|
| V. | doze, rest; (ant.) awaken, wake **1** **2** | |
| N. | nap, rest, slumber **3** | |

| **Word Partnership** | Use sleep with : |
|---|---|
| N. | sleep **deprivation**, sleep **disorder, hours of** sleep, **lack of** sleep **1** sleep **on the floor**, sleep **nights 2** |
| V. | **drift off to** sleep, **get enough get some** sleep, **get some** sleep, **go to** sleep, **need** sleep **1** **can't/couldn't** sleep **2** |
| ADJ. | **deep** sleep **1** **good** sleep **3** |

**sleep|er** /slipər/ (**sleepers**) N-COUNT You can use **sleeper** to indicate how well someone sleeps. For example, if someone is a light **sleeper**, they are easily woken up. ❑ I'm a very light sleeper and the smallest noise wakes me. [from Old English]

**sleep|ing bag** (**sleeping bags**) N-COUNT A **sleeping bag** is a large deep bag with a warm lining, used for sleeping in, especially when you are camping.

**sleep|less** /sliplɪs/ **1** ADJ A **sleepless** night is one during which you do not sleep. ❑ I have sleepless nights worrying about her. **2** ADJ Someone who is **sleepless** is unable to sleep. ❑ She lay there for hours, sleepless. ● **sleep|less|ness** N-UNCOUNT ❑ He suffers from sleeplessness. [from Old English]

**sleep|over** /slipoʊvər/ (**sleepovers**) also sleep-over N-COUNT A **sleepover** is an occasion when someone, especially a child, sleeps for one night in a place such as a friend's home. ❑ Emily asked a friend for a sleepover.

**sleepy** /slipi/ (**sleepier, sleepiest**) **1** ADJ If you are **sleepy**, you are very tired and are almost asleep. ❑ I was feeling sleepy. ● **sleepi|ly** ADV ❑ Joanna sat up, blinking sleepily. **2** ADJ A **sleepy** place is quiet and does not have much activity or excitement. ❑ ...a sleepy little town out in the countryside. [from Old English]

**sleet** /slit/ N-UNCOUNT **Sleet** is rain that is partly frozen. ❑ Today we expect rain, sleet, and snow. [from Germanic]

→ see **precipitation, water**

**sleeve** /sliv/ (**sleeves**) **1** N-COUNT The **sleeves** of a coat, shirt, or other item of clothing are the parts that cover your arms. ❑ She wore a dress with long sleeves. **2** PHRASE If you have something **up** your **sleeve**, you have an idea or plan which you have not told anyone about. You can also say that someone has **an ace, card, or trick up** their **sleeve**. ❑ He wondered what tricks she had up her sleeve. [from Old English]

**sleigh** /sleɪ/ (**sleighs**) N-COUNT A **sleigh** is a vehicle which can slide over snow. Sleighs are usually pulled by horses. [from Dutch]

**slen|der** /slɛndər/ **1** ADJ A **slender** person is attractively thin and graceful. [WRITTEN] ❑ She was tall and slender. **2** ADJ You can use **slender** to describe a situation which exists but only to a very small degree. [WRITTEN] ❑ Clarke had a slender lead in the race.

**slept** /slɛpt/ **Slept** is the past tense and past participle of **sleep**. [from Old English]

**slew** /slu/ (**slews**) **1** **Slew** is the past tense of **slay**. **2** N-COUNT A **slew of** things is a large number of them. ❑ ...a slew of books about American Indians. [Sense 2 from Irish Gaelic]

**slice** /slaɪs/ (**slices, slicing, sliced**) **1** N-COUNT A **slice** of bread, meat, fruit, or other food is a thin piece that has been cut from a larger piece. ❑ Would you like a slice of bread? **2** V-T If you **slice** bread, meat, fruit, or other food, you cut it into thin pieces. ❑ Helen sliced the cake. **3** N-COUNT You can use **slice** to refer to a part of a situation or activity. ❑ Housework takes up a large slice of my time. [from Old French] **4** **slice of the action** → see **action**

→ see **bread, cut**

**Word Web**    sleep

Do you ever go to **bed** and then discover you can't **fall asleep**? You **yawn**. You feel **tired**. But your body isn't ready for **rest**. You **toss** and **turn** and pound the **pillow** for hours. After a while you may **doze**, but then few minutes later you're **wide awake**. The scientific name for this condition is **insomnia**. There are many causes for **sleeplessness**. If you **nap** too late in the day it may change your normal sleep cycle. Worrying can also affect sleep patterns.

S

ADJ.    **small** slice, **thin** slice **1**
N.    slice **of bread**, slice **of pie**,
    slice **of pizza 1**
    slice **a cake 2**
    slice **of life 3**
PREP.    slice **into**, slice **off**, slice **through 2**

**slick** /slɪk/ (**slicker, slickest**) **1** ADJ A **slick**
performance, production, or advertisement is
skillful and impressive. ❑ *They could afford slick TV
ads for their product.* **2** ADJ A **slick** action is done
quickly and smoothly, and without any obvious
effort. ❑ *…the slick way he passed the ball.* **3** ADJ If
you describe a person as **slick**, you dislike them
because they speak easily in a way that is likely
to convince people, but is not sincere. ❑ *Don't be
fooled by slick politicians.* **4** N-COUNT A **slick** is the
same as an **oil slick**. ❑ *Experts are trying to clean up
the huge slick.* [of Scandinavian origin]

**slick|er** /slɪkər/ (**slickers**) N-COUNT A **slicker** is
a long, loose, waterproof coat. [of Scandinavian
origin]

**slide** /slaɪd/ (**slides, sliding, slid**) **1** V-T/V-I
When something **slides** somewhere or when
you **slide** it there, it moves there smoothly over
or against something. ❑ *She slid the door open.*
❑ *I slid the cellphone into my pocket.* **2** V-I If you
**slide** somewhere, you move there smoothly and
quietly. ❑ *He slid into the car.* **3** V-I To **slide into**
a particular mood, attitude, or situation means
to gradually start to have that mood, attitude, or
situation often without intending to. ❑ *She slid
into a depression.* **4** N-COUNT A **slide** is a small piece
of photographic film which you project onto a
screen so that you can see the picture. ❑ *…a slide
show.* **5** N-COUNT A **slide** is a piece of playground
equipment that has a steep slope for children to
go down for fun. ❑ *Two young children were playing
on a slide.* **6** N-COUNT A glass **slide** is a piece of
glass on which you put something that you want
to examine through a microscope. [from Old
English]
→ see **laboratory**

V.    **begin to** slide, **continue to** slide **1** – **3**

**slight** /slaɪt/ (**slighter, slightest, slights,
slighting, slighted**) **1** ADJ Something that is
**slight** is very small in degree or quantity. ❑ *…a
slight change in temperature.* ❑ *He's not the slightest
bit worried.* **2** ADJ A **slight** person has a fairly
thin and delicate looking body. ❑ *She is smaller and
slighter than me.* ● **slight|ly** ADV ❑ *…a slightly built
man.* **3** V-T If you **are slighted**, someone does or
says something that insults you by treating you as
if your views or feelings are not important. ❑ *His
grandson was slighted by the football coach.* ● **Slight** is
also a noun. ❑ *It's not a slight on you that I enjoy being
alone sometimes.* **4** PHRASE You use **in the slightest**
to emphasize a negative statement. ❑ *That doesn't
interest me in the slightest.* [from Old Norse]

**slight|ly** /slaɪtli/ ADV **Slightly** means to some
degree but not to a very large degree. ❑ *His family
moved to a slightly larger house.* ❑ *Each person learns in
a slightly different way.* [from Old Norse]

**slim** /slɪm/ (**slimmer, slimmest, slims, slimming,
slimmed**) **1** ADJ A **slim** person has an attractively
thin and well-shaped body. ❑ *The young woman was
tall and slim.* **2** ADJ A **slim** book, wallet, or other
object is thinner than usual. ❑ *…a slim book of
poetry.* **3** ADJ A **slim** chance or possibility is a very
small one. ❑ *There's a slim chance that he may become
president.* [from Dutch]
▶ **slim down** **1** PHR-VERB If you **slim down**, you
lose weight and become thinner. ❑ *People lose more
weight when they slim down with a friend.* **2** PHR-VERB
If a company or other organization **slims down**
or **is slimmed down**, it employs fewer people, in
order to save money or become more efficient.
[BUSINESS] ❑ *Many firms had to slim down.*

ADJ.    **tall and** slim **1**
ADV.    **pretty** slim, **very** slim **1** – **3**
N.    slim **chance**, slim **lead**, slim **margin 3**

**slime** /slaɪm/ N-UNCOUNT **Slime** is a thick, wet
substance which covers a surface or comes from
the bodies of animals such as snails. ❑ *His feet felt
the slime at the bottom of the pond.* [from Old English]

**sling** /slɪŋ/ (**slings, slinging, slung**) **1** V-T If you
**sling** something somewhere, you throw it there
carelessly. ❑ *She slung the package into the trash can.*
**2** V-T If you **sling** something over your shoulder
or over something such as a chair, you hang it
there loosely. ❑ *She slung her coat over her chair.* ❑ *He
had a backpack slung over one shoulder.* **3** V-T If a
rope, blanket, or other object **is slung** between
two points, someone has hung it loosely between
them. ❑ *…two trees with a blanket slung between
them.* **4** N-COUNT A **sling** is an object made of
ropes, straps, or cloth that is used for carrying
things. ❑ *They used slings of rope to lower us from
the building.* **5** N-COUNT A **sling** is a piece of cloth
which is tied around someone's neck and supports
a broken or injured arm. ❑ *She had her arm in a sling.*
[of Scandinavian origin]

**sling|shot** /slɪŋʃɒt/ (**slingshots**) N-COUNT A
**slingshot** is a device for shooting small stones. It
is made of a Y-shaped stick with a piece of elastic
tied between the two top posts.

**slip** /slɪp/ (**slips, slipping, slipped**) **1** V-I If you
**slip**, you accidentally slide and lose your balance.
❑ *He slipped on the wet grass.* **2** V-I If something
**slips**, it slides out of place or out of your hand.
❑ *His glasses slipped down his nose.* **3** V-I If you **slip**
somewhere, you go there quickly and quietly.
❑ *Amy slipped out of the house without being seen.*
**4** V-T If you **slip** something somewhere, you put
it there quickly in a way that does not attract
attention. ❑ *I slipped a note under Louise's door.*
**5** V-T If you **slip** something **to** someone, or if
you **slip** someone something, you give it to them
secretly. ❑ *Robert slipped her a note in class.* **6** V-I
To **slip into** a particular state or situation means
to pass gradually into it, in a way that is hardly
noticed. ❑ *You soon slip into a routine.* **7** V-I If you
**slip into** or **out of** clothes or shoes, you put them
on or take them off quickly and easily. ❑ *She slipped
out of her shoes and lay down.* **8** N-COUNT A **slip** is a
small or unimportant mistake. ❑ *We can't make any
slips.* **9** N-COUNT A **slip of** paper is a small piece of
paper. ❑ *He wrote our names on slips of paper.* [from
Middle Low German]

S

▶ **slip up** PHR-VERB If you **slip up**, you make a small or unimportant mistake. ❏ *We slipped up a few times.*

| Thesaurus | slip | Also look up : |
|---|---|---|
| V. | fall, slide, trip ■ | |
| N. | blunder, failure, flub, mistake ■ | |
| | leaf, page, paper, sheet ■ | |

| Word Partnership | Use *slip* with : |
|---|---|
| ADJ. | slip **resistant** ■ |
| N. | slip **of paper**, **sales** slip ■ |

**slip|cover** /slɪpkʌvər/ (**slipcovers**) also slip cover N-COUNT A **slipcover** is a piece of cloth that fits over a chair or sofa and can easily be removed. ❏ *…the slipcovers on the dining room chairs.*

**slip|per** /slɪpər/ (**slippers**) **Slippers** are loose, soft shoes that you wear at home. ❏ *…a pair of old slippers.* [from Middle Low German]

**slip|pery** /slɪpəri/ ■ ADJ Something that is **slippery** is smooth, wet, or oily and is therefore difficult to walk on or to hold. ❏ *The kitchen floor was wet and slippery.* ■ PHRASE If someone is on a **slippery slope**, they are involved in a course of action that is difficult to stop and that will eventually lead to failure or trouble. ❏ *We started on the slippery slope of borrowing money.* [from German]

**slit** /slɪt/ (**slits, slitting**)

| The form **slit** is used in the present tense and is the past tense and past participle. |
|---|

■ V-T If you **slit** something, you make a long narrow cut in it. ❏ *Slit the pea pod and take out the peas.* ❏ *He slit open the envelope.* ■ N-COUNT A **slit** is a long narrow cut or opening in something. ❏ *Make a slit about half an inch long.* ❏ *She watched them through a slit in the curtains.* [from Old English] → see **shark**

**slith|er** /slɪðər/ (**slithers, slithering, slithered**) V-I If you **slither** somewhere, you slide along in an uneven way. ❏ *Robert slithered down the muddy bank.* [from Old English]

**sliv|er** /slɪvər/ (**slivers**) N-COUNT A **sliver of** something is a small thin piece or amount of it. ❏ *A sliver of glass got stuck in my foot.*

**slog** /slɒg/ (**slogs, slogging, slogged**) ■ V-I If you **slog through** something, you work hard and steadily through it. [INFORMAL] ❏ *He slogged through five years of study to become a doctor.* ■ N-SING If you describe a task as a **slog**, you mean that it is tiring and requires a lot of effort. [INFORMAL] ❏ *This project has been a hard slog.*

**slo|gan** /sloʊgən/ (**slogans**) N-COUNT A **slogan** is a short phrase that is easy to remember. Slogans are used in advertisements and by political parties. ❏ *They campaigned on the slogan "We'll take less of your money."* [from Gaelic]

**slop** /slɒp/ (**slops, slopping, slopped**) V-T/V-I If liquid **slops** from a container or if you **slop** liquid somewhere, it comes out over the edge of the container, usually accidentally. ❏ *Some water slopped over the edge of the bath.* [from Old English]

**slope** /sloʊp/ (**slopes, sloping, sloped**) ■ N-COUNT A **slope** is the side of a mountain, hill, or valley. ❏ *The village is high on a mountain slope.* ■ N-COUNT A **slope** is a surface that is at an angle, so that one end is higher than the other. ❏ *The table was on a slope.* ■ V-I If a surface **slopes**, it is at an angle, so that one end is higher than the other. ❏ *The land sloped down sharply to the river.* ● **slop|ing** ADJ ❏ *…a building with a sloping roof.* ■ V-I If something **slopes**, it leans to the right or to the left rather than being upright. ❏ *The writing sloped backwards.* ■ N-COUNT The **slope** of something is the angle at which it slopes. ❏ *The slope of the ground was very steep.* [from Old English] ■ **slippery slope** → see **slippery**

**slop|py** /slɒpi/ (**sloppier, sloppiest**) ADJ Something that is **sloppy** has been done in a careless and lazy way. ❏ *He hates sloppy work.* ● **slop|pi|ness** N-UNCOUNT ❏ *Her sloppiness has caused a lot of problems.* [from Old English]

**slop|py joe** /slɒpi dʒoʊ/ (**sloppy joes**) N-COUNT A **sloppy joe** is a sandwich consisting of a bun filled with sauce and cooked meat. [INFORMAL]

**slot** /slɒt/ (**slots, slotting, slotted**) ■ N-COUNT A **slot** is a narrow opening in a machine or container, for example, a hole that you put coins in to make a machine work. ❏ *He dropped a coin into the slot and dialed the number.* ■ V-T/V-I If you **slot** something into something else, or if it **slots** into it, you put it into a space where it fits. ❏ *He slotted a CD into the CD player.* ❏ *The seat belt slotted into place easily.* ■ N-COUNT A **slot** in a schedule or program is a place in it where an activity can take place. ❏ *…a regular time slot when parents can meet with teachers.* [from Old French]

**slouch** /slaʊtʃ/ (**slouches, slouching, slouched**) V-I If someone **slouches**, they sit or stand with their shoulders and head bent so they look lazy and unattractive. ❏ *Sit up — don't slouch.*

**slow** /sloʊ/ (**slower, slowest, slows, slowing, slowed**) ■ ADJ Something that is **slow** moves, happens, or is done without much speed. ❏ *His bike was heavy and slow.* ❏ *He had a slow way of talking.* ❏ *Cleaning up the city has been a slow process.* ● **slow|ly** ADV ❏ *He spoke slowly and clearly.* ● **slow|ness** N-UNCOUNT ❏ *The slowness of our progress was very frustrating.* ■ ADJ If someone is **slow** to do something, they do it after a delay. ❏ *The government was slow to respond to the crisis.* ■ V-T/V-I If something **slows** or if you **slow** it, it starts to move or happen more slowly. ❏ *She slowed the car and turned the corner.* ■ ADJ Someone who is **slow** is not very clever and takes a long time to understand things. ❏ *She thought he was a bit slow.* ■ ADJ If you describe a situation, place, or activity as **slow**, you mean that it is not very exciting. ❏ *Some parts of the movie are a little slow.* ■ ADJ If a clock or watch is **slow**, it shows a time that is earlier than the correct time. ❏ *The clock is about two minutes slow.* [from Old English] ■ **slowly but surely** → see **surely**

▶ **slow down** ■ PHR-VERB If something **slows down** or if something **slows** it **down**, it starts to move or happen more slowly. ❏ *The bus slowed down for the next stop.* ❏ *There is no cure for the disease, although drugs can slow it down.* ■ PHR-VERB If someone **slows down** or if something **slows** them **down**, they become less active. ❏ *He needs to slow down or he will get sick.*

▶ **slow up** PHR-VERB **Slow up** means the same as **slow down** 1. ❏ *Sales are slowing up.*

| Word Partnership | Use *slow* with : |
| --- | --- |
| ADJ. | slow **acting**, slow **moving** 🔟 |
| N. | slow **death**, slow **growth**, slow **movements**, slow **pace**, slow **process**, slow **progress**, slow **recovery**, slow **response**, slow **speed**, slow **start**, slow **stop**, slow **traffic** 🔟 |

**slow mo|tion** also **slow-motion** N-UNCOUNT
When film or television pictures are shown **in slow motion**, they are shown much more slowly than normal. ❑ *They played it again in slow motion.*

**slow|poke** /sloʊpoʊk/ (**slowpokes**) N-COUNT If you call someone a **slowpoke**, you are criticizing the fact that they do something slowly. [INFORMAL] ❑ *Come on, slowpoke.*

**sludge** /slʌdʒ/ (**sludges**) N-VAR **Sludge** is thick mud, sewage, or industrial waste. ❑ *Gallons of sludge have escaped into the river.*

**slug** /slʌg/ (**slugs**) N-COUNT A **slug** is a small slow-moving creature with a long soft body and no legs, like a snail without a shell. [of Scandinavian origin]

**slug|ger** /slʌgər/ (**sluggers**) N-COUNT In baseball, a **slugger** is a player who hits the ball very hard. [of Scandinavian origin]

**slug|gish** /slʌgɪʃ/ ADJ You can describe something as **sluggish** if it moves, works, or reacts much slower than you would like or is normal. ❑ *The economy is sluggish.* [of Scandinavian origin]

**slum** /slʌm/ (**slums**) N-COUNT A **slum** is an area of a city where living conditions are very bad. ❑ *…a slum area of St. Louis.*

**slum|ber** /slʌmbər/ (**slumbers, slumbering, slumbered**) N-VAR **Slumber** is sleep. [LITERARY] ❑ *He fell into exhausted slumber.* ● **Slumber** is also a verb. ❑ *The children were slumbering peacefully.* [from Old English]

**slum|ber par|ty** (**slumber parties**) N-COUNT A **slumber party** is an occasion when a group of young friends spend the night together at the home of one of the group. ❑ *I'm having a slumber party for my birthday.*

**slump** /slʌmp/ (**slumps, slumping, slumped**) 🔟 V-I If something such as the value of something **slumps**, it falls suddenly and by a large amount. ❑ *Profits slumped by 41%.* ● **Slump** is also a noun. ❑ *There has been a slump in house prices.* 🔁 N-COUNT A **slump** is a time when many people in a country are unemployed and poor. ❑ *…the slump of the early 1980s.* 🔢 V-I If you **slump** somewhere, you fall or sit down there heavily. ❑ *She slumped into a chair.* [of Scandinavian origin]

**slung** /slʌŋ/ **Slung** is the past tense and past participle of **sling**.

**slur** /slɜr/ (**slurs, slurring, slurred**) 🔟 N-COUNT A **slur** is an insulting remark which could damage someone's reputation. ❑ *This is a slur on my character.* 🔁 V-T/V-I If someone **slurs** their speech or if their speech **slurs**, they do not pronounce each word clearly, because they are drunk, ill, or sleepy. ❑ *He was slurring his words.* ● **slurred** ADJ ❑ *Her speech was slurred.* [from Middle Low German]

**sly** /slaɪ/ 🔟 ADJ A **sly** look, expression, or remark shows that you know something that other people do not know or that was meant to be a secret. ❑ *He gave a sly smile.* ● **sly|ly** ADV ❑ *Anna grinned slyly.* 🔁 ADJ If you describe someone as **sly**, you disapprove of them because they keep their feelings or intentions hidden and are clever at deceiving people. ❑ *She is sly with other children and adults.* [from Old Norse]

**smack** /smæk/ (**smacks, smacking, smacked**) 🔟 V-T If you **smack** someone, you hit them with your hand. ❑ *She smacked me on the side of the head.* ● **Smack** is also a noun. ❑ *She gave him a smack.* 🔁 V-T If you **smack** something somewhere, you put it or throw it there so that it makes a loud, sharp noise. ❑ *He smacked his hands down on his knees.* 🔢 V-I If one thing **smacks of** another thing that you consider bad, it reminds you of it or is like it. ❑ *She said their comments smacked of racism.* [Senses 1 and 2 from Middle Low German. Sense 3 from Old English.]

**smack dab** ADV **Smack dab** is used in expressions such as "smack dab in the middle" of somewhere to mean exactly in that place. [INFORMAL] ❑ *…an old brick building smack dab in the middle of downtown.*

**small** /smɔl/ (**smaller, smallest**) 🔟 ADJ A **small** person, thing, or amount of something is not large in physical size. ❑ *Use a small amount of glue.* 🔁 ADJ A **small** group or quantity consists of only a few people or things. ❑ *A small group of students sat in the cafeteria.* 🔢 ADJ A **small** child is a young child. ❑ *I have two small children.* 🔴 ADJ You use **small** to describe something that is not significant or great in degree. ❑ *It's easy to make quite small changes to the way that you work.* ❑ *These details are small and unimportant.* 🔵 ADJ **Small** businesses or companies employ a small number of people and do business with a small number of clients. ❑ *…shops, restaurants and other small businesses.* 🔶 ADJ If someone makes you look or feel **small**, they make you look or feel stupid or ashamed. ❑ *I felt very small when I realized what I'd said.* 🔷 N-SING The **small of** your back is the bottom part of your back that curves in slightly. ❑ *Place your hands on the small of your back and breathe in.* [from Old English] 🔸 **small wonder** → see **wonder**

| Thesaurus | *small* | Also look up : |
| --- | --- | --- |
| ADJ. | little, petite, slight; (*ant.*) big, large 🔟 | |
| | minute 🔁 | |
| | young 🔢 | |
| | insignificant, minor; (*ant.*) important, major, significant 🔴 | |

**small claims court** (**small claims courts**) also **small-claims court** N-VAR **Small claims court** is a local law court which settles disputes between people that involve relatively small amounts of money. ❑ *They have the option of taking their case to small claims court.*

**small po|ta|toes** N-UNCOUNT If you say that something is **small potatoes**, you mean that it is unimportant in comparison with something else. [INFORMAL] ❑ *Our everyday worries are usually small potatoes.*

**small print** N-UNCOUNT The **small print** of a contract or agreement is the part of it that is written in very small print. ❑ *Read the small print in your contract.*

S

**small-scale** ADJ A **small-scale** activity or organization is small in size and limited in extent. ❑ ...the small-scale production of cheese.

**small town** ADJ **Small town** is used when referring to small places, usually in the United States, where people are friendly, honest, and polite, or to the people there. **Small town** is also sometimes used to suggest that someone has old-fashioned ideas. ❑ ...a small-town America of neat, middle-class homes.

**smart** /smɑrt/ (**smarter, smartest, smarts, smarting, smarted**) ◼ ADJ You can describe someone who is clever or intelligent as **smart**. ❑ He's very smart and he knows exactly what he's doing. ◻ V-I If a part of your body or a wound **smarts**, you feel a sharp stinging pain in it. ❑ My eyes smarted from the smoke. ◼ V-I If you **are smarting from** something such as criticism or failure, you feel upset about it. ❑ The Americans were still smarting from their defeat in the World Cup. [from Old English]

**smart aleck** (**smart alecks**) also **smart alec** N-COUNT If you describe someone as a **smart aleck**, you dislike the fact that they think they are very clever and always have an answer for everything. [INFORMAL] ❑ ...a smart-aleck TV reporter.

**smart growth** N-UNCOUNT People such as architects and environmentalists use **smart growth** to refer to the construction of new buildings and roads within a town or city so that they are close to people's workplaces and mass transit systems and so that open spaces are not built on.

**smart phone** (**smart phones**) N-COUNT A **smart phone** is a type of cellphone that can perform many of the operations that a computer does, such as accessing the Internet.

**smarts** /smɑrts/ ◼ N-PLURAL You can use **smarts** to mean the skill and intelligence that people need in order to be successful in difficult situations. [INFORMAL] ❑ I didn't think he had the smarts to do something like that. [from Old English] ◻ → see also **street smarts**

**smash** /smæʃ/ (**smashes, smashing, smashed**) ◼ V-T/V-I If you **smash** something or if it **smashes**, it breaks into many pieces, for example, when it is hit or dropped. ❑ The boys started smashing windows. ❑ Someone dropped a bottle and it smashed. ◻ V-I If you **smash** through a wall, gate, or door, you get through it by hitting and breaking it. ❑ They used a car to smash through the gates. ◼ V-T/V-I If something **smashes** or **is smashed** against something solid, it moves very fast and with great force against it. ❑ He smashed his fist down on the table. ◼ V-T To **smash** a political group or system

means to deliberately destroy it. [INFORMAL] ❑ They want to smash our system of government. ▸ **smash up** PHR-VERB If you **smash** something **up**, you completely destroy it by hitting it and breaking it into many pieces. ❑ Someone smashed up the bus stop during the night.

**smear** /smɪər/ (**smears, smearing, smeared**) ◼ V-T If you **smear** a surface **with** an oily or sticky substance or **smear** the substance onto the surface, you spread a layer of the substance over the surface. ❑ My sister smeared herself with suntan oil. ● **smeared** ADJ ❑ The child's face was smeared with dirt. ◻ N-COUNT A **smear** is a dirty or oily mark. ❑ There was a smear of gravy on his chin. ◼ V-T To **smear** someone means to spread unpleasant and untrue rumors or accusations about them in order to damage their reputation. ❑ They planned to smear him by spreading rumors about his private life. ◼ N-COUNT A **smear** is an unpleasant and untrue rumor or accusation that is intended to damage someone's reputation. ❑ ...a smear campaign by another candidate. [from Old English]

**smell** /smɛl/ (**smells, smelling, smelled**) ◼ N-COUNT The **smell** of something is a quality it has which you become aware of when you breathe in through your nose. ❑ ...the smell of freshly baked bread. ❑ ...horrible smells. ◻ N-UNCOUNT Your sense of **smell** is the ability that your nose has to detect things. ❑ She has lost her sense of smell. ◼ V-LINK If something **smells** a particular way, it has a quality which you become aware of through your nose. ❑ The room smelled of lemons. ❑ It smells delicious. ◼ V-I If you say that something **smells**, you mean that it smells unpleasant. ❑ The fish was old and starting to smell. ◼ V-T If you **smell** something, you become aware of it when you breathe in through your nose. ❑ As soon as we opened the door we could smell the gas. ◼ V-T If you **smell** something, you put your nose near it and breathe in, so that you can discover its smell. ❑ I picked a flower, and smelled it. [from Middle Dutch]
→ see Word Web: **smell**
→ see **taste**

| **Thesaurus** | smell | Also look up : |
|---|---|---|
| N. | aroma, fragrance, odor, scent ◼ | |
| V. | reek, stink ◼ | |
| | breathe, inhale, sniff ◼ | |

**smelly** /smɛli/ (**smellier, smelliest**) ADJ Something that is **smelly** has an unpleasant smell. ❑ He had smelly feet. [from Middle Dutch]

**smile** /smaɪl/ (**smiles, smiling, smiled**) ◼ V-I When you **smile**, the corners of your mouth curve

**Word Web** smell

Scientists say that the average person can recognize about 10,000 different **odors**. Until recently we did not understand the **sense** of **smell**. Now we know that most substances send odor molecules into the air. They enter the body through the **nose**. When they reach the **nasal cavity**, they attach to **sensory** cells. The olfactory **nerve** carries the information to the brain. The brain identifies the smell. The eyes, mouth, and throat also contain receptors that add to the olfactory experience. Interestingly, our sense of smell is better later in the day than in the morning.

up, usually because you are pleased or amused. □ *When he saw me, he smiled.* □ *The children were all smiling at her.* ☑ N-COUNT A **smile** is the expression that you have on your face when you smile. □ *She gave a little smile.* □ *"Come in," she said with a smile.* [of Scandinavian origin]

**Word Partnership** Use *smile* with :

| | |
|---|---|
| V. | smile **and laugh**, **make** *someone* smile, smile **and nod**, **see** *someone* smile, **try to** smile ☑ |
| | smile **fades**, **flash** a smile, **give** *someone* a smile ☑ |
| ADJ. | **big/little/small** smile, **broad** smile, **friendly** smile, **half** smile, **sad** smile, **shy** smile, **warm** smile, **wide** smile, **wry** smile ☑ |

**smirk** /smɜrk/ (**smirks, smirking, smirked**) V-I If you **smirk**, you smile in an unpleasant way. □ *The two men looked at me and smirked.* [from Old English]

**smog** /smɒg/ (**smogs**) N-VAR **Smog** is a mixture of fog and smoke which occurs in some busy industrial cities. □ *The smog in London killed 4,000 people.*
→ see **ozone, pollution**

**smoke** /smoʊk/ (**smokes, smoking, smoked**)
☑ N-UNCOUNT **Smoke** consists of gas and small bits of solid material that are sent into the air when something burns. □ *A cloud of black smoke blew over the city.* ☑ V-I If something **is smoking**, smoke is coming from it. □ *The chimney was smoking.* ☑ V-T/V-I When someone **smokes** a cigarette, cigar, or pipe, they suck the smoke from it into their mouth and blow it out again. If you **smoke**, you regularly smoke cigarettes, cigars, or a pipe. □ *He was smoking a big cigar.* ● **smoker** (**smokers**) N-COUNT □ *...a 64-year-old smoker.* ● **smoking** N-UNCOUNT □ *Smoking is banned in many places of work.* ☑ V-T If fish or meat **is smoked**, it is hung over burning wood so that the smoke preserves it and gives it a special flavor. □ *The fish are smoked over a wood fire.* [from Old English]
→ see **fire**

**smoke de|tec|tor** (**smoke detectors**) N-COUNT A **smoke detector** is a device fixed to the ceiling which makes a loud noise if there is smoke in the air, to warn people.

**smoky** /smoʊki/ (**smokier, smokiest**) also **smokey** ☑ ADJ A place that is **smoky** has a lot of smoke in the air. □ *He hated the smoky atmosphere at work.* ☑ ADJ You can use **smoky** to describe something that looks or tastes like smoke. □ *...a piece of smoky glass.* [from Old English]

**smol|der** /smoʊldər/ (**smolders, smoldering, smoldered**) ☑ V-I If something **smolders**, it burns slowly, producing smoke but not flames. □ *The fire was still smoldering the next morning.* ☑ V-I If a feeling such as anger or hatred **smolders** inside you, you continue to feel it but do not show it. □ *Anger smoldered in her heart for many years.*
→ see **fire**

**smooth** /smuð/ (**smoother, smoothest, smooths, smoothing, smoothed**) ☑ ADJ A **smooth** surface has no roughness, lumps, or holes. □ *The baby's skin was soft and smooth.* ● **smooth|ness** N-UNCOUNT □ *...the smoothness of her hands.* ☑ ADJ A **smooth** liquid or mixture has been mixed well

so that it has no lumps. □ *Stir the mixture until it is smooth.* ☑ ADJ If you describe a drink as **smooth**, you mean that it is not bitter and is pleasant to drink. □ *This coffee is really smooth.* ☑ ADJ A **smooth** line or movement has no sudden breaks or changes in direction or speed. □ *Do the exercise in one smooth motion.* ● **smooth|ly** ADV □ *Move your body smoothly, without jerking.* ☑ ADJ You use **smooth** to describe something that is going well and is free of problems or trouble. □ *We hope for a smooth move to our new home.* ● **smooth|ly** ADV □ *So far, our discussions have gone smoothly.* ☑ ADJ If you describe a man as **smooth**, you mean that he is extremely smart, confident, and polite, often in a way that you find rather unpleasant. □ *A smooth young salesman came to talk to us.* ☑ V-T If you **smooth** something, you move your hands over its surface to make it smooth and flat. □ *She stood up and smoothed down her skirt.* [from Old English]
→ see **muscle**

▶ **smooth out** PHR-VERB If you **smooth out** a problem or difficulty, you solve it, especially by talking to the people concerned. □ *He tried to smooth out the problem with his friends.*

▶ **smooth over** PHR-VERB If you **smooth over** a problem or difficulty, you make it less serious and easier to deal with, especially by talking to the people concerned. □ *The president is trying to smooth things over.*

**smooth mus|cle** (**smooth muscles**) N-VAR **Smooth muscle** is muscle that is mainly found inside the organs of your body and that cannot be controlled voluntarily. [TECHNICAL]

**smoth|er** /smʌðər/ (**smothers, smothering, smothered**) ☑ V-T If you **smother** a fire, you cover it with something in order to put it out. □ *She tried to smother the flames with a blanket.* ☑ V-T To **smother** someone means to kill them by covering their face with something so that they cannot breathe. □ *She tried to smother him with a pillow.* ☑ V-T To **smother** something **with** or **in** something means to cover it completely. □ *He smothered his food with ketchup.* ☑ V-T If you **smother** someone, you show your love for them too much and protect them too much. □ *You can love your children without smothering them.* [from Old English]

**smudge** /smʌdʒ/ (**smudges, smudging, smudged**) ☑ N-COUNT A **smudge** is a dirty mark. □ *There was a dark smudge on his forehead.* ☑ V-T If you **smudge** something, you make it dirty or messy by touching it. □ *She rubbed her eyes, smudging her make-up.*

**smug** /smʌg/ ADJ If you say that someone is **smug**, you are criticizing the fact they seem very pleased with how good, clever, or lucky they are. □ *They looked at each other in smug satisfaction.* ● **smug|ly** ADV □ *The captain smiled smugly and sat down.* [from Germanic]

**smug|gle** /smʌgəl/ (**smuggles, smuggling, smuggled**) V-T If someone **smuggles** things or people into a place or out of it, they take them there illegally or secretly. □ *They smuggled goods into the country.* ● **smug|gler** (**smugglers**) N-COUNT □ *...diamond smugglers.* ● **smug|gling** N-UNCOUNT □ *A pilot was arrested and charged with smuggling.* [from Low German]

**snack** /snæk/ (**snacks**) ☑ N-COUNT A **snack** is a simple meal that is quick to cook and to

S

eat. ❑ *The kids have a snack when they come in from school.* ② N-COUNT A **snack** is something such as a chocolate bar that you eat between meals. ❑ *Do you eat sugary snacks?* [from Middle Dutch]
→ see **peanut**

sna|fu /snæfu/ (snafus) N-COUNT If you describe a situation as a **snafu**, you mean that it is disorderly or disorganized and that it is usually like this. [INFORMAL] ❑ *The project was cut short because of a technical snafu.*

snag /snæg/ (snags, snagging, snagged) ① N-COUNT A **snag** is a small problem or disadvantage. ❑ *We hit a snag when we disagreed about money.* ② V-T/V-I If you **snag** part of your clothing **on** a sharp or rough object or if it **snags**, it gets caught on the object and tears. ❑ *She snagged her heel on a root and fell.* ❑ *Thorns snagged his suit.* [of Scandinavian origin]

snail /sne<u>ɪ</u>l/ (snails) N-COUNT A **snail** is a small animal with a long, soft body, no legs, and a spiral-shaped shell. Snails move very slowly. [from Old English]

snake /sne<u>ɪ</u>k/ (snakes, snaking, snaked) ① N-COUNT A **snake** is a long, thin reptile without legs. ② V-I Something that **snakes** in a particular direction goes in that direction in a line with a lot of bends. [LITERARY] ❑ *The road snaked up the mountainside.* [from Old English]
→ see **desert**

snap /snæp/ (snaps, snapping, snapped) ① V-T/V-I If something **snaps** or if you **snap** it, it breaks suddenly, usually with a sharp cracking noise. ❑ *A twig snapped.* ● **Snap** is also a noun. ❑ *I heard a snap and a crash as a tree fell down.* ② V-T/V-I If you **snap** something into a particular position, or if it **snaps** into that position, it moves quickly into that position, with a sharp sound. ❑ *He snapped the notebook shut.* ● **Snap** is also a noun. ❑ *He shut the book with a snap.* ③ V-T/V-I If someone **snaps at** you, they speak to you in a sharp, unfriendly way. ❑ *Sorry, I didn't mean to snap at you.* ❑ *"Of course I don't know," Roger snapped.* ④ V-I If an animal such as a dog **snaps at** you, it opens and shuts its jaws quickly near you, as if it were going to bite you. ❑ *The dog snapped at my ankle.* ⑤ ADJ A **snap** decision or action is one that is taken suddenly, often without careful thought. ❑ *I think this is too important for a snap decision.* ⑥ N-COUNT A **snap** is a photograph. [INFORMAL] ❑ *They showed us some snaps of their vacation.* [from Middle Low German]
→ see **button**

▶ **snap up** PHR-VERB If you **snap** something **up**, you buy it quickly because it is cheap or is just what you want. ❑ *People rushed to the sales to snap up bargains.*

snap|shot /snæpʃɒt/ (snapshots) N-COUNT A **snapshot** is a photograph that is taken quickly and casually. ❑ *Let me take a snapshot of you guys.*

snare /sne<u>ɑ</u>r/ (snares, snaring, snared) ① N-COUNT A **snare** is a trap for catching birds or small animals. ❑ *A bird was caught in the snare.* ② V-T If someone **snares** an animal, they catch it using a snare. ❑ *He went out snaring rabbits.* [from Old English]

snarl /sn<u>ɑ</u>rl/ (snarls, snarling, snarled) V-I When an animal **snarls**, it makes a fierce, rough sound in its throat while showing its teeth. ❑ *The dog ran after them, barking and snarling.* ● **Snarl** is

also a noun. ❑ *With a snarl, the dog bit his leg.* [of Germanic origin]

snatch /snætʃ/ (snatches, snatching, snatched) ① V-T/V-I If you **snatch** something or **snatch at** something, you take it or pull it away quickly. ❑ *Mick snatched the cards from Archie's hand.* ② V-T If you **snatch** an opportunity, you take it quickly. If you **snatch** something to eat or **snatch** a rest, you have it quickly in between doing other things. ❑ *He snatched a few hours to sleep and to read.* ③ N-COUNT A **snatch of** a conversation or a song is a very small piece of it. ❑ *I heard snatches of the conversation.* [from Middle Dutch]

sneak /sni<u>k</u>/ (sneaks, sneaking, sneaked or snuck)

> The form **snuck** is informal.

① V-I If you **sneak** somewhere, you go there very quietly on foot, trying to avoid being seen or heard. ❑ *He sneaked out of his house late at night.* ② V-T If you **sneak** something somewhere, you take it there secretly. ❑ *He smuggled papers out, photocopied them, and snuck them back.* ③ V-T If you **sneak** a look at someone or something, you secretly have a quick look at them. ❑ *She sneaked a look at her watch.* [from Old English]

sneak|er /sni<u>k</u>ər/ (sneakers) N-COUNT **Sneakers** are casual shoes with rubber soles that people wear especially for sports. ❑ *...a new pair of sneakers.* [from Old English]
→ see **clothing**, **shoe**

sneer /sn<u>ɪ</u>ər/ (sneers, sneering, sneered) V-T/V-I If you **sneer at** someone or something, you show you do not like or respect them by the expression on your face or by what you say. ❑ *Critics have sneered at the movie, saying it is boring.* ❑ *"I don't need any help from you," he sneered.* ● **Sneer** is also a noun. ❑ *Her mouth twisted in a sneer.* [from Low Dutch]

sneeze /sni<u>z</u>/ (sneezes, sneezing, sneezed) V-I When you **sneeze**, you suddenly take in your breath and then blow it down your nose noisily without being able to stop yourself, for example, because you have a cold. ❑ *What exactly happens when we sneeze?* ● **Sneeze** is also a noun. ❑ *The disease is passed from person to person by a sneeze.* [from Old English]

sniff /sn<u>ɪ</u>f/ (sniffs, sniffing, sniffed) ① V-I When you **sniff**, you breathe in air through your nose hard enough to make a sound, for example, when you are trying not to cry, or in order to show disapproval. ❑ *She dried her eyes and sniffed loudly.* ❑ *He sniffed. There was a smell of burning.* ● **Sniff** is also a noun. ❑ *I could hear quiet sobs and sniffs.* ② V-T/V-I If you **sniff** something or **sniff at** it, you smell it by sniffing. ❑ *Suddenly, he stopped and sniffed the air.*

snig|ger /sn<u>ɪ</u>gər/ (sniggers, sniggering, sniggered) V-I If someone **sniggers**, they laugh quietly in a disrespectful way, for example at something rude or unkind. ❑ *Three kids sitting near me started sniggering.* ● **Snigger** is also a noun. ❑ *I heard a snigger when I told them I was traveling by bus.*

snip /sn<u>ɪ</u>p/ (snips, snipping, snipped) V-T/V-I If you **snip** something, or if you **snip at** or **through** something, you cut it quickly using sharp scissors. ❑ *He began to snip at the piece of paper.* [from Low German]

snipe /sna<u>ɪ</u>p/ (snipes, sniping, sniped) ① V-I If someone **snipes at** you, they criticize you. ❑ *The* media are still sniping at the president. ● **snip|ing** N-UNCOUNT ❑ *Despite the sniping of critics, most people loved the movie.* **2** V-I To **snipe at** someone means to shoot at them from a hidden position. ❑ *Protestors have sniped at U.S. Army positions many times.* ● **snip|er** (**snipers**) N-COUNT ❑ *Seven soldiers were shot by a sniper on Sunday.* [from Old Norse]

**snip|pet** /snɪpɪt/ (**snippets**) N-COUNT A **snippet** of something is a small piece of it. ❑ *...snippets of classical music.*

**snippy** /snɪpi/ ADJ A **snippy** person is often bad-tempered and speaks rudely to people. [INFORMAL] ❑ *Don't be snippy with me!* [from Low German]

**snob** /snɒb/ (**snobs**) N-COUNT If you call someone a **snob**, you disapprove of them because they behave as if they are superior to other people because of their intelligence, taste, or social status. ❑ *They did not like him because they were snobs.*

**snob|bery** /snɒbəri/ N-UNCOUNT **Snobbery** is the attitude of a snob. ❑ *There is an element of snobbery in golf.*

**snook|er** /snʊkər/ N-UNCOUNT **Snooker** is a game involving balls on a large table. The players use a long stick to hit a white ball, and score points by knocking colored balls into the pockets at the sides of the table. ❑ *...a game of snooker.*

**snoop** /snup/ (**snoops, snooping, snooped**) V-I If someone **snoops** around a place, they secretly look around it in order to find out things. ❑ *She saw a man snooping around.* ● **Snoop** is also a noun. ❑ *I'd love to have a snoop around their house.* ● **snoop|er** (**snoopers**) N-COUNT ❑ *A snooper could find out where you live from the phone book.* [from Dutch]

**snore** /snɔr/ (**snores, snoring, snored**) V-I When someone who is asleep **snores**, they make a loud noise each time they breathe. ❑ *His mouth was open, and he was snoring.* ● **Snore** is also a noun. ❑ *Uncle Arthur, after a loud snore, woke suddenly.* [from Middle Low German]

**snor|kel** /snɔrkᵊl/ (**snorkels, snorkeling, snorkeled**) **1** N-COUNT A **snorkel** is a tube through which a person swimming just under the surface of the ocean can breathe. **2** V-I When someone **snorkels**, they swim under water using a snorkel. ❑ *You can snorkel off the side of the boat.* [from German]

**snort** /snɔrt/ (**snorts, snorting, snorted**) V-I When people or animals **snort**, they breathe air noisily out through their noses. People sometimes snort in order to express disapproval or amusement. ❑ *Harrell snorted with laughter.* ● **Snort** is also a noun. ❑ *...snorts of laughter.*

**snow** /snoʊ/ (**snows, snowing, snowed**) **1** N-UNCOUNT **Snow** consists of a lot of soft white pieces of frozen water that fall from the sky in cold weather. ❑ *Six inches of snow fell.* **2** V-I When **it snows**, snow falls from the sky. ❑ *It snowed all night.* **3** V-T If someone **snows** you, they persuade you to do something or convince you of something by flattering or deceiving you. [INFORMAL] ❑ *I let him snow me with his big ideas.* [from Old English]
→ see Word Web: **snow**
→ see **precipitation, storm, water**

**snow|ball** /snoʊbɔl/ (**snowballs, snowballing, snowballed**) **1** N-COUNT A **snowball** is a ball of snow. **2** V-I If something such as a project **snowballs**, it rapidly increases and grows. ❑ *From those early days the business has snowballed.*

**snow|board** /snoʊbɔrd/ (**snowboards**) N-COUNT A **snowboard** is a narrow board that you stand on in order to slide quickly down snowy hills as a sport or for fun.

**snow|board|ing** /snoʊbɔrdɪŋ/ N-UNCOUNT **Snowboarding** is the sport or activity of traveling down snowy slopes using a snowboard. ❑ *He loves skiing and snowboarding.* ● **snow|board|er** N-COUNT ❑ *Snowboarders whizzed past us.*

**snow pea** (**snow peas**) N-COUNT **Snow peas** are a type of pea whose pods are eaten as well as the peas inside them.

**snow|plow** /snoʊplaʊ/ (**snowplows**) N-COUNT A **snowplow** is a vehicle which is used to push snow off roads or railroad tracks.

**snowy** /snoʊi/ (**snowier, snowiest**) ADJ A **snowy** place is covered in snow. A **snowy** day is a day when a lot of snow has fallen. ❑ *...snowy mountains.* [from Old English]

**snub** /snʌb/ (**snubs, snubbing, snubbed**) **1** V-T If you **snub** someone, you deliberately insult them by ignoring them or by behaving or speaking rudely toward them. ❑ *He snubbed her in public and made her feel an idiot.* **2** N-COUNT If you snub someone, your behavior or your remarks can be referred to as a **snub**. ❑ *They didn't invite her and she took this as a snub.* [from Old Norse]

**snuck** /snʌk/ **Snuck** is a past tense and past participle of **sneak**. [INFORMAL] [from Old English]

**snuff** /snʌf/ (**snuffs, snuffing, snuffed**)
▶ **snuff out** PHR-VERB To **snuff out** something such as a disagreement means to stop it, usually in a forceful or sudden way. ❑ *The government snuffed out all opposition.*

**snug** /snʌg/ (**snugger, snuggest**) **1** ADJ If you feel **snug** or are in a **snug** place, you are very warm and comfortable, especially because you are protected from cold weather. ❑ *They were snug and*

**S**

## Word Web    snow

Some people love winter. They like to watch **snowflakes** falling softly from the sky. The **snow** forms beautiful **drifts** on the ground and trees. A house with **icicles** hanging from the roof and **frost** on the windows looks warm and cosy. But winter has a dangerous side as well. **Ice** and snow on streets and roads causes many accidents. And a **blizzard** can leave behind large amounts of snow in a single day. In the mountains, large amounts of snow can cause **avalanches**. They usually happen when light, new snow falls on top of older, heavy snow.

*warm under the blankets.* **2** ADJ Something such as a piece of clothing that is **snug** fits very closely or tightly. ❑ *He wore a snug black T-shirt.* ● **snug|ly** ADV ❑ *The shoes fitted snugly.* [from Old Icelandic]

**snug|gle** /snʌgʷl/ (**snuggles, snuggling, snuggled**) V-I If you **snuggle** somewhere, you settle yourself into a warm, comfortable position, especially by moving closer to another person. ❑ *Jane snuggled up against his shoulder.*

**so** /soʊ/

> Usually pronounced /soʊ/ for meanings **1**, **4**, **5**, **6**, **12**, and **14**.

**1** ADV You use **so** to refer back to something that has just been mentioned. ❑ *"Do you think they will stay together?" — "I hope so."* ❑ *If you don't like it, then say so.* **2** ADV You use **so** when you are saying that something which has just been said about one person or thing is also true of another one. ❑ *I enjoy Ann's company and so does Martin.* **3** CONJ You use the structures **as...so** and **just as...so** when you want to indicate that two events or situations are similar in some way. ❑ *As computers become more sophisticated, so too do their users.* ❑ *Just as John has changed, so has his wife.* **4** CONJ You use **so** and **so that** to introduce the result of the situation you have just mentioned. ❑ *I am shy and so I find it hard to talk about my feelings.* ❑ *People are living longer, so that even people who are 65 or 70 feel young.* **5** CONJ You use **so**, **so that**, and **so as** to introduce the reason for doing the thing that you have just mentioned. ❑ *Come to dinner so we can talk about what happened.* ❑ *They moved to the corner of the room so that nobody would hear them.* **6** ADV You can use **so** in conversations to introduce a new topic, or to introduce a question or comment about something that has been said. ❑ *So how was your day?* ❑ *So as for your question, Miles, the answer is no.* **7** CONVENTION You say "**So?**" and "**So what?**" to indicate that you think something that someone has said is unimportant. [INFORMAL] ❑ *"I don't like it." — "So?"* **8** ADV You can use **so** in front of adjectives and adverbs to emphasize the quality that they are describing. ❑ *He was surprised they got married — they seemed so different.* **9** ADV You can use **so...that** and **so...as to** emphasize the degree of something by mentioning the result or consequence of it. ❑ *He's not so stupid as to listen to rumors.* **10** → see also **insofar as** **11** PHRASE You use **and so on** or **and so forth** at the end of a list to indicate that there are other items that you could also mention. ❑ *...important issues such as health, education, and so on.* **12** PHRASE You use the structures **not...so much** and **not so much...as to** say that something is one kind of thing rather than another kind. ❑ *I don't object to Will's behavior so much as his personality.* **13** PHRASE You use **or so**

when you are giving an approximate amount. ❑ *A ticket will cost you $20 or so.* **14** PHRASE You use **so much** and **so many** when you are saying that there is a definite limit to something but you are not saying what this limit is. ❑ *You can only do something so many times before you get bored.* ❑ *There is only so much fuel in the tank.* [from Old English] **15** **so far** → see **far** **16** **every so often** → see **often**

**soak** /soʊk/ (**soaks, soaking, soaked**) **1** V-T/V-I If you **soak** something or leave it to **soak**, you put it into a liquid and leave it there. ❑ *Soak the beans for 2 hours.* **2** V-T If a liquid **soaks** something or if you **soak** something **with** a liquid, the liquid makes the thing very wet. ❑ *The water soaked his jacket.* ● **soaked** /soʊkt/ ADJ ❑ *The tent got completely soaked in the storm.* ● **soak|ing** ADJ ❑ *My raincoat was soaking wet.* **3** V-I If a liquid **soaks through** something, it passes through it. ❑ *Blood soaked through the bandages.* **4** V-I If someone **soaks**, they spend a long time in a hot bath, because they enjoy it. ❑ *I need to soak in a hot tub.* ● **Soak** is also a noun. ❑ *I had a long soak in the bath.* [from Old English]

▶ **soak up** PHR-VERB If a soft or dry material **soaks up** a liquid, the liquid goes into the substance. ❑ *The cotton will soak up the water.*

**so-and-so** PRON You use **so-and-so** instead of a word, expression, or name when you are talking generally rather than giving a specific example of a particular thing. [INFORMAL] ❑ *If he tells me to do so-and-so, I do it.*

**soap** /soʊp/ (**soaps**) **1** N-VAR **Soap** is a substance that you use with water for washing yourself or for washing clothes. ❑ *...a bar of soap.* ❑ *...a large box of soap powder.* **2** N-COUNT A **soap** is the same as a **soap opera.** [INFORMAL] [from Old English]
→ see Word Web: **soap**

**soap op|era** (**soap operas**) N-COUNT A **soap opera** is a popular television drama series about the daily lives and problems of a group of people who live in a particular place.

**soar** /sɔr/ (**soars, soaring, soared**) **1** V-I If the amount, value, level, or volume of something **soars**, it quickly increases by a great deal. ❑ *Prices have soared.* **2** V-I If something such as a bird **soars** into the air, it goes quickly up into the air. [LITERARY] ❑ *A golden eagle soared overhead.* [from Old French]

**sob** /sɒb/ (**sobs, sobbing, sobbed**) **1** V-I When someone **sobs**, they cry in a noisy way, breathing in short breaths. ❑ *She began to sob.* ● **sob|bing** N-UNCOUNT ❑ *The room was silent except for her sobbing.* **2** N-COUNT A **sob** is one of the noises that you make when you are crying. ❑ *His sobs grew louder.* [from Low German]

---

### Word Web    soap

**Soap** is important in everyday life. We **wash** our hands before we eat. We lather up with a **bar** of soap in the **shower** or **tub**. We use liquid **detergent** to **clean** our dishes. We use **laundry** detergent to get our clothes clean. But why do we use soap? How does it work? It works almost like a magnet. But soap doesn't **attract** metal. It attracts dirt and grease. It makes a **bubble** around the dirt, and water washes it all away.

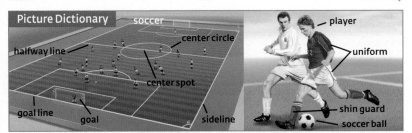

**Picture Dictionary**

soccer

player

center circle

halfway line

uniform

center spot

goal line

goal                                          sideline

shin guard

soccer ball

**so|ber** /soʊbər/ (**sobers, sobering, sobered**)
**1** ADJ When you are **sober**, you are not drunk.
❑ *He was completely sober.* **2** ADJ A **sober** person
is serious and thoughtful. ❑ *He is very sober and
realistic.* ● **so|ber|ly** ADV ❑ *"There's a problem," he said
soberly.* **3** ADJ **Sober** colors and clothes are plain
and rather dull. ❑ *He dresses in sober gray suits.*
● **so|ber|ly** ADV ❑ *She was soberly dressed in a dark
suit.* [from Old French] **4** → see also **sobering**
▸ **sober up** PHR-VERB If someone **sobers up**, or if
something **sobers** them **up**, they become sober
after being drunk. ❑ *He was put in a police cell to
sober up.*

**so|ber|ing** /soʊbərɪŋ/ ADJ You say that
something is a **sobering** thought or has a **sobering**
effect when a situation seems serious and makes
you become serious and thoughtful. ❑ *It is a
sobering thought that we could have been killed.* [from
Old French]

**so-called** also **so called** **1** ADJ You use
**so-called** to indicate that you think a word
or expression used to describe someone or
something is in fact wrong. ❑ *This so-called miracle
never actually happened.* **2** ADJ You use **so-called** to
indicate that something is generally referred to by
the name that you are about to use. ❑ *...the world's
seven largest economies, the so-called G-7.*

**soc|cer** /sɒkər/ N-UNCOUNT **Soccer** is a game
played by two teams of eleven players using a
round ball. Players kick the ball to each other and
try to score goals by kicking the ball into a large
net. Outside the United States, this game is also
referred to as **football**. ❑ *She plays soccer.*
→ see Picture Dictionary: **soccer**

**soc|cer play|er** /sɒkər pleɪər/ (**soccer players**)
N-COUNT A **soccer player** is a person who plays
soccer, especially as a profession.

**so|cia|ble** /soʊʃəbəl/ ADJ **Sociable** people are
friendly and enjoy talking to other people. ❑ *She
was extremely sociable.* [from French]

**Word Link**  *soci ≈ companion : associate, social,
sociology*

**so|cial** /soʊʃəl/ **1** ADJ **Social** means relating to
society. ❑ *...unemployment, and other social problems.*
● **so|cial|ly** ADV ❑ *It wasn't socially acceptable to eat
in the street.* **2** ADJ **Social** means relating to leisure
activities that involve meeting other people. ❑ *We
should organize more social events.* ● **so|cial|ly** ADV
❑ *We have known each other socially for a long time.*
[from Latin]
→ see **kiss, myth**

**so|cial be|hav|ior** N-UNCOUNT **Social behavior**
is the interaction between animals of the same
species or between people.

**so|cial dance** (**social dances**) N-VAR **Social
dance** is any form of dance that is done in a social
setting, for example ballroom dancing.

**so|cial|ism** /soʊʃəlɪzəm/ N-UNCOUNT **Socialism**
is a set of political principles whose general aim is
to create a system in which everyone has an equal
opportunity to benefit from a country's wealth.
Under socialism, the country's main industries
are usually owned by the state. [from Latin]

**so|cial|ist** /soʊʃəlɪst/ (**socialists**) **1** ADJ
**Socialist** means based on socialism or relating
to socialism. ❑ *...members of the Socialist Party.*
**2** N-COUNT A **socialist** is a person who believes in
socialism or who is a member of a socialist party.
❑ *His grandparents were socialists.* [from Latin]

**so|cial|ize** /soʊʃəlaɪz/ (**socializes, socializing,
socialized**) V-I If you **socialize**, you meet other
people socially, for example at parties. ❑ *...an
opportunity to socialize and make friends.* [from Latin]

**so|cial life** (**social lives**) N-COUNT Your **social life**
involves spending time with your friends. ❑ *I was
popular and had a busy social life.*

**so|cial sci|ence** (**social sciences**) N-VAR **Social
science** is the scientific study of society. ❑ *...a
degree in a social science.*

**So|cial Se|cu|rity** N-UNCOUNT **Social Security** is
a system by which workers and employers in the
U.S. have to pay money to the government, which
gives money to people who are retired, who are
disabled, or who cannot work.

**So|cial Se|cu|rity num|ber** (**Social Security
numbers**) N-COUNT A **Social Security number** is
a nine digit number that is given to U.S. citizens
and to people living in the U.S. You need it to get
a job, collect Social Security benefits, and receive
some government services.

**so|cial ser|vices** N-PLURAL **Social services** in
a district are the services provided by the local
authority or government to help people who have
serious family problems or financial problems.
❑ *Social services are trying to help these children.*

**so|cial work** N-UNCOUNT **Social work** is work
which involves giving help and advice to people
with serious family problems or financial
problems.

**so|cial work|er** (**social workers**) N-COUNT A
**social worker** is a person whose job is to do social
work.

**so|ci|ety** /səsaɪɪti/ (**societies**) **1** N-VAR **Society**
consists of all the people in a country or region,
thought of as a large organized group. ❑ *...common
problems in society.* ❑ *We live in an unequal society.*
**2** N-COUNT A **society** is an organization for
people who have the same interest or aim. ❑ *...the*

S

American Historical Society. **3** N-UNCOUNT **Society** is the rich, fashionable people in a particular place who meet on social occasions. ❑ *The couple were well-known in society.* [from Old French]
→ see **culture**

**so|ci|ol|ogy** /soʊsiɒlədʒi/ N-UNCOUNT **Sociology** is the study of society or of the way society is organized. ● **so|cio|logi|cal** /soʊsiəlɒdʒɪkªl/ ADJ ❑ *...a sociological study on the importance of the family.* ● **so|ci|olo|gist** (**sociologists**) N-COUNT ❑ *As a sociologist she is interested in the role of women.* [from French]

**sock** /sɒk/ (**socks**) N-COUNT **Socks** are pieces of clothing which cover your foot and ankle and are worn inside shoes. ❑ *...a pair of red socks.* [from Old English]
→ see **clothing**

**sock|et** /sɒkɪt/ (**sockets**) **1** N-COUNT A **socket** is a device on a piece of electrical equipment into which you can put a bulb or plug. ❑ *He took the light bulb out of the socket.* **2** N-COUNT You can refer to any hollow part or opening in a structure which another part fits into as a **socket**. ❑ *His tooth was loose in its socket.* [from Anglo-Norman]

**soda** /soʊdə/ (**sodas**) **1** N-UNCOUNT **Soda** is a sweet carbonated drink. ❑ *...a glass of soda.* ● A **soda** is a bottle of soda. ❑ *Get sodas for the children.* [from Medieval Latin] **2** → see also **club soda**

**soda pop** (**soda pops**) N-VAR **Soda pop** is the same as **soda 1**.

**sod|den** /sɒdªn/ ADJ Something that is **sodden** is extremely wet. ❑ *Our clothes were sodden.*

**so|dium** /soʊdiəm/ N-UNCOUNT **Sodium** is a silvery white chemical element which combines with other chemicals. Salt is a sodium compound. [from New Latin]

**sofa** /soʊfə/ (**sofas**) N-COUNT A **sofa** is a long, comfortable seat with a back and arms, which two or three people can sit on. [from Arabic]

**soft** /sɒft/ (**softer, softest**) **1** ADJ Something that is **soft** is pleasant to touch, and not rough or hard. ❑ *Body lotion will keep your skin soft.* ❑ *She wiped the baby's face with a soft cloth.* ● **soft|ness** N-UNCOUNT ❑ *He loved the softness of her hair.* **2** ADJ Something that is **soft** changes shape or bends easily when you press it. ❑ *Add milk to form a soft dough.* **3** ADJ Something that is **soft** is very gentle and has no force. For example, a **soft** sound or voice is quiet and not harsh. A **soft** light or color is pleasant to look at because it is not bright. ❑ *There was a soft tapping on my door.* ● **soft|ly** ADV ❑ *She walked into the softly lit room.* **4** ADJ If you are **soft on** someone, you do not treat them as strictly or severely as you should. ❑ *The law is too soft on criminals.* [from Old English]

| **Thesaurus** | soft | Also look up : |
|---|---|---|

ADJ. fluffy, silky; (*ant.*) firm, hard, rough **1**
    faint, gentle, light, low; (*ant.*) clear,
    strong **3**

**soft|cover** /sɒftkʌvər/ (**softcovers**) also soft-cover N-COUNT A **softcover** is a book with a thin cardboard, paper, or plastic cover. ❑ *...a set of 6 softcover books.*

**soft drink** (**soft drinks**) N-COUNT A **soft drink** is a cold, nonalcoholic drink such as lemonade or fruit juice, or a carbonated drink.

**sof|ten** /sɒfªn/ (**softens, softening, softened**) **1** V-T/V-I If you **soften** something or if it **softens**, it becomes less hard, stiff, or firm. ❑ *Soften the butter in a small saucepan.* **2** V-T If one thing **softens** the damaging effect of another thing, it makes the effect less severe. ❑ *He wanted to soften the impact of the new tax on the poor.* **3** V-T/V-I If you **soften** your position, if your position **softens**, or if you **soften**, you become more sympathetic and less hostile or critical. ❑ *The letter shows that they have softened their position.* ❑ *His views have softened a lot in recent years.* [from Old English]

| **Word Link** | ware ≈ merchandise : hardware, software, warehouse |
|---|---|

**soft|ware** /sɒftwɛər/ N-UNCOUNT Computer programs are referred to as **software**. Compare **hardware**. [COMPUTING] ❑ *He writes software.*

**sog|gy** /sɒgi/ (**soggier, soggiest**) ADJ Something that is **soggy** is unpleasantly wet. ❑ *...soggy cheese sandwiches.*

**soil** /sɔɪl/ (**soils**) N-VAR **Soil** is the substance on the surface of the earth in which plants grow. ❑ *The soil here is good for growing vegetables.* [from Anglo-Norman]
→ see **erosion, farm, grassland, photosynthesis**

**sol|ace** /sɒlɪs/ N-UNCOUNT **Solace** is a feeling of comfort that makes you feel less sad. [FORMAL] ❑ *I found solace in writing when my father died.* [from Old French]

**so|lar** /soʊlər/ **1** ADJ **Solar** is used to describe things relating to the sun. ❑ *...solar gases.* ❑ *...solar wind.* **2** ADJ **Solar** power is obtained from the sun's light and heat. ❑ *...the advantages of solar power.* [from Latin]
→ see Word Web: **solar**
→ see **energy, greenhouse effect, photosynthesis**

**so|lar col|lec|tor** (**solar collectors**) N-COUNT A **solar collector** is a device that collects heat from the sun and converts it into electricity. ❑ *Large homes should have solar collectors.*

**so|lar eclipse** (**solar eclipses**) N-COUNT A **solar eclipse** is an occasion when the moon is between the Earth and the sun, so that for a short time you cannot see part or all of the sun. Compare **lunar eclipse**.

**so|lar neb|ula** (**solar nebulae** or **solar nebulas**) N-COUNT The **solar nebula** is the cloud of gas from which our solar system is believed to have developed. [TECHNICAL]

**so|lar sys|tem** (**solar systems**) N-COUNT The **solar system** is the sun and all the planets that go around it. ❑ *Saturn is the second biggest planet in the solar system.*
→ see Picture Dictionary: **solar system**
→ see Word Web: **solar system**
→ see **galaxy**

**sold** /soʊld/ **Sold** is the past tense and past participle of **sell**. [from Old English]

**sol|dier** /soʊldʒər/ (**soldiers**) N-COUNT A **soldier** is a member of an army, especially one who is not an officer. [from Old French]
→ see **war**

**sole** /soʊl/ **1** ADJ The **sole** thing or person of a particular type is the only one of that type. ❑ *Their sole aim is to win.* ● **sole|ly** ADV ❑ *Doctors do not rely solely on what a patient tells them.*

S

## Word Web   solar

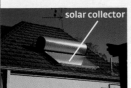

Sources of **fossil fuel energy** are becoming scarce and expensive. They also cause environmental **pollution**. Scientists are studying alternative sources of energy such as **solar power**. There are two ways to use the **sun's energy**. **Thermal** systems produce heat.

**photovoltaic cells**

**Photovoltaic** systems generate

solar collector

electricity. Thermal systems use a **solar collector**. This is an insulated box with a clear cover. It stores the sun's energy for use in household air or water heating systems. Photovoltaic systems have thin layers of **semiconductor** materials to change the sun's heat into electricity. They are often used in calculators and solar-powered watches.

**2** ADJ If you have **sole** charge or ownership of something, you are the only person in charge of it or who owns it. ❏ *She was the sole caregiver for her sick mother.* **3** N-COUNT The **sole** of your foot or of a shoe or sock is the underneath surface of it. ❏ *...shoes with thick soles.* [from Old French] → see **foot**

**sol|emn** /sɒləm/ **1** ADJ Someone or something that is **solemn** is very serious rather than cheerful or humorous. ❏ *His face looked solemn.* ● **sol|emn|ly** ADV ❏ *Her listeners nodded solemnly.* ● **sol|em|nity** /səlɛmnɪti/ N-UNCOUNT ❏ *...the solemnity of the event.* **2** ADJ A **solemn** promise or agreement is one that you make in a very formal, sincere way. ❏ *She made a solemn promise not to tell anyone.* ● **sol|emn|ly** ADV ❏ *Her husband solemnly promised to keep it a secret.* [from Old French]

**sol|fege** /sɒlfɛʒ, soʊl-/ N-UNCOUNT **Solfege** is a system used in the teaching of music and singing,

in which the steps of the musical scale are given the names Do, Re, Me, Fa, Sol, La, Ti, and Do. [TECHNICAL] [from French]

**so|lic|it** /səlɪsɪt/ (solicits, soliciting, solicited) V-T If you **solicit** money, help, support, or an opinion **from** someone, you ask them for it. [FORMAL] ❏ *He solicited the advice of an expert.* ● **so|lic|it|a|tion** N-UNCOUNT ❏ *...the solicitation of money from a foreign government.* [from Old French]

**so|lici|tor** /səlɪsɪtər/ (solicitors) N-COUNT In the United States, a **solicitor** is the chief lawyer in a government or city department. [from Old French]

**sol|id** /sɒlɪd/ (solids) **1** ADJ A **solid** substance or object stays the same shape whether it is in a container or not. ❏ *He did not eat solid food for several weeks.* **2** N-COUNT A **solid** is a substance that stays the same shape whether it is in a container or not. ❏ *Solids turn to liquids at certain temperatures.*

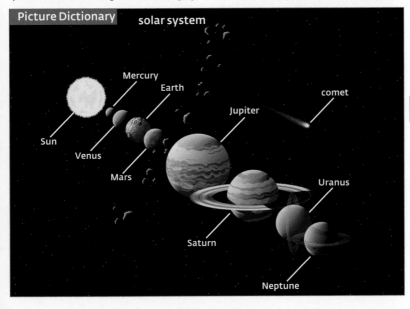

## Picture Dictionary   solar system

- Sun
- Mercury
- Venus
- Earth
- Mars
- Jupiter
- Saturn
- Uranus
- Neptune
- comet

S

## Word Web    solar system

The **sun** formed when a nebula turned into a star almost
5 billion years ago. All the **planets**, **comets**, and asteroids in
our **solar system** came from this nebula. Today they all
**orbit** the sun. The four planets closest to the sun are small
and rocky. The next four consist mostly of **gases**. The
outermost planet, Pluto, is a dwarf planet. It is made of rock
and ice. Many of the planets have **moons** orbiting them.
Most asteroids have irregular shapes and are covered with
**craters**. Only about 200 asteroids have diameters of more than 100 kilometers.

**3** ADJ A substance that is **solid** is very hard or
firm. ❑ *The lake was frozen solid.* **4** ADJ A **solid**
object or mass does not have a space inside it, or
holes or gaps in it. ❑ *…50 feet of solid rock.* **5** ADJ A
structure that is **solid** is strong and is not likely to
collapse or fall over. ❑ *Only the most solid buildings
were still standing after the earthquake.* ● **sol|id|ly** ADV
❑ *Their house was solidly built.* ● **so|lid|ity** /səlɪdɪti/
N-UNCOUNT ❑ *…the solidity of the walls.* **6** ADJ If
you describe someone as **solid**, you mean that they
are very reliable and respectable. ❑ *Her husband is
solid and stable.* ● **sol|id|ly** ADV ❑ *Graham is so solidly
consistent.* ● **so|lid|ity** N-UNCOUNT ❑ *The British
are known for their solidity.* **7** ADJ You use **solid** to
describe something such as advice or information
which is reliable and useful. ❑ *She always gives me
solid advice.* ❑ *We don't have any solid information on
where he is.* ● **sol|id|ly** ADV ❑ *Their claims are solidly
based in good research.* **8** ADJ If you do something
for a **solid** period of time, you do it without any
pause or interruption throughout that time. ❑ *We
worked together for two solid years.* ● **sol|id|ly** ADV
❑ *I've worked solidly since last summer and I need a
break.* [from Old French]
→ see Picture Dictionary: **solid**
→ see **matter, pattern**

**soli|dar|ity** /sɒlɪdæriti/ N-UNCOUNT If a group
of people show **solidarity**, they show support for
each other or for another group, especially in
political or international affairs. ❑ *People marched
to show solidarity with their leaders.* [from French]

**so|lidi|fy** /səlɪdɪfaɪ/ (**solidifies, solidifying,
solidified**) V-T/V-I When a liquid **solidifies** or is

solidified, it changes into a solid. ❑ *The cement took
several days to solidify.* [from Old French]

**soli|taire** /sɒlɪtɛər/ N-UNCOUNT **Solitaire** is a
card game for only one player. [from Old French]

**soli|tary** /sɒlɪteri/ **1** ADJ A person or animal
that is **solitary** spends a lot of time alone. ❑ *Paul
was a shy, solitary man.* **2** ADJ A **solitary** activity
is one that you do alone. ❑ *He spent his evenings in
solitary reading.* **3** ADJ A **solitary** person or object
is alone, with no others near them. ❑ *There was a
solitary house on the hillside.* [from Latin]

**soli|tude** /sɒlɪtud/ N-UNCOUNT **Solitude** is
the state of being alone, especially when this is
peaceful and pleasant. ❑ *He enjoyed his moments of
solitude.* [from Latin]

**solo** /soʊloʊ/ (**solos**) **1** ADJ You use **solo** to
indicate that someone does something alone
rather than with other people. ❑ *He has just
recorded his first solo album.* ● **Solo** is also an adverb.
❑ *Lindbergh was the first person to fly solo across the
Atlantic.* **2** N-COUNT A **solo** is a piece of music or a
dance performed by one person. ❑ *The song featured
a guitar solo.* [from Italian]

**so|lo|ist** /soʊloʊɪst/ (**soloists**) N-COUNT A
**soloist** is a musician or dancer who performs a
solo. ❑ *The conductor looked at the soloist.* [from
Italian]

**sol|ubil|ity** /sɒlyəbɪlɪti/ N-UNCOUNT A
substance's **solubility** is its ability to dissolve in
another substance or the amount of it that will
dissolve in another substance. [from Late Latin]

**sol|uble** /sɒlyəbəl/ ADJ A substance that is

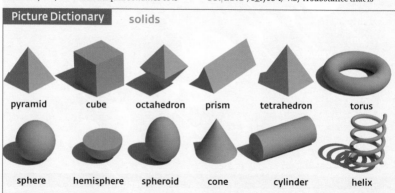

## Picture Dictionary    solids

pyramid    cube    octahedron    prism    tetrahedron    torus

sphere    hemisphere    spheroid    cone    cylinder    helix

S

**soluble** will dissolve in a liquid. ❑ *The red dye is soluble in hot water.* [from Late Latin]

**so|lute** /sɒlyut, soʊlut/ (**solutes**) N-COUNT A **solute** is any substance that dissolves in another substance. [TECHNICAL] [from Latin]

**so|lu|tion** /səluʃ³n/ (**solutions**) **1** N-COUNT A **solution to** a problem is a way of dealing with it so that the difficulty is removed. ❑ *They both want to find a peaceful solution.* **2** N-COUNT The **solution to** a puzzle is the answer to it. ❑ *We asked readers to send in their solutions.* **3** N-COUNT A **solution** is a liquid in which a solid substance has been dissolved. ❑ *...a soapy solution.* [from Latin]
→ see **fraction**

| Word Partnership | Use *solution* with : |
| --- | --- |
| ADJ. | **best** solution, **peaceful** solution, **perfect** solution, **possible** solution, **practical** solution, **temporary** solution **1** |
| | **easy** solution, **obvious** solution, **simple** solution **1** **2** |
| PREP. | solution **to a conflict**, solution **to a crisis 1** |
| | solution **to a problem 1** **2** |
| V. | **propose a** solution, **reach a** solution, **seek a** solution **1** |
| | **find a** solution **1** **2** |

**solve** /sɒlv/ (**solves, solving, solved**) V-T If you **solve** a problem or a question, you find a solution or an answer to it. ❑ *They have not solved the problem of unemployment.* [from Latin]

| Word Partnership | Use *solve* with : |
| --- | --- |
| N. | **ability to** solve *something*, solve **a crisis**, solve **a mystery**, solve **a problem**, solve **a puzzle**, **way to** solve *something* |
| V. | **attempt/try to** solve *something*, **help** solve *something* |

**sol|vent** /sɒlv³nt/ (**solvents**) **1** ADJ If a person or a company is **solvent**, they have enough money to pay all their debts. [BUSINESS] ❑ *The company is now solvent.* **2** N-VAR A **solvent** is a liquid that can dissolve other substances. ❑ *...a small amount of cleaning solvent.* [from Latin]

**som|ber** /sɒmbər/ **1** ADJ If someone is **somber**, they are serious or sad. ❑ *She described the somber mood of her co-workers.* ● **som|ber|ly** ADV ❑ *"I've got bad news for you," he said somberly.* **2** ADJ **Somber** colors and places are dark and dull. ❑ *His room is somber and dark.* [from French]

**some** /səm, STRONG sʌm/ **1** DET You use **some** to refer to a quantity of something or to a number of people or things, when you are not stating the quantity or number precisely. ❑ *Would you like some orange juice?* ❑ *He went to fetch some books.* ● **Some** is also a pronoun. ❑ *The apples are ripe, and we picked some today.* **2** DET You use **some** to emphasize that a quantity or number is fairly large. For example, if an activity takes **some** time, it takes quite a lot of time. ❑ *We have discussed this in some detail.* ❑ *He was silent for some time.* **3** QUANT If you refer to **some of** the people or things in a group, you mean a few of them but not all of them. If you refer to **some of** a particular thing, you mean a part of it but not all of it. ❑ *Some of the workers will*

lose their jobs. ❑ *Put some of the sauce onto a plate.*
● **Some** is also a pronoun. ❑ *When the chicken is cooked I'll freeze some.* **4** DET If you refer to **some** person or thing, you are referring to that person or thing but in a vague way, without stating precisely which person or thing you mean. ❑ *If you are worried about some aspect of your child's health, call us.* **5** ADV You can use **some** in front of a number to indicate that it is approximate. ❑ *I have kept birds for some 30 years.* **6** ADV **Some** is used to mean to a small extent or degree. ❑ *I'll look around some to pass the time.* [from Old English]

**some|body** /sʌmbadi, -bʌdi/ PRON **Somebody** means the same as **someone**.

**some|how** /sʌmhaʊ/ ADV You use **somehow** to say that you do not know or cannot say how something was done or will be done. ❑ *We'll manage somehow, I know we will.*

**some|one** /sʌmwʌn/

| The form **somebody** is also used. |
| --- |

**1** PRON You use **someone** or **somebody** to refer to a person without saying exactly who you mean. ❑ *I got a call from someone who wanted to rent the apartment.* ❑ *I need someone to help me.* **2** PRON If you say that a person is **someone** or **somebody** in a particular kind of work or in a particular place, you mean that they are considered to be important in that kind of work or in that place. ❑ *"Before she arrived," she says, "I was somebody in this town."*

**some|place** /sʌmpleɪs/ ADV **Someplace** means the same as **somewhere**. ❑ *Maybe we could go someplace together.*

**some|thing** /sʌmθɪŋ/ **1** PRON You use **something** to refer to a thing, situation, event, or idea, without saying exactly what it is. ❑ *He knew that there was something wrong.* ❑ *Was there something you wanted to ask me?* **2** PRON You can use **something** in expressions like "that's something" when you think that a situation is not very good but is better than it might have been. ❑ *Well, at least he called. That was something.* **3** PRON If you say that a thing is **something** of a disappointment, you mean that it is quite disappointing. If you say that a person is **something** of an artist, you mean that they are quite good at art. ❑ *The vacation was something of a disappointment.* **4** PRON If you say that there is **something** in an idea or suggestion, you mean that it is quite good and should be considered seriously. ❑ *There could be something in what he said.* **5** **something like** → see **like**

**some|time** /sʌmtaɪm/ ADV You use **sometime** to refer to a time in the future or the past that is unknown or that has not yet been decided. ❑ *We will finish sometime next month.* ❑ *Why don't you come and see me sometime?*

| Usage | **sometime, sometimes,** and **some time** |
| --- | --- |

*Sometime, sometimes,* and *some time* are easy to confuse. *Sometime* means "at some unknown time"; *sometimes* means "occasionally, from time to time"; *some time* means "some amount of time". ❑ *Sometimes Ilya enjoys spending some time catching up on his favorite soap operas; the last time he did that was sometime in August.*

**some|times** /sʌmtaɪmz/ ADV You use **sometimes** to say that something happens on

some occasions rather than all the time. ❑ *I sometimes sit out in the garden and read.* ❑ *Sometimes he's a little rude.*
→ see also **sometime**

**some|what** /sˈʌmwʌt, -wɒt/ ADV You use **somewhat** to indicate that something is true to a limited extent or degree. [FORMAL] ❑ *He sounded somewhat uncertain.*

**some|where** /sˈʌmwɛər/ ◼ ADV You use **somewhere** to refer to a place without saying exactly where you mean. ❑ *I've seen him before somewhere.* ❑ *I'm not going home yet. I have to go somewhere else first.* ❑ *I needed somewhere to live.* ◼ ADV You use **somewhere** when giving an approximate amount, number, or time. ❑ *The house is worth somewhere between $7 million and $10 million.* ❑ *Caray is somewhere between 73 and 80 years of age.* ◼ PHRASE If you say that you **are getting somewhere**, you mean that you are making progress toward achieving something. ❑ *If we can agree on this, we'll be getting somewhere.*

**son** /sˈʌn/ (**sons**) N-COUNT Someone's **son** is their male child. ❑ *He shared a pizza with his son Laurence.* ❑ *Sam is the seven-year-old son of Eric Davies.* [from Old English]
→ see **child**

**so|na|ta** /sənˈɑːtə/ (**sonatas**) N-COUNT A **sonata** is a piece of classical music written either for a single instrument, or for one instrument and a piano. [from Italian]

**sonata-allegro form** /sənˈɑːtəˈæˌlɛɡroʊ fɔrm/ (**sonata-allegro forms**) also **sonata form** N-VAR A **sonata-allegro form** is a piece of classical music that consists of three main sections in which musical themes are introduced, developed, and then repeated. [TECHNICAL]

**song** /sˈɔŋ/ (**songs**) ◼ N-COUNT A **song** is words and music sung together. ❑ *She sang a Spanish song.* ◼ N-UNCOUNT **Song** is the art of singing. ❑ *...a festival of dance, music, and song.* ◼ N-COUNT A bird's **song** is the pleasant, musical sounds that it makes. ❑ *It's lovely to hear a blackbird's song in the evening.* [from Old English]
→ see **concert, music**

<table>
<tr><th colspan="2">Word Partnership    Use song with :</th></tr>
<tr><td>ADJ.</td><td>beautiful song, favorite song, old song, popular song ◼</td></tr>
<tr><td>V.</td><td>hear a song, play a song, record a song, sing a song, write a song ◼</td></tr>
<tr><td>N.</td><td>hit song, love song, song lyrics, song music, pop song, rap song, song title, theme song, words of a song ◼ birds song ◼</td></tr>
</table>

**song|book** /sˈɔŋbʊk/ (**songbooks**) ◼ N-COUNT A songwriter's **songbook** is all the songs that he or she has written. You can also refer to the songs that a singer performs as their **songbook**. ❑ *...hits from the songbook of Bob Dylan.* ◼ N-COUNT A **songbook** is a book containing the words and music of a lot of songs. ❑ *...a pop songbook.*

**song form** (**song forms**) N-VAR **Song form** is a way of describing the structure of a song in which different sections of the song are represented by different letters of the alphabet.

**son|ic** /sˈɒnɪk/ ADJ **Sonic** is used to describe things related to sound. [TECHNICAL] ❑ *...the sonic*

*and visual effects in the show.* [from Latin]
→ see **sound**

**son-in-law** (**sons-in-law**) N-COUNT Someone's **son-in-law** is the husband of their daughter.

**son|net** /sˈɒnɪt/ (**sonnets**) N-COUNT A **sonnet** is a poem that has 14 lines. Each line has 10 syllables, and the poem has a fixed pattern of rhymes. [from Italian]

**soon** /sˈuːn/ (**sooner, soonest**) ◼ ADV If something is going to happen **soon**, it will happen after a short time. If something happened **soon** after a particular time or event, it happened a short time after it. ❑ *I'll call you soon.* ❑ *He arrived sooner than I expected.* ◼ PHRASE If you say that something happens **as soon as** something else happens, you mean that it happens immediately after the other thing. ❑ *As soon as the weather improves we will go.* ◼ PHRASE If you say that you **would just as soon** do something or you**'d just as soon** do it, you mean that you would prefer to do it. ❑ *These people could afford to retire to Florida but they'd just as soon stay here.* ❑ *I'd just as soon not tell anyone about this.* [from Old English]

**soot** /sˈʊt, sˈuːt/ N-UNCOUNT **Soot** is black powder which rises in the smoke from a fire and collects on the inside of chimneys. ❑ *The wall is black with soot.* [from Old English]

**soothe** /sˈuːð/ (**soothes, soothing, soothed**) ◼ V-T If you **soothe** someone who is angry or upset, you make them feel calmer. ❑ *He sang to her to soothe her.* ● **sooth|ing** ADJ ❑ *Put on some nice soothing music.* ◼ V-T Something that **soothes** a part of your body where there is pain or discomfort makes the pain or discomfort less severe. ❑ *...lotion to soothe dry skin.* ● **sooth|ing** ADJ ❑ *Cold tea is very soothing for burns.* [from Old English]

**so|phis|ti|cat|ed** /səfˈɪstɪkeɪtɪd/ ◼ ADJ A **sophisticated** machine, device, or method is more advanced or complex than others. ❑ *Bees use a very sophisticated communication system.* ◼ ADJ Someone who is **sophisticated** is comfortable in social situations and knows about culture, fashion, and other matters that are considered socially important. ❑ *Claude was a charming, sophisticated man.* [from Medieval Latin]

<table>
<tr><th colspan="2">Thesaurus    sophisticated    Also look up :</th></tr>
<tr><td>ADJ.</td><td>advanced, complex, elaborate, intricate ◼ cultured, experienced, refined, worldly; (ant.) backward, crude ◼</td></tr>
</table>

**so|phis|ti|ca|tion** /səfˌɪstɪkeɪʃⁿn/ N-UNCOUNT The **sophistication** of people, places, machines, or methods is their quality of being sophisticated. ❑ *She lacks sophistication, but she is not stupid.* [from Medieval Latin]

**sopho|more** /sˈɒfəmɔr/ (**sophomores**) N-COUNT A **sophomore** is a student in the second year of college or high school.

**so|pra|no** /səprˈænoʊ, -prˈɑn-/ (**sopranos**) N-COUNT A **soprano** is a woman, girl, or boy with a high singing voice. ❑ *She was the main soprano at the theatre.* [from Italian]

**sor|did** /sˈɔrdɪd/ ◼ ADJ If you describe someone's behavior as **sordid**, you mean that it is immoral or dishonest. ❑ *We discovered the sordid truth about his life.* ◼ ADJ If you describe a place as **sordid**, you mean that it is dirty, unpleasant, or

S

depressing. ❑ *...the dirty windows of their sordid little rooms.* [from Latin]

**sore** /sɔr/ (**sorer, sorest, sores**) **1** ADJ If part of your body is **sore**, it causes you pain and discomfort. ❑ *I had a sore throat and a cough.* **2** ADJ If you are **sore** about something, you are angry and upset about it. [INFORMAL] ❑ *Her friends are very sore at her.* **3** N-COUNT A **sore** is a painful place on the body where the skin is infected. ❑ *Our hands were covered with sores from the ropes.* [from Old English]

**sore|ly** /sɔrli/ ADV **Sorely** is used to emphasize that a feeling such as disappointment or need is very strong. ❑ *I was sorely disappointed.* ❑ *He will be sorely missed.* [from Old English]

**sor|row** /sɒroʊ/ (**sorrows**) **1** N-UNCOUNT **Sorrow** is a feeling of deep sadness or regret. ❑ *Words cannot express my sorrow.* **2** N-PLURAL **Sorrows** are events or situations that cause deep sadness. ❑ *...the joys and sorrows of everyday living.* [from Old English]

**sor|ry** /sɒri/ (**sorrier, sorriest**) **1** CONVENTION You say "**Sorry**" or "**I'm sorry**" as a way of apologizing to someone for something that you have done which has upset them or caused them difficulties, or when you bump into them accidentally. ❑ *"You're making too much noise."* — *"Sorry."* ❑ *Sorry I took so long.* ❑ *I'm really sorry if I said anything wrong.* **2** ADJ If you are **sorry** about a situation, you feel regret, sadness, or disappointment about it. ❑ *She was very sorry about all the trouble she'd caused.* ❑ *I'm sorry he's gone.* **3** CONVENTION You say "**I'm sorry**" to express your regret and sadness when you hear sad or unpleasant news. ❑ *"He can't come because he's ill."* — *"I'm sorry to hear that."* **4** ADJ If you feel **sorry for** someone who is unhappy or in an unpleasant situation, you feel sympathy and sadness for them. ❑ *I felt sorry for him because nobody listened to him.* **5** CONVENTION You say "**Sorry?**" when you have not heard something that someone has said and you want them to repeat it. ❑ *Sorry? What did you say?* **6** ADJ If someone or something is in a **sorry** state, they are in a bad state, mentally or physically. ❑ *After the fire, the building was in a sorry state.* [from Old English]

**sort** /sɔrt/ (**sorts, sorting, sorted**) **1** N-COUNT If you talk about a particular **sort of** something, you are talking about a class of things that have particular features in common and that belong to a larger group of related things. ❑ *What sort of school did you go to?* ❑ *There are so many different sorts of mushrooms available these days.* ❑ *A dozen trees of various sorts were planted.* **2** N-SING You describe someone as a particular **sort** when you are describing their character. ❑ *He seemed to be just the right sort for the job.* ❑ *She was a very lively sort of person.* **3** V-T/V-I If you **sort** things, you separate them into different classes, groups, or places. ❑ *He sorted the materials into their folders.* ❑ *He opened the box and sorted through the papers.* **4** PHRASE If you describe something as a thing **of sorts** or as a thing **of a sort**, you are suggesting that the thing is of a rather poor quality or standard. ❑ *He made a living of sorts selling books door-to-door.* **5** PHRASE You use **sort of** when you want to say that your description of something is not very accurate. [INFORMAL] ❑ *They treated us sort of like house pets.* [from Old French] **6** **nothing of the sort** → see **nothing** ▶ **sort out** **1** PHR-VERB If you **sort out** a group of

things, you separate them into different classes, groups, or places. ❑ *Sort out all your bills as quickly as possible.* ❑ *Davina was sorting out scraps of material.* **2** PHR-VERB If you **sort out** a problem or the details of something, you do what is necessary to solve the problem or organize the details. ❑ *India and Nepal have sorted out their disagreement on trade.*

**souf|flé** /sufleɪ/ (**soufflés**) also **souffle** N-VAR A **soufflé** is a light food made from a mixture of beaten egg whites and other ingredients that is baked in the oven. ❑ *...a superb cheese soufflé.* [from French]

**sought** /sɔt/ **Sought** is the past tense and past participle of **seek**. [from Old English]

**sought-after** ADJ Something that is **sought-after** is in great demand, usually because it is rare or of very good quality. ❑ *An Olympic gold medal is the most sought-after prize in world sport.*

**soul** /soʊl/ (**souls**) **1** N-COUNT Your **soul** is the part of you that consists of your mind, character, thoughts, and feelings. Many people believe that your soul continues existing after your body is dead. ❑ *She went to pray for the soul of her late husband.* **2** N-SING You use **soul** in negative statements like **not a soul** to mean nobody at all. ❑ *I've never harmed a soul in my life.* **3** N-UNCOUNT **Soul** is the same as **soul music**. ❑ *...American soul singer Anita Baker.* [from Old English]

**soul food** N-UNCOUNT **Soul food** is used to refer to the kind of food, for example corn bread, ham, and yams, that was traditionally eaten by African-Americans in the southern United States.

**soul music** N-UNCOUNT **Soul music** is a type of pop music performed mainly by African-American musicians. It often expresses deep emotions.

---

**sound**

❶ NOUN AND VERB USES
❷ ADJECTIVE USES

---

❶ **sound** /saʊnd/ (**sounds, sounding, sounded**) **1** N-COUNT A **sound** is something that you hear. ❑ *Peter heard the sound of gunfire.* ❑ *Liza was so frightened she couldn't make a sound.* **2** N-UNCOUNT **Sound** is energy that travels in waves through air, water, or other substances, and can be heard. ❑ *The airplane will travel at twice the speed of sound.* **3** V-T/V-I If something such as a horn or a bell **sounds** or if you **sound** it, it makes a noise. ❑ *The buzzer sounded in Daniel's office.* **4** V-LINK When you are describing a noise, you can talk about the way it **sounds**. ❑ *They heard what sounded like a huge explosion.* ❑ *The creaking of the floorboards sounded very loud in that silence.* **5** V-LINK When you talk about the way someone **sounds**, you are describing the impression you have of them when they speak. ❑ *She sounded a bit worried.* ❑ *Murphy sounds like a child.* **6** V-LINK When you are describing your impression or opinion of something you have heard about or read about, you can talk about the way it **sounds**. ❑ *It sounds like a wonderful idea to me.* ❑ *It sounds as if they made a mistake.* **7** N-SING You can describe your impression of something you have heard about or read about by talking about **the sound of** it. ❑ *Here's a new idea we liked the sound of.* ❑ *I don't like the sound of Toby Osborne.* [from Old French]
→ see Word Web: **sound**
→ see **concert, ear, echo**
▶ **sound out** PHR-VERB If you **sound** someone **out**,

## Word Web    sound

Sound is the only form of energy we can hear. The energy makes molecules in the air **vibrate**. Fast vibrations called high **frequencies** produce high-pitched sounds. Slower vibrations produce lower frequencies. Sound vibrations travel in waves, just like **waves** in water. Each wave has a **crest** and a **trough**. Amplitude measures the size of a wave. It is the vertical distance between the middle of a wave and its crest. When a **sound wave** bounces off something, it creates an **echo**. When an airplane reaches **supersonic** speed, it generates **shock waves**. As these waves move toward the ground, a **sonic boom** occurs.

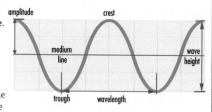

you question them in order to find out what their opinion is about something. ❑ *The management will sound out the views of the employees.*

**❷ sound** /sa͟ʊnd/ (**sounder, soundest**) **1** ADJ If a structure, part of your body, or your mind is **sound**, it is in good condition or healthy. ❑ *When we bought the house, it was structurally sound.* ❑ *The car is basically sound.* **2** ADJ **Sound** advice, reasoning, or evidence is reliable and sensible. ❑ *They are professionals who can give sound advice.* ❑ *Only buy from a company that is financially sound.* **3** ADJ If someone is in a **sound** sleep, they are sleeping very deeply. ❑ *She woke me out of a sound sleep.* ● **Sound** is also an adverb. ❑ *He was lying in bed, sound asleep.* [from Old English] **4** → see also **soundly**

### Thesaurus    sound    Also look up :

ADJ.    safe, sturdy, whole ❷ **1**
        logical, valid, wise; (*ant.*) illogical,
        unreliable ❷ **2**

**sound card** /sa͟ʊndkɑrd/ (**soundcards**) also **sound card** N-COUNT A **soundcard** is a piece of equipment which can be put into a computer so that the computer can produce music or other sounds. [COMPUTING]

**sound en|er|gy** N-UNCOUNT **Sound energy** is energy in the form of sound waves.

**sound|ly** /sa͟ʊndli/ **1** ADV If someone is **soundly** defeated, they are defeated thoroughly. ❑ *The Celtics were soundly beaten by the Pistons in Game 1.* **2** ADV If a decision, opinion, or statement is **soundly** based, there are sensible or reliable reasons behind it. ❑ *Changes must be soundly based in economic reality.* **3** ADV If you sleep **soundly**, you sleep deeply and do not wake during your sleep. ❑ *How can he sleep soundly at night?* [from Old French]

**sound|track** /sa͟ʊndtræk/ (**soundtracks**) also **sound track** N-COUNT The **soundtrack** of a movie is its sound, speech, and especially the music. ❑ *...the soundtrack to a movie called "Casino Royale."*

**sound wave** (**sound waves**) also **soundwave** N-COUNT **Sound waves** are the waves of energy that we hear as sound.

**soup** /su͟p/ (**soups**) N-VAR **Soup** is liquid food made by boiling meat, fish, or vegetables in water. ❑ *...homemade chicken soup.* [from Old French]

**sour** /sa͟ʊər/ (**sours, souring, soured**) **1** ADJ

Something that is **sour** has a sharp, unpleasant taste like the taste of a lemon. ❑ *The stewed apple was sour.* **2** ADJ **Sour** milk is milk that has an unpleasant taste because it is no longer fresh. ❑ *The milk has gone sour.* **3** ADJ Someone who is **sour** is bad-tempered and unfriendly. ❑ *She made a sour face in his direction.* ● **sour|ly** ADV ❑ *"Leave my mother out of it," he said sourly.* **4** ADJ If a situation or relationship **turns sour** or **goes sour**, it stops being enjoyable or satisfactory. ❑ *Everything turned sour for me there.* ❑ *Our friendship slowly began to turn sour.* **5** V-T/V-I If a friendship, situation, or attitude **sours** or if something **sours** it, it becomes less friendly, enjoyable, or hopeful. ❑ *The differences in their world views is likely to sour their relationship.* [from Old English]
→ see **taste**

**source** /sɔ͟rs/ (**sources**) **1** N-COUNT The **source** of something is the person, place, or thing which you get it from. ❑ *Many adults use television as their major source of information.* ❑ *...renewable sources of energy.* **2** N-COUNT A **source** is a person or book that provides information for a news story or for a piece of research. ❑ *Military sources say the boat was heading south.* **3** N-COUNT The **source** of a river or stream is the place where it begins. ❑ *...the source of the Tiber.* [from Old French]
→ see **diary**

**sour|dough** /sa͟ʊərdoʊ/ ADJ **Sourdough** bread is made with fermented dough that has been saved from a previous baking, so that fresh yeast is not needed. ❑ *...big chunks of sourdough bread.* ❑ *...a sourdough bun.*

**south** /sa͟ʊθ/ also **South** **1** N-UNCOUNT The **south** is the direction which is on your right when you are looking toward the direction where the sun rises. ❑ *The town lies ten miles to the south of here.* **2** N-SING The **south of** a place, country, or region is the part which is in the south. ❑ *...vacations in the south of Mexico.* **3** ADV If you go **south**, you travel toward the south. ❑ *I drove south on Highway 9.* **4** ADV Something that is **south of** a place is positioned to the south of it. ❑ *They now live on a farm 50 miles south of Rochester.* **5** ADJ The **south** edge, corner, or part of a place or country is the part which is toward the south. ❑ *...the south coast of Long Island.* **6** ADJ A **south** wind is a wind that blows from the south. ❑ *...a mild south wind.* [from Old English]

**south|east** /sa͟ʊθi͟ːst/ **1** N-UNCOUNT The **southeast** is the direction which is halfway between south and east. ❑ *The train left Colombo for Galle, 70 miles to the southeast.* **2** N-SING The **southeast of** a place, country, or region is the part which is in the southeast. ❑ *There has been a lot of rain in the southeast of the country.* **3** ADV If you go **southeast**, you travel toward the southeast. ❑ *I know we have to go southeast, more or less.* **4** ADV Something that is **southeast of** a place is positioned to the southeast of it. ❑ *The ship sank 500 miles southeast of Nova Scotia.* **5** ADJ The **southeast** part of a place, country, or region is the part which is toward the southeast. ❑ *...rural southeast Kansas.* ❑ *...Southeast Asia.* **6** ADJ A **southeast** wind is a wind that blows from the southeast.

**south|eastern** /sa͟ʊθi͟ːstərn/ ADJ **Southeastern** means in or from the southeast of a region or country. ❑ *...this city on the southeastern edge of the United States.*

**south|er|ly** /sa͟ðərli/ **1** ADJ A **southerly** point, area, or direction is to the south or toward the south. ❑ *We set off in a southerly direction.* **2** ADJ A **southerly** wind is a wind that blows from the south. ❑ *...a strong southerly wind.* [from Old English]

**south|ern** /sa͟ðərn/ also **Southern** ADJ **Southern** means in or from the south of a region, state, or country. ❑ *The Everglades National Park stretches across southern Florida.* [from Old English]

**South|ern|er** /sa͟ðərnər/ (**Southerners**) N-COUNT A **Southerner** is a person who was born in or lives in the south of a country. ❑ *Bob Wilson is a Southerner, from Texas.* [from Old English]

**south|ward** /sa͟ʊθwərd/ also **southwards** ADV **Southward** or **southwards** means toward the south. ❑ *They drove southward.* ● **Southward** is also an adjective. ❑ *We decided on the southward route.* [from Old English]

**south|west** /sa͟ʊθwe͟st/ **1** N-UNCOUNT The **southwest** is the direction which is halfway between south and west. ❑ *...about 500 kilometers to the southwest of Johannesburg.* **2** N-SING The **southwest of** a place, country, or region is the part which is toward the southwest. ❑ *...the southwest of France.* **3** ADV If you go **southwest**, you travel toward the southwest. ❑ *We took a plane southwest to Cappadocia.* **4** ADV Something that is **southwest of** a place is positioned to the southwest of it. ❑ *It's about 65 miles southwest of Houston.* **5** ADJ The **southwest** part of a place, country, or region is the part which is toward the southwest. ❑ *...a Labor Day festival in southwest Louisiana.* **6** ADJ A **southwest** wind is a wind that blows from the southwest. ❑ *Then the southwest wind began to blow.*

**south|western** /sa͟ʊθwe͟stərn/ ADJ **Southwestern** means in or from the southwest of a region or country. ❑ *...small towns in the southwestern part of the country.*

**sou|ve|nir** /su͟ːvənɪ͟ər/ (**souvenirs**) N-COUNT A **souvenir** is something which you buy or keep to remind you of a vacation, place, or event. ❑ *...a souvenir of the summer of 1992.* [from French]

**sov|er|eign** /sɒ͟vrɪn/ (**sovereigns**) **1** ADJ A **sovereign** state or country is independent and not under the authority of any other country. ❑ *They are now independent sovereign states.* **2** ADJ **Sovereign** is used to describe the person or institution that has the highest power in a country. ❑ *Every organized society needs a sovereign power.* **3** N-COUNT A **sovereign** is a king, queen, or other royal ruler of a country. ❑ *In March 1889, she became the first British sovereign to travel to Spain.* [from Old French]

**sov|er|eign|ty** /sɒ͟vrɪnti/ N-UNCOUNT **Sovereignty** is the power that a country has to govern itself or another country or state. ❑ *It is vital to protect our national sovereignty.* [from Old French]

---

**sow**

**1** VERB USES
**2** NOUN USE

---

**1 sow** /so͟ʊ/ (**sows, sowing, sowed, sown**) **1** V-T If you **sow** seeds or **sow** an area of land **with** seeds, you plant the seeds in the ground. ❑ *Sow the seed in a warm place in February/March.* **2** V-T If someone **sows** an undesirable feeling or situation, they cause it to begin and develop. ❑ *...an attempt to sow confusion and terror among the people.* [from Old English]

**2 sow** /sa͟ʊ/ (**sows**) N-COUNT A **sow** is an adult female pig. [from Old English]

**soy** /sɔ͟ɪ/ N-UNCOUNT **Soy** flour, butter, or other food is made from soybeans. [from Japanese]

**soy|bean** /sɔ͟ɪbiːn/ (**soybeans**) also **soy bean** N-COUNT **Soybeans** are beans that can be eaten or used to make flour, oil, or soy sauce.

**soy sauce** N-UNCOUNT **Soy sauce** is a dark brown liquid made from soybeans and is used as a flavoring, especially in Asian cooking.

**spa** /spɑ͟ː/ (**spas**) N-COUNT A **spa** is a place where water with minerals in it comes out of the ground. ❑ *...Fiuggi, a spa town famous for its water.*
→ see **hotel**

**space** /spe͟ɪs/ (**spaces, spacing, spaced**) **1** N-VAR You use **space** to refer to an area of any size that is empty or available. ❑ *They cut down more trees to make space for houses.* ❑ *I had plenty of space to write.* ❑ *The space underneath could be used as a storage area.* **2** N-SING A **space** of time is a period of time. ❑ *They've come a long way in a short space of time.* **3** N-UNCOUNT **Space** is the area beyond the Earth's atmosphere, where the stars and planets are. ❑ *The six astronauts will spend ten days in space.* **4** V-T If you **space** a series of things, you arrange them so that they are not all together but have gaps or intervals of time between them. ❑ *Women are having fewer children and spacing them further apart.* ● **Space out** means the same as **space**. ❑ *He talks quite slowly and spaces his words out.* ● **spac|ing** N-UNCOUNT ❑ *We felt the size of the yards and the spacing between the homes was better here than elsewhere.* **5** N-VAR In dance, **space** refers to the immediate space around the body in all directions. **Space** is also the place where a dance takes place. [from Old French] **6** → see also **airspace, breathing space, outer space, spacing**
→ see **meteor, moon, satellite**

**space|craft** /spe͟ɪskræft/ (**spacecraft**) N-COUNT A **spacecraft** is a rocket or other vehicle that can travel in space. ❑ *...the world's largest and most expensive spacecraft.*

**space probe** (**space probes**) N-COUNT A **space probe** is a spacecraft with no people in it which is sent into space in order to study the planets and send information about them back to Earth.

**space|ship** /speɪsʃɪp/ (**spaceships**) N-COUNT A **spaceship** is the same as a **spacecraft**. [from Old French]

**space shut|tle** (**space shuttles**) N-COUNT A **space shuttle** is a spacecraft that is designed to travel into space and back to Earth several times.

**space sta|tion** (**space stations**) N-COUNT A **space station** is a place built for astronauts to live and work in, which is sent into space and then keeps going around the Earth.
→ see **satellite**

**space suit** (**space suits**) also **space-suit** N-COUNT A **spacesuit** is a special protective suit that is worn by astronauts in space.

**spac|ing** /speɪsɪŋ/ **1** N-UNCOUNT **Spacing** refers to the way that typing or printing is arranged on a page. ❑ *Single spacing is used within paragraphs, double spacing between paragraphs.* [from Old French] **2** → see also **space**

**spa|cious** /speɪʃəs/ ADJ A **spacious** room or other place is large in size or area, so that you can move around freely in it. ❑ *The house has a spacious kitchen and dining area.* [from Latin]

**spade** /speɪd/ (**spades**) **1** N-COUNT A **spade** is a tool used for digging, with a flat metal blade and a long handle. ❑ *...a garden spade.* **2** N-UNCOUNT **Spades** is one of the four suits in a deck of playing cards. Each card in the suit is marked with one or more black symbols: ♠. ❑ *...the ace of spades.* ● A **spade** is a playing card of this suit. ❑ *He should play a spade now.* [Sense 1 from Old English. Sense 2 from Italian.]
→ see **garden**

**spa|ghet|ti** /spəgeɪti/ N-UNCOUNT **Spaghetti** is a type of pasta which looks like long pieces of string. [from Italian]

**spam** /spæm/ (**spams, spamming, spammed**) V-T In computing, to **spam** people or organizations means to send unwanted e-mail to a large number of them, usually as advertising. [COMPUTING] ❑ *...programs that let you spam the newspapers.* ● **Spam** is also a noun. ❑ *People are sick of spam.* ● **spam|mer** /spæmər/ (**spammers**) N-COUNT ❑ *We want to stop the spammers.*

**span** /spæn/ (**spans, spanning, spanned**) **1** N-COUNT A **span** is the period of time between two dates or events during which something exists, functions, or happens. ❑ *The batteries had a life span of six hours.* **2** N-COUNT Your concentration **span** or your attention **span** is the length of time you are able to concentrate on something or be interested in it. ❑ *His concentration span was short.* **3** V-T If something **spans** a long period of time, it lasts throughout that period of time or relates to that whole period of time. ❑ *His professional career spanned 16 years.* **4** N-COUNT The **span** of something that extends or is spread out sideways is the total width of it from one end to the other. ❑ *The butterfly has a 2-inch wing span.* **5** V-T A bridge or other structure that **spans** something such as a river or a valley stretches right across it. ❑ *There is a footbridge that spans the little stream.* [from Old English]
→ see **bridge**

| Word Partnership | Use *span* with : |
|---|---|
| ADJ. | **brief** span **1** |
| | **short** span **1 4** |
| N. | **life** span, **time** span **1** |
| | **attention** span **2** |
| | span **years 3** |

**spank** /spæŋk/ (**spanks, spanking, spanked**) V-T If someone **spanks** a child, they punish them by hitting them on the bottom several times with their hand. ❑ *When we were kids, our mom never spanked us.*

**spar** /spɑr/ (**spars, sparring, sparred**) V-RECIP If you **spar with** someone, you box using fairly gentle blows instead of hitting your opponent hard, for example in training. ❑ *He was sparring with a friend in the boxing ring.* [from Old English]

**spare** /speər/ (**spares, sparing, spared**) **1** ADJ You use **spare** to describe something that is the same as something you are already using, but that you do not need yet and are keeping ready in case another one is needed. ❑ *It's useful to have a spare pair of glasses.* ❑ *I'll give you the spare one.* ● **Spare** is also a noun. ❑ *In case you get a flat tire, you should always carry a spare.* **2** ADJ You use **spare** to describe something that is not being used by anyone, and is therefore available for someone to use. ❑ *They don't have a lot of spare cash.* ❑ *You can stay in the spare bedroom.* **3** V-I If you have something such as time, money, or space **to spare,** you have some extra time, money, or space that you have not used or which you do not need. ❑ *We got to the airport with three hours to spare.* **4** V-T If you **spare** time or another resource **for** a particular purpose, you make it available for that purpose. ❑ *I can only spare 35 minutes for this meeting.* **5** V-T If you **spare** someone an unpleasant experience, you prevent them from suffering it. ❑ *I wanted to spare her the embarrassment of talking about it.* [from Old English] **6** → see also **sparing**

| Thesaurus | spare | Also look up : |
|---|---|---|
| ADJ. | additional, backup, emergency, extra, reserve **1 2** | |

| Word Partnership | Use *spare* with : |
|---|---|
| N. | spare **change**, spare **equipment 1** |
| | spare **bedroom 2** |
| | **a moment to** spare, **time to** spare **3** |

**spare part** (**spare parts**) N-COUNT **Spare parts** are parts that you can buy separately to replace old or broken parts in a piece of equipment. ❑ *They sell spare parts for washing machines.*

**spare time** N-UNCOUNT Your **spare time** is the time during which you do not have to work and you can do whatever you like. ❑ *In her spare time she read books on cooking.*

**spare tire** (**spare tires**) **1** N-COUNT A **spare tire** is a wheel with a tire on it that you keep in your car in case you get a flat tire and need to replace one of your wheels. **2** N-COUNT If you describe someone as having a **spare tire**, you mean that they are fat around the waist. [INFORMAL]

**spar|ing** /speərɪŋ/ ADJ If you are **sparing with** something, you use it or give it only in very small quantities. ❑ *Be sparing with the salt.* ● **spar|ing|ly** ADV ❑ *Medication is used sparingly.* [from Old English]

**spark** /spɑrk/ (**sparks, sparking, sparked**)
■ N-COUNT A **spark** is a tiny bright piece of burning material that flies up from something that is burning. ❑ *Sparks flew out of the fire in all directions.* ■ N-COUNT A **spark** is a flash of light caused by electricity. ❑ *I saw a spark when I connected the wires.* ■ N-COUNT A **spark** of a quality or feeling, especially a desirable one, is a small but noticeable amount of it. ❑ *His music does not have that vital spark of imagination.* ■ V-T If one thing **sparks** another, the first thing causes the second thing to start happening. ❑ *We had a class on space exploration that really sparked my interest.* ● **Spark off** means the same as **spark**. ❑ *What sparked off their quarrel?* [from Old English]
→ see **fire**

**spar|kle** /spɑrkᵊl/ (**sparkles, sparkling, sparkled**) V-I If something **sparkles**, it is clear and bright and shines with a lot of very small points of light. ❑ *The jewels on her fingers sparkled.* ❑ *His bright eyes sparkled.* ● **Sparkle** is also a noun. ❑ *...the sparkle of colored glass.*

**spar|kling** /spɑrklɪŋ/ ■ ADJ **Sparkling** drinks are slightly carbonated. ❑ *...a glass of sparkling water.* ■ → see also **sparkle**

**spar|row** /spæroʊ/ (**sparrows**) N-COUNT A **sparrow** is a small brown bird that is very common in the United States. [from Old English]

**sparse** /spɑrs/ (**sparser, sparsest**) ADJ Something that is **sparse** is small in number or amount and spread out over an area. ❑ *He was a fat little man in his fifties, with sparse hair.* ● **sparse|ly** ADV ❑ *...a sparsely populated mountain region.* [from Latin]

**spar|tan** /spɑrtᵊn/ ADJ A **spartan** lifestyle or existence is very simple or strict, with no luxuries. ❑ *They live a spartan lifestyle, with no TV or phone.* [after Sparta, an ancient Greek city]

**spasm** /spæzəm/ (**spasms**) N-VAR A **spasm** is a sudden tightening of your muscles, which you cannot control. ❑ *He felt a painful spasm in his chest.* [from Latin]

**spat** /spæt/ **Spat** is a past tense and past participle of **spit**.

**spate** /speɪt/ (**spates**) N-COUNT A **spate of** things, especially unpleasant things, is a large number of them that happen or appear within a short period of time. ❑ *...the recent spate of attacks.* [from Northern English and Scottish]

**spa|tial** /speɪʃᵊl/ ADJ **Spatial** is used to describe things relating to the position of things in space. ❑ *...a diagram showing the spatial distribution of the population.* ● **spa|tial|ly** ADV ❑ *...spatially remote cultures.* [from Latin]

**spat|ter** /spætər/ (**spatters, spattering, spattered**) V-T/V-I If a liquid **spatters** a surface or you **spatter** a liquid over a surface, drops of the liquid fall on an area of the surface. ❑ *Rain*

spattered on the window. ❑ *Be careful not to spatter any hot butter on yourself.* ● **-spattered** ADJ ❑ *...mud-spattered boots.* [from Low German]

**speak** /spik/ (**speaks, speaking, spoke, spoken**)
■ V-I When you **speak**, you use your voice in order to say something. ❑ *He opened his mouth to speak.* ❑ *I rang the hotel and spoke to Louie.* ❑ *He often speaks about his mother.* ● **speak|er** (**speakers**) N-COUNT ❑ *You can understand a lot from the speaker's tone of voice.* ● **spo|ken** ADJ ❑ *They took tests in written and spoken English.* ■ V-I When someone **speaks to** a group of people, they make a speech. ❑ *He spoke to an audience at the Denver International Film Festival.* ❑ *He will speak at the Democratic Convention.* ● **speak|er** N-COUNT ❑ *Bruce Wyatt will be the guest speaker at next month's meeting.* ■ V-I If you **speak for** a group of people, you make their views and demands known, or represent them. ❑ *It is the job of the Church to speak for the poor.* ❑ *I speak for all 7,000 members of our organization.* ■ V-T If you **speak** a foreign language, you know the language and are able to have a conversation in it. ❑ *He speaks English.* ● **speak|er** N-COUNT ❑ *A fifth of the population are Russian speakers.* ■ V-RECIP If two people **are not speaking**, they no longer talk to each other because they have argued. ❑ *He is not speaking to his mother because she threw away his TV.* ■ V-I If you say that something **speaks for itself**, you mean that its meaning or quality is so obvious that it does not need explaining or pointing out. ❑ *The facts speak for themselves in this case.* ■ PHRASE If you **speak well of** someone or **speak highly of** someone, you say good things about them. If you **speak ill of** someone, you criticize them. ❑ *Everyone speaks highly of him.* ■ PHRASE You use **so to speak** to draw attention to the fact that you are describing or referring to something in a way that may be amusing or unusual rather than completely accurate. ❑ *He was, so to speak, one of the family.* [from Old English]
▶ **speak out** PHR-VERB If you **speak out** against something or in favor of something, you say publicly that you think it is bad or good. ❑ *He spoke out strongly against the company's plans.*
▶ **speak up** PHR-VERB If you ask someone to **speak up**, you are asking them to speak more loudly. ❑ *I'm quite deaf — you'll have to speak up.*

**speak|er** /spikər/ (**speakers**) ■ N-PROPER; N-VOC In the legislature or parliament of many countries, the **Speaker** is the person who is in charge of meetings. ❑ *He used to be the speaker of the California Assembly.* ■ N-COUNT A **speaker** is a piece of electrical equipment, for example part of a radio or set of equipment for playing CDs or tapes, through which sound comes out. ❑ *I bought a pair*

S

*of speakers for my computer.* [from Old English]

**spear** /spɪər/ (**spears, spearing, speared**)
■ N-COUNT A **spear** is a weapon consisting of a long pole with a sharp metal point attached to the end. ■ V-T If you **spear** something, you push or throw a pointed object into it. ❑ *He speared a piece of chicken with his fork.* [from Old English]
→ see **army**

**spear|head** /spɪərhɛd/ (**spearheads, spearheading, spearheaded**) V-T If someone **spearheads** a campaign or an attack, they lead it. ❑ *She is spearheading a national campaign against bullying.*

**spe|cia|tion** /spiʃieɪʃⁿn/ N-UNCOUNT **Speciation** is the development of new species of animals or plants, which occurs when two populations of the same species develop in different ways. [TECHNICAL]

**spe|cif|ic grav|ity** (**specific gravities**) N-VAR The **specific gravity** of a substance is a measure of its weight, compared to the weight of an equal amount of water. [TECHNICAL]

**spe|cif|ic heat ca|pac|ity** (**specific heat capacities**) N-VAR The **specific heat capacity** of a substance is the amount of heat that is needed in order to change the temperature of the substance by one degree Celsius. [TECHNICAL]

**spe|cial** /spɛʃⁿl/ (**specials**) ■ ADJ Someone or something that is **special** is better or more important than other people or things. ❑ *You're very special to me.* ❑ *My special guest will be Jerry Seinfeld.* ■ ADJ **Special** means different from normal. ❑ *In special cases, a child can be educated at home.* ❑ *Did you notice anything special about him?* ■ ADJ You use **special** to describe something that relates to one particular person, group, or place. ❑ *Every person has his or her own special problems.* [from Old French]

| **Thesaurus** | *special* | Also look up : |
| --- | --- | --- |
| ADJ. | distinctive, exceptional, unique; (ant.) ordinary ■ ■ | |

**spe|cial ef|fect** (**special effects**) N-COUNT In a movie, **special effects** are unusual pictures or sounds that are created by using special techniques. ❑ *...a horror film with amazing special effects.*

**spe|cial|ist** /spɛʃəlɪst/ (**specialists**) N-COUNT A **specialist** is a person who has a particular skill or knows a lot about a particular subject. ❑ *Peckham is a cancer specialist.* [from Old French]

**spe|cial|ize** /spɛʃəlaɪz/ (**specializes, specializing, specialized**) V-I If you **specialize in** a thing, you know a lot about it and concentrate a great deal of your time and energy on it, especially in your work or when you are studying or training. ❑ *...a professor who specializes in Russian history.* ● **spe|cial|i|za|tion** /spɛʃəlɪzeɪʃⁿn/ (**specializations**) N-VAR ❑ *We encourage broad general knowledge rather than specialization.* [from Old French]

**spe|cial|ized** /spɛʃəlaɪzd/ ADJ Someone or something that is **specialized** is trained or developed for a particular purpose or area of knowledge. ❑ *Children with learning difficulties need specialized support.* [from Old French]

**spe|cial|ly** /spɛʃəli/ ■ ADV If something has

been done **specially for** a particular person or purpose, it has been done only for that person or purpose. ❑ *...a soap specially designed for sensitive skin.* ❑ *Patrick needs to use specially adapted computer equipment.* ■ ADV **Specially** is used to mean more than usually or more than other things. [INFORMAL] ❑ *On his birthday I got up specially early.* [from Old French]

**spe|cial|ty** /spɛʃⁿlti/ (**specialties**) ■ N-COUNT Someone's **specialty** is a particular type of work that they do most or do best, or a subject that they know a lot about. ❑ *His specialty is international law.* ■ N-COUNT A **specialty** of a particular place is a special food or product that is always very good there. ❑ *...seafood and other specialties.* [from Old French]

**spe|cies** /spiʃiz/ (**species**) N-COUNT A **species** is a class of plants or animals whose members have the same main characteristics and are able to breed with each other. ❑ *Many species could disappear from our earth.* [from Latin]
→ see **amphibian, evolution, zoo**

**spe|cif|ic** /spɪsɪfɪk/ ■ ADJ You use **specific** to refer to a particular exact area, problem, or subject. ❑ *Do you have pain in any specific part of your body?* ❑ *There are several specific problems.* ■ ADJ If someone is **specific**, they give a description that is precise and exact. You can also use **specific** to describe their description. ❑ *She refused to be more specific about why they left the country.* ■ ADJ Something that is **specific to** a particular thing is connected with that thing only. ❑ *Some problems are specific to a particular job, but some are experienced by everyone.* [from Medieval Latin]

**spe|cifi|cal|ly** /spɪsɪfɪkli/ ■ ADV You use **specifically** to emphasize that something is given special attention and considered separately from other things of the same kind. ❑ *...a nursing home designed specifically for people with cancer.* ❑ *The show is aimed specifically at children.* ■ ADV You use **specifically** to add something more precise or exact to what you have already said. ❑ *Death frightens me, specifically my own death.* ❑ *...the Christian, and specifically Protestant, religion.* ■ ADV If you state or describe something **specifically**, you state or describe it precisely and clearly. ❑ *I specifically asked you to come at 8 o'clock.* [from Medieval Latin]

**speci|fi|ca|tion** /spɛsɪfɪkeɪʃⁿn/ (**specifications**) N-COUNT A **specification** is a requirement which is clearly stated, for example about the necessary features in the design of something. ❑ *They had a house built to their specification.* [from Medieval Latin]

**spe|cif|ics** /spɪsɪfɪks/ N-PLURAL The **specifics** of a subject are the details of it that need to be considered. ❑ *Can you tell me more about the specifics of the project?* [from Medieval Latin]

**speci|fy** /spɛsɪfaɪ/ (**specifies, specifying, specified**) V-T If you **specify** what should happen or be done, you explain it in an exact and detailed way. ❑ *Each recipe specifies the size of egg to be used.* ❑ *A new law specified that houses must be a certain distance from one another.* [from Medieval Latin]

**speci|men** /spɛsɪmɪn/ (**specimens**) N-COUNT A **specimen of** something is an example or a small amount of it which gives an idea of what the whole of it is like. ❑ *Job applicants have to give a* *specimen of handwriting.* [from Latin]

**speck** /spɛk/ (**specks**) N-COUNT A **speck** is a very small stain, mark, or piece. ❑ *There was a speck of dirt on his collar.* [from Old English]

**specs** /spɛks/ N-PLURAL Someone's **specs** are their eyeglasses. [INFORMAL] ❑ *Let me find my specs.*

---

**Word Link**    *spect ≈ looking : spectacle, spectacular, spectator*

---

**spec|ta|cle** /spɛktək³l/ (**spectacles**) N-COUNT A **spectacle** is an interesting or impressive sight or event. ❑ *The fireworks were an amazing spectacle.* [from Old French]

**spec|tacu|lar** /spɛktækyələr/ (**spectaculars**) ◼ ADJ Something that is **spectacular** is very impressive or dramatic. ❑ *...spectacular views of Sugar Loaf Mountain.* ● **spec|tacu|lar|ly** ADV ❑ *Our sales increased spectacularly.* ◻ N-COUNT A **spectacular** is a show or performance which is very grand and impressive. ❑ *...a television spectacular.* [from Old French]

**spec|ta|tor** /spɛkteɪtər/ (**spectators**) N-COUNT A **spectator** is someone who watches something, especially a sports event. ❑ *Thirty thousand spectators watched the game.* [from Latin]

**spec|ter** /spɛktər/ (**specters**) N-COUNT If you refer to the **specter** of something unpleasant, you are referring to something that you are frightened might occur. ❑ *The arrests raised the specter of revenge attacks.* [from Latin]

**spec|trum** /spɛktrəm/ (**spectra** or **spectrums**) ◼ N-SING The **spectrum** is the range of different colors which is produced when light passes through a glass prism or through a drop of water. ◻ N-COUNT A **spectrum** is a range of a particular type of thing. ❑ *His moods covered the entire emotional spectrum.* ❑ *Politicians across the political spectrum have criticized her.* [from Latin]

**specu|late** /spɛkyəleɪt/ (**speculates, speculating, speculated**) ◼ V-T/V-I If you **speculate** about something, you make guesses about its nature or identity, or about what might happen. ❑ *There is no point speculating about why she left.* ❑ *Doctors speculate that his death was caused by a blow on the head.* ● **specu|la|tion** /spɛkyəleɪʃ³n/ (**speculations**) N-VAR ❑ *There has been a lot of speculation in the press about their marriage.* ◻ V-I If someone **speculates** financially, they buy property, stocks, or shares, in the hope of being able to sell them again at a higher price and make a profit. ❑ *The banks speculated in property.* ● **specu|la|tor** (**speculators**) N-COUNT ❑ *He sold the contracts to another speculator for a profit.* [from Latin]

**specu|la|tive** /spɛkyəleɪtɪv, -lətɪv/ ADJ A piece of information that is **speculative** is based on guesses rather than knowledge. ❑ *The papers printed speculative stories about his disappearance.* [from Latin]

**sped** /spɛd/ **Sped** is a past tense and past participle of **speed**.

**speech** /spitʃ/ (**speeches**) ◼ N-UNCOUNT **Speech** is the ability to speak or the act of speaking. ❑ *...the development of speech in children.* ❑ *The medication can affect speech.* ◻ N-UNCOUNT Your **speech** is the way in which you speak. ❑ *His speech became slow and unclear.* ◼ N-UNCOUNT **Speech** is

spoken language. ❑ *She understands written Spanish very well, but not speech.* ◼ N-COUNT A **speech** is a formal talk which someone gives to an audience. ❑ *She made a speech on the economy.* ❑ *He delivered his speech in French.* [from Old English] ◼ → see also **indirect speech**
→ see **election**

---

**Word Partnership**    Use *speech* with :

| | |
|---|---|
| ADJ. | **slurred** speech ◼ <br> **famous** speech, **major** speech, **political** speech, **recent** speech ◼ |
| N. | **acceptance** speech, **campaign** speech, **keynote** speech, speech **writing** ◼ |
| V. | **deliver** a speech, **give** a speech, **make** a speech, **prepare** a speech ◼ |

---

**speech|less** /spitʃlɪs/ ADJ If you are **speechless**, you are temporarily unable to speak, usually because something has shocked you. ❑ *Alex was speechless with rage.* [from Old English]

**speed** /spid/ (**speeds, speeding, sped** or **speeded**)

---

The form of the past tense and past participle is **sped** in meaning ◼ but **speeded** for the phrasal verb.

---

◼ N-VAR The **speed** of something is the rate at which it moves, happens, or is done. ❑ *He drove off at high speed.* ❑ *...a way to measure wind speeds.* ❑ *The speed of technological change has increased.* ◻ N-UNCOUNT **Speed** is very fast movement or travel. ❑ *Speed is essential for all athletes.* ◼ V-I If you **speed** somewhere, you move or travel there quickly, usually in a vehicle. ❑ *Trains speed through the tunnel at 186 mph.* ◼ V-I Someone who is **speeding** is driving a vehicle faster than the legal speed limit. ❑ *Police stopped him because he was speeding.* ● **speed|ing** N-UNCOUNT ❑ *He was fined for speeding.* [from Old English]
▶ **speed up** PHR-VERB When something **speeds up** or when you **speed** it **up**, it moves, happens, or is done more quickly. ❑ *My breathing speeded up a bit.* ❑ *We need to speed up a solution to the problem.*

**speed bump** (**speed bumps**) ◼ N-COUNT A **speed bump** is a raised part in a road that is designed to make the traffic travel more slowly. ◻ N-COUNT A **speed bump** is something that stops a person or thing from progressing. ❑ *It was just a minor speed bump in Anglo-American relations.*

**speed dat|ing** N-UNCOUNT **Speed dating** is a method of introducing single people to potential partners by arranging for them to meet a series of people on a single occasion.

**speed lim|it** (**speed limits**) N-COUNT The **speed limit** on a road is the maximum speed at which you are legally allowed to drive. ❑ *I was fined $158 for breaking the speed limit.*

**speed|way** /spidweɪ/ (**speedways**) ◼ N-UNCOUNT **Speedway** is the sport of racing motorcycles on special tracks. ◻ N-COUNT A **speedway** is a special track for car or motorcycle racing. [from Old English]

**speedy** /spidi/ (**speedier, speediest**) ADJ A **speedy** process, event, or action happens or is done very quickly. ❑ *We wish Bill a speedy recovery.* [from Old English]

**S**

**spell** /spɛl/ (spells, spelling, spelled) **1** V-T When you **spell** a word, you write or speak each letter in the word in the correct order. ❑ He spelled his name. ❑ How do you spell "potato?" ● **Spell out** means the same as **spell**. ❑ If I don't know a word, I ask them to spell it out for me. **2** V-T/V-I Someone who can **spell** knows the correct order of letters in words. ❑ Many of the students can't spell. ❑ He can't even spell his own name. **3** V-T If something **spells** a particular outcome, often an unpleasant one, it suggests that this will be the result. ❑ This plan could spell disaster for local people. **4** N-COUNT A **spell** of a particular type of weather or a particular activity is a short period of time during which this type of weather or activity occurs. ❑ There has been a long spell of dry weather. **5** N-COUNT A **spell** is a situation in which events are controlled by a magical power. ❑ They say a witch cast a spell on her. [Senses 1 to 3 from Old French. Senses 4 and 5 from Old English.] **6** → see also **spelling**
▶ **spell out 1** PHR-VERB If you **spell** something **out**, you explain it in detail or in a very clear way. ❑ You need to spell out exactly how you feel. **2** → see **spell 1**

| Word Partnership | Use *spell* with : |
| --- | --- |
| N. | spell **a name/word** 1 |
| | spell **the end of** *something*, |
| | spell **trouble** 3 |
| V. | **can/can't** spell *something* 2 |
| | **break a** spell, **cast a** spell 5 |

**spell-check** (spell-checks, spell-checking, spell-checked) also **spell check** V-T If you **spell-check** something you have written on a computer, you use a special program to check whether you have made any spelling mistakes. [COMPUTING] ❑ This program allows you to spell-check over 100,000 different words.

**spell-checker** (spell-checkers) also **spell checker** N-COUNT A **spell-checker** is a special program on a computer which you can use to check whether something you have written contains any spelling mistakes. [COMPUTING]

**spell|ing** /spɛlɪŋ/ (spellings) **1** N-COUNT A **spelling** is the correct order of the letters in a word. ❑ I'm not sure about the spelling of his name. **2** N-UNCOUNT **Spelling** is the ability to spell words in the correct way. It is also an attempt to spell a word in the correct way. ❑ His spelling is very bad. [from Old French] **3** → see also **spell**

**spell|ing bee** (spelling bees) N-COUNT A **spelling bee** is a competition in which children try to spell words correctly. Anyone who makes a mistake is out and the competition continues until only one person is left.

**spe|lunk|er** /spɪlʌŋkər/ (spelunkers) N-COUNT A **spelunker** is someone who goes into underground caves and tunnels as a leisure activity. [from Latin]

**spend** /spɛnd/ (spends, spending, spent) **1** V-T When you **spend** money, you pay money for things that you want or need. ❑ I have spent all my money. ❑ Companies spend millions advertising their products. **2** V-T If you **spend** time or energy doing something, you use your time or effort doing it. ❑ She spends a lot of time working on her garden. **3** V-T If you **spend** a period of time in a place, you stay there for a period of time. ❑ We spent the night in a hotel. [from Old English]

| Word Partnership | Use *spend* with : |
| --- | --- |
| N. | spend **billions/millions, companies** |
| | spend, **consumers** spend, |
| | spend **money** 1 |
| | spend **an amount** 1 2 |
| | spend **energy**, spend **time** 2 |
| | spend **a day**, spend **hours/minutes**, |
| | spend **months/years**, spend **a night**, |
| | spend **a weekend** 3 |
| V. | **afford to** spend, **expect to** spend, **going to** spend, **plan to** spend 1 – 3 |

**spent** /spɛnt/ **Spent** is the past tense and past participle of **spend**. [from Old English]

**sperm** /spɜrm/ (sperms)

**Sperm** can also be used as the plural form.

**1** N-COUNT A **sperm** is a cell which is produced in the sex organs of a male animal and can enter a female animal's egg and fertilize it. ❑ A baby is conceived when a sperm joins with an egg. **2** N-UNCOUNT **Sperm** is used to refer to the liquid that contains sperm when it is produced. ❑ ...a test tube of sperm. [from Late Latin]
→ see **reproduction**

**sperm bank** (sperm banks) N-COUNT A **sperm bank** is a place where sperm is frozen and stored so that it can be used to help women become pregnant.

**spew** /spyu/ (spews, spewing, spewed) V-T/V-I When something **spews** out a substance or when a substance **spews** from something, the substance flows out quickly in large quantities. ❑ The volcano spewed out ash, gas, and rocks. [from Old English]

**SPF** /ɛs pi ɛf/ (SPFs) N-COUNT **SPF** is used before a number to indicate the degree of protection from the sun's rays that is provided by a sunscreen or similar product. The higher a product's SPF, the more protection it provides. **SPF** is an abbreviation for "sun protection factor." ❑ Always use sunscreen of at least SPF 15.

**sphere** /sfɪər/ (spheres) **1** N-COUNT A **sphere** is an object that is completely round in shape like a ball. ❑ The Earth is not a perfect sphere. **2** N-COUNT A **sphere of** activity or interest is a particular area of activity or interest. ❑ ...the sphere of international politics. [from Late Latin]
→ see **solid, volume**

**spice** /spaɪs/ (spices) N-VAR A **spice** is a part of a plant, or a powder made from that part, which you put in food to give it flavor. Cinnamon, ginger, and paprika are spices. ❑ ...herbs and spices. [from Old French]
→ see Word Web: **spice**

**spiced** /spaɪst/ ADJ Food that is **spiced** has had spices or other strong-tasting foods added to it. ❑ The food was heavily spiced. [from Old French]

**spicy** /spaɪsi/ (spicier, spiciest) ADJ **Spicy** food is strongly flavored with spices. ❑ Thai food is hot and spicy. [from Old French]
→ see **spice**

**spi|der** /spaɪdər/ (spiders) N-COUNT A **spider** is a small creature with eight legs. [from Old English]

**spif|fy** /spɪfi/ (spiffier, spiffiest) ADJ Something that is **spiffy** is stylish and attractive and often

## Word Web    spice

While studying the use of **spices** in cooking, scientists found that many spices can help prevent disease. Bacteria can grow quickly on food and cause serious illnesses in humans. The researchers found that many spices kill bacteria. For example, **garlic**, **onion**, allspice, and oregano kill almost all common **germs**. **Cinnamon**, tarragon, cumin, and **chili peppers** also stop about 75% of bacteria. And even common, everyday **black pepper** kills about 25% of all germs. The scientists also found that food is connected to climate. **Spicy** food is common in hot climates. **Bland** food is common in cold climates.

garlic          onion          chili pepper

ginger    black pepper    cinnamon    cloves

new. Someone who looks **spiffy** is stylishly and attractively dressed. ❑ *He bought a spiffy new car.*

**spig|ot** /spɪgət/ (**spigots**) N-COUNT A **spigot** is a faucet or tap. [from Old Provençal]

**spike** /spaɪk/ (**spikes**) N-COUNT A **spike** is a long piece of metal with a sharp point. ❑ *...a high wall with iron spikes at the top.* [from Old English]

**spiked** /spaɪkt/ ◼ ADJ Something that is **spiked** has one or more spikes on it. ❑ *...spiked railings.* [from Old English] ◻ → see also **spike**

**spike heels** N-PLURAL **Spike heels** are women's shoes with very high narrow heels.

**spiky** /spaɪki/ ADJ Something that is **spiky** has one or more sharp points. ❑ *She has short spiky hair.* [from Old English]

spill

**spill** /spɪl/ (**spills, spilling, spilled** or **spilt**) ◼ V-T/V-I If a liquid **spills** or if you **spill** it, it accidentally flows over the edge of a container. ❑ *Oil spilled into the sea.* ❑ *He always spilled the drinks.* ◼ V-I If people or things **spill** out of a place, they come out of it in large numbers. ❑ *Tears spilled out of the boy's eyes.* [from Old English]

**spin** /spɪn/ (**spins, spinning, spun**) ◼ V-T/V-I If something **spins** or if you **spin** it, it turns quickly around a central point. ❑ *The disk spins 3,600 times a minute.* ❑ *He spun the steering wheel and turned the car around.* ● **Spin** is also a noun. ❑ *He gave the wheel a spin.* ◼ N-SING If someone puts a certain **spin** on an event or situation, they interpret it and try to present it in a particular way. [INFORMAL] ❑ *Even when they lose, they try to put a positive spin on it.* ◼ V-T/V-I When people **spin**, they make thread by twisting together pieces of a fiber such as wool or cotton using a device or machine. ❑ *...a machine for spinning wool.* ❑ *She never learned how to spin.* [from Old English]
→ see **wheel**

▸ **spin out** PHR-VERB If you **spin** something **out**, you make it last longer than it normally would. ❑ *It seemed that the lawyers were spinning the case out for as long as possible.*

**spin|ach** /spɪnɪtʃ/ N-UNCOUNT **Spinach** is a

vegetable with large dark green leaves. [from Old French]
→ see **vegetable**

**spi|nal** /spaɪnᵊl/ ADJ **Spinal** means relating to your spine. ❑ *...spinal fluid.* [from Old French]

**spine** /spaɪn/ (**spines**) N-COUNT Your **spine** is the row of bones down your back. ❑ *He suffered injuries to his spine.* [from Old French]

**spin|off** /spɪnɒf/ (**spinoffs**) ◼ N-COUNT A **spinoff** is an unexpected but useful or valuable result of an activity that was designed to achieve something else. ❑ *The research could have valuable commercial spinoffs.* ◼ N-COUNT A **spinoff** is a book, film, or television series that comes after and is related to a successful book, film, or television series. ❑ *The movie is a spinoff from the TV series.*

**spi|ral** /spaɪrəl/ (**spirals, spiraling** or **spiralling, spiraled** or **spiralled**) ◼ N-COUNT A **spiral** is a shape which winds around and around, with each curve above or outside the previous one. ❑ *The leaves are in the shape of a spiral.* ● **Spiral** is also an adjective. ❑ *...a spiral staircase.* ◼ V-I If something **spirals** somewhere, it grows or moves in a spiral curve. ❑ *Vines spiraled upward toward the roof.* ❑ *The aircraft began spiraling out of control.* ● **Spiral** is also a noun. ❑ *A spiral of smoke rose from the chimney.* ◼ V-I If an amount or level **spirals**, it rises quickly and at an increasing rate. ❑ *Prices began to spiral.* ❑ *...the spiraling crime rate.* ● **Spiral** is also a noun. ❑ *...a spiral of debt.* [from French]
→ see **circle**

**spi|ral gal|axy** (**spiral galaxies**) N-COUNT A **spiral galaxy** is a galaxy consisting of a flat disk at the center and spiral arms that contain many young stars.

**spire** /spaɪər/ (**spires**) N-COUNT The **spire** of a building such as a church is the tall pointed structure on the top. ❑ *We saw a church spire above the trees.* [from Old English]

**spir|it** /spɪrɪt/ (**spirits**) ◼ N-SING Your **spirit** is the part of you that is not physical and that consists of your character and feelings. ❑ *The human spirit is hard to destroy.* ◼ N-COUNT A person's **spirit** is the non-physical part of them that is believed to remain alive after their death. ❑ *He is gone, but his spirit is still with us.* ◼ N-COUNT A **spirit** is a ghost or supernatural being. ❑ *These*

S

*plants protect us against evil spirits.* **4** N-UNCOUNT **Spirit** is the courage and determination that helps people to survive in difficult times and to keep their way of life and their beliefs. □ *She was very brave and everyone admired her spirit.* **5** N-SING The **spirit** in which you do something is the attitude you have when you are doing it. □ *She took part in the game in a spirit of fun.* **6** N-SING **The spirit of** something such as a law or an agreement is the way that it was intended to be interpreted or applied. □ *These ads go against the spirit of the law.* **7** N-PLURAL Your **spirits** are your feelings at a particular time, especially feelings of happiness or unhappiness. □ *At supper, everyone was in high spirits.* [from Old French]

**spir|it|ed** /spɪrɪtɪd/ **1** ADJ A **spirited** action shows great energy and courage. □ *They made a decision after 12 hours of spirited discussions.* **2** ADJ A **spirited** person is very active, lively, and confident. □ *He was a spirited little boy.* [from Old French]

**spir|itu|al** /spɪrɪtʃuəl/ **1** ADJ **Spiritual** means relating to people's thoughts and beliefs, rather than to their bodies and physical surroundings. □ *She is a very spiritual person, and does not really care about material things.* • **spir|itu|al|ly** ADV □ *We need to feed children spiritually as well as physically.* • **spir|itu|al|ity** /spɪrɪtʃuælɪti/ N-UNCOUNT □ *...the spirituality of Japanese culture.* **2** ADJ **Spiritual** means relating to people's religious beliefs. □ *He is the spiritual leader of the world's Catholics.* [from Old French]

→ see **myth**

**spit** /spɪt/ (**spits, spitting, spit** or **spat**) **1** N-UNCOUNT **Spit** is the watery liquid produced in your mouth. □ *Spit collected in her mouth.* **2** V-I If someone **spits**, they force an amount of liquid out of their mouth, often to show hatred or lack of respect. □ *He turned and spat in disgust.* □ *They spat at me.* **3** V-T If you **spit** liquid or food somewhere, you force a small amount of it out of your mouth. □ *Spit out that gum.* [from Old English]

**spite** /spaɪt/ **1** PHRASE You use **in spite of** to introduce a fact which makes the rest of the statement you are making seem surprising. □ *He hired her in spite of the fact that she had no experience.* **2** PHRASE If you do something **in spite of yourself**, you do it although you did not really intend to or expect to. □ *The comment made Richard laugh in spite of himself.* **3** N-UNCOUNT If you do something cruel out of **spite**, you do it because you want to hurt or upset someone. □ *I didn't help him, out of spite I suppose.* **4** V-T If you do something cruel **to spite** someone, you do it in order to hurt or upset them. □ *He left all his money to his brother, to spite his wife.*

**splash** /splæʃ/ (**splashes, splashing, splashed**) **1** V-I If you **splash** around or **splash** about in water, you hit or disturb the water in a noisy way. □ *People were splashing around in the water.* □ *Children love to splash in puddles.* **2** V-T/V-I If you **splash** a liquid somewhere or if it **splashes**, it hits someone or something and scatters in a lot of small drops. □ *He splashed water on his face.* □ *A little wave splashed in my face.* **3** N-SING A **splash** is the sound made when something hits water or falls into it. □ *There was a splash and something fell into the water.* **4** N-COUNT A **splash** of a liquid is a small quantity of it that falls on something or is added to something. □ *There were splashes on the table cloth.* **5** PHRASE If you **make a splash**, you become

noticed or become popular because of something that you have done. □ *She first made a splash in the television show "Civil Wars."*

**splat|ter** /splætər/ (**splatters, splattering, splattered**) V-T/V-I If a thick wet substance **splatters** on something or is **splattered** on it, it drops or is thrown over it. □ *Rain splattered against the windows.* □ *He splattered the cloth with jam.*

**splen|did** /splɛndɪd/ ADJ If you say that something is **splendid**, you mean that it is very good. □ *The book includes some splendid photographs.* • **splen|did|ly** ADV □ *We get along splendidly.* [from Latin]

**splen|dor** /splɛndər/ (**splendors**) N-VAR The **splendor** of something is its beautiful and impressive appearance or features. □ *...the splendor of the city.* [from Latin]

**splin|ter** /splɪntər/ (**splinters, splintering, splintered**) **1** N-COUNT A **splinter** is a very thin, sharp piece of wood, glass, or other hard substance, which has broken off from a larger piece. □ *...splinters of glass.* **2** V-T/V-I If something **splinters** or **is splintered**, it breaks into thin, sharp pieces. □ *The branch splintered into pieces.* [from Middle Dutch]

**split** /splɪt/ (**splits, splitting**)

> The form **split** is used in the present tense and is the past tense and past participle of the verb.

**1** V-T/V-I If something **splits** or if you **split** it, it is divided into two or more parts. □ *The ship split in two during a storm.* □ *Split the chicken in half.* **2** V-T/V-I If an organization **splits** or **is split**, one group of members disagree strongly with the other members, and may form a group of their own. □ *The party could split over this.* • **Split** is also an adjective. □ *The government is deeply split over foreign policy.* **3** N-COUNT A **split in** an organization is a disagreement between its members. □ *There are rumours of a split in the military.* **4** N-SING A **split between** two things is a division or difference between them. □ *There is a split between what he says and what he feels.* **5** V-T/V-I If something such as wood or a piece of clothing **splits** or **is split**, a long crack or tear appears in it. □ *The seat of his pants split.* □ *He split the log with an ax.* **6** V-T If two or more people **split** something, they share it between them. □ *Let's split the bill.* [from Middle Dutch]

▶ **split up** **1** PHR-VERB If two people **split up**, or if someone or something **splits** them **up**, they end their relationship or marriage. □ *His parents split up when he was ten.* □ *I thought that nothing could ever split us up.* **2** PHR-VERB If a group of people **split up** or **are split up**, they go away in different directions. □ *We split up and searched different parts of the forest.* □ *The war has split up many families.* **3** PHR-VERB If you **split** something **up**, or if it **splits up**, you divide it so that it is in a number of smaller separate sections. □ *We are not planning to split up the company.* □ *Museums have asked to borrow her collection, but she refuses to split it up.*

| Thesaurus | split | Also look up : |
|---|---|---|
| v. | break, divide, part, separate; (ant.) combine **1** **2** **4** | |

**split se|cond** also **split-second** N-SING A **split second** is an extremely short period of time. □ *She looked at Michael for a split second.* □ *We have to make split-second decisions.*

**splut|ter** /splʌtər/ (**splutters, spluttering, spluttered**) 1 V-T/V-I If someone **splutters**, they make short sounds and have difficulty speaking clearly, for example because they are embarrassed or angry. □ *"It can't be true," he spluttered.* □ *Bess spluttered and sat up.* 2 V-I If something **splutters**, it makes a series of short, sharp sounds. □ *The engine spluttered and died.*

**spoil** /spɔɪl/ (**spoils, spoiling, spoiled** or **spoilt**) 1 V-T If you **spoil** something, you prevent it from being successful or satisfactory. □ *Don't let mistakes spoil your life.* 2 V-T If you **spoil** children, you give them everything they want or ask for. □ *Grandparents often like to spoil their grandchildren.* 3 V-T If you **spoil yourself** or **spoil** another person, you give yourself or them something nice as a treat or do something special for them. □ *Spoil yourself with a new perfume.* [from Old French]

**spoke** /spoʊk/ (**spokes**) 1 **Spoke** is the past tense of **speak**. 2 N-COUNT The **spokes** of a wheel are the bars that connect the outer ring to the center. [from Old English]
→ see **bicycle, wheel**

**spo|ken** /spoʊkən/ **Spoken** is the past participle of **speak**. [from Old English]

**spokes|man** /spoʊksmən/ (**spokesmen**) N-COUNT A **spokesman** is a male spokesperson. □ *A spokesman said that food is on its way.*

**spokes|person** /spoʊkspɜrsᵊn/ (**spokespersons** or **spokespeople**) N-COUNT A **spokesperson** is a person who speaks as the representative of a group or organization. □ *...a White House spokesperson.*

**spokes|woman** /spoʊkswʊmən/ (**spokeswomen**) N-COUNT A **spokeswoman** is a female spokesperson. □ *A United Nations spokeswoman said the request would be considered.*

**sponge** /spʌndʒ/ (**sponges, sponging, sponged**) 1 N-UNCOUNT **Sponge** is a very light soft substance with lots of little holes in it, which can be either artificial or natural. It is used to clean things or as a soft layer. □ *...a sponge mattress.* 2 N-COUNT A **sponge** is a piece of sponge that you use for washing yourself or for cleaning things. □ *He wiped the table with a sponge.* 3 V-T If you **sponge** something, you clean it by wiping it with a wet sponge. □ *She gently sponged the baby's face.* 4 V-I If you say that someone **sponges off** other people or **sponges on** them, you disapprove of them because they regularly get money from other people when they should be trying to support themselves. [INFORMAL] □ *He should get a job and stop sponging off the rest of us!* 5 N-COUNT A **sponge** is a sea animal with a soft round body made of natural sponge. [from Old English]

**sponge cake** (**sponge cakes**) N-VAR A **Sponge cake** is a very light cake made from flour, eggs, and sugar, usually without any shortening.

**spon|gy bone** N-UNCOUNT **Spongy bone** is a type of bone that consists of many small pieces with spaces between them. It forms the interior of other bones. [TECHNICAL]

**spon|sor** /spɒnsər/ (**sponsors, sponsoring, sponsored**) 1 V-T If an organization or an individual **sponsors** something such as an event, they pay for it, often in order to get publicity for themselves. □ *A local bank is sponsoring the race.* 2 V-T If you **sponsor** someone who is doing something to raise money for charity, for example trying to walk a certain distance, you agree to give them money for the charity if they succeed in doing it. □ *The children asked friends and family to sponsor them.* 3 V-T If you **sponsor** a proposal or suggestion, you officially introduce it and support it. □ *An animal rights group is sponsoring the proposal to stop animal testing.* 4 N-COUNT A **sponsor** is a person or organization that sponsors something or someone. □ *Our company is proud to be the sponsor of this event.* [from Latin]

**spon|sor|ship** /spɒnsərʃɪp/ N-UNCOUNT **Sponsorship** is financial support given by a sponsor. □ *Athletes can make a lot of money out of sponsorship.* [from Latin]

**spon|ta|neity** /spɒntəniɪti, -neɪ-/ N-UNCOUNT **Spontaneity** is spontaneous, natural behavior. □ *He had the spontaneity of a child.* [from Late Latin]

**spon|ta|neous** /spɒnteɪniəs/ 1 ADJ **Spontaneous** acts are not planned or arranged, but are done because someone suddenly wants to do them. □ *He gave her a spontaneous hug.* ● **spon|ta|neous|ly** ADV □ *People spontaneously stood up and cheered.* 2 ADJ A **spontaneous** event happens because of processes within something, rather than being caused by things outside it. □ *...a spontaneous explosion.* ● **spon|ta|neous|ly** ADV □ *The memories arrived in his head spontaneously.* [from Late Latin]

**spooky** /spuki/ (**spookier, spookiest**) ADJ A place that is **spooky** has a frightening atmosphere, and makes you feel that there are ghosts around. [INFORMAL] □ *The house has a slightly spooky atmosphere.* [from Dutch]

**spool** /spul/ (**spools**) N-COUNT A **spool** is a round object onto which thread, tape, or film can be wound, especially before it is put into a machine. □ *...a spool of film.* [from Germanic]

**spoon** /spun/ (**spoons, spooning, spooned**) 1 N-COUNT A **spoon** is an object used for eating, stirring, and serving food. One end of it is shaped like a shallow bowl and it has a long handle. □ *He stirred his coffee with a spoon.* 2 V-T If you **spoon** food into something, you put it there with a spoon. □ *He spooned sugar into the mug.* [from Old English]
→ see **utensil**

**spo|rad|ic** /spərædɪk/ ADJ **Sporadic** occurrences of something happen at irregular intervals. □ *There was sporadic fighting near the border.* ● **spo|radi|cal|ly** ADV □ *The thunder continued sporadically.* [from Medieval Latin]

**spore** /spɔr/ (**spores**) N-COUNT **Spores** are cells produced by bacteria and fungi which can develop into new bacteria or fungi. [from New Latin]

**spo|ro|phyte** /spɔrəfaɪt/ (**sporophytes**)

S

N-COUNT The **sporophyte** is the stage in the life of a plant when it produces spores. [TECHNICAL]

**sport** /spɔrt/ (**sports**) N-VAR **Sports** are games such as football and basketball and other competitive leisure activities which need physical effort and skill. ❑ *Basketball is my favorite sport.* ❑ *She is very good at sports.*

**sport coat** (**sport coats**) also **sports coat** N-COUNT A **sport coat** is a man's jacket. It is worn on informal occasions with pants of a different material. ❑ *He wore a sport coat and a blue shirt.*

**sport|ing** /spɔrtɪŋ/ ADJ **Sporting** means relating to sports or used for sports. ❑ *...major sporting events, such as the U.S. Open.*

**sport jack|et** (**sport jackets**) N-COUNT A **sport jacket** is the same as a **sport coat**.

**sports|cast** /spɔrtskæst/ (**sportscasts**) N-COUNT A **sportscast** is a radio or television broadcast of a sporting event.

**sports|caster** /spɔrtskæstər/ (**sportscasters**) N-COUNT A **sportscaster** is a radio or television broadcaster who describes or comments on sporting events.

**sports|man** /spɔrtsmən/ (**sportsmen**) N-COUNT A **sportsman** is a man who takes part in sports.

**sports|woman** /spɔrtswʊmən/ (**sportswomen**) N-COUNT A **sportswoman** is a woman who takes part in sports.

**sporty** /spɔrti/ (**sportier, sportiest**) ADJ Someone who is **sporty** likes playing sports. ❑ *I'm an outdoor, sporty type and don't want to sit behind a desk all day.*

**spot** /spɒt/ (**spots, spotting, spotted**) ◻ N-COUNT **Spots** are small, round, colored areas on a surface. ❑ *The leaves are yellow with orange spots.* ◻ N-COUNT **Spots** on a person's skin are small lumps or marks. [AM usually **pimples**] ◻ N-COUNT You can refer to a particular place as a **spot**. ❑ *This is one of the country's top tourist spots.* ◻ V-T If you **spot** something or someone, you notice them. ❑ *I didn't spot the mistake in his essay.* ◻ PHRASE If you do something **on the spot**, you do it immediately. ❑ *They offered him the job on the spot.* [from German]

### Word Partnership   Use *spot* with :

| | |
|---|---|
| ADJ. | **good** spot, **perfect** spot, **popular** spot, **quiet** spot, **the right** spot ◻ |
| N. | **parking** spot, **vacation** spot ◻ |

**spot|light** /spɒtlaɪt/ (**spotlights, spotlighting, spotlighted**) ◻ N-COUNT A **spotlight** is a powerful light, for example in a theater, which can be directed so that it lights up a small area. ◻ V-T If something **spotlights** a particular problem or situation, it makes people notice it and think about it. ❑ *Her comments spotlight the problem of racism.*
→ see **concert**

**spotlight**

**spot|ty** /spɒti/ ADJ Something that is **spotty** does not stay the same but is sometimes good and

sometimes bad. ❑ *His attendance record was spotty.* [from German]

**spous|al** /spaʊzəl/ ADJ **Spousal** means relating to someone's husband or wife. [FORMAL] ❑ *...spousal benefits.* [from Old French]

**spouse** /spaʊs/ (**spouses**) N-COUNT Someone's **spouse** is the person they are married to. ❑ *You and your spouse must both sign the contract.* [from Old French]
→ see **love**

**spout** /spaʊt/ (**spouts, spouting, spouted**) ◻ V-T/V-I If something **spouts** liquid or fire, or if liquid or fire **spout** out of something, it comes out very quickly with a lot of force. ❑ *The engine began to spout flames.* ❑ *...a fountain that spouts water 40 feet into the air.* ◻ V-T If you say that a person **spouts** something, you disapprove of them because they say something which you do not agree with or which you think they do not honestly feel. ❑ *They sit around all day spouting stupid theories.* ◻ N-COUNT A **spout** is a long, hollow part of a container through which liquids can be poured out easily. ❑ *Hot tea came out of the spout.* [from Middle Dutch]

**sprain** /spreɪn/ (**sprains, spraining, sprained**) ◻ V-T If you **sprain** a joint such as your ankle or wrist, you accidentally damage it by twisting it or bending it violently. ❑ *He fell and sprained his ankle.* ◻ N-COUNT A **sprain** is the injury caused by spraining a joint. ❑ *Rubin suffered a right ankle sprain.*

**sprang** /spræŋ/ **Sprang** is the past tense of **spring**. [from Old English]

**sprawl** /sprɔl/ (**sprawls, sprawling, sprawled**) ◻ V-I If you **sprawl** somewhere, you sit or lie down with your legs and arms spread out in a careless way. ❑ *She sprawled on the sofa.* ● **Sprawl out** means the same as **sprawl**. ❑ *He sprawled out on his bed.* ◻ V-I If you say that a place **sprawls**, you mean that it covers a large area of land. ❑ *The park sprawls over 900 acres.* ◻ N-UNCOUNT You can use **sprawl** to refer to an area where a city has grown outward in an uncontrolled way. ❑ *The urban sprawl of Ankara contains over 2.6 million people.* [from Old English]

**spray** /spreɪ/ (**sprays, spraying, sprayed**) ◻ N-VAR **Spray** is a lot of small drops of water which are being thrown into the air. ❑ *We were hit by spray from the waterfall.* ◻ N-VAR A **spray** is a liquid kept under pressure in a can or other container, which you can force out in very small drops. ❑ *...hair spray.* ◻ V-T/V-I If you **spray** a liquid somewhere or if it **sprays** somewhere, drops of the liquid cover a place or shower someone. ❑ *A plane was spraying chemicals over the fields.* ❑ *Police sprayed the crowd with water.* ◻ V-T/V-I If a lot of small things **spray** somewhere or if something **sprays** them, they are scattered somewhere with a lot of force. ❑ *A shower of crumbs sprayed into the air.* ❑ *The window broke, spraying glass on the street below.* [from Middle Dutch]

### Word Partnership   Use *spray* with :

| | |
|---|---|
| N. | spray **bottle**, **bug** spray, spray **can**, **hair** spray, **pepper** spray ◻ |
| PREP. | spray **with water** ◻ |

**spread** /sprɛd/ (**spreads, spreading, spread**) ◻ V-T If you **spread** something somewhere, you open it out or arrange it over a place or surface, so that all of it can be seen or used easily. ❑ *She spread a towel on the sand and lay on it.* ● **Spread out** means the same as **spread.** ❑ *He spread the papers out on a table.* **2** V-T If you **spread** your arms, hands, fingers, or legs, you stretch them out until they are far apart. ❑ *Sitting on the floor, spread your legs as far as they will go.* ● **Spread out** means the same as **spread.** ❑ *David spread out his hands.* **3** V-T If you **spread** a substance on a surface or **spread** the surface **with** the substance, you put a thin layer of the substance over the surface. ❑ *She was spreading butter on the bread.* **4** V-T/V-I If something **spreads** or **is spread** by people, it gradually reaches or affects a larger and larger area or more and more people. ❑ *Information technology has spread across the world.* ❑ *Fear is spreading in the neighborhood.* ● **Spread** is also a noun. ❑ *...the slow spread of information.* **5** V-T If you **spread** something **over** a period of time, it takes place regularly or continuously over that period, rather than happening at one time. ❑ *You can pay the whole amount, or spread your payments over several months.* **6** V-T If you **spread** something such as wealth or work, you distribute it evenly or equally. ❑ *...policies that spread the wealth more evenly.* ● **Spread** is also a noun. ❑ *We need to encourage the even spread of wealth.* **7** N-SING A **spread of** ideas, interests, or other things is a wide variety of them. ❑ *The school has students with a wide spread of ability.* [from Old English] ▶ **spread out** **1** PHR-VERB If people, animals, or vehicles **spread out**, they move apart from each other. ❑ *They spread out to search the area.* **2** → see **spread 1, 2**

**spree** /sprɪ/ (**sprees**) N-COUNT If you spend a period of time doing something in an excessive way, you can say that you are going on a particular kind of **spree.** ❑ *We went on a shopping spree.* [from Scottish]

**sprig** /sprɪg/ (**sprigs**) N-COUNT A **sprig** is a small stem with leaves on it which has been picked from a bush or plant. [from Germanic]

**spring** /sprɪŋ/ (**springs, springing, sprang, sprung**) **1** N-VAR **Spring** is the season between winter and summer when the weather becomes warmer and plants start to grow again. ❑ *They are getting married next spring.* **2** N-COUNT A **spring** is a spiral of wire which returns to its original shape after it is pressed or pulled. ❑ *The springs in the bed were old and soft.* **3** N-COUNT A **spring** is a place where water comes up through the ground. ❑ *The town is famous for its hot springs.* **4** V-I When a person or animal **springs**, they jump upward or forward suddenly or quickly. ❑ *He sprang to his feet.* **5** V-I If something **springs** in a particular direction, it moves suddenly and quickly. ❑ *The*

lid of the box sprang open. **6** V-I If one thing **springs from** another thing, it is the result of it. ❑ *His anger sprang from shock and surprise.* **7** V-T If you **spring** some news or a surprise **on** someone, you tell them something that they did not expect to hear, without warning them. ❑ *Mike sprang a new idea on him.* [from Old English]
→ see **river**
▶ **spring up** PHR-VERB If something **springs up**, it suddenly appears or begins to exist. ❑ *New theaters sprang up all over the country.*

**spring-cleaning** N-UNCOUNT; N-SING **Spring-cleaning** is the process of thoroughly cleaning a place, especially your home. You can also say that you give a place a **spring-cleaning.** ❑ *They were giving the house a good spring-cleaning.*

**spring tide** (**spring tides**) N-COUNT A **spring tide** is an unusually high tide that happens at the time of a new moon or a full moon.

**sprin|kle** /sprɪŋkªl/ (**sprinkles, sprinkling, sprinkled**) **1** V-T If you **sprinkle** a thing **with** something such as a liquid or powder, you scatter the liquid or powder over it. ❑ *Sprinkle the meat with salt before you cook it.* **2** V-I If **it is sprinkling**, it is raining very lightly. [from Middle Dutch]

sprinkle

**sprint** /sprɪnt/ (**sprints, sprinting, sprinted**) **1** N-SING **The sprint** is a short, fast race. ❑ *Rob Harmeling won the sprint.* **2** N-SING A **sprint** is a fast run that someone does, either at the end of a race or because they are in a hurry. ❑ *She made a sprint for the bus.* **3** V-I If you **sprint**, you run or ride as fast as you can over a short distance. ❑ *Sergeant Horne sprinted to the car.* [of Scandinavian origin]

**sprint|er** /sprɪntər/ (**sprinters**) N-COUNT A **sprinter** is a person who takes part in short, fast races. [of Scandinavian origin]

**sprout** /spraʊt/ (**sprouts, sprouting, sprouted**) **1** V-I When plants, vegetables, or seeds **sprout**, they produce new shoots or leaves. ❑ *It only takes a few days for beans to sprout.* **2** V-I When leaves, shoots, or plants **sprout** somewhere, they grow there. ❑ *Leaves were beginning to sprout on the trees.* **3** V-T/V-I If something such as hair **sprouts** from a person or animal, or if they **sprout** it, it grows on them. ❑ *Hair sprouted from his chin.* **4** N-COUNT **Sprouts** are vegetables that look like tiny cabbages. They are also called **Brussels sprouts.** [from Old English]
→ see **tree**

**spruce** /sprus/ (**spruces, sprucing, spruced**)

Spruce is both the singular and the plural form.

N-VAR A **spruce** is a kind of evergreen tree. ❑ *Trees such as spruce, pine, and oak have been planted.* ❑ *...a young spruce.* [from Old French]

▶ **spruce up** PHR-VERB If something **is spruced up**, its appearance is improved. If someone **is spruced up**, they have made themselves look neat and clean. ❑ *The buildings have been spruced up.*

**sprung** /sprʌŋ/ **Sprung** is the past participle of **spring**. [from Old English]

**spun** /spʌn/ **Spun** is the past tense and past participle of **spin**. [from Old English]

**spur** /spɜr/ (**spurs, spurring, spurred**) **1** V-T If one thing **spurs** you **to** do another, it encourages you to do it. ❑ *Money spurs these men to risk their lives.* ● **Spur on** means the same as **spur**. ❑ *The applause seemed to spur him on.* **2** V-T If something **spurs** a change or event, it makes it happen faster or sooner. ❑ *Our aim is to spur economic growth.* **3** N-COUNT Something that acts as a **spur to** something else encourages a person or organization to do that thing or makes it happen more quickly. ❑ *Financial profit can be a spur to progress.* **4** PHRASE If you do something **on the spur of the moment**, you do it suddenly, without planning it beforehand. ❑ *They went to the beach on the spur of the moment.* [from Old English]

**spu|ri|ous** /spyʊəriəs/ ADJ A **spurious** claim or argument seems to be correct or genuine, but is really false or dishonest. ❑ *He was arrested on spurious charges.* [from Latin]

**spurn** /spɜrn/ (**spurns, spurning, spurned**) V-T If you **spurn** someone or something, you reject them. ❑ *He spurned the advice of his boss.* [from Old English]

**spurt** /spɜrt/ (**spurts, spurting, spurted**) **1** V-T/V-I If liquid or fire **spurts** from somewhere, it comes out quickly in a thin, powerful stream. ❑ *The pipe burst, spurting oil.* ❑ *I saw flames spurt from the roof.* **2** N-COUNT A **spurt of** liquid is a stream of it which comes out of something very forcefully. ❑ *There was a spurt of water from his mouth.* **3** N-COUNT A **spurt** of activity, effort, or emotion is a sudden, brief period of it. ❑ *Many children have a growth spurt around the age of 13.* **4** V-I If someone or something **spurts** somewhere, they suddenly increase their speed for a short while in order to get there. ❑ *She spurted to the finish line.* [from Middle High German]

**spy** /spaɪ/ (**spies, spying, spied**) **1** N-COUNT A **spy** is a person whose job is to find out secret information about another country or organization. **2** V-I Someone who **spies for** a country or organization tries to find out secret information about another country or organization. ❑ *He spied for the Soviet Union for more than twenty years.* ❑ *The two countries are still spying on one another.* ● **spy|ing** N-UNCOUNT ❑ *He spent ten years in jail for spying.* **3** V-I If you **spy on** someone, you watch them secretly. ❑ *He spied on her while pretending to work in the yard.* [from Old French]

**sq.** **sq.** is used as a written abbreviation for **square** when you are giving the measurement of an area. ❑ *The building provides about 25,500 sq. ft. of offices.*

**squab|ble** /skwɒbəl/ (**squabbles, squabbling, squabbled**) V-RECIP When people **squabble**, they quarrel about something that is not really important. ❑ *His parents squabble all the time.* ❑ *The children were squabbling over a toy.* ● **Squabble** is also a noun. ❑ *They had a squabble about money.* [of Scandinavian origin]

**squad** /skwɒd/ (**squads**) **1** N-COUNT A **squad** is a section of a police force that is responsible for dealing with a particular type of crime. ❑ *Someone called the bomb squad.* **2** N-COUNT A **squad** is a group of players from which a sports team will be chosen. ❑ *There have been a lot of injuries in the squad.* [from Old French]

**squad|ron** /skwɒdrən/ (**squadrons**) N-COUNT A **squadron** is a section of one of the armed forces, especially the air force. ❑ *...a squadron of fighter planes.* [from Italian]

**squal|id** /skwɒlɪd/ ADJ A **squalid** place is dirty, untidy, and in bad condition. ❑ *They lived in a squalid apartment.* [from Latin]

**squal|or** /skwɒlər/ N-UNCOUNT You can refer to very dirty, unpleasant conditions as **squalor**. ❑ *He was out of work and living in squalor.* [from Latin]

**squan|der** /skwɒndər/ (**squanders, squandering, squandered**) V-T If you **squander** money, resources, or opportunities, you waste them. ❑ *He squandered his money on fancy clothes.*

**square** /skwɛər/ (**squares, squaring, squared**) **1** N-COUNT A **square** is a shape with four sides that are all the same length and four corners that are all right angles. ❑ *Cut the cake in squares.* ❑ *There was a calendar on the wall, with squares around some dates.* **2** N-COUNT In a town or city, a **square** is a flat open place, often in the shape of a square. ❑ *The house is in one of the city's prettiest squares.* **3** ADJ Something that is **square** has a shape the same as a square or similar to a square. ❑ *They sat at a square table.* **4** ADJ **Square** is used before units of length when referring to the area of something. For example, if something is three feet long and two feet wide, its area is six square feet. ❑ *The house covers an area of 3,000 square feet.* **5** V-T To **square** a number means to multiply it by itself. For example, **3 squared** is 3 x 3, or 9. **3 squared** is usually written as 3². ❑ *Find the length of one side and square it.* **6** N-COUNT The **square** of a number is the number produced when you multiply that number by itself. ❑ *The square of 25 is 625.* **7** V-T/V-I If you **square** two different ideas or actions **with** each other or if they **square with** each other, they fit or match each other. ❑ *That explanation doesn't square with the facts.* [from Old French] **8** → see also **squarely**

→ see **shape**

▶ **square away** PHR-VERB If you **square** something or someone **away**, you deal with them so that the situation is satisfactory. ❑ *First we have to square away how much this is going to cost.*

▶ **square off** PHR-VERB If one group or person **squares off against** or **with** another, they prepare to fight or compete against them. ❑ *The two politicians squared off against one another in a TV debate.* ❑ *I saw my brother squaring off with another boy.*

**square|ly** /skwɛərli/ **1** ADV **Squarely** means directly or in the middle, rather than indirectly or at an angle. ❑ *She looked squarely at him.* **2** ADV If something such as blame or responsibility lies

**squarely** with someone, they are definitely the person responsible. ❏ *She put the blame squarely on her husband.* [from Old French]

**square root** (**square roots**) N-COUNT The **square root of** a number is another number which produces the first number when it is multiplied by itself. For example, the square root of 16 is 4.

**squash** /skwɒʃ/ (**squashes, squashing, squashed**) **1** V-T If someone or something **is squashed**, they are pressed or crushed with such force that they become injured or lose their shape. ❏ *Robert was squashed against a fence by a car.* ❏ *Whole neighborhoods have been squashed flat by bombing.* **2** ADJ If people or things are **squashed into** a place, they are put or pushed into a place where there is not enough room for them to be. ❏ *There were 2,000 people squashed into the hall.* **3** N-UNCOUNT **Squash** is a game in which two players hit a small rubber ball against the walls of a court using rackets. ❏ *I play squash once a week.* [from Old French]
→ see **vegetable**

**squat** /skwɒt/ (**squats, squatting, squatted**) **1** V-I If you **squat**, you lower yourself toward the ground, balancing on your feet with your legs bent. ❏ *We squatted beside the pool.* ● **Squat down** means the same as **squat**. ❏ *Albert squatted down to see the bug.* ● **Squat** is also a noun. ❏ *He got down into a squat.* **2** ADJ If you describe someone or something as **squat**, you mean they are short and thick, usually in an unattractive way. ❏ *Eddie was a short squat fellow.* **3** V-I People who **squat** occupy an unused building or unused land without having a legal right to do so. ❏ *Homeless families have been squatting on the land.* [from Old French]

**squatter** /skwɒtər/ (**squatters**) N-COUNT A **squatter** is someone who lives in an unused building without having a legal right to do so and without paying any rent or any property tax. ❏ *Police evicted squatters from empty buildings.* [from Old French]

**squeak** /skwik/ (**squeaks, squeaking, squeaked**) V-I If something or someone **squeaks**, they make a short, high-pitched sound. ❏ *My boots squeaked as I walked.* ❏ *The door squeaked open.* ● **Squeak** is also a noun. ❏ *I heard a squeak, like a mouse.* [of Scandinavian origin]

**squeal** /skwil/ (**squeals, squealing, squealed**) V-I If someone or something **squeals**, they make a long, high-pitched sound. ❏ *Jennifer squealed with delight.* ● **Squeal** is also a noun. ❏ *There was a squeal of brakes as the car suddenly stopped.*

**squeeze** /skwiz/ (**squeezes, squeezing, squeezed**) **1** V-T If you **squeeze** something, you press it firmly, usually with your hands. ❏ *He squeezed her arm gently.* ● **Squeeze** is also a noun. ❏ *She took my hand and gave it a squeeze.* **2** V-T If you **squeeze** a liquid or a soft substance out of an object, you get the liquid or substance out by pressing the object. ❏ *Joe squeezed some toothpaste out of the tube.* **3** V-T/V-I If you **squeeze** a person or thing somewhere or if they **squeeze** there, they manage to get through or into a small space. ❏ *Can you squeeze one more box into your car?* **4** N-SING If you say that squeezing a number of people into a small space is **a squeeze**, you mean that it is only just possible for them all to get into it. [INFORMAL] ❏ *It was a squeeze with five of us in the car.* [from Middle English]

**squid** /skwɪd/ (**squids**)

> **Squid** can also be used as the plural form.

N-COUNT A **squid** is a sea creature with a long soft body and many soft arms called tentacles. ● **Squid** is pieces of this creature eaten as food. ❏ *Cook the squid for 2 minutes.*

**squint** /skwɪnt/ (**squints, squinting, squinted**) **1** V-I If you **squint at** something, you look at it with your eyes partly closed. ❏ *The girl squinted at the photograph.* ❏ *The bright sunlight made me squint.* **2** N-COUNT If someone has a **squint**, their eyes look in different directions from each other. ❏ *The child had a squint.*

**squirm** /skwɜrm/ (**squirms, squirming, squirmed**) V-I If you **squirm**, you move your body from side to side, usually because you are nervous or uncomfortable. ❏ *He squirmed when his father washed his face.* ❏ *He tried to squirm free.*

**squirrel**

**squirrel** /skwɜrəl/ (**squirrels**) N-COUNT A **squirrel** is a small animal with a long furry tail. Squirrels live mainly in trees. [from Old French]

**squirt** /skwɜrt/ (**squirts, squirting, squirted**) V-T/V-I If you **squirt** a liquid somewhere or if it **squirts** somewhere, the liquid comes out of a narrow opening in a thin fast stream. ❏ *Norman squirted tomato sauce onto his plate.* ● **Squirt** is also a noun. ❏ *It needs a little squirt of oil.*

**stab** /stæb/ (**stabs, stabbing, stabbed**) **1** V-T If someone **stabs** you, they push a knife or sharp object into your body. ❏ *Somebody stabbed him in the stomach.* **2** V-T/V-I If you **stab** something or **stab at** it, you push at it with your finger or with something pointed that you are holding. ❏ *Bess stabbed a slice of cucumber.* ❏ *Greg stabbed his finger at the photo he wanted to show me.* **3** N-SING If you have **a stab at** something, you try to do it. [INFORMAL] ❏ *Have you ever had a stab at acting?* **4** N-SING You can refer to a sudden, usually unpleasant feeling as **a stab** of that feeling. [LITERARY] ❏ *He felt a stab of pain above his eye.* [from Middle English]
→ see **carnivore**

**stabbing** /stæbɪŋ/ (**stabbings**) **1** N-COUNT A **stabbing** is an incident in which someone stabs someone else with a knife. ❏ *...the victim of a stabbing.* **2** ADJ A **stabbing** pain is a sudden sharp pain. ❏ *He felt a stabbing pain in his stomach.* [from Middle English]

**stabilize** /steɪbɪlaɪz/ (**stabilizes, stabilizing, stabilized**) V-T/V-I If something **stabilizes**, or **is stabilized**, it becomes stable. ❏ *Doctors say her condition has stabilized.* ● **stabilization** /steɪbɪlɪzeɪʃ³n/ N-UNCOUNT ❏ *...the stabilization of house prices.* [from Old French]

**stable** /steɪb³l/ (**stabler, stablest, stables**) **1** ADJ If something is **stable**, it is not likely to change or come to an end suddenly. ❏ *The price of oil has remained stable this month.* ● **stability** /stəbɪlɪti/ N-UNCOUNT ❏ *It was a time of political stability.* **2** ADJ If an object is **stable**, it is firmly fixed in position and is not likely to move or fall. ❏ *Make sure the ladder is stable.* **3** N-COUNT A **stable**

or **stables** is a building in which horses are kept. [from Old French]

**stack** /stæk/ (**stacks, stacking, stacked**)
■ N-COUNT A **stack of** things is a pile of them. ❑ *There were stacks of books on the floor.* ❷ V-T If you **stack** a number of things, you arrange them in neat piles. ❑ *She was stacking the clean bottles onto the shelf.* ● **Stack up** means the same as **stack.** ❑ *They stacked up pillows behind his back.* ❸ N-PLURAL If you say that **the odds are stacked against** someone, or that particular factors **are stacked against** them, you mean that they are unlikely to succeed in what they want to do because the conditions are not favorable. ❑ *The odds are stacked against him winning the competition.* [from Old Norse]

**stacked** /stækt/ ADJ If a place or surface is **stacked with** objects, it is filled with piles of them. ❑ *Shops in Ho Chi Minh City are stacked with goods.*

**sta|dium** /steɪdiəm/ (**stadiums** or **stadia** /steɪdiə/) N-COUNT A **stadium** is a large sports field with rows of seats all around it. ❑ *...a baseball stadium.* [from Latin]

**staff** /stæf/ (**staffs, staffing, staffed**)

Staves is the usual plural form for meaning ⑤.

■ N-COUNT The **staff** of an organization are the people who work for it. ❑ *The hospital staff were very good.* ❑ *We have a staff of six people.* ❑ *...staff members.* ❷ → see also **chief of staff** ❸ N-PLURAL People who are part of a particular staff are often referred to as **staff.** ❑ *10 staff were moved to different departments.* ❹ V-T If an organization **is staffed by** particular people, they are the people who work for it. ❑ *The office is staffed by volunteers.* ● **staffed** ADJ ❑ *The hotel was pleasant and well staffed.* ⑤ A **staff** is the five lines that music is written on. [from Old English]

**staff|er** /stæfər/ (**staffers**) N-COUNT A **staffer** is a member of a staff, especially in political organizations or in journalism. ❑ *...White House staffers.* [from Old English]

**staff|ing** /stæfɪŋ/ N-UNCOUNT **Staffing** refers to the number of workers employed to work in a particular organization or building. [BUSINESS] ❑ *Staffing levels in prisons are too low.* [from Old English]

**stag** /stæg/ (**stags**) N-COUNT A **stag** is an adult male deer. [from Old English]

**stage** /steɪdʒ/ (**stages, staging, staged**)
■ N-COUNT A **stage of** an activity, process, or period is one part of it. ❑ *...the first stage of the plan to reopen the airport.* ❷ N-COUNT In a theater, the **stage** is an area where actors or other entertainers perform. ❑ *The band walked onto the stage.* ❸ N-COUNT The **stage** on a microscope is the place where you put the specimen that you want to look at. ❹ V-T If someone **stages** a play or other show, they organize and present a performance of it. ❑ *He plans to stage "Hamlet" in Chicago.* ⑤ V-T If you **stage** an event or ceremony, you organize it and usually take part in it. ❑ *Workers are planning to stage a strike.* [from Old French] ⑥ **to set the stage** → see **set**
→ see **concert, drama, theater**

**Word Partnership** Use *stage* with :

| ADJ. | **advanced** stage, **critical** stage, **crucial** stage, **final** stage, **late/later** stage ■ |
| N. | stage **of development**, stage **of a disease**, stage **of a process** ■ **actors on** stage, **center** stage, **concert** stage, stage **fright**, stage **manager** ❷ |
| V. | **reach a** stage ■ **leave the** stage, **take the** stage ❷ |

**stage crew** (**stage crews**) N-COUNT A **stage crew** is a team of workers who move the scenery about in a play or other theatrical production.

**stage left** ADV **Stage left** is the left side of the stage for an actor who is standing facing the audience.

**stage man|ag|er** (**stage managers**) N-COUNT At a theater, a **stage manager** is the person who is responsible for the scenery and lights and for the way that actors or other performers move around and use the stage during a performance.

**stage right** ADV **Stage right** is the right side of the stage for an actor who is standing facing the audience.

**stag|ger** /stægər/ (**staggers, staggering, staggered**) ■ V-I If you **stagger**, you walk very unsteadily, for example because you are ill. ❑ *He staggered back and fell over.* ❷ V-T If something **staggers** you, it surprises you very much. ❑ *Their stupidity staggers me.* ● **stag|gered** ADJ ❑ *I felt staggered by how much everything cost.* ❸ V-T To **stagger** things means to arrange them so that they do not all happen at the same time. ❑ *The university staggers the summer vacation periods for students.* [from Old Norse]

**stag|ger|ing** /stægərɪŋ/ ADJ Something that is **staggering** is very surprising. ❑ *The cost was a staggering $900 million.* [from Old Norse]

**stag|nant** /stægnənt/ ■ ADJ If something such as a business or society is **stagnant**, there is little activity or change. ❑ *When people do the same job for a long time, they get stagnant.* ❷ ADJ **Stagnant** water is not flowing, and therefore often smells unpleasant and is dirty. ❑ *...a stagnant pond.* [from Latin]

**stag|nate** /stægneɪt/ (**stagnates, stagnating, stagnated**) V-I If something such as a business or society **stagnates**, it stops changing or progressing. ❑ *The economy is stagnating.* ● **stag|na|tion** N-UNCOUNT ❑ *...the stagnation of the steel industry.* [from Latin]

**staid** /steɪd/ ADJ If you say that someone or something is **staid**, you mean that they are serious, dull, and rather old-fashioned. ❑ *She shocked her staid neighbors.*

**stain** /steɪn/ (**stains, staining, stained**)
■ N-COUNT A **stain** is a mark on something that is difficult to remove. ❑ *How do you remove tea stains?* ❷ V-T If a liquid **stains** something, the thing becomes colored or marked by the liquid. ❑ *Some foods can stain the teeth.* ● **stained** ADJ ❑ *His clothing was stained with mud.* ❑ *...ink-stained fingers.* [from Old French]

**stained glass** also **stained-glass** N-UNCOUNT **Stained glass** consists of pieces of glass of different colors which are fitted together to make decorative windows or other objects. ❑ ...*the stained glass window in St. John's Cathedral.*

**stain|less steel** /stɛɪnlɪs stil/ N-UNCOUNT **Stainless steel** is a metal made from steel and chromium which does not rust. ❑ ...*a stainless steel sink.*
→ see **pan**

**stair** /stɛər/ (**stairs**) **1** N-PLURAL **Stairs** are a set of steps inside a building which go from one floor to another. ❑ *Nancy began to climb the stairs.* ❑ *We walked up a flight of stairs.* **2** N-COUNT A **stair** is one of the steps in a flight of stairs. ❑ *Terry was sitting on the bottom stair.* [from Old English]

**stair|case** /stɛərkeɪs/ (**staircases**) N-COUNT A **staircase** is a set of stairs inside a building. ❑ *They walked down the staircase together.*
→ see **house**

**stair|lift** /stɛərlɪft/ (**stairlifts**) also **stair lift** N-COUNT A **stairlift** is a device that is attached to a staircase in a house in order to allow an elderly or sick person to go upstairs.

**stair|way** /stɛərweɪ/ (**stairways**) N-COUNT A **stairway** is a staircase or a flight of steps, inside or outside a building. ❑ ...*the stairway leading to the top floor.* [from Old English]

**stake** /steɪk/ (**stakes, staking, staked**) **1** PHRASE If something is **at stake**, it is being risked and might be lost or damaged if you are not successful. ❑ *There was so much at stake in this game.* **2** N-PLURAL The **stakes** involved in a contest or a risky action are the things that can be gained or lost. ❑ *They play cards, but not for high stakes.* **3** V-T If you **stake** something such as your money or your reputation **on** the result of something, you risk your money or reputation on it. ❑ *She staked her reputation as a writer on this article.* **4** N-COUNT If you have a **stake in** something such as a business, it matters to you, for example because you own part of it or because its success or failure will affect you. ❑ *We all have a stake in the success of the next generation of children.* **5** N-COUNT A **stake** is a pointed wooden post which is pushed into the ground, for example in order to support a young tree. ❑ *She hung the clothes on a rope tied between two wooden stakes.* **6** PHRASE If you **stake a claim**, you say that something is yours or that you have a right to it. ❑ *His children have all staked their claim to his money.* [Sense 5 from Old English]

| Word Partnership | Use *stake* with : |
|---|---|
| N. | **interests at** stake, **issues at** stake **1** stake **lives on** *something* **3** stake **in a company/firm**, **majority/minority** stake **4** |
| ADJ. | **controlling** stake, **personal** stake **4** |

**stale** /steɪl/ (**staler, stalest**) **1** ADJ **Stale** food or air is no longer fresh. ❑ ....*stale bread.* **2** ADJ If a place, an activity, or an idea is **stale**, it has become boring because it is always the same. ❑ *Her relationship with Mark has become stale.* [from Old French]

**stale|mate** /steɪlmeɪt/ (**stalemates**) N-VAR **Stalemate** is a situation in which neither side in an argument or contest can win or make progress. ❑ *Relations between the two countries have reached a stalemate.* [from Old French]

**stalk** /stɔk/ (**stalks, stalking, stalked**) **1** N-COUNT The **stalk** of a flower, leaf, or fruit is the thin part that joins it to the plant or tree. ❑ *A single flower grows on each long stalk.* **2** V-T If you **stalk** a person or a wild animal, you follow them quietly in order to kill them, catch them, or observe them carefully. ❑ ...*a picture of a hunter stalking a deer.* **3** V-T If someone **stalks** someone else, they keep following them or contacting them in an annoying and frightening way. ❑ *I see you everywhere I go — are you stalking me?* ● **stalk|er** (**stalkers**) N-COUNT ❑ *She was followed by a stalker.* [from Old English]

**stall** /stɔl/ (**stalls, stalling, stalled**) **1** V-T/V-I If a process **stalls**, or if someone or something **stalls** it, the process stops but may continue at a later time. ❑ *They're trying to stall the meeting.* ❑ *The peace process stalled.* **2** V-I If you **stall**, you try to avoid doing something until later. ❑ *Thomas spent all week stalling over his decision.* **3** V-T/V-I If a vehicle **stalls** or if you accidentally **stall** it, the engine stops suddenly. ❑ *The engine stalled.* **4** N-COUNT A **stall** is a large table on which you put goods that you want to sell, or information that you want to give people. ❑ ...*market stalls selling fruit and vegetables.* **5** N-COUNT A **stall** is a small enclosed area in a room which is used for a particular purpose, for example a shower. ❑ *She went into the shower stall and turned on the water.* [from Old English]
→ see **traffic**

**stal|lion** /stælyən/ (**stallions**) N-COUNT A **stallion** is a male horse, especially one that is used for breeding. [from Old French]

**stal|wart** /stɔlwərt/ (**stalwarts**) N-COUNT A **stalwart** is a loyal worker or supporter of an organization, especially a political party. ❑ *He is a stalwart of the Republican party.* [from Old English]

**sta|men** /steɪmən/ (**stamens**) N-COUNT The **stamen** is the male part of a flower, which produces pollen. Compare **pistil**. [TECHNICAL] [from Latin]
→ see **flower**

**stami|na** /stæmɪnə/ N-UNCOUNT **Stamina** is the physical or mental energy needed to do a tiring activity for a long time. ❑ *You have to have a lot of stamina to be a dancer.* [from Latin]

**stam|mer** /stæmər/ (**stammers, stammering, stammered**) **1** V-T/V-I If you **stammer**, you speak with difficulty, hesitating and repeating words or sounds. ❑ *A lot of children stammer.* ● **stam|mer|ing** N-UNCOUNT ❑ *Stammering can be embarrassing.* **2** N-SING Someone who has a **stammer** tends to stammer when they speak. ❑ *She helps children who have stammers.* [from Old English]

**stamp** /stæmp/ (**stamps, stamping, stamped**) **1** N-COUNT A **stamp** or a **postage stamp** is a small piece of paper which you stick on an envelope or package before you mail it to pay for the cost of the postage. ❑ ...*a book of stamps.* ❑ *She put a stamp on the corner of the envelope.* **2** N-COUNT A **stamp** is a small block of wood or metal with words, numbers or a pattern on it. You press it onto an pad of ink and then onto a piece of paper in order to produce a mark on the paper. The mark is also called a **stamp**. ❑ ...*a date stamp.* **3** V-T If you **stamp** a mark or word on an object, you press the mark or word onto the object using a stamp or other device. ❑ *They stamp a special number on new cars*

S

to help find stolen ones. ◻ v-T/v-I If you **stamp** or **stamp** your **foot**, you put your foot down very hard on the ground, for example because you are angry. ◻ *I stamped my foot in anger.* ◻ *His foot stamped down on my toe.* [from Old English] ◻ → see also **rubber stamp**

▸ **stamp out** PHR-VERB If you **stamp** something **out**, you put an end to it. ◻ *It's impossible to stamp out crime completely.*

**stam|pede** /stæmpiːd/ (**stampedes, stampeding, stampeded**) ◻ N-COUNT If there is a **stampede**, a group of people or animals run in a wild, uncontrolled way. ◻ *There was a stampede for the door.* ◻ v-T/v-I If a group of animals or people **stampede** or if something **stampedes** them, they run in a wild, uncontrolled way. ◻ *The crowd stampeded and many people were injured.* ◻ *…a herd of stampeding cows.* [from American Spanish]

**stance** /stæns/ (**stances**) ◻ N-COUNT Your **stance** on a particular matter is your attitude to it. ◻ *What is your stance on the war?* ◻ N-COUNT Your **stance** is the way that you are standing. [FORMAL] ◻ *Take a wide stance and bend your knees a little.* [from French]

| Word Partnership | Use *stance* with : |
| --- | --- |
| PREP. | stance **against/on/toward** *something* ◻ |
| ADJ. | **aggressive** stance, **critical** stance, **hard-line** stance, **tough** stance ◻ |
| V. | **adopt** a stance, **take** a stance ◻ ◻ |

## stand

① VERB USES
② NOUN USES
③ PHR-VERBS

**① stand** /stænd/ (**stands, standing, stood**)
◻ v-I When you **are standing**, your body is upright, your legs are straight, and your weight is supported by your feet. ◻ *She was standing beside my bed.* ◻ *They told me to stand still and not to turn around.* ● **Stand up** means the same as **stand**. ◻ *We waited, standing up, for an hour.* ◻ v-I When someone who is sitting **stands**, they change their position so that they are upright and on their feet. ◻ *Becker stood and shook hands with Ben.* ● **Stand up** means the same as **stand**. ◻ *When I walked in, they all stood up.* ◻ v-I If you **stand aside** or **stand back**, you move a short distance sideways or backward, so that you are standing in a different place. ◻ *I stood aside to let her pass me.* ◻ v-I If something such as a building or a piece of furniture **stands** somewhere, it is upright in that position. [WRITTEN] ◻ *The house stands alone on top of a hill.* ◻ v-T If you **stand** something somewhere, you put it there in an upright position. ◻ *Stand the plant in a sunny place.* ◻ v-I If you ask someone **where** or **how** they **stand on** a particular issue, you are asking them what their attitude or view is. ◻ *Where do you stand on the issue of private schools?* ◻ v-I If a decision, law, or offer **stands**, it still exists and has not been changed or canceled. ◻ *The rule still stands.* ◻ v-I If something that can be measured **stands at** a particular level, it is at that level. ◻ *The number of missing people now stands at 30.* ◻ v-T If something can **stand** a situation or a test, it is good enough or strong enough to cope with it. ◻ *These shoes can stand a lot of use.* ◻ v-T

If you cannot **stand** someone or something, you dislike them very strongly. [INFORMAL] ◻ *I can't stand that awful man.* ◻ v-T If you **stand to gain** something, you are likely to gain it. If you **stand to lose** something, you are likely to lose it. ◻ *He stands to gain a lot of money if he wins the competition.* [from Old English] ◻ → see also **standing** ◻ to **stand a chance** → see **chance** ◻ to **stand firm** → see **firm** ◻ to **stand on** your **own two feet** → see **foot** ◻ to **stand** your **ground** → see **ground** ◻ to **stand** someone **in good stead** → see **stead** ◻ to **stand trial** → see **trial**

**② stand** /stænd/ (**stands**) ◻ N-COUNT If you take or make a **stand**, you do something or say something in order to make it clear what your attitude to a particular thing is. ◻ *He made a stand against racism.* ◻ N-COUNT A **stand** is a small store or stall, outdoors or in a large public building. ◻ *I bought a magazine from a newspaper stand.* ◻ N-PLURAL The **stands** at a sports stadium or arena are a large structure where people sit or stand to watch what is happening. ◻ *The people in the stands at Candlestick Park stood and cheered.* ◻ N-COUNT A **stand** is an object or piece of furniture that is designed for supporting or holding a particular kind of thing. ◻ *Take the television set off its stand.* ◻ N-COUNT A **stand** is an area where taxis or buses can wait to pick up passengers. ◻ *There was a taxi stand nearby.* ◻ N-SING In a law court, **the stand** is the place where a witness sits to answer questions. ◻ *When the father took the stand today, he said his son was a good man.* [from Old English]
→ see **laboratory**

**③ stand** /stænd/ (**stands, standing, stood**)
▸ **stand by** ◻ PHR-VERB If you **are standing by**, you are ready and waiting to provide help or to take action. ◻ *American ships are standing by to help.* ◻ → see also **standby** ◻ PHR-VERB If you **stand by** and let something bad happen, you do not do anything to stop it; used showing disapproval. ◻ *I will not stand by and let them tells about my friend.*
▸ **stand down** PHR-VERB If someone **stands down**, they resign from an important job or position, often in order to let someone else take their place. ◻ *After ten years, the leader stood down.*
▸ **stand for** ◻ PHR-VERB If you say that a letter **stands for** a particular word, you mean that it is an abbreviation for that word. ◻ *AIDS stands for Acquired Immune Deficiency Syndrome.* ◻ PHR-VERB The ideas or attitudes that someone or something **stands for** are the ones that they support or represent. ◻ *What does the Democratic Party stand for?* ◻ PHR-VERB If you will **not stand for** something, you will not allow it to happen or continue. ◻ *We won't stand for this bad behavior anymore.*
▸ **stand in** ◻ PHR-VERB If you **stand in for** someone, you take their place or do their job, because they are sick or away. ◻ *I had to stand in for her on Tuesday when she was sick.* ◻ → see also **stand-in**
▸ **stand out** PHR-VERB If something **stands out**, it is very noticeable. ◻ *The black necklace stood out against her white dress.*
▸ **stand up** ◻ → see **stand** ① 1, 2 ◻ PHR-VERB If something such as a claim or a piece of evidence **stands up**, it is accepted as true or satisfactory after being carefully examined. ◻ *He gave the police a lot of information, but none of it stood up in court.*

▶ **stand up for** PHR-VERB If you **stand up for** someone or something, you defend them and make your feelings or opinions very clear. ❑ *They stood up for what they believed to be right.*

▶ **stand up to** ■ PHR-VERB If something **stands up to** bad conditions, it is not damaged or harmed by them. ❑ *Is this building going to stand up to the strong winds?* ② PHR-VERB If you **stand up to** someone more powerful than you, you defend yourself against their attacks or demands. ❑ *He was too afraid to stand up to her.*

**stand|ard** /stǽndərd/ (**standards**) ■ N-COUNT A **standard** is a level of quality or achievement, especially a level that is thought to be acceptable. ❑ *The standard of his work is very low.* ② N-PLURAL **Standards** are moral principles which affect people's attitudes and behavior. ❑ *My father always had high moral standards.* ③ ADJ You use **standard** to describe things which are usual and normal. ❑ *It's just a standard size car.* [from Old French]

| Word Partnership | Use *standard* with : |
| --- | --- |
| v. | **become a** standard, **maintain a** standard, **meet a** standard, **raise a** standard, **set a** standard, **use a** standard ■ ② |
| N. | standard **of excellence**, **industry** standard ■ ② standard **English**, standard **equipment**, standard **practice**, standard **procedure** ③ |

**stand|ard Ameri|can Eng|lish** N-UNCOUNT **Standard American English** is the form of English that is spoken by most people in the United States.

**stan|dard de|via|tion** (**standard deviations**) N-VAR The **standard deviation** of a set of data is a statistical measure of how much variation there is in the data. [TECHNICAL]

**stand|ard|ize** /stǽndərdaɪz/ (**standardizes, standardizing, standardized**) V-T To **standardize** things means to change them so that they all have the same features. ❑ *They should standardize the parts so they fit any machine.* ● **stand|ardi|za|tion** /stǽndərdɪzeɪʃⁿn/ N-UNCOUNT ❑ *...the standardization of working hours.* [from Old French]

**stand|ard of liv|ing** (**standards of living**) N-COUNT Your **standard of living** is the level of comfort and wealth which you have. ❑ *We're trying to improve their standard of living.*

**stand|by** /stǽndbaɪ/ (**standbys**) also **stand-by** ■ N-COUNT A **standby** is something or someone that is always ready to be used if they are needed. ❑ *Canned vegetables are a good standby.* ② PHRASE If someone or something is **on standby**, they are ready to be used if they are needed. ❑ *Five ambulances are on standby.* ③ ADJ A **standby** ticket for something such as the theater or a plane trip is a cheap ticket that you buy just before the performance starts or the plane takes off, if there are still some seats left. ❑ *He bought a standby ticket to New York and flew to JFK airport six hours later.* ● **Standby** is also an adverb. ❑ *Magda was going to fly standby.*

**stand-in** (**stand-ins**) N-COUNT A **stand-in** is a person who takes someone else's place or does someone else's job for a while, for example because the other person is sick or away. ❑ *He was*

*a stand-in for my regular doctor.*

**stand|ing** /stǽndɪŋ/ (**standings**) ■ N-UNCOUNT Someone's **standing** is their reputation or status. ❑ *...an artist of international standing.* ❑ *He improved his country's standing abroad.* ② ADJ You use **standing** to describe something which is always there. ❑ *We have a standing invitation to stay at their home.* [from Old English] ③ → see also **long-standing**

**stand|ing wave** (**standing waves**) N-COUNT A **standing wave** is a wave such as a sound wave that appears not to move, because another wave of the same frequency is traveling in the opposite direction. [TECHNICAL]

**stand|off** /stǽndɔf/ (**standoffs**) N-COUNT A **standoff** is a situation in which neither of two opposing groups or forces will make a move until the other one does something, so nothing can happen until one of them gives way. ❑ *There was a standoff between the crowd and the police.*

**stand|point** /stǽndpɔɪnt/ (**standpoints**) N-COUNT From a particular **standpoint** means looking at an event, situation, or idea in a particular way. ❑ *From a business standpoint, this is a great deal.*

**stand|still** /stǽndstɪl/ N-SING If movement or activity comes **to** or is brought to **a standstill**, it stops completely. ❑ *The cars came to a standstill.*

**stand-up** also **standup** ■ ADJ A **stand-up** comic or comedian stands alone in front of an audience and tells jokes. ❑ *He can do jokes — he could be a stand-up comic.* ② N-UNCOUNT **Stand-up** is stand-up comedy. ❑ *It takes a lot of courage to do stand-up.*

**stank** /stǽŋk/ **Stank** is a past tense of **stink**.

**sta|ple** /steɪpⁿl/ (**staples, stapling, stapled**) ■ ADJ A **staple** food, product, or activity is one that is basic and important in people's everyday lives. ❑ *Rice is the staple food of more than half the world's population.* ● **Staple** is also a noun. ❑ *Fish is a staple in the diet of many Africans.* ② N-COUNT **Staples** are small pieces of bent wire that are used mainly for holding sheets of paper together firmly. You put the staples into the paper using a device called a stapler. ③ V-T If you **staple** something, you fasten it to something else or fix it in place using staples. ❑ *Staple some sheets of paper together.* [Sense 1 from Middle Dutch. Senses 2 and 3 from Old English.]

**sta|pler** /steɪplər/ (**plural**) N-COUNT A **stapler** is a device used for putting staples into sheets of paper. [from Old English]

stapler

**star** /stɑr/ (**stars, starring, starred**) ■ N-COUNT A **star** is a large ball of burning gas in space. Stars appear to us as small points of light in the sky on clear nights. ❑ *Stars lit the sky.* ② N-COUNT You can refer to a shape or an object as a **star** when it has four, five, or more points sticking out of it in a regular pattern. ❑ *Children at school receive colored stars for good work.* ③ N-COUNT Famous actors, musicians, and sports players are often referred to as **stars**. ❑ *...star of the TV series "Friends."* ❑ *Murphy is Hollywood's top comedy*

**S**

## Word Web   star

North Star

**Astronomy** is the oldest science. It is the study of **stars** and other objects in the **night sky**. People sometimes confuse astronomy and **astrology**. Astrology is the belief that the stars affect people's lives. Long ago people named groups of stars after gods, heroes, and imaginary animals. One of the most famous of these **constellations** is the Big Dipper. Its original name meant "the big bear." It is easy to find and it points toward the **North Star***. For centuries sailors have used the North Star to **navigate**. The best-known star in our **galaxy** is the **sun**.

Big Dipper

*North Star: the star that the earth's northern axis points toward.*

**star.** 🔄 v-I If an actor or actress **stars in** a play or movie, he or she has one of the most important parts in it. ❑ *Adolphson starred in a play in which Ingrid had a part.* 🔼 v-T If a play or movie **stars** a famous actor or actress, he or she has one of the most important parts in it. ❑ *...a movie starring Anthony Quinn.* 🔼 N-PLURAL Predictions about people's lives which are based on astrology and appear regularly in a newspaper or magazine are sometimes referred to as **the stars**. ❑ *There was nothing in my stars to say I'd have travel problems!* [from Old English]
→ see Word Web: **star**
→ see **galaxy, navigation**

### Word Partnership   Use *star* with :

| | |
|---|---|
| ADJ. | **bright** star 🔟 |
| | **bronze** star, **gold** star 🔼 |
| | **big** star, **former** star, **rising** star 🔼 |
| N. | **all**-star **cast/game**, **basketball/football/tennis** star, **film/movie** star, **guest** star, **pop/rap** star, **TV** star 🔼 |
| | star **in a film/movie/show** 🔼 |

**star|board** /stɑrbərd, -bɔrd/ ADJ The **starboard** side of a ship or an aircraft is the right side when you are facing toward the front. [TECHNICAL] ❑ *He noticed a ship moving down the starboard side of the submarine.* [from Old English]

**starch** /stɑrtʃ/ (**starches**) 🔟 N-VAR **Starch** is a substance that is found in foods such as bread, potatoes, pasta, and rice, and that gives you energy. ❑ *You should eat less starch, salt, and fat.* 🔼 N-UNCOUNT **Starch** is a substance that is used for making cloth stiffer. ❑ *He never puts enough starch in my shirts.* [from Old English]
→ see **rice**

**star|dom** /stɑrdəm/ N-UNCOUNT **Stardom** is the state of being very famous, usually as an actor, musician, or athlete. ❑ *She gave up her chance of stardom when she married her husband.* [from Old English]

**stare** /stɛər/ (**stares, staring, stared**) v-I If you **stare at** someone or something, you look at them for a long time. ❑ *Ben continued to stare out the window.* ● **Stare** is also a noun. ❑ *Harry gave him a long stare.* [from Old English]

### Word Partnership   Use *stare* with :

| | |
|---|---|
| ADJ. | **blank** stare |
| V. | **continue to** stare, **turn to** stare |

**stark** /stɑrk/ (**starker, starkest**) 🔟 ADJ **Stark** choices or statements are harsh and unpleasant. ❑ *Companies face a stark choice if they want to succeed.* ● **stark|ly** ADV ❑ *"She never loved you," he said starkly.* 🔼 ADJ If two things are in **stark** contrast to one another, they are very different from each other. ❑ *His opinions were in stark contrast to my own.* [from Old English]

**Star of David** /stɑr əv deɪvɪd/ (**Stars of David**) N-COUNT The **Star of David** is a six-pointed star that is a symbol of Judaism and the state of Israel. ❑ *Sarah wears a Star of David around her neck.*

**start** /stɑrt/ (**starts, starting, started**) 🔟 v-T If you **start to** do something, you do something that you were not doing before. ❑ *I started to follow him up the stairs.* ❑ *Susanna started the work on the garden in 1956.* ● **Start** is also a noun. ❑ *After several starts, she read the report properly.* 🔼 v-T/v-I When something **starts**, or if someone **starts** it, it takes place from a particular time. ❑ *The fire started in an upstairs room.* ❑ *I started the day with a swim.* ● **Start** is also a noun. ❑ *...1918, four years after the start of the Great War.* 🔼 v-I You use **start** to say what your first job was. ❑ *Betty started as an office girl.* ● **Start off** means the same as **start**. ❑ *Mr. Dambar started off as an assistant to Mrs. Spear's husband.* 🔼 v-T When someone **starts** something such as a new business, they create it or cause it to begin. ❑ *George Granger has started a health center and he's looking for staff.* ● **Start up** means the same as **start**. ❑ *...the cost of starting up a day-care center for children.* 🔼 v-T/v-I If you **start** an engine, car, or machine, or if it **starts**, it begins to work. ❑ *He started the car, which hummed smoothly.* ● **Start up** means the same as **start**. ❑ *He started up the car and drove off.* ❑ *Turn the key to start the car up.* 🔼 v-I If you **start**, your body suddenly moves slightly as a result of surprise or fear. ❑ *She banged the bottle down on the table. He started at the sound.* ● **Start** is also a noun. ❑ *Sylvia woke with a start.* 🔼 → see also **head start, false start** 🔼 PHRASE You use **for a start** or **to start with** to introduce the first of a number of things or reasons that you want to mention or could mention. ❑ *You need her name and address, and that's*

S

a problem for a start. [from Old English] **5** to **get off to a flying start** → see **flying**

▶ **start off 1** PHR-VERB If you **start off by** doing something, you do it as the first part of an activity. ❑ *She started off by clearing some space on the table.* **2** → see **start 3**

▶ **start on** PHR-VERB If you **start on** something that needs to be done, you start dealing with it. ❑ *Before you start on the cleaning, put on some old clothes.*

▶ **start out 1** PHR-VERB If someone or something **starts out as** a particular thing, they are that thing at the beginning although they change later. ❑ *Daly started out as a salesman.* **2** PHR-VERB If you **start out by** doing something, you do it at the beginning of an activity. ❑ *I always start out by saying clearly what I want.*

▶ **start over** PHR-VERB If you **start over** or **start** something **over**, you begin something again from the beginning. ❑ *I did it all wrong and had to start over.*

▶ **start up** → see **start 4, 5**

| Thesaurus | *start* | Also look up : |
| --- | --- | --- |
| v. | begin, commence, originate **1** **2** | |
| | establish, found, launch **4** | |
| n. | beginning, onset **1** **2** | |
| | jump, scare, shock **6** | |

**start|ing point** (**starting points**) also **starting-point** N-COUNT Something that is a **starting point for** a discussion or process can be used to begin it or act as a basis for it. ❑ *It seemed like a good starting point for the book.*

**star|tle** /stɑrt³l/ (**startles, startling, startled**) V-T If something sudden and unexpected **startles** you, it surprises and frightens you slightly. ● *The telephone startled him.* ● **star|tled** ADJ ❑ *Martha gave her a startled look.* [from Old English]

**star|tling** /stɑrt³lɪŋ/ ADJ Something that is **startling** is so different, unexpected, or remarkable that people react to it with surprise. ❑ *Sometimes the results are startling.* [from Old English]

**starve** /stɑrv/ (**starves, starving, starved**) **1** V-I If people **starve**, they suffer greatly from lack of food which sometimes leads to their death. ❑ *A number of the prisoners are starving.* ❑ *In the 1930s, millions of Ukrainians starved to death.* ● **star|va|tion** /stɑrveɪʃ°n/ N-UNCOUNT ❑ *Over three hundred people died of starvation.* **2** V-T To **starve** someone means not to give them any food. ❑ *He was starving himself.* **3** V-T If a person or thing **is starved of** something that they need, they are suffering because they are not getting enough of it. ❑ *She felt awful, starved of his love.* [from Old English]

**starv|ing** /stɑrvɪŋ/ ADJ If you say that you are **starving**, you mean that you are very hungry. [INFORMAL] ❑ *Does anyone have any food? I'm starving.* [from Old English]

**stash** /stæʃ/ (**stashes, stashing, stashed**) **1** V-T If you **stash** something valuable in a secret place, you store it there to keep it safe. [INFORMAL] ❑ *She stashed the money in her bedroom.* **2** N-COUNT A **stash of** something valuable is a secret store of it. [INFORMAL] ❑ *...a stash of diamonds.*

**state** /steɪt/ (**states, stating, stated**) **1** N-COUNT You can refer to countries as **states**, particularly when you are discussing politics.

❑ *...a socialist state.* **2** N-COUNT Some large countries such as the U.S. are divided into smaller areas called **states**. ❑ *Leaders of the Southern states are meeting in Louisville.* **3** N-PROPER The U.S. is sometimes referred to as **the States**. [INFORMAL] ❑ *She bought it in the States.* ❑ *The went on vaction to the States.* **4** N-SING You can refer to the government of a country as **the state**. ❑ *In Sweden, child care is provided by the state.* **5** ADJ A **state** occasion is a formal one involving the head of a country. ❑ *The president of the Czech Republic is in Washington on a state visit.* **6** N-COUNT When you talk about the **state** of someone or something, you are referring to the condition they are in or what they are like at a particular time. ❑ *For the first few months after Daniel died, I was in a state of shock.* **7** V-T If you **state** something, you say or write it in a formal or definite way. ❑ *Clearly state your address and telephone number.* ❑ *The police report stated that he was arrested for stealing a car.* **8** PHRASE **States of matter** are the different physical forms in which substances can exist. The most common states of matter are solid, liquid, and gas. [from Old French] **9** → see also **head of state**

→ see **matter**

| Thesaurus | *state* | Also look up : |
| --- | --- | --- |
| N. | government, land, nation, republic, sovereignty **1** | |
| | attitude, condition, mood, situation **6** | |
| v. | articulate, express, narrate, relate, say, tell **7** | |

**state line** (**state lines**) N-COUNT A **state line** is a border between two states within a country. ❑ *Then they crossed the state line into Mississippi.*

**state|ly** /steɪtli/ ADJ Something or someone that is **stately** is impressive and graceful or dignified. ❑ *He was moving at a stately pace.* [from Old French]

**state|ment** /steɪtmənt/ (**statements**) **1** N-COUNT A **statement** is something that you say or write which gives information in a formal or definite way. ❑ *I was very angry when I made that statement.* **2** N-COUNT A printed document showing how much money has been paid into and taken out of a bank or investment account is called a **statement**. ❑ *...the address at the top of your monthly statement.* [from Old French]

**state of af|fairs** N-SING If you refer to a particular **state of affairs**, you mean the general situation and circumstances connected with someone or something. ❑ *This is a terrible state of affairs.*

**state of emer|gen|cy** (**states of emergency**) N-COUNT If a government declares a **state of emergency** in an area, it introduces special measures such as increased powers for the police or army, usually because of civil disorder or because of a natural disaster such as an earthquake. ❑ *The government declared a state of emergency in New Orleans.*

**state of mind** (**states of mind**) N-COUNT Your **state of mind** is your mood or mental state at a particular time. ❑ *I want you to get into a whole new state of mind.*

**state-of-the-art** ADJ If you describe something as **state-of-the-art**, you mean that it is the best available because it has been made using

**S**

the most modern techniques and technology. ❑ *...a state-of-the-art computer.*
→ see **technology**

**State of the Un|ion** N-UNCOUNT A **State of the Union** speech or address is a speech, given once a year, in which the president of the United States talks about the current political issues that affect the country as a whole and about his plans for the year ahead. ❑ *In his State of the Union message, the president talked about change.*

**state school** (**state schools**) N-COUNT In the United States, a **state school** is a college or university that is part of the public education system provided by the state government.

**states|man** /steɪtsmən/ (**statesmen**) N-COUNT A **statesman** is an important and experienced politician, especially one who is widely known and respected. ❑ *Hamilton is a great statesman and political thinker.*

**state trooper** (**state troopers**) N-COUNT In the U.S., a **state trooper** is a member of the police force in one of the states. ❑ *State troopers said the truck driver was going too fast.*

**state uni|ver|sity** (**state universities**) N-COUNT A **state university** is the same as a **state school**. ❑ *He was a professor at the local state university.*

**Word Link** stat ≈ standing : static, station, stationary

**stat|ic** /stætɪk/ ■ ADJ Something that is **static** does not move or change. ❑ *The number of people without work has remained static.* ■ N-UNCOUNT **Static** or **static electricity** is electricity which collects on things such as your body or metal objects. ❑ *When the weather turns cold and dry, my clothes develop a static problem.* ■ N-UNCOUNT If there is **static** on the radio or television, you hear a series of loud noises which spoils the sound. ❑ *...the static on the radio.* [from New Latin]

**sta|tion** /steɪʃⁿ/ (**stations, stationing, stationed**) ■ N-COUNT A **station** or a train **station** is a building by a railroad track where trains stop so that people can get on or off. ❑ *Ingrid went with him to the train station.* ■ N-COUNT A bus **station** is a building, usually in a town or city, where buses stop, usually for a while, so that people can get on or off. ❑ *I walked to the bus station and bought a ticket home.* ■ N-COUNT If you talk about a particular radio or television **station**, you are referring to the company that broadcasts programs. ❑ *...a local radio station.* ■ V-T PASSIVE If soldiers or officials **are stationed** in a place, they are sent there to do a job or to work for a period of time. ❑ *Troops are stationed on the streets.* [from Old French] ■ → see also **gas station, police station, power station, space station**
→ see **cellphone, radio, television**

**Word Partnership** Use station with :

| | |
|---|---|
| N. | **railroad** station, **subway** station ■ |
| | **radio** station, **television/TV** station ■ |
| ADJ. | **local** station ■ |

**sta|tion|ary** /steɪʃənɛri/ ADJ Something that is **stationary** is not moving. ❑ *...a stationary line of vehicles.* [from Latin]

**sta|tion|ery** /steɪʃənɛri/ N-UNCOUNT **Stationery** is paper, envelopes, and other

materials or equipment used for writing. ❑ *...paper and other office stationery.* [from Old French]
→ see **office**

**sta|tion house** (**station houses**) N-COUNT A **station house** is a police station or a fire station, or a building that is attached to a police station or a fire station. ❑ *They were taken in a police van to the station house.*

**sta|tion mod|el** (**station models**) N-COUNT A **station model** is a weather map containing symbols that represent the weather conditions around a particular weather station. [TECHNICAL]

**sta|tion wag|on** (**station wagons**) N-COUNT A **station wagon** is a car with a long body, a door at the rear, and space behind the back seats.

station wagon

**sta|tis|tic** /stətɪstɪk/ (**statistics**) ■ N-COUNT **Statistics** are facts which are obtained from analyzing information and are expressed in numbers. ❑ *Statistics show that wages are rising.* ● **sta|tis|ti|cal** ADJ ❑ *The report contains a lot of statistical information.* ● **sta|tis|ti|cal|ly** /stətɪstɪkli/ ADV ❑ *The results are not statistically correct.* ■ N-UNCOUNT **Statistics** is a branch of mathematics concerned with the study of information that is expressed in numbers. ❑ *...a professor of mathematical statistics.* [from German]

**statue** /stætʃu/ (**statues**) N-COUNT A **statue** is a large sculpture of a person or an animal, made of stone or metal. ❑ *...a stone statue of a horse.* [from Old French]

**stat|ure** /stætʃər/ ■ N-UNCOUNT Someone's **stature** is their height. ❑ *Mother was of very small stature.* ■ N-UNCOUNT The **stature** of a person is the importance and reputation that they have. ❑ *...his stature as the world's greatest opera singer.* [from Old French]

**sta|tus** /steɪtəs, stæt-/ ■ N-UNCOUNT Your **status** is your social or professional position. ❑ *...women and men of status.* ■ N-UNCOUNT The **status** of someone or something is the importance that people give them. ❑ *Nurses do not have the same status as doctors.* ■ N-UNCOUNT **Status** is an official description that gives a person, organization, or place particular rights or advantages. ❑ *They were proud of their status as guards.* [from Latin]

**Word Partnership** Use status with :

| | |
|---|---|
| V. | **achieve** status, **maintain/preserve** one's status ■ |
| N. | **celebrity** status, **wealth and** status ■ ■ |
| | **change of** status ■ – ■ |
| | **marital** status, **tax** status ■ |
| ADJ. | **current** status ■ – ■ |
| | **economic** status, **financial** status ■ |

**sta|tus quo** /steɪtəs kwoʊ, stæt-/ N-SING The **status quo** is the state of affairs that exists at a particular time. ❑ *They wanted to keep the status quo.*

S

**stat|ute** /stǽtʃut/ (**statutes**) N-VAR A **statute** is a rule or law which has been formally written down. ❑ *The new statute is about the protection of children.* [from Old French]

**stat|ute of limi|ta|tions** (**statutes of limitations**) N-COUNT If there is a **statute of limitations on** a legal case such as a crime, people can no longer be accused after a certain period of time has passed. ❑ *The statute of limitations on most crimes is five years.*

**statu|tory** /stǽtʃutɔri/ ADJ **Statutory** means relating to rules or laws which have been formally written down. [FORMAL] ❑ *...statutory law.* [from Old French]

**staunch** /stɔntʃ/ (**stauncher, staunchest**) ADJ A **staunch** supporter or believer is very loyal to a person, organization, or set of beliefs, and supports them strongly. ❑ *He's a staunch supporter of the Republican party.* ● **staunch|ly** ADV ❑ *He was staunchly against the idea.* [from Old French]

**stave** /steɪv/ (**staves, staving, staved**)
▶ **stave off** PHR-VERB If you **stave off** something bad, or if you **stave** it **off**, you succeed in stopping it from happening for a while. ❑ *He didn't earn enough money to stave off hunger.* ❑ *We'll never be able to solve the problem, we can only stave it off.*

**stay** /steɪ/ (**stays, staying, stayed**) **1** V-I If you **stay** where you are, you continue to be there and do not leave. ❑ *"Stay here," Trish said. "I'll bring the car to you."* **2** V-T/V-I If you **stay** in a city, or hotel, or at someone's house, you live there for a short time. ❑ *Gordon stayed at The Park Hotel, Milan.* ❑ *Can't you stay a few more days?* ● **Stay** is also a noun. ❑ *Please contact the hotel reception if you have any problems during your stay.* **3** V-LINK If someone or something **stays** in a particular state or situation, they continue to be in it. ❑ *If you want to stay ahead you have to work hard.* ❑ *...classes on how to stay healthy.* **4** V-I If you **stay away from** a place, you do not go there. ❑ *Most workers stayed away from work during the strike.* **5** V-I If you **stay out of** something, you do not get involved in it. ❑ *I try to stay out of other people's arguments.* **6** PHRASE If you **stay put**, you remain somewhere. ❑ *I want you to stay put while I go and find out what's happening.* [from Anglo-French]
▶ **stay in** PHR-VERB If you **stay in** during the evening, you remain at home and do not go out. ❑ *We decided to stay in and have dinner at home.*
▶ **stay on** PHR-VERB If you **stay on** somewhere, you remain there after other people have left or after the time when you were going to leave. ❑ *He arranged to stay on in Adelaide.*
▶ **stay out** PHR-VERB If you **stay out** at night, you remain away from home, especially when you are expected to be there. ❑ *That was the first time Elliot stayed out all night.*
▶ **stay up** PHR-VERB If you **stay up**, you remain out of bed at a later time than normal. ❑ *I used to stay up late with my mom and watch movies.*

**stead** /stɛd/ PHRASE If you say that something will **stand** someone **in good stead**, you mean that it will be very useful to them in the future. ❑ *These two games will stand them in good stead for the future.* [from Old English]

**stead|fast** /stɛdfæst/ ADJ If someone is **steadfast** in something that they are doing, they are convinced that what they are doing is right and they refuse to change it or to give up. ❑ *He*

*remains steadfast in his belief that he did the right thing.* ● **stead|fast|ly** ADV ❑ *She steadfastly refused to look at him.* [from Old English]

| **Word Link** | stead ≈ place, stand : home*stead*, in*stead*, stead*y* |
|---|---|

**steady** /stɛdi/ (**steadier, steadiest, steadies, steadying, steadied**) **1** ADJ A **steady** situation continues or develops gradually without any interruptions and is not likely to change quickly. ❑ *...the steady progress of the building work.* ❑ *The improvement in standards has been steady.* ● **steadi|ly** /stɛdɪli/ ADV ❑ *Relax and keep breathing steadily.* **2** ADJ If an object is **steady**, it is firm and does not shake or move around. ❑ *Hold the camera steady.* **3** ADJ If you look at someone or speak to them in a **steady** way, you look or speak in a calm, controlled way. ❑ *"Well, go on," said Camilla, her voice steady.* ● **steadi|ly** ADV ❑ *He stared steadily at Elaine.* **4** V-T/V-I If you **steady** something or if it **steadies**, it stops shaking or moving around. ❑ *Two men were at the back of the house, steadying a ladder.* **5** V-T If you **steady yourself**, you control your voice or expression, so that people will think that you are calm and not nervous. ❑ *Somehow she steadied herself.* [from Old High German]

| **Thesaurus** | steady | Also look up : |
|---|---|---|

| ADJ. | consistent, continuous, uninterrupted **1** constant, fixed, stable **2** calm, cool, reserved, sedate **3** |
|---|---|

| **Word Partnership** | Use *steady* with : |
|---|---|

| N. | steady **decline/increase**, steady **diet**, steady **growth**, steady **improvement**, steady **income**, steady **progress**, steady **rain**, steady **rate**, steady **supply 1** |
|---|---|
| V. | **remain** steady **1 2** **hold/keep** *something* steady **2** |

**steak** /steɪk/ (**steaks**) **1** N-VAR A **steak** is a large flat piece of beef without much fat on it. You cook it by grilling or frying it. ❑ *...a steak cooking on the grill.* **2** N-COUNT A fish **steak** is a large piece of fish that contains few bones. ❑ *...fresh salmon steaks.* [from Old Norse]

**steal** /stil/ (**steals, stealing, stole, stolen**) V-T/ V-I If you **steal** something **from** someone, you take it away from them without their permission and without intending to return it. ❑ *They said he stole a small boy's bicycle.* ❑ *It's wrong to steal.* ● **steal|ing** N-UNCOUNT ❑ *She was put in jail for stealing.* ● **sto|len** /stoʊlən/ ADJ ❑ *We have now found the stolen car.* [from Old English]

**steam** /stim/ (**steams, steaming, steamed**) **1** N-UNCOUNT **Steam** is the hot mist that forms when water boils. **Steam** vehicles and machines are operated using steam as a means of power. ❑ *The heat converts water into steam.* **2** V-I If something **steams**, it gives off steam. ❑ *Coffee pots steamed on their burners.* **3** V-T/V-I If you **steam** food or if it **steams**, you cook it in steam rather than in water. ❑ *Steam the carrots until they are slightly soft.* ❑ *Leave the vegetables to steam over the rice.* **4** PHRASE If you **run out of steam**, you stop doing something because you have no more energy or enthusiasm left. [INFORMAL] ❑ *I decided to paint the bathroom but ran out of steam halfway*

S

*through.* [from Old English]
→ see **cook**

**Word Partnership** Use *steam* with :

N.    steam **bath**, **clouds of** steam, steam
      **engine**, steam **pipes**, steam
      **turbine** 🔢
ADJ.  steam **powered**, **rising** steam 🔢

**steam|er** /stimər/ (**steamers**) 🔢 N-COUNT A
**steamer** is a ship that has an engine powered
by steam. 🔢 N-COUNT A **steamer** is a special
container used for steaming food such as
vegetables and fish. [from Old English]

**steamy** /stimi/ ADJ A **steamy** place has hot, wet
air. ❑ *...a steamy cafe.* [from Old English]

**steel** /stil/ (**steels, steeling, steeled**)
🔢 N-UNCOUNT **Steel** is a very strong metal which
is made mainly from iron. ❑ *...steel pipes.* ❑ *...the
iron and steel industry.* 🔢 → see also **stainless steel**
🔢 If you **steel yourself**, you prepare to deal
with something unpleasant. ❑ *They are steeling
themselves for the coming battle.* [from Old English]
→ see **bridge, train**

**steely** /stili/ ADJ **Steely** is used to emphasize
that a person is strong and determined. ❑ *The
Maryland players had a steely determination.* [from Old
English]

**steep** /stip/ (**steeper, steepest**) 🔢 ADJ A **steep**
slope rises at a very sharp angle and is difficult to
go up. ❑ *Some of the hills in San Francisco are very steep.*
● **steep|ly** ADV ❑ *The road climbs steeply.* 🔢 ADJ A
**steep** increase or decrease in something is a very
big increase or decrease. ❑ *There have been steep
price increases.* ● **steep|ly** ADV ❑ *Unemployment is
rising steeply.* [from Old English]

**steeped** /stipt/ ADJ If a place or person is
**steeped in** a quality or characteristic, they are
surrounded by it or deeply influenced by it. ❑ *The
castle is steeped in history.* [from Old English]

**steer** /stiər/ (**steers, steering, steered**) 🔢 V-T
When you **steer** a car, boat, or plane, you control
it so that it goes in the direction that you want.
❑ *What is it like to steer a big ship?* 🔢 V-T If you **steer**
someone in a particular direction, you guide
them there. ❑ *Nick steered them into the nearest
seats.* 🔢 PHRASE If you **steer clear of** someone or
something, you deliberately avoid them. ❑ *We
steered clear of the subject of religion.* [from Old
English]

**steer|ing wheel** (**steering wheels**) N-COUNT
In a car or other vehicle, the **steering wheel** is the
wheel which the driver holds when he or she is
driving.

**stem** /stɛm/ (**stems, stemming, stemmed**)
🔢 V-I If a condition or problem **stems from**
something, it was caused originally by that
thing. ❑ *All my problems stem from my childhood.*
🔢 V-T If you **stem** something, you stop it from
spreading, increasing, or continuing. [FORMAL]
❑ *She tied some cloth around his arm to try to stem the
flow of blood.* 🔢 N-COUNT The **stem** of a plant is
the thin, upright part on which the flowers and
leaves grow. ❑ *He cut the stem and gave her the flower.*
[Senses 1 and 3 from Old English. Sense 2 from Old
Norse.]
→ see **flower**

**Word Partnership** Use *stem* with :

N.    **charges** stem **from** *something*, **problems**
      stem **from** *something* 🔢
      stem **the flow of** *something*, stem **losses**,
      stem **the** *something* 🔢

**stench** /stɛntʃ/ (**stenches**) N-COUNT A **stench** is
a strong and very unpleasant smell. ❑ *...the stench
of burning rubber.* [from Old English]

**sten|cil** /stɛnsəl/ (**stencils, stenciling,**
**stenciling, stenciled** or **stencilled**) 🔢 N-COUNT A
**stencil** is a piece of paper, plastic, or metal which
has a design cut out of it. You place the stencil on
a surface and paint it so that paint goes through
the holes and leaves a design on the surface. 🔢 V-T
If you **stencil** a design or if you **stencil** a surface
**with** a design, you put a design on a surface using
a stencil. ❑ *He stenciled the ceiling with a moon and
stars.* [from Old French]

**ste|nog|ra|pher** /stənɒgrəfər/ (**stenographers**)
N-COUNT A **stenographer** is a person who types
and writes shorthand, usually in an office.

**step** /stɛp/ (**steps, stepping, stepped**)
🔢 N-COUNT If you take a **step**, you lift your foot
and put it down in a different place, for example
when you are walking. ❑ *I took a step toward
him.* ❑ *She walked on a few steps.* 🔢 V-I If you **step**
**on** something or **step** in a particular direction,
you put your foot on the thing or move your foot
in that direction. ❑ *Neil Armstrong was the first
man to step on the Moon.* ❑ *Doug stepped sideways.*
🔢 N-COUNT A **step** is a raised flat surface, often
one of a series, on which you put your feet in order
to walk up or down to a different level. ❑ *This little
room was along a passage and down some steps.* ❑ *A
little girl was sitting on the step of the house.* 🔢 → see
also **doorstep** 🔢 N-COUNT A **step** is one of a
series of actions that you take in order to achieve
something. ❑ *The agreement is the first step toward
peace.* 🔢 PHRASE If you stay **one step ahead of**
someone or something, you manage to achieve
more than they do or avoid competition or danger
from them. ❑ *Teachers should always keep one step
ahead of their students.* 🔢 PHRASE If people are **in**
**step with** each other, their ideas or opinions are
the same. If they are **out of step with** each other,
their ideas or opinions are different. ❑ *Colorado is
in step with other states around the country.* 🔢 PHRASE
If you do something **step by step**, you do it by
progressing gradually from one stage to the next.
❑ *I am not rushing things and I'm taking it step by step.*
[from Old English]

▶ **step aside** → see **step down**

▶ **step back** PHR-VERB If you **step back** and think
about a situation, you think about it as if you were
not involved in it. ❑ *I stepped back and thought about
the situation.*

▶ **step down** or **step aside** PHR-VERB If someone
**steps down** or **steps aside**, they resign from an
important job or position. ❑ *He stepped down as the
trial judge.*

▶ **step in** PHR-VERB If you **step in**, you get involved
in a difficult situation because you think you
can or should help with it. ❑ *If no agreement was
reached, the army would step in.*

▶ **step up** PHR-VERB If you **step up** something,
you increase it or increase its intensity. ❑ *We need
to step up our efforts to save energy.*

---

| **Word Partnership** | Use *step* with : |
| --- | --- |

ADV. step **outside** 2
step **ahead**, step **backward**, step **closer**,
step **forward** 2 5

ADJ. **big** step, **bold** step, **critical** step, **giant**
step, **important** step, **positive** step, **the**
**right** step 4

N. step **in a process** 4

---

| **Word Link** | *step ≈ related by remarriage :* |
| --- | --- |
| | *stepfamily, stepfather, stepmother* |

**step|family** /stɛpfæmɪli, -fæmli/
(**stepfamilies**) N-COUNT A **stepfamily** is a family
that consists of a husband and wife and one
or more children from a previous marriage or
relationship. ❑ *Stepfamilies are much more common*
*than they used to be.*

**step|father** /stɛpfɑðər/ (**stepfathers**) also
step-father N-COUNT Someone's **stepfather** is
the man who has married their mother after the
death or divorce of their father.

**step|mother** /stɛpmʌðər/ (**stepmothers**) also
step-mother N-COUNT Someone's **stepmother**
is the woman who married their father after
the death or divorce of their mother.

**step|ping stone** (**stepping stones**) also
stepping-stone or steppingstone 1 N-COUNT
You can describe a job or event as a **stepping stone**
when it helps you to make progress, especially in
your career. ❑ *It is a stepping stone to bigger and better*
*things.* 2 N-COUNT **Stepping stones** are a line of
large stones which you can walk on in order to
cross a shallow stream or river.

**ste|reo** /stɛriou, stɪər-/ (**stereos**) 1 ADJ **Stereo**
is used to describe a sound system in which the
sound is played through two speakers. Compare
**mono.** ❑ *…equipment that gives stereo sound.*
2 N-COUNT A **stereo** is a CD player with two
speakers.

**ste|reo|type** /stɛriətaɪp, stɪər-/ (**stereotypes,**
**stereotyping, stereotyped**) 1 N-COUNT A
**stereotype** is a fixed general image or set of
characteristics that a lot of people believe
represents a particular type of person or thing.
❑ *There's always been a stereotype about successful*
*businessmen.* 2 V-T If someone **is stereotyped** as
something, people form a fixed general idea or
image of them, so that it is assumed that they will
behave in a particular way. ❑ *He was stereotyped by*
*some people as a trouble-maker.* [from French]

**ster|ile** /stɛrəl/ 1 ADJ Something that is **sterile**
is completely clean and free from germs. ❑ *Cover*
*the cut with a sterile bandage.* ● **ste|ril|ity** /stərɪlɪti/
N-UNCOUNT ❑ *…the sterility of the hospital.* 2 ADJ A
person or animal that is **sterile** is unable to have
or produce babies. ❑ *George was sterile.* ● **ste|ril|ity**
N-UNCOUNT ❑ *This disease causes sterility in both*
*males and females.* [from Latin]

**ster|i|lize** /stɛrɪlaɪz/ (**sterilizes, sterilizing,**
**sterilized**) 1 V-T If you **sterilize** a thing or a place,
you make it completely clean and free from germs.
❑ *Sterilize the needle by boiling it.* ● **steri|li|za|tion**
/stɛrɪlɪzeɪʃ⁰n/ N-UNCOUNT ❑ *…the sterilization of*
*milk.* 2 V-T If a person or an animal **is sterilized**,
they have a medical operation that makes it
impossible for them to have babies. ❑ *My wife*

*was sterilized after the birth of her fourth child.*
● **steri|li|za|tion** (**sterilizations**) N-VAR ❑ *Doctors*
*advised her to have a sterilization.* [from Latin]

**ster|ling** /stɜrlɪŋ/ 1 ADJ If you describe
someone's work or character as **sterling**, you mean
that it is very good. [FORMAL] ❑ *She has some sterling*
*qualities.* 2 N-UNCOUNT **Sterling** is the British
money system. ❑ *He paid for the goods in sterling.*
[from Old English]

**stern** /stɜrn/ (**sterner, sternest**) 1 ADJ **Stern**
words or actions are very severe. ❑ *He gave a stern*
*warning to people who leave garbage in the streets.*
● **stern|ly** ADV ❑ *"We will punish anyone who breaks*
*the rules," she said sternly.* 2 ADJ Someone who is
**stern** is very serious and strict. ❑ *Her father was a*
*stern man.* [from Old English]

**ster|oid** /stɪrɔɪd, stɛr-/ (**steroids**) N-COUNT A
**steroid** is a type of chemical substance found
in your body. Steroids can also be artificially
introduced into your body.

**stew** /stu/ (**stews, stewing, stewed**) 1 N-VAR A
**stew** is a meal which you make by cooking meat
and vegetables in liquid at a low temperature.
❑ *She gave him a bowl of beef stew.* 2 V-T When you
**stew** meat, vegetables, or fruit, you cook them
slowly in liquid in a covered pot. ❑ *Stew the apples*
*for half an hour.* [from Old French]

**stew|ard** /stuərd/ (**stewards**) 1 N-COUNT A
**steward** is a man who works on a ship, plane,
or train, taking care of passengers and serving
meals to them. 2 N-COUNT A **steward** is a man
or woman who helps to organize a race, march, or
other public event. ❑ *The steward at the march was*
*talking to a police officer.* [from Old English]

**stew|ard|ess** /stuərdɪs/ (**stewardesses**)
N-COUNT A **stewardess** is a woman who works on
a ship, plane, or train, taking care of passengers
and serving meals to them. This term is
considered old-fashioned and people generally
use **steward** when referring to men and women.
[from Old English]

---

**stick**

❶ NOUN USES
❷ VERB USES

---

❶ **stick** /stɪk/ (**sticks**) 1 N-COUNT A **stick** is
a thin branch which has fallen off a tree. ❑ *He*
*put some dry sticks on the fire.* 2 N-COUNT A **stick**
is a long thin piece of wood which is used for a
particular purpose. ❑ *…drum sticks.* 3 N-COUNT
Some long thin objects that are used in sports are
called **sticks.** ❑ *…a hockey stick.* 4 N-COUNT A **stick**
**of** something is a long thin piece of it. ❑ *…a stick of*
*celery.* [from Old English]

❷ **stick** /stɪk/ (**sticks, sticking, stuck**) 1 V-T If
you **stick** something somewhere, you put it there
in a rather casual way. [INFORMAL] ❑ *He folded the*
*papers and stuck them in his desk.* 2 V-T/V-I If you
**stick** a pointed object in something, or if it **sticks**
in something, it goes into it or through it. ❑ *The*
*nurse stuck a needle in my back.* 3 V-T If you **stick** one
thing to another, you attach it using glue, tape, or
another sticky substance. ❑ *Then stick your picture*
*on a piece of paper.* 4 V-I If one thing **sticks to**
another, it becomes attached to it and is difficult
to remove. ❑ *The paper sometimes sticks to the bottom*
*of the cake.* [from Old English] 5 → see also **stuck**
▶ **stick around** PHR-VERB If you **stick around**, you

S

stay where you are. [INFORMAL] ❑ *Stick around a while and see what happens.*

▸ **stick by** PHR-VERB If you **stick by** someone, you continue to give them help or support. ❑ *...friends who stuck by me during the difficult times.*

▸ **stick out** ◧ PHR-VERB If something **sticks out** or if you **stick** it **out**, it extends beyond something else. ❑ *She stuck out her tongue at him.* ◨ PHRASE If someone in an unpleasant or difficult situation **sticks it out**, they do not leave or give up. ❑ *I didn't like New York, but I decided to stick it out a little longer.*

▸ **stick to** ◧ PHR-VERB If you **stick to** something, you stay close to it or with it and do not change to something else. ❑ *Let's stick to the road we know.* ◨ V-VERB If you **stick to** a promise, agreement, decision, or principle, you do what you said you would do, or do not change your mind. ❑ *We are waiting to see if he sticks to his promise.*

▸ **stick together** PHR-VERB If people **stick together**, they stay with each other and support each other. ❑ *If we all stick together, we will be okay.*

▸ **stick up for** PHR-VERB If you **stick up for** a person or a principle, you support or defend them forcefully. ❑ *My father always sticks up for me.*

▸ **stick with** PHR-VERB If you **stick with** someone or something, you stay with them and do not change to something else. ❑ *If you're in a job that keeps you busy, stick with it.*

| Word Partnership | Use *stick* with : |
| --- | --- |
| ADV. | stick **together** ❷ ❸ |
| PREP. | stick **to** *something* ❷ ❹ |

**stick|er** /stɪkər/ (**stickers**) N-COUNT A **sticker** is a small piece of paper or plastic, with writing or a picture on one side, that you can stick onto a surface. ❑ *...a sticker that said, "I love Florida."* [from Old English]

**stick|er price** (**sticker prices**) N-COUNT The **sticker price** of an item, especially a car, is the price at which it is advertised. ❑ *This car has a sticker price of nearly $27,000.*

**stick|er shock** N-UNCOUNT **Sticker shock** is the shock you feel when you find out how expensive something is. ❑ *Get over the sticker shock and buy some good kitchen knives.*

**stick fig|ure** (**stick figures**) N-COUNT A **stick figure** is a simple drawing of a person that uses straight lines to show the arms and legs. ❑ *Claire drew a stick figure on a sheet of paper.*

**stick shift** (**stick shifts**) N-COUNT A **stick shift** is the lever that you use to change gear in a car or other vehicle.

**sticky** /stɪki/ (**stickier, stickiest**) ◧ ADJ A **sticky** substance is soft, or thick and liquid, and can stick to other things. **Sticky** things are covered with a sticky substance. ❑ *...sticky toffee.* ❑ *If the mixture is sticky, add more flour.* ◨ ADJ **Sticky** weather is unpleasantly hot and damp. ❑ *...four hot, sticky days in the middle of August.* ◩ ADJ A **sticky** situation involves problems or is embarrassing. [INFORMAL] ❑ *There were some sticky moments.*

**stiff** /stɪf/ (**stiffer, stiffest**) ◧ ADJ Something that is **stiff** is firm or does not bend easily. ❑ *The furniture was stiff and uncomfortable.* ❑ *His pants were new and stiff.* ● **stiff|ly** ADV ❑ *Moira sat stiffly upright in her chair.* ◨ ADJ Something such as a door or drawer that is **stiff** does not move as easily

as it should. ❑ *Train doors have stiff handles, so you cannot open them accidentally.* ◪ ADJ If you are **stiff**, your muscles or joints hurt when you move. ❑ *A hot bath is good for stiff muscles.* ● **stiff|ly** ADV ❑ *He climbed stiffly from the car.* ● **stiff|ness** N-UNCOUNT ❑ *...stiffness in the neck.* ◫ ADJ **Stiff** behavior is rather formal and not very friendly or relaxed. ❑ *They always seemed stiff and formal with each other.* ● **stiff|ly** ADV ❑ *"Why don't you borrow your sister's car?" said Cassandra stiffly.* ◧ ADJ **Stiff** means difficult or severe. ❑ *Despite stiff competition, they won the game.* ◪ ADV If you are bored **stiff**, worried **stiff**, or scared **stiff**, you are extremely bored, worried, or scared. [INFORMAL] ❑ *Anna tried to look interested, but she was bored stiff.* [from Old English]

**stiff|en** /stɪfᵊn/ (**stiffens, stiffening, stiffened**) ◧ V-I If you **stiffen**, you stop moving and stand or sit with muscles that are suddenly tense, for example because you feel afraid or angry. ❑ *Ada stiffened when she heard his voice.* ◨ V-T/V-I If your muscles or joints **stiffen**, or if something **stiffens** them, they become difficult to bend or move. ❑ *When muscles stiffen this affects the blood supply to your skin.* ● **Stiffen up** means the same as **stiffen**. ❑ *These clothes stiffen up the whole body.* ◩ V-T If something such as cloth **is stiffened**, it is made firm so that it does not bend easily. ❑ *They stiffen the paper with a kind of paste.* [from Old English]

**sti|fle** /staɪfᵊl/ (**stifles, stifling, stifled**) V-T To **stifle** something means to stop it from happening or continuing. ❑ *He stifled a laugh.* ❑ *The clouds did not stifle the heat.* [from Old French]

**sti|fling** /staɪflɪŋ/ ◧ ADJ **Stifling** heat is so intense that it makes you feel uncomfortable. ❑ *The stifling heat of the little room made me feel sick.* ◨ ADJ If a situation is **stifling**, it makes you feel uncomfortable because you cannot do what you want. ❑ *Life at home with her parents was stifling.* [from Old French]

**stig|ma** /stɪgmə/ (**stigmas**) ◧ N-VAR If something has a **stigma** attached to it, people think it is something to be ashamed of. ❑ *There is still a stigma attached to cancer.* ◨ N-COUNT The **stigma** of a flower is the top of the center part which takes in pollen. [TECHNICAL] [from Latin]

**stig|ma|tize** /stɪgmətaɪz/ (**stigmatizes, stigmatizing, stigmatized**) V-T If someone or something **is stigmatized**, they are unfairly regarded by many people as being bad or having something to be ashamed of. ❑ *Although he was not imprisoned, he felt stigmatized at work.* [from Latin]

**sti|let|to** /stɪlɛtoʊ/ (**stilettos**) N-COUNT **Stilettos** are women's shoes that have high, very narrow heels. ❑ *She took off her sneakers and put on a pair of stilettos.* [from Italian]

---

### still

| ❶ ADVERB USES |
| --- |
| ❷ NOT MOVING OR MAKING A NOISE |

**❶ still** /stɪl/ ◧ ADV If a situation that used to exist **still** exists, it has continued and exists now. ❑ *I still love Simon.* ❑ *Brian's toe is still badly swollen.* ◨ ADV If something that has not yet happened could **still** happen, it is possible that it will happen. ❑ *They could still win the game.* ❑ *We could still get there before dinner.* ◩ ADV You use **still** to emphasize that something is true in spite of what you have just said. ❑ *My weight is average. But I still feel I'm fatter than I should be.* **4** ADV You use **still** to indicate that a problem or difficulty is not really worth worrying about. ❑ *I didn't know where I was. Still, I had a map.* **5** ADV You use **still** in expressions such as **still further**, **still another**, and **still more** to show that you find the number or quantity of things you are referring to surprising or excessive. ❑ *We need to improve still further.* **6** ADV You use **still** with comparatives to indicate that something has even more of a quality than something else. ❑ *It's good to travel, but it's better still to come home.* [from Old English]

**❷ still** /stɪl/ (**stiller, stillest**) **1** ADJ If you stay **still**, you stay in the same position and do not move. ❑ *He played the tape through once, then stayed very still for several minutes.* **2** ADJ If something is **still**, there is no movement or activity there. ❑ *Inside the room it was very still.* ● **still|ness** N-UNCOUNT ❑ *...the stillness of the night air.* [from Old English]

**still life** (**still lifes**) N-VAR A **still life** is a painting or drawing of an arrangement of objects such as flowers or fruit. **Still life** refers to this type of painting or drawing. ❑ *...a still life by a French artist.* → see **painting**

**stimu|lant** /stɪmyələnt/ (**stimulants**) N-COUNT A **stimulant** is a drug that makes your body work faster, often increasing your heart rate and making you less likely to sleep. ❑ *It is not a good idea to take stimulants when you are tired.* [from Latin]

**stimu|late** /stɪmyəleɪt/ (**stimulates, stimulating, stimulated**) **1** V-T To **stimulate** something means to encourage it to begin or develop further. ❑ *America is trying to stimulate its economy.* ● **stimu|la|tion** /stɪmyəleɪʃ³n/ N-UNCOUNT ❑ *...an economy in need of stimulation.* **2** V-T If you **are stimulated by** something, it makes you feel full of ideas and enthusiasm. ❑ *Bill was stimulated by the challenge.* ● **stimu|lat|ing** ADJ ❑ *It is a stimulating book.* ● **stimu|la|tion** N-UNCOUNT ❑ *Many people enjoy the stimulation of a difficult job.* **3** V-T If something **stimulates** a part of a person's body, it causes it to move or start working. ❑ *Exercise stimulates your body.* ● **stimu|lat|ing** ADJ ❑ *...the stimulating effect of some drugs.* ● **stimu|la|tion** N-UNCOUNT ❑ *...physical stimulation.* [from Latin]

**stimu|lus** /stɪmyələs/ (**stimuli** /stɪmyəlaɪ/) N-VAR A **stimulus** is something that encourages activity in people or things. ❑ *What was the stimulus that made you take this job?* [from Latin]

**sting** /stɪŋ/ (**stings, stinging, stung**) **1** V-T/V-I If a plant, animal, or insect **stings** you, a sharp part of it, usually covered with poison, is pushed into your skin so that you feel a sharp pain. ❑ *A wasp stung her.* ❑ *This type of bee rarely stings.* **2** N-COUNT The **sting** of an insect or animal is the part that stings you. ❑ *Remove the bee sting from your body.* **3** N-COUNT If you feel a **sting**, you feel a sharp pain in your skin or other part of your body. ❑ *This won't hurt — you will just feel a little sting.* **4** V-T/V-I If a part of your body **stings**, or if a substance **stings** it, you feel a sharp pain there. ❑ *His cheeks were stinging from the cold wind.* **5** V-T If someone's remarks **sting** you, they make you feel hurt and annoyed. ❑ *Some of the criticism stung him.* ● **sting|ing** ADJ ❑ *...a stinging attack on the*

government. [from Old English]
→ see **insect**

**stink** /stɪŋk/ (**stinks, stinking, stank, stunk**) **1** V-I To **stink** means to smell very bad. ❑ *We all stank and nobody cared.* ❑ *The kitchen stinks of fried onions.* ● **Stink** is also a noun. ❑ *He was aware of the stink of garlic on his breath.* **2** V-I If you say that something **stinks**, you disapprove of it because it involves ideas, feelings, or practices that you do not like. [INFORMAL] ❑ *I think their methods stink.* [from Old English]

**stint** /stɪnt/ (**stints**) N-COUNT A **stint** is a period of time which you spend doing a particular job or activity. ❑ *...a five-year stint in Hong Kong.* [from Old English]

**sti|pend** /staɪpɛnd/ (**stipends**) N-COUNT A **stipend** is a sum of money that is paid to a student for their living expenses. [from Old French]

**stipu|late** /stɪpyəleɪt/ (**stipulates, stipulating, stipulated**) V-T If you **stipulate** a condition or **stipulate that** something must be done, you say clearly that it must be done. ❑ *He stipulated that $1 million should go to charity.* ● **stipu|la|tion** /stɪpyəleɪʃ³n/ (**stipulations**) N-COUNT ❑ *Clifford's only stipulation is that his clients must obey his advice.* [from Latin]

**stir** /stɜr/ (**stirs, stirring, stirred**) **1** V-T If you **stir** a liquid or other substance, you mix it in a container using something such as a spoon. ❑ *Stir the soup for a few seconds.* ❑ *Mrs. Bellingham stirred sugar into her tea.* **2** V-I If you **stir**, you move slightly, for example because you are uncomfortable or beginning to wake up. [WRITTEN] ❑ *Eileen shook him, and he started to stir.* **3** V-T/V-I If a particular memory, feeling, or mood **stirs** or **is stirred in** you, you begin to think about it or feel it. [WRITTEN] ❑ *Then a memory stirs in you and you start feeling anxious.* ❑ *Amy remembered the anger he stirred in her.* **4** N-SING If an event causes a **stir**, it causes great excitement, shock, or anger among people. ❑ *His movie caused a stir.* [from Old English] **5** → see also **stirring**

▸ **stir up** **1** PHR-VERB If something **stirs up** dust or **stirs up** mud in water, it causes it to rise up and move around. ❑ *They saw first a cloud of dust and then the car that was stirring it up.* **2** PHR-VERB If someone **stirs up** a particular mood or situation, usually a bad one, they cause it. ❑ *As usual, Harriet is trying to stir up trouble.*

| Word Partnership | Use *stir* with : |
|---|---|
| N. | stir **a mixture**, stir **in sugar 1** |
| V. | **cause** a stir, **create** a stir **4** |

**stir|ring** /stɜrɪŋ/ (**stirrings**) **1** ADJ A **stirring** event, performance, or account of something makes people very excited or enthusiastic. ❑ *The president made a stirring speech.* **2** N-COUNT A **stirring of** a feeling or thought is the beginning of one. ❑ *I feel a stirring of interest.* [from Old English]

**stitch** /stɪtʃ/ (**stitches, stitching, stitched**) **1** V-T/V-I If you **stitch** cloth, you use a needle and thread to join two pieces together or to make a decoration. ❑ *Stitch the two pieces of fabric together.* ❑ *We stitched for hours.* **2** N-COUNT **Stitches** are the short pieces of thread that have been sewn in a piece of cloth. ❑ *...a row of straight stitches.* **3** N-COUNT A **stitch** is a loop made by one turn

S

of wool around a knitting needle. ❑ *Her mother counted the stitches on her knitting needles.* ◪ V-T When doctors **stitch** a wound, they use a special needle and thread to sew the skin together. ❑*Jill washed and stitched the wound.* ◪ N-COUNT A **stitch** is a piece of thread that has been used to sew the skin of a wound together. ❑ *He had six stitches in a head wound.* ◪ N-SING A **stitch** is a sharp pain in your side, usually caused by running or laughing a lot. ❑ *He was laughing so much he got a stitch.* [from Old English]

**stock** /stɒk/ (**stocks, stocking, stocked**) ◪ N-COUNT **Stocks** are shares in the ownership of a company, or investments on which a fixed amount of interest will be paid. [BUSINESS] ❑ *...the buying and selling of stocks.*s ◪ N-UNCOUNT A company's **stock** is the amount of money which the company has made through selling shares. [BUSINESS] ❑ *The company's stock was valued at $38 million.* ◪ V-T If a store **stocks** particular products, it keeps a supply of them to sell. ❑ *The store stocks everything from pens to TV sets.* ◪ N-UNCOUNT A store's **stock** is the total amount of goods which it has available to sell. ❑ *Most of the store's stock was destroyed in the fire.* ◪ N-COUNT A **stock of** things is a supply of them. ❑ *I keep a stock of blank video tapes.* ◪ N-VAR **Stock** is a liquid, usually made by boiling meat, bones, or vegetables in water, that is used to give flavor to soups and sauces. ❑ *Finally, add the beef stock.* ◪ PHRASE If goods are **in stock**, a store has them available to sell. If they are **out of stock**, it does not. ❑ *Check that your size is in stock.* ◪ PHRASE If you **take stock**, you pause to think about all the aspects of a situation or event before deciding what to do next. ❑ *It was time to take stock of the situation.* [from Old English]

▸ **stock up** PHR-VERB If you **stock up on** something, you buy a lot of it, in case you cannot get it later. ❑ *We stocked up on food for the weekend.*

**stock|broker** /stɒkbroʊkər/ (**stockbrokers**) N-COUNT A **stockbroker** is a person whose job is to buy and sell stocks and shares for people who want to invest money. [BUSINESS]

**stock|broking** /stɒkbroʊkɪŋ/ N-UNCOUNT **Stockbroking** is the professional activity of buying and selling stocks and shares for clients. [BUSINESS] ❑ *...his stockbroking firm.*

**stock char|ac|ter** (**stock characters**) N-COUNT A **stock character** is a character in a play or other story who represents a particular type of person, for example the mad scientist or the nosy neighbor, rather than a fully-developed individual.

**stock ex|change** (**stock exchanges**) N-COUNT A **stock exchange** is a place where people buy and sell stocks and shares. [BUSINESS] ❑ *The daily newspapers print a list of stocks trading on the stock exchange.*

**stock|holder** /stɒkhoʊldər/ (**stockholders**) N-COUNT A **stockholder** is a person who owns shares in a company. [BUSINESS] ❑ *He was a stockholder in a hotel corporation.*

**stock|ing** /stɒkɪŋ/ (**stockings**) N-COUNT **Stockings** are items of women's clothing which fit closely over their feet and legs. Stockings are usually made of nylon and are held in place by garters. ❑ *...a pair of silk stockings.*

**stock mar|ket** (**stock markets**) N-COUNT The **stock market** consists of the general activity of buying stocks and shares, and the people and institutions that organize it. [BUSINESS] ❑ *...a practical guide to investing in the stock market.*

**stock op|tion** (**stock options**) N-COUNT A **stock option** is an opportunity for the employees of a company to buy shares at a special price. [BUSINESS] ❑ *He sold shares that he bought under the company's stock option program.*

**stock|pile** /stɒkpaɪl/ (**stockpiles, stockpiling, stockpiled**) ◪ V-T If people **stockpile** things such as food or weapons, they store large quantities of them for future use. ❑ *People are stockpiling food for winter.* ◪ N-COUNT A **stockpile of** things is a large quantity of them that has been stored for future use. ❑ *...an agreement to cut stockpiles of weapons.*

**stocky** /stɒki/ (**stockier, stockiest**) ADJ A **stocky** person has a body that is broad, solid, and often short. ❑ *...a short stocky man.*

**stoke** /stoʊk/ (**stokes, stoking, stoked**) ◪ V-T If you **stoke** a fire, you add coal or wood to it to keep it burning. ❑ *She was stoking the stove.* ● **Stoke up** means the same as **stoke**. ❑ *He stoked up the fire.* ◪ V-T If you **stoke** something such as a feeling, you cause it to be felt more strongly. ❑ *These problems are stoking fears that the business will close.* ● **Stoke up** means the same as **stoke**. ❑ *He was trying to stoke up interest for the idea.* [from Dutch]

**stoked** /stoʊkt/ ADJ If you are **stoked about** something, you are very excited about it. [INFORMAL] ❑ *I am so stoked about this trip.*

**stole** /stoʊl/ **Stole** is the past tense of **steal**.

**sto|len** /stoʊlⁿn/ **Stolen** is the past participle of **steal**. [from Old English]

**sto|ma** (**stomata**) N-COUNT **Stomata** are small holes on the leaves of plants that allow water and air to enter and leave the plant. [TECHNICAL] [from New Latin]

**stom|ach** /stʌmək/ (**stomachs, stomaching, stomached**) ◪ N-COUNT Your **stomach** is the organ inside your body where food is digested. ❑ *He has stomach problems.* ◪ N-COUNT You can refer to the front part of your body below your waist as your **stomach**. ❑ *The children lay down on their stomachs.* ◪ V-T If you cannot **stomach** something, you cannot accept it because you dislike it or disapprove of it. ❑ *I cannot stomach cruelty to animals.* [from Old French]

**stomp** /stɒmp/ (**stomps, stomping, stomped**) V-I If you **stomp** somewhere, you walk there with very heavy steps, often because you are angry. ❑ *He stomped off up the hill.*

**stomp|ing ground** (**stomping grounds**) N-COUNT Someone's **stomping ground** is a place where they like to go often.

**stone** /stoʊn/ (**stones**) ◪ N-VAR **Stone** is a hard solid substance found in the ground and often used for building. ❑ *...a stone floor.* ❑ *Marble is a natural stone.* ◪ N-COUNT A **stone** is a small piece of rock that is found on the ground. ❑ *He removed a stone from his shoe.* ◪ N-COUNT You can refer to a jewel as a **stone**. ❑ *...a diamond ring with three stones.* [from Old English] ◪ → see also **stepping stone, stoned**

**Stone Age** N-PROPER **The Stone Age** is a very early period of human history, when people used tools and weapons made of stone, not metal.

**stony** /stoʊni/ (**stonier, stoniest**) ◪ ADJ **Stony**

ground is rough and contains a lot of stones.
**2** ADJ A **stony** expression or attitude does not show any sympathy or friendliness. ❑ *She gave me a stony look.* [from Old English]

**stood** /stʊd/ **Stood** is the past tense and past participle of **stand.** [from Old English]

**stool** /stul/ (**stools**) N-COUNT A **stool** is a seat with legs but no support for your arms or back. ❑ *O'Brien sat on a stool and leaned on the counter.* [from Old English]

**stoop** /stup/ (**stoops, stooping, stooped**)
**1** V-I If you **stoop,** you stand or walk with your shoulders bent forward. ❑ *She was taller than he was and stooped slightly.* ● **Stoop** is also a noun. ❑ *He was a tall man with a slight stoop.* **2** V-I If you **stoop,** you bend your body forward and downward. ❑ *He stooped to pick up the bag.* ❑ *Two men stooped over the car.* **3** V-I If you say that a person **stoops to** doing something, you are criticizing them because they do something wrong or immoral that they would not normally do. ❑ *He never stooped to insulting people.* **4** N-COUNT A **stoop** is a small platform, porch or staircase at the door of a building, with steps leading up to it. ❑ *They stood on the stoop and rang the bell.* [Senses 1 to 3 from Old English. Sense 4 from Dutch.]

**stop** /stɒp/ (**stops, stopping, stopped**) **1** V-T/V-I If you have been doing something and then you **stop** doing it, you no longer do it. ❑ *Stop throwing those stones!* ❑ *How can we stop the fighting?* ❑ *She stopped and then continued eating.* **2** V-T If you **stop** something from happening, or you **stop** something happening, you prevent it from happening or prevent it from continuing. ❑ *...a way of stopping the war.* ❑ *He must stop her from destroying him.* **3** V-I If an activity or process **stops,** it is no longer happening. ❑ *The rain has stopped.* ❑ *It started snowing and building work had to stop.* **4** V-T/V-I If something such as a machine **stops** or **is stopped,** it is no longer moving or working. ❑ *The clock stopped at 11:59 Saturday night.* ❑ *Arnold stopped the engine and got out of the car.* **5** V-T/V-I When a moving person or vehicle **stops** or **is stopped,** they no longer move. ❑ *The car failed to stop at a stoplight.* ❑ *He stopped and waited for her.* **6** N-SING If something that is moving comes **to a stop,** it is brought **to a stop,** it slows down and no longer moves. ❑ *Do not open the door before the train comes to a stop.* **7** N-COUNT A **stop** is a place where buses or trains regularly stop so that people can get on and off. ❑ *The closest subway stop is Houston Street.* **8** V-I If you **stop** somewhere on a journey, you stay there for a short while. ❑ *We stopped at a small restaurant just outside of Atlanta.* **9** PHRASE If you **put a stop to** something that you do not like or approve of, you prevent it from happening or continuing. ❑ *I'm going to put a stop to all this talk.* [from Old English] **10** to **stop dead** → see **dead** **11** to **stop short of** → see **short**
▸ **stop by** or **stop in** PHR-VERB If you **stop by** somewhere, you make a short visit to a person or place. [INFORMAL] ❑ *Perhaps I'll stop by the hospital.*
▸ **stop off** PHR-VERB If you **stop off** somewhere, you stop for a short time in the middle of a trip. ❑ *The president stopped off in Poland on his way to Munich.*

**stop**|**light** /stɒplaɪt/ (**stoplights**) also **stop light** N-COUNT A **stoplight** is a set of colored lights which controls the flow of traffic on a road.

**stop**|**page** /stɒpɪdʒ/ (**stoppages**) N-COUNT When there is a **stoppage,** people stop working because of a disagreement with their employers. [BUSINESS] ❑ *Mineworkers voted for a one-day stoppage next month.* [from Old English]

**stor**|**age** /stɔrɪdʒ/ N-UNCOUNT **Storage** is the process of keeping something in a special place until it is needed. ❑ *...the storage of fuel.* ❑ *Some of the space is used for storage.* [from Old French]

**store** /stɔr/ (**stores, storing, stored**) **1** N-COUNT A **store** is a building or part of a building where things are sold. ❑ *They are selling them for $10 each at a few stores in Texas.* ❑ *...grocery stores.* **2** V-T When you **store** things, you put them in a container or other place and leave them there until they are needed. ❑ *Store the cookies in a tin.* ● **Store away** means the same as **store.** ❑ *He stored the tapes away.* **3** N-COUNT A **store of** things is a supply of them that you keep somewhere until you need them. ❑ *I have a secret store of chocolate.* **4** N-COUNT A **store** is a place where things are kept while they are not being used. ❑ *...a store for food supplies.* **5** → see also **department store** **6** PHRASE If something is **in store for** you, it is going to happen at some time in the future. ❑ *Surprises were in store for me.* [from Old French]
→ see **city**
▸ **store away** → see **store 2**
▸ **store up** PHR-VERB If you **store** something **up,** you keep it until you think that the time is right to use it. ❑ *I stored up stories about people to use in my book.*

| **Thesaurus** | store | Also look up : |
|---|---|---|
| N. | business, market, shop **1** collection, reserve, stock **3** | |
| V. | accumulate, keep, save **2** | |

**store-bought** ADJ **Store-bought** products are sold in stores, rather than being made at home. ❑ *You can use this sauce with store-bought pasta.*

**store brand** (**store brands**) N-COUNT **Store brands** are products which have the trademark or label of the store which sells them, especially a supermarket chain. ❑ *...a tub of store-brand ice cream.*

**stored en**|**er**|**gy** N-UNCOUNT **Stored energy** is the same as **potential energy.** [TECHNICAL]

**store**|**front** /stɔrfrʌnt/ (**storefronts**) **1** N-COUNT A **storefront** is the outside part of a store which faces the street, including the door and windows. **2** N-COUNT A **storefront** is a small store or office that opens onto the street and is part of a row of stores or offices. ❑ *Main Street has many small storefronts and restaurants.* ❑ *...a tiny storefront office on the main street.*

**store**|**keep**|**er** /stɔrkipər/ (**storekeepers**) N-COUNT A **storekeeper** is a person who owns or manages a small store.

**storm** /stɔrm/ (**storms, storming, stormed**) **1** N-COUNT A **storm** is very bad weather, with heavy rain, strong winds, and often thunder and lightning. ❑ *...the violent storms along the East Coast.* **2** N-COUNT If something causes a **storm,** it causes an angry or excited reaction from a large number of people. ❑ *The photos caused a storm when they were first published.* **3** V-I If you **storm into** or **out of** a place, you enter or leave it quickly and noisily,

S

because you are angry. □ *After an argument, he stormed out.* ◤ v-⟙ If a place that is being defended **is stormed**, a group of people attack it, usually in order to get inside it. □ *Government buildings have been stormed.* ● **storm|ing** N-UNCOUNT □ ...*the storming of the Bastille.* ◤ PHRASE If someone or something **takes** a place or activity **by storm**, they are extremely successful. □ *Kenya's runners have taken the athletics world by storm.* [from Old English]
→ see Word Web: **storm**
→ see **disaster, forecast, hurricane, weather**

**storm surge** (**storm surges**) N-COUNT A **storm surge** is an increase in the sea level along a shore that accompanies a hurricane or storm. [TECHNICAL]

**stormy** /stɔrmi/ (**stormier, stormiest**) ◤ ADJ If there is **stormy** weather, there are strong winds and heavy rain. □ ...*a night of stormy weather, with heavy rain and strong winds.* ◤ ADJ If you describe a situation as **stormy**, you mean it involves a lot of angry argument or criticism. □ *It was a stormy meeting.* [from Old English]

**sto|ry** /stɔri/ (**stories**) ◤ N-COUNT A **story** is a description of imaginary people and events, which is written or told in order to entertain. □ *The story is called "The Student."* □ *I shall tell you a story about four little rabbits.* ◤ N-COUNT A **story** is a description or account of something that has happened. □ *The parents all had interesting stories about their children.* □ ...*the story of the women's movement.* ◤ N-COUNT A news **story** is a piece of news in a newspaper or in a news broadcast. □ *Those are some of the top stories in the news.* ◤ N-COUNT A **story** of a building is one of its different levels, which is situated above or below other levels. □ ...*long buildings, two stories high.* ◤ PHRASE You use **a different story** to refer to a situation, usually a bad one, which exists in one set of circumstances when you have mentioned that it does not exist in another set of circumstances. □ *Where Marcella lives, the rents are cheap, but further north it's a different story.* ◤ PHRASE

If you say **it's the same old story** or **it's the old story**, you mean that something unpleasant or undesirable seems to happen again and again. □ *It's the same old story. They want one person to do three people's jobs.* ◤ PHRASE If you say that something is **only part of the story** or is **not the whole story**, you mean that the explanation or information given is not enough for a situation to be fully understood. □ *This is true but it is only part of the story.* ◤ PHRASE If someone tells you their **side of the story**, they tell you why they behaved in a particular way and why they think they were right, when other people think that person behaved wrongly. □ *He had already decided before even hearing her side of the story.* [Senses 1 to 3 and 5 to 8 from Anglo-French. Sense 4 from Anglo-Latin.]
→ see **myth**

**stout** /staʊt/ (**stouter, stoutest**) ◤ ADJ A **stout** person is quite fat. □ *He was a tall, stout man with gray hair.* ◤ ADJ **Stout** shoes, branches, or other objects are thick and strong. □ *I hope you have stout shoes.* [from Old French]

**stove** /stoʊv/ (**stoves**) N-COUNT A **stove** is a piece of equipment which provides heat, either for cooking or for heating a room. □ *She put the saucepan on the gas stove.* [from Old English]

**stow** /stoʊ/ (**stows, stowing, stowed**) V-⟙ If you **stow** something somewhere, you carefully put it there until it is needed. ❑ *Luke stowed his bags in the trunk of the car.* [from Old English]

**strad|dle** /stræd³l/ (**straddles, straddling, straddled**) **1** V-T If you **straddle** something, you put or have one leg on either side of it. ❑ *He sat down, straddling the chair.* **2** V-T If something **straddles** a river, road, border, or other place, it stretches across it or exists on both sides of it. ❑ *A wooden bridge straddled the stream.* **3** V-T Someone or something that **straddles** different periods, groups, or fields of activity exists in, belongs to, or takes elements from them all. ❑ *He straddles two cultures, because he grew up in the United States but now lives in India.* [from Old English]

**straight** /streɪt/ (**straighter, straightest**) **1** ADJ If something is **straight**, it continues in one direction or line and does not bend or curve. ❑ *Keep the boat in a straight line.* ❑ *Grace had long straight hair.* ● **Straight** is also an adverb. ❑ *Stand straight and stretch the left hand to the right foot.* ❑ *He was looking straight at me.* **2** ADV If you go **straight** to a place, you go there immediately. ❑ *We went straight to Alan for advice.* **3** ADJ If you give someone a **straight** answer, you answer them clearly and honestly. ❑ *Why can't you give a straight answer to a straight question?* ● **Straight** is also an adverb. ❑ *I told him straight that I thought he was wrong.* **4** PHRASE If you **get** something **straight**, you make sure that you understand it properly or that someone else does. [SPOKEN] ❑ *You need to get your facts straight.* [from Old English] **5** a straight face → see **face** → see **hair**

**straight ar|row** (**straight arrows**) N-COUNT A **straight arrow** is someone who is very traditional, honest, and moral. ❑ *…a straight-arrow group of young people.*

**straight away** also **straightaway** ADV If you do something **straight away**, you do it immediately and without delay. ❑ *I should go and see a doctor straight away.*

**straight|en** /streɪt³n/ (**straightens, straightening, straightened**) **1** V-T If you **straighten** something, you make it neat or put it in its proper position. ❑ *She straightened a picture on the wall.* ● **Straighten up** means the same as **straighten**. ❑ *This is my job, to straighten up and keep the offices tidy.* **2** V-I If you are standing and you **straighten**, you make your back or body straight and upright. ❑ *The three men straightened and stood waiting.* ● **Straighten up** means the same as **straighten**. ❑ *He straightened up and put his hands in his pockets.* **3** V-T/V-I If you **straighten** something, or it **straightens**, it becomes straight. ❑ *Straighten both legs.* ● **Straighten out** means the same as **straighten**. ❑ *She straightened out her skirt.* [from Old English]
▶ **straighten out 1** PHR-VERB If you **straighten out** a confused situation, you succeed in getting it organized and cleaned up. ❑ *We need to straighten out a couple of things.* **2** → see **straighten 3**
▶ **straighten up** → see **straighten 2**

**straight|forward** /streɪtfɔrwərd/ **1** ADJ If you describe something as **straightforward**, you approve of it because it is easy to do or understand. ❑ *The computer system is straightforward to use.* ❑ *The question seemed straightforward to me.* ● **straight|forward|ly** ADV ❑ *He never gives his ideas straightforwardly.* **2** ADJ If you describe a person or their behavior as **straightforward**, you approve of them because they are honest and direct, and do not try to hide their feelings. ❑ *She is straightforward, and very honest.* ● **straight|forward|ly** ADV ❑ *Speak straightforwardly but be careful not to offend anyone.*

**strain** /streɪn/ (**strains, straining, strained**) **1** N-VAR If **strain** is put on a person or organization, they have to do more than they are really able to do. ❑ *The prison service is under a lot of strain.* ❑ *…the stresses and strains of a demanding career.* **2** V-T To **strain** something means to make it do more than it is able to do. ❑ *The large number of customers is straining our system.* **3** N-VAR **Strain** is an injury to a muscle in your body, caused by using the muscle too much or twisting it. ❑ *Avoid muscle strain by not doing too much exercise.* **4** V-T If you **strain** a muscle, you injure it by using it too much or twisting it. ❑ *He strained his back playing tennis.* **5** V-T If you **strain to** do something, you make a great effort to do it when it is difficult to do. ❑ *I had to strain to hear.* **6** V-T When you **strain** food, you separate the liquid part of it from the solid parts. ❑ *Strain the soup and put it back into the pan.* [from Old French]

**strained** /streɪnd/ **1** ADJ If your appearance, voice, or behavior is **strained**, you seem worried and nervous. ❑ *She looked a little pale and strained.* **2** ADJ If relations between people are **strained**, those people do not like or trust each other. ❑ *…a period of strained relations between the two countries.* [from Old French]

**strait** /streɪt/ (**straits**) **1** N-COUNT You can refer to a narrow strip of ocean which joins two large areas of ocean as a **strait** or the **straits**. ❑ *1,600 ships pass through the strait every year.* **2** N-PLURAL If someone is in **dire** or desperate **straits**, they are in a very difficult situation. ❑ *Many small businesses are in desperate financial straits.* [from Old French]

**strand** /strænd/ (**strands, stranding, stranded**) **1** N-COUNT A **strand of** something such as hair, wire, or thread is a thin piece of it. ❑ *She tried to blow a strand of hair from her eyes.* **2** V-T If you are **stranded**, you are prevented from leaving a place, for example because of bad weather. ❑ *The climbers were stranded by a storm.* [Sense 2 from Old English]

**strange** /streɪndʒ/ (**stranger, strangest**) **1** ADJ Something that is **strange** is unusual or unexpected. ❑ *There was something strange about the way she spoke.* ● **strange|ly** ADV ❑ *She noticed he was acting strangely.* ● **Strangely**, they didn't invite her to join them. ● **strange|ness** N-UNCOUNT ❑ *…the strangeness of the music.* **2** ADJ A **strange** place is one that you have never been to before. A **strange** person is someone that you have never met before. ❑ *I was alone in a strange city.* [from Old French]

S

## Thesaurus        *strange*        Also look up :

ADJ.    bizarre, different, eccentric, odd, peculiar, unusual, weird; (*ant.*) ordinary, usual **1**
exotic, foreign, unfamiliar **2**

**stran|ger** /stréɪndʒər/ (**strangers**) **1** N-COUNT
A **stranger** is someone you have never met before. ❑ *Telling a complete stranger about your life is difficult.* **2** N-PLURAL If two people are **strangers**, they do not know each other. ❑ *The two women were strangers.* **3** N-COUNT If you are a **stranger to** something, you have had no experience of it or do not understand it. ❑ *He is no stranger to trouble.* [from Old French]

**stran|gle** /stréŋgᵊl/ (**strangles, strangling, strangled**) **1** V-T To **strangle** someone means to kill them by squeezing their throat tightly so that they cannot breathe. ❑ *He tried to strangle a policeman.* **2** V-T To **strangle** something means to prevent it from succeeding or developing. ❑ *The country's economic problems are strangling its development.* [from Old French]

**strangle|hold** /stréŋgᵊlhoʊld/ N-SING To have a **stranglehold on** something means to have control over it and prevent it from being free or from developing. ❑ *These companies have a stranglehold on the banana industry.*

**strap** /stræp/ (**straps, strapping, strapped**) **1** N-COUNT A **strap** is a narrow piece of leather, cloth, or other material. Straps are used to carry things, fasten things together, or to hold a piece of clothing in place. ❑ *Nancy held the strap of her bag.* ❑ *Her shoes had elastic ankle straps.* **2** V-T If you **strap** something somewhere, you fasten it there with a strap. ❑ *She strapped the baby seat into the car.*

**stra|ta** /stréɪtə, strǽtə/ **Strata** is the plural of **stratum.** [from New Latin]

**stra|tegic** /strətídʒɪk/ **1** ADJ **Strategic** means relating to the most important, general aspects of something such as a military operation or political policy. ❑ *We need a strategic plan for reducing crime.* ● **stra|tegi|cal|ly** /strətídʒɪkli/ ADV ❑ *...strategically important roads.* **2** ADJ **Strategic** weapons are very powerful missiles that can be fired only after a decision to use them has been made by a political leader. ❑ *...strategic nuclear weapons.* **3** ADJ If you put something in a **strategic** position, you place it cleverly in a position where it will be most useful or have the most effect. ❑ *Benches are placed at strategic points throughout the gardens.* ● **stra|tegi|cal|ly** ADV ❑ *We hid behind a strategically placed chair.* [from French]

### Word Partnership        Use *strategic* with :

N.    strategic **decisions**, strategic **forces**, strategic **interests**, strategic **planning**, strategic **targets**, strategic **thinking** **1**
strategic **missiles**, strategic **nuclear weapons** **2**
strategic **location**, strategic **position** **3**

**strat|egist** /strǽtədʒɪst/ (**strategists**) N-COUNT
A **strategist** is someone who is skilled in planning the best way to gain an advantage or to achieve success, especially in war. ❑ *...military strategists.* [from French]

**strat|egy** /strǽtədʒi/ (**strategies**) **1** N-VAR A **strategy** is a general plan or set of plans intended to achieve something, especially over a long period. ❑ *Do you have a strategy for solving this problem?* **2** N-UNCOUNT **Strategy** is the art of planning the best way to gain an advantage or achieve success, especially in war. ❑ *...the basic principles of strategy.* [from French]

### Thesaurus        *strategy*        Also look up :

N.    plan, policy, tactic **1**

### Word Partnership        Use *strategy* with :

N.    **campaign** strategy, **investment** strategy, **marketing** strategy, **part of a** strategy, **pricing** strategy, strategy **shift** **1**
V.    **adopt a** strategy, **change a** strategy, **develop a** strategy, **plan a** strategy **1** use (a) strategy **1** **2**
ADJ.    **aggressive** strategy, **new** strategy, **political** strategy, **successful** strategy, **winning** strategy **1**

**strati|fi|ca|tion** /strætɪfɪkéɪʃᵊn/ N-UNCOUNT
In geology, **stratification** is the process by which layers of sediment accumulate over time to produce separate layers of rock. [TECHNICAL] [from New Latin]

**strati|fied drift** N-UNCOUNT **Stratified drift** is layers of sand and gravel that have been deposited by melted ice from a glacier. [TECHNICAL]

**stra|tum** /stréɪtəm, strǽt-/ (**strata**) **1** N-COUNT
A **stratum** of society is a group of people in it who are similar in their education, income, or social status. [FORMAL] ❑ *The changes affected every stratum of society.* **2** N-COUNT **Strata** are different layers of rock. [from New Latin]

**stra|tus** /stréɪtəs, strǽt-/ (**strati**) N-VAR **Stratus** is a type of thick gray cloud that forms at low altitudes. [TECHNICAL] [from New Latin]

**straw** /strɔ/ (**straws**) **1** N-UNCOUNT **Straw** consists of the dried, yellowish stalks from crops such as wheat or barley. ❑ *The floor of the barn was covered with straw.* **2** N-COUNT A **straw** is a thin tube of paper or plastic, which you use to suck a drink into your mouth. ❑ *...a bottle of soda with a straw in it.* **3** PHRASE If an event is **the last straw** or **the straw that broke the camel's back**, it is the latest in a series of unpleasant or undesirable events, and makes you feel that you cannot tolerate a situation any longer. ❑ *When he broke my radio, that was the last straw.* [from Old English]
→ see **rice**

**straw|berry** /strɔ́beri/ (**strawberries**) N-COUNT A **strawberry** is a small red fruit which is soft and juicy and has tiny yellow seeds on its skin. ❑ *...strawberries and cream.* [from Old English]

**strawberries**

**stray** /stréɪ/ (**strays, straying, strayed**) **1** V-I If someone **strays** somewhere, they wander away from where they are supposed to be. ❑ *Be careful not to stray into dangerous parts* of the city. **2** ADJ A **stray** dog or cat has wandered away from its owner's home. □ *A stray dog came up to him.* ● **Stray** is also a noun. □ *The dog was a stray.* **3** V-I If your mind or your eyes **stray**, you do not concentrate on or look at one particular subject, but start thinking about or looking at other things. □ *My mind keeps straying when I'm trying to work.* **4** ADJ **Stray** things have become separated from other similar things. □ *...a few stray hairs.* [from Old French]

**streak** /strik/ (**streaks, streaking, streaked**) **1** N-COUNT A **streak** is a long stripe or mark on a surface. □ *There are dark streaks on the surface of the moon.* **2** V-T If something **streaks** a surface, it makes long stripes or marks on the surface. □ *Rain began to streak the windows.* **3** N-COUNT If someone has a **streak** of a particular type of behavior, they sometimes behave in that way. □ *There is a streak of madness in Christina.* **4** V-I If something or someone **streaks** somewhere, they move there very quickly. □ *A plane streaked across the sky.* **5** N-COUNT In geology, the **streak** of a mineral is the color of the powder that is produced when the mineral is rubbed against a hard, white surface. [TECHNICAL] [from Old English]

**stream** /strim/ (**streams, streaming, streamed**) **1** N-COUNT A **stream** is a small narrow river. □ *There was a small stream at the end of the garden.* **2** N-COUNT A **stream** of things is a large number of them occurring one after another. □ *The TV show caused a stream of complaints.* □ *...a stream of jokes.* **3** V-I If a mass of people, liquid, or light **streams** somewhere, it enters or moves there in large amounts. □ *Tears streamed down their faces.* □ *Sunlight was streaming into the room.* [from Old English]

**stream|line** /strimlaɪn/ (**streamlines, streamlining, streamlined**) V-T To **streamline** an organization or process means to make it more efficient by removing unnecessary parts of it. □ *They are streamlining the tax system.* ● **stream|lined** ADJ □ *...the streamlined organizations of the future.*

**stream|lined** /strimlaɪnd/ ADJ A **streamlined** vehicle, animal, or object has a shape that allows it to move quickly or efficiently through air or water. □ *...these beautifully streamlined cars.*

**street** /strit/ (**streets**) **1** N-COUNT A **street** is a road in a city, town, or village, usually with houses along it. □ *He lived at 66 Bingfield Street.* **2** N-COUNT You can use **street** or **streets** when talking about activities that happen out of doors in a city or town rather than inside a building. □ *You can wear these shoes indoors or outdoors, in the car or on the street.* □ *We need to get homeless people off the streets.* [from Old English]

**street|car** /stritkɑr/ (**streetcars**) N-COUNT A **streetcar** is an electric vehicle for carrying people which travels on rails in the streets of a city or town.
→ see **transportation**

**street crime** N-UNCOUNT **Street crime** refers to crimes such as vandalism, car theft, and mugging that are usually committed outdoors.

**street smart** also **street-smart** ADJ Someone who is **street smart** knows how to deal with

difficult or dangerous situations, especially in big cities. [INFORMAL] □ *He is street smart and is not afraid of this neighborhood.*

**street smarts** N-PLURAL You can use **street smarts** to refer to the skills and intelligence people need to be successful in difficult situations, especially in a city. [INFORMAL] □ *The boys learned their street smarts early.*

**strength** /strɛŋkθ, strɛŋθ/ (**strengths**) **1** N-UNCOUNT Your **strength** is the physical energy that you have, which gives you the ability to perform various actions, such as lifting or moving things. □ *Swimming builds up the strength of your muscles.* □ *He threw the ball forward with all his strength.* **2** N-UNCOUNT; N-SING Someone's **strength** in a difficult situation is their confidence or courage. □ *Something gave me the strength to overcome the difficulty.* □ *He copes with his illness very well. His strength is amazing.* **3** N-VAR The **strength** of an object or material is its ability to be treated roughly, or to carry heavy weights. □ *He checked the strength of the rope.* **4** N-VAR The **strength** of a person, organization, or country is the power or influence that they have. □ *...America's military strength.* **5** N-UNCOUNT If you refer to the **strength** of a feeling, opinion, or belief, you are talking about how deeply it is felt or believed by people, or how much they are influenced by it. □ *He was surprised at the strength of his own feeling.* **6** N-VAR Someone's **strengths** are the qualities and abilities that they have which are an advantage to them, or which make them successful. □ *What are your strengths and weaknesses?* **7** N-UNCOUNT The **strength** of a group of people is the total number of people in it. □ *These soldiers make up one-tenth of the strength of the army.* **8** PHRASE If a person or organization **goes from strength to strength**, they become more and more successful or confident. □ *The company has gone from strength to strength.* **9** PHRASE If one thing is done **on the strength of** another, it is done because of the influence of that other thing. □ *She got the job on the strength of her interview.* [from Old English]
→ see **muscle**

**strength|en** /strɛŋθəʳn/ (**strengthens, strengthening, strengthened**) V-T/V-I If something **strengthens** or if something **strengthens** it, it becomes stronger. □ *Cycling strengthens all the muscles of the body.* □ *The dollar strengthened against most other currencies.* [from Old English]

**strenu|ous** /strɛnyuəs/ ADJ A **strenuous** activity or action involves a lot of energy or effort. □ *Avoid strenuous exercise in the evening.* □ *Strenuous efforts were made to improve conditions in the jail.* ● **strenu|ous|ly** ADV □ *He argued strenuously against the decision.* [from Latin]

**strep** /strɛp/ also **strep throat** N-UNCOUNT **Strep** or **strep throat** is an illness that is caused by bacteria and which gives you a fever and a very sore throat. □ *Nicola had strep.* □ *I have strep throat.*

**stress** /strɛs/ (**stresses, stressing, stressed**) **1** V-T If you **stress** a point in a discussion, you put extra emphasis on it because you think it is important. □ *He stressed that the problem was not serious.* □ *Her teachers stressed the need for her to do more work at home.* ● **Stress** is also a noun. □ *Japanese car makers are putting more stress on overseas sales.* **2** N-VAR If you feel under **stress**, you

S

are worried and tense because of difficulties in your life. ❑ *Katy cannot think clearly when she is under stress.* ❸ V-T If you **stress** a word or part of a word when you say it, you put emphasis on it so that it sounds slightly louder. ❑ *She stressed the words "very important."* ● **Stress** is also a noun. ❑ *The stress is on the first part of this word.* ❹ N-VAR **Stresses** are strong physical pressures applied to an object.
→ see **emotion**

### Word Partnership    Use *stress* with :

| | |
|---|---|
| N. | stress **the importance of** *something* ❶ **anxiety and** stress, **effects of** stress, **job/work-related** stress, stress **management**, stress **reduction**, **response to** stress, **symptoms of** stress, stress **test** ❷ |
| V. | **cause** stress, **cope with** stress, **deal with** stress, **experience** stress, **induce** stress, **reduce** stress, **relieve** stress ❷ |
| ADJ. | **emotional** stress, **excessive** stress, **high** stress, **physical** stress, stress **related**, **severe** stress ❷ |

**stressed** /strɛst/ ADJ If you are **stressed**, you feel tense and anxious because of difficulties in your life. ❑ *What situations make you feel stressed?*

**stress frac|ture** (**stress fractures**) N-COUNT A **stress fracture** is a slight break in a bone that is usually caused by using a part of your body too much, for example, as a result of exercise or sport. ❑ *I had a stress fracture in my left leg.*

**stress|ful** /strɛsfəl/ ADJ If a situation or experience is **stressful**, it causes the person involved to feel stress. ❑ *I've got one of the most stressful jobs there is.*

**stretch** /strɛtʃ/ (**stretches, stretching, stretched**) ❶ V-I Something that **stretches** over an area or distance covers or exists in the whole of that area or distance. ❑ *The line of cars stretched for several miles.* ❷ N-COUNT A **stretch of** road, water, or land is a length or area of it. ❑ *It's a very dangerous stretch of road.* ❸ V-T/V-I When you **stretch**, you put your arms or legs out straight and tighten your muscles. ❑ *He yawned and stretched.* ❑ *Try stretching your legs and pulling your toes upwards.* ● **Stretch** is also a noun. ❑ *At the end of a workout do some slow stretches.* ❹ N-COUNT A **stretch of** time is a period of time. ❑ *...an 18-month stretch in the army.* ❺ V-I If something **stretches from** one time to another, it begins at the first time and ends at the second, which is longer than expected. ❑ *...a working day that stretches from seven in the morning to eight at night.* ❻ V-T/V-I When something soft or elastic **stretches** or **is stretched**, it becomes longer or bigger as well as thinner, usually because it is pulled. ❑ *The rope won't stretch.* ❼ V-T If something **stretches** your money or resources, it uses them up so you have hardly enough for your needs. ❑ *The war was stretching resources.* ● **stretched** ADJ ❑ *...our stretched finances.* [from Old English]
▸ **stretch out** ❶ PHR-VERB If you **stretch out** or **stretch yourself out**, you lie with your legs and body in a straight line. ❑ *The bathtub was too small to stretch out in.* ❷ PHR-VERB If you **stretch out** a part of your body, you hold it out straight. ❑ *He stretched out his hand to touch me.*

### Word Partnership    Use *stretch* with :

| | |
|---|---|
| PREP. | stretch **across** ❶ ❸ **along** a stretch **of road, down the road** a stretch ❷ **during** a stretch ❸ ❹ **at** a stretch ❹ |
| N. | stretch **of highway/road**, stretch **of a river** ❷ stretch **your legs** ❸ |

**stretch|er** /strɛtʃər/ (**stretchers**) N-COUNT A **stretcher** is a long piece of canvas with a pole along each side, which is used to carry an injured or sick person. ❑ *They put him on a stretcher and got him into the ambulance.* [from Old English]

**strewn** /struːn/ ADJ If a place is **strewn with** things, they are lying scattered there. ❑ *The room was strewn with books and clothes.* [from Old English]

**strick|en** /strɪkən/ ADJ If a person or place is **stricken by** something such as an unpleasant feeling, an illness, or a natural disaster, they are severely affected by it. ❑ *He was stricken with illness for several weeks.* ❑ *...hunger-stricken parts of Africa.*

**strict** /strɪkt/ (**stricter, strictest**) ❶ ADJ A **strict** rule or order is very clear and precise or severe and must be obeyed completely. ❑ *Their leader gave them strict instructions not to get out of the car.* ❑ *The school's rules are very strict.* ● **strict|ly** ADV ❑ *The acceptance of new members is strictly controlled.* ❷ ADJ A **strict** person regards many actions as unacceptable and does not allow them. ❑ *My parents were very strict.* ● **strict|ly** ADV ❑ *They brought their children up very strictly.* ❸ ADJ If you talk about the **strict** meaning of something, you mean the precise meaning of it. ❑ *She's not Belgian in the strict sense, but she was born in Belgium.* ● **strict|ly** ADV ❑ *That is not strictly true.* ❹ ADJ You use **strict** to describe someone who never does things that are against their beliefs. ❑ *Millions of Americans are now strict vegetarians.* [from Latin]

**strict|ly** /strɪktli/ ❶ ADV You use **strictly** to emphasize that something is of one particular type, or intended for one particular thing or person, rather than any other. ❑ *The trip was strictly business.* [from Latin] ❷ → see also **strict**

**stride** /straɪd/ (**strides, striding, strode**) ❶ V-I If you **stride** somewhere, you walk there with quick, long steps. ❑ *The farmer came striding across the field.* ❷ N-COUNT A **stride** is a long step which you take when you are walking or running. ❑ *With every stride, runners hit the ground hard.* ❸ N-COUNT If you **make strides** in something that you are doing, you make rapid progress in it. ❑ *The country has made big strides politically.* ❹ PHRASE If you **take** a problem or difficulty **in stride**, you deal with it calmly and easily. ❑ *He took the school tests in stride.* [from Old English]

### Word Partnership    Use *stride* with :

| | |
|---|---|
| V. | **break (your)** stride, **lengthen your** stride ❷ |
| ADJ. | **long** stride ❷ |

**stri|dent** /straɪdᵊnt/ ADJ If you use **strident** to describe someone or the way they express themselves, you are critical of them for making their feelings or opinions known in a very strong way that perhaps makes people uncomfortable. □ *He has very strident views.* [from Latin]

**strife** /straɪf/ N-UNCOUNT **Strife** is strong disagreement or fighting. [FORMAL] □ *Money is a major cause of strife in many marriages.* [from Old French]

---
### strike

❶ NOUN USES
❷ VERB USES
❸ PHR-VERBS
---

❶ **strike** /straɪk/ (**strikes**) ■ N-COUNT When there is a **strike**, workers stop doing their work for a period of time, usually in order to try to get better pay or working conditions. [BUSINESS] □ *Workers began a three-day strike.* □ *Staff at the hospital went on strike.* ■ N-COUNT A military **strike** is a military attack, especially an air attack. □ *...an air strike.* ■ PHRASE If someone has **two strikes against** them, they are in a bad situation or at a disadvantage. [INFORMAL] □ *The Hotel has two strikes against it. One, it's an ugly building. Second, it's in an ugly place.* [from Old English] ■ → see also **hunger strike**
→ see **union**

❷ **strike** /straɪk/ (**strikes, striking, struck**) ■ V-I When workers **strike**, they go on strike. [BUSINESS] □ *Workers have the right to strike.* □ *They shouldn't be striking for more money.* ● **striker** (**strikers**) N-COUNT □ *The strikers want higher wages.* ■ V-T If you **strike** someone or something, you deliberately hit them. [FORMAL] □ *She took two steps forward and struck him across the mouth.* □ *Why did you strike him?* ■ V-T If something that is falling or moving **strikes** something, it hits it. [FORMAL] □ *His head struck the bottom when he dived into the pool.* ■ V-I To **strike** someone or something means to attack or affect them quickly and violently. □ *We hope the killer will not strike again.* □ *A storm struck the northeastern United States on Saturday.* ■ V-T If an idea or thought **strikes** you, it suddenly comes into your mind. □ *A thought struck her. Was she jealous of her mother?* ■ V-T If something **strikes** you as being a particular thing, it gives you the impression of being that thing. □ *He struck me as a very friendly person.* ■ V-T If you **are struck** by something, you think it is very impressive, noticeable, or interesting. □ *She was struck by the kindness in his voice.* ■ V-T If something **strikes** fear **into** people, it makes them very frightened or anxious. [LITERARY] □ *The Brazilians strike fear into opposing teams.* ■ V-T/V-I When a clock **strikes**, its bells make a sound to indicate what the time is. □ *The clock struck nine.* □ *I didn't hear the clock strike.* ■ V-T When you **strike** a match, you make it produce a flame by moving it quickly against something rough. □ *Robina struck a match and lit the fire.* ■ V-T If someone **strikes** oil or gold, they discover it in the ground as a result of mining or drilling. □ *The company has struck oil in Syria.* [from Old English]

❸ **strike** /straɪk/ (**strikes, striking, struck**)
▸ **strike down** ■ PHR-VERB If someone **is struck down**, especially by an illness, they are killed or severely harmed. [WRITTEN] □ *Frank has been struck down by serious illness.* ■ PHR-VERB If a judge or court **strikes down** a law or regulation, they say that it is illegal and end it. □ *The Court struck down*

*a law that prevents criminals from earning money from books about their crimes.*
▸ **strike out** ■ PHR-VERB In baseball, if a pitcher **strikes out**, they fail three times to hit the ball and end their turn. If a pitcher **strikes out**, they throw three balls that the batter fails to hit, and end the batter's turn. □ *Trachsel struck Bonds out seven times.* □ *The third baseman struck out four times.* ■ PHR-VERB If you **strike out**, you begin to do something different, often because you want to become more independent. □ *She wanted me to strike out on my own and buy a business.* ■ PHR-VERB If someone **strikes out**, they fail. [INFORMAL] □ *His first lawyer struck out completely.*
▸ **strike up** PHR-VERB When you **strike up** a conversation or friendship with someone, you begin one. [WRITTEN] □ *I followed her into the store and struck up a conversation.*

**striker** /straɪkər/ (**strikers**) N-COUNT In soccer and some other team sports, a **striker** is a player who mainly attacks and scores goals, rather than defends. □ *The striker scored a great goal.* [from Old English]

**striking** /straɪkɪŋ/ ■ ADJ Something that is **striking** is very noticeable or unusual. □ *The most striking feature of the garden is the swimming pool.* ● **strikingly** ADV □ *The two men were strikingly similar.* ■ ADJ Someone who is **striking** is very attractive, in a noticeable way. □ *She was a striking woman with long blonde hair.* [from Old English]

**string** /strɪŋ/ (**strings**) ■ N-VAR **String** is thin rope made of twisted threads, used for tying things together or tying up packages. □ *He held out a small bag tied with string.* ■ N-COUNT A **string of** things is a number of them on a piece of string, thread, or wire. □ *She wore a string of pearls around her neck.* ■ N-COUNT A **string of** places or objects is a number of them that form a line. □ *We traveled through a string of villages.* ■ N-COUNT The **strings** on a musical instrument such as a violin or guitar are the thin pieces of wire or nylon stretched across it that make sounds when the instrument is played. □ *He changed a guitar string.* ■ N-PLURAL The **strings** are the section of an orchestra which consists of stringed instruments played with a bow. □ *The strings play this section of the music.* ■ PHRASE If something is offered to you with **no strings attached** or with **no strings**, it is offered without any special conditions. □ *We should help them with no strings attached.* [from Old English]
→ see Picture Dictionary: **strings**
→ see **orchestra**

---
| **Thesaurus** | *string* | Also look up : |
|---|---|---|
| N. | cord, fiber, rope ■ | |
| | chain, file, line, row, sequence, series ■ | |
---

---
| **Word Partnership** | | Use *string* with : |
|---|---|---|
| N. | **piece of** string ■ | |
| | string **of pearls** ■ | |
| | **banjo** string, **guitar** string ■ | |
| ADJ. | **long** string ■ – ■ | |
---

**string bean** (**string beans**) N-COUNT **String beans** are long, narrow green vegetables consisting of the cases and seeds of a climbing plant.

**stringent** /strɪndʒ³nt/ ADJ **Stringent** laws,

S

**Picture Dictionary** strings

cello

violin

viola

double bass

electric guitar

acoustic guitar

harp

rules, or conditions are very severe or are strictly controlled. [FORMAL] ❑ *The tests were subject to stringent controls.* [from Latin]

**strip** /strɪp/ (**strips, stripping, stripped**)
■ N-COUNT A **strip of** something such as paper, cloth, or food is a long, narrow piece of it. ❑ *They pressed the two strips of wood together.* ❑ *...rugs made from strips of fabric.* ■ N-COUNT A **strip of** land or water is a long narrow area of it. ❑ *He owns a narrow strip of land on the coast.* ■ N-COUNT A **strip** is a long street in a city or town, where there are a lot of stores, restaurants, and hotels. ❑ *...a busy shopping strip in North Dallas.* ■ V-I If you **strip**, you take off your clothes. ❑ *They stripped and jumped into the pool.* • **Strip off** means the same as **strip**. ❑ *The children were stripping off and running into the ocean.* ■ V-T If someone **is stripped**, their clothes are taken off by another person, for example in order to search for hidden or illegal things. ❑ *He was stripped and searched at the airport.* ■ V-T To **strip** something means to remove everything that covers it. ❑ *I stripped the bed, then put on clean sheets.* ■ V-T To **strip** someone **of** their property, rights, or titles means to take those things away from them. ❑ *They stripped us of our passports.* ■ N-COUNT In a newspaper or magazine, a **strip** is a series of drawings which tell a story. ❑ *...a cartoon strip.* [Senses 1 to 3 and 8 from Middle Dutch. Senses 4 to 7 from Old English.]
▶ **strip away** PHR-VERB To **strip away** something, especially something that hides the true nature of a thing, means to remove it completely. ❑ *Altman strips away the glamor of the film industry.*
▶ **strip off** PHR-VERB If you **strip off** your clothes, you take them off. ❑ *He stripped off his wet clothes.*
→ see also **strip 4**

**stripe** /straɪp/ (**stripes**) N-COUNT A **stripe** is a long line which is a different color from the areas next to it. ❑ *...a skirt with a white stripe down the side.* [from Middle Dutch]
→ see **pattern**

**striped** /straɪpt/ ADJ Something that is **striped** has stripes on it. ❑ *...a green and red striped tie.* [from Middle Dutch]

**strip mall** (**strip malls**) N-COUNT A **strip mall** is a shopping area consisting of one or more long buildings. ❑ *...a parking lot outside a strip mall.*

**strip mine** (**strip mines**) N-COUNT A **strip mine** is a mine in which the coal, metal, or mineral is

near the surface, and so underground passages are not needed.

**strip min|ing** also **strip-mining** N-UNCOUNT **Strip mining** is a method of mining that is used when a mineral is near the surface and underground passages are not needed.

**strive** /straɪv/ (**strives, striving**)

The past tense is either **strove** or **strived**, and the past participle is either **striven** or **strived**.

V-I If you **strive to** do something or **strive for** something, you make a great effort to do it or get it. ❑ *He strives hard to keep himself fit.* [from Old French]

**strode** /stroʊd/ **Strode** is the past tense and past participle of **stride**. [from Old English]

**stroke** /stroʊk/ (**strokes, stroking, stroked**)
■ V-T If you **stroke** someone or something, you move your hand slowly and gently over them. ❑ *Carla was stroking her cat.* ■ N-COUNT If someone has a **stroke**, a blood vessel in their brain bursts or becomes blocked, which may kill them or make them unable to move one side of their body. ❑ *He had a stroke last year, and now cannot walk.* ■ N-COUNT The **strokes** of a pen or brush are the movements or marks that you make with it when you are writing or painting. ❑ *Use short strokes of the pencil.* ■ N-COUNT When you are swimming or rowing, your **strokes** are the repeated movements that you make with your arms or the oars. ❑ *I turned and swam a few strokes further out to sea.* ■ N-COUNT A swimming **stroke** is a particular style or method of swimming. ❑ *Which stroke is the fastest for swimming?* ■ N-COUNT The **strokes** of a clock are the sounds that indicate each hour. ❑ *On the stroke of 12, they ring a bell.* ■ N-COUNT In sports such as tennis, baseball, golf, and cricket, a **stroke** is the action of hitting the ball. ❑ *He hit the ball a long way with each stroke.* ■ N-SING A **stroke of** luck or good fortune is something lucky that happens. ❑ *It didn't rain, which was a stroke of luck.* [from Old English]

**Word Partnership** Use *stroke* with:

| | |
|---|---|
| V. | **die from a** stroke, **have a** stroke, **suffer a** stroke ■ |
| N. | **risk of a** stroke ■ <br> stroke **of a pen** ■ |

**stroll** /stroʊl/ (**strolls, strolling, strolled**) v-ι If you **stroll** somewhere, you walk there in a slow, relaxed way. ❑ *He strolled to the kitchen window.* ● **Stroll** is also a noun. ❑ *After dinner, I took a stroll round the city.* [from German]
→ see **park**

**stroll|er** /stroʊlər/ (**strollers**) N-COUNT A **stroller** is a small chair on wheels, in which a baby or small child can sit and be wheeled around. [from German]

**strong** /strɒŋ/ (**stronger** /strɒŋgər/, **strongest** /strɒŋgɪst/) **1** ADJ Someone who is **strong** is healthy with good muscles. ❑ *I'm not strong enough to carry him.* **2** ADJ Someone who is **strong** is confident and determined. ❑ *He has a very strong character.* ● *You have to be strong and do what you believe is right.* **3** ADJ **Strong** objects or materials are not easily broken. ❑ *The strong plastic will not crack.* ● **strong|ly** ADV ❑ *The wall was very strongly built.* **4** ADJ **Strong** means great in degree or intensity. ❑ *I have very strong feelings for my family.* ❑ *She has strong support from her friends.* ● **strong|ly** ADV ❑ *He is strongly influenced by Spanish painters.* **5** ADJ If you have **strong** opinions on something or express them using **strong** words, you have extreme or very definite opinions which you are willing to express or defend. ❑ *She has strong views on Cuba.* ❑ *I am a strong supporter of the president.* ● **strong|ly** ADV ❑ *Obviously you feel very strongly about this.* **6** ADJ If someone in authority takes **strong** action, they act firmly and severely. ❑ *Congress decided to take strong action.* **7** ADJ Your **strong** points are your best qualities or talents, or the things you are good at. ❑ *Cooking is not Jeremy's strong point.* **8** ADJ A **strong** competitor, candidate, or team is good or likely to succeed. ❑ *This year we have a very strong team.* **9** ADJ You can use **strong** when you are saying how many people there are in a group. For example, if a group is twenty strong, there are twenty people in it. ❑ *The country's army is 400,000 strong.* **10** ADJ A **strong** drink, chemical, or drug contains a lot of the particular substance which makes it effective. ❑ *...a cup of strong coffee.* **11** ADJ A **strong** color, flavor, smell, sound, or light is intense and easily noticed. ❑ *Onions have a strong smell.* ● **strong|ly** ADV ❑ *He smelled strongly of sweat.* **12** PHRASE If someone or something is still **going strong**, they are still alive, in good condition, or popular after a long time. [INFORMAL] ❑ *The old car was still going strong.* [from Old English]

| **Thesaurus** | strong | Also look up : |
| --- | --- | --- |
| ADJ. | mighty, powerful, tough; (*ant.*) weak **1** confident, determined; (*ant.*) cowardly **2** solid, sturdy **3** | |

**strong|hold** /strɒŋhoʊld/ (**strongholds**) N-COUNT If a place or region is a **stronghold** of a particular attitude or belief, most people there share this attitude or belief. ❑ *The city is a stronghold of terrorism.*

**strove** /stroʊv/ **Strove** is a past tense of **strive**. [from Old French]

**struck** /strʌk/ **Struck** is the past tense and past participle of **strike**. [from Old English]

**struc|tur|al** /strʌktʃərəl/ ADJ **Structural** means relating to or affecting the structure of something. ❑ *The bomb caused structural damage to*

the building. ● **struc|tur|al|ly** ADV ❑ *When we bought the house, it was structurally in very good condition.* [from Latin]

**struc|ture** /strʌktʃər/ (**structures, structuring, structured**) **1** N-VAR The **structure of** something is the way in which it is made, built, or organized. ❑ *The typical family structure was two parents and two children.* **2** N-COUNT A **structure** is something that is built from or consists of parts connected together in an ordered way. ❑ *Your feet are structures made up of 26 small bones.* ❑ *...structures such as roads and bridges.* **3** V-T If you **structure** something, you arrange it in a careful, organized pattern or system. ❑ *We structure the class in two parts.* ● **struc|tured** ADJ ❑ *...a more structured training program.* [from Latin]

**strug|gle** /strʌgəl/ (**struggles, struggling, struggled**) **1** V-I If you **struggle to** do something difficult, you try hard to do it. ❑ *They had to struggle against all kinds of problems.* **2** N-VAR A **struggle** is a long and difficult attempt to achieve something such as freedom or political rights. ❑ *...the struggle for power between Nixon and Kennedy.* ❑ *...a young boy's struggle to survive.* **3** V-I If you **struggle** when you are being held, you twist, kick, and move violently in order to get free. ❑ *I struggled, but she was too strong for me.* **4** V-RECIP If two people **struggle with** each other, they fight. ❑ *They struggled on the ground.* ● **Struggle** is also a noun. ❑ *He died in a struggle with prison officers.* **5** V-I If you **struggle to** move yourself or to move a heavy object, you try to do it, but it is difficult. ❑ *I could see the young boy struggling to free himself.* **6** N-SING An action or activity that is **a struggle** is very difficult to do. ❑ *Losing weight was a terrible struggle.*

| **Word Partnership** | Use *struggle* with : |
| --- | --- |
| N. | struggle **for democracy**, struggle **for equality**, struggle **for freedom/ independence**, struggle **for survival 1 2** **power** struggle **2** |
| ADJ. | **bitter** struggle, **internal** struggle, **long** struggle, **political** struggle, **uphill** struggle **2** **locked in a** struggle **2 4** |

**strum** /strʌm/ (**strums, strumming, strummed**) V-T If you **strum** a stringed instrument such as a guitar, you play it by moving your fingers backward and forward across the strings. ❑ *One man sat softly strumming a guitar.*

**strut** /strʌt/ (**struts, strutting, strutted**) **1** V-I Someone who **struts** walks in a proud way, with their head held high and their chest out, as if they are very important. ❑ *He struts around town as if he's really important.* **2** N-COUNT A **strut** is a piece of wood or metal which holds the weight of other pieces in a building or other structure. ❑ *...the struts of a bridge.* [from Old English]

**stub** /stʌb/ (**stubs, stubbing, stubbed**) **1** N-COUNT The **stub** of a pencil is the last short piece of it which remains when the rest has been used. ❑ *He pulled the stub of a pencil from behind his ear.* **2** N-COUNT A ticket or check **stub** is the part that you keep. ❑ *Save the ticket stubs from every game.* ❑ *I have every check stub we've written since 1990.* **3** V-T If you **stub** your **toe**, you hurt it by accidentally kicking something. ❑ *I stubbed my*

**S**

*toes against a table leg.* [from Old English]

▶ **stub out** PHR-VERB When someone **stubs out** a cigarette, they put it out by pressing it against something hard. ❑ *A sign told visitors to stub out their cigarettes.*

**stub|ble** /stʌbəl/ N-UNCOUNT The very short hairs on a man's face when he has not shaved recently are referred to as **stubble**. ❑ *His face was covered with stubble.* [from Old French]

**stub|born** /stʌbərn/ ◼ ADJ Someone who is **stubborn** or who behaves in a **stubborn** way is determined to do what they want and is very unwilling to change their mind. ❑ *He is a stubborn character and always gets what he wants.* ● **stub|born|ly** ADV ❑ *He stubbornly refused to tell her the truth.* ● **stub|born|ness** N-UNCOUNT ❑ *His refusal to talk was simple stubbornness.* ◼ ADJ A **stubborn** stain or problem is difficult to remove or to deal with. ❑ *This product removes the most stubborn stains.* ● **stub|born|ly** ADV ❑ *Prices stayed stubbornly high.*

**stuck** /stʌk/ ◼ **Stuck** is the past tense and past participle of **stick**. ◼ ADJ If something is **stuck** in a particular position, it is fixed tightly in this position and is unable to move. ❑ *His car got stuck in the snow.* ◼ ADJ If you are **stuck** in a place or in a boring or unpleasant situation, you want to get away from it, but are unable to. ❑ *I was stuck at home sick.* ❑ *I don't want to get stuck in another job like that.* ◼ ADJ If you get **stuck** when you are trying to do something, you are unable to continue doing it because it is too difficult. ❑ *They will be there to help if you get stuck.* [from Old English]

**stud** /stʌd/ (**studs**) ◼ N-COUNT **Studs** are small pieces of metal which are attached to a surface for decoration. ❑ *You see studs on lots of front doors.* ◼ N-UNCOUNT Horses or other animals that are kept for **stud** are kept to be used for breeding. ❑ *Most of the young horses are sold, but a few are kept for stud.* [from Old English]

**stud|ded** /stʌdɪd/ ADJ Something that is **studded** is decorated with studs or things that look like studs. ❑ *...studded leather jackets.* [from Old English]

**stu|dent** /studənt/ (**students**) ◼ N-COUNT A **student** is a person who is studying at an elementary school, secondary school, college, or university. ❑ *Warren's eldest son is an art student.* [from Latin] ◼ → see also **graduate student** → see **graduation**

**stu|dent body** (**student bodies**) N-COUNT A **student body** is all the students of a particular school, considered as a group. ❑ *Those groups make up a quarter of the student body.*

**stu|dent coun|cil** (**student councils**) N-VAR A **student council** is an organization of students within a school that represents the interests of the students who study there. ❑ *Jim Blaschek is student council president at Sandburg High School.*

**stu|dent loan** (**student loans**) N-COUNT A **student loan** is a government loan that is available to students at a college or university in order to help them pay their expenses. ❑ *...the government's $12 billion student loan program.*

**stu|dent un|ion** (**student unions**) N-COUNT The **student union** is the building at a college or university which usually has food services, a bookstore, meeting places for leisure activities,

and offices for the student government.

**stu|dio** /studiou/ (**studios**) ◼ N-COUNT A **studio** is a room where a painter, photographer, or designer works. ❑ *She was in her studio painting on a large canvas.* ◼ N-COUNT A **studio** is a room where radio or television programs are recorded, CDs are produced, or movies are made. ❑ *She's much happier performing live than in a recording studio.* [from Italian] → see **art**

| Word Partnership | Use *studio* with : |
|---|---|
| N. | studio **album**, studio **audience**, **music** studio, **recording** studio, **television/TV** studio ◼ |

**study** /stʌdi/ (**studies, studying, studied**) ◼ V-T/V-I If you **study**, you spend time learning about a particular subject or subjects. ❑ *She spends most of her time studying.* ❑ *He studied History and Economics.* ◼ N-VAR **Study** is the activity of studying. ❑ *...the study of local history.* ◼ N-COUNT A **study** of a subject is a piece of research on it. ❑ *Recent studies suggest many new mothers suffer from depression.* ◼ N-PLURAL You can refer to educational subjects or several related courses as **studies** of a particular kind. ❑ *...a center for Islamic studies.* ◼ V-T If you **study** something, you look at it or consider it very carefully. ❑ *Debbie studied her friend's face.* ◼ N-COUNT A **study** is a room in a house which is used for reading, writing, and studying. ❑ *We sat together in his study.* [from Old French] ◼ → see also **case study** → see **laboratory**

**study hall** (**study halls**) N-VAR A **study hall** is a room where students can study during free time between classes, or a period of time during which such study takes place. ❑ *Children are working hard in the study hall.*

**stuff** /stʌf/ (**stuffs, stuffing, stuffed**) ◼ N-UNCOUNT You can use **stuff** to refer to things in a general way without mentioning the thing itself by name. [INFORMAL] ❑ *I like tea, but not that herbal stuff.* ❑ *He pointed to a bag. "That's my stuff."* ◼ V-T If you **stuff** something somewhere, you push it there quickly and roughly. ❑ *I stuffed my hands in my pockets.* ◼ V-T If you **stuff** a container or space **with** something, you fill it with something or with a quantity of things until it is full. ❑ *He took my purse, stuffed it full, then gave it back to me.* ◼ V-T If you **stuff** a bird such as a chicken or a vegetable such as a pepper, you put a mixture of food inside it before cooking it. ❑ *Will you stuff the turkey and put it in the oven for me?* ◼ V-T If a dead animal **is stuffed**, it is filled with a substance so that it can be preserved and displayed. ❑ *...his collection of stuffed birds.* [from Old French]

| Thesaurus | *stuff* | Also look up : |
|---|---|---|
| N. | belongings, goods, material, substance ◼ | |
| V. | crowd, fill, jam, squeeze ◼ ◼ | |

**stuffed ani|mal** (**stuffed animals**) N-COUNT **Stuffed animals** are toys that are made of cloth filled with a soft material and which look like animals.

**stuff|ing** /stʌfɪŋ/ (**stuffings**) ◼ N-VAR **Stuffing** is a mixture of food that is put inside a bird such as a chicken, or a vegetable such as a pepper, before it is cooked. ❑ *…a stuffing for chicken.* **2** N-UNCOUNT **Stuffing** is material that is used to fill things such as cushions or toys in order to make them firm or solid. ❑ *…a doll with all the stuffing coming out.* [from Old French]

**stuffy** /stʌfi/ (**stuffier, stuffiest**) ADJ If it is **stuffy** in a place, it is unpleasantly warm and there is not enough fresh air. ❑ *It was hot and stuffy in the classroom.* [from Old French]

**stum|ble** /stʌmbᵊl/ (**stumbles, stumbling, stumbled**) V-I If you **stumble**, you put your foot down awkwardly while you are walking or running and nearly fall over. ❑ *He stumbled and almost fell.* [from Norwegian]
▶ **stumble across** or **stumble on** PHR-VERB If you **stumble across** something or **stumble on** it, you find it or discover it unexpectedly. ❑ *I stumbled across a good way of saving money.*

**stum|bling block** (**stumbling blocks**) N-COUNT A **stumbling block** is a problem which stops you from achieving something. ❑ *The major stumbling block in the talks was money.*

**stump** /stʌmp/ (**stumps, stumping, stumped**) **1** N-COUNT A **stump** is a small part of something that remains when the rest of it has been removed or broken off. ❑ *…a tree stump.* **2** V-T If you **are stumped** by a question or problem, you cannot think of any solution or answer to it. ❑ *He was stumped by an unexpected question.* [from Middle Low German]

**stun** /stʌn/ (**stuns, stunning, stunned**) **1** V-T If you **are stunned** by something, you are extremely shocked or surprised by it and are therefore unable to speak or do anything. ❑ *He's stunned by today's news.* ● **stunned** ADJ ❑ *When they told me she was missing I was totally stunned.* **2** V-T If something such as a blow on the head **stuns** you, it makes you unconscious or confused and unsteady. ❑ *The blow to his head stunned him.* [from Old French] **3** → see also **stunning**

**stung** /stʌŋ/ **Stung** is the past tense and past participle of **sting**. [from Old English]

**stun gun** (**stun guns**) N-COUNT A **stun gun** is a device that can immobilize a person or animal for a short time without causing them serious injury.

**stunk** /stʌŋk/ **Stunk** is the past participle of **stink**. [from Old English]

**stun|ning** /stʌnɪŋ/ ADJ A **stunning** person or thing is extremely beautiful or impressive. ❑ *She was 55 and still a stunning woman.* ● **stun|ning|ly** ADV ❑ *…stunningly beautiful countryside.* [from Old French]

**stunt** /stʌnt/ (**stunts, stunting, stunted**) **1** N-COUNT A **stunt** is something interesting that is done in order to attract attention and get publicity for the person or company responsible for it. ❑ *She turned her wedding into a publicity stunt.* **2** N-COUNT A **stunt** is a dangerous and exciting piece of action in a movie. ❑ *Sean Connery did his own stunts.* **3** V-T If something **stunts** the growth or development of a person or thing, it prevents it

from growing or developing as much as it should. ❑ *The disease stunted his growth.* ● **stunt|ed** ADJ ❑ *Damage to the plant may result in stunted growth.* [Sense 3 from Old English]

**stu|pid** /stupɪd/ (**stupider, stupidest**) **1** ADJ If you say that someone or something is **stupid**, you mean that they show a lack of good judgment or intelligence and they are not at all sensible. ❑ *I'll never do anything so stupid again.* ❑ *I made a stupid mistake.* ● **stu|pid|ly** ADV ❑ *We were stupidly looking at the wrong information.* ● **stu|pid|ity** /stupɪdɪti/ (**stupidities**) N-VAR ❑ *I was surprised by his stupidity.* **2** ADJ You say that something is **stupid** to indicate that you do not like it or that it annoys you. ❑ *It's not art. It's just stupid and ugly.* [from French]

**stur|dy** /stɜrdi/ (**sturdier, sturdiest**) ADJ Someone or something that is **sturdy** looks strong and is unlikely to be easily injured or damaged. ❑ *She was a short, sturdy woman.* ● **stur|di|ly** ADV ❑ *The table was strong and sturdily built.* [from Old French]

**stut|ter** /stʌtər/ (**stutters, stuttering, stuttered**) **1** N-COUNT If someone has a **stutter**, they find it difficult to say the first sound of a word, and so they often hesitate or repeat it two or three times. ❑ *He spoke with a stutter.* **2** V-I If someone **stutters**, they have difficulty speaking because they find it hard to say the first sound of a word. ❑ *I thought I would stutter when I spoke.* ● **stut|ter|ing** N-UNCOUNT ❑ *Then his stuttering started.* [from Middle Low German]

**style** /staɪl/ (**styles, styling, styled**) **1** N-COUNT The **style** of something is the general way in which it is done or presented. ❑ *Children have different learning styles.* ❑ *I prefer the Indian style of cooking.* **2** N-UNCOUNT If people or places have **style**, they are fashionable and elegant. ❑ *Boston has style.* ❑ *Both women love doing things in style.* **3** N-VAR The **style** of a product is its design. ❑ *He has strong feelings about style.* **4** V-T If something such as a piece of clothing, a vehicle, or your hair **is styled** in a particular way, it is designed or shaped in that way. ❑ *His thick blond hair was styled before his trip.* **5** N-COUNT The **style** of a writer, painter, or other artist is the particular way that their work is constructed and the way that it differs from the

S

work of other artists. **6** N-COUNT A **style** is a set of characteristics which defines a culture, period, or school of art. [from Latin] **7** → see also **self-styled**

**Word Partnership** Use *style* with :

| N. | **leadership** style, **learning** style, style **of life**, style, **music** style, **prose** style, **writing** style **1** |
| | **differences in** style **1** – **3** |
| ADJ. | **distinctive** style, **particular** style, **personal** style **1** – **3** |

**styl|ish** /staɪlɪʃ/ ADJ Someone or something that is **stylish** is elegant and fashionable. ☐ *…a stylish woman of 27.* ● **styl|ish|ly** ADV ☐ *…stylishly dressed men.* [from Latin]

**sty|lis|tic** /staɪlɪstɪk/ ADJ **Stylistic** describes things relating to the methods and techniques used in creating a piece of writing, music, or art. ☐ *There are some stylistic differences in their work.* ● **sty|lis|ti|cal|ly** ADV ☐ *Stylistically, this book is very unusual.* [from Latin]

**sty|lis|tic nu|ance** (**stylistic nuances**) N-VAR The **stylistic nuances** of an artistic performance or work are the small details in the way it is performed or constructed that give it a distinctive style.

**styl|ized** /staɪlaɪzd/ ADJ Something that is **stylized** is shown or done in a way that is not natural in order to create an artistic effect. ☐ *The play is very stylized.* [from Latin]

**suave** /swɑv/ (**suaver, suavest**) ADJ Someone who is **suave** is charming, polite, and elegant, but may be insincere. ☐ *He is a suave man.* [from Latin]

**sub** /sʌb/ (**subs**) **1** N-COUNT A **sub** is a long soft bread roll filled with a combination of foods such as meat, cheese, and salad. **Sub** is an abbreviation for "submarine sandwich." **2** N-COUNT A **sub** is the same as a **substitute teacher. 3** N-COUNT In team games such as football, a **sub** is a player who is brought into a game to replace another player. [INFORMAL] ☐ *A few kids from the youth team were used as subs.* **4** N-COUNT A **sub** is the same as a **submarine.** [INFORMAL]

**sub|com|mit|tee** /sʌbkəmɪti/ (**subcommittees**) N-COUNT A **subcommittee** is a small committee made up of members of a larger committee.

**sub|con|scious** /sʌbkɒnʃəs/ **1** N-SING Your **subconscious** is the part of your mind that can influence you or affect your behavior even though you are not aware of it. ☐ *…the power of the subconscious.* **2** ADJ A **subconscious** feeling or action exists in or is influenced by your subconscious. ☐ *He caught her arm in a subconscious attempt to stop her from leaving.* ● **sub|con|scious|ly** ADV ☐ *Subconsciously I knew that I wasn't in danger.* [from Latin]

**Word Link** *sub ≈ below : subculture, submarine, submerge*

**sub|cul|ture** /sʌbkʌltʃər/ (**subcultures**) N-COUNT A **subculture** is the ideas, art, and way of life of a group of people within a society, which are different from the ideas, arts, and way of life of the rest of the society. ☐ *…the latest American subculture.* [from Old French]
→ see **culture**

**sub|di|vi|sion** /sʌbdɪvɪʒ°n/ (**subdivisions**) **1** N-COUNT A **subdivision** is an area, part, or section of something which is itself a part of something larger. ☐ *Months are a subdivision of the year.* **2** N-COUNT A **subdivision** is an area of land for building houses on. ☐ *Rammick lives in a subdivision of 400 homes.* [from Latin]

**sub|due** /səbdu/ (**subdues, subduing, subdued**) **1** V-T If soldiers or the police **subdue** a group of people, they defeat them or bring them under control by using force. ☐ *They took control of the land by violently subduing its people.* **2** V-T To **subdue** feelings means to make them less strong. ☐ *He forced himself to subdue his fears.* [from Old French]

**sub|dued** /səbdud/ **1** ADJ Someone who is **subdued** is very quiet, often because they are sad or worried about something. ☐ *He was in a subdued mood.* **2** ADJ **Subdued** lights or colors are not very bright. ☐ *The lighting was subdued.* [from Old French]

**sub|ject** (**subjects, subjecting, subjected**)

The noun and adjective are pronounced /sʌbdʒɪkt/. The verb is pronounced /səbdʒɛkt/.

**1** N-COUNT The **subject** of something such as a conversation, letter, or book is the thing that is being discussed or written about. ☐ *I raised the subject of plastic surgery.* ☐ *…the president's own views on the subject.* **2** N-COUNT A **subject** is an area of knowledge or study, especially one that you study in school, or college. ☐ *Math is my favorite subject.* **3** N-COUNT In grammar, the **subject** of a clause is the noun group that refers to the person or thing that is doing the action expressed by the verb. For example, in "My cat keeps catching birds," "my cat" is the subject. **4** ADJ To be **subject to** something means to be affected by it or to be likely to be affected by it. ☐ *Prices may be subject to change.* **5** V-T If you **subject** someone **to** something unpleasant, you make them experience it. ☐ *He subjected her to a life of misery.* **6** N-COUNT The people who live in or belong to a particular country, usually one ruled by a monarch, are the **subjects** of that monarch or country. ☐ *His subjects thought he was a good king.* **7** PHRASE If an event will take place **subject to** a condition, it will take place only if that thing happens. ☐ *They agreed to a meeting, subject to certain conditions.* [from Latin]

**Word Partnership** Use *subject* with :

| ADJ. | **controversial** subject, **favorite** subject, **touchy** subject **1** |
| V. | **change the** subject **1** |
| | **broach** a subject, **study** a subject **1 2** |
| N. | **knowledge of a** subject **1 2** |
| | subject **of a debate**, subject **of an investigation 2** |
| | subject **of a sentence**, subject **of a verb 3** |
| PREP. | subject **to approval**, subject **to availability**, subject **to laws**, subject **to scrutiny**, subject **to a tax 4** |

**sub|jec|tive** /səbdʒɛktɪv/ ADJ Something that is **subjective** is based on personal opinions and feelings rather than on facts. ☐ *Art is very subjective.* ● **sub|jec|tive|ly** ADV ☐ *You are just thinking about this subjectively.* ● **sub|jec|tiv|ity**

/sʌbdʒəktɪviti/ N-UNCOUNT ❑ *They accused her of subjectivity in her reporting of events in their country.* [from Latin]

**sub|ject mat|ter** N-UNCOUNT The **subject matter** of something such as a book, lecture, movie, or painting is the thing that is being written about, discussed, or shown. ❑ *Artists can choose any subject matter.*

**sub|junc|tive** /səbdʒʌŋktɪv/ N-SING In English, a clause expressing a wish or suggestion can be put in the **subjunctive**, or in the **subjunctive** mood, by using the base form of a verb or "were." Examples are "He asked that they be removed" and "I wish I were somewhere else." These structures are formal. [TECHNICAL] [from Late Latin]

**sub|li|ma|tion** /sʌblɪmeɪʃ°n/ (sublimations) N-VAR Sublimation is the change that occurs when a solid substance becomes a gas without first becoming a liquid. [TECHNICAL] [from Latin]

**sub|lime** /səblaɪm/ ADJ If you describe something as **sublime**, you mean that it has a wonderful quality that affects you deeply. [LITERARY] ❑ *…sublime music.* ● You can refer to sublime things as **the sublime**. ❑ *Fear of love is fear of the sublime.* [from Latin]

| Word Link | **sub ≈ below** : sub**culture**, sub**marine**, sub**merge** |
|---|---|

| Word Link | **mar ≈ sea** : **marine**, **maritime**, sub**marine** |
|---|---|

**sub|ma|rine** /sʌbmərin/ (submarines) N-COUNT A **submarine** is a type of ship that can travel both above and below the surface of the ocean. The abbreviation **sub** is also used. ❑ *…a nuclear submarine.* [from Old French]
→ see **tsunami**

| Word Link | **merg ≈ sinking** : e**merge**, **merge**, sub**merge** |
|---|---|

**sub|merge** /səbmɜrdʒ/ (submerges, submerging, submerged) V-T/V-I If something **submerges** or if you **submerge** it, it goes below the surface of water or another liquid. ❑ *The frog submerged.* [from Latin]

**sub|mis|sion** /səbmɪʃ°n/ N-UNCOUNT **Submission** is a state in which people can no longer do what they want to do because they have been brought under the control of someone else. ❑ *She felt that he had bullied her into submission.* [from Latin]

**sub|mis|sive** /səbmɪsɪv/ ADJ If you are **submissive**, you obey someone without arguing. ❑ *He believed that young people should be submissive to their parents.* ● **sub|mis|sive|ly** ADV ❑ *The troops submissively laid down their weapons.* [from Latin]

**sub|mit** /səbmɪt/ (submits, submitting, submitted) ■ V-I If you **submit to** something, you do it unwillingly, for example because you are not powerful enough to resist. ❑ *Mrs. Jones submitted to an operation on her knee to relieve the pain.* ■ V-T If you **submit** a proposal, report, or request **to** someone, you formally send it to them so that they can consider it or decide about it. ❑ *They submitted their reports yesterday.* [from Latin]

**sub|or|di|nate** (subordinates, subordinating, subordinated)

The noun and adjective are pronounced /səbɔrd°nɪt/. The verb is pronounced /səbɔrd°neɪt/.

■ N-COUNT If someone is your **subordinate**, they have a less important position than you in the organization that you both work for. ❑ *Haig did not ask for advice from subordinates.* ■ ADJ Someone who is **subordinate to** you has a less important position than you and has to obey you. ❑ *Sixty of his subordinate officers were with him.* ■ ADJ Something that is **subordinate to** something else is less important than the other thing. ❑ *Science became subordinate to technology.* ■ V-T If you **subordinate** something **to** another thing, you regard it or treat it as less important than the other thing. ❑ *He subordinated everything to his job.* ● **sub|or|di|na|tion** /səbɔrd°neɪʃ°n/ N-UNCOUNT ❑ *…the social subordination of women.* [from Medieval Latin]

**sub|or|di|nate clause** (subordinate clauses) N-COUNT A **subordinate clause** is a clause in a sentence which adds to or completes the information given in the main clause. It cannot usually stand alone as a sentence. Compare **main clause**. [TECHNICAL]

**sub|scribe** /səbskraɪb/ (subscribes, subscribing, subscribed) ■ V-I If you **subscribe to** an opinion or belief, you are one of a number of people who have this opinion or belief. ❑ *I don't subscribe to the view that men are better than women.* ■ V-I If you **subscribe to** a magazine, newspaper, or service, you pay money regularly to receive it. ❑ *Why do you subscribe to "New Scientist"?* ● **sub|scrib|er** (subscribers) N-COUNT ❑ *I am a subscriber to "Newsweek."* ❑ *China has millions of subscribers to cable television.* [from Latin]

**sub|script** /sʌbskrɪpt/ (subscripts) N-COUNT In chemistry and mathematics, a **subscript** is a number or symbol that is written below another number or symbol and to the right of it, for example the '2' in $H_2O$.

**sub|scrip|tion** /səbskrɪpʃ°n/ (subscriptions) ■ N-COUNT A **subscription** is an amount of money that you pay regularly in order to belong to or support an organization, to receive copies of a magazine or newspaper, or to receive a service. ❑ *Members pay a subscription every year.* ■ ADJ **Subscription** television is television that you can watch only if you pay a subscription. A **subscription** channel is a channel that you can watch only if you pay a subscription. ❑ *Premiere is a subscription channel.*

**sub|se|quent** /sʌbsɪkwənt/ ADJ You use **subsequent** to describe something that happened or existed after the time or event that has just been referred to. [FORMAL] ❑ *…the increase of prices in subsequent years.* ● **sub|se|quent|ly** ADV ❑ *He subsequently worked in Canada.* [from Latin]

**sub|ser|vi|ent** /səbsɜrviənt/ ■ ADJ If you are **subservient**, you do whatever someone wants you to do. ❑ *I will not be subservient to my children.* ● **sub|ser|vi|ence** /səbsɜrviəns/ N-UNCOUNT ❑ *…his subservience to authority.* ■ ADJ If you treat one thing as **subservient to** another, you treat it as less important than the other thing. ❑ *He considers my needs to be subservient to his.* [from Latin]

**S**

**sub|side** /səbsaɪd/ (**subsides, subsiding, subsided**) **1** V-I If a feeling or noise **subsides**, it becomes less strong or loud. ❑ *The pain subsided during the night.* **2** V-I If the ground or a building **is subsiding**, it is very slowly sinking to a lower level. ❑ *Is the whole house subsiding?* [from Latin]

**sub|sidi|ary** /səbsɪdiɛri/ (**subsidiaries**) **1** N-COUNT A **subsidiary** or a **subsidiary** company is a company which is part of a larger and more important company. [BUSINESS] ❑ *WM Financial Services is a subsidiary of Washington Mutual.* **2** ADJ If something is **subsidiary**, it is less important than something else with which it is connected. ❑ *The marketing department plays a subsidiary role to the sales department.* [from Latin]

**sub|si|dize** /sʌbsɪdaɪz/ (**subsidizes, subsidizing, subsidized**) V-T If a government or other authority **subsidizes** something, they pay part of the cost of it. ❑ *The government subsidizes farming.* ● **sub|si|dized** ADJ ❑ *...subsidized prices for housing, bread, and meat.* [from Latin]

**sub|si|dy** /sʌbsɪdi/ (**subsidies**) N-COUNT A **subsidy** is money that is paid by a government or other authority in order to help an industry or business, or to pay for a public service. ❑ *...farm subsidies.* [from Latin]

**sub|sist|ence** /səbsɪstəns/ N-UNCOUNT **Subsistence** is the condition of just having enough food or money to stay alive. ❑ *...people living below subsistence level.* [from Latin]

**sub|species** /sʌbspiʃiz/ (**subspecies**) also **sub-species** N-COUNT A **subspecies** of a plant or animal is one of the types that a particular species is divided into. ❑ *Several other subspecies of lavender found in the region.* [from Latin]

**sub|stance** /sʌbstəns/ (**substances**) **1** N-COUNT A **substance** is a solid, powder, liquid, or gas. ❑ *The waste contained several unpleasant substances.* **2** N-UNCOUNT **Substance** is the quality of being important or significant. [FORMAL] ❑ *Was anything of substance achieved?* **3** N-SING **The substance of** what someone says or writes is the main thing that they are trying to say. ❑ *The substance of his discussions doesn't really matter.* **4** N-UNCOUNT If you say that something has no **substance**, you mean that it is not true. [FORMAL] ❑ *There is never any substance to what he says.* [from Old French]

| Word Partnership | Use *substance* with : |
| --- | --- |
| ADJ. | **banned** substance, **chemical** substance, **natural** substance **1** |
| N. | **lack of** substance **2** |

**sub|stance abuse** N-UNCOUNT **Substance abuse** is the use of illegal drugs. ❑ *...accidents caused by substance abuse.*

**sub|stan|tial** /səbstænʃ³l/ ADJ **Substantial** means large in amount or degree. [FORMAL] ❑ *A substantial number of mothers do not go out to work.* ● **sub|stan|tial|ly** /səbstænʃəli/ ADV ❑ *The number of women in engineering has increased substantially.* [from Middle English]

| Word Partnership | Use *substantial* with : |
| --- | --- |
| N. | substantial **amount**, substantial **changes**, substantial **difference**, substantial **evidence**, substantial **increase**, substantial **loss**, substantial **number**, substantial **part**, substantial **progress**, substantial **savings**, substantial **support** |
| ADV. | **fairly** substantial, **very** substantial |

**sub|stan|ti|ate** /səbstænʃieɪt/ (**substantiates, substantiating, substantiated**) V-T To **substantiate** a statement or a story means to supply evidence which proves that it is true. [FORMAL] ❑ *Most research substantiates the idea that the Earth is getting warmer.* [from New Latin]

**sub|stan|tive** /sʌbstəntɪv/ ADJ **Substantive** negotiations or issues deal with the most important and central aspects of a subject. [FORMAL] ❑ *They plan to meet again very soon to begin substantive negotiations.* [from Late Latin]

**sub|sti|tute** /sʌbstɪtut/ (**substitutes, substituting, substituted**) **1** V-T/V-I If you **substitute** one thing **for** another, or if one thing **substitutes for** another, it takes the place or performs the function of the other thing. ❑ *They were substituting argument for discussion.* ❑ *Will you substitute for me?* ● **sub|sti|tu|tion** /sʌbstɪtuʃⁿn/ (**substitutions**) N-VAR ❑ *...the substitution of oil for butter.* **2** N-COUNT A **substitute** is something that you have or use instead of something else. ❑ *She is seeking a substitute for her father.* **3** N-COUNT In team games such as football, a **substitute** is a player who is brought into a game to replace another player. ❑ *Jefferson entered as a substitute in the 60th minute.* [from Latin]

**sub|sti|tute teach|er** (**substitute teachers**) N-COUNT A **substitute teacher** is a teacher whose job is to take the place of other teachers at different schools when they are unable to be there.

| Word Link | terr ≈ earth : sub*terr*anean, *terr*ain, *terr*itory |
| --- | --- |

**sub|ter|ra|nean** /sʌbtəreɪniən/ ADJ A **subterranean** river or tunnel is under the ground. [FORMAL] ❑ *The city has 9 miles of subterranean passages.* [from Latin]

**sub|text** /sʌbtɛkst/ (**subtexts**) N-VAR The **subtext** is the implied message or subject of something that is said or written. [from Medieval Latin]

**sub|tle** /sʌt³l/ (**subtler, subtlest**) **1** ADJ Something that is **subtle** is not immediately obvious or noticeable. ❑ *Subtle changes take place in all living things.* ● **sub|tly** ADV ❑ *The truth is subtly different.* **2** ADJ **Subtle** smells, tastes, sounds, or colors are pleasantly complex and intricate. ❑ *...subtle shades of brown.* ● **sub|tly** ADV ❑ *...subtly colored rugs.* [from Old French]

**sub|tle|ty** /sʌt³lti/ (**subtleties**) **1** N-COUNT **Subtleties** are very small details or differences which are not obvious. ❑ *He has an interest in the subtleties of human behavior.* **2** N-UNCOUNT **Subtlety** is the quality of being not immediately obvious or noticeable, and therefore difficult to describe. ❑ *African dance is lively, but full of subtlety.*

**3** N-UNCOUNT **Subtlety** is the ability to use indirect methods to achieve something, rather than doing something that is obvious. ☐ *They talk about these issues with subtlety.* [from Old French]

> **Word Link** tract ≈ dragging, drawing : contract, subtract, tractor

**sub|tract** /səbtrǽkt/ (**subtracts, subtracting, subtracted**) V-T If you **subtract** one number **from** another, you do a calculation in which you take it away from the other number. For example, if you subtract 3 from 5, you get 2. • **sub|trac|tion** /səbtrǽkʃ³n/ (**subtractions**) N-VAR ☐ *She's ready to learn subtraction.* [from Latin]
→ see **fraction, mathematics**

**sub|trac|tive sculp|ture** /səbtrǽktɪv skʌlptʃər/ (**subtractive sculptures**) N-VAR **Subtractive** sculpture is sculpture that is created by removing material such as clay or wax until the sculpture is complete. Compare **additive**. [TECHNICAL]

**sub|tropi|cal** /sʌbtrɒpɪk³l/ ADJ **Subtropical** places have a climate that is warm and wet, and are often near tropical regions. ☐ *...the subtropical region of the Chapare.*

> **Word Link** urb ≈ city : suburb, suburbia, urban

**sub|urb** /sʌbɜrb/ (**suburbs**) N-COUNT The **suburbs** of a city or large town are the areas on the edge of it where people live. ☐ *Anna was born in a suburb of Philadelphia.* ☐ *His family lived in the suburbs.* [from Latin]
→ see **city, transportation**

**sub|ur|ban** /səbɜrbən/ ADJ **Suburban** means relating to a suburb. ☐ *...a comfortable suburban home.* [from Latin]

**sub|ur|bia** /səbɜrbiə/ N-UNCOUNT Journalists often use **suburbia** to refer to the suburbs of cities and large towns considered as a whole. ☐ *...summer mornings in suburbia.* [from Latin]

**sub|ver|sion** /səbvɜrʒ³n/ N-UNCOUNT **Subversion** is the attempt to weaken or destroy a political system or a government. ☐ *He was arrested for subversion because he organized a demonstration.* [from Late Latin]

**sub|ver|sive** /səbvɜrsɪv/ (**subversives**) **1** ADJ Something that is **subversive** is intended to weaken or destroy a political system or government. ☐ *They banned the play because they said it was subversive.* **2** N-COUNT **Subversives** are people who attempt to weaken or destroy a political system or government. ☐ *The leader thought anyone who disagreed with him was a subversive.* [from Late Latin]

> **Word Link** verg, vert ≈ turning : converge, diverge, subvert

**sub|vert** /səbvɜrt/ (**subverts, subverting, subverted**) V-T To **subvert** something means to destroy its power and influence. [FORMAL] ☐ *...a plan to subvert the state.* [from Latin]

**sub|way** /sʌbweɪ/ (**subways**) N-COUNT A **subway** is an underground railroad. ☐ *I don't ride the subway late at night.* [from Old English]
→ see **transportation**

**suc|ceed** /səksid/ (**succeeds, succeeding, succeeded**) **1** V-I To **succeed** means to achieve the result that you wanted or to perform in a

satisfactory way. ☐ *We have already succeeded in starting our own company.* ☐ *Do you think these talks will succeed?* **2** V-T If you **succeed** another person, you are the next person to have their job or position. ☐ *David Rowland will succeed him as chairman.* [from Latin]

> **Thesaurus** succeed Also look up :
>
> v. accomplish, conquer, master; (ant.) fail **1** displace, replace; (ant.) precede **2**

**suc|cess** /səksɛs/ (**successes**) **1** N-UNCOUNT **Success** is the achievement of something that you have been trying to do. ☐ *It is important for the success of any diet to vary your meals.* ☐ *Hard work is the key to success.* ☐ *We were surprised by the play's success.* **2** N-COUNT Someone or something that is a **success** achieves a high position, makes a lot of money, or is admired a great deal. ☐ *We hope the movie will be a success.* [from Latin]

> **Word Partnership** Use success with :
>
> N. success **of a business 1** **chance for/of** success, success **or failure, key to** success, **lack of** success, **measure of** success **1 2**
> V. **achieve** success, success **depends on something, enjoy** success **1 2**
> ADJ. **great** success, **huge** success, **recent** success, **tremendous** success **1 2**

**suc|cess|ful** /səksɛsfəl/ ADJ Someone or something that is **successful** achieves a desired result or performs in a satisfactory way. ☐ *How successful will this new treatment be?* ☐ *Women do not have to be like men to be successful in business.* • **suc|cess|ful|ly** ADV ☐ *The disease can be successfully treated with drugs.* [from Latin]

**suc|ces|sion** /səksɛʃ³n/ (**successions**) **1** N-SING A **succession of** things of the same kind is a number of them that exist or happen one after the other. ☐ *Adams took a succession of jobs.* **2** N-UNCOUNT **Succession** is the act or right of being the next person to have an important job or position. ☐ *He became king in succession to his father.* [from Latin]

**suc|ces|sive** /səksɛsɪv/ ADJ **Successive** means happening or existing one after another without a break. ☐ *Jackson was the winner for a second successive year.* [from Latin]

**suc|ces|sor** /səksɛsər/ (**successors**) N-COUNT Someone's **successor** is the person who takes their job after they have left. ☐ *His successor is Dr. John Todd.* [from Latin]

**suc|cess sto|ry** (**success stories**) N-COUNT Someone or something that is a **success story** is very successful, often unexpectedly or in spite of unfavorable conditions. ☐ *His company is a success story.*

**suc|cinct** /səksɪŋkt/ ADJ Something that is **succinct** expresses facts or ideas clearly and in few words. ☐ *The book gives a succinct account of the technology and its history.* • **suc|cinct|ly** ADV ☐ *He succinctly explained what he meant.* [from Latin]

> **Word Link** ulent ≈ full of : opulent, succulent, turbulent

**suc|cu|lent** /sʌkyələnt/ ADJ **Succulent** food,

S

especially meat or vegetables, is juicy and good to eat. ❑ …*pieces of succulent chicken.* [from Latin]

**suc|cumb** /səkˈʌm/ (**succumbs, succumbing, succumbed**) V-I If you **succumb to** temptation or pressure, you do something that you want to do, or that other people want you to do, although you feel it might be wrong. [FORMAL] ❑ *Don't succumb to the temptation of just one more piece of cake.* [from Latin]

**such** /sʌtʃ/

When **such** is used as a predeterminer, it is followed by "a" and a count noun in the singular. When it is used as a determiner, it is followed by a count noun in the plural or by an uncountable noun.

■ DET You use **such** to refer back to the thing or person that you have just mentioned or to something similar. ❑ *We each have an account. Such individual accounts are held at the local post office.* ● **Such** is also a predeterminer. ❑ *If I need more information, how do I make such a request?* ❑ *Now he's very satisfied. Unfortunately, not every story has such a happy ending.* ● **Such** is also a pronoun used before **be**. ❑ *We are scared to say anything wrong — such is the atmosphere in our house.* ② DET You use **such…as** or **such as** to introduce one or more examples of something. ❑ …*such careers as teaching and nursing.* ❑ …*serious offenses, such as assault on a police officer.* ③ DET You use **such** to emphasize the degree or extent of something. ❑ *Most of us don't want to read what's in the newspaper in such detail.* ❑ *Why does he feel such anger?* ● **Such** is also a predeterminer. ❑ *It was such a pleasant surprise.* ④ DET You use **such…that** or **such that** in order to say what the result or consequence of something is. ❑ *She looked at him in such distress that he had to look away.* ❑ *His problems are such that he has to go to a special school.* ● **Such** is also a predeterminer. ❑ *He could put an idea in such a way that you would believe it was your own.* ⑤ PHRASE You use **such and such** to refer to a thing or person when you do not want to be exact or precise. [SPOKEN] ❑ *They usually say, "Can you come over tomorrow at such and such a time?"* ⑥ PHRASE You use **as such** with a negative to indicate that a word or expression is not a very accurate description of the actual situation. ❑ *I am not a learner as such — I used to ride a bike years ago.* ⑦ PHRASE You use **as such** after a noun to indicate that you are considering that thing on its own, separately from other things or factors. ❑ *He's not against taxes as such.* [from Old English]

**suck** /sʌk/ (**sucks, sucking, sucked**) ■ V-T/V-I If you **suck** something, you hold it in your mouth and pull at it with the muscles in your cheeks and tongue, for example in order to get liquid out of it. ❑ *They sucked their candies.* ❑ *The baby sucked on his bottle of milk.* ② V-T If something **sucks** a liquid, gas, or object in a particular direction, it draws it there with a powerful force. ❑ *The pump will suck the water out of the basement.* [from Old English]

**suck|er** /sʌkər/ (**suckers**) ■ N-COUNT; N-VOC If you call someone a **sucker**, you mean that it is very easy to cheat them. [INFORMAL] ❑ *Poor Lionel! What a sucker.* ② N-COUNT If you describe someone as a **sucker for** something, you mean that they find it very difficult to resist it. [INFORMAL] ❑ *I'm such a sucker for romance.* ③ N-COUNT The **suckers** on some animals and insects are the parts on the outside of their body which they use in order to

stick to a surface. [from Old English]

**sud|den** /sʌdⁿn/ ■ ADJ **Sudden** means happening quickly and unexpectedly. ❑ *He was shocked by the sudden death of his father.* ❑ *It was all very sudden.* ● **sud|den|ly** ADV ❑ *Suddenly, she looked ten years older.* ❑ *Her expression suddenly changed.* ● **sud|den|ness** N-UNCOUNT ❑ *The enemy seemed surprised by the suddenness of the attack.* ② PHRASE If something happens **all of a sudden**, it happens quickly and unexpectedly. ❑ *All of a sudden she didn't look tired anymore.* [from French]

**sue** /su/ (**sues, suing, sued**) V-T/V-I If you **sue** someone, you start a legal case against them, usually in order to claim money from them because they have harmed you in some way. ❑ *A company that makes toothpaste has been sued for false advertising.* ❑ *The company could be sued for damages.* [from Old French]

**suede** /sweɪd/ N-UNCOUNT **Suede** is leather with a soft, slightly rough surface. ❑ …*a brown suede jacket.* [from French]

**suf|fer** /sʌfər/ (**suffers, suffering, suffered**) ■ V-T/V-I If you **suffer** pain, you feel it in your body or in your mind. ❑ *She was very sick, suffering great pain.* ❑ *He suffered terribly the last few days.* ② V-I If you **suffer from** an illness or from some other bad condition, you are badly affected by it. ❑ *He was suffering from cancer.* ● **suf|fer|er** (**sufferers**) N-COUNT ❑ …*sufferers of mental health problems.* ❑ …*asthma sufferers.* ③ V-T If you **suffer** something bad, you are in a situation in which something painful, harmful, or very unpleasant happens to you. ❑ *They could suffer complete defeat.* ④ V-I If you **suffer**, you are badly affected by an event or situation. ❑ *It is the children who suffer.* ⑤ V-I If something **suffers**, it becomes worse because it has not been given enough attention or is in a bad situation. ❑ *I'm not surprised that your studies are suffering.* [from Old French]

**suf|fer|ing** /sʌfərɪŋ/ (**sufferings**) ■ N-VAR **Suffering** is serious pain which someone feels in their body or their mind. ❑ *They began to recover from their pain and suffering.* [from Old French] ② → see also **long-suffering**

**suf|fice** /səfaɪs/ (**suffices, sufficing, sufficed**) V-I If something will **suffice**, it will be enough to achieve a purpose or to fulfill a need. [FORMAL] ❑ *A short letter will suffice.* [from Old French]

**suf|fi|cient** /səfɪʃⁿnt/ ADJ If something is **sufficient for** a particular purpose, there is enough of it for the purpose. ❑ *The amount of food was sufficient for 12 people.* ● **suf|fi|cient|ly** ADV ❑ *She recovered sufficiently to go on vacation with her family.* [from Latin]

| Word Link | fix ≈ fastening : fixture, prefix, suffix |

**suf|fix** /sʌfɪks/ (**suffixes**) N-COUNT A **suffix** is a letter or group of letters, for example "-ly" or "-ness," which is added to the end of a word in order to form a different word, often of a different word class. For example, the suffix "-ly" is added to "quick" to form "quickly." Compare **affix** and **prefix**. [from New Latin]

**suf|fo|cate** /sʌfəkeɪt/ (**suffocates, suffocating, suffocated**) V-T/V-I If someone **suffocates** or is **suffocated**, they die because there is no air for them to breathe. ❑ *He either suffocated, or froze to death.* ● **suf|fo|ca|tion** /sʌfəkeɪʃⁿn/ N-UNCOUNT

## Word Web    sugar

**Sugar cane** was discovered in prehistoric New Guinea*. As people migrated across the Pacific islands and into India and China, they brought sugar cane with them. At first, people just chewed on the cane. They liked the **sweet taste**. When sugar cane reached the Middle East, people discovered how to **refine** it into **crystals**. **Brown sugar** is created by stopping the refining process earlier. This leaves some of the molasses syrup in the sugar. Today two-fifths of sugar comes from **beets**. Refined sugar is used in many **foods** and **beverages**. Too much sugar can cause health problems, such as **obesity** and **diabetes**.

*New Guinea: a large island in the southern Pacific Ocean.*

❏ *Many of the victims died of suffocation.* [from Latin]

**suf│fra│gist** /sʌ́frədʒɪst/ (**suffragists**) N-COUNT A **suffragist** is a person who is in favor of women having the right to vote, especially in societies where women are not allowed to vote. [from Latin]

**sug│ar** /ʃʊ́gər/ (**sugars**) **1** N-UNCOUNT Sugar is a sweet substance that is used to make food and drinks sweet. It is usually in the form of small white or brown crystals. ❏ *...bags of sugar.* **2** N-COUNT If someone has one **sugar** in their tea or coffee, they have one small spoon of sugar or one sugar lump in it. ❏ *How many sugars do you take?* **3** N-COUNT **Sugars** are substances that occur naturally in food. When you eat them, the body converts them into energy. [from Old French] → see Word Web: **sugar**

**sug│gest** /səgdʒɛ́st/ (**suggests, suggesting, suggested**) **1** V-T If you **suggest** something, you put forward a plan or idea for someone to think about. ❏ *I suggested a walk in the park.* ❏ *I suggest you ask him some questions about his past.* ❏ *No one has suggested how this might happen.* **2** V-T If you **suggest that** something is true, you say something which you believe is true. ❏ *I'm not suggesting that is what is happening.* ❏ *It is wrong to suggest that there is an easy solution.* **3** V-T If one thing **suggests** another, it implies it or makes you think that it might be the case. ❏ *Earlier reports suggested that a meeting would take place on Sunday.* [from Latin]

### Word Partnership    Use *suggest* with :

N.  **analysts** suggest, **experts** suggest, **researchers** suggest **1** **2** **data** suggest, **findings** suggest, **results** suggest, **studies** suggest, **surveys** suggest **3**

**sug│ges│tion** /səgdʒɛ́stʃ°n/ (**suggestions**) **1** N-COUNT If you make a **suggestion**, you put forward an idea or plan for someone to think about. ❏ *She made suggestions as to how I could improve my diet.* ❏ *Perhaps he followed her suggestion of a walk to the river.* **2** N-COUNT A **suggestion** is something that a person says which implies that something is true. ❏ *We reject any suggestion that the law needs changing.* [from Latin]

### Word Partnership    Use *suggestion* with :

V.  **follow** a suggestion, **make a** suggestion **1** **reject** a suggestion **1** **2**

**sug│ges│tive** /səgdʒɛ́stɪv/ ADJ Something that is **suggestive of** something else is quite like it or may be a sign of it. ❏ *...long nails suggestive of animal claws.* [from Latin]

**sui│cid│al** /suːɪsáɪd°l/ ADJ People who are **suicidal** want to kill themselves. ❏ *I was suicidal and just couldn't stop crying.* ❏ *I stayed with him as he seemed suicidal* [from New Latin]

**sui│cide** /suːɪsaɪd/ (**suicides**) N-VAR People who commit **suicide** deliberately kill themselves. ❏ *She tried to commit suicide several times.* ❏ *...a case of attempted suicide.* [from New Latin]

### Word Partnership    Use *suicide* with :

V.  **attempt** suicide, **commit** suicide
N.  suicide **bomber**, suicide **prevention**, suicide **rate**, **risk of** suicide

**suit** /suːt/ (**suits, suiting, suited**) **1** N-COUNT A man's **suit** consists of a jacket, pants, and sometimes a vest, all made from the same fabric. ❏ *...a dark business suit.* **2** N-COUNT A woman's **suit** consists of a jacket and skirt, or sometimes pants, made from the same fabric. ❏ *I was wearing my yellow suit.* **3** N-COUNT A particular type of **suit** is a piece of clothing that you wear for a particular activity. ❏ *The divers wore special rubber suits.* **4** V-T If something **suits** you, it is convenient for you or is the best thing for you in the circumstances. ❏ *They will only release information if it suits them.* **5** V-T If a piece of clothing or a particular style or color **suits** you, it makes you look attractive. ❏ *Green suits you.* **6** N-COUNT In a court of law, a **suit** is a legal action taken by one person or company against another. ❏ *Many former employees filed personal injury suits against the company.* [from Old French] **7** → see also **pantsuit** → see **clothing**

**suit│able** /suːtəb°l/ ADJ Someone or something that is **suitable for** a particular purpose or occasion is right or acceptable for it. ❏ *Employers usually decide within five minutes whether someone is suitable for the job.* ● **suit│abil│ity** /suːtəbɪ́lɪti/ N-UNCOUNT ❏ *...information on the suitability of a product for use in* *the home.* ● **suit|ably** ADV ❑ *We need suitably qualified staff.* [from French]

suitcase

**suit|case** /sutkeɪs/ (**suitcases**) N-COUNT A **suitcase** is a case for carrying your clothes when you are traveling. ❑ *It did not take Andrew long to pack a suitcase to go on vacation.*

**suite** /swit/ (**suites**) **1** N-COUNT A **suite** is a set of rooms in a hotel or other building. ❑ *They stayed in a suite at the Paris Hilton.* **2** N-COUNT A **suite** is a set of matching furniture. ❑ ...*a three-piece suite.* **3** N-COUNT A bathroom **suite** is a matching bathtub, sink, and toilet. ❑ ...*the horrible pink suite in the bathroom.* **4** N-COUNT A **suite** is a piece of instrumental music consisting of several short, related sections. [from French]
→ see **hotel**

**suit|ed** /sutɪd/ ADJ If something or someone is well **suited to** a particular purpose or person, they are right or appropriate for that purpose or person. ❑ *Adriana is well suited to caring for children.* [from French]

**Word Partnership** Use *suited* with :

ADV. **ill** suited, **perfectly** suited, **uniquely** suited, **well** suited
PREP. suited **to** *something*

**sul|fur** /sʌlfər/ N-UNCOUNT **Sulfur** is a yellow chemical which has a strong smell. ❑ *Burning sulfur creates an unpleasant smell.* [from Old French]
→ see **firework**

**sulk** /sʌlk/ (**sulks, sulking, sulked**) V-I If you **sulk**, you are silent and bad-tempered for a while because you are annoyed about something. ❑ *He turned his back and sulked.* ● **Sulk** is also a noun. ❑ *He went off in a sulk.*

**sul|len** /sʌlən/ ADJ Someone who is **sullen** is bad-tempered and does not speak much. ❑ *He sat in a sullen silence.* ● **sul|len|ly** ADV ❑ *"I've never seen it before," Harry said sullenly.* [from Latin]

**sul|tan** /sʌltən/ (**sultans**) N-TITLE; N-COUNT A **sultan** is a ruler in some Muslim countries. ❑ ...*during the reign of Sultan Abdul Hamid.* [from Medieval Latin]

**sul|try** /sʌltri/ **1** ADJ **Sultry** weather is hot and damp. [WRITTEN] ❑ ...*one sultry August evening.* **2** ADJ Someone who is **sultry** is attractive in a way that suggests hidden passion. [WRITTEN] ❑ ...*a dark-haired sultry woman.*

**sum** /sʌm/ (**sums, summing, summed**) **1** N-COUNT A **sum of** money is an amount of money. ❑ *Large sums of money were lost.* **2** N-SING In mathematics, the **sum of** two or more numbers is the number that is obtained when they are added together. ❑ *The sum of all the angles of a triangle is 180 degrees.* [from Old French] **3** → see also **lump sum**
▶ **sum up** PHR-VERB If you **sum** something **up**, you describe it as briefly as possible. ❑ *The story is too complicated to sum up in one or two words.*

**Word Partnership** Use *sum* with :

ADJ. **equal** sum, **large** sum, **substantial** sum, **undisclosed** sum **1**
N. sum **of money** **1**

**sum|ma cum lau|de** /sʊmə kʊm laʊdeɪ/ ADV If a college student graduates **summa cum laude**, they receive the highest honor that is possible. ❑ *Jeremy Heyl graduated summa cum laude with a degree in modern history.* ● **Summa cum laude** is also an adjective. ❑ ...*a summa cum laude graduate of Princeton.* [from Latin]

**sum|ma|rize** /sʌməraɪz/ (**summarizes, summarizing, summarized**) V-T/V-I If you **summarize** something, you give a summary of it. ❑ *Table 3.1 summarizes the information given above.* ❑ *The article can be summarized in three sentences.* ❑ *To summarize, this is a clever solution to the problem.* [from Latin]

**sum|mary** /sʌməri/ (**summaries**) **1** N-COUNT A **summary of** something is a short account of it, which gives the main points but not the details. ❑ *What follows is a brief summary of the process.* **2** PHRASE You use **in summary** to indicate that what you are about to say is a summary of what has just been said. ❑ *In summary, I think the meeting was a success.* [from Latin]

**sum|mer** /sʌmər/ (**summers**) N-VAR **Summer** is the season between spring and fall. In the summer the weather is usually warm or hot. ❑ *I flew to Maine this summer.* ❑ *It was a perfect summer's day.* [from Old English]

**sum|mer camp** (**summer camps**) N-COUNT A **summer camp** is a place in the country where parents can pay to send their children during the school summer vacation.

**sum|mer school** (**summer schools**) N-VAR **Summer school** is a summer term at a school, college, or university, for example for students who need extra teaching or who want to take extra courses.

**sum|mer squash** (**summer squashes**) N-COUNT A **summer squash** is a type of squash that is used after being picked rather than being stored for the winter.

**summer|time** /sʌmərtaɪm/ N-UNCOUNT **Summertime** is the period of time during which the summer lasts. ❑ *It's a very beautiful place in the summertime.*

**sum|mit** /sʌmɪt/ **1** N-COUNT A **summit** is a meeting at which the leaders of two or more countries discuss important matters. ❑ ...*next week's Washington summit.* **2** N-COUNT The **summit** of a mountain is the top of it. ❑ ...*the first man to reach the summit of Mount Everest.* [from Old French]
→ see **mountain**

**sum|mon** /sʌmən/ (**summons, summoning, summoned**) **1** V-T If you **summon** someone, you order them to come to you. [FORMAL] ❑ *Howe summoned a doctor.* ❑ *Suddenly we were summoned to his office.* **2** V-T If you **summon** a quality such as courage or energy, you make a great effort to have it. ❑ *It took her a month to summon the courage to tell her mother.* ● **Summon up** means the same as **summon.** ❑ *He finally summoned up courage to ask her to a game.* [from Latin]

**sum|mons** /sʌmənz/ (**summonses**) ■ N-COUNT A **summons** is an order to come and see someone. ❑ I received a summons to the principal's office. ❷ N-COUNT A **summons** is an official order to appear in court. ❑ She received a summons to appear in court. [from Old French]

**sump|tu|ous** /sʌmptʃuəs/ ADJ Something that is **sumptuous** is grand and obviously very expensive. ❑ ...a sumptuous dinner. [from Old French]

**sun** /sʌn/ ■ N-SING The sun is the ball of fire in the sky that the Earth goes around, and that gives us heat and light. ❑ The sun was now high in the sky. ❑ The sun came out. ❷ N-UNCOUNT You refer to the light and heat that reach us from the sun as **the sun**. ❑ They went outside to sit in the sun. [from Old English]
→ see Word Web: sun
→ see **astronomer, earth, eclipse, navigation, solar, solar system, star**

**sun|bathe** /sʌnbeɪð/ (**sunbathes, sunbathing, sunbathed**) V-I When people **sunbathe**, they sit or lie in a place where the sun shines on them, so that their skin becomes browner. ❑ Frank swam and sunbathed at the pool every morning. ● **sun|bath|ing** N-UNCOUNT ❑ The beach is perfect for sunbathing during the summer.

**sun|burn** /sʌnbɜrn/ (**sunburns**) N-VAR If someone has **sunburn**, their skin is bright pink and sore because they have spent too much time in hot sunshine. ❑ Sunburn can damage your skin.
→ see **skin**

**sun|burned** /sʌnbɜrnd/ also **sunburnt** ADJ Someone who is **sunburned** has sore bright pink skin because they have spent too much time in hot sunshine. ❑ A badly sunburned face is extremely painful.

**Sun|day** /sʌndeɪ, -di/ (**Sundays**) N-VAR **Sunday** is the day after Saturday and before Monday. ❑ We went for a drive on Sunday. [from Old English]

**sun|down** /sʌndaʊn/ N-UNCOUNT **Sundown** is the time when the sun sets. ❑ We got home about two hours after sundown.

**sun|dry** /sʌndri/ ■ ADJ If someone refers to **sundry** people or things, they are referring to several people or things that are all different from each other. [FORMAL] ❑ Scientists, business people, and sundry others were at the opening of the museum. ❷ PHRASE **All and sundry** means everyone. ❑ I made tea for all and sundry at the office. [from Old English]

**sun|flower** /sʌnflaʊər/ (**sunflowers**) N-COUNT A **sunflower** is a very tall plant with large yellow flowers.

**sung** /sʌŋ/ **Sung** is the past participle of **sing**. [from Old English]

**sun|glasses** /sʌnglæsɪz/ N-PLURAL **Sunglasses** are glasses with dark lenses which you wear to protect your eyes from bright sunlight. ❑ She put on a pair of sunglasses.

**sunk** /sʌŋk/ **Sunk** is the past participle of **sink**. [from Old English]

**sunk|en** /sʌŋkən/ ■ ADJ **Sunken** ships have sunk to the bottom of a sea, ocean, or lake. ❑ ...a sunken sailboat. ❷ ADJ **Sunken** gardens, roads, or other features are below the level of their surrounding area. ❑ Steps lead down to the sunken garden. ❸ ADJ **Sunken** eyes, cheeks, or other parts of the body curve inward and make you look thin and unwell. ❑ Her eyes were sunken with black rings around them. [from Old English]

**sun|light** /sʌnlaɪt/ N-UNCOUNT **Sunlight** is the light that comes from the sun during the day. ❑ Sunlight filled the room.
→ see **habitat, photosynthesis, rainbow, skin, sun**

**Sun|ni** /sʊni/ (**Sunnis**) ■ N-UNCOUNT **Sunni** is the main branch of Islam. ❷ N-COUNT A **Sunni** is a Muslim who follows the Sunni branch of Islam. [from Arabic]

**sun|ny** /sʌni/ ■ ADJ When it is **sunny**, the sun is shining brightly. ❑ The weather was warm and sunny. ❷ ADJ **Sunny** places are brightly lit by the sun. ❑ ...a sunny window seat. [from Old English]

**sun|rise** /sʌnraɪz/ (**sunrises**) ■ N-UNCOUNT **Sunrise** is the time in the morning when the sun first appears in the sky. ❑ The rain began before sunrise. ❷ N-COUNT A **sunrise** is the colors and light that you see in the eastern part of the sky when the sun first appears. ❑ There was a beautiful sunrise yesterday.

**sun|screen** /sʌnskrin/ (**sunscreens**) N-VAR A **sunscreen** is a cream that protects your skin from the sun's rays, especially in hot weather. ❑ Use a sunscreen when you go outside.
→ see **skin**

**sun|set** /sʌnsɛt/ (**sunsets**) ■ N-UNCOUNT **Sunset** is the time in the evening when the sun disappears out of sight from the sky. ❑ The party ends at sunset. ❷ N-COUNT A **sunset** is the colors and light that you see in the western part of the sky when the sun disappears in the evening. ❑ There was a red sunset over Paris.

S

---

## Word Web    sun

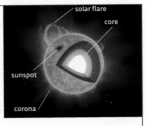

The **sun**'s core contains **hydrogen** atoms. These atoms combine to form helium. This process is called **fusion**. It makes the core very hot. The corona is a layer of hot, glowing gases surrounding the sun. Large flames also burn on the surface of the sun. They are called solar flares. **Infrared** and **ultraviolet** light are **invisible** parts of **sunlight**. Sometimes dark patches called sunspots appear on the sun. They can appear every eleven years. Scientists believe that sunspots affect the growth of plants on Earth. They also affect radio transmissions.

**sun|shine** /sʌnʃaɪn/ N-UNCOUNT **Sunshine** is the light and heat that comes from the sun. ◻ *She was sitting outside a cafe in bright sunshine.*

**sun|spot** /sʌnspɒt/ (**sunspots**) N-COUNT **Sunspots** are dark cool patches that appear on the surface of the sun and last for about a week.

**sun|tan** /sʌntæn/ (**suntans**) ◼ N-UNCOUNT If you have a **suntan**, the sun has turned your skin an attractive brown color. ◻ *They want to go to the Bahamas and get a suntan.* ◼ ADJ **Suntan** lotion, oil, or cream protects your skin from the sun. ◻ *She rubbed suntan lotion on his neck.*
→ see **skin**

**sun-up** also **sunup** N-UNCOUNT **Sun-up** is the time of day when the sun rises. ◻ *We worked from sunup to sunset.*

**su|per** /supər/ ◼ ADV **Super** is used before adjectives to indicate that something has a lot of a quality. ◻ *I want to be super slim.* ◼ ADJ **Super** is used before nouns to indicate that something is larger, better, or more advanced than similar things. ◻ *...a new super plane.* ◼ ADJ Some people use **super** to mean very nice or very good. This use can be regarded as old-fashioned. [INFORMAL] ◻ *We had a super time.* [from Latin]

**su|perb** /supɜrb/ ADJ If something is **superb**, its quality is very good indeed. ◻ *There is a superb golf course 6 miles away.* ● **su|perb|ly** ADV ◻ *The orchestra played superbly.* [from Old French]

**Su|per Bowl** (**Super Bowls**) also **Superbowl** N-COUNT **The Super Bowl** is a football game that is held each year in the United States between the two best professional football teams. ◻ *The Giants won the Super Bowl in 1987.*

**super|cell** /supərsɛl/ (**supercells**) N-COUNT A **supercell** is a powerful thunderstorm that often produces tornadoes. [TECHNICAL]

**Word Link**    super ≈ above : super**ficial**, super**natural**, super**power**

**super|fi|cial** /supərfɪʃəl/ ◼ ADJ If you describe someone as **superficial**, you disapprove of them because they do not think deeply, and have little understanding of anything serious or important. ◻ *This guy is superficial and stupid.* ● **super|fi|cial|ity** /supərfɪʃiæliti/ N-UNCOUNT ◻ *...the superficiality of Hollywood.* ◼ ADJ If you describe something such as an action, feeling, or relationship as **superficial**, you mean that it includes only the simplest and most obvious aspects of that thing, and not those aspects which require more effort to deal with or understand. ◻ *He gave the newspaper a superficial look.* ● **super|fi|cial|ity** N-UNCOUNT ◻ *...the superficiality of the music business.* ● **super|fi|cial|ly** ADV ◻ *The movie deals with these questions, but only superficially.* ◼ ADJ **Superficial** injuries are not very serious, and affect only the surface of the body. You can also describe damage to an object as **superficial**. ◻ *He escaped the crash with superficial injuries.*

**super|flu|ous** /supɜrfluəs/ ADJ Something that is **superfluous** is unnecessary or is no longer needed. ◻ *My presence at the meeting was superfluous.*

**super|gi|ant** /supərdʒaɪənt/ (**supergiants**) N-COUNT A **supergiant** is a very large, bright star. [TECHNICAL]

**super|high|way** /supərhaɪweɪ/ (**superhighways**) ◼ N-COUNT A **superhighway** is a large, fast highway or freeway with several lanes. ◻ *He drove to the city on the superhighway.* ◼ N-COUNT The information **superhighway** is the network of computer links that enables computer users all over the world to communicate with each other.

**super|im|pose** /supərɪmpoʊz/ (**superimposes, superimposing, superimposed**) V-T If one image is **superimposed on** another, it is put on top of it so that you can see the second image through it. ◻ *The features of different faces were superimposed on one another.*

**Word Link**    ent ≈ one who does, has : depend**ent**, resid**ent**, superintend**ent**

**super|in|ten|dent** /supərɪntɛndənt, suprɪn-/ (**superintendents**) ◼ N-COUNT A **superintendent** is a person who is responsible for a particular thing or the work done in a particular department. ◻ *He became superintendent of the bank's East African branches.* ◼ N-COUNT A **superintendent** is a person whose job is to take care of a large building such as a school or an apartment building and deal with small repairs to it. ◻ *The superintendent opened the door with one of his keys.*

**su|peri|or** /supɪəriər/ (**superiors**) ◼ ADJ You use **superior** to describe someone or something that is better than other similar people or things. ◻ *We have a relationship that is superior to those of our friends.* ◻ *...superior quality coffee.* ● **su|peri|or|ity** /supɪəriɔrɪti/ N-UNCOUNT ◻ *...the technical superiority of CDs over tapes.* ◼ ADJ A **superior** person or thing is more important than another person or thing in the same organization or system. ◻ *She complained to her superior officers.* ◼ N-COUNT Your **superior** in an organization that you work for is a person who has a higher rank than you. ◻ *They do not have much communication with their superiors.* ◼ ADJ If you describe someone as **superior**, you dislike them because they behave as if they are better, more important, or more intelligent than other people. ◻ *Fred gave a superior smile.* ● **su|peri|or|ity** /supɪəriɔrɪti/ N-UNCOUNT ◻ *He had a sense of his own superiority.*

**Word Partnership**    Use superior with :

| ADV. | **far** superior, **morally** superior, **vastly** superior ◼ |
| N. | superior **performance**, superior **quality**, superior **service** ◼ |

**su|peri|or court** (**superior courts**) also **Superior Court** N-VAR A **superior court** is a law court that deals with serious or important cases. ◻ *...a Superior Court of the District of Columbia.* ◻ *...a Los Angeles Superior Court judge.*

**super|la|tive** /supɜrlətɪv/ (**superlatives**) ADJ In grammar, the **superlative** form of an adjective or adverb is the form that indicates that something has more of a quality than anything else in a group. For example, "biggest" is the superlative form of "big." Compare **comparative**. ● **Superlative** is also a noun. ◻ *His writing contains many superlatives.*

**super|mar|ket** /supərmɑrkɪt/ (**supermarkets**) N-COUNT A **supermarket** is a large store which sells all kinds of food and some household goods. ◻ *Most of us do our food shopping in the supermarket.* [from Latin]

**super|model** /sˌupərmɒdᵊl/ (**supermodels**)
N-COUNT A **supermodel** is a very famous fashion
model.

**super|natu|ral** /sˌupərnˈætʃərəl, -nˈætʃrəl/
ADJ **Supernatural** creatures, forces, and events
are believed by some people to exist or happen,
although they are impossible according to
scientific laws. ❑ These evil spirits had supernatural
powers. ● **The supernatural** is things that are
supernatural. ❑ He writes stories about the
supernatural.

**super|no|va** /sˌupərnˈouvə/ (**supernovas** or
**supernovae** /sˌupərnˈouvi/) N-COUNT A **supernova**
is an exploding star.

**super|pow|er** /sˌupərpaʊər/ (**superpowers**)
N-COUNT A **superpower** is a very powerful and
influential country, usually one that is rich and
has nuclear weapons. ❑ The United States is a
military and economic superpower.

**super|sede** /sˌupərsˈid/ (**supersedes,
superseding, superseded**) V-T If something is
**superseded by** something newer, it is replaced
because it has become old-fashioned or
unacceptable. ❑ Hand tools have been superseded by
machines.

**super|size** /sˌupərsaɪz/ (**supersizes, supersizing,
supersized**) 1 ADJ **Supersize** or **supersized**
things are very large. ❑ ...a supersize portion of
fries. ❑ ...a supersized mug of coffee. 2 V-T If a fast-
food restaurant **supersizes** a portion of food, it
offers the customer a larger portion. ❑ Fast-food
restaurants encourage people to supersize their orders.

**super|son|ic** /sˌupərsˈɒnɪk/ ADJ **Supersonic**
aircraft travel faster than the speed of sound.
❑ ...a supersonic jet.
→ see sound

**super|star** /sˌupərstɑr/ (**superstars**) N-COUNT A
**superstar** is a very famous entertainer or athlete.
[INFORMAL] ❑ Johnson was a basketball superstar.

**super|sti|tion** /sˌupərstˈɪʃᵊn/ (**superstitions**)
N-VAR **Superstition** is belief in things that are not
real or possible, for example magic. ❑ Many people
have superstitions about numbers.

**super|sti|tious** /sˌupərstˈɪʃəs/ ADJ People who
are **superstitious** believe in things that are not
real or possible, for example magic. ❑ Jean was
superstitious and believed the color green brought bad
luck.

**super|vise** /sˌupərvaɪz/ (**supervises,
supervising, supervised**) V-T If you **supervise**
an activity or a person, you make sure that the
activity is done correctly or that the person is
doing a task or behaving correctly. ❑ I supervised
the packing of orders. ● **super|vi|sion** /sˌupərvˈɪʒᵊn/
N-UNCOUNT ❑ Young children need close supervision.
● **super|vi|sor** (**supervisors**) ❑ ...a job as a
supervisor at a factory.

**super|vi|sory** /sˌupərvaɪzəri/ ADJ **Supervisory**
means involved in supervising people, activities,
or places. ❑ ...staff with supervisory roles.

**sup|per** /sˈʌpər/ (**suppers**) 1 N-VAR Some
people refer to the main meal eaten in the early
part of the evening as **supper**. ❑ Would you like to
join us for supper? 2 N-VAR **Supper** is a simple meal
eaten just before you go to bed at night. ❑ She gives
the children their supper, then puts them to bed. [from
Old French]

**sup|plant** /səplˈænt/ (**supplants, supplanting,
supplanted**) V-T If a person or thing is **supplanted**,
another person or thing takes their place.
[FORMAL] ❑ He was supplanted by a younger man.
❑ CDs have completely supplanted tapes. [from Old
French]

**sup|ple** /sˈʌpᵊl/ (**suppler, supplest**) 1 ADJ A
**supple** object or material bends or changes shape
easily without cracking or breaking. ❑ The leather
is supple and will last for years. 2 ADJ A **supple**
person can move and bend their body very
easily. ❑ Paul was very supple and strong. [from Old
French]

**sup|ple|ment** /sˈʌplɪmənt/ (**supplements,
supplementing, supplemented**) V-T If you
**supplement** something, you add something to it
in order to improve it. ❑ Some people do extra jobs
to supplement their incomes. ● **Supplement** is also a
noun. ❑ These classes are a supplement to school study.
[from Latin]

**sup|ple|men|ta|ry** /sˌʌplɪmˈɛntəri, -tri/ ADJ
**Supplementary** things are added to something
in order to improve it. ❑ Should people take
supplementary vitamins? [from Latin]

**sup|pli|er** /səplˈaɪər/ (**suppliers**) N-COUNT A
**supplier** is a person, company, or organization
that sells or supplies something such as goods or
equipment to customers. [BUSINESS] ❑ ...one of the
country's biggest food suppliers. [from Old French]

**sup|ply** /səplˈaɪ/ (**supplies, supplying, supplied**)
1 V-T If you **supply** someone with something that
they want or need, you give them a quantity of
it. ❑ ...an agreement not to supply chemical weapons.
❑ The pipeline will supply Greece with Russian natural
gas. 2 N-PLURAL You can use **supplies** to refer to
food, equipment, and other essential things that
people need, especially when these are provided in
large quantities. ❑ What happens when there are no
more food supplies? 3 N-VAR A **supply of** something
is an amount of it which someone has or which
is available for them to use. ❑ The brain needs a
constant supply of oxygen. 4 N-UNCOUNT **Supply**
is the quantity of goods and services that can
be made available for people to buy. [BUSINESS]
❑ Prices change according to supply and demand.
5 PHRASE If something is **in short supply**, there is
very little of it available and it is difficult to find
or obtain. ❑ Food is in short supply all over the country.
[from Old French]

| | |
|---|---|
| N. | supply **electricity**, supply **equipment**, supply **information** 1 |
| ADJ. | **abundant** supply, **large** supply, **limited** supply 3 |

**sup|ply chain** (**supply chains**) N-COUNT A
**supply chain** is the entire process of making and
selling commercial goods, including every stage
from the supply of materials and the manufacture
of the goods through to their distribution and
sale.

**sup|port** /səpˈɔrt/ (**supports, supporting,
supported**) 1 V-T If you **support** someone or their
ideas or aims, you agree with them, and perhaps

S

help them because you want them to succeed. ❑ *The vice president said that he supported the people of New York.* • **Support** is also a noun. ❑ *The president gave his full support to the reforms.* • **sup|port|er** (**supporters**) N-COUNT ❑ *...the president's supporters.* **2** N-UNCOUNT If you give **support** to someone during a difficult or unhappy time, you are kind to them and help them. ❑ *She gave me a lot of support when my husband died.* **3** N-UNCOUNT Financial **support** is money provided to enable an organization to continue. ❑ *The company gets support from government.* **4** V-T If you **support** someone, you provide them with money or the things that they need. ❑ *I have three children to support.* **5** V-T If a fact **supports** a statement or a theory, it helps to show that it is true or correct. ❑ *A lot of research supports this theory.* • **Support** is also a noun. ❑ *History offers some support for this view.* **6** V-T If something **supports** an object, it is underneath the object and holding it up. ❑ *Thick wooden posts supported the roof.* **7** N-COUNT A **support** is a bar or other object that supports something. ❑ *Each piece of metal was on wooden supports.* **8** V-T If you **support yourself**, you prevent yourself from falling by holding onto something or by leaning on something. ❑ *He supported himself on a nearby wall.* • **Support** is also a noun. ❑ *Alice leaned against him for support.* [from Old French]

**sup|port|ive** /səpɔrtɪv/ ADJ If you are **supportive**, you are kind and helpful to someone at a difficult or unhappy time in their life. ❑ *They were always supportive of each other.* [from Old French]

**sup|pose** /səpouz/ (**supposes, supposing, supposed**) **1** V-T You can use **suppose** or **supposing** before mentioning a possible situation or action. You usually then go on to consider the effects that this situation or action might have. ❑ *Suppose someone gave you a check for $6 million dollars. What would you do with it?* **2** V-T If you **suppose that** something is true, you believe that it is probably true. ❑ *I suppose you're in high school, too?* ❑ *The problem was more complex than he supposed.* **3** PHRASE You can say "**I suppose**" when you want to express slight uncertainty. [SPOKEN] ❑ *I suppose I'd better do some homework.* ❑ *"Is that the right way?" — "Yeah. I suppose so."* [from Old French]

**sup|posed**

Pronounced /səpouzd/ or /səpoust/ for meanings **1** and **2**, and /səpouzd/ for meaning **3**.

**1** PHRASE If you say that something **is supposed to** happen, you mean that it is planned or expected. Sometimes this use suggests that the thing does not really happen in this way. ❑ *This is the girl he is supposed to marry.* ❑ *He was supposed to go back to Brooklyn on the last bus.* **2** PHRASE If you say that something **is supposed to** be true, you mean that people say it is true but you do not know for certain that it is true. ❑ *"The Whipping Block" is supposed to be a really good poem.* **3** ADJ You can use **supposed** to suggest that something that people talk about or believe in may not in fact exist, happen, or be as it is described. ❑ *...the supposed cause of the accident.* • **sup|pos|ed|ly** /səpouzɪdli/ ADV ❑ *It was supposedly his own work.* [from Old French]

**sup|press** /səprɛs/ (**suppresses, suppressing,**

**suppressed**) **1** V-T If someone in authority **suppresses** an activity, they prevent it from continuing, by using force or making it illegal. ❑ *As we know, it's difficult to suppress crime.* • **sup|pres|sion** /səprɛʃⁿn/ N-UNCOUNT ❑ *...the suppression of protests.* **2** V-T If a natural function or reaction of your body **is suppressed**, it is stopped, for example by drugs or illness. ❑ *The growth of cancer cells can be suppressed by various treatments.* • **sup|pres|sion** N-UNCOUNT ❑ *...suppression of the immune system.* **3** V-T If you **suppress** your feelings or reactions, you do not express them, even though you might want to. ❑ *Liz thought of Barry and suppressed a smile.* • **sup|pres|sion** N-UNCOUNT ❑ *A mother's suppression of her own feelings can cause problems.* **4** V-T If someone **suppresses** a piece of information, they prevent other people from learning it. ❑ *They did not try to suppress the information.* • **sup|pres|sion** N-UNCOUNT ❑ *...the suppression of official documents.* [from Latin]

**su|prema|cy** /supreməsi/ N-UNCOUNT If one group of people has **supremacy** over another group, they have more power. ❑ *...the supremacy of the Supreme Court.* ❑ *...they had re-established their supremacy.* [from Latin]

**su|preme** /suprim/ **1** ADJ **Supreme** is used in the title of a person or an official group to indicate that they are at the highest level in a particular organization or system. ❑ *...the supreme ruler of Eastern Russia.* ❑ *...the Supreme Court.* **2** ADJ You use **supreme** to emphasize that a quality or thing is very great. ❑ *Her happiness was of supreme importance.* • **su|preme|ly** ADV ❑ *She does her job supremely well.* [from Latin]

**sure** /ʃʊər/ (**surer, surest**) **1** ADJ If you are **sure** that something is true, you are certain that it is true. If you are not **sure** about something, you do not know for certain what the true situation is. ❑ *He was not sure that he wanted to be a teacher.* ❑ *I'm not sure where he lives.* **2** ADJ If someone is **sure of** getting something, they will definitely get it or they think they will definitely get it. ❑ *How can you be sure of getting quality?* **3** PHRASE If you say that something **is sure to** happen, you are emphasizing your belief that it will happen. ❑ *With a face like that, she's sure to get a boyfriend.* **4** ADJ **Sure** is used to emphasize that something such as a sign or ability is reliable or accurate. ❑ *There were black clouds in the sky, a sure sign of rain.* **5** CONVENTION **Sure** is an informal way of saying "yes" or "all right." ❑ *"Do you know where she lives?" — "Sure."* **6** PHRASE You say **sure enough**, especially when telling a story, to confirm that something was really true or was actually happening. ❑ *The pie looked good. Sure enough, it tasted great.* **7** PHRASE If you say that something is **for sure** or that you know it **for sure**, you mean that it is definitely true. ❑ *One thing's for sure, women still love Barry Manilow.* **8** PHRASE If you **make sure that** something is done, you take action so that it is done. ❑ *Make sure that you follow the instructions carefully.* **9** PHRASE If you **make sure that** something is the way that you want or expect it to be, you check that it is that way. ❑ *He looked in the bathroom to make sure that he was alone.* **10** PHRASE If you are **sure of yourself**, you are very confident about your own abilities or opinions. ❑ *I've never*

S

seen him so sure of himself. **11** CONVENTION You say "**sure thing**" to show that you agree with someone or will do as they say. [SPOKEN] ❑ *"Be careful!" — "Sure thing, Dad."* [from Old French]

**sure|ly** /ʃʊ̱ərli/ **1** ADV You use **surely** to emphasize that you think something should be true, and you would be surprised if it was not true. ❑ *You're an intelligent woman, surely you realize by now that I'm helping you.* ❑ *You surely haven't forgotten Dr. Walters?* **2** PHRASE If you say that something is happening **slowly but surely**, you mean that it is happening gradually but it is definitely happening. ❑ *Slowly but surely she was starting to like him.* [from Old French]

**surf** /sɜ̱rf/ (**surfs, surfing, surfed**) **1** N-UNCOUNT **Surf** is the mass of white bubbles that is formed by waves as they fall upon the shore. ❑ *...surf rolling onto white sand beaches.* **2** V-I If you **surf**, you ride on big waves in the ocean on a special board. ❑ *I'm going to buy a board and learn to surf.* ● **surf|er** (**surfers**) N-COUNT ❑ *...this small fishing village, which continues to attract surfers.* ● **surf|ing** N-UNCOUNT ❑ *My favorite sport is surfing.* **3** V-T If you **surf** the Internet, you spend time finding and looking at things on the Internet. [COMPUTING] ❑ *No one knows how many people currently surf the Net.* ● **surf|er** (**surfers**) N-COUNT ❑ *Net surfers can use their credit cards to pay for goods.* ● **surf|ing** N-UNCOUNT ❑ *...your surfing habits.*
→ see **beach**

> **Word Link**    *sur ≈ above : surface, surpass, surplus*

**sur|face** /sɜ̱rfɪs/ (**surfaces, surfacing, surfaced**) **1** N-COUNT The **surface** of something is the flat top part of it or the outside of it. ❑ *There were pen marks on the table's surface.* ❑ *...waves on the surface of the water.* **2** N-SING When you refer to **the surface** of a situation, you are talking about what can be seen easily rather than what is hidden or not immediately obvious. ❑ *Back home, things appear, on the surface, simpler.* **3** V-I If someone or something under water **surfaces**, they come up to the surface of the water. ❑ *He surfaced, trying to get air.* [from French]

> **Word Partnership**    Use *surface* with :
>
> | N. | surface **area**, **Earth's** surface, surface **level**, surface **of the water** **1** |
> |---|---|
> | ADJ. | **flat** surface, **rough** surface, **smooth** surface **1** |
> | V. | **break** the surface **1** **scratch** the surface **1** **2** |

**sur|face cur|rent** (**surface currents**) N-COUNT A **surface current** is a current of water that flows at or near the surface of the sea. Compare **deep current**.

**sur|face grav|ity** (**surface gravities**) N-VAR The **surface gravity** of a planet is the gravitational force that exists on the surface of the planet. [TECHNICAL]

**sur|face ten|sion** (**surface tensions**) N-VAR **Surface tension** is the force that acts on the surface of a liquid and causes it to form droplets. [TECHNICAL]

**surface-to-volume ra|tio** (**surface-to-volume ratios**) N-COUNT The **surface-to-volume**

**ratio** of a cell or organ is the difference between the surface area of the cell or organ and its volume. [TECHNICAL]

**sur|face wave** (**surface waves**) N-COUNT In physics, a **surface wave** is a wave that travels along the boundary between two substances with different densities, such as the sea and the air. In geology, a **surface wave** is a vibration from an earthquake that travels close to the Earth's surface. [TECHNICAL]

**surge** /sɜ̱rdʒ/ (**surges, surging, surged**) **1** N-COUNT A **surge** is a sudden large increase in something that has previously been steady, or has only increased or developed slowly. ❑ *...the recent surge in prices.* **2** V-I If something **surges**, it increases suddenly and greatly, after being steady or developing only slowly. ❑ *The Freedom Party's support surged from 10 percent to nearly 17 percent.* **3** V-I If a crowd of people **surge** forward, they suddenly move forward together. ❑ *The crowd was getting angry and suddenly surged forward into the store.* **4** N-COUNT A **surge** is a sudden powerful movement of a physical force such as wind or water. ❑ *The whole car shook with a surge of power.* **5** V-I If a physical force such as water or electricity **surges** through something, it moves through it suddenly and powerfully. ❑ *The wall fell and water surged into the yard.* [from Latin]

**sur|geon** /sɜ̱rdʒ³n/ (**surgeons**) N-COUNT A **surgeon** is a doctor who is specially trained to perform surgery. ❑ *...a heart surgeon.* [from Old French]

**sur|geon gen|er|al** (**surgeons general**) also **Surgeon General** N-COUNT In the United States, the **surgeon general** is the head of the public health service.

**sur|gery** /sɜ̱rdʒəri/ (**surgeries**) **1** N-UNCOUNT **Surgery** is medical treatment in which your body is cut open so that a doctor can repair, remove, or replace a diseased or damaged part. ❑ *His father just had heart surgery.* **2** → see also **plastic surgery** **3** N-COUNT A **surgery** is the area in a hospital with operating rooms where surgeons operate on their patients. [from Old French]
→ see **cancer, laser**

**sur|gi|cal** /sɜ̱rdʒɪk³l/ **1** ADJ **Surgical** equipment and clothing is used in surgery. ❑ *...a collection of surgical instruments.* **2** ADJ **Surgical** treatment involves surgery. ❑ *...a simple surgical operation.* ● **sur|gi|cal|ly** ADV ❑ *The lump on his arm will be surgically removed.* [from Old French]

**sur|mise** /sərma̱ɪz/ (**surmises, surmising, surmised**) V-T If you **surmise** that something is true, you guess it from the available evidence, although you do not know for certain. [FORMAL] ❑ *We can only surmise what happened.* [from Old French]

**sur|name** /sɜ̱rneɪm/ (**surnames**) N-COUNT Your **surname** is the name that you share with other members of your family. In English speaking countries and many other countries it is your last name. ❑ *She didn't know his surname, only his first name.* [from Old French]

**sur|pass** /sərpæ̱s/ (**surpasses, surpassing, surpassed**) V-T If one person or thing **surpasses** another, the first is better than, or has more of a particular quality than, the second. ❑ *He wanted*

**S**

to surpass the achievements of his older brothers. [from French]

**sur|plus** /sɜrplʌs, -pləs/ (**surpluses**) **1** N-VAR If there is a **surplus** of something, there is more than is needed. □ ...countries where there is a surplus of labor. **2** ADJ **Surplus** is used to describe something that is extra or that is more than is needed. □ Few people have large sums of surplus cash. □ I sell my surplus birds to a local pet shop. **3** N-COUNT If a country has a trade **surplus**, it exports more than it imports. □ Japan's annual trade surplus is around 100 billion dollars. **4** N-COUNT If a government has a budget **surplus**, it has spent less than it received in taxes. □ Norway's budget surplus has fallen from 5.9%. [from Old French]

**sur|prise** /sərpraɪz/ (**surprises, surprising, surprised**) **1** N-COUNT A **surprise** is an unexpected event, fact, or piece of news. □ I have a surprise for you: We are moving to Switzerland! □ It may come as a surprise that a child is born with many skills. ● **Surprise** is also an adjective. □ Baxter arrived this afternoon, on a surprise visit. **2** N-UNCOUNT **Surprise** is the feeling that you have when something unexpected happens. □ The Pentagon has expressed surprise at his comments. □ "You mean he's going to vote against her?" Scobie asked in surprise. **3** V-T If something **surprises** you, it gives you a feeling of surprise. □ We'll do the job ourselves and surprise everyone. □ It surprised me that a driver of Alain's experience should make those mistakes. [from Old French] **4** → see also **surprised, surprising**

**sur|prised** /sərpraɪzd/ **1** ADJ If you are **surprised** at something, you have a feeling of surprise, because it is unexpected or unusual. □ I was surprised at how easy it was. [from Old French] **2** → see also **surprise**

**sur|pris|ing** /sərpraɪzɪŋ/ **1** ADJ Something that is **surprising** is unexpected or unusual and makes you feel surprised. □ It is not surprising that children learn to read at different rates. ● **sur|pris|ing|ly** ADV □ The party was surprisingly good. [from Old French] **2** → see also **surprise**

**sur|re|al** /səriəl/ ADJ If you describe something as **surreal**, you mean that it is very strange and like a dream. □ It was a surreal evening. [from French]

**sur|ren|der** /sərɛndər/ (**surrenders, surrendering, surrendered**) **1** V-I If you **surrender**, you stop fighting or resisting someone and agree that you have been beaten. □ The army finally surrendered. ● **Surrender** is also a noun. □ ...the government's surrender to demands made by the people. **2** V-T If you **surrender** something you would rather keep, you give it up or let someone else have it, for example after a struggle. □ Nadja had to surrender all rights to her house. ● **Surrender** is

also a noun. □ ...the surrender of weapons. [from Old French]
→ see **war**

**sur|ro|gate** /sɜrəgeɪt, -gɪt/ (**surrogates**) ADJ You use **surrogate** to describe a person or thing that is given a particular role because the person or thing that should have the role is not available. □ Martin became Howard Cosell's surrogate son. ● **Surrogate** is also a noun. □ He was using her as a surrogate for someone he loved long ago. [from Latin]

**sur|round** /səraʊnd/ (**surrounds, surrounding, surrounded**) **1** V-T If a person or thing **is surrounded** by something, that thing is situated all around them. □ The church was surrounded by a low wall. □ The shell surrounding the egg has many important functions. □ ...Chicago and the surrounding area. **2** V-T If you **are surrounded** by soldiers or police, they spread out so that they are in positions all the way around you. □ When the car stopped it was surrounded by soldiers. **3** V-T The circumstances, feelings, or ideas which **surround** something are those that are closely associated with it. □ A lot of the facts surrounding the case are unknown. **4** V-T If you **surround yourself with** certain people or things, you make sure that you have a lot of them near you all the time. □ He surrounds himself with intelligent people. [from Old French]

**sur|round|ings** /səraʊndɪŋz/ N-PLURAL When you are describing the place where you are at the moment, or the place where you live, you can refer to it as your **surroundings**. □ He soon felt at home in his new surroundings. [from Old French]

**sur|veil|lance** /sərveɪləns/ N-UNCOUNT **Surveillance** is the careful watching of someone, especially by an organization such as the police or the army. □ They kept him under constant surveillance. [from French]

**sur|vey** (**surveys, surveying, surveyed**)

The noun is pronounced /sɜrveɪ/. The verb is pronounced /sərveɪ/, and can also be pronounced /sɜrveɪ/ in meanings **2** and **5**.

**1** N-COUNT If you carry out a **survey**, you try to find out detailed information about a lot of different people or things, usually by asking people a series of questions. □ They conducted a survey to see how students study. **2** V-T If you **survey** a number of people, companies, or organizations, you try to find out information about their opinions or behavior, usually by asking them a series of questions. □ They surveyed 211 companies for the report. **3** V-T If you **survey** something, you look at or consider the whole of it carefully. □ He stood up and surveyed the room. **4** N-COUNT If someone carries out a **survey** of an area of land, they examine it and measure it, usually in order to make a map of it. □ ...a survey of India. **5** V-T If someone **surveys** an area of land, they examine it and measure it, usually in order to make a map of it. □ The area was surveyed in detail. ● **sur|vey|or** /sərveɪər/ (**surveyors**) N-COUNT □ ...surveyor's maps. [from French]

**sur|viv|al** /sərvaɪvəl/ N-UNCOUNT The **survival** of something or someone is the fact that they manage to continue or exist in spite of difficulty or danger. ❑ ...companies which have been struggling for survival. [from Old French]

| **Word Link** | viv ≈ living : revival, survive, vivid |

**sur|vive** /sərvaɪv/ (**survives, surviving, survived**) ■ V-T/V-I If a person or living thing **survives** in a dangerous situation such as an accident or an illness, they do not die. ❑ It's a miracle that anyone survived. ❑ He survived heart surgery. ● **sur|vi|vor** (**survivors**) N-COUNT ❑ Officials said there were no survivors of the plane crash. ☐ V-T/V-I If you **survive** in difficult circumstances, you manage to live or continue in spite of them. ❑ People are struggling to survive without jobs. ❑ How do people survive the pressure of working all the time? ● **sur|vi|vor** (**survivors**) N-COUNT ❑ ...survivors of abuse. ☐ V-T If you **survive** someone, you continue to live after they have died. ❑ Most women will survive their husbands. ● **sur|vi|vor** (**survivors**) N-COUNT ❑ The money will go to him or his survivors. [from Old French]

**sus|cep|tible** /səsɛptɪbªl/ ■ ADJ If you are **susceptible to** something or someone, you are very likely to be influenced by them. ❑ Young people are the most susceptible to advertisements. ❑ James was very susceptible to praise. ☐ ADJ If you are **susceptible to** a disease or injury, you are very likely to be affected by it. ❑ Walking with weights makes the shoulders susceptible to injury. [from Late Latin]

**sus|pect** (**suspects, suspecting, suspected**)

The verb is pronounced /səspɛkt/. The noun and adjective are pronounced /sʌspɛkt/.

■ V-T You use **suspect** when you are stating something that you believe is probably true, in order to make it sound less strong or direct. ❑ I suspect they were right. ❑ He is, I suspect, a very kind man. ☐ V-T If you **suspect** that something dishonest or unpleasant has been done, you believe that it has probably been done. If you **suspect** someone **of** doing an action of this kind, you believe that they probably did it. ❑ He suspected that she was telling lies. ❑ The police did not suspect him of anything. ☐ N-COUNT A **suspect** is a person who the police or authorities think may be guilty of a crime. ❑ Police have arrested a suspect. ☐ ADJ **Suspect** things or people are ones that you think may be dangerous or may be less good or genuine than they appear. ❑ They had to leave the building when a suspect package was found. [from Latin]

**sus|pend** /səspɛnd/ (**suspends, suspending, suspended**) ■ V-T If you **suspend** something, you delay it or stop it from happening for a while or until a decision is made about it. ❑ The company will suspend production June 1st. ☐ V-T If someone **is suspended**, they are prevented from holding a particular job or position for a fixed length of time or until a decision is made about them. ❑ Julie was suspended from her job. ☐ V-T If something **is suspended** from a high place, it is hanging from that place. ❑ A map was suspended from the ceiling. [from Latin]

**sus|pend|ers** /səspɛndərz/ N-PLURAL **Suspenders** are a pair of straps that go over someone's shoulders and are fastened to their pants at the front and back to prevent the pants

from falling down. [from Latin]

**sus|pense** /səspɛns/ N-UNCOUNT **Suspense** is a state of excitement or anxiety about something that is going to happen very soon, for example about some news that you are waiting to hear. ❑ The suspense ended when the judges gave their decision. [from Medieval Latin]

**sus|pen|sion** /səspɛnʃ⁰n/ (**suspensions**) ■ N-UNCOUNT The **suspension** of something is the act of delaying or stopping it for a while or until a decision is made about it. ❑ There was a suspension of flights out of Miami. ☐ N-VAR Someone's **suspension** is their removal from a job or position for a period of time or until a decision is made about them. ❑ No one knows the reason for his suspension. ☐ N-VAR A vehicle's **suspension** consists of the springs and other devices attached to the wheels, which give a smooth ride over uneven ground. ❑ There's a problem with the car's suspension. ☐ N-COUNT In chemistry, a **suspension** is a mixture containing tiny particles floating in a fluid. [TECHNICAL] [from Medieval Latin]
→ see **bridge**

**sus|pi|cion** /səspɪʃ⁰n/ (**suspicions**) ■ N-VAR **Suspicion** or a **suspicion** is a belief or feeling that someone has committed a crime or done something wrong. ❑ There was a suspicion that this student was cheating. ☐ N-VAR If there is **suspicion of** someone or something, people do not trust them or consider them to be reliable. ❑ There is suspicion of police among homeless people. ☐ N-COUNT A **suspicion** is a feeling that something is probably true or is likely to happen. ❑ I have a suspicion that they are going to succeed. [from Old French]

**sus|pi|cious** /səspɪʃəs/ ■ ADJ If you are **suspicious of** someone or something, you do not trust them. ❑ He was suspicious of me until I told him I was not writing about him. ● **sus|pi|cious|ly** ADV ❑ "What is it you want me to do?" Adams asked suspiciously. ☐ ADJ If you describe someone or something as **suspicious**, you mean that there is some aspect of them which makes you think that they are involved in a crime or a dishonest activity. ❑ Two suspicious-looking characters approached him. ● **sus|pi|cious|ly** ADV ❑ Has anyone been acting suspiciously over the last few days? [from Old French]

**sus|tain** /səsteɪn/ (**sustains, sustaining, sustained**) ■ V-T If you **sustain** something, you continue it or maintain it for a period of time. ❑ He sustained his strong political views throughout his life. ☐ V-T If you **sustain** something such as a defeat, loss, or injury, it happens to you. [FORMAL] ❑ The aircraft sustained some damage. ☐ V-T If something **sustains** you, it supports you by giving you help, strength, or encouragement. [FORMAL] ❑ The money his father gave him sustained him for the moment. [from Old French]

**sus|tain|able** /səsteɪnəbªl/ ■ ADJ You use **sustainable** to describe the use of natural resources when this use is kept at a steady level that is not likely to damage the environment. ❑ ...the sustainable development of forests. ● **sus|tain|abil|ity** /səsteɪnəbɪlɪti/ N-UNCOUNT ❑ ...environmental sustainability. ☐ ADJ A **sustainable** plan, method, or system is designed to continue at the same rate or level of activity without any problems. ❑ We need to create a sustainable transport system. ● **sus|tain|abil|ity**

S

N-UNCOUNT □ ...the sustainability of the American economic recovery. [from Old French]

**swab** /swɒb/ (swabs) N-COUNT A **swab** is a small piece of cotton used for cleaning a wound. □ The nurse cleaned the cut with a cotton swab. [from Middle Dutch]

**swag|ger** /swægər/ (swaggers, swaggering, swaggered) V-I If you **swagger**, you walk in a very proud, confident way, holding your body upright and swinging your hips. □ A tall man swaggered in through the door. ● **Swagger** is also a noun. □ He walked with a swagger.

**swal|low** /swɒloʊ/ (swallows, swallowing, swallowed) ◼ V-T/V-I If you **swallow** something, you cause it to go from your mouth down into your stomach. □ I swallowed my coffee. □ Polly took a bite of the apple and swallowed. ● **Swallow** is also a noun. □ Jane lifted her glass and took a quick swallow. ◼ V-T If someone **swallows** a story or a statement, they believe it completely. □ They didn't swallow most of what I said. ◼ N-COUNT A **swallow** is a kind of small bird with pointed wings and a forked tail. [from Old English]

**swam** /swæm/ **Swam** is the past tense of **swim**. [from Old English]

**swamp** /swɒmp/ (swamps, swamping, swamped) ◼ N-VAR A **swamp** is an area of very wet land with wild plants growing in it. □ I spent one night by a swamp listening to frogs. ◼ V-T If something **swamps** a place or object, it fills it with water. □ A big wave swamped the boat. ◼ V-T If you **are swamped** by things or people, you have more of them than you can deal with. □ He is swamped with work. [from Middle Dutch]

**swan** /swɒn/ (swans) N-COUNT A **swan** is a large bird with a very long neck. Swans live on rivers and lakes and are usually white. [from Old English]

**swap** /swɒp/ (swaps, swapping, swapped) ◼ V-RECIP If you **swap** something with someone, you give it to them and receive a different thing in exchange. □ Next week they will swap places. □ I swapped my shirt for one of Karen's. ● **Swap** is also a noun. □ There followed a swap of signed photos. ◼ V-T If you **swap** one thing **for** another, you remove the first thing and replace it with the second, or you stop doing the first thing and start doing the second. □ He swapped his overalls for a suit and tie.

**swarm** /swɔrm/ (swarms, swarming, swarmed) ◼ N-COUNT A **swarm** of bees or other insects is a large group of them flying together. □ The bees traveled in a swarm. ◼ V-I When bees or other insects **swarm**, they move or fly in a large group. □ A group of bees came swarming toward me. ◼ V-I When people **swarm** somewhere, they move there quickly in a large group. □ People swarmed to the stores, buying everything they could. ◼ N-COUNT A **swarm of** people is a large group of them moving about quickly. □ A swarm of people came out of the hotel. ◼ V-I If a place **is swarming with** people, it is full of people moving about in a busy way. □ The place was swarming with police officers. [from Old English]

**swat** /swɒt/ (swats, swatting, swatted) V-T If you **swat** something such as an insect, you hit it with a quick, swinging movement, using your hand or a flat object. □ I use this thing to swat flies. [from northern English dialect]

**swathe** /swɒð/ (swathes, swathing, swathed)

The noun is also spelled **swath**.

◼ N-COUNT A **swathe of** land is a long strip of land. □ Great swathes of countryside have disappeared. ◼ V-T To **swathe** someone or something in cloth means to wrap them in it completely. □ She swathed her enormous body in black fabrics. □ His head was swathed in bandages. [from Old English]

**SWAT team** /swɒt tim/ (SWAT teams) N-COUNT A **SWAT team** is a group of police officers who have been specially trained to deal with very dangerous or violent situations. **SWAT** is an abbreviation for "Special Weapons and Tactics."

**S-wave** /ɛs weiv/ (S-waves) N-COUNT **S-waves** are waves of energy that are released in an earthquake, after the release of waves called P-waves. **S-wave** is an abbreviation for "secondary wave". [TECHNICAL]

**sway** /swei/ (sways, swaying, swayed) ◼ V-I When people or things **sway**, they lean or swing slowly from one side to the other. □ The people swayed back and forth singing. □ The whole boat swayed and tipped. ◼ V-T If you **are swayed by** someone or something, you are influenced by them. □ Don't ever be swayed by fashion. ◼ PHRASE If someone or something **holds sway**, they have great power or influence over a particular place or activity. □ Powerful chiefs hold sway over more than 15 million people. [from Old Norse]

**swear** /swɛər/ (swears, swearing, swore, sworn) ◼ V-I If someone **swears**, they use language that is considered to be vulgar or offensive. □ It's wrong to swear and shout. ◼ V-T If you **swear to** do something, you promise in a serious way that you will do it. □ Alan swore that he would do everything he could to help us. □ We have sworn to fight cruelty. ◼ V-T/V-I If you say that you **swear** that something is true or that you can **swear** to it, you are saying very firmly that it is true. □ I swear I've told you all I know. ◼ V-T If someone **is sworn to** secrecy or **is sworn to** silence, they promise another person that they will not reveal a secret. □ She wanted to tell everyone the news but was sworn to secrecy. [from Old English] ◼ → see also **sworn**
▸ **swear by** PHR-VERB If you **swear by** something, you believe that it can be relied on to have a particular effect. [INFORMAL] □ Many people swear by vitamin C to prevent colds.
▸ **swear in** PHR-VERB When someone **is sworn in**, they formally promise to fulfill the duties of a new job or appointment. □ Mary Robinson was sworn in as Ireland's first woman president.

| Word Partnership | Use *swear* with : |
| --- | --- |
| N. | swear **words** ◼ |
| | swear **allegiance**, swear **an oath** ◼ |
| ADV. | **solemnly** swear ◼ |

**sweat** /swɛt/ (sweats, sweating, sweated) ◼ N-UNCOUNT **Sweat** is the salty colorless liquid which comes through your skin when you are hot, sick, or afraid. □ Both horse and rider were dripping with sweat. ◼ V-I When you **sweat**, sweat comes through your skin. □ It's really hot. I'm sweating. ● **sweat|ing** N-UNCOUNT □ Sweating can be an embarrassing problem. ◼ N-COUNT If someone is **in a sweat**, they are sweating a lot. □ Every morning I break out in a sweat. □ Cool down very gradually after *working up a sweat.* **4** N-PLURAL **Sweats** are loose, warm, stretchy pants or pants and top which people wear to relax and do exercise. [INFORMAL] **5** PHRASE If someone is **in a cold sweat** or **in a sweat**, they feel frightened or embarrassed. ❑ *The thought of talking to him brought me out in a cold sweat.* [from Old English]

**sweat|er** /swɛtər/ (**sweaters**) N-COUNT A **sweater** is a warm knitted piece of clothing which covers the upper part of your body and your arms. [from Old English]
→ see **clothing**

**sweat gland** (**sweat glands**) N-COUNT Your **sweat glands** are the organs in your skin that release sweat.

**sweat|shirt** /swɛtʃɜrt/ (**sweatshirts**) also **sweat shirt** N-COUNT A **sweatshirt** is a loose warm piece of casual clothing, usually made of thick stretchy cotton, which covers the upper part of your body and your arms.
→ see **clothing**

**sweaty** /swɛti/ (**sweatier, sweatiest**) ADJ If parts of your body or your clothes are **sweaty**, they are soaked or covered with sweat. ❑ *...sweaty hands.* [from Old English]

**sweep** /swip/ (**sweeps, sweeping, swept**) **1** V-T/V-I If you **sweep** an area of floor or ground, you push dirt or garbage off it using a brush with a long handle. ❑ *The owner of the store was sweeping his floor.* ❑ *She was in the kitchen sweeping food off the floor.* ❑ *Norma picked up the broom and began sweeping.* **2** V-T If you **sweep** things off something, you push them off with a quick smooth movement of your arm. ❑ *She swept the cards from the table.* **3** V-T If wind, a stormy sea, or another strong force **sweeps** someone or something somewhere, it moves them there quickly. ❑ *The flood swept cars into the sea.* **4** V-T/V-I If events, ideas, or beliefs **sweep** through a place or **sweep** a place, they spread quickly through it. ❑ *Then war swept through Europe.* **5** PHRASE If someone **sweeps** something bad or wrong **under the carpet**, or if they **sweep** it **under the rug**, they try to prevent people from hearing about it. ❑ *For a long time this problem has been swept under the carpet.* [from Old English]
▶ **sweep up** PHR-VERB If you **sweep up** garbage or dirt, you push it together with a brush and then remove it. ❑ *Get a broom and sweep up that glass.*

**sweep|ing** /swipɪŋ/ **1** ADJ A **sweeping** statement or generalization applies to all things of a particular kind, without considering all the relevant facts carefully; used showing disapproval ❑ *She's always making sweeping statements about things.* **2** ADJ **Sweeping** changes are large and very important or significant. ❑ *The new government has started to make sweeping changes in the economy.* [from Old English]

**sweet** /swit/ (**sweeter, sweetest, sweets**) **1** ADJ **Sweet** food and drink contains a lot of sugar. ❑ *...a cup of sweet tea.* ❑ *If the sauce is too sweet, add some salt.* ● **sweet|ness** N-UNCOUNT ❑ *Fruit has a natural sweetness.* **2** ADJ A **sweet** smell is a pleasant one, for example the smell of a flower. ❑ *...the sweet smell of her soap.* **3** ADJ A **sweet** sound is pleasant, smooth, and gentle. ❑ *The young girl's voice was soft and sweet.* ● **sweet|ly** ADV ❑ *He sang sweetly.* **4** ADJ If you describe something as **sweet**, you mean that it gives you great pleasure and satisfaction. [WRITTEN] ❑ *Success is sweet.* **5** ADJ If you describe

someone as **sweet**, you mean that they are pleasant, kind, and gentle toward other people. ❑ *He was a sweet man.* ● **sweet|ly** ADV ❑ *I just smiled sweetly and said no.* **6** ADJ If you describe a small person or thing as **sweet**, you mean they are attractive in a simple or unsophisticated way. [INFORMAL] ❑ *...a sweet little baby.* **7** N-PLURAL **Sweets** are foods that have a lot of sugar. ❑ *Eat more fruit and vegetables and less fats and sweets.* [from Old English]
→ see **sugar, taste**

**sweet|corn** /switkɔrn/ N-UNCOUNT **Sweetcorn** is a long vegetable covered in small yellow seeds. It is part of the corn plant. The seeds themselves can also be referred to as **sweetcorn**.

**sweet|en** /swit³n/ (**sweetens, sweetening, sweetened**) V-T If you **sweeten** food or drink, you add sugar, honey, or another sweet substance to it. ❑ *He sweetened his coffee.* [from Old English]

**sweet|en|er** /swit³nər/ (**sweeteners**) N-VAR A **sweetener** is an artificial substance that can be used in drinks instead of sugar. [from Old English]

**sweet|heart** /swithɑrt/ (**sweethearts**) N-VOC You call someone **sweetheart** if you are very fond of them. ❑ *Happy birthday, sweetheart.*

**swell** /swɛl/ (**swells, swelling, swelled, swollen**)

> The forms **swelled** and **swollen** are both used as the past participle.

**1** V-T/V-I If the amount or size of something **swells** or if something **swells** it, it becomes larger than it was before. ❑ *His army swelled to one hundred thousand men.* ❑ *Sales swelled by 50%.* **2** V-I If something such as a part of your body **swells**, it becomes larger and rounder than normal. ❑ *Do your legs swell at night?* ● **Swell up** means the same as **swell**. ❑ *His neck swelled up.* **3** N-COUNT **Swells** are large, smooth waves on the surface of the sea that are produced by the wind and can travel long distances. [from Old English] **4** → see also **swollen**

**swell|ing** /swɛlɪŋ/ (**swellings**) N-VAR A **swelling** is a raised, curved shape on the surface of your body which appears as a result of an injury or an illness. ❑ *There was a swelling on his eye.* [from Old English]

**swel|ter|ing** /swɛltərɪŋ/ ADJ If you describe the weather as **sweltering**, you mean that it is extremely hot and makes you feel uncomfortable. ❑ *...the sweltering heat of summer.* [from Old English]

**swept** /swɛpt/ **Swept** is the past tense and past participle of **sweep**. [from Old English]

**swerve** /swɜrv/ (**swerves, swerving, swerved**) V-T/V-I If a vehicle or other moving thing **swerves** or if you **swerve** it, it suddenly changes direction, often in order to avoid hitting something. ❑ *Drivers swerved to avoid the tree in the road.* ❑ *Her car swerved off the road.* ● **Swerve** is also a noun. ❑ *He swung the car to the left and that swerve saved his life.* [from Old English]

**swift** /swɪft/ (**swifter, swiftest, swifts**) **1** ADJ A **swift** event or process happens very quickly or without delay. ❑ *We need to make a swift decision.* ● **swift|ly** ADV ❑ *We have to act as swiftly as we can.* ● **swift|ness** N-UNCOUNT ❑ *...the swiftness of the invasion.* **2** ADJ Something that is **swift** moves very quickly. ❑ *With a swift movement, Matthew sat*

S

up. ● **swift|ly** ADV ❑ *Lenny moved swiftly and silently across the grass.* [from Old English]

**swim** /swɪm/ (**swims, swimming, swam, swum**) **1** V-T/V-I When you **swim**, you move through water by making movements with your arms and legs. ❑ *She learned to swim when she was 10.* ❑ *Let's go to the other side of the pool then swim back.* ❑ *I swim a mile a day.* ● **Swim** is also a noun. ❑ *When can we go for a swim?* ● **swim|mer** (**swimmers**) N-COUNT ❑ *I'm a good swimmer.* **2** V-I If your head is **swimming**, you feel unsteady and slightly ill. ❑ *The smell made her head swim.* [from Old English] **3** **sink or swim** → see **sink**

**swim blad|der** (**swim bladders**) N-COUNT A **swim bladder** is an organ in fish that contains air or gas and allows the fish to rise or sink through the water.

**swim|ming** /swɪmɪŋ/ N-UNCOUNT **Swimming** is the activity of swimming, especially as a sport or for pleasure. ❑ *Swimming is a great form of exercise.* [from Old English]

**swim|ming pool** (**swimming pools**) N-COUNT A **swimming pool** is a large hole that has been made and filled with water so that people can swim in it.

**swim|suit** /swɪmsut/ (**swimsuits**) N-COUNT A **swimsuit** is a piece of clothing that is worn for swimming, especially by women and girls. ❑ *...10 different styles of swimsuit for men.*

**swin|dle** /swɪndᵊl/ (**swindles, swindling, swindled**) V-T If someone **swindles** a person or an organization, they deceive them in order to get money from them. ❑ *He swindled people out of millions of dollars.* ● **Swindle** is also a noun. ❑ *He was involved in a tax swindle.* ● **swind|ler** (**swindlers**) N-COUNT ❑ *...an insurance swindler.* [from German]

**swing** /swɪŋ/ (**swings, swinging, swung**) **1** V-T/V-I If something **swings** or if you **swing** it, it moves repeatedly backward and forward or from side to side from a fixed point. ❑ *The sign came loose and started to swing from one side to the other.* ❑ *She was swinging a bottle of soda in her hand.* ● **Swing** is also a noun. ❑ *She walked with a slight swing to her hips.* **2** V-T/V-I If a vehicle **swings** in a particular direction, or if the driver **swings** it, it turns suddenly in that direction. ❑ *Joanna swung back and headed for the airport.* **3** V-I If you **swing at** a person or a fly, you try to hit them with your arm or with something that you are holding. ❑ *Blanche swung at her but missed.* ● **Swing** is also a noun. ❑ *I often want to take a swing at someone to relieve my feelings.* **4** N-COUNT A **swing** is a seat hanging by two ropes or chains from a metal frame or from the branch of a tree. You can sit on the seat and move forward and backward through the air. ❑ *I took the kids to the park to play on the swings.* **5** N-COUNT A **swing** in people's opinions, attitudes, or feelings is a change in them, especially a sudden or big change. ❑ *There are a lot of swings and changes in education.* ❑ *She suffers from mood swings.* **6** V-I If people's opinions, attitudes, or feelings **swing**, they change, especially in a sudden or extreme way. ❑ *In the next election the voters could swing again.* **7** PHRASE If something is **in full swing**, it is operating fully and is no longer in its early stages. ❑ *When we returned, the party was in full swing.* [from Old English]

| N. | swing **a bat, golf** swing **1** |
| | swing **at a ball 3** |
| | **porch** swing **4** |
| | **voters** swing **6** |
| ADJ. | **good** swing, **perfect** swing **1** |
| | **big** swing **1 3 5** |
| | **in full** swing **7** |

**swing vote** (**swing votes**) N-COUNT In a situation when people are about to vote, the **swing vote** is used to talk about the vote of a person or group which is difficult to predict and which will be important in deciding the result. [JOURNALISM] ❑ *...a Democrat who holds the swing vote on the committee.*

**swing vot|er** (**swing voters**) N-COUNT A **swing voter** is a person who is not a firm supporter of any political party, and whose vote in an election is difficult to predict.

**swipe** /swaɪp/ (**swipes, swiping, swiped**) V-I If you **swipe at** a person or thing, you try to hit them with a stick or other object, making a swinging movement with your arm. ❑ *She swiped at Roger as though he was a fly.* ● **Swipe** is also a noun. ❑ *He took a swipe at Andrew that made him fall on the floor.*

**swipe card** (**swipe cards**) also **swipecard** N-COUNT A **swipe card** is a plastic card with a magnetic strip on it which contains information that can be read or transferred by passing the card through a special machine. ❑ *They use a swipe card to go in and out of their offices.*

**swirl** /swɜrl/ (**swirls, swirling, swirled**) V-T/V-I If you **swirl** something liquid or flowing, or if it **swirls**, it moves around and around quickly. ❑ *She swirled the soda in her glass.* ❑ *The black water swirled around his legs.* ● **Swirl** is also a noun. ❑ *...small swirls of paint.* [from Dutch]

**swish** /swɪʃ/ (**swishes, swishing, swished**) V-T/V-I If something **swishes** or if you **swish** it, it moves quickly through the air, making a soft sound. ❑ *A car swished past.* ❑ *He swished his coat around his shoulders.* ● **Swish** is also a noun. ❑ *She turned with a swish of her skirt.*

**switch** /swɪtʃ/ (**switches, switching, switched**) **1** N-COUNT A **switch** is a small control for an electrical device which you use to turn the device on or off. ❑ *She shut the dishwasher and pressed the switch.* **2** N-PLURAL On a railroad track, the **switches** are the levers and rails at a place where two tracks join or separate. The **switches** enable a train to move from one track to another. ❑ *...a set of railroad tracks — including switches — and a model train.* **3** V-T/V-I If you **switch to** something different, for example to a different system, task, or subject of conversation, you change to it from what you were doing or saying before. ❑ *Maybe you should switch to a different medication.* ❑ *The law would help companies to switch from coal to cleaner fuels.* ● **Switch** is also a noun. ❑ *She decided on a switch to part-time work.* **4** V-T If you **switch** two things, you replace one with the other. ❑ *They switched the keys, so Karen*

switch

*had the key to my room and I had the key to hers.* [from Middle Dutch]

▶ **switch off** ■ PHR-VERB If you **switch off** a light or other electrical device, you stop it from working by operating a switch. ❏ *She switched off the coffee machine.* ■ PHR-VERB If you **switch off**, you stop paying attention or stop thinking or worrying about something. [INFORMAL] ❏ *I switch off when he starts complaining.*

▶ **switch on** PHR-VERB If you **switch on** a light or other electrical device, you make it start working by operating a switch. ❏ *He switched on the lamp.*

| Word Partnership | Use *switch* with : |
|---|---|
| V. | **flick** a switch, **flip** a switch, **turn** a switch ■ |
| | **make** a switch ■ |
| N. | **ignition** switch, **light** switch, **power** switch ■ |
| | switch **sides** ■ |

**switch|board** /swɪtʃbɔrd/ (**switchboards**) N-COUNT A **switchboard** is a place in a large office or business where all the telephone calls are connected. ❏ *Can you connect me to the central switchboard?* [from Middle Dutch]

**swiv|el** /swɪvᵊl/ (**swivels, swiveling** or **swivelling, swiveled** or **swivelled**) V-T/V-I If something **swivels** or if you **swivel** it, it turns around a central point so that it is facing in a different direction. ❏ *She swiveled her chair and stared out the window.* [from Old English]

**swol|len** /swoʊlᵊn/ ■ ADJ If a part of your body is **swollen**, it is larger and rounder than normal, usually as a result of injury or illness. ❏ *My eyes were swollen and I could hardly see.* ■ **Swollen** is the past participle of **swell**. [from Old English]

**swoon** /swun/ (**swoons, swooning, swooned**) V-I If you **swoon**, you are strongly affected by your feelings for someone you love or admire very much. ❏ *In the 1920s, women swooned over the stars of the silent movies.* ❏ *The ladies swoon at his every word.* [from Old English]

**swoop** /swup/ (**swoops, swooping, swooped**) ■ V-I If police or soldiers **swoop on** a place, they go there suddenly and quickly, usually in order to arrest someone or to attack the place. ❏ *Police swooped on the car.* ● **Swoop** is also a noun. ❏ *Police arrested five people after a swoop on a Los Angeles home.* ■ V-I When a bird or airplane **swoops**, it suddenly moves downwards through the air in a smooth curving movement. ❏ *The bird swooped in low over the ocean.* [from Old English]

sword

**sword** /sɔrd/ (**swords**) N-COUNT A **sword** is a weapon with a handle and a long sharp blade. [from Old English]
→ see **army**

**swore** /swɔr/ **Swore** is the past tense of **swear**. [from Old English]

**sworn** /swɔrn/ ■ **Sworn** is the past participle of **swear**. ■ ADJ If you make a **sworn** statement or declaration, you swear that everything that you have said in it is true. ❏ *He had to sign a sworn statement.* [from Old English]

**swum** /swʌm/ **Swum** is the past participle of **swim**. [from Old English]

**swung** /swʌŋ/ **Swung** is the past tense and past participle of **swing**. [from Old English]

**syl|labi|ca|tion** /sɪlæbɪkeɪʃᵊn/ also **syllabification** /sɪlæbɪfɪkeɪʃᵊn/ N-UNCOUNT **Syllabication** or **syllabification** is the division of a word into its separate syllables. [TECHNICAL] [from Old French]

**syl|la|ble** /sɪləbᵊl/ (**syllables**) N-COUNT A **syllable** is a part of a word that contains a single vowel sound and that is pronounced as a unit. So, for example, "book" has one syllable, and "reading" has two syllables. ❏ *We children called her Oma, accenting both syllables.* [from Old French]

**syl|la|bus** /sɪləbəs/ (**syllabuses**) N-COUNT A **syllabus** is an outline or summary of the subjects to be covered in a course. ❏ *The course syllabus consisted mainly of novels by African-American writers.* [from Late Latin]

**sym|bio|sis** /sɪmbioʊsɪs, -baɪ-/ N-UNCOUNT **Symbiosis** is a close relationship between two organisms of different kinds which benefits both organisms. [TECHNICAL] ❏ *...the link between bacteria, symbiosis, and the evolution of plants and animals.* [from New Latin]

**sym|bol** /sɪmbᵊl/ (**symbols**) ■ N-COUNT Something that is a **symbol** of a society or an aspect of life seems to represent it because it is very typical of it. ❏ *For her people, she is a symbol of freedom.* ■ N-COUNT A **symbol** of something such as an idea is a shape or design that is used to represent it. ❏ *The rose is an Irish symbol.* ■ N-COUNT A **symbol for** an item in a calculation or scientific formula is a number, letter, or shape that represents that item. ❏ *What's the chemical symbol for oxygen?* [from Church Latin]
→ see **myth**

**sym|bol|ic** /sɪmbɒlɪk/ ■ ADJ If you describe an event, action, or procedure as **symbolic**, you mean that it represents an important change, although it has little practical effect. ❏ *The president's trip is of symbolic importance.* ● **sym|boli|cal|ly** /sɪmbɒlɪkli/ ADV ❏ *Museums symbolically remove paintings to remember when particular artists died.* ■ ADJ **Symbolic** is used to describe things involving or relating to symbols. ❏ *...the symbolic meaning of names.* ● **sym|bol|ism** /sɪmbəlɪzəm/ N-UNCOUNT ❏ *...the writer's use of symbolism.* [from Church Latin]

**sym|bol|ize** /sɪmbəlaɪz/ (**symbolizes, symbolizing, symbolized**) V-T If one thing **symbolizes** another, it is used or regarded as a symbol of it. ❏ *For some people, the old flag symbolizes better times.* [from Church Latin]

**sym|met|ri|cal** /sɪmɛtrɪkᵊl/ ADJ If something is **symmetrical**, it has two halves which are exactly the same, except that one half is the mirror image of the other. ❏ *The rows of windows were perfectly symmetrical.* ● **sym|met|ri|cal|ly** /sɪmɛtrɪkli/ ADV ❏ *She placed the sandwiches symmetrically on a plate.* [from Latin]

**sym|me|try** /sɪmɪtri/ (**symmetries**) ■ N-VAR Something that has **symmetry** is symmetrical in shape, design, or structure. ❏ *...the symmetry of a snowflake.* ■ N-VAR In mathematics, **symmetry** is the relationship between two geometric figures

S

that are the same size and shape. [TECHNICAL] [from Latin]

**sym|pa|thet|ic** /sɪmpəθεtɪk/ **1** ADJ If you are **sympathetic** to someone who is in a bad situation, you are kind to them and show that you understand their feelings. ◻ *She was very sympathetic to the problems of her students.* ● **sym|pa|theti|cal|ly** /sɪmpəθεtɪkli/ ADV ◻ *She nodded sympathetically.* **2** ADJ If you are **sympathetic** to a proposal or action, you approve of it and are willing to support it. ◻ *...judges who are more sympathetic to crime control.* [from Latin]

**sym|pa|thize** /sɪmpəθaɪz/ (**sympathizes, sympathizing, sympathized**) **1** V-I If you **sympathize** with someone who is in a bad situation, you show that you are sorry for them. ◻ *I know what it's like when a parent dies, and I sympathize with you.* **2** V-I If you **sympathize with** someone's feelings, you understand them and are not critical of them. ◻ *Some Europeans sympathize with the Americans over the issue.* **3** V-I If you **sympathize with** a person or group, you approve of them and are willing to support them. ◻ *Most of the people living there sympathized with the government.* ● **sym|pa|thiz|er** (**sympathizers**) N-COUNT ◻ *...a Communist sympathizer.* [from Latin]

> **Word Link** *path ≈ feeling : apathy, empathy, sympathy*

> **Word Link** *sym ≈ together : sympathy, symphony, symposium*

**sym|pa|thy** /sɪmpəθi/ (**sympathies**) **1** N-UNCOUNT If you have **sympathy** for someone who is in a bad situation, you are sorry for them, and show this in the way you behave toward them. ◻ *We expressed our sympathy at the death of her mother.* ◻ *I get no sympathy from my family when I'm sick.* **2** N-UNCOUNT If you have **sympathy** with someone's ideas or opinions, you agree with them. ◻ *I have some sympathy with this point of view.* **3** N-UNCOUNT If you take some action **in sympathy with** someone else, you do it in order to show that you support them. ◻ *Several hundred workers went on strike in sympathy with their colleagues.* [from Latin]

> **Word Partnership** Use *sympathy* with :
>
> ADJ. **deep** sympathy, **great** sympathy, **public** sympathy **1**
> V. **express** sympathy, **feel** sympathy, **gain** sympathy, **have** sympathy **1 2**

> **Word Link** *phon ≈ sound : microphone, symphony, telephone*

**sym|pho|ny** /sɪmfəni/ (**symphonies**) N-COUNT A **symphony** is a piece of music written to be played by an orchestra. Symphonies are usually made up of four separate sections called movements. ◻ *...Beethoven's Ninth Symphony.* [from Old French]
→ see **music, orchestra**

**sym|pho|ny or|ches|tra** (**symphony orchestras**) N-COUNT A **symphony orchestra** is a large orchestra that plays classical music.

**sym|po|sium** /sɪmpoʊziəm/ (**symposia** /sɪmpoʊziə/ or **symposiums**) N-COUNT A **symposium** is a conference in which experts or academics discuss a particular subject. ◻ *He went to an international symposium.* [from Latin]

**symp|tom** /sɪmptəm/ (**symptoms**) **1** N-COUNT A **symptom** of an illness is something wrong with your body or mind that is a sign of the illness. ◻ *One symptom of mental illness is hearing imaginary voices.* ◻ *...patients with flu symptoms.* **2** N-COUNT A **symptom of** a bad situation is something that happens which is considered to be a sign of this situation. ◻ *The food problem is a symptom of a much deeper crisis in the country.* [from Late Latin]
→ see **diagnosis, illness**

**symp|to|mat|ic** /sɪmptəmætɪk/ ADJ If something is **symptomatic** of something else, especially something bad, it is a sign of it. [FORMAL] ◻ *The city's problems are symptomatic of the crisis that is spreading throughout the country.* [from Late Latin]

**syna|gogue** /sɪnəgɒg/ (**synagogues**) N-COUNT A **synagogue** is a building where Jewish people meet to worship or to study their religion. [from Old French]

> **Word Link** *chron ≈ time : chronic, chronicle, synchronize*

> **Word Link** *syn ≈ together : synchronize, syndicate, synthesis*

**syn|chro|nize** /sɪŋkrənaɪz/ (**synchronizes, synchronizing, synchronized**) V-RECIP If you **synchronize** two activities, processes, or movements, or if you **synchronize** one activity, process, or movement **with** another, you cause them to happen at the same time and speed as each other. ◻ *We could not synchronize our lives so we could take vacations together.* ◻ *They have to synchronize the voices with the film action.* [from Late Latin]

**syn|cline** /sɪnklaɪn/ (**synclines**) N-COUNT A **syncline** is a rock formation in which layers of rock are folded so that they resemble the shape of a letter U. [TECHNICAL] [from Greek]

**syn|co|pa|tion** /sɪŋkəpeɪʃⁿn/ (**syncopations**) N-VAR **Syncopation** is the quality that music has when the weak beats in a bar are stressed instead of the strong ones. [from Late Latin]

**syn|di|cate** /sɪndɪkɪt/ (**syndicates**) N-COUNT A **syndicate** is an association of people or organizations that is formed for business purposes or in order to carry out a project. ◻ *They formed a syndicate to buy the car.* ◻ *...a syndicate of 152 banks.* [from Old French]

**syn|drome** /sɪndroʊm/ (**syndromes**) N-COUNT A **syndrome** is a medical condition that is characterized by a particular group of signs and symptoms. ◻ *No one knows what causes Sudden Infant Death Syndrome.* [from New Latin]

> **Word Link** *onym ≈ name : acronym, anonymous, synonym*

**syno|nym** /sɪnənɪm/ (**synonyms**) N-COUNT A **synonym** is a word or expression which means the same as another word or expression. ◻ *"Afraid" is a synonym for "frightened."* [from Late Latin]

**syn|ony|mous** /sɪnɒnɪməs/ ADJ If you say that one thing is **synonymous with** another, you mean that the two things are very closely associated with each other so that one suggests the other or one cannot exist without the other. ❑ *Paris has always been synonymous with style.* [from Late Latin]

| **Word Link** | syn ≈ *together* : synchronize, syndicate, synthesis |
|---|---|

**syn|the|sis** /sɪnθɪsɪs/ (**syntheses** /sɪnθɪsiz/) N-COUNT A **synthesis of** different ideas or styles is a mixture or combination of these ideas or styles. [FORMAL] ❑ *His novels are a synthesis of history and fiction.* [from Latin]

**syn|the|sis re|ac|tion** (**synthesis reactions**) N-COUNT A **synthesis reaction** is a chemical reaction in which two or more substances combine to form a compound. [TECHNICAL]

**syn|the|size** /sɪnθɪsaɪz/ (**synthesizes, synthesizing, synthesized**) V-T If you **synthesize** different ideas, facts, or experiences, you combine them to form a single idea or impression. [FORMAL] ❑ *These artists synthesized different elements of modern art.* [from Latin]

**syn|thet|ic** /sɪnθɛtɪk/ ADJ **Synthetic** products are made from chemicals or artificial substances rather than from natural ones. ❑ *...synthetic rubber.* [from New Latin]

**sy|ringe** /sɪrɪndʒ/ (**syringes**) N-COUNT A **syringe** is a small tube with a thin hollow needle at the end. Syringes are used for injecting drugs or for taking blood from your body. [from Late Latin]

**syr|up** /sɪrəp, sɜr-/ (**syrups**) N-VAR **Syrup** is a sweet liquid made by cooking sugar with water or fruit juice. ❑ *...canned fruit with syrup.* [from Medieval Latin]

**sys|tem** /sɪstəm/ (**systems**) **1** N-COUNT A **system** is a way of working, organizing, or doing something which follows a fixed plan or set of rules. ❑ *You need a better system for organizing your CDs.* **2** N-COUNT A **system** is a set of equipment, parts or devices. ❑ *There's something wrong with the computer system.* ❑ *...a heating system.* **3** N-COUNT A **system** is a network of things that are linked together so that people or things can travel from one place to another or communicate. ❑ *...Australia's road and rail system.* **4** N-COUNT A **system** is a particular set of rules, especially in mathematics or science, which is used to count or measure things. ❑ *...the decimal system of weights and measures.* **5** N-SING People sometimes refer to the government or administration of a country as **the system**. ❑ *These feelings are likely to make people try to overthrow the system.* [from French] **6** → see also **ecosystem, immune system, nervous system, solar system**

**sys|tem|at|ic** /sɪstəmætɪk/ ADJ Something that is done in a **systematic** way is done according to a fixed plan, in a thorough and efficient way. ❑ *The searched the area in a systematic way.* ● **sys|tem|ati|cal|ly** /sɪstəmætɪkli/ ADV ❑ *They have systematically destroyed all our hard work.* [from French]

**sys|tem|ic** /sɪstɛmɪk/ ADJ **Systemic** means affecting the whole of something. [FORMAL] ❑ *The economy is in a systemic crisis.* [from French]

**sys|tem|ic cir|cu|la|tion** N-UNCOUNT **Systemic circulation** is the flow of blood between the heart and the rest of the body except for the lungs. Compare **pulmonary circulation.** [TECHNICAL] → see **cardiovascular system**

S

# Tt

**tab** /tæb/ (tabs) **1** N-COUNT A **tab** is a small piece of cloth or paper that is attached to something, usually with information about that thing written on it. ❑ *The file had the wrong tab on it.* **2** PHRASE If someone **keeps tabs on** you, they make sure that they always know where you are and what you are doing, often in order to control you. [INFORMAL] ❑ *It was obvious Heller was keeping tabs on Johnson.* **3** PHRASE If you **pick up the tab**, you pay a bill for other people or pay for something that is needed. [INFORMAL] ❑ *Pollard picked up the tab for dinner.*

**ta|ble** /teɪbᵊl/ (tables, tabling, tabled) **1** N-COUNT A **table** is a piece of furniture with a flat top that you put things on or sit at. ❑ *She was sitting at the kitchen table eating a peach.* **2** V-T If someone **tables** a proposal or plan, they decide to discuss it at a later date, rather than right away. ❑ *We will table that for later.* **3** N-COUNT A **table** is a written set of facts and figures arranged in columns and rows. ❑ *See the table on page 104.* [from Old French]

**tab|leau** /tæblou, tæbloʊ/ (tableaux) N-COUNT A **tableau** is a scene, often from a picture, that consists of a group of people in costumes who do not speak or move. [from French]

**table|cloth** /teɪbᵊlklɔθ/ (tablecloths) N-COUNT A **tablecloth** is a cloth used to cover a table.

**table|spoon** /teɪbᵊlspun/ (tablespoons) N-COUNT A **tablespoon** is a large spoon used for serving food and in cooking.

**tab|let** /tæblɪt/ (tablets) N-COUNT A **tablet** is a small solid piece of medicine which you swallow. ❑ *...a sleeping tablet.* [from Old French]

**tab|loid** /tæblɔɪd/ (tabloids) N-COUNT A **tabloid** is a newspaper that has small pages, short articles, and a lot of photographs. ❑ *I sometimes read the tabloids.*

**ta|boo** /tæbu/ (taboos) N-COUNT A **taboo** against a subject or activity is a social custom to avoid doing that activity or talking about that subject, because people find it embarrassing or offensive. ● **Taboo** is also an adjective. ❑ *Cancer is a taboo subject.* [from Tongan]

**tac|it** /tæsɪt/ ADJ If you refer to someone's **tacit** agreement or approval, you mean they are agreeing to something or approving it without actually saying so. ❑ *...tacit agreement that mistakes were made.* ● **tac|it|ly** ADV ❑ *He tacitly admitted that they broke the law.* [from Latin]

**tack** /tæk/ (tacks, tacking, tacked) **1** N-COUNT A **tack** or a **thumbtack** is a short pin with a broad, flat top that you can push with your thumb, used especially for fastening papers to a bulletin board. **2** N-COUNT A **tack** is a short nail with a broad, flat top, especially one that is used for fastening carpets to the floor. ❑ *...a box of carpet tacks.* **3** → see also **thumbtack** **4** V-T If you **tack** something to a surface, you pin it there with tacks or thumbtacks. ❑ *He tacked a note to her door.* **5** N-SING If you change **tack** or try a different **tack**, you try a different method for dealing with a situation. ❑ *Seeing the puzzled look on his face, she tried a different tack.* [from Middle Low German] → see **office**

▶ **tack on** PHR-VERB If you say that something **is tacked on** to something else, you think that it is added in a hurry and in an unsatisfactory way. ❑ *A small kitchen is tacked on to the back of the beautiful stone house.*

**tack|le** /tækᵊl/ (tackles, tackling, tackled) **1** V-T If you **tackle** a difficult problem or task, you deal with it in a determined way. ❑ *We must tackle these problems in order to save children's lives.* **2** V-T If you **tackle** someone in a game such as football or rugby, you try to stop them from running or try to take the ball away from them. ❑ *Foley tackled the quarterback.* ● **Tackle** is also a noun. ❑ *Owens ran out of a tackle.* **3** V-T If you **tackle** someone about a particular matter, you speak to them honestly about it, usually in order to get something changed or done. ❑ *I tackled him about his poor work.* **4** N-UNCOUNT **Tackle** is the equipment that you need for a sport or activity, especially fishing. ❑ *...fishing tackle.* [from Middle Low German]

**tacky** /tæki/ (tackier, tackiest) ADJ If you describe something as **tacky**, you dislike it because it is cheap and badly made or vulgar. [INFORMAL] ❑ *...tacky red sunglasses.*

**tact** /tækt/ N-UNCOUNT **Tact** is the ability to avoid upsetting or offending people by being careful not to say or do things that would hurt their feelings. ❑ *Her tact never failed.* [from Latin]

**tact|ful** /tæktfəl/ ADJ If you describe a person or what they say as **tactful**, you approve of them because they are careful not to offend or upset another person. ❑ *He was very tactful in dealing with difficult questions.* ● **tact|ful|ly** ADV ❑ *Alex tactfully said nothing.* [from Latin]

**tac|tic** /tæktɪk/ (tactics) N-COUNT **Tactics** are the methods that you choose to use in order to achieve what you want in a particular situation. ❑ *I decided to change my tactics.* [from New Latin]

**tac|ti|cal** /tæktɪkᵊl/ ADJ A **tactical** action or plan is intended to help someone achieve what they want in the future, rather than immediately. ❑ *His latest offer may simply be a tactical move.* ● **tac|ti|cal|ly** ADV ❑ *Many people voted tactically against the government.* [from New Latin]

**taf|fy** /tæfi/ N-VAR **Taffy** is a sticky candy that you chew. It is made by boiling sugar and butter together with water.

**tag** /tæg/ (**tags, tagging, tagged**) **1** N-COUNT A **tag** is a small piece of cardboard or cloth which is attached to an object or person and has information about that object or person on it. ❑ *The staff wore name tags.* **2** V-T If you **tag** something, you attach something to it or mark it so that it can be identified later. ❑ *He only has a short time to tag the birds before spring.*
▶ **tag along** PHR-VERB If you **tag along** with someone, you go with them, especially when they have not asked you to. ❑ *I let him tag along.*

**tai chi** /taɪ tʃiː/ also Tai Chi N-UNCOUNT **Tai chi** is a type of Chinese physical exercise in which you make slow, controlled movements.

**tai|ga** /taɪɡə/ (**taigas**) N-VAR The **taiga** is an area of thick forest in the far north of Europe, Asia, and North America, situated immediately south of the tundra. [from Russian]

**tail** /teɪl/ (**tails, tailing, tailed**) **1** N-COUNT The **tail** of an animal, bird, or fish is the part extending beyond the end of its body. ❑ *...a black dog with a long tail.* **2** N-COUNT You can use **tail** to refer to the end or back of something, especially something long and thin. ❑ *...the plane's tail.* **3** V-T To **tail** someone means to follow close behind them and watch where they go and what they do. [INFORMAL] ❑ *Officers tailed the gang for weeks.* [from Old English]
→ see **fish, horse**
▶ **tail off** PHR-VERB When something **tails off**, it gradually becomes less, often before coming to an end completely. ❑ *His voice tailed off in the last part of his speech.*

**tail|gate par|ty** /teɪlɡeɪt pɑːrti/ (**tailgate parties**) N-COUNT A **tailgate party** is a social gathering at which food is served from or near a vehicle, especially in a parking lot before a sports game. [INFORMAL]

**tai|lor** /teɪlər/ (**tailors, tailoring, tailored**) **1** N-COUNT A **tailor** is a person whose job is to make and repair clothes. **2** V-T If you **tailor** something such as a plan or system **to** your needs, you make it suitable by changing the details of it. ❑ *We can tailor the program to the patient's needs.* [from Old French]

**tailor-made** ADJ If something is **tailor-made**, it has been specially designed for a particular person or purpose. ❑ *The course is tailor-made for each student.*

**tail|pipe** /teɪlpaɪp/ (**tailpipes**) N-COUNT A **tailpipe** is the end pipe of a car's exhaust system.

**tail|spin** /teɪlspɪn/ **1** N-SING If something such as an industry or an economy goes into a **tailspin**, it begins to perform very badly or to fail. ❑ *The war has thrown the economy into a tailspin.* **2** N-SING If an aircraft goes into a **tailspin**, it falls very rapidly toward the ground in a spiral movement. ❑ *The aircraft went into a tailspin before crashing.*

**taint** /teɪnt/ (**taints, tainting, tainted**) **1** V-T If a person or thing **is tainted by** something bad or undesirable, their status or reputation is harmed because they are associated with it. ❑ *The elections were tainted by violence.* ● **taint|ed** ADJ ❑ *...tainted evidence.* **2** N-COUNT A **taint** is an undesirable quality which ruins the status or reputation of someone or something. ❑ *...the taint of corruption.* [from Old French]

take

❶ USED WITH NOUNS DESCRIBING ACTIONS
❷ OTHER USES

**❶ take** /teɪk/ (**takes, taking, took, taken**)

**Take** is used in combination with a wide range of nouns, where the meaning of the combination is mostly given by the noun. Many of these combinations are common idiomatic expressions whose meanings can be found at the appropriate nouns. For example, the expression **take care** is explained at **care**.

**1** V-T You can use **take** to say that someone does something. For example, you can say "**she took a shower**" instead of "she showered." ❑ *She was too tired to take a shower.* ❑ *Betty took a photograph of us.* **2** V-T You can use **take** with a range of nouns instead of using a more specific and often more formal verb. For example, you can say "**he took control**" or "**she took a positive attitude**" instead of "he assumed control" or "she adopted a positive attitude." ❑ *Castro took power in 1959.* ❑ *Workers should take control of their careers.* [from Maori]

**❷ take** /teɪk/ (**takes, taking, took, taken**)

**1** V-T If you **take** something, you reach out for it and hold it. ❑ *Let me take your coat.* ❑ *He took a handkerchief from his pocket.* **2** V-T If you **take** something with you when you go somewhere, you carry it or have it with you. ❑ *Mark often took his books to Bess's house to study.* ❑ *You should take your passport with you when changing money.* **3** V-T If a person, vehicle, or path **takes** someone somewhere, they transport or lead them there. ❑ *She took me to a Mexican restaurant.* **4** V-T If you **take** something from its owner, you steal it. ❑ *He took my money.* **5** V-T To **take** something or someone means to win or capture them from an enemy or opponent. ❑ *An army unit took the town.* **6** V-T If you cannot **take** something unpleasant, you cannot tolerate it without becoming upset, ill, or angry. ❑ *Don't ever ask me to look after those kids again. I just can't take it!* **7** V-T If something **takes** a certain amount of time, that amount of time is needed in order to do it. ❑ *Since the roads are very bad, the trip took us a long time.* ❑ *Your application could take a couple of months.* ❑ *The sauce takes 25 minutes to prepare.* **8** V-T If something **takes** a particular quality or thing, it requires it. ❑ *Walking across the room took all her strength.* ❑ *It takes courage to say what you think.* **9** V-T If you **take** something that is offered to you, you accept it. ❑ *When I took the job I thought I could change the system.* **10** V-T If you **take** something in a particular way, you react in the way mentioned. ❑ *No one took my opinion seriously.* **11** V-T If you **take** a road or route, you choose to travel along it. ❑ *Take Old Mill Road to the edge of town.* **12** V-T If you **take** a car, train, bus, or plane, you use it to go from one place to another. ❑ *She took the train to New York.* **13** V-T If you **take** a subject or course at school or college, you choose to study it. ❑ *Students can take European history and American history.* **14** V-T If you **take** a test or examination, you do it or take part in it. ❑ *She took her driving test yesterday.* **15** V-T If someone **takes** a drug or medicine, they swallow it. ❑ *She's been taking sleeping pills.* **16** V-T If you **take** a particular size in shoes or clothes, that size fits you. ❑ *"What size do you take?" — "I take a size 7."* **17** CONVENTION If you say to someone **"take it or leave it,"** you are telling them that they can accept something or not accept it, but that you are not prepared to discuss any other alternatives. ❑ *A 72-hour week, 12 hours a day, 6 days a week, take it or leave it.* [from Old English] **18** to **be taken aback** → see **aback 19** to **take up arms** → see **arm 20** to **take the cake** → see **cake 21** to **take** your **hat off to** someone → see **hat 22** to **be taken for a ride** → see **ride 23** to **take** someone **by surprise** → see **surprise**

| **Thesaurus** | *take* | Also look up : |
|---|---|---|
| v. | grab, grasp, hold **2 1** | |
| | drive, escort, transport **2 3** | |
| | steal **2 4** | |
| | capture, seize **2 5** | |

▶ **take after** PHR-VERB If you **take after** a member of your family, you look or behave like them. ❑ *She was a smart, brave woman. You take after her.*

▶ **take apart** PHR-VERB If you **take** something **apart**, you separate it into its different parts. ❑ *When the clock stopped, he took it apart.*

▶ **take away 1** PHR-VERB If you **take** something **away from** someone, you remove it from them. ❑ *They're going to take my chickens away because they are too noisy.* ❑ *They took everything away from him.* **2** PHR-VERB If you **take** one number or amount **away from** another, you subtract one number from the other. ❑ *Add up the bills for each month. Take this away from the income.*

▶ **take back 1** PHR-VERB If you **take** something **back**, you return it. ❑ *If I buy something he doesn't like, I take it back.* **2** PHR-VERB If you **take** something **back**, you admit that something that you said or thought is wrong. ❑ *Take back what you said about Jeremy!*

▶ **take down 1** PHR-VERB If you **take down** a structure, you remove each piece of it. ❑ *The Canadian army took down the fences.* **2** PHR-VERB If you **take down** a piece of information or a statement, you write it down. ❑ *I think we took your number down incorrectly.*

▶ **take in 1** PHR-VERB If you **take** someone **in**, you allow them to stay in your house or your country. ❑ *He persuaded Jo to take him in.* **2** PHR-VERB If you **are taken in** by someone or something, you are deceived or fooled by them. ❑ *I was taken in by his charm.* **3** PHR-VERB If you **take** something **in**, you pay attention to it and understand it when you hear it or read it. ❑ *I could tell she wasn't taking it in.*

▶ **take off 1** PHR-VERB When an airplane **takes off**, it leaves the ground and starts flying. ❑ *We took off at 11 o'clock.* **2** PHR-VERB If you **take** a garment **off**, you remove it. ❑ *He wouldn't take his hat off.* **3** PHR-VERB If you **take** time **off**, you obtain permission not to go to work for a short period of time. ❑ *Mitchel's boss did not allow him to take time off.*

▶ **take on 1** PHR-VERB If you **take on** a job or responsibility, especially a difficult one, you accept it. ❑ *No other organization was willing to take on the job.* **2** PHR-VERB If something **takes on** a new appearance or quality, it develops that appearance or quality. ❑ *His face took on a look of fear.* **3** PHR-VERB If you **take** someone **on**, you employ them to do a job. ❑ *He spoke to a publishing company. They're going to take him on.* **4** PHR-VERB If

you **take** someone **on**, you fight them or compete against them, especially when they are more powerful than you are. ❑ *Democrats were unwilling to take on such a popular president.*

▶ **take out 1** PHR-VERB If you **take out** something such as a loan or an insurance policy, a company agrees to let you have it. ❑ *I'll have to take out a loan.* **2** PHR-VERB If you **take** someone **out**, you take them somewhere enjoyable, and usually you pay for everything. ❑ *Jessica's grandparents took her out for the day.* ❑ *Sophia took me out to lunch.*

▶ **take over 1** PHR-VERB To **take over** something such as a company or country means to gain control of it. [BUSINESS] ❑ *I'm going to take over the company one day.* **2** PHR-VERB If you **take over** a job or if you **take over**, you start doing it after someone else has stopped doing it. ❑ *His widow took over the running of the business after he died.* ❑ *In 2001, I took over from him as mayor.* **3** → see also **takeover**

▶ **take to 1** PHR-VERB If you **take to** someone or something, you start to like them very quickly. ❑ *Did the children take to him?* **2** PHR-VERB If you **take to** doing something, you begin to do it as a regular habit. ❑ *They took to walking through the streets.*

▶ **take up 1** PHR-VERB If you **take up** an activity or a job, you start doing it. ❑ *He did not want to take up a competitive sport.* **2** PHR-VERB If you **take up** a question, problem, or cause, you act on it or discuss how you are going to act on it. ❑ *If you have a problem, take it up with the authorities.* ❑ *The issue will be taken up on Monday when the Russian president arrives.* **3** PHR-VERB If you **take up** an offer or a challenge, you accept it. ❑ *Since she offered to babysit, I took her up on it.* **4** PHR-VERB If something **takes up** a particular amount of time, space, or effort, it uses that amount. ❑ *I don't want to take up too much of your time.*

**tak|en** /ˈteɪkən/ **1** **Taken** is the past participle of **take**. **2** ADJ If you are **taken with** something or someone, you are very interested in them or attracted to them. [INFORMAL] ❑ *She was very taken with the idea.* [from Old English]

**take|off** /ˈteɪkɔf/ (**takeoffs**) also **take-off** N-VAR **Takeoff** is the beginning of a flight, when an aircraft leaves the ground. ❑ *What time is takeoff?*

**take|out** /ˈteɪkaʊt/ (**takeouts**) **1** N-UNCOUNT **Takeout** or **takeout** food is hot cooked food which you buy from a store or restaurant and eat somewhere else. ❑ *...a takeout pizza.* **2** N-COUNT A **takeout** is a store or restaurant that sells hot cooked food that you eat somewhere else. ❑ *...a Chinese takeout.*

**take|over** /ˈteɪkoʊvər/ (**takeovers**) **1** N-COUNT A **takeover** is the act of gaining control of a company by buying more of its shares than anyone else. [BUSINESS] ❑ *He lost his job after the takeover.* **2** N-COUNT A **takeover** is the act of taking control of a country, political party, or movement by force. ❑ *There was a military takeover.*

**tak|er** /ˈteɪkər/ (**takers**) N-COUNT If there are no **takers for** something such as an investment or a challenge, nobody is willing to accept it. ❑ *We approached over 100 buyers, but there were no takers.* [from Old English]

**tale** /ˈteɪl/ (**tales**) **1** N-COUNT A **tale** is a story, often involving magic or exciting events. ❑ *...stories, poems and folk tales.* **2** N-COUNT You

can refer to an interesting, exciting, or dramatic account of a real event as a **tale**. ❑ ...*tales of horror about Monday's earthquake.* [from Old English]
**8** → see also **fairy tale**

**tal|ent** /tǽlənt/ (**talents**) N-VAR **Talent** is the natural ability to do something well. ❑ *Both her children have a talent for music.* ❑ *He's got lots of talent.* [from Old English]

> **Thesaurus**    *talent*    Also look up :
>
> N.    ability, aptitude, gift

> **Word Partnership**    Use *talent* with :
>
> ADJ.    **great** talent, **musical** talent, **natural** talent
> V.    **have (a)** talent, **have got** talent
> N.    talent **pool**, talent **search**

**tal|ent|ed** /tǽləntɪd/ ADJ Someone who is **talented** has a natural ability to do something well. ❑ *Howard is a talented pianist.* [from Old English]

**tal|is|man** /tǽlɪsmən, -ɪz-/ (**talismans**) N-COUNT A **talisman** is an object which you believe has magic powers to protect you or bring you luck. [from French]

**talk** /tɔk/ (**talks, talking, talked**) **1** V-I When you **talk**, you use spoken language to express your thoughts, ideas, or feelings. ❑ *He was too upset to talk.* ❑ *They were talking about American food.* ❑ *I talked to him yesterday.* ● **Talk** is also a noun. ❑ *We had a long talk about her father.* **2** V-I If you **talk on** or **about** something, you make an informal speech about it. ❑ *She will talk on the issues she cares most about.* ● **Talk** is also a noun. ❑ *A guide gave a brief talk on the history of the site.* **3** N-PLURAL **Talks** are formal discussions intended to produce an agreement, usually between different countries or between employers and employees. ❑ ...*the next round of Middle East peace talks.* **4** V-RECIP If one group of people **talks to** another, or if two groups **talk**, they have formal discussions in order to do a deal or produce an agreement. ❑ *We're talking to some people about opening an office in Boston.* ❑ ...*the day when the two sides sit down and talk.* **5** V-I If someone **talks** when they are being held by police or soldiers, they reveal important or secret information, usually unwillingly. ❑ *They'll talk, and say I was involved.* **6** V-T If you **talk** something such as politics or sports, you discuss it. ❑ ...*middle-aged men talking business.* [from Old English] **7** to **talk shop** → see **shop**

▶ **talk down** PHR-VERB If someone **talks down** a particular thing, they reduce its value or importance by saying bad things about it. ❑ *Businessmen are tired of politicians talking the economy down.*

▶ **talk into** PHR-VERB If you **talk** a person **into** doing something, you persuade them to do it. ❑ *He talked me into marrying him.*

▶ **talk out of** PHR-VERB If you **talk** someone **out of** doing something, you persuade them not to do it. ❑ *My mother tried to talk me out of getting a divorce.*

▶ **talk over** PHR-VERB If you **talk** something **over**, you discuss it thoroughly and honestly. ❑ *He always talked things over with his friends.*

▶ **talk through** PHR-VERB If you **talk** something **through** with someone, you discuss it with them

thoroughly. ❑ *He and I have talked through the problem.*

▶ **talk up** PHR-VERB If someone **talks up** a particular thing, they increase its value or importance by saying exaggerated things about it. ❑ *He talked up the area as a great place to live.*

> **Thesaurus**    *talk*    Also look up :
>
> N.    argument, conversation, dialogue, discussion, interview, negotiation; (ant.) silence **1**
> V.    chat, discuss, gossip, say, share, speak, tell; (ant.) listen **1**

**talk ra|dio** N-UNCOUNT **Talk radio** is radio broadcasting which consists mainly of discussions with people who call the show rather than, for example, music or drama. ❑ ...*a talk radio station.*

> **Word Link**    *er ≈ more : bigger, louder, taller*

**tall** /tɔl/ (**taller, tallest**) **1** ADJ Someone or something that is **tall** has a greater height than is normal or average. ❑ *John was very tall.* **2** ADJ You use **tall** to ask or talk about the height of someone or something. ❑ *How tall is the building?* **3** PHRASE If something is **a tall order**, it is very difficult. ❑ *Paying for college may seem like a tall order.* [from Old English]

**tal|ly** /tǽli/ (**tallies, tallying, tallied**) **1** N-COUNT A **tally** is a record of amounts or numbers which you keep changing and adding to as the activity which affects it progresses. ❑ *They keep a tally of visitors to the museum.* **2** V-RECIP If two numbers or statements **tally**, they agree with each other or are exactly the same. ❑ *Their stories tally.* [from Medieval Latin]

**tame** /teɪm/ (**tames, taming, tamed, tamer, tamest**) **1** ADJ A **tame** animal or bird is not afraid of humans. ❑ *Deer never become tame; they will run away if you approach them.* **2** ADJ If you say that something or someone is **tame**, you are criticizing them for being weak and uninteresting. ❑ *Its programs are tame, even boring.* **3** V-T If someone **tames** a wild animal or bird, they train it not to be afraid of humans. ❑ *They were the first people to tame horses.* [from Old English]

**tam|per** /tǽmpər/ (**tampers, tampering, tampered**) V-I If someone **tampers with** something, they interfere with it or try to change it when they have no right to do so. ❑ *I don't want to be accused of tampering with the evidence.*

**tam|pon** /tǽmpɒn/ (**tampons**) N-COUNT A **tampon** is a tube made of cotton that a woman puts inside her vagina in order to absorb blood during menstruation. [from French]

**tan** /tæn/ (**tans, tanning, tanned**) **1** N-SING If you have a **tan**, your skin has become darker than usual because you have been in the sun. ❑ *She is tall and blonde, with a tan.* **2** V-T/V-I If a part of your body **tans** or if you **tan** it, your skin becomes darker than usual because you spend a lot of time in the sun. ❑ *I have very pale skin that never tans.* ● **tanned** ADJ ❑ *Her skin was tanned and glowing.* [from Old English]

**tan|dem** /tǽndəm/ (**tandems**) **1** N-COUNT A **tandem** is a bicycle designed for two riders. **2** PHRASE If one thing happens or is done **in**

t

**tandem with** another thing, the two things happen at the same time. ❑ *They are working in tandem with local police.* [from Latin]
→ see **bicycle**

**tan|gible** /tǽndʒɪbªl/ ADJ If something is **tangible**, it is clear enough to be easily seen, felt, or noticed. ❑ *There is tangible evidence that the economy is starting to recover.* [from Late Latin]

**tan|gle** /tǽngªl/ (**tangles, tangling, tangled**) ■ N-COUNT A **tangle of** something is a mass of it twisted together in a messy way. ❑ *...a tangle of wires.* ■ V-T/V-I If something **is tangled** or **tangles**, it becomes twisted together in a messy way. ❑ *Animals get tangled in fishing nets and drown.* ❑ *Her hair tends to tangle.* [of Scandinavian origin]

**tank** /tǽŋk/ (**tanks**) ■ N-COUNT A **tank** is a large container for holding liquid or gas. ❑ *...an empty fuel tank.* ❑ *Two water tanks have a total capacity of 400 liters.* ■ N-COUNT A **tank** is a large military vehicle that is equipped with weapons and moves along on metal tracks that are fitted over the wheels. [from Gujarati]
→ see **aquarium**

**tank|er** /tǽŋkər/ (**tankers**) N-COUNT A **tanker** is a large ship or truck used for transporting large quantities of gas or liquid, especially oil. ❑ *...a Greek oil tanker.* [from Gujarati]
→ see **oil, ship**

**tank top** (**tank tops**) N-COUNT A **tank top** is a soft cotton shirt with no sleeves, collar, or buttons.

**tan|ning bed** (**tanning beds**) N-COUNT A **tanning bed** is a piece of equipment with ultraviolet lights. You lie on it to make your skin tan.

**tan|ta|lize** /tǽntªlaɪz/ (**tantalizes, tantalizing, tantalized**) V-T If someone or something **tantalizes** you, they make you feel hopeful and excited about getting what you want, usually before disappointing you. ❑ *The memory tantalized her.* ● **tan|ta|liz|ing** ADJ ❑ *...a tantalizing smell of chicken.*

**tan|ta|mount** /tǽntəmaʊnt/ ADJ If you say that one thing is **tantamount to** another, more serious thing, you are emphasizing how bad or unfortunate the first thing is by comparing it to the second thing. [FORMAL] ❑ *Slowing down can seem tantamount to saying you're weak.*

**tan|trum** /tǽntrəm/ (**tantrums**) N-COUNT If someone, especially a child, has a **tantrum**, they suddenly lose their temper in a noisy and uncontrolled way. ❑ *He immediately threw a tantrum, screaming and stomping up and down.*

**tap** /tǽp/ (**taps, tapping, tapped**) ■ V-T/V-I If you **tap** something, you hit it with a quick, light blow or a series of quick, light blows. ❑ *He tapped the table nervously with his fingers.* ❑ *Grace tapped on the bedroom door and went in.* ● **Tap** is also a noun. ❑ *A tap on the door interrupted him.* ■ V-T If someone **taps** your telephone, they attach a special device to the line so that they can secretly listen to your conversations. ❑ *The government passed laws allowing the police to tap telephones.* ● **Tap** is also a noun. ❑ *...phone taps.* [Sense 1 from Old French. Senses 2 and 3 from Old English.]

**tap dance** (**tap dances**) N-VAR A **tap dance** is a dance in which the dancer wears special shoes with pieces of metal on the heels and toes. The shoes make loud sharp sounds when the dancer's feet move.
→ see **dance**

**tape** /teɪp/ (**tapes, taping, taped**) ■ N-UNCOUNT **Tape** is a sticky strip of plastic used for sticking things together. ❑ *...a roll of tape.* ■ N-UNCOUNT **Tape** is a narrow plastic strip covered with a magnetic substance. It is used to record sounds, pictures, and computer information. ❑ *Tape loses sound quality every time it is copied.* ■ V-T/V-I If you **tape** music, sounds, or television pictures, you record them using a tape recorder or a video recorder. ❑ *She has just taped an interview.* ❑ *He shouldn't be taping without the singer's permission.* ■ V-T If you **tape** one thing to another, you stick it on using tape. ❑ *I taped the envelope shut.* ■ N-COUNT A **tape** is a ribbon that is stretched across the finishing line of a race. ❑ *...the finishing tape.* [from Old English] ■ → see also **red tape, videotape**
→ see **office**

**tape meas|ure** (**tape measures**) N-COUNT A **tape measure** is a strip of metal, plastic, or cloth which has numbers marked on it and is used for measuring.

**ta|per** /teɪpər/ (**tapers, tapering, tapered**) V-T/V-I If something **tapers**, or if you **taper** it, it becomes gradually thinner at one end. ❑ *Unlike*

tape measure

*other trees, it doesn't taper very much.* ● **ta|pered** ADJ ❑ *...the tapered legs of the table.* [from Old English]

**tape re|cord|er** (**tape recorders**) also **tape-recorder** N-COUNT A **tape recorder** is a machine used for recording and playing music, speech, or other sounds.

**tap|es|try** /tǽpɪstri/ (**tapestries**) N-VAR A **tapestry** is a large piece of heavy cloth with a picture woven into it using colored threads. [from Old French]

**tape|worm** /teɪpwɜrm/ (**tapeworms**) N-COUNT A **tapeworm** is a long, flat parasite which lives in the stomach and intestines of animals or people.

**tap|root** /tǽprut/ (**taproots**) also **tap root**
N-COUNT Plants that have a **taproot** have one
main root that grows straight downward.
[TECHNICAL]

**tar** /tɑr/ N-UNCOUNT Tar is a thick, black, sticky
substance that is used especially for making
roads. ❑ *The oil has hardened to tar.* [from Old
English]

**tar|get** /tɑrgɪt/ (**targets, targeting** or
**targetting, targeted** or **targetted**) **1** N-COUNT A
**target** is something that someone is trying to
hit with a weapon or other object. ❑ *The village
lies beside a main road, making it an easy target.*
**2** N-COUNT A **target** is a result that you are trying
to achieve. ❑ *...her target of 20 goals this season.*
**3** V-T To **target** a particular person or thing
means to decide to attack or criticize them. ❑ *The
attacks targeted civilians.* ● **Target** is also a noun.
❑ *They have been the target of abuse.* **4** V-T If you
**target** a particular group of people, you try to
appeal to those people or affect them. ❑ *The union
is eager to target young people.* **5** PHRASE If someone
or something is **on target**, they are making good
progress and are likely to achieve the result that is
wanted. ❑ *We were still right on target for our deadline.*
[from Old French]

| Word Partnership | Use *target* with : |
| --- | --- |
| V. | **attack** a target **1** |
| | **hit** a target, **miss a** target **1 2** |
| ADJ. | **easy** target, **moving** target **1** |
| | **intended** target, **likely** target, **possible** |
| | target, **prime** target **1 3** |
| N. | target **practice 1** |
| | target **date 2** |
| | target **of criticism**, target **of an** |
| | **investigation 3** |

**tar|iff** /tǽrɪf/ (**tariffs**) N-COUNT A **tariff** is a
tax on goods coming into a country. [BUSINESS]
❑ *...tariffs on items such as electronics.* [from
Italian]

**tar|mac** /tɑrmæk/ N-SING The **tarmac** is the
area from which planes take off at an airport.

**tar|nish** /tɑrnɪʃ/ (**tarnishes, tarnishing,
tarnished**) **1** V-T If something **tarnishes** your
reputation, it causes people to have a worse
opinion of you than they would otherwise have
had. ❑ *The accusation could tarnish the reputation of
the senator.* ● **tar|nished** ADJ ❑ *He wants to improve
the tarnished image of his country.* **2** V-T/V-I If a
metal **tarnishes** or if something **tarnishes** it, it
becomes stained and loses its brightness. ❑ *It never
rusts or tarnishes.* [from Old French]

**tarp** /tɑrp/ (**tarps**) N-COUNT A **tarp** is a sheet
of heavy waterproof material that is used as a
protective cover.

**tart** /tɑrt/ (**tarts**) **1** N-VAR A **tart** is a shallow
pastry case with a filling of food, especially sweet
food. ❑ *...apple tarts.* **2** ADJ If something such as
fruit is **tart**, it has a sharp taste. ❑ *The blackberries
were too tart.* [Sense 1 from Old French. Sense 2
from Old English.]

**tar|tan** /tɑrtⁿn/ (**tartans**) N-VAR **Tartan** is a type
of cloth traditionally associated with Scotland,
that has different colored stripes crossing each
other at right angles. ❑ *...traditional tartan kilts.*
[from Old French]

**tar|tar sauce** /tɑrtər sɔs/ also **tartare sauce**
N-UNCOUNT **Tartar sauce** is a thick cold sauce
made from mayonnaise and chopped pickles,
usually eaten with fish. [from French]

**task** /tæsk/ (**tasks**) N-COUNT A **task** is an
activity or piece of work which you have to do,
usually as part of a larger project. ❑ *Walden had
the task of breaking the bad news to Mark.* [from Old
French]

| Thesaurus | *task* | Also look up : |
| --- | --- | --- |
| N. | assignment, job, responsibility | |

| Word Partnership | Use *task* with : |
| --- | --- |
| V. | **accomplish** a task, **assign** *someone* a |
| | task, **complete** a task, **face** a task, **give** |
| | *someone* a task, **perform** a task |
| ADJ. | **complex** task, **difficult** task, **easy** task, |
| | **enormous** task, **important** |
| | task, **impossible** task, **main** task, |
| | **simple** task |

**task|bar** /tæskbɑr/ (**taskbars**) also **task bar**
N-COUNT The **taskbar** on a computer screen is a
narrow strip, usually at the bottom of the screen,
that shows you which windows are open and that
allows you to control functions such as the Start
button. [COMPUTING]

**taste** /teɪst/ (**tastes, tasting, tasted**)
**1** N-UNCOUNT Your sense of **taste** is your ability
to recognize the flavor of things with your
tongue. ❑ *...an excellent sense of taste.* **2** N-COUNT
The **taste** of something is the individual quality
that it has when you put it in your mouth, for
example whether it is sweet or salty. ❑ *I like the
taste of chocolate.* **3** V-I If food or something **tastes of**
something, it has that particular flavor. ❑ *The
water tasted of metal.* ❑ *The pizza tastes delicious.*
**4** V-T If you **taste** some food or drink, you eat or
drink a small amount of it in order to see what the
flavor is like. ❑ *Don't add salt until you've tasted the
food.* ● **Taste** is also a noun. ❑ *Once you get a taste
of the pie, you want more.* **5** V-T If you can **taste**
something that you are eating or drinking, you
are aware of its flavor. ❑ *You can taste the green chili
in the dish.* **6** V-T If you **taste** something such as
a way of life or a pleasure, you experience it for a
short period of time. ❑ *Once you have tasted the life
in southern California, it's hard to return to Montana
in winter.* ● **Taste** is also a noun. ❑ *This trip was his
first taste of freedom.* **7** N-SING If you have a **taste
for** something, you enjoy it. ❑ *That gave me a taste
for reading.* **8** N-UNCOUNT A person's **taste** is
their choice in the things that they like or buy,
for example, their clothes, possessions, or music.
❑ *His taste in clothes is extremely good.* **9** PHRASE
If you say that something that is said or done is
**in bad taste** or **in poor taste**, you mean that it is
offensive. ❑ *He rejects the idea that his film is in bad
taste.* [from Old French]
→ see Word Web: **taste**
→ see **sugar**

**taste bud** (**taste buds**) also **tastebud** N-COUNT
Your **taste buds** are the little points on the surface
of your tongue which enable you to recognize the
flavor of a food or drink.
→ see **taste**

**t**

## Word Web    taste

What we think of as **taste** is mostly **odor**. The sense of **smell** controls about 80% of the experience. We taste only four **sensations: sweet, salty, sour,** and **bitter**. We experience sweetness and saltiness through **taste buds** near the tip of the **tongue**. We sense sourness at the sides and bitterness at the back of the tongue. Some people have more taste buds than others. Scientists have discovered some

"supertasters" with 425 taste buds per square centimeter. Most of us have about 184 and some "nontasters" have only about 96.

## Word Partnership    Use *taste* with :

| | |
|---|---|
| N. | **sense of** taste **1** |
| ADJ. | **bitter/salty/sour/sweet** taste **2** |
| | taste **bitter/salty/sour/sweet**, taste **good 3** |
| | **acquired** taste, **bad/good/poor** taste **8** |
| | **in bad/good/poor** taste **9** |
| V. | **like the** taste **of** *something* **2** |
| | **get a** taste **of** *something* **6** |
| ADV. | taste **like** *something* **3** |

**taste|ful** /teɪstfəl/ ADJ If you say that something is **tasteful**, you consider it to be attractive and elegant. ❏ *...a tasteful black dress.* ● **taste|ful|ly** ADV ❏ *...a large and tastefully-decorated home.* [from Old French]

**taste|less** /teɪstlɪs/ **1** ADJ If you describe something as **tasteless**, you consider it to be vulgar and unattractive. ❏ *...a house full of tasteless furniture.* **2** ADJ If you describe something such as a remark or joke as **tasteless**, you mean that it is offensive. ❏ *...the most tasteless remark I have ever heard in my life.* **3** ADJ If you describe food or drink as **tasteless**, you mean that it has very little or no flavor. ❏ *The fish was tasteless.* [from Old French]

**tasty** /teɪsti/ (**tastier, tastiest**) ADJ If you say that food is **tasty**, you mean that it has a pleasant, fairly strong flavor which makes it good to eat. ❏ *Try this tasty dish for supper.* [from Old French]

**tat|tered** /tætərd/ ADJ If something such as clothing is **tattered**, it is damaged or torn, especially because it has been used a lot over a long period of time. ❏ *He wore a gray T-shirt and tattered jeans.* [of Scandinavian origin]

**tat|ters** /tætərz/ **1** N-PLURAL Clothes that are **in tatters** are badly torn in several places. ❏ *His jeans were in tatters.* **2** N-PLURAL If you say that something such as a plan or relationship is **in tatters**, you are emphasizing that it is weak and has suffered a lot of damage. ❏ *The economy is in tatters.* [of Scandinavian origin]

**tat|too** /tætu/ (**tattoos, tattooing, tattooed**) **1** N-COUNT A **tattoo** is a design on a person's skin made using needles to make little holes and filling them with colored dye. ❏ *He has a tattoo of a heart on his arm.* **2** V-T If someone **tattoos** you, they give you a tattoo. ❏ *They painted and tattooed their bodies.* [from Tahitian]

**taught** /tɔt/ **Taught** is the past tense and past participle of **teach**. [from Old English]

**taunt** /tɔnt/ (**taunts, taunting, taunted**) V-T If someone **taunts** you, they say unkind or insulting things to you, especially about your weaknesses or failures. ❏ *A gang taunted a disabled man.* ● **Taunt** is also a noun. ❏ *For years they suffered racist taunts.* [from French]

**taut** /tɔt/ (**tauter, tautest**) ADJ Something that is **taut** is stretched very tight. ❏ *The clothes line is pulled taut.* [from Old English]

**tax** /tæks/ (**taxes, taxing, taxed**) **1** N-VAR **Tax** is an amount of money that you have to pay to the government so that it can pay for public services such as roads and schools. [BUSINESS] ❏ *No one enjoys paying tax.* ❏ *...a promise not to raise taxes.* **2** V-T When a person or company **is taxed**, they have to pay a part of their income or profits to the government. When goods **are taxed**, a percentage of their price has to be paid to the government. [BUSINESS] ❏ *Husband and wife are now taxed separately.* [from Old French] **3** → see also **income tax, taxing**
→ see **citizenship**

**tax|able** /tæksəbəl/ ADJ **Taxable** income is income on which you have to pay tax. [BUSINESS] ❏ *Taxpayers can reduce their taxable income by up to $2,500.* [from Old French]

**taxa|tion** /tækseɪʃən/ **1** N-UNCOUNT **Taxation** is the system by which a government takes money from people and spends it on things such as education, health, and defense. [BUSINESS] ❏ *...changes in taxation.* **2** N-UNCOUNT **Taxation** is the amount of money that people have to pay in taxes. [BUSINESS] ❏ *The result will be higher taxation.* [from Old French]

**tax break** (**tax breaks**) N-COUNT If the government gives a **tax break** to a particular group of people or type of organization, it reduces the amount of tax they have to pay or changes the tax system in a way that benefits them.

**tax-deferred** ADJ If you have savings in a **tax-deferred** account, you do not have to pay tax on them until a later time.

**tax-exempt** ADJ Income or property that is **tax-exempt** is income or property that you do not have to pay tax on. ❏ *About 15 percent of the town's property is tax-exempt.*

**tax-free** ADJ **Tax-free** is used to describe income on which you do not have to pay tax. [BUSINESS] ❑ *...a tax-free investment plan.*

**taxi** /tǽksi/ (**taxis, taxiing, taxied**) **1** N-COUNT A **taxi** is a car driven by a person whose job is

to take people where they want to go in return for money. ❑ *The taxi stopped in front of the club.* **2** V-T/V-I When an aircraft **taxis** along the ground or when a pilot **taxis** a plane

taxi

somewhere, it moves slowly along the ground. ❑ *The plane taxied into position for takeoff.*

**taxi|cab** /tǽksikæb/ (**taxicabs**) also **taxi-cab** N-COUNT A **taxicab** is the same as a **taxi**.

**tax in|cen|tive** (**tax incentives**) N-COUNT A **tax incentive** is a government measure that is intended to encourage individuals and businesses to spend money or to save money by reducing the amount of tax that they have to pay. ❑ *...a new tax incentive to encourage investment.*

**tax|ing** /tǽksɪŋ/ ADJ A **taxing** task or problem is one that requires a lot of mental or physical effort. ❑ *It's unlikely that you will have to do anything too taxing.* [from Old French]

**taxi stand** (**taxi stands**) N-COUNT A **taxi stand** is a place where taxis wait for passengers, for example at an airport.

**tax|ono|my** /tækspnəmi/ (**taxonomies**) N-VAR **Taxonomy** is the process of naming and classifying things such as animals and plants into groups within a larger system, according to their similarities and differences. [TECHNICAL] [from French]

**tax|payer** /tǽkspeɪər/ (**taxpayers**) N-COUNT **Taxpayers** are people who pay a percentage of their income to the government as tax. [BUSINESS] ❑ *This is not going to cost the taxpayer anything.*

**TB** /tiː biː/ N-UNCOUNT **TB** is an extremely serious infectious disease that affects your lungs and other parts of your body. **TB** is an abbreviation for **tuberculosis**.

**TBA** also **tba** **TBA** is sometimes written in announcements to indicate that something such as the place where something will happen or the people who will take part is not yet known and will be announced at a later date. **TBA** is an abbreviation for "to be announced."

**T-ball** N-UNCOUNT **T-ball** is a game for children, similar to baseball, in which the batter hits a ball that has been placed on top of a post.

**TCP/IP** N-UNCOUNT **TCP/IP** is a set of rules for putting data onto the Internet. **TCP/IP** is a written abbreviation for "Transmission Control Protocol/ Internet Protocol." [COMPUTING]

**tea** /tiː/ (**teas**) **1** N-VAR **Tea** is a drink made by pouring boiling water on the chopped dried leaves of a plant called the tea bush. ❑ *...a cup of tea.* ❑ *Would you like some tea?* **2** N-VAR **Tea** is the chopped dried leaves of the plant that tea is made from. ❑ *...a box of tea.* [from Chinese]
→ see Word Web: **tea**

**teach** /tiːtʃ/ (**teaches, teaching, taught**) **1** V-T If you **teach** someone something, you give them instructions so that they know about it or how to do it. ❑ *She taught me to read.* ❑ *George taught him how to ride a horse.* **2** V-T To **teach** someone something means to make them think, feel, or act in a new or different way. ❑ *We have to teach drivers to respect pedestrians.* **3** V-T/V-I If you **teach** or **teach** a subject, you help students to learn about a subject by explaining it or showing them how to do it. ❑ *Ingrid is currently teaching mathematics at the high school.* ❑ *She taught English to Japanese business people.* ❑ *She has taught for 34 years.* • **teach|er** (**teachers**) N-COUNT ❑ *I was a teacher for 21 years.* • **teach|ing** N-UNCOUNT ❑ *The quality of teaching in the school is excellent.* [from Old English] **4** to **teach** someone **a lesson** → see **lesson**
→ see also **learn**

| **Thesaurus** | teach | Also look up : |
|---|---|---|
| v. | educate, train **1** – **3** | |

| **Word Partnership** | Use *teach* with : |
|---|---|
| ADV. | teach *someone* how **1** |
| N. | teach *someone* a skill, teach students **1** |
| | teach children **1** – **3** |
| | teach classes, teach courses, teach English/history/reading/science, teach school **3** |
| | teach *someone* a lesson **4** |
| v. | try to teach **1** – **3** |

**teach|er's aide** (**teacher's aides**) N-COUNT A **teacher's aide** is a person who helps a teacher in a school classroom but who is not a qualified teacher.

**teach|ing** /tiːtʃɪŋ/ (**teachings**) N-COUNT The **teachings** of a particular person, school of thought, or religion are all the ideas and principles that they teach. ❑ *...the teachings of Jesus.* [from Old English]

**teach|ing as|sis|tant** (**teaching assistants**) N-COUNT A **teaching assistant** is a graduate student at a college or university who teaches some classes. ❑ *She is working as a teaching assistant.*

t

---

**Word Web** tea

Do you want to **brew** a good cup of **tea**? Don't use a **tea bag**. For the best taste, use fresh **tea leaves**. First, boil water in a **teakettle**. Use some of the water to warm the inside of a china **teapot**. Empty the pot, and add the tea leaves. Pour in more boiling water. Let the tea steep for at least five minutes. Serve the tea in thin china **cups**. Add milk and sugar if you wish.

**teak** /tik/ N-UNCOUNT Teak is a very hard wood. [from Portuguese]

**tea|kettle** /ˈtiːkɛtˀl/ (**teakettles**) also **tea kettle** N-COUNT A **teakettle** is a kettle that is used for boiling water to make tea.
→ see **tea**

**team** /tim/ (**teams, teaming, teamed**)
**1** N-COUNT A **team** is a group of people who play a particular sport or game together against other similar groups of people. □ …a soccer team. □ The team is close to the bottom of the league. **2** N-COUNT You can refer to any group of people who work together as a **team**. □ …a team of doctors. [from Old English]
▶ **team up** PHR-VERB If you **team up with** someone, you join them in order to work together for a particular purpose. □ A friend asked me to team up with him for a working holiday in Europe.

**team|mate** /ˈtimmeɪt/ (**teammates**) also **team-mate** N-COUNT In a game or sport, your **teammates** are the other members of your team. □ He was a great example to his teammates.

**team|work** /ˈtimwɜrk/ N-UNCOUNT **Teamwork** is the ability a group of people have to work well together. □ She knows the importance of teamwork.

**tea|pot** /ˈtipɒt/ (**teapots**) also **tea pot** N-COUNT A **teapot** is a container with a lid, a handle, and a spout, used for making and serving tea.
→ see **tea**

---
**tear**

**❶** CRYING
**❷** DAMAGING OR MOVING

---

**❶ tear** /tɪər/ (**tears**) **1** N-COUNT **Tears** are the drops of liquid that come out of your eyes when you are crying. □ Her eyes filled with tears. □ I wept tears of joy. **2** N-PLURAL You can use **tears** in expressions such as **in tears, burst into tears**, and **close to tears** to indicate that someone is crying or is almost crying. □ He was in tears. □ She burst into tears and ran from the kitchen. [from Old English]
→ see **cry**

**❷ tear** /tɛər/ (**tears, tearing, tore, torn**) **1** V-T If you **tear** paper, cloth, or another material, you pull it into two pieces or you pull it so that a hole appears in it. □ I tore my coat on a nail. ● **Tear** is also a noun. □ I looked through a tear in the curtains. **2** V-T To **tear** something from somewhere means to remove it violently. □ She tore the windshield wipers from his car. **3** V-I If you **tear** somewhere, you run, drive, or move there very quickly. □ Miranda tore into the room. [from Old English] **4** → see also **torn**
→ see **cut**

The verbs *tear* and *break* both mean "to damage something," but *tear* is used only for paper, cloth, or other thin, flexible materials that you can pull apart: *Philain fell down the stairs; she not only broke her arm, but she also tore a muscle in her leg. When the window broke, a piece of the glass tore Niran's shirt.*

▶ **tear apart** PHR-VERB If something **tears** people **apart**, it causes them to argue or to leave each other. □ The quarrel was tearing the family apart.
▶ **tear away** PHR-VERB If you **tear** someone **away from** a place or activity, you force them to leave the place or stop doing the activity, even though they want to remain there or continue. □ He finally tore himself away from the TV.
▶ **tear down** PHR-VERB If you **tear** something **down**, you destroy it or remove it completely. □ Angry protesters tore down the statue.
▶ **tear off** PHR-VERB If you **tear off** your clothes, you take them off in a rough and quick way. □ He tore his clothes off and fell into bed.
▶ **tear up** PHR-VERB If you **tear up** a piece of paper, you tear it into a lot of small pieces. □ Don't you dare tear up her ticket.

**tear|ful** /ˈtɪərfəl/ ADJ If someone is **tearful**, their face or voice shows signs that they have been crying or that they want to cry. □ She became very tearful. [from Old English]

**tear gas** /ˈtɪər gæs/ N-UNCOUNT **Tear gas** is a gas that causes your eyes to sting and makes it difficult to see. It is sometimes used by police to control crowds.

**tease** /tiz/ (**teases, teasing, teased**) V-T To **tease** someone means to laugh at them or make jokes about them in order to embarrass, annoy, or upset them. □ He teased me about my hair. [from Old English]

| V. | aggravate, bother, provoke |
|---|---|

**tea|spoon** /ˈtispun/ (**teaspoons**) N-COUNT A **teaspoon** is a small spoon used for eating, for putting sugar into tea or coffee, or in cooking. □ Drop the dough onto a baking sheet with a teaspoon.

**tech|ni|cal** /ˈtɛknɪkəl/ **1** ADJ **Technical** means involving the sorts of machines, processes, and materials that are used in industry, transportation, and communications. □ A number of technical problems will have to be solved. ● **tech|ni|cal|ly** /ˈtɛknɪkli/ ADV □ …technically-advanced medical products. **2** ADJ You use **technical** to describe the practical skills and methods used to do an activity such as an art, a craft, or a sport. □ Their technical ability is exceptional. ● **tech|ni|cal|ly** ADV □ …a technically brilliant movie. **3** ADJ **Technical** language involves using special words to describe the details of a specialized activity. □ The technical term for sunburn is "erythema." [from French]

| N. | technical **knowledge** **1** technical **assistance**, technical **difficulties**, technical **expertise**, technical **experts**, technical **information**, technical **issues**, technical **problems**, technical **services**, technical **skills**, technical **support**, technical **training** **2** |
|---|---|
| ADV. | **highly** technical **1** – **3** |

**tech|ni|cal|ity** /ˌtɛknɪˈkælɪti/ (**technicalities**) **1** N-PLURAL The **technicalities** of a process or activity are the detailed methods used to do it or to carry it out. □ …the technicalities of classroom teaching. **2** N-COUNT A **technicality** is a point based on a strict interpretation of the law or of a set of rules. □ They won the case on a legal technicality. [from French]

**tech|ni|cal|ly** /ˈtɛknɪkli/ **1** ADV If something is **technically** true or possible, it is true or possible

## Word Web technology

Innovative **technologies** affect everything in our lives. In new homes, **state-of-the-art** computer systems control heating, lighting, communication, and entertainment systems. **Gadgets** such as **digital** music players are small and easy to carry. But high technology has a serious side, too. **Biotechnology** may help us cure diseases. It also raises many ethical questions. **Cutting-edge** biometric technology is replacing old-fashioned security systems. Soon your ATM will check your identity by scanning the iris of your eye and your laptop will scan your fingerprint.

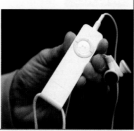

according to a strict interpretation of facts, laws, or rules, but may not be important or relevant in a particular situation. ❏ *More than a third of workers said they called into the office while technically on vacation.* [from French] **2** → see also **technical**

**tech|ni|cian** /tɛknɪʃ⁰n/ (**technicians**) N-COUNT A **technician** is someone whose job involves skilled practical work with scientific or medical equipment, for example, in a laboratory. ❏ *...a laboratory technician.* [from French]

**tech|nique** /tɛknik/ (**techniques**) **1** N-COUNT A **technique** is a particular method of doing an activity, usually a method that involves practical skills. ❏ *...the techniques of modern agriculture.* **2** N-UNCOUNT **Technique** is skill and ability in an artistic, sporting, or other practical activity that you develop through training and practice. ❏ *He went to the Amsterdam Academy to improve his technique.* [from French]

**tech|nol|ogy** /tɛknɒlədʒi/ (**technologies**) N-VAR **Technology** refers to methods, systems, and devices which are the result of scientific knowledge being used for practical purposes. ❏ *Technology is changing fast.* ● **tech|no|logi|cal** /tɛknəlɒdʒɪk⁰l/ ❏ *...a time of rapid technological change.* ● **tech|no|logi|cal|ly** /tɛknəlɒdʒɪkli/ ADV ❏ *...technologically-advanced aircraft.* [from Greek]
→ see Word Web: **technology**

### Word Partnership Use *technology* with :

ADJ. **advanced** technology, **available** technology, **high** technology, **latest** technology, **medical** technology, **modern** technology, **sophisticated** technology, **wireless** technology

N. **computer** technology, **information** technology

**tec|ton|ic plate** /tɛktɒnɪk pleɪt/ (**tectonic plates**) N-COUNT **Tectonic plates** are very large pieces of the Earth's surface or crust. [TECHNICAL]

**ted|dy** /tɛdi/ (**teddies**) N-COUNT A **teddy** or a **teddy bear** is a soft toy that looks like a bear.

**te|di|ous** /tidiəs/ ADJ If you describe something such as a job, task, or situation as **tedious**, you mean it is boring and frustrating. ❏ *The list is long and tedious to read.* ● **te|di|ous|ly** ADV ❏ *Her life was tediously routine.* [from Latin]

**tee** /ti/ (**tees, teeing, teed**) **1** N-COUNT In golf, a **tee** is a small piece of wood or plastic which is used to support the ball before it is hit at the start

of each hole. **2** N-COUNT On a golf course, a **tee** is one of the small flat areas of ground from which people hit the ball at the start of each hole.
▶ **tee off** **1** PHR-VERB If someone or something **tees** you **off**, they make you angry or annoyed. [INFORMAL] ❏ *Something the boy said to him teed him off.* ❏ *That really teed off the old man.* **2** PHR-VERB In golf, when you **tee off**, you hit the ball from a tee at the start of a hole. ❏ *In a few hours most of the world's top golfers tee off in the U.S. Masters.*

**teem** /tim/ (**teems, teeming, teemed**) V-I If you say that a place **is teeming with** people or animals, you mean that there are a lot of people or animals moving around in it. ❏ *The area is teeming with tourists.* [from Old English]

**teen** /tin/ (**teens**) **1** N-PLURAL If you are in your **teens**, you are between thirteen and nineteen years old. ❏ *I met John when I was in my teens.* ● A **teen** is a person in his or her teens. **2** ADJ **Teen** is used to describe things such as movies, magazines, bands, or activities that are aimed at or are done by people who are in their teens. ❏ *...a new teen center.* [from Old English]

**teen|age** /tineɪdʒ/ **1** ADJ **Teenage** children are aged between thirteen and nineteen years old. ❏ *She looked like any other teenage girl.* **2** ADJ **Teenage** is used to describe things such as movies, magazines, or activities that are aimed at or are done by teenage children. ❏ *...a teenage magazine.* [from Old English]

### Word Link teen ≈ plus ten, from 13-19 : *eighteen, seventeen, teenager*

**teen|ager** /tineɪdʒər/ (**teenagers**) N-COUNT A **teenager** is someone who is between thirteen and nineteen years old. [from Old English]
→ see **age, child**

**tee|ter** /titər/ (**teeters, teetering, teetered**) **1** V-I **Teeter** is used in expressions such as **teeter on the brink** to emphasize that something seems to be in a very unstable situation or position. ❏ *She was teetering on the brink of danger.* **2** V-I If someone or something **teeters**, they shake in an unsteady way, and seem to be about to lose their balance and fall over. ❏ *Hyde felt himself teeter forward.* [from Middle English]

**teeth** /tiθ/ **Teeth** is the plural of **tooth**. [from Old English]
→ see Word Web: **teeth**
→ see **face**

**tee|to|tal|er** /titout⁰lər/ (**teetotalers**) N-COUNT A **teetotaler** is someone who does not drink alcohol.

t

### Word Web    teeth

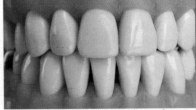

**Dentists** say **brushing** and flossing every day helps prevent **cavities**. Brushing removes food from the surface of the **teeth**. Flossing removes **plaque** from between teeth and **gums**. In many places, the water supply contains fluoride which also helps keep teeth healthy. If **tooth decay** does develop, a dentist can use a metal or plastic **filling** to repair the tooth. A badly damaged or broken tooth may require a **crown**. Orthodontists use **braces** to straighten uneven rows of teeth. Occasionally, a dentist must remove all of a patient's teeth. Then **dentures** take the place of natural teeth.

**TEFL** /tɛfᵊl/ N-UNCOUNT **TEFL** is the teaching of English to people whose first language is not English, especially people from a country where English is not spoken. **TEFL** is an abbreviation for "teaching English as a foreign language."

**Te|ja|no** /tɛhɑnoʊ/ (**Tejanos**) N-COUNT A **Tejano** is a person from Mexico, or a person whose family is from Mexico, who lives in Texas. ● **Tejano** is also an adjective. □ ...the growing popularity of Tejano music. [from American Spanish]

**tele|cast** /tɛlɪkæst/ (**telecasts**) N-COUNT A **telecast** is a program that is broadcast on television, especially a program that is broadcast live.

**tele|com|mu|ni|ca|tions**
/tɛlɪkəmyunɪkeɪʃᵊnz/ N-UNCOUNT
**Telecommunications** is the technology of sending signals and messages over long distances using electronic equipment, for example, by radio and telephone. □ ...the telecommunications industry.

> **Word Link**    gram ≈ writing : diagram, program, telegram

**tele|gram** /tɛlɪgræm/ (**telegrams**) N-COUNT A **telegram** is a message that is sent by telegraph and then printed and delivered to someone. □ The president received the news by telegram.

**tele|mar|ket|ing** /tɛlɪmɑrkɪtɪŋ/ N-UNCOUNT **Telemarketing** is the selling of products or services by telephone. [BUSINESS]

**te|lepa|thy** /tɪlɛpəθi/ N-UNCOUNT **Telepathy** is the direct communication of thoughts and feelings between people's minds, without the need to use speech or writing. ● **tele|path|ic** /tɛlɪpæθɪk/ ADJ □ They had a telepathic understanding. [from Greek]

> **Word Link**    phon ≈ sound : microphone, symphony, telephone

> **Word Link**    tele ≈ distance : telephone, telescope, television

**tele|phone** /tɛlɪfoʊn/ (**telephones, telephoning, telephoned**) **1** N-UNCOUNT The **telephone** is an electrical system of communication used to talk directly to someone else in a different place, by dialing a number on a piece of equipment and speaking into it. □ It's easier to reach her by telephone than by e-mail. □ I hate to think what our telephone bill is going to be. **2** N-COUNT A **telephone** is the piece of equipment that you use when you talk to someone by telephone. □ He got up and answered the telephone. **3** V-T/V-I If you **telephone** someone, you dial their telephone number and speak to them by telephone. □ I had to telephone Owen to say I was sorry. □ They usually telephone first to see if she's home. **4** PHRASE If you are **on the telephone**, you are speaking to someone by telephone. □ Linda was on the telephone for three hours.

**tele|phone pole** (**telephone poles**) N-COUNT A **telephone pole** is a tall wooden pole with telephone wires attached to it, connecting several different buildings to the telephone system.

> **Word Link**    scope ≈ looking : horoscope, microscope, telescope

**tele|scope** /tɛlɪskoʊp/ (**telescopes**) N-COUNT A **telescope** is an instrument shaped like a tube. It has lenses inside it that make distant things seem larger and nearer when you look through it. [from Italian]
→ see Word Web: **telescope**

**tele|vise** /tɛlɪvaɪz/ (**televises, televising, televised**) V-T If an event or program **is televised**, it is filmed and shown on television. □ The game will be televised on TV.

> **Word Link**    vid, vis ≈ seeing : television, videotape, visible

**tele|vi|sion** /tɛlɪvɪʒᵊn, -vɪʒ-/ (**televisions**) **1** N-COUNT A **television** or television set is a piece of electrical equipment consisting of a box with a glass screen on it on which you can watch programs with pictures and sounds. □ She turned the television on. **2** N-UNCOUNT **Television** is the system of sending pictures and sounds over electrical signals over a distance so that people can receive them on a television in their home. □ People will do anything to be on television.
→ see Word Web: **television**

**tell** /tɛl/ (**tells, telling, told**) **1** V-T If you **tell** someone something, you give them information. □ I told Phyllis I got the job. □ I called Andie to tell her how angry I was. □ Claire made me promise to tell her the truth. □ He told his story to The New York Times. **2** V-T If you **tell** someone to do something, you order or advise them to do it. □ Officers told him to get out of his car. **3** V-T If you can **tell** what is happening or what is true, you are able to judge correctly what is happening or what is true. □ You can never tell what life is going to bring you. □ I could tell that he was angry. **4** V-T If facts or events **tell** you something, they

Once, there were only two types of **telescopes**. Refracting telescopes had lenses. **Reflecting** telescopes had a concave **mirror**. The lenses and the mirror had the same purpose. They **focused light rays** and made a clear **image**. Today scientists use **radio telescopes** to study the **universe**. These telescopes can detect **X-rays**, gamma **rays**, and other types of invisible light **waves**. But sometimes a person makes important discoveries without fancy tools. Robert Evans is an amateur **astronomer** in Australia.

He has discovered more supernovas than anyone else in the world. And he uses a very simple 16-inch reflecting telescope set up in his backyard.

reveal certain information to you through ways other than speech. ❑ *The facts tell us that this is not true.* ❑ *The photographs tell a different story.* **5** V-I If an unpleasant or tiring experience begins to **tell**, it begins to have a serious effect. ❑ *The hot weather was beginning to tell on all of us.* [from Old English] **6** → see also **telling**

▶ **tell apart** PHR-VERB If you can **tell** people or things **apart**, you are able to recognize the differences between them and can therefore identify each of them. ❑ *It's easy to tell the sisters apart.*

▶ **tell off** PHR-VERB If you **tell** someone **off**, you speak to them angrily or seriously because they have done something wrong. ❑ *He never listened to us when we told him off.* ❑ *I'm always being told off for being so clumsy.*

**tell|er** /tɛlər/ (**tellers**) N-COUNT A **teller** is someone who works in a bank and who customers pay money to or get money from. ❑ *Every bank pays close attention to the speed and accuracy of its tellers.* [from Old English]

**tell|ing** /tɛlɪŋ/ ADJ If something is **telling**, it shows the true nature of a person or situation. ❑ *August will be a very telling month.* ● **tell|ing|ly** ADV ❑ *Tellingly, they do not all agree with the decision.* [from Old English]

**telo|phase** /tɛləfeɪz/ (**telophases**) N-VAR **Telophase** is the final stage of cell division, when two completely separate cells are formed.

**tem|per** /tɛmpər/ (**tempers**) **1** N-VAR If you say that someone has a **temper**, you mean that they become angry very easily. ❑ *He had a temper and*

could be nasty. **2** N-VAR If you are **in** a particular type of **temper**, that is the way you are feeling. ❑ *I was in a bad temper last night.* **3** PHRASE If you **lose** your **temper**, you become so angry that you shout or lose control of your behavior. ❑ *I've never seen him lose his temper.* [from Old English]

**tem|pera|ment** /tɛmprəmənt/ (**temperaments**) N-VAR Your **temperament** is your basic nature, especially as it is shown in the way that you react to situations or to other people. ❑ *His family doesn't understand the artistic temperament.* [from Latin]

**tem|pera|men|tal** /tɛmprəmɛntᵊl/ **1** ADJ If you say that someone is **temperamental**, you are criticizing them for having moods that change often and suddenly. ❑ *He is very temperamental.* **2** ADJ If you describe something such as a machine or car as **temperamental**, you mean that it often does not work well. ❑ *The boys couldn't start the temperamental motor.* [from Latin]

**tem|per|ate** /tɛmpərɪt, -prɪt/ ADJ A **temperate** climate or a place is never extremely hot nor extremely cold. ❑ *The Nile Valley keeps a temperate climate throughout the year.* [from Latin]

For many years, all **televisions** used cathode **ray tubes**. These tubes made the picture. They shot a stream of **electrons** at a **screen**. When the electrons hit the screen, they made a tiny lighted area. This area is

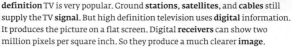

called a pixel. The average cathode ray TV screen has about 200,000 pixels. Today, **high definition** TV is very popular. Ground **stations**, **satellites**, and **cables** still supply the TV **signal**. But high definition television uses **digital** information. It produces the picture on a flat screen. Digital **receivers** can show two million pixels per square inch. So they produce a much clearer **image**.

**tem|per|ate zone** (**temperate zones**) N-COUNT
The Earth's **temperate zones** are the areas where
the climate is never extremely hot nor extremely
cold. The northern temperate zone extends from
the Arctic Circle to the Tropic of Cancer, and the
southern temperate zone extends from the Tropic
of Capricorn to the Antarctic Circle.

**tem|pera|ture** /tɛmprətʃər, -tʃʊər/
(**temperatures**) **1** N-VAR The **temperature**
of something is how hot or cold it is. □ *The
temperature dropped below freezing.* **2** N-UNCOUNT
Your **temperature** is the temperature of your
body, that shows whether you are healthy.
□ *His temperature continued to rise.* **3** PHRASE If
you **are running a temperature** or if you **have a
temperature**, your temperature is higher than
it should be. **4** PHRASE If someone **takes** your
**temperature**, they use an instrument called a
thermometer to measure the temperature of
your body. □ *The doctor will probably take your child's
temperature.* [from Latin]
→ see **calorie, climate, cooking, forecast,
greenhouse effect, habitat, thermometer,
wind**

| **Word Partnership** | Use *temperature* with : |
|---|---|
| ADJ. | **average** temperature, **high/low** temperature, **normal** temperature **1** |
| V. | **reach a** temperature **1** |
| N. | **changes in/of** temperature, temperature **increase, ocean** temperature, **rise in** temperature, **room** temperature, **surface** temperature, **water** temperature **1** <br> **body** temperature **2** |

**tem|plate** /tɛmplɪt/ (**templates**) **1** N-COUNT A
**template** is a thin piece of metal or plastic which
is cut into a particular shape. It is used to help
you cut wood, paper, metal, or other materials
accurately, or to reproduce the same shape many
times. **2** N-COUNT In computing, a **template**
is a model of a document that you can use as a
guide when creating a document of your own.
[COMPUTING] [from French]

**tem|ple** /tɛmpᵊl/ (**temples**) **1** N-VAR A **temple**
is a building used for the worship of a god or gods,
especially in the Buddhist, Jewish, Mormon, and
Hindu religions. □ *...a small Hindu temple.* □ *We go
to temple on Saturdays.* **2** N-COUNT Your **temples**
are the flat parts on each side of the front part of
your head, near your forehead. □ *The hair at his
temples was gray.* [Sense 1 from Old English. Sense 2
from Old French.]

**tem|po** /tɛmpoʊ/ (**tempos**)

Tempi can also be used as the plural form.

**1** N-SING The **tempo** of an event is the speed at
which it happens. □ *...the slow tempo of change in
a rural country.* **2** N-VAR The **tempo** of a piece of
music is the speed at which it is played. [from
Italian]

| **Word Link** | *tempo* ≈ *time* : *contemporary,* *temporal, temporary* |
|---|---|

**tem|po|rary** /tɛmpəreri/ ADJ Something that
is **temporary** lasts for only a limited time. □ *His job
here is only temporary.* □ *...a temporary loss of memory.*
● **tem|po|rari|ly** /tɛmpərɛərɪli/ ADV □ *The peace*

agreement has temporarily halted the civil war. [from
Latin]

**tempt** /tɛmpt/ (**tempts, tempting, tempted**)
V-T Something that **tempts** you attracts you
and makes you want it, even though it may
be wrong or harmful. □ *Cars like that may tempt
drivers into driving too fast.* □ *Don't let credit tempt
you to buy something you can't afford.* ● **tempt|ing**
ADJ □ *...Raoul's tempting offer of a trip to Palm Beach.*
[from Old French]

| **Word Link** | *tempt* ≈ *trying* : *attempt,* *temptation, tempted* |
|---|---|

**temp|ta|tion** /tɛmpteɪʃᵊn/ (**temptations**)
N-VAR **Temptation** is the feeling that you want to
do something or have something, even though
you know you really should avoid it. □ *Will they be
able to resist the temptation to buy?* [from Old
French]

**tempt|ed** /tɛmptɪd/ ADJ If you are **tempted to**
do something, you would like to do it. □ *I'm very
tempted to sell my car.* [from Old French]

**ten** /tɛn/ (**tens**) NUM **Ten** is the number 10.
□ *Over the past ten years things have changed.* [from
Old English]

**te|na|cious** /tɪneɪʃəs/ ADJ A **tenacious** person
is very determined and does not give up easily.
□ *He's a very tenacious guy.* ● **te|na|cious|ly** ADV
□ *The Dodgers clung tenaciously to their lead.* [from
Latin]

**te|nac|ity** /tɪnæsɪti/ N-UNCOUNT If you have
**tenacity**, you are very determined and do not give
up easily. □ *Hard work and tenacity are crucial to career
success.* [from Latin]

**ten|an|cy** /tɛnənsi/ (**tenancies**) N-VAR Tenancy
is the use that you have of land or property
belonging to someone else, for which you pay
rent. □ *His father took over the tenancy of the farm 40
years ago.* [from Old French]

**ten|ant** /tɛnənt/ (**tenants**) N-COUNT A **tenant**
is someone who pays rent for the place they live
in, or for land or buildings that they use. □ *...the
obligations of a landlord to the tenant.* [from Old
French]

**tend** /tɛnd/ (**tends, tending, tended**) **1** V-T
If something **tends** to happen, it usually
happens or it often happens. □ *Smaller cars
tend to be noisy.* **2** V-I If you **tend toward** a
particular characteristic, you often display that
characteristic. □ *Artistic people often tend toward
liberal views.* [from Old French]

| **Word Partnership** | Use *tend* with : |
|---|---|
| V. | tend **to agree**, tend **to avoid**, tend **to become**, tend **to blame**, tend **to develop**, tend **to feel**, tend **to forget**, tend **to happen**, tend **to lose**, tend **to stay**, tend **to think 1** |
| N. | **Americans** tend, **children/men/women** tend, **people** tend **1** **2** |

**ten|den|cy** /tɛndənsi/ (**tendencies**) N-COUNT
A **tendency** is a worrying or unpleasant habit or
action that keeps occurring. □ *...the government's
tendency to secrecy in recent years.* [from Medieval
Latin]

---

**tender**

❶ ADJECTIVE USES
❷ NOUN AND VERB USES

❶ **ten|der** /tɛndər/ (**tenderer, tenderest**)
**1** ADJ Someone or something that is **tender** expresses gentle and caring feelings. ❑ *Her voice was tender.* • **ten|der|ly** ADV ❑ *Mr. Williams tenderly embraced his wife.* • **ten|der|ness** N-UNCOUNT ❑ *She smiled, politely rather than with tenderness.* **2** ADJ If someone does something at a **tender** age, they do it when they are still young and have not had much experience. ❑ *He began playing the game at the tender age of seven.* **3** ADJ Meat or other food that is **tender** is easy to cut or chew. ❑ *Cook for a minimum of 2 hours, until the meat is tender.* **4** ADJ If part of your body is **tender**, it is sensitive and painful when it is touched. ❑ *My tummy felt very tender.* [from Old French]
→ see **cooking**

❷ **ten|der** /tɛndər/ (**tenders, tendering, tendered**) V-I If a company **tenders for** something, it makes a formal offer to supply goods or do a job for a particular price. [BUSINESS] ❑ *The company tendered for contracts in Spain and Germany.* • **Tender** is also a noun. [BUSINESS] ❑ *Builders will be asked to submit a tender for the work.* [from Anglo-French]

**ten|don** /tɛndən/ (**tendons**) N-COUNT A **tendon** is a strong cord of tissue in your body joining a muscle to a bone. ❑ *...a torn tendon in his right shoulder.* [from Medieval Latin]

**ten|ement** /tɛnəmənt/ (**tenements**)
**1** N-COUNT A **tenement** is an old building in poor condition which is divided into individual apartments. ❑ *...streets of low-cost tenements.* **2** N-COUNT A **tenement** is one of the apartments in a tenement. ❑ *He struggled to pay the rent on his tenement.* [from Medieval Latin]

**ten|et** /tɛnɪt/ (**tenets**) N-COUNT The **tenets** of a theory or belief are the main principles on which it is based. [FORMAL] ❑ *Non-violence and patience are*

*the central tenets of their faith.* [from Latin]

**ten|nis** /tɛnɪs/ N-UNCOUNT **Tennis** is a game played by two or four players on a rectangular court with a net across the middle. The players use rackets to hit a ball over the net. [from Old French]
→ see Picture Dictionary: **tennis**
→ see **park**

**ten|or** /tɛnər/ (**tenors**) **1** N-COUNT A **tenor** is a male singer whose voice is fairly high. ❑ *...the Italian tenor, Luciano Pavarotti.* **2** ADJ A **tenor** saxophone or other musical instrument has a range of notes that are of a fairly low pitch. ❑ *...one of the best tenor sax players.* [from Old French]

**tense** /tɛns/ (**tenser, tensest, tenses, tensing, tensed**) **1** ADJ If you are **tense**, you are anxious and nervous and cannot relax. ❑ *Mark was very tense at first.* **2** ADJ If your body is **tense**, your muscles are tight and not relaxed. ❑ *A bath can relax tense muscles.* **3** V-T/V-I If your muscles **tense**, they become tight and stiff, often because you are anxious or frightened. ❑ *Newman's stomach muscles tensed.* • **Tense up** means the same as **tense**. ❑ *When we are under stress our bodies tend to tense up.* **4** N-COUNT The **tense** of a verb is its form, which shows whether you are referring to past, present, or future time. ❑ *They were already speaking of her in the past tense.* [Senses 1 to 3 from Latin. Sense 4 from Old French.]

| **Word Partnership** | Use *tense* with : |
|---|---|
| N. | tense **atmosphere**, tense **moment**, tense **mood**, tense **muscles**, tense **situation** **1** |
| V. | **feel** tense **1** **2** |
| ADV. | **very** tense **1** **2** |
| ADJ. | **future/past/perfect/present** tense **4** |

**ten|sion** /tɛnʃən/ **1** N-UNCOUNT **Tension** is a feeling of worry and anxiety which makes it difficult for you to relax. ❑ *Laughing can relieve tension.* **2** N-UNCOUNT **Tension** is a feeling of

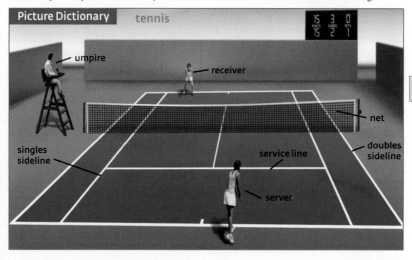

**Picture Dictionary**    tennis

umpire

receiver

net

singles sideline

service line

doubles sideline

server

t

anxiety produced by a difficult or dangerous situation, especially one in which there is a possibility of conflict or violence. ❑ *The tension between the two countries is likely to remain.*
❸ N-UNCOUNT The **tension** in a rope or wire is the extent to which it is stretched tight. ❑ *It is possible to change the tension of the cable.* [from Latin]
→ see **anger**

| Word Partnership | Use *tension* with : |
|---|---|
| v. | **ease** tension, tension **grows**, **relieve** tension ❶ ❷ |
| N. | **source of** tension ❶ ❷ |
| ADJ. | **racial** tension ❷ |

tent

**tent** /tɛnt/ (**tents**)
N-COUNT A **tent** is a shelter made of canvas or nylon which is held up by poles and ropes, and is used mainly by people who are camping. [from Old French]

**ten|ta|cle** /tɛntəkʰl/ (**tentacles**) N-COUNT The **tentacles** of an animal such as an octopus are the long thin parts that are used for feeling and holding things, for getting food, and for moving. [from New Latin]

**ten|ta|tive** /tɛntətɪv/ ❶ ADJ **Tentative** agreements or plans are not definite or certain, but have been made as a first step. ❑ *...a tentative agreement to hold a conference.* ❷ ADJ If someone is **tentative**, they are cautious and not very confident because they are uncertain or afraid. ❑ *My first attempts at complaining were tentative.* ● **ten|ta|tive|ly** ADV ❑ *I tentatively suggested an alternative route.* [from Medieval Latin]

**tenth** /tɛnθ/ ORD The **tenth** item in a series is the one that you count as number ten. ❑ *...her tenth birthday.* [from Old English]

**tenu|ous** /tɛnyuəs/ ADJ If you describe something such as a connection, a reason, or someone's position as **tenuous**, you mean that it is very uncertain or weak. ❑ *The president is in a somewhat tenuous position.* [from Latin]

**ten|ure** /tɛnyər/ ❶ N-UNCOUNT **Tenure** is the legal right to live in a particular building or to use a particular piece of land during a fixed period of time. ❑ *...new laws affecting land tenure.* ❷ N-UNCOUNT **Tenure** is the period of time during which someone holds an important job. ❑ *...his tenure as chief executive officer.* [from Old French]

**tep|id** /tɛpɪd/ ADJ Water or another liquid that is **tepid** is slightly warm. [from Latin]

**term** /tɜrm/ (**terms, terming, termed**)
❶ PHRASE If you talk about something **in terms of** something or **in particular terms**, you are specifying which aspect of it you are considering. ❑ *Our goods compete in terms of quality and price.*
❷ N-COUNT A **term** is a word or expression with a specific meaning. ❑ *"Myocardial infarction" is the medical term for a heart attack.* ❸ V-T If you say that something **is termed** a particular thing, you mean that that is what people call it or consider it to be. ❑ *He was termed a temporary employee.* ❹ N-VAR A **term** is one of the periods of time that a school, college, or university divides the year into. ❑ *...the*

*summer term.* ❺ N-COUNT A **term** is a period of time that someone spends doing a particular job or in a particular place. ❑ *Nixon never completed his term of office.* ❑ *...a 12-month term of service.* ❻ N-PLURAL The **terms** of an agreement or arrangement are the conditions that must be accepted by the people involved in it. ❑ *...the terms of the Helsinki agreement.* ❼ PHRASE If you **come to terms with** something difficult or unpleasant, you learn to accept and deal with it. ❑ *She has come to terms with her husband's death.* ❽ PHRASE If two people or groups compete **on equal terms** or **on the same terms**, neither of them has an advantage over the other. ❑ *I want to compete with men on equal terms.*
❾ PHRASE If two people are **on good terms** or **on friendly terms**, they are friendly with each other. ❑ *Madeleine is on good terms with Sarah.* ❿ PHRASE You use the expressions **in the long term, in the short term**, and **in the medium term** to talk about what will happen over a long period of time, over a short period of time, and over a medium period of time. ❑ *In the long term we hope to open an office in Moscow.* ⓫ PHRASE If you say that you **are thinking in terms of** doing a particular thing, you mean that you are considering it. ❑ *You should be thinking in terms of graduating next year.* [from Old French] ⓬ **in no uncertain terms** → see **uncertain** ⓭ **in real terms** → see **real**

| Word Link | term, termin ≈ limit, end : de**term**ine, **termin**al, **termin**ate |
|---|---|

**ter|mi|nal** /tɜrmɪnʰl/ (**terminals**) ❶ ADJ A **terminal** illness or disease causes death and cannot be cured. ❑ *...terminal cancer.* ● **ter|mi|nal|ly** ADV ❑ *The patient is terminally ill.* ❷ N-COUNT A **terminal** is a place where vehicles, passengers, or goods begin or end a journey. ❑ *...a new terminal at Dulles airport.* ❸ N-COUNT A computer **terminal** is a piece of equipment consisting of a keyboard and a screen connected to a computer. [COMPUTING] ❑ *Carl sits at a computer terminal 40 hours a week.* [from Latin]

**ter|mi|nal ve|loc|ity** (**terminal velocities**) N-VAR The **terminal velocity** of a falling object is the maximum speed it reaches. [TECHNICAL]

**ter|mi|nate** /tɜrmɪneɪt/ (**terminates, terminating, terminated**) ❶ V-T/V-I When you **terminate** something or when it **terminates**, it ends completely. [FORMAL] ❑ *She suddenly terminated the conversation.* ❑ *His contract terminates at the season's end.* ● **ter|mi|na|tion** /tɜrmɪneɪʃʰn/ N-UNCOUNT ❑ *...the sudden termination of electricity.* ❷ V-I When a train or bus **terminates** somewhere, it ends its journey there. [FORMAL] ❑ *This train will terminate at Lamy.* [from Latin]

**ter|mi|nol|ogy** /tɜrmɪnɒlədʒi/ (**terminologies**) N-VAR The **terminology** of a subject is the set of special words and expressions used in connection with it. ❑ *...medical terminology.* [from Medieval Latin]

**ter|mite** /tɜrmaɪt/ (**termites**) N-COUNT **Termites** are small insects that do a lot of damage by eating wood. [from New Latin]

**term pa|per** (**term papers**) N-COUNT A **term paper** is an essay or report which a student writes on a subject that he or she has studied during a term at a school, college, or university.

**ter|race** /tɛrɪs/ (**terraces**) ❶ N-COUNT A **terrace** is a flat area of stone or grass next to a building, where people can sit. ❑ ...*a terrace overlooking the sea.* ❷ N-COUNT **Terraces** are a series of flat areas built like steps on the side of a hill so that crops can be grown there. ❑ ...*terraces on steep mountain slopes.* [from Old French]

**terra|cotta** /tɛrəkɒtə/ also **terra cotta** N-UNCOUNT **Terracotta** is a brownish-red clay that has been baked and is used for making things such as flower pots and tiles. [from Italian]

**ter|rain** /təreɪn/ (**terrains**) N-VAR The **terrain** in an area is the type of land that is there. ❑ ...*mountainous terrain.* [from French]

**ter|res|trial plan|et** /tɪrɛstriəl plænɪt/ (**terrestrial planets**) N-COUNT A **terrestrial planet** is a planet with a rocky surface similar to the Earth's. In our solar system the four planets closest to the sun are **terrestrial planets**. [TECHNICAL]

**ter|ri|ble** /tɛrɪbəl/ ❶ ADJ **Terrible** means extremely bad. ❑ *She admits her French is terrible.* ● **ter|ri|bly** ADV ❑ *My son has suffered terribly.* ❷ ADJ You use **terrible** to emphasize the great extent or degree of something. ❑ *I was a terrible fool.* ● **ter|ri|bly** ADV ❑ *I'm terribly sorry to bother you at this hour.* [from Latin]

**ter|rif|ic** /tərɪfɪk/ ❶ ADJ If you describe something or someone as **terrific**, you are very pleased with them or very impressed by them. [INFORMAL] ❑ *What a terrific idea!* ❷ ADJ **Terrific** means very great in amount, degree, or intensity. ❑ *There was a terrific bang.* [from Latin]

**ter|ri|fy** /tɛrɪfaɪ/ (**terrifies, terrifying, terrified**) ❶ V-T If something **terrifies** you, it makes you feel extremely frightened. ❑ *Flying terrifies him.* ● **ter|ri|fied** ADJ ❑ *He was terrified of heights.* [from Latin] ❷ → see also **terror**

**ter|ri|fy|ing** /tɛrɪfaɪɪŋ/ ADJ If something is **terrifying**, it makes you very frightened. ❑ *It was a terrifying accident.* [from Latin]

**ter|ri|to|rial** /tɛrɪtɔriəl/ ADJ **Territorial** means concerned with the ownership of a particular area of land or water. ❑ ...*territorial disputes.* [from Latin]

**ter|ri|tory** /tɛrɪtɔri/ (**territories**) ❶ N-VAR **Territory** is land which is controlled by a particular country or ruler. ❑ ...*Afghan territory* ❷ N-UNCOUNT You can use **territory** to refer to an area of knowledge or experience. ❑ *Atwood's latest novel returns to more familiar territory.* ❸ N-UNCOUNT **Territory** is land with a particular character. ❑ ...*mountainous territory.* ❹ N-VAR An animal's **territory** is an area which it regards as its own and which it defends when other animals try to enter it. [from Latin]

**ter|ror** /tɛrər/ ❶ N-UNCOUNT **Terror** is very great fear. ❑ *I shook with terror whenever I was about to fly on a plane.* ❷ N-UNCOUNT **Terror** is violence or the threat of violence, especially when it is used for political reasons. ❑ *The president gave a press conference, during which he spoke of the war on terror.* ❑ ...*a campaign of terror.* [from Old French]

**ter|ror|ism** /tɛrərɪzəm/ N-UNCOUNT **Terrorism** is the use of violence in order to achieve political goals or to force a government to do something.

**ter|ror|ist** /tɛrərɪst/ (**terrorists**) N-COUNT A **terrorist** is a person who uses violence, especially murder and bombing, in order to achieve political aims. ❑ ...*terrorist attacks.* ● **ter|ror|ism** N-UNCOUNT ❑ ...*the threat of global terrorism.* [from Old French]

**ter|ror|ize** /tɛrəraɪz/ (**terrorizes, terrorizing, terrorized**) V-T If someone **terrorizes** you, they keep you in a state of fear by making it seem likely that they will attack you. ❑ *Gangs of young men and women terrorized the city's inhabitants.* [from Old French]

**terse** /tɜrs/ (**terser, tersest**) ADJ A **terse** statement or comment is brief and unfriendly. ❑ *He issued a terse statement in response to the media allegations.* ● **terse|ly** ADV ❑ *"It's too late," he said tersely.* [from Latin]

**test** /tɛst/ (**tests, testing, tested**) ❶ V-T When you **test** something, you try using it or touching it in order to find out what it is, what condition it is in, or how well it works. ❑ *Test the temperature of the water with your wrist.* ● **Test** is also a noun. ❑ ...*the banning of nuclear tests.* ❷ V-T If you **test** someone, you ask them questions in order to find out how much they know about something. ❑ *Each teacher spent an hour testing students.* ● **Test** is also a noun. ❑ *Out of 25 students only 15 passed the test.* ❸ → see also **quiz** ❹ N-COUNT If an event or situation is a **test of** a person or thing, it reveals their qualities or effectiveness. ❑ *Vacations are a major test of any relationship.* ❺ V-T If you **are tested for** a particular disease or medical condition, you are examined or go through various procedures in order to find out whether you have that disease or condition. ❑ *After I spoke with her my doctor said she wanted me to be tested for diabetes.* ❻ N-COUNT A medical **test** is an examination of a part of your body in order to check that you are healthy. ❑ ...*blood tests.* ❼ PHRASE If you **put** something **to the test**, you find out how useful or effective it is by using it. ❑ *The team is now putting its theory to the test.* [from Latin]
→ see **experiment**

t

---

**Word Partnership** Use *test* with :

N.    test **a drug, flight** test, test **a hypothesis 1**
     **achievement** test, **aptitude** test, **crash** test, test **data/results,** test **items, math/reading** test, test **preparation,** test **scores, standardized** test, **stress** test, test **takers 2**
     **blood** test, **drug** test, **HIV** test, **pregnancy** test **6**

ADJ.    **nuclear** test **1**
     **diagnostic** test **6**

V.    **administer a** test, test **drive, fail a** test, **give** *someone* **a** test, **study for a** test, **take a** test **2**

---

**tes|ta|ment** /tɛstəmənt/ (**testaments**) N-VAR
If one thing is a **testament** to another, it shows that the other thing exists or is true. [FORMAL] ❑ *For him to win like that is a testament to his courage.* [from Latin]

**test case** (**test cases**) N-COUNT A **test case** is a legal case which becomes an example for deciding other similar cases.

**test drive** (**test drives, test driving, test drove, test driven**) also **test-drive** V-T If you **test drive** a car or other vehicle, you drive it for a short period to help you decide whether to buy it. ❑ *...invitations to test drive expensive cars.* ● **Test drive** is also a noun. ❑ *People are buying cars from websites without ever going for a test drive.*

**tes|ti|cle** /tɛstɪkᵊl/ (**testicles**) N-COUNT A man's **testicles** are the two reproductive glands that produce sperm. [from Latin]

**tes|ti|fy** /tɛstɪfaɪ/ (**testifies, testifying, testified**) V-T/V-I When someone **testifies** in a court of law, they give a statement of what they saw someone do or what they know of a situation, after having promised to tell the truth. ❑ *He testified that he saw the officers hit Milner.* ❑ *Eva testified to seeing Herndon with a gun.* [from Latin]

**tes|ti|mo|nial** /tɛstɪmoʊniəl/ (**testimonials**)
**1** N-COUNT A **testimonial** is a written statement about a person's character and abilities, often written by their employer. **2** N-COUNT A **testimonial** is an event which is held to honor someone for their services or achievements. ❑ *...a testimonial dinner held in New York.* [from Latin]

**tes|ti|mo|ny** /tɛstɪmoʊni/ (**testimonies**)
**1** N-VAR In a court of law, your **testimony** is a formal statement that you make about what you saw someone do or what you know of a situation, after having promised to tell the truth. ❑ *His testimony was an important element of the case.*
**2** N-UNCOUNT; N-SING If one thing is **testimony to** another, it shows clearly that the second thing has a particular quality. ❑ *The environmental movement is testimony to people's love of nature.* [from Latin]
→ see **trial**

**tes|tis** /tɛstɪs/ (**testes** /tɛstiz/) N-COUNT A man's **testes** are his **testicles**. [MEDICAL] [from Latin]

**tes|tos|ter|one** /tɛstɒstəroʊn/ N-UNCOUNT
**Testosterone** is a hormone found in higher levels in men and male animals than in women or female animals.

**test tube** (**test tubes**) also **test-tube** N-COUNT

A **test tube** is a small tube-shaped container made from glass. Test tubes are used in laboratories.

**teth|er** /tɛðər/ (**tethers, tethering, tethered**)
**1** PHRASE If you are **at the end of** your **tether,** you are so worried or unhappy because of your problems that you feel you cannot cope. ❑ *She was emotionally at the end of her tether.* **2** V-T If you **tether** an animal or object **to** something, you attach it there with a rope or chain. ❑ *The officer tethered his horse to a tree.* [from Old Norse]

**Tex-Mex** /tɛksmɛks/ ADJ You use **Tex-Mex** to describe things such as food or music that combine typical elements from Mexico and Texas. [INFORMAL] ❑ *...Tex-Mex restaurants.*

**text** /tɛkst/ (**texts, texting, texted**)
**1** N-UNCOUNT **Text** is any written material. ❑ *The machine can turn handwriting into printed text.* **2** N-COUNT A **text** is a book or other piece of writing, especially one connected with science or learning. ❑ *...his study of religious texts.* **3** N-COUNT A **text** is the same as a **text message.** ❑ *The new system can send a text to a cellphone.* **4** V-T If you **text** someone, you send them a text message on a cellphone. ❑ *Mary texted me when she got home.* **5** N-COUNT The **text** of a speech, broadcast, or recording is the written version of it. [from Medieval Latin]
→ see **diary**

**text|book** /tɛkstbʊk/ (**textbooks**) also **text book** N-COUNT A **textbook** is a book containing facts about a particular subject that is used by people studying that subject. ❑ *...a textbook on international law.*

**tex|tile** /tɛkstaɪl/ (**textiles**) **1** N-COUNT **Textiles** are types of woven cloth. ❑ *...textiles for the home.* **2** N-PLURAL **Textiles** are the industries concerned with the manufacture of cloth. ❑ *75,000 jobs will disappear in textiles.* [from Latin]
→ see **industry, quilt**

**text|ing** /tɛkstɪŋ/ N-UNCOUNT **Texting** is the same as **text messaging.** [from Medieval Latin]

**text mes|sage** (**text messages**) N-COUNT A **text message** is a written message that you send using a cellphone. ❑ *She has sent text messages to her family telling them not to worry.*

**text mes|sag|ing** N-UNCOUNT **Text messaging** is the sending of written messages using a cellphone. ❑ *...the popularity of text messaging.*

**tex|ture** /tɛkstʃər/ (**textures**) **1** N-VAR The **texture** of something is the way that it feels when you touch it. ❑ *Her skin had a smooth texture.* **2** N-VAR The **texture** of a piece of music is the way that the different sounds combine to produce an overall effect. **3** N-VAR The **texture** of something, especially food or soil, is its structure, for example, whether it is light with lots of holes, or very heavy and solid. [from Latin]

**than** /ðən, STRONG ðæn/ **1** PREP You use **than** to link two parts of a comparison or contrast. ❑ *Children learn faster than adults.* ❑ *They talked on the phone for more than an hour.* ❑ *It feels much more like a car than a truck.* ● **Than** is also a conjunction. ❑ *He should have helped her more than he did.* [from Old English] **2** **less than** → see **less** **3** **more than** → see **more** **4** **more often than not** → see **often** **5** **other than** → see **other** **6** **rather than** → see **rather**

*Than* and *then* are often confused. Use *than* to make a comparison. *The unemployment rate is lower now than it was last year. Then* means "at that time" or "next." *There were a lot more unemployed people then. Slice the skin off the fruit and then cut it into quarters.*

**thank** /θæŋk/ **(thanks, thanking, thanked)**
**1** CONVENTION You use **thank you** or, in more informal English, **thanks** to express your gratitude when someone does something for you or gives you what you want. ❑ *Thank you very much for your call.* ❑ *Thanks for the information.* ❑ *"Would you like a cup of coffee?" — "Thank you, I'd love one."* ❑ *"Tea?" — "No thanks."* **2** CONVENTION You use **thank you** or **thank you very much** in order to say firmly that you do not want help or to tell someone that you do not like the way that they are behaving toward you. ❑ *I can find my own way home, thank you.* **3** V-T When you **thank** someone you express your gratitude to them for it. ❑ *I thanked them for their long and loyal service.* **4** N-PLURAL When you express your **thanks** to someone, you express your gratitude to them for something. ❑ *They accepted their certificates with words of thanks.* **5** PHRASE You say **"Thank God," "Thank goodness,"** or **"Thank heavens"** when you are very relieved about something. ❑ *I was wrong, thank God.* **6** PHRASE If you say that something happens **thanks to** a particular person or thing, you mean that they are responsible for it happening or caused it to happen. ❑ *Thanks to this committee, many new supporters have come forward.* [from Old English]

**thank|ful** /θæŋkfəl/ ADJ When you are **thankful**, you are very happy and relieved that something has happened. ❑ *I'm just thankful that I've got a job.* [from Old English]

**thank|ful|ly** /θæŋkfəli/ ADV You use **thankfully** in order to express approval or happiness about a statement that you are making. ❑ *Thankfully, she was not injured.* [from Old English]

**Thanks|giving** /θæŋksgɪvɪŋ/ **(Thanksgivings)**
**1** N-VAR In the United States, **Thanksgiving** or **Thanksgiving Day** is a public holiday on the fourth Thursday in November, when people remember the occasion on which the first European settlers celebrated a successful harvest with the Native Americans. ❑ *He always managed to be home for Thanksgiving.* **2** N-VAR In Canada, **Thanksgiving** or **Thanksgiving Day** is a public holiday on the second Monday in October, when people celebrate a successful harvest.

---

**that**

**❶** DEMONSTRATIVE USES
**❷** CONJUNCTION AND RELATIVE PRONOUN USES

---

**❶ that** /ðæt/ **1** PRON You use **that** to refer back to an idea, situation, or period of time that you have referred to previously. ❑ *They said you wanted to talk to me. Why was that?* ❑ *"There's a party tonight." — "Is that why you're phoning?"* ● **That** is also a determiner. ❑ *She's away; for that reason I'm cooking tonight.* ❑ *The story was published later that week.* **2** DET You use **that** when you are referring to

someone or something which is a distance away from you in position or time, especially when you indicate or point to them. When there are two or more things near you, **that** refers to the more distant one. ❑ *Look at that guy over there.* ● **That** is also a pronoun. ❑ *What's that you're writing?* ❑ *"Who's that with you?" — "A friend of mine."* **3** ADV If something is **not that** bad, funny, or expensive, for example, it is not as bad, funny, or expensive as it might be or as has been suggested. ❑ *Not even Gary is that stupid.* **4** → see also **those** **5** PHRASE You use **that is** or **that is to say** to indicate that you are about to express the same idea more clearly or precisely. ❑ *I am a good student. That is, I do as I'm told.* **6** PHRASE You use **that's that** to say there is nothing more you can do or say about a particular matter. [SPOKEN] ❑ *If that's the way you want it, I guess that's that.* [from Old English] **7** like that → see **like** **8** this and that → see **this** **9** this, that and the other → see **this**

**❷ that** /ðət, STRONG ðæt/ **1** CONJ You can use **that** after many verbs, adjectives, nouns, and expressions to introduce a clause. ❑ *He said that he and his wife were coming to New York.* ❑ *...the news that your contract has ended.* ❑ *It's interesting that you like him.* **2** PRON You use **that** to introduce a clause which gives more information to help identify the person or thing you are talking about. ❑ *...a decision that will make the problem disappear.* **3** CONJ You use **that** after expressions with "so" and "such" in order to introduce the result or effect of something. ❑ *She was so nervous that she started shaking.* [from Old English]

**thatched** /θætʃt/ ADJ A **thatched** house or a house with a **thatched** roof has a roof made of straw or reeds. ❑ *...a 400-year-old thatched cottage.* [from Old English]

**that's** /ðæts/ **That's** is a spoken form of "that is."

**thaw** /θɔ/ **(thaws, thawing, thawed)** **1** V-T/V-I When ice, snow, or something else that is frozen **thaws**, it melts. ❑ *It's so cold the snow doesn't get a chance to thaw.* ❑ *Always thaw chicken thoroughly.* **2** N-COUNT A **thaw** is a period of warmer weather when snow and ice melt. ❑ *...an early spring thaw.* [from Old English]

**the**

**The** is the definite article. It is used at the beginning of noun groups. It is usually pronounced /ðə/ before a consonant and /ði/ before a vowel, but pronounced /ði:/ when you are emphasizing it.

**1** DET You use **the** at the beginning of noun groups to refer to someone or something when they are generally known about or when it is clear which particular person or thing you are referring to. ❑ *Six of the 38 people were U.S. citizens.* ❑ *It's always hard to think about the future.* ❑ *The doctor's on his way.* **2** DET You use **the** in front of a singular noun when you want to make a general statement about things or people of that type. ❑ *The computer has developed very fast in recent years.* **3** DET You use **the** with adjectives and plural nouns to refer to all people of a particular type or nationality. ❑ *...the poor in Los Angeles.* ❑ *We must keep the British and the French involved in this.* **4** DET You use **the** in front of an adjective when you are referring to a particular thing that is described by that adjective. ❑ *He knows he's wishing for the impossible.* **5** DET You use **the** in front of numbers to refer to days and dates. ❏ *The meeting should take place on the fifth of May.* ❏ *It's hard to imagine how bad things were in the thirties.* **6** DET You use **the** in front of superlative adjectives and adverbs. ❏ *Daily walks are the best exercise.* **7** DET You use **the** in front of each of two comparative adjectives or adverbs when you are describing how one amount or quality changes in relation to another. ❏ *The more you learn, the greater your chances of success.* **8** DET When you express rates, prices, and measurements, you can use **the** to say how many units apply to each of the items being measured. ❏ *...cars that get more miles to the gallon.* [from Old English]

**thea|ter** /ˈθiətər/ (**theaters**) also **theatre**
**1** N-COUNT A **theater** is a building with a stage on which plays and other performances take place. ❏ *We went to the theater.* **2** N-COUNT A **theater** or a **movie theater** is a place where people go to watch movies for entertainment. ❏ *...American musical theater.* **3** N-UNCOUNT **Theater** is entertainment that involves the performance of plays. ❏ *...American musical theater.* **4** N-SING You can refer to work in the theater such as acting or writing plays as **the theater**. [from Latin]
→ see Word Web: **theater**
→ see **city, drama**

**thea|ter of the ab|surd** N-SING The **theater of the absurd** is a style of theater that began in the 1950s. It represents life as meaningless or irrational.

**the|at|ri|cal** /θiˈætrɪkəl/ **1** ADJ **Theatrical** means relating to the theater. ❏ *...great theatrical performances.* **2** ADJ **Theatrical** behavior is deliberately exaggerated and unnatural. ❏ *...a theatrical gesture.* ● **the|at|ri|cal|ly** /θiˈætrɪkli/ ADV ❏ *He looked theatrically at his watch.* [from Latin]

**the|at|ri|cal con|ven|tion** (**theatrical conventions**) N-VAR A **theatrical convention** is a part of the style or structure of a play which is traditional and therefore familiar to most audiences.

**the|at|ri|cal ex|peri|ence** (**theatrical experiences**) N-COUNT A **theatrical experience** is an occasion when someone attends a play, musical, or other theatrical production.

**the|at|ri|cal game** (**theatrical games**) N-COUNT **Theatrical games** are exercises, such as role-playing, that are designed to develop people's acting skills.

**theft** /θɛft/ (**thefts**) N-VAR **Theft** is the crime of stealing. ❏ *Auto theft has increased by over 56 percent.*

[from Old English]
→ see **crime**

**their** /ðɛər/

> **Their** is the third person plural possessive determiner.

**1** DET You use **their** to indicate that something belongs or relates to the group of people, animals, or things that you are talking about. ❏ *Janis and Kurt have announced their engagement.* ❏ *They took off their coats.* **2** DET You use **their** instead of "his or her" to indicate that something belongs or relates to a person without saying whether that person is a man or a woman. Some people think this use is incorrect. ❏ *Each student decides their own pace.* [from Old Norse]

**theirs** /ðɛərz/

> **Theirs** is the third person plural possessive pronoun.

**1** PRON You use **theirs** to indicate that something belongs or relates to the group of people, animals, or things that you are talking about. ❏ *...the table next to theirs.* ❏ *Theirs was a happy marriage.* **2** PRON You use **theirs** instead of "his or hers" to indicate that something belongs or relates to a person without saying whether that person is a man or a woman. Some people think this use is incorrect. ❏ *I don't know whose book it is. Somebody must have left theirs.* [from Old Norse]

**them** /ðəm, STRONG ðɛm/

> **Them** is a third person plural pronoun. **Them** is used as the object of a verb or preposition.

**1** PRON You use **them** to refer to a group of people, animals, or things. ❏ *Kids these days have no one to tell them what's right and wrong.* **2** PRON You use **them** instead of "him or her" to refer to a person without saying whether that person is a man or a woman. Some people think this use is incorrect. ❏ *It takes great courage to face your child and tell them the truth.* [from Old English]

---

**Word Web** **theater**

It only takes two hours to watch a **play**. It takes a lot of time, money, and work before the curtain rises on the **stage**. First, a **playwright** writes an interesting story. Then, a **producer** gets the money for the **production** and finds a **theater**. **Actors audition** for the play. The **director casts** the actors in the **roles**. **Rehearsals** sometimes go on for months. The **set, lighting,** and **costumes** all have to be designed and made. Special **props** and **makeup** are usually necessary. A **band** or an **orchestra** is needed if the play is a **musical**. It takes a large **crew** to do all these things.

*A scene from the Broadway play, Les Miserables*

**theme** /θiːm/ (themes) **1** N-COUNT A **theme** in a piece of writing, a discussion, or a work of art is an important idea or subject that runs through it. ❑ *The novel's theme is the conflict between men and women.* **2** N-COUNT A **theme** in an artist's work or in a work of literature is an idea in it that the artist or writer develops or repeats. [from Latin]
→ see **myth**

| Word Partnership | Use *theme* with : |
|---|---|
| N. | theme **of a book/movie/story** |
| ADJ. | **central** theme, **common** theme, **dominant** theme, **main** theme, **major** theme, **new** theme, **recurring** theme |

**theme and variation** (themes and variations) N-VAR Music that uses **theme and variation** begins with a particular musical theme and then repeats the theme with small changes.

**themselves** /ðəmsɛlvz/

Themselves is the third person plural reflexive pronoun.

**1** PRON You use **themselves** to refer to people, animals, or things when the object of a verb or preposition refers to the same people or things as the subject of the verb. ❑ *They all seemed to be enjoying themselves.* ❑ *The men talked among themselves.* **2** PRON You use **themselves** to emphasize the people or things that you are referring to. **Themselves** is also sometimes used instead of "them" as the object of a verb or preposition. ❑ *The games themselves are very popular.* ❑ *...other people who are in the same position as themselves.* **3** PRON You use **themselves** instead of "himself or herself" to refer back to the person who is the subject of a sentence without saying whether it is a man or a woman. Some people think this use is incorrect. ❑ *What can a patient with heart disease do to help themselves?*

**then** /ðɛn/ **1** ADV **Then** means at a particular time in the past or in the future. ❑ *Since then, house prices have fallen.* ❑ *Until then, he won't need any more money.* **2** ADV You use **then** to say that one thing happens after another, or is after another on a list. ❑ *Add the oil and then the onion.* **3** ADV You use **then** to signal the end of a topic or the end of a conversation. ❑ *"I'll talk to you on Friday anyway."* — *"Yes. Okay then."* **4** ADV You use **then** with words like "now," "well," and "okay," to introduce a new topic or a new point of view. ❑ *Now then, I'm going to explain everything to you.* **5** ADV You use **then** to introduce the second part of a sentence which begins with "if." The first part of the sentence describes a possible situation, and **then** introduces the result of the situation. ❑ *If the answer is "yes," then we need to leave now.* **6** ADV You use **then** at the beginning of a sentence or after "and" or "but" to introduce a comment or an extra piece of information to what you have already said. ❑ *He sounded sincere, but then, he always did.* [from Old English] **7** now and then → see now **8** there and then → see there
→ see also **than**

**theologian** /θiːəloʊdʒ³n, -dʒiən/ (theologians) N-COUNT A **theologian** is someone who studies religion and the nature of God. [from Late Latin]

**theology** /θiːɒlədʒi/ N-UNCOUNT **Theology** is the study of religion and the nature of

God. ❑ *...questions of theology.* ● **theological** /θiːəlɒdʒɪk³l/ ADJ ❑ *...theological books.* [from Late Latin]

**theoretical** /θiːərɛtɪk³l/ ADJ **Theoretical** means based on or using the ideas and abstract principles of a particular subject, rather than its practical aspects. ❑ *...theoretical physics.* [from Late Latin]

**theoretically** /θiːərɛtɪkli/ ADV You use **theoretically** to say that although something is supposed to be true or to happen in the way stated, it may not in fact be true or happen in that way. ❑ *Such an event is theoretically possible but highly unlikely.* [from Late Latin]

**theorize** /θiːəraɪz/ (theorizes, theorizing, theorized) V-T/V-I If you **theorize** that something is true or **theorize** about it, you develop an abstract idea or set of ideas about something in order to explain it. ❑ *Police are theorizing that the robbers may be local.* ❑ *By studying the way people behave, we can theorize about what they are thinking.* ● **theorist** /θiːərɪst/ (theorists) N-COUNT ❑ *...a leading political theorist.* ● **theorizing** N-UNCOUNT ❑ *This is no time for theorizing.* [from Late Latin]

**theory** /θiːəri/ (theories) **1** N-VAR A **theory** is a formal idea or set of ideas intended to explain something and which is capable of being tested. ❑ *...a new theory about historical change.* **2** N-COUNT If you have a **theory** about something, you have your own opinion about it which you cannot prove but which you think is true. ❑ *There was a theory that he wanted to marry her.* **3** N-UNCOUNT The **theory** of a practical subject or skill is the set of rules and principles that form the basis of it. ❑ *He taught us music theory.* **4** PHRASE You use **in theory** to say that although something is supposed to be true or to happen in the way stated, it may not in fact be true or happen in that way. ❑ *In theory I'm available day and night.* [from Late Latin]
→ see **evolution, experiment, science**

| Word Partnership | Use *theory* with : |
|---|---|
| N. | theory **and practice** **3** **evidence for a** theory, **support for a** theory **1** **2** **conspiracy** theory **2** **learning** theory **3** |
| V. | **advance a** theory, **develop a** theory, **propose a** theory, **test a** theory **1** **2** |
| ADJ. | **economic** theory, **literary** theory, **scientific** theory **3** |

**therapeutic** /θɛrəpyuːtɪk/ ADJ If something is **therapeutic**, it helps you to relax or feel happier. ❑ *Having a garden is therapeutic.* [from New Latin]

**therapist** /θɛrəpɪst/ (therapists) N-COUNT A **therapist** is a person who is skilled in a particular type of therapy, especially psychotherapy. ❑ *My therapist helped me to deal with my anger.* [from New Latin]

**therapsid** /θəræpsɪd/ (therapsids) N-COUNT **Therapsids** were animals similar to reptiles that lived in prehistoric times and evolved into mammals. [TECHNICAL] [from New Latin]

**therapy** /θɛrəpi/ (therapies) **1** N-UNCOUNT **Therapy** is the process of talking to a trained counselor about your emotional problems and your relationships in order to understand and

t

---

### Word Web — thermometer

The first scientist to **measure** heat was Galileo. He invented a simple water **thermometer** in 1593. But his thermometer did not have a **scale** to show exact **temperatures**. In 1714, a German named Daniel Fahrenheit invented a **mercury** thermometer. In 1724, he added the **Fahrenheit scale** of temperatures with 32°F* as the **freezing** temperature of water. On this scale, water **boils** at 212°F. In 1742, Anders **Celsius** invented the centigrade scale. Centigrade means 'divided into 100 **degrees**.' On this scale, water freezes at 0°C* and boils at 100° C.

*32°F = thirty-two degrees Fahrenheit*
*0°C = zero degrees Celsius or zero degrees centigrade*

---

improve the way you feel and behave. ❑ *Children may need therapy to help them deal with death.*
**2** N-VAR **Therapy** or a **therapy** is a treatment for a particular illness or condition. [MEDICAL] ❑ *...vitamin therapies.* [from New Latin]
→ see **cancer**

**there**

Pronounced /ðər/, STRONG ðer/ for meaning **1**, and /ðɛər/ for meanings **2** to **11**.

**1** PRON **There** is used as the subject of the verb "be" to say that something exists or does not exist, or to draw attention to it. ❑ *There must be another way of doing this.* ❑ *Are there any cookies left?* **2** ADV If something is **there**, it exists or is available. ❑ *The group of old buildings is still there today.* **3** ADV You use **there** to refer to a place which has already been mentioned. ❑ *I'm going back to California. My family have lived there for many years.* ❑ *"Come on over, if you want." — "How do I get there?"* **4** ADV You use **there** to indicate a place that you are pointing to or looking at. ❑ *There it is, on the corner over there.* ❑ *There she is on the left up there.* **5** ADV You use **there** when speaking on the telephone to ask if someone is available to speak to you. ❑ *Hello, is Gordon there please?* **6** ADV You use **there** to refer to a point that someone has made in a conversation. ❑ *I think you're right there, John.* **7** ADV You use **there** to refer to a stage that has been reached in an activity or process. ❑ *We are investigating and will take the matter from there.* **8** ADV You can use **there** in expressions such as **there you go** or **there we are** when accepting that an unsatisfactory situation cannot be changed. [SPOKEN] ❑ *We've had this argument before, but there we are.* **9** ADV You can use **there** in expressions such as **there you go** and **there we are** when emphasizing that something proves that you were right. [SPOKEN] ❑ *There you go. I knew you'd be upset.* **10** PHRASE If something happens **there and then** or **then and there**, it happens immediately. ❑ *Many people thought that he should have resigned there and then.* **11** CONVENTION You say "**there you are**" or "**there you go**" when you are offering something to someone. [SPOKEN] ❑ *"There you go, Mr. Walters," she said, giving him his documents.* [from Old English]
→ see also **their**

**there|after** /ðɛəræftər/ ADV **Thereafter** means after the event or date mentioned. [FORMAL] ❑ *The plan will help you lose 3 – 4 pounds the first week, and 1 – 2 pounds the weeks thereafter.*

**there|by** /ðɛərbaɪ/ ADV You use **thereby** to introduce an important result or consequence of the event or action you have just mentioned.

[FORMAL] ❑ *Our bodies sweat, thereby losing heat.*

**there|fore** /ðɛərfɔr/ ADV You use **therefore** to introduce a logical result or conclusion. ❑ *The process is much quicker and therefore cheaper.*

**there|in** /ðɛərɪn/ ADV **Therein** means in the place that has just been mentioned. [FORMAL] ❑ *...the documents, or the information contained therein.*

**ther|mal** /θɜrmᵊl/ **1** ADJ **Thermal** means relating to or caused by heat. ❑ *...thermal power stations.* **2** ADJ **Thermal** clothes are specially designed to keep you warm. ❑ *...thermal underwear.* [from Greek]
→ see **solar**

**ther|mal en|er|gy** N-UNCOUNT **Thermal energy** is energy in the form of heat.

**ther|mal equi|lib|rium** N-UNCOUNT Two or more substances that are in **thermal equilibrium** have the same temperature. [TECHNICAL]

**ther|mal ex|pan|sion** N-UNCOUNT **Thermal expansion** is the increase in a substance's size or volume that occurs when it is heated. [TECHNICAL]

**ther|mal pol|lu|tion** N-UNCOUNT **Thermal pollution** is an increase in the temperature of a river or lake that is harmful to the organisms living there. Thermal pollution often occurs when water that has been used in industrial processes is returned to a river or lake. [TECHNICAL]

**ther|mo|cline** /θɜrməklaɪn/ (**thermoclines**) N-COUNT A **thermocline** is a layer of water in an ocean or lake that separates the warmer water on the surface from the colder water below it. [TECHNICAL]

**ther|mo|cou|ple** /θɜrməkʌpᵊl/ (**thermocouples**) N-COUNT A **thermocouple** is a kind of thermometer that uses an electric current to measure temperature. [TECHNICAL]

**ther|mom|eter** /θərmɒmɪtər/ (**thermometers**) N-COUNT A **thermometer** is an instrument for measuring the temperature of a place or of a person's body.
→ see Word Web: **thermometer**

**ther|mo|sphere** /θɜrməsfɪər/ (**thermospheres**) N-COUNT The **thermosphere** is the highest layer of the Earth's atmosphere. [TECHNICAL]

**these**

The determiner is pronounced /ðiz/. The pronoun is pronounced /ðiz/.

**1** DET You use **these** to refer to someone or something that you have already mentioned or identified. ❑ *These people can make quick decisions* which would take us months. ● **These** is also a pronoun. ❑ *These are good players.* **2** DET You use **these** to introduce people or things that you are going to talk about. ❑ *If you're looking for a builder, these phone numbers will be useful.* ● **These** is also a pronoun. ❑ *These are some of the things you can do for yourself.* **3** DET In spoken English, people use **these** to introduce people or things into a story. ❑ *I was by myself and these guys suddenly came towards me.* **4** PRON You use **these** when you are identifying a group or asking about their identity. ❑ *These are my children.* **5** DET You use **these** to refer to people or things that are near you, especially when you touch them or point to them. ❑ *These scissors are heavy.* ● **These** is also a pronoun. ❑ *These are the people who are helping us.* **6** DET You use **these** in the expression **these days** to mean "at the present time." ❑ *These days, people appreciate a chance to relax.* [from Old English]

**the|sis** /θíːsɪs/ (**theses** /θíːsiz/) **1** N-COUNT A **thesis** is an idea or theory that is expressed as a statement and is discussed in a logical way. ❑ *This thesis is only partly true.* **2** N-COUNT A **thesis** is a long piece of writing based on your own ideas and research that you do as part of a college degree, especially a higher degree such as a Ph.D. [from Late Latin]
→ see **graduation**

**they** /ðeɪ/

> **They** is a third person plural pronoun. **They** is used as the subject of a verb.

**1** PRON You use **they** to refer to a group of people, animals, or things. ❑ *She said goodbye to the children as they left for school.* ❑ *People matter because of who they are, not what they have.* **2** PRON You use **they** instead of "he or she" to refer to a person without saying whether that person is a man or a woman. Some people think this use is incorrect. ❑ *The teacher is not responsible for the student's success or failure. They are only there to help the student learn.* **3** PRON You use **they** in expressions such as **they say** or **they call it** to refer to people in general when you are making general statements about what people say, think, or do. ❑ *They say there are plenty of opportunities out there.* [from Old Norse]

**they'd** /ðeɪd/ **1** **They'd** is a spoken form of "they had," especially when "had" is an auxiliary verb. ❑ *They'd both lived on this road all their lives.* **2** **They'd** is a spoken form of "they would." ❑ *He agreed that they'd visit her later.*

**they'll** /ðeɪl/ **They'll** is the usual spoken form of "they will." ❑ *They'll probably be here Monday.*

**they're** /ðɛər/ **They're** is the usual spoken form of "they are." ❑ *People eat when they're depressed.*
→ see also **their**

**they've** /ðeɪv/ **They've** is the usual spoken form of "they have," especially when "have" is an auxiliary verb. ❑ *They've gone out.*

**thick** /θɪk/ (**thicker, thickest**) **1** ADJ Something that is **thick** has a large distance between its two opposite sides. ❑ *...a thick slice of bread and butter.* ❑ *He wore thick glasses.* ● **thick|ly** ADV ❑ *Slice the meat thickly.* **2** ADJ You can use **thick** to talk or ask about how wide or deep something is. ❑ *The folder was two inches thick.* ❑ *How thick are these walls?* ● **thick|ness** (**thicknesses**) N-VAR ❑ *The cooking time depends on the thickness of the steaks.* **3** ADJ If something that consists of several things is **thick**,

it has a large number of them very close together. ❑ *...thick, wavy hair.* ● **thick|ly** ADV ❑ *The trees grew thickly.* **4** ADJ **Thick** smoke, fog, or cloud is difficult to see through. ❑ *The smoke was thick and black.* **5** ADJ **Thick** liquids are fairly stiff and solid and do not flow easily. ❑ *It rained last night, so the garden was thick mud.* [from Old English]

| Word Partnership | Use *thick* with : |
|---|---|
| N. | thick **glass**, thick **ice**, thick **layer**, thick **lips**, thick **neck**, thick **slice**, thick **wall** **1** thick **carpet**, **feet/inches** thick **2** thick **beard**, thick **fur**, thick **grass**, thick **hair** **3** thick **air**, thick **clouds**, thick **fog**, thick **smoke** **4** |
| ADV. | so thick, too thick, very thick **1** – **5** |

**thick|en** /θɪkən/ (**thickens, thickening, thickened**) V-T/V-I If something **thickens**, or if you **thicken** it, it becomes more closely grouped together or more solid than it was before. ❑ *The dust thickened into a cloud.* ❑ *Thicken the soup with potato.* [from Old English]

**thief** /θiːf/ (**thieves** /θiːvz/) N-COUNT A **thief** is a person who steals something from another person. ❑ *The thieves took his camera.* [from Old English]

**thigh** /θaɪ/ (**thighs**) N-COUNT Your **thighs** are the top parts of your legs, between your knees and your hips. [from Old English]
→ see **body**

**thin** /θɪn/ (**thinner, thinnest, thins, thinning, thinned**) **1** ADJ If something is **thin**, there is a small distance between its two opposite surfaces. ❑ *...a thin cable.* ❑ *...a book printed on thin paper.* ● **thin|ly** ADV ❑ *Peel and thinly slice the onion.* **2** ADJ A person or animal that is **thin** has no extra fat on their body. ❑ *He was a tall, thin man.* **3** ADJ Liquids that are **thin** are weak and watery. ❑ *The soup was thin and clear.* **4** V-T/V-I When you **thin** something or when it **thins**, it becomes less crowded because people or things have been removed from it. ❑ *By midnight the crowd was thinning.* ● **Thin out** means the same as **thin**. ❑ *Thin out plants if they become crowded.* [from Old English] **5** **on thin ice** → see **ice** **6** **thin air** → see **air**

| Thesaurus | thin | Also look up : |
|---|---|---|
| ADJ. | flimsy, transparent; (*ant.*) dense, solid, thick **1** lean, skinny, slender, slim; (*ant.*) fat, heavy **2** watery, weak; (*ant.*) thick **3** | |

| Word Partnership | Use *thin* with : |
|---|---|
| N. | thin **film**, thin **ice**, thin **layer**, thin **line**, **razor** thin, thin **slice**, thin **smile**, thin **strips** **1** thin **body**, thin **face**, thin **fingers**, thin **legs**, thin **lips**, thin **mouth** **1** **2** thin **man/woman** **2** |
| ADJ. | long and thin **1** tall and thin **2** |
| ADV. | extremely thin, too thin, very thin **1** – **3** |

---
### thing

**①** NOUN USES
**②** PHRASES

---

**① thing** /θɪŋ/ (**things**) **1** N-COUNT You can use **thing** as a substitute for another word when you cannot, need not, or do not want to be more precise. ❑ *What's that thing in the middle of the road?* ❑ *She was clearing away the breakfast things.* ❑ *They spend their money on things like rent and groceries.* **2** N-SING **Thing** is often used instead of the pronouns "anything," or "everything" in order to emphasize what you are saying. ❑ *Don't you worry about a thing.* ❑ *It isn't going to solve a single thing.* **3** N-COUNT A **thing** is a physical object that is considered as having no life of its own. ❑ *It's not a thing. It's a human being!* **4** N-COUNT You can call a person or an animal a particular **thing** when you want to mention a particular quality that they have and express your feelings toward them, usually affectionate feelings. [INFORMAL] ❑ *She is such a cute little thing.* **5** N-PLURAL Your **things** are your clothes or possessions. ❑ *Sara told him to take all his things and not to return.* **6** N-PLURAL **Things** can refer to the situation or life in general and the way it is changing or affecting you. ❑ *Everyone agrees things are getting better.* [from Old Norse]

**② thing** /θɪŋ/ (**things**) **1** PHRASE If you do something **first thing**, you do it at the beginning of the day, before you do anything else. If you do it **last thing**, you do it at the end of the day, before you go to bed or go to sleep. ❑ *I'll go see her, first thing tomorrow.* **2** PHRASE You can say **for one thing** when you are explaining a statement or answering a question, to suggest that you are not giving the whole explanation or answer, and that there are other points that you could add to it. ❑ *She couldn't sell the house because for one thing, it was too big.* **3** PHRASE You say **"the thing is"** to introduce an explanation, comment, or opinion that relates to something that has just been said. **"The thing is"** is often used to identify a problem relating to what has just been said. [SPOKEN] ❑ *I have a place at college. The thing is, I'm not sure I want to go anymore.* [from Old English] **4** **other things being equal** → see **equal**

---
### think

**①** VERB AND NOUN USES
**②** PHRASES
**③** PHRASAL VERBS

---

**① think** /θɪŋk/ (**thinks, thinking, thought**) **1** V-T/V-I If you **think** that something is the case, you believe that it is the case. ❑ *I think you will agree I made the right decision.* ❑ *What do you think of my idea?* ● **think**|**ing** N-UNCOUNT ❑ *...his thinking on education.* **2** V-T If you say that you **think** that something is true or will happen, you mean that you have the impression that it is true or will happen, although you are not certain of the facts. ❑ *Nora thought he was seventeen years old.* **3** V-I When you **think** about ideas or problems, you make a mental effort to consider them. ❑ *She closed her eyes for a moment, trying to think.* ❑ *I have often thought about this problem.* ● **think**|**ing** N-UNCOUNT ❑ *...quick thinking.* **4** V-T/V-I If you **think of** something, it comes into your mind or

you remember it. ❑ *Nobody could think of anything to say.* ❑ *I was trying to think what else we could do.* **5** V-T If you **are thinking** something at a particular moment, you have words or ideas in your mind without saying them out loud. ❑ *She must be sick, Tatiana thought.* ❑ *I remember thinking how lovely he looked.* **6** V-T/V-I If you **think** a lot **of** someone or something, you admire them very much or think they are very good. ❑ *To tell the truth, I don't think much of doctors.* ❑ *Everyone in my family thought very highly of him.* **7** V-I If you **are thinking of** or **are thinking about** taking a particular course of action, you are considering it as a possible course of action. ❑ *Martin was thinking of taking legal action.* [from Old English] **8** → see also **thinking, thought**

| **Thesaurus** | *think* | Also look up : |
|---|---|---|
| V. | believe, consider, feel, judge, understand **①** **1** | |
| | analyze, evaluate, meditate, reflect, study **①** **3** | |
| | recall, remember; (ant.) forget **①** **4** | |

**② think** /θɪŋk/ (**thinks, thinking, thought**) **1** PHRASE You use **"I think"** as a way of being polite when you are explaining or suggesting something, giving your opinion, or responding to an offer. ❑ *I think I'll go home.* ❑ *Thanks, but I think I can do it myself.* **2** PHRASE If you **think nothing of** doing something that other people might consider difficult, strange, or wrong, you consider it to be easy or normal. ❑ *I thought nothing of walking 20 miles.* [from Old English] **3** you **can't hear** yourself **think** → see **hear** **4** to **think better of it** → see **better** **5** to **think big** → see **big**

**③ think** /θɪŋk/ (**thinks, thinking, thought**) ▶ **think back** PHR-VERB If you **think back**, you make an effort to remember things that happened to you in the past. ❑ *I thought back to the time when my son was very ill.* ▶ **think over** PHR-VERB If you **think** something **over**, you consider it carefully before making a decision. ❑ *She said she needs time to think it over.* ▶ **think through** PHR-VERB If you **think** a situation **through**, you consider it thoroughly, together with all its possible effects or consequences. ❑ *He went for a long bike ride to think the problem through.* ❑ *The administration has not thought through what it will do once the war ends.* ▶ **think up** PHR-VERB If you **think** something **up**, for example, an idea or plan, you invent it using mental effort. ❑ *Julian has been thinking up new ways of raising money.*

**think**|**er** /θɪŋkər/ (**thinkers**) N-COUNT A **thinker** is a person who spends a lot of time thinking deeply about important things, especially someone who is famous for thinking of new or interesting ideas. ❑ *...some of the world's greatest thinkers.* [from Old English]

**think**|**ing** /θɪŋkɪŋ/ **1** → see **think** **2** → see also **wishful thinking** **3** **to my way of thinking** → see **way**

**third** /θɜrd/ (**thirds**) **1** ORD The **third** item in a series is the one that you count as number three. ❑ *I sleep on the third floor.* **2** ORD A **third** is one of three equal parts of something. ❑ *A third of the cost went into machinery.* [from Old English]

**third**|**ly** /θɜrdli/ ADV You use **thirdly** when you want to make a third point or give a third reason for something. ❑ *First of all, there are not many of them, secondly, they have little money and, thirdly, they're hungry.* [from Old English]

**third par|ty** (**third parties**) N-COUNT A **third party** is someone who is not one of the main people involved in a business agreement or legal case, but who is involved in it in a minor role. ❑ *They could decide to sell the company to a third party.*

**Third World** N-PROPER Countries that are poor and do not have much industrial development are sometimes referred to together as **the Third World**. Some people find this term offensive. ❑ *…development in the Third World.*

**thirst** /θɜrst/ (**thirsts**) ■ N-VAR **Thirst** is the feeling of wanting to drink something. ❑ *Drink water to quench your thirst.* ② N-UNCOUNT **Thirst** is the condition of not having enough to drink. ❑ *They died of thirst.* [from Old English]

**thirsty** /θɜrsti/ (**thirstier, thirstiest**) ADJ If you are **thirsty**, you feel a need to drink something. ❑ *Drink whenever you feel thirsty.* [from Old English]

**thir|teen** /θɜrtin/ (**thirteens**) NUM **Thirteen** is the number 13. [from Old English]

**thir|teenth** /θɜrtinθ/ ORD The **thirteenth** item in a series is the one that you count as number thirteen. ❑ *…his thirteenth birthday.* [from Old English]

**thir|ti|eth** /θɜrtiəθ/ ORD The **thirtieth** item in a series is the one that you count as number thirty. ❑ *…the thirtieth anniversary of my parents' wedding.* [from Old English]

**thir|ty** /θɜrti/ (**thirties**) ■ NUM **Thirty** is the number 30. ② N-PLURAL When you talk about the **thirties**, you are referring to numbers between 30 and 39. For example, if you are **in** your **thirties**, you are aged between 30 and 39. If the temperature is **in the thirties**, the temperature is between 30 and 39 degrees. ❑ *He lived in Chicago throughout his twenties and early thirties.* ③ N-PLURAL The **thirties** is the decade between 1930 and 1939. ❑ *She was well-known in the thirties.* [from Old English]

**this**

The determiner is pronounced /ðɪs/. In other cases, **this** is pronounced /ðɪs/.

■ DET You use **this** to refer back to a particular person or thing that has been mentioned or implied. ❑ *The president is prepared for this challenge.* ● **This** is also a pronoun. ❑ *I have seen many movies, but never one like this.* ② PRON You use **this** to introduce someone or something that you are going to talk about. ❑ *This is what I will do. I will telephone Anna and explain.* ● **This** is also a determiner. ❑ *This report is from our Science Unit.* ③ DET In spoken English, people use **this** to introduce a person or thing into a story. ❑ *I was watching what was going on, when this girl came up to me.* ④ PRON You use **this** to refer to a person or thing that is near you, especially when you touch them or point to them. When there are two or more people or things near you, **this** refers to the nearest one. ❑ *Is this what you were looking for?* ❑ *"If you'd like a different one I'll gladly change it for you." — "No, this is great."* ● **This** is also a determiner. ❑ *I like this room much better than mine.* ⑤ PRON You use **this** when you refer to a general situation, activity, or event which is happening or has just happened and which you feel involved in. ❑ *I thought, this is why I traveled thousands of miles.* ❑ *Tim, this is awful.*

⑥ DET You use **this** to refer to the next occurrence in the future of a particular day, month, season, or festival. ❑ *…this Sunday's performance.* ❑ *We're getting married this June.* ⑦ PRON You use **this is** in order to say who you are or what organization you are representing, when you are speaking on the telephone, radio, or television. ❑ *Hello, this is John Thompson.* ⑧ → see also **these** ⑨ PHRASE If you say that you are doing or talking about **this and that**, or **this, that, and the other** you mean that you are doing or talking about a variety of things that you do not want to specify. ❑ *"And what are you doing now?" — "Oh this and that."* [from Old English]

**thong** /θɔŋ/ (**thongs**) ■ N-COUNT A **thong** is a piece of underwear worn on the lower part of your body that has a very narrow piece of cloth at the back. ② N-COUNT **Thongs** are open shoes which are held on your foot by a V-shaped strap that goes between your big toe and the toe next to it. [from Old English]

thorn

**thorn** /θɔrn/ (**thorns**) N-COUNT **Thorns** are the sharp points on some plants and trees. ❑ *Most roses have thorns.* [from Old English]

**thorny** /θɔrni/ (**thornier, thorniest**) ■ ADJ A **thorny** plant or tree is covered with thorns. ② ADJ A **thorny** problem or question is difficult to deal with. ❑ *…the thorny issue of immigration.* [from Old English]

**thor|ough** /θɜroʊ/ ■ ADJ A **thorough** action or activity is one that is done very carefully and in a detailed way. ❑ *We are making a thorough investigation.* ● **thor|ough|ly** ADV ❑ *The food must be thoroughly cooked.* ● **thor|ough|ness** N-UNCOUNT ❑ *…the thoroughness of the work.* ② ADJ Someone who is **thorough** is always very careful in their work, so that nothing is forgotten. ❑ *He was calm and thorough.* ● **thor|ough|ness** N-UNCOUNT ❑ *His thoroughness and attention to detail is amazing.* ③ ADJ **Thorough** is used to emphasize the large degree or extent of something. ❑ *This seemed like a thorough waste of time.* ● **thor|ough|ly** ADV ❑ *I thoroughly enjoy your program.* [from Old English]

**those**

The determiner is pronounced /ðoʊz/. The pronoun is pronounced /ðoʊz/.

■ DET You use **those** to refer to people or things which have already been mentioned. ❑ *I don't know any of those people.* ● **Those** is also a pronoun. ❑ *You had some concerns. Tell me about those.* ② DET You use **those** when you are referring to people or things that are a distance away from you in position or time, especially when you indicate or point to them. ❑ *What are those buildings?* ● **Those** is also a pronoun. ❑ *Those are nice shoes.* ③ PRON You use **those** to mean "people." ❑ *Selfish behavior hurts those around us.* [from Old English]

**though** /ðoʊ/ ■ CONJ You use **though** to introduce a statement in a subordinate clause which contrasts with the statement in the main clause, or makes it seem surprising. ❑ *Everything I told them was correct, though I forgot a few things.* ❑ *I like him. Though he makes me angry sometimes.* [from Old English] ② **as though** → see **as** ③ **even though** → see **even**

t

**thought** /θɔt/ (**thoughts**) **1** Thought is the past tense and past participle of **think**. **2** N-COUNT A **thought** is an idea or opinion. ❑ *The thought of Nick made her sad.* ❑ *I just had a thought.* ❑ *Many of you wrote to us to tell us your thoughts.* **3** N-UNCOUNT **Thought** is the activity of thinking, especially deeply, carefully, or logically. ❑ *Alice was deep in thought.* ❑ *He gave some thought to what she told him.* **4** N-UNCOUNT **Thought** is the group of ideas and beliefs which belongs, for example, to a particular religion, philosophy, science, or political party. ❑ *...the history of Western thought.* [from Old English]

**thought|ful** /θɔtfəl/ **1** ADJ If you are **thoughtful**, you are quiet and serious because you are thinking about something. ❑ *Nancy was looking thoughtful.* ● **thought|ful|ly** ADV ❑ *Daniel nodded thoughtfully.* **2** ADJ If you describe someone as **thoughtful**, you approve of them because they remember what other people want, need, or feel, and try not to upset them. ❑ *...a thoughtful and caring man.* ● **thought|ful|ly** ADV ❑ *He thoughtfully brought flowers to the party.* [from Old English]

**thought|less** /θɔtlɪs/ ADJ If you describe someone as **thoughtless**, you are critical of them because they forget or ignore other people's wants, needs, or feelings. ❑ *...a small number of thoughtless people.* ● **thought|less|ly** ADV ❑ *They thoughtlessly planned a picnic without him.* [from Old English]

**thou|sand** /θaʊzªnd/ (**thousands**)

> The plural form is **thousand** after a number, or after a word or expression referring to a number, such as "several" or "a few."

**1** NUM A **thousand** or **one thousand** is the number 1,000. ❑ *...five thousand people.* **2** QUANT If you refer to **thousands of** things or people, you are emphasizing that there are very many of them. ❑ *I must have driven past that place thousands of times.* ● You can also use **thousands** as a pronoun. ❑ *Thousands came to his funeral.* [from Old English] **3 a thousand and one** → see **one**

**thou|sandth** /θaʊzªnθ/ ORD The **thousandth** item in a series is the one that you count as number one thousand. ❑ *The magazine has just published its six thousandth edition.* [from Old English]

**thrash** /θræʃ/ (**thrashes, thrashing, thrashed**) **1** V-T If one player or team **thrashes** another in a game or contest, they defeat them easily or by a large score. [INFORMAL] ❑ *The Kings were thrashed by the Knicks last night.* ● **thrash|ing** (**thrashings**) N-COUNT ❑ *...her thrashing of the former champion.* **2** V-T If you **thrash** someone, you hit them several times as a punishment. ❑ *The guards thrashed people who broke the rules.* ● **thrash|ing** N-COUNT ❑ *If her mother catches her, she will get a thrashing.* **3** V-T/V-I If you **thrash around** or **thrash** your arms or legs **around**, you move in a wild or violent way, often hitting against something. ❑ *She thrashed around in her hospital bed.* [from Old English]

▸ **thrash out** PHR-VERB If people **thrash out** something such as a problem or a plan, they discuss it in detail until a solution is reached. ❑ *I'm not leaving until we've thrashed this thing out.*

**thread** /θrɛd/ (**threads, threading, threaded**) **1** N-VAR **Thread** or a **thread** is a long very thin piece of a material such as cotton, nylon, or silk,

thread

especially one that is used in sewing. ❑ *...a piece of thread.* **2** V-T When you **thread** a needle, you put a piece of thread through the hole in the top of the needle in order to sew with it. ❑ *I sat down and threaded a needle.* **3** N-COUNT The **thread** of a story or a situation is an aspect of it that connects all the different parts together. ❑ *He lost the thread of the story.* **4** N-COUNT The **thread** on a screw, or on something such as a lid, is the raised spiral line around it which allows it to be fixed in place by twisting. **5** V-T/V-I If you **thread** your **way** through a group of people or things, or **thread through** it, you move through it carefully. ❑ *Slowly she threaded her way back through the crowd.* **6** V-T If you **thread** small objects such as beads onto a string or thread, you join them together by pushing the string or thread through them. ❑ *She was threading glass beads on a string.* **7** N-COUNT On websites such as newsgroups, a **thread** is one of the subjects that is being written about. [COMPUTING] ❑ *You can go back to previous threads and read them.* [from Old English]

**threat** /θrɛt/ (**threats**) **1** N-VAR A **threat to** a person or thing is a danger that something bad might happen to them. A **threat** is also the cause of this danger. ❑ *Stress is a threat to people's health.* **2** N-COUNT A **threat** is a statement by someone that they will hurt you in some way, especially if you do not do what they want. ❑ *He may carry out his threat to leave.* [from Old English]

**threat|en** /θrɛtªn/ (**threatens, threatening, threatened**) V-T If a person **threatens** to do something bad to you, or if they **threaten** you, they say or imply that they will hurt you in some way, especially if you do not do what they want. ❑ *Army officers threatened to destroy the town.* ❑ *If you threaten me I will go to the police.* [from Old English]

**threat|en|ing** **1** ADJ ❑ *...threatening behavior.* **2** V-T If something **threatens** people or things, it is likely to harm them. ❑ *The fire threatened a street of houses just off the freeway.* **3** V-T If something bad **threatens to** happen, it seems likely to happen. ❑ *It's threatening to rain.* [from Old English]

**three** /θri/ (**threes**) NUM **Three** is the number 3. ❑ *We waited three months before going back.* [from Old English]

**three-dimensional** ADJ A **three-dimensional** object is solid rather than flat, because it can be measured in three different directions, usually the height, length, and width. ❑ …*a three-dimensional model.*

**three-quarters** QUANT **Three-quarters** is an amount that is three out of four equal parts of something. ❑ *Three-quarters of the students are African-American.* ● **Three-quarters** is also a pronoun. ❑ *Applications have increased by three-quarters.*

**thresh|old** /ˈθrɛʃhoʊld/ (**thresholds**) **1** N-COUNT The **threshold** of a building or room is the floor in the doorway, or the doorway itself. ❑ *He stopped at the threshold of the bedroom.* **2** N-COUNT A **threshold** is an amount, level, or limit on a scale. ❑ *Mathers has a high threshold for pain.* **3** PHRASE If you are **on the threshold of** something exciting or new, you are about to experience it. ❑ *We are on the threshold of a new age of discovery.* [from Old English]

**threw** /θruː/ **Threw** is the past tense of **throw**. [from Old English]

**thrift** /θrɪft/ N-UNCOUNT **Thrift** is the quality and practice of being careful with money and not wasting things. ❑ *Is thrift a thing of the past?* [from Old Norse]

**thrift shop** (**thrift shops**) N-COUNT A **thrift shop** or **thrift store** is a shop that sells used goods cheaply and gives its profits to a charity.

**thrill** /θrɪl/ (**thrills, thrilling, thrilled**) **1** N-COUNT If something gives you a **thrill**, it gives you a sudden feeling of great excitement, pleasure, or fear. ❑ *I can remember the thrill of opening my birthday presents.* **2** V-T If something **thrills** you, it gives you a feeling of great pleasure and excitement. ❑ *The atmosphere both terrified and thrilled him.* [from Old English]

**thrilled** /θrɪld/ ADJ If you are **thrilled**, you are very happy and excited about something. ❑ *I was so thrilled to get a good grade.* [from Old English]

**thrill|er** /ˈθrɪlər/ (**thrillers**) N-COUNT A **thriller** is a book, movie, or play that tells an exciting fictional story about something such as criminal activities or spying. ❑ …*a tense crime thriller.* [from Old English]

**thrill|ing** /ˈθrɪlɪŋ/ ADJ Something that is **thrilling** is very exciting and enjoyable. ❑ …*a thrilling adventure movie.* [from Old English]

**thrive** /θraɪv/ (**thrives, thriving, thrived**) V-I If someone or something **thrives**, they do well and are successful, healthy, or strong. ❑ *He appears to be thriving.* ❑ *Her company continues to thrive.* ❑ *Many people thrive on a stressful lifestyle.* [from Old Norse]

**throat** /θroʊt/ (**throats**) **1** N-COUNT Your **throat** is the back of your mouth and the top part of the tubes that go down into your stomach and your lungs. ❑ *She had a sore throat.* **2** N-COUNT Your **throat** is the front part of your neck. ❑ *His tie was loosened at his throat.* **3** PHRASE If you **clear** your **throat**, you cough once either to make it easier to speak or to attract people's attention. ❑ *Crossley cleared his throat and spoke.* [from Old English] **4** **a lump in** your **throat** → see **lump**

**throb** /θrɒb/ (**throbs, throbbing, throbbed**) **1** V-I If part of your body **throbs**, you feel a series of strong and usually painful beats there. ❑ *His head throbbed.* **2** V-I If something **throbs**, it vibrates and makes a steady noise. [LITERARY] .

**throne** /θroʊn/ (**thrones**) **1** N-COUNT A **throne** is a decorative chair used by a king, queen, or emperor on important official occasions.

**2** N-SING You can talk about **the throne** as a way of referring to the position of being king, queen, or emperor. ❑ …*the queen's 50 years on the throne.* [from Old French]

**throng** /θrɔŋ/ (**throngs, thronging, thronged**) **1** N-COUNT A **throng** is a large crowd of people. [LITERARY] ❑ *An official pushed through the throng.* **2** V-I When people **throng** somewhere, they go there in great numbers. [LITERARY] ❑ *The crowds thronged into the stadium.* [from Old English]

**throt|tle** /ˈθrɒtəl/ (**throttles, throttling, throttled**) **1** V-T To **throttle** someone means to kill or injure them by holding them tightly by the throat so that they cannot breathe. ❑ *The attacker tried to throttle him.* **2** N-COUNT The **throttle** of a motor vehicle or aircraft is the device that controls the quantity of fuel entering the engine and is used to control the vehicle's speed. ❑ *He opened the throttle, and the ship began to move forward.*

---

**through**

❶ ADVERBS AND PREPOSITIONS: PHYSICAL MOVEMENTS AND POSITIONS

❷ ADVERBS AND PREPOSITIONS, ABSTRACT USES: TIMES, EXPERIENCES, CAUSES

❸ ADJECTIVES

---

The preposition is pronounced /θruː/. In other cases, **through** is pronounced /θruː/.

In addition to the uses shown below, **through** is used in phrasal verbs such as "follow through," "see through," and "think through."

❶ **through** **1** PREP To move, cut, or travel **through** something means to move, cut, or travel from one side or end to the other. ❑ *Go straight through that door.* ❑ *We walked through the crowd.* ● **Through** is also an adverb. ❑ *There was a hole in the wall and water was coming through.* **2** PREP If you see, hear, or feel something **through** a particular thing, that thing is between you and the thing you can see, hear, or feel. ❑ *Alice looked through the window.* [from Old English]

❷ **through** **1** PREP If something happens or exists **through** a period of time, it happens or exists from the beginning until the end. ❑ *She kept quiet all through breakfast.* ● **Through** is also an adverb. ❑ *We'll be working right through to the summer.* **2** PREP If something happens from a particular period of time **through** another, it starts at the first period and continues until the end of the second period. ❑ *The office is open Monday through Friday from 9 to 5.* **3** PREP If you go **through** a particular experience or event, you experience it, and if you behave in a particular way **through** it, you behave in that way while it is happening. ❑ *We have been going through a bad time.* **4** PREP If something happens because of something else, you can say that it happens **through** it. ❑ *I only succeeded through hard work.* **5** PREP If someone gets **through** an examination or a round of a competition, they succeed or win. ❑ *I got through my exams.* ● **Through** is also an adverb. ❑ *Only the top four teams go through.* **6** PREP If you look or go **through** a lot of things, you look at them or deal with them one after the other. ❑ *Let's go through the numbers together.* [from Old English]

t

**➌ through** ■ ADJ If you are **through with** something or if it is **through**, you have finished doing it. ❑ *We're through with dinner.* ➋ ADJ If you are **through with** someone, you do not want to have anything to do with them again. ❑ *I'm through with her!* [from Old English]

**through|out** /θruː_aʊt/ ■ PREP If you say that something happens **throughout** a particular period of time, you mean that it happens during the whole of that period. ❑ *The school runs cooking courses throughout the year.* ❑ *The themes are repeated throughout the film.* ● **Throughout** is also an adverb. ❑ *The first song didn't go too badly except that everyone talked throughout.* ➋ PREP If you say that something happens or exists **throughout** a place, you mean that it happens or exists in all parts of that place. ❑ *They run projects throughout Africa.* ● **Throughout** is also an adverb. ❑ *The route is well marked throughout.*

**throw** /θroʊ/ (**throws, throwing, threw, thrown**) ■ V-T When you **throw** an object that you are holding, you move your hand or arm quickly and let go of the object, so that it moves through the air. ❑ *He spent hours throwing a tennis ball against a wall.* ❑ *The crowd began throwing stones.* ● **Throw** is also a noun. ❑ *I made a good throw.* ➋ V-T If you **throw** your body or part of your body into a particular position or place, you move it there suddenly and with a lot of force. ❑ *She threw her arms around his shoulders.* ❑ *She threw herself onto her bed.* ➌ V-T To **throw** something or someone into a particular place or position means to cause them to fall there. ❑ *He threw his jacket onto the back seat.* ❑ *He threw me to the ground.* ➍ V-T If a horse **throws** its rider, it makes the rider fall off. ❑ *The horse stopped suddenly, throwing its rider.* ➎ V-T If a person or thing **is thrown into** a bad situation or state, something causes them to be in it. ❑ *The city was thrown into chaos because of a protest by taxi drivers.* ➏ V-T If you **throw** yourself, your energy, or your money **into** a particular job or activity, you become involved in it very actively or enthusiastically. ❑ *She threw herself into a modeling career.* ➐ V-T If you **throw** a fit or a tantrum, you suddenly start to behave in an uncontrolled way. ❑ *I used to throw tantrums all over the place.* ➑ V-T If something such as a remark or an experience **throws** you, it surprises you or confuses you because it is unexpected. ❑ *Her sudden change in attitude threw me.* ➒ V-T When someone **throws** a party, they organize one. [INFORMAL] ❑ *Why not throw a party for your friends?* [from Old English] ➓ to **throw** someone **in at the deep end** → see **end** ⓫ to **throw down the gauntlet** → see **gauntlet** ⓬ to **throw light on** something → see **light** ⓭ to **throw in the towel** → see **towel**

▸ **throw away** or **throw out** ■ PHR-VERB When you **throw away** or **throw out** something that you do not want, you get rid of it. ❑ *I never throw anything away.* ➋ PHR-VERB If you **throw away** an opportunity, advantage, or benefit, you waste it. ❑ *Don't throw away your chances of finding happiness.*

▸ **throw out** ■ → see **throw away** 1 ➋ PHR-VERB If a judge **throws out** a case, he or she rejects it and the accused person does not have to stand trial. ❑ *The defense wants the judge to throw out the case.* ➌ PHR-VERB If you **throw** someone **out**, you force them to leave a place or group. ❑ *I threw him out of the house.*

▸ **throw up** PHR-VERB When someone **throws up**, they vomit. ❑ *I went to the rest room and threw up.*

| **Word Partnership** | Use *throw* with : |
|---|---|
| N. | throw **a ball**, throw **a pass**, throw **a pitch**, throw **a rock/stone**, throw **strikes** ■ |

**thrown** /θroʊn/ **Thrown** is the past participle of **throw**. [from Old English]

**throw rug** (**throw rugs**) N-COUNT A **throw rug** is a rug that covers a small part of the floor.

**thrush** /θrʌʃ/ (**thrushes**) N-COUNT A **thrush** is a fairly small bird with a brown back and sometimes a spotted breast. [from Old English]

**thrust** /θrʌst/ (**thrusts, thrusting, thrust**) ■ V-T If you **thrust** something or someone somewhere, you push or move them there quickly with a lot of force. ❑ *They thrust him into the back of a car.* ● **Thrust** is also a noun. ❑ *...arm thrusts.* ➋ N-UNCOUNT **Thrust** is the power or force that is required to make a vehicle move in a particular direction. [from Old Norse]

**thru|way** /θruːweɪ/ (**thruways**) also **throughway** N-COUNT A **thruway** is a wide road that is specially designed so that a lot of traffic can move along it very quickly.

**thud** /θʌd/ (**thuds, thudding, thudded**) ■ N-COUNT A **thud** is a dull sound, such as that which a heavy object makes when it hits something soft. ❑ *She tripped and fell with a thud.* ➋ V-I If something **thuds** somewhere, it makes a dull sound, usually when it falls onto or hits something else. ❑ *She ran up the stairs, her feet thudding on the wood.* [from Old English]

**thug** /θʌɡ/ (**thugs**) N-COUNT You can refer to a violent person or criminal as a **thug**. ❑ *...the cowardly thugs who attack old people.* [from Hindi]

**thumb** /θʌm/ (**thumbs**) ■ N-COUNT Your hand has four fingers and one **thumb**. ❑ *...the tip of her left thumb.* [from Old English] ➋ **green thumb** → see **green** ➌ **rule of thumb** → see **rule** → see **hand**

**thumb|tack** /θʌmtæk/ (**thumbtacks**) N-COUNT A **thumbtack** is a short pin with a broad, flat top which is used for fastening papers or pictures to a bulletin board, wall, or other surface.

**thump** /θʌmp/ (**thumps, thumping, thumped**) ■ V-T/V-I If you **thump** something, you hit it hard, usually with your fist. ❑ *He thumped my back affectionately.* ❑ *I heard you thumping on the door.* ● **Thump** is also a noun. ❑ *He felt a thump on his shoulder.* ➋ V-T/V-I If you **thump** something somewhere or if it **thumps** there, it makes a loud, dull sound by hitting something else. ❑ *The teacher thumped her pen on her book.* ● **Thump** is also a noun. ❑ *There was a loud thump.* ➌ V-I When your heart **thumps**, it beats strongly and quickly, usually because you are afraid or excited. ❑ *My heart was thumping wildly.* [from Icelandic]

**thun|der** /θʌndər/ (**thunders, thundering, thundered**) ■ N-UNCOUNT **Thunder** is the loud noise that you hear from the sky after a flash of lightning, especially during a storm. ❑ *There was thunder and lightning.* ➋ V-I When **it thunders**, a loud noise comes from the sky after a flash of lightning. ❑ *It will probably thunder later.* ➌ N-UNCOUNT The **thunder of** something that is moving or making a sound is the loud deep noise it makes. ❑ ...*the thunder of the sea on the rocks.* **4** V-I If something or someone **thunders** somewhere, they move there quickly and with a lot of noise. ❑ *The horses thundered across the valley.* [from Old English]

**thun|der|ous** /θʌ́ndərəs/ ADJ A **thunderous** noise is very loud and deep. ❑ *The sound was thunderous, almost deafening.* [from Old English]

**thunder|storm** /θʌ́ndərstɔrm/ (**thunderstorms**) N-COUNT A **thunderstorm** is a storm with thunder and lightning and a lot of heavy rain.
→ see **erosion**

**Thurs|day** /θɜ́rzdeɪ, -di/ (**Thursdays**) N-VAR **Thursday** is the day after Wednesday and before Friday. ❑ *On Thursday Barrett invited me for a drink.* ❑ *We do the weekly shopping every Thursday morning.* [from Old English]

**thus** /ðʌs/ **1** ADV You use **thus** to show that what you are about to mention is the result of something else that you have just mentioned. [FORMAL] ❑ *Neither of them turned on the TV. Thus they didn't hear the news.* **2** ADV If you say that something is **thus** or happens **thus** you mean that it is, or happens, as you have just described or as you are just about to describe. [FORMAL] ❑ *Joanna was pouring the tea. While she was thus occupied, Charles sat on an armchair.* [from Old English]

**thwart** /θwɔrt/ (**thwarts, thwarting, thwarted**) V-T If you **thwart** someone or **thwart** their plans, you prevent them from doing or getting what they want. ❑ *He does everything he can to thwart me.* [from Old Norse]

**thyme** /taɪm/ (**thymes**) N-VAR **Thyme** is a type of herb used in cooking. [from Old French]

**thy|mine** /θaɪmin, -mɪn/ (**thymines**) N-VAR **Thymine** is one of the four basic components of the DNA molecule. It bonds with adenine. [TECHNICAL]

**thy|mus** /θaɪməs/ (**thymuses** /θaɪməsɪz/ or **thymi** /θaɪmaɪ/) N-COUNT The **thymus** is an organ in your chest that forms part of the body's immune system. [TECHNICAL] [from New Latin]

**tick** /tɪk/ (**ticks, ticking, ticked**) V-I When a clock or watch **ticks**, it makes a regular series of short sounds as it works. ❑ *A clock ticked on the kitchen counter.* • **Tick** is also a noun. ❑ ...*the tick of the clock.* • **tick|ing** N-UNCOUNT ❑ *She could hear the ticking of a clock.* [from Lower German]
▶ **tick off** PHR-VERB If you say that someone or something **ticks** you **off**, you mean that they annoy you. [INFORMAL] ❑ *That ticks me off.*

**tick|et** /tɪkɪt/ (**tickets**) **1** N-COUNT A **ticket** is a small, official piece of paper or card which shows that you have paid to enter a place such as a theater or a sports stadium, or shows that you have paid for a trip. ❑ ...*two tickets for the game.* ❑ ...*a plane ticket to Paris.* **2** N-COUNT A **ticket** is an official piece of paper which orders you to pay a fine or to appear in court because you have committed a driving or parking offense. ❑ *Slow down or you'll*

ticket

*get a ticket.* [from Old French] **3** → see also **season ticket**

**ticket|less** /tɪkɪtlɪs/ **1** ADJ Someone who is **ticketless** does not have a ticket for a particular event such as a concert or a sports game. ❑ *The band begged ticketless fans to stay away.* **2** ADJ A **ticketless** system is a way of buying something, such as a seat on an aircraft, without being given a paper ticket. ❑ ...*a ticketless reservation system.* [from Old French]

**tick|le** /tɪkᵊl/ (**tickles, tickling, tickled**) **1** V-T When you **tickle** someone, you move your fingers lightly over a sensitive part of their body, often in order to make them laugh. ❑ *I was tickling him, and he was laughing.* **2** V-T/V-I If something **tickles** you or **tickles**, it causes an irritating feeling by lightly touching a part of your body. ❑ ...*a hat with a feather that tickled her ear.* [from Old English]

**tic-tac-toe** /tɪktæktoʊ/ also **tick-tack-toe** N-UNCOUNT **Tic-tac-toe** is a game in which two players take turns in drawing either an "O" or an "X" in one square of a grid consisting of nine squares. The winner is the first player to get three of the same symbols in a row.

**tid|al** /taɪdᵊl/ ADJ **Tidal** means relating to or produced by tides. ❑ *Seabirds flew up from the tidal pools.* [from Old English]

**tid|al bore** (**tidal bores**) N-COUNT A **tidal bore** is a large wave that moves up a river as the tide rises.

**tid|al range** (**tidal ranges**) N-COUNT The **tidal range** is the difference in height between the low tide and the high tide at a particular place.

**tid|al wave** (**tidal waves**) N-COUNT A **tidal wave** is a very large wave, often caused by an earthquake, that flows onto the land and destroys things. ❑ *A tidal wave swept the ship away.*

**tide** /taɪd/ (**tides**) **1** N-COUNT The **tide** is the regular change in the level of the ocean on the beach. ❑ *The tide was going out.* **2** N-SING The **tide** of opinion, for example, is what the majority of people think at a particular time. ❑ *The tide of opinion seems to be in his favor.* [from Old English]
→ see Word Web: **tide**
→ see **ocean, tsunami**

**tie** /taɪ/ (**ties, tying, tied**) **1** V-T If you **tie** two things **together** or **tie** them, you fasten them together with a knot. ❑ *He tied the ends of the plastic bag together.* • **Tie up** means the same as **tie**. ❑ *She tied up the bag and took it outside.* **2** V-T If you **tie** something or someone in a particular place or position, you put them there and fasten them using rope or string. ❑ *He tied the dog to one of the trees.* • **Tie up** means the same as **tie**. ❑ *Would you go and tie your horse up please?* **3** V-T If you **tie** a piece of string or cloth around something or **tie** something **with** a piece of string or cloth, you put the piece of string or cloth around it and fasten the ends together. ❑ *She tied her scarf over her head.* ❑ *Roll the meat and tie it with string.* **4** V-T If you **tie**

## Word Web    tide

The **gravitational** pull of the **moon** on the earth's
**oceans** causes **tides**. It moves the water in the earth's
oceans. **High tides** occur twice a day at any given
point on the earth's surface. Then the water **ebbs**
gradually. After six hours, **low tide** occurs. In some
places tidal energy powers hydroelectric **plants**.
Riptides cause the deaths of hundreds of swimmers
each year. But a riptide is not really a tide. It is a strong ocean **current**.

a knot or bow in something or **tie** something in a
knot or bow, you fasten the ends together. ❑ *He
took a short piece of rope and tied a knot.* ❑ *...a large
red ribbon tied in a bow.* **5** N-COUNT A **tie** is a long
narrow piece of cloth that is worn around the
neck under a shirt collar and tied in a knot at the
front. Ties are worn mainly by men. ❑ *Jason took
off his jacket and loosened his tie.* **6** V-T If one thing
**is tied to** another or two things **are tied**, the two
things have a close connection or link. ❑ *My social
life is closely tied to my work.* **7** N-COUNT **Ties** are
the connections you have with people or a place.
❑ *Quebec has close ties to France.* **8** V-RECIP; V-I If
two people **tie** in a competition or game or if they
**tie with** each other, they have the same number
of points or the same degree of success. ❑ *Ronan
Rafferty tied with Frank Nobilo.* ● **Tie** is also a noun.
❑ *The first game ended in a tie.* [from Old English]
**9** your **hands are tied** → see **hand**
→ see **clothing**
▸ **tie up** → see **tie 1** and **2**

**tier** /tɪər/ (tiers) N-COUNT A **tier** is a row or layer
of something that has other layers above or below
it. ❑ *...tiers of seats.* [from Old French]

**ti|ger** /taɪɡər/ (tigers) N-COUNT A **tiger** is a
large fierce animal belonging to the cat family.
Tigers are orange with black stripes. [from Old
French]

**tight** /taɪt/ (tighter, tightest) **1** ADJ **Tight**
clothes or shoes are small and fit closely to your
body. ❑ *She walked off the plane in a tight black dress.*
● **tight|ly** ADV ❑ *He buttoned his collar tightly round
his neck.* **2** ADV If you hold someone or something
**tight**, you hold them firmly and securely. ❑ *She
just fell into my arms, holding me tight.* ❑ *Just hold tight
to my hand and follow me.* ● **Tight** is also an adjective.
❑ *He kept a tight hold of her arm.* ● **tight|ly** ADV ❑ *He
folded his arms tightly across his chest.* **3** ADJ **Tight**
controls or rules are very strict. ❑ *The rules include
tight control of the media.* ❑ *The government is keeping
a tight hold on inflation.* ● **tight|ly** ADV ❑ *The media
was tightly controlled by the government.* **4** ADJ Skin,
cloth, or string that is **tight** is stretched or pulled
so that it is smooth or straight. ❑ *My skin feels tight
and dry.* ● **tight|ly** ADV ❑ *Pull the cloth tightly across
the wooden frame.* **5** ADJ **Tight** is used to describe
a group of things or an amount of something
that is closely packed together. ❑ *She curled up in a
tight ball.* ● **Tight** is also an adverb. ❑ *The socks were
packed tight in the drawer.* ● **tight|ly** ADV ❑ *Many
animals travel in tightly-packed trucks.* **6** ADJ A **tight**
schedule or budget allows very little time or
money for unexpected events or expenses. ❑ *It's
difficult to fit everything into a tight schedule.* ❑ *Emma*

*is on a tight budget for clothes.* [from Old Norse]
**7** → see also **airtight** **8** to **keep a tight rein
on** → see **rein** **9** to **sit tight** → see **sit**

### Word Partnership    Use *tight* with :

| | |
|---|---|
| N. | tight **dress/jeans/pants** **1** |
| | tight **fit** **1** **5** |
| | tight **grip**, tight **hold** **2** |
| | tight **control**, tight **security** **3** |
| ADV. | **extremely** tight, **a little** tight, **so** tight, |
| | **too** tight, **very** tight **1 – 6** |

**tight|en** /taɪtᵊn/ (tightens, tightening,
tightened) **1** V-T/V-I If you **tighten** your grip on
something, or if your grip **tightens**, you hold the
thing more firmly or securely. ❑ *Luke tightened
his hold on her shoulder.* **2** V-T/V-I If you **tighten**
something such as a rope, chain, or belt, or if it
**tightens**, it is stretched or pulled hard until it
is straight. ❑ *The man leaned back, tightening the
rope.* **3** V-T When you **tighten** a screw, nut, or
other device, you turn it or move it so that it is
more firmly in place or holds something more
firmly. ❑ *She tightened one of the screws holding the
gas can in place.* ● **Tighten up** means the same as
**tighten**. ❑ *It's important to tighten up the wheels
properly.* **4** V-T/V-I To **tighten** rules or controls
means to make them stricter. ❑ *The United States
plans to tighten import controls.* ❑ *...an attempt by
management to tighten the rules.* ● **Tighten up** means
the same as **tighten**. ❑ *Every attempt to tighten up
the law has failed.* [from Old Norse] **5** to **tighten
your belt** → see **belt**

**tights** /taɪts/ N-PLURAL **Tights** are a piece of
tight clothing covering the hips and each leg,
worn by women and girls and usually by dancers,
acrobats, or people in exercise classes. [from Old
Norse]

**tile** /taɪl/ (tiles) N-VAR **Tiles** are flat, square
pieces of baked clay, carpet, cork, or other
substance, which are fixed as a covering onto a
floor, wall, or roof. [from Old English]

**till** /tɪl/ (tills) **1** PREP In spoken English and
informal written English, **till** is often used instead
of **until**. ❑ *They had to wait till Monday to phone the
bank.* ● **Till** is also a conjunction. ❑ *I didn't leave home
till I was nineteen.* **2** N-COUNT A **till** is the drawer of
a cash register, where the money is kept. ❑ *There
was money in the till.* **3** N-UNCOUNT **Till** or **glacial
till** is the same as **glacial drift**. [TECHNICAL] [Sense 1
from Old English]

**tilt** /tɪlt/ (tilts, tilting, tilted) **1** V-T/V-I If you
**tilt** an object or if it **tilts**, it moves into a sloping
position with one end or side higher than the

other. ❑ *She tilted the mirror and combed her hair.* ❑ *Leonard tilted his chair back and stretched his legs.* **2** N-UNCOUNT The **tilt** of something is the fact that it tilts or slopes, or the angle at which it tilts or slopes. [from Old English]

**tim|ber** /tɪmbər/ N-UNCOUNT **Timber** is wood that is used for building houses and making furniture. ❑ *…a single-story timber building.* [from Old English]
→ see **forest**

**tim|bre** /tæmbər/ (**timbres**) N-COUNT The **timbre** of someone's voice or of a musical instrument is the particular quality of sound that it has. [from French]

---

### time

❶ NOUN USES
❷ VERB USES
❸ PHRASES

---

❶ **time** /taɪm/ (**times**) **1** N-UNCOUNT **Time** is what we measure in minutes, hours, days, and years. ❑ *…a two-week period of time.* ❑ *Time passed, and still Mary did not come back.* **2** N-SING You use **time** to ask or talk about a specific point in the day, which can be stated in hours and minutes and is shown on clocks. ❑ *"What time is it?" — "Eight o'clock."* ❑ *He asked me the time.* **3** N-COUNT The **time** when something happens is the point in the day when it happens or is supposed to happen. ❑ *Departure times are 08:15 from Baltimore, and 10:15 from Newark.* **4** N-UNCOUNT; N-SING You use **time** to refer to the period that you spend doing something or when something has been happening. ❑ *Adam spent a lot of time in his grandfather's office.* ❑ *He wouldn't have the time or money to take care of me.* ❑ *Listen to me, I haven't got much time.* **5** N-SING If you say that something has been happening for **a time**, you mean that it has been happening for a fairly long period of time. ❑ *I lived for a time in Ontario, Canada.* ❑ *He stayed for quite a time.* **6** N-COUNT You use **time** or **times** to talk about a particular period of time. ❑ *We were in the same college, which was male-only at that time.* ❑ *By this time he was thirty.* ❑ *They were hard times and his parents were struggling to raise their family.* ❑ *It was a time of great uncertainty.* **7** N-COUNT When you describe the **time** that you had on a particular occasion or during a particular part of your life, you are describing the sort of experience that you had then. ❑ *Sarah and I had a great time while the kids were away.* **8** N-UNCOUNT If you say it is **time for** something, **time to** do something, or **time** you did something, you mean that this thing ought to happen or be done now. ❑ *…a feeling among the public that it was time for a change.* ❑ *It was time for him to go to work.* **9** N-COUNT When you talk about a **time** when something happens, you are referring to a specific occasion when it happens. ❑ *Every time she travels on the bus it's late.* **10** N-COUNT You use **time** after numbers to say how often something happens. ❑ *It was her job to make tea three times a day.* **11** N-PLURAL You use **times** after numbers when comparing one thing to another and saying, for example, how much bigger, smaller, better, or worse it is. ❑ *Its profits are rising four times faster than the average company.* **12** CONJ You use **times** to show multiplication. Three **times** five is 3×5. ❑ *Four times six is 24.* **13** N-COUNT

The **time** of a piece of music is the number of beats that the piece has in each bar. The **time** of a dance measures body rhythms such as breath and heartbeat. [from Old English]

❷ **time** /taɪm/ (**times, timing, timed**) **1** V-T If you **time** something **for** a particular hour, day, or period, you plan or decide to do it or cause it to happen at this time. ❑ *I timed our visit for March this year.* **2** V-T If you **time** an action or activity, you measure how long someone takes to do it or how long it lasts. ❑ *He timed the speed of the baseball.* [from Old English] **3** → see also **timing**

❸ **time** /taɪm/ (**times**) **1** PHRASE If you say it is **about time** that something was done, you are saying in an emphatic way that it should happen or be done now, and really should have happened or been done sooner. ❑ *It's about time he learned to behave well.* **2** PHRASE If someone is **ahead of** their **time** or **before** their **time**, they have new ideas a long time before other people start to think in the same way. ❑ *He was ahead of his time in employing women.* **3** PHRASE If something happens or is done **all the time**, it happens or is done continually. ❑ *We can't be together all the time.* **4** PHRASE If you say that something was the case **at one time**, you mean that it was the case during a particular period in the past. ❑ *At one time 400 men, women and children lived in the village.* **5** PHRASE You use **at the same time** to introduce a statement that contrasts with the previous statement. ❑ *I was afraid of her, but at the same time I really liked her.* **6** PHRASE If something is the case or will happen **for the time being**, it is the case or will happen now, but only until something else becomes possible or happens. ❑ *The situation is calm for the time being.* **7** PHRASE If you do something **from time to time**, you do it occasionally. ❑ *Her daughters visited him from time to time.* **8** PHRASE If you are **in time for** something, or if you are **on time**, you are not late. ❑ *I arrived just in time for my flight to Hawaii.* **9** PHRASE If something will happen **in time**, it will happen eventually. ❑ *He will solve his own problems, in time.* **10** PHRASE If you say that something will happen, for example, **in a week's time** or **in two years' time**, you mean that it will happen a week from now or two years from now. ❑ *Presidential elections will be held in ten days' time.* **11** PHRASE If you say that someone or something is, for example, the best writer **of all time**, or the most successful movie **of all time**, you mean that they are the best or most successful that there has ever been. ❑ *"Monopoly" is one of the best-selling games of all time.* **12** PHRASE If you say that something will **take time**, you mean that it will take a long time. ❑ *Change will come, but it will take time.* **13** PHRASE If you **take** your **time** doing something, you do it slowly and do not hurry. ❑ *"Take your time," Ted told him. "I'm in no hurry."* [from Old English] **14** **time and again** → see **again** → see Picture Dictionary: **time**

**time-honored** ADJ A **time-honored** tradition or way of doing something is one that has been used and respected for a very long time. ❑ *Their cheese is made in the time-honored way.*

**time|less** /taɪmlɪs/ ADJ If you describe something as **timeless**, you mean that it is so good or beautiful that it cannot be affected by changes in society or fashion. ❑ *There is a timeless quality to his best work.* [from Old English]

## Picture Dictionary — time

**analog clock**
- second hand
- hour hand
- minute hand

It's 2:30.
It's two-thirty.

**digital clock**
- minutes
- hours

It's 2:45.
It's a quarter to three.

**time line**

noon · evening · midnight

12 am · 6 am · 12 pm · 6 pm · 12 am

morning · afternoon · night

---

**time|ly** /ˈtaɪmli/ ADJ If you describe an event as **timely**, it happens exactly at the moment when it is most useful, effective, or relevant. ❑ *The recent outbreaks of the disease are a timely reminder that it is still a serious danger.* [from Old English]

**time|table** /ˈtaɪmteɪbᵊl/ (**timetables**) N-COUNT A **timetable** is a plan of the times when particular events will take place. ❑ *Don't you realize we're working to a timetable?*

**tim|id** /ˈtɪmɪd/ ADJ **Timid** people are shy, nervous, and lack courage or confidence in themselves. ❑ *Isabella was a timid child.* • **ti|mid|ity** /tɪˈmɪdɪti/ N-UNCOUNT ❑ *He tried to overcome his natural timidity.* • **tim|id|ly** ADV ❑ *The little boy stepped forward timidly.* [from Latin]

**tim|ing** /ˈtaɪmɪŋ/ ■ N-UNCOUNT **Timing** is the skill or action of judging the right moment in a situation or activity at which to do something. ❑ *His photo caught the happy moment with perfect timing.* ■ N-UNCOUNT **Timing** is used to refer to the time at which something happens or is planned to happen, or to the length of time that something takes. ❑ *They are worried about the timing of the report.* [from Old English] ■ → see also **time**

**tin** /ˈtɪn/ (**tins**) ■ N-UNCOUNT **Tin** is a soft, silvery-white metal. ❑ *…tin cans.* ■ N-COUNT A **tin** is a metal container with a lid in which things such as cookies, cakes, or tobacco can be kept. ❑ *Store the cookies in an airtight tin.* ❑ *…a tin of paint.* [from Old English] ■ **to have a tin ear** → see **ear** → see **pan**

**tinge** /ˈtɪndʒ/ (**tinges**) N-COUNT A **tinge** of a color, feeling, or quality is a small amount of it. ❑ *His skin had an unhealthy grayish tinge.* [from Latin]

**tinged** /ˈtɪndʒd/ ADJ If something is **tinged with** a particular color, feeling, or quality, it has a small amount of it. ❑ *His dark hair was tinged with gray.* ❑ *Her homecoming was tinged with sadness.* [from Latin]

**tin|gle** /ˈtɪŋgᵊl/ (**tingles, tingling, tingled**) ■ V-I When a part of your body **tingles**, you have a slight stinging feeling there. ❑ *Hairs tingled at the back of* her neck. • **tin|gling** N-UNCOUNT ❑ *Its effects include tingling in the hands and feet.* ■ V-I If you **tingle with** a feeling such as excitement, you feel it very strongly. ❑ *She tingled with excitement.* • **Tingle** is also a noun. ❑ *…a sudden tingle of fear.*

**tink|er** /ˈtɪŋkər/ (**tinkers, tinkering, tinkered**) V-I If you **tinker with** something, you make some small changes to it, in an attempt to improve it or repair it. ❑ *Instead of admitting their error, they just tinkered with the problem.*

**tint** /ˈtɪnt/ (**tints, tinting, tinted**) ■ N-COUNT A **tint** is a small amount of color. ❑ *Its leaves show a delicate purple tint.* ■ V-T If something is **tinted**, it has a small amount of a particular color or dye in it. ❑ *Eyebrows can be tinted with the same dye.* ■ N-COUNT In painting, a **tint** is a color that has had white added to it in order to make it lighter.

**tiny** /ˈtaɪni/ (**tinier, tiniest**) ADJ Something or someone that is **tiny** is extremely small. ❑ *The living room is tiny.* ❑ *Though she was tiny, she had a very loud voice.*

**tip** /ˈtɪp/ (**tips, tipping, tipped**) ■ N-COUNT The **tip** of something long and narrow is the end of it. ❑ *…the tips of his fingers.* ■ V-T/V-I If you **tip** an object or part of your body or if it **tips**, it moves into a sloping position with one end or side higher than the other. ❑ *She had to tip her head back to see him.* ■ V-T If you **tip** something somewhere, you pour it there. ❑ *Tip the vegetables into a bowl.* ■ V-T If you **tip** someone such as a waiter in a restaurant, you give them some money in order to thank them for their services. ❑ *We usually tip 18–20%.* • **Tip** is also a noun. ❑ *I gave the barber a tip.* ■ N-COUNT A **tip** is a useful piece of advice. ❑ *The article gives tips on applying for jobs.* [Sense 1 from Old Norse. Senses 4 and 5 from Low German.]
▸ **tip off** PHR-VERB If someone **tips** you **off**, they give you information about something that has happened or is going to happen. ❑ *Greg tipped police off about his neighbor.* • **tip-off** (**tip-offs**) N-COUNT ❑ *The man was arrested at his home after a tip-off.*
▸ **tip over** PHR-VERB If you **tip** something **over** or if it **tips over**, it falls over or turns over. ❑ *He tipped the table over in front of him.* ❑ *Don't tip over that glass.*

T

**tip|toe** /tɪptoʊ/ (**tiptoes, tiptoeing, tiptoed**)
■ V-I If you **tiptoe** somewhere, you walk there very quietly without putting your heels on the floor. ❑ *She slipped out of bed and tiptoed to the window.* ■ PHRASE If you do something **on tiptoe** or **on tiptoes**, you do it standing or walking without putting your heels on the ground. ❑ *She stood on tiptoe to look over the wall.*

**ti|rade** /taɪreɪd/ (**tirades**) N-COUNT A **tirade** is a long, angry speech in which someone criticizes a person or thing. ❑ *She left in 2000 after an angry tirade against her boss.* [from French]

**tire** /taɪər/ (**tires, tiring, tired**) ■ N-COUNT A **tire** is a thick piece of rubber which is fitted onto the wheels of vehicles such as cars, buses, and bicycles. ■ V-T/V-I If something **tires** you or you **tire**, you feel that you have used a lot of energy and you want to rest or sleep. ❑ *If driving tires you, take the train.* ■ V-I If you **tire of** something, you no longer wish to do it, because you have become bored with it or unhappy with it. ❑ *He never tired of listening to her stories.* [from Old French]
→ see **bicycle**

**tired** /taɪərd/ ■ ADJ If you are **tired**, you feel that you want to rest or sleep. ❑ *Michael is tired and he has to rest after his long trip.* • **tired|ness** N-UNCOUNT ❑ *He left early because of tiredness.* ■ ADJ If you are **tired of** something, you do not want it to continue because you are bored of it or unhappy with it. ❑ *I am tired of all the uncertainty.* [from Old English]
→ see **sleep**

**tire|less** /taɪərlɪs/ ADJ If you describe someone or their efforts as **tireless**, you approve of the fact that they put a lot of hard work into something, and refuse to give up or take a rest. ❑ *...her tireless efforts to help the poor.* • **tire|less|ly** ADV ❑ *He worked tirelessly for the cause of health and safety.* [from Old English]

**tire|some** /taɪərsəm/ ADJ If you describe someone or something as **tiresome**, you mean that you find them irritating or boring. ❑ *...the tiresome old lady next door.* [from Old English]

**tir|ing** /taɪərɪŋ/ ADJ If you describe something as **tiring**, you mean that it makes you tired so that you want to rest or sleep. ❑ *It was a long and tiring day.* ❑ *Traveling is tiring.* [from Old English]

**tis|sue** /tɪʃu/ (**tissues**) ■ N-VAR In animals and plants, **tissue** consists of cells that are similar to each other in appearance and that have the same function. ❑ *...muscle tissue.* ■ N-UNCOUNT **Tissue** or **tissue paper** is thin paper that is used for

wrapping things that are easily damaged, such as objects made of glass or china. ❑ *...a small package wrapped in tissue paper.* ■ N-COUNT A **tissue** is a piece of thin, soft paper that you use to blow your nose. ❑ *...a box of tissues.* [from Old French]
→ see **cancer**

**ti|tle** /taɪtᵊl/ (**titles**) ■ N-COUNT The **title** of a book, play, movie, or piece of music is its name. ❑ *"Patience and Sarah" was first published under the title "A Place for Us."* ■ N-COUNT Someone's **title** is a word such as "Doctor," "Mr." or "Mrs." that is used before their own name in order to show their status or profession. ❑ *Please fill in your name and title.* ■ N-COUNT A **title** in a sports competition is the position of winner or champion. ❑ *He won the 400-meter title in 1948.* [from Old French]
→ see **graph**

**ti|tled** /taɪtᵊld/ ADJ In Britain, someone who is **titled** has a title such as "Lord," "Lady," "Sir," or "Princess" before their name, showing that they have a high rank in society. ❑ *Her mother was a titled lady.* [from Old French]

**TLC** /tiː ɛl siː/ N-UNCOUNT If someone or something needs some **TLC**, they need to be treated in a kind and caring way. **TLC** is an abbreviation for "tender loving care." [INFORMAL] ❑ *Plants with small, yellow leaves will need some TLC.*

### to

❶ PREPOSITION AND ADVERB USES
❷ USED BEFORE THE BASE FORM OF A VERB

**❶ to**

Usually pronounced /tə/ before a consonant and /tu/ before a vowel, but pronounced /tu/ when you are emphasizing it.

In addition to the uses shown below, **to** is used in phrasal verbs such as "see to" and "come to." It is also used with some verbs that have two objects in order to introduce the second object.

■ PREP You use **to** when indicating the place that someone or something visits, moves toward, or points at. ❑ *Two friends and I drove to Florida.* ❑ *She went to the window and looked out.* ■ PREP If you go **to** an event, you go where it is taking place. ❑ *We went to a party at Kurt's house.* ❑ *He came to dinner.* ■ PREP If something is attached **to** something larger or fixed **to** it, the two things are joined together. ❑ *There was a piece of cloth tied to the dog's collar.* ■ PREP You use **to** when indicating the position of something. For example, if something is **to** your left, it is nearer your left side than your right side. ❑ *The bathroom is to the right.* ■ PREP When you give something **to** someone, they receive it. ❑ *He picked up the knife and gave it to me.* ■ PREP You use **to** to indicate who or what an action or a feeling is directed toward. ❑ *Marcus has been really mean to me today.* ❑ *...troops loyal to the government.* ■ PREP You use **to** when describing someone's reaction to something or someone's feelings about a situation or event. ❑ *To his surprise, the bedroom door was locked.* ■ PREP **To** can show whose opinion is being stated. ❑ *It was clear to me that he respected his boss.* ■ PREP You use **to** when indicating what something or someone is becoming, or the state or situation that they are progressing toward. ❑ *The shouts changed to laughter.* ❑ *…an old house that was converted to a nature center.* **10** PREP **To** can indicate the last thing in a range of things. ❑ *I read everything from fiction to science.* **11** PREP You use **to** when you are stating a time less than thirty minutes before an hour. For example, if it is "five **to** eight," it is five minutes before eight o'clock. ❑ *At twenty to six I was waiting by the entrance to the station.* **12** PREP You use **to** when giving ratios and rates. ❑ *…engines that can run at 60 miles to the gallon.* [from Old English] **13** → see also **according to** **14** → see also **too**

**② to**

Pronounced /tə/ before a consonant and /tu/ before a vowel.

**1** You use **to** before the base form of a verb to indicate the purpose or intention of an action. ❑ *…using the experience of big companies to help small businesses.* **2** You use **to** before the base form of a verb when you are expressing your attitude or intention in making a statement. ❑ *I'm disappointed, to be honest.* **3** You use **to** before the base form of a verb in many other constructions when talking about an action or state. ❑ *The management wanted to know.* ❑ *Nuclear plants are expensive to build.* ❑ *…advice about how to do her job.* ❑ *The president is to visit China.* [from Old English]

**toad** /toʊd/ (**toads**) N-COUNT A **toad** is an animal like a frog, but with drier skin. [from Old English]

**toast** /toʊst/ (**toasts, toasting, toasted**) **1** N-UNCOUNT **Toast** is slices of bread heated until they are brown and crisp. ❑ *…a piece of toast.* **2** V-T When you **toast** bread, you heat it so that it becomes brown and crisp. ❑ *Toast the bread lightly on both sides.* **3** N-COUNT When you drink a **toast to** someone or something, you drink some wine or another alcoholic drink, in order to show your appreciation of them or to wish them success. ❑ *Eleanor and I drank a toast to the bride and groom.* ● **Toast** is also a verb. ❑ *We all toasted his health.* [from Old French] → see **cook**

**toast|er** /toʊstər/ (**toasters**) N-COUNT A **toaster** is a piece of electrical equipment used to toast bread. [from Old French]

**to|bac|co** /təbækoʊ/ (**tobaccos**) N-VAR **Tobacco** is the dried leaves of a plant which people smoke in pipes, cigars, and cigarettes. [from Spanish]

**to|day** /tədeɪ/ **1** ADV You use **today** to refer to this day on which you are speaking or writing. ❑ *How are you feeling today?* ● **Today** is also a noun. ❑ *Today is Friday, September 14th.* **2** → see also **yesterday, tomorrow** **3** ADV You can refer to the present period of history as **today**. ❑ *More and more young people today are working for themselves.* ● **Today** is also a noun. ❑ *In today's America, health care is one of the very biggest businesses.* [from Old English]

**tod|dler** /tɒdlər/ (**toddlers**) N-COUNT A **toddler** is a young child who has only just learned to walk. ❑ *I had a toddler at home and two other children at school.* → see **age, child**

**toe** /toʊ/ (**toes**) N-COUNT Your **toes** are the five movable parts at the end of each foot. ❑ *She wiggled her toes in the sand.* [from Old English] → see **foot**

**toe|nail** /toʊneɪl/ (**toenails**) N-COUNT Your **toenails** are the thin, hard areas at the end of each of your toes. → see **foot**

**tof|fee** /tɔfi/ (**toffees**) N-VAR **Toffee** or **English toffee** is a hard brown candy made with butter and sugar.

**to|fu** /toʊfu/ N-UNCOUNT **Tofu** is a soft, white or brown food made from soybeans. [from Japanese]

**to|geth|er** /təgɛðər/

In addition to the uses shown below, **together** is used in phrasal verbs such as "piece together," "pull together," and "sleep together."

**1** ADV If people do something **together**, they do it with each other. ❑ *We went on long bicycle rides together.* ❑ *He and I worked together on a book.* **2** ADV If things are joined **together**, they are joined with each other so that they touch or form one whole. ❑ *Mix the ingredients together thoroughly.* **3** ADV If things or people are situated **together**, they are in the same place and very near to each other. ❑ *The trees grew close together.* ❑ *Ginette and I gathered our things together.* **4** ADV If two things happen or are done **together**, they happen or are done at the same time. ❑ *Three horses crossed the finish line together.* **5** ADV You use **together** when you are adding two or more amounts or things to each other in order to consider a total amount or effect. ❑ *Together we earn $60,000 per year.* **6** PHRASE You use **together with** to mention someone or something else that is also involved in an action or situation. ❑ *Return the completed form, together with your check for $60.* [from Old English] **7** to **get** your **act together** → see **act** **8** to **put** your **heads together** → see **head** **9** **put together** → see **put**

| Word Partnership | Use *together* with : | |
|---|---|---|
| V. | **go** together, **live** together, **play** together, **spend time** together, **work** together **1** | |
| | **come** together **1** – **4** | |
| | **get** together **1** **3** | |
| | **act** together | |
| | **fit** together, **glue** together, **join** together, **lump** together, **mix** together, **string** together, **stuck** together, **tied** together **2** | |
| | **gather** together, **sit** together, **stand** together **3** | |
| ADJ. | **bound** together **2** | |
| | **close** together **3** **4** | |

**toil** /tɔɪl/ (**toils, toiling, toiled**) V-I When people **toil**, they work very hard doing unpleasant or tiring tasks. [LITERARY] ❑ *…people who toiled in factories.* ❑ *Workers toiled long hours.* [from Anglo-French]

**toi|let** /tɔɪlɪt/ (**toilets**) N-COUNT A **toilet** is a large bowl with a seat, or a platform with a hole, which is connected to a water system and which you use when you want to get rid of urine or feces from your body. [from French] → see **bathroom**

**toi|let pa|per** N-UNCOUNT also **toilet tissue** **Toilet paper** is thin, soft paper that people use to clean themselves after they have gotten rid of urine or feces from their body.

**toi|let|ries** /tɔɪlətriz/ N-PLURAL **Toiletries** are things that you use when washing or taking care of your body, for example, soap and toothpaste. [from French]

**toi|let tissue** → see **toilet paper**

**to|ken** /toʊkən/ (**tokens**) **1** ADJ You use **token** to describe things or actions which are meant to show an intention or feeling, but which are small or unimportant and may not be sincere. ❑ *Please accept this gift as a token of our thanks.* **2** N-COUNT A **token** is a round, flat piece of metal or plastic that is sometimes used instead of money. ❑ *...slot-machine tokens.* **3** PHRASE You use **by the same token** to introduce a statement that you think is true for the same reasons that were given for a previous statement. ❑ *If you give up exercise, your muscles shrink and fat increases. By the same token, if you do more exercise you will lose fat.* [from Old English]

**told** /toʊld/ **1 Told** is the past tense and past participle of **tell**. **2** PHRASE You can use **all told** to introduce or follow a summary, general statement, or total. ❑ *All told, he went to 14 different schools.* [from Old English]

**tol|er|able** /tɒlərəbªl/ ADJ If you describe something as **tolerable**, you mean that you can bear it, even though it is unpleasant or painful. ❑ *Our living conditions are tolerable, but I can't wait to leave.* ● **tol|er|ably** /tɒlərəbli/ ADV ❑ *They were treated tolerably well.* [from Latin]

**tol|er|ant** /tɒlərənt/ ADJ If you describe someone as **tolerant**, you approve of the fact that they allow other people to say and do as they like and that they are willing to accept different races, religions, and lifestyles. ❑ *They need to be tolerant of different points of view.* ● **tol|er|ance** N-UNCOUNT ❑ *...his tolerance and understanding of human nature.* [from Latin]

**tol|er|ate** /tɒləreɪt/ (**tolerates, tolerating, tolerated**) **1** V-T If you **tolerate** a situation or person, you accept them although you do not particularly like them. ❑ *She can no longer tolerate the position that she's in.* **2** V-T If you can **tolerate** something bad or painful, you are able to bear it. ❑ *The ability to tolerate pain varies from person to person.* [from Latin]

**toll** /toʊl/ (**tolls, tolling, tolled**) **1** V-I When a bell **tolls**, it rings slowly and repeatedly, often as a sign that someone has died. ❑ *Church bells tolled as people arrived for the funeral.* **2** N-COUNT A **toll** is a sum of money that you have to pay in order to use a particular bridge or road. ❑ *You can pay a toll to drive on Pikes Peak Highway.* **3** N-COUNT A **toll** road or **toll** bridge is a road or bridge that you have to pay to use. ❑ *Most people who drive the toll roads don't use them every day.* **4** N-COUNT A **toll** is a total number of deaths, accidents, or disasters that occur in a particular period of time. ❑ *There are fears that the toll of dead and injured may be higher.* **5** → see also **death toll 6** PHRASE If you say that something **takes its toll** or **takes a heavy toll**, you mean that it has a bad effect or causes a lot of suffering. ❑ *Winter takes its toll on your health.* [from Old English]

**Word Link** *free ≈ without : care**free**, duty-**free**, toll-**free***

**toll-free** ADJ A **toll-free** telephone number is one which you can dial without having to pay for the call. ● **Toll-free** is also an adverb. ❑ *Call our customer-service staff toll-free.*

**to|ma|to** /təmeɪtoʊ/ (**tomatoes**) N-VAR **Tomatoes** are soft, red fruit that you can eat raw in salads or cooked as a vegetable. [from Spanish] → see **vegetable**

**tomb** /tum/ (**tombs**) N-COUNT A **tomb** is a stone structure containing the body of a dead person. ❑ *...the emperor's tomb.* [from Old French]

**tomb|stone** /tumstoʊn/ (**tombstones**) N-COUNT A **tombstone** is a large stone with words carved into it, which is placed on a grave. [from Old French]

**to|mor|row** /təmɒroʊ/ (**tomorrows**) **1** ADV **Tomorrow** refers to the day after today. ❑ *Bye, see you tomorrow.* ● **Tomorrow** is also a noun. ❑ *What's on your schedule for tomorrow?* **2** ADV You can refer to the future as **tomorrow**. ❑ *What is education going to be like tomorrow?* ● **Tomorrow** is also a noun. ❑ *...tomorrow's computer industry.* [from Old English]

**ton** /tʌn/ (**tons**) N-COUNT A **ton** is a unit of weight that is equal to 2,000 pounds. ❑ *Hundreds of tons of oil spilled into the ocean.*

**to|nal|ity** /toʊnælɪti/ N-VAR **Tonality** is the presence of a musical key in a piece of music. [TECHNICAL] [from Latin]

**tone** /toʊn/ (**tones, toning, toned**) **1** N-COUNT The **tone** of a sound is its particular quality. ❑ *Chris heard them speaking in low tones to Sarah.* **2** N-COUNT Someone's **tone** is a quality in their voice which shows what they are feeling or thinking. ❑ *I didn't like his tone of voice; he sounded angry.* **3** N-SING The **tone** of a speech or piece of writing is its style and the opinions or ideas expressed in it. ❑ *The tone of the letter was very friendly.* **4** V-T/V-I Something that **tones** your body makes it firm and strong. ❑ *This movement lengthens your spine and tones the back muscles.* ● **Tone up** means the same as **tone**. ❑ *Exercise tones up your body.* **5** N-COUNT In painting, a **tone** is a color that has had gray added to it in order to make it darker. [from Latin] ▶ **tone down** PHR-VERB If you **tone down** something that you have written or said, you make it less forceful, severe, or offensive. ❑ *The leader toned down his statements after the meeting.*

**Word Partnership** Use *tone* with :

| | |
|---|---|
| ADJ. | **clear** tone, **low** tone **1** |
| | **different** tone **2** |
| | **serious** tone **2 3** |
| V. | **change your** tone **2** |
| N. | tone **of voice 2** |

**tone poem** (**tone poems**) N-COUNT A **tone poem** is a piece of music for an orchestra that is based upon something such as a novel or painting.

**tongue** /tʌŋ/ (**tongues**) **1** N-COUNT Your **tongue** is the soft movable part inside your mouth which you use for tasting, licking, and speaking. ❑ *I walked over to the mirror and stuck my tongue out.* **2** N-COUNT A **tongue** is a language. [LITERARY] ❑ *English is not her native tongue.* **3** PHRASE A **tongue-in-cheek** remark or attitude is not serious, although it may seem to be. ❑ *...a lighthearted, tongue-in-cheek approach.* [from Old English] **4** to **bite** your **tongue** → see **bite** → see **diagnosis, face, taste**

t

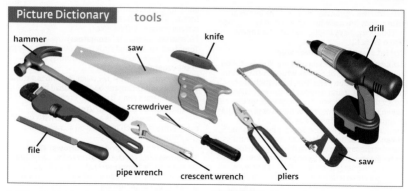

**Picture Dictionary**  tools

hammer

saw

knife

drill

screwdriver

file

pipe wrench    crescent wrench    pliers

saw

**ton|ic** /tɒnɪk/ (tonics) **1** N-VAR **Tonic** or **tonic water** is a colorless carbonated drink that has a slightly bitter flavor. **2** N-VAR A **tonic** is a medicine that makes you feel stronger, healthier, and less tired. □ *People are spending twice as much on health tonics.* [from New Latin]

**to|night** /tənaɪt/ ADV **Tonight** is used to refer to the evening of today or the night that follows today. □ *I'm at home tonight.* □ *Tonight he proved what a great player he was.* ● **Tonight** is also a noun. □ *Tonight is the opening night of the opera.* [from Old English]

**ton|sils** /tɒnsəlz/

The form **tonsil** is used as a modifier.

N-PLURAL Your **tonsils** are the two small soft lumps in your throat at the back of your mouth. [from Latin]

**too**

**❶** ADDING SOMETHING OR RESPONDING
**❷** INDICATING EXCESS

**❶ too** /tu/ **1** ADV You use **too** after mentioning another person, thing, or aspect that a previous statement applies to or includes. □ *"Nice to talk to you." — "Nice to talk to you too."* □ *"I've got a great feeling about it." — "Me too."* **2** ADV You use **too** after adding a piece of information or a comment to a statement, in order to emphasize that it is surprising or important. □ *We learned to read, and quickly too.* [from Old English]

**❷ too** /tu/ **1** ADV You use **too** in order to indicate that there is a greater amount or degree of something than is desirable, necessary, or acceptable. □ *Jeans that are too big will make you look larger.* □ *I'm turning up the heat because it's too cold.* **2** ADV You use **too** with a negative to make what you are saying sound less forceful or more polite or cautious. □ *I'm not too happy with what I've written.* **3** PHRASE You use **all too** or **only too** to emphasize that something happens to a greater extent or degree than is good or desirable. □ *She remembered it all too well.* [from Old English] **4** **none too** → see **none**

**Usage**  **too, two**, and **to**

*Too, two*, and *to* are frequently confused. Their meanings and uses are very different, but they sound exactly the same. *Too* means "also" or "excessively"; *two* is the number 2; and *to* has many different uses as a preposition and in the *to*-infinitive: *Bahati asked Sekou to sit with her on the swing, but it was too small for the two of them, so they went to the movies instead.*

**took** /tʊk/ **Took** is the past tense of **take**. [from Old English]

**tool** /tul/ (tools) **1** N-COUNT A **tool** is any instrument or simple piece of equipment, for example a hammer or a knife, that you hold in your hands and use to do a particular kind of work. □ *The best tool for the purpose is a hammer.* **2** N-COUNT You can refer to anything that you use for a particular purpose as a particular type of **tool**. □ *Writing is a good tool for expressing feelings.* [from Old English]
→ see Picture Dictionary: **tools**

**Word Partnership**  Use *tool* with :

| N. | tool **belt 1** |
| | **communication** tool, **learning** tool, |
| | **management** tool, **marketing** tool, |
| | **teaching** tool **2** |
| V. | **use a** tool **1 2** |
| ADJ. | **effective** tool, **important** tool, **valuable** |
| | tool **1 2** |
| | **powerful** tool **2** |

**tool|bar** /tulbɑr/ (toolbars) N-COUNT A **toolbar** is a narrow strip across a computer screen containing pictures, called icons, which represent different computer functions. [COMPUTING]

**tooth** /tuθ/ (teeth) **1** N-COUNT Your **teeth** are the hard white objects in your mouth, which you use for biting and chewing. □ *She had very straight teeth.* **2** N-PLURAL The **teeth** of something such as a comb, saw, or zipper are the parts that stick out in a row on its edge. □ *...a comb with most of its teeth missing.* [from Old English] **3** **to grit** your **teeth** → see **grit** **4** **a kick in the teeth** → see **kick** → see **teeth**

N.     tooth **decay**, tooth **enamel** ∎
V.     **lose a** tooth, **pull a** tooth ∎

**tooth|brush** /tuːθbrʌʃ/ (**toothbrushes**)
N-COUNT A **toothbrush** is a small brush that you
use for cleaning your teeth.

**tooth|paste** /tuːθpeɪst/ (**toothpastes**) N-VAR
**Toothpaste** is a thick substance which you put
on your toothbrush and use to clean your teeth.
❑ ...*shaving supplies, toothpaste, and soap.*

---

**top**

① NOUN AND ADJECTIVE USES
② PHRASAL VERBS
③ PHRASES

---

① **top** /tɒp/ (**tops**) ∎ N-COUNT The **top** of
something is its highest point or part. ❑ *I waited at
the top of the stairs.* ❑ *Don't fill it up to the top.* • **Top** is
also an adjective. ❑ ...*the top corner of the newspaper.*
② ADJ The **top** thing or layer in a series of things
or layers is the highest one. ❑ *I can't reach the top
shelf.* ③ N-COUNT The **top** of a bottle, jar, or tube is
its cap or lid. ❑ ...*the plastic tops from soda bottles.*
④ N-COUNT A **top** is a piece of clothing that you
wear on the upper half of your body, for example,
a blouse or shirt. [INFORMAL] ❑ *Look at my new top.*
⑤ ADJ You can use **top** to describe the highest
level of a scale or measurement. ❑ *The car has a
top speed of 100 miles per hour.* ⑥ N-SING The **top** of
an organization or career structure is the highest
level in it. ❑ *He joined the company as a salesman and
worked his way to the top.* • **Top** is also an adjective.
❑ ...*the top people in this company.* ⑦ N-SING If
someone is **at the top** of a class or league or is the
**top of** it, their performance is better than that of
all the other people involved. ❑ *She was always top
of the class at school.* • **Top** is also an adjective. ❑ *He
was the top student in physics.* [from Old English]
→ see **hat**

**Thesaurus**     *top*     Also look up :

N.     peak, summit; (*ant.*) base, bottom ① ∎
ADJ.     best ① ⑦

② **top** /tɒp/ (**tops, topping, topped**)
▶ **top out** PHR-VERB If something such as a
price **tops out at** a particular amount, that is the
highest amount that it reaches. ❑ *The temperature
topped out at 99 degrees.*

③ **top** /tɒp/ (**tops**) ∎ PHRASE If you **are on top
of** or **get on top of** something that you are doing,
you are dealing with it successfully. ❑ ...*the
government's inability to get on top of the situation.*
② PHRASE If one thing is **on top** of another, it is
placed over it or on its highest part. ❑ *He was
asleep on top of the covers.* ③ PHRASE You can use
**on top** or **on top of** to indicate that a particular
problem exists in addition to a number of other
problems. ❑ *We have all the problems a normal family
has, with additional problems on top.* [from Old
English]

**top-down** ADJ In a **top-down** organization, all
the important decisions are made by the most
senior people in the organization. ❑ ...*a traditional
top-down company.*

**top|ic** /tɒpɪk/ (**topics**) N-COUNT A **topic** is a
particular subject that you discuss or write about.
❑ *The weather is a constant topic of conversation in
Alaska.* [from Latin]

**topi|cal** /tɒpɪkᵊl/ ADJ **Topical** is used to describe
something that concerns or relates to events that
are happening at the present time. ❑ *The newscast
covers topical events and entertainment.* [from Latin]

**top|ic sen|tence** (**topic sentences**) N-COUNT A
**topic sentence** is a statement that expresses the
main idea in a short piece of writing such as a
paragraph. [TECHNICAL]

**top|less** /tɒplɪs/ ADJ A person who is **topless** is
not wearing anything on the upper half of their
body. [from Old English]

**topo|graph|ic map** /tɒpəgræfɪk mæp/
(**topographic maps**) N-COUNT A **topographic map**
is a map of an area that shows the height of the
land by means of contour lines.

**top|ple** /tɒpᵊl/ (**topples, toppling, toppled**)
∎ V-I If someone or something **topples**
somewhere, they become unsteady or unstable
and fall over. ❑ *He toppled slowly backwards.*
• **Topple over** means the same as **topple**. ❑ *The tree
is so badly damaged they are worried it might topple over.*
② V-T To **topple** a government or leader, especially
one that is not elected by the people, means to
cause them to lose power. ❑ ...*the revolution which
toppled the government.*

**top se|cret** also **top-secret** ADJ **Top-secret**
information or activity is intended to be kept
completely secret. ❑ ...*top-secret documents.*

**top-shelf** ADJ **Top-shelf** things or people are of
a very high standard or quality. ❑ ...*top-shelf hotel
resorts.*

**To|rah** /tɔrə/ N-PROPER In the Jewish religion,
the **Torah** is the first five books of the Old
Testament of the Bible. ❑ ...*the study of the Torah.*
[from Hebrew]

**torch** /tɔrtʃ/ (**torches**) N-COUNT A **torch** is a long
stick or device with a flame at one end, used to
provide light, to set things on fire, or to melt or cut
something. ❑ *They carried torches to light their way.*
[from Old French]

**tore** /tɔr/ **Tore** is the past tense of **tear**.

**tor|ment** (**torments, tormenting, tormented**)

The noun is pronounced /tɔrmɛnt/. The verb is
pronounced /tɔrmɛnt/.

∎ N-VAR **Torment** is extreme suffering, usually
mental suffering. ❑ *After years of torment, she is
finally at peace.* ❑ ...*the torments of being a writer.*
② V-T If something **torments** you, it causes you
extreme mental suffering. ❑ *At times the memories
returned to torment her.* [from Old French]

**torn** /tɔrn/ **Torn** is the past participle of **tear**.
[from Old English]

**tor|na|do** /tɔrneɪdoʊ/ (**tornadoes** or **tornados**)
N-COUNT A **tornado** is a violent wind storm
consisting of a tall column of air which spins
around very fast and causes a lot of damage. [from
Spanish]

**tor|pe|do** /tɔrpidoʊ/ (**torpedoes, torpedoing,
torpedoed**) ∎ N-COUNT A **torpedo** is a bomb that
is shaped like a tube and that travels under water.
② V-T If a ship **is torpedoed**, it is hit, and usually
sunk, by a torpedo or torpedoes. ❑ *More than a*

**t**

*thousand people died when the Lusitania was torpedoed.*
[from Latin]

**tor|rent** /tɔrənt/ (**torrents**) **1** N-COUNT A **torrent** is a lot of water falling or flowing rapidly or violently. ❑ *Torrents of water flooded into the lake.* **2** N-COUNT A **torrent of** abuse or questions is a lot of abuse or questions directed continuously at someone. ❑ *He turned around and directed a torrent of verbal abuse at me.*
[from French]

**tor|ren|tial** /tɔrɛnʃ°l/ ADJ **Torrential** rain falls very fast and very heavily. ❑ *There was torrential rain across the country.*
[from French]

**tor|so** /tɔrsoʊ/ (**torsos**) N-COUNT Your **torso** is the main part of your body, and does not include your head, arms, and legs. [FORMAL] ❑ *The man had a broad, muscular torso.*
[from Italian]

**tor|toise** /tɔrtəs/ (**tortoises**) N-COUNT A **tortoise** is a slow-moving animal with a shell into which it can pull its head and legs for protection.
[from Old French]

**tor|tu|ous** /tɔrtʃuəs/ **1** ADJ A **tortuous** road is full of bends and twists. ❑ *The only road is a tortuous mountain route.* **2** ADJ A **tortuous** process or piece of writing is very long and complicated. ❑ *...these long and tortuous negotiations.*
[from Late Latin]

**tor|ture** /tɔrtʃər/ (**tortures, torturing, tortured**) V-T If someone **is tortured,** another person deliberately causes them terrible pain, in order to punish them or to make them reveal information. ❑ *In many countries soldiers torture captured enemies to get information.* ● **Torture** is also a noun. ❑ *...cases of torture by the guards.* [from Late Latin]

**toss** /tɔs/ (**tosses, tossing, tossed**) **1** V-T If you **toss** something somewhere, you throw it there lightly, often in a careless way. ❑ *Just toss it in the trash.* **2** V-T If you **toss** your head, you move it backward, quickly and suddenly, often as a way of expressing anger or contempt. ❑ *"I'm sure I don't know," Debbie tossed her head.* **3** V-T In sports and informal situations, if you decide something by **tossing** a coin, you spin a coin into the air and guess which side of the coin will face upward when it lands. ❑ *We tossed a coin to decide who would go out and buy the cakes.* ● **Toss** is also a noun. ❑ *It would be better to decide it on the toss of a coin.* [of Scandinavian origin]

**to|tal** /toʊt°l/ (**totals, totaling** or **totalling, totaled** or **totalled**) **1** N-COUNT A **total** is the number that you get when you add several numbers together or when you count how many things there are in a group. ❑ *The companies have a total of 1,776 employees.* ● **Total** is also an adjective. ❑ *The total cost of the project would be more than $240 million.* **2** PHRASE If there are a number of things **in total,** there are that number when you count or add them all together. ❑ *The business lasted eight years in total.* **3** V-T If several numbers or things **total** a certain figure, that figure is the total of all the numbers or all the things. ❑ *The firm's profits will total $5 million this year.* **4** ADJ **Total** means complete. ❑ *I felt like a total failure.* ● **to|tal|ly** ADV ❑ *...something totally different.* [from Old French]

| Word Partnership | Use *total* with : |
|---|---|
| N. | total **area**, total **population**, sum total **1** <br> total **amount**, total **cost**, total **expenses**, total **sales**, total **savings**, total **value 3** |
| ADJ. | **grand** total **1 3** |

**to|tal eclipse** (**total eclipses**) N-COUNT A **total eclipse of** the sun is an occasion when the moon is between the Earth and the sun, so that for a short time you cannot see any part of the sun. A **total eclipse of** the moon is an occasion when the Earth is between the sun and the moon, so that for a short time you cannot see any part of the moon. Compare **partial eclipse**.

| Word Link | *arian* ≈ believing in, having : **humanit**arian, **totalit**arian, **veget**arian |
|---|---|

**to|tali|tar|ian** /toʊtælɪtɛəriən/ ADJ A **totalitarian** political system is one in which there is only one political party which controls everything and does not allow any opposition parties. ❑ *The country won't return to its totalitarian past.*

**tote bag** (**tote bags**) N-COUNT A **tote bag** is a large strong bag. ❑ *She was carrying a tote bag.*

**tot|ter** /tɒtər/ (**totters, tottering, tottered**) V-I If someone **totters** somewhere, they walk there in an unsteady way. ❑ *She came tottering into the room in her mother's high heels.* [from Old English]

**touch**

❶ VERB AND NOUN USES
❷ PHRASES AND PHRASAL VERBS

❶ **touch** /tʌtʃ/ (**touches, touching, touched**) **1** V-T/V-I If you **touch** something, you put your hand onto it in order to feel it or to make contact with it. ❑ *Her tiny hands gently touched my face.* ❑ *Don't touch!* ● **Touch** is also a noun. ❑ *...a light touch on the face.* **2** V-RECIP; V-T If two things **are touching,** or if one thing **touches** another, their surfaces come into contact with each other. ❑ *Their knees were touching.* ❑ *Her feet touched the floor.* **3** N-UNCOUNT Your sense of **touch** is your ability to tell what something is like when you feel it with your hands. ❑ *Our sense of touch declines with age.* **4** V-I If you **touch on** a particular subject, you mention it briefly. ❑ *The film only touches on these issues.* **5** V-T If something that someone says or does **touches** you, it affects you emotionally, often because that person is suffering or is being very kind. ❑ *Their kindness touched me deeply.* ● **touched** ADJ ❑ *He was touched that we came.* ● **touch|ing** ADJ ❑ *...the touching tale of a wife who nursed the husband she loved.* **6** → see also **touch** **7** N-COUNT A **touch** is a detail which is added to something to improve it. ❑ *They called the event "a tribute to heroes," which was a nice touch.* [from Old French] **8** → see also **touching**

| Word Partnership | Use *touch* with : |
|---|---|
| ADJ. | **gentle** touch, **light** touch ❶ **1** <br> **finishing** touch, **nice** touch, **personal** touch, **soft** touch ❶ **7** |

**❷ touch** /tʌtʃ/ (**touches, touching, touched**)
**1** PHRASE If you are **in touch with** someone, you write, phone, or visit each other regularly. ❑ *We have to keep in touch by phone.* ❑ *I will get in touch with my lawyer about this.* **2** PHRASE If you are **in touch with** a subject or situation, or if someone keeps you **in touch with** it, you know the latest news or information about it. If you are **out of touch with** it, you do not know the latest news or information about it. ❑ *I try to keep in touch with what's happening.* **3** PHRASE If you **lose touch with** someone, you gradually stop writing, phoning, or visiting them. ❑ *In my job you often lose touch with friends.* [from Old French] **4 the finishing touch** → see **finish**
▸ **touch down** PHR-VERB When an aircraft **touches down**, it lands. ❑ *The space shuttle touched down yesterday.*

**touch|screen** /tʌtʃskrɪn/ (**touchscreens**) also **touch-screen** N-COUNT A **touchscreen** is a computer screen that allows the user to give commands to the computer by touching parts of the screen rather than by using a keyboard or mouse. [COMPUTING] ❑ *...touchscreen voting machines.*

**touchy** /tʌtʃi/ (**touchier, touchiest**) ADJ A **touchy** person is easily upset, offended, or irritated. ❑ *She is very touchy about her past.* [from Old French]

**tough** /tʌf/ (**tougher, toughest**) **1** ADJ A **tough** person is strong and determined, and can tolerate difficulty or suffering. ❑ *He built up a reputation as a tough businessman.* ● **tough|ness** N-UNCOUNT ❑ *...a reputation for toughness and determination.* **2** ADJ A **tough** task or problem is difficult to do or solve. ❑ *It was a very tough decision, but we feel we made the right one.* **3** ADJ A **tough** substance is strong and difficult to break, cut, or tear. ❑ *The beans have a tough outer skin.* [from Old English]

| Word Partnership | Use *tough* with : |

| | |
|---|---|
| N. | tough **guy** **1** |
| | tough **choices**, tough **competition**, tough **conditions**, tough **decision**, tough **fight**, tough **going**, tough **job**, tough **luck**, tough **question**, tough **sell**, tough **situation**, tough **time** **2** |
| V. | **get** tough, **talk** tough **1** **2** |
| | **make the** tough **decisions** **2** |

**tough|en** /tʌfᵊn/ (**toughens, toughening, toughened**) **1** V-T/V-I If you **toughen** something or if it **toughens**, you make it stronger so that it will not break easily. ❑ *Months of walking barefoot have toughened his feet.* **2** V-T If an experience **toughens** you, it makes you stronger and more independent in character. ❑ *They believe that fighting toughens boys and shows them how to be men.* ● **Toughen up** means the same as **toughen**. ❑ *He thinks boxing is good for kids, that it toughens them up.* [from Old English]

**tour** /tʊər/ (**tours, touring, toured**) **1** V-T/V-I When people such as musicians, politicians, or theater companies **tour**, they go to several different places, stopping to perform or to meet people. ❑ *A few years ago they toured the country.* ● **Tour** is also a noun. ❑ *Their tour was a sell-out.* ❑ *The band will be going on tour.* **2** N-COUNT A **tour** is a trip to an interesting place or around several interesting places. ❑ *...a tour of the major cities of Europe.* **3** V-T If you **tour** a place, you go on a trip

around it. ❑ *You can tour the site on a bicycle.* [from Old French]

| Word Partnership | Use *tour* with : |

| | |
|---|---|
| N. | **concert** tour, **farewell** tour **1** |
| | tour **bus**, tour **guide**, **museum** tour, **walking** tour, **world** tour **2** |
| V. | **begin** a tour, **finish** a tour **1** **2** |
| | **take** a tour **2** |

**tour guide** (**tour guides**) N-COUNT A **tour guide** is someone who helps tourists who are on vacation or shows them around a place. ❑ *A tour guide will organize activities every day.*

**tour|ism** /tʊərɪzəm/ N-UNCOUNT **Tourism** is the business of providing services for people on vacation, for example, hotels, restaurants, and trips. ❑ *Tourism is important economically.* [from Old French]
→ see **industry**

**tour|ist** /tʊərɪst/ (**tourists**) N-COUNT A **tourist** is a person who is visiting a place for pleasure, especially when they are on vacation. ❑ *...a tourist attraction.* [from Old French]
→ see **city**

**tour|na|ment** /tʊərnəmənt, tɜr-/ (**tournaments**) N-COUNT A **tournament** is a sports competition in which players who win a game continue to play further games in the competition until just one person or team is left. ❑ *...the biggest golf tournament in the world.* [from Old French]

**tour of duty** (**tours of duty**) N-COUNT A soldier's **tour of duty** is a period of time when he or she is involved in a particular mission or stationed in a particular place. ❑ *He served two tours of duty in Vietnam.*

**tout** /taʊt/ (**touts, touting, touted**) V-T If someone **touts** something, they try to sell it or convince people that it is good. ❑ *...ads touting price cuts on over 50,000 items.* [from Old English]

**tow** /toʊ/ (**tows, towing, towed**) V-T If one vehicle **tows** another, it pulls it along behind it. ❑ *He uses the truck to tow his work trailer.* [from Old English]

**to|ward** /tɔrd/ also **towards**

In addition to the uses shown below, **toward** is used in phrasal verbs such as "count toward" and "lean toward."

**1** PREP If you move, look, or point **toward** something or someone, you move, look, or point in their direction. ❑ *They were all moving toward him down the stairs.* ❑ *When he looked toward me, I smiled and waved.* **2** PREP If things develop **toward** a particular situation, that situation becomes nearer in time or more likely to happen. ❑ *The agreement is a major step toward peace.* **3** PREP If you have a particular attitude **toward** something or someone, that is the way you feel about them. ❑ *This man changed my attitude toward religion.* **4** PREP If something happens **toward** a particular time, it happens just before that time. ❑ *There was a forecast of cooler weather toward the end of the week.* **5** PREP If something is **toward** part of a place or thing, it is near that part. ❑ *...a small island toward the eastern shore.* **6** PREP If you give money **toward** something, you give it to help pay for that thing. ❑ *He gave them $50,000 toward a house.* [from Old English]

**t**

**tow|el** /taʊəl/ (**towels, toweling** or **towelling, toweled** or **towelled**) **1** N-COUNT A **towel** is a piece of thick soft cloth that you use to dry yourself. □ *…a bath towel.* □ *…a beach towel.* **2** V-T If you **towel** something, you dry it with a towel. □ *James came out of his bedroom, toweling his wet hair.* □ *I toweled myself dry.* **3** PHRASE If you **throw in the towel**, you stop trying to do something because you realize that you cannot succeed. [INFORMAL] □ *The boys only softball league threw in the towel and accepted girls on their teams.*
[from Old French]
→ see **bathroom**

**tow|er** /taʊər/ (**towers, towering, towered**) **1** N-COUNT A **tower** is a tall, narrow building, that either stands alone or forms part of another building such as a church or castle. □ *…a castle with high towers.* **2** V-I Someone or something that **towers** over surrounding people or things is a lot taller than they are. □ *He stood up and towered over her.* [from Old French]
→ see **computer**

**tow|er|ing** /taʊərɪŋ/ ADJ If you describe something such as a mountain or cliff as **towering**, you mean that it is very tall and therefore impressive. [LITERARY] □ *…towering cliffs which rise straight out of the sea.* [from Old French]

**town** /taʊn/ (**towns**) **1** N-COUNT A **town** is a place with streets and buildings, smaller than a city, where people live and work. □ *…the northern California town of Albany.* **2** N-UNCOUNT You use **town** in order to refer to the town where you live. □ *He doesn't even know when his brother is in town.* [from Old English]

**town hall** (**town halls**) also **Town Hall** N-COUNT A **town hall** is a building or hall used for local government business. □ *The meeting was held in the town hall.*

**town meet|ing** (**town meetings**) N-COUNT A **town meeting** is a meeting held by the residents of a town, or by the people who are eligible to vote in a town.

**town|ship** /taʊnʃɪp/ (**townships**) **1** N-COUNT In the United States and Canada, a **township** is an area of land, especially a part of a county which is organized as a unit of local government. □ *…her 20 years of service with the township and county.* **2** N-COUNT In South Africa, a **township** was a town where only black people lived. □ *…the South African township of Soweto.* [from Old English]

**tox|ic** /tɒksɪk/ ADJ A **toxic** substance is poisonous. □ *…the cost of cleaning up toxic waste.* [from Latin]
→ see **cancer**

**toy** /tɔɪ/ (**toys, toying, toyed**) N-COUNT A **toy** is an object that children play with, for example, a doll or a model car. □ *He was really too old for children's toys.*

▶ **toy with** **1** PHR-VERB If you **toy with** an idea, you consider it casually without making any decisions about it. □ *He toyed with the idea of going to China.* **2** PHR-VERB If you **toy with** food or drink, you do not eat or drink it with any enthusiasm, but only take a bite or a little drink from time to time. □ *She had no appetite, and toyed with the bread and cheese.*

**trace** /treɪs/ (**traces, tracing, traced**) **1** V-T If you **trace** the origin or development of something, you find out or describe how it started or developed. • **Trace back** means the same as **trace**. □ *…residents who trace their families back to Dutch settlers.* **2** V-T If you **trace** someone or something, you find them after looking for them. □ *Police are trying to trace two men seen leaving the house just before 8 a.m.* □ *I am trying to trace my sister.* **3** V-T If you **trace** a picture, you copy it by covering it with a piece of transparent paper and drawing over the lines underneath. □ *She learned to draw by tracing pictures out of old storybooks.* **4** N-COUNT A **trace** of something is a very small amount of it. □ *Wash them in cold water to remove all traces of sand.* [from French]
→ see **draw, fossil**

---

### Word Partnership Use *trace* with :

N. trace *your* **ancestry/origins/roots**, trace **the history of** *something*, trace **the origins/roots of** *something* **1**
  trace **of an accent**, trace **amount**, trace **minerals** **4**

---

**trace gas** (**trace gases**) N-COUNT **Trace gases** are gases that make up less than one percent of the Earth's atmosphere, such as carbon dioxide and methane.

**tra|chea** /treɪkiə/ (**tracheas** or **tracheae** /treɪkiiː/) N-COUNT Your **trachea** is the passage from your **larynx** to your **lungs**. [MEDICAL] [from Medieval Latin]

**track** /træk/ (**tracks, tracking, tracked**) **1** N-COUNT A **track** is a rough, unpaved road or path. □ *We set off once more, over a rough mountain track.* **2** N-COUNT A **track** is a piece of ground that is used for races. □ *…the running track and the gym.* **3** N-COUNT Railroad **tracks** are the rails that a train travels along. □ *A cow stood on the tracks.* **4** N-COUNT A **track** is one of the songs or pieces of music on a CD, record, or tape. □ *I only like two of the ten tracks on this CD.* **5** N-PLURAL **Tracks** are marks left in the ground by the feet of animals or people. □ *The only evidence of the animals was their tracks in the snow.* **6** V-T If you **track** animals or people, you try to find them by following their footprints or other signs. □ *He decided to track this wolf and see where it lived.* **7** → see also **racetrack, soundtrack 8** PHRASE If you **keep track of** a situation or a person, you have accurate information about them all the time. □ *With eleven thousand employees, it's very difficult to keep track of them all.* **9** PHRASE If you **lose track of** someone or something, you no longer know where they are or what is happening. □ *I'm sorry, I guess I lost track of time.* **10** PHRASE If you are **on the right track**, you are acting or progressing in a way that is likely to result in success. □ *Guests are returning in increasing numbers — a sure sign that we are on the right track.* [from Old French]
→ see **fossil, transportation**

▶ **track down** PHR-VERB If you **track down** someone or something, you find them after a difficult or long search. □ *She spent years trying to track down her parents.*

## Word Partnership Use *track* with :

N.     **dirt** track **1** **2**
       track **meet**, track **team** **2**
       **train** track **3**

**track meet** (**track meets**) N-COUNT A **track meet** is an event in which athletes come to a particular place in order to take part in a race or races.

**track rec|ord** (**track records**) N-COUNT The **track record** of a person, company, or product is their past performance, achievements, or failures. ❏ *The job needs someone with a good track record in sales.*

**track|suit** /trǽksut/ (**tracksuits**) also **track suit** N-COUNT A **tracksuit** is a loose, warm suit consisting of pants and a top which people wear to do exercise or to relax.

**tract** /trækt/ (**tracts**) **1** N-COUNT A **tract of** land is a very large area of land. ❏ *A vast tract of land is ready for development.* **2** N-COUNT A **tract** is a system of organs and tubes in an animal's or person's body that has a particular function, especially the function of processing a substance in the body. [MEDICAL] ❏ *Foods are broken down in the digestive tract.* [from Latin]

## Word Link     *tract ≈ dragging, drawing : contract, subtract, tractor*

**trac|tor** /trǽktər/ (**tractors**) **1** N-COUNT A **tractor** is a farm vehicle that is used to pull farm machinery. **2** N-COUNT A **tractor** is a short vehicle with a powerful engine and a driver's cab, used to pull a trailer. ❏ *The truck was an 18-wheeler with a white tractor.* [from Late Latin]
→ see **barn**

**tractor-trailer** (**tractor-trailers**) N-COUNT A **tractor-trailer** is a large truck that is made in two separate sections, a tractor and a trailer, which are joined together by metal bars.

**trade** /treɪd/ (**trades, trading, traded**) **1** V-T; V-RECIP If someone **trades** one thing **for** another or if two people **trade** things, they agree to exchange one thing for the other thing. ❏ *They traded land for goods and money.* ❏ *Kids used to trade baseball cards.* ● **Trade** is also a noun. ❏ *I am willing to make a trade with you.* **2** V-T; V-RECIP If you **trade** places **with** someone or if the two of you **trade** places, you move into the other person's position or situation, and they move into yours. ❏ *Mike asked George to trade places with him.* **3** V-I When people, companies, or countries **trade**, they buy, sell, or exchange goods or services between themselves. [BUSINESS] ❏ *They had years of experience of trading with the West.* ● **Trade** is also a noun. ❏ *Texas has a long history of trade with Mexico.* ❏ *...a new international trade agreement.* ● **trad|ing** N-UNCOUNT ❏ *...trading on the stock exchange.* **4** V-T In professional sports, for example football or baseball, if a player **is traded** from one team to another, they leave one team and begin playing for another. ❏ *He was traded from the Giants to the Yankees.* ❏ *The A's have not won a game since they traded him.* [from Old Saxon]

## Thesaurus     *trade*     Also look up :

V.     barter, exchange, swap **1** **3**

**trade defi|cit** (**trade deficits**) N-COUNT A **trade deficit** is a situation in which a country imports goods worth more than the value of the goods that it exports. [BUSINESS]

**trade|mark** /treɪdmɑrk/ (**trademarks**) N-COUNT A **trademark** is a name or symbol that a company uses on its products and that cannot legally be used by another company. [BUSINESS] ❏ *Kodak is a trademark of Eastman Kodak Company.*

**trad|er** /treɪdər/ (**traders**) N-COUNT A **trader** is a person whose job is to trade in goods or stocks. [BUSINESS] ❏ *Market traders display a selection of the island's produce.* [from Old Saxon]

**trade show** (**trade shows**) N-COUNT A **trade show** is an exhibition where manufacturers show their products to other people in industry and try to get business.

**trade wind** (**trade winds**) also **tradewind** N-COUNT The **trade winds** are winds that blow from east to west near the equator.

**trad|ing card** (**trading cards**) N-COUNT A **trading card** is one of a set of thin pieces of cardboard with a picture relating to a particular theme, such as baseball or football, printed on it, for people to collect and trade with other collectors.

**tra|di|tion** /trədɪ̃ʃᵊn/ (**traditions**) N-VAR A **tradition** is a custom or belief that has existed for a long time. ❏ *...the rich traditions of Afro-Cuban music.* ● **tra|di|tion|al** /trədɪ̃ʃənᵊl/ ADJ ❏ *...traditional teaching methods.* ● **tra|di|tion|al|ly** ADV ❏ *December 26 is traditionally one of the busiest days for malls.* [from Latin]

## Thesaurus     *tradition*     Also look up :

N.     culture, custom, practice, ritual

**traf|fic** /trǽfɪk/ (**traffics, trafficking, trafficked**) **1** N-UNCOUNT **Traffic** refers to all the vehicles that are moving along the roads in a particular area. ❏ *There was heavy traffic on the roads.* ❏ *Traffic was unusually light for that time of day.* **2** N-UNCOUNT **Traffic** refers to the movement of ships, trains, or aircraft between one place and another. ❏ *Air traffic has returned to normal.* **3** N-UNCOUNT **Traffic in** something such as stolen goods is an illegal trade in them. ❏ *...the traffic in stolen paintings.* **4** V-I Someone who **traffics in** something such as stolen goods buys and sells them even though it is illegal to do so. ❏ *He was accused of trafficking in stolen vehicles.* ● **traf|fick|ing** N-UNCOUNT ❏ *...charges of gun trafficking.* ● **traf|fick|er** (**traffickers**) N-COUNT ❏ *...suspected drug traffickers.* [from Old French]
→ see Word Web: **traffic**

**traffic circle** (**traffic circles**) N-UNCOUNT A **traffic circle** is a circular structure in the road at a place where several roads meet. You drive around it until you come to the road you want. ❏ *You need to take a left turn at the traffic circle.*

t

## Word Web traffic

Boston's Southeast Expressway opened in 1959. It was built to handle 75,000 **vehicles** a day. But it wasn't enough and **commuter traffic** crawled. Sometimes it **stalled** completely. The 27 entrance **ramps** and no **breakdown lanes** caused frequent **gridlock**. By the 1990s, **traffic congestion** was even worse. Nearly 200,000 cars were using the **highway** every day and there were constant **traffic jams**. In 1994, a ten-year **road** construction project called the Big Dig began. The project built underground roadways, six-**lane** bridges, and improved **tunnels**. As a result of the project, traffic **flows** more smoothly through the city.

## Word Partnership Use *traffic* with :

ADJ.    **heavy** traffic, **light** traffic, **oncoming** traffic, **stuck in** traffic ◼

N.    traffic **accident**, **city** traffic, traffic **congestion**, traffic **flow**, traffic **pollution**, traffic **problems**, **rush hour** traffic, traffic **safety**, traffic **signals**, traffic **violation** ◼
**air** traffic ◻
**drug** traffic ◼

**traf|fic jam** (**traffic jams**) N-COUNT A **traffic jam** is a long line of vehicles that cannot move forward because there is too much traffic, or because the road is blocked.

**traffic light**

**traf|fic light** (**traffic lights**) N-COUNT **Traffic lights** are the colored lights at the places where roads meet, that control the flow of traffic.

**trag|edy** /trædʒɪdi/ (**tragedies**) ◼ N-VAR A **tragedy** is an extremely sad event or situation. ◻ *They have suffered an enormous personal tragedy.* ◻ N-VAR **Tragedy** is a type of serious drama, usually ending in the death of the main character. ◻ *...the tragedies of Shakespeare.* [from Old French]

**trag|ic** /trædʒɪk/ ◼ ADJ A **tragic** event or situation is extremely sad, usually because it involves death or suffering. ◻ *It was a tragic accident.* ◻ *...the tragic loss of so many lives.* ● **tragi|cal|ly** /trædʒɪkli/ ADV ◻ *He died tragically young.* ◻ ADJ **Tragic** is used to refer to tragedy as a type of literature. ◻ *...Shakespeare's tragic hero, Hamlet.* [from Old French]

**trail** /treɪl/ (**trails, trailing, trailed**) ◼ N-COUNT A **trail** is a rough path across open country or through forests. ◻ *He was walking along a trail through the trees.* ◻ N-COUNT A **trail** is a series of marks or other signs of movement or other activities left by someone or something. ◻ *Everywhere in the house was a sticky trail of orange juice.* ◼ V-T If you **trail** someone or something, you follow them secretly, often by finding the marks or signs that they have left. ◻ *Two detectives were trailing him.* ◼ V-T If you **trail** something, it hangs down loosely behind you as you move along. ◻ *She*

came down the stairs slowly, trailing the coat behind her. ◼ PHRASE If you are **on the trail of** a person or thing, you are trying hard to find them or find out about them. ◻ *The police are already on his trail.* [from Old French]

## Word Partnership Use *trail* with :

N.    **hiking** trail ◼
V.    **follow** a trail ◼ ◼
**leave** a trail, **pick up** a trail ◼

**trail|er** /treɪlər/ (**trailers**) ◼ N-COUNT A **trailer** is a long narrow house made to be driven to a home site, where it becomes a permanent home. ◼ N-COUNT A **trailer** is a temporary vacation home that is pulled by a car to each vacation spot. ◼ N-COUNT A **trailer** is a container on wheels which is pulled by a truck, tractor, or other vehicle and which is used for transporting large or heavy items. ◼ N-COUNT A **trailer** for a movie or television program is a set of very short scenes which are shown to advertise it. [from Old French]

**trail|er park** (**trailer parks**) N-COUNT A **trailer park** is an area where people can pay to park their trailers and live in them.

**trail|er truck** (**trailer trucks**) N-COUNT A **trailer truck** is a truck that is made in two or more sections joined together by metal bars, so that the vehicle can turn more easily.

### train
❶ NOUN USES
❷ VERB USES

❶ **train** /treɪn/ (**trains**) ◼ N-COUNT A **train** is a number of cars or trucks pulled by an engine along a railroad. ◻ *We can catch the early morning train.* ◻ *He arrived in New York by train.* ◼ N-COUNT A **train of** thought or a **train of** events is a connected series of thoughts or events. ◻ *He lost his train of thought for a moment.* [from Old French]
→ see Word Web: **train**
→ see **transportation**

❷ **train** /treɪn/ (**trains, training, trained**) ◼ V-T/ V-I If you **train to** do something, or if someone **trains** you **to** do it, you learn the skills that you need in order to do it. ◻ *Stavros was training to be a priest.* ● **-trained** ADJ ◻ *...a professionally-trained chef.* ● **train|er** (**trainers**) N-COUNT ◻ *...teachers and teacher trainers.* ● **train|ing** N-UNCOUNT ◻ *Kennedy*

had no formal training. **2** V-T/V-I If you **train for** an activity such as a race or if someone **trains** you **for** it, you prepare for it by doing particular physical exercises. □ *Strachan is training for the new season.*
● **trainer** (**trainers**) N-COUNT □ *She went to the gym with her trainer.* ● **training** N-UNCOUNT □ *...keeping fit through exercises and training.* [from Old French]

**trainee** /treɪniː/ (**trainees**) N-COUNT A **trainee** is someone who is employed at a low level in a particular job in order to learn the skills needed for that job. [BUSINESS] □ *He is a 24-year-old management trainee.* [from Old French]

**trait** /treɪt/ (**traits**) N-COUNT A **trait** is a particular characteristic, quality, or tendency that someone or something has and which can be inherited. □ *...personality traits.* [from French]
→ see **culture**

**traitor** /treɪtər/ (**traitors**) N-COUNT A **traitor** is someone who betrays their country, friends, or a group of which they are a member by helping its enemies. □ *There were traitors among us who were sending messages to the enemy.* [from Old French]

**tram** /træm/ (**trams**) **1** N-COUNT A **tram** is a public transportation vehicle, usually powered by electricity, which travels along rails laid in the surface of a street. □ *You can get to the beach by tram.* [from Low German] **2** N-COUNT A **tram** is the same as a **cable car**.
→ see **transportation**

**tramp** /træmp/ (**tramps, tramping, tramped**)
**1** N-COUNT A **tramp** is a person who has no home or job, who travels around and gets money by begging or by doing occasional work. □ *...tramps who sleep outdoors.* **2** V-T/V-I If you **tramp** somewhere, you walk there slowly and with regular, heavy steps, for a long time. □ *They put on their coats and tramped through the falling snow.* [from Middle Low German]

**trample** /træmpᵊl/ (**tramples, trampling, trampled**) **1** V-T/V-I To **trample on** someone's rights or values or to **trample** them means to deliberately ignore or disregard them. □ *They are trampling on the rights of local people.* **2** V-T If someone **is trampled**, they are injured or killed by being stepped on by animals or by other people. □ *Many people were trampled in the panic that followed.* **3** V-T/V-I If you **trample** something or **trample on** it, you step heavily on it and damage it. □ *They don't want people trampling the grass.* [from Middle High German]

**trance** /træns/ (**trances**) N-COUNT If someone is in a **trance**, they seem to be asleep, but they still have their eyes open and can see and hear things. □ *Like a man in a trance, Blake found his way back to his rooms.* [from Old French]

**tranquil** /træŋkwɪl/ ADJ **Tranquil** means calm and peaceful. □ *...the tranquil atmosphere of the library.* ● **tranquillity** /træŋkwɪlɪti/ N-UNCOUNT □ *...the tranquillity of village life.* [from Latin]

**tranquilize** /træŋkwɪlaɪz/ (**tranquilizes, tranquilizing, tranquilized**) V-T To **tranquilize** a person or an animal means to make them become calm, sleepy, or unconscious by means of a drug. [from Latin]

**tranquilizer** /træŋkwɪlaɪzər/ (**tranquilizers**) N-COUNT A **tranquilizer** is a drug that is used to tranquilize people or animals. □ *...a horse tranquilizer.* [from Latin]

**transaction** /trænzækʃᵊn/ (**transactions**) N-COUNT A **transaction** is a piece of business, for example, an act of buying or selling something. [FORMAL, BUSINESS] □ *...a cash transaction.* [from Latin]

---

**Word Partnership**   Use *transaction* with :

| | |
|---|---|
| N. | **cash** transaction, transaction **costs**, transaction **fee** |
| V. | **complete** a transaction |

---

**transatlantic** /trænzətlæntɪk/ ADJ **Transatlantic** flights or signals go across the Atlantic Ocean, usually between the United States and Britain. □ *Many transatlantic flights land there.*

**transcend** /trænsɛnd/ (**transcends, transcending, transcended**) V-T Something that **transcends** normal limits or boundaries goes beyond them, because it is more significant than them. □ *...issues that transcend politics.* [from Latin]

---

**Word Link**   scrib ≈ writing : inscribe, scribble, transcribe

---

**transcribe** /trænskraɪb/ (**transcribes, transcribing, transcribed**) V-T If you **transcribe** a speech or text, you write or type it out, for example, from notes or from a tape recording. □ *She is transcribing his diaries.* [from Latin]

t

---

**Word Web**   train

In sixteenth-century Germany, a **railway** was a horse-drawn **wagon** traveling along wooden **rails**. By the 19th century, **steam locomotives** and **steel rails** had replaced the older system. At first, railroads operated only **freight lines**. Later, they began to run **passenger** trains. And soon **Pullman** cars were added to make overnight trips more comfortable. Today, Japan's bullet trains carry people at speeds up to 300 miles per hour. This type of train doesn't have an engine or use tracks. Instead, an electromagnetic field allows the **cars** to float just above the ground. This electromagnetic field also pushes the train ahead.

*A Japanese Bullet Train.*

## Word Link
*script ≈ writing : manu*script, *script*ure, tran*script*

**tran|script** /trǽnskrɪpt/ (**transcripts**) N-COUNT
A **transcript of** a conversation or speech is a
written text of it, based on a recording or notes.
❑ *A transcript of this program is available through our
website.* [from Latin]

## Word Link
*trans ≈ across : trans*fer, tran*sition,
trans*late

**trans|fer** (**transfers, transferring, transferred**)

The verb is pronounced /trænsfɜ́r/. The noun is
pronounced /trǽnsfɜr/.

**1** V-T/V-I If you **transfer** something or someone
**from** one place **to** another, or they **transfer from**
one place **to** another, they go from the first place
to the second. ❑ *Transfer the meat to a plate and leave
in a warm place.* ● **Transfer** is also a noun. ❑ *Arrange
for the transfer of medical records to your new doctor.*
**2** V-T/V-I If you **are transferred**, or if you **transfer**,
**to** a different job or place, you move to a different
job or place within the same organization. ❑ *I was
transferred to the book department.* ● **Transfer** is also
a noun. ❑ *He told me he was unhappy and wanted a
transfer.* [from Latin]

## Word Partnership
Use *transfer* with :

N. **balance** transfer, transfer **funds**,
transfer **money** **1**
transfer **schools, students** transfer **2**

**trans|form** /trænsfɔ́rm/ (**transforms,
transforming, transformed**) V-T To **transform**
someone or something means to change
them completely. ❑ *The railroad transformed
America.* ❑ *Your body transforms food into energy.*
● **trans|for|ma|tion** /trǽnsfərméɪʃᵊn/
(**transformations**) N-VAR ❑ *…the transformation of a
bedroom into an office.* [from Latin]

**trans|form bounda|ry** (**transform
boundaries**) N-COUNT A **transform boundary** is a
place on the Earth's surface where two tectonic
plates meet and slide past each other. Compare
**plate boundary**. [TECHNICAL]

**trans|fu|sion** /trænsfyúʒᵊn/ (**transfusions**)
N-VAR A blood **transfusion** is a process in which
blood is injected into the body of a person who is
sick or badly injured. [from Latin]

**tran|si|ent** (**transients** /trǽnʃənt/) **1** ADJ
**Transient** is used to describe a situation that
lasts only a short time or is constantly changing.
[FORMAL] ❑ *…the transient nature of fashion.*
● **tran|si|ence** /trǽnʃəns/ N-UNCOUNT ❑ *…the
transience of emotions.* **2** N-COUNT **Transients** are
people who stay in a place for only a short time
and then move somewhere else. [FORMAL] ❑ *…a
dormitory for transients.* [from Latin]

**tran|sis|tor** /trænzɪ́stər/ (**transistors**)
N-COUNT A **transistor** is a small electronic part in
something such as a television or radio, which
controls the flow of electricity.

**trans|it** /trǽnzɪt/ **1** N-UNCOUNT **Transit** is the
carrying of goods or people by vehicle from one
place to another. ❑ *…the transit of goods between the
two countries.* ❑ *…a transit of about 42 minutes.*
**2** PHRASE If people or things are **in transit**, they
are traveling or being taken from one place to

another. **3** ADJ A **transit** area is an area where
people wait or where goods are kept between
different stages of a journey. ❑ *…refugees arriving
at the two transit camps.* **4** N-UNCOUNT **Transit** is a
system for moving people or goods from one place
to another, for example, using buses or trains. ❑ *If
fuel prices go up, transit prices go up.* [from Latin]
→ see **transportation**

**tran|si|tion** /trænzɪ́ʃᵊn/ (**transitions**)
**1** N-VAR **Transition** is the process in which
something changes from one state to another.
❑ *…the transition from dictatorship to democracy.*
● **tran|si|tion|al** ADJ ❑ *…the transitional stage
between the old and new methods.* **2** N-COUNT In
dance and music, a **transition** is a part of a dance
or piece of music where one section ends and
another section begins. [from Latin]

**tran|si|tive** /trǽnzɪtɪv/ ADJ A **transitive** verb
has a direct object. [from Late Latin]

## Word Link
*ator ≈ one who does : cre*ator,
narr*ator, trans*lator

**trans|late** /trænzleɪt/ (**translates, translating,
translated**) **1** V-T/V-I If something said or written
**is translated**, it is said or written again in the
second language. ❑ *Only a small number of Kadare's
books have been translated into English.* ❑ *The Spanish
word "acequia" is translated as "irrigation ditch."* ❑ *The
girls waited for Mr. Esch to translate.* ● **trans|la|tion**
N-UNCOUNT ❑ *The papers have been sent for
translation.* ● **trans|la|tor** (**translators**) N-COUNT
❑ *She works as a translator.* **2** V-T To **translate**
one thing into another means to change it into
something else. ❑ *Your decision must be translated
into action.* [from Latin]

**trans|la|tion** /trænzléɪʃᵊn/ (**translations**)
**1** N-COUNT A **translation** is a piece of writing
or speech that has been put into a different
language. ❑ *…a translation of the Bible.* **2** → see
also **translate** **3** N-VAR In geometry, **translation**
is the change of position of a figure such as a
triangle in which all the points of the figure
are moved the same distance and in the same
direction. [TECHNICAL] [from Latin]

## Word Link
*luc ≈ light : hal*luc*ination,* luc*id,
trans*luc*ent*

**trans|lu|cent** /trænzlúsᵊnt/ ADJ If a material is
**translucent**, some light can pass through it. ❑ *The
roof is made of translucent plastic.* [from Latin]
→ see **pottery**

**trans|mis|sion** /trænzmɪ́ʃᵊn/ (**transmissions**)
**1** N-UNCOUNT The **transmission** of something is
the passing or sending of it to a different person
or place. ❑ *….e-mail and other forms of electronic data
transmission.* **2** N-UNCOUNT The **transmission** of
television or radio programs is the broadcasting of
them. ❑ *The transmission of the program was canceled.*
**3** N-COUNT A **transmission** is a broadcast.
❑ *…foreign television transmissions.* **4** N-UNCOUNT
**Transmission** is the passage of light through
matter. [from Latin]

**trans|mit** /trænzmɪ́t/ (**transmits, transmitting,
transmitted**) **1** V-T/V-I When radio and
television programs, computer data, or other
electronic messages **are transmitted**, they are
sent using wires, radio waves, or satellites. ❑ *The
game was transmitted live.* ❑ *…the best way to transmit*

certain types of data. **2** V-T If one person or animal **transmits** a disease to another, they have the disease and cause the other person or animal to have it. [FORMAL] ❑ ...insects that transmit disease to humans. [from Latin]

**trans|mit|ter** /trænzmɪtər/ (**transmitters**) N-COUNT A **transmitter** is a piece of equipment that is used for broadcasting television or radio programs. ❑ ...a homemade radio transmitter. [from Latin]
→ see **cellphone, radio**

**trans|par|en|cy** /trænspɛərənsi, -pær-/ (**transparencies**) **1** N-COUNT A **transparency** is a small piece of photographic film with a frame around it which can be projected onto a screen so that you can see the picture. ❑ ...transparencies of famous places. **2** N-UNCOUNT **Transparency** is the quality that an object or substance has when you can see through it. ❑ ...the transparency of water. [from Medieval Latin]

**trans|par|ent** /trænspɛərənt, -pær-/ **1** ADJ If an object or substance is **transparent**, you can see through it. ❑ ...a sheet of transparent plastic. **2** ADJ If a situation, system, or activity is **transparent**, it is easily understood or recognized. ❑ The company has to make its operations as transparent as possible. [from Medieval Latin]
→ see **glass**

**tran|spi|ra|tion** /trænspɪreɪʃ³n/ N-UNCOUNT **Transpiration** is the process by which plants release water vapor into the air through their leaves. [TECHNICAL] [from Medieval Latin]

**tran|spire** /trænspaɪər/ (**transpires, transpiring, transpired**) **1** V-T When **it transpires that** something is true or correct, people discover that it is true or correct. [FORMAL] ❑ It transpired that there was something wrong with the roof. **2** V-I When something **transpires**, it happens. ❑ I don't know what transpired at the meeting. [from Medieval Latin]
→ see **water**

**trans|plant** (**transplants, transplanting, transplanted**)

The noun is pronounced /trænsplænt/. The verb is pronounced /trænsplænt/.

**1** N-VAR A **transplant** is a medical operation in which a part of a person's body is replaced because it is diseased. ❑ ...a heart transplant. **2** V-T To **transplant** something or someone means to

move them to a different place. ❑ ...an operation to transplant a kidney.
→ see **donor, hospital**

**tran|spond|er** /trænspɒndər/ (**transponders**) N-COUNT A **transponder** is a type of radio transmitter that transmits signals automatically when it receives particular signals.

**trans|port** (**transports, transporting, transported**)

The verb is pronounced /trænspɔrt/. The noun is pronounced /trænspɔrt/.

V-T To **transport** people or goods somewhere is to take them from one place to another in a vehicle. ❑ Buses transported passengers to the town. [from Latin]

**trans|por|ta|tion** /trænspərteɪʃ³n/ **1** N-UNCOUNT **Transportation** refers to any type of vehicle that you can travel in or carry goods in. ❑ The company will provide transportation. **2** N-UNCOUNT **Transportation** is a system for taking people or goods from one place to another, for example, using buses or trains. ❑ ...public transportation. **3** N-UNCOUNT **Transportation** is the activity of taking goods or people from one place to another in a vehicle. ❑ ...transportation costs. [from Latin]
→ see Word Web: **transportation**

**trans|ver|sal** /trænzvɜrs³l/ (**transversals**) N-COUNT A **transversal** is a straight line that crosses two or more other lines. [TECHNICAL] [from Latin]

**trans|verse wave** /trænzvɜrs weɪv/ (**transverse waves**) N-COUNT **Transverse waves** are waves, such as those in water, in which the material that the waves are passing through moves at right angles to the waves. Compare **longitudinal wave**. [TECHNICAL]

**trap** /træp/ (**traps, trapping, trapped**) **1** N-COUNT A **trap** is a device for catching animals. ❑ Nathan's dog got caught in a trap. **2** V-T To **trap** animals means to catch them using traps. ❑ People were encouraged to trap and kill mice. **3** N-COUNT A **trap** is a trick that is intended to catch or deceive someone. ❑ He suspected a police trap. **4** V-T If someone **traps** you, they trick you so that you do or say something that you do not want to. ❑ Were you trying to trap her into making an admission? **5** V-T If you **are trapped** somewhere, something falls onto you or blocks your way and

---

## Word Web    transportation

**Mass transportation** began more than 200 years ago. By 1830, there were horse-drawn **streetcars** in New York City and New Orleans. They ran on **rails** built into the **right of way** of city streets. The first electric **tram** opened in Berlin in 1881. Later, **buses** became more popular because they didn't require **tracks**. Today, **commuter trains** link **suburbs** to cities everywhere. Many large cities also have an underground train system. It may be called the **subway, metro,** or **tube**. In cities with steep hills, **cable cars** are a popular form of mass **transit**.

prevents you from moving. ❏ *The train was trapped underground by a fire.* ❏ *The car turned over, trapping both men.*
[from Old English]

**Word Partnership**    Use *trap* with :

v.    **avoid a** trap, **caught in a** trap, **fall into a** trap, **set a** trap 🔟 🔢

**trap|pings** /trǽpɪŋz/ N-PLURAL The **trappings** of power, wealth, or a particular job are the extra things, such as decorations and luxury items, that go with it. ❏ *The family evidently loved the trappings of power.*

**trash** /trǽʃ/ 🔟 N-UNCOUNT **Trash** consists of unwanted things or waste material such as used paper, empty containers and bottles, and waste food. ❏ *The yards are full of trash.* 🔢 N-UNCOUNT If you say that something such as a book, painting, or movie is **trash**, you mean that it is of very bad quality. [INFORMAL] ❏ *Pop music doesn't have to be trash.* 🔣 N-SING **The trash** means the trash can. ❏ *I threw it in the trash.*

**Thesaurus**    *trash*    Also look up :

N.    debris, garbage, junk, litter 🔟

**trash can** (**trash cans**) N-COUNT A **trash can** is a large round container which people put their trash in and which is usually kept outside their house. ❏ *The trash can is full and needs to be emptied immediately.*

**trash|y** /trǽʃi/ (**trashier, trashiest**) ADJ If you describe something as **trashy**, you think it is of poor quality. [INFORMAL, DISAPPROVAL] ❏ *I was reading some trashy romance novel.*

**trau|ma** /trɔ́umə, trɔ́-/ (**traumas**) N-VAR **Trauma** is a very severe shock or very upsetting experience, which may cause psychological damage. ❏ *I've been through the trauma of divorce.* [from Greek]

**trau|mat|ic** /trəmǽtɪk/ ADJ A **traumatic** experience is very shocking and upsetting, and may cause psychological damage. ❏ *I suffered a nervous breakdown. It was a traumatic experience.* [from Greek]

**trav|el** /trǽvᵊl/ (**travels, traveling** or **travelling, traveled** or **travelled**) 🔟 V-T/V-I If you **travel**, you go from one place to another, often to a place that is far away. ❏ *You could travel to Nova Scotia tomorrow.* ❏ *I've been traveling all day.* ❏ *Students often travel hundreds of miles to get here.* 🔢 N-UNCOUNT **Travel** is the activity of traveling. ❏ *Information on travel in New Zealand is available at the hotel.* ❏ *He hated air travel.* 🔣 V-I When light or sound from one place reaches another, you say that it **travels** to the other place. ❏ *When sound travels through water, strange things can happen.* 🔟 N-PLURAL Someone's **travels** are the trips that they make to places a long way from their home. ❏ *He collects souvenirs on his travels abroad.*
[from Old French]

**Thesaurus**    *travel*    Also look up :

V.    explore, trek, visit 🔟
N.    expedition, journey, trip 🔢

**Word Partnership**    Use *travel* with :

N.    travel **the world** 🔟
     **air** travel, travel **arrangements**, travel **books, car** travel, travel **delays**, travel **expenses**, travel **guide**, travel **industry**, travel **insurance**, travel **plans**, travel **reports**, travel **reservations** 🔢
ADV.    travel **abroad**, travel **overseas** 🔟 🔢

**trav|el agen|cy** (**travel agencies**) N-COUNT A **travel agency** or **travel agent's** is a business which makes arrangements for people's vacations and trips.

**trav|el agent** (**travel agents**) N-COUNT A **travel agent** is a person or business that arranges people's vacations and trips.

**trav|el|er** /trǽvələr/ (**travelers**) also **traveller** N-COUNT A **traveler** is a person who is on a trip or a person who travels a lot. ❏ *...airline travelers.* [from Old French]

**trav|el|er's check** (**traveler's checks**) N-COUNT **Traveler's checks** are special checks that you can use as cash or exchange for the currency of the country that you are in when you travel.

**trav|erse** /trǽvɜrs, trəvɜ́rs/ (**traverses, traversing, traversed**) V-T If someone or something **traverses** an area of land or water, they go across it. [LITERARY] ❏ *I traversed the narrow bridge.* [from Old French]

**trav|es|ty** /trǽvəsti/ (**travesties**) N-COUNT If you describe something as a **travesty of** another thing, you mean that it is a very bad representation of that other thing. ❏ *The movie was a travesty of the book.* [from French]

**trawl|er** /trɔ́lər/ (**trawlers**) N-COUNT A **trawler** is a fishing boat with large nets. [from Middle Dutch]

**tray** /treɪ/ (**trays**) N-COUNT A **tray** is a flat piece of wood, plastic, or metal which is used for carrying things, especially food and drinks. [from Old English]

**treach|er|ous** /trɛ́tʃərəs/ 🔟 ADJ If you describe someone as **treacherous**, you mean that they are likely to betray you and cannot be trusted. ❏ *He left his political party because of its treacherous leaders.* 🔢 ADJ If you say that something is **treacherous**, you mean that it is very dangerous and unpredictable. ❏ *The current of the river is fast flowing and treacherous.* [from Old French]

**treach|ery** /trɛ́tʃəri/ N-UNCOUNT **Treachery** is behavior or an action in which someone betrays their country or betrays a person who trusts them. ❏ *He was deeply wounded by the treachery of old friends.* [from Old French]

**tread** /trɛ́d/ (**treads, treading, trod, trodden**) 🔟 N-VAR The **tread** of a tire or shoe is the pattern of thin lines cut into its surface that stops it from slipping. ❏ *The tires had a good depth of tread.* 🔢 V-I If you **tread** in a particular way, you walk that way. [LITERARY] ❏ *She trod softly up the stairs.* 🔣 V-I If you **tread** carefully, you behave in a careful or cautious way. ❏ *If you are hoping to form a new relationship, tread carefully and slowly to begin with.* [from Old English]

**tread|mill** /trɛ́dmɪl/ (**treadmills**) N-COUNT 🔟 N-COUNT A **treadmill** is a piece of equipment, for example, an exercise machine, consisting of a wheel with steps around its edge or a continuous moving belt. The weight of a person or animal walking on it causes the wheel or belt to turn. **2** You can refer to a task or a job as a **treadmill** when you have to keep doing it although it is unpleasant and exhausting. ❑ ...*an endless treadmill to pay for rent and food.*

**trea|son** /trˈizᵊn/ N-UNCOUNT **Treason** is the crime of betraying your country. ❑ *They were found guilty of treason.* [from Old French]

**treas|ure** /trˈɛʒər/ (**treasures, treasuring, treasured**) **1** N-UNCOUNT In stories, **treasure** is a collection of valuable old objects, such as gold coins and jewels. [LITERARY] ❑ ...*buried treasure.* **2** N-COUNT **Treasures** are valuable objects, especially works of art and items of historical value. ❑ *The house was large and full of art treasures.* **3** V-T If you **treasure** something that you have, you keep it or care for it carefully because it gives you great pleasure and you think it is very special. ❑ *She treasures her memories of those happy days.* ● **treas|ured** ADJ ❑ ...*my most treasured possessions.* [from Old French]

**treas|ur|er** /trˈɛʒərər/ (**treasurers**) N-COUNT The **treasurer** of a society or organization is the person in charge of its finances. [from Old French]

**treas|ury bill** /trˈɛʒəri bɪl/ (**treasury bills**) also **Treasury bill** or **Treasury Bill** N-COUNT A **treasury bill** is a short-term bond that is issued by the United States government in order to raise money.

**treat** /trˈit/ (**treats, treating, treated**) **1** V-T If you **treat** someone or something in a particular way, you behave toward them or deal with them in that way. ❑ *All faiths should be treated with respect.* ❑ *Stop treating me like a child.* **2** V-T When a doctor or nurse **treats** a patient or an illness, he or she tries to make the patient well again. ❑ *Doctors treated her with medication.* ❑ *The boy was treated for a minor head wound.* **3** V-T If something **is treated with** a particular substance, the substance is put onto or into it, for example in order to clean or protect it. ❑ *The fields are treated with insecticide.* **4** V-T If you **treat** someone **to** something special, you buy it or arrange it for them. ❑ *She was always treating him to ice cream.* ❑ *Tomorrow I'll treat myself to a day's gardening.* ● **Treat** is also a noun. ❑ *Lesley returned from town with a special treat for him.* [from Old French]

**Word Partnership** Use *treat* with:

ADV.  treat **differently,** treat **equally,** treat **fairly,** treat **well** **1**
PREP. treat **with contempt/dignity/ respect** **1**
N.    treat **people,** treat **women** **1** **2** treat **AIDS,** treat **cancer,** treat **a disease,** **doctor's** treat **2**

**treat|ment** /trˈitmənt/ (**treatments**) **1** N-VAR **Treatment** is medical attention given to a sick or injured person or animal. ❑ *Many patients are not getting the medical treatment they need.* **2** N-UNCOUNT Your **treatment** of someone is the way you behave toward them or deal with them. ❑ *We don't want any special treatment.* [from Old French]
→ see **cancer, illness**

**Word Partnership** Use *treatment* with:

V.    **get/receive** treatment, **give** treatment, **undergo** treatment **1**
N.    treatment **of addiction, AIDS** treatment, **cancer** treatment, treatment **center,** treatment **of an illness** **1** treatment **of prisoners** **2**
ADJ.  **effective** treatment, **medical** treatment **1** **better** treatment, **equal/unequal** treatment, **fair** treatment, **humane** treatment, **special** treatment **2**

**trea|ty** /trˈiti/ (**treaties**) N-COUNT A **treaty** is a written agreement between countries. ❑ ...*a treaty on global warming.* [from Old French]

**tre|ble** /trˈɛbᵊl/ N-UNCOUNT On a stereo system or radio, the **treble** is the ability to reproduce the higher musical notes. [from Old French]

**tre|ble clef** (**treble clefs**) N-COUNT A **treble clef** is a symbol that you use when writing music in order to show that the notes on the staff are above middle C.

**tree** /trˈi/ (**trees**) N-COUNT A **tree** is a tall plant that has a hard trunk, branches, and leaves. ❑ *I planted those apple trees.* [from Old English]
→ see Word Web: **tree**
→ see **forest, plant**

t

## Word Web    tree

**Trees** are one of the oldest living things. They are also the largest **plant.** Some scientists believe that the largest living thing on Earth is a coniferous giant redwood tree named General Grant. Other scientists think a huge **grove** of **deciduous** aspen trees known as Pando. This grove is a single plant because all of the trees grow from the root system of just one tree. Pando covers more than 106 acres. Some aspen trees **germinate** from seeds, but most come from natural cloning. In this process the parent tree sends up new **sprouts** from its root system. Fossil records show tree clones may live up to a million years.

## Word Web    trial

Many countries have **trial** by jury. The **judge** begins by explaining the **charges** against the **defendant**. Next the defendant **pleads guilty** or not guilty. Then the **lawyers** for the **plaintiff** and the defendant present **evidence**. Both **attorneys** interview **witnesses**. They can also question each other's **clients**. Sometimes the lawyers **cross-examine** witnesses their **testimony**. When the lawyers finish, the **jury** meets to **deliberate**. They deliver their **verdict**. If the jury says the defendant is guilty, the judge **pronounces** the **sentence**. Sometimes the defendant may be able to **appeal** the verdict and ask for a new trial.

**trek** /trɛk/ (**treks, trekking, trekked**) V-I If you **trek** somewhere, you go on a journey across difficult country, usually on foot. ❑ *...trekking through the jungle.* ● **Trek** is also a noun. ❑ *He is on a trek through the desert.* [from Afrikaans]

**trem|ble** /ˈtrɛmbəl/ (**trembles, trembling, trembled**) ◼ V-I If you **tremble**, you shake slightly because you are frightened or cold. ❑ *He began to tremble all over.* ❑ *Lisa was white and trembling with anger.* ◼ V-I If something **trembles**, it shakes slightly. [LITERARY] ❑ *He felt the earth tremble under him.* [from Old French]

**tre|men|dous** /trɪˈmɛndəs/ ◼ ADJ You use **tremendous** to emphasize how strong a feeling or quality is, or how large an amount is. ❑ *I felt a tremendous pressure on my chest.* ● **tre|men|dous|ly** ADV ❑ *I thought they played tremendously well, didn't you?* ◼ ADJ You can describe someone or something as **tremendous** when you think they are very good or very impressive. ❑ *I thought her performance was absolutely tremendous.* [from Latin]

**trem|or** /ˈtrɛmər/ (**tremors**) ◼ N-COUNT A **tremor** is a small earthquake. ❑ *The earthquake sent tremors through the region.* ◼ N-COUNT A **tremor** is a shaking of your body or voice that you cannot control. ❑ *The old man has a tremor in his hands.* [from Latin]

**trench** /trɛntʃ/ (**trenches**) N-COUNT A **trench** is a long narrow channel dug in the ground. [from Old French]

**trend** /trɛnd/ (**trends**) N-COUNT A **trend** is a change or development toward something different. ❑ *...a trend toward part-time employment.* [from Old English]

**trendy** /ˈtrɛndi/ (**trendier, trendiest**) ADJ If you say that something or someone is **trendy**, you mean that they are very fashionable and modern.

[INFORMAL] ❑ *...a trendy Seattle night club.* [from Old English]

**trepi|da|tion** /trɛpɪˈdeɪʃən/ N-UNCOUNT **Trepidation** is fear or anxiety about something that you are going to do or experience. [FORMAL] ❑ *I opened the door with some trepidation.* [from Latin]

**tres|pass** /ˈtrɛspəs, -pæs/ (**trespasses, trespassing, trespassed**) V-I If someone **trespasses**, they go onto someone else's land without their permission. ❑ *They were trespassing on private property.* [from Old French]

**tri|ad** /ˈtraɪæd/ (**triads**) N-COUNT In music, a **triad** is a chord consisting of three notes. [TECHNICAL] [from Late Latin]

**tri|al** /ˈtraɪəl/ (**trials**) ◼ N-VAR A **trial** is a formal meeting in a law court, at which a judge and jury listen to evidence and decide whether a person is guilty of a crime. If someone is **on trial**, they are being judged in this way. ❑ *New evidence showed the witness lied at the trial.* ❑ *He is currently on trial for burglary.* ◼ N-VAR A **trial** is an experiment in which you test something by using it or doing it for a period of time to see how well it works. If something is **on trial**, it is being tested in this way. ❑ *The drug is being tested in clinical trials.* ❑ *I took the car out for a trial on the roads.* ◼ PHRASE If you do something **by trial and error**, you try several different methods of doing it until you find the method that works best. ❑ *Many life-saving drugs were discovered by trial and error.*
→ see Word Web: **trial**

**tri|an|gle** /ˈtraɪæŋgəl/ (**triangles**) N-COUNT A **triangle** is a shape with three straight sides. ❑ *Its outline forms a triangle.* ● **tri|an|gu|lar** /traɪˈæŋgyələr/ ADJ ❑ *...a triangular roof.* [from Latin]
→ see **circle, shape**

T

**tribe** /traɪb/ (**tribes**) N-COUNT **Tribe** is sometimes used to refer to a group of people of the same race, language, and customs, especially in a developing country. Some people disapprove of this use. ❑ ...*three-hundred members of the Xhosa tribe.* ● **trib|al** /traɪbᵊl/ ADJ ❑ ...*tribal lands.* [from Latin]

**tribu|la|tion** /trɪbyəleɪʃᵊn/ (**tribulations**) N-VAR You can refer to the suffering or difficulty that you experience in a particular situation as **tribulations**. [FORMAL] ❑ ...*the trials and tribulations of everyday life.* [from Old French]

**tri|bu|nal** /traɪbyuːnᵊl/ (**tribunals**) N-COUNT A **tribunal** is a special court or committee that is appointed to deal with particular problems. ❑ *His case comes before an industrial tribunal in March.* [from Latin]

**tribu|tary** /trɪbyəteri/ (**tributaries**) N-COUNT A **tributary** is a stream or river that flows into a larger one.

**trib|ute** /trɪbyuːt/ (**tributes**) ■ N-VAR A **tribute** is something that you say, do, or make to show your admiration and respect for someone. ❑ *The song is a tribute to Roy Orbison.* ■ N-SING If one thing is **a tribute to** another, the first thing is the result of the second and shows how good it is. ❑ *His success has been a tribute to hard work.* [from Latin]

**trick** /trɪk/ (**tricks, tricking, tricked**) ■ V-T If someone **tricks** you, they deceive you, often in order to make you do something. ❑ *Stephen is going to be very upset when he finds out how you tricked him.* ❑ *His family tricked him into going camping.* ● **Trick** is also a noun. ❑ *We are playing a trick on a man who keeps bothering me.* ■ N-COUNT A **trick** is a clever or skillful action that someone does in order to entertain people. ❑ *He shows me card tricks.* ■ N-COUNT A **trick** is a clever way of doing something. ❑ *I use a trick of my mother's for perfect mashed potatoes.* ■ PHRASE If something **does the trick**, it achieves what you wanted. [INFORMAL] ❑ *Sometimes a few words will do the trick.* [from Old Northern French]

**trick|le** /trɪkᵊl/ (**trickles, trickling, trickled**) ■ V-T/V-I When a liquid **trickles**, or when you **trickle** it, it flows slowly in a thin stream. ❑ *A tear trickled down the old man's cheek.* ● **Trickle** is also a noun. ❑ *There was not even a trickle of water.* ■ V-I When people or things **trickle** in a particular direction, they move there slowly in small groups or amounts, rather than all together. ❑ *Money is already trickling in.* ● **Trickle** is also a noun. ❑ *The flood of cars has now slowed to a trickle.*

**tricky** /trɪki/ (**trickier, trickiest**) ADJ A **tricky** task or problem is difficult to deal with. ❑ *Parking can be tricky downtown.* [from Old Northern French]

**tri|col|or** /traɪkʌlər/ (**tricolors**) N-COUNT A **tricolor** is a flag which is made up of blocks of three different colors, such as the Mexican flag.

**tried** /traɪd/ ■ ADJ **Tried** is used in the expressions **tried and tested** and **tried and true**, which describe a product or method that has already been used and has been found to be successful. ❑ ...*over 1,000 tried-and-tested recipes.* [from Old French] ■ → see also **try**

**tri|fle** /traɪfᵊl/ (**trifles**) ■ N-COUNT A **trifle** is something that is not considered important. ❑ *He had no money to spare on trifles.* ■ N-VAR **Trifle** is a cold dessert made of layers of sponge cake, fruit gelatin, fruit, and custard, and usually covered with cream. ❑ ...*a bowl of trifle.* [from Old French]

**trig|ger** /trɪgər/ (**triggers, triggering, triggered**) ■ N-COUNT The **trigger** of a gun is a small lever which you pull to fire it. ❑ *A man pointed a gun at them and pulled the trigger.* ■ V-T To **trigger** a bomb or system means to cause it to work. ❑ *The thieves triggered the alarm.* ■ V-T If something **triggers** an event or situation, it causes it to begin to happen or exist. ❑ ...*the incident which triggered the outbreak of the war.* ● **Trigger off** means the same as **trigger**. ❑ *It is still not clear what triggered off the demonstrations.* ■ N-COUNT If something acts as a **trigger for** another thing such as an illness, event, or situation, the first thing causes the second thing to begin to happen or exist. ❑ *Stress may be a trigger for these illnesses.* [from Dutch]

**tril|lion** /trɪlyən/ (**trillions**)

The plural form is **trillion** after a number, or after a word or expression referring to a number, such as "several" or "a few."

NUM A **trillion** is 1,000,000,000,000. ❑ ...*a 4 trillion dollar debt.* [from French]

**tril|ogy** /trɪlədʒi/ (**trilogies**) N-COUNT A **trilogy** is a series of three books, plays, or movies that have the same subject or the same characters. ❑ ...*Tolkien's trilogy, "The Lord of the Rings."* [from Greek]

**trim** /trɪm/ (**trimmer, trimmest, trims, trimming, trimmed**) ■ ADJ Something that is **trim** is neat and attractive. ❑ *The neighbors' gardens were trim and neat.* ■ ADJ If someone has a **trim** figure, they are slim. ❑ ...*a trim young woman.* ■ V-T If you **trim** something, you cut off small amounts of it in order to make it look neater. ❑ *My friend trims my hair every eight weeks.* ● **Trim** is also a noun. ❑ *His hair needed a trim.* ■ V-T If something such as a piece of clothing **is trimmed with** a type of material or design, it is decorated with it, usually along its edges. ❑ ...*jackets which are trimmed with ribbon.* ■ N-VAR The **trim** on something such as a piece of clothing is a decoration along its edges in a different color or material. ❑ ...*a white scarf with black trim.* [from Old English]

**tri|mes|ter** /traɪmɛstər/ (**trimesters**) ■ N-COUNT A **trimester** of a pregnancy is one of the three periods of three months into which it is divided. ❑ ...*the end of the first trimester.* ■ N-COUNT In some colleges and universities, a **trimester** is one of the three main periods into which the year is divided. [from French]

**trim|ming** /trɪmɪŋ/ (**trimmings**) ■ N-VAR The **trimming** on something such as a piece of

**t**

clothing is a decoration in a different color or material. ❑ ...*the lace trimming on her nightgown.* **2** N-PLURAL **Trimmings** are pieces of something, usually food, which are left over after you have cut what you need. ❑ *Use the pastry trimmings to decorate the pie.* [from Old English]

**trio** /trↄʊ/ (**trios**) N-COUNT A **trio** is a group of three people, especially musicians or singers. ❑ ...*American songs from a Texas trio.* [from Italian]

**trip** /trↄp/ (**trips, tripping, tripped**) **1** N-COUNT A **trip** is a journey that you make to a particular place. ❑ *We're taking a trip to Montana.* ❑ *On Thursday we went out on a day trip.* **2** → see also **round trip** **3** V-I If you **trip** when you are walking, you knock your foot against something and fall or nearly fall. ❑ *She tripped and broke her hip.* • **Trip up** means the same as **trip.** ❑ *I tripped up and hurt my foot.* **4** V-T If you **trip** someone who is walking or running, you put your foot or something else in front of them, so that they knock their own foot against it and fall or nearly fall. ❑ *One guy stuck his foot out and tried to trip me.* • **Trip up** means the same as **trip.** ❑ *He made a sudden dive for Uncle Jim's legs to try to trip him up.* [from Old French]

---

**Word Partnership** Use *trip* with :

| | |
|---|---|
| N. | **boat** trip, **bus** trip, **business** trip, **camping** trip, **field** trip, trip **home,** **return** trip, **shopping** trip, **train** trip, **vacation** trip **1** |
| V. | **cancel** a trip, **make** a trip, **plan** a trip, **return from** a trip, **take** a trip **1** |
| ADJ. | **free** trip, **last** trip, **long** trip, **next** trip, **recent** trip, **safe** trip, **short** trip **1** |

---

**tri|ple** /trↄpᵊl/ (**triples, tripling, tripled**) **1** ADJ **Triple** means consisting of three things or parts. ❑ ...*a triple somersault.* **2** V-T/V-I If something **triples** or if you **triple** it, it becomes three times as large in size or number. ❑ *I got a fantastic new job and my salary tripled.* ❑ *The exhibition has tripled in size from last year.* [from Latin]

**tri|ple me|ter** (**triple meters**) N-VAR Music that is written in **triple meter** has a beat that is repeated in groups of three. Compare **duple meter.** [TECHNICAL]

**tri|plet** /trↄplↄt/ (**triplets**) N-COUNT **Triplets** are three children born at the same time to the same mother.

**tri|pod** /trↄpↄd/ (**tripods**) N-COUNT A **tripod** is a stand with three legs that is used to support something such as a camera or a telescope. [from Latin]

**tri|umph** /trↄↄmf/ (**triumphs, triumphing, triumphed**) **1** N-VAR A **triumph** is a great success or achievement. ❑ *The championships were a personal triumph for the coach.* **2** N-UNCOUNT **Triumph** is a feeling of great satisfaction and pride resulting from a success or victory. ❑ ...*her sense of triumph.* **3** V-I If someone or something **triumphs,** they win a great victory or succeed in overcoming something. ❑ *The movie is about good triumphing over evil.* [from Old French]

**tri|um|phant** /trↄↄmfənt/ ADJ Someone who is **triumphant** has gained a victory or succeeded in something and feels very happy about it. ❑ *The captain's voice was triumphant.* • **tri|um|phant|ly**

ADV ❑ *They marched triumphantly into the capital.* [from Old French]

**trivia** /trↄviə/ N-UNCOUNT **Trivia** is unimportant facts or details that are interesting rather than serious or useful. ❑ *The two men chatted about trivia.* [from New Latin]

**triv|ial** /trↄviəl/ ADJ If you describe something as **trivial,** you think that it is unimportant and not serious. ❑ ...*trivial details.* [from Latin]

**trod** /trↄd/ **Trod** is the past tense of **tread.** [from Old English]

**trod|den** /trↄdᵊn/ **Trodden** is the past participle of **tread.** [from Old English]

**trol|ley** /trↄli/ (**trolleys**) N-COUNT A **trolley** or **trolley car** is an electric vehicle for carrying people which travels on rails in the streets of a city or town. ❑ *He took a northbound trolley on State Street.*

**trom|bone** /trↄmboↄn/ (**trombones**) N-VAR A **trombone** is a brass musical instrument which you play by blowing into it and sliding part of it backward and forward. ❑ *Her husband played the trombone.* [from Italian]
→ see **brass, orchestra**

**troop** /trↄp/ (**troops, trooping, trooped**) **1** N-PLURAL **Troops** are soldiers. ❑ ...*35,000 troops from a dozen countries.* **2** N-COUNT A **troop** is a group of soldiers. ❑ ...*a troop of American marines.* **3** V-I If people **troop** somewhere, they walk there in a group. [INFORMAL] ❑ *They all trooped back to the house for a rest.* [from French]
→ see **army**

**troop|er** /trↄpər/ (**troopers**) **1** N-COUNT In the United States, a **trooper** is a police officer in a state police force. ❑ *He considered becoming a state trooper.* **2** N-COUNT; N-TITLE A **trooper** is a soldier of low rank in the cavalry or in an armored regiment in the army. ❑ ...*a trooper from the 7th Cavalry.* [from French]

**tro|phy** /troↄfi/ (**trophies**) N-COUNT A **trophy** is a prize such as a cup, given to the winner of a competition. ❑ *The special trophy for the best rider went to Chris Read.* [from French]

**tropi|cal** /trↄpↄkᵊl/ ADJ **Tropical** means belonging to or typical of the tropics. ❑ ...*tropical diseases.* [from Late Latin]
→ see **disaster, habitat, hurricane**

**tropi|cal de|pres|sion** (**tropical depressions**) N-COUNT A **tropical depression** is a system of thunderstorms that begins in the tropics and has relatively low wind speeds. It is the second stage in the development of a hurricane.

**tropi|cal dis|turb|ance** (**tropical disturbances**) N-COUNT A **tropical disturbance** is a system of thunderstorms that begins in the tropics and lasts for more than 24 hours. It is the first stage in the development of a hurricane.

**tropi|cal storm** (**tropical storms**) N-COUNT A **tropical storm** is a system of thunderstorms that begins in the tropics and has relatively high wind speeds. It is the third stage in the development of a hurricane.

**tropi|cal zone** (**tropical zones**) N-COUNT The **tropical zone** is the part of the Earth's surface near the equator, where the climate is hot and wet.

**trop|ics** /trↄpↄks/ N-PLURAL **The tropics** are the hottest parts of the world, near the equator.

❑ *Being in the tropics meant that insects formed a large part of our life.* [from Late Latin]

**tro|pism** /trʊpɪzəm/ (**tropisms**) N-VAR A **tropism** is the involuntary movement of a plant or other organism in response to an external stimulus such as heat or light. [TECHNICAL] [from Greek]

**tropo|sphere** /trɒpəsfɪər, troʊ-/ N-SING The **troposphere** is the layer of the Earth's atmosphere that is closest to the Earth's surface.

**trot** /trɒt/ (**trots, trotting, trotted**) ◧ V-I If you **trot** somewhere, you move fairly fast at a speed between walking and running, taking quick small steps. ❑ *I trotted down the steps and out to the garden.* ● **Trot** is also a noun. ❑ *He followed at a trot.* ◨ V-I When an animal such as a horse **trots**, it moves fairly fast, taking quick small steps. ❑ *Alan took the reins and the horse started trotting.* ● **Trot** is also a noun. ❑ *He kicked his horse into a trot.* [from Old French]

**trou|ble** /trʌbəl/ (**troubles, troubling, troubled**) ◧ N-VAR You can refer to problems or difficulties as **trouble**. ❑ *I had trouble parking.* ❑ *You've caused us a lot of trouble.* ◨ N-SING If you say that one aspect of a situation is **the trouble**, you mean that it is the aspect which is causing problems or making the situation unsatisfactory. ❑ *The trouble is that he's still sick.* ◩ N-UNCOUNT If you have, for example, kidney trouble or back **trouble**, there is something wrong with your kidneys or your back. ❑ *Her husband has never had any heart trouble.* ◪ N-UNCOUNT If there is **trouble**, people are arguing or fighting. ❑ *Police were sent to the city to prevent trouble.* ◫ V-T If something **troubles** you, it makes you feel worried. ❑ *Is anything troubling you?* ● **trou|bling** ADJ ❑ *Most troubling of all was the fact that nobody knew what was going on.* ◬ PHRASE If someone is **in trouble**, they have broken a rule or law and are likely to be punished by someone in authority. ❑ *He was in trouble with his teachers.* ◭ PHRASE If you **take the trouble to** do something, you do something which requires some time or effort. ❑ *He did not take the trouble to see the movie before he criticized it.* [from Old French]

## Word Partnership  Use *trouble* with :

| | |
|---|---|
| DET. | **no** trouble ◧ |
| V. | **cause** trouble, **make** trouble, **run into** trouble, **spell** trouble, **start** trouble ◧ |
| | **have** trouble ◧ ◩ |
| | **get in/into** trouble, **get out of** trouble, **stay out of** trouble ◬ |
| N. | **engine** trouble ◧ |
| | **sign of** trouble ◧ ◩ ◪ |
| ADJ. | **financial** trouble ◧ |
| | **big** trouble, **deep** trouble, **real** trouble, **serious** trouble ◧ ◪ |
| | **heart** trouble ◩ |
| PREP. | trouble **with** ◧ ◨ ◪ |
| | **in** trouble ◬ |
| ADV. | trouble **ahead** ◧ ◪ |

**trou|bled** /trʌbəld/ ADJ **Troubled** means worried or full of problems. ❑ *Rose sounded deeply troubled.* ❑ *...this troubled country.* [from Old French]

**trouble|maker** /trʌbəlmeɪkər/ (**troublemakers**) N-COUNT A **troublemaker** is someone who causes unpleasantness, quarrels, or fights. ❑ *She has always been a troublemaker.*

## Word Link  *some ≈ causing : awesome, fearsome, troublesome*

**trou|ble|some** /trʌbəlsəm/ ADJ Someone or something that is **troublesome** causes annoying problems or difficulties. ❑ *...a troublesome back injury.* [from Old French]

**trough** /trɒf/ (**troughs**) ◧ N-COUNT A **trough** is a long narrow container from which farm animals drink or eat. ❑ *...the old stone cattle trough.* ◨ N-COUNT A **trough** is a low point in a pattern that has regular high and low points. ❑ *The industry's worst trough was in 2001 and 2002.* ◩ N-COUNT A **trough** is a low area between two big waves on the sea. [from Old English] → see **sound**

**troupe** /truːp/ (**troupes**) N-COUNT A **troupe** is a group of actors, singers, or dancers who work together. [from French]

**trou|sers** /traʊzərz/

The form **trouser** is used as a modifier.

N-PLURAL **Trousers** are a piece of clothing that cover the body from the waist downward, and that cover each leg separately. [FORMAL] ❑ *He was dressed in a shirt, dark trousers and boots.*

**trout** /traʊt/ (**trout** or **trouts**)

The plural can be either **trout** or **trouts**.

N-VAR A **trout** is a fairly large fish that lives in rivers and streams. ● **Trout** is this fish eaten as food. ❑ *...grilled trout.* [from Old English]

**tru|ant** /truːənt/ (**truants**) N-COUNT A **truant** is a student who stays away from school without permission. ❑ *The parents of truants can be put in jail.* [from Old French]

**truce** /truːs/ (**truces**) N-COUNT A **truce** is an agreement between two people or groups of people to stop fighting or arguing for a short time. ❑ *The fighting has given way to an uneasy truce between the two sides.* [from Old English]

**truck** /trʌk/ (**trucks, trucking, trucked**) ◧ N-COUNT A **truck** is a large vehicle that is used to transport goods by road. ❑ *They heard the roar of a heavy truck.* ❑ *My dad is a truck driver.* ◨ N-COUNT A **truck** is a vehicle with a large area in the back for carrying things and with low sides to make it easy to load and unload. ❑ *There are only two seats in the truck.* [from Anglo-Norman]

**truck|er** /trʌkər/ (**truckers**) N-COUNT A **trucker** is someone who drives a truck as their job.

**truck stop** (**truck stops**) N-COUNT A **truck stop** is a place where drivers, especially truck drivers, can stop to rest or to get something to eat.

**trudge** /trʌdʒ/ (**trudges, trudging, trudged**) V-I If you **trudge** somewhere, you walk there with slow heavy steps. ❑ *We had to trudge back to the station.* ● **Trudge** is also a noun. ❑ *...the long trudge home.*

**true** /truː/ (**truer, truest**) ◧ ADJ If something is **true**, it is accurate and based on facts, and is not invented or imagined. ❑ *Everything she said was true.* ❑ *The movie is based on a true story.* ◨ ADJ **True** means real, genuine, or typical. ❑ *This country claims to be a true democracy.* ❑ *Maybe one day you'll find true love.* ◩ ADJ **True north** is the same as the **North Pole**. **True south** is the same as the **South Pole**. [TECHNICAL] ◪ PHRASE If a dream, wish,

**t**

or prediction **comes true**, it actually happens. ❑ *When I was 13, my dream came true and I got my first horse.* **5** PHRASE If a general statement **holds true** in particular circumstances, or if your previous statement **holds true** in different circumstances, it is true or valid in those circumstances. [FORMAL] ❑ *I'm not sure that what you are saying holds true.* [from Old English] **6** to **ring true** → see **ring** **7** **tried and true** → see **tried**

**true-breeding** ADJ A **true-breeding** plant is a plant that fertilizes itself and therefore produces offspring with exactly the same genetic characteristics as itself. [TECHNICAL]

**tru|ly** /trúli/ **1** ADV **Truly** means completely and genuinely. ❑ *...a truly democratic system.* ❑ *Believe me, Susan, I am truly sorry.* **2** ADV You can use **truly** in order to emphasize your description of something. ❑ *...a truly great man.* **3** **well and truly** → see **well** **4** CONVENTION You can write **Yours truly** before your signature at the end of a letter to someone you do not know very well. ❑ *Yours truly, Phil Turner.* [from Old English]

**trump** /trʌmp/ (**trumps**) **1** N-UNCOUNT In a game of cards, **trumps** is the suit which is chosen to have the highest value in one particular game. ❑ *Hearts are trumps.* **2** PHRASE Your **trump card** is something powerful that you can use or do, which gives you an advantage. ❑ *The administration knows that this is their trump card.* [from French]

**trum|pet** /trʌmpɪt/ (**trumpets**) N-VAR A **trumpet** is a brass musical instrument. ❑ *I played the trumpet in the school orchestra.* [from Old French] → see **brass, orchestra**

**trum|pet|er** /trʌmpɪtər/ (**trumpeters**) N-COUNT A **trumpeter** is someone who plays a trumpet. [from Old French]

**trun|dle** /trʌndəl/ (**trundles, trundling, trundled**) **1** V-I If a truck or other heavy vehicle **trundles** somewhere, it moves there slowly. ❑ *The truck was trundling along the valley.* **2** V-T If you **trundle** something somewhere, especially an object with wheels, you move or roll it along slowly. ❑ *The old man lifted the handles of the wheelbarrow and trundled it away.* [from Old English]

**trunk** /trʌŋk/ (**trunks**) **1** N-COUNT The **trunk** of a tree is the large main stem from which the branches grow. ❑ *The trunk of the tree was more than five feet across.* **2** N-COUNT The **trunk** of a car is a covered space at the back in which you put luggage or other things. ❑ *She opened the trunk of the car and took out a bag of groceries.* **3** N-COUNT A **trunk** is a large, strong case or box used for storing things or for taking on a trip. ❑ *Maloney unlocked his trunk and took out some clothing.* **4** N-COUNT An elephant's **trunk** is its long nose. [from Old French]

trunk

**trust** /trʌst/ (**trusts, trusting, trusted**) **1** V-T If you **trust** someone, you believe that they are honest and will not deliberately do anything to harm you. ❑ *I trust you completely," he said.* ● **Trust** is also a noun. ❑ *He destroyed my trust in men.* ❑ *...a shared feeling of trust.* **2** V-T If you **trust** someone **to** do something, you believe that they will do it.

❑ *I trust you to keep this secret.* **3** V-T If you **trust** someone **with** something, you allow them to look after it or deal with it. ❑ *I would trust him with my life.* ● **Trust** is also a noun. ❑ *She holds a position of trust.* **4** V-T If you do not **trust** something, you feel that it is not safe or reliable. ❑ *She nodded, not trusting her own voice.* ❑ *He didn't trust his legs to hold him up.* **5** V-T If you **trust** someone's judgment or advice, you believe that it is good or right. ❑ *Jake has raised two kids and I trust his judgment.* **6** N-COUNT A **trust** is a financial arrangement in which a group of people or an organization keeps and invests money for someone. [BUSINESS] ❑ *You could set up a trust for the children.* [from Old Norse]

| Word Partnership | Use *trust* with : |
| --- | --- |
| V. | **build** trust, **create** trust, **learn to** trust, **place** trust **in** *someone* **1** |
| ADJ. | **mutual** trust **1** **charitable** trust **6** |
| N. | trust *your* **instincts**, trust *someone's* **judgment** **5** **investment** trust **6** |

**trus|tee** /trʌstí/ (**trustees**) N-COUNT A **trustee** is someone with legal control of money or property that is kept or invested for another person, company, or organization. [BUSINESS] [from Old Norse]

**trust|ing** /trʌstɪŋ/ ADJ A **trusting** person believes that people are honest and sincere and do not intend to harm him or her. ❑ *She has an open, trusting nature.* [from Old Norse]

**trust|worthy** /trʌstwɜrði/ ADJ A **trustworthy** person is reliable, responsible, and can be trusted completely. ❑ *He is a trustworthy leader.*

**truth** /truθ/ (**truths**) **1** N-UNCOUNT The **truth** about something is all the facts about it, rather than things that are imagined or invented. ❑ *Is it possible to tell truth from fiction?* ❑ *I must tell you the truth about this business.* **2** N-UNCOUNT If you say that there is some **truth in** a statement or story, you mean that it is true, or at least partly true. ❑ *There is no truth in this story.* **3** N-COUNT A **truth** is something that is believed to be true. ❑ *...a universal truth.* [from Old English]

| Word Partnership | Use *truth* with : |
| --- | --- |
| V. | **accept the** truth, **find the** truth, **know the** truth, **learn the** truth, **search for the** truth, **tell the** truth **1** |
| N. | **a grain of** truth, **the** truth **of the matter 1** |
| ADJ. | **the awful** truth, **the plain** truth, **the sad** truth, **the simple** truth, **the whole** truth **1** **absolute** truth **1 3** |

**truth|ful** /truθfəl/ ADJ If a person or their comments are **truthful**, they are honest and do not tell any lies. ❑ *Most religions teach you to be truthful.* ● **truth|ful|ly** ADV ❑ *I answered all their questions truthfully.* ● **truth|ful|ness** N-UNCOUNT ❑ *I can say, with absolute truthfulness, that I did my best.* [from Old English]

**try** /traɪ/ (**tries, trying, tried**) **1** V-T/V-I If you **try** to do something, you make an effort to do it. ❑ *He tried to help her at work.* ❑ *Does it annoy you if others* *don't seem to try hard enough?* ❑ *I must try and see him.* ● **Try** is also a noun. ❑ *It was worth a try.* **2** V-I If you **try for** something, you make an effort to get it or achieve it. ❑ *I'll just keep trying for a job.* **3** V-T If you **try** something new or different, you use it or do it in order to discover its qualities or effects. ❑ *You could try a little cheese melted on the top.* ● **Try** is also a noun. ❑ *All we're asking is that you give it a try.* **4** V-T If you **try** a particular place or person, you go to that place or person because you think that they may be able to provide you with what you want. ❑ *Have you tried the local music stores?* **5** V-T When a person **is tried**, he or she appears in a law court and is found innocent or guilty after the judge and jury have heard the evidence. ❑ *Those responsible should be tried for war crimes.* [from Old French] **6** → see also **tried, trying** **7** to **try** your **best** → see **best** **8** to **try** your **hand** → see **hand** **9** to **try** someone's **patience** → see **patience**

▶ **try on** PHR-VERB If you **try on** a piece of clothing, you put it on to see if it fits you or if it looks nice. ❑ *Try on clothing and shoes to make sure they fit.*

▶ **try out** PHR-VERB If you **try** something **out**, you test it in order to find out how useful or effective it is. ❑ *I wanted to try the boat out next weekend.*

▶ **try out for** PHR-VERB If you **try out for** a sports team or an acting role, you compete or you perform a test in an attempt to be chosen. ❑ *He should have tried out for the Olympic team.*

**try|ing** /ˈtraɪɪŋ/ **1** ADJ Someone or something that is **trying** is difficult to deal with and makes you feel impatient or annoyed. ❑ *Support from those close to you is important in trying times.* [from Old French] **2** → see also **try**

**T-shirt** (**T-shirts**) also **tee-shirt** N-COUNT A **T-shirt** is a cotton shirt with no collar or buttons. T-shirts usually have short sleeves.
→ see **clothing**

**tsu|na|mi** /tsʊˈnɑmi/ (**tsunamis**) N-COUNT A **tsunami** is a very large wave, often caused by an earthquake, that flows onto the land and can cause widespread death and destruction. [from Japanese]
→ see Word Web: **tsunami**

**tub** /tʌb/ (**tubs**) **1** N-COUNT A **tub** is the same as a **bathtub**. ❑ *She lay back in the tub.* **2** N-COUNT A **tub** is a deep container of any size. ❑ *...four tubs of ice cream.* [from Middle Dutch]
→ see **soap**

**tube** /tub/ (**tubes**) **1** N-COUNT A **tube** is a long hollow object that is usually round, like a pipe. ❑ *He is fed by a tube that enters his nose.* **2** N-COUNT A **tube** of something such as paste is a long, thin container which you squeeze in order to force the substance out. ❑ *...a tube of toothpaste.* [from Latin]
→ see **container, laboratory, transportation**

**tu|ber|cu|lo|sis** /tʊbɜrkyəˈloʊsɪs/ N-UNCOUNT **Tuberculosis** is a serious infectious disease that affects the lungs. The abbreviation **TB** is also used. [from New Latin]

**tube worm** also **tubeworm** (**tube worms**) N-COUNT A **tube worm** is a type of worm that lives in the sea and constructs a tube from sand and other material, which it lives in.

**tub|ing** /ˈtubɪŋ/ N-UNCOUNT **Tubing** is plastic, rubber, or another material in the shape of a tube. ❑ *...three meters of plastic tubing.* [from Latin]

**tuck** /tʌk/ (**tucks, tucking, tucked**) V-T If you **tuck** something somewhere, you put it there so that it is safe, comfortable, or neat. ❑ *He tried to tuck his shirt inside his pants.* [from Old English]

▶ **tuck away** PHR-VERB If you **tuck away** something such as money, you store it in a safe place. ❑ *The extra income means that Phillippa can tuck away the rent.* **2** PHR-VERB If someone or something **is tucked away**, they are well hidden in a quiet place where very few people go. ❑ *We were tucked away in a corner of the room.*

▶ **tuck in** **1** PHR-VERB If you **tuck in** a piece of material, you keep it in position by placing one edge or end of it behind or under something else. ❑ *Tuck your shirt in.* **2** PHR-VERB If you **tuck** a child **in** bed, you make them comfortable in bed by straightening the sheets and blankets and pushing the loose ends under the mattress. ❑ *I read Lily a story and tucked her in.*

**Tues|day** /ˈtuzdeɪ, -di/ (**Tuesdays**) N-VAR **Tuesday** is the day after Monday and before Wednesday. ❑ *He phoned on Tuesday, just before you came.* [from Old English]

**tug** /tʌg/ (**tugs, tugging, tugged**) **1** V-T/V-I If you **tug** something or **tug at** it, you give it a quick and usually strong pull. ❑ *A little boy came running up and tugged at his sleeve excitedly.* ● **Tug** is also a noun. ❑ *I felt a tug at my sleeve.* **2** N-COUNT A **tug** or a **tug boat** is a small powerful boat which pulls large ships, usually when they come into a port. ❑ *...an oil tanker pulled by five tug boats.* [from Old English]

**Word Web** tsunami

Ordinary ocean **waves** are mostly the result of wind. The gigantic waves of a **tsunami**, however, are usually the result of an underwater **earthquake**. A **submarine landslide** or **volcano** can also cause a tsunami. The most destructive recent tsunami occurred in Indonesia in 2004. The earthquake that caused it measured 9.0 on the **Richter scale**. Scientists have found ways of predicting when these huge waves will strike. They use **buoys** in the open ocean and **tide gauges** near the shore. They also use **seismographs** to record earthquake activity. A central station **monitors** all this information and produces a tsunami **forecast**.

t

| Word Web | tunnel |
|---|---|

The Egyptians built the first **tunnels** as entrances to tombs. Later the Babylonians* built a tunnel under the Euphrates River*. It connected the royal palace with the Temple of Jupiter*. The Romans **dug** tunnels when **mining** for gold. By the late 1600s, **explosives** had replaced **digging**. Gunpowder was used to build the **underground** section of a canal in France in 1679. Nitroglycerin explosions helped create a railroad tunnel in Massachusetts in 1867. The longest continuous tunnel in the world is the Delaware Aqueduct. It carries water from the Catskill Mountains* to New York City and is 105 miles long.

*Babylonians: people who lived in the ancient city of Babylon.*
*Euphrates River: a large river in the Middle East.*
*Temple of Jupiter: a religious building.*
*Catskill Mountains: a mountain range in the northeastern U.S.*

**tui|tion** /tuɪʃ°n/ N-UNCOUNT You can use **tuition** to refer to the amount of money that you have to pay for being taught in a university, college, or private school. ☐ *Angela's $35,000 tuition at college this year will be paid for with scholarships.* [from Old French]

**tu|lip** /tuːlɪp/ (**tulips**) N-COUNT **Tulips** are flowers that grow in the spring from bulbs. [from New Latin]

**tum|ble** /tʌmb°l/ (**tumbles, tumbling, tumbled**) V-I If someone or something **tumbles**, they fall with a rolling or bouncing movement. ☐ *A small boy tumbled off the step.* ● **Tumble** is also a noun. ☐ *He broke his leg in a tumble from his horse.* [from Old English]

**tum|my** /tʌmi/ (**tummies**) N-COUNT Your **tummy** is your stomach. ☐ *Your baby's tummy should feel warm, but not hot.*

**tu|mor** /tuːmər/ (**tumors**) N-COUNT A **tumor** is a mass of diseased or abnormal cells that has grown in a person's or animal's body. ☐ *...a brain tumor.* [from Latin]
→ see **cancer**

**tu|mul|tu|ous** /tuːmʌltʃuəs/ **1** ADJ A **tumultuous** event or period of time involves many exciting and confusing events or feelings. ☐ *...the tumultuous changes in Eastern Europe.* **2** ADJ A **tumultuous** reaction to something is very noisy, because the people involved are very happy or excited. ☐ *...a tumultuous welcome from the crowd.* [from Latin]

**tuna** /tuːnə/ (**tuna** or **tunas**)

The plural can be either **tuna** or **tunas**.

N-VAR **Tuna** or **tuna fish** are large fish that live in warm seas. ● **Tuna** or **tuna fish** is this fish eaten as food. ☐ *She opened a can of tuna.* [from American Spanish]

**tun|dra** /tʌndrə/ (**tundras**) N-VAR **Tundra** is one of the large flat areas of land in the north of Europe, Asia, and America. The ground below the top layer of soil is always frozen and no trees grow there. [from Russian]

**tune** /tuːn/ (**tunes, tuning, tuned**) **1** N-COUNT A **tune** is a series of musical notes that is pleasant

to listen to. ☐ *She was humming a little tune.* **2** V-T When someone **tunes** a musical instrument, they adjust it so that it produces the right notes. ☐ *We tune our guitars before we go on stage.* ● **Tune up** means the same as **tune.** ☐ *Others were quietly tuning up their instruments.* **3** V-T If your radio or television **is tuned to** a particular channel or broadcasting station, you are listening to or watching the programs being broadcast by that station. ☐ *A small color television was tuned to a movie channel.* **4** → see also **fine-tune** **5** PHRASE If you say that someone **has changed** their **tune,** you are criticizing them because they have changed their opinion or way of doing things. ☐ *You've changed your tune since this morning, haven't you?* **6** PHRASE A person or musical instrument that is **in tune** produces exactly the right notes. A person or musical instrument that is **out of tune** does not produce exactly the right notes. ☐ *It was just an ordinary voice, but he sang in tune.*
▸ **tune in** PHR-VERB If you **tune in** to a particular television or radio station or program, you watch or listen to it. ☐ *All over the country, youngsters tune in to "Sesame Street" every day.*

**tu|nic** /tuːnɪk/ (**tunics**) N-COUNT A **tunic** is a long sleeveless garment that is worn on the top part of your body. ☐ *...a cotton tunic.* [from Old English]

**tun|nel** /tʌn°l/ (**tunnels, tunneling** or **tunnelling, tunneled** or **tunnelled**) **1** N-COUNT A **tunnel** is a long passage which has been made under the ground, usually through a hill or under the sea. ☐ *Boston drivers love the tunnel.* **2** V-I To **tunnel** somewhere means to make a tunnel there. ☐ *The thieves tunneled deep under the walls.* [from Old French]
→ see Word Web: **tunnel**
→ see **traffic**

**tur|bine** /tɜrbɪn, -baɪn/ (**turbines**) N-COUNT A **turbine** is a machine or engine which uses a stream of air, gas, water, or steam to turn a wheel and produce power. ☐ *The ship will be powered by two gas turbines.* [from French]
→ see **electricity, wheel**

| Word Link | ulent ≈ full of: opulent, succulent, turbulent |
|---|---|

**tur|bu|lent** /tɜrbyələnt/ **1** ADJ A **turbulent** time, place, or relationship is one in which there is a lot of change and confusion. ❑ *...six turbulent years of marriage.* ● **tur|bu|lence** /tɜrbyələns/ N-UNCOUNT ❑ *The 1960s was a time of turbulence.* **2** ADJ **Turbulent** water or air contains strong currents which change direction suddenly. ❑ *...a boat that could handle turbulent seas.* ● **tur|bu|lence** N-UNCOUNT ❑ *Heat waves caused turbulence for airplanes overhead.* [from Latin]

**turf** /tɜrf/ N-UNCOUNT **Turf** is short, thick, even grass. ❑ *...the turf toward the cliff's edge.* [from Old English]

**tur|key** /tɜrki/ (**turkeys**) N-COUNT A **turkey** is a large bird that is kept on a farm for its meat. ● **Turkey** is the meat of this bird eaten as food. ❑ *...a traditional turkey dinner.* [from French]

**tur|moil** /tɜrmɔɪl/ (**turmoils**) N-VAR **Turmoil** is a state of confusion or great anxiety. ❑ *Her feelings were in turmoil.*

turkey

---

### turn

❶ VERB USES
❷ NOUN USES
❸ PHRASAL VERBS

**Turn** is used in a large number of other expressions which are explained under other words in the dictionary. For example, the expression "turn a blind eye" is explained at **blind**.

**❶ turn** /tɜrn/ (**turns, turning, turned**) **1** V-T/V-I To **turn** means to move in a different direction or to move into a different position. ❑ *He turned and walked away.* ❑ *She turned the chair to face the door.* ❑ *He sighed, turning away and looking at the sea.* ● **Turn around** means the same as **turn**. ❑ *I felt a tap on my shoulder and I turned around.* **2** V-T/V-I When something **turns**, or when you **turn** it, it moves around in a circle. ❑ *The wheel turned.* ❑ *Turn the key three times to the right.* **3** V-T/V-I When you **turn** in a particular direction or **turn** a corner, you change the direction in which you are moving or traveling. ❑ *He turned into the narrow street where he lived.* ❑ *Now turn right to follow West Ferry Road.* ● **Turn** is also a noun. ❑ *You can't do a right-hand turn here.* **4** V-I If you **turn to** a particular page in a book or magazine, you open it at that page. ❑ *To order, turn to page 236.* **5** V-T/V-I If you **turn** your attention or thoughts to a particular subject or if you **turn to** it, you start thinking about it or discussing it. ❑ *We turn now to our main question.* **6** V-I If you **turn to** someone, you ask for their help or advice. ❑ *For assistance, they turned to one of the city's museums.* **7** V-T/V-I If something **turns into** something else, or if you **turn** it **into** something else, it becomes something different. ❑ *They plan to turn the country into a one-party state.* ❑ *The sky turned pale pink.* **8** V-T When someone **turns** a particular age, they pass that age. When it

turns a particular time, it passes that time. ❑ *He made a million dollars before he turned thirty.* [from Old English]

**❷ turn** /tɜrn/ (**turns**) **1** N-COUNT If a situation or trend takes a particular kind of **turn**, it changes so that it starts developing in a different or opposite way. ❑ *The situation took a new turn over the weekend.* **2** N-COUNT If it is your **turn to** do something, you now have the duty, chance, or right to do it, when other people have done it before you or will do it after you. ❑ *Tonight it's my turn to cook.* **3** PHRASE You use **in turn** to refer to actions or events that are in a sequence one after the other. ❑ *He told his girlfriend, who in turn told her father.* **4** PHRASE If two or more people **take turns to** do something, they do it one after the other several times, rather than doing it together. ❑ *We took turns driving.* [from Old English]

| Thesaurus | turn | Also look up : |
|---|---|---|
| v. | bend, pivot, revolve, rotate, spin, twist ❶ **1** – **3** | |
| | become ❶ **7** **8** | |
| N. | chance, opportunity ❷ **2** | |

**❸ turn** /tɜrn/ (**turns, turning, turned**)
▶ **turn against** PHR-VERB If you **turn against** someone or something, or if you **are turned against** them, you stop supporting them, trusting them, or liking them. ❑ *One of my friends turned against me.*
▶ **turn around 1** → see **turn ❶ 1** **2** PHR-VERB If you **turn** something **around**, or if it **turns around**, it is moved so that it faces the opposite direction. ❑ *Bud turned the truck around, and started back for Dalton Pond.*
▶ **turn away** PHR-VERB If you **turn** someone **away**, you do not allow them to enter your country, home, or other place. ❑ *Many colleges are turning away students.*
▶ **turn back** PHR-VERB If you **turn back** or if someone **turns** you **back** when you are going somewhere, you change direction and go toward where you started from. ❑ *She turned back toward home.* ❑ *Police attempted to turn back protesters.*
▶ **turn down 1** PHR-VERB If you **turn down** a person or their request or offer, you refuse their request or offer. ❑ *I thanked him for the offer but turned it down.* **2** PHR-VERB When you **turn down** a radio, heater, or other piece of equipment, you reduce the amount of sound or heat being produced, by adjusting the controls. ❑ *He turned the heater down.*
▶ **turn off 1** PHR-VERB If you **turn off** the road or path you are going along, you start going along a different road or path which leads away from it. ❑ *The truck turned off the main road.* **2** PHR-VERB When you **turn off** a piece of equipment or a supply of something, you stop heat, sound, or water from being produced by adjusting the controls. ❑ *The light's a bit bright. Can you turn it off?*
▶ **turn on 1** PHR-VERB When you **turn on** a piece of equipment or a supply of something, you cause heat, sound, or water to be produced by adjusting the controls. ❑ *I want to turn on the television.* **2** PHR-VERB If someone **turns on** you, they suddenly attack you or speak angrily to you. ❑ *Demonstrators turned on police.*
▶ **turn out 1** PHR-VERB If something **turns out** a particular way, it happens in that way or has the

t

result or degree of success indicated. ❑ *I didn't know my life was going to turn out like this.* ❑ *I was certain things were going to turn out fine.* **2** PHR-VERB If something **turns out to** be a particular thing, it is discovered to be that thing. ❑ *The weather forecast turned out to be completely wrong.* **3** PHR-VERB When you **turn out** something such as a light, you move the switch or knob that controls it so that it stops giving out light or heat. ❑ *Turn the lights out.* **4** → see also **turnout**

▶ **turn over** **1** PHR-VERB If you **turn** something **over**, or if it **turns over**, it is moved so that the top part is now facing downward. ❑ *Liz picked up the envelope and turned it over.* ❑ *The car turned over and landed in a ditch.* **2** PHR-VERB If you **turn** something **over in** your mind, you think carefully about it. ❑ *You could see her turning things over in her mind.* **3** PHR-VERB If you **turn** something **over to** someone, you give it to them when they ask for it, because they have a right to it. ❑ *I turned the evidence over to the police.* **4** → see also **turnover**

▶ **turn up** **1** PHR-VERB If you say that someone or something **turns up**, you mean that they arrive unexpectedly or after you have been waiting a long time. ❑ *They finally turned up at nearly midnight.* **2** PHR-VERB When you **turn up** a radio, heater, or other piece of equipment, you increase the amount of sound, heat, or power being produced, by adjusting the controls. ❑ *Can you turn up the TV?* ❑ *I turned the volume up.*

**turn|ing point** (**turning points**) N-COUNT A **turning point** is a time at which an important change takes place which affects the future of a person or thing. ❑ *Yesterday was a turning point in the war.*

**tur|nip** /tɜrnɪp/ (**turnips**) N-VAR A **turnip** is a round root vegetable with a cream-colored skin. [from Latin]

**turn|out** /tɜrnaʊt/ (**turnouts**) N-COUNT The **turnout** at an event is the number of people who go to it. ❑ *It was a great afternoon with a huge turnout of people.*

**turn|over** /tɜrnoʊvər/ (**turnovers**) **1** N-VAR The **turnover** of a company is the value of the goods or services sold during a particular period of time. [BUSINESS] ❑ *The company had a turnover of $3.8 million.* **2** N-VAR The **turnover** of people in an organization or place is the rate at which people leave and are replaced. [BUSINESS] ❑ *Staff turnover is high because they don't pay people very much.*

**turn|pike** /tɜrnpaɪk/ (**turnpikes**) N-COUNT A **turnpike** is a road, especially an expressway, which people have to pay to drive on.

**turn sig|nal** (**turn signals**) N-COUNT A car's **turn signals** are the flashing lights that tell you it is going to turn left or right.

turtle

**tur|quoise** /tɜrkwɔɪz/ (**turquoises**) COLOR **Turquoise** or **turquoise blue** is used to describe things that are of a light greenish-blue color. ❑ *...a clear turquoise sea.* [from Old French]

**tur|tle** /tɜrtᵊl/ (**turtles**) N-COUNT A **turtle** is any reptile that has a thick shell around its body, for example a tortoise, and can pull its whole body into its shell. [from French]

**turtle|neck** /tɜrtᵊlnɛk/ (**turtlenecks**) N-COUNT A **turtleneck** or **turtleneck sweater** is a sweater with a high neck which folds over.

tusk

**tusk** /tʌsk/ (**tusks**) N-COUNT The **tusks** of an elephant, wild boar, or walrus are its two very long, curved, pointed teeth. [from Old English]

**tus|sle** /tʌsᵊl/ (**tussles, tussling, tussled**) V-I; V-RECIP If one person **tussles with** another, or if they **tussle**, they get hold of each other and struggle or fight. ❑ *They ended up tussling with the security staff.* ● **Tussle** is also a noun. ❑ *Two players were taken out after a tussle on the field.* [from Old High German]

**tu|tor** /tutər/ (**tutors**) **1** N-COUNT A **tutor** is someone who gives private lessons to one student or a very small group of students. ❑ *...a Spanish tutor.* **2** N-COUNT In some American universities or colleges, a **tutor** is a teacher of the lowest rank. [from Latin]

**tu|to|rial** /tutɔriəl/ (**tutorials**) **1** N-COUNT In a university or college, a **tutorial** is a regular meeting between a tutor or professor and one or several students, for discussion of a subject that is being studied. **2** N-COUNT A **tutorial** is part of a book or a computer program which helps you learn something step-by-step without a teacher. [from Latin]

tuxedo

**tux|edo** /tʌksidoʊ/ (**tuxedos**) N-COUNT A **tuxedo** is a suit or jacket, usually black, that is worn by men for formal social events. [from New York]

**TV** /ti vi/ (**TVs**) N-VAR **TV** means the same as **television**. ❑ *The TV was on.* ❑ *What's on TV?* ❑ *They watch too much TV.*

**tweed** /twid/ (**tweeds**) N-VAR **Tweed** is a thick woolen cloth, often woven from different colored threads. ❑ *...a tweed jacket.* [from Scottish]

**twelfth** /twɛlfθ/ (**twelfths**) **1** ORD The **twelfth** item in a series is the one that you count as number twelve. ❑ *...the twelfth anniversary of the revolution.* **2** ORD A **twelfth** is one of twelve equal parts of something. ❑ *She will get a twelfth of her father's money.* [from Old English]

**twelve** /twɛlv/ (**twelves**) NUM **Twelve** is the number 12. [from Old English]

**twelve-bar blues** N-UNCOUNT **Twelve-bar blues** is a form of blues music based on a system of twelve bars to each verse.

**twelve-tone** ADJ A **twelve-tone** scale is a musical scale consisting of all twelve notes in an octave. **Twelve-tone** music is music that is composed using a twelve-tone scale. [TECHNICAL]

**twen|ti|eth** /twɛntiəθ/ (**twentieths**) **1** ORD The **twentieth** item in a series is the one that you count as number twenty. ❑ *...the twentieth century.* **2** ORD A **twentieth** is one of twenty equal parts of something. ❑ *...a few twentieths of a gram.* [from Old English]

**twen|ty** /twɛnti/ (**twenties**) ◼ NUM **Twenty** is the number 20. ◢ N-PLURAL When you talk about the **twenties**, you are referring to numbers between 20 and 29. For example, if you are **in** your **twenties**, you are aged between 20 and 29. If the temperature is **in the twenties**, the temperature is between 20 and 29 degrees. ◻ *They're both in their twenties.* ◢ N-PLURAL **The twenties** is the decade between 1920 and 1929. ◻ *It was written in the twenties.* [from Old English]

**24-7** /twɛntifɔrsɛvⁿn/ also **twenty-four seven** ADV If something happens **24-7**, it happens all the time without ever stopping. **24-7** means twenty-four hours a day, seven days a week. [INFORMAL] ◻ *I feel like sleeping 24-7.* ● **24-7** is also an adjective. ◻ *...a 24-7 radio station.*

**Word Link** *twi ≈ two : twice, twilight, twin*

**twice** /twaɪs/ ◼ ADV If something happens **twice**, it happens two times. ◻ *He visited me twice that fall.* ◻ *I phoned twice a day.* ◢ ADV If one thing is, for example, **twice as** big or old **as** another, the first thing is double the size or age of the second. ◻ *The figure of seventy million dollars was twice as big as expected.* ● **Twice** is also a predeterminer. ◻ *Unemployment here is twice the national average.* [from Old English]

**twig** /twɪg/ (**twigs**) N-COUNT A **twig** is a very small thin branch that grows out from a main branch of a tree or bush. ◻ *There is the bird, sitting on a twig.* [from Old English]

**twi|light** /twaɪlaɪt/ N-UNCOUNT **Twilight** is the time just before night when the daylight has almost gone but when it is not completely dark. ◻ *They returned at twilight.* [from Old English]

**twin** /twɪn/ (**twins**) ◼ N-COUNT **Twins** are two people who were born at the same time from the same mother. ◻ *Sarah was looking after the twins.* ◢ ADJ **Twin** is used to describe a pair of things that look the same and are close together. ◻ *...a twin-engined aircraft.* [from Old English]
→ see **clone**

**twin|kle** /twɪŋkⁿl/ (**twinkles, twinkling, twinkled**) ◼ V-I If a star or a light **twinkles**, it shines with an unsteady light which rapidly and constantly changes from bright to faint. ◻ *Lights twinkled across the valley.* ◢ V-I If someone's eyes **twinkle**, they eyes express good humor or amusement. ◻ *Her mother's eyes twinkled with amusement.* ● **Twinkle** is also a noun. ◻ *A twinkle came into her eyes.* [from Old English]

**twirl** /twɜrl/ (**twirls, twirling, twirled**) ◼ V-T/V-I If you **twirl** something or if it **twirls**, it turns around and around with a smooth, fast movement. ◻ *Bonnie twirled her empty glass in her fingers.* ◢ V-I If you **twirl**, you turn around and around quickly, for example, when you are dancing. ◻ *Several hundred people twirled around the dance floor.*

**twist** /twɪst/ (**twists, twisting, twisted**) ◼ V-T If you **twist** something, you turn it to make a spiral shape, for example, by turning the two ends of it in opposite directions. ◻ *She sat twisting the handles of the bag.* ◢ V-T/V-I If you **twist** something, especially a part of your body, or if it **twists**, it moves into an unusual, uncomfortable, or bent position. ◻ *Can you twist your arms behind your back?*

◻ *...the twisted wreckage of a train.* ◢ V-T/V-I If you **twist** part of your body such as your head or your shoulders, you turn that part while keeping the rest of your body still. ◻ *She twisted her head sideways.* ◻ *Susan twisted around in her seat.* ◢ V-T If you **twist** a part of your body such as your ankle or wrist, you injure it by turning it too sharply, or in an unusual direction. ◻ *He fell and twisted his ankle.* ◢ V-T If you **twist** something, you turn it so that it moves around in a circular direction. ◻ *She was twisting the ring on her finger.* ◢ V-T If someone **twists** something that you have said, they repeat it in a way that changes its meaning, in order to harm you or benefit themselves. ◻ *The media can twist your words.* ◢ N-COUNT A **twist** in something is an unexpected and significant development. ◻ *The battle between them took a new twist.* [from Old English]

**Word Partnership** Use *twist* with :

| | |
|---|---|
| ADV. | twist **around** ◢ ◢ |
| ADJ. | **added** twist, **bizarre** twist, **interesting** twist, **new** twist, **unexpected** twist ◢ |
| V. | **plot** twist, **story** twist ◢ |

**twist|ed** /twɪstɪd/ ADJ If you describe a person as **twisted**, you dislike them because you think they are bad or mentally unbalanced. ◻ *He was an evil, twisted man.* [from Old English]

**twitch** /twɪtʃ/ (**twitches, twitching, twitched**) V-T/V-I If something, especially a part of your body, **twitches** or if you **twitch** it, it makes a little jumping movement. ◻ *Her right cheek began to twitch.* ● **Twitch** is also a noun. ◻ *He had a nervous twitch.* [from Old English]

**two** /tu/ (**twos**) NUM **Two** is the number 2. [from Old English]

**two-dimensional** also **two dimensional** ADJ A **two-dimensional** object or figure is flat rather than solid so that only its length and width can be measured.

**two-percent milk** N-UNCOUNT **Two-percent milk** is milk from which some of the fat has been removed.

**two-point per|spec|tive** (**two-point perspectives**) N-VAR A **two-point perspective** is a method of representing three-dimensional space on a two-dimensional surface by the use of two vanishing points on the horizon. [TECHNICAL]

**two-thirds** also **two thirds** QUANT **Two-thirds of** is an amount that is two out of three equal parts of it. ◻ *Two-thirds of families own their own homes.* ● **Two-thirds** is also a pronoun. ◻ *Sales are down by two-thirds.* ● **Two-thirds** is also an adverb. ◻ *Do not fill the container more than two-thirds full.* ● **Two-thirds** is also an adjective. ◻ *A two-thirds majority is needed to make changes.*

**two-way** ADJ **Two-way** means moving or working in two opposite directions. ◻ *The bridge is now open to two-way traffic.* ◻ *...a two-way radio.*

**ty|coon** /taɪkun/ (**tycoons**) N-COUNT A **tycoon** is a person who is successful in business and so has become rich and powerful. ◻ *...a real estate tycoon.* [from Japanese]

t

---

**type**

① SORT OR KIND
② WRITING AND PRINTING

---

**① type** /taɪp/ (**types**) **1** N-COUNT A **type of** something is a group of those things that have particular features in common. ❑ ...*several types of lettuce.* ❑ *There are various types of the disease.* **2** N-COUNT If you refer to a particular thing or person as a **type of** something more general, you are considering that thing or person as an example of that more general group. ❑ *Have you done this type of work before?* ❑ *I am a very determined type of person.* **3** N-COUNT If you refer to a person as a particular **type**, you mean that they have that particular appearance, character, or type of behavior. ❑ *I'm an outdoor type.* [from Latin]

**② type** /taɪp/ (**types, typing, typed**) V-T/V-I If you **type** something, you use a typewriter or computer keyboard to write it. ❑ *I can type your essays for you.* ❑ *I never really learned to type properly.* ● **typing** N-UNCOUNT ❑ *I'm taking a typing class.* [from Latin]
→ see **printing**
▶ **type in** or **type into** PHR-VERB If you **type** information **into** a computer or **type** it **in**, you press keys on the keyboard so that the computer stores or processes the information. ❑ *Officials type each passport number into a computer.* ❑ *You have to type in commands, such as "help" and "print."*
▶ **type up** PHR-VERB If you **type up** a text that has been written by hand, you produce a typed copy of it. ❑ *When the first draft was completed, Nichols typed it up.*

**type|writ|er** /taɪpraɪtər/ (**typewriters**) N-COUNT A **typewriter** is a machine with keys which are pressed in order to print letters, numbers, or other characters onto paper.

**ty|phoon** /taɪfun/ (**typhoons**) N-COUNT A **typhoon** is a very violent tropical storm. [from Chinese]
→ see **disaster, hurricane**

**typi|cal** /tɪpɪkəl/ **1** ADJ You use **typical** to describe someone or something that shows the most usual characteristics of a particular type of person or thing, and is therefore a good example of that type. ❑ *He is everyone's image of a typical cop.* **2** ADJ If a particular action or feature is **typical of** someone or something, it shows their usual qualities or characteristics. ❑ *These boys are typical of children their age.* [from Medieval Latin]

**typi|cal|ly** /tɪpɪkli/ **1** ADV You use **typically** to say that something usually happens in the way that you are describing. ❑ *The day typically begins with swimming.* **2** ADV You use **typically** to say that something shows all the most usual characteristics of a particular type of person or thing. ❑ *The food is typically American.* **3** ADV You use **typically** to indicate that someone has behaved in the way that they normally do. ❑ *Typically, he took her comments in good humor.* [from Medieval Latin]

**typi|fy** /tɪpɪfaɪ/ (**typifies, typifying, typified**) V-T To **typify** something means to be a typical example of it. ❑ *These two buildings typify the local style.* [from Latin]

**typ|ist** /taɪpɪst/ (**typists**) N-COUNT A **typist** is someone who works in an office typing letters and other documents. [from Latin]

**ty|po** /taɪpoʊ/ (**typos**) N-COUNT A **typo** is a typographical error. [INFORMAL] ❑ *There are no typos or misprints.*

**tyr|an|ny** /tɪrəni/ (**tyrannies**) N-VAR **Tyranny** is cruel and unfair rule by a person or small group of people. ❑ ...*the struggle between freedom and tyranny.* [from Latin]

**ty|rant** /taɪrənt/ (**tyrants**) N-COUNT A **tyrant** is someone who treats the people they have authority over in a cruel and unfair way. ❑ ...*families where the father was a tyrant.* [from Old French]

T

# Uu

**ubiqui|tous** /yubɪkwɪtəs/ ADJ If you describe something or someone as **ubiquitous**, you mean that they seem to be everywhere. [FORMAL] ❑ *Sugar is ubiquitous in the diet.* [from Latin]

**ugly** /ʌgli/ (**uglier, ugliest**) **1** ADJ If you say that someone or something is **ugly**, you mean that they are very unattractive and unpleasant to look at. ❑ *...an ugly little hat.* ● **ug|li|ness** N-UNCOUNT ❑ *...the ugliness of his native city.* **2** ADJ If you refer to an event or situation as **ugly**, you mean that it is very unpleasant, usually because it involves violence. ❑ *There have been some ugly scenes.* ❑ *The mood turned ugly.* [from Old Norse]

| Thesaurus | *ugly* | Also look up : |
|---|---|---|
| ADJ. | unattractive; (ant.) beautiful **1** | |
| | offensive, unpleasant **2** | |

**ul|cer** /ʌlsər/ (**ulcers**) N-COUNT An **ulcer** is a sore area on the outside or inside of your body which is very painful and may bleed. ❑ *...stomach ulcers.* [from Latin]

| Word Link | *ultim ≈ end, last : penultimate, ultimate, ultimatum* |
|---|---|

**ul|ti|mate** /ʌltɪmɪt/ **1** ADJ You use **ultimate** to describe the final result or aim of a long series of events. ❑ *The ultimate aim is to keep kids in school.* **2** ADJ You use **ultimate** to describe the most important or extreme thing of a particular kind. ❑ *Our ultimate goal is to win.* **3** PHRASE The **ultimate in** something is the best or most advanced example of it. ❑ *This hotel is the ultimate in luxury.* [from Late Latin]

| Word Partnership | Use *ultimate* with : |
|---|---|
| N. | ultimate **aim/goal/objective**, ultimate **outcome 1** |
| | ultimate **authority**, ultimate **decision**, ultimate **experience**, ultimate **power**, ultimate **weapon 2** |

**ul|ti|mate|ly** /ʌltɪmɪtli/ **1** ADV **Ultimately** means finally, after a long series of events. ❑ *Who, ultimately, is going to pay?* **2** ADV You use **ultimately** to indicate that what you are saying is the most important point in a discussion. ❑ *Ultimately, the judge has the final decision.* [from Late Latin]

**ul|ti|ma|tum** /ʌltɪmeɪtəm/ (**ultimatums**) N-COUNT An **ultimatum** is a warning to someone that unless they act in a particular way, action will be taken against them. ❑ *He gave them an ultimatum to leave the city in 24 hours.* [from New Latin]

**ultra|sound** /ʌltrəsaʊnd/ N-UNCOUNT **Ultrasound** is sound waves which travel at such a high frequency that they cannot be heard by humans. Ultrasound is used in medicine to get pictures of the inside of people's bodies. ❑ *...ultrasound photos of his unborn child.*

**ultra|vio|let** /ʌltrəvaɪəlɪt/ ADJ **Ultraviolet** light or radiation is what causes your skin to become darker in color after you have been in sunlight. ❑ *The sun's ultraviolet rays are responsible for both tanning and burning.*
→ see **ozone, skin, sun, wave**

**um|bili|cal cord** /ʌmbɪlɪkᵊl kɔrd/ (**umbilical cords**) N-COUNT The **umbilical cord** is the tube that connects an unborn baby to its mother, through which it receives oxygen and food.

**um|brel|la** /ʌmbrɛlə/ (**umbrellas**) **1** N-COUNT An **umbrella** is an object which you use to protect yourself from the rain or hot sun. It consists of a long stick with a folding frame covered in plastic or cloth. ❑ *Harry held an umbrella over Denise.* **2** N-SING **Umbrella** is used to refer to a single group or description that includes a lot of different organizations or ideas. ❑ *...a national umbrella group of thirty-five businesses.* [from Italian]

umbrella

**um|pire** /ʌmpaɪr/ (**umpires, umpiring, umpired**) **1** N-COUNT An **umpire** is a person whose job is to make sure that a sports contest or game is played fairly and that the rules are not broken. ❑ *The umpire's decision is final.* **2** V-T/V-I To **umpire** means to be the umpire in a sports contest or game. ❑ *He umpired baseball games.* [from Old French]

**un|able** /ʌneɪbᵊl/ ADJ If you are **unable to** do something, it is impossible for you to do it. ❑ *He was unable to walk.* [from Latin]

| Word Partnership | Use *unable* with : |
|---|---|
| ADV. | **physically** unable |
| V. | unable **to afford**, unable **to agree**, unable **to attend**, unable **to control**, unable **to cope**, unable **to decide**, unable **to explain**, unable **to find**, unable **to hold**, unable **to identify**, unable **to make**, unable **to move**, unable **to pay**, unable **to perform**, unable **to reach**, unable **to speak**, unable **to walk**, unable **to work** |

**un|ac|cep|table** /ʌnəkseptəbᵊl/ ADJ If you describe something as **unacceptable**, you strongly disapprove of it or object to it and feel that it should not be allowed to continue. ❑ *It is unacceptable for children to swear.* [from Latin]

**un|af|fect|ed** /ʌnəfɛktɪd/ **1** ADJ If someone or something is **unaffected by** an event, they are not changed by it in any way. ❑ *Travelers were unaffected*

u

by the bad weather. **2** ADJ If you describe someone as **unaffected**, you like them because they are natural and genuine in their behavior. ❏ ...this unaffected, charming couple.

**un-Ameri|can** /ʌnəmɛrɪkən/ **1** ADJ If you describe someone or something as **un-American**, you think that they do not follow or fit in with American ideals and customs. ❏ This is a deeply un-American attitude. **2** ADJ **Un-American** activities are political activities that are considered to be against the interests of the U.S. ❏ ...the House Un-American Activities Committee.

**una|nim|ity** /yunənɪmɪti/ N-UNCOUNT When there is **unanimity** among a group of people, they all agree about something. ❏ All decisions required unanimity. [from Latin]

**Word Link**   anim ≈ alive, mind : animal, animated, unanimous

**unani|mous** /yunænɪməs/ ADJ When a group of people are **unanimous**, they all agree about something. ❏ Their decision was unanimous. ● **unani|mous|ly** ADV ❏ They unanimously approved the project last week. [from Latin]

**un|an|nounced** /ʌnənaʊnst/ ADJ If someone arrives or does something **unannounced**, they do it unexpectedly and without anyone having been told about it beforehand. ❏ He arrived unannounced from South America.

**un|an|swered** /ʌnænsərd/ ADJ Something such as a question or letter that is **unanswered** has not been answered. ❏ The report leaves a lot of unanswered questions.

**un|armed** /ʌnɑrmd/ ADJ If a person or vehicle is **unarmed**, they are not carrying any weapons. ❏ The soldiers were unarmed. [from Old English]

**un|ashamed** /ʌnəʃeɪmd/ ADJ If you describe someone's behavior or attitude as **unashamed**, you mean that they are open and honest about things that other people might find embarrassing or shocking. ❏ She cried unashamed tears of joy. ● **un|ashamed|ly** /ʌnəʃeɪmɪdli/ ADV ❏ Bernstein was unashamedly American. [from Old English]

**un|at|trac|tive** /ʌnətræktɪv/ **1** ADJ **Unattractive** people and things are unpleasant in appearance. ❏ I felt lonely and unattractive. ❏ ...an unattractive orange color. **2** ADJ If you describe something as **unattractive**, you mean that people do not like it and do not want to be involved with it. ❏ The price is unattractive to most people. [from Latin]

**un|author|ized** /ʌnɔθəraɪzd/ ADJ If something is **unauthorized**, it has been produced or is happening without official permission. ❏ ...an unauthorized biography of the Russian president. ❏ The trip was unauthorized.

**un|avail|able** /ʌnəveɪləbᵊl/ ADJ When things or people are **unavailable**, you cannot obtain them, meet them, or talk to them. ❏ The governor was unavailable for comment last night. [from Old French]

**un|avoid|able** /ʌnəvɔɪdəbᵊl/ ADJ If something is **unavoidable**, it cannot be avoided or prevented. ❏ The delay was unavoidable.

**un|aware** /ʌnəwɛər/ ADJ If you are **unaware of** something, you do not know about it. ❏ Many people are unaware of how much they eat. [from Old English]

**Word Partnership**   Use unaware with :

ADV.   **apparently** unaware, **blissfully** unaware, **completely** unaware, **totally** unaware

**un|bal|anced** /ʌnbælənst/ **1** ADJ If you describe someone as **unbalanced**, you mean that they appear disturbed and upset or they seem to be slightly crazy. ❏ His brother was mentally unbalanced. **2** ADJ If you describe something such as a report or argument as **unbalanced**, you think that it is unfair or inaccurate because it emphasizes some things and ignores others. ❏ The report was unbalanced and unfair. [from Old French]

**un|bal|anced forces** N-PLURAL In physics, **unbalanced forces** are forces that are not equal and opposite to each other, so that an object to which the forces are applied moves.

**un|bear|able** /ʌnbɛərəbᵊl/ ADJ If you describe something as **unbearable**, you mean that it is so unpleasant, painful, or upsetting that you feel unable to accept it or deal with it. ❏ The pain was unbearable. ● **un|bear|ably** /ʌnbɛərəbli/ ADV ❏ In the evening it became unbearably hot. [from Old English]

**un|beat|able** /ʌnbitəbᵊl/ **1** ADJ If you describe something as **unbeatable**, you mean that it is the best thing of its kind. ❏ We're making an unbeatable offer. **2** PHRASE **Unbeatable prices** are the lowest prices you can find. ❏ Their prices are unbeatable.

**un|beat|en** /ʌnbitᵊn/ ADJ In sports, if a person or their performance is **unbeaten**, nobody else has performed well enough to beat them. ❏ He's unbeaten in 20 fights.

**un|be|liev|able** /ʌnbɪlivəbᵊl/ **1** ADJ If you say that something is **unbelievable**, you are emphasizing that it is very extreme, impressive, or shocking. ❏ His guitar solos are just unbelievable. ❏ It's unbelievable that people can accept this sort of behavior. ● **un|be|liev|ably** /ʌnbɪlivəbli/ ADV ❏ What you did was unbelievably stupid. **2** ADJ If an idea or statement is **unbelievable**, it seems so unlikely to be true that you cannot believe it. ❏ This story is both fascinating and unbelievable. ● **un|be|liev|ably** ADV ❏ Unbelievably, I made it to the final twice. [from Old English]

**Thesaurus**   unbelievable   Also look up :

ADJ.   astounding, incredible, remarkable **1** inconceivable, preposterous, unimaginable **2**

**un|born** /ʌnbɔrn/ ADJ An **unborn** child has not yet been born and is still inside its mother's uterus. ❏ ...her unborn baby. ● **The unborn** are children who are not born yet. ❏ ...a law that protects the lives of pregnant women and the unborn.

**un|bro|ken** /ʌnbroʊkən/ ADJ If something is **unbroken**, it is continuous or complete and has not been interrupted or broken. ❏ We had ten days of almost unbroken sunshine.

**un|can|ny** /ʌnkæni/ ADJ If something is **uncanny**, it is strange and difficult to explain. ❏ Cathy had an uncanny feeling that she knew this man. ● **un|can|ni|ly** /ʌnkænɪli/ ADV ❏ They have uncannily similar voices.

U

**un|cer|tain** /ʌnsɜrt³n/ ■ ADJ If you are **uncertain about** something, you do not know what you should do, what is going to happen, or what the truth is about something. ❑ *He was uncertain about his future.* ❑ *They were uncertain of the value of the goods.* ● **un|cer|tain|ly** ADV ❑ *He entered the room and stood uncertainly.* ■ ADJ If something is **uncertain**, it is not known or definite. ❑ *The company's future is uncertain.* ❑ *It's uncertain whether they will accept the plan.* ■ PHRASE If you say that someone tells a person something **in no uncertain terms**, you are emphasizing that they say it strongly and clearly so that there is no doubt about what they mean. ❑ *She told him in no uncertain terms to go away.* [from Old French]

**un|cer|tain|ty** /ʌnsɜrt³nti/ (**uncertainties**) N-VAR **Uncertainty** is a state of doubt about the future or about what is the right thing to do. ❑ *...a time of political uncertainty.*

**un|chal|lenged** /ʌntʃælɪndʒd/ ADJ When something goes **unchallenged** or is **unchallenged**, people accept it without asking questions about whether it is right or wrong. ❑ *That kind of statement cannot go unchallenged.* ❑ *...his unchallenged leadership*

**un|changed** /ʌntʃeɪndʒd/ ADJ If something is **unchanged**, it has stayed the same for a particular period of time. ❑ *For many years prices have remained unchanged.*

**un|char|ac|ter|is|tic** /ʌnkærɪktərɪstɪk/ ADJ If you describe something as **uncharacteristic of** someone, you mean that it is not typical of them. ❑ *It was uncharacteristic of her father to disappear like this.* ● **un|char|ac|ter|is|ti|cal|ly** /ʌnkærɪktərɪstɪkli/ ADV ❑ *Owen has been uncharacteristically silent.*

**un|checked** /ʌntʃɛkt/ ADJ If something harmful or undesirable is left **unchecked**, nobody controls it or prevents it from growing or developing. ❑ *If left unchecked, weeds will spread.* [from Old French]

**un|cle** /ʌŋk³l/ (**uncles**) N-COUNT; N-TITLE Your **uncle** is the brother of your mother or father, or the husband of your aunt. ❑ *My uncle was the mayor of Memphis.* ❑ *An e-mail from Uncle Fred arrived.* [from Old French]
→ see **family**

**un|clear** /ʌnklɪər/ ■ ADJ If something is **unclear**, it is not known or not certain. ❑ *It is unclear how much support they have.* ■ ADJ If you are **unclear** about something, you do not understand it well or are not sure about it. ❑ *He is unclear about his future.* [from Old French]

**Uncle Sam** /ʌŋk³l sæm/ N-PROPER Some people refer to the United States of America or its government as **Uncle Sam**. ❑ *...the best education Uncle Sam could provide.*

**un|com|fort|able** /ʌnkʌmftəb³l, -kʌmfərtə-/ ■ ADJ If you are **uncomfortable**, you are slightly worried or embarrassed, and not relaxed and confident. ❑ *The request for money made them feel uncomfortable.* ❑ *She was uncomfortable with the situation.* ● **un|com|fort|ably**

/ʌnkʌmftəbli, -kʌmfərtə-/ ADV ❑ *Sam's face was uncomfortably close to Brad's.* ■ ADJ Something that is **uncomfortable** makes you feel slight pain or physical discomfort when you experience it or use it. ❑ *...an uncomfortable chair.* ❑ *The ride back to the center of the town was hot and uncomfortable.* ● **un|com|fort|ably** ADV ❑ *The water was uncomfortably cold.* ■ ADJ If you are **uncomfortable**, you are not physically content and relaxed, and feel slight pain or discomfort. ❑ *I sometimes feel uncomfortable after eating in the evening.* ● **un|com|fort|ably** ADV ❑ *He felt uncomfortably hot.* [from Old French]

**un|com|pli|cat|ed** /ʌnkɒmplɪkeɪtɪd/ ADJ **Uncomplicated** people or things are easy to deal with or understand. ❑ *She is a beautiful, uncomplicated girl.* [from Latin]

**un|com|pro|mis|ing** /ʌnkɒmprəmaɪzɪŋ/ ADJ If you describe someone as **uncompromising**, you mean that they are determined not to change their opinions or aims in any way. ❑ *...an uncompromising politician.* [from Old French]

**un|con|cerned** /ʌnkənsɜrnd/ ADJ If a person is **unconcerned about** something, they are not interested in it or worried about it. ❑ *She was unconcerned about her looks.*

**un|con|di|tion|al** /ʌnkəndɪʃən³l/ ADJ Something that is **unconditional** is done or given freely, without anything being required in return. ❑ *Children need unconditional love from their parents.* ● **un|con|di|tion|al|ly** ADV ❑ *They accepted our offer unconditionally.* [from Latin]

**un|con|firmed** /ʌnkənfɜrmd/ ADJ If a report or a rumor is **unconfirmed**, there is no definite proof that it is true. ❑ *...unconfirmed reports of trouble.*

**un|con|nect|ed** /ʌnkənɛktɪd/ ADJ If one thing is **unconnected with** another or the two things are **unconnected**, the things are not related to each other in any way. ❑ *Her problems were unconnected with her marriage.* [from Latin]

**un|con|scious** /ʌnkɒnʃəs/ ■ ADJ Someone who is **unconscious** is in a state similar to sleep, usually as the result of a serious injury or a lack of oxygen. ❑ *By the time the ambulance arrived he was unconscious.* ● **un|con|scious|ness** N-UNCOUNT ❑ *...a knock to the head which led to unconsciousness.* ■ ADJ If you are **unconscious of** something, you are unaware of it. ❑ *He seemed unconscious of his failure.* ● **un|con|scious|ly** ADV ❑ *His hand unconsciously went to the back of his head.* ■ ADJ If feelings or attitudes are **unconscious**, you do not know that you have them, but they show in the way that you behave. ❑ *...my unconscious fear of becoming a mother.* ● **un|con|scious|ly** ADV ❑ *We unconsciously form opinions about people we meet.* [from Latin]
→ see **dream**

**un|con|sti|tu|tion|al** /ʌnkɒnstɪtuʃən³l/ ADJ If something is **unconstitutional**, it breaks the rules of a constitution. ❑ *...laws they believe are unconstitutional.*

**un|con|trol|lable** /ʌnkəntroʊləbᵊl/ ADJ If you describe a feeling or physical action as **uncontrollable**, you mean that you cannot control it or prevent yourself from feeling or doing it. ❑ ...*feelings of uncontrollable anger.* ● **un|con|trol|lably** /ʌnkəntroʊləbli/ ADV ❑ *I started shaking uncontrollably and began to cry.*

**un|con|trolled** /ʌnkəntroʊld/ ADJ If something such as a feeling or activity is **uncontrolled**, no attempt is made to stop it or to make it less extreme. ❑ *His uncontrolled behavior disturbed the entire class.* ❑ ...*uncontrolled immigration.*

**un|con|ven|tion|al** /ʌnkənvɛnʃᵊnᵊl/ ADJ If someone is **unconventional**, they do not behave in the same way as most other people in their society. ❑ *Linus Pauling is an unconventional genius.* [from Latin]

**un|con|vinc|ing** /ʌnkənvɪnsɪŋ/ ADJ If you describe something such as an argument or explanation as **unconvincing**, you find it difficult to believe because it does not seem real. ❑ *His excuses were unconvincing.* ● **un|con|vinc|ing|ly** ADV ❑ *"I believe you, Meg," Jack said, unconvincingly.* [from Latin]

**un|cool** /ʌnkul/ ADJ If you say that a person, thing, or activity is **uncool**, you disapprove of them because they are not fashionable, sophisticated, or attractive. ❑ *He was fat, uncool, and unpopular.* [from Old English]

**un|count noun** /ʌnkaʊnt naʊn/ (**uncount nouns**) N-COUNT An **uncount noun** is a noun such as "gold" or "information" which has only one form and can be used without a determiner (e.g. **a**, **the**, **some** or **this**).

**un|cov|er** /ʌnkʌvər/ (**uncovers, uncovering, uncovered**) **1** V-T If you **uncover** something secret, you find out about it. ❑ *We must uncover every detail.* **2** V-T To **uncover** something means to remove something that is covering it. ❑ *Uncover the dish and cook the chicken for about 15 minutes.* [from Old French]

| Word Partnership | Use *uncover* with : |
| --- | --- |
| N. | uncover **evidence**, uncover **a plot**, uncover **the truth** **1** |
| V. | **help** uncover *something* **1** **2** |

**un|daunt|ed** /ʌndɔntɪd/ ADJ If you are **undaunted**, you are not at all afraid or worried about dealing with something, especially something that would frighten or worry most people. ❑ *She is undaunted by the cost of her program.*

**un|de|cid|ed** /ʌndɪsaɪdɪd/ ADJ If you are **undecided**, you cannot decide about something or have not yet decided about it. ❑ *She was still undecided about her career.* [from Old French]

**un|demo|crat|ic** /ʌndɛməkrætɪk/ ADJ A system, process, or decision that is **undemocratic** is one that is controlled or made by one person or a small number of people, rather than by all the people involved. ❑ ...*undemocratic countries.* [from French]

**un|de|ni|able** /ʌndɪnaɪəbᵊl/ ADJ If you say that something is **undeniable**, you mean that it is definitely true. ❑ *Her charm is undeniable.* ● **un|de|ni|ably** /ʌndɪnaɪəbli/ ADV ❑ *Bringing up a baby is undeniably hard work.*

**un|der** /ʌndər/

In addition to the uses shown below, **under** is also used in phrasal verbs such as "go under" and "knuckle under."

**1** PREP If a person or thing is **under** something, they are directly below or beneath it. ❑ ...*tunnels under the ground.* ❑ *A path runs under the trees.* ❑ *She held her breath for three minutes under the water.* **2** PREP If something happens **under** particular circumstances or conditions, it happens when those circumstances or conditions exist. ❑ *Under the circumstances I think we did well.* ❑ *He was able to work under pressure.* **3** PREP If something happens **under** a particular person or government, it happens when that person or government is in power. ❑ *I hope that there will be a change under this government.* **4** PREP If you study or work **under** a particular person, that person teaches you or tells you what to do. ❑ *I have eight hundred people working under me.* ❑ *General Lewis Hyde served under General Mitchell.* **5** PREP If you do something **under** a particular name, you use that name instead of your real name. ❑ *Did you write any of your books under the name Amanda Fairchild?* **6** PREP You use **under** to say which section of a list, book, or system something is in. ❑ *Look on page 164, under the heading "Top Ten Cities."* **7** PREP If something or someone is **under** a particular age or amount, they are less than that age or amount. ❑ ...*jobs for those under 65.* ● **Under** is also an adverb. ❑ ...*free health insurance for children 13 and under.* [from Old English]
→ see **location**

**under|brush** /ʌndərbrʌʃ/ N-UNCOUNT **Underbrush** consists of bushes and plants growing close together under trees in a forest. ❑ ...*the cool underbrush of the rain forest...* ❑ *The trail was thick with underbrush.*

**under|class** /ʌndərklæs/ (**underclasses**) N-COUNT A country's **underclass** consists of those members of its population who are poor, and who have little chance of improving their situation. ❑ *There is a growing underclass of people in poor neighborhoods.*

**under|cov|er** /ʌndərkʌvər/ ADJ **Undercover** work involves secretly obtaining information for the government or the police. ❑ ...*a five-day undercover operation.* ❑ ...*undercover FBI agents.*

**under|cur|rent** /ʌndərkɜrənt/ (**undercurrents**) N-COUNT If there is an **undercurrent** of a feeling, you are hardly aware of the feeling, but it influences the way you think or behave. ❑ *Most comedy has an undercurrent of truth.*

**under|cut** /ʌndərkʌt/ (**undercuts, undercutting**)

The form **undercut** is used in the present tense and is also the past tense and past participle.

V-T If you **undercut** someone or **undercut** their prices, you sell a product more cheaply than they do. [BUSINESS] ❑ ...*promises to undercut air fares on some routes by 40 percent.*

**under|de|vel|oped** /ʌndərdɪvɛləpt/ ADJ An **underdeveloped** country or region does not have modern industries and usually has a low standard of living. Some people dislike this term and prefer to use **developing**. ❑ ...*the problems of underdeveloped countries.*

**under|dog** /ˈʌndərdɔg/ (**underdogs**) N-COUNT
The **underdog** in a competition or situation is the person who seems least likely to succeed or win. ❑ *Most people were cheering for the underdog to win.*

**under|es|ti|mate** /ˈʌndərˈɛstɪmeɪt/
(**underestimates, underestimating, underestimated**) ◼ V-T If you **underestimate** something, you do not realize how large or great it is or will be. ❑ *Never underestimate the power of anger.* ◻ V-T If you **underestimate** someone, you do not realize what they are capable of doing. ❑ *I think a lot of people still underestimate him.*

**under|go** /ˌʌndərˈgoʊ/ (**undergoes, undergoing, underwent, undergone**) V-T If you **undergo** something necessary or unpleasant, it happens to you. ❑ *She is undergoing treatment for cancer.* [from Old English]

**under|gradu|ate** /ˌʌndərˈgrædʒuɪt/
(**undergraduates**) N-COUNT An **undergraduate** is a student at a university or college who is studying for a bachelor's or associate's degree. ❑ *More than 55 percent of undergraduates are female.*

**under|ground**

> The adverb is pronounced /ˌʌndərˈgraʊnd/.
> The noun and adjective are pronounced /ˈʌndərgraʊnd/.

◼ ADV Something that is **underground** is below the surface of the ground. ❑ *It was unclear whether the water was underground or on the surface.* ● **Underground** is also an adjective. ❑ *...an underground parking garage for 2,100 vehicles.* ◻ ADJ **Underground** groups or activities are secret because their purpose is to oppose the government and they are illegal. ❑ *...an underground terrorist group.*
→ see **tunnel**

**under|growth** /ˈʌndərgroʊθ/ also
**underbrush** N-UNCOUNT **Undergrowth** consists of bushes and plants growing together under the trees in a forest. ❑ *...hidden by trees and undergrowth.*

**under|hand** /ˈʌndərhænd/ also **underhanded**
◼ ADJ If something is done in an **underhand** way, it is done secretly and dishonestly. ❑ *...underhand financial deals.* ◻ ADJ You use **underhand** or **underhanded** to describe actions, such as throwing a ball, in which you do not raise your arm above your shoulder. ❑ *...an underhanded pitch.* ● **Underhand** is also an adverb. ❑ *In softball, pitches are tossed underhand.*

**under|lie** /ˌʌndərˈlaɪ/ (**underlies, underlying, underlay, underlain**) ◼ V-T If something **underlies** a feeling or situation, it is the cause or basis of it. ❑ *Try to figure out what feeling underlies your anger.* ◻ → see also **underlying**

**under|line** /ˈʌndərlaɪn/ (**underlines, underlining, underlined**) ◼ V-T If one thing, for example an action or an event, **underlines** another, it draws attention to it and emphasizes its importance. ❑ *This accident underlines the danger of traveling there.* ◻ V-T If you **underline** something such as a word or a sentence, you draw a line underneath it in order to make people notice it or to give it extra importance. ❑ *She underlined her name.*

---

| **Word Partnership** | Use *underline* with : |
| --- | --- |
| N. | underline **the need for** *something* ◼ underline **passages**, underline **text**, underline **titles**, underline **words** ◻ |

**un|der|ly|ing** /ˌʌndərˈlaɪɪŋ/ ◼ ADJ The **underlying** features of an object, event, or situation are not obvious, and it may be difficult to discover or reveal them. ❑ *You have to understand the underlying causes of the problem.* ◻ → see also **underlie**

**under|mine** /ˌʌndərˈmaɪn/ (**undermines, undermining, undermined**) V-T If you **undermine** something such as a feeling or a system, you make it less strong or less secure. ❑ *He undermined my position.* [from Middle English]

| **Word Partnership** | Use *undermine* with : |
| --- | --- |
| N. | undermine **authority**, undermine **government**, undermine **peace**, undermine **security** |
| V. | **threaten to** undermine, **try to** undermine |

**under|neath** /ˌʌndərˈniθ/ ◼ PREP If one thing is **underneath** another, it is directly under it. ❑ *The bomb exploded underneath a van.* ● **Underneath** is also an adverb. ❑ *He was wearing a long-sleeved blue shirt with a white T-shirt underneath.* ◻ ADV The part of something which is **underneath** is the part which normally touches the ground or faces toward the ground. ❑ *The robin is a brown bird with red underneath.* ● **Underneath** is also a noun. ❑ *Now I know what the underneath of a car looks like.* ◼ ADV You use **underneath** when talking about feelings and emotions that people do not show in their behavior. ❑ *He was a violent man underneath.* ● **Underneath** is also a preposition. ❑ *Underneath his friendly behavior Luke was shy.* ❑ *The idea of getting away from home was underneath my mind.* [from Old English]
→ see **location**

**under|pants** /ˈʌndərpænts/ N-PLURAL
**Underpants** are a piece of underwear which have two holes to put your legs through and elastic around the top to hold them up around your waist or hips. ❑ *...white cotton underpants.*

**under|per|form** /ˌʌndərpərˈfɔrm/ also **under-perform** (**underperforms, underperforming, underperformed**) V-T/V-I If someone **underperforms** in something such as a sports contest, they do not perform as well as they could. If one thing **underperforms** another thing, it performs less well than the other thing. ❑ *Smaller companies have underperformed larger ones in the past several years.* ● **under|per|form|er** /ˌʌndərpərˈfɔrmər/ (**underperformers**) N-COUNT ❑ *They transformed the bank from an underperformer to one of the best in the world.* ● **under|per|for|mance** /ˌʌndərpərˈfɔrməns/ N-UNCOUNT ❑ *...the movie's underperformance in theaters.*

**under|rate** /ˌʌndərˈreɪt/ (**underrates, underrating, underrated**) V-T If you **underrate** someone or something, you do not recognize how intelligent, important, or great they are. ❑ *He has good business skills, although he sometimes underrates himself.* ● **under|rat|ed** ADJ ❑ *He is a very underrated poet.*

u

**under|score** /ˌʌndərskɔːr/ (**underscores, underscoring, underscored**) **1** V-T If something such as an action or an event **underscores** another, it draws attention to the other thing and emphasizes its importance. ❑ *The report underscores a larger problem.* **2** V-T If you **underscore** something such as a word or a sentence, you draw a line underneath it in order to make people notice it or give it extra importance. ❑ *He heavily underscored his note to Shelley.*

**under|shirt** /ˈʌndərʃɜːrt/ (**undershirts**) N-COUNT An **undershirt** is a piece of clothing that you wear on the top half of your body next to your skin in order to keep warm. ❑ *He put on a pair of short pants and an undershirt.*

**under|side** /ˈʌndərsaɪd/ (**undersides**) N-COUNT The **underside** of something is the part of it which normally faces towards the ground. ❑ *...the underside of the car.*

**under|stand** /ˌʌndərstænd/ (**understands, understanding, understood**) **1** V-T If you **understand** someone or **understand** what they are saying, you know what they mean. ❑ *I think you heard and understood me.* ❑ *I don't understand what you are talking about.* **2** V-T To **understand** someone means to know how they feel and why they behave in the way that they do. ❑ *I feel she really understands me.* **3** V-T You say that you **understand** something when you know why or how it happens. ❑ *They are too young to understand what is going on.* **4** V-T If you **understand** that something is true, you think it is true because you have heard or read that it is. ❑ *We understand that she's going to be here all day.* ❑ *As I understand it, she has a house in the city.* [from Old English]
→ see **philosophy**

**Thesaurus**    *understand*    Also look up :

V.  catch on, comprehend, get, grasp; (*ant.*) misunderstand **1**

**under|stand|able** /ˌʌndərstændəbəl/ ADJ If you describe someone's behavior or feelings as **understandable**, you think that they have reacted to a situation in a natural way or in the way you would expect. ❑ *His unhappiness was understandable.* ● **under|stand|ably** /ˌʌndərstændəbli/ ADV ❑ *They are understandably upset.* [from Old English]

**under|stand|ing** /ˌʌndərstændɪŋ/ (**understandings**) **1** N-VAR If you have an **understanding of** something, you know how it works or know what it means. ❑ *Children need an understanding of right and wrong.* **2** ADJ If you are **understanding** toward someone, you are kind and forgiving. ❑ *He was very understanding when we told him about our decision.* **3** N-UNCOUNT If there is **understanding between** people, they are friendly toward each other and trust each other. ❑ *There was complete understanding between Wilson and myself.* **4** N-COUNT An **understanding** is an informal agreement about something. ❑ *We have an understanding about the way we work.* ❑ *He was free to come and go as he wished on the understanding that he would not run away.* [from Old English]

**Word Partnership**   Use *understanding* with :

V.  **develop** an understanding, **lack** an understanding **1**
    **lack** understanding **3**

ADJ.  **basic** understanding, **clear** understanding, **complete** understanding **1**
    **deep/deeper** understanding, understanding **1** **3** **4**
    **better** understanding **1** **4**
    **mutual** understanding **3** **4**

**under|state** /ˌʌndərsteɪt/ (**understates, understating, understated**) V-T If you **understate** something, you describe it in a way that suggests that it is less important or serious than it really is. ❑ *The government understated the increase in prices.*

**under|stat|ed** /ˌʌndərsteɪtɪd/ ADJ If you describe a style, color, or effect as **understated**, you mean that it is simple and plain, and does not attract attention to itself. ❑ *I have always liked understated clothes.*

**under|state|ment** /ˈʌndərsteɪtmənt/ (**understatements**) N-VAR An **understatement** is a statement that does not say fully how true something is. ❑ *To say I'm disappointed is an understatement.*

**un|der|stood** /ˌʌndərstʊd/ **Understood** is the past tense and past participle of **understand**. [from Old English]

**under|take** /ˌʌndərteɪk/ (**undertakes, undertaking, undertook, undertaken**) **1** V-T When you **undertake** a task or job, you start doing it and accept responsibility for it. ❑ *A carpenter will usually undertake this kind of work for you.* ● **under|tak|ing** /ˌʌndərteɪkɪŋ/ (**undertakings**) N-COUNT ❑ *Organizing the show has been a huge undertaking.* **2** V-T If you **undertake** to do something, you promise that you will do it. ❑ *He undertook to write the letter himself.*

**under|tak|er** /ˈʌndərteɪkər/ (**undertakers**) N-COUNT An **undertaker** is a person whose job is to care for the bodies of people who have died and to arrange funerals. ❑ *An undertaker had already taken the body away.*

**un|der|took** /ˌʌndərtʊk/ **Undertook** is the past tense of **undertake**.

**under|value** /ˌʌndərvæljuː/ (**undervalues, undervaluing, undervalued**) V-T If you **undervalue** something or someone, you do not recognize how valuable or important they are. ❑ *We must never undervalue freedom.* ❑ *Even the best teacher can feel undervalued.*

**under|wa|ter** /ˌʌndərwɔːtər/ ADV Something that exists or happens **underwater** exists or happens below the surface of the ocean, a river, or a lake. ❑ *...submarines able to travel at high speeds underwater.* ❑ *Some parts of the beach are completely underwater at high tide.* ● **Underwater** is also an adjective. ❑ *...divers using underwater cameras.*

**under|way** /ˌʌndərweɪ/ ADJ If an activity is **underway**, it has already started. If an activity gets **underway**, it starts. ❑ *Plans are underway to build more homes.* [from Old English]

**under|wear** /ˈʌndərwɛər/ N-UNCOUNT **Underwear** is items of clothing that you wear next to your skin and under your other clothes. ❑ *For*

*Christmas my brother and I got new underwear, a toy, and a book.*

**un|der|went** /ʌndərwɛnt/ **Underwent** is the past tense of **undergo**. [from Old English]

**under|world** /ʌndərwɜrld/ N-SING The **underworld** is organized crime and the people who are involved in it. ❑ *People say that she still has connections to the criminal underworld.*

**under|write** /ʌndərraɪt/ (**underwrites, underwriting, underwrote, underwritten**) V-T If an institution or company **underwrites** an activity or **underwrites** the cost of it, they agree to provide any money that is needed to cover losses or buy special equipment, often for an agreed-upon fee. [BUSINESS] ❑ *The two firms are likely to underwrite the deal.*

**un|de|sir|able** /ʌndɪzaɪərəbəl/ ADJ If you describe something or someone as **undesirable**, you think they are bad or will have harmful effects. ❑ *...undesirable behavior like fighting.* [from Old French]

**un|did** /ʌndɪd/ **Undid** is the past tense of **undo**.

**un|dip|lo|mat|ic** /ʌndɪpləmætɪk/ ADJ If someone is described as **undiplomatic**, they say or do things that offend people, usually not on purpose. ❑ *He's the most undiplomatic man ever to work here.* ● **un|dip|lo|mati|cal|ly** ADV ❑ *He undiplomatically described two years in Dublin as "very, very boring."* [from French]

**un|dis|closed** /ʌndɪskloʊzd/ ADJ **Undisclosed** information is not revealed to the public. ❑ *The company was sold for an undisclosed amount of money.*

**un|dis|put|ed** /ʌndɪspyutɪd/ ADJ If you describe something as **undisputed**, you mean that everyone accepts that it exists or is true. ❑ *...an undisputed fact.* ❑ *Seles was the undisputed world champion.* ❑ *At 78 years of age, he's still undisputed leader of his country.*

**un|dis|turbed** /ʌndɪstɜrbd/ **1** ADJ Something that remains **undisturbed** is not touched, moved, or used by anyone. ❑ *The desk looked undisturbed.* **2** ADJ If you are **undisturbed** in something that you are doing, you are able to continue doing it and are not affected by something that is happening. ❑ *There was a small restaurant on Sullivan Street where we could talk undisturbed.* [from Latin]

**undo** /ʌndu/ (**undoes, undoing, undid, undone**) **1** V-T If you **undo** something, you unfasten, loosen, or untie it. ❑ *I managed to undo a corner of the package.* ❑ *I undid the bottom two buttons of my gray shirt.* **2** V-T To **undo** something that has been done means to reverse its effect. ❑ *A heavy-handed approach from the police could undo that good impression.* ❑ *She knew it would be difficult to undo the damage.* **3** → see also **undoing**

**un|do|ing** /ʌnduɪŋ/ N-SING If something is someone's **undoing**, it is the cause of their failure. ❑ *Greed was his undoing.*

**un|doubt|ed** /ʌndaʊtɪd/ ADJ You can use **undoubted** to emphasize that something exists or is true. ❑ *The event was an undoubted success.* ❑ *...a man of your undoubted ability.* ● **un|doubt|ed|ly** ADV ❑ *He was undoubtedly right.*

**un|dress** /ʌndrɛs/ (**undresses, undressing, undressed**) V-T/V-I When you **undress**, you take off your clothes. If you **undress** someone, you take off their clothes. ❑ *She went out, leaving Rachel to undress and take a shower.* ● **un|dressed** ADJ ❑ *Fifteen minutes later he was undressed and in bed.* [from Old French]

**un|due** /ʌndu/ ADJ If you describe something bad as **undue**, you mean that it is greater or more extreme than you think is reasonable or appropriate. ❑ *I don't want to put any undue pressure on them to win the baseball game.* ● **un|du|ly** ADV ❑ *"But you're not unduly worried about doing this report?" — "No."* [from Old French]

**un|earth** /ʌnɜrθ/ (**unearths, unearthing, unearthed**) **1** V-T If someone **unearths** facts or evidence, they discover them with difficulty. ❑ *Researchers have unearthed documents from the 1600s.* **2** V-T If someone **unearths** something that is buried, they find it by digging in the ground. ❑ *They unearthed the bones of an elephant believed to be 500,000 years old.* [from Old English]

**un|ease** /ʌniz/ N-UNCOUNT If you have a feeling of **unease**, you feel anxious or afraid, because you think that something is wrong. ❑ *A terrible sense of unease came over her.* [from Old French]

**un|easy** /ʌnizi/ **1** ADJ If you are **uneasy**, you feel that something is wrong and you are anxious or uncomfortable about it. ❑ *He looked uneasy and refused to answer questions.* ❑ *I was uneasy about the time.* ● **un|easi|ly** /ʌnizɪli/ ADV ❑ *Meg moved uneasily on her chair.* ● **un|easi|ness** N-UNCOUNT ❑ *Her uneasiness grew as she looked at him.* **2** ADJ If you describe a situation or relationship as **uneasy**, you mean that the situation is not settled and may not last. ❑ *There is an uneasy relationship between us and the politicians.* ● **un|easi|ly** ADV ❑ *The boutique sat uneasily between a butcher's and a shoe store.* [from Old French]

**un|em|ployed** /ʌnɪmplɔɪd/ ADJ Someone who is **unemployed** does not have a job. ❑ *The problem is millions of people are unemployed.* ❑ *This workshop helps young unemployed people.* ● **The unemployed** are people who are unemployed. ❑ *We want to create jobs for the unemployed.*

**un|em|ploy|ment** /ʌnɪmplɔɪmənt/ **1** N-UNCOUNT **Unemployment** is the fact that people who want jobs cannot get them. ❑ *...periods of high unemployment.* **2** N-UNCOUNT **Unemployment** is the same as **unemployment compensation**. ❑ *He's out of work and is getting unemployment.* [from Old French]

**un|em|ploy|ment com|pen|sa|tion** N-UNCOUNT **Unemployment compensation** is money that some people receive from the state, usually for a limited time after losing a job, when they do not have a job and are unable to find one. ❑ *He has to manage on unemployment compensation.*

**un|em|ploy|ment line** (**unemployment lines**) N-COUNT When people talk about **the**

**u**

**un|employment line**, they are talking about the state of being unemployed, especially when saying how many people are unemployed. ☐ *Being without work means standing in the unemployment line.*

**un|equaled** /ʌnˈikwəld/ ADJ If you describe something as **unequaled**, you mean that it is greater, better, or more extreme than anything else of the same kind. ☐ *This record figure was unequaled for 13 years.*

**un|equivo|cal** /ʌnɪˈkwɪvəkəl/ ADJ If you describe someone's attitude as **unequivocal**, you mean that it is completely clear and very firm. [FORMAL] ☐ *The answer is an unequivocal "yes."*
● **un|equivo|cal|ly** /ʌnɪˈkwɪvəkli/ ADV ☐ *They should unequivocally say how they feel.*

**un|ethi|cal** /ʌnˈɛθɪkəl/ ADJ Behavior that is **unethical** is morally wrong. ☐ *It's unethical to advertise such a dangerous product.* ☐ *I thought it was unethical for doctors to operate on their own families.* [from Latin]

**un|even** /ʌnˈivən/ **1** ADJ An **uneven** surface or edge is not smooth, flat, or straight. ☐ *He fell on the uneven surface.* ☐ *The pathways were uneven, broken, and dangerous.* **2** ADJ Something that is **uneven** is not regular or consistent. ☐ *Her breathing was uneven.* [from Old English]

| Thesaurus | *uneven* | Also look up : |
|---|---|---|
| ADJ. | jagged, rough; (*ant.*) even **1** inconsistent, irregular **2** | |

**un|ex|pec|ted** /ʌnɪkˈspɛktɪd/ ADJ If something is **unexpected**, it surprises you because you did not think that it was likely to happen. ☐ *His death was totally unexpected.* ● **un|ex|pect|ed|ly** ADV ☐ *May was unexpectedly hot.*

| Thesaurus | *unexpected* | Also look up : |
|---|---|---|
| ADJ. | startling, surprising | |

**un|ex|plained** /ʌnɪkˈspleɪnd/ ADJ If something is **unexplained**, the reason for it or cause of it is unclear or is not known. ☐ *Colton suffered a terrifying, unexplained illness.* ☐ *The city's water supply was cut for unexplained reasons.*

| Word Link | *un = not : unfair, unreal, unspoken* |
|---|---|

**un|fair** /ʌnˈfɛər/ ADJ An **unfair** action or situation is not right or fair. ☐ *Her position as president gives her an unfair advantage.* ☐ *It was unfair that he should suffer so much.* ● **un|fair|ly** ADV ☐ *He unfairly blamed Frances for his failure.* ● **un|fair|ness** N-UNCOUNT ☐ *...the unfairness of life.* [from Old English]

**un|faith|ful** /ʌnˈfeɪθfəl/ ADJ If someone is **unfaithful to** their lover or to the person they are married to, they have a sexual relationship with someone else. ☐ *James had been unfaithful to Christine for the four years they'd been together.* [from Latin]

**un|fa|mil|iar** /ʌnfəˈmɪlyər/ **1** ADJ If something is **unfamiliar** to you, you know nothing or very little about it, because you have not seen or experienced it before. ☐ *...a voice that was unfamiliar to me.* **2** ADJ If you are **unfamiliar with** something, you know nothing or very little about it. ☐ *She doesn't speak Japanese and is unfamiliar with Japanese culture.* [from Latin]

**un|fash|ion|able** /ʌnˈfæʃənəbəl/ ADJ If something is **unfashionable**, it is not approved of or done by most people because it is out of style. ☐ *He wears unfashionable clothes.* [from Old French]

**un|fa|vor|able** /ʌnˈfeɪvərəbəl/ **1** ADJ **Unfavorable** conditions or circumstances cause problems and reduce the chances of success. ☐ *...unfavorable weather conditions.* ☐ *...an unfavorable result.* **2** ADJ If you have an **unfavorable** reaction to something, you do not like it. ☐ *The president is getting unfavorable comments on his new policy.* ☐ *They have some unfavorable opinions about him.*
● **un|fa|vor|ably** /ʌnˈfeɪvərəbli/ ADV ☐ *Some parents compare their children unfavorably to other children.* [from Latin]

**un|fet|tered** /ʌnˈfɛtərd/ ADJ If you describe something as **unfettered**, you mean that it is not controlled or limited by anyone or anything. [FORMAL] ☐ *He had an unfettered mind.*

**un|fin|ished** /ʌnˈfɪnɪʃt/ ADJ If something is **unfinished**, it is not complete. ☐ *...Jane Austen's unfinished book.* [from Old French]

**un|fit** /ʌnˈfɪt/ **1** ADJ If someone or something is **unfit** for a particular purpose, they are not suitable or not good enough for that purpose. ☐ *The water was unfit for swimming.* ☐ *...tunnels filled with air unfit to breathe.* **2** ADJ If you are **unfit**, your body is not in good condition because you have not been getting regular exercise. ☐ *Many children are so unfit they cannot do even basic exercises.* [from Middle Dutch]

**un|fold** /ʌnˈfoʊld/ (**unfolds, unfolding, unfolded**) **1** V-I If a situation or story **unfolds**, it develops and becomes known or understood. ☐ *We'll see how the situation unfolds in the next 24 hours.* ☐ *The policeman listened carefully as the story unfolded.* **2** V-T/V-I If someone **unfolds** something which has been folded or if it **unfolds**, it is opened out and becomes flat. ☐ *She unfolded the piece of paper.* [from Old English]

**un|fore|seen** /ʌnfɔrˈsin/ ADJ An **unforeseen** event happens unexpectedly. ☐ *...an unforeseen rise in costs.*

**un|for|get|table** /ʌnfərˈgɛtəbəl/ ADJ If something is **unforgettable**, it is so beautiful, enjoyable, or unusual that you remember it for a long time. ☐ *The day was truly unforgettable.* ☐ *...the outdoor activities that will make your vacation unforgettable.*

**un|for|tu|nate** /ʌnˈfɔrtʃənɪt/ **1** ADJ If you describe someone as **unfortunate**, you mean that something unpleasant or unlucky has happened to them. ☐ *I've just been unfortunate to be ill.* **2** ADJ If you describe something that has happened as **unfortunate**, you think that it is inappropriate, embarrassing, awkward, or undesirable. ☐ *It is unfortunate that your flight was canceled.* [from Old French]

**un|for|tu|nate|ly** /ʌnˈfɔrtʃənɪtli/ ADV You can use **unfortunately** to express regret about what you are saying. ☐ *Unfortunately, I don't have time to stay.* [from Old French]

**un|found|ed** /ʌnˈfaʊndɪd/ ADJ If you describe a rumor, belief, or feeling as **unfounded**, you mean that it is wrong and is not based on facts or evidence. ☐ *These unfounded rumors are hurtful to our family.* ☐ *Their fears were unfounded.* [from Old French]

U

**un|friend|ly** /ʌnfrɛndli/ ADJ If you describe someone as **unfriendly**, you mean that they behave in an unkind or hostile way. ❑ *Some people were unfriendly to her.* ❑ *People always complain that banks are unfriendly and unhelpful.* [from Old English]

**un|ful|filled** /ʌnfʊlfɪld/ **1** ADJ If you use **unfulfilled** to describe something such as a promise, ambition, or need, you mean that what was promised, hoped for, or needed has not happened. ❑ *Her wishes were unfulfilled.* ❑ *...angry at unfulfilled promises of jobs.* **2** ADJ If you describe someone as **unfulfilled**, you mean that they feel dissatisfied with life or with what they have done. ❑ *I don't want to die unloved and unfulfilled.*

**un|furl** /ʌnfɜrl/ (unfurls, unfurling, unfurled) V-T/V-I If you **unfurl** something such as an umbrella, sail, or flag, you open it, so that it is spread out. You can also say that it **unfurls**. ❑ *We began to unfurl all the sails.*

**un|gram|mati|cal** /ʌngrəmætɪkəl/ ADJ If someone's language is **ungrammatical**, it is not considered correct because it does not obey the rules of grammar. ❑ *The sentence is unclear but not totally ungrammatical.* ● **un|gram|mati|cal|ly** ADV ❑ *She speaks ungrammatically but fluently.*

**un|hap|py** /ʌnhæpi/ (unhappier, unhappiest) **1** ADJ If you are **unhappy**, you are sad and depressed. ❑ *He was a shy, sometimes unhappy man.* ● **un|hap|pi|ly** ADV ❑ *"I don't have your imagination," Kevin said unhappily.* ● **un|hap|pi|ness** N-UNCOUNT ❑ *There was a lot of unhappiness in my childhood.* **2** ADJ If you are **unhappy about** something, you are not pleased about it or not satisfied with it. ❑ *College students are unhappy with their school bookstores.* ● **un|hap|pi|ness** N-UNCOUNT ❑ *She spoke about her unhappiness with her job.* **3** ADJ An **unhappy** situation or choice is not satisfactory or desirable. ❑ *...his unhappy choice of words.*

**un|harmed** /ʌnhɑrmd/ ADJ If someone or something is **unharmed** after an accident or violent incident, they are not hurt or damaged in any way. ❑ *They both escaped unharmed.*

**un|healthy** /ʌnhɛlθi/ (unhealthier, unhealthiest) **1** ADJ Something that is **unhealthy** is likely to cause illness or bad health. ❑ *Avoid unhealthy foods such as hamburgers and fries.* **2** ADJ If you are **unhealthy**, you are sick or not in good physical condition. ❑ *...an unhealthy looking man.*

**un|heard of** /ʌnhɜrd ʌv/ ADJ An event or situation that is **unheard of** never happens. ❑ *Riots are almost unheard of in Japan.*

**un|help|ful** /ʌnhɛlpfəl/ ADJ If you say that someone or something is **unhelpful**, you mean that they do not help you or improve a situation, and may even make things worse. ❑ *She does not want to sound unhelpful.* [from Old English]

**un|hurt** /ʌnhɜrt/ ADJ If someone who has been attacked, or involved in an accident, is **unhurt**, they are not injured. ❑ *The driver escaped unhurt.* [from Old French]

**uni|cel|lu|lar** /yunɪsɛlyələr/ ADJ **Unicellular** organisms are organisms that consist of a single cell, such as bacteria. Compare **multicellular**. [TECHNICAL]

**un|iden|ti|fied** /ʌnaɪdɛntɪfaɪd/ ADJ If you describe someone or something as **unidentified**, you mean that nobody knows who or what they are. ❑ *An unidentified woman was in the car.*

**uni|fi|ca|tion** /yunɪfɪkeɪʃən/ N-UNCOUNT **Unification** is the process by which two or more countries join together and become one country. ❑ *...the unification of East and West Germany in 1990.* [from Medieval Latin]

**uni|form** /yunɪfɔrm/ (uniforms) **1** N-VAR A **uniform** is a special set of clothes which some people wear to work in and which some children wear in school. ❑ *The police wear dark blue uniforms.* ❑ *He was dressed in his school uniform.* **2** ADJ If something is **uniform**, it is even and regular. ❑ *Plants do not all grow to uniform size.* ● **uni|form|ity** /yunɪfɔrmɪti/ N-UNCOUNT ❑ *...uniformity of color.* ● **uni|form|ly** ADV ❑ *Outside, the November day was uniformly gray.* **3** ADJ If you describe a number of things as **uniform**, you mean that they are all the same. ❑ *Along each wall were uniform green metal filing cabinets.* ● **uni|form|ity** N-UNCOUNT ❑ *...the dull uniformity of the houses.* [from Latin]

uniform

→ see **basketball, football, soccer**

**uni|formed** /yunɪfɔrmd/ ADJ **Uniformed** people are wearing a uniform while they do their job. ❑ *...uniformed policemen.* [from Latin]

**uni|fy** /yunɪfaɪ/ (unifies, unifying, unified) V-T/V-I If someone **unifies** different things or parts, or if the things or parts **unify**, they are brought together to form one thing. ❑ *They are trying to unify boys' and girls' basketball rules in Washington.* ● **uni|fied** ADJ ❑ *You are sending a loud and unified message.* [from Medieval Latin]

**uni|lat|er|al** /yunɪlætərəl/ ADJ A **unilateral** decision is made by only one of the groups, organizations, or countries that are involved in a particular situation, without the agreement of the others. ❑ *...a unilateral decision.*

**un|im|agi|nable** /ʌnɪmædʒɪnəbəl/ ADJ If you describe something as **unimaginable**, you are emphasizing that it is difficult to imagine or understand well, because it is not part of people's normal experience. ❑ *Life without cars is almost unimaginable.* ● **un|im|agi|nably** /ʌnɪmædʒɪnəbli/ ADV ❑ *She was unimaginably rich.* [from Latin]

**un|im|por|tant** /ʌnɪmpɔrtənt/ ADJ Something or someone that is **unimportant** does not have much influence, effect, or value. ❑ *The difference in their ages seemed unimportant.* [from Old Italian]

**un|im|pressed** /ʌnɪmprɛst/ ADJ If you are **unimpressed** by something or someone, you do not think they are very good, intelligent, or useful. ❑ *He was very unimpressed by his teachers.*

**un|in|forma|tive** /ʌnɪnfɔrmətɪv/ ADJ Something that is **uninformative** does not give

u

you enough useful information. ❑ *He was polite but uninformative.* [from French]

**un|in|hib|it|ed** /ˌʌnɪnhɪbɪtɪd/ ADJ If you describe a person or their behavior as **uninhibited**, you mean that they express their opinions and feelings openly, and behave as they want to, without worrying what other people think. ❑ *...a bold and uninhibited entertainer.* ❑ *The dancing grew more and more uninhibited.* [from Latin]

**un|in|stall** /ˌʌnɪnstɔl/ (**uninstalls, uninstalling, uninstalled**) V-T If you **uninstall** a computer program, you remove it permanently from your computer. [COMPUTING] ❑ *If you don't like the program, just uninstall it.* [from Medieval Latin]

**un|in|ten|tion|al** /ˌʌnɪntɛnʃənᵊl/ ADJ Something that is **unintentional** is not done deliberately, but happens by accident. ❑ *They often make unintentional mistakes.* ● **un|in|ten|tion|al|ly** ADV ❑ *There are times when the book is unintentionally funny.* [from Late Latin]

**un|in|ter|rupt|ed** /ˌʌnɪntərʌptɪd/ ADJ If something is **uninterrupted**, it is continuous and has no breaks or interruptions in it. ❑ *...a weekend full of uninterrupted music.* ❑ *I was hoping to work uninterrupted.*

---

**Word Link**　　uni ≈ one : *uniform, unilateral, union*

---

**un|ion** /yunyən/ (**unions**) **1** N-COUNT A **union** is a workers' organization which represents its members and which tries to improve things such as their working conditions and pay. ❑ *Ten new members joined the union.* **2** N-UNCOUNT When the **union** of two or more things occurs, they are joined together and become one thing. ❑ *...the union of Tanganyika and Zanzibar to form Tanzania.* [from Church Latin]
→ see Word Web: **union**
→ see **empire, factory**

**unique** /yunik/ ADJ Something that is **unique** is the only one of its kind. ❑ *Each person's signature is unique.* ● **unique|ly** ADV ❑ *She's a dog with uniquely colored eyes; one is brown and one is blue.* ● **unique|ness** N-UNCOUNT ❑ *I like the uniqueness of flavors in Australian cooking.* **2** ADJ You can use **unique** to describe things that you admire because they are very unusual and special. ❑ *She was a woman of unique talent.* ● **unique|ly** ADV ❑ *...a uniquely beautiful city.* **3** ADJ If something is **unique to** one thing, person, group, or place, it concerns or belongs only to that thing, person, group, or place. ❑ *This animal is unique to Borneo.* ● **unique|ly** ADV

❑ *The problem isn't uniquely American.* [from French]

---

**Thesaurus**　　*unique*　　Also look up :

ADJ.　different, one-of-a-kind, special; (*ant.*) common, standard, usual

---

**uni|son** /yunɪsən, -zən/ **1** PHRASE If two or more people do something **in unison**, they do it together at the same time. ❑ *They were singing in unison.* **2** N-UNCOUNT In dance, **unison** is the performance of a series of movements by two or more dancers at the same time. [TECHNICAL] [from Late Latin]

**unit** /yunɪt/ (**units**) **1** N-COUNT If you consider something as a **unit**, you consider it as a single, complete thing. ❑ *...a happy family unit enjoying the day together.* **2** N-COUNT A **unit** is a group of people who work together at a specific job, often in a particular place. ❑ *...a firefighting unit.* **3** N-COUNT A **unit** is a small machine which has a particular function, often part of a larger machine. ❑ *The unit plugs into any TV set.* **4** N-COUNT A **unit** of measurement is a fixed standard quantity, length, or weight that is used for measuring things. The quart, the inch, and the ounce are all units.
→ see **graph**

**Uni|tar|ian** /yunɪtɛəriən/ (**Unitarians**) **1** N-COUNT **Unitarians** are Christians who reject the idea of the Trinity and believe that God is a single being. ❑ *They were Unitarians.* **2** ADJ **Unitarian** means relating to the religious beliefs or practices of Unitarians. ❑ *...a Unitarian minister.* [from Modern Latin]

**unite** /yunaɪt/ (**unites, uniting, united**) V-T/V-I If a group of people or things **unite** or if something **unites** them, they join together and act as a group. ❑ *Only the president can unite the people.* [from Late Latin]

**unit|ed** /yunaɪtɪd/ **1** ADJ When people are **united** about something, they agree about it and act together. ❑ *They were united by their love of music.* **2** ADJ **United** is used to describe a country which has been formed from two or more states or countries. ❑ *...a united Germany.* [from Late Latin]

**Unit|ed Na|tions** N-PROPER The **United Nations** is an organization which most countries belong to. Its role is to encourage international peace, cooperation, and friendship.

**Unit|ed States of Ameri|ca** N-PROPER The **United States of America** is the official name for the country in North America that consists of fifty

---

**Word Web**　　union

U

In some places, **laborers** work long hours with little chance for a **raise** in **wages. Workdays** of 10 to 12 hours are common. Some people work seven days a week. Conditions like this lead to unhappiness among **workers.** At that point, **organizers** can encourage them to join a **union.** Union leaders do **collective bargaining** with business owners. They may ask for a shorter workday or better working conditions. If the **employees** are not satisfied with the results, they may **strike.** In Sweden, 85% of laborers and 75% of **white-collar** employees belong to unions.

states and the District of Columbia. It is bordered by Canada in the north and Mexico in the south. The form **United States** is also used.

**unit frac|tion** (**unit fractions**) N-COUNT A **unit fraction** is a fraction in which the top part of the fraction is always the number one, for example ½ or ¼. [TECHNICAL]

**unity** /yuniti/ **1** N-UNCOUNT **Unity** is the state of different areas or groups being joined together to form a single country or organization. □ ...the unity of Eastern and Western Europe. **2** N-UNCOUNT When there is **unity**, people are in agreement and act together for a particular purpose. □ The president called for unity between the United States and Europe. **3** N-UNCOUNT The **unity** of a work of art such as a painting or a piece of music is the impression it gives that it is complete and that all the different parts belong together. [from Old French]

**uni|ver|sal** /yunɪvɜrsªl/ ADJ Something that is **universal** relates to everyone in the world or everyone in a particular group or society. □ ...universal health care. ● **uni|ver|sal|ly** /yunɪvɜrsəli/ ADV □ ...a universally-accepted point of view. [from French]

**uni|ver|sal gravi|ta|tion** /yunɪvɜrsªl grævɪteɪʃªn/ N-SING The **law of universal gravitation** is a principle in physics which states that all objects in the universe attract one another because of the force of gravity. [TECHNICAL]

**uni|verse** /yunɪvɜrs/ (**universes**) N-COUNT The **universe** is the whole of space and all the stars, planets, and other forms of matter and energy in it. □ ...all the stars and planets in the universe. [from French]
→ see **biosphere, galaxy, telescope**

**uni|ver|sity** /yunɪvɜrsiti/ (**universities**) N-VAR A **university** is an institution where students study for degrees and where academic research is done. □ ...the University of Washington. □ She goes to Duke University. [from Old French]

**un|just** /ʌndʒʌst/ ADJ If you describe an action, system, or law as **unjust**, you think that it treats a person or group badly in a way that they do not deserve. □ The attack on Charles was unjust. ● **un|just|ly** ADV □ She was unjustly accused of stealing money. [from Latin]

**un|jus|ti|fied** /ʌndʒʌstɪfaɪd/ ADJ If you describe a belief or action as **unjustified**, you think that there is no good reason for having it or doing it. □ "The decision is unjustified," he said. [from Old French]

**un|kind** /ʌnkaɪnd/ (**unkinder, unkindest**) ADJ If someone is **unkind**, they behave in an unpleasant, unfriendly, or slightly cruel way. □ He was unkind to her all evening. □ No one has an unkind word to say about him. ● **un|kind|ly** ADV □ He never spoke unkindly of anyone. ● **un|kind|ness** N-UNCOUNT □ His unkindness upset me. [from Old English]

| **Thesaurus** | unkind | Also look up : |
|---|---|---|
| ADJ. | harsh, mean, unfriendly; (ant.) kind | |

**un|known** /ʌnnoʊn/ (**unknowns**) **1** ADJ If something is **unknown** to you, you have no knowledge of it. □ The child's age is unknown. ● An **unknown** is something that is unknown. □ There

are still a lot of unknowns about the illness. **2** ADJ An **unknown** person is not famous or publicly recognized. □ He was an unknown writer. ● An **unknown** is a person who is unknown. □ ...a group of complete unknowns. **3** N-SING The **unknown** refers generally to things or places that people do not know about or understand. □ ...fear of the unknown.

**un|law|ful** /ʌnlɔfəl/ ADJ If something is **unlawful**, the law does not allow you to do it. [FORMAL] □ ...unlawful copying of DVDs. ● **un|law|ful|ly** ADV □ They acted unlawfully. [from Old English]

**un|lead|ed** /ʌnlɛdɪd/ ADJ **Unleaded** fuel contains a smaller amount of lead than most fuels so that it produces less harmful substances when it is burned. □ He filled up his car with regular unleaded gas. ● **Unleaded** is also a noun. □ All its engines will run happily on unleaded.

**un|leash** /ʌnliʃ/ (**unleashes, unleashing, unleashed**) V-T If someone or something **unleashes** a powerful force, feeling, activity, or group, they suddenly release it. □ She unleashed her anger on him during the meeting.

**un|less** /ʌnlɛs/ CONJ You use **unless** to introduce the only circumstances in which an event you are mentioning will not take place or in which a statement you are making is not true. □ I'm not happy unless I drive every day. [from French]

**un|li|censed** /ʌnlaɪsªnst/ **1** ADJ If you are **unlicensed**, you do not have official permission from the government or from the authorities to do something. □ ...unlicensed cab drivers. **2** ADJ If something that you own or use is **unlicensed**, you do not have official permission to own it or use it. □ Owners of unlicensed cats may face a $250 fine. [from Old French]

**un|like** /ʌnlaɪk/ **1** PREP If one thing is **unlike** another thing, the two things have different qualities or characteristics from each other. □ He's so unlike his father. **2** PREP You can use **unlike** to contrast two people, things, or situations, and show how they are different. □ Unlike most meetings, this one was a lot of fun. **3** PREP If you describe something that a particular person has done as being **unlike** them, you mean that you are surprised by it because it is not typical of their character or normal behavior. □ It was unlike him to say something like that. [from Old English]

**un|like|ly** /ʌnlaɪkli/ (**unlikeliest**) ADJ If you say that something is **unlikely** to happen or **unlikely to** be true, you believe that it will not happen or that it is not true, although you are not completely sure. □ They are unlikely to arrive before nine o'clock. [from Old Norse]

| **Word Partnership** | Use *unlikely* with : |
|---|---|
| N. | unlikely **event** |
| ADV. | **extremely** unlikely, **highly** unlikely, **most** unlikely, **very** unlikely |
| V. | unlikely **to change**, unlikely **to happen**, **seem** unlikely |

**un|lim|it|ed** /ʌnlɪmɪtɪd/ ADJ If there is an **unlimited** quantity of something, you can have as much or as many of that thing as you want. □ You can make an unlimited number of changes. [from Latin]

u

**un|load** /ʌnloʊd/ (unloads, unloading, unloaded) V-T If you **unload** goods from a vehicle, or if you **unload** a vehicle, you remove the goods from the vehicle. ❑ *We unloaded everything from the car.* [from Old English]

**un|lock** /ʌnlɒk/ (unlocks, unlocking, unlocked) V-T If you **unlock** something such as a door, a room, or a container, you open it using a key. ❑ *He unlocked the car and threw the coat on to the back seat.* [from Old English]

**un|lucky** /ʌnlʌki/ (unluckier, unluckiest) **1** ADJ If someone is **unlucky**, they have bad luck. ❑ *She's always been unlucky with cars.* **2** ADJ **Unlucky** is used to describe something that is thought to cause bad luck. ❑ *Sixteen is her unlucky number.*

**un|marked** /ʌnmɑrkt/ **1** ADJ Something that is **unmarked** has no marks on it. ❑ *Her shoes are still white and unmarked.* **2** ADJ Something that is **unmarked** has no marking on it which identifies what it is or whose it is. ❑ *He saw them get into the unmarked police car.* [from Old English]

**un|mis|tak|able** /ʌnmɪsteɪkəbᵊl/ also unmistakeable ADJ If you describe something as **unmistakable**, you mean that it is so obvious that it cannot be mistaken for anything else. ❑ *He didn't say his name, but the voice was unmistakable.* ● **un|mis|tak|ably** /ʌnmɪsteɪkəbli/ ADV ❑ *...an unmistakably American accent.*

**un|moved** /ʌnmuvd/ ADJ If you are **unmoved by** something, you are not emotionally affected by it. ❑ *He seemed unmoved by the news.*

**un|named** /ʌnneɪmd/ ADJ **Unnamed** people or things are talked about but their names are not mentioned. ❑ *Springer was sitting two rows behind the unnamed man.*

**un|natu|ral** /ʌnnætʃərᵊl/ **1** ADJ If you describe something as **unnatural**, you mean that it is strange and often frightening, because it is different from what you normally expect. ❑ *His eyes were an almost unnatural shade of blue.* ● **un|natu|ral|ly** ADV ❑ *The house was unnaturally silent.* **2** ADJ Behavior that is **unnatural** seems artificial and not normal or genuine. ❑ *She gave him a smile which seemed unnatural.* ● **un|natu|ral|ly** ADV ❑ *She smiled, showing a row of unnaturally perfect teeth.* [from Old French]

**un|nec|es|sary** /ʌnnɛsəsɛri/ ADJ If you describe something as **unnecessary**, you mean that it is not needed or does not have to be done. ❑ *It's unnecessary to go until I'm needed.* ● **un|nec|es|sari|ly** /ʌnnɛsəsɛrɪli/ ADV ❑ *I didn't want to upset my husband unnecessarily.* [from Latin]

**un|nerve** /ʌnnɜrv/ (unnerves, unnerving, unnerved) V-T If you say that something **unnerves** you, you mean that it worries or troubles you. ❑ *The news about Dermot unnerved me.* ● **un|nerv|ing** /ʌnnɜrvɪŋ/ ADJ If you describe something as **unnerving**, you mean that it makes you feel worried or uncomfortable. ❑ *Loud noises are unnerving.* [from Latin]

**un|no|ticed** /ʌnnoʊtɪst/ ADJ If something happens or passes **unnoticed**, it is not seen or noticed by anyone. ❑ *I tried to go upstairs unnoticed.*

**un|ob|tru|sive** /ʌnəbtrusɪv/ ADJ If you describe something or someone as **unobtrusive**, you mean that they are not easily noticed or do not draw attention to themselves. [FORMAL] ❑ *She started to cry in a quiet, unobtrusive way.* ● **un|ob|tru|sive|ly**

ADV ❑ *They left unobtrusively.*

**un|of|fi|cial** /ʌnəfɪʃᵊl/ ADJ An **unofficial** action or statement is not organized or approved by a person or group in authority. ❑ *Memorial Day is the unofficial start of summer.* ● **un|of|fi|cial|ly** ADV ❑ *The park has been unofficially open since September.*

**un|ortho|dox** /ʌnɔrθədɒks/ ADJ If you describe someone's behavior, beliefs, or customs as **unorthodox**, you mean that they are different from what is generally accepted. ❑ *...his unorthodox management style.* ❑ *...an unorthodox approach to problems.* [from Church Latin]

**un|pack** /ʌnpæk/ (unpacks, unpacking, unpacked) V-T/V-I When you **unpack** a suitcase, box, or similar container, or when you **unpack**, you take the things out of the container. ❑ *He unpacked his bag.* [from Middle Low German]

**un|paid** /ʌnpeɪd/ **1** ADJ If you do **unpaid** work or are an **unpaid** worker, you do a job without receiving any money for it. ❑ *Most of the work I do is unpaid.* **2** ADJ **Unpaid** taxes or bills have not been paid yet. ❑ *...millions of dollars in unpaid taxes.*

**un|pal|at|able** /ʌnpælɪtəbᵊl/ ADJ If you describe an idea as **unpalatable**, you mean that you find it unpleasant and difficult to accept. ❑ *I began to learn the unpalatable truth about John.* [from Latin]

**un|par|al|leled** /ʌnpærəlɛld/ ADJ If you describe something as **unparalleled**, you are emphasizing that it is, for example, bigger, better, or worse than anything else of its kind. ❑ *...his unparalleled career record.*

**un|pleas|ant** /ʌnplɛzᵊnt/ **1** ADJ If something is **unpleasant**, it gives you bad feelings, for example by making you feel upset or uncomfortable. ❑ *The plant has an unpleasant smell.* ● **un|pleas|ant|ly** ADV ❑ *We were unpleasantly surprised to hear about the problem.* **2** ADJ An **unpleasant** person is very unfriendly and rude. ❑ *She thought he was an unpleasant man.* ● **un|pleas|ant|ly** ADV ❑ *Melissa laughed unpleasantly.* [from Old French]

**un|plug** /ʌnplʌg/ (unplugs, unplugging, unplugged) V-T If you **unplug** an electrical device or telephone, you pull a wire out of an outlet so that it stops working. ❑ *Whenever there's a storm, I unplug my computer.* [from Middle Dutch]

**un|popu|lar** /ʌnpɒpyələr/ ADJ If something or someone is **unpopular**, most people do not like them. ❑ *It was an unpopular decision.* ❑ *I was very unpopular in high school.* ● **un|popu|lar|ity** /ʌnpɒpyəlærɪti/ N-UNCOUNT ❑ *...his unpopularity among his colleagues.* [from Latin]

**un|prec|edent|ed** /ʌnprɛsɪdɛntɪd/ **1** ADJ If something is **unprecedented**, it has never happened before. ❑ *Such an action is rare, but not unprecedented.* **2** ADJ If you describe something as **unprecedented**, you are emphasizing that it is very great in quality or amount. ❑ *...an unprecedented success.*

**un|pre|dict|able** /ʌnprɪdɪktəbᵊl/ ADJ If you describe someone or something as **unpredictable**, you mean that you cannot tell what they are going to do or how they are going to behave. ❑ *He is completely unpredictable.* ● **un|pre|dict|abil|ity** /ʌnprɪdɪktəbɪlɪti/ N-UNCOUNT ❑ *...the unpredictability of the weather.* [from Latin]

**un|pre|pared** /ʌnprɪpɛərd/ **1** ADJ If you are **unprepared for** something, you are not ready for it, and you are therefore surprised when it happens. ❑ *I was totally unprepared for the news.* **2** ADJ If you are **unprepared to** do something, you do not want to do it. ❑ *They are unprepared to work together.* [from Latin]

**un|pro|duc|tive** /ˌʌnprədˈʌktɪv/ ADJ Something that is **unproductive** does not produce any good results. ❑ *...a busy but unproductive night.* [from Latin]

**un|prof|it|able** /ˌʌnˈprɒfɪtəbəl/ ADJ An industry, company, or product that is **unprofitable** does not make enough profit. [BUSINESS] ❑ *...unprofitable, badly-run industries.* [from Latin]

**un|pro|tect|ed** /ˌʌnprəˈtɛktɪd/ **1** ADJ An **unprotected** person or place is not watched over or defended, and so they may be harmed or attacked. ❑ *...a 4,800-kilometer unprotected border.* **2** ADJ If something is **unprotected**, it is not covered or treated with anything, and so it may easily be damaged. ❑ *If we are unprotected from the sun for long enough, our skin will burn.*

**un|pub|lished** /ˌʌnˈpʌblɪʃt/ ADJ An **unpublished** book, letter, or report has never been published. ❑ *Much of his writing is unpublished.*

**un|quali|fied** /ˌʌnˈkwɒlɪfaɪd/ **1** ADJ If you are **unqualified**, you do not have any qualifications, or you do not have the right qualifications for a particular job. ❑ *She was unqualified for the job.* **2** ADJ **Unqualified** means total or unlimited. ❑ *The event was an unqualified success.* [from Old French]

**un|ques|tion|able** /ˌʌnˈkwɛstʃənəbəl/ ADJ If you describe something as **unquestionable**, you are emphasizing that it is so obviously true or real that nobody can doubt it. ❑ *His ability is unquestionable.* ● **un|ques|tion|ably** /ˌʌnˈkwɛstʃənəbli/ ADV ❑ *The next two years were unquestionably the happiest of his life.* [from Old French]

**un|rav|el** /ˌʌnˈrævəl/ (**unravels, unraveling, unraveled**) **1** V-T/V-I If you **unravel** something that is knotted or knitted, or if it **unravels**, it becomes one straight piece again or separates into different threads. ❑ *He could unravel knots others couldn't.* **2** V-T/V-I If you **unravel** a mystery or puzzle, or it **unravels**, it gradually becomes clearer until you can work out the answer to it. ❑ *Carter was still trying to unravel the truth of the woman's story.*

**Word Link** un ≈ not : unfair, unreal, unspoken

**un|real** /ˌʌnˈril/ ADJ If you say that a situation is **unreal**, you mean that it is so strange that you find it difficult to believe it is happening. ❑ *Then we won our next 10 games, which is a record. It was unreal.* [from Old French]

**un|re|al|is|tic** /ˌʌnriəˈlɪstɪk/ ADJ If you say that someone is being **unrealistic**, you mean that they do not recognize the truth about a situation, especially about the difficulties involved. ❑ *It was unrealistic to expect us to finish this in time.* [from Old French]

**un|rea|son|able** /ˌʌnˈrizənəbəl/ **1** ADJ If you say that someone is being **unreasonable**, you mean that they are behaving in a way that is not fair or sensible. ❑ *I know I'm being unreasonable and unfair.* ❑ *It was her unreasonable behavior which ruined her marriage.* ● **un|rea|son|ably** /ˌʌnˈrizənəbli/ ADV

❑ *We unreasonably expect perfect behavior from our children.* **2** ADJ An **unreasonable** decision, action, price, or amount seems unfair and difficult to justify. ❑ *...unreasonable increases in the price of gas.* ● **un|rea|son|ably** ADV ❑ *The banks' charges are unreasonably high.* [from Old French]

**un|re|lat|ed** /ˌʌnrɪˈleɪtɪd/ ADJ If one thing is **unrelated to** another, there is no connection between them. ❑ *My job is unrelated to politics.* [from Latin]

**un|re|lent|ing** /ˌʌnrɪˈlɛntɪŋ/ **1** ADJ If you describe someone's behavior as **unrelenting**, you mean that they are continuing to do something in a very determined way. ❑ *Rosie directed the project, and she was unrelenting.* **2** ADJ If you describe something unpleasant as **unrelenting**, you mean that it continues without stopping. ❑ *...an unrelenting downpour of rain.*

**un|re|li|able** /ˌʌnrɪˈlaɪəbəl/ ADJ If you describe a person, machine, or method as **unreliable**, you mean that you cannot trust them. ❑ *The car was slow and unreliable.* ❑ *His judgment was unreliable.* [from Old French]

**un|re|mark|able** /ˌʌnrɪˈmɑrkəbəl/ ADJ If you describe someone or something as **unremarkable**, you mean that they are very ordinary, without many exciting, original, or attractive qualities. ❑ *...a tall man with an unremarkable face.* [from Old French]

**un|re|pent|ant** /ˌʌnrɪˈpɛntənt/ ADJ If you are **unrepentant**, you are not ashamed of your beliefs or actions. ❑ *Pamela was unrepentant about her strong language.*

**un|re|solved** /ˌʌnrɪˈzɒlvd/ ADJ If a problem or difficulty is **unresolved**, no satisfactory solution has been found to it. ❑ *The dispute remains unresolved.* [from Latin]

**un|rest** /ˌʌnˈrɛst/ N-UNCOUNT If there is **unrest** in a particular place or society, people are expressing anger and dissatisfaction, often by demonstrating or rioting. ❑ *There is growing unrest among students in several major cities.* [from Old English]

**un|re|strict|ed** /ˌʌnrɪˈstrɪktɪd/ ADJ If an activity is **unrestricted**, you are free to do it in the way that you want, without being limited by any rules. ❑ *...unrestricted access to the Internet.*

**un|ri|valed** /ˌʌnˈraɪvəld/ ADJ If you describe something as **unrivaled**, you are emphasizing that it is better than anything else of the same kind. ❑ *She has an unrivaled knowledge of plants.*

**un|ru|ly** /ˌʌnˈruli/ **1** ADJ If you describe people, especially children, as **unruly**, you mean that they behave badly and are difficult to control. ❑ *...unruly behavior.* **2** ADJ **Unruly** hair is difficult to keep tidy. ❑ *The man had remarkably black, unruly hair.*

**un|safe** /ˌʌnˈseɪf/ **1** ADJ If something, such as a building, machine, activity, or area is **unsafe**, it is dangerous. ❑ *The water is unsafe to drink.* **2** ADJ If you are **unsafe**, you are in danger of being harmed. ❑ *They felt unsafe walking there at night.* [from Old French]

**un|sat|is|fac|tory** /ˌʌnsætɪsˈfæktəri/ ADJ If you describe something as **unsatisfactory**, you mean that it is not as good as it should be, and cannot be considered acceptable. ❑ *He called her answer "unsatisfactory and disappointing."* [from French]

**u**

**un|satu|rat|ed hydro|car|bon**
/ʌnsætʃəreɪtɪd haɪdrəkɑrbən/ (**unsaturated hydrocarbons**) N-VAR An **unsaturated hydrocarbon** is a chemical compound consisting of carbon and hydrogen in which there is less than the maximum amount of hydrogen. [TECHNICAL]

**un|sa|vory** /ʌnseɪvəri/ ADJ If you describe a person, place, or thing as **unsavory**, you mean that you find them unpleasant or morally unacceptable. ❑ *Police officers meet more unsavory people in a week than most of us do in a lifetime.* [from Old English]

**un|scathed** /ʌnskeɪðd/ ADJ If you are **unscathed** after a dangerous experience, you have not been injured or harmed by it. ❑ *Tony was unscathed apart from a severely-bruised finger.*

**un|scru|pu|lous** /ʌnskrupyələs/ ADJ If you describe a person as **unscrupulous**, you are critical of the fact that they are prepared to act in a dishonest or immoral way in order to get what they want, and which you do not agree with. ❑ *…a trick used by unscrupulous employers.* [from Latin]

**un|seed|ed** /ʌnsidɪd/ ADJ In tennis and badminton competitions, an **unseeded** player is someone who has not been ranked among the top 16 players by the competition's organizers. ❑ *Venus was the first unseeded woman in history to reach the final round.*

**un|seen** /ʌnsin/ ADJ You can use **unseen** to describe things which people cannot see or have not seen for a long time. ❑ *The boys escaped unseen.*

**un|set|tled** /ʌnsɛtᵊld/ **1** ADJ In an **unsettled** situation, there is a lot of uncertainty about what will happen. ❑ *There is some unsettled business right now.* **2** ADJ If you are **unsettled**, you cannot concentrate on anything because you are worried. ❑ *To tell the truth, I'm a bit unsettled tonight.* [from Old English]

**un|set|tling** /ʌnsɛtəlɪŋ/ ADJ If you describe something as **unsettling**, you mean that it makes you feel worried or uncertain. ❑ *Phil had unsettling dreams every night.*

**un|sight|ly** /ʌnsaɪtli/ ADJ If you describe something as **unsightly**, you mean that it is ugly. ❑ *…an unsightly pile of garbage.*

**un|skilled** /ʌnskɪld/ **1** ADJ People who are **unskilled** do not have any special training for a job. ❑ *He worked as an unskilled laborer.* **2** ADJ **Unskilled** work does not require any special training. ❑ *…low-paid, unskilled jobs.* [from Old Norse]

**un|so|lic|it|ed** /ʌnsəlɪsɪtɪd/ ADJ Something that is **unsolicited** has been given without being asked for and may not have been wanted. ❑ *She's always full of unsolicited advice.*

**un|solved** /ʌnsɒlvd/ ADJ An **unsolved** mystery or problem has never been solved. ❑ *…an unsolved mathematical problem.*

**un|speak|able** /ʌnspikəbᵊl/ ADJ If you describe something as **unspeakable**, you are emphasizing that it is extremely unpleasant. ❑ *The pain is unspeakable.* ● **un|speak|ably** /ʌnspikəbli/ ADV ❑ *The book was unspeakably boring.*

**un|speci|fied** /ʌnspɛsɪfaɪd/ ADJ You say that something is **unspecified** when you are not told exactly what it is. ❑ *An unspecified number of people died.*

**un|spoiled** /ʌnspɔɪld/ ADJ If you describe a place as **unspoiled**, you think it is beautiful because it has not been changed or built on for a long time. ❑ *The town is quiet and unspoiled.*

**Word Link**   un ≈ not : **un**fair, **un**real, **un**spoken

**un|spo|ken** /ʌnspoʊkən/ ADJ If your thoughts, wishes, or feelings are **unspoken**, you do not speak about them. ❑ *There's an unspoken agreement between us.* [from Old English]

**un|sports|man|like** /ʌnspɔrtsmənlaɪk/ **Unsportsmanlike** behavior is behavior that is rude, aggressive or unfair, especially during a game. ❑ *He was sent off for unsportsmanlike conduct.*

**un|sta|ble** /ʌnsteɪbᵊl/ **1** ADJ You can describe something as **unstable** if it is likely to change suddenly, especially if this creates difficulty or danger. ❑ *The country was unstable and unsafe.* **2** ADJ **Unstable** objects are likely to move or fall. ❑ *The roof of the building is unstable.* **3** ADJ If people are **unstable**, their emotions and behavior keep changing because their minds are disturbed or upset. ❑ *He was emotionally unstable.* [from Old French]

**un|steady** /ʌnstɛdi/ **1** ADJ If you are **unsteady**, you have difficulty doing something because you cannot completely control your legs or your body. ❑ *She was unsteady on her feet.* ● **un|steadi|ly** /ʌnstɛdᵊli/ ADV ❑ *She walked unsteadily from the bed to the door.* **2** ADJ If you describe something as **unsteady**, you mean that it is not regular or stable, but unreliable or unpredictable. ❑ *His voice was unsteady.* **3** ADJ **Unsteady** objects are not held, attached, or balanced securely. ❑ *…a slightly unsteady table.* [from Old High German]

**un|sub|scribe** /ʌnsəbskraɪb/ (**unsubscribes, unsubscribing, unsubscribed**) V-I If you **unsubscribe** from an online service, you send a message saying that you no longer wish to receive that service. [COMPUTING] ❑ *Go to the website today and you can unsubscribe online.* [from Latin]

**un|sub|stan|ti|at|ed** /ʌnsəbstænʃieɪtɪd/ ADJ A claim, accusation, or story that is **unsubstantiated** has not been proven to be valid or true. ❑ *Their story is totally unsubstantiated.*

**un|suc|cess|ful** /ʌnsəksɛsfəl/ **1** ADJ Something that is **unsuccessful** does not achieve what it was intended to achieve. ❑ *His efforts were unsuccessful.* ❑ *…a second unsuccessful operation on his knee.* ● **un|suc|cess|ful|ly** ADV ❑ *He tried unsuccessfully to sell the business.* **2** ADJ Someone who is **unsuccessful** does not achieve what they intended to achieve, especially in their career. ❑ *He and his friend Boris were unsuccessful in getting a job.* [from Latin]

**un|suit|able** /ʌnsutəbᵊl/ ADJ Someone or something that is **unsuitable for** a particular purpose or situation does not have the right qualities for it. ❑ *Amy's shoes were unsuitable for walking outside.* [from French]

**un|sure** /ʌnʃʊər/ **1** ADJ If you are **unsure of yourself**, you lack confidence. ❑ *Phyllis was worried and unsure of herself.* **2** ADJ If you are **unsure about** something, you feel uncertain about it. ❑ *Fifty-two percent were unsure about the idea.* [from Old French]

**un|sus|pect|ing** /ʌnsəspɛktɪŋ/ ADJ You can use **unsuspecting** to describe someone who does not know something that is happening or going to happen. ❑ *She threw a surprise party for her unsuspecting husband.*

**un|sym|pa|thet|ic** /ʌnsɪmpəθɛtɪk/ **1** ADJ If someone is **unsympathetic**, they are not kind or helpful to a person in difficulties. ❑ *Her husband was unsympathetic and she felt she had no one to talk to.* **2** ADJ An **unsympathetic** person is unpleasant and difficult to like. ❑ *The book has a very unsympathetic main character.*

**un|ten|able** /ʌntɛnəbəl/ ADJ An argument, theory, or position that is **untenable** cannot be defended successfully against criticism or attack. ❑ *It's an impossible and untenable situation.*

**un|think|able** /ʌnθɪŋkəbəl/ ADJ If you say that something is **unthinkable**, you are emphasizing that it cannot possibly be accepted or imagined as a possibility. ❑ *It is unthinkable for a school to run out of textbooks.* ● **The unthinkable** is something that is hard to believe. ❑ *Ralston did the unthinkable - cutting off his own arm to save his life.*

**Word Link** *un ≈ reversal : untie, unusual, unwrap*

**un|tie** /ʌntaɪ/ (**unties, untying, untied**) **1** V-T If you **untie** something that is tied to another thing or if you **untie** two things that are tied together, you remove the string or rope that holds them or that has been tied around them. ❑ *Please untie my hands.* **2** V-T If you **untie** something such as string or rope, you undo it so that there is no knot in it. ❑ *She untied the laces on one of her shoes.* [from Old English]

**un|til** /ʌntɪl/ **1** PREP If something happens **until** a particular time, it happens during the period before that time and stops at that time. ❑ *Until 2004, she lived in Canada.* ● **Until** is also a conjunction. ❑ *I waited until it got dark.* **2** PREP If something does not happen **until** a particular time, it does not happen before that time and only starts happening at that time. ❑ *I won't know anything until Saturday.* ● **Until** is also a conjunction. ❑ *They'll never be safe until they get out of the country.* [from Old High German] **3 up until →** see **up**

**un|told** /ʌntoʊld/ **1** ADJ You can use **untold** to emphasize how bad or unpleasant something is. ❑ *This could do untold damage to her health.* **2** ADJ You can use **untold** to emphasize that an amount or quantity is very large, especially when you are not sure how large it is. ❑ *...a man with untold millions of dollars in the bank.*

**un|touched** /ʌntʌtʃt/ **1** ADJ If something is **untouched**, it has not been changed or damaged in any way. ❑ *There was one building that remained untouched.* ❑ *The island is still untouched by tourism.* **2** ADJ If food or drink is **untouched**, none of it has been eaten or drunk. ❑ *The coffee was untouched, the toast was cold.*

**un|trained** /ʌntreɪnd/ ADJ Someone who is **untrained** has not been taught the skills that they need for a particular job, activity, or situation. ❑ *...untrained healthcare assistants.*

**un|treat|ed** /ʌntritɪd/ **1** ADJ If an injury or illness is left **untreated**, it is not given medical treatment. ❑ *If left untreated, the condition may become serious.* **2** ADJ **Untreated** materials, water, or chemicals are harmful and have not been made safe. ❑ *...untreated drinking water.*

**un|true** /ʌntru/ ADJ If a statement or idea is

**untrue**, it is false and not based on facts. ❑ *Bryant said the story was untrue.* [from Old English]

**un|used**

Pronounced /ʌnyuzd/ for meaning **1**, and /ʌnyust/ for meaning **2**.

**1** ADJ Something that is **unused** has not been used or is not being used at the moment. ❑ *...unused cans of food.* **2** ADJ If you are **unused to** something, you have not often done it or experienced it before. ❑ *My mother was unused to hard work.*

**un|usu|al** /ʌnyuʒuəl/ ADJ If something is **unusual**, it does not happen very often or you do not see it or hear it very often. ❑ *It's unusual for him to make a mistake.* ● **un|usu|al|ly** /ʌnyuʒuəli/ ADV ❑ *...an unusually cold winter.* [from Late Latin]

**Thesaurus** *unusual* Also look up :

ADJ. abnormal, different, interesting, strange, uncommon, unconventional; (*ant.*) common, conventional, normal, usual

**un|veil** /ʌnveɪl/ (**unveils, unveiling, unveiled**) **1** V-T If someone formally **unveils** something such as a new statue or painting, they open the curtain which is covering it. ❑ *There is a plan to unveil a statue in front of the building.* **2** V-T If you **unveil** a plan, new product, or some other thing that has been kept secret, you introduce it to the public. ❑ *The company unveiled plans to open 100 new stores.* [from Norman French]

**un|want|ed** /ʌnwɒntɪd/ ADJ If you say that something or someone is **unwanted**, you mean that you do not want them, or that nobody wants them. ❑ *...unwanted calls and e-mails.* ❑ *She felt unwanted.*

**un|war|rant|ed** /ʌnwɔrəntɪd/ ADJ If you describe something as **unwarranted**, you are critical of it because there is no need or reason for it. [FORMAL] ❑ *...unwarranted use of force.*

**un|wel|come** /ʌnwɛlkəm/ **1** ADJ An **unwelcome** experience is one that you do not like and did not want. ❑ *The news was an unwelcome surprise to some people.* **2** ADJ If you say that a visitor is **unwelcome**, you mean that you did not want them to come. ❑ *...an unwelcome guest.* [from Old English]

**un|well** /ʌnwɛl/ ADJ If you are **unwell**, you are sick. ❑ *Their grandmother was feeling unwell and had to stay at home.* [from Old English]

**un|wieldy** /ʌnwildi/ **1** ADJ An **unwieldy** object is difficult to move or carry because it is so big or heavy. ❑ *They came to the door with their unwieldy baggage.* **2** ADJ An **unwieldy** system does not work very well because it is too large or badly organized. ❑ *...costly and unwieldy social services.*

**un|will|ing** /ʌnwɪlɪŋ/ ADJ If you are **unwilling** to do something, you do not want to do it. ❑ *Many people are unwilling to change their e-mail addresses.* ● **un|will|ing|ly** ADV ❑ *He accepted his orders very unwillingly.* ● **un|will|ing|ness** N-UNCOUNT ❑ *...their unwillingness to listen to good advice.*

**un|wind** /ʌnwaɪnd/ (**unwinds, unwinding, unwound**) **1** V-I When you **unwind**, you relax after you have done something that makes you tense or tired. ❑ *It helps them to unwind after a busy day at work.* **2** V-T/V-I If you **unwind** something that is wrapped around something else, you

u

loosen it and make it straight. You can also say that it **unwinds**. ❑ *She unwound the scarf from her neck.* [from Old English]

**un|wise** /ʌnwaɪz/ ADJ If you describe something as **unwise**, you think that it is foolish and likely to lead to a bad result. ❑ *I think this is very unwise.* ● **un|wise|ly** ADV ❑ *She acted unwisely.* [from Old English]

**un|wit|ting** /ʌnwɪtɪŋ/ ADJ If you describe a person or their actions as **unwitting**, you mean that the person does something or is involved in something without realizing it. ❑ *It had been an unwitting mistake on his part.* ● **un|wit|ting|ly** ADV ❑ *...people who unwittingly break the law.* [from Old English]

**un|work|able** /ʌnwɜrkəbəl/ ADJ If a plan, law, or system is **unworkable**, it cannot be successful. ❑ *There is a strong possibility that the plan will be unworkable.*

**un|wor|thy** /ʌnwɜrði/ ADJ If a person or thing is **unworthy of** something good, they do not deserve it. ❑ *She felt unworthy of the help people offered her.*

**un|wound** /ʌnwaʊnd/ **Unwound** is the past tense and past participle of **unwind**. [from Old English]

| Word Link | *un ≈ reversal : untie, unusual, unwrap* |
|---|---|

**un|wrap** /ʌnræp/ (**unwraps, unwrapping, unwrapped**) V-T When you **unwrap** something, you take off the paper, plastic, or other covering that is around it. ❑ *I untied the bow and unwrapped the small box.*

**un|writ|ten** /ʌnrɪtən/ **1** ADJ Something such as a book that is **unwritten** has not been printed or written down. ❑ *...a $500,000 offer for two books, both unwritten.* **2** ADJ An **unwritten** rule, law, or agreement is one that is understood and accepted by everyone, although it may not have been formally or officially established. ❑ *They both understood a set of unwritten rules.*

**un|zip** /ʌnzɪp/ (**unzips, unzipping, unzipped**) **1** V-T/V-I When you **unzip** something which is fastened by a zipper or when it **unzips**, you open it by pulling open the zipper. ❑ *James unzipped his bag.* **2** V-T To **unzip** a computer file means to open a file that has been made smaller so that it is quicker and easier to send by e-mail. [COMPUTING] ❑ *Unzip the file with the password.*

---

**up**

❶ PREPOSITION, ADVERB, AND ADJECTIVE USES
❷ USED IN COMBINATION AS A PREPOSITION
❸ VERB USES

---

**❶ up**

The preposition is pronounced /ʌp/. The adverb and adjective are pronounced /ʌp/.

**Up** is often used with verbs of movement such as "jump" and "pull," and also in phrasal verbs such as "give up" and "wash up."

**1** PREP **Up** means toward a higher place or in a higher place. ❑ *They were climbing up a mountain*

*road.* ❑ *I ran up the stairs.* ❑ *He was up a ladder.* ● **Up** is also an adverb. ❑ *Keep your head up.* ❑ *I went up to John's room.* **2** ADV If someone stands **up**, they move so that they are standing. ❑ *He stood up and went to the window.* **3** PREP If you go or look **up** something such as a road or river, you go or look along it. If you are **up** a road or river, you are somewhere along it. ❑ *A dark blue truck came up the road.* ❑ *We stood on the bridge and looked up the river.* **4** ADV If you go **up** to something or someone, you move to the place where they are and stop there. ❑ *The girl ran across the street and up to the car.* **5** ADV If an amount of something goes **up**, it increases. If an amount of something is **up**, it has increased and is at a higher level than it was. ❑ *Gasoline prices went up 1.3 percent in June.* ❑ *Jobs are up, income is up.* **6** ADJ If you are **up**, you are not in bed. ❑ *They were up very early.* **7** ADJ If a period of time is **up**, it has come to an end. ❑ *When the half-hour was up, Brooks left.* **8** PHRASE If you move **up and down** somewhere, you move there repeatedly in one direction and then in the opposite direction. ❑ *I used to jump up and down to keep warm.* ❑ *I walked up and down before calling a taxi.* [from Old English]

**❷ up** /ʌp/ **1** PHRASE If you feel **up to** doing something, you are well enough to do it. ❑ *You have a visitor if you feel up to seeing him.* ❑ *They were not up to running the business without him.* **2** PHRASE If you say that it is **up to** someone to do something, you mean that it is their responsibility to do it. ❑ *It was up to him to tell her what to do.* **3** PHRASE **Up until** or **up to** are used to indicate the latest time at which something can happen. ❑ *Please feel free to call me any time up until 9:30 at night.* **4** PHRASE You use **up to** to say how large something can be or what level it has reached. ❑ *...buildings up to thirty stories high.* **5** PHRASE If someone or something is **up for** election, review, or discussion, they are about to be considered. ❑ *A third of the Senate is up for election every two years.* **6** PHRASE If you are **up against** something, you have a very difficult situation or problem to deal with. ❑ *They were up against a good team but did very well.* [from Old English]

**❸ up** /ʌp/ (**ups, upping, upped**) **1** V-T If you up something such as the amount of money you are offering for something, you increase it. ❑ *He upped his offer for the company.* **2** V-I If you **up** and leave a place, you go away from it, often suddenly or unexpectedly. ❑ *One day he just upped and left.* [from Old English]

**up-and-coming** ADJ **Up-and-coming** people are likely to be successful in the future. ❑ *Their daughter is an up-and-coming tennis player.*

**up|beat** /ʌpbit/ ADJ If people or their opinions are **upbeat**, they are cheerful and hopeful about a situation. [INFORMAL] ❑ *Neil was in an upbeat mood in spite of the bad news.*

**up|bring|ing** /ʌpbrɪŋɪŋ/ N-UNCOUNT Your **upbringing** is the way that your parents treat you and the things that they teach you when you are growing up. ❑ *Her son had a good upbringing.*

**up|com|ing** /ʌpkʌmɪŋ/ ADJ **Upcoming** events will happen in the near future. ❑ *She talked about her upcoming birthday party.*

**up|date** /ʌpdeɪt/ (**updates, updating, updated**)

The verb is pronounced /ʌpdeɪt/. The noun is pronounced /ʌpdeɪt/.

**■** v-T/v-I If you **update**, or **update** something, you make it more modern, usually by adding new parts to it or giving new information. ❑ *We update our records regularly.* ❑ *Experienced teachers need to update.* **■** N-COUNT An **update** is a news item containing the latest information about a particular situation. ❑ *...a weather update.*

**up|draft** /ˈʌpdræft/ (**updrafts**) N-COUNT An **updraft** is a rising current of air, which often produces a cumulus cloud.

**up front** also **up-front** **■** ADJ If you are **up front about** something, you act openly or publicly so that people know what you are doing or what you believe. [INFORMAL] ❑ *I wanted to be up front about it.* **■** ADV If a payment is made **up front**, it is made in advance and openly, so that the person being paid can see that the money is there. ❑ *She paid about $800 up front.*

**up|grade** /ˈʌpgreɪd, -ˈgreɪd/ (**upgrades, upgrading, upgraded**) v-T If equipment or services **are upgraded**, they are improved or made more efficient. ❑ *The road is being upgraded.* ● **Upgrade** is also a noun. ❑ *...equipment which needs expensive upgrades.*
→ see **hotel**

**up|heav|al** /ˌʌpˈhiːvəl/ (**upheavals**) N-COUNT An **upheaval** is a big change which causes a lot of trouble, confusion, and worry. ❑ *...a time of political upheaval.*

**up|held** /ˌʌpˈhɛld/ **Upheld** is the past tense and past participle of **uphold**.

**up|hill** /ˌʌpˈhɪl/ **■** ADV If something or someone is **uphill** or is moving **uphill**, they are near the top of a hill or are going up a slope. ❑ *He ran uphill a long way.* ● **Uphill** is also an adjective. ❑ *...a long, uphill journey.* **■** ADJ If you refer to something as an **uphill** battle or an **uphill** struggle, you mean that it requires a lot of effort and determination, but it should be possible to achieve it. ❑ *It was an uphill battle to get what she wanted.*

**up|hold** /ˌʌpˈhoʊld/ (**upholds, upholding, upheld**) v-T If you **uphold** something such as a law, a principle, or a decision, you support and maintain it. ❑ *Our policy is to uphold the law.*

**up|hol|stery** /ˌʌpˈhoʊlstəri, əˈpoʊl-/ N-UNCOUNT **Upholstery** is the soft covering on chairs and seats that makes them more comfortable to sit on. ❑ *...white leather upholstery.*

**up|keep** /ˈʌpkip/ **■** N-UNCOUNT The **upkeep** of a building or place is the work of keeping it in good condition. ❑ *We will use the money for the upkeep of the park.* **■** N-UNCOUNT The **upkeep** of a group of people or services is the process of providing them with the things that they need. ❑ *He paid $250 a month toward his son's upkeep.*

**up|lift|ing** /ˌʌpˈlɪftɪŋ/ ADJ You describe something as **uplifting** when it makes you feel very cheerful and happy. ❑ *...an uplifting story of hope.*

**upon** /əˈpɒn/

In addition to the uses shown below, **upon** is used in phrasal verbs such as "come upon" and "look upon," and after some other verbs such as "decide" and "depend."

**■** PREP If one thing is **upon** another, it is on it. [LITERARY] ❑ *He put the tray upon the table.* **■** PREP You use **upon** when mentioning an event that is followed immediately by another event. [FORMAL] ❑ *She had to give the store her full name upon entering.* **■** PREP You use **upon** between two occurrences of the same noun in order to say that there are large numbers of the thing mentioned. ❑ *Row upon row of women moved forwards.* **■** PREP If an event is **upon** you, it is just about to happen. [LITERARY] ❑ *The storm was upon us.*

**up|per** /ˈʌpər/ **■** ADJ You use **upper** to describe something that is above something else. ❑ *There is a good restaurant on the upper floor.* **■** ADJ The **upper** part of something is the higher part of it. ❑ *...the upper part of the foot.* ❑ *...the upper back and chest.* **■** PHRASE If you have the **upper hand** in a situation, you have an advantage over other people involved, for example because you have more power or success. ❑ *The home team had the upper hand.* [from Old English]

**up|per class** (**upper classes**) also **upper-class** N-COUNT The **upper class** or the **upper classes** are the group of people in a society who own the most property and have the highest social status. ❑ *...members of the upper class.* ● **Upper class** is also an adjective. ❑ *All of them came from wealthy, upper-class families.*

**upper|class|man** /ˌʌpərˈklæsmən/ (**upperclassmen**) N-COUNT An **upperclassman** is a male junior or senior student in an American high school, college, or university.

**upper|class|woman** /ˌʌpərˈklæswʊmən/ (**upperclasswomen**) N-COUNT An **upperclasswoman** is a female junior or senior student in a high school, college, or university.

**up|per man|tle** N-SING The **upper mantle** is the part of the Earth's interior that lies immediately beneath the crust.

**up|right** /ˈʌpraɪt/ **■** ADJ If you are sitting or standing **upright**, you are sitting or standing with your back straight, rather than bending or lying down. ❑ *Helen sat upright in her chair.* ❑ *He moved into an upright position.* **■** ADJ You can describe people as **upright** when they are careful to follow acceptable rules of behavior and behave in a moral way. ❑ *...a very upright, trustworthy man.*

**up|ris|ing** /ˈʌpraɪzɪŋ/ (**uprisings**) N-COUNT When there is an **uprising**, a group of people start fighting against the people who are in power in their country, because they want to bring about a political change. ❑ *...an uprising against the government.*

**up|roar** /ˈʌprɔːr/ **■** N-UNCOUNT; N-SING If there is **uproar**, there is a lot of shouting and noise because people are very angry or upset about something. ❑ *The uproar was loud and immediate.* **■** N-UNCOUNT; N-SING You can also use **uproar** to refer to a lot of public criticism and debate about something that has made people angry. ❑ *The town is in an uproar over the decision.*

**up|root** /ˌʌpˈrut/ (**uproots, uprooting, uprooted**) **■** v-T If you **uproot yourself** or if you **are uprooted**, you leave, or are made to leave, a place where you have lived for a long time. ❑ *She has just uprooted herself from a 29-year stay in Vancouver.* ❑ *Ms. Jefferson didn't want to uproot her young family.* **■** v-T If someone **uproots** a tree or plant, or if the wind **uproots** it, it is pulled out of the ground. ❑ *They had uprooted their vines.* ❑ *...fallen trees which were uprooted by the storm.*

u

**up|scale** /ʌpskeɪl/ ADJ **Upscale** is used to describe products or services that are expensive, of good quality, and aimed at people in a high social class. ❑ *...sporting goods with an upscale image.* ❑ *...upscale department-store chains such as Bloomingdale's and Saks Fifth Avenue.*

**up|set** (upsets, upsetting, upset)

> The verb and adjective are pronounced /ʌpsɛt/. The noun is pronounced /ʌpsɛt/.

**1** ADJ If you are **upset**, you are unhappy or disappointed because something bad has happened to you. ❑ *After she died I was very, very upset.* ❑ *Marta looked upset.* **2** V-T If something **upsets** you, it makes you feel worried or unhappy. ❑ *Your letter upset me.* ● **up|set|ting** ADJ ❑ *Childhood sickness can be upsetting for children and parents alike.* **3** V-T If events **upset** what normally happens, they make it go wrong. ❑ *Political problems could upset agreements between Moscow and Kabul.* **4** ADJ An **upset** stomach is a slight sickness in your stomach caused by an infection or by something you have eaten. ❑ *Paul was unwell last night with an upset stomach.* [from Middle High German] → see **anger**

| **Thesaurus** | *upset* | Also look up : |
|---|---|---|
| ADJ. | disappointed, hurt, unhappy; *(ant.)* happy **1** ill, sick, unsettled **4** | |

| **Word Partnership** | Use *upset* with : |
|---|---|
| PREP. | upset **about/by/over** *something* **1** |
| V. | **become, feel** upset, **get** upset **1** |
| ADV. | **so** upset, **very** upset, **visibly** upset **1** **really** upset **1** **2** |
| N. | **stomach** upset (or upset **stomach**) **4** |

**up|side down** /ʌpsaɪd daʊn/ also upside-down ADV If something is or has been turned **upside down**, it has been turned around so that the part that is usually lowest is above the part that is usually highest. ❑ *The painting was hung upside down.* ● **Upside down** is also an adjective. ❑ *...an upside-down triangle.*

**up|stage** /ʌpsteɪdʒ/ (upstages, upstaging, upstaged) **1** V-T If someone **upstages** you, they draw attention away from you by being more attractive or interesting. ❑ *He had a younger brother who always upstaged him.* **2** ADV When actors or **upstage** or move **upstage**, they are positioned toward the back of the stage or they move toward the back of the stage. ● **Upstage** is also an adjective. ❑ *...the large upstage box that Noble used for his 1990 production of King Lear.*

**up|stairs** /ʌpstɛərz/ **1** ADV If you go **upstairs** in a building, you go up a staircase toward a higher floor. ❑ *He went upstairs and changed his clothes.* **2** ADV If something or someone is **upstairs** in a building, they are on a floor that is higher than the ground floor. ❑ *The restaurant is upstairs.* **3** ADJ An **upstairs** room or object is on a floor of a building that is higher than the ground floor. ❑ *Marsani lived in the upstairs apartment.* **4** N-SING The **upstairs** of a building is the floor or floors that are higher than the ground floor. ❑ *The upstairs had only two bedrooms.*

**up|start** /ʌpstɑrt/ (upstarts) N-COUNT You can refer to someone as an **upstart** when they behave as if they are important, but you think that they are too new in a place or job to be treated as important. ❑ *A young upstart came to town.*

**up|state** /ʌpsteɪt/ ADJ **Upstate** means belonging or relating to the parts of a state that are furthest to the north or furthest from the main city. ❑ *...a little village in upstate New York.* ● **Upstate** is also an adverb. ADV ❑ *He wants to move upstate to Woodstock.*

**up|stream** /ʌpstrim/ ADV Something that is moving **upstream** is moving toward the source of a river. Something that is **upstream** is toward the source of a river. ❑ *...fish trying to swim upstream.* ● **Upstream** is also an adjective. ❑ *We'll go to the upstream side of that big rock.*

**up|surge** /ʌpsɜrdʒ/ N-SING If there is an **upsurge** in something, there is a sudden, large increase in it. ❑ *...an upsurge in oil prices.*

**up|tight** /ʌptaɪt/ ADJ Someone who is **uptight** is tense, nervous, or annoyed about something. [INFORMAL] ❑ *Penny never got uptight about exams.*

**up-to-date** also up to date **1** ADJ If something is **up-to-date**, it is the newest thing of its kind. ❑ *...up-to-date weather information.* **2** ADJ If you are **up-to-date** about something, you have the latest information about it. ❑ *We'll keep you up to date with any news.*

**up|town** /ʌptaʊn/ ADV If you go **uptown**, or go to a place **uptown**, you go away from the center of a city or town toward the edge. **Uptown** sometimes refers to a part of the city other than the main business district. ❑ *He rode uptown and went to Bob's apartment.* ❑ *Susan lived uptown.* ● **Uptown** is also an adjective. ❑ *...a small uptown radio station.*

**up|turn** /ʌptɜrn/ (upturns) N-COUNT If there is an **upturn** in the economy or in a company or industry, it improves or becomes more successful. [BUSINESS] ❑ *Some companies report an upturn in business.*

**up|ward** /ʌpwərd/

> The form **upwards** is also used for the adverb.

**1** ADJ An **upward** movement or look is directed towards a higher place or a higher level. ❑ *She started on the upward climb.* ❑ *She gave him a quick, upward look, then lowered her eyes.* **2** ADV If someone moves or looks **upward**, they move or look up toward a higher place. ❑ *She turned her face upward.* ❑ *"There," said Jack, pointing upwards.* **3** ADV If an amount or rate moves **upward**, it increases. ❑ *...with prices moving upward in stores.* ❑ *Unemployment will continue upward for much of this year.* **4** PHRASE A quantity that is **upwards of** a particular number is more than that number. ❑ *The package costs upwards of $9.99 a month.* [from Old English]

**up|wards** /ʌpwərdz/ → see **upward**

**up|well|ing** /ʌpwɛlɪŋ/ (upwellings) N-COUNT An **upwelling** is a process in which cold water from deep in the ocean rises to the surface near a shoreline, bringing nutrients with it. [TECHNICAL]

**ura|nium** /yʊreɪniəm/ N-UNCOUNT **Uranium** is a radioactive metal that is used to produce nuclear energy and weapons. [from New Latin]

**Ura|nus** /yʊərənəs, yʊreɪ-/ N-PROPER **Uranus** is the seventh planet from the sun. [from Latin]

U

| Word Link | urb ≈ city : suburb, suburbia, urban |
|---|---|

**ur|ban** /ɜrbən/ ADJ **Urban** means belonging to, or relating to, a city or town. □ *Most urban areas are close to a park.* [from Latin]
→ see **city**

**urethra** /yʊəriθrə/ (**urethras**) N-COUNT The **urethra** is the narrow tube inside a man's penis that carries urine and semen out of the body. [from Late Latin]

**urge** /ɜrdʒ/ (**urges, urging, urged**) ■ V-T If you **urge** someone to do something, you try hard to persuade them to do it. □ *Doctors urged him to change his diet.* ■ N-COUNT If you have an **urge to** do or have something, you have a strong wish to do or have it. □ *He had an urge to laugh.* [from Latin]

| Word Partnership | Use *urge* with : |
|---|---|

| N. | leaders/officials urge, urge people, urge voters ■ |
|---|---|
| ADV. | strongly urge ■ |
| V. | feel an urge, fight an urge, get an urge, resist an urge ■ |

**ur|gent** /ɜrdʒ³nt/ ■ ADJ If something is **urgent**, it needs to be dealt with as soon as possible. □ *There is an urgent need for food and water.* ● **ur|gen|cy** N-UNCOUNT □ *...the urgency of the problem.* ● **ur|gent|ly** ADV □ *The Red Cross said they urgently needed bread and water.* ■ ADJ If you speak in an **urgent** way, you show that you are anxious for people to notice something or to do something. □ *His voice was low and urgent.* ● **ur|gen|cy** N-UNCOUNT □ *She was surprised at the urgency in his voice.* ● **ur|gent|ly** ADV □ *"Did you find it?" he asked urgently.* [from French]

| Word Partnership | Use *urgent* with : |
|---|---|

| N. | urgent action, urgent business, urgent care, urgent matter, urgent meeting, urgent mission, urgent need, urgent problem ■ urgent appeal, urgent message ■ |
|---|---|

**uri|nate** /yʊərɪneɪt/ (**urinates, urinating, urinated**) V-I When you **urinate**, you get rid of urine from your body. [from Old French]

**urine** /yʊərɪn/ N-UNCOUNT **Urine** is the liquid that you get rid of from your body when you go to the toilet. □ *The doctor took a urine sample and a blood sample.* [from Old French]

**URL** /yu ɑr ɛl/ (**URLs**) N-COUNT A **URL** is an address that shows where a particular page can be found on the World Wide Web. **URL** is an abbreviation for "Uniform Resource Locator." [COMPUTING] □ *The URL for Collins Dictionaries is http://www.collinslanguage.com.*

**urn** /ɜrn/ (**urns**) ■ N-COUNT An **urn** is a container in which a dead person's ashes are kept. □ *...a funeral urn.* ■ N-COUNT An **urn** is a metal container used for making a large quantity of tea or coffee and keeping it hot. □ *...a ten-gallon coffee urn.* [from Latin]

**us** /əs, STRONG ʌs/

Us is the first person plural pronoun. Us is used as the object of a verb or a preposition.

PRON A speaker or writer uses **us** to refer both to himself or herself and to one or more other people. □ *Heather went to the kitchen to get drinks for us.* □ *They don't like us much.* [from Old English]

**us|able** /yuzəbᵊl/ ADJ If something is **usable**, it is in a good enough state or condition to be used. □ *The house had eleven usable rooms.* [from Old French]

**us|age** /yusɪdʒ/ ■ N-UNCOUNT **Usage** is the way in which words are actually used in particular contexts, especially with regard to their meanings. □ *...a book on English usage.* ■ N-UNCOUNT **Usage** is the degree to which something is used or the way in which it is used. □ *...an increase in computer usage.* [from Old French]

**USB** /yu ɛs bi/ (**USBs**) N-COUNT A **USB** or **USB port** on a computer is a place where you can attach another piece of equipment, for example a printer. **USB** is an abbreviation for "Universal Serial Bus." [COMPUTING] □ *It plugs into the computer's USB port.*

---

**use**

❶ VERB USES
❷ NOUN USES

---

❶ **use** /yuz/ (**uses, using, used**) ■ V-T If you **use** something, you do something with it in order to do a job or to achieve a particular result or effect. □ *They wouldn't let him use the phone.* □ *She used the money to help her family.* ■ V-T If you **use** a supply of something, you finish it so that none of it is left. □ *She used all the shampoo.* ● **Use up** means the same as **use**. □ *Daisy used up all the hot water.* ■ V-T If you **use** a particular word or expression, you say or write it, because it has the meaning that you want to express. □ *He used the word "sorry" six times.* ■ V-T If you say that someone **uses** people, you disapprove of them because they make others do things for them in order to benefit or gain some advantage from it, and not because they care about the other people. □ *I felt he was using me.* [from Old French] ■ → see also **used**

❷ **use** /yus/ (**uses**) ■ N-UNCOUNT; N-SING Your **use** of something is the action or fact of your using it. □ *...the use of computers in classrooms.* ■ N-VAR If something has a particular **use**, it is intended for a particular purpose. □ *There are many good uses for e-mail.* □ *We can always find a use for the money.* ■ N-UNCOUNT If you have the **use of** something, you have the permission or ability to use it. □ *She has the use of the car one night a week.* □ *...people who have lost the use of their legs.* ■ N-COUNT A **use** of a word is a particular meaning that it has or a particular way in which it can be used. □ *There are new uses of words coming in all the time.* ■ PHRASE If something such as a technique, building, or machine is **in use**, it is used regularly by people. If it has gone **out of use**, it is no longer used regularly by people. □ *...the number of homes with televisions in use.* ■ PHRASE If you **make use of** something, you do something with it in order to do a job or achieve a particular result or effect. [WRITTEN] □ *We made use of the extra time we had.* ■ PHRASE If you say **it's no use**, you mean that you have failed to do something and realize that it is useless to continue trying because it is impossible. □ *"It's no use talking to him," said Kate.* [from Old French]

u

## used

① MODAL USES AND PHRASES
② ADJECTIVE USES

**① used** /yu̇st/ **1** PHRASE If something **used to** be done or **used to** be true, it was done regularly in the past or was true in the past. ❑ *People used to come and visit him every day.* ❑ *He used to be one of my teachers.* **2** PHRASE If you **are used to** something, you are familiar with it because you have done it or experienced it many times before. ❑ *I'm used to hard work.* **3** PHRASE If you **get used to** something or someone, you become familiar with it or get to know them. ❑ *This is how we do things here. You'll soon get used to it.* [from Old French]

### Usage  used to

Used to is often confused with *be/get used to*. *Used to* refers to something in the past: *We used to live in an apartment, but we now live in a house.* *Be/get used to* means "be or become accustomed to": *We're used to living in an apartment, but we're getting used to our new house.*

**② used** /yu̇zd/ **1** ADJ A **used** object is dirty or spoiled because it has been used, and usually needs to be thrown away or washed. ❑ *...a used coffee cup* **2** ADJ A **used** car has already had one or more owners. ❑ *Would you buy a used car from this man?* [from Old French]

**use|ful** /yu̇sfəl/ **1** ADJ If something is **useful**, you can use it to do something or to help you in some way. ❑ *...pages of useful information.* ● **use|ful|ly** ADV ❑ *Adams usefully divides his book into two parts.* ● **use|ful|ness** N-UNCOUNT ❑ *...the usefulness of his work.* **2** PHRASE If an object or skill **comes in useful**, it can help you achieve something in a particular situation. ❑ *Extra paper will probably come in useful.* [from Old French]

### Word Partnership  Use *useful* with :

| | |
|---|---|
| ADV. | **also** useful, **especially** useful, **extremely** useful, **less/more** useful, **particularly** useful, **very** useful **1** |
| N. | useful **information**, useful **knowledge**, useful **life**, useful **purpose**, useful **strategy**, useful **tool 1** |

**use|less** /yu̇slɪs/ **1** ADJ If something is **useless**, you cannot use it. ❑ *Their money was useless in this country.* **2** ADJ If something is **useless**, it does not achieve anything helpful or good. ❑ *She knew it was useless to argue.* **3** ADJ If you say that someone or something is **useless**, you mean that they are no good at all. ❑ *He was useless at any game with a ball.* [from Old French]

**user** /yu̇zər/ (users) N-COUNT A **user** is a person or thing that uses something such as a place, facility, product, or machine. ❑ *...Internet users.* ❑ *...a regular user of the subway.* [from Old French] → see **Internet**

**user-friendly** ADJ If you describe something such as a machine or system as **user-friendly**, you mean that it is well designed and easy to use. ❑ *It is written in simple, user-friendly language.*

**U-shaped val|ley** (U-shaped valleys) N-COUNT A **U-shaped valley** is a valley with steep sides that forms when a glacier is eroded.

**ush|er** /ʌʃər/ (ushers, ushering, ushered) **1** V-T If you **usher** someone somewhere, you show them where they should go by going with them. [FORMAL] ❑ *I ushered him into the office.* **2** N-COUNT An **usher** is a person who shows people where to sit, for example at a wedding or at a concert. ❑ *He did part-time work as an usher in a theater.* [from Old French]

**usu|al** /yu̇ʒuəl/ **1** ADJ **Usual** is used to describe what happens or what is done most often in a particular situation. ❑ *It is a large city with the usual problems.* ❑ *February was warmer than usual.* **2** PHRASE You use **as usual** to indicate that you are describing something that normally happens or that is normally true. ❑ *As usual, there will be the local and regional elections on June twelfth.* **3** PHRASE If something happens **as usual**, it happens in the way that it normally does, especially when other things have changed. ❑ *He's late, as usual.* [from Late Latin]

### Word Partnership  Use *usual* with :

| | |
|---|---|
| ADV. | **less/more than** usual, **longer than** usual **1** |
| N. | usual **place**, usual **routine**, usual **self**, usual **stuff**, usual **suspects**, usual **way 1** |

**usu|al|ly** /yu̇ʒuəli/ ADV If something **usually** happens, it is the thing that most often happens in a particular situation. ❑ *We usually eat in here.* [from Late Latin]

**usurp** /yusɜrp, -zɜrp/ (usurps, usurping, usurped) V-T If you say that someone **usurps** a job, role, title, or position, they take it from someone when they have no right to do this. [FORMAL] ❑ *Did she usurp his place in his mother's heart?* [from Old French]

**uten|sil** /yutɛnsəl/ (utensils) N-COUNT **Utensils** are tools or objects that you use in order to help you to cook, serve food, or eat. ❑ *...utensils such as cooking pots or pans.* [from Old French] → see Picture Dictionary: **kitchen utensils**

**uter|us** /yutərəs/ (uteruses) N-COUNT The **uterus** of a woman or female mammal is the part of her body where babies develop. [MEDICAL] ❑ *...a scan of the uterus.* [from Latin]

**utili|tar|ian** /yutɪlɪtɛəriən/ ADJ **Utilitarian** objects and buildings are designed to be useful rather than attractive. ❑ *Bruce's office is plain and utilitarian.* [from Old French]

**util|ity** /yutɪlɪti/ (utilities) N-COUNT A **utility** is an important service such as water, electricity, or gas that is provided for everyone, and that everyone pays for. ❑ *...public utilities such as gas and electricity.* [from Old French]

**util|ity pole** (utility poles) **1** N-COUNT A **utility pole** is a tall pole with telephone or electrical wires attached to it. ❑ *The bus hit a tree and knocked down a utility pole.* **2** → see also **telephone pole**

**uti|lize** /yutɪlaɪz/ (utilizes, utilizing, utilized) V-T If you **utilize** something, you use it. [FORMAL] ❑ *...how to utilize the knowledge and talent of everyone in the company.* ● **uti|li|za|tion** /yutɪlɪzeɪʃ⁰n/ N-UNCOUNT ❑ *...the best utilization of space.* [from Old French]

| Word Link | most ≈ superlative degree : al most, fore most, ut most |
| --- | --- |

**ut|most** /ʌtmoʊst/ **1** ADJ You can use **utmost** to emphasize the importance or seriousness of something or to emphasize the way that it is done. ❑ *The decision is of the utmost importance.* ❑ *...driving with utmost care.* **2** N-SING If you say that you are doing your **utmost to** do something, you are emphasizing that you are trying as hard as you can to do it. ❑ *He did his utmost to help her.* [from Old English]

**uto|pia** /yutoʊpiə/ (**utopias**) N-VAR If you refer to a real or imaginary situation as a **utopia**, you mean that it is one in which society is perfect and everyone is happy. ❑ *...a relaxing utopia of sea and sand.*

**uto|pian** /yutoʊpiən/ ADJ If you describe a plan or idea as **utopian**, you are criticizing it because it is unrealistic and shows a belief that things can be improved much more than is possible. ❑ *...a utopian dream.* [from New Latin]

**ut|ter** /ʌtər/ (**utters, uttering, uttered**) **1** V-T If someone **utters** sounds or words, they say them. [LITERARY] ❑ *He uttered the words "I'm sorry."* **2** ADJ You use **utter** to emphasize that something is great in extent, degree, or amount. ❑ *This is utter nonsense.* [Sense 1 from Middle Dutch. Sense 2 from Old English]

**ut|ter|ance** /ʌtərəns/ (**utterances**) N-COUNT Someone's **utterances** are the things that they say. [FORMAL] ❑ *"I'm very happy," was his first utterance.* [from Middle Dutch]

**ut|ter|ly** /ʌtərli/ ADV You use **utterly** to emphasize that something is very great in extent, degree, or amount. ❑ *He didn't want to appear utterly stupid.* ❑ *He felt completely and utterly alone.* [from Middle Dutch]

**U-turn** (**U-turns**) **1** N-COUNT If you make a **U-turn** when you are driving or riding a bicycle, you turn in a half circle in one movement, so that you are then going in the opposite direction. ❑ *Dave made a U-turn on North Main and drove back to Depot Street.* **2** N-COUNT If you describe a change in someone's policy, plans, or actions as a **U-turn**, you mean that it is a complete change. ❑ *He did a U-turn and decided not to retire.*

**u**

# Vv

**v.** **v.** is a written abbreviation for **versus**.

**va|can|cy** /veɪkənsi/ (**vacancies**) ◼ N-COUNT A **vacancy** is a job or position that has not been filled. ❑ *We have a vacancy for an assistant.* ◻ N-COUNT If there are **vacancies** at a hotel, some of the rooms are available to stay in. ❑ *The hotel still has a few vacancies.* [from Latin]

| **Word Link** | vac ≈ empty : *e*vacuate, vacant, vacate |

**va|cant** /veɪkənt/ ◼ ADJ If something is **vacant**, it is not being used by anyone. ❑ *…a vacant seat.* ◻ ADJ If a job or position is **vacant**, no one is doing it or in it at present, and people can apply for it. ❑ *The position of chairman has been vacant for three months.* ◼ ADJ A **vacant** look or expression is one that suggests that someone does not understand something or that they are not concentrating. ● **va|cant|ly** ADV ❑ *He looked vacantly out of the window.* [from Latin]

**va|cant lot** (**vacant lots**) N-COUNT A **vacant lot** is a small area of land in a city or town that is not occupied or not being used. ❑ *There is a vacant lot at the corner of the street.*

**va|cate** /veɪkeɪt/ (**vacates, vacating, vacated**) V-T If you **vacate** a place or a job, you leave it, making it available for other people. [FORMAL] ❑ *He vacated his apartment and went to live with a friend.* [from Latin]

**va|ca|tion** /veɪkeɪʃ⁰n/ (**vacations, vacationing, vacationed**) ◼ N-COUNT A **vacation** is a period of time during which you relax and enjoy yourself away from home. ❑ *They planned a vacation in Europe.* ◻ N-COUNT A **vacation** is a period of the year when schools, universities, and colleges are officially closed. ❑ *During his summer vacation he visited Russia.* ◼ N-UNCOUNT If you have a particular number of days' or weeks' **vacation**, you do not have to go to work for that number of days or weeks. ❑ *The French get five to six weeks' vacation a year.* ◼ V-I If you **are vacationing** in a place away from home, you are on vacation there. ❑ *Mike vacationed in Jamaica.* [from Latin]

**va|ca|tion|er** /veɪkeɪʃənər/ (**vacationers**) N-COUNT **Vacationers** are people who are on vacation in a particular place. [from Latin]

**vac|ci|nate** /væksɪneɪt/ (**vaccinates, vaccinating, vaccinated**) V-T If a person or animal **is vaccinated**, they are given a vaccine, usually by injection, to prevent them from getting a disease. ❑ *Has your child been vaccinated against measles?* ● **vac|ci|na|tion** /væksɪneɪʃ⁰n/ (**vaccinations**) N-VAR ❑ *…a flu vaccination.* [from New Latin]

**vac|cine** /væksin/ (**vaccines**) N-VAR A **vaccine** is a substance containing a harmless form of the germs that cause a particular disease. It is given to people to prevent them from getting that disease.

❑ *…flu vaccine.* [from New Latin]
→ see **hospital**

**vacu|ole** /vækyuoʊl/ (**vacuoles**) N-COUNT A **vacuole** is a space within a plant cell that contains water, waste products, or other substances. [TECHNICAL] [from French]

**vacuum** /vækyum, -yuəm/ (**vacuums, vacuuming, vacuumed**) ◼ N-COUNT If someone or something creates a **vacuum**, they leave a place or position that then needs to be filled by another person or thing. ❑ *When she resigned she left a power vacuum in the company.* ◻ N-COUNT A **vacuum** is a space that contains no air or other gas. ❑ *…a vacuum caused by hot air rising.* ◼ V-T/V-I If you **vacuum**, or **vacuum** something, you clean it using a vacuum cleaner. ❑ *It's important to vacuum regularly.* [from Latin]

**vacuum clean|er** (**vacuum cleaners**) N-COUNT A **vacuum cleaner** or a **vacuum** is an electric machine that sucks up dust and dirt from carpets.

vacuum cleaner

**va|gary** /veɪgəri, vəgɛəri/ (**vagaries**) N-COUNT The **vagaries** of something are the unexpected and unpredictable changes in it. [FORMAL] ❑ *…the vagaries of politics.* [from Latin]

**va|gi|na** /vədʒaɪnə/ (**vaginas**) N-COUNT A woman's **vagina** is the passage connecting her outer sex organs to her uterus. ● **vagi|nal** /vædʒɪnⁱl/ ADJ ❑ *…vaginal infections.* [from Latin]

**vague** /veɪg/ (**vaguer, vaguest**) ◼ ADJ If something written or spoken is **vague**, it does not explain or express things clearly. ❑ *The description was pretty vague.* ● **vague|ly** ADV ❑ *"I'm not sure," Liz said vaguely.* ◻ ADJ If you have a **vague** memory or idea of something, the memory or idea is not clear. ❑ *They have only a vague idea of how much money is left.* ● **vague|ly** ADV ❑ *Judith could vaguely remember playing the game as a child.* ◼ ADJ A **vague** shape or outline is not clear and is therefore not easy to see. ❑ *The bus was a vague shape in the distance.* [from French]

**vague|ly** /veɪgli/ ADV **Vaguely** means to a small degree. ❑ *The voice on the phone was vaguely familiar.* [from French]

**vain** /veɪn/ (**vainer, vainest**) ◼ ADJ A **vain** attempt or action is one that fails to achieve what was intended. ❑ *We worked through the night in a vain attempt to finish on time.* ● **vain|ly** ADV ❑ *He looked vainly through his pockets for a piece of paper.* ◻ ADJ If you describe someone as **vain**, you are critical of their extreme pride in their own beauty, intelligence, or other good qualities. ❑ *He was so vain he spent hours in front of the mirror.* ◼ PHRASE If you do something **in vain**, you do not succeed in

V

achieving what you intend. ❏ *She tried in vain to open the door.* [from Old French]

**vale|dic|to|ri|an** /ˌvælɪdɪktɔ̱riən/ (**valedictorians**) N-COUNT A **valedictorian** is the student who has the highest grades in their class when they graduate from high school or college, and who gives a speech at their graduation ceremony. [from Latin]

**va|lence elec|tron** /ve̱ɪləns ɪlɛ̱ktrɒn/ (**valence electrons**) N-COUNT **Valence electrons** are the outermost electrons in an atom, which combine with other atoms to form molecules. [TECHNICAL]

**val|et park|ing** N-UNCOUNT **Valet parking** is a service that operates at places such as hotels and restaurants, in which customers' cars are parked by an attendant.

**val|iant** /væ̱lyənt/ ADJ A **valiant** action is very brave and determined, though it may lead to failure or defeat. ❏ *Despite valiant efforts by paramedics, he died at the scene of the crash.* ● **val|iant|ly** ADV ❏ *He fought valiantly against his disease.* [from Old French]

**val|id** /væ̱lɪd/ ◳ ADJ A **valid** argument, comment, or idea is based on sensible reasoning. ❏ *They gave many valid reasons for not signing the contract.* ● **va|lid|ity** /vəlɪ̱dɪti/ N-UNCOUNT ❏ *I question the validity of this argument.* ◲ ADJ If a ticket or other document is **valid**, it can be used and will be accepted by people in authority. ❏ *All tickets are valid for two months.* [from Latin]

**vali|date** /væ̱lɪdeɪt/ (**validates, validating, validated**) V-T To **validate** something such as a claim or statement means to prove or confirm that it is true or correct. [FORMAL] ❏ *This discovery seems to validate his claims.* ● **vali|da|tion** /væ̱lɪdeɪ̱ʃ⁰n/ (**validations**) N-VAR ❏ *She saw this as a validation of her decision.* [from Latin]

**val|ley** /væ̱li/ (**valleys**) N-COUNT A **valley** is a low stretch of land between hills, especially one that has a river flowing through it. ❏ *...a wooded valley.* [from Old French]
→ see **river**

**val|or** /væ̱lər/ N-UNCOUNT **Valor** is great bravery, especially in battle. [LITERARY] [from Late Latin]

**valu|able** /væ̱lyuəb⁰l/ ◳ ADJ If you describe something or someone as **valuable**, you mean that they are very useful and helpful. ❏ *Television can be a valuable tool in the classroom.* ◲ ADJ **Valuable** objects are worth a lot of money. ❏ *Do not leave any valuable items in your hotel room.* [from Old French]

**valu|ables** /væ̱lyuəb⁰lz/ N-PLURAL **Valuables** are things that you own that are worth a lot of money, especially small objects such as jewelry. ❏ *Lock your valuables in the hotel safe.* [from Old French]

**valua|tion** /væ̱lyueɪ̱ʃ⁰n/ (**valuations**) N-VAR A **valuation** is a judgment that someone makes about how much money something is worth. ❏ *A valuation of the company said it was worth $10 million.* [from Old French]

**value** /væ̱lyu/ (**values, valuing, valued**) ◳ N-UNCOUNT; N-SING The **value** of something such as a quality, attitude, or method is its importance or usefulness. ❏ *Don't underestimate the value of work experience.* ◲ V-T If you **value** something or someone, you think that they are important and you appreciate them. ❏ *I value my husband's opinion.* ◳ N-VAR The **value** of something is how much money it is worth. ❏ *The value of the house rose by $50,000 in a year.* ❏ *...jewelry of high value.* ◳ V-T When experts **value** something, they decide how much money it is worth. ❏ *He valued the property at $130,000.* ◳ N-PLURAL The **values** of a person or group are their moral principles and beliefs. ❏ *The countries of South Asia share many common values.* ◳ N-VAR In painting, the **value** of a color is how light or dark it is. White is the lightest value and black is the darkest value. [TECHNICAL] [from Old French]

**value scale** (**value scales**) N-COUNT A **value scale** is an arrangement of all the different colors used in painting, organized according to their lightness or darkness. [TECHNICAL]

**valve** /væ̱lv/ (**valves**) N-COUNT A **valve** is a device attached to a pipe or a tube that controls the flow of air or liquid through the pipe or tube. [from Latin]
→ see **engine**

**vam|pire** /væ̱mpaɪər/ (**vampires**) N-COUNT In horror stories, **vampires** are creatures that come out of graves at night and suck the blood of living people. [from French]

**van** /væ̱n/ (**vans**) N-COUNT A **van** is a small or medium-sized road vehicle with one row of seats at the front and a space for carrying goods in the back.
→ see **car**

**van|dal** /væ̱nd⁰l/ (**vandals**) N-COUNT A **vandal** is someone who deliberately damages things, especially public property. ❏ *The street lights were*

V

*broken by vandals.* [from Latin]

**van|dal|ism** /vænd°lɪzəm/ N-UNCOUNT
**Vandalism** is the deliberate damaging of things, especially public property. □ *Vandalism, such as breaking windows, is a problem here.* [from Latin]

**van|dal|ize** /vænd°laɪz/ (**vandalizes, vandalizing, vandalized**) V-T If something such as a building or part of a building **is vandalized** by someone, it is damaged on purpose. □ *The walls were vandalized with spray paint.* [from Latin]

**van|guard** /vængɑrd/ N-SING If someone is **in the vanguard of** something such as a revolution or an area of research, they are involved in the most advanced part of it. □ *This university is in the vanguard of scientific research.* [from Old French]

**va|nil|la** /vənɪlə/ N-UNCOUNT **Vanilla** is a flavoring used in ice cream and other sweet food. [from New Latin]

**van|ish** /vænɪʃ/ (**vanishes, vanishing, vanished**) V-I If someone or something **vanishes**, they disappear suddenly or in a way that cannot be explained. □ *He vanished ten years ago and was never seen again.* □ *The car vanished from outside the house.* [from Old French]

**van|ish|ing point** (**vanishing points**) N-COUNT The **vanishing point** is the point in the distance where parallel lines seem to meet.

**van|ity** /vænɪti/ N-UNCOUNT If you refer to someone's **vanity**, you are critical of them because they are too proud of their appearance or abilities. □ *Do you want to lose weight for your health, or out of vanity?* [from Old French]

**van|tage point** /væntɪdʒpɔɪnt/ (**vantage points**) N-COUNT A **vantage point** is a place from which you can see a lot of things. □ *From his vantage point on the hill, he saw a car arrive.*

**va|por** /veɪpər/ (**vapors**) N-VAR **Vapor** consists of tiny drops of water or other liquids in the air, that appear as mist. □ *...water vapor.* [from Latin]
→ see **greenhouse effect, lake, precipitation, water**

**va|por|ize** /veɪpəraɪz/ (**vaporizes, vaporizing, vaporized**) V-T/V-I If a liquid or solid **vaporizes** or if you **vaporize** it, it changes into vapor or gas.
● **va|por|iza|tion** /veɪpərɪzeɪʃ°n/ N-UNCOUNT
□ *...the energy required to cause vaporization of water.* [from Latin]

**va|por|iz|er** /veɪpəraɪzər/ (**vaporizers**) N-COUNT A **vaporizer** is a device that produces steam or that converts liquid medicine into vapor so that it can be breathed in. [from Latin]

**vari|able** /vɛəriəb°l/ (**variables**) ◼ ADJ Something that is **variable** changes quite often, and there usually seems to be no fixed pattern to these changes. □ *The quality of his work is very variable.* ● **vari|abil|ity** /vɛəriəbɪlɪti/ N-UNCOUNT □ *There's a lot of variability between individuals.* ◼ N-COUNT A **variable** is a factor in a situation that can change. □ *Consider variables such as price and delivery dates.* ◼ N-COUNT A **variable** is a quantity that can have any one of a set of values. [TECHNICAL] [from Latin]
→ see **experiment**

**vari|ance** /vɛəriəns/ PHRASE If one thing is **at variance with** another, the two things seem to contradict each other. [FORMAL] □ *His statement was at variance with the facts.* [from Old French]

**vari|ant** /vɛəriənt/ (**variants**) N-COUNT A

**variant** of a particular thing is something that has a different form from that thing, although it is related to it. □ *Doctors have discovered a new variant of the disease.* [from Old French]

**vari|ation** /vɛərieɪʃ°n/ (**variations**) ◼ N-COUNT A **variation on** something is the same thing presented in a slightly different form. □ *...a delicious variation on an omelet.* ◼ N-VAR A **variation** is a change or difference in a level, amount, or quantity. □ *Can you explain the wide variation in your prices?* [from Latin]

**var|ied** /vɛərid/ ◼ ADJ Something that is **varied** consists of things of different types, sizes, or qualities. □ *Your diet should be varied and balanced.* [from Latin] ◼ → see also **vary**

**va|ri|ety** /vəraɪɪti/ (**varieties**) ◼ N-UNCOUNT If something has **variety**, it consists of things that are different from each other. □ *Susan wanted variety in her lifestyle.* ◼ N-SING A **variety of** things is a number of different kinds or examples of the same thing. □ *The West Village has a variety of good stores.* □ *The island has a wide variety of plants.* ◼ N-COUNT A **variety** of something is a type of it. □ *They make 20 varieties of bread every day.* ◼ N-UNCOUNT **Variety** is the quality that something such as a painting or a dance has when it consists of different parts that are combined in an interesting way, for example because some parts contrast with other parts or change them. [from Latin]

| **Word Partnership** | Use *variety* with : |
|---|---|
| N. | variety **of activities,** variety **of colors,** variety **of foods,** variety **of issues,** variety **of problems,** variety **of products,** variety **of reasons,** variety **of sizes,** variety **of styles,** variety **of ways** ◼ |
| V. | **choose a** variety, **offer a** variety, **provide a** variety ◼ |

**va|ri|ety store** (**variety stores**) N-COUNT A **variety store** is a store that sells a wide range of small, inexpensive items.

**vari|ous** /vɛəriəs/ ADJ If you say that there are **various** things, you mean there are several different things of the type mentioned. □ *He spent the day doing various jobs around the house.* [from Latin]

**vari|ous|ly** /vɛəriəsli/ ADV You can use **variously** to introduce a number of different ways that something can be described. □ *He is variously described as a designer and a photographer.* [from Latin]

**var|nish** /vɑrnɪʃ/ (**varnishes, varnishing, varnished**) ◼ N-VAR **Varnish** is an oily liquid that is painted onto wood or other material to give it a hard, clear, shiny surface. ◼ V-T If you **varnish** something, you paint it with varnish. □ *Varnish the table with two or three coats of varnish.* [from Old French]

**var|sity** /vɑrsiti/ (**varsities**) N-COUNT The **varsity** is the main or first team for a particular sport at a high school, college, or university. □ *...the varsity basketball team.*

**vary** /vɛəri/ (**varies, varying, varied**) ◼ V-I If things **vary**, they are different from each other in size, amount, or degree. □ *The jugs are handmade,*

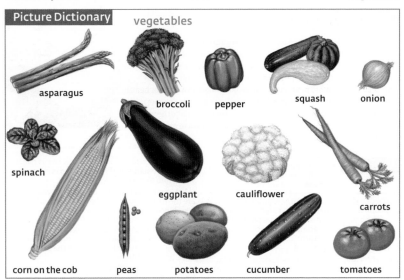

Picture Dictionary

**vegetables**

asparagus

broccoli    pepper     squash    onion

spinach

eggplant    cauliflower

carrots

corn on the cob    peas    potatoes    cucumber    tomatoes

so they vary slightly. ❑ *Her story varies from her friends'*
*accounts.* **2** V-T/V-I If something **varies** or if you
**vary** it, it becomes different or changed. ❑ *The cost*
*of coffee varies according to where it comes from.* [from
Latin] **3** → see also **varied**

---

**Word Partnership**   Use *vary* with :

| | |
|---|---|
| N. | **prices** vary, **rates** vary, **styles** vary **1** vary **by location**, vary **by size**, vary **by state**, vary **by store** **1 2** |
| ADV. | vary **considerably**, vary **greatly**, vary **slightly**, vary **widely** **1 2** |

---

**vas|cu|lar plant** /væskyələr plænt/ (**vascular
plants**) N-COUNT **Vascular plants** are plants that
have tissues which can carry water and other
fluids through the body of the plant. [TECHNICAL]

**vas de|fe|rens** /væs dɛfərɛnz/ (**vasa deferentia**
/veɪzədɛfərɛnʃiə, -ʃə/) N-COUNT The **vas deferens**
is the pair of narrow tubes in a man's body that
carries sperm from his testicles towards his penis.
[TECHNICAL] [from New Latin]

**vase** /veɪs, vɑz/ (**vases**) N-COUNT A **vase** is a jar,
usually made of glass or pottery, used for holding
cut flowers or as an ornament. ❑ *...a vase of red*
*roses.* [from French]
→ see **glass**

**vast** /væst/ (**vaster, vastest**) ADJ Something
that is **vast** is extremely large. ❑ *...farmers who own*
*vast stretches of land.* [from Latin]

---

**Word Partnership**   Use *vast* with :

| | |
|---|---|
| N. | vast **amounts**, vast **distance**, vast **expanse**, vast **knowledge**, vast **majority**, vast **quantities** |

---

**vast|ly** /væstli/ ADV **Vastly** means to an
extremely great degree or extent. ❑ *The jury heard*

*two vastly different accounts.* [from Latin]

**vau|de|ville** /vɔdvɪl, vɔdə-/ N-UNCOUNT
**Vaudeville** is a type of entertainment consisting
of short acts of comedy, singing, and dancing, that
was popular in the early twentieth century. [from
French]

**vault** /vɔlt/ (**vaults, vaulting, vaulted**)
**1** N-COUNT A **vault** is a secure room where money
and other valuable things can be kept safely. ❑ *The*
*jewels were kept in a bank vault.* **2** N-COUNT A **vault**
is a room underneath a church or in a cemetery,
where people are buried. ❑ *Matilda was buried in*
*the family vault.* **3** V-T/V-I If you **vault** something
or **vault over** it, you jump quickly onto or over it,
putting one or both of your hands on it to help
you. ❑ *He could easily vault the wall.* [from Old
French]

**VCR** /vi si ɑr/ (**VCRs**) N-COUNT A **VCR** is a
machine that can be used to record television
programs or movies onto videotapes. **VCR**
is an abbreviation for "video cassette
recorder."

**veal** /vil/ N-UNCOUNT **Veal** is meat from a calf.
❑ *...a veal cutlet.* [from Old French]

**vec|tor** /vɛktər/ (**vectors**) N-COUNT A **vector** is a
variable quantity, such as force, that has size and
direction. [TECHNICAL] [from Latin]

**veer** /vɪər/ (**veers, veering, veered**) V-I If
something **veers** in a certain direction, it suddenly
moves in that direction. ❑ *The plane veered off the*
*runway.* [from Dutch]

**veg|eta|ble** /vɛdʒtəbˀl, vɛdʒɪ-/ (**vegetables**)
N-COUNT **Vegetables** are plants such as cabbages,
potatoes, and onions that you can cook and eat.
[from Late Latin]
→ see Picture Dictionary: **vegetables**
→ see **vegetarian**

V

## Word Web · vegetarian

The Greek philosopher Pythagoras was a **vegetarian**. He believed that if humans killed animals, they would also kill each other. So he did not eat **meat**. Vegetarians eat many kinds of food, not just **vegetables**. They eat fruits, grains, oils, fats, and sugar. Vegans are vegetarians who don't eat eggs or dairy products. Some people choose this **diet** for health reasons. A well-balanced **veggie** diet can be healthy. Some people choose this diet for religious reasons. Others want to make the world's **food** supply go further. It takes fifteen pounds of grain to produce one pound of meat.

### Word Link · arian ≈ believing in, having :
humanit**arian**, totalit**arian**, veget**arian**

**veg|etar|ian** /vɛdʒɪtɛəriən/ (**vegetarians**) ADJ Someone who is **vegetarian** never eats meat or fish. □ …*a strict vegetarian diet.* ● A **vegetarian** is someone who is vegetarian. □ …*a special menu for vegetarians.* [from Late Latin]
→ see Word Web: **vegetarian**

**veg|eta|tion** /vɛdʒɪteɪʃⁿn/ N-UNCOUNT Plants, trees, and flowers can be referred to as **vegetation**. [FORMAL] □ …*tropical vegetation.* [from Late Latin]
→ see **erosion, habitat, herbivore**

**veg|eta|tive re|pro|duc|tion** /vɛdʒɪteɪtɪv riprədʌkʃⁿn/ also **vegetative propagation** N-UNCOUNT **Vegetative reproduction** is a process by which new plants are produced without using seeds, for example by using cuttings instead. [TECHNICAL]

**veg|gie** /vɛdʒi/ (**veggies**) N-COUNT **Veggies** are vegetables. [INFORMAL] □ …*fresh fruit and veggies.*

**ve|he|ment** /viəmənt/ ADJ **Vehement** feelings or opinions are strongly held and forcefully expressed. □ *She became vehement, jumping around and shouting.* ● **ve|he|mence** N-UNCOUNT □ *He spoke with vehemence.* ● **ve|he|ment|ly** ADV □ *Karl vehemently denied stealing.* [from Latin]

**ve|hi|cle** /viɪkⁿl/ (**vehicles**) ■ N-COUNT A **vehicle** is a machine with an engine, such as a bus, car, or truck, that carries people or things from place to place. □ *There are too many vehicles on the road.* ■ N-COUNT You can use **vehicle** to refer to something that you use in order to achieve a particular purpose. □ *Her art became a vehicle for her political beliefs.* [from Latin]
→ see **car, traffic**

**veil** /veɪl/ (**veils**)
■ N-COUNT A **veil** is a piece of thin soft cloth that women sometimes wear over their heads and that can also cover their face. □ *She wore a veil over her face.* ■ N-COUNT You can refer to something that hides or partly hides a situation or activity as a **veil**. □ *It is time for the government to lift the veil of secrecy over this matter.* [from Norman French]

veil

**veiled** /veɪld/ ■ ADJ A **veiled** comment is expressed indirectly rather than directly and openly. □ *He made a veiled reference to human rights.* ■ ADJ A woman or girl who is **veiled** is wearing a veil. [from Norman French]

**vein** /veɪn/ (**veins**) ■ N-COUNT Your **veins** are the thin tubes in your body through which your blood flows toward your heart. ■ N-COUNT Something that is written or spoken in a particular **vein** is written or spoken in that style or mood. □ *Her next book was in a lighter vein.* ■ N-COUNT The **veins** on a leaf are the thin lines on it. [from Old French]
→ see **cardiovascular system**

**ve|loc|ity** /vəlɒsɪti/ (**velocities**) N-VAR **Velocity** is the speed at which something moves in a particular direction. [TECHNICAL] □ *His velocity was a little lower than usual.* [from Latin]

**vel|vet** /vɛlvɪt/ (**velvets**) N-VAR **Velvet** is soft material made from cotton, silk, or nylon, that has a thick layer of short cut threads on one side. [from Old French]

**ven|det|ta** /vɛndɛtə/ (**vendettas**) N-VAR If one person has a **vendetta against** another, the first person wants revenge for something the second person did to them in the past. □ *He has a vendetta against me for some reason.* [from Italian]

**ven|dor** /vɛndər/ (**vendors**) N-COUNT A **vendor** is someone who sells things such as newspapers, drinks, or food from a small stall or cart. □ …*ice cream vendors.* [from Anglo-Norman French]

**ve|neer** /vɪniər/ N-SING If you refer to the pleasant way that someone or something appears as a **veneer**, you are critical of them because you believe that their true, hidden nature is not good. □ *He fooled everyone with his veneer of knowledge.* [from German]

**ven|er|able** /vɛnərəbⁿl/ ■ ADJ A **venerable** person deserves respect because they are old and experienced. □ …*some of the nation's most venerable actors.* ■ ADJ Something that is **venerable** is impressive because it is old or important historically. □ *Yale University is a venerable institution.* [from Latin]

**venge|ance** /vɛndʒⁿns/ ■ N-UNCOUNT **Vengeance** is the act of killing, injuring, or harming someone because they have harmed you. □ *He swore vengeance on everyone involved in the murder.* ■ PHRASE If you say that something happens **with a vengeance**, you are emphasizing that it happens to a great extent. □ *It began to rain with a vengeance.* [from Old French]

**veni|son** /vɛnɪsⁿn, -zⁿn/ N-UNCOUNT **Venison** is the meat of a deer. [from Old French]

**Venn dia|gram** /vɛn daɪəgræm/ (**Venn diagrams**) N-COUNT A **Venn diagram** is a diagram in mathematics that uses overlapping circles to represent features that are common to, or unique to, two or more sets of data. [after John Venn (1834-1923), an English logician]

**ven|om** /vɛnəm/ (**venoms**) ◼ N-UNCOUNT **Venom** refers to feelings of great bitterness and anger toward someone. ❑ *In his speech, he directed most of his venom at his critics.* ◻ N-VAR The **venom** of a creature such as a snake or spider is the poison that it puts into your body when it bites or stings you. [from Old French]

**vent** /vɛnt/ (**vents, venting, vented**) ◼ N-COUNT A **vent** is a hole in something through which air can come in and smoke, gas, or smells can go out. ❑ *Steam escaped from the vent at the front of the machine.* ◻ V-T If you **vent** your feelings, you express your feelings forcefully. ❑ *She telephoned her best friend to vent her frustration.* ◼ N-COUNT A **vent** is a crack in the Earth's surface through which lava and gas are released. [from Old French]

**ven|ti|late** /vɛntᵊleɪt/ (**ventilates, ventilating, ventilated**) V-T If you **ventilate** a room or building, you allow fresh air to get into it. ❑ *You must ventilate the room well when painting.* ● **ven|ti|la|tion** /vɛntᵊleɪʃᵊn/ N-UNCOUNT ❑ *The only ventilation came from one tiny window.* [from Latin]

**ven|tri|cle** /vɛntrɪkᵊl/ (**ventricles**) N-COUNT A **ventricle** is a part of the heart that pumps blood to the arteries. [MEDICAL] [from Latin]

**ven|ture** /vɛntʃər/ (**ventures, venturing, ventured**) ◼ N-COUNT A **venture** is a project or activity that is new, exciting, and difficult because it involves the risk of failure. ❑ *...a joint venture between two schools.* ◻ V-I If you **venture** somewhere, you go somewhere that might be dangerous. [LITERARY] ❑ *People are afraid to venture out at night.* ◼ V-I If you **venture into** an activity, you do something that involves the risk of failure because it is new and different. ❑ *He ventured into business but had no success.*

**venue** /vɛnyu/ (**venues**) N-COUNT The **venue** for an event or activity is the place where it will happen. ❑ *The Convention Center is the venue for a three-day arts festival.* [from Old French]
→ see **concert**

**Ve|nus** /vinəs/ N-PROPER **Venus** is the second planet from the sun, situated between Mercury and the Earth. [from Latin]

**ve|ran|da** /vərændə/ (**verandas**) also **verandah** N-COUNT A **veranda** is a roofed platform along the outside of a house. ❑ *They had their coffee on the veranda.* [from Portuguese]

veranda

**verb** /vɜrb/ (**verbs**) ◼ N-COUNT A **verb** is a word such as "sing," "feel," or "die" that is used with a subject to say what someone or something does or what happens to them, or to give information about them. [from Latin] ◻ → see also **phrasal verb**

**Word Link** verb ≈ word : *adverb, proverb, verbal*

**ver|bal** /vɜrbᵊl/ ◼ ADJ You use **verbal** to indicate that something is expressed in speech rather than in writing or action. ❑ *We will not tolerate verbal or physical abuse of our employees.* ● **ver|bal|ly** ADV ❑ *We complained both verbally and in writing.* ◻ ADJ You use **verbal** to indicate that something is connected with words and the use of words. ❑ *...verbal skills.* [from Latin]

**verb phrase** (**verb phrases**) N-COUNT A **verb phrase** or **verbal phrase** consists of a verb, or of a main verb following a modal or one or more auxiliaries. Examples are "walked," "can see," and "has been waiting."

**Word Link** ver ≈ truth : *verdict, verify, version*

**ver|dict** /vɜrdɪkt/ (**verdicts**) ◼ N-COUNT In a court of law, the **verdict** is the decision that is given by the jury or judge at the end of a trial. ❑ *The jury delivered a verdict of not guilty.* ◻ N-COUNT Someone's **verdict** on something is their opinion of it, after thinking about it or investigating it. ❑ *The doctor's verdict was that he was healthy.* [from Medieval Latin]
→ see **trial**

**verge** /vɜrdʒ/ (**verges, verging, verged**) PHRASE If you are **on the verge of** something, you are going to do it very soon or it is likely to happen or begin very soon. ❑ *Carole was on the verge of tears.* [from Old French]
▶ **verge on** PHR-VERB If someone or something **verges on** a particular state or quality, they are almost the same as that state or quality. ❑ *Her anger verged on madness.*

**veri|fy** /vɛrɪfaɪ/ (**verifies, verifying, verified**) ◼ V-T If you **verify** something, you check that it is true by careful examination or investigation. ❑ *We haven't yet verified his information.* ● **veri|fi|ca|tion** /vɛrɪfɪkeɪʃᵊn/ N-UNCOUNT ❑ *...the verification of her story.* ◻ V-T If you **verify** something, you state or confirm that it is true. ❑ *The government has not verified any of those reports.* [from Old French]

**veri|table** /vɛrɪtəbᵊl/ ADJ You can use **veritable** to emphasize the size, amount, or nature of something. ❑ *He is a veritable hero.* [from Old French]

**ver|nacu|lar** /vərnækyələr/ (**vernaculars**) N-COUNT The **vernacular** is the language or dialect that is most widely spoken by ordinary people in a region or country. ❑ *...plays written in the vernacular.* [from Latin]

**ver|sa|tile** /vɜrsətᵊl/ ◼ ADJ If you say that a person is **versatile**, you approve of them because they have many different skills. ❑ *He was one of our most versatile athletes.* ● **ver|sa|til|ity** /vɜrsətɪlɪti/ N-UNCOUNT ❑ *...her versatility as an actress.* ◻ ADJ A tool, machine, or material that is **versatile** can be used for many different purposes. ❑ *Computers today are so versatile.* ● **ver|sa|til|ity** N-UNCOUNT ❑ *Plastic is known for its versatility.* [from Latin]

**verse** /vɜrs/ (**verses**) ◼ N-UNCOUNT **Verse** is writing arranged in lines that have rhythm and that often rhyme at the end. ❑ *...a few lines of verse.* ◻ N-COUNT A **verse** is one of the parts into which a poem, a song, or a chapter of the Bible or the Koran is divided. [from Old English]

**ver|sion** /vɜrɜᵊn/ (**versions**) ◼ N-COUNT A **version of** something is a particular form of it in which some details are different from earlier or later forms. ❑ *He is bringing out a new version of his*

V

book. **2** N-COUNT Someone's **version of** an event is their own description of it. ❑ *...the official version of events.* [from Medieval Latin]

**ver|sus** /vɜrsəs/ **1** PREP You use **versus** to indicate that two figures, ideas, or choices are opposed. ❑ *They discussed getting a job after graduation versus going to college.* **2** PREP **Versus** is used to indicate that two teams or people are competing against each other in a sports event. ❑ *It will be the U.S. versus Belgium in tomorrow's game.* [from Latin]

**ver|te|bra** /vɜrtɪbrə/ (**vertebrae** /vɜrtɪbreɪ, -bri/) N-COUNT **Vertebrae** are the small circular bones that form the spine of a human being or animal. [from Latin]

**ver|te|brate** /vɜrtɪbrɪt/ (**vertebrates**) N-COUNT A **vertebrate** is a creature that has a skull and a spine. Mammals, birds, reptiles, and fish are vertebrates. [from Latin]

**ver|ti|cal** /vɜrtɪkᵊl/ ADJ Something that is **vertical** stands or points straight up. ❑ *...a vertical wall of rock.* ● **ver|ti|cal|ly** ADV ❑ *Cut each lemon in half vertically.* [from Late Latin]
→ see **graph**

**very** /vɛri/ **1** ADV **Very** is used to give emphasis to an adjective or adverb. ❑ *The answer is very simple.* ❑ *I'm very sorry.* **2** PHRASE **Not very** is used with an adjective or adverb to say that something is not at all true, or that it is true only to a small degree. ❑ *She's not very impressed with them.* ❑ *"How well do you know her?" — "Not very."* **3** ADJ You use **very** with certain nouns in order to specify an extreme position or extreme point in time. ❑ *At the very back of the yard was a tree.* ❑ *I turned to the very end of the book.* **4** ADJ You use **very** with nouns to emphasize that something is exactly the right one or exactly the same one. ❑ *She died in this very house.* **5** PHRASE **Very much so** is an emphatic way of answering "yes" to something or saying that it is true or correct. ❑ *"Are you enjoying your vacation?" — "Very much so."* **6** CONVENTION **Very well** is used to say that you agree to do something or you accept someone's answer, even though you might not be completely satisfied with it. ❑ *"Very well," she said, "you may go."* [from Old French]

| **Thesaurus** | *very* | Also look up : |
| --- | --- | --- |

ADV. absolutely, extremely, greatly, highly **1**

**vesi|cle** /vɛsɪkᵊl/ (**vesicles**) N-COUNT A **vesicle** is a compartment within a living cell in which substances are carried or stored. [TECHNICAL] [from Latin]

**ves|sel** /vɛsᵊl/ (**vessels**) **1** N-COUNT A **vessel** is a ship or large boat. [FORMAL] ❑ *...a New Zealand navy vessel.* [from Old French] **2** → see also **blood vessel**
→ see **ship**

**vest** /vɛst/ (**vests**) N-COUNT A **vest** is a sleeveless piece of clothing with buttons that people usually wear over a shirt. [from Old French]

**vest|ed in|ter|est** /vɛstɪd ɪntrɪst, -tərɪst/ (**vested interests**) N-VAR If you have a **vested interest in** something, you have a very strong reason for acting in a particular way, for example, to protect your money, power, or reputation. ❑ *Society has a vested interest in educating its young people.*

**ves|tige** /vɛstɪdʒ/ (**vestiges**) N-COUNT The

**vestiges of** something are the small parts that still remain after most of it has gone. [FORMAL] ❑ *...vestiges of the past such as castles.* [from French]

**ves|tig|ial struc|ture** /vɛstɪdʒiəl strʌktʃər, -stɪdʒəl/ (**vestigial structures**) also **vestigial organ** N-COUNT A **vestigial structure** or **vestigial organ** is a part of the body of an animal, such as the appendix in humans, that was useful at an earlier stage of the animal's evolution but no longer has any function. [TECHNICAL]

**vet** /vɛt/ (**vets, vetting, vetted**) N-COUNT A **vet** is someone who is qualified to treat sick or injured animals. **Vet** is an abbreviation for **veterinarian**. [INFORMAL]

**vet|er|an** /vɛtərən/ (**veterans**) **1** N-COUNT A **veteran** is someone who has served in the armed forces of their country, especially during a war. ❑ *...veterans of the Vietnam War.* **2** N-COUNT You use **veteran** to refer to someone who has been involved in a particular activity for a long time. ❑ *...a veteran movie critic.* [from Latin]

**vet|eri|nar|ian** /vɛtərɪnɛəriən/ (**veterinarians**) N-COUNT A **veterinarian** is a person who is qualified to treat sick or injured animals. [from Latin]

**vet|eri|nary** /vɛtərənɛri/ ADJ **Veterinary** is used to describe the work of a person whose job is to treat sick or injured animals, or to describe the medical treatment of animals. ❑ *...a veterinary examination.* [from Latin]

**veto** /vitoʊ/ (**vetoes, vetoing, vetoed**) **1** V-T If someone in authority **vetoes** something, they forbid it, or stop it from being put into action. ❑ *The president vetoed the bill passed by Congress.* ● **Veto** is also a noun. ❑ *The chairperson of the committee used her veto.* **2** N-UNCOUNT **Veto** is the right that someone in authority has to forbid something. ❑ *...the president's power of veto.* [from Latin]

**vex** /vɛks/ (**vexes, vexing, vexed**) V-T If someone or something **vexes** you, they make you feel annoyed, puzzled, and frustrated. ❑ *Their attitude vexed him.* ● **vexed** ADJ ❑ *Farmers are vexed and blame the government.* ● **vex|ing** ADJ ❑ *...a vexing problem.* [from Old French]

**via** /vaɪə, viə/ **1** PREP If you go somewhere **via** a particular place, you go through that place on the way to your destination. ❑ *I'm flying to Sweden via New York.* **2** PREP If you do something **via** a particular means or person, you do it by making use of that means or person. ❑ *We can continue the discussion via e-mail.* [from Latin]

**vi|able** /vaɪəbᵊl/ ADJ Something that is **viable** is capable of doing what it is intended to do. ❑ *The business in its current state is not viable.* ● **vi|abil|ity** /vaɪəbɪlɪti/ N-UNCOUNT ❑ *...worries about the company's long-term viability.* [from French]

**vi|brant** /vaɪbrənt/ **1** ADJ Someone or something that is **vibrant** is full of life, energy, and enthusiasm. ❑ *...her vibrant personality.* ● **vi|bran|cy** /vaɪbrənsi/ N-UNCOUNT ❑ *She was a woman with extraordinary vibrancy.* **2** ADJ **Vibrant** colors are very bright and clear. ❑ *The grass was a vibrant green.* ● **vi|brant|ly** ADV ❑ *...vibrantly colored fabrics.* [from Latin]

**vi|brate** /vaɪbreɪt/ (**vibrates, vibrating, vibrated**) V-T/V-I If something **vibrates** or if

you **vibrate** it, it shakes with repeated small, quick movements. ❑ *The ground seemed to vibrate.*
● **vi|bra|tion** /vaɪbreɪᵍn/ (**vibrations**) N-VAR ❑ *The vibration of the trucks rattled the windows.* [from Latin]

→ see **sound, ear**

**vice** /vaɪs/ (**vices**) **1** N-COUNT A **vice** is a habit that is regarded as a weakness in your character, but not usually as a serious fault. ❑ *My only vice is that I spend too much on clothes.* **2** N-UNCOUNT **Vice** refers to criminal activities, especially those connected with pornography or prostitution. [from Old French]

**vice ver|sa** /vaɪsəvɜrsə, vaɪs/ PHRASE **Vice versa** is used to indicate that the reverse of what you have said is true. For example, "women may bring their husbands with them, and vice versa" means that men may also bring their wives with them. [from Latin]

**vi|cin|ity** /vɪsɪnɪti/ N-SING If something is **in the vicinity of** a particular place, it is near it. [FORMAL] ❑ *There were several hotels in the vicinity of the station.* [from Latin]

**vi|cious** /vɪʃəs/ **1** ADJ A **vicious** person or a **vicious** blow is violent and cruel. ❑ *...a cruel and vicious man.* ● **vi|cious|ly** ADV ❑ *He was viciously attacked.* ● **vi|cious|ness** N-UNCOUNT ❑ *...the viciousness of his hatred.* **2** ADJ A **vicious** remark is cruel and intended to upset someone. ❑ *...a vicious comment about his appearance.* ● **vi|cious|ly** ADV ❑ *"He deserved to die," said Penelope viciously.* [from Old French]

**vi|cious cir|cle** (**vicious circles**) also **vicious cycle** N-COUNT A **vicious circle** is a problem or difficult situation that has the effect of creating new problems that then cause the original problem or situation to occur again.

**vic|tim** /vɪktəm/ (**victims**) N-COUNT A **victim** is someone who has been hurt or killed. ❑ *...the victims of violent crime.* [from Latin]

**vic|tim|ize** /vɪktəmaɪz/ (**victimizes, victimizing, victimized**) V-T If someone is **victimized**, they are deliberately treated unfairly. ❑ *The students were victimized because they opposed the government.* ● **vic|timi|za|tion** /vɪktəmɪzeɪᵍn/ N-UNCOUNT ❑ *...society's victimization of women.* [from Latin]

**vic|tor** /vɪktər/ (**victors**) N-COUNT The **victor** in a battle or contest is the person who wins. [LITERARY] [from Latin]

**Vic|to|rian** /vɪktɔriən/ (**Victorians**) **1** ADJ **Victorian** means belonging to, connected with, or typical of Britain in the middle and last parts of the 19th century, when Victoria was Queen. ❑ *...a lovely old Victorian house.* **2** ADJ You can use **Victorian** to describe people who have old-fashioned attitudes, especially about good behavior and morals. ❑ *Victorian attitudes have no place in modern society.* **3** N-COUNT The **Victorians** were the British people who lived in the time of Queen Victoria.

**vic|to|ri|ous** /vɪktɔriəs/ ADJ You use **victorious** to describe someone who has won a victory in a struggle, war, or competition. ❑ *...the victorious*

**vic|to|ry** /vɪktəri, vɪktri/ (**victories**) N-VAR A **victory** is a success in a struggle, war, or competition. ❑ *The Democrats celebrated their victory.* [from Old French]

**video** /vɪdioʊ/ (**videos, videoing, videoed**) **1** N-COUNT A **video** is a movie or television program recorded on tape. ❑ *...sports and exercise videos.* **2** N-UNCOUNT **Video** is the system of recording movies and events on tape. ❑ *She has watched the show on video.* [from Latin]

**video ar|cade** (**video arcades**) N-COUNT A **video arcade** is a place where you can play video games on machines which work when you put money in them.

**video game** (**video games**) N-COUNT A **video game** is an electronic or computerized game that you play on your television or on a computer screen.

**video re|cord|er** (**video recorders**) N-COUNT A **video recorder** or a **video cassette recorder** is the same as a **VCR**.

**video|tape** /vɪdioʊteɪp/ (**videotapes**) also **video tape** N-VAR **Videotape** is magnetic tape that is used to record moving pictures and sounds to be shown on television. ❑ *...the use of videotape in court cases.*

**vie** /vaɪ/ (**vies, vying, vied**) V-RECIP If one person or thing **is vying with** another for something, the people or things are competing for it. [FORMAL] ❑ *The brothers vied with each other to offer help to their parents.* [from Old French]

**view** /vyu/ (**views, viewing, viewed**) **1** N-COUNT Your **views** on something are the beliefs or opinions that you have about it. ❑ *We have similar views on politics.* **2** N-SING Your **view of** a particular subject is the way that you understand and think about it. ❑ *Something happened to change my view of this place and of my work there.* **3** V-T If you **view** something in a particular way, you think of it in that way. ❑ *Immigrants viewed the United States as a land of opportunity.* ❑ *Linda views her daughter's talent with pride.* **4** N-COUNT The **view** from a window or high place is everything that can be seen from that place, especially when it is considered to be beautiful. ❑ *From our hotel room we had a great view of the ocean.* **5** N-SING If you have a **view of** something, you can see it. ❑ *He stood up to get a better view of the blackboard.* **6** N-UNCOUNT You use **view** in expressions to do with being able to see something. For example, if something is **in view**, you can see it. If something is **in full view of everyone**, everyone can see it. ❑ *She was lying there in full view of anyone who walked by.* **7** V-T If you **view** something, you look at it for a particular purpose. [FORMAL] ❑ *They came to view the house again.* **8** PHRASE You use **in view of** when you are taking into consideration facts that have just been mentioned or are just about to be mentioned. ❑ *In view of the heavy rain we are staying at home.* **9** PHRASE If something such as a work of art is

V

**on view**, it is shown in public for people to look at. ❏ *Her paintings are on view at the Portland Gallery.* **10** PHRASE If you do something **with a view to** doing something else, you do it because you hope it will result in that other thing being done. ❏ *We called a meeting with a view to resolving the dispute.* [from Old French]

**view|er** /vyuər/ (**viewers**) N-COUNT **Viewers** are people who watch television, or who are watching a particular program on television. ❏ *19 million viewers watch the show every week.* [from Old French]

**view|point** /vyupɔɪnt/ (**viewpoints**) N-COUNT Someone's **viewpoint** is the way that they think about things in general, or the way they think about a particular thing. ❏ *The book is written from the girl's viewpoint.*

| Word Link | vig ≈ awake, strong : *in*vigorating, *vig*il, *vig*ilant |
| --- | --- |

**vig|il** /vɪdʒɪl/ (**vigils**) N-COUNT A **vigil** is a period of time when people remain quietly in a place, especially at night, for example, because they are praying or are making a political protest. ❏ *Protesters held a vigil outside the jail.* [from Old French]

**vigi|lant** /vɪdʒɪlənt/ ADJ Someone who is **vigilant** gives careful attention to a particular problem or situation and concentrates on noticing any danger or trouble that there might be. ❏ *He warned the public to be vigilant.* ● **vigi|lance** N-UNCOUNT ❏ *We wish to increase vigilance among local police.* [from Latin]

**vigi|lan|te** /vɪdʒɪlænti/ (**vigilantes**) N-COUNT **Vigilantes** are people who organize themselves into an unofficial group to protect their community and to catch and punish criminals. [from Spanish]

**vig|or** /vɪgər/ N-UNCOUNT **Vigor** is physical or mental energy and enthusiasm. ❏ *He approached his new job with vigor.* [from Old French]

**vig|or|ous** /vɪgərəs/ ADJ **Vigorous** physical activities involve using a lot of energy, usually to do short and repeated actions. ❏ *...vigorous exercise.* ● **vig|or|ous|ly** ADV ❏ *He shook his head vigorously.* [from Old French]

**vile** /vaɪl/ (**viler, vilest**) ADJ If you say that someone or something is **vile**, you mean that they are very unpleasant. ❏ *The weather was vile.* [from Old French]

**vil|la** /vɪlə/ (**villas**) N-COUNT A **villa** is a fairly large house, especially one in a hot country or a resort. [from Italian]

**vil|lage** /vɪlɪdʒ/ (**villages**) N-COUNT A **village** consists of a group of houses, together with other buildings such as a church and a school, in a country area. [from Old French]

**vil|lag|er** /vɪlɪdʒər/ (**villagers**) N-COUNT You refer to the people who live in a village, especially the people who have lived there for most or all of their lives, as the **villagers**. [from Old French]

**vil|lain** /vɪlən/ (**villains**) N-COUNT A **villain** is someone who deliberately harms other people or breaks the law in order to get what he or she wants. ❏ *They called him a villain and a murderer.* [from Old French]

**vin|di|cate** /vɪndɪkeɪt/ (**vindicates, vindicating, vindicated**) V-T If a person or their decisions,

actions, or ideas **are vindicated**, they are proved to be correct, after people have said that they were wrong. [FORMAL] ❏ *The court's decision vindicated her claims.* ● **vin|di|ca|tion** /vɪndɪkeɪⁿn/ N-UNCOUNT; N-SING ❏ *He said their success was a vindication of his party's policy.* [from Latin]

**vin|dic|tive** /vɪndɪktɪv/ ADJ If you say that someone is **vindictive**, you are critical of them because they deliberately try to upset or cause trouble for someone who they think has done them harm. ❏ *...a vindictive woman desperate for revenge.* ● **vin|dic|tive|ness** N-UNCOUNT ❏ *He acted out of vindictiveness.* [from Latin]

**vine** /vaɪn/ (**vines**) N-VAR A **vine** is a plant that grows up or over things, especially one that produces grapes. [from Old French]

**vin|egar** /vɪnɪgər/ (**vinegars**) N-VAR **Vinegar** is a sharp-tasting liquid, usually made from sour wine or malt, that is used in cooking to make things such as salad dressing. [from Old French]

**vine|yard** /vɪnyərd/ (**vineyards**) N-COUNT A **vineyard** is an area of land where grape vines are grown in order to produce wine. [from Old English]

**vin|tage** /vɪntɪdʒ/ (**vintages**) **1** N-COUNT The **vintage** of a good quality wine is the year and place that it was made. ❏ *This wine is from one of the best vintages of the decade.* **2** ADJ **Vintage** wine is good quality wine that has been stored for several years in order to improve its quality. **3** ADJ **Vintage** cars or airplanes are old but are admired because they are considered to be the best of their kind. [from Old French]

**vi|nyl** /vaɪnɪl/ N-UNCOUNT **Vinyl** is a strong plastic used for making things such as floor coverings and furniture. ❏ *...vinyl floor covering.*

**vio|la** /vioʊlə/ (**violas**) N-VAR A **viola** is a musical instrument that is like a violin, but is slightly larger. [from Italian]
→ see **orchestra, string**

**vio|late** /vaɪəleɪt/ (**violates, violating, violated**) **1** V-T If someone **violates** an agreement, law, or promise, they break it. [FORMAL] ❏ *They went to prison because they violated the law.* ● **vio|la|tion** /vaɪəleɪⁿn/ (**violations**) N-VAR ❏ *...a violation of state law.* **2** V-T If you **violate** someone's privacy or peace, you disturb it. [FORMAL] **3** V-T If someone **violates** a special place such as a grave, they damage it or treat it with disrespect. ● **vio|la|tion** N-VAR ❏ *...the violation of the graves.* [from Latin]

**vio|lence** /vaɪələns/ **1** N-UNCOUNT **Violence** is behavior that is intended to hurt, injure, or kill people. ❏ *Twenty people died in the violence.* **2** N-UNCOUNT If you do or say something with **violence**, you use a lot of force and energy in doing or saying it, often because you are angry. [LITERARY] ❏ *The violence of her behavior shocked him.* [from Old French]

**vio|lent** /vaɪələnt/ **1** ADJ If someone is **violent**, or if they do something that is **violent**, they use physical force or weapons to hurt, injure, or kill other people. ❏ *These men have committed violent crimes.* ❏ *...violent anti-government demonstrations.* ● **vio|lent|ly** ADV ❏ *Some politicians have been violently attacked.* **2** ADJ A **violent** event happens suddenly and with great force. ❏ *A violent explosion shook the city.* ● **vio|lent|ly** ADV ❏ *The volcano erupted violently.* **3** ADJ If you describe something as **violent**, you mean that it is said, done, or felt very strongly. ❑ *He had violent stomach pains.* ● **vio|lent|ly** ADV ❑ *She protested violently.* [from Latin]

**vio|let** /ˈvaɪələt/ (**violets**) **1** N-COUNT A **violet** is a small plant that has purple or white flowers in the spring. **2** COLOR Something that is **violet** is a bluish-purple color. [from Old French]
→ see **color, rainbow**

**vio|lin** /ˌvaɪəˈlɪn/ (**violins**) N-VAR A **violin** is a musical instrument made of wood with four strings. You play the **violin** by holding it under your chin and moving a bow across the strings. ❑ *Lizzie plays the violin.* ● **vio|lin|ist** (**violinists**) N-COUNT ❑ *Rose's father was a talented violinist.* [from Italian]
→ see **orchestra, string**

**VIP** /ˌviː aɪ ˈpiː/ (**VIPs**) N-COUNT A **VIP** is someone who is given better treatment than ordinary people because they are famous, influential, or important. **VIP** is an abbreviation for "very important person." ❑ *...VIPs such as Prince Charles and Bill Clinton.*

**vir|gin** /ˈvɜrdʒɪn/ (**virgins**) **1** N-COUNT A **virgin** is someone who has never had sex. ● **vir|gin|ity** /vərˈdʒɪnɪti/ N-UNCOUNT ❑ *At American weddings, brides often wear white, the color of purity and virginity.* **2** ADJ You use **virgin** to describe something such as land that has never been used or spoiled. ❑ *...virgin forest.* [from Old French]

**vir|ile** /ˈvɪrᵊl/ ADJ If you describe a man as **virile**, you mean that he has the qualities that a man is traditionally expected to have, such as strength and sexual power. ❑ *He wanted his sons to be strong, virile, and athletic.* ● **vi|ril|ity** /vɪˈrɪlɪti/ N-UNCOUNT ❑ *Children are considered to be proof of a man's virility.* [from Latin]

**vir|tual** /ˈvɜrtʃuəl/ **1** ADJ You can use **virtual** to indicate that something is so nearly true that for most purposes it can be regarded as true. ❑ *He was a virtual prisoner in his own home.* ● **vir|tu|al|ly** /ˈvɜrtʃuəli/ ADV ❑ *She does virtually all the cooking.* **2** ADJ **Virtual** objects and activities are generated by a computer to simulate real objects and activities. ❑ *...a virtual world of role playing.* [from Medieval Latin]

**vir|tual re|al|ity** N-UNCOUNT **Virtual reality** is an environment that is produced by a computer and seems very like reality to the person experiencing it. [COMPUTING]

**vir|tue** /ˈvɜrtʃu/ (**virtues**) **1** N-UNCOUNT **Virtue** is thinking and doing what is right and avoiding what is wrong. ❑ *The priests talked to us about virtue.* **2** N-COUNT A **virtue** is a good quality or way of behaving. ❑ *His greatest virtue is patience.* **3** N-COUNT The **virtue** of something is an advantage or benefit that it has, especially in comparison with something else. ❑ *The virtue of doing it this way is it's very quick and easy.* **4** PHRASE You use **by virtue of** to explain why something happens or is true. [FORMAL] ❑ *We have these rights by virtue of being human.* [from Old French]

**vir|tuo|so** /ˌvɜrtʃuˈoʊsoʊ/ (**virtuosos** or **virtuosi** /ˌvɜrtʃuˈoʊsi/) **1** N-COUNT A **virtuoso** is someone who is extremely good at something, especially at playing a musical instrument. ❑ *...a violin virtuoso.* **2** ADJ A **virtuoso** performance or display shows great skill. [from Italian]

**vir|tu|ous** /ˈvɜrtʃuəs/ **1** ADJ A **virtuous** person behaves in a moral and correct way. ❑ *...a courageous and virtuous man.* **2** ADJ If you describe someone as **virtuous**, you mean that they have done what they ought to do and feel very pleased with themselves, perhaps too pleased. ❑ *I cleaned the apartment, which made me feel virtuous.* ● **vir|tu|ous|ly** ADV ❑ *"I've already done that," said Ronnie virtuously.* [from Old French]

**viru|lent** /ˈvɪryələnt/ **1** ADJ **Virulent** feelings or actions are extremely bitter and hostile. [FORMAL] ❑ *He faced virulent attacks from the media.* ● **viru|lence** /ˈvɪryələns/ N-UNCOUNT ❑ *The virulence of his anger had appalled her.* ● **viru|lent|ly** ADV ❑ *He was virulently hostile to the president.* **2** ADJ A **virulent** disease or poison is extremely powerful and dangerous. ❑ *...a very virulent form of the disease.* ● **viru|lence** N-UNCOUNT ❑ *...the virulence of the epidemic.* [from Latin]

**vi|rus** /ˈvaɪrəs/ (**viruses**) **1** N-COUNT A **virus** is a kind of germ that can cause disease. ❑ *There are many different strains of flu virus.* **2** N-COUNT In computer technology, a **virus** is a program that introduces itself into a system, altering or destroying the information stored in the system. [COMPUTING] ❑ *You should protect yourself against computer viruses.* [from Latin]
→ see **illness**

**visa** /ˈvizə/ (**visas**) N-COUNT A **visa** is an official document, or a stamp put in your passport, that allows you to enter or leave a particular country. [from French]

**vis|cos|ity** /vɪsˈkɒsɪti/ N-UNCOUNT **Viscosity** is the quality that some liquids have of being thick and sticky. [from Late Latin]

**vise** /ˈvaɪs/ (**vises**) N-COUNT A **vise** is a tool with a pair of parts that hold an object tightly while you do work on it. [from Old French]

**vis|ibil|ity** /ˌvɪzɪˈbɪlɪti/ N-UNCOUNT **Visibility** means how far or how clearly you can see in particular weather conditions. ❑ *Visibility was poor.* [from Latin]

**Word Link** vid, vis ≈ seeing : tele**vis**ion, **vid**eotape, **vis**ible

**vis|ible** /ˈvɪzɪbᵊl/ **1** ADJ If something is **visible**, it can be seen. ❑ *The warning lights were clearly visible.* **2** ADJ You use **visible** to describe something or someone that people notice or recognize. ❑ *He made a visible effort to control his temper.* ● **vis|ibly** /ˈvɪzɪbli/ ADV ❑ *She was visibly upset.* [from Latin]
→ see **wave**

**Word Partnership** Use *visible* with :

| | |
|---|---|
| N. | visible **to the naked eye** **1** |
| ADV. | **barely** visible, **clearly** visible, **highly** visible, **less** visible, **more** visible, **still** visible, **very** visible **1** **2** |
| V. | **become** visible **1** **2** |

**vi|sion** /ˈvɪʒᵊn/ (**visions**) **1** N-COUNT Your **vision of** a future situation or society is what you imagine or hope it would be like if things were very different from the way they are now. ❑ *I have a vision of world peace.* **2** N-UNCOUNT Your **vision** is your ability to see clearly with your eyes. ❑ *He's suffering from loss of vision.* [from Latin]

### Word Partnership    Use *vision* with :

| | |
|---|---|
| v. | **have a** vision, **share a** vision **1** |
| N. | vision **of the future**, vision **of peace**, vision **of reality 1** color vision, **field of** vision **2** |
| ADJ. | **clear** vision **1 2** **blurred** vision **2** |

**vi|sion|ary** /vɪʒəneri/ (**visionaries**) **1** N-COUNT If you refer to someone as a **visionary**, you mean that they have strong, original ideas about how things might be different in the future, especially about how things might be improved. ❑ *A great leader needs to be a visionary.* **2** ADJ You use **visionary** to describe the strong, original ideas of a visionary. ❑ *...visionary architectural designs.* [from Latin]

**vis|it** /vɪzɪt/ (**visits, visiting, visited**) **1** V-T/V-I If you **visit** someone, you go to see them and spend time with them. ❑ *He wanted to visit his brother.* ❑ *In the evenings, friends often visit.* ● **Visit** is also a noun. ❑ *Helen recently paid him a visit.* **2** V-T/V-I If you **visit** a place, you go there for a short time. ❑ *He'll be visiting four cities including Cagliari.* ❑ *...a visiting family from Texas.* ● **Visit** is also a noun. ❑ *...the Queen's visit to Canada.* [from Latin]
▸ **visit with** PHR-VERB If you **visit with** someone, you go to see them and spend time talking with them. ❑ *I visited with him in San Francisco.*

### Thesaurus    *visit*    Also look up :

| | |
|---|---|
| v. | call on, go, see, stop by **1** |

### Word Partnership    Use *visit* with :

| | |
|---|---|
| N. | visit **family/relatives**, visit **friends**, visit *your* **mother 1** **weekend** visit **1 2** visit **a museum**, visit **a restaurant 2** |
| v. | **come to** visit, **go to** visit, **invite** *someone* **to** visit, **plan to** visit **1 2** |
| ADJ. | **brief** visit, **last** visit, **next** visit, **recent** visit, **short** visit, **surprise** visit **1 2** **foreign** visit, **official** visit **2** |

**vis|ita|tion rights** /vɪzɪteɪʃⁿn raɪts/ N-PLURAL If a parent who is divorced and does not live with their child has **visitation rights**, they officially have the right to spend time with their child. ❑ *The divorce court did not give him any visitation rights.*

**vis|it|ing hours** N-PLURAL In an institution such as a hospital or prison, **visiting hours** are the times during which people from outside the institution are officially allowed to visit people who are staying at the institution. ❑ *Visiting hours are 3 to 7 p.m.*

**vis|it|ing pro|fes|sor** (**visiting professors**) N-COUNT A **visiting professor** is a professor at a college or university who is invited to teach at another college or university for a short period such as one term or one year.

**visi|tor** /vɪzɪtər/ (**visitors**) N-COUNT A **visitor** is someone who is visiting a person or place. ❑ *We had some visitors from Milwaukee.* [from Latin]

**vis|ta** /vɪstə/ (**vistas**) N-COUNT A **vista** is a view from a particular place, especially a beautiful view from a high place. [WRITTEN] ❑ *From my window*

*I looked out on a vista of hills and rooftops.* [from Italian]

**vis|ual** /vɪʒuəl/ ADJ **Visual** means relating to sight, or to things that you can see. ❑ *...careers in the visual arts.* ● **visu|al|ly** ADV ❑ *The movie is visually spectacular.* [from Late Latin]

### Word Partnership    Use *visual* with :

| | |
|---|---|
| N. | visual **arts**, visual **effects**, visual **information**, visual **memory**, visual **perception** |

**visu|al|ize** /vɪʒuəlaɪz/ (**visualizes, visualizing, visualized**) V-T If you **visualize** something, you imagine what it is like by forming a mental picture of it. ❑ *Susan visualized her wedding day.* ❑ *He could not visualize her as old.* [from Late Latin]

**vis|ual lit|era|cy** N-UNCOUNT **Visual literacy** is the ability to understand and interpret visual images. [TECHNICAL]

**vis|ual meta|phor** (**visual metaphors**) N-VAR A **visual metaphor** is a way of describing something by referring to another thing that shares similar visual qualities to the thing being described. For example, a family tree is a visual metaphor for the history of a family. [TECHNICAL]

### Word Link    vita ≈ life : re**vita**lize, **vita**l, **vita**lity

**vi|tal** /vaɪtᵊl/ ADJ If something is **vital**, it is necessary or very important. ❑ *It is vital that children attend school regularly.* ● **vi|tal|ly** ADV ❑ *Lesley's job is vitally important to her.* [from Old French]

### Thesaurus    *vital*    Also look up :

| | |
|---|---|
| ADJ. | crucial, essential, necessary; (ant.) unimportant |

### Word Partnership    Use *vital* with :

| | |
|---|---|
| ADV. | **absolutely** vital |
| N. | vital **importance**, vital **information**, vital **interests**, vital **link**, vital **organs**, vital **part**, vital **role** |

**vi|tal|ity** /vaɪtælɪti/ N-UNCOUNT If you say that someone or something has **vitality**, you mean that they have great energy and liveliness. ❑ *At 85 years old, he is still full of vitality.* [from Old French]

**vita|min** /vaɪtəmɪn/ (**vitamins**) N-COUNT **Vitamins** are substances in food that you need in order to remain healthy. ❑ *...problems caused by lack of vitamin D.* ❑ *...vitamin pills.* [from Latin]

### Word Link    viv ≈ living : re**viv**al, sur**viv**e, **viv**id

**viv|id** /vɪvɪd/ **1** ADJ If you describe memories and descriptions as **vivid**, you mean that they are very clear and detailed. ❑ *It was a very vivid dream.* ● **viv|id|ly** ADV ❑ *I can vividly remember the first time I saw him.* **2** ADJ Something that is **vivid** is very bright in color. ❑ *...a vivid blue sky.* ● **viv|id|ly** ADV ❑ *...vividly colored birds.* [from Latin]

### Word Link    voc ≈ speaking : a**voc**ate, **voc**abulary, **voc**al

**vo|cabu|lary** /voʊkæbyəleri/ (**vocabularies**) **1** N-VAR Your **vocabulary** is the total number of words you know in a particular language. ❑ *He has a very wide vocabulary.* **2** N-SING The **vocabulary** of a language is all the words in it. ❑ *...a new word in the German vocabulary.* [from Medieval Latin] → see **English**

---

**Word Partnership** Use *vocabulary* with :

N.   **part of** *someone's* vocabulary **1**
     vocabulary **development 1 2**
V.   **learn** vocabulary **2**

---

**Word Link** *voc ≈ speaking : a*voc*ate, *voc*abulary, *voc*al*

---

**vo|cal** /voʊkˀl/ **1** ADJ You say that people are **vocal** when they speak forcefully about something that they feel strongly about. ❑ *Local people were very vocal in their opposition to the plan.* **2** ADJ **Vocal** means involving the use of the human voice, especially in singing. ❑ *...a range of vocal styles.* [from Latin]

**vo|cal cords** also **vocal chords** N-PLURAL **Vocal cords** are the part of your throat that vibrates when you speak.

**vo|cal|ist** /voʊkəlɪst/ (**vocalists**) N-COUNT A **vocalist** is a singer who sings with a group. ❑ *...the band's lead vocalist.* [from Latin]

**vo|cal pro|jec|tion** N-UNCOUNT **Vocal projection** is the same as **projection**.

**vo|cal qual|ity** (**vocal qualities**) N-VAR A person's **vocal quality** is the way their voice sounds, for example whether it is deep or loud or high-pitched.

**vo|cals** /voʊkˀlz/ N-PLURAL In a pop song, the **vocals** are the singing, in contrast to the playing of instruments. ❑ *Johnson sings backing vocals for Mica Paris.* [from Latin]

**vo|ca|tion** /voʊkeɪʃˀn/ (**vocations**) **1** N-VAR If you have a **vocation**, you have a strong feeling that you are especially suited to do a particular job or to fulfill a particular role in life, especially one that involves helping other people. ❑ *She has a real vocation to teach.* **2** N-VAR If you refer to your job or profession as your **vocation**, you feel that you are particularly suited to it. ❑ *Her vocation is her work as an actress.* [from Latin]

**vo|ca|tion|al** /voʊkeɪʃənˀl/ ADJ **Vocational** training and skills are the training and skills needed for a particular job or profession. ❑ *...vocational training in engineering.* [from Latin]

**vo|cif|er|ous** /voʊsɪfərəs/ ADJ If you describe someone as **vociferous**, you mean that they speak with great energy and determination, because they want their views to be heard. ❑ *He was a vociferous opponent of racism.* ● **vo|cif|er|ous|ly** ADV ❑ *He campaigned vociferously for this law.* [from Latin]

**vod|ka** /vɒdkə/ (**vodkas**) N-VAR **Vodka** is a strong, clear, alcoholic drink. [from Russian]

**vogue** /voʊg/ **1** N-SING If there is a **vogue for** something, it is very popular and fashionable. ❑ *...a vogue for herbal teas.* **2** PHRASE If something is **in vogue**, it is very popular and fashionable. If it comes **into vogue**, it becomes very popular and fashionable. ❑ *Pale colors are in vogue.* [from French]

**voice** /vɔɪs/ (**voices**) **1** N-COUNT When someone speaks or sings, you hear their **voice**.

❑ *She spoke in a soft voice.* **2** N-COUNT Someone's **voice** is their opinion on a particular topic and what they say about it. ❑ *The government refuses to listen to the voice of the people.* **3** V-T If you **voice** something such as an opinion or an emotion, you say what you think or feel. ❑ *She voiced her opinion about what was going on.* **4** N-SING In grammar, if a verb is in the **active voice**, the person who performs the action is the subject of the verb. If a verb is in the **passive voice**, the thing or person affected by the action is the subject of the verb. [from Old French]

**void** /vɔɪd/ (**voids**) **1** N-COUNT If you describe a situation or a feeling as a **void**, you mean that it seems empty because there is nothing interesting or worthwhile about it. ❑ *His death left a void in her life.* **2** N-COUNT You can describe a large or frightening space as a **void**. ❑ *He looked over the edge of the mountain into the void.* **3** ADJ Something that is **void** or **null and void** is officially considered to have no value or authority. ❑ *The elections were declared void.* **4** ADJ If you are **void of** something, you do not have any of it. [FORMAL] ❑ *His face was void of emotion.* [from Old French]

**vola|tile** /vɒlətˀl/ **1** ADJ A situation that is **volatile** is likely to change suddenly and unexpectedly. ❑ *There have been riots and the situation is volatile.* **2** ADJ If someone is **volatile**, their mood often changes quickly. ❑ *...a volatile, passionate man.* [from Latin]

**vol|can|ic** /vɒlkænɪk/ ADJ **Volcanic** means coming from or created by volcanoes. ❑ *Over 200 people have been killed by volcanic eruptions.* [from Italian] → see **volcano**

**vol|ca|no** /vɒlkeɪnoʊ/ (**volcanoes**) N-COUNT A **volcano** is a mountain from which hot melted rock, gas, steam, and ash from inside the earth sometimes burst. ❑ *The volcano erupted last year.* [from Italian]
→ see Word Web: **volcano**
→ see **rock, tsunami**

**vol|ley** /vɒli/ (**volleys, volleying, volleyed**) **1** V-T/V-I In sports, if you **volley** the ball or if they **volley**, they hit the ball before it touches the ground. ❑ *He volleyed the ball into the net.* ● **Volley** is also a noun. ❑ *She hit the winning volley.* **2** N-COUNT A **volley of** gunfire is a lot of bullets that travel through the air at the same time. ❑ *A volley of shots was heard.* [from French]

**volley|ball** /vɒlibɔl/ N-UNCOUNT **Volleyball** is a game in which two teams hit a large ball with their hands back and forth over a high net.

**volt** /voʊlt/ (**volts**) N-COUNT A **volt** is a unit used to measure the force of an electric current. [after Count Alessandro Volta (1745-1827), an Italian physicist]

**volt|age** /voʊltɪdʒ/ (**voltages**) N-VAR The **voltage** of an electrical current is its force measured in volts. ❑ *...high-voltage power lines.* [from Italian]

**vol|ume** /vɒlyum/ (**volumes**) **1** N-COUNT The **volume of** something is the amount of it that there is. ❑ *The volume of sales has increased.* **2** N-COUNT The **volume** of an object is the amount of space that it contains or occupies. ❑ *The volume of a cube with sides of length 3 cm is 27 cm* **3** N-COUNT A **volume** is one book in a series of books. ❑ *...the*

V

## Word Web    volcano

The most famous **volcano** in the world is Mount Vesuvius, near Naples, Italy. This mountain sits in the middle of the much older **volcanic cone** of Mount Somma. In 79 AD the sleeping volcano **erupted**, and **magma** rose to the surface. The people of the nearby city of Pompeii were terrified. Huge black clouds of **ash** and pumice came rushing toward them. The clouds blocked out the sun and smothered thousands of people.

Pompeii was buried under hot ash and **molten lava**. Centuries later the remains of the people and town were found. The discovery made this active volcano famous.

*first volume of his autobiography.* ◢ N-UNCOUNT A **volume** is a collection of several issues of a magazine, for example, all the issues for one year. ❑ *...bound volumes of the magazine.* ◣ N-UNCOUNT The **volume** of a radio, television, sound system, or someone's voice is the loudness of the sound it produces. ❑ *He turned down the volume.* [from Old French]
→ see Picture Dictionary: **volume**

**vol|un|tary** /vɒləntɛri/ ◮ ADJ **Voluntary** actions or activities are done because someone chooses to do them and not because they have been forced to do them. ❑ *...classes where attendance is voluntary.* ● **vol|un|tar|ily** /vɒləntɛərɪli/ ADV ❑ *I would never leave here voluntarily.* ◧ ADJ **Voluntary** work is done by people who are not paid for it, but who do it because they want to do it. ◪ ADJ A **voluntary** organization is controlled and organized by the people who have chosen to work for it, often without being paid. ◭ ADJ **Voluntary** movements are movements of your body that you make because you choose to, rather than because they are automatic. [from Latin]
→ see **muscle**

### Word Partnership    Use *voluntary* with :

N.　voluntary **action**, voluntary **basis**, voluntary **compliance**, voluntary **contributions**, voluntary **program**, voluntary **retirement**, voluntary **test** ◮ voluntary **organizations** ◪

### Word Link    *eer ≈ one who does : auctioneer, mountaineer, volunteer*

**vol|un|teer** /vɒləntɪər/ (**volunteers, volunteering, volunteered**) ◮ N-COUNT A **volunteer** is someone who does work without being paid for it, because they want to do it. ❑ *She helps in a local school as a volunteer.* ◧ N-COUNT A **volunteer** is someone who offers to do a particular task or job without being forced to do it. ❑ *I need two volunteers to help me move these tables.* ◪ V-I If you **volunteer** to do something, you offer to do it without being forced to do it. ❑ *Mary volunteered to clean up the kitchen.* ❑ *He volunteered for the army in 1939.* ◭ V-T If you **volunteer** information, you tell someone something without being asked. [FORMAL] ❑ *No one volunteered any information.*

### Picture Dictionary    volume

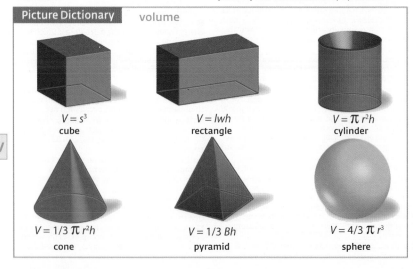

$V = s^3$
cube

$V = lwh$
rectangle

$V = \pi\, r^2 h$
cylinder

$V = 1/3\, \pi\, r^2 h$
cone

$V = 1/3\, Bh$
pyramid

$V = 4/3\, \pi\, r^3$
sphere

V

## Word Web    vote

Today in almost all **democracies** any adult can **vote** for the **candidate** of his or her choice. But years ago women could not vote. Not until the suffrage movement revolutionized voting rights did women have the right to vote. In 1893, New Zealand became the first country to give women full voting rights. Women could finally enter a **polling place** and **cast** a **ballot**. Many countries soon followed. The included Canada, Finland, Germany, Sweden, and the U.S. soon. However, China, France, India, Italy, and Japan didn't grant suffrage until the mid-1900s.

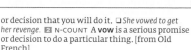

**5** N-COUNT A **volunteer** is someone who chooses to join the armed forces, especially during a war, as opposed to someone who is forced to join by law. ❑ They fought as volunteers. [from French]

### Word Partnership    Use volunteer with :

| | |
|---|---|
| N. | **community** volunteer, **Red Cross** volunteer **1** |
| | volunteer **organization**, volunteer **program**, volunteer **work 1 2** |
| | volunteer **for service**, volunteer **for the army 3** |
| | volunteer **information 4** |
| V. | **need a** volunteer **1 2 5** |
| | volunteer **to help**, volunteer **to work 3** |

**vom|it** /vɒmɪt/ (**vomits, vomiting, vomited**)
**1** V-T/V-I If you **vomit**, food and drink comes back up from your stomach and out through your mouth. ❑ Cow's milk made him vomit. ❑ She vomited everything she ate. **2** N-UNCOUNT **Vomit** is partly digested food and drink that comes out of your mouth when you vomit. [from Latin]

**vo|ra|cious** /vɔreɪʃəs/ ADJ If you describe a person, or their appetite for something, as **voracious**, you mean that they want a lot of something. [LITERARY] [from Latin]

**vote** /voʊt/ (**votes, voting, voted**) **1** N-COUNT A **vote** is a choice made by a particular person or group in a meeting or an election. ❑ He went to the polling place to cast his vote. **2** N-SING The **vote** is the total number of votes or voters in an election, or the number of votes received or cast by a particular group. ❑ The vote was in favour of the Democratic Party. **3** N-SING If you have **the vote** in an election, or have **a vote** in a meeting, you have the legal right to indicate your choice. ❑ At that time, women did not have a vote. **4** V-T/V-I When you **vote**, you indicate your choice officially at a meeting or in an election, for example, by raising your hand or writing on a piece of paper. ❑ Nearly everyone voted for Buchanan. ● **vot|ing** N-UNCOUNT ❑ Voting began about two hours ago. ● **vot|er** (**voters**) N-COUNT ❑ ...registered voters. [from Latin]
→ see Word Web: **vote**
→ see **citizenship, election**

**vouch|er** /vaʊtʃər/ (**vouchers**) N-COUNT A **voucher** is a ticket or piece of paper that can be used instead of money to pay for something. ❑ ...a voucher for two movie tickets. [from Old French]

**vow** /vaʊ/ (**vows, vowing, vowed**) **1** V-T If you **vow** to do something, you make a serious promise

or decision that you will do it. ❑ She vowed to get her revenge. **2** N-COUNT A **vow** is a serious promise or decision to do a particular thing. [from Old French]

**vow|el** /vaʊəl/ (**vowels**) N-COUNT A **vowel** is a sound, such as the ones represented in writing by the letters **a, e, i, o** and **u**, that you pronounce with your mouth open, allowing the air to flow through it. [from Old French]

**voy|age** /vɔɪɪdʒ/ (**voyages**) N-COUNT A **voyage** is a long journey on a ship or in a spacecraft. ❑ ...voyage to the West Indies. [from Old French]

**vs.** vs. is a written abbreviation for **versus**.

**vul|gar** /vʌlgər/ **1** ADJ If you describe something as **vulgar**, you think it is in bad taste or of poor artistic quality. ❑ I think it's a very vulgar house. ● **vul|gar|ity** /vʌlgærɪti/ N-UNCOUNT ❑ I hate the vulgarity of the bright colors in this room. **2** ADJ If you describe pictures, gestures, or remarks as **vulgar**, you dislike them because they refer to sex or parts of the body in an offensive way that you find unpleasant. ❑ ...the comedian's vulgar jokes. ● **vul|gar|ity** N-UNCOUNT ❑ Charles avoided any rudeness or vulgarity. [from Latin]

**vul|ner|able** /vʌlnərəbᵊl/ **1** ADJ Someone who is **vulnerable** is weak and without protection, with the result that they are easily hurt physically or emotionally. ● **vul|ner|abil|ity** /vʌlnərəbɪlɪti/ (**vulnerabilities**) N-VAR ❑ ...the vulnerability of children. **2** ADJ If someone or something is **vulnerable to** something, they have some weakness or disadvantage which makes them more likely to be harmed or affected by that thing. ❑ Children from 6 to 24 months are most vulnerable to the flu. ● **vul|ner|abil|ity** N-UNCOUNT ❑ ...vulnerability to infection. [from Late Latin]

### Word Partnership    Use vulnerable with :

| | |
|---|---|
| N. | vulnerable **children/people/women 1** |
| V. | **feel** vulnerable **1** |
| | **become** vulnerable, **remain** vulnerable **1 2** |
| ADV. | **especially** vulnerable, **extremely** vulnerable, **highly** vulnerable, **particularly** vulnerable, **so** vulnerable, **too** vulnerable, **very** vulnerable **1 2** |

**vul|ture** /vʌltʃər/ (**vultures**) N-COUNT A **vulture** is a large bird that eats the flesh of dead animals. [from Old French]

**vy|ing** /vaɪɪŋ/ **Vying** is the present participle of **vie**. [from Old French]

**V**

# Ww

**wacky** /wǽki/ (**wackier, wackiest**) also
**whacky** ADJ If you describe something or
someone as **wacky**, you mean that they are quirky,
unusual, and often funny. [INFORMAL] ❏ ...a wacky
new television comedy series.

**wad** /wɒd/ (**wads**) N-COUNT A **wad of**
something such as paper or cloth is a tight bundle
or ball of it. ❏ ...a wad of banknotes. [from Late
Latin]

**wade** /weɪd/ (**wades, wading, waded**) ◼ V-I
If you **wade** through water or mud, you walk
through it with difficulty. ❏ Her mother waded
across a river to reach them. ◼ V-I To **wade through**
a lot of documents or pieces of information means
to spend a lot of time and effort reading them or
dealing with them. ❏ It took a long time to wade
through the reports. [from Old English]

**wa|fer** /weɪfər/ (**wafers**) N-COUNT A **wafer** is
a thin crisp cookie that is often eaten with ice
cream. [from Old Northern French]

**waf|fle** /wɒfᵊl/ (**waffles, waffling, waffled**)
◼ N-COUNT A **waffle** is a flat, sweet cake with
a pattern of squares cut into it that is usually
warmed up and eaten with syrup for breakfast
in the United States. ◼ V-I If someone **waffles**
on an issue or question, they cannot decide what
to do or what their opinion is about it. ❏ He said
the president was waffling on the issue. [Sense 1 from
Dutch]

**waft** /wɒft, wæft/ (**wafts, wafting, wafted**) V-T/
V-I If sounds or smells **waft** through the air, or if
something such as a light wind **wafts** them, they
move gently through the air. ❏ The scent of roses
wafted through the window. [from Middle Dutch]

**wag** /wæg/ (**wags, wagging, wagged**) ◼ V-T
When a dog **wags** its tail, it repeatedly waves
its tail from side to side. ◼ V-T If you **wag** your
finger, you shake it repeatedly and quickly from
side to side, usually because you are annoyed with
someone. ❏ He wagged his finger at me. [from Old
English]

**wage** /weɪdʒ/ (**wages, waging, waged**)
◼ N-COUNT Someone's **wages** are the amount of
money that is regularly paid to them for the work
that they do. ❏ His wages have gone up. ◼ V-T To
**wage** a campaign or a war means to start it and
continue it over a period of time. ❏ New York City
officials waged a campaign to host the Olympics. [from
Old Northern French]
→ see **factory, union**

| Thesaurus | | *wage* | Also look up : |
|---|---|---|---|
| N. | earnings, pay, salary ◼ | | |

| Word Partnership | Use *wage* with : |
|---|---|
| ADJ. | **average** wage, **high/higher** wage, **hourly** wage, **low/lower** wage ◼ |
| V. | **offer a** wage, **pay a** wage, **raise a** wage ◼ |
| N. | wage **cuts**, wage **earners**, wage **increases**, wage **rates** ◼ wage **a campaign**, wage **war** ◼ |

**wa|ger** /weɪdʒər/ (**wagers, wagering, wagered**)
V-T/V-I If you **wager on** a horse race, baseball
game, or other event, you bet money on the result.
❏ They wagered a lot of money on the race. ● **Wager** is
also a noun. ❏ He placed a wager on the football game.
[from Old Northern French]

**wag|on** /wǽgən/ (**wagons**) N-COUNT A **wagon**
is a strong vehicle with four wheels, usually
pulled by horses or oxen and used for carrying
heavy loads. [from Dutch]
→ see **train**

**wail** /weɪl/ (**wails, wailing, wailed**) ◼ V-I If
someone **wails**, they make long, loud, high-
pitched cries which express sorrow or pain. ❏ The
women began to wail. ● **Wail** is also a noun. ❏ ...wails
of crying families. ◼ V-I If something such as a siren
or an alarm **wails**, it makes a long, loud, high-
pitched sound. ❏ Police cars, their sirens wailing,
followed the trucks. ● **Wail** is also a noun. ❏ ...the wail
of police sirens. [of Scandinavian origin]

**waist** /weɪst/ (**waists**) ◼ N-COUNT Your **waist**
is the middle part of your body where it narrows
slightly above your hips. ❏ Ricky put his arm around
her waist. ◼ N-COUNT The **waist** of a dress, coat,
or pair of pants is the part of it which covers the
middle part of your body. ❏ The waist of these pants
is a little tight. [from Old English]
→ see **body**

**wait** /weɪt/ (**wait, waiting, waited**) ◼ V-T/V-I
When you **wait** for something or someone,
you spend some time doing very little, before
something happens or someone arrives. ❏ I walked
to the street corner and waited for the school bus. ❏ I
waited to hear what she said. ❏ We had to wait a week
before we got the results. ● **wait|ing** ADJ ❏ She walked
toward the waiting car. ◼ N-COUNT A **wait** is a
period of time in which you do very little, before
something happens. ❏ There was a four-hour wait at
the airport. ◼ V-T/V-I If something **is waiting for**
you, it is ready for you to use, have, or do. ❏ There'll
be a car waiting for you. ❏ When we came home we had a
meal waiting for us. ◼ V-I If you say that something
can **wait**, you mean that it is not important or
urgent and so you will deal with it or do it later.
❏ I want to talk to you, but it can wait. ◼ V-T **Wait** is
used in expressions such as **wait a minute**, **wait a
second**, and **wait a moment** to interrupt someone
when they are speaking, for example, because

you object to what they are saying or because you want them to repeat something. [SPOKEN] ❑ *"Wait a minute!" he interrupted. "This isn't fair!"* ◻ PHRASE If you say that you **can't wait** to do something or **can hardly wait** to do it, you are emphasizing that you are very excited about it and eager to do it. [SPOKEN] ❑ *We can't wait to get started.* [from Old French]

▸ **wait around** PHR-VERB If you **wait around**, you stay in the same place, usually doing very little, because you cannot act before something happens or before someone arrives. ❑ *I'm tired of waiting around for her to call me.* ❑ *I waited around to speak to the doctor.*

| Thesaurus | *wait* | Also look up : |
|---|---|---|
| V. | anticipate, expect, hold on, stand by; (*ant.*) carry out, go ahead ◼ | |
| N. | delay, halt, holdup, pause ◼ | |

| Word Partnership | Use *wait* with : |
|---|---|
| ADV. | wait **forever**, wait **here**, **just** wait, wait **outside**, wait **patiently** ◼ |
| N. | wait **for an answer**, wait **days/hours**, wait **a long time**, wait **your turn** ◼ wait **a minute**, wait **until tomorrow** ◼◼ |
| V. | (**can't**) **afford to** wait ◼ **can/can't/couldn't** wait, **have to** wait, wait ◼◼ wait **to hear**, wait **to say** ◼◼◼ **can't** wait, **can hardly** wait ◻ |
| ADJ. | **worth the** wait ◼ |

**wait|er** /wˈeɪtər/ (**waiters**) N-COUNT A **waiter** is a man whose job is to serve food in a restaurant. [from Old French]

**wait|ing list** (**waiting lists**) N-COUNT A **waiting list** is a list of people who have asked for something that cannot be given to them immediately, such as medical treatment, housing, or training, and who must therefore wait until it is available. ❑ *There were 20,000 people on the waiting list for a home.*

**wait|ress** /wˈeɪtrɪs/ (**waitresses**) N-COUNT A **waitress** is a woman whose job is to serve food in a restaurant. [from Old French]

**wait|staff** /wˈeɪtstæf/ N-COUNT **Waitstaff** are waiters or waitresses. ❑ *The waitstaff are there when you need them.*

**waive** /wˈeɪv/ (**waives, waiving, waived**) ◼ V-T If you **waive** your right to something, you choose not to have it or do it. ❑ *He waived his right to a hearing.* ◼ V-T If someone **waives** a rule, they say that people do not have to obey it in a particular situation. ❑ *The art gallery waives admission charges on Sundays.* [from Old Northern French]

**waiv|er** /wˈeɪvər/ (**waivers**) N-COUNT A **waiver** is an agreement by a person, government, or organization to give up a right or claim, or to not enforce a particular rule or law. ❑ *Non-members do not receive the tax waiver.* [from Old Northern French]

| Word Link | *wak* ≈ being awake : *a*wake, *a*wakening, *wak*e |
|---|---|

**wake** /wˈeɪk/ (**wakes, waking, woke, woken** or **waked**) ◼ V-T/V-I When you **wake** or when someone or something **wakes** you, you become

conscious again after being asleep. ❑ *It was cold and dark when I woke at 6:30.* ❑ *She went upstairs to wake Milton.* ● **Wake up** means the same as **wake**. ❑ *One morning I woke up and felt something was wrong.* ◼ N-COUNT The **wake** of a boat or other object moving in the water is the track of waves it makes behind it as it moves through the water. ❑ *The wake of the boats washed against the shore.* ◻ N-COUNT A **wake** is a gathering or social event that is held before a funeral. ◼ PHRASE If one thing follows **in the wake of** another, it happens after the other thing is over, often as a result of it. ❑ *There are more police on the streets in the wake of last week's attack.* [from Old English]

| Word Partnership | Use *wake* with : |
|---|---|
| PREP. | wake **up during the night**, wake **up in the middle of**, wake **up in the morning** ◼ |
| ADV. | wake (*someone*) **up** ◼ |

**walk** /wˈɔk/ (**walks, walking, walked**) ◼ V-T/V-I When you **walk**, you move forward by putting one foot in front of the other in a regular way. ❑ *Rosanna and Forbes walked in silence.* ❑ *We walked into the hall.* ❑ *I walked a few steps toward the fence.* ◼ N-COUNT A **walk** is a trip that you make by walking, usually for pleasure. ❑ *I went for a walk.* ◻ N-SING A **walk** of a particular distance is the distance that a person has to walk to get somewhere. ❑ *It was only a short walk from there.* ◼ N-SING A **walk** is the action of walking rather than running. ❑ *She slowed to a steady walk.* ◻ V-T If you **walk** someone somewhere, you walk there with them. ❑ *She walked me to my car.* [from Old English] ◻ to **walk tall** → see **tall**

▸ **walk off with** PHR-VERB If you **walk off with** something such as a prize, you win it or get it very easily. ❑ *We'd like to see him walk off with the big prize.*

▸ **walk out** ◼ PHR-VERB If you **walk out of** a meeting, a performance, or an unpleasant situation, you leave it suddenly, usually to show that you are angry or bored. ❑ *Several people walked out of the meeting in protest.* ● **walk|out** /wˈɔkaʊt/ (**walkouts**) N-COUNT ❑ *Hundreds of students held a walkout Thursday.* ◼ PHR-VERB If someone **walks out on** their family or their partner, they leave them suddenly and go to live somewhere else. ❑ *Her husband walked out on her.* ◻ PHR-VERB If workers **walk out**, they stop doing their work for a period of time, usually in order to try to get better pay or conditions for themselves. ❑ *Union workers walked out last Thursday.* ● **walk|out** (**walkouts**) N-COUNT ❑ *Union leaders are calling for a walkout.*

| Thesaurus | *walk* | Also look up : |
|---|---|---|
| V. | amble, hike, stroll ◼ | |
| N. | hike, march, parade, stroll ◼ ◼ | |

| Word Partnership | Use *walk* with : |
|---|---|
| ADV. | walk **alone**, walk **away**, walk **back**, walk **home**, walk **slowly** ◼ |
| V. | **begin to** walk, **start to** walk ◼ **go for a** walk, **take a** walk ◼ ◻ |
| ADJ. | (**un**)**able to** walk ◼ **brisk** walk, **long** walk, **short** walk ◼ ◻ |

**W**

**walk|er** /wɔkər/ (**walkers**) N-COUNT A **walker** is a person who walks, especially in the countryside for pleasure or in order to keep healthy. [from Old English]

**walk|ing** /wɔkɪŋ/ N-UNCOUNT **Walking** is the activity of taking walks for exercise or pleasure, especially in the country. □ *I've started to do a lot of walking and cycling.* [from Old English]

**walk of life** (**walks of life**) N-COUNT The **walk of life** that you come from is the position that you have in society and the kind of job you have. □ *I love meeting people from all walks of life.*

**walk|way** /wɔkweɪ/ (**walkways**) N-COUNT A **walkway** is a passage or path for people to walk along. Walkways are often raised above the ground. □ *...a new walkway between two rows of apartment blocks.* [from Old English]

**wall** /wɔl/ (**walls**) ■ N-COUNT A **wall** is one of the vertical sides of a building or room. □ *...the bedroom walls.* ■ N-COUNT A **wall** is a long narrow vertical structure made of stone or brick that surrounds or divides an area of land. □ *He sat on the wall in the sun.* ■ N-COUNT The **wall** of something hollow is its side. □ *...the stomach wall.* [from Old English]

| | Word Partnership Use *wall* with : |
|---|---|
| PREP. | **against a** wall, **along a** wall, **behind a** wall, **near a** wall, **on a** wall ■ ■ |
| N. | **back to the** wall, **brick** wall, **concrete** wall, **glass** wall, **stone** wall ■ ■ |
| V. | **build a** wall, **climb a** wall, **lean against/on a** wall ■ ■ |

**wall cloud** (**wall clouds**) N-COUNT A **wall cloud** is an area of cloud that extends beneath a thunderstorm and sometimes develops into a tornado. [TECHNICAL]

**walled** /wɔld/ ADJ A **walled** city or area of land is surrounded or enclosed by a wall. [from Old English]

**wal|let** /wɒlɪt/ (**wallets**) N-COUNT A **wallet** is a small, flat folded case, usually made of leather or plastic, in which you can keep money and credit cards. [from Germanic]

**wal|low** /wɒloʊ/ (**wallows, wallowing, wallowed**) ■ V-I If you say that someone is **wallowing in** an unpleasant situation, you are criticizing them for being unhappy on purpose. □ *He continued to wallow in self-pity.* ■ V-I If a person or animal **wallows** in water or mud, they lie or roll about in it slowly for pleasure. □ *I wallowed in a deep warm bath.* [from Old English]

**wall|paper** /wɔlpeɪpər/ (**wallpapers, wallpapering, wallpapered**) ■ N-VAR **Wallpaper** is thick colored or patterned paper that is used for covering and decorating the walls of rooms. ■ V-T If someone **wallpapers** a room, they cover the walls with wallpaper. ■ N-UNCOUNT **Wallpaper** is the background on a computer screen. [COMPUTING]

**wal|nut** /wɔlnʌt, -nət/ (**walnuts**) N-VAR **Walnuts** are edible nuts that have a wrinkled shape and a hard round shell that is light brown in color. [from Old English]

**waltz** /wɔlts, wɑls/ (**waltzes, waltzing, waltzed**) ■ N-COUNT A **waltz** is a piece of music with a rhythm of three beats in each bar, which people can dance to. ■ N-COUNT A **waltz** is a dance in which two people hold each other and move around the floor doing special steps in time to waltz music. □ *Arthur taught me the waltz.* ■ V-RECIP If you **waltz** with someone, you dance a waltz with them. [from German]

**wan|der** /wɒndər/ (**wanders, wandering, wandered**) ■ V-T/V-I If you **wander** in a place, you walk around there in a casual way, often without intending to go in any particular direction. □ *When he got bored he wandered around the park.* □ *People wandered the streets.* ● **Wander** is also a noun. □ *A wander around the garden is a relaxing experience.* ■ V-I If a person or animal **wanders** from a place where they are supposed to stay, they move away from the place without going in a particular direction. □ *We aren't allowed to wander far.* ■ V-I If your mind **wanders** or your thoughts **wander**, you stop concentrating on something and start thinking about other things. □ *His mind was starting to wander.* [from Old English]

**wane** /weɪn/ (**wanes, waning, waned**) V-I If something **wanes**, it becomes gradually weaker or less, often so that it eventually disappears. □ *His interest in these sports began to wane.* [from Old English]

**want** /wɒnt/ (**wants, wanting, wanted**) ■ V-T If you **want** something, you feel a desire or a need for it. □ *I want a drink.* □ *People wanted to know who she was.* □ *They wanted their father to be the same as other dads.* □ *They didn't want people staring at them.* ■ V-T If you tell someone that you **want to** do a particular thing, you are advising them to do it. [INFORMAL] □ *You want to be very careful what you say when interviewed by the police.* ■ V-T If someone is **wanted** by the police, the police are searching for them because they are thought to have committed a crime. □ *He was wanted for the murder of a judge.* ● **want|ed** ADJ □ *He is one of the most wanted criminals in Europe.* ■ PHRASE If you do something **for want of** something else, you do it because the other thing is not available or not possible. □ *When he failed it was not for want of trying.* [from Old Norse]

| | Thesaurus *want* Also look up : |
|---|---|
| V. | covet, desire, long, need, require, wish ■ |

**want ad** (**want ads**) N-COUNT The **want ads** in a newspaper or magazine are small advertisements, usually offering things for sale or offering jobs. □ *I saw the address in a want ad.*

**want|ing** /wɒntɪŋ/ ADJ If you find something or someone **wanting**, they are not of as high a standard as you think they should be. □ *She looked around the room and found it wanting.* [from Old Norse]

**war** /wɔr/ (**wars**) ■ N-VAR A **war** is a period of fighting or conflict between countries. □ *He spent part of the war in France.* ■ N-VAR **War** is intense economic competition between countries or organizations. □ *...a trade war.* [from Old Northern French] ■ → see also **civil war**
→ see Word Web: **war**
→ see **army, history**

**ward** /wɔrd/ (**wards, warding, warded**) N-COUNT A **ward** is a room in a hospital which has beds for many people, often people who need similar

## Word Web    war

The Hague Conventions* and the Geneva Convention* are rules for **war**. They try to make war more humane. First, they say countries should avoid **armed conflict**. They suggest a **neutral mediator** or a 30-day "time out." A country must **declare** war before **combat** can begin. Sneak **attacks** are forbidden. The rules for **firearms** use are quite simple. One rule states it is illegal to **kill** or **injure** a person who **surrenders**. Wounded **soldiers**, **prisoners**, and **civilians** must get medical care immediately. And countries must not use **biological** and **chemical weapons**.

*Hague Conventions: agreements between many nations on rules to limit warfare and weapons.*
*Geneva Convention: an agreement between most nations on treatment of prisoners of war and the sick, injured, or dead.*

treatment. ❑ *They took her to the children's ward.* [from Old English]
→ see **hospital**
▶ **ward off** PHR-VERB To **ward off** a danger or illness means to prevent it from affecting you or harming you. ❑ *We needed warm coats to ward off the winter cold.*

**war|den** /wˈɔrdᵊn/ (**wardens**) **1** N-COUNT A **warden** is a person who is responsible for a particular place or thing, and for making sure that the laws or regulations that relate to it are obeyed. ❑ *He was a warden at the local parish church.* **2** N-COUNT The **warden** of a prison is the person in charge of it. [from Old Northern French]

**ward|robe** /wˈɔrdroʊb/ (**wardrobes**) **1** N-COUNT Someone's **wardrobe** is the total collection of clothes that they have. ❑ *He had no time to think about his wardrobe.* **2** N-COUNT A **wardrobe** is a tall closet or cabinet in which you can hang your clothes. ❑ *She shut the wardrobe door.* [from Old Northern French]

### Word Link    ware ≈ merchandise : hardware, software, warehouse

**ware|house** /wˈɛərhaʊs/ (**warehouses**) N-COUNT A **warehouse** is a large building where raw materials or manufactured goods are stored.

**war|fare** /wˈɔrfɛər/ N-UNCOUNT **Warfare** is the activity of fighting a war. ❑ *...desert warfare.*

**war|head** /wˈɔrhɛd/ (**warheads**) N-COUNT A **warhead** is the front part of a bomb or missile where the explosives are carried. ❑ *...nuclear warheads.*

**warm** /wˈɔrm/ (**warmer, warmest, warms, warming, warmed**) **1** ADJ Something that is **warm** has some heat but not enough to be hot. ❑ *...places which have cold winters and warm, dry summers.* **2** ADJ **Warm** clothes and blankets are made of a material such as wool that protects you from the cold. ● **warm|ly** ADV ❑ *Remember to dress warmly on cold days.* **3** ADJ **Warm** colors have red or yellow in them rather than blue or green, and make you feel comfortable and relaxed. **4** ADJ A **warm** person is friendly and shows a lot of affection or enthusiasm in their behavior. ❑ *She was a warm and loving mother.* ● **warm|ly** ADV ❑ *We warmly welcome new members.* **5** V-T If you **warm** a part of your body or if something hot **warms** it, it

stops feeling cold and starts to feel hotter. ❑ *The sun warmed his back.* **6** V-I If you **warm to** a person or an idea, you become fonder of the person or more interested in the idea. ❑ *Those who got to know him warmed to him.* [from Old English]
▶ **warm up** **1** PHR-VERB If you **warm** something **up** or if it **warms up**, it gets hotter. ❑ *He blew on his hands to warm them up.* ❑ *She warmed up the pie.* **2** PHR-VERB If you **warm up** for an event such as a race, you prepare yourself for it by doing exercises or by practicing just before it starts. ❑ *In an hour the drivers will be warming up for the main event.* ● **warm-up** (**warm-ups**) N-COUNT ❑ *These exercises are a good warm-up.* **3** PHR-VERB When a machine or engine **warms up** or someone **warms** it **up**, it becomes ready for use a little while after being switched on or started. ❑ *He waited for his car to warm up.*

### Word Partnership    Use warm with :

| N. | warm **air**, warm **bath**, warm **breeze**, warm **hands**, warm **water**, warm **weather** **1** |
| | warm **clothes** **2** |
| | warm **smile**, warm **welcome** **4** |
| ADJ. | warm **and sunny** **1** |
| | warm **and cozy**, warm **and dry** **1** **2** |
| | **soft and** warm **2** |
| | warm **and friendly** **4** |

**warm-blooded** ADJ A **warm-blooded** animal, such as a bird or a mammal, has a fairly high body temperature that does not change much and is not affected by the surrounding temperature.

**warmth** /wˈɔrmθ/ **1** N-UNCOUNT The **warmth** of something is the heat that it has or produces. ❑ *...the warmth of the fire.* **2** N-UNCOUNT The **warmth** of something such as clothing or a blanket is the protection that it gives you against the cold. ❑ *The blanket will provide additional warmth and comfort in bed.* [from Old English]

**warn** /wˈɔrn/ (**warns, warning, warned**) **1** V-T/V-I If you **warn** someone about something such as a possible danger or problem, you tell them about it so that they are aware of it. ❑ *The doctor warned her that too much sugar was bad for her health.* ❑ *They warned him of the dangers of sailing alone.* **2** V-T/V-I If you **warn** someone not to do something, you advise them not to do it so that they can avoid possible danger or punishment. ❑ *Mrs. Blount warned me not to interfere.* ❑ *"Don't do anything yet," he warned.* [from Old English]

| **Thesaurus** | *warn* | Also look up : |
|---|---|---|
| v. | alert, caution, notify **1** **2** | |

**Word Link** *war ≈ watchful : aware, beware, warning*

**warn|ing** /wɔrnɪŋ/ (**warnings**) N-VAR A **warning** is something said or written to tell people of a possible danger, problem, or other unpleasant thing that might happen. ❑ *It was a warning that we should be careful.* ❑ *Suddenly and without warning, a car crash changed her life forever.* [from Old English]

| **Word Partnership** | Use *warning* with : |
|---|---|
| ADJ. | **advance** warning, **early** warning, **stern** warning |
| N. | warning **of danger, hurricane** warning, warning **labels,** warning **signs, storm** warning |
| v. | **give (a)** warning, **ignore a** warning, **receive (a)** warning, **send a** warning |

**warp** /wɔrp/ (**warps, warping, warped**) V-T/V-I If something **warps** or **is warped**, it becomes damaged by bending or curving, often because of the effect of heat or water. ❑ *The wood started to warp.* [from Old English]

**war|rant** /wɔrənt/ (**warrants, warranting, warranted**) **1** V-T If something **warrants** a particular action, it makes the action seem necessary or appropriate. ❑ *Her illness was serious enough to warrant being in the hospital.* **2** N-COUNT A **warrant** is a legal document that allows someone to do something, especially one that gives the police permission to arrest someone or search their house. ❑ *Police issued a warrant for his arrest.* [from Old French]

**war|ran|ty** /wɔrənti/ (**warranties**) N-COUNT A **warranty** is a written promise by a company that, if you find a fault in something they have sold you within a certain time, they will repair it or replace it free of charge. ❑ *...a twelve month warranty.* [from Old French]

**war|ri|or** /wɔriər/ (**warriors**) N-COUNT A **warrior** is a fighter or soldier, especially one in former times who was very brave and experienced in fighting. ❑ *...the great warriors of the past.* [from Old Northern French]

**war|ship** /wɔrʃɪp/ (**warships**) N-COUNT A **warship** is a ship with guns that is used for fighting in wars. [from Old Northern French] → see **ship**

**wart** /wɔrt/ (**warts**) N-COUNT A **wart** is a small lump that grows on your skin. [from Old English]

**war|time** /wɔrtaɪm/ N-UNCOUNT **Wartime** is a period of time when a war is being fought. ❑ *He served his country during wartime.*

**wary** /wɛəri/ (**warier, wariest**) ADJ If you are **wary of** something or someone, you are cautious because you do not know much about them and you believe they may be dangerous or cause problems. ❑ *People teach their children to be wary of strangers.* ● **wari|ly** /wɛərɪli/ ADV ❑ *She studied me warily, as if I might become violent.*

**was** /wəz, STRONG wɒz, wʌz/ **Was** is the first and third person singular of the past tense of **be**. [from Old English]

**wash** /wɒʃ/ (**washes, washing, washed**) **1** V-T If you **wash** something, you clean it with water and usually a substance such as soap or detergent. ❑ *She finished her dinner and washed the dishes.* ❑ *It took a long time to wash the dirt out of his hair.* **2** V-T/V-I If you **wash**, or if you **wash** part of your body, especially your hands and face, you clean part of your body using soap and water. ❑ *They look as if they haven't washed in days.* ❑ *She washed her face with cold water.* **3** V-T/V-I If a sea or river **washes** somewhere, it flows there gently. You can also say that something carried by a sea or river **washes** or **is washed** somewhere. ❑ *The sea washed against the shore.* **4** → see also **washing** **5** PHRASE If something such as an item of clothing **is in the wash**, it is being washed, is waiting to be washed, or has just been washed and should therefore not be worn or used. [INFORMAL] ❑ *Your jeans are in the wash.* [from Old English] **6** to **wash** your **hands of** something → see **soap** → see **hand**

▶ **wash away** PHR-VERB If rain or floods **wash away** something, they destroy it and carry it away. ❑ *Flood waters washed away one of the bridges.*

▶ **wash down** PHR-VERB If you **wash** something, especially food, **down** with a drink, you drink the drink after eating the food, especially to make the food easier to swallow or digest. ❑ *...a sandwich washed down with a bottle of lemonade.*

▶ **wash up** PHR-VERB If you **wash up**, you clean part of your body with soap and water, especially your hands and face. ❑ *He went to the bathroom to wash up.* **2** PHR-VERB If something **is washed up on** a piece of land, it is carried by a river or sea and left there. ❑ *Thousands of fish were washed up on the beach during the storm.*

| **Thesaurus** | *wash* | Also look up : |
|---|---|---|
| v. | clean, rinse, scrub **1** clean, bathe, soap **2** | |

| **Word Partnership** | Use *wash* with : |
|---|---|
| N. | wash **a car,** wash **clothes,** wash **dishes 1** wash *your* **face/hair/hands 2** |

**wash|able** /wɒʃəbəl/ ADJ **Washable** clothes or materials can be washed in water without being damaged. ❑ *The floor is washable plastic.* [from Old English]

**wash|cloth** /wɒʃklɔθ/ (**washcloths**) N-COUNT A **washcloth** is a small cloth that you use for washing yourself. → see **bathroom**

**wash|er** /wɒʃər/ (**washers**) **1** N-COUNT A **washer** is a thin flat ring of metal or rubber that is placed over a bolt before the nut is screwed on. **2** N-COUNT A **washer** is the same as a **washing machine.** [INFORMAL] [from Old English]

**wash|ing** /wɒʃɪŋ/ N-UNCOUNT **Washing** is a collection of clothes, sheets, and other things that are waiting to be washed, are being washed, or have just been washed. ❑ *...plastic bags full of dirty washing.* [from Old English]

W

**wash|ing ma|chine** (**washing machines**)
N-COUNT A **washing machine** is a machine that
you use to wash clothes in. ❑ *Dan put his shirts in the
washing machine.*

**wasn't** /wʌz³nt, wɒz-/ **Wasn't** is the usual
spoken form of "was not."

**wasp** /wɒsp/ (**wasps**) N-COUNT A **wasp** is an
insect with wings and yellow and black stripes
across its body. Wasps have a painful sting like a
bee but do not produce honey. [from Old English]

**waste** /weɪst/ (**wastes, wasting, wasted**) **1** V-T
If you **waste** something such as time, money, or
energy, you use too much of it doing something
that is not important or necessary, or is unlikely to
succeed. ❑ *She didn't want to waste time looking at old
cars.* ❑ *I decided not to waste money on a hotel.* ● **Waste**
is also a noun. ❑ *It is a waste of time complaining
about it.* **2** N-UNCOUNT **Waste** is material that has
been used and is no longer wanted, for example,
because the valuable or useful part of it has been
taken out. ❑ *Waste materials such as paper and
aluminum cans can be recycled.* **3** V-T If you **waste**
an opportunity for something, you do not take
advantage of it when it is available. ❑ *Let's not
waste this opportunity.* [from Latin] **4** to **waste no
time** → see **time**
→ see **dump**
▸ **waste away** PHR-VERB If someone **wastes
away**, they become extremely thin or weak
because they are ill or worried and they are not
eating properly. ❑ *She began to waste away.*

| **Thesaurus** | *waste* | Also look up : |
| --- | --- | --- |
| V. | misuse, squander **1** | |
| N. | garbage, junk, trash **2** | |

| **Word Partnership** | Use *waste* with : |
| --- | --- |
| N. | waste **energy**, waste **money**, waste **time**, waste **water 1** |
| V. | **reduce** waste **1 2** **recycle** waste **2** |
| ADJ. | **hazardous** waste, **human** waste, **industrial** waste, **nuclear** waste, **toxic** waste **2** |

**waste|basket** /weɪstbæskɪt/ (**wastebaskets**)
N-COUNT A **wastebasket** is a container for trash,
especially paper.

**waste|ful** /weɪstfəl/ ADJ Action that is **wasteful**
uses too much of something valuable such as
time, money, or energy. ❑ *The senator says he is worried
about wasteful government spending.* [from Latin]

**waste|land** /weɪstlænd/ (**wastelands**) N-VAR A
**wasteland** is an area of land on which not much
can grow or which has been spoiled in some way.
❑ *Richard looked out into the burning wasteland.*

---

**watch**

**①** LOOKING AND PAYING
ATTENTION
**②** INSTRUMENT THAT TELLS THE
TIME

---

**①** **watch** /wɒtʃ/ (**watches, watching, watched**)
**1** V-T/V-I If you **watch** someone or something,
you look at them, usually for a period of time,
and pay attention to what is happening. ❑ *A man*

stood in the doorway, watching him.* ❑ *He seems to
enjoy watching me work.* ❑ *Watch how I do this, OK?*
**2** V-T If you **watch** something on television or
an event such as a sports contest, you spend time
looking at it, especially when you see it from the
beginning to the end. ❑ *I stayed up late to watch
the movie.* **3** V-T/V-I If you **watch** a situation or
event, you pay attention to it or you are aware
of it, but you do not influence it. ❑ *Human rights
groups are closely watching the situation.* **4** V-T If
you tell someone to **watch** a particular person or
thing, you are warning them to be careful that the
person or thing does not get out of control or do
something unpleasant. ❑ *You really have to watch
him.* **5** PHRASE If someone **keeps watch**, they look
and listen all the time, while other people are
asleep or doing something else, so that they can
warn them of danger or an attack. ❑ *Josh climbed a
tree to keep watch.* **6** N-COUNT A hurricane **watch**
or a storm **watch** is an official announcement that
severe weather conditions may soon develop in a
particular area. **7** PHRASE If you **keep watch** on
events or a situation, you pay attention to what
is happening, so that you can take action at the
right moment. ❑ *U.S. officials are keeping watch
on the situation.* **8** PHRASE You say "**watch it**" in
order to warn someone to be careful, especially
when you want to threaten them about what will
happen if they are not careful. ❑ *"Now watch it,
Patsy," said John.* [from Old English] **9** to **watch
your step** → see **step**
▸ **watch for** or **watch out for** PHR-VERB If you
**watch for** something or **watch out for** it, you pay
attention so that you notice it, either because you
do not want to miss it or because you want to avoid
it. ❑ *We'll be watching for any developments.*
▸ **watch out** PHR-VERB If you tell someone to
**watch out**, you are warning them to be careful,
because something unpleasant might happen
to them or they might get into difficulties. ❑ *You
have to watch out because this is a dangerous city.*
▸ **watch out for** → see **watch for**

**②** **watch** /wɒtʃ/ (**watches**) N-COUNT A **watch**
is a small clock that you wear on a strap on your
wrist, or on a chain. [from Old English]
→ see **jewelry**

| **Word Partnership** | Use *watch* with : |
| --- | --- |
| ADV. | watch **carefully**, watch **closely ① 1 3 4** |
| N. | watch **a DVD**, watch **a film/movie**, watch **fireworks**, watch **a game**, watch **the news**, watch **people**, watch **television/TV**, watch **a video ① 2** watch **children ① 4** |
| V. | **check** *your* watch, **glance at** *your* watch, **look at** *your* watch **②** |

**watch|dog** /wɒtʃdɔg/ (**watchdogs**) **1** N-COUNT
A **watchdog** is a person or committee whose job is
to make sure that companies do not act illegally
or irresponsibly. ❑ *…a consumer watchdog group.*
**2** N-COUNT A **watchdog** is a fierce dog that has
been specially trained to protect a particular place.

**watch|ful** /wɒtʃfəl/ ADJ Someone who is
**watchful** notices everything that is happening.
❑ *Be watchful for any change in your health.* [from Old
English]

**wa|ter** /wɔtər/ (**waters, watering, watered**)
**1** N-UNCOUNT **Water** is a clear thin liquid that

W

## Word Web  water

Water changes its form in the **hydrologic cycle**. The sun warms oceans, lakes, and rivers. Some water **evaporates**. Evaporation creates a gas called **water vapor**. Plants also give off water vapor through transpiration. Water vapor rises into the **atmosphere**. It hits cooler air and **condenses** into drops of water. These drops form **clouds**. When these drops get heavy enough, they begin to fall. They form different types of precipitation. Rain forms in warm air. Cold air creates **freezing rain**, **sleet**, and **snow**.

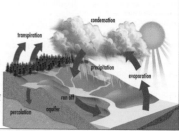

has no color or taste when it is pure. It falls from clouds as rain. ❑ *Get me a glass of water, please.* **2** N-PLURAL You use **waters** to refer to a large area of sea, especially the area of sea that is near to a country and that is regarded as belonging to it. ❑ *The ship will remain outside Australian waters.* **3** V-T If you **water** plants, you pour water over them in order to help them to grow. **4** V-I If your eyes **water**, tears build up in them because they are hurting or because you are upset. **5** V-I If you say that your mouth **is watering**, you mean that you can smell or see some nice food that makes you want to eat it. ❑ *...cookies to make your mouth water.* [from Old English]
→ see **biosphere, erosion, glacier, greenhouse effect, habitat, lake, photosynthesis, precipitation**
▶ **water down** PHR-VERB If something such as a proposal, speech, or statement **is watered down**, it is made much weaker and less forceful, or is less likely to make people angry.
→ see Word Web: **water**

**water|color** /wɔtərkʌlər/ (**watercolors**) **1** N-VAR **Watercolors** are colored paints, used for painting pictures, which you apply with a wet brush or dissolve in water first. ❑ *Campbell painted with watercolors.* **2** N-COUNT A **watercolor** is a picture that has been painted with watercolors. ❑ *...a lovely watercolor by J. M. W. Turner.*

**wa|ter cool|er** (**water coolers**) N-COUNT A **water cooler** is a machine that cools water for people to drink, usually in an office.

**wa|ter cy|cle** (**water cycles**) N-COUNT The **water cycle** is the continuous process in which water from the surface of the Earth evaporates to form clouds and then returns to the surface as rain or snow. [TECHNICAL]

**water|fall** /wɔtərfɔl/ (**waterfalls**) N-COUNT A **waterfall** is a place where water flows over the edge of a steep, high cliff in hills or mountains, and falls into a pool below.

**water|front** /wɔtərfrʌnt/ (**waterfronts**) N-COUNT A **waterfront** is a street or piece of land next to an area of water, such as a harbor or the sea. ❑ *They went for a walk along the waterfront.*

**wa|ter pow|er** also **waterpower** N-UNCOUNT **Water power** is the same as **hydropower**.

**water|proof** /wɔtərpruf/ ADJ Something that is **waterproof** does not let water pass through it. ❑ *Take waterproof clothing — Oregon weather is unpredictable.*

**water|shed** /wɔtərʃɛd/ (**watersheds**) **1** N-COUNT If something such as an event is

a **watershed in** the history or development of something, it is very important because it is the beginning of a new stage. ❑ *He realized that he was at a watershed in his life.* **2** N-COUNT A **watershed** is a high piece of land that divides two river systems. [TECHNICAL]

**water|spout** /wɔtərspaʊt/ (**waterspouts**) N-COUNT A **waterspout** is a small tornado that occurs over water.

**wa|ter ta|ble** (**water tables**) N-COUNT The **water table** is the level below the surface of the ground where water can be found.

**water|tight** /wɔtərtaɪt/ also **water-tight** ADJ Something that is **watertight** does not allow water to pass through it, for example, because it is tightly sealed. ❑ *The container is completely watertight.*

**wa|ter va|por** N-UNCOUNT **Water vapor** is water in the form of gas in the air.

**wa|ter vas|cu|lar sys|tem** (**water vascular systems**) N-COUNT The **water vascular system** is a network of water-filled tubes and pumps in the bodies of animals such as starfish, which helps them to move, eat, and breathe. [TECHNICAL]

**wa|ter wave** (**water waves**) N-COUNT A **water wave** is a wave that occurs in water, especially in the sea.

**water|way** /wɔtərweɪ/ (**waterways**) N-COUNT A **waterway** is a canal, river, or narrow channel of sea which ships or boats can sail along. ❑ *There are more than 400 miles of waterways in the area.* [from Old English]

**wa|tery** /wɔtəri/ **1** ADJ Something that is **watery** is weak or pale. ❑ *A watery light began to show in the sky.* **2** ADJ If you describe food or drink as **watery**, you dislike it because it contains too much water, or has no flavor. ❑ *...a bowl of watery soup.* **3** ADJ Something that is **watery** contains, resembles, or consists of water. ❑ *Emma's eyes were red and watery.* [from Old English]

**watt** /wɒt/ (**watts**) N-COUNT A **watt** is a unit of measurement of electrical power. ❑ *...a 100-watt light bulb.* [from Scottish]

**wave** /weɪv/ (**waves, waving, waved**) **1** V-T/V-I If you **wave** or **wave** your hand, you move your hand from side to side in the air, usually in order to say hello or goodbye to someone. ❑ *Jessica saw Lois and waved to her.* ❑ *He smiled, waved, and said, "Hi!"* ● **Wave** is also a noun. ❑ *Steve stopped him with a wave of the hand.* **2** V-T If you **wave** someone away or **wave** them on, you make a movement

W

with your hand to indicate that they should move in a particular direction. ❑ *Ben waved her away but smiled.* ▪3 V-T If you **wave** something, you hold it up and move it rapidly from side to side. ❑ *More than 4000 people waved flags and sang songs.* ▪4 N-COUNT A **wave** is a raised mass of water on the surface of water, especially the sea, which is caused by the wind or by tides making the surface of the water rise and fall. ❑ *...the sound of the waves breaking on the shore.* ▪5 N-COUNT **Waves** are the form in which things such as sound, light, and radio signals travel. ❑ *...sound waves.* ▪6 N-COUNT If you refer to a **wave of** a particular feeling, you mean that it increases quickly and becomes very intense, and then often decreases again. ❑ *She felt a wave of panic.* ▪7 N-COUNT A **wave** is a sudden increase in a particular activity or type of behavior, especially an undesirable or unpleasant one. ❑ *...the current wave of violence.* [from Old English] ▪8 → see also **tidal wave**
→ see Word Web: **wave**
→ see **beach, ear, earthquake, echo, ocean, radio, sound, tsunami**

**wave height** (**wave heights**) N-VAR The difference in height between the highest point of a water wave and the lowest point of the following wave can be referred to as the **wave height**.

**wave|length** /ˈweɪvlɛŋθ/ (**wavelengths**) ▪1 N-COUNT A **wavelength** is the distance between a part of a wave of energy such as light or sound and the next similar part. ❑ *Short wavelength X-rays are strong enough to pass through the skin.* ▪2 N-COUNT A **wavelength** is the size of radio wave that a particular radio station uses to broadcast its programs. ❑ *She found the station's wavelength on her radio.* ▪3 PHRASE If two people are **on the same wavelength**, they find it easy to understand each other and they tend to agree, because they share similar interests or opinions. ❑ *We finished each other's sentences because we were on the same wavelength.*

**wave pe|ri|od** (**wave periods**) N-COUNT The time difference between the passage of two water waves can be referred to as the **wave period**.

**wa|ver** /ˈweɪvər/ (**wavers, wavering, wavered**) ▪1 V-I If you **waver**, you cannot decide about something or you consider changing your mind about something. ❑ *He has never wavered in his opinion.* ▪2 V-I If something **wavers**, it shakes with very slight movements or changes. ❑ *At first she shook and her voice wavered.* [from Old Norse]

**wave speed** (**wave speeds**) N-VAR **Wave speed** is the speed at which a wave such as a sound wave or a water wave is traveling.

**wavy** /ˈweɪvi/ (**wavier, waviest**) ADJ **Wavy** hair is not straight or curly, but curves slightly. ❑ *She had short, wavy brown hair.* [from Old English]
→ see **hair**

**wax** /wæks/ (**waxes**) N-VAR **Wax** is a solid, slightly shiny substance made of fat or oil that is used to make candles and polish. ❑ *...candle wax.* [from Old English]

**wax pa|per** N-UNCOUNT **Wax paper** is paper that has been covered with a thin layer of wax. It is used mainly in cooking or to wrap food.

---

## way

❶ NOUN AND ADVERB USES
❷ PHRASES: GROUP 1
❸ PHRASES: GROUP 2

---

❶ **way** /weɪ/ (**ways**) ▪1 N-COUNT If you refer to a **way** of doing something, you are referring to how you can do it, for example, the action you can take or the method you can use to achieve it. ❑ *One way of making friends is to go to an evening class.* ▪2 N-COUNT If you talk about the **way** someone does something, you are talking about the qualities their action has. ❑ *She smiled in a friendly way.* ▪3 N-COUNT If a general statement or description is true **in** a particular **way**, this is the form of it that is true in a particular case. ❑ *Airlines have cut costs in several ways.* ❑ *She was afraid in a way that was quite new to her.* ▪4 N-COUNT You use **way** in expressions such as **in some ways**, **in many ways**, and **in every way** to indicate the degree or extent to which a statement is true. ❑ *In some ways, I liked him a lot.* ▪5 N-PLURAL The **ways** of a particular person or group of people are their customs or their usual behavior. ❑ *I'm too old to change my ways.* ▪6 N-SING You use **way** in expressions such as **push your way**, **work your way**, or **eat your way**, followed by a prepositional phrase or adverb, in order to indicate movement, progress, or force as well as the action described by the verb. ❑ *She pushed her way into the crowd.* ▪7 N-COUNT The **way** somewhere consists of the different places that you go through or the route that you take in order to get there. ❑ *Does anybody know the way to the bathroom?* ❑ *I'm afraid I can't remember the way.* ▪8 N-SING If you go or look a particular **way**, you go or look in that direction. ❑ *As he walked into the kitchen, he passed Dad coming*

---

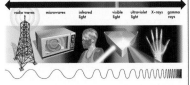

**Word Web** wave **THE ELECTROMAGNETIC SPECTRUM**

As **wind** blows across water, it makes **waves**. It does this by giving energy to the water. If the waves hit an object, they bounce off it. Light also moves in waves and acts the same way. We can see an object only if light waves bounce off it. Light waves have different **frequencies**. Wave frequency is usually the measure of the number of waves per second. **Radio waves** and **microwaves** are examples of low-frequency light waves. **Visible light** has medium-frequency light waves. **Ultraviolet radiation** and **X-rays** are high-frequency light waves.

**W**

the other way. ❑ *They wondered which way to go next.*
**9** N-SING You use **way** in expressions such as **the right way up** and **the other way around** to refer to one of two or more possible positions or arrangements that something can have. ❑ *Hold that bottle the right way up!* **10** ADV You can use **way** to emphasize, for example, that something is a great distance away or is very much below or above a particular level or amount. ❑ *The town of Freiburg is way down in the valley.* ❑ *You've waited way too long.* **11** N-SING **Way** is used in expressions such as **a long way, a little way,** and **quite a way,** to say how far away something is or how far you have traveled. ❑ *…places quite a long way from here.* ❑ *A little way down the road we passed a house.* **12** N-SING You use **way** in expressions such as **all the way, most of the way** and **half the way** to refer to the extent to which an action has been completed. ❑ *I listened to the story all the way through.* [from Old English]

❷ **way** /weɪ/ (**ways**) **1** PHRASE You say **by the way** when you add something to what you are saying, especially something that you have just thought of. [SPOKEN] ❑ *By the way, how is your back?* **2** PHRASE If someone says that you **can't have it both ways,** they are telling you that you have to choose between two things and cannot do or have them both. ❑ *You can't have it both ways: you're either doing it properly or not.* **3** PHRASE **Every which way** and **any which way** are used to emphasize that something happens, or might happen, in a lot of different ways, or using a lot of different methods. [INFORMAL] ❑ *Her short hair stuck up every which way.* **4** PHRASE If someone **gets their way** or **has their way,** nobody stops them from doing what they want to do. You can also say that someone **gets their own way** or **has their own way.** ❑ *She is very good at getting her own way.* **5** PHRASE If one thing **gives way to** another, the first thing is replaced by the second. ❑ *First he felt sad. Then the sadness gave way to anger.* **6** PHRASE If an object that is supporting something **gives way,** it breaks or collapses, so that it can no longer support that thing. ❑ *He fell when the floor gave way beneath him.* [from Old English]

❸ **way** /weɪ/ (**ways**) **1** PHRASE If you say that something is true **in a way,** you mean that although it is not completely true, it is true to a limited extent or in certain respects. You use in **a way** to reduce the force of a statement. ❑ *In a way, I guess I'm frightened of failing.* **2** PHRASE If you say that someone **gets in the way** or **is in the way,** you are annoyed because their presence or their actions stop you from doing something properly. ❑ *"We won't get in the way," Suzanne promised.* **3** PHRASE If one person or thing **makes way for** another, the first is replaced by the second. ❑ *He said he was happy to make way for younger people.* **4** PHRASE If you **go out of** your **way to** do something, for example, to help someone, you make a special effort to do it. ❑ *He went out of his way to help me.* **5** PHRASE If someone **keeps out of** your **way** or **stays out of** your **way,** he or she avoids you or does not get involved with you. ❑ *I kept out of his way as much as I could.* **6** PHRASE When something is **out of the way,** it has finished or you have dealt with it, so that it is no longer a problem or needs no more time spent on it. ❑ *Let's get this out of the way first.* [from Old English] **7** → see also **underway**

**way of life** (**ways of life**) N-COUNT A **way of life** is the behavior and habits that are typical of a particular person or group, or that are chosen by them. ❑ *They're teaching me a lot about their way of life.*

**way|ward** /weɪwərd/ ADJ If you describe a person or their behavior as **wayward,** you mean that they behave in a selfish, bad, or unpredictable way, and are difficult to control. ❑ *…wayward children.*

**we** /wɪ, STRONG wi/

We is the first person plural pronoun. **We** is used as the subject of a verb.

PRON A speaker or writer uses **we** to refer both to himself or herself and to one or more other people as a group. ❑ *We said we'd be friends for ever.* ❑ *We bought a bottle of lemonade.* [from Old English]

**weak** /wik/ (**weaker, weakest**) **1** ADJ If someone is **weak,** they are not healthy or do not have good muscles, so that they cannot move quickly or carry heavy things. ❑ *I was too weak to move.* ● **weak|ly** ADV ❑ *"I'm all right," Max said weakly.* ● **weak|ness** N-UNCOUNT ❑ *The condition can lead to weakness and rash.* **2** ADJ If someone has an organ or sense that is **weak,** it is not very effective or powerful, or is likely to fail. ❑ *She had a weak heart.* **3** ADJ If you describe someone as **weak,** you mean that they are not very confident or determined, so that they are often frightened or worried, or easily influenced by other people. ❑ *He was a good doctor, but a weak man.* ● **weak|ness** N-UNCOUNT ❑ *Some people see crying as a sign of weakness.* **4** ADJ If something such as an argument or case is **weak,** it is not convincing or there is little evidence to support it. ❑ *The argument against him was weak.* **5** ADJ A **weak** drink, chemical, or drug contains very little of a particular substance, for example, because a lot of water has been added to it. ❑ *…a cup of weak tea.* [from Old English] **6** → see also **weakness**
→ see **muscle**

| **Thesaurus** | weak | Also look up : |
|---|---|---|
| ADJ. | feeble, frail; (*ant.*) strong **1** cowardly, insecure; (*ant.*) strong **3** | |

| **Word Partnership** | Use *weak* with : |
|---|---|
| ADV. | **relatively** weak, **still** weak, **too** weak, **very** weak **1**–**5** |

**weak|en** /wikən/ (**weakens, weakening, weakened**) **1** V-T/V-I If you **weaken** something or if it **weakens,** it becomes less strong or less powerful. ❑ *The illness weakened his heart.* ❑ *Families are weakening and breaking up.* **2** V-I If you **weaken,** you become less certain about a decision you have made. ❑ *Jennie weakened, and finally agreed that they could stay another half hour.* [from Old English]

**weak|ness** /wiknɪs/ (**weaknesses**) **1** N-COUNT If you have a **weakness for** something, you like it very much. ❑ *Stephen had a weakness for chocolate.* [from Old English] **2** → see also **weak**

**wealth** /wɛlθ/ **1** N-UNCOUNT **Wealth** is the possession of a large amount of money, property, or other valuable things. You can also refer to a particular person's money or property as their **wealth.** ❑ *His own wealth grew.* **2** N-SING A **wealth**

W

of something is a very large amount of it. [FORMAL] ❑ *The city has a wealth of beautiful churches.*

**wealthy** /wɛlθi/ (**wealthier, wealthiest**) ADJ Someone who is **wealthy** has a large amount of money, property, or valuable possessions. ❑ *...a wealthy businessman.* ● **The wealthy** are people who are wealthy. ❑ *Good education should be available to everyone, not just the wealthy.*

**wean** /win/ (**weans, weaning, weaned**) ■ V-T When a baby or baby animal **is weaned**, its mother stops feeding it milk and starts giving it other food, especially solid food. ❑ *When is the best time to start weaning my baby?* ■ V-T If you **wean** someone **off** a habit or something they like, you gradually make them stop doing it or liking it. ❑ *She is trying to wean herself off coffee.* [from Old English]

**weap|on** /wɛpən/ (**weapons**) N-COUNT A **weapon** is an object such as a gun, a knife, or a missile, which is used to kill or hurt people in a fight or a war. ❑ *...nuclear weapons.* [from Old English]
→ see **army, war**

**weap|ons of mass de|struc|tion** N-PLURAL **Weapons of mass destruction** are biological, chemical, or nuclear weapons. The abbreviation **WMD** is often used.

**wear** /wɛər/ (**wears, wearing, wore, worn**) ■ V-T When you **wear** something such as clothes, shoes, or jewelry, you have them on your body or on part of your body. ❑ *He was wearing a brown shirt.* ■ V-T If you **wear** your hair or beard in a particular way, you have it cut or styled in that way. ❑ *She wore her hair in a long ponytail.* ■ N-UNCOUNT You use **wear** to refer to clothes that are suitable for a certain time or place. ❑ *...a new range of evening wear.* ■ N-UNCOUNT **Wear** is the amount or type of use that something has over a period of time. ❑ *You'll get more wear out of a good quality pair of shoes.* ■ N-UNCOUNT **Wear** is the damage or change that is caused by something being used a lot or for a long time. ❑ *...a large armchair which showed signs of wear.* ■ V-I If something **wears**, it becomes thinner or weaker because it is constantly being used over a long period of time. ❑ *The stone steps are beginning to wear.* [from Old English]
→ see **makeup**

▸ **wear away** PHR-VERB If you **wear** something **away** or if it **wears away**, it becomes thin and eventually disappears because it is used a lot or rubbed a lot. ❑ *The paint has worn away from the edge of the door.*
▸ **wear down** ■ PHR-VERB If you **wear** something **down** or if it **wears down**, it becomes flatter or smoother as a result of constantly rubbing against something else. ❑ *Rivers have worn down the rocks over the years.* ❑ *The heels on his shoes have worn down.* ■ PHR-VERB If you **wear** someone **down**, you make them gradually weaker or less determined until they eventually do what you want. ❑ *She wore him down until he eventually signed the letter.*
▸ **wear off** PHR-VERB If a sensation, or feeling **wears off**, it disappears slowly. ❑ *Now that the shock was wearing off, he was in pain.*
▸ **wear out** ■ PHR-VERB When something **wears out** or when you **wear** it **out**, it is used so much

that it becomes thin or weak and unable to be used anymore. ❑ *The batteries of her watch were wearing out.* ❑ *He wore out his shoes wandering around Mexico City.* ■ PHR-VERB If something **wears** you **out**, it makes you feel extremely tired. [INFORMAL] ❑ *The young people wore themselves out playing soccer.*
■ → see also **worn out**

**wea|ry** /wɪəri/ (**wearier, weariest**) ■ ADJ If you are **weary**, you are very tired. ❑ *Rachel looked pale and weary.* ■ ADJ If you are **weary of** something, you have become tired of it and have lost your enthusiasm for it. ❑ *We're getting very weary of Alan's behavior.* [from Old English]

**weath|er** /wɛðər/ (**weathers, weathering, weathered**) ■ N-UNCOUNT The **weather** is the temperature and condition of the air, for example, if it is raining, hot, or windy. ❑ *The weather was bad.* ❑ *I like cold weather.* ■ V-T/V-I If something such as wood or rock **weathers** or **is weathered**, it changes color or shape as a result of the wind, sun, rain, or cold. ❑ *Unpainted wood weathers to a gray color.* ■ V-T If you **weather** a difficult time or a difficult situation, you survive it. ❑ *The company has weathered the recent difficulties.* [from Old English]
→ see Word Web: **weather**
→ see **forecast, storm**

**weath|er fore|cast** (**weather forecasts**) N-COUNT A **weather forecast** is a statement saying what the weather will be like the next day or for the next few days.

**weath|er|ing** /wɛðərɪŋ/ ■ N-UNCOUNT **Weathering** is a process in which rocks near the Earth's surface are broken into smaller pieces as a result of exposure to rain, wind, and ice. [from Old English] ■ → see also **chemical weathering, mechanical weathering**

**W**

**Word Web** weather

Researchers believe the **weather** affects our bodies and minds. The **barometric pressure** drops before a **storm**. The difference in pressure may change the blood flow in the brain. Some people get migraine headaches. In **damp, humid** weather people have problems with arthritis. A sudden **heat wave** can produce heatstroke. People get seasonal affective disorder or SAD in the winter. They feel depressed during the short, **gloomy** days. As the word "sad" suggests, people with this condition feel depressed. The bitter cold of a **blizzard** can cause frostbite. The **hot, dry** Santa Ana winds* in southern California create confusion and depression in some people.

*Santa Ana winds: strong, hot, dry winds that blow in southern California in autumn and early spring.*

**weath|er map** (**weather maps**) N-COUNT A **weather map** is a chart that shows what the weather is like or what it will be like.

**weave** /wiv/ (**weaves, weaving, wove, woven**)

The form **weaved** is used for the past tense and past participle for meaning **2**.

**1** V-T/V-I If you **weave** cloth or a carpet, you make it by crossing threads over and under each other using a frame or machine called a loom. ❑ *We gathered wool and learned how to weave it into cloth.* ● **weav|er** (**weavers**) N-COUNT ❑ *...a linen weaver from Ireland.* ● **weav|ing** N-UNCOUNT ❑ *I studied weaving.* **2** V-T/V-I If you **weave** your way somewhere, you move between and around things as you go there. ❑ *He weaved around the tables to where she sat with Bob.* [from Old English]
→ see **industry**

**web** /wɛb/ (**webs**) **1** N-PROPER **The Web** is a computer system that links documents and pictures into a database that is stored in computers in many different parts of the world and that people everywhere can use. It is also referred to as the **World Wide Web**. [COMPUTING] ❑ *The handbook is available on the Web.* **2** N-COUNT A **web** is a complicated pattern of connections or relationships, sometimes considered as an obstacle or a danger. ❑ *...a web of lies.* **3** N-COUNT A **web** is the thin net made by a spider from a sticky substance that it produces in its body. ❑ *There's a spider's web in the window.* [from Old English]
→ see **blog**

**web|cam** /wɛbkæm/ (**webcams**) also Webcam N-COUNT A **webcam** is a video camera that takes pictures that can be viewed on a website. [COMPUTING]

**web|cast** /wɛbkæst/ (**webcasts**) also Webcast N-COUNT A **webcast** is an event such as a musical performance that you can listen to or watch on the Internet. [COMPUTING]

**web|log** /wɛblɔg/ (**weblogs**) N-COUNT A **weblog** is a website containing a diary or journal on a particular subject. [COMPUTING] ❑ *...a weblog for writing about New York.* ● **web|log|ger** /wɛblɔgər/ (**webloggers**) N-COUNT ❑ *Many webloggers are getting into blogging for the wrong reasons.*

● **web|log|ging** /wɛblɔgɪŋ/ N-UNCOUNT ❑ *...a popular online diary and weblogging site.*

**web|mas|ter** /wɛbmæstər/ (**webmasters**) N-COUNT A **webmaster** is someone who is in charge of a website, especially someone who does that as their job. [COMPUTING] [from Old English]
→ see **Internet**

**web page** (**web pages**) also Web page N-COUNT A **web page** is a set of data or information that is designed to be viewed as part of a website. [COMPUTING]
→ see **Internet**

**Word Link** site, situ ≈ position, location : campsite, situation, website

**web|site** /wɛbsaɪt/ (**websites**) also Web site, web site N-COUNT A **website** is a set of data and information about a particular subject that is available on the Internet. [COMPUTING]
→ see **blog, Internet**

**wed|ding** /wɛdɪŋ/ (**weddings**) N-COUNT A **wedding** is a marriage ceremony and the party or special meal that often takes place after the ceremony. ❑ *Many couples want a big wedding.* [from Old English]
→ see Word Web: **wedding**

**wedge** /wɛdʒ/ (**wedges, wedging, wedged**) **1** V-T If you **wedge** something, you force it to remain in a particular position by holding it there tightly or by putting something next to it to prevent it from moving. ❑ *I shut the door and wedged it with a piece of wood.* **2** V-T If you **wedge** something somewhere, you fit it there tightly. ❑ *Wedge the plug into the hole.* **3** N-COUNT A **wedge** of something such as fruit or cheese is a piece of it that has a thick triangular shape. ❑ *Serve the fish with a wedge of lemon.* **4** N-COUNT A **wedge** is an object with one pointed edge and one thick edge, which you put under a door to keep it firmly in position. **5** N-COUNT A **wedge** is a piece of metal with a pointed edge which is used for splitting a material such as stone or wood, by being hammered into a crack in the material. [from Old English]

**Wednes|day** /wɛnzdeɪ, -di/ (**Wednesdays**) N-VAR **Wednesday** is the day after Tuesday and before Thursday. ❑ *Come and have supper with us on*

W

## Word Web    wedding

Some **weddings** are fancy, like the one in this picture. Most ceremonies include a similar group of attendants. The **maid of honor** or **matron of honor** helps the **bride** get ready for the ceremony. She also signs the **marriage certificate** as a legal **witness**. The **bridesmaids** plan the bride's wedding **shower**. The **best man** arranges for the **bachelor party** the night before the wedding. He also helps the groom dress for the wedding.

After the **ceremony**, the guests gather for a **reception**. When the party is over, many couples leave on a **honeymoon** trip.

*Wednesday, if you're free.* [from Old English]

**weed** /wiːd/ (**weeds, weeding, weeded**)
■ N-COUNT A **weed** is a wild plant that grows in gardens or fields of crops and prevents the plants that you want from growing properly. ❑ *The garden was full of weeds.* ❷ V-T/V-I If you **weed** an area, you remove the weeds from it. ❑ *Try not to walk on the flowerbeds while weeding.* [from Old English]
→ see **plant**
▶ **weed out** PHR-VERB If you **weed out** things or people that are useless or unwanted in a group, you find them and get rid of them. ❑ *It is difficult to weed out bad employees.*

**week** /wiːk/ (**weeks**) ■ N-COUNT A **week** is a period of seven days. Some people consider that a week starts on Monday and ends on Sunday. ❑ *I had a letter from my mother last week.* ❑ *I thought about it all week.* ❷ N-COUNT Your working **week** is the hours that you spend at work during a week. ❑ *Many women work a 40-hour week.* ❸ N-SING The **week** is the part of the week that does not include Saturday and Sunday. ❑ *Anna looked after the children during the week.* [from Old English]
→ see **year**

**week|day** /wiːkdeɪ/ (**weekdays**) N-COUNT A **weekday** is any of the days of the week except Saturday and Sunday.

**week|end** /wiːkɛnd/ (**weekends**) N-COUNT A **weekend** is Saturday and Sunday. ❑ *I had dinner with him last weekend.*

**week|ly** /wiːkli/ (**weeklies**) ■ ADJ A **weekly** event or publication happens or appears once a week or every week. ❑ *We do the weekly shopping every Thursday.* ● **Weekly** is also an adverb. ❑ *The group meets weekly.* ❷ N-COUNT A **weekly** is a newspaper or magazine that is published once a week. ❑ *Two of the four national daily papers are to become weeklies.* [from Old English]

**weep** /wiːp/ (**weeps, weeping, wept**) V-T/V-I If someone **weeps**, they cry. [LITERARY] ❑ *She wept tears of joy.* [from Old English]
→ see **cry**

**weigh** /weɪ/ (**weighs, weighing, weighed**) ■ V-T If someone or something **weighs** a particular amount, this amount is how heavy they are. ❑ *It weighs nearly 65 pounds.* ❷ V-T If you **weigh** something or someone, you measure how heavy they are. ❑ *Lisa weighed the boxes for postage.* ❸ V-T If you **weigh** the facts about a situation, you consider them very carefully before you make a decision, especially by comparing the various facts involved. ❑ *She weighed her options.* [from Old English]

▶ **weigh down** PHR-VERB If something that you are wearing or carrying **weighs** you **down**, it stops you moving easily by making you heavier. ❑ *I was weighed down by my backpack.*

### Word Partnership   Use *weigh* with :

| | |
|---|---|
| ADV. | weigh **less**, weigh **more** ■<br>weigh **carefully** ❷ ❸ |
| N. | weigh **10 pounds** ■<br>weigh **alternatives**, weigh **benefits**,<br>weigh **costs**, weigh **the evidence**, weigh<br>**risks** ❸ |

**weight** /weɪt/ (**weights**) ■ N-VAR The **weight** of a person or thing is how heavy they are, measured in units such as kilograms, pounds, or tons. ❑ *What is your height and weight?* ❷ PHRASE If someone **loses weight**, they become lighter. If they **gain weight** or **put on weight**, they become heavier. ❑ *I'm lucky because I never put on weight.* ❸ N-COUNT **Weights** are objects that weigh a known amount and that people lift as a form of exercise. ❑ *I was in the gym lifting weights.* ❹ N-COUNT You can refer to a heavy object as a **weight**, especially when you have to lift it. ❑ *Lifting heavy weights can hurt your back.* ❺ N-UNCOUNT The **weight** of something is the vertical force exerted on it as a result of gravitation. Weight is measured in units called "newtons." ❻ PHRASE If you **pull your weight**, you work as hard as everyone else who is involved in the same task or activity. ❑ *We must make sure that everyone is pulling his or her weight.* [from Old English]
→ see **diet**

### Word Partnership   Use *weight* with :

| | |
|---|---|
| V. | add weight, gain/lose weight, put on<br>weight ■ |
| N. | body weight, weight gain/loss, height<br>and weight, size and weight ■<br>weight training ❸ |
| ADJ. | excess weight, healthy weight, ideal<br>weight, weight ■<br>heavy weight, light weight ❷ ❸ |

**weight|ed** /weɪtɪd/ ADJ A system that is **weighted** in favor of a particular person or group is organized so that this person or group has an advantage. ❑ *The test is weighted in favor of students who took the test online.* [from Old English]

**weight|lifting** /weɪtlɪftɪŋ/ N-UNCOUNT **Weightlifting** is a sport in which the competitor who can lift the heaviest weight wins.

**weight train|ing** N-UNCOUNT **Weight training** is a kind of physical exercise in which people lift or heavy weights with their arms and legs in order to strengthen their muscles.

**weighty** /weɪti/ (**weightier, weightiest**) ADJ If you describe something such as an issue or a decision as **weighty**, you mean that it is serious or important. [FORMAL] ❑ *They have to make decisions about such weighty matters as marriage and starting a family.* [from Old English]

**weird** /wɪərd/ (**weirder, weirdest**) ADJ If you describe something or someone as **weird**, you mean that they are strange. [INFORMAL] ❑ *He's a very weird guy.* [from Old English]

**wel|come** /wɛlkəm/ (**welcomes, welcoming, welcomed**) **1** V-T/V-I If you **welcome** someone, you greet them in a friendly way when they arrive somewhere. ❑ *She was there to welcome him home.* ● **Welcome** is also a noun. ❑ *They gave him a fantastic welcome.* **2** CONVENTION You use **welcome** in expressions such as **welcome home, welcome to Boston,** and **welcome back** when you are greeting someone who has just arrived somewhere. ❑ *Welcome to Washington.* **3** V-T If you **welcome** an action, decision, or situation, you approve of it and are pleased that it has occurred. ❑ *She welcomed the decision but said that the changes didn't go far enough.* **4** ADJ If you describe something as **welcome**, you mean that people wanted it and are happy that it has occurred. ❑ *"Any improvement is welcome," he said.* **5** ADJ If you say that someone is **welcome** in a particular place, you are encouraging them to go there by telling them that they will be liked and accepted. ❑ *New members are always welcome.* **6** ADJ If you tell someone that they are **welcome** to do something, you are encouraging them to do it by telling them that they are allowed to do it. ❑ *You are welcome to visit the hospital at any time.* **7** PHRASE If you **make** someone **welcome** or **make** them **feel welcome**, you make them feel happy and accepted in a new place. **8** CONVENTION You say "**You're welcome**" to someone who has thanked you for something in order to acknowledge their thanks in a polite way. ❑ *"Thank you for dinner." — "You're welcome."* [from Old English]

**Word Partnership** Use *welcome* with :

| | |
|---|---|
| ADJ. | **warm** welcome **1** |
| N. | welcome **guests,** welcome **visitors 1 5** |
| ADV. | welcome **home 2** |
| | **always** welcome **4 – 6** |

**weld** /wɛld/ (**welds, welding, welded**) V-T/V-I To **weld** one piece of metal to another means to join them by heating the edges and putting them together so that they cool and harden into one piece. ❑ *It's possible to weld stainless steel to ordinary steel.* [from Old English]

**wel|fare** /wɛlfɛər/ **1** N-UNCOUNT The **welfare** of a person or group is their health, comfort, and happiness. ❑ *I don't believe he is thinking of Emma's welfare.* **2** ADJ **Welfare** services are provided to help with people's living conditions and financial problems. ❑ *...child welfare services.* **3** N-UNCOUNT **Welfare** is money that is paid by the government to people who are unemployed, poor, or sick. ❑ *Some states are making cuts in welfare.* [from Old Norse]

**Word Partnership** Use *welfare* with :

| | |
|---|---|
| ADJ. | **public** welfare, **social** welfare **1** |
| N. | **animal** welfare, **child** welfare, **health and** welfare **1** |
| | welfare **programs,** welfare **reform,** welfare **system 2** |
| | welfare **benefits,** welfare **checks 3** |

---

**well**

**1** DISCOURSE USES
**2** ADVERB USES
**3** PHRASES
**4** ADJECTIVE USE
**5** NOUN USES
**6** VERB USES

---

**1 well** /wɛl/

Well is used mainly in spoken English.

**1** ADV You say **well** to indicate that you are about to say something. ❑ *Well, it's a pleasure to meet you.* **2** ADV You say **well** just before or after you pause, especially to give yourself time to think about what you are going to say. ❑ *I'm sorry I woke you, and, well, I just wanted to tell you I was all right.* **3** ADV You say **well** when you are correcting something that you have just said. ❑ *There was a note. Well, a letter really.* **4** CONVENTION You say **oh well** to indicate that you accept a situation or that someone else should accept it, even though you or they are not very happy about it, because it is not too bad and cannot be changed. ❑ *Oh well, it could be worse.* [from Old English] **5 very well** → see **very**

**2 well** /wɛl/ (**better, best**) **1** ADV If you do something **well**, you do it to a high standard or to a great extent. ❑ *It's important that we play well at home.* ❑ *He speaks English well.* **2** ADV If you do something **well**, you do it thoroughly and completely. ❑ *Mix the butter and sugar well.* **3** ADV You use **well** to ask or talk about the extent or standard of something. ❑ *How well do you remember your mother?* ❑ *She can speak French much better than me.* **4** ADV You use **well** in front of a prepositional phrase to emphasize it. For example, if you say that one thing happened **well before** another, you mean that it happened a long time before it. ❑ *Frank did not arrive until well after midnight.* ❑ *...well over a million people.* **5** ADV You use **well** after verbs such as "may" and "could" when you are saying what you think is likely to happen. ❑ *That could well be the problem.* [from Old English]

**3 well** /wɛl/ **1** PHRASE You use **as well** when mentioning something that happens in the same way as something else already mentioned, or that should be considered at the same time as that thing. ❑ *If you work in the garden in spring you'll have less to do in summer — and a more beautiful garden, as well.* **2** PHRASE You use **as well as** when you want to mention another item connected with the subject you are discussing. ❑ *Adults as well as children will enjoy the movie.* **3** PHRASE If you say that something that has happened **is just as well**, you mean that it is fortunate that it happened in the way it did. ❑ *From what you've said, it's just as well she wasn't there.* **4** PHRASE If you say that you **might as well** do something, or that you **may as**

**well** do it, you mean that you will do it although you do not have a strong desire to do it and may even feel slightly unwilling to do it. ❑ *Anyway, you're here; you might as well stay.* [from Old English] **5** all very well → see **all** **6** to know full well → see **full**

**④ well** /wɛl/ ADJ If you are **well**, you are healthy and not ill. ❑ *I'm not very well today.* [from Old English]

**⑤ well** /wɛl/ (wells) **1** N-COUNT A **well** is a hole in the ground from which a supply of water is extracted. ❑ *I carried the water home from the well.* **2** N-COUNT A **well** is an oil well. ❑ *About 650 wells are on fire.* [from Old English] → see **oil**

**⑥ well** /wɛl/ (wells, welling, welled) V-I If tears **well** in your eyes, they come to the surface. ● **Well up** means the same as well. ❑ *Tears welled up in Annie's eyes.* [from Old English]

**well-balanced** **1** ADJ If you describe someone as **well-balanced**, you mean that they are sensible and do not have many emotional problems. ❑ *...a fun-loving, well-balanced person.* **2** ADJ If you describe something that is made up of several parts as **well-balanced**, you mean that there is a good mixture of each part. ❑ *...a well-balanced diet.*

**well-being** N-UNCOUNT Someone's **well-being** is their health and happiness. ❑ *Singing can create a sense of well-being.*

**well done** **1** CONVENTION You say **Well done** to indicate that you are pleased that someone has done something good. ❑ *"Daddy! I came in second in history" — "Well done, sweetheart!"* **2** ADJ If something that you have cooked, especially meat, is **well done**, it has been cooked thoroughly. ❑ *I like lamb well done.*

**well-dressed** ADJ Someone who is **well-dressed** is wearing fashionable or elegant clothes.

**well-established** ADJ If you say that something is **well-established**, you mean that it has been in existence for a long time and is successful. ❑ *...well-established companies.*

**well-informed** (better-informed) ADJ If you say that someone is **well-informed**, you mean that they know a lot about many different subjects or about one particular subject. ❑ *She's well-informed about our city.*

**well-intentioned** also well intentioned ADJ If you say that a person or their actions are **well-intentioned**, you mean that they intend to be helpful or kind but they are unsuccessful or cause problems. ❑ *He is well-intentioned but disorganized.*

**well-known** ADJ A **well-known** person or thing is known about by a lot of people and is therefore famous or familiar. ❑ *She was a very well-known author.*

**well-meaning** ADJ If you say that a person or their actions are **well-meaning**, you mean that they intend to be helpful or kind but they are unsuccessful or cause problems. ❑ *He is well-meaning but not very smart.*

**well-off** ADJ Someone who is **well-off** is rich enough to be able to buy and do most of the things that they want. [INFORMAL]

**well-paid** ADJ If you say that a person or their job is **well-paid**, you mean that they receive a lot of money for the work that they do.

**well-to-do** ADJ A **well-to-do** person is rich enough to be able to buy and do most of the things that they want. ❑ *...a well-to-do family.*

**well-traveled** ADJ A **well-traveled** person has traveled a lot in foreign countries.

**went** /wɛnt/ Went is the past tense of **go**. [from Old English]

**wept** /wɛpt/ Wept is the past tense and past participle of **weep**. [from Old English]

**were** /wər, STRONG wɜr/ **1** Were is the plural and the second person singular of the past tense of **be**. **2** Were is sometimes used instead of "was" in certain structures, for example, in conditional clauses or after the verb "wish." [FORMAL] ❑ *Jerry wished he were back in Washington.* [from Old English] **3** as it were → see **as**

**weren't** /wɜrnt, wɜrənt/ Weren't is the usual spoken form of "were not."

**west** /wɛst/ also West **1** N-UNCOUNT The **west** is the direction you look toward in the evening in order to see the sun set. ❑ *I drove to Flagstaff, a hundred miles to the west.* **2** N-SING The **west** of a place, country, or region is the part of it which is in the west. ❑ *Many of the buildings in the west of the city are on fire.* **3** ADV **West** means toward the west, or positioned to the west of a place or thing. ❑ *We are going west to California.* ❑ *Penryn is about 60 miles west of Philadelphia.* **4** ADJ A **west** wind blows from the west. **5** N-SING The **West** is used to refer to the United States, Canada, and the countries of Western Europe. ❑ *...relations between Japan and the West.* [from Old English]

**west|er|ly** /wɛstərli/ (westerlies) **1** ADJ A **westerly** point, area, or direction is to the west or toward the west. ❑ *They walked in a westerly direction along the riverbank.* **2** ADJ A **westerly** wind blows from the west. **3** N-COUNT A **westerly** is a wind that blows from the west. [from Old English]

**west|ern** /wɛstərn/ (westerns) also Western **1** ADJ **Western** means in or from the west of a region, state, or country. ❑ *Visitors from Western Europe to the United States rose one percent in 2003.* **2** ADJ **Western** is used to describe things, people, ideas, or ways of life that come from or are associated with the United States, Canada, and the countries of Western Europe. ❑ *They need billions of dollars from Western governments.* **3** N-COUNT A **western** is a book or movie about life in the western United States and territories in the nineteenth century, especially the lives of cowboys. [from Old English]

**west|ern|er** /wɛstərnər/ (westerners) also Westerner N-COUNT A **Westerner** is a person who was born in or lives in the United States, Canada, or Western Europe. ❑ *There are many Westerners living in China.* [from Old English]

**west|ward** /wɛstwərd/

The form **westwards** is also used.

ADV **Westward** or **westwards** means toward the west. ❑ *He sailed westward.* ● **Westward** is also an adjective. ❑ *...the one-hour westward flight over the Andes to Lima.* [from Old English]

**wet** /wɛt/ (wetter, wettest, wets, wetting, wet or wetted) **1** ADJ If something is **wet**, it is covered in water or another liquid. ❑ *He dried his wet hair with a towel.* **2** V-T To **wet** something means to get water or some other liquid over it. ❑ *Wet the*

**W**

Saltwater **wetlands** protect beaches from erosion. These **tidal flats** are homes for shellfish and migrating birds. In some areas, mangrove **swamps** form along the shore. They shelter many kinds of fish. They also filter **groundwater** before it reaches the ocean. Inland wetlands also form along rivers and streams. They become **marshes** and **freshwater** swamps. A **bog** is an unusual type of freshwater wetland. A layer of **peat** forms on the surface of the water. This layer can support shrubs, trees, and small animals. In some places people dry peat to burn. They use it for cooking and heating.

---

*shirts before you iron them.* **3** ADJ If the weather is **wet**, it is raining. ❑ *If the weather is wet or cold, stay indoors.* **4** ADJ If something such as paint, ink, or cement is **wet**, it is not yet dry or solid. **5** V-T If people, especially children, **wet** their beds or clothes or **wet** themselves, they urinate in their beds or in their clothes because they cannot stop themselves. ❑ *Many children wet the bed.* [from Old English]

| | |
|---|---|
| V. | **get** wet **1** |
| N. | wet **clothes**, wet **feet**, wet **grass**, wet **hair**, wet **sand 1**  wet **snow**, wet **weather 3**  wet **the bed 5** |
| ADJ. | **soaking** wet **1**  **cold and** wet **1 3** |

**wet|land** /wɛtlænd/ (**wetlands**) N-VAR A **wetland** is an area of very wet, muddy land with wild plants growing in it. You can also refer to an area like this as **wetlands**. ❑ *...a plan to protect the wetlands.*
→ see Word Web: **wetlands**

**we've** /wiv, STRONG wiv/ **We've** is the usual spoken form of "we have," especially when "have" is an auxiliary verb. ❑ *It's the first time we've been to the cinema together as a family.*

**whack** /wæk/ (**whacks, whacking, whacked**) V-T If you **whack** someone or something, you hit them hard. [INFORMAL] ❑ *Someone whacked him on the head.*

**whacky** /wæki/ → see **wacky**

**whale** /weɪl/ (**whales**) N-COUNT **Whales** are very large mammals that live in the sea. [from Old English]
→ see Word Web: **whale**

**whal|ing** /weɪlɪŋ/ N-UNCOUNT **Whaling** is the activity of hunting and killing whales. ❑ *...a ban on commercial whaling.* [from Old English]

**wharf** /wɔrf/ (**wharves** or **wharfs**) N-COUNT A **wharf** is a platform by a river or the sea where ships can be tied up. [from Old English]

**what** /wʌt, wɒt/

Usually pronounced /wɒt/ for meanings **2** and **4**.

**1** PRON You use **what** in questions when you ask for information. ❑ *What do you want?* ❑ *"Has something happened?" — "Yes." — "What?"* ● **What** is also a determiner. ❑ *What time is it?* **2** CONJ You use **what** after certain words, especially verbs and adjectives, when you are referring to a situation that is unknown or has not been specified. ❑ *I want to know what happened to Norman.* ● **What** is also a determiner. ❑ *I didn't know what else to say.* **3** CONJ You use **what** at the beginning of a clause in structures where you are changing the order of the information to give special emphasis to something. ❑ *What I wanted, more than anything, was a few days' rest.* **4** CONJ You use **what** to indicate that you are talking about the whole of an amount that is available to you. ❑ *He drank what was left in his cup.* ● **What** is also a determiner. ❑ *They spent what money they had.* **5** CONVENTION You say "**What?**" when you ask someone to repeat the thing that they have just said because you did not hear or understand it properly. "What?" is more informal and less polite than expressions such as "Pardon?" and "Excuse me?" [SPOKEN] ❑ *"We could buy this place," she said. "What?" he asked.* **6** CONVENTION You say "**What**" to express surprise. ❑ *"I love you." — "What?"* **7** PREDET You use **what** in exclamations to emphasize an opinion or reaction. ❑ *What a horrible thing to do!* ● **What** is also a determiner. ❑ *What pretty hair she has!*

**W**

**Whales** are part of a group of animals called cetaceans. This group also includes **dolphins** and porpoises. Whales live in the water, but they are **mammals**. They breathe air and are warm-blooded. Whales are adapted to life in the **ocean**. They have a 2-inch thick layer of blubber just under their skin. This insulates them from the cold ocean water. They sing beautiful songs that can be heard miles away. Blue whales are the largest animals in the world. They can become almost 100 feet long and weigh up to 145 tons.

**8** PHRASE In conversation, you say **or what?** after a question as a way of stating an opinion forcefully and showing that you expect other people to agree. ❏ *Look at that moon. Is that beautiful or what?* **9** PHRASE You use **what about** at the beginning of a question when you make a suggestion, offer, or request. ❏ *What about going out with me tomorrow?* **10** PHRASE You say **what if** at the beginning of a question when you ask about the consequences of something happening, especially something undesirable. ❏ *What if this doesn't work?* [from Old English] **11** **what's more** → see **more**

**what|ev|er** /wʌtɛvər, wɒt-/ **1** CONJ You use **whatever** to refer to anything or everything of a particular type. ❏ *Frank was free to do whatever he wanted.* ● **Whatever** is also a determiner. ❏ *Whatever their size or shape, the best gardens have beautiful flowers.* **2** CONJ You use **whatever** to say that something is the case in all circumstances. ❏ *I will always love you, whatever happens.* **3** CONJ You use **whatever** when you are indicating that you do not know the precise identity, meaning, or value of the thing just mentioned. ❏ *I thought that my childhood was "normal," whatever that is.*

**what's** /wʌts, wɒts/ **What's** is the usual spoken form of "what is" or "what has," especially when "has" is an auxiliary verb.

**what|so|ev|er** /wʌtsoʊɛvər, wɒt-/ ADV You use **whatsoever** to emphasize something negative. ❏ *James did nothing whatsoever to help.* ❏ *It made no sense to me whatsoever.*

**wheat** /wit/ (**wheats**) N-UNCOUNT **Wheat** is a cereal crop grown for food, which is ground into flour and used to make bread. [from Old English] → see **bread, grain**

**wheel** /wil/ (**wheels, wheeling, wheeled**) **1** N-COUNT The **wheels** of a vehicle are the circular objects that are attached underneath it and that enable it to move along the ground. ❏ *The car's wheels slipped on the wet road.* **2** N-COUNT The **wheel** of a car or other vehicle is the circular object that is used to steer it. ❏ *Curtis sat behind the wheel and they drove back.* **3** V-T If you **wheel** an object that has wheels somewhere, you push it along. ❏ *He wheeled his bike into the alley.* [from Old English] **4** → see also **steering wheel** → see Word Web: **wheel** → see **bicycle, color**

**wheel|chair** /wiltʃɛər/ (**wheelchairs**) N-COUNT A **wheelchair** is a chair with wheels that you use in order to move around in if you cannot walk properly, for example, because you are disabled or sick. → see **disability**

**wheeze** /wiz/ (**wheezes, wheezing, wheezed**) V-I If someone **wheezes**, they breathe with difficulty and make a whistling sound. ❏ *He had problems with his chest and wheezed and coughed all the time.* [from Old Norse]

**when** /wɛn/ **1** PRON You use **when** to ask questions about the time at which things happen. ❏ *When are you going home?* ❏ *When did you get married?* **2** CONJ You use **when** to introduce a clause in which you mention something that happens at some point during an activity, event, or situation. ❏ *When I met Jill, I was living on my own.* **3** CONJ You use **when** to introduce a clause where you mention the circumstances under which the event in the main clause happened or will happen. ❏ *When he brought Jane her drink she gave him a smile.* **4** CONJ You use **when** after certain words, especially verbs and adjectives, to introduce a clause where you mention the time at which something happens. ❏ *I asked him when he was coming back.* **5** CONJ You use **when** to introduce the reason for an opinion, comment, or question. ❏ *How can you understand when you don't have kids?* **6** CONJ You use **when** in order to introduce a fact or comment which makes the other part of the sentence rather surprising or unlikely. ❏ *Our mothers made us read, when all we really wanted to do was play.* [from Old English]

**when|ever** /wɛnɛvər/ CONJ You use **whenever** to refer to any time or every time that something happens or is true. ❏ *Whenever I talked to him, he seemed like a pretty regular guy.* ❏ *You can stay at my house whenever you like.*

**where** /wɛər/

Usually pronounced /wɛər/ for meanings **2** and **3**.

**1** PRON You use **where** to ask questions about the place something is in, or is coming from or going to. ❏ *Where did you meet him?* ❏ *Where's Anna?* **2** CONJ You use **where** to specify or refer to the

W

place in which something is situated or happens. ❏ *People were looking to see where the noise was coming from.* ❏ *He knew where Henry Carter was.* ● **Where** is also a relative pronoun. ❏ *The police closed off the area where the accident occurred.* **3** ADV You use **where** when you are referring to or asking questions about a situation, a stage in something, or an aspect of something. ❏ *Where will it all end?* ● **Where** is also a relative pronoun. ❏ *I've got to the point where I'll talk to almost anyone.* [from Old English]

**where|abouts**

> Pronounced /wɛərəbaʊts/ for meaning **1**, and /ˌwɛərəbaʊts/ for meaning **2**.

**1** N-SING If you refer to the **whereabouts** of a particular person or thing, you mean the place where that person or thing may be found. ❏ *…a map showing the whereabouts of the hotel.* **2** ADV You use **whereabouts** in questions when you are asking precisely where something is. ❏ *"Whereabouts in France?" — "Normandy."*

**where|as** /wɛərˈæz/ CONJ You use **whereas** to introduce a comment that contrasts with what is said in the main clause. ❏ *She knows her feelings, whereas I don't.*

**where|by** /wɛərˈbaɪ/ PRON A system or action **whereby** something happens is one that makes that thing happen. [FORMAL] ❏ *…an arrangement whereby employees may choose when to start work.*

**where|upon** /ˌwɛərəpɒn/ CONJ You use **whereupon** to say that one thing happens immediately after another thing, and usually as a result of it. [FORMAL] ❏ *"Tell me what happened," said Dobson, whereupon Davies started to explain.*

**wher|ever** /wɛrɛvər/ **1** CONJ You use **wherever** to indicate that something happens or is true in any place or situation. ❏ *Some people enjoy themselves wherever they are.* **2** CONJ You use **wherever** when you indicate that you do not know where a person or place is. ❏ *I'd like to join my children, wherever they are.*

**wheth|er** /wɛðər/ **1** CONJ You use **whether** when you are talking about a choice or doubt between two or more alternatives. ❏ *They now have two weeks to decide whether or not to buy.* **2** CONJ You use **whether** to say that something is true in any of the circumstances that you mention. ❏ *We're in this together, whether we like it or not.* [from Old English]

> **Usage** **whether** and **if**
>
> *Whether* and *if* are often interchangeable: *Jorge wondered whether/if Sania really liked the cake — he wasnt sure whether/if she was being sincere or just polite.* Only *whether* can be used after a preposition: *Sania didnt like the cake, but she wanted Jorge to like her — she was uncertain about whether to be honest.*

**which** /wɪtʃ/

> Usually pronounced /wɪtʃ/ for meanings **2**, **3** and **4**.

**1** PRON You use **which** in questions when there are two or more possible answers or alternatives. ❏ *"You go down that road." — "Which one?"* ❏ *Which man or woman do you like best?* **2** DET You use **which** to refer to a choice between two or more possible answers or alternatives. ❏ *I want to know which*

school you went to. ❏ *I can't remember which teachers I had.* **3** PRON You use **which** at the beginning of a relative clause when specifying the thing that you are talking about. In such clauses, **which** has the same meaning as *that.* ❏ *Police stopped a car which didn't stop at a red light.* **4** PRON You use **which** to refer back to what has just been said. ❏ *They ran out of milk, which didn't bother me because I don't drink milk.* ● **Which** is also a determiner. ❏ *She may be ill, in which case she needs to see a doctor.* [from Old English]

**which|ever** /wɪtʃɛvər/ **1** DET You use **whichever** in order to indicate that it does not matter which of the possible alternatives happens or is chosen. ❏ *Whichever way we do this, it isn't going to work.* ● **Whichever** is also a conjunction. ❏ *We will gladly exchange your purchase, or refund your money, whichever you prefer.* **2** DET You use **whichever** to specify which of a number of possibilities is the right one or the one you mean. ❏ *They ran the seat whichever way you like.* ● **Whichever** is also a conjunction. ❏ *He has been very fortunate or very clever, whichever is the right word.*

**whiff** /wɪf/ (**whiffs**) N-COUNT If there is a **whiff** of a particular smell, their is a faint smell of it. ❏ *He caught a whiff of her perfume.*

> **while**
>
> **❶** CONJUNCTION USES
> **❷** NOUN AND VERB USES

**❶ while** /waɪl/ **1** CONJ If something happens **while** something else is happening, the two things are happening at the same time. ❏ *I sat on the chair to unwrap the package while he stood behind me.* **2** CONJ You use **while** at the beginning of a clause to introduce information that contrasts with information in the main clause. ❏ *The first two services are free, while the third costs $35.* **3** CONJ You use **while** before making a statement in order to introduce information that partly conflicts with your statement. ❏ *While the weather is good today, it may be bad tomorrow.* [from Old English]

> **Usage** **while**
>
> *While* is used to join two verb phrases. *I listen to music while I exercise.*

**❷ while** /waɪl/ (**whiles**, **whiling**, **whiled**) **1** N-SING A **while** is a period of time. ❏ *They walked on in silence for a while.* ❏ *He got married a little while ago.* [from Old English] **2** once in a while → see **once** **3** worth your while → see **worth**
▶ **while away** PHR-VERB If you **while away** the time in a particular way, you spend time in that way, because you are waiting for something else to happen, or because you have nothing else to do. ❏ *They whiled away the hours telling stories.*

**whim** /wɪm/ (**whims**) N-VAR A **whim** is a sudden wish to do or have something that seems to have no serious reason or purpose. ❏ *We decided, on a whim, to fly to Morocco.*

**whim|per** /wɪmpər/ (**whimpers**, **whimpering**, **whimpered**) V-I If someone **whimpers**, they make quiet, unhappy, or frightened sounds, as if they are about to start crying. ❏ *She lay at the bottom of the stairs, whimpering in pain.* ● **Whimper** is also a noun. ❏ *David's cries quieted to a whimper.*

**whim|si|cal** /wɪmzɪkəl/ ADJ A **whimsical** person

or idea is unusual, playful, and unpredictable, rather than serious and practical. ❑ *...his gentle and whimsical humor.*

**whine** /waɪn/ (**whines, whining, whined**) **1** V-I If something or someone **whines**, they make a long, high-pitched noise, especially one that sounds sad or unpleasant. ❑ *He could hear the dog barking and whining in the background.* ● **Whine** is also a noun. ❑ *...the whine of the police siren.* **2** V-T/V-I If someone **whines**, they complain in an annoying way about something unimportant. ❑ *...children who whine that they are bored.* [from Old English]

**whip** /wɪp/ (**whips, whipping, whipped**) **1** N-COUNT A **whip** is a long thin piece of material such as leather or rope, fastened to a stiff handle. It is used for hitting people or animals. **2** V-T If someone **whips** a person or animal, they beat them or hit them with a whip or something like a whip. ❑ *Mr. Melton whipped the horse several times.* ● **whip|ping** (**whippings**) N-COUNT ❑ *His father threatened to give him a whipping.* **3** V-T If someone **whips** something out or **whips** it off, they take it out or take it off very quickly and suddenly. ❑ *Bob whipped out his notebook.* ❑ *She whipped off her skis and ran up the hill.* **4** V-T When you **whip** something liquid such as cream or an egg, you stir it very fast until it is thick or stiff. ❑ *Whip the cream until it is thick.* [from Middle Dutch]
▸ **whip up** PHR-VERB If someone **whips up** an emotion such as hatred, they deliberately cause and encourage people to feel that emotion. ❑ *He blamed politicians for whipping up fear.*

**whir** /wɜr/ (**whirs, whirring, whirred**) also **whirr** V-I When something such as a machine or an insect's wing **whirs**, it makes a series of low sounds so quickly that they seem like one continuous sound. ❑ *Flies whirred around him.* ● **Whir** is also a noun. ❑ *...the whir of a vacuum cleaner.* [of Scandinavian origin]

**whirl** /wɜrl/ (**whirls, whirling, whirled**) **1** V-T/V-I If something or someone **whirls** around or if you **whirl** them around, they move around or turn around very quickly. ❑ *She whirled around to look at him.* ❑ *He was whirling Anne around the floor.* **2** N-COUNT You can refer to a lot of intense activity as a **whirl** of activity. [from Old Norse]

**whirl|wind** /wɜrlwɪnd/ (**whirlwinds**) N-COUNT A **whirlwind** is a tall column of air that spins around and around very fast and moves across the land or sea.

**whirr** /wɜr/ → see **whir**

**whisk** /wɪsk/ (**whisks, whisking, whisked**) **1** V-T If you **whisk** someone or something somewhere, you take them or move them there quickly. ❑ *He whisked her across the dance floor.* **2** V-T If you **whisk** eggs or cream, you stir them very fast, often with an electric device, so that they become full of small bubbles. **3** N-COUNT A **whisk** is a kitchen tool used for whisking eggs or cream.
[from Old Norse]
→ see **utensil**

**whisk|er** /wɪskər/ (**whiskers**) N-COUNT The **whiskers** of an animal such as a cat or a mouse are the long stiff hairs that grow near its mouth. [from Scottish Gaelic]

whisker

**whis|key** /wɪski/ (**whiskeys**) N-VAR **Whiskey** is a strong alcoholic drink made, especially in the United States and Ireland, from grain such as barley or rye. ● A **whiskey** is a glass of whiskey. ❑ *Beattie took two whiskeys from a tray.* [from Scottish Gaelic]

**whis|ky** /wɪski/ (**whiskies**) N-VAR **Whisky** is whiskey that is made in Scotland and Canada. ● A **whisky** is a glass of whisky. [from Scottish Gaelic]

**whis|per** /wɪspər/ (**whispers, whispering, whispered**) V-T/V-I When you **whisper**, you say something very quietly, using your breath rather than your throat, so that only one person can hear you. ❑ *"Be quiet," I whispered.* ❑ *She sat on Ross's knee as he whispered in her ear.* ❑ *He whispered the message to David.* ● **Whisper** is also a noun. ❑ *Men were talking in whispers in every office.* [from Old English]

**whis|tle** /wɪsªl/ (**whistles, whistling, whistled**) **1** V-T/V-I When you **whistle**, you make sounds by forcing your breath out between your lips or teeth. ❑ *He was whistling softly to himself.* **2** V-I If something such as a train or a kettle **whistles**, it makes a loud, high sound. ❑ *Somewhere a train whistled.* **3** V-I If something such as the wind or a bullet **whistles** somewhere, it moves there, making a loud, high sound. ❑ *The wind whistled through the building.* **4** N-COUNT A **whistle** is a small metal or plastic tube that you blow in order to produce a loud sound and attract someone's attention. ❑ *The guard blew his whistle and the train started to move.* [from Old English]

**whistle-blowing** also **whistleblowing** N-UNCOUNT **Whistle-blowing** is the act of telling the authorities or the public that the organization you work for is doing something immoral or illegal.

**white** /waɪt/ (**whiter, whitest, whites**) **1** COLOR Something that is **white** is the color of snow or milk. ❑ *He had nice white teeth.* **2** ADJ A **white** person has a pale skin and belongs to a race of European origin. ❑ *A family of white people moved into a house up the street.* ● **Whites** are white people. ❑ *The school has brought blacks and whites and Hispanics together.* **3** ADJ **White** wine is pale yellow in color. ❑ *Gregory poured me another glass of white wine.* **4** N-VAR The **white** of an egg is the transparent liquid that surrounds the yellow part called the yolk. **5** N-COUNT The **white** of your eye is the white part that surrounds the colored part called the iris. [from Old English]
→ see **color**

**white blood cell** (**white blood cells**) N-COUNT **White blood cells** are the cells in your blood which your body uses to fight infection. Compare **red blood cell**.

**white|cap** /waɪtkæp/ (**whitecaps**) N-COUNT A **whitecap** is a wave in the ocean that is blown by the wind so that the top of the wave appears white.

**white-collar** also **white collar** ADJ **White-collar** workers work in offices rather than doing physical work such as making things in factories or building things. ❑ *White-collar workers now work longer hours.*
→ see **union**

**white dwarf** (**white dwarfs** or **white dwarves**) N-COUNT A **white dwarf** is a very small, dense star that has collapsed.

W

**White House** N-PROPER **The White House** is the official home in Washington DC of the president of the United States. You can also use **the White House** to refer to the president of the United States and his or her officials. ❑ *He drove to the White House.* ❑ *The White House has not yet commented publicly.*

**white light** N-UNCOUNT **White light** is light such as sunlight that contains all the colors of the visible spectrum in roughly equal amounts. [TECHNICAL]

**White Pages** N-PLURAL **White Pages** is used to refer to the section of a telephone directory which lists names and telephone numbers in alphabetical order.

**white|wash** /waɪtwɒʃ/ N-UNCOUNT **Whitewash** is a mixture of lime or chalk and water that is used for painting walls white.

**whit|tle** /wɪtəl/ (**whittles, whittling, whittled**) [from Old English]
▶ **whittle away** PHR-VERB To **whittle** something **away** or to **whittle** it **down** means to make it smaller or less effective. ❑ *She whittled away all her money.*

**whiz** /wɪz/ (**whizzes, whizzing, whizzed**) also **whizz** V-I If something **whizzes** somewhere, it moves there very fast. [INFORMAL] ❑ *Stewart felt a bottle whiz past his head.*

**whiz kid** (**whiz kids**) N-COUNT If you refer to a young person as a **whiz kid**, you mean that they have achieved success at a young age because they are very clever and very good at something. [INFORMAL] ❑ *...a computer whiz kid.*

**who** /hu/

Usually pronounced /hu/ for meanings **2** and **3**.

Who is used as the subject or object of a verb. See entries at **whom** and **whose**.

**1** PRON You use **who** in questions when you ask about the name or identity of a person or group of people. ❑ *Who's there?* ❑ *Who is the least popular man around here?* ❑ *"You remind me of somebody." — "Who?"* **2** CONJ You use **who** to introduce a clause where you talk about the identity of a person or a group of people. ❑ *Police have not found out who did it.* **3** PRON You use **who** at the beginning of a relative clause when specifying the person or group of people you are talking about or when giving more information about them. ❑ *...a woman who is 23 years old and has two children.* [from Old English]

**WHO** /dʌbəlyu eɪtʃoʊ/ N-PROPER **WHO** is an abbreviation for **World Health Organization**.

**who'd** /hud, hud/ **1** **Who'd** is the usual spoken form of "who had," especially when "had" is an auxiliary verb. **2** **Who'd** is a spoken form of "who would."

**who|ever** /huɛvər/ **1** CONJ You use **whoever** to refer to someone when their identity is not yet known. ❑ *Whoever did this will sooner or later be caught.* ❑ *Whoever wins the prize is going to be famous for life.* **2** CONJ You use **whoever** to indicate that the actual identity of the person who does something will not affect a situation. ❑ *You can have whoever you like visit you.*

**whole** /hoʊl/ (**wholes**) **1** QUANT If you refer to **the whole of** something, you mean all of it. ❑ *This is a problem for the whole of the western world.* ● **Whole**

is also an adjective. ❑ *We spent the whole summer in Italy that year.* **2** N-COUNT A **whole** is a single thing that contains several different parts. ❑ *We should look at the writer's work as a whole, not just in parts.* **3** ADJ If something is **whole**, it is in one piece and is not broken or damaged. ❑ *He took an ice cube from the glass and swallowed it whole.* **4** ADV You use **whole** to emphasize what you are saying. [INFORMAL] ❑ *It was like seeing a whole different side of somebody.* ● **Whole** is also an adjective. ❑ *That saved me a whole bunch of money.* **5** PHRASE If you refer to something **as a whole**, you are referring to it generally and as a single unit. ❑ *He said it was a victory for the people of South Africa as a whole.* **6** PHRASE You use **on the whole** to indicate that what you are saying is true in general but may not be true in every case, or that you are giving a general opinion or summary of something. ❑ *On the whole I agree with him.* [from Old English]

**whole|heart|ed** /hoʊlhɑrtɪd/ ADJ If you support or agree to something in a **wholehearted** way, you support or agree to it enthusiastically and completely. ❑ *You have my wholehearted support.* ● **whole|heart|ed|ly** ADV ❑ *I agree wholeheartedl.*

**whole note** (**whole notes**) N-COUNT A **whole note** is a musical note that has a time value equal to two half notes.

**whole|sale** /hoʊlseɪl/ **1** N-UNCOUNT **Wholesale** is the activity of buying and selling goods in large quantities and therefore at cheaper prices, usually to stores who then sell them to the public. Compare **retail**. [BUSINESS] ❑ *Members can buy goods at wholesale prices.* **2** ADV If something is sold **wholesale**, it is sold in large quantities and at cheaper prices, usually to stores. [BUSINESS] ❑ *The goods are sold wholesale.* **3** ADJ You use **wholesale** to describe the destruction, removal, or changing of something when it affects a very large number of things or people. ❑ *...the company's wholesale reorganization.*

**whole|sal|er** /hoʊlseɪlər/ (**wholesalers**) N-COUNT A **wholesaler** is a person whose business is buying large quantities of goods and selling them in smaller amounts to stores. [BUSINESS]

**whole|some** /hoʊlsəm/ **1** ADJ If you describe something as **wholesome**, you approve of it because you think it is likely to have a positive influence on people's behavior or mental state. ❑ *...wholesome family entertainment.* **2** ADJ If you describe food as **wholesome**, you approve of it because you think it is good for your health. ❑ *...fresh, wholesome ingredients.* [from German]

**who'll** /hul, hul/ **Who'll** is a spoken form of "who will" or "who shall."

**Word Link** *hol ≈ whole* : holistic, holocaust, wholly

**whol|ly** /hoʊlli/ ADV **Wholly** means completely. ❑ *This is a wholly new approach.* [from Old English]

**whom** /hum/

Whom is used in formal or written English instead of "who" when it is the object of a verb or preposition.

**1** PRON You use **whom** in questions when you ask about the name or identity of a person or group of people. ❑ *"I want to send a telegram." — "Fine, to whom?"* ❑ *Whom did he expect to answer his phone?* **2** CONJ You use **whom** to introduce a clause where you talk about the name or identity of a person or a group of people. ❏ *He asked whom I'd told.* **3** PRON You use **whom** at the beginning of a relative clause when specifying the person or group of people you are talking about or when giving more information about them. ❏ *She whooped with delight.* • **Whoop** is also a noun. ❏ *Whoops broke out in the crowd.*

**whoop** /huːp/ (**whoops, whooping, whooped**) V-I If you **whoop**, you shout loudly in a very happy or excited way. [WRITTEN] ❏ *One writer in whom I took an interest was John Grisham.* [from Old English]

**whoop|ing crane** (**whooping cranes**) N-COUNT A **whooping crane** is a rare bird belonging to the crane family that lives only in North America.

**who's** /huːz, huz/ **Who's** is the usual spoken form of "who is" or "who has," especially when "has" is an auxiliary verb. ❏ *Who's going to argue with that?*

**whose** /huːz/

> Usually pronounced /huz/ for meanings **2** and **3**.

**1** PRON You use **whose** at the beginning of a relative clause where you mention something that belongs to or is associated with the person or thing mentioned in the previous clause. ❏ *...a driver whose car was blocking the street.* **2** PRON You use **whose** in questions to ask about the person or thing that something belongs to or is associated with. ❏ *"Whose is this?" — "It's mine."* • **Whose** is also a determiner. ❏ *Whose daughter is she?* **3** DET You use **whose** after certain words, especially verbs and adjectives, to introduce a clause where you talk about the person or thing that something belongs to or is associated with. ❏ *I'm wondering whose mother she is.* ❏ *I can't remember whose idea it was.* [from Old English]

> **Usage** whose
>
> *Whose* and *who's* are often confused. *Whose* expresses possession: *Are you the one whose cell phone kept ringing during class today? Who's* means *who is* or *who has: Who's calling you at this hour? Who's been calling you all night?*

**who've** /huːv, huv/ **Who've** is the usual spoken form of "who have," especially when "have" is an auxiliary verb. ❏ *These are people who've never used a computer before.*

**why** /waɪ/

> The conjunction and the pronoun are usually pronounced /waɪ/.

**1** PRON You use **why** in questions when you ask about the reasons for something. ❏ *Why hasn't he brought the money?* ❏ *Why didn't he stop me?* **2** CONJ You use **why** at the beginning of a clause in which you talk about the reasons for something. ❏ *He couldn't say why the elevator was stuck.* • **Why** is also an adverb. ❏ *I don't know why.* **3** ADV You use **why** with "not" in questions in order to introduce a suggestion. ❏ *Why not give Charmaine a call?* **4** CONVENTION You say **why not** in order to agree with what someone has suggested. ❏ *"Would you like to spend the afternoon with me?" — "Why not?"* **5** EXCLAM People say **"Why!"** at the beginning of a sentence when they are surprised, shocked, or angry. ❏ *Why hello, Tom!* [from Old English]

**wick|ed** /wɪkɪd/ ADJ You use **wicked** to describe someone or something that is very bad and deliberately harmful to people. ❏ *She described the shooting as a wicked attack.* • **wickedness** N-UNCOUNT ❏ *...the wickedness of war.* [from Old English]

**wick|er** /wɪkər/ N-UNCOUNT **Wicker** is long thin sticks, stems, or reeds that have been woven together to make things such as baskets and furniture. ❏ *...a wicker basket.* [of Scandinavian origin]

**wide** /waɪd/ (**wider, widest**) **1** ADJ Something that is **wide** measures a large distance from one side or edge to the other. ❏ *...a shirt with wide sleeves.* **2** ADJ If you open or spread something **wide**, you open or spread it as far as possible or to the fullest extent. ❏ *"It was huge," he announced, spreading his arms wide.* **3** ADJ You use **wide** to talk or ask about how much something measures from one side or edge to the other. ❏ *...a strip of land four miles wide.* ❏ *The road is only one lane wide.* **4** ADJ You use **wide** to describe something that includes a large number of different things or people. ❏ *The brochure offers a wide choice of hotels.* • **wide|ly** ADV ❏ *...the most widely read newspaper in Hungary.* **5** ADJ **Wider** is used to describe something that relates to the most important or general parts of a situation, rather than to the smaller parts or to details. ❏ *He spoke about the wider issues.* [from Old English] **6** **wide awake** → see **awake** **7** **wide of the mark** → see **mark** **8** **wide open** → see **open**

> | **Thesaurus** | wide | Also look up : |
> |---|---|---|
> | ADJ. | broad, large; *(ant.)* narrow **1** **4** | |

> | **Word Partnership** | Use *wide* with : | |
> |---|---|---|
> | N. | wide **grin/smile**, wide **margin**, wide **shoulders 1** arms/eyes/mouth open wide **2** wide **array**, wide **audience**, wide **selection**, wide **variety 4** | |

**wide-eyed** ADJ If you describe someone as **wide-eyed**, you mean that they are inexperienced and innocent, and may be easily impressed. ❏ *She gave him a wide-eyed look.*

**wid|en** /waɪdən/ (**widens, widening, widened**) **1** V-T/V-I If you **widen** something or if it **widens**, it becomes greater in measurement from one side or edge to the other. ❏ *They are planning to widen the road.* **2** V-T/V-I If you **widen** something or if it **widens**, it becomes greater in range or it affects a larger number of people or things. ❏ *The search for the missing boy widened.* [from Old English]

**wide-ranging** ADJ If you describe something as **wide-ranging**, you mean it deals with or affects a great variety of different things. ❏ *...wide-ranging knowledge.*

**wide|screen** /waɪdskriːn/ ADJ A **widescreen** television has a screen that is wide in relation to its height.

**wide|spread** /waɪdspred/ ADJ Something that is **widespread** exists or happens over a large area, or to a great extent. ❏ *Food shortages are widespread.*

**wid|ow** /wɪdoʊ/ (**widows**) N-COUNT A **widow** is a woman whose husband has died and who has not married again. ❏ *She became a widow a year ago.* [from Old English]

**W**

**wid|owed** /wɪdoʊd/ V-T PASSIVE If someone **is widowed**, their husband or wife dies. ❑ *She was widowed last year.* [from Old English]

**wid|ow|er** /wɪdoʊər/ (**widowers**) N-COUNT A **widower** is a man whose wife has died and who has not married again. ❑ *He is a widower and lives in Durango.* [from Old English]

**width** /wɪdθ, wɪtθ/ (**widths**) N-VAR The **width** of something is the distance it measures from one side or edge to the other. ❑ *Measure the full width of the window.*

**wield** /wild/ (**wields, wielding, wielded**) **1** V-T If you **wield** a weapon, tool, or piece of equipment, you carry and use it. ❑ *He saw a man wielding a knife.* **2** V-T If someone **wields** power, they have it and are able to use it. ❑ *He is still chairman, but wields little power at the company.* [from Old English]

**wie|ner** /winər/ (**wieners**) also **weenie** or **wienie** N-COUNT **Wieners** are sausages made from smoked beef or pork. [from German]

**wife** /waɪf/ (**wives**) N-COUNT A man's **wife** is the woman he is married to. ❑ *He married his wife Jane 37 years ago.* [from Old English]
→ see **family, love**

**wig** /wɪg/ (**wigs**) N-COUNT A **wig** is a covering of false hair that you wear on your head.

**wig|gle** /wɪgᵊl/ (**wiggles, wiggling, wiggled**) V-T/V-I If you **wiggle** something or if it **wiggles**, it moves up and down or from side to side in small quick movements. ❑ *She wiggled her finger.* ● **Wiggle** is also a noun. ❑ *If you haven't caught a fish yet, try giving the fishing line a wiggle!* [from Middle Low German]

**wild** /waɪld/ (**wilds, wilder, wildest**) **1** ADJ **Wild** animals or plants live or grow in natural surroundings and are not taken care of by people. ❑ *...wild cats.* **2** ADJ **Wild** land is natural and is not used by people. ❑ *...a wild area of woods and lakes.* **3** N-PLURAL **The wilds** of a place are the natural areas that are far away from cities and towns. ❑ *...the wilds of Canada.* **4** ADJ **Wild** behavior is uncontrolled, excited, or energetic. ❑ *The crowds went wild when they saw him.* ● **wild|ly** ADV ❑ *As she finished each song, the crowd clapped wildly.* **5** ADJ A **wild** idea is unusual or extreme. A **wild** guess is one that you make without much thought. ❑ *Go on, take a wild guess.* ● **wild|ly** ADV ❑ *"Thirteen?" he guessed wildly.* **6** → see also **wildly** [from Old English] **7** beyond your **wildest dreams** → see **dream** **8** in your **wildest dreams** → see **dream** **9** to **sow** your **wild oats** → see **oats**
→ see **carnivore**

| Thesaurus | *wild* | Also look up : |
|---|---|---|
| ADJ. | desolate, natural, overgrown **2** excited, rowdy, uncontrolled **4** | |

| Word Partnership | Use *wild* with : |
|---|---|
| N. | wild **animal**, wild **beasts/creatures**, wild **game**, wild **horse**, wild **mushrooms** **1** |
| V. | go wild, run wild **4** |

**wil|der|ness** /wɪldərnɛs/ (**wildernesses**) N-COUNT A **wilderness** is a desert or other area of natural land which is not used by people. ❑ *...the icy Canadian wilderness.* [from Old English]

**wild|life** /waɪldlaɪf/ N-UNCOUNT You can use **wildlife** to refer to the animals and other living things that live in the wild. ❑ *The area is rich in wildlife.*
→ see **zoo**

**wild|ly** /waɪldli/ **1** ADV You use **wildly** to emphasize the degree, amount, or intensity of something. ❑ *Milk costs twice what it should and meat is also wildly over-priced.* [from Old English] **2** → see also **wild**

---
### will

❶ MODAL VERB USES
❷ WANTING SOMETHING TO HAPPEN
---

**❶ will** /wɪl/

> Will is a modal verb. It is used with the base form of a verb. In spoken English and informal written English, the form **won't** is often used in negative statements.

**1** MODAL You use **will** to indicate that you hope, think, or have evidence that something is going to happen or be the case in the future. ❑ *Will you ever be happy here?* ❑ *The ship will not be ready for a month.* **2** MODAL You use **will** to indicate your intention to do something. ❑ *Will you be staying?* ❑ *What will you do next?* **3** MODAL You use **will** in questions in order to make polite invitations or offers. ❑ *Will you stay for supper?* ❑ *Will you have dinner with me?* **4** MODAL You use **will** to say that someone is willing to do something. You use **will not** or **won't** to indicate that someone refuses to do something. ❑ *I'll answer the phone.* [from Old English] **5** → see also **willing**

**❷ will** /wɪl/ (**wills, willing, willed**) **1** N-VAR **Will** is the determination to do something. ❑ *He has lost his will to live.* **2** → see also **free will 3** N-SING If something is **the will of** a person or group of people with authority, they want it to happen. ❑ *...the will of God.* **4** V-T If you **will** something to happen, you try to make it happen by using mental effort rather than physical effort. ❑ *I looked at the telephone, willing it to ring.* **5** N-COUNT A **will** is a document in which you say what you want to happen to your money and property when you die. [from Old English]

**will|ful** /wɪlfəl/ **1** ADJ If you describe actions or attitudes as **willful**, you are critical of them because they are done or expressed deliberately, especially with the intention of causing someone harm. ❑ *...willful damage to property.* ● **willfully** ADV ❑ *They willfully committed the crime.* **2** ADJ If you describe someone as **willful**, you mean that they are determined to do what they want to do, even if it is not a good idea. ❑ *Molly was sometimes impatient and willful.* [from Old English]

**will|ing** /wɪlɪŋ/ **1** ADJ If someone is **willing to** do something, they are fairly happy about doing it and will do it if they are asked or required to do it. ❑ *She's willing to answer questions.* ● **willingly** ADV ❑ *Bryant talked willingly to the police.* ● **willingness** N-UNCOUNT ❑ *She showed her willingness to work hard.* **2** ADJ **Willing** is used to describe someone who does something fairly enthusiastically and because they want to do it rather than because they are forced to do it. ❑ *He was a natural and willing*

W

learner. [from Old English] **3 God willing** → see
**god**

**wil|low** /wɪloʊ/ (**willows**) N-VAR A **willow** or a
**willow tree** is a type of tree with long branches
and long narrow leaves that grows near water.
[from Old English]

**will|power** /wɪlpaʊər/ also **will-power, will
power** N-UNCOUNT **Willpower** is a very strong
determination to do something. □ He has the
willpower to succeed.

**wilt** /wɪlt/ (**wilts, wilting, wilted**) V-I If a plant
**wilts**, it gradually bends downward and becomes
weak because it needs more water or is dying.
[from Middle Dutch]

**wily** /waɪli/ (**wilier, wiliest**) ADJ If you describe
someone or their behavior as **wily**, you mean
that they are clever at achieving what they
want, especially by tricking people. □ He is a wily
politician. [from Old Norse]

**wimp** /wɪmp/ (**wimps**) N-COUNT If you call
someone a **wimp**, you disapprove of them because
they lack confidence or determination, or because
they are often afraid of things. [INFORMAL] □ He
told people I was a wimp.

**win** /wɪn/ (**wins, winning, won**) **1** V-T/V-I If
you **win** something such as a competition, battle,
or argument, you defeat those people you are
competing or fighting against, or you do better
than everyone else involved. □ He does not have
a chance of winning the fight. □ The top four teams
all won. N-COUNT ● **Win** is also a noun. □ They
played eight games without a win. **2** V-T If you **win**
something such as a prize or medal, you get
it because you have defeated everyone else in
something such as an election, competition,
battle, or argument, or have done very well in it.
□ The first correct entry wins the prize. **3** V-T If you
**win** something that you want or need, you succeed
in getting it. □ ...moves to win the support of the poor.
[from Old English] **4** → see also **winning 5** to
**win hands down** → see **hand**

▶ **win over** PHR-VERB If you **win** someone **over**,
you persuade them to support you or agree with
you. □ Not everyone agrees but I am winning them over.

| **Thesaurus** | win | Also look up : |
|---|---|---|
| v. | conquer, succeed, triumph; (ant.) lose **1** | |
| N. | conquest, success, victory; (ant.) defeat **1** | |

**wince** /wɪns/ (**winces, wincing, winced**) V-I
If you **wince**, the muscles of your face tighten
suddenly because you have felt a pain or because
you have experienced something unpleasant.
□ Every time he stepped on his left foot he winced in pain.

[from Old French]

**winch** /wɪntʃ/ (**winches, winching, winched**)
**1** N-COUNT A **winch** is a machine that is used to
lift heavy objects. It consists of a cylinder around
which a rope or chain is wound. **2** V-T If you
**winch** an object or person somewhere, you lift or
lower them using a winch. □ Rescuers winched the
men to safety. [from Old English]

---

## wind

**❶** AIR
**❷** TURNING OR WRAPPING

---

**❶ wind** /wɪnd/ (**winds, winding, winded**)
**1** N-VAR A **wind** is a current of air that is moving
across the Earth's surface. □ A strong wind was
blowing. **2** V-T If you **are winded** by something
such as a blow, the air is suddenly knocked
out of your lungs so that you have difficulty
breathing for a short time. □ He was winded by the
fall. **3** N-UNCOUNT **Wind** energy or **wind** power is
energy or power that is obtained from the wind,
for example by the use of a turbine. [from Old
English]
→ see Word Web: **wind**
→ see **beach, electricity, erosion, hurricane, storm,
wave**

| **Word Partnership** | Use *wind* with : |
|---|---|
| ADJ. | **cold** wind, **hot** wind, **howling** wind, **icy** wind, **warm** wind **❶ 1** |
| N. | **desert** wind, **gust** of wind, **wind** power, **winter** wind **❶ 1** |
| V. | wind **blows, blown/driven by** the wind, wind **whips ❶ 1** |

**❷ wind** /waɪnd/ (**winds, winding, wound**)
**1** V-T/V-I If a road, river, or line of people **winds**
in a particular direction, it goes in that direction
with a lot of bends or twists in it. □ The road winds
along by the river. **2** V-T When you **wind** something
flexible around something else, you wrap it
around it several times. □ She wound the rope around
her waist. **3** V-T When you **wind** a mechanical
device, for example, a watch or a clock, you turn a
knob, key, or handle on it several times in order to
make it operate.

▶ **wind down** PHR-VERB If someone **winds down**
a business or activity, they gradually reduce the
amount of work that is done or the number of
people that are involved, usually before closing
or stopping it completely. □ Aid workers have begun
winding down their operation.

▶ **wind up 1** PHR-VERB When you **wind up**
an activity, you finish it or stop doing it. □ The

---

## Word Web    wind

The earth's surface **temperature** isn't the same everywhere. This temperature
difference causes **air** to move from one area to another. We call this airflow
**wind**. As warm air expands and rises, air pressure goes down. Then denser
cool air **blows** in. The amount of difference in air pressure determines how
strong the wind will be. It can be anything from a **breeze** to a **gale**. The earth's
geography creates **prevailing winds**. For example, air in the warmer areas near
the Equator is always rising, and cooler air from polar regions is always flowing
in to take its place.

*president is winding up his visit to Somalia.* **2** → see also **wound up**

**wind chill fac|tor** also **wind-chill factor** or **windchill factor** N-SING A **wind chill factor** is a measure of the cooling effect of the wind on the temperature of the air. ❑ ...*a wind chill factor of 80 degrees below zero.*

**wind|fall** /wɪndfɔl/ (**windfalls**) N-COUNT A **windfall** is a sum of money that you receive unexpectedly. ❑ *He received a $250,000 windfall.*

**wind|mill** /wɪndmɪl/ (**windmills**) N-COUNT A **windmill** is a building with long pieces of wood on the outside that turn as the wind blows and provide energy. **Windmills** are used to grind grain or pump water.

windmill

**win|dow** /wɪndoʊ/ (**windows**) **1** N-COUNT A **window** is a space in the wall of a building or in the side of a vehicle, which has glass in it so that light can come in and you can see out. ❑ *He looked out of the window.* **2** N-COUNT On a computer screen, a **window** is one of the work areas that the screen can be divided into. [COMPUTING] ❑ *Open the document in a new window.* [from Old Norse]

**win|dow shade** (**window shades**) N-COUNT A **window shade** is a piece of stiff cloth or heavy paper that you can pull down over a window as a covering.

**wind|shield** /wɪndʃild/ (**windshields**) N-COUNT The **windshield** of a car or other vehicle is the glass window at the front through which the driver looks.

**wind|shield wip|er** (**windshield wipers**) N-COUNT A **windshield wiper** is a device that wipes rain from a vehicle's windshield.

**wind|sock** /wɪndsɒk/ (**windsocks**) also **wind sock** N-COUNT A **windsock** is a device, consisting of a tube of cloth mounted on a pole, that is used at airports and airfields to indicate the direction and force of the wind.

**wind vane** (**wind vanes**) N-COUNT A **wind vane** is a metal object on the roof of a building that turns around as the wind blows. It is used to show the direction of the wind.

**windy** /wɪndi/ (**windier, windiest**) ADJ If it is **windy**, the wind is blowing a lot. ❑ *The sun*

*was setting after a day of windy weather.* [from Old English]

**wine** /waɪn/ (**wines**) N-VAR **Wine** is an alcoholic drink made from grapes. ❑ ...*a bottle of white wine.* [from Old English]

**wine bar** (**wine bars**) N-COUNT A **wine bar** is a place where people can buy and drink wine, and sometimes eat food as well.

**win|ery** /waɪnəri/ (**wineries**) N-COUNT A **winery** is a place where wine is made. [from Old English]

**wing** /wɪŋ/ (**wings**) **1** N-COUNT The **wings** of a bird or insect are the two parts of its body that it uses for flying. ❑ *The bird flapped its wings.* **2** N-COUNT The **wings** of an airplane are the long flat parts sticking out of its side which support it while it is flying. ❑ *The plane dipped its wings, then circled back.* **3** N-COUNT A **wing** of a building is a part of it that sticks out from the main part. ❑ *Her office was in the west wing of the building.* **4** N-COUNT A **wing** of an organization, especially a political organization, is a group within it which has a particular function or particular beliefs. ❑ ...*the military wing of the African National Congress.* **5** → see also **left-wing, right-wing** **6** N-PLURAL In a theater, **the wings** are the sides of the stage that are hidden from the audience by curtains or scenery. ❑ *I watched the start of the play from the wings.* [of Scandinavian origin] → see **bird, insect**

**winged** /wɪŋd/ ADJ A **winged** insect or other creature has wings. [of Scandinavian origin]

**wink** /wɪŋk/ (**winks, winking, winked**) V-I When you **wink at** someone, you look toward them and close one eye very briefly, usually as a signal that something is a joke or a secret. ● **Wink** is also a noun. ❑ *I gave her a wink.* [from Old English]

**win|ner** /wɪnər/ (**winners**) N-COUNT The **winner** of a prize, race, or competition is the person, animal, or thing that wins it. ❑ *She will present the prizes to the winners.* [from Old English]

**win|ning** /wɪnɪŋ/ **1** ADJ You can use **winning** to describe a person or thing that wins something such as a competition, game, or election. ❑ ...*the winning ticket.* **2** ADJ You can use **winning** to describe actions or qualities that please other people and make them feel friendly toward you. ❑ *She gave him a winning smile.* [from Old English] **3** → see also **win**

**win|nings** /wɪnɪŋz/ N-PLURAL You can use **winnings** to refer to the money that someone wins in a competition. ❑ *I have come to collect my winnings.* [from Old English]

**win|ter** /wɪntər/ (**winters**) N-VAR **Winter** is the season between fall and spring. In the winter the weather is usually cold. ❑ *In winter the nights are long and cold.* [from Old English]

**wipe** /waɪp/ (**wipes, wiping, wiped**) **1** V-T If you **wipe** something, you rub its surface to remove dirt or liquid from it. ❑ *I'll just wipe my hands.* ● **Wipe** is also a noun. ❑ *I'm going to give the table a good wipe.* **2** V-T If you **wipe** dirt or liquid from something, you remove it by using a cloth or your hand. ❑ *Gary* *wiped the sweat from his face.* [from Old English]

▶ **wipe out** PHR-VERB To **wipe out** something such as a place or a group of people or animals means to destroy them completely. ❏ *The disease wiped out thousands of birds.*

| **Word Partnership** | Use *wipe* with : |
| --- | --- |
| ADJ. | wipe *something* **clean** 1 |
| N. | wipe **blood**, wipe *your* **eyes**, wipe *someone's* **face**, wipe **tears** 2 |

**wire** /waɪər/ (**wires**) 1 N-VAR A **wire** is a long thin piece of metal that is used to fasten things or to carry electric current. ❏ *...fine copper wire.* [from Old English] 2 → see also **barbed wire** → see **metal**

**wired** /waɪərd/ ADJ If someone is **wired**, they are tense, nervous, and unable to relax. [INFORMAL] ❏ *They were so wired with fear that they could not sleep.* [from Old English]

| **Word Link** | less ≈ without : endless, hopeless, wireless |
| --- | --- |

**wire|less** /waɪərlɪs/ ADJ **Wireless** technology uses radio waves rather than electricity and therefore does not require any wires. ❏ *...the fast-growing wireless communication market.* [from Old English] → see **cellphone**

**wir|ing** /waɪərɪŋ/ N-UNCOUNT The **wiring** in a building or machine is the system of wires that supplies electricity to the different parts of it. ❏ *Bad wiring is the main cause of house fires.* [from Old English]

**wiry** /waɪəri/ 1 ADJ Someone who is **wiry** is somewhat thin but is also strong. ❏ *His body is wiry and athletic.* 2 ADJ Something such as hair or grass that is **wiry** is stiff and rough to touch. [from Old English]

| **Word Link** | dom ≈ state of being : boredom, freedom, wisdom |
| --- | --- |

**wis|dom** /wɪzdəm/ 1 N-UNCOUNT **Wisdom** is the ability to use your experience and knowledge in order to make sensible decisions or judgments. ❏ *...the wisdom that comes from old age.* 2 N-SING If you talk about **the wisdom of** a particular decision or action, you are talking about how sensible it is. ❏ *They are questioning the wisdom of the plan.* [from Old English]

**wise** /waɪz/ (**wiser, wisest**) ADJ A **wise** person is able to use their experience and knowledge in order to make sensible decisions and judgments. ❏ *She's a wise woman.* • **wise|ly** ADV ❏ *They spent their money wisely.* [from Old English]

**wish** /wɪʃ/ (**wishes, wishing, wished**) 1 N-COUNT A **wish** is a desire for something. ❏ *Her wish is to become a doctor.* 2 V-T/V-I If you **wish** to do something, you want to do it. [FORMAL] ❏ *I wish to leave a message.* ❏ *We can do as we wish now.* 3 V-T If you **wish** something were true, you would like it to be true, even though you know that it is impossible or unlikely. ❏ *I wish I could do that.* 4 V-I If you **wish for** something, you express the desire for that thing silently to yourself. In fairy tales, when a person wishes for something, the thing they wish for often happens by magic. ❏ *Be careful what you wish for. You might get it!* • **Wish** is also a

noun. ❏ *Did you make a wish?* 5 V-T If you **wish** someone something such as luck or happiness, you express the hope that they will be lucky or happy. ❏ *I wish you both a good trip.* 6 N-PLURAL If you express your good **wishes** toward someone, you are politely expressing your friendly feelings toward them and your hope that they will be successful or happy. ❏ *Please give him my best wishes.* [from Old English]

| **Word Partnership** | Use *wish* with : |
| --- | --- |
| V. | wish **come true**, **get your** wish, **grant a** wish, **have a** wish 1 4 |
| N. | wish *someone* **the best**, wish *someone* **luck** 5 |

**wish|ful think|ing** N-UNCOUNT If you say that an idea or hope is **wishful thinking**, you mean that it is unlikely to come true. ❏ *It is wishful thinking to expect him to change.*

**wist|ful** /wɪstfəl/ ADJ Someone who is **wistful** is sad because they want something and know that they cannot have it. ❏ *He looked a little wistful.* • **wistfully** ADV ❏ *"I wish I had a little brother," said Daphne wistfully.*

**wit** /wɪt/ (**wits**) 1 N-UNCOUNT **Wit** is the ability to use words or ideas in an amusing, clever, and imaginative way. ❏ *He writes with great wit.* 2 N-PLURAL You can refer to your ability to think quickly and effectively in a difficult situation as your **wits**. ❏ *She has used her wits to get to where she is today.* [from Old English]

**witch** /wɪtʃ/ (**witches**) N-COUNT In fairy tales, a **witch** is a woman, usually an old woman, who has evil magic powers. [from Old English]

**witch|craft** /wɪtʃkræft/ N-UNCOUNT **Witchcraft** is the use of magic powers, especially evil ones.

**witch hunt** (**witch hunts**) N-COUNT A **witch hunt** is an attempt to find and punish a particular group of people who are being blamed for something, often simply because of their opinions and not because they have actually done anything wrong. ❏ *...a political witch hunt.*

**with** /wɪð, wɪθ/

In addition to the uses shown below, **with** is used after some verbs, nouns and adjectives in order to introduce extra information. **With** is also used in most reciprocal verbs, such as "agree" or "fight," and in some phrasal verbs, such as "deal with" and "go along with."

1 PREP If one person is **with** another, they are together in one place. ❏ *Her son and daughter were with her.* 2 PREP If you discuss something **with** someone, or if you fight or argue **with** someone, you are both involved in a discussion, fight, or argument. ❏ *We didn't discuss it with each other.* ❏ *About a thousand students fought with police.* 3 PREP If you do something **with** a particular tool, object, or substance, you do it using that tool, object, or substance. ❏ *Turn the meat over with a fork.* ❏ *I don't allow my children to eat with their fingers.* 4 PREP If someone stands or goes somewhere **with** something, they are carrying it. ❏ *A woman came in with a cup of coffee.* 5 PREP Someone or something **with** a particular feature or possession has that feature or possession. ❏ *He was tall, with blue eyes.* 6 PREP If something is filled or covered **with** a substance or **with** things, it has

**W**

that substance or those things in it or on it. ❑ *His legs were covered with dirt.* **7** PREP You use **with** to indicate what a state, quality, or action relates to, involves, or affects. ❑ *He has a problem with money.* ❑ *I'm familiar with the neighborhood.* **8** PREP You use **with** when indicating the way that something is done or the feeling that a person has when they do something. ❑ *He listened with great care.* **9** PREP You use **with** when indicating a sound or gesture that is made when something is done, or an expression that a person has on their face when they do something. ❑ *"It's still early," he said with a smile.* ❑ *The front door closed with a crash.* **10** PREP You use **with** to indicate the feeling that makes someone have a particular appearance or type of behavior. ❑ *Gil was white and shaking with anger.* **11** PREP You use **with** when mentioning the position or appearance of a person or thing at the time that they do something, or what someone else is doing at that time. ❑ *Joanne stood with her hands on the sink, staring out the window.* **12** PREP You use **with** to introduce a current situation that is a factor affecting another situation. ❑ *With all the bad things that have happened, he's had a difficult year.* [from Old English]

> **Word Link** with ≈ against, away : with*draw*, with*hold*, with*stand*

**with|draw** /wɪðdrɔ, wɪθ-/ (**withdraws, withdrawing, withdrew, withdrawn**) **1** V-T If you **withdraw** something from a place, you remove it or take it away. [FORMAL] ❑ *He reached into his pocket and withdrew a sheet of paper.* **2** V-T/V-I When groups of people such as troops **withdraw** or when someone **withdraws** them, they leave the place where they are fighting or where they are based and return nearer home. ❑ *The army will withdraw as soon as the war ends.* **3** V-T If you **withdraw** money from a bank account, you take it out of that account. ❑ *He withdrew $750 from his account.* **4** V-I If you **withdraw from** an activity or organization, you stop taking part in it. ❑ *...the second tennis player to withdraw from the games.*

> **Word Partnership** Use *withdraw* with :
>
> N. withdraw **an offer**, withdraw **support 1**
> **decision to** withdraw **1** – **4**
> **deadline to** withdraw, **forces/troops** withdraw **2**
> withdraw **money 3**

**with|draw|al** /wɪðdrɔəl, wɪθ-/ (**withdrawals**) **1** N-VAR The **withdrawal** of something is the act or process of removing it, or ending it. [FORMAL] ❑ *...the withdrawal of food and medical treatment.* **2** N-UNCOUNT Someone's **withdrawal from** an activity or an organization is their decision to stop taking part in it. ❑ *...his withdrawal from government in 1946.* **3** N-COUNT A **withdrawal** is an amount of money that you take from your bank account. ❑ *I went to the cash machine to make a withdrawal.*

**with|drawn** /wɪðdrɔn, wɪθ-/ **1** Withdrawn is the past participle of **withdraw**. **2** ADJ Someone who is **withdrawn** is very quiet, and does not want to talk to other people. ❑ *Her husband became withdrawn and difficult to talk to.*

**with|drew** /wɪðdru, wɪθ-/ Withdrew is the past tense of **withdraw**.

**with|er** /wɪðər/ (**withers, withering, withered**) **1** V-I If someone or something **withers**, they become very weak. ❑ *Her right arm began to wither as a result of the disease.* **2** V-I If a flower or plant **withers**, it dries up and dies. ❑ *The tree withered all the way down to its roots.* [from German]

**with|ered** /wɪðərd/ ADJ If you describe a person or a part of their body as **withered**, you mean that they are thin and their skin looks old. ❑ *...her withered hands.* [from German]

**with|hold** /wɪðhoʊld, wɪθ-/ (**withholds, withholding, withheld** /wɪðhɛld, wɪθ-/) V-T If you **withhold** something that someone wants, you do not let them have it. [FORMAL] ❑ *Police withheld the man's name until they could tell his family about the accident.*

**with|in** /wɪðɪn, wɪθ-/ **1** PREP If something is **within** a place, area, or object, it is inside it or surrounded by it. [FORMAL] ❑ *The sports fields must be within the city.* ● **Within** is also an adverb. ❑ *A small voice called from within. "Yes, I'm just coming."* **2** PREP Something that happens or exists **within** a society, organization, or system, happens or exists inside it. ❑ *He is working within a system that doesn't allow him to make many changes.* ● **Within** is also an adverb. ❑ *The real dangers came from within.* **3** PREP If something is **within** a particular limit or set of rules, it does not go beyond it or is not more than what is allowed. ❑ *He had to stay within a range of five miles.* **4** PREP If you are **within** a particular distance of a place, you are less than that distance from it. ❑ *The man was within a few feet of him.* **5** PREP **Within** a particular length of time means before that length of time has passed. ❑ *Within twenty-four hours I had the money.* **6** PREP If something is **within sight**, **within earshot**, or **within reach**, you can see it, hear it, or reach it. ❑ *He parked the car within sight of Sandra's house.* **7** **within reason** → see **reason**

**with|out** /wɪðaʊt, wɪθ-/

> In addition to the uses shown below, **without** is used in the phrasal verbs "do without" and "go without".

**1** PREP You use **without** to indicate that someone or something does not have or use the thing mentioned. ❑ *I don't like him without a beard.* ❑ *You shouldn't drive without a seat belt.* **2** PREP If one thing happens **without** another thing, or if you do something **without** doing something else, the second thing does not happen or occur. ❑ *He left without speaking to me.* ❑ *They worked without stopping until about eight in the evening.* **3** PREP If you do something **without** a particular feeling, you do not have that feeling when you do it. ❑ *"Hello, David," he said without surprise.* **4** PREP If you do something **without** someone else, they are not in the same place as you are or are not involved in the same action as you. ❑ *I told Frank to start dinner without me.*

**with|stand** /wɪðstænd, wɪθ-/ (**withstands, withstanding, withstood**) V-T If something or someone **withstands** a force or action, they survive it or do not give in to it. [FORMAL] ❑ *The building should withstand an earthquake.*

**wit|ness** /wɪtnɪs/ (**witnesses, witnessing, witnessed**) **1** N-COUNT A **witness** to an event such as an accident or crime is a person who saw it. ❑ *Witnesses say they saw an explosion.*

**2** V-T If you **witness** something, you see it happen. ❑ *Anyone who witnessed the attack should call the police.* **3** N-COUNT A **witness** is someone who appears in a court of law to say what they know about a crime or other event. ❑ *Eleven witnesses appeared in court.* **4** N-COUNT A **witness** is someone who writes their name on a document that you have signed, to confirm that it really is your signature. ❑ *You must sign the document in front of two witnesses.* **5** V-T If someone **witnesses** your signature on a document, they write their name after it, to confirm that it really is your signature. [from Old English]
→ see **trial, wedding**

**wit|ness stand** N-SING The **witness stand** in a court of law is the place where people stand or sit when they are giving evidence. ❑ *O'Donnell took the witness stand Thursday.*

**wit|ty** /wɪti/ (**wittier, wittiest**) ADJ Someone or something that is **witty** is amusing in a clever way. ❑ *His books were very witty.* [from Old English]

**wives** /waɪvz/ **Wives** is the plural of **wife.** [from Old English]

**wiz|ard** /wɪzərd/ (**wizards**) **1** N-COUNT In legends and fairy tales, a **wizard** is a man who has magic powers. **2** N-COUNT If you admire someone because they are very good at doing a particular thing, you can say that they are a **wizard.** ❑ *...a financial wizard.* **3** N-COUNT A **wizard** is a computer program that guides you through the stages of a particular task. [COMPUTING]
→ see **fantasy**

**WMD** /dʌbªlyu ɛm di/ N-PLURAL **WMD** is an abbreviation for **weapons of mass destruction.**

**wob|ble** /wɒbªl/ (**wobbles, wobbling, wobbled**) V-I If something or someone **wobbles**, they make small movements from side to side, for example, because they are unsteady. ❑ *A cyclist wobbled into my path.* [from Low German]

**wob|bly** /wɒbli/ ADJ Something that is **wobbly** moves unsteadily from side to side. ❑ *...a wobbly plastic chair.* [from Low German]

**woe** /woʊ/ N-UNCOUNT **Woe** is great sadness. [LITERARY] ❑ *He listened to my tale of woe.* [from Old English]

**woe|ful** /woʊfəl/ ADJ You can use **woeful** to emphasize that something is very bad or undesirable. ❑ *...another woeful mistake.* • **woe|ful|ly** ADV ❑ *I have a woefully short time to finish the job.* [from Old English]

**woke** /woʊk/ **Woke** is the past tense of **wake.** [from Old English]

**wok|en** /woʊkən/ **Woken** is the past participle of **wake.** [from Old English]

**wolf** /wʊlf/ (**wolves, wolfs, wolfing, wolfed**) **1** N-COUNT A **wolf** is a wild animal that looks like a large dog. **2** V-T If someone **wolfs** their food, they eat it all very quickly and greedily. [INFORMAL] ❑ *He wolfed doughnuts and pastries.* • **Wolf down** means the same as **wolf.** ❑ *He wolfed down the rest of the sandwich.* [from Old English]

**wolf**

→ see **carnivore**

**wom|an** /wʊmən/ (**women**) N-COUNT A **woman** is an adult female human being. ❑ *My favorite woman is my mother.* [from Old English]
→ see **age**

**wom|an|hood** /wʊmənhʊd/ N-UNCOUNT **Womanhood** is the state of being a woman rather than a girl, or the period of a woman's adult life. ❑ *...young girls approaching womanhood.* [from Old English]

**womb** /wum/ (**wombs**) N-COUNT A woman's **womb** is the part inside her body where a baby grows before it is born. ❑ *...an unborn child in the womb.* [from Old English]

**wom|en** /wɪmɪn/ **Women** is the plural of **woman.** [from Old English]

**wom|en's room** (**women's rooms**) N-COUNT The **women's room** is a toilet for women in a public building.

**wom|en's shel|ter** (**women's shelters**) N-COUNT A **women's shelter** is a place where women can go for safety and protection, for example, if they feel threatened by violence.

**won** /wʌn/ **Won** is the past tense and past participle of **win.**
→ see **election**

**won|der** /wʌndər/ (**wonders, wondering, wondered**) **1** V-T/V-I If you **wonder** about something, you think about it, and try to guess or understand more about it. ❑ *I wondered what the noise was.* ❑ *"We've been wondering about him," said Max.* **2** V-T/V-I If you **wonder at** something, you are very surprised about it or think about it in a very surprised way. ❑ *Angie wondered at her calmness.* **3** N-SING If you say that it is a **wonder** that something happened, you mean that it is very surprising and unexpected. ❑ *It's a wonder that we're still friends.* **4** N-UNCOUNT **Wonder** is a feeling of great surprise and pleasure that you have, for example, when you see something that is very beautiful, or when something happens that you thought was impossible. ❑ *"That's right!" Bobby shouted in wonder.* **5** N-COUNT A **wonder** is something that causes people to feel great surprise or admiration. ❑ *...the wonders of nature.* **6** PHRASE If you say "**no wonder**," "**little wonder,**" or "**small wonder,**" you mean that something is not surprising. ❑ *No wonder my brother wasn't feeling well.* **7** PHRASE If you say that a person or thing **works wonders** or **does wonders,** you mean that they have a very good effect on something. ❑ *A few hours' sleep can work wonders.* [from Old English]

**won|der|ful** /wʌndərfəl/ ADJ If you describe something or someone as **wonderful,** you think they are extremely good. ❑ *The cold air felt wonderful on his face.* ❑ *It's wonderful to see you.* • **won|der|ful|ly** ADV ❑ *The vegetables are wonderfully tasty.* [from Old English]

**won't** /woʊnt/ **Won't** is the usual spoken form of "will not." ❑ *I won't hurt you.*

**woo** /wu/ (**woos, wooing, wooed**) V-T If you **woo** people, you try to encourage them to help you, support you, or vote for you, for example, by promising them things which they would like. ❑ *They wooed them with gifts.* [from Old English]
→ see **love**

**W**

**wood** /wʊd/ (**woods**) **1** N-VAR **Wood** is the material that forms the trunks and branches of trees. ❑ *Some houses are made of wood.* **2** N-COUNT A **wood** or **woods** is a fairly large area of trees growing near each other. ❑ *We went for a walk in the woods.* [from Old English]
→ see **energy, fire, forest**

**wood|ed** /wʊdɪd/ ADJ A **wooded** area is covered in trees. ❑ *...a wooded valley.* [from Old English]

**wood|en** /wʊdᵊn/ ADJ **Wooden** objects are made of wood. ❑ *...wooden chair.* [from Old English]

**wood|land** /wʊdlənd/ (**woodlands**) N-VAR **Woodland** is land with a lot of trees. ❑ *...an area of dense woodland.*

**woods|man** /wʊdzmən/ (**woodsmen**) also **woodman** N-COUNT A **woodsman** is a person who cuts down trees for timber, or a person who lives in a wood.

**wood|work** /wʊdwɜrk/ N-UNCOUNT You can refer to the doors and other wooden parts of a house as the **woodwork**. ❑ *I love the living room, with its dark woodwork.*

woodwork

**wood|work|ing** /wʊdwɜrkɪŋ/ N-UNCOUNT **Woodworking** is the activity or skill of making things out of wood. ❑ *He taught himself woodworking after he retired five years ago.*

**wool** /wʊl/ (**wools**) **1** N-UNCOUNT **Wool** is the hair that grows on sheep and on some other animals. **2** N-VAR **Wool** is a material made from animal's wool that is used to make things such as clothes, blankets, and carpets. ❑ *...a wool coat.* [from Old English]

**wool|en** /wʊlən/ ADJ **Woolen** clothes or materials are made from wool. ❑ *...thick woolen socks.* [from Old English]

**wool|ly** /wʊli/ also **wooly** ADJ Something that is **woolly** is made of wool or looks like wool. ❑ *...a woolly hat.* [from Old English]

---
**word**
**❶** NOUN AND VERB USES
**❷** PHRASES
---

**❶ word** /wɜrd/ (**words, wording, worded**)
**1** N-COUNT A **word** is a single unit of language that can be represented in writing or speech. In English, a word has a space on either side of it when it is written. ❑ *How many words do you see on this page?* **2** N-SING If you have **a word** with someone, you have a short conversation with them, usually in private. [SPOKEN] ❑ *I think you should have a word with him.* **3** N-COUNT If you offer someone **a word of** something such as warning, advice, or praise, you warn, advise, or praise them. ❑ *I'd like to say a word of thanks to all the people who helped me.* **4** N-SING If you say that someone does **not** hear, understand, or say **a word**, you are emphasizing that they hear, understand, or say nothing at all. ❑ *I can't understand a word she says.* **5** N-UNCOUNT If there is **word** of something, people receive news or information about it. ❑ *Is there any word on Joyce's husband?* **6** N-SING If you

give your **word**, you make a sincere promise to someone. ❑ *He gave his word the boy would be safe.* **7** V-T To **word** something in a particular way means to choose or use particular words to express it. ❑ *He worded his letter carefully.* ● **-worded** ADJ ❑ *...a strongly-worded speech.* [from Old English] **8** → see also **wording**

**❷ word** /wɜrd/ (**words**) **1** PHRASE If someone has **the last word** or **the final word** in a discussion, argument, or disagreement, they are the one who wins it or who makes the final decision. ❑ *She likes to have the last word in any discussion.* **2** PHRASE You say **in other words** in order to introduce a different, and usually simpler, explanation or interpretation of something that has just been said. ❑ *Ray is in charge of the office. In other words, he's my boss.* **3** PHRASE If you repeat something **word for word**, you repeat it exactly as it was originally said or written. ❑ *I learned the song word for word.* [from Old English] **4** **the operative word** → see **operative**
→ see **English**

**word|ing** /wɜrdɪŋ/ N-UNCOUNT The **wording** of a piece of writing or a speech are the words used in it, especially when these are chosen to have a particular effect. ❑ *I checked the wording of the report.* [from Old English]

**word pro|cess|ing** also **word-processing** N-UNCOUNT **Word processing** is the work or skill of producing printed documents using a computer. [COMPUTING]

**word pro|ces|sor** (**word processors**) N-COUNT A **word processor** is a computer program or a computer which is used to produce printed documents. [COMPUTING]

**word rec|og|ni|tion** N-UNCOUNT **Word recognition** is the ability to recognize a written word and to know how it is pronounced and what it means.

**wore** /wɔr/ **Wore** is the past tense of **wear**. [from Old English]

---
**work**
**❶** VERB USES AND PHRASES
**❷** NOUN USES AND PHRASES
**❸** PHRASAL VERBS
---

**❶ work** /wɜrk/ (**works, working, worked**) **1** V-I People who **work** have a job, usually one which they are paid to do. ❑ *He worked as a teacher for 40 years.* ❑ *I want to work, I don't want to be on welfare.* **2** V-T/V-I When you **work**, you do the things that you are paid or required to do in your job. ❑ *I can't talk to you right now — I'm working.* ❑ *They work forty hours a week.* **3** V-I If a machine or piece of equipment **works**, it operates and performs a particular function. ❑ *"The phone doesn't work,"* he said. **4** V-I If an idea, system, or way of doing something **works**, it is successful, effective, or satisfactory. ❑ *95 percent of diets do not work.* **5** V-T If you **work** a machine or piece of equipment, you use or control it. ❑ *Do you know how to work the DVD player?* **6** → see also **working 7** PHRASE If you **work** your **way** somewhere, you move or progress there slowly, and with a lot of effort or work. ❑ *Many managers started as assistants and worked their way up.* [from Old English]

**❷ work** /wɜrk/ (**works**) **1** N-UNCOUNT Your

**work** consists of the things you are paid or required to do in your job. ❑ *I've got work to do.* ❑ *I sometimes take work home.* **2** N-UNCOUNT **Work** is the place where you do your job. ❑ *Many people travel to work by car.* **3** N-COUNT A **work** is something such as a painting, book, or piece of music produced by an artist, writer, or composer. ❑ *I think this is his greatest work.* **4** N-UNCOUNT In physics, **work** is the energy that is transferred to a moving object as the result of a force acting upon the object. [from Old English]
→ see **factory**

| Thesaurus | *work* | Also look up : |
|---|---|---|
| v. | labor ❶ **1** **2** |
| | function, go, operate, perform, run ❶ **3** **4** |
| N. | business, craft, job, occupation, profession, trade, vocation; *(ant.)* entertainment, fun, pastime ❷ **1** **2** |

❸ **work** /wɜrk/ (**works, working, worked**)
▶ **work off** PHR-VERB If you **work off** energy, stress, or anger, you get rid of it by doing something that requires a lot of physical effort. ❑ *If I've had a bad day I work it off by cooking.*
▶ **work out** **1** PHR-VERB If you **work out** a solution to a problem or mystery, you manage to find the solution by thinking or talking about it. ❑ *It took me some time to work out the answer.* **2** PHR-VERB If something **works out** at a particular amount, it is calculated to be that amount after all the facts and figures have been considered. ❑ *The price per pound works out to be $3.20.* **3** PHR-VERB If a situation **works out** well or **works out**, it happens or progresses in a satisfactory way. ❑ *Things didn't work out as planned.* **4** PHR-VERB If a process **works** itself **out**, it reaches a conclusion or satisfactory end. ❑ *I'm sure it will all work itself out.* **5** PHR-VERB If you **work out**, you do physical exercises in order to make your body fit and strong. ❑ *I work out at a gym twice a week.* **6** → see also **workout**
▶ **work up** **1** PHR-VERB If you **work** yourself **up**, you make yourself feel very upset or angry about something. ❑ *She worked herself up into a rage.* ● **worked up** ADJ ❑ *Steve shouted at her. He was really worked up now.* **2** PHR-VERB If you **work up** the enthusiasm or courage to do something, you succeed in making yourself feel it. ❑ *We could go for a swim, if you can work up the energy.*

**work|able** /wɜrkəbᵊl/ ADJ A **workable** idea or system is realistic and practical, and likely to be effective. ❑ *This isn't a workable solution.* [from Old English]

**work|day** (**work days**) also **work day** N-COUNT A **workday** is the amount of time during a day which you spend doing your job. ❑ *His workday starts at 3:30 a.m. and lasts 12 hours.*

**work|er** /wɜrkər/ (**workers**) **1** N-COUNT **Workers** are people who are employed in industry or business and who are not managers. ❑ *...factory workers.* **2** N-COUNT You can use **worker** to say how well or badly someone works. ❑ *He is a hard worker.* [from Old English] **3** → see also **social worker**
→ see **factory**, **union**

**work|force** /wɜrkfɔrs/ (**workforces**) **1** N-COUNT The **workforce** is the total number of people in a country or region who are physically able to do a job and are available for work. ❑ *Half the workforce is unemployed.* **2** N-COUNT The **workforce** is the total number of people who are employed by a particular company. ❑ *...an employer of a very large workforce.*

**work|ing** /wɜrkɪŋ/ (**workings**) **1** ADJ **Working** people have jobs that they are paid to do. ❑ *Working women and men come to the evening classes.* **2** ADJ Your **working** life is the period of your life in which you have a job or are the right age to have a job. ❑ *He started his working life as a truck driver.* **3** N-PLURAL The **workings of** a piece of equipment, an organization, or a system are the ways in which it operates and the processes which are involved in it. ❑ *...computer systems which copy the workings of the brain.* [from Old English] **4** in **working order** → see **order**

**work|ing class** (**working classes**) N-COUNT The **working class** or the **working classes** are the group of people in a society who do not own much property, who have low social status, and who often do jobs that involve using physical skills. ● **Working class** is also an adjective. ❑ *...a man from a working class background.*

**work in|put** (**work inputs**) N-VAR In physics, **work input** is the amount of effort that is applied to a machine in order to do work. Compare **work output**.

**work|load** /wɜrkloʊd/ (**workloads**) N-COUNT The **workload** of a person or organization is the amount of work that has to be done by them. ❑ *You need someone to share your workload.*

**work|man** /wɜrkmən/ (**workmen**) N-COUNT A **workman** is a man who works with his hands, for example, building or repairing houses or roads.

**work of art** (**works of art**) N-COUNT A **work of art** is a painting or piece of sculpture of high quality. ❑ *...works of art by local artists.*

**work|out** /wɜrkaʊt/ (**workouts**) N-COUNT A **workout** is a period of physical exercise or training. ❑ *...a 35-minute workout.*
→ see **muscle**

**work out|put** (**work outputs**) N-VAR In physics, **work output** is the amount of work that is done by a machine. Compare **work input**.

**work|place** /wɜrkpleɪs/ (**workplaces**) also **work place** N-COUNT Your **workplace** is the place where you work. ❑ *This decision will make the workplace safer for everyone.*

**work|shop** /wɜrkʃɒp/ (**workshops**) **1** N-COUNT A **workshop** is a period of discussion or practical work on a particular subject in which a group of people share their knowledge or experience. ❑ *...a jazz workshop.* **2** N-COUNT A **workshop** is a building that contains tools or machinery for making or repairing things, especially using wood or metal.

**work|station** /wɜrksteɪʃᵊn/ (**workstations**) also **work station** **1** N-COUNT Your **workstation** is the desk and computer that you sit at when you are at work. **2** N-COUNT A **workstation** is a screen

**W**

and keyboard that are part of an office computer system.

**work week** (**work weeks**) N-COUNT A **work week** is the amount of time during a normal week which you spend doing your job. ❑ *The union wants a shorter work week.*

**world** /wɜrld/ (**worlds**) **1** N-SING **The world** is the planet that we live on. ❑ *It's a beautiful part of the world.* **2** ADJ You can use **world** to describe someone or something that is one of the most important or significant of its kind on earth. ❑ *He's a world expert on heart disease.* **3** N-COUNT Someone's **world** is the life they lead, the people they have contact with, and the things they experience. ❑ *His world was very different from mine.* **4** N-SING You can use **world** to refer to a particular field of activity, and the people involved in it. ❑ *...the latest news from the movie world.* **5** N-SING You can use **world** to refer to a particular group of living things, for example, **the animal world, the plant world,** and **the insect world.** **6** → see also **real world, Third World** **7** PHRASE If you say that someone has **the best of both worlds,** you mean that they have only the benefits of two things and none of the disadvantages. ❑ *I have a lot of friends but I also have my career, so I have the best of both worlds.* **8** PHRASE You can use **the outside world** to refer to all the people who do not live in a particular place or who are not involved in a particular situation. ❑ *I was his only link with the outside world.* [from Old English]

**world-class** ADJ A **world-class** athlete, performer, or organization is one of the best in the world. ❑ *He's a world-class player.*

**world-famous** ADJ Someone or something that is **world-famous** is known about by people all over the world. ❑ *...the world-famous Statue of Liberty.*

**World Health Or|gani|za|tion** N-PROPER The **World Health Organization** is an organization within the United Nations that is responsible for helping governments to improve their health services. The abbreviation **WHO** is also used.

**world|ly** /wɜrldli/ **1** ADJ Someone who is **worldly** is experienced and knows about the practical or social aspects of life. ❑ *Though he was a teenager, Bryant was very worldly.* **2** ADJ You can refer to your possessions, rather than spiritual things, as your **worldly** goods or possessions. [LITERARY] [from Old English]

**world view** (**world views**) also **world-view** N-COUNT A person's **world view** is the way they see and understand the world, especially regarding issues such as politics, philosophy, and religion.

**world war** (**world wars**) N-VAR A **world war** is a war that involves countries all over the world. ❑ *...the second world war.*

**world|wide** /wɜrldwaɪd/ ADV If something exists or happens **worldwide,** it exists or happens throughout the world. ❑ *His books have sold more than 20 million copies worldwide.* ● **Worldwide** is also an adjective. ❑ *...$20 billion in worldwide sales.*

**World Wide Web** N-PROPER The **World Wide Web** is a computer system that links documents and pictures into a database that is stored in computers in many different parts of the world and that people everywhere can use. The abbreviations **WWW** and the **Web** are often used. [COMPUTING]
→ see **Internet**

**worm** /wɜrm/ (**worms**) N-COUNT A **worm** is a small animal with a long thin body, no bones, and no legs. [from Old English]

**worn** /wɔrn/ **1** **Worn** is the past participle of **wear.** **2** ADJ **Worn** is used to describe something that is damaged or thin because it is old and has been used a lot. ❑ *...a worn blue carpet.* [from Old English]

**worn out** also **worn-out** **1** ADJ Something that is **worn out** is so old, damaged, or thin from use that it cannot be used anymore. ❑ *We need to replace the worn out tires on the car.* **2** ADJ Someone who is **worn out** is very tired after hard work or a difficult or unpleasant experience. ❑ *Before the race, he was fine. After the race, he was worn out.*

**wor|ri|some** /wɜrɪsəm/ ADJ Something that is **worrisome** causes people to worry. ❑ *It's Johnson's injury that is the most worrisome.* [from Old English]

**wor|ry** /wɜri, wʌri/ (**worries, worrying, worried**) **1** V-T/V-I If you **worry,** you keep thinking about problems that you have or about unpleasant things that might happen. ❑ *Don't worry, I'm sure he'll be fine.* ❑ *I worry about her all the time.* ❑ *They worry that he works too hard.* ● **wor|ried** ADJ ❑ *He seemed very worried.* **2** V-T If someone or something **worries** you, they make you anxious because you keep thinking about problems or unpleasant things that might be connected with them. ❑ *"Why didn't you tell us?" — "I didn't want to worry you."* **3** N-UNCOUNT **Worry** is the state or feeling of anxiety and unhappiness caused by the problems that you have or by thinking about unpleasant things that might happen. ❑ *Modern life is full of worry.* **4** N-COUNT A **worry** is a problem that you keep thinking about and that makes you unhappy. ❑ *My parents had a lot of worries.* [from Old English]

**worse** /wɜrs/ **1** **Worse** is the comparative of **bad.** **2** **Worse** is the comparative of **badly.** **3** PHRASE If a situation changes **for the worse,** it becomes more unpleasant or more difficult. ❑ *Jackson's life took a turn for the worse.* ❑ *They say that things have changed ffor the worse.* [from Old English]

**wors|en** /w3rsən/ (**worsens, worsening, worsened**) v-T/v-I If a bad situation **worsens** or if something **worsens** it, it becomes more difficult, unpleasant, or unacceptable. □ *The weather was worsening.* [from Old English]

**wor|ship** /w3rʃɪp/ (**worships, worshiping, worshiped**) ◼ v-T/v-I If you **worship** a god, you show your respect to the god, for example, by saying prayers. □ ...*different ways of worshiping God.* □ *He likes to worship in his own home.* ● **Worship** is also a noun. □ ...*places of worship.* □ ...*the worship of the ancient Roman gods.* ● **wor|ship|er** (**worshipers**) N-COUNT □ *The mosque holds 1000 worshipers.* ◻ v-T If you **worship** someone or something, you love them or admire them very much. □ *She worshiped him for many years.* [from Old English]

**worst** /w3rst/ ◼ **Worst** is the superlative of **bad.** ◻ **Worst** is the superlative of **badly.** ◼ N-SING The **worst** is the most unpleasant or unfavorable thing that could happen or does happen. □ *Many people still fear the worst.* ◼ PHRASE You use **at worst** or **at the worst** to indicate that you are mentioning the worst thing that might happen in a situation. □ *At best she will be sick for months; at worst she could die.* ◼ PHRASE When someone is **at their worst,** they are as unpleasant, bad, or unsuccessful as it is possible for them to be. □ *He was at his worst when work wasn't going well.* [from Old English]

> **Usage**    **worst and worse**
>
> *Worst* and *worse* sound very similar. You should avoid substituting one for the other in various expressions: *Emily's plans have changed for the worse; at the worst, she'll have to go to the hospital.*

**worst-case** ADJ The **worst-case** scenario is the worst possible thing that could happen in a particular situation. □ *The worst-case scenario is that the aircraft could crash.*

**worth** /w3rθ/ ◼ v-T If something is **worth** a particular amount of money, it can be sold for that amount or is considered to have that value. □ *The picture is worth $500.* ◻ **Worth** combines with amounts of money, so that when you talk about a particular amount of money's worth of something, you mean the quantity of it that you can buy for that amount of money. □ *I went and bought six dollars' worth of potato chips.* ◼ v-T If you say that something is **worth** having, you mean that it is pleasant or useful, and therefore a good thing to have. □ *He decided to see if the house was worth buying.* ◼ If something is **worth** a particular action, or if an action is **worth** doing, it is considered to be important enough for that action. □ *I spent a lot of money on my kitchen, but I think it was worth it.* □ *This restaurant is well worth a visit.* ◼ PHRASE If an action or activity is **worth** your **while,** it will be helpful, useful, or enjoyable for you if you do it, even though it requires some effort. □ *It might be worth your while to look at their website.* [from Old English]

> **Word Partnership**    Use *worth* with :
>
> N.    worth **five dollars**, worth **a fortune**, worth **money**, worth **the price** ◼
> worth **the effort**, worth **the risk**, worth **the trouble**, worth **a try** ◼
> V.    worth **buying**, worth **having** ◼
> worth **fighting for**, worth **remembering**, worth **saving**, worth **watching** ◼

**worth|less** /w3rθlɪs/ ADJ Something that is **worthless** is of no real value or use. □ ...*a worthless piece of paper.* [from Old English]

**worth|while** /w3rθwaɪl/ ADJ If something is **worthwhile,** it is enjoyable or useful, and worth the time, money, or effort that is spent on it. □ *The president's trip was worthwhile.*

> **Thesaurus**    *worthwhile*    Also look up :
>
> ADJ.    beneficial, helpful, useful; (*ant.*) worthless

**wor|thy** /w3rði/ (**worthier, worthiest**) ADJ If a person or thing is **worthy of** something, they deserve it because they have the qualities or abilities required. [FORMAL] □ *She was a worthy winner.* [from Old English]

**would** /wəd, STRONG wʊd/

> **Would** is a modal verb. It is usually used with the base form of a verb. In spoken English, **would** is often abbreviated to **'d.**

◼ MODAL You use **would** when you are saying what someone believed, hoped, or expected to happen or be the case. □ *No one believed there would actually be a war.* □ *Would he always be like this?* ◻ MODAL You use **would** when you are referring to the result or effect of a possible situation. □ *It would be fun to learn to ski.* ◼ MODAL You use **would** to say that someone was willing to do something. You use **would not** to indicate that they refused to do something. □ *He said he would help her.* □ *She wouldn't say where she bought her shoes.* ◼ MODAL You use **would,** especially with "like," "love," and "wish," when saying that someone wants to do or have a particular thing or wants a particular thing to happen. □ *She asked me what I would like to do.* □ *I'd love to have another baby.* ◼ **would rather** → see **rather** ◼ MODAL You use **would** with "if" clauses in questions when you are asking for permission to do something. □ *Would it be all right if I opened a window?* ◼ MODAL You use **would,** usually in questions with "like," when you are making a polite offer or invitation. □ *Would you like a drink?* ◼ MODAL You say that someone **would** do something when it is typical of them and you are critical of it. You emphasize the word **would** when you use it in this way. □ *Well, you would say that: you're a man.* ◼ MODAL You use **would** or **would have** to express your opinion about something that you think is true. □ *I think you'd agree he's a very good singer.* □ *I would have thought he was too old to do that job.* ◼ MODAL You use **would have** with a past participle when you are referring to the result or effect of a possible event in the past. □ *I would have written to you if I had known your address.* ◼ MODAL If you say that someone **would have** liked or preferred something, you mean that they wanted

**W**

to do it or have it but were unable to. ❑ *I would have liked a little more time.* [from Old English]

**would-be** ADJ You can use **would-be** to describe someone who wants or attempts to do a particular thing. For example, a **would-be** writer is someone who wants to be a writer.

**wouldn't** /wʊdᵊnt/ **Wouldn't** is the usual spoken form of "would not." ❑ *My parents wouldn't allow me to stay up late.*

**would've** /wʊdəv/ **Would've** is a spoken form of "would have," when "have" is an auxiliary verb. ❑ *My mom would've loved one of us to go to college.*

**wound** (**wounds, wounding, wounded**)

Pronounced /waʊnd/ for meaning **1**, and /wund/ for meanings **2**, **3** and **4**.

**1** **Wound** is the past tense and past participle of **wind** ❷. **2** N-COUNT A **wound** is damage to part of your body, especially a cut or a hole in your flesh, which is caused by a gun, knife, or other weapon. ❑ *The wound is healing nicely.* **3** V-T If a weapon or something sharp **wounds** you, it damages your body. ❑ *He killed one man with a knife and wounded five other people.* **4** V-T If you **are wounded** by what someone says or does, your feelings are deeply hurt. ❑ *He was deeply wounded by his son's comments.* [from Old English]
→ see **war**

| Word Partnership | Use *wound* with : |
|---|---|
| N. | **bullet** wound, **chest** wound, **gunshot** wound, **head** wound **2** |
| V. | **die from a** wound, wound **heals, inflict a** wound **2** |
| ADJ. | **fatal** wound, **open** wound **2** |

**wound up** /waʊnd ʌp/ ADJ If someone is **wound up**, they are very tense and nervous or angry. ❑ *Don't get so wound up.*

**wove** /woʊv/ **Wove** is the past tense of **weave**. [from Old English]

**wo|ven** /woʊvᵊn/ **Woven** is a past participle of **weave**. [from Old English]

**wow** /waʊ/ EXCLAM You can say "**wow**" when you are very impressed, surprised, or pleased. [INFORMAL] ❑ *I thought, "Wow, what a good idea."* [of Scottish origin]

**wran|gle** /ræŋgᵊl/ (**wrangles, wrangling, wrangled**) V-RECIP If you say that someone is **wrangling with** someone **over** a question or issue, you mean that they have been arguing angrily for a long time about it. ❑ *The two sides have spent most of their time wrangling over small points.* [from Low German]

**wrap** /ræp/ (**wraps, wrapping, wrapped**) **1** V-T When you **wrap** something, you fold paper or cloth tightly around it to cover it. • **Wrap up** means the same as **wrap**. ❑ *Diana is wrapping up the presents.* **2** V-T When you **wrap** something such as a piece of paper or cloth around another thing, you put it around it. ❑ *She wrapped a cloth around her hand.* **3** → see also **wrapping**
▸ **wrap up** **1** PHR-VERB If you **wrap up**, you put warm clothes on. ❑ *She wrapped up in her warmest clothes.* ❑ *It'll be cold, so wrap up well.* **2** PHR-VERB If you **wrap up** something such as a job or an agreement, you finish it in a satisfactory way. ❑ *The president wrapped up the meeting earlier today.*

**3** → see also **wrap 1, wrapped up**

**wrapped up** ADJ If someone is **wrapped up** in a particular person or thing, they spend nearly all their time thinking about them, so that they forget about other things that may be important. ❑ *He's wrapped up in his career.*

**wrap|per** /ræpər/ (**wrappers**) N-COUNT A **wrapper** is a piece of paper, plastic, or thin metal that covers and protects something that you buy, especially food. ❑ *...candy wrappers.*

**wrap|ping** /ræpɪŋ/ (**wrappings**) N-VAR **Wrapping** is something such as paper or plastic that is used to cover and protect something. ❑ *I pulled off the wrapping and opened the box.*

**wrath** /ræθ/ N-UNCOUNT **Wrath** means the same as anger. [LITERARY] ❑ *...the wrath of an angry crowd.* [from Old English]

**wreak** /rik/ (**wreaks, wreaking, wreaked**)

Some people use the form **wrought** as the past tense and past participle of **wreak**, but many people consider this to be wrong.

V-T Something or someone that **wreaks** havoc or destruction causes a great amount of disorder or damage. [LITERARY] ❑ *Storms wreaked havoc on the Florida coast.* [from Old English]

wreath

**wreath** /riθ/ (**wreaths**) N-COUNT A **wreath** is an arrangement of flowers and leaves in the shape of a circle, which you sometimes put on a grave or by a statue to show that you remember a person who has died or people who have died. [from Old English]

**wreck** /rɛk/ (**wrecks, wrecking, wrecked**) **1** V-T To **wreck** something means to completely destroy or ruin it. ❑ *The storm wrecked the garden.* **2** N-COUNT A **wreck** is something such as a ship, car, plane, or building that has been destroyed, usually in an accident. ❑ *...the wreck of a sailing ship.* [of Scandinavian origin]

**wreck|age** /rɛkɪdʒ/ N-UNCOUNT When something such as a plane, car, or building has been destroyed, you can refer to what remains as **wreckage** or **the wreckage**. ❑ *They pulled Mark from the burning wreckage of his car.* [of Scandinavian origin]

**wren** /rɛn/ (**wrens**) N-COUNT A **wren** is a very small brown bird. [from Old English]

**wrench** /rɛntʃ/ (**wrenches, wrenching, wrenched**) **1** V-T If you **wrench** something that is fixed in a particular position, you pull or twist it violently, in order to move or remove it. ❑ *Two men wrenched the suitcase from his hand.* **2** N-COUNT A **wrench** is an adjustable metal tool used for tightening or loosening metal nuts of different sizes. **3** V-T If you **wrench** your neck, you hurt it by pulling or twisting it in an unusual way. [from Old English]
→ see **tools**

**wres|tle** /rɛsᵊl/ (**wrestles, wrestling, wrestled**) **1** V-I When you **wrestle with** a difficult problem, you try to deal with it. ❑ *They wrestled with the problem for hours.* **2** V-I If you **wrestle with** someone, you fight them by forcing them into painful positions or throwing them to the ground, rather than by hitting them. Some people wrestle as a sport. ❑ *My father taught me to wrestle.* [from Old English] **3** → see also **wrestling**

**wres|tler** /rɛslər/ (**wrestlers**) N-COUNT A **wrestler** is someone who wrestles as a sport. [from Old English]

**wres|tling** /rɛslɪŋ/ N-UNCOUNT **Wrestling** is a sport in which two people wrestle and try to throw each other to the ground. ❑ *...a wrestling match.* [from Old English]

**wretch|ed** /rɛtʃɪd/ **1** ADJ You use **wretched** to describe someone or something that you dislike or feel angry with. [INFORMAL] ❑ *The pay was wretched.* **2** ADJ Someone who feels **wretched** feels very unhappy. [FORMAL] ❑ *I feel wretched thinking of him all alone for Christmas.* [from Old English]

**wrig|gle** /rɪɡ³l/ (**wriggles, wriggling, wriggled**) V-T/V-I If you **wriggle** or **wriggle** part of your body, you twist and turn with quick movements. ❑ *She pulled off her socks and wriggled her toes.* [from Middle Low German]
▸ **wriggle out of** PHR-VERB If you say that someone has **wriggled out of** doing something, you disapprove of the fact that they have managed to avoid doing it. ❑ *He's wriggled out of doing the dishes again.*

**wring** /rɪŋ/ (**wrings, wringing, wrung**) V-T If you **wring** something **out of** someone, you manage to make them give it to you even though they do not want to. ❑ *It is impossible to wring any information out of him.* [from Old English]
▸ **wring out** PHR-VERB When you **wring out** a wet cloth or a wet piece of clothing, you squeeze the water out of it by twisting it strongly. ❑ *He turned away to wring out his wet shirt.*

**wrin|kle** /rɪŋk³l/ (**wrinkles, wrinkling, wrinkled**) **1** N-COUNT **Wrinkles** are lines that form on your face as you grow old. **2** V-T/V-I If cloth **wrinkles**, or if someone or something **wrinkles** it, it gets folds or lines in it. ❑ *Her stockings wrinkled at the ankles.* ● **wrin|kled** ADJ ❑ *His suit was wrinkled and he looked very tired.* **3** V-T/V-I When you **wrinkle** your nose or forehead, or when it **wrinkles**, you tighten the muscles in your face so that the skin folds. [from Old English]
→ see **skin**

**wrist** /rɪst/ (**wrists**) N-COUNT Your **wrist** is the part of your body between your hand and your arm that bends when you move your hand. [from Old English]
→ see **body, hand**

**writ** /rɪt/ (**writs**) N-COUNT A **writ** is a legal document that orders a person to do a particular thing. ❑ *I'll make sure there's a writ against him in every state in this country.* [from Old English]

**write** /raɪt/ (**writes, writing, wrote, written**) **1** V-T/V-I When you **write**, you use something such as a pen or pencil to produce words, letters, or numbers. ❑ *Write your name and address on a postcard and send it to us.* ❑ *I'm teaching her to read and write.* **2** V-T If you **write** something such as a book, a poem, or a piece of music, you create it and record it on paper, on a computer or on a recording device. ❑ *She wrote articles for French newspapers.* **3** V-T/V-I When you **write** someone or to someone or **write** them a letter, you give them information, ask them something, or express your feelings in a letter. You can also **write** someone a note or an

e-mail. ❑ *She wrote to her aunt asking for help.* ❑ *I wrote a letter to the manager.* **4** **nothing to write home about** → see **home** **5** V-T When someone **writes** something such as a check, receipt, or prescription, they put the necessary information on it and usually sign it. ❑ *She got out her checkbook and wrote a check.* [from Old English] **6** → see also **writing, written**
▸ **write down** PHR-VERB When you **write** something **down**, you record it on a piece of paper using a pen or pencil. ❑ *I wrote down what I thought was good about the training course.*
▸ **write in** PHR-VERB If you **write in** to an organization, you send them a letter. ❑ *What's the point in writing in when you only print half the letter anyway?*
▸ **write into** PHR-VERB If a rule or detail **is written into** a contract, law, or agreement, it is included in it when the contract, law, or agreement is made.
▸ **write off** **1** PHR-VERB If someone **writes off** a debt or an amount of money that has been spent on a project, they accept that they are never going to get the money back. [BUSINESS] ❑ *He wrote off the money years ago.* **2** PHR-VERB If you **write** someone or something **off**, you decide that they are unimportant or useless and that they are not worth further serious attention. ❑ *He gets angry when people write him off because of his age.*
▸ **write up** PHR-VERB If you **write up** something that has been done or said, you record it on paper in a neat and complete form, usually using notes that you have made. ❑ *He wrote up his visit in a report.*

**writ|er** /raɪtər/ (**writers**) **1** N-COUNT A **writer** is a person who writes books, stories, or articles as a job. ❑ *...detective stories by American writers.* **2** N-COUNT The **writer** of a particular article, report, letter, or story is the person who wrote it. ❑ *Callie Khouri is the writer of "Thelma and Louise."* [from Old English]

**writhe** /raɪð/ (**writhes, writhing, writhed**) V-I If you **writhe**, your body twists and turns violently backward and forward, usually because you are in great pain or discomfort. ❑ *He was writhing in pain.* [from Old English]

**writ|ing** /raɪtɪŋ/ **1** N-UNCOUNT **Writing** is something that has been written or printed. ❑ *Joe tried to read the writing on the next page.* **2** N-UNCOUNT You can refer to any piece of written work as **writing**, especially when you are considering the style of language used in it. ❑ *The writing is very funny.* **3** N-UNCOUNT **Writing** is the activity of writing, especially of writing books for money. ❑ *She was bored with writing books about the same thing.* **4** N-UNCOUNT Your **writing** is the way that you write with a pen or pencil, which can usually be recognized as belonging to you. ❑ *It's difficult to read your writing.*

**writ|ten** /rɪt³n/ **1** **Written** is the past participle of **write**. **2** ADJ A **written** test or piece of work is one that involves writing rather than doing something practical or giving spoken answers. ❑ *...a short written test.* **3** ADJ A **written** agreement, rule, or law has been officially written down. ❑ *The newspaper broke a written agreement not to sell the photographs.* [from Old English]

**W**

**wrong** /rɔŋ/ (**wrongs**) **1** ADJ If you say there is something **wrong**, you mean there is something unsatisfactory about the situation, person, or thing you are talking about. ❑ *Pain is the body's way of telling us that something is wrong.* ❑ *What's wrong with him?* **2** ADJ If you choose the **wrong** thing, person, or method, you make a mistake and do not choose the one that you really want. ❑ *He went to the wrong house.* • **Wrong** is also an adverb. ❑ *You've done it wrong.* **3** ADJ If something such as a decision, choice, or action is **the wrong** one, it is not the best or most suitable one. ❑ *I made the wrong decision.* **4** ADJ If something is **wrong**, it is incorrect. ❑ *I did not know if Mark's answer was right or wrong.* • **Wrong** is also an adverb. ❑ *I must have added it up wrong.* • **wrong|ly** ADV ❑ *She was wrongly accused of stealing.* **5** ADJ If you are **wrong** about something, what you say or think about it is not correct. ❑ *I was wrong about the time of the meeting.* **6** ADJ If you say that something someone does is **wrong**, you mean that it is bad or immoral. ❑ *She was wrong to leave her child alone.* • **Wrong** is also a noun. ❑ *I did him a great wrong.* **7** N-UNCOUNT **Wrong** is used to refer to activities or actions that are considered to be morally bad and unacceptable. ❑ *He can't tell the difference between right and wrong.* **8** PHRASE If a situation **goes wrong**, it stops progressing in the way that you expected or intended, and becomes much worse. ❑ *My marriage started to go wrong after six months.* **9** PHRASE If someone who is involved in an argument or dispute is **in the wrong**, they have behaved in a way that is morally or legally wrong. ❑ *You were completely in the wrong.*

[from Old English]

---

**Thesaurus**          *wrong*          Also look up :

ADJ.    incorrect; (*ant.*) right **4**
        corrupt, immoral, unjust **6**
N.      abuse, offense, sin **7**

---

**wrong|doing** /rɔŋduɪŋ/ (**wrongdoings**) N-VAR **Wrongdoing** is behavior that is illegal or immoral. ❑ *...criminal wrongdoing.*

**wrote** /roʊt/ **Wrote** is the past tense of **write**. [from Old English]

**wrought** /rɔt/ V-T If something has **wrought** a change, it has made it happen. [LITERARY] ❑ *The events wrought a change in public opinion.* [from Old English]

**wrung** /rʌŋ/ **Wrung** is the past tense of **wring**. [from Old English]

**wry** /raɪ/ **1** ADJ If someone has a **wry** expression, it shows that they find a bad situation or a change in a situation slightly amusing. ❑ *Matthew gave a wry smile.* **2** ADJ A **wry** remark or piece of writing refers to a bad situation or a change in a situation in an amusing way. ❑ *There is a wry sense of humor in his work.* [from Old English]

**wuss** /wʊs/ (**wusses**) N-COUNT If you call someone a **wuss**, you are criticizing them for being afraid. [INFORMAL]

**WWW** /dʌbᵊlyu dʌbᵊlyu dʌbᵊlyu/ **WWW** is an abbreviation for **World Wide Web**. It appears at the beginning of website addresses in the form **www**. [COMPUTING] ❑ *Check our website at www.collinslanguage.com.*

# Xx

**xeno|pho|bia** /zɛnəfoʊbiə/ N-UNCOUNT
**Xenophobia** is strong and unreasonable dislike
or fear of people from other countries. [FORMAL]
❑ ...a tolerant society which rejects xenophobia and
racism. ● **xeno|pho|bic** ADJ ❑ The man was obsessively
xenophobic. [from Greek]

**X-rated** ADJ An **X-rated** movie or video contains
sexual scenes that are considered suitable only
for adults.

**X-ray** (**X-rays, X-raying, X-rayed**) also **x-ray**
**1** N-COUNT **X-rays** are a type of radiation that
can pass through most solid materials. X-rays are
used by doctors to examine the bones or organs
inside your body and are also used at airports to
see inside people's bags. **2** N-COUNT An **X-ray**
is a picture made by sending X-rays through
something, usually someone's body. ❑ She had to
have a chest X-ray. **3** V-T If someone or something
**is X-rayed**, an X-ray picture is taken of them. ❑ All
bags were x-rayed. [from German]
→ see **telescope, wave**

**xy|lem** /zaɪləm, -lɛm/ (**xylems**) N-VAR **Xylem**
is the layer of material in plants that carries
water and nutrients from the roots to the leaves.
Compare **phloem**. [TECHNICAL] [from Greek]

# Yy

yacht

**yacht** /yɒt/ (yachts)
N-COUNT A **yacht** is a large
boat with sails or a motor,
used for racing or pleasure
trips. [from Dutch]

**yacht|ing** /yɒtɪŋ/
N-UNCOUNT **Yachting** is the
sport or activity of sailing
a yacht. ❑ ...the joys of
yachting. [from Dutch]

**yad|da** /yɑdə/ also **yada** CONVENTION You use
**yadda yadda yadda** or **yadda, yadda, yadda** to
refer to something that is said or written without
giving the actual words, because you think that
they are boring or unimportant. [INFORMAL] ❑ Oh,
I know, I know, it's meant to be so sad, yadda yadda
yadda.

**y'all** /yɔl/ In the Southern United States, people
use **y'all** when addressing a two or more people.
**Y'all** is an informal way of saying "you all."
[INFORMAL] ❑ Y'all just talk amongst yourselves.

**yam** /yæm/ (yams) ◼ N-VAR A **yam** is a root
vegetable which is like a potato, and grows in
tropical regions. ◼ N-VAR **Yams** are the same as
**sweet potatoes**. [from Portuguese]

**yang** /yæŋ/ N-UNCOUNT In Chinese philosophy,
**yang** is one of the two opposing principles whose
interaction is believed to influence everything
in the universe. **Yang** is positive, bright, and
masculine while **yin** is negative, dark, and
feminine. ❑ ...a perfect balance of yin and yang. [from
Chinese]

**yank** /yæŋk/ (yanks, yanking, yanked) V-T/V-I If
you **yank** someone or something somewhere, you
pull them there suddenly and with a lot of force.
❑ She yanked open the drawer. ● **Yank** is also a noun.
❑ Shirley grabbed his ponytail and gave it a yank.

**Yan|kee** /yæŋki/ (Yankees) ◼ N-COUNT A
**Yankee** is a person from a northern or northeastern state of the United States. ◼ N-COUNT
Some speakers of British English refer to anyone
from the United States as a **Yankee**. This use could
cause offence. [INFORMAL] [from Dutch]

**yard** /yɑrd/ (yards) ◼ N-COUNT A **yard** is
a unit of length equal to thirty-six inches or
approximately 91.4 centimeters. ❑ ...500 yards
from where he was standing. ◼ N-COUNT A **yard** is
a flat area of concrete or stone that is next to a
building and often has a wall around it. ❑ I saw
him standing in the yard. ◼ N-COUNT You can refer to
a large open area where a particular type of work
is done as a **yard**. ❑ ...a rail yard. ◼ N-COUNT A **yard**
is a piece of land next to a house, with grass and
plants growing in it. [from Old English]
→ see **football, measurement**

**yard|age** /yɑrdɪdʒ/ ◼ N-UNCOUNT **Yardage**
is a measurement of the length or distance

of something, expressed in yards. ❑ Where are
you taking the yardage from — the front or the back?
◼ N-UNCOUNT In a game of football, **yardage** is the
number of yards that a team or player manages
to move the ball forward toward their opponent's
end zone. **Yardage** is measured by lines that cross
the field every five yards. ❑ He made huge yardage
every time he got the ball.

**yard sale** (yard sales) N-COUNT A **yard sale** is a
sale where people sell things they no longer want
from a table outside their house. ❑ ...clothes he'd
picked up at yard sales.

**yard|stick** /yɑrdstɪk/ (yardsticks) N-COUNT If
you use someone or something as a **yardstick**, you
use them as a standard for comparison when you
are judging other people or things. ❑ Sales became
the yardstick for success.

**yarn** /yɑrn/ (yarns) N-VAR **Yarn** is thread used
for knitting or making cloth. ❑ She brought me a bag
of wool yarn and knitting needles. [from Old English]

**yawn** /yɔn/ (yawns, yawning, yawned) V-I If
you **yawn**, you open your mouth very wide and
breathe in more air than usual, often when
you are tired or when you are not interested in
something. ❑ She yawned, and stretched lazily.
● **Yawn** is also a noun. ❑ She woke and gave a huge
yawn. [from Old English]
→ see **sleep**

**yeah** /yɛə/ ◼ CONVENTION **Yeah** means yes.
[INFORMAL, SPOKEN] ❑ "Bring us something to drink."
— "Yeah, yeah." ◼ → see also **yes**

**year** /yɪər/ (years) ◼ N-COUNT A **year** is a
period of twelve months or 365 or 366 days,
beginning on the first of January and ending on
the thirty-first of December. ❑ The year was 1840.
❑ We had an election last year. ◼ → see also **leap
year** ◼ N-COUNT A **year** is any period of twelve
months. ❑ Graceland has more than 650,000 visitors
a year. ◼ N-COUNT A school **year** or academic
**year** is the period of time in each twelve months
when schools or colleges are open and students
are studying there. The school year starts in
August or September. ◼ N-COUNT A financial or
business **year** is an exact period of twelve months
which businesses or institutions use as a basis for
organizing their finances. [BUSINESS] ◼ N-PLURAL
You can use **years** to emphasize that you are
referring to a long time. ❑ I haven't laughed so much
in years. ◼ → see also **calendar year, fiscal year**
◼ PHRASE If you say something happens **all year
round** or **all the year round**, it happens continually
throughout the year. ❑ The gardens produce flowers
nearly all year round. [from Old English]
→ see Word Web: **year**
→ see **season**

**year|ly** /yɪərli/ ◼ ADJ A **yearly** event happens
once a year or every year. ❑ The two sisters looked

## Word Web    year

The earth takes a **year** to orbit the sun. It is about 365 **days**. The exact time is 365.242199 days. To make years come out even, every four years there is a **leap year**. It has 366 days. The **months** on a **calendar** are based on the phases of the moon. The Greeks had a 10-month calendar. About 60 days were left over. So the Romans added two months. The idea of seven-day **weeks** came from the Bible. The Romans named the days. We still use three of these names: Sunday (sun day), Monday (moon day), and Saturday (Saturn day).

forward to their yearly meetings. ● **Yearly** is also an adverb. ❏ Clients normally pay fees yearly. **2** ADJ You use **yearly** to describe something such as an amount that relates to a period of one year. ❏ …your yearly health care costs. ● **Yearly** is also an adverb. ❏ They carried out 20 or more operations yearly. [from Old English]

**yearn** /yɜrn/ (**yearns, yearning, yearned**) V-T/V-I If someone **yearns for** something that they are unlikely to get, they want it very much. ❏ He yearned for freedom. ❏ I yearned to be an actor. ● **yearn|ing** (**yearnings**) N-VAR ❏ …his yearning for another child. [from Old English]

**yeast** /yist/ (**yeasts**) N-VAR **Yeast** is a kind of fungus which is used to make bread rise, and in making alcoholic drinks such as beer. [from Old English]
→ see **fungus**

**yell** /yɛl/ (**yells, yelling, yelled**) V-T/V-I If you **yell**, you shout loudly, usually because you are excited, angry, or in pain. ❏ "Eva!" he yelled. ❏ I'm sorry I yelled at you last night. ● **Yell out** means the same as **yell**. ❏ "Are you coming or not?" they yelled out after him. N-COUNT A **yell** is a loud shout given by someone who is afraid or in pain. ❏ Bob let out a yell. [from Old English]

### Thesaurus    yell    Also look up :

v.    cry, scream, shout; (ant.) whisper

**yel|low** /yɛloʊ/ COLOR Something that is **yellow** is the color of lemons, butter, or the middle part of an egg. ❏ The walls were painted bright yellow. ❏ She was wearing a yellow dress. [from Old English]
→ see **color, rainbow**

**yel|low card** (**yellow cards**) N-COUNT In soccer, if a player is shown the **yellow card**, the referee holds up a yellow card to indicate that the player has broken the rules, and that if they do so again, they will be ordered to leave the field.

**yen** /yɛn/ (**yen**) The **yen** is the unit of currency used in Japan. ❏ …2,000 yen. [from Japanese]

**yes** /yɛs/

In informal English, **yes** is often pronounced in a casual way that is usually written as **yeah**.

**1** CONVENTION You use **yes** to give a positive response to a question. ❏ "Are you a friend of Nick's?" — "Yes." **2** CONVENTION You use **yes** to accept an offer or request, or to give permission. ❏ "More coffee?" — "Yes please." **3** CONVENTION You use **yes** to tell someone that what they have said is correct.

❏ "Well I suppose it's based on fact, isn't it?" — "Yes, that's right." **4** CONVENTION You use **yes** to say that a negative statement or question that the previous speaker has made is wrong or untrue. ❏ "That is not possible," she said. — "Oh, yes, it is!" Mrs. Gruen insisted. [from Old English]

**yes|ter|day** /yɛstərdeɪ, -di/ **1** ADV You use **yesterday** to refer to the day before today. ❏ She left yesterday. ● **Yesterday** is also a noun. ❏ In yesterday's games, Switzerland were the winners. **2** N-UNCOUNT You can refer to the recent past, especially the recent past, as **yesterday**. ❏ The worker of today is different from the worker of yesterday. [from Old English]

**yet** /yɛt/ **1** ADV You use **yet** in negative statements to indicate that something has not happened up to the present time, although it probably will happen. You can also use **yet** in questions to ask if something has happened up to the present time. ❏ They haven't finished yet. ❏ No decision has yet been made. ❏ She hasn't yet set a date for her marriage. **2** ADV If you say that something should not or cannot be done **yet**, you mean that it should not or cannot be done now, although it will have to be done at a later time. ❏ Don't get up yet. ❏ You can't go home just yet. **3** ADV You can use **yet** to say that there is still a possibility that something will happen. ❏ This story may yet have a happy ending. **4** ADV You can use **yet** after expressions that refer to a period of time, when you want to say how much longer a situation will continue for. ❏ Unemployment will go on rising for some time yet. **5** ADV If you say that you have **yet** to do something, you mean that you have never done it, especially when this is surprising or bad. ❏ She has yet to spend a Christmas with her husband. **6** CONJ You can use **yet** to introduce a fact that is rather surprising after the previous fact you have just mentioned. ❏ I don't eat much, yet I am a size 16. **7** ADV You can use **yet** to emphasize a word, especially when something is surprising because it is more extreme than previous things of its kind, or a further case of them. ❏ I saw yet another doctor. [from Old English]
→ see also **but**

**yield** /yild/ (**yields, yielding, yielded**) **1** V-I If you **yield to** someone or something, you stop resisting them. [FORMAL] ❏ Carmen yielded to pressure and took the child to the doctor. **2** V-T If you **yield** something that you have control of or responsibility for, you allow someone else to have control or responsibility for it. [FORMAL] ❏ He may yield control. **3** V-I If a moving person or a vehicle **yields**, they slow down in order to allow other people or vehicles to pass in front of

**V**

them. ❑ *Motorists must yield to buses.* ❑ *…examples of common signs like No Smoking and Yield.* **4** V-I If something **yields**, it breaks or moves position because force or pressure has been put on it. ❑ *He pushed the door and it yielded.* **5** V-T When something **yields** an amount of something such as food or money, it produces that amount. ❑ *400,000 acres of land yielded a crop worth $1.75 billion.* [from Old English]

| **Word Partnership** | Use *yield* with : |
|---|---|
| N. | yield **to pressure**, yield **to temptation** **1** yield **information**, yield **a profit**, yield **results** **5** |
| V. | **refuse to** yield **1** – **4** |
| ADJ. | **annual** yield, **expected** yield, **high/ higher** yield **5** |

**yin** /yɪn/ also **ying** /yɪŋ/ N-UNCOUNT In Chinese philosophy, **yin** is one of the two opposing principles whose interaction is believed to influence everything in the universe. Yin is negative, dark, and feminine, while **yang** is positive, bright, and masculine. ❑ *…a perfect balance of yin and yang.* [from Chinese]

**yip** /yɪp/ (**yips, yipping, yipped**) V-I If a dog or other animal **yips**, it gives a sudden short cry, often because of fear or pain. ❑ *Coyotes yipped in the distance.* ● Yip is also a noun. ❑ *…a yip of pain.*

**yoga** /yoʊgə/ N-UNCOUNT **Yoga** is a type of exercise in which you move your body into various positions in order to become more fit or flexible, to improve your breathing, and to relax your mind. ❑ *I do yoga twice a week.* [from Sanskrit]

**yogurt** /yoʊgərt/ (**yogurts**) also **yoghurt** N-VAR **Yogurt** is a food in the form of a thick, slightly sour liquid that is made by adding bacteria to milk. A **yogurt** is a small container of yogurt. [from Turkish]

**yoke** /yoʊk/ (**yokes, yoking, yoked**) **1** N-SING If you say that people are under the **yoke of** a bad thing or person, you mean they are forced to live in a difficult or unhappy state because of that thing or person. [LITERARY] ❑ *She was no longer under the yoke of her husband.*

**2** V-T If two or more people or things **are yoked together**, they are forced to be closely linked with each other. ❑ *The introduction attempts to yoke the pieces together.* [from Old English]

yoke

**yolk** /yoʊk/ (**yolks**) N-VAR The **yolk** of an egg is the yellow part in the middle. ❑ *Only the yolk contains cholesterol.* [from Old English]

**you** /yu/

> **You** is the second person pronoun. **You** can refer to one or more people and is used as the subject of a verb or the object of a verb or preposition.

**1** PRON A speaker or writer uses **you** to refer to the person or people that they are talking or writing to. ❑ *When I saw you across the room I knew I'd met you before.* ❑ *You two seem very different to me.* **2** PRON In spoken English and informal written English, **you** is sometimes used to refer to people in general. ❑ *Getting good results gives you confidence.*

❑ *In those days you did what you were told.* [from Old English]
→ see also **one**

**you'd** /yʊd, STRONG yud/ **1** **You'd** is the usual spoken form of "you had," when "had" is an auxiliary verb. ❑ *I think you'd better tell us why you're asking these questions.* **2** **You'd** is the usual spoken form of "you would." ❑ *You'd look good in red.*

**you'll** /yʊl, STRONG yul/ **You'll** is the usual spoken form of "you will." ❑ *Promise me you'll take care of yourself.*

**young** /yʌŋ/ (**younger** /yʌŋgər/, **youngest** /yʌŋgɪst/) **1** ADJ A **young** person, animal, or plant has not lived or existed for very long and is not yet mature. ❑ *…information written for young people.* ❑ *…a field of young barley.* ● **The young** are people who are young. ❑ *Everyone from the young to the elderly can enjoy yoga.* **2** N-PLURAL The **young** of an animal are its babies. ❑ *The hen may not be able to feed its young.* [from Old English]
→ see **age, mammal**

| **Thesaurus** | *young* | Also look up : |
|---|---|---|
| ADJ. | childish, immature, youthful; (ant.) mature, old **1** | |
| N. | family, litter **2** | |

**youngster** /yʌŋstər/ (**youngsters**) N-COUNT Young people, especially children, are sometimes referred to as **youngsters**. [from Old English]

**your** /yɔr, yʊər/

> **Your** is the second person possessive determiner. **Your** can refer to one or more people.

**1** DET A speaker or writer uses **your** to indicate that something belongs or relates to the person or people that they are talking or writing to. ❑ *I trust your opinion.* ❑ *I left all of your messages on your desk.* **2** DET In spoken English and informal written English, **your** is sometimes used to indicate that something belongs to or relates to people in general. ❑ *Painkillers are very useful to bring your temperature down.* [from Old English]

| **Usage** | *your* and *you're* |
|---|---|

Be careful not to confuse *your* and *you're*, which are pronounced the same. *Your* is the possessive form of *you*, while *you're* is the contraction of *you are*: *Be careful! You're going to spill your coffee!*

**you're** /yɔr, yʊər/ **You're** is the usual spoken form of "you are." ❑ *Tell him you're sorry.*
→ see also **your**

**yours** /yɔrz, yʊərz/

> **Yours** is the second person possessive pronoun. **Yours** can refer to one or more people.

**1** PRON A speaker or writer uses **yours** to refer to something that belongs or relates to the person or people that they are talking or writing to. ❑ *I believe Paul is a friend of yours.* **2** CONVENTION People write **yours**, **yours sincerely**, **sincerely yours**, or **yours truly** at the end of a letter before they sign their name. ❑ *With best regards, Yours, George.* [from Old English]

**yourself** /yɔrsɛlf, yʊər-, yər-/ (**yourselves**)

> **Yourself** is the second person reflexive pronoun.

**1** PRON A speaker or writer uses **yourself** to refer to the person that they are talking or writing to. **Yourself** is used when the object of a verb or preposition refers to the same person as the subject of the verb. ❑ *Look after yourself.* **2** PRON You use **yourself** to emphasize the person that you are referring to. ❑ *Don't do that yourself — get someone else to do it.* **3** **by yourself** → see **by**

**youth** /yuθ/ (**youths** /yuðz/) **1** N-UNCOUNT Someone's **youth** is the period of their life during which they are a child, before they are a fully mature adult. ❑ *In my youth my ambition was to be a dancer.* **2** N-UNCOUNT **Youth** is the quality or state of being young. ❑ *The team is now a good mixture of experience and youth.* **3** N-COUNT Journalists often refer to young men as **youths**, especially when they are reporting that the young men have caused trouble. ❑ *A 17-year-old youth was arrested yesterday.* **4** N-PLURAL **The youth** are young people considered as a group. ❑ *Tell that to the youth of today and they won't believe you.* [from Old English]

| **Word Partnership** | Use *youth* with : |
| --- | --- |
| N. | youth **center**, youth **culture**, youth **groups**, youth **organizations**, youth **programs**, youth **services** **4** |

**youth|ful** /yuθfəl/ ADJ Someone who is **youthful** behaves as if they are young or younger than they really are. ❑ *I'm a very youthful 50.* ❑ *...youthful energy.* [from Old English]

**you've** /yuv/ **You've** is the usual spoken form of "you have," when "have" is an auxiliary verb. ❑ *You've got to see it to believe it.*

**yuck** /yʌk/ also **yuk** EXCLAM Some people say "**yuck**" when they think something is very unpleasant or disgusting. [INFORMAL] ❑ *"It's corned beef and cabbage," said Malone. "Yuck," said Maureen.*

**yucky** /yʌki/ ADJ If you describe a food or other substance as **yucky**, you mean that it disgusts you. [INFORMAL] ❑ *It tastes yucky, so Mom adds sugar to make it go down easier.*

**yup|pie** /yʌpi/ (**yuppies**) N-COUNT A **yuppie** is a young person who has a well-paid job and likes to show that they have a lot of money by buying expensive things and living in an expensive way. You use **yuppy** when you disapprove of people like this. ❑ *...too old to be a yuppie, or maybe too smart.*

Y

# Zz

**zap** /zæp/ (**zaps, zapping, zapped**) V-T To **zap** someone or something means to kill, destroy, or hit them, for example, with a gun or in a computer game. [INFORMAL] ❑ *It started to rain and the lightning zapped straight down on him.*

**zeal** /ziːl/ N-UNCOUNT **Zeal** is great enthusiasm, especially in connection with work, religion, or politics. ❑ *...his zeal for teaching.* [from Late Latin]

**zeal|ous** /zɛləs/ ADJ Someone who is **zealous** spends a lot of time or energy in supporting something that they believe in very strongly, especially a political or religious ideal. ❑ *She was a zealous worker for charity.* ● **zeal|ous|ly** ADV ❑ *He guards his privacy zealously.* [from Late Latin]

**ze|bra** /ziːbrə/ (**zebras** or **zebra**) N-COUNT A **zebra** is an African wild horse that has black and white stripes. [from Italian]

zebra

**zero** /zɪəroʊ/ (**zeros** or **zeroes**) **1** NUM **Zero** is the number 0. **2** N-UNCOUNT **Zero** is a temperature of 0°. It is freezing point on the Celsius scale, and 32° below freezing point on the Fahrenheit scale. ❑ *...a few degrees above zero.* **3** ADJ You can use **zero** to say that there is none at all of the thing mentioned. ❑ *He has zero personality.* [from Italian]
→ see Word Web: **zero**

**zeros of a func|tion** also **zeroes of a function** N-PLURAL The **zeros of a function** are the points on a graph or in an algebraic expression at which the value of a mathematical function is zero. [TECHNICAL]

**zest** /zɛst/ (**zests**) **1** N-UNCOUNT; N-SING **Zest** is a feeling of pleasure and enthusiasm. ❑ *He has a zest for life.* **2** N-UNCOUNT **Zest** is a quality in an activity or situation which you find exciting. ❑ *Live interviews add zest to any piece of research.* [from French]

**zig|zag** /zɪgzæg/ (**zigzags, zigzagging, zigzagged**) also **zig-zag 1** N-COUNT A **zigzag** is a line that has a series of angles in it like a continuous series of Ws. **2** V-T/V-I If you **zigzag**, you move forward by going at an angle first to one side then to the other. ❑ *He zigzagged his way across the field.* [from French]

**zinc** /zɪŋk/ N-UNCOUNT **Zinc** is a bluish-white metal which is used to make other metals such as brass, or to cover other metals such as iron to stop rust from forming. [from German]

**zip** /zɪp/ (**zips, zipping, zipped**) V-T When you **zip** something, you fasten it using a zipper. ❑ *She zipped her jeans.*
▶ **zip up** PHR-VERB If you **zip up** something such as a piece of clothing or if it **zips up**, you are able to fasten it using its zipper. ❑ *He zipped up his jeans.*

**zip code** (**zip codes**) N-COUNT Your **zip code** is a short sequence of numbers at the end of your address, which helps the post office to sort the mail.

**zip|per** /zɪpər/ (**zippers**) N-COUNT A **zipper** is a device used to open and close parts of clothes and bags. It consists of two rows of metal or plastic teeth which separate or fasten together as you pull a small handle along them.
→ see **button**

**zo|di|ac** /zoʊdiæk/ N-SING The **zodiac** is a diagram used by astrologers to represent the positions of the planets and stars. It is divided into twelve sections, each of which has its own name and symbol. The zodiac is used to try to calculate the influence of the planets on people's lives. ❑ *...the twelve signs of the zodiac.* [from Old French]

---

## Word Web     zero

The **number zero** developed after the other numbers. At first, ancient peoples used numbers for real objects. They **counted** two children or four sheep. Over time they moved from "four sheep" to "four things" to the concept of "four." The idea of a **place** holder like zero came from the Babylonians*. Originally, they wrote numbers like 23 and 203 the same way. The reader had to figure out the difference based on the context. Later, they used zero to represent the idea of null value. It shows that there is no amount of something. For example, the number 203 shows that there are 2 hundreds, no tens, and 3 ones.

*Babylonians: people who lived in the ancient city of Babylon.*

**zone** /zoʊn/ (**zones, zoning, zoned**) **1** N-COUNT A **zone** is an area that has particular features or characteristics. ❑ *The area is a disaster zone.* **2** V-T If an area of land **is zoned**, it is formally set aside for a particular purpose. ❑ *The land was not zoned for commercial use.* ● **zon|ing** N-UNCOUNT ❑ *...city zoning regulations.* [from Latin]
→ see **football**

| Thesaurus | zone | Also look up : |
|---|---|---|
| N. | area, region, section **1** | |

**zoo** /zu/ (**zoos**) N-COUNT A **zoo** is a park where live animals are kept so that people can look at them. ❑ *He took his son to the zoo.* [from Greek]
→ see Word Web: **zoo**
→ see **park**

**zo|ol|ogy** /zoʊɒlədʒi/ N-UNCOUNT **Zoology** is the scientific study of animals. ● **zoo|logi|cal** /zoʊəlɒdʒɪkəl/ ADJ ❑ *...zoological specimens.* ● **zo|olo|gist** /zoʊɒlədʒist/ (**zoologists**) N-COUNT

❑ *...a famous zoologist and writer.* [from Modern Latin]

**zoom** /zum/ (**zooms, zooming, zoomed**) V-I If you **zoom** somewhere, you go there very quickly. [INFORMAL] ❑ *We zoomed through the gallery.*
▶ **zoom in** PHR-VERB If a camera **zooms in on** something that is being filmed or photographed, it gives a close-up picture of it. ❑ *The television cameras zoomed in on me.*

**zoo|plank|ton** /zoʊəplæŋktən/ N-UNCOUNT **Zooplankton** are tiny animals that live in water and are found in plankton. Compare **phytoplankton.** [TECHNICAL]

**zuc|chi|ni** /zukini/ (**zucchini** or **zucchinis**) N-VAR **Zucchini** are long thin vegetables with a dark green skin. [from Italian]

**zy|gote** /zaɪgoʊt/ (**zygotes**) N-COUNT A **zygote** is an egg that has been fertilized by sperm, and which could develop into an embryo. [from Greek]
→ see **reproduction**

### Word Web    zoo

In **zoos** people enjoy looking at animals. But zoos are important for another reason, too. More and more **species** are becoming **extinct**. Zoos help preserve **biological diversity**. They do this through educational programs, **breeding** programs, and **research** studies. One example is the Smithsonian National Zoological Park in Washington, DC. It trains **wildlife** managers from 80 countries.
The Wolong Reserve in China has a breeding program. It has produced 38 **pandas** since 1991. And the Tama Zoo in Hino Japan does research. It studies **chimpanzee** behavior. One chimp has even learned to use a vending machine.

# CONTENTS

## Simple Present Tense

### A. With states, feelings, and perceptions

The simple present tense describes states, feelings, and perceptions that are true at the moment of speaking.

- The box *contains* six cans.     (state)
- Jenny *feels* tired.     (feeling)
- I *see* three stars in the sky.     (perception)

### B. With situations that extend before and after the present moment

The simple present tense can also describe ongoing activities, or things that happen all the time.

- Tina *works* for a large corporation.
- She *lives* in California.
- Jim *goes* to San Francisco State College.

The simple present tense can also describe repeated activities that occur at regular intervals, including people's habits or customs.

- I *exercise* every morning.
- Peter usually *walks* to work.
- Anna often *cooks* dinner.

**NOTE:** Notice the adverbs of frequency *every morning*, *usually*, and *often* in these sentences. Other adverbs of frequency used this way include *always*, *sometimes*, *rarely*, and *never*.

C. **With general facts**
The simple present tense describes things that are always true.
- The Empire State Building *is* in New York City.
- The heart *pumps* blood throughout the body.
- Water *boils* at 100° Celsius.

D. **With future activities**
The simple present tense is sometimes used to talk about scheduled events in the future.
- The train *arrives* at 8:00 tonight.
- We *leave* at 10:00 tomorrow morning.
- The new semester *begins* in September.

## PRESENT CONTINUOUS TENSE

A. **For actions that are happening right now**
The present continuous tense describes an action that is happening at the moment of speaking. These activities started a short time before and will probably end in the near future.

- Ali is *watching* television right now.
- Frank and Lisa *are doing* homework in the library.
- It *is raining*.

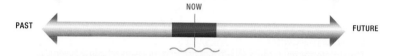

B. **For ongoing activities that aren't necessarily happening at this moment**
The present continuous tense can describe a continuing action that started in the past and will probably continue into the future. However, the action may not be taking place at the exact moment of speaking.

- Mr. Chong *is teaching* a Chinese cooking course.
- We *are practicing* for the soccer championships.
- My sister *is making* a quilt.

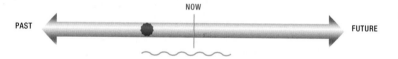

C. **With situations that will happen in the future**
The present continuous tense can also describe planned activities that will happen in the future.

- I *am studying* French next semester.
- We *are having* a party Friday night.
- Raquel *is taking* her driver's test on Saturday.

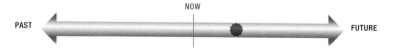

**NOTE:** The use of expressions like *next semester*, *Friday night*, and *on Saturday* help make it clear that the activity is planned and is not happening at the present moment, but will happen in the future.

## Simple past and past continuous

A. **Simple past for one-time and repeated activities that happened in the past**
The simple past tense can describe single or repeated occurrences in the past.
- I *saw* Linda at the post office yesterday.
- Alex *visited* Paris last year.
- We *played* tennis every day last summer. (repeated activity)

B. **Past continuous for continuous actions in the past**
The past continuous tense can describe ongoing activities that went on for a period of time in the past.
- Anna *was living* in Mexico.
- The baby *was sleeping*.
- Snow *was falling*.

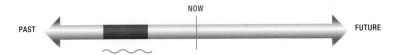

C. **Simple past and past continuous to show a past action that was interrupted**
The simple past tense can describe an action that interrupted an ongoing (past continuous) activity.
- I *met* Alice while I *was living* in New York.
- I *dropped* my purse while I *was crossing* the street.
- The phone *rang* while I *was studying*.

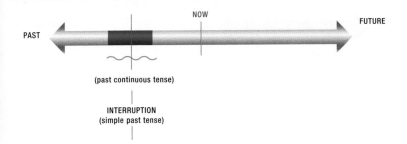

# PRESENT PERFECT AND PRESENT PERFECT CONTINUOUS

A. **Present perfect for actions or situations that started in the past and continue in the present and possibly the future**

The present perfect tense describes an action that started in the past, continues up to the present, and may continue into the future.

- Lee *has collected* stamps for ten years.
- Carmen *has lived* in this country since 1995.
- Yukio *has played* piano since she was four years old.

B. **Present perfect for experience in general, without mentioning when something occurred**

The present perfect tense can show that something happened in the past and the results can be seen in the present.

- We *have caught* several big fish. (they are on the table/in the boat)
- Larry *has met* my family. (they know each other)
- I *have seen* that movie twice. (I can tell you the plot)

C. **Present perfect continuous for ongoing actions that started in the past and continue in the present**

The present perfect continuous tense describes an ongoing activity that went on for a period of time in the past and is still going on.

- It *has been raining* for three days. (it's raining now)
- The baby *has been crying* for ten minutes. (she is still crying)
- We *have been waiting* for the bus since 9:00. (we're still waiting)

## SIMPLE PAST VS. PRESENT PERFECT

A. **Simple past for situations that started and ended in the past vs. present perfect for things that started in the past but continue in the moment**
   The simple past tense describes an action that started and ended in the past, while the present perfect tense describes situations that started in the past but continue up to the present and maybe into the future.

   Past:              John *worked* as a waiter for two years when he was in college.
   Present perfect:   Carol *has worked* as an engineer since 1998.

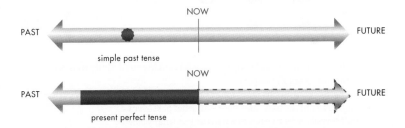

B. **Simple past to emphasize when something happened vs. present perfect to emphasize that something happened, without indicating when**
   The simple past emphasizes when something happened, and the present perfect emphasizes its impact on the present.

   Past:              Peter *graduated* from college in 2007. (at a known point in the past: 2007)
   Present perfect:   Alice *has graduated* from college, and is working in the city. (exactly when is unknown)

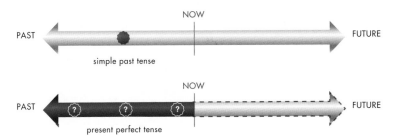

## SIMPLE PAST, PAST PERFECT, AND PAST PERFECT CONTINUOUS

**A.** Past and past perfect tenses with an activity that occurred before another activity in the past

Two simple past tenses are used to show a sequence of events in the past.

Simple past + simple past:   Ali *said* goodbye before he *left*.
I *closed* the door and then *locked* it.

**B.** Past perfect continuous and simple past for a continuous activity that occurred before another event in the past

The past perfect continuous tense followed by the simple past tense shows that an ongoing activity in the past came before another past event.

- We *had been waiting* for two hours when the bus finally *arrived*.
- I *had been thinking* about the problem for days when the answer suddenly *occurred* to me.
- Terry *had been hoping* for the answer that he *got*.

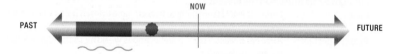

## FUTURE WITH *will* AND *going to*

NOW

PAST — FUTURE

A. Will or *going to* for simple facts
   Either *will* or *going to* can be used to give information about the future. *Will* is used to give definite information.
   - Class *will start* in ten minutes.
   - The class *is going* to use a new textbook.
   - Your teacher *will be* Mr. Ellis.
   - There *is going to* be a final exam.

B. Will or *going to* for prediction
   Either *will* or *going to* can be used to describe things that are likely to happen in the future. *Will* is used when there is evidence that things are likely to happen.
   - It *will rain* this afternoon.
   - You *are going to love* that movie!
   - They *are going to study* a lot the night before the exam.
   - They *will* probably *stay up* all night.

C. Will for promises
   Will is used to give a guarantee concerning a future action.
   - I *will be there* on time.
   - Your father and I *will pay for* your college education.
   - I *won't tell* anyone.
   - I *will save* you a seat.

D. Will for decisions made at the time of speaking
   Will is used for decisions made at the time of speaking.
   - I *will help* you with your homework.
   - We're out of milk. I'*ll go* to the store on my way home.
   - I can't talk right now, but I'*ll call* you later.
   - Danny *will be* happy to wash your car.

## MODALS *can*, *should/ought to*, *must*, AND *have to*

A. *Can* and *can't* for ability, permission, and requests
   *Can* and *can't* are used to:
   - make statements about things people are and are not able to do.
   - describe what people are allowed or not allowed to do.
   - make requests.

   | | |
   |---|---|
   | *Can/can't* **for ability:** | Alan *can swim* very well. |
   | | I *can't run* very fast. |
   | *Can/can't* **for permission:** | You *can leave* whenever you want. |
   | | We *can't use* our dictionaries during the test. |
   | *Can/can't* **for requests:** | *Can* I borrow your laptop? |
   | | *Can't you* turn down the TV? |

B. *Should* and *ought to* for advice and warnings
   *Should* and *ought to* are used to tell people what to do or what to avoid doing.

   | | |
   |---|---|
   | *Should/shouldn't* **for advice/warnings:** | What *should* I *do*? |
   | | You *should ask* questions in class. |
   | | You *shouldn't drive* so fast. |
   | *Ought to* **for advice/warnings:** | You *ought to save* more money. |
   | | He *ought to buy* some new clothes. |

   **NOTE:** *Ought to* is almost never used in questions or negative statements.
   ~~Ought I to go?~~         ~~You ought not see that movie.~~

C. *Must* and *mustn't* for rules and laws
   *Must* and *mustn't* are used in formal situations to show that something is necessary or prohibited.

   | | |
   |---|---|
   | *Must* **for necessity:** | My doctor told me that I *must lose* weight. |
   | *Must* **for obligation:** | Swimmers *must shower* before entering the pool. |
   | *Mustn't* **for prohibition:** | You *mustn't be* late to class. |

   *Must* and *mustn't* are not always opposites. *Needn't (need not)* expresses a lack of obligation to do something, whereas *mustn't* expresses an obligation not to do something.

D. *Have to* and *don't have to* for personal obligations
   *Have to* and *don't have to* are used in informal or personal situations to show that something is necessary or not necessary.

   | | |
   |---|---|
   | *Have to* **for necessity:** | I *have to call* my mother tonight. |
   | | We *have to remember* to buy Jimmy a birthday present. |
   | *Don't/doesn't have to* **for lack of necessity:** | You *don't have to return* the pen. You can keep it. |
   | | Grandpa *doesn't have to comb* his hair. He doesn't have any. |

## MODALS *may*, *might*, *could*, AND *would*

A. *May* and *might* to discuss possibility and permission

*May* and *might* are used to describe future possibilities. *May* is used to give permission in formal situations.

| | |
|---|---|
| *May* for possibility: | We're not sure yet, but we *may leave* tomorrow. |
| | The weather *may not be* good this weekend. |
| *Might* for possibility: | I *might fly* to Florida this weekend, but I probably won't. |
| | We both *might get* 100 on the test. |

NOTE: Sentences with *might* are less definite than sentences with *may*.

| | |
|---|---|
| *May* for permission: | *May I call* you Jimmy? |
| | You *may turn in* your paper Monday if it's not ready today. |
| | No, you *may not have* my telephone number. |
| *Might* for permission: | I wonder if I *might leave* early. |
| | When *might* I *need* to see the doctor again? |

NOTE: *Can* also works in these sentences, but *may* is more polite and formal. Sentences with *might* are often indirect questions.

B. *Could* to show possibility, past ability, and to make requests

*Could* is used to indicate future possibilities, past abilities, and to ask for things.

| | |
|---|---|
| *Could* for future possibilities: | The dog *could have* six or seven puppies. |
| | The movie *could make* a million dollars if it's really popular. |
| *Could* for past ability: | When I was six, I *could* already *speak* two languages. |
| | Tina *could walk* when she was only eight months old. |
| *Could* for requests: | *Could* you *give* me the remote control? |
| | *Could* I *have* another cookie? |

C. *Would* to ask permission and to make requests

*Would* is used to request permission and to ask for things.

| | |
|---|---|
| *Would* to ask permission: | *Would* you *mind* if I asked your age? |
| | *Would* he *mind* if I borrowed his book? |
| *Would* to make requests: | *Would* you *give* me a ride home? |
| | I *would like* two tickets for the 7:00 show. |

## Used to

**A.** *Used to* for statements and questions about past habits or customs
*Used to* shows that something that was true in the past is no longer true.

- Years ago, children *used to be* more polite.
- I *used to hate* broccoli, but now I like it.
- Children *didn't use to have* TVs in their bedrooms.
- Did girls *use to play* on high school football teams?

**NOTE:** When using the negative and question forms with *used to*, drop the past tense -*d* from the word *used*.

**B.** *Used to* for repeated past events
*Used to* also shows that something that happened regularly in the past no longer does.

- We *used to go* to the movies every Friday night.
- Taylor *used to visit* his grandmother every Sunday.
- I didn't *use to sleep* late on Saturday, but now I do.
- Did you *use to walk* home every day?

**C.** *Be used to* for statements and questions about things people have become accustomed to
*Be used to* statements and questions discuss how strange or normal something feels.

- Gail has lived in Chicago and New York. She *is used to living* in big cities.
- I have six brothers and sisters. I *am used to sharing* everything with them.
- Pete *isn't used to doing* homework every night.
- *Are* you *used to* drinking black coffee yet?

**NOTE:** When using the negative and question forms with *be used to*, don't drop the past tense -*d* from the word *used*.

**D.** *Get used to* for statements and questions about becoming accustomed to something new
*Get used to* statements and questions focus on the process of becoming accustomed to something.

- After three weeks, I *got used to* the noise outside my apartment.
- I *am getting used to* living with three roommates.

**NOTE:** The negative form of *get used to* usually employs the modal *can't* or *couldn't*.
I *can't get used to* getting up at 6:00 AM.
Ellen *couldn't get used to* the cold weather in Chicago.

# CONDITIONALS

### A. Unreal conditions in the present

To describe a conditional situation that is unlikely to happen, use a past form in the conditional clause and the modal *would* or *could* in the main clause.

| Conditional clause | Main clause |
|---|---|
| If I *had* enough money, | I *would buy* a boat. |
| If we *went* to Paris, | we *could visit* the Eiffel Tower. |
| If the traffic *got* any worse, | I *wouldn't drive* my car every day. |
| If Shelia *knew* the answer, | she *would tell* us. |

### B. Possible conditions in the future

To describe a conditional situation that is likely to happen, use a present form in the conditional clause and the future with *will* or the modal *can* in the main clause.

| Conditional clause | Main clause |
|---|---|
| If I *have* enough money, | I *will buy* a boat. |
| If we *go* to Paris, | we *can visit* the Eiffel Tower. |
| If the traffic *gets* any worse, | I *won't drive* my car every day. |
| If Shelia *knows* the answer, | she *will tell* us. |

### C. Unreal conditions in the past

To describe a situation from a future point of view, use the past perfect in the conditional clause and *would have* + the past participle in the main clause.

| Conditional clause | Main clause |
|---|---|
| If we *had known* it was raining, | we *would have taken* our umbrellas. |
| If Roberto *had been* home, | he *would have answered* the phone. |
| If you *had known* my grandmother, | you *would have loved* her. |
| If the movie *hadn't been* boring, | I *wouldn't have fallen* asleep. |

### D. Unreal conditions in the present

When discussing unreal conditions, the *if* clause is sometimes not stated; it is implied.

| Conditional statement or question | Implied statement |
|---|---|
| I *would* never *borrow* money from a friend. | (if I had the opportunity) |
| *Would* you *want* to visit the moon? | (if you had the chance) |
| That *wouldn't work*. | (if you tried it) |
| *Would* he *borrow* your car without telling you? | (if he had the opportunity) |

## Passive voice

**A. Passive statements and questions with** *be* **+ past participle**

The passive voice is used when it is not important (or we don't know) who performs the action. The passive can be used with any tense as well as with modals.

| Sentence with passive voice | Verb form |
|---|---|
| The winner *was chosen* last night. | past tense |
| New cures *are being discovered* every day. | present continuous |
| *Will* the renovations *be finished* by next week? | future |
| Aspirin *should be taken* with a full glass of water. | modal *should* |

**B. Passives with an agent**

To put the emphasis on the subject of the sentence and also tell who performed the action, use *by* followed by the agent at the end of the sentence.

- The missing girl was finally found *by her older brother.*
- The theory of relativity was discovered *by Albert Einstein.*
- The modern movie camera was invented *by Thomas Edison.*

**C. Passives with** *get*

In everyday speech, *get* instead of *be* is often used to form the passive. The verb *do* (instead of the verb *be*) is used for questions and negatives with the *get* passive.

- Most hourly workers *get paid* on Thursday or Friday.
- I *got caught* going 40 miles per hour in a 25 mile per hour zone.
- *Did* anyone *get killed* in the accident?
- Roger *didn't get hired* for the job.

# REPORTED SPEECH

**A. Shifting verb tenses in reported speech**

When reporting someone's exact words, the verb in the noun clause usually moves back one tense. Only the past perfect tense remains the same in reported speech.

| Exact quote | Reported speech | Change in verb tense |
|---|---|---|
| I *am* tired. | He said that he *was* tired. | Simple present to simple past |
| We *are waiting*. | They told me that they *were waiting*. | Present continuous to past continuous |
| I *finished* the book last night. | She said that she *had finished* the book the night before. | Simple past to past perfect |
| We *are enjoying* the good weather. | They reported that they *were enjoying* the good weather. | Past continuous to past perfect continuous |
| I *have lived* here for two years. | He added that he *had lived* here for two years. | Present perfect to past perfect |
| We *had eaten* breakfast before we left the house. | They said that they *had eaten* breakfast before they left the house. | Past perfect remains the same |

**B. Shifting modals in reported speech**

Many modals change form in reported speech.

| Exact quote | Reported speech | Change in modal form |
|---|---|---|
| I *can speak* French. | She said that she *could speak* French. | *Can* to *could* |
| We *may need* help. | They said that they *might need* help. | *May* (for possibility) to *might* |
| You *may use* my pencil. | She said that I *could use* her pencil. | *May* (for permission) to *could* |
| I *must make* a phone call. | He said that he *had to make* a phone call. | *Must* to *had to* |
| We *will help* you. | They said that they *would help* me. | *Will* to *would* |
| I *should stop* smoking. | He said that he *should stop* smoking. | *Should* (no change) |
| We *should have left* at 9:00. | They said that they *should have left* at 9:00. | *Should have* (no change) |
| I *could have saved* money with a coupon. | She said that she *could have saved* money with a coupon. | *Could have* (no change) |
| She *must have gone* to bed early. | He said that she *must have gone* to bed early. | *Must have* (no change) |

C. *Say* vs. *tell* in reported speech

The passive voice is used when it is not important (or we don't know) who performs the action. The passive can be used with any tense as well as with modals.

- When using *say* with reported speech, an object is not required. (Other verbs that work this way are *add*, *answer*, *explain*, and *reply*.)
- When using *tell* with reported speech, there is always a direct object. (Other verbs that work this way are *inform*, *notify*, *remind*, and *promise*.)

| Exact quote | Reported speech | Direct object |
|---|---|---|
| It is raining. | He *said* that it was raining. | No |
| I was late to class. | She *explained* that she had been late to class. | No |
| I bought a camera at the mall. | He *told me* that he had bought a camera at the mall. | Yes |
| There is a test on Friday. | She *informed the students* that there was a test on Friday. | Yes |

## COMPARATIVES AND SUPERLATIVES
Comparatives and superlatives have several different forms.

A. With one-syllable adjectives and adverbs
Add *-er* or *-est*.

| Adjective / Adverb | Comparative / superlative form | Example |
|---|---|---|
| cold | colder | December is *colder* than November. |
| hard | harder | The wind blows *harder* in winter than in summer. |
| short | shortest | December 21 is *the shortest* day of the year. |
| fast | fastest | Summer passes *the fastest* of any season. |

B. With two-syllable adjectives ending in *-y*
Change the *-y* to *-i* and add *-er* or *-est*.

| Adjective / Adverb | Comparative / superlative form | Example |
|---|---|---|
| easy | easier | Yesterday's assignment was *easier* than today's. |
| busy | busiest | This is the *busiest* shopping day of the year. |

C. With most adjectives of two or more syllables not ending in -y
Use *more* + adjective for comparatives and *the most* + adjective for superlatives.

| Adjective / Adverb | Comparative / superlative form | Example |
|---|---|---|
| famous | more famous | Amy's Pizza is *more famous* than Bennie's Pizza. |
| frequent | most frequent | Amy's has the *most frequent* specials of any pizzeria. |
| expensive | more expensive | Bennie's pizza is *more expensive* than Amy's. |
| delicious | most delicious | Bennie's makes the *most delicious* pizza in town. |

D. Irregular comparatives and superlatives
Some adjectives and superlatives have irregular forms.

| Adjective / Adverb | Comparative / superlative form | Example |
|---|---|---|
| bad | worse, worst | SUVs have *worse* safety records than sedans. |
| good | better, best | Sedans drive *better* than SUVs. |
| much | more, most | An SUV can carry *the most* people. |
| far | farther, farthest | A sedan can go *the farthest* on a tank of gas. |

E. Comparisons with *as...as*
Use *as . . . as* + adjective or adverb to describe things that are equal, and *not as . . . as* + adjective or adverb to describe inequalities.

| | |
|---|---|
| Adjective | Algebra was *as difficult as* geometry for me. |
| Adjective with negative | However, geometry wasn't *as interesting as* algebra. |
| Adverb | I worked *as hard as* anyone else, but I got a C in algebra. |
| Adverb with negative | I didn't do *as well as* many other students. |

## Infinitives and Gerunds

A verb (or sometimes an adjective) near the beginning of a sentence determines whether a second verb form should be an infinitive or a gerund. Below are lists of some common main verbs (and adjectives) and the type of verb form that follows each.

NOTE: Each list contains several high-frequency items, but the lists are not comprehensive.

A. Verb + infinitive
   These verbs are followed by an infinitive, not a gerund: *ask, attempt, begin, decide, expect, hope, like, plan, promise, start.*
   I *attempted* to start the car.
   They *decided* to stay home last night.
   We *hope* to save at least $1000 by the end of the year.

   WRONG: She plans ~~giving~~ a party this weekend.

B. Causatives + infinitives
   When a person causes something to happen, the causative verb is followed by a direct object plus an infinitive, not a gerund. These causative verbs are followed by an infinitive: *allow, convince, encourage, get, force, persuade, require.*
   We *convinced* the teacher to postpone the test until Monday.
   The teacher *encouraged* us to study over the weekend.
   I *got* my brother to help me with the grammar.

   WRONG: The teacher required us ~~leaving~~ our dictionaries at home.

C. Verb + gerund
   These verbs are followed by a gerund, not an infinitive: *avoid, discuss, dislike, enjoy, finish, imagine, practice, quit, recommend, suggest.*
   The couple *discussed* having another child.
   The children *enjoy* going to the park.
   The couple *can't imagine* having four children.

   WRONG: They avoided ~~to talk~~ about it for a few days.

D. Preposition + infinitive and preposition + gerund
   An infinitive is the preposition *to* and the base of a verb: *to speak.* Gerunds can be used with other prepositions such as *about, at, for, in, of,* and *on.*
   I want *to go* on vacation in August.
   I never even think *about swimming* in the winter.
   This organization plans *on having* a fundraising drive.

   WRONG: They are responsible for ~~help~~ thousands of animals.
   The guests are sorry to ~~leaving~~ the party so early.

## PUNCTUATION

### Apostrophe

• The apostrophe + s is used with singular and plural nouns to show possession.

Jim's computer    the children's toys

my boss' file    the Smiths' house [Only the apostrophe is needed when a word ends in s.]

• The apostrophe + s is used to show ownership.

Pedro and Ana's CDs [The 's on the second name shows they own the CDs together.]

Pedro's and Ana's hats [The 's on both names shows they each own different hats.]

• The apostrophe is used in contractions.

I'm (= I am)    they'll (= they will)

### Brackets

• Brackets are used to add your own information in quoted material.

Jason said, "This is a good time [meaning today] for us to start looking for a new apartment."

• Brackets with three dots are used when you omit words from a quotation.

Jason said, "This is a good time [. . .] for a new apartment."

### Colon

• The colon is used with clock time.

11:30        9:45

• The colon is used to introduce a list.

Jean enjoys all kinds of physical activity: hiking, playing tennis, and even cleaning house.

• The colon is used in the salutation of a business letter.

Dear Ms. Mansfield:

### Comma

• Commas are used with dates and addresses.

Monday, December 1, 1964    16 Terhune Street, Teaneck, NJ 07666

• Commas are used after introductory phrases or clauses.

After finishing school, she joined the Navy.

• Commas are used to set off items in a series.

They served pizza, pasta, lasagna, and salad at the party.

• Commas are used to set off added information in nonrestrictive phrases or clauses.

Mr. Karas, my sister's teacher, comes from Greece.

Rita, who almost never misses class, is absent today.

• Commas are used in the salutation in informal correspondence and at the close of a letter.

Dear Grace,       Sincerely yours,

### Dash

- Dashes are used instead of commas when the added information contains commas.
  The school offers several math courses—algebra, geometry, and trigonometry—as well as a wide variety of science classes.

### Exclamation Point

- An exclamation point is used after a word or group of words to show strong feeling.
  Stop! Don't run over that cat!

### Hyphen

- Hyphens appear in compound words or numbers.
  mother-in-law        twenty-one
- Hyphens are used to divide words at the end of a line.
  After Mrs. Leander finished exploring all her options, she decided the best plan was to return home and start out tomorrow.

### Parentheses

- Parentheses are used with nonessential information and with numbers and letters in lists.
  We left the party (which started at 7:00 P.M.) sometime after midnight.
  My requirements are (1) a room with a view and (2) a working air conditioner.

### Period

- A period is used at the end of any sentence that is not a question or an exclamation.
  Rutgers University offers a wide variety of social science courses.

- A period is used after many abbreviations.
  Mr.   etc.   P.M.   Jr.   i.e.

### Question Mark

- A question mark is used after a word or sentence that asks a question.
  What?                Did you say you don't have a ride home?

### Quotation Marks

- Quotation marks are used to set off a direct quotation but not an indirect quotation.
  Smithers said, "Homer, you must go home now."
  Smithers said Homer must go home.

- Quotation marks are used with the titles of short written material such as poems, short stories, chapters in books, songs, and magazine articles.
  My favorite poem is "A Spider Sewed at Night" by Emily Dickinson.

### Semicolon

- The semicolon is used to link independent clauses when there is no coordinating conjunction (such as *and, but, or, nor,* or *for*) between them.
  Some people like country music; some people don't.

- The semicolon is also used to link independent clauses before a conjunctive adverb (such as *however, furthermore*).

  Some people like country music; however, other people dislike it intensely.

Slash

- The slash separates alternatives.

  and/or
- The slash divides numbers in dates, and divides numerators and denominators in fractions.

  the memorable date 9/11/01        Ten and 50/100 dollars
- The slash is used when quoting lines of poetry to show where each line ends.

  My favorite lines from this poem are, "She slept beneath a tree / remembered but by me."

## CAPITALIZATION

Capitalize proper nouns and proper adjectives.

- Main words in titles: Gone with the Wind

- People: John Lennon, Pelé

- Cities, nations, states, nationalities, and languages: Istanbul, Turkey, California, Brazil, American, Spanish

- Geographical items: Mekong River, Mount Olympus, Central Park

- Companies and organizations: Ford Motor Company, Harvard University, National Organization for Women

- Departments and government offices: English Department, Internal Revenue Service

- Buildings: the Empire State Building

- Trademarked products: Kleenex tissue, Scotch tape

- Days, months, and holidays: Tuesday, January, Ramadan

- Some abbreviations without periods: **USA, UN, YMCA**

- Religions and related words: Hindu, Bible, Muslim

- Historical periods, events, and documents: Civil War, Declaration of Independence

- Titles of people: Professor Jones, President Lincoln, Ms. Tanaka, Dr. Lee

- Titles of printed matter: *Collins COBUILD Student's Dictionary of American English*

## ITALICIZATION

In handwritten or typed copy, italics are shown by underlining.

**Use italics for the following types of material.**

- Words or phrases you wish to emphasize.

  Is this *really* your first time in an airplane?

  She feeds her dog *T-bone steak*. [It's best not to use italics for emphasis very often.]

- A publication that is not part of a larger publication.

  *The Daily News* (newspaper)
  *The Sun Also Rises* (book)
  *Newsweek* (magazine)
  *Titanic* (movie)

- Foreign words in an English sentence.

  The first four numbers in Turkish are *bir, iki, üc, dört*.
  The French have a saying: *Plus ça change . . .*

- Letters used in algebraic equations.

  $E = mc^2$

## SPELLING

Frequently Misspelled Words

**People sometimes confuse the spelling of the following words:**

| | | |
|---|---|---|
| accept, except | conscience, conscious | lay, lie |
| access, excess | council, counsel | lead, led |
| advice, advise | diary, dairy | lessen, lesson |
| affect, effect | decent, descent, dissent | lightning, lightening |
| aisles, isles | desert, dessert | lose, loose |
| alley, ally | device, devise | marital, martial |
| already, all ready | discreet, discrete | maybe, may be |
| altar, alter | dyeing, dying | miner, minor |
| altogether, all together | elicit, illicit | moral, morale |
| always, all ways | emigrate, immigrate | of, off |
| amoral, immoral | envelop, envelope | passed, past |
| angel, angle | fair, fare | patience, patients |
| ask, ax | faze, phase | peace, piece |
| assistance, assistants | fine, find | personal, personnel |
| baring, barring, bearing | formerly, formally | plain, plane |
| began, begin | forth, fourth | pray, prey |
| believe, belief | forward, foreword | precede, proceed |
| board, bored | gorilla, guerrilla | presence, presents |
| break, brake | have, of | principle, principal |
| breath, breathe | hear, here | prophecy, prophesy |
| buy, by, bye | heard, herd | purpose, propose |
| capital, capitol | heroin, heroine | quiet, quit, quite |
| censor, censure, sensor | hole, whole | raise, rise |
| choose, chose | holy, wholly | respectfully, respectively |
| cite, site, sight | horse, hoarse | right, rite, write |
| clothes, cloths | human, humane | road, rode |
| coarse, course | its, it's | sat, set |
| complement, compliment | later, latter | sense, since |

| | | |
|---|---|---|
| shown, shone | throne, thrown | were, wear, where, we're |
| stationary, stationery | to, too, two | which, witch |
| straight, strait | tract, track | who's, whose |
| than, then | waist, waste | your, you're |
| their, there, they're, there're | weak, week | |
| threw, through, thorough | weather, whether | |

**NOTE:** The following summary will answer many spelling questions. However, there are many more rules and also many exceptions. Always check your dictionary if in doubt.

### Ei and ie

There is an old saying that says: "I before e, except after c, or when pronounced like ay as in neighbor and weigh."

- I before e: brief, niece, fierce
- E before i after the letter c: receive, conceit, ceiling
- E before i when pronounced like ay: eight, weight, their

### Prefixes

A prefix changes the meaning of a word but no letters are added or dropped.

- usual, **un**usual
- interested, **dis**interested
- use, **re**use

### Suffixes

- Drop the final e on the base word when a suffix beginning with a vowel is added.
  drive, driv**ing**    combine, combin**ation**
- Keep the silent e on the base word when a suffix beginning with a consonant is added.
  live, live**ly**    safe, safe**ly** [Exceptions: truly, ninth]
- If the base word (1) ends in a final consonant, (2) is a one-syllable word or a stressed syllable, and (3) the final consonant is preceded by a vowel, double the final consonant.
  hit, hi**tt**ing    drop, dro**pp**ing
- Change a final y on a base word to i when adding any suffix except -ing.
  day, da**i**ly    try, tr**i**ed    BUT: play, pla**ying**

## GRAMMAR

### Conjunctions

Conjunctions are words that connect words, phrases, or clauses.

### Coordinating Conjunctions

The coordinating conjunctions are: and, but, for, nor, or, so, yet

- Sarah **and** Michael
- on vacation **for** three weeks
- You can borrow the book from a library **or** you can buy it at a bookstore.

Correlative Conjunctions

Correlative conjunctions are used in pairs.

The correlative conjunctions are: *both ... and, either ... or, neither ... nor, not only ... but also, whether ... or*

- **Neither** Sam **nor** Madeleine could attend the party.
- The singer was **both** out of tune **and** too loud.
- Oscar **not only** ate too much, **but also** fell asleep at the table.

Subordinating Conjunctions

Subordinating conjunctions are used to connect a subordinate clause to a main clause.

- Antonia sighed loudly **as if** she were really exhausted.
- Uri arrived late **because** his car broke down.

**Here is a list of subordinating conjunctions:**

| | | | | |
|---|---|---|---|---|
| after | before | no matter how | than | where |
| although | even if | now that | though | wherever |
| as far as | even though | once | till | whether |
| as if | how | provided that | unless | while |
| as soon as | if | since | until | why |
| as though | in as much as | so that | when | |
| because | in case | supposing that | whenever | |

Conjunctive Adverbs

Two independent clauses can be connected using a semicolon, plus a conjunctive adverb and a comma. The conjunctive adverb often comes right after the semicolon.

- Kham wanted to buy a car; **however,** he hadn't saved up enough money.
- Larry didn't go right home; **instead,** he stopped at the health club.

Some conjunctive adverbs can appear in different positions in the second clause.

- Kham wanted to buy a car; he hadn't, **however,** saved up enough money.
- Larry didn't go right home; he stopped at the health club **instead.**

**Here is a list of conjunctive adverbs:**

| | | | | |
|---|---|---|---|---|
| also | finally | indeed | nevertheless | then |
| anyhow | furthermore | instead | next | therefore |
| anyway | hence | likewise | otherwise | thus |
| besides | however | meanwhile | similarly | |
| consequently | incidentally | moreover | still | |

Transitional Phrases

If all the sentences in a passage begin with subject + verb, the effect can be boring. To add variety, use a transitional phrase, followed by a comma, at the beginning of some sentences.

- Rita needed to study for the test. **On the other hand,** she didn't want to miss the party.
- Yuki stayed up all night studying. **As a result,** he overslept and missed the test.

**Here is a list of transitional phrases:**

| | |
|---|---|
| after all | for example |
| as a result | in addition |
| at any rate | in fact |
| at the same time | in other words |
| by the way | on the contrary |
| even so | on the other hand |

Common Prepositions

A preposition describes a relationship to another part of speech; it is usually used before a noun or pronoun.

- Sancho was waiting **outside** the club.
- I gave the money **to** him.

**Here is a list of common prepositions:**

| | | |
|---|---|---|
| about | by | out |
| above | concerning | outside |
| across | despite | over |
| after | during | past |
| against | down | regarding |
| among | except | round |
| around | for | since |
| as | from | through |
| at | in | to |
| before | inside | toward |
| behind | into | under |
| below | lie | unlike |
| beneath | near | until |
| beside | of | up |
| between | off | upon |
| beyond | on | with |

Phrasal Prepositions

**Here is a list of phrasal prepositions:**

| | | |
|---|---|---|
| according to | by way of | in spite of |
| along with | due to | instead of |
| apart from | except for | on account of |
| as for | in addition to | out of |
| as regards | in case of | up to |
| as to | in front of | with reference to |
| because of | in lieu of | with regard to |
| by means of | in place of | with respect to |
| by reason of | in regard to | with the exception of |

## DOCUMENTATION

College instructors usually require one of three formats (APA, Chicago, or MLA) to document the information you use in research papers and essays. The following pages compare and contrast the highlights of these three styles.

**APA Style** (American Psychological Association style)

1.  General Endnote Format

    Title the page "References." Double-space the page and arrange the names alphabetically by authors' last names, the date in parentheses, followed by the rest of the information about the publication.

2.  Citation for a Single Author

    Moore, (1992). *The care of the soul*. New York: HarperPerennial.

3.  Citation for Multiple Authors

    List the last names first followed by initials and use the "&" sign before the last author.

    Spinosa, C., Flores, F., & Dreyfus, H.L. (1997). *Disclosing new worlds: Entrepreneurship, democratic action, and the cultivation of solidarity*. Cambridge, MA: MIT Press.

4.  Citation for an Editor as Author

    Wellwood, J. (Ed.). (1992). *Ordinary magic: Everyday life as a spiritual path*. Boston: Shambhala Publications.

5.  Citation for an Article in a Periodical

    List the author, last name first, the year and month (and day if applicable) of the publication. Then list the title of the article (not underlined), the name of the publication (followed by the volume number if there is one) and the page number or numbers.

    Gibson, S. (2001, November). Hanging wallpaper. *This Old House*, 77.

6. Citation of Online Materials

   Provide enough information so that readers can find the information you refer to. Try to include the date on the posting, the title, the original print source (if any), a description of where you found the information, and the date you found the material.

   Arnold, W. (April 26, 2002). "State senate announces new tax relief." *Seattle Post-Intelligencer*. Retrieved May 1, 2002, from http://seattle.pi.nwsource.com/printer2/index.asp?ploc=b

7. General In-text Citation Format

   Include two pieces of information: the last name of the author or authors of the work cited in the References and the year of publication.
   (Moore, 1992).

**Chicago Style** (from *The Chicago Manual of Style*)

1. General Endnote Format

   Title the page "Notes." Double-space the page. Number and indent the first line of each entry. Use full authors' names, not initials. Include page references at the end of the entry.

2. Citation for a Single Author

   Thomas Moore, *The Care of the Soul* (New York: HarperPerennial, 1992), 7–9.

3. Citation for Multiple Authors

   Charles Spinosa, Ferdinand Flores, and Hubert L. Dreyfus, *Disclosing New Worlds: Entrepreneurship, Democratic Action, and the Cultivation of Solidarity* (Cambridge: MIT Press, 1997), 66.

4. Citation for an Editor as Author

   John Wellwood, ed. 1992. *Ordinary Magic: Everyday Life as Spiritual Path* (Boston: Shambhala Publications).

5. Citation for an Article in a Periodical

   List the author, last name first. Then put the title of the article in quotation marks, the name of the publication, the volume number (if one is given), the month, and the page number or numbers.

   Gibson, Stephen, "Hanging Wallpaper," *This Old House* 53 (2001): 77.

6. Citation of Online Materials

   Number and indent each entry and provide enough information so that readers can find the information you refer to. Try to include the author (first name first), the date on the posting (in parentheses), the title, the original print source (if any), a description of where you found the information, the URL, and the date you found the material (in parentheses).

1. William Arnold, "State Senate Announces New Tax Relief," *Seattle Post-Intelligencer*, April 26, 2002, http://seattle.pi.nwsource.com/printer2/index.asp?ploc=b

7. General In-text Citation Format

Number all in-text notes. The first time you cite a work within the text, use all the information as shown in 2. above. When citing the same work again, include only the last name of the author or authors and the page or pages you refer to.

(Moore, 8)

MLA Style (Modern Language Association style)

1. General Endnote Format

Title the page "Works Cited." Double-space the page and arrange the names alphabetically by authors' last names, followed by the rest of the information about the publication as shown below.

2. Citation for a Single Author

Moore, Thomas. *The Care of the Soul*. New York: HarperPerennial, 1992.

3. Citation for Multiple Authors

List the authors' names in the same order as on the title page. List only the first author's last name first.

Spinosa, Charles, Ferdinand Flores, and Hubert L. Dreyfus. *Disclosing New Worlds: Entrepreneurship, Democratic Action, and the Cultivation of Solidarity*. Cambridge: MIT, 1997.

4. Citation for an Editor as Author

Wellwood, John, ed. *Ordinary Magic: Everyday Life as Spiritual Path*. Boston; Shambhala, 1992.

5. Citation for an Article in a Periodical

List the author (last name first), the title of the article (using quotation marks), the title of the magazine (with no period), the volume number, the date (followed by a colon), and the page number.

Gibson, Stephen. "Hanging Wallpaper." *This Old House* 53 (2001): 77.

6. Citation of Online Materials

Provide enough information so that readers can find the information you refer to. Try to include the date on the information, the title, the original print source (if any), the date you found the material, and the URL (if possible).

1. Arnold, William. "State Senate Announces New Tax Relief." *Seattle Post-Intelligencer* 26 Apr. 2002 http://seattle.pi.nwsource.com/printer2/index.asp?ploc=b

7. General In-text Citation Format

Do not number entries. When citing a work listed in the "Works Cited" section, include only the last name of the author or authors and the page or pages you refer to. (Moore 7-8)

## BLOCK LETTER FORMAT

Using the block letter format, there are no indented lines.

| | |
|---|---|
| Return address | 77 Lincoln Avenue<br>Wellesley, MA 02480 |
| Date | May 10, 2009 |
| Inside address | Dr. Rita Bennett<br>Midland Hospital Senior Care Center<br>5000 Poe Avenue<br>Dayton, OH 45414 |
| Salutation | Dear Dr. Bennett: |
| Body of the letter | I am responding to your advertisement for a dietitian in the May 5 edition of the *New York Times*. I graduated from Boston University two years ago. Since graduation, I have been working at Brigham and Women's Hospital and have also earned additional certificates in nutritional support and diabetes education.<br><br>I am interested in locating to the Midwest and will be happy to arrange for an interview at your convenience. |
| Complimentary close | Sincerely, |
| Signature | *Daniel Chin* |
| Typed name | Daniel Chin |

## INDENTED LETTER FORMAT

Using the indented format, the return address, the date, and the closing appear at the far right side of the paper. The first line of each paragraph is also indented.

| | |
|---|---|
| Return address | 77 Lincoln Avenue<br>Wellesley, MA 02480 |
| Date | May 15, 2009 |
| Inside address | Dr. Rita Bennett<br>Senior Care Center<br>5000 Poe Avenue<br>Dayton, OH 45414 |
| Salutation | Dear Dr. Bennett: |
| Body of the letter | It was a pleasure to meet you and learn more about the programs offered at the Senior Care Center. I appreciate your taking time out to show me around and introduce me to the staff.<br><br>I am excited about the possibility of working at the Senior Care Center and I look forward to talking with you again soon. |
| Complimentary close | Sincerely, |
| Signature | *Daniel Chin* |
| Typed name | Daniel Chin |

# RESUMES

Successful resume strategies

- **Length:** One page
- **Honesty:** Never say something that is untrue
- **Inclusiveness:** Include information about your experience and qualifications. You do not have to include your age, religion, marital status, race or citizenship. It is not necessary to include a photo.

Heading
Include name, address, e-mail, and phone number.

Objective
Include your goals or skills or both.

Skills
Include any skills that you have that may be helpful in the job that you are applying for.

Experience
Describe the jobs you've held. Include your accomplishments and awards. Use positive, action-oriented words with strong verbs. Use present-tense verbs for your current job and past-tense verbs for jobs you've had in the past. Include the job titles that you've held.

Education
Include schools attended. If you are a college graduate, don't include high school. List degrees with most recent first.

Interests
This is not required, but can help a potential employer see you as a well-rounded person.

Sample Resume

There are several different acceptable resume formats. Here is one example.

**Maria Gonzales**
9166 Main Street, Apartment 3G
Los Angeles, CA 93001
gonzales@email.com
213-555-9878

| | |
|---|---|
| **OBJECTIVE:** | Experienced manager seeks a management position in retail sales |

**EXPERIENCE:**

**Assistant Director of Retail**

2005 – Present   Shopmart, Los Angeles, CA
Manage relationships with vendors to complete orders, create accounts, and resolve issues. Maintain inventory and generate monthly inventory reports. Plan weekly promotions. Communicate with all retail employees to improve product knowledge and selling techniques. Implemented new customer service procedures.

**Server**

2005 – Present   Chuy's Grill, Santa Monica, CA
Greet and seat guests. Bus tables. Answer phones and take and prepare in-house, phone, or fax orders. Train new and existing employees. Awarded Employee of the Month five times for exceeding company expectations for quality and service.

**Store Supervisor**

1999 – 2005   Impact Photography Systems, Waco, TX
Oversaw daily operations, including customer and employee relations, counter sales, inventory management, maintaining store appearance, banking transactions, and equipment maintenance. Managed, trained, and scheduled staff of 35.

**SKILLS:**   Fluent in English and Spanish. Expert in MS Word and Excel.

**EDUCATION:**

**Associate of Arts Degree**

1997 – 2000   Los Angeles Community College, Los Angeles, CA
Coursework in business management, marketing, studio art, communication, psychology, and sociology.

**Study Abroad**

2000 – 2001   University of Valencia, Valencia, Spain
Coursework in Spanish and international business.

**INTERESTS:**   Backpacking, playing softball, and volunteering as a tutor for Literacy First.

## PROOFREADING MARKS

Teachers often use the following correction abbreviations and symbols on students' papers.

| Problem area | Symbol | Example |
|---|---|---|
| agreement | **agr** | He **go** to work at 8:00. |
| capital letters | **cap** | the United states |
| word division or | **div** | disorientati |
| hyphenation | **hy** | -on |
| sentence fragment | **frag** | **Where she found the book.** |
| grammar | **gr** | It's the **bigger** house on the street. |
| need italics | **ital** | I read it in **The Daily News.** |
| need lower case | **lc** | I don't like Peanut Butter. |
| punctuation error | **p** | Where did you find that coat. |
| plural needed | **pl** | I bought the **grocery** on my way home. |
| spelling error | **sp** | Did you recieve my letter yet? |
| wrong tense | **t** | I **see** her yesterday. |
| wrong word | **ww** | My family used to **rise** corn and wheat. |
| need an apostrophe | ⌣ | I don⌣t know her name. |
| need a comma | ⌃ | However⌄we will probably arrive on time. |
| delete something | ⸿ | We had the most best meal of our lives. |
| start a new | ¶ | … since last Friday. |
| paragraph | | ¶ Oh, by the way … |
| transpose words | ⌒ | They live on the floor first. |

## 1. GREETINGS, INTRODUCTIONS, AND LEAVE-TAKING

**Greeting someone you know**
Hello.
Hi.
Hey.
Morning.
How's it going?   [Informal]
What's up?   [Informal]

**Greeting someone you haven't
seen for a while**
It's good to see you again.
It's been a long time.
How long has it been?
Long time no see!   [Informal]
You look great!   [Informal]
So what have you been up to?   [Informal]

**Greeting someone you don't know**
Hello.
Good morning.
Good afternoon.
Good evening.
Hi, there!   [Informal]

**Saying goodbye**
Goodbye.
Bye.
Bye-bye.
See you.
See you later.
Have a good day.
Take care.
Good night. [Only when saying goodbye]

**Introducing yourself**
Hi, I'm Tom.
Hello, my name is Tom.
Excuse me.
We haven't met.
My name is Tom.   [Formal]
I saw you in (science) class.
I met you at Jane's party.

**Introducing other people**
Have you two met?
Have you met Maria?
I'd like you to meet Maria.
There's someone I'd like you to meet.
Let me introduce you to Maria.

> **You:** This is my friend Maria.
> **Ali:** Glad to meet you, Maria.
> **You:** Maria, this is Ali.
> **Maria:** Nice to meet you, Ali.

I've been wanting to meet you.
Tom has told me a lot about you.

**Greeting guests**
Welcome.
Oh, hi.
How are you?
Please come in.
Glad you could make it.
Did you have any trouble finding us?
Can I take your coat?
Have a seat.
Please make yourself at home.

> **You:** Can I get you something
> to drink?
> **Guest:** Yes, please.
> **You:** What would you like?
> **Guest:** I'll have some orange juice.

What can I get you to drink?
Would you like some ...?

**Saying goodbye to guests**
Thanks for coming.
Thanks for joining us.
I'm so glad you could come.
It wouldn't have been the same without
   you.
Let me get your things.
Stop by anytime.

## 2. HAVING A CONVERSATION

**Starting a conversation**
Nice weather, huh?
Aren't you a friend of Jim's?
Did you see last night's game?
What's your favorite TV show?
So, what do you think about (the situation in Europe)?
So how do you like (your new car)?
Guess what I did last night.

**Showing that you are listening**
Uh-huh.
Right.
Exactly.
Yeah.
OK...
I know what you mean.

**Giving yourself time to think**
Well...
Um...
Uh...
Let me think.
Just a minute.

> **Other:** We should ride our bikes.
> **You:** It's too far. And, I mean ...,
> it's raining and we're already
> late.

**Checking for comprehension**
Do you see what I mean?
Are you with me?
Does that make sense?

**Checking for agreement**
Don't you agree?
So what do you think?
We have to (act fast), you know?

**Expressing agreement**
You're right.
I couldn't agree with you more.
Good thinking!  [Informal]
You said it!  [Informal]
You're absolutely right.
Absolutely!  [Informal]

**Expressing disagreement**
I'm afraid I disagree.
Yeah, but ...
I see your point, but ...
That's not true.
You must be joking!  [Informal]
No way!  [Informal]

**Asking someone to repeat something**
Excuse me?
Sorry?
I didn't quite get that.
Could you repeat that?
Could you say that again?
Say again? [Informal]

**Interrupting someone**
Excuse me.
Yes, but (we don't have enough time).
I know, but (that will take hours).
Wait a minute.  [Informal]
Just hold it right there!  [Impolite]

**Changing the topic**
By the way, what do you think about (the new teacher)?
Before I forget, (there's a free concert on Friday night).
Whatever ... (Did you see David's new car?)
Enough about me. Let's talk about you.

**Ending a conversation**
It was nice talking with you.
Good seeing you.
Sorry, I have to go now.

## 3. USING THE TELEPHONE

### Making personal calls
Hi, this is David.
Is this Alice?
Is Alice there?
May I speak with Alice, please?    [Formal]
I work with her.
We're in the same science class.
Could you tell her I called?
Would you ask her to call me?

### Answering personal calls
Hello?
Who's calling, please?
Oh, hi David. How are you?
I can't hear you.
Sorry, we got cut off.
I'm in the middle of something.
Can I call you back?
What's your number again?
Listen. I have to go now.
It was nice talking to you.

### Answering machine greetings
You've reached 212-555-6701.
Please leave a message after the beep.
Hi, this is Carlos.
I can't take your call right now.
Sorry I missed your call.
Please leave your name and number.
I'll call you back as soon as I can.

### Answering machine messages
This is Magda. Call me back when you
    get a chance.   [Informal]
Call me back on my cell.
I'll call you back later.
Talk to you later.
If you get this message before 11:00, please
    call me back.

### Making business calls
Hello. This is Andy Larson.
I'm calling about ...
Is this an OK time?

### Answering business calls
Apex Electronics. Rosa Baker speaking.
    [Formal]
Hello, Rosa Baker.
May I help you?
Who's calling, please?

| Caller: | May I speak with Mr. Hafner, please? |
| **Businessperson:** | This is he. |

| Caller: | Mr. Hafner, please. |
| **Businessperson:** | Speaking. |

### Talking to an office assistant
Extension 716, please.
Customer Service, please.
May I speak with Sheila Spink, please?
She's expecting my call.
I'm returning her call.
I'd like to leave a message for Ms. Spink.

### Making appointments on the phone
| **You:** | I'd like to make an appointment to see Ms. Spink. |
| **Assistant:** | How's 11:00 on Wednesday? |
| **You:** | Wednesday is really bad for me. |
| **Assistant:** | Can you make it Thursday at 9:00? |
| **You:** | That would be perfect! |
| **Assistant:** | OK. I have you down for Thursday at 9:00. |

### Special explanations
I'm sorry. She's not available.
Is there something I can help you with?
Can I put you on hold?
I'll transfer you to that extension.
If you'll leave your number, I'll have Ms. Spink
    call you back.
I'll tell her you called.

## 4. INTERVIEWING FOR A JOB

**Small talk by the interviewer**
Thanks for coming in today.
Did you have any trouble finding us?
How was the drive?
Would you like a cup of coffee?
Do you happen to know (Terry Mendham)?

**Small talk by the candidate**
What a great view!
Thanks for arranging to see me.
I've been looking forward to meeting you.
I spent some time exploring the company's web site.
My friend, Dale, has worked here for several years.

**Getting serious**
OK, shall we get started?
So, anyway . . .
Let's get down to business.

**General questions for a candidate**
Tell me a little about yourself.
How did you get into this line of work?
How long have you been in this country?
How did you learn about the opening?
What do you know about this company?
Why are you interested in working for us?

**General answers to an interviewer**
I've always been interested in (finance).
I enjoy (working with numbers).
My (uncle) was (an accountant) and encouraged me to try it.
I saw your ad in the paper.
This company has a great reputation in the field.

**Job-related questions for a candidate**
What are you qualifications for this job?
Describe your work experience.
What were your responsibilities on your last job?
I'd like to hear more about (your supervisory experience).

**Interviewer:** Have you taken any courses in (bookkeeping)?
**You:** Yes, I took two courses in business school and another online course last year.

What interests you about this particular job?
Why do you think it's a good fit?
Why did you leave your last job?
Do you have any experience with (HTML)?
Would you be willing to (travel eight weeks a year)?
What sort of salary are you looking for?

**Describing job qualifications to an interviewer**
In (2000), I started working for (Booker's) as a (sales rep).
After (two years), I was promoted to (sales manager).
You'll notice on my resumé that (I supervised six people).
I was responsible for (three territories).
I was in charge of (planning sales meetings).
I have experience in all areas of (sales).
I helped implement (online sales reports).
I had to (contact my reps) on a daily basis.
I speak (Spanish) fluently.
I think my strong points are (organization and punctuality).

**Ending the interview**
I'm impressed with your experience.
I'd like to arrange a second interview.
When would you be able to start?
You'll hear from us by (next Wednesday).
We'll be in touch.

## 5. PRESENTATIONS

### Introducing yourself

Hello, everyone. I'd like to thank you all for coming.

Let me tell you a little bit about myself.

My name is (Rita Nazario).

I am president of (Catco International).

Hi. I'm (Ivan Wolf) from (Peekskill Incorporated).

Two years ago (I started out as a salesperson at Peekskill).

Today (I supervise the West Coast sales team).

### Introducing someone else

This is (Tina Gorman), a (woman) who needs no introduction.

(Tina) is one of America's best-known (lawyers).

(She) is going to talk to us about (car insurance).

Let's give (her) a warm welcome.

We are lucky to have with us today (Barry Rogers).

As you know, (he) is (the president of Ranger Incorporated).

It gives me great pleasure to present (Barry Rogers).

And so without further ado, I'd like to present (Barry Rogers).

### Stating the purpose

Today I'd like to talk to you about (managing your money).

Today I'm going to show you how to (save a lot of money).

I'll begin by (outlining the basics).

Then I'll (go into more detail).

I'll tell you (everything you need to know about savings accounts).

I'll provide an overview of (different types of investments).

I also hope to interest you in (some safe investments).

I'll list (the three biggest mistakes people make).

By the end, you'll (feel like an expert).

### Relating to the audience

Can everyone hear me?

Raise your hand if you need me to repeat anything.

Please stop me at any point if you have a question.

How many people here (plan to continue their education)?

If you're like me, (you haven't saved up enough money).

We all know what that's like, don't we?

Does this ring a bell?

Don't you hate it when (people tell you what you should do)?

### Citing sources

According to the New York Times, ...

A study conducted by Harvard University showed that ...

Recent research shows that ...

Medical researchers have discovered that ...

Peter Butler said, and I quote, "..."

I read somewhere that ...

(The federal government) released a report stating that ...

### Making transitions

I'd like to expand on that before we move on.

The next thing I'd like to talk about is ...

Now let's take a look at ...

Moving right along ...

To sum up what I've said so far, ...

Now let's move on to the question of ...

Now that you have an overview, let's look at some of the specifics.

Recapping the main points, ...

I'm afraid we have to move on.

### Emphasizing important points

I'd like to emphasize that ...

Never forget that ...

This is a key concept.

The bottom line is ...

If you remember only one thing I've said today, ...

I can't stress enough the importance of ...

### Using visuals

Take a look at (the chart on the screen).

I'd like to draw your attention to (the poster over there).

You'll notice that ...

Pay special attention to the ...

If you look closely, you'll see that ...

So what does this tell us?

### Closing

And in conclusion, ...

Let's open the floor to questions.

It's been a pleasure being with you today.

## 6. Agreeing and Disagreeing

**Agreeing**
Yeah, that's right.
I know it.
I agree with you.
You're right.
That's true.
I think so, too.
That's what I think.
Me, too.
Me neither.

**Agreeing strongly**
You're absolutely right!
Definitely!
Certainly!
Exactly!
Absolutely!
Of course!
I couldn't agree more.
You're telling me!   [Informal]
You said it!   [Informal]

**Agreeing weakly**
I suppose so.
Yeah, I guess so.
It would seem that way.

**Remaining neutral**
I see your point.
You have a point there.
I understand what you're saying.
I see what you mean.
I'd have to think about that.
I've never thought about it that way before.
Maybe yes, maybe no.
Could be.

**Disagreeing**
No, I don't think so.
I agree up to a point.
I really don't see it that way.
That's not what I think.
I agree that (going by car is faster), but . . .
But what about (the expense involved)?
Yes, but . . .
I know, but . . .
No, it wasn't. / No, they don't. / etc.

| | |
|---|---|
| **Other person:** | We could save a lot of money by taking the bus. |
| **You:** | Not really. It would cost almost the same as driving. |

**Disagreeing strongly**
I disagree completely.
That's not true.
That is not an option.
Definitely not!
Absolutely not!
You've made your point, but . . .
No way!   [Informal]
You can't be serious.   [Informal]
You've got to be kidding!   [Informal]
Where did you get that idea?   [Impolite]
Are you out of your mind!   [Impolite]

**Disagreeing politely**
I'm afraid I have to disagree with you.
I'm not so sure.
I'm not sure that's such a good idea.
I see what you're saying, but . . .
I'm sure many people feel that way, but . . .
But don't you think we should consider (other alternatives)?

## 7. INTERRUPTING, CLARIFYING, CHECKING FOR UNDERSTANDING

### Informal interruptions
Ummm.

Sir? / Ma'am?

Just a minute.

Can I stop you for a minute?

Wait a minute! [Impolite]

Hold it right there! [Impolite]

### Formal interruptions
Excuse me, sir / ma'am.

Excuse me for interrupting.

Forgive me for interrupting you, but . . .

I'm sorry to break in like this, but . . .

Could I interrupt you for a minute?

Could I ask a question, please?

### Asking for clarification—Informal
What did you say?

I didn't catch that.

Sorry, I didn't get that.

I missed that.

Could you repeat that?

Could you say that again?

Say again?

I'm lost.

Could you run that by me one more time?

Did you say . . . ?

Do you mean . . . ?

### Asking for clarification—Formal
I beg your pardon?

I'm not sure I understand what you're saying.

I can't make sense of what you just said.

Could you explain that in different words?

Could you please repeat that?

Could you go over that again?

### Giving clarification—Informal
I'll go over it again.

I'll take it step by step.

I'll take a different tack this time.

Stop me if you get lost.

OK, here's a recap.

Maybe this will clarify things.

To put it another way, . . .

In other words, . . .

### Giving clarification—Formal
Let me put it another way.

Let me give you some examples.

Here are the main points again.

I'm afraid you didn't understand what I said.

I'm afraid you've missed the point.

What I meant was . . .

I hope you didn't think that . . .

I didn't mean to imply that . . .

I hope that clears things up.

### Checking for understanding
Do you understand now?

Is it clearer now?

Do you see what I'm getting at?

Does that help?

Is there anything that still isn't clear?

What other questions do you have?

> **Speaker:** What else?
>
> **Listener:** I'm still not clear on the difference between a preposition and a conjunction.

Now explain it to me in your own words.

## 8. APOLOGIZING

**Apologizing for a small accident or mistake**

Sorry.

I'm sorry.

Excuse me.

It was an accident.

Pardon me.   [Formal]

Oops!   [Informal]

My mistake.   [Informal]

I'm terrible with (names).

I've never been good with (numbers).

I can't believe I (did) that.

**Apologizing for a serious accident or mistake**

I'm so sorry.

I am really sorry that I (damaged your car).

I am so sorry about (damaging your car).

I feel terrible about (the accident).

I'm really sorry but (I was being very careful).

I'm sorry for (causing you a problem).

Please accept my apologies for . . .   [Formal]

I sincerely apologize for . . .   [Formal]

**Apologizing for upsetting someone**

I'm sorry I upset you.

I didn't mean to make you feel bad.

Please forgive me.   [Formal]

I just wasn't thinking straight.

That's not what I meant to say.

I didn't mean it personally.

I'm sorry. I'm having a rough day.

**Apologizing for having to say** *no*

I'm sorry. I can't.

Sorry, I never (lend anyone my car).

I wish I could say *yes*.

I'm going to have to say *no*.

I can't. I have to (work that evening).

Maybe some other time.

**Responding to an apology**

Don't worry about it.

Oh, that's OK.

Think nothing of it.   [Formal]

Don't mention it.   [Formal]

> **Other person:** I'm afraid I lost the pen you lent me.
>
> **You:** No big thing.

It doesn't matter.

It's not important.

Never mind.

No problem.

It happens.

Forget it.

Don't sweat it.   [Informal]

Apology accepted.   [Formal]

**Showing regret**

I feel really bad.

It won't happen again.

I wish I could go back and start all over again.

I don't know what came over me.

I don't know what to say.

Now I know better.

Too bad I didn't . . .

It was inexcusable of me.   [Formal]

It's not like me to . . .

I hope I can make it up to you.

That didn't come out right.

I didn't mean to take it out on you.

**Sympathizing**

This must be very difficult for you.

I know what you mean.

I know how you're feeling.

I know how upset you must be.

I can imagine how difficult this is for you.

## 9. Suggestions, Advice, Insistence

**Making informal suggestions**
Here's what I suggest.
I know what you should do.
Why don't you (go to the movies with Jane)?
What about (having lunch with Bob)?
Try (the French fries next time).
Have you thought about (riding your bike to work)?

**Accepting suggestions**
Thanks, I'll do that.
Good idea!
That's a great idea.
Sounds good to me.
That's a plan.
I'll give it a try.
Guess it's worth a try.

**Refusing suggestions**
No. I don't like (French fries).
That's not for me.
I don't think so.
That might work for some people, but . . .
Nawww. [Informal]
I don't feel like it. [Impolite]

**Giving serious advice—Informal**
Listen!
Here's the plan.
Take my advice.
Take it from one who knows.
Take it from someone who's been there.
Here's what I think you should do.
Hey! Here's an idea.
How about (waiting until you're 30 to get married)?
Don't (settle down too quickly).
Why don't you (see the world while you're young)?
You can always (settle down later).
Don't forget—(you only live once).

**Giving serious advice—formal**
Have you ever thought about (becoming a doctor)?
Maybe it would be a good idea if you (went back to school).
It looks to me like (Harvard) would be your best choice.
If I were you, I'd study (medicine).
In my opinion, you should (consider it seriously).
Be sure to (get your application in early).
I always advise people to (check that it was received).
The best idea is (to study hard).
If you're really smart, you'll (start right away).

**Accepting advice**
You're right.
Thanks for the advice.
That makes a lot of sense.
I see what you mean.
That sounds like good advice.
I'll give it a try.
I'll do my best.
You've given me something to think about.
I'll try it and get back to you.

**Refusing advice**
I don't think that that would work for me.
That doesn't make sense to me.
I'm not sure that would be such a good idea.
I could never (become a doctor).
Thanks for the input.
Thanks, but no thanks. [Informal]
You don't know what you're talking about. [Impolite]
I think I know what's best for myself. [Impolite]
Back off! [Impolite]

**Insisting**
You have to (become a doctor).
Try to see it my way.
I know what I'm talking about.
If you don't (go to medical school), I won't (pay for your college).
I don't care what you think. [Impolite]

## 10. DESCRIBING FEELINGS

### Happiness

I'm doing great.
This is the best day of my life.
I've never been so happy in my life.
I'm so pleased for you.
Aren't you thrilled?
What could be better?
Life is good.

### Sadness

Are you OK?
Why the long face?
I'm not doing so well.
I feel awful.
I'm devastated.
I'm depressed.
I'm feeling kind of blue.
I just want to crawl in a hole.
Oh, what's the use?

### Fear

I'm worried about (money).
He dreads (going to the dentist).
I'm afraid to (drive over bridges).
She can't stand (snakes).
This anxiety is killing me.
He's scared of (big dogs).
How will I ever (pass Friday's test)?
I have a phobia about (germs).

### Anger

I'm really mad at (you).
They resent (such high taxes).
How could she (do) that?
I'm annoyed with (the neighbors).
(The noise of car alarms) infuriates her.
He was furious with (the children).

### Boredom

I'm so bored.
There's nothing to do around here.
What a bore!
Nothing ever happens.
She was bored to tears.
They were bored to death.
I was bored stiff.
It was such a monotonous (movie).
(That TV show) was so dull.

### Disgust

That's disgusting.
Eeew! Yuck!    [Informal]
I hate (raw fish).
How can you stand it?
I almost vomited.
I thought I'd puke.    [Impolite]
I don't even like to think about it.
How can you say something like that?
I wouldn't be caught dead (wearing that
    dirty old coat).

### Compassion

I'm sorry.
I understand what you're going through.
Tell me about it.
How can I help?
Is there anything I can do?
She is concerned about him.
He worries about the children.
He cares for her deeply.
My heart goes out to them.
    [Old-fashioned]

### Guilt

I feel terrible that I (lost your mother's
    necklace).
I never should have (borrowed it).
I feel so guilty!
It's all my fault.
I blame myself.
I make a mess of everything.
I'll never forgive myself.

# TEXT MESSAGING AND EMOTICONS

| | |
|---|---|
| 1 | used to replace "-one": NE1 = anyone |
| 2 | to or too: it's up 2 U = it's up to you; me 2 = me too |
| | used to replace "to-": 2day = today |
| 2DAY | today |
| 2MORO | tomorrow |
| 2NITE | tonight |
| 4 | for: 4 U = for you |
| | used to replace "-fore": B4 = before |
| 411 | information: TNX 4 the 411 |
| 8 | used to replace "-ate" or "-eat": GR8 = great; C U L8R = see you later |
| 86 | discard, get rid of |
| AFAIK | as far as I know |
| B | be: used to replace "be-" in other words: B4 = before |
| B4 | before |
| B4N | bye for now |
| BRB | be right back |
| BTW | by the way |
| C | see: C U 2moro = see you tomorrow |
| CID | consider it done |
| CU | see you |
| CUL8R | call you later |
| D8 | date |
| EZ | easy |
| FWIW | for what it's worth: used for saying that someone may or may not be interested in what you have to say |
| FYI | for your information: used as a way of introducing useful information |
| GR8 | great |
| G2G | got to go |
| HHIS | hanging head in shame: used for showing that you are embarassed |

| | |
|---|---|
| IB | I'm back |
| IYSS | if you say so |
| K | OK |
| L8 | late |
| L8R | later: CUL8R = see you later |
| LOL | laughing out loud: used for showing that you think something is funny |
| MSG | message |
| MYOB | mind your own business: for telling people not to ask questions about something that you do not want them to know about |
| NE | any |
| NE1 | anyone |
| NO1 | no one |
| NETHING | anything |
| OIC | Oh, I see |
| OTOH | on the other hand |
| PCM | please call me |
| PLS | please |
| prolly | probably |
| R | are: RU free 2nite = Are you free tonight? |
| RUCMNG | Are you coming? |
| RUOK? | Are you OK? |
| SPK | speak |
| SRY | sorry |
| THNQ | thank you: THNQ for visiting my home page. |
| THX/TX | thanks: THX 4 the info. |
| TTUL/TTYL | talk to you later |
| U | you: CUL8R = see you later |
| URW | You're welcome. |
| W8 | wait |
| WAN2 | want to |
| WRK | work |
| XLNT | excellent |
| YR | your |
| ZZZZ | sleeping |

## EMOTICONS HORIZONTAL →

| | |
|---|---|
| :-) | smiling; agreeing |
| :-D | laughing |
| \|-) | hee hee |
| \|-D | ho ho |
| '-) or ;-) | winking; just kidding |
| :*) | clowning |
| :-( | frowning; sad |
| :( | sad |
| :'-( | crying and really sad |
| >:-< or :-\|\| | angry |
| :-@ | screaming |
| :-V | shouting |
| :-p or :-r | sticking tongue out |
| \|-O | yawning |
| : * | kiss |
| ((((name)))) | hug |
| @-{---- | rose |
| <3 | heart |
| </3 | broken heart |

## EMOTICONS VERTICAL ↓

| | |
|---|---|
| (^_^) | smiling |
| (`_^) or (^_~) | winking |
| (>_<) | angry, or ouch |
| (-_-)zzz | sleeping |
| \(^o^)/ | very excited (raising hands) |
| (-_-;) or (^_^') | nervous, or sweatdrop (embarrassed; semicolon can be repeated) |
| d-_-b title.mp3 | listening to music, labelling title afterwards |
| \m/ | rocker fingers |
| \m/(>_<)\m/ | rocker dude |

# DEFINING VOCABULARY

| | | | | |
|---|---|---|---|---|
| a | adjust | all | anything | assess |
| abandon | administration | allegation | anyway | asset |
| ability | admire | alliance | anywhere | assist |
| able | admit | allied | apart | assistance |
| abortion | adopt | allow | apartment | assistant |
| about | adult | all right | apparent | associate |
| above | advance | ally | apparently | association |
| abroad | advanced | almost | appeal | assume |
| absence | advantage | alone | appear | assumption |
| absolute | advertise | along | appearance | assured |
| absolutely | advice | alongside | apple | at |
| abuse | advise | already | application | athlete |
| academic | adviser | also | apply | atmosphere |
| accept | advocate | alter | appoint | attach |
| acceptable | affair | alternative | appointment | attack |
| accepted | affect | although | appreciate | attempt |
| access | afford | altogether | approach | attend |
| accident | afraid | always | appropriate | attention |
| accompany | after | amateur | approval | attitude |
| accord | afternoon | amazing | approve | attorney |
| according to | afterward | ambassador | April | attract |
| account | again | ambition | area | attractive |
| accurate | against | amendment | aren't | auction |
| accuse | age | among | argue | audience |
| achieve | agency | amount | argument | audio |
| achievement | agenda | analysis | arise | August |
| acid | agent | analyst | arm | aunt |
| acknowledge | aggressive | ancient | armed | author |
| acquire | ago | and | armed forces | authority |
| acquisition | agree | anger | army | automatic |
| acre | agreement | angle | around | autumn |
| across | agriculture | angry | arrange | available |
| act | ahead | animal | arrangement | avenue |
| action | ahead of | anniversary | arrest | average |
| active | aid | announce | arrival | avoid |
| activist | aim | announcement | arrive | await |
| activity | air | annual | art | award |
| actor | aircraft | another | article | aware |
| actress | air force | answer | artist | away |
| actual | airline | antique | as | awful |
| actually | airport | anxiety | Asian | |
| ad | alarm | anxious | aside | baby |
| add | album | any | ask | back |
| addition | alcohol | anybody | aspect | background |
| address | alert | anymore | assault | backing |
| adequate | alive | anyone | assembly | bad |

| | | | | |
|---|---|---|---|---|
| badly | behave | bone | burst | cat |
| bag | behavior | book | bury | catch |
| bake | behind | boom | bus | category |
| balance | being | boost | business | Catholic |
| ball | belief | boot | businessman | cause |
| ballot | believe | border | busy | cautious |
| ban | bell | bore | but | cave |
| band | belong | born | butter | cease |
| bank | below | borrow | button | ceasefire |
| banker | belt | boss | buy | celebrate |
| banking | bend | both | by | cell |
| bar | beneath | bother | bye | center |
| bare | benefit | bottle | | central |
| barely | beside | bottom | cabinet | century |
| bargain | besides | bound | cable | ceremony |
| barrel | best | bowl | cake | certain |
| barrier | bet | box | call | certainly |
| base | better | boy | calm | chain |
| baseball | between | brain | camera | chair |
| basic | beyond | branch | camp | chairman |
| basically | bid | brand | campaign | challenge |
| basis | big | brave | can | chamber |
| basketball | bike | bread | cancel | champion |
| bass | bill | break | cancer | championship |
| bat | billion | breakfast | candidate | chance |
| bath | bird | breast | cap | chancellor |
| bathroom | birth | breath | capable | change |
| battle | birthday | breathe | capacity | channel |
| bay | bit | breed | capital | chaos |
| be | bite | bridge | captain | chapter |
| beach | bitter | brief | caption | character |
| bean | black | bright | capture | characteristic |
| bear | blame | brilliant | car | charge |
| bearing | blast | bring | carbon | charity |
| beat | blind | broad | card | chart |
| beautiful | block | broadcast | care | charter |
| beauty | blood | broker | career | chase |
| because | bloody | brother | careful | chat |
| become | blow | brown | caring | cheap |
| bed | blue | brush | carrier | check |
| bedroom | board | budget | carry | cheer |
| beer | boat | build | case | cheese |
| before | body | building | cash | chemical |
| begin | boil | bunch | cast | chest |
| beginning | bomb | burden | castle | chicken |
| behalf | bond | burn | casualty | chief |

| | | | | |
|---|---|---|---|---|
| child | cold | complete | contain | county |
| childhood | collapse | complex | contemporary | coup |
| chip | colleague | complicated | content | couple |
| chocolate | collect | component | contest | courage |
| choice | collection | comprehensive | context | course |
| choose | collective | compromise | continent | court |
| chop | college | computer | continue | cousin |
| Christian | colonel | concede | contract | cover |
| Christmas | color | concentrate | contrast | coverage |
| church | colored | concentration | contribute | cow |
| cigarette | column | concept | contribution | crack |
| cinema | combat | concern | control | craft |
| circle | combination | concert | controversial | crash |
| circuit | combine | concession | controversy | crazy |
| circumstance | come | conclude | convention | cream |
| cite | comedy | conclusion | conventional | create |
| citizen | comfort | concrete | conversation | creative |
| city | comfortable | condemn | convert | credit |
| civil | coming | condition | convict | crew |
| civilian | command | conduct | conviction | cricket |
| civil war | commander | conference | convince | crime |
| claim | comment | confidence | cook | criminal |
| clash | commentator | confident | cooking | crisis |
| class | commerce | confirm | cool | critic |
| classic | commercial | conflict | cooperate | critical |
| classical | commission | confront | cope | criticism |
| clean | commissioner | confrontation | copy | criticize |
| clear | commit | Congress | core | crop |
| clever | commitment | connection | corner | cross |
| client | committee | conscious | corporate | crowd |
| climate | common | consciousness | corporation | crown |
| climb | communicate | consequence | correct | crucial |
| clinic | communication | conservative | correspondent | cruise |
| clock | communism | consider | corruption | cry |
| close | community | considerable | cost | crystal |
| clothes | company | consideration | cottage | cue |
| clothing | compare | considering | cotton | cultural |
| cloud | compared | consist | cough | culture |
| club | comparison | consistent | could | cup |
| coach | compensation | constant | council | cure |
| coal | compete | constitution | counsel | curious |
| coalition | competition | construction | count | currency |
| coast | competitive | consult | counter | current |
| coat | competitor | consultant | counterpart | curtain |
| code | complain | consumer | country | customer |
| coffee | complaint | contact | countryside | cut |

| | | | | |
|---|---|---|---|---|
| cutting | delighted | dinner | drama | effective |
| cycle | deliver | diplomat | dramatic | efficient |
| | delivery | diplomatic | draw | effort |
| dad | demand | direct | dream | egg |
| daily | democracy | direction | dress | eight |
| damage | democrat | director | dressed | eighteen |
| dance | democratic | dirty | drift | eighteenth |
| danger | demonstrate | disappear | drink | eighth |
| dangerous | deny | disappointed | drive | eightieth |
| dare | department | disaster | driver | eighty |
| dark | departure | discipline | drop | either |
| data | depend | discount | drug | elderly |
| date | deposit | discover | drum | elect |
| daughter | depression | discovery | dry | election |
| day | depth | discuss | due | electoral |
| dead | deputy | discussion | dump | electric |
| deadline | describe | disease | during | electricity |
| deal | description | dish | dust | electronic |
| dear | desert | dismiss | duty | elegant |
| death | deserve | display | | element |
| debate | design | dispute | each | eleven |
| debt | designer | distance | eager | eleventh |
| debut | desire | distribution | ear | eliminate |
| decade | desk | district | earlier | else |
| December | desperate | divide | early | elsewhere |
| decide | despite | dividend | earn | embassy |
| decision | destroy | division | earnings | emerge |
| deck | detail | divorce | earth | emergency |
| declaration | detailed | do | ease | emotion |
| declare | detective | doctor | easily | emotional |
| decline | determine | document | east | emphasis |
| decorate | determined | doesn't | eastern | emphasize |
| deep | develop | dog | easy | empire |
| defeat | development | dollar | eat | employ |
| defend | device | domestic | echo | employee |
| defense | dialogue | dominate | economic | employer |
| deficit | diary | done | economics | employment |
| define | didn't | door | economist | empty |
| definitely | die | double | economy | enable |
| definition | diet | doubt | edge | encounter |
| degree | difference | down | edit | encourage |
| delay | different | downtown | edition | end |
| delegate | difficult | dozen | editor | enemy |
| delegation | difficulty | draft | editorial | energy |
| deliberate | dig | drag | education | engage |
| delight | digital | drain | effect | engine |

| | | | | |
|---|---|---|---|---|
| engineer | evil | extra | feeling | flood |
| engineering | exact | extraordinary | fellow | floor |
| English | exactly | extreme | female | flow |
| enhance | examination | eye | fence | flower |
| enjoy | examine | | festival | fly |
| enormous | example | fabric | few | focus |
| enough | excellent | face | field | fold |
| ensure | except | facility | fierce | folk |
| enter | exception | fact | fifteen | follow |
| enterprise | excerpt | faction | fifteenth | following |
| entertain | excess | factor | fifth | food |
| entertainment | exchange | factory | fiftieth | fool |
| enthusiasm | exchange rate | fade | fifty | foot |
| entire | exciting | fail | fight | football |
| entirely | excuse | failure | fighter | for |
| entitle | execute | fair | figure | force |
| entrance | executive | fairly | file | forecast |
| entry | exercise | faith | fill | foreign |
| environment | exhaust | fall | film | foreigner |
| equal | exhibition | false | final | forest |
| equally | exile | familiar | finally | forget |
| equipment | exist | family | finance | form |
| equivalent | existence | famous | financial | form |
| era | existing | fan | find | formal |
| error | expand | fancy | fine | former |
| escape | expect | fantasy | finger | formula |
| especially | expectation | far | finish | forth |
| essential | expense | fare | fire | fortieth |
| essentially | expensive | farm | firm | fortune |
| establish | experience | farmer | first | forty |
| establishment | experiment | fashion | fiscal | forward |
| estate | expert | fast | fish | found |
| estimate | explain | fat | fishing | foundation |
| ethnic | explanation | fate | fit | founder |
| European | explode | father | five | four |
| even | exploit | fault | fix | fourteen |
| evening | explore | favor | fixed | fourteenth |
| event | explosion | favorite | flag | fourth |
| eventually | export | fear | flash | frame |
| ever | expose | feature | flat | fraud |
| every | exposure | February | flavor | free |
| everybody | express | federal | flee | freedom |
| everyone | expression | federation | fleet | freeze |
| everything | extend | fee | flexible | frequent |
| everywhere | extensive | feed | flight | fresh |
| evidence | extent | feel | float | Friday |

| | | | | |
|---|---|---|---|---|
| friend | gift | guilty | hide | hundred |
| friendly | girl | guitar | high | hundredth |
| friendship | give | gun | highlight | hunt |
| from | give | guy | highly | hunter |
| front | given | | high school | hurt |
| fruit | glad | habit | highway | husband |
| frustrate | glance | hair | hill | |
| fry | glass | half | him | I |
| fuel | global | hall | himself | ice |
| fulfil | go | halt | hint | idea |
| full | goal | hand | hip | ideal |
| fully | god | handle | hire | identify |
| fun | going | hang | his | identity |
| function | gold | happen | historic | if |
| fund | golden | happy | historical | ignore |
| fundamental | golf | harbor | history | ill |
| funding | gone | hard | hit | illegal |
| funny | good | hardly | hold | illness |
| furniture | goods | harm | holder | illustrate |
| further | got | hat | hole | image |
| future | govern | hate | holiday | imagination |
| | government | have | holy | imagine |
| gain | governor | he | home | immediate |
| gallery | grab | head | homeless | immediately |
| game | grade | headline | homosexual | immigrant |
| gang | graduate | headquarters | honest | immigration |
| gap | grain | heal | honor | immune |
| garden | grand | health | hook | impact |
| gas | grant | health care | hope | implement |
| gate | grass | healthy | horror | implication |
| gather | grave | hear | horse | imply |
| gay | gray | hearing | hospital | import |
| gear | great | heart | host | important |
| gene | green | heat | hostage | impose |
| general | grip | heaven | hot | impossible |
| general election | gross | heavy | hotel | impress |
| generally | ground | height | hour | impression |
| generate | group | helicopter | house | impressive |
| generation | grow | hell | household | improve |
| generous | growth | hello | housing | in |
| gentle | guarantee | help | how | inch |
| gentleman | guard | her | however | incident |
| genuine | guerrilla | here | huge | include |
| gesture | guess | hero | human | including |
| get | guest | herself | human rights | income |
| giant | guide | hi | humor | increase |

| | | | | |
|---|---|---|---|---|
| increasingly | interest | judge | later | life |
| incredible | interested | judgment | latest | lift |
| indeed | interesting | juice | latter | light |
| independent | interim | July | laugh | like |
| index | interior | jump | laughter | likely |
| indicate | internal | June | launch | limit |
| indication | international | junior | law | limited |
| individual | Internet | jury | lawsuit | line |
| industrial | interview | just | lawyer | link |
| industry | into | justice | lay | lip |
| inevitable | introduce | justify | layer | list |
| infect | invasion | | lead | listen |
| infection | invest | keen | leader | literary |
| inflation | investigate | keep | leadership | literature |
| influence | investment | key | leading | little |
| inform | invitation | kick | leaf | live |
| information | invite | kid | league | living |
| ingredient | involve | kill | leak | load |
| initial | involved | killer | lean | loan |
| initially | involvement | kilometer | leap | lobby |
| initiative | iron | kind | learn | local |
| injured | Islam | king | lease | location |
| injury | island | kiss | least | lock |
| inner | issue | kitchen | leather | long |
| innocent | it | knee | leave | long-time |
| inquiry | item | knife | lecture | look |
| inside | its | knock | left | loose |
| insist | itself | know | leg | lord |
| inspect | | know-how | legal | lose |
| inspector | jacket | knowledge | legislation | loss |
| install | jail | | lend | lost |
| instance | January | label | length | lot |
| instant | jazz | labor | lens | loud |
| instead | jersey | laboratory | lesbian | love |
| institute | Jesus | lack | less | lovely |
| institution | jet | lady | lesson | lover |
| instruction | Jew | lake | let | low |
| instrument | Jewish | land | let's | lower |
| insurance | job | landscape | letter | luck |
| integrate | join | lane | level | lucky |
| intellectual | joint | language | liberal | lunch |
| intelligence | joke | lap | liberate | luxury |
| intelligent | journal | large | liberty | |
| intend | journalist | largely | library | machine |
| intense | journey | last | license | mad |
| intention | joy | late | lie | magazine |

| | | | | |
|---|---|---|---|---|
| magic | meaning | minute | murder | newly |
| mail | means | mirror | muscle | news |
| main | meanwhile | miss | museum | news agency |
| mainly | measure | missile | music | newscaster |
| maintain | meat | missing | musical | newspaper |
| major | mechanism | mission | musician | next |
| majority | medal | mistake | Muslim | nice |
| make | media | mix | must | night |
| maker | medical | mixed | mutual | nightmare |
| makeup | medicine | mixture | my | nine |
| male | medium | mobile | myself | nineteen |
| man | meet | model | mystery | nineteenth |
| manage | meeting | moderate | myth | ninetieth |
| management | member | modern | | ninety |
| manager | membership | modest | name | ninth |
| manner | memory | mom | narrow | no |
| manufacture | mental | moment | nation | nobody |
| manufacturer | mention | Monday | national | nod |
| many | merchant | monetary | nationalist | noise |
| map | mere | money | native | none |
| march | merely | monitor | natural | no one |
| March | merger | month | naturally | nor |
| margin | mess | monthly | nature | normal |
| marine | message | mood | naval | normally |
| mark | metal | moon | navy | north |
| marked | method | moral | near | northeast |
| market | middle | more | nearby | northern |
| marriage | middle class | moreover | nearly | nose |
| married | Middle East | morning | neat | not |
| marry | midnight | mortgage | necessarily | note |
| mask | might | most | necessary | noted |
| mass | mild | mostly | neck | nothing |
| massive | mile | mother | need | notice |
| master | militant | motion | negative | notion |
| match | military | motivate | negotiate | novel |
| mate | milk | motor | negotiation | November |
| material | mill | mount | neighbor | now |
| matter | million | mountain | neighborhood | nowhere |
| maximum | millionth | mouth | neither | nuclear |
| may | mind | move | nerve | number |
| May | mine | movement | nervous | numerous |
| maybe | minimum | movie | net | nurse |
| mayor | minister | Mr. | network | |
| me | ministry | Mrs. | never | object |
| meal | minor | Ms. | nevertheless | objective |
| mean | minority | much | new | observe |

| | | | | |
|---|---|---|---|---|
| observer | opposed | pair | perhaps | please |
| obtain | opposite | palace | period | pleased |
| obvious | opposition | pale | permanent | pleasure |
| obviously | opt | pan | permission | pledge |
| occasion | optimistic | panel | permit | plenty |
| occasional | option | panic | person | plot |
| occupation | or | paper | personal | plunge |
| occupy | orange | parent | personality | plus |
| occur | order | park | personally | pocket |
| ocean | ordinary | parliament | personnel | poem |
| o'clock | organization | parliamentary | perspective | poet |
| October | organize | part | persuade | poetry |
| odd | organized | participate | pet | point |
| of | origin | particular | phase | point of view |
| of course | original | particularly | philosophy | pole |
| off | other | partly | phone | police |
| offense | otherwise | partner | photo | policeman |
| offensive | ought | partnership | photograph | police officer |
| offer | our | party | photographer | policy |
| offering | ourselves | pass | phrase | political |
| office | out | passage | physical | politician |
| officer | outcome | passenger | pick | politics |
| official | outline | passion | picture | poll |
| often | output | past | piece | pollution |
| oh | outside | path | pile | pool |
| oil | outstanding | patient | pill | poor |
| okay | over | pattern | pilot | pop |
| old | overall | pause | pin | popular |
| Olympic | overcome | pay | pink | population |
| on | overnight | payment | pipe | port |
| once | overseas | peace | pit | portrait |
| one | overwhelming | peaceful | pitch | pose |
| one's | owe | peak | place | position |
| online | own | peer | plain | positive |
| only | owner | peg | plan | possibility |
| onto | ownership | pen | plane | possible |
| open | | penalty | planet | possibly |
| opening | pace | penny | planning | post |
| opera | pack | pension | plant | pot |
| operate | package | people | plastic | potato |
| operation | pact | pepper | plate | potential |
| operator | page | per | platform | pound |
| opinion | pain | percentage | play | pour |
| opponent | painful | perfect | player | poverty |
| opportunity | paint | perform | playoff | power |
| oppose | painting | performance | pleasant | powerful |

| | | | | |
|---|---|---|---|---|
| practical | proceed | purchase | reaction | regulator |
| practice | process | pure | read | reject |
| praise | produce | purple | reader | relate |
| precisely | product | purpose | reading | related |
| predict | production | pursue | ready | relation |
| prefer | profession | push | real | relationship |
| pregnant | professional | put | real estate | relative |
| premier | professor | | reality | relax |
| premium | profile | qualified | realize | release |
| preparation | profit | qualify | really | reliable |
| prepare | program | quality | rear | relief |
| prepared | progress | quantity | reason | religion |
| presence | project | quarter | reasonable | religious |
| present | prominent | quarterback | rebel | reluctant |
| preserve | promise | queen | recall | rely |
| presidency | promote | question | receive | remain |
| president | prompt | quick | recent | remaining |
| presidential | proof | quiet | recently | remark |
| press | proper | quite | recession | remarkable |
| pressure | property | quote | reckon | remember |
| presumably | proportion | | recognition | remind |
| pretty | proposal | race | recognize | remote |
| prevent | propose | racial | recommend | remove |
| previous | prosecution | racing | record | renew |
| previously | prospect | radical | recording | rent |
| price | protect | radio | recover | repair |
| pride | protection | rage | recovery | repeat |
| priest | protein | raid | recruit | replace |
| primary | protest | rail | red | replacement |
| prime | proud | railway | reduce | reply |
| prime minister | prove | rain | reduction | report |
| prince | provide | raise | reel | reporter |
| princess | province | rally | refer | reporting |
| principal | provision | range | reference | represent |
| principle | provoke | rank | referendum | representative |
| print | psychological | rape | reflect | republic |
| prior | public | rapid | reform | republican |
| priority | publication | rare | refugee | reputation |
| prison | publicity | rarely | refuse | request |
| prisoner | publish | rate | regard | require |
| private | publisher | rather | regime | requirement |
| privatize | publishing | rating | region | rescue |
| prize | pull | raw | register | research |
| probably | pump | ray | regret | reserve |
| problem | punch | reach | regular | resident |
| procedure | pupil | react | regulation | resign |

resignation
resist
resistance
resolution
resolve
resort
resource
respect
respond
response
responsibility
responsible
rest
restaurant
restore
result
resume
retail
retain
retire
retirement
retreat
return
reveal
revenue
reverse
review
revolution
revolutionary
reward
rhythm
rice
rich
rid
ride
rider
right
right wing
ring
riot
rise
risk
rival
river
road
rock

rocket
role
roll
Roman
romantic
roof
room
root
rose
rough
round
route
routine
row
royal
rugby
ruin
rule
ruling
rumor
run
runner
running
rural
rush

sack
sacrifice
sad
safe
safety
sail
saint
sake
salary
sale
salt
same
sample
sanction
sand
satellite
satisfied
Saturday
sauce
save

savings
say
scale
scandal
scene
schedule
scheme
school
science
scientific
scientist
score
scream
screen
script
sea
seal
search
season
seat
second
secret
secretary
Secretary of
    State
section
sector
secure
security
see
seed
seek
seem
segment
seize
select
selection
self
sell
Senate
senator
send
senior
sense
sensible
sensitive

sentence
separate
September
series
serious
seriously
servant
serve
service
session
set
settle
settlement
setup
seven
seventeen
seventeenth
seventh
seventieth
seventy
several
severe
sex
sexual
shade
shadow
shake
shall
shame
shape
shaped
share
shareholder
sharp
she
shed
sheet
shell
shelter
shift
ship
shirt
shock
shoe
shoot
shop

shopping
shore
short
shortage
shortly
short-term
shot
should
shoulder
shout
show
shut
sick
side
sigh
sight
sign
signal
significant
silence
silent
silver
similar
simple
simply
since
sing
singer
single
sink
sir
sister
sit
site
situation
six
sixteen
sixteenth
sixth
sixtieth
sixty
size
ski
skill
skin
sky

| | | | | |
|---|---|---|---|---|
| sleep | sound | stand | strip | surgery |
| slice | source | standard | stroke | surplus |
| slide | south | star | strong | surprise |
| slight | southeast | stare | structure | surprised |
| slightly | southern | start | struggle | surprising |
| slim | southwest | state | student | surrender |
| slip | space | statement | studio | surround |
| slow | spare | station | study | survey |
| small | spark | statistic | stuff | survival |
| smart | speak | status | stupid | survive |
| smash | speaker | stay | style | suspect |
| smell | special | steady | subject | suspend |
| smile | specialist | steal | subsequent | suspicion |
| smoke | specialize | steam | subsidy | sustain |
| smooth | species | steel | substance | sweep |
| snap | specific | stem | substantial | sweet |
| snow | specifically | step | substitute | swim |
| so | spectacular | sterling | succeed | swing |
| so-called | speculate | stick | success | switch |
| soccer | speech | still | successful | symbol |
| social | speed | stimulate | such | sympathy |
| socialist | spell | stir | sudden | symptom |
| society | spend | stock | suffer | system |
| soft | spin | stock exchange | sufficient | |
| software | spirit | stock market | sugar | table |
| soil | spiritual | stomach | suggest | tackle |
| soldier | spite | stone | suggestion | tactic |
| solicitor | split | stop | suicide | tail |
| solid | spokesman | store | suit | take |
| solution | spokeswoman | storm | suitable | takeover |
| solve | sponsor | story | sum | tale |
| some | sport | straight | summer | talent |
| somebody | spot | strain | summit | talk |
| somehow | spray | strange | sun | tall |
| someone | spread | strategic | Sunday | tank |
| something | spring | strategy | super | tap |
| sometimes | spur | stream | superb | tape |
| somewhat | squad | street | superior | target |
| somewhere | square | strength | supply | task |
| son | squeeze | strengthen | support | taste |
| song | stable | stress | suppose | tax |
| soon | stadium | stretch | supposed | tea |
| sophisticated | staff | strict | supreme | teach |
| sorry | stage | strike | sure | teaching |
| sort | stake | striking | surely | team |
| soul | stamp | string | surface | tear |

| | | | | |
|---|---|---|---|---|
| technical | thirteen | tour | tunnel | upper |
| technique | thirteenth | tourist | turn | upset |
| technology | thirtieth | tournament | TV | urban |
| teenager | thirty | toward | twelfth | urge |
| telephone | this | tower | twelve | urgent |
| television | thorough | town | twentieth | us |
| tell | those | toy | twenty | use |
| temperature | though | trace | twice | used |
| temple | thought | track | twin | useful |
| temporary | thousand | trade | twist | user |
| ten | threat | trader | two | usual |
| tend | threaten | tradition | type | usually |
| tendency | three | traffic | typical | |
| tennis | throat | tragedy | | valley |
| tension | through | trail | ultimate | valuable |
| tenth | throughout | train | ultimately | value |
| term | throw | transaction | unable | van |
| terrible | Thursday | transfer | uncle | variety |
| territory | thus | transform | under | various |
| terror | ticket | transition | underground | vary |
| terrorist | tide | transport | undermine | vast |
| test | tie | trap | understand | vegetable |
| text | tight | travel | understanding | vehicle |
| than | till | traveler | unemployment | venture |
| thank | time | treat | unexpected | venue |
| that | tiny | treatment | unfair | verdict |
| the | tip | treaty | unfortunately | version |
| theater | tired | tree | unhappy | very |
| their | tissue | tremendous | unidentified | vessel |
| them | title | trend | uniform | veteran |
| theme | titled | trial | union | via |
| themselves | to | trick | unique | vice |
| then | today | trigger | unit | victim |
| theory | together | trip | united | victimize |
| therapy | tomorrow | triumph | United Nations | victory |
| there | ton | troop | unity | video |
| therefore | tone | trouble | universe | view |
| these | tonight | truck | university | village |
| they | too | true | unknown | violate |
| thick | tool | truly | unless | violence |
| thin | tooth | trust | unlike | violent |
| thing | top | truth | unlikely | virus |
| think | torture | try | until | visible |
| thinking | total | tube | unusual | vision |
| third | touch | Tuesday | up | visit |
| Third World | tough | tune | upon | visitor |

| | | | | |
|---|---|---|---|---|
| vital | weaken | whereas | wipe | wrap |
| vitamin | wealth | whether | wire | write |
| voice | weapon | which | wireless | writer |
| volume | wear | while | wise | writing |
| voluntary | weather | whip | wish | written |
| volunteer | web | whisper | with | wrong |
| vote | website | white | withdraw | |
| vulnerable | wedding | White House | withdrawal | yard |
| | Wednesday | who | within | yeah |
| wage | week | whole | without | year |
| wait | weekend | whom | witness | yellow |
| wake | weekly | whose | woman | yen |
| walk | weigh | why | wonder | yes |
| wall | weight | wide | wonderful | yesterday |
| want | welcome | widespread | wood | yet |
| war | welfare | wife | wooden | yield |
| warm | well | wild | word | you |
| warn | well-known | will | work | young |
| warning | west | willing | worker | youngster |
| wash | western | win | working | your |
| waste | wet | wind | world | yours |
| watch | what | window | world war | yourself |
| water | whatever | wine | worldwide | youth |
| wave | wheel | wing | worry | |
| way | when | winner | worth | zone |
| we | whenever | winning | would | |
| weak | where | winter | wound | |

# ACADEMIC WORD LIST

This list contains the head words of the families in the Academic Word List. The numbers indicate the sublist of the Academic Word List, with Sublist 1 containing the most frequent words, Sublist 2 the next most frequent and so on. For example, *abandon* and its family members are in Sublist 8 of the Academic Word List.

| | | | | | |
|---|---|---|---|---|---|
| abandon | 8 | arbitrary | 8 | classic | 7 |
| abstract | 6 | area | 1 | clause | 5 |
| academy | 5 | aspect | 2 | code | 4 |
| access | 4 | assemble | 10 | coherent | 9 |
| accommodate | 9 | assess | 1 | coincide | 9 |
| accompany | 8 | assign | 6 | collapse | 10 |
| accumulate | 8 | assist | 2 | colleague | 10 |
| accurate | 6 | assume | 1 | commence | 9 |
| achieve | 2 | assure | 9 | comment | 3 |
| acknowledge | 6 | attach | 6 | commission | 2 |
| acquire | 2 | attain | 9 | commit | 4 |
| adapt | 7 | attitude | 4 | commodity | 8 |
| adequate | 4 | attribute | 4 | communicate | 4 |
| adjacent | 10 | author | 6 | community | 2 |
| adjust | 5 | authority | 1 | compatible | 9 |
| administrate | 2 | automate | 8 | compensate | 3 |
| adult | 7 | available | 1 | compile | 10 |
| advocate | 7 | aware | 5 | complement | 8 |
| affect | 2 | behalf | 9 | complex | 2 |
| aggregate | 6 | benefit | 1 | component | 3 |
| aid | 7 | bias | 8 | compound | 5 |
| albeit | 10 | bond | 6 | comprehensive | 7 |
| allocate | 6 | brief | 6 | comprise | 7 |
| alter | 5 | bulk | 9 | compute | 2 |
| alternative | 3 | capable | 6 | conceive | 10 |
| ambiguous | 8 | capacity | 5 | concentrate | 4 |
| amend | 5 | category | 2 | concept | 1 |
| analogy | 9 | cease | 9 | conclude | 2 |
| analyze | 1 | challenge | 5 | concurrent | 9 |
| annual | 4 | channel | 7 | conduct | 2 |
| anticipate | 9 | chapter | 2 | confer | 4 |
| apparent | 4 | chart | 8 | confine | 9 |
| append | 8 | chemical | 7 | confirm | 7 |
| appreciate | 8 | circumstance | 3 | conflict | 5 |
| approach | 1 | cite | 6 | conform | 8 |
| appropriate | 2 | civil | 4 | consent | 3 |
| approximate | 4 | clarify | 8 | consequent | 2 |

1119

| | | | | | |
|---|---|---|---|---|---|
| considerable | 3 | denote | 8 | enormous | 10 |
| consist | 1 | deny | 7 | ensure | 3 |
| constant | 3 | depress | 10 | entity | 5 |
| constitute | 1 | derive | 1 | environment | 1 |
| constrain | 3 | design | 2 | equate | 2 |
| construct | 2 | despite | 4 | equip | 7 |
| consult | 5 | detect | 8 | equivalent | 5 |
| consume | 2 | deviate | 8 | erode | 9 |
| contact | 5 | device | 9 | error | 4 |
| contemporary | 8 | devote | 9 | establish | 1 |
| context | 1 | differentiate | 7 | estate | 6 |
| contract | 1 | dimension | 4 | estimate | 1 |
| contradict | 8 | diminish | 9 | ethic | 9 |
| contrary | 7 | discrete | 5 | ethnic | 4 |
| contrast | 4 | discriminate | 6 | evaluate | 2 |
| contribute | 3 | displace | 8 | eventual | 8 |
| controversy | 9 | display | 6 | evident | 1 |
| convene | 3 | dispose | 7 | evolve | 5 |
| converse | 9 | distinct | 2 | exceed | 6 |
| convert | 7 | distort | 9 | exclude | 3 |
| convince | 10 | distribute | 1 | exhibit | 8 |
| cooperate | 6 | diverse | 6 | expand | 5 |
| coordinate | 3 | document | 3 | expert | 6 |
| core | 3 | domain | 6 | explicit | 6 |
| corporate | 3 | domestic | 4 | exploit | 8 |
| correspond | 3 | dominate | 3 | export | 1 |
| couple | 7 | draft | 5 | expose | 5 |
| create | 1 | drama | 8 | external | 5 |
| credit | 2 | duration | 9 | extract | 7 |
| criteria | 3 | dynamic | 7 | facilitate | 5 |
| crucial | 8 | economy | 1 | factor | 1 |
| culture | 2 | edit | 6 | feature | 2 |
| currency | 8 | element | 2 | federal | 6 |
| cycle | 4 | eliminate | 7 | fee | 6 |
| data | 1 | emerge | 4 | file | 7 |
| debate | 4 | emphasis | 3 | final | 2 |
| decade | 7 | empirical | 7 | finance | 1 |
| decline | 5 | enable | 5 | finite | 7 |
| deduce | 3 | encounter | 10 | flexible | 6 |
| define | 1 | energy | 5 | fluctuate | 8 |
| definite | 7 | enforce | 5 | focus | 2 |
| demonstrate | 3 | enhance | 6 | format | 9 |

| | | | | | |
|---|---|---|---|---|---|
| formula | 1 | individual | 1 | layer | 3 |
| forthcoming | 10 | induce | 8 | lecture | 6 |
| foundation | 7 | inevitable | 8 | legal | 1 |
| found | 9 | infer | 7 | legislate | 1 |
| framework | 3 | infrastructure | 8 | levy | 10 |
| function | 1 | inherent | 9 | liberal | 5 |
| fund | 3 | inhibit | 6 | license | 5 |
| fundamental | 5 | initial | 3 | likewise | 10 |
| furthermore | 6 | initiate | 6 | link | 3 |
| gender | 6 | injure | 2 | locate | 3 |
| generate | 5 | innovate | 7 | logic | 5 |
| generation | 5 | input | 6 | maintain | 2 |
| globe | 7 | insert | 7 | major | 1 |
| goal | 4 | insight | 9 | manipulate | 8 |
| grade | 7 | inspect | 8 | manual | 9 |
| grant | 4 | instance | 3 | margin | 5 |
| guarantee | 7 | institute | 2 | mature | 9 |
| guideline | 8 | instruct | 6 | maximize | 3 |
| hence | 4 | integral | 9 | mechanism | 4 |
| hierarchy | 7 | integrate | 4 | media | 7 |
| highlight | 8 | integrity | 10 | mediate | 9 |
| hypothesis | 4 | intelligence | 6 | medical | 5 |
| identical | 7 | intense | 8 | medium | 9 |
| identify | 1 | interact | 3 | mental | 5 |
| ideology | 7 | intermediate | 9 | method | 1 |
| ignorance | 6 | internal | 4 | migrate | 6 |
| illustrate | 3 | interpret | 1 | military | 9 |
| image | 5 | interval | 6 | minimal | 9 |
| immigrate | 3 | intervene | 7 | minimize | 8 |
| impact | 2 | intrinsic | 10 | minimum | 6 |
| implement | 4 | invest | 2 | ministry | 6 |
| implicate | 4 | investigate | 4 | minor | 3 |
| implicit | 8 | invoke | 10 | mode | 7 |
| imply | 3 | involve | 1 | modify | 5 |
| impose | 4 | isolate | 7 | monitor | 5 |
| incentive | 6 | issue | 1 | motive | 6 |
| incidence | 6 | item | 2 | mutual | 9 |
| incline | 10 | job | 4 | negate | 3 |
| income | 1 | journal | 2 | network | 5 |
| incorporate | 6 | justify | 3 | neutral | 6 |
| index | 6 | label | 4 | nevertheless | 6 |
| indicate | 1 | labor | 1 | nonetheless | 10 |

| | | | | | |
|---|---|---|---|---|---|
| norm | 9 | potential | 2 | regulate | 2 |
| normal | 2 | practitioner | 8 | reinforce | 8 |
| notion | 5 | precede | 6 | reject | 5 |
| notwithstanding | 10 | precise | 5 | relax | 9 |
| nuclear | 8 | predict | 4 | release | 7 |
| objective | 5 | predominant | 8 | relevant | 2 |
| obtain | 2 | preliminary | 9 | reluctance | 10 |
| obvious | 4 | presume | 6 | rely | 3 |
| occupy | 4 | previous | 2 | remove | 3 |
| occur | 1 | primary | 2 | require | 1 |
| odd | 10 | prime | 5 | research | 1 |
| offset | 8 | principal | 4 | reside | 2 |
| ongoing | 10 | principle | 1 | resolve | 4 |
| option | 4 | prior | 4 | resource | 2 |
| orient | 5 | priority | 7 | respond | 1 |
| outcome | 3 | proceed | 1 | restore | 8 |
| output | 4 | process | 1 | restrain | 9 |
| overall | 4 | professional | 4 | restrict | 2 |
| overlap | 9 | prohibit | 7 | retain | 4 |
| overseas | 6 | project | 4 | reveal | 6 |
| panel | 10 | promote | 4 | revenue | 5 |
| paradigm | 7 | proportion | 3 | reverse | 7 |
| paragraph | 8 | prospect | 8 | revise | 8 |
| parallel | 4 | protocol | 9 | revolution | 9 |
| parameter | 4 | psychology | 5 | rigid | 9 |
| participate | 2 | publication | 7 | role | 1 |
| partner | 3 | publish | 3 | route | 9 |
| passive | 9 | purchase | 2 | scenario | 9 |
| perceive | 2 | pursue | 5 | schedule | 8 |
| percent | 1 | qualitative | 9 | scheme | 3 |
| period | 1 | quote | 7 | scope | 6 |
| persist | 10 | radical | 8 | section | 1 |
| perspective | 5 | random | 8 | sector | 1 |
| phase | 4 | range | 2 | secure | 2 |
| phenomenon | 7 | ratio | 5 | seek | 2 |
| philosophy | 3 | rational | 6 | select | 2 |
| physical | 3 | react | 3 | sequence | 3 |
| plus | 8 | recover | 6 | series | 4 |
| policy | 1 | refine | 9 | sex | 3 |
| portion | 9 | regime | 4 | shift | 3 |
| pose | 10 | region | 2 | significant | 1 |
| positive | 2 | register | 3 | similar | 1 |

| | | | | | |
|---|---|---|---|---|---|
| simulate | 7 | survey | 2 | transport | 6 |
| site | 2 | survive | 7 | trend | 5 |
| so-called | 10 | suspend | 9 | trigger | 9 |
| sole | 7 | sustain | 5 | ultimate | 7 |
| somewhat | 7 | symbol | 5 | undergo | 10 |
| source | 1 | tape | 6 | underlie | 6 |
| specific | 1 | target | 5 | undertake | 4 |
| specify | 3 | task | 3 | uniform | 8 |
| sphere | 9 | team | 9 | unify | 9 |
| stable | 5 | technical | 3 | unique | 7 |
| statistic | 4 | technique | 3 | utilize | 6 |
| status | 4 | technology | 3 | valid | 3 |
| straightforward | 10 | temporary | 9 | vary | 1 |
| strategy | 2 | tense | 8 | vehicle | 8 |
| stress | 4 | terminate | 8 | version | 5 |
| structure | 1 | text | 2 | via | 8 |
| style | 5 | theme | 8 | violate | 9 |
| submit | 7 | theory | 1 | virtual | 8 |
| subordinate | 9 | thereby | 8 | visible | 7 |
| subsequent | 4 | thesis | 7 | vision | 9 |
| subsidy | 6 | topic | 7 | visual | 8 |
| substitute | 5 | trace | 6 | volume | 3 |
| successor | 7 | tradition | 2 | voluntary | 7 |
| sufficient | 3 | transfer | 2 | welfare | 5 |
| sum | 4 | transform | 6 | whereas | 5 |
| summary | 4 | transit | 5 | whereby | 10 |
| supplement | 9 | transmit | 7 | widespread | 8 |

# PRESIDENTS OF THE UNITED STATES OF AMERICA

| | |
|---|---|
| 44. Barak Obama | 2009-Present |
| 43. George W. Bush | 2001-2009 |
| 42. William J. Clinton | 1993-2001 |
| 41. George H.W. Bush | 1989-1993 |
| 40. Ronald Reagan | 1981-1989 |
| 39. Jimmy Carter | 1977-1981 |
| 38. Gerald Ford | 1974-1977 |
| 37. Richard Nixon | 1969-1974 |
| 36. Lyndon Johnson | 1963-1969 |
| 35. John F. Kennedy | 1961-1963 |
| 34. Dwight Eisenhower | 1953-1961 |
| 33. Harry Truman | 1945-1953 |
| 32. Franklin D. Roosevelt | 1933-1945 |
| 31. Herbert Hoover | 1929-1933 |
| 30. Calvin Coolidge | 1923-1929 |
| 29. Warren Harding | 1921-1923 |
| 28. Woodrow Wilson | 1913-1921 |
| 27. William H. Taft | 1909-1913 |
| 26. Theodore Roosevelt | 1901-1909 |
| 25. William McKinley | 1897-1901 |
| 24. Grover Cleveland | 1893-1897 |
| 23. Benjamin Harrison | 1889-1893 |
| 22. Grover Cleveland | 1885-1889 |
| 21. Chester Arthur | 1881-1885 |
| 20. James Garfield | 1881 |
| 19. Rutherford B. Hayes | 1887-1881 |
| 18. Ulysses S. Grant | 1869-1877 |
| 17. Andrew Johnson | 1865-1869 |
| 16. Abraham Lincoln | 1861-1865 |
| 15. James Buchanan | 1857-1861 |
| 14. Franklin Pierce | 1853-1857 |
| 13. Millard Fillmore | 1850-1853 |
| 12. Zachary Taylor | 1849-1850 |
| 11. James Polk | 1845-1849 |
| 10. John Tyler | 1841-1845 |
| 9. William Henry Harrison | 1841 |
| 8. Martin Van Buren | 1837-1841 |
| 7. Andrew Jackson | 1829-1837 |
| 6. John Adams | 1825-1829 |
| 5. James Monroe | 1817-1825 |
| 4. James Madison | 1809-1825 |
| 3. Thomas Jefferson | 1801-1809 |
| 2. John Adams | 1797-1801 |
| 1. George Washington | 1789-1797 |

# USA States, Abbreviations, and Capitals

| State | Capital |
|---|---|
| Alabama (AL) | Montgomery |
| Alaska (AK) | Juneau |
| Arizona (AZ) | Phoenix |
| Arkansas (AR) | Little Rock |
| California (CA) | Sacramento |
| Colorado (CO) | Denver |
| Connecticut (CT) | Hartford |
| Delaware (DE) | Dover |
| Florida (FL) | Tallahassee |
| Georgia (GA) | Atlanta |
| Hawaii (HI) | Honolulu |
| Idaho (ID) | Boise |
| Illinois (IL) | Springfield |
| Indiana (IN) | Indianapolis |
| Iowa (IA) | Des Moines |
| Kansas (KS) | Topeka |
| Kentucky (KY) | Frankfort |
| Louisiana (LA) | Baton Rouge |
| Maine (ME) | Augusta |
| Maryland (MD) | Annapolis |
| Massachusetts (MA) | Boston |
| Michigan (MI) | Lansing |
| Minnesota (MN) | Saint Paul |
| Mississippi (MS) | Jackson |
| Missouri (MO) | Jefferson City |
| Montana (MT) | Helena |
| Nebraska (NE) | Lincoln |
| Nevada (NV) | Carson City |
| New Hampshire (NH) | Concord |
| New Jersey (NJ) | Trenton |
| New Mexico (NM) | Santa Fe |
| New York (NY) | Albany |
| North Carolina (NC) | Raleigh |
| North Dakota (ND) | Bismarck |
| Ohio (OH) | Columbus |
| Oklahoma (OK) | Oklahoma City |
| Oregon (OR) | Salem |
| Pennsylvania (PA) | Harrisburg |
| Rhode Island (RI) | Providence |
| South Carolina (SC) | Columbia |
| South Dakota (SD) | Pierre |
| Tennessee (TN) | Nashville |
| Texas (TX) | Austin |
| Utah (UT) | Salt Lake City |
| Vermont (VT) | Montpelier |
| Virginia (VA) | Richmond |
| Washington (WA) | Olympia |
| West Virginia (WV) | Charleston |
| Wisconsin (WI) | Madison |
| Wyoming (WY) | Cheyenne |

**Capital of the United States of America (USA)**

| | |
|---|---|
| District of Columbia (DC) | Washington (commonly abbreviated: Washington, D.C.) |

# Geographical Places and Nationalities

This list shows the spelling and pronunciation of geographical names. If a country has different words for the country, adjective, and person, these are all shown. Inclusion in this list does not imply status as a sovereign nation.

**Af|ghan|i|stan** /æfgænɪstæn/; Af|ghan, Af|ghani /æfgæn/, /æfgæni, -gani/

**Af|ri|ca** /æfrɪkə/; Af|ri|can /æfrɪkən/

**Al|ba|nia** /ælbeɪniə/; Al|ba|ni|an /ælbeɪniən/

**Al|ge|ria** /ældʒɪəriə/; Al|ge|ri|an /ældʒɪəriən/

**An|dor|ra** /ændɔrə/; An|dor|ran /ændɔrən/

**An|go|la** /æŋɡoʊlə/; An|go|lan /æŋɡoʊlən/

**Ant|arc|ti|ca** /æntarktɪkə, -artɪ-/; Ant|arc|tic /æntarktɪk, -artɪk/

**An|ti|gua and Bar|bu|da** /æntigə ən barbudə/; An|ti|guan, Bar|bu|dan /æntigən/, /barbudən/

**(the) Arc|tic Ocean** /(ði) arktɪk oʊʃən, artɪk/; Arc|tic /arktɪk, artɪk/

**Ar|gen|ti|na** /arjəntinə/; Ar|gen|tine, Ar|gen|tin|ian, or Ar|gen|tin|ean /arjəntin, -taɪn/, /arjəntɪniən/

**Ar|me|nia** /arminiə/; Ar|me|nian /arminiən/

**A|sia** /eɪʒə/; A|sian /eɪʒən/

**(the) At|lan|tic Ocean** /(ði) ætlæntɪk oʊʃən/

**Aus|tra|lia** /ɔstreɪlyə/; Aus|tra|lian /ɔstreɪlyən/

**Aus|tria** /ɔstriə/; Aus|tri|an /ɔstriən/

**Azer|bai|jan** /æzərbaɪdʒan, azər-/; Azer|bai|ja|ni, Azeri /æzərbaɪdʒani, azər-/, /əzɛri/

**(the) Ba|ha|mas** /(ðə) bəhaməz/; Ba|ha|mian /bəheɪmiən, -ha-/

**Bah|rain** /bareɪn/; Bah|raini /bareɪni/

**Ban|gla|desh** /baŋɡlədɛʃ, bæŋ-/; Ban|gla|deshi /baŋɡlədɛʃi, bæŋ-/

**Bar|ba|dos** /barbeɪdoʊs/; Bar|ba|di|an /barbeɪdiən/

**Be|la|rus** /bɛlərus, byɛl-/; Be|la|ru|si|an /bɛlərʌʃən, byɛl-/

**Bel|gium** /bɛldʒəm/; Bel|gian /bɛldʒən/

**Be|lize** /bəliz/; Be|liz|ean /bəliziən/

**Be|nin** /bənin/; Be|ni|nese /beniniz/

**Bhu|tan** /butan, -tæn/; Bhu|tani, Bhu|ta|nese /butani, -tæni/, /butᵊniz/

**Bo|liv|ia** /bəlɪviə/; Bo|liv|i|an /bəlɪviən/

**Bos|nia and Her|ze|go|vi|na** /bɒzniə ən hɛrtsəɡoʊvinə/; Bos|ni|an, Her|ze|go|vi|ni|an /bɒzniən/, /hɛrtsəɡoʊvinian/

**Bo|tswa|na** /bɒtswanə/; Ba|tswa|nan/ bɒtswanən/; Mo|tswan|a (person), Ba|tswa|na (people) /mɒtswanə/, /batswanə/

**Bra|zil** /brəzɪl/; Bra|zil|ian /brəzɪlyən/

**Bru|nei Da|rus|sa|lam** /brunaɪ darusaləm/; Bru|nei, Bru|nei|an /brunaɪ/, /brunaɪən/

**Bul|gar|ia** /bʌlɡɛəriə/; Bul|gar|i|an /bʌlɡɛəriən/

**Bur|ki|na Fa|so** /bərkinə fasoʊ/; Bur|kin|abe, Bur|kin|ese /bərkɪnabeɪ/, /bərkɪniz/

**Bur|ma—See Myanmar** /bərmə/; Bur|mese—/bərmiz/

**Bu|run|di** /burundi/; Bu|run|di|an /burundiən/

**Cam|bo|dia** /kæmboʊdiə/; Cam|bo|di|an /kæmboʊdiən/

**Cam|er|oon** /kæmərun/; Cam|er|oo|ni|an /kæməruniən/

**Can|a|da** /kænədə/; Ca|na|di|an /kəneɪdiən/

**Cape Verde** /keɪp vɜrd/; Cape Verd|ean /keɪp vɜrdiən/

**Cen|tral Af|ri|can Re|pub|lic** /sɛntrəl æfrɪkən rɪpʌblɪk/; Cen|tral Af|ri|can /sɛntrəl æfrɪkən/

**Chad** /tʃæd/; Chad|ian /tʃædiən/

**Chi|le** /tʃɪli, -leɪ/; Chil|ean /tʃɪliən, tʃɪleɪ-/

**Chi|na** /tʃaɪnə/; Chi|nese /tʃaɪniz/

**Co|lom|bia** /kəlʌmbiə/; Co|lom|bi|an /kəlʌmbiən/

**Com|o|ros** /kɒmərouz/; Com|or|an /kəmɔrən/
**Cos|ta Ri|ca** /kɒstə rikə/; Cos|ta Ri|can /kɒstə
rikən/
**Côte d'Ivoire** /kout divwar/; Ivoir|i|an
/ivwariən/
**Cro|a|tia** /krouɛɪʃə/; Cro|a|tian /krouɛɪʃən/
**Cu|ba** /kyubə/; Cu|ban /kyubən/
**Cy|prus** /saɪprəs/; Cyp|riot /sɪpriət/
**(the) Czech Re|pub|lic** /(ðə) tʃɛk rɪpʌblɪk/;
Czech /tʃɛk/
**Dem|o|crat|ic Re|pub|lic of the Con|go,
or (the) Con|go** /dɛməkrætɪk rɪpʌblɪk
əv ðə kɒŋgou/, /(ðə) kɒŋgou/; Con|go|lese
/kɒŋgəliz, -lis/
**Den|mark** /dɛnmark/; Dan|ish, Dane /deɪnɪʃ,
/deɪn/
**Dji|bou|ti** /dʒɪbuti/; Dji|bou|tian /dʒɪbutiən/
**Dom|i|ni|ca** /dɒmɪnɪkə, dəmɪnɪkə/;
Do|mi|ni|can /dɒmɪnikən/
**(the) Do|min|i|can Re|pub|lic** /(ðə)
dəmɪnɪkən rɪpʌblɪk; Do|mi|ni|can
/dəmɪnɪkən/
**East Ti|mor** /ist timɔr/; East Ti|mor|ese /ist
timɔriz/
**Ec|ua|dor** /ɛkwədɔr/; Ec|ua|dor|ian /
ɛkwədɔriən/
**Egypt** /idʒɪpt/; Egyp|tian /ɪdʒɪpʃən/
**El Sal|va|dor** /ɛl sælvədɔr/; Sal|va|do|ran,
Sal|va|do|rean /sælvədɔrən/, /sælvədɔriən/
**Eng|land** /ɪŋglənd/; Eng|lish /ɪŋglɪʃ/
**Equi|to|ri|al Guinea** /ɛkwɪtɔriəl gɪni/;
Equi|to|ri|al Guin|ean, Equi|to|guinean
/ɛkwɪtɔriəl gɪniən/, /ɛkwɪtouginiən/
**Er|i|trea** /ɛrɪtriə/; Er|i|tre|an /ɛrɪtriən/
**Es|to|nia** /ɛstouniə/; Es|to|ni|an /ɛstouniən/
**Ethi|o|pia** /iθioupiə/; Ethi|o|pi|an /iθioupiən/
**Eu|rope** /yuərəp/; Eu|ro|pe|an /yuərəpiən/
**Fi|ji** /fidʒi/; Fi|ji|an /fidʒiən, fiji-/
**Fin|land** /fɪnlənd/; Fin|nish, Finn, Fin|land|er
/fɪnɪʃ/, /fɪn/, /fɪnləndər, -lændər/

**France** /fræns/; French /frɛntʃ/
**Ga|bon** /gaboun/; Gab|o|nese /gæbəniz/
**(the) Gam|bia** /(ðə) gæmbiə/; Gam|bi|an
/gæmbiən/
**Geor|gia** /dʒɔrdʒə/; Geor|gian /dʒɔrdʒən/
**Ger|ma|ny** /dʒɜrməni/; Ger|man /dʒɜrmən/
**Gha|na** /ganə/; Gha|na|ian /ganiən, gəneɪən/
**Greece** /gris/; Greek /grik/
**Gre|na|da** /grɪneɪdə/; Gre|na|di|an /grɪneɪdiən/
**Gua|te|ma|la** /gwatəmalə/; Gua|te|ma|lan
/gwatəmalən/
**Guin|ea** /gɪni/; Guin|ean /gɪniən/
**Guin|ea-Bis|sau** /gɪni bɪsau/; Guin|ean
/gɪniən/
**Guy|ana** /gaɪænə, -anə/; Guy|a|nese /gaɪəniz/
**Hai|ti** /heɪti/; Hai|tian /heɪʃən/
**Hon|du|ras** /hɒnduərəs/; Hon|du|ran
/hɒnduərən/
**Hun|ga|ry** /hʌŋgəri/; Hun|gar|i|an /hʌŋgɛəriən/
**Ice|land** /aɪslənd/; Ice|lan|dic, Ice|land|er
/aɪslændɪk/, /aɪsləndər, -lændər/
**In|dia** /ɪndiə/; In|di|an /ɪndiən/
**(the) In|di|an Ocean** /(ði) ɪndiən ouʃən/
**In|do|ne|sia** /ɪndəniʒə/; In|do|ne|sian
/ɪndəniʒən/
**Iran** /ɪran, ɪræn, aɪræn/; Ira|ni|an, Iran|i
/ɪreɪniən, ɪra-, aɪreɪ-/, /ɪrani/
**I|raq** /ɪræk, ɪrak/; I|raq|i /ɪræki, ɪraki/
**Ire|land** /aɪərlənd/; Ir|ish /aɪrɪʃ/
**Is|ra|el** /ɪzriəl, -reɪəl/; Is|rae|li /ɪzreɪli/
**It|a|ly** /ɪtəli/; Ital|ian /ɪtælyən/
**Ja|mai|ca** /dʒəmeɪkə/; Ja|mai|can /dʒəmeɪkən/
**Ja|pan** /dʒəpæn/; Jap|a|nese /dʒæpəniz/
**Jor|dan** /dʒɔrdən/; Jor|da|ni|an /dʒɔrdeɪniən/
**Ka|zakh|stan** /kazakstan, -stæn/;
Ka|zakh|stan|i, Ka|zakh /kazakstani,
-stæni/, /kazak, kəzæk/
**Ken|ya** /kɛnyə, kin-/; Ken|yan /kɛnyən, kin-/
**Ki|ri|bati** /kɪərəbati, -bæs/; I-Ki|ri|bati /i
kɪərəbati, -bæs/

**Ko|rea, South Ko|rea, North Ko|rea**
/kəriə, kɔ-/, /souθ kəriə, kɔ-/, /nɔrθ kəriə,
kɔ-/; Ko|rean /kəriən, kɔ-/, /souθ kəriən,
kɔ-/, /nɔrθ kəriən, kɔ/

**Ku|wait** /kuweɪt/; Ku|wai|ti /kuweɪti/

**Kyr|gyz|stan** /kɪərgɪstan, -stæn/;
Kyr|gyz|sta|ni /kɪərgɪstani, -stæni/

**Laos** /laʊs, laʊs/; Lao, Lao|tian /laʊ, laʊ/,
/leɪoʊʃən/

**Lat|via** /lætviə, lɑt-/; Lat|vi|an /lætviən, lɑt-/

**Leb|a|non** /lɛbənən, -nɒn/; Leb|a|nese /lɛbəniz/

**Le|so|tho** /ləsoutou, -sutu/ So|tho, Mo|so|tho
(person), Ba|so|tho (people) /soutou, sutu/,
/mɔsoutou, -sutu/, /basoutou, -sutu/

**Li|be|ria** /laɪbɪəriə/; Li|be|ri|an /laɪbɪəriən/

**Lib|ya** /lɪbiə/; Lib|y|an /lɪbiən/

**Liech|ten|stein** /lɪktənstaɪn/; Liech|ten|stein,
Liech|ten|stein|er /lɪktənstaɪn/, /lɪktənstaɪnər/

**Lith|u|a|nia** /lɪθuemiə/; Lith|u|a|ni|an
/lɪθuemiən/

**Lux|em|bourg** /lʌksəmbɜrg/;
Lux|em|bourger /lʌksəmbɜrgər/

**Mac|e|do|nia** /mæsɪdouniə/; Mac|e|do|ni|an
/mæsɪdouniən/

**Mad|a|gas|car** /mædəgæskər/; Mad|a|gas|can,
Mala|gasy /mædəgæskən/, /mæləgæsi/

**Ma|la|wi** /məlawi/; Ma|la|wi|an /məlawiən/

**Ma|lay|sia** /məleɪʒə/; Ma|lay|sian /məleɪʒən/

**Mal|dives** /mɔldivz, -daɪvz/; Mal|div|ian
/mɔldɪviən/

**Ma|li** /mɑli/; Ma|lian /mɑliən/

**Mal|ta** /mɔltə/; Mal|tese /mɔltiz/

**(the) Mar|shall Is|lands** /(ðə) mɑrʃəl
aɪləndz/; Mar|shall|ese /mɑrʃəliz/

**Mau|ri|ta|nia** /mɔrɪteɪniə/; Mau|ri|ta|ni|an
/mɔrɪteɪniən/

**Mau|ri|ti|us** /mɔrɪʃəs/; Mau|ri|tian /mɔrɪʃən/

**Mex|i|co** /mɛksɪkou/; Mex|i|can /mɛksɪkən/

**Mi|cro|ne|sia** /maɪkrəniʒə/; Mi|cro|ne|sian
/maɪkrəniʒən/

**Mol|do|va** /mɔldouvə/; Mol|do|van /
mɔldouvən/

**Mo|na|co** /mɒnəkou/; Mo|na|can,
Mon|e|gasque /mɒnəkən/, /mɒnɪgæsk/

**Mon|go|lia** /mɒŋgouliə/; Mon|go|li|an
/mɒŋgouliən/

**Mo|roc|co** /mərɒkou/; Mo|roc|can /mərɒkən/

**Mo|zam|bique** /mouzæmbik, -zəm-/;
Mo|zam|bi|can /mouzæmbikən, -zəm-/

**Myan|mar** (Burma) /myanmar (bɜrmə)/;
Bur|mese /bɜrmiz/

**Na|mib|ia** /nəmibiə/; Na|mib|ian /nəmibiən/

**Na|u|ru** /nauru/; Na|u|ru|an /nauruən/

**Ne|pal** /nəpɔl/; Nep|a|lese /nɛpəliz/

**(the) Neth|er|lands** /(ðə) nɛðərləndz/; Dutch
/dʌtʃ/

**New Zea|land** /nu zilənd/; New Zea|land,
New Zea|land|er /nu zilənd/, /nu ziləndər/

**Nic|a|ra|gua** /nɪkəragwə/; Nic|a|ra|guan
/nɪkəragwən/

**Ni|ger** /naɪdʒər, niʒɛər/; Ni|ge|rien, Ni|ger|ois
/naɪdʒɪəriən, niʒɛryɛn/, /niʒɛrwa/

**Ni|ge|ria** /naɪdʒɪəriə/; Ni|ge|ri|an /naɪdʒɪəriən/

**Nor|way** /nɔrweɪ/; Nor|we|gian /nɔrwidʒən/

**Oman** /ouman/; Omani /oumani/

**(the) Pa|cif|ic Ocean** /(ðə) pəsɪfɪk ouʃən/

**Pa|ki|stan** /pækɪstæn, pakɪstan/; Pa|ki|sta|ni
/pækɪstæni, pakɪstani/

**Pa|lau** /palaʊ, pə-/; Pa|lau|an /palaʊən, pə-/

**Pan|a|ma** /pænəmə, -mɔ/; Pan|a|ma|ni|an
/pænəmeɪniən/

**Pap|ua New Guin|ea** /pæpyuə nu gɪni,
papua/; Pa|p|ua New Guin|ean, Pap|uan
/pæpyuə nu gɪniən, papua/, /pæpyuən, papuən/

**Par|a|guay** /pærəgwaɪ, -gweɪ/; Par|a|guay|an
/pærəgwaɪən, -gweɪən/

**Pe|ru** /pəru/; Pe|ru|vi|an /pəruviən/

**(the) Phil|ip|pines** /(ðə) fɪlɪpinz/;
Phil|ip|pine, Fi|li|pi|no, Fi|li|pi|na /fɪlɪpin/,
/fɪlɪpinou/, /fɪlɪpinə/

Po|land /ˈpoʊlənd/; Po|lish, Pole /ˈpoʊlɪʃ, /poʊl/

Por|tu|gal /ˈpɔːrtʃəgəl/; Por|tu|guese / pɔːrtʃəgiz/

Qa|tar /ˈkətɑːr/; Qa|tari /kəˈtɑːri/

Ro|ma|nia /roʊˈmeɪniə/; Ro|ma|nian / roʊˈmeɪniən/

Rus|sia /ˈrʌʃə/; Rus|sian /ˈrʌʃən/

Rwan|da /ruˈɑndə/; Rwan|dan /ruˈɑndən/

Saint Kitts–Ne|vis /seɪnt kɪts ˈnivɪs/; Kit|ti|tian, Ne|vis|ian /ˈkɪtɪʃən/, /ˈnɪvɪʒən/

Saint Lu|cia /seɪnt ˈluʃə/; Saint Lu|cian /seɪnt ˈluʃən/

Saint Vin|cent and the Gren|a|dines /seɪnt ˈvɪnsənt ən ðə ˈgrenədɪnz/; Saint Vin|cen|tian, Vin|cen|tian /seɪnt ˈvɪnsenʃən/, /ˈvɪnsenʃən/

Sa|moa /səˈmoʊə/; Sa|mo|an /səˈmoʊən/

San Ma|ri|no /sæn məˈrinoʊ/; Sam|ma|ri|nese, San Ma|ri|nese /sæmˈmærɪniz/, /ˌsæn ˈmærɪniz/

São To|mé and Prin|ci|pe /soʊn təˈmeɪ ən ˈprɪnsɪpi/; Sao To|me|an /soʊn təˈmeɪən/

Sau|di Ara|bia /ˈsoʊdi əˈreɪbiə/; Sau|di Ara|bi|an /ˈsoʊdi əˈreɪbiən/

Scot|land /ˈskɒtlənd/; Scot|tish, Scot(s) /ˈskɒtɪʃ/, /skɒts/

Sen|egal /ˈsenɪgɔl, -gɑl/; Sen|e|gal|ese /ˌsenɪgəˈliz/

Ser|bia and Mon|te|negro /ˈsɜːrbiə ən mɒntɪˈnegroʊ/ Ser|bi|an, Serb, Mon|te|ne|grin /ˈsɜːrbiən/, /sɜːrb/, /ˌmɒntɪˈnegrɪn/

(the) Sey|chelles /(ðə) seɪˈʃelz/; Sey|chel|lois /ˌseɪʃelˈwɑ/

Sier|ra Le|one /siˈerə liˈoʊn/; Sier|ra Le|on|ean /siˈerə liˈoʊniən/

Sin|ga|pore /ˈsɪŋəpɔr, ˈsɪŋgə-/; Sin|ga|por|ean /ˌsɪŋəˈpɔriən, ˌsɪŋgə-/

Slo|va|kia /sloʊˈvɑkiə, -ˈvækiə/; Slo|vak, Slo|va|ki|an /ˈsloʊvæk/, /sloʊˈvɑkiən, -ˈvæk-/

Slo|ve|nia /sloʊˈviniə/; Slo|vene /sloʊˈvin/; Slo|ve|nian /sloʊˈviniən/

Sol|o|mon Is|lands /ˈsɒləmən ˈaɪləndz/; Sol|o|mon Is|land|er /ˈsɒləmən ˈaɪləndər/

So|ma|lia /səˈmɑliə, soʊ-/; So|ma|li, So|ma|lian /səˈmɑli, soʊ-/, /səˈmɑliən, soʊ-/

South Af|rica /ˈsoʊθ ˈæfrɪkə/; South Af|ri|can /ˈsoʊθ ˈæfrɪkən/

(the Re|pub|lic of) Spain (ðə rɪˈpʌblɪk əv) speɪn/; Span|ish, Span|iard /ˈspænɪʃ/, /ˈspænyərd/

Sri Lan|ka /sri ˈlɑŋkə, ʃri/; Sri Lan|kan /sri ˈlɑŋkən, ʃri/

Su|dan /suˈdæn, -ˈdan/; Su|da|nese /ˌsudᵊˈniz/

Su|ri|na|me /ˈsʊərɪnɑm/; Su|ri|na|mer, Su|ri|na|mese /ˈsʊərɪnɑmər/, /ˌsʊərɪnəˈmiz/

Swa|zi|land /ˈswɑzilænd/; Swazi /ˈswɑzi/

Swe|den /ˈswidᵊn/; Swe|dish, Swede /ˈswidɪʃ/, /swid/

Swit|zer|land /ˈswɪtsərlənd/; Swiss /swɪs/

Syr|ia /ˈsɪəriə/; Syr|ian /ˈsɪəriən/

Tai|wan /ˈtaɪwɑn/; Tai|wan|ese /ˌtaɪwɑˈniz/

Ta|jik|i|stan /tɑˈdʒɪkɪstæn, -stɑn/; Ta|jik|i|stan|i, Ta|jik /tɑˈdʒɪkɪstæni, -stɑni/, /tɑˈdʒɪk, -ˈdʒik/

Tan|za|nia /ˌtænzəˈniə/; Tan|za|nian / tænzəˈniən/

Thai|land /ˈtaɪlænd, -lənd/; Thai /taɪ/

To|go /ˈtoʊgoʊ/; To|go|lese /ˌtoʊgəˈliz/

Ton|ga /ˈtɒŋə/; Ton|gan /ˈtɒŋgən/

Trin|i|dad and To|ba|go /ˈtrɪnɪdæd ən təˈbeɪgoʊ/; Trin|i|da|di|an, To|ba|go|ni|an /ˌtrɪnɪˈdeɪdiən/, /ˌtoʊbəˈgoʊniən/

Tu|ni|sia /tuˈniʒə/; Tu|ni|sian /tuˈniʒən/

Tur|key /ˈtɜːrki/; Turk|ish, Turk /ˈtɜːrkɪʃ/, /tɜːrk/

Turk|men|i|stan /ˈtɜːrkmenɪstæn, -stɑn/; Turk|men /ˈtɜːrkmen, -mən/

**Tu|va|lu** /tuvɑlu, tuvəlu/; **Tu|va|luan** /tuvəluən/

**Ugan|da** /yugændə, ugan-/; **Ugan|dan** /yugændən, ugan-/

**Ukraine** /yukreɪn/; **Ukrai|ni|an** /yukreɪmiən/

**(the) Unit|ed Ar|ab Emir|ates** /(ðə) yunaɪtɪd ærəb ɛmərɪts, -əreɪts/; **Emir|ati** /ɛmərati/

**(the) Unit|ed King|dom of Great Brit|ain and North|ern Ire|land** /(ðə) yunaɪtɪd kɪŋdəm əv greɪt brɪtᵊn ən nɔrðərn aɪərlənd/; **Brit|ish** /brɪtɪʃ/

**(the) Unit|ed States of Amer|i|ca** /(ðə) yunaɪtɪd steɪts əv əmerɪkə/; **Amer|i|can** /əmerɪkən/

**Uru|guay** /yuərəgweɪ, -gwaɪ/; **Uru|guay|an** /yuərəgweɪən, -gwaɪən/

**Uz|bek|i|stan** /ʊzbɛkɪstæn, -stan, uz-/; **Uz|bek|i|stani,**

**Uz|bek** /ʊzbɛkɪstæni, -stani, uz-/, /ʊzbɛk, uz-/

**Va|nua|tu** /vænwatu/; **Ni-Va|nua|tu** /ni vænwatu/

**Vat|i|can City** /vætɪkən sɪti/

**Ven|e|zue|la** /venɪzweɪlə/; **Ven|e|zue|lan** /venɪzweɪlən/

**Vi|et|nam** /vietnam, vyɛt-/; **Vi|et|nam|ese** /vietnəmiz, vyɛt-/

**Wales** /weɪlz/; **Welsh** /wɛlʃ/

**Ye|men** /yemən/; **Ye|meni, Ye|men|ite** /yeməni/, /yemənaɪt/

**Zam|bia** /zæmbiə/; **Zam|bi|an** /zæmbiən/

**Zim|ba|bwe** /zɪmbabweɪ, -wi/; **Zim|ba|bwe|an** /zɪmbabweɪən, -wiən/

# CREDITS

## Illustrations:

**Higgins Bond:** pp. 190, 316, 350, 356, 383, 423, 445, 478, 506, 540, 577, 667, 832, 1007;
© Higgins Bond/Anita Grien

**Richard Carbajal:** pp. 168, 285, 350, 565, 603, 657, 843, 911, 956, 1016 (bottom); © Richard
Carbajal/illustrationOnLine.com

**Ron Carboni:** pp. 121, 145, 179, 275, 369, 510, 569, 653, 835, 863 (bottom), 956;
© Ron Carboni/Anita Grien

**Todd Daman:** pp. 22, 77; © Todd Daman/illustrationOnLine.com

**Dick Gage:** pp. 87, 104, 130, 289 (top); © Dick Gage/illustrationOnLine.com

**Patrick Gnan:** pp. 31, 163, 304 (top), 497, 597, 631 (right), 681 (bottom), 785;
© Patrick Gnan/illustrationOnLine.com

**Sharon and Joel Harris:** pp. 96, 97, 220, 249, 361 (top), 419, 612, 769 (fetus), 773, 850;
© Sharon and Joel Harris/illustrationOnLine.com

**Philip Howe:** pp. 125, 160, 329, 605, 658, 808, 1039; © Philip Howe/illustrationOnLine.com

**Robert Kayganich:** pp. 72, 87, 106, 245, 289 (bottom), 294, 381, 392, 437, 513, 577 (bottom), 813,
886, 913, 1053; © Robert Kayganich/illustrationOnLine.com

**Robert Kemp:** pp. 192, 204, 300, 404, 629; © Robert Kemp/illustrationOnLine.com

**Stephen Peringer:** pp. 196, 244, 283, 292, 360, 387; © Stephen Peringer/
illustrationOnLine.com

**Alan Reingold:** pp. 210, 276, 416; © Alan Reingold/Anita Grien

**Mark Ryan:** pp. 829, 864 (bottom), 1016 (top); © Mark Ryan/illustrationOnLine.com

**Simon Shaw:** pp. 84, 295, 531, 674, 740; © Simon Shaw/illustrationOnLine.com

**Daniel M. Short:** pp. 304 (bottom); © Daniel M. Short

**Gerard Taylor:** pp. 75, 137, 333, 486, 868, 1024, 1025; © Gerard Taylor/illustrationOnLine.com

**Ralph Voltz:** pp. 46, 71, 334, 361 (bottom), 399, 448, 566, 571, 641, 861, 939; © Ralph Voltz/
illustrationOnLine.com

**Cam Wilson:** pp. 105, 199, 260, 358, 368, 407, 503, 515, 557, 673, 864 (top), 902, 977;
© Cam Wilson/illustrationOnLine.com